TOOL AND MANUFACTURING ENGINEERS HANDBOOK

DESK EDITION

TOOL AND MANUFACTURING ENGINEERS HANDBOOK

DESK EDITION

From the complete five-volume Fourth Edition

William H. Cubberly
Consulting Editor

Ramon Bakerjian, CMfgT
Staff Editor

Produced under the supervision of the SME Reference Publications Committee in cooperation with the SME Technical Divisions

Society of Manufacturing Engineers
One SME Drive
Dearborn, Michigan

TMΞH ® *Desk Edition*

ISBN No. 0-87263-351-9

Library of Congress Catalog No. 88-63758

Society of Manufacturing Engineers (SME)

Copyright © 1989, 1976, 1959, 1949 by Society of Manufacturing Engineers, One SME Drive, P.O. Box 930, Dearborn, Michigan 48121

First edition published 1949 by McGraw-Hill Book Co. in cooperation with SME under earlier Society name, American Society of Tool Engineers (ASTE), and under title *Tool Engineers Handbook*. Second edition published 1959 by McGrawHill Book Co. in cooperation with SME under earlier Society name, American Society of Tool and Manufacturing Engineers (ASTME), and under title *Tool Engineers Handbook*. Third edition published 1976 by McGraw-Hill Book Co. in cooperation with SME under current Society name and under title *Tool and Manufacturing Engineers Handbook*.

Printed in the United States of America.

PREFACE

This Desk Edition of the *Tool and Manufacturing Engineers Handbook* presents a unique collection of manufacturing information in one convenient source. In addition to three entirely new chapters (robotics, CAD/CAM and flexible manufacturing), this book contains selected information from the five volumes of the Fourth Edition of the TMEH. Those volumes are:

- Volume 1, *Machining*, published in 1983
- Volume 2, *Forming*, published in 1984
- Volume 3, *Materials, Finishing and Coating*, published in 1985
- Volume 4, *Quality Control and Assembly*, published in 1987
- Volume 5, *Manufacturing Management*, published in 1988.

The scope of this edition is multifaceted—authoritative manufacturing information for daily use by engineers, managers, consultants, and technicians, yet it also provides coverage of the fundamentals of manufacturing processes for study by the novice engineer or student. This blend of coverage has characterized the proven usefulness and reputation of SME Handbooks in previous editions (dating back to 1949) and continues in this Desk Edition to provide the basis for acceptance across all segments of manufacturing.

The reference material contained in this volume is the product of incalculable hours of unselfish contribution by hundreds of individuals and organizations who provided reference material for the five volumes of the Handbook. These individuals and organizations are listed at the beginning of this book. No written words of appreciation can sufficiently express the special thanks due to these many forward thinking professionals and their companies. But more importantly, their contributions will undoubtedly serve to advance the understanding of manufacturing by management throughout industry and will certainly help to spur major gains in competitiveness in the years ahead. It should be noted that company affiliations listed with each individual contributor are the contributor's affiliation at the time they donated their expertise to the development of the five volume set.

Further recognition is due to the members of the SME Reference Publications Committee for their expert guidance and support and recognition is due to the members of the Publications Development Department at SME for their efforts on this volume.

The Editors

CONTRIBUTORS

CHAPTER 1: **Ted J. Egan**, Div. of American Financial Consulting Co., Greenwich Technologies; **Alice Greene**, Arthur D. Little, Inc.

CHAPTER 2: **Dr. Max E. Kanagy, CMfgT**, Eastern Michigan University.

CHAPTER 3: **Carl M. Jacobson**, Computervision.

CHAPTER 4: **Glenn A. Graham**, Coopers & Lybrand.

CHAPTER 5: **James Pearse**, Leviton Manufacturing Co.; **Henry W. Stoll**, Design for Manufacturing, Industrial Technology Institute.

CHAPTER 6: **Michael Burstein**, Center for Social and Economic Issues, Industrial Technology Institute; **Pearson Graham**, Consultant; **Jay Baron**, Industrial Technology Institute.

CHAPTER 7: **James R. Bingham**, Facilities Location, The Austin Co.; **Daniel R. Bradley**, Coopers & Lybrand; **William L. Duncan**, Coopers & Lybrand; **W. David Lasater**, K.W. Tunnell Co., Inc.; **Robert Lasecki**, Austin Consulting; **A. Leonard Schade**, Automation and Productivity, The Austin Co.; **Robert L. Shumaker**, The Austin Co.; **William Taylor**, The Austin Co.; **Kenneth W. Tunnell**, K.W. Tunnell Co., Inc.; **William R. Welter**, Austin Consulting; **Richard W. White**, K.W. Tunnell Co., Inc.; **Robert A. Will**, Technical Services Div., The Austin Co.; **Steven S. Zagor**, EDP Facilities, The Austin Co.; **Dale H. Zempel**, Coopers & Lybrand.

CHAPTER 8: **Oliver Wade**, Tolerance Chart Services Co., Inc.

CHAPTER 9: **Dino Emanuelli**, Greenfield Tap and Die, TRW; **Lowell W. Foster**, Lowell W. Foster Associates, Inc.; **John W. Geier**, Consultant-Instructor; **Gary K. Griffith**, AiResearch Mfg. Co.; **Bill Janninck**, ITW Illitron; **Stanley P. Johnson**, Johnson Gage Co.; **Max A Kickhofel**, Invospline, Inc.; **Richard S. Marrelli**, Mechanical Design Consultant; **George Pruitt**, Technical Documents Consultants; **Ronald M. Pruitt**, Technical Documents Consultants; **Edward S. Roth**, Productivity Services, Inc.; **Warner Weniger**, Rank Precision Industries, Inc.; **Gary Whitmire**, Tec/Trend.

CHAPTER 10: **Roger W. Berger**, Iowa State University; **Richard Copp**, Holley Automotive Div.; **Richard B. Stump**, National Computer Systems, Inc.; **William O. Winchell**, Department of Industrial Engineering, Alfred University.

CHAPTER 11: **Dr. T.H. Chang**, Dept. of Industrial and Systems Engineering, University of Wisconsin-Milwaukee; **Dr. Richard E. DeVor**, Dept. of Mechanical and Industrial Engineering, University of Illinois at Urbana-Champaign.

CHAPTER 12: **B. J. Brown**, Control Gaging, Inc.; **William E. Drews**, Rank Precision Industries, Inc.; **Don Marchand**, Autoflex, Inc.; **Craig McLanahan**, McLanahan & Co., Inc. and Salem State College; **William C. Mullin**, Edmunds Gages; **Dr.**

Walt Pastorius, Diffracto, Ltd.; **William Planick**, Techwrite; **Richard H. Searle**, Bridgeport Machines Co.

CHAPTER 13: **Ray Achterberg**, Gilman Engrg. & Mfg. Co., A Unit of AMCA; **Harold Berger**, Industrial Quality, Inc.; **Sam Currie**, Ardrox, Inc.; **Donald C. Gates**, Reliance Industries; **Allen T. Green**, Acoustic Emission Technology Corp.; **John Johnston**, Staveley NDT Technologies, Inc., Sonic Systems Div.; **William J. Lang**, Lenox Instrument Co., Inc.; **William E. Mooz**, Met-L-Chek Co.; **James Pellicer**, Staveley NDT Technologies, Inc., Nortec Div.; **Robert T. Pitlak**, Pitlak Corp.; **Michael David Stebel**, UPA Technology, Inc.; **Fred Wiesinger**, Uson Corp.

CHAPTER 14: **Guy Bellows**, Metcut Research Associates, Inc.; **Dr. Marvin F. DeVries**, University of Wisconsin—Madison; **William E. Drews**, Rank Precision Industries; **Michael Field**, Metcut Research Associates, Inc.; **Brian K. Lambert, PhD, P.E.**, Department of Industrial Engineering, Texas Tech University; **David Nixon**, LaSalle Steel Co.; **Milton C. Shaw**, Arizona State University; **E. J. Weller, CMfgE, P.E.**, Consultant.

CHAPTER 15: **D. C. Agarwal**, Cabot Corp.; **Dr. George Aggen**, Research Center, Allegheny Ludlum Steel Corp.; **James W. Barr**, The Aluminum Association, Inc.; **Alan M. Bayer**, Teledyne Vasco; **John T. Benedict**, Consultant; **H. M. Butler**, Special Metals Corp.; **Arthur Cohen**, Copper Development Association, Inc.; **Calvin Cooley**, American Iron and Steel Institute; **V. Samuel Hill**, Dow Chemical Co.; **William B. Hampshire**, Tin Research Institute, Inc.; **Anthony D. Ippolito**, Lead Industries Association, Inc.; **Lyle R. Jenkins**, Ductile Iron Society; **Richard L. Kennedy**, Teledyne Allvac; **Ted Kosa**, Stainless Alloy Research and Development Dept.; Carpenter Technology Corp.; **Dwaine L. Klarstrom**, Product Development, Cabot Corp.; **Daniel Lea**, International Magnesium Association; **W. C. Leslie**, Dept. of Materials and Metallurgical Engineering, University of Michigan; **L. W. Lherbier**, Universal Cyclops; **Roy W. Lobenhofer**, American Foundrymen's Society; **Dr. Paul E. Manning**, Cabot Corp.; **Paul J. Mikelonis**, General Casting Corp.; **Kurt H. Miska**, Climax Molybdenum Co. of Michigan; **Hugh Morrow III**, Zinc Institute, Inc.; **Tom Oakwood**, Wrought Alloy Steel Development, Climax Molybdenum, AMAX Inc.; **Phil Ranson**, Huntington Alloys, Inc.; **Wayne M. Riggle**, Castwell Div., Wells Manufacturing Co.; **Dr. Harry W. Rosenberg**, TIMET; **John Svoboda**, Steel Founders' Society of America; **Donald J. Tillack**, Huntington Alloys, Inc.; **Charles F. Walton**, Specialist in Iron Castings;

CHAPTER 16: **Robert W. Bainbridge**, Bainbridge Consultants, Inc.; **Glenn L. Beall**, Glenn Beall/Engineering Inc.; **John T. Benedict**, Consultant; **D. M. Bigg**, Battelle Columbus Laboratories; **Frank D. Diodato**, Engineering Resins Div., Celanese Corp.; **Christopher M. Hall**, Plastics Machinery Div., Cincinnati Milacron Marketing Co.; **Joseph Hansmann**, Magna International, Inc., Concord; **Jack Hill**, J. Hill Associates; **Roy S. Klein**, American Sterilizer Co.; **John Kovalchuck**, Firelands College, Bowling Green State University; **Blaise A. LeWark, Sr.**, Polytech, Ltd.; **Roy L. Manns**, Boston Plastics Group, Medical

Electronic Independent Plastics Engineering Centre, Inc. (MEIPEC); **William K. McConnell, Jr.** McConnell Co., Inc.; **Travis H. Meister**, Consultant—Plastics; **Dario Ramazzotti**, Ramazzotti Design and Engineering.

CHAPTER 17: Loren C. Bone, Manufacturing & Materials Development, Caterpillar Tractor Co.; **Samuel Bradbury**, Hoeganaes Corp.; **R. W. Bratt**, Specialty Metals Div., Crucible Inc., Colt Industries Inc.; **Robert Burns**, Cincinnati Incorporated; **A. P. Crease, Jr.**, Drever Co.; **Raymond P. De Santis**, PTX-Pentronix Inc.; **Frank Emley**, Applied Metallurgical Co.; **John D. Generous**, American Powdered Metals Co.; **Myron I. Jaffe**, Sintered Metals Inc.; **Peter K. Johnson**, Metal Powder Industries Federation; **Walter V. Knopp**, P/M Engineering and Consulting; **Bruce G. McMordie**, Materials Div., SermeTel Inc.; **Robert K. Owens**, Hoeganaes Corp; **Kempton H. Roll**, Metal Powder Industries Federation; **Richard J. Smith**, Process Equipment Div., Patterson-Kelley Co.; **Milton W. Toaz**, Technology Center, Imperial Clevite Inc.

CHAPTER 18: Roger L. Baas, Machinery Div., Prince Corp.; **William M. Barron**, Waukesha Foundry Div., Abex Corp.; **Timothy L. Coghill**, Precision Metalsmiths, Inc.; **Ronald E. Greenwood**, Unicast Development Corp.; **Jeffrey T. Heinen**, Corporate Research and Development, General Electric Co.; **Leo J. LeBlanc**, Enterprise Brass Works, Inc.; **Raymond W. Monroe**, Steel Founders' Society of America; **Rodney L. Naro**, Ashland Chemical Div., Ashland Oil, Inc.; **John M. Svoboda**, Steel Founders' Society of America; **Fred E. Weil**, SRI International.

CHAPTER 19: Guy Bellows, Metcut Research Associates, Inc.; **Edward J. Berger**, Tool and Alloy Metallurgy, Carpenter Technology Corp.; **Richard W. Bratt**, Crucible Specialty Metals Div., Colt Industries; **E. J. Buchanan**, Petroleum Products Research, Texaco Inc.; **Dr. Marvin F. DeVries**, University of Wisconsin—Madison; **I. R. Dolich**, Quaker Chemical Corp.; **Michael Field**, Metcut Research Associates, Inc.; **Greg Foltz**, Products Div., Cincinnati Milacron; **Gerald B. Franklin**, E.F. Houghton & Co.; **Dr. Bernard Hamrock**, Tribology Branch, NASA-Lewis Research Center; **R. E. Hatton**, Monsanto Industrial Chemicals Co.; **T. V. Hazelton**, Hydraulic Fluids, Quaker Chemical Corp.; **Joseph Ivaska, Jr.**, Tower Oil & Technology Co.; **Herbert S. Kalish**, Adamas Carbide Corp.; **William Katzenstein, Michigan Petroleum Co.; Paul J. Kenney**, Acheson Colloids Co.; **Daniel J. Klaphaak**, Sandvik, Inc.; **Erich W. Krumrei**, Specialty Materials Dept., General Electric Co.; **Richard C. Ladd**, Specialty Materials Dept., General Electric Co.; **Brian K. Lambert, PhD, P.E.**, Department of Industrial Engineering, Texas Tech University; **Harold R. Lebrecht**, VR/Wesson Div., Fansteel, Inc.; **Geoffrey L. Manna**, Machining and Grinding Fluids, Quaker Chemical Corp.; **Nick L. Matthews**, Lubrication Div., Russell Products; **William H. Millett**, Fluid Power Products, E. F. Houghton & Co., (retired); **David Moskowitz**, Ford Motor Co.; **Dr. Elliot S. Nachtman**, Tower Oil and Technology Co.; **Ronald J. Newhouse**, Franklin Oil Corp.; **David Nixon**, LaSalle Steel Co.; **Andrew G. Papay**, Edwin Cooper Div., Ethyl Corp.; **Dr. Harold W. Rossmoore**, Wayne State University; **Donald J. Sargent**, E/M Lubricants, Inc.; **Milton C. Shaw**, Arizona State University; **Albert F. Shuster**, Kennametal, Inc.; **Kathryn F. Strang**, Quaker Chemical Corp.; **Herman F. Weindel**, Mobil Oil Corp., **E. J. Weller**,

CMfgE, P.E., Consultant; **J. George Wills**, Mobil Oil Corp.; **Donald O. Wood**, The Lodge & Shipley Co.; **Marino Zapico**, Carmet Materials Div., Allegheny Ludlum Industries, Inc.

CHAPTER 20: Thomas M. Austin, Electronics Div., Giddings & Lewis Machiine Tool Co.; **John A. Blaeser**, Modicon Div., Gould Inc.; **Vincent F. Bobrowicz**, MDSI, a Schlumberger Co.; **Gary Cavano**, Systems Div., AllenBradley; **Robert M. Elliott**, MDSI; **Lloyd Fogg**, MDSI; **Donald R. Fontecchio**, Giddings & Lewis Machine Tool Co.; **James Gilgenbach**, Giddings & Lewis Machine Tool Co.; **Hillary A. Handwerger**, MDSI; **Golden E. Herrin**, Cincinnati Milacron; **John H. Kidd**, MDSI; **Robert J. Samson**, MDSI; **Michael K. Savelyev**, Modicon Div., Gould Inc.; **Arne L. Watland**, Modicon Div., Gould Inc.; **David R. Witt**, Electronics Div., Giddings & Lewis Machine Tool Co.

CHAPTER 21: Merlin D. Nord, DoALL Co.; **Ted A Slezak**, Armstrong-Blum Mfg. Co.; **James E. Wolf**, Kaltenbach, Inc.

CHAPTER 22: Steven J. Hamm, The Ohio Broach & Machine Co.; **Robert E. Roseliep**, General Broach and Engineering Co.; **Leonard J. Smith**, Ty Miles, Inc.; **Christopher Van DeMotter**, The Ohio Broach & Machine Co.

CHAPTER 23: Steve Cole, LeBlond Makino Machine Tool Co.; **Arthur S. Dinsmore**, Seneca Falls Machine Co.; **Thomas C. Doud**, Hardinge Brothers, Inc.; **Frank Ferdinand**, Wadell Equipment Co. Inc.; **Geoffrey Y. Gill**, Muskegon Tool Industries; **Theodore W. Judson**, General Motors Institute; **Jack S. Larson**, Olofsson Corp.; **Robert M. Perry**, Moore Special Tool Co. Inc.; **James M. Sullivan**, Cushman Industries, Inc.

CHAPTER 24: Robert H. Allen, Charles G. Allen Co.; **Paul D. Bober**, Chicago-Latrobe Div., TRW, Inc.; **Sebastian Ebenhoch**, Waukesha Cutting Tools, Inc.; **Geoffrey Y. Gill**, Muskegon Tool Industries; **DeWitt F. Goodemote, CMfgE, P.E.**, Aerospace Div., Moog Inc.; **Edward G. Hoffman**, E. G. Hoffman Co.; **Michael J. McGinty**, Cleveland Twist Drill Co., Div. of Acme-Cleveland Corp,; **Donald C. Noble**, The Weldon Tool Co.; **Roger J. Reddin**, Burgmaster Div., Houdaille Industries, Inc.; **A. J. Reitenbach**, Metallurgical Quality Control, Cleveland Twist Drill Co.; **J. K. Scholz**, Cleereman Machine Tool Div., Appleton Machine Co.; **Ernest E. Torkilsen**, Industrial Products Div., Dumore Corp.; **Charles J. Trost**, C.J.T. Industries, Inc.; **Cyrus T. Wax**, Engineering Industrial Tools Div., The Bendix Corp.; **Howard Whalley**, The George Whalley Co.; **Jon A. Wolfe**, Coromant Div., Sandvik Inc.; **Lou Yane**, Zagar, Inc.

CHAPTER 25: Henry Gill, Cincinnati Milacron Inc.; **William R. Jahnke, P.E.**, Bridgeport Machines Div., Textron Inc.; **Ralph Lacey**, Carboloy Systems Dept., General Electric Co.; **John Mitchell**, Carboloy Systems Dept., General Electric Co.; **David J. Rivard**, Valenite Metals Milling Div., Valeron Corp.

CHAPTER 26: John G. Burgess, Brown & Sharpe Mfg. Co.; **Gerald C. Cotter**, Industrial Tools Div., Bendix Corp.; **Paul H. DeRamo**, The Hill Acme Co.; **Everett W. Emery**, Cone-Blanchard Machine Co.; **Dr. Francis T. Farago, CMfgE**, General Motors Corp., (retired); **Robert M. Gauvreau**, Coated Abrasives Div., Norton Co.; **Don Greenburg**, Barnes Drill Co.; **Robert S. Hahn, DSc., P.E., CMfgE**, Hahn Associates; **Edward G. Hoffman**, E.G. Hoffman Co.; **Burton R. Leathley**, Oliver

Instrument Co.; **Dr. Richard Lindsay**, Norton Co.; **Robert M. Perry**, Moore Special Tool Co., Inc.; **W. D. Pollard**, Diamond Products Branch, Carborundum Co.; **Thomas Z. Richards**, Grinding Wheel Operations, Norton Co.; **William A. Sluhan**, Master Chemical Corp.; **D. M. Syed**, Rollway Bearing International; **Thomas J. Turner**, AirTronics Div., American Gage & Machine Co., A Katy Industries, Inc., Co.

CHAPTER 27: Judith F. Enden, Sales Engineering Dept., Teledyne Landis Machine; **Arthur Fitzwater**, Reed Rolled Thread Die Co., Div. of Litton Industries; **Alan R. Hails**, Morse Cutting Tools Div., Gulf & Western Mfg. Co.; **Allan S. Johnson**, Tapmatic Corp.; **Spencer I. Kanter, P.E.** The Hanson Whitney Co.; **Adolph V. Klancnik**, Universal-Automatic Corp.; **David L. Lewis**, Universal Engineering Div., Houdaille Industries, Inc.; **Richard J. Miller**, H.E.S. Machine Tool, Inc.; **Ronald J. Sabatos**, The Cleveland Twist Drill Co., Div. of Acme-Cleveland Corp.; **David L. Turner**, Prutton Corp.; **Joseph B. Yuryan, P.E.**, The Cleveland Tapping Machine Co.; **Raymond J. Zeman**, Normac Inc.

CHAPTER 28: Russel A. Brezler, Jr., Teledyne Landis Machine; **Brian W. Cluff**, American Pfauter Corp.; **Richard B. Goodrum**, Fellows Corp.; **Ernest R. Hugenbruch**, Gleason Machine Div., Gleason Works, (retired).

CHAPTER 29: D. G. Anderson, Linde Div., Union Carbide Corp.; **David A. Belforte**, AVCO Everett Metalworking Lasers; **Terry Bryce**, Charmilles Corp. of America; **R. E. Fromson**, Westinghouse Electric Corp.; **Robert N. Harris**, Charmilles Corp. of America; **T. J. Kujawa**, Apollo Lasers Inc.; **F. J. McGee**, Vought Corp., LTV, Inc.; **Hugh H. Muller**, Adcoat, Inc.; **Jill V. Paul**, Sonobond Corp; **Dean A. Pollack**, Hansvedt Engineering, Inc.; **William H. Shiner**, Laser Inc., A Subsidiary of Coherent, Inc.; **Israel Weber**, Lectrokem Sales Div., Everite Machine Products Co.

CHAPTER 30: Engineering Dept., The Bullard Co., Div. of White Consolidated Industries, Inc.; **Arthur S. Dinsmore**, Seneca Falls Machine Co.; **Thomas A. Powell**, Greenlee, Manufacturing Systems Div., Ex-Cell-O Corp.; **Larry E. Warnock**, Machine Tool Div., Brown & Sharpe Manufacturing Co.

CHAPTER 31: John L. Duncan, Mechanical Engineering Department, McMaster University; **C. Howard Hamilton**, Science Center, Rockwell International; **Stuart P. Keeler**, Great Lakes Steel Div., National Steel Corp.; **Harmon D. Nine**, Physics Dept., Research Laboratories, General Motors Corp.; **Philip A. Stine**, Applied Science and Technology Laboratory, General Electric Co.; **William L. Weeks**, Sheet Metal Forming Consultant; **Michael L. Wenner**, Research Laboratories, General Motors Corp.

CHAPTER 32: Lewis F. Bogart, Tool Chemical Co., Inc.; **Peter B. Hopper**, Crucible Specialty Metals Div., Colt Industries; **Herbert S. Kalish**, Adamas Carbide Corp.; **Russell M. Melvin**, The Budd Co.; **Raymond J. Severson**, Ampco Metals Div., Ampco-Pittsburgh Corp; **J. F. Thompson**, Universal-Cyclops Specialty Steel Div., Cyclops Corp.; **David C. Vale**, Specialty Products Group, Kennametal Inc.; **William H. Wills**, AL Tech Specialty Steel Corp., Zinc Institute Inc., Fraser Industrial Mall.

CHAPTER 33: Frohman C. Anderson, Anderson Industries, Inc.; **James W. Bowman**, Pacific Press & Shear Co.; **Thomas P. Conmay**, Arrowsmith Industries, Inc.; **Sokka M. Doraivelu**, AFWAL/MLLM, Wright-Patterson Air Force Base; **Daniel B. Dallas**, Consultant; **M. F. Einecker**, Danly Machine Corp.; **Lowell W. Foster**, Lowell W. Foster Associates, Inc.; **Harold L. Gelgel**, AFWAL/MLLM, Wright-Patterson Air Force Base; **Jay S. Gunasekera**, AFWAL/MLLM, Wright-Patterson Air Force Base; **C. Howard Hamilton**, Science Center, Rockwell International; **Thomas F. Hill**, Grotnes Metalforming Systems, Inc.; **Harding R. Hugo**, Consultant; **Kenneth F. James**, Manufacturing Engineering and Development, Technical Center, General Motors Corp.; **Karl A. Keyes**, Consultant; **Cor Langewis, P.E.** Langewis Consulting & Engineering Inc.; **Robert Charles McFarland**, The Cyril Bath Co.; **Arthur Joseph Moser**, Consultant; **George E. Murray**, Aircraft Hydro-Forming, Inc.; **Alvin G. Neumann**, Technical Consultants International; **Jerome B. Pfeffer**, Quintus Department, ASEA Pressure Systems Inc.; **Richard I. Phillips**, Department of Industrial Education and Technology, Southwest Missouri State University; **Ralph E. Roper**, Wallace Expanding Machines, Inc.; **Felix T. Sasso**, Arrowsmith Industries, Inc.; **Robert Soman, P.E.**, Consulting Engineer; **George Tann**, Congress Tool & Die, Div. of Tann Co.;

CHAPTER 34: Henry F. Classe, P.E., J.D., Cupples Products Div., H. H. Robertson Co.; **Eugene F. Gorman, P.E.**, Teledyne Metal Forming; **Timothy A. Gutowski**, Contour Roll Co.; **George T. Halmos**, Delta Engineering Ltd./LTEE; **Donald R. Hill**, Hill Engineering, Inc.; **Richard O. Pearson**, Roll Form Consultant Services; **Donald D. Penick**, Kirsch Co.; **Charles Prochaska**, Roll Design Services.

CHAPTER 35: Jeffrey M. Downing, Lake Geneva Spindustries, Inc.; **Gary Gates**, Kansas City Div., The Bendix Corp.; **Tony Hudson**, Electrologic, Inc.; **Burton F. Lewis**, BFL Associates.

CHAPTER 36: Rune G. Adolfsson, Technical Dept. HK, ASEA, AB; **Reed Bertolette**, Bertolette Machines, Inc.; **John A. Gillanders**, International Piping Systems, Ltd.; **David A. Johnson**, Fabricating Manufacturers Association; **Norman R. Judge**, Industrial Metal Products Corp.; **George M. Kimmel**, Machine Tool Div., Conrac Corp.; **Patrick E. Oldenburg**, Di-Acro Div., Houdaille Industries, Inc.; **Dale D. Oliver**, Di-Acro Div., Houdaille Industries, Inc.; **Richard I Phillips**, Department of Industrial Education and Technology, Southwest Missouri State University; **Ralph Scroggins**, Tower Oil and Technology Corp.; **Richard A. Sprick**, Di-Acro Div., Houdaille Industries, Inc.; **Ronald R. Stange**, Tools for Bending, Inc.; **Alan Williamson**, Machine Tool Div., Conrac Corp.

CHAPTER 37: Howard Abbott, C. Behrens Machinery Co., Inc.; **James W. Bowman**, Pacific Press and Shear Co.; **John Buta**, Paxson Machine Co.; **R. L. Butchart, Jr.**, Wysong and Miles Co.; **Victor Carbone**, Strippit Div., Houdaille Industries, Inc.; **John Gehring**, Paxson Machine Co.; **Jim Mishek**, Wilson Tool; **Patrick E. Oldenburg**, Di-Arco Div., Houdaille Industries, Inc.; **Dale D. Oliver**, Di-Arco Div., Houdaille Industries, Inc.; **Gary Pappas**, Raskin, Datason Corporation; **Robert L. Rachor**, Lynch Machinery Co., Inc.; **Jerry Rush**, U.S. Amada, Ltd.; **Jack Schneider**, Mate Punch and Die Co.; **Richard A. Sprick**, Di-Arco Div., Houdaille Ind., Inc.; **Richard M. Stein, P.E.**, Strippit Div., Houdaille, Industries, Inc.; **Ronald E. Van**

Wieringen, Wiedemann Div., Warner & Swasey Co.; **Frederic J. Vezina, Jr.**, Strippit Div., Houdaille Industries, Inc.; **Laurie Videle**, W. A. Whitney Corp.

CHAPTER 38: **Robert G. Backus**, The Ajax Manufacturing Co.; **R. F. Boshold**, Mannesmann Demag Wean Co., Hydraulic Machinery Div.; **Thomas G. Johannisson**, ASEA AB; **Paul D. Noble**, Tubular and Bar Div., Mannesmann Demag Wean Co., Engineering Center; **Jerome B. Pfeffer**, Quintus Dept., ASEA Pressure Systems; **Ted A. Schiebold**, Imerman Industries, Inc.; **J. E. Spearman**, Vaughn Div., Wean United, Inc.

CHAPTER 39: **R. S. Dusseau, CMfgE**, Abbey Etna Machine Co.; **Clarence Miller**, Abbey Etna Machine Co.

CHAPTER 40: **Dr. Taylan Altan**, Battelle Columbus Laboratories; **Gene G. Bates**, Acme Div., The Hill Acme Co.; **Kay H. Beseler**, Girard Associates, Inc.; **David A. Dickinson**, Girard Associates, Inc.; **Richard Edmonson**, National Machinery Co.; **Mario Farina**, Erie Press Systems; **Charles W. Frame**, Chambersburg Engineering Co.; **Dale W. Hutchinson**, Metalworking Products Acheson Colloids Co.; **Otto Knapp**, COSA Corp.; **Joseph Leitersdorf, P.E.** Consulting Engineer; **Nick L. Matthews**, Lubricant Div., Russell Products; **Dr. Charles C. Reynolds**, GESCO Inc.; **Robert W. Stansbury**, Metalprep Dept., Pennwalt Corp.

CHAPTER 41: **Gary E. Armour**, Sunbeam Equipment Corp.; **Mary Anton**, Leybold-Heraeus Vacuum Systems Inc.; **Steve Balme**, C. I. Hayes Inc.; **Alan M. Bayer**, Teledyne Vasco; **Robert L. Chaney**, Industrial Furnace Div., Wellman Thermal Systems Corp.; **D. Michael Donovan**, Lindberg Corp.; **Charles A. Divine**, AL Tech Specialty Steel Corp.; **James R. Easterday**, Kolene Corp.; **Anthony G. Fennell**, Fennell Corp.; **Dr. Robert W. Foreman**, Park Chemical Co.; **Edward F. Grady**, C. I. Hayes Inc.; **Richard E. Haimbaugh**, Induction Heat Treating Corp.; **Ronald C. Hanson**, E. B. Systems, Sciaky Bros., Inc., Alleghency International; **V. Sam Hill**, Lake Jackson Research Center, Dow Chemical Co.; **C. N. Hubbard, Jr.** Domestic Sales, Thermatool Corp.; **L. E. Jones**, Lindberg Heat Treating Co.; **Gary LaFlamme**, Leybold-Heraeus Vacuum Systems, Inc.; **W. James Laird, Jr.** Upton Industries, Inc.; **William A. Leeper**, GH-Thornhill Craver; **Q. D. Mehrkam**, Ajax Electric Co.; **J. Howard Mendenhall**, Olin Brass; **Paul J. Mikelonis**, General Casting Corp., **Randall A. Oertel**, AL Tech Specialty Steel Corp.; **John E. O'Neil**, Leeds & Northup Co., A Unit of General Signal Corp.; **George D. Pfaffman**, TOCCO Div., Park-Ohio Industries, Inc.; **Professor Karl B. Rundman**, Dept., of Metallurgical Engineering, Michigan Technological University; **Harry W. Rosenberg**, Technical Services, TIMET; **Michael J. Rothman**, High Temperature Alloys, Cabot Wrought Products Div., Cabot Corp.; **Ole A. Sandven**, Avco Everett Research Laboratory, Inc.; **John W. Smith**, Holcroft/Loftus Div., Thermo Electron Corp.; **Ronald W. Sustich**, Fennell Corp.; **Donald J. Tillack**, Huntington Alloys, Inc.; **George P. Welch**, Ajax Magnethermic Corp.; **Daniel S. Zamborsky**, Research Div., Bendix Corp.; **Stanley Zinn**, Ferrotherm Inc.

CHAPTER 42: **Frank Arsenault**, Bostitch Div., Textron, Inc.; **Richard C. Baubles**, Jacobson Mfg. Co., Inc.; **Wallace Berliner**, Truarc Retaining Rings Div., Waldes Kohinoor, Inc.; **Joseph J. Braychak**, POP Fasteners Div., Emhart Fastener Group; **Lawrence B. Curtis**, Equipment Div., Fisher Gauge Ltd.;

Richard L. Davis, Heli-Coil Products, Div. of Mite Corp.; **W. E. Duffey**, Driv-Lok, Inc.; **Robert S. Eckles**, Brainard Rivet Co.; **Richard B. Ernest**, Penn Engrg & Mfg. Corp.; **Dr. John L. Frater**, Cleveland State University; **Girard S. Haviland**, Engineering Center, Loctite Corp., Industrial Group; **Donald Johnston**, GEMCOR Drivmatic Div.; **Michael M. Joseph**, Southern Screw Div. Farley Metals, Inc.; **Kenneth E. McCullough**, SPS Technologies; **Dr. J. Dean Minford**, Minford Consulting; **John Nasiatka**, Duo-Fast Corp.; **Michael M. Plum**, Maxwell Laboratories, Inc.; **James F. Sullivan**, Acme Packaging, Div. of Interlake, Inc.; **Dr. H. E. Trucks**, Consultant; **Paul W. Wallace**, Aerospace Div., SPS Technologies; **Stephen M. Ward**, Ramsey Piston Ring Div., TRW Automotive Products Inc.

CHAPTER 43: **Professor William Baeslack**, Ohio State University; **Joseph A. Bagley**, Beamo Welding; **Stephen R. Baron**, MG Industries; **Roy E. Beal**, Amalgamated Technolgies, Inc.; **Howard B. Cary**, Advanced Welding Systems Div., Hobart Brother Co.; **Janet Devine**, Sonobond Ultrasonics; **David E. Ferguson**, Duffers Scientific, Inc.; **Hans D. Fricke**, Orgo-Thermit Inc.; **Richard D. Green**, MAPP Products; **Gregory Hall**, Unimation Inc.; **Roy Hardwick**, Explosive Fabricators, Inc.; **Tim Hirthe**, Lucas-Milhaupt, Inc.; **Gene Meyer**, Victor Equipment Co.; **Carl B. Miller**, U.S. Laser Corp.; **Charles C. Pease**, KSM Fastening Systems; **Robert L. Peaslee**, Wall Colmonoy Corp.; **C. W. Philp**, Brazing Products, Handy & Harman; **Michael M. Plum**, Maxwell Laboratories, Inc.; **Andrew Pocalyko**, Detaclad Operations, E.I. duPont deNemours & Co., (retired); **Donald E. Powers**, Leybold-Heraeus Vacuum Systems Inc.; **Jim Powers**, Sciaky Bros., Allegheny International; **Terry N. Raymond**, Plasma Welding Product Specialist, Thermal Dynamics Corp.; **Frederic D. Seaman**, Materials and Manufacturing Technology, IIT Research Institute; **Richard D. Smith**, The Lincoln Electric Co.; **Dietmar E. Spindler**, Manufacturing Technology Inc.; **Richard E. Trillwood**, E. B. Engineering, Inc.; **Terry L. VanderWert**, Laserdyne Div., Data Card Corp.; **Bruce R. Williams**, Fusion, Inc.; **Cecil C. Wristen**, Advanced Robotics Corp.

CHAPTER 44: **Steven A. Cousins**, DuPont Engineering Development Laboratory, E. I. duPont deNemours & Co., Inc.; **Harold R. Marcotte**, Defense Systems Div., Honeywell, Inc.; **Malcolm Mills**, GMF Robotics; **Art Pietrzyk**, Programmable Controller Div., Industrial Computer Group, AllenBradley Co; **Charles K. Watters**, Assembly Machines, Inc.

CHAPTER 45: **Walter G. Bainbridge**, Roto-Finish Co., Inc.; **Davis L. Baughman**, Pangborn Co., A Sohio Co.; **E. W. Bendziunas**, Lea Manufacturing Co.; **Michael C. Burr**, Cogsdill Tool Products, Inc.; **James J. Daly**, Metal Improvement Co.; **Warren B. Depperman**, Cogsdill Tool Products, Inc.; **Thomas R. Dombrowski**, S. S. White Industrial Products, Pennwalt Corp.; **Mike Ferrara**, Ultramatic Equipment Co.; **George A. Gazan**, French Enterprises, Inc.; **L. K. Gillespie**, Kansas City Div., Bendix Corporation.*; **Richard Gillott**, Sales Engineer Spadone Machine Co., Inc.; **Tom Hankins**, Sunnen Products Co.; **R. Z. Herr**, Airblast & Shot Peening, Pangborn Co., A Sohio Co.; **Frank J. Hettes**, Weiler Brush Co., Inc.; **J. Bernard Hignett**, Harper Co.; **John H. Indge**, Peter Wolters of America, Inc.; **William J. Miller**, Jackson Buff Co., A Div. of AMCA International Corp.; **Roy B. Pleiman**, United Technologies Elliott; **Lawrence J. Rhoades**, Extrude Hone Corp.; **Richard R.**

Robinson, Ex-Cell-O Corp., Micromatic Operations; **Robert C. Sasena**, Anderson Operations, Dresser Industries, Inc.; **Alfred F. Scheider**, Osborn Manufacturing Corp., A Div. of AMCA International Corp.; **Dr. William J. Westerman**, Cogsdill Tool Products, Inc.
*Operated for the U.S. Department of energy by The Bendix Corporation, Kansas City Div., under Contract No. DE-AC04-76DPO0613.

CHAPTER 46: **John F. Jumer**, Alchemize Corp. and Electro Glo Co.; **Jerome F. Miller**, Chemtool, Inc.; **Daniel E. Duffy**, Automated Chemical Systems; **Joseph V. Otrhalek**, Industrial Chemical Specialties Div., Detrex Chemical Industries, Inc.; **Graham Pendleton**, Kleer-Flo Co.; **H. M. Sadwith**, Industrial Washing Machine Corp.; **Avery B. Smith**, Automated Chemical Systems.

CHAPTER 47: **Alan Brooks**, Waldes Kohinoor, Inc.; **Mike D'Angelo**, Metal Finishing, MacDermid, Inc.; **Dr. George D. DiBari**, International Nickel, Inc.; **Max DiMarco**, Plating on Plastics, MacDermid, Inc; **Dr. Otto Kardos**, M & T Chemicals, Inc.; **Joe A. Miglionico**, Sifco Selective Plating Div., Sifco Industries, Inc.; **Joe C. Norris**, Sifco Selective Plating Div., Sifco Industries, Inc.; **Richard F. Rapids**, Rapid Electroplating Process, Inc.; **Hal Thrasher**, MacDermid, Inc.; **Phil Stapleton**, Stapleton Co. & Associates.

CHAPTER 48: **C. H. Alexander**, Technical Enterprises, Inc.; **John Alexander**, Eastern Steel Div., Armco, Inc.; **Charles A. Baer**, Charles A. Baer Associates; **Mirza Baig**, Aldoa Co.; **Clark Bergman**, Multi-Arc Vacuum Systems, Inc.; **Norman F. Callahan**, Cidona, Inc.; **Manek Dustoor**, Powder Metal Products Div., Imperial Clevite, Inc.; **John H. Eggleston**, Lindberg, A Unit of General Signal Corp.; **Robert D. Fisher**, Lindberg, A Unit of General Signal Corp.; **Doug H. Harris**, APS-Materials, Inc.; **Russell J. Hill**, Temescal, Div. of the BOC Group, Inc.; **Frederick C. Hornbeck**, Southwall Technologies, Inc.; **Dr. B. L. Kindberg**, American Hoechst Corp.; **Thomas C. Leister**, SPS Technologies; **Lee H. Miller**, Elitine Corp.; **Ken Moyer**, Hoegenaes Corp.; **Ed Meyer**, Barrett Centrifugals, Inc.; **Dennis R. Nichols**, Thin Film Technology Div., Varian Associates; **Dr. Stefan Reineck**, Leybold-Heraeus Technologies; **Gary T. Satterfield**, American Hot Dip Galvanizers Assn., Inc.; **George E. Stephens**, USA, Ltd.; **Kenneth E. Steube**, Ivadizing Technology, McDonnell Aircraft Co.; **Merle L. Thorpe**, TAFA, Inc.; **George Updike**, Porcelain Enamel Coatings, Ferro Corp.; **Richard P. Vento**, Bernex Div., Sylvester & Co.; **Dr. Wesley H. Weisenberger**, Ion Implant Services.

CHAPTER 49: **George E. F. Brewer**, Coatings Consultants; **Dr. John C. Graham**, Dept. of Interdisciplinary Technology, Eastern Michigan University; **Glen L. Muir**, Finishing Div., Graco, Inc.; **Daniel C. Riter**, Powder Coatings Dept., Coatings Div., Ferro Corp.

CHAPTER 50: **Lewis H. Bell**, Bell and Associates, Inc.; **George E. F. Brewer**, Coating Consultants; **Benjamin J. Cieslik**, General Motors Corp.; **Steven A. Cousins**, DuPont Engineering Development, Laboratory, E.I. DuPont de Nemours & Co., Inc.; **Hillman E. Deaton**, Riley-Beird Co., Div. of U.S. Riley Corp.; **Eugene J. Dreger**, Occupational Safety and Health Administration, U.S. Department of Labor; **William E. Gaskin**, American Metal Stamping Association; **Herbert W. Goetz**, Product Safety, Cincinnati Incorporated; **Susan Hanke**, Wausau Insurance Companies; **Roger P. Harrison**, Rockford Safety Equipment Co.; **Joseph W. Hart**, Loss Prevention Department, Liberty Mutual Insurance Co.; **Harold R. Mull**, Bell and Associates, Inc.; **Frederick W. Lang**, General Motors Corp.; **Harry C. Lein**, Pyrotronics; **Douglas E. Morse**, Deere & Co.; **Cathy Shutway**, Safety & Health, Forging Industry Association.

The editorial development and production of this volume involved many sources both within and outside of SME. This group includes:

EDITORIAL

Thomas J. Drozda
Director of Reference
Publications
Society of Manufacturing
Engineers

William H. Cubberly
Consulting Editor
W. H. Cubberly & Associates

Ramon Bakerjian
Staff Editor
Society of Manufacturing
Engineers

Kurt Miska
Consulting Editor
Creative Communications

Frances Kania
Editorial Secretary
Society of Manufacturing
Engineers

TYPESETTING

Gary Price
Typesetter
Graphis 6

Shari L. Smith
Supervisor
Society of Manufacturing
Engineers

GRAPHICS

Frank Bania
Assistant Manager
Society of Manufacturing
Engineers

Kevin Rinna
Illustrator/Keyliner
Society of Manufacturing
Engineers

Ann Doman
Illustrator/Keyliner
Society of Manufacturing
Engineers

Jill Stevenson
Illustrator/Keyliner
Society of Manufacturing
Engineers

Special acknowledgements to the staffs of:

Art Works
Dearborn, Michigan

Truzzi & Treer
Ann Arbor, Michigan

M. G. Advertising
Farmington Hills,
Michigan

**W. H. Cubberly &
Associates**
Aurora, Ohio

SME

The Society of Manufacturing Engineers is a professional society dedicated to advancing manufacturing through the continuing education of manufacturing managers, engineers, technicians, and other manufacturing professionals. The specific goal of the Society is to advance scientific knowledge in the field of manufacturing and to apply its resources to research, writing, publishing, and disseminating information. "The purpose of SME is to serve the professional needs of the many types of practitioners that make up the manufacturing community...The collective goal of the membership is the sharing and advancement of knowledge in the field of manufacturing for the good of humanity."

The Society was founded in 1932 as the American Society of Tool Engineers (ASTE). From 1960 to 1969 it was known as the American Society of Tool and Manufacturing Engineers (ASTME), and in January 1970 it became the Society of Manufacturing Engineers. The changes in name reflect the evolution of the manufacturing engineering profession and the growth and increasing sophistication of a technical society that has gained an international reputation for being the most knowledgeable and progressive voice in the field.

Associations of SME—The Society provides complete technical services and membership benefits through a number of associations. Each serves a special interest area. Members may join these associations in addition to SME. The associations are:

Association for Finishing Processes of SME (AFP/SME)
Computer and Automated Systems Association of SME (CASA/SME)
Machine Vision Association of SME (MVA/SME)
North American Manufacturing Research Institute of SME
(NAMRI/SME)

Users Group of SME (MAP/TOP)
Composites Group of SME (CoGSME)
Electronics Manufacturing Group of SME (EM/SME)

Members and Chapters — The Society and its associations have 80,000 members in 73 countries, most of whom are affiliated with SME's 300-plus senior chapters. The Society also has some 8,000 student members and more than 150 student chapters at colleges and universities.

Publications—The Society is involved in various publication activities encompassing handbooks, textbooks, videotapes, and magazines. Current periodicals include:

Manufacturing Engineering
Manufacturing Insights (a video magazine)
SME Technical Digest
SME News
Journal of Manufacturing Systems

Certification—This SME program formally recognizes manufacturing managers, engineers, and technologists based on experience and knowledge. The key certification requirement is successful completion of a two-part written examination covering (1) engineering fundamentals and (2) an area of manufacturing specialization.

Educational Programs—The Society sponsors a wide range of educational activities, including conferences, clinics, in-plant courses, expositions, publications and other educational/training media, professional certification, and the SME Manufacturing Engineering Education Foundation.

CONTENTS

DESK EDITION

SYMBOLS AND ABBREVIATIONS

The following is a list of symbols and abbreviations in general use throughout this volume. Supplementary and/or derived units, symbols, and abbreviations which are peculiar to specific subject matter are listed within chapters.

A

A	Ampere
AA	Arithmetic average
ABN	Amber boron nitride
ABS	Acrylonitrile butadiene styrene
a-c	Alternating current
AC	Adaptive control
ACC	Adaptive control for constraint
ACD	Annealed cold drawn
A/cm^2	Ampere per square centimeter
ACO	Adaptive control for optimization
A/D	Analog/digital
AFM	Abrasive flow machining
AFMDC	Air Force Machinability Data Center
AGMA	American Gear Manufacturers Association
$A/in.^2$	Ampere per square inch
AISI	American Iron and Steel Institute
Al	Aluminum
ALGOL	Algorithmic language
Al_2O_3	Aluminum oxide (alumina)
ANSI	American National Standards Institute
API	American Petroleum Institute
APT	Automatic programming tool
ASLE	American Society of Lubrication Engineers
ASM	American Society for Metals
ASME	American Society of Mechanical Engineers
ASP	Antisegregation process
ASTM	American Society for Testing and Materials
AUTOSPOT	Automatic system for positioning of tools
AWG	American wire gauge

B

BASIC	Beginner's all-purpose symbolic instruction code
B_4C	Boron carbide
BCD	Binary coded data
Be'	Baume' specific gravity scale
Bhn	Brinell hardness
BOD	Biological oxidation demand
B/P	Blueprint
BTR	Behind the tape reader
BTU	British thermal unit
$BTU/in.^2$	British thermal unit per square inch
BUE	Built-up edge
BZN	Borazon brand cubic boron nitride (G.E.)

C

C	Coulomb, Celsius or carbon
CAD/CAM	Computer aided design/Computer aided manufacturing
cal	Calorie
CAL	Conversional algebraic language
cal/cm^3	Calorie per cubic centimeter
$cal/in.^3$	Calorie per cubic inch
CAMI	Coated Abrasive Manufacturers Institute
CAPP	Computer aided process planning
Cb	Columbium
CbC	Columbium carbide
CBN	Cubic boron nitride
cfm	Cubic foot per minute
CIMS	Computer integrated manufacturing system
CL	Cutter location
cm	Centimeter
cm^2	Square centimeter
$cm^3/A{\cdot}s$	Cubic centimeter per ampere second
CMfgE	Certified manufacturing engineer
cm^2/hr	Square centimeter per hour
cm^2/m	Square centimeter per meter
cm^2/min	Square centimeter per minute
cm^3/min	Cubic centimeter per minute
CMOS	Complementary metal oxide semiconductor
cm/s	Centimeter per second
cm^3/s	Cubic centimeter per second
CNC	Computer numerical control
Co	Cobalt
Co.	Company
CO	Compliance officer
CO_2	Carbon dioxide
COBOL	Common Business Oriented Language
COD	Chemical oxidation demand
COM	Computer output microfilm
Corp.	Corporation
cP	Centipoise
CPM	Crucible Particle Metallurgy
cps	Cycle per second
CPU	Central processing unit
Cr	Chromium
CRT	Cathode ray tube
CSA	Canadian Standards Association
cSt	Centistoke
Ctbr	Counterbore
Cu	Copper
CVD	Chemical vapor deposition

D

dB	Decibel
d-c	Direct current
DC	Data communication
DCF	Discounted cash flow
DCTL	Direct-coupled transistor logic
DDA	Digital differential analyzer
DEC	Digital Equipment Corp.
deg or °	Degree
diam	Diameter
DIN	Deutscher Normenausschuss (German Standards Organization)
Div.	Division
DNC	Direct numerical control
DRO	Digital readout
DTL	Diode transistor logic
DX	Data transfer

E

E	Modulus of elasticity
EBG	Electrolytic belt grinding
EBM	Electron beam machining
EBW	Electron beam welding
ECD	Electrochemical deburring
ECDG	Electrochemical discharge grinding
ECEA	End cutting edge angle
ECG	Electrochemical grinding
ECH	Electrochemical honing
ECM	Electrochemical machining
ECP	Electrochemical polishing
ECT	Electrochemical turning
ECVT	Electrochemical vibratory tumbling
EDC	Extended data comparison
EDG	Electrical discharge grinding
EDM	Electrical discharge machining
EDP	Electronic data processing
EDWC	Electrical discharge wire cutting
EEM	Electrolytic end milling
EHD	Elastohydrodynamic
EIA	Electronic Industries Association
ELP	Electropolishing
EMD	Electromechanical drilling
EMM	Electromechanical machining
EMT	Electromechanical turning
EOB	End of block
EOP	End of program
EOT	End of tape
EP	Extreme pressure
EPA	Environmental Protection Agency
EPROM	Erasable programmable read only memory
Eq.	Equation
ER	Electro-Ream
ESCM	Electro-Stream chemical milling
ESM	Electro-Stream milling
ESR	Electroslag remelting
EVM	Electrovapor machining
EXAPT	Extended subset of APT

F-G-H

F	Fahrenheit
FCI	Flux changes per inch
fd	Farad
FDX	Full duplex
$FeCl_3$	Ferric chloride
FIFO	First in, first out
Fig.	Figure
fpm	Foot per minute
fps	Foot per second
fpt	Feed per tooth
FRN	Feed rate number
FSK	Frequency shift keying
ft	Foot
ft^2	Square foot
ft^3	Cubic foot
ft^3/hr	Cubic foot per hour
FTS	Full top skive

gal	Gallon
g/cm^3	Gram per cubic centimeter
GDM	Glow discharge machining
GJ/m^3	Giga Joule per cubic meter
g/L	Gram per liter
GP	General purpose
GPa	Giga pascal
GPAC	General purpose aqueous coolant
GPG	Grain per gallon
gpm	Gallon per minute
GPO	General purpose oil
GPS	General purpose soluble oil
GR	Grinding ratio
GT	Group technology

H	Henry
HAZ	Heat-affected zone
HBM	Horizontal boring machine
HCl	Hydrochloric acid
H_2CrO_4	Chromic acid
HD	Heavy duty
HDAC	Heavy duty aqueous coolant
HDM	Hydrodynamic machining
HDO	Heavy duty oil
HDX	Half duplex
Hf	Hafnium
HF	Hone-Forming
HfC	Hafnium carbide
Hg	Mercury
HI-E	High efficiency
H_2O	Water
hp	Horsepower
hp/in.	Horsepower per inch
$hp/in.^3/min$	Horsepower per cubic inch per minute
hr	Hour
H_2S_4	Sulphuric acid
HSS	High speed steel
HTM	High technology materials
Hz	Cycles per second

I-J

I	Current or Moment of inertia
IC	Inscribed circle or Integrated circuit
ID	Inside diameter
IGA	Intergranular attack
in. or "	Inch
in.^{2}	Square inch
in.^{3}	Cubic inch
in./ft	Inch per linear foot
in.^{2}/ft	Square inch per foot
in.^{2}/hr	Square inch per hour
in.^{3}/hr	Cubic inch per hour
in./in.	Inch per inch
in.-lbf	Inch pound force
in./min	Inch per minute
in.^{2}/min	Square inch per minute
in.^{3}/min	Cubic inch per minute
in.^{3}/min/in.	Cubic inch per minute per inch
in./pass	Inch per pass
in./s	Inch per second
I/O	Input-output
IP	Index of performance or United Kingdom Standard
ipm	Inch per minute
ipr	Inch per revolution
IRR	Internal rate of return
IRS	Internal Revenue Service
ISO	International Standards Organization
J	Joule
J/cm^2	Joule per square centimeter
JIC	Joint Industry Conference

K-L

kc	Kilocycles
kg	Kilogram
kg/mm^2	Kilogram per square millimeter
kg/mm^3	Kilogram per cubic millimeter
kHz	Kilohertz
kl	Kiloliter
kN	KiloNewton
kN·m	KiloNewton meter
kohm	Kilo-ohm
kPa	Kilopascal
ksi	1000 pounds per square inch
kV	Kilovolt
kW	Kilowatt
kW/cm^3/min	Kilowatt per cubic centimeter per minute
L	Liter
lb	Pound mass
lbf	Pound force
lbf-ft	Foot pound
lbf/in.	Pound force per inch
lb/gal	Pound mass per gallon
lb/in.^{3}	Pound mass per cubic inch

LBM	Laser beam machining
L/d	Length to diameter
LD	Light duty
LED	Light emitting diode
LH	Left hand
lin	Linear
LMC	Least material condition
L/min	Liter per minute
LPM	Lines per minute
LS	Low stress
LSD	Least significant digit
LSI	Large scale integration

M

m	Meter
m^2	Square meter
m^3	Cubic meter
mA	Milliampere
mach	Machine
man	Manual
max	Maximum
MC	Molybdenum carbide
MCR	Master control relay
MCTI	Metal Cutting Tool Institute
MCU	Machine control unit
MD	Medium duty
MDI	Manual data input
MFM	Magnetic field machining
Mg	Magnesium
MgO	Magnesium Oxide
m^3/hr	Cubic meter per hour
MHz	Megahertz
min	Minimum or Minute
MIS	Management information system
ml	Milliliter
mm	Millimeter
mm^2	Square millimeter
mm^3	Cubic millimeter
MMC	Maximum material condition
mm^3/hr	Cubic millimeter per hour
m/min	Meter per minute
mm/m	Millimeter per linear meter
mm/min	Millimeter per minute
mm^2/min	Square millimeter per minute
mm^3/min	Cubic millimeter per minute
mm/mm	Millimeter per millimeter
mm/pass	Millimeter per pass
mm/rev	Millimeter per revolution
mm/s	Millimeter per second
mm^2/s	Square millimeter per second
mm^3/s	Cubic millimeter per second
mm^3/s/mm	Cubic millimeter per second per millimeter
Mn	Manganese
MnS	Manganese sulfide
Mo	Molybdenum
MODEM	MODulator DEModulator
MOS	Metal oxide semiconductor
MoS$_2$	Molybdenum disulfide

MPa	Megapascal
MR	Machinability rating
MRP	Material requirements planning
ms	Millisecond
M/s	Meter per second
MSI	Medium scale integration
MTBF	Mean time between failure
MTS	Medium top skive
MTTR	Mean time to repair
mV	Millivolt

N

N	Newton or Nitrogen
N_2	Nitrogen
NaCl	Sodium chloride
$NaClO_3$	Sodium chlorate
$NaNO_2$	Sodium nitrite
$NaNO_3$	Sodium nitrate
NaOH	Sodium hydroxide
NAS	National Aerospace Standards
Na_2SO_4	Sodium sulphate
NbN	Niobium nitride
NBR	Nitrile rubber
NC	Numerical control
NCD	Normalized cold drawn
Nd:YAG	Neodymium-doped, yttrium aluminum garnet
NEC	National Electrical Code
neg	negative
NEMA	National Electrical Manufacturers Association
NFPA	National Fire Protection Association
Ni	Nickel
NIOSH	National Institute for Occupational Safety and Health
NLGI	National Lubricating Grease Institute
N·m	Newton meter
N/mm	Newton per millimeter
N/mm^2	Newton per square millimeter
N·m/s	Newton meter per second (Watt)
NMTBA	National Machine Tool Builders Association
No.	Number
Nontrad	Nontraditional
NPV	Net present value
NR	Nose radius
NS	Nonstaining
NTS	No top skive

O-P

O_2	Oxygen
OA	Overaging
OD	Outside diameter
OEM	Original equipment manufacturer
OSHA	Occupational Safety and Health Administration
OTM	Overtempered martensite

oz	Ounce
P	Phosphorus or Poise
Pa	Pascal
PAM	Plasma arc machining
Pa·s	Pascal second
PAU	Position analog unit
Pb	Lead
PC	Programmable controller
PCB	Printed circuit board
pcs/hr	Pieces per hour
pcs/shift	Pieces per shift
PD	Plastic deformation or Pitch diameter
PD^2	Plastically deformed debris
PE	Professional engineer
PERA	Production Engineering Research Association
pH	Acidity measure
PID	Proportional, integral derivative
PM or P/M	Powder metallurgy
pos	Positive
PPD	Pour point depressant
ppm	Parts per million
PROM	Programmable read only memory
PRS	Product relative step
psi	Pound per square inch
pt	Part
PTC	Programmed turning center
PVD	Physical vapor deposition
PWM	Pulse width modulated

R-S

R	Resistance
R_a	Arithmetic average roughness
$R_{A, B, or C}$	Rockwell hardness—A, B, or C scale
RAM	Random access memory
R_B	Rockwell hardness—B scale
R_C	Rockwell hardness—C scale
RCTL	Resistor capacitor transistor logic
Ref	Reference
R/O	Reverse osmosis
R&O	Rust and oxidation inhibited
ROM	Read only memory
rpm	Revolution per minute
RTL	Resistor transistor logic
RUM	Rotary ultrasonic machining

s or sec	Second
S	Sulfur
SACD	Spheroidized annealed cold drawn
SAE	Society of Automotive Engineers
s/cm^2	Second per square centimeter
SCR	Silicon controlled rectifier
SE	Selective etch
SES	Stationary ElectroStream
sfm	Surface feet per minute
SHF	Synthetic hydrocarbon fluids
Si	Silicon
SI	International System of Units

s/in.^{2}	Second per square inch		yr	Year
SiO$_2$	Silicon dioxide			
SME	Society of Manufacturing Engineers		ZFM	Zero force machining
Sn	Tin		Zn	Zinc
S-N	Stress vs. number of cycles until failure		Zr	Zirconium
SSI	Small scale integration		ZrO$_2$	Zirconium oxide
SSU	Seconds Saybolt Universal			
St	Stoke			
STEM	Shaped Tube Electrolytic Machining			

T-U-V

t	Metric ton
Ta	Tantalum
TaC	Tantalum carbide
Ti	Titanium
TiC	Titanium carbide
TiN	Titanium nitride
TIR	Total indicator runout or Total indicator reading
TJ	Thin joint
TLV	Threshold limit valve
TMEH	Tool and Manufacturing Engineers Handbook
tol	Tolerance
tpi	Threads per inch
TPI	Teeth per inch
TRS	Transverse rupture strength
TSCA	Toxic Substances Control Act
TTL	Transistor transistor logic
TWA	Time weighted average
UAM	Ultrasonically assisted machining
uhp	Unit horsepower
UNC	Unified coarse thread
UNF	Unified fine thread
USM	Ultrasonic machining
UTM	Untempered martensite
UTS	Ultimate tensile strength
V	Vanadium or Volt
VBM	Vertical boring machine
VC	Vanadium carbide
VI	Viscosity index
VII	Viscosity index improver
vol	Volume
VTL	Vertical turret lathe

μ	Coefficient of friction
μ A	Microampere
μ fd	MicroFarad
μ in.	Microinch (micron)
μ m	Micrometer
μ s	Microsecond
Ω	Ohm
π	Pi (3.14159...)
$	Dollar
$\approx$	Approximately
$\pm$	Plus or minus
$/hr	Dollar per hour
$	Dollar
%	Percent
$\perp$	Perpendicular to
//	Parallel to

W-Y-Z

W	Watt or Tungsten
WB$_2$	Tungsten boride
WC	Tungsten carbide
WC-Co	Tungsten carbide with cobalt binder
W/cm^2	Watt per square centimeter
W/in.^{2}	Watt per square inch
WJM	Water jet machining
W/mm	Watt per millimeter

COMPUTER-INTEGRATED MANUFACTURING

INTRODUCTION

The importance of computer-integrated manufacturing (CIM) to the future of U.S. manufacturing cannot be overstated. It is a key ingredient in improving the productivity, efficiency, and profitability of the U.S. industrial base and in regaining a competitive position in the world marketplace.

Computer-integrated manufacturing is the view of manufacturing that recognizes that the different steps in the development of a manufactured product are interrelated and can be accomplished more effectively and efficiently with computers. These relationships are based not simply on the physical part or product being produced but also on the data that define and direct each step in the process. Controlling, organizing, and integrating the data that drive the manufacturing process through the application of modern computer technology effectively integrates all the steps in the manufacturing process into one coherent entity. Such integration should yield efficiencies not possible from a more segmented approach to manufacturing.

Although CIM implies integrating *all* steps in the manufacturing process, in practice many companies have achieved significant benefits from implementing only partial CIM systems (those in which only some manufacturing steps are integrated). In fact, it is likely that no company has achieved full integration to date. Both situations—those in which all or only some manufacturing sequences are integrated—are accurately called CIM systems.

DEFINITION OF CIM

To translate CIM from a manufacturing theory to a manufacturing tool, a comprehensive definition is required. The interrelationships that exist in any manufacturing environment are many. Technical disciplines such as design engineering and manufacturing engineering interact; departmental issues such as marketing schedules and production schedules interact; and business interests such as financial concerns and strategic concerns interact. All these relationships and many more must be part of a workable definition of CIM.

The National Research Council defines CIM as follows:

> CIM includes all activities from the perception of a need for a product; through the conception, design, and development of the product; and on through production, marketing, and support of the product in use. Every action involved in these activities uses data, whether textual, graphic, or numeric. The computer, today's prime tool for manipulating data, offers the real possibility of integrating the now often fragmented operations of manufacturing into a

single, smoothly operating system. This approach is generally termed computer-integrated manufacturing.

Because of the complexity of CIM, some organizations that promote the understanding and implementation of CIM have found it useful to define CIM graphically by diagramming how technologies and disciplines work together as a unified whole. One of the most inclusive representations is the CIM Wheel developed by the Computer and Automated Systems Association of the Society of Manufacturing Engineers (CASA/SME), as in Fig. 1-1.

The CIM Wheel is composed of five fundamental dimensions:[1] (1) general business management, (2) product and process definition, (3) manufacturing planning and control, (4) factory automation, and (5) information resource management. Each of these five dimensions is a composite of other more specific manufacturing processes that have shown a natural affinity to each other. As a result, each dimension is seen to be a family of automated CIM processes that has emerged naturally because of an affinity among what used to be independent, stand-alone "islands of automation."

The general business management family of processes is arrayed around the periphery of the Wheel. Although seen as an integral part of the manufacturing enterprise, this family of processes was viewed as being the primary link between the rest of the enterprise and the outside world. The general business management family of applications includes a wide range of automated processes from general and cost accounting to marketing, sales, order entry, human relations, decision support, program scheduling, cost status reporting, and labor collection.

The second, third, and fourth families have been arrayed as thirds of the inner circle of the CIM Wheel. The processes represented in these families, however, do not occur in series, moving clockwise from the product and process definition dimension. In reality, all these activities are happening at the same time. It is important to recognize that even though the individual processes in each family of manufacturing processes have a natural affinity for one another, they also are closely tied to processes in other families represented in the Wheel. Most of the interfamily integration occurs through information resource management, the Wheel Hub. Because of the way the technology has grown in most manufacturing environments, *inter*family integration is much more difficult than *intra*family integration.

In many ways, the hub is the most difficult part of the Wheel to comprehend. It has to do with a set

INTRODUCTION

of functions that are called information resource management (IRM).

At the heart of CIM information resource management is the concept of data management. Manufacturing productivity is believed to be linked to the notion of shared or common data, especially between engineering and manufacturing. One of the objectives of CIM information resource management is to break down the walls that have traditionally existed between those two organizations, rendering them, in effect, into one organization through a common database. There are basically two aspects to CIM information resource management. One aspect is intangible and the other is tangible. The intangible (or logical) aspect is the information itself. The tangible (or physical) aspect includes the tools of information such as the computers themselves and also the disk storage devices, printers, plotters, tapes, communication devices, operating systems, and terminals that are used to store, exchange, and process the information.

INDUSTRIES IN THE FOREFRONT OF CIM IMPLEMENTATION

The first industries to take advantage of the potential benefits of partial CIM implementation were aerospace, off-highway equipment, electronics, and automotive, as well as several government facilities. Although the relative size of the companies within these industries varied, as did the number and type of products produced, they all had pressures to be competitive, productive, and responsive. The early participants were companies with the knowledge and the resources to invest in a new methodology. They believed in CIM and planned a systematic approach to its implementation. In addition, the more successful companies had specific improvement areas that were targeted. To this day, larger companies have more readily accepted CIM, although the benefits of CIM apply equally to smaller manufacturers.

Although no company has successfully implemented CIM in its entirety, many companies have made great strides toward that goal. In fact, partial CIM systems have proven very cost effective for many manufacturers. Partial CIM systems may be: those in which a number of key functions are supported by stand-alone computer systems or are still performed manually; those in which there is only some shared data and it is not widely shared throughout the organization; or those in which the integration is limited to linking only some of the functions of engineering, design, manufacturing, marketing, purchasing, and distribution. Essentially all CIM systems today fall into the

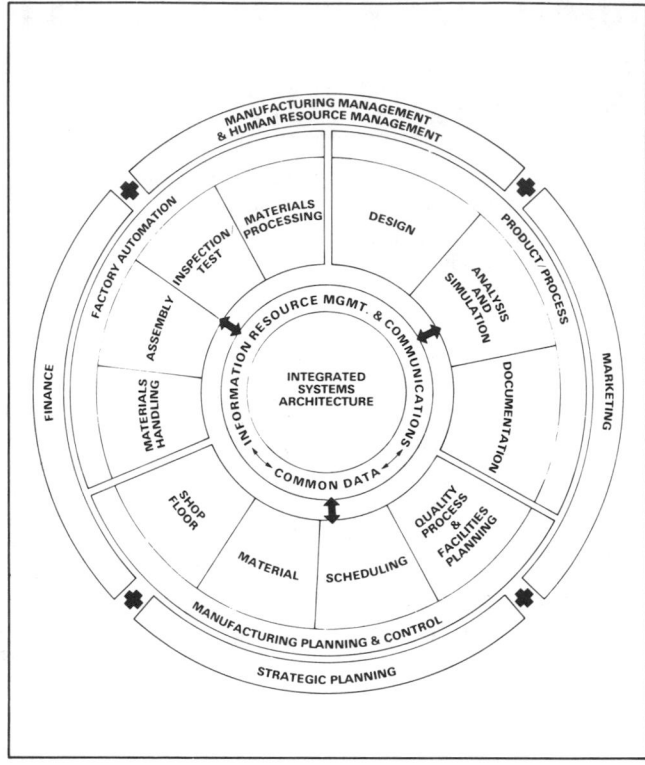

Fig. 1-1 The CIM Wheel emphasizes that CIM encompasses the total manufacturing enterprise. (*CASA/SME*)

latter category. For many companies this is a useful and viable solution that is usually easier to implement and less expensive than full CIM implementation.

A 1984 study by the Committee on the CAD/CAM Interface, formed by the Manufacturing Studies Board of the Commission on Engineering and Technical Systems of the National Research Council, described the experience of leading companies that have made significant progress toward integration.[3] In this study, the CIM efforts of five companies were examined. The benefits realized by these companies during the integration process are shown in Table 1-1. These results are preliminary, representative of 10 to 20-year efforts at integration. Further benefits are expected to accrue as companies approach full integration.

TABLE 1-1
The Benefits of CIM Implementation

Reduction in engineering design cost	15-30%	Increased productivity of production operations (complete assemblies)	40-70%
Reduction in overall lead time	30-60%		
Increased product quality as measured by yield of acceptable product	2-5 times previous level	Increased productivity (operating time) of capital equipment	2-3 times
		Reduction of work in process	30-60%
Increased capability of engineers as measured by extent and depth of analysis in same or less time than previously	3-35 times	Reduction of personnel costs	5-20%

CIM TECHNOLOGIES

The technologies or building blocks that comprise CIM are discussed in this section in four groups: (1) those that relate to the beginning of the product cycle, (2) those that relate to the physical manufacture of the product, (3) those that plan and control the manufacturing process, and (4) those technologies that tie all the others together. It is important to remember that although each technology is discussed as an entity, its operation in a CIM environment enhances the benefits the technology has to offer a manufacturer.

BEGINNING THE PRODUCT CYCLE

Computer-aided design (CAD) is the principal technology that begins a product design cycle. Computer-aided design actually comprises a number of technologies involved in the creation and analysis of a design—whether that design is a three-dimensional part to be machined, a printed circuit board, or a plant layout. In the CIM environment, the design data generated on the CAD system is used by other CIM technologies in the manufacture of the product.

Computer-Aided Design

Computer-aided design equipment allows a designer to create images of parts, integrated circuits, assemblies, and models of virtually anything else—from molecules to manufacturing facilities—at a graphics workstation connected to a computer. These images become the definition of a new design, or the modification of an existing one, and are assigned geometric, mass, kinematic, material, and other properties simply by the user interacting with the computer.

The image on the screen replaces the paper on the drawing board. The data that describes and defines the geometry displayed on the screen is calculated by the computer and stored in the computer's database. CAD allows the designer to be more creative by making it easier to experiment with many different designs and to be more efficient by using existing design data already stored in the same computer database.

In simpler applications, CAD reduces the amount of paperwork for drafting and design. Complete engineering drawings can be created without ever lifting a pen. The savings in drafting time and expense alone have often paid for a CAD system in a very short time. More important than the reduction in the direct cost of drafting is the reduction in the possibility for error that exists when different versions of a drawing are circulating throughout an organization.

Mechanical CAD systems. Mechanical design software allows a user to translate ideas on a product design into a geometric model of that design through the use of interactive graphics. The model can be created in two, two and one half, or three dimensions, depending on the capability of the CAD system and the type of part to be modeled. While two dimensions are usually adequate for flat parts, two and one half give more information for parts that don't need the side walls detailed; the most sophisticated modeling is done in three dimensions. Three-dimensional models are required to describe the three-dimensional features of most mechanical parts. Three dimensional capability is also necessary for multi-axis machining, and gives better accuracy in later NC programming.

Geometric information is stored in a database that can then be used for other manufacturing functions by other software. The geometric database is critical to the implementation of the CIM concept through proper database and data flow management. In the ideal CIM environment, the same data that describes one part, for example, can be used to create the sequence of operations that will make that part; the data can be used to design the fixtures that will hold the part; and the data can input other programs to aid in scheduling shop floor operations or in ordering raw materials. In other words, the data can be used not only by design engineering, but by manufacturing, administration, purchasing, and maintenance personnel. And because that data is entered once and is invariant, the opportunity for error throughout an organization is dramatically decreased.

Solids modeling is a relatively new feature of CAD systems. This capability goes well beyond the visualization of a solid shape on the screen. Solids modeling provides the most complete geometric and mathematical description of a part geometry possible to date. This data is particularly important if the model is to be used as the basis for computer-aided engineering (CAE), for generating mass properties of the part, or for generating the NC data to machine the part.

Electrical/electronics CAD systems. The electrical/electronics design area includes the printed circuit board (PCB), integrated circuit (IC), large scale integrated circuit (LSI), and very large scale integrated circuit (VLSI) industries. As recently as 5 years ago, this area was served mostly by some of the two-dimensional CAD systems available. These systems largely concentrated on the layout of these electronics devices. Since that time, the electronics CAE industry has emerged to address the more complex tasks associated with electronic design.

Traditional CAD systems for electronics design handled the schematic capture, component placement and routing, and the generation of the artwork as well as the necessary documentation. Circuit analysis and simulation was done on a mainframe computer or by hand. Today's electronics CAE systems can encompass all the tasks involved in electronics design, from circuit design to analysis, design verification, and simulation. The ability to handle the complete design cycle, plus the flexibility of analyzing different designs, determining the cost differential associated with substituting different components in a design, is driving the market from CAD to CAE.

Architecture, engineering and construction CAD systems. CAD systems applied to architectural applications provide the tools to model a design concept, produce the architectural production drawings, perform space and facilities planning, produce the contract drawings, and to produce schedules and bills of materials that are required for the electrical, plumbing, and structural work in a facility.

Technical publications. Technical publications is a growing area of importance for CAD systems. Almost every manufacturer is faced with the need to provide technical documentation on products, write proposals for sales or other business activities, and to publish product literature as well as annual reports.

Specialized software allows a CAD system to take a design (a product design or an illustrated parts breakdown) that resides in the CAD engineering database, merge that design with text on the CAD screen, and through this merger, develop

CIM TECHNOLOGIES

the exact format of a document that can then be printed out on a laser printer or sent to a phototypesetter for subsequent publishing. CAD system software exists that also allows business graphics to be generated and halftone photographs to be merged with text.

Computer-Aided Engineering

Computer-aided engineering (CAE) is the technology that analyzes a design and simulates its operation to determine its adherence to design rules and its performance characteristics. Today, CAE is almost two separate technologies: one is CAE applied to mechanical design and one is CAE applied to electronics design. Common elements, however, do exist. Both of these subdivisions involve subjecting a design to extensive analyses, simulating its performance, and verifying the design against physical laws and/or accepted industry standards. But the differences that lie in performing these steps on a mechanical design and on an electronics design are quite significant. Until recently, different companies supplied CAD software and systems for mechanical CAE and electronics CAE. In fact, the growing demand for electronics CAE spawned a new industry with new participants and new hardware/software concepts.

Mechanical CAE. As was mentioned previously, mechanical CAE takes the mechanical part design and subjects it to a variety of engineering analyses. While analyses have been performed by computer for many years (CAE is actually the oldest aspect of CAD), the preprocessing required to put design data in an acceptable form for a computer was a lengthy procedure. With computer assistance, these techniques are easier and faster to execute. Color graphics also simplifies interpretation.

Mechanical CAE programs include finite element analysis (FEA) to evaluate the structural characteristics of a part and advanced kinematics programs to study complex motions of linkages and mechanisms. Other programs might evaluate thermal stress or fluid mechanics. The CAE analysis data may be displayed in graphic form.

The ability to design a part and test it before ever cutting a piece of metal has obvious economies. Less tangible are the benefits in design freedom, the benefits of allowing a designer the flexibility to look at several alternate designs, and the ability to use existing designs of similar parts stored in the same computer database. The more critical the structural integrity of the product, the more important is the use of mechanical CAE technology.

Electronics CAE. If CAE is an option in mechanical design, CAE is a necessity in electronics design. It would be impossible to design a complex integrated circuit without the benefit of a computer. And more and more, complex printed circuit board designs are being captured and simulated on CAE systems.

Electrical/electronics CAE capabilities include design capture, design verification, functional simulation, circuit simulation, timing verification, and netlist generation. Each one of these technical analyses are required to make sure that a printed circuit board or a VLSI operate properly. These functions had traditionally been performed by computer, but until recently on a mainframe in a batch mode. CAE systems provide the engineer with the ability to interact with the design and see the effects in a graphical form.

Computer-Aided Process Planning

One of the bigger hurdles that CIM must overcome is closing the gap between CAD and CAM. Technologies exist to minimize this hurdle, one of the most important being computer-aided process planning (CAPP).

Computer-aided process planning systems are, in effect, expert systems that capture the knowledge of a specific manufacturing environment plus generic manufacturing engineering principles. This knowledge is then applied to a new part design to create the plan for the physical manufacture of the part. This plan specifies the actual machinery employed in the part production, the sequence of operations to be performed, the tooling, speed and feeds, and any other data that is required to transform the design to a finished product. To use CAPP most effectively in a CIM environment, the design should originate on a CAD system and be electronically transferred to the CAPP system from the database.

CAPP draws on the geometric model of the part to be produced, generated in the CAD system, and matches the characteristics and components of that part to the production machinery on the factory floor. This technology will develop the process sheets or routings needed to manufacture a part.

Because a computer-aided process planning system contains information on all parts being produced at any given time, it is able to contribute to more efficient machinery utilization. Because CAPP determines how a part will be made, it is a factor in determining the cost of manufacturing the product.

A CAPP system will provide a set of instructions on how to make a part, in what sequence the process steps shall be executed, and what machines, tools/fixtures, workcenters, and labor skills will be required. A process planning system, manual or automatic, must be constantly updated to reflect a company's total manufacturing capability. Process plans must change as, for example, new machinery is procured and new quality control procedures or robots are introduced.

Computer-aided process planning systems are of two basic types: variant and generative. The variant method of process planning is the most commonly used method today. This method develops a process plan by modifying an existing plan that is selected using group technology principles, namely coding and classification. Some form of parts classification and coding is essential to expedite the location of previously developed plans, which are to be adopted as is or modified and adopted, and to specify the processing plan for a new part.

Generative process planning systems incorporate into their database a body of manufacturing logic, the capacities of existing machinery, standards, specifications, and the like. Based on the part description (geometry and material) and finished specifications, the computer then selects from this stored knowledge the optimum method of producing the part and automatically generates the process plan.

MANUFACTURING THE PRODUCT

The physical manufacture of a product involves a number of interrelated technologies. By using CAD and CAE to create and analyze the design and by using CAPP and GT to organize, plan, and control the individual manufacturing steps, the manufacturing enterprise must now control the processing of the physical materials that will become a product or a part.

The production process is complex. Raw materials, fixtures, tools, or components must be delivered to the specified production machinery in a timely fashion, dictated by a production control system. Materials and/or components must be accurately loaded and fixtured, if necessary, onto a machine bed or other work surface. The production machinery itself must be properly tooled for the part to be made, and it must have directions on how to perform the required operation. After machining, assembly, or whatever other operation is performed, the finished or semifinished part must be moved to the next logical step in its production, be that another machine station, a test stand, a packaging operation, a loading dock for shipment, or a storage location.

In an automated environment, all these operations must be monitored and controlled. Progress, as well as discrepancies, through the production process must be reported, at least in summary fashion, to manufacturing management.

Unlike the design technologies, which are predominantly software related, the physical manufacturing or production operations are a combination of hardware and software. The hardware has been around for as long as manufacturing has existed. Refinements have advanced conventional machine tools into complex machining centers or flexible manufacturing systems (FMSs), lift trucks into automated guided vehicles (AGVs), and shop floor data collection devices from clipboards into data entry terminals and bar code readers.

Manufacturing Machinery

Manufacturing machinery encompasses machine tools, manufacturing cells, flexible manufacturing systems, automated assembly equipment, transfer lines, and inspection equipment.

Machine tools include machinery for metalcutting operations such as drilling, milling, and boring and for metalforming machinery such as presses, forges, and extrusion machinery.

Manufacturing cells and flexible manufacturing systems are

so closely related that it is difficult to discuss them separately. Computer technology was first applied to very high volume and very low volume production operations. High-volume repetitive manufacturing implemented "hard automation," typified by automotive transfer lines. Low-volume aerospace-type industries were pioneers of numerically controlled machine tools. The middle ground of manufacturing, with volumes too high for stand-alone machine tools and too low for dedicated automation systems such as transfer lines, went for a long time before adapting existing automation technologies to its particular production requirements.

Historically, machining cells are small groups of machine tools linked by material handling equipment. All elements of the cell may be computer controlled, and the individual controls may be able to communicate with each other as necessary to coordinate the operation of the cell. It is possible to have a cell of co-located machines with manual material transfer and without common computer control, although current usage of the term *machining cell* most often refers to more automated configurations. A manufacturing cell may or may not have a central control, depending on its complexity. In most cases, cells are configured to machine/process a variety of parts in a batch mode. Lot sizes are typically small to medium.

Flexible manufacturing systems, like manufacturing cells, are groups of computer-controlled machine tools linked by an automated material handling system, controlled by a common supervisory computer control, and capable of processing parts in random order. Variations in the parts handled are accommodated by the FMS machinery directed by the supervisory control. Figure 1-2 illustrates a typical FMS installation that combines machining centers with head-indexing machines.

The successful implementation of the concept of flexible manufacturing involves proficiency not only in the level of

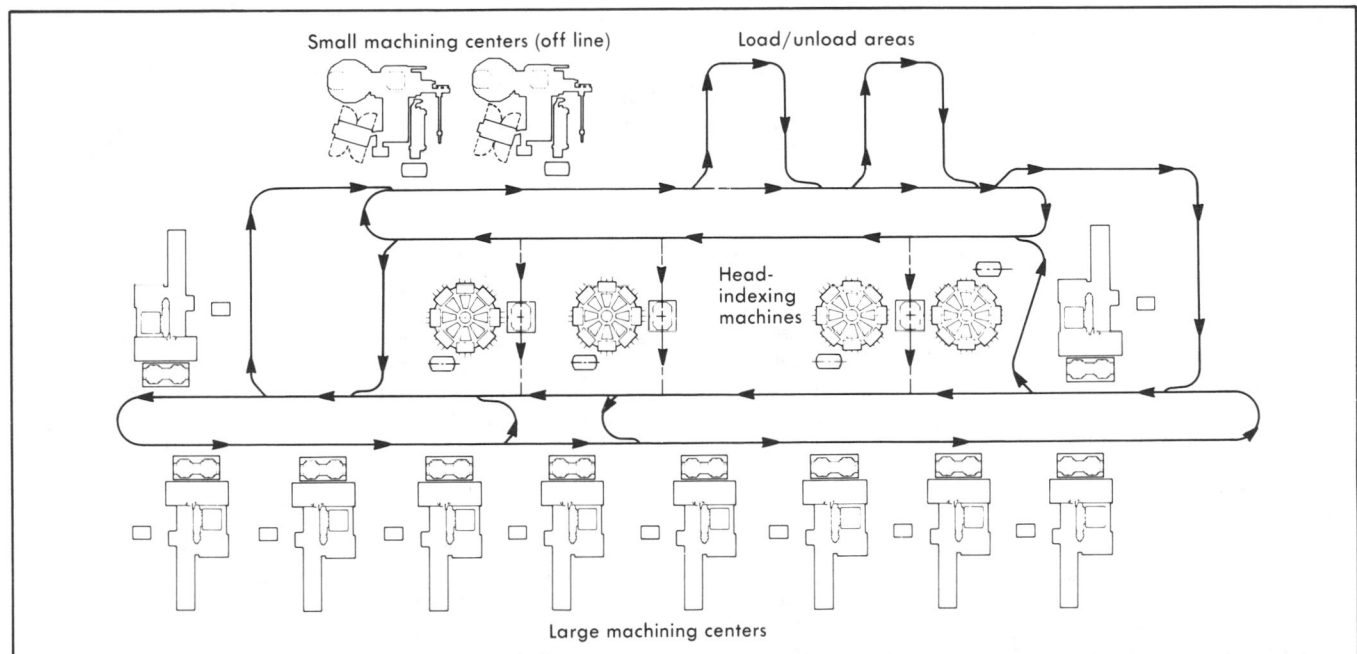

Fig. 1-2 Plan view of typical flexible manufacturing system (FMS). Large machining centers and head-indexing machines are linked through an automated fixture cart transportation system under computer control. NC part programs are downloaded to CNC machining centers from memory of the central computer. (*Kearney & Trecker Corp.*)

CIM TECHNOLOGIES

integrating the physical material or part processing (machining and transporting), but in the level of integrating the information flow that determines the physical operation of the system. For optimum efficiency, the operation of an FMS is integrated into a broader automation environment. In this environment, which is not yet a reality, parts to be produced are designed on a CAD system that produces both the bill of materials to allow a manufacturing management and control system to schedule production and the NC part programs to accomplish that production. Also part of that environment is feedback from the FMS to management on the quality and productivity of the system's operation.

Auxiliary Manufacturing Machinery

Auxiliary manufacturing machinery is the machinery that enhances the efficiency of machine tools and assembly equipment by coordinating material movement and machine loading and unloading so that the overall production flow is smooth. These technologies include automated material handling equipment and robotics.

Automated material handling is the technology that is responsible for the physical integration of the production process. It includes the computer-based systems that store materials and parts before, after, and sometimes during processing and the systems that transport materials, parts, and assemblies from the time they enter the plant, through the various production stations, and until they leave the plant as finished assemblies or products. As such, this technology plays a very important role in a CIM environment, a role that is very often underestimated and undervalued.

The principal system that automates material storage in a manufacturing environment is the automated storage and retrieval system (AS/RS). These types of systems are the modern counterparts of storage racks and storage bins. Adding computer control to the storage function permits faster retrieval, more efficient use of storage space, buffer storage to feed machine tools, and, most importantly, better control.

On the transportation side of automated material handling, there are many technologies such as automated guided vehicles (AGVs), conveyors, towlines, and cart systems. Automated guided vehicles are not constrained in their movement by rigid travel paths (chains or tracks in the floor) and therefore have the potential to contribute more to a modern manufacturing environment where flexibility is important.

Automated storage and retrieval systems. Automated storage and retrieval systems fall into two categories based on their size and the size of the goods they store. The larger high-rise AS/RS is often referred to as a unit loader, while smaller versions that handle binnable materials are called miniloaders. Storage carousels are similar in concept to AS/RS. They are often used for tool, fixture, and fastener storage.

An AS/RS is really a rack into which parts are loaded and from which parts are unloaded automatically. It typically consists of input/output staging areas, the storage/retrieval (S/R) machines which shuttle loads in and out of storage, the control system, and the storage racks themselves. Some system designs require humans to perform the picking function (physically removing material from a rack), but the state of the art is the unmanned system. Newer systems make use of bar code readers and optical character readers to identify the correct load to be picked. Stored parts may be palletized or placed in bins or pans.

The devices that service the input/output staging areas may be conveyors, lift trucks, automated guided vehicles, or other transport devices. It is important that these devices mesh well with the operation of the AS/RS to get the maximum efficiency from the system. The size and configuration of the AS/RS and of the individual storage compartments in it are customized to the specific installation.

Control of an AS/RS can vary widely. A manual input station controls storage and retrieval through prepunched cards or pushbuttons. In a more sophisticated system, AS/RS controls can be a combination of computers, microprocessor controls, and programmable controllers working together under a supervisory control, which is normally a computer. This type of system not only controls the moving of loads in and out of storage, but can provide a host of data to other computers for managing inventory, for coordinating other plant activities, or for providing management information systems.

Automated guided vehicles. Automated guided vehicles (AGVs) are driverless trucks that operate under computer control. Most systems in use today follow a path defined either by a wire embedded in the plant floor or by a reflective stripe of paint or tape. Because of the computer control, they are able to interface automatically with a variety of other factory floor equipment, including machine tools, production machinery, the AS/RS, and robots. Their principal advantage is that AGVs are able to move over "flexible" routes to deliver materials.

Guided vehicles can perform a variety of tasks in a factory environment. They can be used to tow trailers that hold rolling loads up to 50,000 lb (25 tons) or they can be used as unit load transporters and carry loads up to 12,000 lb (6 tons). Lift tables can be built into some AGVs to increase their flexibility in delivering loads; some vehicles can place loads in elevated storage locations, up to 30′ (9 m) high. Vehicles with integral forklifts can transport pallets. Vehicle controls can trigger other activities such as opening doors or signaling elevators, if desired. AGVs can be either unidirectional or bidirectional.

Robotics. Robotics technology is one of the most versatile of the CIM technologies. Robots can function as material handling devices to load and unload machinery; they can function as manufacturing machines to perform machining, painting, or welding operations; equipped with vision capabilities, they are performing assembly operations for small parts manufacturing, particularly in the electronics industry, and in inspection tasks for a variety of industries.

Robots do not function alone; they must be integrated into plant operations. To be most successful, their operation must be integrated with other computer-based systems in the plant. Integration, even the limited systems development required to load and unload a machine tool, takes planning to be most effective. That simple operation must fit into an overall manufacturing strategy that governs production flow. Robots are very flexible, but a company must be ready to use that flexibility properly.

Within the concept of CIM, robots serve many functions. They are both manufacturing machinery and auxiliary manufacturing machinery. They range in complexity from very simple pick-and-place types to complex, sensor-based systems. They are an integral part of computer-aided manufacturing and of automated material handling. Their operation in a manufacturing cell or FMS can be simulated on some CAD systems, and some robotic programming can be performed on some CAD systems. Newer developments in programming languages will allow the robot and the workcell in which it operates to be programmed at the same time. Clearly this has the potential to simplify workcell programming and improve the cell performance. In this environment, the robot control, like a machine tool control, can be linked with other controls in a DNC-type arrangement.

Controls for Manufacturing Machinery

Computer control enables manufacturing machinery to communicate and coordinate its activities with other computer-based systems in the CIM environment. A variety of control types exist; all rely on the power of the microprocessor. Microprocessors allow sophisticated controls to be small enough to be embedded in machinery if required, to operate on the factory floor, and to communicate the status and performance of the equipment they control to other machine controls on the floor and to supervisory-level control systems.

Computer numerical control. Computer numerical controls (CNC) are outgrowths of the hard-wired numerical control systems first developed in the 1950s. Today the terms *NC* and *CNC* are used interchangeably.

Although the addition of a computer added considerably to the capability of NC control, the basic function of the systems is the same: to control the operation of a machine tool through a series of coded instructions that represent the tool path to be followed, the depth of cut, coolant flow start, tool change, the machine speeds and feeds associated with the operation, and emergency stop. NC and CNC took some of the art out of machining and put it in the machine control so that repeatability and consistency were achievable from part to part.

Modern CNC technology can go beyond controlling a single machining sequence on a particular workpiece to encompass multimachining operations. It can direct an automatic tool-changer to replace a cutting tool in preparation for the next operation. Instructions are also included that trigger the operation of a robot to load and unload the workpiece and then signal to the cell controller the successful completion of the operation, the condition of the cutting tool, the time elapsed, and a host of other data that can be used to refine the operation of the cell. Computer control has changed manufacturing technology more than any other single development. It introduced the concept of automated machine control. In so doing, it broke the ground that enabled manufacturing cells, FMS, robots, coordinate measuring machines, and programmable logic controllers to be developed.

Distributed numerical control. Distributed numerical control (DNC) is the outgrowth of direct numerical control, which is the concept of linking a computer containing the part programs and associated information to the NC control attached to a machine tool. In this concept, the computer would download programs as needed. Unfortunately, computer technology was not as reliable in the early days, and if the DNC computer went down, so did the machine tool.

Distributed numerical control is a much more practical concept because it connects several CNC machine tools to a higher level DNC computer. A DNC system allows all the part programs for one facility to reside in one central location and be downloaded as required to individual CNC machine tools. This arrangement facilitates management of part programs and part program revisions. At the same time, a DNC installation can allow data from the machine operation to be automatically passed to a higher level computer for management information and interaction. Such data can include production piece counts, machine downtime, quality control information, or part

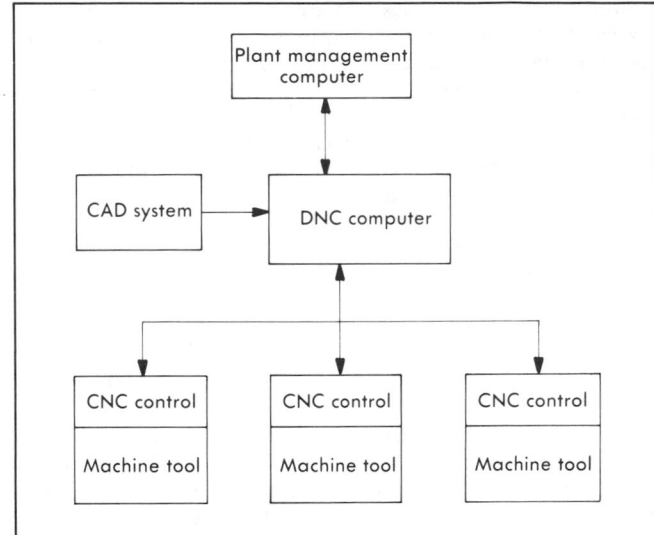

Fig. 1-3 Typical distributed numerical control layout.

program enhancements. Figure 1-3 depicts a typical DNC hierarchy.

Programmable logic controllers. Programmable logic controllers are a very important control element in a factory automation environment. PLCs are computers specifically designed to be rugged and to withstand the heat, dirt, and electrical noise that is endemic to the factory floor. PLCs originally replaced relay panels in the automotive industry and were primarily used as sequencing controls. Developed at the request of General Motors Corp., they were designed to be programmed in relay ladder logic so that they could be programmed and maintained by electricians. Built-in diagnostic capabilities further simplified maintenance.

The acceptance of programmable logic controllers was so strong that the devices were enhanced by more and more features, such as arithmetic functions, timing, data storage and processing capabilities, and subroutine capabilities. All these features made PLCs more computer-like. Newer higher level languages have replaced the ladder diagrams in some applications, and sophisticated computer graphics provide a window into the operation being controlled.

PLANNING AND CONTROLLING THE MANUFACTURING PROCESS

No matter how efficient the physical production operation appears to be with computer-aided machinery cutting and shaping metal, assembling components, and moving material and parts around, they may not add up to real efficiency unless all these operations are planned, scheduled, and coordinated in view of the overall business objectives. The CIM technologies that perform these manufacturing management functions are manufacturing resource planning (MRP II) and, more recently, just-in-time (JIT) systems.

Manufacturing Resource Planning Systems

Manufacturing resource planning systems have been called the central nervous system of the manufacturing enterprise.

CIM TECHNOLOGIES

Contained within these systems are the software modules that plan and schedule manufacturing operations, allow production and material schedules to be explored for better alternatives, monitor operations against the plan, allow operating results to be projected, and tie financial reporting to operating figures.

These manufacturing systems allow management to control an entire organization and give management the timely information it needs to control and direct the organization in accordance with its established business plan. In a CIM environment, modern MRP II systems have the ability to tie real-time information from virtually the entire business enterprise together—design engineering, manufacturing, accounting and finance, marketing, distribution—so that this data may be used to support the overall business strategy. Relatively few of the installed systems take advantage of the full capabilities of the MRP II software.

The importance of such systems to successful CIM implementation is obvious; through the data they generate, collect, and manage, MRP II systems establish and maintain links between the shop floor, the engineering department, and the front office. At this point in time, very few commercial MRP II systems have established direct links with CAD systems, NC programming, or CAPP. However, this integration is currently being discussed by most of the leading MRP II vendors.

Just-in-Time Systems

Just-in-time (JIT) production, a technology related to MRP II, has caused many U.S. companies to rethink their approach to material management; many have experienced significant benefits after adopting this philosophy.

One of the basic tenets of JIT is to produce only what is needed when it is needed, thereby reducing inventory, particularly work-in-process (WIP) inventory, and inventory costs. Purchased parts or raw materials are delivered directly to the production line, several times a day if necessary. Internally, one production area makes only as many components or subassemblies as the next portion of the production operation can use that day or that shift. The philosophy turns inventory into products as quickly as possible. It's a 180° change from the philosophy of keeping a full supply of spare parts in storage just in case they were needed.

To be successful, however, JIT requires close working arrangements with suppliers; quality must be assured because poor quality parts or materials result in manufacturing problems, and JIT allows no time for checking incoming parts. When properly applied, JIT can mean reductions of inventory of more than 75% and equivalent improvements in product quality.

CONNECTING THE ISLANDS OF AUTOMATION

The previous sections of this chapter have attempted to describe the CIM concept and how its component technologies fit into that concept. This section will discuss the technologies and the technological trends that are enabling integration to be realized. These technologies center around computer technology and telecommunications standards; trends include the drive toward integration of all business activities.

Computing Technology

Computing technology is the technology that integrates all of the other CIM technologies. Computing technology includes the range of hardware configurations as they are used in the CIM environment and the software-related functions that effect integration, namely, database management systems, linkages between technologies, and telecommunications. Figure 1-4 illustrates the control hierarchy in a manufacturing environment.

The lowest level in the control hierarchy is the machine control level. This level consists of microprocessor-based products that directly control machinery. These products can be PLCs or other microprocessor-based controls.

The next level is the cell level. At this level, several machines act together, and although they may each have their own control, their operation is coordinated by a central computer. At this level, the control computer may be a sophisticated PLC or a microcomputer. A small manufacturing cell is typical of this level of complexity.

Moving up the control hierarchy is the area control. This computer will monitor the operation of an area of a plant such as an assembly line or a robotic welding line. These control products are typically minicomputers or superminicomputers. The VAX line of products from Digital Equipment Corp. is very strong at this level of control. The area computer can direct the operation of a number of controls. In turn, it can collect data from a number of operations and synthesize this data for transfer to a plant-wide computer, the next level of control.

The plant-level computer serves more of a management function. Although planning must be done at several levels, the plant level has responsibility to plan and schedule shop floor operations. The plant-level computers collect operations data, including machinery and personnel performance data, and direct and manage maintenance operations. The process planning system resides at this level also; however, it interacts with several other levels.

At the top of the control hierarchy is the corporate computer wherein resides the corporate database and the financial and administrative programs that run the company. One of the most important functions of the corporate computer is to organize the corporate database so that data can easily be stored, retrieved, and manipulated.

Communications between systems is vital in a modern manufacturing environment. A hierarchy of computers that communicate with each other implies at least commonality in communications protocols. One of the most significant trends in computer and control communications is the recent initiative by General Motors Corp. to develop the Manufacturing Auto-

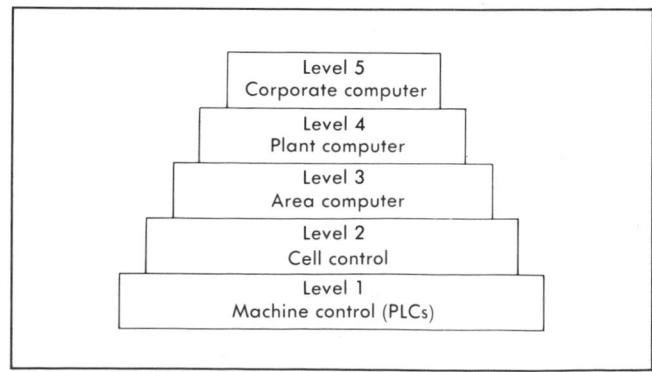

Fig. 1-4 Computer control hierarchy. (*Arthur D. Little, Inc.*)

mation Protocol (MAP). This subject is so important that it is discussed in a separate section in this chapter.

Computer-Integrated Business

Computer-integrated business is the logical extension of the trend toward communications and integration in a manufacturing enterprise. Considering that all the operations of a facility depend to some degree on the same data, it is shortsighted to limit CIM-type activities to the design and manufacturing technologies. If Dr. Joseph Harrington's definition of computer-integrated manufacturing is accepted, then all business activities, direct or indirect, that are involved in the transition of a product from concept to after-sales service are part of CIM. They are linked by the data that defines the business.

MAP/TOP

Computer-integrated manufacturing is the art of integrating computers into the manufacturing process. How well this integration is accomplished is directly related to the quality of the communications network design. The Manufacturing Automation Protocol and Technical and Office Protocol (MAP/TOP) networking standards provide a framework that can be used to integrate computers, and the software which runs on those computers, into the manufacturing process. While MAP specifies functional network protocols for the factory floor, TOP specifies them for information processing in technical and business environments. Protocols are rules governing the interaction between communicating entities.

Internal View of MAP and TOP

MAP and TOP are the first network standards that conform to the OSI seven-layer reference model introduced in 1977. This model presents a structure that can be used to organize the services provided by a network into seven layers or modules. The reason behind organizing the services into modules is that a module can be replaced as long as the functionality of the module is not compromised. For example, a network that conforms to the OSI model could use fiber-optics as the transmission medium in place of broadband without affecting the ability to detect and correct transmission errors.

To be as useful as possible, network protocols must provide a variety of services. These services are as follows:

- Allow the transmission of data between application programs or processes on the network.
- Provide for control mechanisms between software and hardware on the network.
- Insulate programmers from the intricacies of communicating over the network.
- Be modular so that choices between alternate protocols can be made with minimal impact.
- Allow for communication with other networks.

One of the first tasks faced by the International Organization for Standardization (ISO) was to produce a framework for the establishment of these standards. It agreed to produce a layered model, with each layer representing a set of services so that the implementation of services at one layer could be changed without affecting the other layers. The seven-layer model for Open Systems Interconnect, or OSI reference model, was proposed and eventually adopted by the ISO.

As shown in Fig. 1-5, the layers are organized in a very specific way. The services provided by the model can be thought

of as user services at the top layers: application, presentation, and session. The network services are provided by the bottom four layers: transport, network, data link, and physical.

User services are those services that are concerned with providing a uniform method for communicating processes to use the network, a method of converting the way data is represented on one device to the way data is represented on another, and some means to establish and control the dialog between communicating entities.

Network services are those services that are concerned with the details of the network: control the flow of data between end systems, route messages, prioritize messages, access to the network, represent data electronically on the network, and physically attach devices to the network medium.

Services Provided by the Seven-Layer Model

It is important to note that the seven-layer model is still functional even if the services provided by one or more layers are left undefined. The idea behind the use of a seven-layer model was that it could provide a path for migration toward OSI compatibility for all networking systems then in existence, even though the layered network architectures that were available at the time did not use all seven layers.

Physical layer protocols. If devices are to communicate with one another through a communication medium, some standard means must exist for connecting those devices to the medium and for representing data electronically on that medium. The protocols governing attachment to the medium and the modulation techniques are found in the standards for the physical layer.

MAP and TOP have chosen different protocols for the physical layer. The designers of the MAP protocols chose broadband coaxial cable as the preferred physical medium because of the superior immunity to electromagnetic interference and multichannel capability found in this medium. Broadband can best be thought of as a way to guide radio waves along a piece of cable. Devices attached to a broadband system transmit all messages at low frequencies and receive all messages at high frequencies. The conversion between low and high-frequency transmissions takes place at a headend or translation device. Broadband is the system used in cable television systems (CATV).

The designers of the TOP protocols took a different approach than that chosen by the designers of the MAP protocols. Because very few factories had networks in place (and those who did usually had broadband closed-circuit TV systems), the MAP Task Force was free to specify any medium it felt was appropriate. The designers of the TOP protocols, on the other hand, were faced with a large installed base of baseband coaxial cable. The use of baseband simplifies the process of installing a TOP network in those offices that are contemplating replacing their existing network.

Data link layer. In a networking method that uses a single communications medium shared between the devices on the network, a method must be specified for controlling access to the physical medium and for identifying stations on the network. Control mechanisms have to be found to ensure that a station does not transmit more data than the receiver can digest at one time, and to detect and recover from errors caused by problems on the physical medium. In the OSI seven-layer reference model, the standards for these areas are found in the standards for the data link layer.

CIM TECHNOLOGIES

The data link layer is organized into two sublayers: media access control (MAC) and logical link control (LLC). The MAC sublayer is concerned with controlling access to the medium; the LLC sublayer is concerned with the size of frames, or chunks of data transmitted on the network, and the priority of transmissions.

Media access control. The standards for controlling access to the medium and for identifying stations on the network are functions of the MAC sublayer. There is a heated debate about whether this sublayer should be a part of the data link layer or the physical layer. The debate is really meaningless from an implementation point of view because the sequence of layers and sublayers is unaffected by the placement of the MAC sublayer at the top of the physical layer or the bottom of the data link layer.

MAP and TOP use different protocols for controlling access to the medium. MAP uses a method called Token Passing on a Bus (specified in IEEE 802.4), while TOP uses Carrier Sense Multiple Access with Collision Detection (CSMA/CD, specified in IEEE 802.3). Once again, the reasons for the difference in choices has to do with the different environments where the networks will be used.

Under the Token Passing on a Bus protocols, a special control frame called a "token" is passed from station to station on the network. When a station has the token, it can transmit messages on the network for a preset time. Because access to the network can be determined by calculating the length of time it takes the token to be passed around the network, token-passing networks are considered deterministic.

The TOP standard, CSMA/CD, allows any device that wishes to transmit a message to do so at any time, providing the medium is not busy. Because it is possible for two or more stations to perceive silence (nonuse) on the medium at the same time, each station must listen to its own transmission to determine if another station began transmitting at the same time. If another station also began transmitting, both stations detect the collision, cease transmitting, and wait a random amount of time before trying to transmit a second time.

While CSMA/CD works very well on lightly loaded networks, it can result in very long delays when the network is busy, because there will be fewer periods of silence, and the probability of collisions during nonsilence will increase. As a result, the network is nondeterministic; there is no way to predict how long it will take to transmit a message because access to the network is essentially random.

CSMA/CD does have several advantages. If the network is lightly loaded, access can be instantaneous. Because the protocols that govern the access method are very easy to implement, the cost of connecting a station to the network is considerably lower than the cost of implementing other access schemes. The designers of the TOP protocols felt that an access delay of a few seconds under heavy network loads is offset by the lower cost of CSMA/CD.

Logical link control. The second sublayer of the data link layer is the logical link control (LLC) sublayer, which is always found in the data link layer. This sublayer is concerned primarily with frame size and access class, or priority. MAP and TOP both use the Class 1, Type 1 LLC protocols specified in IEEE 802.2. Class 1, Type 1 allows the exchange of messages between stations without the need to first establish a connection and without flow control.

The designers of the MAP protocols realized that some factory networking applications would need faster response

times than could be achieved with the overhead of the full seven-layer stack. They designed an option to the MAP protocols that allows a station with a short, time-critical message to bypass the upper layers of the stack and interface directly to the data link layer. This high-performance option is known as enhanced performance architecture (EPA). The EPA option specifies Class 3, Type 3 LLC protocols that use single, frame-acknowledged services to achieve faster response times.

Network layer. It is sometimes desirable for a device on one network to communicate with a device on another network. This can happen in a large network that is divided into smaller subnetworks or when the communicating devices are on different local area networks (LAN) connected by a wide area network (WAN).

Because the addresses used at the data link layer (or more correctly, the MAC sublayer) are not sufficient for this purpose, there must be standards for accomplishing this internetwork routing over public data networks. The protocols that standardize the methods used for this global routing are found at the network layer.

TOP and MAP both use the protocols specified in the ISO internet standard 8473 for the network layer. This specification establishes formats for network addresses that are unique on a global scale and provides a base for resolving protocol differences between different OSI seven-layer networks as well as providing an internetwork routing capability.

Transport layer. There are often several routes a message can take to arrive at its destination. It is not unusual in these situations for a portion of a message to arrive at its destination before earlier portions that took different, and longer, routes and thus were delayed in arriving at their destination. In real life, this happens when a passenger's luggage takes a different airline route than does the passenger. As a result, the receive buffer on a device attached to the network must be divided into frames, with each frame corresponding to an anticipated message packet. Some means must be provided to ensure that packets are not lost in transit or reassembled in the wrong order. The standards for these transport problems are addressed in the protocols for the transport layer.

MAP and TOP both use Class 4 transport protocols. Class 4 is the largest and most complex class of transport protocols; it allows for connection establishment, data transfer, and connection disestablishment. Class 4 handles flow control, detection of protocol data units that are missing or received out of sequence, and the transfer of a limited amount of expedited data. The specific options to the protocols are negotiated between stations during connection establishment.

Session layer. Two communicating application programs or processes must have some means to create and control the connection between themselves. This control involves establishing, maintaining, and terminating the connection between the application programs. The standards for these services are covered in the protocols for the session layer.

Both MAP and TOP specify the use of the session kernel protocols with the full duplex option at the session layer. The session kernel contains the minimal subset of session layer functionality; it allows the establishment of a connection, the transmission of data over the connection, and the release, either orderly (normal) or through an "abort" service.

Presentation layer. Different computer manufacturers use different sequences of binary digits to represent characters and numbers. If an IBM computer using EBCDIC wants to talk to a DEC computer using ASCII, some translation must occur so

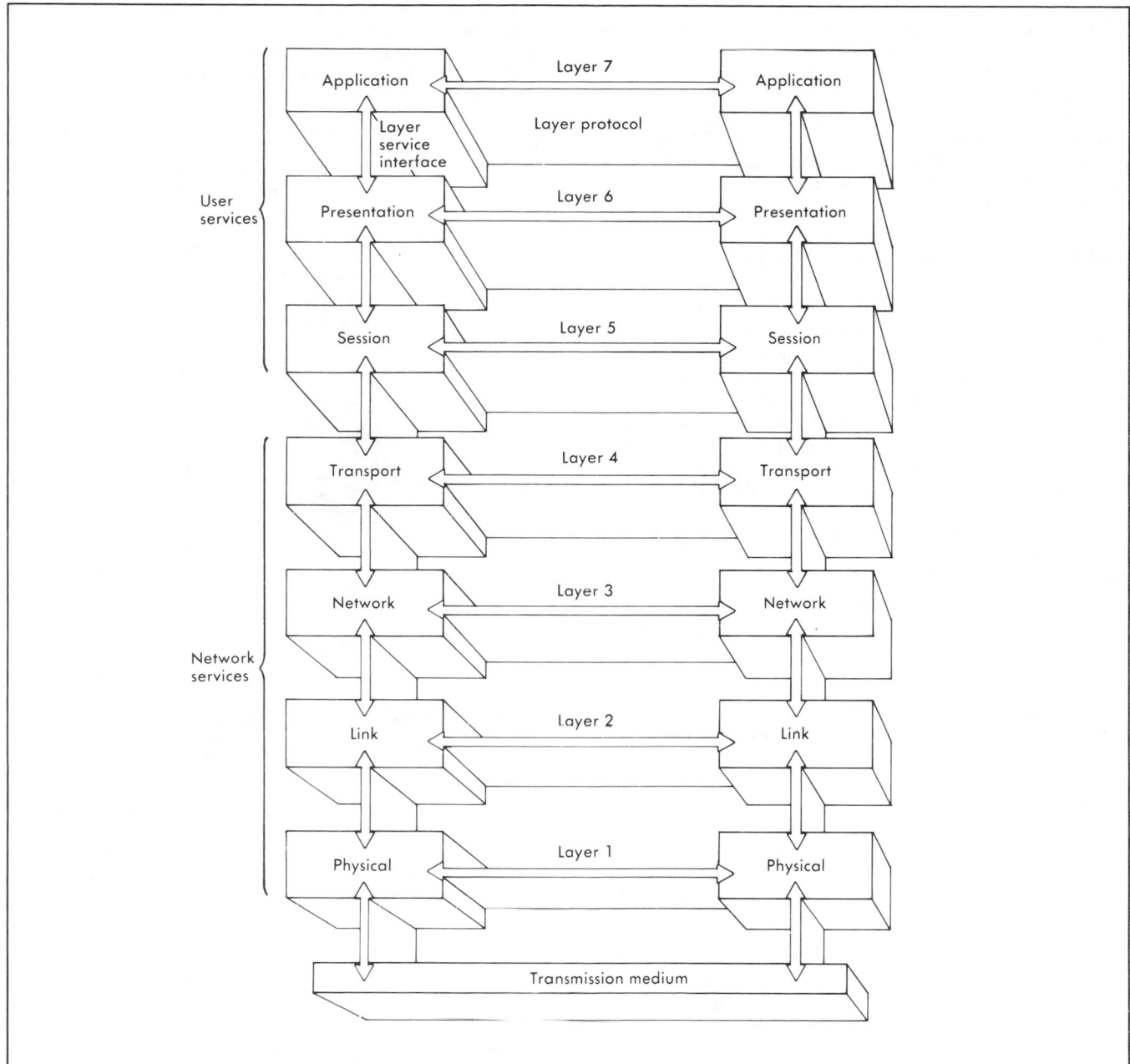

Fig. 1-5 Open Systems Interconnection (OSI) reference model.

the data will be meaningful to the computer receiving the message. Translation services such as this are covered in the standards for the presentation layer.

At the present time (Version 2.2 of MAP and Version 1.0 of TOP), the presentation layer is null; translation services must be handled by the application programs that are involved in the dialog.

Application layer. Finally, standards need to be established for specifying the interface to the seven-layer stack and for establishing the context, or meaning of the data, of an information exchange. The protocols for the application layer standard-

ize this interface and allow communicating application processes to specify the context for the communication session.

An Application View of MAP and TOP

When two application processes communicate with one another, they have an association in OSI terminology. The services available at the application layer are standardized for some of the more common types of associations. There is a great deal of work still going on to further define the context of application associations.

TOP Version 1.0 and MAP Version 2.2 specify the protocols

CIM TECHNOLOGIES

for a small subset of the possible application associations. When Version 3.0 is released in 1988 for both network standards, there will be a great deal of functionality added to the application layer.

Currently, both MAP and TOP specify a limited subset of file transfer access method (FTAM), which specifies the protocols for transferring files between systems. MAP Version 2.2 and TOP Version 1.0 allow only bulk file transfers using FTAM. When Version 3.0 is available, FTAM will be upgraded to allow record-level access as well as bulk file transfer.

Building Blocks and Future Options

Both the TOP and MAP Version 3.0 specifications will include optional media and access methods. TOP will have an option for a token passing bus on broadband; the MAP specification will include token passing on a bus with carrierband as the medium. There is some pressure on the MAP Users Group to include CSMA/CD as an optional access method in the factory. Both groups are considering fiber-optics, which will probably use the token ring access method. The token ring access method is very similar to token passing on a bus.

The set of application layer protocols available on TOP networks will allow network designers to select "building blocks" of application layer options (see Fig. 1-6). These building blocks will be described by their names and three attributes: function, specification reference, and binding rules. The shaded areas in Fig. 1-6 represent the building blocks, superimposed over the OSI model layers and elements of the TOP specification. There are two sets of these building blocks: (1) user building blocks at the upper layers and (2) network building blocks at the lower four layers. A complete TOP end system will include one or more network building blocks from the bottom four layers and at least one user building block covering the upper three layers.

Selections from the user network building blocks are optional. If two end systems that use different selections at the bottom layers want to intercommunicate, they can do so through a device called a router as long as the protocols used above the data link layer are compatible. A router is a device that translates between different protocols at the physical and data link layers as long as the protocols used at the network layer and above are compatible.

The network designer is also free to choose from the building blocks available at the upper layers, as long as two communicating application processes have at least one building block in common. These sets of standardized building blocks are what give MAP and TOP networks their functionality. A network

designer can select building blocks that complement the functionality of application processes without relying on a single vendor to supply all data processing and equipment needs—the true promise of international standardization is freedom from dependence on vendors.

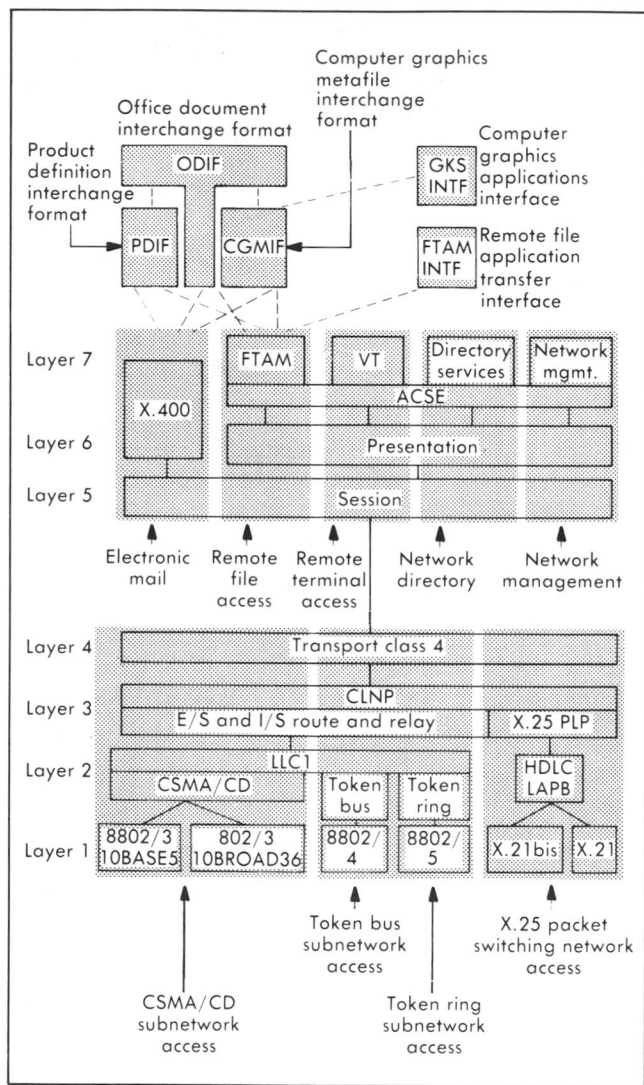

Fig. 1-6 Building blocks available on TOP 3.0.

IMPLEMENTATION OF CIM

Computer-integrated manufacturing is the way of the future for U.S. manufacturing. It has the promise to restore the competitive advantage the U.S. enjoyed for so many years. But CIM is not an easy cure. It requires careful planning; it requires an enlightened management to weigh the investment in CIM in terms of its value as a strategic tool, not just another capital investment. For those companies who choose CIM, the benefits of CIM are real; it can mean the difference between success and failure.

PLANNING FOR CIM

CIM is a manufacturing philosophy adopted by organizations to remain competitive or increase market share. As such, CIM is more of a direction or a management program that may involve the planning for and implementation of a great many technologies in a time-phased manner. Planning for CIM involves planning for its component technologies with CIM as the goal or reference.

The objective of CIM planning is to focus individual projects toward a well-defined set of goals usually established at the highest management level. Ultimately, all systems are expected to work synergistically, supported by information systems, i.e., computer hardware, system and application software, and tele-communications technology and common databases.

A CIM checklist has been developed that may be useful for companies contemplating CIM implementation.[2] The list that follows reflects the types of issues companies must address:

- Clear statement of business strategy and goals.
- List of critical success factors (CSF) to support the business strategy. What key things must go right to achieve this strategy?
- Clear statement of CIM strategy that supports business strategy and CSF.
- CEO/GM charter for CIM strategy and implementation program and top support from all functions.
- Identification of the company's starting point:
  1. Level I—Integration, policy and data architecture.
  2. Level II—Interfacing, standards.
  3. Level III—Isolated islands.
- Strong commitment to overall integration, not just excellence in functional islands or convenience in interfacing activities.
- Survey existing systems to determine levels of compatibility. How are many software and hardware systems capable of communicating together?
- Agreement to manage data as a corporate asset.
- Support from the MIS department and good cooperation with engineering and manufacturing.
- Commitment to move information between all functions in digital form.
- Agreement on standards and protocols.
- Use of integration methodologies like those that have grown out of the USAF's ICAM Program.
- Development of an architecture for a common logical database.
- Development of phased process to support the transition to CIM:
  1. Goals/plans.
  2. Conceptual design.
  3. Detailed design.
  4. Implementation.
  5. Benefits tracking and finetuning.
- Ability to learn from and receive support from the hardware and software vendors.
- Ability to learn from experiences of other companies.
- Willingness to streamline or simplify existing operations. (Reduce the complexity index.)
- Reviewing use of just in time and group technology.
- Adjust departmental charters and work assignments to support a networked organization.
- Ability to move from an individual application-bound approach to a data-driven approach, where the same data can be used by different functions for their own unique needs.
- Use of outside resources (universities, professional associations, and consultants).
- Identify potential financial benefits.
- Develop new ways of working with and exchanging information with vendors and customers/clients.
- Make use of public-domain information from the various federal projects, such as NASA's IPAD, USAF's ICAM,

and the Advanced Manufacturing Program of the National Bureau of Standards.

JUSTIFYING CIM

In too many cases, company management looks at CIM investments as decisions with only short-term implications. They are, in fact, strategic decisions that will affect the future, perhaps the existence, of the organization. Some of the problems associated with using traditional justification methods include failure to consider the changing business environment and failure to recognize the intangible benefits of CIM.

In the first case, capital expenditure requests are oftentimes evaluated against a "base case" of no new investment. Moreover, the base case typically assumes a continuation of the status quo regarding the external competitive environment. In reality, the external environment is constantly changing, and many of the more important changes are quite predictable. Some of these changes are as follows:

- *Adoption of new technology*. Once new process technology becomes available, it will likely be adopted by leading domestic and international manufacturers. In particular, new process technology tends to be rapidly introduced into the manufacturing operations of companies participating within the international marketplace in the so-called "early adopter" industries of automotive, electronics, and aerospace. These companies are likely to reap benefits in terms of quality, flexibility, responsiveness to customer requests, and the ability to attract and retain engineering talent.
- *Market share changes*. Companies adopting new process technology are likely to reap benefits in terms of quality, flexibility, and responsiveness to customer requests. These companies will enjoy, at least temporarily, comparative advantages over their competitors.
- *Prices*. History has taught that, in other than depressed markets, prices tend to increase over long periods of time. Ignoring the virtual certainty of price increases leads to underestimates of revenue and more difficulty in justifying the new investment.

A valid cost/benefit analysis taken over a reasonable length of time, say 10 or so years, must incorporate "best judgment" estimates of changes in the external environment. The assumption of continued cash flows for the base case is not realistic. A more valid assumption is that the base case of no new investment will result in declining cash flows as the company falls behind its competitors.

Perhaps a better approach to justifying CIM investments lies in developing a system model of the business, using ICAM Definition Method (IDEF) or other available simulation modeling methodologies. Any such model should include the various functions and transactions that typically take place in a manufacturing enterprise.

BENEFITS OF CIM

Although the qualitative benefits of CIM are not often factored into a cost justification equation, it is well accepted that CIM technology yields many unquantifiable benefits. Among the most important benefits of CIM are improved productivity, faster introduction of new and/or modified prod-

IMPLEMENTATION OF CIM

ucts, and improved traceability of specific jobs and processes. Some of the more important strategic benefits of CIM are contained in Table 1-2.

TABLE 1-2
Strategic Benefits of CIM

Benefit	Description
Flexibility	Ability to respond more quickly to changing mix/volume requirements
Quality	Resulting from automated inspection and greater consistency in manufacturing
Lead times	Substantial reductions resulting from information integration efficiencies
Inventories	Reduced WIP and finished goods inventories due to lead time reductions and timely access to accurate information
Managerial control	Reduced control resulting from information access and computer implementation of production decisions
Floor space	Reductions resulting from more efficient layouts and integration of operations
Options	Prevents potential pre-emption by competitors by maintaining option to exploit new technology

References

1. *Introducing the New CIM Enterprise Wheel* (Dearborn, MI: The Computer and Automated Systems Association of the Society of Manufacturing Engineers, 1985).
2. Dr. Charles M. Savage, ed., *A Program Guide for CIM Implementation* (Dearborn, MI: The Computer and Automated Systems Association of the Society of Manufacturing Engineers, 1985).

INTRODUCTION TO INDUSTRIAL ROBOTICS

This chapter focuses on basic robotics for manufacturing. The topics include robotic systems, specifications, standards, programming, end-of-arm tooling, operations, implementation, applications, communications, integrated vision, performance runoffs, safety maintenance, and service. This chapter is directed towards actual use of the robot as one of a variety of manufacturing tools.

ROLE OF ROBOTS

The Robotic Industries Association defines a robot as follows:

A robot is a reprogrammable, multifunctional manipulator designed to move material, parts, tools, or specialized devices through variable programmed motions for the performance of a variety of tasks.

Robots are automated machines, primarily automated tools for materials handling or process machines (such as spraying or welding), and are to be justified and used in accordance with good manufacturing practices. Successful implementation of automation occurs when good manufacturing engineering and engineering economics are used. "Keeping up with the Joneses" does not justify requesting robots. Robots, selected and implemented according to good manufacturing engineering practices, can be successful applications, while those used just to keep up with competitors tend not to be successful.

Personnel working with robots need to be sensitive to the issues of comparing robots to people (terminology) and of robots displacing people ("Robots don't buy products"). Robots are not made any more or less human by using terminology that is also used to describe human anatomy. It is a common practice to refer to arms, legs, fingers, and feet when describing features of equipment, but this has not made robotics any more human by doing so. The controversy over robots "stealing" jobs raises valid social concerns, but robots are not any more or less guilty of displacing people in the work force than are other forms of automation. This is not meant to dismiss the issue lightly, rather it is meant to put it in the broad context of automation, where it belongs.

DESCRIPTION OF ROBOTIC SYSTEMS

A robot is a complex machine and, like most equipment of this type, it consists of a number of subsystems. The operation of a robot is a result of the performance of each of its subsystems. The four major subsystems are the manipulator, power system, control system, and end-of-arm tooling (twist and end effector). The manipulator, or arm, is the physical device used to move the end-of-arm tooling and payload from place to place. It is driven by the power system through a programmed motion stored in the control system. The wrist provide small changes in orientation of the end effector mounted on the stub of the robot arm and supports the end effector, which is the interface between the robot and the manufacturing operation. The wrist is considered as part of the end-of-arm tooling because it is almost as application-specific as the end effector.

MANIPULATOR SUBSYSTEMS

A robot manipulator is an assembly of links and joints. A manipulator link is solid, and a joint provides rotational or translatory (linear) movement between two links. The links are supported by a base (the base may be horizontal, vertical, or suspended) with a joint between the base and the first link. This motion is called a "degree of freedom" and each additional joint adds another degree of freedom. A typical robot arm has three degrees of freedom, with an additional one to three degrees of freedom being performed at the wrist as part of the end-of-arm tooling for a total of from four to six axes (or degrees of freedom). Some fairly sophisticated robots have from seven to nine degrees of freedom.

The base is rigid and attached to a supporting member (not always the floor). If it has movement, it generally is limited to a single axis and is used to move the robot in a synchronized motion with other equipment. It is common for a robot to have three links and three joints. Generally, the robot manipulator can move in three-dimensional space, or three degrees of freedom. If the base can move, then it has four degrees of freedom.

The manipulator moves in various motions with the different link/joint relationships. The volume through which the end of the manipulator is capable of moving is called the work envelope, and it is

DESCRIPTION OF ROBOTIC SYSTEMS

one of the methods used to describe the configuration of the robot. Robot work envelopes are either Cartesian, cylindrical, or spherical.

If all three degrees of freedom are linear moves, they are called Cartesian and the work envelope is a rectangular prism (see Fig. 2-1). The combination of a rotational joint with the base and two linear movements is identified as cylindrical, and it has a cylinder-shaped work envelope (see Fig. 2-2). Having rotational axes perpendicular to each other and one linear movement is called polar, and it has a spherical work envelope (see Fig. 2-3). When all three moves are rotational (with the base axis of rotation perpendicular to the other two axes), it is called an articulated arm (also a jointed arm or an anthropomorphic arm). This type of manipulator also moves through a spherical work envelope (see Fig. 2-4).

There are variations of each of these four configurations, but the robots are still classed by their individual work envelopes. In most cases, the gantry is classified as a Cartesian type. The "selective compliance assembly robot arm" (SCARA) is viewed as a cylindrical type with three rotational movements and one linear motion, instead of one rotational and two linear. It was designed primarily for assembly applications. Unlike the articulated arm, all three of SCARA's rotational motions are around parallel axes and the work envelope is that of a cylindrical robot (see Fig. 2-5).

The popularity of the polar and, to an even greater extent, the articulated (jointed) arm is due partially to their greater flexibility. What is especially appealing about the articulated arm is its larger work envelope. Many articulated models can reach back over themselves and change the orientation of the

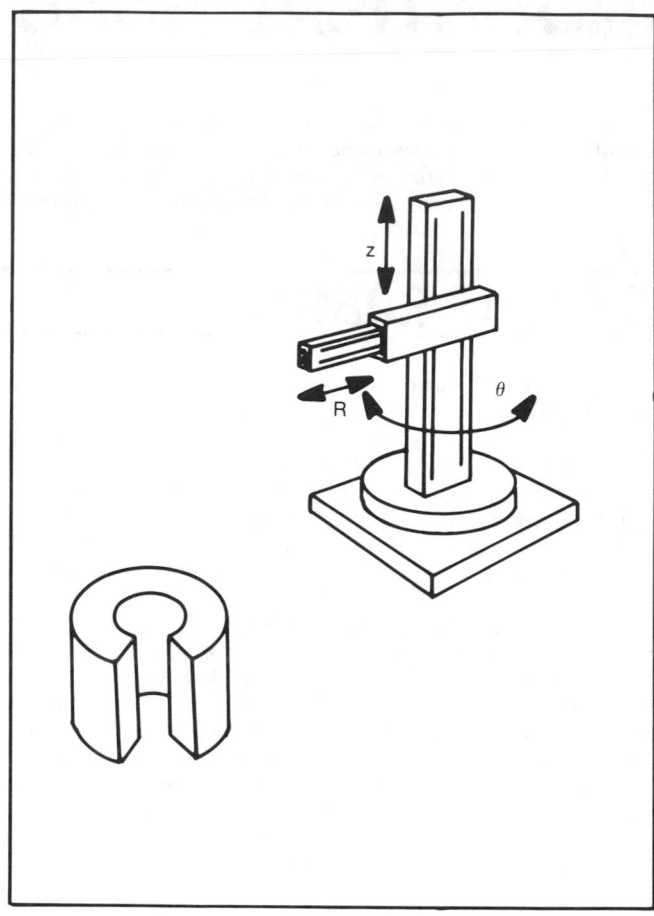

Fig. 2-2 Cylindrical work envelope (Cylindrical arm).

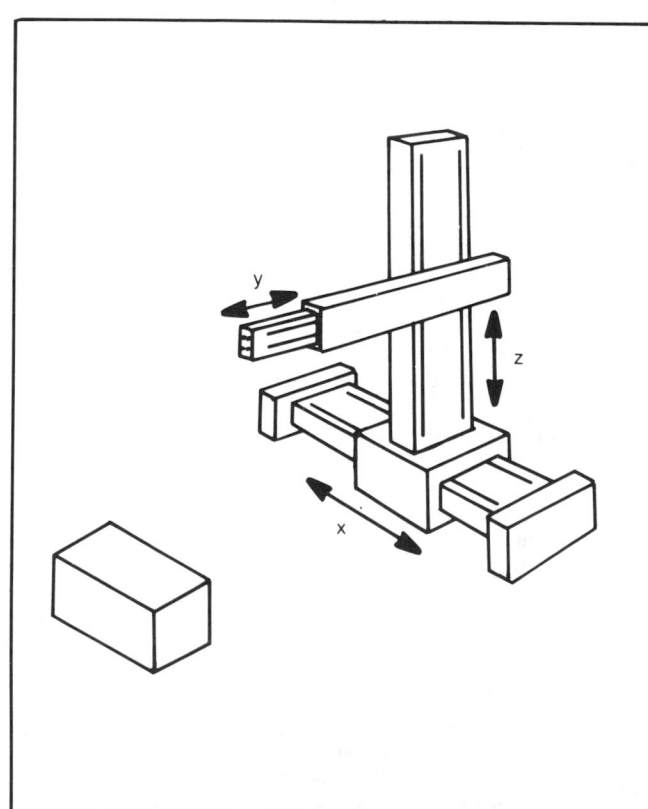

Fig. 2-1 Cartesian work envelope (Cartesian arm).

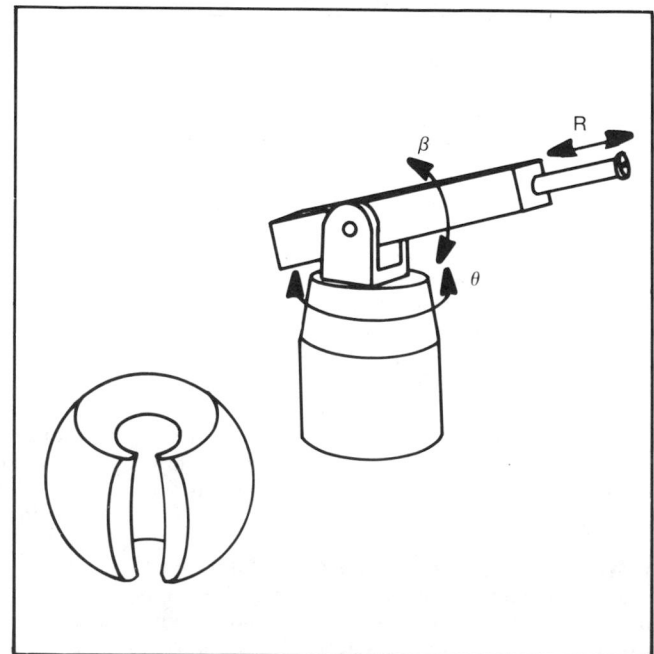

Fig. 2-3 Spherical work envelope (Polar arm).

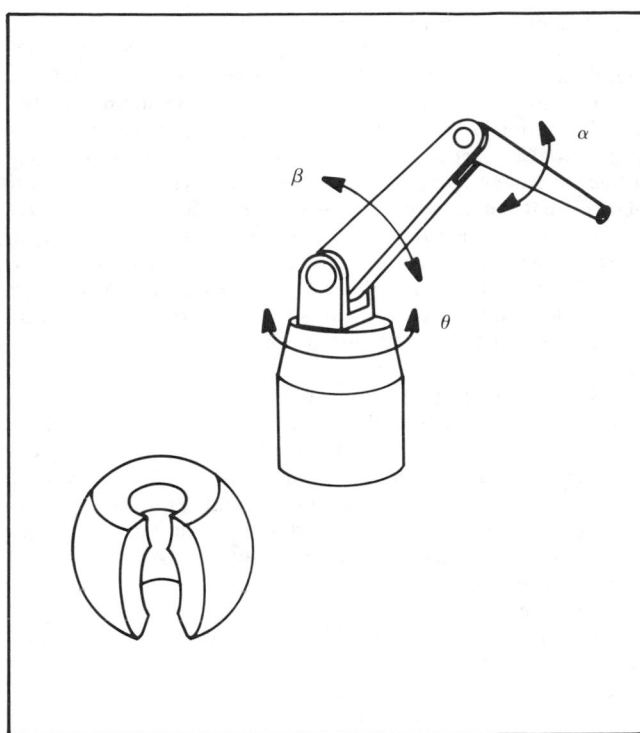

Fig. 2-4 Spherical work envelope (Articulated arm).

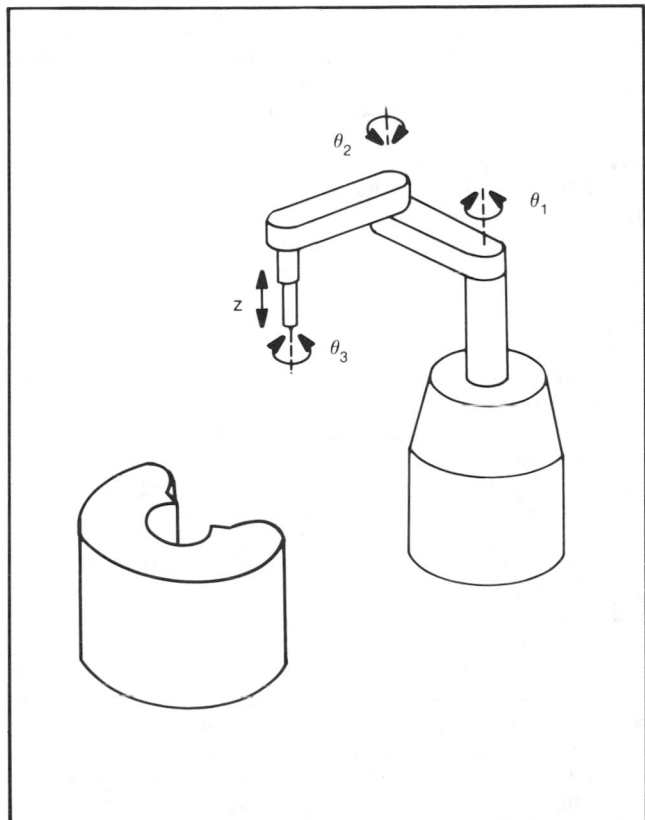

Fig. 2-5 Cylindrical work envelope (SCARA).

mount for the end-of-arm tooling, something the other three configurations can not achieve in their standard or modified versions. For these reasons, most finishing and spot-welding robots used in the manufacturing of automobiles are of the polar or articulated arm styles.

The second method of classifying robot manipulators is by joint motion (see Fig. 2-6). The translatory joint motions are transverse or linear (the link motion is perpendicular to the supporting link) and telescopic or extension (the link motion is parallel to the supporting link), and the rotational joint motions are hinge or rotational (the link axis is perpendicular to the axis of rotation) and pivot or twist (the link axis is parallel to the axis of rotation).[1] Starting with the base, one can describe a robot having a cylindrical work envelope by identifying its motions:

1. Rotational (hinge)
2. Pivot (twist)
3. Transverse (linear)
4. Telescopic (extension)

POWER SUBSYSTEMS

The power subsystem provides the energy to move the manipulator. Power subsystems are either electric, hydraulic, or pneumatic. More than 65% of the robots in use are electrically powered, and that percentage will probably increase in the future. They are clean, reliable, and well understood.

Electric motor-driven robots have an acceptable operating load-velocity capability, and they are economical. Explosion-proof and intrinsically safe electric robots are available and can be used safely in flammable environments, but these added safety features are more expensive. The required precision mechanical power transmission equipment (geartrains) tend to be expensive, and with wear it adds inaccuracies to the system. Harmonic drives tend to be more accurate than conventional geartrains.

Hydraulic power subsystems are used in about 25% of the robots. Hydraulics have been, and continue to be, used in large robots with heavy payloads and in those that are operating in flammable environments.

Pneumatic power subsystems are rather limited in their applications and typically are used only in nonservo (pick-and-place) types of robots. Pneumatic units constitute approximately 10% of the robots manufactured. One can have a pick-and-place robot using any of the three power subsystems, but pneumatics are very economical with comparably short cycle times for light duty applications.

Electric Motor Drives

Most electric robots use stepper motors, direct current (DC) servo motors, or alternating current (AC) servo motors. The control and feedback systems may be different depending on the motors being used.

The stepper motor-driven robot may be an open-loop system. A given stepper motor has a specific angular displacement for each electrical step it receives. These motors vary from 15 degrees/step (24 steps/revolution) to .5 degrees/step (720 steps/revolution). The premise is that a stepper motor driver accelerates the motor through a number of steps, drives the motor through the appropriate number of steps, and decelerates the motor to a stop to achieve the desired angular displacement with a specific number of steps. The control system determines both the desired angular displacement and the number of steps, and the motor design determines the magnitude of the steps. The

DESCRIPTION OF ROBOTIC SYSTEMS

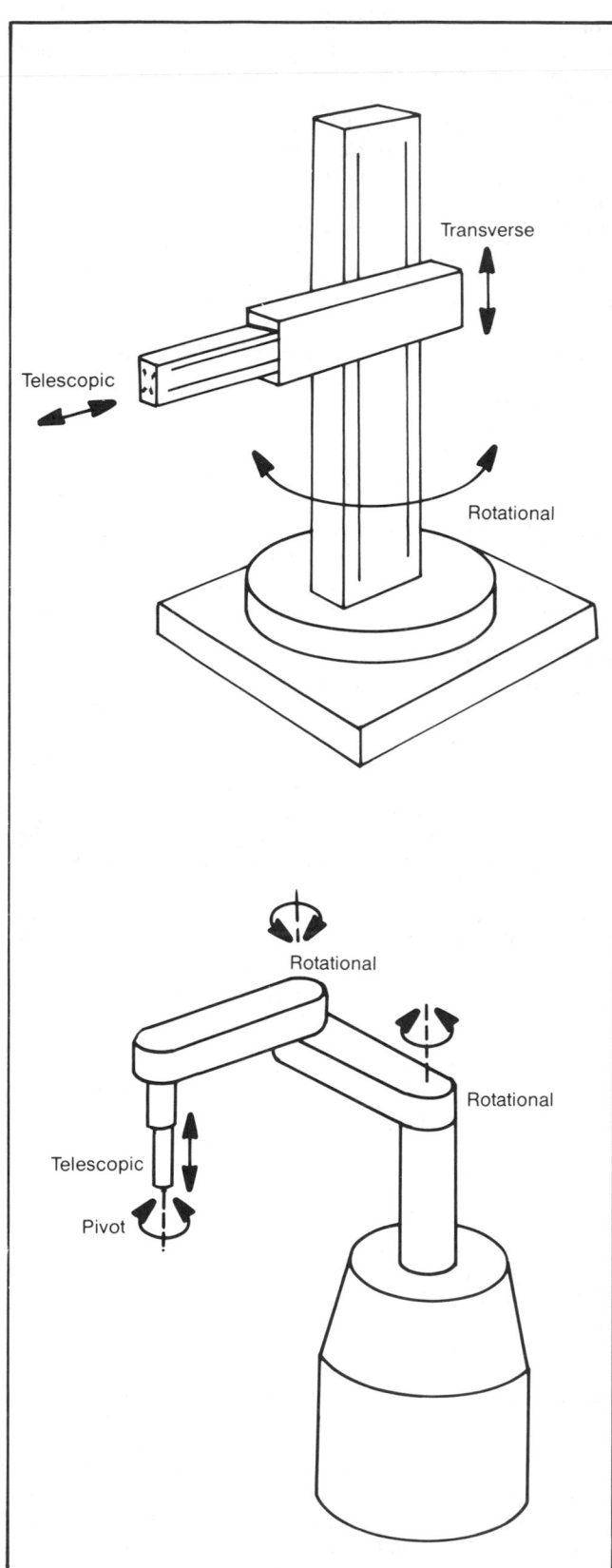

Fig. 2-6 Robot joint motions

stepper motor driver ramps up the motor speed (acceleration), maintains motor speed, and ramps down the motor speed (deceleration). The underlying assumption is that the robot will always move in the manner prescribed by the stepper motor driver. As long as this assumption holds true, the robot will be accurate. If a stepper motor does not rotate through the prescribed angular displacement, then the robot will incur a margin of error that is determined by the difference between the actual and the programmed angular displacements. Since most stepper motor systems are open-loop, the controller is unaware of the missed steps and the inaccuracy. This is the major disadvantage of open-loop stepper motor drives. Closed-loop stepper motor systems do not have the limitation just described and can be every bit as accurate as servo systems.

DC and AC motors are both used for closed-loop servo systems. These motors tend to have the same characteristics as the nonservo motors of the same classification. The differences are due to rotor design (smaller diameter for smaller moments of inertia and better response), larger wire diameter in the windings for less power loss (heat gain), and more sensitivity to voltage change for speed and torque control, especially when starting.[2]

DC permanent magnet servo motors are used extensively in light and medium-duty robots. These motors have very linear speed-torque characteristics. There are a variety of AC servo motors and these are often brushless DC motors. They also have linear speed-torque characteristics. In addition to the desirability of linear speed-torque characteristics, a sensitive, linear response to voltage change is desirable in a servo motor. Some nonlinearity may be compensated for by the control system, but it is preferred not to use software to correct hardware performance problems. These DC permanent magnet motors are economical and readily available in fractional and small integral horsepower sizes. The controllers for the AC servos are slightly more expensive, but AC servo motors do not have the brush commutator wear and maintenance requirements.

Hydraulic Drives

Hydraulic drives or power units were used in the original Unimate robots, but they are less common today than in the early 1980s. Hydraulic power units are able to move heavy payloads at relatively high velocities using smaller and less expensive components than electrically driven units, and this makes them better suited for flammable environments. While hydraulic power systems do not have to be noisy, leaky, and messy, they sometimes have problems.

The servo control system directs the hydraulic power system through servo valves. These servo valves require either (60 Hz oscillation) and have low voltage (0 to ± 3 volts DC) and current requirements (100 mA or less). This provides good sensitivity to voltage changes from the control system and good response time.

Pressure surges in the hydraulic lines may be five or more times greater than the operating pressure due to the rapid valve position changes and the hysteresis of the system. The fluctuation of oil temperatures is a limiting factor for hydraulic robot accuracy and repeatability. In some robot designs the hydraulics are as accurate as the electric motor drives, but the lead-through teaching method used for many continuous-path machines requires a certain mechanical freedom (play) that results in lower accuracy and repeatability when the robot is operated. For welding and spray finishing, this limited accuracy is not a problem. Fine assembly or painting trim stripes requires greater accuracy than most hydraulic units can provide. On slow moves, rod friction may cause an undesirable jerky motion. Weekly maintenance can minimize this problem. On point-to-point, or any move other than a slow one, rod friction is not a significant factor. Filtration of hydraulic fluid must be maintained at high levels, specifically within 80 to 160 μin. (2 to 4 μm).

There are many servo valve designs, but two types—flapper (most common) and jet pipe—are used in robots. Flapper servo valves are more common for point-to-point machines that have high velocity moves. Jet pipe servo valves are used in continuous-path machines for more accurate slow speed control.

The servo control hydraulic system is extremely sensitive to sludge, varnish, and small particles of dirt; 80 to 160 μin. (2 to 4 μm) versus the traditional 1000-1600 μin. (25 to 40 μm) level for conventional hydraulics. This contamination is caused by oxidation which is accelerated by heat and the presence of water and dirt in the oil. Oxidation will occur over time, but the cleaner the oil, the less rapid the oxidation. Oxidation causes carbon to be separated from the oil molecules, leaving the common varnish and sludge. Varnish and sludge cause component wear, increased heating, and further oxidation. This circuitous action results in even more wear, heating, and oxidation. The varnish and sludge deposits, causes of servo valve failure, not the traditional dirt type of contamination, are the most common manufacturers of electrostatic liquid cleaner (ELC) have reported good results in minimizing the problems of lubrication contamination.

Fewer people are trained to service hydraulic servo systems than electric servos, and hydraulic systems are not as well understood as electric motor—even though their controllers and power amplifiers are similar. Electricians tend to know electric motors better than hydraulic valves.

Pneumatic Drives

Commercial pneumatic drives or power units are limited to the nonservo (pick-and-place) type of robot. This is approximately 10% of the market. The pneumatic power system can be used on a servo basis, but it is not a common practice. These power systems usually work against mechanical stops or with air motor-driven, mechanical drivetrain systems that are positioned by limit switches. Pneumatic power systems consist of low-power systems (less energy intensive than electric or hydraulic drives) and drive robots with light payloads. Pneumatics can be economical and can operate at high speed, but they are limited to pick-and-place machines with light payloads. In smaller robots with lighter payloads, pneumatics have the edge. For larger systems the hydraulic or electric drives may be used.

CONTROL SUBSYSTEMS

The control subsystem has three functions. First, it directs the robot power system to cause the manipulator to move in a prescribed path. Second, the control system stores one or more programs and any data collected as a function of the program. Third, the control system communicates with the outside world through the teach pendant, programming terminal, computer interface, and either magnetic tape plays, or floppy disk drives, or discrete inputs and outputs (I/O).

The fundamental standard used to classify control subsystems is nonservo vs. servo. Another common criterion is to classify the control system by the technology (low, medium, high, and adaptive). A short discussion of computer numerical-control robot controllers follows.

Controller Technology

Low technology controllers are of the relay, air logic, drum sequencer, electromechanical or programmable logic controllers (PLC) types for nonservo, pick-and-place robots. These controllers may use, but do not require, microprocessors. Reprogramming, which is done on-line, is time consuming and may include mechanical adjustments. Typically, these pick-and-place units have only four degrees of freedom. Such units tend to be islands of automation that are not integrated into a larger communications network.

Medium technology robots are used with servo robots with point-to-point control. These robots may have six degrees of freedom. They do not have computer communications capability, but they do have discrete inputs and outputs (I/O). Program storage and retrieval may make use of cassette magnetic tapes or floppy disks. Conditional branching is common. Linear and circular interpolation, computer communications, palletizing firmware, and off-line programming may be options.

The high-technology robot controller has continuous path capability, co-processors, computer communications interface capability, additional memory, rapid program changes, and additional sensing capability smart grippers or vision.

Adaptive robots are high-technology robots with additional sensing capability, computer interfacing capability, appropriate software, and a higher level of intelligence; they can be programmed to act in an adaptive mode. This will permit a robot to locate, grasp, orient, inspect, move, and release randomly placed workpieces. During this activity, the robot controller can correct its position, touch, velocity, and force. In short, the adaptive-technology robot could, within certain parameters, adapt to its environment and interact smoothly with the computer-controlled equipment.[3]

The controller architecture for medium, high, and adaptive-technology robots consists of a central processing unit (CPU), memory, input/output (I/O) connections for transfer of programs or data, program display, and program execution. Communication with cell controllers, PLCs, or other computer equipment is through RS-232C, RS-422, or a local area network communications card.

Programs are stored in the controller's memory by either 1) creating them on-line with a teach pendant or with the lead-through technique or 2) having them down-loaded from a computer through a communications channel. Many robot controllers can store at least four programs in their on-board memory.

Numerical Control

Computer numerical-controlled (CNC) machine tools are related to robot systems. A CNC part program is similar to a robot task program. CNC controllers have sometimes been used to drive robot systems, and the robots are programmed much like a five- or six-axis CNC machine tool. Machine tools and robots do have a significant difference in the required number of degrees (axes) of freedom. Machine tools require three axes to position the tool, and they have one to three axes on a table with the tool orientation being fixed with respect to the axes. Robots require five or six axes to position and orient the tool. Tool orientation is especially significant in welding, finishing, and some material handling applications.

The use of CNC controllers on robots has the major advantage of utilizing the three-dimensional computer-aided design (CAD) software to generate the tool path geometry and the associated computer-aided manufacturing (CAM) software to

DESCRIPTION OF ROBOTIC SYSTEMS

convert the tool path through post-processing into an NC code for the controller. The CNC robot controller, like the CNC machine tool, is programmed in the world coordinate system (WCS), rather than the tool coordinate system used with teach pendants or lead-through programming. This feature makes this type of controller more restrictive and cumbersome for programming robots on- or off-line, except when one is using CAD/CAM software that supports the CNC.

Manipulator Sensing

Robotic sensing can be divided into two area, manipulator positioning and end-effector sensing. This section on manipulator sensing will focus on the current common manipulator sensors (encoders, resolvers, tachometer generators, and linear variable differential transformers, LVDT). All of these sensing devices are evaluated for their capabilities to give resolution, accuracy, linearity, range, response time, and repeatability.

Optical encoders are digital devices, generally 5-12 volts DC; they use infrared light emitting diodes (LEDs) for transmitters and receivers, although other light sources and receivers are available, and they are designed either for incremental positioning or absolute positioning operation. Resolvers, tachometer generators, and LVDT are analog devices operating at higher voltages and absolute positioning. Since encoders are digital, they require less electronic signal processing than analog devices that require analog-to-digital conversion (ADC) hardware. All of these sensors are used in robot manipulator systems.

The relationship between the output data from the encoders, resolvers, and LVDTs and the displacement in the Cartesian coordinate system—usually based on the WCS of the robot-is calculated by the controller. For Cartesian robots, this is a relatively straightforward calculation. The computing power required to determine XYZ coordinates for the cylindrical and polar robot configurations are slightly more involved than for the Cartesian robot. The jointed arm robots require the greatest computational power of the different robot arm configurations.

Robot controllers, and other equipment with incremental encoders, always count the number of OFF-ON signals from the encoder's previous position to the current position in order to indicate displacement, which can be angular or linear. Quadrature encoders have a 90-degree phase difference between pulse signals, and they can also indicate to the robot controller the direction in which an actuator (motor or cylinder) is moving. If the controller is going to indicate rectilinear velocity (angular velocity) or acceleration (angular acceleration), then the "ds/dt (dθ/dt)" or "dv/dt (dω/dt)" values, respectively, must be calculated by the controller. The incremental encoder gives only the displacement count, which must then be processed by the controller for more precise and varied information.

The control system with incremental encoders generally does not know where the robot is positioned, or where "HOME" is, when the robot is turned on. The encoder marker (a single slot on a different radius from the incremental slots) can be used in conjunction with limit switches to find an accurate HOME position. This requires that the robot identify its HOME position before any programs are executed or taught. The approximate HOME position for each axis is identified by limit switches to get the encoder within one revolution of its accurate HOME. After the limit switch HOMEs are identified, the various motors are rotated until the single marker on each encoder is identified for the accurate HOME position of each axis (see Fig. 2-7). Once HOME is established, software limits are initialized. Generally, it is better to have the hardware limit switches outside

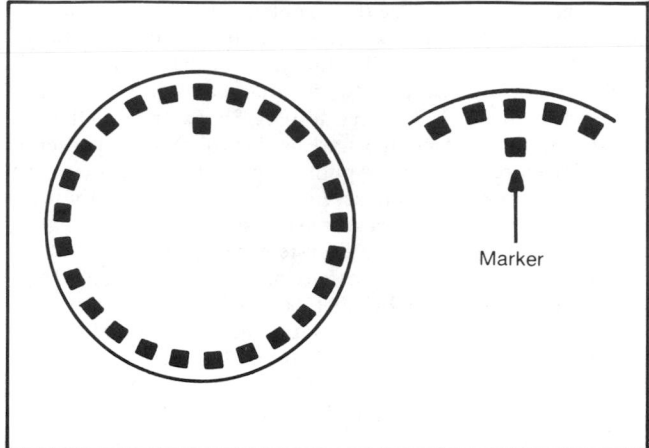

Fig. 2-7 Incremental encoder.

the work envelope setup by the software limits. Software limits do not activate EMERGENCY STOP (E-STOP) circuitry, while hardware limit switches may give E-STOP conditions. The hard-wired limit switches can be moved, but they should be kept outside the work envelope established by the software limits. One some controllers, the software limits are programmable.

Robot controllers with absolute encoders generally know the position of each joint, even at start-up, because of the information given by the encoder. Absolute encoders can be binary, binary-coded decimal, or gray code. The reliability of the gray code is much higher than that of the binary encoder because at any given displacement, only one bit is changing its ON-OFF status, and thus error-checking capability is much greater (see Fig. 2-8). The absolute encoder is only valid for one revolution. Other techniques need to be used or included to maintain complete absolute positioning. One method is to use two absolute encoders with an appropriate gear train between the two encoders. A second method uses a constant memory-counting circuit with the absolute encoder. In the first method the gear train does not affect accuracy since the gear train and second encoder are used to count the number of revolutions made by the first one.

The resolver is a rotary transformer with a primary consisting of one rotor (rotating primary field) one and two pairs of stator coils (secondary field winding) that are displaced 90 electrical degrees from each other. The output will be a sine wave for the one winding and a cosine wave for the other (see Fig. 2-9). At any point in time, a given rotor position will generate a specific voltage

$$e = E \sin(\theta t) \qquad (1)$$

in stator winding #1 on the sine wave and a second point on the cosine wave

$$e = E \cos(\theta t) \qquad (2)$$

or

$$e = E \sin(\omega t + \theta) \qquad (3)$$

in stator winding #2. The information from the data in the two

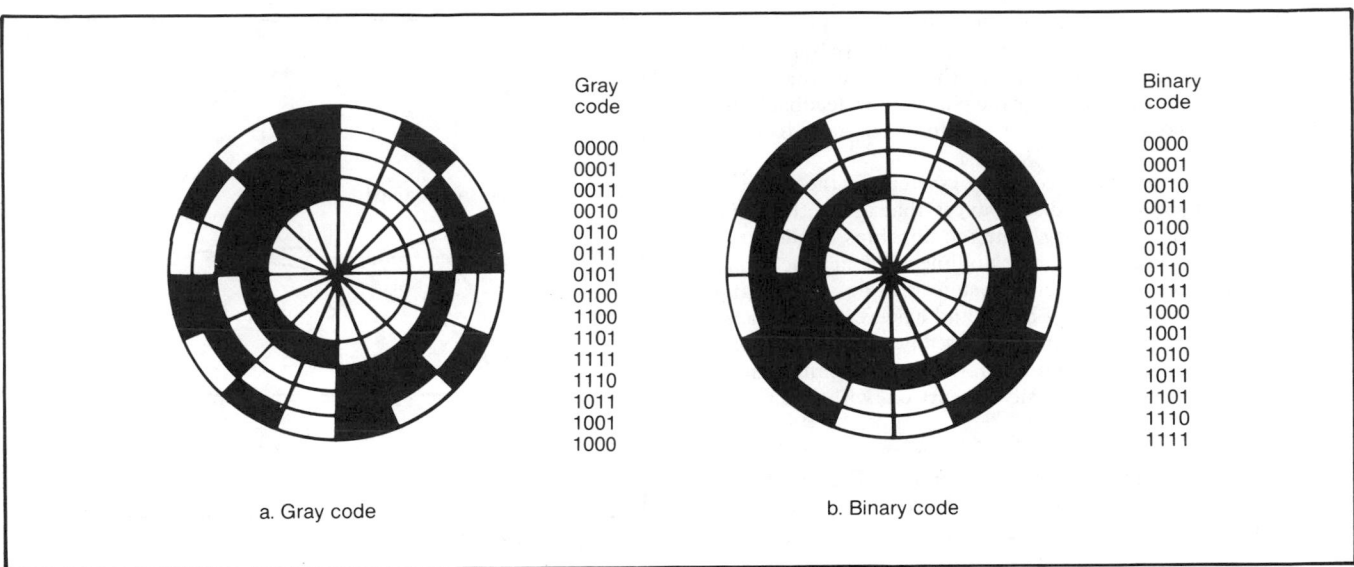

Fig. 2-8 Gray and binary absolute encoders and codes.

sinusoidal waves, processed together will distinguish the absolute rotor position. Also, the direction of rotation can be determined from the two waves and velocity from the frequency of the AC output.

The advantages of resolver include reliability, low noise to signal ratio with output signals of 0 to 120 volts AC, velocity output, and good vibration toleration. Their disadvantages are physical size, impedance changes with a change in temperature, and the cost of the ADC electronics (12 bit) required to give absolute positioning of the same order of resolution that is possible with optical encoders. Resolvers, like absolute encoders, can only distinguish a position for one revolution. When resolvers are used for absolute positioning in multiturn operations, a gear train generally is included.

Open-Loop Control Systems

Open-loop control systems are not common in robotics and are restricted to two types: 1) pick-and-place pneumatically actuated robots driven by a controller on a timed sequential basis or, at a higher level, 2) stepper motor-driven robot axes using a microprocessor controller with a stepping motor driver for each axis. The stepper motor-driven robots are also not very common. The advantage of the open-loop system is the apparent economical initial price of the robot. The price of accessory items for part presentation will probably be greater than the price for robots with more capable controllers. The open-loop stepper motor-driven robots can be accurate, but they have two problems: 1) knowing the location of a HOME position and 2) if an axis misses a step for any reason, then the remaining movements will be offset by that missed displacement. These two problems cause a robot to wander in its tool coordinate system, reducing its repeatability and its practical use.

Closed-Loop Control Systems

The majority of robots are closed-loop control machines. The assurance of accuracy and repeatability of closed-loop control is not matched by open-loop machines. The closed-loop control system uses the microprocessor to generate the servo signal for a given axis, and a servo amplifier to amplify the signal

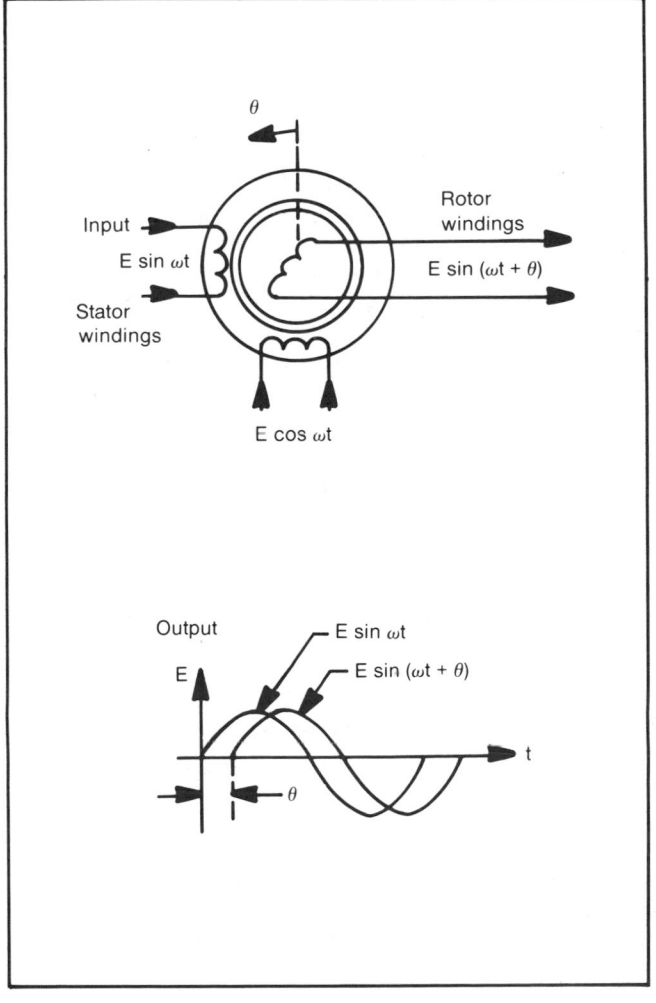

Fig. 2-9 Resolver circuitry.

and drive the actuator (electric motor or hydraulic valve to control a motor, cylinder or rotary actuator) for that axis. The microprocessor receives as an input the manipulator sensor signal (encoders or resolvers) for the closed-loop feedback signal. The servo control is shown in block diagram form in Fig. 2-10.

The significance of the servo control system for the user is in the two areas of nonlinear disturbances that affect the servo system and the gain/damping/time relationships of the servo amplifier for each axis. Common nonlinear disturbances that affect the operation of the servo system include stiction and friction, viscous friction, dead band, and hysteresis (and backlash). These specific disturbances affect any servo system and can be minimized but not eliminated. Other disturbances, such as temperature, are more easily linearized with electronic circuitry.

Classical servo system operation shows overdamped, critically damped, and underdamped operation (see Fig. 2-11). The gain adjustment in the controller is related to the damping by the amplification of the error feedback signal. The higher the gain for a given axis is set:

1. The larger the signal to the servo amplifier.
2. The amplifier's output to the actuator is larger.
3. The greater the slope of the curve in the servo system for that specific axis.

Each servo axis has a separate gain control for that servo feedback signal amplifier.

If the gain is too high, underdamping and oscillation will result. This underdamping is related to the hysteresis of the system and the load. The greater the speed, the greater the kinetic energy ($KE = .5mv^2$). Since the robot controller has less time to decelerate that axis, overshooting occurs. If the gain is too low, the error signal is minimized and the servo amplifier will give a smaller output signal. In turn the system will react at a

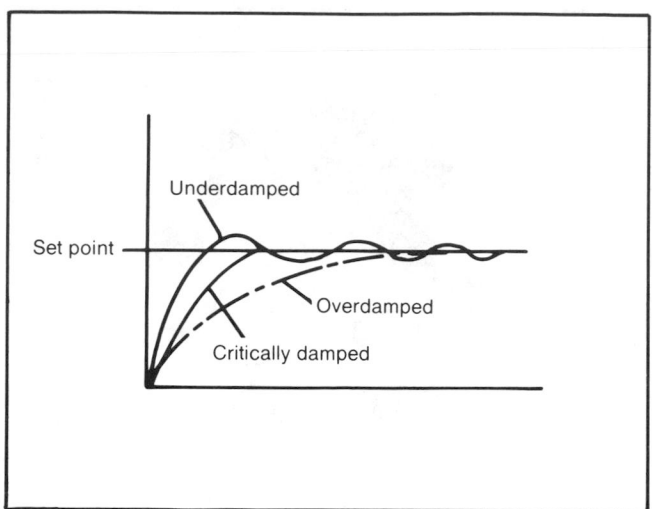

Fig. 2-11 Response of servo systems.

slower rate, with overdamping and a longer time to complete the move.

In most robotic systems, a critically damped operation is desired. Whenever the servo is not critically damped, the time for the robot to execute a step will probably be longer than the critically damped time. Obviously, overdamped systems are slower. The oscillation and settling time for an underdamped system may require a longer time period than a critically damped system.

The oscillations of an underdamped system may not be a problem for some gross material handling applications, but oscillations are a problem for fine assembly work, continuous-path processing operations, and any other applications where precise, accurate movements are required. The damping/time relationship is important for minimizing robot cycle time and for having accurate, smooth robotic arm and wrist movements at the full range of robot operation speeds at the specified loads.

The servo valves in hydraulic systems need to be nulled frequently; electric systems need to be balanced. In each case, gain and balancing adjustments are part of the servo tuning that needs to be done periodically, even if the robot is given only light use.

The optical encoders, resolvers, tachometer generators, and LVDTs or other sensors in the manipulator generate the feedback signal for the servo amplifier. High-quality signals with a low signal-to-noise ratio are an advantage in this environment.

SPECIFICATIONS

The general specifications for robots include the requirements for the robot and controller operating environment, physical dimensions and characteristics, electrical requirements, dimensions of its work envelope, weight of the payload the arm will carry (this includes the weight of the wrist), and the velocity, accuracy, and repeatability of each of the axes under different load conditions. The end of arm tooling, including the wrist, is specified separately from the robot. The specifications for the wrist are similar to those of the robot manipulator. The specifications of the controller include the type (servo vs. non-servo), inputs and outputs, program storage, program recording, teaching procedures, memory size, program panel display, and communications capability.

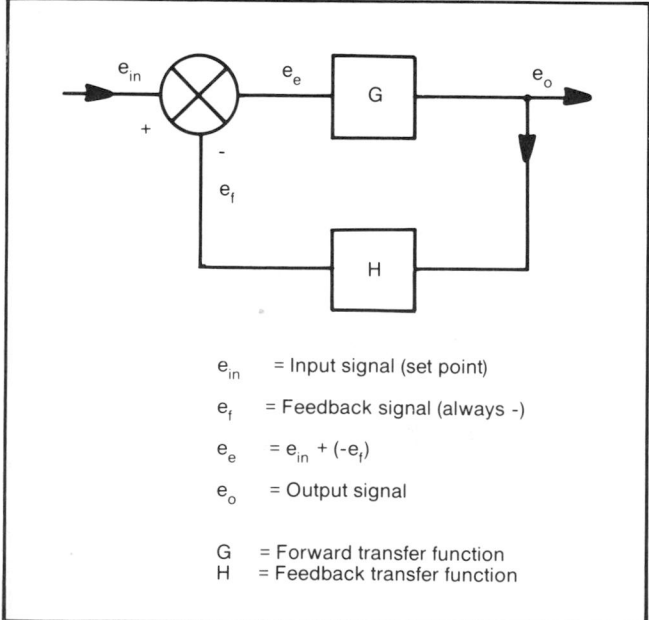

e_{in} = Input signal (set point)

e_f = Feedback signal (always -)

e_e = $e_{in} + (-e_f)$

e_o = Output signal

G = Forward transfer function
H = Feedback transfer function

Fig. 2-10 Block diagram representation of closed loop servo system.

STANDARDS

The purpose of standards in the robotics industry is to improve the following:

- safety of robot operation.
- exchange of technical information.
- accuracy in processing statistics about robot usage.
- importation and exportation of robots.
- education and training.

Standards support these goals when manufacturers use similar designations and procedures for describing the operation of the robot. When robot operators may have to contend with several robots from several countries, confusion, and unsafe conditions, can occur. Terms should have the same definitions for robots, regardless of country of origin. To date, the ISO has standard graphic symbols for robots, while the Robotic Industries Association (RIA) does not.[4]

PROGRAMMING ROBOTS

The most ommon practice in programming robots has been to use on-line programming with either a teach pendant with some pick-and-place and point-to-point robots or lead-through for point-to-point and continuous-path robots. Teach pendant and lead-through programming have many advantages, primarily the ability to do direct programming, ease of learning to program, and economy. Workers who are familiar with the manufacturing process (manual painting, welding, or dispensing routines) are the best candidates for programming the continuous-path moves that require expertise in the movement.

On-line and off-line programming require knowledge of different coordinate systems. The world frame or world coordinate system (WCS) is a fixed base, Cartesian coordinate system, with its origin at the center of the manipulator base or some other fixed location. The tool frame or tool coordinate system (TCS) is a coordinate system used with end-of-arm tooling. Teach pendant and lead-through programming are done in the TCS. The tool center point (TCP) is often the center of the TCS. The joint frame or joint coordinate system (JCS) identifies the joint position values for each position. Point-to-point robots store each TCS point by saving the JCS values for that position. The sensor frame or sensor coordinate system (SCS) is the coordinate system for the sensing system in the manipulator or a vision system if integrated with the robot. The goal frame or user coordinate system (UCS) is the coordinate system for the part that is to be handled by the robot. In material handling, the TCS and the UCS must be used to move the part correctly.[5] These coordinate systems are more significant when off-line programming is used. NC machine tools use only the Cartesian coordinate system.

On-Line Programming

Teach pendant programming for point-to-point or continuous-path machines is relatively easy to learn, especially if the programming is direct without subroutines or conditional branching. Teach pendant programming does not require a conscious awareness of different coordinate systems. Teach-pendant programming can deal in a relative world and not the absolute world required for off-line programming. On-line programming with a teach pendant is more economical. In any case, one needs the teach pendant, whereas software for off-line programming is several thousand dollars.

On-line programming is most appropriate when:

- Robot programs are not changed very often.
- The programming is direct.
- There are trades people who enjoy this technical challenge.
- The programming can be done on-line in off hours.
- The programming can be done quickly during production.
- The programs can be saved once they are developed and perfected.

On-line programming that frequently shuts down production for long periods of time or requires excessive lead time to develop is not acceptable.

Off-Line Programming

Off-line programming is typically an engineering department function. It requires knowledge of the absolute positions of all the stations in the work cell with the WCS, learning a new proprietary language, a computer plus an additional $1000.00 to $10,000.00 for the software and is available only for the more sophisticated point-to-point or continuous-path robot controllers.

At this time, most robot companies that have off-line programming capability have their own proprietary programming languages. Examples of these proprietary languages are Unimate's VAL, IBM's A Manufacturing Language (AML), and GMF's Karel. The most common nonproprietary languages involve the use of a CNC controller and NC code, with their inherent disadvantages, or a little-known language developed in academia. Several CAD/CAM programs have off-line simulation programs for robots. Off-line programming is valuable in modeling the objects in a work cell, modeling the robot's kinematics, simulation of the robot movements and other devices in the work cell, and in developing the robot program. The off-line programming system and robot controller need to have two-way communication capability (up-loading and down-loading). This up-loading is most significant when a large complex program has been developed and requires on-line adjustment with a teach pendant and off-line storage. The modified and acceptable program needs to be up-loaded and stored for easy recall and use. A work cell will include the robot(s) workpieces, end-of-arm tooling, materials handling equipment, and any other equipment significant to the application. One advantage of off-line programming is that with a large number of complex programs (over ten) one or two programs may be written off-line, verified, modified until they are acceptable, and implemented while the remaining programs are being written. In many cases, verification and modification will still need to be done on-line, but in much less time than with total on-line programming.

Off-line programming is appropriate in applications where on-line programming is not accessible or dangerous, when multiple robots can be programmed from one off-line system, when CAD/CAM data bases can be integrated, when complex tasks can be simplified compared to on-line procedures, and when suitable simulation and verification can be used for the program.[6,7]

Users of off-line programming will need to learn the specific proprietary language for that robot controllers, to allow for on-line program verification and modification in many applications, and to be thorough in checking the meaning of terms used in the programming language the different coordinate systems or world, robot, and tool).[8] Generally, off-line programming often models or simulates the robot's kinematics but not its

CHAPTER 2

DESCRIPTION OF ROBOTIC SYSTEMS

dynamics. In the off-line program it is possible to program a move in the off-line program that the robot can perform in an acceptably kinematically but not dynamically.

Off-line programming requires construction of a geometric model. This has often been time consuming, inaccurate, and error prone. If CAD system data can be used, the process can be minimized. International Graphic Exchange Specification (IGES) can be effective in exchanging graphics data between hardware systems. The off-line programming system should be able to model the robot kinematics. Unless software is written specifically for a given robot, its accuracy will be limited in simulating the robot's kinematics. The accuracy of the software representation of robot's kinematic characteristics needs to be verified for specific software and robots. Some off-line programs do not include robot modeling, and others include it under kinematics, path control, or generalized operation.

Four levels of off-line programming have been identified:[9]

1. Joint level, where each robot joint is programmed, the robotic equivalent to programming a microcomputer in machine language.
2. Manipulator level, using the world coordinate system (WCS) and mathematical techniques to determine individual joint values in the Cartesian coordinate system.
3. Object level, specifies task movement in a WCS, involves structured programming with data structures and a higher level of programming.
4. Objective level, states the task in general form in conversational language.

Most off-line programs today are still at the manipulator level with a few at the object level.[10] The off-line programs for robotics parallel NC computer-assisted programs in that they are either textual or graphic.

Desirable options for off-line programming software include the capability to program, control, perform collision detection of multiple robots; model both kinematics and dynamics of the robots, model joint constraints and reach testing and communicate with a specific controller.[11]

END-OF-ARM TOOLING

The purpose of a robot is to perform reprogrammable tasks, which may require a variety of tools on the end of the robot manipulator. The wide range of tools used on any given robot has led some manufacturers to market robots without wrists or end-of-arm tooling. The wrist plus the end effector (also called end-of arm tooling) are mounted on the end of the robot manipulator arm. End-of-arm tooling includes grasping tools (mechanical fingers, vacuum suckers, and electromagnets) and nongrasping tooling (spraying, welding, and dispensing).

In conceiving an end of arm tool, it is useful to consider three variables: the level of existing technology in the overall facility, the degree of flexibility desired in the tooling, and the role of the end of arm tooling within the system.[12]

End of arm tooling needs to be designed as one of the components of the robotic work cell. Consideration of dual grippers for removing a finished part and placing a new one can decrease robot unload/load cycle time. Dual grippers may be necessary to accommodate the changes in the part due to the process (such as, machining or welding processes). If a large number of payloads requiring different types of grippers are being included in the work cell, then either a universal gripper or

quick exchange grippers should be included in the design. As the interface between the robot and the parts to be handled, the design of the end-of-arm tooling is critical to the success of the work cell.

The robot controller, or cell controller if one is used, and its accompanying software should be specified. If vision, automatic identification (AID), or the frequent development of new robot programs are planned, the robot controller and software should provide for the vision integration, AID input, or the development of off-line programs.

The Wrist.

The wrist will have one, two, or three axes of motion. The three axes—roll, pitch, and yaw—give the end effector orientation while the manipulator gives it position (see Fig. 2-12). Most robots have at least one of these three axes, with either roll or pitch being the most common; many robots have two of the three, with roll and pitch being the most common motions. Others have a full three-axes wrist that utilizes all three motions, and this gives the robot the greatest flexibility in positioning the end effector. As implied, yaw is the least common motion utilized. On servo controlled systems, each wrist axis has its own servo amplifier, and gain and damping adjustment. The weight of the wrist, with its actuators and sensors, is included in the specifications given for the robot manipulator's lifting capacity, or payload.

The end effectors are mounted on the wrist. The center of gravity for both the end effector and the load changes both the wrist's load capacity and the performance of the servo control system. The wrist actuators must be capable of handling the forces generated by the payload. The bending moments imposed by the wrist and the work load must be considered in the selection of a robot to move a given load at a given velocity both within a specified cycle time (including settling time) and at a specified quality of movement (no overshooting or underdamping on continuous-path machines).

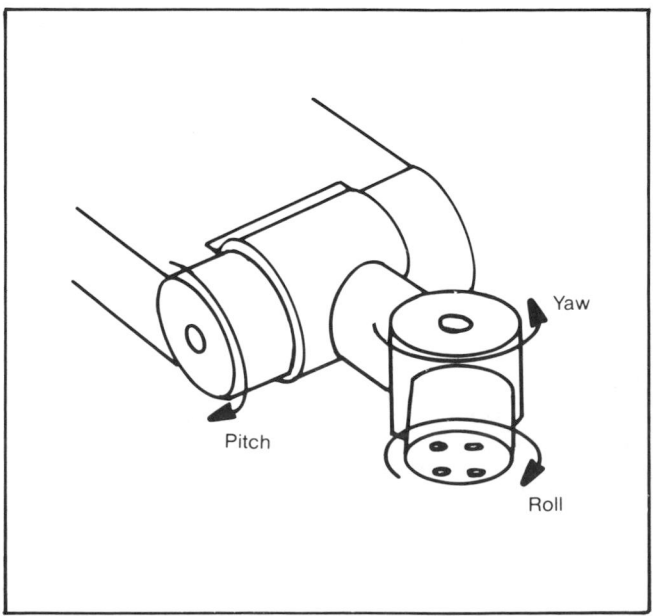

Fig. 2-12 Robot wrist motions.

End Effectors

The end effector is the interface device between the manipulator/wrist and the workpiece. Most end effectors have a mounting plate, a power device for operating the tooling, and mechanical linkages. Sensors are optional. There are literally thousands of gripper and end effector designs available today. While most grippers are mechanical, some jobs require vacuum or magnetic grippers. There are generic end effectors available, and there are companies who just make end effectors and sell them to robot manufacturers or sophisticated end users. Still, most end effectors are designed for a specific application.

The mounting plate may provide for a bolted mount and orientation of the end effector. The mounting plate may be designed to enhance programmed, quick-change tooling to be secured by a coupling mechanism to give multiple end effectors for a given robot in a work cell. Similar to manipulator power supplies, end effector power sources are either electrical, hydraulic, or pneumatic. Unlike the manipulator power source, pneumatic is the most common type because of lightweight actuators, low cost, and ease of installation and maintenance. It is possible to program changes in gripping force by changing regulators or regulator pressure. When larger gripping forces are necessary, hydraulic power can be used. Electrically operated end effectors are used, but they tend to have a larger footprint than pneumatically operated ones for equivalent forces.

Each end effectors should be evaluated for weight, the lighter the better; size, the smaller the better; flexibility in part handling, the more the better; rigidity, the stronger the more accurate with less vibration; holding force, the more available the larger the safety factor (but without damaging the workpiece); and installation and maintenance, the easier and quicker the better for getting a robot back into production.[13]

The design of the end effectors should start with the analysis of the workpiece, proceed to process analysis, and conclude with a robot system consideration. The end effectors must be designed to successfully grasp or process the workpiece. Two scissors or parallel jaw grippers may be more appropriate than highly articulated fingers.

The actual robot configuration and specifications should not be chosen until workpiece analysis is completed, or the design of the end effector may have to be changed to correct for problems with the specific robot. the latter often leads to an unsuccessful installation.

Similarly, a complete understanding of the manufacturing process is critical to correctly designing the end effectors. Relevant considerations include changes in part size, changes in oiliness, presentation and deposition of the part, variances from part model to part model, changes in part temperature, sequence of operations, and the environment of the robot.[14]

Grasping Tools

End effectors used to grasp parts have grippers with two or more fingers, vacuum suckers, electromagnets, multipurpose grippers, one of a variety of less common devices (single inflatable fingers), or special tooling. The ideal gripper is strong, flexible, universal, small, lightweight, and economical. This combination is not always possible and compromises are required.

The basic question in the selection of a gripper is, How well can it do the specified task? The task (moving a workpiece) must be completed successfully without damaging the workpiece or the processing equipment.[15] Often, the robot does not grasp a part directly, but it grips a pallet instead and may move one or more workpieces. In such as case, the terms workpiece, part, and pallet are considered as interchangeable. The analysis of mechanical grasping introduces the concept of prehension (seizing or grasping).

There are several basic concerns for gripper design. The common features a gripper and work cell must possess are:

1. The part must be accessible to the gripper.
2. The gripper must be able to accommodate the manufacturing processes performed on the workpiece between the robot loading and unloading operations (changes in diameter during a turning operation).
3. The work holder and gripper must be compatible so the gripper can successfully grasp the workpiece in the workholder.
4. The gripper should grasp the workpiece near the part's center of gravity. This reduces the bending moments on the gripper and wrist. As the weight of the workpiece increases with respect to robot and wrist payload capacity, so does the significance of where to grasp the part.
5. The gripper should grasp the largest possible dimension of the part, when there is a choice of sizes. Grasping the larger dimension should improve gripper control of the part.[16]

Grasping an object can be done with several forms of prehension: 1) cylindrical, 2) tip, 3) hook or snap, 4) palmar, 5) spherical, or 6) lateral.[17] The industrial mechanical grippers have either rigid or articulated fingers, grasping of external or internal surfaces, scissors or parallel movement, and single or multiple-gripper mountings. The two-fingered gripper is the most popular for industry.[18] The relationship between the number of fingers, rigid versus one-joint articulation, and selected capabilities of the gripper are given in Table 2-1.

TABLE 2-1
Approximate Relationship Between Finger, Articulation, and Function[19]

Type of Gripper Finger	Functions		
	Grasping	Shape Accommodation	Manipulation
2 Fingers, Rigid	Possible	Not Possible	Not Possible
2 Fingers, Articulated	Possible	Possible	Not Possible
3 Fingers, Rigid	Possible	Possible	Not Possible
3 Fingers, Articulated	Possible	Possible	Possible
5 Fingers, Rigid	Possible	Possible	Not Possible
5 Fingers, Articulated	Possible	Possible	Possible

CHAPTER 2

DESCRIPTION OF ROBOTIC SYSTEMS

Vacuum and electromagnetic grippers are standard types of grasping tools. Vacuum suckers are used to handle a variety of nonporous flexible and rigid materials. They are usually gentle with the workpiece, and function best when the sucker and workpiece are vertical and not horizontal and when the surfaces are clean and dry (definitely not oily). Vacuum suckers use proven designs and have blow-off capability.[20]

Industrial vacuum systems operate between 10-25″ Hg (254-635 torrs). High vacuums, above 25″ Hg (635 torr), are not as economical. Further more, most industrial robotic vacuums are developed by venturis, not motor-driven pumps, and will not produce the high vacuum characteristic of a pump.

The electromagnetic gripper is somewhat comparable to vacuum-operated systems with one limitation, it can grasp only ferromagnetic materials. The part shape/electromagnet fit must be good, single or multiple magnets must support sheet material to prevent curling and pulling away from the magnets, and the workpiece must always be of dirt, scale, or other substances that would increase the gap between the electromagnet and the part.

Universal grippers are defined as computer-controlled grippers that are able to grasp a number of different sized and shaped parts firmly and rigidly and, upon command, present the part in a specified orientation. These grippers can have multiple degrees of freedom that are similar to the human hand. Several different designs have been developed and tested. Very few are commercially available or in production use. The demands on a controller for moving each joint of each finger in a coordinated manner for screwing a nut on a bolt are very large. It is difficult to get the necessary amount of force into a joint of a finger by any actuator small enough to allow for the number of actuators required for a three or five-fingered multijointed hand. To date, most designs have incorporated cables from the actuator to the finger joint. There is no need for robot end effectors to look and operate like human hands.[21] A two or three-finger rigid gripper may be appropriate and may be able to exert more force than if it were articulated.

An almost infinite number of special grasping tools has been designed to achieve specific capabilities. The limitations in special tooling are based on economic factors and the creativity of the designers.

As the robot and end effectors become more sophisticated, the requirements placed on the equipment that presents the part to the robot decrease. The converse is also true; if the robot technology is low, the part presentation technology must be higher.

Passive remote center compliance (RCC) devices are available and they permit angular as well as parallel misalignment. The specification for RCC devices indicate the amount of misalignment they will accommodate.

Non-Grasping Tools

Two of the most common uses of robots have been in spot-welding and paint spraying—examples of nongrasping end effectors. Other nongrasping end-of-arm tools include various kinds of welding and sealant and adhesive dispensing, deburring, green sand mold drying, and some other less-common applications.

Nongrasping end effectors such as spot welding and arc welding, and paint spraying require at least five—and often six—degrees of freedom in the robot and wrist. These complex motions are necessary to orient the tool at the correct angle to the workpiece. Also, most of these applications, especially automotive ones, require polar or articulated manipulators to achieve the necessary flexibility. Arc welding, spraying, and dispensing are normally continuous-path operations compared to the point-to-point operation that is adequate for most grasping or spot-welding applications. Selected paths can be followed with point-to-point robots with linear and circular interpolation capabilities in contrast to full continuous-path capabilities. Whether the arc welding, spraying, dispensing, or deburring, the path between end points is as important as the end points themselves. Mounting the process equipment on the robot wrist and programming the robot require that the robot applications people and the programmers understand the technology of the applications as well as of robotics.

APPLICATION

The corporate goal for any expenditure is to "get the most for the investment." Management may define a successful robotic installation as one that achieves 100% of the planned objectives. Not every robotic installation will be 100% successful.[22]

Robotics, more than some forms of automation, cause concerns of job security among the labor force. The short history of robotics has shown that a robotics installation that forgoes early and thorough communication with labor will tend to be significantly less than successful.

The statement that "automation should be planned from the top down and implemented from the bottom up" also continues to be advocated for robotics. Top-level corporate officers are expected to know the company's strategic plans, projected plans for current and new products, production costs, reinvestment plans, and manufacturing needs. They are also in a position to commit resources for a major investment in robotics. Without top-level support, middle-management is often reluctant to introduce new technology until they are assured of top-level management's support. Support is shown through corporate statements, communications between people, communications with labor, and corresponding actions capital expenditures for robotics equipment and the allocation of resources for robotics projects). If there is no long-term corporate commitment, any major automation project—including robotics—has little chance of success.

A robotics project should be more than an engineering project by engineers. It should involve the engineers, but also representatives from both management and labor. The role of management and labor is not intended to diminish that of the manufacturing and other engineering personnel, but rather to emphasize the necessary team effort and the communications required for the acceptance of the robot by all levels of hourly and salaried personnel. One-way communications from engineering to production and maintenance people is not adequate; the successful implementation of robots needs to include two-way communication. Three different approaches to organizing a robotics project team are recommended. One approach is to use a team from corporate headquarters to serve all plants. A second practice is to have individual teams at each plant. The third method is to have a combination of the first two with representatives from headquarters working with the local team.

Following is an outline for a four-phase, sixteen-step process for the implementation of robots:[23]

Phase I
1. Top management commitment.
2. Communication with organized labor.
3. Establishment of robotics team.
4. Familiarization with robotic technology.
5. Familiarization with commercially available equipment.
6. Knowledge of manufacturing operations and processes.
7. Initial plant survey.
8. Detailed analysis.
9. Selection and prioritization of applications.

Phase II
1. Preliminary design.
2. Detailed design.

Phase III
1. Fabrication of the system.
2. Pre-installation activities.

Phase IV
1. Monitoring.
2. Downtime logging.
3. Final cost/benefit analysis.

PHASE I

Robots are implemented for different reasons. One scenario is a corporate mandate to automate, and engineering people try to find the best places to do this automation. In another scenario engineering personnel are trying to solve a difficult manufacturing problem, with robots as part of one potential solution. Still another situation occurs when a company is replacing production equipment or adding to current capacity, and robots are included as a possible solution. Occasionally, a manager observes that other division have robots and he/she wants some in his/her division, too, but this scenario does not usually result in successful installations and will not be discussed any further. The following procedures have value for any of the above scenarios. Any application, whether it is a single-potential application being considered as part of expanding capability or one installation site of several, should be implemented within the following guidelines.

The first three points of Phase I have been discussed in the first paragraphs of this section. The familiarization of personnel with robotic technology and commercially available equipment can and should happen through participation in local Robotic Industries Association meetings; courses at community colleges, vocational tech schools, and universities; and attendance at automated manufacturing and robotic trade shows and conference presentations such as "AUTOFACT" and "Robotics." A knowledge of a company's manufacturing operations and processes is an absolute must. Knowledge of why certain operations are done the way they are, must be understood before a project team can realistically plan changes.

The preliminary site survey for placing a robot, selection of

sites for robot, prioritization of sites, engineering of a site, implementation of the robot(s), and evaluation will be discussed in the following sections.

Preliminary Site Survey

The preliminary site survey should identify tasks a robot could accomplish, tasks that do not require judgement, and tasks that can justify the use of a robot. These preliminary criteria are used to identify potential sites to install robots. If labor and management can agree to video taping or photographs of present operations done manually, it is a good time to get them on file for later reference. The above criteria can be used in either a plant survey or a specific site survey such as the suggestion: "Let's put a robot here." Some rules of thumb for preliminary survey include:[24]

1. Looking for hazardous, repetitive, and boring jobs—perhaps ones with a history of workmen's compensation claims or jobs which have a high rate of personnel turnover. The labor members of a robotic project team may have input about how workers feel about given work assignments.
2. A projected robot cycle time of more than five seconds.
3. The planned lot size should be greater than twenty-five.
4. Accurate, consistent presentation of the part to the robot is possible.
5. Precision placement of the part by the robot is not required (higher accuracy than + 0.0004″, 0.1 mm).
6. The working volume for the potential robot is less than 1060 ft^3 (30 m^3).
7. The payloads are less than 1100 lbs (500 kg.).
8. The number of parts per cycle are less than ten.
9. The process can be structured.
10. The number of program subroutine options for a given program is less than five, depending on how many programs a robot can have in active memory at one time. One needs to remember that rules of thumb are not absolutes, especially as robot technology changes, specifically the smaller SCARA-type robots can have high arm velocities, short cycle times, and extremely accurate functions.

Site Selection

The preliminary survey does some screening of potential sites, but it is cursory. After several potential sites are identified, a more thorough survey needs to be done before a site is selected and the engineering study is done. The criteria used to determine the qualifications of a site should be at least a seven-step process. These qualifying criteria are especially appropriate for individuals in corporations without a large robotics knowledge base.[25]

Complexity. Robots should not be used in extremely simple or extremely complex operations. Extremely simple operations may use pick-and-place robots, but simpler and cheaper shop fabricated systems with relay or microprogrammable logic controllers may work just as well. Operations requiring a combination of judgement, feel, and control should be avoided. If the human sensing abilities are the only practical ones, then the robot is not appropriate. In the area of complexity of operations, many times new or modified equipment can be purchased to eliminate the problem of "feel" from the operation. This additional equipment can raise the cost of the robot installation,

CHAPTER 2

APPLICATION

but the new equipment may improve the manufacturing processes as well as making it possible to automate the process with or without robots.

Repeatability. The process must have repeatability and disorder must be eliminated.

Part position and attitude should be consistent. If consistency is not attained, additional systems—including vision—may be required. This follows the rule of thumb that simple robots require repeatability from the accessory equipment, while sophisticated robots can tolerate some types of disorders in the accessory equipment. For example, a stack of parts may vary in height as they are used. Vision equipment can deal with this variation in height. Bin picking of overlapping parts, however, is too disordered and ambiguous with the vision equipment that is available today.

Speed. Robots are generally not any faster than people when measured cycle by cycle, but robots do work at a consistent pace better than people.

Pick-and-place robots can be very fast. Smaller servo controlled robots with lighter payloads can also be fast and move at speeds up to 4.3 ft/sec (1.3 m/sec). As payloads become larger, either speed or accuracy drops off. Good accuracies can be achieved, but this is generally with slower speeds, and at the end of a faster move. The result is a longer cycle time. Robot production over a longer period of time (an eight-hour shift for example), is usually higher than production with people because people tire, have work breaks, and are inconsistent.

Utilization. Robots are best utilized when small batches are 25 cycles or more, and large continuous production runs are less than 25 million cycles per year.

If fewer than 25 cycles per set-up are run, the setup time may become too time-consuming, and people may prove to be a more productive alternative. Changeover time should be less than 10% of the time required to produce a batch of parts. If more than 25 million cycles per year are run, then special purpose automation should be considered for better economy and production rates. Part, product, and process obsolescence, an excessive amount of time required to go from engineering to production using automated equipment, or the desire for flexibility in the future may suggest installation of robots. If these issues are not factors, then hard automation should be considered.

Cost Justification. If approximate savings are more than 50% of approximate costs, then the installation of a robot in the application can probably be justified economically (assuming a two-year payoff criterion).

This criterion is used as a rough estimate and not the final economic justification. For this purpose the following formula is appropriate:

$$P = \frac{I}{S - E} \qquad (4)$$

Where:
P = Payback in years
I = Total investment for the project
S = Total savings per year (labor, material, scrap rework, etc.)
E = Total expenses per year (maintenance, education, etc.)

The final economic justification cannot be completed until the engineering analysis is completed, but this analysis indicates whether or not the project will be close to a two-year payoff. If a particular company uses criterion other than a two-year payoff, the above figure should be changed to reflect the specific situation.

Acceptance. A robot should be accepted by workers for a specific operation in a specific location.

It is common for people to say they favor using robots, but these same people always find negative reasons for not using them in applications that may affect them directly. Involvement of labor during the planning and implementation of a robot technology is necessary to ensure acceptance of the robots, for specific installations. If this does not happen, the chances of success for the installation are low.

Prioritization

A number of authors have developed quantifiable lists and ordinal-based scoring systems for ranking and qualifying robot installations. These are helpful in objectively evaluating different sites for installing robots. Videotapes and photographs can be very helpful to the project team in these deliberations. If a quantifiable process has been used previously, then its results should be inserted here for a historical comparison. Otherwise, the evaluation chart (as seen in Table 2-2) should be completed to serve as a source of data for evaluation after the installation is completed. Even though the following selection criteria chart may not be of specific value for this application before the installation, it should be completed to start developing the data base for evaluation of future robot sites and evaluation of the robot selection process.

When the prioritization and screening have been completed, the robot selection team should select from the prioritized list one of the top two or three applications. Final on-site inspections of the top selections are recommended. Other factors not measured in the qualifications process may be considered, but if these new factors are very significant they should be included in the qualifying criteria.

Proponents of robotics recommend that the first installation is relatively simple, that it will be successful, and that robots should not be used to solve manufacturing problems.

Once the selection step is completed and approved, the engineering work can begin.

PHASE II

The purpose of this phase is to do the manufacturing engineering, (process and material handling and simulation and work cell interfacing, for example) and it requires that the manufacturing engineers in communication with the robot project team—develop a familiarity with the manufacturing work site, the standard operations involved, production data, and any random disturbances to the process. This familiarity requires on-the-floor observation and conversation with labor personnel.

The first analysis should include start-of-shift activities, normal operating activities, and end-of-shift activities. The analysis should include conversations with the workers about normal and random activities—procedures they may have to do either once an hour, a day, or a week.

A second analysis of the work site should include a thorough examination of alternatives. The alternatives consist of the following questions:

1. Is there equipment other than a robot that would be better suited for the task at hand?
2. Is there a better way to mount the robot than the conventional foot of the robot to the floor?

TABLE 2-2
Robot Application Evaluation Chart [25]

ELEMENT	MEASURED BY	POINTS	
1. Complexity of task	One to five parts	1 part	10
		5 parts	5
	One to ten operations	1 oper.	10
		10 opers.	5
	One to five batches	1 batch	5
		5 batches	1
2. Complexity of tooling and peripherals	One to ten parts	1 part	10
		5 parts	5
	Parts delivery orientation	Single	10
		Matrix	5
		Random	0
	Ease of orienting parts	Easy	10
		Difficult	5
3. Facility and equipment	Relocation required	No	2
		Yes	0
	Utilities availability	At site	5
		Nearby	3
		Not Avail.	0
	Floor loading	Adequate	3
		Need new	0
4. Product and/or process changes	Product changes required	None	10
		Minor	5
		Major	0
	Process changes	None	10
		Minor	5
		Major	0
5. Impact on related operations	Synchronized with previous operations	No	3
		Yes	0
	Synchronized with following operations	No	3
		Yes	0
	Bottleneck	No	3
		Yes	0

ELEMENT	MEASURED BY	POINTS	
	Backup/buffer	Easy	3
		Hard	1
		Impossible	0
6. Impact on work force	Current work: Monotonous	Yes	3
		No	0
	Bad environment	Yes	3
		No	0
	Safety hazard	Yes	5
		No	0
	Fast pace or heavy load	Yes	3
		No	0
	Labor turnover	High	3
		Low	1
7. Risk of unforseen or random problems	Number of potential different occurences	One	10
		Ten	1
	Attitude/expectations of management	Understanding	10
		Unrealistic	0
8. Potential benefits	Labor savings per shift	Per 10 people	1
	Production shifts per day	Per shift	5
	Quality improvement	Yes	5
		No	0
	Productivity improvement	Per % increase	1
	Reduce repair and rework	Yes	5
		No	0
		—	
Total*			

*The higher the score the more desirable the installation.

APPLICATION

3. Is there a better way to do the process? What are the other ways to do the job? Which is best? Why?

Other engineering questions that could be considered and answered are listed below:

1. How will backup be provided if the robot is down?
2. What is the effect of the environment on the robot? Temperature, chemicals in fumes, vibration, and explosive atmospheres are some examples.
3. How will the robot affect the space currently allocated for the work site? Will it use more space, if so, is more space available?
4. How will the robot (or other equipment) affect the layout of the work site, the accessibility to servicing the equipment in the cell, and the material handling in the work cell?
5. How will people be protected from the robot, or the robot from people?

Engineering people are now ready to develop a scale layout drawing of the work site, including the robot and its work envelope, conveyors, buffers (if any), process equipment, and anything else that is involved in the cell. The description of the robot task, at the step level, needs to be documented. These two activities work site engineering and robot tasks with steps listed—may require that either one or the other or both need to be optimized to achieve an finely tuned manufacturing process.

The robot performance specifications can now be developed. If the robot specifications are done earlier than this, personnel may tend to be constrained by them, rather than use them in selecting a robot for the application. The robot specifications should be done for commercially available equipment based on economic and performance reliability reasons. Unless a corporation has sufficient robotic engineering skill in-house, it may be wise to employ an objective consultant to help with the specifications. Regardless of the approach used, performance specifications (and the manufacturer's fiscal stability) rather than manufacturer's brand and model should be specified. Standards are being developed by the Robotics Industries Association (RIA) for performance runoff as well as other robotic specifications. These are available from RIA.

The procedure for selecting a vendor depends on the company purchasing the robot, the software, and the accessory equipment for the work site. Fortune 500 corporations may have the personnel capable of doing the entire project internally, and they purchase the components. Smaller firms may want to consider a turnkey operation provided by a systems house. In between these two extremes are either contracts with systems houses where the purchasing corporation provides some of the services, or contracts with manufacturers of a specific robotic product line for the products and services they can provide.

The selection of a vendor and the resulting robot are extremely significant issues for assuring that the engineering will be successful and that both the vendor and the robot company will remain in business for years to come. The robot business is not a very mature industry, and it still has a large number of small vendors and system houses with some, but limited, experience. In the late 1980s there has been a consolidation in the number of robot manufacturers. These two players, vendors and manufacturers, remain critical considerations for a purchaser of robots.

The robotic project team shold evaluate not just the performance of the vendors' robots but also the financial statements of the potential vendors and manufacturers. This criterion should increase (it will not guarantee) the probability that both the vendor and the manufacturer will be around to provide service for the robot in future years. Purchasing agents and managers, who look only for the low bid, may not appreciate now that in five years their low bid vendor may be gone and there is only one knowledgeable service person or parts supplier for that robot left in the United States. This may be true for robots built either domestically or off-shore. If the corporation purchasing the robot has an adequately trained maintenance crew, this may not present any difficulties. But if the corporation is planning to have the manufacturer or distributor provide the major service, it can be a problem.

PHASE III

Phase III involves the work site fabrication at either the vendor's location or on-site. In each case a performance runoff acceptance clause, indicating that the robotic system should meet specifications, should be in the contract. The performance runoff/acceptance feature is a standard part of most contracts today. Still there are occasions when the runoff is acceptable according to the specifications, but final performance is not determined by the desired performance. Training for operators, maintenance, and manufacturing engineering people should also occur during this phase.

PHASE IV

Phase IV involves the project evaluation activities. Current and future cooperation between robotics teams, manufacturing, and maintenance rests on the robotics team. Representatives of the robotics team must stay in communication and support of the newly operational system.

SPECIFIC RELATED EQUIPMENT

Robots are not used in isolation, they are used with other equipment. This related equipment must be selected to form as efficient a robotic work cell as possible. In many instances the downtime in a work cell is caused by the related equipment and not the robot, yet the robot is referred to as being down again. This related equipment needs to be at least as reliable as the robot, if the robot system is to maintain a 98% or better mean-time-between-failures (MTBF).

The robot work cell requires a good knowledge base of the production operations involved. Basic low-tech manufacturing equipment (one example being a rotary table) is often used in the cell along with the high-tech equipment. The equipment selected for a work cell and the layout designed for the work cell depend on the function, or objectives, and the activities for the cell. Engineers and robot project teams need to evaluate the specified production task and restructure the task as necessary to accomplish it with the new robotic equipment. As stated earlier, task restructuring does impose a different constraint regarding robot backup when the robot is down and a human cannot perform the task as the robot was doing it.

There are four different relationships between robot work cells and the product being processed. These are identified by the method utilized in presenting the workpiece to the robot.

The first method, used typically with a large workpiece such as an automobile, has the workpiece moving past the robot on a material handling device conveyor or automatic guided vehicle (AGV), while the robot operates (spot welds, spray paints, or dispenses sealant) on it. These cells are often linear in flow with robots on one or both sides of the material handling equipment.

The second approach has the product being presented to the robot by input equipment (die cast machines, conveyors, or rotary tables). The robot moves the part through a variety of processes (machining by machine tools, tools grasped and manipulated by the robot, inspection equipment, and/or fastening stations) and deposits it on an output or transfer device. These types of cells are often circular to accommodate a variety of machines within the reach of the robot.

The third approach involves a part or pallet being transported to the area of the robot and being off-loaded to a stationary position. If it is an assembly operation, the robot selects the programmed component parts from the various feeders and assembles these parts onto the original workpiece or pallet. It then reloads the assembled unit onto the material handling equipment. When parts are placed on a pallet, but not on the original part in an assembly mode, the operation is called "kitting." Work cells doing kitting or assembly work may be circular, but typically they are arranged parallel to a power-and-free conveyor or other types of programmable materials handling systems.

The fourth relationship of the robot to the workpiece is for the part to be either manually or automatically loaded onto and unloaded from a turn table. In between, the part is presented to the robot for a value adding process (that is, arc welding, paint spraying, scalant dispensing or kitting). These types of cells are often "I" shaped.

It should be obvious that more than one configuration will support most of the processes. It is engineering's responsibility to assess the manufacturing facility, manufacturing operations, and projected cost/benefit analysis to determine the appropriate cell configuration.

These robot work cells will use the related equipment as well as the robots. Paint spraying, welding, sealant dispensing, materials handling, machine tending, kitting and assembly require simple types of related equipment. Vibratory hoppers, vibratory bowl feeders, brush feeders, centrifugal bowl feeders, magazine feeders, coil feeders, blow feeders and indexing conveyors are only a few of the conventional materials handling and part presentation types of machines that are often used with assembly robots.[26]

Not all of the above part presentation devices will work consistently without jamming or interlocking. Extensive knowledge of good materials handling practices is critical to achieving a successful robotics installation.

Part orientation is highly desirable, if no longer an absolute necessity, for robotic handling. Part orientation should be maintained when the workpiece leaves the work cell. Generally, the effort required to maintain correct part orientation is small compared to the effort required to achieve it.

One of the roles of the robot project team is to evaluate the design for the work cell. If operators are excluded from evaluation but asked to "work with the robot", the relationship generally will not be as good as when operators have meaningful input.

Robot Functions

The reprogrammable nature of a robot has implied that, as long as a robot met the specifications, it could be programmed and reprogrammed to perform different types of tasks. Now the dynamics of robots and robot controllers are viewed to be sufficiently different to warrant caution in using robots in applications other than the ones they were designed for. This means that one should not assume that a robot can be taken from spot welding, retooled and reprogrammed, then perform adequately as a finishing robot. Similarly, a material handling robot may not be a good spot welding robot. Performance may be acceptable in the new application, but the robot will not perform as well as a robot designed for that application. The dynamics and accessory control options vary for different applications and end-of-arm tooling loads. Robots should be used for the general applications for which they were designed.

The common functions for robots have been mentioned in variety of sections in the chapter. Specifically, these are:

- Material handling
  1. Machine tending
  2. Material movement
  3. Palletizing
  4. Kitting

- Assembly
  1. Mechanical assembly
  2. Electronic assembly

- Inspection
  1. Contact
  2. Non-Contact

- Welding
  1. Spot welding
  2. Arc welding

- Cutting
  1. Oxy-Acetylene cutting
  2. Laser-Oxygen cutting

- Finishing
  1. Air spraying of finishes
  2. Airless spraying of finishes

- Sealant and Adhesive dispensing

- Foundry
  1. Mold preparation
  2. Fettling

- Machining (deburring)

Laser Beam Machining

The laser machining robot is a unique, fully integrated adaptive system, designed with two-or three-axis coordinates. Other designs allow for up to five-axis systems, covering every plane and angle depending upon their applications. The robots are driven by controllers based on a microprocessor, can usually be interfaced with a teach pendant control panel, and can interlock with other machines in the industry, factory or shop. The laser machining robot is designed to cut specialty items such as plain carbon steel. It can perform jobs such as drilling tiny holes in aerospace composites and diamond or carbide wire drawing dies.[27]

CHAPTER 2

APPLICATION

In order to cope with the escalating overheads and the fast ever-changing requirements of the manufacturing industry today, modern industry needs automatic machinery which can increase production. The rationale for the design of the laser beam machining robot centers around the usefulness of robots in hot, heavy-duty, hazardous, and boring work environments. To this end, laser beam machining robots are useful for high-speed cutting and profiling deep penetration welding, micro-trimming, microwelding, microdrilling, scribing, engraving, heat treatment, and surfacing. With the use of laser beam machining robots all these techniques can be carried out rapidly and uniquely on a vast range of materials including metal, plastics, timber composites, and even diamonds.

A laser beam machining robot, like any other robot, is made up of basically two most important features: The robot manipulator arm which in the case of this application culminated in a drilling, welding, or scribing torch and the robot controller, which is typically the brain of the laser beam machining robot. The controller operates the manipulator arm which provides the necessary commands and other data needed by the support equipment. The robot controller memory contains a program of series of programs which contains data to complete a specific laser operation such as drilling, welding, etc.

Materials Handling

The traditional materials handling robots have often been pick-and-place or servo units with point-to-point control. Material handling moves are strictly point-to-point moves. Robots are doing material handling when they pick-up and place the payload in each cycle. Robotic material handling includes part feeding, material delivery, machine tending, machine loading and unloading, storage and retrieval, kitting, bin picking, case packing and palletizing and depalletizing, (loading and unloading products or containers on pallets).[28] One should remember that material handling robots should follow the fundamentals of material handling (these are listed in most materials handling handbooks and texts). Further, any-time a part is handled by any means, its movement is a production cost. The performance of these work cells depends on the reliability of the equipment used to present the parts to the robots; how well the physical characteristics of the part accommodate automated handling; the reliability of the end effector to grasp the part every time and the speed, payload and software capability of the robots themselves.

When robots are used for machine tending (that is, machine tools, plastics molding equipment, or press work), part or pallet transfer or palletizing/depalletizing; they can work consistently and constantly. This use of robots is justified by direct labor replacement, because there are no major improvements in quality and the moves add minimal value to the workpieces. Heavier payloads are easier to justify. The pick-and-place units have limited points and have not been used for palletizing. The more powerful controllers for palletizing robots permit the location of a few parts and the remainder of the program is executed with information entered at the controller.

Dual end effectors are used to improve robot performance in part loading and unloading in machine tending. One hand secures and removes the finished part from the machine and the second hand loads the next part into the machine. The dual hand is valuable whenever two parts are to be handled at one location. The dual hand is also appropriate when the process changes are so significant that the same gripper cannot load and unload the workpiece.

More sophisticated control systems can be used to locate parts, identify the orientation of the part and provide adaptive control. But this level of sophistication carries high costs. If the robot task can be done without the additional sensing, the installation will be less expensive, have longer mean-time-between-failures, be easier to service and to program. Keep the process as simple as possible.

Foundry and Molding

Since their inception robots have been used in die casting foundry operations. Investment casting is not a common as die casting, but robots have been very successful in making invest-ment molds. They have been used in green sand mold prepara-tion for flame curing, processing of cores, and spur and gate cutting. After the casting has cooled, robots have been used for fettling. The fettling of castings and injection molded parts are extremely similar and are covered in this section. Die casting is still the largest foundry application for robots.

Industrial robots used for either fettling or deburring are selected based on tool and part weight, burr accessibility, forces involved, dexterity required, part complexity and the require-ments of work space. There are some significant differences between deburring and fettling. Fettling requires cutting through thick sections of cast metal and smoothing wide sections of flash. Fettling requires high-power tools and large forces occur. Therefore, more powerful robots are needed.[29]

The tasks for robots in die cast cells vary, but generally involves unloading the hot casting from the die cast machine. The robot then quenches the part in a cooling tank. In some applications the robot places the part in a trimming press to remove the spur and flash while other operations involve trim-ming at another location. If trimming is done elsewhere in the plant (the more common method), the cooled die cast will be placed in a material handling device for transport to the trim press. Other potential functions performed by the robot are cleaning, die lubrication and installation of any cores into the die.

The major advantages to using robots in die casting cells is a reduction in labor, consistency in cycle times, more cycles per shift without the various breaks, and the removal of personnel from unpleasant and potentially dangerous tasks.

The robot tended die casting machines have consistent unload, die cleaning, die lube and die closing times. Consistency keeps the dies at the same temperature each time the shot (molten metal) is forced into the die and this yields parts of the same quality.

Tending a die casting machine is a hot and hazardous job. This type of operation does not require great precision. This is an operation a basic robot can do fairly weil. As the possible operations (loading and unloading the trim press, cleaning and lubricating of the die and installing cores in the die) are increased, the layout of the die casting cell will need to be designed so the robot can perform all of its tasks. Reengineering becomes even more significant if only one robot is used to tend two die casting machines and/or a trim press is moved into the work cell for the robot to load and unload.

The use of robots to assist investment casting generally involves dipping a wax tree (multiple molds connected with sprues and gates), into a slurry, coating it with sand and allow-ing the slurry-sand shell to dry. This process is repeated seven to twelve times per mold to give the sand shell the strength neces-sary to hold the molten metal during casting.

Use of robots in green sand mold preparation is similar to

other robotic applications in which the robot has a tool in its end effector (sprue cutter, gate cutter or flame dryer) and performs the designated task for each cope and drag. Robots for these tasks can be point-to-point type machines capable of executing several different programs, depending on which mold is being cast.

The fettling of a casting and injection molded parts requires higher level robot control to guide the robot in removing the gates, sprues, and flash. These operations add value to the part and prepare it for further processing. The fettling of ferrous castings can be accomplished with saws, cutoff abrasive wheels or oxygen fuel cutting torches. The oxygen fuel (that is, acetylene MAPP gas) are faster than the chip forming processes. The control of the flow of both gases and an electric igniter can be performed by the robot controller or separate programmable logic controller (PLC), if one is warranted.[30]

COMMUNICATIONS

The function of robot communications is to input programs, up-load and down-load programs from a computer and to exchange data. If the data exchange is to be interractive real time (that is, vision system input), the communications should be at a high speed.

Robot controller communications capabilities start with the teach pendant, keyboard/CRT, and tape or disc drives, and then expand to a specified number of serial communications ports, parallel ports, and a modem port. Not all robots have all of these, but all robots should have at least one of them. Robots control systems designed to incorporate vision and other peripheral equipment will have multiple serial, and sometimes a parallel, communications ports.

If a robot does not have sensing capability or the work cell is an island, additional communications capability is not needed. If the robot or island is to be part of a system that is local area network or data status reporting), serial communications, other than to the teach pendant, keyboard/CRT, and data storage devices, becomes necessary. If a vision system is to be interfaced to the system, parallel communications ports are desirable for faster communications to enhance realtime operation. Interfacing with cell controller sand other equipment, such as bar code or other automatic identification equipment, requires serial communications ports at least to a microcomputer to handle bar code reading.

Robot communications can occur at several levels. The lowest level, least expensive form and least capable (generally not included in communications) are the inputs and outputs (I/O) of the robot. The output provides a signal to indicate that the robot has completed a task and is ready for some other machine to execute its operation. The input to the robot controller provides a signal to the robot to indicate that some activity has been completed and the robot should execute a given program or subroutine. This form of communication is satisfactory only when the robot is an island of automation and a few programs (typically four or less in realtime) are being used interchangeably. This level of "communication" limits future uses of the robot and integration of island of automation into a computer-aided manufacturing or computer integrated manufacturing (CIM) system.

True communications with robots controllers are either parallel or serial, but generally serial. Serial communications lines are used between many pieces of micro-mainframe computer hardware, since many hardware items cannot process data as fast as a serial line can transmit it. RS-232C and RS-422 are two defined serial communications standards for interfacing computer hardware. RS-232C is the older, more widely used standard and works well in home, office and educational settings. A second, newer serial interface standard is RS-422 which accepts longer transmission lines, higher baud rates, multiple host control and offers greater flexibility.

LOCAL AREA NETWORKS

The current trend in world class manufacturing is to use Manufacturing Information Systems (MIS) and CIM to improve manufacturing, from conception through shipping and billing. Local area networks (LAN) are used to transfer computer data in both MIS and CIM.

The purchase of a robot, that is to be part of corporate automation strategy (not and island of automation), should be considered in terms of its relationship to a LAN. This may mean a more powerful controller on the robot or the purchase of an intelligent terminal to interface between the robot and the LAN. In either case, RS-232C or RS-422 communications interface capability needs to be part of the robot controller. Fifteen or fewer nodes can be connected together with an RS-232C serial communications system. This falls outside of the general definition of a LAN, a LAN being a high speed, medium distance communications network. A LAN generally supports a minimum of 100 stations (nodes), at 56 kilobaud to 10 megabaud and at distances up to several miles. In addition to the above features, industrial LANs are to be capable of real-time control, high data integrity (detection of transmission errors), high immunity to noise and high reliability in harsh environments.[31]

This is not to suggest that the robot should be controlled by the LAN. Robot control should remain local, i.e. at the work site. The LAN may permit message communication between the robot and another node, the up- and down- loading of programs and communicating data between the work cell and another node.

Some of the software to operate a LAN is commercially available and some must be written for each specific application. The special software can be designed by a systems house or by the LAN company's computer analysts and programmers.

LAN configurations and operating characteristics that should be considered before choosing a system include:

1. Topologies (star, ring, star shaped ring and bus).
2. Network access (polling, collision detection or token passing).
3. Communications medium (twisted pair, baseband coaxial cable, broadband coaxial cable and fiber optics).
4. Maximum number of devices (nodes) on the LAN.
5. Types of devices accepted by the LAN.
6. Response time (time for input at one node and corresponding output at another node).
7. Response time (time for input at one node and corresponding output at another node).
8. Throughput (the number of I/O points that can be updated per second through the LAN).
9. Devices supported (microcomputers, intelligent terminals, programmable controllers, gateways, hosts and other microprocessor hardware).
10. Applications interface (How do the nodes communicate with each other?)

Most industrial control equipment manufacturers have

APPLICATION

designed, installed, and proven proprietary networks. The purchase of any of these networks should be analyzed by manufacturing and computer people as to their pros and cons in terms of costs, corporate goals, manufacturing or computer operations goals, develop the specifications, and select the appropriate system and vendor. Some of these LAN use twisted pair conductors, master/slave relationships vs. peer-to-peer and maximum length of less than 0.5 mile (0.8 km).

Manufacturing Automation Protocol (MAP) is a LAN that has received the most attention in recent years. It is one of a number of networks, has an open architecture, is ISO based, has proven to be expensive to implement and is to provide the capability for all participating vendors of computerized equipment to have their equipment communicate with each others' equipment on the LAN. In terms of the above, it is a bus-based, token-passing and broadband LAN. It is often shown as an umbrella network to provide the top levels of the corporation with information. A variety of baseband, RS-422, RS-232C and parallel communications occur at lower levels. Ideally all computerized equipment should communicate with each other. But, if each device is on the broadband bus, each device would have to transmit and receive the ASCII data at the broadband frequencies and in a format it can understand, and this capability to communicate on MAP is expensive. The host computer and software to manage MAP is currently five to ten times greater than the cost for the smaller proprietary networks. A primary reason for using MAP is to be able to utilize computer based communications with material suppliers and buyers of a company's products in the world economy. MAP has now progressed to the point that additional equipment can be added to

the network with many times fewer man-hours than in the past.

The communications capabilities of robot controllers are an important component in their selection and in the operation of a work cell. The controller's communications capabilities determine the extent to which data and programs can be shared with a host computer or a local area network.

Options that the selection team should consider when selecting a system:

1. If off-line programming should be included as part of the system.
2. If programs are to be stored or accessed by a process other than magnetic tape.
3. If robotic program steps as well as coordinates are to be visible to the on-line programmer and operator.
4. If sensors (especially vision) are to part of the cell.
5. If a robot needs to communicate with a cell controller.

These issues should all be resolved as part of the equipment selection process. The specifications for communications capability need to be more specific than whether they are RS-232C compatible or not. Some controllers do not accept retrofitted communications hardware or may require additional expense to make two RS-232C systems compatible. RS-232C versus RS-422, baud rates, data format (5, 6, 7 or 8 bits; parity and the number of stop bits) and the distance the communications need to travel should be specified to insure that two pieces of computer equipment can communicate with each other without additional expense and frustration.

IMPLEMENTATION

Whenever a vendor has responsibility for more than shipping an operating robot and control system there should be acceptance runoffs. Manufacturers and vendors should use acceptance runoffs to verify specific features at the time the robot is accepted. These runoffs should be defined in the purchasing contract and generally specifies that the buyer supplies the vendor with a number of real parts to be used in the runoffs.

The runoff specified by the buyer should, as closely as possible, duplicate the planned manufacturing operation. The vendor is required to demonstrate that the robot(s) and other peripheral hardware in the work cell can execute the specified robot movements, with required payloads, in the stated cycle time, with synchronized paths of all the work cell equipment and with acceptable overshoot and settling time. in addition to maintaining a cycle time with a given payload, accuracy, repeatability and maintainability are common issues. Accuracy can be checked by teaching the robot a position or continuous path move or constructing an off-line program and downloading the program, and operating the robot with programmed moves. The other qualities can be checked by operating the robots at less than, equal to, and greater than full payload at less than, equal to and, greater than the specified speed over a period of time that may be 40 hours or longer in length. During the runoff, data acquisition systems should record the performance of the equipment (robot and peripheral equipment) for later review of consistency of performance and trends in the measured data.

Many contracts stipulate that if the equipment being tested fails to meet the specifications, the vendor makes the necessary modifications and restarts the test.

The runoff should, as closely as possible, duplicate exact contractual conditions. Variances from these conditions do not necessarily mean problems, but all too often what is foreseen as a minor change requires a major effort. This is expecially true when a little higher speed or a little heavier payload is required than is used in the runoff. The results of accepting variances during an acceptance runoff will probably delay production start-up, non-compliance to specifications during production, and a loss in confidence and credibility in the project engineers within the organization.[32]

The robot acceptance testing team should, prior to receipt of robot:[33]

1. Analyze Repeatability data.
2. Restart any test that fails.
3. Run robot at 25% to 150% of nominal speed for more repeatability data.
4. Run tests with largest parts to be used by robot once in facility.
5. Do as much testing of software as possible prior to receipt of robot to insure high level of confidence in the programs once they are installed.

INSTALLATION

Once the performance runoff is completed and approved at the vendor site, the work cell is disassembled and shipped to the buyer. If a this work cell is one of several, installation on-site should be done in stages. The pilot installation can be used as a guide for the remaining stations to verify that the design is appropriate or if design modifications are necessary. Often there is only one installation and the pilot scenario is not viable.

The installation should take place with guidance from a vendor representative. If service personnel have been properly trained by the vendor or the vendor's agent to install and service the robot and peripheral equipment the installation process will probably go more smoothly. The training of the service personnel should occur during the work cell fabrication and testing so they are ready to install the robot when it arrives.

Operators of the robotic equipment can be trained on- or off-site in the cell operating procedures during or just after installation. If maintenance people and technicians are sent to class prior to installation, installation may go easier. When installation is completed, service personnel and operators should be ready to conduct the final acceptance test. If off-line programmed software is involved, it should be loaded and tested. If engineering work was completed thoroughly, any problems encountered at this level should be minor.

It is a good practice order selected spares of critical components for servicing the robot. These parts can be shipped so the electronic cards can be tested and all the inventory stored at the time the robot is installed. This can help to keep the mean-time-to-repair short and build confidence in use of the robotic work cell.

The robot may be run for one week dry with no production to familiarize workers with system. This also allows some last minute bugs to show up. Monitoring the performance of the robot(s) and peripheral equipment for start-up and operating procedures and personnel for safety compliance and maintenance procedures should be assigned to a specific individual. This should assure manufacturing and maintenance personnel that they are not forgotten once the work cell is in operation. The same individual should be able to log and analyze downtime and complete cost/benefit analysis. After the initial period of operation, the work cell should be operating at the 98% or better mean-time-between-failure (MTBF), and it should gain the confidence of production and maintenance personnel and require less attention.

SAFETY

Industrial safety practices and regulation have and should focus on providing good, non-injurious workplaces in which people can work. For manufacturing engineers, safety rules include but go beyond the human dimension. The first rule states that personnel safety is the top priority. People should be able to work under conditions that neither threatens their lives nor their health. The second rule, equipment should be protected from itself. Equipment should be setup, operated and controlled so that it will not harm itself. The third rule is that equipment should be setup and controlled so that it does not harm other equipment.

The operation of a robot has several distinctive features.

1. It appears to behave in a repetitive manner.
2. It is microprocessor or computer controlled and subject to unannounced changes in its routines.
3. It has hidden interlock conditions that may cause unan-

nounced or alternative actions such that, time delays or the termination of a time delay) for reasons that are not visible.
4. It may extend, beyond normal movements into unsecured areas.

The repetitive characteristic listed above is one that may cause people to becomelax around the operation of the robot and think they can enter a restricted area without endangering themselves. The invisibility of the computer programming makes the robot unpredictable and yet it can appear to most personnel as being very repetitive. Three areas of safety that need to be considered are normal working conditions, programming, and maintenance and service.

One safety device, a fence, is common to all three and is the most basic and cost effective safety device available areas of safety. Working conditions on a factory floor virtually require a fenced barrier type of enclosure around robots. In addition to preventing accidental and deliberate movement into a robot's workspace by people, it prevents objects or vehicles from being placed or parked in the work space when the robot is not operating and it prevents or reduces the probability of an object being thrown out of the work cell. Depending upon the application, other protective measures may be necessary (such as, eye protection from arc welding processes). The fenced barrier generally has openings for conveyors or equipment that is part of the work cell.

Protecting the robot from other equipment and other equipment from the robot is a very significant and complex issue. There are at least four conditions that need to be considered by the designers of the control systems. These conditions involve:

1. Interfacing the robot with other pieces of equipment and the resulting interlock conditions.
2. The effect of E-stop and space intrusion type control switches not only on the robot but the other equipment as well during the shutdown phase.
3. The effect of power failure or the E-stop of the startup conditions.
4. The use of programmable controllers with robot controllers in the control of the equipment in a cell.

The first condition in protecting the robot from other processing equipment requires that the robot be out of a specific space for the next step in the sequential process to occur. Shuttling conveyors or power-and-free conveyors have damaged products and robots by moving when a robot arm was still in the conveyor/load path. These situations are fairly easy to control with limit switches that interlock the two sequences.

The second condition is a more difficult one to solve, because involves use of the E-stop switch or STEP mode on the robot or another E-stop switch on peripheral equipment in the work cell. The E-stop will stop the robot or a different piece of equipment reliably. The problem occurs when a second device is in mid-cycle and does not stop. The image of the press crushing the robot arm comes to mind when the robot stops and the press does not. A similar problem may occur if the robot is in a STEP mode and other equipment cycles are triggered and the robot arm or tooling may be damaged.

The third condition involves the power-up after a planned, emergency or power failure type of shutdown. What will the equipment do in power-up situation, especially when it was not shutdown in the normal planned procedure? Another dimen-

IMPLEMENTATION

sion to this problem occurs when an E-stop or space intrusion switch is activated, what happens on start-up after the emergency shutdown?

In the fourth condition, many robot work cells have programmable logic controllers (PLC) to orchestrate the work cell and communicate with the robot. It does present an additional safety issue in the are of a PLC (or any microprocessor) failure. A major difficulty with the failure of microprocessor-based equipment is the lack of predictability of the outputs when the CPU fails. Many PLC manufacturers attempt to build in an OFF output status when the CPU fails. Yet, all too often the output may stay ON and a press crushes some hardware. Most PLC manufacturers recommend that at least one hardwired relay safety circuit be included in the control circuit besides the hardwired E-STOP switches and relays to shut down the system if specific conditions are not maintained or met.

Safety during programming and setup has a few problems in addition to those already mentioned relative to normal operation. The operator doing on-line programming may need to be in the vicinity of the end-effector for accurate positioning. One method used to minimize the danger of this human proximity is to reduce the power and speed of the robot arm when it moves in the TEACH mode. The speed should be low enough so that a programmer can escape from the robot's path if there is a failure, and if he is trapped that the robot will not have enough force to cause physical harm. This type of control must be done so the robot is in a fail-safe condition. Typically, this suggests normally open circuits for relays. Many of the so-called safety circuits or operating modes for the TEACH mode will not prove to be safe under certain failure conditions.

Other equipment in the work cell should not be operating during the programming cycle. During the programming routine, it is good practice to have an assistant monitor the activity ready to operate the E-STOP switch if something does not go according to the plan. The dry run of a new program should be treated as a normal operating condition regarding the robot work envelope (personnel should be out of the envelope) and the work cell.

Maintenance and service constitute the third area of operation in which safety needs to addressed. As people become familiar with equipment, they tend to take short cuts from safe operation. Knowledge of and strict adherence to the recommended safe servicing practices need to be followed by service personnel. Troubleshooting and repair can be extremely dangerous when testing systems and subsystems. Warnings and cautions need to be observed. As with programming, it is good practice to shutdown other work cell equipment and have a second person ready to shut the robot system down if something goes wrong.

MAINTENANCE

A robot is a piece of equipment that is electrical, mechanical, and often pneumatic, and it will have wear and degradation of performance with use. Scheduled and unscheduled maintenance of automated equipment will occur; it is only a question of which and when. You will have to provide maintenance work on robots and other automated equipment, the question is under what conditions. Will it be done in a scheduled manner or will it be done under crisis conditions with management personnel worrying about production schedules and demanding that trades people or technicians "get the work done by yesterday".

Just-in-time (JIT) manufacturing works best when the maintenance is done in a scheduled manner. Unscheduled mainten-

ance is disruptive to JIT manufacturing schedules. As U.S. manufacturing adopts the more competitive management and manufacturing techniques, such as JIT, it must also adopt the maintenance practices that made these techniques work for off-shore manufacturing people. JIT requires scheduled (preventive) maintenance.

Scheduled Maintenance

Four elements of scheduled maintenance are training, inventory of spare parts, special tools, and an acceptable schedule. The trades people and technicians responsible for servicing the automated equipment, specifically robots, need to be trained to do the work. This training should not just be in general two-year technical schools or seminars, but in specific programs conducted by the manufacturers of the respective robots. An appropriate inventory of spare parts should be kept on hand for these machines, and this inventory should be in an orderly manner so the parts can be located when they are needed. Any special tools or instruments needed to service the robots should be purchased and stored so they are available on demand for the specific robot. This control of special tools will probably require creative techniques, as most of the traditional procedures have not been successful in keeping the special tools or having them available for the right people at the right time. The robot project team, including the vendor, should assist production and maintenance managers and in the development of a scheduled maintenance schedule. This way every one knows what to expect from the respective service groups and when to expect starting with the first day of operations. The follow-up checking when maintenance is completed can be one of the responsibilities of the robot project team person who monitors and evaluates the performance of the robot and work cell during the first months of production.

Obviously, the tasks that should be completed for any given robot and the specific schedule cannot be presented here. The robot project team and the vendor should work together to be certain that the appropriate maintenance groups know the schedule that they are trained to perform the maintenance and that they are given time by management to do it. This cannot be over emphasized.

There are a few general points on scheduled robot maintenance that can and should be made. These are applicable to most robots. The purpose of schedules maintenance is to do those activities that are necessary for optimum operation of the equipment. Lubrication and filter changes are two jobs that are common to electric, hydraulic, and pneumatic powered robots. Many electric and hydraulic servo robots use pneumatics for the end effectors or arm counter-balances.

Lubrication is a scheduled maintenance activity for all electric-powered robots having gear, harmonic, or ballscrew drives. Usually the lubricant is a specific grease that will loose its oiliness with operation over time and the higher the temperature, the shorter the lubricating period. Generally, a grease has a carrier that remains after the lubricating qualities have disappeared and the carrier, traditionally a chemical soap, increases the friction in the mechanical transmission. This residue needs to be cleaned out (of gear and harmonic drives) and the specified grease applied on the recommended schedules and more often if the environment (temperature, solvent fumes, or other factors) causes the lubricant to degrade more rapidly. Where the grease is pumped in (for example, ball screws), regular greasing is easily done and will help the robot provide long trouble-free service.

Pneumatic systems generally use lubricators to put the

desired quantity and type of lubrication in the system. This may appear to be straight forward, but occasionally the type of short stroke cylinders found on robots do not receive the desired amount of lubricant if the directional control valves are mounted too far from the cylinder. Quick exhaust valves at the cylinders can help get the lubricant into the cylinder. The lubricators for pneumatic systems need to be filled and the filters changed on a regularly scheduled basis.

Any servo system needs to be readjusted or tuned on a periodic basis (12-24 months). The servo system will perform better if this service is done. In addition, a servo amplifier for a given axis can, in certain failure modes, cause a CPU board to fail as well and add to the repair problems. Hydraulic servo valves need additional maintenance, and if this maintenance is performed as recommended, or more often if experience shows a need, a given robot will meet the objectives that are expected of it.

Hydraulic and pneumatic filters need to be changed on schedule. Dirty filters still pass fluid, but as the pressure drop across the filter increases, the quantity and size of the contaminants that pass through the filter also increase. The correct installation of pneumatic lines (take-off are to go up and then down and drip legs) can help filter the air. Also excess oil in the air can be removed with coalescing filters.

Contaminants are a major problem for hydraulic servo systems. Dirt, even as small as 80 to 160 μin. (2 to 4 μm), ingested through the normal cycling of the cylinders is not the only problem. Varnishes and sludge that passes through normal filters cause more servo valve failures than dirt.

Electrostatic liquid cleaners (ELC), common in European and Asian countries but relatively new to the USA, can remove not only the traditional dirt but also the varnish, sludge, and carbonaceous deposits from the oil that traditional filtration techniques cannot remove. The performance, (up time and reliability) of hydraulic servo systems reportedly have improved when ELC has been used on a regular, preventive maintenance schedule. ELC is used as an external cleaning system with its own circulating system and can operate whether or not the hydraulic system is in operation. The ELC cleaning schedule should be developed in terms of the specific hydraulic system operating characteristics. ELC units may be mobile and shared between a number of hydraulic systems.[34]

The oil and hydraulic companies have informed their customers that new hydraulic oil in sealed drums is not clean. Oil transferred from those drums is not at the recommended 1000 to 1600 μin. (25 to 40 μm) level for conventional hydraulic systems, and definitely not clean enough for servo systems. It should be filtered when it is transferred to the reservoir.

Unscheduled Maintenance

If scheduled maintenance is done correctly, then unscheduled maintenance should be rare. Murphy's Law suggests that unscheduled maintenance will need to be done. This maintenance may require a few minutes to a few weeks. The robot project team should have developed a contingency strategy for this situation. The task of the project team is not complete without such a back-up strategy. The strategy should be discussed, not just approved, by manufacturing, maintenance, and management. Robots will fail and acceptable contingency plans need to be prepared, understood, and accepted by management, manufacturing, and maintenance people as a part of the robot and work cell engineering plans. Common items that have higher probability of failure should be inventoried. This is

another reason to have good early communications by a variety of people and the people on the robot project team to see potential problems from different viewpoints.

References

1. H. Warnecke, R. Schraft and M. Wanner, "Mechanical Design of the Robot System," *Handbook of Industrial Robotics*, ed. S. Nof (New York: John Wiley and Sons, 1985), pp. 44.
2. C. Bodine, *Small Motor, Gearmotor, and Control Handbook*, 4th ed., (Chicago: Bodine Electric Company, 1978), pp. 73-74.
3. C. A Rosen, "Robots and Machine Intelligence," *Handbook of Industrial Robotics*, ed. S. Nof (New York: John Wiley and Sons, 1985), pp. 22-23.
4. Y. Hasegawa, "Industrial Robot Standardization," *Handbook of Industrial Robotics*, ed. S. Nof (New York: John Wiley and Sons, 1985), p. 518.
5. Y. Koren, "Numerical Control and Robots," *Handbook of Industrial Robotics*, ed. S. Nof (New York: John Wiley and Sons, 1985), p. 204.
6. Y. F. Yong, J. A. Gleave, J. L. Green and M. C. Bonney, "Off-Line Programming of Robots," *Handbook of Industrial Robotics*, ed. S. Nof (New York: John Wiley and Sons, 1985), pp. 368, 379.
7. D. F. Stephanic and M. P. Jacobs, *Conference Proceedings for Robotics Machine Vision 88* (Dearborn, MI: Society of Manufacturing Engineers, 1988), pp. 4-127 to 4-143.
8. *Ibid.*, pp. 4-127 to 4-142.
9. Yong, Gleave, Green and Bonney, loc. cit. p. 367.
10. S. J. Buckley and G. F. Collins, "A Structured-Programming Robot Language," *Handbook of Industrial Robotics*, ed. S. Nof (New York: John Wiley and Sons, 1985), pp. 381-382.
11. Yong, Gleave, Green and Bonney, loc. cit. pp. 374-375.
12. Graham, Glenn A., *Encyclopedia of Industrial Automation* (Dearborn, MI: Society of Manufacturing Engineers, 1988), p. 214.
13. R. D. Potter, "End-of-Arm Tooling," *Handbook of Industrial Robotics*, ed. S. Nof (New York: John Wiley and Sons, 1985), pp. 782-784.
14. *Ibid.*, pp. 784-786.
15. D. R. Malcom, Jr., *Robotics, An Introduction*. (Boston: PWS-Kent Publishing Co., 1988), p. 266.
16. *Ibid.*, p. 266.
17. K. Tanie, "Design of Robot Hands," *Handbook of Industrial Robotics*, ed. S. Nof (New York: John Wiley and Sons, 1985), pp. 112-113.
18. *Ibid.*, p. 114.
19. *Ibid.*, p. 113.
20. K. Gore, H. Lipkin and S. Dickerson, *Conference Proceedings for Robotics 12 and Machine Vision 88* (Dearborn, MI: Society of Manufacturing Engineers, 1988), pp. 15-13 to 15-20.
21. Potter, loc. cit. p. 775.
22. G. V. Soska, *Conference Proceedings for Robotics 12 and Machine Vision 88*, (Dearborn, MI: Society of Manufacturing Engineers, 1988), pp. 1-7.
23. *Ibid.*, pp. 1-11.
24. W. R. Tanner, "Product Design and Produciton Planning," *Handbook of Industrial Robotics*, ed. S. Nof (New York: John Wiley and Sons, 1985), pp. 537-538.
25. *Ibid.*, pp. 539-542.
26. R. Gilchrist, *Conference Proceedings for Robotics 12 and Machine Vision 88*, (Dearborn, MI: Society of Manufacturing Engineers, 1988), pp. 9-4 to 9-9.
27. Graham, op. cit., pp. 348-349.
28. J. A. White and J. M. Apple, "Robots in Material Handling," *Handbook of Industrial Robotics*, ed. S. Nof (New York: John Wiley and Sons, 1985), pp. 955-956.
29. Graham, op. cit., p. 229.
30. G. E. Munson, *Industrial Robots, Vol. 2/Applications*. W. R. Tanner, ed. (Dearborn, MI: Society of Manufacturing Engineers), pp. 207-210.

CHAPTER 2

REFERENCES

31. L. A. Bryan and E. A. Bryan, *Programmable Controllers , Theory and Practice* (Chicago: Industrial Text Co., 1988), pp. 437, 444-448.
32. Soska, loc. cit., p. 1-10.
33. Riske, Gordon E., "Sensor-Guided Robotic Arc Welding," *Conference Proceedings for Robotics/Machine Vision 88* (Dearborn, MI: Society of Manufacturing Engineers), p. 14-101.
34. K. Wood, *Conference Proceedings for Robotics 12 and Machine Vision 88* (Dearborn, MI: Society of Manufacturing Engineers, 1988), pp. 4-59 to 4-61.

COMPUTER-AIDED DESIGN AND MANUFACTURING

GENERAL INFORMATION

Design and manufacturing have been a basic part of human life ever since the first wheel was conceived and then carved out of stone. Communicating in written form, using symbols and graphics, has existed since early man. When man needed to convey his idea for another to build, the design through manufacturing process was born. Needless to say, the process and problems of communicating and sharing design and manufacturing information have been around for a long time.

This chapter addresses computer-aided design and computer-aided manufacturing (CAD/CAM) - its concepts, tools, applications, and methods of implementation and use. In addition to basic CAD/CAM functionalities, such as design, drafting, and numerical control, machining descriptions are provided for the full range of automation tools available to serve today's engineering and manufacturing environments.

Today, CAD/CAM has become a signification factor in the design and manufacturing process. No longer a tool for only the Fortune 500 the price, performance and functionality of CAD/CAM now has become affordable by all.

In this chapter various key factors are presented that govern selection and use of CAD/CAM technology at various levels of industry. No attempt has been made to recommend specific solutions, but rather to allow the reader to effectively decide on CAD/CAM implementation and use as these affect his/her individual job or the company where he/she works.

The chapter is also intended to help managers, engineers, designers, drafters, and manufacturing personnel in best choosing the levels and methods to be used in performing specific tasks or jobs on a CAD/CAM system.

CONCEPTS

Most CAD/CAM systems today are designed and intended to automate manual functions, whether the particular function represents engineering analysis, conceptual design, drafting, documentation, or the programming of manufacturing and inspection machinery.

Frequently, these automated functions may either be loosely or closely linked through software or common data files. However, this coupling is usually limited to the passing or sharing of information currently communicated in the manual world through paper processes and written communications.

As in the manual world, this information normally flows from the designer (concept) to and through manufacturing. The information flow from manufacturing back into the design process relies on verbal communications, training, and the knowledge of key individuals. Today the CAD/CAM industry is only just beginning to work on the capturing and passing of manufacturing knowledge back into the design process through CAD/CAM implementation.

The key to implementing CAD/CAM is a fundamental decision that depends on how much of the technology applies to an individual's job or the functioning of a business or company. If drawings have to be produced, or if the resulting products are one-time production items, and few, if any, changes will be required once the design is completed, a simple computer-aided drafting system will probably suffice. However, if the product has multiple parts or components with a need for interchangeability and fit, or documentation and life-cycle support are requirements, then a more comprehensive CAD/CAM system will probably be required.

Another factor to be considered in implementing CAD/CAM is selection or availability of hardware. Today's CAD/CAM capability is available on various platforms ranging from simple personal computers to sophisticated engineering (32-bit) workstations and mainframe computers. The selection or availability of hardware often a controls the power, performance, and cost of the systems and application software the end user of a CAD/CAM system will choose from.

The cost and life-cycle management of CAD/CAM technology itself are often overlooked. Today, the training and implementation costs associated with CAD/CAM represent a major portion of a company's initial investment. However, within months of implementation it is the data created and stored in the system and the experience of the CAD/CAM users/operators which represent the greatest asset resulting from the customers initial investment.

Unfortunately, when resources of data and trained personnel begin to represent a major company CAD/CAM asset, they also become a tie-that-binds. Too often companies become locked into platforms and technologies through the selection of their initial CAD/CAM systems. At any level, the key to selection of CAD/CAM technology, should therefore be based on life-cycle costs and needs and not on the intial investment.

Selecting the right technology is critical factor both for major corporations and small businesses. While open systems architectures, improved communications, and standards for the storage and exchange of data are emerging in the computer industry, they can never replace or recreate data

GENERAL INFORMATION

that has been stored or technological training that has never been received.

In the world of CAD/CAM, therefore, the ability to achieve results is a combination of available tools, user experience, and the volume of data and engineering knowledge created and stored in the CAD/CAM system.

PLATFORMS

One of the most rapidly changing aspects of CAD/CAM implementation is that of platforms. In the past, most major CAD/CAM products ran on restricted hardware or mainframe computers. Systems capable of providing and/or supporting hardware and software architectures were not common on general purpose computing systems.

Most of the early computers, with exception of some high-cost processors, lacked the processing speed and graphics support necessary for interactive engineering, design, and manufacturing operations.

Today, the concept of adequate platforms has changed drastically. Now most major CAD/CAM applications are no longer limited to specific hardware. Therefore, a broader definition of platform is required when discussing the CAD/CAM environment. The concept of platforms can be separated into hardware and software. This distinction is necessary because:

1. The number and range of hardware platforms capable of supporting CAD/CAM applications today.
2. The range of CAD/CAM software products available in the market.
3. The number of software products or applications in the CAD/CAM industry which run on more than one hardware platform.

This separation of the core architecture (software platform) of CAD/CAM products from technical applications allows for the discussion of basic CAD/CAM architectures as a part of product capability and selection.

A second aspect of software platform discussions deals with operating systems. Systems tools and capabilities include hardware, peripheral devices and communications as they affect the CAD/CAM process. Figure 3-1 shows hardware and software platforms and their relationships.

It is critical in the purchase or upgrades of any CAD/CAM system, from the simplest to the most complex, to consider the full long-range scope of a company's CAD/CAM endeavors. What may be right for a simple 2D personal computer based "start-up" system today, might not be able to support more advanced applications as company needs and ambitions grow.

Hardware Platforms

One of the most significant changes in computer hardware and architectures today is networked computing. Distributed processing and powerful desktop processors have created unlimited options in computer flexibility and processing power. However, a question remains, as to the full effect of this new distributed processing capability on the engineering and manufacturing. To examine the potential for real change brought about by distributed processing, it is necessary to examine available hardware options.

Mainframe computing continues to dominate many engineering and business environments today. Heart and core of the mainframe environment is its manageability. Major mainframes with sufficient capacity and processing power allow for a centralized computing environment. Computer terminals, ranging from basic entry systems and alpha-numeric terminals for simplified graphics to high-end graphics terminals and display devices linked to a mainframe, permit various of uses on a low cost per operator basis after the initial purchase of computing resources.

A major key to mainframe computing is the consolidation of overhead supporting functions for the computing environment including systems operation, administration, maintenance, and support. Also, centralized management facilitates required, often routine, operations such as backup, archiving, input/output control, and distribution.

A disadvantage of mainframe computing is the broad range of applications and functions sharing a common processing capability. Often the processing and computing priorities of business and management applications conflict with those of the CAD/CAM users in terms of current or immediate needs or local department priorities.

Minicomputers or mainframes can often serve to decentralize the mainframe solution and minimize the number of users on a specific processor. To some degree this reduces the effect of multiple processes on the specific end-users priorities. However, it often increases the overall administrative costs of computer implementation at the company level. It was the advent of the minicomputers, customized for engineering and graphics applications, that led to early CAD/CAM turnkey systems.

Personal computing soon changed the role and vision of computers both in day to day life and in business. Since their introduction PCs have grown in power and performance to a level capable of supporting engineering and graphics applications.

An additional effect of personal computing, has been the widening of the CAD/CAM market, a widening made possible by providing technical computing solutions at small-business (low-entry cost) prices.

However, personal computer CAD/CAM solutions have created an administrative problem in the engineering environment. File management and housekeeping on personal computers has become the responsibility of the individual user, often leading to lost files and data, especially when PCs are shared by more than one individual.

The freedom of personal computing and the demand for more powerful desktop computing led to a new form of hardware architecture known as the workstation, moving from 8- and 16-bit dedicated processors of the personal computing world to high-performance 32-bit computing in desktop and deskside environments required for the CAD/CAM and engineering technology.

Concurrent with the growth of personal computing and workstations, improvements in networked computing, network file systems and the performance of computer network architectures has used the maintenance of data and file systems on high performance distributed processing solutions.

The result of these changes in computing technology have directly effected CAD/CAM implementation and use. No longer are mainframes, mini-computers or specialized turnkey systems necessary to the CAD/CAM environment. Nor distributed processors such as personal computers and workstations significantly affect the ability to perform centralized file management in a distributed environment.

Networking and Mixing Systems

The ideal solution to effective CAD/CAM implementation and integration is to have identical or fully compatible hardware

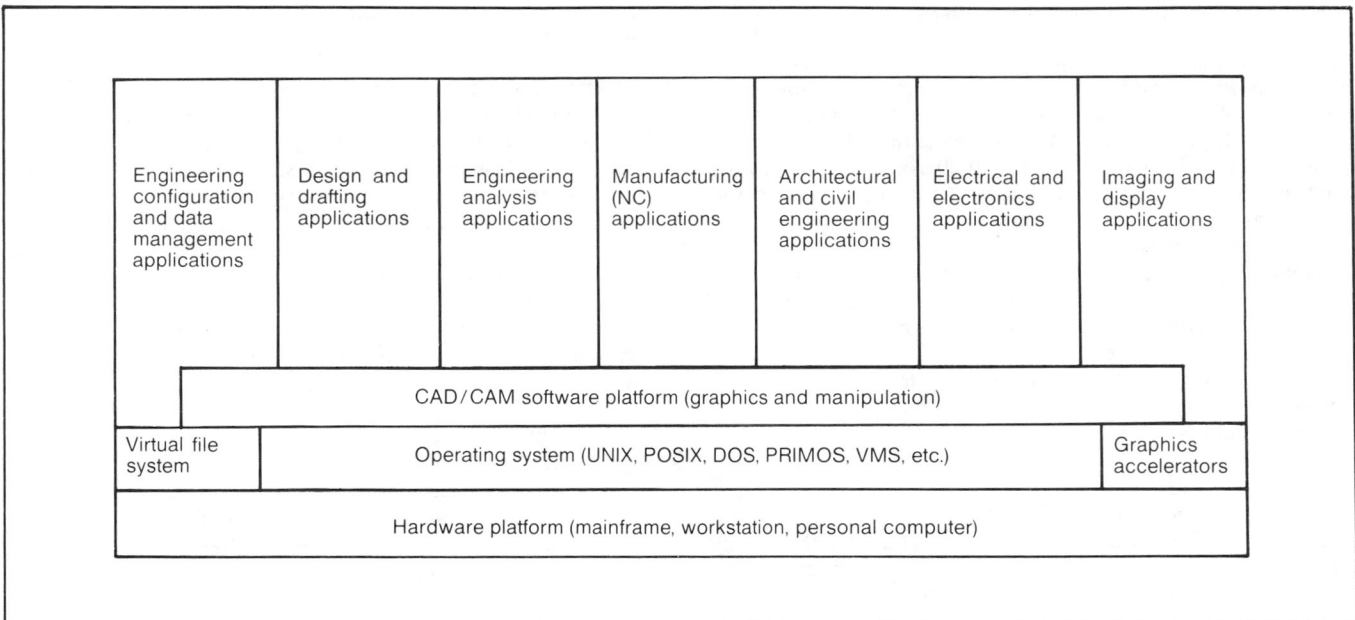

Engineering configuration and data management applications	Design and drafting applications	Engineering analysis applications	Manufacturing (NC) applications	Architectural and civil engineering applications	Electrical and electronics applications	Imaging and display applications
CAD/CAM software platform (graphics and manipulation)						
Virtual file system	Operating system (UNIX, POSIX, DOS, PRIMOS, VMS, etc.)					Graphics accelerators
Hardware platform (mainframe, workstation, personal computer)						

Fig. 3-1 CAD/CAM hardware and software platform relationships.

and software systems. However, this is not an ideal world. Computers are evolving rapidly and in most companies today there exists, or will exist, the need to mix systems based on price, performance, and technology.

The variety and power of systems today range from mainframes and supercomputers to workstations (often referred to as number crunchers or compute nodes) and low end PCs well suited to less complex computing tasks. Therefore price, functionality, and performance have become the key in selecting systems. The result is a need to communicate in a common language.

This common language is called the computing environment. Equating the need for communications to the well known world of telephones, the wire through which information flows is the network and the languages which allow common communication are protocols. The instruments at the end of the wire which allow communications are the controllers, network file systems, operating systems, and application software.

There are various vendor and industry standards which affect this communications process at the software and hardware level, including: ETHERNET, TCP/IP, MAP/TOP, ASCII, NFS, FTP, and numerous others. Considering these standards while selecting systems and hardware is the key to eventual success in integrating CAD/CAM solutions.

Use of these tools can range from total transparency for the average engineering and manufacturing user to simple or very complex user operations. In general, when dealing with networks and network communications the amount of work required by the user and the speed of response when using the network is inversely proportional to the cost of the systems and networking tools. The less expensive the system the more work for the users.

The key to communications is not necessarily in the hardware platform itself, but in the quality of networking and network file systems it supports. Therefore, when choosing a system look for transparency. Transparency for the user in

communications and transparency in the file system search and retrieval system. Today there should only be the need for one copy of a given file anywhere on a network, and not on every machine where needed. In design and manufacturing this can be equated to the idea that there should only be one master drawing or certification document, the original. It should also be possible to centrally manage all files from a given node and centralize plotting independent of where the file exists or the user plot command is issued.

Peripherals

To define the full hardware platform with its peripherals for CAD/CAM, various options are provided by system and solution vendors. Understanding the abilities and limitations of these options can positively affect total CAD/CAM implementation.

It would do well to consider hardware resources and capabilities when planning for short and long term CAD/CAM implementation and growth.

Graphic Displays and Accelerators

If there is one factor which has contributed to CAD/CAM today, it has been the development of high performance, high quality computer graphics. It was the development of graphics and display devices which was the key to the early development and success of many of today's CAD/CAM companies. The marriage of computer graphics with computing platforms and application software was the basis of most "turnkey" CAD/CAM systems.

Today, quality computer graphics are becoming standard computing technology, ranging from low resolution, monochromatic devices to high resolution displays supporting full color rendering. Today, high performance CAD/CAM systems can develop and display colored images of design models with the look and realism of a photograph.

As in the case of networking, it is critical to examine needs

GENERAL INFORMATION

when evaluating the graphics capabilities of prospective CAD/CAM system. While low resolution, monochrome devices can provide adequate pictures for working purposes, most companies are finding that systems with a minimum of 64 colors and a resolution of approximately 1000 x 1000 pixels, are more conducive to effective production use systems. In addition, systems with resolutions in access of 4000 x 4000 pixels, and 256 colors are found in many design and styling areas of automotive and other consumer products companies.

While graphics systems and display devices today are a key element in system selection, they also restrict the portability of CAD/CAM applications from one vendor's computer platform to another. It is the graphics system which is both the differentiator and competitive edge between many CAD/CAM systems. Efforts are now underway to reduce the interdependency between CAD/CAM and computer graphics software and the platforms on which they run through the development of graphics software display standards, such as PHIGS, CGM, GKS, and other.

It is important to choose carefully. Better color and resolution are becoming rapidly less expensive technology than in the past, and often letting cost govern selection can reduce productivity and affect the long term cost savings made possible by more high quality systems.

Plotters, Scanners and Other Devices

There are a number of commercially available peripheral devices for CAD/CAM systems, as well as machinery driven by the output of the system and its application software. A key to the effective use of peripheral devices lies as much in the CAD/CAM application and operating system software as in the devices an device drivers themselves.

For example, in the area of plotters:

1. The plotter may be driven directly by the CAD/CAM application software through the device driver.
2. The CAD/CAM application software may write a file in plotter format for off-line or batch plotting.
3. The CAD/CAM application software may produce a plot spooler file at operating system level. The operating system plot/print software would then route the file to the appropriate system and plotting devices.
4. In an effort to standardize plotting, some CAD/CAM systems today output plotting information in a standard output form, such as the Computer Graphic Metafile (CGM). In these cases, the job of producing information for specific plotters may be generated at the operating system level, or it may be left to the tool provided directly by the plotter manufacturer.

Among the various devices required or supported by CAD/CAM systems are:

- Tablets.
- Mouse-type devices.
- Function key pads.
- Large-scale digitizers.
- Printers.
- Plotters.
- Raster and raster-to-vector scanners.

These devices can range from very basic tools to laser printer/plotters and color print or plot output devices. Applications run from design and analysis, through process planning, to finally, the manufacturing of products themselves.

Software Platforms

The concept of software platforms is new to the CAD/CAM industry. CAD/CAM software platforms have come to play an important role in engineering and manufacturing. This concept of software platforms and their scope and content should be consideration in acquiring CAD/CAM technology.

The term software platform, when applied to a CAD/CAM product, is intended to describe the basic software architecture including database, methodology, graphics capabilities, and geometric tools upon which a vendor's applications are based. It is intended to describe a basic level of functionality, which can be directly linked to:

1. Hardware requirements and performance.
2. Basic CAD/CAM capabilities and limitations.
3. User flexibility, functions, and options.
4. (Implementation) of future tools and technology.
5. Effects on implementation and training.
6. Availability of vendor provided application support.

Given this definition of platform, there are three basic classifications which can be defined for CAD/CAM platforms: 2D, 2-½D, and 3D. Within these classifications are a various tools for generating and using various symbol and part libraries, as well as for adding various levels of intelligence. Surrounding these classifications are various additional tools for customizing, access, input/output, peripheral devices, and display technology. Beyond these basic classifications are various definitions of geometry used for curves, surfaces, and solids. Figure 3-2 shows the relationships and functional differences in platform geometry.

It is the total (combination aggregate) of these tools from any given vendor's systems that comprise what is called the CAD/CAM software platform.

In turn, applications are in turn software packages which make use of and expand upon these basic capabilities.

Limitations in a software platform are also limiting factors in an end-user's technological growth and increase the cost of implementing new or emerging technologies.

In addition to CAD/CAM software platforms, operating systems have become the key to open systems architectures and the portability of CAD/CAM software and tools. UNIX (mainframes and workstations), DOS (personal computers) and their equivalents on various hardware platforms have become standards in the computing industry. The majority of today's engineering and manufacturing software is available for one or more of these operating systems. The introduction of hardware capable of supporting both UNIX and DOS environments has been another step in the evolution of CAD/CAM technology.

To best understand the effect of the CAD/CAM software platform on CAD/CAM capabilities, a detailed discussion of tools and applications follows.

TOOLS

Basic modeling, assembly modeling, detailing, drafting, and documentation are the tools which comprise the software platform of the CAD/CAM environment. They comprise the basic content of the majority of today's CAD/CAM offerings.

Discussions on modeling methods, precision, units of measurement, drafting, dimensioning, and text editing and insertion

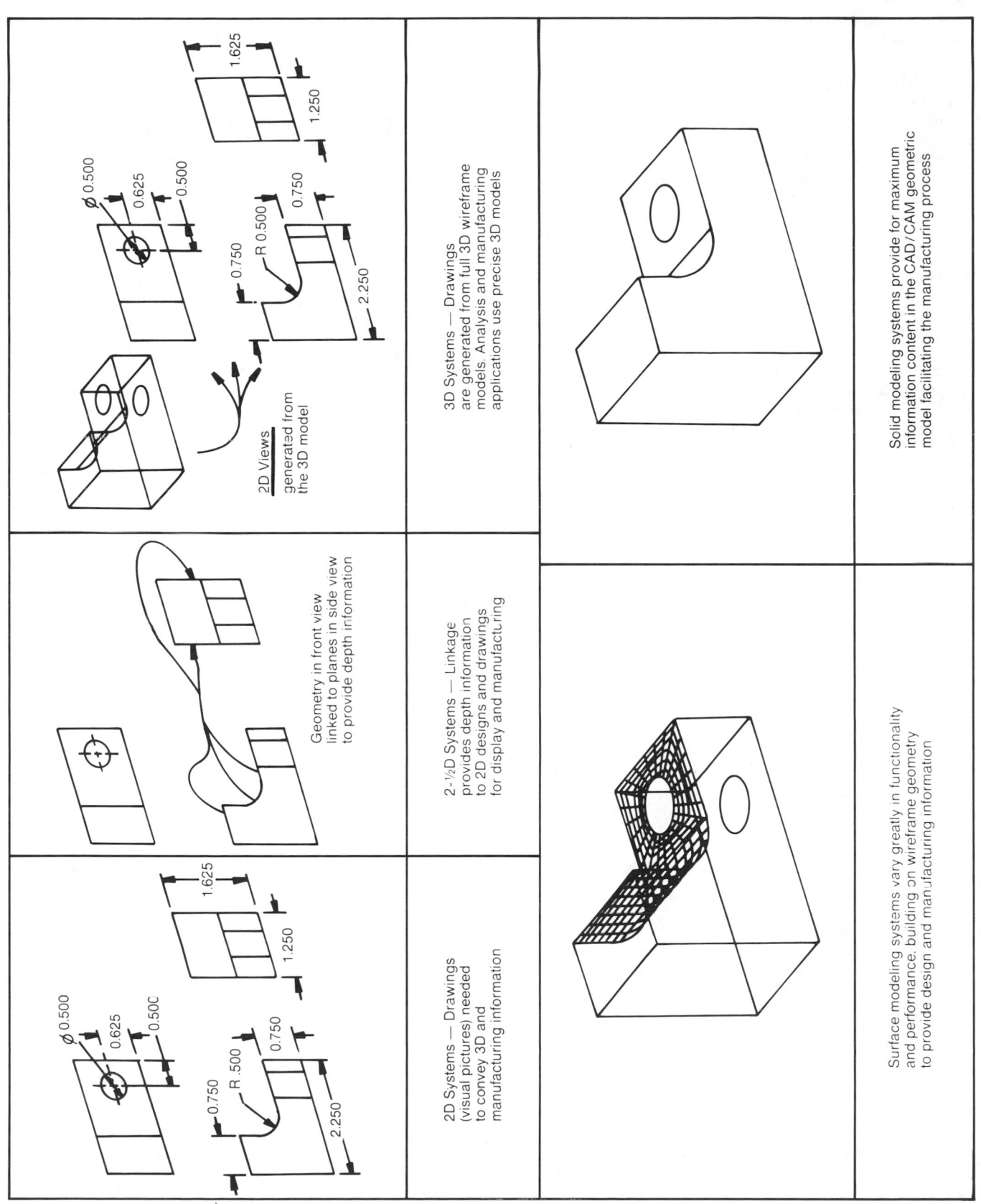

2D Views
generated from
the 3D model

3D Systems — Drawings
are generated from full 3D wireframe
models. Analysis and manufacturing
applications use precise 3D models

Solid modeling systems provide for maximum
information content in the CAD/CAM geometric
model facilitating the manufacturing process

Geometry in front view
linked to planes in side view
to provide depth information

2-½D Systems — Linkage
provides depth information
to 2D designs and drawings
for display and manufacturing

2D Systems — Drawings
(visual pictures) needed
to convey 3D and
manufacturing information

Surface modeling systems vary greatly in functionality
and performance, building on wireframe geometry
to provide design and manufacturing information

Fig. 3-2 Comparison of geometric modeling methods.

GENERAL INFORMATION

are included. Standards affecting the CAD/CAM industry are also discussed.

Basic Modeling

In the world of CAD/CAM the primary focus of the system is on geometry. It is both the tool upon which the system is built and the primary constraint on any of its associated applications. Many available CAD/CAM systems are confined to the creation of designs and drawings through computer graphics. Others provide the most comprehensive suite of tools and geometry possible based on current technology.

Basic modeling methods employed by CAD/CAM systems that most affect their price, performance, and user productivity. For example, two-dimensional drafting systems require simpler mathematical algorithms, and produce simpler display generation software and smaller databases. Two and a half dimensions require additional computer power, but it provides depth information, three-dimensional image display, and view generation capabilities that increase productivity. In both cases, however, methods generally replicate current manual design methods. Three dimension provide the highest productivity, quality, and design gains of all methods, but require considerable more computing power and database storage. With three dimensional solids modeling systems gains in productivity can be seen which far exceed that of 2D, 2-½D, 3D and solids modeling applications. If the only products are drawings, a low cost 2D system would likely suffice. On the other hand, a 2D system will likely never be expanded to support newer high-end technology.

Two-dimensions. With few exceptions most early CAD/CAM systems started with the implementation of two-dimensional geometric tools. Two dimension enabled replication of manual design, detailing, and drafting. Today, two-dimensional systems continue to have a place in the CAD/CAM environment. (This does not imply that they're the best productivity wise for producing 2D drawings.)

A good two-dimensional system is made up of the following:

1. The availability of drafting construction line methods for insuring proper view alignment and orthographic projection.
2. A strong line-font capability for drawing preparation and representation as described later in this chapter.
3. Full support of ANSI and international standard drawing sizes including "E" size (34" × 44").
4. High interactive response speeds. Users should never have to wait on the machine.
5. Tools for creating and storing libraries containing drawing and drafting symbols, parts, and drawing formats.
6. A strong dimensioning package supporting ANSI, international (ISO, JIS, AFNOR, DIN), and other standards.
7. Tools supporting English and metric dimensioning.
8. Tools supporting geometric dimensioning and tolerancing methods.
9. High quality (scaleable) text fonts.
10. Separate view and drawing scales.
11. Entity/drawing layering capability.

Things to watch out for in two-dimensional systems:

1. Is the system vector or raster based? Vector based systems provide intelligent 2D systems capable of supporting more advanced CAD/CAM and manufacturing applications, while raster-based systems are best suited for scanning in, displaying, and editing previous paper drawings.
2. How are curves represented? (Are they precise?)
3. Can the output be scaled (if required)?
4. Is there an upgrade path to three-dimensional systems?
5. Can the system be used to detail three-dimensional models?

Why choose a two-dimensional system?

1. If a company's only output are drawings there may be no need for three dimensional modeling.
2. A two-dimensional system require can run on the lower cost hardware platforms and require the least amount of disk storage, if cost is a critical selection factor.

Two and one-half dimensions. One might ask what is a half of a dimension? In the CAD/CAM world this implies that the system has a knowledge of depth and often the ability to display three-dimensional appearances of models developed using two-dimensional techniques, yet without the overhead of storing the full geometric representations of the model.

The 2-½D system creates and displays 3D representations of 2D orthographic drawings by linking the geometry in two orthographic views to provide depth related information. This linking information is then used in an interactive or batch mode to provide depth information for imaging or manufacturing processes. Often, 2-½D systems are well suited for simple component and sheet metal design and manufacturing applications. In addition, they are often suited to companies whose products consist more of purchased, standard parts than manufactured parts, where interface, interaction, and interference between parts is a given rather than a design function. However, 2-½D systems provide limited increases in quality and productivity for minimum increased costs over 2D systems.

In general, features to look for in a 2-½D system are the same as those associated with 2D systems. One might also look for simple (easy to use) methods for view and geometry linking and editing.

Three-dimensions. Three dimensional modeling is the key to a full and complete CAD/CAM environment. While 3D systems may not be required for all design, engineering, and manufacturing environments, most three-dimensional CAD/CAM systems can replicate the functions of 2 and 2-½ D systems if required.

Three-dimensional CAD/CAM systems can be broken down into three classes of modeling systems:

Wireframe. In wireframe system the 3D model is created and stored only as geometry representing points and edges within the model. 3D wireframe models are transparent in nature and therefore require user experience and knowledge of the model before representations can be clearly understood.

In a wireframe model points on a surface are implied. Any precise surface representations or information must be passed through line and offset type information similar to previous manual drafting techniques.

A major advantage of 3D systems is the automated generation of an infinite number of drawing and views of a part from a single geometric model. This helps in quality, productivity, readability, and producibility of the drawings and the products. However, in wireframe modeling, there are few tools for cleaning up these views for drawing representation purposes. Therefore a weakness of 3D wireframe modeling systems is the amount of effort required to produce clean finished engineering drawings from the fully completed 3D model.

Surfaces. The addition of surface information to the 3D model results in improved graphical imaging when linking it to 2-½, 3, and 5-axis manufacturing application and numerical control processes, and sometimes to improvements in hidden line removal and drawing generation.

Surface modeling provides for varying degrees of accuracy in the CAD/CAM model from very precise, as in the case of planer and ruled surfaces or surfaces of revolution, to lesser degrees of accuracy such as on sculptured surfaces.

Various mathematical surface models developed during the past decade allow for highly precise modeling of sculptured and trimmed surfaces, with non-uniform, rational, bezier splines providing the most common of high-end surfacing technology.

Solids. Solids modeling provides the ultimate geometric modeling method for the CAD/CAM environment. A key factor to automating the design through manufacturing process, this tool permits storage of precise and complete information about a given part, component, or assembly designed on a CAD/CAM system.

Solid models (or the representation in which CAD/CAM solid models are stored) can be broken down into two primary categories: constructive solid geometry (CSG) and boundary representation (BREP) solids.

Constructive solid geometry implies the use of general case primitives, such as cubes, cylinder, cones, tori, etc., to create a solid image. In these types of systems, solids are created by storing size and construction parameters applying to a given set of primitives to create a composite solid object. These methods are often well suited to more regular prismatic components, and while limited, the number of primitives on many systems is growing rapidly.

BREP solids can be stored in two forms: true surfaced and faceted. In the first instance the true surfaces representation and topology of the solid is stored. In the latter faceted surface representation is stored and true surface data is generated when needed by other applications. In most cases BREP solids also store data on the construction sequence associated with the BREP solid.

Data on the sequence in which Boolean operations were performed to create a solid indicate the order in which holes were drilled in a block when only the bounding geometry is retained on the system. In this way, when one hole of a pair of intersecting holes is deleted or moved the other hole is patched or restored to reflect this change. It is this storage of constructive data associated with a solid model allows minor changes such as moving a hole or feature in the original model to be accomplished easily. Solid model applications which fail to store the constructive data require the generation of new geometry and the execution of Booleans which were not a part of the original solid modeling process in order to affect the change.

Solid modeling brings a great deal of knceowledge into the CAD/CAM environment. Topological models allow software applications to understand the inside and outside of a model. In the mechanical world dimensional information linked to a solid model can provide precise information about maximum and least material condition models.

In analysis, solids allow for rapid calculation and extraction of physical property information such as volume, area, centroid, moment of inertia, and so on.

In drafting, comprehensive solids models allow for the rapid generation of drawings through automated hidden line removal and view fonting.

In addition, solid modeling techniques eliminate one of the last remaining arguments over two-dimensional versus three dimensional CAD/CAM, that is, the cleanup of wireframe models. Key arguments given for 2D versus 3D include the time to generate the total design geometry and the time to edit drawings. Solids, while requiring more computer power and storage, can generate models faster than wireframe and surfacing methods. They can also produce drawings from these models in a combined modeling and drawing generation in less time than 2D drawing methods. The result is improved product quality in less time at a level which can more than justify the cost of today's workstation platforms.

Coordinate systems. Another key and critical feature of 3D systems is that of auxiliary coordinate systems (see Fig. 3-3) when working in either model or drawing space. A differentiator between many 3D systems is the ability to work in one or more Cartesian or polar coordinate systems affecting the same model database. This allows the user to enter coordinates for specific geometry or features relative to a particular planer surface within a model. Stronger systems allow the user to specify any number of coordinate systems for modeling purposes, either through explicit coordinates and instructions or through the use of existing model geometry. Any coordinate system established in this way can be displaced and rotated to any required orientation from the original model space.

Assembly Modeling

One of the most significant paybacks in the CAD/CAM environment is in the area of checking, design verification, and product producibility. This is one of the key values today of 3D vs. 2D systems, where a physical part or product is to be the final output.

There are several ways in which assembly models are generated on CAD/CAM systems today.

Models in models. Two of the earliest forms of assembly modeling, and still among the most effective for small scale operations, are the concept of layering and technique such as the draw/model.

In these methods, all of the parts of an assembly are developed using three-dimensional modeling methods in a single common database. Individual parts are separated using layering techniques in the database. Layering allows only selected layers to be displayed on the CAD/CAM terminal or plotted by an output device at any given time. By separating components on layers, with adjoining geometry on common layers, they can be displayed individually or as a part of the total assembly.

The draw/model concept then allows multiple drawings to be combined from the model database; either for a single component or for an assembly or sub-assembly. Line fonting, hidden line removal, and dimensions will apply only to specific drawings and views. In this way drawings of each component can then be produced, displayed, and output separately from a single common assembly model database.

This method represents the minimum of technology and overhead required to develop and produce a complete design of assemblies and their components.

Components or figures. The next level of assembly technology deals with the use of component models or figures. This method applies to both two and three dimensional geometric construction and is an extension of the use of symbol libraries for schematics, mapping, printed circuit board, and other 2D

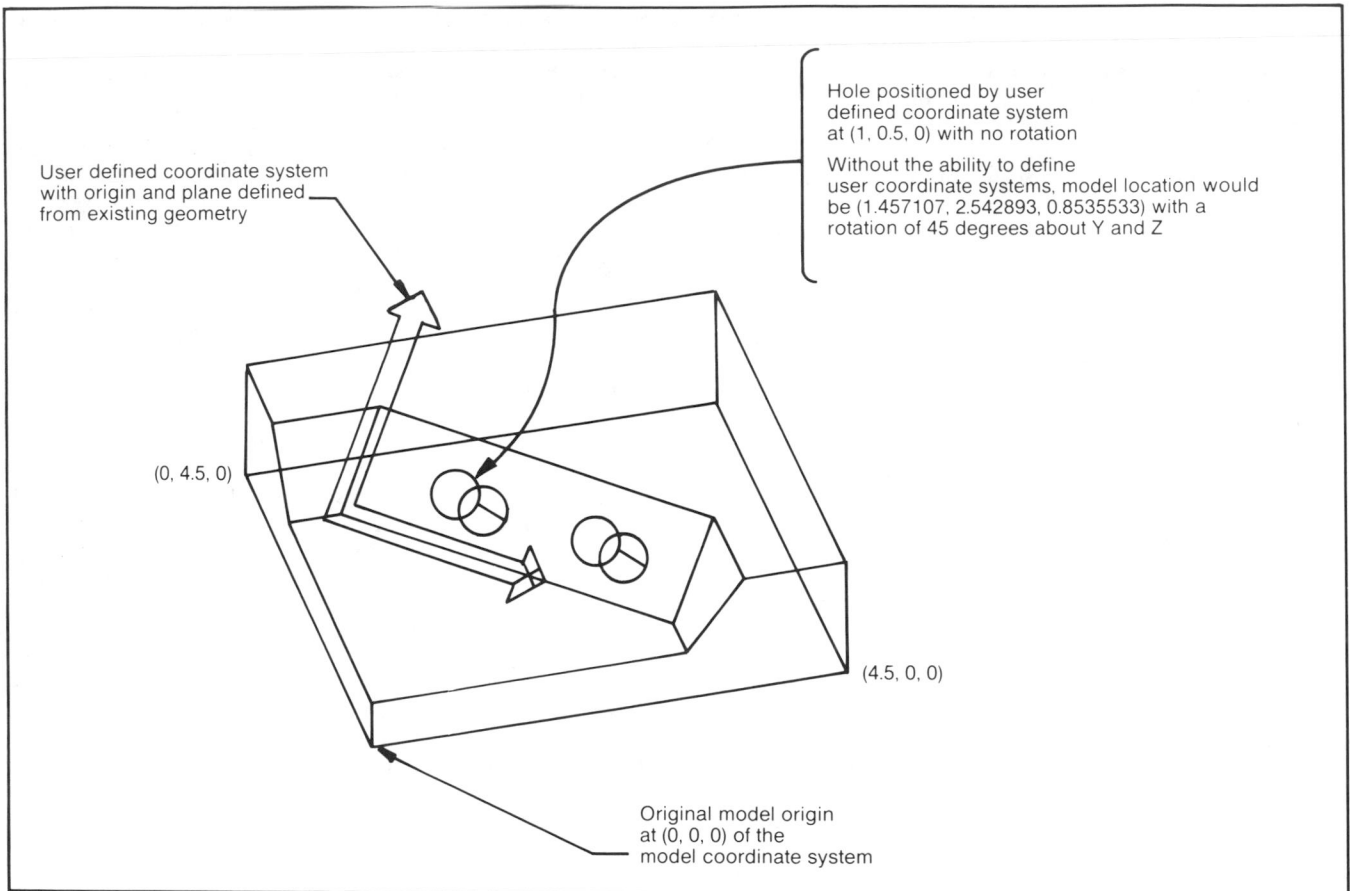

Hole positioned by user
defined coordinate system
at (1, 0.5, 0) with no rotation

Without the ability to define
user coordinate systems, model location would
be (1.457107, 2.542893, 0.8535533) with a
rotation of 45 degrees about Y and Z

User defined coordinate system
with origin and plane defined
from existing geometry

(0, 4.5, 0)

(4.5, 0, 0)

Original model origin
at (0, 0, 0) of the
model coordinate system

Fig. 3-3 Creation and use of coordinate systems.

and 3D applications. In this method each object or components is developed as a separate CAD/CAM model.

Two methods exist for the development and generation of designs using component or figure libraries on CAD/CAM systems; top-down and bottom-up.

In the top-down method the assembly is designed as a complete and comprehensive model in a single, common database. Components are then constructed from the parent assembly in a way that creates separate component databases with intelligent instances in the assembly from which they were created. The resulting single component databases are then used to detail and document the individual components.

In the bottom-up method the components are each designed and detailed in their own individual databases. Assemblies are then created by instancing (or "referencing" external part or component information) the previously created components in the assembly database.

In addition to geometry, component databases can contain non-graphic data such as part names, descriptions, and so on, for each individual component.

In this method, displayed output and engineering drawings depicting the group comprising an assembly are joined by the application, through relationships or instancing, while each component continues to reside in its own separate database.

The advantage to this method is improved configuration and change management and automated or semi-automated updates of assemblies when component parts are changed.

A disadvantage is that each assembly drawing must be individually enhanced and detailed for documentation purposes. It is time consuming process with other than solid modeling or without advanced methods of automated hidden line removal.

Intelligent assemblies. Intelligent assemblies represent a tool of more modern generation platforms. They have been made possible by hardware and software platforms which have been input/output channels and facilitate the sharing of data files among applications and users.

In this method, the existence of an actual assembly database is replaced by references to a non-graphical database containing assembly modeling relationships and information. The resulting display and output of assembly models, when required, is based on an edited composite of all of the databases (or models) represented in the assembly. Assembly drawing edit information is then applied to the resulting composite of geometric part models comprising the assembly. Figure 3-4 presents an illustration of various assembly methods.

Elements that make up a good three-dimensional system include:

1. Multiple to unlimited user illustration systems.
2. Precise curve and surface representations (NURBS/ EZIER).
3. Strong multiple drawing and multiple view per drawing capabilities.
4. Separate draw and model coordinate systems and units.

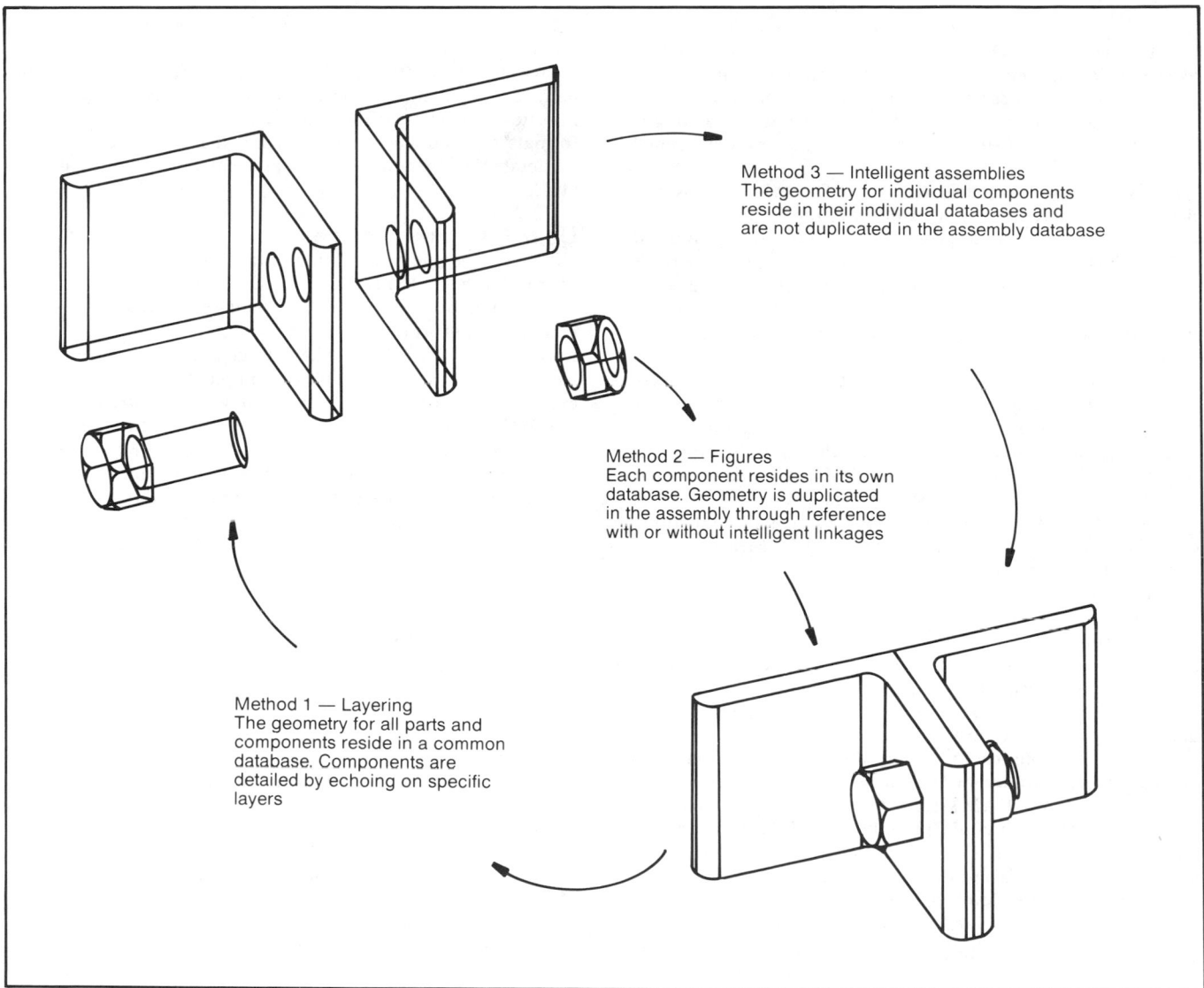

Fig. 3-4 Assembling of CAD/CAM models.

5. View and model associative dimensions and drawing entities.
6. Strong support of both 2D and 3D design and drafting methods.
7. A strong family of integrated analysis and manufacturing applications (with upward migration paths).
8. Strong assembly design and documentation tools.
9. Ease-of-generation of 2D drawings from 3D models.

Things to watch out for in three dimensional systems include:

1. Low interactive response in identifying, selecting, and displaying graphics.
2. Limited graphic entity capabilities (less than 50,000) where assemblies or complex designs are involved.
3. Lack of dimension associativity.
4. Lack of intelligent tools and libraries for assemblies and material list generation or extraction.

5. Limited expandability and available integrated applications.

A three-dimensional system should be chosen for the following reasons:

1. Improvements in product quality and in part-to-part tolerances and alignment.
2. Reduction in design time and in potential manufacturing problems.
3. Support of improved automation of design, analysis, manufacturing, and inspection processes.
4. Support of 2D when required without restricting future methods or expansion.

Detailing, Drafting and Documentation
Producing drawings and documentation for engineering, manufacturing, sales, and service is an important requirement

GENERAL INFORMATION

of any engineering and manufacturing organization.

This process will continue to exist until such time that all aspects of design, manufacturing, inspection, documentation, and service are reduced to a controlled (automated) environment. This level of automation will probably not exist as long as products are sold, distributed, and used on an international basis.

This implies that much of the CAD/CAM process will become automated in the next decade, replacing paper with digital information and process planning with automated machine instructions. However, documentation, in some readable form, must exist, or be capable of being generated, if anyone is to work on or understand the concepts of a product, or it's workings, when separated from a working computer device or display.

Forms and formats. A great deal of the process of engineering and product documentation is tied to the use of forms and formats for the presentation of graphic and textural material. The ability to create, customize, and utilize prepared forms is therefore a key portion of CAD/CAM functionality which should exist in any CAD/CAM platform.

Formating systems allow for the development of stand-alone or composite forms and formats (see Fig. 3-5). Fields in forms allow for the definition of separate text fonts, sizes, and positions as required to serve the function of each block on the form. In addition, tools are provided to allow for automated annotation of forms for material lists and other key functions. Many form systems allow for pre-identification of specific blocks in a format so that information inserted in a block during the drafting or design process can be extracted programmatically for data management and business applications.

Fonting and hidden lines. The ability to hide, erase, or change the appearance of specific geometry in a drawing is critical to any CAD/CAM system. It would be ideal if solid lines of a consistent width could provide the full level of graphic communication required in an engineering drawing. However, visual perception and established documentation standards, require more detailed levels of presentation.

Line fonting capabilities of CAD/CAM systems allow for the partial or complete fonting of lines or curves for presentation purposes without breaking a line or curve into separate segments.

Most systems provide standard fonts and line widths for hidden lines, phantom lines, centerlines, borders, and other line fonts required by U.S. and international standards. More advanced systems provide both scaleable and fixed fonts, where scaleable fonts are tied directly to the scale of the model in the CAD/CAM system, while fixed fonts provide a given an predefined appearance in a drawing or document when plotted at full scale.

User definable fonts are available for many of today's systems such that line fonts critical to an application or use can be created by user.

Text and notes. A picture may be worth a thousand words, but text is still a critical portion of any CAD/CAM system. The ability to create, edit, manipulate, and modify the appearance of text on a CAD/CAM system is a very important function of the system.

Most major CAD/CAM systems now provide standard and user defined text fonts. Text fonts meeting required presentation standard stipulated by U.S. and international organizations are usually provided on the system. Text may or may not be editable once placed in a document, however, many systems allow for the editing of graphical drawing or documentation text without removing the original text from the database.

Text height, width, slant, and other attributes can usually be defined at a global level, and changed if required at the time of insertion or at a later time. More advanced systems allow forms, formats, and nodes pre-inserted in drawings and documentation to dictate the appearance of text associated with the document at a later time.

User Aids and Devices

No two people work or think exactly alike. This fact carries over when they interact with a CAD/CAM system.

It would be a simple world if all of today's design and manufacturing processes could be automated in the same way in which the end user did not have to change the way he or she works or interfaces with today's computer technology. However, just as no two people think or work exactly alike, few CAD/CAM systems work or are configured in the same way.

Likewise, while most engineering drawings and documents may look very similar at a basic level (lines on paper), the information they represent and the features and functions they document vary greatly from industry to industry.

Most CAD/CAM systems provide only a subset (although often a very complete subset) of the process interfacing requirements for a given end user or industry. As a result, most CAD/CAM systems today offer only a subset of all the tools and interfaces users would like to have to support their day-to-day operations.

It is therefore essential that CAD/CAM systems provide the maximum possible openness for customization of the system by its eventual user. The following aids and devices are associated with many CAD/CAM systems:

Digitizing tablets and menus. A common device found on many CAD/CAM systems is the digitizing tablet. It provides a means to:

- Control the cursor on the display of a CAD/CAM system.
- Allow for command input through graphic tablet menus and user or system provided macros.
- Input data from previous paper documents through digitizing.

The most commonly used tablets on most CAD/CAM systems vary from "A" (8-½" × 11") to "C" (17" × 22") size in common use. However, larger tablets through "E" (34" × 44") size, and beyond, are available from most major systems for precise digitizing of input data. For precise digitizing, most high-end CAD/CAM systems allow for variable tablet calibration to allow for paper shrinkage or for paper not mounted precisely normal to the digitizer grid.

While widely used in early CAD/CAM systems, the digitizing tablet is now being replaced by the mouse and screen menus for user interactive input, and by scanner technology for data input on many newer CAD/CAM systems.

User definable and programmable tablet menus today are valuable elements in customization and productivity on many CAD/CAM systems. It is possible for each department in a company to develop their own individual tablet menus.

Screen menus and icons. Innovations and creativity by companies such as Xerox and Apple Computer have brought many changes to modern computing. Coupled with new graphics display and screen management technology, their use of gra-

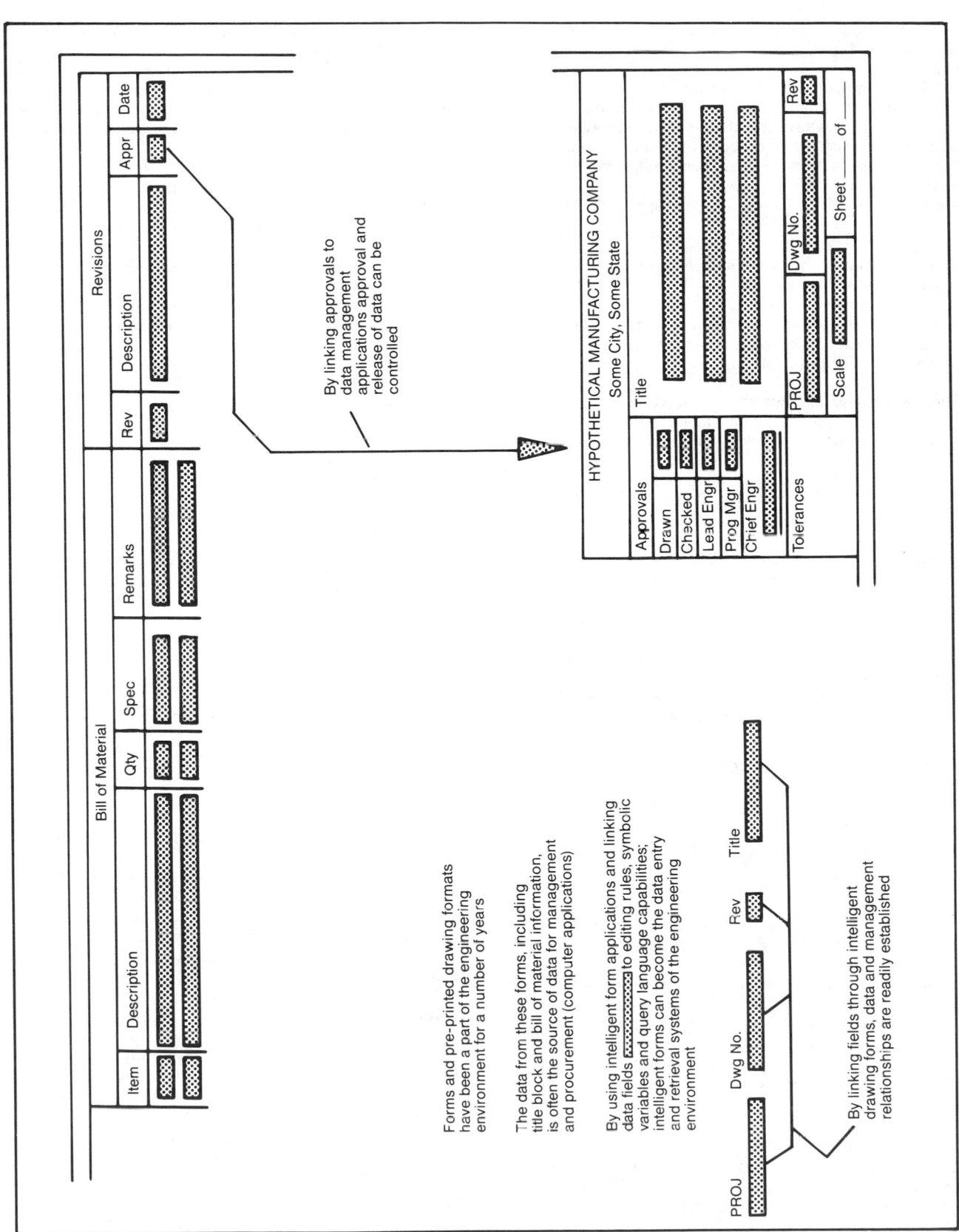

Forms and pre-printed drawing formats have been a part of the engineering environment for a number of years

The data from these forms, including title block and bill of material information, is often the source of data for management and procurement (computer applications)

By using intelligent form applications and linking data fields *************** to editing rules, symbolic variables and query language capabilities; intelligent forms can become the data entry and retrieval systems of the engineering environment

By linking fields through intelligent drawing forms, data and management relationships are readily established

By linking approvals to data management applications approval and release of data can be controlled

Fig. 3-5 Intelligent forms and formats.

GENERAL INFORMATION

phics and presentation in the user interface area have changed the demand and expectations computer users today.

The primary function of a screen menu, however, is not unlike that of tablet. An important feature to look for is the ability to edit and customize screen interfaces and commands to suit individual users. Only through customization can true productivity be achieved. Most of today's advanced systems provide easy methods for editing screen menus and screen layout or presentation.

Among the interface features to look for in a CAD/CAM system are:

1. Standard and consistent command syntax.
2. Consistent layout and flow of all screen interfaces provided by the same vendor.
3. Ready access to on-line help menus and tutorial information from the text or icon level of the interface.
4. Ability to edit the display and associated macros.

Command fields and macros. No CAD/CAM system is complete without some type of batch, macro-language, or programming tool dedicated to the systems user. No CAD/CAM vendor can easily define, produce, or sell for a profit every tool required by all of the industries and companies they serve.

For instance, only a hypothetical squicket manufacturer might need CAD/CAM commands like "INSERT SQUICKET GUIDE" or "POCKET SQUICKET". The result of executing these commands might be the processing of a string of predefined commands, a macro language program with interactive input, or a user developed program. These tools, when programmed, would then be accessible as a typed (keyboard entry) command or from screen or tablet menus.

Now quality command and macro-language packages provide for compiled or interpretive modes, symbolic variables, external file references, branching, looping, and conditional expressions as minimum levels of functionality.

Languages and Data Access

Beyond simple user customization, many companies need to interface their CAD/CAM systems to in-house design, manufacturing, or management systems. This requires access to CAD/CAM applications and data from higher level programming languages such as FORTRAN and C.

Major CAD/CAM vendors provide extensive application (software) libraries and documentation to support access to their CAD/CAM environments, and many of their systems allow integration of customer developed code directly into the CAD/CAM command interface processor.

While there are many other features, such as cross hatching and schematic diagram creation tools, of CAD/CAM systems which could be considered a portion of the software platform, they might also be considered a portion of specific application software. Many of these value added tools, provided by CAD/CAM vendors, should be evaluated when a company is selecting a new system.

APPLICATIONS

The foundation of any CAD/CAM system is the software platform used in generating and documenting of the drawing or model of a part or component. With limited exceptions, all vendors provide support and performance in this area; while some have made their software platform their entire product

strategy. Others have chosen to build upon the basic software platform of their core systems.

Software platforms, might be considered the core or heart of CAD/CAM systems, while applications represent the soul. It is through applications that the true efficencies of CAD/CAM in terms of savings in production and process related costs can be realized.

In looking at the full spectrum of CAD/CAM applications, it is difficult to define, or even constrain, the range of computer-aided tools for engineering, design, and manufacturing which reside under the CAD/CAM umbrella. CAD/CAM applications can be defined as all of those software tools which "utilize" or "specialize in the creation of" parts, drawing or models developed on CAD/CAM systems.

Applications in the CAD/CAM environment can be broken down in three ways: function, discipline and industry.

- Function.
  1. Design
  2. Analysis
  3. Documentation
  4. Production planning
  5. Manufacturing
  6. Quality assurance
  7. Simulation
  8. Logistic support.

- Disciplines.
  1. Structural
  2. Mechanical
  3. Electrical
  4. Electronics
  5. Architecture
  6. Civil
  7. Other

- Industry.
  1. Aerospace
  2. Automotive
  3. Consumer electronics
  4. Other

In relating CAD/CAM applications to function, discipline, and industry:

Functions are normally those operations, tools, or actions supported by the underlying CAD/CAM software platform such as wireframe geometry insertion or surface modeling.

Disciplines are created through the addition of specialized application software, libraries, user interfaces, and tools on top of the basic functions to create schematic diagram applications from wireframes and surface definition, or styling applications from surface modeling software.

Industries applications are then created through the packaging of software for a specific discipline with industry specific additional application software, libraries, and tools to change schematic applications into electrical/electronic, hydraulic, or plant design applications, and surface applications into airframe design or automotive body styling packages.

Applications are therefore the result of software customization, tools, and packaging as follows:

Design

The creation and basic documentation of CAD/CAM models is a part of the software platform, while design applications are the tools used to automate the total design process. A brief listing of applications might include:

- Mechanical.
  1. Linkage and mechanisms
  2. Gears and drive systems
  3. Hydraulics and pneumatics
  4. Sheet metal
  5. Mold design
  6. Casting design
  7. Surfaces and styling

- Electrical/Electronics Design.
  1. Wiring diagrams
  2. Schematic and Logic design
  3. Cabling and routing
  4. Wire Harness design
  5. Lighting systems
  6. Power distribution
  7. Mount and enclosure design

- Architectural/Civil.
  1. Steel design
  2. Building design
  3. Piping and plant design
  4. Topography and surveying
  5. Mapping
  6. Concrete design
  7. Space planning

- Electronic Components Designs.
  1. Printed circuit boards
  2. LSI and VLSI design
  3. Hybrid design
  4. Wave guide design

Engineering Analysis

Engineering analysis can be broken down into a number of discrete areas, however, more general classifications are:

Closed-form solutions. Analysis based on the usage of a single or fixed set of equations applicable to a particular engineering or design problem.

Logic and simulation analysis. The use of computer-based methods to analyze a particular system design for form fit, and function. This type of analysis is found in a number of engineering disciplines including mechanics, fluids, and electrical/electronics.

Finite element and finite difference analysis. Computer-based modeling and analysis techniques are used for structural, mechanical, and thermal analysis, and include static and dynamic state analysis. This type of analysis is readily integrated with CAD/CAM applications software to take advantage of a single design model concept and reduce errors in translation or recreation.

Kinematic analysis. A major advantage of high-end CAD/CAM systems is their ability to be linked to kinematic analysis packages. It is now possible for engineers and designers to visually observe the operation of a component part or of a piece of machinery early in the design stage. Kinematics can actually model the forces acting on a part or a machine. Other test parameters may include velocity, acceleration thermal gradients, etc. Conditions and stress due to the actual operation of a designed component or piece of machinery can be analyzed without the need for full or reduced scale prototypes.

The key to a productive design and analysis process is to look for close interacting between the design and analysis models. Concurrent access to the model and analysis packages at a single terminal is a desirable feature. The ability to pre and post process model and analysis data to a off-line batch mode process is desirable for large scale (high degree of freedom) analysis problems. However, with new high-powered engineering workstations, 60-70% of the analysis process should co-reside with the design application for best results.

DOCUMENTATION

It is important to look now at a major set of functionalities required to completely automate the design process.

The concept of automated documentation in today's technology is not limited to engineering drawings. An equal part of the design through manufacturing process is the necessary documentation of the associated product information.

Included in these documents are scores of engineering documents to produce the product and user, service, sales, and marketing documents to support the finished product.

The development of high quality printers, plotters and other output devices, as well as higher standards for the storage of raster and vector data produced by graphic systems, has resulted in increasingly better publishing and documentation systems.

Word-processing, documentation, and publishing packages can be found as stand-alone, associated, or integrated products in the CAD/CAM environment. Most stand-alone packages for engineering and product documentation rely on a computer assisted cut and paste process to combine text and CAD/CAM graphic data in a finished form. Associative packages normally used for internal engineering documentation, are produced programmatically be merging independent graphics and text to produce a composite document. Associative packages use programmatic tools that can recreate the merged document if changes are made. Integrated documentation products merge active engineering CAD/CAM applications and active work-processing to form packages into a composite engineering documentation process. This permits separate editing of text and document graphics as well as CAD/CAM graphics in a common process for manipulation, output, or display.

PRODUCTION PLANNING

A major growing application area in the CAD/CAM environment is that of process planning. Linked to more intelligent CAD/CAM databases, applications, and feature-based modeling techniques, the goal is to move the planning process earlier into the design cycle.

To understand process planning applications one must first understand a little of what intelligent databases of feature-based modeling brings to the CAD/CAM equation.

In essence, intelligent databases and applications imply that in a CAD/CAM database information is stored which defines portions of geometry as to function or purpose (i.e. hole, pocket, boss, taper, thread, etc.). Along with this information data on size, depth, type, etc. might also be stored. In this way process planning and manufacturing applications can access and use his information stored in the CAD/CAM database.

Feature-based modeling, a reasonably new concept brought about by advancements in computer technology and geometric modeling, is a method of inserting features with the intelligence

CHAPTER 3

GENERAL INFORMATION

previously mentioned as a portion of the actual design and modeling process.

The more basic process planning applications utilize methods similar to existing manual processes, but use computer-aided tools to assist in the planning and presentation process. In some cases preparation includes the merging of CAD/CAM graphics with process planning documents. Then the documents and data generated in this way are integrated with or linked to the CAD/CAM databases. In this way process planning information can be kept or conveyed with the part data for current or future planning and production purposes.

Now, more advanced applications using a process known as generative process planning, are beginning to reach the market. In this process, intelligence is created in the design process through inclusion of planned or intended manufacturing information and the use of feature-based modeling. Process planning applications can then generate process plan information based on querying information in the design database. This process plan information can then be used to generate process plans based on a set of user developed rules and the database information obtained.

While initially limited to simple processes and applications, this is a growing CAD/CAM area.

MANUFACTURING

As in the case of design applications, the number of manufacturing applications available today is growing rapidly. Unlike some of the current design tools, however, many of the manufacturing applications have matured over considerable time.

In addressing manufacturing applications, the process can be divided into two categories: generation and use. In discussing manufacturing as it relates to CAD/CAM, the main thrust is on the generation of data. The transmission to an use of the information at the machine level is a broader part of the overall implementation of CAD/CAM in the computer integrated manufacturing process.

The CAM in CAD/CAM implies that the design and manufacturing processes are closely tied. It is this relationship that provides for productivity in the design of tooling, jig, and fixtures and the generation of machine instructions for manufacturing, inspection, and robotics. In the electronics world, manufacturing tools based on CAD/CAM technology support printed circuit board, hybrid, LSI and VLSI manufacturing, and auto-insertion and wire wrap processes. Other industry applications support pipe and tubing fabrication and assembly.

The key is that CAM products utilize CAD data. They are processes that rely on the graphics of the design to drive, with the help of CAM applications, the manufacturing process.

The range and depth of CAM applications today vary greatly. They range from highly automated tools which are predominantly graphics driven to pure language based tools where machine tool programmers use APT, COMPACT II, and other programming languages to drive the machine.

The more advanced products now allow the use and integration of both graphic and language based methods in a concurrent application to maximize user productivity. In addition, more recent applications allow for parametric or family of parts programming for the manufacturing process, eliminating the constant programming and reprogramming of parts with similar designs or features.

A partial list of current manufacturing applications which utilize CAD/CAM geometric databases to drive process includes:

- Flame-cutting.
- Drilling.
- Punching.
- Pressing.
- 2-½, 3 and 5-axis machining.
- Welding.
- Photo etching.
- Part placement and assembly.
- Tool design.
- Mold design.
- Pipe and tube bending.
- Extrusion.
- Stamping and die design.
- Robotics programming.
- Printed circuit boards.
- Wire wrap.

In addition to physical manufacturing functions, there are also CAD/CAM products supporting factory floor operations through direct applications. These include graphic display devices for CAD/CAM and processing planning information on the factory floor, and interactive information systems for graphic and non-graphic two-way communications between design and manufacturing.

INTEGRATION

The breath of life in the CAD/CAM world is integration. In CAD/CAM, integration implies the close coupling of functions and disciplines through data sharing, communication, and exchange. In the following section on methods and implementation the need for, and advantages of, integration will become better understood.

QUALITY ASSURANCE

A key element in product quality is the test and verification process for design, manufacturing, and assembly. In every case, the intent is to verify that the as-built part meets design specifications, and that the final product performs as designed. There are a number of tools in the CAD/CAM and CAE arena designed to test and verify products.

Soft gaging, or coordinate measuring machine technology, is a major area of emerging technology. Here automated or computer-assisted technology is coupled with design geometric dimensioning and tolerancing information to create machine instructions for inspection of finished parts. Integration of CAD/CAM systems to automate this process is a progressing technology. However, until the use of geometric dimensioning and tolerancing methods, is more universal and close coupling of this dimensioning information to CAD/CAM geometry is accomplished the process will remain only a computer-assisted rather than fully automated.

In test and inspection, data and its documentation are being integrated or associated with CAD/CAM model and geometry information. Both CAD/CAM drawing and reporting capabilities, as well as documentation products previously discussed, are used to support the test and inspection process.

A third area of testing deals with the physical testing of products. Here CAM applications, such as jig and fixture design, are coupled with design and analysis functions for physical destructive and non-destructive testing. In addition, drawings for the specification and mapping of joints and components for inspection are directly tied to the design and fabrication databases.

In dynamic testing, there are application and industry products available today with finite element type analysis to compare analysis data with physical test results in order to refine and improve product designs and concepts.

DATA MANAGEMENT

A key to successful CAD/CAM implementation is the proper management, control, and re-use of existing information and knowledge. This applies to basic business management processes, engineering and configuration management and total product life-cycle support.

In many companies, where CAD/CAM systems have been implemented, it is the ability of the company to successfully implement proper data management and logistics processes that is the key to maximum productivity and return on their CAD/

CAM investment.

A variety of data management applications those based on personal computers to mainframes, have emerged on the market in recent years. These applications range from basic file management to comprehensive engineering and change management. More advanced applications provide for signature and approval authority, as well as document security. A major requirement in today's environment is the ability to manage data on large scale distributed systems.

Another important feature of good data management application is a close coupling to planning, design purchasing, and business management systems to insure single source entry and maximum control of information. A drawing title, number, and so on, should have to be entered only once at any point in the process, whether at time of planning or creation, be utilized by other applications requiring the information.

METHODS OF IMPLEMENTATION AND USE

The method and quality of implementation of CAD/CAM in various industry environments is a critical factor in the successful use of the technology. CAD/CAM and automation technologies are critical to corporate success in today's highly competitive world economy.

In the following paragraphs various aspects of CAD/CAM implementation and use are discussed including:

- Local functional requirements.
- Management.
- Training.
- Services.
- Support.
- Archiving backup and recovery.
- Local, partial, and fully integrated solutions.

In discussing implementation and use of CAD/CAM, one major premise must be considered. The major benefits of CAD/CAM technology are derived from improvements in the entire product process from concept through production, distribution, and support. Reduced time to market and improved product quality are major returns on a customer's investment. The improved productivity of individuals performing a given task is one by-product or contributing factor in the total equation.

A key in implementing CAD/CAM is to not let today's CAD/CAM decisions affect on future planning and implementation of tomorrow's technology.

It may not be necessary, for instance, to purchase all the CAD/CAM software a vendor has to offer a company evaluating CAD/CAM. If a company fails to buy hardware, operating systems, and peripherals capable to expanding to more robust use, its first system could be first inadequate, and second be a throw away if more powerful or flexible tools are required.

Also to be considered are the values and discounts or price breaks to be gained by purchasing an entire system up-front. In addition the integration of CAD/CAM comes first from the purchase of integrated, common platform systems.

THE DESIGN PROCESS

All aspects of the CAD/CAM process start with the basic concept for a product. The earlier design and manufacturing

information can be entered into the process, the more effective and productive the overall CAD/CAM cycle will be.

In considering product design, it is important to remember that most design processes are evolutionary rather than revolutionary. They rely on the use of previous designs and products in the development of newer products.

Also, many of the components used in the design of a product are standard purchased parts such as fasteners, bearings, bushings, motors, switches, ducts, beams, etc.

As a result of this evolutionary design process and the use of standard components, the following should be considered when implementing CAD/CAM design systems:

1. Development or availability of part libraries for standard components.
2. The use of classification and coding systems for previously designed and manufactured families of parts for their future retrieval and use.
3. Use of CAD/CAM translator systems to allow sharing of precise CAD/CAM data between vendors and suppliers.
4. Capture of existing designs and drawings in raster or vector mode depending on the design life and use of the product.
5. Requirements for maintenance of precious design documentation using automated methods.
6. Use of parametric and feature-based modeling tools for standard components and design features.
7. The use of automated and semi-automated tools to produce 3D models from 2D drawings and designs where use and life-cycle of the product dictate.
8. The use of previously or simultaneously created external geometry (part or component) data in the design of new or adjoining components.

In the revolutionary or conceptual design process, key elements to look for include:

1. The use of high speed conceptual design tools for sketching, modeling, and layout work.
2. Close coupling of sketching and conceptual design tools to the eventual system to be used for detailed design.
3. Linkage to front-end analysis tools.

CHAPTER 3

METHODS OF IMPLEMENTATION AND USE

The following are common to both evolutionary or revolutionary design concepts and should be considered in selecting and implementing the design process to be used for a given product or project:

1. Consider all aspects of the product process and insure that models, geometry, and other information input at one point in the process are useable at all points. (Having to rebuild or reenter geometry or data for any process reduces product throughput and increases the potential for errors or quality degradation.)
2. Remember that for automated processes, the more intelligent the design process or the initially generated database, the chance for a shortened product cycle and reduced design and manufacturing costs are greatly enhanced. Do not use 2D wireframes if sculptured surface machining is required in the future. Likewise, question the use of solids modeling if the only output requirement is a simple source control drawing of a purchased bushing.
3. Work towards totally integrated solutions. Remember that analysis, as well as its background manufacturing data captured in an initial design, can reduce the product design and manufacturing times for future product development.
4. Remember the solid modeling methods used to design parts with a minimum number of operations (subtractions or additional of individual solid primitives) will probably lead to a less expensive part through reduced manufacturing processes (see Fig. 3-6).
5. The methods, platforms, and systems to be used for a specific project, product, or program should be selected based on the total product process and the intended life of the product including manufacturer services and warrantees.
6. Remember that it is usually possible to accomplish low end documentation tasks on high end CAD/CAM systems but not the reverse.

ENGINEERING ANALYSIS

As previously noted, engineering analysis applications can be divided into basic classifications: Closed-form solutions, Logic and Simulation Analysis, Finite Element and Finite Difference Analysis, and Kinematics.

The key to implementation and use of analysis packages is not so much in their functionality, but in their accessibility and level of integration and management.

In most design engineering environments, the processes of design and analysis are closely knit. In the manual world, early sketches are often used as the basis for rough analysis, sizing, and material selection; while detailed analysis is more closely linked to the finished physical design of the product. Geometry and/or system configurations are the basis for early analysis, while finished analysis is based on the final design and often reevaluation or verification for the prior analyzed data.

Based on this close link between design and analysis, the following should be considered in implementation and use of CAD/CAM-based analysis packages:

1. In selecting CAD/CAM systems or platforms, look for multi-processing systems where analysis and graphics packages can be used and accessed concurrently on a common device.
2. Look for CAD/CAM systems where basic analysis formulas and solutions are integrated with the product, if appropriate.
3. In the areas of finite element analysis, insure that the system used is linked to the model geometry. In this way later design changes will not require the recreation or modification of unbundled finite element models.
4. Analysis and CAD/CAM systems should be chosen where design, drafting, documentation, and analysis can be performed at a common site. As a basic rule, 70% of most engineering analysis should reside on and be used in conjunction with CAD/CAM applications.
5. Direct CAD/CAM input of technical data and geometric information to analysis programs.
6. Where integrated analysis packages cannot perform large scale solutions, systems should allow for model data from local packages to be pre- and post-processed to larger computational programs and machines without modification.
7. Data management applications should be implemented based on their ability to tie and cross manage the data and results of both analysis and design applications, including revision and change control.

DRAFTING/DETAILING

The drafting and detailing process is a critical part of any design process. At this stage conceptual designs are converted into documented designs suitable for manufacturing or construction.

For discussion purposes it is presumed that the majority of conceptual design work is accomplished independently and prior to detailed design and drafting. It is also assumed that most initial design work has been based on nominal dimensioning rather than refined for actual detailed manufacturing. In other works, in a design model one might find geometry representing a 2″ (51 mm) shaft passing through a 2″ hole where both the shaft and hole models were precisely 2″ in diameter. In the initial design and analysis phase this may be adequate, however, if the part database is to be precisely documented, or the model is to be used for automated manufacturing, the true dimensions should likely have been: Shaft 1.9996 +.0000/-.0004; Hole 2.000 +.0007/-.0000 (Running Class 2 Fit).

Regardless of the design stage at which nominal geometry is turned into detailed manufacturing data, the process and requirements are much the same:

1. Insure that the system supports required engineering and documentation standards (ANSI, ISO, JIS, and so forth).
2. Look for systems with adequate line fonting capabilities and hidden line or drawing cleanup facilities. (Remember that cleanup of 3D models can be costly).
3. Look for strong dimensioning packages which allow maximum automated or semi-automated dimensioning and dimension editing.
4. Choose initial design and drafting methods with the final product in mind. Solids modeling can yield products and designs faster, and resulting products often cost less to manufacture.
5. Associative dimensioning capability (dimensional data linked to part geometry) yields reduced costs where design changes or future family of parts requirements exist.
6. Look for strong, and if possible, associative geometric dimensioning and tolerancing capability (see Fig. 3-7). Remember that reliable and interchangeable parts are a product of properly toleranced geometry. Support of

METHODS OF IMPLEMENTATION AND USE

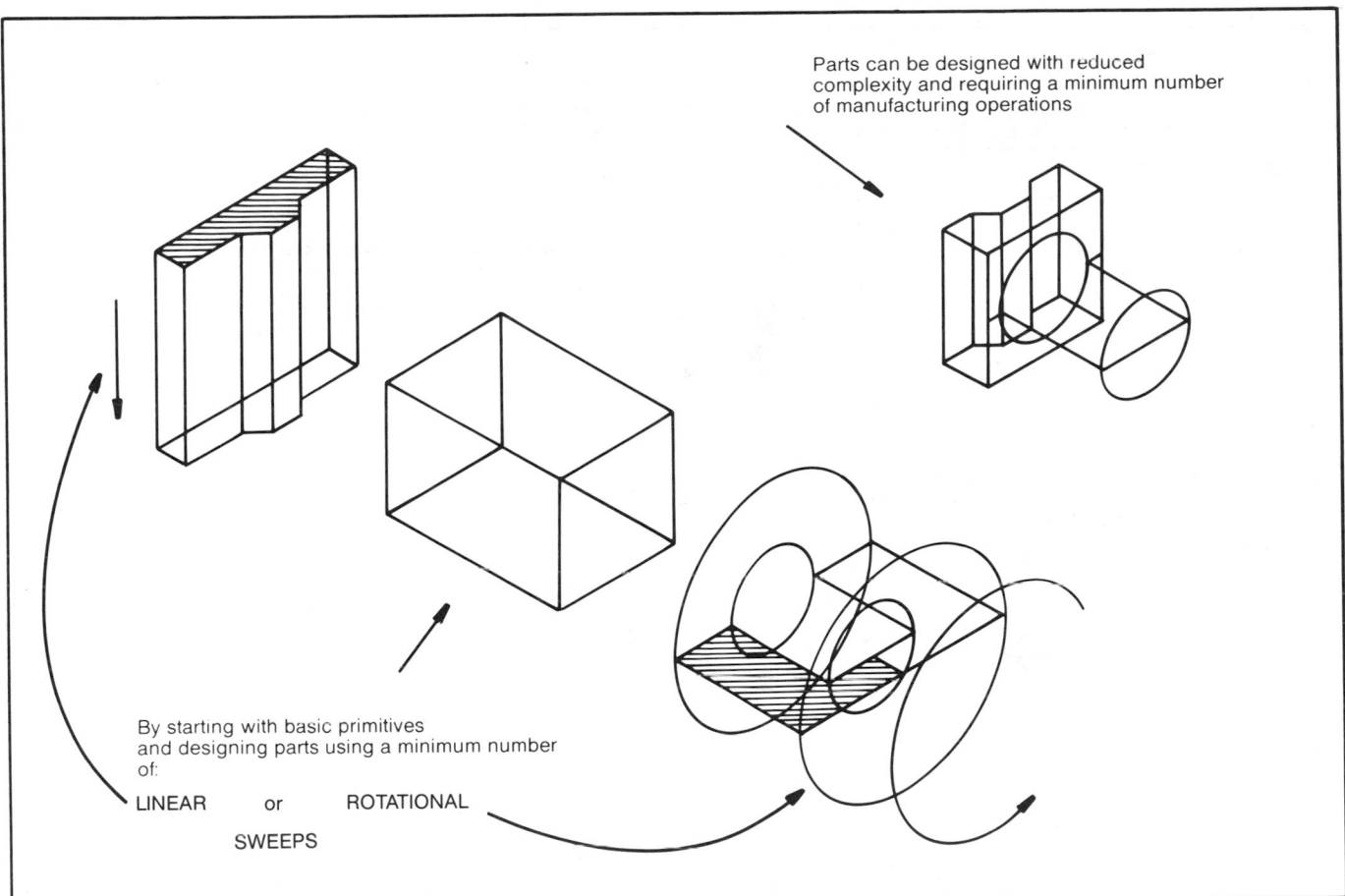

Parts can be designed with reduced complexity and requiring a minimum number of manufacturing operations

By starting with basic primitives and designing parts using a minimum number of:

LINEAR   or   ROTATIONAL

SWEEPS

Fig. 3-6 Improved manufacturing through solids.

today's geometric dimensioning and tolerancing methods insure non-ambiguous part definition and truly interchangeable parts.

7. A great deal of the drafting process has to do with the use of forms, tables, and text. Strong CAD/CAM systems support strong text editing and customizable and intelligent form capabilities in their design and drafting products.

8. Remember that a great deal of drawing data is used for procurement and manufacturing. Good drafting systems should support intelligent bill of material and table preparation.

DOCUMENTATION

There are several previously discussed applications which effect the non-engineering-drawing portion of engineering and manufacturing documentation. In selecting and implementing documentation packages the goal should be the maximum avoidance of redundant efforts in the illustrating and documentation process.

In establishing and implementing documentation processes within the CAD/CAM environment, the following areas should be considered:

1. Design, drafting, and detailing processes should consider eventual documentation needs when developing and enhancing the initial design models.

2. If exploded views without hidden lines are required for documentation then solids model methods may be desirable for the overall product effort.

3. If shaded pictures or colored and textured images are required, and solids modeling is not considered a viable design tool, then surfacing should be considered in designing the model.

4. When wireframe modeling methods are chosen for CAD/CAM design and manufacturing tools, select a documentation system that insures the hidden line and fonting information can be passed from the design to the documentation process.

5. When selecting CAD/CAM and documentation systems the availability of intelligent or semi-intelligent forms systems should be considered.

6. Whatever system is used, direct cut and paste between CAD/CAM and documentation systems should be a basic requirement. Mixed mode CAD/CAM graphics and word processing are also highly desirable features.

7. Whatever publishing and documentation systems are used, the system should be able to support standard output and display processed in raster and vector form.

PROCESS PLANNING

Process planners and manufacturing and industrial engineers are likely to play key roles in future CAD/CAM produc-

METHODS OF IMPLEMENTATION AND USE

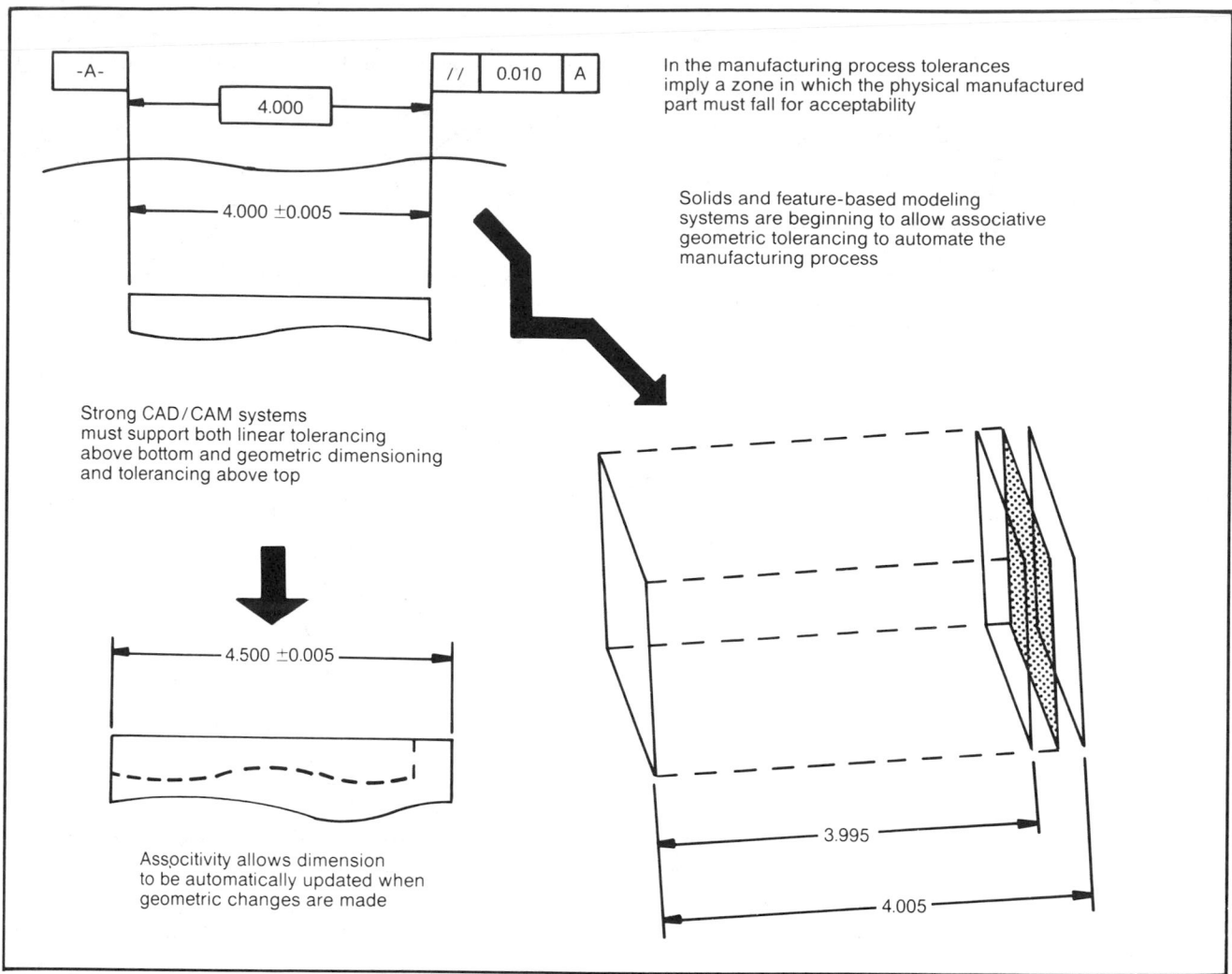

Fig. 3-7 Geometric tolerancing in CAD/CAM.

tivity improvements.

The level of intelligence of applications products and CAD/CAM databases has now reached a point where manufacturing data and processes can be linked directly to the design process.

Now, solid, parametric, and feature-based modeling systems, offered with current CAD/CAM technology, can be used to generate process planning and manufacturing data directly from the design database.

However, a key factor in this process, is knowledge of a company's manufacturing capabilities and methods. Thus, while automated systems may be able to extract information directly from CAD/CAM databases on machine or manufacturing processes, such as drilling, cutting, stamping, boring, etc., the rules for local processes must still be developed based on a company's tools, machine processes, and available capacity.

Assuming that processes can be defined and rules developed, lastly it must be insured that designers learn when and how to include manufacturing information as part of the design process.

Key factors to look for in the integrated process planning are the ability:

1. Of the CAD/CAM systems to accept and store manufacturing and process information in the CAD/CAM database.
2. To adapt the system to local processes and administrative procedures for purchasing, tacking, and so on.
3. To customize the planning system based on local company manufacturing capabilities and processes.
4. For the system to product emerged graphics from the CAD/CAM design and manufacturing processes with text and information generated by the process planning tools.
5. Of the process planning application to support factory floor display and controls systems and to link to other CIM applications.

MANUFACTURING

If CAD/CAM is to be implemented successfully implemented, then the CAM (manufacturing) portion of the equation, next to data management and control, is probably the most critical issue from an implementation standpoint.

Without going into great detail about any particular manufacturing application, certain considerations are critical to implementation.

First, know what manufacturing facilities processes and tooling are available to support the CAM process, whether local, remote, or furnished by a supplier.

Then ask the following questions:

1. Can the CAD/CAM system being implemented support automated manufacturing of the product, and is it feasible?
2. Are the required peripheral devices available to support the process. (That is, photo plotters for reproducing printed circuit boards, etc.)
3. Are there CAM post-processors available to support the NC machines in use?
4. Are the necessary CNC or DNC capabilities of the CAD/CAM and factory floor systems compatible?
5. Are all required factory floor support tools provided?

While these are only a few questions, manufacturing is a large portion of the CAD/CAM world. Therefore, look at the processes, look at the tools, examine the total environment and shop carefully for the right CAD/CAM solutions.

QUALITY ASSURANCE

One of the least recognized, and yet most drastically affected areas, in fully automating the design through manufacturing process is quality assurance. This occurs not necessarily in post-manufacturing test and inspection, but in the integrated design and manufacturing process.

CAD/CAM technology is moving rapidly towards a truly integrated and automated manufacturing environment. Many programs and success stories have emerged where parts were manufactured directly from design databases without the generation of engineering drawings.

The paper world and the checking of numbers is gone, but how are form, fit, and function checked in a binary CAD/CAM database.

Needless to say if properly and adequately checked during the design process, both for manufacturability and form, fit, and function, the part is virtually guaranteed to be a success.

An important question is what happened to the design and drawing checker, that experienced designer or technician who could spot design and potential product manufacturing problems with just a brief glimpse at engineering drawings.

While drawing and design checkers will still check drawings produced manually and with CAD/CAM systems, a new breed of database checker is being born. Quality assurance technicians and engineers are being trained to input or monitor database information relative to inspection, testing, and soft and hard gaging.

Now checking entails building and verifying design databases in nominal as well as minimum and maximum material conditions for quality, manufacturability, and useability. It is no longer possible just to look at graphics. Now, manufacturing, process planning, material, and other information contained in the database must be checked during the early design phases without the benefit of drawings.

As the quality and dependability of embedded manufacturing information in CAD/CAM databases improves, and checkers learn to provide quality assurance of data in digital form post-manufacture gaging may perhaps become less of a requirement in the product cycle.

ENGINEERING AND MANUFACTURING DATA MANAGEMENT

Assuming that all of the necessary CAD/CAM, CAE, and CIM tools needed to automate a company's operations are in place, it is time to address the real issues of making CAD/CAM work.

If any major industry operation were examined today, the one thing that would be obvious at in any stage of the operation is paper. Automated processes are linked by reams of paper for management and process control. This flow of paper often accompanies CAD/CAM databases to convey information the CAD/CAM system cannot process or manage.

Enter one of the most critical and least implemented applications of the CAD/CAM environment, data management (see Fig. 3-8).

Notice the term is data management and not file management. The term data management does not just refer to any unspecified or non-manufacturing related data either. Companies have business and MIS applications to deal with that.

Data management in the CAD/CAM environment refers to all of the miscellaneous information and knowledge about the design through manufacturing process required to produce and support product. These include:

- Information and knowledge associated with product approval and control.
- Configuration management.
- Engineering change control.
- Waivers and deviations.
- Interface control.
- Material purchasing and receipt control.
- Work orders.
- Testing.
- Inspection and certification.
- Product documentation.

Of course the paper process is there and in some cases it may even be linked to a local management information system, but depends on man to insure a link between the paper world and CAD/CAM. However, this need not be the case, for there are engineering data management products which are linked to or designed to be linked to a CAD/CAM process.

It is important to insure that any data management product selected meets the entire needs of an integrated design and manufacturing environment. Some things to look for might include:

1. Whether the system can connect any and all documents associated with a given product for future use.
2. Whether all active change documents for a given product can be accurately tracked against all associated product documentation and databases (design and analysis through test and inspection).
3. Whether the data management application can process, track, control, and manage configuration data embedded in the engineering model and drawing databases.
4. Does the data management product provide user oriented customer query and programmatic access to the information contained in and managed by the application?
5. Is there a strong review, approval, release, and security process which can manage approval and voting processes on CAD/CAM documents generated on the CAD/CAM systems?

METHODS OF IMPLEMENTATION AND USE

	Low-end systems	Mid-range systems	High-end systems
System types	Personal Computers Low-end workstations Some minis and mainframes	2-4 mip workstations Minis and mainframes Some high-end PC's	Workstations over 4 mips Some mainframes Some mini-super computers
Breadth of CAD/CAM	2D and 3D wireframe and surfaces Numerical control and some manufacturing Limited assembly capability	2D and 3D wireframe and surfaces Numerical control and some manufacturing Limited assembly capability	Integrated wireframe, surface and solid modeling Full manufacturing suite Technical publishing capability Full engineering data management
Tools generally provided	File management Limited naming conventions Limited networking General file transfer capability Local peripherals	File management Expanded naming conventions Full file management suite Transparent networking Distributed file management Remote peripheral management	File and data management Unrestricted naming convention Full engineering data and change management Full security, approval and release controls
Required management functions	Localized backup Manual file security on external media Manual archiving and recovery	Initial system configuration Centralized but manual backup and archiving Manual security management	Initial system configuration Initial configuration of engineering management and security software
Limitations	Highly limited security No centralized file management Easy to create duplicate files (parts or drawings) Difficult design/production environment to manage	Lacks high level application integration Lacks adequate engineering change and configuration management	

The measure of a CAD/CAM system is more than technical functionality

Fig. 3-8 The data management factor.

6. Does the vendor provide a two-way close coupling between the CAD/CAM and data management applications so that the data can be initiated, accessed or modified for both technical and management applications?
7. Is the application limited to the documentation management and control side, or does it support data distribution and display in the production environment?
8. Can data managed by application be classified and retrieved based on geometry, configuration, material, process, etc.?

Finding the right data management application, establishing methods that maximize evolutionary design and manufacturing processes, eliminating the need to duplicate work previously performed at some point in time. These are important in successful CAD/CAM implementation.

STANDARDS

In implementing CAD/CAM for the 1990s with the current pace of technological change two factors can be critical to the CAD/CAM future: 1) selecting quality and extendable hardware and CAD/CAM software on open systems that support current industry standards, and 2) selecting survivable vendors who will still be around to support future database and technical needs.

In coming years CAD/CAM systems should support standards PHIGS, CGM, CCITT, IGES, and PDES. The first three deal with 3D, 2D, and raster graphics. IGES is a data exchange package for CAD/CAM information. PDES stands for Product Data Exchange Standard. PDES is the first major attempt to define all aspects of data management, model data, engineering data, manufacturing data, material data, etc., in a single common data exchange format. Planned for tomorrow's solid modeling and feature-based world of integrated CAD/CAM, it holds the key to ultimate integration.

PUTTING IT ALL TOGETHER

Regardless of the type of CAD/CAM systems installed, the bottom line is making maximum use of the hardware and software while increasing management and productivity and decreasing cost.

It is a simple world where there is only one computer and only one CAD/CAM vendor. There is one operating system, one method of facing up and restoring files, one method to provide system and file security, and one (or no) methods for

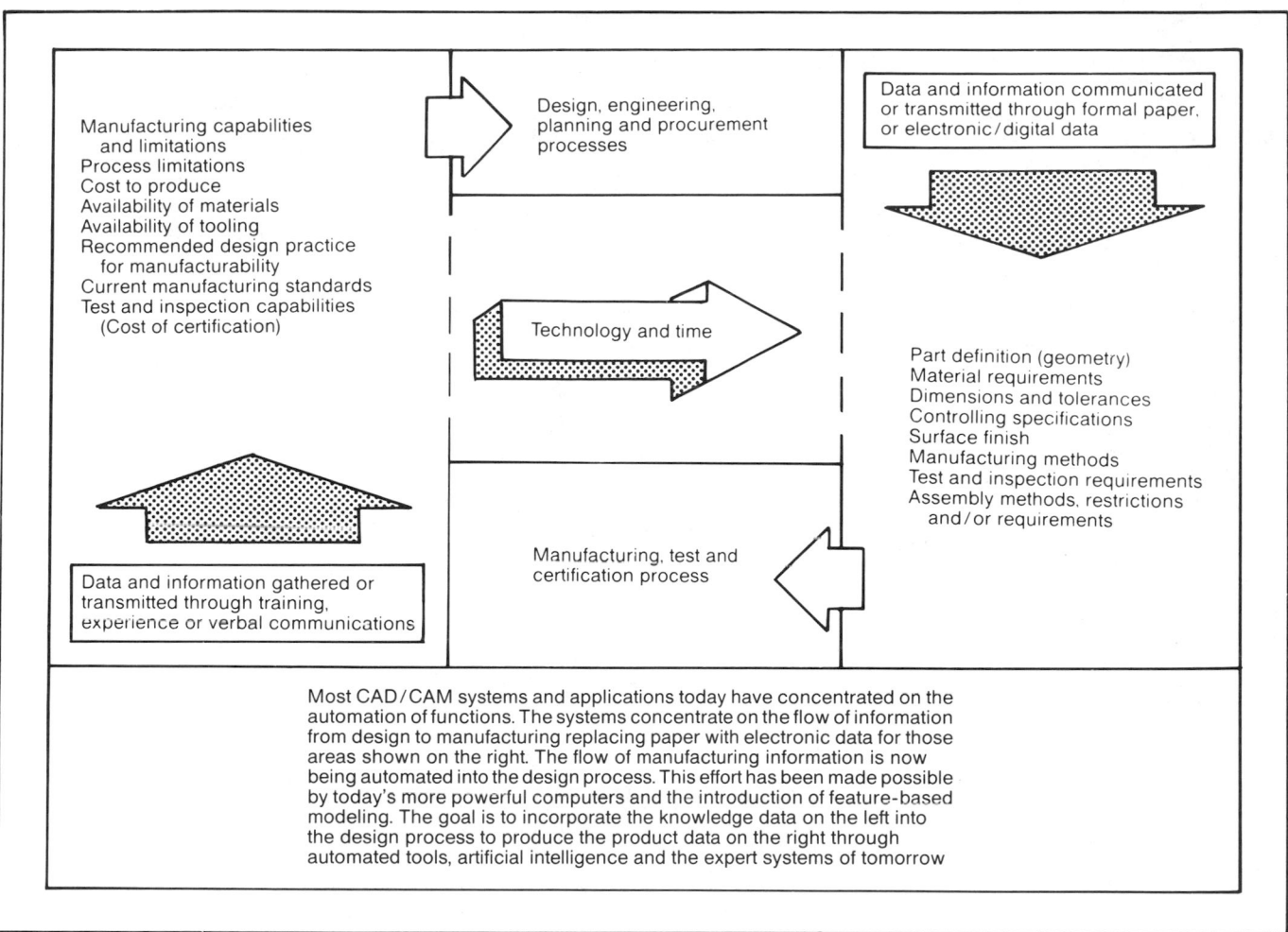

Fig. 3-9 The recycling of knowledge.

inter-computer communications and data exchange.

In this simple world there is likely a single system manager responsible for supporting and maintaining the CAD/CAM environment, and he or she defines and enforces all the company policies and rules on use of the CAD/CAM systems.

Unfortunately in most large corporations the systems and the rules are far from simple. Sending and managing CAD/CAM files across several different systems, and transferring data to and from other company divisions, customers, and contractors or suppliers are facts of life. Open networks and network file systems create an environment where files can be moved readily and often duplicated at several points in a network. Security is complex, and in a multi-processing environment it may never be known who or what processes are sharing the system the users are working on.

In this more complex environment, system management is an important factor in successful CAD/CAM implementations. Also, common hardware and software platforms support and simplify the management and use of CAD/CAM. However, if this is not possible, insuring the existence of open systems and standards for operating systems, networks, file systems, and engineering and manufacturing data exchange is the best way to provide maximum security and efficiencies at minimum costs.

FORGING THE FUTURE

Feature-based modeling systems, object oriented databases and programming, artificial intelligence and expert systems have become key phrases in any discussion of the future of CAD/CAM. It is these and other technologies which will have a major bearing on the design, engineering and manufacturing of tomorrow. The CAD/CAM industry is in transition from the automation of manual functions to the automation of process.

The goal of future technology is to capture and combine the design, engineering, and manufacturing knowledge of yesterday and today to assist in to automating of the processes of tomorrow (see Fig. 3-9).

FLEXIBLE MANUFACTURING

Flexible manufacturing technology holds a great deal of promise for manufacturing. Potential benefits include an improvement in quality, the reduction of costs and inventory, and improved product turnaround. The technology might well be divided into two segments; the flexible manufacturing system (FMS) and the flexible manufacturing cell (FMC).

FLEXIBLE MANUFACTURING SYSTEMS

An FMS has many definitions as people attempt to describe an FMS from their perspective. At a higher level, an FMS is a collection of flexible manufacturing cells. It also can be a group of dedicated, singlepurpose manufacturing machines, providing flexibility due to both the variable flow of material between stations and the different combinations of using the various single-operation stations. In both cases, the end result is the ability to manufacture multiple parts or assemblies using the same collection of machines. A transfer line with variable usage and operation of the stations can function as an FMS. Therefore, flexible manufacturing describes any collection of machines or centers with a means to move material between them. The entire system is controlled by computers, which collectively can manufacture different parts and products from start to finish. Figure 4-1 shows a typical FMS configuration.

Although the acronym FMS is considered to be somewhat generic, many other terms and acronyms are used to describe this general class of manufacturing equipment—Computer Integrated Manufacturing System (CIMS), Computer Managed Parts Manufacturing (CMPM), Variable Mission Manufacturing (VMM), for example. In countries other than the United States, terms such as Flexible Automation, Flexible Manufacturing System Complex (FMC), and Computer Integrated and Automated Manufacturing Systems (CIAM) are used.

Machine tools employed in an FMS usually are CNC machining centers or headchangers, but may also be other production equipment such as lathes, automated testing or assembly stations, or even forming or finishing equipment. The FMS concept of manufacturing is characterized by the ability to bring together in an integrated fashion, work stations, automated material handling, and computer control.

The unique feature of an FMS is its capability to manufacture more than one part, or in some cases, more than one family of parts in midvolume output rates. Some systems require batching of workpiece families, while other systems accept workpieces from various families of parts in random order. The use of Group Technology (GT), as a way of classifying parts with similarly manufactured features, helps determine the manufacturing capabilities required for a collection of parts. It also allows the grouping of similar functions to minimize changeover and setup time between parts. Group technology sequencing is sometimes adversely affected by just-in-time (JIT) product and material scheduling, because the latter does not sequence parts based on similarity of manufacturing operations, but on priority assembly sequence. This apparent contradiction of objectives only exists if the changeover and setup time is significant when changing between parts. If the FMS has essentially zero setup time, a lot size of one is an economic lot size and the objectives of JIT do not suboptimize the FMS. If this can be achieved when trying to follow a rigid JIT plan, the benefits of an FMS are greatly visible since there are more frequent changeovers in the parts being manufactured.

The FMS, in contrast to an FMC, usually requires a larger capital investment and more sophisticated control. The flexible manufacturing system is usually more difficult for people to understand. Productivity and cost-saving returns of the FMS hold great potential.

An FMS is not totally flexible, due to being limited by the cube size and general shape of a part which any machine can accommodate, and also part configuration—round, flat, square, rectangular, and so on. Therefore, a plant totally operating with the FMS concept would have multiple FMSs to make all parts for a complex assembly. The concept of focused manufacturing might allow for multiple small plants each with a single FMS producing a single type of product.

An FMS must usually be tied to a material requirements planning (MRP) system to ensure incoming material is scheduled properly to appear at the correct time and place. Integrating an FMS with a computer-aided design (CAD) database allows the use of design data and tolerance specifications for Numerical Control (NC) machine programming and automated inspection.

Since an FMS contains various machines with computer based controls, workcell controllers and factory controllers are used to link these individual machine controllers. Part program selection and NC program data is downloaded to the machine controllers, while inspection, maintenance, and production reporting data is uploaded to the factory control system. Manufacturing Automation Protocol (MAP) and other local area networks were conceived as common communications protocols to make possible the development of an integrated, interconnected system using machines and controllers from different manufacturers.

About 200 systems were in use in 1987 (excluding Eastern bloc nations), about half are in Europe. The rest are split between the United States and

FLEXIBLE MANUFACTURING SYSTEMS

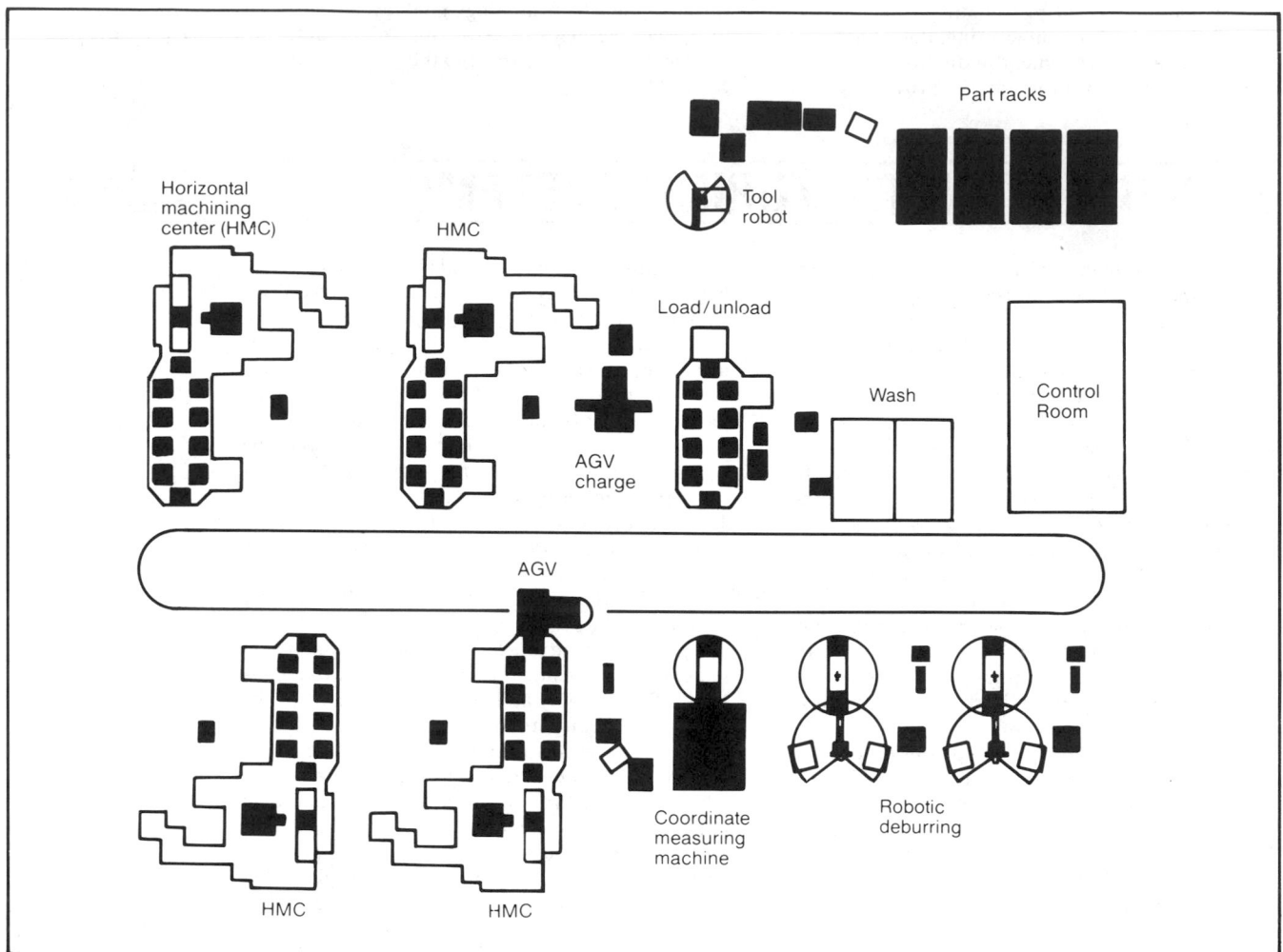

Fig. 4-1 A sample FMS layout.

Japan. The automotive industry (including truck and farm equipment) was the first industry to use FMS, and it remains the major user in the United States and Europe. In Japan, the major user is the machine tool industry.

Many early installations were in very large companies. The reason was not related to the larger manufacturing volume or the greater financial resources of these firms as it was to their greater sophistication in applying computers to various business and manufacturing functions, including numerical control.

ADVANTAGES AND JUSTIFICATION

For many years, so-called midvolume, midvariety manufacturing processes have exhibited rather unique problems not the least of which has been the rationalization of the tradeoff between flexibility in manufacturing and efficiency. Transfer machines have long provided the established and most productive method for machining high-volume, low-variety workpieces. Low-volume, high-variety workpieces traditionally have been produced in a cost-effective manner using stand-alone, single-purpose machine tools or NC or CNC machining centers. The special problems of midvolume manufacturing, until the advent of FMS concepts, have not been solvable with the technologies employed for strictly high or low-volume output.

This lack of appropriate technologies for midvolume manufacturing over the years has spurred an array of special problems. In the past, lead times and in-process inventories in midvolume manufacturing were often excessive. This was caused primarily by the large amount of handling of the workpieces during their respective manufacturing processes. Batch processing of midvolume parts loaded machine tools fully for lengthy periods of time, causing other lower priority jobs to wait in-process for available machines tools. The large number of stand-alone machine tools required to handle midvolume manufacturing requirements utilized a disproportionate amount of floor space in relation to the machine's productivity, in many cases. These and other problems associated with midvolume manufacturing have been intensified by the fact that mass production accounted, as the 1980s began, for at most 25% of the total value of metalworking production in all industrialized nations; the remaining 75% is nonmass-produced, with at least half of these workpieces produced in batches of less than 50 parts.[1]

The FMS concept is viewed by many experts as at least a partial solution to the problems of batch or midvolume manufacturing, as shown in Table 4-1.[2] One source suggests that the FMS concept is particularly well suited to workpieces produced in volumes of about 1000 to 100,000 units per year.[3] Other

FLEXIBLE MANUFACTURING SYSTEMS

TABLE 4-1

Comparison of Machine Tool Systems for Production at Various Volumes

	Piece Production	Batch Production	Mass Production
Annual volume per year*	1 to 10,000	5000 to 200,000	over 100,000
No. of part pieces per lot*	1 to 100	100 to 50,000	over 50,000
Primary motivation	Ability	Flexibility	Volume
Manufacturing cost per part at full utilization	Highest	Lower	Lowest
Cutting tools	Standard	Some special	Custom
Automatic part handling	Seldom	Some cases	Always
Flexibility to change to a completely different part	Yes	Possible	Impossible
Flexibility to change to a similar but somewhat different part	Yes	Yes, if previously planned	Very limited
Ability to change materials	Yes	Limited	Extremely limited
Ability to implement gradually	Yes	Possible	Difficult
Machine tools best suited to the job	Tool shop: several machine tools or NC machining centers	Job shop: NC machining centers, cell of machines, FMS networks	Transfer lines
Typical applications	Aircraft, tool and die shop, maintenance shop, repair shop, specialty machinery for industrial-process equipment (centrifuges, filters, etc.)	Agricultural machinery, off-road vehicles, mining machinery, trucks, furniture, truck diesel engines, associated subcontract shops, aerospace propulsion	Automotive factory, automotive part supplier, metal fasteners, appliances

Source: *Iron Age,* September 28, 1981, p. 85.
* Typical case; numbers vary with size, complexity, and cost of workpieces.

sources indicate that aggregate production should range between 15,000 and 35,000 units per year. Yearly production volumes for individual parts may range between 100 and 8000 units. A graphical representation of production flexibility versus productive capacity for FMS, as well as other machines and machining systems, is presented in Fig. 4-2.

The FMS concept is most applicable to family-of-parts processing; a range of midvolume workpieces such as axle housings, air compressor housings, or engine blocks are typical examples. Workpieces which are part of a family of parts that feature a significant number of processing options are good candidates for FMS manufacturing.

Most existing FMS installations are employed to manufacture prismatic parts that require operations such as drilling, milling, tapping, boring, or grooving.

Labor Costs

The direct labor component of the total cost of manufacturing a workpiece is said to be decreased through the use of FMS technology because of the high degree of automation employed. Indirect labor (maintenance, etc.) may be increased due to the higher level of hardware complexity employed, however.

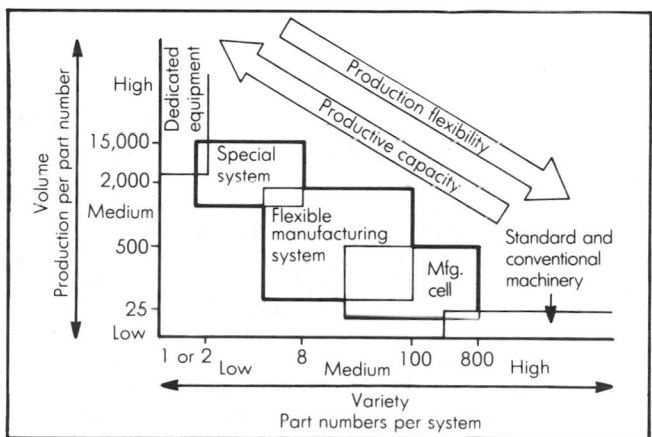

Fig. 4-2 Production flexibility vs. productive capacity for FMS, as well as other machines and machining systems. (*Kearney & Trecker Corp.*)

Equipment Utilization

Many claims have been made concerning the ability of FMSs to increase machine utilization. Proponents of the con-

FLEXIBLE MANUFACTURING SYSTEMS

cept suggest that the pacing effect of computer control and optimization effects provided by computer algorithms spur increased machine tool utilization. It is also stated that utilization is improved by the flexibility of FMSs because downtime of individual work stations usually does not shut down the entire production process. Utilization rates of up to 80-90% are cited.[4] However, some studies show considerably less average machine tool utilization with FMS equipment. One study of FMS performance explored system utilization (the ratio of machine hours actually used to theoretical capacity) and found actual operating utilization to be only 50-60%.[5]

Manufacturing Flexibility

An FMS installation is capable of accommodating changes in part volumes and/or product mix, design changes, etc., with fewer problems than conventional equipment. Because FMS equipment is flexible with respect to part design, the useful life of the equipment is considered to be longer than specially tooled conventional equipment; thus, increased flexibility can eliminate the need for some future capital outlays for new equipment.

Because an FMS can process a wide variety of workpieces at random, downtime associated with traditional changeover techniques is eliminated. Computer control allows more flexibility in part routing to minimize production time.

Inventory

In many cases, processing of workpieces through the shop is considerably faster with FMS than with conventional equipment. For this reason, in-process inventory can be greatly reduced. When using transfer line production methods, in cases in which more than one workpiece is produced on the line, setup time and costs may dictate that workpieces be run in rather large batches, thus increasing inventory costs.

Management Control

Computer control of FMS installations affords greater production control than that possible with conventional, standalone machine tools. Accuracy of short-term decision making can be increased through generation of timely management reports, and changes in production schedules, etc., are more easily handled.

Acquisition Cost Justification

The justification of the costs of an FMS can be broken down into the acquisition costs (site preparation, system design, and initial operator training) and the operating costs (usage scheduling, maintenance, reprogramming, and ongoing quality assurance activities).

The acquisition cost justification of an FMS was at one time, done the same as for any manufacturing capital equipment. This was to list the direct costs of acquisition, scheduled maintenance, with allowances for overhead and burden, and compare to the revenues generated from the net sales of the product produced by the system over a specified time period. The discounted effects of inflation and depreciation were factored into the equation, and if the resulting payback period was within the guidelines of the corporate specifications and sufficient capital was available, the acquisition was approved.

Sometimes, in this traditional approach, there was no similar financial detailing of alternative approaches, and typically there was never any inclusion of the cost of quality of the product, the financial effects of time-to-market capabilities of current or new designs, the inventory carrying costs, the effects of designing the product for easier manufacturing, the cost effects on and requirements of the design engineering environment, nor the ability to manufacture an inherently higher quality product.

Contemporary cost justification and manufacturing accounting methods are changing to include many of the other factors and effects which must be considered in today's worldwide market and manufacturing environment. Cost justification of large capital expenditures is being made more in terms of what are the strategic implications if the expenditure is not made. Competitiveness and ability to respond to a dynamic market maintain market share with offshore manufacturing and foreign competition. The quality of a product and a long MTBF (mean time between failure) are highly desirable attributes, which can be enhanced by greater and more flexible manufacturing capabilities.

One of the main problems with justification of flexible manufacturing is that the reason a company should investigate flexible manufacturing is because it does not have stability in its product design or in the product mix. Therefore, the products and the quantity of products to be manufactured are both unknown. Assumptions about either can be very difficult to make with much reliability.[6]

It is difficult to justify new technology by traditional cost benefit methods. The costs are current and easily measured, while the benefits are often realized in the future and not easily quantified.[7]

ROI methodology assumes stability in the economy, technology, labor, and most important, the marketplace behavior of competitors—assumptions that have proven time and again to be false. In addition it stresses short run returns rather than long-run strategy. The difficulty lies in the disparity between the apparent ease of quantifying costs and the difficulty of quantifying benefits.[8]

The value of an FMS rests on its application. Furthermore, its value can be extended or optimized if such a system is properly integrated with conventional machinery which constitutes the main-stream of today's manufacturing environment. Misapplication is often a result of lack of business vision. In the case of an FMS deployment, the project definition which represents the goal of the system must be clearly understood. Such definition should remain as the absolute measuring index throughout the project cycle. Redefining the project is permitted and encouraged, but one must realize that such redefinition often means additional expenditures.[9]

BENEFITS OF AN FMS

There are many reasons for using an FMS. It supplies greater utilization of expensive machine tools or other special purpose equipment. Another reason is to minimize the need to buy additional capital equipment each time a new part or product is developed. The ability to limit the manufacturing effect of new products to only new tooling requirements for existing machines provides significant savings in time (the lead time required for delivery of new machine tools could be 6 to 12 months for a sophisticated machine, as opposed to a few weeks or months for new tooling) and money. This was primarily because the cost of these machines was such that machine tool builders did not deliver from stock, but rather built machines essentially to order. The current trend is to use more modular designs which enable machine tool builders to have some of the basic functional modules pre-built, or to use more standard purchased parts and subassemblies, which also cuts delivery time significantly.

The use of FMSs have provided a new concept in factories—the FMS factory—which has a greatly simplified material flow. The raw materials flow directly to the manufacturing operation where they are converted into the finished assembly. Handling is decreased, labor content is reduced, and manufacturing cost is favorably affected. Since the raw materials have a much shorter life span in the factory, the inventory costs are decreased. In the best scenarios, the finished product can be sold and payment received before the payment becomes due for the raw materials.

PLANNING FMS INSTALLATIONS

One example of planning took place in October 1986 at the U.S. Department of Energy/Albuquerque Operations Office (DOE/AL) which established a cooperative Precision Flexible Manufacturing Systems (PFMS) effort among the nuclear weapons production plants, design laboratories, the National Bureau of Standards (NBS) and U.S. private industry. Its intentions to develop and implement critical technologies for the automated manufacturing and certification of precision hemishell components. The DOE structured a three-phase approach to achieve the PFMS objectives. The near-term phase focuses on defining, developing, and demonstrating critical PFMS technolgies. These are defined as: demonstrating precision part and fixture transfers in a machining environment, identifying and demonstrating in-process technologies that will minimize, monitor, and control process variability, and developing and demonstrating a PFMS in-process quality (IPQ) architecture system. To develop and demonstrate these critical technologies, cooperative working groups have been organized.

Table 4-2 traces the various stages of planning, specifying, purchasing, and installing a new FMS. Both FMS builders and users suggest that successful application is assured only through extensive planning from the outset. Some of the stages presented in Table 4-2 are complex; some may be routine. The emphasis any one stage receives depends upon the people and the situation at the specific plant performing the analysis. However, experience has shown that it is best not to bypass any of the cited stages entirely.

Specifications

Figure 4-3 illustrates one possible architecture for a flexible manufacturing system project. This architecture, along with the associated detailed description, physical layout, data structure, control scenarios, and organizational relationships, are included in the system specification. For some multiplant or large-scale applications, it is more effective to define a standard system architecture or platform. The platform consists of standard system building blocks and conventions that provide specified functions through well-defined interfaces. Following are some examples:
- Guidelines should be established for developing common subsystems such as statistical process control, maintenance management, and data acquisition so that they can be integrated with other subsystems and do not themselves become inseparably locked into larger subsystems.
- Common interface software for integrating existing systems.
- Common man/machine interface conventions (forms management software) so that operators, equipment attendants, inspection, test, and maintenance personnel moving about the factory can use the same procedure to interact with any subsystem on any terminal.

- Standard database management system.
- Selection of common computer equipment and terminals for text and graphics information display.
- Equipment control programming specifications to suppliers should contain standards for incorporating communications interfaces.
- Standard control equipment for ease of application and use as well as component repair, part stocking, and maintenance procedures.

The actual implementation approach of the building block is of secondary importance as long as functional, interface, and performance specifications are met. Such a building block approach allows the business to do the following:
- Plug in new technology building blocks without disrupting the overall system (technology transparency).
- Procure equipment from any vendor capable of meeting building block specifications.
- Incrementally expand a system implementation in both functionality and scope.

Several typical building blocks are illustrated in Fig. 4-4.

CAD/CAM/CAE

Computer-aided design (CAD) has an effect on design and use of an FMS. Design rules for easier—or even simply allowable—manufacturing can be incorporated into a CAD system. Features, tolerances, and shapes which are difficult to manufacture can be indicated as the design engineer first creates them, allowing an immediate change without costing time and product integrity. With the emergence of simultaneous engineering, all the required manufacturing processes can be determined as soon as the basic design is generated.

As the design is finalized and computer-aided engineering (CAE) tools are used to ensure the product is properly designed with all necessary characteristics and properties. The design data can be utilized by the computer-aided manufacturing (CAM) systems to develop the NC programs for controlling the machines within the cells of the FMS. This design database which starts with the CAD system, must be compatible with and usable by the successive CAE and CAM systems. Several emerging and proposed standards exist to support this compatibility. A Product Data Exchange Specification (PDES) is being developed by the National Institute of Standards and Technology (NIST, formerly the National Bureau of Standards) to provide a standard database specification for mechanical part descriptions. The specification can be used from design through manufacturing. The Center for Manufacturing Engineering of the NIST has been conducting a Research Associate Program with over 40 industry sponsors to develop and test in a simulated manufacturing environment many aspects of a totally integrated and flexible manufacturing environment.

Robot Usage in an FMS

Industrial robots are now seen as simply flexible computer numerical control (CNC) machine tools, which are incorporated into FMSs and FMCs. When appropriate, robots are used for material handling, machine loading, and other processes which are done better by the robot than by a dedicated CNC machine. One of the major obstacles to more fully utilizing robots is the disparity of not being able to perform off-line programming for them directly from CAD data in the same, easy way as can be done for CNC machine tools.

FLEXIBLE MANUFACTURING SYSTEMS

TABLE 4-2
Stages in Planning an FMS Installation

Stage* 1	Stage 2	Stage 3	Stage** 4	Stage† 5
Define the "cadence" of your machine shop: • You produce a variety of parts in mid-volume—neither continuous production nor prototype and one-of-a-kinds. • People in your plant can handle computers, NC, and machining problems. • Your products, and therefore the component parts, will be made in relatively short runs, repeated during the year. • Your inventory turns are low. • Several (or many) of the machined components are of roughly the same size, with similar geometries requiring similar processing and machining operations. • Setup time is high. • Machining cycles are long. • Tolerances are close for multisetup processing. • Floor space requirements are reduced. • Other: _____ _____	**Establish "families" of parts among your products or components:** Classical families are: **1. By assembly:** grouping parts together that would be required to make up a single assembly, such as all the major casting housings of a tractor assembly, or an engine assembly. The system would be designed to allow the user to order these castings against an assembly schedule, rather than in batch order quantity. **2. By type:** categorizing parts by type that would go into the system by a production volume range, such as transmissions or torque converters. This family represents the relieving of low to mid-volume part numbers from higher volume production lines, eliminating the line changeover generated by the lower volume parts. **3. By size and similar operations:** In this family a group technology study could be applied to selected workpieces, categorizing them by production and volume range and by machining operations. For instance, all parts below a determined volume rate requiring milling, drilling, boring, and tapping might become the basis for a system.	• Determine your current (anticipated) annual requirement for each of the parts in a family. • Determine the total annual requirements for the total number of parts in the family.	• Define the annual requirements for these parts over the next five years. Over the next 10 years. • Define changes in those parts through redesign or other changes during the next five years. Next 10 years. • Define new products that might fit the "family" as you can best perceive them for the next 5 and 10 years. Changing customer wants means changes for you. • Analyze how the product mix might change during those periods. • Evaluate your need for, and use of, automatic flexibility.	•Analyze in depth the capabilities of your personnel (or of the personnel you may need to hire) to run an FMS at optimum utilization and effectiveness. • Determine whether your present labor agreements or contracts will permit you to properly manage and staff the FMS department. If not, you will need to consult with the workers or with the union regarding special agreements that will permit utilization of best skills and that will result in worker continuity. • Make certain that you have a person competent to become Project Manager of the FMS system, from the time the order is placed through installation and run-in. Then make certain that you have supervisors qualified to run the line in production—one per shift. If these capabilities are missing from your staff, know that your company is willing to acquire such capabilities.

Source: Reprinted by permission; *Production*, August 1981, p. 5-76.
  * These conditions would typify (but not exclusively define) plants that are users of or prime candidates for FMS.
 ** An analysis of these kinds of factors will be essential to your justification procedures; it also is vital if your machine suppliers are to do a thorough job of engineering the proper system for your needs.
  † These first five steps can assure you that you either are, or are not, a candidate for FMS. If you are, the information you have developed will be invaluable in implementing the rest of the program.
  ‡ Adequate preparation during preparatory stages will make this a routine evaluation.

FLEXIBLE MANUFACTURING SYSTEMS

TABLE 4-2—*Continued*

Stage‡ 6	Stage 7	Stage 8	Stage 9	Stage 10	Stage 11	Stage 12
• Work with system suppliers to determine alternative system solutions to your problems. • Pick the best possible (and economical) solution which will meet all of your requirements. • Ask for proposals from two or three builders. (You may have to pay for some engineering.)	• Cost justify the investment with normal plant or company procedures. Systems can cost from $1 million (very small) to $20 million or more. Include a consideration of gains not always quantified, such as: reduced work-in-process and finished products inventory, reduction of scrap, shorter leadtimes, higher utilization rates, reduced setup times, closer tolerances, optimum balance of components delivered to assembly, ability to accommodate design changes and future products (vs. dedicated methods). Marketing benefits would include shorter product leadtimes, ability to accommodate design changes and reduced product cost. FMS major disadvantage may be the time and the cost of total process planning and implementation (including staffing) that are needed to make it work properly. Further, it may be difficult or impossible to retain the level of skills you need, due to the shortage of qualified NC and computer-control skills for upgrading and maintaining programs. It should also be noted that where the skills exist, supplier training will provide the necessary specific knowledge, usually without additional cost. Be certain to consider cost avoidance, comparing the FMS cost vs. the cost of achieving the same output, efficiencies and benefits via either dedicated special machines or stand-alone standard machines. With its high utilization rates, FMS often will be the least costly method.	ORDER THE SYSTEM	**Project Manager** • Set up programs to explain the FMS to plant employees, selling them on the need for the new system. Explain just what it will mean in terms of their jobs and in terms of the company's economic health. Follow through to assure union support when it is a factor. • Work with all other departments, including marketing, product design, purchasing, quality control, plant engineering, personnel and finance. • Meet with suppliers to explain requirements for delivery schedules, maintenance of proper stock allowance and of tolerances (including machinability variations), etc., and of all quality characteristics.	**Project Manager** • Work with all necessary departments to develop production scheduling and process routines for each part to be machined on the FMS. • Establish tool maintenance and replacement facilities and procedures for the FMS. (Consider having the FMS capability separate from the rest of the plant's tooling department.) • Select FMS operators, technicians and supervisors, and schedule them for training at the control/system suppliers' plants. • Clear the appropriate area(s), and undertake the construction stages that precede installation. • At an appropriate time, check out FMS machines, tooling, controls, programs, etc., at builder plant. Acquaint and train operators and demonstrate system to other persons who will work with it.	INSTALLATION	**Post Audit** • It is essential that your original plans include a detailed specification of what the system is to do. It also is recommended by every builder contacted that a post audit be conducted so that everyone involved knows how and when performance (success?) will be measured.

Many FMS suppliers provide the robots as part of the turnkey system. In some cases, a customer can select the brand of robot desired from a provided list of machines capable of the task. In most cases, however, the customer cannot select robots in the same way as for cell controllers or NC machine controllers. Due to the many unique qualities of each vendor's robots, an FMS is typically designed to utilize a particular make and model of robot.

With the continuing improvement in the accuracy, speed, and repeatability of industrial robots, as well as the advances in programming, robots are more and more being used as a component of sophisticated manufacturing systems.

FLEXIBLE MANUFACTURING SYSTEMS

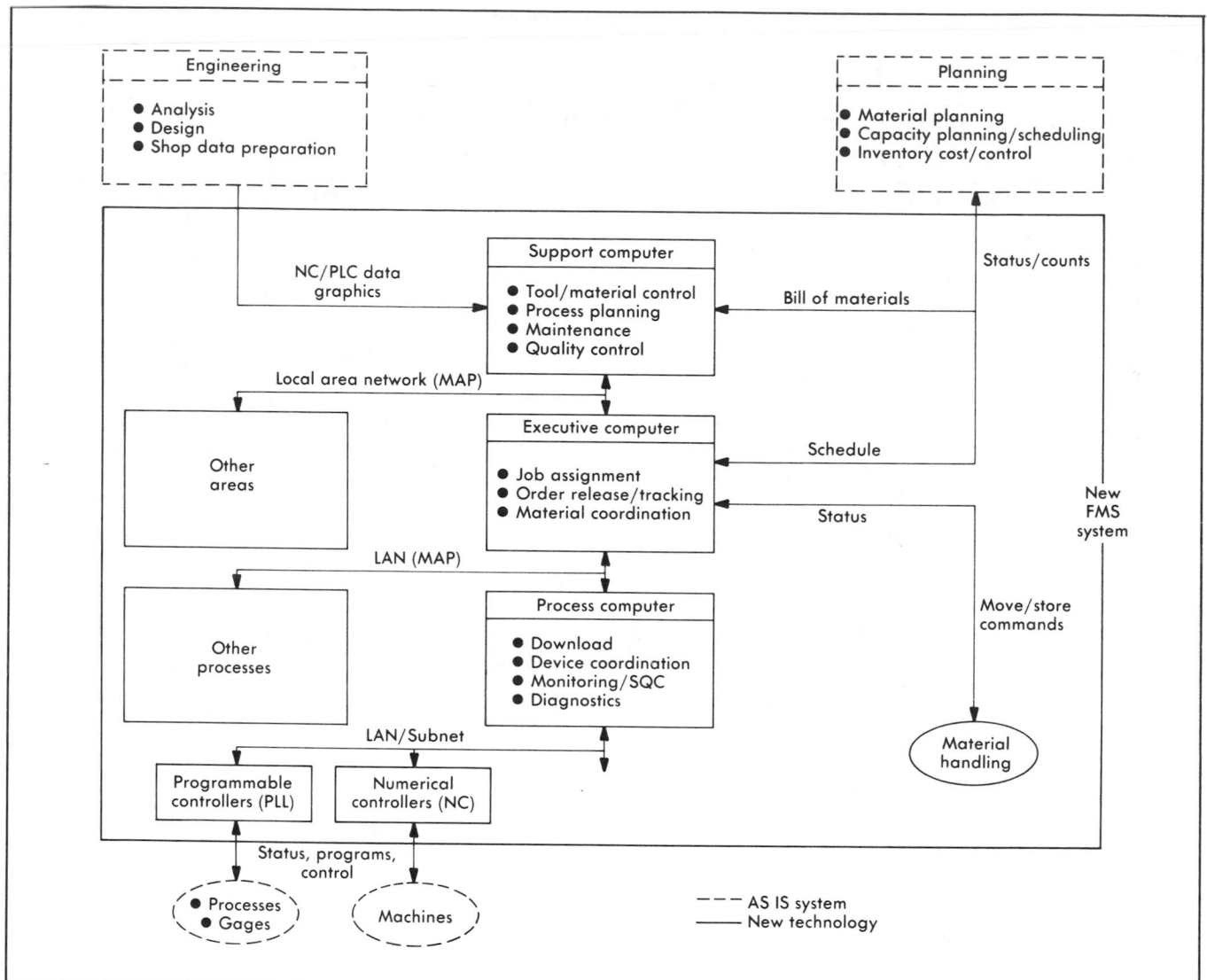

Fig. 4-3 Diagram of a flexible manufacturing system specification.

Requirements For An Effective FMS

The FMS software and hardware have to correctly work together in a real-time mode and simulation can be effectively utilized to insure that this will occur.[10] An overall simplistic view of the information flow is given in Fig. 4-5. The vertical structure gives a rough hierarchical computer arrangement with the plant mainframe at the top and the FMS and shop floor information system computers begin at the bottom. A brief discussion of the hierarchical components follows.

Capacity (aggregate) planning. Based on forecasted and known demand as well as current and projected operating conditions, management develops a macroschedule over a relatively long-range horizon. Basically, this indicates which facilities will be utilized for what products over specified time frames. The output of capacity planning then becomes the master schedule which is input to the MRP planning phase.

MRP I/MRP II. Based on current inventory levels and planned macro-demand, material requirements planning (MRP I) evolves a detailed product/time schedule for both vendor and in-house production. Manufacturing resource planning (MRP II) allows feedback of current conditions (vendor and manufacturing) to allow the master schedule to be changed while minimizing disruption when problems accrue at the lower levels. This detailed schedule is still independent of specific machine assignment (routing) and so the output of the MRP function feeds into a computerized scheduling module. It should be mentioned that long-run assembly processes might be feasible to schedule directly from the MRP phase. If machine loading (shop floor schedule) is required then routings, and alternate routings in case of equipment malfunction, are needed in addition to the MRP output. However, MRP will only function effectively if shop floor control keeps accurate tallies on part location and machine status.

CAPP. Computer-aided process planning has as its aim the development of a machine routing sheet, including time standards, directly from design; thus allowing the feasibility for computer-aided manufacturing and computer-aided design integration. In electronics assembly this integration is even more

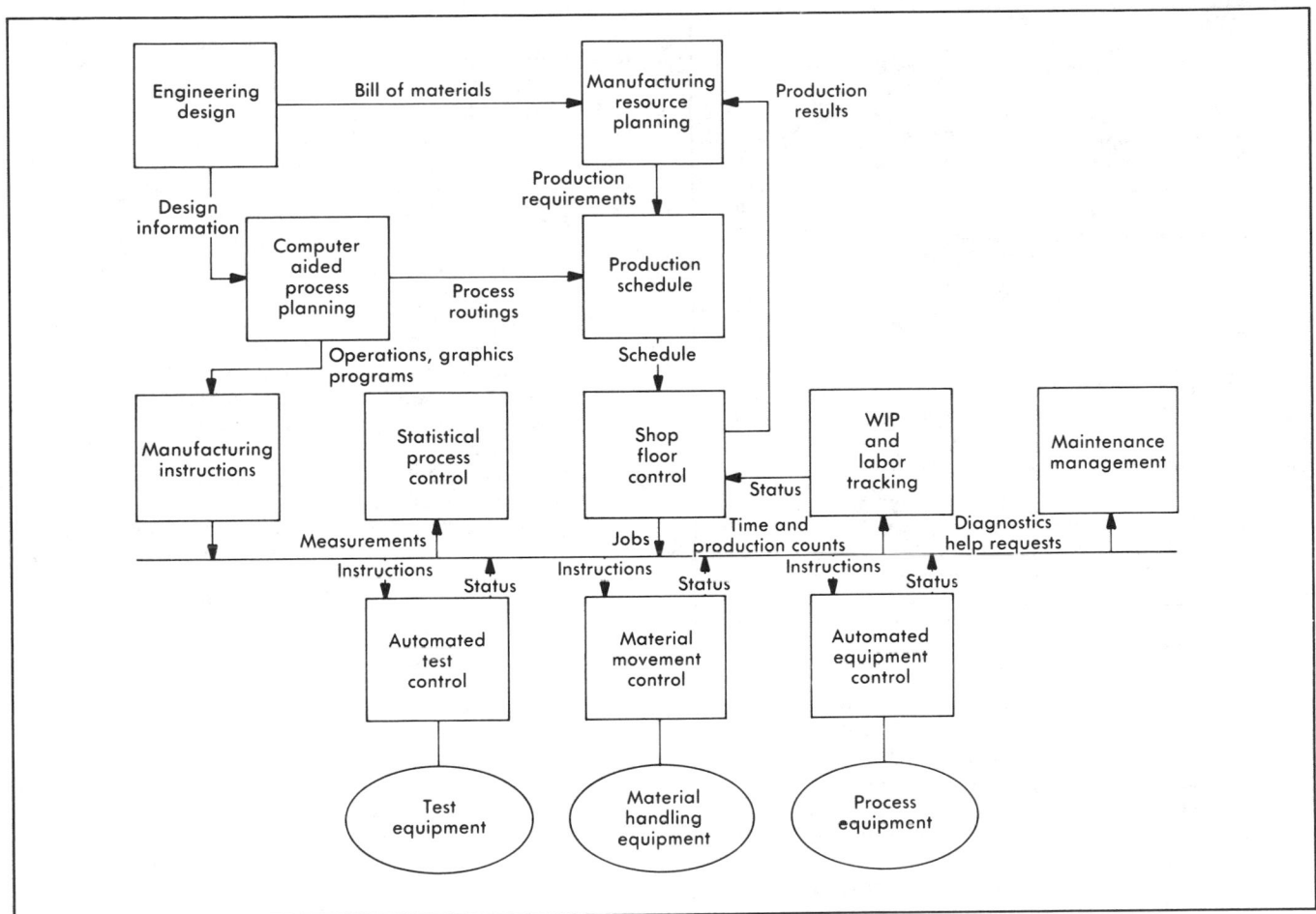

Fig. 4-4 Typical system building blocks.

feasible due to the relative sameness (ignoring rework) of PCBA insertion processes.

Computerized scheduling. If the FMS is to operate in an automatic real-time mode then shop floor scheduling has to be reactive in real-time. This implies an algorithm that allows for alternate routings when conditions change on the shop floor, such as machine breakdowns, components not available, material handling breakdowns, and so on. Further, a fully computerized system offers potential benefits of schedule optimization based on an objective function that might include cost minimization.

Effective, cost-conscious planning is the goal that should be sought in early stages of project design. The project team needs to evaluate many varied alternatives at this early stage in the project so as not to exclude any of the potential solutions, regardless of how infeasible or far-fetched they appear. As the project takes shape a clearer direction will emerge and non-feasible alternatives can be eliminated. The design team must at this point begin a detailed analysis of the different proposed scenarios. Simulation is a tool that permits evaluation of the various scenarios without ever developing a physical system.

Simulation

Simulation tools are increasingly being used to aid in the planning, design, and management of FMSs. Only by utilizing the capability of a computer to model several scenarios and

configurations can a planner be assured of selecting the most effective solution for the system's particular needs. Capacity planning and machine balancing of numerous parts, being manufactured in many different lot sizes using several different machines, are tasks which are next to impossible when using manual methods.

The design of an integrated FMS with its complexity and large variations in system design, choice of hardware, communication protocols, and material flow, require thorough planning. While a number of equally capable solutions could be used in individual cells and flexible manufacturing centers, care should be taken to use machines and centers that are incompatible with each other when the time comes to integrate them.

For today's designer of an FMS, several specialized simulation packages are available which provide pre-designed and tailorable routines for simulating a manufacturing process. Some of the more robust packages provide real-time graphical depictions of the product moving along conveyors and use color coding to show machine status. Not only are the dynamic graphics useful for the person involved with the details of the design, but they are sometimes useful to demonstrate the features and benefits of various solutions to individuals who are not knowledgeable in the details of an FMS.

A variety of simulation modeling theories and methodologies have been introduced over the years. Conventional simula-

FLEXIBLE MANUFACTURING SYSTEMS

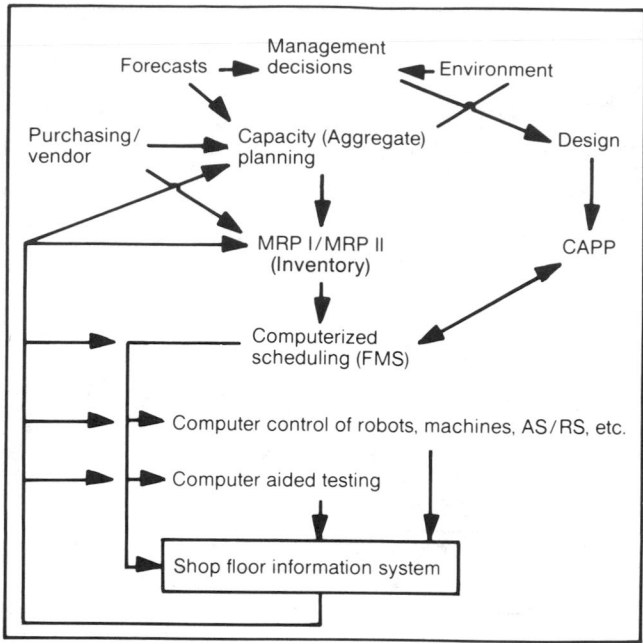

Fig. 4-5 Information flow.

tions though suffer from many drawbacks. Try to use a conventional simulation package for modeling an FMS that has:

1. Flexibility in expressing model structure and attributes. For example, in GPSS, the programmer is restricted to the concepts of facility, transaction, and queue. Behavior representation is done by the use of entity blocks which cannot be altered easily.
2. Lower expertise requirements in the programming language. Due to the programming knowledge requirements, a model which is generally conceived by management personnel often requires the services of a special programmer to translate the model into a program. This generates problems in verifying and analyzing the many assumptions involved in both modeling and programming because the programmer often has little understanding of the system being modeled.
3. Ability to provide aid in a real-time decision making environment. The state-of-the-art in current simulation systems requires an iterative process to find an answer to a problem. A typical iterative process follows these procedures: the modeler designs the model, decides upon a scenario (input), runs the experiment, analyzes the results, decides upon another scenario, runs the experiment, and so on, until the analysis is complete.
4. Ease in modifying the model for a new environment. Most simulation models today have integrated information and control modules specifically built around a particular problem domain. Modification of a certain portion of the module may adversely alter the others in the model so that problems are incorrectly characterized.
5. Time requirements for building, processing and interpreting. Some of the common characteristics of conventional simulations are special knowledge of computer programming, iterative processing, a primarily numeric-based model and customizing knowledge for appropriately analyzing the results.

Currently, simulation researchers are exploring the use of artificial intelligence (AI) concepts to design real-time simulation environments.

Characteristics of proposed simulators. Among the several issues affecting the development and application of manufacturing simulation languages and models, the resolution of real-time application for process monitoring and feedback seem to be dominant. However, with the current development in Cell Management Language (CML) by Westinghouse as an AI-based simulation language dedicated to FMS applications, these problems are expected to be reduced. A decision-support simulator as a knowledge-based system, which has been proposed as a development project, should provide the following characteristics to achieve better user accessibility:

1. The model construction should require as little programming knowledge and effort as possible.
2. The model creation and alteration interface should be interactive.
3. The model should allow the modeler to declare essential knowledge about the system, define goals, and let the system find the solution in a nonprogramming mode.
4. Model alterations should be done without affecting the overall program.
5. The model should have the capability of heuristically training and adapting itself to the problem solving domain.
6. The model should be selectively instrumentable to gather and analyze data, and to provide run-time output and update domain knowledge bases if necessary.
7. The model should allow real-time testing of what-if questions. For example, what might happen if a process change were initiated.
8. The model should aid in defining classes of entities in the system.
9. The model should provide conceptual guidance and a means of differentiating entities by characteristics.
10. The model should describe the relationship of entities to one another and their environment.
11. The model should have predefined report modules and allow a user to define a report module which permits the user to generate certain information for the selection of system parameters.

System structures. The main emphasis of using the proposed simulation system for real-time decision support will be to:

1. Help users to determine a desirable configuration of the FMS.
2. Identify inadequate or excessive production capacities.
3. Control system design parameters.
4. Debug/optimize manufacturing processes.
5. Suggest appropriate sequencing rules and procedures.
6. Provide real-time, on-line scheduling and routing.
7. Provide what-if, input-output scenarios for decision making.
8. Animate manufacturing scenarios.

The system which provides those functions consists of five main modules:

1. User interface.
2. Global database.
3. System specialist (knowledge base).
4. Production optimizer.
5. Plant database interface and monitor.

The system is completely closed-loop as shown in Fig. 4-6.

User interface. The user interface is a module for data acquisition and transmission capabilities with the simulation executive. This module permits users to define the specification of a manufacturing system along with a system of interest, goals, objectives, and the form of answer desired in a natural, meaningful language interactively. This module also provides facilities for interactive model creation and alteration and allows the user to define and simulate at different levels of abstraction.

Global database. The global database contains all of the necessary data such as types of system configuration, manufacturing system elements and associated cost information, storage areas and actual production information for designing, planning, and controlling flexible manufacturing systems. During the manufacturing phase, this knowledge database is automatically updated through knowledge base generation by the system specialist and new data gathered by the monitor.

Specialist. The specialist is a knowledge-based module which contains expert decision and control strategies, and inference and reasoning capabilities. This module has not only the expertise of manufacturing and production planning engineers, but also the following items:

1. Multi-plant related product data.
2. Plant operation procedures.
3. Factory management strategies.

The engineer's expertise includes knowledge of facilities planning, group technology, aggregate productive planning, manufacturing resource planning, process planning, capacity planning, scheduling and dispatching, material handling, and cost planning and control.

Production optimizer. The production optimizer module keeps monitoring the global database to identify any abnormalities and then match the symptoms with prior experiences. This module may consult with the system specialist and/or analyze the simulator's output for taking appropriate action.

Plant database interface and monitor. The plant database interface and monitor is a knowledge acquisition mechanism which collects production data. The sampling period and/or strategy, which could be on request, periodic, and by exception, can be defined in this module. The collected data are compared with built-in assumptions and influence updating of the global database.

The complexity of an FMS and the large number of functions which are occurring simultaneously at any one time, make the tracking and reporting of production and various statuses difficult and time consuming. The same simulation tools which were used to plan the FMS can also be used as information management tools. Real-time graphical representations of the FMS can provide a dynamic pictorial overview of the FMS as it functions.

FMS TOOL MANAGEMENT

Tool management is a key area in metal-cutting FMSs. Although tooling poses problems in any low-manned machining system, it is especially important in systems with high accuracy and flexibility requirements. Tool management is an example of a function that is critical to overall system performance and requires careful integration in a a number of dimensions.[11]

Physical integration and automation of tool management

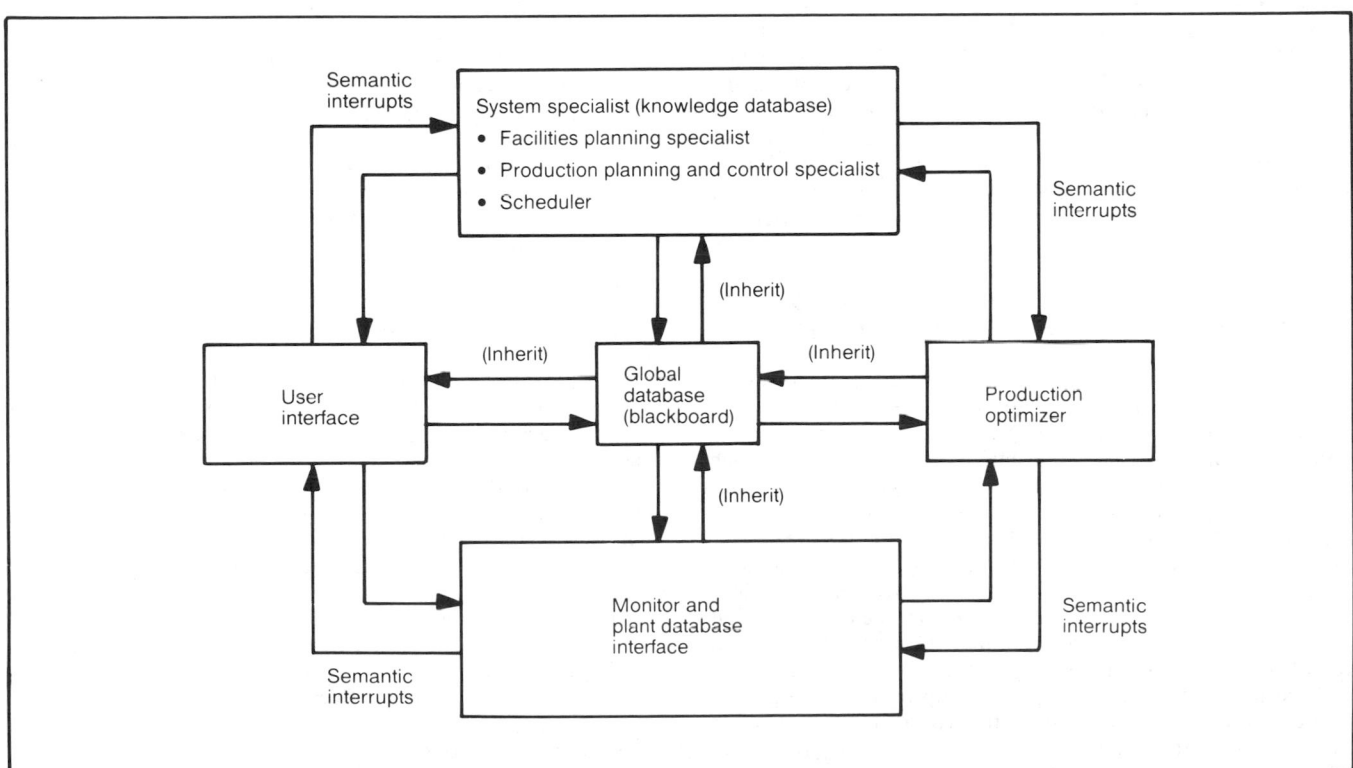

Fig. 4-6 Architecture of a knowledge-based simulator.

CHAPTER 4

FLEXIBLE MANUFACTURING SYSTEMS

involves moving of tools among the various components of the system, from tool shop to machine and back again. Tool control involves a number of different layers of control, ranging from real-time control on the CNC up to corporate planning functions. A third integration area is to provide more efficient links from process planning and part programming to simplify the use of the advanced capabilities of new machines and CNC controllers.

Without an operator watching each operation, it is important to have broken tool sensors to detect problems as they occur. They are typically provided on machines for FMSs. The search for a reliable, widely applicable tool wear method goes on. Changing tools at conservative, predetermined intervals continues to be the normal approach, but this is costly in terms of wasted tool life. Workpiece measurements are useful wear detectors in some applications. Force (and power) sensors and fixed touch probes are starting to be useful, and optical approaches show promise.

Quality tooling is essential to precision operations. Without setup at the machine, the presetting of tools in the tool room becomes more important. A variety of presetting machines are now available to support accurate and efficient presetting of tools and recording of tool offset measurements. But is good presetting sufficient? Precision grinding of tools in their holders can improve the dimensional accuracy of the tool and, in some cases, their accuracy in operation. Part accuracy depends on the combination of tool and machine, and tuning of precision tools, such as boring bars, may be required to match the characteristics of a specific machine spindle. Tools can be controlled to ensure their use on only one machine, but this reduces the flexibility of the system. Another approach is the use of adjustable tooling, in-process measurement, and special control procedures to automatically tune tools.

Special tooling can add to the productivity and flexibility of an FMS in several ways. For repeated characteristics, such as hole patterns, the use of multi-spindle tools on the tool changer can increase productivity and repeatability, but at the cost of flexibility. On the other hand, flexibility can be greatly enhanced with the use of programmable tooling. Controlling the diameter of a point tool under CNC control can allow a machining center to perform lathe operations, thus reducing the variety of machines required in an FMS.

New presetting machines can perform many functions automatically or semi-automatically, for greater productivity in the tool room. Some machines will move the tool to the predefined alignment position on the viewing screen and then vision systems can measure the offset. Offsets are automatically recorded and sent to the FMS computer for later downloading.

Tool magazines on machining centers come in a variety of configurations. Each machine supplier has its own approach and will typically offer several different configurations, depending on the application and capacity required. A single chain or disk is often the most economical approach, but its dimensions grow as capacity increases so that access can begin to be a problem. Use of multiple tool chains can provide more flexibility of access and better overlapping of machine operation and tool loading. The tool magazine should at least be large enough to hold all the tools required for a single part. If it is large enough to hold all the tools for two parts, setup time can be greatly reduced, since tools for one operation can be loaded while the preceding operation is in progress. Larger tool magazines can allow for longer times without tool changes (such as an unmanned shift) or can eliminate changes of the tool mix if they can hold all tools required for all parts served by the system. A discussion of various tooling strategies and a study of tool magazine size for a variety of different part mixes is provided by reference 12. Tool magazines holding ninety or more tools are now commonly offered on machining centers.

CONTROL

Functions of the FMS control subsystem include:[13]
1. Command and monitor tool path and machine movement.
2. Command the routing, moving, and transfer of parts to different stations (material handling).
3. Control machine tool/system operations (coolant flow, lubrication, chip removal, etc.).
4. Diagnostics for sensing drastic failure.
5. Emergency stops or chnages in operating conditions, if failure is sensed.
6. Automatic recovery from failure.
7. Redundancy to enhance reliability.
8. Diagnostics to identify cause of failure prior to repair.
9. Data flow control.
10. Monitoring condition/status of machines, material handling, and inventory.
11. Command tool change, control tool inventory or tool condition.
12. Data manipulation for desired outputs (alarms, reports, displays, shutdown).
13. Store, remove, and/or add programs.
14. Accept specific operator/management inputs (manual control, priorotiy, or re-route around downed machine).

Control System Requirements

The control system requirements of an FMS are much more demanding than a stand-alone NC machine. The need for coordination and integration of all facets of the manufacturing operation includes material handling systems, manufacturing machines, inspection and gaging equipment, and data collection and reporting equipment. The informational and data needs of these various devices must be managed by the control system of the FMS. With all the obvious complexity, the control system must also have a simple user interface to allow easy interaction by an operator. A complex, ungainly, and temperamental control system negates most of the time savings and other benefits of the FMS with the effort required to interact with the system. The continuous evolution of computer hardware and software capability makes functions which were next to impossible a short time ago, now well within the realm of practicality.

As more functionality is designed into the software controls of an FMS, greater processing capability is required of the control hardware. The trend toward real-time, dynamic graphics requires a substantial increase in computing capabilities and graphics processing. Object-oriented programming requires interaction between the off-line programming environment and the FMS control system as an expert system programming routine queries the FMS controller to determine the best selection of programming primitives. With the critical nature of any JIT based system, a high availability, or fault-tolerant control system is preferred. Since there are no queues or stockpiled finished product, unscheduled downtime of an FMS has an immediate and substantial effect.

Production Control

The production control of an FMS is done by a hierarchy of computers, starting at the highest levels with the factory control systems and being driven by an MRP system. This provides the need for product to be manufactured. In a JIT environment, product is only made to fill orders, not build-to-stock. The high-level requests for product are distributed to the appropriate cell controllers to be translated into the operational sequence controls for the discrete NC machines. In an FMS which optimizes use of available resources, the required machine capabilities may be compared to alternative utilizations of the machines in the FMS to select the most desirable allocation of machine tasking.

Once the production sequence is established, the required control programs for the different machines are requested, and if not already in the NC machines, they are downloaded, as needed, by the cell controller. To minimize setup time, the next program to be used is downloaded to a machine while it is still performing the previous operation. Anything which is done in parallel within the cycle time of a critical path operation has no additional contribution of its own to the overall cycle time.

In more sophisticated FMSs, tasks can be dynamically re-allocated as certain processes require longer time than expected to complete. This dynamic re-allocation is completely controlled by the supervisory computers. Expert system rules are utilized when the need arises, and by conducting simulations of alternative task distributions, a more efficient allocation of tasks is determined.

Not only are the standard tasks and processes controlled by the computers, but exception handling and reporting is also done automatically. Many errors and problems, such as cutting tool breakage, improperly chucked parts, or stock depletion, are non-fatal. By featuring automatic calibration of tools, as well as utilizing off-line, pre-setup of tooling, the FMS can function unattended for long periods of time.

Control Hierarchy

Most FMS controller designs utilize three levels of control. Different levels of the control operate at different time scales and make different operational decisions, from aggregated parameters to more detailed ones. Thus, the control system can efficiently handle the enormous amount of static and dynamic data and decisions required to automatically operate a complex system, like an FMS.

The control system shown in Fig. 4-7 is divided into user interface, databases, a control part, and communication. By using a manufacturing input language, the user enters the system representation to the various databases. Two major databases define the manufacturing system and the processes. Merging the two results in alternative process plans for a particular FMS type. Current development projects are attempting to eliminate the need for this manual input of data. Instead they are trying to be able to use the CAD description of a part, together with expert system software, to develop the control program for the entire cell.

The first of the three levels is the dynamic scheduler, which determines the instantaneous production rate of each part type to best utilize the varying capacity of the system.

The second is the process sequencer level determines the details of the internal movement of parts. To cut the number of possibilities to evaluate at this level, some of the interdependent conflicts are solved at a lower level by a faster mechanism to determine the timing of the machine operation.

Finally, the dynamic resource allocation, or communication, level transmits the decisions and receives feedback from the direct machine controllers. Part of this level is also in charge of

collecting statistical data, monitoring options of the system, and providing run time services. An event processor coordinates the overall activities in the controller.

FMS OPERATION

The operations of a FMS are relatively simple. Typically, an FMS is programmed to operate according to predefined objectives; for example, the optimization of material flow or the maximizing of station utilization. The central computer selects a specific workpiece to be machined according to production schedules stored in computer memory. An appropriate fixture cart is sent via the workpiece handling system to the load/unload station. The load/unload station operator receives instructions (via teletype or CRT) from the computer as to which workpiece to position in the fixture cart. When the operator has loaded the workpiece, he signals the computer to move the fixture cart to the first operation.

Stored in the central computer is an ordered listing of processing steps for each workpiece. This listing is used by the computer to select an appropriate station (machine tool) for the first processing step. Upon command by the computer, the fixture cart is directed to an appropriate station to begin processing. An optimum route through the system is selected as calculated by the control system. At the first processing station, the workpiece may be required to wait; when the station is clear, the workpiece is shuttled into it to begin processing. When the first operation is complete, the workpiece is automatically moved to the next appropriate station as defined by the ordered list of processing steps stored in computer memory. Thus, workpieces simultaneously travel through the system in random order stopping only at selected stations. When processing is complete, the workpieces are sent to the load/unload station for removal by the operator. At this stage, the workpiece may be complete or may require further processing using a different fixture cart; in the latter case, an appropriate fixture cart is automatically sent to the load/unload station for loading by the operator, and a new sequence of processing steps through the FMS is initiated by the computer.

Loading and unloading of workpieces in fixture carts is the only manual function required in the operation of an FMS (except of course, normal tool setup, monitoring, and maintenance); all other functions are automatic in most cases.

FMS APPLICATIONS

Figures 4-8 and 4-9 illustrate and briefly describe FMS installations that are in current use in various plants and system that are proposed for production.

One company's FMS is made up of four horizontal machining centers each with a 10-pallet carousel, two robot deburr stations, one dual position wash station, a coordinate measuring machine, a load/unload carousel, an AGV for material handling, and the hardware to support a tool management system including tool set and an AGV with robot arm for tool delivery (refer to Fig. 4-1).[14]

A unique feature of the FMS is the 10-pallet carousels attached to each machine. The additional hardware cost was easily justified by the benefits provided which include:
- Reduced the number of AGVs from three to one. (Control system significantly simpler for single versus multiple AGVs.)
- Eliminate risk of material handling system problems affecting machine utilization.

FLEXIBLE MANUFACTURING SYSTEMS

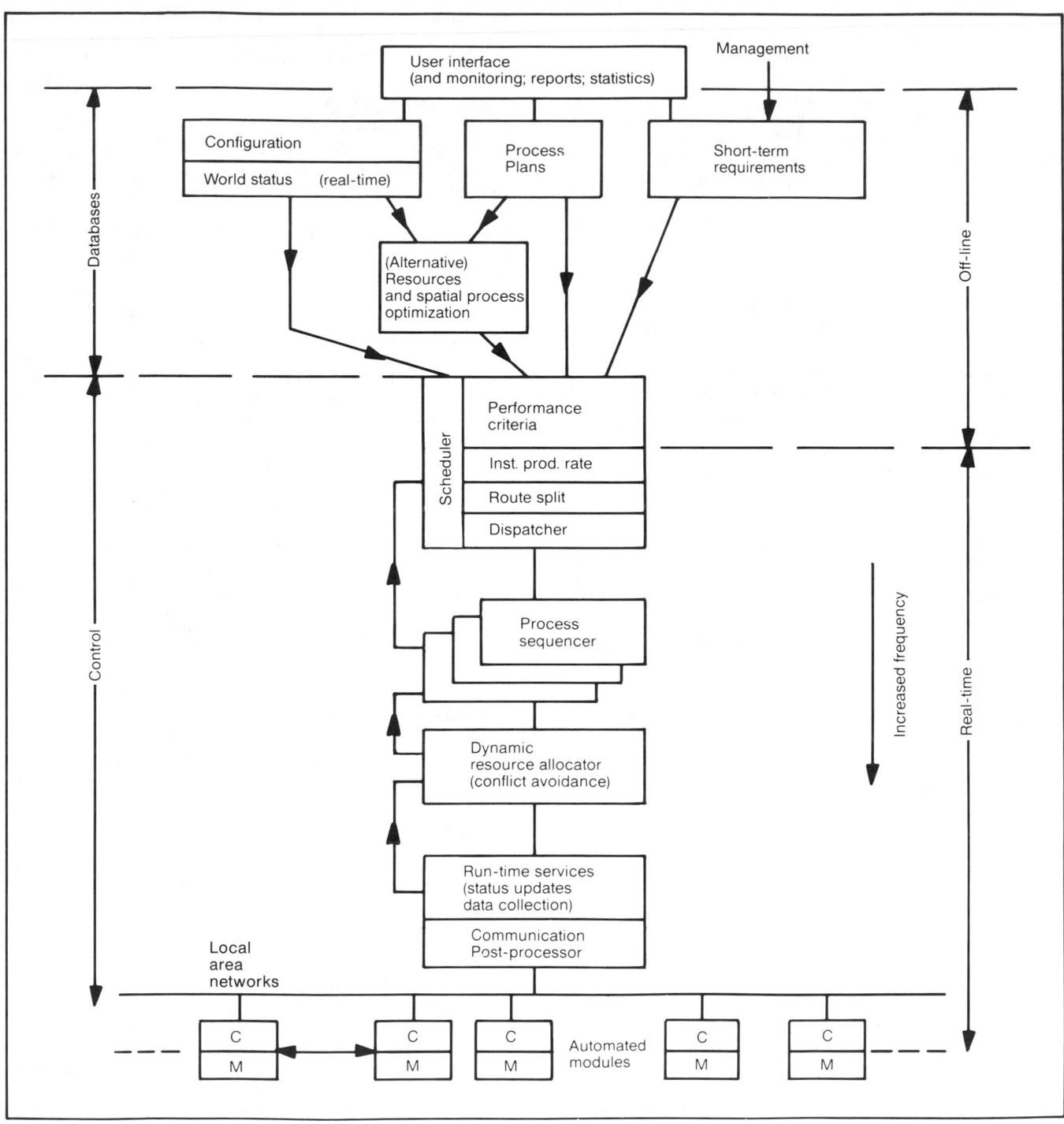

Fig. 4-7 Flexible manufacturer system controller scheme.

- Provide additional flexibility to run any one of 45 different operations without requiring an AS/RS.

The horizontal machining centers are of four-axis configuration with 90 tool storage capacity and 6000 rpm spindles.

Tooling concepts, refined over several years of experience with robotic deburr systems, facilitate efficient burr removal while maximizing tool life. Process consistency and elimination of manual deburr costs are the main advantages of this approach.

A coordinate measuring machine (CMM) verifies part features based on statistical sampling plans and process characteristics. The CMM operates within the shop environment and

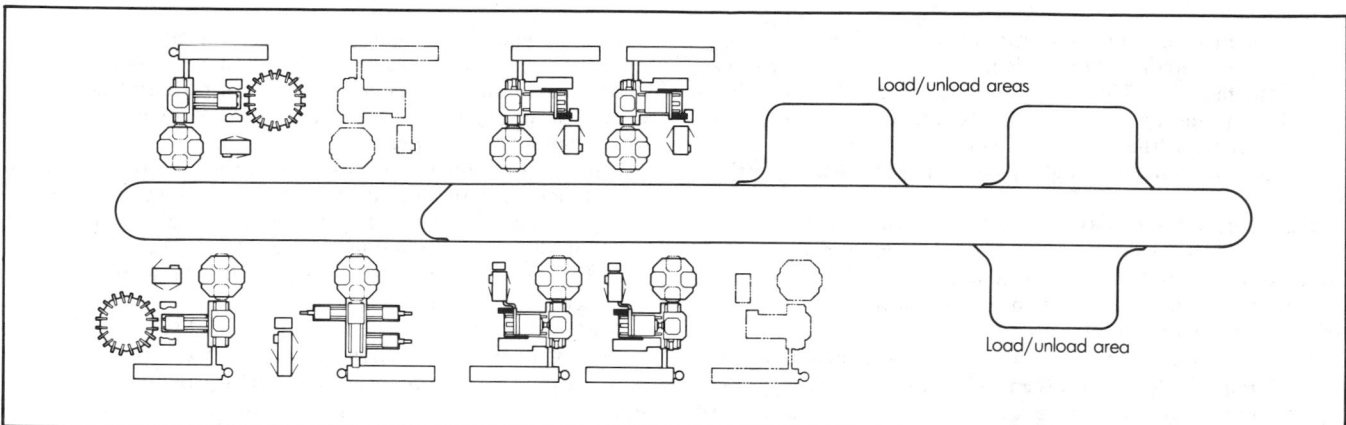

Fig. 4-8   Plan view of Multistation,   Towline Material Handling System,   Computer-Controlled Flexible Manufacturing System featuring two system component phases. Phase 1: Four Milwaukee-matic 800's; two horizontal head changers; and a special finish-boring station. Phase 2: Two Milwaukee-matic 800's. Overall system size: 200 ft (60.96 m) x 58 ft (17.68 m). (*Kearney & Trecker Corp.*)

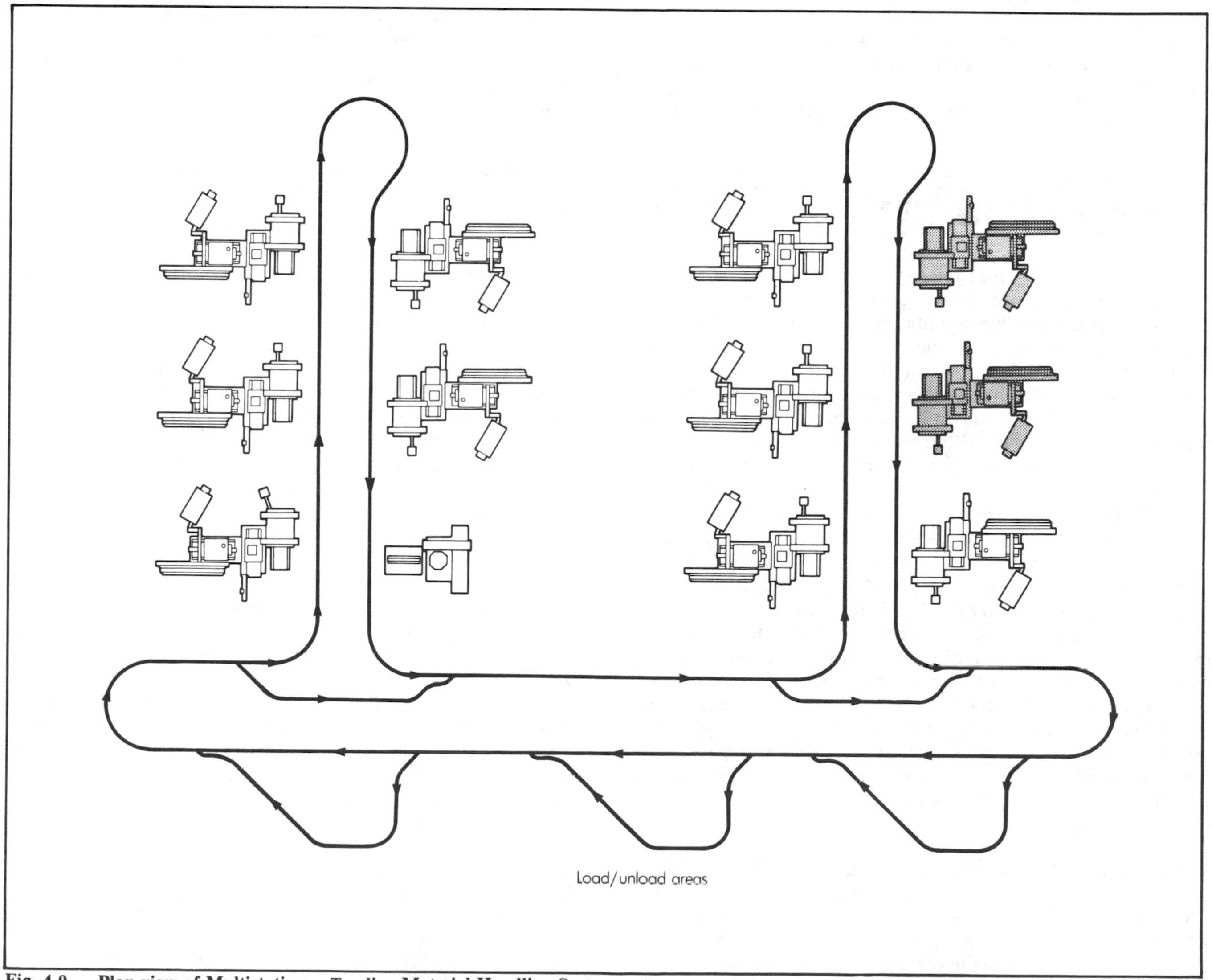

Fig. 4-9   Plan view of Multistation,   Towline Material Handling System,   Computer-Controlled Flexible Manufacturing System with on-line inspection and featuring two system component phases. Phase 1: Nine Milwaukee-matic 600's; one cordax inspection station; a Towline Material Handling System; and a central computer. Phase 2: Two Milwaukee-matic 600's. Overall system size: 122 ft (37.19 m) x 92 ft (28.04 m). (*Kearney & Trecker Corp.*)

FLEXIBLE MANUFACTURING CELLS

utilizes the production fixtures for part positioning.

The load/unload station is identical to the 10-pallet carousels on the machine. This station provides the operator with a central location for loading parts to the fixtures based on instructions from the scheduling system. Fixtures with completed parts also move through this station for unloading by the operator.

Transport of the pallets in the FMS is handled by the AGV. The AGV is designed to interface to varying equipment heights using floor mounted positioning cones.

The tool management system includes a tool set machine, storage area, and queue station.

The operator receives information via a terminal as to which tools are required to support the production schedule as well as replacement tools that will exceed their predetermined life within certain time periods.

The FMS control system combines mature manufacturing systems for realtime factory control and NC program support with artificial intelligence (AI) for planning, scheduling, and dispatching.

AI tools were selected over conventional programming approaches because the development costs were significantly reduced.

NC program support is provided by a CAD/CAM graphics system, a mainframe, and a terminal interface at the NC machine. Together, these systems provide a means of developing and maintaining NC programs in a central database under configuration management control and downloading to a specific machine upon request.

The cell controller provides the real-time interface to automated material handling equipment. It receives point-to-point move commands from the dispatcher and coordinates the operation of all material handling devices. This includes the automated guided vehicle which transports pallets between machines and secondary operations.

Instructions to the operator for part loading and tool replacement are conveyed using personal computers (PCs). Application specific programs in the PCs provide instructions upon command from the dispatcher to drive a highly visible message center.

The early phases of software development concentrated on creation of a test bed capable of modeling each machine and the material handling system. This model was used to test the dispatching subsystem before integration with other systems.

The emulator was constructed to interact with the dispatcher, providing a simulated real world environment in a laboratory setting. In this configuration, the test bed exactly duplicated the message protocol of the cell controller.

FLEXIBLE MANUFACTURING CELLS

An FMC is a group of related machines which perform a particular process or step in a larger manufacturing process. It may be a part of a flexible manufacturing system. A cell may be segregated due to noise, chemical requirements, raw material needs, operator requirements, or manufacturing cycle times. The flexible aspect of a flexible manufacturing cell indicates that the cell is not restricted to just one type of part or process, but can easily accommodate different parts and products, usually within families of similar physical properties and dimensional characteristics.

An FMC is a single center or small collection of machines which together produce a part, subassembly, or product. One of the distinctions between a cell and a system is the lack of major material movement systems such as AGVs between machines in a cell. The machines in an FMC are usually in a roughly circular pattern, with often a robot or manual operator in the center who moves the parts from machine to machine. The collection of machines in a cell support each other to perform a basic related activity, such as machining, drilling, finishing, and inspection of a part. An FMS may contain multiple cells, which can perform different and varied functions in each cell or at a particular machine or center. Figures 4-10 and 4-11 show two typical cell layouts; the former a simple turning cell and the latter a shaft manufacturing cell.[15]

FMC ADVANTAGES AND JUSTIFICATION

Some manufacturers have reported that the first benefit of FMC is in the area of production control. Cells can reduce work-in-process time and inventory.

In addition, by moving many processes into a single cell, the tracking of different operations by production control have been eliminated. Several production orders can be consolidated into one production order. Improved product scheduling results.

Improved material movement is also reported. By producing parts in only one department, there is a large reduction in forklift movement of parts. Incorporated just-in-time principles in connection with FMC means that inventory costs are cut.

In the area of statistical process control (SPC), it has been found that cells and SPC complement one another. Cells need quality parts and SPC helps define process capability and maintains process control.[16] Also, with most of the processes in a cell with the same quality personnel, the processes which need SPC charts get them. The cell itself helps quality by having different operations next to one another. If a part is mis-machined, it will not go together properly and the operator discovers this on an immediate basis. For example, parts damaged by operator carelessness or by moving between departments.

A manufacturing cell can accomplish much in improving efficiency and productivity for machining operations. The most popular cell configuration is two or more machining centers tied together with a dedicated parts transfer device, usually a shuttle mechanism. Such flexible machining cells provide the advantages of random parts processing without the use of complex software that is often associated with large, traditional FMS configurations. Machining cells are generally less expensive to install and debug, allowing the user to implement flexible manufacturing technology in a step-by-step program.

The current opinion of many users regarding an FMC is that simpler is better. Many manufacturers are implementing flexible manufacturing cells, and then integrating the cells, but without the intertwined constraints and interdependencies of a full-blown FMS. Many FMS users have never achieved full functionality in their FMS due to improperly functioning segments or a lack of true integration. FMS software is usually cited as a large problem area. The disappointments have caused some users to decide that the goal of implementing a single, large

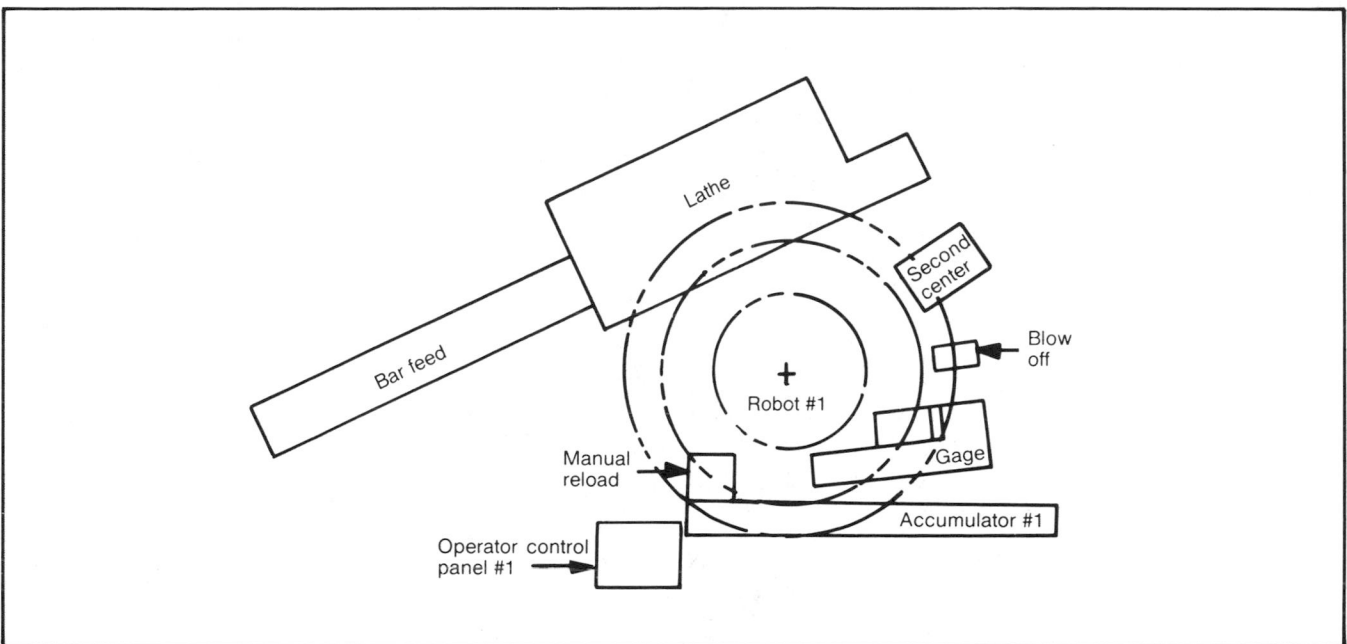

Fig. 4-10 Turning cell.

FMS for their operations is impractical. The emergence of standards now allows the integration of cells into fully functioning, flexible systems. The trend today is toward the implementation of flexible cells.

The distinction between an FMS and an FMC can be somewhat cloudy. The significant difference is not the final result—which may be identical—but the path which is traveled to reach the end result. Implementation of an FMS usually requires an all encompassing CIM plan, whereas in some circumstances, a single FMC can be planned and implemented without completing a comprehensive CIM plan. The use of simulation techniques does much to prevent undesirable results, without a major expenditure of resources.

One company's cell project began with meetings between its employees and the labor union.[17] Meetings were held with members of the union bargaining committee, the cell team, and the company bargaining team. The cell had strong selling points for the union employees as well as for company management:

- Work would be brought back in-house from outside. Operations that were once performed in-house and then out-sourced to cut costs would be returned.
- Operators working in the cell would have a new classification.
- Operators would work under lower levels of supervision. The operators work as a team to meet the production requirement for their shift. Operators report to the cell foreman, but the foreman will not dictate individual tasks to the operators.
- Operators would participate in reviews of design for fixturing, gaging, and floor plans.
- It was an important project for the plant. The cell would give job security for the immediate future, and this concept makes the company more competitive for future contracts.

PLANNING FMC INSTALLATIONS

In planning for an FMC, a number of areas need to be targeted for consideration. In the area of direct labor, this includes:

- Selection of machines to run unattended.
- The elimination or minimization of setup time.
- Downtime.

In the area of indirect labor, considerations include:
- Inspection.
- Shipping and handling.

In the area of machine cycle times:
- Tooling.
- Coolants and lubricants.

In the area of scrap and rework:
- Setups.
- Inspection.

In the area of material handling and paperwork:
- Part movements.
- Part scheduling.
- Leadtimes.

Simulation

A flexible manufacturing system is a collection of programmable and non-programmable equipment.[18] The cell is computer controlled and the cell's components communicate with each other. Elements of an FMS include numerical control (NC) machine tools, robots, programmable logic controllers/ computers, transfer devices (conveyors), pallets, sensor systems, automated guided vehicles, storage devices, etc. However, the most important elements are the workpieces and the operations performed on them. Designing an FMS and optimizing its tasks is not intuitively obvious. Thus, use of a CAD/CAE system can be a valuable aid in effectively modelling and simulating of flexible manufacturing systems.

FLEXIBLE MANUFACTURING CELLS

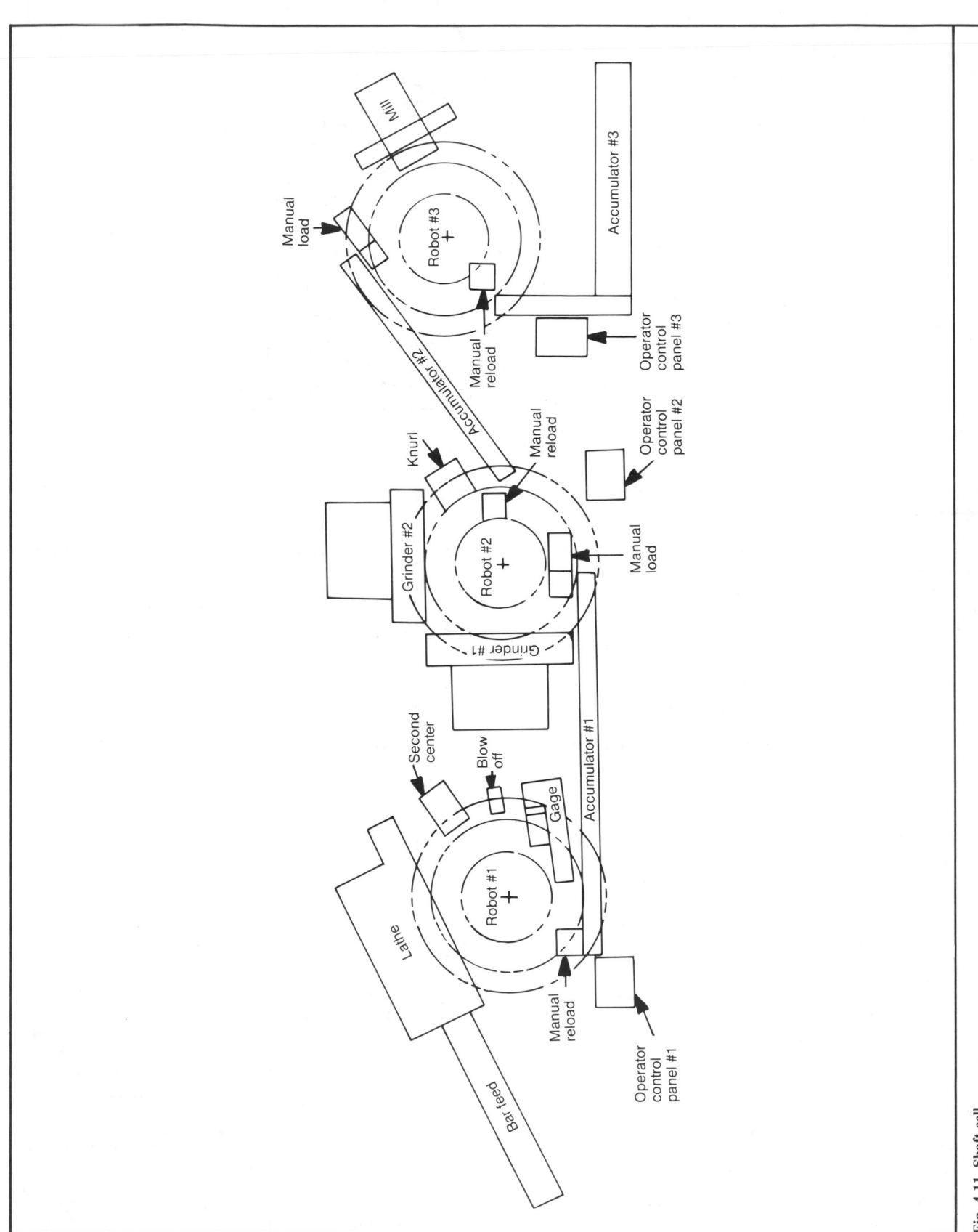

Fig. 4-11 Shaft cell.

FLEXIBLE MANUFACTURING CELLS

Simulation concepts in production—Discrete vs Continuous. There are two basic types of simulation employed for modeling manufacturing systems: "discrete" and "continuous" simulation. Discrete simulation is "event" oriented and is based on network concepts. Cell components such as machine tools, robots, conveyors, etc., are modeled as black boxes. Discrete changes of state of these boxes are of interest. This type of simulation is used for overall factory layout and planning, optimization of scheduling strategies, determination of batch size and bottlenecks, etc. Examples of simulation packages based on discrete simulation concepts are described in references 19-21.

The continuous simulation concept is used for the detailed modeling of a cell containing a limited number of components. A continuous simulation, for example, should not be used to simulate a complete factory, because it would be computationally overwhelming. The continuous simulation is based on detailed CAE/CAD modeling of its elements through geometric, kinematic, and dynamic parameters. This method is then used for detailed workcell layout, programming, synchronization, cycle time calculation, cell design, process optimization, and off-line programming.[22,23,24] Figure 4-12 shows comparisons of the two simulation concepts.

Hierarchy of simulation. The lowest level of simulation, based on a continuous concept, involves the detailed simulation of individual elements. This level of simulation allows for different levels of sophistication. Modeling of cell layout also requires considerable dimensional and geometric details.

The highest level is used for simulation of a complete factory. The factory simulation is event oriented and is based on the discrete concept of simulation. In this simulation, details of the cell components are not modeled, instead the component are modeled as black boxes. Similarly, the floor layout planning also requires only a minimum of geometric information as this

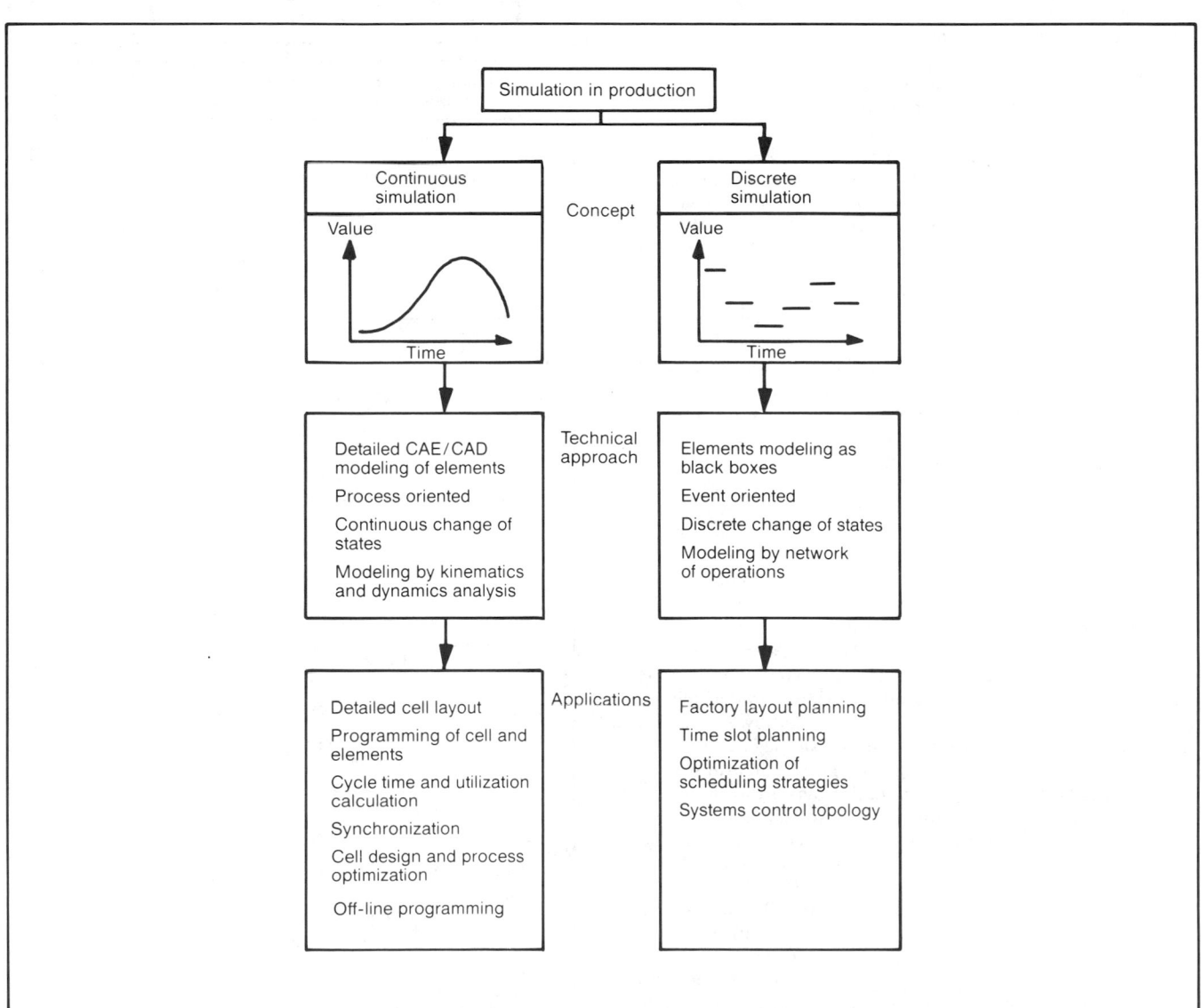

Fig. 4-12 Simulation in production.

FLEXIBLE MANUFACTURING CELLS

information is not intended for use in interference checking during operation of the cell. The primary applications of factory simulation are for layout planning, time slot planning and preliminary design of production and scheduling strategies. Furthermore, analysis and reduction of in-process inventory can also be determined.

A manufacturing cell simulation lies in between these two simulation methods and will incorporate the simulation analysis types featured in both factory and element simulation. A discrete simulation is suited for the initial phase of a cell design when a wide range of possibilities must be investigated. Detailed simulation is suited when the system configuration is nearly complete and the detailed design is being evaluated. Figures 4-13 and 4-14 show the interrelationship and basic functionalities of the different levels of simulation.

Workcell simulation. There are several main uses for workcell simulation:[25]

- Workcell layout.
- Process design.
- Off-line program generation.
- Collision detection studies.
- Workcell cycle time determination.
- Safety equipment considerations.

Workcell layout and process design. The design stage of manufacturing workcells is the ideal time to apply simulation. It is here that the most time and effort may be saved over conventional methods, particularly with regard to the avoidance of revision and redesign. In addition, design confidence can be much higher, with more realistic expectations for the capabilities of a particular robot or device which cannot be gained from 2D hand drawings, and such confidence can be had in a comparably short time.

The workcell process plan can be checked for conceptual integrity as well as efficiency. Modifications to the plan based on workcell layout constraints can be attempted several ways to establish the optimal solution. During the layout and process planning stage, it is possible to explore custom-gripper designs, safety equipment issues, and controller placement to insure unexpected conflicts do not arise after the concrete is set. Operations which unduly extend the cell cycle time can easily be identified and potentially improved. Ideally, the workcell simulator can be a powerful tool in the hands of the designer to keep the workcell design fluid so that several prototypes may be evaluated to converge on the best design.

Once a robot is selected, the cell is laid out, and the process plan is established accurate cycle time estimates can easily be generated and used by the material flow simulation, which are also usually done at design time. The material flow simulation requires cell cycle times as input to establish the characteristic behavior for each workcell. Using a workcell simulator in conjunction with the material flow simulation makes this characteristic more than an assumption. Note also that the workcell simulator is useful in this way during product change-overs and line re-design, when cell process plans and cycle times are likely to change.

Collision detection. Of all the capabilities that a workcell simulator should possess, one of the most significant is an automatic collision detection facility. This type of feature single-handedly makes the concept of off-line program verification a reality. Simply observing a simulation on a screen is inadequate for 100% verification. Ideally, a near miss version of the collision detection can also be employed to insure user defined

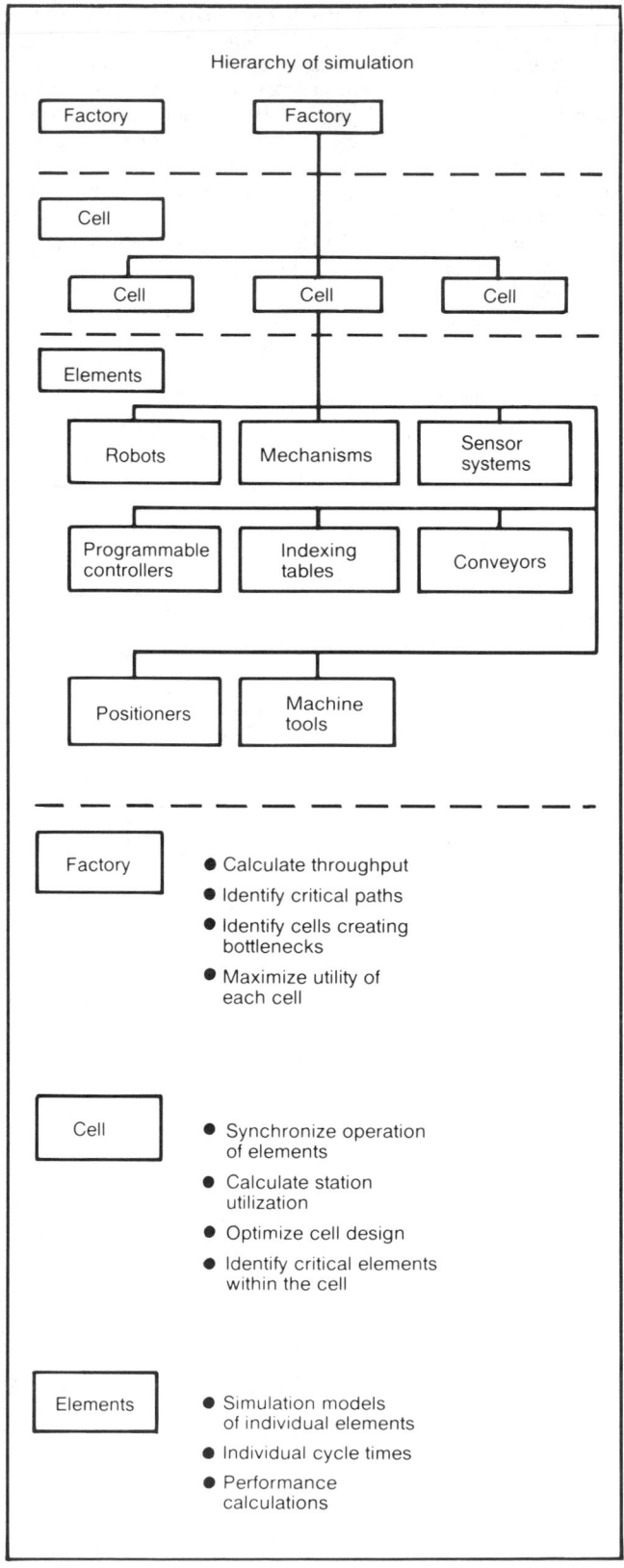

Fig. 4-13 Hierarchy of simulation.

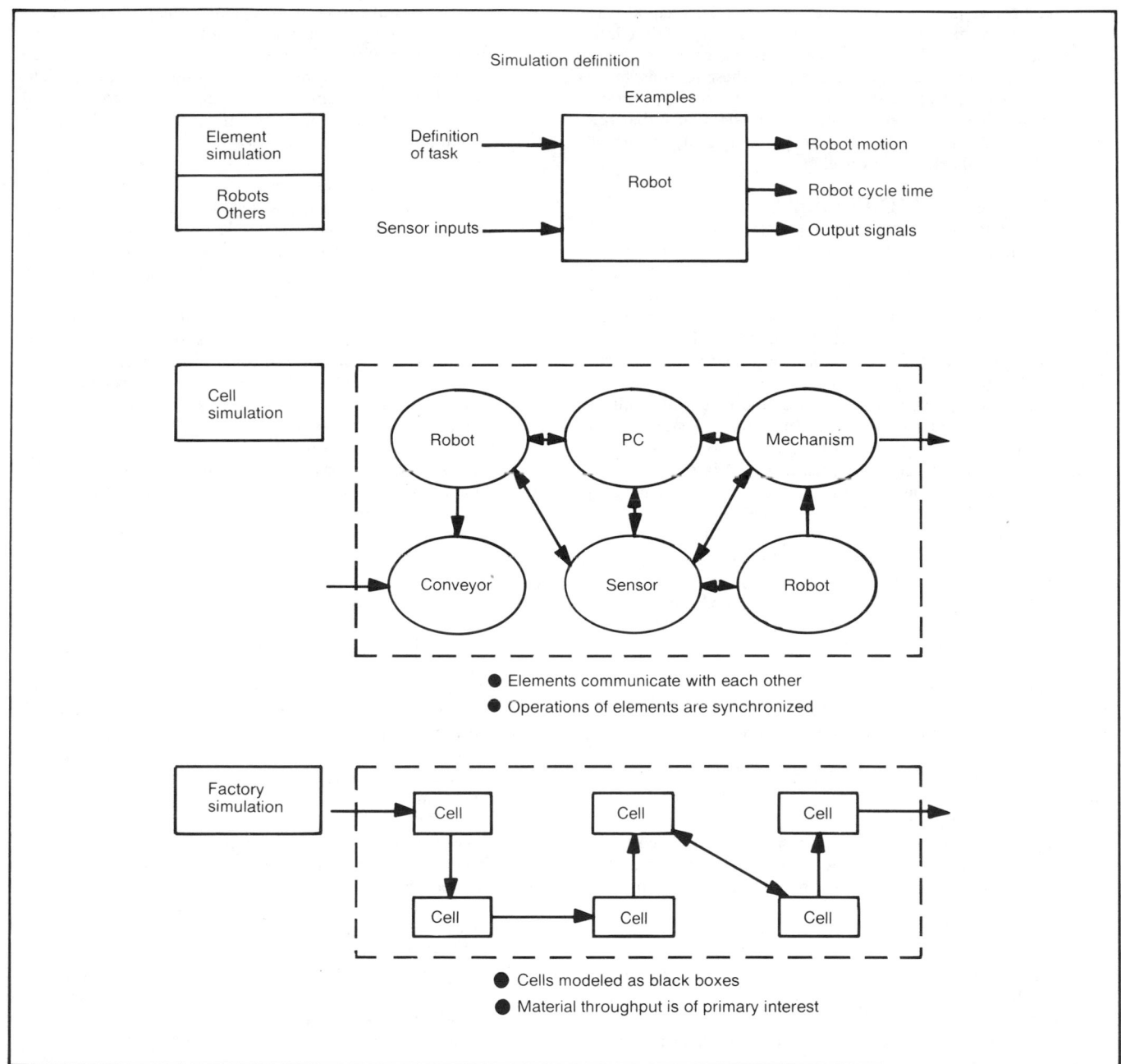

Fig. 4-14 Simulation definition.

tolerances are maintained throughout the motion. This type of insurance is not available from a purely visual simulation. Certainly wireframe, as well as solid shaded displays, suffer from visual ambiguities since the motion cannot be viewed from all angles at once during each step of the simulation.

Off-line programming. Off-line programming is a technique utilizing workcell simulation to generate and verify a robot's program within the simulation environment. This has several distinct advantages. First, the down time for the actual robot is greatly reduced since 95% of the work is accomplished in the simulation environment. Second, mistakes and programming

errors occur in the simulation, thus reducing the risks of personal injury, as well as damage or excessive wear on the actual device. Third, the resulting program can be verified at full speed to be free of collisions and to have correct I/O logic before the actual device(s) runs the program. Lastly, the off-line programmer must only master one language regardless of the number of robots from different vendors actually used by the manufacturing facility.

The other 5% of the work in off-line programming is cell calibration. Inaccuracies arise from several sources such as geometrical modeling errors, blueprint errors, device placement

FLEXIBLE MANUFACTURING CELLS

errors, and robot motion inaccuracies. The simulation quality is dependent on the data used, and the correspondence of that data to the real workcell. Unfortunately, final design data is not always available to the simulation user. For these reasons, techniques for recalibration of the data points in a robot program are essential. The net effect is to modify the data such that the robot base and/or the workpiece is relocated slightly to correct for several possible effects at once.

An Example of FMC Planning

One company's implementation of a manual FMC involved "selling" cellular manufacturing to the union as well as management.[26] After just five months, a post audit report showed a fourteen week reduction in lead time, 27% in labor hours, and 60% in work-in-process. Combined operations were reduced from thirteen to seven. Work previously outsourced was brought back in-house. Setup time was virtually eliminated, while scrap and rework were drastically reduced.

A team was formed to create a flexible-machining cell to produce parts for the largest product line. The team started with a project manager, two manufacturing engineers, an industrial engineer, and tool designer. The team would later expand to include a quality engineer, a production foreman, and two machine operators. Team meetings were held daily in the early stages of planning and implementation of the cell. Meetings are held bi-weekly on a permanent basis for operator input on problems, possible improvements, etc.

The team looked within the product line for a family of parts suitable for cellular manufacturing, parts that could benefit most from a reprocessing and retooling effort. The parts had to meet the following requirements:

1. relatively high part-quantities.
2. multi-year production schedule.
3. parts for which the prices were fixed or reduced.

New methods would be utilized in each of the areas targeted for improvement.

To reduce direct labor costs:
- Machines in the cell would run unattended. The role of the operators would change from actively operating the equipment to loading, unloading, deburring, and inspecting the workpiece.
- Setups would be eliminated or minimized by using dedicated setups.
- Down time waiting for first piece layout inspections would be eliminated. Centerline type dimensions are checked by layout inspection. The workpiece is taken to the layout room, where it must wait its turn in line for inspection. If the part fails the layout inspection, corrections are made at the machine; another part is run and submitted to layout. This process is repeated until all dimension meet specifications.

In the past, there was time lost waiting for first piece layout inspection for each operation performed. During much of the time a part is in layout, the machine and operator are idle. In the new cell operators will perform layout inspections internal to the machine cycle time. The machine operators would deburr parts. This deburring would be performed internal to the machine cycle.

To reduce indirect labor costs:
- Elimination of a minimum of two hundred sixteen layout inspections. Waiting time for each layout consists of time

for the layout inspector to perform the layout as well as the machine operator in down time waiting for layout.
- Elimination of shipping and handling cost. The cell would perform all machining of the cylinders in-house. This would eliminate shipping out to vendors for partial machining. Inspections done at receiving would be also eliminated.

To reduce machine cycle times:
- State of the art tooling would be utilized. The latest in carbide indexable tooling would be used in place of high speed steel, and cemented carbide tooling. These tools have much higher metal removal rates, and require only that the inserts be indexed when dull.
- Water based coolants would be used. Before the cell, all machining centers used cutting oils for coolant. This was required for the machining of aluminum manifolds. With the cell dedicated to the machining of steel cylinders, water based coolants with their greater capacity to remove heat could be used.

The use of new tooling with water-based coolant would give an estimated twenty-five percent reduction in machine cycle times. This with the proposed reductions in machine down time due to layout inspection, would allow running all operations to machine these cylinders in-house. The thirteen operations now performed by outside vendors would be included in the new cell.

To reduce scrap and rework:
- A high percent of scrap and rework is caused during setup. Eliminations of setups would prevent this scrap and rework.
- Ability to inspect all dimensions would minimize non setup-related defects. After the first piece layout is approved, all layout dimensions are assumed good for the remainder of the part run. Layout dimensions that go out during the part run are not detected until final inspection or assembly.

Reduce material handling and paperwork cost:
- The total number of part movements reduced. Subcontracted operations are considered one move.
- Within the cell, parts are moved between machine types by operators, not expediters.
- Production scheduling between departments eliminated. All cylinder machining is performed in one location. Raw forgings are delivered to the "front door" and completed cylinders are picked up at the "back door."
- Handling effort reduced. Parts lose 50% of rough forging weight at the first machining operation.
- Leadtime for major machining operations reduced from fourteen to three weeks. Because of reductions in lead-time, inprocess inventory would also be cut by thirty-one percent.

TOOL MANAGEMENT

The tool management function provides control of reusable resources used in the manufacturing process. Tools include things such as drill bits, fixtures, gages, dies, robot grippers, etc.

The tool management function includes keeping an inventory of tools, monitoring tool wear, performing kitting, and having tools delivered to the cell.

The inventory subfunction is responsible for tracking the status and position of tools. It provides an operator interface for manual entry and interfaces to external systems such as CAD/ CAM and MRP for computerized data entry and inventory updating.

The kitting subfunction is responsible for collecting the required tools and having them delivered to the cell on time. This requires interfacing with the operator, material handling, and schedule execution.

CONTROL

Flexible machining cells can be a combination of machines with two commonalities. First, the machines are operated under common control. Second, there is common material handling.

Machine Control

Control of many machining center operations is handled by a central processing unit (CPU). Schedule data is input and modified, and the location and status of pallets is displayed in real-time. Scheduled time, required program numbers, and the accumulated total of uncompleted machining is also relayed.

Some controllers also handle the selection of tools, the monitoring of cutting condition, and the generation of optimum tool paths.

Management Control

By moving many processes into the cell, some firms have found a decrease in tracking the different operations by production control. In this case, all production orders are consolidated into a single production order. This step may improve scheduling of products. With less time dedicated toward the tracking of parts, an improvement is shown in securing raw materials.

Control System Requirements

These requirements can be broken into three areas: a) interface requirements, b) functional requirements, and c) operational requirements.[27] The cell control system needs to interface with a variety of stations in the cell for monitoring and control of cell operation. Typically these stations are:

- Process stations (CNC machines, robots).
- Material handling stations (AGV, robots).
- Test stations (CMM, inspection machines).
- Storage stations (AS/RS, buffers).
- Manual stations (CRT, bar code readers).

A combination of these stations forms a cell which generally has equipment manufactured by different vendors. The controls and communication capability of this equipment varies significantly from practically nonexistent to a fairly sophisticated implementation. Yet, they all need to be integrated cohesively into the cell control system for the desired flexibility.

Functionally, the control system needs to be capable of the following:

Equipment monitoring. Extends an operator's capability to monitor all pieces of equipment in the cell at one place and take corrective actions should problems occur. This helps improve the equipment up-time.

Alarm monitoring. Detects and reports error conditions, and can respond by taking alternative actions automatically. This helps in early detection of defective parts or equipment reducing repair and scrap costs.

Program management. Allows storage, uploading, and downloading of programs for programmable equipment in the cell, as well as operator instructions for manual stations. This reduces the setup time when handling a mix of parts and also keeps better track of the programs.

Production control. Tracks work-in-process and results of machine operations, and then accordingly dispatches work to stations to maximize production. This capability improves machines utilization and reduces work-in-process inventory.

Adaptive Controls

Adaptive controls should be used to detect and correct RPM's, feed rates; for maximizing machining while minimizing machine and cutter wear.

Tooling

Tooling should be designed and purchased around the following parameters.
1. Use of indexable carbide tooling whenever possible. This eliminates finding size after tool changes, regrinding cutters, and allows higher cutting speeds.
2. Coolant through whenever possible. High pressure coolant through tooling aids chip removal and insures against catastrophic tool failure during unattended machining.
3. Build tooling assemblies for maximum rigidity.

Cell Controllers

Today's programmable controllers can log and store the large amounts of data needed to perform statistical analysis.[28] The memories found in today's programmable controllers extend into the megaword range. Micro-disk and hard-disk peripheral storage devices can store up to 20 megabytes of production data each. Co-processors found in programmable controllers perform such computer functions as:
- Floating point math.
- Special instructions for data analysis and control algorithms.
- Interactive report generation for operator interaction.
- BASIC programming for greater flexibility.
- Connectivity to multiple devices for peripheral communication.

FMC APPLICATIONS

Cells are finding their way to factory floors with greater variation.

Machining

One manufacturer has a flexible, palletized cell, which permits the production of a family of components, in random order, on a to-order basis.[29] Basically, the cell links two machining centers with a linear transport module and cell controller. It also includes a 120-tool change magazine, with broken tool identification system. The shuttle car has two arms to handle delivery to the machining centers, as well as 30 cue stations on both sides of the track. Cell control is handled by computer, for which there are two data entry stations. Jobs can be entered at production control, where the operator schedules each job, including part number, part quantity, and start and finish dates. This information is then downloaded to the cell controller.

The computer prioritizes the jobs on the system, assigns the route batch, and then—depending on the part sequence—the shuttle car pulls the fixtures, delivers to load or unload, or takes them to the correct station for machining.

The former method involved thirteen people, while the current cell requires just three and a half people. Even though the cell is processing some 75 parts, all set up has been virtually eliminated, and the average cycle time has been reduced by 33%.

FLEXIBLE MANUFACTURING CELLS

In terms of total time making parts versus machine availability, the cell has improved utilization from 55% to 85%.

One systems integrator designed and built an FMC for one of the automotive "Big Three" to machine a family of exhaust manifolds for a V6 engine.

Gross production rates are twenty pairs of standard manifold, and twelve service parts, every hour.

After parts are manually loaded, a load assist mechanism is used to make sure the locating pads on the part are firmly in contact with the fixture locaters.

At the load station, an identification system using proximity sensors determines part identity. This data is then fed into the CNC controller to select the correct machining program for the part.

Depending on the part, this may range from a simple milling operation on the joint faces, to a complex series of operations, including drilling, and tapping several holes.

The heart of the CNC machining center is a three-axis traveling column unit—a machine well suited to this production application. It features a recirculating oil system to lubricate and cool the precision cartridge-type spindle.

The machining center is equipped with a 30-tool capacity, stationary toolchanger. This provides ample storage for all necessary tools, plus spares to support long production runs.

The toolchanger is totally enclosed, so tools are protected from chips and coolant, as a part of overall chip management to improve uptime of the system.

The design of the toolchanger also permits tools to be loaded or unloaded for maintenance with complete safety, even while the machine is operating.

Programming, and control functions such as overrides are easily accomplished by floor-level personnel, without extensive computer training.

Fabrication

Robotic FMC technology is being used to manufacture outerwing ribcaps for military transport aircraft by a leading aerospace/defense company.[30]

The 54 ribcaps are made from aluminum extrusions—stretch-formed to the contours of the upper and lower wing.

The extrusions are pre-formed, heat treated, and then finish-formed before arriving at the FMC.

In the past, fabrication had taken five days—even though the actual production time was only twenty minutes. The rest of the five days the parts were being transferred—or waiting to be transferred—to 10 different machining workstations for drilling, routing, and cutting operations.

The solution to the costly process was an FMC, developed by the company itself as a multi-function robotic workcell that could produce—on one machine—the same ribcap in *five minutes* by eliminating redundant setups and transportation time.

The FMC, in daily operation, was programmed by a regular production NC programmer and run by specially trained production operators.

The two main components of the cell are the robot with a multi-functional end-of-arm tooling, and the workholding table, which is part of the workstation shuttle. The robot's unique end-of-arm tooling includes an airpower drill, router, and saw.

The robot's work area is protected by a fence, and the gates are electronically interlocked with the robot's hold signal. The operator selects the correct pair of templates—or router blocks—for the new work order and positions them in the workstation.

After the corresponding program data is loaded into the robot controller's memory, the operator positions a stretch-formed extrusion on the router blocks and clamps it into place.

When ready, the operator initializes the robot to begin machining the part. The robot turns its end-of-arm tooling to the router and begins routing the profile of the part.

The robot also cuts the lightening holes with its router and when it has completed this task, it turns its saw to the precise angle and cuts off each end of the extrusion.

The workstation shuttles are cycled, bringing the completed part back to the load position for removal. The next extrusion ready for machining is then sent forward to the robot.

A record 98.4% uptime was established during the first month of production of this cell. Research indicates the cell has produced other significant benefits, including a 75% savings on total production time, which includes more consistent quality, increased safety, and reduced scrap rework time.

Old Equipment-New Life

The Engineering Technology Department at Texas A&M University assembled a full scale flexible manufacturing cell for use in research and teaching.[31] In its present configuration, this widely varying collection of equipment is used to perform turning, milling, drilling and related material handling operations under the direction of a single cell controller. Originally, the cell control was provided by a standard programmable logic controller (PLC) without program storage or communications features. Although adequate during development of the cell, the data communications limitations of this controller quickly became a bottleneck in the new dynamic environment. Within this configuration, the cell devices were programmed individually under operator control, the PLC had to be reprogrammed for each new application and even minor part changes were difficult to implement. Several methods of alleviating this situation were considered including:

- Upgrading to a PLC with data communications capability.
- Combining the PLC with a micro- or minicomputer supervisory system to handle data communications.
- Eliminating the PLC and developing a custom micro- or minicomputer based controller/supervisor.

The final choice was selected in an effort to maximize flexibility, provide ease of use and allow for customization to augment the capabilities of the older equipment in the cell. The accessibility of the technical know-how and budgetary constraints were strong considerations. The result of this decision is the cell manager system (CMS), a microcomputer based cell control and configuration management system.

The complete CMS is an integrated hardware and software system with part routing programming, data communications, production control, and configuration management components. The data communication and production control components incorporate custom hardware for the cell devices and the CMS computer. Designed for flexibility, CMS provides for rapid changes in both part types and cell configuration.

Configuration flexibility is a key feature in supporting the older equipment comprising this cell.

As a point of reference, the current cell configuration is composed of:

- A 3-axis, CNC vertical mill with automatic tool changer.
- A 19-inch CNC lathe with a 4-station automatic turret.
- A 5-axis, polar coordinate robotic machine server.

- A semi-automatic drilling station.
- Two conveyors.
- Various parts feeders and fixtures.

The daily operation of this facility may be compared to a typical job shop. The jobs handled by this cell arise from long and short term research and several small projects from upper level manufacturing and robotics courses. CMS allows many different users to apply essentially the same set of equipment for different projects. All fixtures may use the same PLC connections which may serve different purposes for each application and fixture. Wiring, programming, and production are simplified by this integrated controller.

The development of the system can be viewed as a collection of smaller problems each of which must be solved to integrate these devices into a manufacturing cell. The subproblems include implementation of automatic computer-to-machine program transfers for all programmable devices, cell control computer-to-host communications for network hierarchy, digital input/output (I/O) handling, application and part process plan program development, and a flexible configuration management scheme.

Program and data transfer for the devices was the foremost problem. With a usable cell controller already in place, the data communications with the individual devices was the first problem attacked. With each machine in the cell representing a different point in the history of data communications hardware and software standards, communication presented the greatest challenge to the integration effort.

Digital I/O presented the next challenge. In the interest of conversion time and a limited budget, it was decided that the new cell controller could be designed to connect directly to the existing PLC I/O modules. This approach allows continued use of the existing system during development and testing of its replacement. The solutions, like data communications, consist of hardware and software components.

The two other sub-problems have strictly software solutions. Within the software environment, the problem of programming the controller for a particular part is managed by a specialized program compiler. A part program similar to a part process plan or route sheet is developed and compiled within CMS, this program is then used by the production controller. The production controller monitors the digital inputs and generates output responses according to the program for the part in process.

The majority of the CMS software is written in PASCAL with several assembly language support routines. The selection of PASCAL over other languages was based on the availability of graphics, windowing, and menu "toolbox" routines which simplified the development of a user-oriented system interface.

Generic Assembly Robot Cells

The following approaches, both past and present, are examples of the conceptual development pursued by different end users, and system integrators:[32]

1. In the electronic, odd-shaped component and surface mount industry several system integrators have taken the approach of a two robot workcell; one robot performs component preparation, and the other performs insertion. The cells generally utilize fixed, inflexible tooling, and standard feeding devices that were developed in-house. Those feeding devices took advantage of pre-packaging from electronic component manufacturers.

2. Several manufacturers developed single robot cells that were very flexible. They utilized vision dependent architecture and either indexing turret end-of-arm tooling, or exchange tooling (with either fixed vision-dependent feeders, or flexible, simplistic feeders), and a control technology that utilized a powerful robot controller.

3. Several large Fortune 100 companies developed in-house, generic robot cells with very generic material transporters, a small overall cell footprint, and standard material handling pallets whose outside footprint was identical, but whose inside component insert was interchangeable. These cells generally utilized exchange end-of-arm tooling, moveable fixtures, and generic software.

4. Between late 1986 and early 1988, five factory automation manufacturing integrators introduced standard modular (and to varying degrees) generic robotic cells. The majority of these cells are directly applied to electronic assembly, and more specifically to odd-shaped components and surface mount technology for printed circuit and printed wiring boards. Depending on which cell chosen, they continue to have either single or multiple robots, turret or exchange hand end-of-arm tooling, very fixed dedicated work place fixtures, and shared/dedicated transporters and tooling. Finally, most are robot processor controlled and vision dependent.

5. During the 1980s, slow acceptance of new cell technology, the reluctance of U. S. manufacturers to reinvest in productivity producing capital goods, and the influence of competing technologies have forced system suppliers to hone their conceptual approaches to be extremely cost competitive and highly reliable.

Typical mechanical assembly tasks can be divided into the following major categories:

1. Mechanical sub-assembly. Consisting of the modular construction of mechanical components to create a sub-assembly or major assembly. These tasks are usually material presentation pick and place where an assembly fits together without mechanical fastening and process fastening.

2. Mechanical fastening workcells. Where the tasks include (but, are not limited to) screw feeding/screw driving, riveting, ultrasonic bonding, swedging, or other mechanical fastening.

3. Electronic sub-assembly. These assembly tasks include the material feeding, lead preparation, and placement of electronic components, generally odd-shaped components and surface mount devices. Normally, these cells are used to supplement or replace dedicated, high-volume, component placement devices.

4. Process fastening. These assembly tasks include chemical or physical fastening techniques such as flux/soldering, epoxy bonding, resistance welding, gas welding, and other processes that generally require a transfer of chemical or physical material to other components in the assembly.

5. Post-assembly testing. These tasks are generally performed either between mechanical assembly tasks or after an assembly is completed, and include mechanical testing to ensure assembly strength, electrical testing such as continuity, "high pot" electric resistance, or saturation tests. This testing can also include vision inspection to ensure quality and reliability of located components, the

FLEXIBLE MANUFACTURING CELLS

quality of chemical/mechanical processes such as solder joints, epoxy bonding, or other joining techniques. Depending on system architecture, the post-assembly testing may be stand-alone data, or may be integrated with statistical process control and statistical quality control programs to determine process control or assembly cell performance, either in real time or using batch data.

The above description in no way includes all the possibilities for assembly tasks to be accomplished with a generic cell. These tasks are only limited by the imagination, and ability to define the assembly problem in terms of techniques which can be utilized within a generic cell.

FMC SUMMARY

The need for long, stable runs of standard products may necessitate moving back to traditional transfer lines, but the need for flexible and dynamic scheduling, high product variations, and customization to customer requirements, will lead many companies into the use of flexible manufacturing cells or systems.[33]

Born of necessity to compete against global pressures, and made possible by industrial restructuring and rapid changes in technology, flexible manufacturing cells are providing clear-cut solutions for many manufacturers. And most industry observers see a good future ahead—a future in which FMCs will not only solve difficult manufacturing problems, but also serve as the stepping stone to FMS and, perhaps, a "factory of the future."[34]

References

1. Kenneth Fox, *Variable Mission Manufacturing Systems*, SME Technical Paper MS81-158, p. 1.
2. Raymond J. Larsen, "Flexible Manufacturing: More Companies Make Competition Intense," *Iron Age* (September 28, 1981), p. 85.
3. Robert F. Huber, "Flexible Machining Systems," Manufacturing Planbook Supplement, *Production* (August 1981), p. 5-68.
4. *Ibid.*, p. 5-65.
5. Melvin Blumberg and Antone Alber, "The Human Element: Its Impact on the Productivity of Advanced Manufacturing Systems," *Journal of Manufacturing Systeems*, vol. 1, no. 1 (1982).
6. Gary Lueck, "Financial Justification of FMS Compared to Conventional Equipment," *Management Guide for CIM*, Nathan A. Chiantella, ed. (Dearborn, MI: Society of Manufacturing Engineers, 1986), p. 62.
7. Computer Integration of Engineering Design and Production, Committee on the CAD/CAM Interface, Manufacturing Studies Board, and Commission on Engineering and Technical Systems (Washington, D.C.: National Academy Press, 1984), p. 12.
8. *Ibid.*, p. 35-38.
9. Kwok-sang Chui, *Case Report on Integrating FMS and Traditional Machine Tools*, SME Technical Paper MS88-106 (Dearborn, MI: Society of Manufacturing Engineers, 1988).
10. David D. Bedworth and Gerald T. Mackulak, "FMS Planning Evaluation Through Simulation," SME Technical Paper EE85-131 (Dearborn, MI: Society of Manufacturing Engineers, 1985), pp. 3-4.
11. J. Scott Rhodes, "The Development of Integrated Control Systems for Flexible Manufacturing Systems," SME Technical Paper (Dearborn, MI: Society of Manufacturing Engineers, 1985), p. 7.
12. *Ibid*, p. 9.
13. Joel A. Schnur, *Implementing the FMS in Your Enterprise*, '87 AUTOFACT Conference & Exposition (Dearborn, MI: Society of Manufacturing Engineers, 1987).
14. Glenn A. Graham, *Automation Encyclopedia* (Dearborn, MI: Society of Manufacturing Engineers, 1988), 248.
15. Sheff Bryant, "Flexible Manufacturing Cell Control Functions," *Flexible Manufacturing Cells '86*, August 26-28, 1986 (Dearborn, MI: Society of Manufacturing Engineers, 1986), p. 10.
16. Gene D. Kelly, "Cellular Manufacturing A.B. Chance's "Factory Within a Factory'," SME Technical Paper MS88-788 (Dearborn, MI: Society of Manufacturing Engineers, 1988), p. 7.
17. Howard Carpenter, Jr., "Flexible Manual Machining Cell at NWL Control Systems: A Case History," SME Technical Paper MS88-787 (Dearborn, MI: Society of Manufacturing Engineers, 1988), p. 8.
18. I. Imam, T.J. Fougere, and J.E. Davis, "Flexible Manufacturing Cell Simulation," SME Technical Paper (Dearborn, MI: Society of Manufacturing Engineers, 1987), p. 1.
19. A.A.B. Pritsker and C.D. Pegden, *Introduction to Simulation and SLAM* (Halstead Press/J. Wiley & Sons, 1979).
20. R.R. Duersch and M.A. Laymon, "A Graphic Workflow Simulator," *Proc. 1983 Summer Computer Simulation Conf.*, pp. 141-144.
21. R.R. Duersch and M.A. Laymon, "A Graphic Workflow Simulator for Factory Simulation," *Proceedings, 17th Annual Sim. Conf.* (1984), pp. 37-48.
22. I. Imam and S. Levy, "Application of Advanced Computer-Aided Engineering Tools for Kinematic and Dynamic Analysis of Robot Systems," *AUTOFACT4—Conference Proceedings* (Philadelphia, PA, November 30—December 2, 1982), pp. 3-28 to 3-51.
23. I. Imam, L. Sweet, J.E. Davis, M. Good, and L. Strobel, "A Simulation and Display of Dynamic Path Errors for Robot Motion," *ROBOT—8 Conference Proceedings*, Vol. 1 (Detroit, MI, June 4-7, 1984), pp. 4-28 to 4-44.
24. T.J. Fougere, S.D. Chawla, and J.J. Kanerva, "Robot-Sim: A CAD Based Workcell Design and Off-line Programming System," *ASME Proceedings of Robotics and Manufacturing Automation*, PED-Vol. 15, (Miami, FL, November 17-22, 1985), pp. 211-217.
25. Charles E. Fuller, "An Introduction to Workcell Simulation," SME Technical Paper MS88-248 (Dearborn, MI: Society of Manufacturing Engineers, 1988), p. 2.
26. Carpenter, *op. cit.*, pp. 2-5.
27. Arun K. Agrawal, "Distributed Control System for Flexible Manufacturing Cells," SME Technical Paper (Dearborn, MI: Society of Manufacturing Engineers, 1986), p.1
28. Art Pietrzyk, "Programmable Logic Controllers for Supervision of Flexible Manufacturing Cells," *Flexible Manufacturing Cells '86*, August 26-28, 1986 (Dearborn, MI: Society of Manufacturing Engineers, 1986), p. 4.
29. *Flexible Manufacturing Cells*, SME Manufacturing Insights Video Series (Dearborn, MI: Society of Manufacturing Engineers, 1987)
30. *Ibid*
31. Roy A. Harrington and Jon F. Botsford, "Integrating Older Technology with Emerging Technology: A Microprocessor-Based Flexible Manufacturing Cell Controller," SME Technical Paper MS87-662 (Dearborn, MI: Society of Manufacturing Engineers, 1987), p. 2.
32. Terrence E. McGinn, "Generic Robot Cells for Flexible, Multicomponent Assembly," SME Technical Paper MS88-320 (Dearborn, MI: Society of Manufacturing Engineers, 1988), pp. 2-3.
33. *Flexible Manufacturing Cells, op. cit.*
34. *Ibid.*

DESIGN FOR MANUFACTURE

Continual and rapid change is one of the leading characteristics of the modern Information Age. New materials, process refinements, and customer requirements are emerging and evolving at ever-increasing rates. Coping with rapid change has become a major problem for industry. In industries driven by technological change, coming to market 9-12 months late can cost a new product half of its potential revenues. Even in calmer businesses, companies that drive from lab to market more swiftly than the competition have the luxury of starting later so they can employ up-to-date manufacturing methods and the latest customer requirements.

Business goals, on the other hand, have not changed. The business goals of most companies are twofold: (1) make as good a product as possible, in as short a time as possible, and for as little cost as possible; and (2) sell as many as possible, as fast as possible, for as much as possible. Accomplishing these goals under today's conditions of rapid change requires change in many of the ways that companies currently make decisions and operate.

Embedded within the manufacturing system are a large number of distinct processes or stages that, individually and collectively, affect product quality and cost, as well as the time and effort required to produce the product and the time required to introduce a new version of the product. The interactions between the various facets of the manufacturing system are complex, and decisions made concerning one aspect have ramifications that extend to the others (see Fig. 5-1).

In its broadest sense, design for manufacture (DFM) is concerned with comprehending these interactions and using this knowledge to optimize the manufacturing system for effective quality, cost, and delivery. More specifically, DFM is concerned with:

1. Understanding how the process by which a product is designed interacts with the other components of the manufacturing system and using this understanding to design better quality products that can be produced for lower cost and brought to market more quickly.
2. Understanding how the physical design of the product itself interacts with the components of the manufacturing system and using this understanding to define product design alternatives that help facilitate "global" optimization of the manufacturing system as a whole.

Ultimately, the goal of design for manufacture is to facilitate the design of functionally and visually appealing products with mechanical reliability, to manufacture these products effectively, to introduce the products, and to market them in a timely manner.

DESIGN BASICS

A study of design basics reveals much about design. It shows why conceptual product design is such a pivotal step in the lifecycle of a product, where current practices have gone wrong, and what steps need to be taken to get back on track. As was mentioned previously, the heart and foundation of DFM is a fundamental understanding of the design process.

THE DESIGN PROCESS

The essential purpose of design is to satisfy need. Need arises in many forms and may be for many markets, U.S. and otherwise. Products ranging from ball bearings to satellite communication systems, from deep sea oil drilling platforms to manufacturing systems all fulfill human needs. Often the particular needs involved determine the design strategy followed. For example, the needs to be satisfied in the design of a simple welding fixture are far different from those of a mass-produced washing machine or multifunctional interplanetary space probe. Needs also exact various prices. Certain functions require certain materials and various amounts of energy. Safety, ecological, and societal considerations increase complexity. Light weight often implies costly materials as well as extensive analysis, research, and development. Quality implies consistency and adherence to design intent. Efficient design requires an optimal balance between cost, function, appearance, convenience, maintainability, and life. This balance is generally determined by the needs the design is intended to fulfill.

In general, engineering design begins with the recognition of a need and the conception of an idea to meet this need. It proceeds with the definition of the problem; continues through a program of directed research, analysis, and development; and often leads to the construction and evaluation of a prototype. It concludes with the effective manufacture and distribution of a product or system so that the original need may be met wherever it exists. Because many decisions made along the way must be made in the absence of needed information, the engineer seldom arrives at an acceptable solution the first time around. As the final design evolves, many decisions are reexamined because additional information becomes available. This process of reexamination is the iterative nature of design and is recognized as an essential part of the process. Iteration permits inadequate decisions to be improved under increasing knowledge.

Engineering design is accomplished through a process of problem solving. Problem solving in design is a process that follows a logical sequence. The complete process, from start to finish, is

DESIGN BASICS

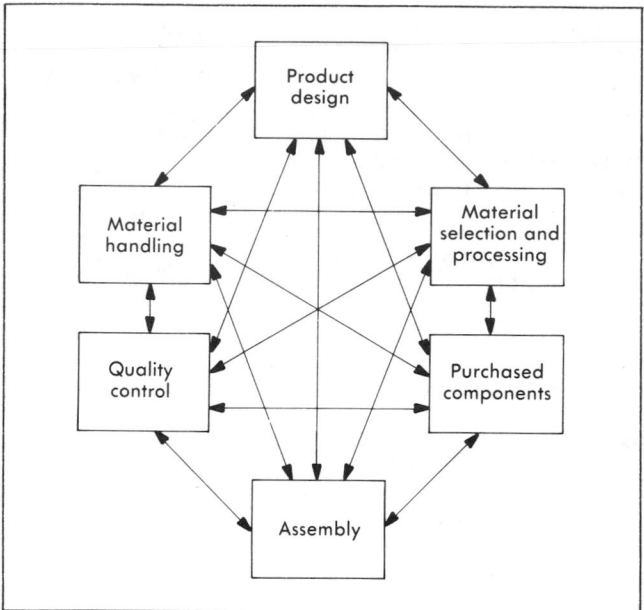

Fig. 5-1 Manufacturing interactions. (*Industrial Technology Institute*)

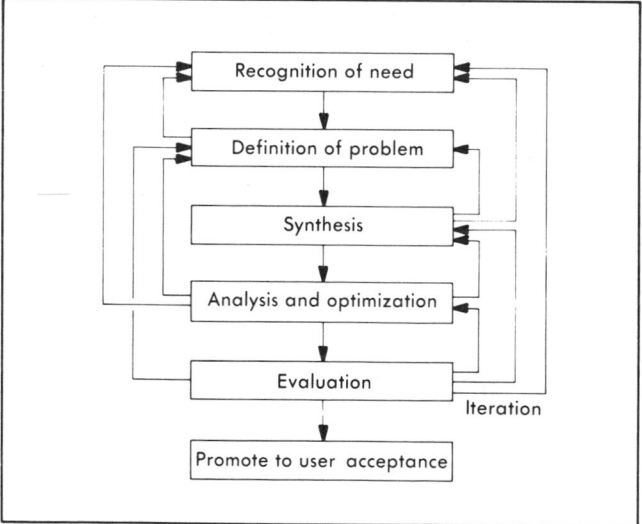

Fig. 5-2 Schematic diagram showing the different phases of design.

often outlined as shown in Fig. 5-2.[1] The process begins with a decision maker—the engineer or manager—recognizing a need and making a decision to do something about it. After performing many iterations, the process ends with plans for satisfying the need.

GOVERNING CHARACTERISTICS

The design process previously discussed can be summarized by the following definition:

Design is an *iterative, decision-making* activity involving the use of scientific and technological information to produce a system, device, or process intended to meet *specified needs*.

The italicized words in this definition represent intrinsic,

governing characteristics of the design process. At the outset of a design project, usually very little is known about the design problem and what the eventual design solution will actually consist of. Hence, early design decisions must often be made under a great deal of uncertainty. Two mechanisms are available to offset this uncertainty: (1) accurate problem definition (careful and thorough specification of needs, examination of past experience, and a study of the competition) and (2) iteration.

Problem Definition

Problem definition is the process of going from a primitive statement of need to a clear, exact statement of the problem to be solved expressed in engineering terms. In most cases, the solution to a design problem is directly determined by the problem definition. For this reason, it is essential to understand and define the problem before any solutions are sought. Developing an accurate and thorough definition of the problem before any lines are put on paper avoids much of the uncertainty associated with early design decisions.

The Iterative Nature of Design

Iteration allows the design to be continuously improved and optimized over time as better and more complete design information becomes available. What constitutes "more complete information" can vary depending on circumstance. For example, more complete information could come in the form of improved understanding gained from a prototype test or revealed through analysis or innovation; it could be a better definition of customer or market needs or a change in those needs; or it could involve a new material or emerging manufacturing technology or some other new discovery.

Accompanying iteration are local design changes made to improve the design. These local changes generally propagate in a "ripple effect" throughout the design because they require that each part of the design affected by the change be reexamined. An unavoidable consequence of design iteration is therefore "engineering change," caused both by the design iteration itself and the ripple effect it produces. In the early phases of a design project, engineering changes are handled fairly easily because the design is fluid, hardware is still remote, few people are involved, and constraints and interactions have not become

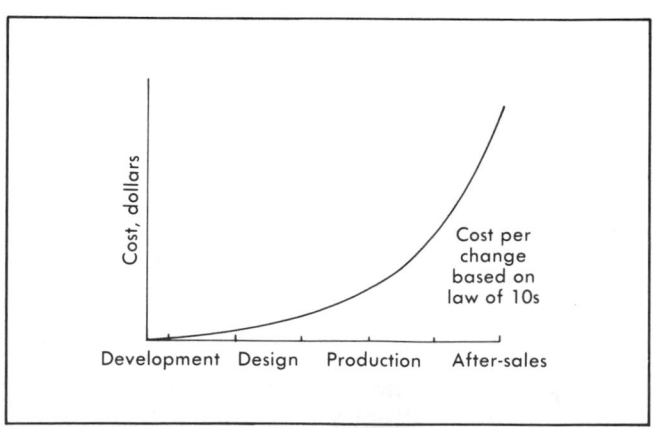

Fig. 5-3 Real cost of engineering changes based on the law of 10s. (*Industrial Technology Institute*)

tight. The cost of engineering changes in the early stages of design is usually just the direct labor costs involved.

In the later stages of the project, engineering changes become much more difficult and costly to handle; many engineers, designers, and drafting personnel are committed, several components of the manufacturing system are usually actively involved, and much has been designed and irrevocably fixed. Because of the ripple effect, an ill-chosen solution for even a relatively minor problem can put the whole project in jeopardy. For these reasons, the range of solutions to a problem discovered late in a project are severely limited, and even minor changes are likely to result in both undesirable deviations from the original design intent and in suboptimal design.

The cost of engineering changes can be plotted as a function of product lifecycle (see Fig. 5-3). This curve is based on the "law of 10s," which assumes that the cost of an engineering change increases by a factor of 10 with each subsequent stage in the product development cycle following concept decision. Recognizing that iteration is an inherent part of the design process, Fig. 5-3 shows that a concerted attempt should be made to converge quickly to the desired solution in the early stages of the design project.

NEED FOR CHANGE AND CHANGING NEEDS

Awareness that there is a need for change in the basic way industry accomplishes product delivery began to surface in the late 1970s. It was at this time that many established and successful manufacturers realized that their preeminent position in the global marketplace was being challenged by declining productivity, shortening product lifecycles, global competition, and the emergence of new manufacturing technologies. This precipitated a quest for short-term solutions that quickly focused on fledgling technologies such as robotics, vision and optical processing, and flexible manufacturing systems. Failure to achieve promised productivity improvements using these and other advanced manufacturing technologies in a variety of industrial settings has taught much about product design and its relation to the rest of the manufacturing system.

Implicit in this experience is the realization that there is both a need to change and changing needs; that is, coping with the demands of the present-day market requires that changes be made in the way companies do work. In addition, this same market is imposing new product requirements that also demand a new approach to design. Along with market demands is the availability of advanced manufacturing technologies that promise highly desirable productivity improvements that cannot be fully realized without changes in design practice. In the following sections, some of the needed changes in current practices are discussed along with some of the changing needs that are making it imperative for changes in the design approach.

ORGANIZATIONAL AND PROCEDURAL ISSUES

Perhaps the most important lesson learned from the failures of the late 1970s is that the design, function, and implementation of advanced manufacturing technology is directly related to the product being manufactured. When implementing these technologies, design of the product and design of the equipment processes that produce it can no longer be treated as separate entities. Manufacturing goals and requirements must be included, from the very beginning of the project, as part of the product plan (problem definition). To minimize design iteration and move engineering changes back into the early stages of design, the product and process design must also proceed, from the start, hand in hand as one common, integrated activity.

Recognizing the need to integrate product and process design is only the first step. The pivotal second step—actually doing it within the constraints imposed by an organization's structure and procedural processes—is the challenge.

Complexity is perhaps the main underlying cause of the problem. Prior to the Industrial Revolution, a single craftworker understood and implemented all of the functions of the manufacturing system. With the onset of the Industrial Revolution, complexity of the manufacturing system grew to the point where the work, skills, and knowledge required to go from design to production had to be split up into a multitude of specializations, each organized and compartmentalized within different companies, divisions, and departments. As businesses grew and further specialized, many companies became organized along lines of functional specialization.

Because of the complexity of the products that are now required and desired, and because of the complexity of the manufacturing systems that are needed to produce these products, it is unlikely that meaningful reductions in specialization can be made. Also, even though the need exists for restructuring many industrial organizations and operational procedures, the immense cultural and social inertia that must be overcome makes rapid change in this area unlikely. Nevertheless, to maximize the quality of early design decisions and thereby minimize the amount of engineering change, input is needed from as many manufacturing systems activities as possible and as early in the design process as possible.

COST REDUCTION, QUALITY AND PRODUCTIVITY

The importance of manufacturability in product design has been recognized for years. Just how important is illustrated by the well-known fact that up to 80% or more of production decisions are directly determined by the product design. This leaves little freedom of choice for process planning, especially when process planning is often performed downstream of concept decisions.

What this all-too-frequent scenario shows is that truly effective cost reduction begins when the first inklings of a new product or product enhancement or product redesign begin to emerge into the corporate consciousness. As shown in Fig. 5-4, early design decisions affect lifecycle cost far more than years of manufacturing improvements made subsequent to concept decision and detail product design. The elimination of a part, for example, or a machining direction or separate fasteners, by design can result in the elimination of stations, operations, fixturing, and quality risks, in addition to the direct costs accompanying them, for the life of the product. No amount of

CHANGE AND CHANGING NEEDS

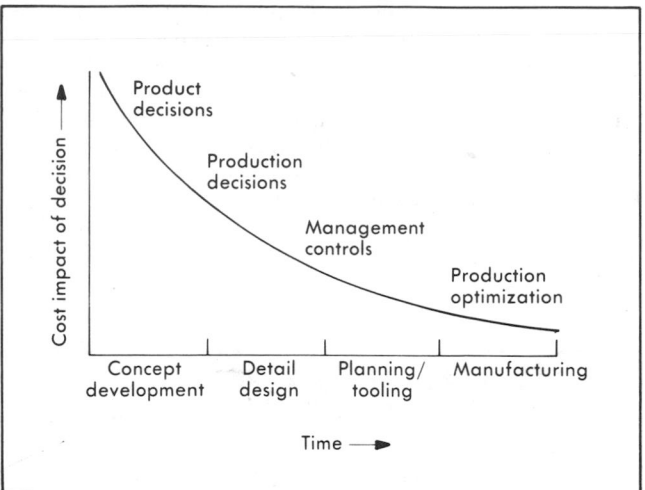

Fig. 5-4 Cost impact of decisions. (*Industrial Technology Institute*)

optimization of speeds and feeds or work simplification or advanced manufacturing technology can match the overwhelming benefits of a product correctly designed, from the start, for manufacture.

A major reason why early design decisions affect product lifecycle cost so heavily is that they directly affect manufacturing system productivity. Product designs that are based on a design concept selected for its inherent ease of manufacture and composed of components that have been carefully designed to be easy to make, easy to fixture and handle, easy to assemble, and are carefully matched in process and materials to the manufacturing processes that produce them naturally result in productivity improvements. Along with lower cost and enhanced productivity comes quality improvements. Quality is the third term in the cost reduction equation. Improved productivity requires error-free manufacture, which in turn requires design for quality and leads to quality improvements, both real and perceived.

The synergism between cost, productivity, and quality is the real key to cost reduction. Taking the time to properly plan and design the product right the first time makes it easier to manufacture. Ease of manufacture reduces both direct and indirect manufacturing costs. Because the product is easy to manufacture, there is less quality risk and deviation from design intent. This results in a better, more desirable product, which in turn leads to increased sales and market share. Also, because the product has more perceived quality, it can be sold for a higher price. Lower total manufacturing cost plus increased sales and sale price translate into bigger profits, the ultimate goal of business.

FLEXIBILITY

The modern Information Age, together with ever-increasing electronic computing capabilities and applications, has created an entirely new manufacturing system dimension that significantly affects the design process. This new dimension is flexibility, the ability to adapt quickly and easily to changes in product or production conditions and/or requirements. Flexibility is manifested on the manufacturing floor in the form of programmable automation and new approaches to material handling and part fixturing.

A robot is a typical example of flexible automation. Because it is programmable (under software control), the robot can be programmed to perform a variety of different tasks within its envelope of capability, without change or modification to its physical form. Hence, in a new manufacturing application, instead of designing a special piece of equipment, a standard robot, programmed to perform the new task, can be readily placed on line.

The ability to manufacture to customer order, produce a correct first part, manufacture a variety of different products or product models in any sequence and/or quantity, and rapidly introduce a new product or change an existing design are a few of many important capabilities promised by flexible, computer-based manufacturing. Realization of this promise requires a process-driven product design methodology (model) together with a viable means for electronically transferring design and process planning information between the computer-aided design (CAD) environment in which the product is designed and the computer-integrated manufacturing (CIM) environment in which it is manufactured, assembled, and tested.

MAINTAINING OPTIONS

From the standpoint of design, flexibility implies more than the ability to manufacture to customer order in any sequence and lot sizes of one or more. It also implies the ability to maintain product and process options over time. As discussed previously, change is an inherent and fundamental property of the design process. Customer needs and perceptions change, new product innovations and technology breakthroughs occur regularly, competition is constantly challenging and pushing current products, and new materials and processes are continually emerging. Maintaining options under these conditions means designing the product and process so that either can be easily and quickly changed without major cost or timing consequences.

Designing this kind of flexibility into the manufacturing system is fast becoming a primary design requirement, especially in industries involving very high volume production. In these industries, economies of scale have historically dictated fixed (nonprogrammable) automation, dedicated transfer lines, specialized fixturing and tooling, and continuous motion assembly lines. Any change to the product under these conditions implies costly and time-consuming changes to the production system. Similarly, introduction of new manufacturing technologies or innovations is often hampered by the fact that the product was never designed with the new technology in mind.

PROCESS-DRIVEN DESIGN

Process-driven design is implemented by specifying process requirements and the preferred methods of manufacture as design requirements before design of the product begins. The product is then designed so that it can be manufactured in this most desirable way. For example, by telling the engineer (or designer) beforehand that the assembly is to be assembled using SCARA (selective compliance assembly robot arm) type robots, the designer can provide the features to make easy use of this type of assembly equipment. As the product design evolves, it is often necessary to modify the proposed method of manufacture. The result is a refined and carefully matched product design and process plan which, by meeting the requirements of both, achieves the goal of "doing it right the first time."

THE DFM APPROACH

Design for manufacture has evolved out of the need to change the way a company performs design and the changing needs of design. The objectives of the design for manufacture approach are:

- Identify product concepts that are inherently easy to manufacture.
- Focus on component design for ease of manufacture and assembly.
- Integrate manufacturing process design and product design to ensure the best matching of needs and requirements.

Meeting these objectives requires the integration of an immense amount of diverse and complex information. This information not only includes considerations of product form, function, and fabrication, but also the organizational and administrative procedures that underly the design process and the human psychology and cognitive processes that make it possible.

Because of the complexity of the issues involved, it is convenient to divide the subject of DFM into two considerations:

1. The DFM approach or process by which a product can be effectively designed for manufacture.
2. The methodologies and tools that can be used to help enable the DFM approach and help ensure that the physical design meets the DFM objectives.

A DFM PROCESS

Many different versions of the DFM process can be proposed. Each version is likely to be similar in the issues addressed and the concepts embodied. Differences would likely reflect idiosyncrasies imposed by the organization in which a particular version originated and the type of design problem it was meant to address. With this in mind, one proposed version of the DFM process is shown in Fig. 5-5.[2]

This process begins with a proposed product concept, a proposed process concept, and a set of design goals. All three of these inputs would be generated by a thorough, well thought out product plan developed using the team approach. Design goals would include both manufacturing and product goals. For example, the design goals may include goals for product performance improvements and added conveniences as well as manufacturing goals such as the elimination of a particular number of assembly workers and/or processing operations and the ability to substitute alternative manufacturing technologies.

Four activities, each addressing particular aspects of the DFM approach, are included within the process itself. Optimization of the product/process concept is concerned with integrating the proposed product and process plan to ensure that product and process flexibility goals are maintained, that the best match between product and process requirements is attained, and that the integrated product/process developed ensures inherent ease of manufacture. With the integrated product concept and process plan specified, the next activity focuses on component design for ease of assembly and handling and on the simplification of components to further promote ease of manufacture, improve quality, and reduce manufacturing cost.

The third activity is aimed at ensuring conformance of the design to processing needs. For example, if a particular part is to be a plastic injection molding, this step would seek to make

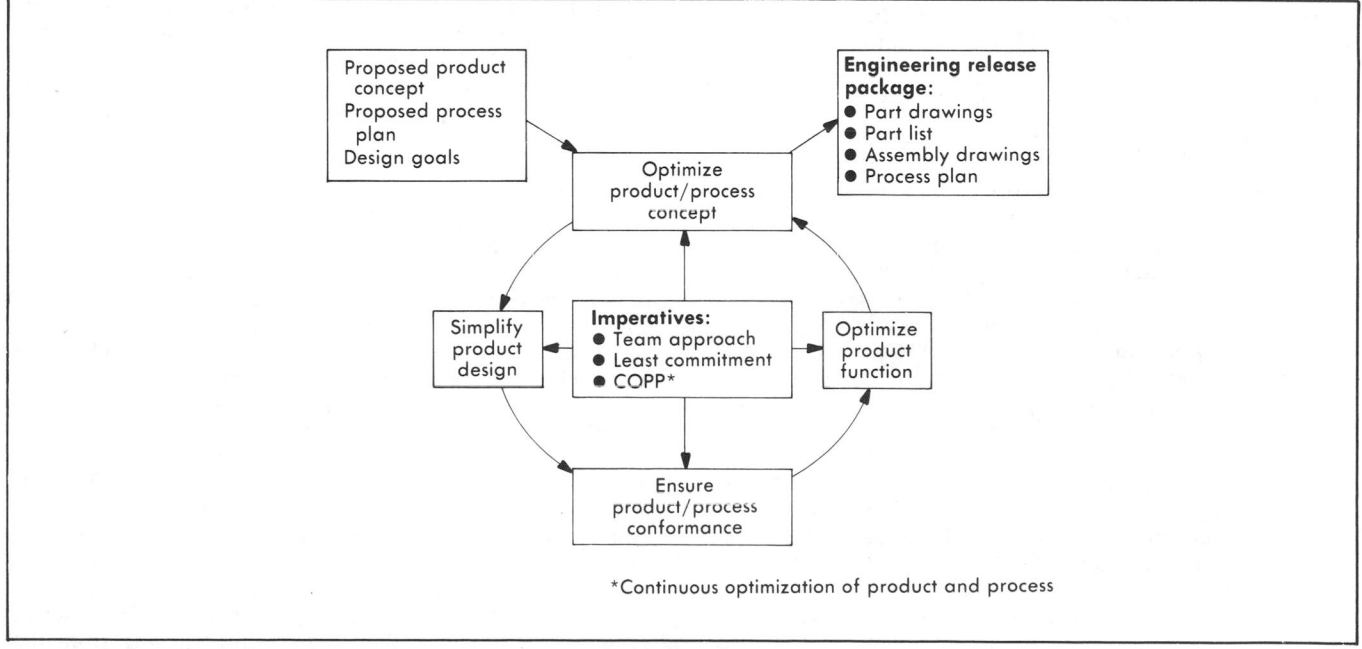

Fig. 5-5 Diagram of one type of DFM process. (*Industrial Technology Institute*)

DFM APPROACH

sure the part is properly designed for the particular process involved. This would not only include designing the part for ease of injection molding, but also designing the part to simplify the tooling, fixturing, and material handling required to support the process. The last activity, which in the traditional approach has often been one of the first steps, is to optimize the product function. This activity is saved until last to ensure that all of the design constraints, including assembly, processing, and material handling requirements, are known before the optimization is attempted.

Figure 5-5 shows the four activities arranged in a circular fashion. This is to emphasize the iterative nature of the process. For instance, as a result of performing the first three activities, imagine that an approach to optimizing the product function is identified that necessitates changing one or many aspects of the design. Implementing these changes implies a second iteration through the loop. Similarly, as a result of going through the four activities, a means may be found for eliminating camming in a mold, a fastening operation, or a fixture flow. Again, these opportunities would be implemented in the next design iteration. The key is to consider all aspects of the product's design and manufacture in the early stages of the design cycle so that design iteration and accompanying engineering changes are easy and cost effective to make.

IMPERATIVES FOR EFFECTIVE DFM

Product design is only one of many complex activities that comprise the manufacturing system. From the very beginnings of an idea for a new product or product model to the last step in retiring it from production and use, a great deal of product knowledge, originating within all components and activities of the manufacturing system, is gained. This interdependency between time, design knowledge, and the manufacturing system in which the product is conceived, designed, produced, and eventually brought to the marketplace to be sold and serviced makes it imperative that there be effective communication within the manufacturing system and that there is flexibility to adapt and modify the design during each product stage as new knowledge becomes available. These imperatives, which are essential for good design in the modern Information Age, can be formalized as the following design principles:

1. *Simultaneous engineering.* The design project should, from the beginning, have continued input from all aspects of the manufacturing system because product function, cost, and quality result from the combined efforts of all components of the manufacturing system. To enable this, all relevant manufacturing system components (process planning, facilities planning, manufacturing equipment design, material handling, marketing and sales, distribution, and service) should be designed and/or planned concurrently with the product design.

2. *Principle of least commitment.* The designer or design team should pursue a policy of least commitment because of the iterative nature of design, the ripple effect, and the real cost of engineering change; that is, in progressing from step to step or phase to phase in the realization of a design, *no irreversible decision should be made until it must be made.* This principle permits maximum flexibility in each step, ensures that better alternatives can be implemented if they become available, and when necessary, makes it easier to accommodate engineering changes. Planning for change by designing flexibility into the product and/or process as well as designing in a means for maintaining options are natural extensions of this principle.

3. *Continuous optimization of product and process.* The best design for mass production is seldom arrived at the first time because of incomplete knowledge. Hence, a policy of improvement and simplification of the product and process should be pursued. That is, for mass-produced products, changes that are directionally correct (help optimize the product design together with the other components of the manufacturing system as a whole) should be implemented on a continuing basis. This principle essentially acknowledges that the benefits of global optimization (lower lifecycle cost, better quality, increased market share, and flexibility) always justify, in the long run, the incremental cost required to achieve it. It also implies that incremental changes are usually the most effective. Introducing frequent small improvements based on customer's reactions or improved manufacturability is less risky than taking one great leap forward based on market researcher's prognostications or the need to cut manufacturing costs. To be practical, continuous optimization of product and process (COPP) should be pursued in conjunction with simultaneous engineering and the principle of least commitment.

IMPLEMENTING THE DFM IMPERATIVES

As shown in Fig. 5-5, the design imperatives underly the entire DFM process and are pivotal to its successful implementation. Implementation of these imperatives tends to be hierarchical in nature; that is, the team approach (simultaneous engineering) generally needs to be adopted before the principle of least commitment can be made to work well. Both of these principles need to be operative for continuous optimization of product and process to work.

In general, the team should be multifunctional, and efforts should be made to keep the same people on the project from start to finish; in reality, however, this does not always happen. As the design evolves, each team member stays in close communication so that changes and fast-breaking developments are quickly relayed to each component of the manufacturing system as they occur. This allows all activities to progress in parallel, thereby shortening the development cycle and increasing the completeness of information on which design decisions are based. Engineers and designers start work before feasibility testing is complete, and manufacturing and sales begin gearing up well before the design is finished.

In making up the team, it is important that there be a balance of skills and personalities. Team members should be technically excellent, but broad enough to understand what others have to say, share goals, and exercise good people skills. The team approach also depends strongly on the presence of an experienced, strong team leader (champion).

Once the team approach is in place, the secret to quick product development is exhaustive product planning, including technology planning and planning for the future. Establishment of checkpoints for a technology's robustness and readiness is essential before letting engineers and designers use it. The key is to make sure that every technological risk has a potential market payoff. Unnecessary risks should not be taken. Often the best course is to reconfigure components already proven in mass production instead of designing everything from the ground up. Also, it is often wise to test new technologies in existing products before putting them all together in a new product. Ultimately, minimizing risk associated with new technology is best done by judicious application of the principle of least commitment.

DFM METHODOLOGIES AND TOOLS

In addition to the DFM process, there are a variety of DFM methodologies and tools that help promote the objectives of DFM by guiding the designer in making better informed design decisions. Figure 5-6 gives a selected list of DFM tools and shows where they might logically fit into the DFM process. The purpose of this section is to review these tools by describing what they are and how they might be used.

DFM PRINCIPLES AND RULES

Over the years, a wealth of product design approaches, techniques, short cuts (rules of thumb), and design tips have evolved out of product design and manufacturing experience that help show the way to good design for manufacture. Knowledge of this information and the ability to correctly apply it has always been one of the hallmarks of the expert design engineer and manufacturing engineer. DFM principles and rules are codifications of this empirical experience into forms that can be directly used to help guide the designer in the early stages of design. The great advantage of using concisely stated design for manufacture principles and guidelines is that they explicitly state what is intuitively obvious to experienced designers and commonly used by good designers. Such a system of principles and guidelines, therefore, provide a firm basis on which design knowledge can be expanded in a systematic way.

A study of many successful designs by several individuals in 1977 led them to propose a set of hypothetical axioms for design and manufacturing.[3] Analysis and refinement of the initial axioms has shown that good design embodies two basic concepts. The first of these is that each functional requirement of a product should be satisfied independently by some aspect, feature, or component within the design. The second basic concept is that good designs maximize simplicity; in other words, they provide the required functions with minimal complexity. These two concepts have been formalized as follows:[4]

- *Axiom 1:* In good design, the independence of functional requirements is maintained.
- *Axiom 2:* Among the designs that satisfy Axiom 1, the best design is the one that has the minimum information content.

Use of the design axioms in design is a two-step process. The first step is to identify the functional requirements (FRs) and constraints. Each FR should be specified such that the FRs are neither redundant nor inconsistent. It is also useful in this step to order the FRs in a hierarchical structure, starting with the primary FR and proceeding to the FR of least importance. Once the functional requirements and constraints are specified for a given product or design problem, the second step is to proceed with the design, applying the axioms to each individual design decision.

One of the important reasons why the axiomatic approach leads to good design is that independence of functional requirements effectively short-circuits the ripple effect. By uncoupling or decoupling functional requirements, changes in a particular requirement or changes made to the design solution affecting that requirement do not affect the other functional requirements satisfied by the design.

The design axioms can be used to both explain and provide insight into many well-known product design strategies and tactics. For example, standardization is a way of separating or decoupling product and marketing needs from manufacturing. Standardization also reduces the amount of information required for product manufacture. This can be illustrated by considering modular design. A module is a self-contained component with standardized interfaces to other product modules and to the production equipment and tooling used in the prod-

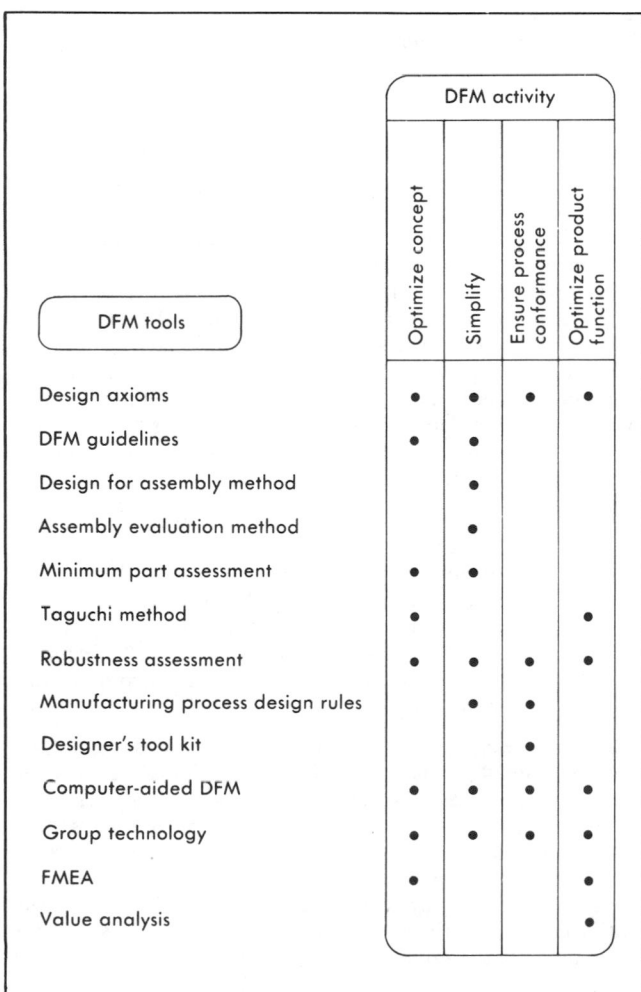

Fig. 5-6 Design for manufacture tools. (*Industrial Technology Institute*)

DFM PRINCIPLES

uct manufacture. Individual modules can be varied to provide functional and styling diversity. Similar diversity can be provided by using different combinations of standard modules. All of this has no effect on the production line as long as the module/process equipment and tooling interfaces are standardized. Modular design also reduces final assembly information content because there are fewer parts to assemble and each module can be fully checked prior to final assembly.

DFM GUIDELINES

DFM guidelines are systematic and codified statements of good design practice that have been empirically derived from years of design and manufacturing experience. Typically, the guidelines are stated as directives that act to both stimulate creativity and show the way to good design for manufacture. If correctly followed, they should result in a product that is inherently easier to manufacture. Various forms of the design guidelines have been stated by different authors,[5,6,7] a sampling of which are provided as follows:

1. Design for a minimum number of parts.
2. Develop a modular design.
3. Minimize part variations.
4. Design parts to be multifunctional.
5. Design parts for multiuse.
6. Design parts for ease of fabrication.
7. Avoid separate fasteners.
8. Minimize assembly directions; design for top-down assembly.
9. Maximize compliance; design for ease of assembly.
10. Minimize handling; design for handling and presentation.
11. Evaluate assembly methods.
12. Eliminate or simplify adjustments.
13. Avoid flexible components.

It should be noted that DFM guideline number 13, "avoid flexible components," is really a subset of guideline number 10. In general, most of the guidelines given can be subdivided into an almost endless list of additional rules that become more and more specific to particular applications and situations. For this reason, many companies have found it advantageous to develop a distinct set of rules that apply more specifically to their particular business.

APPLYING THE GUIDELINES

Application of the DFM guidelines is not always easy or straightforward. They show the way, but do not replace the talent, innovation, and experience of the product development team. They must also be applied in a manner that maintains and, if possible, enhances product performance and marketing goals. Design guidelines should be thought of as "optimal suggestions," which, if successfully followed, will result in a high-quality, low-cost, and manufacture-friendly design.

Minimize Total Number of Parts

A part is a good candidate for elimination if there is (1) no need for relative motion, (2) no need for subsequent adjustment between parts, (3) no need for service or repairability, and (4) no need for materials to be different. However, part reduction should not exceed the point of diminishing return, where further part elimination adds cost and complexity because the remaining parts are too heavy, too complicated to make, etc.

Perhaps the best way to eliminate parts is to identify a design concept that requires few parts. Integral design, or the combining of two or more parts into one, is another approach. Besides the advantages previously given, integral design reduces the amount of interfacing information required, and decreases weight and complexity. One-piece structures have no fasteners, no joints, and fewer points of stress concentration. Conversely, structural continuity leads to high strength and light weight. An example of a single stamping that replaced a two-part assembly is shown in Fig. 5-7.

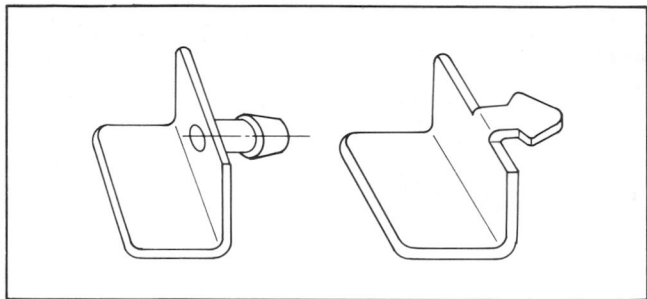

Fig. 5-7 Two part assembly (left) is replaced by a single stamping.

Develop a Modular Design

Designing for modularity requires careful consideration of a variety of needs. To decouple the product from the method of manufacture, it is essential that stable groups be identified and that the interfacing information be specified in a way that facilitates the desired decoupling.

In seeking to identify the minimum number of stable groups, it is useful to look at the distribution of functional requirements among different product models and lines to see if a particular function could be satisfied everywhere by one module. Looking for common problems within different models and product lines is another approach. Will the same solution work everywhere? Other questions to ask include the following:

- Can customization (diversity) requirements be satisfied using add-on modules?
- How will future product(s) differ from the current design? What commonalities will exist?
- What modular configuration will simplify material handling? Decouple quality from production? Decouple variation in vendor-supplied components from production? Decouple style from production?

Experience has shown that products consisting of 4-8 modules with 4-12 parts per module are most automation friendly. A good design strategy is to keep the product generic for as long as possible during assembly by saving the specialized modules for last. If possible, the modules should be designed to add up to the final product, thereby eliminating the need for a housing or other integrating structure. Also, information content is reduced if all modules (except perhaps the base) are approximately the same size.

Minimize Part Variations

Information content of the product and quality risks are reduced when part variations (such as the types of screws used) are kept to a minimum. It is seldom justifiable, for example, to use several screw sizes or types of metal in one part. Minimizing part variations also simplifies manufacturing by reducing the information content of the production system required to produce the part.

Use of standard (off-the-shelf) components also helps reduce part variations as well as total information content of the manufacturing system. A stock item is always less expensive than a custom-made item. Standard components require little or no lead time and are more reliable because characteristics and weaknesses are well known. They can be ordered in any quantity at any time. They are usually easier to repair, and replacements are easier to find. Use of standardized components enables the supplier to become a part of the design team.

The many advantages of standardization can be further amplified through the concept of standardization and rationalization (S&R). In the S&R approach, standardization is defined as the reduction in number of part numbers used in current and former designs. Rationalization is the identification of the fewest number of parts required for use in future designs.

Design Parts to be Multifunctional

Combine function wherever possible. For example, design a part to act both as a spring and a structural member or to act both as an electrical conductor and structural member. An electronic chassis can be made to act as an electrical ground, a heat sink, and a structural member. Less obvious combinations of function might involve adding guiding, aligning, and/or self-fixturing features to a part to aid in assembly or providing a reflective surface or recognizable feature to facilitate vision inspection. These latter examples illustrate inclusion of functions that are only needed during manufacture. Such function combinations are often the result of design for manufacture awareness produced by the team approach.

Design Parts for Multiuse

Many parts can be designed for multiuse. For example, the same mounting plate can be designed to mount a variety of components. The same gear can be used for different applications in different products. A spacer can also serve as an axle, lever, or standoff. Multiuse parts reduce manufacturing system information content by reducing the number of different parts or part variations that need to be manufactured. They also produce economies of scale because of increased production volume of fewer parts and economies of scope because the same part is being used in a variety of applications and products.

The key to multiuse part design is the identification of part candidates. Multiuse parts can be created using a group technology database (discussed subsequently) by first sorting all parts (or a statistical sample) manufactured or purchased by the company into two groups consisting of (1) parts that are unique to a particular product or model (such as crankshafts and housings) and (2) "building block" parts that are generally used in all products and/or models (shafts, flanges, bushings, spacers, levers, ball bearings, switches, connectors, and hardware). Each group is then divided into categories of similar parts (part families). Multiuse parts are created by standardization and rationalization of similar parts. This process consists of sequentially seeking to (1) minimize the number of part categories, (2) minimize the number of variations within each category, and (3) minimize the number of design features within each variation. Once developed, the rationalized family of standard parts

should be used exclusively in new product designs. Also, manufacturing processes and tooling based on a composite part containing all design features found in a particular part family should be developed. Individual parts can then be obtained by skipping some steps and features during the manufacturing process.

Design Parts for Ease of Fabrication

This guideline requires that individual parts be designed using the least costly material that just satisfies functional requirements (including style and appearance) and such that both material waste and cycle time are minimized. This in turn requires that the most suitable fabrication process available be used to make each part and that the part be properly designed for the chosen process. Use of near net shape processes are preferred whenever possible. Likewise, secondary processing (such as finish machining and painting) should be avoided whenever possible. Secondary processing can be avoided by specifying tolerances and surface finish carefully and then selecting primary processes (such as precision casting, PM) that meet these requirements. Also, material alternatives that avoid painting, plating, or buffing should be considered. This guideline is based on the recognition that higher material and/or unit process cost can be accepted if it leads to lower overall production cost. In other words, adding information content to a particular part is acceptable as long as total information content of the product/process is reduced.

Avoid Separate Fasteners

Separate fasteners involve large amounts of information. Even in manual assembly, the cost of driving a screw can be 6-10 times the cost of the screw. One of the easiest things to do is eliminate fasteners in assembly by using snap fits. If fasteners must be used, cost as well as quality risks can be significantly reduced by minimizing the number, size, and variations used and by using standard fasteners whenever possible. Screws that are too short or too long, separate washers, tapped holes, and round and flat heads (not good for vacuum pickup) should be avoided. Conversely, captured washers should be used for reduced part placement risk and improved blow feeding. Self-tapping/forming/locking fasteners are preferred as are screws with dog or cone (chamfered) points for improved placement success. Also, screw heads designed to reduce "cam-out" problems, bit wear, and fastener damage should be used. For vacuum pickup, screw heads having flat vertical sides should be used (socket head, fillister head, and hex head).

Minimize Assembly Directions

All parts should be assembled from one direction. Extra directions mean wasted time and motion as well as more transfer stations, inspection stations, and fixture nests. This in turn leads to increased cost, increased wear and tear on equipment due to added weight and inertia load, and increased reliability and quality risks. The best possible assembly is when all parts are added in a top-down fashion to create a Z-axis stack. Multimotion insertion should be avoided. Ideally, the product should resemble a Z-axis "club sandwich," with all parts positively located as they are added.

Maximize Compliance

Because parts are not always identical and perfectly made, misalignment and tolerance stackup can produce excessive

DFM PRINCIPLES

assembly force leading to sporadic automation failures and/or product unreliability. Major factors affecting rigid part mating include part geometry (accuracy, consistency), stiffness of assembly tool, stiffness of jigs and fixtures holding the parts, and friction between parts. To guard against this, compliance should be built into both the product and production process.

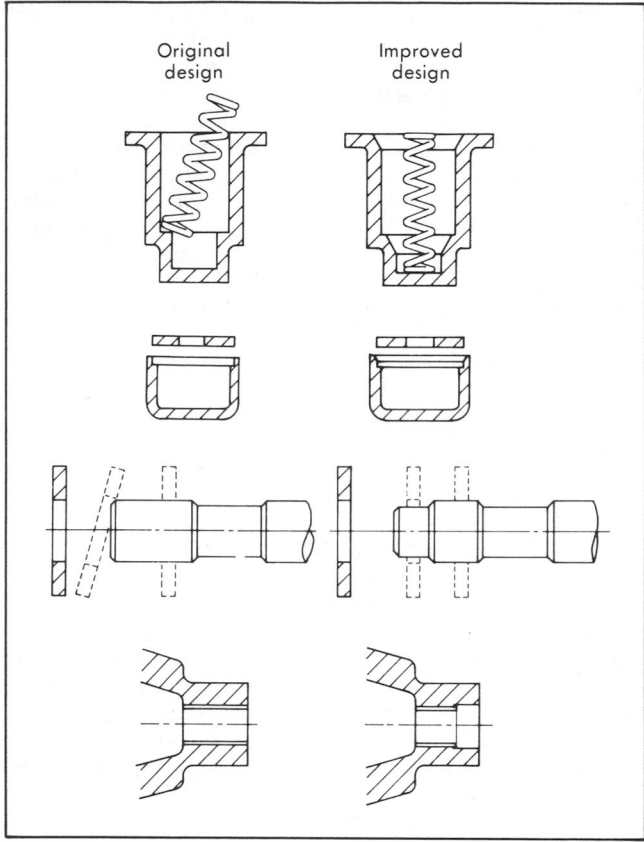

Fig. 5-8 Changes in design that facilitate inserting and mounting of components.

Designed-in compliance features include the use of generous tapers or chamfers for easy insertion, use of leads and other guiding features, and use of generous radii when possible (see Fig. 5-8). A nice approach, if possible, is to design one of the product components, perhaps the largest, to act both as the part base (part to which other parts are added) and as the assembly fixture (avoid need for a special fixture to hold the assembly). A good base design may include features that aid manufacturability, but are not needed for product function. In any case, the part base should be made as stable and rigid as possible to improve insertion accuracy and simplify handling. If fixturing is required, "fixture-friendly" features such as accurate location points, generous tapers, and other guiding features that provide easy compliance between base part and fixture should be provided. Gravity is an extremely useful external effect that assists compliance and costs nothing. In addition to assisting with insertion, gravity is useful for feeding parts and for ejecting finished and defective product.

Minimize Handling

Position is the sum of location (X, Y, Z) and orientation (α, β, γ). Position costs money. Therefore, parts should be designed to make position easy to achieve, and the production process should maintain position once it is achieved. The number of orientations required during production equates with increased equipment expense, greater quality risk, slower feed rates, and slower cycle times. To assist in orientation, parts should be made as symmetrical as possible (see Fig. 5-9). If polarity is important, then an existing asymmetry should be accentuated, or a very obvious asymmetry should be designed in, or a clear identifying mark provided. Orientation can also be assisted by designing in features that help guide and locate parts in the

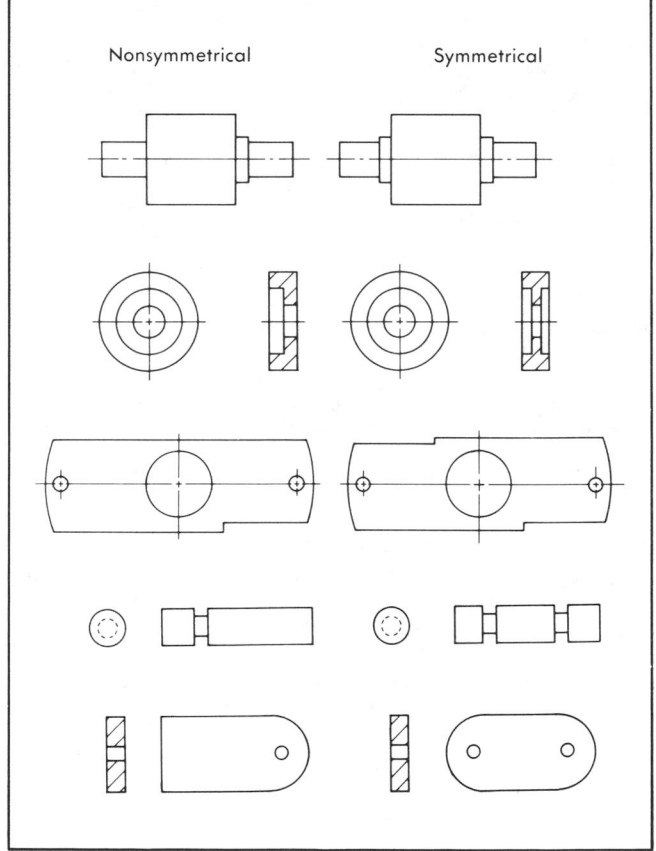

Fig. 5-9 Parts made symmetrical for easier orientation.

proper position (see Fig. 5-10). Parts should also be designed to avoid tangling, nesting, and shingling in vibratory part feeders.

Robotic part handling can be facilitated by providing a large, flat, smooth top surface for vacuum pickup, an inner hole for spearing, or a cylindrical surface or other feature of sufficient length for gripper pickup. Because parts usually come off the production line properly oriented, this orientation should be preserved by using magazines, tube feeders, or part strips. Palletized trays and kitting are methods for supplying properly oriented parts to the assembly line.

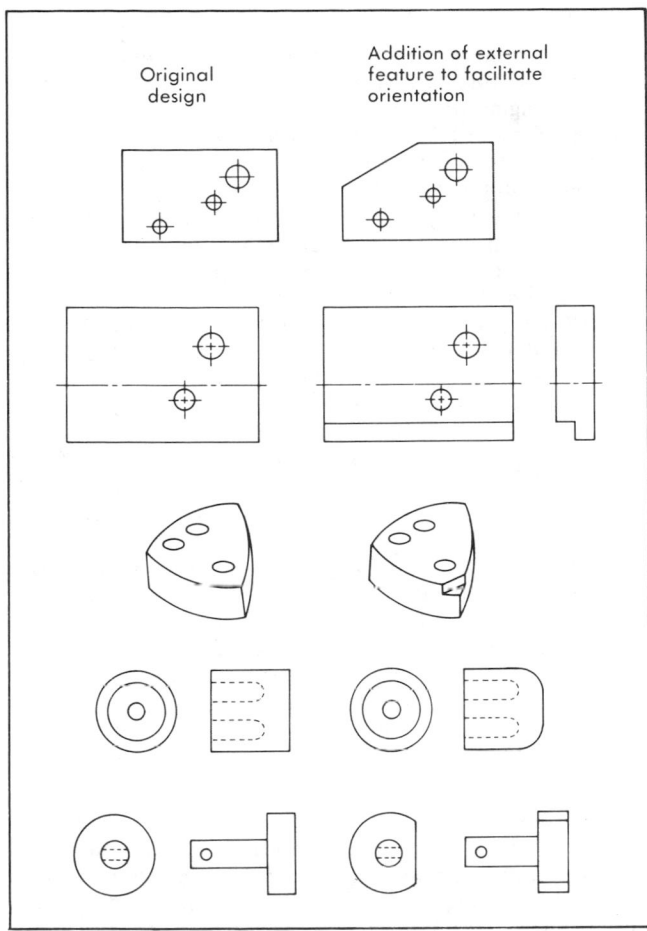

Original design

Addition of external feature to facilitate orientation

Fig. 5-10 Adding external features such as chamfers, slots, shoulders, radii, or flats can facilitate orientation.

Eliminate or Simplify Adjustments

Manual and automated mechanical adjustments are expensive and a continual source of assembly, reliability, test, and service problems. Also, equipment that goes out of adjustment is one of the biggest causes of customer dissatisfaction. Avoiding adjustments reduces assembly cost, enables automation, and improves service of the product as well as reducing service costs. The need for adjustment can be avoided in a variety of ways by providing natural stopping points, notches, and spring-mounted components, which ensure a preferred location as well as compensate for wear. Often, by understanding the nature of the difficulty caused by a particular adjustment, the designer can find an innovative way to reduce or eliminate the need for the adjustment. Process-driven design combined with the team approach can solve many of these problems.

Avoid Flexible Components

Electrical wires and other flexible components are difficult to assemble because their flexibility makes handling difficult. Connectors in fixed position are good for robotic assembly. Rigid or process-applied gaskets should be used whenever possible. Plugs and connectors can be used to eliminate lead wires. Also, consider using circuit boards in place of cables. Often,

locating all connectors at one end of the assembly helps simplify assembly operations. If a cable cannot be avoided, it is often helpful to locate the cable end by having the cable plugged into a dummy connector. A reduction in the use of flexible components can also reduce information content in other ways. For example, a reduction in the number of electrical cables will also reduce cable wiring errors, thereby reducing a major source of assembly test problems.

QUANTITATIVE EVALUATION METHODS

Quantitative evaluation methods form a major part of the arsenal of DFM tools that have been developed in recent years. These methodologies allow the design engineer to rate the manufacturability of the design quantitatively and, in so doing, provide a systematic, step-by-step procedure that helps ensure that the DFM guidelines are being correctly applied. These methods encourage the designer to improve manufacturability of the design by providing insight, stimulating creativity, and rewarding the designer with improved quantitative scores if the DFM guidelines are correctly applied. An important added benefit of these methodologies is that they teach good design practice. Consequently, the need for repetitive use of the methodology diminishes with use.

At present, there are two quantitative evaluation methodologies in widespread use, both of which focus on ease of product assembly. The design for assembly (DFA) method developed by G. Boothroyd and P. Dewhurst is perhaps the most widely used of these methods. The second quantitative methodology, known as the Hitachi assemblability evaluation method (AEM), is less widely used domestically because of its proprietary nature. Available from General Electric Co. through a license from Hitachi, Ltd. (Tokyo), modified versions of this methodology are being used by Hewlett-Packard, General Motors Corp., Caterpillar, and several other companies in the U.S.

Boothroyd-Dewhurst DFA Method

The design for assembly (DFA) method was developed by G. Boothroyd and P. Dewhurst while at the University of Massachusetts. They are presently at the University of Rhode Island. Details of the methodology are presented in the *Design for Assembly Handbook.*[8] The DFA methodology has been adopted by a number of large U.S. manufacturers, among them Ford Motor Co., Xerox Corp., and Whirlpool Corp.

Based largely on industrial engineering time study methods, the DFA method developed by Boothroyd and Dewhurst seeks to minimize cost of assembly within constraints imposed by other design requirements. This is done by first reducing the number of parts and then ensuring that the remaining parts are easy to assemble. Essentially, the method is a systematic, step-by-step implementation of the DFM guideline numbers 1, 7, 8, 9, and 10.

The *DFA Handbook* is divided into three sections dealing with choice of assembly method, design for manual assembly, and design for automatic assembly. The first section provides a procedure for choosing between manual, special-purpose automatic, or programmable automatic assembly. Basic information required includes production volume per shift, number of parts in the assembly, single product or a variety of products, number of additional parts required for different styles of the product, number of major design changes expected during the product life, and the company investment policy regarding labor-saving machinery. This basic information is used to

CHAPTER 5

DFM PRINCIPLES

choose the appropriate row and column on a color-coded chart. The recommended assembly method is given at the row-column intersection on the chart. By varying the basic information slightly, different intersections are obtained, thereby giving a feel for what parameters are driving the assembly method choice.

The design for manual assembly procedure consists of comparing an "ideal" assembly time with an estimated "actual" assembly time required for a particular product design. To calculate the ideal assembly time, the theoretical minimum number of parts is first determined by questioning whether each part needs to be separate for good reasons regarding relative motion, whether there is a need for differing materials, and whether there is a need for manufacture and repair. The ideal assembly time is calculated assuming an assembly containing the theoretical minimum number of parts, each of which can be assembled in an ideal time of 3 seconds. This ideal time assumes that each part is easy to handle and insert and that about one third of the parts are secured immediately on insertion with well-designed snap-fit elements.

Assembly for each part is divided into handling and insertion operations. To estimate the actual assembly time for each part, penalties in seconds are assessed for difficulties associated with each operation. The penalties are based on a compilation of standard time study data as well as dedicated time study experiments. This data is tabulated in chart form as a function of part geometry, orientation features, handling features, and method of attachment. Actual assembly time is the sum of handling and insertion times obtained from the charts for each part contained in the actual assembly. The manual assembly efficiency rating is computed as the ratio of ideal assembly time to actual assembly time.

Following evaluation, the assembly is redesigned for ease of assembly by first eliminating and combining parts using the insights gained from the theoretical minimum part count determination. The remaining parts are then designed to provide features that reduce assembly time, again using insights gained from the evaluation. To gage improvements, assemblability efficiencies calculated for the new and old designs can be compared.

The design for automatic assembly analysis consists of four steps: (1) estimate the cost of automated bulk handling and oriented delivery, (2) estimate cost of automatic part insertion, (3) decide whether the part must be separate from all other parts in the assembly, and (4) combine the results of steps 1-3 to estimate the total cost of assembly. Although more computations are involved, the basis for the design efficiency calculation and procedure for product redesign is essentially the same as for manual assembly.

Minimum Part Assessment

Once the basic ideas behind quantitative evaluation methodologies are understood, it is not difficult to begin to imagine other design measures and/or methods for rating a design's manufacturability. The reader is encouraged to consider the following procedure as one way of implementing DFM within his or her organization. The basis for the minimum part assessment is the part count ratio, which is defined as:

$$\text{part count ratio} = \frac{\text{theoretical minimum number of parts}}{\text{actual number of parts}}$$

A procedure for determining the theoretical minimum number of parts, based on the Boothroyd-Dewhurst questions,

could be developed as follows:

1. Obtain the best information about the product or assembly. Useful items include:
   - Engineering drawings.
   - Exploded three-dimensional views.
   - An existing version of the product.
   - A prototype.
2. Take the assembly apart (or imagine how this might be done). If the assembly contains subassemblies, treat these, at first, as "parts" and then analyze them later as assemblies.
3. Begin reassembling the product in the reverse order from which it was disassembled. As each part is added to the assembly and regardless of practical or functional limitations, answer each of the following questions:
   a. Does the part move relative to other parts?
   b. Must the part, for good reasons, be made of a different material?
   c. Does the part need to be separate for manufacture or repair?
4. If the answer to any of these questions is yes, then the part under consideration must be a separate part and cannot be eliminated. If the answer to all three questions is no, then the part is a candidate for elimination.
5. The theoretical minimum number of parts for the product is equal to the total number of parts that must be separate as determined by yes answers to the previous critical questions.

Summary

Once a set of design measures such as the Boothroyd-Dewhurst assemblability efficiency or the proposed part count ratio have been agreed on, it might be possible to begin including target values for these measures as part of the design goals of a project (refer to Fig. 5-5). Such an approach could be beneficial both by giving the design team some quantitative design goals to aim at and by providing added basis for judging the acceptability of a particular design. One cautionary note is in order. It is important to remember that the quantitative DFM methodologies are only design tools and not ends in themselves. It is, therefore, very important that such measures are used for what they are—a means for improving the DFM quality of the design—and that they do not become just one more "hoop" the design department must jump through to get a design released. DFM practice must become a natural, not an additional, part of the design process.

ROBUST DESIGN

Robust design implies a product designed to perform its intended function no matter what the circumstances. A rifle that continues to fire reliably even after being dropped in mud might be considered robust with respect to external or environmental factors such as intrusion of dirt and moisture. Similarly, if the rifle continues to fire reliably in spite of years of mistreatment and neglect, it might be considered robust with respect to deterioration over time.

Although the concept of robust design is well known and its importance is well understood by consumers and manufacturers alike, little has been done to provide the manufacturing or product design engineer with formalized methodologies for doing robust design. Perhaps the greatest contribution in this area to date has been the work of Genichi Taguchi. Better known as the Taguchi methods, the on-line and off-line quality control methodology developed by Taguchi in the early 1950s is, for the most part, a formalized approach to robust design based largely on statistical design of experiment theory.

Much of Taguchi's ideas about robust design directly addresses the problem of off-line quality control.[9] In this work, Taguchi calls variables that disturb the function of a product noise. Noises are classified as follows:

1. *Outer noise.* Outer noise consists of those variables that are operative during product use, such as temperature, humidity, input voltage, dust, external load, time rate of load application, and type of use.

2. *Inner noise, or deteriorating noise.* Inner noise consists of those properties or variables of a product that influence the benefits or function of the product and change during use of the product. Examples include loss of strength due to corrosion or fatigue, wear of mating parts, and deterioration due to operation at elevated temperature.

3. *Variational noise or between product noise.* Variational noise consists of those properties or variables of a product that influence the performance or function of the product and vary from product to product manufactured under the same specifications. Examples include variations in part dimensions, stackup tolerances, and calibration variations.

Functional variation due to deterioration and variation between products are actually, in Taguchi's view, two types of inner noise. The former is referred to as "timewise noise" and the latter as "spacewise noise." For Taguchi,

> Good functional quality means less functional variation due to inner and outer noise, and that the product always functions correctly under a wide range of conditions. Quality is measured by the degree of variation from the target value (design intent)—the nominal value or ideal value identified in the specification.[10]

In performing robust design, the design team seeks to minimize the effects caused by these noise sources. Several strategies for robust design are possible:

- Identify product concepts and process concepts that are inherently insensitive to variation and change (robust).
- For a given product design and process plan, determine the optimum values for the design parameters and process parameters to maximize robustness.
- Minimize the source and cause of variation.
- Provide design and process features that are variation tolerant.

TOOLS FOR PROCESS-DRIVEN DESIGN

Process-driven design seeks to ensure that parts and products are correctly designed to be produced using a particular production process or method. Design requirements for a given process are often stated in the form of design guidelines and rules of thumb. Typically, these guidelines are highly specialized for a given industry or particular process implementation or particular plant or particular equipment installation within a particular plant. Making the designer aware of these process requirements and constraints early in the design process, before concepts are finalized and lines are put irreversibly on paper, is a key goal of design for manufacture. Design tools that help

ensure product/process conformance and enable process-driven design can generally be classified either as process specific or facility specific. Each of these categories are discussed in the following sections.

Process-Specific Tools

Process-specific DFM has to do with the design of parts to be manufactured using particular methods or processes such as casting, forging, injection molding, and stamping. Typically, these tools facilitate systematic application of specialized process knowledge in the form of codified statements of design guidelines and rules to the design of parts to be made using a particular manufacturing process or method. Examples include design for casting, design for injection molding, and design for metal stamping.

This area of design for manufacture recognizes that manufacturing variables such as cost and life of dies, time and cost to build tools and fixtures, configuration and complexity of material flows, throughput of the process, process capability, and number of stations and workers required are often established and heavily influenced by detail design of the parts to be produced. It also recognizes that knowledge of the interaction between the product and process is crucial when the designer first puts lines on paper and that many designers, at this stage, must of necessity be more concerned with function than fabrication details. Hence, these tools generally seek to provide the designer with guidance as he or she makes these critical decisions and to help evaluate the suitability of the design once it has been specified.

Facility-Specific Tools

The second general category of activity involves the development of DFM tools that facilitate correct design of products intended to be manufactured using highly specialized or unique advanced manufacturing facilities. Such tools, which could be aptly described as "designer tool kits," provide design rules, physical examples and models, various design aids, and other specific information about a specialized manufacturing facility in a readily usable form to the designer.

To illustrate a facility-specific application, suppose a company has a flexible assembly system (FAS) that can be programmed to automatically assemble a variety of different subassemblies used in various products manufactured by the company. Such a system would likely consist of several stations designed to perform certain classes of assembly operations. Parts might be handled and inserted by robots using programmable "gripper engines" and fixtured using "flexible fixtures" specially designed for the FAS. For a particular subassembly to be built on a specific FAS facility of this kind, the subassembly and parts making up the subassembly must be correctly designed to be compatible with the assembly operations available, the work envelopes available, and the associated flexible tooling that interfaces the parts and in-process assembly to each station and to the material handling system. The "designer's tool kit" for such a FAS would provide needed process specific information to ensure conformance of the product design to the FAS requirements. It would also facilitate "what-if" optimization and experimentation with alternative design concepts and forms.

COMPUTER-AIDED DFM

A major barrier to DFM is usually time. Design and manu-

DFM PRINCIPLES

facturing engineers are typically operating under very tight schedules and are, therefore, reluctant to spend time learning and using DFM approaches. Computer-aided DFM helps simplify the effort and shortens the time required to implement DFM on a daily basis. Computer-aided DFM also enables the design team to consider a multitude of product/process alternatives easily and quickly. "What-if" optimization allows each alternative to be refined and fine tuned. Together, these capabilities greatly increase the probability of identifying the most desirable solutions during the early stages of design. When properly implemented and applied, computer-aided DFM has the potential to vastly improve quality of early product/process decisions and thereby enhance the design team's ability to do design for effective quality, cost, and delivery.

TRADITIONAL DESIGN METHODOLOGIES

In this section, some widely used, but more traditional design tools that can also offer assistance and insight into the problems of design for manufacture will be reviewed. They are group technology (GT), failure mode and effects analysis (FMEA), and value engineering.

Group Technology

Group technology (GT) is an approach to design and manufacturing that seeks to reduce manufacturing system information content by identifying and exploiting the sameness or similarity of parts based on their geometrical shape and/or similarities in their produciton process. GT is implemented by utilizing classification and coding systems needed to identify and understand part similarities and to establish parameters for action.

As a DFM tool, group technology can be used in a variety of ways to produce significant design efficiency and product performance and quality improvements. One of the most rapidly effective of these is the use of GT to help facilitate significant reductions in design time and effort. Often in design, it is easier to design new parts, tooling, and jigs rather than try to locate a similarly designed part.

The grouping of related parts into part families is the key to group technology implementation. The family of parts concept not only provides the information necessary to design individual parts in an incremental or modular manner, but also provides information for rationalizing process planning and forming the machine groups or cells that process the designated part family.

Failure Mode and Effects Analysis

Failure mode and effects analysis (FMEA) is an important design and manufacturing engineering tool intended to help prevent failures and defects from occurring and reaching the customer. It provides the design team with a methodical way of studying the causes and effects of failures before the design is finalized. Similarly, it helps manufacturing engineers identify and correct potential manufacturing and/or process failures. In performing an FMEA, the product and/or production system is examined for all the ways in which failure can occur. For each failure, an estimate is made of its effect on the total system, of its seriousness, and its occurrence frequency. Corrective actions are then identified to prevent failures from occurring or reaching the customer. FMEA asks the following principal questions:

1. How can each part or process conceivably fail?
2. What mechanisms might produce these modes of failure?
3. What would the effects be if the failures did occur?
4. Is the failure in the high-risk direction?
5. How is the failure detected?
6. What inherent provisions are provided in the design to compensate for the failure?
7. What corrective actions should be taken to prevent the failure?

In FMEA, function is defined as the task that a component, subsystem, or product must perform, stated in a way that is concise, exact, and easy to understand for all users. Functions are typically actions such as position, support, seal, retain, and lubricate. Failure is defined as the inability of a component/subsystem/system to perform the intended function (design intent).

Failure modes are the ways in which components/subsystems/system could fail to perform their intended functions. Typical failure modes would be fatigue, fracture, excessive deformation, buckling, leakage, fail to open, fails to close, and requires excessive force. Asking what could happen to cause loss of function is often an effective way to identify failure modes. Such questioning of a simple electrical on-off switch, for instance, leads to failure modes such as fails to switch on, fails to switch off, difficult or impossible to actuate, inadvertent switching, blows fuse, and produces electric shock. Other examples of failure modes could be listed as:

- Component parts: Broken, deformed, worn, or corroded.
- Assembly: Noise level, loose fit, tight fit, or imbalance.
- Process: Oversize, undersize, cracked, omitted, or improper finish.

For each failure mode, there are possible mechanisms and/or causes of failure. Identification of these are an important part of FMEA because it points the way to preventive or corrective action. Examples of design-caused failures include improper tolerancing, improper stress calculations or the use of wrong or unrealistic loads, wrong material specification, vibration, or improper fits. Process-caused failures include broken or worn tools, worn bearings, inadequate gating, insufficient cooling, heat treat shrinkage, improper locating, improper setup, inaccurate gaging, operator error, voltage drop, and pressure drop.

Value Engineering

Value engineering provides a systematic approach to evaluating design alternatives that is often very useful and may even point the way to innovative new design approaches or ideas. Also called value analysis, value control, or value management, value engineering utilizes a multidisciplinary team to analyze the functions provided by the product and the cost of each function. Based on results of the analysis, creative ways are sought to eliminate unnecessary features and functions and to achieve required functions at the lowest possible cost while optimizing manufacturability, quality, and delivery.

In value engineering, value is defined as a numerical ratio, the ratio of function, or performance to the cost. Because cost is a measure of effort, value of a product using this definition is seen to be simply the ratio of output (function or performance) to input (cost) commonly used in engineering studies. In a complicated product design or system, every component contributes both to the cost and the performance of the entire

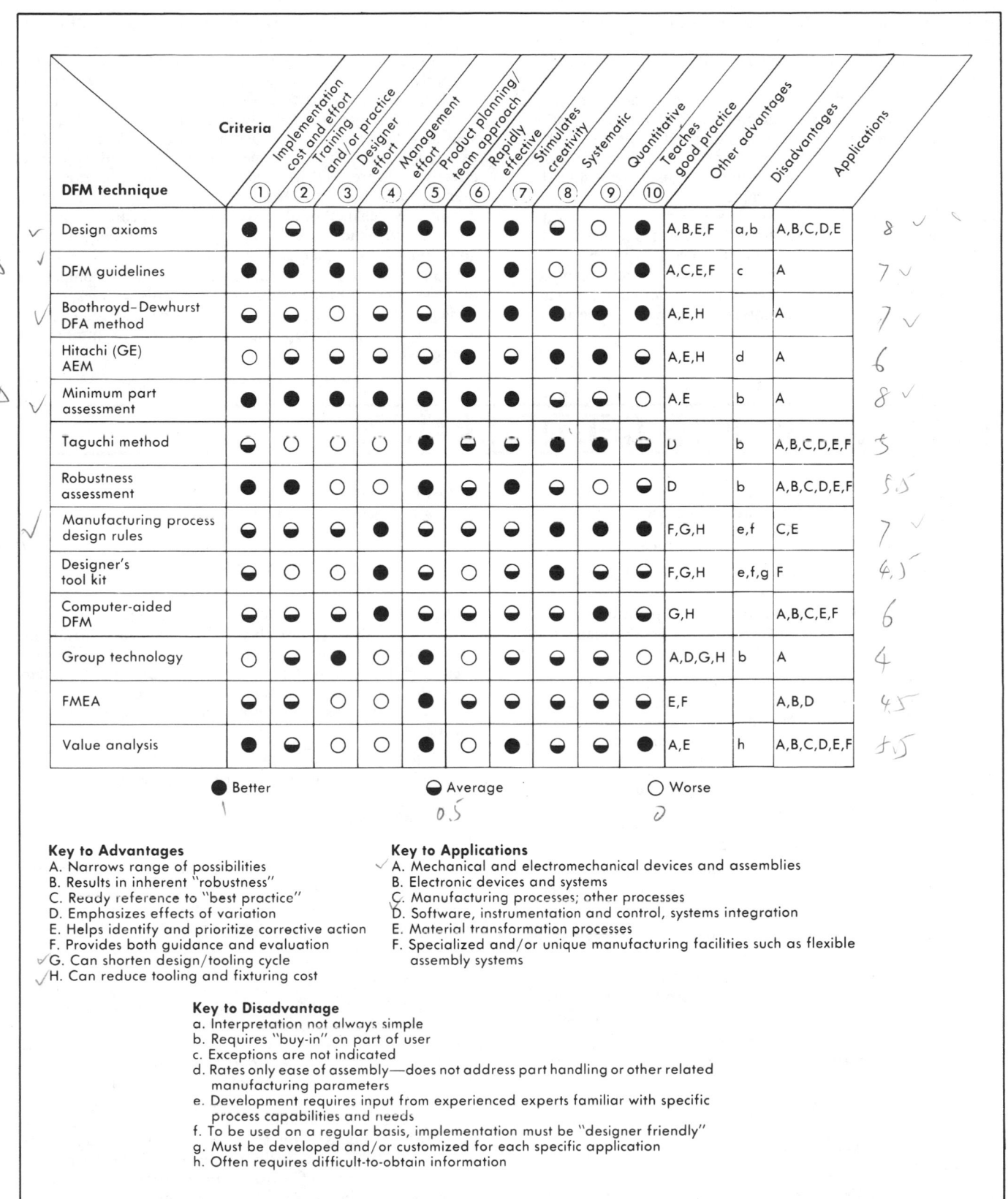

DFM technique	Implementation cost and effort (1)	Training and/or practice (2)	Designer effort (3)	Management effort (4)	Product planning/team approach (5)	Rapidly effective (6)	Stimulates creativity (7)	Systematic (8)	Quantitative (9)	Teaches good practice (10)	Other advantages	Disadvantages	Applications
Design axioms	●	◐	●	●	●	●	◐	○	●	●	A,B,E,F	a,b	A,B,C,D,E
DFM guidelines	●	●	●	○	●	●	○	○	●	●	A,C,E,F	c	A
Boothroyd–Dewhurst DFA method	◐	◐	○	◐	●	●	●	●	●	●	A,E,H		A
Hitachi (GE) AEM	○	◐	◐	◐	●	●	●	●	●	◐	A,E,H	d	A
Minimum part assessment	●	●	●	●	●	●	●	◐	◐	○	A,E	b	A
Taguchi method	◐	○	○	○	●	◐	◐	●	●	◐	D	b	A,B,C,D,E,F
Robustness assessment	●	●	○	○	◐	◐	●	◐	○	◐	D	b	A,B,C,D,E,F
Manufacturing process design rules	◐	◐	◐	●	◐	◐	◐	●	●	●	F,G,H	e,f	C,E
Designer's tool kit	◐	○	○	●	◐	○	◐	●	◐	◐	F,G,H	e,f,g	F
Computer-aided DFM	◐	◐	◐	◐	◐	◐	◐	◐	●	◐	G,H		A,B,C,E,F
Group technology	○	◐	●	○	●	○	◐	◐	◐	○	A,D,G,H	b	A
FMEA	◐	◐	◐	◐	●	◐	◐	◐	◐	◐	E,F		A,B,D
Value analysis	●	◐	○	○	●	○	●	◐	◐	●	A,E	h	A,B,C,D,E,F

● Better　　　　◒ Average　　　　○ Worse

Key to Advantages
A. Narrows range of possibilities
B. Results in inherent "robustness"
C. Ready reference to "best practice"
D. Emphasizes effects of variation
E. Helps identify and prioritize corrective action
F. Provides both guidance and evaluation
G. Can shorten design/tooling cycle
H. Can reduce tooling and fixturing cost

Key to Applications
A. Mechanical and electromechanical devices and assemblies
B. Electronic devices and systems
C. Manufacturing processes; other processes
D. Software, instrumentation and control, systems integration
E. Material transformation processes
F. Specialized and/or unique manufacturing facilities such as flexible assembly systems

Key to Disadvantage
a. Interpretation not always simple
b. Requires "buy-in" on part of user
c. Exceptions are not indicated
d. Rates only ease of assembly—does not address part handling or other related manufacturing parameters
e. Development requires input from experienced experts familiar with specific process capabilities and needs
f. To be used on a regular basis, implementation must be "designer friendly"
g. Must be developed and/or customized for each specific application
h. Often requires difficult-to-obtain information

Fig. 5-11 Comparison of DFM methodologies. (*Industrial Technology Institute*)

STANDARDS AND CERTIFICATION

system. The ratio of performance to cost of each component indicates the relative value of individual components. Obtaining the maximum performance per unit cost is the basic objective of value analysis.

For any expenditure or cost, two kinds of value are received: use (functional) value and esteem (prestige) value. Use value reflects the properties or qualities of a product or system that accomplish the intended work or service. To achieve maximum use value is to achieve the lowest possible cost in providing the performance function. Esteem value is composed of properties, features, or attractiveness that makes ownership of the product desirable. To achieve maximum esteem value is to achieve the lowest possible cost in providing the necessary appearance, attractiveness, and features that the customer wants. Examples of prestige items include surface finish, streamlining, packaging, decorative trim, ornamentation, attachments, special features, and adjustments.

COMPARISON OF DFM METHODOLOGIES

A number of different DFM methodologies and tools have been discussed. All of these techniques are effective and, if properly applied, can produce significant improvements in product quality and performance, manufacturing system productivity, and lifecycle cost. Ideally, these methodologies, as well as others that are just beginning to be developed (AI/expert systems), should all be implemented and applied to effectively address DFM needs. The question that arises for many managers is how to begin to do this in as effective a way as possible. Which methodologies can be implemented most easily and quickly? Which are most rapidly effective? What would be a good long-range implementation plan?

To help provide insight into these questions, a comparison of the various DFM methodologies and tools with respect to a variety of different criteria along with specific advantages, disadvantages, and appropriate applications are summarized in Fig. 5-11.

STANDARDS AND CERTIFICATION

The definitions of terms commonly used when dealing with the subject of standards and certification are as follows:

certification An offer of proof of conformance to a standard.

self-certification Certification offered by a party attesting to its own conformance to a standard.

third-party certification Certification offered by an independent party with respect to another's conformance to a standard.

consensus Substantial agreement reached by concerned interests according to the judgment of a duly-appointed authority, after a concerted attempt at resolving objections. Consensus implies much more than the concept of a simple majority, but not necessarily unanimity.

standard A standard is usually a written document that aims at achieving the optimum degree of order in a given context. It may define terms and establish definitions, set test methods and requirements, or specify performance and safety.

external standard A standard established by a national or international coordinating organizatiod; technical, trade, or professional group; or government agency.

internal standard A standard established by a company, organization, or agency for its own use.

international standard A standard developed under a process open to relevant bodies from all countries, adopted by an international standardizing/standards organization, and made available to the public.

mandatory standard A standard adopted by an authoritative body that requires compliance.

national standard A standard that is adopted by a national standards body and made available to the public.

voluntary standard A standard for which compliance is obtained by consent of the users.

standardization Establishing provisions for common and repeated use, aimed at the achievement of the optimum degree of order in a given context. Involves the processes of formulating, issuing, and implementing standards.

COMPANY STANDARDS PROGRAM

The nature and activity of the standards program depends on the company size. For a very small company, it is not unusual to find this responsibility as a part-time job split among a few individuals. In very large companies, there may be several specialized standards departments that coordinate activities to ensure that duplicate effort does not take place.

A good standards program has the following five distinct aspects:

1. Internal standards development.
2. (External) voluntary standards participation.
3. Certification.
4. Standardization programs (compliance).
5. Communications.

Prior to proceeding with these different aspects of a standards program, it is necessary to determine the cost and return (justification) of this activity and to ensure that qualified people are in positions of leadership for the program.

Justification

A vigorous standards program affords a competitive advantage to the modern manufacturer. It serves to minimize product cost as well as the overhead activity necessary to manufacture and bring the product to market. The manufacturer who minimizes the number of raw materials and purchased items in a product or process and makes use of standard industry items as well not only benefits from the lowest possible purchase cost, but also from the ability to obtain materials and other purchased items quickly from vendors. The net result is lower product cost and less investment for work-in-process inventory. It is important to keep in mind the distinction between standards and the process of standardization (or

Internal Standards Development

The distinction between a company with a good internal standards program and one with a bad program is quite simple. Questions to ask regarding an internal standards program are as follows:

1. Do the standards respond to the current needs of users?
2. Documentation.
   - Are the internal standards in written form?
   - Are the documents clear, concise, and well prepared?
3. Communication.
   - Are the standards available to the people who should use them?
   - Do designers have a loose-leaf book of standard company practices?
4. Control.
   - Does management control internal standards or are they "developed by custom"?
   - Does the company have a periodic review of internal standards?
   - Are the standards being used? If not, why not?

The existence of internal standards should not be equated with the assumption that the company has been "standardized." For example, a company may have an internal standard that specifies the requirements for machine screws and further mandates that all machine screws must meet this standard. The machine screw standard may be a variation of an external standard or one that was prepared in-house to suit particular requirements. Compliance with this standard is the measure of the company's degree of standardization.

adoption of a standard). The savings that come from standardization may be lost by a poor choice of standards.

Internal standards. Obviously, it is a good idea to standardize on fasteners such as screws, nuts, bolts, rivets, and eyelets. It would also be obvious to minimize the different varieties of these fasteners, as well as the materials and finishes. In this computer age, one should attempt to standardize on the computer hardware and software necessary to carry out business activities. These things can be quantified, costs assigned to the standardization activity, and benefits calculated to determine payback. This is usually true of most company internal standards activity.

For example, consider the steps required to standardize machine screws. Basically, the end use of each type and quantity of screw should be reviewed. If a screw is required, the least expensive one that will do the job should be used. The objective is to minimize the number of screws in inventory and the cost of this inventory. The proper screw standard must be chosen or developed. Product design changes may be required, so the engineering department will be involved. A bill of material for all screws, "where-used" lists, costs, and the ability to project the cost of a change to the screw will be needed.

External standards. External standards activity in areas that affect a company's business may proceed in a manner that appears satisfactory regardless of whether or not the company participates. Management may reason that good standards activity is not designed to show a competitive advantage to any particular manufacturer. While it is true that the purpose of standards activity is never to limit competition, competitors do not know another company's products and processes as well as that company does and may fail to include material that is important. As a general rule, companies should take a leadership role in the development of industry standards where they are a significant factor in that industry and should monitor standards development where they are an insignificant factor.

External standards activity affords opportunity to participate and influence standards that affect a company's product, operations, and business. It also is an image builder that pays off in long-term benefits. It indicates a "good corporate citizen" who is concerned with quality, technology, and safety—the kind of company customers want to deal with.

Organization and Personnel

In selecting personnel for a standards department, the overriding concern should be knowledge of the company's operations, products, and processes. Unfortunately, standards engineering is not included as a college-level course at technical institutions, with perhaps the exception of one or two. There are no undergraduate or graduate courses that will lead to recognition as a standards engineer for newly graduated technical personnel. Hence, the best source for the recruitment of a good standards engineer from within the company is a person who has the knowledge of the company and products. It is also possible to hire an experienced standards engineer or contract with a consultant to set up a standards program and provide training.

External Standards Development

As indicated earlier, the choice of whether or not a manufacturer should participate in a voluntary standards program is a long-range issue. Before a decision can be made as to participation and before a budget can be developed, it is necessary to know what standards affect the company's operation. Development of this type of list will usually lead to the identification of an incredible number of industry, trade, and professional organizations that develop standards affecting every facet of the business. To aid in this identification, the reader should review NBS Special Publication 681, "Standards Activities of Organizations in the United States." Some of the developers of industrial standards are listed in Table 5-1.

TABLE 5-1
Developers of Industrial Standards

	No. of Standards
American Society for Testing and Materials	8400
Society of Automotive Engineers	4600
Aerospace Industries Association	2900
American National Standards Institute	1900*
Association of American Railways	1350
Factory Mutual	600
American Society of Mechanical Engineers	590
Electronic Industries Association	550
Institute of Electrical and Electronics Engineers	550
Underwriters' Laboratories	520
American Railway Engineers Association	400
American Petroleum Institute	350
Technical Association of the Pulp and Paper Industry	270
Industry	260
National Fire Protection Association	220

* Copyright assigned to the American National Standards Institute.

CHAPTER 5

STANDARDS AND CERTIFICATION

Determining whether to participate in the development of external standards is straightforward. As in the development of internal standards, the company should make a chart listing its component parts, products, processes, procedures, markets, and means of distribution. For each of the general classifications on the list, a search should be made for a particular standard that might affect that item, along with the organization that sponsors that standard. This information should be listed in a second column on the chart. In a third column, the relative importance of that standard should be entered using a

CERTIFICATION

A manufacturer may be asked for proof that a certain product complies with specific standards and that the product is suitable for the customer's intended application. This proof is referred to as certification. Certification may be either self-certification or third-party certification.

With self-certification, the manufacturer sends a letter on company letterhead to the customer stating that the product in question does indeed comply with the requirements of a specific standard(s). Sometimes this letter will have to be notarized and signed by a company officer. It may also be appropriate to include test data showing compliance, references to particular construction requirements, or drawings. Enough information should be included with the self-certification letter, and it should be worded in the proper form, to satisfy the needs of the customer.

Third-party certification brings someone else into the act. This is usually an independent testing laboratory or agency such as Underwriters Laboratories Inc. (UL), the Canadian Standards Association, or even a government agency. For example, UL will accept applications to investigate products; if the investigation and testing shows a product to be in compliance with the applicable standards, UL will authorize the manufacturer to use the UL Listing Mark as evidence (third-party certification) of this fact.

The UL procedure starts with an application and submittal of samples of a product or component to UL for investigation. UL will determine whether or not the product complies with its requirements. In most cases, these requirements will be published in an existing UL standard. UL produces product standards in response to perceived need, generally three or more clients with products in a specific area. When a standard does not exist, a "desk drawer" standard may be put together by UL staff detailing construction requirements and tests that will be necessary to investigate the product for safety and compliance with NEC requirements and other installation standards.

COMMUNICATIONS

An essential part of communications with respect to a program of standards and certification is to assure that management has the information needed to authorize and control the activity. "Reporting up" means answering the following questions:

1. What's being done?
   * Internal standards.
   * External standards.
   * Standardization programs.
   * Status of certification.

2. Why is it being done?
   * Justification.
3. Who's involved?
   * List programs and active personnel.
   * Time involvement.
4. How much is it costing?
   * Original budgets.
   * Performance to budget.
5. Where's the return?
   * Cost savings.
   * Market penetration.
   * Corporate image.
   * Effect on operations.

"Reporting down" is equally important. Management must be prepared to perform its traditional duties as follows:

1. Set policy and give clear direction.
2. Set goals, both internal and external.
3. Authorize activities.
4. Delegate responsibility.
5. Evaluate performance and hold personnel accountable for their work.
6. Offer support and leadership.

References

1. J. Shigley and L. Mitchell, *Mechanical Engineering Design*, 4th ed. (New York: McGraw-Hill Book Co., 1983).
2. H.W. Stoll, "A Design Backwards Approach to Product Optimization," presented at the *SME Simultaneous Engineering Conference*, held June 1, 1987 (Dearborn, MI: Society of Manufacturing Engineers).
3. N.P. Suh, A.C. Bell, and D.C. Gossard, "On an Axiomatic Approach to Manufacturing and Manufacturing Systems," *ASME Journal of Engineering for Industry*, vol. 100, no. 2 (May 1978).
4. M. Yasuhara and N.P. Suh, "A Quantitative Analysis of Design Based on Axiomatic Approach," *Computer Applications in Manufacturing Systems*, ASME Production Engineering Div. Publication, PED-vol. 2 (1980).
5. H.W. Stoll, "Design for Manufacture: An Overview," ASME Applied Mechanics Reviews, vol. 39, no. 9 (September 1986).
6. M.M. Andreasen, S. Kahler, and T. Lund, *Design for Assembly* (Bedford, UK: IFS Publications, Ltd., 1983).
7. S.N. Dwivedi and B.R. Klein, "Design for Manufacturability Makes Dollars and Sense," *CIM Review* (Spring 1986).
8. G. Boothroyd and P. Dewhurst, *Design for Assembly—A Designers Handbook*, Department of Mechanical Engineering, University of Massachusetts-Amherst (1983).
9. G. Taguchi and W. Yuin, *Introduction to Off-Line Quality Control* (Nagaya, Japan: Central Japan Quality Control Association, 1979).
10. *Ibid.*

PLANNING AND ANALYSIS OF MANUFACTURING INVESTMENTS

Manufacturing firms are companies created by people to facilitate the manufacture of goods. While these firms have many social effects, they are for the most part created and managed to increase the wealth of the owner or owners. This is true whether the firm is a small garage shop owned by one individual producing a single, simple product or a world-wide conglomerate owned by thousands of shareholders producing a wide variety of different products in factories throughout the world.

The way manufacturing firms increase the wealth of their owners is first to invest in resources that are used to make products. The resources generally include raw material and machines that are purchased, as well as people who are paid salaries and wages. The resources are then used to produce products that are sold in various markets to people and firms to whom the product has a value greater than the cost of the resources used to make it. Thus, the manufacturing firm can sell the product for a price greater than the cost of the resources used and earn a profit. Ordinarily, the investments must be made and the goods produced some time before any money is received from their sale.

Because this is the main thrust of most manufacturing firms, the analysis of investments, their costs, and the benefits that are likely to accrue to firms and their owners is an important part of managing these firms, and selling in U.S. and world markets.

INVESTMENT ANALYSIS AS PART OF A STRATEGIC DECISION

This section briefly describes the business planning process, with particular emphasis on the relationship between business planning and manufacturing investment. It is the intent of this section to broaden the approach of the investment analyst from the financial analysis of specific investments as isolated opportunities for cost reduction to the analysis of investments relative to the strategic plan of the business with the objective of meeting the functional requirements demanded of the manufacturing system to respond to the strategic needs of the business. In so doing, it is necessary to relate the investment being considered to the entire manufacturing system as it exists at the time, and as it is likely to evolve in the future as products, markets, and manufacturing technologies evolve.

BUSINESS STRATEGY

Historically, capital budgets have begun in many firms as the list of capital investments requested by operations for the coming year. This list was reviewed and revised at various levels and ultimately became the capital budget for the firm. These investments in total represented an implicit strategy of some sort that might or might not have been internally consistent. Very often the implicit strategy was to continue doing whatever the firm had been doing in the past.

While this may have been adequate in a simpler and less competitive world, in recent years firms have found that their need to compete more aggressively requires an explicit statement of objectives to be achieved, a definition of the strategy intended to achieve the objectives, and a plan to put the strategy into action, usually covering a period of several years. The capital budget in these firms has become a part of this plan.

MANUFACTURING STRATEGY

Just as managers once relied on implicit business strategies, they also tended to oversimplify their manufacturing requirements by assuming that such demands could be defined in a simple phrase such as "efficient manufacturing" or "high productivity." There is growing recognition that the diverse demands placed on manufacturing require a more thoughtful consideration of the functionality of the manufacturing system if it is to be responsive to the strategic needs of the firm. Thus, once the business strategy is established, the next task is to prepare a manufacturing strategy that broadly defines the firm's manufacturing function in a way that is consistent with and complementary to the business strategy. While the firm's business strategy is based on the characteristics of the industry and on the position of the firm in the U.S. and world markets, the manufacturing strategy is based on the requirements of the business strategy for manufacturing and the ability of the manufacturing system to respond. It is, in effect, the trace of the business strategy on the manufacturing plane. It deals with the following internal manufacturing issues:

- What are the possible collections of product families and variants of each family that the

system should be capable of handling at a given time?
● At what rate should the system produce good product?
● How readily should the system be changed over
—from one variant to another within a family?
—from one current family to another?
—from the current set of families to some range of possible future families?
● What should the firm's involvement be over the product lifecycle?
—Engineering models.
—Production prototypes.
—Pilot production.
—Production.
—Aftermarket.
● What should be the process span of the firm?

● What is the best organization for manufacturing?
—Multi-plant or single plant? If multi-plant, by geography, product, or process? If single plant, how to obtain focus?
—Relationship to marketing, engineering, and other functions.
—Ongoing employee involvement programs.

These are the internal issues that define the relationship of manufacturing to the business strategy of the firm and establish the functional requirements of the manufacturing system. While they are generally proposed by manufacturing, they relate closely to other functions, as well as to the overall management of the firm. Thus, they should have the agreement of other functional areas as well as approval and support of top management of the firm.

DYNAMIC MODELING OF MANUFACTURING SYSTEMS

If alternative systems for manufacturing are being considered to achieve the objectives of the firm, and these alternative systems have different characteristics, require different investments, and are likely to result in different cost patterns, it is helpful to define the alternative systems in such a way that as many as possible of the important characteristics of the systems be captured prior to making the investment. If the systems are defined in terms of a dynamic modeling technique, they are likely to display the tangible effects of the investment in terms of these important characteristics. This will allow the manufacturing engineer to be more thorough in evaluating the costs and benefits of each alternative than if he or she had to consider many of them as "intangibles." In turn, thorough evaluation facilitates a better answer as to which alternative will best meet the needs of the company.

As a first step in making modeling of manufacturing systems more feasible, three somewhat more specialized types of computer programs have been developed. One path has used queueing theory and modeled the manufacturing system as a network of servers with queues of work in process at each server. A second has developed general simulation languages, such as GPSS and SIMSCRIPT, that simulate the discrete events that occur in a manufacturing network on a timed basis. A third path, stochastic activity network software, has been developed permitting the modeling of communication and control systems in conjunction with manufacturing; METASAN, from the Industrial Technology Institute, is one of these packages. These three types of modeling techniques have been found to be useful and are widely used. The disadvantage has been that they require special training, and few manufacturing engineers find it feasible to maintain their professional standards in both manufacturing and programming skills. Some of these disadvantages have been overcome in the last few years by general manufacturing simulation software such as SLAM II from Pritsker & Associates and SIMAN from Systems Modeling.

ROUGH-CUT ESTIMATION OF SYSTEM PERFORMANCE

For rough-cut estimation of the performance of an existing or proposed system, available programs based on queueing network theory allow the manufacturing engineer to check the feasibility of a manufacturing system without a great deal of effort. A queueing network conceives of a manufacturing system as a collection of servers and waiting lines at each of those servers, with movement of entities from the waiting line of a server into the server and then into the waiting line of the next server in the network or to completion. In a queueing system, there are arrivals to the system, according to a particular distribution of time between arrivals, and there are operations each with a particular distribution of performance time. Parts arrive at receiving and then go to a waiting line, a station, on to another waiting line, to another station, and so forth according to a specified operation routing until they are complete and ready for shipment. Queueing models are typically used to (1) reduce the risk of expending time and effort in simulating an infeasible manufacturing system and (2) assist in establishing the design specifications for a system that will subsequently be simulated.

Queueing models are useful in dealing with the following issues:

● How a product redesign may affect a manufacturing process.
● How a process may be designed so as to accommodate future increases in production requirements.
● How a process may be designed so as to accommodate future production of additional designs.
● Whether a synchronous or nonsynchronous material handling process is desirable in a particular manufacturing system.
● Where major maintenance emphasis should be placed in a manufacturing system.
● How a redesigned product and process might best be phased in.
● Where defect detection capabilities might best be placed.
● How job redesign might increase labor productivity.

However, queueing models yield only average values, and provide no information on high or low values. Work in process, for example, may yield identical averages for two systems, but be very stable for one and fluctuate greatly for the other. Thus, queueing models arc rarely used for a final choice among alternative manufacturing systems. Nonetheless, their value is great, relative to the time and effort required, as a way of screening undesirable alternatives prior to performing a simulation analysis.

HIGH-RESOLUTION ESTIMATION OF SYSTEM PERFORMANCE

Simulation models are similar to queueing models in that they require input data about the parts to be produced, machine groups, and processes, and in that they yield information about

---

XCELL: Cellular Simulation System

Results of run of factory named "FACTORY"

Current time is: 2000.00
Period started: 1500.00

Receiving areas:
  rl
    Current period
      Units started: 366
      Units/unit time: 0.73
    Cumulative
      Units started: 1452
      Units/unit time: 0.73

Shipping areas:
  SHP
    Current period
      Units finished: 343
      Units/unit time: 0.69
    Cumulative
      Units finished: 1326
      Units/unit time: 0.66
  SCR
    Current period
      Units finished: 40
      Units/unit time: 0.08
    Cumulative
      Units finished: 139
      Units/unit time: 0.07

Workcenters:
  MIL
    Current period
      Current state
        Busy until 2000.03 on part "B"
      Percent of time busy: 73.69
      Percent of time in set-up: 10.00
    Cumulative
      Percent of time busy: 72.75
      Percent of time in set-up: 10.00
  GRD
    Current period
      Current state
        Busy until 2000.06 on part "B"
      Percent of time busy: 70.40
      Percent to time in set-up: 10.00
    Cumulative
      Percent of time busy: 69.66
      Percent of time in set-up: 10.00

DRL
  Current period
    Current state
      Busy until 2000.15 on part "B"
    Percent of time busy: 69.61
    Percent of time in set-up: 10.00
  Cumulative
    Percent of time busy: 68.28
    Percent of time in set-up: 10.00

TAP
  Current period
    Current state
      Being repaired
    Percent of time busy: 70.24
    Percent of timc in set-up: 10.00
  Cumulative
    Percent of time busy: 67.70
    Percent of time in set-up: 10.00

Buffers:
  b1
    Current period
      Current stock: 10
      Max stock this period: 10
      Avg stock this period: 5.23
    Cumulative
      Maximum stock level: 10
      Avg stock to date: 6.36
  b2
    Current period
      Current stock: 0
      Max stock this period: 10
      Avg stock this period: 5.67
    Cumulative
      Maximum stock level: 10
      Avg stock to date: 6.41
  b3
    Current period
      Current stock: 3
      Max stock this period: 10
      Avg stock this period: 5.11
    Cumulative
      Maximum stock level: 10
      Avg stock to date: 5.31

Maintenance facilities:
  m1
    Number of repairmen: 1
    Number currently available: 0

Fig. 6-1 Summary printout of simple factory operation simulated on XCELL. (*Industrial Technology Institute*)

CHAPTER 6

DYNAMIC MODELING

the physical operation of the factory. The difference is that they move specific parts through a defined manufacturing process according to a clock instead of performing calculations based on queueing theory. Thus, a simulation model keeps track of time, and when an operation performed on a part by a machine is finished, the part moves on to the queue for the next operation. Randomness can be built into the system with specification of service times, machine failures and repairs, queue sizes, and defects in terms of statistical distributions. Because the clock moves much more quickly than a conventional clock, it is possible to gain a great deal of experience running a manufacturing system very quickly, thereby obtaining a large sample of the random events that occur during the actual operation of the factory.

The nature of a discrete event simulation is such that output data include full information on the sample of events during the run rather than just averages. Thus, if one wishes to know storage requirements for a bank of in-process inventory, simulation provides not only average work in process, but the full distribution that occurred during the run. Further, with a discrete event simulation, one is able to estimate the effect on other production variables of restricting the size of the work-in-process bank to a specified maximum. This, of course, gives better and more useful information for estimating the effects of investment in new machinery and inventories. The price that must be paid for this information is time. The amount and accuracy of data requirements are also greater; the time to obtain the data and structure the model, although greatly reduced from earlier days, is still much more than that which is needed for a queueing model.

Several programs, such as XCELL (a program offered by Pritsker & Associates, Inc. of West Lafayette, IN), are available for high-resolution estimation of system performance. XCELL operates in the following six modes:

1. Design, for model construction.
2. Run, for running the model.
3. File manager, for storage and retrieval of models.
4. Analysis, for checking out models.
5. New factory, for clearing the workspace.
6. Change display, for altering scale, position, and contents of screen.

The model is run in periods of time units. The default value is 500 units. During the run mode, the user may view events during a simulation run on the screen displaying the various elements of the factory. Workcenters are shown as operating, idle because of shortages of material upstream, blocked because of excess material downstream, in set-up, or in repair. Quantity of material is shown in each buffer. Cumulative receipts and shipments are shown below receiving and shipping areas. Alternatively, during the run mode, the user may view a Gantt chart summarizing operation of the factory or concentrate on a specific buffer and view a plot of the contents of that buffer.

Output of the model is in two forms. The run may be paused, and the screen image at a particular point may be printed. This may be the trace, the Gantt chart, or the buffer plot. Alternatively, a summary chart may be printed. The information obtained from an XCELL run provides the user with the capacity of the system under specified operating conditions, work-in-process inventory requirements, and can be used to determine the sensitivity of the system to changes in conditions.

The summary printout of this simple run is shown in Fig. 6-1 with the trace at the end of the run corresponding to the summary in Fig. 6-1 shown in Fig. 6-2. In a real-life situation, the program would not be used for a single simple line such as this, but would be used to model alternative systems for accomplishing a specified task.

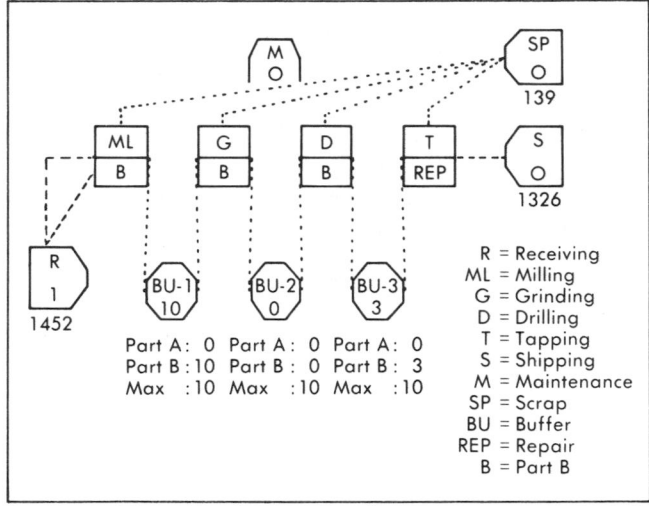

Fig. 6-2 Trace of factory operation at the end of the run.
(*Industrial Technology Institute*)

ECONOMIC TRANSLATION

A simulation model, such as the XCELL program, can keep actual tallies of parts that traverse a particular process link. The implication of such differences in types of performance measures among tools for modeling manufacturing systems is that economic translation formulas must be specific to the system modeling tool. However, neither basic concerns of the manufacturing engineer about the cost accumulation in a system configuration nor the generic contributors (such as labor and materials) to this accumulation vary much by system modeling tool. These basic concerns and manufacturing-generic contributors are the focus of this section on economic translation.

SELECTION OF THE BENCHMARK ALTERNATIVE

Three basic situations for manufacturing investment are the following: the "brownfield" where an existing plant is to be enhanced; the "greenfield" where a new plant is to be constructed for purposes of providing essential capacity; and the "greenhouse" where an experimental facility is to be built for purposes of acquiring valuable experience with new manufacturing technology and/or new product technology. Construction of a benchmark case is quite different from one of these situations to another.

INCREMENTAL COMPARISON OF ALTERNATIVES

All scenarios will be evaluated against the benchmark alternative. The procedure for deciding between two alternatives is through incremental analysis. That is, the incremental difference is evaluated to decide which alternative to choose. The economic spreadsheet reflects the difference between the benchmark and an alternative on a line-item basis over the planning horizon for the analysis (see Fig. 6-3). The example in Table 6-1 looks at just the equipment costs for two alternatives.

It is the last line, the difference, that is used in the economic comparison of the two alternatives. Each line item on the economic spreadsheet must reflect the difference between a benchmark and proposed alternative. When there is no difference between the alternatives, the line item will contain zeros. For example, if one assumes that sales will remain constant regardless of which alternative is implemented, the incremental sales revenue line will be 0.

The Economic Spreadsheet

An economic spreadsheet of incremental cash flows is provided in Fig. 6-3. This spreadsheet identifies a "shopping list" of line items that might be considered for the economic analysis of manufacturing systems. Each line item reflects the incremental economic impact of introducing the alternative vs. using the benchmark alternative. Certain line items may not be applicable to some evaluations, while others may need to be added. Therefore, the actual spreadsheet for a given analysis must be "customized" for the given technology under consideration.

The timeline across the top of the spreadsheet begins with year 0 (the time of the first expenditure for the system) and runs through the expected life of the system. Generally, the life of the system is determined by the product(s) it is expected to make. Any sequence of changes that the system goes through while producing the product should be captured within the spreadsheet. This might include, for example, technology upgrades and equipment enhancements. If the life of the benchmark is different than the alternative, then an adjustment is required so that each scenario meets the functional requirements over the entire life of the system.

Also along the top of the spreadsheet is a line showing an estimate for the annual inflation rate for each year on the spreadsheet. This line is used as an aid with some of the line items to estimate future-year cash flows. For example, new product revenue may perhaps be easily estimated for year 1. After year 1, if the level of output is expected to be constant, then one could assume that the revenue from future sales will increase with inflation. By stating an expected inflation line, values in the spreadsheet can use the line to adjust future sales revenue. There may be other types of annual adjustment assumptions to make. The following are a few commonly used adjustment factors and some line items that might use the factor:

- Inflation—sales revenue, labor rates, material costs, replacement equipment and tooling.
- Learning curve—to reflect the start-up inefficiencies of new technologies, level of output, labor hours, scrap/rework rates.
- Controlled level of capacity—to reflect the controlled level of activity in the system, level of output, labor hours, material usage.

Explanation of Spreadsheet Categories

An advantage of performing incremental analysis is that when a particular line item is constant for all of the alternatives being evaluated, the incremental line on the spreadsheet is 0. Therefore, the value (revenue or expense) of the line item does not have to be computed explicitly for any of the alternatives. This is important to keep in mind when constructing a specific list of line items for incremental analysis; only line items with non-zero incremental entries over the life of the system are used.

The major spreadsheet categories are revenues, direct product expenses, capital equipment expenses, and indirect expenses.

Revenues. Revenues can come from several sources. Revenues from operations result from product sales and are simply the number of units sold times the selling price. If an economic analysis is being performed for a "piece" of a manufacturing system that doesn't actually produce a final product, then some other value of output must be determined (assuming the level of output of the two alternatives is different). For example, when the system produces a subcomponent, the value of that subcomponent must be determined. Its value can be determined by one of the following ways:

- Its market value if the subcomponent were sold on the open market.
- The price that would have to be paid to an outside contractor if the subcomponent were outsourced.
- A percentage of the final product's market value. The percentage could represent the portion of subcomponent cost (to produce) to the total cost to produce the final product. Therefore, the margin of the final product would be used for the margin of the subcomponent.

If the alternative being analyzed has no market effects, then revenue will be unchanged. That is, regardless of the alternative finally selected, there will be no impact on revenue. The objective of the analysis then is minimization of costs.

Other revenue line items shown in Fig. 6-3 might occur depending on the system alternatives. For example, plant sale might occur if one alternative uses an existing facility and another one does not. Therefore, the alternative that does not use the existing facility might provide revenue through the sale of that facility, although this revenue could be offset by teardown costs. The expense of purchasing a new facility will be captured under expenses. The other revenue line items are used for similar purposes.

Direct product expenses. Direct product expenses include direct labor and material, other direct product costs (outside services), and inventory holding costs. Figure 6-3 shows these costs broken down by product for good, scrap, and rework parts; however, this detail may not be necessary for the financial

TABLE 6-1
Comparison of Equipment Costs for Two Alternatives

	Year 0	Year 1	Year 2	Year 3
Alternative A:	$1000	$800	$800	$500
Benchmark:	700	700	700	700
Alternative A minus benchmark:	$ 300	$100	$100	($200)

(*Industrial Technology Institute*)

ECONOMIC TRANSLATION

End of year:	0	1	2	3	4	5
Annual inflation:	0.0%	0.0%	5.0%	5.0%	5.0%	5.0%
	Jun-87	Jun-88	Jun 89	Jun-90	Jun-91	May-92
I. REVENUES						
FROM OPERATIONS						
A. Existing product sales	$0	$0	$0	$0	$0	$0
B. New product sales	$0	$20,000,000	$21,000,000	$22,050,000	$23,152,500	$24,310,125
C. Other sales	$0	$0	$0	$0	$0	$0
OTHER REVENUES						
D. Capital equipment revenue						
— Plant sale	$0	$0	$0	$0	$0	$0
— Plant lease	$0	$0	$0	$0	$0	$0
— Equipment sale	$0	$0	$0	$0	$0	$0
— Equipment lease	$0	$0	$0	$0	$0	$0
— Computer sale	$0	$0	$0	$0	$0	$0
— Computer lease	$0	$0	$0	$0	$0	$0
— Other sale	$0	$0	$0	$0	$0	$0
— Other lease	$0	$0	$0	$0	$0	$0
E. Miscellaneous revenue						
— Miscellaneous	$0	$0	$0	$0	$0	$0
TOTAL REVENUES	$0	$20,000,000	$21,000,000	$22,050,000	$23,152,500	$24,310,125
II. DIRECT PRODUCT EXPENSES						
A. Product labor & material & outside services						
Product A						
— Good production						
— Labor	$0	$2,000,000	$2,100,000	$2,205,000	$2,315,250	$2,431,013
— Material	$0	$1,000,000	$1,050,000	$1,102,500	$1,157,625	$1,215,506
— Scrap production						
— Labor	$0	$225,000	$236,250	$248,063	$260,466	$273,489
— Material	$0	$112,500	$118,125	$124.031	$130,233	$136,744
— Rework production						
— Labor	$0	$475,000	$498,750	$523,688	$549,872	$577,365
— Material	$0	$237,500	$249,375	$261,844	$274,936	$288,683
— Inventory holding	$0	$3,500	$3,675	$3,859	$4,052	$4,254
— Other production costs	$0	$0	$0	$0	$0	$0
Product B						
— Good production						
— Labor	$0	$2,500,000	$2,625,000	$2,756,250	$2,894,063	$3,038,766
— Material	$0	$1,250,000	$1,132,500	$1,378,125	$1,447,031	$1,519,383
— Scrap production						
— Labor	$0	$250,000	$262,500	$275,625	$289,406	$303,877
— Material	$0	$125,000	$131,250	$137,813	$144,703	$151,938
— Rework production						
— Labor	$0	$400,000	$420,000	$441,000	$463,050	$486,203
— Material	$0	$200,000	$210,000	$220,500	$231,525	$243,101
— Inventory holding	$0	$2,900	$3,045	$3,197	$3,357	$3,525
— Other production costs	$0	$0	$0	$0	$0	$0
Total product labor & Material & outside services	$0	$8,781,400	$9,220,470	$9,681,494	$10,165,568	$10,673,847
B. Other product material & labor & outside services	$0	$0	$0	$0	$0	$0
TOTAL DIRECT PRODUCT EXPENSE	$0	$8,781,400	$9,220,470	$9,681,494	$10,165,568	$10,673,847

Fig. 6-3 Incremental cash-flow comparison between a benchmark case and a proposed alternative. (*Industrial Technology Institiute*)

End of year:	0	1	2	3	4	5
Annual inflation:	0.0%	0.0%	5.0%	5.0%	5.0%	5.0%
	Jun-87	Jun-88	Jun 89	Jun-90	Jun-91	May-92

III. CAPITAL EQUIPMENT EXPENSES

A. Purchases

	0	1	2	3	4	5
— Plant	$2,000,000	$150,000	$0	$0	$0	$0
— Equipment	$1,000,000	$100,000	$50,000			
— Nonperishable tooling	$50,000	$5,000	$2,500	$0	$0	$0
— Computer hardware	$225,000	$22,500	$23,625	$24,806	$26,047	$27,349
— Computer software	$75,000	$10,000	$10,500	$11,025	$11,576	$12,155
— Other	$33,000	$5,000	$5,250	$5,513	$5,788	$6,078

B. Improvements

	0	1	2	3	4	5
— Plant	$0	$0	$0	$0	$0	$0
— Equipment & tooling	$0	$0	$0	$0	$0	$0
— Nonperishable tooling	$0	$0	$0	$0	$0	$0
— Computer hardware	$0	$0	$0	$0	$0	$0
— Computer software	$0	$0	$0	$0	$0	$0
— Other	$0	$0	$0	$0	$0	$0
Total capital equipment purchases & improvements	$3,383,000	$292,500	$91,875	$41,344	$43,411	$45,581

C. Leases

	0	1	2	3	4	5
— Plant	$0	$0	$0	$0	$0	$0
— Equipment	$0	$0	$0	$0	$0	$0
— Nonperishable tooing	$0	$0	$0	$0	$0	$0
— Computer hardware	$10,000	$10,000	$10,500	$11,025	$11,576	$12,155
— Computer software	$10,000	$10,000	$10,500	$11,025	$11,576	$12,155
— Other	$5,500	$5,500	$5,775	$6,064	$6,367	$6,685
Total capital equipment lease expense	$25,500	$25,500	$26,775	$28,114	$29,519	$30,995
TOTAL CAPITAL EQUIPMENT EXPENSES	$3,408,500	$318,000	$118,650	$69,458	$72,930	$76,577

D. Manufacturing supplies

Existing product

	0	1	2	3	4	5
— Perishable tooling	$0	$0	$0	$0	$0	$0
— Fixtures	$0	$0	$0	$0	$0	$0
— Other	$0	$0	$0	$0	$0	$0

New product

	0	1	2	3	4	5
— Perishable tooling	$130,000	$260,000	$273,000	$286,650	$300,983	$316,032
— Fixtures	$150,000	$300,000	$315,000	$330,750	$347,288	$364,652
— Other	$0	$0	$0	$0	$0	$0
Total indirect manufacturing supplies	$280,000	$560,000	$588,000	$617,400	$648,270	$680,684

GENERAL & ADMINISTRATIVE

E. Selling expenses

	0	1	2	3	4	5
— Freight out	$0	$275,000	$288,750	$303,188	$318,347	$334,264
— Sales salaries	$0	$0	$0	$0	$0	$0
— Sales commission	$0	$0	$0	$0	$0	$0
— Advertising	$0	$0	$0	$0	$0	$0
— Travel	$0	$0	$0	$0	$0	$0
— Other	$0	$0	$0	$0	$0	$0
Total selling expenses	$0	$275,000	$288,750	$303,188	$318,347	$334,264

Fig. 6-3—*Continued*

ECONOMIC TRANSLATION

End of year:	0	1	2	3	4	5
Annual inflation:	0.0%	0.0%	5.0%	5.0%	5.0%	5.0%
	Jun-87	Jun-88	Jun 89	Jun-90	Jun-91	May-92
F. Business Office						
— Salaries						
— Product managers	$87,500	$175,000	$183,750	$192,938	$202,584	$212,714
— Purchasing	$112,500	$225,000	$236,250	$248,063	$260,466	$273,489
— Expediting	$62,500	$125,000	$131,250	$137,813	$144,703	$151,938
— Computer support	$87,500	$175,000	$183,750	$192,938	$202,584	$212,714
— Office	$42,500	$85,000	$89,250	$93,713	$98,398	$103,318
— Other	$44,000	$88,000	$92,400	$97,020	$101,871	$106,965
— Insurance	$225,000	$225,000	$236,250	$248,063	$260,466	$273,489
— Telephone	$125,000	$125,000	$131,250	$137,813	$144,703	$151,938
— Accounting & legal	$200,000	$200,000	$210,000	$220,500	$231,525	$243,101
— Bad debts	$0	$0	$0	$0	$0	$0
— Interest	$0	$0	$0	$0	$0	$0
— Other G & A	$100,000	$1,500,00	$1,575,000	$1,653,750	$1,736,438	$1,823,259
Total business office	$1,086,500	$2,923,000	$3,069,150	$3,222,608	$3,383,738	$3,552,925
G. Miscellaneous						
— Heat & electricity	$275,000	$275,000	$288,750	$303,188	$318,347	$334,264
— Supplies	$55,000	$55,000	$57,750	$60,638	$63,669	$66,853
— Repair & maintenance parts	$400,000	$400,000	$420,000	$441,000	$463,050	$486,203
— Vehicle expense	$0	$0	$0	$0	$0	$0
— Training equipment	$120,000	$120,000	$126,000	$132,300	$138,915	$145,861
— Other	$0	$250,000	$262,500	$275,625	$289,406	$303,877
Total indirect miscellaneous	$850,000	$1,100,000	$1,155,000	$1,212,750	$1,273,388	$1,337,057
TOTAL INDIRECT EXPENSES	$3,759,000	$8,143,000	$8,550,150	$8,977,658	$9,426,540	$9,897,867
IV. INDIRECT EXPENSES MANUFACTURING						
A. Product warranty						
— Existing product	$0	$0	$0	$0	$0	$0
— New product	$0	$200,000	$210,000	$220,500	$231,525	$243,101
Total product warranty	$0	$200,000	$210,000	$220,500	$231,525	$243,101
B. Product liability						
New product						
— Insurance	$0	$0	$0	$0	$0	$0
— Expected loss	$0	$0	$0	$0	$0	$0
Existing product						
— Insurance	$0	$0	$0	$0	$0	$0
— Expected loss	$0	$0	$0	$0	$0	$0
Total product liability	$0	$0	$0	$0	$0	$0
C. Manufacturing labor						
— Engineering	$250,000	$500,000	$525,000	$551,250	$578,813	$607,753
— Custodial	$100,000	$200,000	$210,000	$220,500	$231,525	$243,101
— Maintenance	$175,000	$350,000	$367,500	$385,875	$405,169	$425,427
— Management	$100,000	$200,000	$210,000	$220,500	$231,525	$243,101
— Material handling	$0	$0	$0	$0	$0	$0
— Production control	$62,500	$125,000	$131,250	$137,813	$144,703	$151,938
— Quality control	$75,000	$150,000	$157,500	$165,375	$173,644	$182,326
— Software specialists	$50,000	$100,000	$105,000	$110,250	$115,763	$121,551
— Stores control	$50,000	$100,000	$105,000	$110,250	$115,763	$121,551
— Supervisory	$75,000	$150,000	$157,500	$165,375	$173,644	$182,326
— Tooling preparation	$62,‸00	$125,000	$131,250	$137,813	$144,703	$151,938
— Trainers	$42,500	$85,000	$89,250	$93,713	$98,398	$103,318
— Other	$500,000	$1,000,000	$1,050,000	$1,102,500	$1,157,625	$1,215,506
Total indirect manufacturing labor	$1,542,500	$3,085,000	$3,239,250	$3,401,213	$3,571,273	$3,749,837

Fig. 6-3—*Continued*

analyst to whom only the total of product costs is important in justification. However, the product cost structure is important to the system designer when looking for opportune areas for cost reduction and for system improvements. The product cost structure can show the savings by eliminating or reducing scrap or rework for a particular product.

Inventory holding costs result from the raw material, work-in-process (WIP), and finished goods' inventories for each of the products produced. Each inventory cost is adjusted by an inventory holding rate to reflect the required financing to maintain that inventory. If a company's before-tax cost of capital is 20%, then the total inventory cost is multiplied by 0.20 to determine the inventory holding cost. Inventory-related labor and equipment costs, such as storage/retrieval systems and transporters, are captured separately under indirect manufacturing labor and capital equipment categories, respectively. The inventory cost is generally determined as follows:

- Raw material. Cost of raw materials (times quantity), including costs for shrinkage.
- Work-in-process. Cumulative part cost of labor and materials at every point in production (times average quantity at every point). Other related costs such as required floor space, inventory holding equipment, and even job accounting/tracking costs could be considered WIP costs, but are generally captured under other categories.
- Finished goods. Similar to work-in-process inventory, only all the products are finished.

Capital equipment expenses. Capital equipment expenses reflect investments in depreciable assets. The definition of depreciable assets varies with IRS rulings and should be checked when preparing an economic analysis. Also, the depreciation schedule for a particular asset is necessary to determine taxes and will be needed later to determine after-tax cash flows. All start-up costs, including freight, installation of the equipment, facilities modifications, and special industrial engineering studies, are added to the cost of the equipment to determine its total cost. Each start-up cost should be classified as expense or capital for cash flow calculations. Capital equipment improvements such as retrofits are sometimes depreciated and are treated like capital equipment purchases.

There are many types of leases; some treat the asset as depreciable, and some treat it as an expense, with the expense equal to the amount of the periodic payment. Expensed purchases belong in the direct expenses section of the spreadsheet (refer to Section II of Fig. 6-3). The particular lease under consideration may require the assistance of a tax specialist.

The capital equipment expenditures, regardless of taxes and depreciation, should be entered on the spreadsheet in the appropriate time column.

Indirect expenses. Quality and volume (of output) are the two key attributes affecting product warranty and liability. Therefore, if the alternatives being compared do not differ in these attributes, the incremental impact will be 0. Generally, product warranty and liability will vary proportionally with level of output. The impact of quality on warranty and liability costs requires a careful analysis as to their root cause(s) in the benchmark case. It is quite possible that improvements in quality do not change warranty or liability. A determination should be made to see if changes in quality affect sales levels or price and to see if the change affects the manufacturing system's performance through reduced downtime, less rework, and so on.

Indirect manufacturing labor includes direct manufacturing support such as floor supervision, tool crib costs, quality control, and other similar costs that are shared across multiple product lines. These costs cannot be easily traced to any one product. Manufacturing supplies are similar in that they cannot be traced to any one product and might include perishable tooling, packaging, and coolant, to name a few.

Indirect general and administrative costs are not directly tied to manufacturing. They typically do not change significantly between alternative manufacturing scenarios unless there prove to be major differences in the output or in the way the business operates.

The Financial Summary

The financial summary pulls together the incremental analysis, determines taxes, and then calculates several economic measures on the incremental cash flow analysis (see Fig. 6-4). The sequence of calculations is self-explanatory. A new category, depreciation, is necessary to determine the after-tax cash flow analysis. Because different assets have different depreciable lives as set by IRS rulings, a tax consultant should help derive the depreciation schedule. Every piece of equipment listed in the capital equipment section must have a depreciation schedule. Similarly, if the incremental analysis calls for the sale of any existing capital assets, the effect on depreciation must be considered here as well. The selection of an appropriate tax rate should be obtained from the accounting/tax department.

The measures of merit shown in Fig. 6-4 include the payback period, present value, and return-on-investment calculations. Both present value and return on investment have been calculated over two different planning horizons: 5 years and 10 years. The period that should be used depends on the firm's planning horizon and the life of the project.

Obtaining Estimates for Indirect Costs

Indirect manufacturing labor can constitute a significant portion of overall production costs. Traditional approaches have related indirect costs as a proportion to direct manufacturing costs. With traditional manufacturing, this approximation was adequate because indirect costs were heavily outweighed by direct costs, and small errors in estimating direct costs did not significantly affect the indirect cost estimate. New, more advanced manufacturing technologies, however, have redistributed manufacturing costs to the indirect areas. Traditional relationships have been breaking down because the indirect costs commonly exceed direct costs by several hundred percent. Therefore, estimating indirect costs can now be more important than estimating direct costs.

One approach to estimating indirect costs is through transaction analysis. A transaction is defined as some signal to do something, either initiated by the manufacturing system or by a support/indirect function external to the manufacturing system. For a particular manufacturing system, transactions can be categorized as follows:

- Logistical. Transactions that relate to the location and movement of resources such as material, jobs, equipment, and personnel in the manufacturing system.
- Balancing. Transactions that control the available amounts/volumes of resources at given periods of time.
- Quality. Transactions that pertain to process and product quality, including the operating systems necessary to carry

ECONOMIC TRANSLATION

	Jun-87	Jun-88	Jun 89	Jun-90	Jun-91	May-92
A. REVENUES	$0	$20,000,000	$21,000,000	$22,050,000	$23,152,500	$24,310,125
B. EXPENSES						
1. Total direct product	$0	$8,781,400	$9,220,470	$9,681,494	$10,165,568	$10,673,847
2. Total equipment purc. & inprov.	$3,383,000	$292,500	$91,875	$41,344	$43,411	$45,581
3. Total equipment leases	$25,500	$25,500	$26,775	$28,114	$29,519	$30,995
4. Total indirect	$3,759,000	$8,143,000	$8,550,150	$8,977,658	$9,426,540	$9,897,867
TOTAL EXPENSES	$7,167,500	$17,242,400	$17,889,270	$18,728,609	$19,665,039	$20,648,291
C. BEFORE-TAX CASH FLOW (A. LESS B.)	($7,167,500)	$2,757,600	$3,110,730	$3,321,392	$3,487,461	$3,661,834
D. TAXABLE INCOME/(LOSS) BEFORE DEPRECIATION (C. LESS B.4)	($3,784,500)	$3,050,100	$3,202,605	$3,362,735	$3,530,872	$3,707,416
E. DEPRECIATION						
3-year assets	$0	$0	$0	$0	$0	$0
5-year assets	$0	$0	$0	$0	$0	$0
10-year assets	$0	$0	$0	$0	$0	$0
F. TAXABLE INCOME/(LOSS) (D. LESS E.)	($3,784,500)	$3,050,100	$3,202,605	$3,362,735	$3,530,872	$3,707,416
G. TAXES (TAX RATE TIMES F.)	($1,324,575)	$1,067,535	$1,120,912	$1,176,957	$1,235,805	$1,297,595
H. NET AFTER-TAX CASH FLOW (C. MINUS G.)	($5,842,925)	$1,690,065	$1,989,818	$2,144,434	$2,251,656	$2,364,239
I. CUMULATIVE NET AFTER-TAX CASH FLOW	($5,842,925)	($4,152,860)	($2,163,042)	($18,608)	$2,233,048	$4,597,287

FINANCIAL MEASURES
* Payback period (years): 3.0
* Present value (10 years/10%): $7,593,442
* Present value (5 years/10%): $1,777,307
* Return on investment (10 years): 34.4%
* Return on investment (5 years): 21.6%

Fig. 6-4 Financial summary of benchmark and proposed alternative comparison. (*Industrial Technology Institute*)

out the transactions such as personnel, file systems, audit systems, and specifications.

When there are significant differences between alternatives in indirect cost areas, a transaction analysis can be helpful in estimating the incremental economic difference. Indirect support areas include manufacturing technical support, maintenance personnel and parts, expeditors, system auditors, and information systems. A few key occurrences (transaction sources) calling for action, and some of the support functions affected, include:

- Equipment failure—maintenance, engineering, expeditors, and schedulers.
- Production fluctuations—expeditors, scheduling, purchasing, and sales.
- Product defect detection—quality control, purchasing, and scheduling.

- Engineering change orders—engineering, expediting, scheduling, supervision, and purchasing.
- New job arrivals—engineering, purchasing, scheduling, purchasing, and auditors.

The transaction analysis in Fig. 6-5 compares the economic impact of manually generating engineering designs vs. use of a computer-aided design and manufacturing (CAD/CAM) system. This analysis lists the activities (transactions) down the left column for the occurrence of a new job arrival. Only those transactions that differ between manual and CAD/CAM processing are listed; of course, many more transactions are involved to completely process a job. The data in the table (average processing time, average labor rates, average volume of jobs, and the productivity ratios) come from a variety of sources. For example, good sources of this type of information come from the personnel involved, industrial engineering, vendors, and studies such as simulation. The resultant annual savings ($834,581) might now be adjusted to reflect a learning curve for the introduction of CAD/CAM if full realization of this benefit is not expected until a start-up period is completed. Also, this benefit reflects current-year savings that might be adjusted for changes in labor rates.

Obtaining Estimates for Direct Costs

Direct manufacturing costs can be directly traced to a single product. If it is a cost that is shared across two or more product lines, then some "fair" means of cost sharing is necessary or else the cost becomes indirect. Typically, direct cost categories include line items for labor, material, and outside services. The economic spreadsheet in Fig. 6-3 includes these categories and has also added inventory holding cost. Whether or not these costs will be direct when the manufacturing system becomes operational should not affect the economic analysis. In performing an economic comparison of alternatives, one should track costs as closely as possible with the products that incur them. Figure 6-3 goes one step further and breaks down these direct costs according to good, scrap, and rework production for each product. This detail is generally helpful if the breakdown is readily available. Detailed manufacturing models (simulation or queuing networks) are often capable of this information. If this resolution of direct costs is not available, then the total "system" costs should be lumped together, preferably by product.

Direct labor. Determination of direct labor requires the hourly rate (usually an average will do, and it should include wages and taxes paid by the company), the overtime rate (if applicable), annual fringe benefit costs, and total hours worked. The total amount of production time (one, two, or three shifts, and the amount of overtime) is then used as a multipler for labor costs. If the amount of labor that goes into rework and scrap is available, then this breakdown can be included on the spreadsheet.

Direct material. The cost of raw materials to produce a finished product needs to be determined. Usually the purchase price including shipping is sufficient.

When a material comes into a manufacturing subsystem from another subsystem (for example, a subassembly), a transfer price must be determined. If a price has been determined by accounting, then that price represents the cost. Otherwise, the same method used for revenue determination (see the subhead entitled "Revenues" earlier) can be used for cost determination: market value, equivalent outsourcing cost, or manufacturing cost plus some markup for shared profit (margin). A balance must be maintained where the cost of a material to one system/department must represent the revenue (transfer price) to the source system/department. When both systems (the subassembly and assembly systems) are in the scope of the analysis, the subassembly is treated as work in process and is valued according to its total raw materials and direct labor. This is described subsequently.

Inventories. There are three types of inventories: raw mate-

Activity (Transaction List)	No. of Jobs Per Year: 171 Manual			Alternative A: CAD/CAM		
	Total Hours (per job)	Average Labor Rate, $/hr	Produc-tivity Ratio	CAD/CAM Hours	Time Saved, hours	Savings, $
1.0 Project management						
1.1 Project planning	20	30	1.50	2213	1107	33,200
2.0 Design						
2.1 Schematics	22	25	1.40	2609	1043	26,086
2.2 Feasibility analysis	5	25	5.00	166	664	16,600
2.3 Design and layout	40	25	2.00	3320	3320	83,000
2.4 Fabrication drawing	6	25	3.00	332	664	16,600
2.5 Assembly drawing	32	25	10.00	531	4781	119,520
2.6 Artwork	40	25	40.00	166	6474	161,850
2.7 Checking	30	25	2.75	1811	3169	79,227
3.0 Development	20	30	1.25	2656	664	19,920
4.0 Manufacturing—support						
4.1 Production planning	5	30	1.25	664	166	4,980
4.2 Scheduling & expediting	5	30	1.25	664	166	4,980
4.3 Engineering	5	30	1.25	664	166	4,980
4.4 Quality control	10	25	1.25	1328	332	8,300
4.5 NC & CNC programming	10	25	3.00	553	1107	27,667
5.0 Manufacturing—operations						
5.1 Inventory reduction						
5.2 Additional capacity						
					Total:	

Fig. 6-5 Sample transaction analysis comparing the economic impact of manually generated designs to computer-aided design. (*Industrial Technology Institute*)

ECONOMIC TRANSLATION

rial, work-in-process (WIP), and finished goods. It is generally acceptable to determine an average inventory level for each of these three and then to assign a cost based on the average value of that inventory. This approach may not be acceptable when inventories fluctuate widely, when costs vary significantly, or if the makeup of the inventory (distribution of part/product types) varies broadly. In these cases, a more detailed breakdown may be necessary.

Once an inventory value is derived, an inventory holding rate can be used to reflect the cost to the business for carrying the inventory. In essence, the holding rate times the inventory value represents the annual investment cost to the business. This method accounts for the investment capital the firm has tied up in inventory. The inventory holding rate can be the firm's cost of capital or, if available, the interest rate at which capital is borrowed against inventories. If the economic spreadsheet has annual cash flow summaries, then the inventory holding rate should be an annual rate; the inventory holding cost is calculated each year for the life of the system.

Raw materials are generally valued according to the material purchase price plus any additional costs for freight.

Work-in-process cost is less straightforward to estimate because it occurs throughout the manufacturing process and represents an investment of direct materials and labor. A generally accepted approach to value WIP is to accumulate direct product costs (labor, material, and services) throughout the production process for each part. Therefore, a part near the end of the production process would have a greater value than a part near the beginning of the process. The resolution of valuation that is needed depends on the volume of parts, location(s) of WIP inventories in the process, and the complexity of the process (many alternative processes require more analysis).

In general, it is helpful to identify the major WIP locations in a process (buffers) and then to assign a WIP value based on the accumulated direct costs. A distinction may have to be made between physical buffers and logical buffers. On the floor, one storage location (physical buffer) may store parts at several different levels of completion (logical buffer—one for each level of completion). An average accumulation of direct costs needs to be made for each level of completion. In general, this would occur after each process. This process is complicated if parts at the same level of completion may have gone through different series of operations, such as rework, mixture of outsourcing, and in-house processes. When there are alternative routings for a particular part, a good approach for valuation is to set up a table that accumulates the costs by operation and then weigh the

accumulated WIP according to the proportion of parts through different routes.

The information in Table 6-2 shows a process sequence with process 3 going through either workcenter A or B at 40 and 60% proportions, respectively. Also, the direct material and labor vary for process 3 depending on which workcenter performs the process. The total cost column represents the total direct costs added to a part at each process. The cumulative value column adds the costs from all processes up to the current process, plus the value added at the current process. However, for process 4, the cumulative value must account for the proportion of parts that went different routes in process 3. Therefore, a weighted cumulative value is 0.4 x $4800 + 0.6 x $4900 = $4860. The average value of a WIP part waiting for process 4 is $4860.

Once this table of cumulative costs has been derived for each part in the system, the average buffer quantity, by process, can be used to estimate the average in-process value by process. Total WIP value is the sum of all buffer values and can be totaled by process or by part. The total is multiplied by the inventory holding rate to represent the company's cost of WIP inventory.

Finished goods are valued the same as raw material, based on direct costs. Finished goods, however, have direct material plus labor added. Therefore, the cost of finished goods is simply the average cumulative value of direct costs for completed product in inventory. This figure is the last value in the cumulative value column in Table 6-2. Again, the value is multiplied by the quantity and then by the inventory holding rate to represent the firm's holding cost for finished goods inventory.

Assembling Economic Spreadsheets for System Evolutions

Manufacturing systems/subsystems with significant evolution over time will have changing performance and, consequently, changing economic behavior. Averages like inventory levels, throughput, and product cost structure can change significantly with modifications to an existing system. Averages may be acceptable in one phase of the manufacturing system/subsystem, but not in the next. The effect of planned changes, such as the evolution from NC to CNC to DNC/FMS, should be estimated as part of the economic justification/planning process, even if the planned changes won't happen for several years. Different performance and economic estimates should be developed for each phase of the system. After the economic spreadsheets are developed for each phase, they should be assembled into one overall estimate with the performance measures calculated for the lifecycle of the system.

TABLE 6-2
Cumulative Costs of a Process Sequence

Process	Work-center	Propor-tion	Material	Labor	Services	Total Cost	Cumulative Value
1	A	100%	$2000	$800		$2800	$2800
2	A	100%	$0	$1200		$1200	$4000
3	A	40%	$500	$300		$800	$4800
	B	60%	$200	$700		$900	$4900
4	A	100%	$0	$500		$500	$5360
5	—	100%	$0	$0	$500	$500	$5860
Finish							

(Industrial Technology Institute)

CAPITAL INVESTMENT ANALYSIS EXAMPLE

While there is no such thing as a fully comprehensive example of a capital investment analysis, this example is relatively complete. It illustrates an investment where benefits are not only spread throughout a manufacturing system as it exists at a point in time, but also throughout the lifecycle of the manufacturing system. Further, the example is of an investment in support of a business strategy in which the objective of the firm is explicitly defined. Under these circumstances, it is the responsibility of production management to devise and implement a manufacturing strategy that is part of an integrated effort by all parts of the firm to achieve the firm's objective.

It has been necessary to simplify the example in certain places and to show typical analyses, such as one year and one alternative rather than every year and each alternative, to avoid excessive length. The intention, however, is an example in sufficient detail to serve as a model for analysis of actual investment alternatives.

BUSINESS STRATEGY

The process has started with a strategic planning exercise to define the product and market position of the firm in light of its perceived threats and opportunities as well as its strengths and weaknesses. The exercise has involved all functional areas, including manufacturing, marketing, engineering, and others.

The firm presently produces and markets two products, A and B. They are engineered products, and the product design changes about every 4 years, as product technology is changing rapidly. Superior engineering and consistent quality are very important to the users of the product, and the firm has the reputation of being the technical leader in the industry and a producer of a high-quality product. The product was originally developed and introduced to the market by the firm, and until recently, the firm dominated the market. It is still the market leader with a market share of about 70%. Recently, however, a competitor emerged that is now threatening the firm's market leadership. Examination of how the competitor was able to secure market entry reveals two weaknesses of the firm relative to the competition:

- A year ago, when product B was redesigned, the competitor brought out a product which, while not as good as the new product B, was better than the old product B, and the competitor was able to get it to market 10 months before the firm's new product. Thus, for 10 months, while the firm had a better product on the drawing board, the competitor had a better product on the market. This is believed to be the primary reason for the success of the competitor, reflecting the importance of timely introduction of up-to-date engineering.
- There has been a disturbing increase in the number of customer complaints. Warranty expenses have increased as well, in spite of more stringent inspection and increased rework in the plant. It is believed that the competitor is selling a quality product and that this is playing a secondary role in its success, reflecting the importance of quality to the market.

The firm has certain strong advantages as well. The engineering department is recognized as the best in the industry. It is still the market leader, with good distribution and an excellent reputation among users of its product, in spite of the recent complaints it has received.

The firm recognizes that completely eliminating a competitor with an initial market success is probably not feasible; but there is agreement that the firm could initiate actions which, if successful, will maintain its 70% market share or even increase it somewhat, restricting the competitor to a secondary position in the market. To do so, the firm must take certain actions, particularly with regard to getting newly engineered products on the market more quickly and restoring product quality. This will place the firm securely in the position of competing on the basis of engineering and quality once again, forcing the competitor to accept some other attribute—probably price—as its basis for competing. Management believes that this will occupy the full attention of the key people in the firm so they will not attempt to enter any new markets at this time, but will concentrate on solidifying their firm's position in the markets for A and B. This is agreed on by all departments as a feasible strategy, particularly in view of the strength of the engineering department.

The outlook for the future based on this strategy has been discussed extensively by the people working on the plan. After a great deal of discussion, general agreement has been reached, and the result is laid out qualitatively in the form of a decision tree (see Fig. 6-6). At the root of the tree is the firm's present position, which has been defined as holding a 70% share of the market with the best engineering in the business, with quality that is still good but with problems starting to show up, with an outmoded plant, and with difficulty getting new products in production and to market on a timely basis. A decision must be made whether or not the firm should make a major investment at this time. At issue is, on the one hand, whether the firm can accomplish its objective without such an investment and, on the other, whether the firm can maintain a profitable position if it goes ahead with a major investment.

The upper half of the tree deals with the chance occurrences and decisions that must be made if the firm goes ahead with a major investment at this time. In the judgment of key members of the firm, the major issue is whether or not the competitor will counter the actions of the firm with a competitive action of its own. This might be a price reduction, an increase in quality, or copying the firm's new product and getting it to market quickly. These are actions that might logically follow from the strengths of the competitor—it is believed unlikely that the competitor would be able to engineer a product superior to that of the firm. By taking one or more of the actions that are open to it, however, the competitor might continue to gain market share.

This leads to a decision about how to deal with such a competitive threat. One response would be to ignore it, to continue producing the product as planned, introducing a new product at the end of the normal 4-year product lifecycle. A more costly alternative would be to accelerate the introduction of a new product after 2 years. It is believed that an accelerated new product introduction would allow the firm either to recover or maintain market share. A normal introduction might allow the firm to maintain share, but could cause continued loss of share.

If no competitive threat was forthcoming, it is believed the firm would maintain its current market share with the new

CAPITAL INVESTMENT EXAMPLE

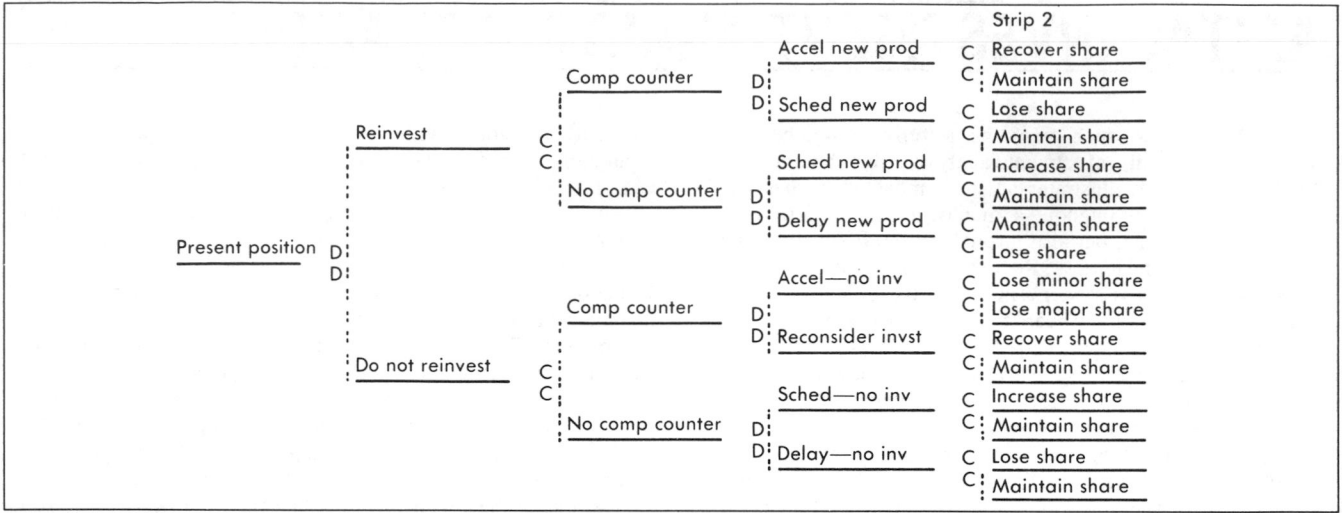

Fig. 6-6 Decision tree showing the qualitative decision of a company to solidify its position in the market. (*Industrial Technology Institute*).

product currently being introduced. It might introduce a new product as scheduled at the end of 4 years, or it might possibly extend the life of the product from 4 to 6 years, using the investment for an additional 2 years to improve cash flow. It is believed that a normal new product introduction would allow the firm either to gain or to maintain market share. A delayed new product introduction might allow the firm to maintain share, but could cause loss of share.

The lower half of the tree deals with the chance occurrences and decisions that must be made if the firm decides not to make a major investment at this time. In the judgment of key members of the firm, the major issue is the same as if the firm reinvests—whether or not the competitor will take this opportunity to initiate a competitive action to gain share. The actions open to the competitor are the same as noted previously—a price reduction, an increase in quality, or copying the firm's new product and getting it to market quickly. By taking one or more of these actions, it is believed the competitor could continue to gain market share.

The firm could deal with such a threat by accelerating the introduction of a new product after 2 years, still without a major investment. Manufacturing questioned the feasibility of such a move, but engineering insisted that it be included in the tree as a potential course of action. Alternatively, manufacturing suggested that a more feasible move would be to accelerate the introduction of the new product, at the same time reconsidering the original decision not to invest and make the major investment at that time. It is believed that an accelerated new product introduction without investment would result in a lack of responsiveness to the market that would inevitably lead to loss of market share. Whether the loss would be major or minor is an issue. Accelerating the new product introduction with a major investment might allow the firm to recover share or at least to maintain share.

If no competitive threat was forthcoming, it is believed the firm would maintain its current market share with the new product currently being introduced. It might introduce a new product as scheduled at the end of 4 years, or it might possibly extend the life of the product from 4 to 6 years. In either event, no major investment would be considered. It is believed that a normal new product introduction would allow the firm either to

gain or maintain market share. A delayed new product introduction might allow the firm to maintain share, but could cause loss of share.

This entire range of decisions, chance events, and outcomes is laid out qualitatively in Fig. 6-6. At this stage, the tree is only a visual aid for the key people in the firm to help them foresee possible future decisions and chance events and to reach agreement on the most important of these potential decisions and events so they can plan for them. Later, the tree will be refined, further detail added, and quantitative data inserted.

MANUFACTURING STRATEGY

Building on this business strategy, each department is examining its own function with the objective of defining what it must do to support the business strategy and what organization, activities, tools, technologies, and investments will enable it to do so. While this example focuses principally on the investments necessary to implement the business strategy, it is important to recognize that investment alone is rarely sufficient. Successful investments to implement business strategies are usually integrated with other actions. For instance, the inability of the firm to get products to the market quickly might be partly a result of a manufacturing system that lacks adaptability and needs extensive retooling each time a new product is introduced and might be partly a result of poor organization leading to inadequate communications between engineering and manufacturing. For an investment in flexible manufacturing to be fully effective, the organization problems must be solved as well.

One of the taskforces established to implement the strategy consists of manufacturing engineers who have the responsibility of defining the functional requirements for the manufacturing system that will be able to support the strategy. After examining the requirements of the business strategy for manufacturing, they decide that the manufacturing system best able to respond to these requirements has the following characteristics:

- Accuracy of shape and size. The demand in the marketplace for quality, the present high level of rework, the increasing customer quality complaints, and increasing warranty costs all point to the need for improved process control.

CAPITAL INVESTMENT EXAMPLE

● Adaptability of shape. The need to redesign the product every few years means that manufacturing can expect a high volume of engineering changes. Future configurations cannot be predicted, so the firm needs to be prepared for whatever comes along. Further, the loss of market share a year ago points out the importance of adapting quickly so the new product can be produced with minimal lead times.

Naturally, there are other functional requirements to which the manufacturing system must respond. It must be able to produce parts of the necessary configurations, it must produce enough of them to meet demand, it must have sufficient flexibility to be able to handle the mix of parts, and it must produce parts at a cost that allows the firm to earn a profit.

OPERATIONAL PLAN

Specific questions must be asked to come up with a viable operational plan. Examples of such questions are: What are the shapes and sizes of the parts to be produced? What manufacturing technologies are available that might produce these shapes and sizes? What is the possible range of shapes and sizes that might need to be produced? Can the range be reduced and other benefits achieved as well by introducing group technology? What quantities must be produced? What is the lot size? Might both lot size and inventories be reduced by increasing the flexibility of the system, allowing more rapid and less expensive changeover from one part to another?

In this example, both parts A and B require four operations: rough mill, grind, drill, and tap. A certain number of pieces must be reworked at each operation, and a certain number are scrapped. A diagram of the process is shown in Fig. 6-7. The firm is presently operating with an antiquated and inadequate manufacturing system. Throughput is insufficient to meet demand, estimated to be 100,000 units of each part this year. The market is expected to grow by 10% each year. Costs are high, changeover times are long, and work-in-process inventory is high. A change is clearly overdue.

A new generation of products is now being designed. They will also be identified as A and B and will require the same four operations. It is anticipated that, under normal circumstances, another generation of parts will come along 4 years from now. Management knows it cannot compete with the existing plant, so keeping the existing plant is not a viable alternative. Three alternatives are under consideration. The example does not concern itself with the physical characteristics of the three alternatives so much as it does with their performance.

The first alternative, which is considered the baseline, requires an investment of $1,000,000. It consists of selectively replacing existing conventional manufacturing equipment with similar new equipment of adequate capacity. Cycle times will remain about as at present. It is believed that with new equipment properly tooled for the next generation of parts, quality problems will become manageable. However, it is estimated that scrap will run at about 8%.

The second alternative is a highly automated system, requiring an investment of $4,250,000. It will be designed specifically for the geometry of the parts presently in design and will require extensive modification when the new parts are again redesigned. Cycle times will be substantially reduced. Changeover time will be high, resulting in a high economic lot size. The cycle time to produce parts will be very low. Part quality will be high, and it is anticipated that the scrap rate will be lowered to 2%.

The third alternative is a flexible manufacturing system costing $5,000,000. Cycle time will be shorter than with conventional equipment, but somewhat longer than with the highly automated system. However, changeover time is low, yielding a low economic batch size. It is anticipated that only a few modifications will be required by the next generation of parts in 2 years. Like the highly automated system, part quality will be high with a 2% scrap rate.

CONVENTIONAL FINANCIAL ANALYSIS

At this point, the traditional approach would be to perform an economic analysis based on direct labor savings and scrap reduction. An investment in either the hard automation manufacturing system or the flexible manufacturing system would be compared with the baseline, which is the investment in conventional equipment. The investment numbers, cycle times, scrap rates, material cost, labor rates, the firm's after-tax cost of capital, and its tax rate are shown at the top of Fig. 6-8.

These figures are then used as inputs for a conventional discounted cash flow analysis, shown at the bottom of the figure, in which incremental cash flows are calculated for the investment in hard automation and the investment in flexible manufacturing, both in comparison with conventional equipment. This analysis shows negative net present values for both hard automation and flexible manufacturing in comparison with the baseline conventional system.

This analysis is based on many assumptions, one of the most questionable being that all of the relative advantages of the

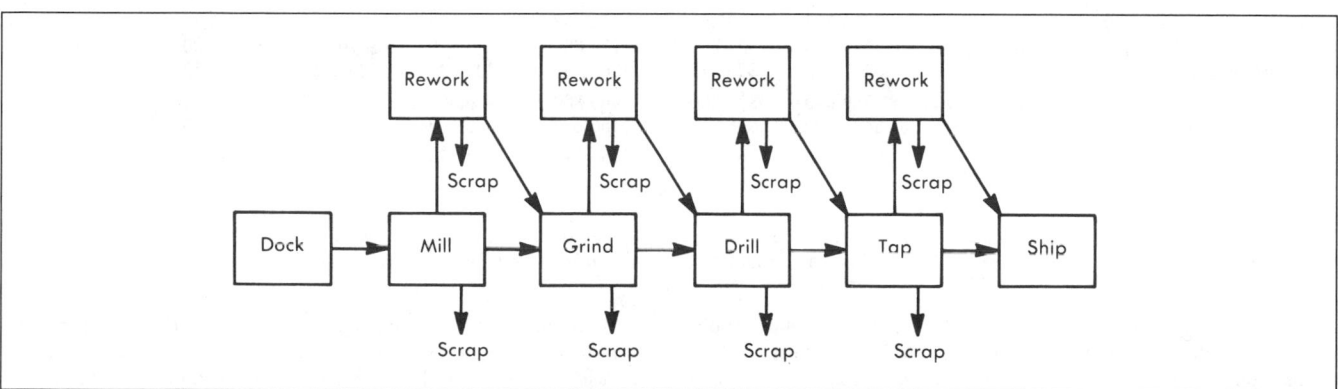

Fig. 6-7 Process diagram for parts A and B of current operation. (*Industrial Technology Institute*)

CAPITAL INVESTMENT EXAMPLE

	Conventional	Hard Automation	Flexible Manufacturing
Cycle time			
Part A	18	4	8
Part B	20	5	10
Annual production			
Part A	100,000	100,000	100,000
Part B	100,000	100,000	100,000
Hours per year			
Part A	30,000	6667	13,333
Part B	33,333	8333	16,667
Total	63,333	15,000	30,000
Dollars per year	$633,333	$150,000	$300,000
Scrap rate			
Part A	8%	2%	2%
Part B	8%	2%	2%
Units scrapped per year			
Part A	8000	2000	2000
Part B	8000	2000	2000
Material cost			
Part A	$25	$25	$25
Part B	$20	$20	$20
Dollars per year			
Part A	$200,000	$50,000	$50,000
Part B	$160,000	$40,000	$40,000
Total	$360,000	$90,000	$90,000
Investment	$1,000,000	$4,250,000	$5,000,000
Annual depreciation			
Year 0	200,000	850,000	1,000,000
Year 1	320,000	1,360,000	1,600,000
Year 2	192,000	816,000	960,000
Year 3	115,200	489,600	576,000
Year 4	115,200	489,600	576,000
Year 5	57,600	244,800	288,000
Year 6	0	0	0

Year	0	1	2	3	4	5	6	NPV
HARD AUTOMATION COMPARED TO CONVENTIONAL								
Incremental investment	$3,250,000							
Labor savings		$483,333	$483,333	$483,333	$483,333	$483,333	$483,333	
Scrap material savings		$270,000	$270,000	$270,000	$270,000	$270,000	$270,000	
Tax on savings		$256,133	$256,133	$256,133	$256,133	$256,133	$256,133	
Increase in depreciation	$650,000	$1,040,000	$624,000	$374,400	$374,400	$187,200	$0	
Depreciation tax shelter	$221,000	$353,600	$212,160	$127,296	$127,296	$63,648	$0	
After-tax cash flow	($3,029,000)	$850,800	$709,360	$624,496	$624,496	$560,848	$497,200	($144,666)
FLEXIBLE MANUFACTURING COMPARED TO CONVENTIONAL								
Incremental Investment	$4,000,000							
Labor savings		$333,333	$333,333	$333,333	$333,333	$333,333	$333,333	
Scrap material savings		$270,000	$270,000	$270,000	$270,000	$270,000	$270,000	
Tax on savings		$205,133	$205,133	$205,133	$205,133	$205,133	$205,133	
Increase in depreciation	$800,000	$1,280,000	$768,000	$460,800	$460,800	$230,400	$0	
Depreciation tax shelter	$272,000	$435,200	$261,120	$156,672	$156,672	$78,336	$0	
After-tax cash flow	($3,728,000)	$833,400	$659,320	$554,872	$554,872	$476,536	$398,200	($1,108,938)

Fig. 6-8 Analysis of investments based on direct labor saving and scrap. (*Industrial Technology Institute*)

alternative investments are captured in the direct labor and scrap numbers. Other assumptions include constant labor savings over a 6-year period and no further investment requirements over this period of time.

This approach, although superficial, is used by many firms. It fails to capture the benefits of flexible manufacturing that are diffused throughout the manufacturing system at a particular point in time, as well as those that occur throughout the lifecycle of the investment. Furthermore, the analysis has failed to recognize the strategic objectives of the firm and the characteristics required of the manufacturing system to respond to these objectives. Yet many firms perform an analysis like this on proposed investments. As a result, these firms find it all but impossible to justify the purchase of equipment they know they need. To identify and quantify some of these hidden benefits and see what happens to the financial analysis, a dynamic model of the alternative manufacturing system will be made.

DYNAMIC MODELING

Before running Manuplan, XCELL, or one of the other models, one must define the manufacturing systems in greater detail than simply in terms of direct labor. The operating characteristics of the three systems are defined in Table 6-3. With the process shown in Fig. 6-7, the operating characteristics shown in Table 6-3, and a little additional data on rework outcome, it is possible to model the manufacturing system with Manuplan. The output of Manuplan indicates that all proposed systems are capable of meeting production requirements of 100,000 units of each part next year, and it provides additional information as shown at the top of Table 6-4.

Some of the advantages of flexible manufacturing are apparent in the summary. Although one cannot yet put dollars and cents on it, the work-in-process inventory will be increased somewhat with hard automation and will be reduced significantly with flexible manufacturing. In addition, the flow times suggest that the factory's response to orders will be slowed somewhat with hard automation and accelerated significantly with flexible manufacturing. Scrap rates and rework are lower for both hard automation and flexible manufacturing. This implies that costs of noncompliance will be lower for automated processes, as is usual because of the greater process control achieved.

Further, a dynamic model of the system provides a more accurate assessment of the number of stations needed for each operation to yield a given level of throughput. Not only does this allow one to estimate the investment more closely, but it also gives better direct labor figure. When the investment is made, one is able to buy either fewer machines than thought necessary with a static analysis or, more significantly, to avoid the serious problems of adding stations after the manufacturing system is in place as a result of unanticipated line shortages and blockages.

ECONOMIC TRANSLATION OF THE MODEL

To capture the benefits and costs of either hard automation or flexible manufacturing in terms useable for evaluating the alternative investments, translation of model output into economic terms is necessary. This may be done by combining the output of the model along with additional inputs, also shown in Table 6-4. The results may be calculated manually, or they may be performed on a computer. The model may include a translator as an integral part of the model, or it may be an attachment to it.

Some of the key calculations performed by the translator are shown at the bottom of Table 6-4. These, along with other figures, are used as inputs to a calculation of net present value in Table 6-5. This analysis is more complete than the analysis performed earlier in that it includes the following:

- It deals with the entire manufacturing system and all the benefits of each investment that are realized throughout the system.
- Because the output of the model calculates not only the material content of scrapped parts, but also the labor

content of both scrapped and reworked parts, one is able to assess the cost savings more completely.
- An estimate has been made of the residual value of the investment—the value the investment would have to the firm at the end of the analysis period. A "going concern" approach has been used to recognize that the assets are unlikely to be sold at the end of the period, but will continue to be used for production. The residual value has been estimated in this example and henceforth as the present value of 4 additional years of cash flows that are equal to the average of the last 4 years, discounted at the firm's cost of capital of 10%.

By incorporating these benefits, both the hard automation and flexible manufacturing investments show a positive net present value in comparison with the baseline conventional system. Hard automation has higher net present value, indicating that, by this analysis, an investment in hard automation will create more value for the firm than an investment in flexible manufacturing.

The analysis still fails to capture the following key benefits:

- It fails to deal with changes in the character and overall volume of output that may occur over time.
- It fails to take into account future investments that may be required.

PUTTING QUANTITATIVE DATA ON THE DECISION TREE

To include anticipated costs and benefits over time, it is necessary to consider the future, which is uncertain. One way of dealing with an uncertain future is through the use of a decision tree, with the objective of using it as the basis for a quantitative decision analysis.

The decision tree in Fig. 6-9 is a modification of the one in Fig. 6-6 as a result of the addition of further detail and the insertion of quantitative data. It has also been modified to show the subjective probabilities of the chance occurrences. These probabilities are based on the best subjective judgment of knowledgeable people—they are not based on statistical tests, such as those used for statistical process control. Further, values have been assigned to the qualitative expressions used earlier, such as "lose market share" or "gain market share." By running these figures for the total market and the firm's share of market, along with resulting levels of production and sales, through the model and translator to determine the financial impacts of these levels of sales on investment requirements and manufacturing costs, it is possible to calculate cash flows by year for each branch of the decision tree and thus to calculate a present value for each branch. Because probabilities for each branch have already been established, the tools discussed in the earlier sections can be used to calculate expected values for each branch, as well as measures of dispersion.

To go through the calculations for each year and each branch would require many pages of calculations that are quick and simple with personal computers, but tedious to read. Figure 6-10 shows the calculations for one branch for a single year and a summary of the results of performing numerous similar calculations on all the branches.

The markets for both products A and B have been forecasted to grow at an annual rate of 10%. These figures are shown at the top of Fig. 6-10. The price for both products is forecast to remain constant, as shown. Path 1, shown as an example, is the top path on the decision tree in Fig. 6-9. It has been defined as the path in which one invests in a flexible manufacturing system, the

CAPITAL INVESTMENT EXAMPLE

TABLE 6-3
Operating Characteristics of Alternative Manufacturing Systems
Used as Inputs to Manuplan

	Conventional		Hard Automation		Flexible Manufacturing	
Number of milling units	7	units	3	units	5	units
Mean time to failure	9600	minutes	9600	minutes	9600	minutes
Mean time to repair	120	minutes	120	minutes	120	minutes
Part A cycle time	6	minutes	1	minute	2	minutes
set-up time	120	minutes	240	minutes	0.1	minute
scrap rate	1.5	%	0.4	%	0.4	%
rework rate	1.5	%	1	%	1	%
Part B cycle time	4	minutes	1	minute	2	minutes
set-up time	120	minutes	240	minutes	0.1	minute
scrap rate	1.5	%	0.4	%	0.4	%
rework rate	1.5	%	1	%	1	%
Number of drilling units	5	units	2	units	4	units
Mean time to failure	9600	minutes	9600	minutes	9600	minutes
Mean time to repair	60	minutes	60	minutes	60	minutes
Part A cycle time	7	minutes	1	minute	2	minutes
set-up time	60	minutes	120	minutes	0.1	minutes
scrap rate	2	%	0.6	%	0.6	%
rework rate	2	%	1.5	%	1.5	%
Part B cycle time	6	minutes	1.5	minutes	3	minutes
set-up time	60	minutes	120	minutes	0.1	minute
scrap rate	2	%	0.6	%	0.6	%
rework rate	2	%	1.5	%	1.5	%
Number of grinding units	8	units	3	units	6	units
Mean time to failure	9600	minutes	9600	minutes	9600	minutes
Mean time to repair	60	minutes	60	minutes	60	minutes
Part A cycle time	2	minutes	1	minute	2	minutes
set-up time	60	minutes	120	minutes	0.1	minute
scrap rate	2	%	0.6	%	0.6	%
rework rate	1	%	0.5	%	0.5	%
Part B cycle time	4	minutes	1	minute	2	minutes
set-up time	60	minutes	120	minutes	0.1	minute
scrap rate	2	%	0.6	%	0.6	%
rework rate	1	%	0.5	%	0.5	%
Number of tapping units	5	units	3	units	5	units
Mean time to failure	12,000	minutes	12,000	minutes	12,000	minutes
Mean time to repair	30	minutes	30	minutes	30	minutes
Part A cycle time	3	minutes	1	minute	2	minutes
set-up time	30	minutes	60	minutes	0.1	minute
scrap rate	2	%	0.6	%	0.6	%
rework rate	2	%	1.5	%	1.5	%
Part B cycle time	6	minutes	1.5	minutes	3	minutes
set-up time	30	minutes	60	minutes	0.1	minute
scrap rate	2	%	0.6	%	0.6	%
rework rate	2	%	1.5	%	1.5	%

(*Industrial Technology Institute*)

competition counters with a competitive move, and one in turn counters by accelerating the introduction of the next generation of product. While the market share of 70% drops temporarily, the company's strategy is successful, and the market share is regained by year 6.

These market shares are applied to the market forecasts to calculate unit sales, which are then multiplied by unit prices to obtain revenue. Production cost is derived from the model—the figure shown for year 1 is identical with that shown for flexible manufacturing in Table 6-5, the analysis of investments based on the manufacturing system model. Investments are based on the need to reinvest only when new products are introduced, as sufficient capacity exists for normal sales growth. Other variable and other fixed costs have been estimated outside the model. In this example, identical fixed costs have been estimated for all three alternatives, with somewhat lower variable costs for

CAPITAL INVESTMENT EXAMPLE

TABLE 6-4
Economic Translation of Manuplan Model

	Conventional	Hard Automation	Flexible Manufacturing
SUMMARY OF MODEL OUTPUTS FROM MANUPLAN MODEL			
Shipments (pieces)			
Product A	100000	100000	100000
Product B	100000	100000	100000
Scrap production (pieces)			
Product A	7595	2087	2087
Product B	7595	2087	2087
Average work in process (pieces)			
Product A	2620	3635	9
Product B	2806	3873	10
Equipment utilization summary (percent)			
Mill			
Set-up	8.7%	12.0%	2.0%
Run	73.9%	62.9%	67.4%
Repair	1.0%	0.9%	0.9%
Total utilization	83.6%	75.8%	70.3%
Drill			
Set-up	5.9%	11.6%	3.3%
Run	60.0%	74.1%	65.6%
Repair	0.4%	0.5%	0.4%
Total utilization	66.3%	86.2%	69.3%
Grind			
Set-up	3.8%	5.9%	2.0%
Run	83.0%	81.3%	87.0%
Repair	0.5%	0.5%	0.6%
Total utilization	87.3%	87.7%	89.6%
Tap			
Set-up	2.9%	3.9%	2.4%
Run	88.9%	73.3%	73.3%
Repair	0.2%	0.2%	0.2%
Total utilization	92.0%	77.4%	75.9%
Flow time (days)			
Part A	5.49	7.72	0.02
Part B	5.91	8.26	0.02
FINANCIAL INPUTS			
Firm's cost of capital (after-tax) (%)	10%	10%	10%
Firm's incremental tax rate (%)	34%	34%	34%
Initial investment ($)	$1,000,000	$4,250,000	$5,000,000
Tax life (yrs)	5	5	5
Material cost by product ($/unit)			
Product A	$20.00	$20.00	$20.00
Product B	$25.00	$25.00	$25.00
Labor cost by code ($/hr)			
Operation	$10.00	$10.00	$10.00
Set-up	$10.00	$10.00	$10.00
Maintenance	$10.00	$10.00	$10.00
Selling price by product			
Product A	$45.00	$45.00	$45.00
Product B	$55.00	$55.00	$55.00
Other variable costs per unit	$8.00	$5.00	$5.00
Other fixed costs per year	$100,000	$100,000	$100,000
SUMMARY OF FINANCIAL CALCULATIONS			
Revenue	$10,000,000	$10,000,000	$10,000,000
Cost of good production	$3,850,641	$3,267,308	$3,417,308
Cost of scrap	$259,401	$64,850	$72,632

CAPITAL INVESTMENT EXAMPLE

TABLE 6-4—Continued

	Conventional	Hard Automation	Flexible Manufacturing
Cost of rework	$41,763	$23,805	$25,893
Depreciation			
Year 0	$200,000	$850,000	$1,000,000
Year 1	$320,000	$1,360,000	$1,600,000
Year 2	$192,000	$816,000	$960,000
Year 3	$115,200	$489,600	$576,000
Year 4	$115,200	$489,600	$576,000
Year 5	$57,600	$244,800	$288,000
Work-in-process inventory	$145,931	$198,997	$511

(Industrial Technology Institute)

TABLE 6-5
Analysis of Investments Based on Manufacturing System Model

Year	0	1	2	3	4	5	6	NPV	NPV Relative to Baseline
CONVENTIONAL									
A unit sales		100,000	100,000	100,000	100,000	100,000	100,000		
B unit sales		100,000	100,000	100,000	100,000	100,000	100,000		
Revenue		10,000,000	10,000,000	10,000,000	10,000,000	10,000,000	10,000,000		
Production cost		4,151,805	4,151,805	4,151,805	4,151,805	4,151,805	4,151,805		
Other variable		1,600,000	1,600,000	1,600,000	1,600,000	1,600,000	1,600,000		
Depreciation	200,000	320,000	192,000	115,200	115,200	57,600	0		
Other fixed		100,000	100,000	100,000	100,000	100,000	100,000		
PBT		3828195	3,956,195	4,032,995	4,032,995	4,090,595	4,148,195		
PAT		2,526,609	2,611,089		2,661,777	2,699,793	2,737,809		
Fixed invest	1,000,00								
Inventory invest		145,931	0	0	0	0	0		
Residual value							12,817,020		
Cash flow	-800,000	2,700,678	2,803,089	2,776,977	2,776,977	2,757,393	15,554,828	18,447,278	0
HARD AUTOMATION									
A unit sales		100,000	100,000	100,000	100,000	100,000	100,000		
B unit sales		100,000	100,000	100,000	100,000	100,000	100,000		
Revenue		10,000,000	10,000,000	10,000,000	10,000,000	10,000,000	10,000,000		
Production cost		3,355,963	3,355,963	3,355,963	3,355,963	3,355,963	3,355,963		
Other variable		1,000,000	1,000,000	1,000,000	1,000,000	1,000,000	1,000,000		
Depreciation	850,000	1,360,000	816,000	489,600	489,600	244,800	0		
Other fixed		100,000	100,000	100,000	100,000	100,000	100,000		
PBT		4,184,037	4,728,037	5,054,437	5,054,437	5,299,237	5,544,037		
PAT		2,761,464	3,120,504	3,335,928	3,335,928	3,497,496	3,659,064		
Fixed invest	4,250,000								
Inventory invest		198,997	0	0	0	0	0		
Residual value							17,460,804		
Cash flow	-3,400,000	3,922,467	3,936,504	3,825,528	3,825,528	3,742,296	21,119,868	23,151,538	4,704,260
FLEXIBLE MANUFACTURING									
A unit sales		100,000	100,000	100,000	100,000	100,000	100,000		
B unit sales		100,000	100,000	100,000	100,000	100,000	100,000		
Revenue		10,000,000	10,000,000	10,000,000	10,000,000	10,000,000	10000000		
Production cost		3,515,833	3,515,833	3,515,833	3,515,833	3,515,833	3,515,833		
Other variable		1,000,000	1,000,000	1,000,000	1,000,000	1,000,000	1,000,000		
Depreciation	1,000,000	1,600,000	960,000	576,000	576,000	288,000	0		
Other fixed		100,000	100,000	100,000	100,000	100,000	100,000		
PBT		3784167	4,424,167	4,808,167	4,808,167	5,096,167	5,384,167		
PAT		2,497,550	2,919,950	3,173,390	3,173,390	3,363,470	3,553,550		
Fixed invest	5000000								
Inventory invest		511	0	0	0	0	0		
Residual value							17056408		
Cash flow	-4,000,000	4,097,039	3,879,950	3,749,390	3,749,390	3,651,470	20,609,958	22,210,067	3,762,788

(Industrial Technology Institute)

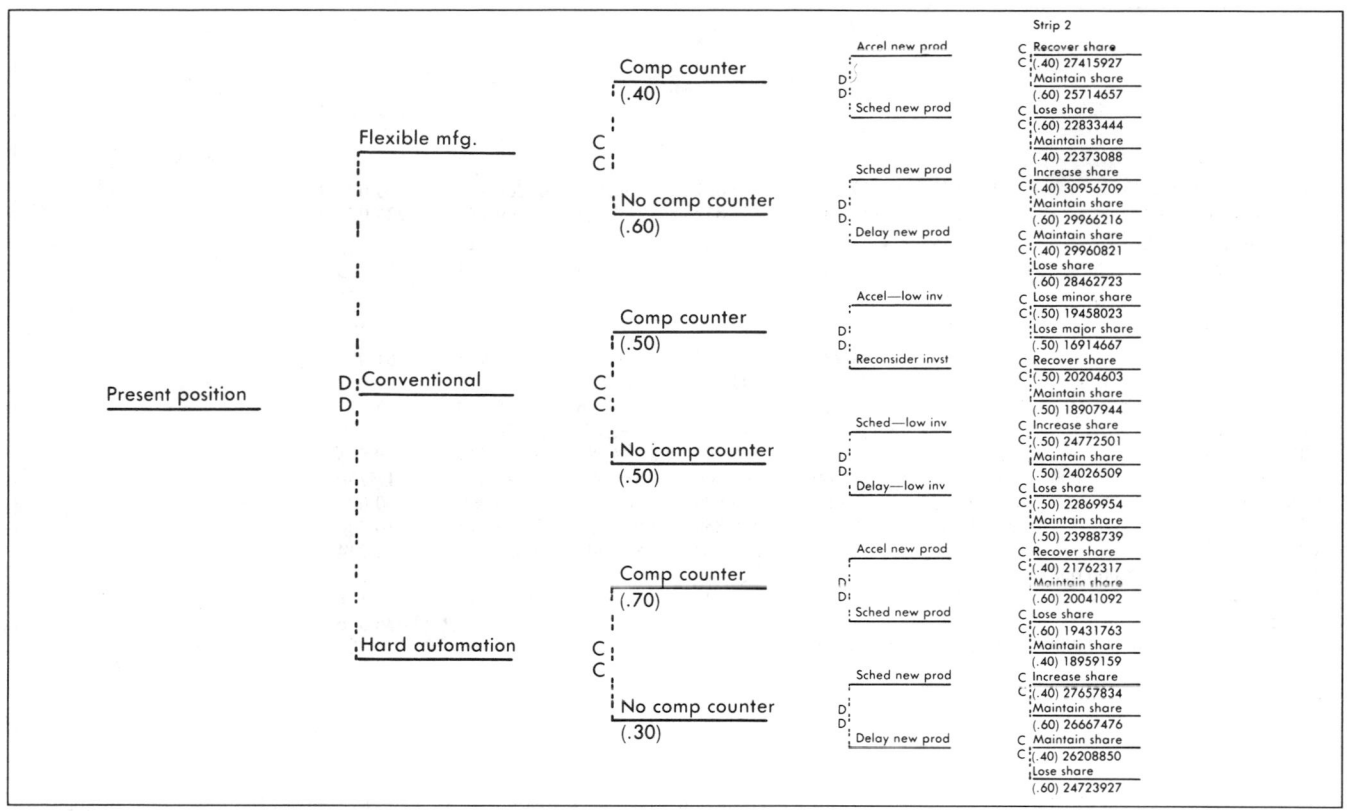

Fig. 6-9 Modified decision tree. (*Industrial Technology Institute*)

flexible manufacturing and hard automation than for the conventional system. Inventory investment is based on varying requirements for work in process in the model as volume changes with market size and the firm's share. Cash flow and net present value are calculated as defined in the appendixes.

The net present value of each branch, as determined by similar calculations, is shown along with its probability of occurrence, given that particular investment. These probabilities are calculated on the basis that the subsequent decision in response to a competitive counter is always made to the branch with the higher expected value. Based on this, the expected value is calculated for each alternative investment.

To calculate incremental costs and benefits, the investment in conventional equipment has been considered as the baseline. The baseline in this more complex example is less clear. It might be considered the expected value of the center branch of the tree; however, this value is influenced by the branch in which major investment is reconsidered.

Philosophically, the baseline is best represented by the branch that reflects a passive response to the business environment. The course of action identified as branch 14, with a net present value of $24,026,509, is probably as good as any to choose as the baseline, although it is not a perfect choice because it depends on the competition not making a competitive counter to a new product offering.

As one can see, when incremental cash flows are calculated over the life of the product, the analysis strongly favors the flexible manufacturing approach. In fact, the minimum value of the flexible manufacturing system is only slightly less than the maximum value of the hard automation system in this example.

Thus, the flexible manufacturing system not only has a higher expected value, but appears to be a more robust investment in the sense that it is the only branch in which the firm has the opportunity to increase value by making good decisions even in the event of adverse chance events.

INVESTMENT DECISION

If the decision analysis had indicated a course of action not meeting some needs of the business strategy to be a better course of action than one that did, it might cast doubt on the viability of the strategy. It is likely in this event, however, that the analysis failed to capture certain categories of costs and benefits. In general, the firm would want to invest in the machinery that will help it achieve its strategic objectives. If, for example, an investment consistent with the firm's strategic needs falls short of some less suitable investment by $10,000 per year, an appropriate question is whether one has overlooked categories of benefits that will yield cash flows of $10,000 per year. If one can define such benefits convincingly, they should be added to the investment analysis. There is no need to do that with this investment example because the flexible manufacturing system that best meets the needs of the strategy also yields the highest net present value. The analysis reflects this value only because the benefits that flexibility yields have been captured, both throughout the entire manufacturing system and also throughout the lifecycle of the system. That is not to say, however, that one has necessarily captured all of its benefits. As the system runs, one might well find unexpected benefits; one might find unexpected costs as well. This is valuable information and should be retained for use when the next investment proposal is analyzed.

CAPITAL INVESTMENT EXAMPLE

Year	0	1	2	3	4	5	6	NPV
Market for product A		142,857	157,143	172,857	190,143	209,157	230,073	
Market for product B		142,857	157,143	172,857	190,143	209,157	230,073	
Price for product A		45	45	45	45	45	45	
Price for product B		55	55	55	55	55	55	
Path 1								
Market share		0.7	0.6	0.6	0.625	0.65	0.7	
A unit sales		100,000	94,286	103,714	118,839	135,952	161,051	
B unit sales		100,000	94,286	103,714	118,839	135,952	161,051	
Revenue		10,000,000	9,428,562	10,371,418	11,883,916	13,595,200	16,105,083	
Production cost		3,515,833.	3,314,925	3,646,418	4,178,187.	4,779,845.	5,662,279.	
Other variable		1,000,000	94,2856	1,037,142	1,188,392	1,359,520	1,610,508	
Depreciation	1,000,000	1,600,000	97,0000	592,000	585,600	2,937,60	1,5760	
Other fixed		100,000	100,000	100,000	100,000	100,000	100,000	
PBT		3,784,167	4,100,781	4,995,859	5,831,738	7,062,075	8,716,536	
PAT		2,497,550	2,706,515	3,297,267	3,848,947	4,660,969	5,752,914	
Fixed invest	5,000,000		50,000				50,000	
Inventory invest		511	-29	48	77	87	128	
Residual value							22,036,376	
Cash flow	-4,000,000	4,097,039	3,626,544	3,889,219	4,434,470	4,954,642	27,754,922	27,415,927

SUMMARY OF OUTCOMES	NPV	Incremental NPV	Probability of Occurrence	Expected Incremental Value	Max and min Incremental Value
Flexible manufacturing					
Path 1	27,415,927	3,389,419	0.16	4,749,006	
Path 2	25,714,657	16,881,49	0.24		1,688,149
Path 3	22,833,444	-1,193,065			
Path 4	22,373,088	-1,653,420			
Path 5	30,956,709	6,930,201	0.24		6,930,201
Path 6	29,966,216	5,939,708	0.36		
Path 7	29,960,821	5,934,312			
Path 8	28,462,723	4,436,214			
Conventional:					
Path 9	19,458,023	-4,568,486		-2,048,619	
Path 10	16,914,667	-7,111,841			
Path 11	20,204,603	-3,821,906	0.25		
Path 12	18,907,944	-5,118,565	0.25		-5,118,565
Path 13	24,772,501	745,993	0.25		745,993
Path 14	24,026,509	0	0.25		
Path 15	22,869,954	-1,156,555			
Path 16	23,988,739	-37,769			
Hard automation:					
Path 17	21,762,317	-2,264,192	0.28	-1,396,715	
Path 18	20,041,092	-3,985,416	0.42		-3,985,416
Path 19	19,431,763	-4,594,746			
Path 20	18,959,159	-5,067,350			
Path 21	27,657,834	3,631,326	0.12		3,631,326
Path 22	26,667,476	2,640,968	0.18		
Path 23	26,208,850	2,182,342			
Path 24	24,723,927	697,419			

Fig. 6-10 Summary of analysis of investments based on decision tree in Fig. 6-9. (*Industrial Technology Institute*)

APPENDIX A—FINANCIAL ANALYSIS OF INVESTMENTS

Financial analysis of investments is sometimes referred to as engineering economics. By itself, it represents the traditional approach to investment evaluation. Embedded in a business planning process, this analysis is a key element in analyzing investment decisions.

THE COST OF CAPITAL

As noted in the main body of this chapter, manufacturing firms are generally formed to create wealth by producing goods. The firm hires people and purchases machinery and raw materials, produces the goods, then sells them. To do so, the firm must have sufficient money to hire the people and purchase the machinery and raw materials until such time as the goods are sold. This money is known as the firm's capital. Capital is always provided by the owners of the firm. The owners may also be the managers of the firm, as with a small job shop, or they may be separate, as with major corporations in which most of the shareholders (or owners) have no other connection with the firm. Capital may also be loaned to the firm by banks, by insurance companies, by individual investors, by other companies, and occasionally by the government.

To induce investors to purchase shares or loan money, the firm must provide compensation to them. Borrowed money requires that interest payments be made. Individuals who invest in shares may be compensated for the use of their funds by dividends, by growth in the value of the shares, or by a combination of both. This compensation provides a yield or return to the investors. Investors have a minimum required rate of return. From the perspective of the firm, this is a cost and is called the cost of capital.

The significance of the cost of capital is that if a firm earns exactly its cost of capital on its investments, it will neither create nor destroy wealth for its owners. If it earns more than its cost of capital, it will create wealth; if it earns less, it will destroy wealth. If a firm's cost of capital is 10%, it will create wealth by earning 11% on its investments; it will destroy wealth by earning 9%, even though it is operating "in the black." Thus the cost of capital is a very important figure when evaluating investments.

In most firms, the calculation of cost of capital is performed by the finance department. Even though the calculation of cost of capital is ordinarily performed by financial people rather than engineers, its significance is so great that calculation of this figure is discussed in Appendix B.

COMPOUND INTEREST

Nearly everyone is familiar with compound interest. A dollar invested at an interest rate of 10% compounded annually earns 10 cents interest the first year. The second year interest is earned not only on the dollar but also on the first year's interest of 10 cents, so the investment earns 11 cents the second year. Each year the interest compounds or is added to the principal and the interest that has already accumulated. Invested at 10% compounded annually, at the end of 10 years the dollar will have increased to $2.59. It is useful to think of this figure of $2.59 as the future value of a dollar invested at 10%, 10 years hence.

The compound interest equation is a simple one and is as follows:

$$FV = PV(1+r)^n \qquad (1)$$

where:

FV = future value
PV = present value
r = interest rate
n = number of years (periods)

Thus, when the present value is $1.00 and the interest rate is 10%, the future value calculation is as follows:

$$
\begin{aligned}
FV &= \$1.00\,(1 + 0.10)^{10}\\
&= \$1.00\,(1.10)^{10}\\
&= \$1.00 \times 2.59\\
&= \$2.59
\end{aligned}
$$

This calculation shows that a dollar now is worth more than a dollar at some time in the future as long as interest is earned. For example, if one can earn interest at a rate of 10% compounded annually, a dollar now would have the same value as $2.59 in 10 years from now.

It is also possible to make the same calculations in reverse. If one knows that a transaction of some specified amount at some particular time in the future will take place and what the proper interest rate is, the future value can be discounted to obtain the present value. The equation for this calculation is as follows:

$$PV = FV/(1+r)^n \qquad (2)$$

Thus, if one will receive a dollar 10 years hence, and the interest rate is 10% compounded annually, the present value is:

$$
\begin{aligned}
PV &= \$1.00/(1 + 0.10)^{10}\\
&= \$1.00/2.59\\
&= \$0.39
\end{aligned}
$$

Tables of compound interest and present value at various interest rates are shown in Appendix D. Compound interest tables show the future value of $1.00 compounded periodically, and discounting tables show the present value of $1.00 from some time in the future discounted periodically. Alternatively, it is sometimes more useful to calculate future and present values directly with a calculator or computer.

The concepts of compounding and discounting, representing the time value of money, are of particular use in evaluating investments because investments typically require an immediate cash outlay for a factory or machine, and yield cash inflows to the firm over some period in the future. By using these concepts, one can account for both the value of a dollar at present and a dollar at some time in the future.

TRADITIONAL CAPITAL INVESTMENT ANALYSIS

Years ago, there were no methods for analyzing and evaluating potential investments. Managers simply did what seemed right. In response to need, several rough techniques evolved for

APPENDIX A—FINANCIAL ANALYSIS

supplementing the manager's intuition with a more analytical approach. While these methods have value, they fail to consider whether the investment creates or destroys value.

Payback Period

Payback period is among the earliest measures that attempted to arrive at a figure of merit for investment projects. Payback period is the time required for the cash outflow for an investment to be offset by the cash inflows resulting from the investment. The concept of cash flow is discussed in some detail in Appendix C. If an investment of $100,000 resulted in cash inflows of $50,000 per year, the payback period of the investment would be 2 years. The presumption is that the investment with the shortest payback period is the best investment.

Throughout the chapter cash outflows from a firm will be referred to as negative cash flows, and cash inflows to a firm are positive cash flows; negative cash flows will be shown inparentheses. A comparison of the cash flows of two investments is shown in Table 6-6. Investment 1 has a payback period of about 3.1 years, while investment 2 has a payback period of about 2.6 years. By this criterion, investment 2 with the shorter payback period is the preferred investment.

Although payback period remains in use, it has two severe shortcomings as a criterion on which to base investments. First, it ignores cash flows in the years following the payback period, and second, it ignores the time value of money.

Accounting Rate of Return

Accounting rate of return is another traditional method for analyzing investments. Return on investment is a standard financial measure equal to net after-tax income divided by total investment. Applied to investments, an estimate is made of the increase in net after-tax income resulting from a specific investment, and this figure is divided by the value of the investment.

Typically, the effect of an investment on income varies from year to year. Further, because capital investments are depreciated over their lives, the value of the investment shown on the accounting books varies from year to year as well. This may be handled by calculating an estimated accounting rate of return for each year or by calculating a single average accounting rate of return over the life of the investment.

The accounting rate of return pattern for an investment of $20,000 depreciated on a straight-line basis over 4 years is shown in Table 6-7. Over the 4-year period, average net income is $4250, and the average value of the investment is $10,000, yielding an average accounting return of 42.5%. The difficulty of using annual accounting rate of return as an investment criterion is that the wide variation from year to year shown in Table 6-7 is typical, making it difficult to appraise the value of an investment. Using the average figure eliminates this problem, but fails to divulge the $2000 loss anticipated in year 1—a potentially important piece of information.

THE MAPI METHOD

In an effort to overcome the serious shortcomings of traditional investment analyses, George Terborgh of the Machinery and Allied Products Institute (MAPI) devised a method of analyzing machinery replacement directed toward selection of only those investments creating value.[1] This approach measures the annual benefits of keeping an existing machine vs. the benefits of replacing it with a new machine. The investment required to replace the asset is considered, as well as the present value of future operating costs and the potential salvage value of the new investment at the end of its life. Operating costs of the old machine are taken into account, as well as its salvage value, and the operating advantage that would result from replacing the old machine is compared with the costs of doing so.

The principal advantage of the MAPI method is its convenience; the principal disadvantage is its narrow focus on machinery replacement. To overcome this, MAPI subsequently incorporated into its methodology the investment analysis described in the following section. The resulting approach is the basis for the treatment of replacement decisions in many, if not all, current textbooks on engineering economy.

TABLE 6-6
Comparison of Cash Flows in Two Investments

Year	Investment 1 Cash Flow, $ Annual	Cumulative	Investment 2 Cash Flow, $ Annual	Cumulative
Investment	(20,000)	(20,000)	(10,000)	(10,000)
1	3000	(17,000)	2000	(8000)
2	7000	(10,000)	5000	(3000)
3	9000	(1000)	5000	2000
4	18,000	17,000	5000	7000

(Industrial Technology Institute)
Note: Values in parentheses are negative.

TABLE 6-7
Example of an Accounting Rate of Return Pattern for a $20,000 Investment

Year	Beginning of Year Investment, $	Annual Depreciation, $	End of Year Investment, $	Average Investment, $	Net Income, $	Accounting Rate of Return, %
1	20,000	5000	15,000	17,500	(2000)	-11
2	15,000	5000	10,000	12,500	2000	16
3	10,000	5000	5000	7500	4000	53
4	5000	5000	-0-	2500	13,000	520

Note: Values in parentheses are negative.

(Industrial Technology Institute)

INVESTMENT ANALYSIS BASED ON CASH FLOWS AND THE COST OF CAPITAL

In recent years, managers have recognized that it is sometimes possible to use the technique of discounting cash flows, long used to value financial assets, to value potential capital investments as well. The three most widely used investment evaluation techniques using discounted cash flows are net present value, profitability index, and internal rate of return. While the details of net present value, profitability index, and internal rate of return differ, all use the same fundamental approach, as follows:

1. Define the cash flows.
2. Define the interest rate.
3. Discount the cash flows to present value.

Net Present Value

Net present value (NPV) is based on the proposition that the value created by making an investment can be calculated by setting benefits equal to the positive cash flows generated by the investment. Costs are negative cash flows associated with making the investment itself, and net present value is the present value of the benefits less the costs. If the net present value is greater than 0, the investment will create value for the firm. Mathematically, NPV can be expressed as follows:

$$NPV = \sum_{j=0}^{n} X_j/(1 + r)^j \qquad (3)$$

where:

NPV = net present value, dollars
Σ = the sum of
X_j = net cash flow at the end of year j, dollars
n = number of years of cash flow
j = the year
r = the company's cost of capital

For example, a machine costing $10,000 results in positive cash flows of $3000 per year for 5 years commencing 1 year after the investment is made. The firm's cost of capital is 10%. As stated previously, cash outflows from the firm are negative, and cash inflows to the firm are positive. Compared with not making the investment, the value created by making the investment is shown in Table 6-8..

Some simplifying assumptions have been made for this calculation. In particular, the cash flows in years 1 through 5 arrive in lump payments, each conveniently arriving exactly at year-end. This is known as the "year-end convention," and it is common to use such a convention in calculating net present value. Other conventions have the cash flows occurring at the beginning of the year, at mid-year, or continuously throughout the year. Unless cash flows can be forecast with great accuracy, the differences in net present value resulting from using different conventions for cash flow patterns during the year are much smaller than the usual forecasting errors and are therefore unimportant.

Profitability Index

Some managers are accustomed to managing by using ratios or percents and would prefer to use a ratio for evaluating capital investment projects. The profitability index (PI) was designed for such managers. Its numerator is equal to the present value of future cash flows from operation with the investment where the relevant interest rate is the firm's cost of capital. The denominator is the present value of investment outlays. If the profitability index is greater than 1, the investment will create value for the firm. In calculation of the profitability index, the negative sign on the present value of investment outlays is typically ignored so that a positive ratio will result. Table 6-9 shows the calculation for an initial investment of $10,000.

Internal Rate of Return

For managers who wish to know the rate at which the investment is earning, the internal rate of return (IRR) may be calculated. The internal rate of return is a "cut-and-try" calculation in which the interest rate at which net present value is equal to 0 is found. That rate is defined as the internal rate of return. If the internal rate of return is greater than the firm's cost of capital, the investment will create value for the firm.

Once cash flows have been defined, the next step is to pick a rate. Very often, analysts pick the firm's cost of capital and calculate the net present value. If the net present value is positive, they know the internal rate of return is higher than the cost of capital. That is, future cash flows must be discounted at a higher rate to reduce the net present value to 0. In the example shown in Table 6-8, the net present value of the investment was found to be $1372 when discounted at 10%, which was the firm's cost of capital. Several tries may be required to find that the internal rate of return of this investment is 15.24% (see Tables 6-10 and 6-11).

TABLE 6-8
Example of Calculations for Determining Net Present Values

Year	Cash Flow, $	Present Value at 10%, $
0	-10,000	= -10,000
1	3000	$3000 \times 1/(1.10)$ = 2727
2	3000	$3000 \times 1/(1.10)^2$ = 2479
3	3000	$3000 \times 1/(1.10)^3$ = 2254
4	3000	$3000 \times 1/(1.10)^4$ = 2049
5	3000	$3000 \times 1/(1.10)^5$ = 1863
		Net present value = 1372

(Industrial Technology Institute)

TABLE 6-9
Example of Calculations for Determining the Profitability Index of an Investment

Year	Cash Flow, $	Present Value at 10%, $
1	3000	$3000 \times 1/(1.10)$ = 2727
2	3000	$3000 \times 1/(1.10)^2$ = 2479
3	3000	$3000 \times 1/(1.10)^3$ = 2254
4	3000	$3000 \times 1/(1.10)^4$ = 2049
5	3000	$3000 \times 1/(1.10)^5$ = 1863
		Present value = 11,372

Profitability index = 11,372 / 10,000 = 1.137

(Industrial Technology Institute)

CHAPTER 6

APPENDIX A—FINANCIAL ANALYSIS

By looking at Tables 6-10 and 6-11, one can conclude that the project IRR is between 15 and 16%. Through the use of linear interpolation, the actual internal rate of return is as follows:

i	NPV
15%	57
IRR	0
16%	-178

$$IRR = 15\% + \left(\frac{57-0}{57-(-178)}\right)(16-15\%) = 15.24\%.$$

TWO EXAMPLES OF SIMPLE CAPITAL INVESTMENT PROJECTS

Prior to the mid-1970s, business strategies were typically simple, and investments were made because they reduced manufacturing costs, provided capacity to produce additional product to be sold on the market, or a combination of both. The first example will be of an investment intended to reduce manufacturing costs with no change in production volume. The second example will be an investment intended to provide manufacturing capacity needed for additional sales volume.

A Cost Reduction Investment

Several years ago, a firm was producing its product on a small, 20-ton press. It could have continued to use this equipment, but its engineers saw a potential opportunity to reduce costs by acquiring a new higher speed press with more rapid changeover capabilities and lower maintenance requirements. The new press delivered, installed, and tooled would cost $33,500. Before buying the new press, however, they were asked to analyze the investment by calculating the net present value, profitability index, and internal rate of return of the investment.

They realized that any such analysis is a comparison of two alternatives, and the alternatives were apparent in this case—continuing to use the old press vs. purchasing the new press. Thus, to make a comparison, they needed to do the following:

1. Estimate the cash flows that would occur if they continued to operate with the old press vs. those that would occur if they invested in the new press.
2. Define the interest rate.
3. Discount future cash flows to present value at the appropriate interest rate.

Their first task was to estimate cash flows. The machinery dealer informed them that their old press could not be resold and had no value and that the new press delivered and installed would cost $33,500. Naturally, if they continued to operate the old press, there was no initial outlay.

The new press would have no effect on sales (they produced and sold 12,000,000 units per year at present), the old press provided adequate capacity to continue, and the sales department saw neither a significant increase nor decrease in volume in future years. Thus, the future cash flows that would result from a new investment would be due only to operating savings.

Engineering discussed what operating savings it might expect from the new investment—a critical step in the evaluation—and decided that it could expect savings in direct labor, set-up labor, maintenance, and tooling. From existing records of standard costs and of performance to standard, the production rates and set-up times of existing equipment were found. Maintenance records yielded annual maintenance costs for the existing press, and purchasing records showed annual tooling expenditures. From financial records, it was determined that labor rates were $3.15 per hour for both press operators and set-up people, to which $1.42 per hour of fringe benefits were added for a total labor cost of $4.57 per hour.

For the new press, engineering studied the specifications and estimated both operating performance and set-up. Likewise, it was necessary for engineering to estimate maintenance and tooling costs.

A comparison of the estimated operating costs yielded by these studies is shown in Table 6-12.

Property records showed that the old press was fully depreciated. The finance department indicated that the new press would be depreciated over 5 years on a straight-line basis. As discussed in Appendix C, while depreciation is not of itself a cash flow, it affects taxes, and taxes are cash flows. The finance department indicated that the firm's tax rate was 34%, and the after-tax cost of capital (as discussed in Appendix A) was 10%.

Management indicated that there was little business risk for the next 5 years, but after the 5-year period they could not foresee what might happen. Thus, they suggested that a 5-year period would be a reasonable period to analyze cash flows. Engineering estimated that the press might be sold for around $10,000 at the end of 5 years if the firm no longer needed it.

With this information, it is possible to define initial outlay and annual cash flows in succeeding years. In this example, initial outlay is simple. There was no equipment to sell, nor were there expenses associated with the investment. Thus, the initial

TABLE 6-10
Calculation of Internal Rate of Return Using 15% as an Estimate

Year	Cash Flow, $	Present Value at 15%, $
0	-10,000	= -10,000
1	3000	$3000 \times 1/(1 + 0.15)$ = 2608
2	3000	$3000 \times 1/(1 + 0.15)^2$ = 2268
3	3000	$3000 \times 1/(1 + 0.15)^3$ = 1974
4	3000	$3000 \times 1/(1 + 0.15)^4$ = 1716
5	3000	$3000 \times 1/(1 + 0.15)^5$ = 1491
		Net present value at 15% = 57

(Industrial Technology Institute)

TABLE 6-11
Calculation of Internal Rate of Return Using 16% as an Estimate

Year	Cash Flow, $	Present Value at 16%, $
0	-10,000	= -10,000
1	3000	$3000 \times 1/(1 + 0.16)$ = 2586
2	3000	$3000 \times 1/(1 + 0.16)^2$ = 2229
3	3000	$3000 \times 1/(1 + 0.16)^3$ = 1923
4	3000	$3000 \times 1/(1 + 0.16)^4$ = 1656
5	3000	$3000 \times 1/(1 + 0.16)^5$ = 1428
		Net present value at 16% = -178

(Industrial Technology Institute)

TABLE 6-12
Comparison of Operating Costs

Category	Present	Proposed
Direct labor	0.017 hours/100 pieces	0.009 hours/100 pieces
	12,000,000 pieces/year	12,000,000 pieces/year
	$4.57/hour	$4.57/hour
	$9322.80/year	$4935.60/year
Set-up	2 hours/set-up	0.5 hours/set-up
	145 set-ups/year	60 set-ups/year
	$4.57/hour	$4.57/hour
	$1325.30/year	$137.10/year
Maintenance	$1700.00/year	$300.00/year
Tooling	$33,600/year	$18,000/year

(*Industrial Technology Institute*)

outlay was equal to the investment itself, or $33,500. In keeping with the cash flow convention, cash outflow is shown as a negative number.

The calculation of annual cash flows is facilitated by a spreadsheet, as shown in Table 6-13. It is assumed that each category of annual savings in this example will occur without change through the years. This might not necessarily be true. For example, it could be assumed that direct labor savings would be less the first year because of the need for operators to learn how to use the new press. Accelerated depreciation could also be assumed, causing depreciation to be greater in earlier years and less in later years.

For each of the four savings categories—operators, set-up, maintenance, tooling—the proposed annual cost (rounded to the nearest dollar) is subtracted from the present annual cost to obtain the difference. When the difference is a reduction in cost that will result in an increase in earnings, the difference is shown as a positive amount. These four differences will flow to profit before tax, where their effect will be to increase the amount of profit. Tax must be paid on this added profit, so the tax is calculated at 34% in the next column and the effect on profit after tax in the final column.

Because expense reductions result in cash savings and the added tax will be a cash outlay, the effect on profit after tax is the same as the cash flow. This is not true of depreciation. Depreciation is not a cash expense but an accrual. It will, however, have an effect on taxes, which do affect cash flow. The increase in depreciation will have a negative effect on profit,

reducing taxes by 34% of the profit reduction. This reduction in taxes will affect cash flow, so the final column in the depreciation row shows only the positive effect on cash flow resulting from the tax reduction.

By adding the various cash flow items, it is found that the annual cash flow resulting from operations will be $17,177 greater in each of the 5 years of use for the new press. There is one additional cash flow that must be taken into account. At the end of the 5-year period, the press, while fully depreciated on the books, will still have a market value estimated at $10,000. The press could be sold and an additional $10,000 of cash recovered. Taxes would have to be paid on the gain, the difference between selling price and book value; in this case, taxes would be due on the entire $10,000. If the tax rate of 34% applies, the after-tax cash flow would be +$6,600. This is often called the "residual value" of the asset being considered. The difference in after-tax cash flows between making the investment in the new press and continuing to use the old press is shown in Table 6-14.

It is assumed that an initial cash outlay of $33,500 at the end of year 0 is required if the new press is purchased, and no outlay is required if the old press is retained. If the new press is purchased, cash flows from operations will be $17,177 greater at the end of each year from year 1 to year 5. The new press could also be sold at the end of year 5 for a cash inflow net after taxes of $6600. Because the year-end convention is used, an assumption can be made stating that cash flows from operations in year 5 and the cash flow resulting from sale of the press can simply be added together. The last column in Table 6-14 is the end result of step 1 of the analysis and defines the cash flows that will result from making the investment.

The next step is to define the interest rate. For net present value and profitability index calculations, it is the firm's after-tax cost of capital; for the internal rate of return calculation, it is the discount rate at which net present value is equal to 0. For this example, the net present value will be calculated first. The profitability index can then be calculated by discounting the cash flows defined as the firm's cost of capital. Finally, the internal rate of return can be calculated.

The firm's after-tax cost of capital was stated to be 10% by the finance department, presumably after making an analysis such as that described in Appendix B. To calculate the net present value of the investment in the new press, the cash flows can be discounted at a rate of 10% by multiplying the after-tax cash flow each year by the discount factor for that year (see Table 6-15).

TABLE 6-13
Spreadsheet Used to Facilitate the Calculation of Cash Flows

Cost Category	Present, $	Proposed, $	Difference, $	Tax Effect, $	After-Tax Cash Flow, $
Operators	9323	4936	4387	(1492)	2895
Set-up	1325	137	1188	(404)	784
Maintenance	1700	300	1400	(476)	924
Tooling	33,600	18,000	15,600	(5304)	10,296
Depreciation	0	6700	(6700)	2278	2278

Annual cash flows from operations = 17,177

(*Industrial Technology Institute*)

Note: Values in parentheses are negative.

CHAPTER 6

APPENDIX A—FINANCIAL ANALYSIS

TABLE 6-14
After-Tax Cash Flow Summary

Year	Initial Outlay, $	Cash Flow from Operations, $	Residual Value After Tax, $	Total After-Tax Cash Flow, $
0	(33,500)	- - -	- - -	(33,500)
1	- - -	17,177	- - -	17,177
2	- - -	17,177	- - -	17,177
3	- - -	17,177	- - -	17,177
4	- - -	17,177	- - -	17,177
5	- - -	17,177	6600	23,777

(Industrial Technology Institute)

Note: Values in parentheses are negative.

TABLE 6-15
Calculations of Net Present Value for A Cost Reduction Investment

Year	After-Tax Cash Flows, $	10% Discount Factor	Presnt Value, $
0	-33,500	1.0	-33,500
1	17,177	$1/1.10 = 0.909$	15,614
2	17,177	$1/(1.10)^2 = 0.826$	14,188
3	17,177	$1/(1.10)^3 = 0.751$	12,900
4	17,177	$1/(1.10)^4 = 0.683$	11,732
5	23,777	$1/(1.10)^5 = 0.621$	14,766
		Net present value at 10% = 35,700	

(Industrial Technology Institute)

The net present value of $35,700 is the algebraic sum of the present values of the cash flows in all years, including the initial outlay. This indicates that investment in the new press will increase the value of the firm by $35,700 over the value the firm would have if no investment were made. Because the net present value is greater than 0, a recommendation to proceed with the investment should be made to management.

Most of the calculations have already been done for the profitability index, which is equal to the present value of operating cash flows at the firm's cost of capital, divided by the initial outlay. The initial outlay is $33,500, and the present value of cash flows in years 1 through 5 is equal to $69,200. The calculation for the profitability index is as follows:

Profitability index = 69,200/33,500 = 2.07

Because the profitability index is greater than 1.0, this calculation also leads engineering to recommend that management proceed with the investment.

Finding the interest rate at which net present value is 0 is a cut-and-try process. The internal rate of return is greater than 10%, because the net present value was positive at a 10% interest rate. It might require several tries to find that the internal rate of return is approximately 45% (see Table 6-16).

The internal rate of return is greater than the firm's cost of capital, so by this criterion as well a recommendation should be made to management that it proceed with the investment. Some pocket calculators and many spreadsheet software packages for personal computers include programs for performing all three calculations or may be readily programmed to do so.

An Investment to Add Capacity

At about the same time, the firm found that its capacity to produce another product was limited to 23,100 units, equal to sales during the current year. Sales were forecast to continue to grow as long as capacity could be added, and the sales department projected a loss of market share in coming years unless the firm added capacity to produce additional product. At present, the product sold for $100 per unit, with an after-tax margin of 12.2%, resulting in profit after tax of $281,500. Management did not want to lose market share in such a profitable product line, so the engineering, marketing, and finance departments were asked to forecast the market for the product, the investment that would be required to meet the demands of the market, and the economics of making such an investment.

The market outlook in Table 6-17 was provided by the marketing department. This outlook was based on an increase in capacity. There was general agreement that if no capacity was added, the current volume of 23,100 units would continue to be sold at the prices forecast for each year. Table 6-18 compares the volume output without an additional investment to the volume output with an investment and also shows the difference in sales. Thus, incremental sales with the investment increase from 0 in the current year to more than $1,000,000 in year 5.

The next step was to estimate the investment to produce the added sales and the incremental earnings from these added sales. This required a joint effort by the engineering and finance departments.

The engineering department found that $200,000 would buy the machinery to produce the additional product. No building

APPENDIX A—FINANCIAL ANALYSIS

TABLE 6-16
Internal Rate of Return Calculations for A Cost
Reduction Investment

Year	After-Tax Cash Flows, $	44.537% Discount Factor	Presnt Value, $
0	-33.500	1.0	-33.500
1	17,177	$1/1.44537 = 0.692$	11,886
2	17,177	$1/(1.44537)^2 = 0.479$	8228
3	17,177	$1/(1.44537)^3 = 0.331$	5686
4	17,177	$1/(1.44537)^4 = 0.229$	3934
5	23,777	$1/(1.44537)^5 = 0.159$	3781
		Net present value at 44.537% =	15

(Industrial Technology Institute)

TABLE 6-17
Market Outlook for an Investment to Add Capacity Example

Year	Total Market	Firm's Market Share, %	Volume, Units	Price, $	Sales, $
0	66,000	35	23,100	100	2,310,000
1	76,000	35	26,600	104	2,766,400
2	80,000	35	28,000	108	3,024,000
3	74,000	35	29,400	112	3,292,800
4	88,000	35	30,800	117	3,603,600
5	92,000	35	32,200	122	3,928,400

(Industrial Technology Institute)

TABLE 6-18
Comparison of Volume Output for Example to Add Production Capacity

Year	Volume Without Investment, Units	Volume With Investment, Units	Volume Difference	Price, $	Sales Difference, $
0	23,100	23,100	0	100	0
1	23,100	26,600	3500	104	364,000
2	23,100	28,000	4900	108	529,200
3	23,100	29,400	6300	112	705,600
4	23,100	30,800	7700	117	900,900
5	23,100	32,200	9100	122	1,110,200

(Industrial Technology Institute)

addition would be required. Finance noted that the machinery would be depreciated on a straight-line basis over 5 years, with zero book value at the end of the period.

Engineering estimated standards, performance to standards, and labor requirements. It also took into account the changes that were likely to occur in fixed and variable costs, the costs of starting up the added machines, the effects of changes in wages, and the cost of raw materials over the years. The incremental earnings that would result from the added sales are shown in Table 6-19.

Additionally, finance estimated additional working capital requirements for inventory and accounts receivable to be equal to 18% of any additional sales (see Table 6-20).

Because the equipment to be purchased was special-purpose machinery, engineering estimated a residual value of only $10,000 at the end of 5 years. Finance informed engineering that the firm's cost of capital was 10% and that the tax rate on income was 34%.

With this information, engineering was ready to begin the analysis. The initial outlay of $200,000 for new machinery was straightforward, but with this investment, as with many investments to provide for additional sales, the investment process continued with increases in working capital throughout the entire period. Thus, the outlay is shown in Table 6-21. The cast inflow from operations is estimated to be equal to profit after tax plus depreciation and is shown in Table 6-22.

APPENDIX A—FINANCIAL ANALYSIS

TABLE 6-19
Summary of Incremental Earnings Resulting
From Added Sales

Year	Added Volume, Units	Price, $	Added Sales, $	Added Profit After Tax, $
0	0	100	0	0
1	3500	104	364,000	(35,000)
2	4900	108	529,200	26,000
3	6300	112	705,600	85,000
4	7700	117	900,900	126,000
5	9100	122	1,110,200	156,000

(*Industrial Technology Institute*)

Note: Values in parenthesis is negative.

Residual value was then considered. This includes not only the value of the machinery at the end of the analysis period, but also the value of working capital to be liquidated if the firm were to stop producing the product. The cumulative value of working capital additions due to the increased sales volume is $198,100. From the estimated $10,000 value of the machinery at the end of the period, $3400 must be subtracted for taxes that would be paid if it were sold, for a net value of $6600. Thus, the total residual value is $204,700.

The difference in after-tax cash flows between making the investment to increase capacity vs. continuing to produce and sell 23,100 units per year is shown in Table 6-23.

The next step is to define the interest rate. For net present value and profitability index calculations, it is the firm's after-tax cost of capital; for the internal rate of return calculation, it is the interest rate at which net present value is equal to 0. Net present value is calculated first, then the profitability index by discounting the cash flows defined at the firm's cost of capital. Finally, the internal rate of return can be calculated.

The firm's after-tax cost of capital was stated to be 10% by the finance department, presumably after making an analysis such as that described in Appendix B. To calculate the net present value of the investment in the new equipment, the after-tax cash flow is multiplied each year by the discount factor for that year (see Table 6-24). The net present value of $160,488 is the algebraic sum of discounted cash flows from all years, including the initial outlay. This indicates that investment in the new equipment will increase the value of the firm by $160,488 over the value the firm would have if no investment were made. Because the net present value is greater than 0, a

recommendation would be made to management to proceed with the investment.

Table 6-23 contains the data for computing the profitability index. The present value of cash flows from operations at the 10% after-tax cost of capital is $387,260. A similar calculation for the investment cash flows is straightforward except that net investment in year 5 is $204,700 - $35,900. Thus, the present value for net investment cash flows over the 5-year period is -$226,850. The profitability index is calculated as follows:

Profitability index = 387,260/226,850 = 1.7

Because the profitability index is greater than 1.0, this calculation also leads to the recommendation that management proceed with the investment.

As was stated previously, the internal rate of return is a cut-and-try process. The internal rate of return is greater than 10% percent because the net present value was positive at an interest rate of 10%. Several tries may be required to find that the internal rate of return is approximately 24%. Because the internal rate of return is greater than the firm's cost of capital, a recommendation would be made to management to proceed with the investment.

Preparing a Capital Budget

The process for establishing a capital budget presented in most textbooks and generally more or less followed in practice is discussed in this section. Engineering, marketing, and operations people put together a complete list of desired capital investment opportunities and analyze them according to net

TABLE 6-20
Estimate of Additional Working Capital for
Investment to Add Capacity

Year	Sales Increase, $	Working Capital, $
0	0	0
1	364,000	65,500
2	165,200	29,700
3	176,400	31,800
4	195,300	35,200
5	199,300	35,900

(*Industrial Technology Institute*)

TABLE 6-21
Investment Cash Flow Over 5-Year Period

Year	Investment Cash Flow, $
0	(200,000)
1	(65,500)
2	(29,700)
3	(31,800)
4	(35,200)
5	(35,900)

(*Industrial Technology Institute*)

Note: Values in parentheses are negative.

TABLE 6-22
Cash Inflow Over Five Years for
Investment to Add Capacity Example

Year	Profit After Tax, $	Depreciation, $	Operations Cash Flow, $
0	0	0	0
1	(35,000)	40,000	5000
2	25,000	40,000	65,000
3	85,000	40,000	125,000
4	126,000	40,000	166,000
5	156,000	40,000	196,000

(Industrial Technology Institute)

Note: Value in parenthesis is negative.

TABLE 6-23
After-Tax Cash Flow for Investment to
Add Capacity

Year	Investment Cash Flow, $	Cash Flow From Operations, $	Residual Value After Tax, $	Total After-Tax Cash Flow
0	(200,000)	0	- - -	(200,000)
1	(65,500)	5000	- - -	(60,000)
2	(29,700)	65,000	- - -	35,300
3	(31,800)	125,000	- - -	93,200
4	(35,200)	166,000	- - -	130,800
5	(35,900)	196,000	204,700	364,800

(Industrial Technology Institute)

Note: Values in parentheses are negative.

TABLE 6-24
Calculations of Net Present Value for an Investment to Add Capacity

Year	After-Tax Cash Flows, $	10% Discount Factor	Present Value, $
0	(200,000)	1.0	(200,000)
1	(60,000)	$1/1.10 = 0.909$	(54,540)
2	35,300	$1/(1.10)^2 = 0.826$	29,158
3	93,200	$1/(1.10)^3 = 0.751$	69,993
4	130,800	$1/(1.10)^4 = 0.683$	89,336
5	364,800	$1/(1.10)^5 = 0.621$	226,541
		Net present value at 10% =	160,488

(Industrial Technology Institute)

Note: Values in parentheses are negative.

present value, profitability index, or internal rate of return. These opportunities should be constructed to be independent in the sense that each of them could be implemented with any combination of the others. Total investment cost would be equal to the sum of the investments for the individual opportunities. Simultaneously, finance people analyze the availability of money for capital investment. Projects are ranked with the best investments at the top of the list. If adequate funds are available, all the investments meeting the firm's criterion for acceptance are made. Otherwise, only the best investments are made, with the less attractive investments either rejected or deferred until another time.

When following such a practice, one must choose a valid criterion for ranking potential investments. Otherwise, it is likely that some of the rejected investments will be better than those that are accepted.

The preceding section reviewed three techniques for evaluating capital investments by discounted cash flows. They are net present value, profitability index, and internal rate of return. It was noted that an investment acceptable by one criterion will be acceptable by both of the others. Thus, if the net present value of an investment project is positive, the profitability index will be greater than 1 and the internal rate of return will be greater than the firm's cost of capital. The investment projects, however, will not necessarily be ranked in the same order.

APPENDIX A—FINANCIAL ANALYSIS

If the firm ranks projects by either profitability index or internal rate of return, the cost reduction project ranks higher than the capacity increase and, if capital is constrained, has a better chance of being accepted. If the firm ranks projects by net present value, the capacity increase project ranks higher and has a better chance of being accepted. Which is best? Because the objective of the firm is to create value or wealth and net present value measures the creation of value quantitatively, it is generally accepted as the correct criterion for ranking projects. Profitability index and internal rate of return indicate whether or not a potential investment will create value, but they do not indicate how much. It is possible, as in the case of the cost reduction, to have an investment that is a very good one, as shown by the high profitability index and internal rate of return, but too small for the creation of much value. The capacity increase is not as profitable per dollar invested, but is large enough to create more value. For this reason, net present value is generally accepted as the preferred evaluation criterion. Furthermore, while most investments have an initial cash outflow followed by cash inflows resulting in one change of sign with respect to cash flow from negative to positive, cash outflows in later years result in more than one sign change. Therefore, the internal rate of return calculation yields multiple answers that are not valid.

Issues

While theoreticians agree that net present value is the best technique available for evaluating investment projects, it is not always easy to apply. To use any of the discounted cash flow methods of investment analysis, one must forecast cash flows. At times it may be impossible to do so with sufficient accuracy to make the analysis worthwhile.

It was noted earlier that cash flow forecasts may have as their source financial and management reports and engineering, marketing, or financial studies. When one seeks to use financial data as a source of cash flow forecasts, one of the greatest barriers is the problem of allocation. When an investment is made to increase capacity, one must ask what will happen to overhead expenses. Will they increase? Probably. Will they increase proportionately with direct labor? Ordinarily, there is no reason to expect that they will, but many analysts make the assumption that they will and are surprised when they do not. For investment analysis, it is best that all costs be considered direct and addressed individually. Will additional supervision be needed? Inspection? And how about tooling maintenance? In many companies, all these costs are hidden in the overhead. Thus, engineering and financial studies are needed to define the specific cost elements affected by the potential investment.

An even more difficult task is to seek out the effects on costs and revenues where customers are involved. If new machinery is acquired to maintain statistical process control, it may be difficult to determine the reductions achieved in scrap and rework. However, it is typically even more difficult to estimate what will happen to warranty costs, not to mention increases in revenue as a result of increased market share from greater consumer satisfaction.

Much of the material that follows in this chapter deals with forecasting cash flows. One section covers manufacturing system modeling as a tool for evaluating the cash flow effects of complex investments. System modeling is a great help in arriving at the economics of complex investments, but the tools currently both available and easy to use are limited in their ability to handle support activities and do not take markets into account explicitly.

A second issue closely related to defining cash flows deals with a realistic alternative to making the investment. As noted earlier, every investment analysis is a comparison of alternatives. An investment can be compared with an alternative investment or with making no investment at all. If the alternative with which an investment is compared is bad enough, any investment will look good. Every investment analyst has to deal at one time or another with the "weeping" manager who claims dire consequences unless a favorite investment project is approved. On the other hand, making unrealistically favorable assumptions concerning the alternative to investing can sometimes keep managers from investing when they should. Often, analysts compare new investments with the status quo, which is all right when the status quo is a viable alternative. In these times of rapidly changing markets, technologies, and international politics, however, maintaining the status quo is not always a possibility.

The difficulty of making accurate forecasts under certain circumstances has already been mentioned, but risk and uncertainty are so intimately interwoven with capital investments that they should be noted separately as the third issue. Because capital investments are inevitably made for future benefits and it is impossible to know the future, investment inevitably means taking risk.

There are numerous definitions of risk and uncertainty, but a good working definition is the possibility that things may not turn out as expected. This does not necessarily mean that things may be worse—they may be better or they may be worse. While risk is inevitable, it can sometimes be dealt with constructively. Some approaches to dealing with risk are discussed in the section on decision analysis.

APPENDIX B—THE COMPOSITE COST OF CAPITAL

In many firms, capital is provided from equity provided by the owners or shareholders leveraged with a certain amount of debt. Firms generally have a target ratio of debt to equity and try not to stray too far from this ratio.

It was stated earlier in this chapter that the yield or return to the investor must be regarded as a cost by the firm. If there were no taxes, the cost to the firm would be equal to the yield to the investor. There are taxes, however, and they must be paid before

the owners of the firm can increase their wealth. Therefore, it is necessary to deal with after-tax numbers in evaluating activities, including investments, that have as their objective increasing the wealth of the owners .

Because of a peculiarity of tax laws in the United States and most other countries, the firm's income taxes are calculated on the basis of an income from which interest payments have been subtracted as a cost, but from which dividends have not. An

APPENDIX B—COMPOSITE COST OF CAPITAL

example of the profit and loss statement of a company is shown in Fig. 6-11.

As indicated in Fig. 6-11, the firm has sold goods during some period of time for $1,000,000 and spent $500,000 for the material, labor, and overhead to produce those goods. This leaves a gross profit of $500,000. Administrative costs, which generally include selling expenses as well, were $100,000, leaving net operating income of $400,000. Interest expenses on borrowings were $50,000, leaving pre-tax income of $350,000 on which federal income taxes of 34% must be paid ($119,000), leaving after-tax income of $231,000. Of this, $150,000 was paid out in dividends, and the remaining $81,000 was retained and reinvested by the firm.

COST OF DEBT

One question that a manager may ask is "where on the profit and loss statement does the firm's cost of capital appear?" The bewildering answer is that it does not. However, part of the cost of capital can be obtained from this statement. Interest expense was $50,000. If the firm had borrowed no money at all, it would have had no interest payments, in which case pre tax earnings would have been $500,000. Taxes in this case would have been 34% ($136,000), leaving a profit after tax of $264,000. Instead of increasing profit by $50,000, it would have only increased profit by $33,000. Likewise, increasing interest payments by $50,000 will reduce profit by only $33,000. The interest payments may be said to have "sheltered" taxes by an amount equal to the interest payment multiplied by the tax rate as shown in the following equation:

$$\text{Tax shelter} = \text{Interest payment} \times \text{tax rate} \qquad (4)$$

Thus, the cost to the firm of interest payments is equal to the interest payment minus the tax shelter provided as shown in the following equation:

$$\text{Cost to firm} = \text{Interest payment} - \text{tax shelter} \qquad (5)$$

The after-tax cost of debt to the firm is as follows:

$$\text{After-tax cost of debt} = \text{Interest rate} \times (1 - \text{tax rate}) \qquad (6)$$

Sales	$1,000,000
Cost of goods sold	500,000
Gross profit	500,000
General and administrative expenses	100,000
Net operating income	400,000
Interest expense	50,000
Pre-tax income	350,000
Income taxes at 34%	119,000
Net after-tax income	231,000
Dividends	150,000
Reinvested earnings	81,000

Fig. 6-11 Example of a company's profit and loss statement. (*Industrial Technology Institute*)

Thus, if the firm is paying an interest rate of 10% and the tax rate is 34%, the after-tax cost to the firm is:

$$\begin{aligned} \text{After-tax cost of debt} &= 0.10 \times (1 - 0.34) \\ &= 0.10 \times 0.66 \\ &= 0.066 \text{ or } 6.6\% \end{aligned}$$

COST OF EQUITY

The cost of equity is a little more difficult to compute because the concepts are a little more complex and because the data are not always readily available. There are a number of methods for calculating cost of equity, two of which are discussed.

The first approach to calculating the cost of equity is based on the observation noted earlier in Appendix A that some shareholders receive a return in the form of dividends, some in the form of increased share value, and some a combination of the two. If a firm exhibited no growth but had the same level of sales, earnings, and dividends year after year, the shareholder would receive a constant stream of dividends, the share price would be unlikely to increase, and the return to the investor (and the cost to the firm) would be equal to the annual dividend divided by the share price. The cost of equity could be calculated as follows:

$$\text{Cost of equity} = \text{Dividend} / \text{share price} \qquad (7)$$

If the firm were to grow at some constant growth rate year after year, the sales, earnings, and dividends would increase each year. The price of the share would reflect the buyers' expectations that dividends would continue to increase each year, and it can be calculated that the cost of equity would be equal to the current dividend divided by the share price, plus the growth rate. In this instance, the cost of equity would be calculated as follows:

$$\text{Cost of equity} = (\text{Dividend} / \text{share price}) + \text{growth rate} \qquad (8)$$

Thus, if a firm paid a dividend of $1.00, the shares sold for $10.00, and the market expected the firm to grow at a rate of 5% annually, the cost of equity may be calculated as follows:

$$\begin{aligned} \text{Cost of equity} &= (\$1.00 / \$10.00) + (0.05) \\ &= 0.10 + 0.05 \\ &= 0.15 \text{ or } 15\% \end{aligned}$$

Because dividends are paid out of after-tax earnings, they provide the firm with no tax shelter, and the tax rate plays no role in the calculation of cost of equity.

The second approach to calculating cost of equity is based on the observation that investors demand a higher return on higher risk investments. A U.S. Treasury bill, for example, attracts investors with a relatively low rate, while securities in firms with shaky financing must pay a high rate to attract investors. The significant risk for shareholders has been defined as the fluctuation of prices in the stock markets. As the markets fluctuate, some stocks fluctuate more than others, and the extent to which they fluctuate (and hence a measure of their risk) can be calculated. The relationship between the required rate of return for a particular stock and the risk-free rate of return is known as beta (β). The required rate of return can be calculated as follows:

$$R_j = R_f + \beta (R_m - R_f) \qquad (9)$$

where:

R_j = return on stock j
R_f = risk-free return
R_m = return on stock market

APPENDIX B—COMPOSITE COST OF CAPITAL

Stock j is, of course, the stock of the firm in question; for the risk-free return, the U.S. Treasury Bill rate is often used; and for the return on the stock market, the yield of the Standard & Poor's 500 is often used.

If the Treasury bill rate were 7%, the market as a whole were yielding 12%, and stock j had a beta of 1.6, the cost of equity could be calculated as follows:

$$R_j = 0.07 + 1.6 \ (0.12{-}0.07)$$
$$= 0.07 + 1.6 \ (0.05)$$
$$= 0.07 + 0.08$$
$$= 0.15$$

This approach is known as the capital asset pricing model, or CAPM. While CAPM and beta are widely used, in a strict sense the statistical concepts that underlie the model limit its validity to cases where cash flows are uncorrelated from period to period.[2] In practice, this is a situation rarely encountered. Because of this limitation, caution should be exercised, and CAPM should be used in conjunction with one or more other approaches to calculating cost of equity.

COMPOSITE COST OF CAPITAL

As noted in the beginning of the appendix, firms generally have a target ratio of debt to equity to which they adhere as closely as possible. The composite cost of capital is simply the cost of the two forms of financing, equity and debt, weighted by the proportions in which they are used.

The weighted cost of capital is expressed mathematically by the following equation:

$$k_b = k_d c + (1{-}c)k_e \qquad (10)$$

where:

k_b = composite cost of capital
k_d = after-tax cost of debt capital
c = proportion of investment financed by debt capital
$(1{-}c)$ = proportion of investment financed by equity capital
k_e = required return on equity (cost of equity capital)

Thus if a firm has an after-tax cost of debt of 6.6%, a cost of equity of 15%, and a target capitalization ratio of 30% debt and 70% equity, the calculation of the composite cost of capital is as follows:

	Cost	Weight	Weighted Average Cost
Debt	0.066 (k_d)	0.30 (c)	0.066 × 0.30 = 0.0198
Equity	0.16 (k_e)	0.70 ($1{-}c$)	0.15 × 0.70 = 0.105

Composite cost of capital = 0.1248 (k_b) or about 12.5%

The firm's composite cost of capital is about 12.5%. Sometimes this approach is refined to incorporate various forms of debt, or to approximate the cost of capital to a part of a firm, particularly when the firm is in various types of businesses.

INFLATION AND THE COST OF CAPITAL

Generally speaking, if inflation is eroding the value of money by some amount each year, investors will demand a higher rate of return by an amount equal to the rate of inflation. When discounting cash flows by the firm's cost of capital, it is absolutely necesssary that inflation be included in both cash flows and the cost of capital, or that it be excluded from both.

It may be easier to remove inflation from the firm's cost of capital than to try and inflate cash flows. If the anticipated inflation rate is 4%, the firm's real (noninflated) cost of capital is calculated as follows:

$$1 + \text{real cost} = (1 + \text{actual cost}) \ / \ (1 + \text{inflation})$$
$$= 1.1248 \ / \ 1.04$$
$$= 1.08$$

Thus the firm's real (noninflated) cost of capital is 8%. For a discussion of the use of the real cost of capital, refer to reference 3 cited at the end of this chapter.

APPENDIX C—CASH FLOWS

The most widely used and most modern methods of evaluating capital investments involve discounting cash flows to present value. To do so, the analyst needs to know both cash flows and the firm's cost of capital. Cost of capital was discussed in Appendix B, and cash flows are discussed in this appendix. This section will deal with defining cash flows, the mechanics of dealing with them (particularly as taxes affect cash flows), and with making estimates of cash flows.

DEFINING CASH FLOWS

Most homes run on the basis of a cash budget. The paycheck comes in on payday, and the groceries, rent, and other payments are also made by cash or check. Cash flow is easy to calculate. Federal income taxes are paid on the basis of cash receipts and cash payments.

Most businesses, however, run on the basis of an accrual budget, and income includes not only cash receipts for sales, but also sales that are billed even though the cash has not yet been received. Likewise, expenses are booked as they are accrued, even though the check has not been issued.

Sometimes, firms spend money for things that will last for several years, such as capital investments. Capital investments are not charged as expenses at the time the investment is made. Instead, the entire amount of the investment is put on the books as an asset, and then, as the capital asset is used to produce goods, the wear and tear on the asset is charged or accrued as an expense over the estimated life of the asset. This accrual is called depreciation, and it is ordinarily charged as a predetermined annual amount regardless of how much or how little the asset is used in any specific year.

Thus, if one looks at the income statement of a firm, the figures are not cash figures, but a mixture of cash and accruals. To define the cash outflows and inflows that occur as the result of making an investment, the accruals must be eliminated.

Cash flow is now being recognized to a much greater extent than it was at one time. Many firms include with their financial statements not only a balance sheet and income statement but also a "source and application of funds" or "flow of funds" statement, which is a statement of cash received and paid out during the year.

DEALING WITH CASH FLOWS

Taxes are cash flows. As was mentioned in the introduction of this chapter, the only cash flows that count to the owners of the firm are the after-tax cash flows. While a firm is concerned with taxes, in this situation the only interest is in determining the after-tax cash flows into and out of the firm.

Sales taxes are simple. When a piece of equipment is purchased, the buyer may be charged sales tax on the value of the equipment. If so, the sales tax is a cash outflow.

Income taxes are less simple. Income taxes are charged by the federal (and often state) government on the basis of income that depends on both cash expenses and accruals, but does not depend directly on investments. Income taxes are cash outflows. Thus, to define after-tax cash flows, it is necessary to define taxes. To define taxes, the accruals that affect taxes must be defined. For most investments, the one accrual that is significant is depreciation. It is large, its effect on taxes is important, and it is specifically dependent on the capital investment being made.

With respect to investments, there are three important ways in which income taxes affect cash flow as follows:

1. If the investment reduces costs, income and therefore taxes will be increased; if it increases costs, income and therefore taxes will be reduced. Both must be taken into account.
2. If the investment increases sales, it will probably increase income. Therefore, taxes will be increased and must be taken into account.
3. If an asset is sold for an amount greater than the amount for which it is valued as an asset on the books, it results in a gain that is taxable. If sold for an amount less than the amount for which it is valued on the books, the loss will reduce taxes. For discussion purposes, the rate is assumed to be the same as the rate on income.

To explain how one deals with cash flows, an example of a cost reduction investment will be discussed. If an investment of $10,000 is made and then depreciated on a straight-line basis (the same amount each year) over 5 years while reducing direct labor by $3000 per year, there will be no effect on pre-tax earnings at the time the investment is made. In each of the next 5 years, direct labor will be reduced by $3000, and a depreciation expense will be charged against earnings in the amount of $2000. The net effect will be an increase of pre-tax earnings in the amount of $1000 per year. If the firm is paying income taxes equal to 34% of earnings, this increase of income will increase taxes by 34% of the income change. Thus, the increase in after-tax income is only 0.66 (1-0.34) x $1000, or $660. This is because the $1000 increase in income is offset by a tax increase in the amount of $340.

A question that may arise is "What will be the effect on after-tax cash flow?" There will be an initial outlay of $10,000 at the time the investment is made. Direct labor is not only an expense, but a cash expense. Therefore, the firm will save the $3000 per year it no longer has to pay. Depreciation in each of the following 5 years is not a cash flow—it will not have to be paid out—so it does not have to be subtracted from the direct labor saving. The tax effect, however, is as calculated in the effect on after-tax earnings. The increase in taxes will be only

$340, resulting in an annual cash flow of $3000-$340 = $2660. Thus, assuming that the investment is made in year 0, the effect on earnings compared with the effect on cash flow is shown in Table 6-25.

Next, consider what will happen if the investment results in an increase in sales. Another investment of $10,000 is made that will again be depreciated on a straight-line basis over the next 5 years. This time the purpose will be to provide the capacity to increase sales by $8000 per year for the next 5 years, on which an after-tax profit of $1500 each year will be earned.

It would be possible to go through the income statement and pick out those expenses that are cash flows and those that are accruals, but as noted earlier, the single most important accrual is depreciation expense, and it is possible to approximate annual operating cash flows with the following equation:

$$\text{Cash flow} = \text{Profit after tax} + \text{depreciation} \qquad (11)$$

This is not accurate enough for the finance department to perform its cash management activities, but ordinarily it is close enough for capital investment analysis. Thus, if annual after-tax earnings are $1500 and depreciation is $2000, annual after-tax cash flows are $3500 per year. The effect on earnings compared with the effect on cash flow is shown in Table 6-26.

Finally, consider the cash flows if the initial investment of $10,000 were offset by sale of an old asset, no longer needed, for $1000. To do so, it is necessary to know the value of the asset

TABLE 6-25
Earnings Compared With Cash Flow for
a Reduction Investment Example

Year	Effect on After-Tax Earnings, $	Effect on After-Tax Cash Flow, $
0	0	(10,000)
1	660	2660
2	660	2660
3	660	2660
4	660	2660
5	660	2660

(*Industrial Technology Institute*)
Note: Value in parenthesis is negative.

TABLE 6-26
Earnings Compared With Cash Flow for
an Investment to Increase Capacity

Year	Effect on After-Tax Earnings, $	Effect on After-Tax Cash Flow, $
0	0	(10,000)
1	1500	3500
2	1500	3500
3	1500	3500
4	1500	3500
5	1500	3500

(*Industrial Technology Institute*)
Note: Value in parenthesis is negative.

APPENDIX C—CASH FLOWS

on the books and the annual depreciation charges that would have been accrued in coming years had the old asset been kept.

First, assume the old asset had been fully depreciated and had a book value of 0. The sale of the old asset for $1000 is considered to result in a gain to the firm equal to the difference between the sale price and the book value. In this case, the full $1000 is considered a gain and is taxable. Assuming a 34% rate, the result would be a $340 increase in taxes. Thus, the initial outlay is equal to $10,000 paid for the new machine less $1000 received for the old machine plus $340 taxes paid on the gain from sale of the old machine. The initial outlay is: $10,000- $1000 + $340 = $9340. Because the old machine had been fully depreciated, the sale of the machine will have no effect on future depreciation expense, and the depreciation on the new machine of $2000 per year will be considered in the calculation of the annual cash flows.

What if, however, the old machine had a book value of $3000 and were to be depreciated at a rate of $1500 per year for the next 2 years. If the old machine is sold for $1000, a loss of $2000 would be incurred, and taxes would be reduced for the current year by 0.34 x $2000 = $680. The initial outlay is $10,000- $1000 - $680 = $8320. By incurring a loss, taxes have thus been sheltered.

By selling the old machine, the depreciation expense that would have accrued in each of the next 2 years was eliminated. The net effect on depreciation when comparing the new investment with the old is shown in Table 6-27.

RESIDUAL VALUE AS A CASH FLOW

When one forecasts future cash flows to analyze a potential investment, one cannot look for an indefinite period into the future. The further into the future one tries to forecast, the more uncertain the view. As a result, it is practical only to forecast for some finite period—perhaps as few as 3 years or perhaps as many as 20. At the end of the forecast period, whatever it is, it is likely that the assets will have some value. This is generally

TABLE 6-27
Effect of Depreciation When Making an Investment

Year	Effect on Depreciation
1	+ $2000 - $1500 = + $500
2	+ $2000 - $1500 = + $500
3	+ $2000
4	+ $2000
5	+ $2000

(*Industrial Technology Institute*)

called the "residual value" of the assets. The firm could realize the market value of these assets by selling them. Inventories could be sold as raw material or finished goods; machinery could be sold as used machinery or scrap, and land and buildings could be sold as real estate. Alternatively, the firm could realize value by continuing to use the assets to produce goods to be sold, in which case the value of the assets would be the discounted value of future cash flows generated by the production and sale of product. In calculating the value of potential investments, this residual value needs to be considered. Once it has been estimated as the value of both inventory and fixed assets at the end of the analysis period, it is treated in the analysis as a cash inflow.

ESTIMATING CASH FLOWS

Estimating cash flows is, almost without exception, the most difficult and time-consuming task when evaluating potential investments. First, one must think through carefully what cash flows will be affected by the investment, and then one must seek an estimate of how great or small the cash flows will be. The importance of the first step—thinking through what cash flows will be affected by the investment—cannot be overemphasized. If something is overlooked, in effect, it is estimated to be 0. If it is other than 0, management may make an incorrect decision based on the analysis. Even a very inaccurate estimate is likely to be better than an assumption of 0.

There are three broad categories of sources for estimates of cash flow. The company's financial and management reporting system is an important source of data. It is rarely sufficient, however. For estimates of cash flows as a result of activities within the firm, such as changes in performance standards or work-in-process inventories, it is often necessary to supplement such information with engineering studies. Sometimes these are based on simulations of manufacturing systems. For estimates of cash flows of activities that reach beyond the firm and involve the responses of customers, such as changes in price, quality, or delivery, it is often necessary to use market studies.

Estimating a realistic residual value is particularly difficult. Book value is sometimes used, and while book value is often a good approximation of the residual value of inventories, it is less likely to be a good approximation of the value of fixed assets. Because accounting rules for determining book value of fixed assets do not consider market forces, book value is unlikely to represent either market value or present value of fixed assets. Difficult as it may be, it is best to estimate directly either the market value or the present value of fixed assets at the end of the analysis period. Fortunately, this value is often small relative to the other cash flows under consideration, so the results of the analysis are typically not greatly biased by an error in forecasting residual value.

References

1. George Terborgh, *Business Investment Management* (Washington, DC: Machinery and Allied Products Institute, 1967).
2. Eugene F. Fama, "Risk-Adjusted Discount Rates and Capital Budgeting Under Uncertainty," *Journal of Financial Economics* (August 1977), pp. 3-24.
3. Robert S. Kaplan, "Must CIM Be Justified By Faith Alone?" *Harvard Business Review* (March-April 1986), pp. 87-95.

APPENDIX D—COMPOUND INTEREST AND PRESENT VALUE TABLES

Present Value of $1.00 N Periods Hence Discounted at Rate R

$N\,R=$	5%	6%	7%	8%	9%	10%	11%	12%	13%	14%	15%	16%	18%	20%	24%	28%	30%	32%	34%	36%
1	0.952	0.943	0.935	0.926	0.917	0.909	0.901	0.893	0.885	0.877	0.870	0.862	0.847	0.833	0.806	0.781	0.769	0.758	0.746	0.735
2	0.907	0.890	0.873	0.857	0.842	0.826	0.812	0.797	0.783	0.769	0.756	0.743	0.718	0.694	0.650	0.610	0.592	0.574	0.557	0.541
3	0.864	0.840	0.816	0.794	0.772	0.751	0.731	0.712	0.693	0.675	0.658	0.641	0.609	0.579	0.524	0.477	0.455	0.435	0.416	0.398
4	0.823	0.792	0.763	0.735	0.708	0.683	0.659	0.636	0.613	0.592	0.572	0.552	0.516	0.482	0.423	0.373	0.350	0.329	0.310	0.292
5	0.784	0.747	0.713	0.681	0.650	0.621	0.593	0.567	0.543	0.519	0.497	0.476	0.437	0.402	0.341	0.291	0.269	0.250	0.231	0.215
6	0.746	0.705	0.666	0.630	0.596	0.564	0.535	0.507	0.480	0.456	0.432	0.410	0.370	0.335	0.275	0.227	0.207	0.189	0.173	0.158
7	0.711	0.665	0.623	0.583	0.547	0.513	0.482	0.452	0.425	0.400	0.376	0.354	0.314	0.279	0.222	0.178	0.159	0.143	0.129	0.116
8	0.677	0.627	0.582	0.540	0.502	0.467	0.434	0.404	0.376	0.351	0.327	0.305	0.266	0.233	0.179	0.139	0.123	0.108	0.096	0.085
9	0.645	0.592	0.544	0.500	0.460	0.424	0.391	0.361	0.333	0.308	0.284	0.263	0.225	0.194	0.144	0.108	0.094	0.082	0.072	0.063
10	0.614	0.558	0.508	0.463	0.422	0.386	0.352	0.322	0.295	0.270	0.247	0.227	0.191	0.162	0.116	0.085	0.073	0.062	0.054	0.046
11	0.585	0.527	0.475	0.429	0.388	0.350	0.317	0.287	0.261	0.237	0.215	0.195	0.162	0.135	0.094	0.066	0.056	0.047	0.040	0.034
12	0.557	0.497	0.444	0.397	0.356	0.319	0.286	0.257	0.231	0.208	0.187	0.168	0.137	0.112	0.076	0.052	0.043	0.036	0.030	0.025
13	0.530	0.469	0.415	0.368	0.326	0.290	0.258	0.229	0.204	0.182	0.163	0.145	0.116	0.093	0.061	0.040	0.033	0.027	0.022	0.018
14	0.505	0.442	0.388	0.340	0.299	0.263	0.232	0.205	0.181	0.160	0.141	0.125	0.099	0.078	0.049	0.032	0.025	0.021	0.017	0.014
15	0.481	0.417	0.362	0.315	0.275	0.239	0.209	0.183	0.160	0.140	0.123	0.108	0.084	0.065	0.040	0.025	0.020	0.016	0.012	0.010
16	0.458	0.394	0.339	0.292	0.252	0.218	0.188	0.163	0.141	0.123	0.107	0.093	0.071	0.054	0.032	0.019	0.015	0.012	0.009	0.007
17	0.436	0.371	0.317	0.270	0.231	0.198	0.170	0.146	0.125	0.108	0.093	0.080	0.060	0.045	0.026	0.015	0.012	0.009	0.007	0.005
18	0.416	0.350	0.296	0.250	0.212	0.180	0.153	0.130	0.111	0.095	0.081	0.069	0.051	0.038	0.021	0.012	0.009	0.007	0.005	0.004
19	0.396	0.331	0.277	0.232	0.194	0.164	0.138	0.116	0.098	0.083	0.070	0.060	0.043	0.031	0.017	0.009	0.007	0.005	0.004	0.003
20	0.377	0.312	0.258	0.215	0.178	0.149	0.124	0.104	0.087	0.073	0.061	0.051	0.037	0.026	0.014	0.007	0.005	0.004	0.003	0.002
21	0.359	0.294	0.242	0.199	0.164	0.135	0.112	0.093	0.077	0.064	0.053	0.044	0.031	0.022	0.011	0.006	0.004	0.003	0.002	0.002
22	0.342	0.278	0.226	0.184	0.150	0.123	0.101	0.083	0.068	0.056	0.046	0.038	0.026	0.018	0.009	0.004	0.003	0.002	0.002	0.001
23	0.326	0.262	0.211	0.170	0.138	0.112	0.091	0.074	0.060	0.049	0.040	0.033	0.022	0.015	0.007	0.003	0.002	0.002	0.001	0.001
24	0.310	0.247	0.197	0.158	0.126	0.102	0.082	0.066	0.053	0.043	0.035	0.028	0.019	0.013	0.006	0.003	0.002	0.001	0.001	0.001
25	0.295	0.233	0.184	0.146	0.116	0.092	0.074	0.059	0.047	0.038	0.030	0.024	0.016	0.010	0.005	0.002	0.001	0.001	0.001	0.000
26	0.281	0.220	0.172	0.135	0.106	0.084	0.066	0.053	0.042	0.033	0.026	0.021	0.014	0.009	0.004	0.002	0.001	0.001	0.000	0.000
27	0.268	0.207	0.161	0.125	0.098	0.076	0.060	0.047	0.037	0.029	0.023	0.018	0.011	0.007	0.003	0.001	0.001	0.001	0.000	0.000
28	0.255	0.196	0.150	0.116	0.090	0.069	0.054	0.042	0.033	0.026	0.020	0.016	0.010	0.006	0.002	0.001	0.001	0.000	0.000	0.000
29	0.243	0.185	0.141	0.107	0.082	0.063	0.048	0.037	0.029	0.022	0.017	0.014	0.008	0.005	0.002	0.001	0.000	0.000	0.000	0.000
30	0.231	0.174	0.131	0.099	0.075	0.057	0.044	0.033	0.026	0.020	0.015	0.012	0.007	0.004	0.002	0.001	0.000	0.000	0.000	0.000

APPENDIX D—TABLES

APPENDIX D—Continued

Future Value of $1.00 Compound at Rate R for N Periods

N R=	5%	6%	7%	8%	9%	10%	11%	12%	13%	14%	15%	16%	18%	20%	24%	28%	30%	32%	34%	36%
1	1.050	1.060	1.070	1.080	1.090	1.100	1.110	1.120	1.130	1.140	1.150	1.160	1.180	1.200	1.240	1.280	1.300	1.320	1.340	1.360
2	1.103	1.124	1.145	1.166	1.188	1.210	1.232	1.254	1.277	1.300	1.323	1.346	1.392	1.440	1.538	1.638	1.690	1.742	1.796	1.850
3	1.158	1.191	1.225	1.260	1.295	1.331	1.368	1.405	1.443	1.482	1.521	1.561	1.643	1.728	1.907	2.097	2.197	2.300	2.406	2.515
4	1.216	1.262	1.311	1.360	1.412	1.464	1.518	1.574	1.630	1.689	1.749	1.811	1.939	2.074	2.364	2.684	2.856	3.036	3.224	3.421
5	1.276	1.338	1.403	1.469	1.539	1.611	1.685	1.762	1.842	1.925	2.011	2.100	2.288	2.488	2.932	3.436	3.713	4.007	4.320	4.653
6	1.340	1.419	1.501	1.587	1.677	1.772	1.870	1.974	2.082	2.195	2.313	2.436	2.700	2.986	3.635	4.398	4.827	5.290	5.789	6.328
7	1.407	1.504	1.606	1.714	1.828	1.949	2.076	2.211	2.353	2.502	2.660	2.826	3.185	3.583	4.508	5.629	6.275	6.983	7.758	8.605
8	1.477	1.594	1.718	1.851	1.993	2.144	2.305	2.476	2.658	2.853	3.059	3.278	3.759	4.300	5.590	7.206	8.157	9.217	10.40	11.70
9	1.551	1.689	1.838	1.999	2.172	2.358	2.558	2.773	3.004	3.252	3.518	3.803	4.435	5.160	6.931	9.223	10.60	12.17	13.93	15.92
10	1.629	1.791	1.967	2.159	2.367	2.594	2.839	3.106	3.395	3.707	4.046	4.411	5.234	6.192	8.594	11.81	13.79	16.06	18.67	21.65
11	1.710	1.898	2.105	2.332	2.580	2.853	3.152	3.479	3.836	4.226	4.652	5.117	6.176	7.430	10.66	15.11	17.92	21.20	25.01	29.44
12	1.796	2.012	2.252	2.518	2.813	3.138	3.498	3.896	4.335	4.818	5.350	5.936	7.288	8.916	13.21	19.34	23.30	27.98	33.52	40.04
13	1.886	2.133	2.410	2.720	3.066	3.452	3.883	4.363	4.898	5.492	6.153	6.886	8.599	10.70	16.39	24.76	30.29	36.94	44.91	54.45
14	1.980	2.261	2.579	2.937	3.342	3.797	4.310	4.887	5.535	6.261	7.076	7.988	10.15	12.84	20.32	31.69	39.37	48.76	60.18	74.05
15	2.079	2.397	2.759	3.172	3.642	4.177	4.785	5.474	6.254	7.138	8.137	9.266	11.97	15.41	25.20	40.56	51.19	64.36	80.64	100.7
16	2.183	2.540	2.952	3.426	3.970	4.595	5.311	6.130	7.067	8.137	9.358	10.75	14.13	18.49	31.24	51.92	66.54	84.95	108.1	137.0
17	2.292	2.693	3.159	3.700	4.328	5.054	5.895	6.866	7.986	9.276	10.76	12.47	16.67	22.19	38.74	66.46	86.50	112.1	144.8	186.3
18	2.407	2.854	3.380	3.996	4.717	5.560	6.544	7.690	9.024	10.58	12.38	14.46	19.67	26.62	48.04	85.07	112.5	148.0	194.0	253.3
19	2.527	3.026	3.617	4.316	5.142	6.116	7.263	8.613	10.20	12.06	14.23	16.78	23.21	31.95	59.57	108.9	146.2	195.4	260.0	344.5
20	2.653	3.207	3.870	4.661	5.604	6.727	8.062	9.646	11.52	13.74	16.37	19.46	27.39	38.34	73.86	139.4	190.0	257.9	348.4	468.6
21	2.786	3.400	4.141	5.034	6.109	7.400	8.949	10.80	13.02	15.67	18.82	22.57	32.32	46.01	91.59	178.4	247.1	340.4	466.9	637.3
22	2.925	3.604	4.430	5.437	6.659	8.140	9.934	12.10	14.71	17.86	21.64	26.19	38.14	55.21	113.6	228.4	321.2	449.4	625.6	866.7
23	3.072	3.820	4.741	5.871	7.258	8.954	11.03	13.55	16.63	20.36	24.89	30.38	45.01	66.25	140.8	292.3	417.5	593.2	838.3	1179
24	3.225	4.049	5.072	6.341	7.911	9.850	12.24	15.18	18.79	23.21	28.63	35.24	53.11	79.50	174.6	374.1	542.8	783.0	1123	1603
25	3.386	4.292	5.427	6.848	8.623	10.83	13.59	17.00	21.23	26.46	32.92	40.87	62.67	95.40	216.5	478.9	705.6	1034	1505	2180
26	3.556	4.549	5.807	7.396	9.399	11.92	15.08	19.04	23.99	30.17	37.86	47.41	73.95	114.5	268.5	613.0	917.3	1364	2017	2965
27	3.733	4.822	6.214	7.988	10.25	13.11	16.74	21.32	27.11	34.39	43.54	55.00	87.26	137.4	333.0	784.6	1193	1801	2703	4032
28	3.920	5.112	6.649	8.627	11.17	14.42	18.58	23.88	30.63	39.20	50.07	63.80	103.0	164.8	412.9	1004	1550	2377	3622	5484
29	4.116	5.418	7.114	9.317	12.17	15.86	20.62	26.75	34.62	44.69	57.58	74.01	121.5	197.8	512.0	1286	2015	3138	4853	7458
30	4.322	5.743	7.612	10.06	13.27	17.45	22.89	29.96	39.12	50.95	66.21	85.85	143.4	237.4	634.8	1646	2620	4142	6503	10,143

PRODUCTION PLANNING AND CONTROL

One of the essential manufacturing support activities is that of production planning and control. Very often, the principal group of personnel involved in these processes is in a group called production and inventory control. They may be a part of an overall materials management department or they may report directly to the manufacturing manager.

The required interfaces for this group include essentially every other department in the organization. Its coordination of planning and control activities requires knowledge and skills related to demand forecasting, aggregate production and inventory planning, material requirements, and personnel/machine capacity planning for shop functions.

The tools used by this support group may or may not include the use of material requirements planning (MRP) or manufacturing resource planning (MRP II) systems. If an organization is implementing or using just-in-time manufacturing techniques, its focus is reduced relative to shop floor control activities, but its planning and communication roles remain essential.

The main topics in this chapter discuss the various techniques that constitute key tools used in performance of the coordination activities that support the performance of the operations group.

FORECASTING

The production and inventory planning process begins with forecasting. All techniques of production and inventory control require some calculation of quantities, which represent future demand. The specific needs of each application are determined by the lead times inherent in the manufacturing processes being supported. Short lead time processes, including material procurement, may be supported quite well utilizing current open orders and only a few weeks' worth of estimated demand. Very long process requirements (12 months or longer) are most likely supported by a contractual order process, and all material planning and workcenter planning will be based on values calculated to support the more or less "known" requirements. Most manufacturing applications fall somewhere in between.

Both types of business operations, including combinations of the two, require some technique of forecasting for business planning and personnel decisions. The anticipated demands, and the forecast error rates experienced, will determine the basis for the systems, inventory policies, purchasing practices, and shop scheduling techniques used to support production requirements.

THEORY

Several general principles can be described regarding forecasts, regardless of their origin. It is important that both marketing and manufacturing staffs understand the importance of these principles and the impact they should have on routine decision processes. Four key concepts and principles describing forecasts are as follows:

1. Accuracy of the forecast is indirectly proportional to the length of time to the forecasted period; the shorter the forecast period, the more accurate the forecast.
2. Accuracy of the forecast is directly proportional to the number of items in the forecast group. The total company forecast can be expected to be more accurate than the corresponding forecast for a given product line, which, in turn, will be more accurate than the corresponding forecast for a single part number in that product line.
3. Forecast error is always present and should be estimated and measured on all forecasts.
4. No single forecast method is best; alternate methods should be tested periodically to determine if another method would result in a smaller forecast error.

For those companies using computerized forecasts, some software packages will vary the model for an item using calculations based on the forecast error experience on the item.

SEASONALITY

A study of seasonality for a forecast group, whether it is an individual part, product line, or company total, requires a sufficient amount of historical data to support the calculation. The result of the calculation is referred to as a deseasonalized demand pattern. Very simply, the removal of the seasonal component of the demand pattern is accomplished by using the average of the historical period percentages (divided by 1/12) as corresponding divisors to calculate the theoretical demand pattern that would be present if no seasonality influence existed. It is not possible to test the randomness of variation without first removing the impact of the seasonal variable, if one is present.

FORECASTING

STATISTICS

Statistical approaches can also range from quite simple to extremely complex. The basic premise of statistical forecasting lies in the assumption that the behavior of individual part demand variations will be random. This is expected whether or not the total forecast is stable or is subject to trend and seasonal factors. Such factors must be treated separately to expose the underlying randomness of individual part demand variations. The basic statistical techniques used in intrinsic forecasts will be examined in the paragraphs that follow. The principles involved also apply to extrinsic forecasting, but the statistical treatments appropriate to multiva riate analysis are beyond the scope of this discussion. All of the components of a demand model are shown graphically in Fig. 7-1.

Trend Patterns

The deseasonalized demand pattern can likewise be calculated for the prior year's data by month in preparation for an analysis of any trend pattern that may exist. This requires the selection of a method or calculation technique for the linear curve-fitting problem. The 12-month moving average can provide the data points for this calculation. Simple techniques of determining the slope of a line include the use of graphical methods and solving for an equation based on two points on the plotted trend line (see Fig. 7-2).

Another method of calculating the trend line for use in a forecasting model is to use the least square regression technique on the deseasonalized monthly data in the previous example. If the number of months is plotted as the X variable and the monthly quantities as the Y data, the graph in Fig. 7-3 results. To solve for the slope of the line using linear regression, the following calculation can be made:

$$Y = 159.0 + (1.389 \times X)$$

Graphically, the apparent linear relationship representing growth of volume over time is demonstrated by also plotting the equation on the same graph. By assigning the values 1 to 42 to the X variable, the trend line can be extended 6 months beyond the 36-month history as a trend forecast of deseasonalized demand.

When the equation for this model is used to project future months' deseasonalized demand and is multiplied by the appropriate monthly season factors, a forecast quantity can be determined. Table 7-1 shows results of the calculations extended for a 6-month period.

Residual Variation—Randomness

The example set of data in Table 7-1 can also be used to look at residual variation not explained by the model. This data can then be studied through a simple histogram to determine if the variation appears to be random. If so, the model depicts the statistical definition of the demand pattern. If not, it is necessary to look for other causes that are contributing to the demand pattern. The goal is to establish a tool or technique that can be expected to yield good results until new variables enter the statistical population that makes up the demand universe. This testing of the model, or any set of techniques used to prepare a forecast, must be reviewed routinely to determine if further improvement can be made. This will be measured by the forecast error rate actually experienced.

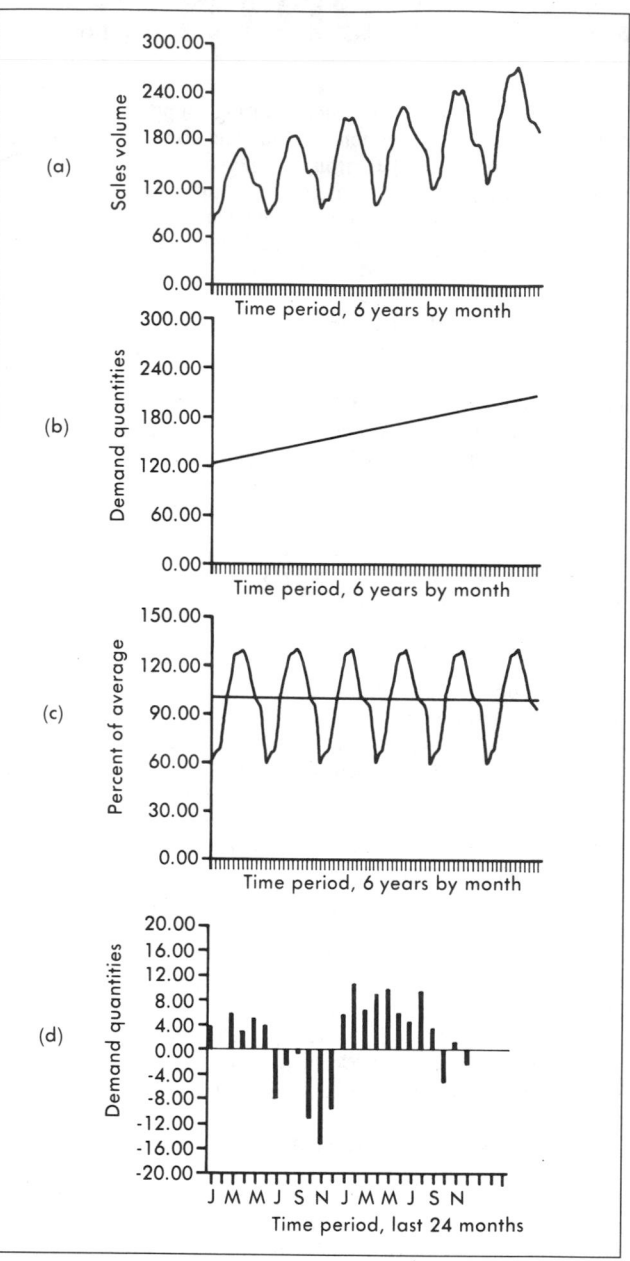

Fig. 7-1 Components of demand: (a) sales history, (b) trend line of demand, (c) seasonal factors, and (d) residual error. (*K.W. Tunnell Company, Inc.*)

DEMAND/ORDERS

It is important to reconcile the forecast generated with the likely impact it may have on the company using the forecast. The most straightforward usage results from using order history data in preparing a forecast of order demand. This gives the best measure of the marketplace demand that can be expected to be presented to the manufacturer as new orders.

If the order history data is based on shipments and the shipping performance is poor, or if there is a significant offset between order receipt and order shipment, a similar offset must be used to arrive at an appropriate timing for the predicted order

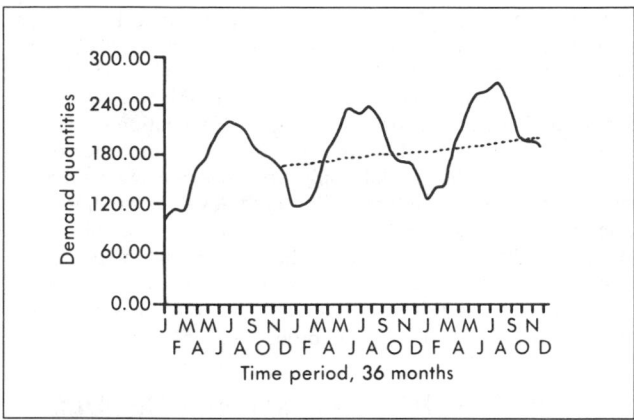

Fig. 7-2 Trend line graph from 12-month moving average. (*K.W. Tunnell Company, Inc.*)

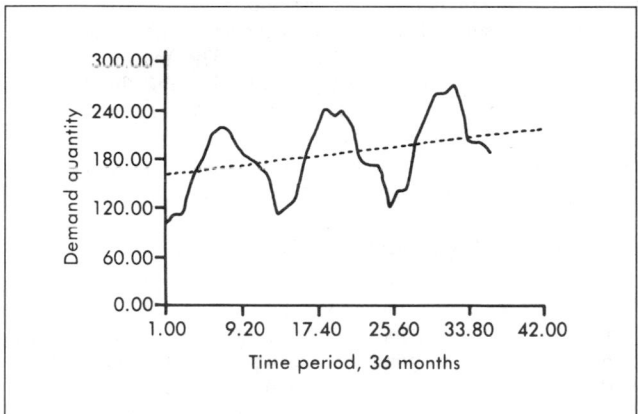

Fig. 7-3 Trend line forecast using the least square regression technique. (*K.W. Tunnell Company, Inc.*)

volume. The best measures of true demand will also include input that corresponds to lost sales volumes.

It is always important to "consume" a forecast with incoming orders to calculate a balance expected in the projection period. This allows for early detection of forecast errors and appropriate reaction. It is equally important to measure error percentages as a part of the learning experience that is essential to an ongoing improvement of prognostication ability. The only way that forecasts ever improve is by forecasters using their forecast errors as signals to guide the improvement of the methods applied.

TABLE 7-1
Product Quantity Forecast Extended for Six Months

Future Month	Deseasonalized Demand Forecast	Seasonal Factor	Resulting Forecast
37—JAN	210	0.595	125
38—FEB	212	0.668	142
39—MAR	213	0.686	146
40—APR	215	0.974	209
41—MAY	216	1.119	242
42—JUN	217	1.281	278

(*K.W. Tunnell Company, Inc.*)

SPARES/SERVICE PARTS

To most manufacturers, the most troublesome independent demands are those that partially overlap with the core of dependent demand items. Spare parts requirements that do not overlap with the calculated requirements for components are often prone to be small in quantity and infrequent in occurrence. For low-volume, infrequent-demand items, an expert opinion forecast manually loaded into the system by period is usually the best approach. Demand patterns of similar items or groups are also useful in some cases.

For service parts or spare parts that have a history of repetitive demand, the same techniques of forecasting used for the primary products are appropriate. Some form of lifecycle analysis is also useful in understanding the demise of service parts requirements. It is important that the historical data representing this form of demand be maintained separately from the usage history on the same parts that is associated with dependent demand patterns that have been exploded (calculated) through a bill of materials.

AGGREGATE PLANNING AND MASTER SCHEDULING

Top-level planning in a manufacturing organization is essential to the smoothness of both its floor and support operations. The performance of actual shop order completions vs. the detail plan as well as the material flow generated through the combination of the production/inventory control and purchasing functions can only be as successful as the top management direction that guides those detail processes.

SALES PLAN

A myth has long existed that the master schedule is the business plan. The source of the master schedule must begin at an executive group level that operates with product group data only and must be finalized by a top management review process. This responsibility may be vested in a single executive or it may be a formal mechanism for negotiation tied to the sales forecasting processes.

If it is a formal process that involves sales and marketing negotiations with production management, ideally with finance providing the link to the overall business plan, it utilizes the chief operating executive as arbitrator for the natural conflicts arising from the specific objectives of each function. The master schedule itself is not the business plan, but should be formally

AGGREGATE PLANNING AND MASTER SCHEDULING

developed to meet the objectives set forth in the plan proposed by top management.

The sales plan begins with a shipments forecast, but should end with a process that recognizes the need for tradeoffs withproduction management and matching of flexibility requirements with true factory capability. This is necessary to achieve a reliable plan that supports the customer service requirements, objectives, and delivery commitment communication needs. The most important sales advantage of reliable planning is the consistent achievement of deliveries made on the promised ship dates. Customers, usually seen as another company's purchasing department, judge the reliability of a suppliers' promises as a critical factor in determining the choice of a supplier.

INVENTORY PLAN

The inventory plan element of the top-level planning process is a critical tool in a management negotiation process. By considering the variations in requirements of the marketplace, inventory policies and overall inventory levels can be set that will allow the operations unit to satisfactorily meet those requirements. Further, this allows the investment in inventory to be managed, not just happen as a collective result of detail-level policies and procedures.

The level of inventory investment should be determined by the amount of mismatch between current manufacturing capability and current market flexibility requirements. If the manufacturing operation can quickly change to meet the needs demonstrated by orders entered, little finished or semifinished product inventory is required. If there is a large seasonal component in the demand function, it may be necessary to build up significant inventories to level the production requirement.

PRODUCTION PLAN

The production plan is the final result of the top-level planning process. Once the changes in anticipated demand are recognized through analysis of the product group forecasts and once the major inventory planning decisions are determined, the production plan is essentially decided. In truth, this is the final test of the decisions already made. If the production plan, so derived, is still not feasible, other changes will need to be negotiated. If shortfalls to certain forecasted demands are still predicted in the final plan, sales and marketing may need to make direct contacts with customers in search of opportunities to delay some of the problem demands without harm. This method of reconciliation of demand to capacity is far superior to order delays caused by missed shipping dates.

Given the stability of a firm plan that has been equated to a realistic assessment of production capability, there is a responsibility to measure actual results against the plan, just as one would measure forecast error for each of the product groups. An excellent indication that good management ability is available, demonstrating skills in both planning and execution, is if both measures attain an accuracy record of 90-95% or better on all product groups (when actual results are measured against the last month's plan). Until such reliability is achieved in the short-term planning processes, the deviations from plan can be utilized as indexes of the weaknesses in predictive capacity of those that control the processes. This form of discipline in top-level planning leads to prioritization of need resolution regarding opportunities for stabilizing the production environment.

AUTHORIZATION OF MASTER SCHEDULE

The key link between a management team's negotiated plan and the detail processes is the *master production schedule* (MPS). The purpose of the MPS is to plan the replenishments for the lower level components and assemblies to meet the production plan. The latter plan is usually expected to be updated on a weekly, but sometimes monthly, basis. The master schedule must translate the product group-level plan into one that operates at a part number level. This plan will consider open orders and will use part number level independent demand forecasts that may or may not be derived using the same techniques as those used for the product group forecasts.

ROUGH-CUT CAPACITY PLANNING

The detail-level tests of the feasibility of the master schedule must include an evaluation of the production resource consumption by day or week. This is referred to as rough-cut capacity planning. It may be conducted using product group data if workcenter loading factors have been developed accordingly. This testing of capacity gives an indication of the loading levels, both for personnel and for machine groups involved. The concept of underscheduling may be introduced at this point, allowing a small portion of capacity to be allocated to emergency or other orders.

FUNCTION OF THE MASTER SCHEDULE

The primary documentation of a factory plan of operation for a period of time equal to its longest lead times is the master schedule (see Fig. 7-4). The master production schedule, sometimes abbreviated MPS, is the actual top level of input into an MRP system. This technique uncouples factory demands from the sales forecasts and order entry elements of the planning information chain. Before this process can be effective, the

Part Number	Periods.........												
	1	2	3	4	5	6	7	8	9	10	11	12	13
A1	35	40	45	55	45	35	30	25	30	30	30	30	30
A2	50	45	35	30	35	45	45	50	50	50	50	50	50
Totals	85	85	80	85	80	80	75	75	80	80	80	80	80
	| Released ||		.... Firm .... ||				.... Planned .... |						

Fig. 7-4 Example of a master production schedule. (*K.W. Tunnell Company, Inc.*)

planning exercise at the management level that determines in broad terms what will go into the master schedule must be completed. This framework, or production, sales, and inventory plan, is the basis for the master scheduler's actions in allocating specific orders and stock units to time slots for production.

PLANNING TIME FENCES

A final definition is required to understand the elements of the factory production planning process. "Time fences" are merely designations of time periods that allow different rules to be related to production planning and scheduling. The first time fence, or end date of a period beginning with the current day, defines the duration of the period for which shop orders have or can be released. This implies that whatever documentation is required on the shop floor to initiate and control the performance of work is already published to cover this period.

The second time fence defines the end of the period that begins immediately after the released period and includes the time in which all orders are firmed. The orders in both the released and firmed period are expected to be completed on time and without the interference of schedule changes. Both periods

are usually only a few weeks in duration. Purchasing support must provide material for both "released" and "firm" orders.

The final time fence is the same as the end of the planning horizon. This planned order period begins immediately after the "firmed" period.

PULL METHOD DIFFERENCES

The discussions of master scheduling and time fences assume that an MRP system is used as the tool to develop part schedules. Another way to schedule the part replenishment release authorization is with a pull system. Pull systems focus on the production of only those parts the next period or to replace those that have just been taken for another area. If the pull methods are used to schedule the part replenishment release authorization for parts supply, master scheduling will be used to drive only the demand planning functions related to capacity planning and supplier communications regarding materials forecasts. It is not necessary to implement full-blown MRP systems to gain the benefits of aggregate planning (PSI planning), master scheduling, and rough-cut capacity planning.

REQUIREMENTS AND CAPACITY PLANNING

The detail planning elements associated with production and material control are essentially those efforts that contribute to the balancing of limited resources with requirements that are generated through the sales activities. Timing is always the critical variable. Costs associated with any set of alternatives are a function of the time elements. Materials can be expedited at additional costs. Labor resource levels can usually be fluctuated significantly in short periods of time, but this adds costs related to hiring, training, and the loss of quality and productivity during training periods.

DETAIL PRODUCTION PLANNING

The process of production planning involves tradeoffs between changes in production rates and inventory investment. Seasonal demands require that a choice be made from the alternatives available. Some of the alternatives are as follows:

- Hold a level production rate and build up an inventory sufficient to cover the period of peak demand.
- Hold a near-level inventory investment and fluctuate the labor supply to meet the sales rates.
- A combination of the previous two, which allows some use of overtime instead of hiring for a portion of the labor fluctuation.

Production plans must consider the economics and feasibility of the alternatives as they relate to inventory investment, storage capacity, purchased component availability, and personnel availability.

PERSONNEL PLANNING

Because personnel requirements vary with the inherent productivity of the resources and the processes used, shifts in mix

can be equally as important as major changes in the processes. The top-level index of personnel required may be as simple as a calculation of the number of direct (or touch) labor resource hours required to produce a standard level of output—for example, 1000 units, $100,000 in sales, or 1000 "standard" process hours. A separate index for the amount of indirect support labor may be defined using the same factors or using a secondary factor such as the number of indirect hours required per 1000 direct hours or number of indirect "heads" per direct "head." An extremely useful refinement of these gross measures may be developed by using a similar set of factors for each product group contributing to the total.

MACHINE LOADING

Loading of machine groups may be treated in a similar fashion for early warning of potential short-term capacity problems, which might be easily overcome by the use of outside resources if sufficient time is available to make such arrangements. If the manufacturing environment is one that combines make-to-stock on its higher volume items with its basic make-to-order operations, additional flexibility is available at the expense of additional inventory.

The ultimate solution to the production planning process as it relates to machine loading may well be in the development of cellular flows that have a primary focus on minimizing set-up time and overall lead times. The concept of the unitary lot size is as well founded in reducing the coordination and planning costs associated with functional alternatives as it is with the floor control simplicity. The fundamental difference in the JIT manufacturing philosophy from that of batch processing oriented MRP approaches is related to the manufacturing logistic problems that are never solved when lead times and lot sizes are allowed to exist at greater than the lowest possible levels.

MRP

CAPACITY ALTERNATIVES

The long-term view of capacity considerations requires decisions that are strategic in nature. In a world economy that has numerous examples of overcapacity situations, more is not necessarily better. Short-term capacity alternatives must consider outside vendors as potential solutions. The possibility also exists for improvement of the productivity of current facilities through efforts involving all employees using techniques for set-up reduction.

PURCHASED PARTS PLANNING

In the 1950s, many purchased parts planning techniques that had not been feasible because of the clerical and/or analytical time required became possible for many manufacturers because of the decreasing cost of the computer. Time-phased order-point techniques were an outgrowth of this new business capability. From this beginning, the techniques called material requirements planning (MRP) and eventually manufacturing resource planning (MRP II) evolved.

MRP

The planning and control systems techniques that are based on computer-aided manipulation of data in time-phased "buckets" are now about 25 years old. It has become common practice to refer to such systems as some form of an MRP system. The introduction of just-in-time manufacturing principles into U.S. manufacturing facilities during the past few years has created a different set of needs for such tools than those concentrated on before 1980.

This section describes the elements, evolution, and application of the popular time-phased manufacturing control systems, usually referred to as material requirements planning (MRP).

TYPICAL MRP SYSTEMS

The *material requirements plan* is the source of the name of the techniques based on time-phased planning, and it originates from the components requirements planning needs of a manufacturing organization.

It is important to recognize that MRP is not for all businesses. There are single-product firms with simple bills of materials that do not require MRP for manufacturing management activities related to planning and scheduling.

MRP is not just for replenishing inventories. The past decade

has seen the focus shift from simpler material requirements planning systems to total integrated manufacturing control systems. Most current references are to "MRP II," implying *manufacturing resource planning*. Most of the implementation efforts that are in process today are utilizing MRP II software resources.

MRP is an exception-message, action-oriented system (see Fig. 7-5). It is not a clerical-burdened system unless it is improperly implemented. The discipline required in the management of this process becomes one of managing the variables' data associated with the control process. MRP techniques provide a method for routine calculation of:

- The "when" (timing of an order release).
- The "how much" (quantity required for order release).
- "Priorities" updated with the results of all purchasing and shop activities in a traditional or functional environment.

Properly utilized, this systems approach provides shop loading data to help plan capacity and to make judgments about the alternative uses of available capacity. It allows for the varying of demands and/or rules and/or lead times as a means of simulating results by asking "what if" questions.

MRP is a set of procedures, a set of decision rules and

Part #	Period	Action Required	Quantity
..	..	..	..
..	..	..	..
..	..	..	..
CC	Week 3	Place order for delivery in Week 5	45
CC	Week 4	Place order for delivery in Week 6	35
CC	Week 5	Place order for delivery in Week 7	30
CC	Week 6	Place order for delivery in Week 8	25
CC	Week 7	Place order for delivery in Week 9	30
CC	Week 8	Place order for delivery in Week 10	30
DD	De-expedite	Reschedule order due in Week 2 to Week 3	125
DD	De-expedite	Reschedule order due in Week 3 to Week 4	125
DD	De-expedite	Reschedule order due in Week 4 to Week 6	125
DD	Expedite	Reschedule order due in Week 10 to Week 8	150
DD	Week 7	Place order for delivery in Week 9	100
DD	Week 8	Place order for delivery in Week 10	100
..	..	..	..
..	..	..	..
..	..	..	..

Fig. 7-5 Examples of MRP exception messages. (*K.W. Tunnell Company, Inc.*)

policies that govern many of the routine decisions required in setting the manufacturing schedule. As such, it provides a highly disciplined approach for arranging lower level factory schedules. Its exception-action orientation is not a clerical system in nature, although when out of control, an MRP system can become a tremendous clerical burden. One of the critical aspects of the definition is that it is a highly disciplined management process; MRP depends on shop events happening just as they were simulated by the computer system based on the plans entered as the MPS and the policies and operations data loaded in their databases.

Given the rules and procedures that have been implemented for a given company, MRP determines the time and the quantity for order releases at lower levels and part manufacture requirements supporting the finished product schedules. MRP is not for controlling finished goods. All MRP systems are driven by a master scheduling approach, which is a finished product scheduling technique that must be developed in some manner to create the top-level demands that will be supported by MRP's subsequent arithmetic calculations.

The first calculations that must be performed are those that explode the demands into requirements by time period for all lower level subassemblies and component requirements. All demands are netted against available orders and committed replenishments (both shop orders and purchase orders), to calculate the actions that are required to support the master schedule. Two types of messages with associated quantity calculations result: (1) new order requirements and (2) changes required to existing orders. Order change messages may indicate data change needs only, quantity change requirements, or both.

The basis for improving operations with the use of an MRP system requires that the functions related to scheduling be integrated and that it be driven by a valid master production schedule. The people who operate and manage the variables of the MRP system must also be qualified—that means educated and trained in not only the techniques of a given system, but also in terms of the principles that they are dealing with.

Procedures and controls for data accuracy are primarily operating discipline issues. The single largest failing in most MRP systems is the lack of discipline in the day-to-day activities that maintain data integrity within the system. A system that attempts to emulate the total production environment within the computer depends on accurate data in the following elements:

- Inventory balances.
- Bills of materials.
- Process routings.

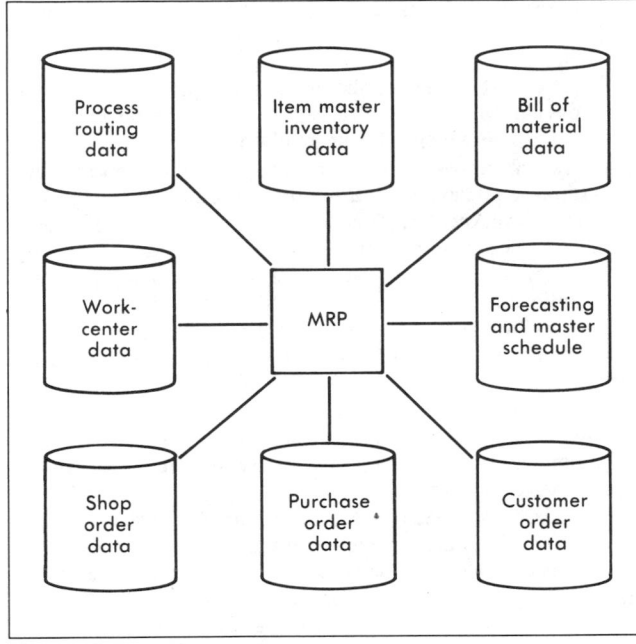

Fig. 7-6 Diagram of elements in an MRP database. (*K.W. Tunnell Company, Inc.*)

- Shop order status by operation.
- Purchase order status by item and date.

MRP does not, in and of itself, reduce inventory or cause a reduction in inventory, nor can it improve customer service or productivity or reduce costs. As a tool, however, it can provide the means for management to gain those benefits.

DATABASE CONSIDERATIONS

MRP databases require integration. Not only do they have to be more accurate than other systems, the magnitude of the functions affected also requires that efforts be made to allow a single reporting of an event to cover all needs for that data. Often, inventories and production activities depend on this tool to control millions of dollars. In a multiplant, multilocation environment, the management of the MRP database is most often controlled by data processing specialists. This administrative function controls the integrity of the system by managing the database elements (see Fig. 7-6).

SCHEDULING AND PRODUCTION ACTIVITY CONTROL

PRIORITIES

The first order of business for the production scheduler and the production and inventory control department is the establishment of the "right" sequence of jobs to be run in the shop.

The requirements of a good priority system are as follows:

1. A priority system should specify which jobs should be done first, second, third, and so on.
2. A priority system should allow for easy and fast updating

SCHEDULING AND PRODUCTION ACTIVITY CONTROL

of priorities, inasmuch as priorities will change after a very short period of time because actual conditions change.

3. A priority system should be objective. If jobs are overstated, an "informal system" will be developed to determine which jobs are really needed.

A major objective of any computer-supported shop scheduling system is to develop the relative priorities of every shop order in a workcenter. Some companies use sophisticated schemes, while others do not. Examples of the most commonly used priority schemes are first in/first out, start date, due date, critical ratio rule, slack time ratio, and queue ratio.

First in/first out method. The first in/first out (FIFO) method is the simplest priority rule. It assumes that the first shop order to enter a workcenter is the first shop order to be worked on. The major advantage of this rule is that it does not require a computer or other sophisticated system to determine priorities. The major disadvantage is that it assumes that all jobs have the same relative priority.

Start date method. The start date priority rule is really a subset of the FIFO rule insofar as the shop order with the earliest start date is the first job to be worked on, and so forth. Naturally, this scheme assumes that all shop orders are released on time. The start date can be calculated from a backward rather than a forward scheduling technique. Forward scheduling is "a scheduling technique in which the scheduler proceeds from a known start date and computes the completion date for an order usually proceeding from the first operation to the last."[1] Backward scheduling, on the other hand, is "a scheduling technique in which the schedule is computed starting with the due date for the order and working backward to determine the required start date. This can generate negative times, thereby identifying where time must be made up."

Due date method. The due date is the date when the material is needed to be available. The due date priority rule is the most popular priority technique that is used in manufacturing industry, particularly with the advent of MRP-type systems. When properly used and kept up to date, the due date rule can be very effective. It is, of course, possible to overstate the master production schedule in an MRP system and destroy the credibility of the due date priority. If the master schedule is well maintained and kept up to date with actual conditions from the shop floor as feedback into the planning and scheduling system, the due date technique is a straightforward tool to determine shop priorities.

Critical ratio rule. The critical ratio priority considers the total standard lead time remaining to complete the job relative to the total time remaining to the due date of the order. The control ratio is computed as follows:

$$\text{Critical ratio} = \frac{\text{Due date - today's date}}{\text{Lead time remaining}} \quad (1)$$

Lead time is defined as the sum of the processing time, set-up time, move time, and queue time. Any order with a critical ratio of less than 1.0 is behind schedule, while an order with a critical ratio of more than 1.0 is ahead of schedule. An order with a critical ratio of 1.0 is right on schedule. Using this technique, shop orders with the lowest ratio have the highest priority. Conversely, the orders with the higher ratios have the lowest priority.

Slack time ratio method. The purpose of the slack time ratio is to assign priorities to jobs in queues at various workcenters. The slack time ratio is computed as follows:

$$\text{Slack time} = \frac{\text{Due date - today's date - processing time}}{\text{Time remaining}} \quad (2)$$

If two or more orders have the same slack time ratio, the computations may be modified to consider the number of operations remaining as follows:

$$\text{Slack time} = \frac{\text{Due date - today's date - processing time left}}{\text{Number of operations remaining}} \quad (3)$$

This alternative encourages the completion of orders having the most operations remaining.

Queue ratio method. The same queue ratio calculates the relationship between its slack time remaining and the queue line originally scheduled between the start of the operations being considered at the scheduled due date. The ratio decreases as the shop order becomes late. The queue ratio is calculated as follows:

$$\text{Queue ratio} = \frac{\text{Slack time remaining}}{\text{Original queue time}} \quad (4)$$

where:

Slack time = Due date - today's date process time remaining

and

Original queue time = Due date - scheduled date - standard process time remaining

Work Authorization

The method used to authorize work will often depend on both the type of production (whether it is job shop, process, or repetitive manufacturing) and on the degree of sophistication in the manufacturing planning and control system. There are generally three ways that work is authorized in the shop: (1) verbal, (2) shop order, and (3) dispatch list.

Verbal. Verbal authorization is the oldest method of assigning work. Using this method, the person responsible for the work assignment simply tells the appropriate supervisor which jobs to work on next. The method is straightforward, but is often based on limited information. It is also subject to loss of control and generally depends on expediting to get critical jobs done.

Shop order. Many companies use shop orders to authorize and track the production of parts, subassemblies, and end products through the plant. In many systems, every workcenter is specified in the writing of a shop order. At the time the order is released, the quantity to be produced is shown, as well as the time the part is expected to arrive at a given workcenter. These dates depend on the start time, process times, and move times associated with the particular job. These work orders are generally used for planning personnel, set-up, and machine loading levels. Specific operation due dates can be used in calculations relative to the shop order due date and expediting that is communicated to the individual workcenters.

Dispatch list. Manufacturing companies frequently issue "dispatch lists" or "shop schedules" at regular time intervals, particularly if a computerized system is being used. The dispatch list shows all shop orders to be worked on by the various workcenters in a priority sequence. Normally, companies that

SCHEDULING AND PRODUCTION ACTIVITY CONTROL

issue dispatch lists will not show any start date or due date on their shop orders when they are released to the individual workcenters because all copies of the work order would have to be collected and the dates modified as the dispatch list dates were reviewed and revised.

Order Launching and Expediting

This "launching" or release of the shop orders involves the actual dispatch of the shop order to the workcenters that will be involved in production activities. Workcenters receive copies of each shop order when the order is released to the workcenter for the first operation specified in the routing. Only orders with a high probability of being completed on time should be released. Typically, shop orders are not released to the first operation until the following conditions are met:

1. All of the material required to produce the part is available.
2. Sufficient capacity for the job is available.
3. Tooling at the first operation is available.

The releasing of the order authorizes the start of production and/or the distribution of the routing to the shop floor. Components and materials can now be moved to the work areas.

Operation Scheduling and Tracking

To accomplish production scheduling, the production control department must have methods to know what to make, when to start it, where to make it, how to make it, what to make it from, how much time is necessary to make it, and when the order is due. The scheduling methodology can be expected to differ by the basic type of manufacturing processes that are involved.

Continuous-process manufacturing. In a continuous-process manufacturing company, work flows through the manufacturing process. The rate of flow can usually be varied, although there are processes in which the rate can be varied little if at all. The production rate in continuous-process production can be varied in several ways:

- The line equipment may be operated for more or fewer hours per day.
- The line rates may be varied, faster or slower.
- The production line may be operated intermittently.
- The line may be operated with more or fewer personnel.
- The line may be operated continuously or only in stages by accumulating in-process inventory within the process.

Generally, the scheduling of a continuous manufacturing process is simpler than scheduling an intermittent production shop because production can be monitored more accurately by utilizing automatic means to continuously measure the flow in terms of weight and length.

Job shop production. A plant with intermittent production is defined as a job shop (see Fig. 7-7). Intermittent production is defined as "a production system in which jobs pass through a functional department in lots."[2] There are a number of problems that must be faced in scheduling and controlling a job shop operation that are different from a continuous flow manufacturer. Examples of the information to be collected manually include:

- When will the order be finished?
- Is it behind schedule?
- Where is it in the process?
- How long will the next operation take?
- Is the machine down for repair?

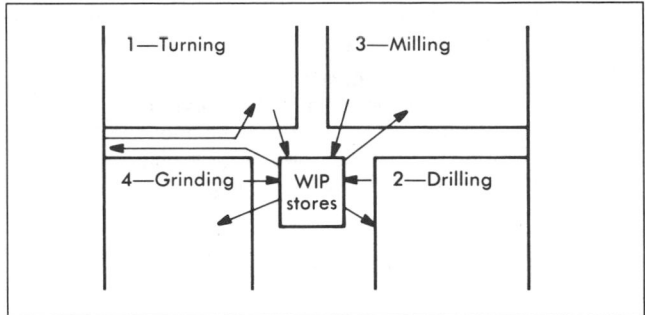

Fig. 7-7 Diagram of a plant with intermittent production. (*K.W. Tunnell Company, Inc.*)

- How are the dies or tools replaced?

Other basic problems are how does one decide what to schedule and how does one determine the best way to schedule the choices. Should products be scheduled? Or should machines be scheduled? Perhaps a combination of both methods? These decisions determine how data must be grouped from the forecasts and orders to allow the production activity scheduling group to visualize the potential load on existing capacity.

Repetitive manufacturing. Repetitive manufacturing involves the production of discrete units that are planned and executed according to a schedule and involve manufacturing at a relatively high volume and speed. Material moves in a sequential flow. Production feedback for control is based on the number of items that pass a predetermined control point. Regardless of the type of industry process that is being scheduled, there are several basic rules that should always be followed in a repetitive manufacturing environment:

1. Process similar orders in an appropriate sequence to minimize set-up time and reduce changeover times.
2. Schedule the input (released shop orders) to meet the planned production rates. If an individual workcenter is consistently not producing to meet its plan, the amount of work released to that center should not exceed the actual "experienced" capacity.
3. Keep released backlogs off the plant floor. On-floor work order backlogs are more difficult to control, make engineering changes more difficult to implement, generate more expediting, and create space problems.
4. Sequence the orders based on the latest requirements, not the requirements data estimated when the shop order was first written.
5. Schedule to the shortest cycle possible, daily if possible, to obtain the latest and most accurate feedback and requirements data on the orders released.

Performance Measurements

The prerequisite for the evaluation and measurement of performance to a predetermined expectation includes clearly defined objectives, clearly defined time elements for measuring performance, reasonable delegation of authority adequate to the performance of the tasks to be measured, and mutual agreement that the measure can be attained between the person being measured and the person doing the measuring. It is the responsibility of management to measure the performance of its production resources. Ideal measurements are quantitative, but

SCHEDULING AND PRODUCTION ACTIVITY CONTROL

should extend beyond simple output quantity measures. The three basic tasks of performance measurement are as follows:

1. An evaluation of individual performance in a manner resulting in the motivation of the workforce.
2. An evaluation of the general assumptions used as the basis for performance measures (assumptions that are really an estimate of overall capabilities).
3. An evaluation of the system as a whole, recognizing that performance measures are based on an estimate and that the overall performance of the systems may require a restating of the original goals.

One of the most critical measurement activities in a manufacturing company is related to its production operations. Typically, the production department will be measured on some of the following objectives:

- Shop orders completed on time.
- Output hours vs. plan.
- Direct labor productivity.
- Machine utilization.
- Actual costs vs. budget.
- Customer service vs. stated plan.
- Quality level vs. plan.
- Production rates vs. capacity plan.
- Personnel vs. plan.
- Input/output backlog vs. plan.

It should be recognized that performance measurement, particularly individual productivity measurements, may become so important internally as to sacrifice the objectives established for overall company inventory and/or customer service objectives. In fact, the measurement of production productivity can in some cases contribute directly to the failure of time-phased material planning systems, usually referred to as material requirements planning (MRP) or manufacturing resource planning (MRP II) systems. Scheduling for operations using just-in-time (JIT) manufacturing philosophies requires that measurements be made at the team level to maintain the focus of employee involvement in problem-solving processes.

WORK FLOW PATTERNS

The physical organization of the manufacturing facility has a dramatic impact on the expected costs of production. In recent years, a variety of changes affecting the direct labor resource have been implemented. Layout and flow can also contribute greatly to the reduction of indirect labor costs associated with material movement and on-floor work-in-process materials.

Traditional/Functional Layouts

The traditional layout of a factory is based on groupings of operations according to manufacturing function, such as drills in one department and lathes in another. This form of plant layout results in a back-and-forth type of physical flow of material throughout the factory. It is not a flow-oriented design. Operations may be spaced as far apart as from one end of the facility to the other. Functional layouts tend to demonstrate the poorest flow patterns after many years of operation.

Production is scheduled in batches that move from one operation to another. There is generally no overlap in operations, inasmuch as a succeeding operation will not begin production of its first piece until the entire batch or lot has been processed at the previous operation and the material physically transported to the next operation.

Cellular/Focused Layouts

Cellular manufacturing is based on the linking of operations according to part families or according to similarities of the manufacturing processes employed in production of a group of parts. Some companies have created cellular manufacturing units to form a complete production operation, from raw material to finished part, subassembly, or final product. The linking of manufacturing operations reduces work-in-process inventory between operations and permits the overlapping of production between operations, although the production may still be scheduled in batches or lots. Cellular flow distances are usually quite short when compared to the functional process routings replaced.

Cellular manufacturing is based on techniques usually described as group technology. This is basically a set of methods whereby functionally oriented production plants are studied for rearrangement into process layouts. Manufacturing cells are those equipment arrangements generally established to produce one or more families of parts. Manufacturing cell layouts permit the parts to be manufactured from start to finish in one location rather than being transported around the factory from workcenter to workcenter or department to department.

In-Process Queues

One of the reasons that manufacturing companies in the United States have large work-in-process inventories is their emphasis on producing "economic lot sizes," which seek to balance inventory costs against the set-up costs created by changing from one part to another. In contrast, the Japanese believe that inventory is, by definition, a liability and a creator of waste costs. Therefore, they strive to avoid the rationale of large batch production by directing their attention and ingenuity to reduction of set-up costs, thereby permitting the economic production of smaller lots. As set-up and ordering costs approach zero, the calculated economic lot size also approaches zero or, for practical purposes, a lot size of 1.

A secondary reason for large in-process inventories in American companies is the method of scheduling operators somewhat independently, which results in batches of in-process work sitting in front of machines, particularly bottleneck operations, waiting to be worked on. This is commonly referred to as a push system. In contrast, pull systems focus on the production of only those parts that are required for use in the next period or to replace those that have just been taken for use in another area.

SIMULATION

As a planning tool, simulation of operations activities aids in the testing of alternatives. MRP systems software usually offers some level of capability to assist in tactical planning evaluation through simulation. This is most often accomplished by allowing the system user to execute functional portions of the system using temporary work files and/or "no update" options. Software for small systems is more likely to require that unique sets of files be established for use in "alternative testing," or simulation runs, of the production programs.

Demand

If demand at the MPS level is varied between a minimum and maximum level around the live production planning forecast, the shop loading and material requirements changes required to respond to such a change in demand can be reviewed. This can be extremely important in developing specific plans for coping with an opportunity to handle unusually high demand patterns that might result from a competitor's strike or closure. To effectively respond in the shortest possible time period without diminishing service to existing customers, specific planning must be done to support decisions regarding the acquisition of additional labor and material resources.

Using simulation techniques, it is possible to load a new forecast into the system and measure the amount of change in processing requirements by workcenter. The amount of material that needs to be expedited and the additional material ordering activity required by that forecasted demand can be calculated. If the output gives strong indication that the level of increase being considered cannot be supported, a second execution of the simulation calculations with different timing and volumes in the trial forecast can be tried. The goal of any simulation activity is to give visibility of the likely results of a set of decisions without committing financial resources to the decision.

Production

Given any level of forecasted demands, another tactical planning support activity is required in anticipation of major changes in the production environment. The addition of new capacity through the installation of some new level of automation in a process requires an assessment of the work-in-process flow that will be expected in the new environment. Likewise, variations in worker-hours and machine-hours for the new operation can be calculated using modified process routing data that must, in any case, be prepared before implementation.

If product group data is to be used for these "what if" exercises, data must be prepared that corresponds to the average load profiles represented by each group. If product-level forecasted demands are to be used, the calculations will be based on product structures and process routings that are loaded into the manufacturing control system database.

Another common use of simulation techniques is in the assessment of the likely impact on a manufacturing facility that would result from a major shift in product mix. Changes in material flow, in-process queues, and existing workcenter loading can be predicted through such calculations. This can be valuable input to the marketing organization in determining the risks associated with a proposed change in their strategies and tactics related to the promotion of certain product groups.

Standard Costs/Standard Hours

Because most MRP application packages include modular support for the standard costing requirements of a manufacturer, changes in structures, routings, and material costs can be used to derive forecasts of financial results related to the changes in any of these database elements. This may be as simple as the calculation of a new cost for an individual product caused by a change proposed in any of those elements. It could also be a prediction of new product group margins that should be expected from the set of alternatives being evaluated. Purchasing departments often need such information to justify a potential change in a material alternative when the change being considered affects a large array of products. Standard costs changes also affect inventory investment levels in raw material, work in process, and finished goods. These too can be estimated through the simulation processes.

Modeling

More complex approaches to simulation include the use of various modeling techniques. In a manufacturing environment, these include the study of moves and queues. Specialized computer software exists, allowing an engineer or analyst to describe the elements of a process for simulation tests. These software packages use statistical approaches based on random number generation and probability distribution patterns to study a set of production demand and flow alternatives.

EQUIPMENT SELECTION AND SEQUENCE

How does one know what equipment is needed for a particular operation? What are the variables with which one has to contend? Why and how should one use consultants and vendors? What is the selection process for equipping or modernizing a manufacturing facility, and finally, how can one plan for the evolution of the equipment in one's facility? This section will provide some insight into these questions.

CRITERIA DEVELOPMENT

How does one know if they are making a good or bad equipment decision? Simply, what criteria is used to evaluate the decision process?

In general, all criteria can be expressed in terms of the following four general criteria (not necessarily listed in order of importance):

- Total product.

- Quality.
- Product flexibility.
- Process (volume) flexibility.

Safety is actually a fifth and absolute criteria.

Cost has to be thought of in terms of total cost, which means that it is not enough to simply consider the cost of production. The cost of rework and warranty work have to be included, as well as the cost of all overhead, including inventory carrying cost. Therefore, the criteria of cost has to consider the total impact of new equipment.

Quality used to be the usual tradeoff to cost; you could either get a good part or you could get it for less cost. This tradeoff no longer exists. Quality is no longer a "nice-to-have" feature; a manufacturer either has quality or loses business.

Just what is product flexibility? It's the ability to make or produce something different than what is currently being made in a time frame that is acceptable to the customer. "Making

EQUIPMENT SELECTION

something different" may mean customized products or even brand new products; and, depending on the product, the acceptable time frame, which is determined by one's customers and competitors, could be anywhere from weeks to years. It is important to keep in mind that this flexibility is itself bounded by the basic process technologies in place.

Volume flexibility is the basic tenet behind the just-in-time movement —make what you need, no more and no less. The real difficulty here is handling all of the perceived and real tradeoffs that are associated with good volume flexibility. U.S. companies have thousands upon thousands of manufacturing managers who were trained by the "economic lot size" theory. This theory simply states that the most economical unit cost for a manufactured item is found at that quantity where the cost of setting up the piece of equipment is balanced against the generally unknown but assumed cost of carrying inventory.

THE SELECTION PROCESS

The equipment selection process shown in Fig. 7-8 has both managerial and technical aspects. Therefore, it is rarely carried through by just one person.

The first two steps are fundamental to the process engineering function and answer the questions "What does this part have to look like?" (What features are needed?) and "With what material do I have to work?" To keep this whole methodology in a broad context, the features should be thought of in a wide range of terms from actual physical features such as profiles and

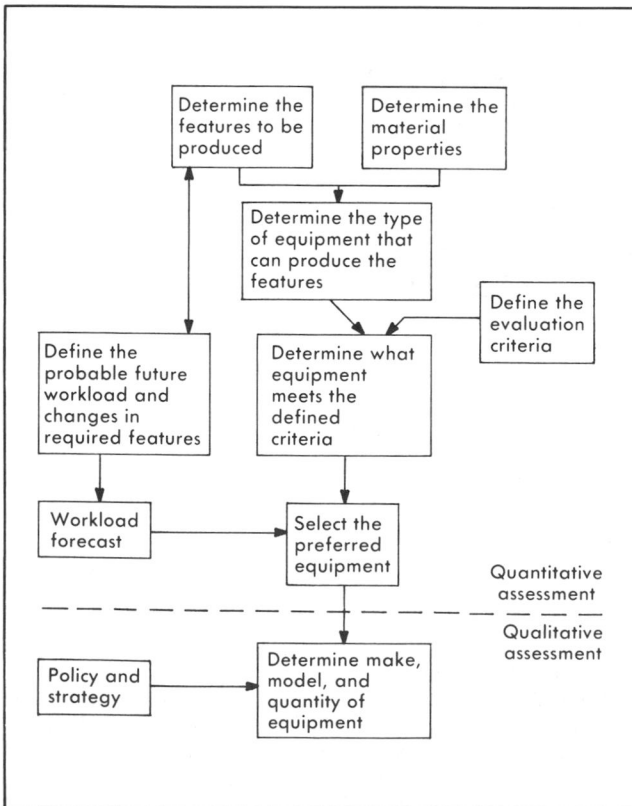

Fig. 7-8 Diagram of steps in equipment selection process. (*Austin Consulting*)

splines to such features as location when planning for material handling equipment. Likewise, the material properties could range from the metalworking properties associated with 9310 steel to such things as "transport in small tote" for material handling.

The next step, determining the type of equipment, is essentially a research step and, as such, one in which there is likely to be considerable involvement with equipment vendors. Another good source of information is trade publications. During this step, the evaluation needs to be as open as possible to nontraditional techniques and technologies. For example, have the advantages and limitations of electrical discharge machining (EDM) been considered? If not, why not?

Evaluation criteria are then applied to the candidate list of equipment. The critical point here is that management should either have defined the criteria or should be aware of them and support them. Remember, these criteria should be the same that will be used to evaluate the ultimate success of the selected equipment.

The process of selecting the make and model of the needed equipment now has to consider the future. For example, an NC lathe with an X-inch (mm) swing may serve today's needs, but with a little market research, it may be determined that an $X + 2$ swing is what will be needed in the near future. After all, most equipment has a useful life measured in decades, not months. It always pays to spend some time to assess the future impact of present decisions.

Determining the required quantity of equipment is another prime area for technical and managerial assessment. Equipment utilization projections can be made based on standard industrial engineering techniques. These techniques do not, however, take management policy into account. For example, management may not allow single quantities of unique/special equipment as insurance against breakdown. Likewise, the adoption of a cellular manufacturing philosophy may require multiple pieces of underutilized equipment to fully develop needed cells. The key here is understanding and appreciating the fallacy of high equipment utilization as the primary criteria. This has, in fact, been one of the biggest problems with adoption of the JIT manufacturing philosophy. Many conventional managers just can't see the advantage of letting equipment sit idle so as to *not* build inventory.

The final big step before signing the purchase order is to assess how this particular solution will fit with policies and strategies of the company and, therefore, move the whole process from the realm of quantitative assessment to the managerial realm of qualitative assessment.

EQUIPMENT PROFILE EVOLUTION

Many manufacturing managers are or will be faced with the problem of shorter and shorter product lifecycles and, consequently, the need for flexible manufacturing capabilities. This need has led, in turn, to the call for more programmable automation and less fixed automation. At the same time there has been a general call to move away from "islands of automation" and to address the need for integrated operations.

The response is to address the needs for manufacturing within an "envelope" of capabilities. As mentioned previously, manufacturing managers have to look at the probable future requirements when addressing the specific needs of today. In light of this, some leading manufacturers have defined their manufacturing capabilities in terms of such statements as "we can manufacture prismatic parts that fall within a dimensional cube of X x Y x Z inches. This sets the limits on what they are prepared to fabricate and forces the need to react rapidly within those limits. In fact, fast reaction time is rapidly becoming a manufacturing requirement.

Rapid response is inherent in the capabilities of a networked manufacturing environment. General Motors saw this in its historic move to force the development of devices adhering to a specific manufacturing protocol on the vendor community. General Motors had tens of thousands of computer-based manufacturing devices and found that, for the most part, they could not communicate with each other. Rather than wait for an industry standard, which might never appear, GM forced the issue with its buying power "either adhere to the standard or we won't buy from you", and forced the development of MAP, Manufacturing Automation Protocol.

MANUFACTURING AUTOMATION PROTOCOL

Integrated manufacturing, specifically computer-integrated manufacturing, requires communication capabilities if the devices and the humans using the devices are to share information. Doing this in a factory setting requires the development and use of a local area network. Simplistically, this is just the data "circuit" that the computer-based tools use to transfer and share data.

In the early 1980s, General Motors found itself with about 40,000 programmable tools, controls, and systems installed at its facilities. The major problem with this situation was that only 15% of these devices could communicate with one another. The basis of this problem was that noncompatible methods of communication existed among the various vendors, and no one was going to change. IBM could communicate with IBM, DEC could communicate with DEC, HP with HP, and on and on.

General Motors was faced with the desire to increase the amount of programmable equipment by 400-500% during the next 5 years; the communications problem would quickly get out of hand.

Assessing the situation led to the following three alternatives:

1. Continue to buy equipment from different vendors and develop custom solutions.
2. Buy all equipment from a single supplier.
3. Develop a standardized approach to plant floor communication.

GM chose the third alternative and set up a taskforce in 1980 to investigate the use of a model developed by the International Organization for Standardization (ISO) as the basis for the third alternative. GM representatives met with various computer manufacturers in 1981 and began to explore solving the problem through the use of local area networks based on the model; this model was to describe a set of communications protocols that would become known as the Manufacturing Automation Protocol. A protocol is a set of rules that govern the format and timing of messages that are exchanged between two communicating devices. In 1982 the GM taskforce developed an initial model composed of existing and newly defined layers for the protocol. (Without going into the architecture of MAP, just consider these levels as modules for the protocol.) The first MAP users meeting was held in 1984, and the development continues today.

As MAP becomes more of a reality, GM and the other users of MAP will have a standard set of protocols with which to access the networks that tie their machines into flexible manufacturing systems; the basic building block of CIM. The end result is that GM is slowly changing its equipment profile to an integrated manufacturing capability.

MATERIAL HANDLING

In the development of manufacturing facilities, the material handling operations must be considered as a critical factor in the design process. Material delivery and product movement philosophies have a dramatic effect on quality, facility requirements, equipment layout, and the physical integration of the operation. Manufacturing operations that are developed without consideration to material handling most often result in compromised performance well below the potential that could have otherwise been achieved. The implementation of complex systems that result in world-class operations is infrequent because of the lack of planning needed for the required coordination and interaction between production, material handling, and facility departments within a company.

The key to developing a successful integrated system is to rigorously follow a structured system development methodology. One such approach that has proven quite successful is shown in the flow chart in Fig. 7-9. This methodology works equally well independent of the operations performed within a facility. The seven steps begin by segmenting the facility into logical operations and conclude by restructuring the facility

with definitive subsystems that can be implemented in a time-phased manner.

SEGMENTATION

The first critical step is to segment the facility into logical operations that require or interface with material handling functions. These may include, but are not limited to: receiving storage, process workstations, packaging, and kitting. Each operation must then be defined in terms of internal function, requirements, and interrelationships with adjacent areas. Essentially, a minisystem functional specification is prepared for each segment or subsystem. The development of these accurate operational performance specifications is a critical element most often overlooked or ignored. Attention to detail at this point generally results in significant reduction in effort required in the later stages of facility development. The most significant benefit in segmentation of the facility into logical operations is that the design tasks are divided into manageable sections. In addition, the engineer is not faced with a monumental database that could result in losing sight of the original objective.

MATERIAL HANDLING

FLOW DEVELOPMENT

An accurate representation of material flows cannot be developed without a clear understanding of the functional operation and requirements of the subsystem. This understanding is the earliest benefit realized from the preparation of performance specifications. Steps 2 through 4 are performed independently for each subsystem.

In these steps, the material flows and the data flows are independently developed, although the data flow definition generally is preceded by the material flow development. All load movements are first defined in a "From-To" matrix for each subsystem as well as the complete facility. These movements are then plotted on a layout of the facility if for a retrofit situation, or as a functional block diagram (see Fig. 7-10) for a new facility development. Consideration must be given to volumes transported, frequencies of moves, and the envelope and characteristics of the items being moved.

Implementation tradeoffs can be evaluated, and significant benefits can be attained if process and material handling operation approaches remain somewhat flexible. Once the material and product movement flows have been determined, including peak and cyclical factors, the required data transactions and flows can be established to effectively support the material and product flows. The data flows will account for inventory monitoring, material dispatch, and tracking.

IDENTIFY IMPLEMENTATION CANDIDATES

For each subsystem, a range of implementation techniques can be defined as alternatives for evaluation. Various candidate technologies may be applicable for any given implementation. All potential candidates should be evaluated for cost, flexibility, performance, and ease of implementation tradeoffs. Alterna-

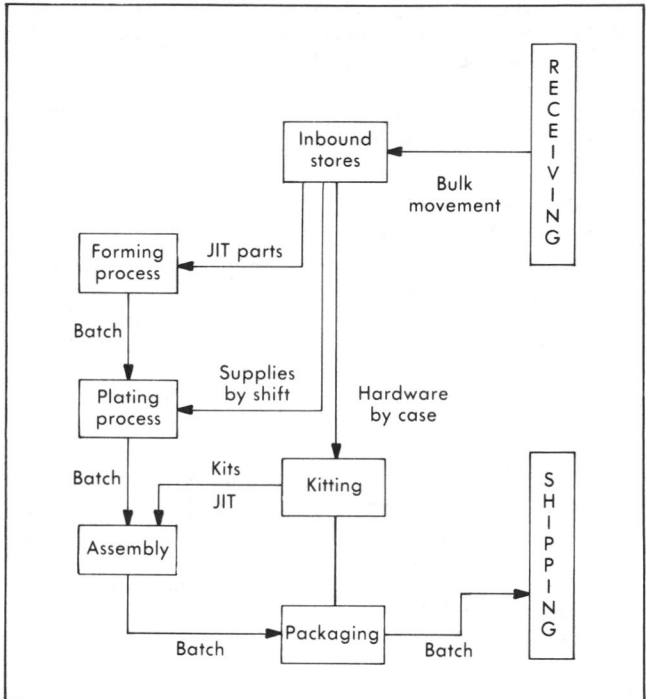

Fig. 7-10 Functional block diagram of material flow in a manufacturing facility. (*Austin Consulting*)

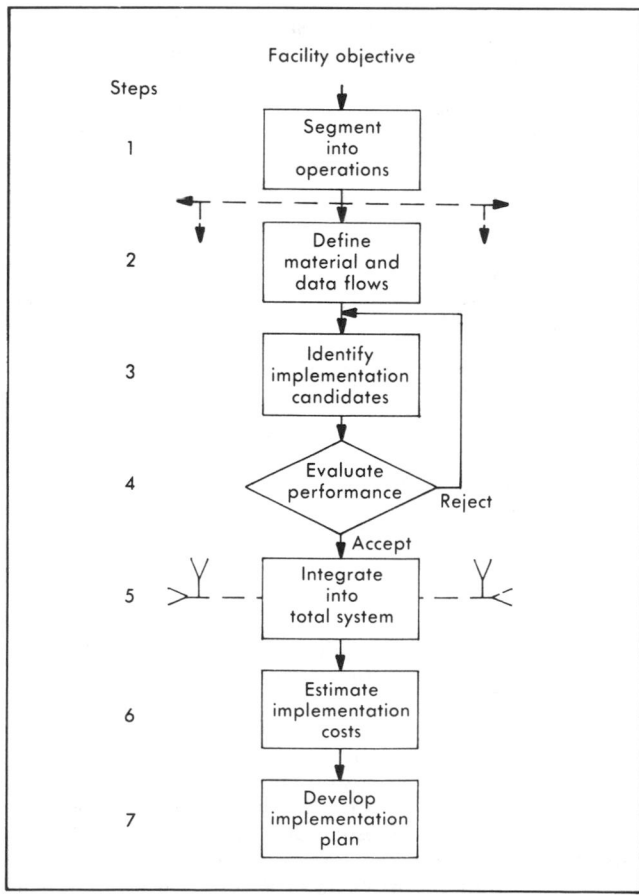

Fig. 7-9 Proposed system methodology for developing an integrated material handling system. (*Austin Consulting*)

TABLE 7-2
Material Handling Movement Implementation Candidates

Manual	Semiautomated	Fully Automated
Pallet jack	Automatic guided vehicle (AGV) pallet jack	Towline
Fork truck		Conveyor
Fork truck with data terminal	AGV tugger	Power-and-free monorail
	AGV stock selector	Automated monorail
		AGV tugger with automatic trailers
		Unit-load AGV
		Multiple-load AGV
		AGV fork truck
		Specialty AGV

(*Austin Consulting*)

tive implementation candidates can be manual, semiautomated, or fully automated. Examples of candidate technologies in each of these classifications are shown in Table 7-2.

Multiple factors must be considered when selecting implementation candidates for evaluation. Local configuration, orientation, and delivery frequencies can restrict traffic because of throughput limitations of load and unload stations. Process requirements at the manufacturing workstations, such as precise load positioning, can also affect material handling choices. The key consideration is to develop a series of candidate configurations that will provide the appropriate balance between delivery frequencies and work in process on the production floor. Facility configuration may also significantly affect the range of candidates available for evaluation. A facility that has low internal ceilings or one that cannot support structures from overhead would probably not be able to accept power-and-free monorail or automated monorail systems.

EVALUATE PERFORMANCE

Once candidate technologies are chosen, a preliminary implementation layout is formulated. Performance is evaluated against the performance specifications developed when the subsystem segmentation was performed. Operational performance is best characterized through the use of computer simulation. Simple operations can be modeled using mathematical networks that only yield statistical results. More complex subsystem implementations require analysis of detailed flows in areas such as critical intersections and subsystem interfaces. This detailed analysis cannot readily be determined from statistical data. Animated graphics are then implemented to visually depict the operation so that flows may be observed and conditions leading to bottleneck situations can be identified. The benefit of using simulation as a design verification tool is the ability to test and evaluate conditional performance before committing to expensive hardware.

Having established conformance with operational criteria, an assessment can be made of cost effectiveness of the final implementation. If the performance, either in flows or cost, is deemed unsatisfactory, another implementation is chosen and the process repeated.

This process is performed for all subsystems individually. The estimated performance of each subsystem can be used as a benchmark at the time of installation test at the subsystem level.

INTEGRATION OF SUBSYSTEMS

Having completed the definition of all subsystems, the process of system integration begins. This process begins with the interface evaluation when any two subsystems are interconnected. The interfaces that must be evaluated are both informational and physical. Care must be taken to ensure that appropriate and timely information transfer is provided and that data handling means are not overloaded. In terms of physical aspects, load transfer mechanisms, orientation, positioning, and transfer times that could restrict flows must be considered. Individual subsystems are then added to the initial integrated pair one at a time. System performance should be reviewed after each subsystem integration definition is completed.

ESTIMATE COSTS

Overall costs for the system can now be considered. The costs for implementation should include not only the purchase price of the hardware and software, but project management, installation, and various administrative costs such as purchasing the installation supervision. The ongoing cost of personnel and maintenance should also be considered. These estimates can be evaluated against improvements in production and displacement of personnel to ascertain the payback rate and cost effectiveness of the facility. If the cost effectiveness is determined to be acceptable, then implementation funding can be pursued.

PLAN IMPLEMENTATION

The implementation plan should be developed to provide installation and testing in a phased manner. This will permit a smooth transition into full system operation, minimize risk, and provide early payback on portions of the installed system resulting from the benefits of early usage.

Material handling system development is still an art as much as it is a science. This is because of the applied creativity of the people who develop the systems. There are as many options and tradeoffs as there are opportunities. Virtually every installation is unique and, as such, will have unique solutions that depend as much on the operating business issues as on the facility. System development and evaluation should be performed or at least supervised by experienced professionals.

SYSTEMS INTEGRATION

Consider how the dictionary defines the terms *integrate* and *integration*:

Integrate—to make into a whole by bringing all the parts together.
Integration—the act of integrating.

The definitions sound so simple. Why then is this concept so difficult to comprehend and perform when it is put into the phrase "computer-integrated manufacturing" or "systems integration"?

What then is systems integration? One concept is that it's using a computer and some wires to connect the various parts of the manufacturing operation together so that the manufacturer can respond to and interrupt and prioritize tasks very fast. A more accurate description is that it is the gathering of dissimilar computer-based products or technologies of multiple vendors into an operating entity. Easy? Only if the person can understand a new language that includes terms like protocol, token ring, twisted pair, and controllers. These terms define elements of the needed local area networks.

SYSTEMS INTEGRATION

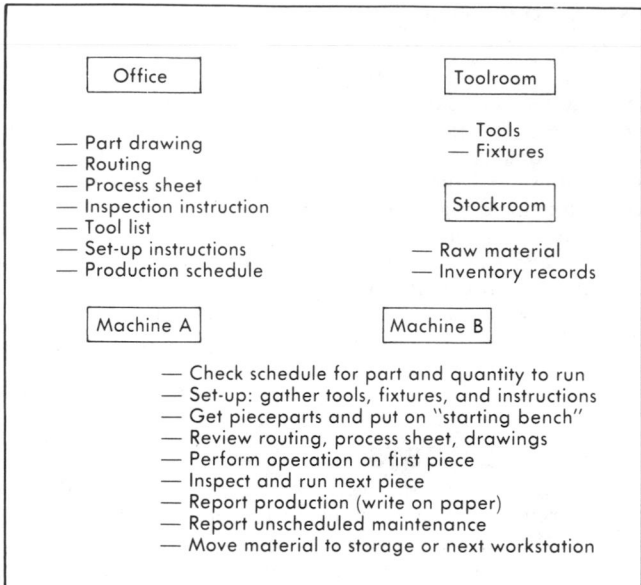

Fig. 7-11 Schematic of a small machine shop operation. (*Austin Consulting*)

The purpose of this section, then, is to lend a bit of understanding to this new language. To do this, a very small shop will be created to work with and integrate. Let's assume that the shop has two machines, a front office, a tool crib, and a stockroom. A schematic of this operation and a listing of the kinds of things that go on in this arrangement is shown in Fig. 7-11.

This little machine shop will work all right as long as there are only a few parts to contend with and a good job is done of keeping all of the paperwork up to date and matched among the shop floor, office, and stockroom. However, as the business grows, the number of parts and tools and the amount of paper will grow at a phenomenal rate. It now becomes harder to keep things up to date—it becomes harder to run the operation in an integrated fashion. What then are some of the key facets of integration and how might they be accomplished?

INTEGRATION

One integration need is to make sure that the shop floor makes the products to the latest specification. Face it, it's a waste of time, material, and labor to make "revision A" when the office has just released "revision B." Under the manual method of integration, drawings are hand drawn, filed, passed to the manufacturing engineer for the development of instructions, and finally passed to the shop floor for the operator to use. Problems arise when the design engineers start to respond to the marketplace with changes or when the machine operator realizes that the part can't be made the way it's shown on the drawing and changes the actual part without informing the design engineers.

If the drawings are created on a computer-aided design (CAD) system, run off on the plotter, and then passed to the manufacturing engineer and the shop floor, the only thing that has been accomplished is a slight reduction in drafting time. However, what if the paper drawings could be eliminated and one electronic master maintained for use by all functions? This

may sound very simplistic, but that is the essence of integrating CAD with numerical control tools—use the computer to "file" the matching set of drawing and NC instructions and a network to send the data to the appropriate machine tool. This is a good start, but it may not be enough.

Integrating CAD with NC machine tools allows the manufacturer to make the correct parts, but it doesn't necessarily help to make the parts that are needed or make them when they are needed. This involves another kind of integration, the integration of schedule requirements with the status of inventory and work in process in a timely manner. To do this, a manufacturer might look at the applicability of software packages designed to do manufacturing resource planning (often referred to as MRP II).

The use of MRP II is an attempt to integrate the current production requirements with the status of the factory and the company vendors. The essential objective is to have accurate data to ensure the accomplishment of the production schedule and to determine the ability to change the schedule.

EXAMPLE

Probably the major cause of integration failure is that the concept is so easily understood and is so very agreeable—"of *course* we need to integrate this operation, let's hook up the machines and go for it!" While the concept is easily understood, the implementation is rarely grasped by manufacturing management because so much of systems integration is really a major data processing project. The example in this section is based on the earlier scenario of a two-machine tool operation, the difference is that there is a distributed numerical control (DNC) environment. The phase or steps in this process are product introduction, downloading, operator functions, and machine monitoring. Different software modules are also used to support the DNC operation.

Figure 7-12 shows the conceptual design for a DNC system for the small operation in this example. Part designs are created and maintained on a CAD system, NC tape images are maintained in the office, tool and inventory information is maintained in the production database, and the machine tools have been fitted with machine controllers capable of accepting NC directions.

Product Introduction

After the design of the part has been finalized by the design engineering department and released to manufacturing engineering, a process plan is prepared, tooling fixtures are designed, NC tool path is generated, and cutting tools are selected. The parts programmer specifies the type of operation, the tool path, and the cutter. Verification of the tool path is usually visual, and changes are made interactively. Once the parts programmer is satisfied that the tool path is correct, a request will be made to convert the tool path to automatically programmed tool (APT) source language. The APT statements are processed through the language processor and subsequently on to the NC machine-specific post processors. The tool path is then reverified. The output from the post processor and coded machine instructions are saved in the Tape Image Database.

Downloading to the Shop Floor Workstation

When a work order for a particular part is issued by production control, the manufacturing engineering department will transmit the tape image file and the other elements of the NC package to the DNC file server. The status of the NC tape

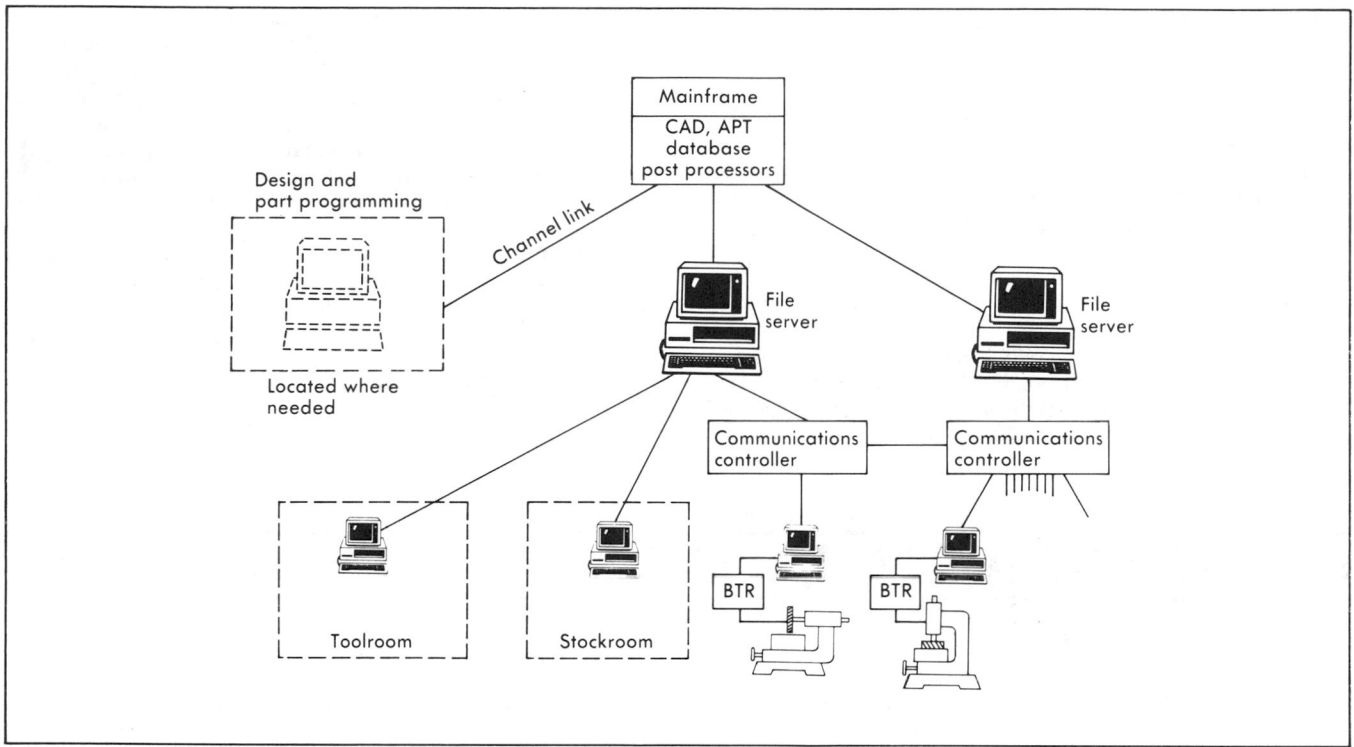

Fig. 7-12 Conceptual design for a DNC system for a small machine shop operation. (*Austin Consulting*)

image stored on the DNC file server will be easily identified as either production (proven) or unreleased. Unproven programs will not be loaded to the operator's workstation. Transmitted data is checked for integrity and is retransmitted in the event of an error.

Operator Functions

The machine operator may query the shop floor workstation to list those jobs ready for production. Once a particular job is selected, the operator may display part geometry with dimensions, part number, program image, program length, cutting tool descriptions, fixture numbers, and set-up instructions.

The operator is allowed to load NC program images designated for that specific machine authorized by NC programming. The downloaded NC program package is stored at the shop floor workstation until the operator is ready to transmit it to the machine controller. Once the operator begins loading the program image into the machine controller, he or she continues the machine tool operations as usual.

Software Modules

A variety of functions are performed by software in support of the DNC operation. The shop traveler software builds the relationship between tool lists, graphic images, machine tool number, job history, and tape number. All of the associated documents can be referenced by the part number and downloaded to the shop floor workstation.

Machine maintenance software automates repair requests and assigns priority levels. It also schedules preventive maintenance for each machine tool. Maintenance management software should also be capable of keeping historical records by machine of repairs and modifications made as well as perform-

ing the scheduling function. These historical records are essential to the establishment of an efficient predictive maintenance program.

Automated tool presetting software ties toolroom operations with the DNC host computer. As a tool is measured, the program updates the tool number and tool description in the cutting tool database. When the tool presetter enters the tool number, the program updates the database with the measurement of the actual tool dimensions.

Operational Machine Monitoring

Operational monitoring of NC machines is accomplished by collecting data from the machine control, capturing data from sensors, or from manual data entry by the operator. The electronic signals being monitored are sampled and stored as raw data values. Both analog and digital information is recorded. At periodic intervals, the shop floor workstation polls the data and transfers it to the DNC file server where it is converted into a more usable format. This converted data is used to produce management reports.

Manual data entry by the operator is initiated through a menu display on the shop floor workstation. The operator specifies machine tool status information by selecting an option from a list such as the following:

- Job set-up.
- Tape tryout.
- Fixture problem.
- Time out.
- No work.
- Work in production.
- Part inspection.

EQUIPMENT INSTALLATION

- Tool inspection.
- No tools, material, operator, or tape.
- Maintenance problem.

Each time the operator selects one of the menu items, the system clock records the "start time" of that event. The event is stopped whenever the operator selects the next event. The elapsed time is computed and recorded by event and is used to produce a variety of machine tool utilization reports.

RESULTS

The integration of the factory has implications beyond simply eliminating the need for punched tape or manual keyboard/console entry. One only has to think of the implications of the manufacturing engineer being able to answer fundamental questions, such as "If we make this design change, what will be affected?" By accessing the material requirements database (containing the item master, "where used," and inventory data) the engineer will be able to assess the impact that the change will have over the expected life and volumes of the part. By accessing the CAD database, the engineer will be able to determine whether or not this change will require changes to other parts (such as mating parts). By accessing the purchasing database, the engineer will be able to assess the impact that the change might have on purchase agreements and blanket orders. And the process goes on and on.

In the final analysis, the integration of the factory will result in the ability to exchange information and share resources. Doing this means being able to leverage manufacturing capabilities and makes the shop more responsive to changes that are made in the product. With CAD/CAM files and integrated systems, changes may be integrated into the product itself more rapidly.

EQUIPMENT INSTALLATION

The purpose of this section is to look at the relationship between equipment and the facility. Although some of this can be considered from the plant engineering point of view, it is more appropriate here to consider it from the plant management point of view. This is best accomplished by answering a series of broad questions about the equipment under consideration. Consider the following questions:

- What does this equipment need?
- What does this equipment produce?
- Where should this equipment fit in the manufacturing flow?
- What is needed if it breaks?

NEEDS

Consider the list of equipment needs and realize that someone from the organization will have to supply those needs. These needs include the following:

- A floor strong enough to support the weight of the equipment in operation.
- Enough clear height to allow access to the workpiece.
- Enough operator space to allow maintenance and operation of the equipment.
- Power, water, and air.
- Floor drains for cleaning purposes.
- Elevators strong enough to move the equipment into place.
- Doorways with enough height and width to allow movement.
- Access to automated material handling equipment.
- A level floor for the required material handling and storage equipment.
- Isolation from vibration caused by other equipment.
- Vent hoods and drains.

PRODUCTION

Another aspect of the equipment installation process is answered by addressing what the equipment produces. Consider the following topics and questions:

- Product.
  How will the product be moved from the machine?
  Where will the product be stored?
- Chips and waste cutting oils.
  Will underfloor chip conveyor tote pans be used?
  How would chip conveyors help or hinder equipment movement flexibility?
- Heat.
  What heat load will this equipment place on the air conditioning system?
- Fumes.
  Are hoods needed?
  Are air scrubbers needed?
- Waste water and tramp oils.
  Can the waste water and tramp oils enter the municipal or company sewer system or will it have to be treated first?
- Noise.
  Are baffles needed?
  Will ear protection and operator screening be required?
- Vibration.
  Is this a high-tolerance machine? Will this machine need to be isolated from the vibration of nearby machines?

MANUFACTURING FLOW

Answering the question of fit in the manufacturing flow is not as easy or as straightforward as the earlier questions. Nevertheless, it is important and often overlooked. For example, most companies find the open space when new equipment is considered. The impact of the new equipment on the overall layout is usually not considered. Likewise, a company rarely updates its layout as the products change over time. What might have been an ideal layout for the old product line may be inappropriate for the present or future products. Whether one looks at the operation from a product or process point of view, it is more easily understood when considered in light of "From-To" considerations and the application of group technology principles. Consider the following questions:

- Where do the workpieces originate?
- Where do the workpieces go?
- How is the tooling delivered?
- Does work in process stay at the machine or does it go to inventory?

MAINTENANCE PLANNING

Deciding what to do when the equipment breaks is a form of contingency planning. It raises the following issues:

- Who will repair the equipment? Does the organization

have the needed skills or will people have to be trained?

For example, are the electricians in need of electronics knowledge?

- What repair inventory is needed? How long are the lead times for the critical repair items? What are the unique items needed for repair and should they be on hand to prevent a shutdown of the production line?

- How does this equipment fit in the scheme of the preventive maintenance program? What aspects of the equipment have to be considered for a predictive maintenance program?

MAINTENANCE

Past manufacturing practices have taken the position of "if it's not broken, then don't fix it." A more enlightened approach, however, is to recognize the relationship between maintenance costs and the cost of production losses caused by equipment failures. This has led managers away from the older assumption of equating maintenance with emergency repairs to the acceptance of the principles of preventive and predictive maintenance.

MAINTENANCE PRINCIPLES

The maintenance function in a factory has four basic resources with which it must be concerned: (1) maintenance labor, (2) plant equipment, (3) maintenance inventory, and (4) maintenance information. Considering the role of these resources in the management of a manufacturing enterprise leads to four fundamental principles.

Principle One

Maintenance labor can only be used in an efficient and effective manner if it is considered in light of a scheduled maintenance program. A policy of "repair maintenance only" leaves this resource in a reactive mode. The three types of maintenance efforts are repair, preventive, and predictive maintenance.

Repair maintenance is the unscheduled servicing of equipment after a problem is discovered. Preventive maintenance (PM) is the application of scheduled work to reduce maintenance costs through a reduction in repair needs. Predictive maintenance is the application of analytical techniques to reduce both maintenance costs and production downtime through identification of upcoming equipment failures. This is accomplished through measuring devices and the use of statistical techniques. In the future, this approach may be fertile ground for the application of artificial intelligence techniques.

Principle Two

The dictates of increased productivity require maintenance workers to know and understand the way in which a task is to be accomplished and how long it should take to accomplish it. This requires a work order system that organizes and maintains the following information:

- Description of the work to be accomplished and where it's to be done.

- Time estimates developed through experience, historical data, or standard data.
- Material and equipment requirements.
- Priority designation.
- Authorization.

Principle Three

Like manufacturing, the organization of the maintenance function has to respond to the needs of advanced technology by supplying the skills that are needed. The maintenance organization must provide those skills based on the existing structure and job descriptions as well as from the standpoint of determining the best qualified person or group from a trained skill viewpoint. Consider the "traditional" crafts associated with a maintenance organization: electricians, millwrights, pipefitters, carpenters, painters, sheet metal workers, and general laborers. The question today is who will be called when a fiber-optic cable has been severed or when a solid-state machine controller is malfunctioning. The maintenance department will also need its share of computer-literate (and trained) workers. Determining who does what may be a function of who is properly trained for the task and is not assigned another equal-priority task.

Principle Four

Principle Four is the requirement for properly documenting any and all actions taken with respect to maintenance or modification of a piece of equipment. This documentation assists other maintenance personnel in troubleshooting similar pieces of equipment as well as providing the statistical basis for a sound predictive maintenance program and for justification of replacement equipment in the future. Such documentation can also assist in personnel planning and scheduling of maintenance personnel and actions.

BENEFITS

Many studies of maintenance expenditures have shown that the total cost of maintenance is subject to improvement through the proper application of maintenance efforts. As shown in Fig. 7-13, by reducing costs due to equipment being out of service and repair costs, an effective predictive and preventive maintenance (PPM) program reduces total controllable maintenance costs. The savings are accrued through extended equipment life, lower repair frequency, reduced lost production time, and reduced employee exposure to malfunctioning equipment.

INVENTORY MANAGEMENT

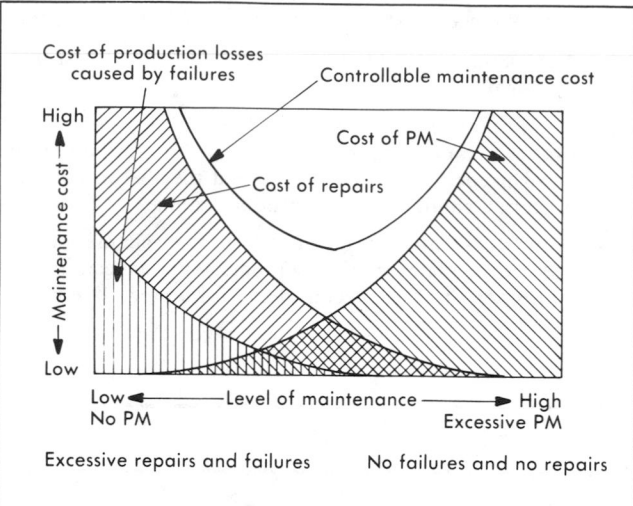

Fig. 7-13 Cost tradeoffs of a maintenance management program. (*Austin Consulting*)

DEVELOPMENT AND IMPLEMENTATION

The development and implementation of a productive and cost effective PM function is a two-step process. The first step involves the determination of the facility's actual equipment PM requirements and the methods and procedures needed to ensure proper results. Step two involves the implementation of a formal PM program that meets the equipment needs for ensuring maximum reliability and minimum emergency breakdowns. The steps require an understanding of the cost of equipment downtime and the ability to forecast the resources required to avoid an unacceptable level of downtime. Although it would be prohibitively expensive to avoid all emergency repairs, a properly designed PM program will return its annual cost many times over.

INVENTORY MANAGEMENT

Of all the disciplines represented by the field of materials management, none is more prominent than inventory management. But inventory management is, itself, a varied collection of many disciplines. In its simplest forms, the inventory management responsibilities may include the establishment of policies and procedures as well as the maintenance of manually posted card records. Thousands of materials managers depend heavily on computerized forecasting and manufacturing resource planning (MRP II) systems to control the flow of inventories. In the most competitive and innovative manufacturing companies today, newer methods utilizing the pull concepts of just-in-time (JIT) and frequent supplier communications orchestrate the management of inventories that may be turning over 20, 40, or more times per year.

USE OF FORECASTING

Inventory is one of the most important financial assets present in manufacturing companies. Stocks of raw materials, work-in-process inventory, and finished goods constitute the focus of control for the time they are held before being converted into sales dollars. The shorter the period that inventory is held, the more productive the asset. Inventory affects the financial health of a company in the following two ways:

1. As an asset representing stored value that, when sold, will produce income and, hopefully, a profit.
2. As a major investment that is financed by equity or debt.

Therefore, inventory levels directly affect a company's rate of return on its total assets.

Inventory may also exist as a result of lot sizing rules. For example, it may be more economical to produce more of a product or work-in-process item than is immediately required.

Another cause for inventory results from discrepancies between supply and demand. Types of inventories usually found include the following:

- Work-in-process and in-transit inventories.
- Raw material.
- Finished goods or semifinished products, manufactured to cover anticipated demand and prone to significant forecast error.
- Inventory buildup in anticipation of a new product introduction or special promotion.
- Purchase of a stockpile inventory in anticipation of a supply interruption such as an impending strike, or in anticipation of a substantial price increase.
- Manufactured products to cover seasonal demands that exceed near-level production requirements.

Therefore, forecast accuracy is a key determinant of the size of the inventory asset. Demand for products and parts inventories present themselves in a variety of ways. Some inventory items have only one source of demand. Other items receive demands from multiple sources. The following paragraphs discuss the nature and importance of the demand functions on the management and control of the inventory resource.

Independent Demand

Demand for an item is considered to be "independent" when that demand is unrelated to the demand for other items. Demands for finished products arriving through orders are the principal element of this type of demand. This form of demand is usually associated with the primary revenue source for the manufacturer and is the subject of the bulk of the forecasting effort. Demand for items that will be consumed in destructive testing and service parts requirements are likewise independent demands.

Level			Part Number			Description	Quantity per Unit	
1			A1			Make—final assembly	1	Each
	2			CC		Make—subassembly	1	Each
		3			EE	Purchased component	2	Each
		3			FF	Make—fabrication	2	Each
			4		HH	Purchased raw material	10	Feet
	2			BB		Purchased component	2	Each
1			A2			Make—final assembly	1	Each
	2			DD		Make—subassembly	2	Each
		3			EE	Purchased component	2	Each
		3			GG	Make—fabrication	2	Each
	2			BB		Purchased component	4	Each

Fig. 7-14 Example of an indented bill of material (explosion). *(K.W. Tunnell Company, Inc.)*

Dependent Demand

Demand for parts or raw materials are considered to be "dependent" demands when they are derived directly from the demands for other items. The usual source of these requirements is the output of a bill of material "explosion" (see Fig. 7-14). These demands are then accumulated as component and material requirements by time period. Such demands are, therefore, calculated and should not be forecasted independently. Some items are subject to both independent and dependent demands.

Demand Variability

The demand for products, parts, components, and materials is almost never stable over time. Forecasting addresses the trend and seasonal causes of variation and anticipates additional random variation in actual demands. Demands may vary from plan as a result of forecast error and lead time variation. Forecast error is always anticipated. Response to this demand variability may be dealt with either by inventory buffers or by improvement in the capability and flexibility of the manufacturing processes. Lead time variation may occur in both the input and output sides of the manufacturing processes. In both cases, the best efforts toward good management of the inventory investment are those that are applied to minimizing demand variation. Forecast error variation is difficult to control, but through meaningful feedback and involvement of people contributing to the variation, such error can be minimized.

Lead time variation is automatically minimized as lead times are shortened. It is possible to theorize that lead time and the lack of reliability in the flow of quality products are the only real causes of problems with variation.

Replenishment Policies

Inventory is always replenished according to some set of rules, either formal or informal. In small companies, there is a tendency to use variations of the simple two-bin system. When one bin is emptied, the second is pulled into the picking position and a signal is given to begin the production or procurement cycle to replenish the first. Bins or storage containers in a pure two-bin system must be able to hold enough inventory to cover all demands that are expected during replenishment lead time.

The objective of inventory policies must always be to balance the cost of carrying inventory with the service level required. The principal measure related to this activity is called inventory "turns." Inventory policies and procedures determine what turns can be achieved. The turns ratios experienced by companies using conventional manufacturing philosophies, functional lay-outs, and large lot sizes will be far less than those experienced by companies using JIT manufacturing methodologies. The difference in ratios might be expected to fall in the range of 2 to 10 for the conventional manufacturer vs. ratios of 10 to 50 or more for the latter. Calculating inventory turns is simply a measure of annual usage at cost divided by the average inventory usage, also at cost. The equation for this calculation is as follows:

$$\text{Inventory turns} = \frac{\text{Annual inventory usage \$ at cost}}{\text{Average inventory \$ at cost}} \qquad (5)$$

Safety Stocks

Minimum inventory balances may be specified as protection against stockouts when the cost of such an event is quite high. Protection may be purchased with additional inventory investment against an anticipation of an unusually large upward swing in demand or lead time. If safety stocks are specified by the inventory replenishment policy, such stocks should be given separate stocking locations.

Safety stock should always be considered an "added-cost" investment, and methods of reducing the risk of stockouts, such as improving the associated lead time, should be considered first. The use of safety stocks can always be expected to lower the inventory turns ratios while increasing the probability of higher customer service measures. The technique should only be considered to be equivalent to an insurance policy, not a cure for the underlying lead time related problems that are inherent in the manufacturing environment being protected.

ORDER POINTS/ORDER QUANTITIES

Of the key quantitative tools used in production and inventory control procedures designed to carry out the execution of stated inventory policies, various forms of reorder point (ROP)/reorder quantity (ROQ) logic are used. Many processes can be described as variations of generic ROP/ROQ logic.

The simple two-bin system may be said to have an order point of "one bin full (remaining)" and an order quantity equivalent to the volume of one bin or container. The old manual inventory card methods gave the names for the logic and used a handwritten or typed pair of numbers: order point and order quantity. Material requirements planning (MRP) logic uses a set of rules that is capable of describing the quantity of zero or any time-dependent quantity like "two weeks" supply as ROPs and many varieties of fixed and variable quantity statements as ROQs. Further, MRP extends the arithmetic calculations out into future periods so as to give a projection of all the times that an ordering action must occur during the planning horizon, often as

INVENTORY MANAGEMENT

much as 12 months in advance.

Empirical Assignments

Both order points and order quantities are subject to the application of empirical quantity or time period assignments. In manual and computerized systems alike, all methods of inventory replenishment require the establishment of rules (policies and procedures) governing the signal to begin replenishment (when to reorder) and rules determining the quantity for the next addition to inventory (how much to order).

Empirical rules may be simple quantity measures or they may be time and demand data dependent. Quantitative rules can be expressed in a manner similar to the following statements: "when the inventory balance drops below 100, order 200 more" or "when the last container is pulled from the warehouse, notify X to order 3 more containers." This type of rule is just as easily implemented in a small manufacturing operation with all manual systems as it is in those with computerized support.

Theoretical Basis

The basis for inventory management theory and replenishment calculations is the basic sawtooth model describing inventory consumption and replenishment (see Fig. 7-15). Order points are shown as signal points on the straight-line curve showing the diminishing total of inventory on hand. The amount of the replenishment is the order quantity. All methods and systems attempt to start the replenishment process at a point in time where there is sufficient inventory to cover the demands that will occur during the replenishment lead time.

The order quantity used determines the height of the inventory curve upon stock receipt. The effect of halving order quantity or cutting lead time is easily visualized in this model. In the statistical model shown in Fig. 7-16, the inventory requirements are reduced toward 1 when lead time and set-up and ordering costs approach zero.

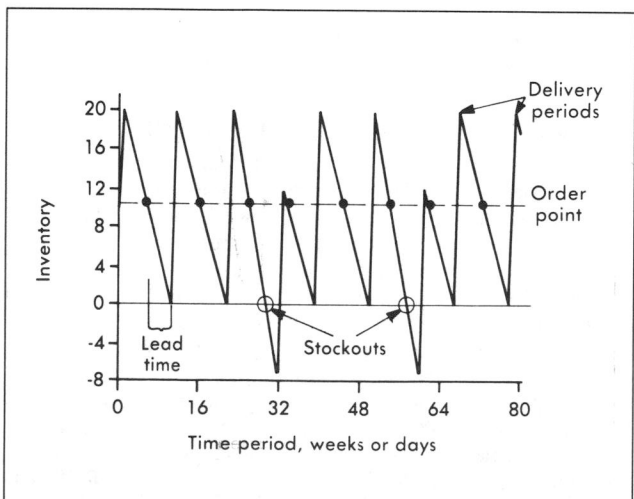

Fig. 7-15 Example of a sawtooth inventory curve having an order quantity of 22, an order point of 10, and a lead time of 6. (*K. W. Tunnell Company, Inc.*)

Statistical Calculations

It is helpful for the practitioner to explore several practical methods related to the calculation of the ROP/ROQ quantities. These methods are based on the statistics that are suitable to the sawtooth models described in Figs. 7-15 and 7-16.

Order point. The statistical basis for order point is the Poisson distribution, which has had its primary application in studies involving random arrivals. In the inventory control application, both the average number of orders received during the lead time period (N) and the average number of units on each order (D) can be tracked. Then, using Table 7-3, a service factor variable (F) can be extracted and a value to be used as the order point (OP) can be calculated using the following equation:

$$OP = D\,(N \times F \times \sqrt{N}) \qquad (6)$$

where:

OP = order point
D = average demand
N = average number of orders in lead time
F = service factor (from Table 7-3)

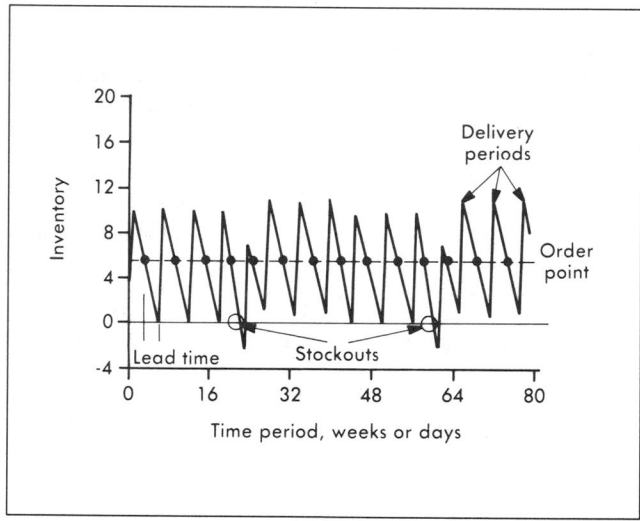

Fig. 7-16 Example of a sawtooth inventory curve when order quantity is reduced to 12, order point is reduced to 5, and lead time is reduced to 3. (*K. W. Tunnell Company, Inc.*)

TABLE 7-3
Poisson Service Factor Table

Backorder Acceptable, %	Service Factor	Customer Service Expected, %
20	0.8	80
15	1.0	85
10	1.3	90
5	1.7	95
2	2.1	98
1	2.3	99
0.1	3.1	99.9

(*K.W. Tunnell Company, Inc.*)

INVENTORY MANAGEMENT

The Poisson distribution can only be used to estimate the number of orders that will arrive during lead time, not the total demand that will occur during that period. Further, Eq. (6) is extremely sensitive to the average order quantity experienced because it is the primary multiplier. Finally, the shorter the lead time, the lower the inventory required due to the reduction in the average number of orders occurring during that period.

Order quantity. The most common use of a statistical calculation in inventory control has, for several decades, been that of the standard economic order quantity (EOQ) formula, which is based on the model shown in Fig. 7-17. This formula attempts to balance inventory carrying costs, with the ordering costs. Annual usage in pieces is required as the first estimate in the calculation. The approximation of ordering costs must include set-up costs if the part is a manufactured item rather than a purchased one. Inventory carrying costs result from the multiplication of the cost of one item by the management policy variable. This last factor describes the interest rate percentage believed to be appropriate as a forecast of appropriate costs, including the cost of money, the cost of storage, the cost of handling, the cost of storage loss, and the costs associated with inventory obsolescence.

Although the EOQ formula serves as a near-perfect model of the theoretical inventory management problem, it has grown to be accurately criticized as the square root of an estimate times an approximation divided by the product of an average unit cost and a management variable (a guess). It is included in this discussion to help understand inventory cost variables and because it is useful in certain preliminary analyses. It is not recommended as a practical shortcut to order quantity calculation because it depends on estimated values. Yet it is calculated in a manner that gives rise to the delusion of scientific "accuracy." The formula for EOQ is as follows:

$$EOQ = \sqrt{(2AS)/(ic)} \tag{7}$$

where:

EOQ = economic order quantity
A = annual usage

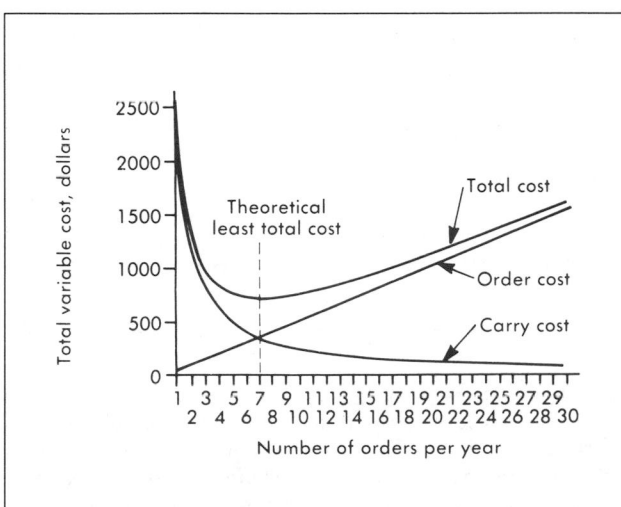

Fig. 7-17 Order cost vs. inventory carry cost curve. (*K. W. Tunnell Company, Inc.*)

TABLE 7-4
Economic Order Quantity Calculation
Results for a $20 Item

Annual Usage	Order and Set-Up Costs	Carry Cost Rate Estimate, %	Economic Order Quantity
20,000	$50.00	12	913
20,000	$50.00	20	707
20,000	$50.00	30	577
20,000	$200.00	20	1414
20,000	$500.00	20	2236
50,000	$50.00	20	1581
100,000	$50.00	20	2236

(*K.W. Tunnell Company, Inc.*)

S = order and set-up costs per order
i = interest and storage costs percentage
c = unit cost of one part

Example calculation results are shown in Table 7-4.

ABC Analysis

A popular technique that lends itself to good management of the inventory asset dollars is the classical "ABC" analysis, which results in the coding of items by categories called A, B, and C (see Table 7-5). This technique requires the sorting of all items by the amount of dollar demand (at cost) recorded over some past period or from the output of an MRP system projected over some future period. It is based on the principles set forth by the Italian economist Vilfredo Pareto (1848-1923). The policies associated with the use of the ABC analysis technique focus on maximizing the human resource attention on the "vital few" described by Pareto. It is usually observed that only about 20% of the items in any inventory will be involved in 80% of the usage measured by dollars. If this top 20% is managed carefully, the lower dollar items can be handled less often with little effect on the total dollar investment. Therefore, it is appropriate to base inventory policy statements on the basis of ABC analyses as a method of establishing an inventory plan. Basing inventory policies on the ABC analysis results in items being given replenishment rules like the following:

1. Review A items weekly, and order 1 week's supply when less than a lead time plus 1 week's supply remains.
2. Review B items biweekly, and order 4 week's supply when less than a lead time plus 2 week's supply remains.
3. Review C items monthly and order 12 week's supply when less than a lead time plus 3 week's supply remains.

The result of such policies and procedures is that the high dollar volume items get the most attention. In this example, the A items will be individually reviewed 4 times as frequently as the B items and 12 times as frequently as the C items.

Manufactured Parts

In manufacturing, the attainment of near-perfect quality requires small lots to allow early detection of problems and prompt corrective actions. The focus of quality assurance efforts becomes supportive defect prevention instead of defect detection.

CHAPTER 7

INVENTORY MANAGEMENT

TABLE 7-5
ABC Analysis of a $1,000,000 Inventory Usage at Cost

Number of Parts	Annual Usage		Cumulative Usage		Inventory Category
	Cost	Percent	Cost	Percent	
6	$681,000	68	$ 681,000	68	A
15	$182,000	18	$ 863,000	82	B
79	$137,000	14	$1,000,000	100	C

(K.W. Tunnell Company, Inc.)

Low-cost approaches for detecting defects during the process followed by immediate root-cause analysis are critical elements of this approach. The achievement of the targeted near-zero inventory depends totally on reliable and predictable processes. This requires an ever-present mode of operation that takes every possible action to prevent defects. When defects do occur, they must be caught almost immediately and used to help isolate the causes so that a cure can be implemented to prevent a recurrence. In any manufacturing environment, it is soon learned that inventory exists for only the following two reasons:

1. To cover the uncertainties associated with material flow related to lead times.
2. To cover the risks associated with the failure of prior processes to deliver quality materials.

Therefore, to eliminate the inventories, one must eliminate the reasons for their existence.

The first cause is approached through a continuous reduction in the lot size requirements. Because of the impact of "economic" job sizing, the factors contributing to order costs must be eliminated.

The second cause is appropriately addressed by implementing methods that allow the manufacturer to gain control of a process and make its output statistically predictable as "good" parts. This requires the use of statistical process control (SPC) techniques in the manufacturing workplace.

Purchased Parts

To achieve near-zero inventories on purchased materials, suppliers must use the same statistical quality management techniques in their operations as does the manufacturer. Defects, or missed delivery dates, on vendor-supplied parts and materials can very quickly shut down a production activity that is not buffered by inventory.

Supplier programs are likely to take even longer to implement than the internal programs because support is made more difficult by the typical remoteness of the supplying facilities. There are several steps that can improve the opportunity for near-zero inventory on purchased materials:

1. A reduction in the overall quantity of suppliers.
2. Long-term partnership programs designed to make both vendor and customer more profitable.
3. Devoting human resources in the purchasing department to long-term cost and quality gains, not adversarial negotiating and expediting.
4. Concentration of the supplier base near the manufacturing facility.

Reliability of Supply

The elimination of causes of defects includes the control of processes used to generate the materials manufactured. Statistical process control (SPC) is the most likely candidate as a technique to support this endeavor, but many management processes come into play. Prevention of defects, not after-the-fact detection, is the focus.

Visual Control

The increased responsibility for quality and production placed in the hands of the operator requires that the control mechanisms become increasingly simple. Visual control methods are the most effective. If a count is needed, a container should be created that makes the count instantly visible; this can be accomplished in a variety of ways. Some of the containers use pins, or holes, each designed to hold one part. By lining up rows of 2 by 5, 4 by 5, or 5 by 10, it is easy to arrive at total counts per "deck" at a glance. This also provides a method of communicating production and move authorizations as well, an improvement over kanban cards.

PROCUREMENT

For many manufacturers, the most significant portion of their total costs lies in the material cost. Often in today's environment, the material component of the cost of goods sold will range from 80 to 90% of the total (see Fig. 7-18). This may amount to a total of 30-70% of every sales dollar. Purchasing management is in the process of change. For decades, the tradition has been an adversarial relationship between supplier

and customer, each trying to get "a little extra" for their side. Negotiation and leverage were the only tools considered to be important in the professional buyer's toolbag. The pressures of world competition have made manufacturers realize that partnerships with suppliers can be far more productive than the price-only posture of the past.

VENDOR SELECTION

The process of procurement begins with the selection of a supplier. The tools used include the "request for quotation," often referred to as the RFQ, but the use is changing the nature of the tool. The vendor interview, the plant visits, and the information requested on the quotation are beginning to be oriented to a view that there are many elements of total cost that are difficult to measure. The focus of most enlightened manufacturers today is to employ a smaller and smaller total number of vendors, but to work with them on a continuous basis toward mutual advantages in profitability and competitiveness.

Quality

If the first concern is quality instead of price, how does one begin the process? The real need is to establish whether or not the potential supplier has processes that are capable of supplying the desired quality and reliability of flow. For vendors to be considered as potential candidates, they must be able to do the following:

● Prove the capability of controlling processes with SPC.
● Show that the operators are responsible for the quality of their own output.
● Demonstrate that the manufacturing environment is one that uses SPC to drive out any waste costs in the processes.
● Communicate an attitude of continuous improvement.

A supplier that meets these criteria can contribute annually to decreased costs as a long-term partner with the customer. In the recent start-up of a new foreign-owned plant, some of the parts were sourced in the United States. The primary reason for selecting particular American suppliers was the perception of the "right" attitude on the part of the potential supplier's plant or general manager.

During the past 15 years, it has been proven by Japanese manufacturers that it does not cost more to have fewer defects, and it is not possible to inspect quality into a product. Since 1980, a growing number of American manufacturers are proving to themselves that these truths are universal.

Delivery

If minimum inventory and least total manufacturing costs are the objectives, reliability of flow is a key element in the sourcing of any part or material. If the manufacturer seeking a vendor is in the process of implementing just-in-time manufacturing philosophies, it is absolutely essential. The flow of parts and materials cannot be reliable at low costs unless the same JIT techniques of achieving quality are used. If the alternative approach of carrying lots of just-in-case inventory is chosen, then the lowest cost production objective must be sacrificed. Quality described by a supplier in terms of parts per million instead of percent defective is evidence of the capability to deliver on time, without rejects, without rework, even without receiving inspection, and with a minimum delivery lead time.

Price

Price is important, not just this year's price, but the price that is expected in the years to come. If the supplier chosen adopts the partnership mode of operation, value engineering approaches will become a standard element of the relationship. Often, "partnership" suppliers bring opportunities for standardization, simplification, and minor design changes into the process of cost reduction year after year. Only a few years ago it was common

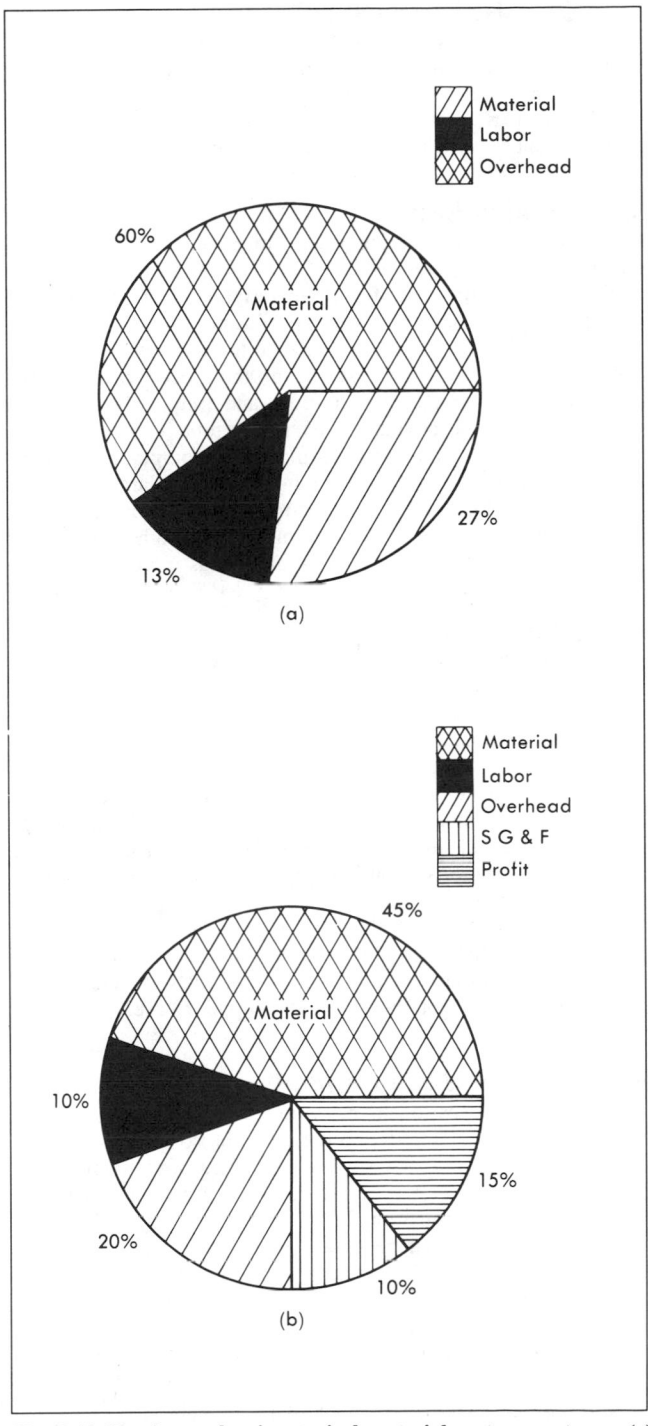

Fig. 7-18 Pie charts showing typical material cost percentages: (a) manufacturing costs and (b) total revenue. (*K. W. Tunnell Company, Inc.*)

among American manufacturers to speak of the expected average price increase for the current year over the past. Now it is possible to interview many purchasing managers who tell of receiving successive price decreases on those same parts three or more years in a row.

PROCUREMENT

VENDOR RELATIONSHIPS

To achieve new standards of partnership with one's suppliers, new tools and practices must be introduced into the process. As more manufacturers attempt this change in their mode of purchasing parts and materials, the potential of nonadversarial procurement becomes known in the marketplace.

Communications

Supplier communications are an important part of the satisfactory long-term relationship. Contracts and purchase orders will provide the umbrella for the material acquisition communication, but the daily or weekly routine of communicating releases or those "infrequent" expedites is another matter of concern. Many companies have begun the process of improving their ability to communicate rapidly and frequently with their suppliers. Another advantage of fewer total suppliers is the reduced cost for this activity. Computer-to-computer communications began between large companies and their larger suppliers in the 1970s. Now all sizes of companies communicate their requirements from one personal computer to another. Telex and facsimile transmission are used by thousands more.

Long-Term Considerations

The change in the procurement focus to long-term relationships with a smaller number of total suppliers is, perhaps, the most important change in the psychology of purchasing today. As more and more companies seek profitable partnerships with a small portion of their supplier base, competition increases and the ineffective vendor is driven out of the marketplace.

The biggest concern expressed by most procurement managers, as the material supply environment changes again, is that of assurance that there is enough competitive pressure in this new mode of operation to ensure that the "best" price is being obtained. It is true that there is a great deal more "trust" involved in this new customer-supplier relationship, but it is also true that price was never a total measure of costs associated with parts and materials obtained from the supplier base.

Performance Measurement

The overall success of the procurement activity is best judged as it relates to the competitive position of the company served. It is appropriate to note that some of the measures, such as the buyer ratios, may get worse before they start to improve. To make a significant transition in the culture of a manufacturing organization, it is often necessary to increase purchasing and manufacturing engineering resources during the implementation period. These increases are usually temporary in nature and are always offset with decreases in other areas, such as quality control. The focus must be changed from defect detection to defect prevention.

Supplier measures. For each part or material purchased, records of certain statistics need to be maintained for each supplier. A few of those that can be related to specific parts or materials are as follows:

- Number of shipments received.
- Number of shipments received on time.
- Quantity of items received.
- Quantity of items received on time.
- Defects incurred in subsequent operations.
- Subsequent costs incurred due to defects.

- Cost-reducing suggestions received/implemented.
- Process improvement or design changes suggested/implemented.
- Manufacturing interruptions caused, if any.
- Periodic process capability measurements.
- Tracking of actual prices billed.

Internal measures. The new approach to purchasing becomes a mixture of those elements that have been in use and those that may have been previously thought of as belonging to either quality assurance, accounting, or some other staff function. If the buyer is held responsible for the quality of the parts purchased, just as the operator is held responsible for his or her output, there is less and less dependence on other overhead functions. The following list suggests that the potential impact of the buyer is, indeed, significant to the total operation:

- Total dollars of sales revenue per buyer.
- Total number of suppliers.
- Total dollars of purchases per buyer.
- Total cost of scrap and rework on vendor material.
- Total number of receiving inspection personnel.
- Material cost percentage of sales revenue.
- Inventory turns on raw materials and purchased parts.
- Number of parts eliminated through standardization.

CONTRACTS

The traditional purchasing tool used in conjunction with the repetitive acquisition of materials or parts from a given supplier is the purchasing contract. Contracts may be used to define the result of negotiations covering a given quantity, a year's procurement plan, or a longer term agreement. Contracts are used as an attempt to establish a definition for all of the obligations of both the supplier and the customer for a stated procurement situation. The legal implications of formal contracts in purchasing include not only the expectations regarding price and delivery, but also the penalties to be suffered by each party in the event of any default to the conditions of the agreement. Simple forms of contracts used for the procurement of goods and services include those discussed in the following paragraphs.

Blanket Orders

One simple form of a purchasing contract is the document referred to as a blanket order. It is sufficient in its usual content to define both the details of a specific procurement requirement and the pricing and delivery schedules or rules covering a period of weeks or months.

The nature of a blanket order is very much like a standard purchase order in content. The key difference is that delivery schedules are relegated to a separate purchasing release process or they are spelled out in a manner that indicates that revisions may be made to the initial quantities and dates through subsequent change orders. Quite often, blanket orders are issued once a year for the purpose of documenting overall planning volumes and price agreements covering that period.

Umbrella Agreements

Umbrella agreements represent another form of purchase contract documentation. Again, the actual documentation will most likely appear quite similar to a standard purchase order. The function is very much like that of the blanket order, but this form of agreement covers not just a single part or material, but rather an entire commodity or a group of similar parts. The reason for selecting an umbrella agreement is usually one of providing standardized documentation for the results of negotiated prices and terms. Very often, the umbrella agreement is a sufficient contract to support the agreement on terms and conditions for procurement of a commodity or a family of parts.

Purchase Orders/Releases

Any purchase order can constitute a valid procurement contract. It is typical for simple purchase order documents to specify a single delivery and the current price purchase order document for infrequently ordered production materials not eligible for coverage under a blanket or an umbrella agreement. Standard purchase order documents are also used frequently for services, tools, lubricants, machinery, and equipment, and for various "maintenance, repair, and other (MRO)" items that are required by a manufacturer.

Supplier Scheduling

The critical need for each manufacturer regarding the scheduling of suppliers is related to the need to minimize inventory investment without loss of the ability to respond to marketplace requirements. The use of various forms of contracts in purchasing increases the flexibility of the parties regarding the subsequent manufacture and delivery requirements support without causing undue risk for either party.

Reliability of flow of materials becomes increasingly important as buffer inventories are squeezed toward zero. The purchasing contract, which provides the guidelines for the constant communication of the "best" knowledge available as to requirements, is critical to this process. As contractual arrangements cover longer and longer periods of time, the supplier is increasingly willing to make specific investments that will help to drive out unnecessary costs in the material being supplied. The added benefit of close communication in the supplier scheduling process is in the improvement in the management of manufacturing flexibility, which results in reduced overtime and production interruptions.

QUALITY AND CERTIFICATION

Part of the vendor qualification effort must deal with the true capabilities that can be demonstrated. This requires specific analysis and a thorough understanding of a potential supplier's processes and procedures.

Process Capability Studies

As quality requirements are redefined from the old standard acceptable quality level (AQL) definition toward zero defects, purchasing agreements and specifications are beginning to aim toward defects targeted in terms of a new measure, parts per million (PPM). A goal of 100 PPM is 100 times better than an acceptance specification of 1% AQL. Purchasing programs striving to achieve quality levels of this order of magnitude require significant changes in approach. One of the specific techniques used is the process capability study.

Explicit part or material design and specification requirements documentation is absolutely critical to this technique. The processes (including personnel, machine, material, and methods) that are targeted for production of the parts or material to be procured must be tested using statistical management techniques to determine whether or not those processes are capable of meeting the specifications essentially 100% of the time. The supplier must use SPC techniques to hold the processes in control

all of the time to ensure the predictability of the process. Thus, the operators of such processes must be given the tools and training required to produce "perfect parts" all the time. Gages, test equipment, and sampling procedures must be in place to maintain a process that is well centered near the nominal values that were targeted.

Supplier Quality Assurance

For the manufacturer, the buyer must be held responsible for the quality of procured materials, just as the operator in both the manufacturer's and the supplier's plant must be held responsible for the quality of production. The method by which the supplier ensures quality is its continuing program of process control. It is no longer appropriate to consider that incoming inspection at the receiving location is a suitable method of providing vendor quality assurance. U.S. manufacturing's failure to remain competitive has proven that "inspecting quality in" is a costly and ineffective technique.

Documentation

With process-controlled quality assurance methods, the documentation is different from the old inspection sampling records. It is more important to understand how well the manufacturing processes are being controlled and the capability weaknesses that need to be worked on than it is to know the statistics of inspection sampling. Therefore, the meaningful documentation sought is provided by copies of SPC charts that were prepared by the operators while the parts were being produced and by the problem-solving documentation that supports the continuous improvement efforts of the employee teams involved in those operator-controlled processes.

OFFSHORE PROCUREMENT

From the 1960s until the recent new beginnings of a "Buy American" mentality, importation of parts and materials by manufacturers increased dramatically. The ability to buy quality products at substantial savings in cost influenced many companies to engage in considerable foreign sourcing activity.

Direct Contact

Large manufacturing companies around the world, particularly in the Far East, established an effective sales presence within the United States to assist in the handling of the direct contact demand. Thus, direct contact in many commodities was made quite easy for the purchasing departments of many manufacturing enterprises. In many cases, inventories were brought into the U.S. as stock for foreign-owned distribution centers. This further increased the attractiveness of the international sourcing because the lead time concern related to ocean shipment delays had been removed.

Trading Companies

Smaller manufacturers on both sides of the ocean found that trading companies have been extremely useful in expanding the supply base to those foreign companies that could not afford a resident representation in the United States. Operating as an agent for a number of foreign plants, trading company organizations made local contact and representation conveniently available to U.S. purchasing professionals.

Trading companies have also established warehousing and distribution stateside, but not to the same degree as the larger foreign manufacturing enterprises. Trading companies are more likely to use a U.S. warehousing site as a means of consolidating ocean freight to a break-bulk type of operation than they are to provide ''off-the-shelf'' stock for domestic consumption.

Offshore Buying Offices

Large U.S. corporations, particularly those that operate as multinational manufacturers and sellers, have found it beneficial to establish foreign buying offices in support of their purchasing contract negotiation and administration activities.

RECEIVING, INSPECTION AND STORAGE

Physical control of parts and components is responsible for one of the largest groups of indirect manufacturing labor usage and frequently occupies as much space as the direct manufacturing activity. Receiving and storage typically constitute the closest contact services to operations of all the materials management functions. This results in these functions being viewed internally as the principal materials services rendered. Inspection usually rests with a quality control or quality assurance department that polices the quality of incoming materials through inspection sampling.

DOCUMENTATION ACCURACY

From a materials management standpoint, physical control activities represent the front lines of count control. Not only must the records related to receipts be completely accurate to control the associated accounts payable function, the usual purchasing activity depends on a very rapid response from its affiliated receiving group.

The accuracy of recordkeeping in the receiving function must include all of the inputs from the inspection activity as part of its support to the manufacturing operation. Its records documenting quantities received must be totally accurate as to the part numbers or material identification numbers, as well as to the purchase order data, if that information is to be depended on by the planning and procurement arms of the overall materials support organization.

CONTROL DISCIPLINES

Control disciplines include the maintenance of data related to a wide variety of documentation. These may be principally seen as computer records accessible through terminal screens, or they may be a collection of manually posted records. Included in the controls are the following:

- Purchase requisitions.
- Receiving reports.
- Production and assembly orders.
- Material withdrawal requisitions.
- Material movement transactions.
- Stock production or put-away records.
- Customer order shipping records.

The standard measure for sufficiently accurate inventory data useful in the production and inventory planning and control activities is 95% or greater.

INSPECTION SAMPLING

The critical need for inspection may come from a variety of reasons, the chief one being the procurement from sources that cannot or do not choose to use statistical quality management techniques in controlling their processes. The highest risks to the manufacturer using such materials exist when:

- The manufacturer of the supplied materials is known to experience low process yields.
- Materials have been supplied by a supplier known to include significant quantities of parts in shipments that do not meet specifications.
- Operations are about to be performed in the manufacturing process where relatively high value is added.
- Operations are about to be performed that make component or material defects difficult to find or repair.
- New designs or new sources are being introduced into the manufacturing processes at the supplying or using location.

In these cases, some receiving inspection and the added cost of quality control inspection is usually more effective than reliance on the performance of the supplier. As much care as possible should be taken to ensure that the materials being sampled are from homogeneous lots, including size, producing machine, operator, and tooling.

MATERIAL HANDLING

The shorter the cycle times, the less opportunity exists for material handling and storage to become an added element of cost. It has already been described how just-in-time manufacturing approaches recognize these effects and minimize the costs of inventory storage and movement. In traditional manufacturing environments, there is often a significant investment in material handling equipment. Forklifts, cranes, and specialized conveyors represent expensive alternatives that are related to conventional manufacturing. Material handlers are usually critical elements of the move-and-wait job queues that are always present in the traditional job shop and some repetitive manufacturing environments.

The shorter the distances, the lower the overall costs of material handling alternatives. As cycles and distances are decreased in approaching a just-in-time manufacturing environment, it is often possible to change the unit quantities and weights of the material receipt to allow specialized carts to become the primary one-move conveyance into the manufacturing area.

Finally, order picking, accumulation, and containerization for shipment to customers represent the last opportunity a manufacturer has to ensure the quality of its products. This requires skills in packaging, the choice of packing materials, and the tactics required for safe loading of the transportation vehicle. Material handling cannot contribute to the value of the product, but, in more ways than one, it can contribute to the cost and to the delivered condition.

WAREHOUSING FACILITIES

Storage space should be planned for the highest volume of activity to occur with the minimum distances traveled. This can be achieved through a study of the anticipated transaction volumes on all materials and components. If an ABC analysis is available, any A materials that will travel through the warehouse should be stored near the "front" of the warehouse space (nearest the manufacturing space). In contrast, the slower moving C items should be allocated space in the remotest sections of the floor plan. Final layout of storage equipment will depend to some degree on the placement of any columns that are present in the building.

Handling equipment may vary from overhead cranes to small pushcarts. There are many different types of forklift equipment for handling loading and unloading of pallet loads of material from both transportation equipment and storage racks. Standard forklift equipment may be customized for specific nonpallet handling assignments requiring large clamps (barrel or drum handlers, paper roll handlers, and large case clamps). Fixed-base varieties including narrow-aisle sideloaders are available if tall reach requirements call for equipment to be dedicated to one or more warehouse aisles.

WAREHOUSING CONTROLS

Physical control should include accurate identification and location of the materials stored. As material withdrawal occurs, the most satisfactory approach is to adhere to a physical first-in-first-out (FIFO) discipline. The custodial responsibility also includes the appropriate care of all materials free from any form of handling damage. The receiving duties associated with most warehousing activities require that the warehouse personnel ensure that no damage to packages and materials has occurred when the material is unloaded from the carrier and then that no damage occurs thereafter.

The administrative controls will likely include various transactions that drive the material control and accounting support functions associated with both replenishment of stock used and with the shipment of product. Specific tasks may include verification of the quantities received to orders and to packing lists. This is usually followed by an updating of inventory records. Both receipt and put-away transactions require the updating of location records. Finally, all accounting inputs for payable activities on receipts and billing on shipments must be judiciously managed.

JUST-IN-TIME MANUFACTURING

Just-in-time is a philosophy that has the elimination of waste as its objective. Waste may appear in the form of rejected parts, excessive inventory levels, interoperation queues, excessive material handling, long set-up and changeover times, and a number of others. Just-in-time highlights the need to match production rate to actual demand and eliminate non-value-adding activities.

While the just-in-time philosophy of waste elimination proves helpful in virtually all types of manufacturing (and service) environments, some types of manufacturing offer more opportunity than other. Table 7-6 lists the estimated improvements for different types of manufacturing.[3]

Generally, process industries (paper mills, chemical manufacturers, and food producers) pose a greater challenge in terms of set-up time reduction and process flow improvements because of the "connected" nature of their operations. Repetitive and discrete manufacturers (metal stamping and machining) tend to encompass more opportunity in these areas because of

TABLE 7-6
Estimated Percent Improvements for Different Industries
as a Result of JIT Implementation

Reductions	Automotive Supplier	Printer	Fashion Goods	Mechanical Equipment	Electric Components	Range
Manufacturing lead time	89	86	92	83	85	83-92
Inventory						
Raw	35	70	70	73	50	35-73
WIP	89	82	85	70	85	70-89
Finished goods	61	71	70	0	100	0-100
Changeover time	75	75	91	75	94	75-94
Labor						
Direct	19	50		5	0	0-50
Indirect	60	50	29	21	38	21-60
Exempt	?	?	22	?	?	?-22
Space	53	N/A	39	?	80(Est.)	39-80
Cost of quality	50	63	61	33	26	26-63
Purchased material (Net)	?	7	11	6	N/A	6-11
Additional capacity	N/A	36	42	N/A	0	0-42

(Coopers & Lybrand)

JUST-IN-TIME MANUFACTURING

their predisposition toward functional area layouts and extensive/frequent machine set-ups. Conversely, process industries generally have a great deal of opportunity in the areas connected with material planning and procurement. These industries often use relatively large quantities of raw materials and may have significant advantages in leverage to negotiate supplier improvements such as delivery, quality, and cost.

JIT THEMES AND MODULES

Based on the improvements made through the application of JIT, a sound JIT program should include the following modules:

- Planning and assessing.
- Organization.
- Awareness and education.
- Housekeeping.
- Quality improvement.
- Uniform plant loading.
- Process flow.
- Set-up and changeover reduction.
- Pull system implementation.
- Supplier integration.

Jit Themes

Before discussing the JIT modules in detail, it is advantageous to identify a few underlying JIT themes. These themes are at the center of the JIT wheel illustration shown in Fig. 15-2. The five basic themes are as follows:

1. *JIT is a philosophy and a continuous program.* It is extremely important to understand that just-in-time is *not* a project, because it has no end. Once JIT improvement activities are under way, they should continue indefinitely. The environment should be transformed to one of continuous improvement and of cooperative management/labor endeavor.
2. *The importance of visibility.* JIT involves an aversion to hidden problems. It increases visibility (and encourages elimination) of these problems by gradually reducing work-in-process inventory, queues, and lead times.
3. *The benefits of synchronization, or balance.* This process involves the matching of throughput times from operation to operation during the course of manufacturing and support functions. Production then occurs at a common rate, or "drum beat."
4. *Simplicity—the view that simpler is better.* A continuous effort is made to perform required operations with fewer resources (time, personnel, and equipment) and in a less complicated fashion.
5. *A holistic approach to the program.* It must cross disciplinary lines and deal with the manufacturing process as a whole, rather than with separate parts.

Planning and Assessing

Experience with the implementation and support of JIT programs indicates that knowing what to do, when to do it, and what results can be expected can only come about through thorough, intelligent planning. It is also important to obtain management commitment to the program before starting.

JIT programs generally involve the following progressive phases:

- Diagnostic review.
- Conceptual design.
- Implementation planning.
- Implementation.
- Continuous improvement.

These phases will be discussed in more detail under the section "JIT Program Phases."

Organization

An effective just-in-time program can be initiated only after an adequate plan encompassing all of the disciplines of the organization has been drawn up and after a group of people has been assembled and committed to the enterprise. From initiation of the program through the implementation phase, a strong leader (or "champion") and a steering committee will be required to direct the JIT team's efforts. Participants on the steering committee are usually senior-level management personnel and could include the general manager, engineering manager, manufacturing manager, MIS manager, and any assistant managers. If a company is unionized, it is also beneficial to have the involvement of upper-level labor leaders, such as a union president, on this committee. This will usually help to resolve the concerns of labor and encourage acceptance during implementation.

Another group of individuals indigenous to the just-in-time environment is the task group, or problem-solving work group. This group is often formed around a nucleus of people devoted to a specific functional area or process. Included with the area-oriented or process-oriented nucleus are representatives from other disciplines that may affect the process being studied by the group, along with a "ringer." A "ringer" is someone who is completely uninvolved or isolated from the process under normal circumstances and can be counted on to ask questions that would be considered or "dumb" by the other group members.

Awareness and Education

The need for awareness, education, and training cannot be overstated. The education and training of all personnel (including direct labor) is essential to the correct application of JIT.

Awareness is comprised of the introduction of JIT concepts, how they have helped other companies, and speculation about how they could prove useful in the current manufacturing environment.

Among the tailored training sessions that can be utilized are the following:

- Set-up reduction.
- Statistical process control.
- Specific machine maintenance.
- Cost accounting in a JIT environment.
- Make vs. buy analysis.
- "Designing in" manufacturability and standardization.
- Forecasting/order entry in a JIT environment.
- Production planning/scheduling in a JIT environment.

- Purchasing:
  "Co-op" contracting.
  Vendor analysis evaluation.
  Procurement strategy.
  Breakeven analysis.
  Methods of payment.
  Negotiation skills.
  Contractual law.
  Specific commodity training.
- Cost of quality.
- Distribution in a JIT environment.

Housekeeping

Housekeeping in a just-in-time environment is far more than what has been referred to as a "clean broom award" program. It is an effort to establish the attitude that each individual "owns" and is responsible for his or her equipment and environs. The worker is accountable for ensuring that necessary tools are in the right places and that those places are effective locations. Tools and materials must be visible and accessible. Lighting, heating and ventilation, and workcenter equipment (racks and trays) must be properly designed and located to minimize reach-

ing, bending, and fatigue. Trash and debris should not be present.

Quality Improvement

The just-in-time philosophy emphasizes the fact that workers are responsible for the capability and quality of their own processes and for inspecting the work of the previous operation. Typical responsibilities for various workforce levels are listed in Table 7-7. In this manner, all defects become visible quickly, and less scrap/rework is produced. Defects uncovered during JIT production operations may result in the stopping of the production line while the source of the problem is discovered and addressed.

Another aspect of quality control in a JIT production environment is the statistical tracking and tightening of process controls using statistical process control (SPC). A major objective of SPC is to recognize the occurrence of special causes of variance in the presence of the constant system of common-cause variances and to shed light on the nature of special causes, thereby providing a basis for corrective actions. Control charts are one of the tools used to accomplish this objective.

The control chart builds a model that describes the way the

TABLE 7-7
Quality Control Management Responsibilities

Group	Responsibilities
Top management	— Allocate adequate resources to fulfill long-range quality needs of the company and the customers — Convey an attitude that quality problems are to be prevented rather than inspected in — Convey an attitude that "low quality is unacceptable" throughout the organization — Overtly encourage the development and maintenance of high quality standards throughout the organization — Hold regular meetings to review quality levels and quality performance
Quality control manager	— Initiate and maintain a defect prevention program — Identify and organize the quality objectives of the various departments within the organization. Ensure that they are consistent and support overall corporate quality goals — Provide adequate inspection, testing, and other quality monitoring equipment and training required by the organization to meet quality objectives — Monitor the performance of the various departments within the organization with regard to their quality objectives and report these findings to top management
Quality control engineers	— Reliability analysis — Develop operator controlled inspection and testing procedures where applicable — Design/specification of test and inspection equipment — Supplier quality evaluation — Reporting of quality performance data — Verification of corrective action — Statistical analysis and defect cause identification — Inspector and operator training
Quality circle members	— Monitor all critical quality specifications — Track frequency and severity of defects via SPC charting, results, and prioritizing occurrences by frequency — Investigate and eliminate defect causes
Other department managers	— Understand, define, and communicate their individual department responsibilities for quality to their subordinates — Regularly monitor the quality performance levels of their staff and take corrective action when defects are identified

(Coopers & Lybrand)

JUST-IN-TIME MANUFACTURING

process variability pattern is expected to appear when only common causes of variation are at work. Once this model is established through appropriate sampling and statistical data characterization methods, a basis is formed for identifying the occurrence of a variation that does not fit the pattern of common-cause variation.

Another important aspect of quality in a JIT production environment is the quality level of purchased goods. This subject will be discussed further under the heading "Purchasing Review" in the section "Diagnostic Review" of this chapter.

The last aspect of quality in a JIT production environment to discuss is fail-safing. Fail-safing is a technique that can be applied in both design and process. Simply stated, a fail-safe design does not allow parts to fit together in any way except the correct way. Wrong parts or the wrong orientation of correct parts do not fit together. In terms of the process, special checking devices and locking devices are utilized (built into the set-up) to ensure that the process produces correctly to specifications. These techniques have been extremely successful in both Japanese and U.S. just-in-time installations.

Uniform Plant Load

The concept of uniform plant load (UPL) at its most basic level is simply this: if one sells daily, build daily. Each model that is sold is manufactured on a daily basis in relatively small lots, so build rates match demand rates. An underlying precept of just-in-time manufacturing is that the organization is moving from a "make-to-stock" to a "make-to-demand" environment. Uniform plant load is the cycle time required to match (not exceed) demand. The result of applying UPL is a production rate that is *not* tied to machine rate, current capacity, or some annualized average demand based on forecast or history. It is a picture of demand per day divided by hours of production per day.

Process Flow

The major benefits of UPL can usually be realized best when the process flow is redesigned. This is true because most manu-

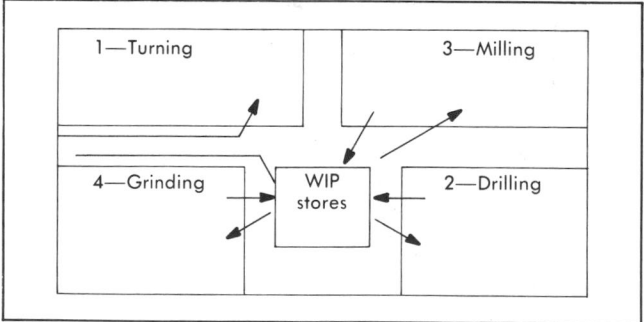

Fig. 7-19 Traditional functional layout of a manufacturing company. (*Coopers & Lybrand*)

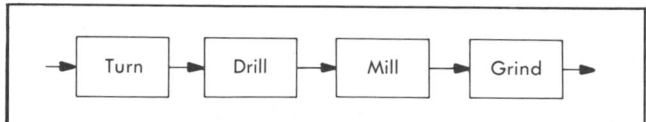

Fig. 7-20 Schematic of typical JIT workcenter layouts. (*Coopers & Lybrand*)

facturing layouts are designed in a functional manner (see Fig. 7-19). The functional approach does not lend itself to rapid throughput times because of the travel distances, material handling, WIP, and storage/retrieval activities involved.

In some respects, JIT layout for repetitive manufacturers is an attempt to turn the production operations into a process. Just-in-time layouts are typified by workcenters that are in close proximity and have little or no inventory between the separate operations (see Fig. 7-20). These smaller process-oriented layouts within the larger production facilities are referred to as cells. One or more cells that comprise all of the product of a given product family may be isolated and run effectively as an autonomous entity from the other factory operations. When this is done, the entity is referred to as a "focus factory" or a "factory within a factory."

The organization of individual cells can be made much more efficient, and provide much greater flexibility in terms of personnel, by designing layouts in U-shape or serpentine configurations (see Fig. 7-21). These designs, and others like them, allow operators to move between individual production operations, performing more or fewer functions as required to meet demand. An important principle to remember here is that the operators must be kept busy, not necessarily the equipment.

Set-up and Changeover Reduction

In those cases where multiple components must share the same manufacturing resources, JIT's orientation to small lot sizes and frequent runs will make it very important to the reduction of set-up times. Reduced set-up times will also yield benefits in uniform plant loading, workcenter organization, and pull system installation. Set-up time means the time from when the last good piece is produced on the old set-up to the time when the first good piece is produced on the new set-up. It includes teardown, installation of the new job, and any required first-piece inspection. Reduction refers to reduced time, but not necessarily to reduced cost. Cost is usually, but not always, reduced.

Set-up reduction in the JIT environment is not an engineering project. It should be performed by a set-up reduction team comprised of the following individuals:

- The machine operators.
- The technical people as required from process engineering, tool design, tool maintenance, and general maintenance.
- A "ringer."

The team should have complete implementation responsibilities, including a small budget for equipment purchases and revisions. One of the set-up reduction group members will need to function as a group leader, keeping the activities on track and communicating constantly with the area supervisor. The area supervisor will need to be directly involved or kept closely informed of group activities to facilitate "buy-in" and ensure successful use of the improvements over time.

The Pull System

The pull system is the next logical step in a JIT program when uniform plant loading and process flow revisions have been installed. The pull system has dramatic effects on inventory levels because it does not provide for production of any inventory until it is needed. Pull systems do not allow parts to be

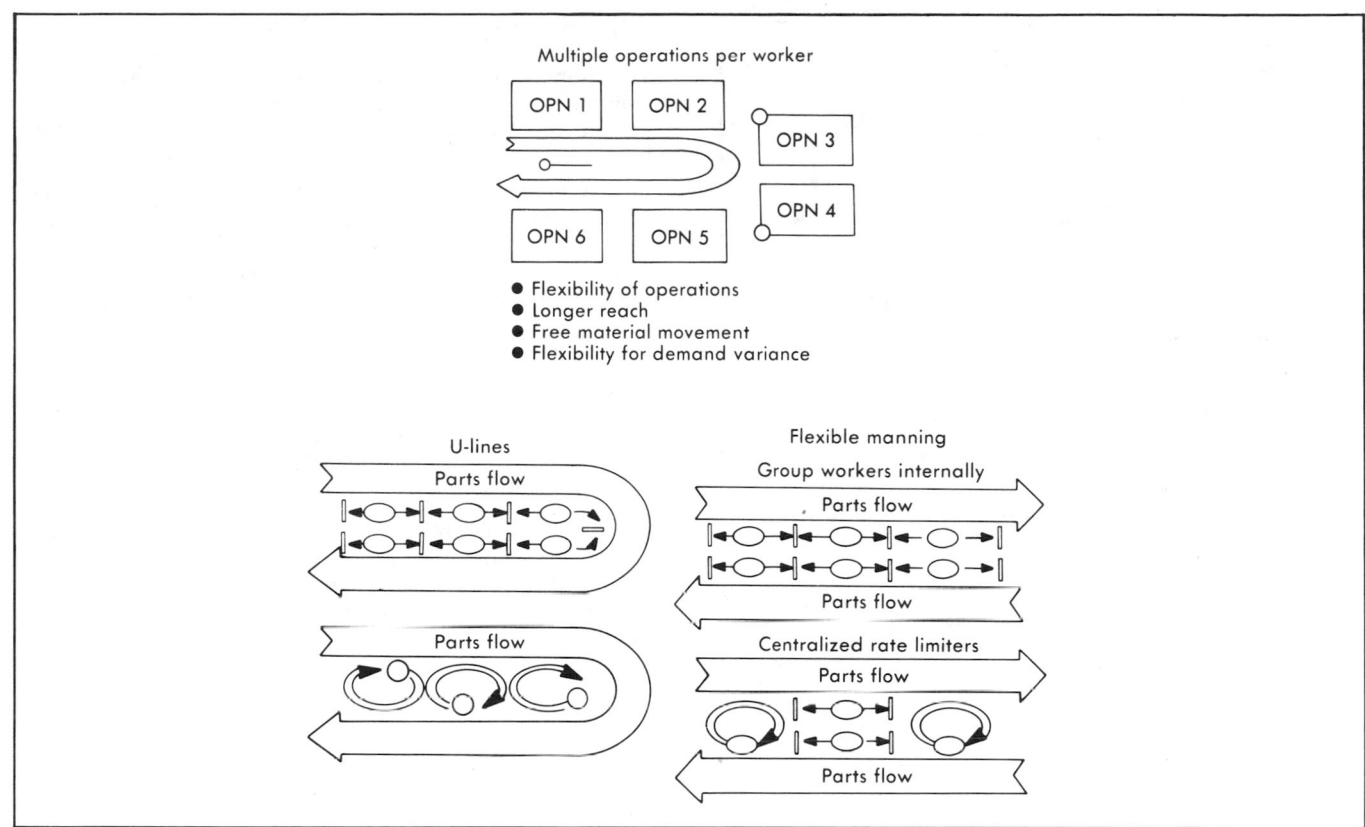

Fig. 7-21 Workcenter configurations in a just-in-time environment. (*Coopers & Lybrand*)

produced until "authorization (pull signal)" is received from the subsequent operation. To visualize this situation, and the contrast between traditional "push" and just-in-time "pull" systems, refer to Fig. 7-22.

If product A was produced in a traditional push production environment, the following sequence of events could occur:

1. A problem arises with part B1.
2. Unaware that B1 production is experiencing difficulty, production continues on C1, C2, B2, C3, and C4 in other areas of the factory.
3. Unable to produce part A, the assembly department switches to another product. Expediting of other components occurs, and surplus inventory of C1, C2, B2, C3, and C4 must be moved to a storage area.
4. When B1's are able to be produced again, priorities will need to be realigned, and work will need to be rescheduled on all workcenters involved to compensate for WIP level imbalance and timing discrepancies.

If product A was produced in a just-in-time pull system environment, the following sequence of events could occur:

1. A problem arises with part B1.
2. Because B1 is unavailable, production of A stops.
3. Because production of A stops, demand for (and therefore production of) B2, C1, C2, C3, and C4 stops. Operators converge from these workcenters on B1 to assist in resolving the problem.
4. When B1's are able to be produced again, priorities are

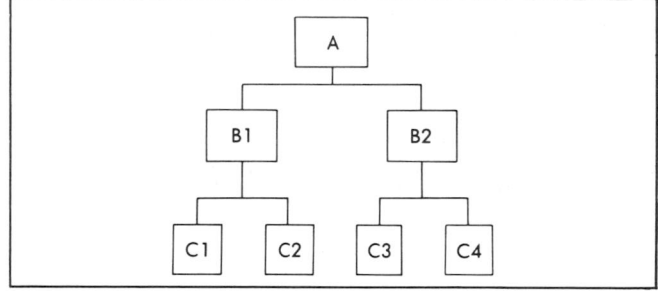

Fig. 7-22 Diagram for comparison between "push" and "pull" production system. (*Coopers & Lybrand*)

correctly aligned and no surplus WIP inventory has been produced.

Pull systems generally take one of two possible forms: overlapped or linked (see Fig. 7-23). Overlapped pull systems utilize empty space as the pull signal or communication device between production operations. This technique is best applied when operations are in close physical proximity.

Linked pull systems are typically utilized when parts compete for the same resource and cannot be made on a one-for-one basis with end-item demand, or when they have to travel significant distances between operations in a lot (or batch) mode. In these situations, it is typical to utilize a pull signal (or kanban) to trigger the production of components from operation to previous operation. The card or kanban is issued by an operator as

JUST-IN-TIME MANUFACTURING

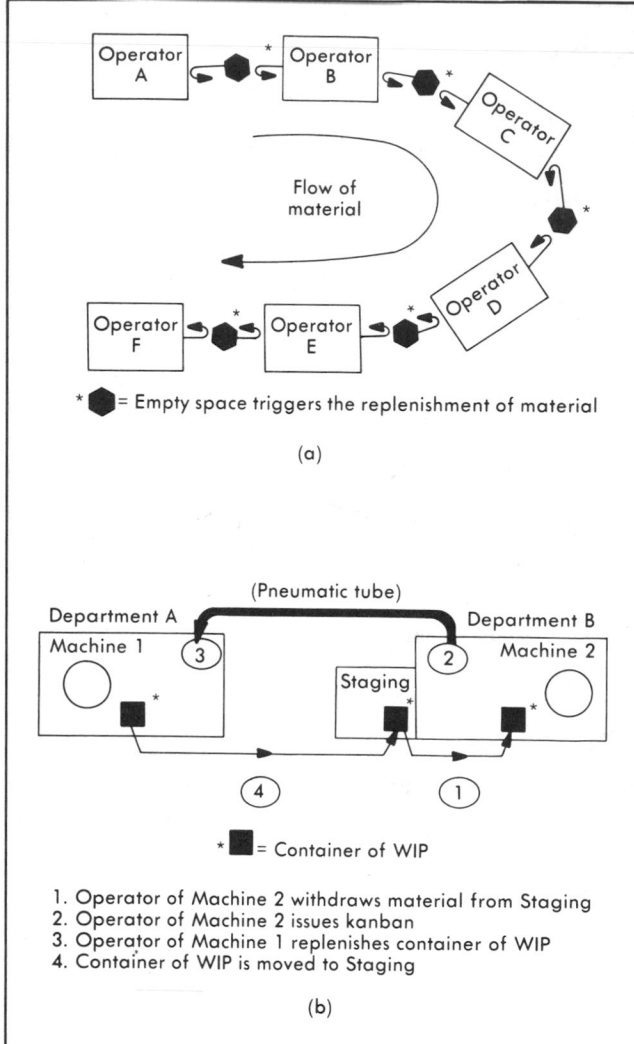

* ⬢ = Empty space triggers the replenishment of material

(a)

(Pneumatic tube)

Department A

Machine 1

Department B

Machine 2

Staging

* ■ = Container of WIP

1. Operator of Machine 2 withdraws material from Staging
2. Operator of Machine 2 issues kanban
3. Operator of Machine 1 replenishes container of WIP
4. Container of WIP is moved to Staging

(b)

Fig. 7-23 Production system in a JIT environment is usually by the pull system, which can be of the (a) overlapped or (b) linked form. (*Coopers & Lybrand*)

a container of material is picked up. The material must be used in a "first-in, first-out" (FIFO) sequence. The kanban is the only authorization for additional material to be produced at the previous operation. When no kanban is issued, no additional components are made. Kanbans may be cards, colored golf balls, or even empty containers. They may be moved by hand, slotted slide, or pneumatic tube. An important principle with regard to the use of a kanban is that it is employed in a FIFO manner.

Regardless of whether the linked or overlapped system is used, the pull system becomes the vehicle for communicating short-range parts requirements and scheduling close-in production. Manufacturing resource planning (MRP II) is still required to perform the longer range planning of material requirements, capacity requirements, and personnel requirements. In short, MRP II is the planning side of production, and just-in-time's pull system is the execution side.

Supplier Network Integration

Achieving a close relationship between the manufacturer and supplier is not an easy task. When it comes time to approach this aspect of just-in-time, it is important for the manufacturer to have a clear understanding of the following items:

- What is wanted. Typically, this can be broken down into quality levels, delivery performance, responsiveness, packaging, and price.
- What devices will be used to measure whether what is wanted is actually received. Performance measures need to be defined for quality, delivery, response, packaging, and price.
- What will be provided to assist the suppliers in becoming just-in-time manufacturers so that they in turn can support the manufacturer's goals. For example, manufacturers with vendor certification and zero inspection goals should be willing to provide suppliers with SPC training.

With these factors clearly defined, purchased commodities and volumes can be identified. A commodity is defined as a group or family of parts that requires the same resources for their production and/or the same raw material processing. The things that are wanted during this identification phase are those commodities currently purchased, their dollar and quantity volumes, the supplier base currently providing each commodity, lead times, and quality levels, by commodity and by supplier.

Buying supplier capacity in lieu of contracting for actual part numbers and volumes is a just-in-time objective. It is, therefore, important to reach the point in JIT supplier relationships where that portion of the supplier's capacity that is attributable to one's products may be regarded as an extension of one's own manufacturing facility. This objective can be achieved through co-op contracting. Co-op contracting rests on the following nine principles:

1. The supplier knows the product best.
2. Forecasts are always wrong.
3. A theoretical goal is zero lead time.
4. Single-source resource management.
5. Elimination of non-value-adding activities.
6. A theoretical goal of lot size is 1.
7. Rejects are intolerable.
8. Mutual (supplier and manufacturer) habit of continuous improvement.
9. Open-door policy between supplier and manufacturer.

In the co-op contracting environment, the user in effect controls the manufacturing schedule of the supplier. The supplier is assured of a long-term number of jobs and, given this commitment, will invest in operation improvements. Whenever possible, the user shares long-term schedules with its supplier.

Aside from the co-op contract, there are other aspects of just-in-time that may be applied in the purchasing environment. These include the following:

- *Supplier certification.* A systematic reduction in the sampling of incoming material from suppliers as their quality levels improve, until no inspection is required at all. At this point, the supplier is "certified."

- *Supplier performance evaluation.* The establishment of specific goals and milestones against which suppliers will be measured as to their performance in the areas of quality, delivery, lead time, and price.

- *Revised ordering mechanisms.* An evaluation of how close-in requirements can most effectively be communicated to suppliers (a kind of linked pull system).

- *Buyer training.* A program involving the identification of buyer training needs and compensating for those needs through the development of individual training modules.

- *Restructured buyer performance evaluation.* A review and revision of buyer performance evaluation based on JIT concepts such as vendor delivery performance, lead-time reductions, inventory reduction, and material quality levels.

- *Supplier training programs.* A group of training programs developed to assist suppliers in the adoption of JIT in their own organizations. If this is not feasible, consideration should be given to bringing suppliers into JIT training sessions for the manufacturer.

- *Review and revision of the purchasing organization.* An analysis of how purchasing functions and roles will change and how the purchasing organization can best be structured to take advantage of those changes.

JIT PROGRAM PHASES

As mentioned previously, a JIT program involves a series of progressive phases: diagnostic review, conceptual design, implementation planning, implementation, and continuous improvement. The subsequent sections discuss these phases in general and also provide manufacturers with specific guidelines to follow when performing the particular phase.

Diagnostic Review

The diagnostic review is that portion of the just-in-time program that allows a manufacturer to identify, assess, and prioritize improvement opportunities. The opportunities can be found in current organizations, current operations, and current layouts. The three fundamental purposes for the diagnostic phase are as follows:

1. Establish a baseline of data (a "benchmark") against which future progress can be measured.

2. Identify gross opportunities for analysis and prioritization.

3. Establish goals and objectives for use during the conceptual design phase.

The diagnostic review should include the development of a project team and an analysis of all of the functional areas.

Project Team Selection. The objective of the project team is to assume full responsibility for the success of the project. A steering committee oversees the progress of the project and intercedes (as appropriate) to resolve any conflicts that may hinder project success.

Organization Assessment. The objective of the organization assessment is to determine the readiness of company personnel to convert to a just-in-time environment and to develop recommendations that will support desired levels of success. The following steps are usually required for this assessment:

1. Compile a list of candidates to be interviewed. This list should include top management as well as middle and lower management personnel and some direct labor employees. Several interviews are usually required to get an accurate picture of most organizations.

2. Schedule and perform the interviews. Questions should include the areas of:
   - Assignment clarity/definition.
   - Performance standards/measurements.
   - Autonomy levels.
   - Perception of the company.
   - Policies/procedures, accuracy, adequacy, and use.
   - Perceived need to improve.
   - Current problem-solving techniques.
   - Consistency of objectives.
   - Reward/recognition levels.
   - Levels of trust.
   - Levels of participation in decision making.
   - Pride in work.
   - Perceptions of management.
   - Levels/frequency of conflict.
   - Ability to exchange ideas.
   - Receptivity to change.

3. Summarize the findings from the interviews.

4. Develop a list of recommendations based on summarized findings.

5. Report recommendations to project manager and senior management.

Design Engineering Review. The objective of the design engineering review is to understand the current role of the design engineer, especially as it relates to throughput times, bottlenecks, market response, interaction with manufacturing and purchasing, use of standardization, and levels of manufacturability. The following four steps are usually required for this review:

1. Chart the flow of the current design process from conception to adoption and implementation in the factory.

2. Summarize the findings in step 1, identifying "long-lead" activities, major costs, external department involvements, and levels of standardization and manufacturability. Identify all activities that do not add value to the process.

3. Develop recommendations based on the summarized findings, oriented toward reducing product design throughput times/costs, queues, and non-value-added activities.

4. Establish a list of preferred manufacturing and purchasing practices for later use in conceptual design and implementation phases.

Forecasting Review. The objective of the forecasting review is to identify current forecasting throughput times, delays, costs, close-in change levels, and reasons for close-in changes. Another objective is to determine the adequacy and/or reliability of the forecast as related to actual demand and to identify resources/methods currently used. As in the design review, the forecasting review requires the following four steps:

JUST-IN-TIME MANUFACTURING

1. Chart the flow of current forecasting processes, identifying area functions, non-value-adding activities, amounts of time expended, and what leading indicators are used.
2. Summarize the results from step 1. Calculate total throughput time, identify any bottlenecks, develop costs associated with the processes, and identify accuracy levels of the leading indicators used (compare actual vs. forecasted schedules). Identify non-value-adding steps involved in the forecasting processes.
3. Develop recommendations regarding what steps might be improved, reduced, or eliminated, how bottlenecks might be resolved, and how close-in changes can be reduced or eliminated.
4. Summarize the recommendations for later use during the conceptual design and implementation phases.

Order Entry Review. The objective of the order entry review is to gain an understanding of the current order entry processes, including throughput times, queues, and costs. It will be important to identify the appropriateness of orders entered as they relate to actual demand. Any orders that are lost or inadvertently omitted should also be identified. The four steps in the review are as follows:

1. Chart the flow of current order entry processes, identifying functions by area, non-value-adding operations, and times/costs associated with each operation. Identify total throughput times/costs, bottlenecks, and any cushions built into the orders for shrink, scrap, and processing delays. Review orders generated against actual historical demand levels to determine their appropriateness.
2. Summarize the findings from step 1.
3. Based on the summarized findings, develop a list of recommendations for reducing throughput times, eliminating cushions, dissolving bottlenecks, and improving ordering accuracy.
4. Summarize the recommendations for use during the conceptual design and implementation phases.

Production Planning Review. The objective of the production planning review is to assess the production planning processes, including their throughput times, delays, and costs. It also determines the adequacy and appropriateness of the data, the methods used, and the value of the output. In summary, the production planning review determines the impact of lot sizing techniques, set-up times, production resource allocation, and process planning in the manufacturing environment.

The diagnostic review of the production planning department is performed primarily to develop an understanding of all functions being performed. This will be of use during the conceptual design and implementation phases when recommendations are made that may dramatically affect current production planning responsibilities.

The five steps required for this review are as follows:

1. Identify all functions currently performed by the production planning department, such as master scheduling, capacity requirements planning, order launching, economic order quantity (EOQ) and lot sizing techniques, and inventory adjustments.
2. Chart the flow of all of the production planning processes, identifying throughput times, functions and responsibilities, non-value-adding activities, and costs associated with each operation. Identify any bottlenecks

or queues.
3. Summarize the findings from step 2.
4. Based on the summarized findings, develop recommendations regarding reductions in throughput times, queues, and costs. Also, consider which functions will need to change in a just-in-time environment, and how. For example, will order launching still be done by production planners? How can the demand most quickly and effectively be translated into shop floor production?
5. Summarize the recommendations for later use during conceptual design and implementation phases.

Production Scheduling Review. The basis for the diagnostic review of this area is to develop an understanding of all functions performed in the current scheduling environment. This study will be of use during the conceptual design and implementation phases of the project when recommendations may be made that dramatically change traditional production scheduling functions.

The four steps in this review are as follows:

1. Identify and chart the flow of all functions currently performed by the production scheduling department. Identify functions by area, time expended at each activity, total throughput times, and bottlenecks. Also identify non-value-adding activities and costs associated with the process. Identify imbalances between work content levels from activity to activity in the scheduling processes.
2. Summarize the findings from step 1.
3. Develop and summarize general recommendations from these findings concerning how/where the process can more efficiently be performed employing JIT principles. Maintain this list of recommendations for use during the conceptual design and implementation sections of the program.
4. Collect data on all shortages or hot jobs that occur over a two-week period. Identify the root causes for each shortage. Summarize the list by reason for shortage using a Pareto diagram. Maintain this listing for later use with the summarized findings described in step 3. The listing should include a summary of general recommendations about how the root causes identified should be addressed.

Purchasing Review. An effective just-in-time purchasing program can be one of the most important elements of the entire project. A great deal of analysis must be performed to develop a real understanding of the entire purchasing process.

The diagnostic for this section is broken down into the following tasks:

- Buyer time distribution study.
- Commodity analysis.
- "ABC" analysis.
- Vendor analysis.
- Buyer interviews (concerns/issues).

These studies will be of use during the conceptual design and implementation phases of the project when gross opportunities have been identified and recommendations may be made that dramatically change traditional purchasing functions.

Manufacturing Review. The objective of the manufacturing review is to identify potential opportunity levels with regard to changeover time reduction, quality improvement, layout improvement and capacity requirements, and housekeeping improvements.

Changeover time review. The objective of the changeover time review is to identify existing set-up/changeover times and assess their impacts on workcenter layouts, capacity, personnel requirements, and queues. The four steps in this review are as follows:

1. Obtain a listing of all machine centers and associated set-up/changeover times by product. Summarize the findings by product, longest to shortest.
2. Review how order quantities are calculated based on time allocated to set-ups/changeovers. Review how capacity planning is performed based on set-ups/changeovers. Identify amount of people required to accommodate set-ups/changeovers.
3. Recalculate order quantities, capacity requirements, and personnel level requirements based on set-up/changeover time reductions of 75%.
4. Summarize the resulting opportunity levels for use in the later conceptual design and implementation planning phases.

Quality level review. The objective of the quality level review is to assess current reject rates and their causes, assess current disposition procedures for rejected parts, and calculate current costs associated with maintaining quality levels. The five steps involved in this review are as follows:

1. Obtain a listing of reject rates over the last 6 months and indicate failure causes in each instance. Develop a chart summarizing findings, categorized by cause and listed in descending order by frequency within cause.
2. Obtain a listing of defective parts over the last 6 months and indicate dispositions in each instance. Calculate costs associated with the dispositions.
3. Identify all costs associated with the maintenance of quality over the previous year. These costs include prevention, appraisal, internal failure, and external failure.
4. Obtain the cost-of-production figures for the previous year. Obtain gross sales figures for the previous year. Calculate the quality cost as a percentage of the cost of production and as a percentage of the cost of sales. Compare these figures with prior years, if available. Develop a chart summarizing these figures.
5. Identify methods used and parties responsible for measuring/plotting defects. Identify course of action taken on defects (where defect notices go, what is done with them, by whom, and how quickly). Summarize gross opportunities for use in conceptual design and implementation phases of the program.

Process flow review. The objectives of the process flow review are to develop a clear understanding of the operations required to produce a specific product; document distances of product travel in the current layout; determine the levels of value added to the product at each stage of the process; identify personnel, work-in-process, and capacity levels at each stage of the process; identify queue levels and causes in the process; identify the lead-time distribution by product within the process; and to evaluate work content at each stage of the process.

The seven steps in this process are as follows:

1. Follow each product through its processes, documenting all major steps. Develop a straight-line flowchart of the process, highlighting all major operations.
2. Obtain a facilities layout (scale drawing or blueprint) of

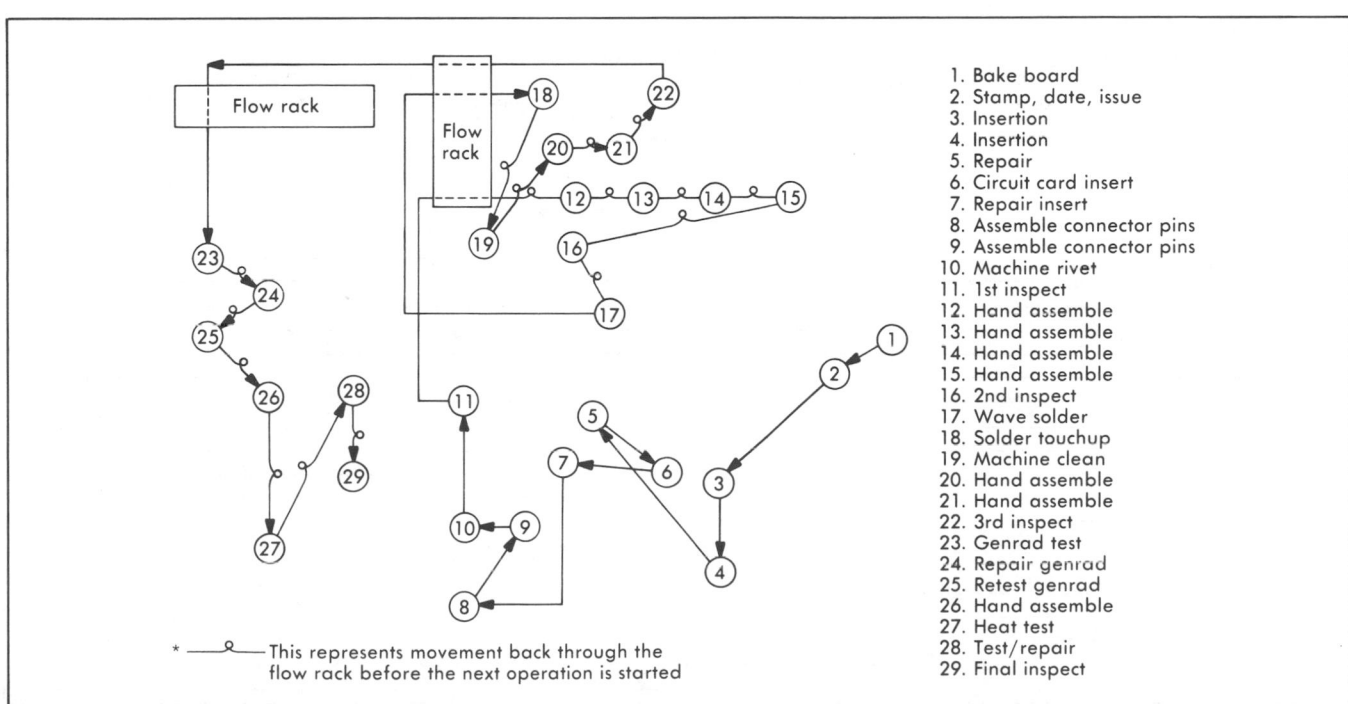

1. Bake board
2. Stamp, date, issue
3. Insertion
4. Insertion
5. Repair
6. Circuit card insert
7. Repair insert
8. Assemble connector pins
9. Assemble connector pins
10. Machine rivet
11. 1st inspect
12. Hand assemble
13. Hand assemble
14. Hand assemble
15. Hand assemble
16. 2nd inspect
17. Wave solder
18. Solder touchup
19. Machine clean
20. Hand assemble
21. Hand assemble
22. 3rd inspect
23. Genrad test
24. Repair genrad
25. Retest genrad
26. Hand assemble
27. Heat test
28. Test/repair
29. Final inspect

* ——o—— This represents movement back through the flow rack before the next operation is started

Fig. 7-24 Actual flowchart of a production process. (*Coopers & Lybrand*)

JUST-IN-TIME MANUFACTURING

the facility in which all production processes occur. Identify the location of each process on the layout and show routes/distances traveled between each step (see Fig. 7-24). Transfer data to a separate sheet.

3. Document everything that happens to a given part before, during, and after each major operation in the process. Indicate whether each step in the process adds value to the product.

4. Select a part that is representative of its entire product line in terms of its processes and complete the information designated in Fig 7-25. From this chart, the following information can be obtained:

   • A comparison of the days-on-hand figure with the throughput figure. The days-on-hand figure represents how long it will take to get a part completely through the process (lead time) after utilizing the WIP currently on the floor. The throughput figure represents how long it will take if lot sizes of 1 are utilized and the part moves immediately from one operation to the next without any interruptions. If larger lot sizes will be used, multiply the throughput figure by the new lot size number to get a new throughput time.

   • The identification of bottlenecks, which are those areas with the greatest number of days-on-hand inventories.

   • A comparison of the machines required with the current number of machines available. This comparison is a quick way to identify underutilized (machines that could be used elsewhere) and overutilized (bottleneck) machine applications that can be addressed immediately.

   • The fundamental data required for the calculation of the uniform plant load.

5. Develop a listing of WIP inventory levels between and at each workcenter, listing quantities and reasons for the queues. Call out the equivalent days or hours of production represented by each queue (see Fig. 7-26). Identify potential methods of reducing the levels of queue.

6. Utilizing an operation-by-operation listing of manufacturing throughput time per piece, graphically depict the lead time in the production process. Use X's to represent appropriate units of time such as $X = 1$ hour or $X = 1$ day (see Fig. 7-27). Use this review to identify operations. that appear to be logical targets for lead-time reduction.

7. As the part moves through its production process, observe direct and indirect labor activities. Review the data gathered and accumulate times by activity. Then accumulate times attributed to activities that add value to the product. Calculate the percentage of labor time (by operation and in total) that is attributable to value-adding activity.

Retain the data from steps 1 through 7 for use in the conceptual design and implementation phases.

Housekeeping review. The objectives of the housekeeping review are the following:

Daily demand _____ Hourly demand_____
Hours per shift_____ Cycle time_____

Item_____ Number of shifts_____

Operation	Standard (hours per 100 pieces)	Rate Per Hour (RPH) (100/standard)	Throughput (TP) (60/RPH), min	Number of Machines	Machines Required (hourly demand/RPH)	Machine Status, Current Required	Personnel Required Per Shift (hourly demand/RPH)	WIP Inventory	Inventory, dollars on hand	Inventory, days on hand
1.										
2.										
3.										
4.										
5.										
6.										
7.										
8.										
9.										
10.										
11.										
12.										
13.										
14.										
15.										
16.										
17.										
18.										
19.										
20.										
21.										
22.										

Fig. 7-25 Sample capacity requirements spreadsheet. (*Coopers & Lybrand*)

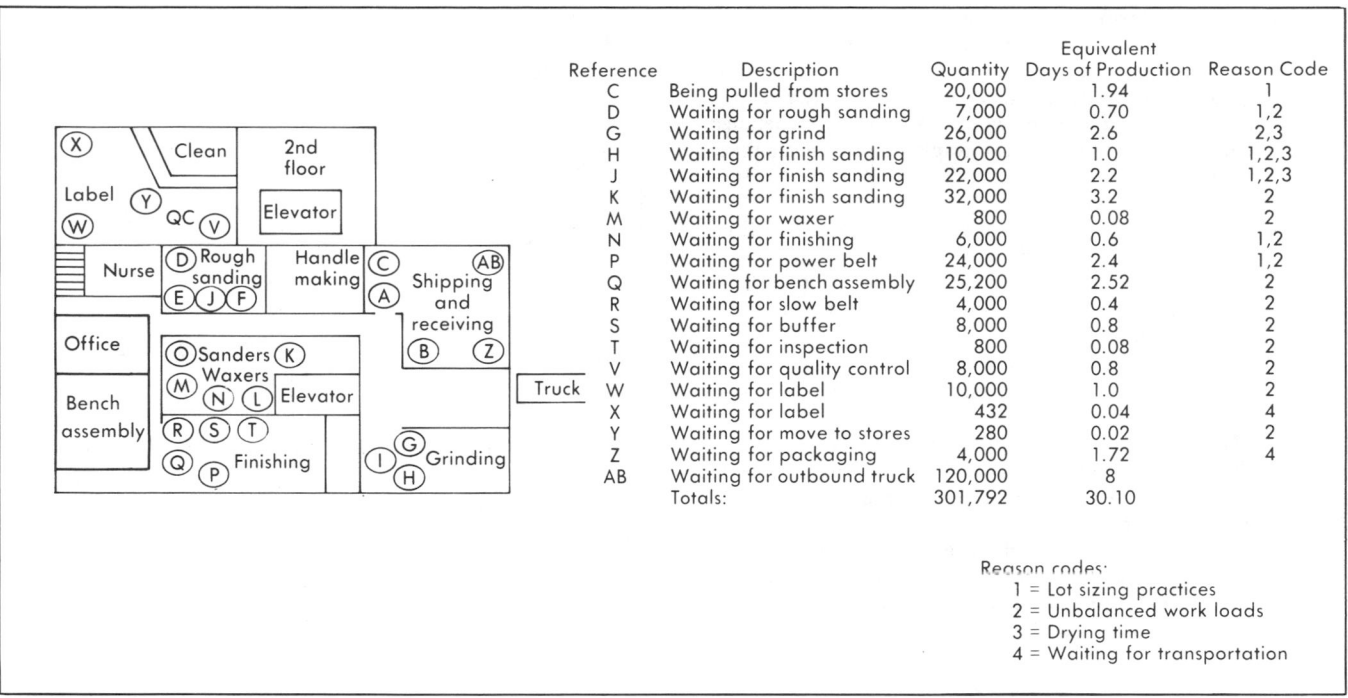

Reference	Description	Quantity	Equivalent Days of Production	Reason Code
C	Being pulled from stores	20,000	1.94	1
D	Waiting for rough sanding	7,000	0.70	1,2
G	Waiting for grind	26,000	2.6	2,3
H	Waiting for finish sanding	10,000	1.0	1,2,3
J	Waiting for finish sanding	22,000	2.2	1,2,3
K	Waiting for finish sanding	32,000	3.2	2
M	Waiting for waxer	800	0.08	2
N	Waiting for finishing	6,000	0.6	1,2
P	Waiting for power belt	24,000	2.4	1,2
Q	Waiting for bench assembly	25,200	2.52	2
R	Waiting for slow belt	4,000	0.4	2
S	Waiting for buffer	8,000	0.8	2
T	Waiting for inspection	800	0.08	2
V	Waiting for quality control	8,000	0.8	2
W	Waiting for label	10,000	1.0	2
X	Waiting for label	432	0.04	4
Y	Waiting for move to stores	280	0.02	2
Z	Waiting for packaging	4,000	1.72	4
AB	Waiting for outbound truck	120,000	8	
	Totals:	301,792	30.10	

Reason codes:
1 = Lot sizing practices
2 = Unbalanced work loads
3 = Drying time
4 = Waiting for transportation

Fig. 7-26 Sample queue causality listing. (*Coopers & Lybrand*)

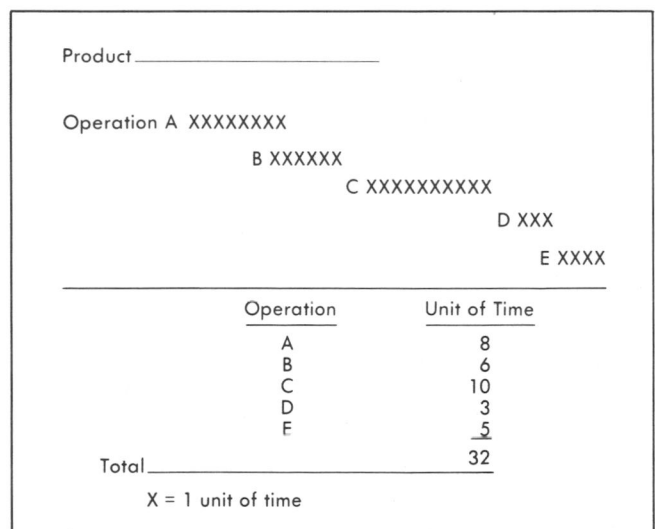

Fig. 7-27 Example of a lead-time distribution depiction. (*Coopers & Lybrand*)

- Identify current tooling/fixturing requirements.
- Identify current WIP storage requirements and how WIP is identified.
- Determine whether all tooling and fixtures have designated locations and if the equipment is kept in those locations.
- Assess current housekeeping practices in regard to general cleanliness and upkeep of the equipment and facility.

The following two steps are recommended when performing a housekeeping review:

1. Develop a chart that lists all workcenters under review. Break the chart down into the following categories:
   - Dies and fixtures required by machine workcenter.
   - Tools required to perform all set-ups on the specific machines.
2. Tour the production area and look for trash on the floor, personal items on or near workstations, WIP inventory lying around, and poor upkeep of machinery, such as fluid leaks and squeaks/rattles. Develop a list of recommendations to be used during the implementation phase of the project. Typical recommendations include the following:
   - Make operators responsible for the general cleanliness of their work area, including picking up trash, placing personal items in lockers, not allowing inventory in their area until it is required, and cleaning machines during idle times.
   - Awarding a prize for the employee(s) keeping their area the cleanest.

Retain this data for later use during the conceptual design and implementation phases of the project.

Distribution Review. The objective of the distribution review is to review current distribution practices and procedures and assess their appropriateness in light of just-in-time manufacturing/distribution concepts. It is also used to identify gross opportunity levels that may be achieved through the application of JIT techniques. The following nine steps can be performed when conducting a distribution review:

1. Develop flowcharts depicting current distribution processes and functions. At least one chart should describe material flow, and another should reflect paperwork processing activities. In the charts, or on a separate listing attached to the charts, identify the following:

JUST-IN-TIME MANUFACTURING

- Areas performing each function.
- Number of reviews/approvals in each flow.
- Amount of time spent in each activity. Queue time (and inventory levels, as appropriate) between each activity should be noted when available. More detailed analysis will follow in the implementation planning phase.
- Distances traveled.
- Number of stores. Areas and/or distribution facilities involved and their actions.

2. Summarize the data gathered and review it with all affected personnel to ensure its accuracy. Include estimates of the following:
   - Total throughput times.
   - Percent of throughput times that is queue.
   - Bottlenecks in the flows.
   - Rough cost data associated with the flow.
   - Percent/cost of functions within the flow that do not add value to the documents or material involved and/or are not critical.

3. Assess the gross opportunity levels in these processes for general efficiency/productivity improvements through the reduction of non-value-adding activities and bottlenecks.

4. Document the estimated opportunity levels (potential for improvement) and retain the data for use during conceptual design and implementation phases later in the program.

5. Conduct interviews with distribution management to determine their perception of:
   - Current customer base.
   - Current service level requirements.
   - Nature/use of the product.
   - Special constraints such as packaging, handling, and contracts.
   - Profit contribution by product.
   - Geographic and distribution channel contribution levels.
   - Areas of needed improvement.
   - Appropriate/desirable carriers and distribution channels.

6. Review historical and current data to identify actual customer base and service levels. Compare the results with the data gathered previously.

7. Conduct a cursory review of distributed end item contribution levels and perform the following tasks:
   - Determine those parts making the greatest contribution to sales.
   - List those parts in descending order (if reasonable).
   - On a chart, plot the parts against the cumulative percentage of sales (see Fig. 7-28). The intent of this chart is to highlight (if applicable) the number of parts that comprise the greatest percentage of sales. In the example shown in Fig. 7-28, less than 50% of the part number population represents 95% of total sales.

8. Considering any special constraints and product characteristics, estimate the improvement potential of JIT concepts (queue elimination, travel distance reduction, and simplification) applied to the existing distribution environment. Quantify the improvement potentials to the extent possible and practical.

9. Summarize and document the findings and retain this

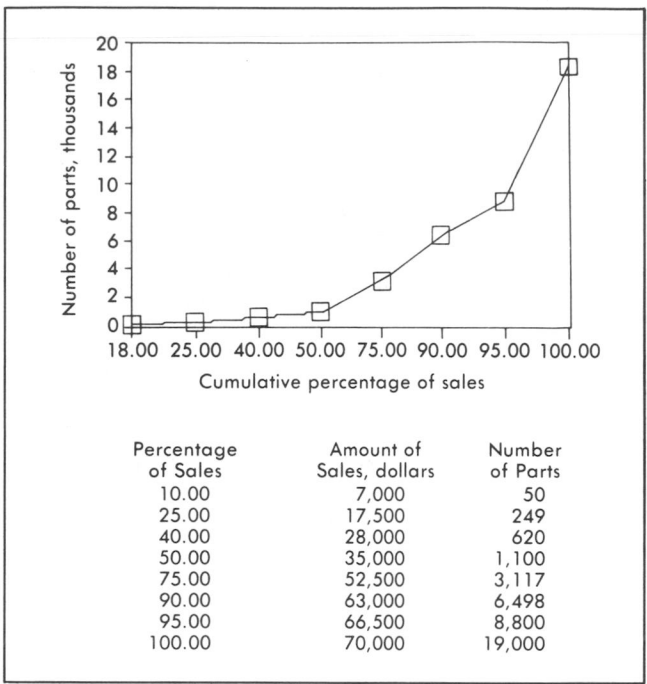

Percentage of Sales	Amount of Sales, dollars	Number of Parts
10.00	7,000	50
25.00	17,500	249
40.00	28,000	620
50.00	35,000	1,100
75.00	52,500	3,117
90.00	63,000	6,498
95.00	66,500	8,800
100.00	70,000	19,000

Fig. 7-28 Graph showing relationship of cumulative sales percentage to number of parts. (*Coopers & Lybrand*)

data for use in the conceptual design and implementation phases later in the program.

Accounting Review. The objective of the accounting review is to review current accounting practices and procedures and assess their applicability to JIT manufacturing operations. Also, it identifies opportunities for general productivity improvement in the existing accounting activities that may be addressed through the application of JIT methodology.

Implementation Planning

The diagnostic review establishes where the organization is today, thus establishing benchmarks against which future progress can be measured. To provide the company with a target of where it should be in 1 to 5 years, a conceptual design of the entire organization is performed. The implementation plan, along with a lot of hard work, provides the means for the organization to move from point A to point B.

To obtain a proper perspective on the various tasks in the implementation plan, and the sequence in which they should be performed, a Gantt chart should be developed. Figure 7-29 shows a Gantt chart of one manufacturer's approach to the implementation plan. Although this particular chart covers a period of 94 weeks, the time frame will vary in other organizations based on the size and the scope of the JIT program.

Conceptual Design Activities

To obtain a sound conceptual picture of the future in a manufacturing organization incorporating JIT, a number of important factors need to be addressed. Table 7-8 lists the factors that need to be addressed in various departments, along with the desired goal. For each factor, the question to be asked is, "How will each factor be measured?"

The question must be answered in both a 5-year and 1-year time frame. The resulting "snapshot" of future operations is comprised of important milestones for the balance of the JIT program. Each milestone must be measurable. For example, improved employee morale is not measurable and, therefore, does not qualify. Milestones are an important indicator of whether planned improvements relate correctly to overall corporate goals and objectives and provide a good infrastructure for divisional and departmental goals and objectives.

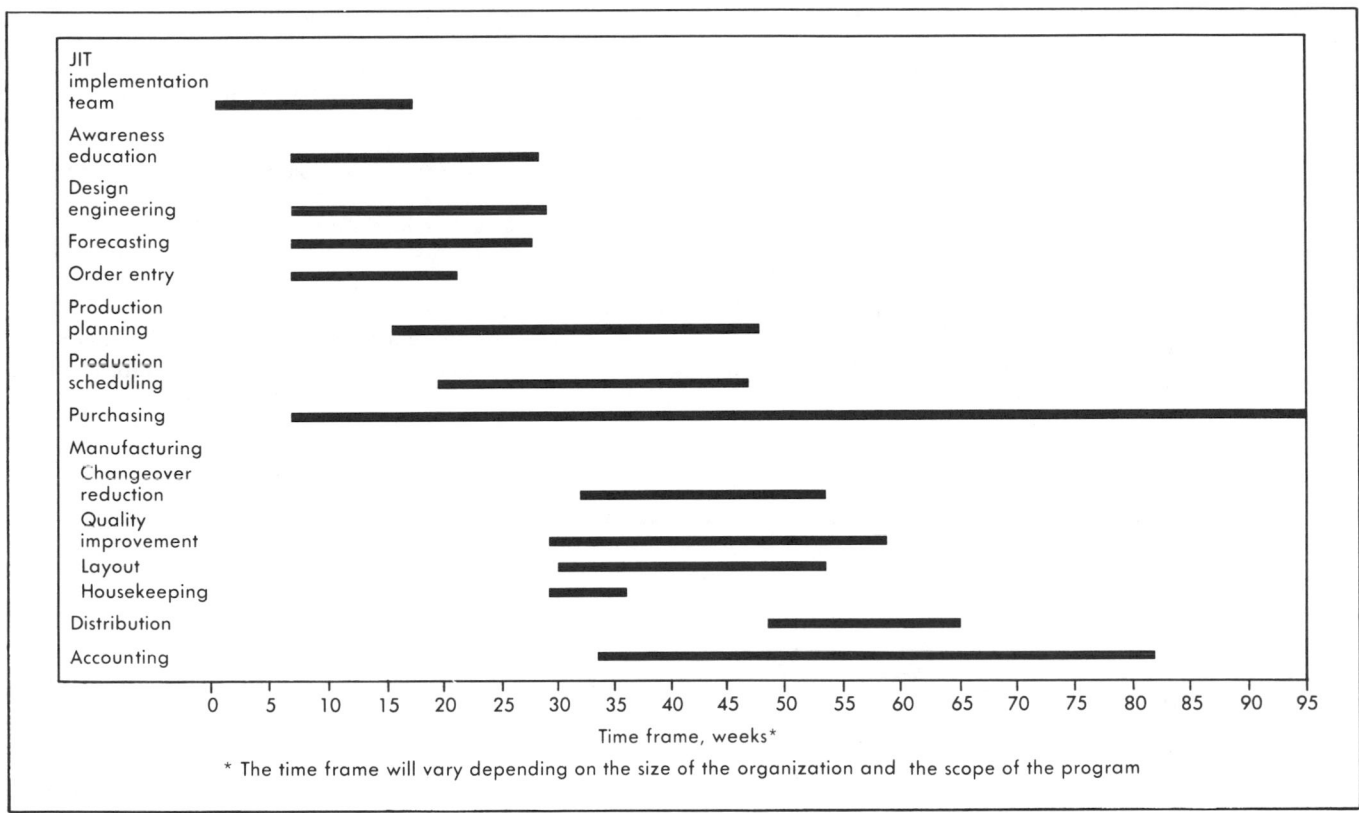

Fig. 7-29 Gantt chart of a generic implementation workplan. (*Coopers & Lybrand*)

TABLE 7-8
Factors to be Addressed During Conceptual Design Phase

Department	Desired Goal	Factors
Design engineering	Reduced design throughput time	Design change throughput time
	Accurate designs that support zero defects and manufacturability	Levels of manufacturability
		Levels of standardization
Forecasting	Reduced forecast generation throughput time	Level of forecast accuracy
Order entry	Reduced order entry throughput time	Order entry accuracy levels
	Defect-free order entry	
Production planning	Reduced production planning throughput time	Average lot size
Production scheduling	Reduced production scheduling throughput time	Requirements communication efficiency and effectiveness levels
Purchasing	Reduced supplier base	Geographic location
	Zero defects in purchased goods	Multiplicity by commodity
	Reduced purchase costs	Delivery performance
	Point-of-use delivery	Appropriateness of price
	Frequent deliveries	Quality levels
	Willingness to do electronic data interchange (EDI)	Willingness to adopt JIT techniques

TABLE 7-8 — *Continued*

Department	Desired Goal	Factors
Manufacturing	Reduced setup and changeover times Zero defects Zero inventory Reduced throughput times Reduced cost of goods sold	Quality levels Quality standards Product flow Pull system mechanisms and procedures WIP levels Manufacturing throughput time Production reporting methods, frequencies, and locations Layout attributes Level of work center commonality and utilization Efficiency levels Designation level for materials and tooling Level of trash, personal effects, and debris at work centers
Distribution	Reduced distribution throughput time Zero	Finished goods levels Transportation costs, frequencies, and volumes
Accounting	Reduced accounts payable throughput time Zero errors in payments	Philosophical and operational changes for accounts payable Accounts receivable throughput times Cost accounting throughput times Philosophical and operational changes for cost accounting

(Coopers & Lybrand)

References

1. *APICS Dictionary*, 5th ed. (Falls Church, VA: American Production and Inventory Control Society, 1984).
2. *Ibid.*
3. William A. Wheeler III, *Straight Talk on Just-in-Time* (New York: Coopers & Lybrand).

TOLERANCE CONTROL

The economy of any industrialized nation simply cannot afford to squander vast sums of money represented by the scrap, rework, and debugging time generated by uncontrolled tolerances. Competition, both internal and external to the country, puts a premium on quality of design and quality of manufacturing, and this quality in large part is based on control of tolerances.

Hand-in-hand with this need to systematically control tolerances walks the need to control manufacturing costs—and one way to minimize production costs is to ensure that no tolerance is held tighter than required by the product-design drawing or by the nature of the manufacturing process concepts covering sequencing, choice of location surfaces, dimensioning schemes on the cuts, workholding principles, etc.

TOLERANCE VS. COST

Figure 8-1 illustrates typical size holding tolerances for various material-removal production processes. The relationship between tightness of tolerance and manufacturing cost is shown in Fig. 8-2. The cost of production increases geometrically for uniform incremental tightening of tolerances. If the truth of this relationship is accepted—and it has been found to be correct in numerous writings by different specialists in a number of countries—then a systematic approach to tolerancing will have as one of its main thrusts the maximizing of production tolerances within the framework of manufacturing process concepts.

TOLERANCE SPECIFICATIONS

Until this point the term *tolerance* has been used in an all-inclusive sense. However, tolerances can be defined as being concerned either with physical sizes of features on a part or with the geometric characteristics of those features. Complete coverage of standard practices for dimensioning of sizes and geometric characteristics is given in the ANSI Standard Y14.5-1973.[1]

Many companies find it desirable, however, to develop and assign their own in-house specification numbers to this same body of methodology. Comparison of most in-house specifications on dimensioning and tolerancing with specifications in the ANSI Standard Y14.5 will show almost complete correspondence except in those special situations unique to the company's product line.

In this chapter the ANSI Standard Y14.5 is used for definitions and symbols to identify geometric characteristics. Figure 8-3 is based on the ANSI Standard Y14.5 presentation of geometric symbols.[2]

Most, but not all, of the 14 geometric characteristics shown in Fig. 8-3 are controlled by correct operation sequencing, by correct application of workholding principles, by properly designed tooling and gaging compatible with the end result accuracies to be controlled, and by the machine tool accuracies themselves. Four of the 14 characteristics: profile of a surface, position, concentricity, and symmetry are handled within tolerance control of sizes. This is covered in detail later in this chapter in the material on tolerance charting.

CONTROL OF SIZE TOLERANCES AND TOLERANCE STACKUPS

Given a drawing of a component and the raw material and told to make one piece, a toolmaker will machine the part and upon inspection will find that it conforms very closely to the mean dimensions on the drawing. This is a result of machining from one feature to another, zeroing out each completed feature, and using that zeroed out condition as the datum to machine the next feature. Tolerance stackups are then bypassed.

In production planning for quantity runs, however, the part cannot always be machined dimensionally as shown on the drawing, so datum surfaces must be set up by the production engineer based on a selection of locating surfaces for fixturing and on cutting tool design layout decisions. As a result, the problem of tolerance stackups is encountered.

The principle of tolerance stackups—or buildup of tolerances or accumulation of tolerances—is illustrated in Fig. 8-4. Simply, addition or subtraction of length dimensions is always characterized by the adding of tolerances on the individual lengths. This principle applies with equal force whenever lengths are added or subtracted.

THE TOLERANCE CHART

Whether a part is made completely to print in one operation or routed over a series of machines, some of which may be NC, the process engineer must be capable of recognizing that a tolerance stackup situation has been created which will affect the tolerances assigned to the machining cuts. When tolerance stackup problems must be handled, the easiest, quickest, and most foolproof way is by use of the tolerance chart.

Whether the tolerance chart is built manually or by a computer program, it is only built after all the initial engineering decisions have been made concerning the process. These decisions include:

1. The sequence of operations to be performed.
2. The machine selection for each operation, based on its capacities and known accuracies. (Note: If a transfer line is to be designed, the same considerations apply except that the stations of the line will be custom designed to accuracy levels based

TOLERANCE CONTROL

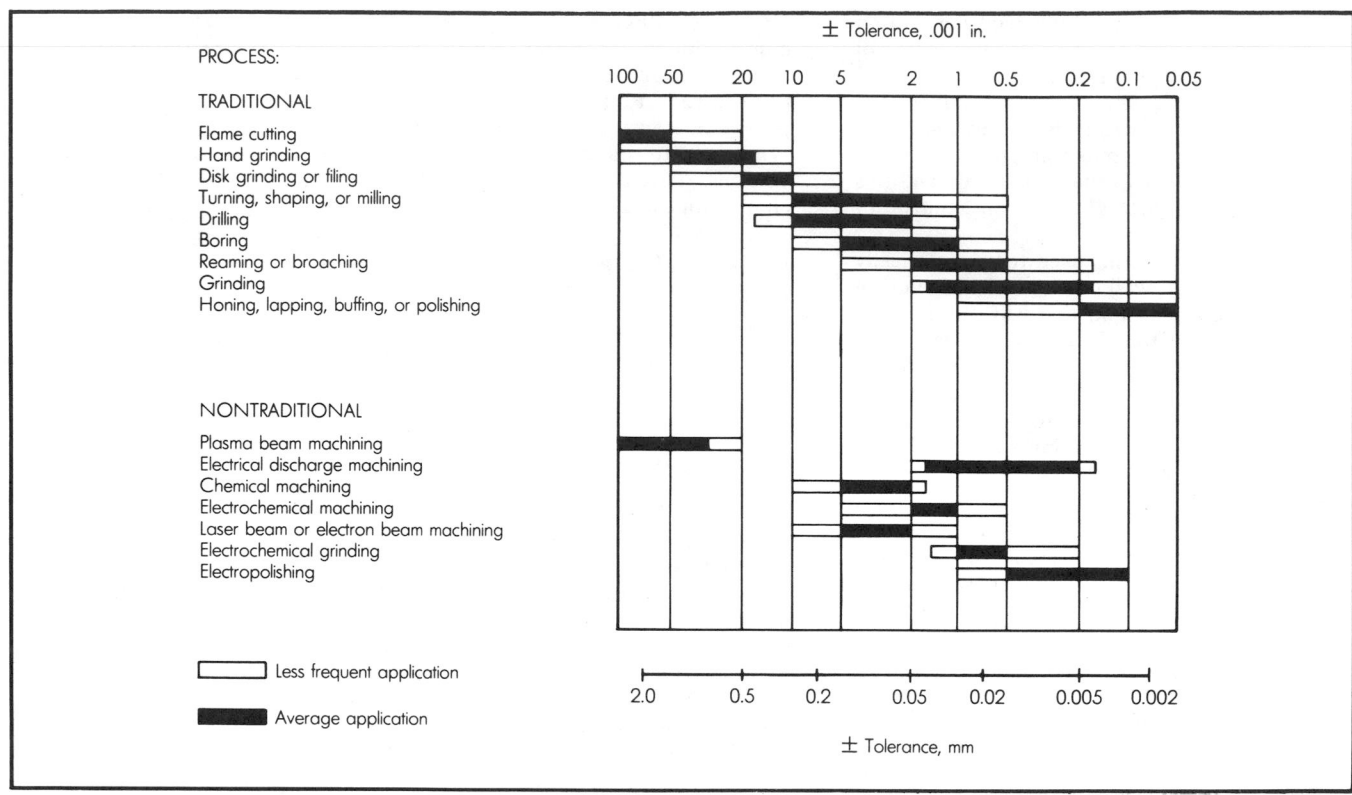

Fig. 8-1 Typical tolerances for material removal production processes. (*Reprinted by permission of the Machinability Data Center, Metcut Research Associates, Inc.*)

on the tolerances developed by construction of the tolerance chart.)

3. The dimensioning patterns for the cuts to be made in each operation. (These patterns do not always correspond to the blueprint.)

4. The selection of the locating surface to be used in each operation. (These datum surfaces do not always conform to those shown on the blueprint.)

5. The kind and type of tooling to be used in each operation to control geometric characteristics such as squareness, parallelism, concentricity, symmetry, etc.

Once these decisions have been made, and possibly subjected to critiquing by tool engineers, the master mechanic, etc., a tolerance chart can be constructed to generate the dimensions and tolerances required by each process cut. Properly constructed, the tolerance chart will verify that the following criteria for economical production have been satisfied:

1. Within the framework of the process/tooling decisions, as much as possible of the blueprint maximum tolerance has been allocated among the in-process cuts, which results in the maximum possible tolerance being assigned to each cut in the process.

2. The minimum and maximum stock removals on secondary cuts are practical and acceptable to the shop.

3. Every tolerance assigned is equal to and preferably larger than the estimated process capability for the cut in question. Since the relationship between the working tolerance and the process capability has a direct bearing

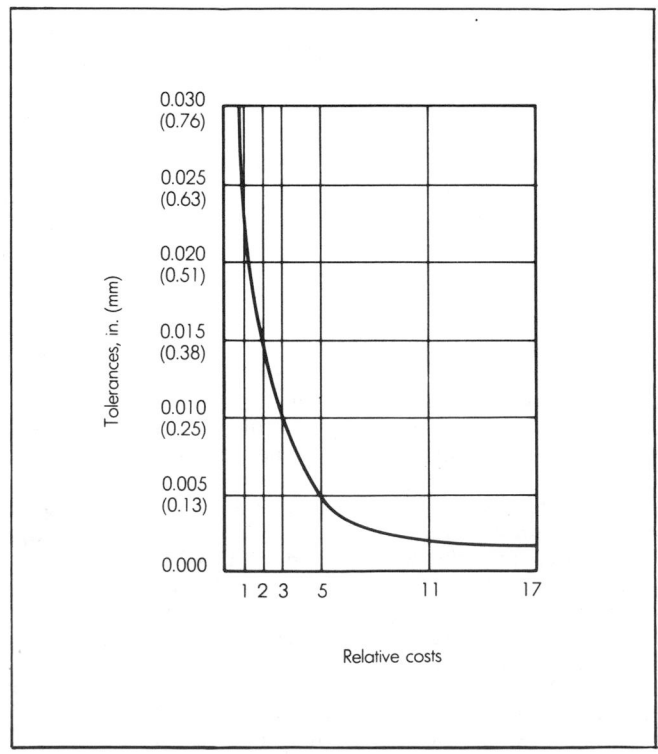

Fig. 8-2 Relationship between tolerances and production costs.

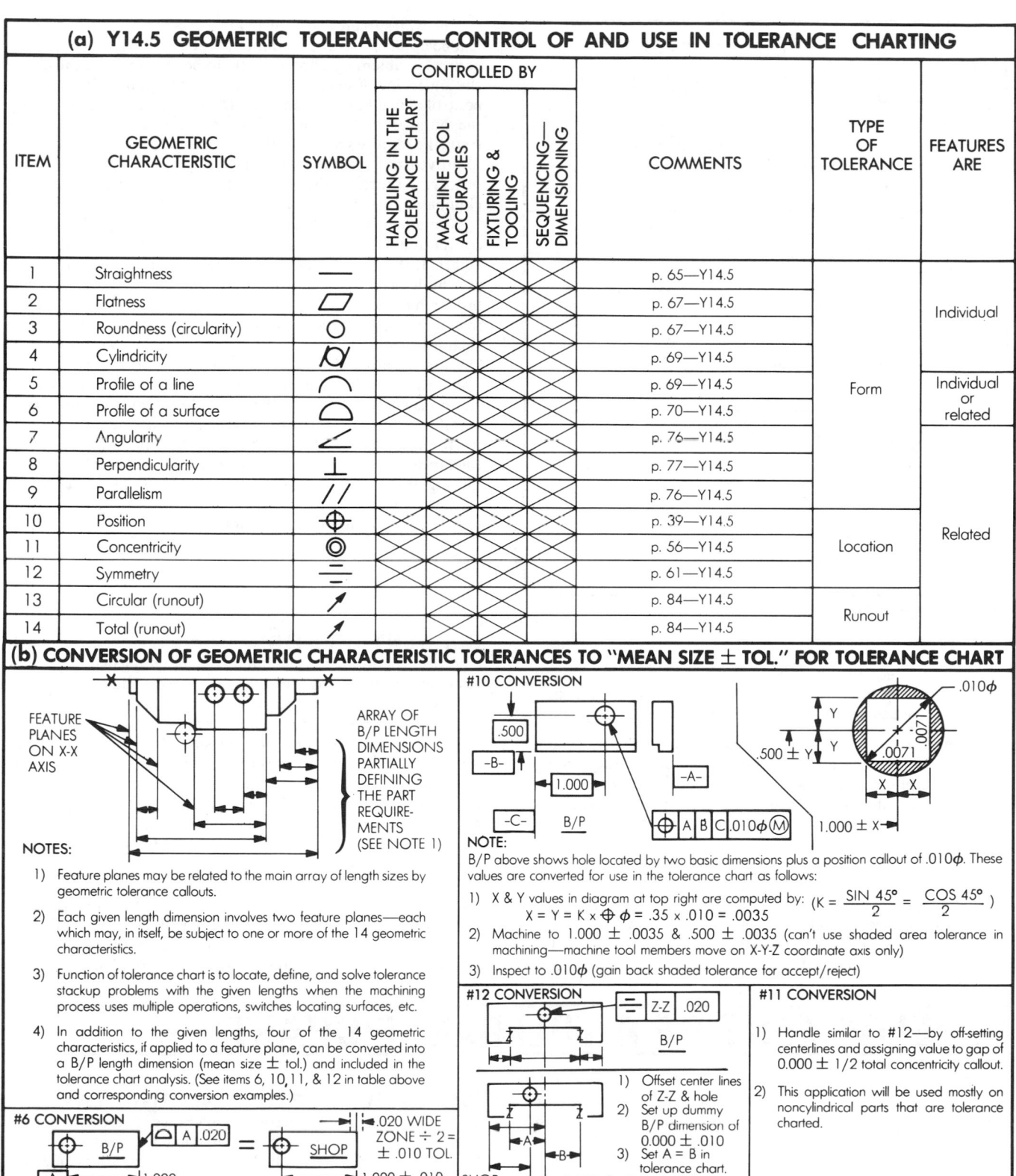

Fig. 8-3 (a) Definitions and symbols to identify geometric characteristics, and **(b)** conversion of geometric characteristic tolerances to mean size tolerance for use in tolerance charting.[2]

TOLERANCE CONTROL

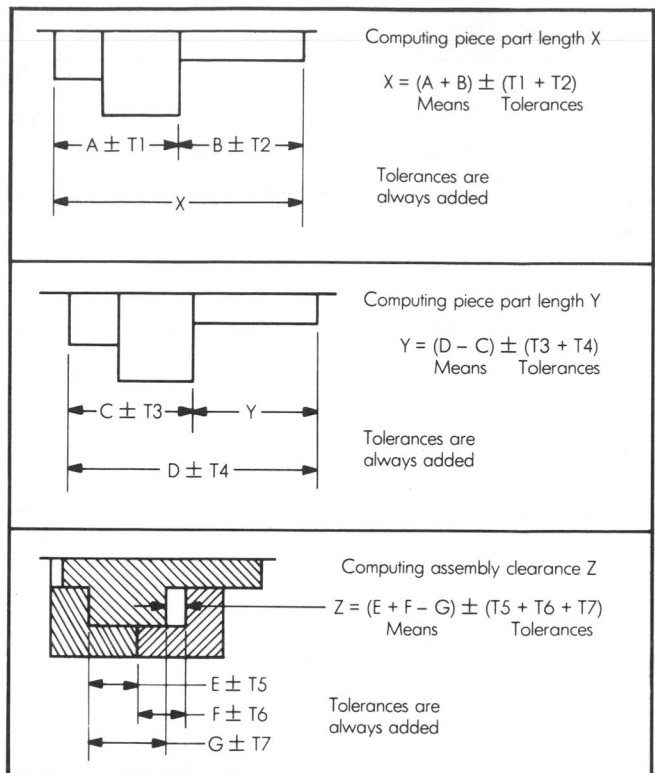

Fig. 8-4 The nature of tolerance stackups.

Computing piece part length X

$$X = (A + B) \pm (T1 + T2)$$
Means   Tolerances

Tolerances are always added

$A \pm T1$ $B \pm T2$ X

Computing piece part length Y

$$Y = (D - C) \pm (T3 + T4)$$
Means   Tolerances

Tolerances are always added

$C \pm T3$ Y $D \pm T4$

Computing assembly clearance Z

$$Z = (E + F - G) \pm (T5 + T6 + T7)$$
Means   Tolerances

$E \pm T5$

$F \pm T6$ Tolerances are always added

$G \pm T7$

The widespread and growing use of NC machining, when it can be applied, has reduced the extent of the tolerance stackup control problem by allowing cuts to be machined as shown on the blueprint dimensioning schemes, by eliminating manual control of machine decisions affecting the cuts, and by reducing the number of location surface changes and the attendant fixturing required by non-NC machining. In general, it has also improved size control and control of geometric characteristics of part features. However, not all tolerance stackups are eliminated by using NC machines.

Numerical Control machines are often combined with conventional machines to form a grouping of machines to make a part. If the volume justifies it, special-purpose transfer lines are built which incorporate all milling, drilling, boring, broaching, etc., so that the transfer line is equivalent to a selection from a large inventory of machine tools. Designing such a transfer line without basing the design on a tolerance chart is far more risky than processing a part on the basis of stand-alone machines selected from a large inventory since each station is custom built for that part alone. Imagine the excess cost if, when the last stations of the machine are built and tested, it is found that failure to meet blueprint specifications is due to a tolerance stackup problem that traces back to the early stations. During testing is no time to find out that the sequence of stations is wrong or that the selection of locating surfaces is responsible for the tolerance stackup problem, etc.

on the frequency of tool changes or adjustments, many companies have in-house rules that call for the working tolerance to be 1.5-2.0 times the process capability value.

During the course of building the tolerance chart, it may become obvious that one or more of the initial process/tooling decisions results in assigning an impossibly tight tolerance to an in-process dimension. When this happens, it is necessary to change these decisions to satisfy the criteria for economic production.

Since all these decisions are still in the paper stage, that is, no tooling has yet been designed, no great time or dollar loss will occur if a process change is required. However, failure to respond to the clear signals from the tolerance chart will result in the problems on paper being transferred into iron on the shop floor.

CURRENT TRENDS

Process planning for machining is undergoing major changes as computer programs are being developed to do the complete processing job on either the basis of a family design of parts or the basis of a true generative approach.

These programs, to be complete, should include subroutines that will handle the tolerance charting function for development of required mean sizes and tolerances for machining cuts, and that will also analyze the process and tooling capabilities relative to control of squareness, parallelism, roundness, etc.

If predictions are correct, it will come about in time—near, not far, that the design engineer's job will fuse with the production engineer's job. A common data base will be in computer memory, along with design and production methodologies. From this amalgam will flow not only the product design but all production engineering outputs of operation sheets, tool designs, tolerance charts, NC tapes, etc.

DEVELOPMENT OF A TOLERANCE CHART

The tolerance chart assumes the character of an accountant's worksheet except that tolerances are manipulated rather than dollars. Just as entries in the accountant's worksheet are entered in strict conformance to rules and procedures to arrive at an ironclad picture of the results and the manner in which they were obtained, every numerical entry in the tolerance chart is also based on rules and procedures. In this section, procedures for tolerance chart construction are described, defined, and demonstrated.

WORKPIECE SKETCH AND STRIP LAYOUT

To facilitate the explanation of tolerance chart construction, a sample workpiece, Fig. 8-5, *a*, is used and a strip layout Fig. 8-5, *b*, is set up to illustrate how an engineer might organize his ideas for machining a part.

Both Fig. 8-5, *a* and Fig. 8-5, *b*, layouts are simplified to highlight those dimensional and tolerance aspects that are involved with the tolerance chart. For example, Fig. 8-5,*a*, blueprint shows four length dimensions measured along the

X-X axis of the part. While there is a Y-Y axis understood at right angles to the X-X axis, the Y-Y axis is of no concern in this analysis. This discussion involves analysis of the stackup of tolerances among the shoulders along the X-X axis.

The Fig. 8-5, b, strip layout provides the following vital information required before a tolerance chart can be produced:

1. Sequence of operations to be performed—chronologically by operation number.
2. The surfaces machined in each operation, as shown by the heavy black lines.
3. The location surfaces chosen for purposes of fixture design or gaging.

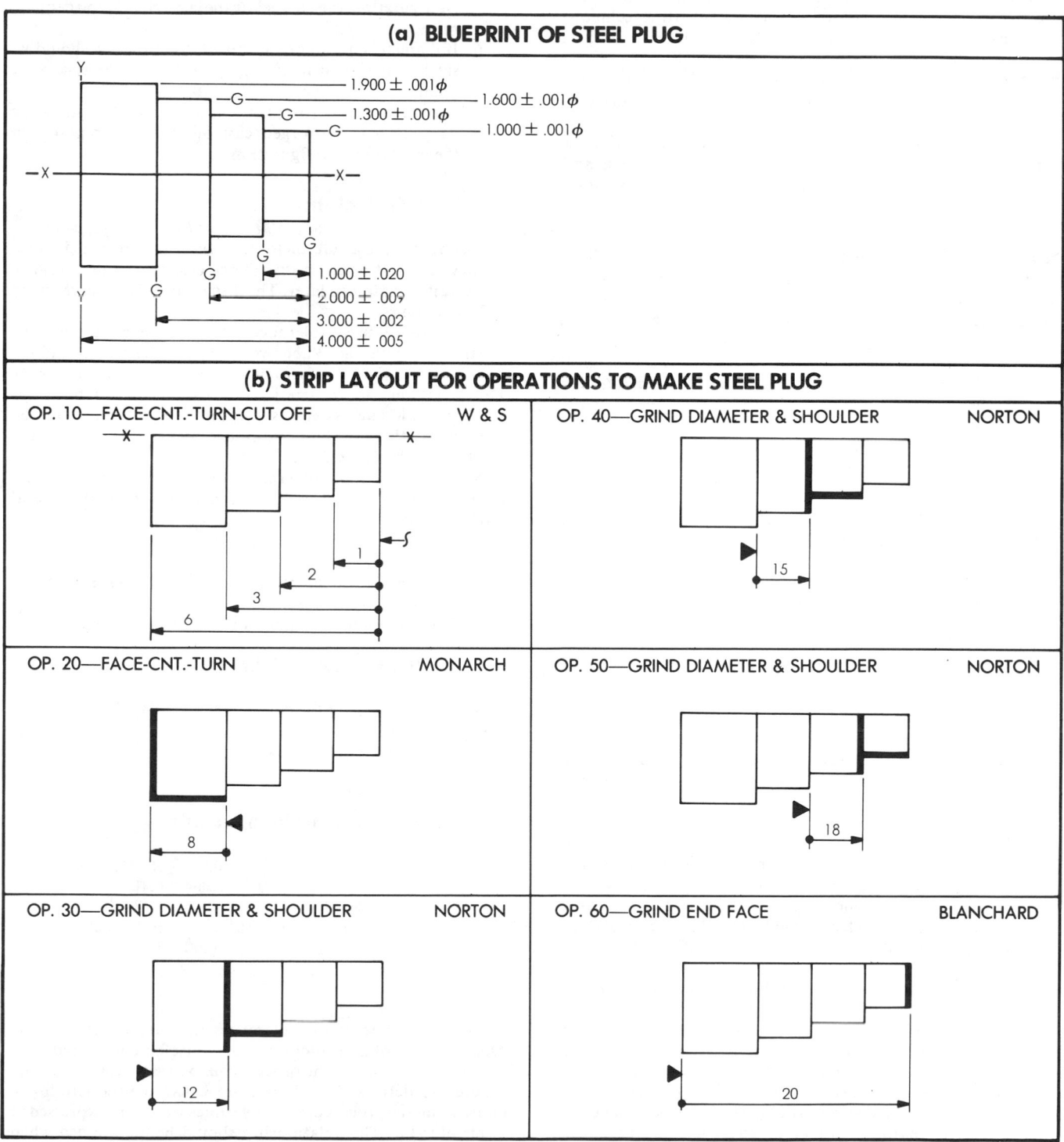

Fig. 8-5 (a) Blueprint dimensions and tolerances for sample part—steel plug. (b) Workpiece strip layout—operations to machine steel plug.

TOLERANCE CHART DEVELOPMENT

4. The dimensioning scheme employed for each cut in each operation.
5. The machine chosen for each operation.

With respect to the strip layout (Fig. 8-5, *b*), it has been deliberately designed to violate sound machining practices and sound tolerance charting principles to reveal as many problems as possible. Many of the deficiencies in the sample strip layout are highlighted by the nature of the tolerance charting technique and are commented on in terms of possible corrective actions.

ELEMENTS OF A TOLERANCE CHART

The tolerance chart represented in Fig. 8-6 is constructed to suit the Fig. 8-5, *a*, blueprint and its matching strip layout, Fig. 8-5, *b*. The Fig. 8-6 tolerance chart is used here to describe the various elements of a tolerance chart and the design and function of the elements. When appropriate, it also provides detailed information on handling these elements.

Blueprint Dimensions

Below the heavy black line, under the heading *Blueprint,* the length dimensions from Fig. 8-5, *a*, are listed. (They are not in the same order as shown in Fig. 8-5, *a*, because order makes no difference. In contrast, the machining cut lines from Fig. 8-5, *b*, must be drawn and numbered on the chart in chronological order by operation number and within the proper operation in accordance with certain restrictions to be described later.) A double-dot heavy black line is drawn between the planes for each blueprint dimension.

Resultant Dimensions

To the right side of the tolerance chart, under the heavy black line, the heading *Resultants* is printed. Recorded under this heading are the same mean blueprint values as shown at the left under *Blueprint,* but the resultant tolerances are either equal to or less than the blueprint tolerances.

Process Sketch

The following points concern the process sketch at the top of a tolerance chart (see Fig. 8-7):

1. When possible, the process sketch should be set up so that its attitude matches that of the blueprint machining configuration. (This presumes that the strip layout sketches were also set up that way—although this is not mandatory.)
2. The sketch does not have to be to scale, but it should have the same general configuration as the blueprint. As a matter of fact, there will be many occasions when the sketch will be exaggerated to more clearly depict features that would be jammed together if drawn to scale. As a rule, the part sketch should resemble the blueprint enough to avoid confusion as to its identification with the print.
3. The part sketch should be laid out on the basis of mean blueprint length dimensions, even if the blueprint dimensions are not displayed in the equal bilateral tolerance system. The result of laying the sketch out on the basis of mean dimensions is that all planes will be in the correct left-to-right relationship to one another. If not done this way, for certain conditions of design in which planes of different features are close together, faulty plane relationships (reversed left-to-right or vice-versa) can

lead to faulty numerical relationships in the tolerance chart.
4. If two features are in line with one another on the basis of mean dimensions, one should be offset from the other, leaving 3/16" to 1/4" between the features.
5. As with the Fig. 8-6 sketch, since the workpiece is cylindrical, it is not necessary to draw the full Fig. 8-5, *a*, configuration; the half below the centerline is an adequate representation.
6. If diameters are to be machined, the balloons should be set up, as shown in Fig. 8-6, to display the successive diameter size changes.
7. If a forging or casting is used, it is helpful to show, by dashed lines, the forged/cast outline superimposed on the machining configuration.

Machine To Column

Under the column heading *Machine To* in Fig. 8-6, a column for *mean sizes* and a column for *tolerances* are presented. Since the development of *mean sizes* is the easiest part of tolerance charting it is explained later. The discussion now centers on the ± *Tol.* column.

All tolerances in the tolerance chart must be expressed in the equal bilateral system. When two or more dimensions are added or subtracted, the tolerances are always added (see Fig. 8-4). This simplifies the arithmetic. In the event that a blueprint dimension tolerance is expressed by any other system, it must be converted to the equal bilateral system before it is entered in the chart under the *Blueprint* column.

No matter how the tolerances are displayed, the following steps can be performed to convert them to the equal bilateral system:

1. If it is not given, compute the maximum dimension.
2. If it is not given, compute the minimum dimension.
3. Then compute the equal bilateral mean dimension

$$MEAN = (MAX + MIN) \div 2.$$

4. Finally compute the equal bilateral tolerance

$$\pm TOL. = (MAX - MIN) \div 2.$$

Example (inches):

Given: 0.105 + 0.010/-0.004

$$MAX = 0.105 + 0.010 = 0.115$$
$$MIN = 0.105 - 0.004 = 0.101$$
$$MEAN = (0.115 + 0.101) \div 2 = 0.108$$
$$\pm TOL. = (0.115 - 0.101) \div 2 = 0.007$$
$$MEAN \pm TOL. = 0.108 \pm 0.007$$

The magnitude of the tolerances that are inserted in the *Machine To* column under ± *Tol.* must be considered very carefully in relation to the process capabilities of the operation. Figure 8-8 defines the relationship between production tolerances and the process capability values which are expressed in terms of ±3 σ. This relationship should be maintained when assigning the *Machine To* tolerances.

TOLERANCE CHART DEVELOPMENT

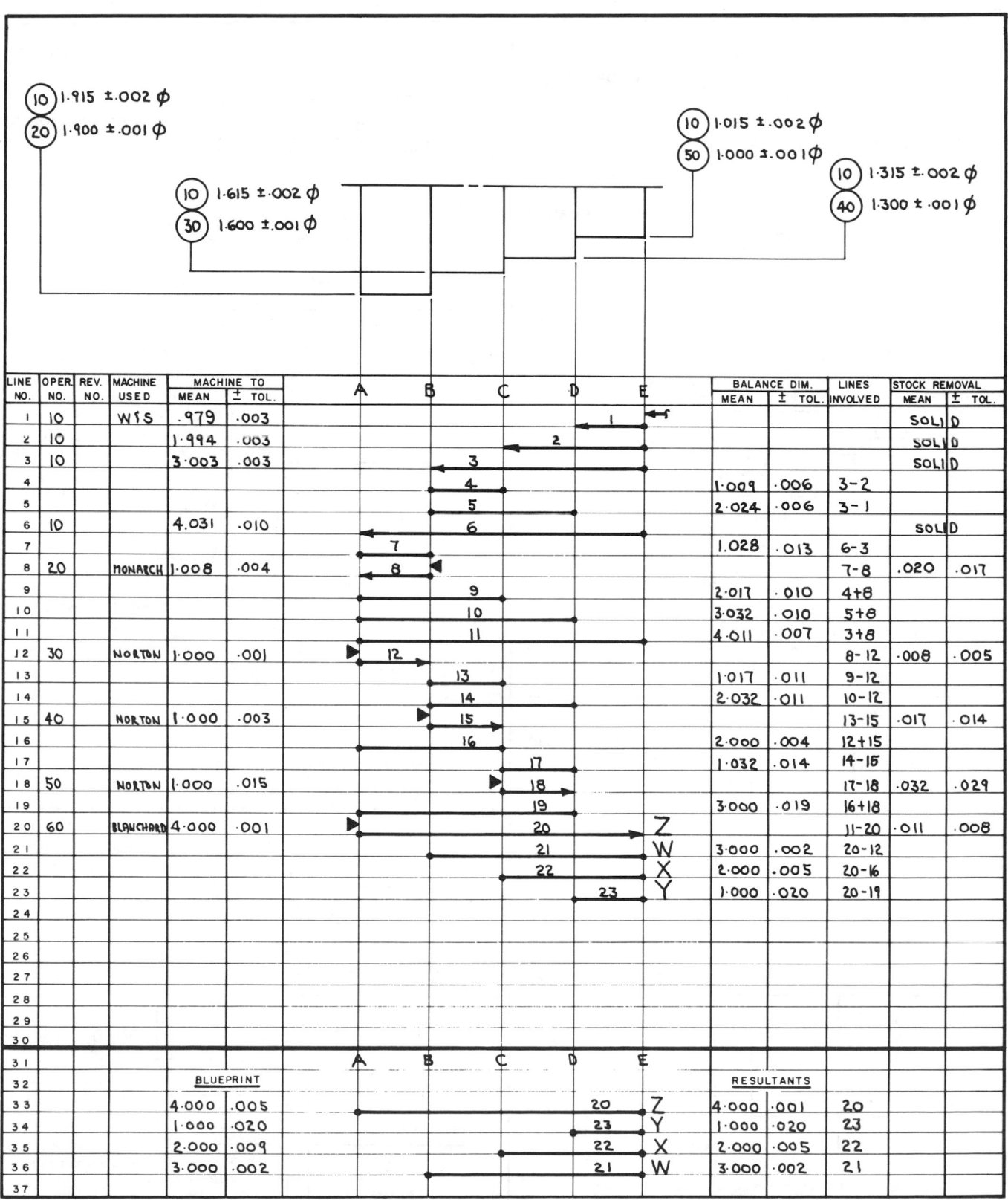

Fig. 8-6 Sample tolerance chart developed from *blueprint dimensions* and *tolerances* given in Fig. 8-5, *a*, and production sequence given in strip layout Fig. 8-5, b.

TOLERANCE CHART DEVELOPMENT

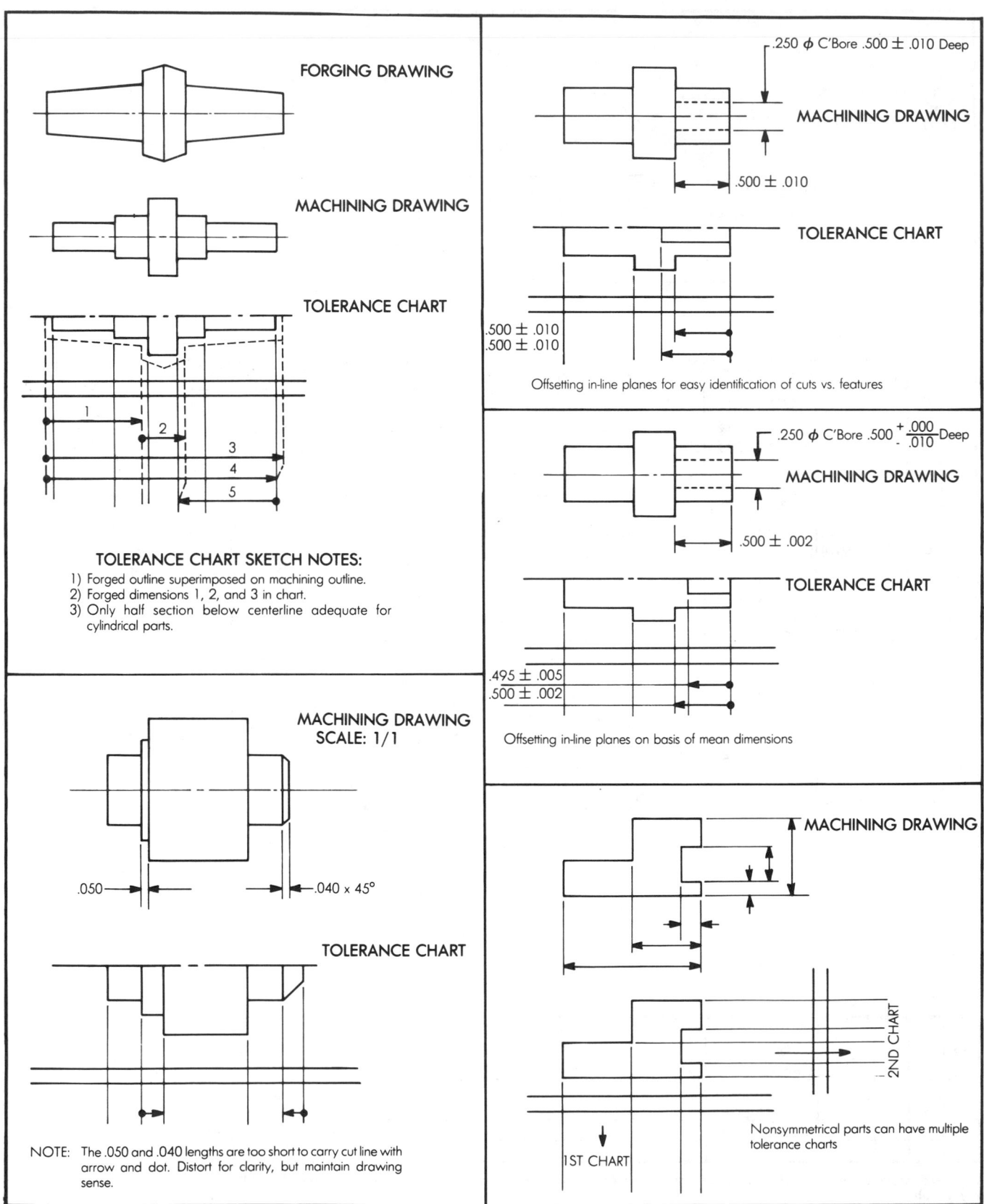

FORGING DRAWING

MACHINING DRAWING

TOLERANCE CHART

TOLERANCE CHART SKETCH NOTES:
1) Forged outline superimposed on machining outline.
2) Forged dimensions 1, 2, and 3 in chart.
3) Only half section below centerline adequate for cylindrical parts.

MACHINING DRAWING
SCALE: 1/1

.050   .040 x 45°

TOLERANCE CHART

NOTE: The .050 and .040 lengths are too short to carry cut line with arrow and dot. Distort for clarity, but maintain drawing sense.

.250 φ C'Bore .500 ± .010 Deep

MACHINING DRAWING

.500 ± .010

TOLERANCE CHART

.500 ± .010
.500 ± .010

Offsetting in-line planes for easy identification of cuts vs. features

.250 φ C'Bore .500 $^{+\ .000}_{-\ .010}$ Deep

MACHINING DRAWING

.500 ± .002

TOLERANCE CHART

.495 ± .005
.500 ± .002

Offsetting in-line planes on basis of mean dimensions

MACHINING DRAWING

2ND CHART

1ST CHART

Nonsymmetrical parts can have multiple tolerance charts

Fig. 8-7 Workpiece sketches for tolerance charts.

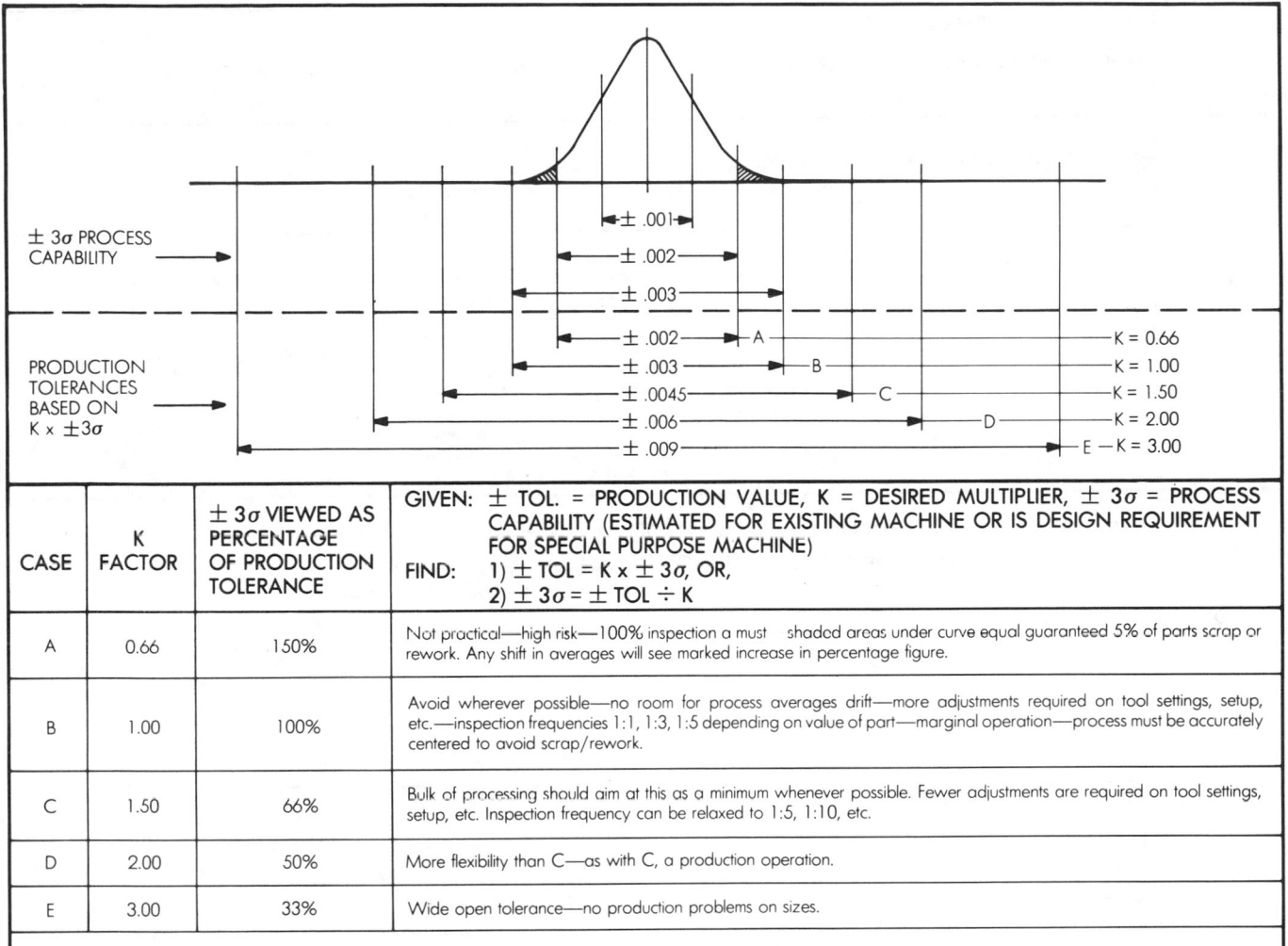

CASE	K FACTOR	± 3σ VIEWED AS PERCENTAGE OF PRODUCTION TOLERANCE	GIVEN: ± TOL. = PRODUCTION VALUE, K = DESIRED MULTIPLIER, ± 3σ = PROCESS CAPABILITY (ESTIMATED FOR EXISTING MACHINE OR IS DESIGN REQUIREMENT FOR SPECIAL PURPOSE MACHINE) FIND: 1) ± TOL = K x ± 3σ, OR, 2) ± 3σ = ± TOL ÷ K
A	0.66	150%	Not practical—high risk—100% inspection a must shaded areas under curve equal guaranteed 5% of parts scrap or rework. Any shift in averages will see marked increase in percentage figure.
B	1.00	100%	Avoid wherever possible—no room for process averages drift—more adjustments required on tool settings, setup, etc.—inspection frequencies 1:1, 1:3, 1:5 depending on value of part—marginal operation—process must be accurately centered to avoid scrap/rework.
C	1.50	66%	Bulk of processing should aim at this as a minimum whenever possible. Fewer adjustments are required on tool settings, setup, etc. Inspection frequency can be relaxed to 1:5, 1:10, etc.
D	2.00	50%	More flexibility than C—as with C, a production operation.
E	3.00	33%	Wide open tolerance—no production problems on sizes.

The above considerations play a role in tolerance charting in that tolerances assigned to cuts must be attainable in production. For example, assume a ± .004 tolerance is assigned in the chart to a cut and it is desired that a K = 2 factor prevail. To determine how capable the machine selected must be, or if a transfer line is being designed, what ± 3σ limits (process capability) the machine must be built for, .004 ÷ 2 = .002 = ± 3σ and process capability tests should produce this ± .002 value if presence of K = 2 factor is to be verified.

This does not mean that production will be held to ± .002. Only the machine selected or the custom-built transfer line station must demonstrate the ± .002 capability if the K = 2 factor (or 50%) is to be made available to the shop. Production will work to ± .004.

If tolerances dictated by the tolerance chart place undue burden on machine selection or special purpose machine design (i.e., transfer lines), relief may come from:
    1) Opening up product tolerances.
    2) Changing process (locating surfaces, operation sequence, etc.).
    3) Statistical tolerancing.
    4) Accepting a K = 1, .9, .8, etc., knowing there will be scrap/rework fallout.

Fig. 8-8 Production tolerances vs. ± 3 σ process capabilities.

Symbols Used in Tolerance Charting

The symbols used in tolerance charting are defined in Fig. 8-9 and do not require amplification here. Figure 8-9 should be referenced for all definitions and explanations.

Balance Dimension Column

Figure 8-9 defines a balance dimension and explains the reasons it is needed. Furthermore, Fig. 8-9 explains that a balance dimension results from subtracting or adding two machine cuts or a balance dimension and a machine cut. The line numbers of the two elements composing each balance dimension are recorded in the *Lines Involved* column.

Figure 8-10 presents a step-by-step technique on the derivation of balance dimensions using schematics. Mastery of the technique laid out in Fig. 8-10 is absolutely vital if correct tolerance charts are to be constructed.

TOLERANCE CHART DEVELOPMENT

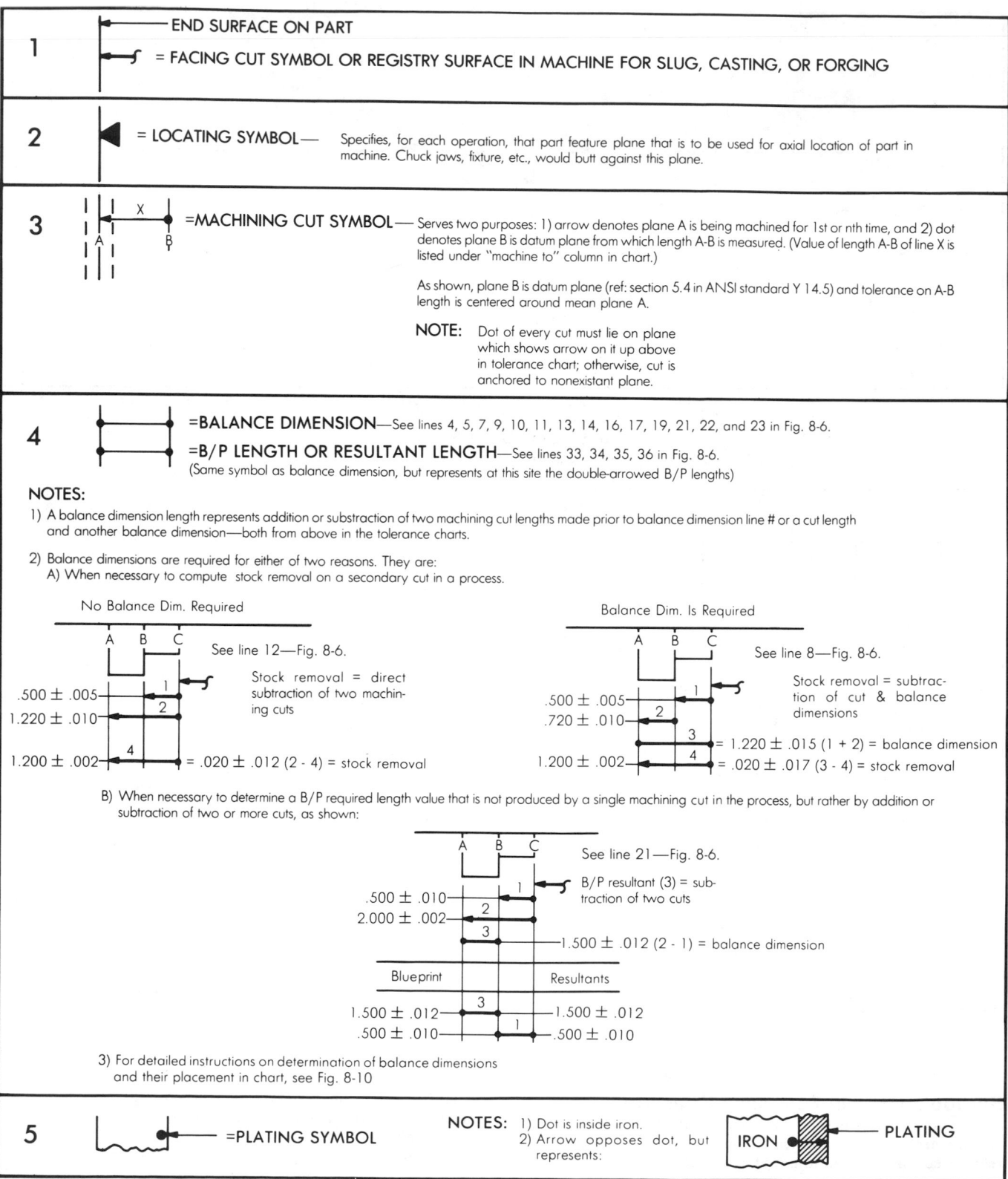

1 = FACING CUT SYMBOL OR REGISTRY SURFACE IN MACHINE FOR SLUG, CASTING, OR FORGING

END SURFACE ON PART

2 = LOCATING SYMBOL— Specifies, for each operation, that part feature plane that is to be used for axial location of part in machine. Chuck jaws, fixture, etc., would butt against this plane.

3 X A B =MACHINING CUT SYMBOL— Serves two purposes: 1) arrow denotes plane A is being machined for 1st or nth time, and 2) dot denotes plane B is datum plane from which length A-B is measured. (Value of length A-B of line X is listed under "machine to" column in chart.)

As shown, plane B is datum plane (ref: section 5.4 in ANSI standard Y 14.5) and tolerance on A-B length is centered around mean plane A.

NOTE: Dot of every cut must lie on plane which shows arrow on it up above in tolerance chart; otherwise, cut is anchored to nonexistant plane.

4 =BALANCE DIMENSION—See lines 4, 5, 7, 9, 10, 11, 13, 14, 16, 17, 19, 21, 22, and 23 in Fig. 8-6.

=B/P LENGTH OR RESULTANT LENGTH—See lines 33, 34, 35, 36 in Fig. 8-6.
(Same symbol as balance dimension, but represents at this site the double-arrowed B/P lengths)

NOTES:

1) A balance dimension length represents addition or substraction of two machining cut lengths made prior to balance dimension line # or a cut length and another balance dimension—both from above in the tolerance charts.

2) Balance dimensions are required for either of two reasons. They are:
A) When necessary to compute stock removal on a secondary cut in a process.

No Balance Dim. Required

A B C   See line 12—Fig. 8-6.

.500 ± .005   Stock removal = direct subtraction of two machining cuts
1.220 ± .010
1.200 ± .002 = .020 ± .012 (2 - 4) = stock removal

Balance Dim. Is Required

A B C   See line 8—Fig. 8-6.

.500 ± .005   Stock removal = subtraction of cut & balance dimensions
.720 ± .010
= 1.220 ± .015 (1 + 2) = balance dimension
1.200 ± .002 = .020 ± .017 (3 - 4) = stock removal

B) When necessary to determine a B/P required length value that is not produced by a single machining cut in the process, but rather by addition or subtraction of two or more cuts, as shown:

A B C   See line 21—Fig. 8-6.

.500 ± .010   B/P resultant (3) = subtraction of two cuts
2.000 ± .002
= 1.500 ± .012 (2 - 1) = balance dimension

Blueprint		Resultants
1.500 ± .012	3	1.500 ± .012
.500 ± .010	1	.500 ± .010

3) For detailed instructions on determination of balance dimensions and their placement in chart, see Fig. 8-10

5 =PLATING SYMBOL   NOTES: 1) Dot is inside iron.
2) Arrow opposes dot, but represents: IRON   PLATING

Fig. 8-9 Symbols used in tolerance charting (reference Figs. 8-6 and 8-10).

TOLERANCE CHART DEVELOPMENT

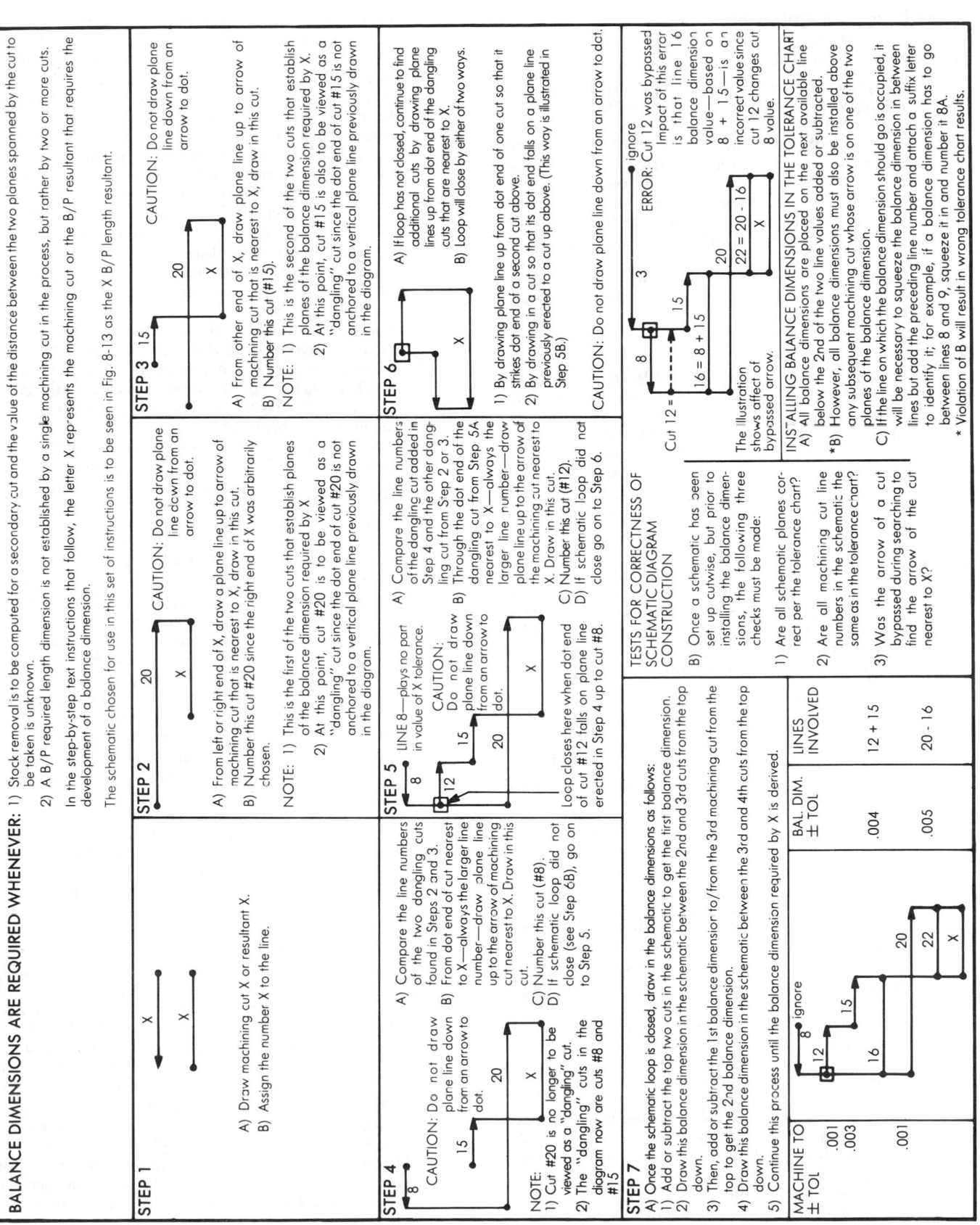

Fig. 8-10 Derivation of *balance dimensions* using schematics.

TOLERANCE CHART DEVELOPMENT

Lines Involved Column

The following comments are made relative to the entries in the *Lines Involved* column (see Fig. 8-6):

1. On any line, only two line numbers are listed, indicating that only two line-numbered values are being added or subtracted at one time.
2. The line-numbered values may be either two listed *Machine To* values (*Means + Tolerances*) or a single *Machine To* value and a single *Balance Dimension* value—but never two *Balance Dimension* values.
3. These two numbers permit immediate tracing of any dimensional relationship without having to reinvent the analysis of the line relationship. The value of this is evident after the process has been released. These numbers (the *Lines Involved* numbers) can be used to track discrepant dimensions in a process.

Stock Removal Column

The *Stock Removal* column consists of a *Mean* column and a ± *Tol.* column. Each stock removal is calculated by subtracting two *machining cuts* or a *balance dimension* and a *machining cut*. Like the balance dimension, the line numbers of the two elements composing each stock removal are recorded in the *Lines Involved* column. To understand the *Stock Removal* column entries, and the considerations involved, see Fig. 8-11, in which two different methods for controlling stock removals are defined.

MECHANICS OF CHART CONSTRUCTION

The components of the tolerance chart have been dissected and analyzed in detail concerning form and function. Now these components are combined to construct Fig. 8-6 from scratch.

Six distinct steps are involved. They are shown, in chronological order of construction, starting with Fig. 8-12 and ending with Fig. 8-17.

Tolerance Chart Construction—Step 1

Figure 8-12 summarizes and displays, within the framework of the tolerance chart format, all information from Fig. 8-5, *a*, and Fig. 8-5, *b*, that is required to construct the Fig. 8-6 chart. The specifics of this information are:

1. The machining configuration from Fig. 8-5, *a*, blueprint is drawn at the top of the form in the space provided between the borders of the *Machine To* and *Balance Dimension* columns. It does not extend beyond them.
2. Feature plane lines are drawn to the bottom of the form only for those features whose length dimensions will be included in the chart.
3. Machining cut lines are installed as shown in Fig. 8-5, *b*. The facing cut symbol must be used—even on castings or forgings.
4. Cut lines are numbered. These line numbers match those of preprinted line numbers on the chart form.
5. Operation numbers are added.
6. The machine to be used in each operation is listed.
7. All solid cuts are labeled *Solid* to indicate that each of these cuts are the first cuts (as shown by an arrow) to be shown on these planes. *Solid* is written in the *Stock Removal* column, and, in effect, shows that no problem exists concerning stock removal since these cuts are the initial or primary cuts on the plane, not the secondary cuts. Caution: The datum dot of any *Solid* cut must be

anchored to an existing plane at that point in the process. The datum dot plane of a *Solid* cut exists if the arrow of a previously made cut is found on the plane in question above the *Solid* cut.

8. Normally, the location symbols would be added just before the first cut in each operation or between the last cut in an operation and the first cut in the next operation, as shown in Fig. 8-6, but they are omitted here for convenience. The location symbols in the chart must match those shown in the strip layout of Fig. 8-5, *b*.
9. If the part is cylindrical, balloons are drawn off the diameters in the sketch, as shown in Fig. 8-6, to record the diameter sizes established in each operation. They too are omitted here for convenience since they play no role in the tolerance calculations for the cuts shown below in the chart.
10. Space is provided after the last cut line for the possible inclusion of *blueprint balance dimensions*, and a heavy black line is drawn across the chart.
11. The headings *Blueprint* and *Resultants* are printed, as shown in Fig. 8-12, in line with the *Machine To* and *Balance Dimension* columns.
12. Under *Blueprint* are listed the mean sizes of the length dimensions that are to be handled in the chart. This list must not include reference, duplicate, or double dimensions. Violation of this rule is a major source of charting problems. To ensure that this condition is satisfied, the listed *blueprint dimensions* should be checked using the following procedures:

    Step 1. Consecutively number/letter the feature planes passing through each *blueprint dimension* dot (Reference Fig. 8-6). Note: If a feature plane line passes through the *blueprint dimension* area, but does not intersect the dot end of a *blueprint dimension*, do not assign a number/letter to that plane.

    Step 2. Make a list of step 1 plane numbers/letters.

    Step 3. Taking each *blueprint dimension* in turn, strike its two plane numbers from the step 2 list.

    Step 4. When all plane numbers/letters are crossed off the step 2 list, all remaining *blueprint dimensions* are reference, duplicate, or double dimensions. Delete these dimensions.

    Step 5. Count the number N of *blueprint dimensions* remaining after the step 4 deletions. These are the *blueprint dimensions* to be handled in the chart.

    Step 6. Count the number of numbered/lettered planes on the step 2 list. This number must equal $N + 1$ planes—if not, recheck steps 1 through 6 for errors.

    Step 7. Finally, verify that each of these $N + 1$ planes (same as step 2 list) has a machining cut arrow on it. If an arrow is not found on a plane, the *blueprint dimension(s)* to that plane cannot be produced. To find the arrow, (a) review the strip layout sketches to locate the missing cut and add it to the chart or (b) add a cut on that plane in an appropriate strip layout sketch, then add it to the tolerance chart. Otherwise, delete the *blueprint dimension(s)* to that plane.

13. Under *Blueprint* are listed the maximum *blueprint tolerances*. Now and then, it might be advantageous to tighten this tolerance for machining or tooling or for assembly reasons, but normally, the maximum tolerance should be used to conform to the goals of economic production.

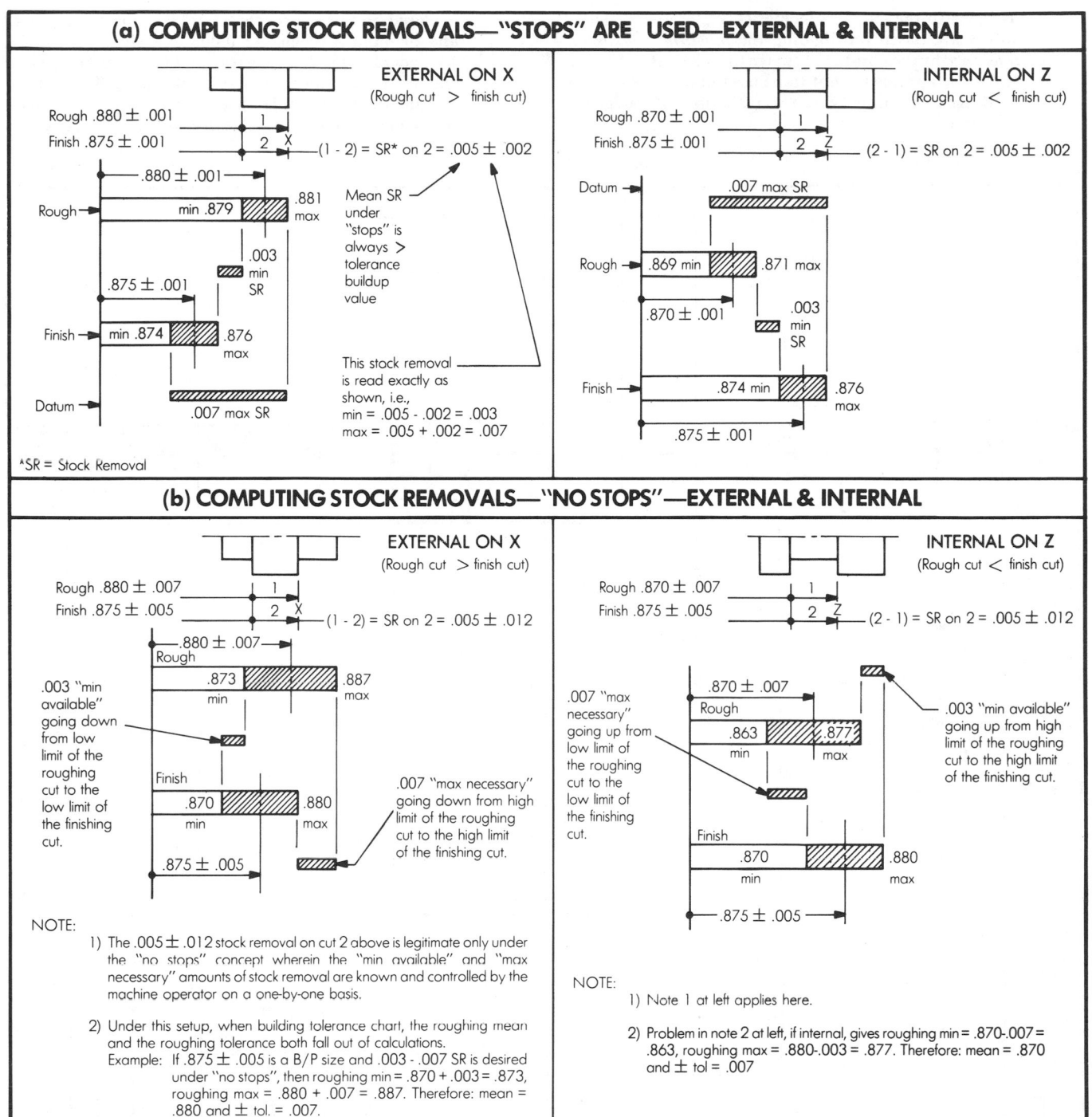

Fig. 8-11 (a) Computing stock removals—"Stops" are used—External and Internal. (b) Computing stock removals—"No Stops" are used—External and Internal.

14. The blueprint length lines are drawn, using the *balance dimension* symbol.

Tolerance Chart Construction—Step 2

Figure 8-13 shows construction of all schematics necessary to determine required *balance dimensions*.

In addition, *blueprint tolerances* are budgeted among the blueprint resultant schematic cuts and then are optimized to ensure maximum economics.

Optimizing of *blueprint resultant tolerances* takes place in the following three stages:

1. In Fig. 8-13 the column titled *Initial Tolerances—Stand Alone Schematic Basis—Ref.* shows the initial tolerances

TOLERANCE CHART DEVELOPMENT

assigned to the cuts in schematics W, X, and Y. These values are based on dividing the *blueprint maximum tolerance* by the number of cuts in the schematic. This is a simplistic approach—not to be used in practice—and is used here to simplify the explanation of budgeting tolerances.

Based on this approach, 0.001″ is assigned to cuts 12 and 20 in the W schematic, 0.003″ is assigned to cuts 12, 15, and 20 in the X schematic, and 0.005″ is assigned to cuts 12, 15, 18, and 20 in the Y schematic. The result is that the total of cut tolerances in each schematic equals the blueprint maximum value in schematics W, X, and Y.

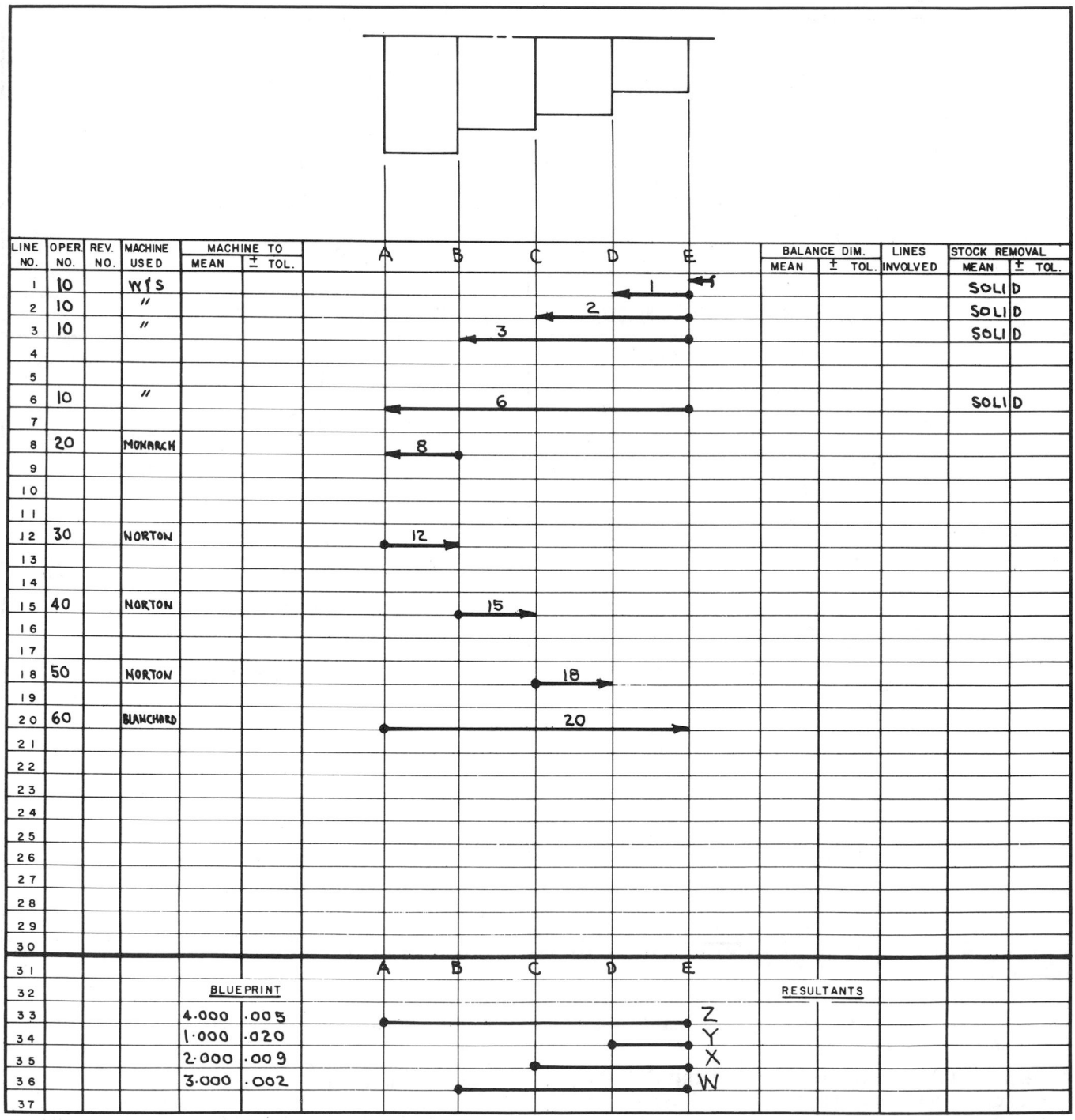

Fig. 8-12 Constructing a tolerance chart—Step 1. Setup of blueprint and strip layout data from Figs. 8-5, *a*, and 8-5, *b*, in tolerance chart framework.

TOLERANCE CHART DEVELOPMENT

BLUEPRINT RESULTANT SCHEMATICS				STOCK REMOVAL SCHEMATICS		
Initial tolerances—stand-alone schematic basis—ref.	Adjusted tolerances due to common cuts, etc.—ref.	Optimized tolerances—use these tolerances in chart				
.001 .001 .002 B/P max	.001 .001 .002 No changes	.001 .001 .002 = B/P max	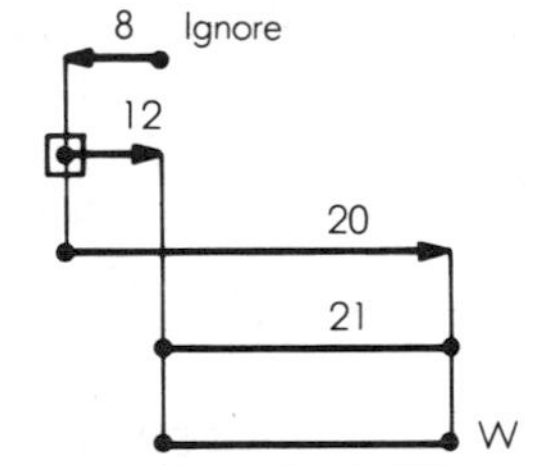	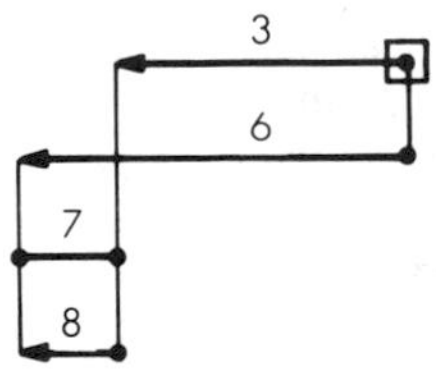 CUT 8	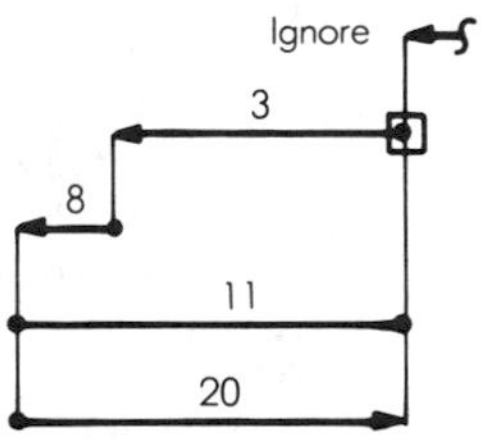 CUT 20	
.003 .003 .003 .009 B/P max	.001 .003 .001 .005 Max possible < B/P max	.001 .003 .001 .005 < B/P max	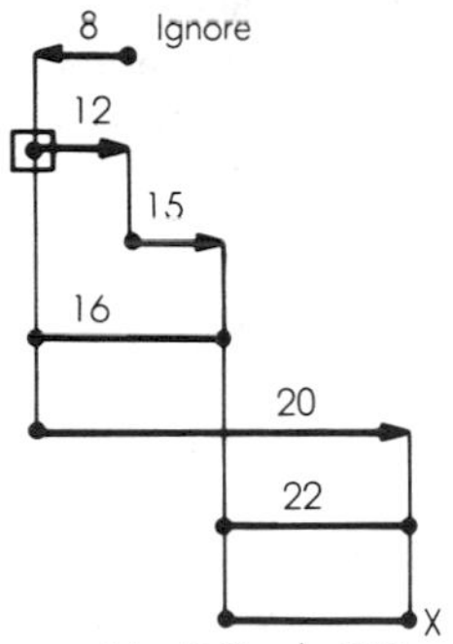	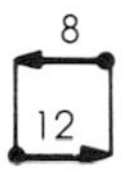 As with the Z schematic, no schematic is needed for cut 12 since direct subtraction between 8-12 yields the tolerance buildup value on 12. CUT 12		
.005 .005 .005 .005 .020 B/P max	.001 .003 .005 .001 .010 Max possible < B/P max	.001 .003 .015 .001 .020 = B/P max		CUT 15		
			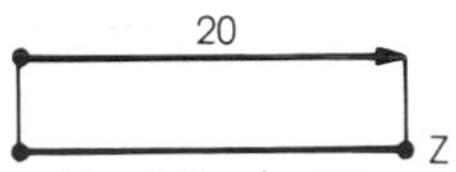 NOTE: Since cut 20 is a direct B/P cut, schematic for Z = a rectangle—and is not needed. Value for 20 tolerance in chart is set in W.	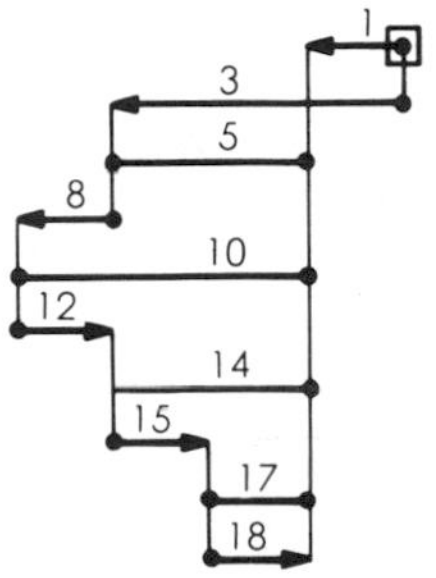 CUT 18		

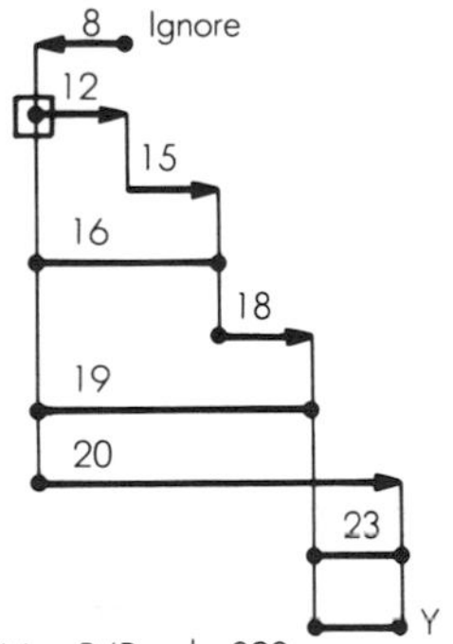

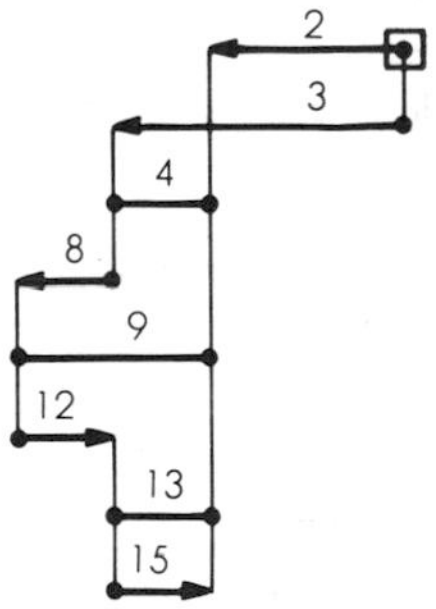

Fig. 8-13 Constructing a tolerance chart—Step 2. Construct schematics and optimize blueprint resultant cut tolerances.

TOLERANCE CHART DEVELOPMENT

2. Note that cut 12 is common to W, X, and Y, cut 15 is common to X and Y, and cut 20 is common to W, X, and Y. Let us consider now the significance of cut 12 being common to W, X, and Y. Cut 12, having been assigned 0.001″ in W, 0.003″ in X, and 0.005″ in Y, cannot, in the tolerance chart, use but one of these three values. Which one will be selected for use? Obviously, the tightest tolerance of 0.001″ must prevail over the 0.003″ and 0.005″ values or schematic W would be violated if 0.003″ or 0.005″ were assigned to 12.

Based on this reasoning, tolerances in the second column titled *Adjusted Tolerances Due to Common Cuts, Etc.—Ref.* are changed as follows: 0.001″ still stands on cuts 12 and 20 in W, but in X, 12 is reduced to 0.001″ from 0.003″, 15 stands at 0.003″, and 20 is reduced to 0.001″ from 0.003″. In Y, the same changes are made as in X plus cut 15 is reduced to 0.003″ since 15 is set at 0.003″ in X.

The result of these tolerance reductions is that the sum of tolerances in X is equal to 0.005″—or 0.004″ less than the blueprint maximum of 0.009″, and in Y, the sum of tolerances is equal to 0.010″—or 0.010″ less than blueprint maximum of 0.020″. Do we want to live with these losses of *blueprint tolerance*?

3. The third column is titled *Optimized Tolerances—Use These Tolerances in Chart.* How are the tolerances optimized? Note that cut 18 in Y is not common, it is not a direct blueprint cut subject to a specific maximum tolerance by blueprint, etc. It is free to be assigned any value; so, since 0.010″ tolerance has been lost in this schematic, 0.010″ is added to 0.005″ (cut 18), resulting in a tolerance of 0.015″ on cut 18, and the sum of the tolerances on Y cuts now equals 0.020″—the schematic cuts are optimized in Y.

The same could be done in X schematic, but is not presented here to illustrate how easy it is to build a chart that does not use all possible tolerance allowed by print.

How might X be optimized also? Simply, if 15 were made 0.007″ in X, the sum of tolerances in X would equal the blueprint maximum of 0.009″, but then 15 in Y would go up to 0.007″ and 18 in Y would go down to 0.011″, while still holding the sum of tolerances in Y to 0.020″, which equals blueprint.

As pointed out earlier, this is a simplistic approach that does not consider differing process capabilities of the cuts performed on different machines. The realities of actual shop conditions are better served if either of the following two methods (which are essentially equal in philosophy) is used to generate the initial startup tolerances in the first column:

Method 1: The *blueprint maximum tolerances* should be proportionately budgeted among the schematic cuts in terms of the estimated process capabilities on the cuts. For example, in schematic X, 12 is a rough milling operation, 15 is a finish milling operation, and 20 is a grinding operation. They have differing process capabilities as shown in Table 8-1. As illustrated in Table 8-1, this "fair-sharing" method conforms to shop realities.

Method 2: If company standards exist in tabulated form covering the minimum tolerance to assign to machining cuts when processing, then headings in Table 8-1 of the first method would change to *Minimum Cut Tolerances, Computed Tolerances on Cuts,* and *Schematics* and the same apportioning scheme would be used.

The difference between the two methods is a time savings advantage for the second method—and probably a higher degree of uniformity exists for a body of engineers—since no individual cut-by-cut evaluations would have to be made by each engineer.

Obviously, for the second method to be reliable, maintenance of tabulated process capability data would

TABLE 8-1
Apportionment of Blueprint Maximum Tolerances

K x 3 SIGMA VALUES ON THE CUTS, IN.	COMPUTED TOLERANCES ON CUTS, IN.	SCHEMATICS
0.003″	0.0045″	
0.002″	0.0030″	
0.001″	0.0015″	
0.006″	0.0090″	

Maximum blueprint = ± 0.009″

NOTE:

Cut 12 tolerance = $\frac{.003}{.006} \times .009 = .0045″$

Cut 15 tolerance = $\frac{.002}{.006} \times .009 = .0030″$

Cut 20 tolerance = $\frac{.001}{.006} \times .009 = .0015″$

rely on support systems (machine maintenance, quality control, etc.) monitoring and correcting data on a periodic, controlled basis. Feedbacks from the shop and inspection become important if integrity of standard data is to be maintained.

Of all steps in tolerance chart construction, step 2 is the most critical—and determines in large part the cost picture for the process insofar as tolerances are responsible.

At this time in tolerance chart construction, it can be recognized that the process/tooling decisions around which the schematics are built can, in themselves, be responsible for excessively tight tolerances. At this time, optional changes can be made in sequence, dimensioning patterns, or location surfaces to optimize the indiviual tolerances assigned.

Tolerance Chart Construction—Step 3

Figure 8-14 transfers to the tolerance chart the Fig. 8-13 results:

1. Cut tolerances.
2. *Balance Dimension* lines and numbers.
3. *Lines Involved* factors for all secondary cuts and *balance dimensions*.
4. Mean blueprint values and their tolerances under the *Machine To, Balance Dimension,* and *Resultant* columns.

With respect to the *Lines Involved* for stock removal on secondary cuts, it should be noted that a subtraction is always involved. If this is so, then the question arises: Which of the line lengths involved is physically (in the iron) longer (or larger numerically) than the other? For example, stock removal for cut 8 is equal to 7 minus 8. Why not 8 minus 7? The only way to determine this is to examine the end planes A/B of cut 8 above in the part sketch and ask the question: When cut 8 is taken, does the physical distance between A and B increase or decrease when stock is removed?

If cut 8 would cause a decrease in the A/B length—as it does in this chart—then length 7 must be longer than length 8 if stock is to come off due to the cut 8. Hence, lines involved for cut 8 should read: 7 minus 8.

If a mistake is made on this decision, chart dimensions above cut 8 will incorporate mean size errors based on two times the mean stock removal on cut 8. The chart will therefore be useless for production since parts, if not immediately scrapped by excessive stock coming off above cut 8, will have to be reworked on a salvage basis.

Tolerance Chart Construction—Step 4

Figure 8-15 assigns tolerances to remaining cuts in the process. These tolerances play no role in *blueprint resultant lengths,* but do have an impact on stock removal tolerance buildups. Therefore, one can be generous in these tolerance assignments in order to ensure trouble-free production—but not so generous as to cause excessively large tolerance buildups on subsequent secondary cuts.

Once all cuts have a working tolerance, all tolerance buildups should be computed in the *Balance Dimension* column, then—and only then—the tolerance buildups should be completed on stock removals.

This is the second place where it can be seen that excessively large tolerance buildups are due to the nature of the sequence, dimensioning patterns, or choice of location surfaces. (Actually,

in Fig. 8-13, schematics for cuts 15 and 18 show involvement of cuts 5 and 6 respectively—and that should be the point for alarm bells to go off.)

For example, cut 18 has a tolerance buildup ±0.029″. Why is it so big? First, examine cut 18 schematic. It has 6 cuts in it and cut 18 was assigned ±0.015″ to optimize a blueprint resultant. This suggests that cut 18 might be reduced to, say, ± 0.005″, thus eliminating ± 0.010″ of the ± 0.029″ on cut 18. Or, as shown in "Do's and Don'ts in Tolerance Charting" later in this chapter, it might be more economical to live with the ± 0.029″ stock removal tolerance by adding a qualifying operation prior to cut 18 to wipe out the tolerance buildup.

As explained once the schematics are available, the builder of the tolerance chart is in position to adjust tolerances freely to satisfy a host of desirable end conditions—and under this system (tolerance charting), the engineer stays in positive control of what is happening at all stages of manipulation and, thus, can make the best tradeoffs between conflicting factors.

Tolerance Chart Construction—Step 5

Figure 8-16 shows the setup of the *mean stock removals.* These values were obtained by merely adding a uniform 0.003″ value to each tolerance buildup in order to get the mean value for *stock removal.*

This approach of adding a uniform amount would also not be used in practice—but serves to simplify the discussion at this point.

Going back to cut 18 in Fig. 8-16, the maximum possible stock removal could be 0.032″ + 0.029″ = 0.061″—a most impractical value since shoulder grinding is being performed by cut 18.

Tolerance Chart Construction—Step 6

Figure 8-17 is the final step in chart construction and is the easiest step of all. No decision making is involved. Only straightforward calculations are required as shown at the top of Fig. 8-17. Having reached this point, no more thinking is required about tolerances; only *mean dimensions* are dealt with. The steps involved with these calculations are based on following these rules:

1. Whenever a mean *machining* cut size is known—in this case, line 20 is equal to the blueprint length 4.000″—use its mean stock removal (a nonsolid, secondary cut) to compute the value of its related *balance dimension* (as in this case) or its related roughing *machining* cut as shown by the *Lines Involved* column (see Fig. 8-17).

    A simple equation is set up that reads: SR 20 = 11 - 20, which is interpreted as: mean stock removal on cut 20 = mean length of line 11 - mean length of cut 20 (0.011″ = mean length line 11 - 4.000″; mean length line 11 = 4.011″). The mean length of line 11, 4.011″, is installed in the chart on line 11.

    Then, because in this chart at this stage, no more mean sizes are available in the *Machine To* column, the second rule by which mean sizes can be developed is used.

2. In following the second rule, take the bottom-most of the *blueprint balance dimensions*—in this case line 23—and set up another kind of simple equation that reads: 23 = 20 - 19, which is interpreted as: mean length of line 23 = mean length of line 20 - mean length of line 19 (1.000″ = 4.000″ -mean length of line 19). The mean length of line 19, 3.000″, is installed on line 19, and the same process is

TOLERANCE CHART DEVELOPMENT

employed for the next blueprint resultant line 22, etc., until finally, line 12, a *machining cut*, is developed for mean size. At this point, rule 1 is used to solve the machining cut 8 mean size. Note: In the box 9 calculation in Fig. 8-17, mean dimensions were not available for lines

14-15. The instruction "stop-go on-return" indicates that one of the subsequent box calculations will produce one of the two missing values and, once developed, the box 9 calculation can be completed. In the case shown, box 10 produced a value for line 15, and in box 11, the box 9

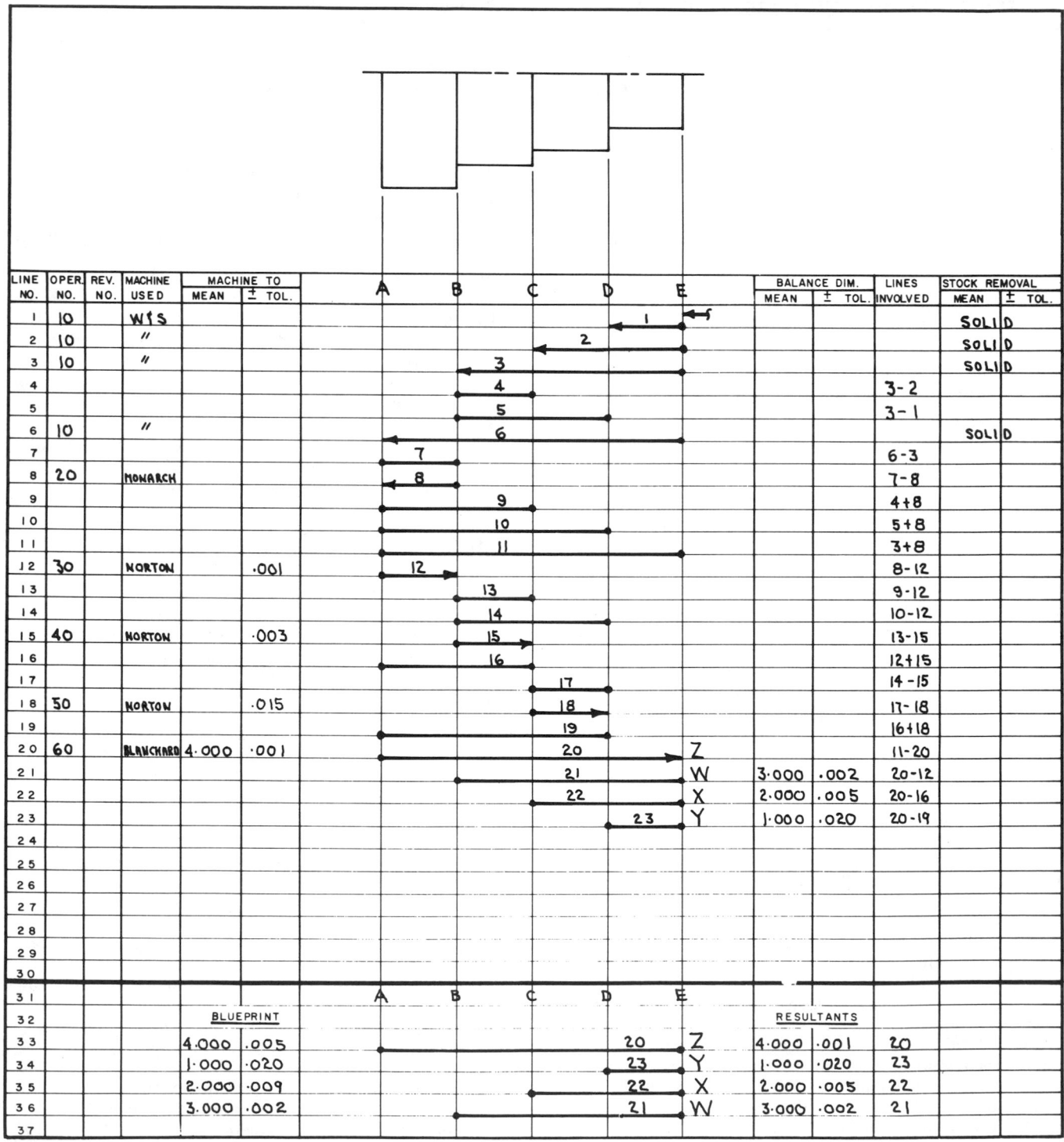

Fig. 8-14 Constructing a tolerance chart—Step 3. (a) Add cut tolerances developed in Step 2. (2) Add *balance dimension* lines. (3) Add *Lines Involved* data. (4) Add all *blueprint* mean values.

calculation is repeated to produce a mean dimension for line 14.

The process of developing the mean sizes is characterized by this alternating from known *machining cut* means to known *balance dimension* means and then back to the cuts until all the unknown mean sizes are developed.

The instructions on building the Fig. 8-6 tolerance chart, as presented heretofore, represent the basic process of tolerance charting. This basic process can be used to chart tolerances on about 75% of the dimensions and part configurations commonly

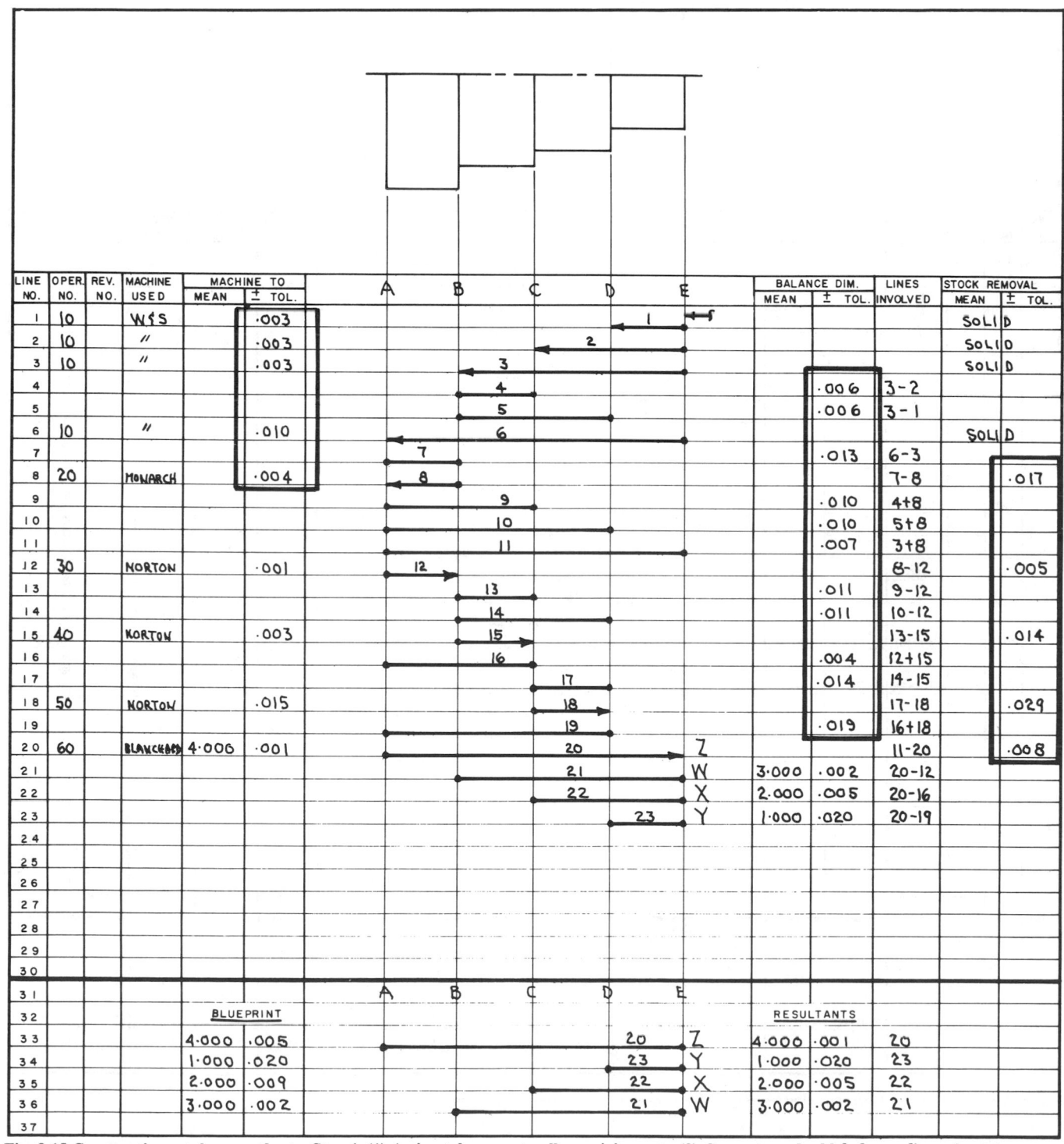

Fig. 8-15 Constructing a tolerance chart—Step 4. (1) Assign tolerances to all remaining cuts. (2) Compute and add *balance dimension* tolerance buildups. (3) Compute and add *stock removal* tolerance buildups.

TOLERANCE CHART DEVELOPMENT

found in industry.

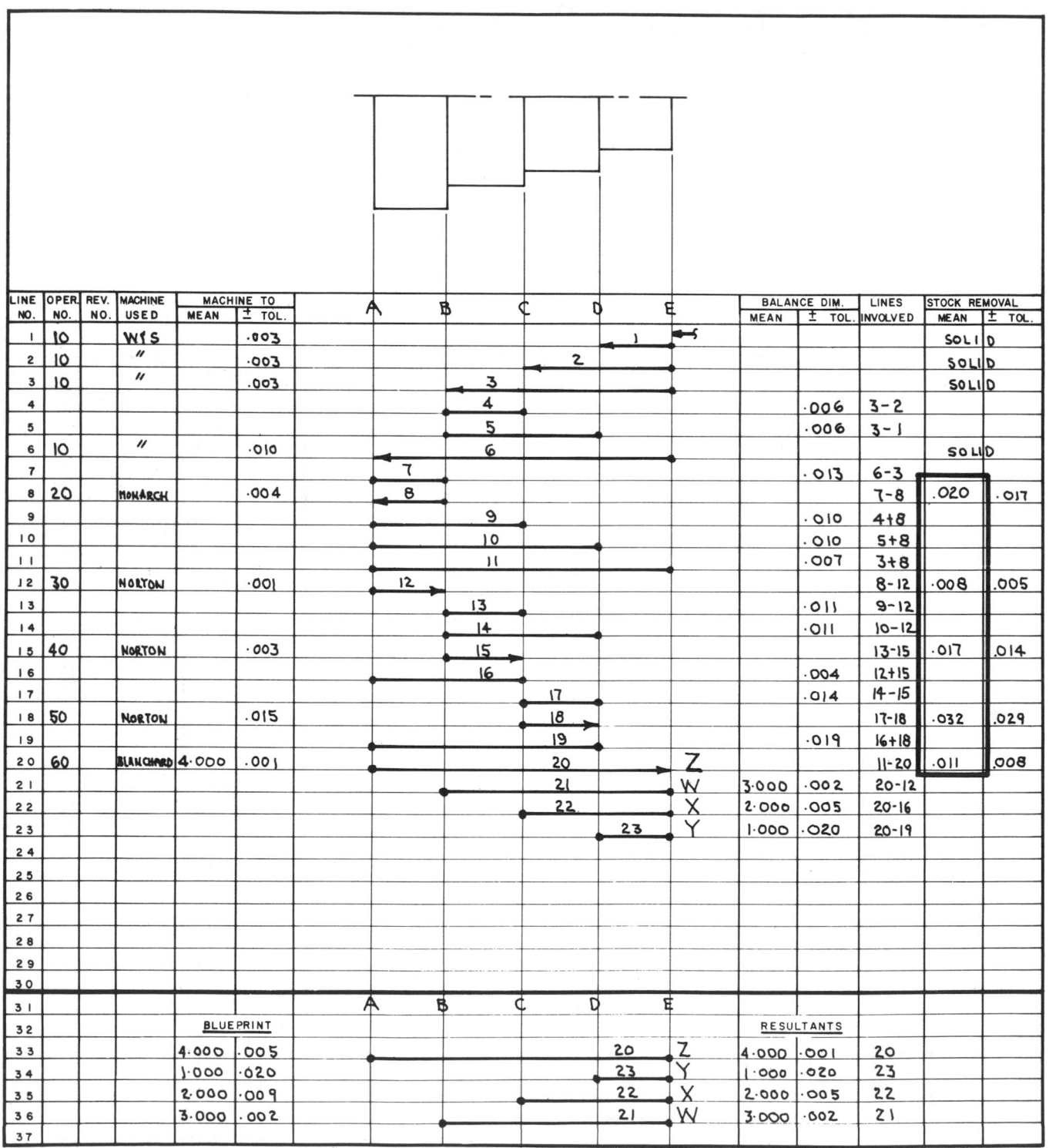

Fig. 8-16 Constructing a tolerance chart—Step 5. Determine and add mean *stock removal* values.

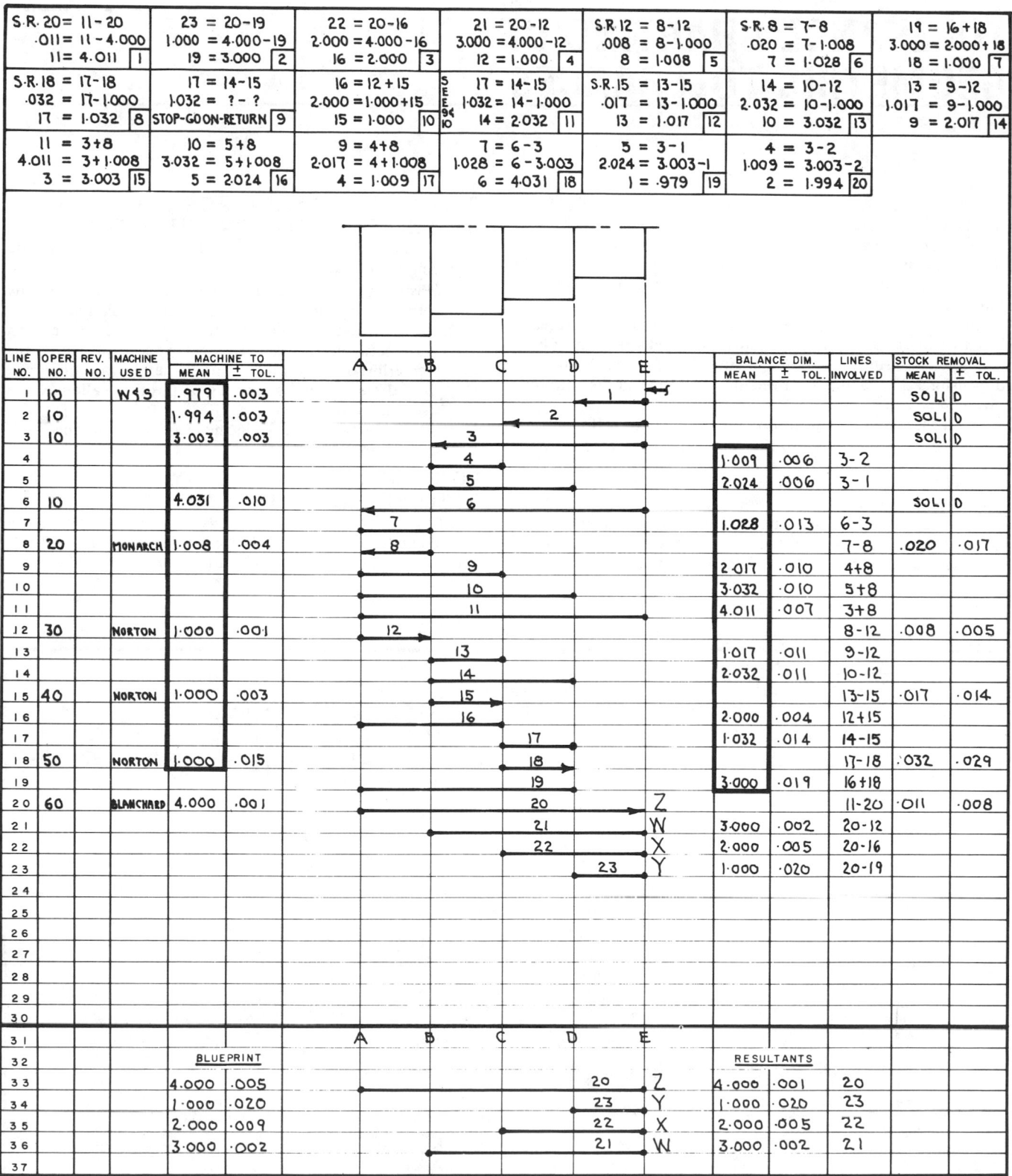

Fig. 8-17 Constructing a tolerance chart—Step 6. (1) Compute and add missing cut and *balance dimension* means. (2) Follow text instructions and model calculations shown above.

TOLERANCE CHARTING OF GEOMETRIC TOLERANCES

Four of the 14 geometric tolerances shown in Fig. 8-3 (items 6, 10, 11, and 12) are controlled in the tolerance chart. These four tolerances are: profile of a plane, position, concentricity, and symmetry. The remaining ten tolerances shown in Fig. 8-3 depend solely on the tooling, sequencing, and machine tool accuracies.

In order for these four geometric tolerances to be factored into the tolerance chart, the blueprint-defined values must be converted into equivalent, equal bilateral form coupled to basic dimensions. The required conversions are shown at the bottom of Fig. 8-3.

With respect to the position conversion note (#10) at the bottom on Fig. 8-3, the position conversion is based on an implied 45° condition so that the X tolerances equal the Y tolerances. In practice, however, the 45° setup may not be practical or desirable because of the nature of the tooling. Or, sequencing may require that a tighter tolerance be held on the X axis—or the Y axis—so that the radial tolerance value will be based on the equation $C^2 = X^2 + Y^2$ instead of the equation $C^2 = 2X^2$ or $C^2 = 2Y^2$.

PROFILE OF A PLANE, POSITION, SYMMETRY AND CONCENTRICITY

With respect to tolerance charting, note the following regarding these characteristics:

1. Profile of a plane. Treat in the tolerance chart like any other dimension with an equal bilateral tolerance.
2. Position and symmetry. Control in the tolerance chart a gap between the centerline of one feature and the centerline of the second feature so that the gap equals one half the converted symmetry or position callout value (see the following section).
3. Concentricity. Control in the chart in accordance with calculation values shown in Fig. 8-18, *a*.

POSITION AND SYMMETRY IN TOLERANCE CHARTING

Of the four characteristics, position and symmetry require special handling in the chart. For purposes of explaining these handling methods, an example of symmetry calculation is provided.

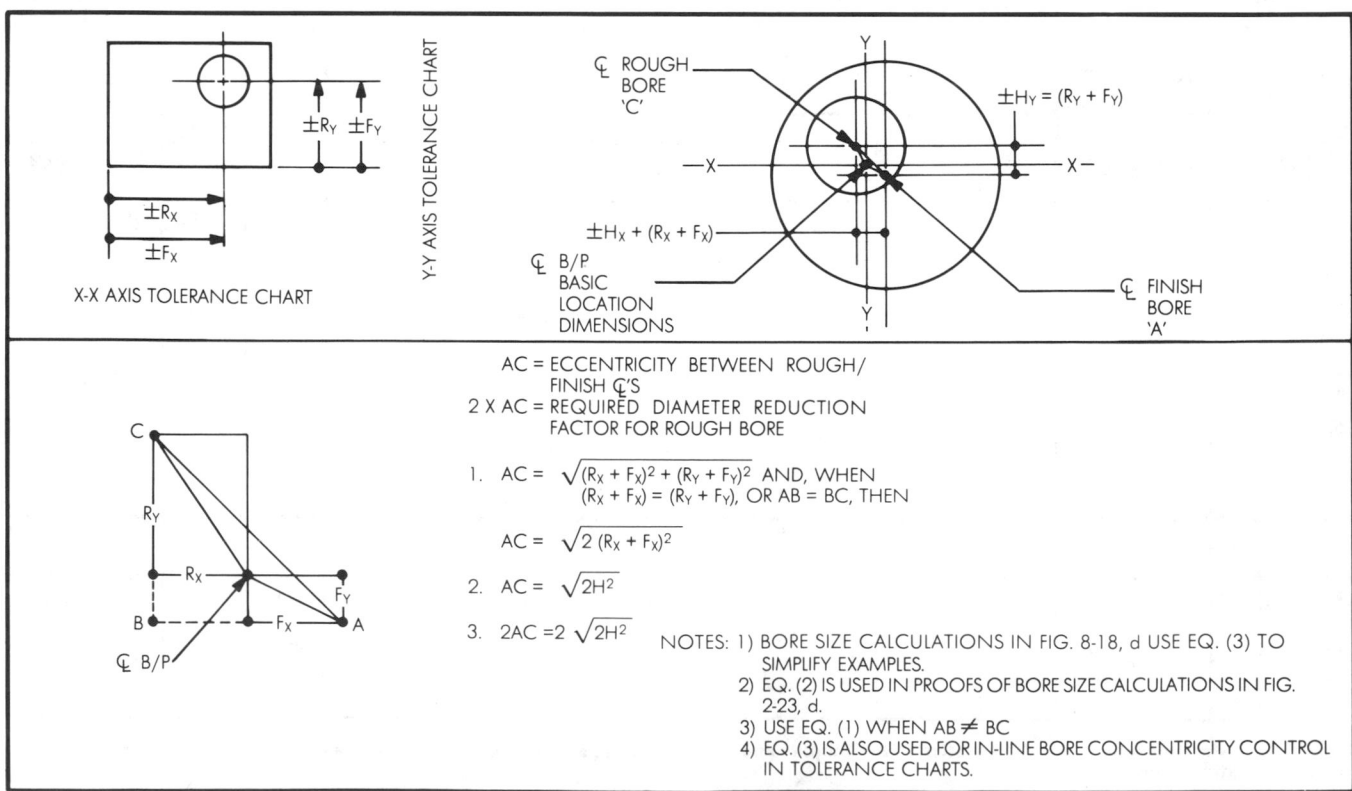

AC = ECCENTRICITY BETWEEN ROUGH/FINISH $\mathcal{C}$'S

$2 \times AC$ = REQUIRED DIAMETER REDUCTION FACTOR FOR ROUGH BORE

1. $AC = \sqrt{(R_X + F_X)^2 + (R_Y + F_Y)^2}$ AND, WHEN $(R_X + F_X) = (R_Y + F_Y)$, OR AB = BC, THEN

   $AC = \sqrt{2(R_X + F_X)^2}$

2. $AC = \sqrt{2H^2}$

3. $2AC = 2\sqrt{2H^2}$

NOTES: 1) BORE SIZE CALCULATIONS IN FIG. 8-18, d USE EQ. (3) TO SIMPLIFY EXAMPLES.
2) EQ. (2) IS USED IN PROOFS OF BORE SIZE CALCULATIONS IN FIG. 2-23, d.
3) USE EQ. (1) WHEN AB ≠ BC
4) EQ. (3) IS ALSO USED FOR IN-LINE BORE CONCENTRICITY CONTROL IN TOLERANCE CHARTS.

Fig. 8-18, *a* Concentricity control in the tolerance chart—calculation of axis eccentricities.

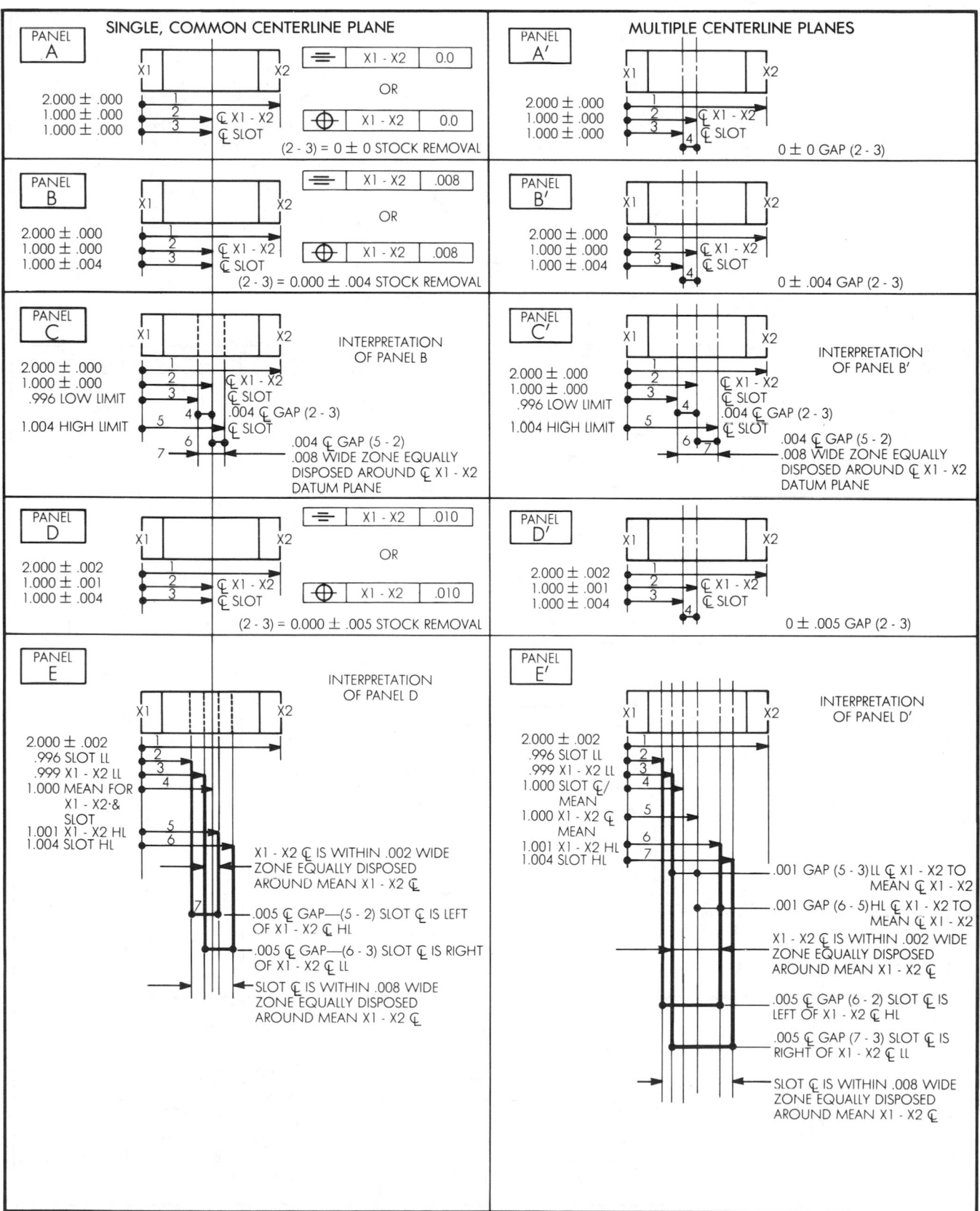

Fig. 8-18, *b* Two methods of symmetry control in the tolerance chart, LL = low limit; HL = high limit.

GEOMETRIC TOLERANCES

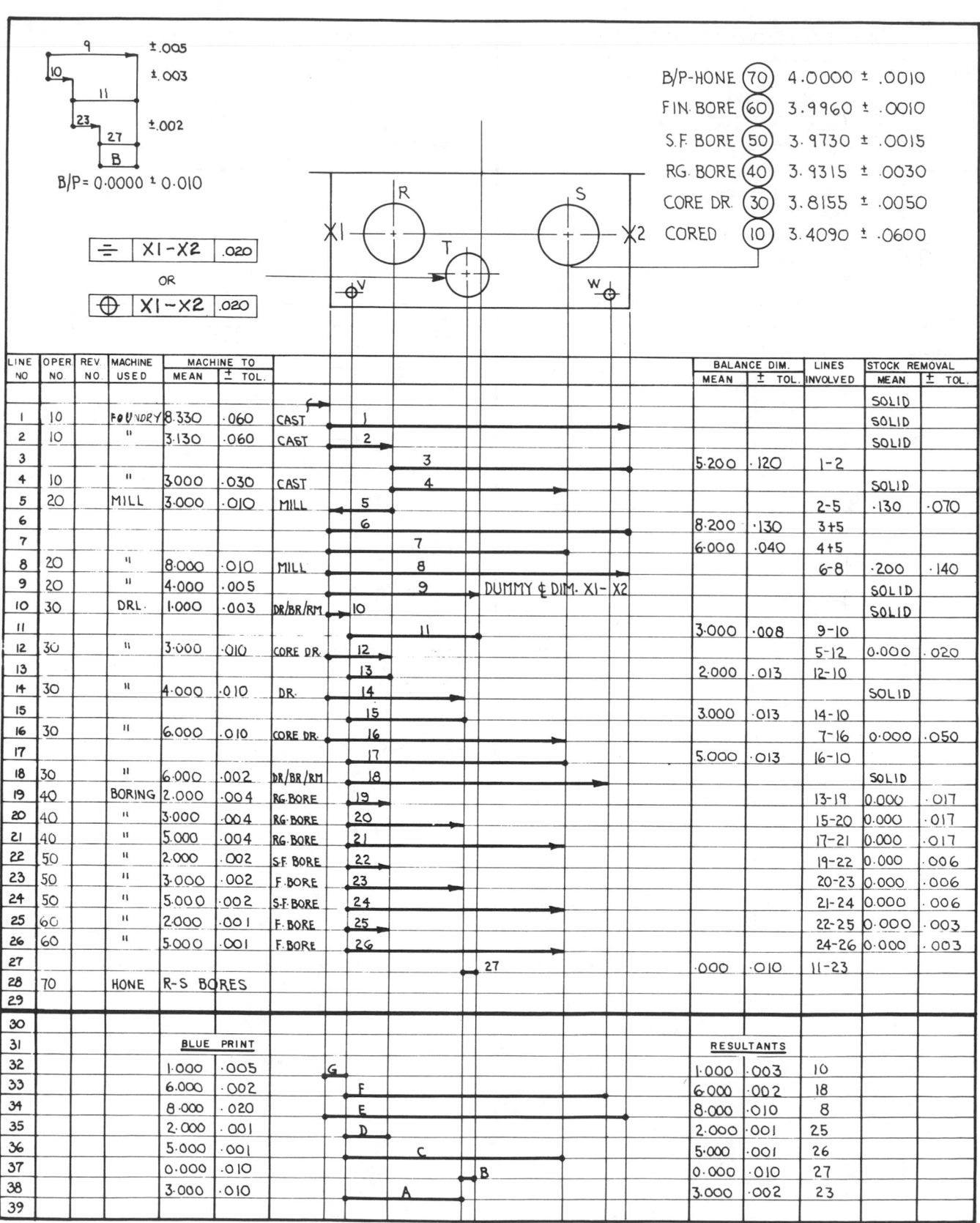

Fig. 8-18, *c* Example of how symmetry condition is handled in the tolerance chart (see also Fig. 8-18, *d*).

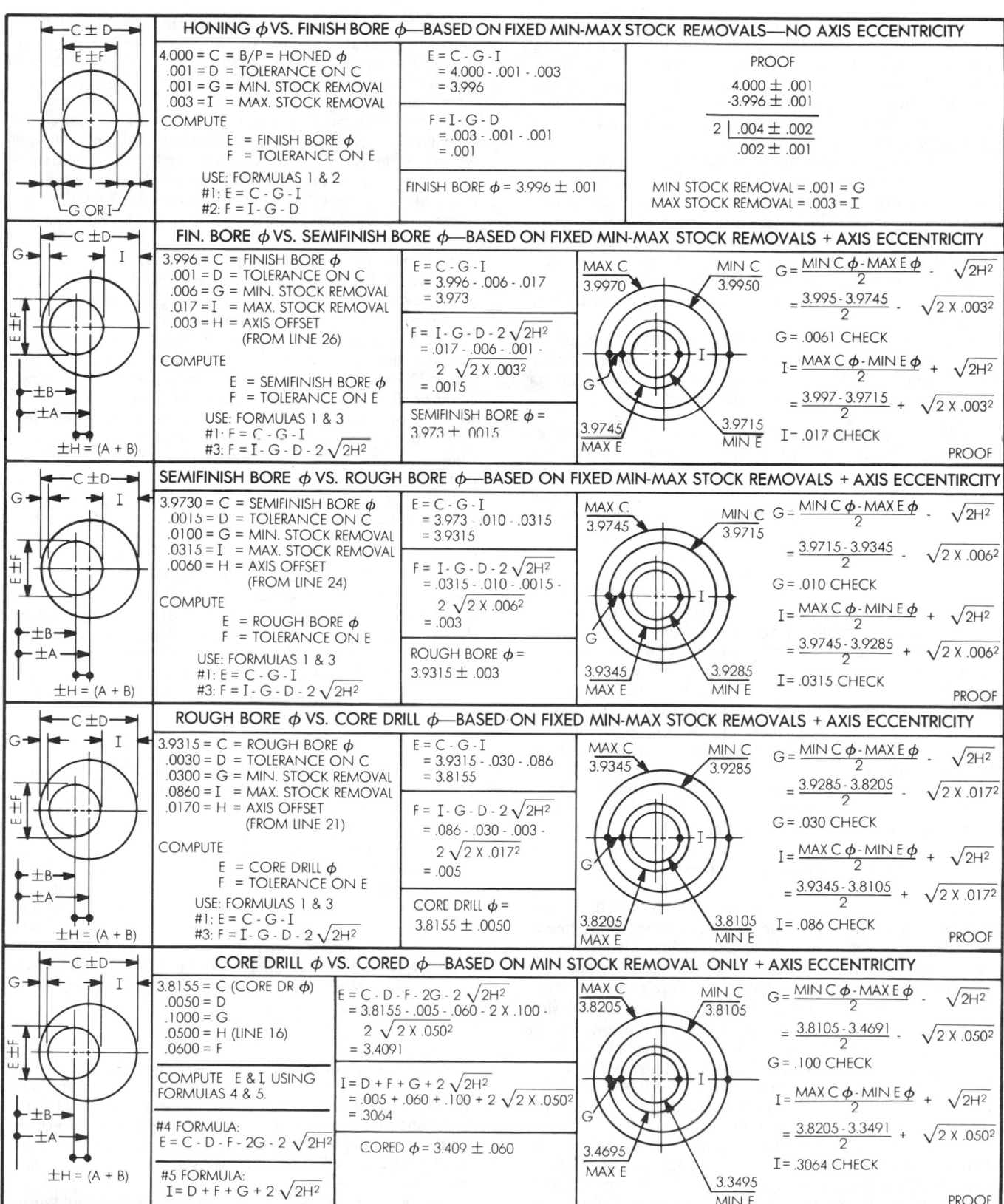

Fig. 8-18, *d* **Calculation of progressive bore sizes used in the tolerance chart illustrated in Fig. 8-18,** *c.*

CHAPTER 8

GEOMETRIC TOLERANCES

At this writing, Y14.5-1973 is being readied for reissuance in an updated version. When the new version is printed it will be found that the symmetry symbol and characteristic have been replaced by the position characteristic. Elimination of the symmetry characteristic does not invalidate the treatment offered here since, for tolerance charting, position and symmetry are handled in the same manner.

If two features are symmetrical to one another, their centerlines will coincide. As one feature shifts with respect to the other, a gap develops between their centerlines and it is said that symmetry error exists between the two features.

Inspection of a machined part for conformance to a blueprint symmetry condition is a routine matter. However, setup of the machining cuts and tolerances to control a specific amount of centerline gap—or symmetry—is not always a routine task.

Two different techniques are presented here for handling symmetry conditions. Selection of one technique over the other will depend on the nature of the part and the problem conditions. These two techniques are described as:

1. Single, common centerline plane to represent two or more features related by a symmetry callout in the blueprint.
2. Multiple feature centerline planes to represent two or more features related by a symmetry callout in the blueprint.

When the first technique is used—a single, common centerline plane—the symmetry values will be shown in the *Stock Removal* columns in the tolerance chart; but when the second technique is used—multiple centerline planes—the symmetry values are shown as dummy blueprint length dimensions.

Figure 8-18, *b*, shows these two methods side by side so that their equivalency, panel A-A', B-B' etc. can be verified.

For symmetry to exist between two features, the centerline of one feature must lie in the plane of the centerline of the other feature; or, expressing it differently, the two centerlines must be coincidental.

Panel A in Fig. 8-18, *b*, shows a 2.000 0.0" block (perfect 2.000" size). The line 2 centerline dimension is located exactly 1.000 ± 0.0" distance from X1 (or X2).

Line 2 in panel A shows a block centerline dimension of 1.000"—a dummy cut whose mean value is one half the X1 to X2 mean block dimension.

If a slot were machined in this block at exactly 1.000 ± 0.0" from X1 (or X2), its centerline would fall on the centerline of X1/X2 (the two centerlines would be coincidental) and the two features would then be considered to be symmetrical since *stock removal* on line 3 equals 0.0 ± 0.0", or a zero gap would exist between the centerline of X1/X2 and the centerline of the slot.

Panel B in Fig. 8-18, *b*, duplicates panel A conditions, except that the slot location is now assigned a tolerance of ±0.004".

The *stock removal* on line 3 in panel B is now 0.0 ± 0.004", which means that the centerline of the slot lies 0.004" to the left or 0.004" to the right of the X1/X2 centerline or, as shown in panel C, within a zone that is 0.008" wide.

Panel D in Fig. 8-18, *b*, duplicates panel B conditions, except that the 2.000" block is now assigned a tolerance of ± 0.002", which results in the addition of a ± 0.001" tolerance to line 2, and the *stock removal* on line 3 now equals 0.0 ± 0.005". Once again, the centerline of the slot is either 0.005" to the left or 0.005" to the right of the X1/X2 centerline.

Panel E in Fig. 8-18, *b*, interprets the panel D relationships—but note that a single 0.010" wide zone does not exist. Instead two zones of 0.005" width which overlap are shown. This is due to the X1/X2 length now having a tolerance on it other than 0.0".

From the foregoing it can be seen that if the slot feature were shown in the blueprint with a symmetry callout of 0.010" relative to the X1/X2 feature, a dummy line 2 (centerline of X1/X2) cut would be set up, and then tolerances would be assigned to line 2 and line 3 cuts based on a 0.0 ± 0.005" stock removal on cut 3—satisfying the 0.010" symmetry requirement. And then, the tolerance on the X1/X2 feature would be set equal to twice the tolerance assigned to the line 2 cut—since its tolerance must be twice that of its centerline dimension.

If the X1/X2 block were allowed a tolerance of ± 0.015" by the blueprint, then ± 0.013" tolerance would be lost to the shop under the conditions listed in panels D and E in Fig. 8-18, *b*. This is a direct result of locating the milling of the slot from surface X1 instead of from the centerline of X1/X2—which could be done by designing centralizing jaws or fixtures that would zero out the centerline of X1/X2 for all parts to be milled.

Further complications can result when one feature plane centerline is machined from a datum that is not one of the end planes of the feature to which it is to be symmetrical. When this is done, schematics are involved in order to compute the final value of 0.0 ± 0.XXX" and then three or more cut tolerances will be involved with the result that the symmetry budget tolerance is split into smaller and smaller values.

Note in Fig. 8-18, *c*, that tolerance chart blueprint condition B represents a symmetry condition of 0.020"—hole T to X1/X2. It is installed in the chart as a 0.000 ± 0.010" dummy blueprint condition. It is established on line 27 and involves a schematic which fixes tolerances on lines 9, 10, and 23. Note also that line 8 value for X1/X2 is set at twice line 9 of 0.005".

Two other aspects of the tolerance chart in Fig. 8-18, *c*, should be noted. They are:

1. Lines 16, 21, 24, and 26 have been assigned a 0.000" *mean stock removal*—contrary to what has been done up to this point—to insure that when mean sizes are being built, the bore axis for successive boring cuts are not eccentric to one another due to mismatch of mean boring dimensions.
2. The boring sizes for hole S were developed by calculations that took into account the possible axis eccentricities between every two successive boring cuts (see Fig. 8-18, *d*). These values were pulled off the chart from lines 16, 21, 24, and 26, and represent the ± $H = (A + B)$ factor used in the bore size calculations; shown in Fig. 8-18, *a*, and Fig. 8-18, *d*.

Failure to include axis eccentricities in bore size calculations can result in hole cleanup problems, problems in handling close tolerances on finish bores, or problems meeting surface texture requirements—all due to eccentric *stock removals*. Since the tolerance chart provides these eccentricity values as a by-product of chart construction, use should be made of them as shown.

Progressive bore sizes based on these methods should prove of major value in the processing of engine blocks, heads, housings, and other components featuring a multitude of holes.

DO'S AND DON'TS FOR COST EFFECTIVE TOLERANCE CHARTING

Construction of tolerance charts can be time consuming and costly. However, the costs in time and money required for construction of the charts are often monies well spent toward the important goal of developing the most cost effective set of tolerances for use in the shop. Observance of what might be termed "good standard practices" tends to keep the costs in time and money to a minimum.

Presented in this section are tactics to keep the cost of tolerance chart construction to a minimum while satisfying shop requirements for practical tolerances.

TOLERANCES ASSIGNED TO CUTS

The following suggestions will help optimize the advantages of tolerance charting when assigning tolerances to cuts:

1. Plan to use as much of the blueprint tolerance as is possible, considering the nature of the process/tooling concepts. Do not hesitate to scrap the original set of ideas and start over if the tolerance chart shows a tendency to produce overtight tolerances.
2. Keep the relationship of the K and $\pm 3\sigma$ values in mind when developing tolerances (see Fig. 8-8).
3. No operation sketch should reflect machining instructions to the operator that cannot be included in the tolerance chart. Such instructions are often single-valued dimensions or they offer the operator the option of removing an indeterminate amount of material. Examples:

   - Skim cut to clean up.
   - Skim cut—remove 0.010" stock.
   - Grind to clean up 80%.
   - A size with a tolerance is shown but a note pointing to the dimension says: "Hold to the high side."

   These examples illustrate that a problem is recognized but they do not represent an acceptable solution since, once this kind of cut is made, it is not possible to verify how much material came off. Instead, the *No Stops* methods described in Fig. 8-11 should be used.
4. It is expected that shop supervision will not arbitrarily work to closer tolerances than are shown on the operation sheet sketch. (Note: Where *precontrol*, *X* and *range* charts, or other statistical techniques are used to verify the correct centering of tools and to control the process, it is understood that this expectation is not being violated.)

LOCATION SURFACES

The following suggestions relating to location surfaces will help maximize process effectiveness:

1. All location surfaces should be shown on the tolerance chart, the strip layout sketches, and in the operation sheet sketches.
2. The tool designer must design fixtures and gages to conform with the dimensions and locating surfaces shown in the operation sheet sketches.
3. As an operating principle in choosing a process sequence, never change the locating surfaces from one operation to the next unless it is absolutely unavoidable.

Every time a previously used locating surface is abandoned or remachined, additional tolerance buildup takes place. The larger the tolerance buildups the larger the *mean stock removals*, or the tighter the machining tolerances must be held to achieve a *blueprint resultant tolerance*. In Fig. 8-19, the left side is concerned with two processes, X and Y, for producing the simple shaft gear. Study the two strip layout processes at the top, the two tolerance charts in the middle, and the two sets of schematics for the processes X and Y.

With respect to the two machining processes shown at the top of Fig. 8-19, they are identical for operations 10 and 20 with respect to the dimensioning of the cuts and the selection of the locating surface in operation 20. However, after heat treatment, shoulders B and C must be ground. The process engineer can specify to grind either shoulder B before C or shoulder C before B. This is a very simple situation that, on the surface, does not require much thinking, yet can have profound effects on the manufacturing costs.

In process X at the top of Fig. 8-19, the process engineer uses the same locating surface in operation 20 and operation 40. In the X process tolerance chart (as shown by the X schematics at the bottom), the process engineer developed tolerances of 0.003", 0.001", 0.001", and 0.001" on cuts 1, 6, 8, and 10 respectively.

However, in process Y at the top of Fig. 8-19, the process engineer reversed the locating surfaces, and ground C before B. As a result, in the Y process (as shown by the Y schematics at the bottom), the process engineer developed tolerances of 0.0025", 0.0005", 0.0005", 0.0005" and 0.0005" on cuts 14, 18, 19, 22 and 25 respectively. These tolerance values are tabulated in Table 8-2.

The cost of process Y is obviously much more than twice the cost of process X—solely due to indiscriminate switching of the locating surfaces in operation 40 of process Y.

TABLE 8-2
Tabulation of Tolerances for Two Processing Methods— X & Y—Shown in Fig. 8-19

Process X		Process Y	
Line #	Tolerance (in.)	Line #	Tolerance (in.)
1	0.0030	14	0.0025
6	0.0010	18	0.0005
8	0.0010	19	0.0005
10	0.0010	22	0.0005
		25	0.0005

DIMENSIONING PATTERNS—SELECTION OF DATUM SURFACES FOR CUTS

Panel A of Fig. 8-19 shows chain dimensioning on the blueprint and the use of a single datum in the strip layout sketches. Certainly, if surfaces A, B, C, D, E, and F are to be remachined, and possibly in separate operations, excessive tolerance buildups may be encountered if chain-type dimensioning is used in the strip layouts.

COST EFFECTIVE CHARTING

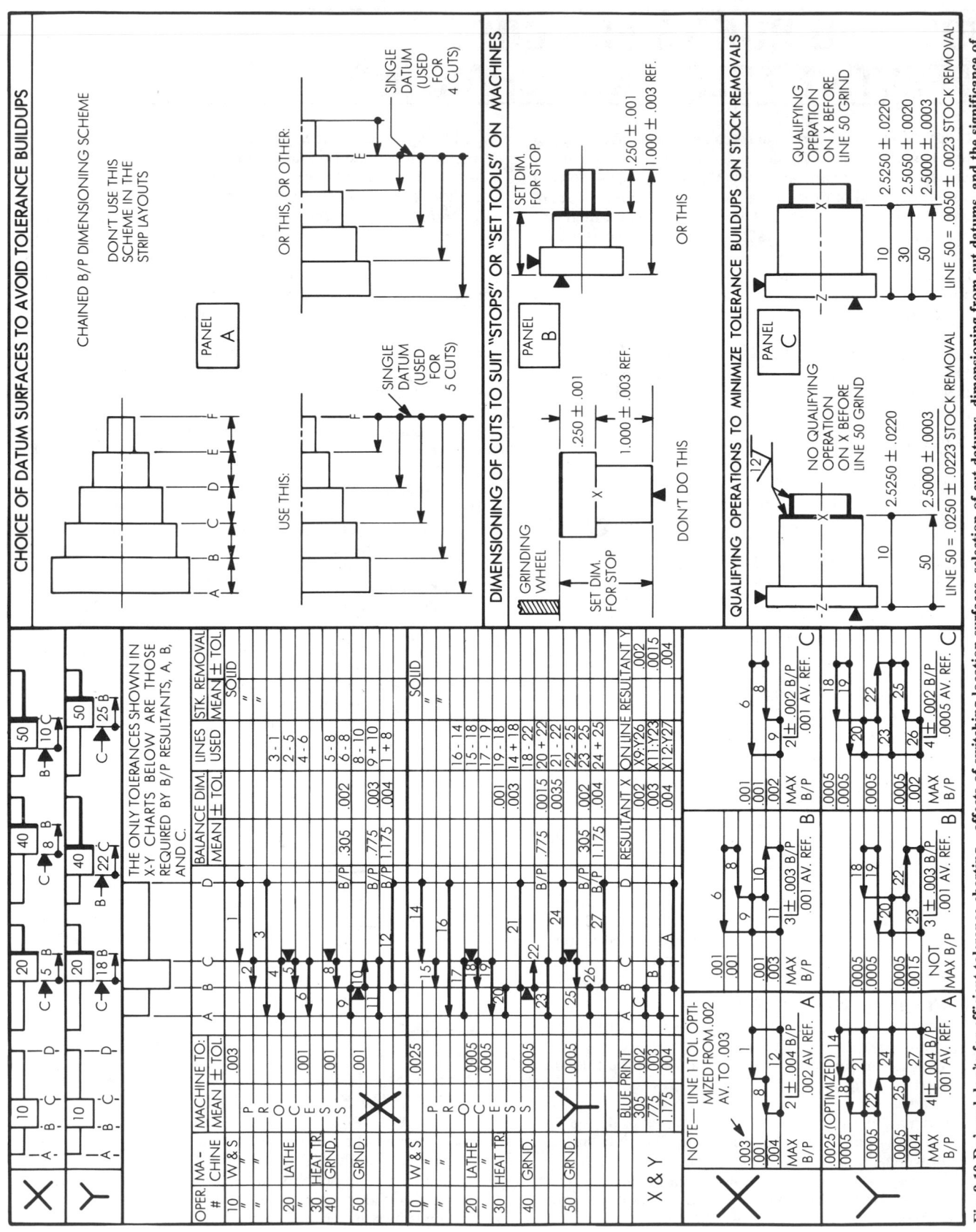

Fig. 8-19 Do's and don'ts for efficient tolerance charting—affects of switching location surfaces, selection of cut datums, dimensioning from cut datums, and the significance of qualifying operations.

Panel B of Fig. 8-19 shows the importance of selecting datum surfaces for cuts that tie in with the location surface to be used in the operation. In both examples, the 0.250 ± 0.001" dimension is measured from a surface that floats ± 0.003" from the locating surface, making it impossible to set stops; or, as shown in the Blanchard operation, making it impossible to load the table to capacity.

QUALIFYING OPERATIONS

Panel C of Fig. 8-19 shows the kind of situation wherein the excessive tolerance buildup of 0.0250 ± 0.0223" (max = 0.047") makes it impossible to hold tolerance or surface finish. For this kind of situation, it may pay to add a qualifying operation (op. 30) to remove the bulk of the stock prior to the final operation.

FORGING/CASTING TOLERANCES

Forging/casting tolerances are normally large compared to machining tolerances. Based on how the machining cuts are dimensioned (and the schematics), it may happen that two or more forged/cast tolerances are added and a monumental tolerance buildup is shown, which if accepted as a real possibility, produces major problems in stock removal.

However, the situation of massive tolerance buildup may not occur. While dies wash out and patterns degrade, the changes in the dies and patterns may still show that massive tolerance buildups are not possible. Check with foundry/supplier people to find out what will really be true of the variations in the forgings/castings. One or two dimensions may vary as broadly as the forging/casting drawing allows, but the others may be fairly stable and uniform within much smaller limits—and these smaller limits are the ones that should be considered for use in the chart.

MISCELLANEOUS SUGGESTIONS

No single operations sheet sketch should require two setups to machine the part. Given such an option by a sketch, the shop would have a 50-50 chance of destroying the sense of the tolerance chart. All heat treating, plating, shot peening, in-process inspections, or other non-chipmaking operations should be indicated on the tolerance chart so that the complete process is visible in the chart. Calculations and scale layouts should be stored in a history file.

References

1. *American National Standard on Dimensioning and Tolerancing*, ANSI Standard Y14.5-1973, American National Standards Institute, New York. [Note: At this writing, a revised version of Y14.5 called Y14.5M is being reviewed for publication. Written in metric units and presenting some rather significant changes in symbology, the new standard is written to provide more commonality with European practice. Changes in the standard do not impact the validity of concepts presented in this chapter on tolerance charting, although some modifications in technique may be required to suit company practice or in-house standards where they apply. See also: Richard S. Marrelli, "New Rules for Dimensioning and Tolerancing Drawings," *Machine Design* (March 11, 1982), p. 215.]

2. *Ibid*, p. 26.

DIMENSIONAL METROLOGY AND GEOMETRIC CONFORMANCE

MEASUREMENT OF GEOMETRIC DIMENSIONING AND TOLERANCING

Geometric dimensioning and tolerancing can be described in its simplest terms as a means of specifying the geometry or shape of a piece of hardware on an engineering drawing.[1] It provides the designer with a clear way of expressing design intent and part requirements, which in turn enables the manufacturer to choose the proper method to produce the part. Geometric dimensioning and tolerancing also indicates how the part should be inspected and gaged, thus protecting the design intent.

Geometric dimensioning and tolerancing is rapidly becoming a universal engineering drawing language and technique that manufacturing industries and government agencies are finding essential to their operational well-being. Over the past 30 years, this subject has matured to become an indispensable tool; it assists productivity, quality, and economics in building and marketing products.

PRINCIPLES

To properly understand and implement geometrics it is important to understand the principles or fundamentals of the concept of geometric dimensioning and tolerancing. Figure 9-1 illustrates the 13 basic geometric characteristic symbols that are defined in ANSI Y14.5M. These symbols are divided into five types of controls, which will be discussed subsequently. Other related symbols and terms are shown in Fig. 9-2.

Basic Dimensions

A basic dimension is a theoretical, exact dimension without tolerance. When used in conjunction with geometric tolerance specification, the basic dimension locates the exact center of the tolerance zone. The center plane or axis of an acceptable feature is allowed to vary within the basic located tolerance zone as shown in Fig. 9-3. Basic dimensions on drawings are enclosed by a rectangular box around the dimension (refer to Fig. 9-2). On older drawings, basic dimensions are identified by the word BASIC or the abbreviation BSC near the dimension.

When features are located by basic chain dimensioning on the drawing, there is no accumulation of tolerance between features (see Fig. 9-4). Basic dimensions are absolute values, and, when added together, they equal an absolute value. The basic dimensions locate the tolerance zone and not the manufactured feature. The manufactured feature can float within the perfectly located tolerance zone.

Material Condition Modifiers

The three material condition modifiers used with geometric dimensioning are maximum material condition (MMC), regardless of feature size (RFS), and least material condition (LMC). The accepted symbols for these modifiers are shown in Fig. 9-2. Material condition modifiers can only be used with size features such as holes, shafts, pins, and slots rather than surface features.

Maximum material condition. The maximum material condition is the condition in which a feature of size contains the maximum amount of material within the stated limits of size. When the MMC symbol is associated with the tolerance or a datum reference letter in the feature control frame, the specified tolerance only applies to the feature if the feature is manufactured at its maximum material condition size.

Regardless of feature size. Regardless of feature size is the term used to indicate that a geometric tolerance or datum reference applies at any increment of size of the feature within its size tolerance. When the RFS symbol is selected to modify the tolerance or datum reference in the feature control frame, the specified tolerance applies to the location of the feature regardless of the feature's size.

Least material condition. Least material condition is the condition in which a feature of size contains the least amount of material within the stated limit of size. Examples of LMC are a shaft made to the smallest size and a hole drilled to the largest size.

Feature Control Frame

The feature control frame (formerly called the feature control symbol) specifies the type, shape, and size of the geometric tolerance zone, dictates the datum surfaces and order precedence for part setup, and assigns material condition modifiers to the tolerance and datum reference letters when applicable. A typical feature control frame is shown in Fig. 9-5.

The symbol Ⓜ in the feature control frame in Fig. 9-5 indicates that the 0.014" tolerance only applies when the feature being verified is produced at its maximum material condition size. The symbol ∅ preceding the tolerance value indicates that the tolerance zone has a cylindrical shape. If no symbol precedes the tolerance value, the tolerance zone is the total area between two parallel planes or two parallel line 0.014" apart.

The order of specified datum reference letters in the feature control frame is very important (refer to Fig. 9-5). The primary datum reference is shown at the left; the least important datum reference is

GEOMETRIC DIMENSIONING AND TOLERANCING

shown at the right. The datum precedence allows manufacturing and inspection personnel to determine the correct part orientation for their respective functions. The part is fixtured to allow a minimum of three points of contact on the primary datum surface, a minimum of two points of contact for the secondary datum feature, and a minimum of one point of contact for the tertiary datum feature. With respect to functional datums, these points of contact must be the highest points on the surface when brought into contact with a simulated datum plane (surface plate).

TYPE OF FEATURE	TYPE OF TOLERANCE	CHARACTERISTIC	SYMBOL
Individual (no datum reference)	Form	Flatness	▱
		Straightness	—
		Circularity (roundness)	○
		Cylindricity	⌭
Individual or related	Profile	Profile of a line	⌒
		Profile of a surface	⌓
Related (datum reference required)	Orientation	Perpendicularity	⊥
		Angularity	∠
		Parallelism	//
	Location	Position	⌖
		Concentricity	◎
	Runout	Circular runout	↗
		Total runout	↗↗

Fig. 9-1 Geometric characteristic symbols. (*American Society of Mechanical Engineers*)

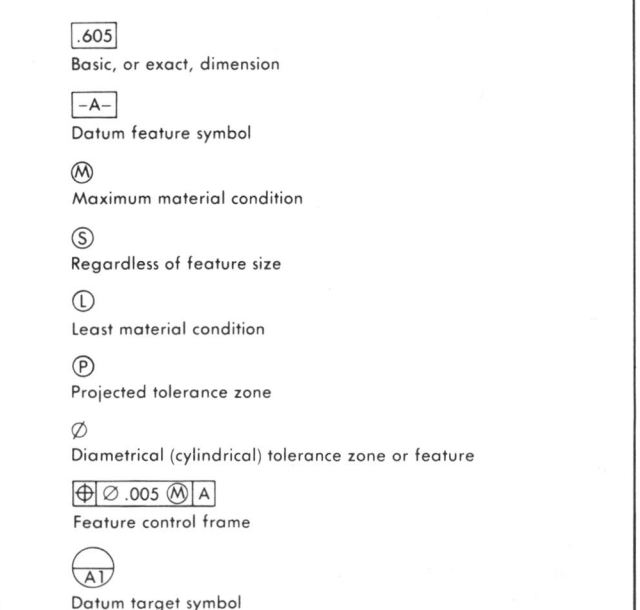

Fig. 9-2 Related geometric characteristic symbols and terms.

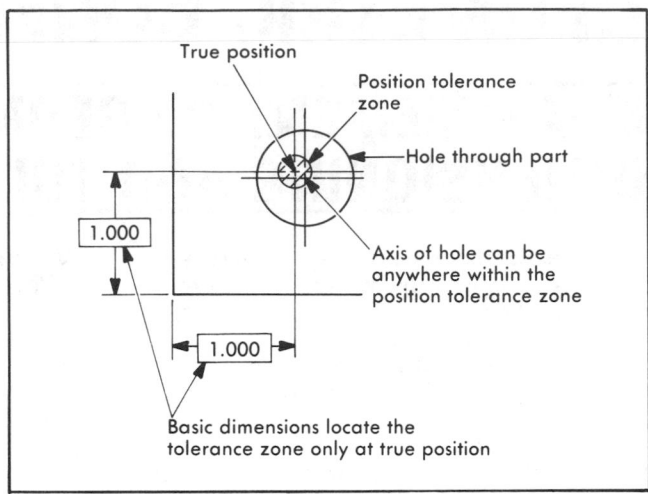

Fig. 9-3 Positional tolerance zone.

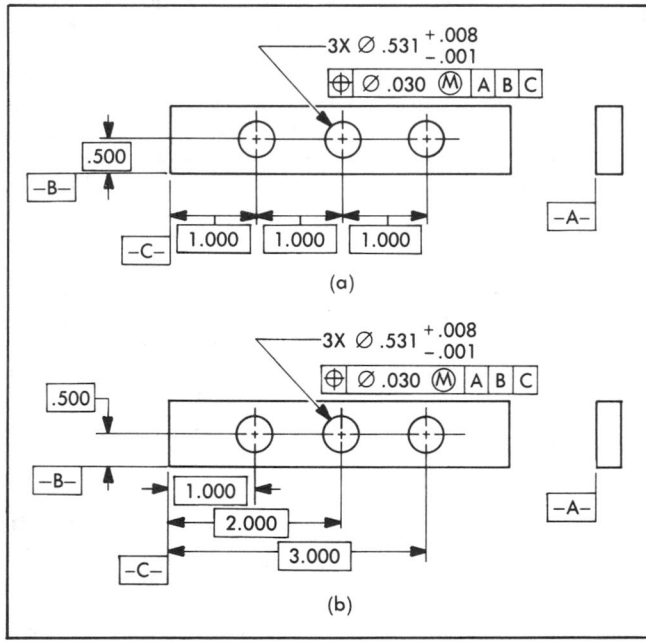

Fig. 9-4 Chain dimensioning versus baseline dimensioning: (a) chain dimensioning and (b) baseline dimensioning. The .531 diam holes can be dimensioned with chain dimensioning or baseline dimensioning and retain the identical interpretation.

Bonus and Additional Tolerances

When a tolerance or datum reference letter is modified with the MMC symbol, the specified tolerance in the feature control frame only applies if the feature is manufactured at its MMC size. As the feature departs from MMC size, the geometric tolerance increases. The amount that the feature deviates from MMC size is added to the geometric tolerance specified in the feature control frame. This extra tolerance is called *bonus* tolerance.

As shown in Fig. 9-6, the 0.014″ diam position tolerance applies when the hole is drilled at 0.515″ diam. If hole number two was drilled at 0.525″ diam, a departure of 0.010″ from the MMC size of the hole, a bonus tolerance of 0.010″ would be gained. The 0.010″ bonus tolerance is added directly to the original 0.014″ positional tolerance to give a total positional tolerance of 0.024″ for the 0.525″ diam hole. The axis of hole two must be within the 0.024″ diam tolerance zone. The total positional tolerance zone size for each hole must be determined in conjunction with the actual manufactured hole size.

An *additional* locational tolerance can be gained as a datum feature of size departs from MMC size. For example, in Fig. 9-7 a bonus tolerance of up to 0.005″ could be gained for the 0.010″ positional tolerance specification if the 0.260″ diam hole is not made at MMC. An additional tolerance of up to 0.020″ could also be gained if datum B departs from MMC. However, this additional tolerance does not add directly to the original positional tolerance as a bonus tolerance would. The additional tolerance must be applied to the hole pattern as a group, allowing the four-hole pattern to shift off center as a group. No additional hole-to-hole tolerance gain is realized within the four-hole pattern.

The rules and principles of MMC bonus and additional tolerances also apply to tolerances and datum references that are specified at LMC. The only difference is that the bonus and additional tolerances are determined from the feature's departure from LMC size.

Datums

The three-plane datum reference frame is necessary to ensure correct drawing interpretation. For noncylindrical parts, the manufacturing/inspection fixture shown in Fig. 9-8 can be constructed to ensure uniformity during manufacturing and inspection operations. All related measurements of the part originate from the fixture datum planes.

For cylindrical parts, the three-plane reference frame is more difficult to visualize. The primary datum is often described as a flat surface perpendicular to the axis of the cylindrical datum feature as shown in Fig. 9-9. This axis can be defined as the intersection of two planes, 90° to each other, at the midpoint of the cylindrical feature. The tertiary datum is used if rotational orientation of the cylindrical feature is required due to interrelationship of radially located features. The tertiary datum is often a locating hole, slot, or pin. If no angular located features are involved in the hardware requirements, the tertiary datum is omitted.

The two types of datum features are datums of size and nonsize datums. Datums of size are established from features that have size tolerance, such as holes, outside diameters, and slot widths. The center plane or axis of a simulated datum contacting or representing MMC size of the feature is the actual datum. For example, a 0.250±0.005″ hole specified as a datum would be a datum feature of size. The centerline or axis of the simulated datum contacting the manufactured hole is the actual datum. Nonsize datums are established from surfaces. A datum surface has no size tolerance because it is a plane from which dimensions or relationships originate.

Screw Thread Specification

When geometric tolerancing is expressed for the control of a screw thread, or when a screw thread is specified as a datum reference, the application shall be applied to the pitch cylinder. If design requirements necessitate an exception to this rule, the notation MINOR DIA or MAJOR DIA shall be shown beneath the feature control frame or datum reference as applicable.

Gears and Splines Specification

When geometric tolerancing is expressed for the control of a gear or spline, a specific feature of the gear or spline must be designated to derive a datum axis. This information is stated beneath the feature control frame or beneath the datum feature symbol.

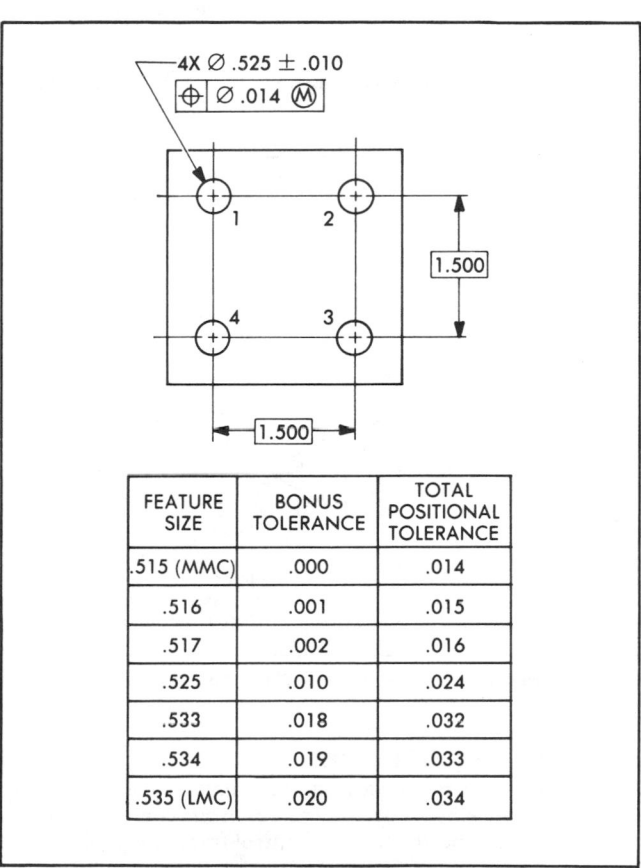

FEATURE SIZE	BONUS TOLERANCE	TOTAL POSITIONAL TOLERANCE
.515 (MMC)	.000	.014
.516	.001	.015
.517	.002	.016
.525	.010	.024
.533	.018	.032
.534	.019	.033
.535 (LMC)	.020	.034

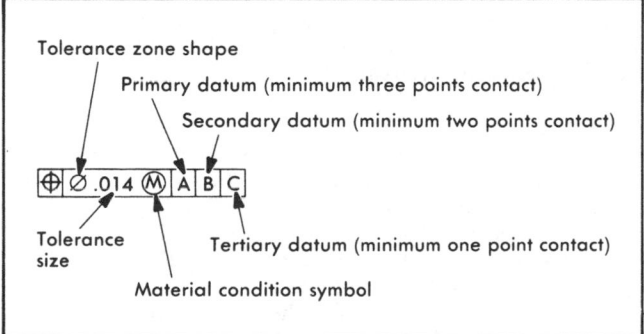

Fig. 9-5 Feature control frame for a noncylindrical part.

Fig. 9-6 Application of bonus tolerances to a part.

GEOMETRIC DIMENSIONING AND TOLERANCING

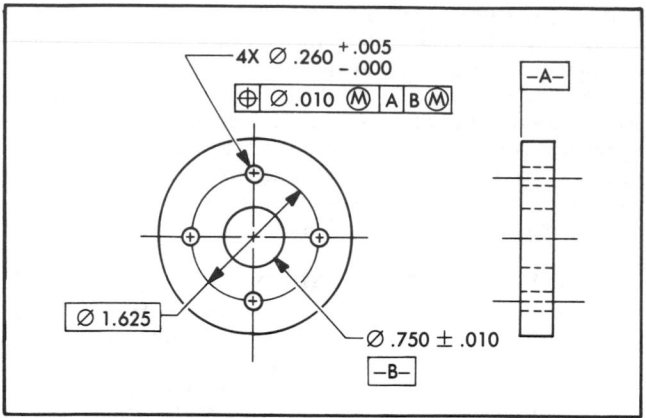

Fig. 9-7 Application of additional tolerances to a part.

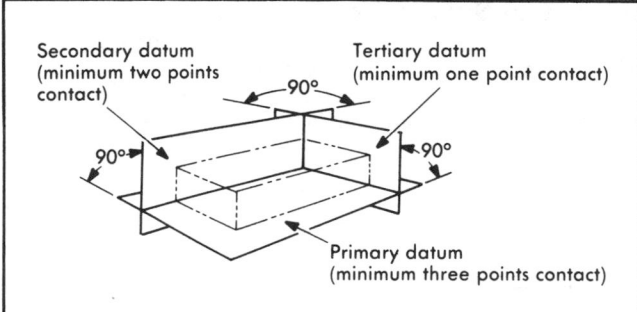

Fig. 9-8 Three-plane datum reference frame for noncylindrical features.

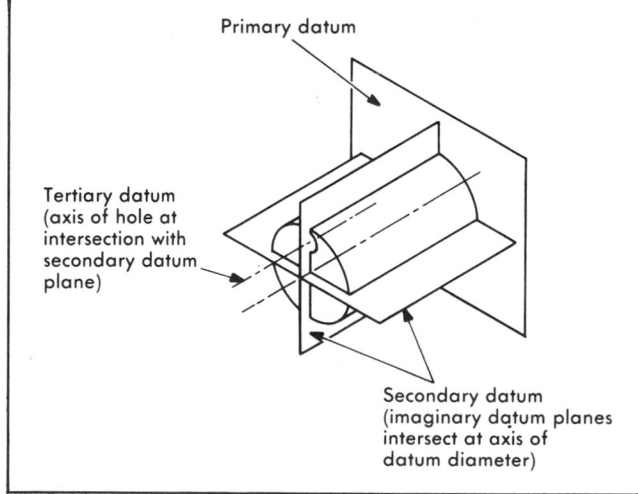

Fig. 9-9 Three-plane datum reference frame for cylindrical features.

Separate Requirements

When more than one pattern of features such as holes and slots are located by basic dimensions from common datum features of size, and the feature control frame for each of the patterns contains the same datums in the same order of precedence and at the same material condition, all the features

are considered as one single pattern. In Fig. 9-10, the two 0.221″ diam holes appear as one pattern, and the two 0.391″ diam holes are a separate pattern. Because the location feature control frame for both hole patterns contain the same datums, in the same order of precedence and at the same material condition, the patterns are considered one pattern of four holes. The parts inspector must verify the dimensional conformance of both hole patterns simultaneously. If the designer had felt this interrelationship of the four holes was not required between the two patterns of features in Fig. 9-10, a notation such as *SEPARATE REQUIREMENTS* would have been placed beneath the feature control frames. This would allow each pattern of features to shift independently in relationship to the common datum system. The parts inspector would then verify each pattern of holes separately.

Envelope Rule

The envelope rule specifies the limit of size of an individual feature and controls variations of geometric shape (form) within the envelope created by the specified size at MMC. A feature produced at the MMC size must have perfect form (straightness, circularity, cylindricity, or flatness) to remain within the MMC size envelope as shown in Fig. 9-11.

As a feature deviates from the MMC size, the form is allowed to vary within the MMC envelope. The quality control inspector is required to verify envelope rule conformance of shape when drawings conform with ANSI Y14.5.

Virtual Condition

Virtual condition is a size representing the worst possible assembly condition of mating parts resulting from the collective effects of size and the geometric tolerance specified to control the feature (see Fig. 9-12). Virtual condition is primarily a size used by product and tool/gage designers for calculating basic gage element size or performing tolerance analysis to ensure assembly of mating parts. The following formulas are used to determine virtual conditions:

EXTERNAL FEATURES =
MMC SIZE + TOLERANCE OF FORM,
ORIENTATION, OR LOCATION

INTERNAL FEATURES =
MMC SIZE - TOLERANCE OF FORM,
ORIENTATION, OR LOCATION

FORM CONTROL TOLERANCES

The four form control symbols—flatness, surface straightness, circularity, and cylindricity—are applied to control the shape of the finished item. These symbols tell the inspector the amount a feature can vary from the perfect shape specified on the drawing. Refer to Fig. 9-1 for the symbols used to represent these geometric characteristics.

Flatness

Flatness is the condition of a surface having all elements in one plane.[2] A flatness tolerance specifies a tolerance zone defined by two parallel planes within which the entire surface must lie. When a flatness tolerance is specified, the feature control frame is attached to a leader directed to the surface or to an extension line of the surface (see Fig. 9-13).

In Fig. 9-13, the outer limit of the 0.005″ flatness tolerance zone is established by the extremities of the manufactured surface. If the surface being verified for flatness was placed on

GEOMETRIC DIMENSIONING AND TOLERANCING

an inspection surface plate, the high points of the surface would make contact with the surface plate, creating the outer tolerance zone limit (see Fig. 9-14). The upper limit of the tolerance would be 0.005″ above the surface plate. Every element of the surface must be within this tolerance band zone to be an acceptable part. No surface valley or peak could violate the two parallel planes that are 0.005″ apart. The flatness tolerance must be contained within the boundary of perfect form at MMC.

Another method of checking flatness requirements is shown in Fig. 9-15. In this method, the surface to be inspected is placed on three stacks of gage blocks; each stack is the same height. A test indicator is then traversed over the entire underside of the part, comparing the part's surface to that of the theoretical flat plane generated by the gage block stacks. The full indicator movement must not exceed the 0.005″ flatness tolerance specified in the feature control frame.

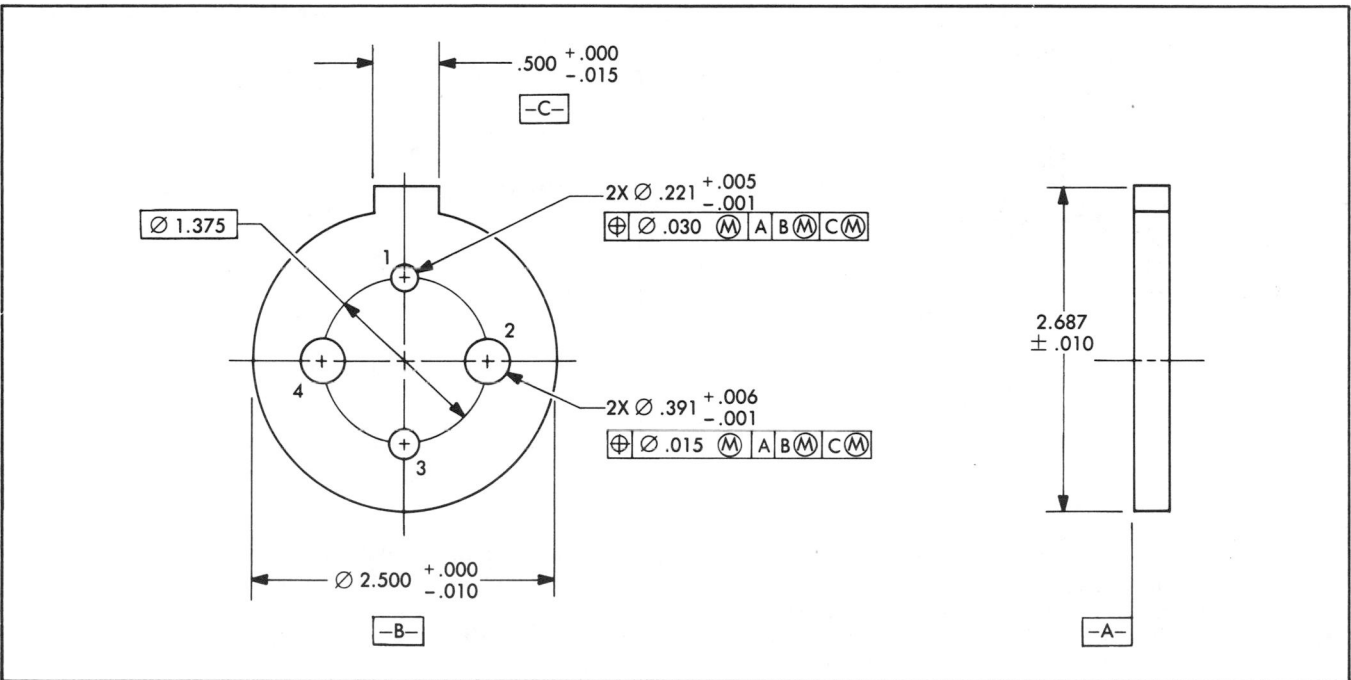

Fig. 9-10 Composite feature patterns.

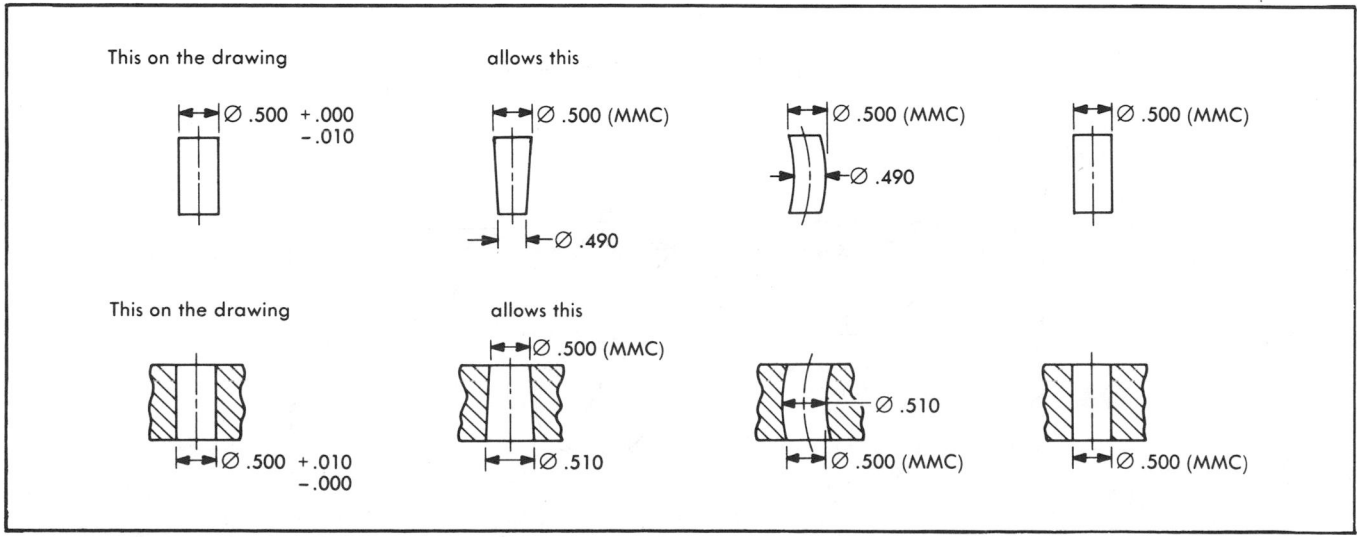

Fig. 9-11 Extreme variations of form allowed by size tolerance.

GEOMETRIC DIMENSIONING AND TOLERANCING

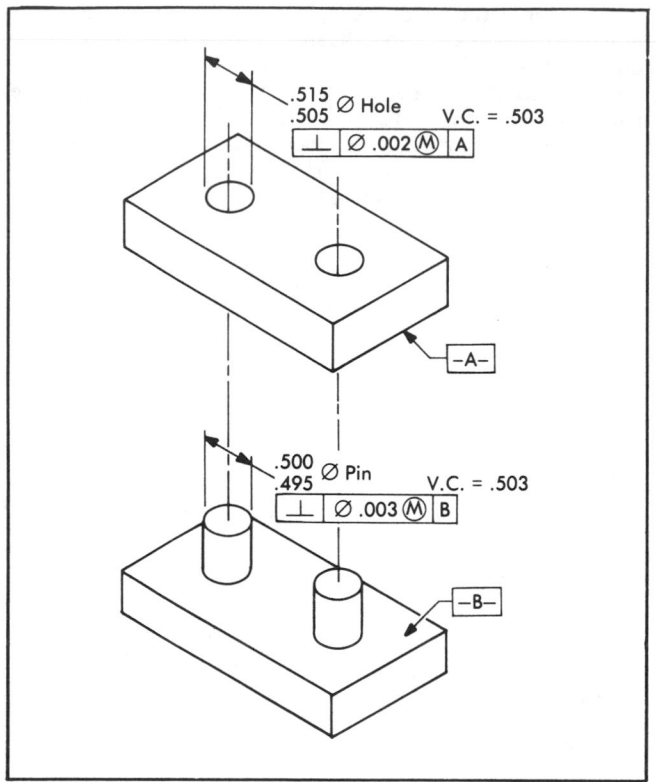

Fig. 9-12 Virtual condition of mating parts.

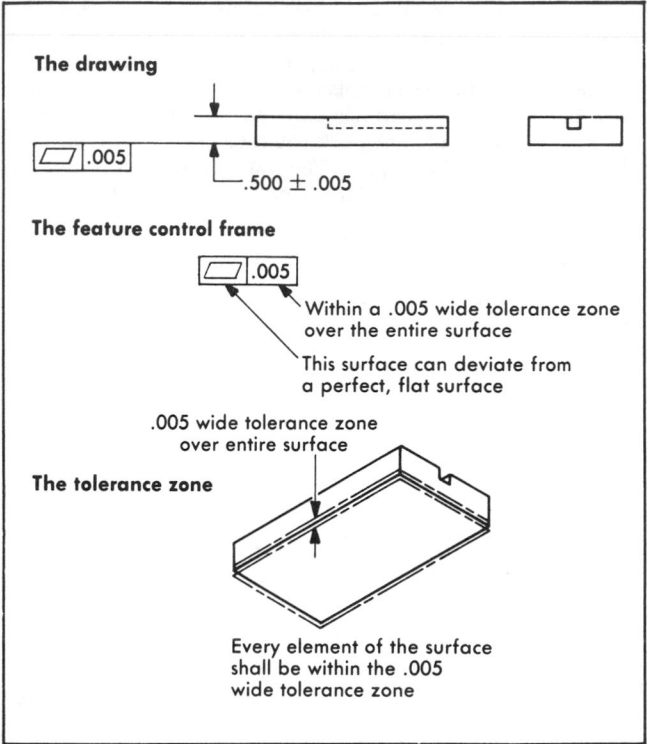

Fig. 9-13 Flatness control.

When flatness must be verified on the upward side of the part due to part size or configuration, the allowable part thickness variation must be nullified. The part thickness variation can be nullified by using leveling screws as shown in Fig. 9-16. The screws are adjusted so that the upper surface extremities of the part establish the upper limit of the flatness tolerance zone. The dial indicator is then traversed over the upper surface of the part. The full indicator movement over the entire surface must not vary greater than the flatness requirement.

Straightness

Straightness is a condition where an element of a surface or an axis is a straight line.[3] A straightness tolerance specifies a tolerance zone within which the considered element or axis must lie.

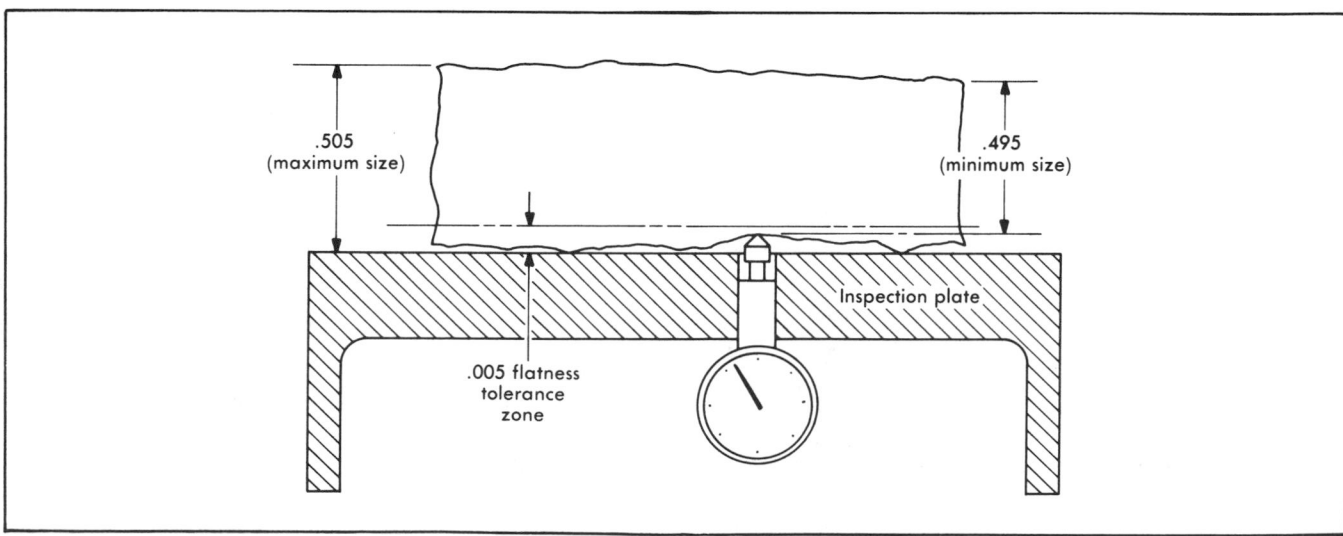

Fig. 9-14 Inspecting flatness on a surface plate.

GEOMETRIC DIMENSIONING AND TOLERANCING

Straightness specifications are divided into surface straightness and axis straightness.

Surface straightness. Figure 9-17 shows the surface straightness tolerance specification on an engineering drawing and then illustrates the tolerance zone for each line element of the surface. To verify surface straightness, the part is placed on two equal stacks of gage blocks that are spaced apart as far as possible (see Fig. 9-18). A test indicator is passed under and perpendicular to the shaft at a number of locations while noting the full indicator movement. For the part to be acceptable, the variation in the maximum indicator reading cannot exceed the straightness specification. This procedure is repeated as the part is rotated a sufficient number of times to ensure that the part meets the drawing requirement.

Axis straightness. The straightness specification in Fig. 9-19 allows the axis of the shaft to vary within a 0.005" diam cylindrical tolerance zone. Because an axis or centerline cannot be seen on an actual part, the external surface of the feature is used to verify the axis straightness specification. To determine the axis straightness conformance, surface straightness, taper, and circularity verification methods are used.

Because the feature control frame does not designate a material condition modifier, the regardless of feature size (RFS) material condition is implied. If the maximum material condition (MMC) modifier were designated, the bonus tolerance would have to be evaluated.

When the MMC symbol is indicated with an axis straightness tolerance, a bonus tolerance is gained as the feature departs from MMC size. An example of this condition is shown in Fig. 9-20. The part can also be functionally gaged; the gage would be at least 3.030" long with a hole at the virtual condition of the feature (see Fig. 9-21). It should be noted that this gage can verify form only, size must be verified separately. It is also necessary to consider gage makers' tolerances and wear allowances when using functional gages.

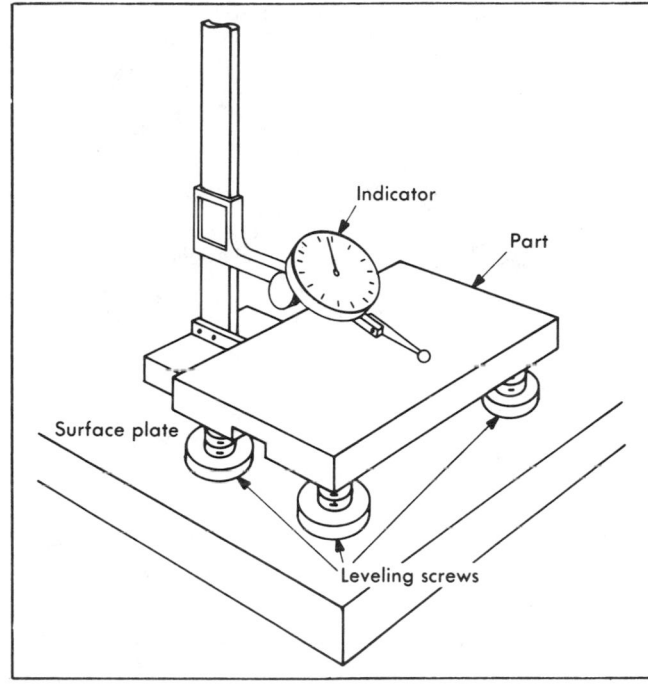

Fig. 9-16 Checking flatness on top surface by nullifying part thickness variation with leveling screws.

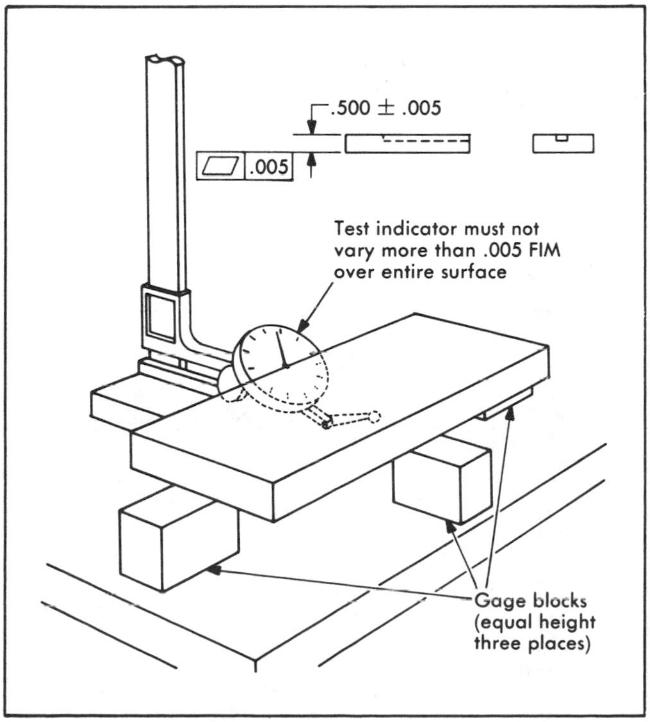

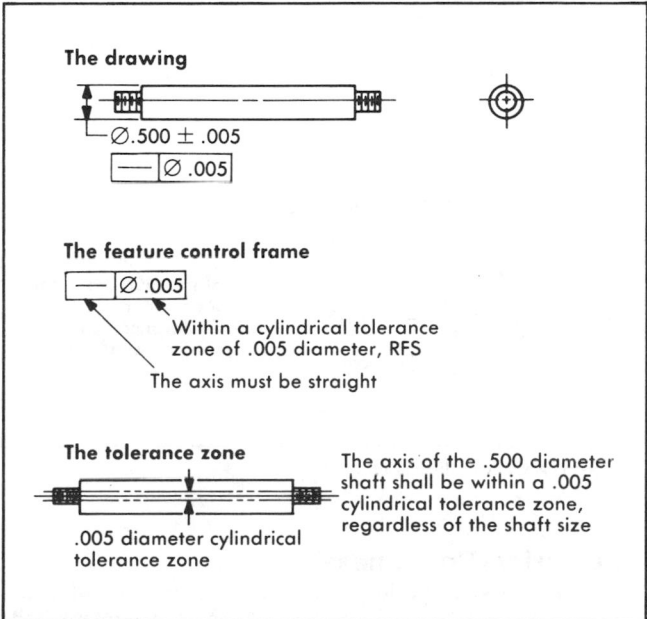

Fig. 9-15 Inspecting flatness by placing the workpiece on gage blocks and checking full indicator movement.

Fig. 9-17 Surface straightness tolerance.

GEOMETRIC DIMENSIONING AND TOLERANCING

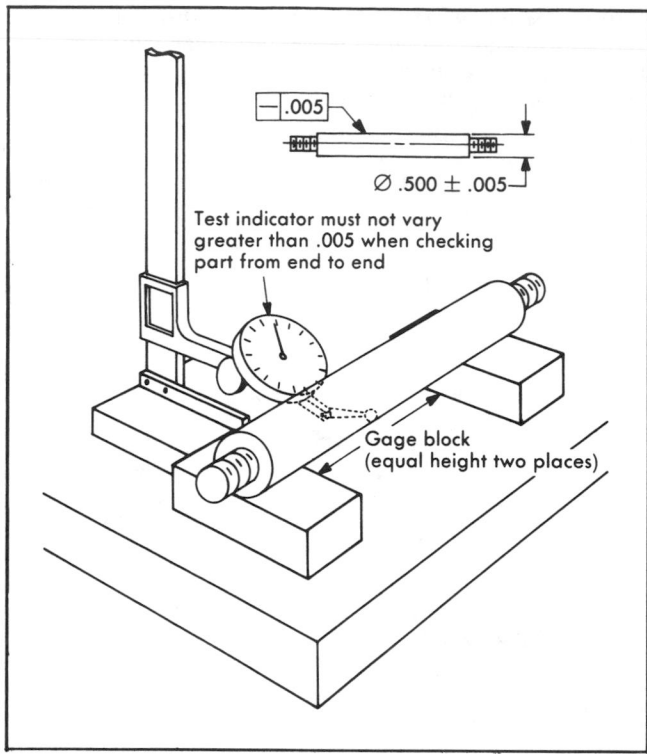

Fig. 9-18 Verifying surface straightness on bottom of part surface.

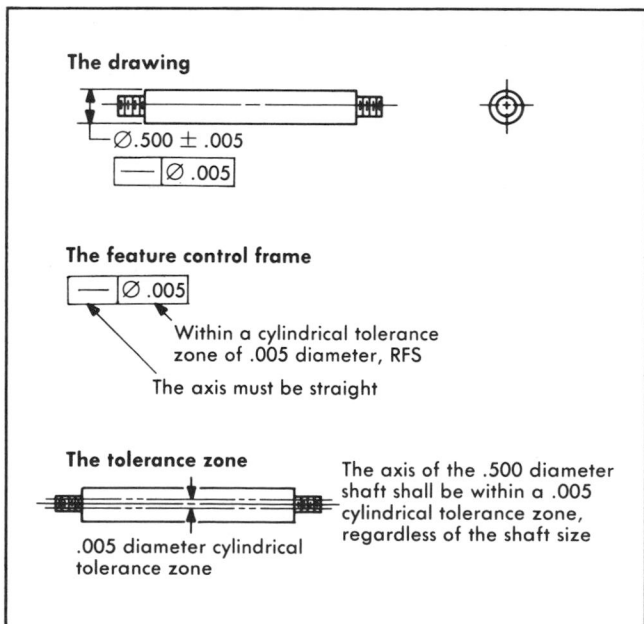

Fig. 9-19 Axis straightness control.

Circularity (Roundness)

Circularity is a condition of a surface of revolution (cylinder, cone, or sphere) where all the points of the surface intersected by any plane perpendicular to a common axis (cylinder or cone)

or passing through a common center (sphere) are equidistant from the center.[4] A circularity tolerance specifies a tolerance zone bounded by two concentric circles within which each circular element of the surface must lie, and it applies independently at each cross section.

The outer tolerance zone boundary is established by the extremities of the manufactured surface of the part (see Fig. 9-22). The inner tolerance zone diameter is less than the outer tolerance zone diameter by two times the tolerance value specified in the circularity feature control frame. The tolerance value specified in the feature control frame is a radial requirement. The circularity tolerance zone applies independently at every cross section perpendicular to the common axis of the feature. Several cross-sectional checks should be made to ensure part conformance. Circularity verification is discussed subsequently under "Measurement of Circularity."

Tapered parts are also occasionally specified with circularity control. Because the circularity tolerance zone applies independently at each cross section and the outer tolerance zone limit is established by the manufactured surface, each outer tolerance zone limit will be a different size from the others. Several cross-sectional checks should be made to ensure part conformance.

Cylindricity

Cylindricity is a condition of a surface of revolution in which all points of the surface are equidistant from a common axis.[5]

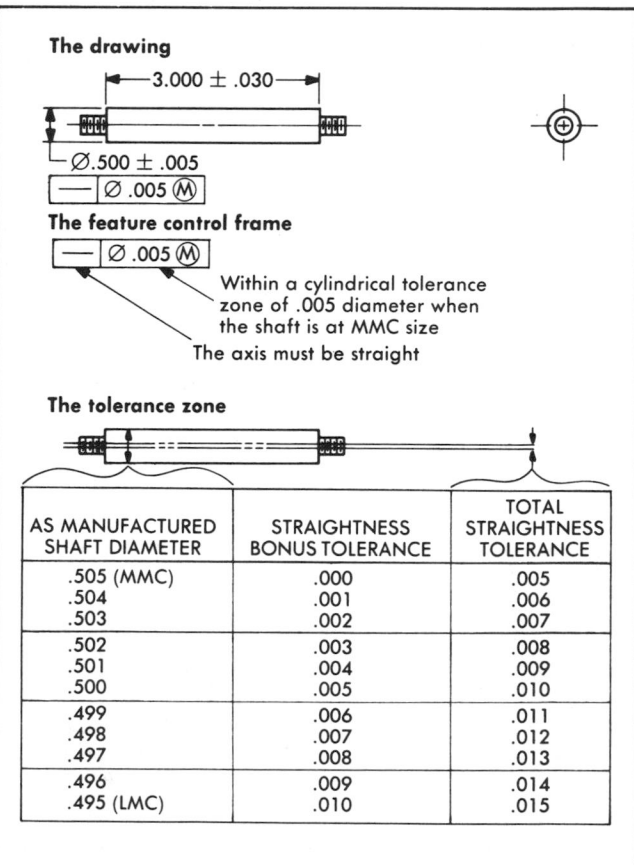

AS MANUFACTURED SHAFT DIAMETER	STRAIGHTNESS BONUS TOLERANCE	TOTAL STRAIGHTNESS TOLERANCE
.505 (MMC)	.000	.005
.504	.001	.006
.503	.002	.007
.502	.003	.008
.501	.004	.009
.500	.005	.010
.499	.006	.011
.498	.007	.012
.497	.008	.013
.496	.009	.014
.495 (LMC)	.010	.015

Fig. 9-20 Axis straightness control at MMC.

A cylindricity tolerance specifies a tolerance zone bounded by two concentric cylinders within which the surface must lie (see Fig. 9-23).

Cylindricity control stretches the circularity tolerance requirement over the length of the part. Cylindricity tolerance applies simultaneously to both circular and longitudinal elements of the part's surface.

Some of the common ways to verify circularity and cylindricity are with a micrometer, with a V-block and test indicator, and between bench centers.

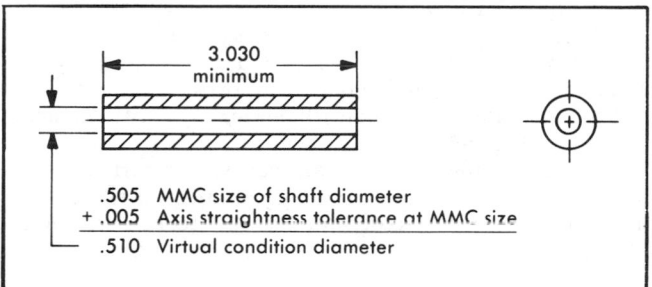

.505 MMC size of shaft diameter
+ .005 Axis straightness tolerance at MMC size
.510 Virtual condition diameter

Fig. 9-21 Functional gage at the virtual condition of the part in Fig. 9-20.

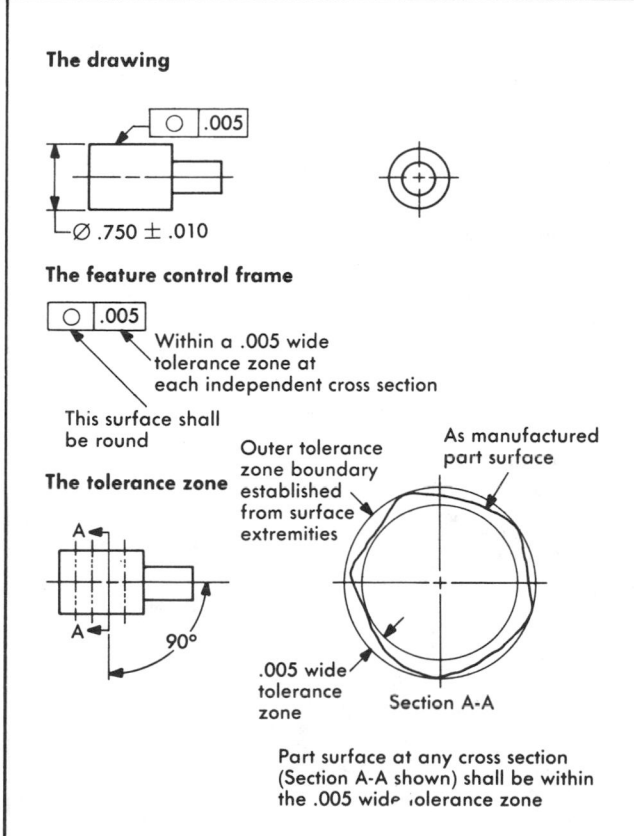

Fig. 9-22 Circularity control.

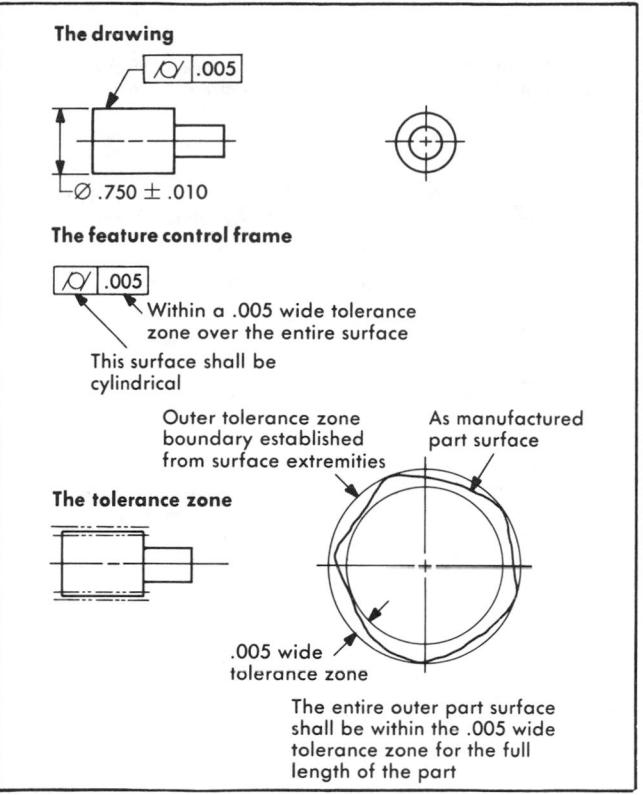

Fig. 9-23 Cylindricity control.

PROFILE CONTROL TOLERANCE

Profile tolerancing is a method of controlling irregular surfaces, lines, arcs, or unusual shapes as well as regular shapes. Profiles can be applied to individual line elements (profile of a line) or to the entire surface (profile of a surface) of a part. Refer to Fig. 9-1 for the symbols used to represent these geometric characteristics.

Definition

The profile tolerance specifies a uniform boundary along the true profile within which the elements of the surface must lie.[6] Profile of surface tolerances are three-dimensional extending along the length and width of the considered feature or features. On the other hand, line tolerances are two-dimensional, extending along the length of the considered feature.

The profile tolerance zone is the distance between two boundaries shaped to the true configuration indicated on the drawing by basic dimensions. The profile tolerance specified in the feature control frame can be applied to the drawing to indicate that the tolerance zone is divided on both sides of the true profile (bilateral tolerance). It can also be used to indicate that the tolerance zone only applies to one side of the true profile (unilateral tolerance). The two methods of indicating the profile tolerance zones are illustrated in Fig. 9-24.

Verification

Several inspection methods are commonly used to verify profile acceptance. One method uses hard tooling. In this method, the part is moved in relationship to a mastered test

GEOMETRIC DIMENSIONING AND TOLERANCING

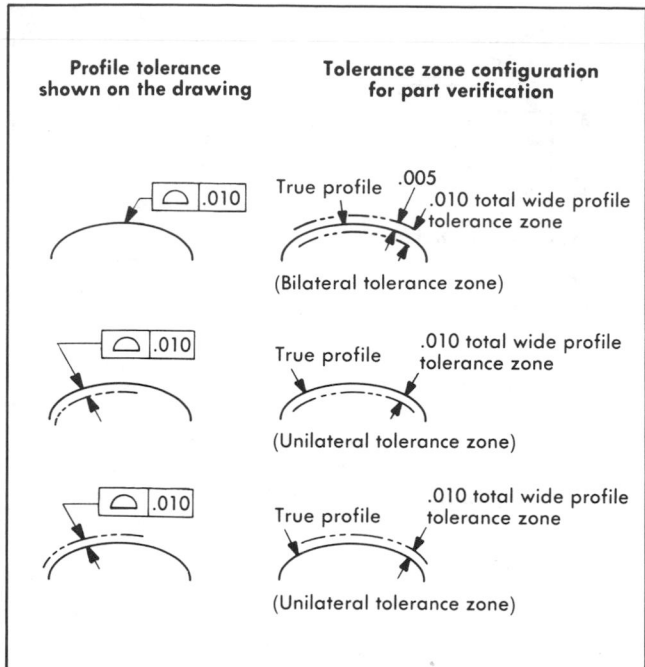

Fig. 9-24 Profile tolerance zones.

indicator at the specified part profile configuration from a datum reference frame.

Another method uses an optical comparator in conjunction with an overlay gage to verify profile requirements. This inspection method is limited to smaller parts that can be enlarged on the comparator screen. The part shadow must fall completely within the acceptable tolerance zone area of the overlay gage to be accepted. The image, visible on the screen, represents the maximum envelope of the part. The minimum envelope of the part should also be verified to make sure that it is within the tolerance requirements.

ORIENTATION TOLERANCES

Perpendicularity, angularity, and parallelism controls are referred to as orientation tolerances. These tolerance specifications control the orientation or attitude of a feature to a datum feature or features. Refer to Fig. 9-1 for the symbols used to represent these geometric characteristics.

Perpendicularity Tolerance

Perpendicularity is the condition of a surface, median plane, or axis at a right angle to a datum plane or axis.[7] Perpendicularity specifications can be applied to a surface or to a feature of size. When a feature of size is controlled, the tolerance zone value applies at RFS unless the MMC symbol is included in the feature control frame. If MMC is utilized, the inspector must take into account allowable bonus tolerances as the controlled feature departs from the MMC size.

In Fig. 9-25, the end of the part is required to be square to datum surface A within a 0.005″ wide tolerance zone. The tolerance zone is exactly 90° to datum surface A. The entire end surface of the part must be within the tolerance zone to meet the drawing requirements.

Perpendicularity requirements are normally verified with a test indicator and angle plate as shown in Fig. 9-26. The datum feature is placed against the angle plate to provide proper orientation of the part for inspection, and the test indicator is traversed over the entire end surface. The perpendicularity is acceptable if the full indicator movement does not exceed the 0.005″ perpendicularity specification. Caution should be exercised when aligning the part to the angle plate to ensure that only perpendicularity error is measured.

Angularity Tolerance

Angularity is the condition of a surface or axis at a specified angle (other than 90°) from a datum plane or axis.[8] Angularity can be specified at all angles except 90°. The 90° case of angularity is perpendicularity, which was previously discussed. The tolerance zones for angularity and perpendicularity are essentially the same for surface and two-dimensional axis controls. A typical feature control frame for angularity tolerance is shown in Fig. 9-27.

When inspecting parts for angularity, the part must be placed on the datum surface(s). The specified tolerance zone limits must not be exceeded for the part to be acceptable.

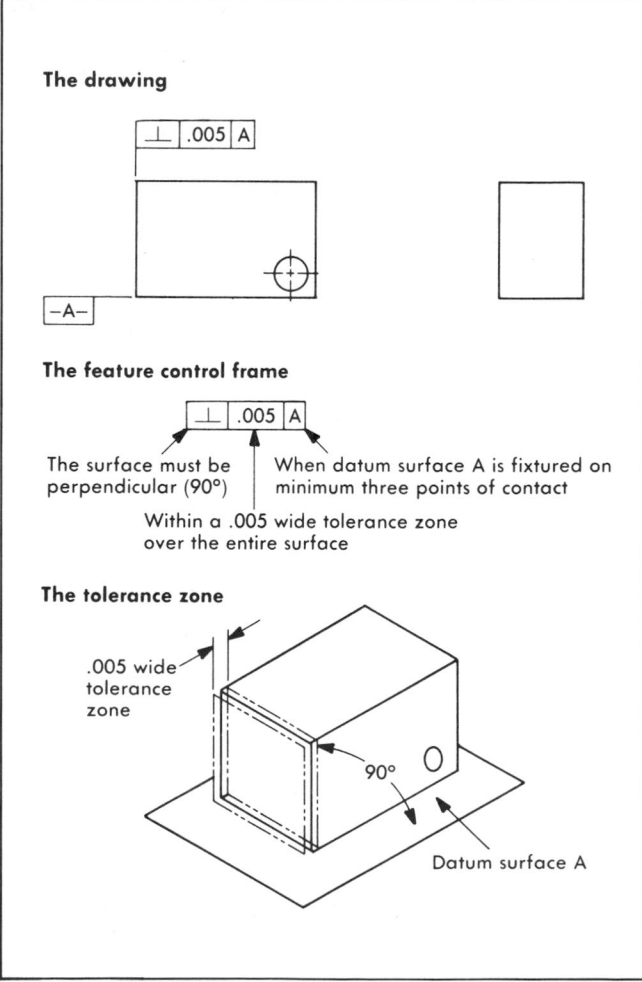

Fig. 9-25 Perpendicularity control.

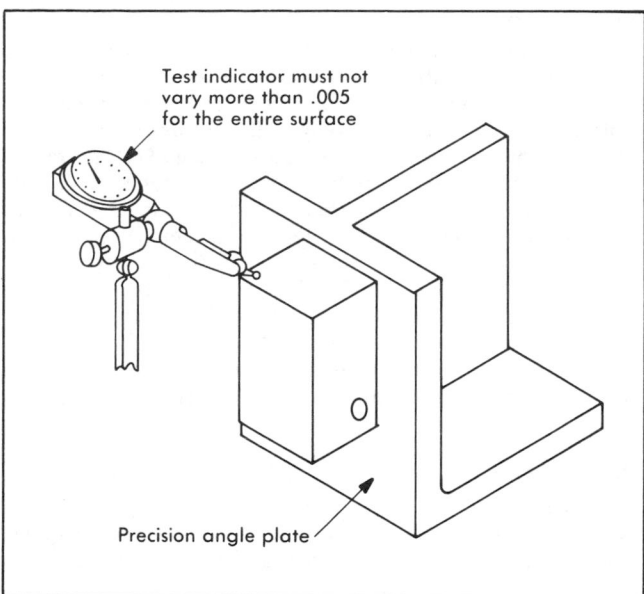

Fig. 9-26 Verifying perpendicularity using a test indicator and a precision angle plate.

Parallelism Tolerance

Parallelism is the condition of a surface equidistant at all points from a datum plane or an axis equidistant along its length to a datum axis.[9] The feature control frame in Fig. 9-28 specifies that the part surface must be parallel within a 0.001″ wide tolerance zone. The tolerance zone is parallel (equidistant) to the inspection table, which establishes datum plane A. The part thickness is allowed to vary within the part size tolerance (±0.005″). The parallelism specification refines the parallelism control allowed by the envelope rule, therefore the parallelism error allowed must be contained inside the boundary of perfect form at MMC.

Figure 9-29 shows a test indicator being used to check the parallelism specification of the part's upper surface. The lower surface, datum reference A, must make a minimum of three points of contact with the surface plate. Because datum planes exist in the manufacturing and inspection tooling and not the actual part, the real datum plane A is the surface plate. According to the ANSI definition, parallelism must be validated in relationship to the extremities of surface A as it contacts the surface plate or inspection table.

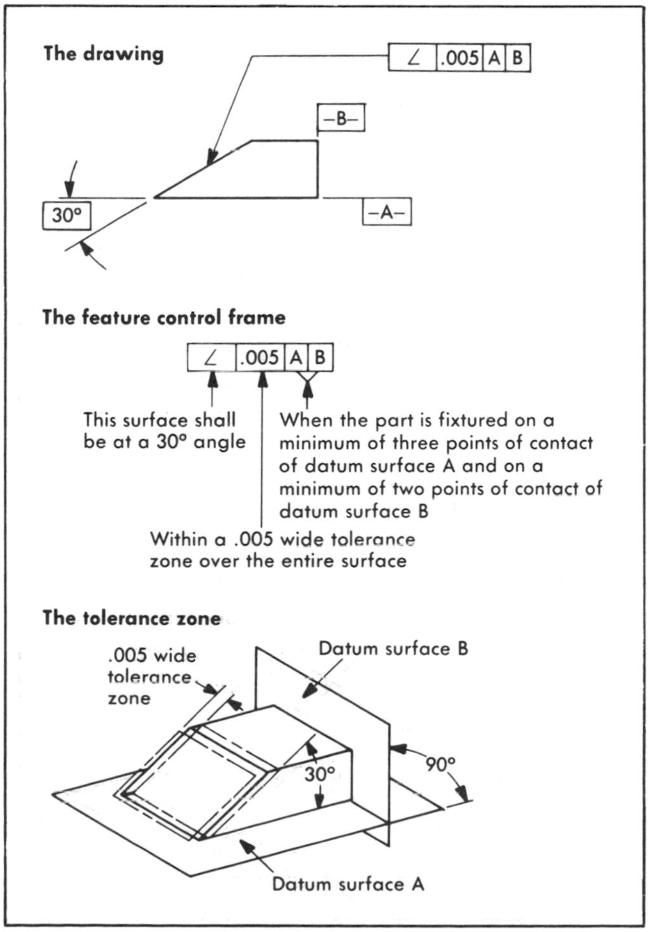

Fig. 9-27 Angularity control.

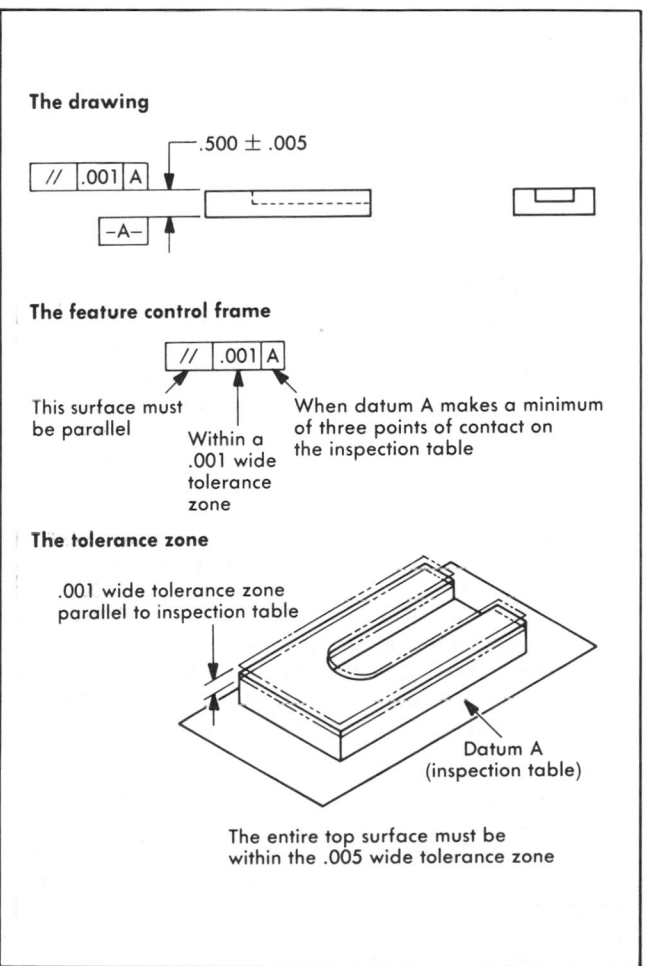

Fig. 9-28 Parallelism control.

GEOMETRIC DIMENSIONING AND TOLERANCING

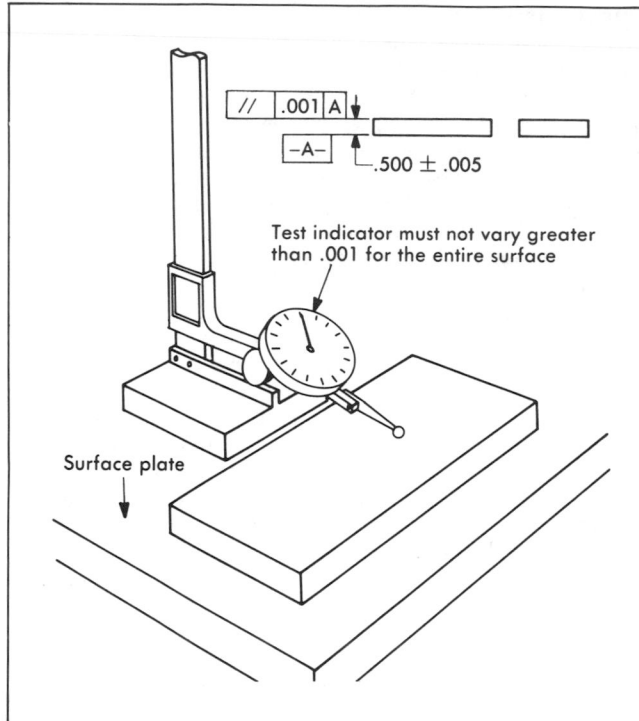

Fig. 9-29 Verifying parallelism by placing datum A on a surface plate and checking full indicator movement.

LOCATION TOLERANCES

The two locational tolerance controls in the ANSI Y14.5M-1982 standard are position and concentricity.

Positional Tolerance

A positional tolerance defines a zone within which the center, axis, or center plane of a feature of size is permitted to vary from true (theoretically exact) position.[10] Basic dimensions establish the true position from datum features and between interrelated features. A positional tolerance is indicated by the position symbol, a tolerance, and appropriate datum references placed in a feature control frame.

Positional tolerance zones are three-dimensional and apply through the thickness of the part. As shown in Fig. 9-30, a diameter position tolerance zone is 90° from the specified primary datum reference surface. It is important to note that the tolerance zone will also control perpendicularity of the feature within the position tolerance requirement.

The three methods used for verifying positional tolerances are functional gages, coordinate analysis, and graphical inspection analysis. Functional gages are three-dimensional mating parts at virtual condition and can only be used if MMC is specified. If the gage assembles to the part being inspected, then all other conforming parts will assemble.

Coordinate analysis is basically a two-step procedure used to verify the positional tolerances of a part. In the first step, the position features are measured using standard inspection instruments while the part is mounted on the specified datum surfaces. The data from these measurements are recorded and then analyzed to determine if the features are within the specified circular positional tolerance zones.

Symmetry

Symmetry is the quality of being the same on both sides in size, shape, and relative position from a center plane.

To check for symmetry, the part is placed on the inspection table as shown in Fig. 9-31, view *a*. If the sides of the datum feature are not parallel, they must be shimmed to centralize the center plane of the datum feature. The distance from the inspection table to the top surface of the tab is measured, and the maximum value is recorded. The part is then turned over to allow the opposite side of the datum feature to rest on the inspection table (see Fig. 9-31, view *b*). Again the maximum distance from the inspection table to the top surface of the tab should be measured and recorded. The difference between the two recorded values is compared. Symmetry control has been met if the difference between the two recorded values does not exceed the specification.

Concentricity

Concentricity is the condition where the axes of all cross-sectional elements of a surface of revolution are common to the axis of a datum feature.[11] Figure 9-32 illustrates how concen-

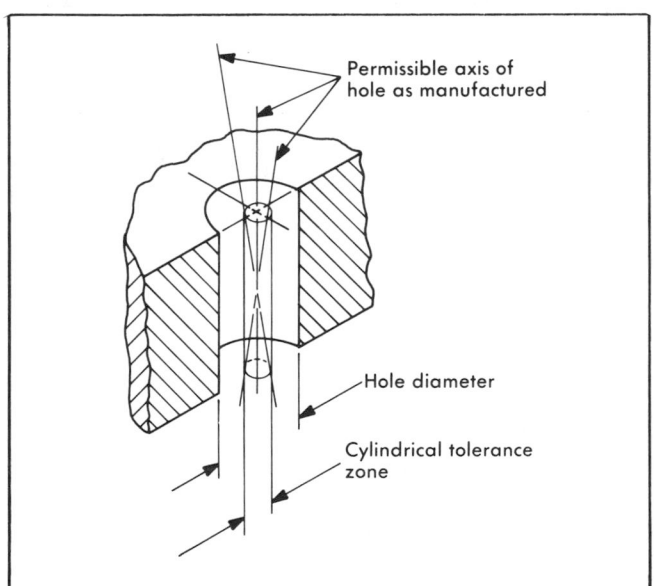

Fig. 9-30 Position tolerance cylindrical zone.

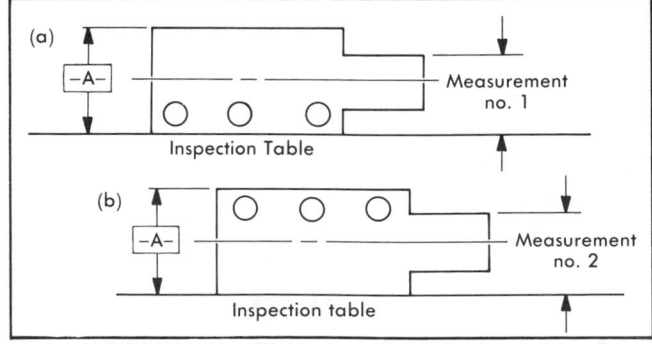

Fig. 9-31 Verifying symmetry.

tricity control is noted on a typical drawing and explains what is required for the part to be in conformance. When concentricity is verified, the feature axis must be evaluated in relationship to the datum axis. The datum axis is established by tooling (precision chucks, collets, expanding mandrels, or gage pins) making contact with the surface of the datum feature. The axis of the controlled feature may, however, be difficult to identify because it must be established from the feature surface, which may be bowed or out-of-round in addition to being eccentric to the datum axis. To establish the true feature axis, an analysis of the surface irregularities may be required.

Concentricity can be verified (not measured) by rotating the part on the datum axis with a dial indicator in contact with the controlled feature surface (see Fig. 9-33). For the part to be in conformance, the entire feature surface must rotate within the concentricity specification. This inspection procedure actually verifies runout control. Parts that check within tolerance specifications are acceptable, but parts exceeding acceptance criteria may also be acceptable.

In addition to excessive feature axis eccentricity, failure to meet the concentricity specification can also be attributed to excessive surface irregularity. Parts having excessive surface irregularities such as out-of-roundness or bow can be within concentricity specifications. Therefore, it is necessary to nullify the surface irregularities in the inspection process.

Out-of-roundness can be nullified by inspecting the part as shown in Fig. 9-34. In view *a*, dial indicator readings are taken at 0° and 180°. If the readings are equal, the feature axis is exactly coincident with the datum axis in this rotational plane. In view *b*, measurements are made at 90° and 270°. Although

the readings are 0.003″ (which is greater than the specification), they are equal, indicating that the part is also concentric in this plane.

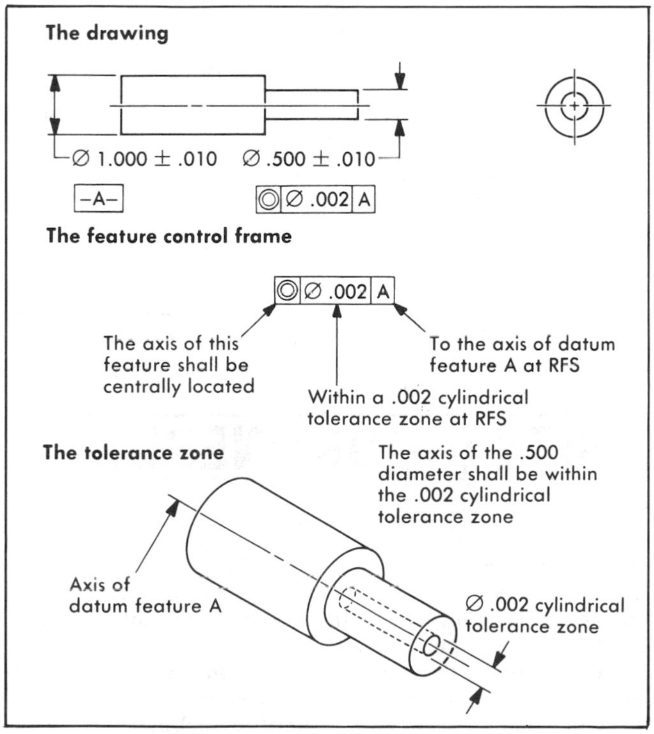

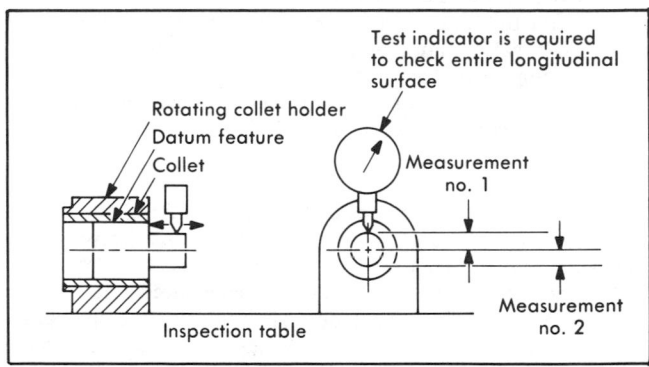

Fig. 9-33 Verifying concentricity using runout.

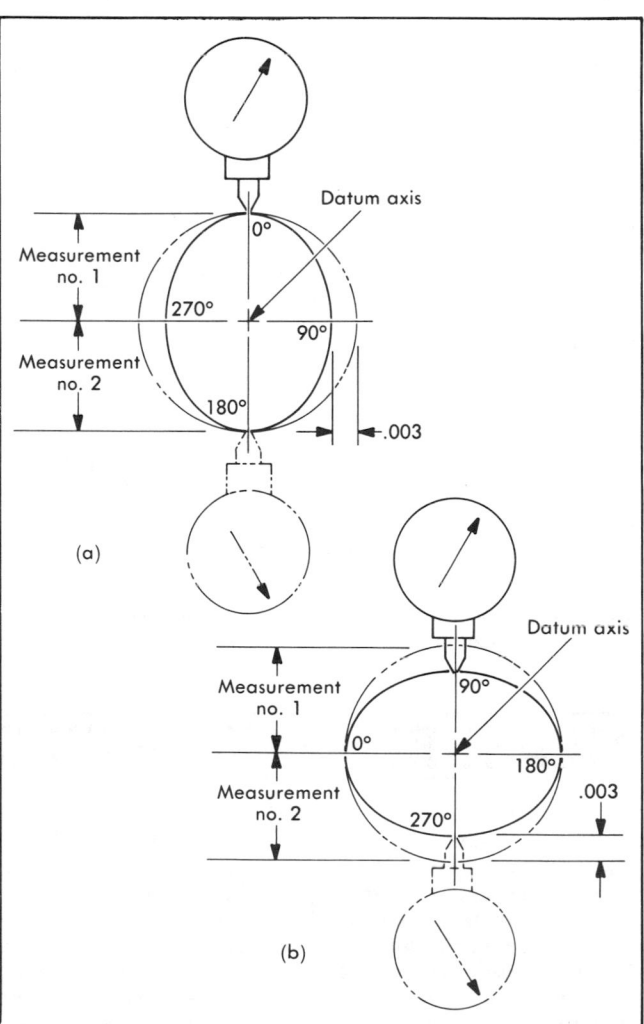

Fig. 9-34 Verifying concentricity by nullifying out-of-roundness.

The drawing

Ø 1.000 ± .010   Ø .500 ± .010

─A─   ◎ Ø .002 A

The feature control frame

◎ Ø .002 A

The axis of this feature shall be centrally located

To the axis of datum feature A at RFS

Within a .002 cylindrical tolerance zone at RFS

The tolerance zone

The axis of the .500 diameter shall be within the .002 cylindrical tolerance zone

Axis of datum feature A

Ø .002 cylindrical tolerance zone

Fig. 9-32 Concentricity control.

GEOMETRIC DIMENSIONING AND TOLERANCING

If the part were trilobed, the dial indicator readings would be verified at 120° increments. When nonsymmetrical lobing and bowing is combined, the inspection process is extremely difficult.

RUNOUT TOLERANCE

Runout tolerance is a combination of surface (form) and position (location) control. Runout can be specified to control surfaces constructed around a datum axis and surfaces perpendicular to the datum axis. Runout tolerances are always applied at RFS and cannot be applied at MMC.

Circular Runout

Circular runout provides control of circular elements of a surface.[12] The tolerance is applied independently at any circular measuring position as the part is rotated 360°. A circular runout tolerance applied to surfaces constructed around a datum axis controls the cumulative variances of circularity and coaxiality. When it is applied to surfaces constructed at right angles to the datum axis, it controls circular elements of a plane surface. The feature control frame specifying circular runout is shown in Fig. 9-35. The tolerance indicates the amount of full indicator movement that is permitted for the feature to be acceptable.

To verify the circular runout of the part in Fig. 9-35, the datum feature is mounted in a precision rotating device to allow the part to rotate on the datum axis. A part mounted on one functional diameter is shown in Fig. 9-36. A test indicator is then placed in contact with the part surface and the part is rotated 360°. Several independent checks should be made along the part's surface to ensure that the entire feature is within tolerance. The indicator should be reset to zero for each circular measurement. For the part to be acceptable, the full indicator movement must be within the specified tolerance.

Total Runout

Total runout provides composite control of all surface elements.[13] The tolerance is applied simultaneously to circular and longitudinal elements as the part is rotated 360°. Total runout controls the cumulative variations of circularity, cylindricity, straightness, coaxiality, angularity, taper, and profile when it is applied to surfaces constructed around a datum axis. When it is applied to surfaces constructed at right angles to a datum axis, it controls cumulative variations of perpendicularity (to limit wobble) and flatness (to limit concavity or convexity).

Total runout is verified in a similar manner as circular runout. The only difference in the inspection process is that when testing total runout, while the part is rotated, the test indicator is moved parallel to the datum axis (for circular surfaces) or perpendicular to the axis (for perpendicular plane surfaces). In addition, the indicator does not have to be reset to zero during the entire testing procedure.

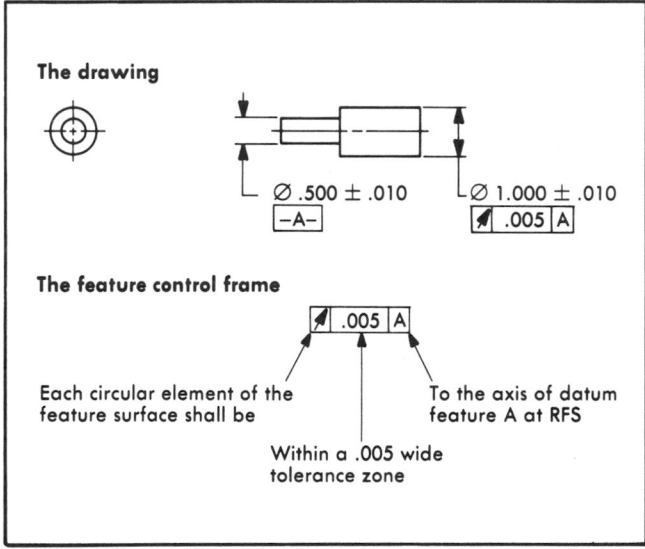

Fig. 9-35 Circular runout control.

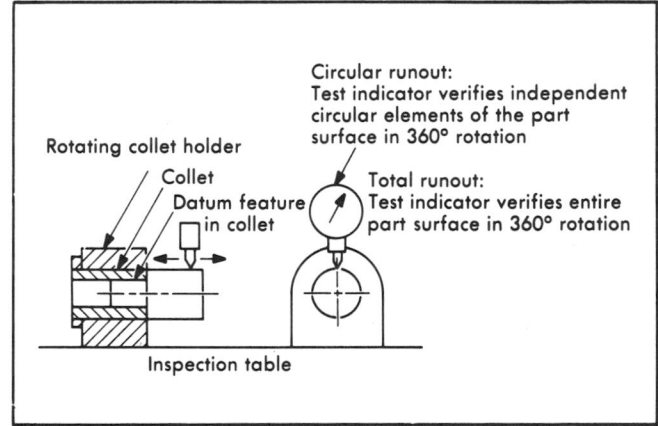

Fig. 9-36 Circular and total runout verification.

MEASUREMENT OF CIRCULARITY (ROUNDNESS)

Geometrically, a part can be said to be round (circular), in a given cross section, if there exists within the section a point from which all points on the periphery are equidistant. In practice, however, the radius of nominally round parts tends to vary from point to point around the periphery. Thus the problem encountered by the manufacturing engineer is one of displaying and assessing these variations and correctly interpreting the results.

The symbol for circularity is based on and used in accordance with the feature control criteria established in ANSI Y14.5M-1982, "Dimensioning and Tolerancing," Figure 9-37 shows the

feature control frame for a round part. The control frame specifies the size of the required tolerance zone for the manufactured part. It does not specify the measuring method to use nor the method of evaluating the data obtained from the measuring method. The method of measurement is selected based on the accuracy required.

Most surfaces of circular cross section are originally generated by revolving about, or with reference to, fixed points, axes, or lines of contact in a machine tool such as centers, work spindles, steady rests, tool edges, and grinding wheel surfaces.

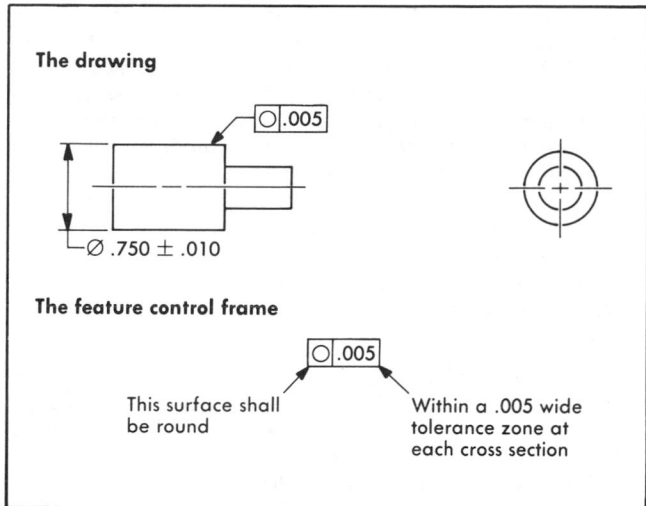

The drawing

Ø .750 ± .010

The feature control frame

⊖ .005

This surface shall be round

Within a .005 wide tolerance zone at each cross section

Fig. 9-37 Feature control frame of a circular part.

However, the relationships of these points, axes, and lines of contact with the part are never perfect. Variable deflections and imperfect rotation occur as the surface is generated because of unbalance, erratic cutting action, inadequate lubrication, wear, defective or incorrect machine parts, and poor part geometry.

The result of these deflections is usually a deviation from circularity, referred to as out-of-roundness, in the form of lobes, waves, or undulations about the circumference of the part. The number of lobes or waves can vary from two to several hundred; two to fifteen lobes are generally generated by the manufacturing process. Out-of-roundness may also result from distortion of the part by chuck jaws, fixturing, localized heating, excessive feeds, and warped or out-of-round stock. Table 9-1 lists the typical causes for parts containing various numbers of lobes.

It is important to know the characteristics of the lobes present so that the correct measuring method can be selected. For example, the out-of-roundness of a part with an odd number of evenly spaced lobes cannot be detected by diametrical

TABLE 9-1
Typical Causes of Lobing Conditions on Circular Parts

Number of Lobes	Causes
2	Inaccuracy in tooling (elliptical). Part not square in machine. Part not square in measuring machine
3-4	Distortion of part due to clamping in machine or measuring system. Commonly caused by three or four-jaw chuck
5-15	Machining process (centerless grinding produces an odd number of lobes)
>15	Process and material parameters. Common process parameters include vibrations, tool condition, spindle speed, feed rates, and medium to high-frequency chatter

methods. Out-of-roundness is also distorted in magnitude when V-block methods are used. In addition, certain lobing patterns cannot be detected in a V-block.

Direct evaluation of a circular surface as a whole is difficult, and assessment is simplified by measuring a series of cross-sectional profiles. For most applications, this approach provides sufficient information about the form of the entire surface.

MEASURING METHODS

The conditions of circularity, external and internal, demand the most attention of any form or shape measurement because this type of geometry comprises the great majority of mechanical form conditions in manufacturing operations. Two primary methods of gaging are currently being used to determine the form trueness and to measure the form irregularities of nominally circular objects.

Intrinsic Datum Method

The measurement of circularity using one of the intrinsic datum methods is extensively used throughout industry. The most commonly used intrinsic datum methods are diametrical measurements, V-block measurements, and bench center measurements. However, it is important to understand that none of these methods will supply information in complete agreement with the standard specifications of circularity.

Diametrical measurements. One of the most common methods of measuring out-of-roundness is by the comparison of diameter measurements made in a common, cross-sectional plane. Measurements are made between two contact points. Two-point measurement methods can only determine the out-of-roundness value when the part is known to have an even number of uniformly spaced and uniformly sized lobes or undulations around its periphery.

When diametrical measurements are used as an indication of out-of-roundness, the lobing condition must be taken into consideration. For parts having an odd number of lobes, the difference in diametrical measurements is generally smaller than the true radial out-of-roundness. The difference will diminish to zero for uniform, symmetrically shaped lobes. Parts having an even lobed surface will produce diametrical out-of-roundness values larger than the true value.

V-block measurements. The V-block measurement method is a three-point method suitable for measuring parts with an odd number of lobes. It is not suitable for parts with an even number of lobes because supporting the part in a V-block will conceal the out-of-roundness condition. The part is placed in the vee and then rotated slowly to keep from disturbing the V-block and gage stand while the test indicator tip is in contact with the part (see Fig. 9-38, view a). If the part is truly round with negligible irregularity, the pointer of the indicator will not move. If, however, the part is out-of-round, the irregularities or lobes will displace the plunger of the test indicator as they are passed under it.

For large parts, an inverted arrangement is sometimes used (see Fig. 9-38, view b). The indicator is mounted in a frame that can be moved around the part; the feet of the frame represent the arms of the vee. A similar arrangement can be used to check the circularity of bores (see Fig. 9-38, view c).

MEASUREMENT OF CIRCULARITY

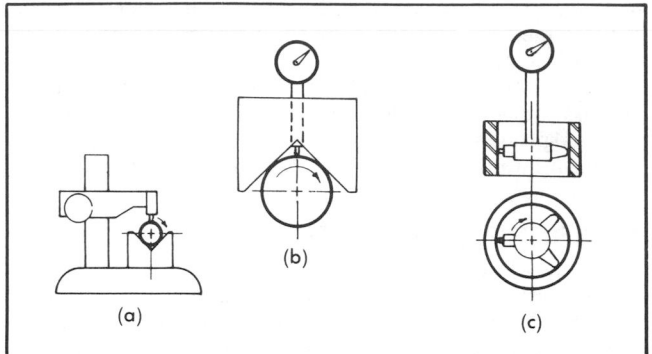

Fig. 9-38 Out-of-roundness can be checked on parts with a V-block and test indicator.

The amount that the pointer on the test indicator moves depends on the height and angular spacing of the lobes as well as the angle of the V-block. The amount of out-of-roundness is actually exaggerated so a conversion factor must be used with the measured value. To determine the angular spacing or the number of lobes on the surface of the parts, it is necessary to employ one of the extrinsic datum methods discussed subsequently. The ideal included angle of the V-block can be determined by the equation:

$$A = 180 - 360/n \qquad (1)$$

where:

A = included angle of the V-block, deg
n = number of lobes

Bench center measurements. The bench center method is only suitable for parts that are manufactured with machine centers. In this method, the part to be measured is mounted between the centers of a bench center and then rotated while a test indicator (mechanical or electronic) is in contact with the surface (see Fig. 9-39).

With the bench center measurement method, parts that are within the tolerance specification are acceptable. However, parts that are not within the tolerance specification may also be acceptable because of errors inherent in this method. Out-of-roundness error can be caused by an improper alignment of the bench centers and/or center holes. The angles of the centers may also be different than the center holes. Other sources of error include out-of-round center holes and centers, inadequate surface condition of centers and center holes, and bowed parts.

Extrinsic Datum Method

In the extrinsic datum method, precision spindle instruments are used to measure part circularity. The part is mounted on either a stationary or rotating table, depending on the instrument design, with an electronic probe (stylus) contacting the surface of the part. When the part or spindle is rotated, the instrument prints an enlarged scale representation of the surface configuration on a polar graph chart. In addition to printing the surface configuration, most precision spindle instruments also print a reference circle for verification.

Measuring circularity with precision spindle instruments supplies a true image of the geometric condition of the part by selective magnification. Magnification rates and suppression of inconsequential features can be varied to enhance the most meaningful aspects of the circularity condition.

The trace produced by the polar graphing instrument is simply a graphical record, suitably magnified, of the displacement of the stylus of the measuring instrument. The out-of-roundness value can be assessed by the differences between the maximum and minimum radial ordinates of the profile measured from a specific center. The four methods by which this center can be located are:

1. Minimum radial separations (MRS).
2. Least squares circle (LSC).
3. Maximum inscribed circle (MIC).
4. Minimum circumscribed circle (MCC).

Minimum radial separation. In the minimum radial separation or minimum zone circles method, two concentric circles are chosen so as to have the least radial separation and yet contain between them, all of the polar trace (see Fig. 9-40, view *a*). The radial separation is the measure of the out-of-roundness value.

Least squares circle. In the least squares circle method, a theoretical circle is located within the polar profile such that the sum of the squares of the radial ordinates between the circle and the profile is a minimum. The center of this circle is then used to draw a circumscribed and inscribed circle on the profile graph (see Fig. 9-40, view *b*). The out-of-roundness value is then the radial separation of these two circles.

The least squares circle (LSC) and its center are unique because there is only one circle that meets the definition. The accuracy of the center and radial zone width depends on the number of ordinates taken.

Maximum inscribed circle. In the maximum inscribed circle method, the profile center is determined by the largest circle that can be fitted inside the profile (see Fig. 9-40, view *c*). The center can be determined by trial-and-error with a bow compass or with engraved circles on a transparent template. The out-of-roundness of the part is the maximum outward departure from the inscribed circle.

Minimum circumscribed circle. In the minimum circumscribed circle method, the profile center is determined by the smallest circle that contains the measured profile (see Fig. 9-40, view *d*). From this center point, an inscribed circle fitted inside the profile is drawn. The out-of-roundness is the maximum inward departure from the circumscribed circle.

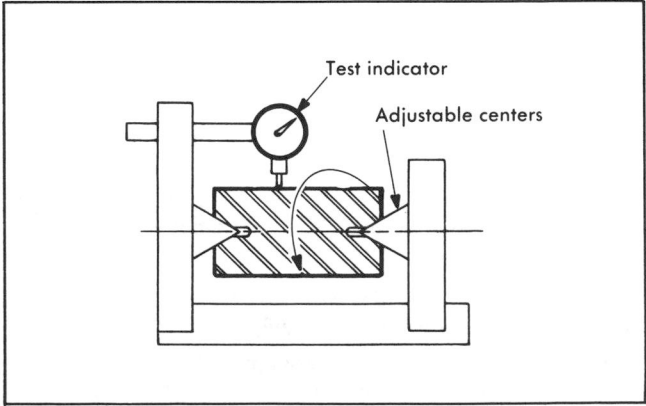

Fig. 9-39 Measurement of out-of-roundness using the bench-center method.

MEASUREMENT OF CIRCULARITY

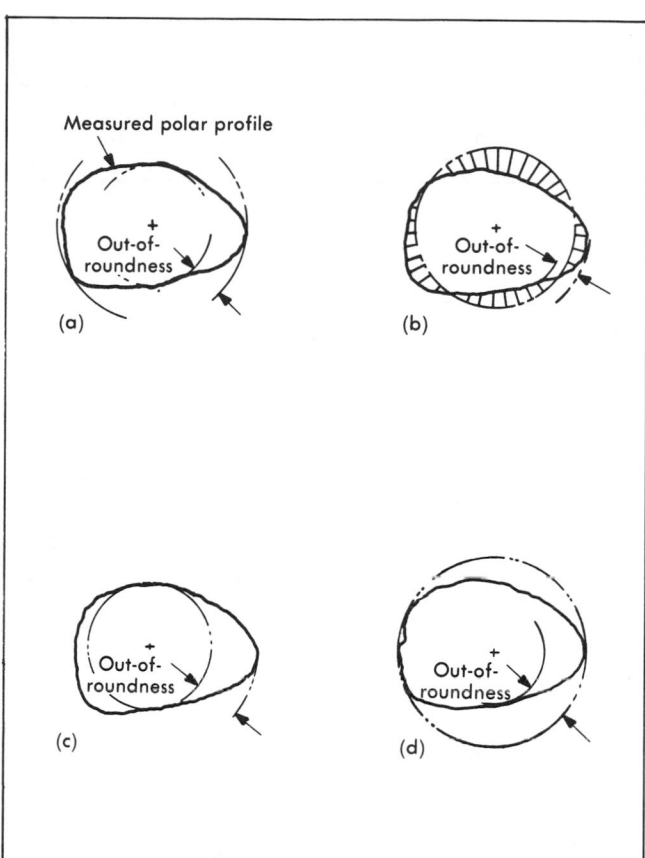

Fig. 9-40 Different methods are used for determining the center of measured profile when measuring out-of-roundness: (a) minimum radial separation, (b) least squares circle, (c) maximum inscribed circle, and (d) minimum circumscribed circle.

EQUIPMENT

In addition to micrometers, V-blocks, and indicators, precision spindle instruments are commonly used to measure circularity. The two types of these instruments are: (1) those in which the part rotates while the stylus and pickup remain stationary and (2) those in which the stylus and pickup rotate while the part remains stationary (see Fig. 9-41). Each type has its advantages and is more suitable for certain types of measurement; the choice depends on the measurements to be made and the size and shape of the parts being measured.

The rotary table instruments are generally used to measure circularity on small parts and with the center of rotation close to the part center because large eccentric loads can adversely affect the accuracy of the machine. These machines are also used to measure any relationships relative to the part axis such as concentricity, eccentricity, perpendicularity, parallelism, and coaxiality because changes in the pickup configuration and position do not affect the spindle to the part relationship. Rotating pickup instruments are the most accurate because the load on the spindle bearings is constant; part weight and configuration do not affect accuracy.

In operation, the stylus of the pickup is brought into contact with a point along the selected surface element of the part and adjusted to a position of zero indication.[14] The rotary displace-

ment movement of the machine is started while the stylus remains in contact with the part surface. An uninterrupted succession of an infinite number of contact points is thus created, describing a complete circle around the surface of the part.

Variations in the distance between the axis of rotation and the contacted points along the surface element cause the stylus to deflect. These deflections produce electrical signals in the pickup that are electronically amplified at a preset rate and then displayed on a meter or by a recorder. The recorder reproduces the deflections on a polar or linear graph. The distance between the axis of rotation and any contact point on the part surface is considered to represent the radius to the momentarily contacted surface point. The variations of the consecutive radii are the measure of departure from perfect circularity as represented by the displacement path of the stylus.

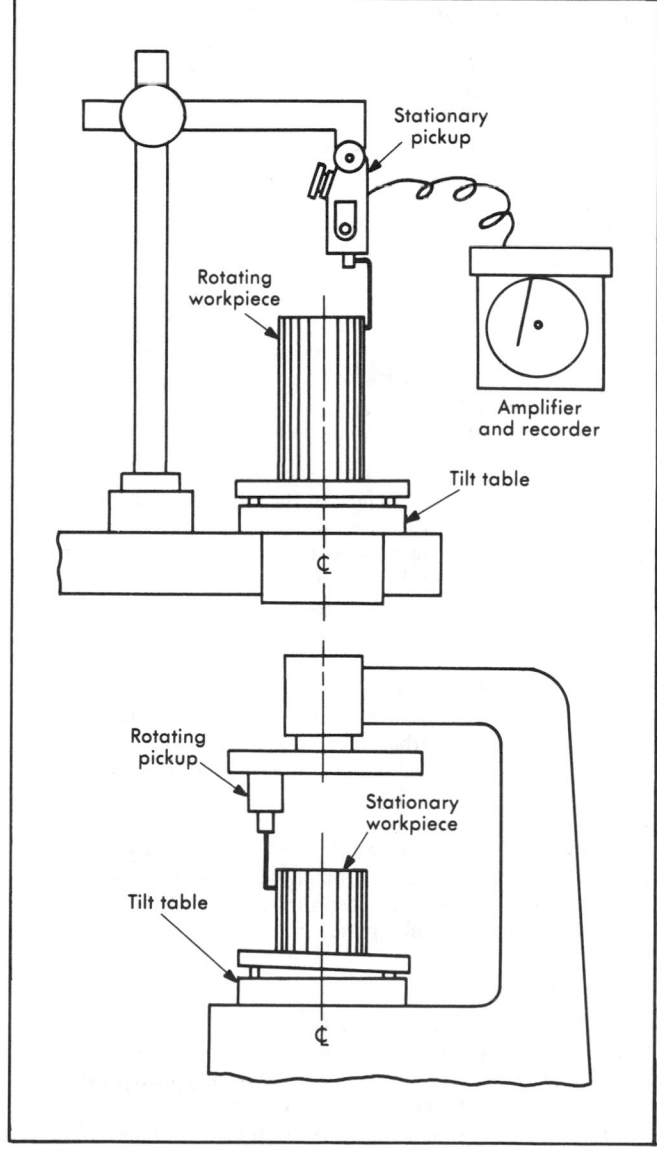

Fig. 9-41 Rotating-workpiece and rotating-pickup types of precision spindle instruments for measuring roundness.

MEASUREMENT OF ANGLES

MEASUREMENT OF ANGLES

One of the most widely used general groups of angle measurements is based on comparing the angular conditions of a part or of a feature to an angle of known size. Angular measurements can also be measured directly using an instrument that is equipped with a scale graduated in angular units. The third general group consists of devices that can be rotated in controlled angular units.

INDIRECT MEASUREMENT

In indirect measurements, the angular surface of the part is compared to an angle of known size.

Adjustable Gages

The main gages used in this group are sine bars and sine plates. A sine bar consists of a hardened steel bar to which two support rolls are attached. The fixed distance between the two rolls is usually 5 or 10″. The sine bar is always used in conjunction with a flat surface and gage blocks.

Angles are generated by placing gage block(s) of known height under one end of the sine bar (see Fig. 9-42). The height of the gage blocks required for a specific angle can be determined by the equation:

$$h = \sin \alpha \times c \qquad (2)$$

where:

    h = height of gage block stack, in.
    α = angle to be measured, deg
    c = length of sine bar between roll centers, in.

Once the angle has been established, the part to be measured is placed on the sloping surface of the sine bar. A height gage with a test indicator is then used to check if the plane of the part's top surface is parallel to the plane of the supporting surface plate. It is generally recommended that sine bars should not be used for checking angles greater than 45° because of the decrease in accuracy resulting from trigonometric relations.

Angle Gage Blocks

Angle gage blocks are comprised of solid blocks having two flat working surfaces that are inclined to each other by a specified angle. The blocks are wrung together to produce the desired angle. Angle blocks are always used in conjunction with flat surfaces.

Once the angle has been established, the part may be placed on the blocks or vice versa. A height gage can then be used to check if the plane of the part's top surface is parallel to the plane of the supporting surface plate.

DIRECT MEASUREMENT

The most commonly used instrument for the direct measurement of angles is the vernier protractor. A typical protractor contains one fixed blade and another blade attached to a rotating turret or dial. The dial is graduated in degrees and a vernier is graduated in five minute increments (one-twelfth of one degree).

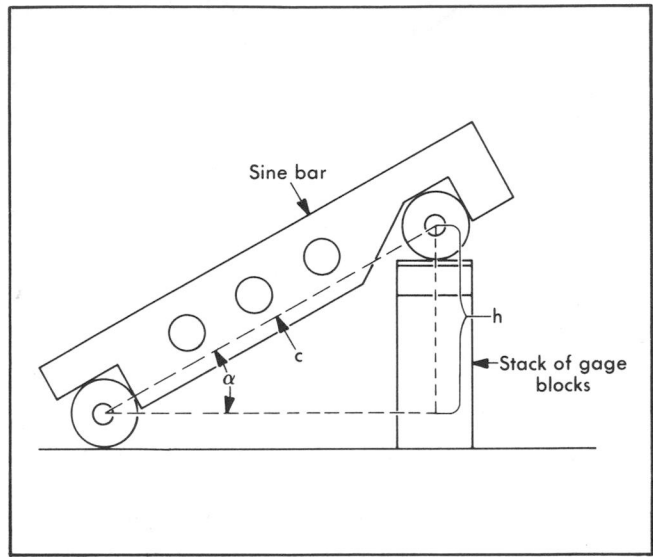

Fig. 9-42 Measuring the angular surface of a part using a sine bar and gage blocks.

Because the protractor measures only the angle between its blades, contact between the blade and the part being measured must be maintained. Intimate contact can be checked by placing a light source behind the protractor. If the contact is good, there will not be any light passing through the blades and the part being measured.

ROTATIONAL MEASUREMENT

Many parts are designed with features arranged in locations that result from the division of a common reference circle.[15] The spacing of these features is determined by associating them with the pertinent radii of the reference circle and specifying the central angles that intercept the radii.

To check the correctness of the angular positions, these features must be presented to the sensing member of a measuring instrument in precise correspondence with the basic values of the specified angle spacings. Common devices for rotating the part by the required angular increments are rotary tables and dividing or indexing heads. The main difference between these two devices is the position of the rotational axis—vertical for the rotary tables and horizontal for the dividing heads. The actual measurement is taken by a mechanical or electronic indicator that references from one of the features at a point contained in a circular path common to all of the features to be inspected.

OPTICAL MEASUREMENT

The three primary methods of optical angle measurement are optical comparators, toolmakers' microscopes, and autocollimators.

Optical Comparators

The optical comparator (projector) displays magnified images on an appropriate viewing screen, with the magnified image used to measure angular relationships. An optical comparator normally contains a high-intensity light source that illuminates the objects either by forming a shadow image on the screen, or by magnifying the object's illuminated surface. An object lens then focuses the enlarged image onto the screen after reflection on one or more mirrors.

To achieve a high accuracy of measurement, the plane of measurement must be perpendicular to the optical axis of the projector. Perpendicularity can be ensured by maintaining sharp focus of all portions of the measured angle. The image should be enlarged to fill as much of the screen as possible. The angle measurement can be made using protractor rings, angular chart gages, or a rotation stage.

Toolmakers' Microscope

A toolmakers' microscope can be used in a similar manner to an optical comparator, except that the eye observes the image through a microscope instead of a screen. The eyepiece reticle is used in a similar fashion to the rear projection screen of an optical comparator. Toolmakers' microscopes are normally supplied with a goniometric eyepiece containing a reticle that can be rotated through 360°. Readout of rotation is then made by reading the circular graduations.

Autocollimators and Reflectors

An autocollimator measures, remotely, the angle of a reflector (mirror). Because of the instrument's extreme sensitivity (1/10 second of arc), it is used to measure small angles and as a nulling accessory when employed with angular gage blocks and rotary tables.

The autocollimator is a modified form of telescope that has an illuminated target or reticle located in the focal plane of an objective lens (Fig. 9-43). The illumination emanating from the autocollimator is directed to the mirror that is used to reflect the image back on itself. Any rotation of the mirror by a small angle deflects the beam by twice this angle, which in turn displaces the image of the cross hairs, as observed through the eyepiece. The motion of the image is verified using a standard driven by a micrometer and slide. The micrometer scale is graduated in 0.1 second of arc increments, with the measuring range normally being 10 minutes of arc. In addition to micrometer readout, electronic readouts are available that operate by photoelectrically sensing the motion of the image of the reticle. In this manner, higher sensitivity and repeatability are realized.

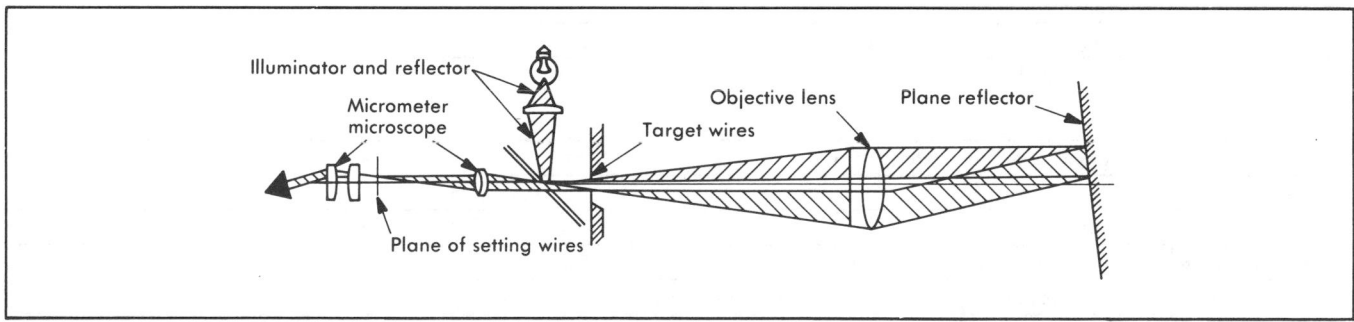

Fig. 9-43 Optical configuration of typical autocollimator.

SCREW THREAD GAGING AND MEASUREMENT

Screw threads are important elements of mechanical design with wide and varied applications, particularly for controlled translational motion and for fasteners providing disengageable connections.[16] The dimensional accuracy of screw threads is necessary to ensure the dependable assembly of threaded mating components, the interchangeability of the corresponding threaded parts, the consistent proportional relationship between the imparted rotational and resulting translational movements, and the mechanical strength of the threaded connection.

MEASURING METHODS

One of the basic fundamentals of thread gaging is to select gaging that is as consistent as possible with the requirements of the application and threading process. The proper gage selection ensures the highest degree of repeatability and reduces the probability of generating sort, scrap, rework, and selective assembly conditions.

Tables 9-2 and 9-3 list the gages, gaging elements, and measuring equipment that can be used in the measurement of screw threads on external and internal products, respectively. The horizontal column contains the various screw thread dimensions and the vertical column contains the gages or equipment currently being used to gage or measure product screw thread dimensions. The horizontal column is also subdivided, where appropriate, into functional limit and size columns. Functional limit refers to attributes inspection and is a qualitative assessment, which only determines if a characteristic is in conformance. Functional size refers to variables inspection and is a quantitative and qualitative assessment. The assessment is then compared with tabled values to determine if the characteristic is in conformance. The type of gage or measuring equipment that could be used to determine a specific screw thread characteristic is designated by a black dot in the body of the appropriate table.

Tables 9-4 and 9-5 list the dimensions that must be inspected to determine thread acceptability by the difference gaging sys-

SCREW THREAD GAGING AND MEASUREMENT

TABLE 9-2
Screw Thread Gages and Equipment for External Product Thread Characteristics

Thread Gages and Measuring Equipment	Maximum Material — GO — Func. Limit A_1	Maximum Material — GO — Func. Size A_2	LO Functional Diameter — Func. Limit B_1	LO Functional Diameter — Func. Size B_2	Minimum Material — Pitch Diameter — Limit C_1	Minimum Material — Pitch Diameter — Size C_2	Minimum Material — Thread Groove Diameter — Limit D_1	Minimum Material — Thread Groove Diameter — Size D_2
1. Threaded rings (ANSI B47.1 split or solid): 1.1 GO	●							
1.2 LO			●					
2. Thread snap gages: 2.1 GO segments	●							
2.2 LO segments—two pitches approximately			●					
2.3 GO rolls	●							
2.4 LO rolls—two pitches approximately			●					
2.5 Minimum material—pitch diameter type—cone and vee					●			
2.6 Minimum material—thread groove diameter type—cone only							●	
3. Plain diameter gages: 3.1 Maximum plain cylindrical ring for major diameter								
3.2 Major diameter snap type								
3.3 Minor diameter snap type								
3.4 Maximum/minimum major diameter snap type								
3.5 Maximum/minimum minor diameter snap type								
4. Indicating thread gages having either two contacts each at 180° or three contacts each at 120°: 4.1 GO segments	●	●	●	●				
4.2 LO segments—two pitches approximately			●	●				
4.3 GO rolls	●	●	●	●				
4.4 LO rolls—two pitches approximately			●	●				
4.5 Minimum material—pitch diameter type—cone and vee					●	●		
4.6 Minimum material—thread groove diameter type—cone only							●	●
4.7 Major diameter/pitch diameter eccentricity gage								
4.8 Differential segment or roll**								
5. Indicating plain diameter gages: 5.1 Major diameter type								
5.2 Minor diameter type								
6. Pitch micrometer with standard contacts (approximately LO profile) cone and vee			●	●				
7. Pitch micrometer with modified contacts (approximately P.D. contact) cone and vee					●	●		
8. Thread measuring wires with suitable measuring means							●	●
9. Optical comparator/toolmakers' microscope with suitable fixturing					●	●		
10. Profile tracing equipment with suitable fixturing								
11. Lead measuring machine with suitable fixturing								
12. Helical path attachment used with GO type indicating gages								
13. Helical path analyzer								
14. Plain micrometer/calipers—modified as required								
15. Surface measuring equipment								
16. Roundness equipment								

* Maximum minor diameter limit is acceptable when product passes GO gage.
** GO profile for one pitch in length used in combination with a GO indicating gage to yield a diameter equivalent for deviation in lead including uniformity of helix; and a minimum material indicating gage to yield a diameter equivalent for deviation in flank angle.

SCREW THREAD GAGING AND MEASUREMENT

TABLE 9-2—*Continued*

Roundness of Pitch Cylinder				Taper of Pitch Cylinder		Lead Including Helix Deviation	Flank Angle Deviation	Major Diameter		Minor Diameter		Root Radius	Diameter Runout Major to Pitch	Surface Texture
Oval 180°		Multilobe 120°												
Limit	Size	Limit	Size	Limit	Size			Limit	Size	Limit	Size			
E_1	E_2	F_1	F_2	G_1	G_2	H	I	J_1	J_2	K_1	K_2	L	M	N
										*				
•										*				
•				•										
•										*				
•				•										
•				•										
•				•										
								•						
								•						
										•				
								•						
										•				
•	•	•	•							*				
•	•	•	•	•	•									
•	•	•	•							*				
•	•	•	•	•	•									
•	•	•	•	•	•									
•	•	•	•	•	•									
													•	
•	•	•	•	•	•	•	•							
								•	•					
										•	•			
•	•			•	•									
•	•			•	•									
•	•			•	•									
•	•	•	•			•	•	•	•	•	•	•	•	
							•					•		•
						•								
						•								
						•								
								•	•					
														•
•	•	•	•											

(ANSI)

SCREW THREAD GAGING AND MEASUREMENT

TABLE 9-3
Screw Thread Gages and Equipment for Internal Product Thread Characteristics

Thread Gages and Measuring Equipment	Maximum Material GO		HI Functional Diameter		Minimum Material Pitch Diameter		Minimum Material Thread Groove Diameter	
	Func. Limit A_1	Func. Size A_2	Func. Limit B_1	Func. Size B_2	Limit C_1	Size C_2	Limit D_1	Size D_2
1. Threaded plugs (ANSI B47.1): 1.1 GO	•							
1.2 HI			•					
1.3 Full-form gage GO plug (UNJ only)	•							
2. Thread snap gages: 2.1 GO segments	•							
2.2 HI segments—two pitches approximately			•					
2.3 GO rolls	•							
2.4 HI rolls—two pitches approximately			•					
2.5 Minimum material—pitch diameter type—cone and vee					•			
2.6 Minimum material—thread groove diameter type—cone only							•	
3. Plain diameter gages: 3.1 Minimum plain cylindrical plug for minor diameter								
3.2 Major diameter snap type								
3.3 Minor diameter snap type								
3.4 Maximum/minimum major diameter snap type								
3.5 Maximum/minimum minor diameter snap type								
4. Indicating thread gages having either two contacts each at 180° or three contacts each at 120°: 4.1 GO segments	•	•						
4.2 HI segments—two pitches approximately			•	•				
4.3 GO rolls	•	•						
4.4 HI rolls—two pitches approximately			•	•				
4.5 Minimum material—pitch diameter type—cone and vee					•	•		
4.6 Minimum material—thread groove diameter type—cone only							•	•
4.7 Minor diameter/pitch diameter runout gage								
4.8 Differential segment or roll**								
5. Indicating plain diameter gages: 5.1 Major diameter type								
5.2 Minor diameter type								
6. Pitch micrometer with standard contacts (approximately HI profile) cone and vee			•	•				
7. Pitch micrometer with modified contacts (approximately P.D. contact) cone and vee					•	•		
8. Thread measuring balls with suitable measuring means							•	•
9. Optical comparator/toolmakers' microscope with suitable fixturing and cast replica					•	•		
10. Profile tracing equipment with suitable fixturing								
11. Lead measuring machine with suitable fixturing								
12. Helical path analyzer								
13. Plain micrometer/calipers—modified as required								
14. Surface measuring equipment								
15. Roundness equipment								

* Minimum major diameter limit is acceptable when product passes GO gage.
** GO profile for one pitch in length used in combination with a GO indicating gage to yield a diameter equivalent for deviation in lead including uniformity of helix; and a minimum material indicating gage to yield a diameter equivalent for deviation in flank angle.

SCREW THREAD GAGING AND MEASUREMENT

TABLE 9-3—Continued

Thread Characteristics														
Roundness of Pitch Cylinder				Taper of Pitch Cylinder		Lead Including Helix Variation	Flank Angle Variation	Major Diameter		Minor Diameter		Root Radius	Diameter Runout Minor to Pitch	Surface Texture
Oval 180°		Multilobe 120°												
Limit	Size	Limit	Size	Limit	Size			Limit	Size	Limit	Size			
E₁	E₂	F₁	F₂	G₁	G₂	H	I	J₁	J₂	K₁	K₂	L	M	N
								*						
								*		•				
•								*						
•				•										
•								*						
•				•										
•				•										
•				•										
										•				
								•						
										•				
								•						
										•				
•	•	•	•					*						
•	•	•	•	•	•									
•	•	•	•					*						
•	•	•	•	•	•									
•	•	•	•	•	•									
•	•	•	•	•	•									
													•	
•	•	•	•	•	•	•	•							
								•	•					
										•	•			
•	•			•	•									
•	•			•	•									
•	•			•	•									
						•	•	•	•				•	
							•						•	•
						•								
						•								
								•	•	•	•			
														•
•	•	•	•											

(ANSI)

SCREW THREAD GAGING AND MEASUREMENT

TABLE 9-4
Gaging Systems for External Threads

System	Dimensions Inspected	Applicable Thread Gages and Measuring Equipment			
		Attributes/Fixed Limit		Variables/Indicating	
	For dimension/gage combinations to be used, refer to Table 4-6	Control	Column	Control	Column
21	GO maximum material	1.1, 2.1, 2.3, 4.1, 4.3	A1	4.1, 4.3	A2
	LO functional diameter	1.2, 2.2, 2.4, 4.1, 4.2, 4.3, 4.4, 6	B1	4.1, 4.2, 4.3, 4.4, 6	B2
	Major diameter	3.1, 3.2, 3.4, 5.1, 14	J1	5.1, 14	J2
22	GO maximum material	1.1, 2.1, 2.3, 4.1, 4.3	A1	4.1, 4.3	A2
	Minimum material: Pitch diameter	2.5, 4.5, 7	C1	4.5, 7	C2
	or Thread groove diameter	2.6, 4.6, 8	D1	4.6, 8	D2
	LO functional diameter combined with mandatory examination of:	1.2, 2.2, 2.4, 4.1, 4.2, 4.3, 4.4, 6	B1	4.1, 4.2, 4.3, 4.4, 6	B2
	or Lead (including helix) and			4.8, 9, 11, 12, 13	H
	Flank angle over the length of full thread			4.8, 9, 10	I
	Major diameter	3.1, 3.2, 3.4, 5.1, 14	J1	5.1, 14	J2
	Minor diameter (UNJ only)	3.3, 3.5, 5.2, 9	K1	5.2, 9	K2
	Root profile (UNJ only)			9, 10	L
23	GO maximum material	1.1, 2.1, 2.3, 4.1, 4.3	A1	4.1, 4.3	A2
	Minimum material: Pitch diameter	2.5, 4.5, 7	C1	4.5, 7	C2
	or Thread groove diameter	2.6, 4.6, 8	D1	4.6, 8	D2
	Major diameter	3.1, 3.2, 3.4, 5.1, 14	J1	5.1, 14	J2
	Minor diameter (UNJ only)	3.3, 3.5, 5.2, 9	K1	5.2, 9	K2
	Root profile (UNJ only)			9, 10	L
	Roundness of pitch cylinder: Oval 180°	2.1, 2.2, 2.3, 2.4, 2.5, 2.6, 4.1, 4.2, 4.3, 4.4, 4.5, 4.6, 4.8, 6, 7, 8, 9, 16	E1	4.1, 4.2, 4.3, 4.4, 4.5, 4.6, 4.8, 6, 7, 8, 9, 16	E2
	Multilobe 120°	4.1, 4.2, 4.3, 4.4, 4.5, 4.6, 4.8, 9, 16	F1	4.1, 4.2, 4.3, 4.4, 4.5, 4.6, 4.8, 9, 16	F2
	Taper of pitch cylinder	2.2, 2.4, 2.5, 2.6, 4.2, 4.4, 4.5, 4.6, 4.8, 6, 7, 8	G1	4.2, 4.4, 4.5, 4.6, 4.8, 6, 7, 8	G2
	Lead including helix deviation			4.8, 9, 11, 12, 13	H
	Flank angle deviation			4.8, 9, 10	I
	Major/pitch diameters			4.7	M
	Surface texture			10, 15	N

(ANSI)

SCREW THREAD GAGING AND MEASUREMENT

TABLE 9-5
Gaging Systems for Internal Threads

System	Dimensions Inspected	Applicable Thread Gages and Measuring Equipment			
		Attributes/ Fixed Limit		Variables/ Indicating	
	For dimension/gage combinations to be used, refer to Table 4-7	Control	Column	Control	Column
21	GO maximum material	1.1, 1.3, 2.1, 2.3, 4.1, 4.3	A1	4.1, 4.3	A2
	HI functional diameter	1.2, 2.2, 2.4, 4.2, 4.4, 6	B1	4.2, 4.4, 6	B2
	Minor diameter	1.3, 3.1, 3.3, 3.5, 5.2, 13	K1	5.2, 13	K2
22	GO maximum material	1.1, 1.3, 2.1, 2.3, 4.1, 4.3	A1	4.1, 4.3	A2
	Minimum material: Direct method: Pitch diameter	2.5, 4.5, 7	C1	4.5, 7	C2
	or Thread groove diameter	2.6, 4.6, 8	D1	4.6, 8	D2
	Indirect method: HI functional diameter combined with control of:	1.2, 2.2, 2.4, 4.2, 4.4, 6	B1	4.2, 4.4, 6	B2
	Lead (including helix)			4.8, 9, 11, 12	H
	Flank angle			4.8, 9, 10	I
		1.3, 3.1, 3.3, 3.5, 5.2, 13	K1	5.2, 13	K2
	Roundness of pitch cylinder: Oval 180°	2.1, 2.2, 2.3, 2.4, 2.5, 2.6, 4.1, 4.2, 4.3, 4.4, 4.5, 4.6, 4.8, 6, 7, 8, 15	E1	4.1, 4.2, 4.3, 4.4, 4.5, 4.6, 4.8, 6, 7, 8, 15	E2
	Multilobe 120°	4.1, 4.2, 4.3, 4.4, 4.5, 4.6, 4.8, 15	F1	4.1, 4.2, 4.3, 4.4, 4.5, 4.6, 4.8, 15	F2
	Taper of pitch cylinder	2.2, 2.4, 2.5, 2.6, 4.2, 4.4, 4.5, 4.6, 4.8, 6, 7, 8	G1	4.2, 4.4, 4.5, 4.6, 4.8, 6, 7, 8	G2
23	GO maximum material	1.1, 1.3, 2.1, 2.3, 4.1, 4.3	A1	4.1, 4.3	
	Minimum material: Pitch diameter	2.5, 4.5, 7	C1	4.5, 7	C2
	or Thread groove diameter	2.6, 4.6, 8	D1	4.6, 8	D2
	Major diameter	1.3, 3.1, 3.3, 3.5, 5.2, 13	K1	5.2, 13	K2
	Roundness of pitch cylinder: Oval 180°	2.1, 2.2, 2.3, 2.4, 2.5, 2.6, 4.1, 4.2, 4.3, 4.4, 4.5, 4.6, 4.8, 6, 7, 8, 15	E1	4.1, 4.2, 4.3, 4.4, 4.5, 4.6, 4.8, 6, 7, 8, 15	E2
	Multilobe 120°	4.1, 4.2, 4.3, 4.4, 4.5, 4.6, 4.8, 15	F1	4.1, 4.2, 4.3, 4.4, 4.5, 4.6, 4.8, 15	F2
	Taper of pitch cylinder	2.2, 2.4, 2.5, 2.6, 4.2, 4.4, 4.5, 4.6, 4.8, 6, 7, 8	G1	4.2, 4.4, 4.5, 4.6, 4.8, 6, 7, 8	G2
	Lead including helix deviation			4.8, 9, 11, 12	H
	Flank angle deviation			4.8, 9, 10	I
	Major/pitch diameters runout			4.7	M
	Surface texture			10, 14	N

(ANSI)

SCREW THREAD GAGING AND MEASUREMENT

tems along with the gages and gaging equipment that can be used. The numbers in the attributes and variables columns correspond to the numbers in the thread gages and measuring equipment column of Tables 9-2 and 9-3. Gages and gaging equipment are manufactured for various thread types, sizes, and classes.

MEASURING EQUIPMENT

A variety of thread gages and gaging equipment is currently being used by industry for the measurement of product screw threads. The type of gage or equipment used depends primarily on the thread characteristics being measured and the accuracy required. Some of the commonly used gages are micrometers, fixed-limit gages, and indicating gages.

Screw Thread Micrometers

Screw thread micrometers have a specially designed spindle and anvil so that externally threaded products can be measured. The end of the spindle of this type of micrometer is pointed to form a 60° cone, and the anvil has the form of a vee to fit over the thread (see Fig. 9-44). The sharp tip of the spindle is ground off to make sure that only the pitch diameter is measured rather than the root or minor diameter.

Flats are ground on the peaks of the vee, and the root of the vee is ground out. The anvil can be fixed in the frame or it can be free to rotate, permitting the anvil to adjust to the helix of the thread being measured. Specially designed anvils and spindles are also available for Whitworth and metric threads.

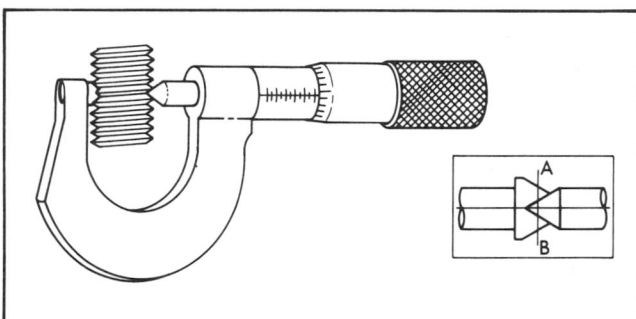

Fig. 9-44 Screw thread micrometer. (*L.S. Starrett*)

Fixed-Limit Gages

Fixed-limit gages are single-purpose gages in that they are made for a specific thread system, form, size, and class. These gages incorporate the essential functional dimensions of the thread and are used primarily to ensure the ability to assemble the product thread with its mating part.

Thread plug gages. Working thread plug gages are similar in design to cylindrical plug gages except that they are threaded.

A typical thread plug gage consists of a handle and one or two thread gaging members (see Fig. 9-45). Depending on the gaging member size, the member can be held in the handle using a threaded collet and bushing design (view *a*), a taperlock design (view *b*), or by a trilock design (view *c*).

The two members in a thread plug gage are referred to as the GO and NOT-GO members. The NOT-GO member is some-times referred to as the HI member. The GO gaging member is generally longer than the NOT-GO member and is used to

check the maximum material functional limit of the product thread. The NOT-GO member checks the NOT-GO (HI) functional diameter limit of the threaded product.

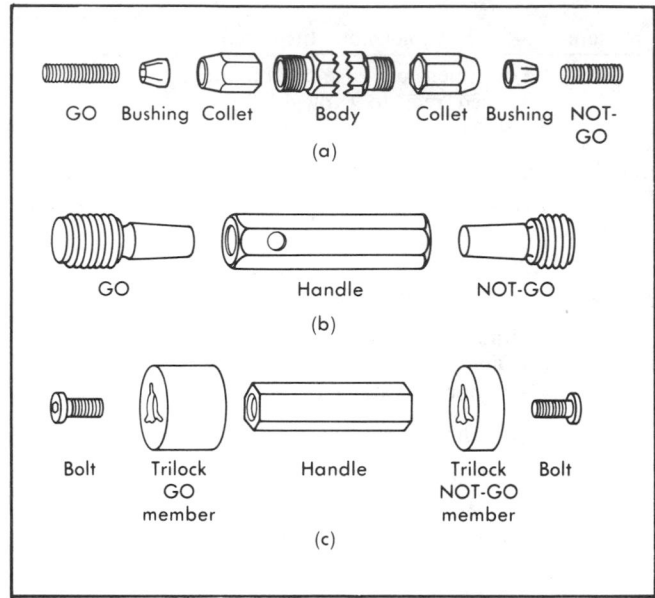

Fig. 9-45 Thread plug gages: (a) threaded collet and bushing design, (b) taperlock design, and (c) trilock design. (*The Van Keuren Co.*)

Thread ring gages. Thread ring gages are similar in design to cylindrical ring gages except that the internal surface is threaded. They are available in both solid and adjustable or split designs.

Thread ring gages are supplied in pairs as GO and NOT-GO gages. The NOT-GO ring is sometimes referred to as a LO ring gage. The GO gage checks the maximum material functional limit of the threaded part. The NOT-GO gage checks the NOT-GO (LO) functional diameter limit of the threaded part and usually has an annular groove machined on the periphery of the ring to differentiate it from the GO ring.

Thread Snap Gages

Thread snap gages have two pair of gaging elements combined in one gage. With proper gaging elements, these gages can check the maximum and minimum material limit of external product screw threads in a single pass. One style of thread snap gage is shown in Fig. 9-46.

The functional or GO portion of the gage may incorporate either functional segments or functional rolls. Rolls rotate when the part is inserted, thus reducing wear. The length of the segments or rolls is approximately equal to the applicational length of engagement of the product thread. The NOT-GO portion of the gage generally contains cone and vee profile rolls.

Indicating Thread Gages

Several different designs of indicating thread gages are available for either internal or external screw thread measurement. Indicating thread gages must be set to the proper thread setting using master thread plug or thread ring gages before checking the threaded parts. Indicating thread gages for internal threads are made in sizes for measuring threads from 0.138 to 40" (3.5 to 1000 mm) diam and for external threads in sizes from 0.06 to 20" (1.5 to 500 mm) diam. A typical gage consists of a frame, a set of contact elements, and a dial indicator (see Fig. 9-47).

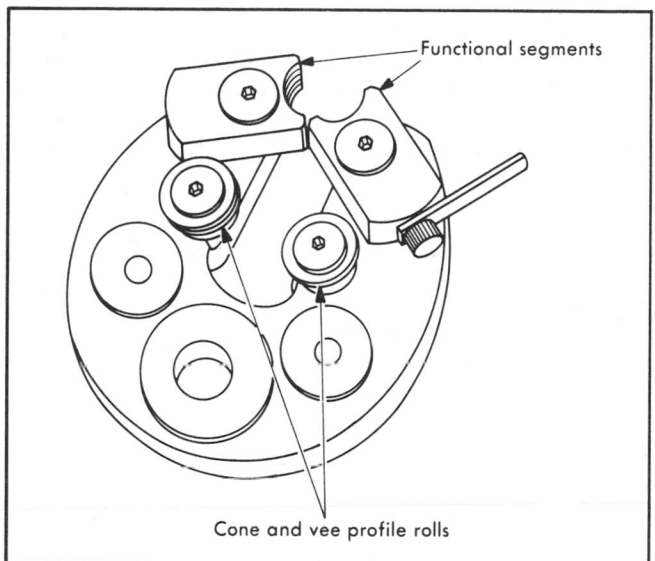

Fig. 9-46 Thread snap gage with functional segments and cone and vee profile rolls. (*The Johnson Gage Co.*)

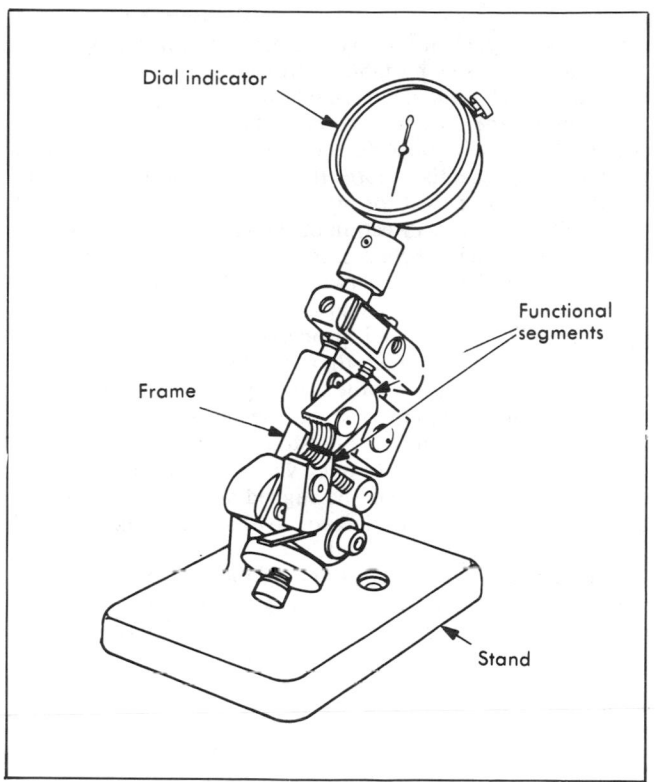

Fig. 9-47 Indicating thread gage with full-form segments. (*The Johnson Gage Co.*)

MEASUREMENT OF GEARS AND SPLINES

Gears and involute splines are important drive elements used in a variety of machines and mechanical devices. Gears are available in various types such as spur, helical, bevel, and worm, each having individual advantages for specific applications.

A splined shaft is a shaft having a series of parallel keys formed integrally with the shaft and mating with corresponding grooves cut in a hub or fitting.[17] They are available in 30°, 37.5°, and 45° pressure angles and are based on the involute form. Splined shafts are commonly used for coupling shafts when heavy torques are to be transmitted without slipping; for transmitting power to gears, pulleys, and other rotating members; and for attaching parts that may require removal for indexing or changing angular position.

This subchapter has been designed to familiarize the manufacturing engineer with the various measurements made on gears and splines. It also provides some practical information on how the measurements are made and a description of the equipment used.

ANALYTICAL GEAR CHECKING

From a diagnostic standpoint, the functional check cannot show the specific amount of variation that would be attributed individually to the various gear tooth parameters. Tooth-to-tooth variations revealed in the functional check are usually a combination of these different parameter variations; therefore a separate check or a series of checks is required to determine the

accuracy of each parameter. The parameters commonly inspected by analytical gear checking are runout, pitch variation, accumulated pitch variation, profile variation, tooth alignment (lead) variation, and tooth thickness.

Runout

Runout is the total variation of the distance between a datum surface and an indicated surface. The datum and indicated surfaces must be specified or identified. The two commonly specified runouts are axial and radial.

Axial runout (wobble) is formed when an angle exists between the datum surface and an indicated surface. It is normally measured in a direction parallel to the axis of rotation between the indicated and datum surfaces.

Radial runout is formed by variations between the datum and indicated surfaces. It is measured in a direction perpendicular to the axis of rotation. Radial runout measurements may include the effects of eccentricity, out-of-roundness, tooth alignment variation, profile variation, pitch variation, and tooth thickness variation.

Pitch Variation

Pitch, spacing, and accumulative pitch or index variations are elemental parameters relating to the accuracy of tooth locations around a gear. Measurements for determining the variations are made (1) at or near the center of the profile, (2) in

MEASUREMENT OF GEARS AND SPLINES

the transverse plane, or (3) relative to the gear datum axis of rotation with bench or floor-type instruments or relative to the top lands when using portable instruments.

With helical gears, the pitch measurement may be made in the normal plane. The values obtained are then divided by the cosine of the helix angle for comparison with the specified tolerances. Sequential tooth flanks in both directions of rotation should be used for pitch measurements. However, if the specific operating direction of the gear is known, only the loaded flanks need to be measured.

Two-probe device. The two-probe device has one fixed probe contacting a flank on a datum circle near the center of tooth profile. The second probe, either a mechanical or electronic indicator, contacts the adjacent tooth flank at or near the same point on the profile (see Fig. 9-48). As the gear is rotated around its datum axis, the two-probe device moves in and out on a precision slide and stop and indicates successive adjacent pitches. If the base pitch variation is to be measured, the two-probe device should be aligned along a tangent to the base circle. Two-probe devices are available as bench or floor models as well as portable models.

Single-probe devices. On single-probe devices, a precision indexing device is used to index the gear exactly $360°/N$ (N = number of teeth) or one pitch for each tooth. Typical indexing

devices are an index plate, a circle divider, an optical or electronic encoder, and a polygon and autocollimator.

In operation, a single probe on a precision slide mechanism is brought into contact with the first and each successive tooth flank around the gear (see Fig. 9-49). The readings from this series of measurements are recorded as the actual value of index variation.

Profile

Profile is the shape of the tooth flank from its root to its tip (see Fig. 9-50). The functional profile is the operating portion that is in actual contact during mesh and cannot extend below the base cylinder. Profile measurements are commonly made using generative, coordinate (nongenerative), or portable involute checking instruments.

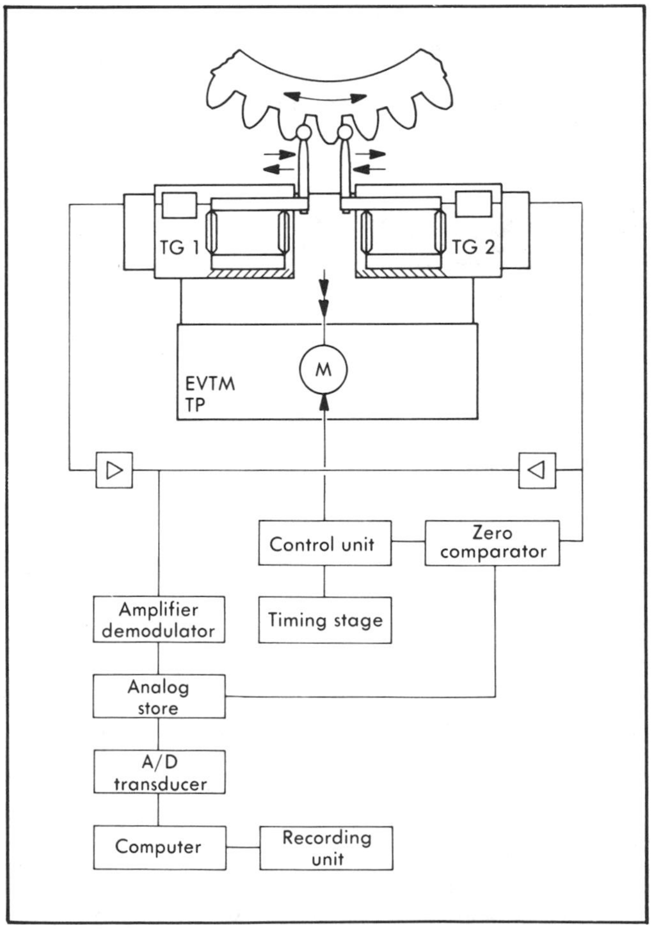

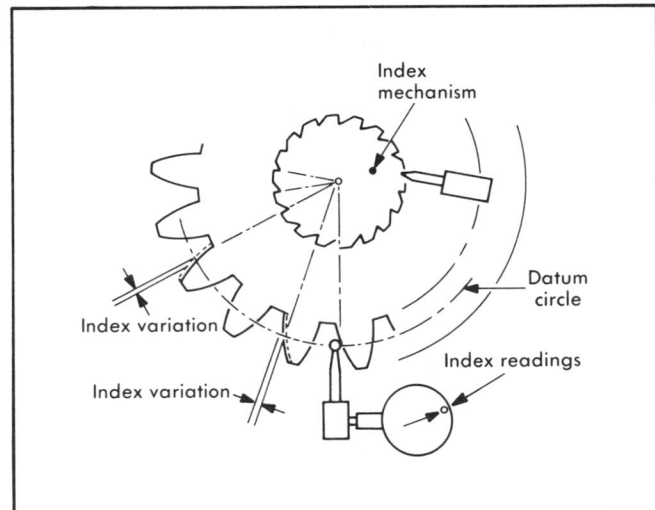

Fig. 9-49 Schematic of single-probe measuring device. (*American Gear Manufacturers Association*)

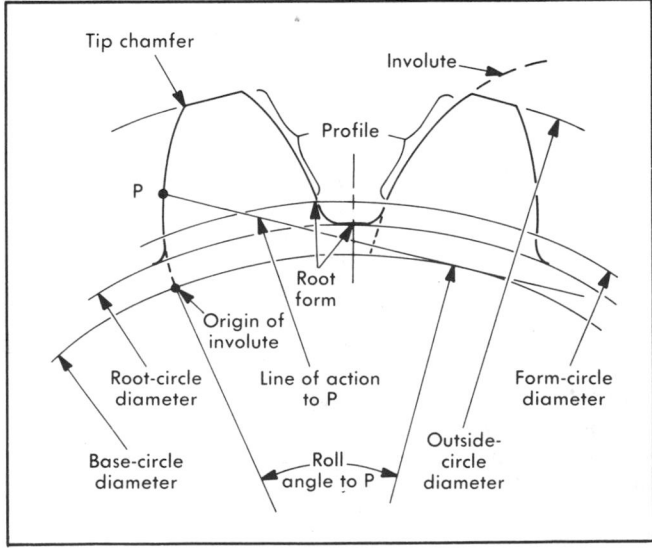

Fig. 9-50 Involute tooth profile.

Fig. 9-48 Schematic of portable two-probe pitch testing unit. (*American Pfauter Limited*)

Generative instruments. The most common instruments used for profile inspection are generative involute checking instruments. These instruments measure the variation of the actual profile from a nominal involute profile that is generated by the instrument. Generating the nominal involute requires a tangential movement of a measurement probe on the involute surface in a synchronized, linear relationship with the rotational movement of a gear mounted on the instrument spindle.

Coordinate instruments. Coordinate measurement inspection instruments indicate the tooth profile by a series of discrete points. The variation of the actual profile from the nominal profile is then determined by comparison of the stored test-point coordinates against calculated coordinates of the theoretical nominal profile.

Portable instruments. Profile measuring instruments are generally fixed-type machines. Gears to be tested must be brought to the instrument and accurately mounted between centers or on a face plate. However, for large gears it may be preferable to use a portable involute checking instrument that can be taken to the gear. These instruments operate on a variety of generative or nongenerative (coordinate) principles.

Profile charts. Amplified traces of profile inspection test results should be presented on charts that are calibrated for degrees of roll or rolling path length as well as magnification of measured variation (see Fig. 9-51). An unmodified profile with no variations will be charted as a straight line. Excess material on the profile is considered a plus variation, while insufficient material is considered a minus variation. In addition to identifying the location and magnitude of the highest points on the profile or the maximum profile variation, these charts are valuable for determining profile characteristics such as tip round, undercut, and tip or root relief.

Tooth Alignment

Tooth alignment is the lengthwise alignment of the tooth flank across the face from one end to the other. The theoretical tooth alignment of a spur gear is a straight line parallel to its rotating axis. On helical or herringbone gears, the tooth alignment is a helix contained on the surface of a cylinder that is concentric with the datum axis of the gear's rotation. Tooth alignment is restricted to the portion of the gear tooth that is in contact with the drive tooth when loaded. It does not include edge rounds or chamfers.

Generative instruments. Generative tooth alignment checking instruments are the most common instruments for checking tooth alignment. These instruments measure the variation of the actual tooth alignment from a nominal tooth alignment generated by the instrument. Generation of the nominal tooth alignment requires the axial movement of a measurement probe in a synchronized, linear relationship with rotational movement of the gear mounted on the instrument spindle. When measuring spur gears, the rotational movement is not required.

During inspection, the gear must be accurately positioned with its axis of rotation coincident with the instrument spindle axis. In addition, the probe tip should be positioned to operate normal to the tooth surface at or near the pitch diameter. The most commonly used probe tips are spherical or disc-shaped.

Coordinate instruments. Coordinate measurement instruments probe the tooth lengthwise at a series of discrete points, storing the rectangular coordinates of each point. The variation of the actual tooth alignment is determined by comparing the stored test-point coordinates against calculated coordinates of the theoretical, nominal tooth alignment.

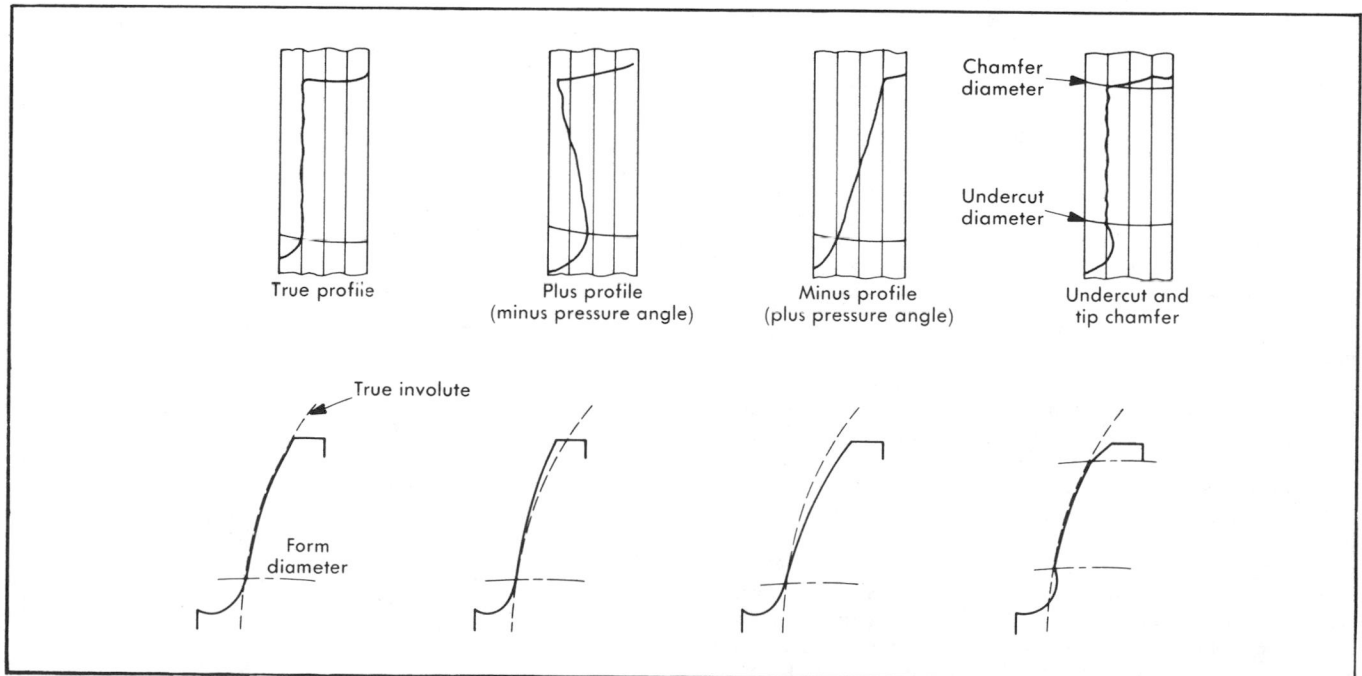

Fig. 9-51 Typical tooth profile tolerance charts. (*American Gear Manufacturers Association*)

MEASUREMENT OF GEARS AND SPLINES

Tooth alignment charts. Amplified traces of test results from tooth alignment inspection should be presented on charts (see Fig. 9-52). The charts should be calibrated for axial displacement and the magnification of the measured tooth alignment variation.

Alignment of an unmodified tooth, free of any variations, will be charted as a straight line. Excess material is considered a plus variation, while insufficient material is considered a minus variation. In addition to identifying the location and magnitude of tooth alignment variations, these charts are valuable for identifying tooth alignment characteristics such as edge chamfers, end relief, crown, and taper.

Tooth Thickness

Tooth thickness can be measured using gear tooth calipers, addendum comparators, micrometers with pins, balls, or blocks, and vernier or plate micrometers. It can also be measured using functional checking techniques.

Gear tooth vernier caliper. The gear tooth vernier caliper combines in one tool the function of both a vernier depth gage and a vernier caliper (Fig. 9-53). The vertical slide is set to depth so that when it rests on top of the gear tooth, the caliper jaws will be correctly positioned to measure across the datum circle of the gear tooth. The gear tooth vernier caliper is generally used only when checking the first gear of a production lot. Once the gear cutting machine has been set to size, all the other gears in the lot are cut to the same size.

Addendum comparator. The addendum comparator measures tooth thickness by comparing the gear addendum with that of a basic rack (see Fig. 9-54). The comparator jaws have the same angle as the normal pressure angle of the gear being inspected. Before measuring a gear, the comparator jaws are set to the proper width using a steel block that corresponds to a rack tooth of the proper normal pitch. With the block in place, the dial indicator is set to read zero for the standard addendum. Correction must be made for taper and dimensional variation of the outside diameter of the gear blank because it is used as a reference point.

Span measurement. In the span measurement method, a vernier caliper or plate micrometer is used to measure the distance across several teeth along a line tangent to the base cylinder (see Fig. 9-55). The distance measured is the sum of the base pitches of the spanned teeth minus one (n-1), plus the thickness of one tooth at the base cylinder. The number of teeth included between the vernier caliper or plate micrometer when measuring dimension M as shown in Fig. 9-55 is based on the number of teeth and pressure angle of the gear being measured.

Measurement over pins. The pin or wire method of checking gear tooth thickness is an accurate method because the measurements are not influenced by the outside diameter or runout of the gear. Measurements are affected, however, by variations in tooth spacing and profile. Tooth thickness measurements can also be made over one pin in a proper fixture, but the result will be influenced by runout.

In practice, two or three cylindrical pins or wires of a specified diameter are placed in diametrically opposite tooth spaces for gears with an even number of teeth (see Fig. 9-56). If the gear has an odd number of teeth, the pins or wires are located as nearly opposite as possible. The overall dimension M is measured using the appropriate-sized micrometer. The pin diameter is based on the diametral pitch of the gear and whether the gear is internal or external.

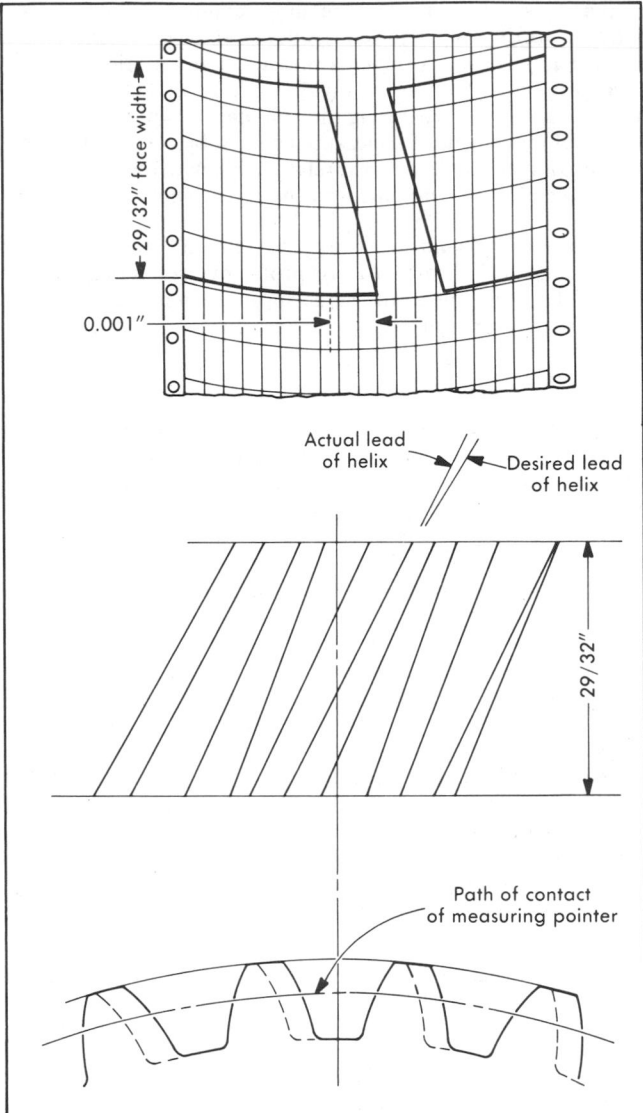

Fig. 9-52 Typical tooth alignment inspection chart.

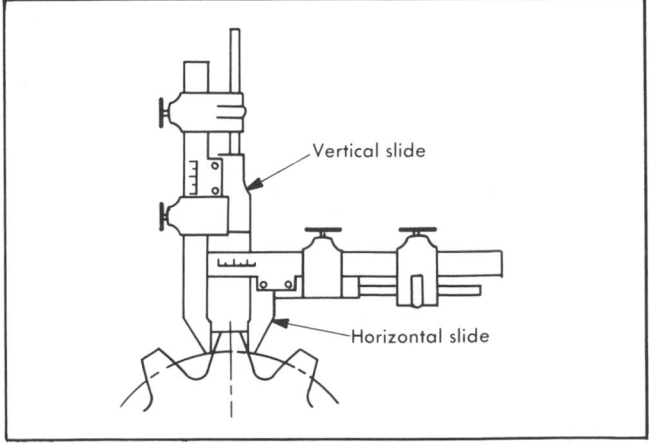

Fig. 9-53 Gear tooth caliper used in tooth thickness inspection.

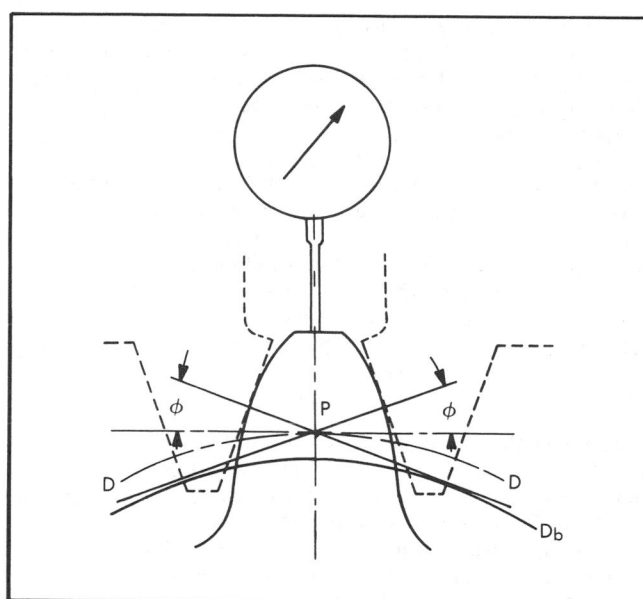

Fig. 9-54 Gear tooth comparator used in tooth thickness inspection.

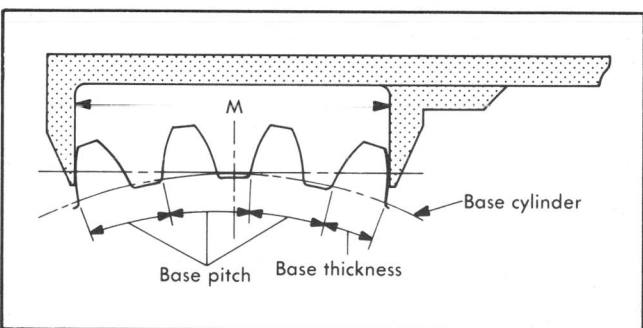

Fig. 9-55 Span-measurement tooth thickness inspection method.

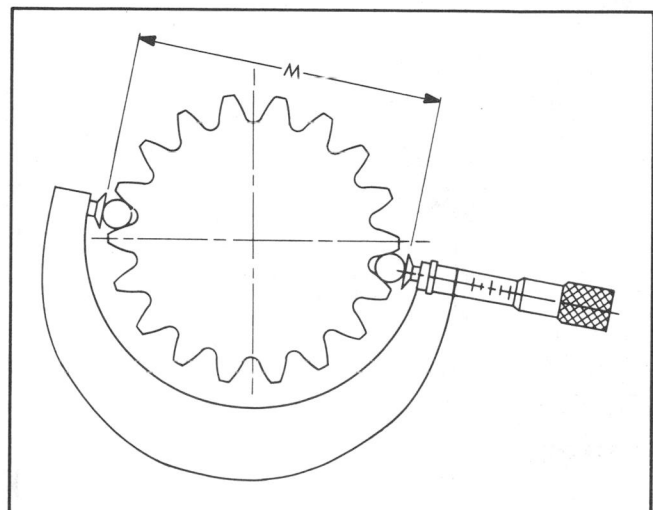

Fig. 9-56 Measurement-over-pins tooth thickness inspection method.

Backlash

Backlash in gears is the play between mating tooth surfaces; a single gear cannot have backlash. For purposes of measurement and calculation, backlash is defined as the amount by which a tooth space exceeds the thickness of an engaging tooth (see Fig. 9-57). The actual backlash is a function of the variations in runout, tooth thicknesses, profile, and tooth alignment. It does not include the effect of center-distance changes of the mountings and variations in bearings. Numerical values of backlash are understood to be measured at the tightest point of mesh on the pitch circle, unless otherwise specified.

One method used to measure backlash is to hold one gear solidly against rotation while permitting the other gear to rotate. An indicator is then mounted against the tooth surface of the gear that is free to rotate. The indicator axis of motion should be perpendicular to this surface (at the large end in the case of bevel gears). Normal backlash can be read on the indicator by turning the gear back and forth. The range over which the gear can be moved is the backlash. Several checks are usually necessary to determine the minimum backlash of the gear.

In spur gears, parallel helical gears, and bevel gears, it is immaterial whether the pinion or gear is held stationary for the test. In crossed helical and hypoid gears, backlash readings may vary depending on which gear is held stationary. It is therefore customary to hold the pinion stationary.

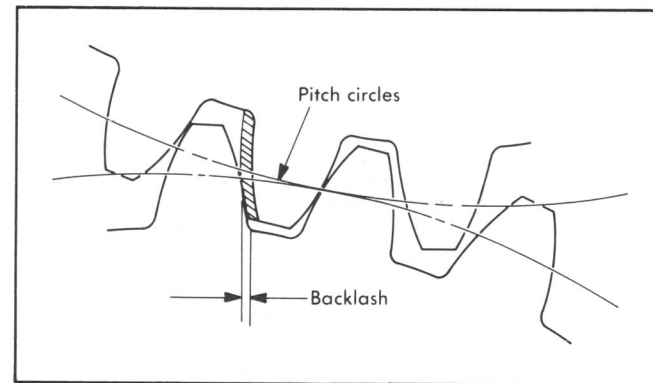

Fig. 9-57 Backlash in the plane of rotation. (*Fellows Corp.*)

FUNCTIONAL GEAR CHECKING

Functional or composite gear checking involves rolling two gears together and measuring the resultant motion. The gears rolled together can be either work and master gears or two work gears. The two commonly used functional checking methods are double-flank testing and single-flank testing. Another checking method related to functional checking is tooth contact or bearing pattern checking.

Double-Flank Testing

In double-flank testing, the gear to be tested (work gear) is mounted on a gear-rolling tester and then run in tight mesh (double-flank contact) against a master gear (see Fig. 9-58). The work gear is constrained from all motion other than rotary while the master gear is mounted on a fixture with a variable center distance. The variations in center distance (or mounting

MEASUREMENT OF GEARS AND SPLINES

distance) that occur as the meshed gears rotate are either recorded on a strip chart or indicated by means of a dial indicator.

Operation. When performing a double-flank test, the master gear and gear-rolling fixture should be calibrated. The work

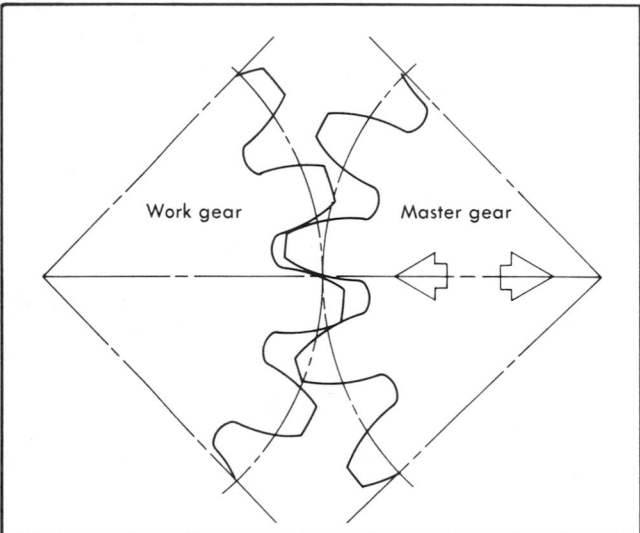

Fig. 9-58 Contact of gear teeth in a double-flank gear test. (*The Gleason Works*)

gear and master gear should then be mounted on their respective fixture. If mounting surfaces are specified on the drawing, they should be used. When the gears are in double-flank contact, the work gear should be rotated at least one complete revolution.

The amount of applied load is important when checking gears on a gear-rolling fixture. For example, excessive loads on fine-pitch gears of narrow face width, on gears made of soft materials, or on journal-type gears having slender shafts result in incorrect readings. The incorrect readings are caused by the deflection of the teeth or blanks. Conversely, too light a load on coarse-pitch gears of relatively wide face width results in incorrect readings caused by variations in contact between the work gear and the master gear.

Equipment. A schematic diagram of a gear-rolling instrument is shown in Fig. 9-59. The diagram shows the kinematic and mechanical requirements of the instrument, but does not imply that this is the only acceptable construction.

For any gear-rolling instrument, provision should be made for the master gear to rotate with a minimum of runout or lateral wobble. Fixed, hardened and ground studs are generally used for master gears with bores. Hardened and ground bushings, precision-interference ball bushings, or centers for use with shank-type master gears should be considered for more accurate use. Any clearance between the master gear bore or hub and its mounting stud or bushing will be reflected in the inspection results.

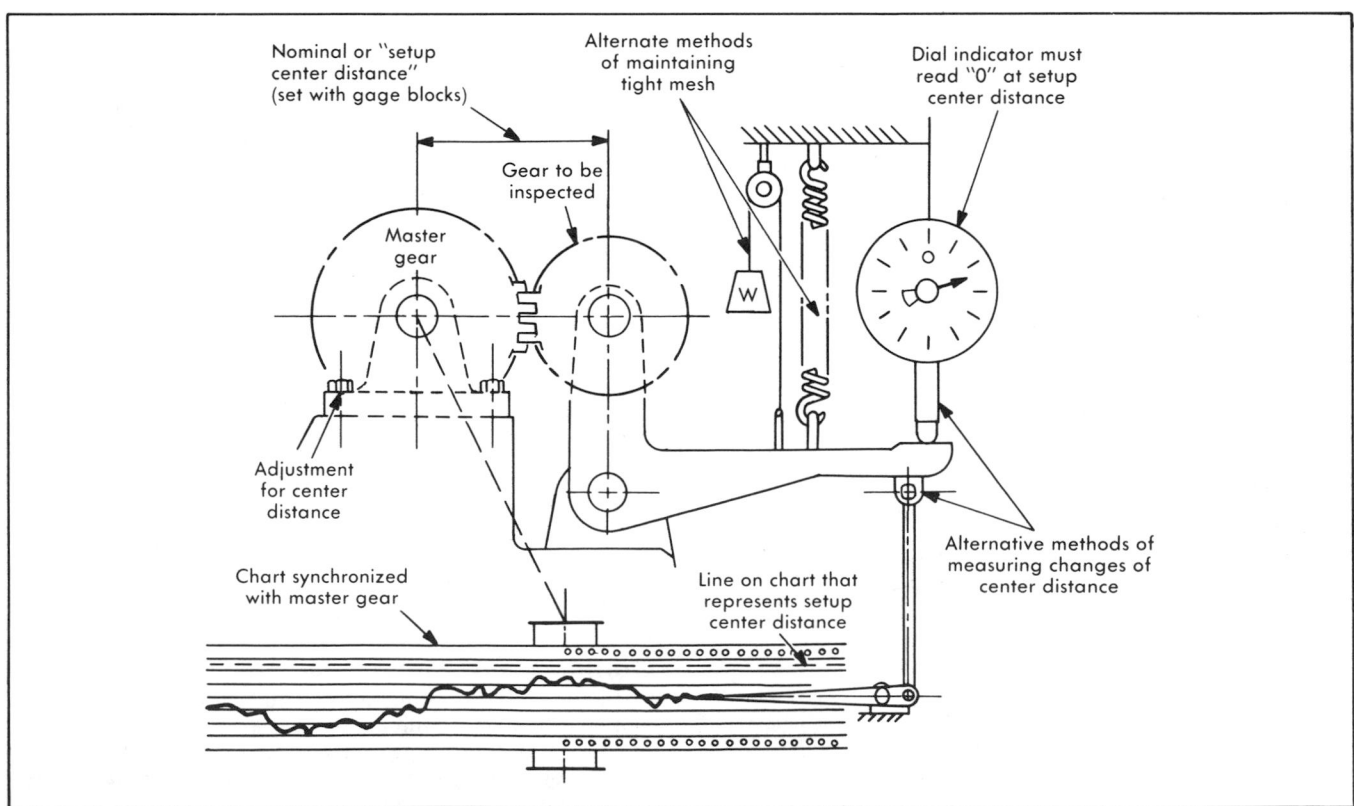

Fig. 9-59 Schematic diagram showing mechanical and kinematic requirements of a gear-rolling fixture.

MEASUREMENT OF GEARS AND SPLINES

Single-Flank Testing

Single-flank testing simulates the actual operating conditions of a gear pair. The mating gears roll together at their proper center distance with backlash and with only one flank in contact (see Fig. 9-60). The driven gear generally has a slight drag. Gears can be tested by pairs or with master gears. Single-flank testing is used for checking parallel axis, bevel, worm, crossed helical, and offset conical gears.

The single-flank test is run using encoders or other devices to measure rotational motion. Encoders may be attached to the input and output shafts of a special machine for testing pairs of gears. The encoders may also be used portably by attaching them directly to the input and output shafts of an actual gear box so as to inspect the quality of a complete train of gears.

Operation. Figure 9-61 shows schematically the operation of a single-flank measuring machine. The two motions being compared are monitored by circular optical gratings. The gratings give a train of impulses having a frequency that is a measure of the angular movements of the two shafts. Because most gear ratios are not 1:1, one or both of the trains of impulses is processed.

The phase difference of the two processed pulse trains is converted to an analog waveform proportional to variations in transmission motion. Motion variations of less than one arc second can be detected.

Data interpretation. Gears with perfect involute tooth forms roll together with uniform motion. Nonuniform motion results when pitch variations or involute modifications exist.

Figure 9-62 shows three typical tooth shapes and their resulting motion curves. The tooth shape and curve in view *a* is of a perfect involute. Because the teeth are perfect involutes, the motion between the teeth is smooth, resulting in an angular motion curve that is a straight line. View *b* shows a gear tooth with a profile modification. The modification is indicated by the dotted line. As the gear revolves on its center, the contact progresses from the tip to the root of one member. The lack of stock at the root and the tip results in a parabola-like motion

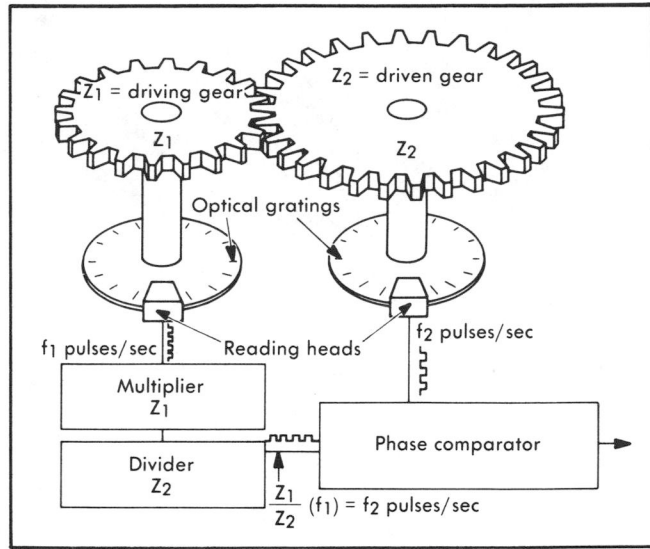

Fig. 9-61 Schematic diagram of the operating principle of a single-flank measuring machine. (*The Gleason Works*)

curve. The tooth in view *c* has a pressure angle variation indicated by the dotted line. As the contact progresses from the tip to the root, the tooth form gets closer to the correct shape. This type of tooth variation results in a ramp or sawtooth type of motion curve.

Data analysis. Much of the information about the gear teeth can be read directly from the graph described previously. However, in many cases, this data becomes complex and difficult to read. Techniques available to aid in this analysis include Fourier analysis (real-time analyzers), time history averaging, and computer-aided data analysis.

Contact Pattern Check

Contact checking is used for the inspection of mating gear sets to determine their operational compatability. It is also used for the inspection of gears that will not fit into available checking machines because of size and weight limits. Contact checking is commonly used on bevel, mill, marine, and high-speed gears.

In practice, the teeth of the gears being checked are coated with a thin film of marking compound. The mating gears are then run under a light load for a few seconds. The contact pattern developed on the gear tooth surface is observed and then evaluated. Contact pattern acceptability is specified by defining the area in which contact may not occur, the areas in which contact should occur, and the percentage of contact required in the desired area. In most applications, a uniform contact pattern extending over the entire area of the tooth surface is desirable. Diagrams of typical contact patterns, indicating different types of errors, can be obtained from AGMA.

MEASUREMENT OF INVOLUTE SPLINES

Involute splines provide a positive rotational coupling between a shaft with external teeth and a related outer member with internal spline teeth. The use of splines permits ease of assembly or disassembly for replacement or servicing and permits fixed or sliding connections. Splined products also permit compact

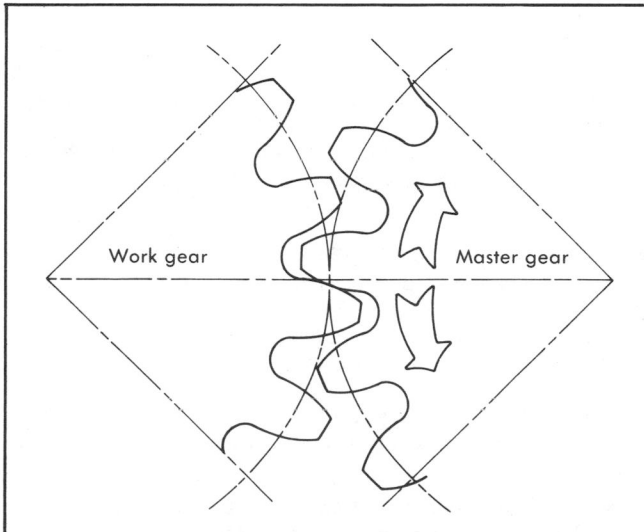

Fig. 9-60 Contact of gear teeth in a single-flank gear test. (*The Gleason Works*)

MEASUREMENT OF GEARS AND SPLINES

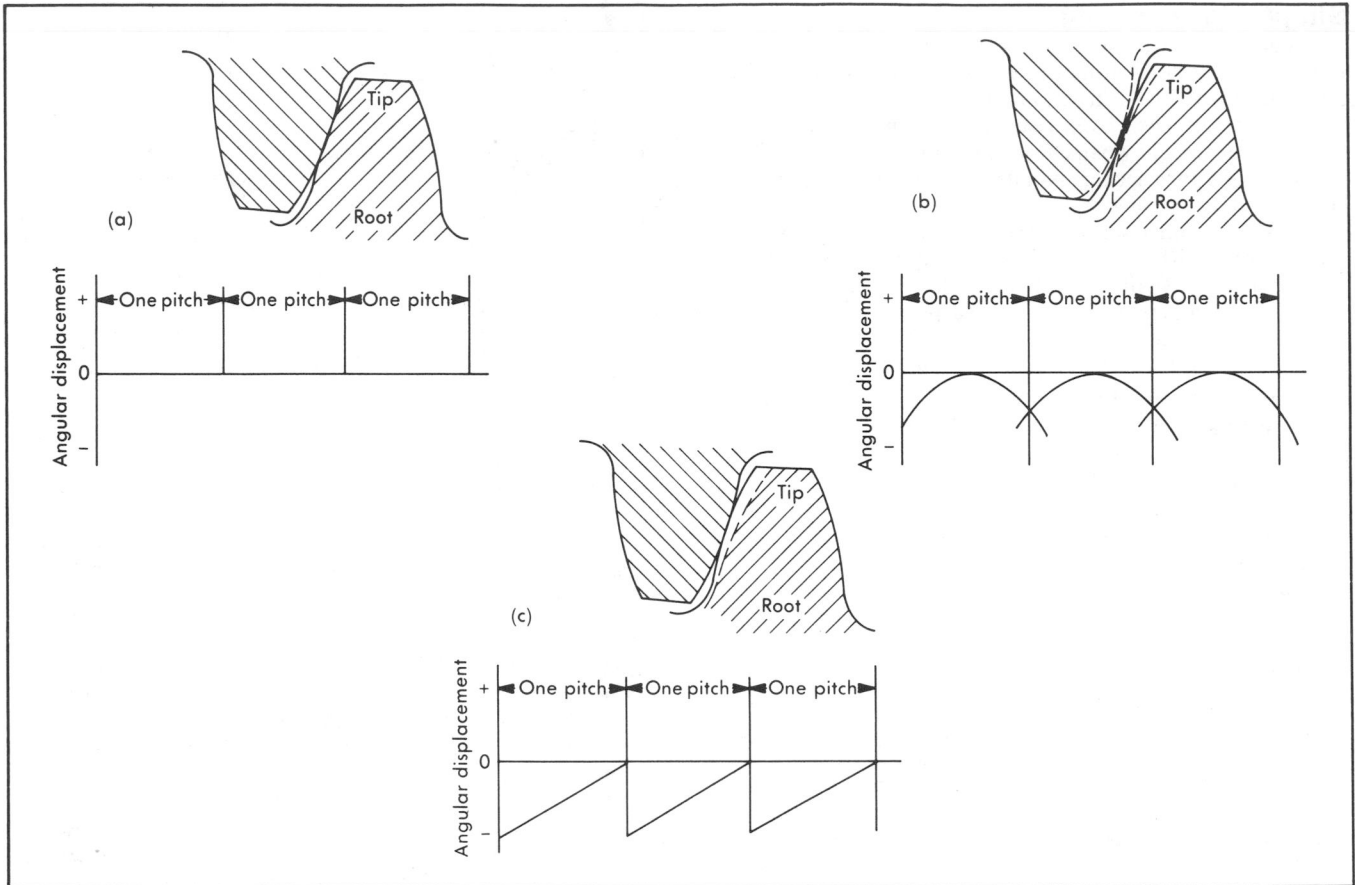

Fig. 9-62 Three typical tooth shapes and their corresponding motion curves: (a) perfect involute, (b) modified tooth shape, and (c) pressure angle variation. (*The Gleason Works*)

assembly of parts or, by use of standardized fittings, the intercoupling of motors with gearboxes or other loads.

Because there is no rolling action between the mating members as there is between meshing gears, all of the spline teeth are expected to fit together. Although various internal and external fits are available, the final goal of involute splines is to achieve a self-centering condition with full contact bearing. The result of this would be equalized load-sharing and stress on all the teeth.

Fixed-Limit Gaging

A common way of inspecting splined workpieces prior to assembly is with fixed-limit gages. External splines are checked with internal-toothed rings whereas internal splines are checked with external-toothed plugs.

Basically there are only two types of fixed-limit spline gages, composite and sector. Composite gages have the same number of teeth as that of the part (see Fig. 9-63, view *a*). Sector gages have only two sectors of teeth 180° apart (see Fig. 4-116, view *b*). These gages are further subdivided into GO and NOT-GO gages. Figure 9-64 illustrates the relationship between the various space width and tooth thickness limits and the main type of gages used for their inspection.

The GO gages are used to inspect maximum material conditions (maximum external or minimum internal dimen-

sions). They may be used to inspect an individual dimension or the relationship between two or more functional dimensions. In addition, they control the minimum looseness or maximum interference.

The NOT-GO gages are used to inspect minimum material conditions (minimum external, maximum internal dimensions), thereby controlling the maximum looseness or minimum interference. Unless otherwise agreed on, a part is only acceptable if the NOT-GO gage does not enter or go on the part. A NOT-GO gage can only check one dimension.

Analytical Spline Inspection

Analytical spline inspection is the measurement of individual dimensions and variations. The variations measured are size, index, profile, lead (tooth alignment), roundness, and eccentricity. Profile inspection also covers the form diameter and tooth tip chamfer.

Analytical spline inspection is performed in the same manner as analytical gear inspection, discussed previously, and may be required:

- To supplement inspection by gages.
- To evaluate parts rejected by gages.
- For prototype parts or short runs when spline gages are not used.

MEASUREMENT OF GEARS AND SPLINES

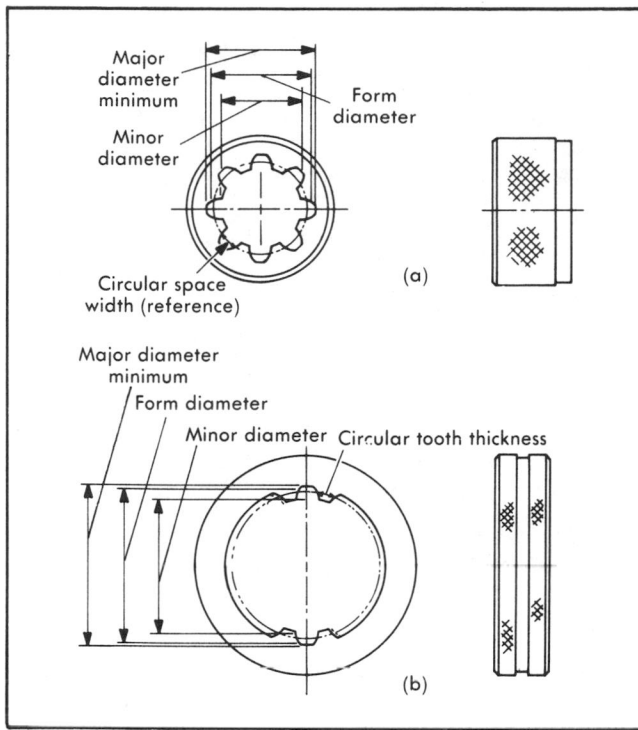

Fig. 9-63 Fixed-limit spline gages: (a) GO composite ring gage and (b) NOT-GO sector ring gage. (*Society of Automotive Engineers*)

- To supplement inspection by gages when each individual variation must be restrained from assuming too great a portion of the tolerance between the minimum material actual and the maximum material effective dimensions.

Measurement with pins. Actual space width and actual tooth thickness may be measured with pins. These measurements do not determine the fit between mating parts but may be used to approximate the actual space width or tooth thickness.

Total index variation. Index variations are the variations in the spacing of all corresponding tooth profiles with respect to one arbitrarily selected tooth side. The total index variation is the spread between the two greatest opposite index variations.

Profile variation. Profile is the shape of the spline tooth flank from its root to its tip. Profile variation is the difference between the measured and the specified functional profile.

Lead variation. Lead variation (tooth variation) is the variation of the direction of the spline tooth from its intended

Composite Spline Inspection

An automated method for involute spline inspection has been developed for high-volume spline production. Its purpose is to permit a higher percent of product inspection as a supplement to the continued use of fixed gaging. The composite spline inspection method uses a dynamic means for span measurement that duplicates the principle of a flange micrometer on block measurement.

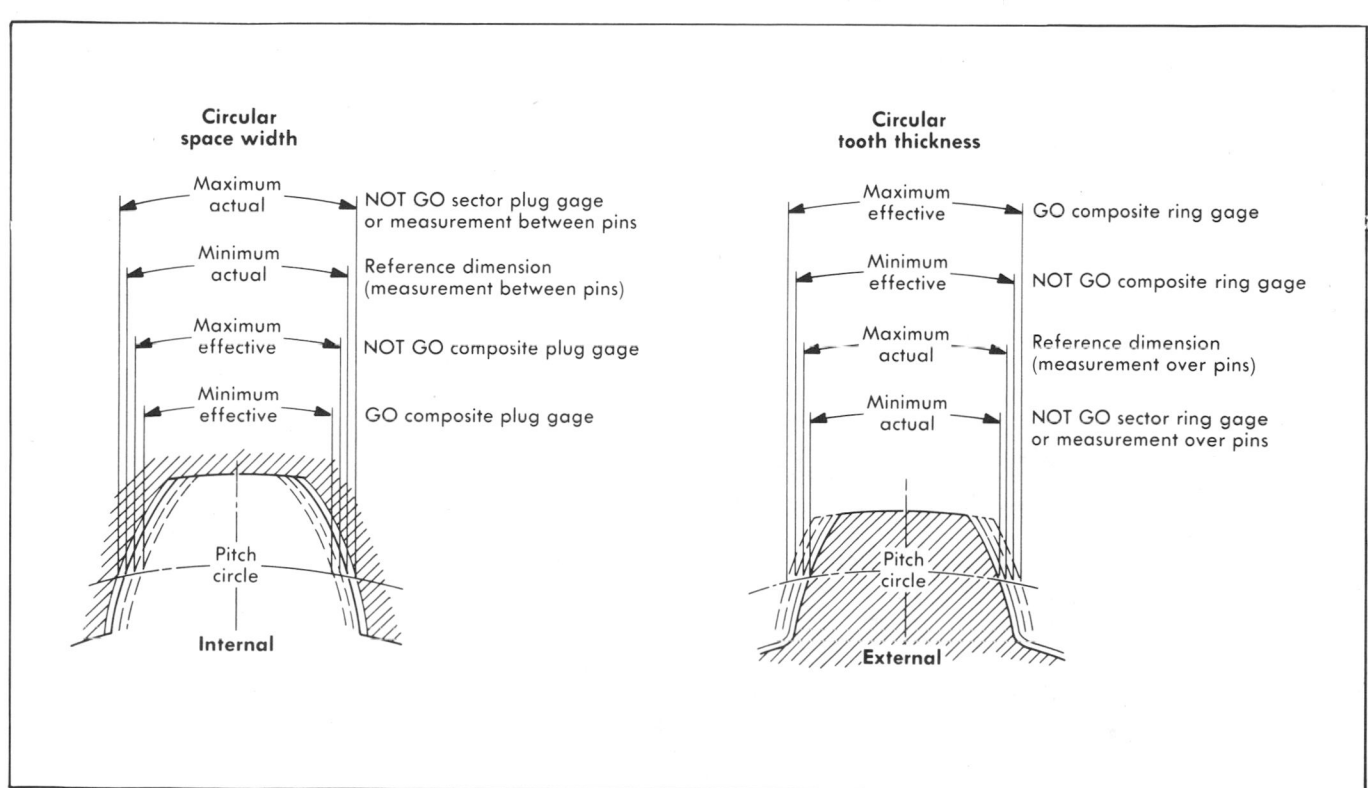

Fig. 9-64 Space width and tooth thickness inspection. (*Society of Automotive Engineers*)

CHAPTER 9

REFERENCES

References

1. Lowell W. Foster, *Modern Geometric Dimensioning and Tolerancing*, 2nd ed. (Fort Washington, MD: National Tooling and Machining Association, 1982), p. 1.
2. "Dimensioning and Tolerancing," ANSI Y14.5M—1982 (New York: American Society of Mechanical Engineers, 1982), p. 94.
3. *Ibid*, p. 91.
4. *Ibid*, p. 95.
5. *Ibid*, p. 96.
6. *Ibid*, p. 97.
7. *Ibid*, p. 106.
8. *Ibid*.
9. *Ibid*.
10. *Ibid.*, p. 53.
11. *Ibid.*, p. 84.
12. *Ibid.*, p. 109.
13. *Ibid*.
14. Francis T. Farago, *Handbook of Dimensional Measurement*, 2nd ed. (New York: Industrial Press, Inc. 1982), p. 352.
15. *Ibid.*, p. 229.
16. *Ibid.*, p. 397.
17. Henry H. Ryffel, ed., *Machinery's Handbook*, 22nd ed. (New York: Industrial Press, Inc. 1984), p. 895.

QUALITY MANAGEMENT AND PLANNING

When a company contracts to deliver the right product, on time, and with the proper quality, but fails to do so, something has gone wrong with the quality planning process during one or more of the planning time frames. The time frames and questions that should be asked within the time frames are as follows:

1. Short Term (recent days)
   - Were the inspection instructions adequate?
   - Did the manufacturing plans provide proper inspection and test steps?
   - Did the manufacturing and inspection personnel have proper tools and adequate training?
2. Intermediate Term (recent weeks)
   - Was adequate notice given to acquire necessary inspection gages and fixtures?
   - Were the customer's requirements properly conveyed to the manufacturing and QA departments?
3. Long Term (recent months or years)
   - Were trained and educated personnel available, having capabilities sufficient to meet the needs of the manufacturing and inspection tasks?
   - Did upper management continually convey a clear message that all QC steps, for all departments, would be properly performed and not bypassed?

The answers to these and many more questions necessary to carry out the execution of quality management and planning will be covered in this chapter.

QUALITY PLANNING HIERARCHY

Considerations for and emphasis on quality can and should enter into every major planning output of the organization. At each position level of the organizational structure, the individual must focus an appropriate portion of his or her planning output toward the effect that quality has on the desired results. Key managers in the chain of command for the quality organization (preferably starting with a vice president at the executive management level, but in practice typically starting at the middle management level) must provide the starting point of the thought process for product and service quality, influencing thought upward; directing thought downward to meet the needs generated by policies, strategies, and goals; and receiving upward thrusts of ideas through participative management practices.

The key issue is that each position level understands what must be integrated into planning so that their version of quality planning contains a well thought out relationship to the quality issues and goals for the company and separate divisions.

These understandings—the relationships between the position levels in the organization, the quality planning output at each level, and the definition of quality at each level in the organization—set the stage for many of the quality management and planning topics to be considered in this chapter. Quality missions, policies, and plans can be placed on this framework.

MISSIONS, POLICIES AND PLANS

Starting with the company planning efforts and cascading on to those who actually carry out the supporting detailed actions, a thorough understanding of the key terms is needed. The impact of the entire quality planning process can be lost if those involved, at each position level, lose direction of their own objectives.

QUALITY MISSION

The statements of purpose needed to formulate the quality mission can be determined once the corporation answers two initial questions:[1]

- What business are we in?
- Why are we in business?

Ideally, the quality mission will include or reflect on portions of the overall company mission or charter statements, adapting them, as they are needed, to the description of the specific quality positions taken.

Once the overall statements of purpose are provided, another set of questions must be asked to cause focus on the objectives of the company quality mission:

- What particular quality needs of the "business we are in" affect how we address quality issues?
- How do we view the quality function as it intertwines in the various people-oriented beliefs and actions?
- What part does the quality function play in support of our competitive edge in the marketplace?

MISSIONS, POLICIES AND PLANS

QUALITY POLICY

Evans and Evans indicate the word *policy*, when properly used, should "refer not to permanent principles but to courses of action. Primarily, it means a definite course of action adopted as expedient or from other considerations (our policy is to give the customer what he wants)..."[2] This is an excellent starting point. For no matter how a company chooses to describe and apply policy (and this can be varied depending on preference) the "course of action" considerations should be the primary focus. The courses of action should establish the long-term, overall intents of the company while focusing on the quality function (as contrasted to the short-term, specific day-to-day decisions). It must describe how people at all position levels will interact both within and without of the company in the interests of product and service quality.[3]

QUALITY PLANS

Quality plans can appear in many forms. Most commonly they include the following:

- The quality assurance manual, which sets the directions for the total quality program.
- Quality plans for special programs.
- Quality planning for control of processing.
- Quality objectives in personal appraisal planning.

The Quality Assurance Manual

The quality assurance manual is the cornerstone of planning for the quality function that is under primary control of the QA management. Contents cover the major areas of concern for quality-related activities, whether performed by personnel in or out of the quality-titled departments.

A well thought out, well-maintained QA manual provides the following:

- Descriptions of how each organizational department or function views and acts on its quality-related assignments and responds to the needs of its interface groups.
- Specific detail for inspection, test, and audit activities, including tools and equipment used; sampling plans; product characteristics to consider; sequence of events; and documentation needed for all employees, not just those in the QA/QC departments.
- Quality reports to be provided.
- Various coverage provided by QA, QC, inspection, and audit personnel.
- Means for attracting prospective customers and portions of proposals for those actively pursued.
- A constant reminder of quality-related activities to all reviewers of draft proposals and recipients of final copies.
- A thought-provoking document, requiring various levels of employees to think carefully about current and potential applications for quality activities.
- A training tool for new or transferred personnel.
- A description of the commitment to customer quality requirements and how the company will strive to fulfill them.

Typically, the QA manual contains two types of documents: policies and procedures. Quality policies explain how the company views the quality function as it applies to the area of interest and what will be done to provide a quality product or service. Quality procedures support a specific policy and explain how the company will carry out the policy.

Quality Planning for Control of Processing

This type of quality planning usually is provided in support of systemic programs initiated by departments that interface with the quality assurance department. Often the systems involved include the manufacturing-sequence quality control program for internal activities and purchase order quality requirements for purchased goods and services.

The quality SOPs provided by the QA manual and supplemented by quality plans for special programs is translated from the more general descriptions and applied to the specific part, process, or service. As the manufacturing sequence-of-events is provided by manufacturing SOPs, so are the inspection needs for each operator at each step, plus specific inspection station, patrol inspection, testing, and audit requirements.

ORGANIZATION

Many events have occurred since the early 1970s that have affected the way manufacturing companies now look at the quality function. The impact of change has improved the way that the quality function is organized. Perhaps the best conceptual description of how the quality function can be organized for maximum effectiveness is found in three related functions that together form an extended, uniform network, though each has its own entity. This is referred to as the Juran Trilogy. Each of these organizational processes of the quality function are described as follows:[4]

1. *Quality planning function.* The group responsible for preparations to meet quality goals. The end result is a process that can meet quality goals under operating conditions. The quality planning activities emphasize efforts that:
    - Identify the customers, external and internal.
    - Develop product features that respond to customer needs. Products include both goods and services.
    - Establish quality goals that meet the needs of customers and suppliers alike and do so at lowest combined costs (combined in the sense that quite often the total cost is not just the purchase price, but includes maintenance, repairs, and downtime).
    - Develop a process that can produce the needed product features.
    - Prove that the process is capable, that it can meet the quality goals during operation.

2. *Quality control function.* The group responsible for documenting or certifying attainment of quality goals during manufacturing operations. The result is conduct of manufacturing operations in accordance with the quality plan. The quality control activities emphasize efforts that:

- Choose control subjects (what to control).
- Choose units of measure.
- Establish measurement methods.
- Establish standards of performance.
- Measure real performance.
- Interpret the difference, real vs. standard.
- Act on the difference.

3. *Quality improvement function.* The group responsible for breaking through to unprecedented performance levels. The results provide operations at levels of quality distinctly superior to planned performance of previous periods. The quality improvement activities emphasize efforts that:
- Identify specific projects for improvement.
- Organize to guide the projects.
- Organize for diagnosis, for discovery of causes.
- Diagnose to find causes.
- Provide remedies in the forms of corrective and preventive actions.
- Prove that the remedies are effective in operation.
- Provide for control to hold the gains.

An up-to-date company will be structured to provide groups responsible for each of the three functions—planning, control, and improvement. With the addition of a group responsible for vendor quality, the coverage is complete. The vendor quality group ensures that the vendors have replicated the three quality functions (planning, control, and improvement) within their own organizations.

A graph using Dr. J.M. Juran's model for optimum quality costs is shown in Fig. 10-1. It is the company's decision where to establish the optimization point. In recent years, companies have moved the optimization point closer to 100% good product as reject rates have been lowered to parts per million for some products. This analysis, even in rough form, can help a company determine how much will be spent both on quality maintenance costs and improvement efforts to attack the avoidable costs of poor quality.

Recently, it has been recognized that emphasis on prevention during product design and process development has resulted in drastic reduction (in some cases elimination) of defectives, thereby driving appraisal costs toward zero and approaching "perfection" at a bounded cost, contrary to the graph in Fig. 10-1. Therefore, Juran's model of optimum quality costs can be misleading because it indicates that appraisal and prevention costs are infinite at 100% quality and thus a program of zero defects cannot succeed. Juran's model, established in earlier years of quality assurance theory, assumes

that no feedback to product design or process controls occurs to eliminate errors at their source, thus requiring appraisal methods to screen out defectives.

As Schneiderman points out, these assumptions may not be valid in many industries today, and therefore a minimum (if not optimum) in total quality costs can occur at 100% quality levels as shown in Fig. 10-2.[5]

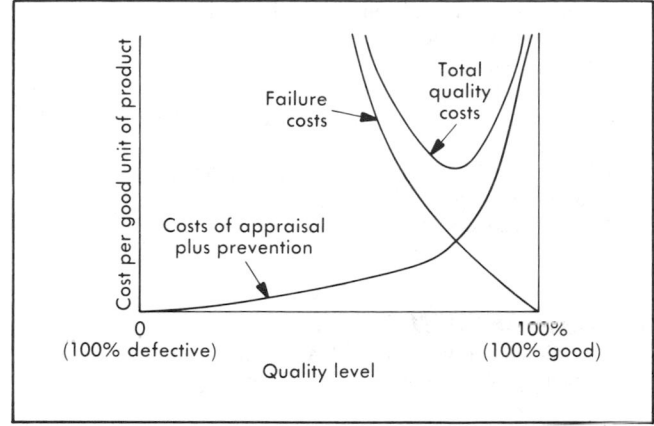

Fig. 10-1 Juran's model for optimum quality costs. (*Reproduced with permission from McGraw-Hill Book Co. from* Quality Control Handbook, *3rd ed., by J.M. Juran*)

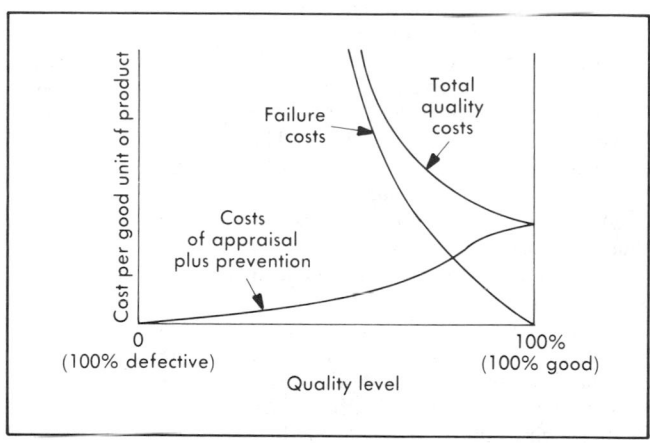

Fig. 10-2 Schneiderman's model for zero defects optimum quality level. (*Copyright American Society for Quality Control, Inc. Reprinted with permission*)

ACHIEVING QUALITY

Quality professionals use a variety of definitions for quality. One school of thought equates quality with satisfying the customer's needs. Another adopts a more modest goal and states that quality is conformance to specifications. Joseph Juran has popularized the concept "fitness for use" as the primary interpretation. W. Edwards Deming says, "Good quality means a predictable degree of uniformity and dependability, with quality suited to the market."

Achieving quality requires manufacturers to put one foot in the technical camp of specifications and processes and the other foot in the managerial camp of plans and people. The manufacturing engineer must at times work as a quality engineer, and at other times call upon a specialized quality engineer, to achieve the desired end result — a quality product delivered on time at a reasonable price.

ACHIEVING QUALITY

ASSURANCE OF QUALITY IN NEW DESIGNS

For projects relating to new products, services, or processes, management should prepare, as appropriate, written quality plans consistent with all other requirements of a company's quality management system.[6]

Quality plans should define the following elements:

- The quality objectives to be attained.
- The specific allocation of responsibilities and authority during the different phases of the project.
- The specific procedures, methods, and work instructions to be applied.
- Suitable testing, inspection, examination, and audit programs at appropriate stages (such as design and development).
- A method for changes and modifications in a quality plan as projects proceed.
- Other measures necessary to meet objectives.

DESIGN REVIEW

As indicated previously, high achieved quality is the result of solid quality plans. One powerful planning technique is the design review.

A schedule of design reviews should be included in the new product development plan. Depending on the complexity of the product, the number will range from one to five formal reviews. Although product and process design reviews may be done separately, at some preselected points in the new product development cycle the reviews must be conducted jointly.

The primary focus of the design review is on how the product will perform. But consideration must also be given to what happens if the product does not function properly. In addition, consideration must be given to the kinds of consequences that may occur and how likely they are to occur. A fault tree analysis (FTA) addresses these issues.

A fault tree analysis first identifies all of the undesired events that might occur. It then works backward to determine the cause of each event. This gives a trouble-and-remedy diagram that shows the probable causes of each symptom of system failure. The FTA then provides a checklist for managers to seek corrective action or develop improvement programs.

Fault tree analysis is used primarily with products demanding high reliability, having significant safety considerations, and having high technological content. Besides helping to design a superior product, FTA can significantly reduce the probability of product liability.

QUALITY FUNCTION DEPLOYMENT

Quality function deployment (QFD), a relatively new planning technique, is one of the most all-encompassing and is especially suited to large-scale consumer items such as automobiles and appliances. These products have heavy tooling and design costs as well as many optional features.

QFD begins with market research to obtain consumer feedback on product features, performance, and service.[7] This feedback, referred to as "the voice of the customer," is then put into part specifications and manufacturing parameters upon which an engineer can act. Thus, QFD ensures that engineering activities focus on meeting customers' likes rather than on the dictates of upper management.

MATERIAL REVIEW BOARD

In early production, there are frequently adjustments that must be made in the use of material. Often, specifications are assigned in haste, without sufficient preliminary data. As a result, material outside specifications is not necessarily defective; it must be reviewed for suitability. If the specifications are wrong and the item will suit the purpose, then it should not be rejected. However, the specification should be reviewed and then changed. These tasks are the function of the material review board (MRB).

PROCESS CAPABILITY AND SPECIFICATIONS

The output from a process will frequently result from the collective effect of numerous sequential operations on different pieces of machinery, or multiple streams of product coming off of the same machine. The first step in performing a capability study is to break the process down into the subprocesses and operations requiring study. For the sake of explanation, the discussion of capability studies will begin with the simplest case, a single operation with a single stream of product, and then move to some special cases.

Capability studies fall into two broad categories—short-term studies and long-term studies. Short-term studies are usually conducted on new products and processes where no opportunity exists to collect data during actual production. Consequently, the short-term study uses relatively small sample sizes (30-100 pieces) to keep costs down. The short-term study is sometimes called a "machine capability study" because all variables are held constant in an attempt to isolate the inherent variability of a particular machine. Long-term studies, on the other hand, consist of analyzing data collected from a current production process. Sample sizes are generally larger than those from a short-term study. The analysis must take into account those factors that change with time and may affect the process output.

THE 14-STEP QUALITY PROGRAM

One of America's leading quality consultants is Phil Crosby. Over a period of years, he developed a 14-step program for building a quality workforce. The 14 steps are shown as follows:[8]

1. Management commitment. Decide that serious change is going to occur and prepare communications to that effect.
2. Quality improvement team. Bring together representatives of each department, select a chairman, define roles. Explain the program to the team.
3. Quality measurement. Find out just what kind of quality now exists. To accomplish this, a quality maturity grid can be used.
4. Cost of quality evaluation. Make rough preliminary estimates, using the controller's office.
5. Quality awareness. Share the results of quality measurement with all employees. Keep the focus on information *sharing*, not manipulation or force.
6. Corrective action. Bring problems to light, solve them, or formally pass them up to the next level of management.
7. Ad hoc committee for zero defects program. The quality improvement team should develop a strategy to create an awareness of zero defects and how to accomplish it. Beware that this will take a good deal of time and will require firm support by the company's thought leaders.

8. Supervisor training. Formal orientation with all levels of management is essential. All supervisors must be tuned in and able to explain their role to their people.
9. Zero Defects Day. This is a major event where the "new attitude" is put on display. Make it special so people will remember.
10. Goal setting. Each supervisor gets employees to set goals for 30, 60, and 90 days. All goals should be measurable and attainable.
11. Error cause removal. Each person should describe any problem that keeps him or her from performing error-free work. Managers and staff must respond with ways that these problems can be removed.
12. Recognition. Provide rewards and ceremonies that focus attention on effective contributors. The rewards should not emphasize the financial aspect, but should be highly visible.
13. Quality councils. The quality professionals and the team chairpersons should come together to communicate and identify actions to upgrade the program being installed.
14. Do it all over again. A year or more is required to accomplish the first 13 steps. By then it is time to start over with new situations and, often, due to turnover, new people as well.

These steps constitute a sound procedure for upgrading quality attitudes and capabilities throughout an organization. Many variations of this procedure have been developed in the literature.

GAGE AND MEASUREMENT SYSTEM CAPABILITY

Capability of gages and measurement equipment presents some special concerns. When assessing the suitability of a measuring system, four characteristics of the system must be evaluated: (1) accuracy, (2) precision (often called repeatability), (3) reproducibility, and (4) stability. Accuracy is how well the entire set of repeated readings on the gage agrees with a known standard. Precision is the amount of dispersion of repeated readings. Reproducibility reflects how well readings made by one operator agree with those made by another. Stability addresses how constant the accuracy and precision remain with time, and it determines the required calibration and maintenance intervals.

RELATION OF STANDARDS TO QUALITY

A question that arises in the discussion of standards is: How do standards relate to the attainment or achievement of quality? The standard provides a basis for comparing a measured result against an agreed-on reference. Conceptually, the standard is a communications medium between (1) buyers and sellers, (2) manufacturing and quality control, (3) customers and quality assurance, and (4) preparers and users. It gives the intent of the design, instruction, requirement, criteria, and method.

Another question that may arise is: How does one know what standards are needed? To answer that question, it is necessary to become familiar with the field, talk to the quality control and quality assurance departments or standards coordinator. The American Society for Quality Control (ASQC) has an information service (414/272-8575) that individuals can call for ideas about what standards are available on quality-related topics. The American National Standards Institute (ANSI) also has an

overview of all available national standards. In addition, a study of various handbooks reveals many applicable standards for each aspect of the manufacturing process.

By referring to the applicable standard, a manufacturer can minimize the time and effort of building up specifications from scratch. Of course, this requires that the manufacturer understands what the standard is.

Standards allow the manufacturer to reduce the number of required varieties in stock and help maintain a uniform product. They are invaluable for purchasing agents to secure truly competitive bids and to compare bids.

Standards allow the designer to specify standard materials that are readily available and provide uniform procedures for testing products in different laboratories. Customers can specify a product based on established standards.

A standard specification implies standard methods of testing and standard definitions. In some instances, methods of testing are incorporated within a materials specification, while in other cases some standardizing agencies establish standard methods of testing separately from the materials specifications and make reference to the test methods.

QUALITY AUDITS

Quality audits are becoming more and more popular with companies as they realize the advantages offered. Some of the benefits of a quality audit system are as follows:[9]

- Fosters quality system development.
- Provides information to help management make good decisions.
- Aids in the allocation of resources.
- Spreads technology.
- Reduces product liability costs.
- Reduces overhead.
- Improves morale.
- Increases capacity.
- Generates profit.

Procedures audit, product audit, and process audit are the three major categories of audits. Each has a distinct purpose and should be used only for that purpose.

A procedures audit evaluates the effectiveness of the quality assurance program or system. The standard used during this audit would include the quality assurance policy and procedures manual and the operating manual for each department, including purchasing, receiving, inspection, shipping, material review board, and calibration.

A product audit is a quantitative assessment of conformance to required product characteristics. Product quality audits are generally performed for the following reasons:[10]

- To evaluate the outgoing quality level of the product or group of products.
- To determine if the outgoing quality product meets a predetermined standard level of quality for a product or a group of products.
- To estimate the level of quality originally submitted to inspection.
- To measure the ability of inspection to make valid quality decisions.
- To determine the suitability of the controls.

APPLICATIONS OF QUALITY COSTS

A process audit provides an independent assessment of the effectiveness of a quality system through the evaluation of the knowledge of adherence to and adequacy of specific production methods used either in the performance or in the control of the work. The major items for evaluation are:

- Existence of procedures for performing the work as well as for inspecting or testing the work.
- Knowledge that production and quality personnel have about the procedures and specified requirements.
- Conformance of these personnel to the requirements.
- Reasons for deviation from the specified procedures.

APPLICATIONS OF QUALITY COSTS

Quality cost techniques can be used as an effective tool for such things as strategic quality planning, continuous improvement efforts, budgeting purposes, product cost estimating, specific department improvements, and supplier quality relationships. It has rather broadbased applications in the business environment because it uses financial terms that are familiar to all disciplines.

STRATEGIC QUALITY PLANNING

The strategic quality planning process focuses on costs. Because of this, knowledge of the existing quality system defined through quality costs is a vital input to the planning process. Knowledge of these costs can provide the basis for direction leading to the optimum integration of resources in the company. It can also prove invaluable in identifying those short-term activities that lead to the achievement of the strategic goals.

As a result of implementing strategic quality planning, one company identified that inconsistent quality was the result of reworked processes to match changed product designs when it was too late to order new equipment that was needed. To avoid this, product development, manufacturing planning, and supplier commitments were scheduled concurrently instead of in series. Producibility problems in this company are now handled at the same time that laboratory and prototype assessments are evaluated. This minimizes the need to solve manufacturing and supplier problems at the time the product is released for production.

PRODUCT IMPROVEMENT

In the past, quality cost reporting was used in improvement efforts, but it often achieved inadequate results. The main reason for this shortcoming was that the reporting was not accompanied by an improvement action. It is now recognized that a far more realistic objective is for quality cost reporting to support an improvement team whose effort is directed toward improving quality and productivity. Multidiscipline improvement teams can use quality cost reports to point out the strengths and weaknesses of a quality system. These improvement teams can also describe the benefits and ramifications of changes in financial terms. Return on investment (ROI) models and other financial analyses can be constructed directly from quality cost data. These models and analyses can be used to justify improvements to management. Those on the improvement teams can also use this information to rank problems in order of priority, seek out root causes, and implement the most effective, irreversible corrective action. The teams can also track results to ensure that they are headed in the right direction.

Companies who collect and report quality costs recognize the value of this information to those making the improvements. They also recognize that reporting will accomplish nothing without someone "making it happen."[11]

DEPARTMENTAL IMPROVEMENT

Quality costs have recently been used as a tool for aiding in the improvement of staff departments. In this application, each department is looked on as a separate business with customers usually internal to the company. The department furnishes

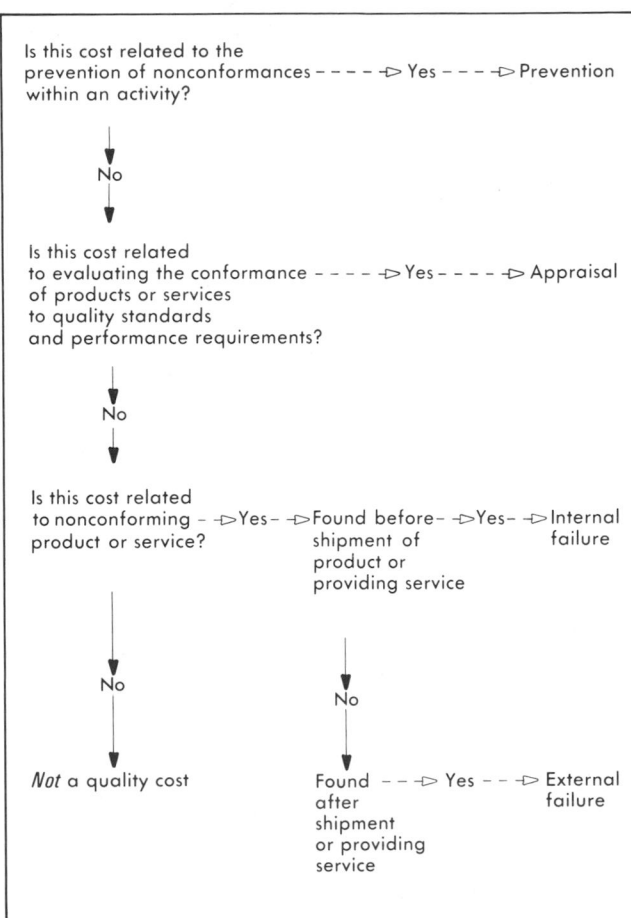

Fig. 10-3 Process for determining quality cost categories in office departments. (*Copyright American Society for Quality Control, Inc. Reprinted with permission*)

products or services to these customers. Each department should also have a quality system to ensure that these products or services meet the needs of the customers. As in the traditional use of quality costs, this tool can document the quality system used in each staff department. Except in a general way, it has been found that the definitions used for manufacturing products are not appropriate for the activities in staff departments. Figure 10-3 illustrates a process that may be useful in defining the quality cost categories after the product or service has been identified.[12]

MANUFACTURING FOCUS

As has been previously mentioned, the costs in a quality system are divided into prevention, appraisal, internal failure, and external failure costs. To assist the user, these four main categories are further divided into different activities applicable to manufacturing and service industries. This subdivision is not meant to be all inclusive, but to provide a general idea of the activities under each cost category. The words used to describe these activities should be changed to reflect the specific language and meanings in use at each company. This will help to ensure a common understanding by those in the company.

Prevention Costs

Prevention is the cost of all activities in a company specifically designed to prevent defects in deliverable products or services. Many of the activities under the prevention costs category are completed before the product is released to production. Activities considered part of the prevention costs category are listed in Table 10-1.

The initial effort in prevention costs is to identify customer or product user needs through customer or user surveys. This work is normally performed by the marketing department. These needs are then translated into quality standards and requirements by the product design department. In addition to the marketing and product design departments, many other departments are also involved at this stage, such as quality, purchasing, manufacturing, and service.

Appraisal Costs

Appraisal costs are the costs of all activities in a company that are associated with measuring, evaluating, or auditing the products or services to ensure conformance with quality standards and performance requirements. Activities under appraisal costs usually occur after the product is in production. Some of the activities in this category include receiving inspection of materials from suppliers, checking performed by production operators, and audits. Other activities included in this category are listed in Table 10-2.

Internal Failure Costs

Whenever quality appraisals are performed, there exists the possibility of discovering products that fail to meet requirements. When this happens, unscheduled and possibly unbudgeted expenses are automatically incurred. For example, when a complete lot of metal parts is rejected for being oversize, the possibility for rework must first be evaluated. Then the cost of rework may be compared to the cost of scrapping the parts and completely replacing them. Finally, a disposition is made and the action is carried out. The total cost of this evaluation, disposition, and subsequent action is an integral part of internal failure costs.

Internal failure costs have been defined to basically include all costs required to evaluate and either correct or replace products or services not conforming to requirements or user needs prior to shipment to the customer. These costs only occur after the product is in production. In general, this includes all the material and labor expenses that are lost or wasted due to defective or otherwise unacceptable work affecting the quality of products or services discovered anywhere during the entire operational sequence. However, corrective action directed toward elimination of the problem in the future is preventive action and may be classified as prevention. Activities performed in various departments as a part of internal failure costs are listed in Table 10-3.

External Failure Costs

External failure costs are those costs due to products or

TABLE 10-1
Typical Activities Performed by Various Departments
That Affect Prevention Costs in a Quality System

Marketing	Product Design and Development	Purchasing	Operations	Quality Administration
Marketing research	Quality progress reviews	Supplier reviews	Process validation	Administrative salaries
Customer perception surveys	Support activities	Supplier rating	Operations quality planning	Administrative expenses
Contract review	Qualification test	Purchase order technical data reviews	Operations support quality planning	Quality program planning
	Field trials	Supplier quality planning	Operator quality education	Quality performance reporting
			Operator SPC/process control	Quality education
			Design and development	Quality improvement
			Quality related equipment	Quality audits

APPLICATIONS OF QUALITY COSTS

TABLE 10-2
Typical Activities Performed by Various Departments
That Affect Appraisal Costs in a Quality System

Purchasing	Operations	External
Receiving or incoming inspection and tests	Performance of planned inspections, tests and audits	Field performance evaluation
Inspection equipment for purchased material	• labor operations	Special product evaluations
Supplier product qualification	• quality audits	Field stock and spare parts evaluation
Source inspection and control program	• inspection and test materials	Test and inspection data review
	Set-up and first-piece inspection	
	Special tests (manufacturing)	
	Process control measurements	
	Laboratory support	
	Inspection and test equipment	
	• depreciation allowances	
	• measurement equipment expenses	
	• maintenance and calibration labor	
	Endorsement and certification by outside agencies	

services not meeting customer requirements or needs after they are shipped to the customer. As is obvious, these costs only occur after the product is in production. The elements included in this category are listed in Table 10-4.

BASELINES FOR ANALYSIS

One difficulty encountered in tracking the progress of improvement efforts is that many things vary from one time period to another. This includes such things as the volume produced and wage adjustments. Because of this, quality cost can be best compared when it is a percentage of some appropriate baseline as shown in Fig. 10-4.[13]

For long-term analysis, net sales is the base most often used for presentations to top management. While this measurement may be important from a strategic point of view, individuals doing the analysis and improvement efforts require a baseline that is more related to the amount of work performed, such as operating costs or value-added costs.

Different baselines and their advantages and limitations are given in Table 10-5.[14] Because no one baseline is ideal for all situations, the use of more than one baseline is often required to meet the diverse needs of those reviewing or using the information.

COSTS AFTER DELIVERY

In some instances, there are costs to the company and the consumer that occur after delivery to the customer. These costs depend on the effectiveness of the quality system. Yet they can be easily looked on as being vague by those in the manufacturing environment. This vagueness is often because the costs can only be predicted based on historical records such as warranty. In some cases, such as product liability, cost prediction may not even be possible. Even with warranty that is predictable, only a very small percentage of the quantity shipped usually requires

TABLE 10-3
Typical Activities Performed by Various Departments That Affect Internal Failure Costs in a Quality System

Product Design	Purchasing	Operations
Corrective action	Purchased material reject disposition costs	Disposition
Rework due to design changes		Troubleshooting or failure analysis
Scrap due to design changes	Purchased material replacement costs	Investigation support
Production liaison costs	Supplier corrective action	Corrective action
	Rework of supplier rejects	Rework
	Uncontrolled material losses	Repair
		Reinspection/retest
		Extra operations
		Scrap
		Downgraded end product or service
		Internal failure labor losses

field service. Catching this small percentage with inspection prior to shipping is simply a futile task. Only through prevention—preventing the problems from occurring in the first place—can these costs be minimized to the company and the consumer. The purpose of this section is to explain in a general way the conditions under which these costs may occur so that they may be better understood and dealt with.

APPLICATIONS OF QUALITY COSTS

TABLE 10-4
Typical Elements That Affect External Failure Costs in a Quality System

Customer complaint investigation and resolution
Returned goods evaluation and repair or replace
Retrofit costs
Recall costs
Warranty claims
Liability costs
Penalties
Customer goodwill
Lost sales

Costs to the Company

After the product is delivered to the customer, costs to the company occur because of warranties, negligence claims, product liabilities, violations of government acts, and lost sales. The two primary types of warranties are express warranties and implied warranties.

Express warranties. In general, express warranties mean that the goods furnished must conform to the description given or sample or model shown when the agreement was made. It also applies to any promises or other statements of fact made at this time.[15] As an example of the broadness of this remedy, a breech of express warranty was found based on a representation in an advertisement about the life of the product.[16]

The federal government has enacted the Magnuson-Moss Act to apply to the warranty of consumer products and service contracts. This act does not require a warranty to be given, but regulates the means of disclosing the warranty terms, places limits on disclaimers, promotes informal settlement procedures, and provides some civil remedies if a warranty is given.[17]

TABLE 10-5
Measurement Bases Used for Determining Quality Costs

Base	Advantages	Disadvantages
Direct labor hour	Readily available and understood	Can be drastically influenced by automation
Direct labor dollars	Available and understood; tends to balance any inflation effect	Can be drastically influenced by automation
Standard manufacturing cost dollars	More stability than direct labor dollars	Includes overhead costs both fixed and variable
Value-added dollars	Useful when processing costs are important	Not useful for relating different types of manufacturing departments
Sales dollars	Appeals to higher management	Sales dollars can be influenced by changes in prices, marketing costs, and demand
Product units	Simplicity	Not appropriate when different products are made unless an "equivalent" item can be offered

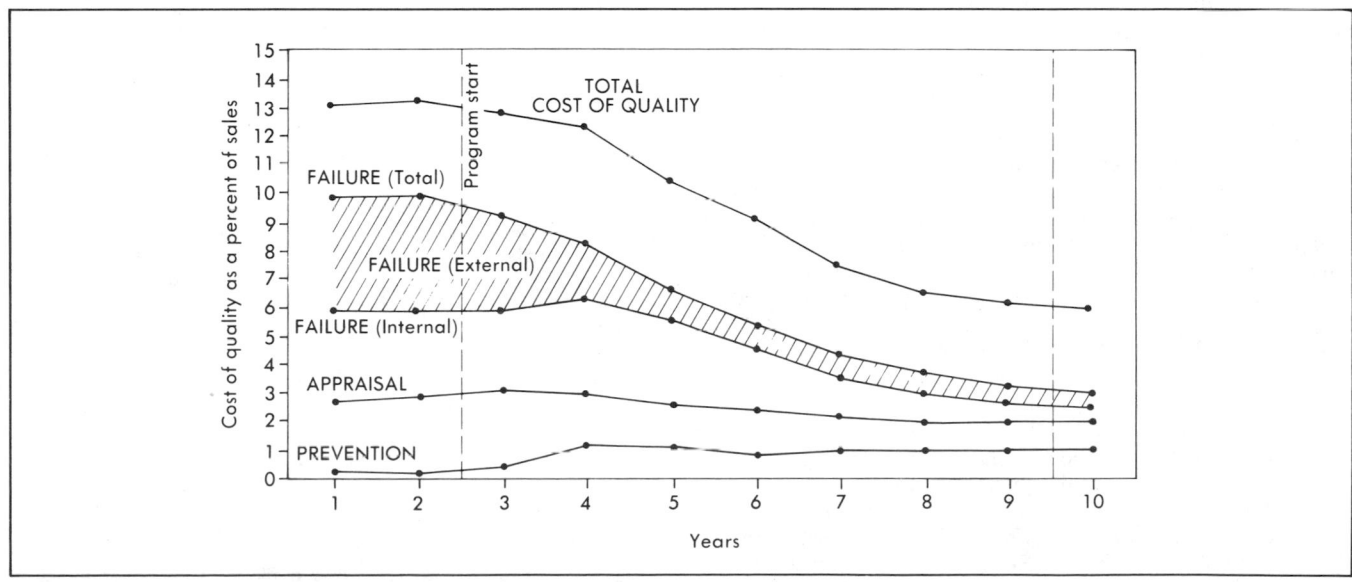

Fig. 10-4 Typical baseline used when comparing quality costs over a period of time. *(Copyright American Society for Quality Control, Inc. Reprinted by permission.)*

APPLICATIONS OF QUALITY COSTS

Many states have enacted so-called "lemon laws" as an indirect consequence of the Magnuson-Moss Act. These laws set standards between consumers and manufacturers that create a statutory warranty modifying the manufacturer's express warranty.[18]

Implied warranties. Implied warranties differ from express warranties in that they are implicit in any agreement when certain conditions are met.[19] In other words, a manufacturer may be obligated for warranty in this manner even though there was no express warranty given to the buyer. Although there are several implied warranties, only the implied warranty of merchantability and the implied warranty of fitness for particular purpose will be discussed.

The implied warranty of merchantability warrants that the goods sold are of average quality within the industry. Appearance as well as the structural safety and durability of a product are important factors. Products must be fit for any ordinary purposes for which they are used. In addition, they must be adequately contained, packaged, and labeled. The products must also conform to any statements made on the container or label.

The implied warranty of fitness for particular purpose is a much stronger warranty than that of merchantability. The products sold must be fit for the purpose for which they are intended. This warranty is implicit in an agreement that specifies how the products are to be used. The agreement is made known to the seller, and the buyer relies on the skill and expertise of the seller.

In certain circumstances, implied warranties can be excluded from an agreement by disclaimers or inspection by the buyer. But if they are not excluded, remedies for breach may in some situations also include damages for personal injuries.

Negligence. The theory of negligence involves the recovery for injuries suffered when the manufacturer fails to exercise reasonable or prudent care in manufacturing a product.[20] A manufacturer also has a duty to design its product so that it does not present an unreasonable risk of harm to the user. The manufacturer's duty is limited under this theory to consequences reasonably foreseeable. Also, the failure to exercise reasonable and prudent care during production of the product must be the cause of the injury. In some cases, this duty extends to providing warnings to users of the product and installing safety devices to protect them from injury.[21]

Product liability. Product liability is the law imposed on the manufacturer in favor of a customer/user for loss suffered by reason of a defective product.[22] The defect could occur from the manufacture, design, construction, formula, development of standards, preparation, processing, assembly, inspection, testing, listing, certifying, warning, instructing, marketing, advertising, packaging, or the labeling of a product. The customer/user must prove that a defect existed when the product was shipped and that this defect caused the injury. It is not necessary to prove any negligence on the part of the manufacturer. The product can also be proved defective by drawing reasonable inferences from circumstantial evidence.[23]

Safety acts violations. Violations of government safety acts are potential sources of unnecessary cost for the manufacturer.[24,25] Besides the federal statutes concerning OSHA, 29 USC 651, and the motor vehicle and tire safety standards under 15 USC 1390, there are many more enacted by both the federal and state governments. For the Federal Consumer Products Safety Act, under 15 USC 2052, the promulgation of standards may be to prevent unreasonable risk of injury associated with a product. In some cases, such acts have the power to make producers recall products having substantial hazards. Violators in some cases may be subject to civil penalties and also criminal penalties.

Recalls. From time to time, even well-managed companies call back quantities of products from the field to correct problems that they have been unable, for one reason or the other, to anticipate.[26] Recent years have seen voluntary recall of products as diverse as automobiles, adhesives, bicycles, chemical sprays, paint removers, and pacemakers. Mandated recalls initiated by the government are not uncommon. Recent consumer legislation requires that in some cases all parties in the distribution chain be reimbursed by the manufacturer in the event of a recall. The government may also publicize the potential hazard. This publicity may be potentially harmful to the manufacturer's reputation.

Lost sales. Lost sales due to the customer's perception of poor product quality is often an abstract concept for most companies to place in perspective. A company that supplies its product to another firm may find it easier to visualize this concept. It is reflected by the cash flow lost because the customer perceives that better quality could be obtained elsewhere and therefore chooses to cancel or not reward a contract. Another example is the cash flow lost because the customer chooses to reduce the portion of the order "pie" for a similar reason.

Costs to the Customer

Lifecycle costs are costs of the product over the entire life of the product from the customer's viewpoint.[27,28] They include the initial cost of purchasing the product, as well as operating

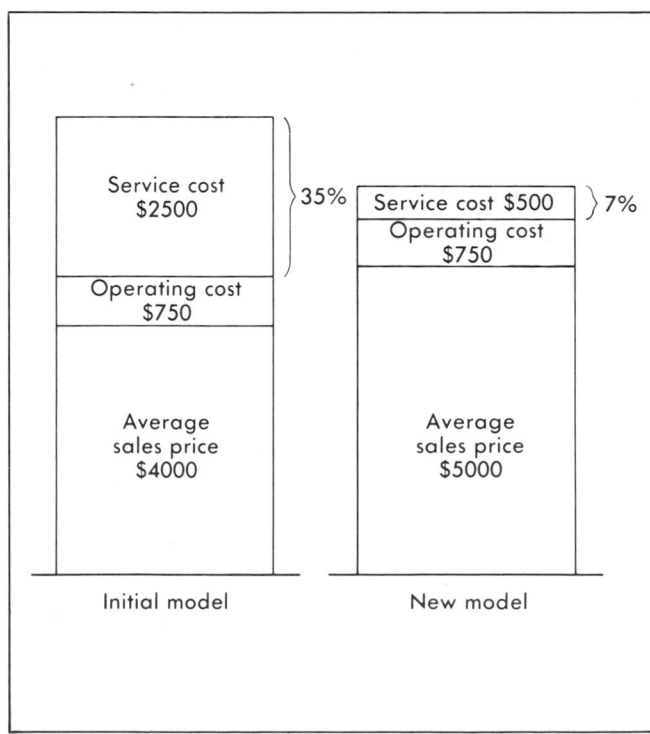

Fig. 10-5 Lifecycle costs for a new model of a computer accessory compared to the initial model. *(Copyright McGraw-Hill Book Co. Reproduced with permission.)*

and disposal costs. Operating costs include, among others, maintenance costs, repair costs, and often the time and expense of the consumer in getting these things done. When the perspective is broadened to include the cost to society, disposal cost may also include the effort to restore the materials in the product to raw material that can be recycled.

Figure 10-5 is an example of the lifecycle costs for a computer accessory. Shortly after the initial model was introduced, sales fell off sharply when the consumers found that service cost was forcing the lifecycle cost to be excessive. A new model that had a higher initial cost but lower lifecycle cost was introduced.

The Taguchi loss function is noted because of its similarity to lifecycle cost.[29] This function furnishes the framework around which Taguchi methods are used to gain improvements in products. It is defined as the financial loss imparted to society after a product is shipped (including any internal costs whether the product is shipped or not). The real power of the Taguchi loss function is its impact on changing the way quality is viewed and the methods that are used to justify improvements that do not meet traditional payback guidelines. Interestingly, it has been found that the manufacturer's cost improvements are often less than the loss to society that may be a result of that change. Therefore, the real value to society of making changes can be evaluated by this concept. This value may be a better indication of the long-term effect of the change on the company's future competitive status.

CONTINUOUS IMPROVEMENT

A systems-oriented approach to quality has been popular for many years in U.S. companies.[30] In some cases the organization of the company has changed to reflect this thinking by adding a systems engineering function. This function was typically assigned the responsibility of pulling together activities associated with the design, manufacture, and assembly of products. Success with this approach has been limited for several reasons.

The first reason concerns a traditional approach widely used in problem solving. For example, a list of the top problems along with corrective action plans is requested. This often leads the whole organization, in a splintered fashion, on a witch hunt to find causal factors and corrective actions. With this approach, the basic problems with systems are often overlooked. Unless these basic problems are solved, a similar list of top problems will be found the next time this information is requested. This approach is often detrimental to continuous quality improvement.

A second reason for the limited success in continuous improvement is related to the way companies are organized. When viewing an organizational chart, a strong vertical relationship typically exists within each department because of the performance objectives. Horizontally among departments a much weaker relationship exists due to many factors, including those same individual department performance objectives. To achieve continuous quality improvement, the horizontal relationship in all departments must be strengthened.[31]

To strengthen the horizontal ties among activities in departments, multidiscipline improvement teams can be used. These teams direct their effort toward improving productivity and quality. As discussed previously, quality cost reports are used as a tool to point out the strengths and weaknesses of the quality system. Those on the teams can also use this information to rank problems in order of priority, seek out root causes,

and to implement the most effective, irreversible corrective action. Financial analyses can be constructed directly from cost data. The teams can also track results to ensure that they are headed in the right direction. Companies who collect and report quality cost recognize the value of this information to those directly involved in making the improvements. They also recognize that reporting will accomplish nothing without someone making it happen.[32]

Reporting

As discussed previously, the initial quality report can be used to allow the improvement team to understand the quality system. A summary page for such a report is depicted in Fig. 10-6.[33] The actual format used should be chosen by the improvement team. In using the report, for example, the improvement team may want to examine various relationships for improvement such as:

- The activity identifying customer perceptions compared to the cost of customer complaints.
- Supplier quality planning activity compared to the cost of required supplier corrective action.
- Operations planning activities compared to operations rework and repair cost.

These are just a few of the comparisons that may lead to improvement efforts in the quality system.

After the initial quality cost study, a decision must be made as to when the study should be repeated. If quality cost reporting is to support the improvement team, then it is logical to assume that specific parts of the study should be repeated when the improvement team needs new or additional information. This should be, for example, when an improvement is in place and a change in results is expected. To generate reports on a regular basis may be wasted effort if no new useful information is provided. Regular reports in the past were perceived as "control" type reports and, in many cases, were not well accepted in the long run by management.

To determine how a situation is doing over time, trend charts can be used. Failure costs, in particular, lend themselves to this type of analysis. Historical data is plotted versus time after normalizing the data by dividing by an appropriate baseline. It is then possible to project trends into the future in view of the improvement projects that have been identified.

There are two types of trend analyses. The first is long range and is principally used for strategic planning and management updates. The second is short range and is usually done in areas of specific interest (see Fig. 10-7).[34]

Failure costs could also be organized in Pareto fashion (the vital few as opposed to the trivial many). This approach provides direction as to the order in which problems should be solved to gain the greatest improvement (see Fig. 10-8).[35]

Problem Solving

Although quality costs are valuable tools for identifying improvement areas, they do not solve any problems. Other tools must be used to find the root causes of problems so that irreversible corrective action can be implemented.

The root cause can be defined as the real cause of a problem. This is often quite different than the apparent cause, which appears after a superficial investigation. A frequently asked

APPLICATIONS OF QUALITY COSTS

Company_____ Product_____ Prepared by_____

Prevention costs	$ (000)
Marketing/customer	
Product/service development	
Purchasing	
Operations	
Quality administration	
Total	

	Year-to-Date	
	Current	Prior year

Appraisal costs	$ (000)
Product/service development	
Purchasing	
Operations	
External appraisal costs	
Total	

	Year-to-Date	
	Current	Prior year

Internal failure costs	$ (000)
Product/service design	
Purchasing	
Operations (subtotal)	
Material review	
Rework	
Repair	
Reappraisal	
Extra operations	
Scrap	
Total	

	Year-to-Date	
	Current	Prior year

External failure costs	$ (000)
Customer complaints	
Returned goods	
Retrofit costs	
Warranty claims	
Liability costs	
Penalties	
Customer goodwill	
Total	

	Year-to-Date	
	Current	Prior year

Baseline data	
Net sales	
Production costs	
Material costs	
Design costs	

	Year-to-Date	
	Current	Prior year

Quality cost ratios	
External failure cost/net sales	
Operations failure costs/production costs	
Operations appraisal costs/Production costs	
Purchasing quality costs/material costs	
Design quality costs/design costs	

	Year-to-Date	
	Current	Prior year

Fig. 10-6 Typical quality cost summary report for a product. *(Copyright American Society for Quality Control, Inc. Reprinted by permission.)*

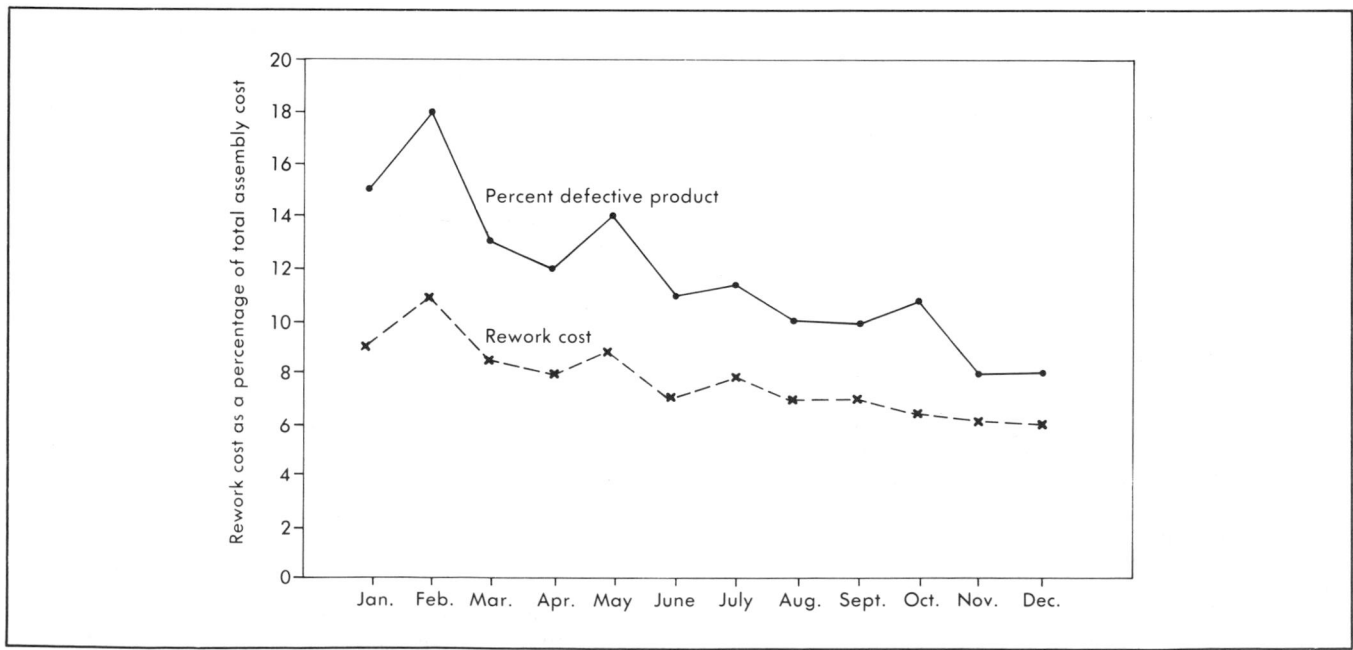

Fig. 10-7 Short-term trend analysis for assembly area quality performance. *(Copyright American Society for Quality Control, Inc. Reprinted by permission.)*

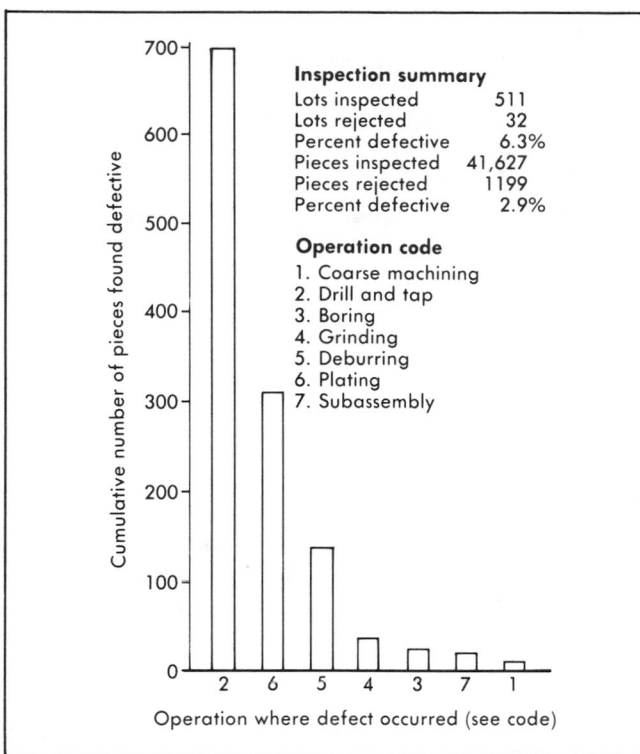

Fig. 10-8 Pareto analysis of eight operations on 11 key part numbers over a two-week period. (*Copyright American Society for Quality Control, Inc. Reprinted with permission*)

question is how can a person know when the root cause of the problem has been found. It has been found when the problem can be turned on or off by adding or removing the cause.

Once the root cause has been found, an irreversible corrective action must be implemented so that there is no foreseeable situation in which the root cause can return. Adhering to this practice ensures permanent improvement.

A problem-solving approach used by one company is illustrated in Fig. 10-9.[36] This system is very effective for several reasons. First, it recognizes that a problem may be solved by a single person when the problem is obvious after some investigation (Phase I). It also recognizes that help may be needed from others to determine potential causes and suggests brainstorming and cause-and-effect analysis by those knowledgeable about the situation (Phase II).

Another important aspect of the problem resolution system is that it recognizes the existence of system or management problems. Quality professionals have consistently maintained that only 15-20% of the problems that occur in manufacturing are within the control of production operators. The remainder of the problems can only be solved by management because they are largely system problems (Phase III and IV).

A commonly used technique for cause-and-effect analysis is called the Ishikawa diagram (see Fig. 10-10).[37] This diagram enables the analysis of an effect or problem for causes by considering the many diverse and complex relationships that exist. The weakness of this approach, as well as other approaches, is that root causes are not distinguishable among all the causes identified. Other methods must be used, such as detailed investigations, comprehensive data analyses, and design of experiments to discover the root causes.

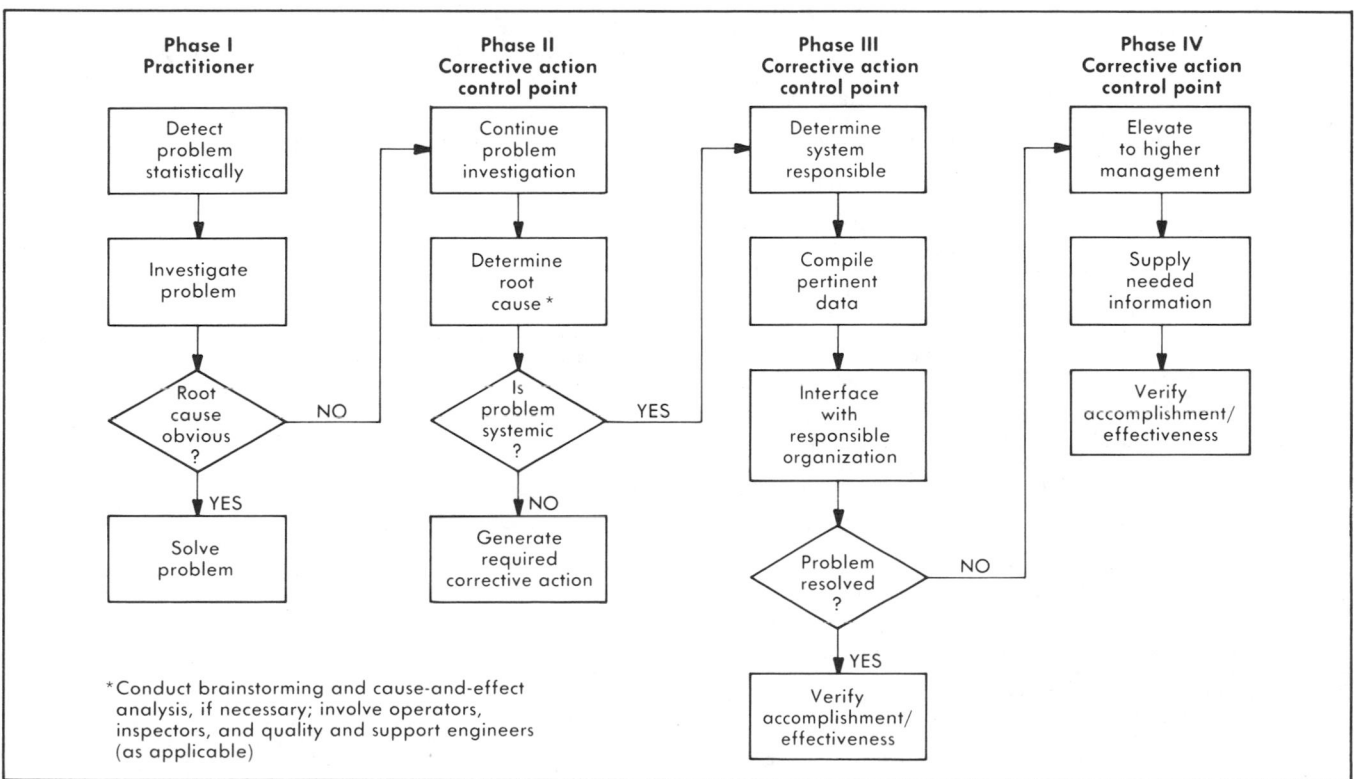

Fig. 10-9 Diagram of a problem-solving approach. (*Copyright American Society for Quality Control, Inc. Reprinted by permission.*)

APPLICATIONS OF QUALITY COSTS

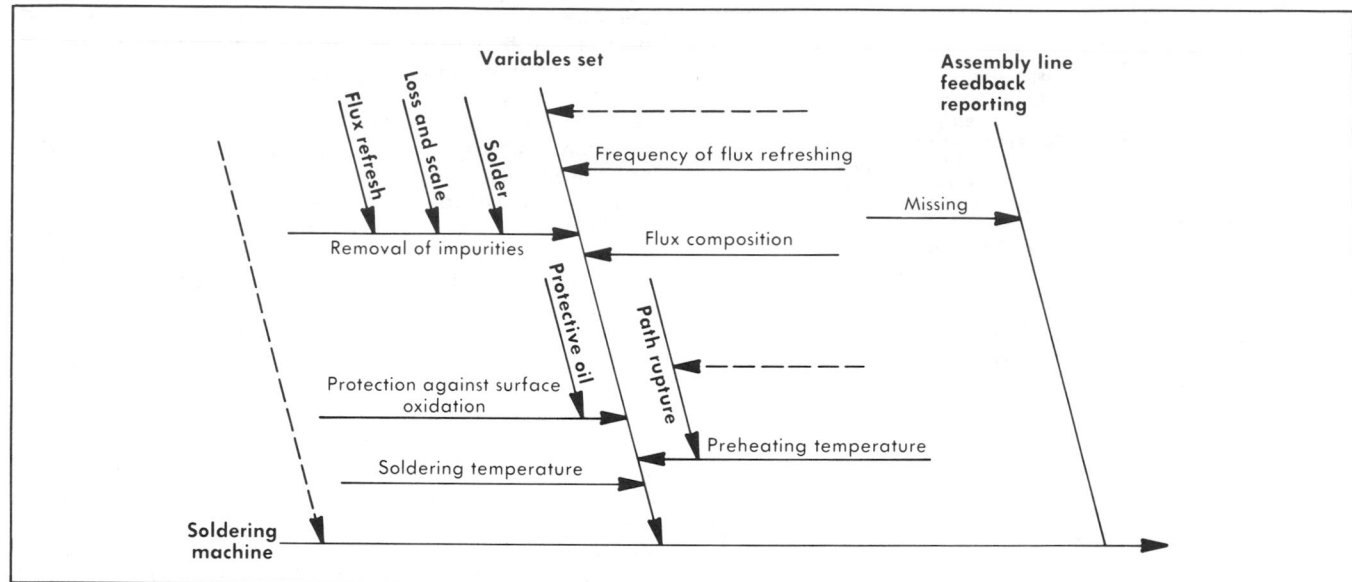

Fig. 10-10 An Ishikawa diagram of a process. *(Copyright American Society for Quality Control, Inc. Reprinted by permission.)*

References

1. W.F. Glueck and L.R. Jauch, *Business Policy and Strategic Management*, 4th ed. (New York: McGraw-Hill Book Co., 1984), p. 51.
2. B. Evans and C. Evans, *A Dictionary of Contemporary American Usage* (New York: Random House, 1957), p. 377.
3. _____ "What is Quality?" *Quality* (March 1979).
4. "New Course for Quality: The Glory Road?" *Production Engineering* (October 1986).
5. A.M. Schneiderman, "Optimum Quality Costs and Zero Defects: Are They Contradictory Concepts?" *Quality Progress* (November 1986).
6. "Quality Management and Quality System Elements—Guidelines," ANSI/ASQC Q94 (New York: American National Standards Institute, 1987).
7. L. P. Sullivan, "Quality Function Deployment," *Quality Progress*, (June 1986), pp. 39-50.
8. Phil Crosby, *Quality is Free* (New York: McGraw-Hill Book Co., 1979).
9. John H. Farrow, "Quality Audits: An Invitation to Management," *Quality Progress* (January 1987), pp. 11-13.
10. Armando Lopes Pereira, "Quality Audits and International Standards," *Quality Progress* (January 1987), pp. 27-29.
11. Jeffrey P. Kalin, "Quality, Stockless Production and Manufacturing," *38th Annual Quality Congress Transactions* (Milwaukee: American Society for Quality Control, 1984).
12. *Principles of Quality Cost* (Milwaukee: American Society for Quality Control, 1986).
13. *Ibid.*
14. Lawrence J. Schrader, "An Engineering Organization's Quality Cost Program," *Quality Progress* (January 1986).
15. Sales under the UCC, *Callaghan's Michigan Civil Jurisprudence* (Callaghan & Co., 1986).
16. Herbert E. Greenstone, "A Lawyer's View of Manufacturer's Responsibility," *34th Annual Technical Conference Transactions* (Milwaukee: American Society for Quality Control, 1980).
17. Business Transactions, *Federal Lawyer's Manual* (Callaghan & Co., 1986).
18. Roger D. Billings, Jr., "Automobile Warranty Law: The Quiet Revolution," *Case and Comment* (January-February 1985).
19. Sales Under the UCC, *loc. cit.*
20. Negligence, *Callaghan's Michigan Civil Jurisprudence* (Callaghan & Co., 1986).
21. Greenstone, *loc. cit.*
22. Products Liability, *Callaghan's Michigan Civil Jurisprudence* (Callaghan & Co., 1986).
23. Edward M. Swartz, "The Search for Product Defect," *Case and Comment* (January-February 1986).
24. Business Transactions, *loc. cit.*
25. Consumer Protection, *Callaghan's Michigan Civil Jurisprudence* (Callaghan & Co., 1986).
26. A.V. Feigenbaum, *Total Quality Control*, 3rd ed. (New York: McGraw-Hill Book Co., 1983).
27. *Ibid.*
28. T. David Kiang, "Life Cycle Costing—A New Dimension for Reliability Engineering Challenge," *1976 ASQC Technical Conference Transactions* (Milwaukee: American Society for Quality Control, 1976).
29. L.P. Sullivan, "The Seven Stages of Company-Wide Quality Control," *Quality Progress* (May 1986).
30. *Guide for Reducing Quality Costs*, *loc. cit.*
31. Sullivan, *loc. cit.*
32. William O. Winchell, "Organizing Quality Cost Efforts to Minimize Difficulties," *39th North East Quality Control Conference Transactions* (Milwaukee: American Society for Quality Control, 1985).
33. *Principles of Quality Cost*, *loc. cit.*
34. *Ibid.*
35. *Ibid.*
36. Billie Ruth Marcum, "An Updated Framework for Problem Resolution," *Quality Progress* (July 1985).
37. Edward Kindlarski, "Ishikawa Diagrams for Problem Solving," *Quality Progress* (December 1984).

STATISTICAL METHODS FOR QUALITY AND PRODUCTIVITY DESIGN AND IMPROVEMENT

Often the stability of a process (that is, a process in good statistical control) signals but the *beginning* of a major improvement effort aimed more fundamentally at determining appropriate system changes to effect overall performance improvements. In this regard, the role of statistical design of experiments in both product and process design is now becoming better understood as a tool to reveal significant opportunities for improvement of performance.

The presence of statistical control provides the condition of stability or predictability of the system under study. It provides a measure of *constancy* with respect to average performance and *consistency* in terms of variation in performance. Statistical control suggests that the process performance is free of special or sporadic variation causes and is governed only by a constant system of common or chronic causes of variation. Design of experiments concepts and methods provide a powerful approach to the discovery of improvement opportunities for already stabilized processes. The manner and extent to which a set of factors may singly or in concert influence the process mean level (location effects) and/or process variability level (dispersion effects) can be efficiently revealed using statistically designed experiments. Conversely, design of experiments techniques can be of great help in identifying the root cause(s) of special causes of variation in unstable processes so that actions may be taken to bring such processes into statistical control.

Figure 11-1 contrasts the two views of quality that are currently being subjected to considerable study and discussion. In the more traditional view of quality (view *a*), part A would be a good part, part B a bad part, and no real distinction would be made between parts A and C; however, such an interpretation may be questionable from a functional point of view. Such an interpretation puts quality strictly on an attribute basis (view *b*).

On part function grounds, if the nominal is really a true reflection of design intent, then it seems more reasonable to consider that: (1) part C must be better that part A and (2) parts A and B are not much different at all. Such an approach to the understanding of quality can be quantified through the use of the "loss function" idea shown in Fig. 11-1, view *c*. Under this representation of quality performance, the closer the part characteristic is to the design intent (the nominal value), the smaller will be the variation in its performance (smaller functional variation), and so the quality of the part should be considered better. It is important to note that given two products that both function at about the same level of performance, the product

that performs more consistently (less variation about the nominal) is considered a better product (higher quality). This is because the product will ultimately experience less trouble in the field and exhibit longer life.

As was pointed out previously, quality is a matter of product function, and in general, the failure to meet intended function can stem from either failure to achieve the nominal performance mandated by engineering design or excessive variation about the intended nominal performance level. These two problems are graphically depicted in Fig. 11-2.

In terms of improvement strategies, these two problems have often tended to be somewhat separated both conceptually and methodologically. For example, design of experiments methods have generally focused on the "average" problem, seeking to understand the ways in which purposeful changes in design/control factors can improve performance on the average. On the other hand, the techniques of statistical process control have emphasized the identification of sources of variation so that remedial actions can be taken to continually reduce variation.

Of course, the world is not divided into these two types of problems; in fact, producing a product on target with the smallest variation is not two separate problems, but a single twofold problem. The following example illustrates how this joint problem can be approached through the use of experimental design techniques.

To control part weight of a molded plastic product, a simple two-level factorial experiment may be conducted to determine how two molding machine parameters influence part weight. The experiment results are shown in Fig. 11-3. Each response weight is the average of 25 parts molded consecutively under each of the four given process conditions.

The results of the experiment seem to indicate that by manipulating control variable 1, average part weight can be controlled. Control variable 2 seems to have little effect on average part weight; that is, changing the level of control variable 2 does not cause average part weight to vary much. As a result, control variable 2 may be set according to some other process performance criterion such as minimum energy consumption.

In addition to evaluating the molding process performance "on the average," the variation in performance about the average can and should also be examined as a process response. Figure 11-4 shows the results of each test in the two-level factorial design as viewed as a time plot of the individual part weight under each machine condi-

STATISTICAL METHODS FOR DESIGN

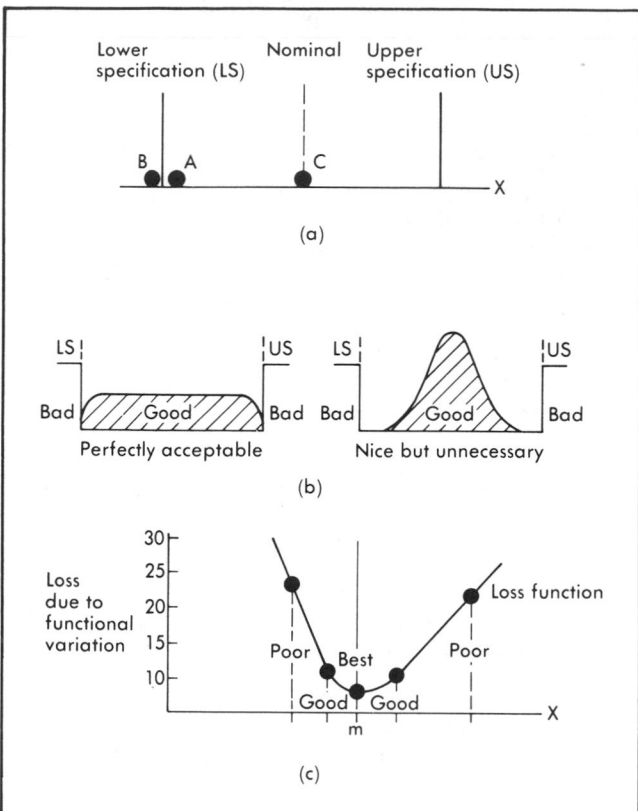

Fig. 11-1 Different views of specifications: (a) conformance to bilateral specification, (b) process performance relative to traditional views of quality needs, and (c) quality as measured by the loss function.

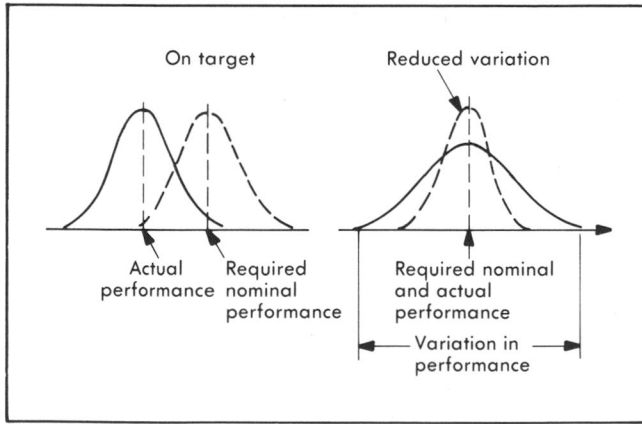

Fig. 11-2 Two problems in meeting intended functions.

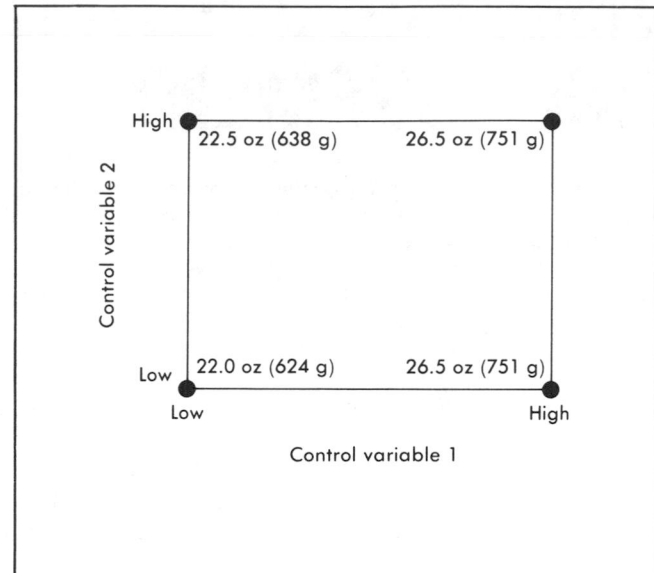

Fig. 11-3 Experimental results of molded part weights.

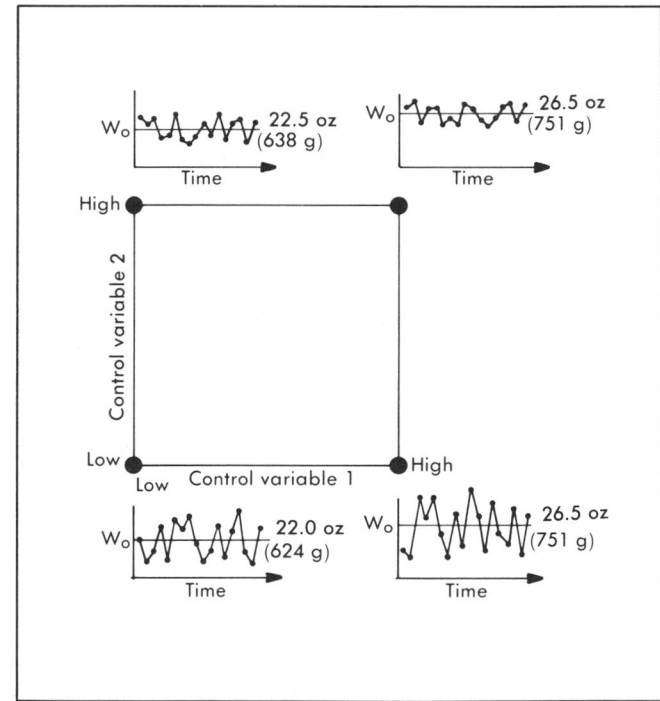

Fig. 11-4 Time plots of part weights.

tion. This process variation response could be summarized in a single statistic for each test such as the standard deviation or the range.

Reexamination of the experimental results reveals something important that was not apparent previously. Although control variable 2 does not affect part weight on the average, it does appear to affect variation in part weight. The complete results of the experiment indicate that not only average weight can be controlled by manipulating control variable 1, but also the variation in weight can be reduced by setting control variable 2 at its high level. In the past, it has been less common to use variation as an experimental design response and to seek ways to reduce variation in product/process performance through designed experimentation.

SOURCES OF VARIATION AND THEIR COUNTERMEASURES

It has been suggested that a product's performance is influenced by three basic sources of variation or three basic types of noise factors.[1] These noise factors are outer noise, inner noise, and variational noise. Outer noise factors describe the conditions such as temperature, humidity, and material contamination operating during product use. These factors generally cannot be easily controlled and, by their presence, generally degrade performance through increased functional variation. Inner noise factors describe internal product change during use. An example of internal product change is deterioration as precipitated by mechanical wear, material aging, or fatigue. Variational noise refers to manufacturing imperfection and is the variation that occurs between like products manufactured to the same specifications.

The basic countermeasures required to mitigate the forces of noise/variation sources may be quite different in nature. Outer noise is clearly a design issue and can only be effectively dealt with at the engineering design stage using off-line quality control methods such as design of experiments. Inner noise is also most effectively dealt with at the design stage.

Variational noise is basically a manufacturing problem and, although product design may play a significant role here, it does so from the relationship between design and the manufacturing process. Because variational noise is based on manufacturing imperfection, the techniques of statistical process control can provide an effective means to identify special and common causes of variation in the process, thus providing a sound basis for action.

QUALITY PERSPECTIVE IN ENGINEERING DESIGN

One important aspect of the study of product performance is the evaluation of the ability of the product to operate within a specified envelope of conditions for a designed life. For many products this may reduce to "normal" operation for a given number of cycles, miles, or hours without failure. The body of knowledge often referred to as reliability engineering involves basically the activities of reliability modeling and prediction and life testing. Reliability modeling encompasses the study and development of probabilistic models for predicting the probability of survival for individual components as well as complex systems of components. Life testing may be used to estimate the failure distributions and test the validity of claims or verify conformance to design requirements. Life testing may also be employed in the estimation of various reliability parameters associated with one or more failure modes.

The characteristic of reliability testing that seems to separate it from other uses of experimentation is that it examines performance over time under a fixed set of design parameters and operating conditions. Reliability testing focuses on the simultaneous operation of many identical units for the purpose of examining the probabilistic nature of failure. Physical study of failed units may give some clues to the underlying nature of the failure mechanism, but may neither pinpoint the root cause nor suggest design modifications for improvement.

In contrast, the field of design of experiments grew out of the need to efficiently evaluate alternate treatments in agricultural research. Particular attention was directed toward not only comparing the yields of competing fertilizers or hybrid seeds, but to doing so under a wide range of conditions such as soil condition, rainfall, sunlight, and drainage conditions that define the operating envelope. Later, design of experiments concepts suggested by Fisher[2] and others were adapted, extended, and refined for use in the industrial sector.[3] Many new techniques were also developed for industrial experimentation. The purpose of such experimental work was to discover those factors that govern ultimate product/process performance so that action toward improvement could be taken off-line (at engineering design) or on-line (process control). In contrast to performing many tests under fixed conditions for many cycles, an experimental strategy can be directed at performing one or a few tests at each of many combinations of design and operating variables over a number of variables for a few cycles to observe performance.

STATISTICAL PROCESS CONTROL

The techniques of SPC, as put forth more than 60 years ago by Dr. Walter Shewhart, employ basic probability laws and statistical methods to develop models for the behavior of the variations witnessed in the quality characteristics of manufactured goods during production.[4] Through the statistical study of these patterns of variation, it is possible to attribute certain types of variations to certain types of fault sources and hence develop a knowledge and understanding of what types of cor-

STATISTICAL PROCESS CONTROL

rective actions may be required. In this regard, the most fundamental principle in the application of SPC methods is the partitioning of the total variation pattern into two major sources: (1) the system sources (chronic problems or common causes) and (2) more localized sources (sporadic problems or special causes). Because system variation comes from many ever-present sources, it appears as a stable, random, and well-behaved pattern of variation. On the other hand, sporadic problems being of external disturbance origin produce unusual patterns of variation that are visible when statistical methods are used to study the total variation pattern.

It is important to recognize the proper assignment of responsibility for corrective action of common and special causes. Because common causes are system faults, they require the attention of management. It is likely that some major breakthrough is required to affect a significant improvement in quality and productivity when common causes are involved. Only management can institute the changes required to remove major sources of common cause variability.

Every fault or source of variation not only erodes quality, but is a source of waste and inefficiency in one form or another. As a result, the elimination of each and every source of variation leads to improvements in productivity as well as in quality. It is therefore advantageous to adopt the philosophy of never-ending improvement using SPC rather than the notion of attaining and then maintaining an acceptable level of improvement. The quality/productivity relationship is a clear motivation for the continual pursuit of process stability.

A stable process is a predictable process, and hence the management of scheduling, inventory control, and maintenance management are all directly influenced by the presence (or absence) of process control. Improvements in the efficiency of production management can obviously be a tremendous force in the attainment of a positive competitive position. The lack of process control/stability will always have a deleterious effect on the ability to efficiently manage and control the total resources of a manufacturing operation.

Statistical control is also essential to the proper evaluation of process capability. Process capability is a measure of the consistent ability of the process to produce at a certain level. Consistency means stability, the ability to extrapolate performance into the future with a strong degree of belief that predictions of future performance levels will be realized. If the process is behaving in an erratic and unstable fashion, it is impossible to assess the process capability. Process data collected at different times may give totally different pictures of the process capability.

Attaining process stability is by no means sufficient to ensure high levels of quality and productivity. A process may be stable or predictable, but not at all capable in terms of its ability to produce a high percentage of acceptable product. A process in a state of good statistical control simply means that the best is being done under the present system. Because a controlled process means that the process is subject only to common causes of variation, the system will have to be changed to make any additional improvement.

DATA CHARACTERIZATION

To find out how the process is behaving in terms of an output quality characteristic, samples can be drawn from the process, and the information can be used to estimate process behavior as a whole. The whole unique process, if it exists, is often referred to in statistical terms as a population. It may be described by a set of measures called population parameters. A process (population) is said to exist if all the elements of the population are subject to a fixed set of common causes of variation. Usually a population can be adequately characterized by a few simple measures such as the mean and standard deviation and a probability distribution. These measures are defined by population parameters that are seldom known and hence are estimated by corresponding measures calculated from sample data. Because sample measures, called statistics, are based on only part of the population, they are uncertain estimates of the population parameters. Consequently, each kind of statistic follows a sampling distribution of its own, which is different from the parent population of individual measurements.

TYPES OF DATA
Data that are collected for quality design and improvement purposes are obtained by direct observation of the process and are classified as either variable data or attribute data. Variable data are characteristics that are measurable along a continuous scale. Examples of these characteristics are length, weight, resistance, temperature, and force. Attribute data are characteristics that are countable or are categorized into discrete classes.

Examples of these characteristics are number of scratches and defective or nondefective items.

FREQUENCY DISTRIBUTION
Table 11-1 gives the data from 50 samples/subgroups of size $n = 5$ each, obtained by measuring soft gasket sheets from one production line over a two-week period. The table records the individual thickness measurements as well as the average and range for each sample/subgroup.

When plotting a frequency histogram of the individual sheet thicknesses, the data are first grouped into cells or intervals. The frequency of observations falling within each cell is tallied (see Fig. 11-5).

To convert the tally sheet to a histogram, the number of observations within each cell is represented by the height of a rectangle; the width of the rectangle represents the cell or interval size. The histogram for the data of Fig. 11-5 is shown in Fig. 11-6. From the frequency histogram, the following three specific things can be noted about the data:

1. The data tend to cluster about a certain value (central tendency).

2. The data exhibit a spread or variation about the central value.

3. The frequencies are approximately symmetric about the center and fall off rapidly from the center.

TABLE 11-1
Thickness of Gasket Sheet Samples, in. x 10^{-4}

Sample Number	Observations					Avg.	Range	Sample Number	Observations					Avg.	Range
1	427	428	457	430	450	438.40	30	26	429	438	444	433	437	436.20	15
2	456	448	442	459	440	449.00	19	27	456	437	436	440	458	445.40	22
3	425	415	441	440	422	428.60	25	28	426	456	428	443	429	436.40	30
4	465	450	438	437	439	445.80	28	29	442	446	447	431	441	441.40	16
5	464	438	439	453	440	446.80	25	30	456	435	436	463	440	446.00	28
6	435	427	418	431	439	430.00	21	31	429	458	439	432	442	440.00	29
7	437	429	444	443	432	437.00	15	32	433	437	462	457	434	444.60	29
8	451	433	461	435	462	448.40	29	33	430	433	429	459	431	436.40	30
9	438	417	426	436	429	429.20	21	34	446	444	425	434	443	438.40	21
10	415	439	425	438	427	428.80	24	35	430	451	457	429	450	443.40	28
11	431	456	441	457	431	443.20	26	36	437	440	432	415	434	431.60	25
12	429	418	425	426	444	428.40	26	37	447	444	443	445	449	445.60	6
13	437	449	436	461	456	447.80	25	38	463	439	440	441	445	445.60	24
14	427	437	436	432	421	430.60	16	39	437	433	432	434	440	435.20	8
15	423	448	435	434	446	437.20	25	40	427	427	426	456	436	434.40	30
16	461	446	450	437	436	446.00	25	41	433	437	423	450	440	436.60	27
17	435	433	443	442	437	438.00	10	42	457	448	434	433	437	441.80	24
18	433	427	442	420	429	430.20	22	43	440	448	433	449	432	440.40	17
19	435	438	431	439	432	435.00	8	44	436	449	440	448	451	444.80	15
20	435	442	463	437	457	446.80	28	45	436	418	444	427	440	433.00	26
21	434	435	457	432	436	438.80	25	46	424	450	439	456	432	440.20	32
22	423	432	441	431	414	428.20	27	47	443	458	456	428	433	443.60	30
23	425	416	439	423	441	428.80	25	48	438	441	446	434	433	438.40	13
24	435	436	439	462	451	444.60	27	49	430	457	442	446	453	445.60	27
25	437	435	457	436	438	440.60	22	50	437	423	426	447	435	433.60	24

MEASURES OF CENTRAL TENDENCY

A measure of central tendency of a distribution is a numerical value that describes the central position or location of the data. The most commonly used measure is the arithmetic average or mean value of all the data in the sample or population.

The true mean of a population (a parameter) can be calculated by the equation:

$$\mu = \sum_{i=1}^{N} X_i / N \tag{1}$$

where:

μ = true mean of the population
Σ = the sum of
N = the total number of observations in the population

X_i = the i-th value of the individual observation

In practice, however, the true mean of the population is seldom calculated because it is rarely possible and unnecessary to measure or count all items in the population. In most instances, the true mean is estimated by the sample mean or average (a statistic). The sample mean can be calculated by the equation:

$$\bar{X} = \sum_{i=1}^{n} X_i / n \tag{2}$$

where:

$\bar{X}$ = the sample mean (pronounced X-bar)
n = the total number of observations in the sample

DATA CHARACTERIZATION

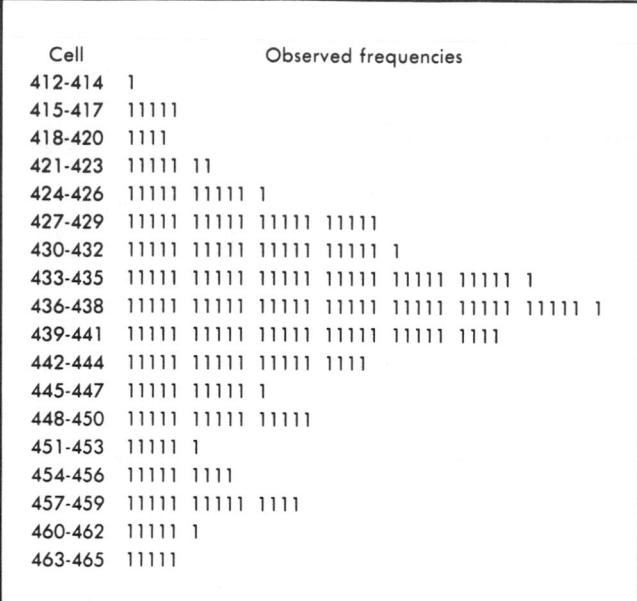

Cell	Observed frequencies
412-414	1
415-417	11111
418-420	1111
421-423	11111 11
424-426	11111 11111 1
427-429	11111 11111 11111 11111
430-432	11111 11111 11111 11111 1
433-435	11111 11111 11111 11111 11111 11111 1
436-438	11111 11111 11111 11111 11111 11111 11111 1
439-441	11111 11111 11111 11111 11111 1111
442-444	11111 11111 11111 1111
445-447	11111 11111 1
448-450	11111 11111 11111
451-453	11111 1
454-456	11111 1111
457-459	11111 11111 1111
460-462	11111 1
463-465	11111

Fig. 11-5 Tally sheet of gasket thicknesses.

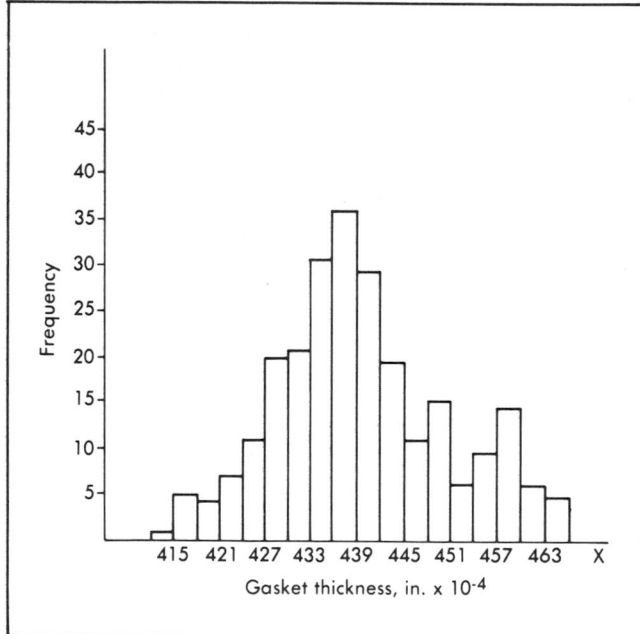

Fig. 11-6 Histogram of gasket data.

MEASURES OF DISPERSION OR VARIABILITY

The variance is an important measure of the variability in data. It is the average of the sum of the squared deviations of the data from their mean. The true variance, σ_X^2, can be calculated by the equation:

$$\sigma_X^2 = \sum_{i=1}^{N} (X_i - \mu)^2 / N \tag{3}$$

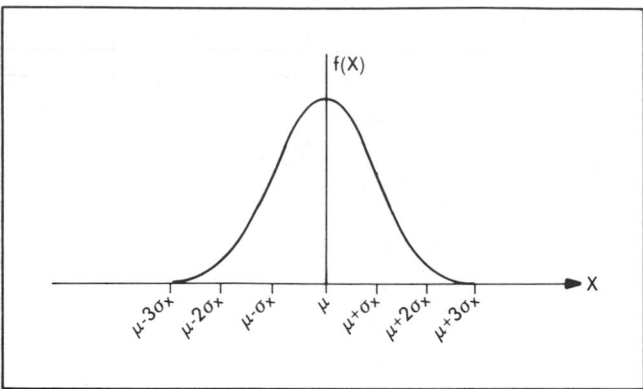

Fig. 11-7 Normal curve.

The square root of the variance called the standard deviation, σ_X, is a more commonly used measure of variation.

In practice, both the true mean and true variance of the population are seldom known and are therefore estimated from sample data. The sample variance, s^2, can be calculated by the equation:

$$s_X^2 = \sum_{i=1}^{n} (X_i - \bar{X})^2 / (n-1) \tag{4}$$

In Eq. (4), the denominator $(n-1)$ is often a source of confusion. Mathematically, it can be shown that the estimate of the true variance using the sample variance has desirable statistical properties and therefore is commonly used. It is important to realize that the sample observations $X_1, X_2, ..., X_n$ are independent. In Eq. (4), there are n deviations $(X_i - \bar{X})$, but only $(n-1)$ of them are independent.

Another important measurement of variability is the range, which is the difference between the largest value and the smallest value of the data within a sample. The range is calculated by the equation:

$$R = X_l - X_s \tag{5}$$

where:

$R =$ the range
$X_l =$ largest value in the sample
$X_s =$ smallest value in the sample

The range is often used to obtain an estimate of the population standard deviation (σ_X). Mathematically, an exact relationship between R and σ_X has been established by the equation:

$$\sigma_X = R / d_2 \tag{6}$$

The value of d_2 varies depending on the size n of the sample/subgroup. This relationship also depends on the assumption that the observations of X come from the normal distribution. Moderate departures from this assumption, however, do not markedly erode the effectiveness of this relationship.

THE NORMAL DISTRIBUTION CURVE

About 200 years ago it was observed that errors of measurement seemed to follow a definite pattern with respect to their relative frequency of occurrence. For example, repeated measurements of the length of certain objects seemed to rise in a frequency sense according to a bell-shaped curve, symmetric about the mean. The frequency of these measurements also falls off rapidly beyond a distance of about one standard deviation from the mean.

This frequency distribution is referred to as the normal distribution. Mathematically, the normal distribution curve is defined by the equation:

$$f(X) = \frac{1}{\sqrt{2\pi}\,\sigma_X}\ e^{-\frac{1}{2}\left(\frac{X-\mu}{\sigma_X}\right)^2} \tag{7}$$

where:

$f(X)$ = probability density function of the random variable X

Figure 11-7 shows the appearance of the normal curve and the relationship between the shape of the curve and the parameters μ_X and σ_X. Strictly speaking, the curve stretches from minus infinity to plus infinity; however, much of it is distributed over a relatively narrow range. In a normal distribution, 68.26% of the observations fall between $\mu - \sigma_X$ and $\mu + \sigma_X$; 95.46% of the observations fall between $\mu - 2\sigma_X$ and $\mu + 2\sigma_X$; and 99.73% of the observations fall between $\mu - 3\sigma_X$ and $\mu + 3\sigma_X$.

Standard Normal Distribution

Because the mean and standard deviation of the normal distribution can take on many different values from situation to situation, it is convenient to define and work with a standardized normal distribution.

The standard normal variable is generally denoted by the letter z and the standard normal probability density function by $f(z)$. Because the standard normal distribution has a standard deviation (σ_z) equal to 1, the value for z can be interpreted as representing the number of standard deviations from the mean (μ_z), which is 0. In terms of any normal distribution with a mean (μ_X) and a standard deviation (σ_X), the z value (number of standard deviations) can be calculated by the equation:

$$z = (X - \mu)/\sigma_X \tag{8}$$

Figure 11-8 illustrates the relationship between the normal distribution curve and the standardized distribution curve.

Example Calculation

Figure 11-9 graphically illustrates the diameter of shafts turned on a lathe. The diameters are normally distributed and have a mean of 1.00″ and a standard deviation of 0.01″. To determine the probability that a given shaft will have a diameter between 0.985 and 1.005″, it is necessary to find the areas under the curve denoted as areas 2 and 1; area 3 (the desired probability) is then the difference between area 2 and area 1. The calculations shown in Fig. 11-9 indicate that 62.47% of the shafts will have a diameter between 0.985 and 1.005″.

DISTRIBUTION OF SAMPLE MEANS

It has been shown that the sample mean, $\overline{X}$, provides an estimate of the population mean, μ. Because $\overline{X}$ is calculated from a sample from the population, it is an uncertain estimate of μ. That is, if a number of samples of size n are drawn from the

population, each time calculating an $\overline{X}$, then these $\overline{X}$ values will vary simply because of sampling variation. The precision of $\overline{X}$ as an estimate of μ depends on the amount of process (population) variation and the size of the sample. In particular, as n increases, the sample variance of the $\overline{X}$s decreases according to the equation:

$$\sigma_{\overline{X}}^2 = \sigma_X^2/n \tag{9}$$

The *central limit theorem* states that sample means have a distribution that approaches the normal distribution for a sufficiently large sample size. As the sample size increases, the tendency to the normal distribution improves. Furthermore, the population from which the samples are drawn generally does not need to be normally distributed for the sample means to be approximately normal.

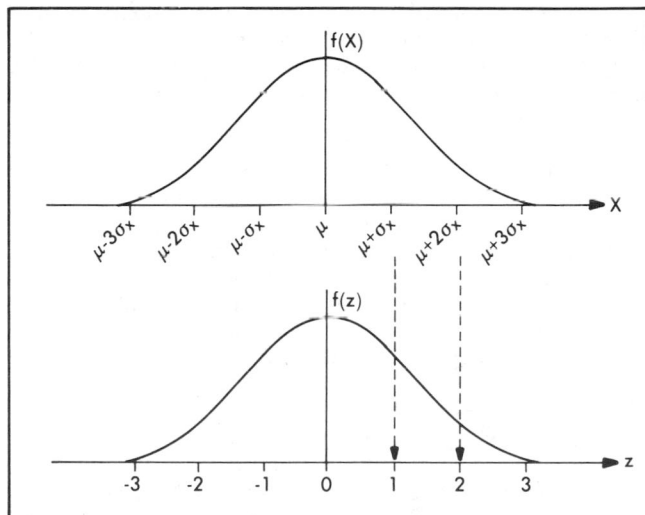

Fig. 11-8 Standardized normal curve.

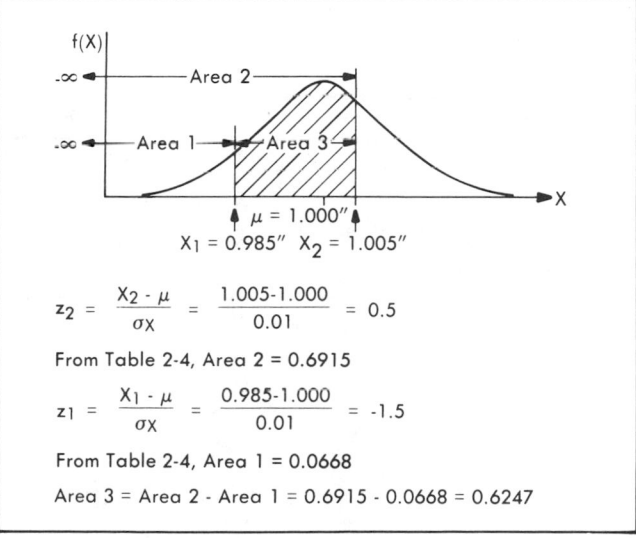

Fig. 11-9 Normal probability calculations.

CONTROL CHARTS

CONTROL CHARTS

A major objective of statistical process control is to recognize the occurrence of special causes in the presence of the constant system of common cause and to shed light on the nature of the special cause, thereby providing a basis for corrective actions. Control charts are one of the tools used to accomplish this objective.

The control chart builds a model that describes the way the process variability pattern is expected to appear when only common causes of variation are at work. Once this model is established through appropriate sampling and statistical data characterization methods, a basis is formed for identifying the occurrence of a variation that does not fit the pattern of common cause variation.

A variety of control charts are available for monitoring and improving a production operation. The charts are generally classified according to the type of data they are based on. The charts most frequently used are presented in Table 11-2.[5]

VARIABLE CONTROL CHARTS

Generally, chaotic disturbances manifest themselves in two possible ways: (1) shifts or changes in the mean level of the process and (2) shifts or changes in the amount of process variability. Sample means ($\bar{X}$) may be used to determine when the former has occurred. The sample ranges, as well as other variability measures such as the standard deviation, can be tracked over time to detect possible changes in process consistency.

Chart Construction

Once the quality characteristic to be studied has been determined, data are collected. When collecting the data, the samples must be properly selected, which is often described by the principles of rational sampling. Rational samples are groups of measurements, the variation among which is attributable to only one system of causes. In other words, the samples should be chosen in such a way to minimize the chances of mixing within the sample measurements that reflect only common cause variations and measurements that have been contaminated by additional special cause variations. By selecting rational samples, the ability of the chart to detect special causes when they occur is enhanced.

As a good rule of thumb, 25 to 50 samples should be selected to provide a solid basis for the initiation of the control chart. Once the process is in a good state of statistical control, periodic recalculation of the control limits is necessary to update the information.

Given a set of rational samples from the process, the following six steps can be used as a guide when constructing control $\bar{X}$,R charts:

1. Calculate the average ($\bar{X}$) for each sample using Eq. (2).

2. Calculate the range within the sample using Eq. (5).

3. Calculate the grand average ($\bar{\bar{X}}$). This is the arithmetic mean of all the sample averages and is an estimate of the process mean (μ). The grand average becomes the centerline of the $\bar{X}$ control chart.

4. Calculate the average of the sample ranges ($\bar{R}$). $\bar{R}$ is the arithmetic average of the sample ranges and becomes the centerline of the R control chart.

5. Calculate the control limits for the $\bar{X}$ chart. The three standard deviation control limits are given by $\bar{\bar{X}} \pm 3\, \sigma_{\bar{X}}$. Because $\sigma_{\bar{X}}$ is equal to $\sigma_X / \sqrt{n}$, the control limits take the form:

$$UCL/LCL = \bar{\bar{X}} \pm 3\, \sigma_X / \sqrt{n} \qquad (10)$$

where:

UCL = upper control limit
LCL = lower control limit

TABLE 11-2
Commonly Used Control Charts

Data Type	Chart Name	Value Charted
Variables	$\bar{X}$ and R chart	Sample averages and ranges
	$\bar{X}$ and s chart	Sample averages and standard deviations
	X and moving R chart	Individual observations and moving ranges
	Median and R chart	Sample medians and ranges
Attribute	p chart	Proportion or percent of units nonconforming (defective) per sample
	np chart	Number of units nonconforming (defective) per sample
	c chart	Number of nonconformities (defects) per inspection unit
	u chart	Average number of nonconformities (defects) per production unit

As was shown in Eq. (6), the value for σ_X can be estimated by $\bar{R}/d_2$, and therefore Eq. (10) can be written as:

$$UCL/LCL = \bar{\bar{X}} \pm 3\bar{R}/(d_2\sqrt{n}) \qquad (11)$$

The term $3/(d_2\sqrt{n})$, which depends only on the sample size n, can be combined into a single constant, A_2. Equation (11) then changes to:

$$UCL/LCL = \bar{\bar{X}} \pm A_2\bar{R} \qquad (12)$$

Values for A_2 for varying sample sizes n are conveniently tabulated in Table 2-3.

6. Calculate the control limits for the R chart. Although the distribution of sample ranges is not normal and not symmetric, the symmetrical $\bar{R} \pm 3\,\sigma_R$ limits are conventionally used for the R chart. If the lower limit is less than 0, the lower control limit is assigned a value of 0. The control limits can be calculated by the equations:

$$UCL = D_4\bar{R} \qquad (13)$$

$$LCL = D_3\bar{R} \qquad (14)$$

Values for D_3 and D_4 have been tabulated as a function of sample size n and are also given in Table 2-3.

The following techniques should be used when plotting the charts:

- Place the R chart directly below the $\bar{X}$ chart using the same horizontal axis. This makes it easy to compare $\bar{X}$ and R results for individual samples.
- Use a heavy solid line to denote the centerline of each chart.
- Plot the individual $\bar{X}$ and R values as solid dots. Connecting these dots helps to clearly see the patterns in the data.
- Use a heavy dashed line to denote the control limits.
- Write the specific numerical values for the control limits on the charts as well as for the centerlines.
- Circle any points that indicate the presence of special causes such as points beyond the control limits.

Chart Interpretation

The purpose of the control chart is to monitor and evaluate the process performance over time. Initial chart use is directed toward identifying the presence of all special causes so that the process can be brought into a state of statistical control. Once control is established, continuing examination of the data patterns helps to indicate further opportunities for quality and productivity improvement.

When interpreting the charts, it is important to start with the R chart and get it under statistical control first because the limits of the $\bar{X}$ chart depend on the magnitude of the common cause variation of the process measured by $\bar{R}$. If some points on the R chart are initially out of control (special causes present), the limits on the $\bar{X}$ chart will be inflated.

Figure 11-10 shows $\bar{X}$ and R charts constructed from 50 samples of size $n = 5$. The charts show good statistical control because:

- No points exceed the control limits.
- The points are approximately normally distributed about the centerline on the $\bar{X}$ chart.
- The points show no evidence of trends or recurring cycles.

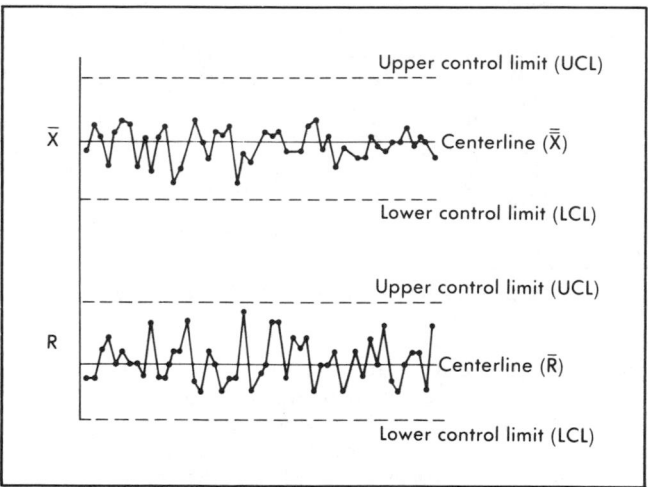

Fig. 11-10 X and R charts in good statistical control.

- The points look quite random with time. No patterns such as runs above or below the centerline are evident.

When just one subgroup average (or range) is beyond a control limit, the process is considered out of control. Further, because the distribution of $\bar{X}$ tends to be normal, serious departures from normality can signal the presence of special causes even if all points are within the control limits. Too many points near the limits or near the centerline may signal problems with the process such as overcontrol or with improper methods of sampling.

The occurrence of a trend or reoccurring cycles in the data pattern can indicate that the system is experiencing a drift or cyclical change with respect to its mean or range. Runs of points above or below the centerline may indicate small shifts in the mean or level of variability.

Whenever an out-of-control condition is indicated, it is important to determine the basic process fault that is producing it. Some useful generic conditions to look for include the following:

Trends/cycles: Systematic changes in the process environment, worker fatigue, maintenance schedules, wear conditions, accumulation of waste material, and contamination.

High proportion of points near or beyond control limits: Overcontrol of the process, large differences in incoming raw material, and charting more than one process on a single chart.

Sudden shifts in level: New machine, die, or tooling; new worker; new batch of raw material; change in measurement system; and change in production method.

Up to this point, a number of general control chart patterns have been discussed, indicating various types of unnatural process behaviors. The unnatural patterns were fairly obvious even through the most cursory examination of the charts. Often, however, special causes of variation produce patterns that are less obvious. Therefore a more rigorous pattern analysis should generally be conducted.

Several useful tests for the presence of unnatural patterns (special causes) can be performed by dividing the distance between the upper and lower control limits into six zones; each

CHAPTER 11

CONTROL CHARTS

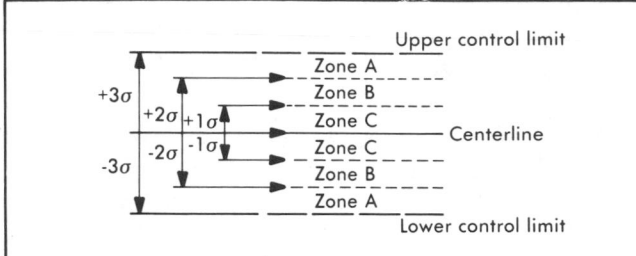

Fig. 11-11 Representation of dividing control regions into zones.

zone is one standard deviation wide (see Fig. 11-11). The zones for the upper half of the chart are referred to as *A* (outer third), *B* (middle third), and *C* (inner third); the lower half is considered a mirror image. The probabilistic basis for the tests to be discussed using the zones is derived from the normal distribution. These tests are therefore applicable to an $\bar{X}$ chart and may be applied to the chart for individuals if it can be assumed that the data follow a normal distribution.

The various tests are illustrated in Fig. 11-12.[6] Although these tests can be considered as basic, they are not totally comprehensive. Analysts should be alert to any patterns of points that might indicate the influences of other special causes in their particular process. Tests 1, 2, 5, and 6 are separately applied to the upper and lower halves of the chart; tests 3, 4, 7, and 8 are applied to the entire chart.

When the existence of a special cause is signaled by a test, the last point should be circled. Points can contribute to more than one test. In this case, however, a point should be circled each time a test is satisfied.

SELECTION OF SAMPLES

Rational subgroups or samples are collections of individual measurements, the variation among which is attributable only to a constant system of common causes. In the development and continuing use of control charts, subgroups or samples should be chosen in a way that provides the maximum opportunity for the measurements within each subgroup to be subject only to common causes, thus providing the maximum chance for special causes arising between subgroups to be detected.

Sample Size

The size of the rational sample is governed by the following considerations:

- The sample size should be small enough to achieve the objective that all members of the sample are subject to one fixed system of variation causes. A sample that is too large may include some members that are subject to one or more different systems of causes, such as one with added variations due to special causes. If the sample size is large enough to allow this to happen often, the sensitivity of the control chart will be eroded.
- The sample size should be large enough to ensure the presence of a normal distribution for the sample means. In general, the larger the sample size, the better the $\bar{X}$ distribution is represented by the normal curve. In practice, sample sizes of 4 or more ensure a good approximation to normality.
- The sample size should be large enough to enhance the

sensitivity to the detection of special causes, particularly for detecting small shifts in the mean.

When these considerations are taken into account, a sample size of 4 to 6 is likely to emerge. The most commonly used size is 5 because of the relative ease of further computations.

Sampling Methods

Consecutive sampling. The most common basis of selecting subgroups is the time order of production. One method of selecting subgroups by production time is to sample parts all produced at approximately the same time. An example of this method is as follows:

5 consecutive measurements at 9:00 a.m.,
5 consecutive measurements at 9:45 a.m.,
5 consecutive measurements at 10:30 a.m., etc.

In this example, the interval between samples is approximately 45 minutes, but each sample is randomly selected over a much smaller time period within this interval. Taking measurements of samples produced at the same time minimizes the chance for other than common cause variation within subgroups to occur and maximizes the chance for special cause variation arising between the subgroups to be detected.

Distributed sampling. If a process is subject to abrupt shifts in the mean level or variability and those shifts are sustained, then the method of consecutive sampling may be preferred. This is because the shift will be more easily seen from one sample result to another; however, if a process is subject to frequent abrupt but short-lived shifts in the mean, then a distributed sample may be preferred. Distributed sampling provides a better opportunity for detecting the shift through the *R* chart with more sensitivity than consecutive sampling. In the distributed sampling method, the various units in a sample are taken at approximately equally spaced time periods within each sampling interval. Distributed sampling can also be used to detect gradual changes in the mean because the opportunity is greater to observe large sample ranges and more rapid changes in the sample means.

There is often a tendency to focus greater attention on the $\bar{X}$ chart and to be on the lookout for changes in process mean level. With this in mind, consecutive sampling may be preferred because it tends to have greater sensitivity to the detection of shifts in the mean. This is so because within-sample variability is a more likely reflection of only common cause variation.

ATTRIBUTE CONTROL CHARTS

Many quality characteristics of manufactured goods are not of the variable measurement type. Instead, they are more logically defined in a "presence of" or "absence of" sense. Examples of instances when this approach would be used include surface flaws on a sheet metal panel, cracks in drawn wire, color inconsistencies on a painted surface, voids, flash or spray on an injection molded part, or wrinkles on a sheet of vinyl. These defects or nonconformities are often simply observed visually or by some sensory device and cause a part to be classified as being defective. In these cases, it is said that the product quality is being assessed by attributes.

Two primary types of control charts exist for attribute data. The first type of chart is for nonconforming parts (defectives) and is called the *p* chart. The *p* chart is based on the binomial probability distribution. This chart plots the fraction defective

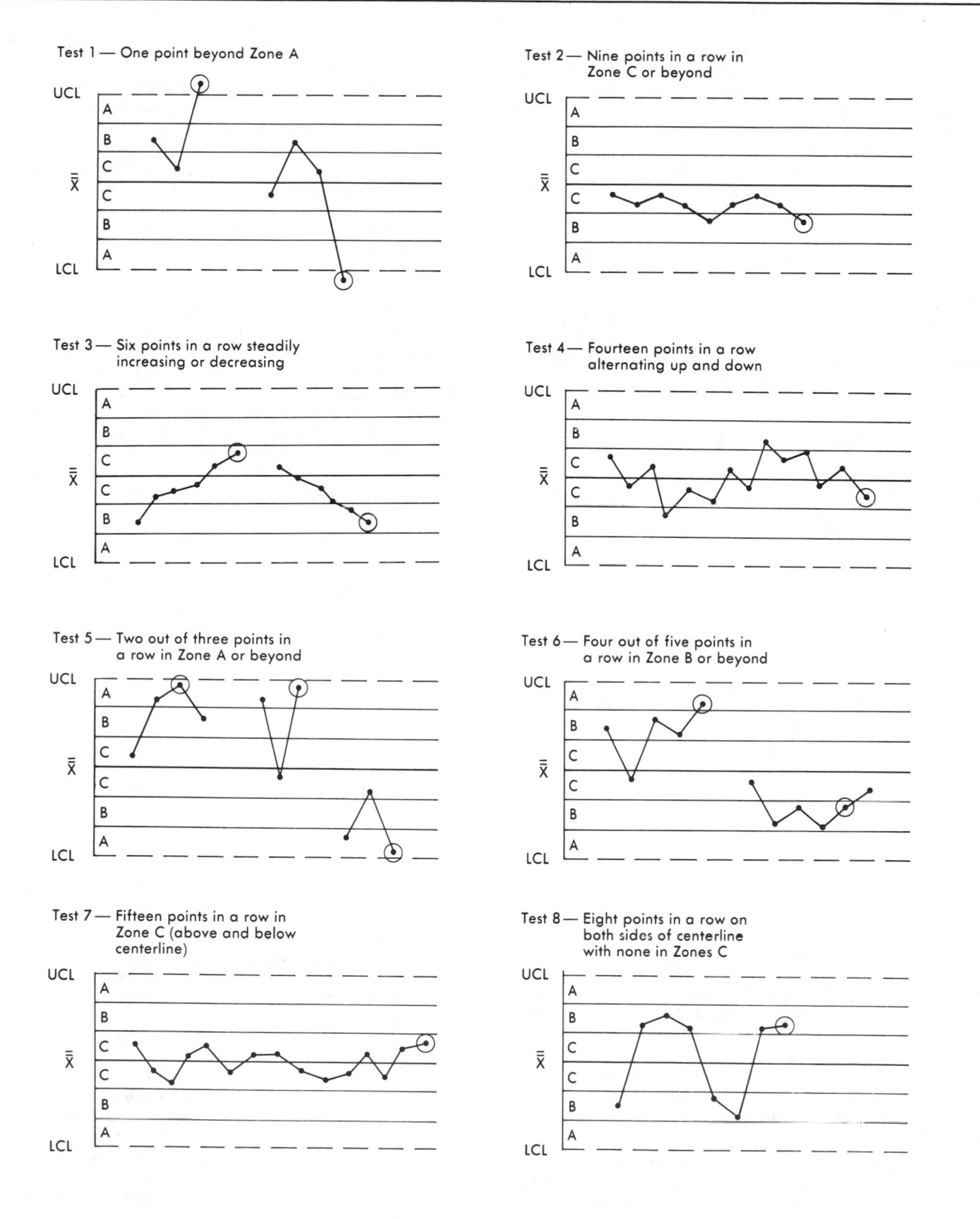

Fig. 11-12 Pattern analysis of $\overline{X}$ charts.

CONTROL CHARTS

in a sample over a succession of samples. A defective is a part or unit with one or more defects.

The other type of attribute control chart is for nonconformities per sample (defects). This type of chart is based on the Poisson probability distribution and is called a c chart. A defect is any fault that causes a part or unit to fail to meet specification requirements. Another closely related chart is the u chart, which is a chart for defects per unit rather than defects per sample.

The general chart construction procedures that apply to variable control charts also apply to attribute control charts.

p Chart

The p chart measures the output of a process as the number of nonconforming or defective units (d) in a subgroup of size n. Each unit is recorded as being either conforming or nonconforming even if the unit has more than one defect. The process characteristic of interest is the true process fraction defective, p'. Because of this, each sample is converted to a fraction defective using the equation:

$$p = d/n \qquad (15)$$

The data fraction defective p are the plotted quantity on the p chart.

The p chart is composed of a centerline and upper and lower control limits. The centerline (p') represents the mean value for p and the control limits are set at ± 3 standard deviations (of p) about p'. Because the mean value p' is generally not known, the trial centerline for a p chart can be calculated from the data:

$$\bar{p} = \sum_{i=1}^{k} d_i / \sum n_i \qquad (16)$$

where:

$\bar{p}$ = average fraction defective in k subgroups
d_i = number of defective units in the i-th subgroup
n_i = number of items inspected in the i-th subgroup
k = number of subgroups

The control limits for the p chart are calculated using the equations:

$$UCL_p = \bar{p} + 3\sqrt{\overline{p}(1-\overline{p})/n} \qquad (17)$$

$$LCL_p = \bar{p} - 3\sqrt{\overline{p}(1-\overline{p})/n} \qquad (18)$$

Because the binomial distribution is generally not symmetric, Eq. (18) may yield a value for the lower control limit of less than 0. When this occurs, a lower control limit of 0 is used.

Whenever possible, p charts should be used with a constant subgroup size; however, there are situations when the subgroup size varies. Because the control limits of the p chart depend on the subgroup size, some adjustments must be made to ensure that the proper interpretation of the chart is made. Some of the more common approaches used to handle variable subgroup size are the following:

1. Compute separate limits for each individual subgroup. This approach leads to a correct set of limits for each sample, but requires continual calculation of the control limits and a somewhat messy looking control chart.
2. Determine an average subgroup size and set the limits

based on this size. This method may be appropriate if the subgroup sizes do not vary greatly, perhaps no more than about 20%; however, if the actual sample size is less than the average subgroup size, a point above the control limit based on that size may not be above its own true upper control limit. Conversely, if the actual subgroup size is greater than the average subgroup size, a point may not show out of control when in fact it really is.

3. A third procedure for varying subgroup size is to express the fraction defective as normalized quantity on a control chart where the centerline is 0 and the control limits are simply ± 3.0. This stabilizes the plotted value even though the subgroup size may be varying.

c Chart

While the p chart monitors the fraction defective of the process, the c chart monitors the number of nonconformities (defects) per sample. A sample could only be one part, particularly if the part is an assembled item such as an automobile, a lift truck, or a washing machine. Examples of defects on a part are missing rivets on an aircraft wing and flash, splay, voids, and knit lines on an injection-molded truck grille.

Because c charts are based on the Poisson distribution, two conditions must be met to collect data and set up the control chart. First, the opportunity for the occurrence of a defect must be large. The second condition requires the probability of getting a defect at a specific point to be small. It is also important that the opportunity space for defects to occur is constant from sample to sample. Examples of a constant opportunity space are fixed length, area, and quantity.

In most applications, the centerline of the c chart is based on the estimate of the average number of defects per sample. This estimate can be calculated by the equation:

$$\bar{c} = \sum_{i=1}^{k} c_i / k \qquad (19)$$

where:

$\bar{c}$ = average number of defects per sample
c_i = observed number of defects in the i-th sample
k = number of samples

The trial control limits are determined from the equations:

$$UCL_c = \bar{c} + 3\sqrt{\bar{c}} \qquad (20)$$

$$LCL_c = \bar{c} - 3\sqrt{\bar{c}} \qquad (21)$$

u Chart

Although in most c-chart applications it is common to comprise a sample of only a single unit or item, the sample or subgroup may be comprised of several units. Further, from subgroup to subgroup, the number of units per subgroup may vary, particularly if a subgroup is an amount of production for the shift or day.

In these applications, the opportunity space for the occurrence of defects per subgroup changes from subgroup to subgroup, violating the equal opportunity space assumption on which the c chart is based. In this case, it is necessary to create some standardized statistic, and such a statistic may be the average number of defects per unit or item.

The average number of defects per unit is calculated using the equation:

$$u = c/n \qquad (22)$$

where:

u = number of defects per unit in a subgroup
c = number of defects per subgroup
n = the number of units per subgroup

When a certain number of subgroups are gathered, the centerline on the u chart is calculated using the equation:

$$\bar{u} = \sum_{i=1}^{k} c_i \Big/ \sum_{i=1}^{k} n_i \qquad (23)$$

where:

$\bar{u}$ = average number of defects per unit (centerline)

The trial control limits for the u chart are calculated using the equations:

$$UCL_u = \bar{u} + 3\sqrt{\bar{u}/n} \qquad (24)$$
$$LCL_u = \bar{u} - 3\sqrt{\bar{u}/n} \qquad (25)$$

PROCESS CAPABILITY

Two issues need to be discussed when process data are statistically represented: (1) the ability of the process to produce parts that conform to specifications and (2) the ability of the process to maintain a state of good statistical control. These two process characteristics are linked together because it is not valid to determine process capability with respect to conformance to specifications without the process being in a state of good statistical control. Although statistical control does not imply conformance, it is a necessary prerequisite for assessing conformance.

In a statistical sense, conformance to specifications involves the process as a whole, and therefore attention must be focused on the distribution of individual measurements.

Because of the distinction between populations and samples, part specifications should not be confused with or compared to control limits. In fact, specification limits should never be placed on a control chart because the control chart monitors sample statistics such as $\bar{X}$ and R, not individual measurements. Placing specification limits on the control chart may give the impression that good conformance exists when it does not.

Occasionally parts produced by a certain process may not meet the specified production standards even though the process itself is in statistical control. One possible reason for this problem is that the process is not centered properly. This means that the actual mean value of the parts produced may be significantly different from the specified nominal value of the part. If this is the case, the machine should be adjusted to move the mean closer to the nominal value. Another possible reason for lack of conformance to specifications is that a statistically stable process may be producing parts with a high level of common cause variation.

To illustrate how a process capability study is performed, the following example will be used. For the process under study, many of the parts were being rejected when inspected using a GO/NOT-GO gage because they did not conform to the specified dimension of $0.140 \pm 0.003''$. It was then decided to study the capability of the process using $\bar{X}$ and R charts. Data were collected from the same machine and operator at a rate of one sample per hour. Table 11-3 gives the results of 27 samples, each having a subgroup size of 5.

After the data were collected, $\bar{X}$ and R charts were constructed to determine whether the process was in statistical control. The calculations for the centerlines and upper control limits are shown in Fig. 11-13 along with the plotted charts.

TABLE 11-3
Data Collected from a Machine for a Process Capability Study

Sample Number	Measurement on Each Item of 5 Items Per Hour*					Average,* $\bar{X}$	Range,* R
1	140	143	137	134	135	137.8	9
2	138	143	143	145	146	143.0	8
3	139	133	147	148	139	141.2	15
4	143	141	137	138	140	139.8	6
5	142	142	145	135	136	140.4	10
6	136	144	143	136	137	139.2	8
7	142	147	137	142	138	141.2	10
8	143	137	145	137	138	140.0	8
9	141	142	147	140	140	142.0	7
10	142	137	145	140	132	139.2	13
11	137	147	142	137	135	139.6	12
12	137	146	142	142	140	141.4	9
13	142	142	139	141	142	141.2	3
14	137	145	144	137	140	140.6	8
15	144	142	143	135	144	141.6	9
16	140	132	144	145	141	140.4	13
17	137	137	142	143	141	140.0	6
18	137	142	142	145	143	131.8	8
19	142	142	143	140	135	140.4	8
20	136	142	140	139	137	138.8	6
21	142	144	140	138	143	141.4	6

(*continued*)

PROCESS CAPABILITY

TABLE 11-3—Continued

Sample Number	Measurement on Each Item of 5 Items Per Hour*					Average,* X	Range,* R
22	139	146	143	140	139	141.4	7
23	140	145	142	139	137	140.6	8
24	134	147	143	141	142	141.4	13
25	138	145	141	137	141	140.4	8
26	140	145	143	144	138	142.0	7
27	145	145	137	138	140	141.0	8

*The values for the measurements are expressed in units of 0.001″.

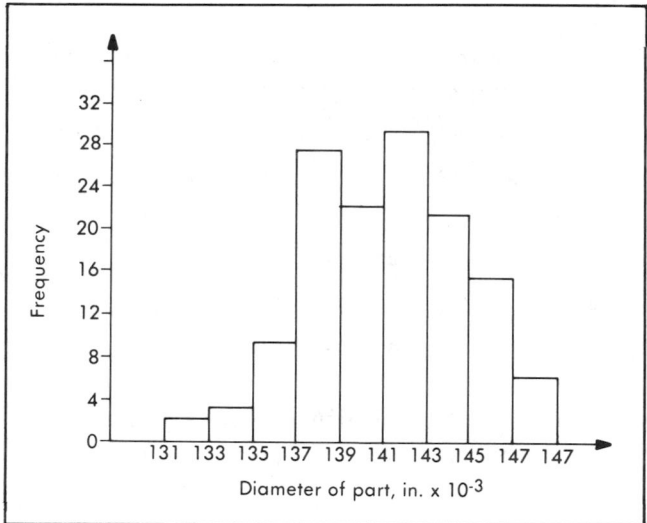

Fig. 11-14 Frequency diagram used in a process capability study.

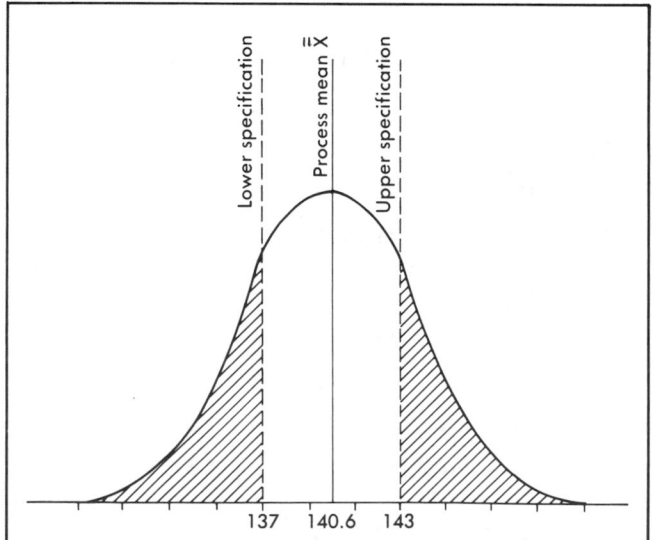

Fig. 11-15 Approximated normal curve.

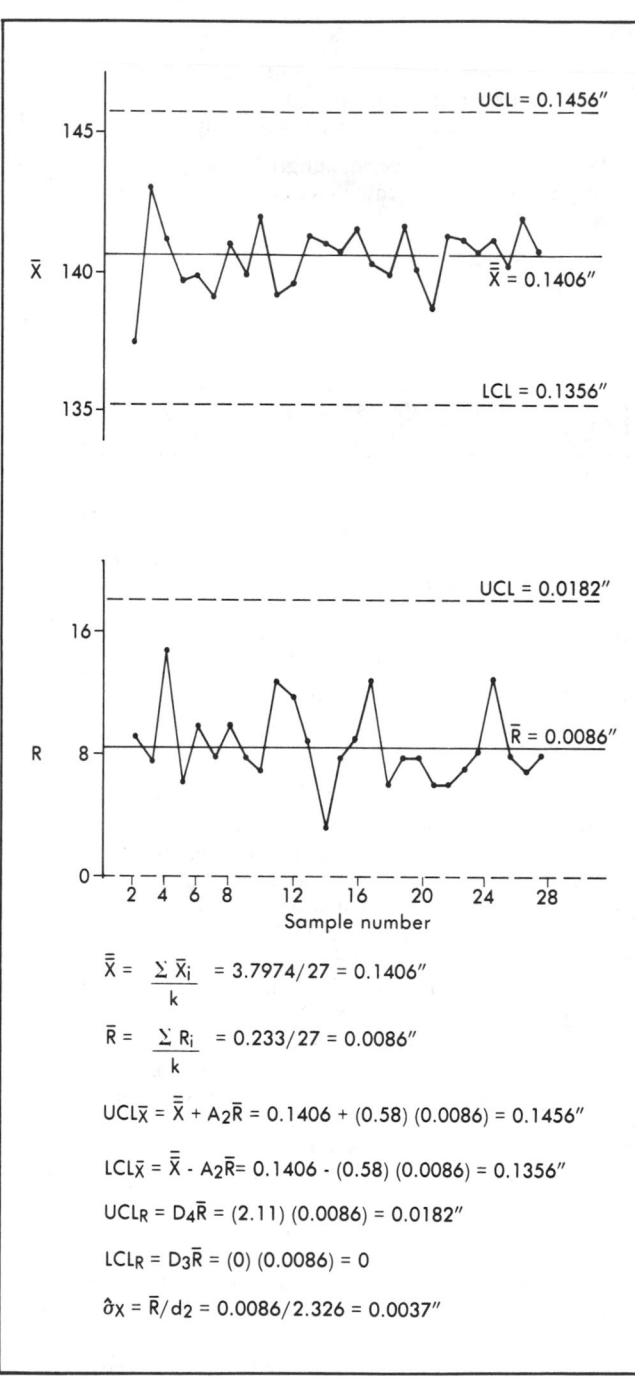

$$\bar{\bar{X}} = \frac{\Sigma \bar{X}_i}{k} = 3.7974/27 = 0.1406''$$

$$\bar{R} = \frac{\Sigma R_i}{k} = 0.233/27 = 0.0086''$$

$$UCL_{\bar{X}} = \bar{\bar{X}} + A_2\bar{R} = 0.1406 + (0.58)(0.0086) = 0.1456''$$

$$LCL_{\bar{X}} = \bar{\bar{X}} - A_2\bar{R} = 0.1406 - (0.58)(0.0086) = 0.1356''$$

$$UCL_R = D_4\bar{R} = (2.11)(0.0086) = 0.0182''$$

$$LCL_R = D_3\bar{R} = (0)(0.0086) = 0$$

$$\hat{\sigma}_X = \bar{R}/d_2 = 0.0086/2.326 = 0.0037''$$

Fig. 11-13 $\bar{X}$ and R control charts for process capability study.

The existence of statistical control is an essential condition for the continuation of the assessment of the process capability. If the process at this point is found not to be in control, no further meaningful statistical analysis of the individual measurements can be made. Attention should immediately be directed toward the identification of specific causes of variation.

Examining the control charts for this example indicates that the process is in statistical control; no points exceed the 3 standard deviation (3σ) limit, a reasonably normal distribution of points exists between the limits, and there are no trends or cycles in the data. The good control of the R chart indicates that the estimate of the process variation ($\sigma_X = 0.0037''$) is a reflection of the forces of common cause variation alone. Based on these results, the process can now be evaluated with respect to its conformance to specifications.

The first step in evaluating the data with respect to conformance to specifications is plotting a frequency histogram (see Fig.

11-14. Examining the histogram reveals that the data appear to be normally distributed with a mean slightly higher than the specified dimension of 0.140''.

Using the estimate of the process mean ($\bar{\bar{X}}$) and the process standard deviation ($\hat{\sigma}_X$) as well as the assumption of normality, the population distribution curve of the individual measurements can be sketched (see Fig. 11-15). The shaded area under the curve represents the probability of obtaining a part that does not meet the specifications.

ASSIGNMENT OF TOLERANCES

It is often necessary to consider how tolerances on individual components in an assembly are to be combined to determine the variations that will result in the assembled unit. Conversely, it may be necessary to partition an allowable assembly variation to assign the required tolerances to the individual components. Statistical models for variations can be very useful in approaching these problems.

STATISTICAL TOLERANCES

The following two examples illustrate some important statistical principles that will help determine how to combine or partition tolerances.

Example 1

The three-part assembly for example 1 is illustrated in Fig. 11-16.[7] Individual part tolerances for part 1, part 2, and part 3 are established to be $\pm0.0040''$, $\pm0.0032''$, and $\pm0.0028''$, respectively. The nominal dimension AD of the assembly is the sum of the component nominal dimensions ($AB + BC + CD$). The processes producing the components are assumed to be in statistical control and normally distributed, and the process capability is ±4 standard deviations ($\pm\sigma_x$); the bilateral specification for each part is therefore $8\sigma_x$ wide. This is often referred to as the natural tolerance of the process.

When the tolerance of the assembly must be determined, it is sometimes incorrectly assumed that the individual part tolerances are added together, yielding in this case an assembly tolerance of $\pm0.010''$. However, if several assemblies were made and then measured, a smaller natural spread would be observed. When the assembly tolerance must be determined, it is necessary to take into consideration the statistical distribution of individual part measurements and the fact that the parts are assembled through random selection.

When parts in question are drawn randomly from their respective normal distributions, the chance of getting any single part with a measurement 4 standard deviations below the nominal is about 0.0005. The chance of getting all three parts having measurements at $-4\sigma_X$ is therefore extremely small (see Fig. 11-17).

Further, the additive law of variances states that for independently selected parts the square of the standard deviation of the assembly is equal to the sum of the squares of the standard deviations of the individual parts. In equation form, this law is represented by:

$$\sigma^2_{Assembly} = \sigma_1^2 + \sigma_2^2 + \ldots + \sigma_n^2 \tag{26}$$

where:

$\sigma^2_{Assembly}$ = variance of the assembly

$\sigma_1^2, \sigma_2^2, \sigma_n^2$ = individual part variances

Based on this law, the standard deviation of the assembly in Fig. 2-28 is calculated to be 0.0015''. If the assembly's natural tolerance is also set at $\pm4\sigma_X$, then virtually all assemblies will fall within $\pm0.006''$ of the nominal assembly dimension. In fact, 99.73% of all the assemblies will fall within $\pm0.0045''$ of the nominal assembly dimension; this value is less than one half of the value obtained by adding part tolerances.

Example 2

The reverse problem of the previous example is a problem of greater practical importance. Instead of trying to determine the assembly tolerance when individual part tolerances are given, this example will discuss how to determine individual part tolerances when an assembly tolerance is given.

The assembly tolerance of three identical parts is designated

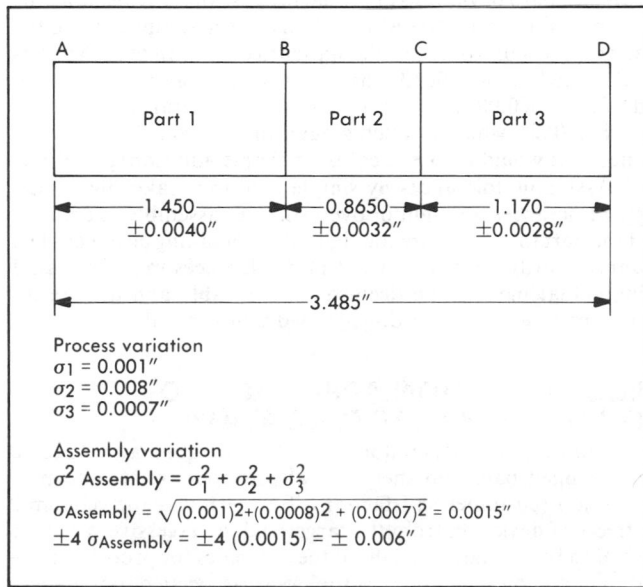

Fig. 11-16 Determining assembly tolerances.

ASSIGNMENT OF TOLERANCES

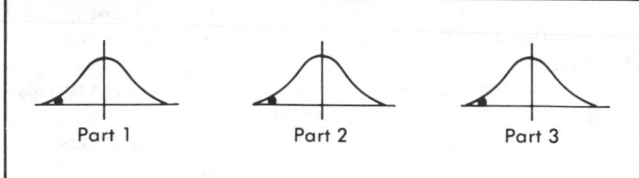

Fig. 11-17 The possibility of selecting three parts all in the far left tail of their respective distributions is small.

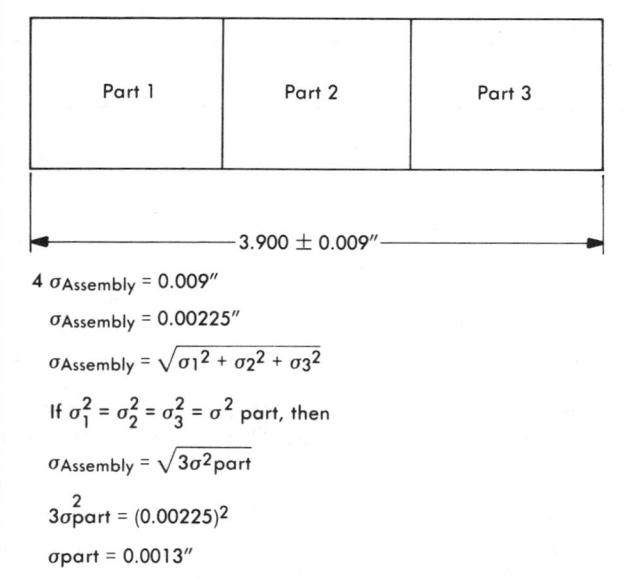

Fig. 11-18 Determining part tolerances.

to be ±0.009" (see Fig. 11-18). It is assumed that the natural part and assembly tolerances are ±4σ_X. It is also assumed that the part standard deviations are equal because they are made by the same or similar processes. Based on these assumptions and the additive law of variances, the standard deviation of each part is calculated to be 0.0013", based on given assembly standard deviation of 0.00225". The individual part tolerance would then be ±0.0052", which is much greater than a ±0.003" part tolerance that would be specified using simple addition/partition.

Assigning tolerances by simple addition makes individual part tolerances too tight or overestimates assembly tolerances. If the part tolerances are too tight, the machining costs could be unnecessarily increased. Tight part tolerances may also cause individual parts to be deemed unacceptable and as a result scrapped, reworked, or downgraded unnecessarily.

LOSS FUNCTION APPROACH TO QUALITY CHARACTERIZATION

From a practical standpoint, part tolerances may need to be determined based on their cost effectiveness relative to part function (customer satisfaction). Furthermore, the economic effects of deviation from the target and/or excessive variation need to be evaluated in light of the strategies for process operation including such things as tool wear, associated tool change, die maintenance, and die repair. This is the role of tolerance

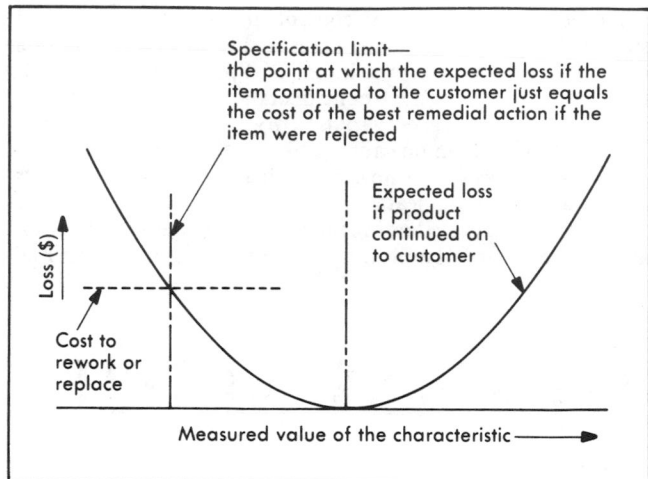

Fig. 11-19 Loss function curve.

design. The following example will be used to demonstrate how the concept of loss function is applied in the evaluation of process capability to the engineering specifications.[8] The quality characteristic of interest is the lever effort on a heater control. Very low efforts would cause customer complaints of flimsy feel or rattle, while very high efforts would cause customer complaints of stiffness. And in each case, the more extreme the condition, the more likely it would prompt a customer complaint. The total complaint rate is the sum of these two individual kinds of complaints. Between the extremes the net complaints from the two conditions drops low. A loss function of the sum of losses from both complaints can be developed as the curve illustrated in Fig. 11-19.

By choosing the point with the minimum loss as the target, it is possible to use the continuous loss function to give an economic interpretation to a specification limit (see Fig. 11-19). There are two possible choices at each measured part quality level X: (1) letting the part pass on to customer with an expected loss as determined by the loss function or (2) reworking or replacing the part at a cost. To minimize the total costs, the alternative with the lower cost should be chosen. The point of indifference between the two choices determines the specification limit.

Defining a Loss Function

In general, a loss function may be defined by evaluating the expected losses for several values of the quality characteristic. Assuming that a quadratic equation approximates the true loss function, then the loss function can be derived from the expected losses estimated from any two points, such as the loss at the target and the loss at one other point. The quadratic loss function together with the statistical distribution of the actual process output can be used to evaluate the expected loss per piece using the equation:

$$L(X) = k\,(\sigma_X^2 + (\mu - m)^2) \tag{27}$$

where:

$L(X)$	=	expected loss per piece of quantity X
k	=	loss coefficient
σ_X	=	standard deviation of the process
μ	=	the actual process mean
m	=	the target process mean

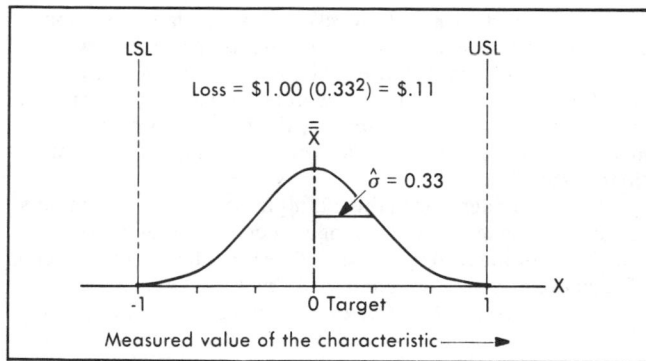

Fig. 11-20 Process distribution of X.

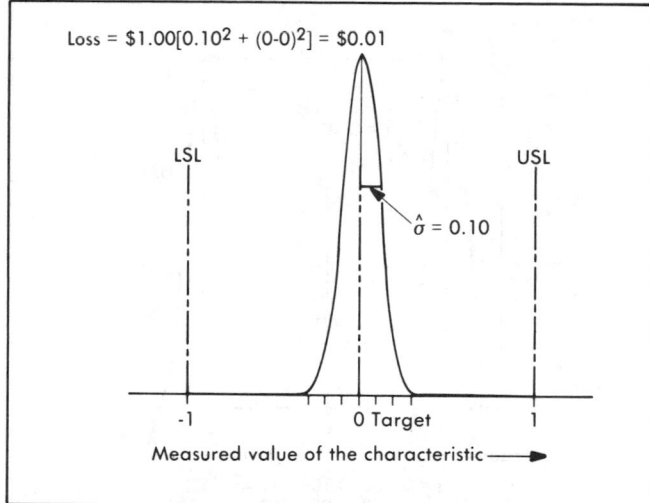

Fig. 11-21 Process distribution of X with reduced variability.

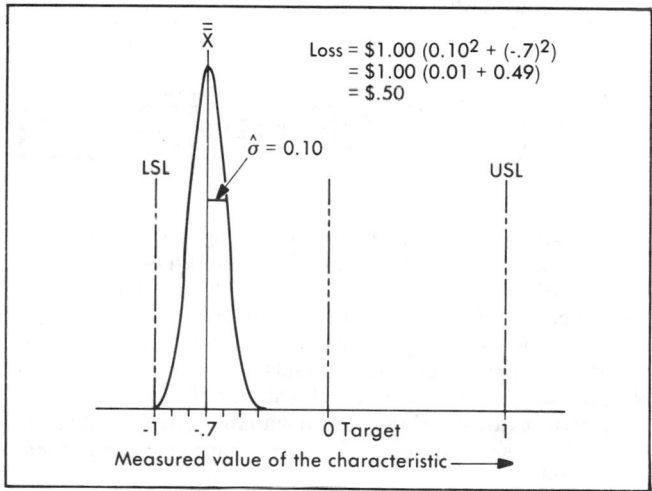

Fig. 11-22 Noncentered process.

Centered Process

The example in Fig. 11-20 considers a process that is assumed to be in good statistical control and centered between a bilateral specification of ±1.0. The standard deviation of the process is $\sigma_X = 0.33$ so that, in terms of the traditional process capability analysis, the process is 6 σ capable. The replacement cost (k) of the part is equal to $1.00.

By applying the quadratic loss function, it is found that the $1.00 part carries with it an additional loss of about $0.11. This is a hidden loss above and beyond direct costs for materials, labor, and processing. It is experienced first by the downstream customers in terms of additional costs that they will incur or by decreased utility of the product.

The hidden loss of $0.11 could be reduced through some process improvement. Because the loss $L(X)$ is proportional to the square of the process standard deviation (σ_X), it is possible to reduce the incremental loss by reducing the process variation; that is, identify and remove one or more common causes of variability. Figure 11-21 shows the effects of reducing the process standard deviation to 0.10. The loss beyond the replacement cost of $1.00 is now only $0.01. It can be seen that a reduction in process variation by a factor of 3 has led to a reduction in the hidden loss by a factor of 11.

Traditional manufacturing wisdom values such "better-than-necessary" performance in terms of process variability primarily because such a process can absorb some shocks from special causes of variation without generating nonconforming output. This example, however, shows that additional benefits can be gained from reduced variation even when the process is already stable, centered on the target, and has a natural spread well within the specification limits.

Noncentered Process

When a process shows a great deal more than just marginal capability, one way of capitalizing on this potential is to seek a short-term benefit by running the process toward one side of the specifications that minimizes, for example, material usage or cycle time. By taking the preceding example (standard deviation = 0.10) and locating the process mean as far to the low side as possible, Figure 11-22 shows the results of such an approach. This process, which generated only $0.01 in hidden losses when centered on the target, now causes $0.50 in customer losses when run close to the lower specification limit. Very few pieces do not conform to specifications, and such a process would meet the explicit requirements of conventional purchase

agreements. However, the loss arises because the output is consistently mediocre; in this situation, the customer suffers loss first.

Linear Drift Processes

Another common approach used to take advantage of small process variation relative to the specifications is to reduce labor or tooling costs by allowing the process to drift across the specification range. A tool change discipline that involves setting the process 3 standard deviations away from one specification limit and then letting the tool wear continue until the process is 3 standard deviations away from the other specification limit seems rational. For those who regularly must deal with the problems of tool wear, die wear, chemical solution replenishment, and the like, it appears uneconomical to think in any other terms. However, these apparent savings are not achieved without risk of hidden customer loss.

DESIGN OF EXPERIMENTS

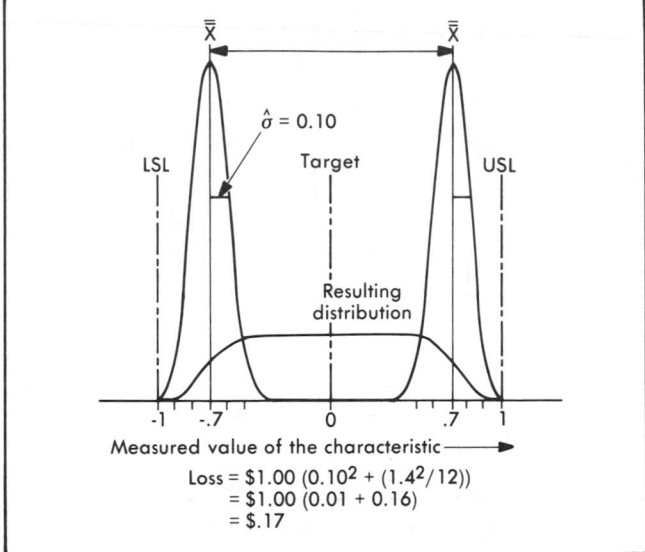

Fig. 11-23 Process with linear drift in the mean.

A normally distributed process with a standard deviation of 0.10 may be allowed to drift to its maximum extent, with its centers moving from -0.7 to +0.7. Figure 11-23 shows the process distributions at these extreme centers, as well as the resulting product distribution of a complete drift cycle. As can be seen, this net distribution is no longer "bell-shaped," but more "loaf-shaped."

The total hidden loss in this example is $0.17, coming mainly because the lengthy tool change interval causes marginally acceptable products to be produced near the beginning and end of each cycle. If the tool change interval was reduced by 30%, for instance, with set and change points at -0.5 and +0.5, the hidden loss would be reduced by almost half, to $0.09. It is apparent that tool change policy should really balance the economies of longer change intervals against the downstream losses to achieve the lowest total cost. It is also apparent that when a process with relatively small variations is allowed to vary within the relatively wide specifications, rather than being maintained in statistical control near the target, this lack of shop discipline is not cost-free, but comes at the expense of the customer's and the producer's own downstream processes.

THE ROLE OF DESIGN OF EXPERIMENTS

In conducting experiments and analyzing product and process performance, difficulties may arise as a result of the environment under study or the manner in which the study is being conducted. Some simple but powerful experimental design strategies and tools may be invoked to mitigate these difficulties. It is beyond the scope and bounds of this chapter to discuss all of these issues or even some of them in any depth. However, a few key issues are briefly presented with the hope that attention to these considerations will lead to more meaningful experimental work.

When designing experiments, there are a number of important factors that must be considered. Some of these are involved with the forces of process variability and external noise that may cloud the experimental results if countermeasures are not properly planned for the experiments. In this section, certain key concepts in planned experimentation and the relationship between design of experiments and SPC are discussed.

EFFECTS OF CHANGE

In many instances, the variables of importance are not clearly known without examination or analysis. It is desirable to be able to study several variables together, but "independently" estimate the effect of a change in each of the variables. Furthermore, it may be deemed important to know if a variable effect varies when other variables take on different levels. When such information on the interactions among the factors is sought, the arrangement of the tests becomes very important.

For example, suppose a chemical reaction is to be studied and the influence of concentration and temperature on reaction time is to be determined.[9] Two possible test arrangements are shown in Fig. 11-24.

The arrangement in view *a* is somewhat haphazard and cannot be used to observe the effect of changing temperature only because no two tests exist for which temperature changes but concentration remains fixed. When the outcome of any two trials is compared, both temperature and concentration change simultaneously. It is therefore difficult to sort out exactly what is effecting change and what is not.

The arrangement in view *b*, however, provides for the opportunity to learn much about the relationships between the two variables and the reaction time. In particular:

1. The effect of changing either of the two variables alone can be observed.
2. It can be observed that the possibility that the effect of one of the variables altered can change as the fixed conditions of the other variable are altered. That is, variable interactions can be revealed.
3. In the case of temperature, it can be observed that the possibility that the effect of temperature can vary over the range of temperature (curvilinear behavior) for fixed levels of concentration.

The arrangement in view *b* is generally referred to as a *factorial* arrangement of test points and is particularly useful for comparison and modeling purposes.

FORCES OF EXPERIMENT VARIATION

It is essential that an experiment is designed to provide for the opportunity to observe the amount of variation inherent in the test environment so that inferences on the magnitude and direction of variable effects can be made in light of the noise in the system. The amount of system noise can best be estimated from results of replicated experimental trials. Replication, not to

DESIGN OF EXPERIMENTS

be confused with repetition, is necessary to reduce risks associated with drawing a wrong conclusion from the experiment.

Replication of an experiment means that the factors under study, which define a unique trial, are separately and independently established or set on more than one occasion and the observed result is recorded in each case. Repetition, on the other hand, refers to the multiple observation of an experiment under a given set of conditions. If on two separate occasions the control settings on a machine are set to the same conditions and a single part is made each time, two replicates exist for a given test condition. If on one occasion the machine is set to those conditions and two parts are made, we have two repetitions. In studying a process in control, for example, repetition could

provide a measure of the common cause variation in the process under a given set of conditions. In trying to draw conclusions about the results of comparative experiments, however, replication is necessary to provide a realistic estimate of experimental errors resulting from errors in the settings of the independent variables and from variation due to fluctuating environmental conditions over the course of completing all experiment trials. Variation in repetitions would likely underestimate this total experimental error.

RELATIONSHIP OF DESIGN OF EXPERIMENTS WITH SPC

If the phenomenon under study is already a viable and ongoing process, the pursuit of improvement opportunities through experimentation can be considerably enhanced by employing the techniques of statistical process control discussed previously. In such a way, sporadic sources of variation can be identified and then removed through remedial action. A stable process contributes to the ability of observing the effects of purposeful process change. Continued study in this fashion will further help to observe the persistence of changes that might be introduced.

Once a process is stabilized, continued attack on the common cause system leads to a progressively quieter process, further enhancing the ability to observe the forces of purposeful process change through experimentation. For example, a simple experiment can be run to see if a change in raw material viscosity has any real effect on the quality of a certain chemical product. Suppose that this change in viscosity actually does increase the

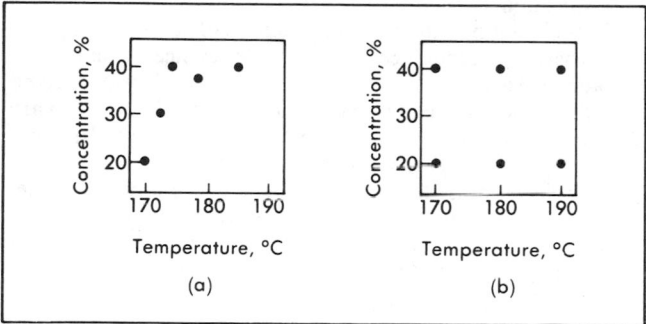

Fig. 11-24 Illustration of two test arrangements.

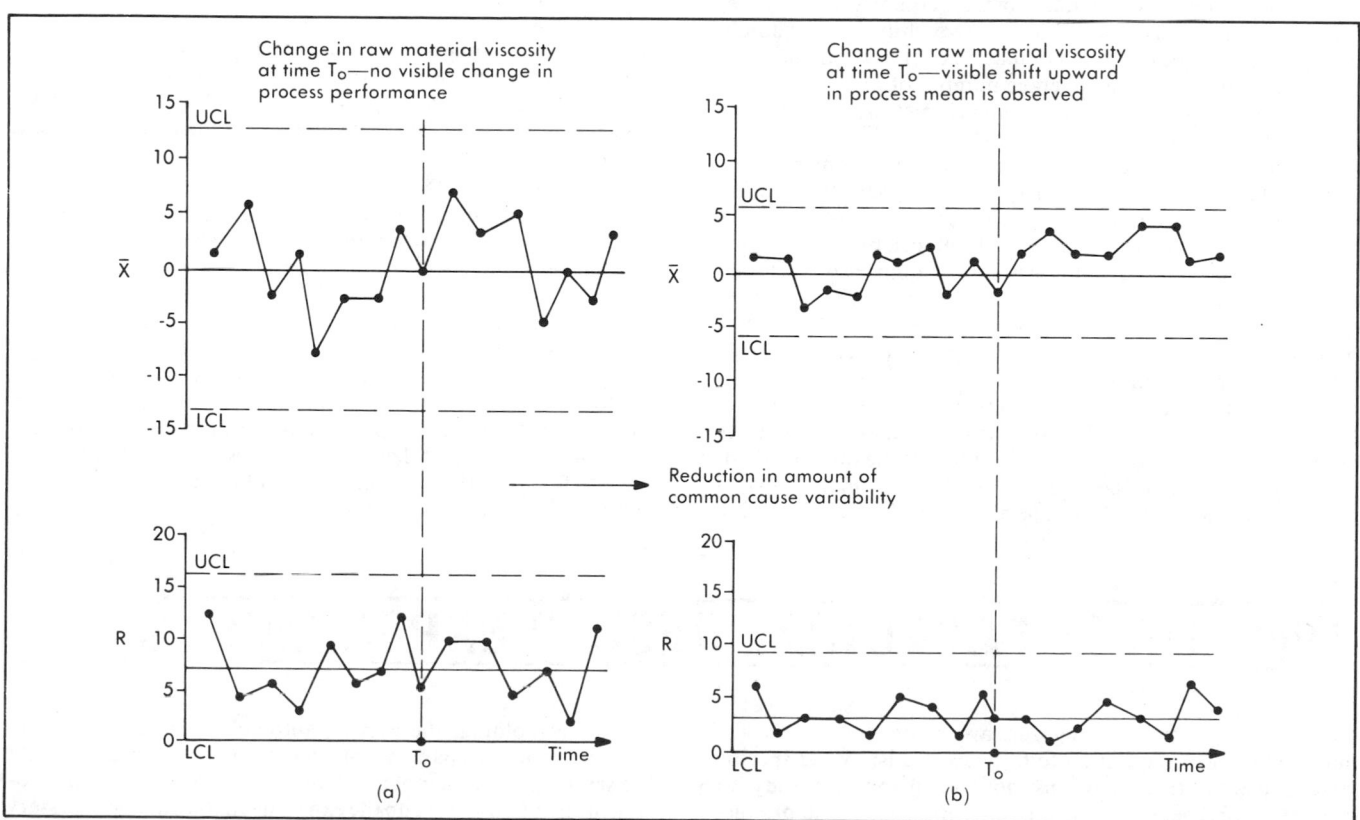

Fig. 11-25 Increased sensitivity of control charts due to reduced common cause variability.

DESIGN OF EXPERIMENTS

average of the quality characteristic; $\overline{X}$ and R control charts are kept on the quality characteristic to monitor possible changes in mean level or amount of variability. Figure 11-25 shows two possible scenarios for this example. The time T_o is the time when the raw material viscosity is purposely changed. In view *a*, the level of common cause variation is so large that the increase in the process mean due to the change in viscosity cannot be seen on the $\overline{X}$ chart. The signal-to-noise ratio of the process is low because of excessive variation. In view *b*, however, it appears that the reduced level of common cause variation has provided the ability to detect the change in product quality (a run above the centerline is evident on the $\overline{X}$ chart).

COUNTERING NUISANCE VARIATION

Emphasis on the fact that experiments ought to be comparative internally helps to counter the problems associated with the fact that the systems under study may not be particularly stable. Instead, their performance may drift in average level over time. For many processes under study, the notion of statistical control or stability may be of little meaning, especially when research and development work on new products and processes is being considered.

When certain factors cause a process to undergo systematic change, the technique of randomization can be used to avoid the problems of nonsense correlation and the aliasing of the effects of factors under study with extraneous factor effects.

The following discussion demonstrates how the techniques of blocking and randomization may improve the sensitivity and validity of an experiment. Suppose two different methods of assembly of a certain subsystem are to be compared. The response of interest is the number of units completed per worker per shift. Twelve assemblers across two shifts are randomly assigned to one of the two methods, six for each method. To make the comparison, an average number of units per shift is determined for the six workers for each method, and the two averages are compared.

The previously described design of experiments may constitute a valid comparison, but it may not be very sensitive because of large differences in skill level from one worker to another. A more sensitive comparison might be developed by using only six workers, each testing both methods. Comparison between methods could then be made for each worker and then averaged across all workers. The worker becomes the experimental subunit or block. Using this design, worker-to-worker variation is blocked from the comparison of methods.

Now suppose the initial experiment (12 workers) was run using the six workers on the day shift to test one of the methods and the six workers on the night shift to test the other method. Now shift-to-shift difference in overall performance due to worker skill level, level of supervision, and type of training could bias the results. The issue now is one of design validity, not simply sensitivity. In this case, shift differences would be confounded with method differences, and as a result, the comparison may not be valid. Randomization of the assignment of method type to worker across both shifts would solve this problem.

TAGUCHI'S APPROACH TO EXTRANEOUS VARIATION

Logic may dictate that comparative experiments can provide more efficient and reliable results if blocking is employed as an experiment design tool; however, there is another side to this coin. Central to Taguchi's definition of quality as loss due to functional variation in product/process performance is the notion of outer noise as a major contributor to performance variation.

Taguchi defines outer noise as sources of variation in product/process performance due to the presence of external/extraneous variables such as temperature, wind velocity, and humidity. The argument is that as these outer noise factors vary they produce functional variation in performance. In other words, they increase the amount of scatter/dispersion of the process. Outer noise factors could include incoming raw material variation, operator-to-operator differences, changing ambient conditions, or even differences in the performance of maintenance. The important things to remember are that:

- The variation sources are somewhat difficult to control or regulate.
- The variation sources are a real part of the environment in which the product/process functions.

Taguchi's approach is to employ design of experiments and often process simulation to understand how the forces of outer noise may be mitigated through the adroit manipulation of controllable variables (process/product design factors). Taguchi refers to this as the method of parameter design. It is a totally different way of thinking about extraneous/external or nuisance noise factors.

When outer noise sources can be identified and "controlled" either in a physical experiment or through simulation, Taguchi has suggested the use of inner and outer array experimental design structures. Through such experiments, adjustments in design/control factors are sought that temper the effects of outer noise factors. In other words, a robust design/process is sought. The emphasis here is on achieving more consistent performance in the face of the inevitable presence of noise in the environment in which the product/process functions. An examination of experimental design structures and how they can be used to facilitate the development of robust products and processes is discussed subsequently.

TWO-LEVEL FACTORIAL DESIGN EXPERIMENTS

When experimental programs are to be undertaken, the most fundamental question to be answered is: "What specific arrangement of test conditions should be planned to study the way in which a set of factors influence the quality and productivity measures of interest?" For example, the process might be injection molding, the part an automobile grille, the quality response could be part weight, and the factors of interest might be screw speed, material melt flow index, cycle time, and holding pressure. In setting up the experiment, it would be necessary to determine what set of varying process conditions ought to be considered as an experiment design to evaluate how these four factors influence part weight.

One common approach to the problem is to first select a range of interest for each of the factors and then run a series of experiments varying only one factor at a time. The results for tests varying only cycle time may appear as seen in Fig. 11-26. The procedure is then repeated for each of the other three factors (screw speed, melt flow index, holding pressure) and their curves developed.

Some of the problems that exist with this one-factor-at-a-time approach to experimentation are the following:

1. Too many tests required. Usually the number of levels for each factor is chosen to be many more than is reasonably required. For example, in Fig. 11-26, seven different cycle times are considered, but the resulting relationship is roughly a straight line, which could have been determined using only two cycle times. Even if the relationship was strongly curvilinear, using three or four different cycle times over the range would probably be adequate.

2. Poor long-range planning. With this approach there is a tendency to focus on one factor, study it, and, if a solution to the problem is not found, then some other factor is studied. The resulting experimental program often becomes a random walk across the product/process factor environment.

3. Failure to recognize factor interactions. Often the way in which a certain factor influences the test outcome depends on the level/setting of one or more other factors. For example, in Fig. 11-27, increasing holding pressure increases weight when the screw speed is 20 fpm, but decreases

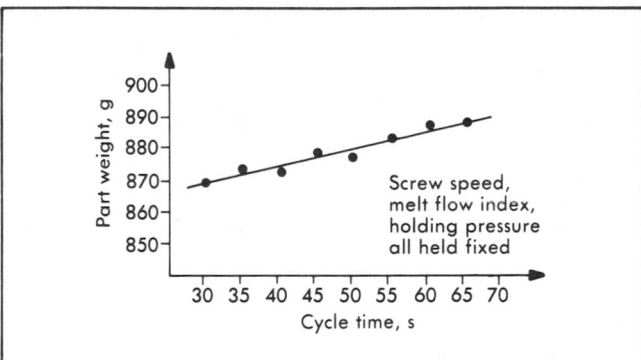

Fig. 11-26 Experiments of one factor at a time.

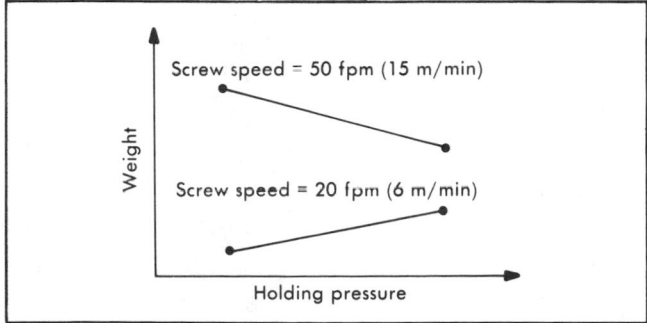

Fig. 11-27 A two-way diagram for interaction analysis.

weight when the screw speed is 50 fpm. It is difficult to clearly see these interactions when experiments are performed by varying only one variable at a time.

4. Difficult to control. When experiments are conducted in a systematic fashion, conducted over a long period of time, or when they proceed in a somewhat ad hoc fashion, it becomes difficult to deal with the presence of nuisance factors in the experimental environment such as accommodating blocking and/or randomization. Experiments involving several factors require thoughtful advance planning and a unified approach.

FEATURES OF TWO-LEVEL FACTORIALS

In an effort to overcome the problems previously discussed, a simple but powerful class of experiments commonly referred to as *two-level factorial designs* can be used. These experimental designs jointly examine a group of factors (k = the number of factors), with each factor taking on two distinct levels or settings. All possible combinations of the k factors over two levels each are considered; there are a total of 2^k unique test conditions.

Some of the advantages of two-level factorials are that they:

- Provide for the independent determination of the average effect that each factor has on the response.
- Provide a structure that can easily reveal variable interactions.
- Provide a structure amenable to the techniques of blocking and randomization.
- Do not require many tests (as long as k is not large).
- Have an appealing geometric representation that makes them simple to visualize, explain to others, and interpret.
- Constitute a basic building block for further experimentation.
- Have an associated mathematical model that explicitly relates the process response to the factors under study.

Although a 2^k factorial may have up to a k factor interaction effect, most problems only require consideration of main effects and two-factor interaction effects. The main effect is a measure of how much change occurs in the process response on the average when a given factor is varied from one level to the other level. It is the average change in the response in the sense that the individual measures of change are averaged over the high and low levels of all the other variables. The two-factor interaction effect is a measure of the extent to which the individual (main) effect of any given factor depends on the specific levels of some other factor. The two-factor interaction is also an average in that it is averaged over the two levels of all other variables.

In the effect definitions previously mentioned, consideration is given to how changes in the factor(s) influence the mean of the process (mean response). Sometimes such effects are referred to as location effects. In a subsequent section, the manner in which changes in the factors influence the variability of the process (variation response) will be discussed. These effects are referred to as dispersion effects.

TWO-LEVEL FACTORIAL EXPERIMENT EXAMPLE

High-carbon steel has been extensively used for railway track because of its high strength and low cost; however, because of its high carbon content it is not easy to weld, thus making repair and reinforcement in the field difficult. Accord-

TWO-LEVEL FACTORIALS

TABLE 11-4
Data for Two-Level, Three-Variable Factorial Design

Variable	Unit	Low Level	High Level
Ambient temperature, T	°F	0	70
Wind velocity, V	mph	0	20
Bar size, B	⅛″	4	11

ing to the code of the American Welding Society (AWS), additional steps of preheating and postheating are required to obtain good-quality welds. Several years ago the Rail Steel Bar Association sponsored a research project at the Welding Research Laboratory of the University of Wisconsin to study whether preheating and postheating were really needed.[10]

A statistical experimental design that was formulated for this study was a two-level, three-variable factorial design, simply designated as a 2^3 *factorial design*. Two levels were chosen for each variable based on desired field conditions to be simulated. The high and low levels of the three variables are given in Table 11-4.

The test condition matrix in both coded and uncoded form is shown in Table 11-5. The eight sets of test conditions are given by the eight rows corresponding to test numbers 1-8. The three factors being studied are represented by X_1, X_2, and X_3. The actual levels of the factors are coded to -1 and +1 values; a -1 represents the low level, and a +1 represents the high level. Other coding notations are also used for the test condition matrix of a two-level factorial. In place of -1, a minus sign (-) or zero (0) can be used; in place of +1, a plus sign (+) or one (1) can be used. Although the tests are written down (1-8) in a systematic order, they should be performed in a random order for the reasons previously discussed.

If the three variables are considered as three mutually perpendicular coordinate axes (X_1, X_2, and X_3), the 2^3 factorial design can be represented geometrically as a cube (see Fig. 11-28). The numbers encircled at the eight corners of the cube represent the corresponding test numbers in standard order. The eight actual test conditions are given in brackets.

Each of the eight tests performed in this example were replicated for a total of sixteen tests (see Table 11-6). The main purpose of running replicated tests is to provide for the estimation of the experimental error. The response for each of these welding experiments is the ultimate tensile strength of the welds, and the average responses for each test condition are also provided in Fig. 11-28.

Geometrically, the main effect of the ambient temperature on the ultimate tensile strength of the welds is the difference between the average test result on plane II and the average test result on plane I (refer to Fig. 11-28); therefore, the main effect equation for ambient temperature is:

$$E_1 = \left(\frac{\overline{Y}_2 + \overline{Y}_4 + \overline{Y}_6 + \overline{Y}_8}{4} \right) - \left(\frac{\overline{Y}_1 + \overline{Y}_3 + \overline{Y}_5 + \overline{Y}_7}{4} \right)$$

where:

E_1 = the main effect of temperature, ksi (MPa)
$\overline{Y}_i$ = the average response (i = 1 through 8), ksi (MPa)

Substituting the date from Table 11-6 into this equation yields main effect of temperature of +9.15 ksi (63 MPa). The interpretation of this main effect is that, on the average, increasing the ambient temperature from its low level to its high level causes an increase in ultimate tensile strength of 9.15 ksi (63 MPa). In a similar fashion, the main effects of wind velocity (X_2) and bar size (X_3) are calculated to be -5.10 ksi (-35 MPa) and 0.85 ksi (5.9 MPa), respectively. These main effects are graphically depicted in Fig. 11-28.

An alternate way to view the main effect of temperature is to compare or contrast pairs of tests that vary in ambient temperature setting, but have fixed levels of wind velocity and bar size. Such contrasts are evident in Fig. 11-28 as results are compared from left to right on the cube. The average of the four contrasts is equivalent to the main effect and the main effect of the ambient temperature would be represented by the equation:

$$E_1 = [(\overline{Y}_2 - \overline{Y}_1) + (\overline{Y}_4 - \overline{Y}_3) + (\overline{Y}_6 - \overline{Y}_5) + (\overline{Y}_8 - \overline{Y}_7)]/4$$

The main effect of wind velocity and bar size could be viewed in a similar manner.

In calculating the main effect of ambient temperature, both the amount and direction of change in weld strength with a

TABLE 11-5
Test Condition Matrix for a Two-Level, Three-Variable Factorial Design

Test Number	Coded Test Conditions			Actual Test Conditions		
	X_1	X_2	X_3	T, °F	V, mph	B, ⅛″
1	-1	-1	-1	0	0	
2	1	-1	-1	70	0	4
3	-1	1	-1	0	20	4
4	1	1	-1	70	20	4
5	-1	-1	1	0	0	11
6	1	-1	1	70	0	11
7	-1	1	1	0	20	11
8	1	1	1	70	20	11

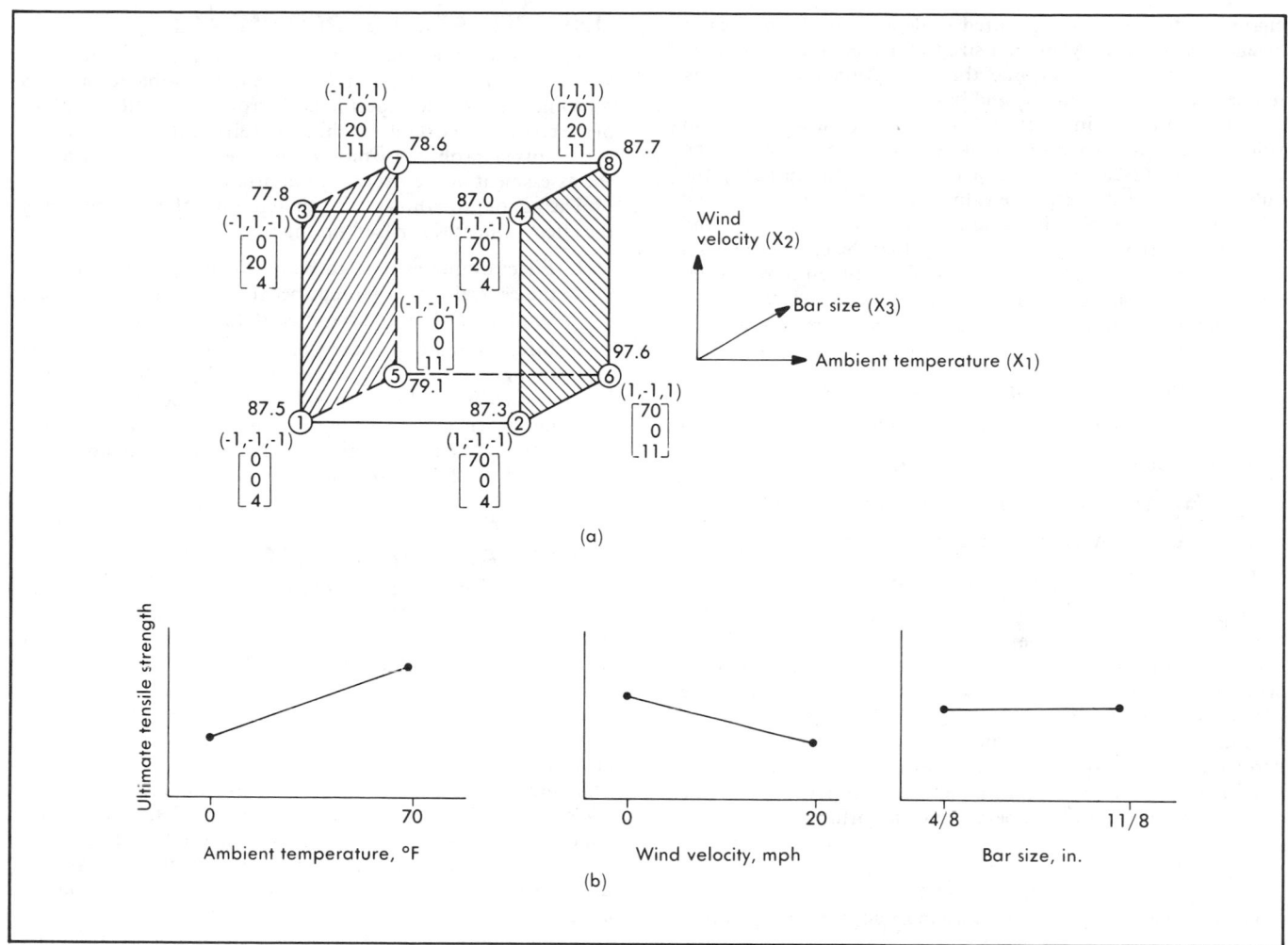

Fig. 11-28 Average response for each test condition: (a) geometric representation of a 2^3 factorial design and (b) two-way diagrams for main effects.

TABLE 11-6
Results of the 16 Welding Experiments

Test Number (i)	Ambient Temperature X_1	Wind Velocity X_2	Bar Size X_3	Test Order for Y_{ai}	Ultimate Tensile Strength, ksi (MPa) Y_{ai}	Y_{bi}	Test Order for Y_{bi}	Average Response, ksi (MPa) $\overline{Y}_i = (Y_{ai} + Y_{bi})/2$
1	-1	-1	-1	6	84.0(579)	91.0(627)	3	87.5(603)
2	1	-1	-1	8	90.6(625)	84.0(579)	7	87.3(602)
3	-1	1	-1	1	69.6(480)	86.0(593)	5	77.8(536)
4	1	1	-1	2	76.0(524)	98.0(676)	4	87.0(600)
5	-1	-1	1	5	77.7(536)	80.5(555)	8	79.1(545)
6	1	-1	1	3	99.7(687)	95.5(658)	1	97.6(673)
7	-1	1	1	4	82.7(570)	74.5(514)	2	78.6(542)
8	1	1	1	7	93.7(646)	81.7(563)	6	87.7(605)

CHAPTER 11

TWO-LEVEL FACTORIALS

change in temperature appeared to depend on the particular levels of wind velocity and bar size (see Table 11-7). It is therefore important to determine the interaction effects among temperature, wind velocity, and bar size.

To examine the interaction between temperature and wind velocity, it is convenient to think in terms of compressing the cube of Fig. 11-28 in the bar size direction. Compressing the cube means that the response values for given temperature and wind velocity combinations are averaged across the high and low levels of the bar size. The result is that the cube becomes a square (see Fig. 11-29). The interaction between temperature and bar size and wind velocity and bar size can also be examined in a similar manner. The calculation of these interactions is as follows:

Interaction between temperature and wind velocity:

$$E_{12} = [(87.35-78.20) - (92.45-83.30)]/2 = 0$$

Interaction between temperature and bar size:

$$E_{13} = [(92.65 - 78.85) - (87.15-82.65)]/2 = 4.65$$

Interaction between wind velocity and bar size:

$$E_{23} = [(83.15-88.35) - (82.40-87.40)]/2 = -0.1$$

A graphical summary of all the factor effects for this two-level factorial experiment is given in Fig. 11-30.

It is important to note that nothing has been said about the size of the estimated variable effects relative to the level of the experimental error. Error analysis can be based on the replication in the experiment. For this problem, it turns out that the error (standard error) of an effect estimate is about 4.11 ksi (28.3 MPa). As a result, it would appear that perhaps only the average main effect of temperature is important.

TABLE 11-7
Change in Weld Strength as Related to Changes in Temperature

Wind Velocity	Bar Size	Effect of Temperature
0 mph	4/8″	-0.2 ksi
20 mph	4/8″	+9.2 ksi
0 mph	11/8″	+18.5 ksi
20 mph	11/8″	+9.1 ksi

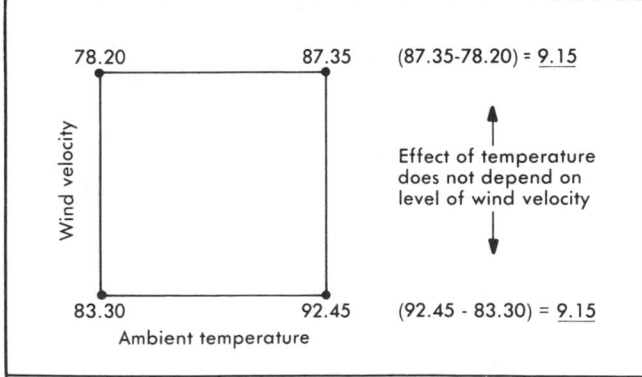

Fig. 11-29 Two-way diagram of temperature to wind velocity interaction effect.

UNREPLICATED EXPERIMENTS

When it is not feasible or desirable to include replications in a two-level factorial experiment, it is not possible to obtain a direct measure of the experimental error for statistical analysis of the relative importance of the factor effects. In such cases, the use of normal probability plots of the effect estimates will aid in the assessment of their relative importance.[11,12]

The use of probability plots to determine the importance of the effect estimates is based on the following two facts:

1. Effect estimates tend to be normally distributed due to the central limit theorem because they represent linear combinations of the response data.
2. Effect estimates that are small (the true effect is 0) may be thought of as arising from a normal distribution with a mean of 0 and therefore will fall about a common straight line when plotted on normal probability paper. Effect estimates that are significant have a true mean other than 0 and will fall off this line.

ALGEBRAIC REPRESENTATION

Although the geometric representation of the two-level factorial provides a useful basis for analysis and interpretation, it is not a convenient way to estimate the factor effects, particularly if four or more factors are involved. However, a simple algebraic method can be employed using a matrix representation (see Table 11-8). The first three columns (from the left, X_1, X_2, X_3) are referred to as the *design matrix*. They define the test conditions for the eight tests in this 2^3 factorial design. The next four columns (X_1X_2 through $X_1X_2X_3$) are obtained by forming all possible cross-product combinations of the first three columns. Together, all seven columns are referred to as the *calculation matrix*. Each column in the calculation matrix is used together with the data (last column) to estimate the factor effects.

To obtain the estimate of the main effect of X_1, the inner product of column X_1 and the Y column is formed, summed, and then divided by $N/2$. The calculation would appear as follows:

$$E_1 = [-Y_1 + Y_2 - Y_3 + Y_4 - Y_5 + Y_6 - Y_7 + Y_8]/4$$

The two-factor interaction effects and the three-factor interaction effects would be obtained in a similar fashion.

In general, for a 2^k factorial design:

- A total of 2^k unique test conditions exist and hence the calculation matrix will have 2^k rows.
- The calculation matrix will have 2^k-1 columns representing the k main effects and $2^k-(k+1)$ interaction effects.
- There will be k main effects, $k!/(k-1)!1!$ two-factor interactions, $k!/(k-2)!2!$ three-factor interactions,...., and one k-factor interactions.
- The i-th effect estimate is given by $E_i = (2/n)[\pm Y_1 \pm Y_2 \pm ... \pm Y_n]$, where $n = 2^k$ and $i = 1, 2, ..., 2^k-1$.

DETERMINATION OF DISPERSION EFFECTS

In addition to location effects (effects on the process average), changes in certain variables may give rise to changes in the amount of process/product performance variation. These

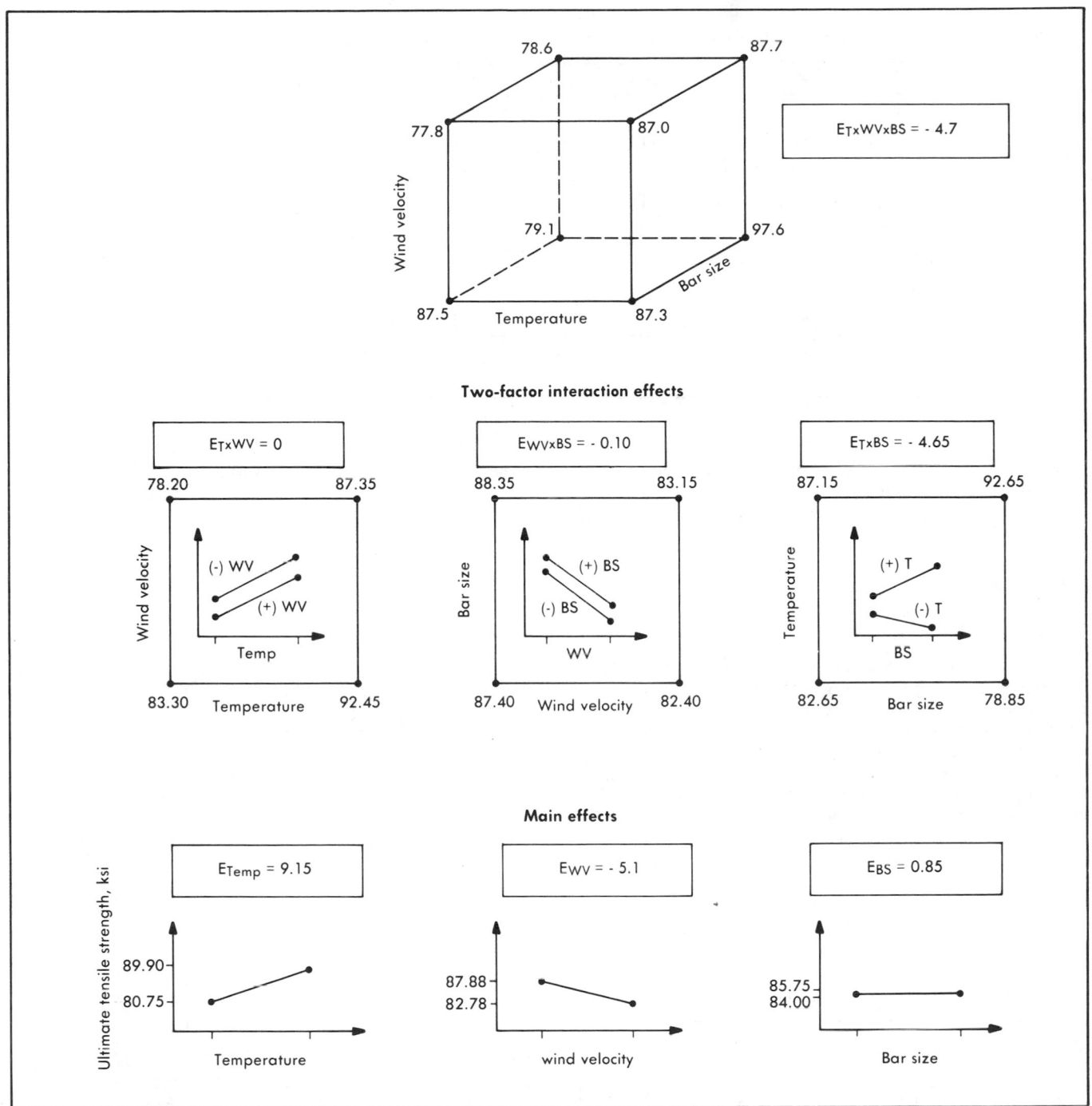

Fig. 11-30 Summary diagrams of variable effects.

changes are referred to as dispersion effects (see Fig. 11-31).[13] In Fig. 11-31, it is seen that increases in X_1 cause an increase in the average performance (a location effect), while increases in X_2 cause an increase in the variation in performance (a dispersion effect).

The graphical representation of the results of a 2^3 factorial experiment are shown in Fig. 11-32. An estimate of the main effect of variable X_1 on location is obtained by calculating the average responses on planes I and II and then taking the difference ($E_1 = Y_{II} - Y_I$). However, the calculation of effects of variable X_1 on dispersion requires some thought because a significant portion of the variation in the data on plane I and in the data on plane II may be attributed to the presence of a location effect due to X_2 and/or X_3. Therefore, important location effects must be removed (filtered out) from the data before the dispersion effects are calculated. One way to accom-

TWO-LEVEL FACTORIALS

TABLE 11-8
Matrix Used for Algebraic Estimation of Variable Effects

Test	X_1	X_2	X_3	X_1X_2	X_1X_3	X_2X_3	$X_1X_2X_3$	Y
1	-1	-1	-1	+1	+1	+1	-1	Y_1
2	+1	-1	-1	-1	-1	+1	+1	Y_2
3	-1	+1	-1	-1	+1	-1	+1	Y_3
4	+1	+1	-1	+1	-1	-1	-1	Y_4
5	-1	-1	+1	+1	-1	-1	-1	Y_5
6	+1	-1	+1	-1	+1	-1	-1	Y_6
7	-1	+1	+1	-1	-1	+1	-1	Y_7
8	+1	+1	+1	+1	+1	+1	+1	Y_8
Divisor	4	4	4	4	4	4	4	
Effect	E_1	E_2	E_3	E_{12}	E_{13}	E_{23}	E_{123}	

plish this is through the mathematical model, which can be expressed in general form as:

$$Y = \hat{Y} + \epsilon \tag{28}$$

where:

Y = data
$\hat{Y}$ = model prediction
ϵ = residual error

The model prediction, $\hat{Y}$, is an expression of all relevant location effects including the average ($\overline{Y}$), and is also the expected result in the long term (a prediction of the average response). Therefore, the residual errors ($\epsilon = Y - \hat{Y}$) constitute the data after the location effects have been removed from consideration. Any important dispersion effects, however, remain within the data.

Using the data given in Fig. 11-32, the main and interaction effects on location were determined. It was found that only E_1, E_3, and E_{23} are significant location effects. To prevent the location effects from being aliased with the dispersion effects, it is necessary to determine the model residuals based on the mathematical model. The model residuals are as follows:

$$Y - \hat{Y} = Y - (14.5 + 3.75\,X_1 + 1.0\,X_3 + 1.25\,X_2X_3)$$

The model residuals associated with the geometric representation of the 2^3 factorial design under consideration are shown in Fig. 11-33.

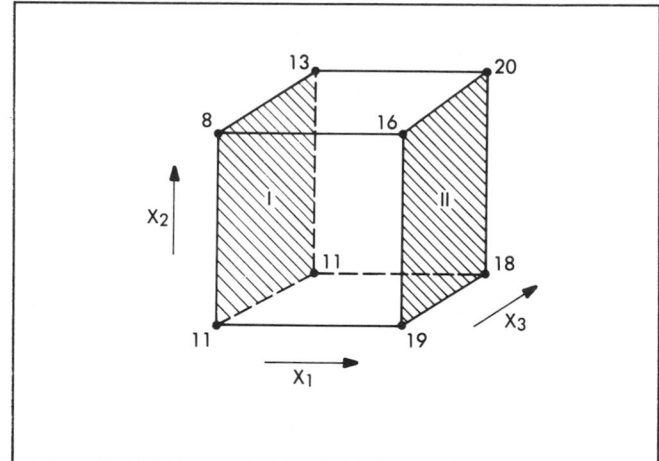

Fig. 11-32 Calculation of average response on plane I and plane II.

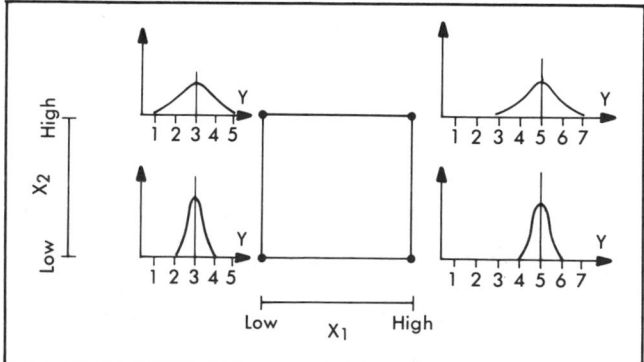

Fig. 11-31 Change in performance variations.

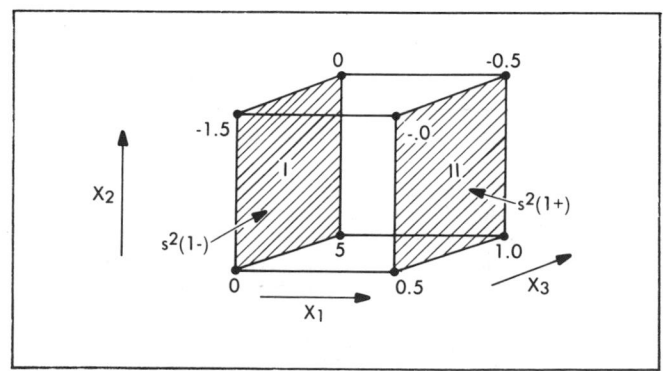

Fig. 11-33 Model residuals.

TWO-LEVEL FRACTIONAL FACTORIAL DESIGNS

Although the class of two-level factorial designs appears to be an efficient way to deal simultaneously with several factors, this efficiency seems to disappear as the number of variables to be studied grows. Because the two-level factorial requires the consideration of all possible combinations of k variables at two levels each, a 10-variable experiment would require $2^{10} = 1024$ tests. Such a test plan is obviously prohibitive in size. Furthermore, although the volume of information from the experiment may on the surface seem impressive, the practical significance of the majority of this information is in question.

CONSEQUENCES OF FRACTIONATION

In the rail steel bar problem discussed in the section on two-level factorial design experiments, three variables were studied to determine their possible effect on the ultimate tensile strength of the welded bars. A 2^3 full factorial design was performed, and the three main effects, the three two-factor interaction effects, and the one three-factor interaction effect were all separately estimated.

Suppose now that the investigator had wished to consider the effects of the type of welding flux (a fourth variable), but the full factorial ($2^4 = 16$ tests) could not be considered; rather only eight tests could be performed.

Based on the assumption about the negligible importance of third and higher order interaction effects, the column of plus and minus signs associated with the 123 interaction in the calculation matrix could be assigned to the fourth variable. This should be acceptable because it is believed that the 123 interaction is very small in magnitude; therefore, this column can be used to define the levels of variable 4 for the eight separate tests. The main effect of variable 4 can therefore be estimated using this column.

In using the 123 column to introduce a fourth variable to the experiment, the new design matrix, which defines the eight tests to be conducted, is shown in Table 11-9. Expanding the design matrix in Table 2-18, the calculation matrix for all possible products of columns 1 through 4 can be obtained (see Table 11-10).

Examination of this calculation matrix reveals, however, that many of the columns are identical. The pairs of variable effects represented in the calculation matrix by the same column of plus and minus signs are:

1 and 234	12 and 34
2 and 134	13 and 24
3 and 124	23 and 14
4 and 123	Avg. and 1234

The effects represented by the columns that have the same plus and minus signs are said to be confounded or confused; they are "aliases" of a unique column of plus and minus signs. That is, one cannot definitively assign the column estimate to one specific main effect or interaction. The tradeoff for the reduced number of tests performed in a fractional factorial experiment over the full factorial is called confounding. To minimize the practical effect of confounding, a good experimental design confounds main effects with higher-order interactions, which may be assumed to be of lesser importance and can be subsequently neglected.

TABLE 11-9
Design Matrix for a Two-Level Fractional Factorial Design

Test	1	2	3	123 4
1	-	-	-	-
2	+	-	-	+
3	-	+	-	+
4	+	+	-	-
5	-	-	+	+
6	+	-	+	-
7	-	+	+	-
8	+	+	+	+

DESIGN GENERATORS AND DEFINING RELATIONSHIP

In any two-level fractional factorial experiment involving n unique test conditions, there will exist only $n-1$ unique columns of plus and minus signs available for the independent estimation of effects. Therefore, if $n-1$ is less than 2^k-1, some degree of confounding among the effects will be present. For example, if five variables are studied in a two-level experiment with only eight tests, then each of the seven independent columns in the calculation matrix is simultaneously representing several effects. If five variables are to be studied in eight tests, which normally would accommodate only three variables as a full factorial, two additional variables need to be assigned to any two of the interaction columns 12, 13, 23, and 123 in the 2^3 calculation matrix. To illustrate this, suppose variables 4 and 5 are assigned to the 12 and 13 columns, respectively (see Table 11-11).

In the matrix of plus (+) and minus (-) signs, the first five columns (excluding I) represent the eight unique test conditions for the five variables. These five columns constitute the design matrix for the 2^{5-2} fractional factorial design. All seven $n-1$ columns, plus a column of all plus signs (column I) constitute the complete calculation matrix for this 2^{5-2} design. This means that all main and interaction effects among the five variables will be contained within these eight linear combinations of the data. The question that remains is to precisely determine which effects are confounded with each other.

Design Generators

Whenever a column heading is referred to as 1, 23, or 123, a column of plus (+) and minus (-) signs should be imagined directly under it. Now, if any column of plus (+) and minus (-) signs is multiplied by itself, a column of all plus signs is produced. This column is referred to as the identity column and has the heading I.

The 2^{5-2} design was generated by setting column 4 equal to column 12 (4 = 12) and column 5 equal to 13 (5 = 13). Given the definition of I, if both sides of the two equations are multiplied by 4 and 5, respectively, the result is:

TWO-LEVEL FRACTIONAL FACTORIALS

TABLE 11-10
Confounding in a Calculation Matrix When Studying Five Variables with Eight Tests

Test	1	2	3	4	12	13	14	23	24	34	123	124	134	234	1234
1	-	-	-	-	+	+	+	+	+	+	-	-	-	-	+
2	+	-	-	+	-	-	+	+	-	-	+	-	-	+	+
3	-	+	-	+	-	+	-	-	+	-	+	-	+	-	+
4	+	+	-	-	+	-	-	-	-	+	-	-	+	+	+
5	-	-	+	+	+	-	-	-	-	+	+	+	-	-	+
6	+	-	+	-	-	+	-	-	+	-	-	+	-	+	+
7	-	+	+	-	-	-	+	+	-	-	-	+	+	-	+
8	+	+	+	+	+	+	+	+	+	+	+	+	+	+	+

$$4 \times 4 = 12 \times 4$$
$$5 \times 5 = 13 \times 5$$

which reduces to $I = \underline{124}$ and $I = \underline{135}$. These two identities are referred to as *design generators*.

Defining Relationship

As was just mentioned, columns $\underline{124}$ and $\underline{135}$ are equal to I. Because of this identity, the product of columns $\underline{123}$ and $\underline{135}$ would also be equal to I. The identity (in the current example, $I = \underline{124} = \underline{135} = \underline{2345}$), which is comprised of the design generators and their products in all possible combinations, is referred to as the *defining relationship*. The defining relationship reveals the complete confounding structure of any two-level fractional factorial design.

Confounding Pattern

For the current example the calculation matrix has seven independent columns of plus and minus signs and one identity column. By letting column $\underline{4}$ equal to $\underline{12}$ and $\underline{5}$ equal to $\underline{13}$, much confounding among the variable effects has been created. To find out what are the aliases of the column headings in the example, each column heading is multiplied by every term

TABLE 11-11
Calculation Matrix for a Two-Level Fractional Factorial Design

Test	I*	1	2	3	4 12	5 13	23	123	Y
1	+	-	-	-	+	+	+	-	Y_1
2	+	+	-	-	-	-	+	+	Y_2
3	+	-	+	-	-	+	-	+	Y_3
4	+	+	+	-	+	-	-	-	Y_4
5	+	-	-	+	+	-	-	+	Y_5
6	+	+	-	+	-	+	-	-	Y_6
7	+	-	+	+	-	-	+	-	Y_7
8	+	+	+	+	+	+	+	+	Y_8

*The column denoted I (all plus signs) is used to estimate the mean response ($\overline{Y}$).

(including I) in the defining relation. For example, in column heading 1 (main effect of variable 1) this would be as follows:

$$I(1) = (1)124 = (1)135 = (1)2345$$

Removing all I's $[(1)(1) = I]$ yields:

$$1 = 24 = 35 = 12345$$

This means that the aliases of 1 are $\underline{24}$, $\underline{35}$, and $\underline{12345}$. Therefore, when the 1 column is multiplied by the Y column, summed, and divided by 4, an estimate of the sum (linear combination) of E_1, E_{24}, E_{35}, E_{12345} is obtained. This sum of confounded variable effects is denoted as l_1 (l stands for the linear combination of the effects). A summary of the confounding pattern and linear combinations of aliased effects that can be estimated from this experiment is given in Table 11-12.

The five-variable, eight-test two-level experiment is referred to as a two-level fractional factorial design because it considers only a fraction of the tests defined by the full factorial. In this case, a one-fourth fraction design has been created. It is commonly referred to as a 2^{5-2} fractional factorial design. It is a member of the general class of 2^{k-p} fractional factorial designs. For such designs, k variables are examined in 2^{k-p} tests requiring that p of the variables be introduced into full factorial in $k-p$ variables by assigning them to interaction effects in the first $k-p$ variables.

2^{k-p} fractional factorial designs are very useful in screening large numbers of potentially important factors in an effort to identify those few factors that actually are important. Two-level fractional factorials may also be usefully employed sequen-

TABLE 11-12
Summary of the Confound Pattern, Linear Combinations and Aliased Effects for a 2^{5-2} Fractional Factorial Design

l_i estimates $I + 124 + 135 + 2345$
l_1 estimates $1 + 24 + 35 + 12345$
l_2 estimates $2 + 14 + 1235 + 345$
l_3 estimates $3 + 1234 + 15 + 245$
l_4 estimates $12 + 4 + 235 + 1345$
l_5 estimates $13 + 234 + 5 + 1245$
l_6 estimates $23 + 134 + 125 + 45$
l_7 estimates $123 + 25 + 34 + 145$

tially, by selecting designs from the same family and combining them in a series of two or perhaps three successive experiments.[14] The idea of sequential and iterative experimentation is important from the standpoint of converging to a state of considerable knowledge and understanding about product or process performance in an efficient and reliable manner.

References

1. G. Taguchi and Y. Wu, *Introduction to Off-Line Quality Control* (Japan: Central Japan Quality Control Association, 1979).
2. R. A. Fisher, *The Design of Experiments*, 8th ed. (New York: Hafner Publishing Co., 1966).
3. G.E.P. Box, W. G. Hunter, and J. S. Hunter, *Statistics for Experimenters* (New York: John Wiley and Sons, Inc., 1978).
4. W. A. Shewhart, *The Economical Control of Quality of Manufactured Product* (New York: McGraw-Hill Book Co., 1931).
5. Jacob Frimenko, *Statistical Process Control: Fundamental Concepts*, SME Technical Paper MF84-472 (Dearborn, MI: Society of Manufacturing Engineers, 1984).
6. L. S. Nelson, "The Shewhart Control Chart—Tests for Special Causes," *Journal of Quality Technology*, vol. 16, no. 4 (1984), pp. 237-239.
7. E. L. Grant, *Statistical Quality Control*, 3rd. ed. (New York: McGraw-Hill Book. Co., 1964).
8. P. T. Jessup, "The Value of Continuing Improvement," *Proceedings of IEEE International Communications Conference*, ICC 85, 1985.
9. Box, Hunter, and Hunter, *op. cit.*
10. S. M. Wu, "Analysis of Rail Steel Bar Welds By Two-Level Factorial Design," *Welding Journal Research Supplement* (1964), pp. 179s-183s.
11. Box, Hunter, and Hunter, *op. cit.*
12. C. Daniel, *Applications of Statistics to Industrial Experimentation* (New York: John Wiley and Sons, Inc., 1976).
13. G.E.P. Box and R. D. Meyer, "Studies in Quality Improvement I: Dispersion Effects From Fractional Designs," *Technometrics* (February 1986), pp. 19-28.
14. G.E.P. Box and J.S. Hunter, "The 2^{k-p} Fractional Factorial Designs," Part I and Part II, *Technometrics*, Vol. 3 (1961), pp. 331-351 and 449-458.

INSPECTION EQUIPMENT AND TECHNIQUES

Although the level of quality control is determined in large part by probability theory and statistical calculations, it is very important that the data collection processes on which these procedures depend be appropriate and accurate.

The best statistical procedure is worthless if fed faulty data, and like machine processes, inspection data collection is itself a process with practical limits of accuracy, precision, resolution, and repeatability.

FUNDAMENTAL UNITS AND STANDARDS

Two major systems of units are in use throughout the world today, the English or Imperial system and the metric system. English units are now defined in terms of the metric units, making the latter the primary system of units; in this way, consistency of units is assured. It should be noted that the metric system by virtue of its greater simplicity, is supplanting the English system in many countries, even in England where the system originated.

A second requirement of units is that they be of convenient and practical size. It is cumbersome, for instance, to express all length measurements in miles or even in meters. The English system employs an assortment of units such as the inch, the foot, and so on up to the mile to cover the wide range of length measurement. In the metric system there is one primary unit of each parameter.

Units are defined and embodies in standards. Units are the language of measurement, and standards are the hardware. For example, the meter was originally defined as the distance between two lines on a specific bar maintained at the International Bureau of Weights and Measures in Paris; that bar was the standard for the meter.

One of the primary requirements of a basic standard is that it be unchangeable. To satisfy this condition, the standard must be indestructible (or if destroyed it should be capable of exact reproduction) and it must be stable. It was this consideration of immutability that led to the adoption of the new basic standard of length, the wavelength of a certain radiation of light. The radiation is produced by a krypton lamp; the wavelength of light produced by the lamp is an atomic constant and thus never changes.

A second requirement for a basic standard is that it be reproducible and not singular, as is the case of the meter bar or the kilogram. Any laboratory with adequate facilities can maintain a krypton lamp, and many do. No longer are they dependent on the meter bar at Paris to define their unit of length.

Yet another requirement of standards is that of practicality. This requirement is particularly dominant in working standards used throughout industry. The popularity of gage blocks as standards of length is in no small measure due to their simplicity and practicality. It is also important that standards be as insensitive as possible to outside influences such as temperature ture and pressure. This requirement is particularly difficult to satisfy and has led to the adoption of standard measuring conditions.

CALIBRATION

The process of comparing one standard or measuring device against a higher-order standard of greater accuracy is know as calibration. Through the process of calibration, all measurements are related back to the primary standard. In other words, traceability is maintained to ensure that all measurements are consistent. The requirements for traceability go hand in hand with requirements for interchangeability, a feature of modern-day production.

CHARACTERISTICS OF A MEASUREMENT

In making a measurement, one of the first considerations is the resolution of the measuring instrument. Resolution refers to the minimum change in value that the instrument can reliably indicate. For instance, many dial gages are graduated in 0.001" (0.01 mm) divisions, but can be read to 0.0005" (0.005 mm). If it is necessary to measure a dimension to only 0.005" (0.15 mm), there is no advantage in using an instrument with a resolution to 0.0005" (0.015 mm); in fact it is likely to be a disadvantage.

There is considerable confusion between the terms *repeatability* and *accuracy* as they relate to measurement. Often, too, repeatability and *resolution* are equated.

Accuracy means closeness to truth. In discussing the accuracy of a micrometer or an electronic gage, reference is to the degree to which it can measure the true size of a part.

The first requirement of any measuring system is that it have adequate repeatability. For instance, if widely varying results are obtained with each measure of the length of a gage block, these results are meaningless, and the measuring system is ineffective.

The difference between repeatability and accuracy is illustrated by the target analogy in Fig. 12-1, which shows that a group of measurements can be repeatable (precise) but not necessarily accurate, and vice versa. In this analogy, which compares the 10-shot groups of five marksmen, accuracy is

---

FUNDAMENTAL UNITS AND STANDARDS

judged by closeness to the "bull's-eye," which represents true value. The shooting of marksman A is neither accurate nor precise. Marksman B is precise (his shots are close together) but inaccurate. Marksman C is no more precise than A, but has greater accuracy. Marksmen D and E are equally precise, but E is more accurate.[1]

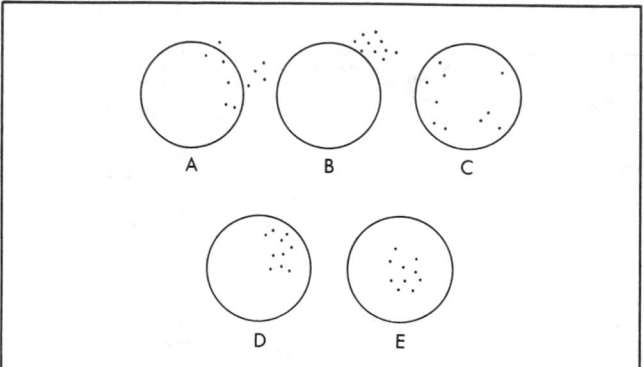

Fig. 12-1 Target analogy: precision and accuracy compared.

Various sources of error can affect the accuracy of a measurement, and various influences can affect the repeatability. There are two types of errors: fixed or systematic errors and random errors. Fixed errors, as the name implies, do not vary between one measurement and the next; they remain constant during a set of measurements. One example might be a zero error on an electronic meter. Another error of this type would be the error in a master block used for calibrating another gage block. The difference of a few degrees in the mean temperature of the two blocks during the course of the measurements is another fixed error that could affect results. Fixed errors affect the accuracy of a measurement, so every effort should be made to isolate and quantify these errors. Once their magnitudes are known, the results can be corrected to allow for them.

Random errors, on the other hand, result from changing conditions during a set of measurements. The conditions under which a measurement is made, such as temperature and gaging force, should be clearly defined, and every effort should be made to maintain these conditions constant or at least reduce fluctuation to an insignificant level.

Two basic types of measurement exist: absolute or direct measurement and comparative measurement. Although all measurements are comparative in nature, the term is normally reserved for situations where like or essentially like items are compared. The comparison of two 3″ (75 mm) gage blocks is a good example of comparative measurement. If the length of a gage block is measured with a micrometer, or in terms of the wavelength of light, the measurement is classified as direct. Comparative measurements have the advantage of being considerably more accurate than direct measurements. The relative size of two similar gage blocks is known with much greater accuracy than the absolute size of either. The principal reason for this is that in comparative measurement many systematic errors are eliminated.

MEASURING CONDITIONS

All measurements should be made under standard conditions. If the measurements are not made under standard conditions, results must be referenced to standard conditions by correcting for any deviations. Because all materials have different coefficients of expansion, it is not sufficient to simply say that a shaft is so many inches (millimeters) in diameter. It is necessary to know at what temperature it has that value.

It is internationally agreed that all dimensional measurements should be referenced to 68° F or 20° C. The temperature in most metrology laboratories is controlled to a nominal value of 68° F (20° C). A temperature-controlled environment eliminates the worry of temperature drifts and ensures that the test pieces and the standards are at the same temperature. In this regard, it should be mentioned that it is essential to allow sufficient time for this equilibrium state to be achieved.

Another environmental condition to be concerned with is humidity. High humidity causes rusting, and variations in humidity can cause condensation and evaporation, which affect the temperature of a part.

The wavelength of light varies with barometric pressure because of changes in the index of refraction of air. Consequently, when making measurements in terms of the wavelength of light, it is necessary to measure the barometric pressure and correct for any deviations from 760 mm of mercury, which is the international standard for barometric pressure.

Prior to measurement, part cleanliness must be ensured. Another requirement often overlooked is that of compatible geometry. It is not meaningful to report the diameter of a hole to 0.0001″ (0.0025 mm) if the hole is out of round by 0.0003″ (0.008 mm). Neither is it meaningful to measure the length of a gage block to 5 μin. (130 μm) if the two faces are out of parallel by 10 μin. (250 μm) or if either face is not flat within 5 μin. (130 μm).

All materials deform when subjected to a load. The initial deformation is elastic, and its extent is determined by the Young's modulus of the material, the geometry of the contact, and the magnitude of the load.

GENERAL-PURPOSE MEASURING DEVICES

Long the mainstay of the inspector, general-purpose measuring devices are still used in toolrooms, receiving inspection areas, and calibration labs for taking many precision measurements. They are often used in conjunction with a surface plate and are capable of measurements with accuracies of 0.001″ (0.02 mm). Instruments with high resolution permit measurements of 0.0001″ (0.002 mm) to be determined. General-purpose measuring devices are usually fabricated of hardened tool steel and are subject to error because of mishandling and the introduction of dirt or cutting chips. It is therefore necessary to calibrate these devices periodically to ensure their integrity.

NONGRADUATED TOOLS OR INSTRUMENTS

As their name implies, nongraduated measuring tools do not have linear or angular graduations incorporated in the tool.

GENERAL PURPOSE MEASURING DEVICES

These tools are generally used when comparing measurements, and their size must be verified by a graduated measuring device.

Calipers and Dividers

Various types of calipers and dividers are available for contact measurement. They are particularly useful for measuring distances between or over surfaces or for comparing dimensions or sizes with standards such as steel rules.

Calipers. Calipers consist of two movable metal legs with formed contacts at one end. The legs are joined by a strong spring hinge and linked together by a screw and adjusting nut. When the contacts are pointed out, the caliper is designed for taking inside measurements and is referred to as an inside caliper. When the contacts are facing in, the caliper is designed for taking outside measurements and is referred to as an outside caliper.

A variation of the standard caliper is the hermaphrodite caliper. This type of caliper has one straight leg ending in a sharp point and one bow leg. Hermaphrodite calipers are used in layout work for scribing parallel lines from an edge or for locating the center of cylindrical work.

Dividers. Dividers are somewhat similar to calipers, but both of the legs are straight and have sharply pointed contacts. They are used for measuring distances between lines or points, transferring lengths taken from a steel rule, and for scribing circles or arcs. Dividers are restricted in range by the opening span of the legs. They become less effective for scribing and similar uses when the points are sharply inclined to the surface on which the scribing is performed.

Telescope Gages

The telescope gage is a T-shaped tool in which the shaft of the tee acts as a handle. The cross arms have hardened spherical forms on the ends to serve as contact elements. The cross arms telescope into each other and are held out by a light spring.

During use, the cross arms are compressed, placed in the hole, and then allowed to expand. A locknut on the top of the handle is turned to lock the cross arms, and then the gage is withdrawn from the hole. The distance across the arms is measured with a micrometer.

When the measurement of holes smaller than 5/16″ (8 mm) is required, small-hole gages can be used. Small-hole gages consist of a small, split, ball-shaped member mounted on the end of a handle. The ball is expanded by turning a knob on the handle until the proper feel is obtained. Once the gage is withdrawn from the hole or recess, the size is measured with a micrometer.

Straightedges and Squares

Straightedges are flat lengths of tool steel or granite finished to extremely fine tolerances. They are used for scribing straight lines and to check surfaces for straightness.

The steel square is one of the most accurate hand tools available for right-angle measurement. It consists of a base into which a blade is set; the blade may be beveled or nonbeveled. Precision squares are so accurate that when they are placed against a master square on a surface plate, they will shut out a vertical source of light.

Surface Plates

A surface plate is a flat plane that is used as a reference surface from which final dimensions are taken. They should be inspected periodically with an autocollimator to ensure flatness. When an overall unilateral flatness of 0.00005″ (0.0013 mm) or finer is required, toolmakers' flats or optical flats are used as a reference surface.

Sine Bars and Plates

The sine bar is a hardened, stabilized, precision ground and lapped tool for accurate angle setting or measuring. It consists of a bar to which two cylinders are attached. When the cylinders are brought in contact with a flat surface, the top of the bar is parallel to that surface.

Sine bars are used in conjunction with gage blocks and a surface plate. The operation of the sine bar is based on known trigonometric relationships between the sides and angles of a right-angled triangle.

Sine blocks and plates are similar in design to sine bars. The primary difference is the width of the instrument and whether it has an attached base or not. Sine blocks are generally wider than 1″ (25 mm) and have tapped holes in the bar for attaching parts as well as a stop to keep the parts from sliding off.

GRADUATED TOOLS OR INSTRUMENTS

Graduated measuring tools have either linear or angular graduations incorporated into the measuring system of the tool. These tools are applied directly to the part being measured, and the dimension is read by the user.

Rules

The rule is a basic measuring tool from which many other tools have been developed. Because rules are so frequently used on a variety of work, a wide selection exists to suit the needs of the precision worker. They range in size from as small as 1/4″ (6 mm) in length for measuring in grooves, recesses, and keyways to as large as 12′ (3.5 m) in length for large work.

Calipers

Slide calipers. Slide calipers are a refinement of the steel rule and are capable of more accurate measurements. With these tools, a head or pair of jaws is added to the rule; one jaw is fixed at the end and the other movable along the scale. Provision is made for clamping the movable jaw to lock the setting. The slide is graduated to read inside or outside measurements.

Vernier calipers. A typical vernier caliper consists of a stationary bar and a movable vernier slide assembly. The stationary rule is a graduated bar with a fixed measuring jaw.

The vernier slide assembly combines a movable jaw, vernier plate, clamp screws, and adjusting nut. It moves as a unit along the graduations of the bar to bring both jaws in contact with the workpiece.

Caliper height gages. Like the vernier caliper, the caliper height gage consists of a stationary bar or beam and a movable slide. The graduated, hardened and ground beam is combined with a hardened, ground and lapped base. The vernier slide assembly can be raised or lowered to any position along the bar.

Vernier depth gage. The vernier depth gage differs slightly from the vernier caliper and the caliper height gage in that the vernier slide assembly remains fixed while the steel rule is moved to obtain the desired measurements. The vernier slide also forms the base that is held on the work by one hand while the blade is operated with the other.

CHAPTER 12

GENERAL PURPOSE MEASURING DEVICES

Gear tooth vernier caliper. The gear tooth vernier caliper measures chordal thickness or thickness at the datum circle of a gear tooth to an accuracy of 0.001″ or 0.01 mm, depending on the units. It can also measure hobs and form and thread tools. Its construction combines in one tool the function of both the vernier depth gage and vernier caliper.

Dial calipers. Similar to vernier calipers, dial calipers have a stationary bar and a movable slide assembly.

Digital calipers. Because gaging is a vital part of SPC, a new generation of electronic instruments has been produced. These instruments incorporate liquid crystal displays (LCD) and are capable of interfacing with a data collection device. Both inch and metric units are incorporated in one tool. The electronic feature is available on calipers, height gages, and depth gages.

Micrometers

A variety of micrometers exist for different applications. The three major types of micrometers are outside, inside, and depth. All micrometers operate based on the principle that an accurately made screw will advance a specified distance with each complete turn. Micrometers graduated in the inch system advance 0.025″ for each turn; those graduated in the metric system advance 0.5 mm for each turn.

Micrometers have both a linear and circumferential scale. The linear scale measures the axial advance of the spindle. It is generally graduated in increments identical to the pitch of the micrometer screw. The circumferential scale indicates the amount of partial rotation that has occurred since the last complete revolution.

Outside micrometers. An outside micrometer consists of a C-shaped frame with an anvil and a threaded spindle. The thread is precision ground to ensure uniform movement of the spindle toward or away from the anvil. The spindle moves as it is rotated in the stationary spindle nut. A graduated stationary sleeve and a graduated rotating thimble are the bases for determining measurement. A locking mechanism can be provided for holding an established reading. A friction thimble or ratchet stop is also available to establish a uniform feel among individual users.

In addition to the standard outside micrometers, micrometers also exist with different anvil and spindle shapes for specialized applications. Blade micrometers are used for measuring narrow slots and grooves. The disc micrometer is used for measuring thin materials such as paper as well as for measuring the distance from a slot to an edge. Hub micrometers can be put through a hole or bore to permit the measurement of the hub thickness of a gear or sprocket. Screw thread micrometers measure the pitch diameter of screw threads.

Inside micrometers. An inside micrometer consists of a micrometer head with one permanent contact. The other contact consists of accurate rods in various increments that are seated snugly in the opposite end of the head against a shoulder and securely locked in place. Inside micrometers are available with solid or tubular rods. Handles can be attached to the micrometer head for measuring into deep holes.

Another type of internal micrometer consists of a specially designed micrometer head and three self-aligning measuring points on the other end. The self-aligning property of this instrument is particularly useful when measuring deep bores.

Depth gages. Depth gages consist of a hardened, ground and lapped base with a micrometer head. Measuring rods are inserted through a hole in the micrometer screw and brought to a positive seat by a knurled nut.

Bench micrometer. The bench micrometer is a precision instrument ideal for bench use either in the shop or inspection laboratory. It can be used as a comparator measuring to 50 μin. (1 μm) or for direct measuring to 0.0001″ (0.001 mm). It can also be adapted for electronic readout.

Protractors

Protractors are used to directly measure angular surfaces. The tools most commonly used are the simple protractor, the protractor head, and the universal bevel protractor.

Simple protractor. A simple protractor consists of a rectangular head graduated in degrees along a semicircle with a blade pivoted on the center pin. By rotating the blade on the center pin, any angle from 0 to 180° can be set.

Protractor head. The protractor head is one of several tools on the combination square. It has revolving turrets with direct-reading double graduations a full 0-180° in opposite directions. This permits direct reading of angles above or below the blade.

Universal bevel protractor. The universal bevel protractor consists of a round body with a fixed blade on which a graduated protractor dial rotates. The turret is slotted to accommodate a 7 or 12″ (180 or 300 mm) nongraduated blade. The blade and dial may be rotated as a unit to any desired position and locked in place by means of the dial clamp nut. The blade may also be independently extended in either direction from the protractor dial.

COMPARATIVE INSTRUMENTS

Comparative instruments compare the workpiece being measured against a master that was used to calibrate the instrument. Because these instruments are compared against a master, they are generally only capable of measuring the amount of deviation as well as the direction of deviation from the calibrated size. The range of the deviation that can be measured depends on the type of comparative gage used. The three most commonly used comparative or indicating gages are mechanical, pneumatic, and electronic.

Mechanical Indicating Gages

Mechanical indicating gages mechanically amplify or magnify variations or displacements in dimensions for the purpose of making precise observations. This magnification may be accomplished by gear trains, levers, cams, torsion strips, reeds, or a combination of these.

Indicator types. Indicators are mechanical instruments for sensing and measuring distance variations. The mechanism of the indicator converts the axial displacement of the measurement spindle into rotational movement. This rotational movement is mechanically amplified and then displayed by a pointer rotating over the face of a circular dial with evenly spaced graduations. Some indicators have hands that can be moved around the face to indicate the permissible tolerance being measured.

Dial indicators. The magnification of a dial-type indicator is obtained by means of a gear train. This type of indicator is most commonly used because its magnification accuracy meets the large majority of requirements. A typical dial indicator is shown in Fig. 12-2.

In operation, a sensitive contact or point is attached to a rack that transfers the motion to the rack gear. A train of three to five gears, depending on the magnification desired, magnifies and transmits the movement of the contact to the pinion gear on which the indicator hand is mounted with a hairspring and takeup gear to eliminate backlash.

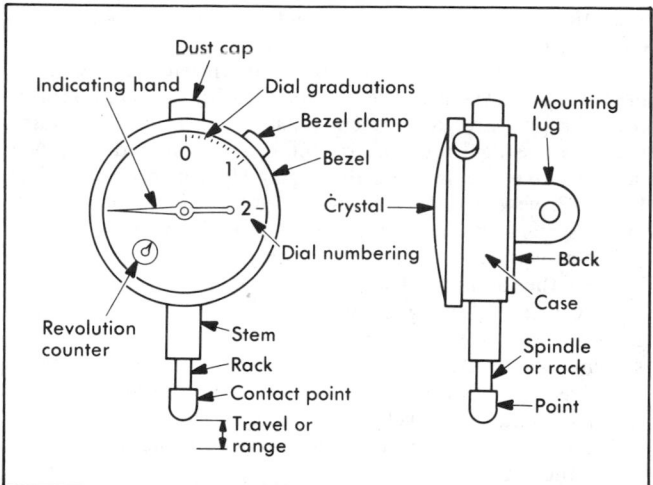

Fig. 12-2 Nomenclature used in describing dial indicator components.

Test indicators. Test indicators sense and measure displacements that occur in a direction perpendicular to the shaft of the contact point (see Fig. 12-3). Magnification is obtained by gears and levers. Because they are small, test indicators are particularly useful in setup inspection and toolroom work.

Reed-type indicators. In this type of indicator, the reed magnifying mechanism uses various combinations of flat steel reeds to obtain mechanical amplification (see Fig. 12-4). The sensitive spindle is mounted on a block that floats on reeds connected to a fixed block that is attached to the mounting. Extending from the top of the two blocks is a vertical member consisting of a pair of reeds, one of which is attached to each of the fixed and the floating blocks; a hand or pointer is mounted on this member. Slight motion of the sensitive contact flexes the reeds and moves the hand along a vertical arc.

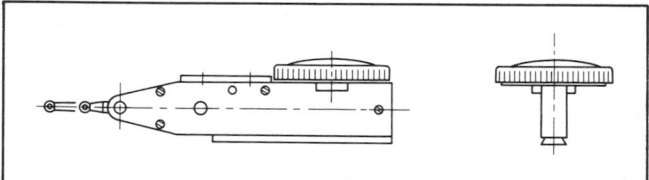

Fig. 12-3 Typical test indicator.

Applications. Dial indicators are designed for use on a wide range of standard measuring devices such as bench comparators, indicator plug gages, depth-indicating gages, indicator snap gages, bore indicator gages, and thread-indicating gages.

Pneumatic Indicating Gages

Pneumatic or air gaging uses the restriction of airflow between a nozzle tip and the part being tested to determine part size. Although a variety of instrument designs and modes of operation exist, a pneumatic gage cannot operate without a regulated air supply, a flow metering device, and at least one or more nozzles.

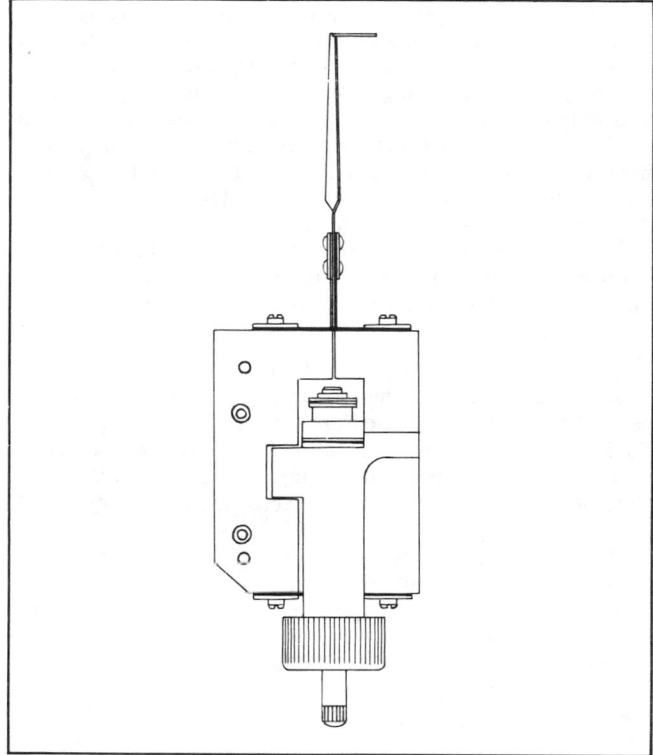

Fig. 12-4 Reed-type dial indicator.

In operation, the air from the regulated supply flows through the restriction and then through the nozzle. When the nozzle is free and open to the atmosphere, there will be a maximum flow of air through the nozzle. In addition, there will be a minimum of pressure in the system downstream of the restriction. If a plate is moved in front on the nozzle and slowly brought toward it, the airflow will gradually be restricted until the nozzle is shut off. At this point, the airflow would be 0. When the nozzle has been completely closed off, the pressure downstream of the restriction will build up until it becomes the same as the regulated supply.

Figure 12-5 shows a plot of both airflow and air pressure versus the distance between the plate and nozzle. With the exception of the extremes of flow and pressure, the curve is virtually a straight line. Because of this linearity, the distance of the plate from the nozzle can be determined.

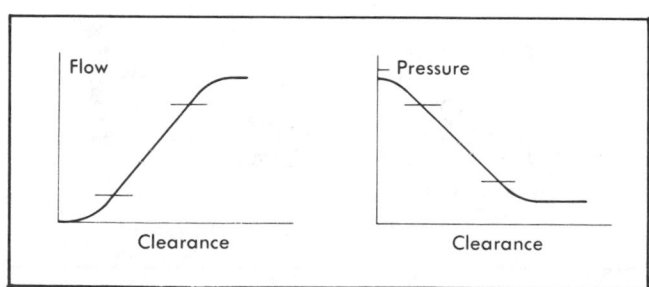

Fig. 12-5 Graph comparing airflow and air pressure with clearance between plate and nozzle. (*Edmunds Gages*)

GENERAL PURPOSE MEASURING DEVICES

Advantages. Air gaging is not the answer to all gaging problems, but it does offer many advantages.[2] In the measurement of hole conditions, air gaging is unsurpassed for speed and accuracy. In addition, air gaging offers sufficient magnification and reliability to measure small tolerances. An air gage can easily determine a size difference of 5 μin. (0.13 μm) and can measure holes as small as 0.040" (1.02 mm). The linear range and resolution of the pneumatic circuit depend on the orifice diameter of the air nozzle and part diameter.

Simplicity is one of the biggest advantages of air gaging. Production workers do not require special training, for using an air gage is as simple as inserting the air probe into a hole and then reading the meter.

Air gage systems. Air gage systems are usually divided and classified according to their operating principles. The two general types of circuits used are freeflow and back pressure. Each type of circuit has individual advantages and areas of performance. Back-pressure gaging is used with an air-to-electronic converter to generate electrical signals for control and analysis.

Flow gage system. The flow gage system is characterized by freedom from restricting orifices and mechanical wearing elements. In principle, air under constant pressure enters the bottom of an internally tapered glass column and flows to the gaging element or tooling (see Fig. 12-6, view *a*). A lightweight float moves up or down in direct ratio to the flow of air between the tooling and the workpiece.

A limitation to this type of system is that the float and tapered glass column tend to get loaded down with the oil in the shop-supplied air. This requires scheduled cleaning of the flow monitoring system.

A modification of the basic flow gage system is shown in Fig. 12-6, view *b*. In operation, air under constant pressure passes through a venturi tube into the gaging element or tooling. Each chamber of the venturi has a pressure tube connected to the opposite sides of a bellows or diaphragm. A difference in pressure existing between the two sections of the venturi tube actuates this bellows, which in turn operates a mechanical amplifier.

Variations of air escaping between the tooling and workpiece effect a change in pressure differential in the venturi.

Back-pressure gage system. Several different types of back-pressure gage systems have been developed. In its basic form, the back-pressure gage system consists of air under constant pressure passing through a controlling orifice of predetermined or adjustable size and into the gaging element or tooling (see Fig. 12-7, view *a*). A suitable pressure-indicating device inserted in the system between the controlling orifice and the tooling indicates changes in pressure resulting from the air escaping between the tooling and workpiece.

The water-column gage system was first developed to determine the size of carburetor jets (see Fig. 12-7, view *b*). This system uses the self-balancing properties of connected vessels, the constant pressure being maintained by the height of the water column. The level of the liquid in the graduated tube indicates the amount of obstruction that is facing the escaping jets in the gage head.

Another modification of the basic back-pressure circuit is the differential air gage system, which employs a parallel circuit as shown in Fig. 12-7, view *c*. In this system, air under constant

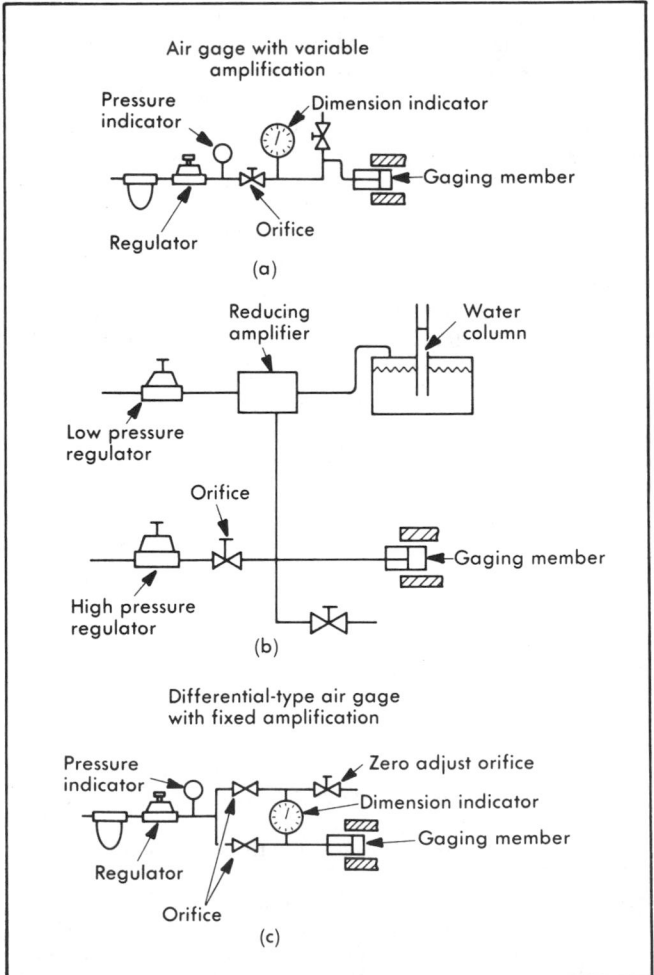

Fig. 12-7 Diagram of basic types of back-pressure gage systems: (a) air gage with variable amplification (b) water-column gage system, and (c) differential-type air gage with fixed amplification. (*Western Gage Corp.*)

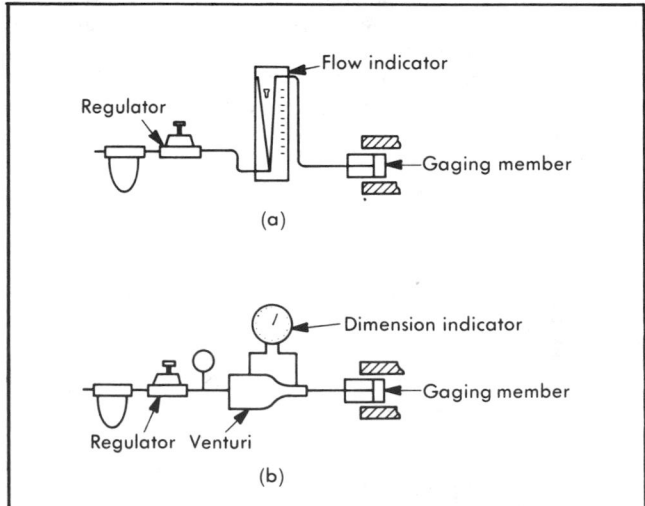

Fig. 12-6 Diagram of basic types of airflow gage systems: (a) airflow gage with rotameter tube and (b) velocity-type air gage with venturi chamber.

GENERAL PURPOSE MEASURING DEVICES

pressure enters two separate channels and passes into opposite sections of a bellows cavity and housing. Air in one of the channels is allowed to escape through the gaging plug. In the other channel, air can escape through the zero setting valve.

Air gage tooling. The tooling used in air gaging is classified as either noncontact or contact.

Noncontact. Noncontact tooling, also referred to as open-jet tooling, uses the direct flow of air from the air escapement orifice to contact the part. The rate of flow depends on the diameter of the nozzle hole and the clearance between the jet and the part.

Dual-jet tooling is used in air probes for internal diameter inspection and in air snap and air ring gages for outside diameter measurements. This type of tooling eliminates the need for precise placement of the workpiece and the use of semiskilled personnel.

Contact. Contact tooling has a mechanical member between the air escapement orifice and the part. This mechanical member can be freely rotating balls, a plunger, or levers. The movement of the mechanical member may be in an axial or a radial direction. Contact-type tooling is generally used for the measurement of rough and porous surfaces or extending the linear measuring range of the air nozzle.

A typical air cartridge is shown in Fig. 12-8. It consists of a plunger that moves in a radial direction and a poppet-type air valve. Any change in the plunger position changes the airflow and the reading on the pneumatic comparator. Because the tapered plunger moves in and out of the air nozzle, the escape area of the air nozzle changes more gradually with the position of the measured surface.

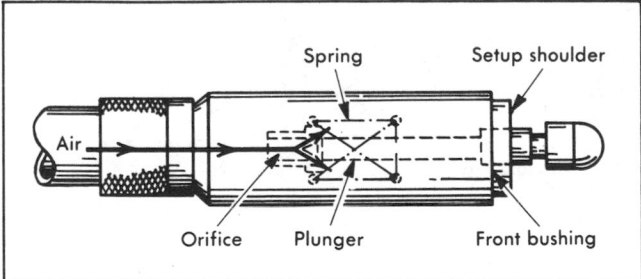

Fig. 12-8 Basic parts of an air cartridge.

Air gage mastering. Because air gages are not direct measuring instruments, the comparator instrument and gaging member must be calibrated with a master of known size. When this calibration is achieved, a certain point on the instrument's scale indicates a particular size. Obtaining accurate data at other points also requires that the correct scale factor be established. That is, the comparator must be adjusted so that the span indicated by the display corresponds identically to a corresponding variation in workpiece size. The two methods used to ensure correct calibration of the gaging system are single master calibration and dual master calibration.

Single master calibration. In single master calibration, both the comparator and the gaging member are manufactured to predetermined pneumatic scale factors. No span adjustments are required or available to the user. Comparators designed for

single master operation utilize fixed orifices for flow restriction or variable restrictors that are factory set and sealed. Precise calibration of these instruments is done at the factory before shipment using master orifice standards.

Dual master calibration. In dual master calibration, the system sensitivity (scale factor) is set by adjusting the span displayed by the comparator instrument to correspond to the difference between minimum and maximum setting masters. This method directly sets the combined sensitivity of all the components of the gaging system. Sensitivities of such items as flow restrictors, amplifiers, pressure indicators, flowmeter tubes, and gaging nozzles as well as restrictive effects of air lines are included in one overall setting. Utilizing the two-master method, stringent control of these individual components is not necessary to obtain highly accurate overall results.

Machine control. Air gaging can be used on external grinders, surface grinders, and centerless grinding machines to locate parts precisely, indicate grinding wheel position if needed, measure wheel wear, and measure and control part size. Figure 12-9 shows an air cartridge mounted to the infeed slide of an external grinder. The cartridge indicates against a fixed adjustable stop attached to the stationary part of the machine. As the part is ground, infeed slide movement is shown by the falling float in the air column. When the float reaches a preset position in the column, the operator knows that the part is at final size.

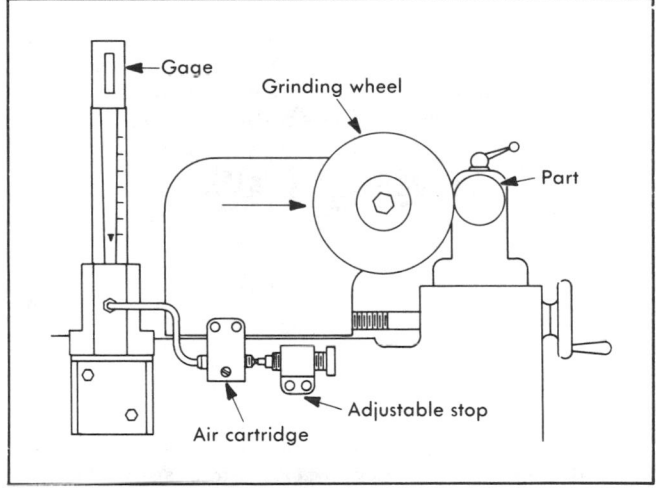

Fig. 12-9 Schematic of air gage machine control. (*Sheffield Measurement Div., Warner & Swasey*)

Electronic Indicating Gages

The three characteristics most responsible for the ever-widening use of electronic gaging equipment are its ability to sense size differences as small as 1 μin. (0.025 μm), its ability to amplify these small measurements as much as 100,000 times, and its ability to generate an electronic signal that can be computer processed. Systems measuring dimensions having very tight tolerances [10 μin. (0.25 μm)] are best put to use in laboratory measuring instruments such as gage block comparators and in comparators and height gages for shop applications. Electronic gages also find their way into automatic sizing and automatic gaging and sorting systems.

CHAPTER 12

GENERAL PURPOSE MEASURING DEVICES

Equipment. As was previously mentioned, the most common types of electronic gaging equipment are the electronic comparator and the height gage. An electronic comparator usually consists of the gaging head(s) (transducer), the stand or support to which the head is attached, the indicator, and the amplifier. The basic difference between the comparator and the height gage is that the comparator has a built-in work support or reference surface. Height gages require a surface plate or some other reference base to support the workpiece and the stand.

Gaging head. Gaging heads transform a displacement of a measuring tip into a proportional electrical signal. They come in a variety of sizes and configurations and are built around different types of transducers.

The three most common head configurations are the lever type, cartridge type, and frictionless type[3] (see Fig. 12-10). The lever-type head, probably the most versatile, features an angularly adjustable, clutch-mounted contact finger. This allows the head to be set at the most convenient gaging angle and protects it against accidental blows. A reversing mechanism allows most of these heads to be used for measuring from above or below

without turning the head upside down. Lever-type heads are most often used in height-gage setups.

The cartridge head is generally used in production gaging fixtures, snap gages, and in jobs involving space and mounting restrictions. Many of them are designed to fit into clamps normally used to hold dial indicators.

The "frictionless" head is the most accurate of these gaging heads and is used mainly in comparator setups. The spindle is suspended from two reeds, assuring virtually frictionless operation.

Applications. Most electronic gages of the comparator type are used in a manner similar to dial indicators. The major difference is that the electronic gage can read much smaller deviations because the signal is digitized.

Because electronic instruments are highly stable, they can be used as absolute measuring devices. Thin parts, up to the maximum range of the instrument, can be measured directly without the use of a master. The accuracy depends on the type of probe and gaging system. For the best accuracy, one master is always required.

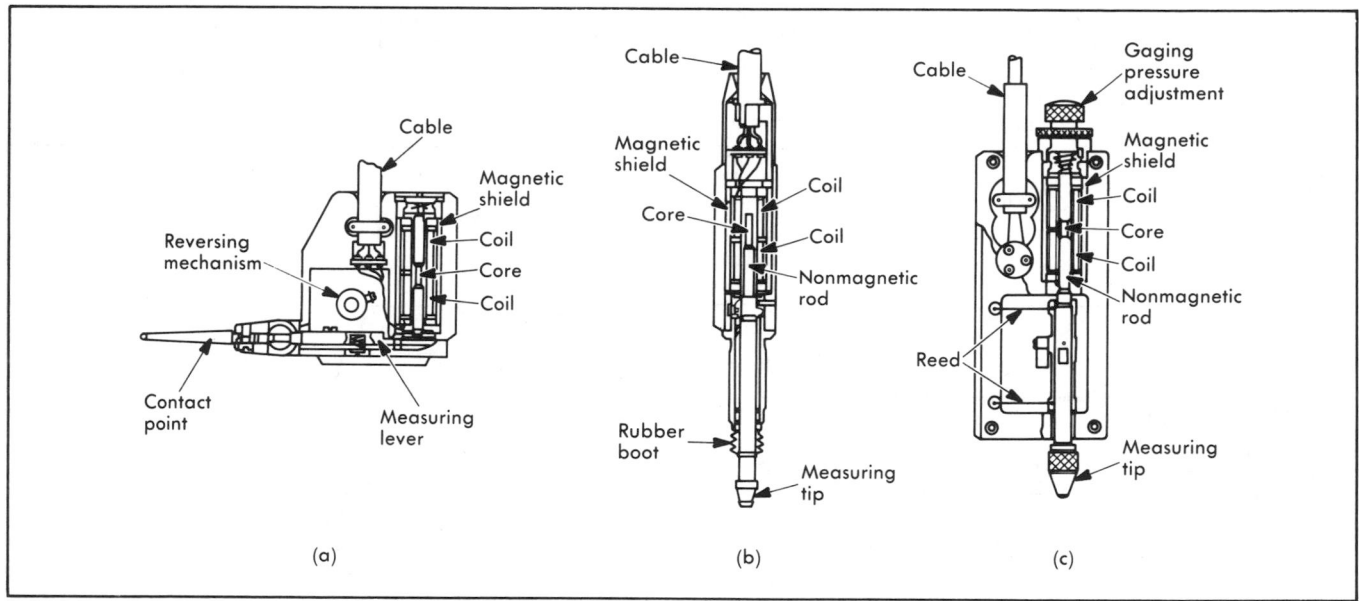

Fig. 12-10 Common gage heads used in electronic gaging: (a) lever-type, (b) cartridge type, and (c) frictionless type.

GAGE BLOCKS

Linear measurement and size agreement of parts, tools, and gages manufactured by various companies in different locations is essential to interchangeability. Gage blocks are the master gages providing the reference standard for comparison in linear measurement. They are made of steel, carbide, or chromium-plated steel that has been stabilized for dimensional stability. The measuring surfaces of these blocks are plane, parallel, and at a specified distance apart. Common shapes for the gaging surfaces of these blocks are rectangular and square; most square blocks have a hole in the center.

USING GAGE BLOCKS

When using gage blocks, it is extremely important that the individual blocks and any associated tooling be free of dirt, grease, and foreign matter. The block faces should, however, have a light film of oil on them. The complete set of blocks should be taken to the location where the inspection will be performed to minimize the potential of scratching or nicking the individual blocks. The blocks selected for a specific application should be removed from the box and placed on clean paper, cloth, or chamois.

Temperature Considerations

The universally accepted standard measuring temperature is 68° F (20° C). Each particular gage block and work material has its own coefficient of expansion. If measured and used at this temperature, these differences are not of consequence. By necessity, however, measurements are often made under uncontrolled temperature. In this case, for accurate results, the coefficient of expansion of both gages and the workpiece must be considered (see Table 12-1).

TABLE 12-1
Expansion of Gage Block Materials

Gage Material	Linear Expansion, μin./in./° F (μm/m/° C)
Tool steel	6.4 (11.5)
Stainless steel (410)	5.5 (9.9)
Tungsten carbide	3.3 (5.9)
Chromium carbide	4.5 (8.1)

Wringing Gage Blocks

When individual gage blocks are combined to provide a specific measurement, they are assembled together using a technique known as "wringing." Wringing is achieved by sliding the mating gaging surfaces on each other until they adhere to such a degree that considerable force must be exerted to break the wring (see Fig. 12-11). A slight pressure is used when sliding the blocks together to prevent any moisture and airborne dust from being trapped between the blocks that could cause scratches and inaccurate measurements.

Blocks are usually wrung in the reverse order of selection, with the largest block on the bottom of the stack. Thin blocks should be wrung to heavier blocks to remove any deflection in the thin block. The wringing operation is repeated until all the necessary blocks needed to form the combination desired are assembled. After completing the combination, the temperature of the blocks should be allowed to stabilize. This can be aided by a cooling plate. This problem can be minimized by the use of forceps, gloves, or other insulating factors, making as little contact as possible. Avoid touching the gaging surfaces, because an overacidic condition can result in etching the steel.

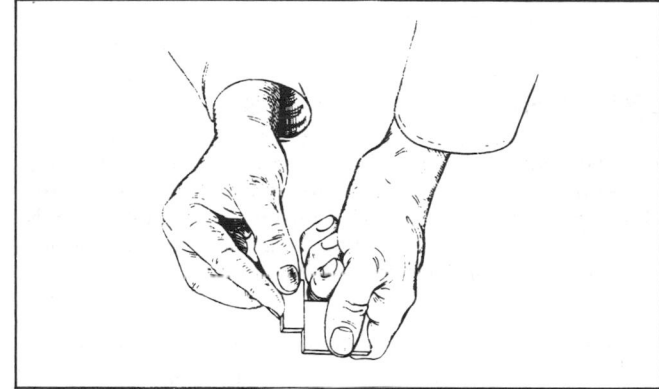

Fig. 12-11 Wringing gage blocks together.

Gage Block Calibration

Because gage blocks are subject to wear, corrosion, and damage, which affect their size or measuring ability, they must be checked periodically to verify their accuracy. The frequency of this check depends on the tolerance requirements of the job, the amount of use, and the conditions under which they are used.

FIXED FUNCTIONAL GAGES

Fixed functional gages are the direct or reverse physical replica of the workpiece dimension being measured.[4] They are usually designed to measure a single dimension. The gage may represent the part in its nominal condition or in one of its limit conditions.

Gages manufactured to the nominal size are referred to as master gages. They are primarily used for setting up comparator-type measuring instruments. Another application of master gages is calibrating measuring tools.

Limit gages check the dimension of the workpiece at one of the specified design limits. For most dimensions checked, two separate gages are required. The GO limit gage checks the part dimension at its maximum material condition and ensures the ability of the part to be assembled. For an inside feature such as a hole, this would be the smallest diameter permissible; for outside features, this would represent the maximum size. If the gage can enter the part feature or the part feature can enter the gage, the dimension is considered acceptable.

To ensure the part's functional adequacy, the minimum material condition must also be checked. This is done with the NOT-GO gage. If the NOT-GO gage enters the part feature, the dimension is considered unacceptable.

CYLINDRICAL PLUG GAGES

A cylindrical plug gage is a hardened and accurately ground steel pin. A typical plug gage consists of a handle and two gage members; one is the GO gage member and the other the NOT-GO (see Fig. 12-12, view *a*). Plug gages larger than 2 ½″ (64 mm) usually only have one gage member attached to the handle. Another style of plug gage combines both gage members into one and is referred to as progressive plug gage (Fig. 12-12, view *b*). The front two thirds of the gage is ground to the GO size, and the remaining portion is ground to the NOT-GO size.

FIXED FUNCTIONAL GAGES

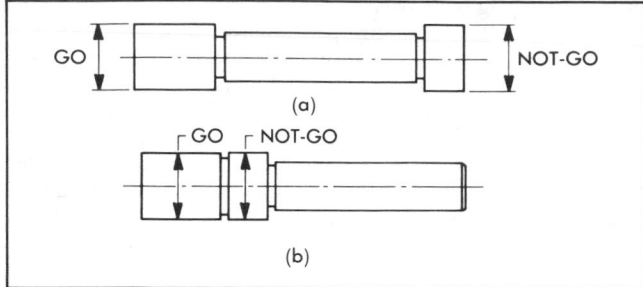

Fig. 12-12 Typical plug gage.

CYLINDRICAL RING GAGES

Cylindrical ring gages are used for checking the limit sizes of a round shaft. They are generally used in pairs—one gage checks the upper limit of the part tolerance (GO gage) while the other checks the lower limit (NOT-GO). The NOT-GO ring is distinguished from the GO ring by a groove in the outside diameter of the gage (see Fig. 12-13).

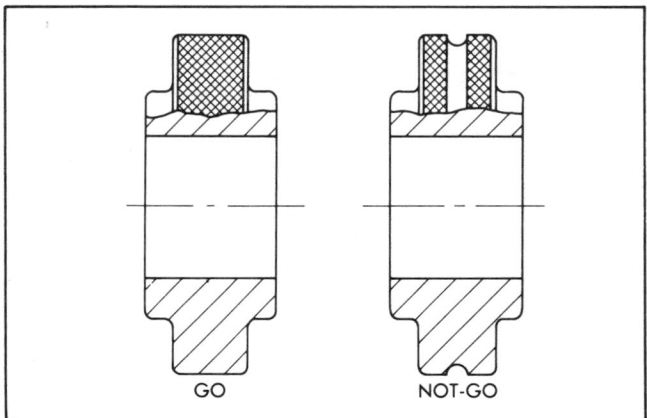

Fig. 12-13 Ring gage set used to inspect the diameter of shafts.

SNAP GAGES

A snap gage is a fixed gage that has the gaging members arranged for measuring diameters, lengths, thicknesses, or widths. An external-measuring snap gage consists of a C-frame with gaging members in the jaw of the frame (see Fig. 12-14). The form of the gaging members may be selected to fit the particular part configuration. These members can usually be adjusted within a specific range to provide two gage sizes corresponding to the dimensions being measured. The outer gaging button, where the workpiece enters the gage, is set at the GO dimension. Snap gages are generally not recommended for inspecting part dimensions if the tolerance is smaller than 0.002″ (0.05 mm).

TAPER GAGES

Taper body forms are commonly used to achieve a precise alignment yet detachable connection between mechanical members. The critical dimensions of machine tapers are the included angle and the diameter at a specific reference level.

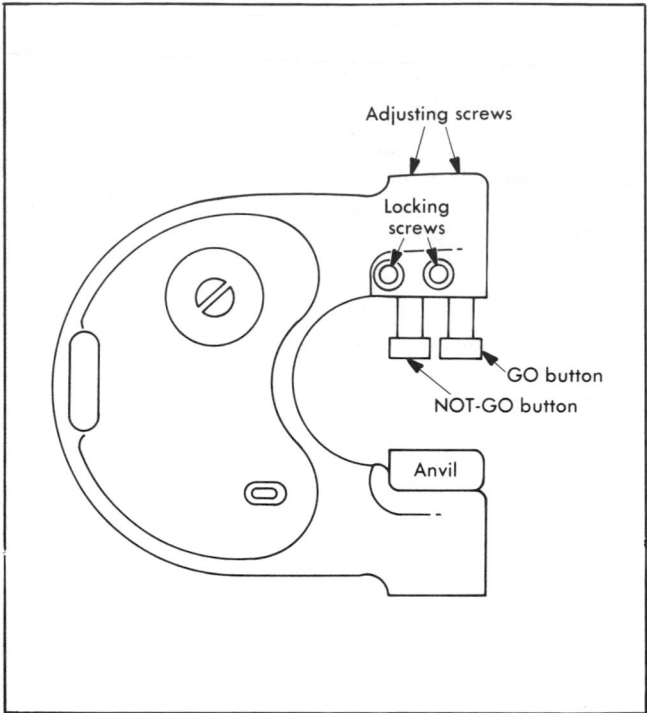

Fig. 12-14 Typical snap gage. (*Southern Gage Co.*)

Taper gages are made for both internal and external tapers in the form of plug and ring gages, respectively. They are also made to inspect machine tapers with or without tangs.

THREAD GAGES

Fixed-limit thread gages are single-purpose gages in that they are made for a specific thread system, form, size, and class. Each designation is stamped or marked on the gage. These gages incorporate the essential functional dimensions of the thread and are used primarily to ensure the ability to assemble the product thread with its mating part.

Thread Plug Gages

Working thread plug gages are similar in design to cylindrical plug gages except that they are threaded. They are designed to check internally threaded products. Thread plug gages are made with either a full thread profile or with their flanks reduced by truncation. The style of the thread profile selected depends on the application.

The types of thread systems for which thread plug gages are available include unified, American National, metric, Whitworth, acme, buttress, and pipe. When thread plug gages are manufactured to W tolerances, they are used as reference or master gages for setting adjustable thread ring gages, thread snap gages, and indicating gages.

VISUAL REFERENCE GAGING

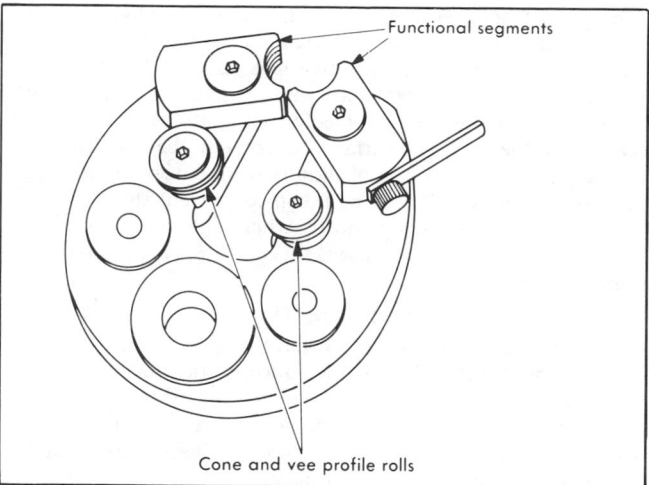

Fig. 12-15 Thread snap gage with functional segments and cone and vee profile rolls. (*The Johnson Gage Co.*)

Thread Ring Gages

Thread ring gages are similar in design to cylindrical ring gages except that the internal surface is threaded. They are available in both solid and adjustable or split designs.

Thread Snap Gages

Thread snap gages have two pair of gaging elements combined in one gage. With proper gaging elements, these gages can check the maximum and minimum material limit of external product screw threads in a single pass. One style of thread snap gage is shown in Fig. 12-15.

SPLINE GAGES

A common way of inspecting splined workpieces prior to assembly is with fixed-limit gages. External splines are checked with internal-toothed rings, whereas internal splines are checked with external-toothed plugs.

VISUAL REFERENCE GAGING

Visual references consist of transparent materials that are dimensionally stable and can be either engraved or marked with reference lines to accurately show feature sizes and/or position; typical materials are glass and plastic. Examples of visual references are optical comparator charts, microscope reticles, and engraved plastic overlay templates. These gages can be made to show a large number of features on the same piece of glass or plastic, and even parts that are oversized for the available visual field can be "stepped" into view using precisely controlled positioning stages or fixtures.

The advantages of visual reference gaging, together with some examples, include the following:

- Many dimensions can be checked simultaneously because they can appear together on the gage. (The inspection of gaskets, stampings, and die-cut parts benefit from this.)
- Complete contours, including irregular or mathematically defined shapes, may be checked for total form instead of probed at specific points. (Cam surfaces and form-ground parts are examples.)
- Unskilled personnel may be used as inspectors, or process operators may quickly and simply verify their own work because the part outline and associated tolerances are usually obvious on the gage. Written instructions can appear on the gage when necessary.
- Gage setup and calibration are facilitated because instructions may be incorporated into the gage, and calibration measurements may be directly verified with an optical comparator or coordinate measuring machine having a video pickup or microscope viewing head.
- Zero gaging pressure is required because contact probes are not used. (The inspection of soft and/or delicate parts such as foamed plastic, small springs, rubber, foil, or paper parts benefits because of this feature.)

OVERLAY TEMPLATES

Overlay templates are transparent plates that are often used in the inspection of flat parts made of paper, rubber, plastic, fabric, and metal as well as other materials. They are also used to check out processes such as the registration of printing on paper and plastic, the legibility and quality of text coming off of computer printout devices, and the size and positioning of test images in photographic processes.

Overlay templates are made of a transparent material onto which is engraved or scribed the min-max profile of the part or feature to be inspected. Incorporated into the overlay may be fixturing devices such as stops, dowel pins, or other machined features to promote precise positioning of the overlay and the part being inspected.

Major advantages of overlay templates, in addition to those for all visual reference gaging, are low cost, ready acceptance by operators and inspectors, and physical toughness, except for those made of glass. The physical toughness characteristic permits overlay templates to be used on the shop floor without extra precautions.

TOOLMAKERS' MICROSCOPES

The toolmakers' microscope consists of a microscope mounted to a base that carries an adjustable stage, a stage transport mechanism, and optionally supplementary lighting for the objects mounted on the stage. Micrometer barrels are often incorporated into the stage transport mechanism to permit precisely controlled movements, and digital readouts of stage positioning are becoming increasingly available. Various objective lenses provide magnifications ranging from 10 to 200X.

Engraved glass reticles, mounted in a reticle holder in the eyepiece of the microscope, can be used to measure parts or to inspect parts on a GO/NOT-GO basis just as overlay templates

VISUAL REFERENCE GAGING

are used. In some microscope setups, other types of reticles can more easily be introduced into the optical path of the microscope by a light-splitting arrangement that lets the reticle be mounted outside the microscope barrel. Here, film or engraved plastic reticles may also be used to check parts.

OPTICAL COMPARATORS AND COMPARATOR CHARTS

An optical comparator (sometimes also called an optical or profile projector) is basically a small parts-measuring microscope, similar in many functions to a toolmakers' microscope, but using a large projection screen instead of eyepieces. It has a stage for mounting parts to be measured and/or inspected, stage transport mechanisms, stage lighting, an optical path that is usually folded by means of mirrors within the machine itself, and a viewing and control area where the operator/inspector works. The image appears on the screen as either an inverted (reversed) or erect image where the part is seen exactly as it is staged. The comparator bounces the image off of one or more mirrors to reverse the inverted image.

There are often two lighting systems in an optical comparator. One permits silhouette viewing of an outside profile of a part. A second surface illuminator permits viewing of the area within the silhouette outline. A schematic sketch of the operation of a direct-lighted optical comparator is seen in Fig. 12-16. The silhouette image is formed on the screen by placing the

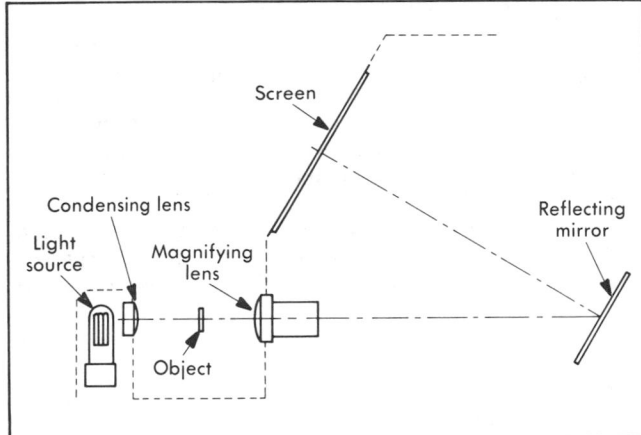

Fig. 12-16 Schematic arrangement of a horizontal shadow lighted optical comparator.

sample part between the light source and the objective lens. Surface illumination requires that light be projected onto the part either through the objective lens using a 1/2 reflecting mirror or from a supplementary oblique lighting system. With sufficient illumination, the objective lens can "see" the surface features of the part. The surface features can then be measured on the screen. Both types of illumination can be used simultaneously, but care should be taken to prevent the part from being subject to high temperatures when high-wattage mercury or xenon illuminators are used; special filters are available to eliminate heat.

Optical Comparator Charts

The comparator chart for inspecting a specific workpiece is a very accurately scribed, magnified outline drawing of the workpiece to be gaged containing all the contours, dimensions, and tolerance limits necessary for the purpose and mounted in an appropriate way on the viewing screen. Chart gages may be made on glass, certain types of plastics, paper, or vellum and laid out by hand drafting methods, special scribing, or chart layout devices. The material and method of layout are such that the chart gage will not significantly add to or detract from manufacturing tolerances. Glass offers the greatest dimensional stability; paper or vellum is suitable only for temporary use.

Measurement by Translation

Many parts can be successfully gaged on optical comparators even though the part configuration cannot be projected by the light beam. Parts having recessed contours such as actuator cam tracks, ball sockets, and the internal grooves of ball nuts can all be gaged by means of tracer techniques. A tracer, as the term is used in projection gaging, is a one-to-one pantograph. On one arm of the pantograph is a stylus that freely traces over the part contour in a given plane. The other arm carries a follower, visible in the light path, that is projected by the light beam as it moves. Three types of followers are used (see Fig. 12-17):

1. Probe follower (view a)—an exact duplicate of the stylus tracer in size and shape.
2. Dot follower (view b)—a glass reticle having an opaque dot of the same diameter as the stylus tracer.
3. Reticle-gage follower (view c)—a glass reticle having an exact one-to-one actual-size reproduction of the part profile.

The choice of follower for a given gaging problem depends on the size of the path and the magnification to be used. In general, the probe or dot is used if the size of the part is less than the field of view of the projector at the given magnification. In some cases, larger parts are gaged by using two followers suit-

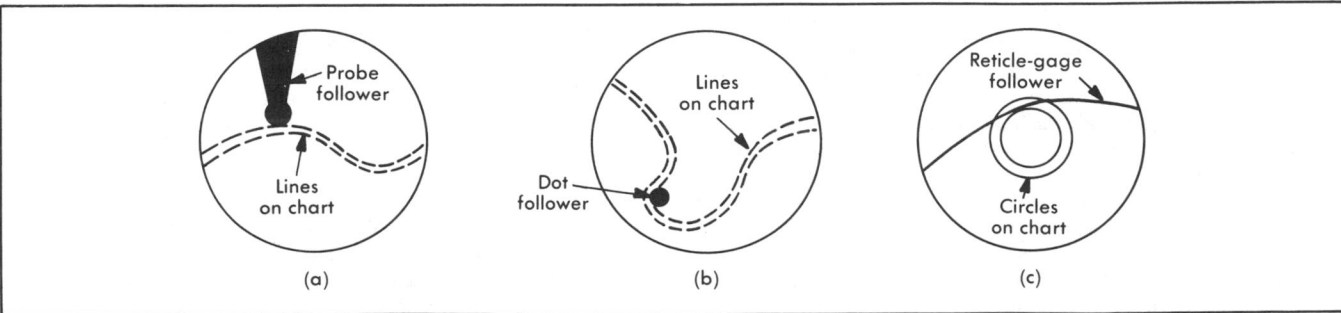

Fig. 12-17 Projector tracer followers: (a) probe type, (b) dot type, and (c) recticle-gage type.

ably spaced to correlate with a special type of chart in which one section of the contour is superimposed on another section. For some purposes, the dot follower is preferred to the probe because it provides a complete circle shadow unrestricted by the shadow of the supporting stem.

The reticle gage follower is more versatile in its application because it is not restricted by part size or magnification. Large parts can be gaged with reticle gages using high magnification.

MAGNIFIERS

Hand loupes fitted with measuring or toleranced GO/NOT-GO reticles are often used as "pocket comparators." A typical loupe consists of an eyepiece, magnifying lens, and a reticle in contact with the part being inspected. These devices are most often used to evaluate small parts, printing or photographic images, and details on larger parts.

Bench magnifiers add magnification and sometimes illumination to an existing inspection setup. They consist of a magnifying lens, a light source, and sometimes a transport mechanism for either the part or the lens.

OPTICAL FLATS

The simplest method of applying interference phenomena to metrology employs optical flats. It may provide the most advantageous combination of precision and accuracy of any readily available measurement method. Precision is sufficient for the closest tolerances. Because light waves are used for a standard, they have accuracy to match precision.

For practical application, three things are needed in addition to the part to be measured. These are the optical flat, a monochromatic light source, and a suitable surface from which to work.

Factors That Control Accuracy

The supporting surface on which optical flat measurements are made must provide a clean, rigid platform. If the measurements consist of the changes on one surface, little more is needed. If, however, the measurement involves comparison of two surfaces, the supporting surface becomes the factor limiting the precision of the measurements.

For the latter reason, optical flats are often used as support for the part. Steel flats, known as toolmakers' flats, are also available. These are simply optical flats to which parts and gage blocks may be wrung for measurement. Glass flats should not be used to wring gage members or parts. Other precision-finished surfaces may also be used. The errors contributed by the supporting surface are of the independent type. They may combine with the measurement errors, thereby increasing the uncertainty of the overall system. Cleanliness is of tremendous importance in optical flat measurements. Even a stray particle of dust that might settle on the part before the flat is placed over it can completely destroy any chance for reliable measurement.

Temperature changes are more apparent when using optical flats than with most other kinds of measurement. Fortunately, they usually involve relatively small parts that normalize quickly. Most optical flats have a lower coefficient of thermal conductivity than the metal parts with which they are used. They are heated rapidly by handling, and once heated or cooled, the flat requires a longer time to regain the ambient temperature. Fused quartz is more stable than Pyrex.

When viewing, the more nearly perpendicular the line of sight is to the surface, the more accurate the measurement will be. To achieve maximum clarity, the measurement surface should be as close to the light source as convenient. The reflex

type of monochromatic light provides this automatically. In this type, a beam-splitter mirror is used to permit both the line of sight and the monochromatic illumination to be reasonably perpendicular to the measurement surface.

A gage block will begin to wring to an optical flat almost immediately unless one of three conditions prevent it. These conditions are: (1) insufficiently flat surfaces, (2) insufficiently fine surface finish, and (3) improperly cleaned surfaces. A gage block, a part, or another flat should never be left wrung to an optical flat beyond the time required for measurement. If left overnight or longer, the flat might be broken in separating them. If they must be forced apart, a wood block should be used.

As soon as the part has begun to wring, fringe bands will appear. Continued wringing can cause the bands to run in any direction across the part. Because of wear to the optical flat and the danger of scratching, wringing should be as slight as possible to obtain the desired fringe pattern.

Optical Flat Convention

Actually, the fringe bands form in the air between the observer and the measurement surface. Therefore, to make fringe bands a practical measurement tool, a convention must be adopted. This is known as parallel-separation-planes concept. Although theoretically nonexistent, it is a great aid in actual measurement.

The convention consists of a set of imaginary planes all parallel to the working surface of the flat and one-half wavelength apart (see Fig. 12-18). The intersections of these planes and the part are the dark fringe lines. The number of fringes thus represents separation between the surfaces in units of half wavelengths. Because the two surfaces are so nearly parallel, the cosine error is in billionths of an inch.

The air-wedge configuration is easily demonstrated. After thorough cleaning, the part and the optical flat are placed together until the fringe pattern crosses the part sidewise as shown in Fig. 12-19. The five dark banks or fringes show that there is an air wedge of five half-wavelengths height separating the flat from the part. At the moment it is not known which way the wedge is facing. The open end is found by applying force to the ends. If there is no change, as in view b, the force is being exerted along the line of contact (wedge point). When the force causes the fringes to spread out, the open end of the wedge is being squeezed closed (view c). The situation, greatly exaggerated, is shown by comparing Fig. 12-18 with Fig. 12-20. Another method is to lower the line of sight. The bands then appear to

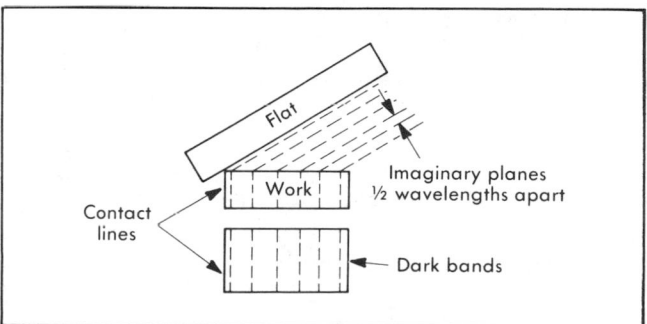

Fig. 12-18 Parallel-separation-planes concept envisions planes parallel to the working surface of the flat and one-half wavelength apart. Dark fringes occur at their intersection with the part.

VISUAL REFERENCE GAGING

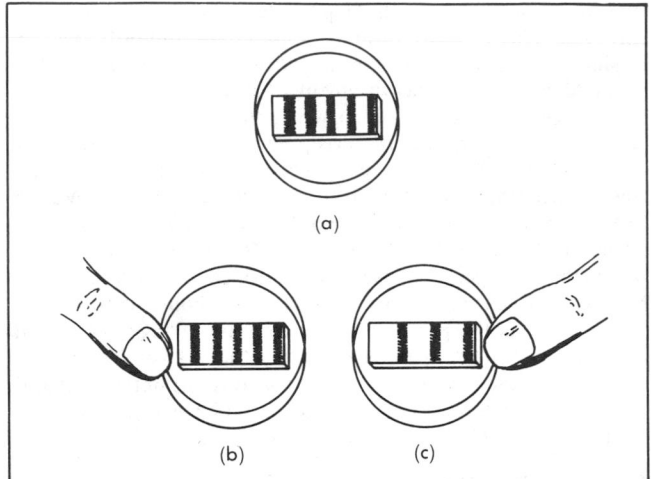

Fig. 12-19 The five fringes shown in view *a* represent an air wedge with a height of five half wavelengths. Pressure at the left as shown in view *b* does not change the pattern, but pressure at the right as shown in view *c* does. The broadening of the fringes shows that the wedge is being closed. Thus the open portion of the wedge is at the right.

move toward the open end of the air wedge. However, the band "value" increases as the line of sight decreases from perpendicular viewing.

The air-wedge configuration would have applied equally well if the fringes were oriented lengthwise along the part (see Fig. 12-21). After the contact has been found, the height can be determined by multiplying the number of fringes by one half the wavelength of the light used. The general relationships are: the fewer the bands, the narrower the angle; the more numerous the bands, the greater the angle. More important is the understanding that the number of bands is a measure of height difference, not of absolute height.

As in all measurement, there must be a reference from which every length is expressed. In surface inspection, the matter of reference is easy. Some part of the surface is arbitrarily chosen as the reference from which the other parts are expressed. In Fig. 12-21, the fringe pattern shows that the surface is flat because the fringe bands are straight and uniformly spaced. A

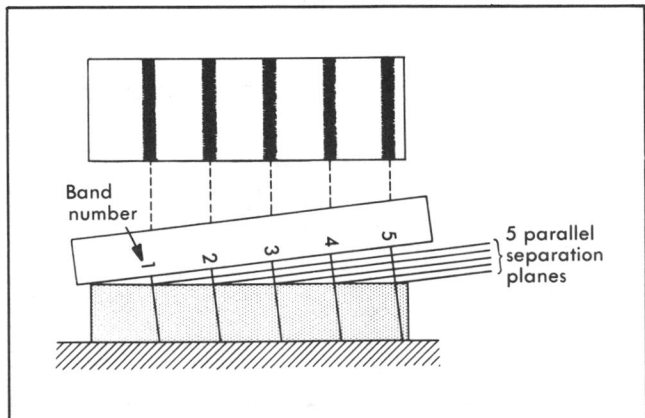

Fig. 12-20 When the wedge is closed down tighter, the number of parallel separation planes decreases.

sharp dropoff would have shown as a change in the pattern. Thus in Fig. 12-22 the closely spaced bands at the right show that the angle is larger along the right-hand edge of the test surface than along the other edge. The actual height change could be measured from this.

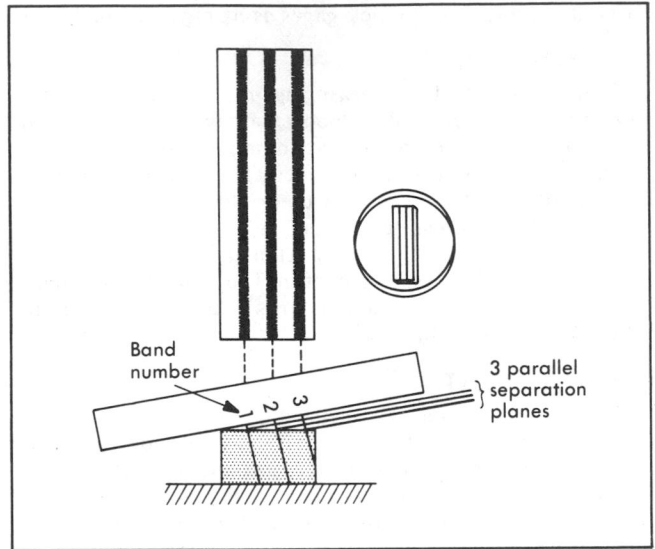

Fig. 12-21 When the fringe bands run lengthwise, the contact is found by applied force.

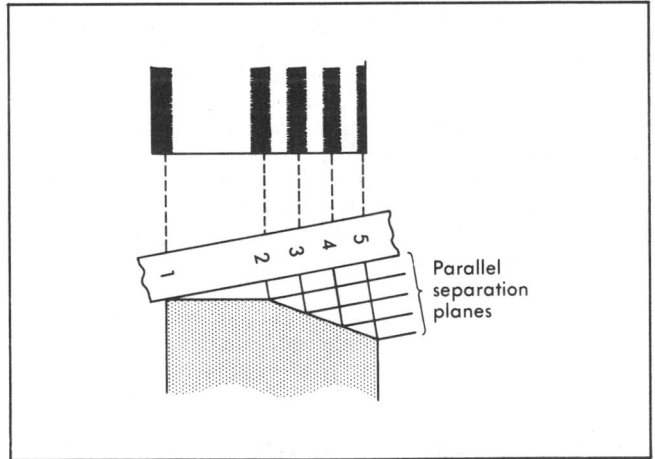

Fig. 12-22 The sharp dropoff is clearly shown by the close bands on the right.

Checking Parallelism

The example in Fig. 12-23 reveals three facts. First, the unknown surface U is parallel longitudinally to the known surface M because it produces the same number of bands. Second, it is not parallel across the width because the bands on the unknown surface are at an angle to those on the known surface. Third, the amount that the unknown surface is out of parallel to the known surface is one-half band in one width.

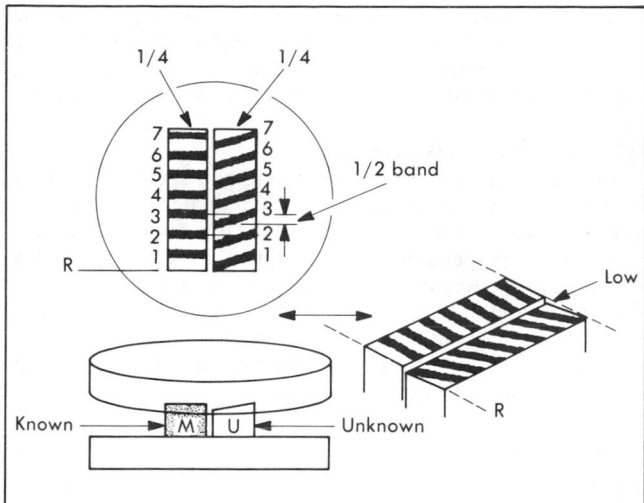

Fig. 12-23 Both surfaces have the same number of bands, but those on the unknown surface slant.

These differences may be measured in much the same way that the fringe patterns were read to evaluate flatness.

In the example shown in Fig. 12-23, an assumption was made that the unknown part had the same basic size as the known part. In most cases there would be a small difference in height. The effect of this is shown in Fig. 12-24. After the known and the

unknown parts have been wrung tightly to a flat and are positioned alongside each other, it is necessary to determine which one is the higher. This is done by placing the second optical flat over them, orienting the fringe pattern to run lengthwise, and then applying force to a point above the center of each part. If force applied at X in Fig. 12-24 does not spread out the pattern but force applied at Y does, then the known part is the higher. In this example, the air-wedge triangles formed over each part are identical. Therefore the fringe patterns are identical. Counting the fringes across the unknown part shows that it is two bands lower than the known.

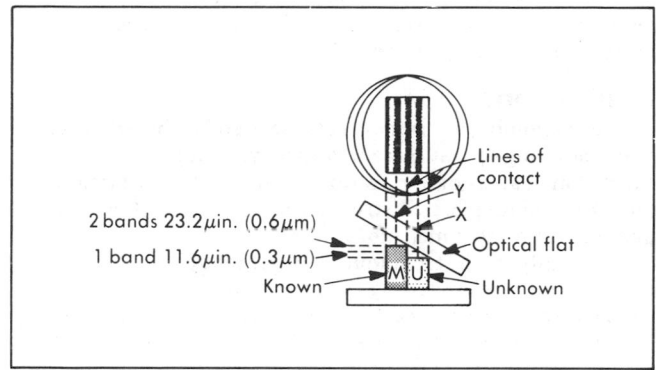

Fig. 12-24 Counting the number of bands on the unknown part provides the measurement of the height difference. Force is applied at points X and Y.

LASER INSPECTION DEVICES

The uses of the laser in metrology arise from the characteristics of laser light that differentiate it from ordinary light. Those characteristics are the extreme intensity, the highly directional, small, collimated beam, the monochromaticity, and the coherent nature of the light.

These same properties are fundamental for the high-speed measuring devices that employ a scanning laser beam. The transmitter section of the gage emits a moving beam of light that scans at a regular speed. The object being measured interrupts the beam, and the detector determines the time that the beam took to traverse the part. The electronic controller converts the data into discrete dimensional readings for end use. The inherent stability of these devices have led to their being used in harsh industrial environments such as steel bar mills.

Again, the intensity and directional properties are fundamental to high-speed contour gages that measure by optical triangulation. These gages direct a small, intense beam of light onto the workpiece. A lens system and photodetector are located at a known angle with respect to the incident beam axis. As the part is moved in the Y direction, the gage determines the change in location of the spot in the X direction. To avoid the problems involved in having the image of the spot move across the detector, the gage moves the part in the X direction to the original location using a null-seeking system. The resulting data are a series of X-Y locations that can be plotted or compared to master data by the gage's computer.

The laser is used in the measurement of straightness deviation, such as in the inspection of surface plates and for machine tool alignment. Before the availability of the laser, it was necessary to use a measuring autocollimator, which requires a high degree of skill on the part of the operator. The laser autocollimator unit is much simpler and easier to use. It directs a collimated laser beam to a flat target mirror that can be at varying distances from the light source.

LASER SCANNING INSTRUMENTS

For the accurate measurement of the diameter of soft, delicate, hot, or moving objects, noncontacting sensors must be used. Devices of this character include capacitive gages, eddy-current gages, air gages, and optical sensors.

Optical sensors have advantages over these other gages because of the nature of light itself. The principal advantages are the following:

1. They do not require direct mechanical contact between the sensor and the object to be measured.
2. The distance from the sensor to the object to be measured can be large.
3. The response time is limited only to that of the photodetector and its electronics.
4. Light variations or interruptions are directly converted to electrical signals.

LASER INSPECTION DEVICES

System Components and Operation

A typical laser scanning instrument consists of a transmitter module, a receiver module, and processor electronics (see Fig. 12-25). The transmitter contains a low-power HeNe gas laser, a power supply, a collimating lens, a multifaceted reflector prism, a synchronizing pulse photodetector, and a protective window. In operation, the transmitter module produces a collimated, parallel, scanning laser beam moving at a high, constant, linear speed. The scanning beam appears as a line of red light and sweeps across its measurement field. When a part is placed in the field, it interrupts the beam. The receiver module collects and photoelectrically senses the laser light transmitted past the part being measured. The processor electronics process the receiver signals, converting them to a convenient form and then displaying the dimension being measured.

Applications

Laser scanning instruments can be used in a broad range of manufacturing operations and a variety of industries. Some of the potential areas of application are wire manufacturing, centerless grinding, plastic extrusion, metal product fabrication, and nuclear reactor metrology.

By modifying the techniques by which the detector output is digitized and interpreted by the processor unit, measurements can be made on translucent material such as fiber-optic cables or transparent material such as glass tubing. In addition to simple diameter measurement, product position, gap size, and multiple dimensions, measurements are possible by examining the detector output in different ways. More elaborate scanner geometries can be used to achieve dual-axis inspection. In these applications, the laser beam is alternately swept across the measurement field in two axes 90° apart. By stacking individual scanners back to back or detecting only the edge of a product and relating it to the position of a reference edge, products

much larger than the range of an individual scanner can be measured. Extra-high-speed scanners, which measure at four to six times the normal rate, allow detection of smaller defects, such as lumps or neckdowns, in moving product applications.

AUTOCOLLIMATORS

Optically, an autocollimator is simply a special form of a telescope. It consists basically of an illuminated target pattern or reticle located in the focal plane of the telescope objective. A plane mirror perpendicular to the optical axis in front of this telescope will reflect an image of the pattern back on itself in the same plane and in focus. A rotation of the mirror by an angle about its perpendicular position causes the return image to be displaced by a specific amount. The amount of displacement can be calculated using the equation:

$$d = 2f\theta \tag{1}$$

where:

d = displacement, in. (mm)
f = focal length of the autocollimator objective, in. (mm)
θ = angular rotation of the mirror

A viewing system is required to observe the relative position of the image, which can be in the form of an illuminated slit or cross line or cross hair in an illuminated field. A simple eyepiece may serve or a compound microscope can be used as shown in Fig. 12-26. The fiducial index should be designed for maximum precision in zeroing the image; for example, a double line to frame a single line. Measurement is made by moving either the image or the index under micrometer control. Although most autocollimators measure around one axis only, a suitable target pattern and a two-axial index micrometer system are all that is required to make readings about two axes.

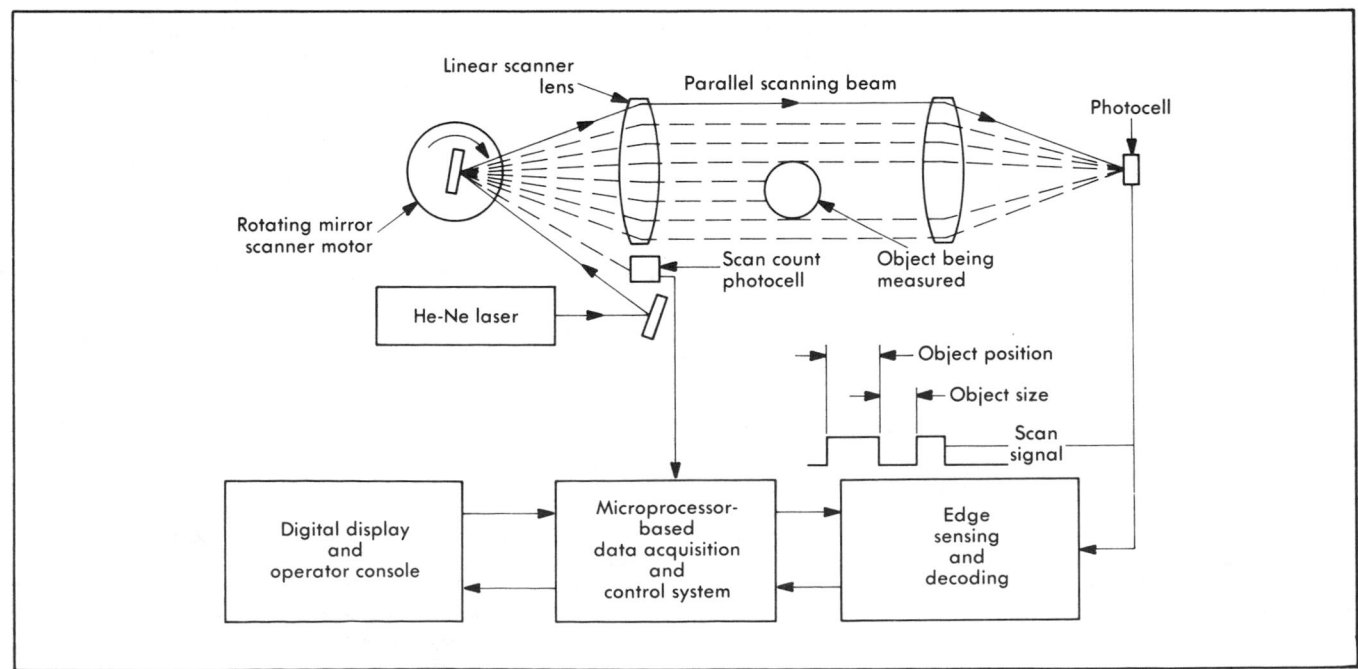

Fig. 12-25 Schematic of laser scanning instrument. (*Lasermike Division, Techmet Co.*)

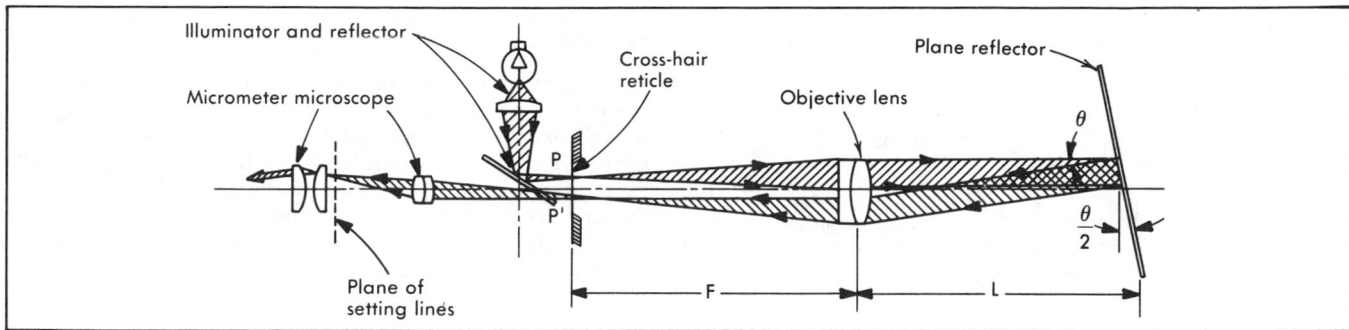

Fig. 12-26 Principle of autocollimation.

Photoelectric Autocollimators

Autocollimators that replace the judgment of the human eye with appropriate photoelectric systems have some important advantages that can outweigh their increased cost and complexity. Setting accuracy is improved and no longer differs between observers. Readings can be made remotely and monitored cotinuously when required. Such autocollimators come in sizes from 1″ (25 mm) (with null-setting sensitivity better than 0.1 arc second) to very large instruments with 10″ (250 mm) objectives. Some provide merely a photoelectric null setting without measuring capability, while others have analog or digital readout with ranges from 10 seconds to a full degree or more.

Calibration

The only effective method for calibrating autocollimators is to monitor output or readings as the reference mirror is tilted through accurately controlled angles. The problem of how to generate small angles accurate to 1 arc second or better has been solved by designing special sine-bar fixtures with a precisely defined axis at one end, while at the other end a well-defined cylinder is raised or lowered with a special micrometer or with gage blocks. A fixed wedge can also be used to calibrate an autocollimator; however, a fixed wedge only gives a specific angle whereas a sine bar can give an infinite number of angles.

Checking Way Straightness

Checking the straightness and flatness of a way or equivalent surface is one of the most frequent applications of an autocollimator. The first objective is to convert deviation from straightness stepwise into successive tilts of a mirror carriage as it is moved along a straight line in increments just equal to the distance between locating pads. At each point, readings are taken from a rigidly mounted autocollimator. These readings are then converted back to a profile curve.

The photoelectric autocollimator can be interfaced to a computer that enables the time for straightness checks and calibration of surface plates for flatness to be considerably reduced. The computer with an interactive program permits three X, three Y, and two diagonal generator lines to be used with a printout of results including a straightness graph and an isometric plot of the surface plate.

INTERFEROMETERS

Interferometric testing has long been used in optical metrology. The advent of the laser has not only made interferometry more convenient to use, but has also extended its range of application. Interferometry is used as a tool in optical fabrication, precision metal finishing, microlithography, and optical and electro-optical systems alignment.

For most interferometry, the output of the test is an interference fringe pattern that can be observed in real time and photographed to produce an interferogram. The type of pattern is determined by the particular measurement configuration and by the errors in the part under test. The quantitative reduction of an interference fringe pattern is usually based on ascertaining the fractional deviation of the interference fringe pattern from some ideal, best-fitting pattern. The denominator of the fractional deviation is the measured spacing between a pair of fringes in the ideal pattern.

Operating Principles

The reason why interference is not observed generally is that it can occur only when two wavefronts, or light rays, come together in a compatible condition known as coherence. Coherence means that the two rays that meet at any given point in a field of view maintain whatever phase relationship they have for an appreciable length of time. This condition is possible only when the two rays have originated from the same point in the light source at the same time. As a result, all practical interferometers make use of some type of beam divider that splits an incoming ray into two parts that travel different paths until they are recombined, usually in the same beam divider. An exception to the above is the gas laser, whose light output under special conditions is sufficiently coherent to interfere with light from another laser.

The most common interference effect, known as Fizeau interference, is that associated with thin, transparent films or wedges bounded on at least one side by a transparent surface. Soap bubbles, oil films on water, and optical flats fall into this category. Light is usually from an extended "white" light source, such as the sky, but for measuring purposes a single-wavelength source is preferred. Helium lamps meet this reasonably well and are therefore the most widely used. The dominant wavelength is 23.4 μin. (0.59 μm), an orange color.

Types of Interferometers

Several types of interferometers are in use today; Michelson, Fabry-Perot, spherical, fringe counting, and gage block.

Michelson interferometers. The basic Michelson interferometer is shown in Fig. 12-27. Light from an extended source,

LASER INSPECTION DEVICES

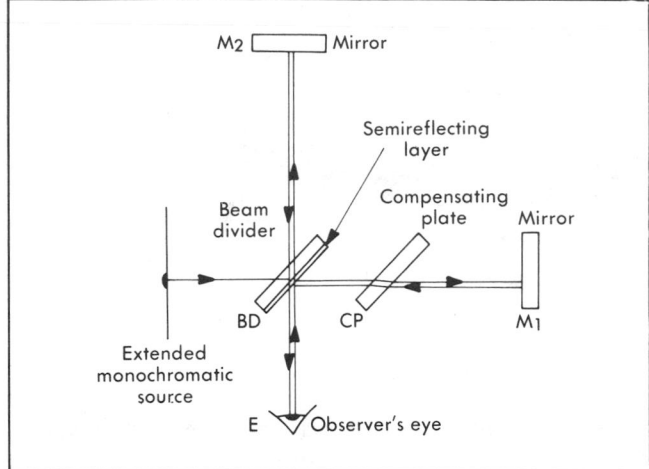

Fig. 12-27 Michelson interferometer.

most often monochromatic (single wavelength), falls onto a plane-parallel plate *BD*, which has on its back a semitransparent layer of silver or a more efficient multilayer film. This divides the light into two rays of equal intensity, one of which is transmitted through compensating plate *CP* to mirror M_1 and the other of which is reflected through *BD* to mirror M_2. The rays are reflected back from the mirrors and reunite at the beam-splitter surface. There they are transmitted to the eye at *E*, where fringes can be observed.

The only purpose of the compensator plate is to introduce exactly the same amount of glass in each of the paths, which is important mainly when a white light source is used. However, so-called white light fringes can be seen only if both ray paths are exactly equal (to a few wavelengths) in total length. The path lengths themselves are not important; only their differences affect fringe formation. Monochromatic sources allow

fringes to be seen over a range of path difference that may vary from a few to a million wavelengths, depending on the source.

Fabry-Perot interferometers. Fabry-Perot interferometers, or etalons, are made up of two optical flats, flat to 1/20 fringe or better, coated with a high-efficiency, semitransparent film on the two facing surfaces. The flats must be kept exactly parallel by means of a carefully designed spacer. When illuminated, as shown in Fig. 12-28, a series of very sharply defined bright circles are seen on a screen that result from interference between rays that are multiply reflected between the two working faces of the etalon.

Spherical interferometers. Commercially produced interferometers are capable of measuring spherical as well as planer surfaces when configured with the proper reference accessories. The spherical accessory generates a cone of light that converges to a focus point and then diverges as the focus point is passed. Within the two cones of light (converging and diverging) there are an infinite number of spherical wavefronts of different radius. To test a spherical part it is only necessary to place the center of curvature of the part in such a way that it is concentric with the focus of the reference. At this point, a wavefront of the same radius as the part will be reflected back into the interferometer system where it interferes with the reference wavefront producing the fringe pattern.

Fringe-counting interferometers. If in a Twyman-Green type interferometer, with both end mirrors perpendicular to the optical axis, one mirror is displaced slowly, exactly parallel to itself, the observer will note periodic changes from bright to dark in the intensity of the field being viewed. Measurement will show the intensity variation to be sinusoidal, with a period that corresponds to mirror motion of exactly half the wavelength of the light source used. If one of the end mirrors is slightly inclined to the optical axis, parallel fringes will be seen that move parallel to themselves by just one fringe for every $\lambda/2$ mirror motion. Counting of such fringes by eye, or with photodetectors hooked up to high-speed counters, enables meas-

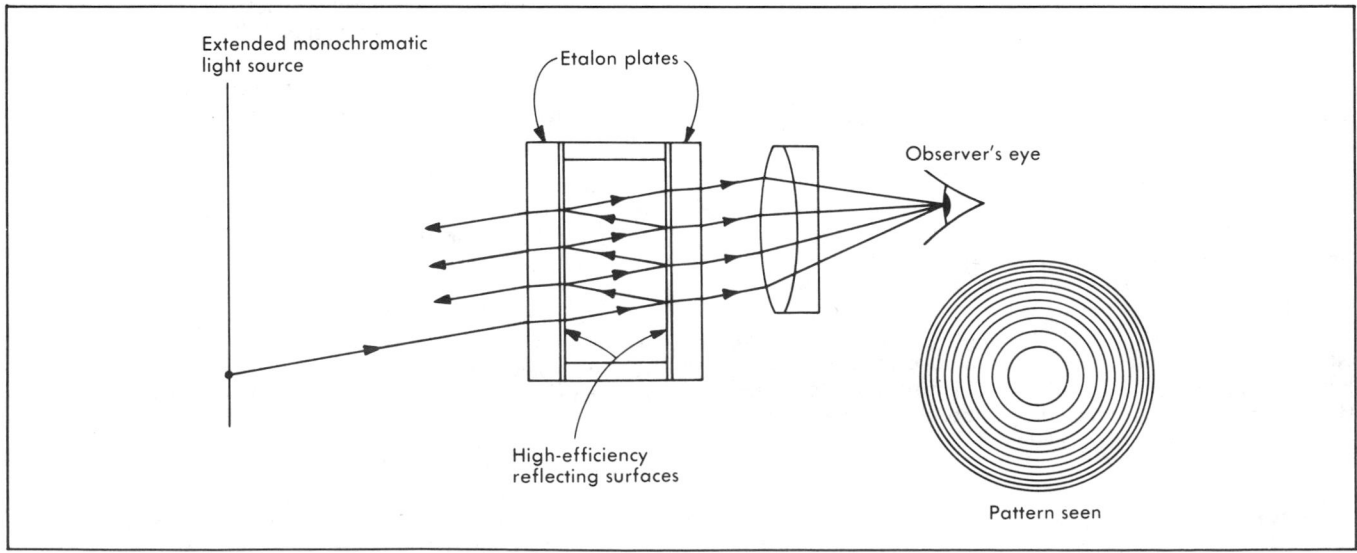

Fig. 12-28 Fabry-Perot etalon.

urement of linear mechanical motion directly in terms of the wavelength of light (see Fig. 12-29). Accuracy of one part in one million should be attainable and has in fact been attained. A

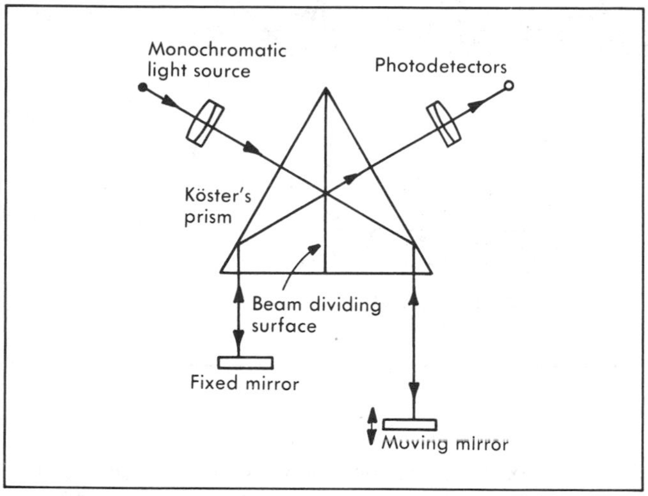

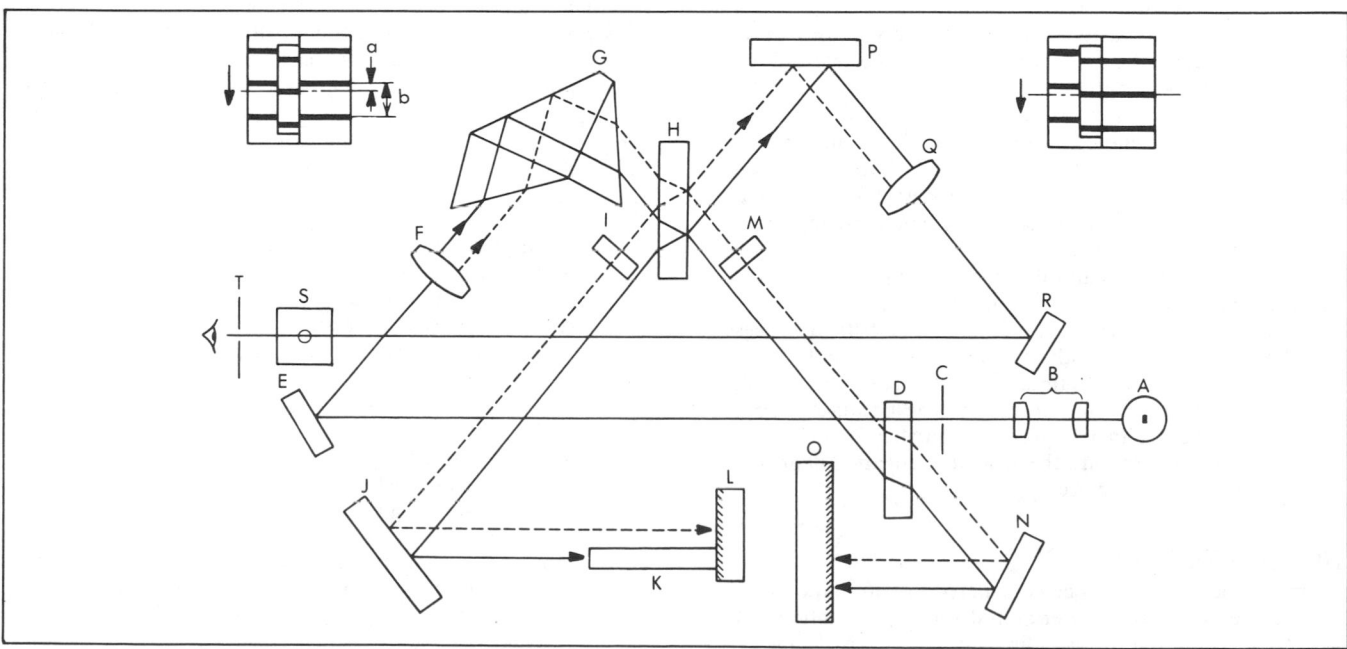

Fig. 12-29 Fringe-count system based on Köster's prism.

number of conditions, however, must be met and understood before such results can be realized.

Gage block interferometers. All gage block interferometers are variations of the Fizeau or Twyman-Green (or Köster's prism equivalent) interferometers. Optical diagrams of two types are shown in Figs. 12-30 and 12-31.

Fundamentally, these interferometers measure the length of a gage block with respect to a baseplate, to which the block is wrung, by arranging the baseplate almost perpendicular to the interferometer axis and determining the number of fringes between the baseplate and the surface of the block.

Interference microscopes. Checking the finish of finely polished or lapped surfaces can be done qualitatively with any good microscope equipped with proper illumination. However, when quantitative information is desired concerning scratch depth and shape, it becomes highly desirable to superimpose interference fringes over the field. Instruments designed for this purpose are called interference microscopes. Fringe patterns are interpreted exactly as in any other case.

Two basic types of interference microscopes are available. The simpler one makes use of Fizeau fringes, often the multiple-beam sharpened fringes that occur between a very small, optically flat reference surface in contact with the workpiece. The flat is not only small but thin, to make room for it in the limited space between the microscope objective and the workpiece. Most microscopes of this type are limited in magnification to 150X, sometimes up to 300X, by the presence of the reference flat. Fortunately this is enough for many purposes, but not for all. Like all such systems, monochromatic light is required, filtered mercury being preferred because very small lamps are available.

Light Sources of Interferometry

Many light sources are used in various interferometers, with the choice based on cost, convenience, and the type of application. Nearly all modern interferometer systems use some type of laser because the longer coherence length offers distinct advantages with respect to fringe visibility, instrument flexibility, and freedom from path length restrictions.

Fig. 12-30 Zeiss gage block interferometer.

AUTOMATIC GAGING AND PROCESS CONTROL

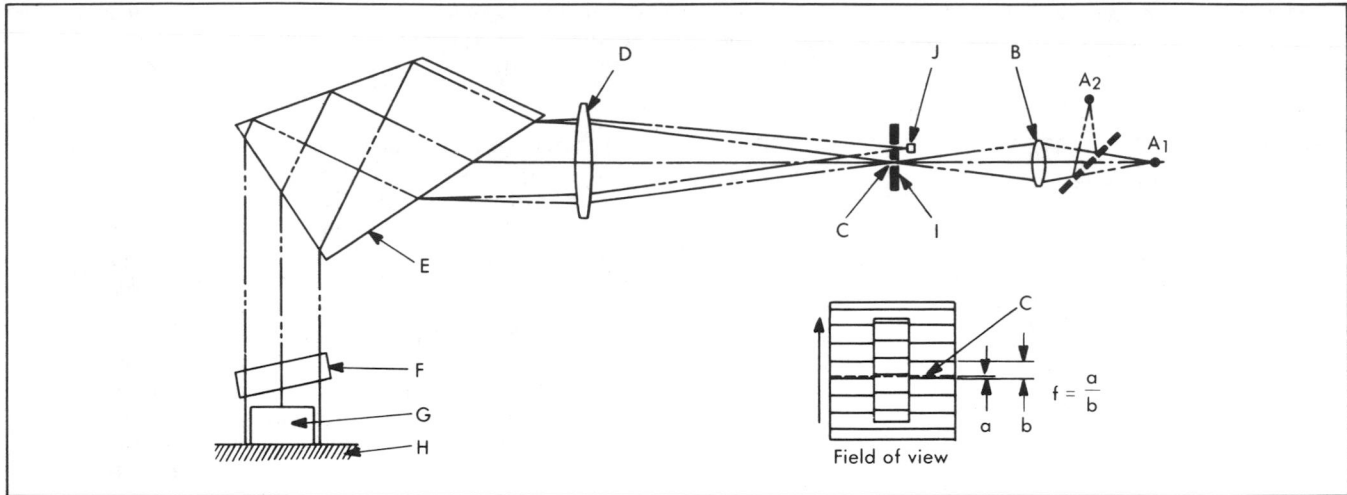

Fig. 12-31 N.P.L. gage block interferometer.

Other nonlaser sources utilize the excitation of atoms of certain elements, which then radiate light at certain discrete wavelengths. These are generally a discharge lamp that is charged with one or sometimes two elements, and a means to electrically excite it. The commonly used types of sources are mercury, mercury 198, cadmium, krypton 86, thallium, sodium, helium, neon, and gas lasers.

AUTOMATIC GAGING AND PROCESS CONTROL

Automatic control over forming, machining, inspection, and assembly ensures greater productivity and lower costs, higher quality, and maximum use of machine capability. Control units must be accurate, have high-speed response, and be unaffected by vibration, oil, dirt, and coolant.

Practically all dimensions, conditions, or spatial relationships can be automatically inspected, including internal and external diameters, length, depth, taper, out of round, and geometrical conditions such as squareness, parallelism, concentricity, and center distance. Advances in electronic circuitry permit almost all configurations of workpieces to be inspected during all stages of the manufacturing process. Parts with large interruptions can be moved or rotated through gage fingers and measured to an accuracy of 20 μin. (0.5 μm) by damping, filtering, or by electronically detecting the interruptions and disregarding the resulting size change.

Automatic gage systems often include statistical process control features to ensure that corrections are made to the process only when the corrections are warranted. For example, if one workpiece in 100 measures oversize because of some periodic malfunction in the process, statistical controls will cause the system to disregard the measurement and not provide a correction to the workpiece.

GAGING FEASIBILITY

Among the variables to be considered in automatic gaging are part size and shape, material and finish, production rate, tolerances, part handling, cleanliness of part, type of gage element, and inspection rate. Interchangeable and adjustable tooling enable a gage to handle different parts, sizes, and tolerances. To accommodate slightly misaligned holes or locations, automatic gages are sometimes designed with floating-type gaging elements. If a part's size or shape prevents it from being gaged in one operation, it is better to inspect the close tolerances first. This prevents wasting the expense of checking the broader tolerances first only to have the part rejected later.

The following questions are presented as a guide to assist the manufacturing engineer in deciding on the exact type of process control to use. The questions highlight some of the distinctions used in defining the connections between the product measurement and the process correction.

1. What part variability is to be processed?
    a. Dedicated to single part.
    b. For family of parts.
    c. For batches of unrelated parts.
2. What type of machine tool is to be used?
    a. Single-purpose.
    b. Machining center.
    c. CNC lathe.
    d. Dial machine.
    e. Linear transfer line.
    f. Manufacturing cell.
    g. FMS.
3. How is part to be transferred?
    a. Into the machine tool.
    b. Into the gage.
    c. Out of the system.
4. What are the objectives of gaging and process control?

AUTOMATIC GAGING AND PROCESS CONTROL

5. How timely is the correction to the process?
    a. Corrections are made on that very piece.
    b. Corrections are made on the very next piece.
    c. Corrections are made several pieces later.
    d. Corrections are made on a statistical basis.
6. When is the measuring done?
    a. While cutting the workpiece.
    b. While not cutting.
7. Where is the measuring done?
    a. On the machine tool.
    b. Off the machine tool.
8. What is the environment?
    a. Shop floor—"in-process."
    b. Clean room/QC area.
9. What is the measuring capability?
    a. Dedicated gaging—specialized for a given part.
    b. Flexible gaging—suited for a family of parts.
    c. General-purpose—suited for almost any part produced on the machine tool.
10. How good does the gage have to be?
    a. Repeatability.
    b. Accuracy.
11. How much processing is performed on the measured data?
    a. Makes a single measurement and displays it.
    b. Makes measurements of different product features and calculates their relationships.
    c. Makes many measurements and stores the readings.
    d. Measures, stores, and processes many data points statistically.
12. How is gaging information linked to the process control?
    a. Measurements are taken for historical purposes only.
    b. Measurements are taken and QC tells operations about the results.
    c. Measurements are taken by manufacturing personnel and they make corrections.
    d. Measurements are taken and automatically fed into the machine tool for correction.

TYPES OF SYSTEMS

Automatic gaging devices are usually referred to by function or position in the manufacturing process: as preprocess gages (inspection before machining), in-process gages (inspection during machining), postprocess gages (inspection after machining), final inspection gages, and assembly gages. Combinations of various types of gaging can provide fully automatic control over dimensional size from the moment the part enters the manufacturing process through assembly.

GAGE TRANSDUCERS

The most common type of transducer used for automatic measurement and process control systems is the linear variable differential transformer (see Fig. 12-32). This device produces an electrical output proportional to the displacement of a separate movable core. Three coils are equally spaced on a cylindrical coil form. A rod-shaped magnetic core positioned axially inside this coil assembly provides a path for the magnetic flux linking the coils. When the primary or center coil is energized with alternating current, voltages are induced in the two outer coils.

In the wiring installation of the transformer, the outer or secondary coils are connected in series opposition so that the

two voltages in the secondary circuit are opposite in phase, the net output of the transformer being the difference of these voltages. For one central position of the core, this output voltage will be essentially 0. This is called the balance point or null position (see Fig. 12-33).

When the core is moved from this balance point, the voltage induced in the coil toward which the core is moved increases while the voltage induced in the opposite coil decreases. This produces a differential voltage output from the transformer that, with proper design, varies linearly with change in core position. Motion of the core in the opposite direction, beyond the null position, produces a similar linear voltage characteristic, but with the phase shifted 180°. A continuous plot of voltage output versus core position (within the linear range limits) appears as a straight line through the origin if opposite algebraic signs are used to indicate opposite phases.

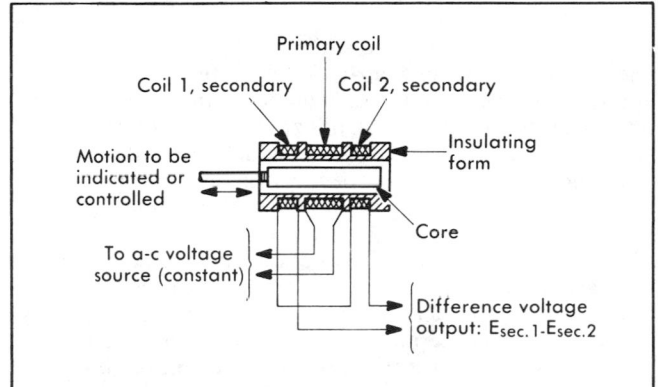

Fig. 12-32 Schematic of linear variable differential transformer. (*Schaevitz Engineering*)

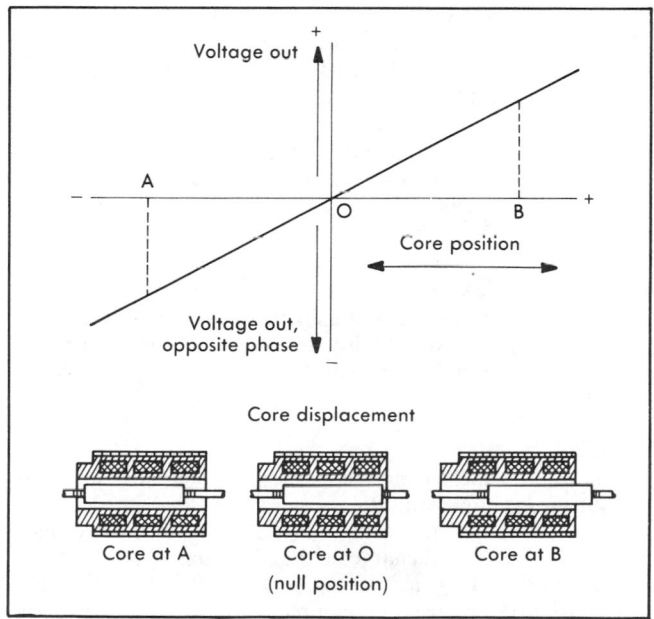

Fig. 12-33 Schematic of linear variable differential transformer operation. (*Schaevitz Engineering*)

COORDINATE MEASURING MACHINES

PROCESS CONTROL

Gaging systems used for machine size control are most often used on external grinders, ID grinders, centerless grinders, and double disc grinders to precisely locate parts, indicate wheel infeed, measure wheel wear, and measure and control part size. They are also used extensively in automatic transfer lines to monitor each station and correct for size variations or to halt the process in the event that catastrophies caused by tool breakage occur.

There are two types of process control systems in use: in-process and postprocess. In-process gages are used to measure the workpiece during grinding and control the grinder wheel slide to produce workpieces within the desired tolerance limits. Postprocess gages measure the workpiece after it has been ground and provide a size offset that will apply a correction to the next workpiece to be ground.

An increasing number of gaging systems are also being used for turning applications and for automatic assembly equipment. In turning, the gage is often used to measure the location of the cutting tool in reference to the workpiece and correct for variations that occur. It is also used in postprocess applications to measure the workpiece after it has been turned, then provide any necessary correction to the cutting tool that will apply to the subsequent workpiece.

COORDINATE MEASURING MACHINES

Currently, coordinate measuring machines are being used in one of three ways in a manufacturing firm. The simplest approach is to place the CMM at the end of the production line or in an inspection area. With this approach, the CMM is used to inspect the first part of a production run to verify the machine setup. Once the setup is verified, it then measures parts on a random basis. For many applications, this permits the best approach to inspection.

Another approach is to incorporate the coordinate measuring machine between two workcenters and then measure 100% of the parts produced at the first center before any secondary operations are performed at the second workcenter. This approach is possible because CMMs are capable of measuring three-dimensional geometry and making many different measurements within a short period of time. When this approach is used, the CMM indirectly controls the production process. In this setting, however, the CMM must be "hardened" to perform in the shop environment or it must be completely enclosed to provide an optimum environment for part inspection.

A third approach integrates the CMM into the production line. This permits the CMM to directly control the production process. In operation, an integrated system would measure the workpiece, compare the measurements with required dimensions, and, if necessary, automatically adjust the machine controls so that the part is manufactured within the required specifications.

ADVANTAGES

Some of the advantages of using CMMs over conventional gaging techniques are flexibility, reduced setup time, improved accuracy, reduced operator influence, and improved productivity.[5]

Flexibility

Coordinate measuring machines are essentially universal measuring machines and do not need to be dedicated to any single or particular measuring task. They can measure practically any dimensional characteristic of virtually any part configuration, including cams, gears, and contoured surfaces. No special fixtures or gages are required; because electronic probe contact is light, most parts can be inspected without being clamped to a surface plate.

Reduced Setup Time

Establishing part alignment and appropriate reference points are very time consuming with conventional surface-plate inspection techniques. These procedures are greatly simplified or virtually eliminated through software available on computer-assisted or computer-controlled CMMs.

Such software allows the operator to define the part's orientation on the CMM, and all coordinate data are subsequently automatically corrected for any misalignment between the part reference system and the machine coordinates. A CMM with sophisticated software can inspect parts in a single setup without the need to orient the part for access to all features even when a fourth axis (rotary table) is employed.

Improved Accuracy

All measurements on a CMM are taken from a common geometrically fixed measuring system, eliminating the introduction and accumulation of errors that can result with hard-gage inspection methods and transfer techniques. Moreover, measuring all significant features of a part in one setup prevents the introduction of errors due to setup changes.

Reduced Operator Influence

The use of digital readouts eliminates the subjective interpretation of readings common with dial or vernier-type measuring devices. Operator "feel" is virtually eliminated with modern electronic probe systems. All CMMs have canned software routines for typical part features, such as bores or center distances. In the part-program-assisted mode, the operator positions the machine; once the initial position has been set, the machine is under the control of a program that eliminates operator choice. In the computer numerically controlled (CNC) mode, motor-driven machines run totally unattended by operators. Also, automatic data recording, available on most machines, prevents errors in transcribing readings to the inspection report. This all adds up to the fact that less skilled operators can be readily instructed to perform relatively complex inspection procedures.

Improved Productivity

All the factors previously mentioned help to make CMMs more productive than conventional inspection techniques.

COORDINATE MEASURING MACHINES

Further dramatic productivity improvements are realized through the computational and analytical capabilities of associated data handling systems, including calculators and all levels of computers.

PROBES

The utility of a coordinate measuring machine depends largely on the nature of the probing device. Three types of probes are commonly used: (1) hard, (2) electronic, and (3) noncontact. A probe is selected according to the dimensional and geometrical requirements of the inspection process.

Hard Probes

Hard probes consist of a shaft and a probe tip mounted in various ways to the probe arm. A variety of probe tip shapes and sizes are available; the shape of the probe determines its application. Conical probes are used for locating holes; ball probes for establishing surface locations; cylindrical probes for checking slots and holes in sheet metal parts; and edge-finder probes are used for part alignment and measurement of flat surfaces or edges of parts. Hard probes can only be used in small, manually operated CMMs when inspecting simple parts of a short production run.

Electronic Probes

Electronic probes are commonly classified into one of three categories: (1) switching, (2) proportional, and (3) nulling probes. Switching probes are the most popular probes in use. This electronic probe, also called a touch probe, is an omnidirectional triggering device consisting of a probe body and a stylus; multiple stylus arrangements are also available. When the stylus is brought into contact with the workpiece, a signal is sent to the computer interface, indicating the instantaneous three-dimensional location of the stylus. All probe designs allow stylus overtravel, some by as much as 0.04" (1.0 mm) normal to probe axis and 0.08" (2.0 mm) perpendicular to the probe axis. When the deflection force is removed, the stylus returns to its initial position. Switching-type probes suffer from lobing due to stylus bending. This lobing effect is exacerbated by high trigger forces and long stylus extensions. Electronic touch probes are used on all CMMs.

Because of their design, proportional-type probes are used exclusively on CMMs that are controlled by direct computer control (DCC). This type of probe is designed for automatic scanning of profiles contained in section planes passing through the probe axis. The probe consists of a transducer and a motor-powered, servocontrolled axis and carries on its tip a servo-assisted feeler that is kept in contact with the surface to be inspected. The feeler generates an error signal, proportional to the pressure exerted on the surface, for the control of the probe motor. During the scanning operation, the probe applies a very light contact pressure to the part and reacts with its motor to profile variations whose amplitudes are smaller than the probe axis working stroke. Longer profile variations are in turn followed by the CMM axes that are coupled to the probe axis position through the control system. A typical proportional probe stroke is ±0.5" (±12.5 mm) from the center of probe axis stroke. Other probes with simultaneous radial and axial scanning capabilities are designed with the above concept.

Nulling probes are basically the same as the proportional probe with two major differences. First of all, it is more accurate than the proportional probe because the control system indi-cates the three-dimensional location of the stylus when the probe is at null condition (machine axis at rest). The second major difference is that the probe must leave the surface to proceed to the next inspection location whereas the proportional probe does not.

Noncontact Probes

Noncontact probes are used when fast, accurate measurements are required with no physical contact with the part. Several types of noncontact probes are used.

Optical probes are used when inspecting drawings, printed circuit boards, and small, fragile workpieces. When these probes are used, the basic measuring programs can still be used.

The two types of optical probes used on manual CMMs are a projection microscope and a centering microscope. On the projection microscope, the image under inspection is displayed on the screen. Part feature locations are obtained by moving the CMM to align the screen reticle to the feature. With the centering microscope, part feature locations are obtained in the same way as the projection microscope as the user looks through the eyepiece.

Another manufacturer has developed an acoustical probe that senses contact with the workpiece by the sound wave generated by the touch rather than by any physical displacement of the probe. At contact, vibration travels up the probe and is picked up by a sensitive acoustic microphone inside the head.

A third type of noncontact probe contains a laser light source that projects a small diameter spot on the part surface. A digital solid-state sensor detects the position of this spot and computes part surface location by optical triangulation. Because of the intrinsic nature of these probes, part insinceiton is generally limited to two dimensions.

MACHINE CONTROL

Besides their physical configurations, coordinate measuring machines can also be classified according to their mode of operation: manual, manual computer-assisted, motorized computer-assisted, and direct computer controlled.[6] Manual machines have a free-floating, solid probe that the operator moves along the machine's coordinate axes to establish each measurement. Digital readouts, associated with each axis, provide the measurement values that the operator notes and records manually. In some instances, a simple digital printout device may be used to record the readings.

Manual computer-assisted CMMs use a data processing system to manipulate the measurements, which are still made by manually moving the probe through a series of measurement locations. Solid or electronic probes may be used on this type of machine. The data processing may be accomplished by a special microprocessor-based digital readout, a programmable calculator, or a full-fledged computer.

Depending on the sophistication of the data processing system and associated software, computer-assisted CMMs perform functions ranging from simple inch/millimeter conversion to automatic three-dimensional compensation for misalignment and a host of geometric and analytical measuring tasks. Storing of predetermined program sequences and operator prompting are also available to create part programs.

In effect, the computer system can carry out all the calculations and analyses required to arrive at dimensional and tolerance evaluations and can lead the operator through a prescribed series of positioning and measuring moves. Data recording is usually included with computer-assisted CMMs.

COORDINATE MEASURING MACHINES

A motorized computer-assisted CMM has all the features of a computer-assisted CMM, but uses power-operated motions under the control of the operator, who uses a joystick. The part program is generated and stored in the computer, which determines the inspection sequence and compares measured results with nominal values and tolerances for automatic GO/NOT-GO decisionmaking. Most motorized CMMs also provide means for disengaging the power drive to permit manual manipulation of the machine motions. Some machines use direct-current servomotors and pneumatically operated friction clutches to reduce the effect of collisions, and all permit drive disengagement for manual movements.

Direct computer controlled (DCC) CMMs are equivalent to CNC machine tools. A computer controls all the motions of a motorized CMM. In addition, the computer also performs all the data processing functions of the most sophisticated computer-assisted CMM. Both control and measuring cycles are under program control. Most DCC machines offer various programming options, including program storage and, in some instances, off-line programming capability.

SOFTWARE

The key to the productivity of all forms of computer-assisted CMMs lies in the sophistication and ease of use of the associated software. Software is the most important element in any coordinate measuring system because its power determines how many part features can be measured, and its ease of use determines the extent to which the machine is used.

The functional capabilities of CMM software depend on the number and type of application programs available. Virtually all CMMs offer some means of compensation for misalignment between the part reference system and the machine coordinates by probing selected points; some are limited to alignment in one plane, while most machines provide full three-dimensional alignment. Once the designated points have been taken, the program calculates the misalignment and applies the appropriate correction to all subsequent measurement readings.

Conversion between Cartesian, polar, and, in some instances, spherical coordinate systems is also commonly handled. Most systems also calculate the deviation of measurements from nominal dimensions of the part stored in memory and flag out-of-tolerance conditions.

Geometric functions handled by CMM software define geometric elements—such as points, lines, planes, circles, cylinders, spheres, and cones—from a series of point measurements and solve measurement problems dealing with the interaction of such geometric elements. Such software can determine, for example, the intersection of two circles established on the basis of a selected number of measurements or it can establish the angle of intersection of two surfaces.

Many software packages also provide a means for evaluating geometric tolerance conditions by determining various types of form and positional relationships (such as flatness, straightness, circularity, parallelism, or squareness) for single features and related groups of features.

Best-fit programs can identify the location of a part finished to size within a rough part from which it is to be made, to optimize the machining-allowance distribution; maximum material condition (MMC) programs evaluate features dimensioned according to MMC principles.

Other application programs include automatic part scanning for digitizing profiles and a variety of special programs to handle the inspection of special shapes such as gears and cams. Statistical analysis software available provides for graphic data display, including histograms.

The accuracy of some CMMs is enhanced beyond the mechanical rigidity and stability of the machine with the aid of software geometry error compensation. A typical compensation package automatically interpolates the probe position throughout the measurement envelope. It corrects each axis for inaccuracies in pitch, yaw, scale errors, straightness, and squareness to the other axes. This software package is usually an integral part of the system software provided with the machine.

MACHINE VISION SYSTEMS

To be classified as machine vision, the system must be capable of performing four primary functions.[7] The first function is image formation. In image formation, incoming light is received from an object or scene and then converted into electrical signals. In the next step, the signals are organized in a form compatible with computer processing capabilities. The third function is to analyze and measure various features or characteristics of these signals that represent the image. Finally, a machine vision system interprets the data so that some useful decisions can be made about the object or scene being studied.

This description of machine vision makes a clear distinction between several broad categories of optical sensing equipment currently used in manufacturing applications. For example, optical comparators, which are used to project silhouettes of a workpiece on a viewing screen, would not fall under this classification because they do not possess the image analysis and interpretation capability normally associated with a machine vision system. Similarly excluded would be equipment such as photocells and other light-beam equipment for measuring presence or dimensions and closed-circuit television systems where the monitors are observed by human operators for off-line inspection applications.

APPLICATIONS

Machine vision as applied to manufacturing extracts information from visual sensors to enable machines to make intelligent decisions. Such decisions are needed in quality control (detection of defects), process monitoring (prevention of defects), product routing (parts acquisition and sorting), and statistical reporting (performance evaluation).

The three main industrial application categories are inspection, identification, and machine guidance. Among the inspection tasks are the following:

- *Gaging.* Checking to make sure that dimensions fall within acceptable tolerance bands.
- *Verification.* Checking to make sure that a product is present, complete, or the right one in the proper orientation.

- *Flaw detection.* Checking for unwanted features of unknown shape anywhere on the observed portion of the product.

Among the identification tasks are the following:

- *Symbol recognition.* Deciding which one of many possible symbols is present in a given location. Examples of this application are reading serial numbers or bar codes.
- *Object recognition.* Deciding which of many possible objects is present by examining features of the object under test.

Among the guidance functions performed by machine vision are the following:

- *Object location.* Two or three-dimensional determination of position and orientation for purposes of part acquisition, transfer, and assembly.
- *Tracking.* Continuously updating the position of a feature relative to a tool to control continuous processes such as gluing or welding.

SYSTEM OPERATION

The machine vision process consists of four basic steps (see Fig. 12-34).[8] In the first step, an image of the scene is formed. The formed image is usually transformed into digital data that can be used by the computer. In the third step, the characteristics of the image are enhanced and analyzed. Finally, the image is interpreted, conclusions are drawn, and a decision is made so that some action can be taken.

Image Formation

Image formation frequently involves a combination of lenses, mirrors, and prisms that image the relevant portion of the object on the photodetector. The important parameters in image formation are lens focal length, aperture, depth of field, and magnification. In addition to these parameters, the object must be properly illuminated to provide good image contrast and properly oriented to obtain a quality image.

Image Preprocessing

The initial sensing operation performed by the camera results in a series of voltage levels that represent light intensities over the area of the image. This preliminary image must then be processed so that it is presented to the microcomputer in a form suitable for analysis. A camera typically forms an image 30 or 60 times per second or once every 33 or 17 milliseconds. At selected time intervals, the image is captured or frozen for processing by an image preprocessor. The image preprocessor transforms the analog voltage values for the image into corresponding digital values by means of an analog-to-digital converter. The result is an array of digital numbers that represent a light intensity distribution over the image area. This digital pixel array is then stored in memory until it is analyzed and interpreted.

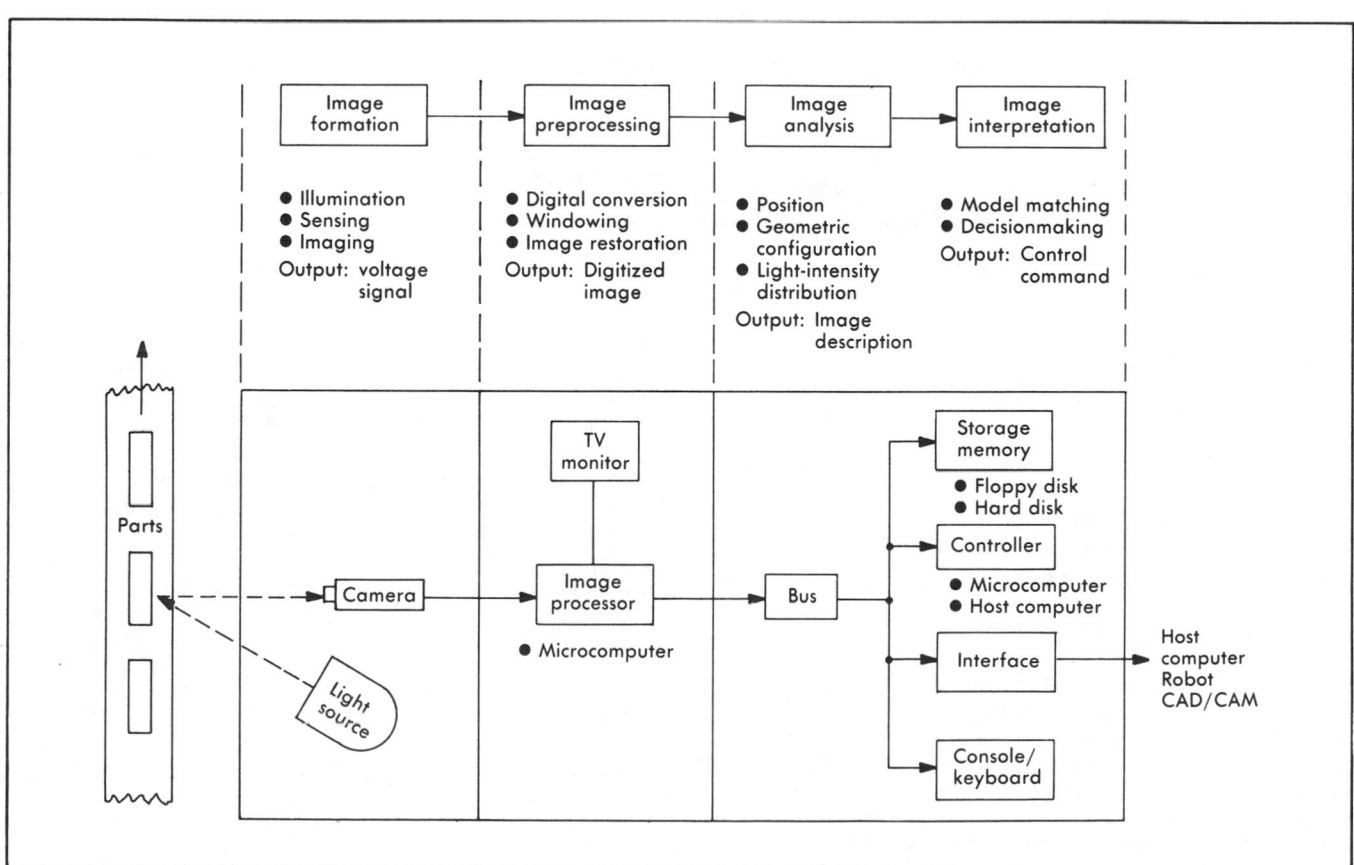

Fig. 12-34 Typical machine vision process. (*Tech Tran Consultants*)

MACHINE VISION SYSTEMS

Image Analysis

The third general step in the vision sensing process is to analyze the digital image that has been formed so that conclusions can be drawn and decisions can be made. This can be performed in the system's central processing unit (CPU) or in custom hardware. The image is analyzed by describing and measuring the properties of several image features. These features may belong to the image as a whole or to regions of the image. In general, machine vision systems begin the process of image interpretation by analyzing the simplest features and then adding more complicated features until the image is clearly identified. A large number of different techniques are either used or being developed for use in commercial vision systems to analyze the image features describing the object's position, its geometric configuration, and the distribution of light intensity over the visible surface of the object.

Some simple geometric features may be area, perimeter, diameter, centroid, curvatures, or angles. More complex features may be edge gradients, spatial frequency content, projections, histograms, or convolutions.

Image Interpretation

When the system has completed the process of analyzing image features, some conclusion must be made about the findings, such as the verification that a part is or is not present, the identification of an object based on recognition of its image, or the establishment that certain parameters of the object fall within acceptable limits. Based on these conclusions, certain decisions can then be made about the object or the production process. These conclusions are formed by comparing the results of the analysis with a prestored set of standard criteria. These standard criteria describe the expected characteristics of the image and are developed either through a programmed model of the image or by building an average profile of previously examined objects. The two most commonly used methods of image interpretation are feature weighting and template matching.

Feature weighting. In cases in which several image features must be measured to interpret an image, a simple factor weighting method may be used to consider the relative contribution of each feature to the analysis. For example, when identifying a valve stem from among a group of stems of several sizes, the image area may not be sufficient by itself to ensure a positive identification. The measurement of height may add some additional information, as may the determination of the centroid of the image. Each feature would be compared with a standard for a goodness-of-fit measurement. Features that are known to be the most likely indicators of a match would be weighted more than others. A weighted total goodness-of-fit score could then be determined to indicate the likelihood that the object has been correctly identified.

Template matching. In template matching, a mask is electronically generated to match a standard image of an object. When the system inspects other objects in an attempt to recognize them, it aligns the image of each object with that of the standard object. In the case of a perfect match, all pixels would align perfectly. If the objects are not precisely the same, some pixels will fall outside of the standard image. The percentage of pixels in the two images that match is a measure of the goodness of fit. A threshold value can then be assigned to test for "pass" (positive match) or "reject" (no match). A probability factor, which presents the degree of confidence that a correct interpretation has been made, is normally calculated along with the GO/NOT-GO conclusion.

ROBOTIC INSPECTION SYSTEMS

With the recent introduction of sophisticated machine vision systems into the workplace, it is now possible to expand the role of robots in flexible inspection.[9,10] Recent advances in CAD/CAM technology now make possible the integration of CAD/CAM into robotic systems.[11] This marriage of CAD/CAM with robotics significantly improves the productivity and economies of robot inspection systems.

The application areas for robotic inspection systems can be generalized as follows:

- Moderate throughput rates.
- Frequent part or model changes or model mix.
- Off-line part inspection requiring a large number of measurements.
- Large parts with complex geometry such as cavities.

ADVANTAGES AND LIMITATIONS

Robot-based inspection systems can provide the maximum in flexibility. A variety of sensors can be mounted on the robot wrist. Robots with articulated arms can reach inside of parts with cavities, such as car bodies and appliances. Robots can be programmed to measure reference datum points and planes on a part. Algorithms, using these reference point measurements, can calibrate the part coordinate system, which allows the CAD/CAM database to be integrated into the robotic measuring system. This integration eliminates the need for precision part fixturing, allows real-time adaptive robot path trajectory control, and provides off-line programming of robot path trajectories.

Inspection robots have a number of limitations. As previously pointed out, they can inspect parts only at moderate throughput rates; about 100 parts per hour would be a nominal rate. They are, therefore, not well suited for very high speed production lines where 1000 parts per hour are common. Gaging accuracy is another concern. At the present time, robot gaging systems rely on the repeatability of the robot for the gaging tolerance. Positioning repeatabilities of commercially available robots suitable for inspection applications range from ±0.001 to 0.008" (±0.025 to 0.20 mm). The sensors are typically accurate to one part in 500 to one part in 1000 of the total field of view, which is usually 2" (50 mm).

SYSTEM COMPONENTS

The main components in a robotic inspection system are the robot, sensors, part presentation device, computer/control system, and software.

Selection

In selecting a robot-based inspection system for a particular application, the following factors must be considered:

- Robot size, repeatability, resolution, and reach.
- Sensor selection.
- Accuracy requirements.
- Process inspection times.

For inspection applications, the Cartesian-style robot appears most appropriate. Because of its geometric design, the Cartesian robot can provide higher repeatable positioning accuracy than other articulated arm robot styles. Experience has shown that a five-axis robot is adequate for most inspection work. This is because coordinate transformation algorithms can be used to correct sensor limitations imposed by a five-degree-of-freedom robot.

Vision Sensors

There are three types of sensors typically used in gaging systems: (1) one-dimensional sensors, (2) contour sensors, and (3) array sensors.

Sensor selection is determined by the geometry of the part. Range sensors can be used for point information only and cannot be used to analyze edges, holes, or contours. Structured light sensors are used for edges and contours, but are not well suited for holes. Area sensors work well on holes, but need additional information for use on surfaces and contours. Depending on the part geometry of the application, one or more sensors (either different types or different focal lengths) are mounted on the robot arm to make the measurements.

Computer/Control Systems

A robotic inspection system may be composed of two to four small computers that are required to perform different distributed processing functions. These computers are interconnected by a data communication and control network. This configuration allows a host computer to coordinate and control the robot and sensor(s).

System Software

The host computer required by the robotic inspection system can range from a small microcomputer or programmable controller to a powerful minicomputer, depending on the degree of flexibility desired and level of data processing and storage required. Consequently, the system software can range from a 64-byte package for a small microcomputer to several million bytes for a large minicomputer. Even the smallest software package should provide, as a minimum, the following functions:

- Initiate and coordinate the process inspection cycle.
- Read in and store sensor measurement data during inspection cycle execution.
- Transform measured data points into real-world coordinates and compare to desired measurement.
- Output process data results in some acceptable report format.
- Provide a limited operator interface to handle calibration and diagnostic requirements.
- Output warning and diagnostic messages to indicate system malfunction and type of error(s).

References

1. T. Busch, *Industrial Quality Control*, vol. 23, no. 1 (July 1966).
2. William M. Stocker, Jr., and Diane Heiberg, *Tools of Our Metalworking Trade* (New York: McGraw-Hill, Inc., 1982), p. 93.
3. *Ibid.*, p. 96.
4. Francis T. Farago, *Handbook of Dimensional Measurement*, 2nd ed. (New York: Industrial Press, Inc., 1982), p. 27.
5. George Schaffer, "Taking the Measure of CMMs," *American Machinist* (October 1982), pp. 146-147.
6. *Ibid.*, p. 153.
7. *Machine Vision Systems: A Summary and Forecast*, 2nd ed. (Lake Geneva, WI: Tech Tran Consultants, 1985), pp. 26-27.
8. *Ibid.*, pp. 29-66.
9. P. Villers, *Recent Proliferation of Industrial Artificial Vision Applications*, SME Technical Paper MS83-311 (Dearborn, MI: Society of Manufacturing Engineers, 1983).
10. T. Pryor and W. Pastorius, *Applications of Machine Vision to Parts Inspection and Machine Control in the Piece Part Manufacturing Industries*, SME Technical Paper MS83-312 (Dearborn, MI: Society of Manufacturing Engineers 1983).
11. R. L. Simon, "The Marriage Between CAD/CAM System and Robotics" (Bedford, MA: Computer-Vision Corp.).

TESTING AND BALANCING

One purpose of this chapter is to provide manufacturing engineers with an overview of the various test methods that are commonly used in industry, along with their potential applications. It is not intended to provide step-by-step guidelines for how a test should be conducted for a particular application. Tables 13-1 and 13-2 summarize the principal features of various test methods.[1]

Nondestructive testing is the examination of an object or material in a manner that will not impair its future usefulness. The purpose of the actual test may be to detect internal or surface flaws, measure thickness, determine material structure or composition, or measure or detect any of the object's or material's properties. The three primary reasons for non-destructive testing are (1) to prevent accidents and save human lives, (2) to ensure product reliability, and (3) to make a profit for the user.[2]

Nondestructive testing is also referred to as nondestructive evaluation (NDE), nondestructive inspection (NDI), and nondestructive testing and inspection (NDTI). In this chapter, the term *nondestructive testing* (NDT) will be used because it is generally the most commonly accepted term.

All nondestructive tests include the following five basic elements:[3]

1. A source that supplies a suitable form and distribution of probing medium to appropriate regions of the test objects.

2. A modification of the probing medium or its distribution within test objects as a result of discontinuities or variations in material properties.
3. A sensitive detector responsive to changes in distribution or character of the probing medium.
4. A means of indicating or recording signals from the detector in forms useful for interpretation.
5. An observer or device capable of interpreting the indications or records in terms of test material properties or discontinuities.

Material testing is needed to learn about existing material properties and to develop new materials. Various tests are performed to explain why something works or does not work, or to meet a need not satisfied by existing materials. Material selection implies a choice to be made from several different materials. Testing is necessary to properly evaluate a material's potential for meeting the desired properties, as well as to identify any inherent shortcomings that may affect its performance. Quality control testing is done by the producer to control composition and uniformity of a specific material and by the manufacturer to confirm the specified properties and compare competing materials or sources of a given material.

VISUAL INSPECTION

Visual inspection is probably the most widely used of all the nondestructive tests.[4] It is simple, easy to apply, quickly carried out, and usually low in cost. The basic principle used in visual inspection is to illuminate the test specimen with light and then examine the specimen with the eye. In many instances, optical aids are used to assist in the examination.

The effectiveness of visual inspection is influenced by the quality of lighting. The inspector is responsible for ensuring that adequate lighting is available. The type of examination being performed determines how much illumination is necessary. Adequate illumination levels for different types of examinations have been defined and are referenced in some standards and specifications.

The information obtained from visual inspection can be permanently recorded in hard copy form with photographs, videotapes, or motion picture films. The hard copy permits comparison of the inspected specimen to a known normal or abnormal standard. In addition, several experts can study the record to obtain a more objective interpretation and evaluation. Comparisons can also be made with prior

inspections to determine whether there has been crack growth or progressive changes. However, most evaluations are made immediately based solely on what is seen. Any comparisons made are done from memory. With this approach, a valid inspection is based on the inspector's visual acuity and competence.

Some of the optical aids used in visual inspection are mirrors, magnifiers, borescopes, video devices, microscopes, and optical comparators.

MIRRORS AND MAGNIFIERS

Mirrors are invaluable to the inspector because they permit visual inspection inside pipes, threaded and bored holes, and castings, as well as around corners when necessary. The two main types of mirrors commonly used are the dental mirror and the movable end mirror.

BORESCOPES

The two primary types of industrial borescopes are rigid borescopes and flexible borescopes or fiberscopes. The type used depends on the application. In addition to the rigid and flexible borescope, other type of borescopes are made for

VISUAL INSPECTION

TABLE 13-1
General Description of Common NDT Methods

Method	Principle	Material
Visual inspection	Illuminate the test specimen with light and then examine the specimen with the eye. May include the use of optical aids	Most materials
Liquid penetrant	A liquid penetrant is drawn into surface flaws by capillary action, then revealed by developer material to aid in visual inspection	Nonporous materials, metals, plastics, and glazed ceramics
Magnetic particle	Magnetic particles, attracted by leakage flux at surface flaws of magnetic object, aid visual inspection	Magnetic materials
Ultrasonic	Sound vibration waves are introduced into a test object. This energy is reflected and scattered by inhomogeneities or becomes resonant. Information is interpreted from cathode ray tube or read from a meter	Metals, plastics, ceramics, glass, rubber, graphite, and concrete
Radiographic	General—penetrating radiation is differentially absorbed by materials, depending on thickness and type of material	Most materials
Eddy-current	Alternating-current coil induces eddy currents in test object. Flaws and material properties affect flow of current. Information derived from meter or cathode ray tube indications	Metals
Leak testing	Material flows across an interface at a leak site. Rate of flow is pressure, time, and leak size dependent. Detection of the trans-interface migration is done using one of several techniques	Totally independent of materials
Infrared	Electromagnetic radiation from test object above a temperature of absolute zero is detected and correlated to quality. Information is displayed by meter, recorder, photograph, or cathode ray tube	Most materials
Acoustic emission	Acoustic emission is a transient elastic wave generated by the rapid release of energy from a localized source within a solid material. Rate and amplitude of high-frequency acoustic emissions are noted and correlated to structure or object characteristics	Solid materials as well as liquids and fluids
Neutron radiography	Neutron beam is attenuated by test object; attenuation pattern of test object is recorded at image plane after conversion of transmitted neutron beam and subsequent detection by film or other imaging device	Neutrons are especially sensitive to hydrogenous materials (adhesives, explosives, and moisture), lithium, boron, cadmium, and several rare-earth materials

TABLE 13-1—*Continued*

Applications	Advantages	Limitations
Inspecting accessible surfaces. Internal surfaces may be inspected using a rigid or flexible borescope	Simple, easy to perform, low in cost	Dependent on inspector; can only detect surface flaws
Detect surface flaws such as cracks, porosity, pits, seams, and laps	Simple to perform, applicable to complex shapes, and inspection can be made on site	Can only detect surface flaws. Surfaces must be clean. The penetrant washes out of large defects. Standards are difficult to establish
Detect surface flaws such as cracks, laps, and seams. Capable of detecting some subsurface flaws	Easy to interpret, fast, and simple to perform	Material must be ferromagnetic. Parts must be relatively clean. Usually requires high current source. Parts must be demagnetized. Standards are difficult to establish
Detect inclusions, cracks, porosity, bursts, laminations, structure, lack of bond, thickness measurement, and weld defects	Variety of inspection elements and circuitry permits selective high sensitivity. High-speed test. Can be automated and recorded. Penetrates up to 60' (18 m) in steel. Indicates flaw location. Access to only one surface usually needed	Difficult to use with complex shapes. Surface may affect test. Defect orientation affects test. Comparative standards only. Requires couplant
Can detect internal defects such as inclusions, porosity, shrink, hot tears, cracks, cold shuts, and coarse structure in cast metals; lack of fusion and penetration in welds. Detection of missing parts in an assembly	More standards established than for other methods. Internal defects detected. Permanent film record. Automatic thickness gaging	Health precautions necessary. Defect must be at least 2% of total section thickness. Film processing requires time, facilities, and care. Difficult to use on complex shapes. Most costly NDT method
Material composition, structure, hardness changes, cracks, case depth, voids, large inclusions, tubing weld defects, laminations, coating thickness, porosity	Intimate contact between coil and material not required. Versatile. Special coils can be easily made. Operation can be automated. Electric circuit design variations permit selective sensitivity and function. Sensitive to surface and near-surface inhomogeneities	Sensitive to many variables. Sensitivity varies with depth. Reference standards needed. Response often comparative
Any vessel containing a product at a pressure different from ambient or a vessel in which a pressure different from ambient can be created for evaluation	Provides assurance that the vessel will contain contents as designed. Advantages vary for the technique used	Varies from technique to technique
Discontinuities that interrupt heat flow such as flaws, voids, inclusions, lack of bond. Higher or lower than normal resistances in circuitry	High sensitivity. One-sided inspection possible. Applicable to complex shapes and assemblies of dissimilar components. Active or passive specimens	Emissivity variations in materials, coatings, and colors must be considered. In multilayer assemblies, hot spots can be hidden behind cool surface component. Relatively slow
Determine or monitor integrity of structures such as weldments or castings	Remote and continuous real-time surveillance of structures is possible. Inaccessible flaws can be determined. Permanent record can be made	Part must be stressed. Nonpropagating flaws cannot be detected. Nonrelevant noise must be filtered out. Transducers must be placed on the object being tested
Detects cracks, voids, and density changes. Presence, absence, or mislocation of internal components of suitable composition	Good penetration of most structural metals. High sensitivity to favorable materials. Permanent record. Complementary to X-ray information	Cost. Not readily portable. Potential health hazard for operators

(continued)

VISUAL INSPECTION

TABLE 13-1—Continued

Method	Principle	Material
Holographic	An optical means of capturing and recording the wavefronts resulting from a distorted object and then comparing them with the image of an undistorted object	Bonded and composite structures. Automotive or aircraft tires. Three-dimensional imaging

TABLE 13-2
Mechanical Tests and Determined Properties

Tension	Compression	Flexure	Direct Shear	Torsion
Elongation	Compressive strength	Modulus of rupture	Shear strength	Angle of twist
Reduction in area	Yield strength	Transverse strength		Modulus of rupture
Tensile strength	Drop-of-the-beam	Flexural strength		Shear strength
Yield strength	"Dividers" method	Proportional limit		Yield strength
Drop-of-the-beam	Stated offset	Tangent		Stated offset
"Dividers" method	Proportional limit	Modulus of elasticity		Proportional limit
Stated offset	Tangent	Initial modulus		Tangent
Proportional limit	Stated offset			Modulus of elasticity
Tangent	Elastic limit			Modulus of rigidity
Stated offset	Modulus of elasticity			Initial modulus
Elastic limit	Initial modulus			
Modulus of elasticity	Tangent modulus			
Initial modulus	Secant modulus			
Tangent modulus				
Secant modulus				

Notched-Bar Impact	Hardness	Fatigue	Creep	Stress-Rupture*
Notch sensitivity	Hardness number	Fatigue strength	Rate of elongation	Time to fracture
Charpy	Brinell	Endurance strength	Minimum creep rate	Total elongation
Izod	Rockwell	Endurance limit	Total elongation	Reduction in area
Notch temperature sensitivity	Rockwell (superficial)	Endurance ratio		
Charpy	Vickers	Notch sensitivity ratio		
% Shear	Knoop			
Ductility	Scleroscope			
	Microcharacter and others			

* If time-elongation measurements also are made, the properties listed under Creep also may be determined.

specialized applications. Another borescope option that has been recently developed is the video device, described subsequently. Like industrial borescopes, it can be either rigid or flexible in design.

Rigid Borescopes

The rigid borescope is generally selected for applications in which a straight line path exists between the viewer and the object to be inspected. It is similar in design to a telescope, but while a telescope narrows the field of view for observation at a distance, the borescope spreads the view for closeup work.

The main components of a rigid borescope are a tubular shell, eyepiece, optical lenses, viewing head, and a light source (Fig. 13-1). The shell can be made in one piece or in modular sections, depending on the length of the borescope.

Flexible Borescopes

Flexible borescopes or fiberscopes are primarily used in applications that do not have a straight passageway to the point of observation. A typical fiberscope consists of an image guide fiber bundle, an objective lens, protective sheath, eyepiece lens, focus and diopter rings, and remote controls for the top articulation (Fig. 13-2). These components are then connected to any one of a variety of light sources.

The optical bundles carry up to 40,000 glass fibers. Each individual fiber consists of a central core of high-quality optical glass coated with a thin layer or cladding of another glass having a different reflective index. The cladding prevents the light entering the end of the fiber from escaping or passing through the sides to an adjacent fiber in the bundle. The number of fibers used is determined by the diameter of the image guide.

VIDEO DEVICES

Video devices used for visual inspection incorporate a probe, video processor, and a color display monitor. The probe can be flexible or rigid and is available in sizes from 3/8 to 9/16" (9.5 to 14 mm) diam and in lengths from 4.9 to 100' (1.5 to 30 m). An

TABLE 13-1—*Continued*

Applications	Advantages	Limitations
Detects strain, plastic deformation, cracks, debonded areas, voids, and inclusions. Measures vibration	Contact or special surface preparations are not required. Applicable to complex shapes	Vibration-free environment is required. Difficult to identify type of flaw detected.

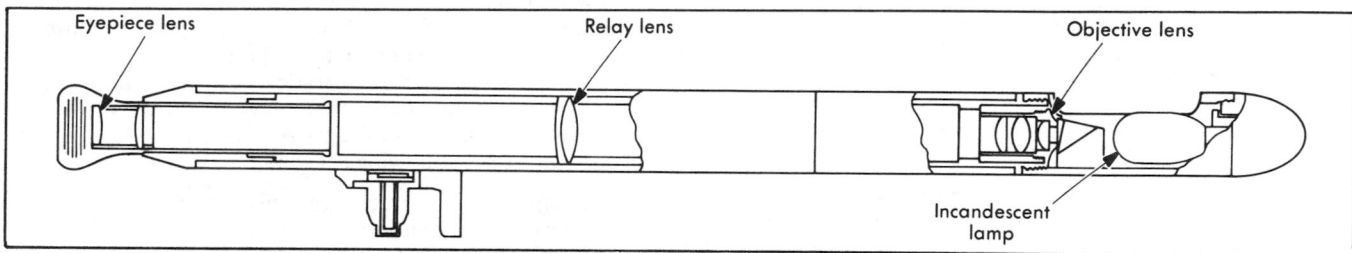

Fig. 13-1 Typical components in a rigid borescope with incandescent illumination. (*Lenox Instrument Co.*)

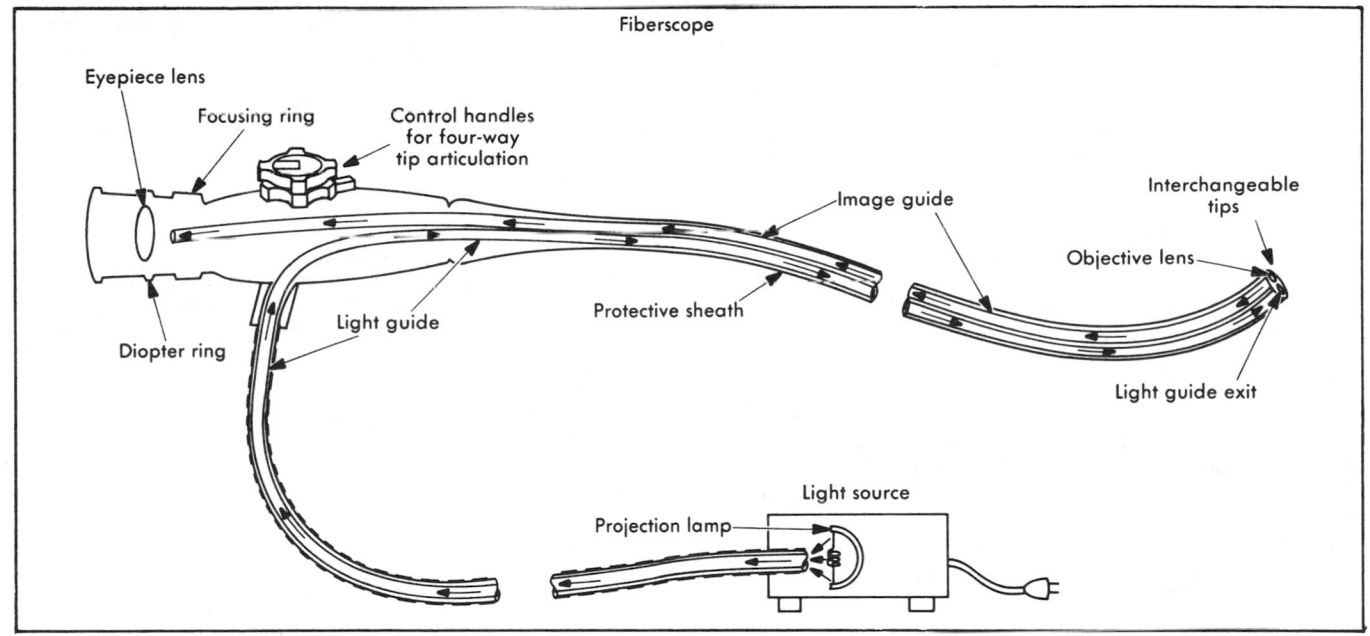

Fig. 13-2 Typical components in a flexible borescope. (*Olympus Corp.*)

electronic sensor, located in the tip of the probe, transfers the object image electronically to the processor. The probe also houses a fiber-optic bundle for illuminating the area being inspected.

LIQUID PENETRANT INSPECTION

The liquid penetrant inspection process is a simple method of locating defects on the surface of metals or other nonporous materials. It is based on the oil and whiting process used by the railroad industry until the mid-1930s. In practice, a dyed liquid penetrant is applied to the surface of the prepared workpiece (Fig. 13-3). After a period of time, the excess penetrant is removed and an absorbent developer is applied. The developer causes the penetrant to be drawn out of any cracks or discontinuities, indicating the locations of defects.

Liquid penetrant inspection can be used to inspect all types of surface cracks, porosity, laminations, and bond joints. In addition, it can be used to inspect for leaks in tubing, pipes, tanks, and welds. Liquid penetrant inspection is effective on any relatively hard, nonporous material.[5] Its widest usefulness is in

LIQUID PENETRANT INSPECTION

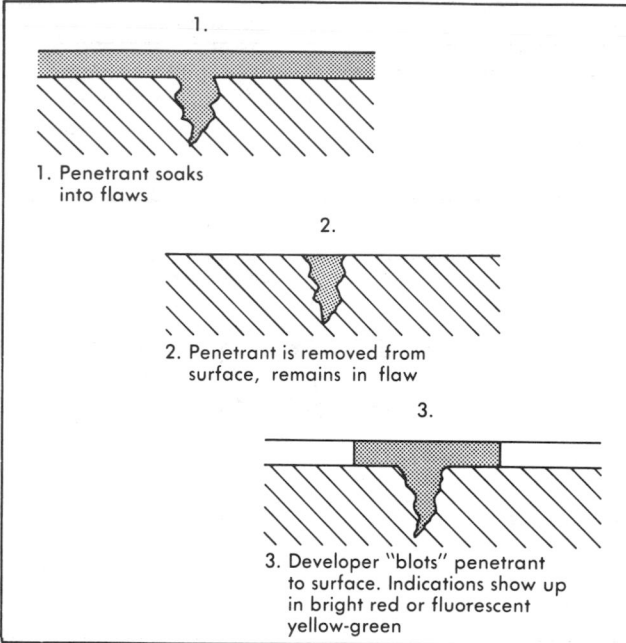

1. Penetrant soaks into flaws

2. Penetrant is removed from surface, remains in flaw

3. Developer "blots" penetrant to surface. Indications show up in bright red or fluorescent yellow-green

Fig. 13-3 Picture diagram of liquid penetrant inspection: (a) penetrant soaks into flaws, (b) penetrant is removed from surface but remains in flaws, and (c) developer blots penetrant to surface. Indications show up in bright red or fluorescent yellow-green.

finding flaws in nonmagnetic metals such as aluminum, magnesium, stainless steels, copper, brass, and various other metals and alloys, including titanium, beryllium, and zirconium. It is also applicable on magnetic metals, vitrified ceramics, powdered metals, glass, and some plastics.

ADVANTAGES AND LIMITATIONS

The versatility of the liquid penetrant process is responsible for its many advantages. For example, portable penetrant kits consisting of aerosol spray cans of penetrant materials can be used in the field to detect small flaws. In field applications, electricity or special equipment may not be required, and the inspection is reliable, inexpensive, and rapid. Liquid penetrant inspection can also be used in a production line setting. High-

sensitivity fluorescent penetrants are capable of identifying extremely small flaws.

Because of the way the process works, liquid penetrant inspection only finds flaws that are open to the surface of the part being tested. Flaws beneath the surface require a different detection method. The part must also be clean and dry because the penetrant cannot enter surface defects that are already filled with dirt, oil, grease, paint, water, or other contamination.

EQUIPMENT

The type of equipment selected for liquid penetrant inspection determines whether or not the inspection method will be an economical and productive operation or a costly and wasteful means of discarding parts that may not be defective.[6] In general, liquid penetrant inspection equipment can be classified in one of the three following categories:

1. Simple, hand-operated, portable equipment that can be moved about easily as needed.
2. Stationary equipment that is somewhat universal in the variety of parts it can accommodate.
3. Specialized high-volume units built to accommodate one or a very few specific parts. The equipment is generally designed to function as an integral part of a production line.

The components that are included in a complete system depend on the number of processing steps required for the penetrant. Typical components in a given system would include:[7]

- Precleaning station; this is usually separated from the penetrant equipment line.
- Penetrant application station, including drain rack.
- Emulsifier station, used only for postemulsifiable penetrants.
- Solvent-remover station, used only with visible-dye penetrants.
- Washing station, used with water-washable and postemulsifiable penetrants.
- Wet-developer station.
- Dryer.
- Dry-developer station.
- Inspection station.
- Postcleaning station.

MAGNETIC PARTICLE TESTING

Magnetic particle testing (MT) is one of the oldest and most widely used nondestructive test methods. It is used for locating surface and subsurface flaws in ferromagnetic materials such as iron, steel, and nickel and cobalt alloys.

Typically, the part being tested is magnetized, and then finely divided magnetic particles are applied to its surface either during or immediately following magnetization. Any discontinuities that generally lie in a direction perpendicular to the magnetic field cause a leakage field to be formed at and above the surface of the part (see Fig. 13-4). The leakage field gathers and holds the magnetic particles at the location of the discontinuity so that it can be visually evaluated. The gathered particles not only indicate the location of the discontinuity, but also provide some indication of its size, shape, and extent.

The principal industrial uses of MT are in-process and final product inspection, maintenance and overhaul of equipment, and machinery maintenance. Although in-process magnetic particle testing is used to detect discontinuities and imperfections in material and parts as early as possible in the sequence of operations, final inspection is needed to ensure that rejectable discontinuities or imperfections detrimental to the use or function of the part have not developed during processing.

Portions of this subchapter are abstracted with permission from *Classroom Training Handbook, Magnetic Particle Testing.*[8]

ADVANTAGES AND LIMITATIONS

The magnetic particle method is a sensitive means of locating surface and near-surface cracks in ferromagnetic materials. Indications may be produced by very small cracks as well as those large enough to be seen by the naked eye. Exceedingly wide cracks will produce a particle pattern at the corner of the surface and crack even if the surface opening is too wide for the particles to bridge.

Discontinuities that do not actually break through the surface also are indicated in many instances by this method, although certain limitations must be recognized and understood. If a discontinuity has reasonable depth and is close to the surface, a sharp indication can be produced. If the discontinuity lies deeper, the indication is less distinct.

The size and shape of the parts inspected by this method are almost unlimited. However, abrupt changes in dimension can cause problems with indication interpretation. In general, elaborate precleaning is not necessary, and cracks filled with nonmagnetic foreign materials can also be detected.

Magnetic particle testing has certain limitations that must be taken into consideration. For example, thin coatings of paint and other nonmagnetic coverings, such as plating, can adversely affect the sensitivity of MT. Other limitations are the following:

- Magnetic particle testing will only work on ferromagnetic materials. Nonmagnetic materials such as aluminum, magnesium, copper, lead, tin, titanium, and their alloys, as well as austenitic stainless steels, cannot be inspected by this method.
- For best results, the magnetic field must be in a direction that will intercept the principal plane of the discontinuity at right angles. This may require two or more sequential inspections with different magnetizations.
- Demagnetization after inspection is often necessary.

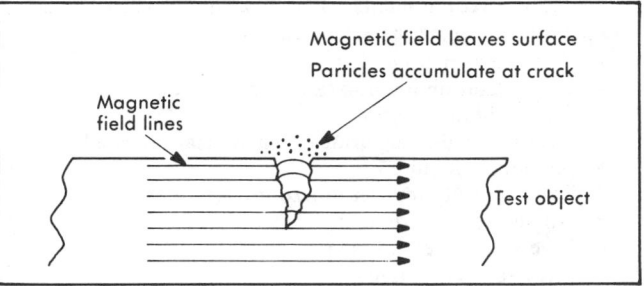

Fig. 13-4 Cross section of a part undergoing magnetic particle testing.

On aircraft parts, demagnetization is required 100% of the time.

- Postcleaning to remove remnants of the magnetic particles or carrying solutions clinging to the surface may sometimes be required after inspection and demagnetization. On aircraft parts, postcleaning is required 100% of the time.
- High currents arc sometimes required.
- Care is necessary to avoid local heating and burning of finished parts or surfaces at the points of electrical contact.
- Although magnetic particle indications are easily seen, experience and skill are required to interpret their significance.

EQUIPMENT

The equipment used to process articles for magnetic particle testing ranges from heavy, complex, and automated systems weighing several tons to small, lightweight, portable units. The

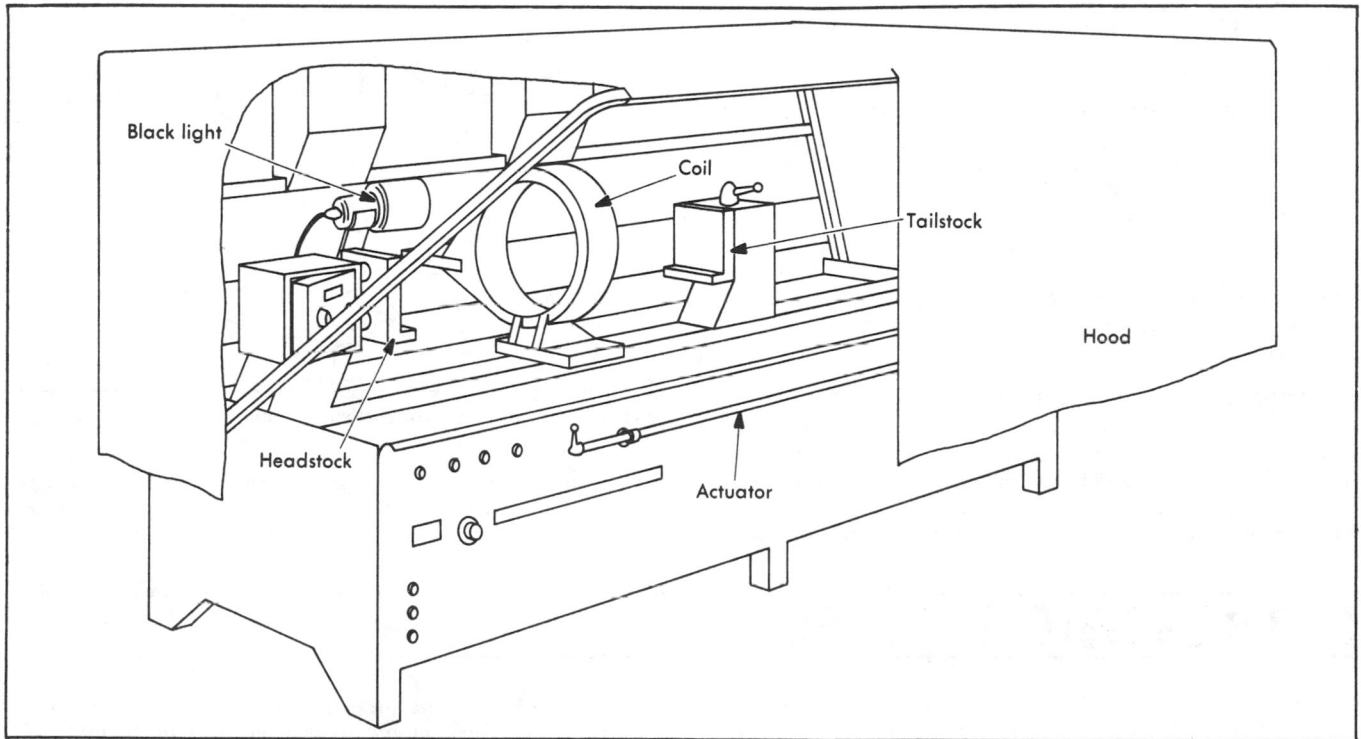

Fig. 13-5 Wet horizontal magnetic particle test equipment. (*Ardrox, Inc.*)

MAGNETIC PARTICLE TESTING

following are requirements to be considered when selecting equipment for magnetic particle testing:

- Wet or dry method.
- Magnetization method (a-c, d-c, or both).
- Degree of automation.
- Incorporated or separate demagnetization capability.
- Amperage required.
- Tank capacity for wet horizontal equipment.
- Air supply requirements.
- Line voltage requirements.
- Accessories required.

Wet Horizontal Equipment

Wet magnetic particle equipment is available or can be built to handle parts of almost any length. The type of equipment illustrated in Fig. 13-5 enables magnetization of parts ranging from a few inches (centimeters) to approximately 12′ (3.6 m) in length. Head openings of 54-144″ (1370-3660 mm) are commonly available.

Mobile Equipment

It is often necessary to bring the test equipment to a part located in another area. The type of equipment used is mobile and sturdy and is able to provide various types and methods of required tests.

A typical mobile piece of magnetic particle equipment is illustrated in Fig. 13-6. This type of equipment operates on 220 or 440 V a-c and provides both a-c and half-wave d-c variable up to approximately 6000 A. Selection of a-c or half-wave d-c is accomplished by switching cables on output lugs located on the front of the unit. Cables ranging in length from 15 to 30′ (4.5 to 9 m) may be further extended to as long as 100′ (30 m) by additional lengths.

Portable Equipment

Figure 13-7 shows a typical portable magnetic particle testing unit. Portable equipment is available in a variety of sizes, shapes, and weights, with a variety of input voltages and amperage outputs. Portable equipment makes testing possible in formerly inaccessible areas. Portable equipment operates on the same principles as stationary equipment; however, the compactness and ample amperage output makes portable equipment a prime tool for testing a variety of articles. Portable equipment is usually operated on 110/220 V a-c and is rated between 500 and 1000 A output depending on model and type. Some models provide only a-c output, others provide only d-c output, and others have the capability of providing both a-c and d-c.

Demagnetizing Equipment

Most common types of demagnetization equipment consist of an open, tunnel-like coil utilizing a-c at the incoming frequency, usually 60 Hz. The larger equipment incorporates a track or carriage to facilitate moving large and heavy articles. Smaller demagnetization equipment such as tabletop units,

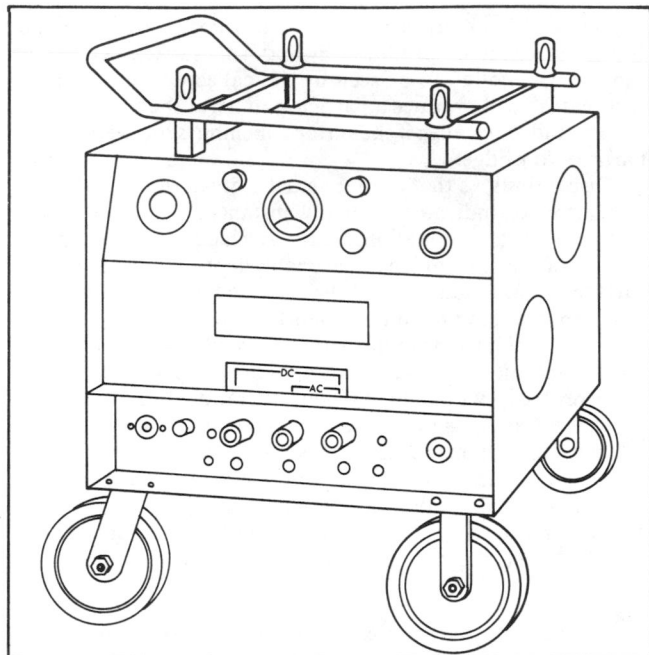

Fig. 13-6 Mobile magnetic particle test equipment. (*Ardrox, Inc.*)

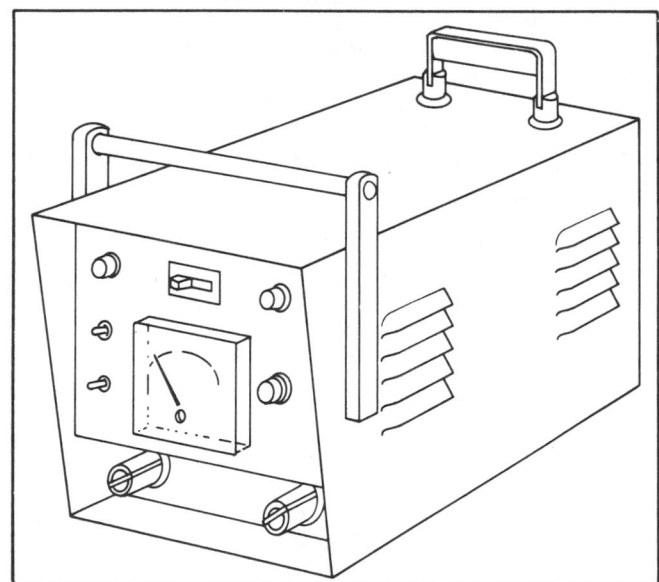

Fig. 13-7 Portable magnetic particle test equipment. (*Ardrox, Inc.*)

yokes, or plug-in cable coils may be feasible for demagnetization of small articles. The large stationary equipment, however, is preferable when multidimensional articles are involved.

ULTRASONIC TESTING

Ultrasonic testing (UT) is a widely used nondestructive method of testing materials. It involves the use of beams of high-frequency sound waves introduced into the material being inspected to detect flaws, measure thickness, or evaluate material properties. The sound waves travel through the material and are reflected back by a material discontinuity to the source of the sound. The reflected beam is then detected and analyzed to define the presence and location of flaws.

Portions of this subchapter are abstracted with permission from *Classroom Training Handbook, Ultrasonic Testing.*[9]

APPLICATIONS

Materials capable of being tested by ultrasonic energy are those that transmit vibrational energy. Metals can be tested by UT in thicknesses up to 30′ (9 m). Noncellular plastics, ceramics, glass, new concrete, organic materials, and rubber can also be tested.

The three main areas in which UT is currently being used are (1) determination of structural integrity, (2) thickness measurement, and (3) evaluation of material properties.

Determining Structural Integrity

When checking parts for structural integrity, the inspector is looking for discontinuities or flaws in the part. Some of the flaws that can be detected by UT include cracks, gross porosity, lack of fusion, laminations, inclusions, segregates, stringers, and bonding faults. Subsurface flaws are usually of primary importance, but UT can also be used to detect surface-breaking discontinuities such as cracks in tubing.

Some of the major types of components that are ultrasonically inspected for the presence of flaws are the following:[10]

- Mill components—rolls, shafts, drives, and press columns.
- Power equipment—turbine forgings, generator rotors, pressure piping, weldments, pressure vessels, nuclear fuel elements, and other reactor components.
- Jet engine parts—turbine and compressor forgings and gear blanks.
- Aircraft components—forging stock, frame sections, and honeycomb sandwich assemblies.
- Machinery materials—die blocks, tool steels, and drill pipe.
- Railroad parts—axles, wheels, and bolted and welded rail.
- Automotive parts—forgings, ductile iron castings, and brazed and/or welded components.

Thickness Measurement

The thickness of a part can be determined from transit time measurements or resonance techniques. When measuring thickness, either the material velocity must be known or appropriate reference standards must be used. Access to only one surface is required, but opposite surfaces must be nearly parallel with the entry surface.

Ultrasonic thickness gaging is widely used in the plastics industry to nondestructively check the wall thickness of molded containers, in the foundry industry to check casting thickness, and in the metal fabrication industry to measure thickness of rolled or machined parts.

Material Property Evaluation

Evaluation of material properties is generally applicable to those elastic or structural properties that affect the propagation of acoustic waves such as hardness, elasticity, density, grain structure, and crystal orientation. Applications range from laboratory investigations, such as the measurement of dynamic elastic moduli, to in-process monitoring of nodular iron castings.

ADVANTAGES AND LIMITATIONS

The principal advantages of ultrasonic testing in comparison with other methods of nondestructive testing are the following:[11]

- Superior penetrating power, permitting detection of flaws deep in the part.
- Ability to detect extremely small flaws.
- Greater accuracy than other nondestructive methods in determining the position of internal flaws, estimating their sizes, and characterizing them in terms of nature, orientation, and shape.
- Only one surface need be accessible.
- Operation is electronic, providing almost instantaneous indications of flaws. This makes the method suitable for immediate interpretation, automation, rapid scanning, in-line production monitoring, and process control.
- With most systems, a permanent record of inspection results can be made.
- Volumetric scanning ability, permitting inspection of a volume of material extending from the front surface to the back surface of a part.
- Presents no radiation hazard to operations or nearby personnel and has no effect on nearby equipment and materials.
- Portability.

Disadvantages of UT include the following:[12]

- Operation requires careful attention by experienced technicians.
- Technical knowledge is required for development of inspection procedures.
- Parts that are rough, irregular in shape, very small or thin, or not homogeneous are difficult to inspect.
- Discontinuities that are present in a shallow layer immediately beneath the surface may not be detectable.
- Couplant is needed to provide effective transfer of the ultrasonic beam between the transducer and part being tested.
- Reference standards are required, both for calibrating the equipment and for characterizing flaws.

EQUIPMENT

Ultrasonic test equipment consists of the transducer, which converts electrical pulses into sound waves; related transmission cables; and the ultrasonic test instrument, which generates the initial electric pulse to the transducer and also electronically processes and interprets the received pulses from the transducer. The great majority of ultrasonic testing is accomplished with the pulse-echo method. In this method, individual pulses of sound with high frequency and short duration are sent into the test material. A small amount of testing is also done by the resonance method. In the resonance method, continuous, rather than pulsed, ultrasound is used.

Transducers

In ultrasonic testing, the ear of the system is the transducer. It consists of a specially prepared piezoelectric element that transforms electrical pulses into high-frequency sound and vice versa. The resonant frequency of the transducer may be between 100 kHz and 100 MHz; the most commonly used frequencies are 1, 2.25, 5, 10, and 15 MHz.

The shape of the transducer crystal or element may be circu-

CHAPTER 13

ULTRASONIC TESTING

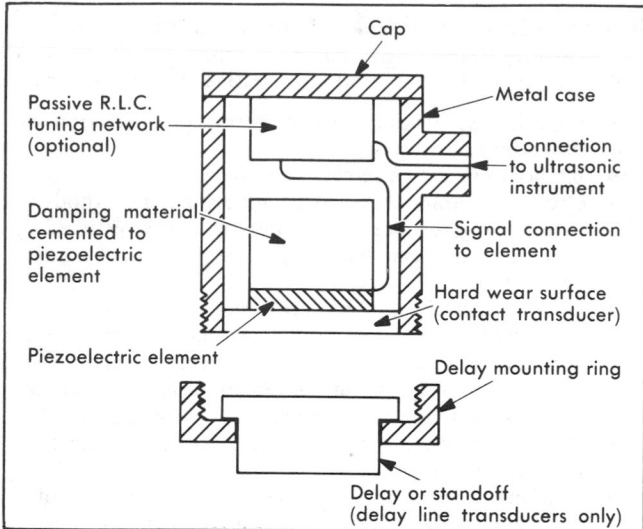

Fig. 13-8 Cross section of a typical transducer. (*Staveley Ultrasonic NDT Technologies, Inc., Sonic Div.*)

lar, square, or rectangular. Common circular sizes are 1/8, 1/4, 3/8, 1/2, 3/4, and 1″ (3, 6, 9, 12, 18, and 25 mm). Square or rectangular transducers range in size from 1/4 x 1/4 to 1 x 1 (6 x 6 mm to 25 x 25 mm) in 1/4″ (6 mm) increments. Construction of a typical transducer is shown in Fig. 13-8.

Materials. The three most common piezoelectric materials that have been used in ultrasonic transducers are quartz, lithium sulfate, and polarized ceramics. Virtually all modern transducers are made from polarized ceramics. With the replacement of crystalline quartz and lithium sulfate with polarized ceramics, it is no longer proper to refer to the transducer element as the crystal.

Types of transducers. Several different types of transducers are currently being used. The type of transducer selected depends on the specific application.

Contact transducers. Contact transducers are placed directly on the part to be tested and introduce sound into the part at 90° to the surface. The elements are protected from the surface by a durable wear plate, and the shape of the element is generally circular.

Either broad-band or narrow-band transducers may be used for flaw testing, while broad-band transducers are chosen for thickness gaging because of superior resolution. Low-frequency (about 1 MHz) narrow-band transducers can penetrate more than 10′ (3 m) in most metallic substances. High-frequency (up to 20 MHz) broad-band transducers can perform precise thickness gaging on thin materials or detect close proximity flaws because of the short pulse duration.

Delay-line transducers. Delay-line transducers are also used in direct contact with the surface. The piezoelectric element is separated from the surface by a delay line of plastic or metal to either protect the element from high-temperature surfaces or to improve the resolution on thin materials by separating the returned sound from the large initial pulse produced by the transducer and ultrasonic test instrument. Delay-line transducers can be used to accurately gage the thickness of materials as thin as 0.005″ (0.13 mm).

Dual transducers. Dual transducers have one element to transmit the initial pulse and a separate element to receive the ultrasonic pulses reflected from internal flaws or from the other

side of the test specimen. Dual transducers often have the sending and receiving elements angled slightly toward each other so that the ultrasound can focus on flaws in the test specimen that are just below the surface. The focusing effect also allows dual transducers to effectively measure pitting and corrosion on the inside surface of pipes.

Angle beam transducers. The angle beam transducer is constructed with an integral or removable wedge that causes the sound to be introduced at an angle other than 90° to the surface of the test specimen. These transducers generally have square or rectangular elements. The commonly used angles are 45, 60, and 70° away from normal to the surface.

When angle beam transducers are used, mode conversion occurs when the sound enters the test specimen; thus the ultrasonic wave is no longer a longitudinal sound wave, but is a shear sound wave. The velocity and wavelength of shear waves are approximately one half that of corresponding longitudinal waves.

Angle beam transducers are used for testing welded materials when the weld bead prevents use of contact transducers being placed on top of the weld or when angular sound waves provide a better beam orientation for flaw testing.

A special type of angle beam transducer is a surface wave transducer. With these transducers, mode conversion causes the ultrasound to travel along the surface of the test specimen and detect surface or near-subsurface discontinuities. The surface wave can also travel around radiused areas of the surface as long as the sound wavelength is smaller than the radius of curvature.

Immersion transducers. Immersion transducers are not held in direct contact with the test specimen, but are separated by a liquid transmitting medium such as water or oil. The use of immersion transducers offers a number of advantages over the contact transducer, although the associated equipment necessary to perform the scanning and immerse the test specimen increases the initial cost. Among the advantages and features of immersion transducer testing are the following:

- Mechanical scanning of the transducer is possible because the liquid in which the specimen is immersed reliably couples the ultrasonic waves to the tested part, regardless of the surface condition of the test specimen.
- The direction of the sound beam can be easily altered as required by the geometry of the part being tested.
- Through-transmission techniques can be used. With these techniques, separate transmitting and receiving transducers are on opposite sides of the test part.
- The ultrasonic beam can be easily focused with immersion transducers. With available focusing techniques, the sound beam can have a cross section as small as 0.005″ (0.13 mm), and the detectability of minute flaws [0.001″ (0.03 mm) or smaller] is possible. In focusing, however, the depth of field of the sound beam is restricted, and the transducer will lose penetrating capability for thick sections. In addition, the smaller beam size requires more scanning time if 100% inspection is required. In some cases, the sound beam is focused into an elongated rectangular area known as a line focus so that small-flaw detectability is optimized while the scanning speed is maintained because of the width of the sound beam.

Multielement transducers. A multielement or array transducer consists of a number of elements individually pulsed in an appropriate pattern. With appropriate synchronization of the pulses to each individual element, these transducers can either improve scanning speed while maintaining small-flaw detectability or dynamically focus or angulate the sound beam because of the acoustic interaction of the separate elements. Multielement transducers, however, require additional expense and complexity in the associated ultrasonic test instrument.

Couplants

One of the practical problems in ultrasonic testing is the transmission of the ultrasonic energy from the source into the test specimen. If a transducer is placed in contact with the surface of a dry part, very little energy is transmitted through the interface into the material because of the presence of air between the transducer and the test material. The air causes a great difference in acoustic impedance (impedance mismatch) at the interface.

A couplant is used between the transducer face and the test surface to ensure efficient sound transmission from transducer to test surface. The couplant, as the name implies, couples the transducer ultrasonically to the surface of the test specimen by smoothing out the irregularities of the test surface and by excluding all air from between the transducer and the test surface. The couplant can be any of a vast variety of liquids, semiliquids, pastes, and even some solids, that will satisfy the following requirements:

- A couplant wets (fully contacts) both the surface of the test specimen and the face of the transducer and excludes all air from between them.
- A couplant is easy to apply.
- A couplant is homogeneous and free of air bubbles or of solid particles, in the case of a nonsolid.
- A couplant is harmless to the test specimen, transducer, and operator.
- A couplant has a tendency to stay on the test surface, but is easy to remove.
- A couplant has an acoustic impedance value between the

impedance value of the transducer face and the impedance value of the test specimen, preferably approaching that of the test surface.

Test Instrument

The ultrasonic test instrument must be capable of producing the individual pulses to the transducer and electronically processing the returned pulses from the transducer. A block diagram of a typical instrument is shown in Fig. 13-9.

The main components of the test instrument are the clock, pulser, receiver, gate, and CRT display.

Computerized Ultrasonic Testing

In recent years the reduction in cost for micro and minicomputers has made computer-controlled ultrasonic testing economically viable. A computerized system may involve either digital acquisition and storage of ultrasonic data or additional computerized automation to control the setting of the ultrasonic instrument, control the scan pattern of the transducer (typically an immersion test), and digitize, process, and store the resulting data. A block diagram of a computerized ultrasonic testing system is shown in Fig. 13-10. Test time may be greatly reduced and operator error minimized with the use of automated systems.

High-Speed Scanning Equipment

Ultrasonic tanks and bridge/manipulators are necessary equipment for high-speed scanning of immersed test specimens. Modern units consist of a bridge and manipulator, mounted over a fairly large water tank, to support a pulse-echo testing unit and a recorder. Drive power units move the bridge along the tank side rails, while traversing power units move the manipulator from side to side along the bridge. Most of these units are automated, although some early units are manually operated. On most automatic units, a C-scan recorder is also

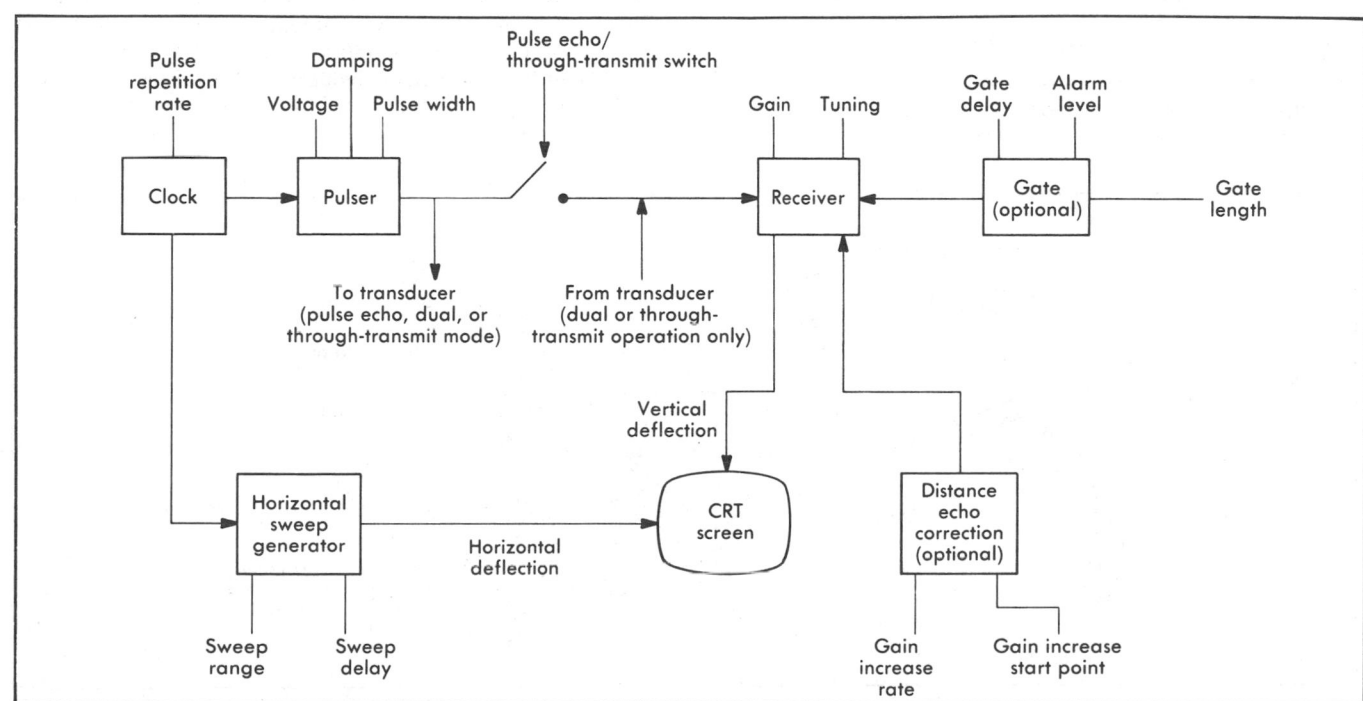

Fig. 13-9 Ultrasonic instrument block diagram. (*Staveley Ultrasonic NDT Technologies, Inc., Sonic Div.*)

ULTRASONIC TESTING

mounted on the bridge.

Ultrasonic tank. The ultrasonic tank may be of any size or shape required to accommodate the test specimen. Coverage of the specimen by a foot or more of water is usually sufficient. Adjustable brackets and variable-speed turntables are provided on the tank bottom for support of the test specimen. The water couplant in the tank is clean, de-aerated water containing a wetting agent. For operator comfort, the water temperature is usually maintained at 70°F (21°C) by automatic controls.

Bridge/manipulator. The bridge/manipulator unit is primarily intended to provide a means of scanning the test specimen with an immersed transducer. The version shown in Fig. 13-11 has a bridge with a carriage unit at each end so the bridge may be easily moved along the tank side rails. The manipulator is mounted on a traversing mechanism that allows movement of the manipulator from side to side. The traversing mechanism is an integral component of the bridge assembly. The search tube

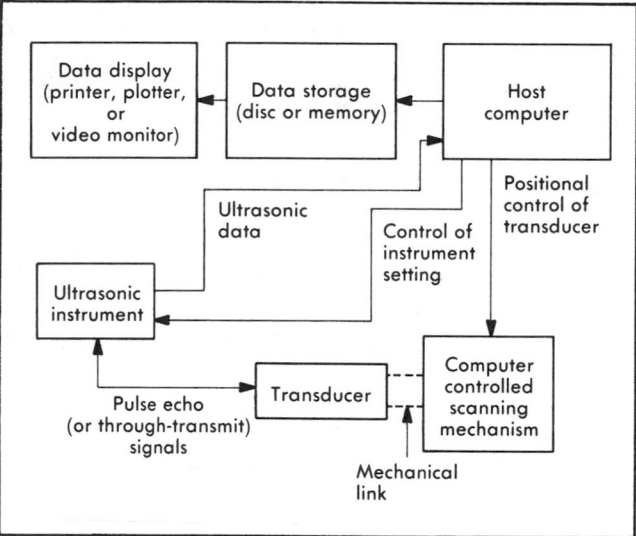

Fig. 13-10 Computerized ultrasonic testing system. (*Staveley Ultrasonic NDT Technologies, Inc., Sonic Div.*)

is usually held rigid, as shown, at right angles to the surface of the test specimen. Locking knobs are provided on the manipulator to allow positioning of the search tube in two planes for angle beam testing.

When the equipment is automated, electric motors are added to power the bridge carriage, the traversing mechanism, and the up-down movement of the search tube. The pulse-echo unit and the recording unit are also mounted on the bridge, with all power cords secured overhead to allow movement of the bridge along the full length of the tank.

Standard Reference Blocks

In ultrasonic testing, all discontinuity indications are compared to indications received from testing a reference standard. The reference standard may be any one of many reference blocks, or sets of blocks, specified for a given test. Ultrasonic standard reference blocks, often called test blocks, are used in ultrasonic testing to standardize the ultrasonic equipment and to evaluate the discontinuity indication received from the test part. Standardizing does two things: (1) it verifies that the instrument/transducer combination is performing as required, and (2) it establishes a sensitivity, or gain, setting at which all discontinuities of the size specified, or larger, will be detected. Evaluation of discontinuities within the test specimen is accomplished by comparing their indications with the indication received from an artificial discontinuity of known size and at the same depth in a standard reference block of the same material.

Standard test blocks are made from carefully selected ultrasonically inspected stock that meets a predetermined standard of sound attenuation, grain size, and heat treatment. Discontinuities are represented by carefully drilled flat-bottomed holes. Test blocks are carefully made and tested so that the only discontinuity present is the one that was added intentionally. The three most familiar sets of amplitude reference blocks are: the Alcoa-Series A area/amplitude blocks; the Alcoa-Series B, or Hitt, distance/amplitude blocks; and the ASTM basic set of blocks that combine area/amplitude and distance/amplitude blocks in one set.

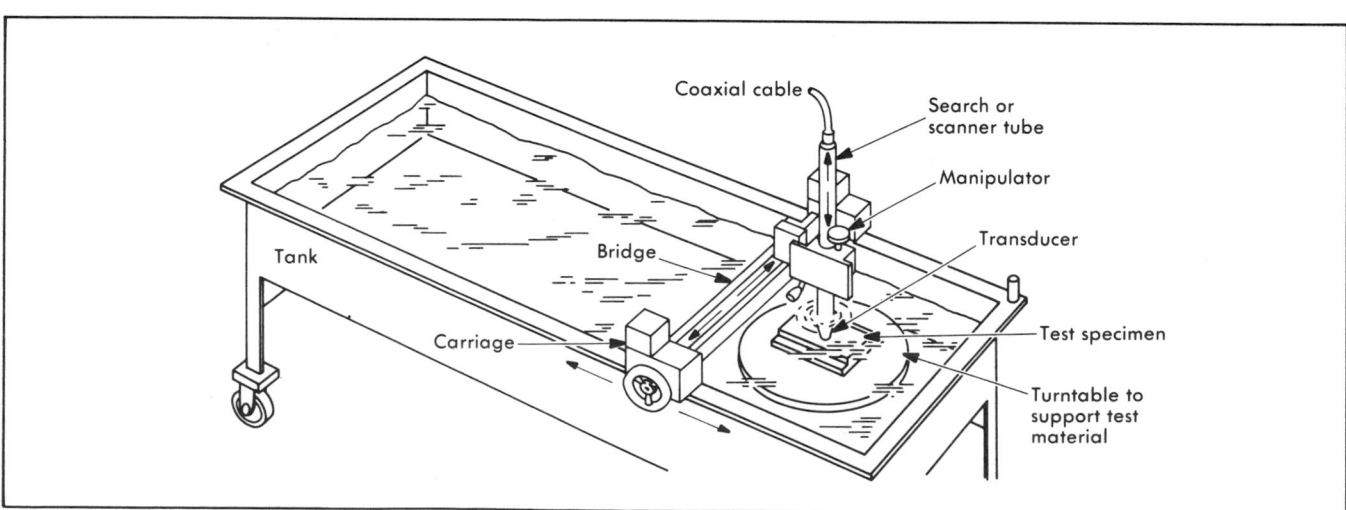

Fig. 13-11 Bridge/manipulator unit in a high-speed scanning system used in computerized ultrasonic testing.

RADIOGRAPHIC TESTING

Radiographic testing (RT) is a versatile nondestructive test method for use in modern industry. A radiograph is similar to a photographic record produced by the passage of X-rays or gamma rays through an object onto a film. When film is exposed to X-rays, gamma rays, or light, an invisible change, called a latent image, is produced in the film emulsion. The areas exposed darken when the film is immersed in a developing solution; the degree of darkening depends on the amount of exposure and the amount of developing. After development, the film is rinsed, preferably in a special bath, to stop development. The film is next put into a fixing bath, which dissolves the undarkened portions of the sensitive salt and hardens the emulsion. It is then washed to remove the fixer and dried so that it may be handled, interpreted, and filed.

Portions of this subchapter are abstracted with permission from *Classroom Training Handbook, Radiographic Testing*[13] and *Radiography in Modern Industry*.[14]

APPLICATIONS

The ability of X-ray and gamma ray radiation to penetrate all engineering materials and the differential rates of absorption for different materials is responsible for the extensive use of this nondestructive inspection technique throughout industry.[15] Accordingly, radiographic inspection methods are extensively used for flaw detection in castings, weldments, solid propellants, missile hardware, and finished assemblies as well as some other applications. The parts inspected by radiographic testing range in size from microminiature electronic parts to large missile rocket motors.

ADVANTAGES AND LIMITATIONS

Some of the advantages of radiographic testing as a quality assurance procedure are the following:

- Can be used with most materials.
- Provides a permanent visual-image record of the test specimen on film when desired.
- Reveals most discontinuities of a material.
- Discloses fabrication errors and often indicates necessary corrective action.
- Reveals assembly errors.

There are both physical and economic limitations to the use of radiographic testing. Geometric exposure requirements make it difficult to use radiographic testing on specimens of complex geometry. When proper orientation of radiation source, specimen, and film cannot be obtained, radiographic testing is of little use. Similarly, any specimen that does not lend itself readily to two-side accessibility cannot be inspected by this method. Because radiographs are patterned by material density differences in the specimen, they are of little value in detecting small discontinuities not parallel to the lines of radiation. Laminar-type discontinuities are therefore often undetected by radiographic testing. If laminar-type discontinuities are suspected in a specimen, the radiation source, the specimen, and the film must be oriented to present the greatest possible discontinuity density difference to the rays. The greatest dimension of the suspected discontinuity must be parallel to the radiation beam and equal to about 2% of the material thickness.

Safety considerations imposed by the use of X-rays and gamma rays must also be considered as a limitation. Compliance with safety regulations, mandatory in radiographic testing, is time consuming and requires costly space utilization and construction practices. Radiographic testing is a relatively expensive means of nondestructive testing. It is most economical when it is used to inspect easily handled material of simple geometry with high rates of test. It becomes expensive when it is used to examine thick specimens that require high energy potential equipment.

EQUIPMENT

Before selecting any equipment for radiographic testing, an analysis of the specimen for inspection should be performed. This analysis would involve determining the types of material being tested and the maximum and minimum thicknesses. The types of material and specimen thicknesses being tested dictate the X-ray potential or gamma ray energy required to achieve sufficient penetration. Consideration must also be given to the size and weight of the specimen, the steps in the production process where inspection is best suited, and the quantity to be inspected in a given time. The type of manufacturing facility and the size, weight, and quantity of products to be inspected establish equipment requirements.

Selection

Because of its flexibility and fewer radiation hazards, X-radiography is preferred to gamma radiography. Gamma radiography is usually selected for industrial applications that involve the following:

- High radiation energy requirements when high-energy X-ray machines are not available.
- Low testing rates.
- Simultaneous exposure of many specimens.
- Confined areas where X-ray cannot be used.
- Field inspections in areas where electrical power is difficult to obtain.

Selection of equipment for a particular test consists of the following related decisions:

- Selection of RT as a test method.
- Selection of X-radiography or gamma radiography.
- Selection of specific X-ray or gamma ray equipment.

Additional factors to consider are available equipment, the time allotted for the test, and the number or frequency of similar specimen tests.

Ideally, there is a best equipment selection for any radiographic test. Practically, most radiography is accomplished by using the equipment available. The equipment lends itself to numerous adaptations, and by knowledgeable choice of film and exposure, any particular equipment can be used for a variety of tasks. For this reason, the capabilities of individual X-ray machines and isotope cameras overlap in many areas of test. Except in large production installations or in a test laboratory, it is impractical to have multiple radiographic equipment. Therefore, it is the responsibility of radiographic test and quality assurance personnel to ensure that the equipment and techniques selected are capable of performing the required task.

X-Ray Equipment

The generation of X-rays requires a source of free electrons, a means of moving the electrons in the right direction, and a

RADIOGRAPHIC TESTING

suitable material for the electrons to strike. The two primary elements in any X-ray machine are the X-ray tube and the power supply. Other components such as shielding, tubeheads, control panels, and coolers are designed to support the function of the tube or to meet safety requirements.

Factors to consider when selecting X-ray equipment are radiation energy, radiation output, source size, and range of operation. It is usually best to obtain a unit that emits a spectrum containing a large portion of the short wavelengths. Longer wavelength X-rays that improve radiographic contrast can be obtained by operating the equipment at low energies. With the designs being equal, an X-ray machine that has the highest output in roentgens per minute at a given distance is the best selection. Machines with the smallest target area, yet capable of providing a useful quantity of radiation, have the best sensitivity. A tradeoff must be made regarding the operating range of the machine and its cost; machines with large ranges are the most expensive.

X-ray tube. The productive portion of X-ray equipment is the tube. It consists of two electrodes, the cathode and the anode, enclosed in a tube envelope (see Fig. 13-12). When current is applied, the filament portion of the cathode functions as a source of free electrons and the anode as the target on which the electrons strike. X-ray tubes that are equipped to produce two size focal spots have two filaments; one of the filaments is larger than the other.

Gamma Ray Equipment

Gamma rays are produced by the nuclei of isotopes undergoing disintegration because of their instability. Radiation from these materials cannot be shut off. Therefore, gamma ray equipment is designed to provide radiation-safe storage and remote handling of the radioisotope source. Most equipment used in the production of gamma rays consists of the radioactive source and the gamma ray projector.

Sources. The three most commonly used sources are cobalt 60, iridium 192, and thulium 170. Cobalt 60 is supplied in the form of a capsuled pellet and may be obtained in different sizes. It is used for radiography of steel, copper, brass, and other medium weight metals of thicknesses ranging from 1 to 10″ (25-250 mm).

Iridium 192 is used for radiography of steel and similar metals of thicknesses between 1/4 and 3″ (6 and 75 mm). Its relatively low-energy radiation and its high specific activity combine to make it an easily shielded, strong radiation source of small physical size. Like cobalt 60, iridium 192 is also available in capsuled pellet.

Thulium 170 is the best isotope known for the radiography of thin metals. Because it has soft-wave radiation, thulium 170 can be contained in small cameras. It is usually supplied in capsules containing thulium oxide (Tm_2O_3) powder.

Because all the radioisotope material is producing gamma rays, the focal spot in gamma radiography is the surface area of the material as viewed from the specimen. For this reason, it is desirable that the gamma ray source be as small as possible. Most isotopes in gamma radiography are cylinders whose diameter and length are approximately equal. When the isotope source is not a right cylinder, it is necessary to place the smallest area of the source parallel to the plane of the specimen for maximum sharpness of film image.

Gamma ray projector. Gamma ray projectors store the radioactive source when not in use and provide a means of exposing the specimen and film to radiation. Most projectors are made from a mass of heavy metal, such as lead or uranium, and contain a passage leading to its geometric center. The amount of metal used is predetermined to reduce the radiation at the surface to a safe level.

Two styles of projectors are commonly used in gamma radiography. The first style stores the radioactive source in a shield case assembly when it is not being used. When exposure is required, the source is moved to the tip of the guide tube with a reel assembly (see Fig. 13-13).

The second style of projector does not require the source to be moved from the shield case assembly for exposure. Instead, a cone section of the case is designed to swing away, permitting the unobstructed escape of radiation (see Fig. 13-14). Both styles of projectors are also referred to as a radioisotope camera.

SAFETY

One of the most important considerations in the X-ray or gamma ray laboratory is the provision and exercise of adequate safeguards for the personnel. Because radiation cannot be detected by any of the human senses and its damaging effects do not become immediately apparent, personnel protection is dependent on detection devices and adequate shielding.

Any of the body tissues may be injured by excessive exposure to X-rays or gamma rays, the blood, the lens of the eye, and

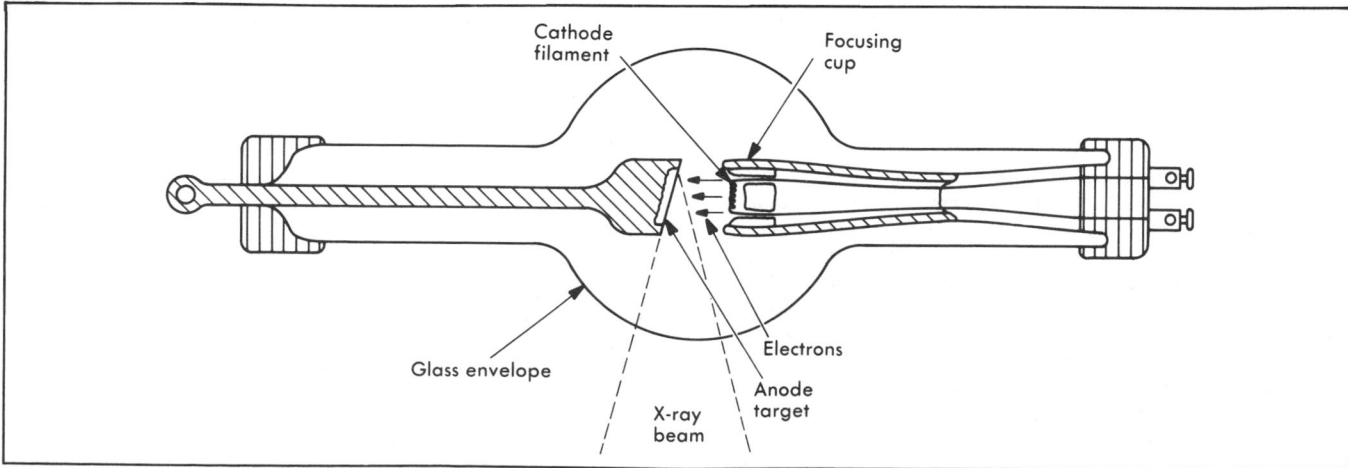

Fig. 13-12 Basic X-ray tube. (*General Dynamics, Convair Div.*)

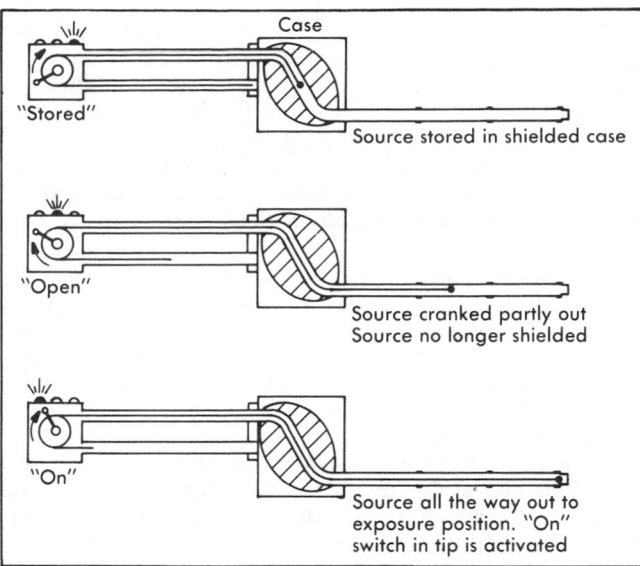

Fig. 13-13 Operation of a typical gamma ray emitter. (*General Dynamics, Convair Div.*)

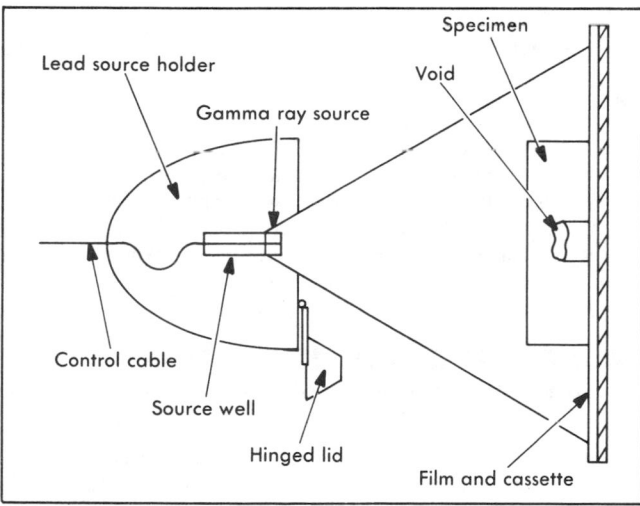

Fig. 13-14 Schematic of a typical gamma ray projector. (*Eastman Kodak Co.*)

some internal organs being particularly sensitive. Unless exposure to X-rays or gamma rays is kept at a minimum, the cumulative effect may cause injury to the body. It is, therefore, essential that workers in the radiographic department be adequately protected against radiation at all times. Furthermore, protective measures should be so arranged that persons in nearby areas are also safe. Precautions should be particularly observed when radiography is done in the work areas of the shop rather than in a specially constructed department.

Detection and Measurement Instruments

Various techniques, based on the characteristic effects of radiant energy on matter, are employed in detection and measurement devices. Chemical and photographic detection methods are used, as well as methods that measure the excitation effect of radiation on certain materials. In radiography, however, the

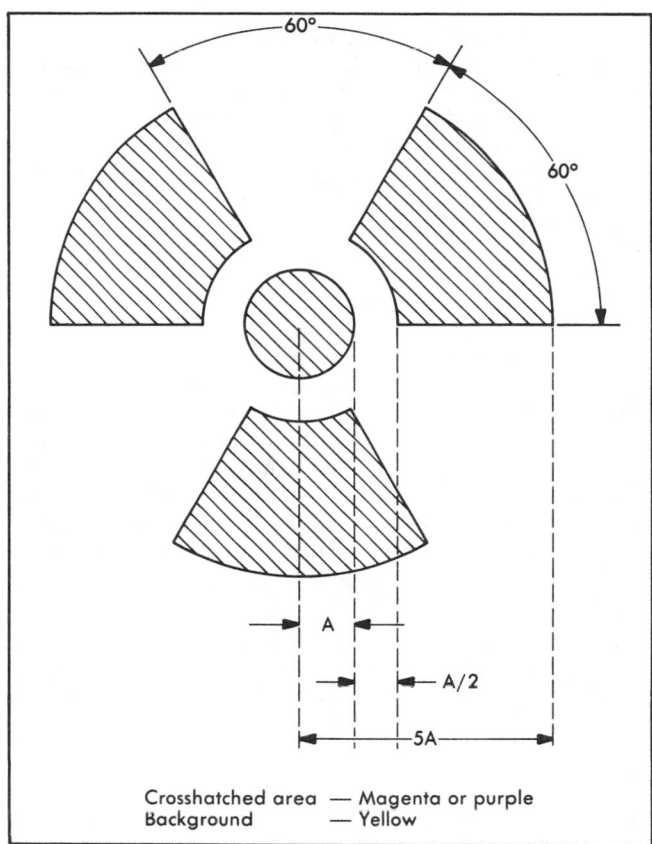

Crosshatched area — Magenta or purple
Background — Yellow

Fig. 13-15 Radiation symbol. (*General Dynamics, Convair Div.*)

instruments most commonly used for radiation detection and measurement rely on the ionization produced in a gas by radiation. Because the hazard of radiation is calculated in terms of total dose and dose rate, the instruments used for detection and measurement logically fall into two categories: (1) instruments that measure total dose exposure and (2) instruments that measure dose rate (radiation intensity).

Radiation Protection

Exposure to radiation may be caused by the direct beam from the X-ray tube or by scattered radiation arising from objects in the direct beam. The three primary means of controlling body exposure to radiation are time, distance, and shielding. In addition, it is important to clearly designate containers of radioactive materials, areas housing those containers, and areas exposed to radiation.

The USNRC requires a sign with the symbol shown in Fig. 13-15 to be placed in conspicuous locations in all exposure areas and on all containers in which radioactive materials are transported, stored, or used. On each sign, the word "Caution" or the word "Danger" must appear. Other wording required is determined by specific sign use. Area signs bear the phrases "Radiation Area," "High-Radiation Area," or "Airborne Radioactivity Area" as appropriate. Containers of radioactive materials and areas housing such containers must be marked with signs or labels bearing the radiation symbol and the words "Radioactive Material(s)." Special tags bearing the radiation symbol and the phrase "Danger—Radioactive Material—Do Not Handle. Notify Civil Authorities If Found" must be attached to sealed

EDDY-CURRENT TESTING

sources not fastened to or contained in an exposure device.

Allowable working time. The amount of radiation absorbed by the human body is directly proportional to the time the body is exposed to the radiation. A person receiving 2 mr in 1 minute at a given point in a radiation field would receive 10 mr in 5 minutes. Allowable working time can be calculated by the following equation:

$$W_A = E_P/E_R \qquad (1)$$

where:

W_A = allowable working time, hr/wk
E_P = permissible exposure, mr/wk
E_R = exposure rate, mr/hr

The exposure rate is determined by measuring radiation intensity with an ionization chamber instrument. The value for permissible exposure is different for monitored radiation workers than for unmonitored nonradiation workers.

Working distance. The greater the distance from a radiation source, the lower the exposure received. The inverse square law is used to calculate radiation intensities at various distances from a source.

Shielding. The most common material used to protect against radiation is lead. It is easily available and comparatively low in cost. Shielding protective measurements are usually expressed in terms of lead thickness. Particular care must be exercised to ensure leakproof shielding. Adjacent sheets of lead must be overlapped, and nails or screws that pass through the lead must also be covered with lead. Pipes, conduits, and air ducts passing through the walls of the shielded area must be completely shielded.

Gamma ray requirements. Gamma radiation cannot be shut off, and protection must be provided at all times. The penetrating capability of gamma radiation makes it impractical to rely on shielding for protection during gamma radiography; a combination of distance and shielding is usually employed. The radiation danger zone is roped off and clearly marked with conspicuous signs; only those persons making the radiograph are permitted in the zone. The extent of the danger zone is based on calculations of safe distance as determined by the source strength. In calculating the area of the danger zone, the possible effects of scatter radiation are considered, and the calculations are confirmed by intensity measurements.

EDDY-CURRENT TESTING

Electromagnetic testing is a term that describes the broad spectrum of electronic test methods involving the interaction of magnetic fields and circulating currents. A widely applied technique within this category is eddy-current testing.

Eddy-current testing (ET) involves the use of a varying magnetic field produced by a test coil to induce small, circulating currents called eddy currents into electrically conductive materials. Certain properties within the material have an effect on the eddy currents thus induced. The eddy currents themselves set up a magnetic field that interacts with the magnetic field of the coil in such a way that the electrical signal of the test coil is changed. Any change in the eddy currents is reflected by a change in the test coil electrical signal. Because the electrical signal of the test coil can be monitored by instruments, any factor existing in the material under test that affects the eddy currents can be detected.

Portions of this subchapter are abstracted with permission from *Classroom Training Handbook, Eddy Current Testing.*[16]

APPLICATIONS

In ET, the word *flaw* has a much wider meaning than it does for other forms of nondestructive testing. Applications of eddy-current testing fall into one of four general categories: (1) metal sorting, (2) surface or subsurface discontinuity detection, (3) thickness measurement, and (4) inside diameter tube inspection. Because a continuous indication is a part of the basic testing system, automatic production testing is feasible. Depending on the equipment and test conditions, ET has been used to:[17]

- Detect discontinuities such as seams, laps, slivers, scabs, pits, cracks, voids, inclusions, and cold shuts.
- Sort for chemical composition on a qualitative basis.
- Sort for physical properties such as hardness, case depth,

and heat damage.
- Measure conductivity and related properties.
- Measure dimensions such as the thickness of metallic coatings, plating, cladding, wall thickness, inside or outside diameter of tubing, corrosion depth, and wear.
- Measure the thickness of nonmetals when a metallic backing sheet can be employed.

ADVANTAGES AND LIMITATIONS

Some of the advantages of eddy-current testing include the following:

- The signal indicating the status of the material is obtained almost instantaneously. There is no requirement for allowing time for the indication to develop.
- The testing procedures are readily adaptable to GO/NOT-GO situations.
- The method is sensitive to many physical and metallurgical variables.
- The only link between the test equipment and the item under test is a magnetic field.
- The equipment for the most part can be self-powered and therefore portable.
- Automatic production testing is feasible.
- On-site, in-service inspection capability.

Some of the limitations include the following:

- Success of the testing procedure is directly related to suppressing variables not of interest.
- Variations in test procedures may be required to determine which variable is being indicated.
- The procedures are applicable to conductive materials only.
- The depth of penetration is restricted—approximately

1/2" (13 mm) in aluminum with standard probes.
- Testing of ferromagnetic metals is sometimes difficult.

EQUIPMENT

Eddy-current test equipment ranges from simple portable units to complex automatic or console-type apparatus.[18] Regardless of the complexity, each system must have at least the following elements:

- A source of magnetic field capable of inducing eddy currents in conductive materials.
- A sensor or probe that is capable of sensing minute changes in the magnetic fields caused by eddy currents.
- A means of interpreting the measured changes in magnetic field.

Instruments

Many different types of eddy-current instruments are currently available; they are all similar in principle, but vary in function and accessories. Every test instrument contains a source of alternating current. In some instruments the source is at a fixed frequency, but in others the frequency can be varied. Multifrequency instruments can be employed to achieve high resolution in more than one area of interest. The test instrument also contains a means of interpreting the signal received from the test coil. Interpretation of the change may be achieved by impedance analysis, phase analysis, or modulation analysis. The procedure used depends on the manufacturer of the instrument and the intended application.

Test Coils

The test coil is an essential part of every eddy-current test system. The test coil induces eddy currents in the material being tested in such a way as to produce a signal indicating the presence of a discontinuity and possible information about the nature of the discontinuity. With most commercial equipment, various sizes and shapes of test coils are supplied and are expressly designed for use with that equipment. From these coils, the operator must choose the one that is most closely suited to the geometry of the part being tested and is capable of establishing an eddy-current pattern of a size sufficiently small to be consistent with the dimensions of the smallest flaw of interest.

The characteristics of the test coil are affected by the part's conductivity, permeability, mass, and homogeneity. The electrical characteristics of the test coil are also affected by the test system's frequency, coil size, current, and spacing.

Three basic types of test coils are used in ET: (1) surface coil, (2) encircling coil, and (3) internal or bobbin-type coil (see Fig. 13-16). Special coil configuration are also available from equipment manufacturers for specialized applications.

Indicating Devices

An important part of the eddy-current test system is the part of the instrument that gives the technician the indication of the change in electrical charge. Several different types of devices are commonly used. The device may be an integral part of the test set, it may be a module that is plugged into the test set, or it may be a separate unit connected to the test set with a cable. The indicating device used should be of adequate speed, accuracy, and range to meet the requirements of the test system.

Two types of meters are commonly used as indicating devices: (1) analog meters and (2) digital meters. The visual output of an analog meter varies as a continuous function of the input to the meter. Response is immediate and the scales can usually be calibrated to read specific values directly. The output of a digital meter is shown in discrete steps in time; input is measured at a given moment and the value is numerically displayed. Because the output of a digital meter is in numbers, possible reading error is less likely than with an analog meter, but the output is relatively slow. Digital meters are used mainly with conductivity measurements.

Another type of indicating device used to display the output of a test circuit is an oscilloscope. Oscilloscopes give an instantaneous, continuous presentation, are highly accurate, provide calibration capabilities so that values may be read directly, have a broad range, and the presentation is adjustable so that parameters of particular interest may be studied more closely.

Strip-chart recorders provide an analog recording of values at reasonably high speeds. The strip-chart recorder is one method that produces a permanent, fairly accurate record. Several channels can be recorded at the same time.

For most inspection systems, a visible or audio alarm can be used to indicate when the specified values have not been attained. Cathode ray tubes with a storage capability are also available and allow visual comparison of indications.

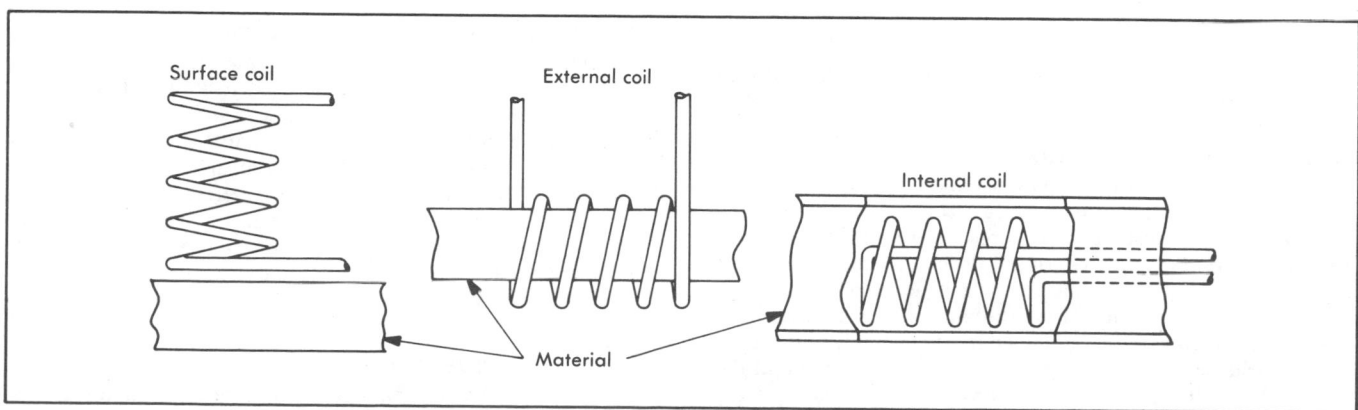

Fig. 13-16 Basic test coil types for eddy-current testing. (*General Dynamics, Convair Div.*)

EDDY-CURRENT TESTING

Standards

As in other types of nondestructive testing, the most useful data is obtained by comparing the data from an item under test with data from a reference standard. Standards furnish an exact value that has been established by authority, custom, or agreement as the norm by which other like parts may be judged. Standards also help in the design of procedures developed to measure those quantities that are represented by the standard. Standards often define the limits of acceptability of an item and serve to ascertain that the equipment being used is capable of measuring that quantity to the required degree of accuracy. A standard is also used to make sure that the equipment provides consistent sensitivity each time the equipment is used.

In eddy-current testing, standards are most often manufactured to fit a particular test situation; however, commercially prepared standards for use in checking the conductivity of a material are available and are usually supplied with conductivity measuring instruments. Discontinuity standards should duplicate the test situation for material type and geometry. In addition, they should include discontinuities that establish the maximum discontinuity that is acceptable and also establish the sensitivity of the system. The two types of discontinuity standards used are natural discontinuity standards and artificial discontinuity standards. When external comparison techniques are used, the reference standard must be free of discontinuities.

TESTING TECHNIQUES

As was mentioned previously, ET can be used in a variety of applications. Each specific application, in turn, has specific techniques that must be followed to ensure accurate results. The success of an eddy-current test depends on the following.[19]

- Proper coil design and arrangement.
- Selection of the proper test frequency or frequencies.
- Selection of the proper instrument.
- Use of proper technique procedures.
- Optimization and maintenance of electromagnetic coupling (liftoff) between the coil and the test piece.
- Selection of the most suitable stage in the manufacturing process for the test procedure.

Because ET involves the use of magnetic fields and conductive materials, the operator must make sure that the tests are performed in areas that are free of any magnetic or electrical disturbances; for example, any conductive material, including all parts other than the part being tested, should be kept at least 12″ (300 mm) away from the test coil. Tabletops that are made of a conductive material are a common source of error. Test coils must also be kept away from the magnetic fields produced by large motors and transformers.

Discontinuity Detection

When the test coil of an eddy-current test system is placed on an electrically conductive material, a certain impedance value is established in the test circuit that results from the presence of the eddy currents in the material. If the coil is then moved over an area that has a discontinuity, the eddy-current flow will be impeded by the presence of the discontinuity. This change in eddy-current flow causes a change in the test coil as it moves across the discontinuity. Care must be taken to ensure that the coil is always in contact with or consistently spaced from the material at all times because any change in the space between the coil and the material will also cause a change. Readings are calibrated with standards having known defects, either natural or manufactured, in the same kind of material.

Material Sorting

When the test coil is placed on a particular kind of conductive material, a specific electrical signal is established in the test circuit. Any other specimens of the same kind of conductive material will cause the same signal in the test circuit provided that the thickness of all the specimens of the material exceeds the depth of penetration of the eddy currents. Readings should be taken at different locations on a particular piece of material to be certain that the reading is not affected by a discontinuity. Liftoff is a factor to be avoided. Signal values are established on a sample of known material, and then the readings obtained from test samples are compared with the reading obtained from the known sample.

Nonconductive Coating Thickness Measurement

To obtain measurements of the thickness of a nonconductive coating on conductive material, the test coil is placed on a sample of the same material that has a known thickness of nonconductive coating. When the test coil is placed on this standard, an electrical signal is established in the test circuit that represents that specific coating thickness. Any variation in the thickness of the nonconductive coating on the test samples will be indicated as a change in this signal. Maximum and minimum coating thickness limits may be established in the same manner.

Conductive Coating Thickness Measurement

The procedure for measuring the thickness of conductive coatings, or cladding, over conductive material is similar to the procedure for measuring the thickness of nonconductive coatings. The test coil is first placed on standards that have a coating of the correct thickness (or that represent the maximum and minimum allowable thicknesses of the coating); thus the electrical signals for these standards are established. When the test coil is placed on the samples to be tested, variations in the thickness of the cladding are shown by variations in this signal. Any readings obtained that fall outside the established limits indicate that the conductive coating is not within allowable tolerances. Liftoff is a factor to be avoided, and the operator should be aware of the effect of discontinuities on the readings obtained.

Material Thickness Measurement

To measure the thickness of thin materials, standards of the same material are carefully machined to known thicknesses. Meter readings obtained from these standards establish the reference points for those thicknesses of that material. Variations in thickness of the test material are then reflected by changes in the meter reading. The meter scales may be calibrated so that a particular reading indicates a particular thickness, but the operator must be continually aware of the possibility of the existence of other factors that would also affect the reading on the meter.

Hardness Measurement

During age hardening of aluminum or titanium alloys, the hardness and conductivity of the material change simultaneously so that the degree of hardening may be obtained by measuring the conductivity of the test specimen and comparing it with a standard of that material with a known hardness. The operator must be aware of the effects of discontinuities and liftoff on the meter readings.

LEAK TESTING

Leak testing is a form of nondestructive testing capable of determining the existence of leak sites and, under proper conditions, measuring the quantity of material passing through these sites.[20] The term *leak* refers to a hole or passage through which a fluid passes in either a pressurized or evacuated system. Two types of leaks exist: real leaks and virtual leaks. A real leak is a discrete hole or passage through which a fluid may flow. Virtual leaks are sources of gradual desorption of gases from surfaces or components within a vacuum system.

Leakage refers to the mass flow of fluid regardless of the size of the leak. Leakage rate is the quantity of fluid per unit of time that flows through the leak at a given temperature as a result of a specified pressure difference across the leak.

The correct choice of the leak test method/technique should optimize cost, sensitivity, and reliability of the test. By applying a number of selection criteria, the choice can often be narrowed to two or three methods, with the final choices being determined by special circumstances or cost effectiveness. Some of the general factors that should be considered when selecting a leak test method are the following:

- The design and specification requirements.
- The nature and accuracy of test information needed.
- The type or size of the leak to be inspected.
- The size and accessibility of the system.

BUBBLE EMISSION TESTING

Bubble emission testing is the oldest documented method used to detect leaks. In recent years, this method often has been displaced by more modern methods; however, bubble emission testing will continue to be used by industry, especially when the permissible leakage is large, the production rate is low, and operator subjectivity is allowable.

TRACER GAS LEAK TESTING

Tracer gas leak testing is one of the many ways that have been devised to test products for leakage. A typical tracer gas leak test consists of the following three basic steps:

1. A tracer gas in a detectable amount is introduced to one side of the surface to be tested.
2. A differential pressure is produced across the surface with the higher pressure at the tracer gas side.
3. A suitable instrument is used to detect the presence of tracer gas on the lower pressure side.

When performing a tracer gas leak test, it is advisable to use the highest test pressure possible within the design safety factor. This is because a leak rate in the laminar flow range varies with the difference of the squares of the absolute pressures across the leak. If the pressure of tracer gas is not changed, an increase of backup pressure with air or a neutral gas dilutes the tracer gas linearly, but increases the total flow rate by nearly the square of the pressure. Thus, by using a high test pressure, it is possible to either reduce the amount of tracer gas used per test or, if the concentration of tracer gas is maintained, increase the test sensitivity. The test part must be dry because small leaks are easily plugged by any liquid. Dryness is also important because some tracer gas detectors are adversely affected by high amounts of water or hydrocarbon vapors.

Advantages and Limitations

The major advantages of tracer gas leak testing in general are the following:

- Lower leak rates can be detected than with any other method.
- Leak sensing times can be short, often ranging from 1 to 8 seconds for production systems.
- Production systems can be automated.
- Test time does not increase greatly with part volume.
- Part temperature does not affect testing, although in some instances the leak path may be affected.

The major limitations of tracer gas leak testing are the following:

- Equipment is more expensive than that of other methods. Cost of gas varies with fill volume, partial pressure requirement (percentage used with a neutral or safe gas), fill pressure, and required leak rate sensitivity.
- The exact location of a leak can be determined with manually operated probes, but cannot be found in automatic production machines. Some parts, however, permit automatic location of a leak "zone."
- Periodic calibration is required; for some equipment this is performed automatically.

Equipment

Helium mass spectrometer. Helium mass spectrometer equipment is all based on the principle of sorting charged particles under vacuum. Depending on the manufacturer, the design, function, and operation of the various components of the spectrometer may vary.

The diagram in Fig. 13-17 shows the general arrangement of one mass spectrometer design. Entering gas molecules are positively ionized by electrons from a heated filament and are accelerated toward an exit slit in the extractor plate. The narrow beam of molecules enters a magnetic field that, because of its imparting a curved path to the molecules, sorts them by mass. The path of a molecule is determined by its speed, mass/charge ratio, and the geometry and strength of the magnetic field. Ions with a specific mass/charge ratio will pass through a slit in the intermediate target plate and then through a final slit to enter the 90° electrostatic field. Ions passing through the electrostatic field strike the collector plate, causing a small current to flow, which is amplified. The resultant is a measurement of helium presence.

Halogen diode detector. The heart of the halogen detector

LEAK TESTING

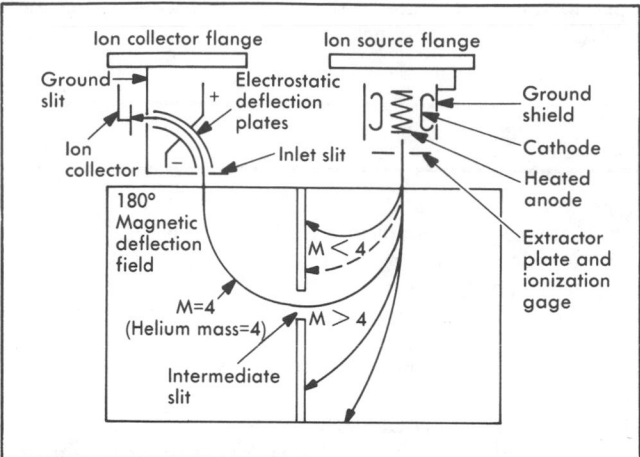

Fig. 13-17 Diagram of a modern mass spectrometer sensor. (*Inficon, Leybold-Heraeus, Inc.*)

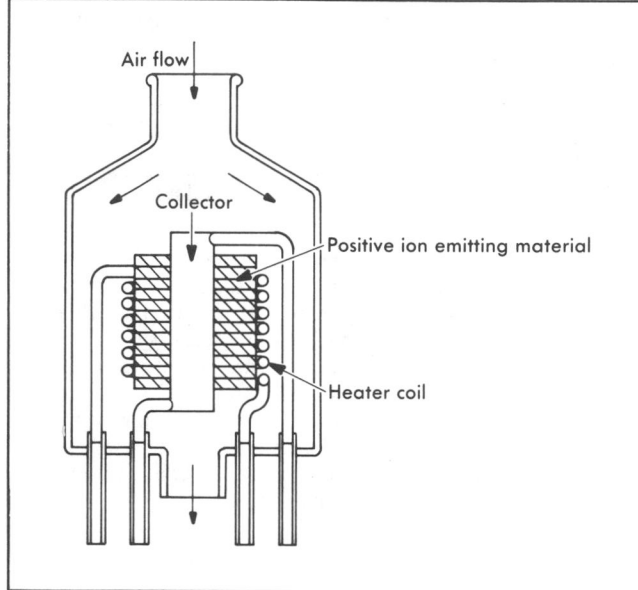

Fig. 13-18 Cross section of halogen diode sensor. (*Inficon, Leybold-Heraeus, Inc.*)

instrument is the sensor (sometimes called a halogen diode), which is a small device of typically less than 1 in.^{3} (16.4 cm^3) in size and structurally simple. The three major elements of the sensor are a platinum wire heater, positive ion emitting material at a positive voltage, and a grounded collector (see Fig. 13-18). These elements are contained within a cylinder having electrical connector pins at one end and small ports at each end for inlet and outlet airflow. An airflow of approximately 5 std·cm^3/s (0.5 Pa·m^3) at atmospheric pressure is drawn through the sensor. The presence of less than one part halide gas per million parts of air will cause a marked increase in ion emission. The resultant increase in current is amplified for meter reading and audiovisual signal actuation. The halogen sensor is nonlinear when the sensed gas exceeds more than a few parts per million in air. Exposure to a high gas concentration will affect sensitivity temporarily; when the detector is used in a system, this effect can be reduced or eliminated.

Safety

The safety aspects of tracer gas leak testing are the following:

1. Toxicity of gases.
2. Flammability or combustibility of gases.
3. Atmospheric oxygen deficiency.
4. Explosion or implosion.
5. Mechanical machinery hazards.
6. Electrical hazards.
7. Cleaning hazards.
8. Temperature hazards.

AIR LEAK TESTING

In air leak testing, the test part, whether it is an engine block, artificial kidney, water faucet, or simple casting, can be simplified to represent a sealed pressure vessel (see Fig. 13-19). During the test, regulated air pressure or vacuum is applied to the part through a manual or automatic operating valve. Leakage within the part is detected by loss of pressure or vacuum (pressure/vacuum decay) or by the need to continually add air to make up for air escaping from the test part.

Applications

When deciding whether a part is a candidate for air leak testing, it is necessary to consider the type of liquid or gas used in service as well as the operating pressure of this liquid or gas. Components that operate with liquid are excellent candidates for air leak testing. The primary advantage of using air over liquid is the speed at which the test can be performed; however, it is necessary to keep in mind that air will pass through some leaks that will not pass liquid. Because of this, a maximum allowable air leakage rate should be specified.

Components and assemblies that operate with gas or vacuum are also applicable for air leak testing; however stringent air leak test specifications are required. For some applications, such as air conditioning and refrigeration components, air leak testing is used as a pretest to identify units that have large leaks.

Automatic Leak Testers

Advanced-design testers are capable of performing air leak flow testing using all of the common automatic leak testing techniques previously described. The versatility of these microprocessor-based leak testers allows testing with various pressure, flow, or vacuum sensors. These testers can manually or automatically select multiple testing routines, such as sequential or simultaneous testing of leak, flow, and pressure.

Advantages. The advantage of automatic leak testing equipment is that no judgment decision for the amount of

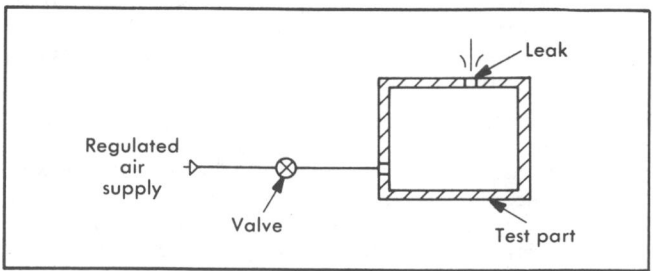

Fig. 13-19 Typical air leak testing diagram. (*Uson Corporation*)

leakage or the accept/reject decision is required of the operator. Additionally, air pressure is relatively inexpensive, easy to apply, easy to remove, noncontaminating, and normally available in most manufacturing facilities. Air leak testing is also clean and dry, eliminating messy and dangerous workstations, part cleanup, and drying associated with water immersion stands and hydrostatic testing.

Limitations. Automatic air leak testing is only as good as the mechanical structure and seals of the automatic test fixture. Minute movements of seals and structures during the leak test cycle can change the pressure inside the test part in excess of the leakage (pressure loss) being measured. Properly designed test fixtures can eliminate this problem. Improperly designed fixtures can go unnoticed because of the lack of understanding of their importance.

Automatic air leak testing does not show the leak location. Normally, rejected parts go to a repair station where leak location (for repair) is revealed by the use of bubble emission.

Another limitation to air leak testing may be an undesirable combination of the test parameters. All leak testing cannot be performed using automatic air leak testers. A test part with a small maximum allowable air leak rate specification, high test pressure, and large test volume is normally not a good candidate for pressure decay leak testing.

Safety

In general, air leak testing is considered safe for workers and the environment; however, hazards in leak testing do exist.

Because typical shop air compressors normally maintain an air supply of approximately 80-100 psig (550-690 kPa), most air leak testing is performed at pressures between 0-80 psig (0-550 kPa). When testing above 30 psig (200 kPa), automatic exhausting of the test pressure prior to opening the test fixture should be considered. The exhausted air should be diverted to a safe area. The exhaust function prevents the possibility of injury that may occur when the test fixture opens and allows a large quantity of air and chips to escape suddenly. When testing in higher pressures such as 500-2000 psig (3.5-14 MPa), safety shields should cover the station prior to the pressurization. Vessels containing large volumes that require leak testing near their yield strength should not be tested with air.

Automatic testing and clamping fixtures should have safety shields that prevent people from placing their hands into an unsafe area. On manual load/unload fixtures, the use of a two-hand safety start system should be utilized. This system requires that both of the operator's hands push individual start buttons and maintain the pushed position until the fixture is completely closed.

THERMAL NONDESTRUCTIVE TESTING

Thermal nondestructive testing is a general term for the various methods used to detect flaws and an undesirable distribution of heat during service.[21,22,23] The methods used normally can be classified as either noncontact or contact. Noncontact methods depend on thermally generated electromagnetic energy radiated from the part being tested. At moderate temperatures this is predominantly the infrared region. Because of this, infrared testing is the most important branch of noncontact thermal testing. Direct contact methods place a thermally sensitive device or material in physical and thermal contact with the test part.

The noncontact and contact methods can be further classified as either thermographic or thermometric methods. Thermographic methods depend on the thermal gradients that occur on the surface of the part. When these methods are used, a map of the equal temperature contours is obtained. With thermometric methods, a precise value of the temperature is obtained. Figure 13-20 shows the various devices or materials that are used for these methods.

A frequent use of infrared detection in NDT is the examination of microcircuits and small electronic components. Printed circuit boards must be coated before inspection because the components in the board have different emissivity values. If the boards are not coated, the data obtained by scanning is of little value. Infrared techniques are also useful for detecting defects/delaminations in composite materials and for in-process quality

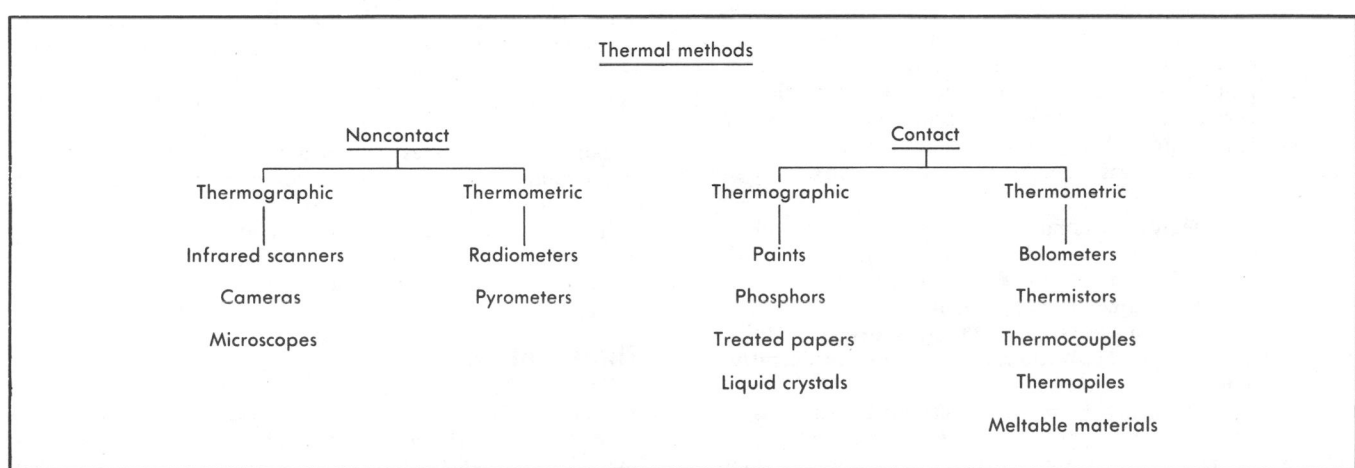

Fig. 13-20 Devices or materials used for thermal nondestructive testing.

THERMAL NONDESTRUCTIVE TESTING

control during plastic processing and composite manufacturing.[24] In the automotive industry, these techniques have been used to detect blocked water tubes and fin-to-tube disbonds in aluminum radiators.[25] They are also used to quantitatively examine temperatures on die surfaces of semipermanent mold die castings for improved casting quality.[26]

NONCONTACT METHODS

Any object at a temperature above absolute zero radiates energy in the infrared bandwidth. Several devices are available that detect this radiation and then convert it to a proportional electric signal for display. The display may be a numerical readout, a line graph of temperature versus position, or a thermal picture.

The greatest advantage of using noncontact methods is that the output can be detected without disturbing the thermal pattern; measurements can also be made rapidly and accurately. The major limitation is that the surface emissivity of the part being tested must be known because the amount of radiation is a direct function of emissivity.

Thermographic

Noncontact thermographic methods are probably the most universally applied technique, and in addition to presenting a thermal contour map of the surface being inspected, these methods also provide detailed thermometric information. Two basic types of infrared detectors are commonly being used in thermography: (1) photon detectors and (2) thermal detectors. Most modern thermal imaging systems use either photon detectors or pyroelectrics, a type of thermal detector, as the infrared sensor. The sensor receives the radiation from the scene or target and converts it into an electrical signal for processing and display.

Photon detectors use solid-state materials that produce voltage, current, or resistance changes when irradiated by photons. These semiconductor materials are wavelength dependent and are generally classified as either photoconductive or photovoltaic detectors. Photoconductive devices are semiconductors whose conductivity changes when irradiated by photons. Photons of sufficient energy will cause bound electrons to jump into the conduction band and hence to become available as charge carriers. The response time of photoconductor materials is fast; times shorter than 1 +s have been reported. Photovoltaic cells are composed of p-n junction semiconductor materials. These cells produce a voltage when irradiated by photons. These devices also are characterized by a rapid response time. For maximum sensitivity, and to reduce extraneous thermal noise, it is usually necessary to cool the semiconductor material to low temperatures. Many commercially available thermographic detector systems require that liquid nitrogen be used for this purpose.

Thermal detectors respond to total radiant energy and are thus wavelength independent. In addition, these detectors do not require cooling as do photon detectors. Therefore the size, weight, cost, and complexity can be reduced. Pyroelectrics are a special class of thermal detector. Unlike the others, they respond only to a change in temperature, rather than to the temperature itself.

Although the heart of a thermal-imaging system is its infrared detector, the detector is but one of several interacting subsystems. The other subsystems incorporated in a thermal-imaging system are: optical system for collecting the radiance from the target, spectrally filtering, and focusing it onto the detector; scanning system for dissecting the target or a chopper for modulating the radiance; detector system including any preamplifiers and ancillary circuits; signal processor system for receiving the low-level signal from the detector(s), amplifying it, limiting the bandwidth, extracting the information contained in the signal, and delivering this information to the display system; and a display system, which is generally a video monitor.

Thermometric

Noncontact thermometric measuring devices depend on the response of a thermal detector to infrared radiation. These devices are particularly useful when monitoring or measuring surface temperatures remotely. Thermometric devices are used in applications where a single component is under evaluation or when the cost limitation precludes the use of thermographic devices. The two most commonly used devices are radiometers and pyrometers.

Radiometers. Radiometers measure incident radiation. A typical radiometer consists of some type of hollow cavity with an aperture in one end and a thermal detector mounted internally. The thermal detector is located in such a position that radiation is focused on it. Because thermal detectors have a uniform response without regard to infrared wavelength, the radiometer is often used to measure total radiation. If the radiometer has a lens system, it will be restricted to the infrared transmission characteristics of the lenses. Current-imaging radiometers operate in the 3-5 μm or 8-12 μm spectral range and have temperature sensitivities of 0.9° F (0.1° C). They can measure temperatures up to 1800° F (1000° C) and are TV compatible.

Pyrometers. Pyrometers are used in nondestructive testing in much the same way as the noncontact thermographic devices. These instruments are not as accurate as other scanning devices, but they are simpler, more rugged, more portable, and less expensive.

Pyrometers are available in the form of infrared microscopes, medium focusing range thermometers, and long-distance focusing thermometers. Depending on the instrument, temperature can be measured from below -32° F (0° C) to 212° F (100° C).

CONTACT METHODS

As was the case with noncontact methods, contact methods can be further divided into those devices and materials that detect the temperature thermographically or thermometrically. The primary advantage of using contact-type materials or devices is the low initial investment, particularly if small areas are being inspected; however, this cost advantage disappears as the area or number of pieces examined increases. The operator skill required and the effectiveness of contact and noncontact methods in detecting flaws are about equivalent.

The major limitation of contact materials is that they alter the heat flow in the surface being tested. Another limitation is that their use is not readily automated.

Thermographic

Contact thermographic methods require the surface being tested to be coated with a temperature-sensitive material. These materials react to thermal change by changing color or appearance. The type of coating material selected for a particular application depends on its characteristics as well as the characteristics of the part being tested. The coating materials commonly used are paints, thermal phosphors, treated papers, liquid crystals, and other temperature-sensitive coatings.

Paints. Temperature-sensitive paints are available to cover a temperature range of 100-2900° F (40-1600° C). As the temperature of the part increases, the coating undergoes several color transitions. Under favorable circumstances, the temperature of the part can be estimated with an accuracy of ±9° F (5° C).

These coatings can be applied by brushing, spraying, or dipping. In general, only a thin film is required. Temperature-sensitive paints have been used to observe the isotherms in the vicinity of a welding operation, for determining the preheat temperature of weldments, and for the inspection of porosity in castings.

Thermal phosphors. Thermal phosphors are organic compounds that emit visible light when excited by ultraviolet radiation. The amount of light emitted is inversely proportional to the temperature of the phosphor. The sensitivity of the phosphor varies according to the intensity of illumination. Sensitivity is also affected by flaw size, location, and test material characteristics. Thermal phosphors can be applied as a paint, in a tape, in a strippable coating, or as a phosphor powder.

Treated papers. Several different types of thermally sensitive papers can be used for thermographic inspection. They are usually bonded to the test surface with an adhesive or with a vacuum hold-down arrangement.

One type of treated paper has an organic coating on it that melts once a certain temperature is achieved. The paper is black and the coating is white. When the melting temperature is reached, the coating is absorbed into the paper, causing it to change colors.

Another type of paper is coated with a plastic film containing a large number of air bubbles. The paper is black and the plastic film has the appearance of being white. Like the organic coating, the plastic film melts when a certain temperature is reached, revealing the black paper beneath it.

Liquid crystals. Liquid crystals exhibit the properties of both a liquid and a crystal at certain temperatures. As these crystals undergo a temperature change, they appear to change in color. When the crystals are heated to their melting point, they become a liquid and are essentially colorless. Any additional heat causes the crystals to undergo a "color play," which is a certain color change sequence. For most nondestructive tests, this color play occurs at a point slightly above room temperature. Under typical conditions, liquid crystals can detect a temperature difference of approximately 0.4° F (0.2° C).

Liquid crystals may be applied by brushing, spraying, or dipping. The applied film is usually between 0.010 and 0.020″ (0.25 and 0.50 mm) thick. Because liquid crystals function by reflecting light, they are more easily seen against a dark background.

The primary advantages of liquid crystals are their initial low cost in comparison to infrared detectors and the low operator skill required. However, liquid crystals are normally not used on large structures because their cost would be prohibitive.

Thermometric

Several different types of contact devices are used to measure surface temperatures. For certain applications, these devices may be used in direct contact with the part being tested or as a radiation detector.

Bolometers. Bolometers are thermal detectors that are based on the principle that the resistance of a material changes as it is heated. The bolometer allows the radiation to impinge on a very fine wire or a thin metallic film, blackened to increase absorption. The resistance change is then a direct function of the radiation absorbed. The temperature coefficient of a bolometer is from 0.15 to 2%/° F (0.3 to 0.5%/° C).

Thermistors. Thermistors, or thermally sensitive resistors, are semiconductors that undergo a reduction in resistance as their temperature rises. Their temperature coefficient is approximately 2%/° F (4%/° C). The limiting factor of the thermistor is thermal noise.

Thermocouples and thermopiles. Thermocouples consist of a junction of two dissimilar metals. As the junction temperature is raised, a thermoelectric electromotive force (emf) is produced. Thermocouples are always used in pairs in a bridge circuit so that the measured temperature is a direct function of the emf produced by the sensing thermocouple as subtracted from the emf produced by a reference thermocouple that is held at a known temperature. As with all thermal detectors, thermocouples may be used as a contact sensor or they can be used in noncontact applications to sense infrared radiation only.

Thermopiles are merely a series of thermocouple junctions; they produce an increase in electromotive force as a direct function of the number of junctions. Although thermopiles do have a higher output signal, the response time is reduced because of the increased mass that must be heated.

Meltable materials. Wax-like crayons rated to melt at various temperature increments between 100 and 3200° F (38 and 1760° C) are commercially available. These crayons have a melting point within a nominal tolerance of ±1% of the rated temperature value. They are normally used by making a mark with one or more of them on a surface before it is heated. The true temperature indication occurs only when the mark melts. Color or color intensity of the crayon may change during heating, but this is not an indication of temperature. By using an appropriate range of these crayons arranged in a suitable pattern, general observations can be made regarding the isothermal pattern (or thermograph) of a heated area.

TESTING CONSIDERATIONS

When performing thermal testing, several precautions should be observed to obtain accurate results. First of all, the surface being tested should be uniformly clean. Oily surfaces may reduce or prevent the adherence of contact materials. Some contact materials, such as liquid crystals, are very sensitive to contamination. Any contamination on the surface may reduce the overall response or cause a shift in color. Contamination will also change the surface emissivity and result in spurious infrared responses.

All contact materials and infrared detectors should be periodically calibrated or checked for sensitivity. Although most contact materials have a rather long shelf life, contamination, exposure to strong light, or high humidity, for example, can sharply reduce shelf life. Infrared instruments are subject to drift over time and therefore should be calibrated against known temperature standards.

When testing passive devices, heating and/or cooling should be as uniform as possible and identical on each piece. Reversible coatings (those which may be cycled back and forth through their response temperature) should neither be held for extended periods above their response temperature nor severely overheated; loss in sensitivity will result.

The radiation from a device usually represents only a fraction of the total heat dissipated. Convection and conduction may be responsible for much larger heat losses than radiation; hence they should be held constant during the test. Active devices should be allowed to warm up and stabilize prior to making temperature measurements.

ACOUSTIC EMISSION TESTING

Almost all materials produce an acoustic emission (AE) when they are stressed. Other terms used to describe this phenomenon are stress-wave emission and microseismic emission. An acoustic emission is a sound wave or, more properly, a stress wave that travels through a material. An acoustic emission may be generated by the following:

- Cracking or delaminations in composite structures such as aircraft parts, industrial storage tanks, pipes, and circuit boards.
- Fracture and crack propagation in metallic structures such as piping, pressure vessels, and weldments.
- Deformation of materials during testing or manufacturing.
- Nugget formation or overwelding during spot welding.
- Leaking gases and fluids in steam traps or valves.
- Bearing failure and lack of lubrication.

Acoustic emission testing is a recent nondestructive test method that has application in a variety of industries. During a typical test, a sensor is mounted on the test piece, which is subsequently subjected to a load. If a defect grows in the test piece, distinct acoustic emission signals are generated by the resulting fracture or deformation. The sensor converts the acoustic emission signals into electrical signals, which are then amplified, filtered, and processed to obtain predetermined types of information. A cathode ray tube, video display tube, or another type of device is used to display the processed data as a function of test duration, applied load, or signal location.

Acoustic emission testing is related in many ways to ultrasonic testing because both methods measure sound waves to detect defects. The main difference between the two methods is the source of the sound waves. In ultrasonic testing, the sound waves are transmitted into the test piece through the sensor. Defects are then detected and located based on the interaction between the sound wave and defect. In AE testing, the sound waves are generated from within the test piece in the course of the relaxation of the stored strain energy.

APPLICATIONS

With the continual improvement in electronic detection equipment, the use of AE testing has increased. Perhaps the greatest attribute to the technology is its ability to be utilized in an extremely broad range of applications. The types of materials for which AE testing can be used are virtually unlimited. Industries currently using this technique include aerospace, nuclear, medical, and transportation. Acoustic emission testing can also be used to help understand and evaluate fabrication methods such as welding, spot welding, bonding, machining, drilling, cutting, and sawing.

ADVANTAGES AND LIMITATIONS

Like the other test methods, AE testing is not a panacea for all applications. It does, however, provide certain advantages over some of the other methods such as radiographic and ultrasonic testing. Some of the advantages of acoustic emission testing are the following:

- The ability to monitor a complete structure in real time.
- The sensitivity to the presence of active flaws, although it requires other methods to characterize the exact size of flaws.
- The ability to detect discontinuities that may be inaccessible to other NDT methods.
- The ability to be used in harsh environments.
- The applicability for use during proof testing of structures that will be stressed sufficiently to produce defect extension or gross plastic deformation.

The main limitation of AE testing as a nondestructive test method is that it can only detect flaws that are growing; the mere presence of defects, however large, is not detected. Either an external or internal force must act on the flaw, causing it to grow. The type and amount of acoustic emission generated is dependent on the behavior of the material. Other limitations of this method are the following:

- Spurious signals may be difficult to separate.
- Limited quantitative information is provided.
- Experience required for proper usage and data interpretation.

INSTRUMENTATION AND SIGNAL PROCESSING

Acoustic emission signals coming from a sensor are first prepared for processing by suitable amplification and filtering. The signals are then processed to extract the data that they contain. Once the data are processed, they are displayed for evaluation or they are recorded, permitting analysis at a later date. A diagram of a typical acoustic emission system is shown in Fig. 13-21.

Sensors

An acoustic emission sensor works on the same principle as a contact microphone on a guitar or other musical instrument. The essential parts of an acoustic emission sensor are a piezoelectric element, wear plate or shoe, and a metal case. The case supports and protects the transducer as well as provides shielding from unwanted electrical interference.

The active part of the sensor is a piezoelectric transducer element. The piezoelectric element converts the stress wave received into an electrical signal that is picked up by the elec-

ACOUSTIC EMISSION TESTING

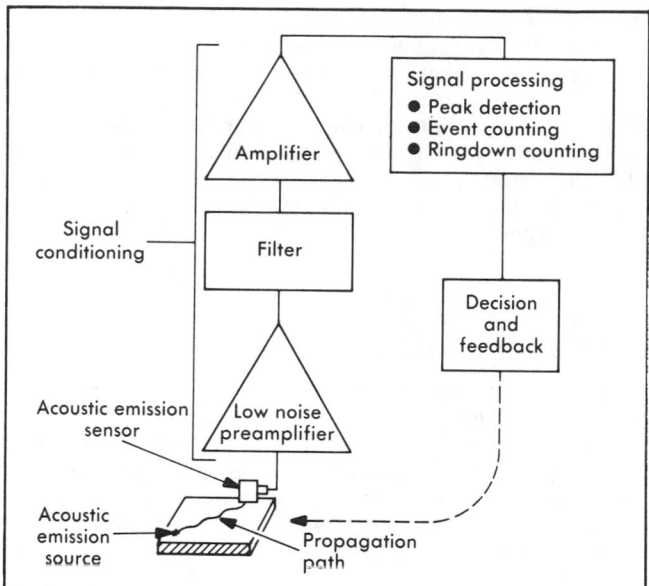

Fig. 13-21 Typical acoustic emission detection system. (*Acoustic Emission Technology Corp.*)

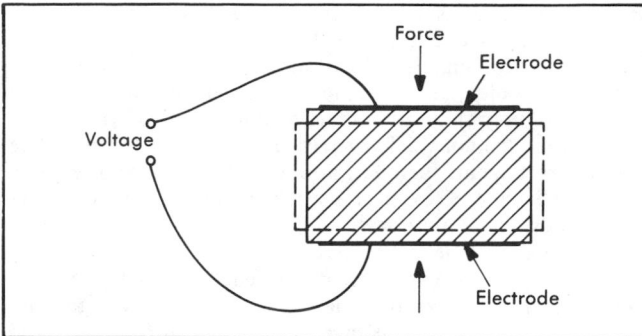

Fig. 13-22 Sound pressure received from the test specimen is picked up by the electrodes on the sensor and then converted into an electrical signal. (*Acoustic Emission Technology Corp.*)

trodes (see Fig. 13-22). The electrical signal is then amplified and fed into suitable instrumentation.

Signal Conditioning

The signal from a sensor must be amplified and unnecessary frequencies filtered out prior to processing. Commonly, it is necessary to amplify the signal to approximately 1 V. Amplification is usually done with a low noise level preamplifier located next to the sensor or sometimes contained in the sensor housing, especially when:

- The spurious electrical noise is high.
- The distance between the sensor and the instrumentation must be more than a few feet.

Signal Processing

The amplified and filtered acoustic emission signals are processed to do one or more of the following:

- Specify the amount of acoustic emission activity by a number.
- Accept acoustic emission signals and reject all other acoustic signals.
- Identify some waveform characteristic of the signal that will help to determine the type of acoustic emission source.
- Obtain a number that is proportional to the energy in the acoustic emission.
- Locate the source of the acoustic emission.

Acoustic emission activity can be interpreted either by measuring the characteristics of the waveform, including ringdown counts, or by measuring the root-mean-square (rms) voltage of the continuous-type signal. Both techniques are relatively simple. The advantage of the counting technique is that it is possible to record a limited number of acoustic emission events in test specimens that show only a small amount of activity over a long period of time.

NEUTRON RADIOGRAPHY

Neutron radiography is a form of nondestructive testing that uses a neutron beam to form a radiographic image of a test piece. Neutrons are subatomic particles that are characterized by relatively large mass and a neutral electric charge. They are constituents of all atomic nuclei except ordinary hydrogen. The pertinent difference between X-rays or gamma rays and neutrons is that the neutron does not interact with the electrons in matter. Instead, it interacts directly with the atomic nucleus, either by scattering or by being absorbed by the nucleus.[27] For example, in radiography (X-ray or gamma ray) the attenuation of the rays increases as the atomic number of the test specimen increases. In neutron radiography, however, some low atomic number elements attenuate a beam of neutrons more strongly than some high atomic number elements. Also, elements having adjacent atomic numbers can vary widely in attenuation.

APPLICATIONS

With the increasing use of composite materials and honeycomb structures in the aircraft and aerospace industries, neutron radiography can offer advantages because of the excellent sensitivity to adhesives and resins. In some cases, combinations of materials are well suited for neutron inspection. For example, the high strength of a boron aluminum composite metal depends on the distribution and continuity of the boron fibers. Because the neutron beam is absorbed more readily by the boron fibers than the aluminum, a neutron radiograph will show the position of the boron in the aluminum matrix.

ADVANTAGES AND LIMITATIONS

Neutron radiography can provide image information that is difficult or impossible to obtain by other methods. Although the technique tends to be relatively expensive compared to other nondestructive testing methods, the unique capability of the method for imaging items such as corrosion, adhesives, explosives, fluids, and ceramics in metallic assemblies makes neutron radiography a valuable technique. It can be used to outline the extent of cracks or delaminations open to the surface if a contrast agent, such as a liquid penetrant, is applied. The method also offers isotopic sensitivity and capability to inspect highly radioactive materials.

A user should be aware that neutron irradiation of objects usually leads to some level of radioactivity. Therefore the objects inspected may become radioactive; however, this has not been a serious problem because the neutron levels and exposure times are relatively low. Irradiated objects may sometimes be retained for an hour or so until they have decayed to safe levels. One of the main deterrents to using neutron radiography is the need to transport the test pieces to a nuclear reactor when high-quality radiographs are required. Portable sources described later produce lower quality radiographs than nuclear reactor sources or require long exposures (hours to days) to obtain the equivalent high grade.

DETECTION METHODS

A neutron radiograph is made by passing a beam of neutrons through a test object. If the neutrons react with any of the material's atomic nuclei, they are absorbed or scattered, attenuating the beam. The beam emerges from the test sample with information about the object's internal structure in the form of differences in attenuation. The principles that govern exposure and processing of neutron radiographs are similar to those for X-ray or gamma ray radiographs.

SPECIFICATIONS AND STANDARDS

Standards are available to address the important parameters of a neutron radiography system. Three standards are available from the American Society for Testing and Materials (ASTM). Document E748 is a tutorial document that describes the general method and provides guidance when performing the test.[28] Image quality measurements for thermal neutron radiography are outlined in ASTM E545.[29]

HOLOGRAPHIC NONDESTRUCTIVE TESTING

Holographic nondestructive testing (HNDT) or holographic interferometry combines holography with interferometry, permitting the detection of material defects and impending fatigue failure, the measurement of residual stress, and vibration mode analysis. Holography is a two-step process that permits the reconstruction of three-dimensional images. A hologram of an object is formed in the first step of the process. In the second step, the original image is recreated, thus permitting the observer to see an exact replica of the image in size and position. The recreated image also displays depth of field and parallax.

When producing a hologram, light emitted by a laser source is split into an object beam and a reference beam (see Fig. 13-23). The object beam is expanded and directed toward the object,

where part of it is reflected toward the recording medium, which is usually a high-resolution photographic film. In recent years, thermoplastic emulsions have become available. Although the reference beam travels directly to the film, it is diverted so that the optical paths of both beams are approximately equal. Because the two beams are from the same coherent source, they interfere with each other as they pass through each other. The film emulsion receives exposure wherever constructive interference occurs and virtually no exposure where destructive interference occurs. The varying exposure results in a very fine pattern in the emulsion of the film. This fine pattern diffracts the beam to form a reconstruction of the object beam when the film is illuminated after development by a replica of the reference beam. The replica of the object can be viewed or photographed.

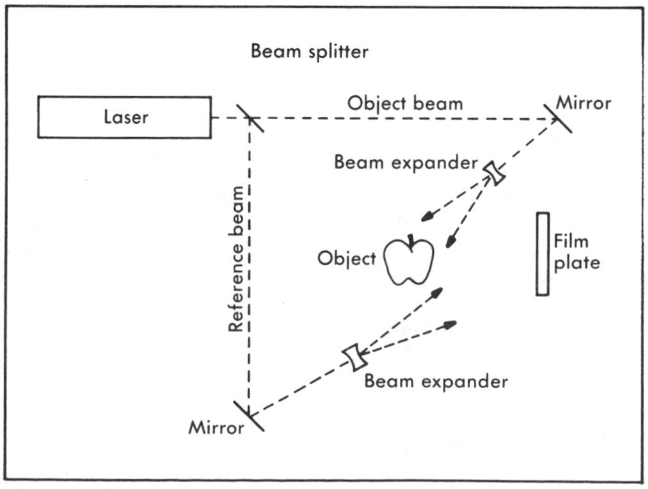

APPLICATIONS

Holographic nondestructive testing has made the precision of interferometric measurements—previously restricted to regular, specularly reflecting surfaces under laboratory conditions—applicable to generalized objects in industrial environments. As a result, the technique has been utilized in a wide range of nondestructive testing applications. For example, in the area of structural analysis, HNDT has been used for nondestructive testing of aircraft panels and honeycomb structures; aircraft wing assemblies and fins; detection of cracks, delaminations, and disbonds; and rotating structures such as turbine blades and naval propellers, small arms barrels, vibrating vehicle components, rock mechanics, and computer components. Holographic techniques have been used to record flowfields associated with turbine blades, projectiles, wind tunnels, rocket engines, and plasmas, as well as to analyze particle fields associated with aerosols, liquid droplets, pollutants, and

Fig. 13-23 Recording a hologram. (*Apollo Lasers*)

spacecraft waste tanks. Finally, in the life sciences, HNDT has been applied to studies in dentistry, chest motions, hearing mechanisms, and pelvic movements.

ADVANTAGES AND LIMITATIONS

The advantages of HNDT are many. It is, first of all, a noncontact technique; thus objects may be studied without disturbing their motions by adding accelerometers or strain gages. Furthermore, sharply curved surfaces or other areas where the addition of such devices is awkward may be readily studied. It is a full-field technique; thus displacements may be studied across an entire surface rather than at discrete points. It offers interferometric precision; therefore, although a variety of techniques can be used to study much larger motions, HNDT can resolve displacements of less than one micrometer.

Pulsed lasers can provide sufficient energy to record double-pulse holographic interferograms of large objects. Furthermore, extremely short exposure times (approximately 30 nanoseconds) and pulse separations (approximately 1 microsecond) permit studies of fast transient events in the presence of relatively large general motions.

The limitations of HNDT fall into three general areas. First, the technology is different and relatively new. The equipment required is expensive, and while a high skill level is not required to operate a holographic laser, some training is required. Secondly, the technique measures only displacements. Strain must be calculated from displacement data and material properties. Finally, the holographic interferogram does not give quantitative data directly. While a number of applications such as crack detection can be conducted with only visual inspection of a hologram, a variety of others rely on quantitative evaluation of the fringes in the hologram. Great progress has been made in development of techniques that produce quantitative results.

EQUIPMENT

Basic equipment required for holographic nondestructive testing consists of a laser with sufficient output and coherence length, an assortment of mirrors, beamsplitters and simple lenses, and a film plate. The optical elements should be housed in mounts that provide sufficient fine adjustment to accurately align the system. If continuous-wave lasers are to be used, the system must be mounted on a rigid platform that isolates the

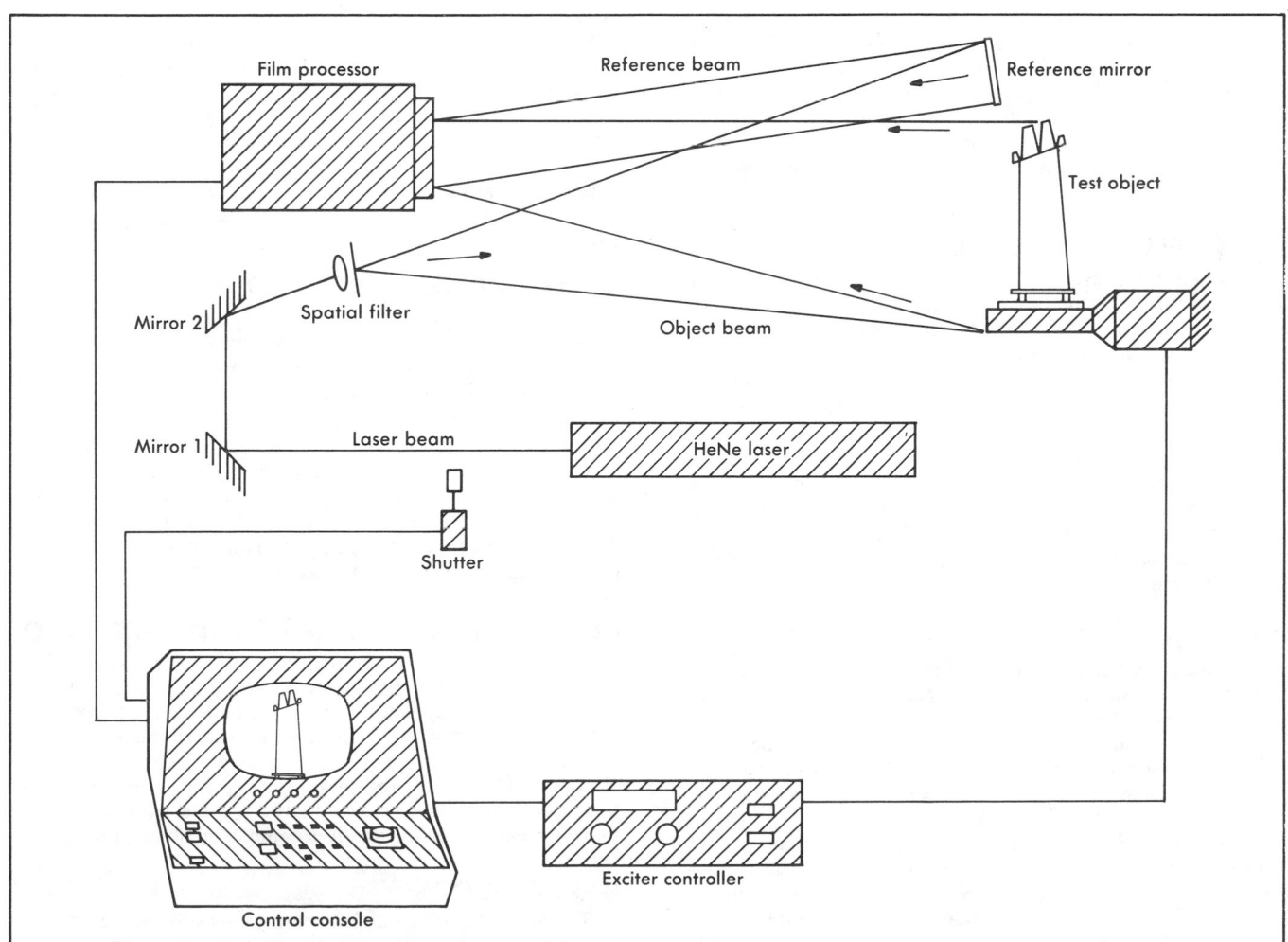

Fig. 13-24 Diagram of a modular holographic camera system. (*Laser Technology, Inc.*)

PLATING AND COATING MEASUREMENT

system from ambient vibrations. Pulsed lasers, because of their very short exposure times, need only be isolated enough to ensure long-term alignment.

A diagram of a modular holographic camera system is shown in Fig. 13-24. The camera contains a HeNe polarized laser, electronic laser beam shutter, spatial filter, and test part mounting stage. During exposure, an electromagnetic shutter passes the beam to a series of mirrors and through the spatial filter. At the filter, the beam is expanded and optically filtered to remove any "noise" caused by dust on the lens and mirrors. The expanded beam illuminates the test part being inspected; a portion of the beam strikes the mirror/polarizer assembly, thus generating the reference beam. Beam ratio can be adjusted by rotating the polarizer. A microprocessor-based photodetector determines and displays the set beam ratio. The exposure and processing of the hologram is completely automatic; the hologram can also be displayed on the video monitor. With this system, holograms can be made using double exposure, real-time, and time-average methods.

SAFETY

The laser exhibits a number of characteristics, some of which are rather unique, that must be understood to ensure safe use. First of all, it must be recognized that most lasers utilize power supplies that usually develop high voltages. Although virtually all high-power lasers are designed with electrical interlocks that turn off the voltage if the cabinet is opened, normal precautions associated with similar electronic equipment should be observed. In addition, only well-trained personnel should be allowed to attempt to service the laser.

A unique characteristic of the holographic laser is its high degree of coherence. Because of this, very high optical intensities can be obtained, and beams can travel great distances with very little change in intensity; thus the potential for ocular damage exists not only from the direct output of the laser but from reflections off distant objects as well. A comprehensive review of laser safety considerations has been prepared by Sliney and Wolbarsht.[30]

PLATING AND COATING THICKNESS MEASUREMENT

Several methods are currently being used for the non-destructive measurement of plating and coating thickness. The most widely used methods are X-ray fluorescence (XRF), beta ray backscatter (BBS), eddy current, electromagnetic induction, electrical resistance, and Hall effect. The instruments that employ these methods are essentially comparators and must be calibrated with reference standards having known coating thicknesses.

X-RAY FLUORESCENCE

The X-ray fluorescence (XRF) method is widely used in the measurement of plating and coating thickness because of its versatility, accuracy, and precision and its capability to rapidly measure small surface areas.

X-ray fluorescence instruments are used predominantly in the electronic field to measure the coating/plating thickness on parts such as electrical connectors, silicon wafers, integrated circuit leadframes, hybrid circuits, printed wiring boards, computer memory discs, wire, contacts, relays, and chip carriers. Typical coatings measured by XRF instruments are gold, silver, nickel, palladium, rhodium, tin-lead, cobalt, iron oxide, and tin plated over substrates such as copper alloys, nickel alloys, silicon, and aluminum.

BETA RAY BACKSCATTER

The beta ray backscatter (BBS) method has been used for more than 20 years to measure the plating thickness of gold, silver, tin, tin-lead, copper, and photoresist coatings on printed wiring boards and small electronic parts. For a given coating to be measurable with BBS instruments, there must be at least a 20% difference in atomic number between the coating and base materials. The thickness of nickel on copper, copper on zinc, chrome on steel, and nickel on Kovar cannot be measured with BBS instruments because the atomic numbers of these combinations are too close. Although the BBS method is not as versatile as the XRF method and cannot measure small surface areas, the BBS method does have certain advantages over the XRF method.

One advantage is that BBS instruments generally cost much less than an equivalent XRF instrument. Beta ray backscatter instruments are also capable of measuring the thickness of materials with low atomic numbers, such as photoresist and organic membranes, but XRF instruments cannot measure these materials. In addition, BBS instruments can often measure thicker deposits than XRF instruments. For example, the maximum gold-plating thickness that can be measured by XRF is approximately 8 μm (300 μin.), and BBS can measure thicknesses more than 25 μm (1000 μin.).

EDDY-CURRENT METHOD

Instruments operating on the eddy-current principle are commonly used to measure nonconductive coatings on nonmagnetic metals. Examples of these applications are anodized coatings on aluminum and coatings of paint, epoxy, or Teflon on aluminum, copper, or brass substrates. The eddy-current technique may also be used for measuring plated metals on conductive or nonconductive substrates as long as there is a significant difference in electrical conductivity between the coating and base materials. Examples of these applications are zinc, cadmium, tin, copper, and nickel on steel as well as copper on plastics and aluminum on silicon.

ELECTROMAGNETIC INDUCTION METHOD

The electromagnetic induction method is a very simple method and is used in measuring the thickness of any nonmagnetic coating on magnetic steel, iron, or Kovar. Electromagnetic induction measures the liftoff distance of the probe from the magnetic substrate. The technique is relatively insensitive to electrical conductivity and total insensitive to other properties of nonmagnetic platings and coatings; therefore any coating may be measured as long as it is completely nonmagnetic.

HALL EFFECT

The measurement of nickel coatings over copper substrates poses some peculiar problems that make measurement by eddy currents or electromagnetic induction undesirable.

The Hall-effect method uses direct current that is applied through a semiconductor. A magnet provides a source of magnetic flux through the semiconductor at right angles to the current flow. This results in a d-c voltage at right angles to both the current flow and magnetic lines of force.

As the magnetic flux becomes concentrated because of the presence of a magnetic layer, the Hall voltage increases. Thus, instruments utilizing the Hall-effect principle are well suited to measuring nickel over copper. As mentioned earlier, XRF can accurately measure nickel coatings over copper substrates, but it is more expensive.

MICRORESISTANCE METHOD

The microresistance method is used for measuring the thickness and quality of copper plating in printed circuit board through-holes (see Fig. 13-25). The method depends on the precise measurement of the true resistance of the cylinder of copper lining the hole. The resistances involved are on the order of a few hundred microhms.

A good microresistance instrument must be capable of injecting d c current uniformly through the hole and then pick ing up the resulting voltage drop. Advanced instruments use pulsed direct current to eliminate the effects of electromagnetic interference. The current is also uniformly introduced by means

of conical contacts that cover as much of the circumference of the hole as possible, leaving a small gap for the voltage pick-up contacts.

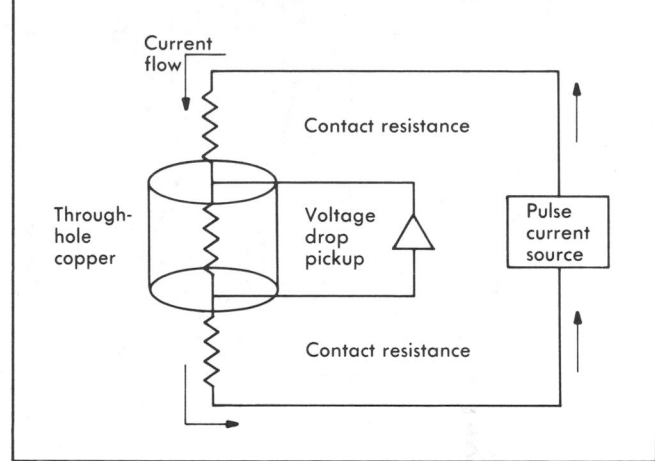

Fig. 13-25 Microresistance testing of printed circuit board through-holes. (*UPA Technology, Inc.*)

MECHANICAL TESTING

Mechanical testing can benefit from automated data acquisition and analysis systems. Computer-aided systems have been developed and used for many types of tests, tension and fatigue test in particular. A suitable computer-aided testing system can perform one or all of the following functions: (1) calibrate and control the equipment that excites the specimen or structure, (2) monitor and record the data generated during the test, and (3) manipulate the data for analysis and automatically summarize the information in suitable tables, graphs, or frequency distributions.

HARDNESS TESTS

Most hardness tests yield numerical values that are based on a material's resistance to indentation under the conditions imposed by the particular test. Resistance to scratching is another measure of hardness, as is the measurement of the energy absorbed by a material when struck by a falling object. Hardness numbers alone, because they indicate characteristics more than properties of materials, have practical significance only when correlated with service experience or a particular material property.

Perhaps the most common use of hardness tests is in quality control, where they are used to check material uniformity or processing treatment. Hardness numbers also provide a quick indication of the numerical value of a particular property of a material; before a hardness number can be used in this way, a relationship to the property must be established, and a comparison range must be defined. By correlating a series of hardness numbers with the corresponding service experience of a material in a particular use, it is possible to evaluate similar materials for use in the same application.

In most applications, the hardness of the material as a whole—the general hardness—can be used for comparison with service experience or a particular property; applicable methods are the Brinell, Rockwell, scleroscope, and Vickers hardness tests, which are carried out on a macroscale. In some applications, such as the testing of metals for bearings, the hardness of the constituents or grains of the metal provides the most useful information for correlation with other data. Hardness tests must then be carried out on a microscale and might be considered measurements of particle hardness; the Knoop and microcharacter hardness tests are particularly applicable to, although not limited to, these measurements. Other methods have also been developed to permit testing on special applications such as aircraft skins (ASTM B 7). These methods generally yield results that correlate to a common scale such as Rockwell C.

In selecting a hardness test, consideration must be given to the thickness of the specimen to be tested. The thickness must be such that the backing material or anvil on which the specimen rests has no effect on the indentation of the penetrator in the specimen. An imprint on the undersurface of a specimen after a test is a definite indication that the specimen was too thin for the particular hardness test used. Satisfactory hardness tests for various minimum thicknesses of uniformly hardened steel can be determined from the curves in Fig. 13-26. If a certain specimen is too thin, a test using a lighter load or a larger indentor should be selected.

The Brinell test finds wide use on large parts such as castings and forgings of low to medium hardness; the Rockwell and Vickers tests on small parts and those of low, medium, or high hardness; and the scleroscope test for quick, routine inspection

MECHANICAL TESTING

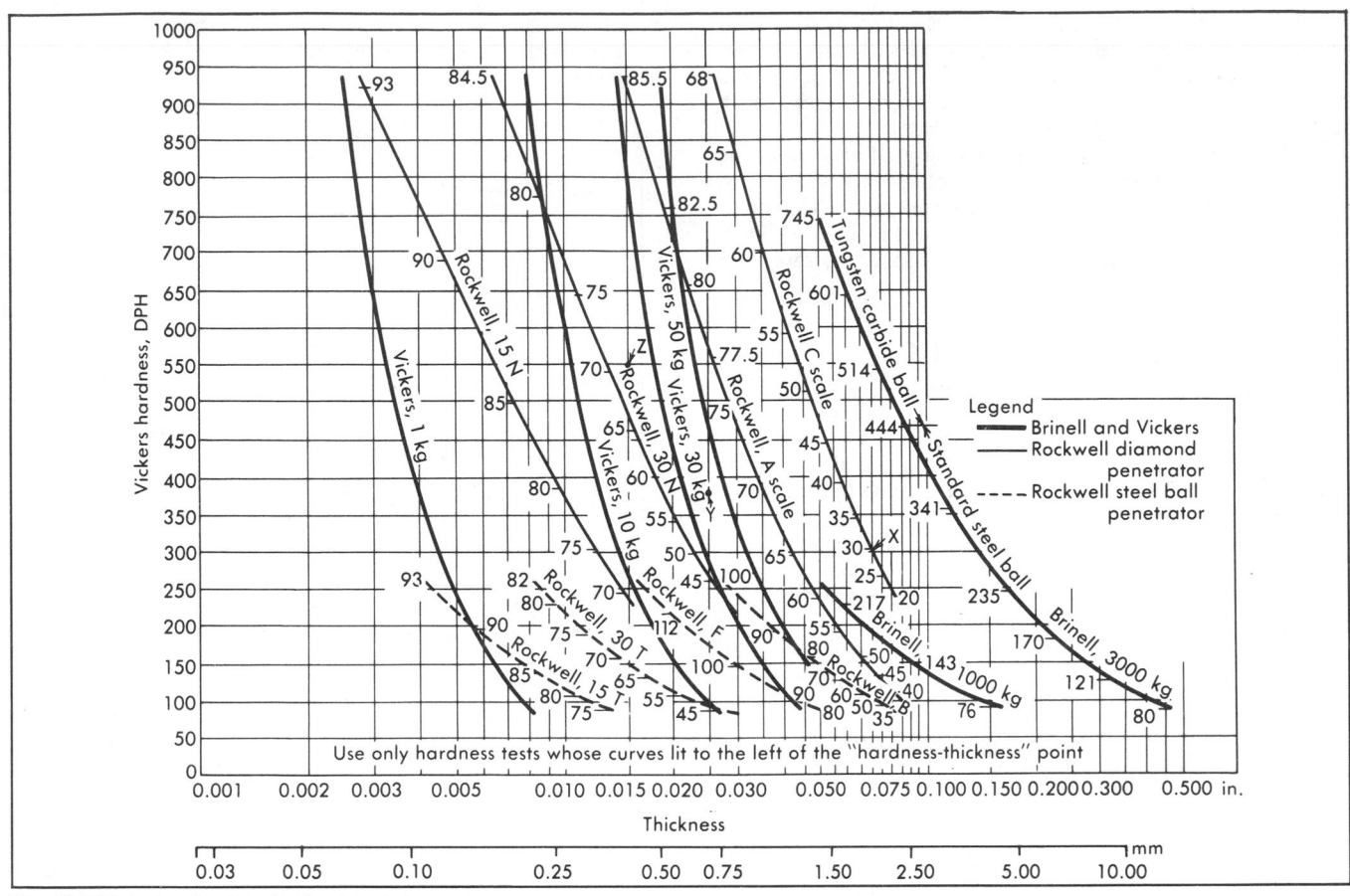

Fig. 13-26 Selector chart for hardness tests for steel.

and for shop tests. The Vickers test is particularly versatile because it has a wide uniform scale and permits the use of an extensive range of loads. Durometers are widely used for quick checks on rubber and plastics. Shore scales are generally used for plastics testing and the international rubber hardness degrees (IRHD) are used for rubber.

Brinell Hardness Test

In the Brinell hardness test, a known load is applied for a given length of time to the surface of the specimen through a hardened-steel or carbide ball of known diameter. The diameter of the resulting permanent indentation is measured and is usually converted to a Brinell hardness number by the use of standard tables.

Rockwell and Rockwell Superficial Hardness Tests

The Rockwell and the Rockwell superficial hardness tests are both based on the same principle. The tests yield an arbitrary number that is related to the difference in the depth of penetration of a penetrator subjected to a minor (initial) and a major (final) load under specified conditions. The Rockwell superficial hardness test is designed particularly for measuring the hardness of thin materials or case-hardened metals. The primary differences between the Rockwell and the Rockwell superficial hardness tests are lighter minor and major loads and

a tester of higher sensitivity in the Rockwell superficial hardness test. The depth of penetration for the Rockwell superficial hardness test is approximately 0.00004″ (0.001 mm) for each scale division. For the Rockwell hardness test, the penetration is approximately 0.00008″ (0.0002 mm) for each scale division.

Vickers Hardness Test

The Vickers hardness test consists of applying a known load for a specified time to the surface of a material through a square-base-pyramid diamond having 136° between opposite faces. The Vickers hardness number, also known as the diamond pyramid hardness, is the applied load in kilograms divided by the area of the permanent indentation in square millimeters. The test is very similar to the Brinell test except for the indentor used.

The two diagonals of the resulting square permanent indentation are measured with a micrometer microscope and then averaged. The average diagonal is usually converted to a Vickers hardness number by the use of tables supplied with the testing machine.

Scleroscope Hardness Tests

Scleroscope hardness is based on the height of rebound of a steel "hammer" falling on a specimen from a fixed height. The hammer is approximately 1/4″ (6 mm) in diameter and 3/4″ (19 mm) long with a rounded striking tip on its normally downward end. The hammer falls freely in a glass tube that has a scale graduated into 140 divisions. The height of the first rebound, which is the scleroscope hardness, is determined by visual observation or a dial indicating device. Repeat tests should not be made in the same location.

Other Tests

Other methods employing machines, but secondary in importance for the manufacturing engineer, are the Knoop hardness, microcharacter hardness, and durometer tests.

Knoop hardness test. The Knoop hardness test may be classed as a microhardness test because the impressions are usually extremely small. It is particularly suited for making hardness surveys and measuring the hardness of very small parts, thin sections, thin cases, and individual grains or particles. The test consists of applying a known load for a specified time to the surface of the material through a diamond having unequal longitudinal and transverse included angles. The Knoop hardness number is the applied load divided by the unrecovered projected area. Often a tester will be used for both Knoop and light-load Vickers testing merely by switching penetrators.

Microcharacter hardness test. The microcharacter hardness test is particularly suited for microscopic hardness surveys and hardness measurements on extremely thin metal parts and constituents of alloys. The standard load ranges from only 3 g up to 9 g for extremely hard materials. The combination of lenses used with the microscope should permit reading to 1 μm (0.00004") with reasonable accuracy.

Durometer test. The durometer measures hardness in a number of scales in terms of the amount of indentation of a spring-loaded indentor beyond the hardness tester's presser foot or stop ring while the latter is firmly pressed against a specimen. The hardness number is read from a scale graduated from 0 to 100. Different types of hardness numbers are obtained by the use of different indentors and loads. The durometer is a portable hardness tester used extensively for hardness measurements on rubber, plastics, and, in a number of instances, soft metals.

Hot Hardness Tests

The hardness of metals at elevated temperatures can be determined by a number of different methods. In some cases, conventional room temperature hardness testers have been modified so that the specimen and the penetrator are both at the test temperature. Zmeskal described the use of the Rockwell hardness tester using a Brale penetrator in which both specimen and penetrator are heated and mentioned that a series H Brale is particularly suited for tests at elevated temperatures.[31] The hardness numbers are reported in the conventional Rockwell scales (Fig. 13-26) for a Brale penetrator.

The Brinell hardness tester also has been modified to perform hardness tests with a heated specimen and penetrator.[32] A sintered carbide ball penetrator is used for this type of hardness test at elevated temperatures. In each case the specimen and the penetrator were surrounded by an electrically heated furnace.

Another method of measuring hot hardness makes use of the mutual indentation produced on two cylinders of the same metal under a known load.[33] In this method, two cylinders of the same metal are placed in an electrically heated furnace and mounted one above the other with their longitudinal axes parallel. A known load is applied to the cylinders at test temperature through hardened-steel backing blocks using a modified Brinell hardness testing machine.

Traverse Tests

Often a series of hardness tests at regularly specified intervals along an axis of hardness variation is called a traverse test. This test may be performed to determine the rate of quenching or the case-hardening depth of a specimen. Generally, a case-hardness traverse test is performed of a sectional sample and a measurement made for the depth of hardness to R_C50, which is the effective case depth, or the total depth of the case.

Hardness Conversions

Hardness tests are made under arbitrary conditions; hence there is no basic correlation for converting hardness numbers from one scale to another. The best that can be done is to calibrate one scale in terms of another, but the hardness conversion relation for one type of material or metal does not usually apply to another type of material or metal. Hardness conversion tables for steel, cartridge brass, nickel, and high-nickel alloys are given in ASTM E 140.

TENSION TEST

The tension test, as the name implies, is used to determine the properties of a material under tension. The properties determined are applicable when an applied load is in the direction perpendicular to the cross-sectional area carrying the load.

Tensile Strength

The *tensile or ultimate strength* is the maximum load applied during a test divided by the original cross-sectional area of the specimen. It is generally reported in pounds per square inch (psi) or megapascals (MPa).

Percent Elongation

The *percent elongation* is the percentage increase in the original gage length as determined from the assembled fractured specimen. The two pieces of a fractured round tensile specimen are generally clamped together between mounted centers for measuring the final distance between the points marking the gage length. Sometimes specimens are held together as closely as possible by manual means. It is customary to report the gage length actually used.

Reduction in Area

The *reduction in area* is the percentage decrease in cross-sectional area at the fracture area of the specimen. The final dimension is measured with the fractured specimen clamped or held together in the same manner described for elongation measurements.

Yield Strength

Yield strength is the stress at which a material exhibits a specified limiting permanent set. There are three methods for determining this value: (1) Under a constant rate of loading, some materials exhibit a sudden arrest in the load being applied. The load at the time of arrest is converted to stress and is termed the yield strength by the "drop-of-the-beam" method. (2) Another method is to use a pair of dividers set at the initial gage length and watch for a visible elongation between two gage

MECHANICAL TESTING

marks. The load at the instant any elongation is observed is converted to stress and is termed the yield strength by the "dividers" method. The yield strength determined by either of these two methods is sometimes called the "yield point." (3) The third method of determining the yield strength is known as the "offset" method. The yield strength is determined from the stress-strain diagram (curves starting at zero stress, zero strain) by drawing a line parallel to the straight or elastic portion of the curve starting at zero stress and the prescribed strain, usually 0.2%. The yield strength for the prescribed offset is taken as the stress corresponding to the intersection of this straight line and the stress-strain curve.

Elastic Limit

The *elastic limit* is the greatest stress that a material is capable of withstanding without a permanent deformation remaining upon complete release of the stress. It is seldom determined for metals as a routine test because the values do not differ widely from values found for the proportional limit.

Proportional Limit

The *proportional limit* is the greatest stress that a material is capable of withstanding without deviating from the law of proportionality of stress to strain. The "tangent proportional limit" is determined by visual examination as the stress at the tangent point of the straight-line section of the stress-strain diagram to the remainder of the curve. The proportional limit is also determined by the offset method used for determining yield strength. The offset used for the proportional limit is generally 0.01%. The proportional limit is sometimes called the "proportional elastic limit" and is reported in psi or MPa.

Modulus of Elasticity

The *modulus of elasticity* is the ratio, within the elastic limit of a material, of stress to corresponding strain. It is the slope (stress divided by strain) of the initial straight portion of the stress strain curve and is designated by the line *OA* in Fig. 13-27. The tangent modulus of elasticity is the slope of a straight line drawn tangent at *B* to the stress-strain curve at a stated stress. Up to the proportional limit of a material, the tangent modulus and the modulus of elasticity are equal; therefore, the former is used only above the elastic limit. The secant modulus of elasticity is the slope of the line *OC* drawn from the origin of the stress-strain diagram (zero stress, zero strain) to some stated stress on the curve above the elastic limit.

COMPRESSION TESTS

Compressive strength is generally defined as the maximum stress in compression that a metal will withstand before rupture. However, when a metal fails in this manner, it is usually accompanied by shearing stress in a diagonal direction. In the case of a material that does not fail by fracture, the compressive stress is usually regarded as an arbitrary value that produces sufficient permanent distortion to make the material unusable. The values of yield point and elastic limit in compression are usually about 110-115% of their values in tension.

Although it would appear that compressive properties are no more difficult to determine than tensile properties, this is far from the fact. Parallelism of the testing machine platens and of specimen ends is a factor of great importance and is frequently overlooked or underestimated. If special care is not exercised to ensure a high degree of parallelism of the platens and specimen

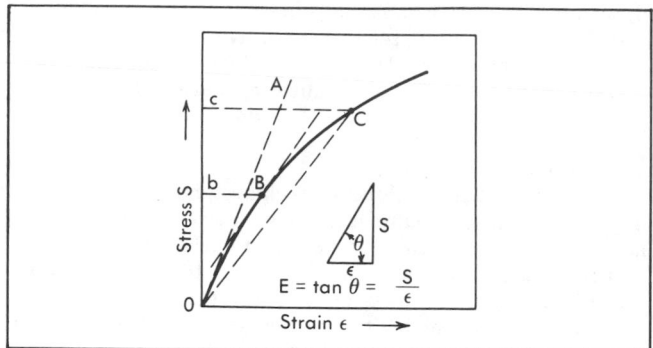

Fig. 13-27 Diagram for determining moduli of elasticity.[34]

ends, uniform axial loading will not be obtained. The latter is necessary for reliable results. Self-aligning hemispherical or ball-mounted platens are desirable for such work.

TRANSVERSE BENDING TESTS

A beam supported at both ends and carrying a transverse load at the center is referred to as being in bending. Similarly, a column carrying an eccentric load parallel to its longitudinal axis is in bending. In each case, one part of the cross section of the material is under tension, and the other part is under compression. Tests involving bending usually are made on materials under the type of loading for a beam. Bending tests are classified into two groups, the distinguishing feature being the type of information obtained from each. Tests to identify the strength properties of the material in bending are generally called flexural tests. Tests to determine the relative response of the material to bending are called bend tests.

Flexural Tests

Flexural tests, to determine the strength properties of metals in bending, are most widely used for the more brittle metals such as cast iron. For cast iron, these tests are more commonly referred to as transverse tests. The general setup for a transverse test is quite similar to that of a beam supported at both ends and loaded transversely at the center with means provided for measuring the deflection at the beam's midpoint. The beam or specimen is loaded to failure in the transverse direction. After the applied load exceeds that corresponding to the proportional limit of the metal under test, the deflection measuring device is removed. Observations of the applied loads and the corresponding deflections provide data for a load-deflection diagram. A coordinate plot of simultaneous load and deflection observations gives a curve similar to a stress-strain curve for a tension or compression test. Load is generally plotted as the ordinate. Values for the various properties are determined by prescribed methods from the diagram and direct load observations.

Bend Tests

Bend tests yield no property useful in design calculations. They are instead a control test to determine the relative abilities of materials to withstand bending. A measure of ductility is usually associated with them. In brief, the tests generally consist of bending a specimen about a radius or upon itself and making observations to determine if it was sufficiently ductile in bending to withstand the conditions imposed by the test.

Two other bend tests are worthy of mention. One consists of determining the number of degrees a specimen will bend around a given radius before failure occurs by cracking. The other consists of determining by trial the minimum radius over which the specimen may be bent by 180° without cracking. The bending operation in these tests may be carried out by any available means as long as the specimen is made to conform to the radius about which it is being bent.

DIRECT SHEAR TESTS

Shear stresses result from the application of a load in the plane or line of the cross section bearing the load. Direct shear is present when one layer of a material is made to move on the adjacent layer in a linear direction. Transverse loading of a rivet or bolt in a plate produces shearing stresses in it. When the load is carried by one plane or cross section of the rivet, as in a single-lap riveted joint, it is called single shear. When the load is carried by two cross sections as in a double-lap riveted joint, it is called double shear. If the opposing forces producing shear do not act in the same plane or line, bending stresses are set up. Therefore, in a direct shear test it is important to have the opposing forces at the cross section, which transmits the load, act in the same plane or line, at least with reasonable precision.

A jig with a specimen in place is mounted between the platens of a universal testing machine and loaded to failure of the specimen in shear. The tensile loading features of the testing machine, including self-aligning drawbars, are used with the jig shown in Fig. 13-28. The compressive loading features are used with the jigs shown in Fig. 13-29. With the latter jigs, it is important that the specimens are firmly clamped and that the load is distributed uniformly over the specimen in the direction normal to the cross section under shear. The maximum load at failure is observed.

The shear strength is the maximum observed load divided by the cross-sectional area that is sheared. For example, the shear strength of a cylindrical specimen sheared in the jig shown in Fig. 13-28 is the maximum observed load up to failure divided by twice the cross-sectional area of the cylinder.

TORSION TESTS

Torsion shear is produced by rotation or by torque. In this type of shear, one layer of a material is made to rotate on an adjacent layer. This type of shear is present in rotating shafts,

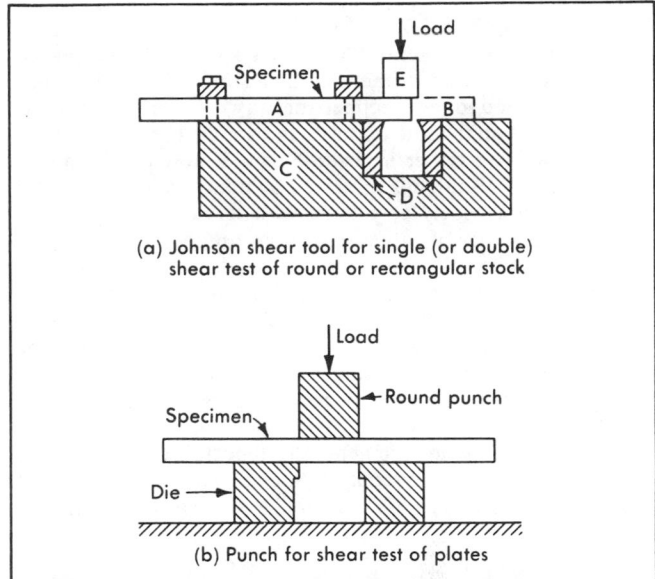

(a) Johnson shear tool for single (or double) shear test of round or rectangular stock

(b) Punch for shear test of plates

Fig. 13-29 Shear jigs for compressive loading. In the field of plasticity, the term "shear strength" refers to the stress acting on the plane under consideration. (*Davis, Troxell, and Wiscocil*)

such as crankshafts or driveshafts. when power is being transmitted.

In a torsion test, equal and opposing moments are applied at opposite ends of a suitable specimen in planes perpendicular to the specimen's longitudinal axis. When placing the specimen in the testing machine, it is important that the longitudinal axis of the specimen coincides with the common axis about which the heads of the testing machine rotate. The applied torque is generally increased until the specimen fractures. A device known as a troptometer is usually attached to the specimen to measure the amount of twist during the application of torque. Observations of the applied torque and corresponding twist of rotation, which are converted to stress in the outer fiber and strain in the outer fiber, respectively, provide the data for plotting a stress-strain diagram. The properties commonly determined are shear strength or modulus of rupture, yield strength, proportional limit, modulus of elasticity or modulus of rigidity, and angle of twist.

NOTCHED-BAR IMPACT TESTS

Notched-bar impact tests are commonly called impact tests, implying that the test results are applicable to problems involving shock loading or impact. Unfortunately, this is not the case because practically all specimens used in impact tests are notched. The type of specimen and the method of breaking it were originally designed and used to show a variation in notch sensitivity for steels that exhibit a ductile fracture in the tensile test. Impact tests are, in reality, notched-bar tests. There are true impact tests, such as ballistics tests, but these are performed infrequently.

Impact tests, such as the Charpy and Izod tests with notched specimens, measure the amount of energy absorbed in fracturing the specimen. The true worth of these values is to determine the relative notch toughness of two or more materials under the particular test conditions. Values determined under one set of test conditions are not convertible to values for other test conditions.

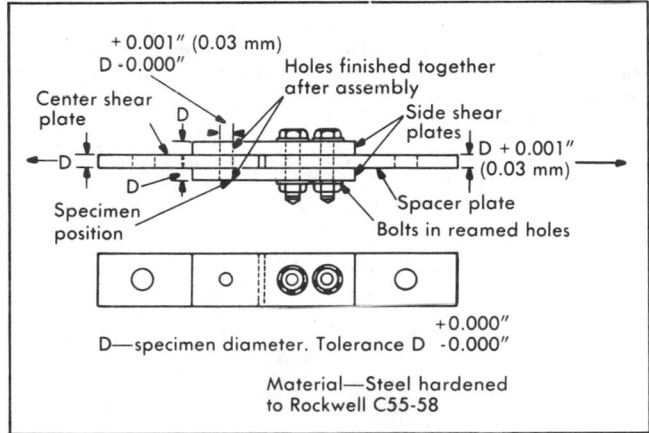

Fig. 13-28 Shear jig for tensile loading in self-aligning fixtures.

MECHANICAL TESTING

Charpy Impact Test

In the Charpy impact test, a notched specimen is supported as a simple beam and is fractured by a single blow. The single blow is delivered to the specimen midway between the supporting anvils and on the side opposite the notch. The specimens in general use have either a keyhole or a V-notch of standard dimensions. A V-notch is preferred by many testers because it has been more widely correlated with service and because it gives a wider range of values. However, tougher materials give false values when the bar does not break fully because they absorb energy when the bar is forced through the anvil.

In the test, the specimen is placed on the anvils horizontally. The line of impact is on the face of the specimen opposite the notch and in the plane bisecting it. The specimen is broken with a single blow delivered by a pendulum from a raised position, and energy absorbed is read directly from a scale (Fig. 13-30). Charpy impact values are generally reported in foot-pounds (newton-meters). When reporting the impact value, it is necessary to include the type of notch used and the test temperature.

Izod Impact Test

In the Izod impact test, a notched specimen of square or round cross section is used, having the V-notch with a fixed radius at the bottom. It is supported as a cantilever with the root of the notch in line with the edge of the vise in which the specimen is clamped. It is broken with a single blow, which is delivered to the notched face of the specimen at a specified distance above the vise.

The standard pendulum type of Izod impact testing machine is used. The general features of this type of machine are the same as those for the Charpy impact testing machine shown in Fig. 13-30. The chief differences are: (1) a vise is used to hold the specimen in the vertical position, and (2) the hammer of the pendulum is shaped to clear the vise and strike the specimen a specified distance above it.

A template is used for aligning the root of the notch with the top of the vise. Izod impact values are generally reported in foot-pounds or newton-meters. It is necessary to report the type of specimen and the test temperature used.

Drop-Weight Test

The drop-weight test has been used extensively to investigate factors affecting the initiation of brittle fractures in structural steels. The test determines the nil ductility transition (NDT) temperature under standardized conditions. The techniques were devised for measuring the fracture initiation of ferritic plates in thicknesses of 5/8″ (16 mm) or more. The test has seldom been used for thin plates and is not recommended for steel sections less than 1/2″ (12 mm) thick. Procedures for conducting the test are described in ASTM E 208.

The drop-weight test employs a small weld bead on the specimen surface as a crack starter. The weld deposit develops a small cleavage-crack flaw in a weld notch during testing. The method of testing is illustrated in Fig. 13-31. Nil ductility transition temperatures determined for a particular steel with any of the standard specimens are expected to agree within $\pm 10^\circ$ F (5.6° C).

Drop-Weight Tear Test

The drop-weight tear test employs full-thickness plate specimens with the dimensions shown in Fig. 13-32 and has been used successfully in recent years by several laboratories in studies on pipeline steels and some other materials. A sharp-pointed tool-steel chisel is pressed into the specimen with a hydraulic ram to produce a notch 0.200″ (5.08 mm) deep with a root radius of 0.0003-0.001″ (0.008-0.03 mm). The small radius combined with cold work ensures that a cleavage fracture will be initiated during testing. The specimens are stood on edge and broken rapidly, as simple beams such as large Charpy bars are broken. The energy can be provided by a dropping weight or by a large pendulum. The latter method permits measurement of breaking energies. The usual practice is to judge the performance of a specimen on the basis of the average percentage of shear texture on the fractured surface.

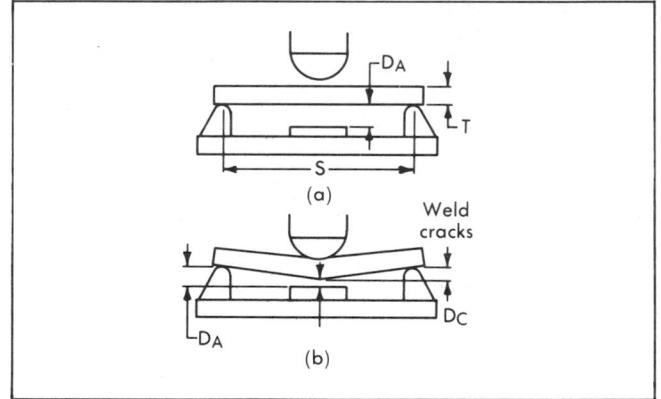

Fig. 13-31 Method for Naval Research Lab drop-weight test: (a) setup and (b) in presence of small crack during test, yield-point loading is terminated by contact with a stop.[35]

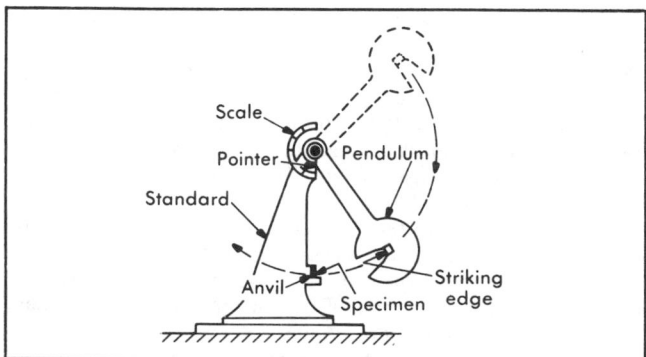

Fig. 13-30 Charpy impact testing machine.

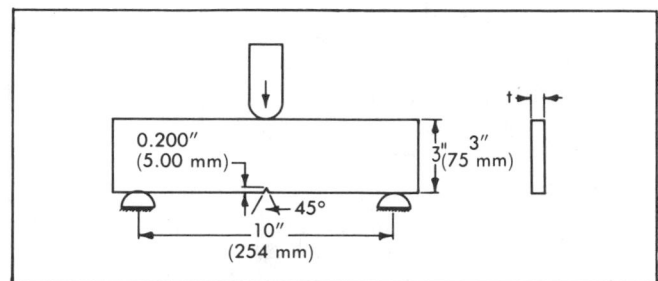

Fig. 13-32 Drop-weight tear test specimen.[36]

Tensile Impact Tests

Tensile impact tests generally are made with a Charpy-type impact machine, modified to satisfy the conditions of the test. A round specimen with a central reduced section approximately 0.25″ (6 mm) in diameter is most commonly used. One end of the specimen is attached to the pendulum of the testing machine. A "dog," attached to the other end of the specimen in a horizontal position, contacts a pair of anvils at the time of impact. Care must be taken to adjust the dog to the specimen so that the impact occurs when the pendulum is in the position of "zero" energy and that all parts of the dog contact the anvils at the same time. The specimen is broken with a single blow delivered in the direction of its longitudinal axis, and the energy absorbed is reported in foot-pounds or newton-meters. Sometimes gage marks are placed on the reduced section, and the elongation of the assembled fractured specimen is determined. It is good practice to give all the details of the test when reporting tensile impact data.

FRACTURE TOUGHNESS TESTS

The linear elastic fracture mechanics approach to judging fracture toughness has been studied intensively for many years. It is appropriate for quantifying fracture and crack growth resistance of materials. Fracture mechanics leads to parametric values that can be used in design if careful consideration is given to differences between testing and service conditions.

Toughness tests based on fracture mechanics characterize strong materials on the basis of their tolerance for cracks and resistance to brittle fracture. It is based on the assumption and experience that cracks or flaws exist in materials and grow when the intensity of the stress field near the edge of the crack reaches a critical value. It is also assumed that the stress intensity is proportional to the square root of the crack parameter. The crack parameter is usually taken as half the crack length because the calculations are usually concerned with disc-like flaws growing to a free surface, such as through-thickness failures in plates. The fracture toughness value for quasi-plane strain, termed K_{IC}, is reported in units of kpsi $\sqrt{\text{inch}}$; higher values indicate better toughness.

The fracture toughness value is also known as the critical stress intensity factor for the opening mode of cracking in the stress state of quasi-plane-strain. The critical stress intensity factor characterizes the resistance of a material to fracture in the presence of a sharp crack under severe tensile constraint when the plastic region at the tip of the crack is small compared with the size of the crack and the specimen. The K_{IC} value is believed to represent a lower limiting value of fracture toughness; it varies with testing temperature and speed.

FATIGUE TESTS

Fatigue tests are concerned with the progressive failure of materials under repeated loading. Fatigue properties of a material are usually determined from a series of tests on a number of similar specimens. In one kind of test, a specimen is subjected to cycles of fully reversed (tension to equal compression) nominal stress and the number of cycles withstood to rupture is recorded. Then other specimens are subjected to cycles of other different stress ranges. A plot known as an *S-N* curve, is then made of stress, *S*, against number of cycles, *N*, to failure (Fig. 13-33).

Usually *S* is plotted as the ordinate on either a Cartesian or a logarithmic scale and *N* as the abscissa on a logarithmic scale.

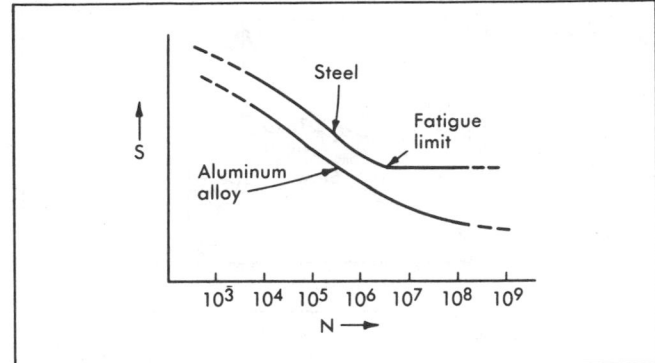

Fig. 13-33 Typical endurance curves for aluminum.

Some materials (particularly steels) show curves that flatten out at large values of *N*. The stress level at which this occurs, and below which fatigue lifetime would presumably be infinite, is called a fatigue limit. Some materials may not exhibit well-defined fatigue limits; hence, the stress level at an arbitrary long lifetime (say, more than 10^7 cycles) is used as a design fatigue limit for such a material. It should be kept in mind that, in the presence of other deteriorating factors (such as corrosion and elevated temperature), a material may not have a fatigue limit.

The *fatigue or endurance strength* is taken from the *S-N* curve by reading the stress corresponding to a stated number of cycles. The *endurance limit*, when such is present, is the limiting stress below which the material will withstand an indefinitely large number of stress cycles without failure. In general, steels have true endurance limits while most other materials do not. The above-mentioned fatigue strength is generally used for materials other than steel, and the number of stress cycles for which it holds must be stated.

The *endurance ratio* is the endurance limit divided by the tensile strength of the material. If the material does not have an endurance limit, the ratio is the fatigue strength divided by the tensile strength. In the latter case, the number of cycles corresponding to the fatigue strength used should be stated.

The *notch sensitivity ratio in fatigue* is the endurance limit for polished unnotched specimens divided by the endurance limit for notched specimens. If the material has no true endurance limit, fatigue strengths are used in this ratio, and the number of cycles corresponding to the stresses used should be stated. Partially or totally reversed flexure tests are used for sheet materials which cannot be tested by means of the rotating-beam method.

CREEP TESTS

Creep is the continuing change in dimension with time of a material under stress. Materials exhibit creep, particularly at elevated temperatures, even at stresses below their short-time proportional limits.

Creep tests are usually made under a constant tensile load. A selected constant tensile load is applied to a specimen at a selected elevated temperature, and the resulting elongation is observed at sufficient intervals of time to define the relationship between elongation and time. When the observed data are plotted, elongation is usually made the ordinate and time the abscissa. Because the load is not applied until the specimen has reached temperature, there is an initial elastic elongation. If the load is above the proportional limit, the initial elongation will

MECHANICAL TESTING

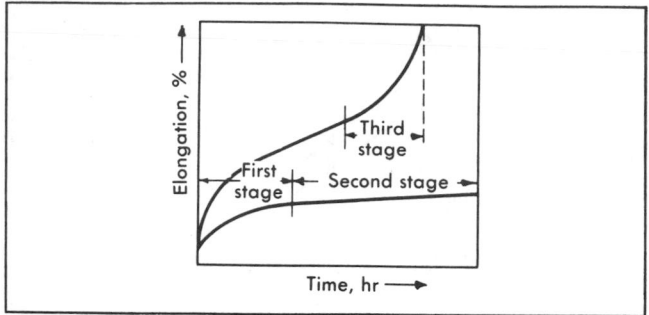

Fig 13-34 Typical creep curves.

also include some plastic deformation. Some plots of creep-time-elongation data include the initial elongation that occurs on application of the load and some do not.

Figure 13-34 shows two typical creep curves in which initial elastic elongations are included. The lower curve in the figure illustrates the type of creep curve obtained when the combination of stress and temperature used in the test does not cause failure of the specimen during the test. The first stage of creep is evidenced by a high but decreasing rate of elongation. The second stage is characterized by an approximately constant rate of elongation. Usually a total test time in excess of 1000 hr is required to establish the approximately constant rate of elongation. The minimum creep rate is observed during the second stage. The upper curve of Fig. 13-34 illustrates the type of creep curve obtained when the combination of stress and temperature used in the test produces failure of the specimen. This curve shows the third, or final, stage of creep, which is characterized by an increased rate of elongation. The time and

elongation at which second-stage creep changes to the third stage of increasing creep rate is called the transition point.

Creep-Rupture Tests

Creep-rupture tests are similar to creep tests. They differ only in being intentionally continued until the test specimen ruptures. In addition to the conventional creep data, rupture time, elongation, and reduction in area are also obtained from creep-rupture tests.

Stress-Rupture Tests

Stress-rupture tests are made by loading a test specimen to failure as in a creep test, but without the use of an extensometer. No strain data are obtained, only time to rupture, elongation, and reduction in area values. Stress-rupture tests are often made using circumferential V-notches in the specimen to determine notch sensitivity under the testing conditions.

STRESS ANALYSIS

Experimental stress analysis is the term applied to the determination of the location, direction, and approximate intensity of stress in a part; no mechanical properties are determined. In practice, strains are measured and the corresponding stresses are obtained by multiplying the known modulus of elasticity of the material under test by the observed strains.

Practical stress analysis methods include photoelasticity, brittle coatings, resin-based coatings, ceramic-based coatings, and strain gages. These methods are generally applicable to parts of any size, shape, or material.

BALANCING

Balancing is an operation whereby the mass distribution of a rotating body or rotor is altered to minimize first-order vibrations at the support bearings. Portions of this subchapter are abstracted with permission from the publications *Balancing Made Simple,*[37] *Fundamentals of Balancing,*[38] and *Balance Engineering Manual #31.*[39]

The word rotor is used throughout this discussion to describe any rotating body requiring balancing. Balancing is normally performed by placing the rotor into a machine specifically designed for that purpose. However, a rotor can also be balanced in its own bearings and supporting structure.

An unbalanced rotor will cause vibrations and stress in the rotor itself and in its supporting structure. Rotors are balanced to achieve one or more of the following purposes:

- Increase bearing life.
- Minimize vibration.
- Minimize audible and signal noises.
- Minimize operating stresses.
- Minimize operator annoyance and fatigue.
- Minimize power losses.
- Increase product quality.
- Satisfy customers.

UNBALANCE

A rotating element having an uneven mass distribution or unbalance will vibrate because of the excess centrifugal forces exerted during rotation by the heavier side of the rotor. Unbalance causes centrifugal force, which in turn causes vibration. Common units used for expressing unbalance are oz.in., g.in., and g.mm. Each of these units expresses a mass multiplied by its distance from the shaft axis.

Types of Unbalance

The two most frequently encountered types of unbalance are static unbalance and dynamic unbalance. Two other types of unbalance found in rotating parts are couple unbalance and quasi-static unbalance.

Static unbalance. Static unbalance, at one time referred to as force unbalance, exists when the principal axis of inertia is displaced parallel to the shaft axis. Figure 13-35 shows an eccentric rotor on knife-edges. If the knife-edges are level, the rotor will turn until the heavy or unbalanced spot reaches the lowest position.

Static unbalance can be corrected by a single mass correction placed opposite the center of gravity in a plane perpendicular to

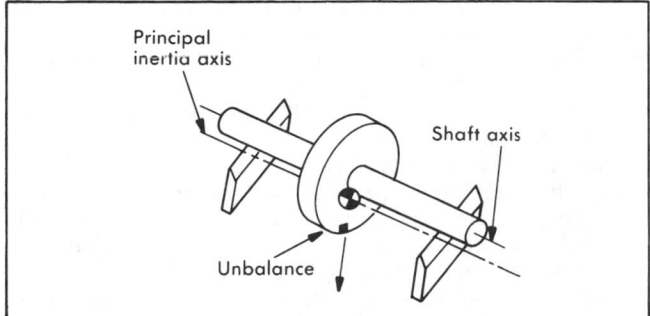

Fig. 13-35 Concentric disc with static unbalance. (*Schenck Trebel Corp.*)

the shaft axis and intersecting the center of gravity. If the unbalance is large enough, it can be detected with conventional gravity-type balancing machines. This type of unbalance is found primarily in narrow, disc-shaped parts such as flywheels and turbine wheels.

Dynamic unbalance. Dynamic unbalance is the most common type of unbalance and exists when the central principal axis of inertia is neither parallel to nor coincident with the shaft axis (Fig. 13-36). It can only be corrected by mass correction in at least two planes perpendicular to the shaft axis.

Couple unbalance. Couple unbalance, at one time called moment unbalance, occurs when two equal unbalance masses are positioned at opposite ends of a rotor and spaced 180° from each other (Fig. 13-37). Unlike dynamic unbalance, the principal axis of inertia intersects the shaft axis at the center of gravity in couple unbalance.

Common units for expressing couple unbalance are g·in.^{2} (gram·inch·inch) or oz·in.^{2}; the second inch dimension refers to the distance between the two planes of unbalance. This type of unbalance cannot be corrected by a single mass in a single correction plane. At least two masses are required, each mass in a different transverse plane and 180° opposite to each other.

Quasi-static unbalance. Quasi-static unbalance is a special case of dynamic unbalance. It exists when the central principal axis of inertia intersects the shaft axis at a point other than the center of gravity (Fig. 13-38). Quasi-static unbalance represents the specific combination of static and couple unbalance when the angular position of one couple component coincides with the angular position of the static unbalance.

Causes of Unbalance

Unbalance in rotating parts and assemblies can be caused by one or more of many factors, some of which are not readily apparent. If proper consideration is given to balance requirements in the design, processing, and manufacturing stages, the unbalance in the finished part can be kept to a minimum and the cost of balancing operations reduced. Some of the causes of unbalance in manufactured parts are:

- Tolerances in fabrication, including casting, machining, forging, and assembly.
- Variation within the material such as voids, porosity, inclusions, grain size, density, and finishes.
- Nonsymmetrical part design.
- Nonsymmetry in use, including distortion, dimensional changes, and shifting of parts due to rotational stress, aerodynamic forces, and temperature changes.

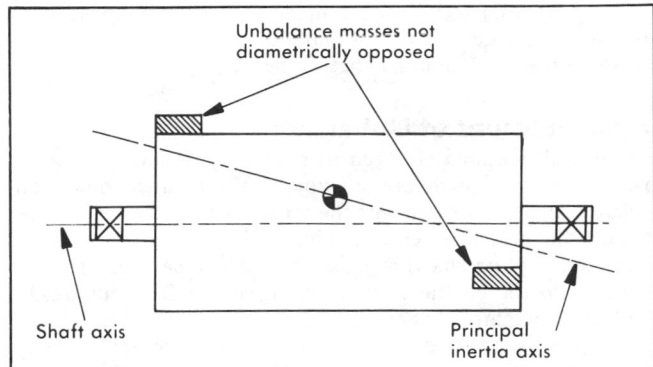

Fig. 13-36 Dynamic unbalance. (*Schenck Trebel Corp.*)

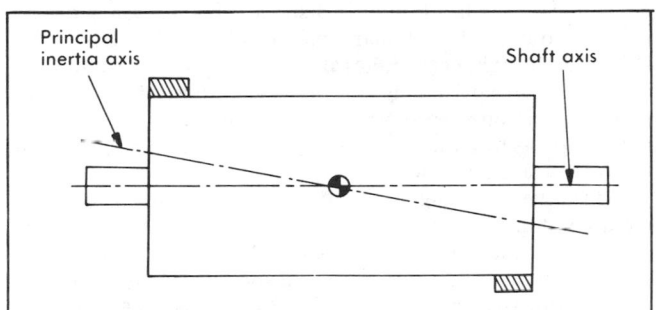

Fig. 13-37 Couple unbalance. (*Schenck Trebel Corp.*)

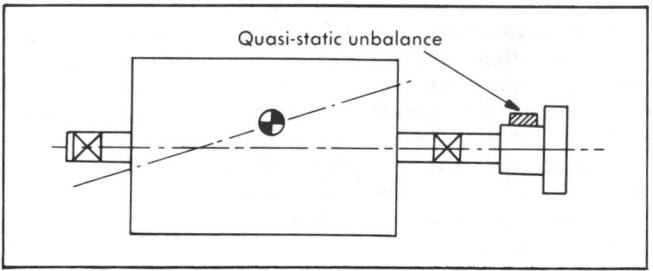

Fig. 13-38 Unbalance in coupling causes quasi-static unbalance in rotor assembly. (*Schenck Trebel Corp.*)

Effects of Unbalance

Unbalance in just one rotating component of an assembly may cause the entire assembly to vibrate. This induced vibration in turn may cause excessive wear in bearings, bushings, shafts, spindles, and gears, resulting in a reduction of their service life. Vibrations set up highly undesirable alternating stresses in structural supports and frames that may eventually lead to their complete failure. Performance is decreased because the unbalance force is absorbed by the supporting structure. Vibrations may also be transmitted to adjacent machinery and seriously impair their accuracy or proper functioning.

BALANCING PROCESS

The balancing process usually consists of three general operations. In the first operation, the unbalance is measured to determine the amount and angle of unbalance in the correction plane or planes. The part is then corrected using a variety of

CHAPTER 13

BALANCING

methods. The correction can be made on the balancing machine or on a separate machine. Finally a second measurement is made of the residual unbalance in the part.

Measurement of Unbalance

Several methods are used to obtain a reference signal by which the phase angle of the amount-of-unbalance indication signal may be correlated with the rotor. On end-drive machines (where the rotor is driven by a universal-joint driver or similarly flexible coupling shaft) a phase reference generator, directly coupled to the balancing machine drive spindle, is used. On belt-drive machines (where the rotor is driven by a belt over the rotor periphery) or on self-driven machines, a stroboscopic lamp flashing once per rotor revolution or a scanning head (photoelectric cell with light source) is employed to obtain the phase reference.

The scanning head requires a single reference mark on the rotor to obtain the angular position of unbalance, but the stroboscopic light necessitates attachment of an angle reference disc to the rotor or placing an adhesive numbered band around it. Under the once-per-revolution flash of the strobe light the rotor appears to stand still so that an angle reading can be taken opposite a stationary mark.

With the scanning head, an additional angle indicating circuit and instrument must be employed. The output from the phase reference sensor (scanning head) and the pickups at the rotor-bearing supports are processed and result in an indication representing the amount of unbalance and its angular position.

Correcting Unbalance

Unbalanced conditions in a rotor can be corrected by material removal, material addition, or by moving the center-line of rotation (mass centering). The selected correction method should ensure that there is sufficient capacity to allow correction of the maximum unbalance that may occur. In many cases, the design of the part or the material itself will determine the method of correction, but in other cases there will be a choice of methods. The residual unbalance and the cost of the correction method should also be considered when selecting a particular method.

Material removal. If the design of the part permits, unbalance correction by removal of material is generally preferred over addition of material. To facilitate balancing, an extra volume of material should be incorporated in the part's design. Conventional machining methods are generally used to remove any material, with drilling, milling, and grinding being the most common. When balancing jet engine components, it is preferable to use hand-operated tools because of the cost of sophisticated rotors.

Material addition. As stated previously, unbalance correction by removal of material is preferable if at all possible, but in many cases this method cannot be used. Some of the disadvantages of correcting unbalance conditions by material addition are: (1) the cost of providing the necessary material; (2) the material must be supplied in increments, which limits the accuracy; (3) the added material may come off unless securely fastened; and (4) the cost of purchasing some material addition equipment is greater than material removal equipment. However, in the case of balancing jet engine rotors, balancing by material addition is preferred because individual components are commonly replaced during maintenance.

Mass centering. Mass centering is a process whereby a rough forging or casting is rotated in a specially designed balancing machine prior to any machining. Provision is made in the mass centering machine to move the workpiece in relation to its axis of rotation until balance is obtained. The workpiece is then centered in this position and all subsequent machining is performed from these centers.

Because material removal is uneven at different parts of the shaft, the machining operation will introduce some new unbalance. A final balancing operation is therefore still required. In general, the more machining or material that must be removed after the initial centering, the less effective the mass centering operation becomes. Although the main application of mass centering has been in the fabrication of crankshafts, the process can be applied to a variety of parts.

Selecting correction points. The three factors that need to be taken into consideration when selecting the point or plane of correction are:

- The proposed correction must not interfere with the function of the part.
- The correction must not weaken or distort the part.
- The correction should not distract from the appearance of the part.

For static unbalance corrections, the correction plane should generally be as close as possible to the part's center of gravity to minimize the introduction of couple unbalance. If there are large unmachined areas on the part, it is better to make the correction at or near the center of gravity of the unmachined areas. It is usually better to correct one half of the unbalance on each side of a narrow part than to make the correction only on one side of the part.

Correction planes for dynamic unbalance should be as close as possible to the ends of the part. By doing so, the amounts of correction required will be reduced. The effect of unbalance correction at one end on the unbalance at the other end is also reduced by separating the correction planes as far as the part allows.

BALANCING MACHINES AND EQUIPMENT

Balancing machines and equipment are divided into two general categories, gravity (nonrotating) and centrifugal (rotating), as shown in Table 13-3. These two general categories can be further subdivided based on the type of unbalance the machine can measure, the attitude of the rotor axis with respect to the machine, the design of the machine, and the class of the machine. Balancing machines can also be categorized based on their intended application.

Gravity Balancing Machines

Gravity balancing machines, also called nonrotating or static balancing machines, measure the unbalance in a rotor by means of gravity. As indicated in Table 13-3, these machines are only capable of measuring static unbalance. The three basic designs are knife-edges, roller stand, and pendulum.

Static balancing is satisfactory for rotors having relatively low service speeds and axial lengths that are small in comparison with the rotor diameter. A preliminary static unbalance correction may be required on rotors having a combined unbalance so large that it is impossible in a dynamic, soft suspension balancing machine to bring the rotor up to its proper balancing speed without damaging the machine. If the rotor is first balanced statically, it is usually possible to decrease

TABLE 13-3
Classification of Balancing Machines

Principle Employed	Unbalance Indicated	Attitude of Shaft Axis	Type of Machine	Available Classes
Gravity (nonrotating)	Static (single-plane)	Vertical	Pendulum	
		Horizontal	Knife-edges	
			Roller sets	
Centrifugal (rotating)	Static (single-plane)	Vertical	Soft suspension	Not classified
			Hard suspension	
		Horizontal	Not commercially available	
	Dynamic (two-plane); also suitable for static (single-plane)	Vertical	Soft suspension	II, III
			Hard suspension	III, IV
		Horizontal	Soft suspension	I, II, III
			Hard suspension	IV

the initial unbalance to a level where the rotor may be brought up to balancing speed and the residual unbalance measured. Such preliminary static correction may not be required on hard suspension balancing machines. For some applications, static balancing is also performed on narrow, high-speed rotors that are subsequently assembled to a shaft and balanced again dynamically.

Centrifugal Balancing Machines

The two types of centrifugal balancing machines in use today are soft and hard bearing machines. These two types are also divided into classes based on the method of calibrating the machine for various parts.

Soft bearing machines. Soft bearing balancing machines are the oldest type of balancers. They derive their name from the soft or flexible vibratory suspension system used in the work-support structures of the machine.

The flexible suspension system permits the rotor to vibrate freely in one direction, which is horizontal and perpendicular to the rotor shaft axis under certain conditions.

Hard bearing machines. Hard bearing balancing machines are essentially of the same construction as soft balancing machines, except that their supports are significantly stiffer in the transverse horizontal direction. As a result of the stiffer supports, the horizontal frequency for these machines occurs at a frequency several orders of magnitude higher than that for a comparable soft suspension machine.

Classes. Centrifugal balancing machines may be categorized by the type of unbalance they can measure (static or dynamic), the attitude of the journal axis of the workpiece (vertical or horizontal), or the type of rotor support system employed (soft or hard suspension). In each category, one or more classes of machines are commercially built (refer to Table 13-3).

Class I. Machines in the Class I category are of the soft suspension type. They do not indicate unbalance directly in weight units (such as ounces or grams in the actual correction planes), but indicate only displacement and/or velocity of vibration at the bearings. The instrumentation does not indicate the amount of weight that must be added or removed in each of the correction planes.

Class II. Machines in the Class II category are of the soft bearing type using instrumentation that permits plane separation and calibration for a given rotor type, if a balanced master or prototype rotor with calibration masses is available. However, the same trial-and-error procedure as for Class I machines is required for the first of a series of identical rotors.

Class III. Machines in the Class III category are of the soft suspension type using instrumentation that includes an integral electronic unbalance compensator. Any unbalanced rotor may be used in place of a balanced master rotor without the need for trial-and-error correction. Plane separation and calibration can be achieved in one or more runs with the help of calibration masses. This class also includes soft suspension machines with electrically driven shakers fitted to the vibratory part of their rotor supports. New digital electronics allow storage of the initial calibration values, permitting simple, one-number recall if an identical rotor is to be balanced.

Class IV. Machines in the Class IV are of the hard bearing type. They are permanently calibrated by the manufacturer for all rotors falling within the weight and speed range of a given machine size. Unlike the machines in other classes, these machines indicate unbalance in the first run without individual rotor calibration. This is accomplished by the incorporation of an analog or digital computer into the instrumentation associated with the machine. The instrumentation then indicates the magnitude and angular position of the required correction mass for each of the two selected planes.

Safety

The design of balancing machines aims to minimize hazards from the use of the machine itself. Rising demand for still greater safety in the work environment calls for additional protection, especially with respect to the rotor to be balanced. Special-purpose balancing machines, such as those used in the mass production automotive industry, normally provide all the necessary measures of safety because the workpiece as well as the operating conditions of the machine can be taken into account by the machine manufacturer. However, when multi-purpose balancing machines are used, the workpieces to be

CHAPTER 13

REFERENCES

balanced are generally unknown and beyond the control of the machine manufacturer; safety measures are limited to covering the end-drive coupling and/or the drive belt.

National and local safety codes generally cover the hazards from machine components. Hazards associated with the spinning rotor in a balancing machine may be separated into several different categories and resolved by a variety of measures.

References

1. "Nondestructive Test," SAE J358, *SAE Handbook* (Warrendale, PA: Society of Automotive Engineers, 1983), p. 3.46.
2. Robert C. McMaster, ed., *Nondestructive Testing Handbook*, Vol. I (New York: The Ronald Press Co., 1959), p. 1.1.
3. *Ibid.*, p. 4.8.
4. Warren J. McGonnagle, *Nondestructive Testing* (New York: McGraw-Hill Book Co., 1961), p. 16.
5. Carl E. Betz, *Principles of Penetrants* (Chicago, IL: Magnaflux Corp., 1963), p. 23.
6. McMaster, *op. cit.*, pp. 7.1 to 7.8.
7. Betz, *op. cit.*, p. 242.
8. *Classroom Training Handbook, Magnetic Particle Testing*, CT-6-3 (San Diego: General Dynamics, Convair Div., 1977).
9. *Classroom Training Handbook, Ultrasonic Testing*, CT-6-4 (San Diego: General Dynamics, Convair Div., 1981).
10. Howard E. Boyer and Timothy L. Gall, eds., *Metals Handbook, Desk Edition* (Metals Park, OH: American Society for Metals, 1985), p. 33-40.
11. *Ibid.*
12. *Ibid.*
13. *Classroom Training Handbook, Radiographic Testing*, CT-6-6 (San Diego: General Dynamics, Convair Div., 1983).
14. Richard A. Quinn and Claire C. Sigl, eds., *Radiography in Modern Industry*, 4th ed. (Rochester, NY: Eastman Kodak Co., 1980).
15. "Penetrating Radiation Inspection," SAE J427b, *SAE Handbook*, Vol. I, (Warrendale, PA: Society of Automotive Engineers, 1983), p. 3.53.
16. *Classroom Training Handbook, Eddy Current Testing*, CT-6-5 (San Diego: General Dynamics, Convair Div., 1979).
17. "Eddy Current Testing by Electromagnetic Methods," SAE J425, *SAE Handbook*, Vol. I (Warrendale, PA: Society of Automotive Engineers, 1983), p. 3.49.
18. Richard L. Pasley and James A. Birdwell, "Eddy Current Testing," *Nondestructive Testing, A Survey*, NASA SP-5113 (Washington, DC: National Aeronautics and Space Administration, 1973), p. 108.
19. "Eddy Current Testing by Electromagnetic Methods," *loc. cit.*
20. "Leakage Testing," SAE J1267, *SAE Handbook*, Vol. I (Warrendale, PA: Society of Automotive Engineers, 1983), p. 3.50.
21. Robert E. Englehardt and William A. Hewgley, "Thermal and Infrared Testing," *Nondestructive Testing, A Survey*, NASA SP-5113 (Washington, DC: National Aeronautics and Space Administration, 1973), pp. 119-140.
22. E. G. Henneke and K. L. Reifsnider, *Quality Control and Nondestructive Evaluation Techniques for Composites - Part VII: Thermography—A State-of-the-Art Review*, AVRADCOM Report No. TR 82-F-5 (Watertown, MA: Army Materials Technology Laboratory, 1982).
23. J. Cohen, *Elements of Thermography for Nondestructive Testing*, NBS Technical Note 1177 (Washington, DC: National Bureau of Standards, 1983).
24. "Infrared Heat Measurement Finds New Uses in Plastics," *Plastics Technology* (August 1983), pp. 13-15.
25. E. P. Papadakis, H. L. Chesney, and R. G. Hurley, "Quality Assurance of Aluminum Radiators by Infrared Thermography," *Materials Evaluation* (March 1984), pp. 333-336.
26. Ronald G. Hurley, "Temperature Measurements on Semipermanent Mold Surfaces Using Infrared Thermography," *Thermosense V Conference Proceedings*, held October 25, 1982, Detroit, MI (Bellingham, WA: Society of Photo-Optical Instrumentation Engineers), pp. 89-91.
27. C. Gerald Gardner, "Radiography," *Nondestructive Testing, A Survey* NASA SP-5113 (Washington, DC: National Aeronautics and Space Administration, 1973), p. 89.
28. "Standard Practices for Thermal Neutron Radiography of Materials," ASTM E 748-85 (Philadelphia: American Society for Testing and Materials, 1985).
29. "Standard Method for Determining Image Quality in Thermal Neutron Radiographic Testing," ASTM E 545 (Philadelphia: American Society for Testing and Materials, 1981).
30. David Sliney and Myron Wolbarsht, *Safety with Lasers and Other Optical Sources* (New York: Plenum, 1980).
31. O. Zmeskal, "Hot Hardness Testing," *Metal Progress*, Vol. 51, no. 1 (1947).
32. P. Rabbe and G. Pomme, "La Durete' a Chaud," *Revue de Metallurgie*, Vol. 63 (1966), pp. 719-725.
33. O. E. Harder and H. A. Grove, "Hot Hardness of High Speed Steel and Related Alloys, *Transactions of American Institute of Mining and Metallurgical Engineers*, I and S Division, Vol. 105 (1933).
34. H. E. Davis, G. E. Troxell, and G. T. Wiscocil, *The Testing and Inspection of Engineering Materials*, 2nd ed. (New York: McGraw-Hill Book Co., 1955).
35. P. P. Puzak and W. S. Pellini, *U.S. Naval Research Laboratory Report 5831* (Washington, DC: 1962).
36. G. M. McClure, A. R. Duffy, and R. D. Eiber, "Fracture Resistance in Line Pipe," *ASME Transactions Series B*, Vol. 87, no. 3 (August 1965) pp. 265-278.
37. *Balancing Made Simple* (Janesville, WI: Gilman Manufacturing and Engineering Co., 1980).
38. *Fundamentals of Balancing*, 2nd ed. (New York: Schenck Trebel Corp., 1983).
39. *Balance Engineering Manual No. 31*, 3rd ed. (Warren, MI: Balance Engineering, General Motors Corp., 1962).

SURFACE TECHNOLOGY

Surface technology is the activity that describes, details, and evaluates both the surface and subsurface layers of manufactured components.[1] Traditionally, surface texture has been accepted as the criterion that controls the quality of a surface. Direct relationships are widely assumed to exist between surface roughness and fatigue strength as well as other properties. However, test have indicated that

surface texture is only part of the consideration.[2] Metallurgical and other alterations below the surface, referred to as surface integrity, also have a major influence on material performance. The performance of a material becomes particularly important when high stresses or severe environments are encountered by the workpiece. Surface technology components are shown in Fig. 14-1.

SURFACE TEXTURE

Surface texture is a term used to describe the general quality of a workpiece surface. The term *surface finish* is colloquial, used widely to denote the general quality of a surface.[3] It is not specifically tied to the texture or characteristic pattern of the surface nor is it tied to the specific roughness values. However, a good "finish" implies low roughness values and vice versa.

The texture on a workpiece can be important for both cosmetic and functional performance reasons. In addition, surface texture and dimensional tolerances go hand in hand. For example, bearing surfaces and locating surfaces usually require close dimensional and surface finish control for proper operation and for ensuring that functional dimensions are maintained throughout the useful life of the workpiece.

Other surface texture requirements exist that are not related to dimensional tolerance. For example, surface texture is important for surfaces to be painted to ensure good adherence; for surfaces that are to be marked to ensure legibility; for surfaces over which gases or fluids are to flow; for surfaces having special appearance requirements; and for surfaces that have specific heat or light reflectivity requirements. In some cases, specific surface patterns must also be maintained.

In many instances relating to mechanical parts, the design engineer specifies the surface texture requirements for various workpiece surfaces. The designer must have a thorough understanding of surface quality to correctly specify the surface texture that will provide optimum properties for service, life, appearance, performance, and other desired mechanical functions. In addition, it is important to recognize the relationship between surface texture and the cost of producing parts. In general, as the quality of surface texture increases, the cost of producing the part also increases.

Manufacturing, process control, and inspection personnel must also have a good understanding of surface texture. For these individuals, a special emphasis should be made to understand the capabilities of the various manufacturing methods at their disposal and the methods available for measuring surface texture.

SURFACE TEXTURE COMPONENTS

The repetitive or random deviations from the nominal surface form the three-dimensional tex-

ture of the surface. This does not include errors of form, which are those components of surface topography caused by such things as warping of parts or straightness errors in the machines that produce the surface. A traditionally machined workpiece surface is composed of many surface texture components created during the manufacturing process. These components become superimposed over one another, forming a complex pattern called the profile. The common components of surface texture are roughness, waviness, and lay. They are shown individually and collectively in Fig. 14-2.

Another component of surface texture is a flaw. Flaws are unintentional, unexpected, and unwanted interruptions in the part surface. They are usually caused by nonuniformity of the material, or they may result from damage to the surface after processing, including scratches, dents, pits, and cracks. If acceptable/nonacceptable flaws are defined in advance by the buyer and seller, the workpieces should be inspected for flaws prior to performing final surface roughness measurements. If defined flaws are not present, or if flaws are not defined, then interruptions in the part surface may be included in roughness measurements.

Roughness

Roughness consists of the finer irregularities of the surface texture, usually including those irregularities that result from the inherent action of the production process. The roughness component of surface texture is generally quantified by the parameter roughness average, R_a.

Roughness average is the arithmetic average of the absolute values of the measured profile height taken within the sampling length and measured from the centerline (see Fig. 14-3). Because R_a is an arithmetic average, it only provides a general description of the actual surface. A large R_a value indicates that the actual surface is rough, and a small R_a value indicates that the actual surface is smooth.

Roughness range. Surfaces produced by a given type of machining or finishing operation vary widely in their roughness. This variation is due partly to factors that the operator has control over, partly to factors beyond the operator's control, and largely to differences in shop practices of the individual plants.

CHAPTER 14

SURFACE TEXTURE

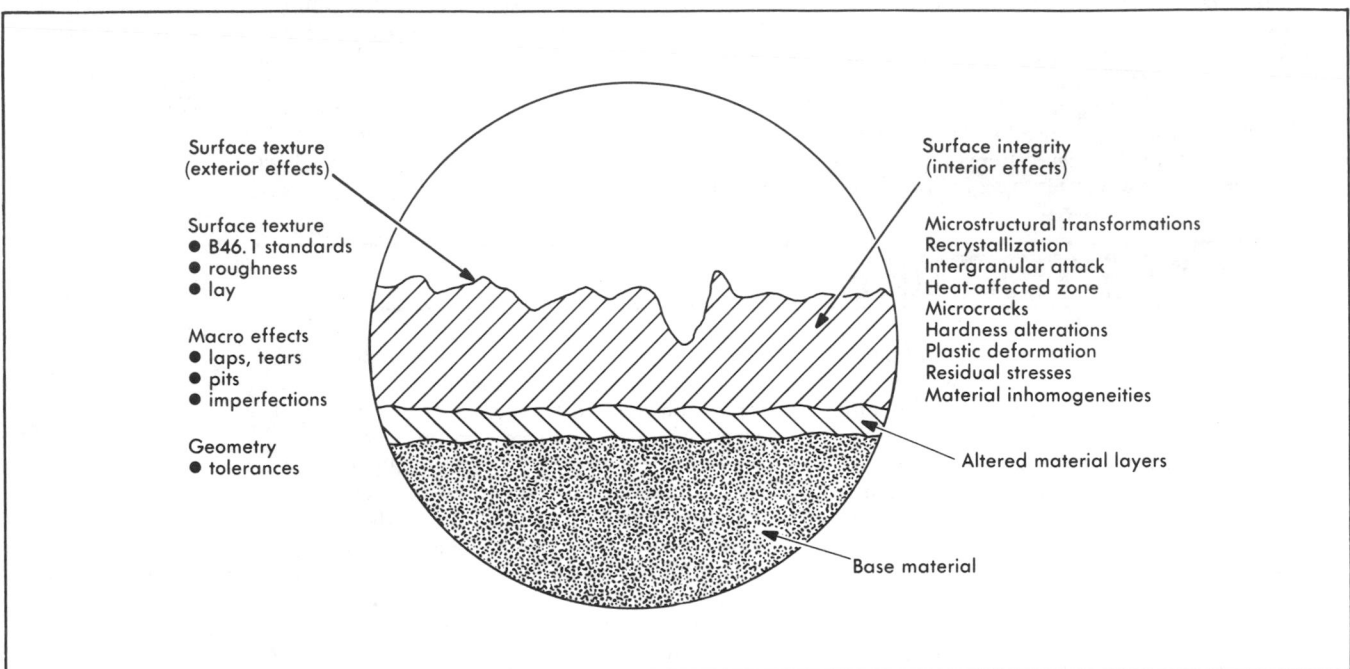

Fig. 14-1 Simulated section of the surface and surface layers of a manufactured workpiece. (*Used with permission of the Machinability Data Center*)

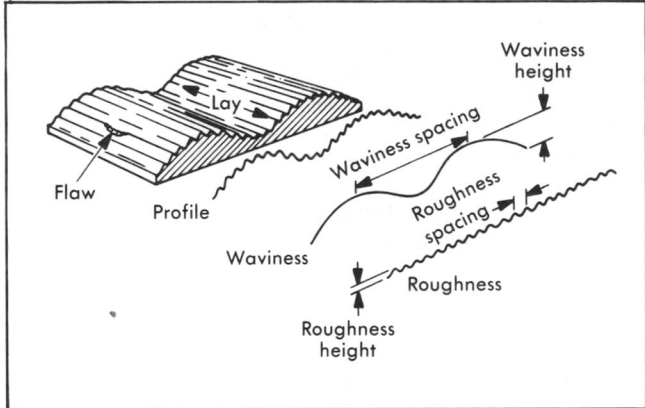

Fig. 14-2 Components of surface texture.

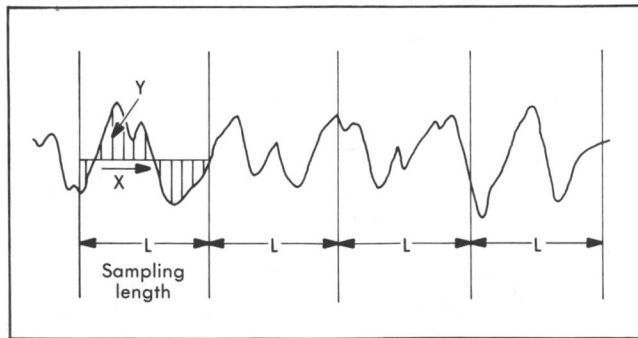

Fig. 14-3 Profile trace of roughness average measurement.

Figure 14-4 shows the typical range of the roughness average values that can be produced by common production methods. It is also evident from the figure that higher or lower values may be obtained under special conditions.

Relation of surface roughness to tolerances. Because the measurement of surface roughness involves the determination of the average deviation of the actual surface from the nominal surface, there is a direct relationship between the dimensional tolerance on a part and the permissible surface roughness. If the deviations induced by the surface roughness exceed those permitted by the dimensional tolerance, the dimension will be subject to an uncertainty beyond the tolerance.

On many surfaces, the total profile height of the surface roughness (peak-to-valley height) can vary from 4 to 10 times the measured roughness average. These values may vary somewhat with the character of the surface under consideration, but they may be used to establish approximate profile heights. Accordingly, the specified tolerance on a diameter should be at least 8 to 20 times the roughness average value. If the tolerance is less, the deviation in surface roughness could exceed the allowable tolerance.

Waviness

Waviness is the more widely spaced component of surface texture. Unless otherwise noted, waviness includes all irregularities whose spacing is greater than the roughness sampling length and less than the waviness sampling length. Waviness may result from such factors as machine or work deflections, vibration, chatter, heat treatment, or warping strains. Roughness may be considered as superimposed on a wavy surface.

Waviness is frequently confused with profile straightness.[4] Straightness is usually specified to ensure the function of a part, whereas waviness is specified to control and limit the sources of

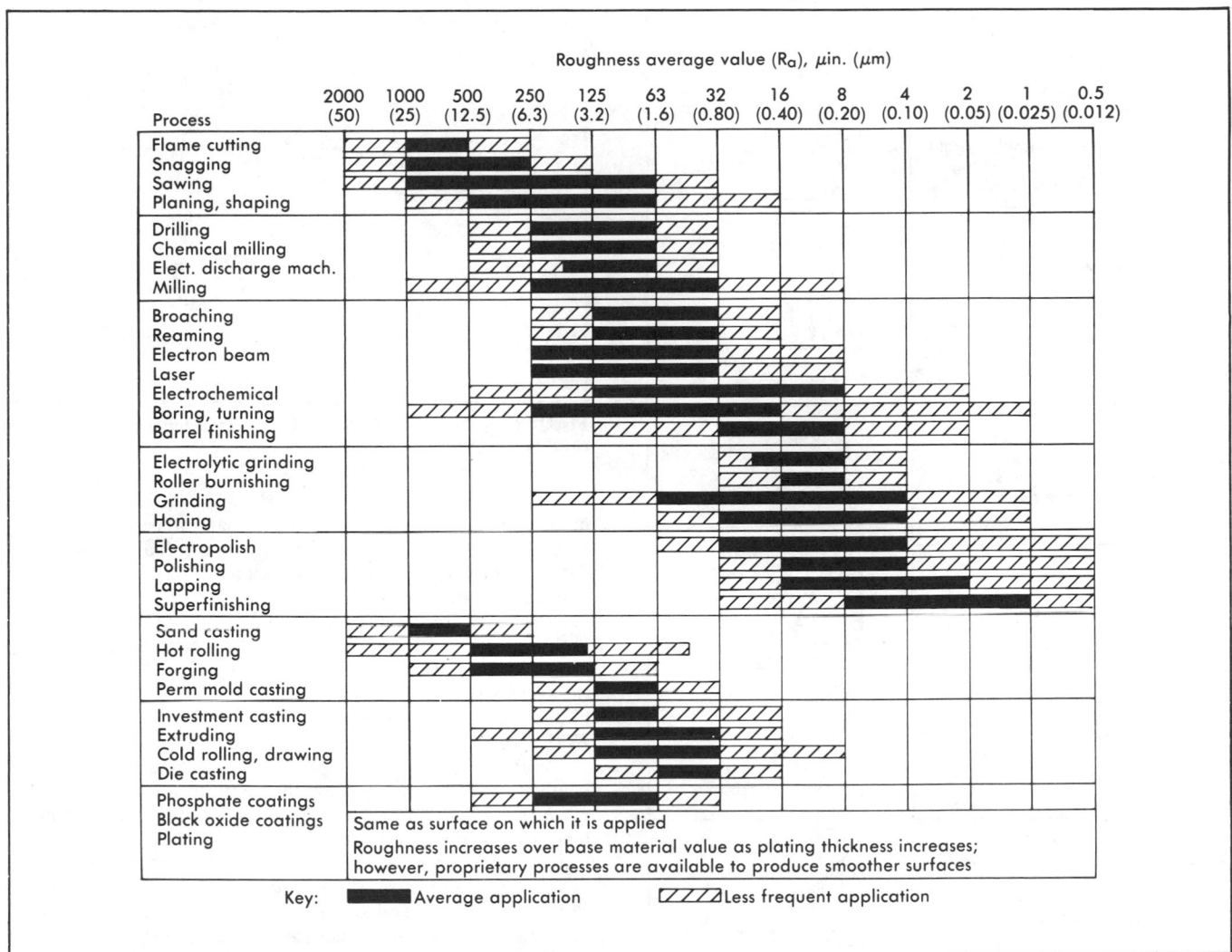

Fig. 14-4 Surface roughness produced by common production methods. (*Based on ANSI B46. 1-1978; used with permission of the American Society of Mechanical Engineers*)

vibration and imperfections of the machine tool and of the environment that might affect the accuracy of the machine tool.

Lay

Lay is the direction of the predominant pattern on the surface of the workpiece. These patterns are generally determined by the production method used. Processes such as turning, milling, grinding, and drawing produce a pattern that is regular and repetitive, providing an observable directionality to the surface texture pattern. The pattern from etching, electrical discharge machining, or rolling between grit-blasted rolls is irregular and random, resulting in no observable directionality. Commonly used lay symbols and their meanings are given in Fig. 14-5.

Surface Texture Parameters

A parameter is a method of assigning a numerical value to typify a surface. The most commonly used parameter for speci-

fying surface texture is roughness average, R_a. However, the value of this parameter does not always adequately indicate how the surface will function for its intended use.

Figure 14-6 shows the profile traces of two different surfaces having the same roughness average. Although the R_a readings are almost identical, the surfaces will function quite differently. It is therefore necessary to consider the function of the part when determining the surface texture parameters to be measured.

For example, if a part is being prepared for painting, the surface must be finished in such a way that the paint adheres in a smooth manner. On the other hand, a part surface that oils or wipes another surface requires a completely different surface texture.

Amplitude parameters. Amplitude parameters are sensitive to variations in the profile height of the surface. The parameters generally included in this grouping are roughness average, geometric roughness average, peak-to-valley height, profile height, skewness, and ten-point height.

Fig. 14-5 Lay symbols. (*Based on ANSI Y14.36-1978; used with permission of the American Society of Mechanical Engineers*)

Lay symbol	Meaning	Example showing direction of tool marks
—	Lay approximately parallel to the line representing the surface to which the symbol is applied	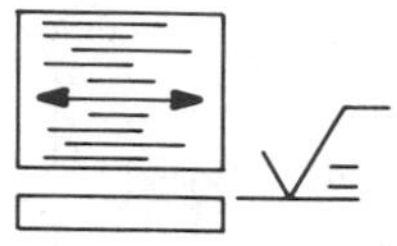
⊥	Lay approximately perpendicular to the line representing the surface to which the symbol is applied	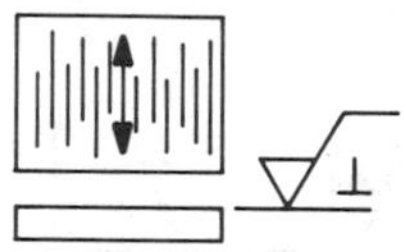
X	Lay angular in both directions to line representing the surface to which the symbol is applied	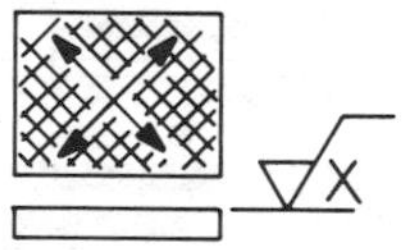
M	Lay multidirectional	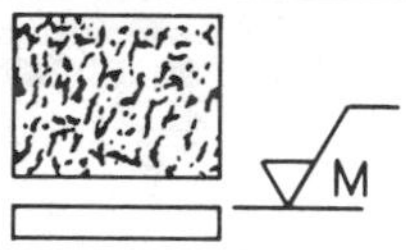
C	Lay approximately circular relative to the center of the surface to which the symbol is applied	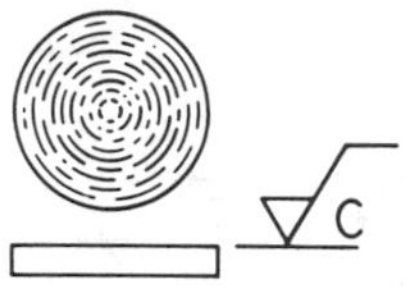
R	Lay approximately radial relative to the center of the surface to which the symbol is applied	
P	Lay particulate, nondirectional, or protuberant	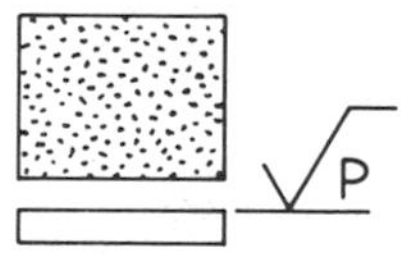

Geometric roughness average. The geometric roughness average, R_q, is an alternative to roughness average that is more sensitive to occasional highs and lows. It is defined as the root mean square (RMS) value of a profile calculated over a single sampling length. The geometric roughness average can also be expressed as the mean result of measurement over five consecutive sampling lengths.

Peak-to-valley height. The peak-to-valley height of a surface can be characterized by several different parameters. The maximum peak-to-valley height within the assessment length is represented by R_t (see Fig. 14-7, view a). The R_t measurement is valuable for analyzing finish to provide guidance for planning subsequent metal removal operations such as honing or lap-

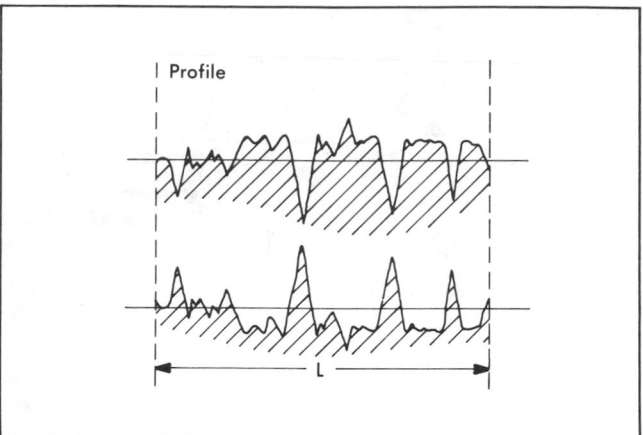

Fig. 14-6 Profile traces of two different surfaces having the same roughness average.

ping. This value indicates how much material can be removed before the part size reaches a particular limit. It also is useful in determining when continued processing of the part would produce little or no effect.

R_{max} or R_y represents the maximum peak-to-valley height within a sampling length L. Because R_{max} can be affected by a scratch or particle of dirt on the surface, it is more usual to use the average peak-to-valley height (R_{tm}) of five consecutive sampling lengths in the German DIN Standard, R_{tm} is designated R_z (DIN).

Profile height. Like the peak-to-valley height, the profile height is characterized by more than one parameter. The maximum profile height from the meanline within the sampling length is represented by R_p (see Fig. 14-7, view b). The mean value of R_p determined over five sampling lengths is R_{pm} .

Skewness. Skewness, R_{sk}, is a measure of the symmetry of the profile about the meanline (see Fig. 14-7, view c). It distinguishes between asymmetrical profiles having the same R_a or R_q values.

Skewness shows whether a porous sintered and cast surface will yield a meaningful R_a value. A positive skew indicates an abundance of peaks, and a negative skew indicates valleys. Skewness provides a criterion for judging bearing surfaces. A good bearing surface should have negative skew.

Ten-point height. The ten-point height, R_z (ISO), is the average height difference between the five highest peaks and the five lowest valleys (see Fig. 14-7, view d). It is measured over a single sampling length from a line parallel to the meanline and not crossing the profile.

The ten-point height can be combined with R_a for a more complete characterization of surface texture. Measuring R_z (ISO) is one preferred method for analyzing short surfaces.

Spacing parameters. Spacing parameters are sensitive to variations in the profile wavelength. The parameters generally included in this grouping are peak count, high spot count, and mean spacing.

Peak count. Peak count, P_c, is the number of peak-and-valley pairs per inch projecting through an arbitrarily specified band width centered about the meanline (see Fig. 14-8, view a). It is an important parameter for surfaces that are formed or are intended to accept a coating such as a polymer or paint. When used in conjunction with R_a, P_c provides essential information about the quality of surfaces prior to coating.

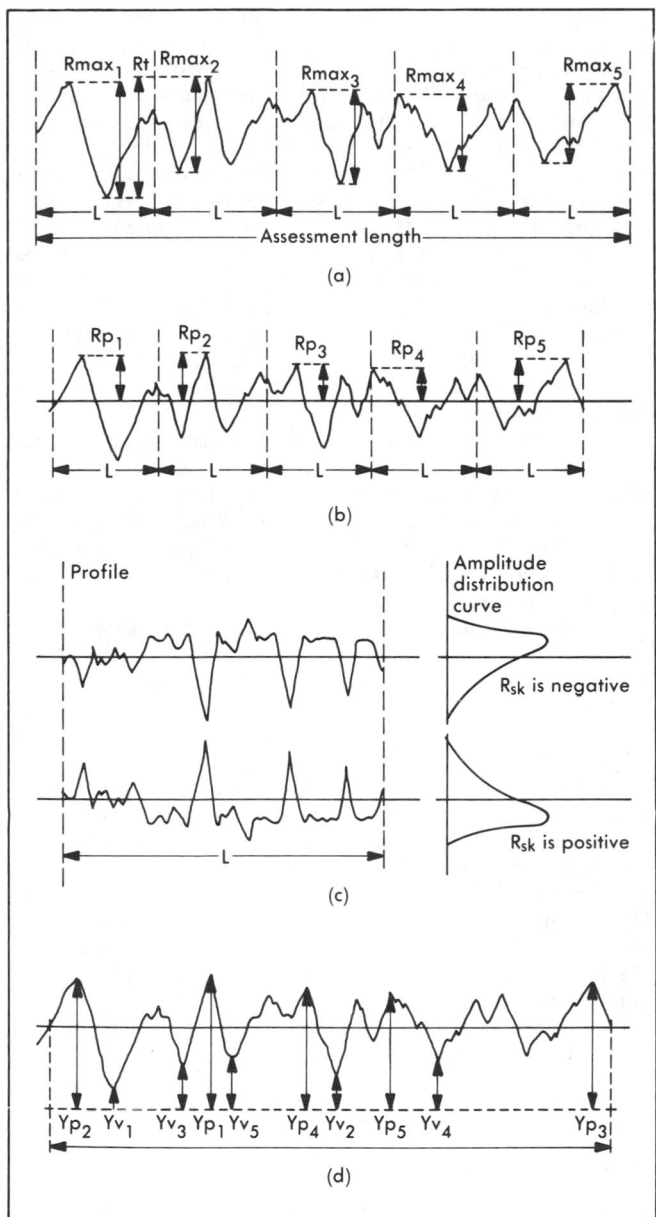

Fig. 14-7 Amplitude parameters used in the measurement of surface texture: (a) peak-to-valley height, (b) profile height, (c) skewness, and (d) ten-point height.

High spot count. The high spot count, HSC, is an alternative peak count (see Fig. 14-8, view *b*). It is the number of profile peaks projecting above the meanline or a line parallel to the meanline at a preset distance from it or from the highest peak. The count of the profile peaks projecting above the meanline is made over five cutoffs.

Mean spacing. Mean spacing, S_m, is the mean spacing between profile peaks at the meanline, assessed over one sampling length L (see Fig. 14-8, view *c*). It is a peak count parameter independent of amplitude.

Hybrid parameters. Hybrid parameters are sensitive to variations in the profile height of the surface as well as profile

wavelength. The parameters generally included in this grouping are wavelength, slope, bearing length ratio, and bearing area.

Wavelength. Average wavelength, λ_a, or RMS wavelength, λ_q, is a measure of the spacings between local peaks and valleys. This measurement takes into account the relative peak-to-valley amplitudes and individual spatial frequencies. Being a hybrid parameter, it is more useful than a parameter based solely on amplitude or spacing for some applications.

Slope. The average or RMS value of the slope of the profile throughout its length is characterized by Δ_a or Δ_q, respectively. From this value, the ratio of the actual profile length to the nominal measured length can be obtained.

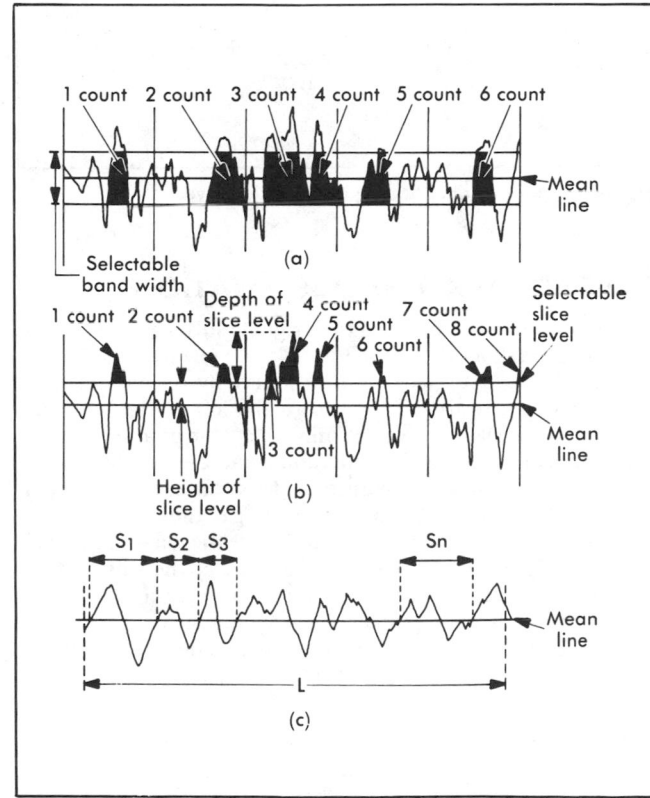

Fig. 14-8 Spacing parameters used in the measurement of surface texture: (a) peak count, (b) high spot count, and (c) mean spacing.

Bearing length ratio. Bearing length ratio, t_p, is the length of the bearing surface, expressed as a percentage of the assessment length L, at a depth p below the highest peak (see Fig. 14-9). It simulates wear at various cutting depths of surface. The bearing length ratio is useful whenever bearing surfaces must be analyzed and qualified for lubrication and wear properties.

The bearing length ratio is also known as the bearing area. In microprocessor-based instruments, the bearing area can be expressed quantitatively as the percent relationship of material surface area to the evaluation length of specific cutting depths. It can also be expressed graphically using the "Abbott Firestone bearing curve." The slope of the Abbott Firestone bearing curve is helpful in analyzing how fast a surface will wear and the dimensional size change after wear-in. A typical bearing area curve is shown in Fig. 14-9.

CHAPTER 14

SURFACE TEXTURE

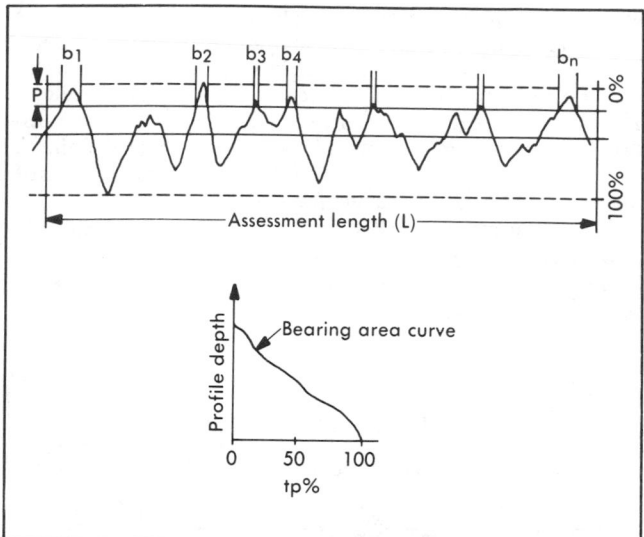

Fig. 14-9 Profile trace of bearing length ratio curve.

SURFACE TEXTURE DESIGNATION

The standard symbol used to designate surface roughness is the check mark as shown in Fig. 14-10, view *a*. This symbol indicates that the surface may be produced by any method. The roughness specification is placed to the left of the long leg. Specifications may be given as only one value or as a range. If two values are specified, the maximum value is usually critical for the function or performance of the surface; the minimum value would prevent costly overmachining of the surface. When only one value is given, the value indicates the maximum value that is acceptable for roughness. Implied in the single value specification is the understanding that a value less than the maximum is also acceptable. The roughness specification is given in either microinches or micrometers depending on the units used for the drawing.

On occasion, the surface texture symbol is modified to indicate whether material removal is required or prohibited and if other surface characteristics must be controlled. When the surface must be produced by machining, the symbol shown in Fig. 14-10, view *b*, is used. The horizontal bar indicates that machining is required and that material must be provided for that purpose. The number to the left of the symbol indicates the amount of stock to be removed (see Fig. 14-10, view *c*). Tolerances may be added to the basic value or given in a note.

The circle in the vee indicates that the surface must be produced by forming processes such as casting, forging, hot finishing, cold finishing, die casting, powder metallurgy, or injection molding without subsequent removal of material (see Fig. 14-10, view *d*). When surface texture characteristics other than roughness are specified, the symbol is drawn with a horizontal extension as shown in Fig. 14-10, view *e*.

For parts requiring extensive and uniform roughness control, a general note may be added to the drawing (see Fig. 14-11). The surface texture value in the note applies to each surface texture symbol specified without values. When surface roughness control of several operations is required within a given area or on a given surface, surface qualities may be designated as shown in Fig. 14-12.

As was previously mentioned, the surface texture symbol is also used to specify waviness and lay. Waviness specifications are indicated above the horizontal extension of the surface texture symbol. The first value given is the maximum waviness height rating, and the second value is the maximum waviness spacing. These values are given either in inches or millimeters. A measured value less than the specified maximum is acceptable. The lay symbol is placed to the right of the surface texture symbol. Refer to Fig. 14-5 for commonly used lay symbols and their meanings.

Figure 14-13 illustrates examples of roughness, waviness, and lay designation by inserting values in appropriate positions relative to the symbol. If the symbol of Fig. 14-14 was applied to the surface of a given part, its surface quality would have to conform to the following specification:

Roughness average, as measured across the lay by an electronic instrument set for a roughness-width cutoff of 0.030",

	Symbol	Meaning
(a)		Basic surface texture symbol. Surface may be produced by any method except when the bar or circle (view b or d), is specified
(b)		Material removal by machining is required. The horizontal bar indicates that material removal by machining is required to produce the surface and that material must be provided for that purpose
(c)	3.5	Material removal allowance. The number indicates the amount of stock to be removed by machining in inches or millimeters. Tolerances may be added to the basic value shown or in a general note
(d)		Material removal prohibited. The circle in the vee indicates that the surface must be produced by processes such as casting, forging, hot finishing, cold finishing, die casting, powder metallurgy, or injection molding without subsequent removal of material
(e)		Surface texture symbol. To be used when any surface characteristics are specified above the horizontal line or to the right of the symbol. Surface may be produced by any method except when the bar or circle (view b and d), is specified

Fig. 14-10 Surface texture symbols. (*Based on ANSI Y14.36-1978; used with permission of the American Society of Mechanical Engineers*)

may be either 63 or 32 μin. deviation from the meanline or any value between 63 and 32. The roughness-width rating must not be greater than 0.015″. The waviness height, measured peak-to-valley, should not exceed 0.002″. The waviness width between adjacent waves (peak-to-peak or valley-to-valley) should not exceed 2.000″.

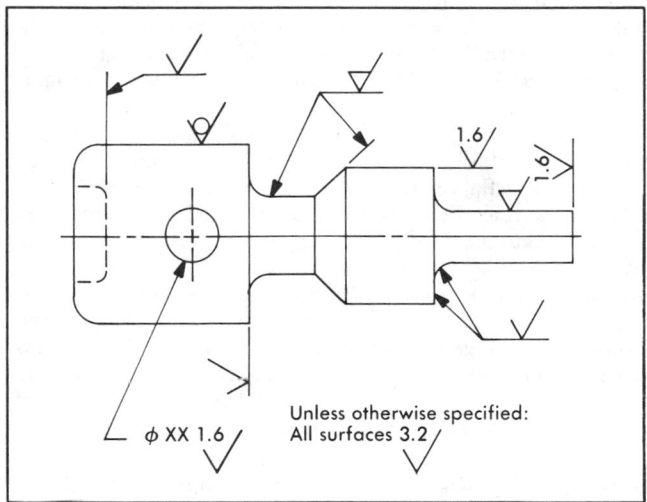

Fig. 14-11 Application of surface texture symbols. (*Based on ANSI Y14.36-1978; used with permission of the American Society of Mechanical Engineers*)

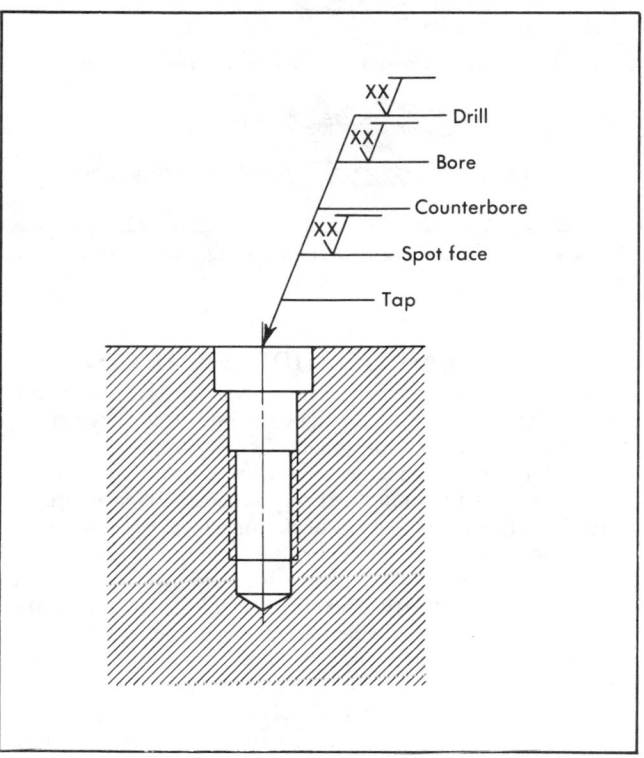

Fig. 14-12 Method of indicating surface texture symbols for several related operations within a given area.

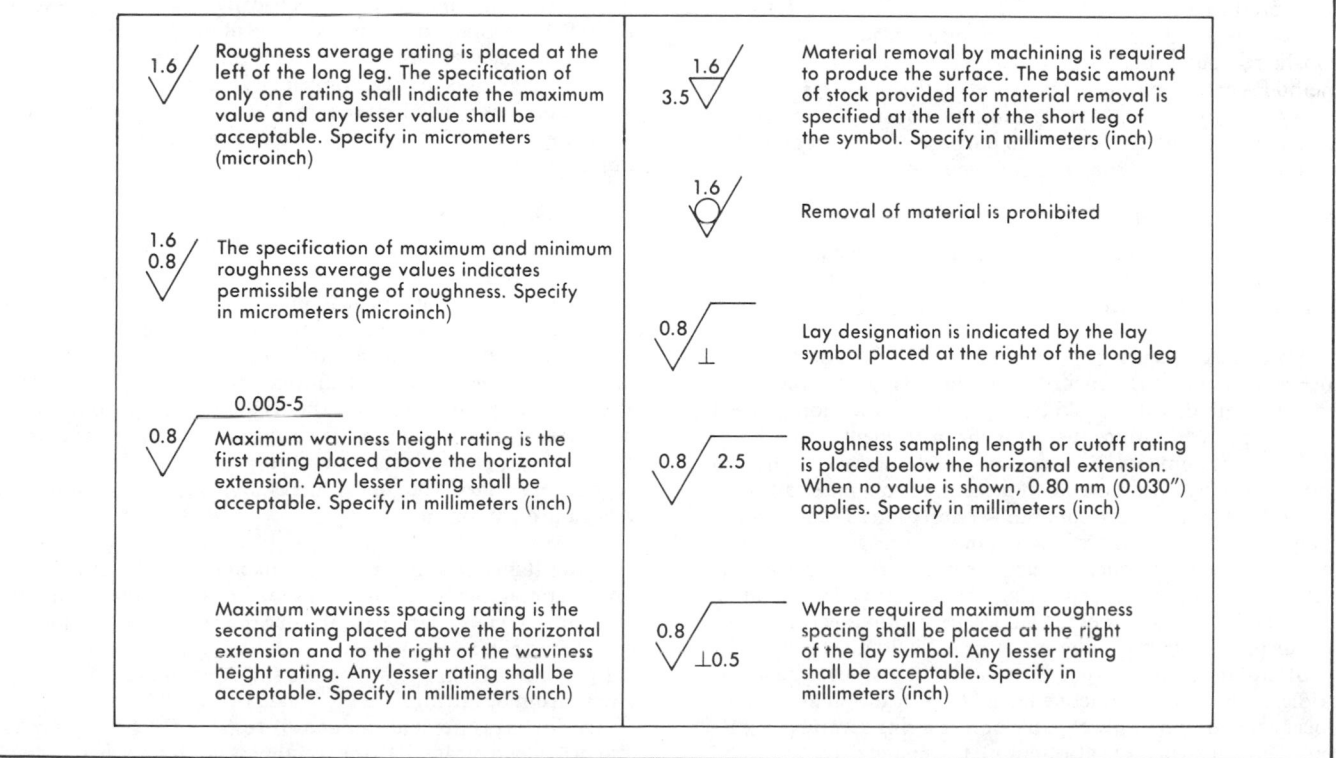

Fig. 14-13 Application of surface texture values to symbols. (*Based on ANSI Y14.36; used with permission of the American Society of Mechanical Engineers*)

SURFACE TEXTURE

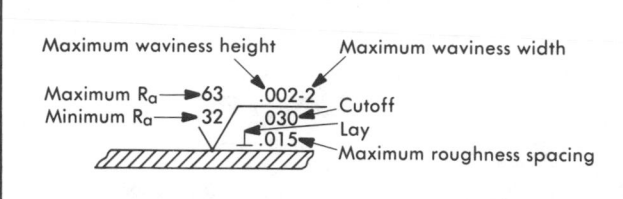

Fig. 14-14 Placement of various surface texture components on the symbol.

MEASUREMENT OF SURFACE TEXTURE

Surfaces and their measurement provide a vital link between the manufacturing of engineering components and their suitability for an intended performance. The measurement of surface texture is not purely a means of quality control, but forms an essential part of the manufacturing process. When it is used correctly, it facilitates control of performance, process, material, and machine.

Three methods of surface texture measurement are currently used throughout industry. The most widely used method is the profile method. In the profile method, the topographic information is derived from a point-by-point scan of surface height as a function of a distance along a straight line on the surface. The resulting profile must be analyzed by either analog or digital methods to derive parameters. The second method is referred to as the area method. Area methods directly produce a measurable parameter that represents some property of the surface topography averaged over the illuminated area. The third method compares sample parts to the other parts produced.

No general method of surface texture measurement may be considered superior to all others. The choice as to which method is employed should be based on the characteristics and parameters to be measured. In addition, considerations should be made regarding the functional purpose of the part as well as technical feasibility of the measurements.

Profile Methods

The profile method of surface texture measurement defines a single line that represents the entire surface. The two types of instruments widely used for this method are stylus and optical.

Stylus instruments. Stylus instrumentation for surface texture measurement is generally classified based on whether it operates with or without skids. Another classification is based on the type of transducer used for the instrument.

Stylus instruments that use skids are the simpler of the two and are usually only capable of measuring roughness average. For this reason, they are commonly referred to as roughness or roughness average meters. Roughness average meters may incorporate either a piezoelectric or inductive linear variable differential transducer, depending on the instrument manufacturer. The roughness average values are continuously updated and displayed on an analog meter or a digital display.

Stylus instruments that do not use skids, referred to as skidless, always use inductive linear variable differential transducers and are generally capable of measuring several parameters. These instruments also require traversing drive units and an accurate datum reference to permit the measurement of waviness and surface profile.

The main components of a typical stylus instrument are the stylus, transducer, skids and shoes, traversing drive, and the amplifier.[5] When setting up a stylus-type instrument for use, it is necessary to adjust the traversing length and cutoff. It is also necessary to periodically check the calibration of the instrument and the condition of the stylus.

Optical instruments. The optical instruments used commonly in profiling methods of surface texture measurement are based on interferometry. Interferometry is an important technique for determining the roughness and figure of high-quality optical surfaces. The schematic of a two-beam interferometer is shown in Fig. 14-15.

A collimated optical wavefront is split into two coherent beams by a partially transmitting mirror. One beam is reflected from a smooth flat reference surface, while the other is reflected from the surface being tested; the reflected beams are then recombined at the mirror. An image of the surface is produced by the lens at 0. Under conditions of perfect alignment, a circular pattern of parallel light and dark fringes is observed.

When the reflected beams are not aligned properly, variations in the fringe patterns occur. Waviness and roughness features can be determined by counting the number of fringes and measuring any deflections within a fringe. The accuracy of this technique depends on the type of light source used.

Another type of optical profiling instrument is based on the Mirau interferometer (see Fig. 14-16). In this design, a beam splitter and reference surface are placed close to the surface to be scanned. Instead of moving either the workpiece or the instrument to develop the surface profile, the surface image is detected by a linear photodiode detector array. The phase information on each element of the array is developed by vibrating the reference mirror piezoelectrically and then processing the reference modulated signals in the photodiode elements.

The accuracy of the output surface profiles does not depend on the straightness of travel or velocity stability of any moving stage, but does depend on the quality of the reference mirror. Scanning length is limited by the magnifications of the available objective lenses.

Area Methods

The term *area methods* is used to denote those techniques that measure a representative area of a surface and produce quantitative results that depend on area averaged properties of the surface texture. Some of the more common techniques used include capacitance, optical, and pneumatic. When carefully used in conjunction with calibrated roughness comparison specimens or pilot specimens, these techniques may be used as comparators to distinguish the surface texture of parts manufactured by a similar process and to produce useful results in repetitive surface roughness measurements of components from a production run.

Capacitance techniques. The capacitance technique uses a probe containing a sensor of predetermined area (typically circular or rectangular) to establish capacitance with an identical area on a surface. An insulator covers the sensor to electrically isolate it from the workpiece surface and prevent a short circuit from occurring (see Fig. 14-17).

During measurement, the sensor rests on the surface peaks and provides a measure of the roughness voids between the two surfaces. The sensor's shape is designed to conform with the surface being measured. For example, a concave or convex

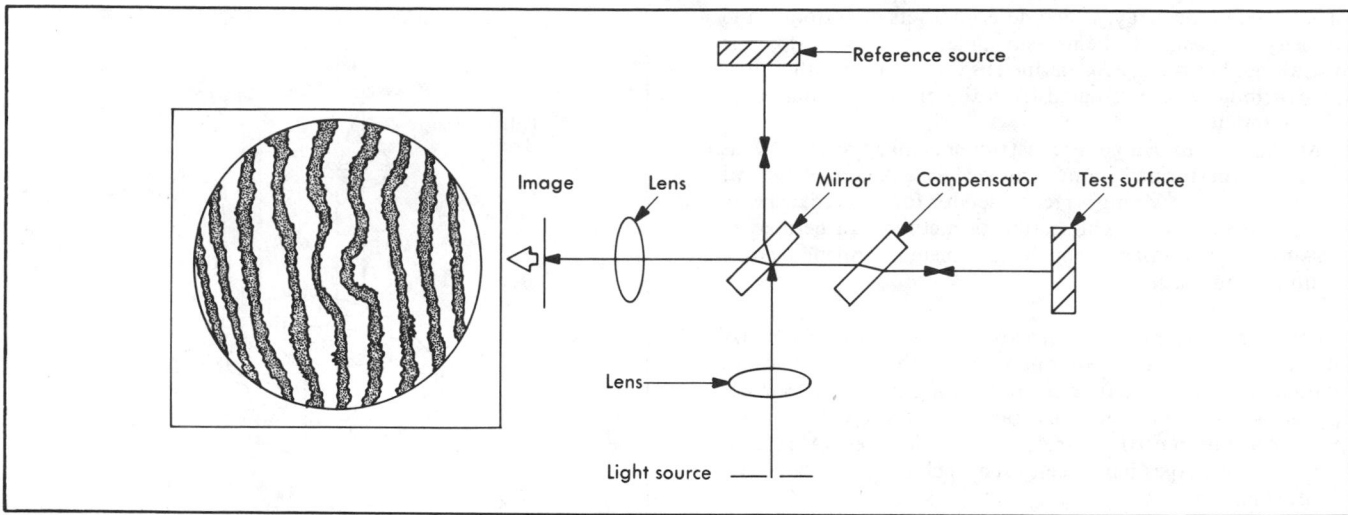

Fig. 14-15 Schematic of a two-beam interferometer.

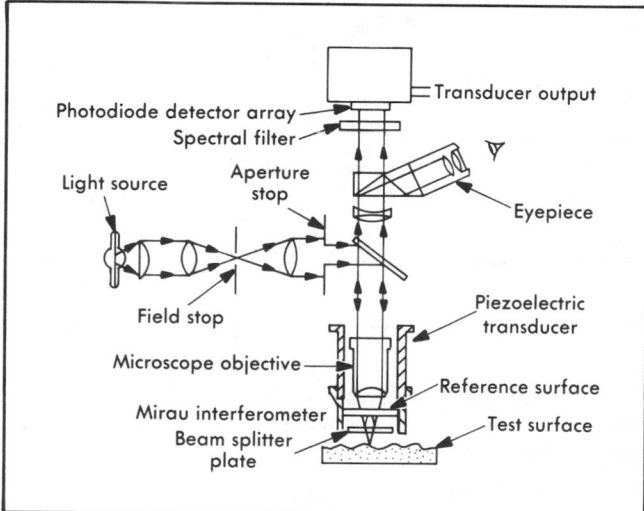

Fig. 14-16 Schematic diagram of optical profiling instrument developed by Wyant, et al.[6, 7]

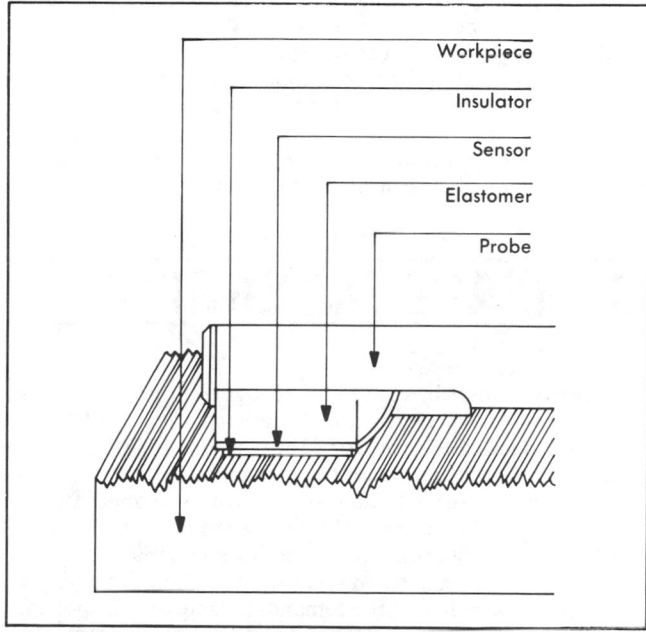

Fig. 14-17 Capacitance is established by placing a probe against the workpiece surface. (*Extrude Hone Corp.*)

sensor would be used to measure circular surfaces. When the probe is pressed against the workpiece, capacitance is established, and a signal is transmitted to the system's electronic circuitry. A readout device displays a roughness average of the area that can be compared to R_a values obtained by stylus instruments.

Capacitance instruments are relatively insensitive to surface lay because an area is measured. Because of this, these instruments can be used for measuring workpieces produced by electrical discharge machining and casting. Generally, these instruments are calibrated to the type of surface texture being measured. The surface to be assessed and the sensor should be clean before measuring. Because insulated and nonconductive surfaces cannot establish capacitance, this technique is limited to conductive or semiconductive workpieces.

Optical techniques. According to the laws of physical optics, the radiation from a collimated beam of laser light reflected by a

rough surface is scattered into an angular distribution. The resulting specular intensity, angular scattering pattern, speckle pattern, and polarization state depend on the roughness heights, the spatial wavelengths, and the wavelength of light. Because of this, a class of techniques has been developed to monitor the roughness condition of the surface optically. This class of techniques does not include the optical profiling techniques discussed previously.

The light-scattering method makes use of the scattering property of rough surfaces to determine a characteristic quantity for roughness. In practice, the surface to be tested is illuminated by an infrared light. Some of the radiation is scattered

SURFACE TEXTURE

back to the diode array, which determines its distribution and intensity, by means of the measuring lens (see Fig. 14-18). The optical roughness value S_N, defined as the variance of the intensity distribution, is calculated from the measured values by a microcomputer.

Measurements using these instruments take less than 50 ms and can be performed on moving surfaces. A compressed air cleaning or simple wiping is recommended for parts coated with a thick oil film. The light-scattering method can be used to measure roughness of parts made from metals, semiconductors, ceramics, and plastics.

Pneumatic techniques. When an air jet is held in close proximity and perpendicular to a rough surface, the resultant flow of air out of the orifice is a function of the roughness of the surface against which it impinges. Instruments based on this phenomenon have been used to assess surface roughness. Many different orifice shapes have been used, including circular, oval, square, and long slit.

Comparison Methods

When the roughness average, R_a, requirements exceed 63 μin. (1.6 μm), most companies use a visual check rather than a measurement of the roughness profile.[8] Often the visual check is aided through the use of sample parts (pilot specimens) that have proper surface finish and are known to perform satisfactorily. These parts are set aside from production and referred to by machine operators so the finishes may be duplicated. To ensure reasonable accuracy, pilot specimens should be rated by properly calibrated measuring instruments.

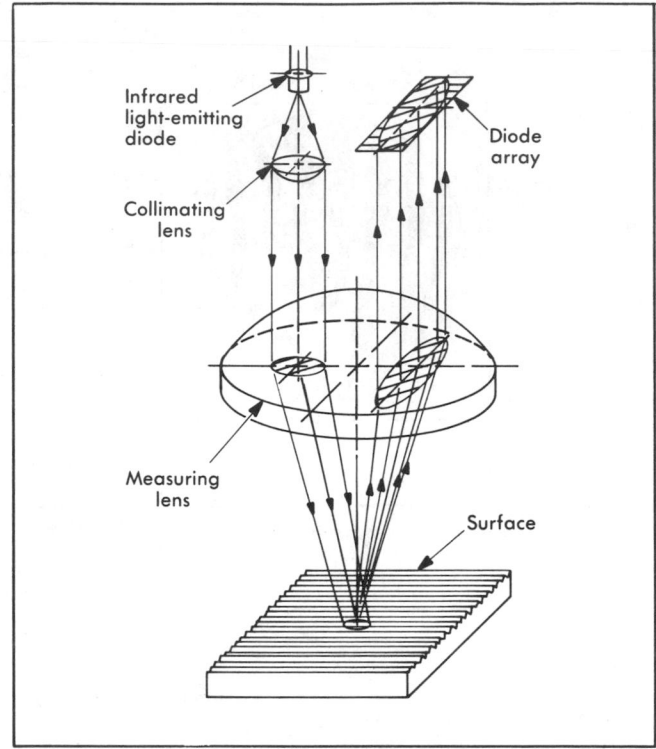

Fig. 14-18 Schematic of scattered-light sensor used in light-scattering method. (*Rodenstock Precision Optics, Inc.*)

SURFACE INTEGRITY

In components subject to contact fatigue, surface integrity is critically related to performance. Surface integrity is a relatively new term covering the nature of the surface condition that is developed in hardware by controlled manufacturing processes. It is achieved by the selection and control of manufacturing processes according to the evaluation of the process effects on specific engineering properties of the work materials.

The quality of a machined surface is becoming increasingly more critical for satisfying the demands for superior component performance, longevity, and reliability. Structures for commercial and military aerospace, automotive, and capital goods industries are being subjected to more severe conditions of stress, temperature, and hostile environments. In addition, section size is being reduced in response to the goal of reduced weight. Thus the surface condition of a component has an ever-increasing influence on its performance.

SURFACE ALTERATIONS

Surface integrity is concerned primarily with the host of effects a manufacturing process produces below the visible surface of a component. The subsurface characteristics occur in various layers or zones.[9] The altered material zones (AMZ) can be as simple as a stress condition different from that in the bulk of the material or as complex as a microstructure change interlaced with intergranular attack. Changes can be caused by chemical, thermal, electrical, or mechanical energy and may

affect both the physical and the mechanical properties of the material. The principal causes of alterations to a surface during material removal operations are as follows:

- High temperatures and high-temperature gradients.
- Chemical reactions or absorption on recently machined surfaces.
- Excessive electrical currents.
- Excessive energy densities during processing.
- Mechanical deformation by cutting tool edge.

The subsurface material zones can be grouped by the principal energy modes that produce them (see Table 14-1).

Machining Processes

In machining processes such as milling or drilling, the gentle operations are those employing machining conditions that provide long tool life and use a sharp tool (the tool is removed before it gets too dull). Abusive machining operations are those in which a tool is used even after it has become dull. It is also promoted by employing improper tools, speeds, feeds, and cutting fluids. In general, abusive machining conditions tend to promote higher temperature and/or excessive plastic deformation.

Many of the adverse effects of abusive machining are readily evaluated by examination of the surface layer microstructure.

TABLE 14-1
Altered Material Zones by Principal Energy Mode[10]

MECHANICAL:
- Plastic deformations (as result of hot or cold working)
- Tears and laps and crevice-like defects (associated with "built-up edge" produced in machining)
- Hardness alterations
- Cracks (macroscopic and microscopic)
- Residual stress distribution in surface layer
- Processing inclusions introduced
- Plastically deformed debris as a result of grinding
- Voids, pits, burrs, or foreign material inclusions in surface

METALLURGICAL:
- Transformation of phases
- Grain size and distribution
- Precipitate size and distribution
- Foreign inclusions in material
- Twinning
- Recrystallization
- Untempered martensite (UTM) or overtempered martensite (OTM)
- Resolutioning or austenite reversion

CHEMICAL:
- Intergranular attack (IGA)
- Intergranular corrosion (IGC)
- Intergranular oxidation (IGO)
- Preferential dissolution of microconstituents
- Contamination
- Embrittlement—by chemical absorption of elements such as hydrogen, chlorine, etc.
- Pits or selective etch
- Corrosion
- Stress corrosion

THERMAL:
- Heat-affected zone (HAZ)
- Recast or redeposited material
- Resolidified material
- Splattered particles or remelted metal deposited on surface

ELECTRICAL:
- Conductivity change
- Magnetic change
- Resistive heating or overheating

Because the microstructural alterations are usually quite shallow, in many cases less than 0.001" (0.02 mm), it is necessary to employ special procedures for sectioning and mounting specimens. These special procedures maintain edge retention of the critical surface that is to be examined.[11]

Figure 14-19 is a typical data sheet illustrating the metallurgical and microhardness changes that occur in drilling 4340 steel, quenched and tempered to R_C52. The gently drilled hole has essentially the same structure at the surface as in the base metal (view a). The abusively drilled hole has an untempered martensitic layer, R_C61, about 0.001" (0.025 mm) deep (view b). An overtempered martensitic layer with a hardness as low as R_C43 is found below the untempered martensite (UTM). The total altered layer is 0.010" (0.25 mm) deep. Microhardness traverses are shown for both gentle and abusive drilling conditions in view c.

The surface alterations and microhardness changes that occur when milling are similar to those previously described for drilling. Abusive milling of 4340 steel often produces streaks of untempered martensite (see Fig. 14-20). These streaks are produced by a dull tooth. The interval of the patches of untempered martensite correspond to the feed per tooth.

Abusive drilling, milling, or grinding of aged R_C52 18% nickel maraging steel tends to produce a soft (R_C30) layer on the surface. This soft layer is caused by resolution of the aged maraging steel due to the high temperature produced by machining (see Fig. 14-21). This phenomenon has been given the name austenite reversion.

When drilling is permitted to continue with an especially dull drill, microcracking has been found sometimes to accompany the formation of UTM (see Fig. 14-22). Drilling of steels as well as other alloys with a high-speed steel drill that "burns out" during the drilling operation can actually result in a portion of the drill bit becoming friction welded to the bottom of the hole (see Fig. 14-23). The hardness of the friction-welded layer is almost R_C70.

SURFACE INTEGRITY

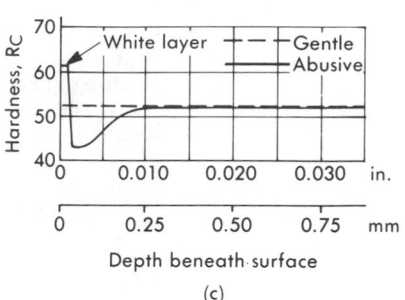

(a)   (b)   (c)

Fig. 14-19 Surface characteristics of AISI 4340 (quenched and tempered, R_C52) produced by drilling; magnification is 250X: (a) gentle conditions, no noticeable microstructural surface alterations; (b) abusive conditions, rehardened primary martensite layer R_C61 approaching 0.001″ (0.025 mm) deep and subsurface overtempered zone having hardness as low as R_C43. Total depth of effect is 0.010″ (0.25 mm); and (c) microhardness traverse for both gentle and abusive drilling conditions.[12]

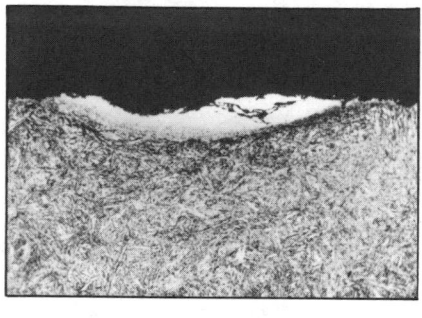

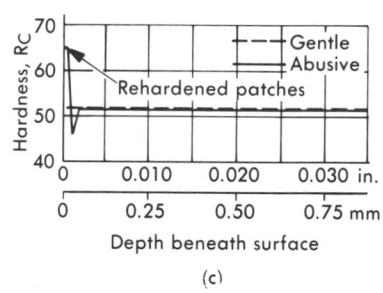

(a)   (b)   (c)

Fig. 14-20 Surface characteristics of AISI 4340 (quenched and tempered, R_C52) produced by face milling: (a) photomicrographs of abusive conditions magnified 250X showing white rehardened patches of martensite; (b) photomicrographs of abusive conditions magnified 500X; and (c) microhardness traverse for both gentle and abusive conditions. Thin zones of overtempered martensite 0.001″ (0.025 mm) deep, with hardness as low as R_C46 are found beneath each patch.[13]

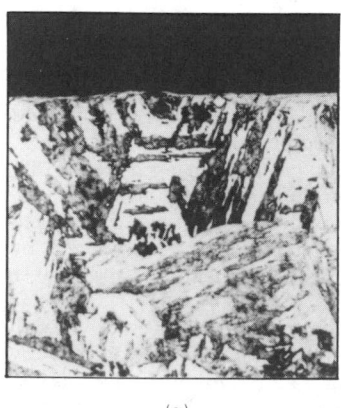

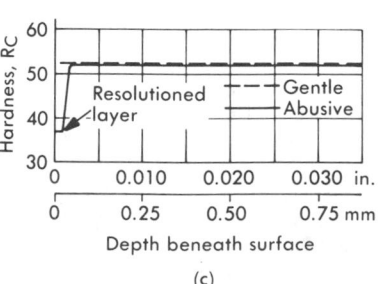

(a)   (b)   (c)

Fig. 14-21 Surface characteristics of 18% nickel maraging steel (grade 250, aged R_C52) produced by drilling: (a) gentle conditions—thin trace of cold work can be seen on surface with magnification at 250X; (b) abusive conditions—an averaged or resolutioned layer 0.001″ (0.025 mm) deep at R_C37 is found on the surface with magnification at 250X, total affected depth is approximately 0.002″ (0.05 mm); and (c) microhardness traverse for gentle and abusive drilling conditions.[14]

SURFACE INTEGRITY

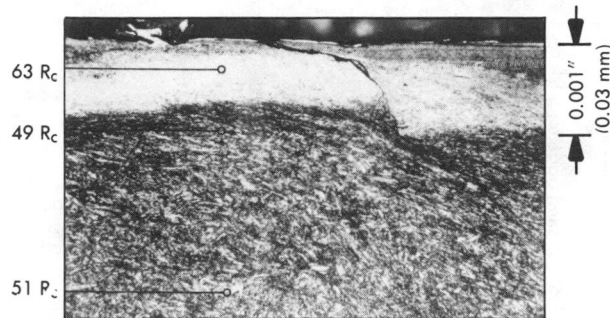

Fig. 14-22 Cross section of hole, perpendicular to hole axis, drilled with a dull drill in 4340 steel hardened to R$_C$48.[15]

63 R$_c$
49 R$_c$
51 P$_c$

0.001″ (0.03 mm)

Fig. 14-23 Cross section of a hole in 410 stainless steel drilled with a dull drill; wearland was 0.060″ (1.52 mm). The drill broke down at the corner during test, and friction welded a portion of the high-speed steel drill bit to the workpiece. The base metal exhibits a hardened and subsequent overtempered zone as a result of the high localized heating. Magnification is approximately 10X.[16]

Grinding Processes

In surface grinding, gentle conditions are those that keep the grinding wheel sharp, while abusive conditions are those that promote wheel dulling. The important operating parameters that influence whether a grinding operation is gentle or abusive include grain size, wheel grade, wheel speed, depth of cut, grinding fluid, and the wheel dressing procedure. Figure 14-24 shows surfaces produced by gentle, conventional, and abusive grinding of 4340 steel hardened to R$_C$50. Gentle grinding produced no visible surface alterations, whereas conventional grinding showed evidence of spotty surface rehardening and underlying overtempering or softening. Abusive grinding produced a rehardened surface layer averaging 0.001″ (0.025 mm) deep and an underlying overtempered zone approximately 0.004″ (0.01 mm) deep.

Nontraditional Machining Processes

Electrical discharge machining (EDM) tends to produce a surface that contains a layer of recast splattered metal. This recast layer is hard, frequently porous, and, in many cases, contains cracks. Below the splattered and recast metal it is possible to have the same surface alterations and microstructure that occur in abusive machining. The effects are more pronounced when using roughing EDM conditions such as high power input.

Residual Stress and Distortion

Conventional machining processes develop a residual stress in the surface layer. This residual stress has been found to be a major cause of workpiece distortion.

In grinding, the residual stress tends to be tensile when abusive conditions are used. Figure 14-25 shows that the stress may be zero or even compressive at the surface, but becomes tensile below the surface. By using gentle grinding conditions, the stress can be reduced in magnitude and can even become compressive. The greater the area under the residual stress curve, the greater the distortion of the workpiece (see Figs. 14-25 and 14-26).

In milling, the residual stress tends to be compressive. For example, when face milling 4340 steel hardened to R$_C$52, the stresses are tensile at the surface, but go into compression below the surface.

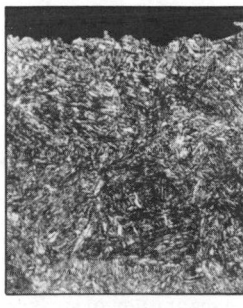
(a)

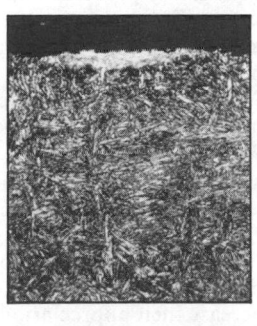
(b)

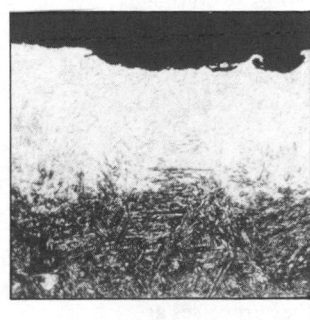
(c)

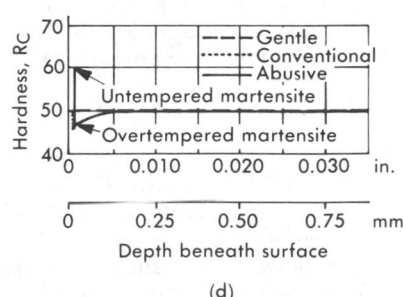
(d)

Fig. 14-24 Surface characteristics of AISI 4340 (quenced and tempered, R$_C$50) produced by grinding: (a) gentle conditions, surface texture is R$_a$40; (b) conventional conditions, surface texture is R$_a$40; (c) abusive conditions, surface texture is R$_a$50: and (d) microhardness traverse for gentle, conventional, and abusive grinding conditions.[17]

SURFACE INTEGRITY

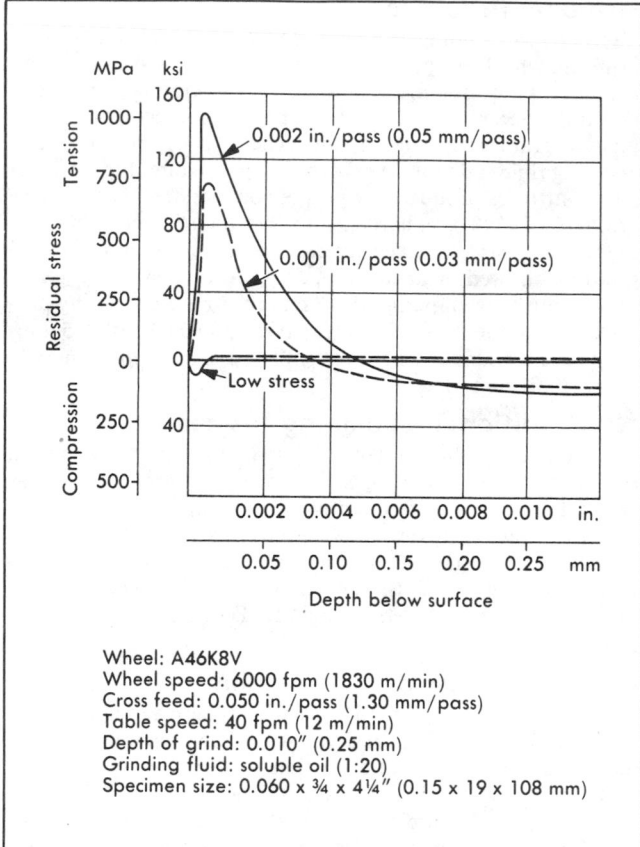

Fig. 14-25 Residual stress in surface-ground D6AC steel, R_C56, and effect of downfeed.[18]

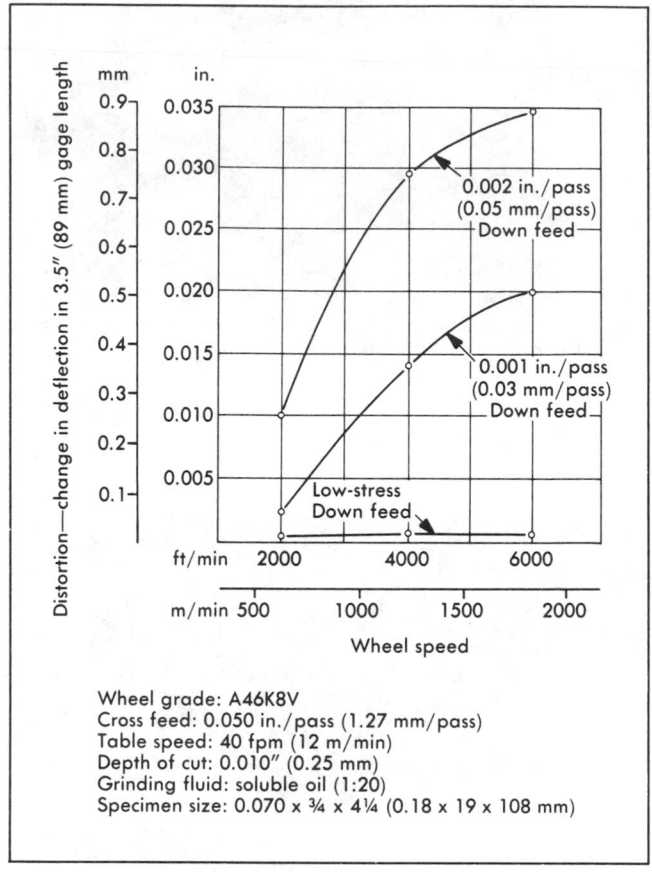

Fig. 14-26 Change in deflection versus wheel speed when surface grinding D6AC steel, R_C56, and the effect of downfeed.[19]

Mechanical Properties

The characteristics of the surface alterations produced in machining are known to affect fatigue and stress-corrosion properties of many materials. From investigations on high-strength steels, it has been found that abusive grinding of 4340 steel at R_C50 can reduce the endurance limit by 35% with respect to low-stress gentle grinding. During abusive grinding, there is a tendency to form patches or streaks of untempered martensite or overtempered martensite on the surface. When either of these two microconstituents are present, the fatigue strength drops significantly. For example, it has been found that the presence of a depth of untempered martensite from 0.0005 to 0.0035" (0.013 to 0.089 mm) produces a drop in endurance limit from 110 ksi (758 MPa) to 70 or 75 ksi (482 or 517 MPa).

PROCESS GUIDELINES

Currently, most of the surface integrity investigations and data collections have involved material removal processes. This does not indicate that forming, coating, or other processes are exempt from surface integrity considerations, only that insufficient data are available for these processes.

Some general guidelines for all material removal processes are as follows:

1. Thorough component or product testing is one of the best assurances/checks of surface integrity. The tests should be run with surfaces produced by the complete and exact sequence of production operations.
2. Surface integrity requirements should only apply to the critical or highly stressed zones of the component part. The requirements should not be applied "all over."
3. Highly stressed areas of critical components should be evaluated carefully to assess the impact of the full sequence of processes that generate the "as shipped" surface. The control of the sequence of processes is as important to surface integrity as is the selection and maintenance of operating parameters.
4. Control of the metallurgical state of the material is as important as control of the process parameters.
5. Material inhomogeneities or anomalies (sometimes even those within specification limits) can have component integrity effects as serious as the surface integrity effects from manufacturing processes.
6. Designers, shop supervisors, and quality control and process engineers must be educated and trained to increase their appreciation of the magnitude of surface integrity effects from manufacturing processes.
7. The surface integrity from processes other than material removal or machining processes should also be evaluated.

8. The surface integrity effects from conventional machining are of the same magnitude as those from nontraditional machining.
9. Metallographic sections at high magnification taken parallel and perpendicular to the lay pattern provide an effective early alert to potential surface integrity problems.
10. Postprocessing treatments such as heat treatment, shot peening, roller burnishing, and low-stress grinding may offset some, but not necessarily all, of the otherwise detrimental surface integrity effects.
11. Hand-controlled operations have a tendency to produce variability in surface effects and should be considered suspect.
12. Low process energy intensities and low material removal rates are characteristic of most, but not all, material removal processes that provide acceptable surface integrity.
13. Rigid, high-quality machine tools and fixtures are desirable.
14. Cutting fluids should be fresh or well controlled and carefully, completely, and quickly removed from the workpiece when the operation is complete.
15. Deburring of all machined edges is desirable.
16. Parts stored for extended periods should be covered with a protective coating to prevent corrosion.

References

1. *Machining Data Handbook*, vol. 2, 3rd ed. (Cincinnati: Metcut Research Associates Inc., Machinability Data Center, 1980), p. 18-3.
2. W. P. Koster and J. F. Kahles, "Surface Finish—Not a Definitive Measure of Part Quality," *Machining Briefs*, No. 2, 1985.
3. *Machining Data Handbook*, *op. cit.*, p. 18-6.
4. Alex N. Tabenkin, "The Growing Importance of Surface-Finish Specs," *Machine Design* (September 20, 1984), pp. 99-102.
5. *1983 SAE Handbook*, vol. 1 (Warrendale, PA: Society of Automotive Engineers, 1983), p. 6.12.
6. J. C. Wyant, et al., "An Optical Profilometer for Surface Characterization of Magnetic Media," *ASLE Trans 27* (Park Ridge, IL: American Society of Lubrication Engineers, 1984), pp. 101-113.
7. B. Bhushan, J. C. Wyant, and C. L. Koliopoulos, "Measurement of Surface Topography of Magnetic Tapes by Mirau Interferometry," *Applied Optics*, vol 24, 1985, pp. 1489-1497.
8. *Machining Data Handbook*, *op. cit.*, p. 18-5.
9. *Ibid.*, p. 18-40.
10. G. Bellows and D. N. Tishler, *Introduction to Surface Integrity*, Report TM70 974 (Cincinnati: General Electric Co., 1970).
11. L. R. Gatto and T. D. DiLullo, *Metallographic Techniques for Determining Surface Alterations in Machining*, SME Technical Paper IQ71-225 (Dearborn, MI: Society of Manufacturing Engineers, 1971).
12. M. Field, "Surface Integrity in Conventional and Nonconventional Machining," *Seminar on Advancements in Machine Tools and Production Trends* (State College, PA: Pennsylvania State University, July 1969).
13. M. Field, W. P. Koster, and J. B. Kohls, *Machining of High Strength Steels with Emphasis on Surface Integrity*, AFMDC 70-1 (Cincinnati, OH: Air Force Machinability Center, 1970).
14. M. Field, *op. cit.*
15. *Ibid.*
16. M. Field, W. P. Koster, and J. B. Kohls, *op. cit.*
17. M. Field, *op. cit.*
18. M. Field and J. F. Kahles, *The Surface Integrity of Machined and Ground High Strength Steels*, DMIC Report 210, October 1964, pp. 54-77.
19. *Ibid.*

METALS

CARBON STEELS

Iron and carbon are the predominant elements in steels. Carbon content ranges from a few hundredths to about one percent. The amount of additional alloying elements determines whether the steel is considered to be a carbon or an alloy steel.

Steel is considered a carbon steel when no minimum content is specified or required for aluminum (except for oxidation or to control grain size), chromium, cobalt, columbium, molybdenum, nickel, titanium, tungsten, vanadium, zirconium, or any other element to obtain a desired alloying effect: when the specified minimum for copper does not exceed 0.40%; or when the addition of manganese, silicon, and copper is limited to a maximum of 1.65%, 0.60%, and 0.60% respectively.

On the basis of carbon content, carbon steels can be divided into three groups. The first group contains 0.001-0.30% carbon and is considered low-carbon steel. The second group contains 0.30%-0.70% carbon and is considered medium-carbon steel. The third group contains 0.70-1.30% carbon and is considered high-carbon steel.

Certain grades may also specify the addition of boron to improve hardenability and aluminum for deoxidation and to control grain size. Carbon steels also contain small quantities of residual elements or impurities from the raw material such as copper, nickel, molybdenum, chromium, phosphorus, and sulfur, which are considered incidental.

Carbon steels may be classified according to chemical composition, deoxidation practice, quality, and end-product forms. Common end-product forms include bar, sheet/strip, plate, wire, tubing, and structural shapes. Carbon steel may also be classified as hot rolled or cold drawn (cold rolled when referring to sheets). Cold finished steels are produced from hot rolled steel by several cold finishing processes, resulting in improved surface finishes, dimensional accuracy, alignment, or machinability; elongation and yield and tensile strengths are increased. Cold rolled sheets are available in different tempers and can be precoated with zinc, aluminum, terne (lead-tin alloy), tin, and organic coatings.

TYPES OF STEEL

The principal reaction in steelmaking is the removal of excess carbon by the combination of carbon and oxygen to form a gas. If the extra oxygen remaining after this reaction is not removed prior to or during casting, the gaseous products continue to evolve during solidification. The type of steel produced is determined by the amount of deoxidation that takes place before casting. The four types of carbon steels produced are killed, semikilled, rimmed, and capped.

Killed Steels

Killed steels are strongly deoxidized by the addition of aluminum and/or silicon to the ladle before pouring. These elements combine with the oxygen; thus, only a negligible evolution of gases occurs during solidification. Killed steels are characterized by a high degree of uniformity in chemical composition and mechanical properties, which render them suitable for applications requiring forging, extrusion, severe cold forming, carburizing, and heat treatment. However, there may be variations in composition depending on the steelmaking practice used.

Semikilled Steels

Semikilled steels have characteristics intermediate between those of killed and rimmed steels. During solidification, the evolved gas is entrapped within the body of the ingot and counteracts the skrinkage.

Rimmed Steels

Rimmed steels are generally low-carbon steels that do not contain significant percentages of easily oxidized elements such as aluminum, silicon, or titanium. Since deoxidation is minimal, the carbon and residual oxygen react during solidification. The reaction stirs the liquid metal causing the metal that solidifies at the outer rim of the ingot to be lower in carbon, phosphorus, and sulfur than the average composition, whereas the inner portion, or core, is higher than average in those elements. The rimming action may continue until the reactions stop and the top of the ingot solidifies, or it may be stopped mechanically or chemically.

Rimmed steels have good surface and ductility characteristics. Because of their ductility, rimmed steels are suitable for moderate cold forming applications.

Capped Steels

Capped steels have characteristics similar to those of rimmed steel. The rimming action is controlled when the steel is cast so that gas produced during solidification causes the metal to rise in the mold. Capping occurs when the rising metal contacts a heavy metal cap placed on the bottle-top mold (mechanical capping). Adding ferrosilicon or aluminum to the ingot top after the ingot has rimmed for the desired period of time is another method of producing capped steel (chemical capping).

GRADES OF STEEL

Grade usually denotes the chemical composition of a particular steel. The grades may vary in chemical composition from almost pure iron to a

CARBON STEELS

material of complex constitution. A particular grade of carbon steel usually has specified limits for various elements, but the properties of products made from that grade can be diverse.

Grade Designation

A four-numeral series, adopted by the AISI and the SAE, is used to designate standard carbon steels specified to chemical composition ranges. It is important to note that these designations do not indicate specifications. The prefix M is used to designate a series of merchantquality steels and the suffix H designates standard hardenability steels.

The first two digits indicate the steel type and identifying elements as shown in Table 15-1. The last two digits indicate the approximate mean of the carbon range. For example, in the grade designation 1035, 35 represents a carbon range of 0.32 to 0.38%. It is necessary to deviate from this system and to interpolate numbers in the case of some carbon ranges and for variations in manganese, phosphorus, or sulfur with the same range. Special-purpose elements such as lead and boron are designated by inserting the letter L or B, respectively, between the second and third numerals.

In 1975, the Unified Numbering System (UNS) for Metals and Alloys was established by the American Society for Testing and Materials (ASTM) and the SAE. The UNS number consists of a single letter prefix followed by five digits. The letter G indicates standard carbon steels, and H indicates standard hardenability steels. The first four digits usually correspond to standard AISI, ASTM, or SAE steel designations, and the last digit usually indicates that an additional element such as lead or boron is specified. The number four indicates that lead is added, the number one indicates boron, and the number six indicates that an electric furnace is used for melting.

Hardenability Grades

Hardenability is a term used to designate that property of steel that determines the depth and distribution of hardness induced by quenching from the austenitizing temperature.[1] Hardenability is mainly determined by allowing elements in the steel, whereas maximum attainable hardness is dependent upon carbon content and cooling rate.

Methods of specifying hardenability requirements. The recommended method and equipment used to determine the hardenability of steel is described in SAE Standard J406,

"Methods of Determining Hardenability of Steels." The hardenability bands are tabulated in SAE Standard J1268, "Hardenability Bands for Carbon and Alloy H Steels." Rockwell hardness C-scale (R_C) is used to designate the minimum and maximum hardnesses of the test bar at specified distances.

Hardenability bands. In the AISI/SAE grade designation system, steels specified to hardenability band limits are identified by the suffix letter H. In the UNS, the prefix letter H indicates steels specified to hardenability band limits. The chemical composition limits of these steels have been modified somewhat from those in the same grade of steel without specified hardenability band limits. The modifications permit adjustments in chemical composition to reflect individual plant melting characteristics that may influence the level and widths of the hardenability bands. The hardenability bands are applicable to killed, fine-grain carbon steels.

CARBON STEEL QUALITY

The term quality is indicative of internal soundness, relative uniformity of composition, relative freedom from detrimental surface imperfections, and finish for any given steel. Steel quality also relates to general suitability for particular applications. For example, cold rolled sheet steel is available in classes for either exposed or unexposed applications. Exposed applications require a good painted surface, whereas the surface finish is not important in unexposed applications.

Carbon steels can be obtained in a number of qualities that reflect various degrees of the conditions mentioned above.

MECHANICAL PROPERTIES

Mechanical properties are those properties of the material that are associated with the material's reaction when a force is applied. Mechanical properties are usually determined from tension, bend, and hardness tests. The properties most commonly specified are tensile and yield strengths, total elongation, reduction in area, and hardness.

Hot rolled and cold drawn bars are usually produced to meet mechanical property requirements as well as limited compositional requirements. The tensile characteristics of hot rolled bars are mainly influenced by chemical composition, thickness or cross-sectional area, and variables in hot rolling and cooling practices. The effect of cold working on cold drawn bars depends on chemical composition, cross-sectional area, amount of cold reduction, and thermal treatment. During cold working, the yield strength of a material will increase more that the tensile strength.

Data from tension tests are used to determine the mechanical properties of sheet steel that influence drawing and stretching. The two main properties are the plastic strain ratio (r) and the work-hardening exponent (n).

The plastic strain ratio is indicative of the ability of a sheet to resist thinning during drawing and is defined as the ratio of width strain to thickness strain in the tensile test. Since the properties of the sheet are different in different directions, the average strain ratio ($\bar{r}$) is given. As the $\bar{r}$ value increases, the depth of permissible draw increases.

The work-hardening exponent (n) is a measure of the ability of the sheet to resist localized straining and thus increase uniform deformation. A metal with a high n value tends to strain uniformly even under nonuniform stress conditions. Typical n values for low-carbon steels are 0.20-0.22.

TABLE 15-1
Grade Designations of Standard Carbon Steels

Series Designation*	Type and Approximate Percentages of Identifying Elements
10XX	Nonresulfurized, 1.00% manganese maximum
11XX	Resulfurized
12XX	Rephosphorized and resulfurized
15XX	Nonresulfurized, over 1.00% manganese

* XX indicates carbon content in hundredths of a percent.

APPLICATIONS

The selection of a carbon steel for a particular application is largely determined by its carbon content. As previously stated, carbon steels can be divided into three main groups: low, medium, and high-carbon steels.

Low-Carbon Steels

In general, low-carbon steels are used for industrial products such as nuts, bolts, sheet, strip, plates, shapes, tubes, and many machined components that are subject to low stresses. An important group of low-carbon steels are free-cutting or free-machining steels. In many instances, the products made from this class of steel are machined from hot or cold formed bars; products requiring a hard, wear-resistant surface can be subsequently surface (case) hardened.

Medium-Carbon Steels

The medium-carbon grades of steel are used when the strength and hardness requirements are greater than can be adequately met by low-carbon steels. The mechanical properties of this class of steel can be improved by quenching and tempering.

Medium-carbon grades are used in producing rails, railroad equipment, parts for lathes and presses, machined parts requiring moderate-to-high strength, heavy stamped or pressed products, crankshafts, connecting rods, axles, gears, and many other automotive parts. In addition, many items in the agricultural equipment and petroleum industries are made from medium-carbon steels.

High-Carbon Steels

High-carbon steels are used for manufacturing products that require high strength, high hardness, and, in certain instances, good wear resistance. Typical applications for high-carbon steels include cutting tools such as drills, reamers, taps and dies, and cutlery. High-carbon steels are also used for high-strength rope, cable, music wire, and springs. High-carbon steels are generally purchased in the annealed condition; the manufactured parts are then heat treated to obtain the desired properties.

MACHINING AND FABRICATING CHARACTERISTICS

The machining and fabricating characteristics of carbon steels depend on the properties of the particular grade of steel being machined or fabricated, as well as the specific equipment and tooling employed. The following sections provide general information to assist the manufacturing engineer in machining, forming, welding, and heat treating carbon steels. Detailed information on the various operations can be obtained from the references mentioned in each section.

Machinability

Machinability concerns the relative ease with which a steel can be cut in turning, drilling, milling, broaching, threading, reaming, or sawing. Machinability is influenced by machine and work material variables. Some common machine variables are cutting speed, dimensions of the cut, tool geometry and material, cutting fluid, condition of the machine, and type of tool engagement with the workpiece. Work material variables include hardness, tensile properties, chemical composition, microstructure, degree of cold work, strain hardenability, shape and dimension of workpiece, and rigidity of the workpiece.

Hot rolled carbon steels containing less than 0.25% carbon tend to be tough and gummy in machining. Increasing carbon and manganese content increases strength and hardness and results in improved surface finish and chip character. Increasing sulfur, phosphorus, or nitrogen content and adding lead also improves the machinability of carbon steels.

If carbon content is approximately 0.20-0.25%, machinability is improved over lower carbon grades in both hot rolled and cold drawn steels. Carbon content greater than 0.25% decreases machinability. Most carbon steels containing less than 0.35% carbon are machined in the as-rolled or as-rolled, cold drawn condition. Cold drawn grades containing greater amounts of carbon are usually annealed to improve machinability. In comparison to hot rolled bars of similar composition and microstructure, cold drawn bars have improved machinability because of the higher yield-tensile strength ratio.

When machining both hot rolled and cold drawn carbon steels, it is necessary to allow for surface finishing. Resulfurized grades have a poorer surface finish and require more material to be removed to form the porper surface finish than nonresulfurized grades.

Formability

Carbon steel bars and sheets are readily formed by a variety of processes. For bars and wires, these processes include forging, wire drawing, extruding, heading, and swaging. Sheet metal forming processes include bending, flanging, hemming, drawing, expanding, shrinking, stretch forming, roll forming, spinning, and several special forming processes.

Low-carbon steels are the most easily formed because they contain less carbon and fewer alloying elements. Medium-carbon steels are usually not formed cold but can be successfully formed warm or hot. Both bar and sheet carbon steels are produced in special qualities that facilitate forming.

Weldability

Weldability is the capacity of a metal or combination of metals to be welded under fabrication conditions into a specific, suitably designed structure, and to perform satisfactorily in the intended service.[2] The weldability of carbon steel depends primarily on the carbon content or carbon equivalent, which in turn controls hardenability and the susceptibility of the welded structure to cracking or to hardening during thermal cycles induced by welding. Carbon equivalent is determined by the combined amount of carbon and other alloying elements present in steel.

Carbon steels with up to 0.30% carbon or with a carbon equivalent not over 0.40% are easily welded by arc, resistance, flash, oxyfuel gas, solid state, electron beam, or laser processes. The selection of the process is usually determined by the section thickness and the quality requirements of the weld. For carbon content over 0.15% and section thicknesses over 1.0" (25 mm), it

ALLOY STEELS

may be necessary to preheat the workpiece, control interpass temperature, and stress relieve the workpiece after welding. Resulfurized carbon steels have poor weldability due to their high sulfur content.

Carbon steels containing more than 0.30% carbon are weldable, but special techniques must be employed to prevent weld cracking.

Heat Treatment

The versatility of steel can be attributed to its response to heat treatment. While the major percentage of steel is used in the as-rolled condition, heat treatment greatly broadens the spectrum of properties attainable.

Heat treatments fall into two general categories: (1) those that increase the strength, hardness, and toughness by virtue of rapid cooling from above the transformation range, and (2) those that decrease hardness and promote uniformity by slow cooling from above the transformation range, or by prolonged heating within or below the transformation range, followed by slow cooling. The first category can involve through hardening by quenching and tempering, or a variety of specialized treatments undertaken to enhance surface hardness to a controlled depth. The second category encompasses normalizing and various types of annealing to improve machinability, toughness, or cold forming characteristics.[3] Annealing after cold forming relieves stresses and restores ductility.

ALLOY STEELS

Simply stated, an alloy steel is a steel that has one or more alloying elements added to it to obtain properties not obtainable in carbon steels. Steel is considered to be an alloy steel when the maximum range for manganese, silicon, or copper exceeds 1.65, 0.60, and 0.60% respectively. A steel is also considered an alloy when a definite range or a minimum quantity is specified or required for aluminum, chromium (up to 3.99%), cobalt, columbium, molybdenum, nickel, titanium, tungsten, vanadium, zirconium, or any other alloying element.

The alloy steels discussed in this section are the low-alloy steels. These steels may be divided into the structural grades and those listed by the American Iron and Steel Institute (AISI) and the Society of Automotive Engineers (SAE). In the structural grades, the alloying elements are the principal means of strengthening the ferrite matrix. The structural grade alloy steels are generally used in the as-rolled condition, the quenched and tempered condition, and in the normalized or annealed condition. In the AISI/SAE grades, the alloying elements serve primarily to improve the mechanical properties over equivalent carbon steel and to enhance the response of the steel to heat treatment.

ALLOY STEEL GRADES

The grade of a particular alloy steel is commonly indicated by the percentage of the various elements that comprise its chemical composition. The composition may be specified by a maximum limit, a minimum limit, or by both minimum and maximum limits, which are referred to as the range. Lists of standard alloy steels designed to serve the needs of fabricators and users of steel products are published by the AISI and SAE. Specialized grades, steels not on the standard alloy steel lists, are also produced.

Grade Designation

As with low-carbon steels, a four-numeral series designates alloy steels specified to chemical composition ranges. For certain grades, a five-numeral series is used.

The last two digits of the four-numeral series indicate the approximate middle of the carbon range; for example, 20 represents a range of 0.18 to 0.23% carbon. In the five-numeral series, the last three digits represent the carbon range. The first two digits of both the four and five-numeral series indicate the primary alloying elements used in the grade, along with their approximate percentages.

The prefix letter E is used to designate steels normally made by the basic electric furnace practice. Steels without the prefix are normally manufactured by the basic open-hearth or basic oxygen processes.

In 1975, the Unified Numbering System (UNS) for Metals and Alloys was established by the ASTM and the SAE. The UNS designates the various alloy steel grades using a single letter prefix followed by five digits. The letter G indicates standard alloy or carbon steels, and the first four digits usually correspond to the AISI/SAE steel designations. The fifth digit indicates an additional element, such as boron (indicated by the number one), or a particular manufacturing practice.

Hardenability Grades

As a result of cooperative work done by the SAE and the AISI, hardenability bands have been developed for many of the constructional alloy steels. The hardenability limits were determined from data obtained by conducting standard 1″ (25.4 mm) Jominy end-quench hardenability tests (ASTM Standard A 256) on many heats of each composition.

As a means of identifying steels specified to hardenability requirements, the suffix letter H has been added to the conventional series number. The UNS designates these steels with the prefix letter H instead of G which is used to designate standard alloy or carbon steels.

ALLOY STEEL QUALITY

Alloy steels are made with more than ordinary care throughout their manufacture. They are more sensitive to thermal and mechanical operations, the control of which is complicated by the varying effects of different chemical combinations.

The quality characteristics of alloy steel include, among others, internal soundness, uniformity of chemical composition, and freedom from injurious surface imperfections. The degree to which these characteristics can be obtained is limited by existing raw materials, manufacturing methods, and the technological nature of the alloy steel. Quality characteristics are related to the suitability of the steel to make a particular part.

ALLOYING ELEMENTS

Alloying elements are added to ordinary steels for the purpose of modifying their behavior during heat treatment, which in turn results in improvement of the mechanical and physical properties. Specifically, the additions are made for one or more of the following reasons:

- Improve tensile strength without lowering material ductility.
- Improve toughness.
- Increase hardenability, which permits the hardening of larger sections than possible with plain carbon steels or allows successful quenching with less drastic cooling rates, reducing the hazard of distortion and quench cracking.
- Retain physical properties at elevated temperatures.
- Obtain better corrosion resistance.
- Improve wear resistance.
- Impart a fine grain size to the steel.
- Improve surface (case) hardening characteristics.

MECHANICAL PROPERTIES

Alloy steels are not directly produced to specific mechanical properties, but are usually heat treated to achieve desired properties. Cold finished alloy steel bars usually require thermal treatments in order to meet definite limitations for tensile or hardness values. Alloy steels in the annealed and cold finished condition can be produced to specified maximum hardness limits. For steels in the normalized and cold finished condition, minimum hardness or minimum tensile strength may be specified. If the steels are normalized and tempered before cold finishing, either maximum and minimum hardnesses or maximum and minimum tensile values can be produced to a range that varies with the tensile strength level and is equivalent to a Brinell indentation diameter range of four-tenths of a millimeter (e.g., 4.0 to 4.4) at any specified location. If the steels are quenched and tempered before cold finishing, either maximum and minimum hardnesses or maximum and minimum tensile strength values can be produced to a range that varies with the tensile strength level and is equivalent to a Brinell indentation diameter range of three-tenths of a millimeter (e.g., 3.6 to 3.9) at any specified location.

When both hardness and tensile values are specified at the same position, the limits should be consistent with each other. In many cases, when the Brinell limits are specified as surface values, the tensile test results, which are of necessity obtained below the surface, and the surface hardness results will not be consistent because they vary according to the size of bar and the hardenability of the steel involved. For that reason the purchaser should recognize inconsistencies between the two and specify limits accordingly. In either case, it is essential that the position at which Brinell hardness values are taken be specified by the purchaser.

Generally the yield, elongation, and reduction of area are specified as minimums for steel in the quenched and tempered

or normalized and tempered conditions, and they should be consistent with the tensile strength or Brinell hardness.

APPLICATIONS

As was stated previously, low-alloy steels can be divided into the structural and AISI/SAE groups. The structural group is produced according to ASTM specifications.

Structural Grades

The high-strength structural steels are used principally in the transportation and construction industries for applications that require moderately high strength and weight reduction. An alloy combination for a common low-alloy structural steel is usually balanced to produce a minimum tensile strength of about 70 ksi (483 MPa), with a corresponding minimum yield strength of about 55 ksi (379 MPa).

AISI/SAE Grades

The AISI alloy steels are used particularly in the automotive and aircraft industries for highly stressed members such as gears, studs, and axles and moving engine parts such as cams, crankshafts, and valves. Certain combinations of the various alloying elements, after appropriate heat treatment, can impart to any one steel certain specialized characteristics for use in specific applications. For example, carbon-molybdenum and several other molybdenum-bearing steels possess good creep characteristics and therefore find useful application for moderately high-temperature service, when oxidation is not too severe. Typical applications are found in piping for steam and oil refineries.

The nickel-chromium steels as a group exhibit excellent hardenability, high strength, good wear resistance, and toughness. The various nickel-chromium combinations, properly heat treated, demonstrate tensile properties embracing the entire range available with alloy steels.

The chromium-vanadium steels, after heat treatment, show remarkable toughness and good fatigue resistance. As such, they find wide application when the part is subjected to reversing cycles such as with leaf and coil springs.

The low-alloy machinery steels are generally characterized by high tensile strength, good ductility, and excellent toughness when appropriately heat treated. The alloy content in these steels imparts good hardenability to the steel and permits the steel to be oil quenched to obtain these characteristics and air quenched when the mass of the section is small enough. This combination of characteristics is also desirable from the standpoint of preventing serious distortion during heat treatment.

MACHINING AND FABRICATING CHARACTERISTICS

To secure the most satisfactory results, purchasers normally consult with the steel producers regarding the working, machining, heat treating, or other operations to be used in fabricating the steel ordered, the mechanical properties to be obtained, and the conditions of service for which the finished parts are intended. Particular attention should be given to informing the producer regarding the details of the first operation to which the steel will be subjected and subsequent operations when significant.

HIGH-STRENGTH LOW-ALLOY STEELS

Alloy steels containing over 0.38% carbon are customarily given a thermal treatment prior to cold finishing. For best results when machining, cold heading, or performing other fabricating operations, thermal treatment of alloy steels having lower carbon content may be required.

Machining

Machinability concerns the relative ease with which a steel is cut by sharp tools in various operations, such as turning, drilling, milling, broaching, threading, reaming, or sawing. Machinability involves the concepts of tool life and surface finish and is influenced in an important way by cutting speed, tool geometry, cutting fluid, rigidity of the workpiece, and mechanical condition of the machine tool.

The characteristics of steel that influence machinability are composition, special additives, treatment, and structure. The chemical composition has a major influence since it affects the microstructure and mechanical properties.

Most low-carbon alloy steels are machined in the as-rolled or as-rolled and cold drawn condition. Higher carbon alloy steels and high-hardenability, low-carbon alloy steels may be conditioned for machining by annealing, either for softening or for producing a specified microstructure.

Forming

Alloy steels are not widely used in forming operations other than forging and heading. Special quality designations are assigned to those alloy steels that are used in different forming operations.

Welding

Alloy steels with a carbon content lower than 0.10% can be readily welded by most welding techniques. Since their carbon content is low, preheating or postheating is not required. Alloy steels containing between 0.10 and 0.30% carbon are slightly more difficult to weld than the steels with lower carbon content. Preheating and postheating of these steels are recommended to reduce internal stresses. Alloy steels containing more than 0.30% carbon are difficult to weld, and preheating and post-heating techniques are required.

Heat treating the alloy steels with a higher carbon content helps to produce a uniform structure in the weld metal and the parent metal. Low-hydrogen electrodes are recommended when arc welding these steels to reduce brittleness in the weld.

Heat Treatment

Alloy steels are usually heat treated to achieve the required properties for a given application.

HIGH-STRENGTH LOW-ALLOY STEELS

High-strength low-alloy (HSLA) steels are a group of steels that exhibit and develop strengths significantly higher than carbon steels owing to the addition of small amounts of alloying elements, coupled with special steel processing methods. The carbon content of these steels is usually less than 0.30% by weight. Small amounts of manganese, silicon, phosphorus, copper, aluminum, chromium, niobium, vanadium, titanium, molybdenum, nickel, zirconium, nitrogen, calcium, and rare earth elements are used singly or in combination to increase strength, toughness, formability, and corrosion resistance.

The total alloy content of a few grades of HSLA steel is high enough to qualify them as alloy steels. However, HSLA steels are considered distinct from traditional alloy steels, such as constructional alloy steels, since, with a few exceptions, they achieve their high strength without separate heat treatment after finishing.

PRODUCT FORMS AND APPLICATIONS

High-strength low-alloy steels are produced in a variety of product forms. Most HSLA steels are produced as hot rolled products including sheet and strip, plates, structural shapes, and bars. A few grades are also produced as cold rolled sheet and strip. Flat rolled product forms are also available with protective coatings, such as zinc, for corrosion resistance.

Sheet and strip products, either in the form of coils or cut lengths, are used in automobiles, trucks and trailers, agricultural equipment, mining equipment, railway equipment, tanks and containers, and in other miscellaneous industrial applications. Plate products are also used in these applications, and, in addition, they are used in bridges, ships, buildings, line pipe, and other structural applications. Structural shapes, which include I-beams, H-beams, channels, angles, tees, and zees, find a wide range of structural applications. Bars are used in applications that require cold and hot forming for the manufacture of structural parts for diverse industrial equipment and machinery.

TYPES OF HSLA STEELS

High-strength low-alloy steels have been categorized or grouped largely on composition.[4,5] Several types can often achieve a given strength level, but with varying degrees of toughness, formability, weldability, and corrosion resistance. In addition, the strength, toughness, and formability of a given type of HSLA steel can vary depending on the rolling and finishing practices used during production.

HSLA steels are typified by a high strength-to-weight ratio, and, as a result, yield strength is an important consideration. Hot rolled grades exhibit yield strengths ranging from 42 to 90 ksi (290 to 620 MPa). Cold rolled sheet and strip grades develop yield strengths from 40 to 140 ksi (276 to 965 MPa).

Niobium (Columbium)/Vanadium Steels

This category of HSLA steels contains niobium and/or vanadium additions in amounts of approximately 0.1% by weight or less. These alloying elements combine with carbon and/or nitrogen to form fine precipitates in the microstructure during controlled rolling with the result that fine ferrite grain size is obtained. Subsequent precipitation hardening during cooling results in high strength. The steels are available in all product forms, are readily weldable, and have good formability. Toughness of hot rolled products is poor when this type of alloy steel is semikilled and conventionally rolled. When fully killed, toughness, along with formability and fatigue resistance, is significantly improved. These steels can also be controlled rolled to obtain excellent toughness along with high strength.

Manganese-Copper Steels

This group of HSLA steels contains higher amounts of manganese along with additions of copper to improve strength and corrosion resistance. Resistance to corrosion is about twice that of carbon steels. This type is produced largely as plates; however, a few grades are available as sheet, strip, bars, and shapes. Weldability is relatively poor, and, as a result, this group of HSLA steels is not recommended for use in welded structures.

Manganese Steels (Heat Treated)

These steels contain additional amounts of manganese for increased strength. Some grades also contain various combinations of nickel, chromium, molybdenum, niobium, and vanadium. In some cases copper is an optional addition. They are available as plates, and, in some cases, as hot rolled sheets. Plate grades are usually normalized to obtain optimum toughness, or, in some instances, quenched and tempered to maximize both strength and toughness. These steels are weldable by filler metal methods.

Manganese-Vanadium and Manganese-Titanium Steels

This group of HSLA steels contains additions of vanadium or titanium in order to improve strength by precipitation hardening and grain refinement. Manganese-vanadium grades may also contain additions of nitrogen or niobium. Manganese-vanadium steels are plate grades, and manganese-titanium steels are available as hot rolled and cold rolled sheet and strip. These steels have good formability and toughness, and are weldable by both filler metal and resistance methods.

Manganese-Vanadium-Copper Steels

These steels contain additions of manganese and vanadium for increased strength, as well as copper for increased corrosion resistance. They have good notch toughness and formability, and exhibit a corrosion resistance about twice that of carbon steel. These steels are weldable by both filler metal and resistance methods. They are available in all product forms.

Multiple Alloy Steels with Copper

These grades contain additions of silicon, copper, chromium, molybdenum, and nickel for improved strength and corrosion resistance. Niobium and vanadium are also added. These steels are weathering steels with corrosion resistance two to six times that of carbon steel. They are primarily plate steels, but a few grades are available as bars, sheets, or shapes. They have good formability, excellent notch toughness, and are readily weldable.

Multiple Alloy Steels with Copper and High Phosphorus

These HSLA steels are also weathering steels that contain additions of copper and phosphorus along with nickel, chromium, and molybdenum. Corrosion resistance is four to eight times that of carbon steel. They exhibit fairly good formability and are weldable; however, notch toughness is poor. These grades are available in most product forms.

HSLA Steels with Special Formability

These steels contain very low carbon contents (0.18% max), are usually fully killed, and often use additions of niobium or vanadium to increase strength. To achieve excellent formability and notch toughness, ladle desulfurization and/or sulfide inclusion shape control using calcium, zirconium, or rare earth elements are employed. These grades are produced primarily as hot and cold rolled sheet and strip; however, a few plate grades are available.

Precipitation-Hardening Steels

This category of HSLA steels contains significant amounts of copper, nickel, and molybdenum. Niobium or vanadium is also added in some instances. These steels develop their strength as a result of low-temperature aging treatments following hot rolling, normalizing, or quenching. They exhibit excellent corrosion resistance (four to six times that of carbon steel) and notch toughness. Product forms include plates, structural shapes, and bars.

Dual-Phase Steels

Dual-phase steels are a special category of high-strength steels that have been recently developed. Their properties result from a mixed ferrite plus martensite microstructure. They are characterized by relatively low yield strengths, 40-50 ksi (275-345 MPa), but work harden rapidly during straining, and develop high tensile strengths on the order of 85 to 100 ksi (585 to 690 MPa). As a result, very high strengths are obtained in fabricated parts. They exhibit significantly higher ductility and formability than more conventional HSLA steels. Dual-phase steels are produced as hot and cold rolled sheet and strip with very small amounts of alloy additions using intercritical annealing. A more highly alloyed version can be produced as directly hot rolled sheet and strip using additions of silicon, chromium, and molybdenum. Where needed, the low yield strengths of dual-phase steels can be increased by low-temperature aging or straining and aging treatments.

Rephosphorized and Renitrogenized Steels

The strength of carbon steels can be increased to the levels exhibited by many HSLA steels through additions of phosphorus or nitrogen. These types of steels are produced as hot and cold rolled sheet and strip products. Nitrogen-containing steels respond to straining and aging treatments resulting in high strength following fabrication. These steels can be obtained with yield strengths ranging from 35 to 140 ksi (240 to 965 MPa).

SPECIFICATIONS

The ASTM, the SAE, and the American Petroleum Institute (API) have developed specifications applicable to high-strength low-alloy steels. In addition, the AISI has developed a designation system applicable to high-strength sheet steels. It is important to note, however, that not all HSLA grades produced by all steel producers are covered by the various specifications. Many grades that are produced as proprietary grades by various manufacturers do not qualify for coverage by any specification.

CHAPTER 15

HIGH-STRENGTH LOW-ALLOY STEELS

API Specifications

The American Pipe Institute Specification 5LX covers high test-line pipe and includes both seamless and welded pipe. This specification includes yield strengths ranging from 42 to 70 ksi (290 to 483 MPa); for example, X42 to X70. Specification 5LS for spiral-weld line-pipe covers these same grades and two lower strength grades. Steel compositions other than those shown in the specifications may be supplied by agreement between purchaser and manufacturer. Niobium and vanadium are often used for higher strength grades, and the pipe skelp is often controlled rolled. Further information may be obtained from the specifications.

AISI Sheet Designation System

The AISI designation system of high-strength sheet steels contains three basic components: (1) the minimum yield strength, (2) the chemical composition, and (3) the deoxidation practice. A five-character code is used to describe these components.

The first three characters give the yield strength of a given grade. Yield strength is categorized in 5 ksi (35 MPa) increments from 35 to 60 ksi (241 to 414 MPa), in 10 ksi (70 MPa) increments from 60 to 80 ksi (414 to 550 MPa), and in 20 ksi (140 MPa) increments from 80 to 140 ksi (550 to 965 MPa). Thus, the designation "050" refers to a steel with a yield strength of 50 ksi (345 MPa).

The chemical composition of each grade is designated by a letter classification: S, X, W, or D. The letter S refers to structural-quality steels that contain carbon plus manganese; carbon plus manganese and phosphorus; carbon plus manganese and nitrogen; or carbon plus manganese, phosphorus, and nitrogen. Recovery-annealed steels, except those with the designation X, are included in this category. The letter X refers to low-alloy steel grades containing niobium, chromium, copper, molybdenum, nickel, silicon, titanium, vanadium, and zirconium either singly or in combination. Weathering steels containing silicon, phosphorus, copper, nickel, and chromium in various combinations are indicated by the letter W. Dual-phase steels containing martensite or other transformation products in a ferrite matrix are designated by the letter D. Dual-phase steels exhibit very high work-hardening rates, and, as a result, formed parts have significantly higher strengths than the original flat rolled sheets. Consequently, the yield strength of a dual-phase steel is designated as the strength after a 5% strain; for example, an 80D grade exhibits an 80 ksi (550 MPa) yield strength after 5% strain.

Deoxidation practice is also designated by a letter classification. The letter F means killed plus sulfide inclusion controlled, K means killed, and O means nonkilled. For example, the steel designation 040SF would mean a minimum yield strength of 40 ksi (275 MPa), structural quality, killed.

SELECTION FACTORS

Selection of an HSLA steel for use in a given application involves an evaluation of (1) properties in relation to the requirements for the application, and (2) manufacturing characteristics needed for the production of the part. Properties to be considered include strength, toughness, weldability, and corrosion resistance. In some instances, fatigue behavior also becomes important. Manufacturing characteristics include formability and weldability.

Strength Characteristics

The strength of an HSLA steel depends on steel composition and production processing. However, a characteristic common to all HSLA steels is their high strength-to-weight ratio. As was mentioned earlier, yield strength is an important criterion for selection. Figure 15-1 shows partial stress-strain diagrams for low-carbon mild steel (SAE 1010) and an HSLA steel (SAE 950X).[6] The higher yield strength and greater elastic range of the HSLA grade permit its use in thinner gages, resulting in weight savings. It should be noted, however, that the modulus of elasticity (Young's modulus) is the same for both grades. Thus, where stiffness, deflection, or buckling is a design consideration, it may not be possible to take full advantage of the increased strength of HSLA steels.

Toughness Characteristics

Toughness of a steel is the ability of the steel to absorb impact loads by plastically deforming prior to fracture.[7] The toughness of HSLA steels can vary considerably depending on steel composition and processing. In general, toughness decreases as strength increases. Toughness can be improved by using fully killed steels and through the use of desulfurization and sulfide inclusion shape control. The use of controlled rolling practices or heat treatment will also result in good toughness.

Corrosion Characteristics

The corrosion resistance of HSLA steels depends primarily on alloy content as well as on the environment. With the exception of steels containing copper and weathering steels, HSLA steels exhibit a corrosion resistance approximately equal to that of carbon steel.

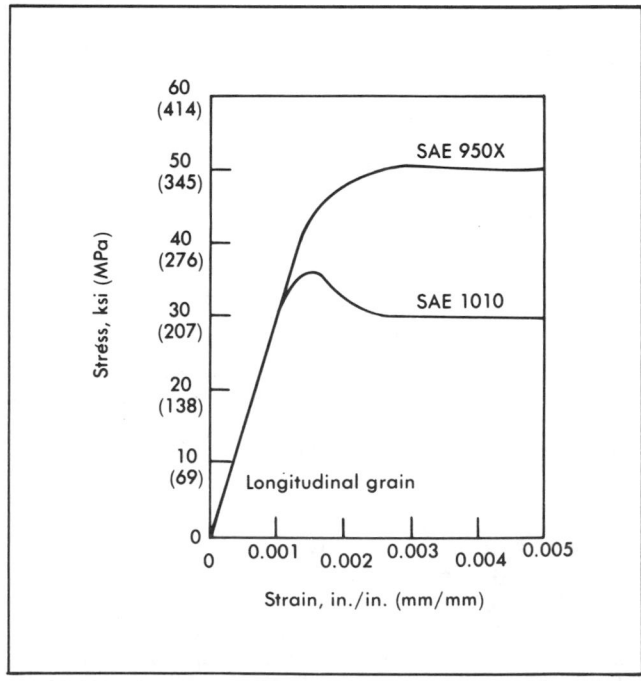

Fig. 15-1 Partial stress-strain diagrams for a low-carbon mild steel (SAE 1010) and an HSLA steel (SAE 950X). (*American Society for Metals*)

Fatigue Strength

Fatigue performance depends on a number of factors including loading cycle, material properties, design of the part, surface condition, and environment.[8] In general, fatigue strength increases as tensile strength increases.

Formability

Formability of a steel may be defined as the capability of the steel to be formed into a useful shape.[9] In general, formability increases as uniform and total elongation and reduction in area increase. As strength increases, formability generally decreases. Thus, while the HSLA steels exhibit good formability for their strength, they are not as formable as the ordinary low-carbon steels.

Weldability

The weldability of HSLA steels is measured in many different ways. It takes into consideration the susceptibility of a steel to cracking during welding and the properties of the weld and heat-affected zone. In structural applications, most welding is carried out by metal arc welding.

When welding HSLA steels, five serious problems may occur. Three of these—hydrogen cracking (cold cracking), solidification cracking (hot cracking), and lamellar tearing—are fabrication problems. The other two—weld metal toughness and heat-affects zone toughness—are service problems.[10]

STAINLESS STEELS

Stainless steels are iron-based alloys containing 10.50% or more chromium. These steels achieve their "stainless" characteristics as a result of the invisible and adherent, chromium-rich oxide film that forms on the material's surface. The oxide film is self-forming and self-healing in the presence of oxygen. Other elements added to improve corrosion resistance, fabricating and machining characteristics, or strength include nickel, molybdenum, copper, titanium, silicon, manganese, columbium, aluminum, nitrogen, and sulfur. Carbon is normally present in amounts from 0.03% to over 1.00% in certain martensitic grades, which improves the alloy's strength.

The selection of stainless steels is based on corrosion or heat resistance, mechanical properties, fabrication characteristics, availability, and the total product cost. Generally, corrosion resistance and mechanical properties are the predominant factors in selecting the appropriate grade of stainless steel for a given application.

TYPES OF STAINLESS STEELS

Stainless steels possess resistance to attack by many corrosive media at room and elevated temperatures, and are produced in a variety of grades to cover a wide range of mechanical and physical properties for specific applications. Currently, over 57 standard grades of stainless are produced as well as proprietary stainless steels with special characteristics. The standard grades are those identified in the American Iron and Steel Institute (AISI) products manual entitled *Stainless and Heat Resisting Steels*.

The AISI classifies the different types of stainless steels according to a three-digit numbering system. The first digit indicates the type of stainless steel that is suggestive of the material's microstructure. The last two digits indicate the specific grade in the group. Letters following the last two digits indicate modifications of a specific grade. The Unified Numbering System (UNS), developed by the American Society for Testing and Materials (ASTM) and the Society of Automotive Engineers (SAE), uses six characters to designate a particular material type and grade. All stainless steels in this system are identified by the letter "S" and followed by five digits. In this Handbook, material designations are given using the three-digit and six character numbering systems whenever they are applicable.

The five main types of stainless steels include austenitic, ferritic, martensitic, precipitation hardening and duplex. Austenitic, ferritic, martensitic, and duplex stainless steels are classified according to the three-digit and six-character number systems. Precipitation-hardening stainless steels are generally classified according to the six-character number system.

Austenitic

Austenitic stainless steels are characterized by their austenitic (face-centered cubic) structure. Austenitic stainless steels are essentially nonmagnetic in the annealed condition and can only be hardened by cold working. They possess excellent cryogenic characteristics and the greatest corrosion resistance and best high-temperature strength of all stainless steels produced. However, some of the newer duplex stainless steels possess better corrosion and strength properties.

Austenitic stainless steels are composed of iron-chromium-nickel and iron-chromium-manganese-nickel alloys. Chromium content is from 16 to 26%, nickel 6 to 22%, and manganese 1 to 15%. Nickel improves the corrosion resistance of the alloy in some environments. The 2xx stainless steels contain nitrogen and 4-15.5% manganese to promote the austenitic structure and reduce the amount of nickel required. The 3xx stainless steels may contain up to 2% manganese. Carbon and, more importantly, nitrogen are also added to promote the austenitic structure. Molybdenum improves the high-temperature strength and increases the resistance to chloride pitting and crevice corrosion. Sulfur or selenium may be added to certain grades to improve machinability.

Cold working austenitic stainless steels significantly increases their tensile and yield strengths. In many—but not all—austenitic steels, cold working partially transforms the austenitic structure to a martensitic structure. The actual rate of work hardening is determined by the total alloy content. At room temperature, yield strengths range from 30 to 200 ksi (200 to 1379 MPa) depending on composition and the amount of cold working performed.

CHAPTER 15

STAINLESS STEELS

Ferritic

Ferritic stainless steels are chromium alloys with body-centered cubic microstructures. Chromium content is usually from 10.5 to 27%, and some grades may contain up to 4% molybdenum to improve pitting and crevice corrosion resistance. Ferritic alloys are magnetic, have good ductility, and resist corrosion and oxidation; however, toughness may be limited. High-temperature strength is poor, and hardening can only be performed by cold working.

Martensitic

Martensitic stainless steels are chromium alloys that possess a martensitic microstructure in the hardened condition. These alloys are magnetic, resistant to corrosion in mild environments, and hardenable by heat treatment. They are also less ductile than the other types of stainless steels, but their ductility is improved in the fully solution annealed condition.

Chromium content ranges from 10.5 to 18% and carbon content may be as high as 1.20%. However, a proper ratio of carbon to chromium must be maintained to ensure a fully austenitic structure during hardening. Chromium increases corrosion resistance, but increasing carbon lowers it. High-carbon, high-chromium alloys provide increased hardness for cutting and wearing applications, as well as improved strength for highly stressed parts such as bolts and nuts. However, toughness will not be as high as that obtained with lower-carbon martensitic stainless steels. Adding sulfur and selenium to the alloy improves machinability, and adding nickel improves corrosion resistance in some media but may hinder full hardening.

Mechanical properties of martensitic stainless steels fall into two groups. The first group consists of grades containing up to 0.15% carbon and are generally referred to as low-carbon alloys. This group can attain a maximum hardness of R_C45. High-carbon alloys, with carbon content greater than 0.15%, can attain a maximum hardness of R_C60. The maximum hardness of both groups in the annealed condition is R_C26. The tensile strength of heat-treated martensitic stainless steels may exceed 200 ksi (1379 MPa).

Precipitation-Hardening

Development of precipitation-hardening (PH) stainless steel alloys began in the 1940s for use in the aerospace industry. Currently, PH alloys are used in a wide variety of applications because of their high strength-to-weight ratio, ductility, and corrosion resistance at temperatures up to their precipitation temperature.

Precipitation-hardening stainless steels are chromium-nickel alloys with the addition of elements such as copper, aluminum, titanium, or molybdenum. Precipitation-hardening stainless steels can be classified as martensitic or austenitic based on the microstructure of the steel. The predominant microstructure is martensitic.

Hardening PH stainless steels to high strengths is accomplished by solution treatment and an aging process. In the precipitation-hardened condition, PH stainless steels are magnetic and attain tensile strengths up to 260 ksi (1790 MPa).

Duplex

Another type of stainless steel that has been widely used in Europe and is now becoming popular in the U.S. and Canada is classified as duplex stainless steel and has a mixed structure of both austenite and ferrite. The exact amount of each phase is varied by the introduction of austenite and ferrite stablizers, but most compositions usually contain 50% austenite and 50% ferrite. The principal alloying elements are chromium and nickel with the addition of molybdenum, copper, and nitrogen in certain grades.

The corrosion resistance of duplex stainless steels is similar to austenitic stainless steels. However, they have improved resistance to stress-corrosion cracking and higher tensile and yield strengths in the annealed condition. They also offer good fabricability and toughness.

APPLICATIONS

Since their introduction over 50 years ago, stainless steels have been used in many different industries for a variety of applications. Some of the industries include chemical, petroleum, textile, nuclear power, pulp and paper, marine, fertilizer, and transportation. Stainless steels are also being used in hospitals, laboratories, cafeterias, dairies, breweries, food processing plants, and residential homes.

Austenitic alloys are the most widely used of the stainless steel alloys due to their resistance to corrosion, ease of fabrication, and wide range of mechanical properties in both elevated temperature and cryogenic environments. Ferritic alloys are frequently used in nonstructural applications that require good corrosion resistance and bright, highly polished finishes. Structural applications include automotive exhaust systems and farm equipment. Martensitic alloys are used in applications that require not only moderate corrosion resistance but high strength, high hardness, and good fatigue properties such as in cutlery. Precipitation-hardening alloys are used predominantly in aerospace and aircraft structural components. Duplex stainless steels are finding increasing use in industries where the 300 series stainless steels are susceptible to localized forms of corrosion such as pitting/crevice corrosion and chloride stress-corrosion cracking.

MACHINING AND FABRICATING CHARACTERISTICS

Care must be exercised in the fabrication of stainless steels because they are sensitive to thermal and mechanical operations. The following sections give general information to assist the manufacturing engineer when machining, forming, welding, or heat treating stainless steels. To obtain the best results, it is advisable to consult with the steel producer regarding the specific stainless steel grade.

Machining

The machining characteristics of austenitic stainless steels are substantially different from those of carbon and alloy steels. Generally, most austenitic stainless steels are tough, gummy, and tend to seize and gall. However, recent modifications in melting and refining practices have improved the machinability of stainless steels.

Austenitic stainless steels are the most difficult to machine because they work harden at a very rapid rate. The 400 series, ferritic and martensitic alloys, are the easiest to machine but the stringy chip produced by these alloys can slow productivity. Machining stainless steels in a slightly hardened condition results in improved machinability and productivity.

Machinability improvements have also been made by modifying the chemical compositions of certain grades referred to as free-machining stainless steels. Sulfur, selenium, lead, copper, aluminum, or phosphorus are added to improve machinability by a variety of mechanisms. These mechanisms include reducing friction between the tool, workpiece, and chip; reducing the tendency for pressure welding of chips to the tool; and increasing the brittleness of the chip. However, the free-machining alloying elements can adversely affect corrosion resistance, transverse ductility, and other qualities, such as weldability.

Forming

Stainless steels can be successfully formed by hot and cold processes. Hot forming processes include forging, extruding, and heading. Cold forming processes include blanking, brake forming, bending, drawing, embossing, heading, punching, roll forming, and spinning.

Hot forming. Most of the stainless steel grades have a moderately restricted hot-working temperature range. The temperature is largely determined by the alloy's composition. In most applications, the lowest feasible temperature is recommended. Since stainless steels possess greater yield strengths than carbon and low-alloy steels, the equipment employed must be capable of delivering greater force. The number of blows must also be increased when using hammers. Heat treatment is generally necessary after hot forming to obtain optimum corrosion resistance and mechanical properties. Austenitic alloys should be reheated to approximately 1900°F (1040°C) and water quenched for optimum corrosion resistance. To prevent cracking, martensitic alloys require slow cooling after forging followed by annealing. Ferritic alloys also require annealing for best corrosion protection.

Cold forming. Stainless steels exhibit maximum ductility in the fully annealed condition. Austenitic alloys have greater ductility than ferritic and martensitic alloys. The formability of the particular grade can be estimated from the room temperature ductility, which is often measured as percent elongation or percent reduction of area. As ductility increases, the formability of the material increases. In general, higher carbon alloys have reduced formability. All stainless steel grades can be slightly heated to improve their formability.

Since the shear strength of most stainless steels is 50-75% greater than mild steel, the press or shear must be capable of delivering the additional force required. Generally press or shear speed is reduced to 75% of normal operating speeds. Proper lubricants are also required to obtain the best cold forming results. Austenitic alloys work harden during cold forming and often require annealing between deep drawing operations.

Welding

All stainless steels can be welded employing the various welding methods available today. The two main methods employed are arc welding and resistance welding. However, the actual techniques followed when using these methods are modified slightly to preserve corrosion resistance in the weld and heat-affected zone (HAZ), to maintain optimum mechanical properties in the joint, and to minimize heat distortion.

When welding joints made with a stainless steel and a low-alloy steel or with dissimilar stainless steels, a highly alloyed welding rod should be used to counteract dilution effects and preserve corrosion resistance. The slow cooling of heavy sections of austenitic stainless steels often results in chromium-carbide precipitation, which reduces corrosion resistance. This precipitation of carbides or sensitizing process can be corrected by solution annealing. Optimum mechanical properties in the joint can be achieved by using the proper weld rod. Following recommended practices by the American Welding Society or consulting with the rod manufacturer will ensure proper rod selection.

The heat generated by the welding process is dissipated at a slower rate in stainless steels than in other steels. The slow cooling rate may result in workpiece distortion. Distortion can be minimized by lowering weld current settings, employing skip-weld techniques, using backup chill bars or other cooling techniques, or by incorporating bevel joints in the design instead of square-end butt joints.

Preheating and postheating martensitic alloys slows the cooling rate. If the cooling rate is too fast, metallurgical changes may occur in the material that could result in cracking. Ferritic alloys are usually heat treated following welding operations to minimize sensitization and losses in ductility. Austenitic alloys do not generally require pre or postheating. In heavy sections that cannot be solution annealed, stabilized or low-carbon grades such as 321, 347, 304L, or 316L are recommended. Postheating is also performed to stress relieve components that may contain high residual stresses. In some chemical environments, residual stresses increase susceptibility to stress-corrosion cracking. Postheating treatments are normally employed for precipitation-hardening alloys to restore or improve their mechanical properties.

Stainless steels can also be joined together by employing brazing and soldering techniques. Brazing is usually preferred when joining stainless steel to another metal. Chloride fluxes must be avoided, or chlorides must be completely removed after brazing to avoid pitting or stress-corrosion problems. Phosphoric acid type fluxes are recommended when preparing stainless steel surfaces for soldering.

Heat Treating

Annealing and other forms of heat treatment are usually performed on all stainless steel grades to improve their corrosion resistance and mechanical properties. In certain high-temperature applications, stainless steels are used in the as-rolled or forged condition. The chemical composition influences how each particular grade responds to the treatment. Austenitic, ferritic, and duplex alloys are not capable of being hardened by heat treatment. These alloys are hardened by cold working. Martensitic alloys and precipitation-hardening alloys are hardened through heat treatment.

Heat-treating methods for stainless steels are similar to those used with other steels and special equipment is not required. Conventional electric, gas-fired, oil-fired, salt bath, or induction furnaces are used to heat the steel. The steel should not be directly exposed to the flame, and slightly oxidizing furnace atmospheres are preferred.

MARAGING STEELS

Maraging steels, developed by the International Nickel Company in the 1960s, comprise a special class of high-strength steels that use nickel as the main alloying element. The term "maraging" is derived from "martensite age hardening" and denotes age hardening of a low-carbon, iron-nickel martensitic matrix.

The annealed microstructure of maraging steel is essentially a carbon-free, iron-nickel lath martensite. In the annealed condition, the material is soft and can be readily machined or formed. The material is martensitic at room temperature but reverts to an austenitic, face-centered cubic structure when heated to 1500° F (815° C). During cooling, martensite starts to form at 310° F (155° C) and is 99% complete at 210° F (100° C). The material is heated to 900° F (480° C) for aging and then cooled to room temperature. During aging, the martensite is strengthened by short-range ordering and subsequent precipitation of nickel-molybdenum and nickel-titanium intermetallic compounds.

Maraging steels are produced by a double-vacuum melting process to maintain high purity and to reduce residual elements. The first process is usually vacuum induction melting which is then followed by a vacuum-arc remelting process. Maraging steels are produced in wrought steel compositions. Common wrought forms are bar, plate, and sheet.

ALLOYS

Currently only 18% nickel maraging steel alloys are being produced. The 20% and 25% nickel alloys were the two original maraging alloys developed, but they were discontinued because of their brittleness at high-temperature strength levels and the complexity of the annealing and aging treatments.

APPLICATIONS

The 18% nickel maraging steels were developed to meet the exacting requirements of the aerospace industry. This class of steels filled the need for ultrahigh-strength steels that had high fracture toughness and high fatigue, tensile, and yield strengths.

Shortly after their development, the great potential of the maraging steels in tooling applications was realized. Some of the initial applications in the tooling area included aluminum die casting dies, aluminum die casting die core pins, plastic molding dies, extrusion tooling, punches, blanking dies, and cold forming dies. These materials continue to be used in tooling areas because of:

1. Excellent machinability.
2. Good polishability.
3. A simple, precipitation-hardening, aging heat treatment.
4. Uniform, predictable shrinkage during heat treatment.
5. Through hardening without quenching.
6. Minimal distortion during heat treatment.

7. Total freedom from decarburization.
8. Good weldability without preheating.

FABRICATING CHARACTERISTICS

Maraging steels can be readily processed by machining, forming, welding, and heat-treating methods.

Machining

Machinability of maraging steels in the annealed condition is approximately comparable to steels such as prehardened AISI 4340. However, after aging, the choice of cutting tools and machining conditions becomes increasingly important. During machining operations, rigid equipment, firm tool supports, sharp tools, and an adequate coolant are essential.

Forming

Maraging steels can be readily formed using cold, warm, and hot-working methods. Cold working is performed in the annealed condition, and large reductions can be made without significantly increasing the tensile strength or hardness of the material. When necessary, annealing can be performed between forming operations. Warm forming can be performed below 600° F (315° C). Forming above 600° F may cause maraging to occur. Hot forming may be performed by forging, forming, or rolling operations between 1500 and 2100° F (815 and 1150° C).

Welding

The 18% nickel maraging steels have high weldability in both the solution annealed and the full-aged conditions. Most conventional welding procedures achieve sound, crack-free welds.

Best results for structural welding have been obtained by either using tungsten inert gas (TIG) or electron-beam welding. Although the metal inert gas (MIG) process may be employed, it does result in a loss of ductility. Preheating is not only unnecessary but should not be performed because of the hardening mechanism of these grades. Gas shielding with pure argon is recommended for either TIG or MIG welding. Thorough cleaning of the as-welded deposit and a maximum interpass temperature of 250° F (120° C) are essential.

To obtain the best possible weld microstructure, and thus the highest joint efficiency, the material should be solution annealed after welding and prior to aging. However, joint efficiencies of better than 90% have been obtained with the 200, 250, and 300 level material by merely aging after welding.

Heat Treatment

Maraging steels are supplied in the solution annealed condition by the steel supplier in the hardness range of R_C 30-35. Aging is performed to develop the material's high strength, toughness, and hardness. The aging process may be performed in an air atmosphere or in a liquid salt-bath solution.

CAST STEELS

In wrought steel production, the various alloying elements are melted together in a furnace and then poured into ingots to cool and subsequently be hot and/or cold worked until the desired form and size has been achieved. When steel castings are produced, the various alloying elements are melted together and then poured directly into a mold cavity having the proper design. The cast part is allowed to cool and then removed from the mold.

The compositions of steel castings are similar to those of wrought steels, with the exception of higher silicon and manganese content to ensure thorough deoxidation. Cast steels may contain alloying elements such as nickel, chromium, vanadium, and copper to give desirable combinations of hardness, tensile strength, and toughness not readily available in plain carbon grades. The total alloy content may be as high as 30% or greater. Chemical compositions of the various alloys are usually based on specifications of the American Society of Testing and Materials (ASTM). Cast steels are also available in American Iron and Steel Institute (AISI) designations, but the silicon and manganese percentages are higher than in wrought steels. The hardness of cast steels is measured by the Brinell test method because of the coarseness of their microstructure.

CAST STEEL ALLOYS AND APPLICATIONS

Cast steels are available in carbon, low-alloy, corrosion-resistant, and heat-resistant alloys. The following material briefly describes the more commonly used alloys and includes the various areas and industries where these alloys are being used. Also included are tables of the mechanical properties that are most useful for manufacturing engineers.

Carbon and Low-Alloy Cast Steels

Cast carbon steels have carbon as the main alloying element, although other alloying elements are also present. They are usually classified by the amount of carbon contained in the steel; low-carbon steel castings contain up to 0.20% carbon, medium-carbon steel castings contain from 0.20 to 0.50% carbon, and high-carbon steel castings contain more than 0.50% carbon. Cast steels containing more than 1.00% manganese, 0.80% silicon, 0.50% nickel, 0.50% copper, 0.25% chromium, 0.10% molybdenum, 0.05% vanadium, and 0.05% tungsten are normally considered alloy steel castings. When the percentage of alloying elements, including carbon, is 8% or less, the cast steel is considered low-alloy cast steel. In low-alloy cast steel, carbon content is generally less than 0.45%.

Carbon steel castings. Medium-carbon steel is used predominantly in carbon steel castings for a variety of applications. Some of these applications include equipment for machinery and tools, rolling mills, mining, road building, and building construction, and in the railroad and other transportation industries. Low-carbon steel castings are used in the automotive industry for components that are case carburized and also in manufacturing electrical components, which require good magnetic properties.

Low-alloy steel castings. Several types of low-alloy steel castings are currently being produced. Carbon-manganese steel castings are widely used for producing parts that are subject to dynamic loading and abrasion. Manganese-molybdenum steel castings are used when producing parts for agricultural machinery and equipment, construction equipment, road building machinery, and mining equipment. Manganese-nickel-chromium-molybdenum steel castings are used in structural and dynamic applications that require high yield-strength steels. Nickel steel castings are being used in the production of components operating in low-temperature

environments. Nickel-chromium-molybdenum steel castings are used when producing large castings and parts that are subject to high static and dynamic stresses as in the aircraft industries. Chromium-molybdenum steel castings are used extensively for oil refinery equipment castings. Copper alloy steel castings are used in the logging and excavating industries.

Corrosion-Resistant Cast Steels

Corrosion-resistant, high-alloy steel castings are commonly referred to as cast stainless steels. Alloy composition is based on the alloy designation system adopted by the Alloy Casting Institute (ACI), and the various alloys produced are covered by ASTM A743, A744, A747, and A494 standards.

The principal grades are martensitic, ferritic, precipitation-hardening, austenitic-ferritic, and austenitic. These steels are generally used when manufacturing chemical processing and power generating equipment to resist corrosion in aqueous or liquid-vapor environments at temperatures below 600° F (315° C).

Martensitic grades. Martensitic cast stainless steels are those alloys beginning with the designation CA. This type of steel has good resistance to atmospheric corrosion and organic media in mild service. Resistance to seawater corrosion increases with the addition of molybdenum. Martensitic cast stainless steels are used when manufacturing pumps, compressors, valves, hydraulic turbines, propellers, and machinery components.

Ferritic grades. Ferritic cast stainless steels are usually those alloys beginning with the designations CB and CC. However, there are also precipitation-hardening alloys designated with CB. The ferritic grade is nonhardenable.

Alloys beginning with CB have a greater resistance to corrosives than alloys beginning with CA, but have a low impact strength. They are generally used when manufacturing valve bodies and trim for chemical production and food processing industries. Alloys beginning with CC have good resistance to oxidizing corrosives, mixed nitric and sulfuric acids, and alkaline liquors. They are frequently used when manufacturing components that are in contact with acid mine waters and are used in nitrocellulose production.

Precipitation-hardening grades. Precipitation-hardening cast stainless steels are those alloys designated by CB and CD that are hardenable. Alloy-type CB-7Cu has better corrosion resistance than CA alloys and is generally used when manufacturing components that require high strength and good corrosion resistance, such as components in the aircraft and food processing industries.

Alloy CD-4MCu has approximately twice the strength of the austenitic-ferritic grade of cast stainless steels as well as equal or better corrosion resistance. This alloy is used for pumps, valves, and stressed components in the marine, chemical, textile, and paper industries.

Austenitic-ferritic grades. Cast stainless steel alloys in this grade are designated by CE, CF, and CG. The CF alloys comprise the majority of the corrosion-resistant cast steels currently being produced and are used in a variety of general purpose applications as well as in applications requiring resistance to nitric acid and other oxidizing agents.

Alloys designated by CE have good resistance to sulfurous acid and to stress-corrosion cracking in polythionic acid. The CG alloys have better corrosion resistance to sulfuric and sulfurous acid solutions than certain CF alloys but are not suitable for applications requiring resistance to nitric acid or

CAST STEELS

other strongly oxidizing environments.

Austenitic grade. Cast stainless steel alloys in the austenitic grade are designated by *CH*, *CK*, and *CN*. Alloys CH and CK are high-chromium, high-carbon alloys and are used for components that are in contact with paper pulp solutions and nitric acid. The CN-7M alloy contains molybdenum and copper and is used for components in steel mills handling nitric-hydrofluoric pickling solutions and other components that operate in severe service environments.

Heat-Resistant Steel Castings

Cast steels discussed in this section are divided into two groups: (1) those that can be used for service up to 1150°F (620°C) and (2) those that can be used for service above 1150°F (620°C). The steels for use below 1150°F (620°C) are made up of carbon and low-alloy cast steels, and the alloys for service above 1150°F (620°C) are made up of high-alloy cast steels.

Carbon and low-alloy steel castings. The two elements common to this group of cast steels and that contribute to creep resistance are molybdenum and chromium. These steels are covered by ASTM A216, A217, A356, and A389 standards.

High-alloy steel castings. To provide effective resistance to oxidation (scaling) or to corrosive gases, these alloys contain chromium content in excess of 12%. Except for their higher carbon content, these cast steels are similar to corrosion-resistant cast steels. The three principal grades in this group are iron-chromium, iron-chromium-nickel, and iron-nickel-chromium. Various alloys are listed in ASTM standard A297.

Iron-chromium. The alloys belonging to this grade are designated by *HC* and *HD*. Alloy HD has greater strength because of its high nickel content. Iron-chromium alloys can be used for components in load-bearing applications up to 1200°F (649°C) and in lighter load-bearing applications up to 1900°F (1038°C). Some typical components are rabble arms and blades for ore-roasting furnaces, salt pots, and grate bars.

Iron-chromium-nickel. The alloys in this grade are partially or completely austenitic and have higher strength and ductility than iron-chromium alloys. These alloys are designated by *HE*, *HF*, *HH*, *HI*, *HK*, and *HL*. Satisfactory results are obtained in either oxidizing or reducing atmospheres.

Typical applications for HE alloys are ore-roasting furnaces and steel mill furnaces. Alloy HF is used for tube supports and beams in oil refinery heaters, in cement kilns, and in ore-roasting and heat-treating furnaces. Alloy HH is used for manufacturing furnace parts that are not subjected to severe temperature cycling. Alloy HI is used in cast retorts for calcium and magnesium production. Alloy HK is used in the production of jet engines, gas turbines, hydrogen reformer tubes, and furnace parts. Alloy HL exhibits the best resistance to high-sulfur environments up to 1800°F (980°C) and is used in gas dissociation equipment.

Iron-nickel-chromium. These alloys—HN, HP, HT, HU, HW, and HX—are high-nickel steels and normally constitute about 40% of the total production of heat-resistant castings. Nickel is either the predominant alloying element or, in some cases, the base metal. The alloys can be used for most applications up to 2100°F (1150°C) and give excellent service life when subject to rapid heating and cooling. Resistance to thermal fatigue is excellent, but they are not recommended in atmospheres with high sulfur content.

Typical applications for alloy HN are brazing fixtures and highly stressed parts. Alloy HP is used for heat-treat fixtures, radiant tubes, and coils for ethylene pyrolysis heaters. Alloy HT is used for parts in heat-treating furnaces, glass rolls, enameling racks, and radiant heater tubes. Alloy HU is used for manufacturing burner tubes, lead and cyanide pots, retorts, and furnace parts. Alloy HW is used for hearths, mufflers, retorts, trays, boxes, burner parts, enameling fixtures, quenching fixtures, and containers for molten lead. Alloy HX finds the same applications as HW, particularly when improved resistance to hot gas corrosion is required.

PROCESSING STEEL CASTINGS

In order to produce a finished casting with specified dimensions and mechanical properties, several secondary processes are employed. These processes include machining, welding, and heat treating.

Machinability

In general, steel castings have the same machinability as comparable wrought steels. Machinability of carbon and low-alloy steel castings can be improved by altering the microstructure through heat treatment. However, this is only recommended when the production quantity and tool and time savings offset the cost of heat treatment. Plain carbon steel castings usually possess better machining properties than low-alloy steel castings.

The oxide scale or skin of the casting should be removed by abrasive blasting prior to any machining operation. The initial cut should be as deep as possible; for large castings the depth should be 1/4 to 3/8″ (6 to 9.5 mm).

Weldability

Weldability of steel castings is mainly determined by the composition of the steel and the heat treatment performed. Generally, steel castings can be welded by the same processes used when welding wrought steels. These processes include shielded metal arc welding, gas tungsten arc welding, gas metal arc welding, flux-cored arc welding, submerged arc welding, and electroslag welding.

Preheating is usually recommended for carbon or low-alloy steels containing over 0.30% carbon to reduce the rate at which heat is extracted from the heat-affected zone (HAZ), relieve mechanical stress, prevent underbead cracking, and minimize hardening in the HAZ. Preheat temperatures are given in the ASTM specifications for the particular grade of steel. Corrosion-resistant cast steels do not generally require preheating; but in many cases, the weld is cooled between passes. Reheat treatment is usually required after welding to restore corrosion resistance at the welds.

Heat Treatment

Steel castings are heat treated to improve the as-cast structure and the mechanical properties. The customary heat treatments are annealing, normalizing, and normalizing and tempering. It is also common to quench and temper steel castings when the size, shape, and composition are not prone to serious distortion and cracking during quenching.

CAST IRONS

The term "cast iron" is a generic term that designates an entire family of cast ferrous metals. These metals possess a wide variety of properties that distinguish them from the family of steels. In composition, both steels and cast irons are primarily iron that is alloyed with carbon. However, steels always contain less than 2% combined carbon (and usually less than 1%), while cast irons contain more than 2% carbon. The carbon in cast iron is generally in the free state except for a maximum 0.65% combined carbon. Cast irons must also contain appreciable amounts of silicon, usually from 1 to 3%. These differences are not arbitrary, but have a metallurgical basis and effect the differing useful properties of these two families of ferrous alloys.

Because of the high carbon and silicon content, cast irons possess excellent casting characteristics and can be melted more easily than steels. Molten cast iron also flows better than molten steel and is less reactive with the molding material because of a lower pouring temperature. Shrinkage and contraction of cast iron during solidification are nominal and easily compensated for. High-strength parts can be cast close to machine dimensions with minimum material to machine off and discard. Machinability is very good since most of the carbon is in the free state. Since most cast irons are not as ductile as steels, they are not usually rolled or forged.

TYPES OF CAST IRON

In most irons, an appreciable portion of the carbon content precipitates during solidification and appears as a separate constituent in the microstructure of the iron. The form and shape in which the excess carbon occurs determine the type of cast iron and establish the nature of its properties. The structure of the matrix metal around the carbon-rich constituent establishes the class of iron within each category.

The five basic types of cast iron are white iron, malleable iron, gray iron, ductile iron, and compacted graphite iron. In white iron, the majority of carbon occurs as the compound iron-carbide, which is a very hard constituent. Malleable iron is characterized by having most of the contained carbon present in irregularly shaped nodules of temper carbon that forms after annealing. Gray iron has the carbon occurring as graphite flakes. In ductile iron, the graphite occurs in spheres; and in compacted graphite iron, the graphite occurs primarily as stubby flakes with some spheres possible.

A sixth type of iron is composed of the high-alloy irons. High-alloy irons are white, gray, or ductile irons containing appreciable amounts of alloying elements, generally in excess of 3%. Their properties are not just modified, but may be essentially different from those of the base iron. Because of the high alloy content, special facilities are usually required for producing high-alloy iron castings.

White Cast Iron

White cast irons differ from other irons in that they contain little or no graphite due to their chemical composition and rapid cooling rate during solidification. Virtually all the carbon present is chemically combined with the iron as iron carbide, a very hard and brittle substance. Since the iron carbide, also called cementite, dominates the microstructure, white iron is essentially hard and brittle and has a white crystalline fracture.

White irons are very high in compressive strength, excellent in wear resistance, and retain their hardness even up to a red heat. However, they are brittle and are not machinable under normal circumstances. The properties can be varied within a limited range by the amount of iron carbide in the structure and the nature of the matrix structure that surrounds it.

Applications. White cast iron is used in applications requiring good wear and abrasive-resistant characteristics. Certain compositions of white iron are used as base metals in the production of malleable cast iron.

Specifications. Standard specifications for unalloyed and low-alloy white cast irons have not been established. Generally, unalloyed and low-alloy white irons can be specified by hardness ranging from 300 to 600 Bhn. The lower hardness values are characteristic of the lower carbon content irons that are a little tougher, but not as wear resistant as the harder irons. Maximum hardness and wear resistance can be obtained with the high-alloy white irons.

Malleable Iron

Malleable iron has the major portion of its carbon content occurring in the microstructure as irregularly shaped nodules of temper carbon. The structure is obtained by first producing a white cast iron casting having the correct composition. The casting is then heat treated at a temperature over 1750° F (950° C) for an extended period of time. During the heat treatment, the iron carbide dissociates and graphite precipitates in the iron matrix. This form of graphite has been called "temper carbon" because it is formed in the solid state during heat treatment. Heat treatment is done in a controlled atmosphere to prevent loss of carbon from the surface. Depending on the type of heat treatment performed, the matrix obtained after heat treatment gives ferritic or pearlitic malleable iron, each of which serves specific purposes and possesses a variety of typical characteristics.

Malleable iron is comparatively strong, ductile, and tough and has machining characteristics comparable to gray iron. It has higher toughness and fatigue strength than gray iron and can be surface hardened to produce good wear resistance. The rapid solidification required to form the preliminary white iron limits the thickness that is practical for a malleable iron casting to about 3" (75 mm).

Malleable iron castings are widely used in the automotive, agricultural equipment, and railroad industries. Some typical applications include universal joint yokes, rear axle housings, crankshafts, connecting rods, rocker arms, transmission gear components, hand tools, and plumbing fittings. Specifications for the composition and heat-treating practices when producing malleable iron can be found in the American Society for Testing and Materials (ASTM) Standards A47, A197, A220, A338, and A602.

Gray Iron

Because most of the iron castings produced are of gray iron, the generic term cast iron is commonly used when gray iron is intended. The name comes from the characteristic gray color of the metal on a fractured surface. The gray color is caused by the

CAST IRONS

presence of graphite flakes in the iron that are formed when the carbon in the iron separates during solidification. Special foundry practices are necessary to obtain the correct form of graphite.

The amount of graphite present, as well as its size and distribution, is important to the properties of gray iron. The different sizes of graphite tend to enhance certain properties of gray iron. The large (Type C) graphite flakes improve thermal shock resistance by increasing the thermal conductivity and lower the modulus of elasticity to minimize thermal stresses. Coarse flakes, on the other hand, are not conducive to a good machine finish or to strength. A very small size of flake graphite (Type D) promotes a fine machine finish by minimizing surface pitting, but it is difficult to obtain a pearlitic matrix with this type of graphite. There are, of course, many casting applications in which the type of graphite is of lesser consequence as long as the mechanical property requirements are met.

The size and shape of the graphite have no direct influence on the soundness of the casting. An iron with coarse graphite, often referred to as open-grained iron, may have a pitted surface when machined because of the breakout of material in machining, but this condition is not an indication of unsoundness or porosity.

A classification system for graphite in iron castings has been established by the ASTM. Specification A-247 is entitled "Standard Method for Evaluating the Microstructure of Graphite in Iron Casting."

Applications. Gray cast irons are used in a variety of structural steel applications that do not require impact resistance and high tensile strength. Some of these applications include engine blocks, cylinder heads, housings, manifolds, hydraulic valve bodies, and other components having complex design. Gray cast irons are also used in manufacturing components requiring vibration damping characteristics and resistance to heat checking and heat shock. Typical examples of these components are clutch plates, brake drums, ingot and pig molds, machine tool members, and piano plates.

Specifications. Gray irons are usually specified by their hardness or tensile strength. Chemical analysis is specified only for special types of irons such as those used in elevated temperatures.

The most commonly used gray iron specification for general engineering application is the ASTM A-48. This specification designates the minimum tensile strength of the iron as determined in a test bar of the size that is comparable with the critical section of the casting.

Ductile Iron

Ductile iron is similar in composition to gray iron but has a very restricted content on minor elements. A very small but definite amount of magnesium with cerium is added to the molten iron, which causes the graphite to nucleate in spheres or spherulites rather than individual flakes. Special control procedures must be employed when processing ductile iron to prevent excessive losses of magnesium. Magnesium prevents the free carbon from precipitating in nonspheroidal shapes.

The high carbon and silicon contents of ductile iron retain the advantages of the casting processes and the excellent machinability of gray iron; but the number, shape, and size of the graphite spheroids have an important influence on the functional properties of the casting. Ductile iron has a higher modulus of elasticity than gray iron, with a somewhat linear stress/strain relationship; a very good range of yield strength, fatigue strength, and impact resistance; and, as its name implies, excellent ductility. Castings are made in a wide range of sizes and in very thin to very thick sections.

Applications. Ductile iron castings combine strength, durability, and toughness with good machinability and low cost. In the automotive and allied industries, ductile iron is used in the production of crankshafts, connecting rods, gears, steering knuckles, idler arms, disc brake calipers, and rocker arms. In the chemical industry, ductile iron is used in both subzero and elevated temperature environments to produce valves, fittings, and pump bodies. Ductile iron castings are also used in the production of machinery for a variety of industries. The controllability and reliability of ductile iron has produced successful applications in safety-related products. Low-cost silicon alloys are used for high-temperature oxidation resistance and thermal stability such as in turbo-charger housings.

Specifications. The various grades of regular, unalloyed ductile iron are designated by their tensile properties. Different grades are produced by obtaining different matrix microstructures in the iron as cast or by subsequent heat treatment. The chemical analyses of the different grades are essentially the same, but may be varied to ensure the formation of the desired matrix microstructure. Alloying elements may be added to ductile iron to enhance as-cast properties and hardenability and to facilitate heat treatment. High-alloy ductile irons are also produced for special requirements.

The common grades of ductile iron based on tensile strength are covered by ASTM A536 and several other specifications. The SAE specification for ductile iron casting, J434c, covers similar grades but specifies them only by Brinell hardness and microstructure. There are a number of other specifications for ductile iron in special service castings such as at elevated temperatures or with a maximum impact resistance at low temperatures.

Compacted Graphite Iron

Compacted graphite (CG) iron is the newest member of the cast iron family. Although it was originally identified as a distinct type of cast iron at the same time ductile iron was discovered, it was not until improved production techniques became available in the late 1970s that the material attracted widespread commercial interest. Other names for CG iron are compacted flake graphite (CFG) iron, quasi-flake graphite iron, vermicular graphite iron, and compacted vermicular graphite iron (CVI). These names refer to the stubby, interconnected graphite flake structure.

Compacted graphite irons possess lower strength and ductility levels than ductile irons, but have machinability characteristics and thermal conductivity values that are close to gray irons. The casting properties of CG iron, such as shrinkage and mold yield, are superior to those of ductile iron if the amount of spheroidal graphite is restricted.

Applications. Compacted graphite irons are being used in the production of engine parts, hydraulic components, and ingot molds. Typical engine components include cylinder heads and blocks, flywheels, bearing caps, and exhaust manifolds.

Specifications. While compacted graphite irons are being used for a number of casting applications, the material does not, as yet, have any specifications by national organizations. Both the SAE and the ASTM have committees working on the formulation of specifications for this material at the time of this writing.

High-Alloy Irons

High-alloy irons are a special group of irons consisting of high-alloy gray irons, high-alloy ductile irons, and high-alloy white irons. Alloy content of these irons ranges from 3 to 40%, modifying the properties of the base iron. Malleable irons are not highly alloyed because this would interfere with the metallurgy of the malleable process. Currently, compacted graphite iron has not been highly alloyed.

Applications. High-alloy irons are used in applications requiring excellent corrosion resistance, high heat resistance, and maximum wear resistance. They are also chosen when special magnetic and electrical properties or low thermal expansion are needed.

Specifications. Because the special property requirements of high-alloy irons are often too difficult to establish and verify for specification, these irons are usually specified by their chemical analysis. Mechanical property requirements may also be included when they are critical.

Eight different grades of high nickel content, austenitic gray iron are specified by ASTM A436. The gray irons with high silicon content used for extreme corrosion resistance are specified by ASTM A518. Eight different grades of high nickel content, austenitic ductile irons are specified by ASTM A439. Castings for low-temperature and nonmagnetic services are specified in ASTM A571. Seven different grades of high-alloy white irons are specified by ASTM A532.

MECHANICAL PROPERTIES

Hardness and tensile strength are the most commonly specified properties for iron castings. While hardness and tensile strength relate directly to many useful characteristics in metals, there are two aspects of mechanical properties in general that should be discussed.

1. Dynamic properties relate closer to part function than static tensile properties. Low-temperature capability cannot be measured by tensile tests nor can high strain rate applications be indicated by tensile tests.
2. The mechanical properties of metal, especially iron, are not specific to a particular batch or heat as is the chemical analysis of metal. Properties are also influenced by the section thickness in which the metal solidifies and the manner in which the metal cools.

As an example of the first qualification, hardness is a relatively good indication of machinability; however, gray iron and ductile iron with the same hardness can exhibit appreciable differences in tool life. That is, if the microstructure of either contains some free carbides, machinability is reduced much more than indicated by the small increase in hardness.

The second qualification results from the fact that the properties of iron are directly influenced by the rate of solidification and subsequent cooling. Appreciably different properties in various portions of a casting are apt to occur if the sections have sufficiently large differences in thickness or shape to cause a significant variation in cooling rate. With modern technology, however, castings can be more uniform throughout variously sized sections. Thus, both large and small castings from the same ladle of metal will have similar mechanical properties.

Cast iron test bars should have a cooling rate and composition that is relatively similar to the casting sections they represent. If the casting is of sufficient size, test bars should be cut from the critical areas of the casting and then tested. Test bars that are different in cooling rate than the castings they represent can be used to establish the relative quality of the metal being poured rather than to indicate the actual properties to be obtained in the casting. Often the tensile properties of the metal in a casting can be related to the properties of the test bar by the hardness of each. This is a valid but not a precise relationship when the microstructures are similar.

As a basic concept, hardness is resistance to abrasion or scratching. As it applies to metals, the measurement of hardness is based on the relative resistance to the penetration of an indenter. The most common testing methods for iron—Brinell, Rockwell, Knoop, and Vickers—use this principle. Hardness is the most frequently used test for metal because it is convenient, it is usually nondestructive, and the test results can be related to a number of other properties.

Hardness is not an absolute value, and test results can vary even under ideal conditions. Some impressions of Brinell diameters can vary 0.15 mm in reading when measured by different individuals. In specifying a required hardness, it is important to stipulate where on the casting the hardness is to be determined and a range to allow for variations when reading the impression. Because of the difference in solidification and cooling rate, different portions of the casting may vary in hardness. Edges and thin sections may be of a higher hardness but usually cannot be measured with conventional instruments.

PROCESSING CHARACTERISTICS

One or more secondary operations or processes are usually performed before the casting is placed in service. The most common are machining, welding, and heat treatment. Coining is performed on malleable and ductile iron castings to eliminate or reduce machining. Iron castings can also be coated successfully using organic and inorganic coatings. For additional information on the various coatings and techniques used, refer to the appropriate section in this volume.

Machining

The machinability of iron relates specifically to its microstructure whether the evaluation is tool life, surface finish, or power. The presence of graphite provides the free-machining characteristics of iron, and the shape and amount of graphite establish the potential surface finish obtainable with a cutting process and the necessary cutting force. The microstructure of the metal around the graphite determines the tool life and establishes the most advantageous cutting speeds and feeds.

The relative ease with which iron castings can be machined is one of their important advantages. The annealed grades can be cut at very high speeds without generating burrs and without chip breakers. Coated carbide inserts and ceramic inserts can be used at rates as high as 3000 sfm (915 m/min) with adequate tool life. The harder grades of iron can also be machined economically and at reasonable rates of speed. White irons and high-alloyed irons are usually machined abrasively.[11]

Welding

Iron castings are successfully welded to assemble parts, to correct casting discontinuities, and to make repairs in-service. Welding is also used to apply wear or corrosion-resisting surfaces to iron castings and to rebuild worn or corroded surfaces.[12] Because welding of cast iron is difficult, the proper

CAST IRONS

techniques must be carefully followed.

Gray, ductile, and malleable iron castings are weldable by standard welding processes including shielded metal-arc, oxy-fuel gas, braze, and gas metal-arc welding. White iron castings are considered unweldable. The selection of the welding process and the welding filler metal depends on the type of weld properties desired and the service life that is expected.[13]

The welding techniques employed when welding iron castings are designed to restrict penetration to the minimum depth required for proper fusion. This practice minimizes or prevents the base metal from forming a brittle zone at the weld due to the rapid freezing and cooling of the weld metal in the heat-affected zone (HAZ).[14] Preheating is desirable for welding iron castings using any of the welding processes in order to reduce the thermal gradient between the weld and the remainder of the casting. The selection of a preheat temperature is based on the welding process, type of filler metal, and the mass and complexity of the casting. After welding, the casting should be cooled slowly or stress relieved to prevent cracks from occurring and to improve the machinability of the HAZ.

Heat Treatment

Most iron castings respond to heat treatment, and several types are heat treated in the course of their manufacture. Iron castings are heat treated to relieve internal stresses, improve machinability, and increase toughness, ductility, strength, and wear resistance. The three categories of heat treatment for iron castings are stress relieving, annealing, and hardening. Localized surface hardening can also be performed by induction, flame, laser, or electron-beam hardening techniques.

Stress relief. Castings are often of complex shape and can contain, under some circumstances, appreciable internal or locked-in stress. If allowed to cool in the sand mold in which it is made, a casting will usually be quite free of internal stresses because molding sand is a good insulator. However, this arrangement is not always possible because of the production method or the need for air cooling to obtain a desired hardness range. Stresses can also result from subsequent processing.

Stress relieving involves heating the casting to a high enough temperature to permit the stresses to relax. For the lower classes of gray iron, 900-1100°F (480-590°C) is generally satisfactory. The high-strength irons and alloyed irons usually require a temperature of 1200°F (650°C) for satisfactory relief of the stresses. After a suitable time and temperature, usually one hour after complete equalization of temperature, the casting must be slowly cooled so that the stresses are not reintroduced. Stress relieving can decrease the hardness and strength of higher hardness castings.

Annealing. Annealing of irons provides minimum hardness and maximum machinability. Some types of iron are fully annealed when they are produced. The annealing of other grades will, of course, reduce their mechanical properties as well as their hardness.

Hardening. The hardness of iron castings can be increased by heat treatment to provide excellent wear resistance or higher strength. The hardening of iron is similar to that for steel except that the critical temperature for iron is increased by its silicon content. Low-silicon irons, such as some malleable irons, should be quenched from temperatures high enough to redissolve the carbon and to provide good depth of quench, varying from 1600 to 1650°F (870 to 900°C). Austempering may require temperatures up to 1700°F (925°C). Ductile iron with 2.5% silicon may require a hardening temperature over 1650°F (900°C). Because of their high carbon content, irons have relatively high hardenability, which can be further increased by alloy additions. Malleable iron requires a lower temperature of quenching media than ductile iron since it possesses a lower hardenability.

Surface hardening by induction heating, laser heating, electron-beam heating, or flame heating plus quenching of working surfaces is commonly performed on iron castings to provide a full, hard working surface with a minimum of internal stress and distortion. Surface hardening creates surface stresses on the workpiece that help to improve fatigue strength. For this process, the casting should not be of the fully annealed type but should have a pearlitic or tempered martensite matrix. Although ferritic irons can be satisfactorily furnace hardened with special processing techniques, the short time at temperature in the flame or induction heating does not allow sufficient time for adequate carbon to diffuse across the ferrite matrix.

Air hardening or normalizing of small and moderately sized castings after furnace heating usually results in a pearlitic matrix with higher hardness and strength than castings in the as-cast or annealed condition. Some castings, depending on size and shape, may require a higher manganese content or other alloy additions to achieve these characteristics with air cooling. Complex castings should generally be stress relieved after normalizing. Oil quenching is practical for crankshafts, gear blanks, and similar castings. More complex castings may be subject to quench cracking. Quenching should be followed immediately by tempering.

HIGH-PERFORMANCE ALLOYS

High-performance alloys are a group of alloys used in applications requiring high strength and/or corrosion resistance over a wide range of temperatures. The high-strength, heat-resistant alloys are commonly referred to as superalloys in the aircraft and aerospace industries.

High-performance alloys achieve some of their high-temperature strength characteristics through solid-solution strengthening or a combination of solid-solution strengthening and precipitation hardening. However, high-temperature strength as well as ambient temperature strengths are also improved by second-phase particle strengthening. Carbides and gamma-prime-type precipitates function as second-phase strengtheners, with carbides playing a minor role in alloys of the gamma prime precipitate type and a major role in the solid-solution type.

The solid-solution strengthening in high-performance alloys comes from the presence of cobalt, chromium, iron, molybdenum, columbium, and tungsten elements in the face-centered cubic structure of the matrix. Of these elements, tungsten, molybdenum, cobalt, and chromium have the greatest strengthening effect.

The carbides in high-performance alloys are of various

types depending on the particular alloy composition and the thermal conditions to which the material has been exposed. The carbides change from one form to another as the thermal conditions vary with time. Titanium carbides tend to be very stable; molybdenum, tungsten, and columbium carbides are moderately stable; and chromium carbides tend to be somewhat unstable. In some alloys used primarily for corrosion-resistant applications, carbon is kept at very low levels because carbides tend to lower corrosion resistance; in particular, intergranular corrosion resistance is lowered when the carbides precipitate at grain boundaries.

Gamma-prime-type precipitates are used in iron, iron-nickel, and nickel-based alloys that contain from 1 to 10% by weight of combinations of aluminum, titanium, and/or columbium. The alloys with the higher amounts of gamma prime formers can be strengthened most.

In high-temperature applications, the oxidation resistance of high-performance alloys is as important as high-temperature strength. Oxidation behavior is complex due to the number of elements involved. In simple terms, the oxidation resistance is primarily due to the adherent surface oxide film that forms as a result of the added elements. Chromium plays a large role in the high-oxidation resistance. Chromium levels of over 15% by weight are normally required to achieve acceptable oxidation resistance. Aluminum and titanium can add to the oxidation resistance at any given chromium level. However, high-performance alloys with the highest strengths above 1200°F (650°C) must have the highest chromium contents in order to have adequate oxidation resistance at such high temperatures. Excessively high chromium can cause reversals in gamma-primetype strengthening. Therefore, chromium levels above 20% are not used in these alloys.

For uniform corrosion resistance, molybdenum, chromium, and nickel contents are increased. Molybdenum improves resistance in nonoxidizing acids, chromium improves resistance in oxidizing environments, and nickel improves resistance in alkaline environments. Pitting corrosion can be improved by additional amounts of molybdenum and chromium. Increased amounts of nickel and molybdenum improve resistance to stress-corrosion cracking.[15]

TYPES OF HIGH-PERFORMANCE ALLOYS

High-performance alloys encompass a wide range of complex materials.[16] It is difficult to define the term "high performance" precisely because it has broader or narrower limits depending upon who is using the word. In this chapter, a high-performance alloy is defined as one developed for elevated temperature, above 1000°F (535°C), and/or corrosion plus oxidation resistance service, usually based on Group VIII A elements. The high-strength, heat-resistant alloys encounter relatively severe multidirectional, often cyclical fatigue-type mechanical stressing and require high surface stability as well as internal structure quality.

Nickel-Based Alloys

Nickel-based alloys generally have greater resistance to high temperatures than low-alloy steels and stainless steels. These alloys contain 30-75% nickel and up to 35% of both chromium and cobalt. Iron content ranges from relatively small amounts to as much as 35% in certain alloys. Aluminum, titanium,

niobium, molybdenum, and tungsten are added to enhance either strength and/or corrosion plus oxidation resistance.

Cobalt-Based Alloys

Cobalt-based alloys contain over 38% cobalt, 20% chromium, usually some nickel, and substantial percentages of molybdenum and/or tungsten for strengthening. These alloys are divided into three main groups. The first group consists of those alloys used in high-temperature applications. They maintain their strength at temperatures from 1200 to 2100°F (650 to 1150°C).

Iron-Based Alloys

Iron-based alloys contain over 12% chromium, at least 9% nickel, and varying amounts of molybdenum, tungsten, cobalt, and titanium. Strengthening of these alloys is usually by precipitation hardening; however, some of these alloys are solid-solution strengthened.

APPLICATIONS

High-performance alloys are relatively expensive and are therefore used only in applications where their special properties are essential to the satisfactory performance of the component. Their special properties include excellent strength and toughness at elevated temperatures and superior resistance to oxidation and corrosion. The maximum temperature for high-performance alloys usually does not exceed 1740°F (950°C). Each alloy has different levels of properties, and selection for a particular application is based on the match between its properties and the needs of the service to be performed.[17]

High-performance alloys are used for chemical and petrochemical processing equipment, industrial furnaces and related heat treating equipment, jet engines, rocket engines, and a variety of other applications involving strenuous service conditions imposed by oxidizing and corrosive atmospheres over a wide range of temperatures.

MACHINING AND FABRICATING CHARACTERISTICS

High-performance alloys are difficult to machine and fabricate because they are designed to have high strengths and excellent surface stability even in aggressive environments.[18] The mechanical properties that make them particularly useful in such environments also make high-performance alloys difficult to machine, form, or weld. However, if careful attention is paid to the metallurgical factors involved, these special materials can be fabricated effectively.

Machining

In comparison to steel, high-performance alloys have low machinability ratings (Fig. 15-2). Some of the characteristics that contribute to difficulty in machining include high strength at elevated temperatures, high resistance to shear loads, presence of abrasive particles in the microstructure, low thermal conductivity, and rapid work hardening. Because of severe work hardening, very high surface stresses may remain in machined components. The stresses can cause distortion and/or premature service failure. Therefore, careful attention to the recommended machining practices is important. Machining

HIGH PERFORMANCE ALLOYS

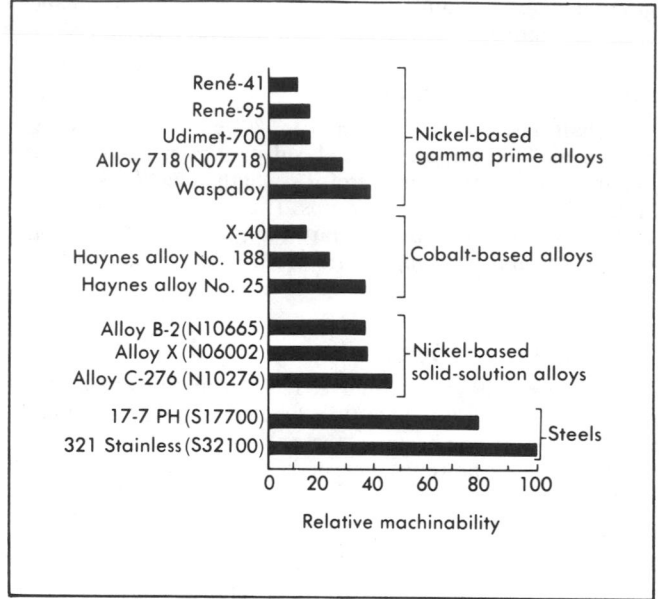

Fig. 15-2 Relative machinability ratings of high-performance alloys.

high-performance alloys typically requires high torques, slow cutting speeds, and machine tools with a high degree of rigidity.

Machinability can be improved by a solution anneal followed by a rapid cool down to ambient temperature. Cutting tools made from high-speed steels containing generous amounts of cobalt are recommended for drilling, tapping, milling, and broaching. Carbide cutting tools tend to be more satisfactory for turning, reaming, and face milling. The carbide grades containing modest amounts of tantalum carbide (TaC) have better abrasion resistance than straight carbide grades. Ceramic (aluminum oxide) cutting tools are not normally used because they are too fragile and chips adhere to the aluminum oxide, thus shortening tool life.

Machining operations on high-performance alloys should be continuous because they work harden, which accelerates tool deterioration for interrupted machining. For most alloys, cutting depths of 0.040 to 0.080″ (1.0 to 2.0 mm) and cutting speeds of 32 to 130 sfm (10 to 40 m/min) are generally satisfactory. Premature tool failure results from too fast a cutting speed.

High-performance alloys can also be ground using bonded aluminum oxide or silicon carbide wheels. Wheel wear can be from 3 to 30 times greater than for steels, depending upon the specific alloy and other operating parameters.

Nontraditional machining methods such as electrochemical machining, electrical discharge machining, and electrochemical grinding can also be used in the machining of high-performance alloys.

Hot Working

High-performance alloys are quite resistant to hot deformation and thus require large forces to work them. In the initial breakdown of ingots to make wrought products, these alloys tend to have relatively narrow ranges of temperatures in which they may be worked. The range is usually around ±270° F (150° C), the recommended temperature. Too high a temperature

causes incipient melting, and too low a temperature results in poor workability. Some precipitation-hardenable, nickel-based alloys are occasionally encased in other less sensitive alloys during primary breakdown to minimize surface cracking. In general, most high-performance alloys require more reheating operations during forming than do the more common alloys.

Once the cast structure is thoroughly broken up by deformation processing, the working temperature range is broader. However, it is important to keep the workpiece within relatively narrow temperature limits because the required working forces rapidly increase as the temperature decreases.

Cold Working

Cold working of high-performance alloys is common, and there are no major difficulties associated with this popular fabrication technique. These alloys work harden more rapidly than steels, and some care is necessary to ensure that they are not worked extensively before annealing. High forces are generally required to form these materials. A high-temperature anneal, followed by a rapid cool down to ambient temperature, is usually recommended for best cold working results. The anneal temperature, however, must be carefully selected; too high a temperature will dissolve carbides that can cause cracking in the heat-affected zone if the component is to be subsequently welded.

Welding

Welding is an essential step in the fabrication of high-performance alloys because it permits the joining of subcomponents into high-integrity fabricated parts with very little increase in weight, and at reasonable cost. In joining high-performance alloys, it is important that the joint area have properties as nearly like those of the base material as practical. Although some degradation of properties from those of the base material is to be expected in a weld, the overall properties of a welded joint are generally as good as, or better than, the properties of joints made by nonwelding methods.

In general, solid-solution-strengthened alloys have welding characteristics similar to those of austenitic stainless steels and can be welded by a variety of methods; shielded metal arc is the most popular. Gas metal arc, gas tungsten arc, and resistance welding techniques can also be employed. Oxyacetylene welding is not normally used because of the susceptibility of these alloys to carbon and oxygen pickup.

Precipitation-hardening alloys are usually welded by the gas tungsten arc method, but several other methods are also used. Heat input should be held to a moderately low level to obtain the highest joint efficiency. For multiple-bead or multiple-layer welds, several small beads should be used instead of a few large, heavy beads. The oxide films should be removed to ensure good fusion and to prevent laminar oxide inclusions.

Rigid or complex structures must be assembled and welded with care to avoid excessively high stress levels. Units or subassemblies should be given sufficient annealing treatments to ensure a low level of residual stress when they are precipitation hardened. Any part that has been subjected to severe bending, drawing, or other forming operations should be annealed before it is welded.

Heat Treatment

The heat treatment of high-performance alloys depends on their composition, the size and shape of the products, and the

REFRACTORY METALS AND TITANIUM

application. Some of the most common treatments performed include solution treating, solution treating and aging, stress relieving, and annealing.

Precipitation-strengthened alloys are solution treated prior to and after cold working to reduce the strength and increase the formability. Aging after a solution treatment strengthens these alloys. Optimum strengthening of the heavily alloyed, solid-solution-strengthened alloys is achieved by a full solution treatment and rapid cooling. Stress relieving is performed on alloys that are not age hardenable to remove residual stresses caused by hot or cold working. Annealing is generally improves high-performance alloy machinability.

REFRACTORY METALS AND TITANIUM

Tungsten and molybdenum are included among the refractory metals, all of which have exceptionally high melting points. A drawback is that tungsten and molybdenum oxidize readily above 1400° F (600° C). Other common characteristics of tungsten and molybdenum (and other refractory metals) are:

- Excellent strength at high temperatures.
- Low coefficient of expansion.
- High elastic modulus.
- Exceptional resistance to corrosion.
- High resistance to thermal shock.
- Good electrical and heat conducting properties.
- High density and specific gravity (tungsten, not molybdenum).
- High hardness properties at elevated temperatures.

In general terms, "refractory" means resistant to heat or capable of enduring high temperatures.

Titanium is not classified as a refractory metal; however, it does have a unique set of characteristics and properties, including a high melting point and a high strength-to-weight ratio at elevated temperatures. It also has good stiffness properties, having a much higher modulus than the other light metals, aluminum and magnesium. Titanium alloys generally exhibit good creep strengths, over a wide range of temperatures.

TUNGSTEN

Chemically, tungsten is relatively inert. It is not readily attacked by the common acids, alkalies, or aqua regia (mixture of nitric and hydrochloric acids). It reacts with a mixture of concentrated nitric acid an hydrofluoric acid. Molten oxidizing salts such as sodium nitrite attack tungsten rapidly. Gaseous chlorine, bromine, iodine, carbon dioxide, carbon monoxide, and sulfur react with tungsten only at high temperatures. Carbon, boron, silicon, and nitrogen also form compounds with tungsten at elevated temperatures; hydrogen does not.

Applications

When added to iron or steel, tungsten improves high-temperature strength and hardness. More than 75% of the tungsten produced is used in ferrous and aluminum alloys and in tungsten carbide for cutting tools.

A well-known use for tungsten is in the filament material for electric light bulbs. Pure tungsten metal in the form of wire, rod, and sheet is important in the electric lamp and electrical industries. Industrial applications include electrodes for inert gas welding and electrical discharge machining.

Small shapes of tungsten sintered to various densities and porosities are used as filters and in probes for ultrasonic nondestructive testing. Tungsten is also used for high inertia devices and for balancing masses. Because of tungsten's high density, a flywheel or balance weight made from tungsten requires only one-third as much space as a steel component.

Some inertial devices use a tungsten-nickel-copper alloy that is more machinable than pure tungsten.

Welding and Bonding

Manganese containing 16% (by weight) of nickel, 16% cobalt, and 1% boron is an effective tungsten-to-tungsten vacuum-brazing alloy. If tungsten parts are to be soft-soldered, they should be precoated with copper. To minimize loss of ductility in tungsten-to-tungsten spot welds, the spot welding is sometimes done with the parts under water. Tungsten surfaces to be joined should be mechanically cleaned, chemically etched, or preheated in hydrogen at 1200° F (650° C).

Arc welds or electron-beam welds in powder-metallurgy tungsten have considerable porosity. Welding should be done at a high speed to avoid excessive heat input.

Tungsten is embrittled more by melting during welding than by high-temperature exposure in a protective atmosphere or under a protective coating. Pressure-diffusion bonding can therefore join the metal without damaging it. Two pieces of tungsten can be united in the fraction of a second necessary for resistance welding or for impulse bonding, or joining by autoclave pressure bonding may require 24 hours.

Fabrication

Deformation processing of tungsten usually begins with primary reduction and ingot breakdown by a compressive process, such as extrusion, before secondary fabrication, machining, and surface finishing are feasible. The reduction process is usually the only means of working an ingot of tungsten without cracking it. The crude metal is converted into a shape such as tube stock or sheet, or bar stock suitable for secondary working by rolling, swaging, or drawing into final shape.

MOLYBDENUM

Molybdenum is similar to tungsten in most of its properties. Its most serious limitation is the ready formation of a volatile oxide at a temperature of approximately 1400° F (760° C). In the worked form, molybdenum is inferior to tungsten in melting point, tensile strength, vapor pressure, and hardness. But, in the recrystallized condition, molybdenum's ultimate strength and elongation are higher.

REFRACTORY METALS AND TITANIUM

Alloys

Molybdenum can be alloyed with several other metals to enhance its special properties, but only two alloy groups are produced commercially: (a) TZM, which is molybdenum alloyed with 0.5% titanium and 0.1% zirconium, for high-temperature structural applications and (b) an alloy comprising 70% molybdenum and 30% tungsten, which is resistant to attack by molten zinc.

Unalloyed molybdenum and its two principal alloys cannot be hardened by heat treatment. The hardness and strength of mill products and forgings are developed by working the metal below its recrystallization temperature. To develop an optimum combination of strength and toughness, the technically "cold worked" products are usually stress relieved by heating them to temperatures below the recrystallization temperature. Unalloyed molybdenum and its two commercial alloys are available in the various common wrought, mill product forms: forging billets, tubes, bars, rods, wire, plate, sheet, strip, and foil.

Applications

The high-temperature strength of molybdenum is responsible for most of the metal's industrial applications. As shown in Fig. 15-3, TZM molybdenum alloy retains good tensile strength properties at temperatures in excess of 2000° F (1093° C). Steels and nickel-based superalloys are inferior to molybdenum in this respect. As stated previously, molybdenum and its alloys do, however, oxidize rapidly in air at temperatures above 1400° F (760° C); hence, they are suitable for high-temperature usage only in vacuum or inert atmospheres.

Unalloyed molybdenum. The principal uses for unalloyed molybdenum are in mandrels for the production of coiled tungsten filaments and the support wires for these filaments in incandescent light bulbs; semiconductor support disc; electrodes for heating molten glass; reflectors (heat shields) and heating elements for vacuum furnaces or special atmosphere furnaces; magnetron components; resistance welding electrodes; electrodes for electrical discharge machines; anodes, grids and supports in vacuum tubes; X-ray targets; and mirrors for laser beams.

Alloy applications. Where high strength and resistance to thermal fatigue are required at high temperatures, the TZM alloy is used. The elevated temperature tensile strength of TZM is compared to the elevated temperature strengths of two popular steels recommended for high-temperature applications in Fig. 15-3. It can be observed that TZM in the fully recrystallized (annealed) condition is superior to the 2.25% Cr-1% Mo steel at temperatures over 400° F (200° C) and the austenitic Type 316 stainless steel at temperatures above 1500° F (815° C).

The 70% molybdenum-30% tungsten alloy has excellent resistance to corrosive attack by molten zinc, but it exhibits no significant improvement over unalloyed molybdenum with respect to mechanical properties at elevated temperatures. For this reason its principal commercial applications are limited to the processing and transfer of molten zinc. Zinc processors and industries concerned with galvanizing use the 70-30 alloy for stirrers, pump impellers and shafts, and piping.

Fabrication

Sheet products can be formed, deep drawn, or spun to produce the desired shapes. Forming, drawing, and spinning are best performed with the metal at temperatures in the range of 300 to 800° F (149 to 427° C). For spinning operations that require large amounts of plastic deformation, or for roll forming of thin-walled tubes, temperatures near 1600° F (871° C) may be advantageous.

If sheet is to be cut to shape by shearing, punching, or blanking, it is recommended that the dies be kept sharp. Thin sheet can be handled at room temperature, but for thick sheet the metal should be heated to about 800° F (427° C) to prevent delamination at the edges. If molybdenum sheet is to be cut to shape with a bandsaw, friction saw, or abrasive wheel, the operation can be accomplished readily at room temperature, but it will be found advantageous to back up the workpiece with a piece of wood or mild-steel plate to reduce chattering and delamination.

Machining

Molybdenum can be machined readily by conventional operations such as sawing, turning, boring, shaping, milling (face milling and end milling), drilling, topping, and threading.

General considerations. No special machines are required to produce parts to accurate dimensions with excellent finishes. With respect to depth of cuts and feeds and speeds, molybdenum and TZM, at hardness levels of 220 to 300 HV50, may be characterized as machining like medium-carbon, low-alloy steel (such as AISI 4340), heat treated to the hardness of R_C 30-35 (300-345 HV50); the chips, however, are generally like the chips generated in the machining of gray cast iron. The hardness values of unalloyed molybdenum and its alloys fall within a fairly narrow range, 160-320 HV; powder metallurgy products and arc-melted products machine similarly, although the arc-cast products have less tendency to chip out at edges and usually develop smoother finishes.

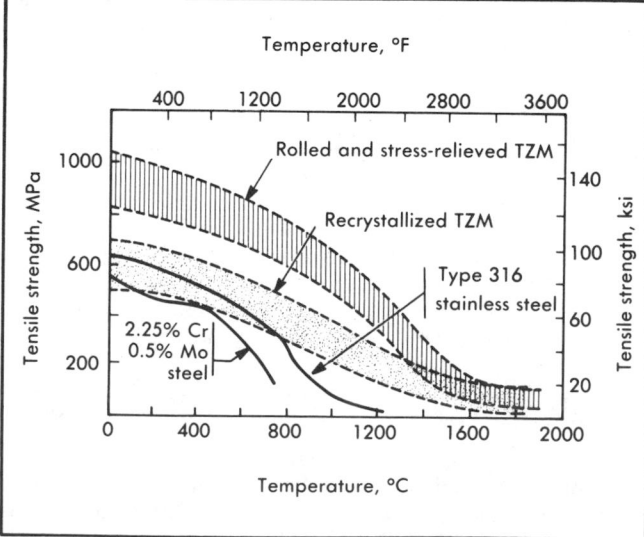

Fig. 15-3 Scatter bands of tensile strength versus temperature for rolled TZM molybdenum bar and curves for two steels that are commonly used at elevated temperatures.

It is important when machining molybdenum that the machines be rigid and free from vibration. The workpieces should be gripped tightly in chucks or vises. For turning and face milling operations, positive rake angles are recommended: near 0° for carbide tools, and up to 20° for high-speed steel tools.

Tooling factors. All molybdenum products may be characterized as "abrasive" due to the generation of fine particles (dust or grit) that separate from the chips during machining. These fine particles wear the cutting edges of high-speed steel tools; therefore, tool life is substantially shorter for a given machine operation on molybdenum than it is for steel. Removal of the chips by an air jet, soluble oils, or cutting fluids can mitigate the decreased tool life, but will not eliminate it. High-speed steel tools usually require more frequent regrinds when they are used to machine molybdenum.

TITANIUM

Titanium has a lower coefficient of expansion and lower thermal conductivity than either steel or aluminum alloys and is nonmagnetic. Titanium exhibits outstanding corrosion resistance to chlorine and its derivatives in oxidizing or neutral aqueous solutions. It resists organic compounds, oxidizing acids, and nonoxidizing acids in low concentrations.

Alloys

In metallurgical terms, the two crystalline forms of titanium are called alpha and beta. The alpha form, which exists at temperatures below 1620° F (882° C), is a close-packed hexagonal crystal structure. The beta phase, which is formed at temperatures above 1620° F, is body-centered cubic.

Pure titanium is soft, weak, and extremely ductile, hence is easily fabricated. With appropriate additions of other elements (mostly metals), the titanium base metal is converted into an engineering material that has unique characteristics, including high strength and stiffness, corrosion resistance, and ductility.

For convenience in differentiating between the various titanium and titanium alloy compositions, the available commercial grades are classified (depending upon the phases that are present in the metal's microstructure at room temperature) as commercially pure (CP) titanium, all-alpha (single phase) weldable alloys, alpha-beta (two phase) weldable alloys, alpha-beta nonweldable alloys, all-beta alloys, beta-lean alpha alloys, and corrosion-resistant alloys.

Commercially pure titanium. This group consists of the unalloyed compositions containing over 99% titanium. The remaining percentage is made up of carbon, nitrogen, oxygen, hydrogen, and iron. Strength levels are influenced significantly by the amounts of oxygen and nitrogen that are present. All of the grades are available in billets, bars, wire, sheet, strip, and tubing, and some can be found in extruded forms.

All-alpha weldable alloys. The hexagonal structure compositions generally have the highest strength at elevated temperatures, 600-1100° F (316-590° C); the best weldability; and, depending on type, the best corrosion resistance. However, in general, these alloys have the lowest room temperature strength and are not heat treatable.

Alpha-beta weldable alloys. The majority of the titanium alloys are of the alpha-beta type. As a group, the alpha-beta alloys have higher strength and respond to heat treatment but are less formable than the commercially pure titanium. All of the alpha-beta alloys are available in bars and billets, and most of the alloys also are offered in sheet form. This class of alloy accounts for more than half of all titanium metal products.

The alpha-beta alloys vary widely in their composition and in their characteristics such as strength, heat treatability, and ductility. The titanium alloy containing 6% Al and 4% V was developed as a forging alloy and is now available in all wrought mill shapes. By far the most commonly used alpha-beta alloy, it is readily weldable (with some sacrifice of joint strength) and is the basic alloy for jet engines and airframes. Through heat treatment, the tensile strength of the 6% Al 4% V alloy can be varied from 120,000 to 180,000 psi (827 to 1241 MPa).

Other alpha-beta weldable alloys include Ti-8Al-1Mo-1V, Ti-6Al-2Sn-4Zr-2Mo, Ti-6Al-2Cb-1Ta-1Mo, Ti-3Al-2.5V, and the new beta-lean alpha alloys.

Alpha-beta nonweldable alloys. The remainder of the alphabeta and the alpha-lean beta alloys are nonweldable by fusion welding, although flash or resistance welding techniques may be used successfully in some cases.

Beta alloys. The titanium beta alloy group formulations contain large amounts of alloying metals. As a result, the beta alloys typically are denser than other titanium alloys. The titanium beta class of alloys is fully heat treatable and cold workable in the solution-treated condition. Welding feasibility has been established for the newer beta alloys, and technical information is available from the suppliers.

Applications

The unique properties of titanium make it the most cost-effective and satisfactory engineering material for many applications. Titanium product uses range from heat exchangers to geothermal power equipment, and from liquefied natural gas condensors to piping and instrumentation for oil exploration. Additional uses include steam turbine blades and nuclear waste containers.

Titanium oxide, TiO_2, a white compound, is used in the production of paint pigment, paper, plastics, glass, and ceramics. Titanium is also added to other metals, such as steel, aluminum, and copper, to attain certain desired properties. About 94% of the titanium raw material produced or imported into the United States is processed into titanium oxide for use as pigment and filler. Only about 6% is used in the production of titanium metal and alloys.

Titanium and its alloys are widely used in aircraft airframes and engines for their strength and fatigue resistance. Since both light weight and medium temperature strength retention are important factors in alloy selection for aerospace, these qualities, plus corrosion resistance, have led to increasing usage of titanium in the aerospace field. Compared with other structural metals, the superior resistance of titanium to the chloride ion accounts for much of the use of titanium in corrosion-resistant applications. This quality, combined with titanium's electrochemical characteristics, has led to many applications in electrochemical devices.

On industrial machines, titanium finds application where high strength is needed and mass effects must be reduced. Examples include high-speed rolls, frames for flying shears, pump shafting, and quick-acting latches. Increasing applications are being made of a recently developed nickel-titanium alloy

REFRACTORY METALS AND TITANIUM

(Nitinol), which has the unusual property of regaining its previous shape when heated.

Fabrication

The use of various metalworking processes for titanium fabrication into end products is handled much like the processing of other high-performance engineering materials, with due regard for titanium's distinctive properties. There are several important differences between titanium and steel or nickel-based alloys. Awareness of these differences enables titanium to be fabricated by techniques similar to those used for stainless steel and nickel-based alloys. Titanium's distinctive characteristics include:

- Lower modulus of elasticity.
- Higher melting point.
- Lower ductility.
- A tendency to gall.
- Sensitivity to welding contamination.

The fabrication of titanium demands close attention to cleanliness. It is not uncommon for metalworking shops that handle several metals to isolate an area solely for titanium. Welding, in particular, requires complete freedom from contaminants that could degrade the properties of titanium. Thus, the work area set aside for titanium should be free of air drafts, moisture, dust, grease, and other contaminants that might affect the weld metal.

Machining. The following are guidelines for machining titanium:

1. Use low cutting speeds. Tool tip temperature is strongly affected by cutting speed, and a low cutting speed will help to minimize tool edge temperature and maximize tool life. Lower speeds are required for titanium alloys than for pure titanium.
2. Maintain high feed rates. Tool temperature is affected less by feed rate than by speed, and the highest rate of feed consistent with good practice should be used. The depth of cut should be greater than the work-hardened layer resulting from the previous cut.
3. Use a generous quantity of cutting fluid. The coolant carries away heat in addition to washing away chips and reducing cutting forces.
4. Maintain sharp tools. Tool wear results in buildup of metal on cutting edges and causes poor surface finish, tearing, and deflection of the workpiece.
5. Do not stop feeding while tool and work are in moving contact. Permitting a tool to dwell in moving contact with titanium can cause work hardening and promote smearing, galling, and seizing. This could lead to total tool breakdown.
6. Use rigid setups. Rigidity of machine tool and workpiece ensures a controlled depth of cut.

Cutting tools for titanium require abrasion resistance and adequate hot hardness, and general-purpose high-speed tool steels (such as Grades M1, M2, M7, and M10) often are suitable. Best results can generally be obtained with more highly alloyed grades (such as Carbide Grades C-2 and C-3).

Forming. The conversion of titanium ingots into mill products such as forging billet, plate, sheet, and tubing is usually done on conventional metalworking equipment. Mills designed to roll and shape stainless or alloy steel are used with only slight modifications. Consequently, titanium and its structural alloys are available in most of the same forms and shapes as stainless steel.

Heating. Fabricating titanium mill products into finished parts is performed on conventional metalworking machinery. During titanium heating operations, it is necessary to avoid the contaminating and embrittling effects of hydrogen, nitrogen, and oxygen. It is critically important to maintain close control of furnace temperatures and atmospheres for heating titanium prior to forging and forming, or for heat treating. During welding operations, the hot and molten titanium metal must be shielded from the atmosphere to avoid brittle welds. Argon or helium gas-shielding techniques are usually used. Titanium and its alloys cannot be welded in air. They cannot be welded to steel, nickel-based alloys, or aluminum. Titanium alloys, however, can be welded to the other reactive metals and to some of the refractory metals for which suitable technical information is available.

Formability. The lowest strength unalloyed grades of titanium have moderately good formability; however, the high-strength unalloyed grades and the alloys require bend radii up to five times the metal thickness. Forming operations must often be done in the temperature range of 400 to 1200° F (204 to 650°C). The beta alloys are an exception; they combine formability and high strength. The low-strength grades of pure titanium have annealed hardnesses in the range of soft steels. Titanium alloys, however, typically have a hardness greater than $R_C 30$ and are difficult to machine. Turning operations are performed readily, but milling and drilling are more difficult.

Powder Metallurgy. The powder metallurgy (PM) process has been instrumental in expanding the applications for titanium. the PM process is attractive from a raw material cost viewpoint because the basic ore refining process produces a sponge product from the magnesium or sodium reduction of $TiCl_4$. Powder metallurgy processing temperatures are a fraction of the melting point of the metal, thus reducing the reactivity problem. A further PM advantage is that substantially fewer processing steps may be needed.

The PM process offers the generic attributes of powder metallurgy products, including fine grain size and homogeneous composition. A further significant advantage of the PM titanium process is its ability to produce near-net-shape components. This advantage may result in lower initial material cost than for ingot metallurgy material and also reduced machining cost.

ALUMINUM

A unique combination of properties makes aluminum a versatile engineering and construction material. It is light in weight, yet some of its alloys have strengths greater than that of structural steel. It has high resistance to corrosion under the majority of service conditions, and no colored salts are formed to stain adjacent surfaces or discolor products that it comes into contact with, such as fabrics in textile operations and solutions in chemical equipment. It has no toxic reaction. The metal can easily be worked into many forms and readily accepts a wide variety of surface finishes.

ALLOY AND TEMPER DESIGNATION[19]

The aluminum alloy and temper designation systems are completely set forth in the American National Standard ANSI H35.1 and in various publications issued by The Aluminum Association. Two numbering formats are employed for designating the individual alloys: one for wrought alloys and another for casting alloys.

In format, the two numbering systems differ only slightly. Designations for wrought alloys consist of four-digit numbers, while casting alloys are designated by a three-digit number followed by a decimal point and a fourth digit. In both systems, the basic temper designation (consisting of capital letters and numerals) follows the alloy designation and is separated from it by a hyphen.

These systems provide a standard means for designating aluminum and its alloys in all product forms   wrought, cast, and ingot—and the tempers in which they are produced.

Wrought Aluminum and Alloys

In the four-digit system used to identify wrought aluminum and aluminum alloys, the first digit indicates the alloy group or principal alloying element. As shown in Table 15-2, the 1xxx series is for minimum aluminum purities of 99.00% and greater, and the 2xxx through 8xxx series group aluminum alloys by major alloying elements. The last two digits identify a specific alloy within a given series or indicate the aluminum purity. The second digit indicates modifications of the original alloy or impurity limits. For codification purposes, an alloying element is any element that is intentionally added for any purpose other than grain refinement and for which minimum and maximum limits are specified.

TABLE 15-2
Designations for Wrought Aluminum Alloy Groups

Group	Alloy Number
Aluminum, 99.00% min and greater	1xxx
Aluminum alloys grouped by major alloying elements:	
Copper	2xxx
Manganese	3xxx
Silicon	4xxx
Magnesium	5xxx
Magnesium and silicon	6xxx
Zinc	7xxx
Other element	8xxx
Unused series	9xxx

Cast Aluminum and Alloys

A system of four-digit numerical designations is used to identify aluminum casting alloys. The first digit indicates the alloy group, as shown in Table 15-3. The 1xx.x series is for aluminum purities of 99.00% and greater, and the 2xx.x through 9xx.x series group aluminum alloys by major alloying

elements. The second two digits identify the aluminum alloy or indicate the aluminum purity. The last digit, which is separated from the others by a decimal point, indicates the product form, i.e., castings or ingot. A modification of the original alloy or impurity limits is indicated by a serial letter before the numerical designation. The serial letters are assigned in alphabetical sequence starting with A but omitting I, O, Q, and X—the X being reserved for experimental alloys. For codification purposes, an alloying element is any element that is intentionally added for any purpose other than grain refinement and for which minimum and maximum limits are specified.

TABLE 15-3
Designations for Aluminum Casting Alloy Groups

Group	Alloy Number
Aluminum, 99.00% min and greater	1xx.x
Aluminum alloys grouped by major alloying elements:	
Copper	2xx.x
Silicon, with added copper and/or magnesium	3xx.x
Silicon	4xx.x
Magnesium	5xx.x
Zinc	7xx.x
Tin	8xx.x
Other element	9xx.x
Unused series	6xx.x

Temper Designation

The temper designation system is used for all forms of wrought and cast aluminum and aluminum alloys except ingot. Significant information about the characteristics and properties of an aluminum alloy is given by the alphanumeric coding that is based on the sequences of basic treatments used to produce the various tempers.

F: As fabricated. Applies to the products of shaping processes in which no special control over thermal conditions or strain hardening is employed. For wrought products, there are no mechanical property limits.

O: Annealed. Applies to wrought products that are annealed to obtain the lowest strength temper, and to cast products that are annealed to improve ductility and dimensional stability. The O may be followed by a digit other than zero.

H: Strain hardened (wrought products only). Applies to products that have their strength increased by strain hardening, with or without supplementary thermal treatments to produce some reduction in strength. The H is always followed by two or more digits.

W: Solution heat treated. An unstable temper applicable only to alloys that spontaneously age at room temperature after solution heat treatment. This designation is specific only when the period of natural aging is indicated—for example, W 1/2 hr.

T: Thermally treated to produce stable tempers other than F, O, or H. Applies to products that are thermally treated, with or without supplementary strain hardening, to produce stable tempers. The T is always followed by one or more digits.

CHAPTER 15

ALUMINUM

PROPERTIES

For aluminum, as for other metals, effective product engineering and manufacturing require an understanding of the material's physical and mechanical properties, its corrosion resistance, and its fabrication, joining, and finishing characteristics.

Typical tensile strengths of aluminum range from as low as 5 ksi (34.5 MPa) for some commercially pure aluminum grades to 90 ksi (620 MPa) or more for high-strength alloys. In the automotive field, commonly used alloys have yield strengths from 18 to 60 ksi (124 to 414 MPa). Young's modulus, an important factor in a material's stiffness and bending strength, is 10×10^6 psi (68.9 GPa) for aluminum.

Aluminum, like steel and the various nonferrous metals, is not a single metal but a family of alloys, each of which has been formulated and developed to provide properties suitable for separate classes or fields of applications.

Effect of Alloying Elements for 1000 Series

The aluminum is of 99% or higher purity. This type has many applications, especially in the electrical and chemical fields. These alloys are characterized by excellent corrosion resistance, high thermal and electrical conductivity, excellent workability, but low strength and mechanical properties. Moderate increases in strength may be obtained by strain hardening. Iron and silicon are the major impurities.

Effect of Alloying Elements for 2000 Series

Copper is the principal alloying elements in this group. These alloys require solution heat treatment to obtain optimum properties. In the heat-treated condition, mechanical properties are similar to, and sometimes exceed, those of mild steel. In some instances, artificial aging is employed to further increase the mechanical properties. This treatment materially increases yield strength, with attendant loss in elongation; its effect on ultimate tensile strength is not as great. The alloys in the 2000 series do not have corrosion resistance as good as most other aluminum alloys, and under certain conditions they may be subject to intergranular corrosion. Therefore, these alloys in the form of sheet are usually clad with a high-purity alloy or a magnesium-silicon alloy of the 6000 series that provides galvanic protection to the core material and thus greatly increases resistance to corrosion. Alloy 2024 is perhaps the best known and most widely used aircraft alloy.

Effect of Alloying Elements for 3000 Series

Manganese is the major alloying element of alloys in this group, which are nonheat-treatable. Because only about 1.5% manganese can be effectively added to aluminum, it is used as a major element in only a few instances. One of these, however, is the popular 3003, which is widely used as a general-purpose alloy for moderate-strength applications requiring good workability. Alloy 3004 is widely used for aluminum can body stock, formed by drawing and ironing operations.

Effect of Alloying Elements for 4000 Series

The major alloying element of this group is silicon, which can be added in sufficient quantities to cause substantial lowering of the melting point without producing brittleness in the resulting alloys. For this reason, aluminum-silicon alloys are used in welding wire and as brazing alloys where a melting point lower than that of the parent metal is required. Most alloys in this series are nonheat-treatable; but when used in welding heat-treatable alloys, they pick up some of the alloying constituents of the latter and respond to heat treatment to a limited extent. The alloys containing appreciable amounts of silicon become dark gray when anodic oxide finishes are applied and hence are in demand for architectural applications.

Effect of Alloying Elements for 5000 Series

Magnesium is one of the most effective and widely used alloying elements for aluminum. When it is used as the major alloying element or with manganese, the result is a moderate-to-high-strength, nonheat-treatable alloy. Magnesium is considerably more effective than manganese as a hardener, about 0.8% magnesium being equal to 1.25% manganese, and it can be added in considerably higher quantities. Alloys in this series possess good welding characteristics and good resistance to corrosion in a marine atmosphere. However, because of possible stress corrosion susceptibility, the higher magnesium content alloys (more than 3% Mg) should not be used in the as-rolled (-HIX) tempers when service temperature above approximately 150°F (66°C) are expected. For such applications, special-H3X tempers are necessary to avoid susceptibility to stress corrosion.

Effect of Alloying Elements for 6000 Series

Alloys in this group contain silicon and magnesium in appropriate proportions to form magnesium silicide, thus making them heat treatable. The major alloy in this series 6061, one of the most versatile of the heat-treatable alloys. Although less strong than most the 2000 or 7000 alloys, the magnesium-silicon (or magnesium-silicide) alloys possess good formability and corrosion resistance, with medium strength. Alloys in this heat treated group may be formed in the T4 temper (solution heat treated but not artificially aged) and then reach full T6 properties by artificial aging.

Effect of Alloying Elements for 7000 Series

Zinc is the major alloying element in this group. When coupled with a smaller percentage of magnesium, the result is a heattreatable alloy of very high strength. Usually other elements such as copper and chromium are also added in small quantities. An outstanding member of this group is 7075, which is among the highest strength alloys available and is used in airframe structures and for parts that are highly stressed.

Effect of Alloying Elements for Cast Alloys

The cast alloys are essentially of two types: (1) alloys wherein the desired mechanical properties are secured by virtue of alloy additions alone and (2) alloys that are subsequently heat treated to improve the properties.

The alloys containing silicon are not only characterized by excellent casting qualities but also exhibit good weldability and freedom from hot-shortness. They are somewhat difficult to machine and, from the standpoint of tool wear, are similar to cast iron.

Many of the sand-casting alloys can be successfully used in

permanent-mold casting, although precise alloy combinations have been developed for this and for die-casting purposes.

Characteristics of Aluminum

Commonly used commercially pure aluminum has a tensile strength of about 13 ksi (90 MPa). Its usefulness as a structural material in this form is thus somewhat limited. By working the metal, as by cold rolling, its strength can be approximately doubled. Much larger increases in strength can be obtained by alloying aluminum with small percentages of one or more other metals such as manganese, silicon, copper, magnesium, or zinc. Like pure aluminum, the alloys are also made stronger by cold working. Some of the alloys are further strengthened and hardened by heat treatments so that aluminum alloys having tensile strengths approaching 100 ksi (690 MPa) are available.

Tempers. A wide variety of mechanical characteristics, or tempers, is available in aluminum alloys through various combinations of cold working and heat treatment. In specifying the temper for any given product, the fabricating process and the amount of cold working involved should be kept in mind. In general, the temper specified should be such that the amount of cold working the metal will receive during fabrication will develop the desired characteristics in the finished products.

Temperature effects. Aluminum and its alloys lose part of their strength at elevated temperatures, although some alloys retain good strength at temperatures from 400 to 500° F (204 to 260° C).

Corrosion Resistance. When aluminum surfaces are exposed to the atmosphere, a thin, invisible oxide skin forms immediately and protects the metal from further oxidation. This self-protecting characteristic gives aluminum its high resistance to corrosion. Unless exposed to some substance or condition that destroys this protective oxide coating, the metal remains fully protected against corrosion. Aluminum is highly resistant to weathering, even in industrial atmospheres that often corrode other metals. It is also corrosion resistant to many acids. Alkalies are among the few substances that attack the oxide skin and therefore are corrosive to aluminum.

Conductivity. Aluminum is one of the two common metals having an electrical conductivity high enough for use as an electric conductor. The conductivity of electric conductor grade 1350 is about 62% of the International Annealed Copper Standard (IACS). Because aluminum has less than one-third the specific gravity of copper, however, a pound of aluminum will go about twice as far as a pound of copper when used for this purpose. Alloying lowers the conductivity somewhat, so that wherever possible the 1350 aluminum is used in electric conductor applications.

Other properties. Aluminum is also an excellent reflector of radiant energy in the entire range of wavelengths from ultraviolet through the visible spectrum to infrared and heat waves, as well as for electromagnetic waves of radio and radar. Aluminum has a light reflectivity of over 80%, which has led to its wide use in lighting fixtures. Aluminum roofing reflects a high percentage of solar radiation; consequently, buildings roofed with this material may be cooler in summer.

Not so well known are the nonmagnetic characteristics of aluminum. Nevertheless, these properties are of great importance for some uses. For example, its nonmagnetic properties make the metal useful for electrical shielding purposes such as in bus-bar housings or enclosures for other electrical equipment.

APPLICATIONS

Aluminum is used extensively in the construction of motor vehicles, railway cars, aircraft, and aerospace equipment. In automobiles, aluminum is used in exterior and interior sheet metal and for trim, grilles, wheels, bumpers, radiators, and air conditioners. A major application is in automatic transmissions. Aluminum alloy castings are used for engine cylinder heads and blocks, crankcases, oil pans, pistons, and many other components of internal combustion engines, including jet engines. Aluminum alloy forgings are widely used in aircraft parts such as propellers and landing gear struts. Toughness, light weight, and heat reflective characteristics have led to aluminum's use for space satellites, moon rockets, and vehicles such as the lunar rover.

In electrical applications, aluminum wire and cable are major products. Underground electrical cables account for a large amount of aluminum usage. Aluminum wiring in residential, commercial, and industrial buildings is also gaining acceptance.

As stated previously, the packaging industry is a large and fast-growing field of application for aluminum. It is used in processing and storage equipment for foods and beverages, as well as in cans, foil, pouches, bags, and other containers. Consumer use includes kitchen utensils, hardware, tools, home appliances, and sporting equipment such as skis, baseball bats, and tennis rackets.

FABRICATION

The ease with which aluminum may be fabricated into any form is one of its most important assets. Often it can compete successfully with lower cost materials having less workability. The metal can be cast by any method known to foundries; it can be rolled to any desired thickness down to foil thinner than paper; aluminum sheet can be stamped, drawn, spun, or roll formed. The metal can also be hammered or forged. Aluminum wire, drawn from rolled rod, can be stranded into cable of any desired size and type. Aluminum's inherent characteristics make it well suited to the extrusion processes, and there is almost no limit to the different shapes in which the metal can be extruded.

Machining

The ease and speed with which aluminum can be machined significantly contributes to the low cost of finished aluminum parts. The metal can be turned, milled, bored, or machined in other ways at the maximum speeds of which most machines are capable. Another advantage of its flexible machining characteristics is that aluminum rod and bar can readily be used in the high-speed manufacture of parts by automatic screw machines.

Joining

Almost any method of joining is applicable to aluminum—riveting, welding, brazing, or soldering. A wide variety of mechanical aluminum fasteners simplifies the assembly of many products. Adhesive bonding of aluminum parts is widely employed, particularly in joining aircraft components.

COPPER

COPPER

Copper is a comparatively heavy metal, with a specific gravity of 8.96 at 68°F (20°C). The melting point is 1981°F (1083°C). The pure element is salmon pink in color and has a bright metallic luster when polished. Copper is nonmagnetic and has very high thermal conductivity and electrical conductivity. Among metals, only silver has a greater electrical conductivity. On a relative basis, with silver rated 100, copper is 95, aluminum 57, and iron 16. The usefulness of copper is derived from its combination of chemical, physical, electrical, and mechanical properties and its abundant supply.

The copper alloys also have the advantages of corrosion resistance, ease of forming, ease of joining, and are available in colors. On the other hand, copper and its alloys have relatively low strength-to-weight ratios and low strengths at elevated temperatures. Some alloys are susceptible to stress-corrosion cracking unless they are stress relieved. Copper and its alloys tend to work harden, and they can be hot or cold worked to increase strength. Ductility can be restored by annealing or in the heating that accompanies welding or brazing operations.

ALLOY DESIGNATION SYSTEM[20]

The Unified Numbering System for Metals and Alloys (UNS) applied to wrought and cast copper and copper alloys evolved from the three-digit system developed by the U.S. copper and brass industry. The original three-digit designations were expanded to five digits, following a prefix letter C.

Alloy Designation Groups

The UNS designation system is an orderly method of identifying and defining coppers and copper alloys. It is not a metallurgical specification system, and the alloy designation numbers have no direct significance with regard to composition and properties. Numbers from C10000 through C79999 denote wrought alloys. Cast alloys are numbered from C80000 through C99999. Within these two categories, the compositions are grouped into the following families of coppers and copper alloys:

Coppers. Pure copper is metal that has a designated minimum copper content of 99.3% or higher and is essentially unalloyed copper.

High-copper alloys. For the wrought products, these are alloys with a designated copper content less than 99.3% but more than 96% that do not fall into any other copper alloy group. The cast high-copper alloys have a designated copper content in excess of 94%, to which silver may be added to create special properties.

Brasses. These alloys contain zinc as the principal alloying element with or without other designated alloying elements such as iron, aluminum, nickel, and silicon.

Wrought. The wrought alloys comprise three main families of brasses: copper-zinc alloys, copper-zinc-lead alloys (leaded brasses), and copper-zinc-tin alloys (tin brasses).

Cast. The cast alloys contain four main families of brasses: copper-tin-zinc alloys (red, semi-red, and yellow brasses); "manganese bronze" alloys (high-strength yellow brasses); leaded "manganese bronze" alloys (leaded high-strength yellow brasses); and copper-zinc-silicon alloys (silicon brasses and bronzes).

Bronzes. Broadly speaking, bronzes are copper alloys in which the major alloying element is not zinc or nickel. Originally "bronze" described alloys with tin as the only or principal alloying element. Today the term is generally used not by itself but with a modifying adjective.

Wrought. For wrought alloys, there are four main families of bronzes: copper-tin-phosphorus alloys (phosphor bronzes), copper-tin-lead-phosphorus alloys (leaded phosphor bronzes), copper-aluminum alloys (aluminum bronzes), and copper-silicon alloys (silicon bronzes).

Cast. The cast alloys have four main families of bronzes: copper-tin alloys (tin bronzes), copper-tin-lead alloys (leaded and high-leaded tin bronzes), copper-tin-nickel alloys (nickel-tin bronzes), and copper-aluminum alloys (aluminum bronzes). The family of alloys known as "manganese bronzes," in which zinc is the major alloying element, is included in the brasses.

Copper nickels. These are alloys with nickel as the principal alloying element, with or without other designated alloying elements.

Copper-nickel-zinc alloys. Known commonly as "nickel silvers," these are alloys that contain zinc and nickel as the principal and secondary alloying elements, with or without other designated elements.

Leaded coppers. These include a series of cast alloys of copper with 20% or more lead, usually with a small amount of silver present, but without tin or zinc.

Special alloys. Alloys with chemical compositions that do not fall into any of the above categories are combined in the category "special alloys."

COPPER AND COPPER ALLOYS

More than 300 standard coppers and alloys are produced by the United States copper and brass industry. As a group, these alloys encompass a wide range of wrought and cast materials that are available in virtually all of the commercial mill and product forms. The fabricated forms will include strip, plate, sheet, pipe, tube, rod, forgings, wire, bar, foil, extrusions, and castings.

Mill Product Terminology

Copper and copper alloy mill products in all their forms are defined in ASTM General Requirements Specifications. ASTM B248 defines plate, sheet, strip, and rolled bar; ASTM B249 defines rod, bar, and shapes; ASTM B250 defines wire; ASTM B251 defines tube; and ASTM B224 contains a classification of copper refinery products. The terminology for copper and copper alloys is unique to the industry and its products.

In some instances, conflicting terminology is employed by various industries. For example, the product known as *bar* in the steel industry is, in specific cases, designated as *rod* by the brass mill industry. In the latter industry, a *rod* is a round, hexagonal, or octagonal solid section in a straight length. A *bar* is a square or rectangular solid section in a straight length. And a *shape* denotes a solid section that is oval, half oval, half round, triangular, pentagonal, or of any special cross section in a straight length. *Wire* is a solid section furnished in coils, on spools, or on reels.

Commonly Used Alloys

For applications requiring maximum electrical conductivity, the most widely used copper is C11000, "tough pitch," which contains approximately 0.03-0.06% oxygen and a minimum of 99.90% copper (including silver). In addition to high electrical conductivity, oxygen-free grades C10100 and C10200 provide immunity to embrittlement at high temperature. The addition of phosphorus produces grade C12200—the standard water-tube copper.

The high-copper alloys contain small amounts of alloying elements that improve strength with minimal loss in electrical conductivity. For example, cadmium in amounts up to 1% can increase strength by 50%, with a decline in conductivity to 85%. Small amounts of cadmium raise the softening temperature in alloy C14300, which is used widely for radiator fin stock. Tellurium, lead, or sulfur—present in small amounts in grades C14500, C14700, and C18700—increase machinability.

For machined products, the most used material is copper alloy C36000, which is called free-cutting brass. This alloy has a combination of good physical, mechanical, and fabrication properties, plus an acceptable cost level for a majority of screw machine product applications. A wide variety of alloys is available to provide other properties and characteristics for various applications. For example, alloy C46400, naval brass, provides higher strength and ductility, but has a lower machinability rating than free-cutting brass.

Pure Copper

Pure copper is alloyed with many other elements to produce minor changes in properties. Tellurium, sulfur, and lead are added to improve machinability. These elements are insoluble in small amounts, and machinability is improved by the action of dispersed tellurides, sulfides, and lead inclusions. Chromium is added for strengthening, as are other elements such as zirconium, cadmium, and tin. Some American copper ores contain silver as a natural impurity. Silver has excellent solubility with copper, and it remains with the copper during refining to produce silver-bearing pure copper, which has improved resistance to softening and grain growth at elevated temperatures. Total alloy additions in pure copper are usually less than 1%.

Commercially pure copper is available in several grades, all of which have essentially the same mechanical properties. The three most commonly used are all of the same purity but vary in some respects.

1. Electrolytic tough-pitch copper, containing nominally about 0.03-0.06% oxygen, has high electrical conductivity. It is susceptible to embrittlement when heated in reducing atmospheres.
2. Deoxidized copper, containing nominally about 0.02% phosphorus as a residual deoxidant, has substantially lower electrical conductivity than electrolytic tough-pitch copper. It has improved cold working characteristics and is not susceptible to embrittlement at elevated temperatures. It has better welding and brazing characteristics than the other grades.
3. Oxygen-free copper is thoroughly deoxidized but contains no residual deoxidants. It possesses exceptional plasticity and is not prone to embrittlement when heated in reducing atmospheres. It has the same high electrical conductivity as electrolytic tough-pitch copper.

Modified Copper

Copper can be modified by the addition of small amounts of other elements to achieve special characteristics. The two principal types of modified copper are:

1. Tellurium copper, a free-cutting copper containing 0.4-0.7% tellurium. It is somewhat less ductile and plastic than the commercially pure coppers. Selenium is occasionally used instead of tellurium. Leaded copper, another free-cutting copper, has been largely superseded by tellurium copper.
2. Tellurium-nickel copper, an age-hardenable alloy combining high strength, high conductivity, and excellent machinability.

Copper-Based Alloys

Binary alloys of copper and zinc are known as brasses, while alloys of copper and tin are bronzes. From long established usage, some true brasses are called bronzes solely because their color is similar to that of the copper-tin alloys. Likewise, the term "bronze" is also used in modern metallurgy to refer to copper in which elements other than tin are the principal alloying material but that has the characteristic bronze color.

Nonleaded Copper-Zinc Alloys

The brasses are the most widely used and least expensive of the copper-based alloys. They possess relatively good corrosion resistance, moderately high strength, and in some compositions exceptionally good ductility and excellent forming characteristics when shaped by pressing, deep drawing, rolling, machining, etc. Cold working results in improved tensile properties. After cold working, they can be softened and recrystallized by appropriate annealing.

Alpha. Brasses with copper content above approximately 64% are called alpha brasses and are best known for their ability to withstand considerable cold working without annealing. These brasses may also be hot worked with reasonable ease.

Beta. The beta brasses, with copper content of 60% and less, are characterized by excellent hot working characteristics. They are not so adaptable to cold working as are the alpha brasses; and at the lower part of the range, about 55% copper, the strengths and elongations of the alpha and beta brasses vary according to the zinc and copper content.

Leaded Brass

Adding lead to the brasses in amounts from 0.5 to 4% results in free-cutting or free-machining alloys in which the elemental lead is present as uniformly dispersed particles. When the lead content is high, these brasses have relatively low ductility and plasticity. The mechanical properties of corrosion resistance and color are not materially affected by the presence of lead.

Casting Brass

While the wrought copper-zinc alloys are essentially simple binary alloys, the casting brasses contain substantial amounts of other elements, added principally to enhance the casting qualities of the alloy and to impart suitable strength properties. The usual elements, added either alone or in combination with one another, are tin (1-6%), lead (1-10%), iron (0.5-3%), and varying amounts of nickel, antimony, and aluminum.

COPPER

Tin Bronze

Copper-tin alloys (phosphor bronzes) containing from about 1.25 to 10% tin possess good strength and cold forming characteristics and the typical bronze color.

The most important copper-tin alloys are those that have been deoxidized with phosphorus during the refining process and hence are known as phosphor bronze. The amount of residual phosphorus may range from a trace to about 0.35% or even higher in some special grades. The excess phosphorus, which exists in solid solution, materially increases the hardness and strength of the alloy, but it does so at the expense of ductility and electrical conductivity. It improves the toughness, elevated temperature properties, and resistance to corrosion. In amounts greater than 1.0%, phosphorus causes excessive brittleness and impairs surface appearance but affords a good bearing surface, as is evident by the use of high-phosphorus bronze compositions for gears and other machine parts subject to wear.

The phosphor bronzes include a variety of distinctive metals, characterized by strength, high resistance to corrosion and fatigue, and high yield strength.

Casting bronzes frequently contain as much as 10% lead, and some bearing compositions as much as 25%. The high lead content precludes the use of cold forming operations and limits the use of such alloys to temperatures below the melting point of lead.

The substitution of zinc for tin in the tin bronzes improves casting qualities, but zinc is seldom added in amounts greater than about 5% because of unattractive color and lower corrosion resistance to some media. A phosphor bronze containing approximately 4% each of tin, lead, and zinc has excellent free-cutting characteristics.

Nickel Silver

The nickel-silver alloys (once known as "German silver") are essentially brasses containing substantial amounts of nickel in addition to the copper and zinc. The designation of nickel silver—for instance, "65-18"—indicates the nominal percentages of copper and nickel. The addition of small amounts of lead produces nickel silvers with free-cutting characteristics. The color of the alloy varies from white with a yellowish tinge to a silvery white as the amount of nickel is increased.

Nickel-silver alloys are generally characterized by a pleasing color, high strength and ductility, good corrosion resistance, and ease in working by stamping, rolling, drawing, etc. Some compositions may be cold worked; others are best formed by hot working.

Copper Nickel

Copper-based alloys containing nickel but no zinc are known as copper nickels. They have good strength and plasticity and are particularly noted for their high resistance to corrosion. They can be cold worked to a considerable degree and are readily hot worked.

Manganese Bronze

Manganese bronzes are essentially high-strength, modified copper-zinc casting alloys containing 55-60% copper, 38-42% zinc, 0-1.5% tin, 0-2% iron, 0-1.5% aluminum, and up to about 3.5% manganese. These alloys are available in various wrought forms and are characterized by good mechanical properties and corrosion resistance. Manganese bronzes have poor cold forming

characteristics, but they can be readily hot worked. Their principal uses are for ship propellers, rudders, and other marine fittings.

Silicon Bronze

These alloys possess high strength (similar to mild steel) and good toughness, plus they exhibit excellent resistance to corrosion by brine and sulfite solutions, nonoxidizing inorganic acids, alkalies, and other media. They are readily hot worked, and the low-silicon alloys particularly have good cold working characteristics. The high-silicon alloys have excellent casting qualities and are superior in this respect to other high-strength nonferrous alloys such as aluminum bronze.

The composition of the silicon bronzes may vary over rather wide limits and may contain about 1-4% silicon, 0.25-1.5% manganese, 0.5-1.0% iron when present, and zinc as high as 22%. The addition of about 0.5% lead produces alloys with good machining characteristics.

Aluminum Bronzes

Aluminum bronzes have high strengths (comparable to medium-carbon steel), high hardnesses in the as-cast state, and excellent corrosion-resistance properties. They possess good antifrictional characteristics and resist scaling and oxidation at elevated temperatures. Aluminum bronzes can be hot worked readily, and some grades possess good cold forming characteristics and respond to a form of precipitation hardening.

The aluminum bronzes are essentially copper-aluminum alloys, containing up to about 13.5% aluminum, small amounts of manganese and nickel, and up to 4% iron for the purpose of hardening the alloys. The presence of iron in these alloys, in the form of an intermetallic compound ($FeAl_3$), contributes to wear resistance and hardness.

The good antifrictional characteristics of these alloys suit them for bearings, bushings, rollers, gears, etc. They resist scaling and oxidation at high temperatures and can be hot worked readily.

Beryllium Coppers

The addition of small amounts of beryllium to copper creates a family of high-copper alloys with strengths as high as alloy steel. The high strength is obtained by precipitation hardening, similar to the PH stainless steels. The commercial grades of beryllium-copper alloys contain from 0.4 to 2.0 weight percent beryllium in the wrought products, and up to 2.75 weight percent in the casting alloys. Small amounts of cobalt or nickel are also added to aid in the precipitation-hardening process and in grain refinement.

There are basically two families of beryllium-copper alloys: (1) high strength with moderate conductivity and (2) high conductivity with moderate strength. The principal characteristics of these alloys are their excellent response to precipitation-hardening treatments, excellent corrosion and fatigue resistance, moderate-to-good electrical and thermal conductivity, and resistance to stress relaxation. Elevated temperature performance is very good; however, the maximum long-time operating temperature should not exceed 400° F (204° C).

Their high strength and ease of manufacture make beryllium-copper alloys particularly suited for bellows, bourdon tubing, diaphragms, fasteners, lock washers, springs, switch parts, relay parts, electrical and electronic components, retaining rings, roll pins, valves, pump parts, spline shafts, rolling mill parts, welding equipment, and instrument housings.

PROPERTIES

Copper is among the toughest of pure metals. It is moderately wear resistant and highly malleable and ductile. As shown in Fig. 15-4, the principal alloy groups have hardness and tensile strength values that are higher than those for pure copper.

Copper alloys do not have a sharply defined yield point. Yield strength is reported either as 0.5% extension under load or as 0.2% offset. On the most common basis (0.5% extension), yield strength of annealed material is approximately one-third the tensile strength. As the material is cold worked or hardened, yield strength approaches tensile strength.

Temper Specification

Wrought coppers and copper-based alloys are available and

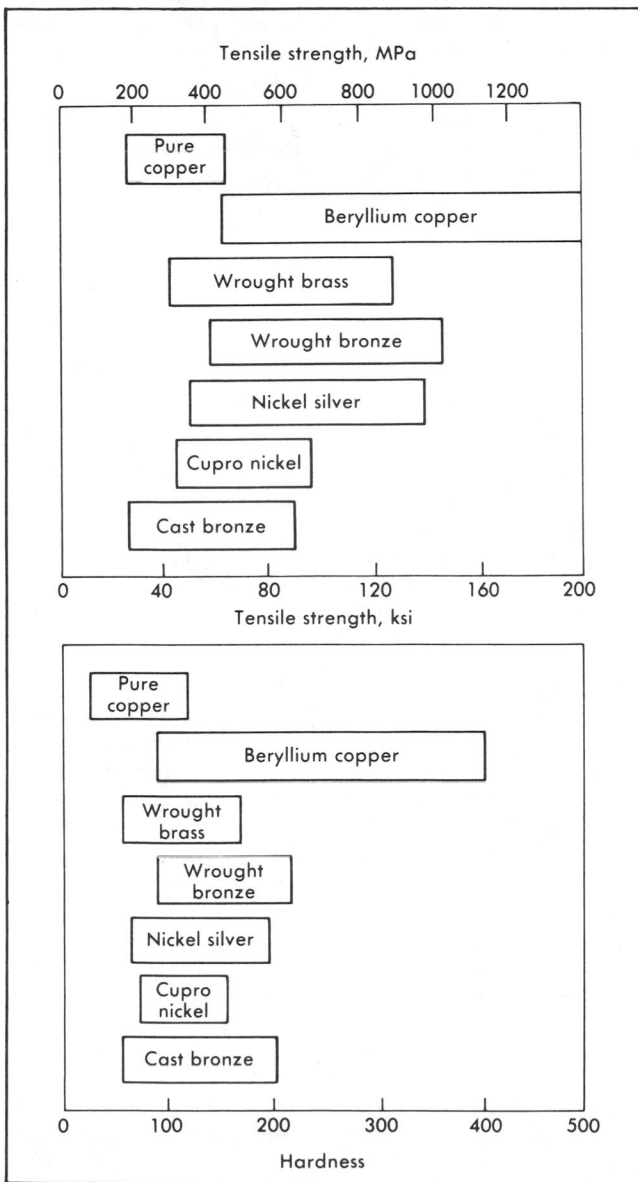

Fig. 15-4 Typical hardness and tensile strength ranges for various copper alloy groups. (*Engineering Materials, Kenneth Budinski, Reston Publishing Co.*)

specified in various degrees of temper, which are established by cold working or annealing. Typical temper levels for flat products are soft, half hard, hard, spring, and extra-spring. The yield strength of a hard temper copper is approximately two thirds of its tensile strength. In the annealed or soft condition, the temper is based on grain size, which is a key factor in successful forming by deep drawing operations.

For brasses, phosphor bronzes, or other commonly cold worked alloy grades, the hardest available tempers are also the strongest. Ductility is sacrificed to gain strength. Beryllium-copper alloys such as C17000 to C17200 can be precipitation hardened to increase strength.

Wrought Copper Properties

The role of the various alloying elements used in copper systems is usually to increase strength and hardness. All of the ductile copper alloys can be cold worked to improve strength, but beryllium copper is the strongest. In the age-hardened condition, the tensile strength can be as high as 200 ksi (1379 MPa).

The ductility of wrought copper alloys depends on the amount of cold work. In the annealed condition, they all have high elongations and good formability. Wrought beryllium copper after heat treatment has poor ductility, but forming can usually be done in the annealed or cold worked condition. The ductility of some of the cast bronzes can be as low as 5% elongation.

Low temperatures have little effect on the ductility of copper alloys; that is, they do not get brittle. Most copper alloys soften at temperatures over 400° F (200° C), and the oxygen-bearing coppers embrittle in reducing atmospheres. Use at elevated temperatures requires careful consideration of elevated temperature property data. The ability to cold work the wrought alloys extensively produces a wide variety of strength ranges within each major alloy system.

Cast Copper Alloy Properties

Copper alloy castings of irregular or complex, internal and external shapes can be produced by sand casting, die casting, and various other casting methods. Alloy and process selection are guided by the need for castings that have superior corrosion resistance, good electrical conductivity, good bearing quality, or other useful properties.

Corrosion Resistance

Copper and its alloys resist corrosion. They are inherently noble (chemically inert) because of their low driving force toward the oxidized state, as measured by the electromotive force or galvanic series. Their corrosion products form adherent surface films in various media.

Copper's performance in the atmosphere, in contact with both potable water and seawater, and in underground applications is well known. In all these media, copper performs well because its noble character keeps corrosion to a minimum even when the surface is disturbed.

Under outdoor atmospheric conditions, the protective oxide film eventually takes on the familiar blue-green color or patina; under indoor and manufacturing plant conditions, the film may consist of oxides, sulfides, or other salts. In potable water, protective films of oxides or of basic copper carbonates generally are formed.

All of the alloys have high resistance to fresh water and

COPPER

steam. Most of the bronzes, copper nickels, and nickel silvers have high resistance to corrosion by salt water but are subject to limitations at high water velocities due to breakdown of the passivating film.

Copper alloys have good resistance to alkalies and organic acids but not to inorganic acids. Alloys with high zinc content may corrode by dezincification, selectively removing zinc from the alloys and leaving the remaining metal with a spongy structure. Copper alloys are attacked by even trace quantities of mercury and by moist ammonia or ammoniacal compounds. Several of the alloy systems are subject to stress-corrosion cracking, which can be avoided in part by the stress relieving of fabricated parts prior to exposure to the corrodent.

Electrical Conductivity

In the electronic and electrical industry, a large user of copper, high electrical conductivity is the single most important material property; although for industrial use, conductivity must be accompanied by other suitable characteristics and properties.

The conductivity of commercial copper is commonly rated on a percentage basis. This method affords a convenient standard for buying and selling, for comparison of quality for electrical purposes, and for comparison with other metals. The rating is based on percentage of a mass conductivity, adopted as a standard by the International Electrotechnical Commission in 1913 and subsequently by the American National Standards Institute, American Society for Testing and Materials, and other organizations.

Wear Resistance

Copper alloys have been used in wear applications for centuries. Today these applications remain among the most important uses of copper alloys. Plain bearings of copper alloys are widely used in fractional horsepower motors, in marine applications, and in very large, heavily loaded journals such as paper mill rolls, railroad train bearings, and steel mill roll bearings. Wrought copper alloys are used for stamped gears, cams, and escapements in clocks, timing mechanisms, switch gears, and cameras.

Brasses, bronzes, and beryllium coppers are the most widely used copper alloys for wear components. Copper alloys are often subjected to cavitation and other forms of corrosive wear, but in machine applications the most important modes of wear are abrasion and metal-to-metal.

APPLICATIONS

Copper's corrosion resistance is an important property that adapts the metal to widespread commercial use. Copper resists oxidation while carrying water, and it does not pick up a mineral deposit from the water. This advantage accounts for the extensive use of copper for water pipes and valves and other fittings in plumbing systems. Copper alloys are widely used in marine applications, specified for propellers, bushings, hardware, and heat exchangers that must resist attack by salt water. In the chemical process industry, copper alloys withstand a wide range of acids, bases, and organic solutions. About one third of all the copper alloy material produced is used for tubing and pipe that carry corrosive fluids of one form or another.

Low Temperature

Copper and copper alloys were the first metals used in the construction of low-temperature equipment for liquefaction and storage of cryogenic fluids. Copper and many copper alloys retain excellent ductility at low temperatures. This characteristic plus good thermal conductivity provides a combination of properties needed for heat exchangers and other components in cryogenic plants and in low-temperature processing and storage facilities.

High Temperature

For applications involving elevated temperatures, the American Society of Mechanical Engineers (ASME) Boiler and Pressure Vessel Code is used to specify critical copper alloy components. The code recommendations make allowances for a falloff in creep or rupture strength, a relatively low strength on a strength-to-weight basis, and susceptibility to stress-corrosion cracking in certain environments. Silicon bronzes, aluminum brass, and copper-nickel alloys are widely used in high-temperature equipment applications.

FABRICATION

Copper and copper alloys have always been noted for their excellent formability and ease of fabrication into utensils and products.

Casting

Pure copper has poor casting qualities caused mainly by the release of gases from the molten metal when it solidifies. Machining is also difficult. Castings of intricate shapes are seldom made of pure copper, although there are exceptions where high thermal or electrical conductivity is a primary consideration. Wirebars, cakes, billets, and similar objects of regular or simple shape intended for working are readily cast if the oxygen content of the molten metal is controlled. In such applications, some porosity is allowable because it will be closed up during working.

Most copper alloys have excellent casting qualities, and some of the bronzes and brasses are outstanding in their suitability for the casting processes. Die castings are made with some compositions of brass.

Forming

Pure copper is highly workable, as are many of the wrought copper alloys. The commonly used methods of working include rolling, extrusion, wire drawing, piercing, and stamping. Other processes that are used include forming by forging, pressing, deep drawing, flanging, spinning, and cupping, as well as various machining operations.

Machining[21]

Most copper alloys are readily machined by usual methods using standard tools designed for steel, but at higher speeds. Consideration of the wide range of characteristics presented by various types of copper alloys and the adaptation of the machining practice to the particular material concerned will provide greatly improved results.

Characteristics. Copper and each of its alloys have individual characteristics such as ductility, hardness, tensile strength, and type of chip produced. Metal to be machined must be rigid enough to stand up against the turning tool without distortion. This demand requires a temper in the wrought copper alloys for automatic screw machining, yet the alloys may need to be soft enough to withstand subsequent cold working. Because of their varying characteristics, care must be taken with copper alloys to clearly define speed, rate of feed, and form of tool to be used in machining, whether it be a single-point tool, form tool, milling cutter, drill, tap, chaser, reamer, or saw.

Groupings. Copper and its alloys can be grouped into classifications for which broad ranges of speeds, feeds, and tool geometry can be established. These general groupings may be summarized as follows: Tellurium and sulfur are added to enhance the machinability of copper with minimum sacrifice in conductivity. The effect of adding controlled quantities of lead may be illustrated by considering C27000 (yellow brass, 65%), an alloy of 65% copper with 35% zinc. When cut, this alloy produces long, stringy chips. By replacing a like amount of copper with lead, a leaded brass results that speeds machining by producing an easily broken chip. This alloy—61.5% copper, 35.5% zinc, 3% lead, known as C36000 (free-cutting brass)—ranks as the finest machining alloy. It is given a rating of 100 and provides the standard to which other alloys are compared when discussing machinability.

Heat Treatment

Pure copper and the copper alloys are usually used in the as-received condition; however, in some applications, heat treatments are used to modify the properties. Annealing may be done to soften wrought alloys when extensive drawing is required.[22]

Stress relieving is performed to provide dimensional stability for parts that are subjected to significant amounts of machining, or to reduce residual stress level on parts that may be exposed to atmospheres that cause stress-corrosion cracking.

Beryllium copper and certain other alloys can be solution treated and age hardened. Included in this group are aluminum bronzes, nickel-copper alloys, chromium copper, and zirconium copper. All of the cast age-hardenable alloys (except C82000 and C82200) attain a hardness of about R_C40 or more when age hardened to maximum strength.

MAGNESIUM

Magnesium (Mg) is a silvery white metal with a specific gravity of 1.74. In the pure state, magnesium's melting point is 1202° F (650° C), which is approximately the same temperature required to melt aluminum.

Most pure metals, including magnesium, are soft and are not suitable for structural use. However, strength properties comparable to those of many aluminum alloys are obtained by alloying magnesium with other metals, and, in some cases, by heat treating or cold or hot working.

With a unit weight of $0.063 \, lb/in.^3$ ($1.74 \, g/cm^3$), magnesium is the lightest of the commonly used metals. For engineering applications, magnesium is usually alloyed with one or more elements, including aluminum, manganese, rare earth metals, lithium, thorium, zinc, and zirconium. The resultant alloys have very high strength-to-weight ratios.

While its light weight is magnesium's best known characteristic (aluminum weighs 1 1/2 times more than magnesium; iron and steel, 4 times more; copper, 5 times more), there are also other desirable properties. Magnesium's excellent machinability, for example, makes it economical in parts where weight saving may not be of primary importance, but where much costly machining is required. Parts made of magnesium can be machined at higher speeds, with fewer cuts, and with greater economies than are possible with most other metals.

ALLOY DESIGNATION SYSTEM

Primary magnesium, like most metals, lacks sufficient strength in its elemental state to be used as a structural metal. Therefore, it must be alloyed with various other metals, such as aluminum, manganese, thorium, rare earth metals, lithium, tin, zinc, and zirconium. Magnesium alloys are most commonly designated by a system established by the American Society for Testing and Materials (ASTM), which covers both chemical compositions and tempers.

The ASTM designations for alloys are based on chemical composition and consist of two letters representing the two alloying elements specified in the greatest amount, arranged either in decreasing percentages or—if of equal percentage—alphabetically. The letters are followed by the respective percentages rounded off to whole numbers, with a serial letter at the end. The serial letter indicates some variation in composition. Experimental alloys have the letter X between the alloy and serial numbers.

The following letters designate various alloying elements: A—aluminum, B—bismuth, C—copper, D—cadmium, E—rare earths, F—iron, G—magnesium, H—thorium, K—zirconium, L—lithium, M—manganese, N—nickel, P—lead, Q—silver, R—chromium, S—silicon, T—tin, Z—zinc.

Primary magnesium metal and alloys have also been assigned UNS (unified numbering system) designations according to the Unified Numbering System for Metals and Alloys, SAE HS1086a and ASTM DS-56A. The UNS designation for a metal or alloy consists of a letter followed by five numbers. The UNS system is intended to provide a nationally accepted means of correlating the many alloy designation numbers used by various organizations, and an improved system for indexing, record keeping, data storage and retrieval, and cross referencing. The numbers M10001 through M19999 have been reserved for magnesium and magnesium alloys.

ASTM Specification B 296 designates tempers for magnesium alloys. Temper designation is separated from alloy designation by a dash.

ALLOYS AND PRODUCT FORMS

The common alloying elements for magnesium are aluminum, zinc, and manganese. The addition of 3 to 10% aluminum increases the hardness and strength about in proportion to the amount added. Magnesium castings with 5 to 10% aluminum respond well to heat treatment. Manganese added in small amounts improves corrosion resistance but has little effect on mechanical properties. Zinc is used up to 3% in the magnesium aluminum alloys, improving strength and saline corrosion resistance. Magnesium-zinc-zirconium alloys with up to 6% zinc provide high strength with good ductility. Where strength and creep resistance are required at moderately elevated temperatures, rare earth or thorium is added, along with zinc and zirconium. For high-temperature strength, a silver addition (2.5%) is used in combination with rare earth or thorium and zirconium.

CHAPTER 15

MAGNESIUM

General forms

Magnesium alloys are available in virtually all of the usual metal forms, including cast ingots, slabs, and billets; sand, permanent-mold, die, and investment castings; forgings, extruded bars, rods, tubes, structural shapes, and special hollow and solid shapes; and rolled sheet and plate.

Wrought Products

Wrought products of various magnesium alloys are available in plate, sheet, strip, rods, bars, irregular extruded shapes, and forgings. Wrought forms can be cold worked to a limited degree, but are usually heated before they are shaped, drawn, forged, or spun. Significant weight and structural savings are gained by using magnesium sheet, plate, and extrusions. High rigidity with reduced weight is possible, permitting diminished lateral and horizontal bracing and reduced fastening.

PROPERTIES

Magnesium alloys do not have the sharp yield point characteristic of carbon steels. Instead, the metal yields gradually when stressed, and the term "yield strength" is used. Yield strength has been defined as the stress at which the stress-strain curve deviates 0.2% from the modulus line. In cast form, the tensile and compressive yield strengths of most magnesium alloys are substantially equal. In most wrought alloys, however, the compressive yield strength is less than that of the tensile yield. Magnesium alloys have a modulus of elasticity of approximately 6.5×10^6 psi (45 GPa), and Poisson's ratio is 0.35.

Magnesium provides high-speed machinability, good thermal and electrical conductivity, fatigue resistance and damping properties of a high order, high impact and dent resistance, and the ability to be cast and formed by a variety of standard metalworking processes. These factors allow the design of large yet light and rigid tools, and jigs and fixtures of ready portability. Moving machine elements made of magnesium have low inertia forces compared with those of steel or aluminum.

APPLICATIONS

The principal industrial and commercial uses of magnesium and its alloys are in nonstructural metallurgical, chemical, and electrochemical applications, as well as in structural components for aircraft, missiles, motor vehicles, portable tools, machinery parts, computers, and office equipment.

Nonstructural

In the metallurgical field, magnesium is an important constituent in aluminum alloys; in fact, the largest usage of magnesium is for alloying with aluminum. Additions of up to 10% magnesium result in aluminum alloys having favorable combinations of strength properties, formability, and corrosion resistance.

Magnesium also improves the properties and stability of zinc die-casting alloys and is used as a reducing agent in the manufacture of titanium and zirconium and as a desulfurization agent for iron and steel. Nodular or ductile cast iron is made by treatment of the molten alloy with magnesium, leaving a few hundredths of a percent magnesium in the nodular iron.

In electrochemical applications, magnesium anodes are used to prevent galvanic corrosion of steel in certain installations, such as underground pipelines, storage tanks, and domestic water heaters. Magnesium is also used in dry cell batteries.

Organic chemistry applications of magnesium include industrial synthesis processes such as the production of tetraethyl lead, an antiknock additive in gasoline.

In the printing industry, magnesium alloy plates are used for photoengraving. Magnesium etches rapidly to provide a sharp impression, and the byproducts do not require extensive effluent treatment for removal. When ignited, finely divided magnesium burns with intensive blue-white light. The powder is used in the pyrotechnical industry in making fireworks, military flares, and various incendiary devices.

Structural

In structural applications, magnesium is used primarily because of its low density. When stiffness or elastic buckling is the main design criterion, a structure will have the least weight when constructed of magnesium.

Structural uses of magnesium generally take advantage of the weight savings over other metals and alloys, especially in aircraft and aerospace applications, and military and electronic equipment. Special magnesium alloys containing zinc, zirconium, thorium, silver, and rare earth metals are used for components operating up to 572° F (300° C). Typical applications include gear boxes, jet engine housings, aircraft landing wheels, and cockpit canopy frames.

A large number of magnesium alloys are used. The most common contain up to 9% aluminum, up to 2% zinc, and small amounts of manganese. The alloys of lower aluminum content are used for the production of sheet and extrusions, while those of higher aluminum content are used mainly for castings.

While sand and permanent-mold castings are used, the major application is in the form of pressure die castings, such as for a variety of automobile and truck components where weight reduction is an important factor. Examples include air-cooled engine blocks and heads, clutch and transaxle housings, wheels, brackets, and grilles. Other examples of pressure die-casting applications include chain saw housings, rotary lawn-mower decks, computers and peripheral equipment, housings for office machines, loudspeakers, luggage, tennis racquets, and archery bows.

In addition to strength and lightness, properties desirable for structural applications include damping capacity, thermal and electrical characteristics, dent resistance, and the ability to be formed and joined. Rods, tubing, and other sections are produced by extrusion, and magnesium is also rolled into sheet and plate. Applications for these mill products range from fuel element containers to materials handling ramps, hand trucks, ladders, and garden tools.

FABRICATION

Magnesium alloys are fabricated by common methods, including melting followed by casting, rolling, extrusion, and forging. Further fabrication includes forming, joining, and machining, after which standard assembly and finishing methods are used.

Magnesium alloys are highly formable at elevated temperature, and they can be readily cast into complex forms with a high degree of accuracy. Drilling, turning, and other machining operations can be performed at higher rates than with other metals; and strong joints between magnesium parts are possible through welding, adhesive bonding, and the use of mechanical joints such as rivets and threaded fasteners.

Die Castings

Magnesium is ideally suited for die casting. The low latent heat allows rapid solidification in the die, with resultant high production rates. Molten magnesium does not react with or solder to die steels, resulting in longer die life and increased productivity. Draft and tape requirements are 20-25% less than those for aluminum die castings. Shrinkage rates are consistent and predictable, and parts are ejected from the die with minimum distortion and residual stress. Maximum mechanical properties of magnesium die-casting alloys are achieved in wall thicknesses ranging from 0.075″ to 0.150″ (1.91 to 3.81 mm), but walls thinner than 0.050″ (1.27 mm) are practicable in localized and unstressed areas.

Sand and Permanent-Mold Castings

Sand and permanent-mold castings in magnesium alloys are produced in a large variety of sizes and shapes for many uses. Typical alloys with good casting qualities are ZE41, AZ63A, AZ91C, and AZ92A. The last provides the optimum combination of high yield strength and moderate elongation with good pressure tightness. Casting alloys containing zirconium, such as ZK51A and ZK61A, have been developed for their improved properties. Alloys containing thorium or rare earths, such as HK31A and EZ33A, respectively, are specified for elevated temperature service [for example, 345 to 600° F (175 to 315° C)], depending on alloy composition. Another relatively new casting alloy, QE22A, contains silver and didymium (cerium-free rare earth metals). This composition provides good room temperature properties, tensile yield, and creep properties up to about 600° F (315° C).

Sand and permanent-mold castings are usually heat treated (solution treated and age hardened, or age hardened alone) in order to achieve the desired properties.

Extrusions

The extrusion process starts with cast extrusion ingots that can be made by casting in thick-walled iron or steel molds, or preferably by means of the direct chill (DC) casting process, which gives a fine grain and less compound segregate.

For ordinary temperature applications, an alloy of the AZ type, such as AZ31B, is used. The heat-treatable alloy ZK60A provides high strength and good toughness. If hot strength and creep resistance is needed, the 3% thorium alloy HM31A can be selected.

Forging

Magnesium forgings are usually made by the press forging process in closed dies, less often by hammer forging. The size of magnesium forgings seems to be limited only by the size of available equipment.

The principal forging alloys are AZ31B, AZ61A, AZ80A, and ZK60A. HM21A, a sheet and plate alloy, is also a good forging alloy. It is used where creep strength is required at temperatures as high as 800° F (427° C).

Forming

The forming of magnesium sheet or extrusions can be done by practically all the methods commonly used. Forming operations involve bending around generous radii. Relatively mild deformation can be performed on magnesium at room temperature. The formability at elevated temperatures of 400 to 600° F (204 to 316° C) is so greatly improved, however, that most magnesium forming is done in this temperature range.

This improved formability at elevated temperature is due to magnesium's hexagonal crystalline structure. When the metal is heated, additional slip planes become available, and plastic deformation characteristics improve. High-speed mechanical presses can be used to make draws in one step up to 59% reduction and at speeds up to 80 fpm (24.4 m/min). Magnesium alloys are also formed by bending, stretch forming, spinning, impact extrusion, drop hammer forging, and other common methods.

Joining

All the standard methods of joining are used with magnesium, including arc welding, electric resistance welding, brazing, riveting, bolting, and adhesive bonding.

Welding. For general welding, the inert-gas-shielded arc welding processes are used. Helium or argon can be used as the inert protective gas. In gas tungsten arc welding, a tungsten electrode is used to maintain the arc that melts the separate magnesium filler rod. Another process called gas metal arc welding uses a coil of magnesium wire that functions as both an electrode and filler rod. This method is sometimes described as consumable-electrode arc welding.

Inert-gas-shielded arc welding is preferred over gas flame welding processes because it requires no corrosive flux. Magnesium can be welded with oxyacetylene, oxyhydrogen, and oxyhydrocarbon gas, but a chloride-based flux is necessary to prevent oxidation. This flux is very corrosive and difficult to completely remove after welding. As a consequence, gas welding of magnesium alloys is usually limited to emergency repair to put broken parts back into service until replacement parts can be obtained.

Other methods. Spot welding is the most frequently used method of electric resistance welding. In addition, forge welding and stud welding can be used. Magnesium alloys can also be joined by furnace, flux-dip, and torch brazing. Soldering is not used as a method of joining because of the brittle joint that is formed; its use is limited to making electrical connections and to the filling of imperfections in the surface. Before soldering electrical connections to magnesium, the metal can be prepared by plating with electroless nickel, or with zinc followed by copper and tin.

Riveting. Riveting is a commonly used method of making mechanical joints in magnesium. Aluminum alloy 5056 rivets in the H32 temper are commonly used, although rivets of 6053-T61 or 6061-T6 can be substituted. These aluminum alloys minimize the possibility of galvanic corrosion. Rivets of steel, brass, copper, and certain aluminum alloys should not be used in magnesium because of the possibility of serious galvanic corrosion. Rivet holes in magnesium should be drilled rather than punched, and squeeze riveters are preferred over pneumatic riveting hammers. The latter are more likely to damage the magnesium sheet by overdriving. Optimum rivet-joint design calls for a minimum spacing in any direction of three times the rivet diameter. Similarly, a minimum edge distance of 2.5 times the rivet diameter is suggested. Riveted joints should preferably be protected with a sealing compound to prevent water entrapment; one or more coats of a chromate-pigmented primer are desirable.

Adhesive Bonding. Adhesive bonding has become a popular method of joining magnesium sheet in certain applications. It is

LEAD

often desirable when joining material too thin to be effectively riveted or welded. A large variety of adhesives are available. Most of them require heat, although in some cases the temperature can be as low as 200° F (93° C). Curing times will range from a few minutes to an hour or more. Certain adhesives require the application of pressure, but many of them require only contact. The shear strength of adhesive-bonded joints in magnesium will range from about 1000 to 4000 psi (6.9 to 27.6 MPa). Most bonded joints are useful at temperatures up to about 150° F (66° C). There is, however, an epoxy-phenolic adhesive that has shown good joint strength retention up to 500° F (260° C).

Machining

Magnesium is the easiest of all structural metals to machine. Its excellent machinability has often been the reason for its use in applications where a large number of machining operations were required. Appropriate procedures and controls should be applied to avoid a fire hazard in high-speed machining operations, especially in the presence of water liquid or vapor. Magnesium is normally machined dry; but, where very high cutting speeds are involved and there is a possibility of igniting fine turnings, it may be necessary to use a coolant. Mineral oils are used because water-based coolants may react chemically with the swarf.

Some advantages of magnesium's excellent machinability include reduced machining time (which can mean fewer machine tools and thus lower capital investment and less floor space to do a given job); four to five times greater tool life; an excellent surface finish with only one cut; well-broken chips that minimize handling cost; and less tool buildup. High-speed routers are standard tools for cutting and trimming magnesium.

LEAD

Pure lead (Pb) is a bluish gray metal that takes on a silvery gray patina with atmospheric exposure. In industrial atmospheres, it may change to a dark gray to black color. The density of cast lead is 0.409 lb/in.^{3} (11.34 g/cm^3), and the melting point is 621° F (327° C).

Lead is readily and inexpensively fabricated into a great variety of useful forms. The diveristy of available forms combined with lead's advantageous properties-high density, low melting point, corrosion resistance, chemical stability, malleability, lubricity, electrical properties, and ability to form useful alloys and chemical compounds— provide a material suitable for a wide range of applications.[23]

Although lead is widely known as a heavy metal, only about 10% of lead applications are based primarily on its high density. In many other applications, lead is selected because it melts at low temperatures, is easy to cast and form, is useful for generating electric current in electrochemical reactions, is a good absorber of sound and vibration, or is among the easiest of metals to salvage from scrap. Lead also resists attack by many corrosive chemicals and acids, most types of soil, and marine and industrial environments. It is the most impervious of all common metals to X-rays and gamma radiation.

Nearly three fourths of all U.S. lead consumption is for chemical applications such as paint pigments, gasoline additives, and storage batteries.

LEAD ALLOY DESIGNATION

Pure lead is available with a purity of 99.999%. By agreement between purchaser and supplier, limits are established for specified elements, and the percentages of unspecified elements may be raised or lowered, depending on the particular application.

The Unified Numbering System (UNS) is a means of describing metal and alloy composition in a logical, numerical manner that is useful to industry and government operations. The format Lxxxxx is used in the UNS number series for "Low Melting Metals and Alloys."

LEAD PRODUCT FORMS

Lead forms a wide range of low-melting alloys. Lead and the various low-melting-point lead alloys are widely available in a large number of product forms, including castings, extrusions, shot, powder, rope, coatings, and sheet, strip and plate products. When lead is added to other alloys, such as steel, brass and bronze, it promotes machinability, corrosion resistance, or other special properties.

PROPERTIES

The properties of lead that make it useful in a wide variety of applications are its density, malleability, lubricity, flexibility, and coefficient of thermal expansion, all of which are high; and elastic modulus, elastic limit, strength, hardness, melting point, and electrical conductivity, all of which are low. Lead also has good resistance to corrosion under a wide variety of conditions, is easily alloyed with many other metals, and is easily cast.

Density

The high density of lead makes it very effective in shielding against X-rays and gamma radiation. In large installations, it is often used in conjunction with concrete structures to reduce the mass of concrete that otherwise would be required.

The combination of high density, high "limpness" (low stiffness), and high damping capacity makes lead an excellent material for deadening sound and for isolating equipment and structures from mechanical vibrations.

Malleability, Softness and Lubricity

These three related properties account for the extensive use of lead in many applications. For example, high malleability is largely responsible for the value of lead as a caulking material, enabling it to fill caulked joints completely. The softness and self-lubricating properties of lead account in substantial part for its use in bearing alloys, gaskets, washers, and lead-headed nails. As a coating on wire or sheet metal, lead acts as a drawing lubricant; and in the form of powder or wire, it imparts lubricity to friction materials, such as brake linings.

Strength

The fact that lead has low tensile strength and low creep strength must always be considered in lead components. However, even when good strength is an essential design criterion, the low strength of lead does not necessarily preclude its use. Lead products can be designed to be self-supporting, or inserts or supports of other materials can be provided. Alloying with certain other metals, notably antimony and calcium, is a common method of strengthening lead for many applications.

Thermal Expansion

The relatively high coefficient of thermal expansion of lead is another important property. In lead roofing and flashing, thermal expansion is a key factor and is provided for by using small sheets and loose-locking each sheet to the next, thus minimizing both individual and cumulative expansion. In pipelines subject to wide variations in temperature, provision must be made for free expansion. The flexibility of lead can be used to advantage in such systems.

Corrosion Resistance

Lead is highly resistant to corrosion by the atmosphere, by water, and by a wide range of chemicals in common use. Where resistance to corrosion must be combined with long service life, the limitations imposed by the mechanical properties of lead must be carefully considered.

For chemical corrosion resistance, lead is usually chosen from the ASTM grades of chemical and acid-copper lead.

APPLICATIONS FOR LEAD AND LEAD ALLOYS

In the metallic form, lead is used extensively in building construction as both sheet and pipe and in solder. Lead is also widely used in alloys such as type metal, antimonial lead, calcium lead for storage batteries, bearing alloys, foil, and collapsible tubes; as a coating for other materials; as lead weight, caulking lead, gaskets, seals, cable sheathing, bullets, and shotgun pellets.

Pure Lead

Lead in various forms and combinations is recognized as an effective material for controlling sound and vibration, and, as such, lead has a significant role in noise control. Its high internal damping characteristics make it one of the most efficient sound attenuators for industrial, commercial, and residential applications. Sheet lead, lead-loaded vinyls, lead composites, and lead laminates are frequently used to reduce machinery noise. Also, lead is important as a shielding material against X-rays and, in the nuclear industry, against gamma radiation.

In addition to its physical and mechanical properties, lead's chemical properties, mainly corrosion resistance, account for many of its uses. Lead is durable under varying weather conditions and when exposed to most types of soil, marine and industrial atmospheres, and the action of many corrosive chemicals. Its resistance to sulfuric acid is used advantageously in the manufacture of the acid and in the most common method of storing electricity—the storage battery.

Lead Alloys

Lead alloyed with other metals is used commercially in large tonnages. Antimony, calcium, and tin are the alloying metals most commonly used. Antimony and calcium provide greater hardness and strength, as in storage battery plates, sheets, pipes, and castings. Tin also increases hardness slightly, but the lead-tin alloys are most commonly used for their low melting characteristics and ability to join other metals, as in solder. In solder, terne metal, and other lead-alloy coatings, tin imparts the ability to bond with metals like steel and copper. High-purity lead has no such bonding ability. Both tin and antimony improve the casting qualities of lead. Bismuth and tin are often alloyed with lead to obtain extremely low-melting fusible alloys.

Although lead does not alloy readily with copper, it is combined in rather high percentages in bronzes and free-machining brasses. Also, while lead is difficult to alloy with steel, fractional percentages of lead are used in the production of free-machining steel. Calcium, magnesium, and sodium in fractional percentages are sometimes alloyed with lead in special bearing alloys and cable sheathing. Cadmium additions prove helpful in coating copper wires with lead.

Compounds

Lead monoxide or Litharge (PbO) is the most important compound of lead. It is used in storage batteries, crystal glass, ceramics, and leaded-glass radiation-shielding windows, as well as in pigments and to vulcanize rubber.

Lead tetraoxide (Pb_3O_4) or "red lead" is prepared by the controlled oxidation of Litharge. It is commonly used for corrosion resistant pigments and storage batteries. Lead chromates—yellow, orange, and red—are used as corrosion-resistant, colored pigments. Lead carbonate, the familiar white lead, is sometimes used in plastics and nacreous coatings; lead azide is a standard explosive detonator; lead arsenate is an insecticide and herbicide; and lead silicates are paint pigments and enameling frits. Lead diamyldithiocarbonate (LDAC) is being investigated as an antioxidant for asphalt roads and roofing shingles. Some lead compounds are used to stabilize plastics resins.

TIN

Tin (Sn) is a soft, ductile, silvery-white metal. It is highly malleable (similar to silver and gold) and can be hammered into very thin, flat sheets or drawn into thin wire. Tin does not tarnish in air, and it melts at a relatively low temperature, 449.4° F (231.9°C). The specific gravity is 5.77 in alpha form (gray tin), and 7.29 in the normal beta form (white tin). The Brinell hardness at room temperature is 3.9, which is somewhat harder than lead.

The largest use of tin is for tin-coated steel containers used to preserve foods. The next largest uses are in solder alloys, babbitt (bearing metal), bronzes, fusible alloys, type metals, pewter, and dental amalgams. Tin chemical compounds, both inorganic and organic, find extensive use in the electroplating, ceramic, plastics, pesticidal, and antifungal industries.

TIN ALLOY DESIGNATION

Tin alloys are included in the Unified Numbering System (UNS) for Metals and Alloys under the "L" designation for "Low Melting Metals and Alloys." Many of these alloys are solders and often are lead based. Other tin-containing alloys appear in the aluminum alloy section of the UNS, throughout the copper section, and in the reactive and refractory metals section, as well as under miscellaneous alloys.

CHAPTER 15

TIN

GRADES OF TIN

Most applications for tin begin with the metal in ingot form. The purity of the ingot usually conforms to the ASTM B339 Standard Classification "Grade A," with 99.80% minimum tin.

PROPERTIES

Because tin is mechanically weak, there are few uses for the pure metal. Tin easily forms alloys with many metals, however, and is used to increase resistance to corrosion and fatigue and to improve malleability. The metals most commonly alloyed with tin are antimony, copper, lead, zinc, and silver to produce the common tin alloys of bronze, pewter, solder, type metal, and babbitt metal. Some brasses also contain a small amount of tin.

Nontoxic

The useful properties of tin that figure prominently in the commercial uses of the metal include nontoxicity, which allows tin coatings to be used on surfaces that come in contact with food or beverages, or in certain applications that require contact with the human body.

Corrosion Resistance

An equally important property for commercial application is the good corrosion resistance of tin. A suitable coating thickness of tin on steel, as in tinplate, gives sufficient protection for most applications.

Low Melting Point

The low melting point of tin makes it suitable for coating a variety of metals by simple hot dipping. Where greater control of thickness uniformity is required and where hot dipping is not feasible, tin can be readily electroplated onto a variety of surfaces. Overall, including the worldwide production of tinplate, tin is the most commonly electroplated metal.

Alloying and Reactive Ability

Another important property of tin is its ability to alloy with or react with many other metals. For this reason, tin coatings adhere well when applied to metallic surfaces, allowing forming, spinning, and deep drawing operations to follow coating without degradation of the coating protection. Furthermore, tin is the active ingredient in solders because of its low melting point and its ability to wet a wide range of surfaces.

Other Properties

Other properties of tin are important for certain applications. For example, the ability of tin and many tin alloys to hold a film of lubricant leads to their use in a variety of commercial bearing alloys. Tin provides useful, improved properties when alloyed with copper (to form bronze) or when added to various titanium and titanium-aluminum alloys.

Limitations

A phenomenon with tin may require precautions in some circumstances. As is the case for several other metals, tin-plated surfaces can grow whiskers, which are single-crystal, thin filaments of metal that grow spontaneously. The exact mechanism is not fully understood, but it appears that the growth is stress driven. Tin whiskers occur most often on thin electroplated layers, especially on brass or when plating organics are codeposited in large amounts. Hot dipping or reflowing an electroplated coating greatly lowers the risk of tin whiskers, as does the codeposition of small amounts of certain metals, such as lead.

Another precaution is for tin use at low temperatures. The allotropic transformation (beta to alpha) is detrimental when it occurs. Several common impurities retard this transformation, even at the low levels found in commercially pure tin, so that the transformation in practical terms is little more than a laboratory curiosity.

APPLICATIONS

Tin is rarely used alone, but usually in metallurgical combination with another metal or as a coating. Coatings, alloys, and compounds are the largest uses for tin.

Pure tin and alloys of tin can be applied as coatings to all of the common metals by hot dipping or electrodeposition. Tin coatings give protection to metal surfaces that oxidize or corrode readily. They also aid in fabricating and joining metals, and provide a clean, adherent base for paints or lacquers.

Solder

About one third of United States tin consumption goes into the production of solder alloys, roughly as much tin as is consumed for tinplate. While solders for food container and radiator manufacture represent large tonnage markets, the tin content of the solder alloys used in those applications is low, so that the most important solders from a tin consumption viewpoint are used for electrical and electronics soldering. The low melting point of tin that minimizes thermal exposure of delicate components and the wetting ability of tin that speeds soldering are both particularly important properties in the latter applications. Molten solder readily penetrates and fills the capillary space of a well-designed joint.

Bearing Alloys

Tin-based bearing alloys are also called tin-based babbitt alloys, named for the 19th century inventor. They are primarily tin with 5-12% antimony and 1-5% copper. The alloying elements form a hard particulate framework, while the soft tin-based matrix offers excellent resistance to seizure, high corrosion resistance, embeddability, and conformability. This combination of properties has led to diverse uses for these alloys. The best examples of such applications are for large, slow-speed diesel engines and machinery, where temperatures are not very high and conformability is particularly important.

Bronzes

In addition to bearing applications, the uses of tin bronzes are quite varied, some of these predating recorded history. Tin additions improve the mechanical and corrosion properties of copper, while maintaining good workability. Chemical hardware, friction surfaces, mechanical hardware, and gear parts are some of the uses of bronzes containing up to 12% tin. Bell metal, which is used in bell founding, is typically 23% tin. Cymbals and glockenspiels are also made from bronzes with a high tin content.

Additions of zinc and/or lead produce the so-called gunmetals. Leaded bronzes are used to cast valves, gears, pump parts, and various fittings. Adding nickel to copper-tin produces a useful family of alloys with excellent corrosion resistance and good solderability.

Pewter

Modern pewter is nearly pure tin, typically 92% tin with 6% antimony and 2% copper. The alloy is easily spun or cast to make a variety of decorative and useful items, such as drinking vessels, candlesticks, trays, and jewelry. Unlike silver items, pewterware requires only occasional polishing in normal use, although regular rinsing in warm soapy water is recommended.

Tin Coatings

As exemplified by tinplate, tin coatings are useful because they are nontoxic, corrosion resistant, solderable, and easy to apply. Coatings can be electroplated from acid or alkaline electrolytes or applied by dipping in molten tin. They are used on electrical and electronic parts, food handling equipment, automotive parts, and a wide range of consumer goods.

Alloy Coatings

Tin-lead alloys are electroplated in various compositions, including as overlays on bearings surfaces, as corrosion-resistant coatings on steel wire or strip, and as solderable coatings. Tin-lead coatings for these same applications can also be produced by hot dipping. Terneplate is the name for lead-tin coatings containing 4-20% tin. These rely on the wetting ability of tin for good adhesion and on the high-lead alloy for improved corrosion resistance. Terneplate can also be produced electrolytically.

Tin-copper in the form of red bronze plating (7-20% tin) is used for its high wear resistance and excellent corrosion resistance. It has been used in hydraulic mining equipment where such properties are most useful, and for jewelry coatings.

Tin-nickel can be electroplated in an alloy of 65% tin and 35% nickel. It is hard and corrosion resistant with good frictional and lubrication-holding properties. Applications include watch parts, drawing instruments, automobile brake pistons, costume jewelry, and electrical contacts.

Tin-zinc (65-80% tin) also exhibits excellent corrosion resistance as needed for specific situations, and has been used in applications where cadmium can no longer be used. For example, tin-zinc's resistance to corrosion by mineral oil has led to its use as a coating for automotive brake-fluid reservoirs. Tin-cobalt (about 80% tin) has been considered a competitor for chromium plating and does have several advantages in the application process, although the plate itself is not quite so wear resistant. Still other binary and ternary tin alloys are plated, but only for specialized applications.

Chemicals

Inorganic tin chemicals have several important uses in the ceramics and glass industries. Stannic oxide is an opacifier in glass and enamels, as well as one of the oxides that constitute some common pigments. Stannic oxide is also used as a coating on glass in various thicknesses for different purposes. Very thin coatings strengthen glass and improve its abrasion resistance, important in extending the life of glass items that are subjected to rigorous use as in restaurant and catering businesses. Thicker coatings, greater than 39 μin. (1 μm), provide electrical conductivity and retain optical transparency. These properties are used for display signs and lighting, for aircraft deicing windows, and for controls in cathode ray tubes. Since these coatings reflect infrared radiation, they are also useful for heat insulating windows. Stannic oxide is used for glass-melting electrodes and as an electrical capacitor dielectric material.

Other inorganic tin chemical applications include the use of chlorides as reaction catalysts and stannous fluoride as a decay-preventative in toothpastes. Other chemicals find use as flame retardants and for certain biocidal applications.

ZINC

Zinc (Zn), in its unalloyed form, is a bluish-white metal with a specific gravity of 7.1, a melting temperature of 787° F (419°C), and a boiling temperature of 1661°F (905°C). It is readily cast and crystallizes in a hexagonal close-packed structure. The tensile strength of as-cast, unalloyed zinc is about 9000 psi (62 MPa), with an elongation of 1%. It can also be readily fabricated into a variety of wrought products such as rolled zinc sheet, which exhibits a tensile strength of 24,000 psi (165 MPa) with 35% elongation. Zinc is highly active in the electromotive series and forms a thin, complex oxide-carbonate-hydroxide film when exposed to air. This property accounts for its wide use in the corrosion protection of steel, in processes such as galvanizing and metallizing, and for zinc-rich paints.

ALLOY DESIGNATION SYSTEM

The Unified Numbering System (UNS) numbers and American Society for Testing and Materials (ASTM) cross-references specifications for zinc and zinc alloys.

PRODUCT FORMS AND ALLOY TYPES

Cast zinc reaches the market primarily in the form of nominal 50 lb (22.7 kg) slabs, 1 to 1½″ (25.4 to 38.1 mm) thick, 8½ to 10″ (210 to 254 mm) wide, and 18 to 20″ (457 to 508 mm) long. This form of cast zinc is called zinc slab or spelter. Wrought zinc is produced in sheets, plates, ribbon, wire, extrusions, and forgings.

Pure Zinc

Unalloyed zinc containing normal trace impurities from its ores or its smelting and refining processes is generally available in the United States in three grades that are defined by the ASTM Specification B6 for zinc (slab zinc).

Zinc Alloys

The zinc alloy family—which includes pressure die cast, gravity cast, and sheet alloys—provides alloys suitable for the production of cast and wrought components.[24]

Casting alloys. There are two basic groups of zinc casting alloys. The first consists of the traditional zinc-4% aluminum alloys, designated as alloy numbers 3, 5, and 7. These are also commonly known as Zamak 3, 5, and 7, and are cast by pressure die casting. The second group is made up of the new zinc-aluminum ZA alloys ZA-8, ZA-12, and ZA-27, which can be successfully cast by a variety of gravity casting processes, as well as by cold chamber die casting. ZA is a registered trademark of

CHAPTER 15

ZINC

the Zinc Institute. The properties of these two groups of zinc alloys provide a broad flexibility in the design and processing of cast products.

Wrought alloys. Wrought zinc alloy products can be divided into three main categories of semifinished materials according to the deformation techniques used to shape them:

- Flat rolled products (rolled zinc).
- Wire drawn products.
- Forged or extruded products.

Rolled sheet and strip are the predominant forms of wrought zinc. They offer economic advantages for high production quantities, sometimes reaching levels of hundreds of millions of parts per year. Forgings add further flexibility to production with zinc and zinc alloys, and are another alternative when maximum strength and precise tolerances, as well as other well-known forging advantages, are required.

Superplastic Zinc-Aluminum Alloys

The term "superplastic," as applied to alloys in general, refers to a metallurgical condition in which the material's properties resemble those of the plastic state of thermoplastic polymers. In this condition, such alloys can be uniformly and plastically elongated, employing technology resembling that used in forming molten glass and plastics. These superplastic properties are found in many alloy systems, and usually occur within a narrow range of composition and depend upon the processing history.

The useful alloys are those that are superplastic at moderately elevated temperatures but that can be heat treated to exhibit good mechanical and physical properties at room temperature. At their forming temperatures, superplastic alloys exhibit no elastic behavior and do not work harden. The commercially available superplastic alloys have compositions with 78% zinc and 22% aluminum, often with minor additions.

PROPERTIES

Aside from zinc coatings, the casting alloys are the most widely used form of zinc. Zinc-based die-casting alloys were introduced in the late 1920s to meet the demand for strong, stable die castings. These alloys, familiarly known as the Zamak or Mazak alloys, show a unique combination of properties that permit rapid, economic casting of strong, durable, accurate parts, and hence have dominated the market since their inception. They have many advantages over other die-casting materials, such as aluminum and magnesium alloys. The zinc alloys are more easily cast, are stronger and more ductile, require less finishing, can be held to closer tolerances, and can be cast in thinner sections. Because of low casting temperatures, die life for zinc die castings exceeds that for other die-cast metals. The production rate (shots per hour) is also higher.

Die casting with zinc-based alloys is one of the most efficient and versatile production methods for the manufacture of accurate, complex metal components. In general, the mechanical properties of zinc alloy die castings used at normal temperatures are superior to those of sand-cast gray iron, brass, and aluminum, particularly fracture toughness and impact strength. Zinc alloy die castings are stronger, tougher, and more dimensionally stable than some injection molded plastics, and can be produced at a higher rate.

Creep Behavior

When specifying and processing materials, it is customary to rely on tensile strength as a significant and useful property. Specifying this property is usually adequate for most metal alloys. However, when zinc alloys are involved and are expected to perform under constant tensile-load conditions or at elevated temperatures, the creep strength will be the determining factor for specifying the alloys.

Foundry alloys. Creep limitations exist with respect to conventional zinc die-casting alloys. However, the new ZA foundry alloys offer improved creep strengths for higher strength designs. Many applications do not impose constant stress at elevated temperatures, and so creep may not be their limiting factor.

Wrought alloys. Rolled unalloyed zinc creeps readily at room temperature; and although the addition of copper is beneficial, the improvement in creep resistance is small. However, the addition of a small amount (0.1-0.2%) of titanium to zinc or zinc-copper alloys provides a substantial improvement in the creep resistance, particularly in the case of the zinc-copper alloys.

Mechanical Properties

Superplastic alloys. The commercially available superplastic zinc alloys can be divided into three general groups, based on their compositions and mechanical properties. These groups have been arbitrarily designated A, B, and C, since no generally accepted nomenclature has been established to date. Alloy A is the basic binary zinc-aluminum alloy; alloy B contains copper, which has been added to improve the tensile and creep strengths; alloy C has magnesium added as well as copper to further improve these properties. The mechanical properties are tabulated under two conditions:

1. As rolled—the alloy in the superplastic condition.
2. Annealed and air cooled—the alloy in the finished condition after heat treatment to remove the superplasticity and reestablish good room temperature mechanical properties.

Wire drawn products. Zinc alloys in the form of wire are largely used for flame or arc-spray metallizing. Certain zinc alloy wire grades are also used either as filler metal for soldering or for their mechanical properties.

Forging and extruded alloys. Although the applications of extruded and forged zinc products have been relatively limited, the inherent advantages of the extrusion and forging processes are applicable to zinc alloys. Zinc extrusions and forgings can be readily machined; can be joined by soldering, welding, or adhesives; and can be finished with paints, polymers, or with electroplated coatings. Because of the ductility of zinc extrusions and forgings, secondary operations—such as bending, swaging, flaring, stamping, and coining—can be readily performed, as required. Zinc extrusions and forgings can be produced to meet the requirements for a variety of applications.

The zinc-based forging alloys can be divided into two groups, the zinc-titanium family and the zinc-aluminum family. The zinc-titanium alloys are recommended for most forging applications. The zinc-aluminum alloys were developed for specialty applications, particularly where high impact strength at low temperatures is required.

Zinc-titanium. The zinc-titanium alloys possess good

strength and ductility, are easily forged and machined, are dimensionally stable, have excellent creep characteristics, and offer unusual resistance to dimensional growth at elevated temperatures. Joining can be accomplished by any of the standard methods, and finishing characteristics are good.

Zinc-aluminum. The zinc-aluminum alloys are low density, two-phase materials having superior strength and impact properties at very low temperatures, -60° F (-50° C). They have somewhat better machine turning characteristics and have better bearing properties. Like the zinc-titanium alloys, joining properties and finishing characteristics are excellent.

APPLICATIONS

Unalloyed zinc is widely used for protective coatings and in engineering applications as anodes for the cathodic protection of structures immersed in an electrolyte, such as seawater or moist soil. Zinc alloys, on the other hand, traditionally have been used extensively in decorative, nonload-bearing applications, but typically were not specified for engineered load-bearing components and structures. However, recent advances in fabricating technology, combined with active and fruitful programs in alloy development, have established the viability of zinc alloys in the field of engineering load-bearing materials.

The principal end uses for zinc are: (1) unalloyed zinc coatings or anodes for corrosion protection; (2) casting alloys; (3) as the alloying element in copper, aluminum, magnesium, or other-based alloys; (4) wrought alloys; and (5) zinc chemicals. In the corrosion protection category, hot-dip or continuous galvanizing accounts for the majority of zinc consumption. In casting alloys, it is the die-casting compositions that consume most of the zinc. In the zinc-containing alloys, the copper-based materials, such as the brasses, are the largest zinc consumers. Rolled zinc is the major form in which wrough zinc products are supplied, although drawn zinc wire for metalizing is gaining increasing usage. In the zinc chemical division, zinc oxide represents the compound of major importance.

For galvanizing applications, the less pure or higher lead content grades are generally used; however, the impurities (lead aluminum, and iron) must be controlled for the various galvanizing processes. The grade of zinc used for die-casting alloys and anodes is usually special high grade, while both high grade and special high grade are employed for brasses and rolled alloys, depending on the specific application.

Zinc oxide is used in rubber, paints, ceramics, chemicals, agriculture, photocopying, floor coverings, and coated fabrics and textiles. Both the French process and the American process grades are used in most of these applications, depending upon the specific character of the end product. Zinc oxide's largest use is found in rubber products where it is an activator for the accelerators used to speed up the vulcanization process. It is a pigment in paints and ceramics, a soil nutrient in the agricultural field, a stabilizer in plastics, and provides the photosensitive character for coated papers used in some photocopying techniques.

FABRICATION

Zinc alloys can be fabricated into parts using a broad range of production processes that are capable of supplying components in quantities anywhere from millions a year down to a single part. Zinc alloys are used in more production casting processes than any other ferrous or nonferrous metal and,

hence, fill a major role in industrial parts manufacture.

Die casting, permanent-mold casting, graphite permanent-mold casting, sand casting, and shell-mold casting are the methods most widely used in commercial zinc alloy components manufacture. Plaster-mold casting is used for prototyping zinc castings to allow testing of new component designs.

References

1. *Modern Steels and Their Properties* (Bethlehem, PA: Bethlehem Steel Corp., 1980), p 43.
2. *American Welding Society, Welding Handbook*, 7th ed., vol 1 (Miami, FL: American Welding Society, 1976), p. 137.
3. *Modern Steels and Their Properties, op. cit.*, p. 61.
4. E. E. Fletcher, *"A Review of the Status, Selection, and Physical Metallurgy of High-Strength, Low-Alloy Steels,"* Battelle Report MCIC-79-39 (Columbus, OH: Battelle Columbus Laboratories, March 1979), pp. 5-110.
5. *Metals Progress 1978 Databook* (Metals Park, OH: American Society for Metals, 1979), pp. 47-59.
6. D. G. Younger, "How Ford Evaluates Conversions to HSLA," *Metal Progress* (May 1975), pp. 43-47.
7. Fletcher, *op. cit.*, p. 40.
8. *Ibid.*, p. 93.
9. *Ibid.*, p. 75.
10. *Ibid.*, p. 49.
11. Charles F. Walton, ed., *Iron Castings Handbook* (Des Plaines, IL: Iron Castings Society, Inc., 1981), pp. 667-668.
12. *Ibid.*, p. 509.
13. Howard B. Cary, *Modern Welding Technology* (Englewood Cliffs, NJ: Prentice-Hall, Inc., 1979), p. 463.
14. Henry Horwitz, *Welding: Principles and Practice* (Boston: Houghton Mifflin Company, 1979), p. 570.
15. Juri Kolts, James B.C. Wu, and Aziz I. Asphahani, "Highly Alloyed Austenitic Materials for Corrosion Resistance," *Metal Progress* (September 1983), p. 34.
16. Eugene W. Kelley, *The Fabrication of Superalloys*, SME Technical Paper MF78-642 (Dearborn, MI: Society of Manufacturing Engineers, 1978), p.1.
17. *Ibid.*
18. Kelley, *op.cit.*, pp. 3-10.
19. The Aluminum Association, Inc., *Aluminum Standards and Data*, 7th ed. (Washington,DC: 1982).
20. Copper Development Association, Inc., *Standard Designations for Copper and Copper Alloys*, Application Data Sheet 101/3.
21. Copper Development Association, Inc., *Machining Rod Handbook: Copper Brass, Bronze*, 702/9.
22. Kenneth Budinski, *Engineering Materials, Properties, and Selection*, 2nd ed. (Reston, VA: Reston Publishing Co., Inc., 1983).
23. Lead Industries Association, Inc., "Properties of Lead and Lead Alloys" (New York: 1983).
24. International Lead Zinc Research Organization, Inc. and Zinc Institute, Inc., *Designing in Zinc*, 1st ed. (New York: 1982).

PLASTICS AND COMPOSITES

PLASTICS

Plastics are nonmetallic materials that can be formed and shaped by many methods. Plastics can be made from such natural resins as shellac; however, most plastics used in industrial applications are produced from man-made synthetic resins.

Plastics have become one of the most common classes of engineering materials in the past decade. For the last five years, the production of plastics, on a volume basis, exceeded steel output. Engineering plastics, those grades devised to resist severe service conditions or structural loads are in widespread use and their applications are increasing rapidly.[1]

To assure selection of the most suitable plastics material from among hundreds that are available, it is advisable to develop direct sources of information, including contacts with resin manufacturers. Table 16-1 lists representative properties for selected thermoplastics and thermosets commonly used in industrial applications.

ASTM CLASSIFICATION SYSTEM

The American Society of Testing and Materials (ASTM) is a technical organization bringing manufacturers, specifiers, and users together to standardize specifications and test methods. Several individual types of plastics have been covered by specific ASTM standards; D 789 for polyamide (nylon) and D 788 for acrylic are two examples. Standards are useful for two reasons: First, the specifier can be assured of minimum strengths and properties for design calculations. Second, competitive manufacturers' resins can be used. Unfortunately, the rapid growth of the plastics industry also limits the usefulness of single standards. As mentioned previously, there is considerable competition between different types of resins. New and modified grades of resins are being developed, more quickly than ASTM standards can be set.

To remedy this situation by establishing an industry-wide designation system, in 1982 the ASTM issued the Standard D 4000 "Guide for Identification of Plastic Materials" to "adequately identify plastic materials in order to give industry a system that can be used universally." In D 4000, ASTM is attempting to establish a single designation system for all types and grades of plastics. In essence, D 4000 combines generic designations with a unified system of identifying important modifications to the generic resin and significant engineering property minimums. Figure 16-1 describes a typical line callout for ASTM Standard D 4000 application. A regular designation for a glass-filled polyamide (PA) or nylon resin is the ASTM D 4000 specification for 33% glassfilled nylon (polyamide) resin grade, that

is, ASTM D 4000 PA120G33A53380GA140 where:

ASTM D 4000 = Plastics material
PA120G33 = Basic—generic resin and modifications
A53380 = Cell—mechanical (physical) properties
GA140 = Suffix—special properties and tests

BASIC TERMINOLOGY

The term "polymer" is commonly used interchangeably with the term "plastics." Neither term is entirely accurate in its delineation. Plastic means pliable, yet most engineering polymers are not plastic at room temperature. Polymer, on the other hand, can include every kind of material made by polymerization with repeating molecules. The ASTM definition (D 883) of a plastic is : "A material that contains as an essential ingredient an organic substance of large molecular weight, is solid in its finished state, and, at some stage in its manufacture or in its processing into finished articles, can be shaped by flow."

In broad terms, plastics are man-made polymers. Polymer is the generic name for all materials composed of long, chainlike molecules. Most living tissue and cells are polymeric. Plastics are created either by modifying natural polymers, such as cellulose fibers, or by causing small synthetic molecules to bond together into a chain. Compared to other classes of materials, the plastics molecular chain is enormous, giving it the term "macromolecule." Millions of macromolecular chains must be put together to make industrially useful quantities.

MECHANICAL PROPERTIES

Both metals and plastics are characterized by similar types of mechanical properties. Metals, however, tend to be consistent in the sense that their behavior is adequately characterized by stress-strain relationships. In contrast, while the individual plastics materials also display distinctive stress-strain characteristics, the mechanical properties of plastics are more dependent on the additional factors of temperature and time (under load). In the design application, and to some extent in processing, creep data are of significant importance in the field of plastics materials.

The engineering plastics materials have ultimate tensile and compressive strengths and stiffness properties that are significantly lower than those of metals. This difference is especially true when comparing plastics to tool steels and high-strength steels. However, the differential in ultimate mechanical strength is much less when plastics are compared with metals such as aluminum,

PLASTICS

TABLE 16-1
Properties of Selected Industrial Plastics

Type of Plastics	Molecular Packing	Specific Gravity	ASTM D-638 Tensile Strength, psi (MPa)	ASTM D-638 Elongation, percent	ASTM D-695 Compressive Strength, psi (MPa)	ASTM D-256 Impact Strength (Izod), ft · lb/in. (J/cm)
Polystyrene	Amorphous	1.10	7500 (51.7)	2	14,000 (96.5)	0.3 (0.2)
High-impact polystyrene	Amorphous	1.15	5000 (34.5)	10	7500 (51.7)	0.6-10.0 (0.3-5.3)
Acrylics	Amorphous	1.15	10,000 (69.0)	6	15,000 (103.4)	0.4 (0.2)
Polycarbonate	Amorphous	1.20	9000 (62.1)	100	10,000 (69.0)	15.0 (8.0)
ABS	Amorphous	1.05	6000 (41.4)	30	8000 (55.2)	6.0 (3.2)
Acetal (homopolymer)	Crystalline	1.40	10,000 (69.0)	40	18,000 (124.1)	1.8 (1.0)
Nylon 6/6 at 50% RH*	Crystalline	1.15	11,000 (75.8)	400	10,000 (69.0)	2.1 (1.1)
Polypropylene	Crystalline	0.91	4500 (31.0)	500	7000 (48.3)	1.0 (0.5)
Polyethylene (high density)	Crystalline	0.95	4000 (27.6)	600	3000 (20.7)	10.0 (5.3)
Polyethylene (medium density)	Crystalline with amorphous regions	0.93	2400 (16.5)	600	3000 (20.7)	8.0 (4.3)
Polyethylene (low density)	Semi-crystalline	0.91	1500 (10.3)	700	3000 (20.7)	No break
Epoxy	Cross-linked network	1.25	10,000 (69.0)	3	20,000 (137.9)	0.8 (0.4)
Phenolic	Cross-linked network	1.35	7000 (4-8.3)	2	10,000 (69.0)	0.4 (0.2)

*RH = relative humidity

magnesium, zinc, and copper. Strength ranges of typical plastics are compared in Fig. 16-2.

Plastics are too new to have a well-defined, standard set of generic properties. As with metals, tensile, compressive, and impact tests are routine. Unlike metals, at room temperature visco-elastic effects dominate the behavior of plastics in service and are an important consideration in parts processing and manufacture. A second dissimilarity is the wide range of differences in property values between metals and plastics. Thus, special tests had to be devised for plastics. To account for visco-elasticity, creep testing data and thermal properties are routinely shown. For standard mechanical tests, special pro-

cedures have been developed to account for both the differences in value ranges and for visco-elasticity. The temperature, humidity, and rate of deformation must be carefully controlled to attain meaningful test results.

Reliable information on mechanical properties and other important characteristics of plastics can be obtained from various sources. The resin manufacturers publish technical information and data for the polymers they produce. Publications and reports are available from the Society of Plastics Engineers (SPE) and the Society of the Plastics Industry (SPI). Additional data sources are the tabulations published by technical periodicals and trade journals in the plastics field.

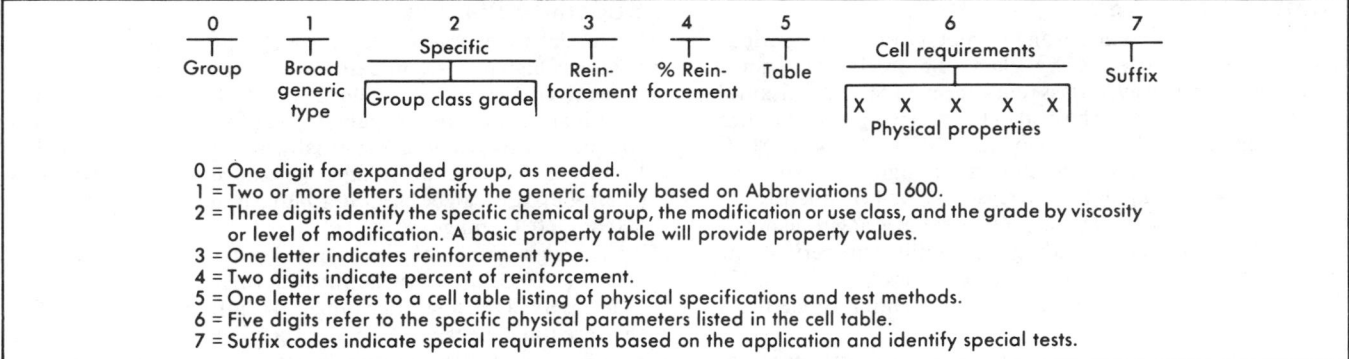

Fig. 16-1 ASTM D 4000 coding system. Line callout to designate a plastics material. (*ASTM*)

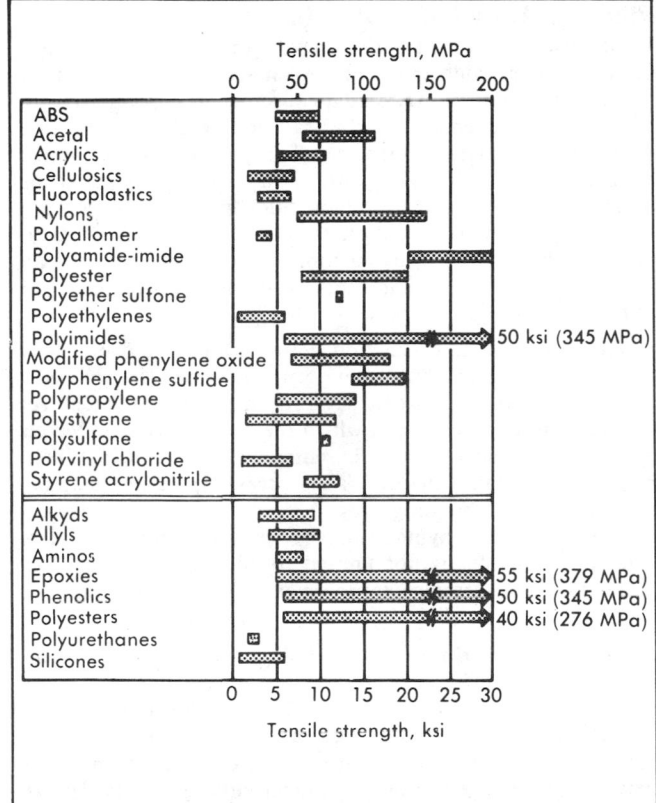

Fig. 16-2 Tensile strength of selected plastics at 68°F (20°C) per ASTM D 638. (*"Engineering Materials, Properties and Selection," Kenneth Budinski*)

ENGINEERING PLASTICS[2]

The thermoplastic engineering resins are usually characterized as those resins having the following combination of properties:

- Thermal, mechanical, chemical, corrosion resistance, and fabricability.
- Ability to sustain high mechanical loads, in harsh environments, for long periods of time.
- Predictable, reliable performance.

The term "engineering plastics" is neither rigorously defined nor restrictive in the sense that implies there is also a well-defined group of nonengineering plastics. Instead, some industry experts advocate a practical definition of engineering plastics that includes not only the property/performance criteria, but also market/pricing criteria.

The above two sets of criteria, taken together, place certain resins in the engineering category to the exclusion of others. The principal resins of the past decade that meet both sets of criteria are: nylon, acetal, thermoplastic polyester, modified phenylene oxide, and polycarbonate. In the 1980s, new materials, including some grades of acrylonitrile butadiene styrene (ABS), are being developed that can be categorized as engineering plastics.

Balance of Properties

The engineering plastics have a good balance of high tensile properties, stiffness, compressive and shear strength, as well as impact resistance, and they are easily moldable. Their high physical strength properties are reproducible and predictable, and they retain their physical and electrical properties over a wide range of environmental conditions (hot, cold, chemicals). The engineering plastics can resist mechanical stress with good retention of properties for long periods of time. Flame retardance, which formerly had not been an essential requirement, has now become an important attribute for many applications.

Advantages and Limitations

The advantageous characteristics of engineering plastics include high strength per unit weight, inherent corrosion resistance, little or no maintenance, and good retention of mechanical properties. Depending on the reinforcements or fillers added (such as glass or graphite), stiffness, lubricity, and other properties can be enhanced.

Because the end products typically are molded, design flexibility enables multiple functions to be combined into a single part, thus reducing the total parts count (as well as assembly time and labor), while eliminating finish grinding and machining. Also, because resins can be pigmented, painting is often not required.

The main inherent problem with engineering plastics is creep deformation under load. Glass reinforcement is commonly used to control and limit the creep characteristics of some plastics. In some applications, abrasion resistance and wear resistance are other limitations that must be taken into consideration.

CHAPTER 16

PLASTICS

Reinforced Resins

As revealed by a comparison of property values, the various resin groups are affected by glass reinforcement in some markedly different ways. Glass reinforcement raises the flexural modulus for all of them. The heat deflection temperatures all go up as well, especially for nylon and PBT. Nylon's 480°F (249°C) HDT qualifies it for short-term high-heat exposure, and its long-term capability increases as well. In the case of PBT, glass reinforcement makes a true engineering resin out of a material that is not outstanding in its unfilled properties. The thermal index of 284°F (140°C) (the highest of all resins in this group) is important in relation to retention of electrical properties.

Glass reinforcement improves the various properties of acetal, compared to the unfilled resin; but, in comparison with other glass-reinforced materials, it is not outstanding. Glass reinforcement of modified phenylene oxide resin and polycarbonate results in decreased impact resistance; and, in the case of polycarbonate, it also causes a loss of transparency. Properties that are generally improved by the use of glass-reinforced resins include dimensional stability, moisture resistance, and flammability ratings.

Glass reinforcement reduces the ductility and unnotched Izod impact resistance of most thermoplastic resins. The use of reinforced resins is growing rapidly, and they are being increasingly specified for engineering applications that replace metal stampings, die castings, and, in some instances, cast iron.

Other Plastics Used
for Engineering Applications

In some product applications, the five principal groups of engineering plastics compete with other plastics such as ABS, polystyrene, and various thermosetting plastics. Glass and/or mineral-filled polypropylene and flame-retardant ABS are widely used where their special characteristics are needed, and modified phenylene oxide (Noryl) must compete against flame-retardant ABS in some electronic cabinetry where a relatively low thermal index is acceptable. Ultrahigh molecular weight polyethylene (UHMWPE) offers excellent wear resistance, but limited processability.

Thermosets. Thermosets have long been available as insulators in electric/electronic applications, offering a wide range of capabilities in resistance to heat and other environmental conditions. Thermoset molding compounds may be formulated to satisfy one or more important uses. Typical distinctive properties of thermosets include dimensional stability, low-to-zero creep, low water absorption, maximum physical strength, good electrical properties, high heat deflection temperatures, high heat resistance, minimal values of coefficient of thermal expansion, low heat transfer, and specific gravities in the 1.35 to 2.00 range.

Fluoropolymers. Fluoropolymers are often categorized along with the engineering plastics, but the two groups seldom directly compete. As a class, fluoropolymers do not offer the load-bearing capability of the engineering plastics, and load-bearing is generally one of the demands placed on plastics in product engineering specifications. In nonload-bearing uses, however, fluoropolymers have outstanding and unique properties, including resistance to very high and low temperatures, exceptional electrical properties, and a low coefficient of friction.

Specialty Plastics

Specialty plastics include a mixed group of materials sold at relatively high prices, compared to the engineering plastics, and in relatively low volumes. The members of this group generally have high-temperature capability, but this capability involves complex, costly synthesis and usually some processing difficulty. In this group, the polyimides (thermoset) and polyamides (thermoplastic) can be used continuously at temperatures in the 500°F (260°C) range.

The significance of thermoplastics that can operate over 302°F (150°C) does not lie in their role as replacements for thermosets in the low-price range. With the exception of PPS, they are too expensive. They can function as replacements for metals, glass, epoxies, fluoropolymers, and specialty thermosets in areas where thermoplastic processing advantages make the cost worthwhile.

Plastics Alloys and Blends

Because of the high cost to develop and introduce a new plastics and provide the necessary marketing and technical support, new materials tailored for specific sets of properties are often made by chemical or physical modifications of existing resins. Desirable characteristics and properties can be obtained by blending or alloying resins, or by adding inorganic or organic fillers and reinforcements. Such modification is being done by primary resin suppliers who use these methods to produce special grades, by custom compounders, and—to an increasing extent—by end-users who tailor-make resins to fulfill their own specific needs.

Description. The distinction between alloys and blends is not clearly defined, but both terms are used for physical mixtures of two or more structurally different polymers. As compared to copolymers, in which the components are linked by strong chemical bonds, the components in alloys adhere primarily through Van der Waals forces, dipole interactions, and/or hydrogen bonding.

The process of alloying to improve certain desired characteristics of a polymer is not limited to adding only one other polymer. There are also terpolymers (three monomers in a chain) and plastics alloys with several polymer additives.

Polymer networks. A new technology that combines incompatible plastics to form interpenetrating polymer networks (IPNs) has been developed by Shell Chemical and other companies. This technique produces a new type of alloy consisting of intimate mixtures of two or more polymer networks held together by permanent entanglements. Unlike conventional alloys, the polymers need not be miscible, and the networks can be devised for optimum properties when they are needed, while using lower cost materials as the predominant ingredient when the property requirements are less severe.

PROCESSING AND APPLICATIONS
OVERVIEW

The melt-processability of thermoplastic resins is a basic characteristic that distinguishes them from thermosets. This fact pertains not only to the advantages of injection molding as compared to compression or transfer molding, but also to the variety of processing alternatives that extend the utility of the thermoplastics. There are thermosets that can be injection molded; but only the thermoplastics offer the options of extrusion into sheet, film and profiles, or blow molding.

The degree to which each of the engineering plastics is amenable to alternative processing methods varies, and the relative potential of each of them depends also on their potential in alternative processes, not just on their utility in injection molding. Tables 16-2 and 16-3 generally relate the thermosets and thermoplastics and their respective parts production processes.

In addition to its use in injection molding, nylon is extruded into monofilament and brush filament. Nylon-6 is used for sewing thread, fishing line, household/industrial brushes, and level-filament paint brushes. Nylon-6,6, stiffer than nylon-6, is used for sewing thread and household/industrial brushes. Nylon-6,12 dominates in personal-care brushes, although poly-

TABLE 16-2
Thermoplastics Parts Manufacturing Processes

Thermoplastics	Compression molding	Transfer molding	Injection molding	Extrusion	Rotational molding	Blow molding	Thermoforming	Reaction injection molding	Casting	Forging	Foam molding	Reinforced plastic molding	Vacuum molding	Pultrusion	Calendering
Acetal			•	•	•	•	•				•	•			•
ABS			•	•	•	•	•			•					•
Acrylic	•		•	•		•	•		•						•
Cellulose acetate	•		•	•			•								•
Cellulose acetate-butyrate	•		•	•	•		•								•
Cellulose nitrate	•		•	•			•								•
Cellulose propionate	•		•	•			•								•
Ethyl cellulose			•	•			•					•			•
Chlorinated polyether			•	•	•	•	•								
CTFE	•	•	•	•			•								•
Tetrafluoroethylene (TFE)	•	•	•	•											•
FEP	•	•	•	•		•									•
CTFE-VF$_2$	•	•	•	•	•	•									•
Nylon			•	•	•	•		•	•	•		•			•
Phenoxy			•	•		•									
Polyimide			•												
Polycarbonate			•	•		•	•								•
Polyethylene			•	•	•	•	•			•	•	•			•
Polyphenylene oxide (PPO)			•	•		•						•			
Polypropylene (PP)	•		•	•	•	•	•		•	•		•			•
Polystyrene			•	•	•	•	•				•	•			•
Polysulfone			•	•		•	•					•		•	
Polyurethane			•	•	•						•	•	•		•
SAN			•	•		•									
PVC	•	•	•	•	•	•	•				•	•	•		•
Polyvinyl acetate	•	•	•	•	•	•	•				•				•
Polyvinylidene chloride			•												

PLASTICS

TABLE 16-3
Thermoset Plastics Parts Manufacturing Processes

Thermosetting Plastics	Compression molding	Transfer molding	Injection molding	Rotational molding	Thermoforming	Reaction injection molding	Casting	Foam molding	Reinforced plastics molding	Laminating
Alkyd	•	•	•				•		•	
Allyl					•		•		•	•
Epoxy				•		•	•	•	•	•
Melamine	•	•	•				•	•	•	
Phenolic	•	•	•				•	•	•	•
Polyester (unsaturated)	•					•	•	•	•	
Polyurethane						•				
Silicone							•	•	•	
Urea	•	•	•						•	

ethylene terephthalate (PET) competes in these applications. In tapered-filament paint brushes, nylon-6,12's leading position has been taken over by PBT, a more expensive but more versatile filament.

Nylon is used as a wire coating, primarily as a protective abrasion-resistant coating over PVC-insulated wire. Nylon film can be cast or blown, or extrusion coated onto various substrates. Most nylon film is cast, and virtually all is sold to converters who add a sealant layer of low-density polyethylene (LDPE), ethylene-vinyl acetate copolymer (EVA), or ionomer. Its major market is vacuum packages of processed meats and cheese, usually combined with a PET-sealant cover web. Nylon film is also used for fresh-meat packaging, and a new market has opened in medical device packaging using techniques similar to those for formed-meat packaging. The most important properties in these applications are formability and heat resistance.

Nylon strapping began replacing steel strapping in the early 1960s, even at higher cost, because of the general advantages of nonmetallic strapping. In recent years, nylon has met increasing competition in this market from polypropylene and PET.

Nylon is also extruded into rods, tubes, and shapes for machining, an important option for low-volume runs. The blow molding of nylon has been restrained partly by cost and partly by the difficulties inherent in crystalline resins because of their sharp melting point. Nylon blow-molding resins have been developed with high melt strengths for parison forming and are used to some extent for monolayer and coextruded bottles and for gas tanks in small equipment. Nylon-6 is also cast to produce very large bearings.

Nylon-11 is used for powder coatings and for flexible tubing. Nylon-12 is used for the same purposes, but to a greater extent in Europe than in the U.S. These resins have exceptional moisture resistance, but they are considerably less stiff than nylon-6 or -6,6. They are used to some extent in rotational molding.

In contrast to nylon, acetal offers few options outside of the injection molding category. An acetal terpolymer is available for injection blow molding; but, apart from some carburetor floats and rod extrusions, it has found little usage. Although acetal is difficult to extrude, it is extruded into shapes, as is nylon, for subsequent machining. Almost all acetal consumption is in injection molding, a factor that limits its total consumption.

The PET thermoplastic polyesters used for film, sheet, and blow molding are not the same as those used for injection-molded engineering applications. PBT can be blow molded, but rarely is. While used almost entirely in injection molding, PBT does find some use in tapered brush filaments and in extruded strip for small electrical parts.

Noryl resin's use in extrusion is relatively minor compared to injection molding, but it is used to some extent for stock shapes and to an increasing extent for sheet and profiles. Noryl (General Electric's PPO) sheet competes with flame-retardant ABS as it does in injection molding, and it can compete with less expensive resins like ABS and PVC where its properties permit the extrusion of thinner walls.

The transparency of polycarbonate, combined with its extrudability and impact resistance, makes it a strong competitor for acrylic sheet in replacement of flat glass. Extruded sheet for glazing, lighting, and signs accounts for approximately 25% of polycarbonate's volume. Its use in extruded profiles is minor, but polycarbonate is widely used in blow molding for water bottles, milk bottles, baby nursing bottles, and miscellaneous packaging.

THERMOSET PLASTICS MOLDING

Types of thermoset materials that are capable of being molded include phenolic, urea, melamine, melamine-phenolic, diallyl phthalate, alkyd, polyester, epoxy, and the silicones. Thermosetting molding compounds processed from the individual heat-reactive resin systems are available in a wide range of formulations to satisfy specific end-use requirements. Depending upon the type of material, products may be supplied in granular, nodular, flaked, diced, or pelletized form. Polyester materials are supplied in granular, bulk, log, rope, or sheet form, and polyurethanes are made in many forms, ranging from flexible and rigid foams to rigid solids and abrasion-resistant coatings.

As the term implies, thermoset molding compounds when placed within the confines of a mold (generally hardened steel) are subjected to heat to plasticize and cure the material, and to pressure to form the desired shape. The mold is held closed, under pressure, sufficiently long to polymerize or cure the material into a hard, infusible mass.

Compression Molding

In compression molding, the plastics compound is placed in a heated mold. The compound softens and becomes plastic as the upper part of the die moves (down or up, depending on the movable platen location), compressing the material to the required shape and density. Continued heat and pressure produce the chemical reaction that hardens the thermosetting material.

Transfer Molding

Transfer molding, as the name implies, is a method of molding specific parts when it is desirable that the two halves of the mold, containing the shape of the part, are closed before any material is introduced. The material is loaded into a pot or transfer sleeve, and transfer pressure is applied to cause material to flow into the closed section of the mold. In a single-cavity mold, the material flows generally through a sprue bushing and is gated directly into the part. In the case of a multicavity mold, it flows from a sprue bushing or transfer sleeve into a runner system and is gated into each cavity and part.

There are two distinct transfer methods of molding. One is known as pot-type transfer, and the other (more widely used) is the plunger transfer method.

INJECTION MOLDING

Injection molding is a versatile process for forming thermoplastic and thermoset materials into molded products of intricate shapes, at high production rates and with good dimensional accuracy. Injection molding makes use of the heat-softening characteristics of thermoplastic materials. These materials soften when heated and reharden when cooled. No chemical changes take place when the material is heated or cooled, the change being entirely physical. For this reason the softening and rehardening cycle can be repeated several times. While this is true for thermoplastics, with certain thermosets and rubbers that can be injection molded, a chemical reaction does occur.

The basic injection molding process involves the injection, under high pressure, of a metered quantity of heated and plasticized material into a relatively cool mold—in which the plastics material solidifies.

EXTRUSION FORMING

The extrusion process is a continuous operation in which hot plasticized material is forced through a die opening that produces an extrudate of the desired shape. The most commonly extruded materials are rigid and flexible vinyl, ABS, polystyrene, polypropylene, and polyethylene. Nylon, polycarbonate, polysulfone, acetal, and polyphenylene are included among other plastics that can be extruded.

The extrusion process is used to produce film (thinner than 0.030"; 0.76 mm), sheets (thicker than 0.030", 0.76 mm), filaments, tubes, and a variety of profiles. The process of

plastics extrusion also is used to coat cables, wires, and metal strips.

In the profile extrusion process, the material in pellet, granular, or powder form is placed into a feed hopper which feeds the cylinder of the extruding machine as required (see Fig. 16-3). The cylinder is heated by electricity, oil, or steam, and closely controlled temperature zones are set up along its length. A rotating screw carries the material through the cylinder, mixing and working the material where necessary, and forcing it through a die orifice of the proper shape.

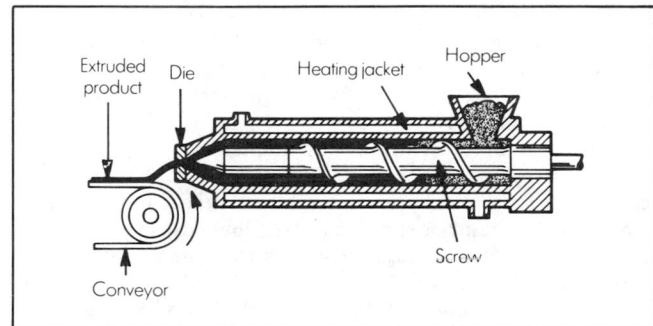

Fig. 16-3 Schematic arrangement of a plastic extrusion machine.

REACTION INJECTION MOLDING

Reaction injection molding (RIM) is a form of injection molding that brings temperature and ratio-controlled, liquid-reactant streams together under high-pressure impingement mixing to form a polymer directly in the mold. Two liquid reactants (monomers) are mixed together as they enter the mold. A chemical reaction produces the plastics as it forms the part.

When compared to other molding systems, RIM offers more design flexibility, lower energy requirements, lower pressures, lower tooling costs, and lower capital investment. Significant advantages in design and production are gained from the RIM fabricating capability for incorporating a load-bearing, structural skin and a lightweight, rigid, cellular core into a part in one processing operation.

While initial RIM applications were primarily automotive, nonautomotive uses are increasing in industrial, business, and consumer-product applications. Recent production applications include business machine cabinets and vacuum cleaner housings. Thermosetting polyurethanes are the most commonly used RIM materials. Recently, however, the successful completion of development and testing programs on other plastics, such as nylons and epoxies, has led to RIM production usage of these materials.

Urethanes currently dominate commercial RIM production and can be formulated to produce a wide range of densities, flexible or rigid, from low-density foam to rigid structural foam and from low to high-modulus elastomers.

Reaction injection molding urethane elastomers provide design freedom combining damage resistance, corrosion resistance, and parts consolidation with large and complex shapes. Current automotive applications include front and rear fascia, bumpers, fenders, and spoilers. Other transportation uses of urethane RIM products include bus bumpers, truck fender extensions, and interior trim panels.

PLASTICS

Nonautomotive urethane RIM applications are increasing and include electronic equipment enclosures; recreation items; shoes; and products for the construction, furniture, agriculture, and appliance fields. Specific product applications include hay rollers, tractor grilles and cab roofs, water-bed frames, tennis backboards, window frames, office furniture, work surfaces, marine boarding ladders, shoe soles, boots, beer kegs, oar blades, file cabinets, bookshelves, computer housings, snowmobiles, golf carts, television screens, and lawn and garden equipment housings.

REINFORCED THERMOSET PLASTICS

The reinforced plastics described in this chapter primarily encompass polyester and fiberglass systems. The most commonly used processes can be divided into two categories: high and low volume. Several less-common intermediate volume processes also are described in this chapter.

The low-volume processes fall in the 2000-25,000 parts per year range. They are characterized by essentially low-pressure to pressureless hand or spray lay-up in low-cost molds with a high labor cost. High-volume processes are those in which more than 30,000 parts per year are produced (100,000 parts per tool for automotive components). They involve an initial high cost for tooling and equipment, but the labor intensity is low. These processes are not competitive with the metal stamping process unless they eliminate the need for multipiece assembly operations.

The high-volume processes for reinforced thermoset plastics are sheet molding compound (SMC), thick molding compound (TMC), bulk molding compound (BMC), pultrusion, and pulforming.

Sheet Molding Compound

Sheet molding compound is a mixture of chopped fiberglass and thermosetting polyester resins that is formed into a sheet up to 1/4" (6.4 mm) thick. This sheet can be easily handled and can be cut into strips or squares and used as a compression molding compound.

Thick Molding Compound (TMC)

This manufacturing process uses a mixture of chopped fiberglass and thermosetting polyester resins that is formed into a sheet up to 2" (51 mm) thick or into a billet shape for compression and injection molding.

The thick molding compound system has a 50% advantage in production rates over SMC systems. Greater filler contents can also be tolerated. The production of thick sheets reduces handling costs and consumption of carrier sheets.

The use of the TMC process for some large automotive parts (grille opening panels) has been successful in providing good strength and improved surfaces (in comparison to the use of the SMC process). The injection-molding method is used.

Bulk Molding Compound

The bulk molding compound (BMC) manufacturing process predates the SMC and TMC systems and has been used to produce a large number of automotive and electrical parts. The automotive companies use large amounts of BMC for heater and air conditioning housings. Some compounders have used sisal as the primary reinforcing fiber.

Pultrusion Manufacturing Process

Pultrusion is a continuous method of manufacturing various reinforced plastic shapes of uniform cross sections (rods, tubes, and I beams). This method consists of pulling various reinforcing materials through a resin bath and subsequently forming and curing them. The cured section of material is then cut to any predetermined length. Figure 16-4 is a schematic drawing of this process.

Pulforming Manufacturing Process

Pulforming (see Fig. 16-5) is a continuous process similar to pultrusion, except the finished product is not a uniform, straight section cut to length. This process is used to produce a curved part that has a constant volume, yet also has a changing geometry. An example is an automotive monoleaf spring which has a square cross section in the center and a flat, rectangular shape at each end. This is a recent development to meet high strength requirements.

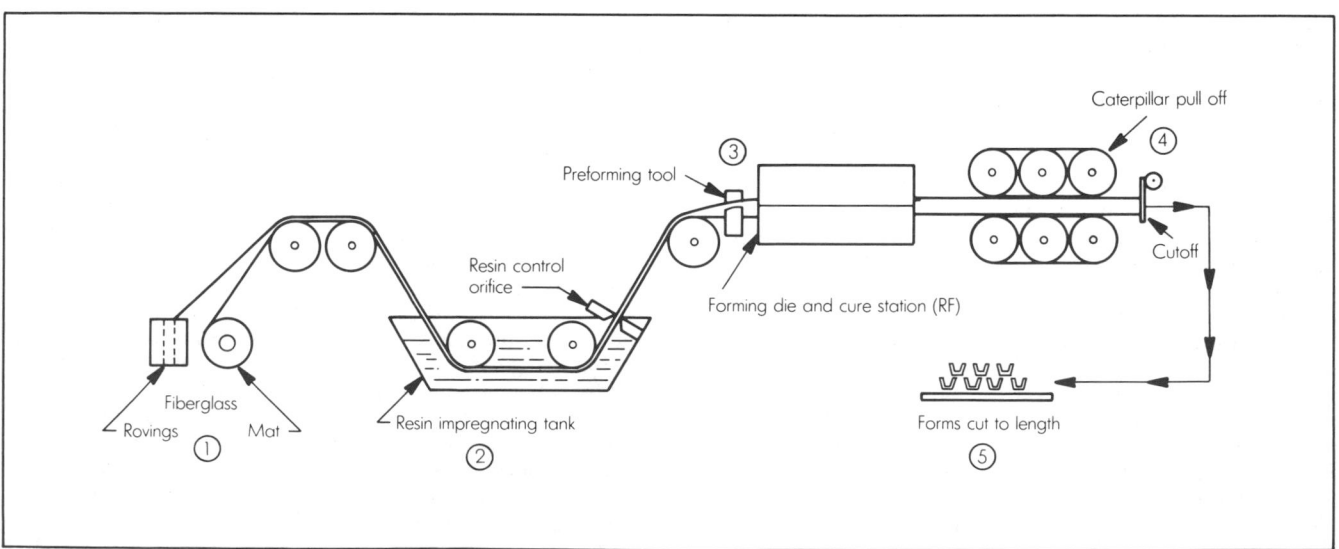

Fig. 16-4 Pultrusion manufacturing process. (*T.H. Meister*)

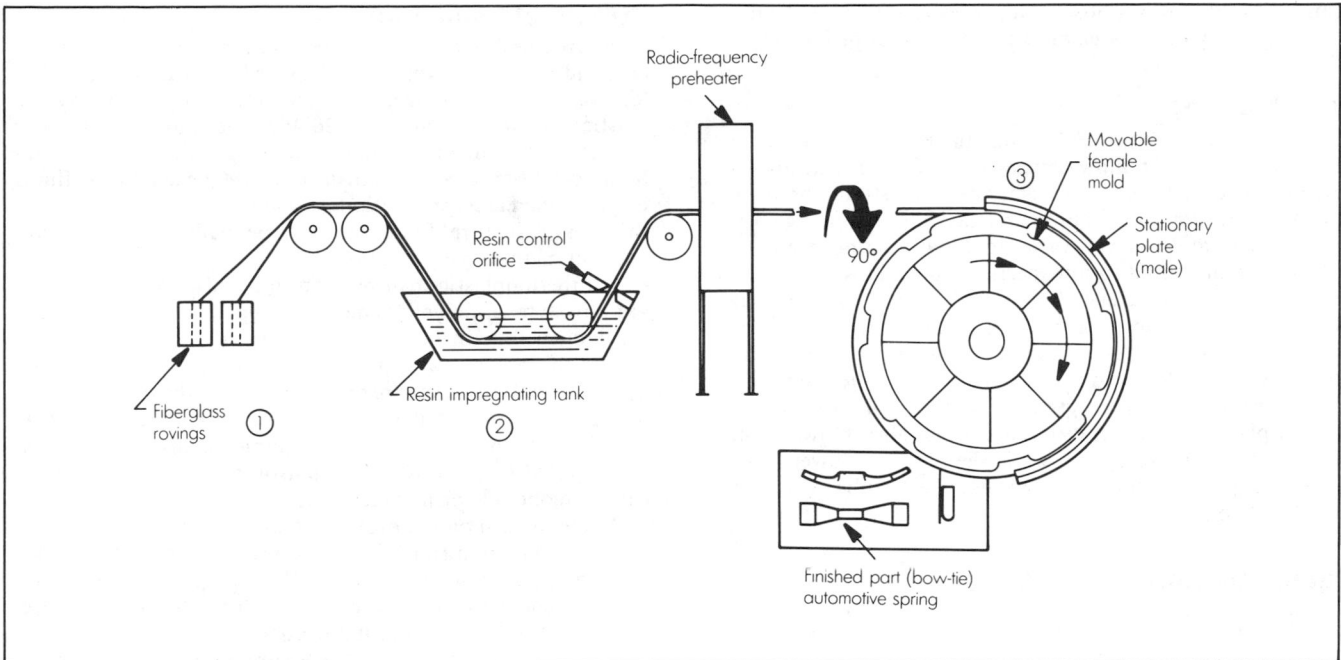

Fig. 16-5 Pulforming manufacturing process. (*T.H. Meister*)

Low-Volume Processes

Commonly used low-volume processes include (1) hand or spray lay-up, (2) vacuum bag, (3) pressure bag, (4) autoclave, (5) wet preform, (6) resin injection, and (7) filament winding. The second and third processes make use of the hand or spray lay-up, but embody a low-pressure system to improve glass content. The wet preform, resin injection, and filament winding processes also are suitable for intermediate-volume operations.

THERMOFORMING PLASTIC SHEET AND FILM

Thermoforming consists of heating a thermoplastic sheet to its processing temperature and forcing the hot, flexible material against the contours of a mold. This pliable material is rapidly moved either mechanically with tools, plugs, matched molds, etc., or pneumatically with differentials in pressure created by a vacuum or by compressed air.

Thermoforming has several advantages including (1) low costs for machinery and tooling because of low processing pressures; (2) low internal stresses and good physical properties in finished parts; (3) capability of being predecorated, laminated, or coextruded to obtain different finishes, properties, etc.; (4) capability of forming light, thin, and strong parts for packaging and other uses; and (5) capability of making large, one-piece parts with relatively inexpensive machinery and tooling. The main disadvantages are: (1) higher cost of using sheet or film instead of plastics pellets and (2) necessity of trimming the finished part.

Machinery Requirements

Equipment for thermoforming ranges from the widely used, hand-fed type of machine utilizing a straight vacuum forming cycle to sophisticated equipment that is capable of converting thermoplastic pellets to the finished thermoformed product.

Typical facilities consist of a sheet extruder, sheet cooling equipment, a reheat oven to bring the sheet to the proper thermoforming state, an automatic thermoforming press, and a die-cutting machine to cut the finished product from the sheet web. Waste material from the web is reground automatically and then pneumatically conveyed to the raw material bin, where it is mixed with virgin pellets for the start of another cycle. Products such as refrigerator door liners are made by this method.

High-Pressure Laminates

High pressure laminates consist of superimposed layers of a thermoset, resin-impregnated or resin-coated filler polymerized (fused) together by heat and pressure. A minimum of 1100 psi (7.6 MPa) and maximum of 2000 psi (13.8 MPa) pressure is used for high-pressure laminating. Fillers and reinforcements are composed of various materials, such as cotton mats, paper, glass fibers or fabric, glass mats, graphite, boron fibers, felted asbestos, and nylon fabric.

These sheets or mats are macerated with such thermosetting resins as phenolic, melamine, polyester, epoxy, and silicone. The heat and pressure during lamination creates a chemical reaction that causes the entire laminate to cure into a hard, nearly homogeneous, insoluble mass. Sheets, tubes, rod, and molded forms are produced. After thermoset resins have polymerized, they cannot be resoftened or reshaped by heat or solvents. Large volumes of decorative, high-pressure laminates are used in the furniture and building industries. Industrial laminates are used throughout industry in aircraft, auto, electronic, and appliance fields, as well as in other fields.

OTHER PROCESSING METHODS

A variety of special techniques is used in processing plastics, in addition to the basic procedures described previously in this

PLASTICS

chapter. Combinations of several processes often may be used advantageously for producing specialty plastics products.

Blow Molding

Blow molding is a process for shaping thermoplastic materials into one-piece, hollow articles by means of heat and air pressure. The method consists basically of stretching a hot thermoplastic tube with air pressure, then hardening it against a relatively cool mold. A wide variety of blow molding techniques and equipment is used to suit specific applications.

The principal difference between blow molding glass and blow molding plastics is attributed to the different material properties. Molten glass is much less sensitive than plastics—not only in the melt viscosity, but also in its chemical stability. For this reason, modified glass blowing machines cannot be used for plastics. Another difference is that glass blowers start with a drop of molten glass, while the plastics blowers use a preformed plastics part, which usually is a tube of molten plastics called a parison.

Liquid Injection Molding

In comparison to other processes, the new liquid injection molding (LIM) method has the potential necessary to replace compression and transfer molding of thermoset plastics in some applications.

Instead of being charged into the cavity of a compression mold or a transfer pot as powder, pellets, or other molding compound, two LIM material components are pumped directly from the shipping containers through a mixing device and injected into a heated mold, where they cure.

Liquid injection molding differs considerably from reaction injection molding (RIM), with which it sometimes is confused. The pumping systems used in LIM are generally lower pressure systems than those used for RIM, and mixing in LIM is accomplished more often mechanically than by impingement. Also, while RIM parts usually are large, LIM parts typically are quite small.

Rotational Molding

Rotational molding is a process for forming hollow plastics parts. The process utilizes the principle that finely divided plastics material becomes molten in contact with a hot metal surface, and then takes the shape of that surface. When the polymer is cooled while in contact with the metal, a reproduction of the mold's interior surface is produced.

Rotational molding employs the simultaneous rotation of thin-walled molds about two axes, primary and secondary, which are perpendicular to each other. After being charged with plastics material, the molds are heated externally while rotating. This causes the particles to melt on the inner surface of the mold as they tumble. Successive layers are deposited until all of the material is uniformly distributed and fused. The molds are cooled by air or external water spray while still rotating. They are then opened for removal of the finished article and recharged.

The process is employed for the production of hollow objects from thermoplastic materials. The main benefit of the rotational molding process is its versatility and applicability to the production of parts ranging from small, intricate products, to larger items such as automobile fuel tanks, to very large (5000 gal; 19 000 L) liquid storage tanks.

Structural Foam Molding

A structural foam is a plastics product with a rigid cellular core and an integral skin. The solid skin is typically 0.030-0.080" (0.76-2.03 mm) thick. Density reductions compared with solid plastics are in the range of 20-40%, depending upon part configuration, thickness, and molding conditions. Structural foams can be molded and extruded. Since the bending stiffness of parts increases proportionately to the cube of the part's thickness, structural foam parts can be made quite rigid, with good strength-to-weight ratios.

All thermoplastics can be foam-molded. Typical materials are polystyrene, polyethylene, polypropylene, polycarbonate, acrylonitrile butadiene styrene (ABS), and vinyl. The plastics used in this process range from preblended resins and foaming agents, to materials that are dry blended with the foaming agent in a machine-mounted hopper blender. The foaming agents usually are combined with inorganic solids which when decomposed by the heat in the plasticizing cylinder, generate carbon monoxide or nitrogen gases.

In the foam-molding process, the solid skin is formed when the injected foaming mass is chilled by cool mold surfaces. This skin creates an insulating barrier that still permits the central mass to complete its expansion to form the foamed core. Because of the heat insulating properties of the foam-molded products, the molding cycle times are slower than the cycle times normally attained in injection molding operations.

Casting

Casting processes are applicable to some thermoplastics and thermosets. These materials can be cast at atmospheric pressure in inexpensive molds to form large parts with section thicknesses that would be impracticable for other manufacturing processes. Casting resins are molded on a production basis in lead, plaster, rubber, and glass molds.

In a typical operation, the liquid resin is poured into the mold and the product is cured in an oven by applying heat, or it is cured exothermically with a catalyst. Shrinkage during curing facilitates removal of the product from the mold. Finishing operations include the removal of flash and, in cold molds, removal of the gate. In some instances, the parts are buffed or tumble polished to improve the appearance.

Plastics products made by the casting process include sheets, rods, tubes, and profile shapes. Embedments and encapsulations are also accomplished by casting. Other important uses of casting resins are for tooling such as draw, bending, and drop-hammer dies.

Forging

The forging process sometimes is used in manufacturing thermoplastic parts that would be difficult to produce by other processes. The forging technique is capable of producing thick parts with abrupt changes in sections. An example of the application of forging is its use to produce thick, large-diameter gears from polypropylene.

Although identified by the term *forging*, this process is misnamed since it is not truly a forging process, but rather a reforming operation. In this process, a preheated blank or billet of the required shape and volume is placed between a pair of forging dies, which are then closed to deform the work blank and fill the die cavity. The dies remain closed for 16-60 seconds to minimize elastic recovery of the part when it is released from the dies.

MACHINING

For low-volume production or prototypes, most plastics can be machined with standard woodworking and metalworking equipment and cutting tools; however, different tool angles are necessary when high-volume production of parts is required. When more than a few pieces are to be machined, the need for cooling should be given careful consideration.

Although most plastics can be machined dry, some require a coolant, particularly when machined at high speeds and feeds. The machining process results in the generation of frictional heat. Virtually all the heat generated by the cutting friction of the plastics and the metal cutting tool is absorbed by the cutting tool. Therefore, very little heat is transferred to the core of the material. This heat must be kept to a minimum or must be removed by a coolant for optimum results. Cooling by air jets, vapor mists, or a solution of between 10-20% soluble oil and water may be necessary.

Guidelines For Machining

Adhering to the following guidelines will facilitate the plastics machining process:

1. Machining and finishing of plastics parts should be avoided or minimized wherever possible through careful design of the part and the mold. Proper positioning of gates and flash lines helps to simplify finishing.
2. In many applications, the part can be redesigned to eliminate or minimize the need for machining. In all (or most) cases of design, this is a desirable objective.
3. Tools must be sharp, with proper chipbreakers or relief, to allow the efficient removal of chips.
4. Water-soluble oil and water, vapor mists or an air jet can be used to aid the machining process. Vacuums can be utilized to collect the chips at or near the point of machining.
5. Cutting tools should be ground with no rake or 2-3° negative rake to allow a scraping action, rather than a cutting action.
6. Plastics are relatively resilient when compared to metals. Stock material should be properly supported to minimize distortion.
7. Elastic recovery occurs in thermoplastics both during and after machining, so provisions must be made in tool geometry for sufficient clearance to provide relief.

Filing

While one of the primary considerations in the production of plastics is limited postprocessing, it is often necessary to remove flash and gates from the body of some parts. Some manufacturers have production employees who use scrapers on parts after removing them from machines. The scrapers are often a piece of brass shaped to allow efficient material removal.

Many parts removed from molds and other processing methods are warm, and this property allows easier removal of flash. For soft thermoplastics, a coarse, single-cut, shear-tooth file having teeth set at a 45° angle should be used. The combination of coarse teeth and long angle promotes self-cleaning. Milled tooth files are recommended for filing edges of sheet stock.

Routing and Shaping

Shapers are used for a variety of operations, such as machining of rabbetted edges to permit flush mounting, machining to predetermined cross sections, and cutting of both flat and formed parts to size.

Routers should have a no-load spindle speed of 10,000-20,000 rpm. Two or three-flute cutters under 1 1/2″ (38 mm) diam running at these speeds produces the smoothest cut. At slower spindle speeds, the cutter should have more flutes or blades and should be larger in diameter to produce the necessary peripheral speed. Cutters should be kept sharp and should have a back clearance angle of 10° and a 0° rake angle.

Gear Cutting

When cutting laminated gear blanks, the feed should be the maximum that is possible without showing marks on the teeth. A coarse feed tends to reduce wear on the cutter edges. In hobbing, it is not necessary to make roughing and finishing cuts; a single cut to the required depth is sufficient. Hobs of 3-4″ (76-102 mm) pitch diam may be run at 140-210 rpm with feeds of 0.040-0.080 ipr (1.02-2.03 mm/rev).

Sawing

Circular saws and bandsaws are the most common tools used for sawing operations. While table saws used in woodworking successfully cut plastics up to 1″ (25 mm) thick with speeds at 10,000-12,000 fpm (3050-3660 m/min), carbide-tipped blades are recommended for production jobs. The carbide-tipped blades should be hollow ground, with zero rake (or slightly negative) and 12-15 teeth/in. (0.5-0.6 teeth/mm) depending on the thickness of the material.

Threading and Tapping

High-speed, nitrided, chromium-plated taps are best for threading small holes. Speeds used range from 40-54 rpm. Tools have three flutes rather than the four commonly used in metalworking. A negative rake of about 5° on the front face of the land helps prevent binding of the tap in the holes when the tap is backed out. Small holes can be tapped dry. Water is a better tapping medium than lard oil or kerosene. Machine taps 0.002-0.006″ (0.05-0.15 mm) oversize are recommended; these give 75% of full thread. A slight chamfer or countersink minimizes uplifting of material around the edge of the hole. Holes larger than 1/4″ (6 mm) diam should be molded rather than threaded or tapped, except when very thin sections are involved.

Drilling

For maximum efficiency in drilling holes up to 1/4″ (6 mm) diam, it is recommended that drills especially designed for plastics be used. These drills are available in 60-90° included-angle points with polished flutes; they are wider than the standard machine drill and have a slow helix. A 60° included angle is desirable for sections up to 3/16″ (5 mm) thick, and a 90° point is desirable for thicker sections. A slow helix works best for through holes; a fast helix is best on blind holes. A 15° lip clearance is provided on the tool.

Drills must be backed out and cleared frequently. This frees chips, especially during the drilling of deep blind holes. Speeds of 100-300 sfm (30-91 m/min) are ordinarily used for drilling; but for materials containing inert or abrasive fillers, a slow speed of approximately 75 sfm (23 m/min) should be used.

When cast phenolics are drilled, the drills sometimes cut 0.003″ (0.08 mm) undersize. Speed should be as high as possible without burning, and the tool should be backed out often. Negative rake helps the drill to clear.

ADVANCED COMPOSITES

Punching

Punching, blanking, shearing, and shaving are done extensively on laminated plastics. Punching grades of phenolic laminates have a letter *P* in the designation standardized by the National Electrical Manufacturers Association (NEMA). Thickness of sheet, character of filler, and temperature of the sheet are factors that determine the operations employed.

Some sheets can be punched cold, up to a certain thickness; others require heating. Usually the thickness that can be punched is greater when the sheet is hot. Heating can be done on hot plates or in ovens. The recommendations of the supplier of laminated stock, as to both temperature and length of heating, should be followed. Some materials can be heated to 380°F

(193°C) without damage, and others only to 250°F (121°C). Too high a temperature may affect the finish of the sheet; heating for too long may make it brittle. Punching would be done within two minutes or less after heating.

Embossing

Embossing, as a stamping or letter pressing operation, often is done in branding parts of plastics materials. Heated brass dies are used; and in some cases, the stock is also heated. Letters are often filled in with paint or enamel by wiping after embossing. However, they can be made to stand out readily by covering the area to be marked with metal leaf before embossing; the pressure causes the leaf to cling in the recesses.

ADVANCED COMPOSITES

A composite material is created by the combination of two or more materials—a reinforcing element and a compatible resin binder (matrix)—to obtain specific characteristics and properties. The components do not dissolve completely into each other or otherwise chemically merge, although they do act synergistically. Normally, the separate components can be physically identified, as well as the interface between components.

A common example of a composite material is fiberglass. Glass fibers are very strong. If notched, however, they fracture readily; or if put in compression, they buckle easily. By encapsulating the glass fibers in a resin matrix, they are protected from damage; at the same time, the resin matrix transfers applied loads to the unified fibers so that their stiffness and strength can be fully utilized in both tension and compression.

The more advanced structural composites use fibers of glass, carbon/graphite, boron, Kevlar (aramid), and other organic materials. These fibers are very stiff and strong, yet lightweight. The strengthening effects of the fiber reinforcements in composites are derived from (a) the percentage of fibers (fiber-resin ratio), (b) the type of fibers, and (c) the fiber orientation with respect to the direction of the loads.

While advanced fiber, resin matrix composites are classified as reinforced thermosets, a special technology has developed involving these materials that sets them somewhat apart from other reinforced thermosets. Called "advanced composites," resin matrix composites can include hybrids, mixtures of fibers in various forms in the resin (usually epoxy) matrix.

GENERAL DESCRIPTION OF ADVANCED COMPOSITES

To engineers in the field, an advanced composite has come to denote a resin matrix material that is reinforced with high-strength, high-modulus fibers of carbon, aramid, or boron, and is usually fabricated in layers to form an engineered component. More specifically, the term is applied principally to epoxy-resin matrix materials reinforced with oriented, continuous fibers of carbon and fabricated in a multilayer form to make extremely rigid, strong structures. Another characteristic that distinguishes composites from reinforced plastics is the fiber-to-resin ratio. This ratio is generally greater than 50% fiber by weight; however, the ratio is sometimes indicated by volume since the weight and volume in composites are similar.

THE MATRIX

The matrix serves two important functions in a composite: (1) it holds the fibers in place; and (2) under an applied force, it deforms and distributes the stress to the high-modulus fibrous constituent. The matrix material for a structural fiber composite must have a greater elongation at break than the fibers for maximum efficiency. Also, the matrix must transmit the force to the fibers and change shape as required to accomplish this, placing the majority of the load on the fibers. Furthermore, during processing, the matrix should encapsulate the fibrous phase with minimum shrinkage, which places an internal strain on the fibers. Other properties of the composite, such as chemical, thermal, electrical, and corrosion resistance, are also influenced significantly by the type of matrix used.

The two main classes of polymer resin matrices are thermoset and thermoplastic. The principal thermosets are epoxy, phenolic, bismaleimide, and polyimide. Thermoplastic matrices are many and varied, including nylon (polyamide), polysulfone, polyphenylene sulfide, and polyether etherketone. The matrix material must be carefully matched for compatibility with the fiber material and for application requirements. The selection process should cover factors such as thermal stability, impact strength, environmental resistance, processability, and surface treatment of the reinforcing fibers (sizing).

Depending on the application, it is possible to view the role of the matrix in two different ways: either as the binder that contains the major structural elements (the fibers) and transfers load between them, or as the primary phase that is merely reinforced by the secondary fiber phase. The first concept is traditional since most composites have used a relatively soft matrix (such as a thermosetting plastics of the polyester, phenolic, or epoxide type). The strength of such composites is almost entirely that of the fibers; hence, for efficiency, it is desirable to optimize the fiber content. Thus, in most instances, small improvements in the structural properties of the matrix are of little value; its adhesion and processing characteristics, however, are of paramount importance.

Most structural composite components are produced with thermosetting resin matrix materials. In metal matrix composites, the most frequently used matrix material is aluminum, while alloys of titanium, magnesium, and copper are being developed. Boron and graphite fibers are generally used as the reinforcement for metal matrix materials.

FIBER TYPES

The unique geometry of a fiber provides many of the advantages in an advanced composite. In their fiber form, materials such as carbon/graphite and boron (which are also known as polycrystalline ceramic fibers) show near-perfect crystalline structure. Parallel alignment of these crystals along the filament axis provides the superior strengths and stiffnesses that characterize advanced composites. Various production methods are used for the different fiber types.

FIBER FORMS AND FABRICS

Composites can be classified in a number of different ways. The accepted classification types are fibrous (composed of fibers in a matrix), laminar (made from layers of materials), and particulate (made from particles in a matrix). Within the particulate type are flake and skeletal subcategories.

Continuous Fibers

Continuous fibers in yarns or tows (untwisted yarns) are used in filament windings and in unidirectional tape form. Tapes as wide as 48″ (1220 mm) are formed by collimating continuous fibers, applying a resin-compatible sizing, and impregnating the fibers with resin. The materials are partially cured (B-staged), then separated with a backing material to prevent them from sticking, and are referred to as prepregs. Prepreg tapes are usually processed by laminating them together in a desired configuration, then final curing them with heat and pressure.

Woven-fiber fabrics, or broadgoods, can be easily laid atop complex mold structures. Weaves of carbon/graphite fibers are available in unidirectional orientations that are sometimes bound with nonstructural tie yarns. Hybrid forms may include Kevlar as a locking element. Hybridizing can also be used to combine the impact resistance of Kevlar or cost savings of fiberglass with the superior strength and stiffness of carbon or boron. Multidirectional weaves of single-material fibers and/or multi-material fibers (hybrids) are available in dry or prepregged forms.

Fabrics

Generally, the fibers are woven into fabrics that come in roll form. Fabrics can be woven for specific part requirements. There are various ways of placing the fibers and fabrics in the matrix; when the fibers are oriented to run in one direction, the resulting material is anisotropic in its strength properties.

Hybrid Composites

Hybrid composites, which combine two or more different fibers in a common matrix, greatly expand the range of properties that can be achieved with advanced composites. They also increase the potential for cost-effective applications since hybrids may cost less than materials reinforced only with graphite, aramid, or boron.

Characteristics. The term *hybrid* generally applies to advanced composites and refers to the use of various combinations of continuous graphite, boron, aramid, and glass filaments in thermoset matrices. Hybrids have unique features that can be used to meet diverse design requirements in a more cost-effective way than either advanced or conventional composites. Some of the advantages of hybrids over conventional composites are balanced strength and stiffness, optimum mechanical properties, thermal-distortion stability, reduced weight and/or cost, improved fatigue resistance, reduced notch sensitivity, improved fracture toughness, improved impact resistance, and, most of all, optimum cost as related to performance.

Fibers. Various types of graphite, boron, glass, and aramid fibers are used in hybrids, as are cloth and fabric woven from the fibers. Fibers are available with the following ranges of mechanical properties: tensile strength from 2500 to 5000 ksi (17.2 to 34.4 GPa) and tensile modulus from 10 to 60 x 10^6 psi (69 to 414 GPa).

COMPOSITE CONSTRUCTION

Composites can be divided into laminates and sandwiches. Laminates are composite materials consisting of two or more layers bonded together. Sandwiches are multiple-layer structural materials that contain a low-density core between thin faces (skins) of composite materials. In some applications, particularly in the field of advanced structural composites, the constituents (the individual layers) may themselves be composites (usually of the fiber-matrix type).

Laminates

In the context of this Handbook section, laminates are the general form in which component parts and end products are fabricated from advanced high-strength structural composite materials. Theoretically, there are as many different types of laminates as there are possible combinations of two or more materials. If materials are divided into metals and nonmetals, and if nonmetals divide into organic and inorganic, there are six possible combinations in which laminates can be produced: metal-metal, metal-organic, metal-inorganic, organic-organic, organic-inorganic, and inorganic-inorganic. In laminates containing more than two layers, there are considerably more possibilities, and one or more of the layers may be a composite.

Sandwiches

As was previously stated, sandwiches consist of a relatively thick, low-density core (such as a honeycomb or foamed material) between thin faces of a material with higher strength and density. Although this distinction between laminates and sandwiches is more descriptive than technical, some general observations can be made. In sandwich composites, for example, a primary objective is improved structural performance, or, more specifically, high strength-to-weight ratio. The core serves to separate and stabilize the faces against buckling under edgewise compression, torsion, or bending, and provides a rigid and highly efficient structure. Other considerations, such as thermal insulation, heat resistance, corrosion resistance, and vibration damping, dictate the particular choice of materials used. While the choice of materials is an important consideration in sandwich composites, it is the configuration of the structure that controls the essential properties. In laminates, however, properties depend much more upon the combination of materials used than in sandwiches.[3]

PROPERTIES

Composite structures, with their capability for tailoring of properties, open new dimensions of freedom not available with isotropic materials. Modulus of elasticity, tensile strength, and thickness can be varied within a single component; parts can be "softened" locally so that loads are transferred from highly stressed areas; and large one-piece structures can be produced without the need for a multitude of fasteners and parts.

Design and production considerations for composites are different from those for homogeneous, isotropic materials having well-defined elastic and plastic stress-strain behavior. For structural parts, all failure modes must be investigated, and

ADVANCED COMPOSITES

particular attention must be paid to interlaminar tensile and shear stresses because the strength of composites depends principally on the matrix resin, not on the reinforcing fiber.

Components made from fiber-resin combinations, often called advanced composites, are usually of laminated construction. They can be essentially isotropic, quasi-isotropic, or anisotropic, depending on material form, lay-up configuration, and fabrication method. Most parts are designed to be anisotropic to exploit the directional properties of the fibers.[4]

Key Factors

Carbon, glass, and aramid fiber composites have outstanding stiffness and strength properties, along with low weight. These composite materials afford a new, wider latitude in the parameters of design, production, and performance.

Stiffness. A major advantage of using various forms of reinforcing fibers in structural parts is that these composite systems can be tailored to suit specific needs. Stiffness, for example, can be varied significantly in different areas of a composite part by selecting the type and form of fiber, by judicious orientation, and by controlling local concentrations of fibers.

Ductility. Like most rigid materials, carbon-reinforced plastics are relatively brittle because carbon fibers are brittle. This characteristic requires close attention to cutouts and areas involving fasteners, where stress concentrations can cause failure. Carbon-fiber composites have a low yield strength, and resistance to impact is low.

Conductivity. Incorporating carbon fibers into plastic resins makes the compounds conductive, both electrically and thermally. Electrical conductivity provides the benefits of static drain and radio-frequency suppression in such applications as electronic equipment enclosures, automotive ignition system devices, and small-appliance housings. This property is also an advantage in providing electrostatic paintability. Thermal conductivity provides the benefits of heat dissipation in such components as gears, bearings, brake pads, composites tooling, and other friction-related products and cryogenic processing equipment.

Thermal expansion. The coefficient of thermal expansion of a composite depends not only on the orientation of the fibers, but also on the fiber content and on the thermal behavior of the matrix material. Thus, care must be exercised to ensure that volumetric expansion of the composite in the usually unrestrained direction does not exceed a tolerable limit. Relative to metals, however, the thermal characteristics of composites are more stable.

APPLICATIONS

By tailoring the materials and fabrication methods, and by modifying structural designs to accommodate their unique properties, advanced composites can be used for applications requiring high strength, high stiffness, or low thermal conductivity. The common feature of many aerospace uses is that the new materials weigh less than the metallic materials that they replace.

Applications Overview

Although advanced composites containing such materials as carbon/graphite or aramid fibers in an organic resin matrix are currently used mainly by the aerospace industries, these stiff, strong, lightweight materials are also used in various other commercial and industrial applications, ranging from aircraft structures to automobiles and trucks, from spacecraft to printed circuit boards, and from prosthetic devices to sports equipment. Products run the gamut from boat hulls and hockey shinguards to an advanced composites hinge for the retractable arm of the space shuttle.

Carbon/graphite cloth reinforced plastics are used in a variety of applications requiring thermal stability, high-temperature strength, good ablation characteristics, and good insulating capability. Since graphite possesses greater heat resistance than carbon and is physically stable at elevated temperatures, graphite reinforcements are used in rocket nozzle throats and ablation chambers. Carbon-carbon composites are used when greater strength and lower conductivity is required, such as in re-entry vehicles, rocket nozzle entrance sections and exit cones, and critical insulation areas.

Tailoring

Composites are often considered as lightweight alternatives for more traditional structural materials. Innovation with composites can lead to higher production efficiency and lower life cycle costs. For example, creativity in the use of raw materials allows the product design-to-production team to build the composite at the same time the structure is fabricated and to use the anisotropy of the materials to tailor the properties of the composite to meet specific structural requirements.

Proper tailoring of material properties to provide greater local strength and stiffness around fastener holes, for example, increases the load-carrying efficiency of the structure and, at the same time, reduces the amount of material and time needed to manufacture a part. Selective arrangement of plies in a composite laminate may also be used to introduce prestrain during the fabrication process, which produces desired shapes and curvatures in panels and parts while eliminating secondary forming operations.

The desirable features of tailorability and fabrication efficiency are illustrated by the use of composites materials in space structures. Graphite-epoxy tubes are used as structural members in space structures because they are lightweight, stiff, strong, and relatively easy to fabricate. They are selected because many space structures must be dimensionally stable, even when exposed to extreme thermal gradients. Because graphite fibers have a negative coefficient of thermal expansion, they can be embedded in matrix materials having a positive coefficient of thermal expansion and selectively oriented in the laminate to produce a structure with a thermal expansion coefficient of zero to satisfy a stringent functional requirement of the space structure. The dimensional and orientational stability of the communications platform allows the space antennae to receive and send signals to stations on earth precisely and accurately.

FABRICATION

Current composites fabrication techniques are similar to those used for producing fiberglass, including hand and automated tape lay-up resin injection, compression molding, vacuum bag and autoclave molding, matched die molding, pultrusion, and filament winding. Organic matrix composites are made primarily by molding in autoclaves, while metal (aluminum, titanium, etc.) matrix composites are formed mainly by diffusion bonding.

Lamination, filament winding, pultrusion, and resin transfer (injection) molding are four widely used methods of producing continuous-fiber composites with closely controlled properties. The shape, size, and type of part and the quantity to be manufactured determine construction techniques. The lamination method is used for comparatively flat pieces. Filament winding is a powerful and potentially high-speed process for making tubes and other cylindrical structures. So-called *pultrusion* and *pulmolding* can be used for parts with constant cross-sectional shapes. Injection molding can be used for small, nonload-bearing parts. A new epoxy injection process, called URTRI (Ultimately Reinforced Thermoset Reaction Injection), is used for making load-bearing structures, sandwiches, and torsion boxes.

Laminating

Advanced composites are typically used in the form of laminates and are processed by starting with a prepreg material (partially cured composite with the fibers aligned parallel to each other). A pattern of the product's shape is cut out, and the prepreg material is then stacked in layers into the desired laminate geometry.

A final product is obtained by curing the stacked plies under pressure and heat in an autoclave. Graphite-epoxy composites are cured at approximately 350°F (175°C) and with a pressure of 100 psi (690 kPa). The new high-temperature composites, such as bismaleimides, are cured at 600°F (316°C). The tooling is essentially a mold that follows a part through the lay-up and autoclaving processes. Tooling materials commonly used when manufacturing composite parts include aluminum, steel, electroplated nickel, a high-temperature epoxy-resin system casting, and fabricated graphite composite tools.

Filament Winding

In the filament winding process, illustrated in Fig. 16-6, fibers or tape are drawn through a resin bath and wound onto a rotating mandrel. Filament winding is a relatively slow process; but the fiber direction can be controlled, and the diameter can be varied along the length of the piece. In some versions of the process, the fiber bundle, which may be made up of several thousand carbon fibers, is first coated with the matrix material to make a prepreg tape. The tape is an endless strip with a width that may vary from an inch to a yard (several centimeters to a meter). With both the fiber and tape winding processes, the finished part is cured in an autoclave and later removed from the mandrel.

For strength-critical aerospace structures, carbon fibers are usually wound with epoxy-based resin systems. The polyesters, phenolics, and bismaleimides are limited to special applications. Filament winding is used to produce round or cylindrical objects such as pressure bottles, missile canisters, and industrial storage tanks. It also has been used to make automobile driveshafts.

Pultrusion

In composites technology, pultrusion is the equivalent of metals extrusion. Pultrusion (also called pultruding), depicted in Fig. 16-7, consists of transporting a continuous fiber bundle through a resin matrix bath and then pulling it through a heated die. The process can be used to make complex shapes; however, it has been limited to items with constant cross sections, such as tubing, channels, I-beams, Z-sections, and flat bars. Developmental activity is progressing on variable-section pultrusion, in which the geometry can be controlled by an articulating die. "Pulmolding" is a process variation that begins with pultruding; then the part is placed in a compression mold.

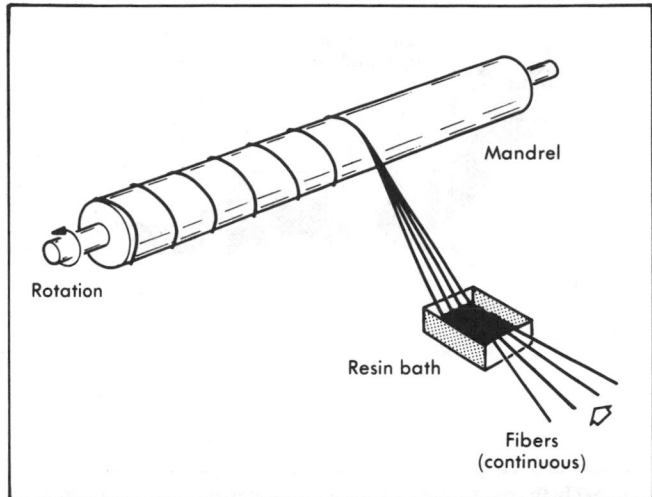

Fig. 16-6 Fundamental elements of the filament winding process for fabricating advanced composites structures. (*Polytech, Ltd.*)

Resin Transfer Molding

Filling a niche between hand manufacturing lay-up or spray-up of parts and compression molding in matched metal molds is resin transfer molding (RTM), also called resin injection molding.

Conventional process. In the conventional RTM process, two-piece matched cavity molds are used with one or multiple injection points and breather holes. The key to RTM is low pressure in the mold, which allows the use of low-cost tooling. The reinforcing material, which is either chopped or continuous-strand mat, is cut to shape and draped in the mold cavity. The mold halves are clamped together, and a polyester resin is pumped through an injection port in the mold. Polyester, glassmat, and conventional RTM are not considered to be in the family of composites.

Compared with the spray-up method, RTM permits faster cycle times and usually requires less labor. The RTM cycle times are longer than for compression molding, but the low cost of RTM tooling often compensates for the differential when the production run is less than 50,000 parts per year.

Advanced RTM. In the advanced RTM process, called URTRI (Ultimately Reinforced Thermoset Reaction Injection), reinforcements are placed in the mold, and cores can be handled as inserts. In this process, shown schematically in Fig. 16-8, a core is cast from syntactic foam (high-temperature epoxy with hollow glass microspheres) around a fitting. The core is then wrapped with multiple layers of bidirectional graphite fabric in 7 and 14 mil (0.18 and 0.36 mm) thicknesses and placed in the mold. Epoxy resin is next injected into the heated mold. Curing time is five minutes.

Potential benefits of URTRI include reduced part weight and cost, and improved quality for items such as aircraft wings, fins, elevons, passenger seat shells, landing-gear beams, and other high-performance structures.

Machining, Cutting, and Joining

The advanced composites materials generally are unsuited for the direct application of equipment, tools, and techniques used for machining, cutting, trimming, and joining metals; hence, special methods are applied to the final processing operations.

ADVANCED COMPOSITES

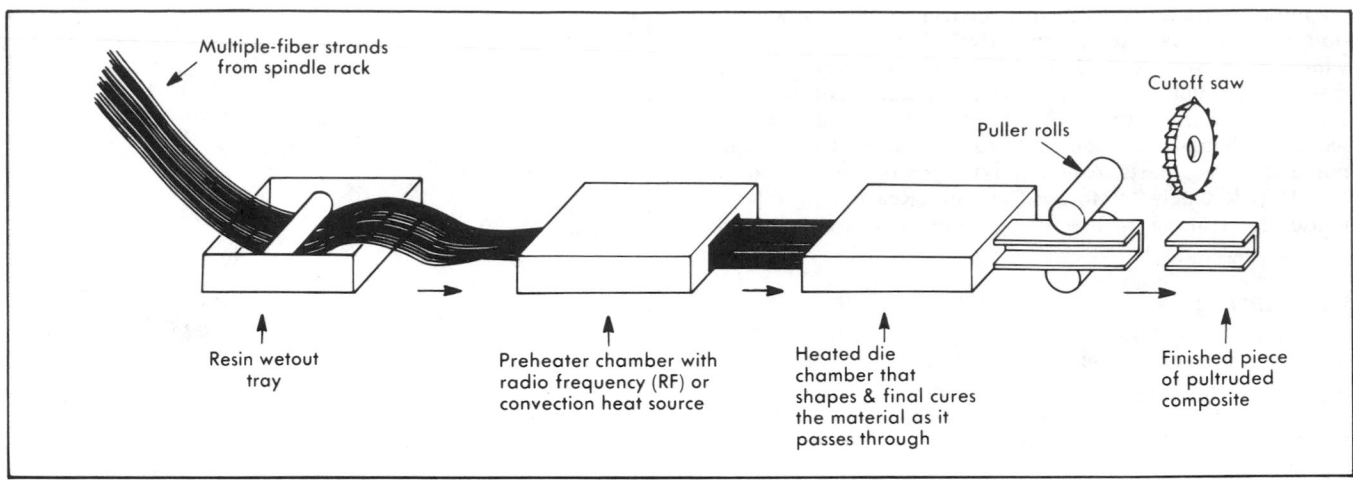

Fig. 16-7 In the pultrusion process, resin-impregnated fibers are pulled through a heated die to produce shapes of constant cross section. (*Polytech, Ltd.*)

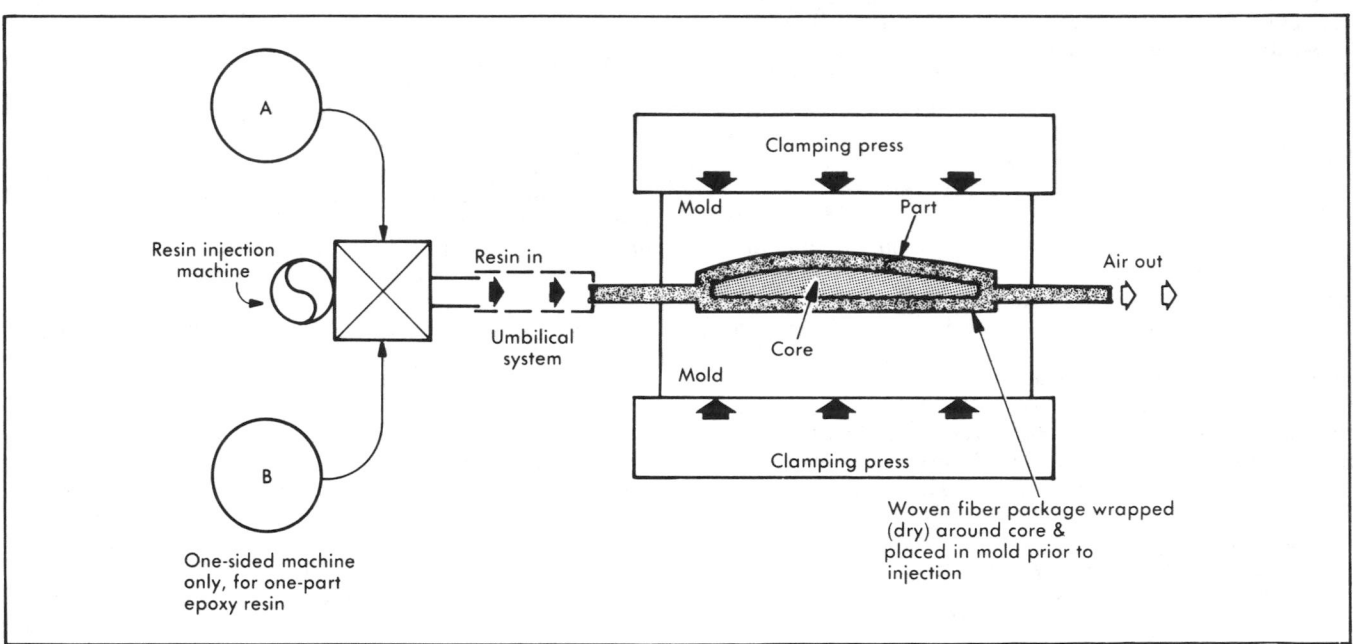

Fig. 16-8 Key features of the Ultimately Reinforced Thermoset Resin Injection (URTRI) process are identified in this schematic diagram. (*Polytech, Ltd.*)

Machining. Acceptable-quality machining of composite materials must ensure that there is no splintering, cracking, fraying, or delamination of cured composite edges. Standard machining equipment can often be used with appropriate modifications. In general, the spindle speeds and feeds depend upon the type of laminate material, its thickness, and the cutting method. Cutting tools for machining operations include countersinks, cutoff wheels, router bits, high-speed steel drills, and reamers. While tungsten carbides and high-speed steel tools are generally used, a polycrystalline diamond insert tool performs satisfactorily and is cost effective.

Tools must be kept sharp to provide quality cuts and avoid delamination. Careful attention must be paid to factors such as tool selection and tool geometry because a composite material comprises two separate types of materials (fiber and matrix) with differing mechanical properties and different machining characteristics. Selective stitching around areas for holes and cutouts prevents delamination of plies while drilling, cutting, or router trimming.

Cutting. The conventional methods for cutting uncured composite materials, such as prepreg plys, involve manual cutting with a carbide disk cutter, scissors, or power shears. For cutting cured composites, principal techniques for production applications include reciprocating knife cutting, high-pressure waterjet cutting, ultrasonic knife cutting, and laser cutting.

The particular choice of cutters must be balanced between required performances and the problems created by advanced composites in each operation. Lasers perform the best for cured composites, but may burn or carbonize uncured materials; they are also limited by ply thicknesses. Knife cutters may create rough edges and may become clogged, while water cutters may lead to moisture problems and delamination.

Waterjet process. The waterjet process cuts material by forcing water through a small-diameter jet at high velocities. A typical waterjet cutter cuts from one to ten plies of carbon, aramid, or glass prepregs in cured form. Maximum cutting speed is typically 13″ (330 mm) per second. Cutting performance of waterjet equipment is affected by factors such as jet pressure, nozzle orifice diameter, traverse speed, and the types and thicknesses of materials that are being cut. In some operations, the cutting head is mounted on automated indexing and positioning equipment. Because of water contamination, the waterjet process has been used only on cured parts.

Joining. Advanced composites introduce engineering and production problems different than those common to metal and conventional molded plastics construction, particularly where components must be fastened together. Because most types of composite joints—whether they are adhesively bonded or mechanically fastened—involve some cutting or machining of the strength-providing fibers, joint configurations and joining operations require careful planning to minimize the possibility of failure.

Since structural composites are usually made with thermosetting resins, they cannot be joined by welding methods as can thermoplastics and metals. The choice for joining composites is between mechanical methods and adhesive bonding. Each technique produces a joint with significant differences in both function and production; each method has advantages and limitations. The best permanent joint incorporates both mechanical fasteners and adhesive bonding.

References

1. Roy S. Klein, "Manufacturing Technology for Designing Plastic Parts," seminar materials (Dearborn, MI: Society of Manufacturing Engineers, 1983).
2. John Hill, Jr., *Engineering Thermoplastics*, Business Opportunity Report P-015R (Stamford, CT: Business Communications Co., Inc., 1983).
3. Mel H. Schwartz, *Composite Materials Handbook* (NY: McGraw-Hill Book Co., 1984), p. 1.40.
4. *Ibid*., p. 3.1.

POWDER METALLURGY

GENERAL CONSIDERATIONS

Powder metallurgy (PM in this text, although P/M is also widely used in the industry) is a metalworking process for forming precision metal components and shapes from metal powders. One accepted definition describes powder metallurgy as "the material processing technique used to consolidate particulate matter, both metals and/or nonmetals, into discrete shapes."[1] Although the scope of this chapter is confined to metallic materials, the principles of the process apply to ceramics and other types of nonmetallic materials. Complex composite materials that combine metallic and nonmetallic powders are also fabricated by this technique, especially to provide the properties required in certain aerospace, electronic, and nuclear applications.

Another authoritative source defines the term *powder metallurgy* by comparing it with fusion metallurgy. In fusion metallurgy, a metal or alloy is melted and cast in a mold. The mold may have the shape of the desired product; if not, an ingot is cast and then is formed into the desired wrought product by rolling, forging, extruding, drawing, machining, etc. In powder metallurgy, metal powders, i.e. metals in finely divided form rather than molten metal, are the starting material. The powders are consolidated into products with a specified shape.[2] Consolidation or pressing is performed at ambient temperature and is followed by heating (sintering) that fuses the particles together without melting.

Powder metallurgy can be broadly defined as the technology of manufacturing articles from metal powders and of producing those powders, which range in diameter from 4 μin. to 0.04" (0.1 to 1000 μm). The powders are smaller than shot and larger than dust. The PM technique is one of the oldest kinds of metallurgy, going back 5000 years to the manufacture of Egyptian implements.

Modern powder metallurgy began in the early 1900's when incandescent lamp filaments were fabricated from tungsten powder—the same way they are made today. Other important products followed, such as cemented carbide cutting tools, friction materials, and self-lubricating bearings. Today, structural PM parts and products are used widely in automobiles, trucks, farm machinery, diesel engines, home appliances, power tools, aircraft engines, lawn and garden equipment, business machines, and wherever small mass-produced metal components can be utilized.

It is instructive to ask: Why would it be desirable to produce a metal product with a given shape starting with metal powders rather than molten metal? One important reason has an economic basis. The cost of producing a product of a particular shape and the required dimensional tolerances by powder metallurgy may be lower than the cost of casting or making it as a wrought product, because of scrap reduction and the fewer processing steps that are needed. The production equipment and processes for these PM structural parts are the principal subjects of this chapter. Such parts must, of course, have adequate physical and mechanical properties and completely fulfill functional performance specifications. But, in many instances, the cost advantage, rather than significantly different or unusual properties, is the main reason for fabricating the part from powder.

Producing structural parts is, however, not the only application of powder metallurgy. Other diverse applications are based on the unusual properties that can be obtained by this technique. These applications range from metals with very high melting points, to materials for which high wear resistance is needed, to porous material (filters, oil-impregnated bearings, etc.), to products with special frictional, magnetic, or electrical properties, to many other applications. In general, PM products of these kinds are outside the scope of this chapter; hence, they are not covered in depth.

The history of PM technology is rooted in the technical advances and the rapid industrial growth that occurred during World War II. In the ensuing decades, PM has been one of the fastest growing metal fabricating processes. The principal reason is that the PM process is an economical, high-volume production method for making parts exactly to, or close to, final dimensions and finishing them with few or no machining operations. When desired, parts can be sized, coined, or repressed to close tolerances. They can be impregnated with oil or plastic, or infiltrated with a lower melting metal. They can be heat treated, plated, and when necessary, machined. Production rates range from several hundred to several thousand per hour.

Properties of PM forgings are comparable to wrought steel, yet production costs may be lower. PM forgings have improved detail and surface finish, hence minimal final machining is required. Accurate control of preform weight results in a minimum of flash and reduces material losses.

Powder metallurgy is a highly developed method of manufacturing reliable ferrous and nonferrous parts. Made by mixing elemental or alloy powders and compacting the mixture in a die, the resultant shapes are then sintered or heated in a controlled atmosphere furnace to metallurgically bond the particles. Basically a "chipless" metalworking process, PM typically uses more than 97% of the original raw material in the finished part; therefore, the PM process conserves both energy and materials.

Shapes that can be fabricated in conventional PM equipment range in weight up to about 35 lb (16 kg).

GENERAL CONSIDERATIONS

Parts of over 100 lb (45 kg) can be produced with special techniques such as hot or cold isostatic compacting. However, most PM parts weigh less than 10 lb (4.5 kg). While many of the early PM parts were simple shapes such as washers and self-lubricating bearings, developments in processing equipment and raw materials have made the production of stronger and more intricate parts feasible and economically practical. Components with flanges, hubs, cores, counterbores, cam surfaces, and combinations of such design features now are commonplace.

Product and production engineers and materials and machinery suppliers now collaborate to design and manufacture PM parts and assemblies and specify them for critical engineering applications. The available PM equipment, techniques, and powders, such as high-strength and high-compressibility powders make it feasible to design and produce PM parts that are stronger, or larger, or both.

Powder metallurgy parts are made from a wide range of materials, including some combinations that are not attainable in wrought or cast forms. These materials can be processed to provide preselected densities in parts ranging from porous components, to high-density, structural and mechanical parts with properties comparable to those attained in other metal forms.

Industrial applications of PM parts fall into two main groups. The first group comprises those applications in which the part cannot be made by other methods. For example, parts made of refractory metals, such as tungsten and molybdenum, or of materials such as tungsten carbide, are not producible efficiently by other means. Self-lubricating bearings and various types of porous metal filters are exclusively products of the powder metallurgy process. The second group of uses consists of mechanical and structural parts that compete with other types of metal forms such as machined parts, castings, stampings, and forgings.

The PM process is primarily a rapid, high-volume production method for making precision metal components. However, PM is not restricted solely to high-volume production. The minimum run of parts that can be produced economically is lowered by a number of conditions. These include production of simple parts with low tool costs, use of some or all of the tooling for more than one part, use of a special part design that is peculiarly suited to PM, minimal need for secondary processing operations, and consideration of machining operations that would be needed if the part were to be produced by a different method. When these factors are taken into account, PM parts can (in certain applications) offer cost and performance advantages in runs producing as few as 1000 parts.

Basically, the PM process involves pressure followed in a separate operation by heat to form metal powder particles into a broad range of engineered shapes, such as gears, cams, sprockets, bearings, brackets, etc. Metal powders are pressed automatically into a precise shape in a rigid precision die in a mechanical or hydraulic press. After compacting, the parts are conveyed through a special controlled-atmosphere furnace to bond the particles together (metallurgically fused without melting). Processes other than die pressing are also used to consolidate metal powders into shapes. These special processes include cold and hot isostatic pressing, roll compacting, gravity sintering, PM forging, consolidating by atmospheric pressure, and injection molding.

PROCESS FUNDAMENTALS

As diagrammed in Fig. 17-1, there are three basic steps in the most widely used conventional powder metallurgy process. These steps are mixing or blending, compacting, and sintering.

Mixing

In this first step of the conventional PM process, elemental metal powders or alloy powders are mixed together with lubricants or other alloy additions to produce a homogeneous mix of ingredients.

Compacting

Compacting is the second step of the conventional PM process. In it, a controlled amount of mixed powder is automatically fed into a precision die and compacted or pressed, usually at room temperature, at pressures as low as 10 tons/in.^{2} (138 MPa) or as high as 60 tons/in.^{2} (827 MPa) or more.

Compacting consolidates and densifies the loose powder into a shape called a "green compact." With conventional pressing techniques, the compact has the size and shape of the finished product when ejected from the die. It has sufficient strength for in-process handling and transport to the sintering furnace.

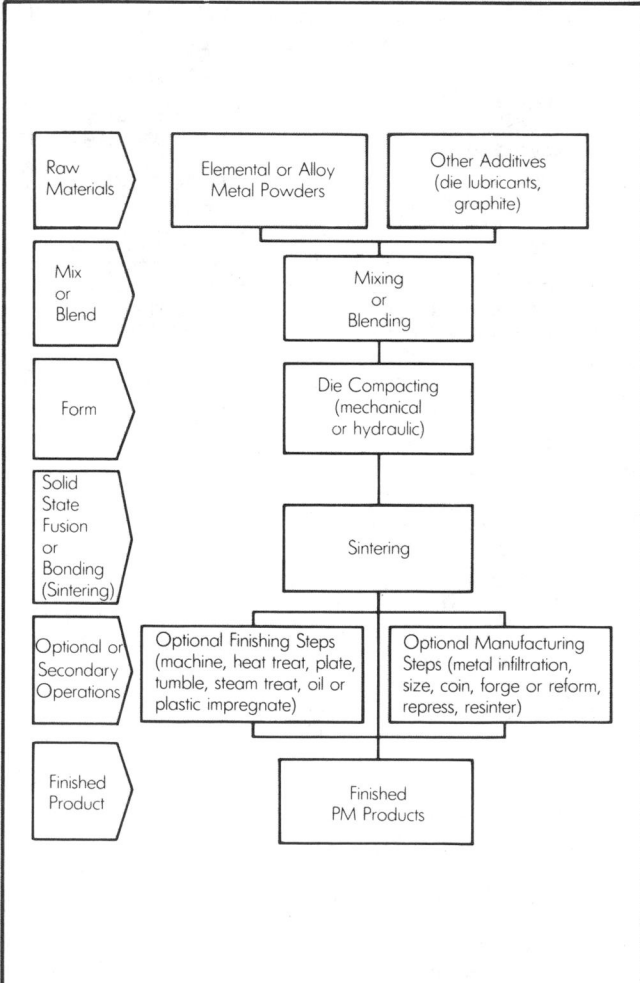

Fig. 17-1 Powder metallurgy process.

Dies and tools, made of either hardened steel and/or carbides, consist of at least a die body or mold, an upper punch, a lower punch and in some cases one or more core rods to provide for holes parallel to the pressing direction. A typical set of tools for producing a straight cylindrical part such as a sleeve bearing is shown in Fig. 17-2. The pressing cycle for this simple part, illustrated in Fig. 17-3 is as follows: (1) The empty die cavity is filled with mixed powder. (2) Both top and bottom punches simultaneously press the metal powder in the die. (3) The top punch is withdrawn, and the green compact is ejected from the die by the bottom punch. (4) The green compact is pushed out of the pressing area to make ready for another operating cycle.

In general, this compacting cycle is essentially the same for all parts. However, when more than one pressing level is needed, as for example in producing flanged shapes, multiple punches are used and separate pressing action may be required. This point is amplified under "Tooling Design Factors" in this chapter.

Sintering

The third step of the conventional PM process is sintering. During sintering, the green compact is heated in a protective-atmosphere furnace to a relatively high temperature, but below the melting point of the metal. Representative temperatures: ferrous PM, 2050°F (1120°C); bronze PM, 1500°F (815°C); stainless steel PM, 2200°F (1200°C). Sintering, which is mainly

a solid-state process, develops metallurgical bonds among the powder particles and thus produces the PM part's mechanical and physical properties. It also serves to prevent oxidation, removes the lubricant from the powder, reduces oxides and controls carbon content on the surface of the part and inside of it. Typical sintering atmospheres are endothermic gas, exothermic gas, dissociated ammonia or nitrogen.

SECONDARY OPERATIONS

For many applications, PM parts are ready for use after sintering. However, any one of several secondary operations can be applied to provide specific or special properties. Parts can be repressed, infiltrated with oil, or impregnated with

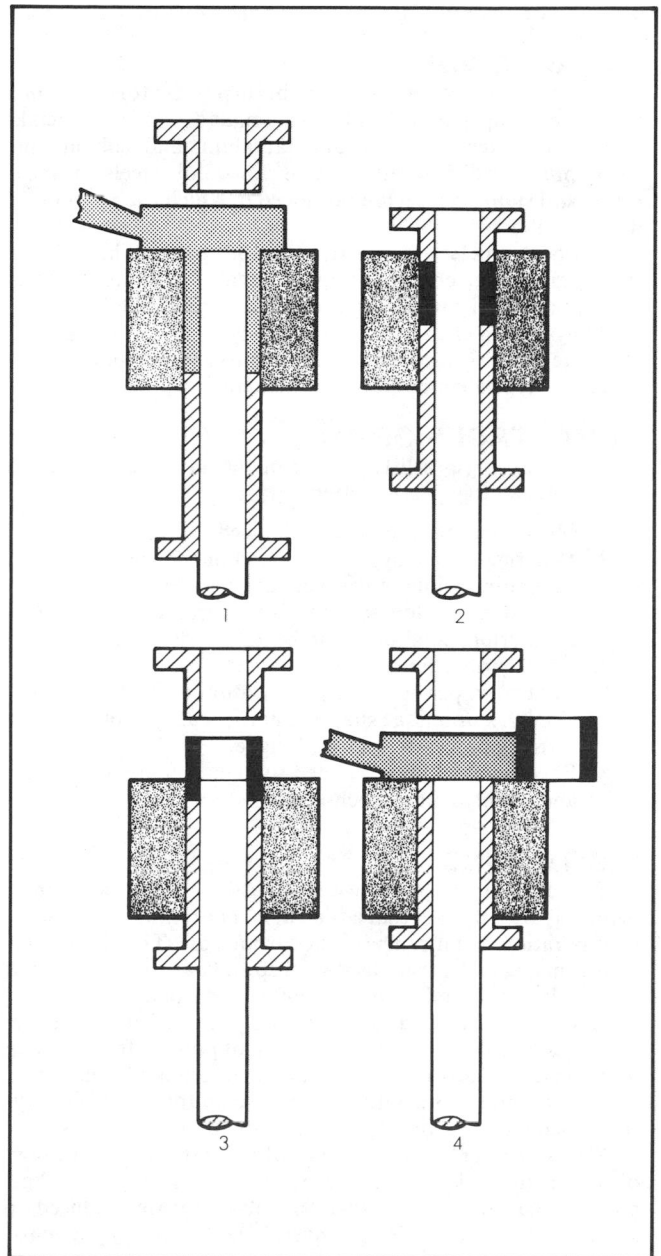

Fig. 17-3 Powder metallurgy pressing cycle.

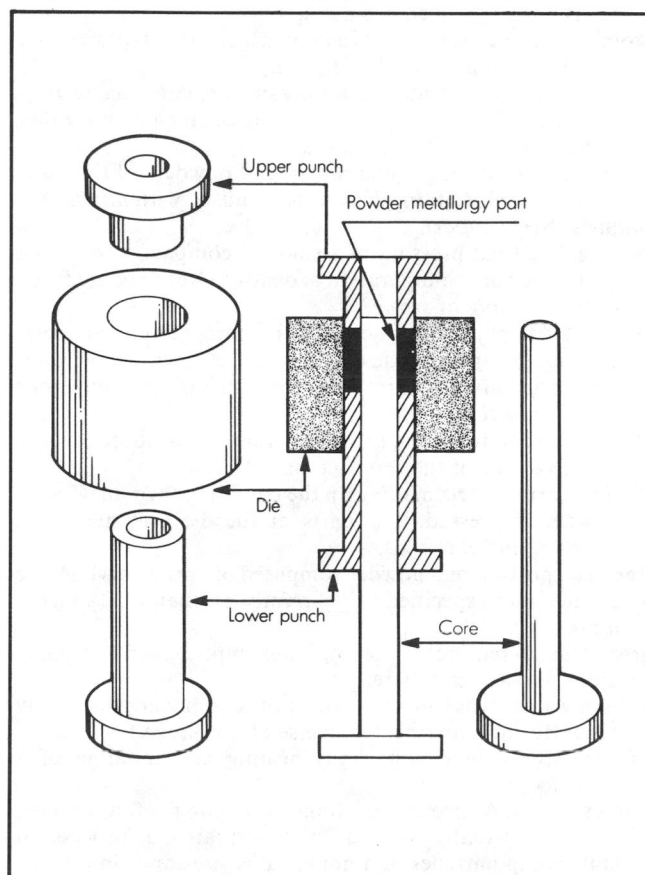

Fig. 17-2 Typical set of PM tools.

GENERAL CONSIDERATIONS

plastic. They can be modified by coining, sizing, machining, tumbling, plating, and heat treating.

The controlled porosity of PM parts makes it possible to infiltrate them with another metal or impregnate them with oil or a resin to either improve mechanical properties or provide additional performance characteristics such as self-lubrication.

The oil-impregnated PM bearing, which has been used in automobiles since the late 1920's, is one of the best known examples of the use of impregnation. Conventional PM bearings can hold from 10-30% by volume of oil. Generally, additive-free oils (nonautomotive engine oils) are used. Impregnation is accomplished by soaking the parts in heated oil or by vacuum techniques. During use, when the parts heat up from friction, the oil expands and flows to the bearing surface. Upon cooling, the oil returns into the metal mass by capillary action.

METAL POWDERS

The most common metals available in powder form are iron, tin, nickel, copper, aluminum, titanium, and refractory metals such as tungsten, molybdenum, tantalum, and columbium. Also, prealloyed powders such as low-alloy steels, bronze, brass, and stainless steel are produced in which each particle is itself an alloy.

Powder particles are specific sizes and shapes. They are not merely ground-up chips or scraps of metal. The major methods for making metal powders are atomization, reduction of oxides, electrolysis, and chemical reduction. Shape and other particle characteristics—whether spherical, irregular, porous, or dense—is dependent upon the manufacturing process.

ADVANTAGES OF PM

The following is a list of some of the advantages that the powder metallurgy process offers:

1. Machining is eliminated or reduced.
2. Material loss (scrap) is eliminated or reduced.
3. Close dimensional tolerances can be maintained.
4. Almost any alloy system under equilibrium or non-equilibrium conditions can be achieved.
5. Good surface finishes are obtained.
6. Controlled permeability for filtration is available.
7. Complex or unique shapes, impractical with other metal forming processes, can be designed.
8. Powder metallurgy is suited to high-volume production and quality control techniques.

LIMITATIONS

The limitations of powder metallurgy are concerned primarily with the fact that a typical PM part must be of such a configuration that it can be ejected from a die. This means that reentrant angles, featheredges, or deep and narrow splines must be handled as secondary operations at additional cost.

In pressing a PM part, the powder does not flow laterally; thus, in a multilevel part, each column of powder for each part level must be controlled independently or unequal density will result. Equipment is available to ensure uniformity of density, thus opening a new field in high-quality, multilevel parts.

Size is another limitation. Typical PM parts are in the range of 1-2 lb (0.5-1 kg) or less; most are under 10 lb (4.5 kg), although parts as heavy as 70-100 lb (32-45 kg) are produced by special PM processes. Using conventional compacting systems, the costs of the equipment and the power necessary to compress the part increase greatly as the size and surface area of the part

increase to the point at which a 3000 ton (26 668 kN) press represents the state-of-the-art maximum.

The main limitations of PM include the following:

1. Initial tool costs are relatively high. Production volume of less than 10,000 identical parts is normally not practical. However, part applications must be evaluated on an individual basis rather than on a strict quantity basis, because some case histories have shown lesser quantities to be economical.
2. Shapes requiring weak, thin sections should be avoided.
3. Featheredges and narrow and deep splines should be avoided.
4. Internal angles must be provided with lands.
5. Length of part in pressing direction is normally limited to 3-6 times cross-sectional dimension.
6. Corrosion protection requires special attention and precaution, depending upon the material used.

NOMENCLATURE

The following definitions of selected terms used in powder metallurgy is provided courtesy of the American Society for Testing and Materials, adapted from ASTM Standard, B243.[3]

alloy powder A powder, all particles of which are composed of the same alloy of two or more metals.

apparent density The weight of a unit volume of powder, usually expressed as grams per cubic centimeter (g/cm^3), determined by a specified method.

atomization The dispersion of a molten metal into particles by a rapidly moving gas or liquid stream.

blank A pressed, presintered, or fully sintered compact, usually in the unfinished condition, requiring cutting or some other operation to give it its final shape.

blending The thorough intermingling of powders of the same nominal composition. (Not to be confused with *mixing*.)

briquette See *compact*.

coining The final pressing of a sintered compact to obtain a definite surface configuration or density. (Not to be confused with *repressing* or *sizing*.)

compact An object produced by the compression of metal powder, generally while confined in a die, with or without the inclusion of nonmetallic constituents. (Synonymous with *briquette*.)

compression ratio The ratio of the volume of the loose powder to the volume of the compact made from it.

die The part or parts making up the confining form in which a powder is pressed. The parts of the die are: die body, punches, and core rods.

fines The portion of a powder composed of particles which are smaller than a specified size, currently less than 1732 μ in. (44 μ m).

green Unsintered (not sintered); for example, green compact, green density, green strength.

growth An increase in dimensions of a compact which may occur during sintering. (Converse of *shrinkage*.)

hot pressing The simultaneous heating and molding of a compact.

impregnation A process of filling the pores of a sintered compact, usually with a lubricant; also a process of embedding particles of a nonmetallic substance in a metal powder matrix as in diamond-impregnated tools.

infiltration A process of filling the pores of a sintered or unsintered compact with a metal or alloy of lower melting point.

milling The mechanical treatment of metal powder, or metal powder mixtures, as in a ball mill, to alter the size or shape of the individual particles or to coat one component of the mixture with another.

mixing The thorough intermingling of powders of two or more materials.

particle-size distribution The percentage by weight, or by number, of each fraction into which a powder sample has been classified with respect to sieve number or micrometers (microns).

powder An aggregate of discrete particles that are usually within the size range 1-1000 micrometers (microns).

preforming The initial pressing of a metal powder to form a compact which is subjected to a subsequent pressing operation other than coining or sizing. Also, the preliminary shaping of a refractory metal compact after presintering and before the final sintering.

presintering The heating of a compact at a temperature below the normal final sintering temperature, usually to increase the ease of handling or shaping of the compact or to remove a lubricant or binder prior to sintering.

pressed density The weight per unit volume of an unsintered compact. (Synonymous with *green density*.)

pulverization The reduction of metal powder by mechanical means; a specific type of disintegration.

repressing The application of pressure to a previously pressed and sintered compact, usually for the purpose of improving some physical property.

roll compacting Passing metal powder continuously through a rolling mill so as to form relatively long sheets of pressed material.

shrinkage A decrease in dimensions of a compact which may occur during sintering. (Converse of *growth*.)

sieve analysis The testing of a powder for particle-size distribution by passing the powder through a series of standard sieves.

sintering The bonding of adjacent surfaces of particles in a mass of powder, or a compact, by heating.

sizing A final pressing of a sintered compact to secure desired size.

slip crack A rupture in the pressed compact caused by the mass slippage of a part of the compact.

METAL POWDERS

The first consideration in powder metallurgy is the powder itself. Metal powders are highly engineered materials. The availability of numerous types and grades of powders designed specifically for PM makes possible the production of parts to meet a wide range of specifications and performance requirements. Although all metals can be produced in powder form, some lack the desired characteristics that are necessary for application feasibility and economical PM production. A substantial number and variety of powders, such as listed in Table 17-1, are used widely, however, in manufacturing PM parts. The particle size, shape, and size distribution of metal powder affect the physical properties and characteristics of the compacted product. Powders are produced to specifications such as shape, fineness, particle size distribution, specific gravity, and sintering properties. Table 17-2 presents a list of the significant characteristics of metal powders.[4]

The two principal kinds of powder in terms of volume usage are iron and copper-based powders. Both are well suited to powder metallurgy. The principal use of iron powders is for PM structural parts, both those processed conventionally by cold compacting followed by sintering without pressure application and those produced as preforms and then hot forged into components. Bronze is used in porous bearings, while brass and iron are usually used in structural parts. Other powders of nickel, silver, aluminum, tungsten, and titanium also have important and growing application in the field of powder metallurgy.

POWDER PRODUCTION

Seven general methods are used to produce metal powders. These include atomization of molten metals, chemical reduction of metallic compounds, and mechanical comminution of solid metals. Some commercial methods, together with the raw materials they use and the product characteristics, advantages, and disadvantages of each are given in Table 17-3.[5]

Most metal powders are mainly produced by atomization, reduction of oxides, electrolysis, or chemical reduction.

Atomization

Atomization, a molten metal spraying operation, is an excellent and widely used means of producing metal powder. The first methods for producing metal powders by atomizing were those for low-melting-point metals, such as lead, aluminum, zinc, and tin. The molten metal is held in the liquid state in a tank and is raised by the suction produced by the atomizing medium, commonly hot air, through a pipe to the atomizing nozzle. A stream of molten metal is broken into droplets, which freeze (solidify) into metal powder particles. The particles are irregular in shape and can be produced in many sizes. For higher melting point metals and alloys, such as copper, iron, and nickel-based alloys, a stream of molten metal issuing from an orifice at the bottom of a tundish (reservoir) is broken up by a jet of atomizing fluid, which may be water, air, steam, or an inert gas. The properties of the powder; average particle size; particle size distribution; particle shape; particle chemistry; and particle structure are controlled in the atomizing process by the major variables such as temperature, stream velocity, and alloy composition.

Reduction

Reduction processes reduce metal oxides to powder form through contact with a reducing gas at temperatures below the melting point. In one method, beneficiated iron ore is reduced in a bed of coke and limestone to form porous, sponge-like iron cakes which are ground into powder. In another method, mill scale (a form of iron oxide) is ground and passed through an atmosphere furnace. The hydrogen atmosphere reacts with the oxygen at a temperature of approximately 1900°F (1050°C). The product of both methods is a relatively pure iron with

METAL POWDERS

TABLE 17-1
Representative Metal Powders

Pure Metals:	Alloys and Dispersions:
Aluminum	Aluminum-iron
Antimony	Brass
Berylium	Bronze
Bismuth	Copper-zinc-nickel
Cadmium	Nickel-chromium
Chromium	Nickel-chromium-iron
Cobalt	Nickel-copper
Columbium	Nickel-iron
Copper	Silicon-iron
Indium	Solder
Iron	Stainless steel
Lead	Steel
Magnesium	Thoria dispersed in nickel
Manganese	
Molybdenum	Compounds:
Nickel	Borides (chromium, tungsten, etc.)
Precious metals (gold, silver, platinum)	Carbides (molybdenum, tungsten, etc.)
Rhenium	Lithium hydride
Silicon	Molybdenum disilicide
Tantalum	Nitrides (silicon, titanium, etc.)
Tellurium	Zirconium hydride
Tin	
Titanium	
Tungsten	
Vanadium	
Zinc	

sponge-like structure. Other metals produced commercially by this process include cobalt, nickel, molybdenum, and tungsten.

Electrolysis

Electrolysis or electrolytic deposition is a means for processing iron, copper, silver, tantalum, and several other metals. For producing iron, steel plates are placed as anodes in tanks containing an electrolyte. Stainless steel sheets are also put in the tanks to act as cathodes upon which the iron is deposited. Direct current is used, and after about 48 hours, a deposit of approximately 0.08" (2 mm) thickness is obtained. The cathode plates then are removed, and the electrolytic iron is stripped from them. The iron, which is brittle, is washed, screened, and sized. Most powder then goes through an annealing operation to soften the particles.

Chemical Reduction

Chemical methods of powder production are those in which a metal powder is produced by chemical decomposition of a compound of the metal. This includes a large group of reduction reactions. Oxides in the form of finely divided solid powder particles may be reduced with hydrogen, as used in the reduction of tungsten oxide to tungsten powder and of copper oxide to copper powder; or they may be reduced with carbon monoxide, as used in making iron powder from iron oxide. An aqueous solution of a metal compound also may be reduced.

POWDER TYPES

The most commonly used metals include iron, nickel, copper, tin, aluminum, and titanium, as well as the refractory metals. These metals can be mixed to produce different alloy compositions during sintering. Also produced are prealloyed powders, such as low-alloy steels, bronze, brass, nickel silver, and stainless steel powders, in which each particle is an alloy. The section "Nonferrous PM Metals" presented later in this chapter provides additional information on this subject.

It is possible to combine metal and nonmetal powders to provide composite materials with the desirable properties of both ingredients in the finished part. Sintered metal friction materials are an example. They contain iron and copper powders for strength and heat conductivity, plus powdered silica or other nonmetallics for frictional characteristics.

The major types of PM materials commonly used for structural parts and bearings are covered by MPIF Standard 35, available from the Metal Powder Industries Federation. This document provides information for specifying those PM materials that have been developed and accepted by the parts manufacturing industry as representative of their capabilities and commercial practices. A listing of specifications applicable to powder metallurgy is shown in Table 17-4.[6]

TABLE 17-2
Metal Powder Characteristics

Apparent Density
  The apparent density or specific gravity of a powder is expressed in grams per cubic centimeter. It should be kept constant so that the same amount of powder can be fed into the die each time.

Chemical Properties
  Such a specification has to do with the *purity* of the powder, amount of oxides permitted, and the percentage of other elements allowed.

Compressibility
  Compressibility is the ratio of the volume of initial powder to the volume of the compressed piece. It varies considerably and is affected by the particle-size distribution and shape. The green strength of a compact is dependent on compressibility.

Fineness
  Fineness refers to the particle size and is determined by passing the powder through a standard sieve or by microscopic measurement. Standard sieves ranging from 36-850 μm are used for checking size, and for determining particle-size distribution.

Flowability
  Flowability is the characteristic of a powder that permits it to flow readily and conform to the mold cavity. It can be described as the rate of flow through a fixed orifice.

Particle-Size Distribution
  Particle-size distribution refers to the amount of each standard particle size in the powder. It has considerable influence in determining the flowability and apparent density as well as porosity of the product.

Sintering Ability
  Sintering ability is the suitability of a powder for bonding of particles by the application of heat.

TABLE 17-3
Methods of Producing Metal Powders

	Atomization	Gaseous Reduction of Oxides	Gaseous Reduction of Solutions	Reduction with Carbon	Electrolytic	Carbonyl Decomposition	Grinding
Raw materials	Scrap or virgin melting stock or metal or alloy powder desired	Oxides of metals such as Cu_2O, NiO, Fe_3O_4	Ore for leaching or other metal salt solution	Ore or mill scale	Soluble anodes	Selected scrap, sponge mattes	Brittle materials such as beryllium, high sulfur nickel, high carbon iron, antimony, bismuth, iron and manganese cathode
Type of powders produced	Stainless steel, brass, bronze, other alloy powders, aluminum, tin, lead, iron, zinc	Iron, copper, nickel, cobalt, tungsten, molybdenum	Nickel, cobalt, copper	Iron	Iron, copper, nickel, silver, titanium	Iron, nickel, cobalt	Iron, beryllium, manganese, nickel, antimony, bismuth, titanium
Typical purity	High, 99.5+	Medium, 98.5 to 99.0+	High, 99.2 to 99.8	Medium, 98.5 to 99.0+	High, 99.5+	High, 99.5+	Medium, 99.0+
Particle shape	Irregular to smooth rounded dense particles	Irregular, spongy	Irregular, spongy	Irregular, spongy	Irregular, flaky to dense	Spherical	Flaky and dense
Meshes available	Coarse shot to mesh	Usually 100 mesh and finer	Usually 100 mesh and finer	Most meshes from 8 down	All mesh sizes	Usually in low micron ranges	All mesh sizes
Compressibility (softness)	Low to high	Medium	Medium	Medium	High	Medium	Medium
Apparent density	Generally high	Low to medium	Low to medium	Medium	Medium to high	Medium to high	Medium to high
Strength	High to medium	Generally low	High	Medium to high	Medium	Low	Low
Advantages	Best method for alloy powders. Applicable to any metal or alloy melting below 3000° F	Easy to control particle size of powder. Good compacting powder	Ore can be used. Purification during leaching. Fine particles	Low cost. Control of particle size. Controlled variation in properties possible	High purity of product. Easy to control	Produces fine, pure powders	Controlled size of powder
Disadvantages	Wide range of particle sizes, not all salable. Particles too spherical for some applications	Requires high grade oxides. Restricted to reducible oxides	Applicable to few metals such as nickel, cobalt, copper	Requires high grade ore or mill scale. Applicable mainly to iron	Limited to few metals, high cost	Limited to few powders, high cost	Limited to brittle or embrittled materials. Quality of powder limits use. Slow

METAL POWDERS

TABLE 17-4
Specifications for P M Materials

Material	MPIF Designation	ASTM Specifications	Material	MPIF Designation	ASTM Specifications
Ferrous:					
Copper steel	FC-0808-N	B426, Grade 3 Type I	Nickel steel	FN-0408-T	B484, Grade 2, Type III, Class C
Iron copper	FC-1000-N	B222, B439, Grade 3	Iron nickel	FN-0700-T	B484, Grade 3, Type I, Class A
Iron nickel	FN-0200-R	B484, Grade 1, Type I, Class A	Iron nickel	FN-0700-S	B484, Grade 3, Type II, Class A
Iron nickel	FN-0200-S	B484, Grade 1, Type II, Class A	Iron nickel	FN-0700-T	B484, Grade 3, Type III, Class A
Iron nickel	FN-0200-T	B484, Grade 1, Type III, Class A	Nickel steel	FN-0705-R	B484, Grade 3, Type I, Class B
Nickel steel	FN-0205-R	B484, Grade 1, Type I, Class B	Nickel steel	FN-0705-S	B484, Grade 3, Type II, Class B
Nickel steel	FN-0205-S	B484, Grade 1 Type II, Class B	Nickel steel	FN-0705-T	B484, Grade 3, Type III, Class B
Nickel steel	FN-0205-T	B484, Grade 1, Type III, Class B	Nickel steel	FN-0708-R	B484, Grade 3, Type I, Class C
Nickel steel	FN-0208-R	B484, Grade 1, Type I, Class C	Nickel steel	FN-0708-S	B484, Grade 3, Type II, Class C
Nickel steel	FN-0208-S	B484, Grade 1, Type II, Class C	Nickel steel	FN-0708-T	B484, Grade 3, Type III, Class C
Nickel steel	FN-0208-T	B484, Grade 1, Type III, Class C	Infiltrated iron	FX-2000-T	B303, Class A
Iron nickel	FN-0400-R	B484, Grade 2, Type I, Class A	**Nonferrous:**		
Iron nickel	FN-0400-S	B484, Grade 2, Type II, Class A	Aluminum	---	B595
			Bronze	CT-0010-N	B438, Grade 1, Type I
Iron nickel	FN-0400-T	B484, Grade 2, Type III, Class A	Bronze	CT-0010-R	B438, Grade 1, Type II
Nickel steel	FN-0405-R	B484, Grade 2, Type I, Class B	Bronze	CT-0010-S	B255, Type II
Nickel steel	FN-0405-S	B484, Grade 2, Type II, Class B	Nickel silver	CZN-1818-U	B458, Grade 1, Type I
Nickel steel	FN-0405-T	B484, Grade 2, Type III, Class B	Nickel silver	CZN-1818-W	B458, Grade 1, Type II
Nickel steel	FN-0408-R	B484, Grade 2, Type I, Class C	Nickel silver, leaded	CZNP-1618-U	B458, Grade 2, Type I
Nickel steel	FN-0408-S	B484, Grade 2, Type II, Class C	Nickel silver, leaded	CZNP-1618-W	B458, Grade 2, Type II

Ferrous Powder Metallurgy

As previously stated, iron powders are the most widely used PM material for structural parts. While iron powder is used alone in some applications, most frequently, small additions of other powders, such as carbon, copper, or nickel, are included singly or in combination to improve mechanical properties of the pressed and sintered part. Plain carbon steels are made from mixtures of iron and graphite. When the parts are sintered, carburization produces a carbon steel structure with carbon that can range up to about 0.75%.

Low, medium, and high-density parts can be produced from the iron/graphite powders, giving a range in tensile strength from 16,000-60,000 psi (110-414 MPa). By heat treatment, strengths can be increased to over 90,000 psi (620 MPa). Prealloyed low-carbon steel is also available. Detailed information and data on the extensive variety of available PM materials is contained in "Powder Metallurgy Design Guidebook," issued by the Metal Powder Industries Federation. This publication contains information on density, porosity, permeability, mechanical properties, strength properties, ductility, hardness, corrosion resistance, surface finish, sound damping, and physical properties.

Adding copper to iron powder increases strength and tends to increase hardness. However, copper additions decrease ductility. Copper steels, covered by MPIF Standard 35, contain from 1.5-10.5% copper and up to 1.0% carbon. Low, medium, and high-density parts, and bearings are produced from copper steels.

Nickel steels contain from 2-8% nickel, with or without copper. In general, the nickel steels are used to produce parts of exceptionally high strength, combined with toughness and fatigue strength.

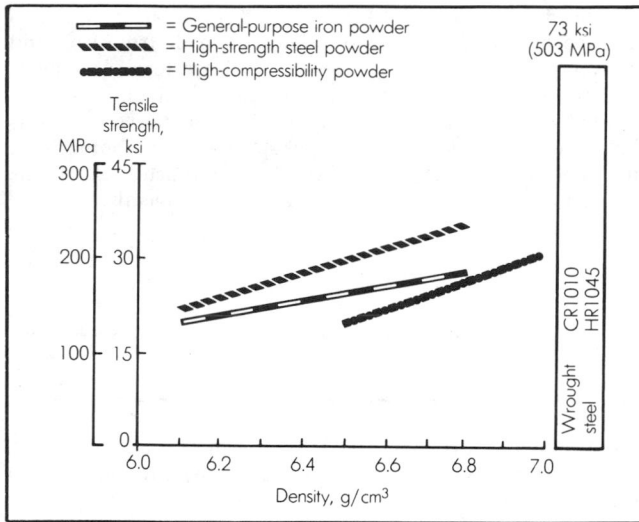

Fig. 17-4 Tensile strength vs. density: straight iron and steel powder.

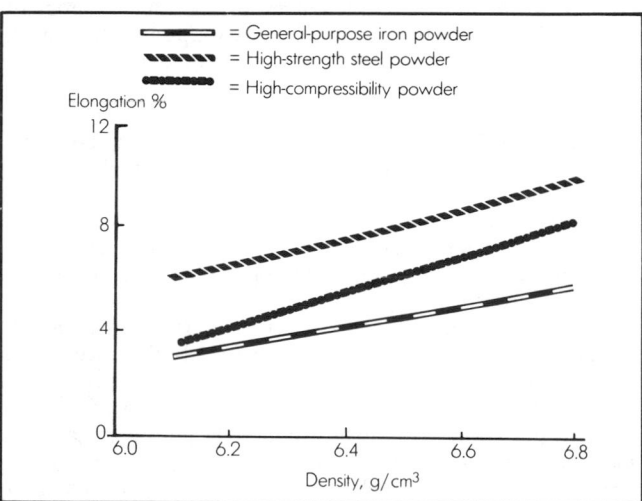

Fig. 17-5 Elongation vs. density: straight iron and steel powder.

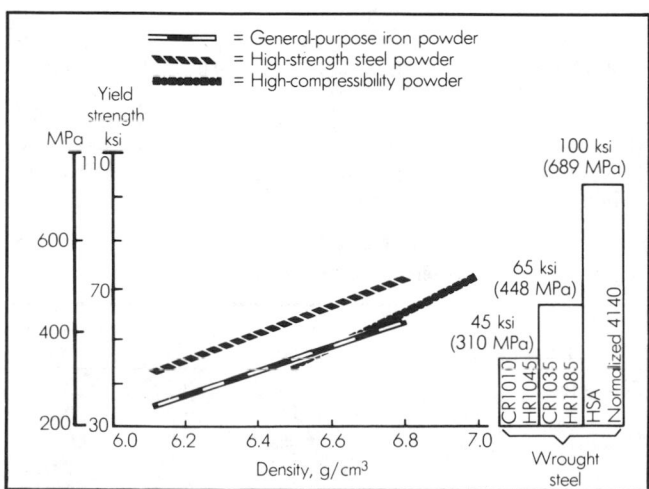

Fig. 17-6 Yield strength vs. density: iron and steel powder with 2 Cu and 1 C added.

Steel powders for PM forging include AISI grades 1025, 1080, 4620 and 4650. Modifications of 4600-type, Ni-Mo, prealloyed steel powders contain either 0.40-0.60% nickel or 1.75-1.90% nickel.

Austenitic and martensitic stainless steels, conforming to AISI compositional limits, are specified widely in applications requiring good corrosion resistance. AISI grades 303, 316, and 410 are covered by MPIF Standard 35. Other stainless steels for PM parts are AISI grades 304 and 434.

Ferrous parts of high porosity can be infiltrated with lower melting materials, such as copper or some brasses. Copper content in parts such as these can range from about 8-25%, reducing residual porosity virtually to zero. Besides improving

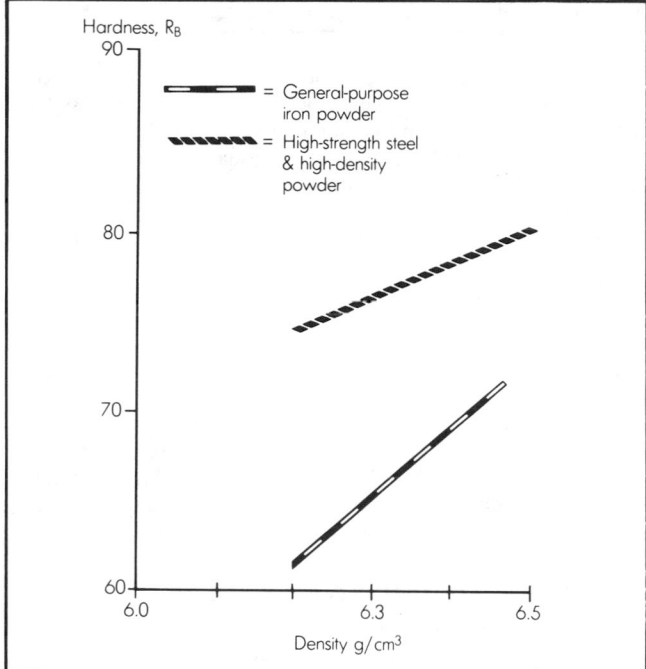

Fig. 17-7 Hardness vs. density: iron and steel powder.

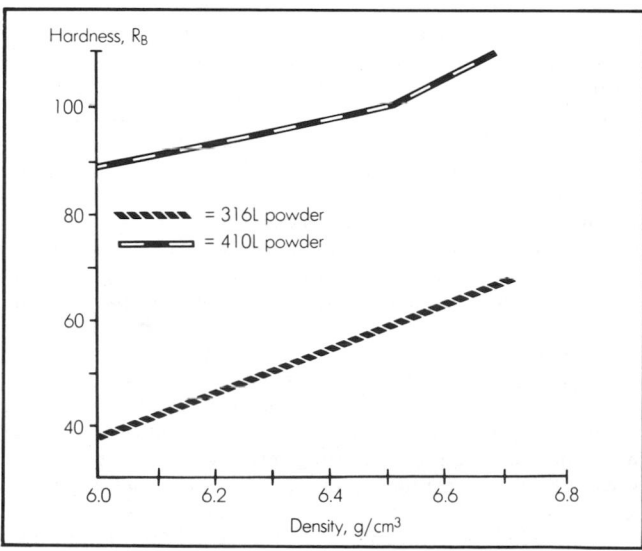

Fig. 17-8 Hardness vs. density: stainless steel powder.

PM PRODUCT DESIGN

strength, infiltration also is used to obtain more uniform density in parts that are difficult to press to uniform density.

Ferrous PM Properties

The physical and mechanical properties of ferrous metal powdered parts can be varied over a wide range and tailor-made for specific applications. Physical properties can range from the properties of low-density, porous parts having a tensile strength as low as 10,000 psi (69 MPa) to those of high-density, minimal-porosity parts with a tensile strength of 180,000 psi (1241 MPa) or more.

The graphs in Fig. 17-4 to Fig. 17-8 show various physical and mechanical properties of PM parts made from iron and alloy powders.[7] The properties covered are tensile strength, elongation, yield strength, and hardness—all of which are plotted against density. This data is representative of results obtained with powders of the types specified. For comparison, it may be noted that the indicated values approach or exceed the corresponding properties for similar wrought metals.

PM PRODUCT DESIGN

From the manufacturing standpoint, product design is the key to PM productivity. The powder metallurgy process has distinct design capabilities, and there are specific guidelines that must be followed to produce functional, economical parts. The practicable maximum part size is set by available presses and powder characteristics. Most parts range in area from 0.125-25 in.^{2} (80.64-16 129 mm^2) and are from 0.031-6" (0.79-150 mm) long.

Maximum surface area depends on the type of powder, part density, and press capacity. The most suitable shapes are those that have uniform dimensions in the direction of pressing. These include simple cylindrical, square, and rectangular shapes, as well as odd shapes in which the contour is a plane at right angles to the direction of pressing. Perfect spheres cannot be made by the PM process. Spherical PM parts are designed with straight or flat areas around the "equator." Parts that must fit into ball sockets are repressed to produce a more spherical shape. Spherical depressions up to a hemisphere are feasible.

GENERAL CONSIDERATIONS

In product design for powder metallurgy, it is important to keep in mind that powders do not follow the laws of hydro-dynamics and do not flow around corners. The required uniform density of a sintered part depends upon uniform powder distribution in the die as well as in the pressed compact. For high production rates, other design limitations are imposed by the required automatic ejection of the compact from the die.

Pressures are applied from the top and from the bottom. Cross holes, reentrant angles, undercuts, and circumferential slots, cannot be molded, but must be machined.

Some shapes would require dies and punches of very weak design, having featheredges or knife-edges, very small punch sections, or very narrow, deep splines. For some contours it is often necessary to leave certain areas for subsequent machining.

It is generally desirable to provide corners and edges with a 45° chamfer, but chamfers of the outside edges of a part should be provided with flats of 0.005-0.015" (0.13-0.38 mm) to avoid feathered punch edges.

Large and abrupt changes in height should be avoided, since the powder distribution would not be uniform and control of shrinkage during sintering would be difficult. If abrupt changes in height are required, it is frequently possible to press the powder to a preform having more gradual changes and then attain final shape, after sintering, by coining.

Complicated radial contours can be readily produced, but excessively narrow sections should be avoided since they contribute to insufficient powder flow and punch weakness. A narrow section can, in many instances, be eliminated by a simple redesign.

On flanged parts, a flange taper of approximately 0.8% of flange thickness is sometimes used to facilitate ejection. For corners on the underside of flanges, a relief on the order of 0.005-0.001" (0.13-0.03 mm) is necessary for parts to be coined, and a radius of about 0.01" (0.3 mm) for parts which are not coined.

Parts with projections in both directions parallel to the axis of compaction can be produced. As a general rule, however, complex profiles on one side only are preferred. Curved surfaces are obtainable, but spherical shapes can only be approximated.

Many of the previously mentioned design limitations can be overcome, but the complicated tooling required may render the process uneconomical.

Since minor design changes frequently transform an undesirable part to one which can be readily pressed, close cooperation between designers and powder metallurgists can considerably widen the applications of sintered parts. A good example of a part which can be produced by powder metallurgy more economically than by other methods is the true involute gear tooth, which cannot be hobbed because of the undercut profile. This feature can be incorporated in the die design, and thus in the sintered gear, without difficulty.

Tolerances depend on the material and also on the size of the part. In general, very close tolerances are obtainable. The tolerance values listed in Table 17-5 for parts not larger than 2" (51 mm) in diameter are typical.

Occasionally tolerances as close as ±0.0001" (0.003 mm) on the diameter of coined parts are possible. In many instances, however, a final grinding operation is more economical than the coining required for such close tolerances.

TABLE 17-5
Tolerances for Small Parts

Dimension	Process	Tolerance in.	mm
Diameter	As sintered	±0.003	±0.08
	Coined	±0.0005	±0.013
Height	As sintered	±0.005	±0.13
	Coined	±0.001	±0.03
Concentricity of holes		0.001	0.03
Parallelism of gear teeth		0.003	0.08

The "Compacting" section of this chapter provides detailed information on the Metal Powder Industries Federation (MPIF) system for classifying PM parts according to their increasing complexity.

Figure 17-9 shows schematically how powder metal part processing, tolerances, and physical properties are interrelated.

DESIGN FACTORS

To assure manufacturing productivity and end-product quality and performance, the design of metal powder parts requires thorough consideration of four factors:

1. The quantity—is it sufficient to justify the necessary investment in tools and dies?
2. The dimensional specifications and shape of the part—can it be made by PM techniques?
3. The required physical and mechanical properties—are they within the limits of powder metallurgy?
4. The cost of the part—is PM processing more economical than methods previously used or than other possible methods of processing?

A well-founded decision to select PM design and processing, based on examination of these key points, can result in functional and economical benefits in part production.

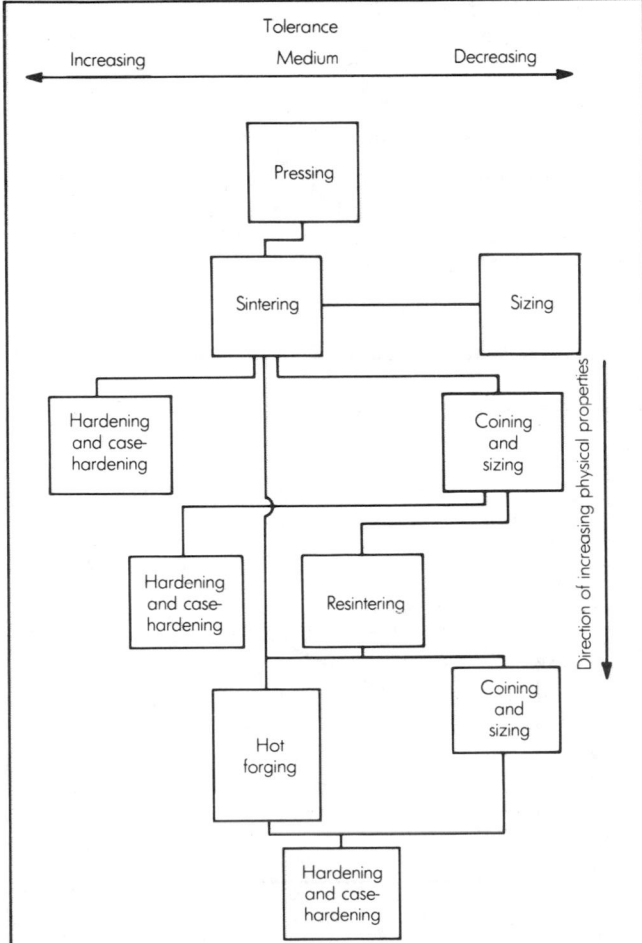

Fig. 17-9 Processing methods influence the tolerances and physical properties of PM parts.

Quantity

The complexity of the part and its adaptability are the most important factors in determining whether a part should be made by the PM process. Generally, production volumes of less than 10,000 identical parts are not practical. However, prospective part applications must be evaluated on an individual basis as well as a quantity basis.

Dimensional Specifications

The possibility of obtaining a high rate of production of finished or semifinished parts with narrow tolerances is one of the economic advantages of the PM process.

The narrowest tolerances are applicable only if the last step involves a sizing or coining operation. Roughly expressed, sizing tolerances can be compared with medium grinding or broaching tolerances.

The tolerances for a part which is sintered, but not sized, can be compared with medium to wide tolerances normally obtained when common machining processes such as turning, milling, and boring are used.

The tolerances of carburized and hardened structural PM parts are comparable with those of similarly treated alloy steel parts; with the tolerances of diecast light alloys; and with the narrowest class tolerances for small items produced by investment casting.

For iron-based parts, the normal range of dimensional tolerances of diameters or dimensions at right angles to the direction of compacting is ±0.1%. Through the use of sizing procedures, it is practical to hold these dimensions within ±0.05% or less. Dimensions in the direction of compacting can be held within ±0.4% without sizing, and about ±0.2% with sizing.

When machining processes are used, narrow tolerances mean high costs. It is more economical to use the PM cycle—pressing. . .sintering. . .sizing—in cases in which narrow tolerances are specified.

Properties

The engineering properties of PM parts depend on the material, design configuration, density, and whether or not the material can be heat treated. Table 17-6 lists typical properties of PM products made from various metals.

Density. Most properties of PM parts are related to final density, which is expressed in grams per cubic centimeter (g/cm^3). Density of structural parts usually is specified on a dry, unimpregnated basis, while the density of bearings is cited on a fully oil-impregnated basis. The method for density computation is described in MPIF Standard 42.

Density also is expressed as a percent of theoretical density. This is defined as the ratio of the PM part's density to that of its wrought counterpart. Powder metallurgy structural parts usually have densities ranging from 80% to above 95%. Oil-impregnated bearing density is approximately 75%, and filters may have densities as low as 50%.

Porosity and permeability. Porosity is the percentage of void volume in a PM part. For example, a part of 90% theoretical density has 10% porosity. Porosity is controllable and depends on the materials and how they are processed. Permeability, which allows passage of liquids and gases, is a special characteristic of certain types of PM parts. This design capability is

PM PRODUCT DESIGN

TABLE 17-6
Physical Properties of Sintered Products

Material	Density, g/cm³	Hardness	Tensile Strength		Yield Strength		Elongation, %
			1000 psi	MPa	1000 psi	MPa	
Aluminum (12-14 oxide)	---	---	48	331	35	241	7
Brass	7.92-8.36	Bhn 39	32-37	220-255	---	---	12-48
Bronze:							
Porous (bearing)	6.0-6.5	Bhn 25-40	11-16.5	76-114	10	69	2
Nonporous	7.0-8.0	Bhn 54	25-35	172-241	13-18	90-124	15
Bronze (friction agents)	---	---	Aprox. 5	---	---	---	---
Copper	7.6	Bhn 45	22.7	157	---	---	3-4
Copper-graphite	3.5	Bhn 32	---	---	---	---	---
Cupronickel	5.8-6.2	R_H 70-90	34-47	234-324	---	---	10-12
Iron:							
Porous	5.6-6.5	Bhn 40-50	14-35	97-241	10-28	69-193	1/2 to 4
Pure, nonporous	7.0-7.6	Bhn 60-70	30-48	207-331	25-30	172-207	7-23
Molybdenum	10.3	Bhn 230-300	200-350	1379-2413	---	---	2.5
Molybdenum-silver	10.3	R_B 80-90	---	---	---	---	---
Steel:							
Low-C	6.0-7.0	Bhn 80	40-50	276-345	25-30	172-207	2.5
1060	4.2% por.	R_C 37	198	1365	---	---	4
1080	2.0% por.	R_C 35	156	1076	---	---	13
Cr-Ni	6.68-7.10	R_B 60-98	63-105	434-724	---	---	4-32
Cu-steel	---	---	37-88	255-607	---	---	8-37
Cu-infiltrated	7.9-8.0	R_B 75-100	70-185	482-1276	60-120	414-827	6.2-11.3
Tantalum	16.6	Bhn 50-350	50-170	345-1172	---	---	1-25
Titanium							
Ti-64 B/E	4.4	R_A 24	133	917	120	827	12
Tungsten	19.3	Bhn 350	250-600	1724-4137	---	---	1-4
Tungsten-copper	13-16.5	R_B 60-110	---	---	---	---	---
Tungsten-silver	12-17	R_B 80-95	---	---	---	---	---

derived from the ability to control porosity. Depending on design, forming, and sintering methods, a part can have any desired permeability from 60% to 0%.

Physical properties. Density, pore size, shape, and distribution and the extent of sintering strongly affect tensile properties. Because of this close relationship, mechanical property data is commonly shown in graphs depicting the variation of strength with density. A typical graph (Fig. 17-10) shows the increase of strength with density for a part made from a PM copper and steel powder blend.

Fatigue strength versus density is plotted in Fig. 17-11. Fatigue strength is best at high densities. For similar PM and wrought parts, the ultimate tensile strength to fatigue strength ratios are the same. However, fatigue strengths of PM parts generally are more uniform and stable than those for wrought parts. Parts containing nickel show improved fatigue resistance compared to iron-carbon steels. High-density nickel steel parts can be case hardened to improve wear and fatigue properties.

Ductility. Ductility of PM parts tends to be relatively low because of the presence of pores. Measured in terms of percentage of elongation, values for ductility usually are less than 10% for ferrous PM material. However, some PM brasses

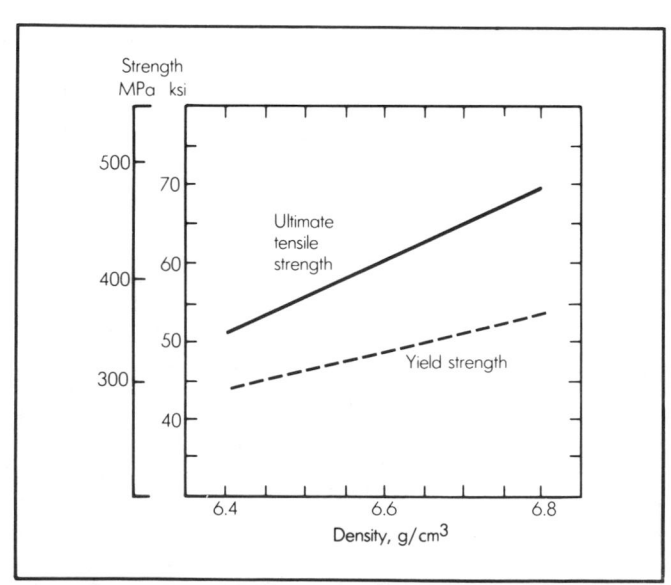

Fig. 17-10 Tensile and yield strengths for typical PM copper steel parts.

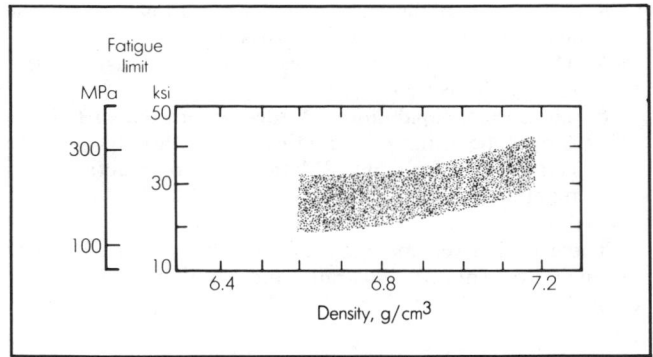

Fig. 17-11 Fatigue strength of PM parts increases with density.

reach 15-20% elongation. Ductility can be increased by hot or cold repressing followed by additional sintering.

Hardness. Because of the difference in metallurgical structure, gross indentation hardness values of PM parts and wrought parts should not be compared directly. The hardness value of a PM part is referred to as "apparent hardness." The apparent hardness is a result of powder particle hardness and porosity, as described in MPIF Standard 43.

Corrosion resistance. Corrosion resistance of PM parts is affected by voids. Entrapment of corrosives can lead to internal corrosion. Corrosion resistance is improved by compacting to higher density. Stainless steel and titanium PM parts have relatively good corrosion resistance in the atmosphere and in weak acids. Nonferrous PM formulations have good atmospheric corrosion resistance. Steam treating of ferrous PM parts creates a corrosion resistant, blue-black, iron oxide surface. Finishes, plating, and coatings also are applied to improve corrosion resistance. Impregnation with a resin or infiltration with metal to seal the pores against entry of plating solutions usually is recommended.

Cost

In evaluating producibility of PM part designs and in specifying the processes to be used, the manufacturing engineer takes into account the cost-effectiveness of the processing options that are available. Figure 17-12 shows the different processes normally used for the production of structural PM parts of iron powder. When making technical judgments that balance cost against physical properties of proposed iron powder parts, the objective is to stay as far as possible toward the left-hand portion of the chart.

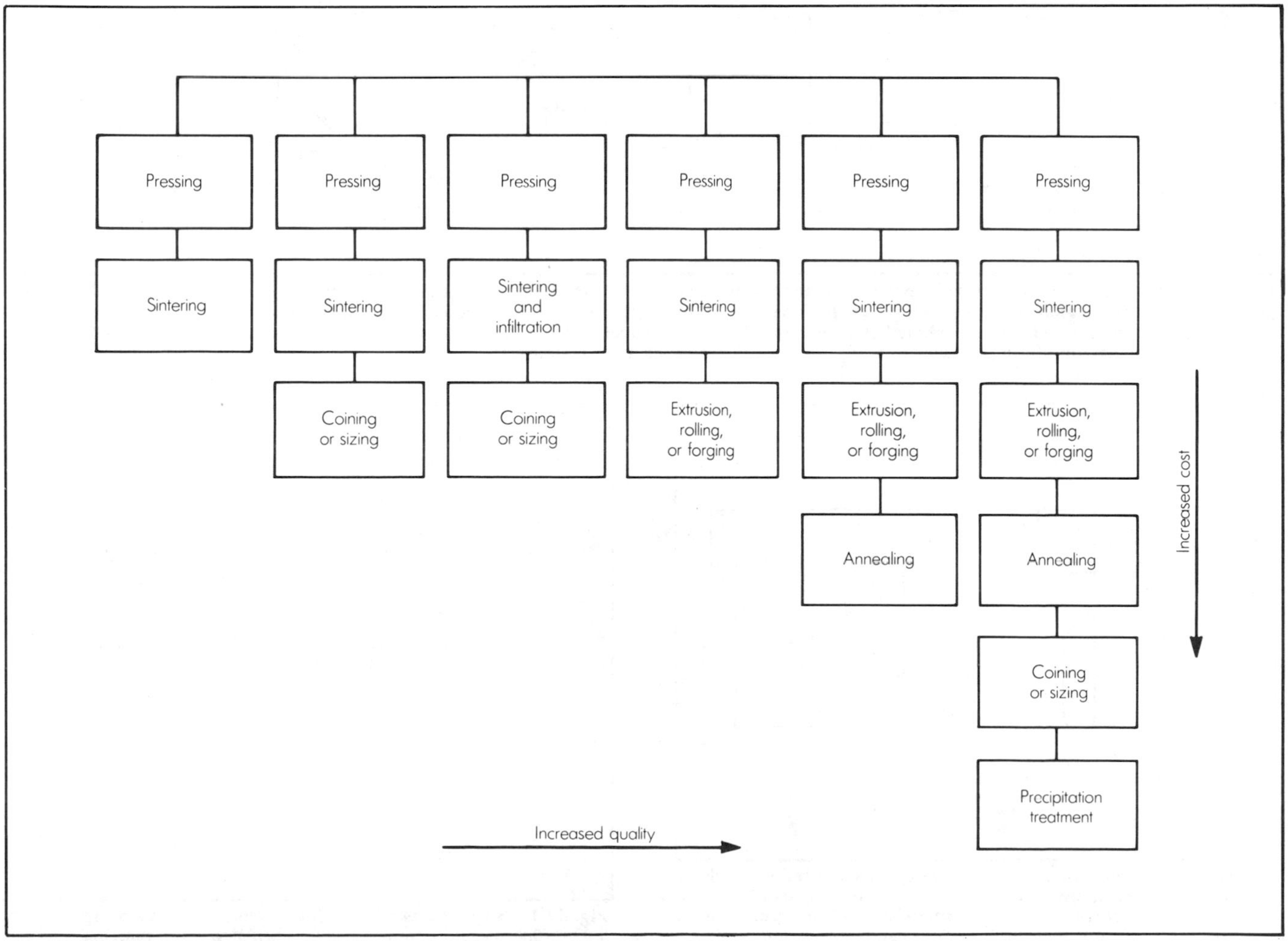

Fig. 17-12 PM process selection determines part quality and cost.

PM PRODUCT DESIGN

Guidelines

Parts should be designed specifically for fabrication by powder metallurgy, rather than adapting designs originally intended for production by other methods. For attainment of appropriate design configurations, simplified tooling, satisfactory parts, and low production costs, the key PM design recommendations may be summarized in the following six guidelines:

1. The shape of the part must permit ejection from the die.
2. The part shape must be such that the powder is not required to flow into thin walls, narrow splines, or sharp corners.
3. The part shape should permit construction of strong, durable tooling.

4. The shape of the part should make allowance for the length to which thin-walled parts can be compacted.
5. The part should be designed with the fewest possible changes in section.
6. The special capabilities afforded by powder metallurgy should be utilized, including the ability to produce certain part forms by PM that are not practicable to manufacture by other methods.

These design recommendations are the key to PM part producibility. They are illustrated and amplified in Fig. 17-13 through Fig. 17-22.

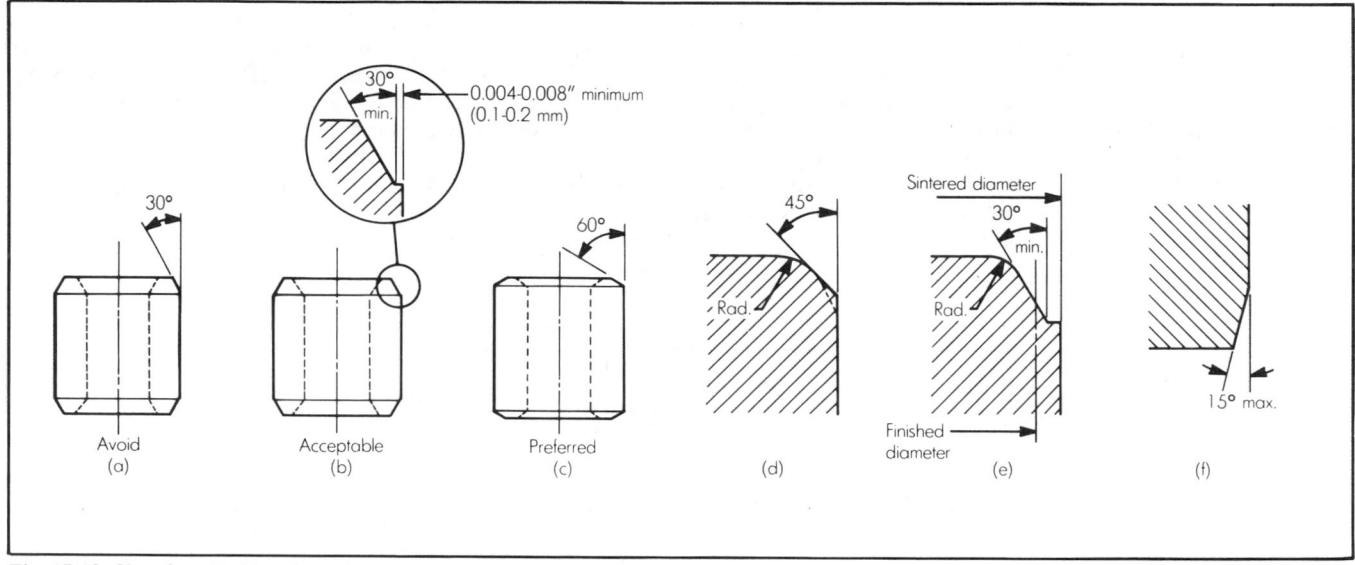

Fig. 17-13 Chamfers: (a) Chamfers with angles less than 45° should be avoided. (b) Chamfers with angles of 45° or less require a flat land to avoid punch breakage. (c) Chamfers greater than 45° are preferred. (d) Where a radius is essential, a useful compromise is a combination of radius and chamfer. (e) When the part is to be machined or ground on the outside diameter, the form shown is practical. (f) An acute angle for a lead-in can be formed in the compacting die, or produced by a coining operation if the chamfer is short.

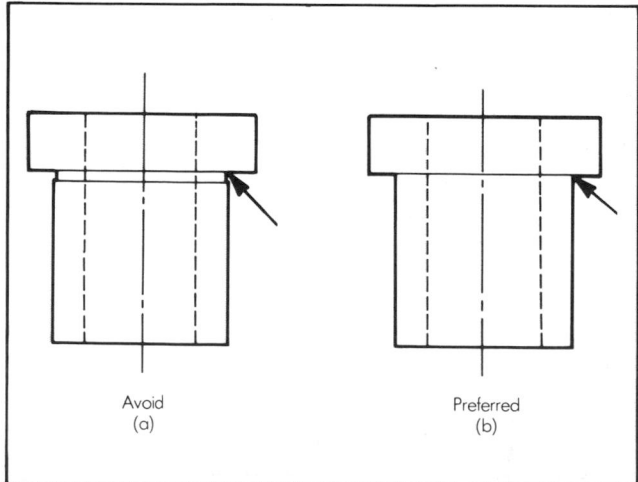

Fig. 17-14 Undercuts: Undercuts cannot be molded. A radius should be provided between flange and body, and the housing should have a corresponding radius or chamfer. Otherwise, the undercut must be machined. If necessary, a radiused groove can be formed in the flange where it meets the hub.

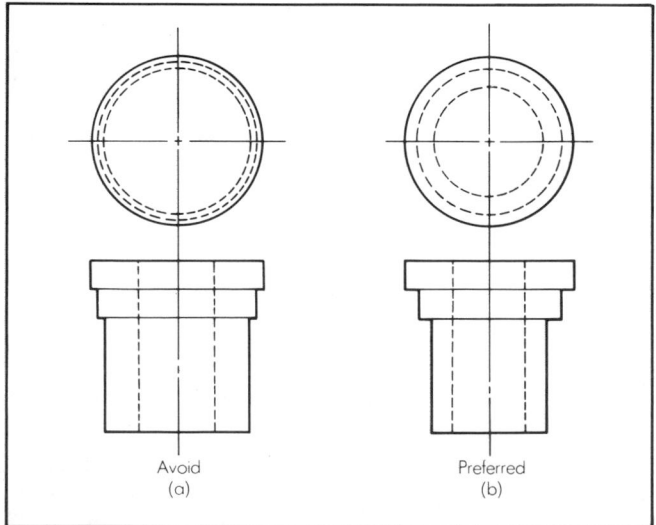

Fig. 17-15 Steps: Parts with multiple steps should be designed with 0.035" (0.9 mm) minimum width for each step. Thin punches increase breakdown time.

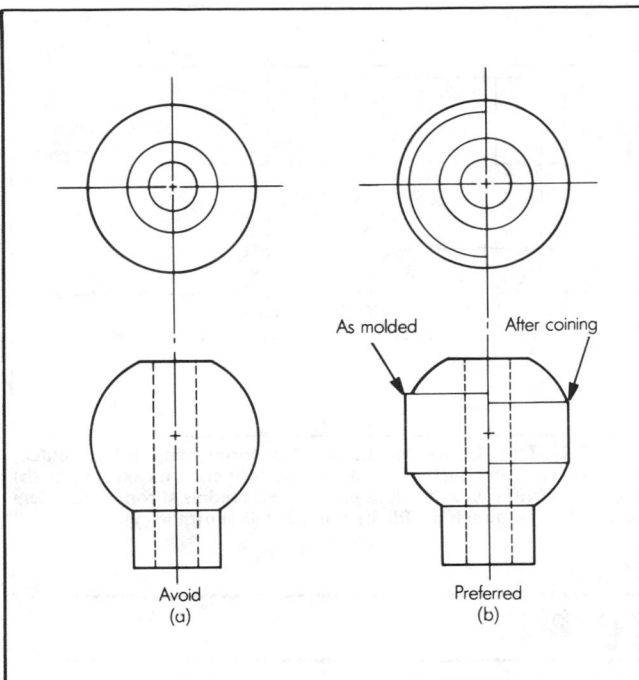

Fig. 17-16 Spheres: (a) Complete spheres cannot be molded, because sharp edges on punches would touch and break. (b) A cylindrical section between two spherical sections can be molded. The cylindrical section will lie within the sphere after coining. If the cylindrical portion is less in height than 25% of the spherical diameter, the punches become weak.

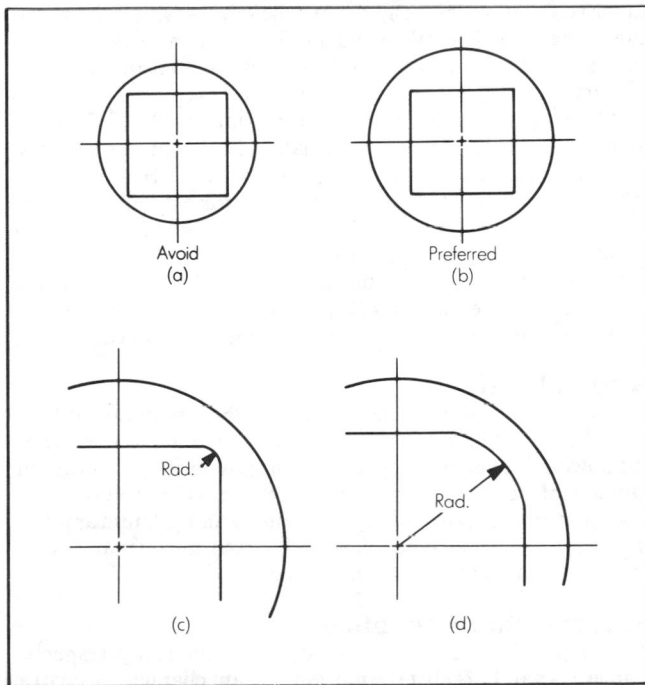

Fig. 17-17 Wall thickness: (a) Avoid parts with a minimum wall thickness less than 0.030″ (0.75 mm). For heavy, rigid, and long parts this limit must be increased. (b) The outside diameter has been increased to give reasonable strength. (c and d) Designs to increase wall thickness where a square bore is required. (d) Practical where flats are machined on a round spindle.

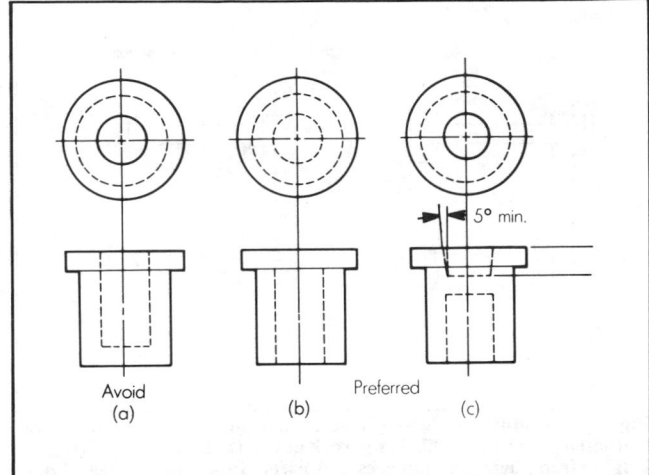

Fig. 17-18 Flanges and holes: (a) If a flange or any projection is opposite the blind end, the design must be modified. (b) Blind hole as shown can be molded. (c) Short counterbores can be molded on the flanged face without complicating the tooling, if the area of the counterbore is not more than 20% of the total pressed area, the depth (x) is not more than 25% of the total thickness, and a minimum taper of 5° is permissible.

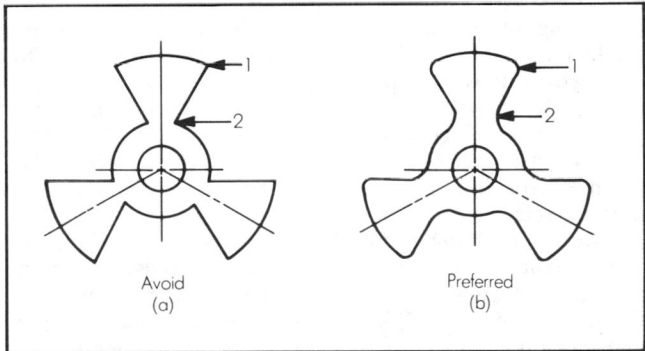

Fig. 17-19 Edges and corners: (a) Avoid sharp edges which weaken the die (1) and corners which weaken parts (2). (b) Radiused edges (1) and radiused corners (2) add strength to tools and parts.

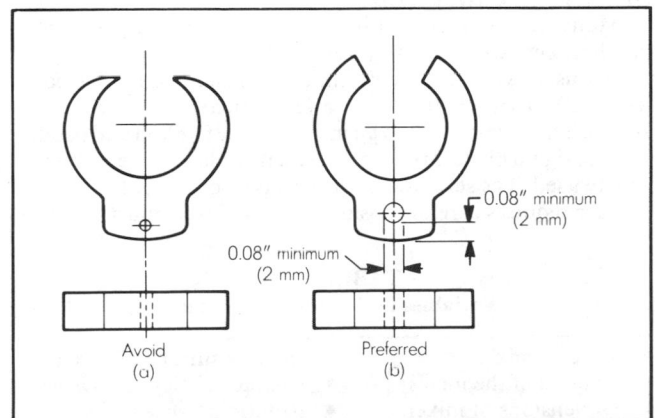

Fig. 17-20 Featheredges: (a) Profiles requiring featheredges on punches should be avoided. Holes should not be less in diameter than 20-25% of their length. The practical minimum diameter for holes is considered to be 0.08″ (2 mm). (b) Redesigned for stronger punches and hole large enough for molding.

POWDER MIXING AND BLENDING

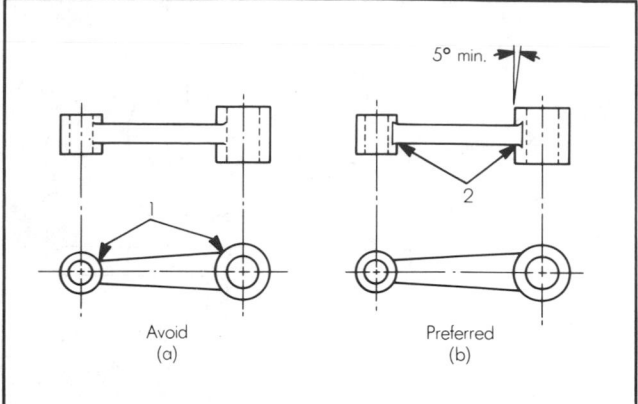

Fig.17-21 Radii: (a) Radii (1) at change in profile require weak, featheredged punches, likely to break down. **(b)** Radii (2) at change in height strengthen both punches and parts. Taper on portion of boss formed by top punch assists extraction. Remainder of boss, formed by die, must be parallel.

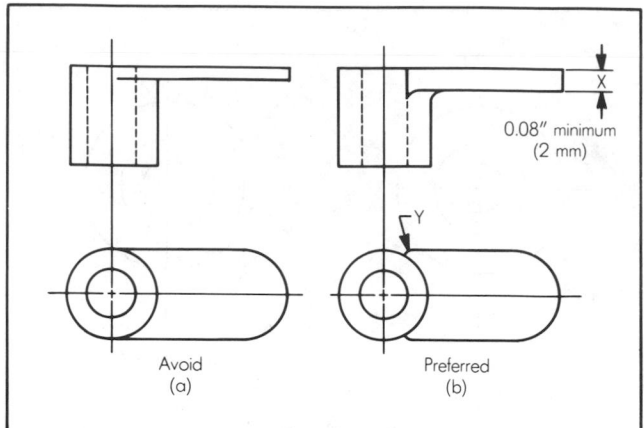

Fig. 17-22 Thin forms: (a) Large, thin forms cannot be molded, particularly when attached to long forms. Parts crack on extraction. **(b)** Make projection (x) as thick as possible, add radius at root, and delete sharp edges on punch profile by radiusing as shown at (y).

POWDER MIXING AND BLENDING

Mixing of powders precedes compacting and includes producing mixtures of different metal powders. In addition to mixing of various metal powders, this section covers mixing of metal powders with lubricants, a procedure that almost universally precedes compacting of parts in rigid dies. Also discussed are some of the numerous variables involved in this complex process and their effects on the degree of mixing that is obtainable.

The term *mixing* of powders refers to "...the thorough intermingling of powders of two or more materials."[8] The term *blending* refers to "...the thorough intermingling of powders of the same composition."[9] In the literature concerning the science and technology of powders, these terms are frequently used interchangeably. In the following short discussion, the term *mixing* will be used exclusively.

MIXER VARIABLES

Many different types of blenders and mixers are available. Batch mixers are commonly used in PM operations. The most widely used types include drum, cubical-shaped, double-cone (conical), twin-shell ("V"), and conical-screw (rotating auger). These types are shown in Fig. 17-23. Ribbon and paddle mixers, sigma blade mixers, and planetary blade mixers also are widely used. The selection of the best type of mixer for a given powder requires careful consideration, and tests must be made in each case.

TABLE 17-7
Variables in the Mixing Process

• Type of mixer	• Interior surface of mixer
• Volume of the mixer	• Characteristics of powders
• Dimensions of mixer	• Rotational speed of mixer
• Volume of powder in the mixer	• Mixing temperature
• Volume ratio of component powders	• Mixing time
	• Mixing medium (gaseous or liquid)

The most common mixing equipment for base metal powder mixes is the double-cone type, as shown in Fig. 17-24. An important consideration in mixing is that the powder must not fall freely during any stage of mixing, because this causes segregation. For this reason, the cylindrical part of double-cone mixers is kept short. This point must also be considered when other types of mixers, e.g. drum-type mixers with baffles, are used. The twin-shell "V" blender offers advantages that should be evaluated when powder uniformity is essential and precisely repeatable, predictable performance is necessary.

Many variables are involved in mixing. Table 17-7 shows some of the most important variables in the mixing process. Mixers can be characterized by their volume. However, two cylindrical mixers of identical volume perform differently when their length to diameter ratios differ. Although they may be of identical volume, the interior surface area of the two mixers is different, thereby changing the frictional effect, and the movement of the particles is quite different. It is the interior surface of the mixer that gives movement to the powder mass.

Size of Load

For every type and size of mixer, the optimum powder charge varies. The ratio of the mixer volume to the volume of the powder is of great importance. There is always an optimum amount of powder for a given mixer, below and above this optimum amount, the mixing is inferior. This optimum amount depends on the type of powders to be mixed and on many other factors that affect the frictional behavior of the powder.

Powder Characteristics

The powders to be mixed may differ in many respects. Tables 17-8 and 17-9 list the most important characteristics of a powder. If the powders differ significantly in density, segregation of the heavier powder may occur because gravitational forces may be stronger than the frictional forces. A change in the type of mixer and in the mixing procedure may be helpful to avoid segregation.

POWDER MIXING AND BLENDING

Powders of identical materials and identical particle size and particle size distribution may mix differently when the particle shape differs. Metal powders with oxidized surfaces flow faster and mix differently than identical metal powders with pure metallic surfaces. All these differences in the mixing behavior are due to the various friction conditions in the powders.

Friction

Friction occurs between the particles in a powder mass. This friction and the manner of mixing determine the movement of

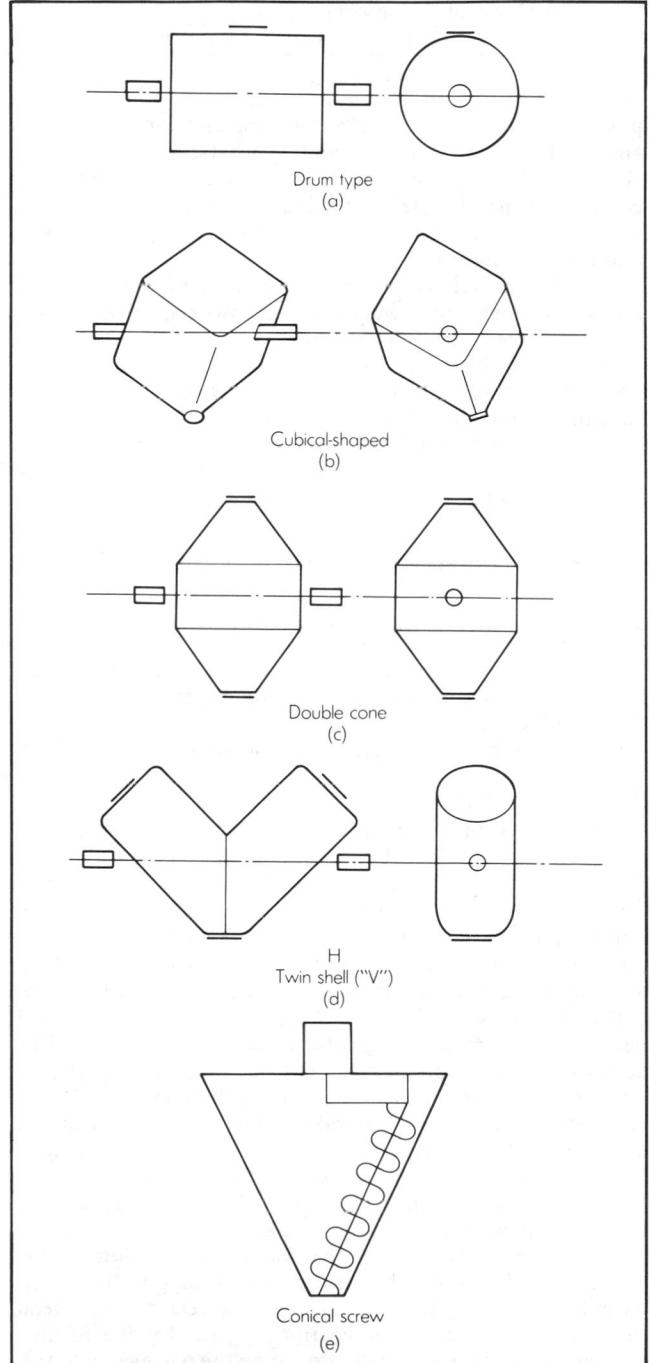

Fig. 17-23 Diagrammatic outlines of powder mixers.

powder particles. Studies of friction in a powder mass provide a better understanding of mixing problems.

During mixing, friction occurs between the powder particles and between the powder and the mixer wall. Friction causes an increase in temperature. If this increase in temperature occurs in an oxygen-containing atmosphere, and if some of the powders to be mixed oxidize, the mixed powders will contain particles with an oxide film. This is highly undesirable in some cases, especially when the oxide film affects further processing of the mixed powder.

The temperature during mixing has a significant effect on friction between powder particles, because the friction coefficient between most materials increases with increasing temperature. The flow of a powder is not as good at an elevated temperature as it is at a lower temperature. If it should be desirable to improve the flow or movement of powder particles during mixing, a lowering of the mixing temperature will lower friction and may improve the mixing.

Rotational Speed

The rotational speed of a mixer greatly affects the mixing. Increasing the speed up to a certain point is useful in shortening the mixing time. However, for practically all types of mixers and powders, there is an optimal speed. Above this speed, the effectiveness decreases because the centrifugal forces are too strong and the powders do not move away from the wall of the mixer.

Mixing Time

The optimum mixing time cannot be determined in advance without some testing. It is difficult to draw useful conclusions from the optimum time for one powder and to apply them to another powder in the same mixer. Mixing time strongly affects quality of the mix. Some powders are well mixed in some equipment after a relatively short time, whereas, other powders and/or other equipment require a prolonged mixing time to achieve the same degree of mixing; in other cases, a prolonged mixing time results in an even lower effectiveness.

LUBRICANT

When parts are pressed in rigid dies, lubrication must be provided to reduce friction between powder particles and between the compact being pressed and the die wall and core

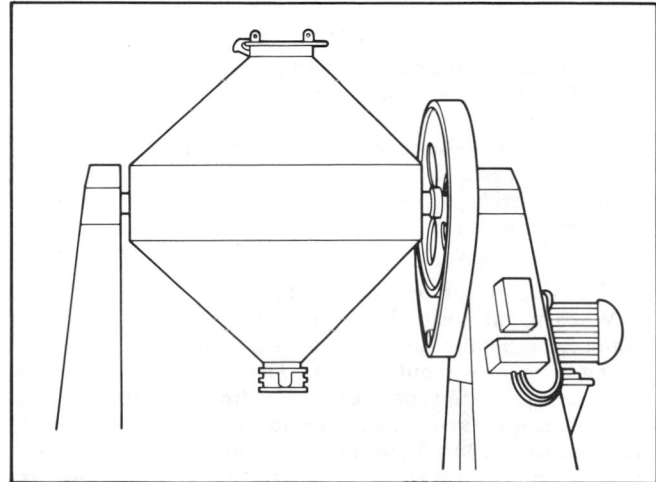

Fig. 17-24 Double cone mixer.

CHAPTER 17

POWDER MIXING AND BLENDING

TABLE 17-8
Characteristics of a Powder Particle

Material characteristics
- Structure
- Theoretical density
- Melting point
- Plasticity
- Elasticity
- Purity (impurities)

Characteristics due to fabrication process
- Density (porosity)
- Particle size (diameter)
- Particle shape
- Particle surface area
- Surface conditions
- Microstructure
- Type of lattice defects
- Gas content within a particle
- Adsorbed gas layer
- Amount of surface oxide
- Reactivity
- Conductivity

TABLE 17-9
Characteristics of a Mass of Powder

- Particle characteristics
- Average particle size
- Particle size distribution
- Average particle shape
- Particle shape distribution
- Specific surface (surface area per 1 gram)
- Apparent density
- Tap density
- Flow of the powder
- Friction conditions between the particles

rod. The lubricant has a low shear strength and keeps the metal surfaces apart. Complete separation is not possible even with well-lubricated surfaces, and there is friction due to contacts between metal asperities which puncture the lubricant film. Lubricants are chosen which attach themselves strongly to the metal surfaces and are not easily penetrated. The base metal powders are stearic acid; graphite; metal stearates, such as zinc and lithium stearate; and synthetic waxes, such as accrawax. Without lubrication, the pressure necessary to eject compacts from the die would increase rapidly; after a few compacts had been pressed, they would seize in the die during automatic compacting.

The lubricant is commonly introduced as a fine powder mixed with the metal powder or metal powders. The amount of lubricant added (generally 1/2 to 1% by weight) depends upon the shape of the compact. Complex shapes require larger amounts of lubricant to achieve a reasonably low ejection pressure. The mixing time and the intensity of mixing powder and lubricant affect such properties of the powder mixture as flow and apparent density. For most base metal powder mixes, mixing times of 20-40 minutes are common.

COMPACTING

To facilitate an orderly presentation of subject matter, this section on "Compacting" is limited to conventional die pressing. Other pressure compacting techniques, including isostatic, forging, high energy rate forming, extrusion, and continuous powder rolling; are discussed subsequently in this chapter under "Special PM Processes." Slip casting and gravity compacting pressureless methods also are presented in that section.

The words *pressing, compacting,* and *briquetting* are synonymous and imply cold pressing powders into a green compact. The objectives in pressing are:

1. To achieve the required part shape.
2. To obtain the required green density (pressed, but not sintered).
3. To secure sufficient green strength to permit safe handling of the part.
4. To provide particle-to-particle contact which is necessary for sintering.

BEHAVIOR OF POWDERS[10]

When metal powders are pressed in a die, the resulting compacts generally have enough adhesion and strength to permit handling without breaking. The green strength depends upon the type of metal powders—those from soft metals having higher strength—and upon the pressure that is applied. For soft metal powders, low pressures less than 35 MPa (5000 psi) produce compacts that can be handled. For harder powders, higher pressures are necessary. The question as to which

"mechanisms" or physical forces produce adhesion between metal particles is basic to an understanding of the green strength of PM compacts. Two basic processes—bulk movement and deformation—occur during compaction under pressure.

Bulk Movement

Bulk movement and rearrangement of particles results in a more efficient packing of the powder; that is, densification. Such movement is limited by frictional forces developed between neighboring particles and between particles and die, punch, and core rod surfaces. The relative ease of such motion increases with decreasing apparent density of the powder. With low apparent densities there is less particle-to-particle contact and more free space into which particles may move. Small particles move relatively greater distances because of their ability to pass through the small channels among the particles. Although most of the motion is in the direction of pressure application, there is some lateral motion due to the restraining action of blocking particles and the availability of free spaces. Powder characteristics that increase frictional forces reduce the extent of bulk particle movement. Movement of particles within the powder mass tends to take place at relatively low pressures and accounts for the early densification of the material. Additionally, the rate of pressure application influences bulk movement. High rates of pressure application tend to cause premature immobilization of particles due to high compressive stresses being developed on the particles, and this tends to block open passages.

COMPACTING

Deformation of Particles

Deformation of individual particles can also reduce the amount of porosity in the compact. Certainly with regard to the production of high-density parts, it is the major mechanism of densification. Both elastic and plastic deformation may occur. Most elastic deformation will be recovered when the stress is removed from the compact. This may take place before, during, and after ejection from the die cavity. It is for this reason that compacts usually have dimensions slightly greater than the die dimensions. The extent of elastic deformation increases with decreasing values of elastic modulus and increasing values of particle stress relative to the yield stress or elastic limit of the material.

When clean metal surfaces are made to touch each other, the adhesion between them is small because the area of contact is small. The area of contact between the surfaces increases when pressure is applied. The pressure produces some elastic deformation. For most practical cases of adhesion of surfaces under pressure, the amount of elastic deformation is negligibly small, since the weight of the powder alone causes plastic flow. Under these circumstances, the area of contact, regardless of the particle type or shape of surface asperities, is roughly proportional to the force applied; however, to produce complete contact, extremely high loads are required. The analysis of adhesion on a fundamental basis is complicated by the fact that metal surfaces, and in particular, the surfaces of metal powder particles, generally are covered with an oxide film. In addition, layers of gas molecules are absorbed on these surfaces. The oxides themselves can be cold welded, but the strength of the bond is generally low compared with that of metals. On the other hand, when metals are rubbed together, which is what happens during compacting of metal powders, the oxide films are penetrated or rubbed off and metal-to-metal contact is established.

Except for porous types of parts, plastic deformation of individual particles usually represents the most important mechanism of densification during compaction. It is evident that the greater the actual pressures on the particles, the greater the degree of plastic deformation. Rapid rates of pressure application may affect this process, but exactly how is not certain. Most materials work harden significantly so that it becomes increasingly more difficult to improve densification by increasing the pressure on the compact. On this basis, the effectiveness of the external pressure is greatest at low pressures where plastic deformation occurs relatively easily, and becomes progressively less effective with increasing pressure.

PRESSES

There are three basic types of compacting presses. The first and most widely used is the mechanical press, which includes (a) opposed-ram pressing, (b) single-action pressing, (c) multiple-action pressing, (d) anvil-type pressing, and (e) rotary-type pressing. The second type, the hydraulic press, also can be obtained with (a) opposed-ram pressing, (b) single-action (with floating die) or withdrawal-type pressing, (c) multiple-action pressing using (a) or (b). The third major type of press, which is finding increasing usage, is the hybrid press. This press uses a combination of mechanical, hydraulic, and pneumatic forces to compact a part.

Tonnage and Stroke Capacity

The capacity in tons, or in kilonewtons (kN) or meganewtons (MN) that a press must have to produce compacts in rigid dies at a given pressure in tons/in.^{2} or MPa depends upon the size of the part to be pressed and is equal to the pressure multiplied by the projected area of the part in in.^{2} or m^2. The compacting pressure depends upon the desired green density of the part which, in turn, is determined by the requirements for the physical and mechanical properties of the sintered part. In addition to tonnage capacity of a press, the stroke capacity of a press, i.e., the maximum ram travel, is important, because it determines the length of a part that can be pressed and ejected. In presses used for automatic compacting, the stroke capacity is related to the length available for diefill and for the ejection stroke.

Green density is the density of the part after it has been pressed, but before it has been put through the next process—sintering in the case of metal powders, or firing in the case of ceramics or ferrites. The most common way of expressing density is grams per cubic centimeter (g/cm^3). The amount of force required to obtain a given green density depends upon the material being pressed. It can range from 3-60 tons/in.^{2} (41.4-827 MPa). The upper limit is usually held to 60 tons/in.^{2} to provide a safety factor against premature tool failure under load. Table 17-10 gives some examples.

Die Pressing

The powder metal compacting press using die compaction is the most widely accepted high-production method of producing components by the powder metallurgy process. This is regarded as the conventional technique. The press is a machine that consolidates loose powdered material into a useful form or shape by compacting the powder under high pressures. The component being produced is formed within the confines of hard tooling, comprising dies, punches, and core rods. The process is called PM die pressing. The part produced is known as a briquette and is said to be in the "green" or unsintered state after ejection from the tooling. While the presses are known as powdered metal compacting presses, they are not limited to the pressing of metal powders. Almost any material, alloys or mixture, that can be provided in powder form can be compacted.

High-production PM compacting presses are available as standard production machines and are built in a wide range of

TABLE 17-10
Press Tonnage for Various Materials

Material	Tons per In.^{2}	MPa
Aluminum	5-20	69-276
Brass	30-50	414-689
Bronze	15-20	207-276
Carbon	10-12	138-165
Carbides	10-30	138-414
Alumina	8-10	110-138
Steatites	3-5	41-69
Ferrites	8-12	110-165
Iron Parts:		
low denisty	25-30	345-414
medium density	30-40	414-552
high density	35-60	483-827
Tungsten	5-10	69-138
Tantalum	5-10	69-138

Note: Tonnage requirements are approximations and vary with changes in chemical, metallurgical, and sieve characteristics; with the amount of die lubricants used; and with mixing procedures.

COMPACTING

capacity and production rate capabilities. Presses are designed to have the capability of producing parts of a specific classification. The Metal Powder Industries Federation (MPIF) has classified PM parts in terms of their complexity, the Class I being the least complex through Class IV, the most complex.

Press Selection

Selection must be based primarily on the type of work to be done, whether parts are large or small, whether they are simple or complex in shape, whether high or low-volume production is required, and numerous other factors related specifically to the job.

In some situations, simple tools and versatile, multiple-action presses are more suitable than complex tools and simple presses. The availability of toolmaking facilities must be considered, as well as the economics involved as far as tool cost and maintenance are concerned. As in selecting equipment for any other process, a thorough analysis of all the conditions involved is essential to ensure the best results.

The requirements for a powder metal compacting press should include the following:

- Adequate pressure capability in the direction of pressing, and sufficient part ejection capacity.
- Controlled length and speed of compression and ejection strokes.
- Synchronized timing of press strokes.
- Capability of producing a part of the desired classification.
- Adjustable powder filling arrangements.
- Material feeding and part removal system.
- Machine safety interlocks to prevent machine and/or tooling damage in the event of a malfunction.
- Necessary safety devices for operating personnel.

In order to better understand the types of commercially available PM compacting presses and their advantages and limitations, an explanation of PM part classification and tooling systems used to produce these parts is necessary.

MPIF Part Classification

Class I parts. As shown in Fig. 17-25, *a*, these parts are thin, are a single level, and are pressed with a force from one direction. A slight density variation within the part results from the single direction pressing. The highest density is on the surface in contact with the moving punch, the lowest density on the opposite side. Parts with a finished thickness of approximately 0.3" (7.6 mm) can be produced by this method without significant density variation.

Class II parts. Figure 17-25, *b*, illustrates parts that are single level of any thickness and are pressed from both top and bottom. The lowest density region of these parts is near the center, with higher density on the top and bottom.

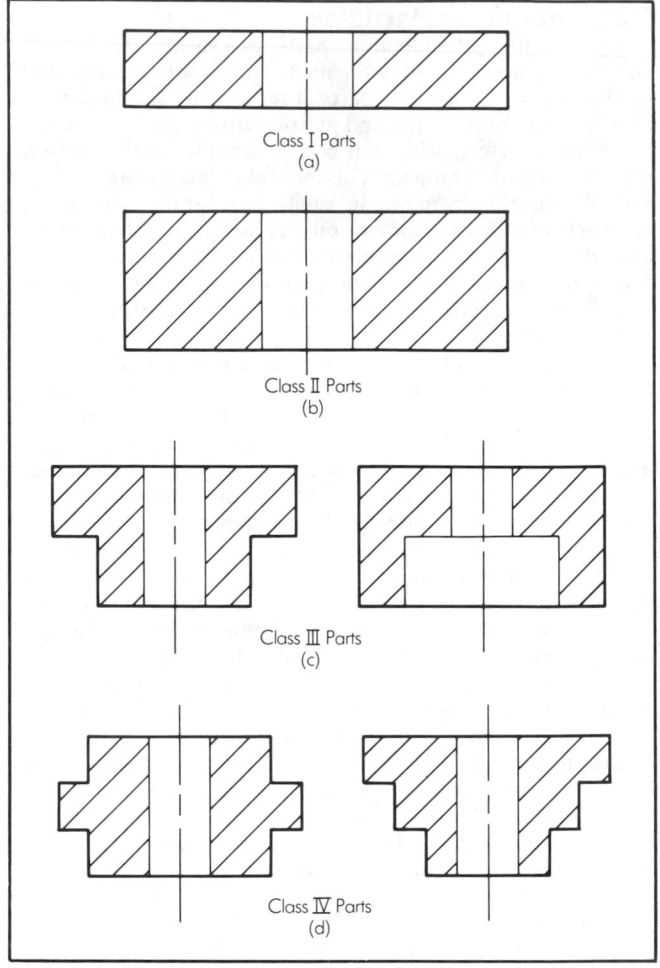

Fig. 17-25 MPIF parts classification.

Class III parts. Figure 17-25, *c*, illustrates parts with two levels of any thickness that are pressed from both top and bottom. Individual punches are required for each of the levels to control powder fill and density in each of the two levels.

Class IV parts. As illustrated in Figure 17-25, *d*, these parts have multiple levels of any thickness and are pressed from both top and bottom. Individual punches are required for each level to control powder fill and density in each of the levels.

The contour of the part does not enter into the determination of part complexity classification. The part may be a gear, cam, lever, or some other configuration and may have the same classification. Only part thickness and the number of distinct levels determine classification.

SINTERING

The briquetting or compacting of PM structural parts is followed by one or more sintering operations in which the green compacts are heated in a controlled-atmosphere furnace. The most commonly used furnaces are of the continuous type, equipped with a pusher, a conveyer belt, or other mechanical means of transporting the workpieces. A cooling section, containing the same protective atmosphere, is provided, enabling removal of the compacts from the furnace at approximately room temperature. Figure 17-26 shows a typical temperature profile in a continuous sintering furnace.

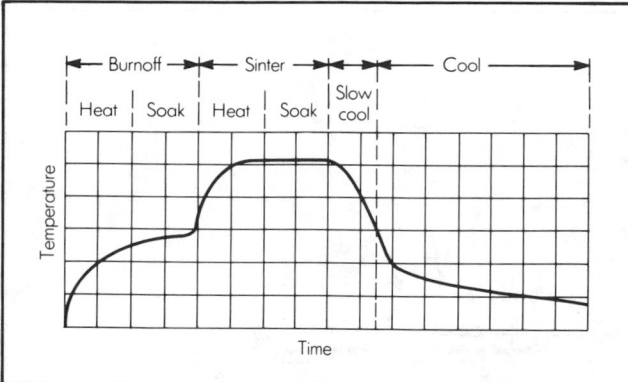

Fig. 17-26 Temperature profile in a continuous sintering furnace.

TABLE 17-11
Sintering Temperature and Time

Material	Time, Minutes	Temperature °F	Temperature °C
Bronze	10-20	1400-1600	760-871
Copper	12-45	1550-1650	843-899
Brass	10-45	1550-1650	843-899
Iron, iron graphite	20-45	1850-2100	1010-1149
Nickel	30-45	1850-2100	1010-1149
Stainless steel	30-60	2000-2350	1093-1288
Alnico magnets	120-150	2200-2375	1204-1302
Ferrites	10-600	2200-2700	1204-1482
90-W, 6-Ni, 4-Cu	10-120	2450-2900	1343-1593
Tungsten carbide	20-30	2600-2700	1427-1482
Molybdenum	120	3730	2054
Tungsten	480	4250	2343
Tantalum	480	4350	2399

In its simplest application, sintering is intended to impart strength to the part. This is accomplished using thermal treatments to promote spontaneous bonding and agglomeration reactions between particles. Sintering can also be employed to introduce alloying elements since the diffusional processes which tend to homogenize the distribution of alloying elements are the same ones that control sintering reactions.

Two basic types of sintering processes are commercially important: solid-phase sintering and liquid-phase sintering. Solid-phase sintering involves only atomic diffusion mechanisms and is, by nature, relatively slow at temperatures less than about 80% of the melting point. Time cycles for sintering and the furnace temperature are determined by the composition of the powders and by the properties desired in the finished product. Representative sintering temperatures and times for various materials are listed in Table 17-11. For a specific metal, the temperature is below the melting point; with mixtures of metals to produce alloys, the temperature is below the melting point of the major constituent.

Furnace atmospheres are produced in cryogenic distillation or gas-reforming equipment and include partially combusted natural gas, propane, dissociated ammonia, byproduct hydrogen, and vacuum. In many installations, sufficient heat is furnished by resistance-wound or silicon carbide element electric furnaces. When gas or oil-fired equipment is used, the furnace is provided with a muffle.

SINTERING METHODS

Sintering methods differ in such respects as the manner in which heat is applied; the medium surrounding the compact (liquid, gas, vacuum, air, powder, or a mold); conditions created by the composition of the compact; and the state of the constituents during sintering. Among the numerous methods employed are treating in a liquid salt bath, for very dense parts; treating in a liquid metal bath, for metal powder blanks that are machined after sintering; imbedding the compact in a heated powder pack of an inert or partially reducing material; and heating in a ceramic or graphite mold. All of these methods have disadvantages that limit their application to special parts.

The most common method of sintering structural parts is by externally heating the compact inside a box, or muffle, that is filled with a protective atmosphere to prevent oxidation.

In high-volume production sintering, continuous furnaces of the type used in heat treating are used. A steady stream of protective atmosphere is retained in the muffle, while the charge of work is passed through the furnace by a stoker arrangement.

The parts may be loaded in trays that are carried on a conveyor belt; frequently, the work itself is placed directly on the conveyor belt.

In addition to the conventional form of sintering, involving heating the original powder mass to a high temperature, but below its melting point, in a protective atmosphere; there are two major variations.

Hot Pressing

This technique identifies the application of both elevated temperature (below the melting point) and an external pressure to the compact. This technique is widely used for ceramic materials and refractory metals, but not for conventional ferrous and nonferrous materials.

Liquid Phase

Sintering usually is considered a solid-state process; that is, no molten or liquid phase is present. However, liquid-phase sintering is a process variation in which sintering temperature is high enough that one or more components of the material is liquefied. Liquid-phase sintering utilizes a second powder, mechanically mixed with the first, which has a melting point lower than the sintering temperature. The presence of a liquid phase during sintering not only enhances the bonding and agglomeration reactions between the solid particles, but also freezes upon cooling and acts in much the same manner as a solder to provide additional strength.

FURNACES

The mesh belt conveyor furnace (Fig. 17-27)[11] is the most commonly used furnace for sintering. It usually consists of the following components:

- Charge table and belt drive.
- Burn-off furnace.
- Sintering furnace.
- Slow cooler.
- Final cooling section.
- Discharge table.

This type of furnace is commonly used for sintering nonferrous and ferrous parts up to a maximum temperature of 2100° F (1150° C).

SINTERING

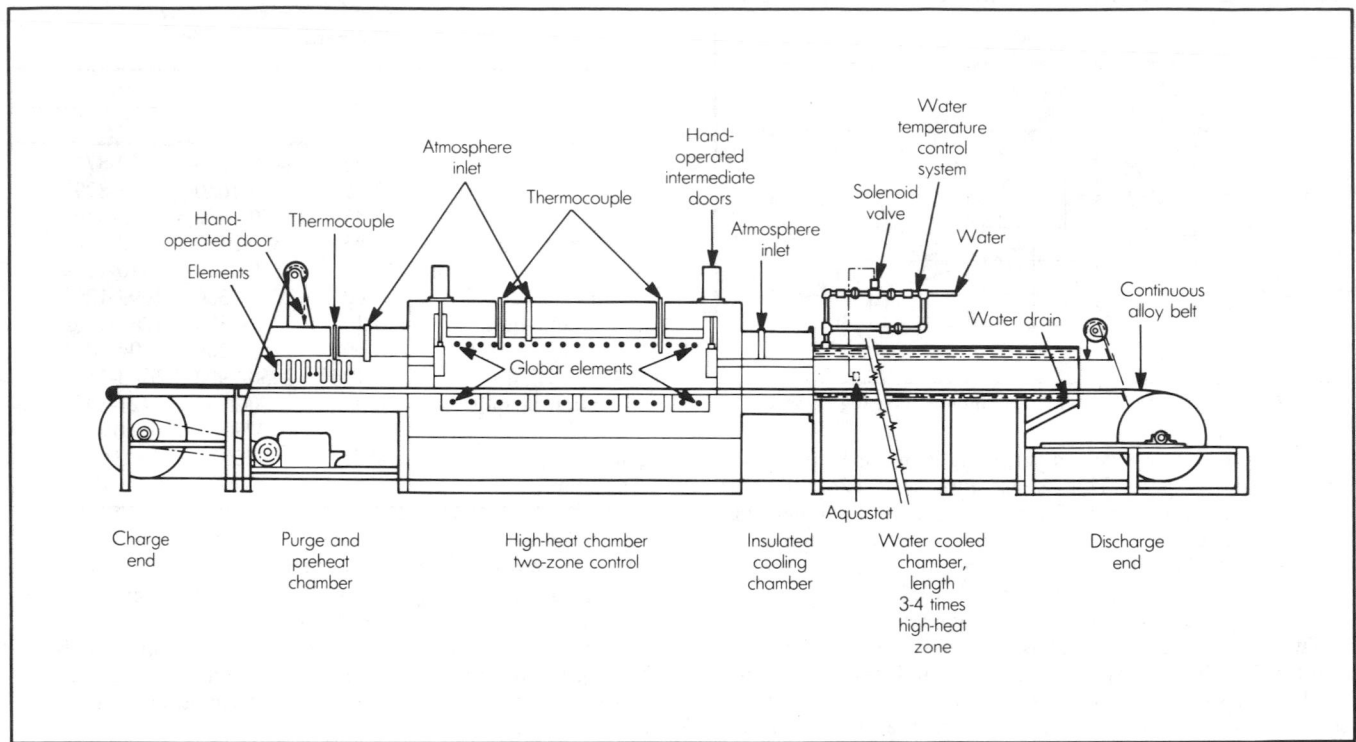

Fig. 17-27 Mesh-belt continuous-type sintering furnace.

When higher sintering temperatures are required, different types of furnaces are used. In the 3150° F (1732° C) temperature range, molybdenum-heated pusher furnaces may be used. In the 2100-2500° F (1150-1371° C) temperature range, walking beam furnaces may be used; and in the maximum temperature range of about 5000° F (2760° C), vacuum furnaces may be used.

When molybdenum heating elements are employed for temperatures of 2200-3150° F (1204-1730° C), it is important that hydrocarbon residues from the lubricant burn-off do not come in contact with the heating elements as they will carburize. For the hydrogen sintering of cemented carbides which is usually performed in a molybdenum-heated pusher furnace, a separate presinter and burn-off furnace is used. This keeps lubricant residues out of the molybdenum heated furnace.

Since the atmosphere in a furnace may react with brickwork or insulation, many furnaces are constructed with a metallic muffle to isolate the atmosphere from the lining. Muffle-type construction gives the best control of atmosphere and atmosphere velocity, but it is limited to a top temperature of 2200° F (1200° C) by the alloy materials that are available.

When the atmosphere is in contact with the refractories, certain precautions must be taken. When endothermic gas is used in contact with the lining materials, the lining must be of special low iron and reducible oxide composition, or carbon nodules will form at certain temperature gradients in the insulation and spall the brickwork. When low dew point reducing atmospheres such as dissociated ammonia or hydrogen are used at high temperatures, they can reduce the silica, which is the major constituent of most refractories. Under these conditions, high-alumina insulating materials are required.

Vacuum sintering is commonly used for such materials as stainless steel, tungsten carbides, tool steels, and titanium.

LUBRICANT PURGING

Since most PM parts are compacted with a lubricant to reduce compacting pressure and to assist in ejection of the part from the die, this lubricant must be burned out of the part before it can be sintered. The removal of the lubricant is normally accomplished in a burn-off furnace, under a protective atmosphere, at temperatures ranging from 800-1500° F (427-816° C) and for a typical time of 20-30 minutes. After lubricant burn-off, the part is conveyed into the sintering furnace for the appropriate period of time at the desired temperature.

ATMOSPHERES

During the burn-off, sintering, and subsequent cooling operations, the parts are maintained in a protective atmosphere. The purpose of this atmosphere is to prevent oxidation; to reduce oxides in the metals; to carburize, decarburize, or maintain a neutrality to carbon; and to assist in flushing lubricant residues from the furnace.

The most commonly used protective atmospheres are:

- Endothermic gas.
- Nitrogen blended with other reducing gases.
- Dissociated ammonia.
- Exothermic gas.
- Hydrogen.

A decision as to the atmosphere to select must take into consideration the atmosphere's compatibility with the materials being processed, the type of furnace needed, and the cost of the furnace. Typical sintering atmospheres are listed in Table 17-12.

TABLE 17-12
Relative Cost and Uses of Sintering Atmospheres

Atmosphere	Relative Cost Index per 1000 ft³ (28.3 m³)	Uses
Cylinder hydrogen	50	All-purpose sintering atmosphere. Most powerful reducing atmosphere. Must be used for tungsten and tantalum carbides, Alnico, and stainless steels or alloys in excess of 2% chromium. Decarburizing to iron powders
Cracked anhydrous ammonia, 75% H_2 -25% N_2. Dew point -60° F	10	Used for brass sintering. Used in place of cylinder hydrogen to reduce cost. Not suitable for metals that absorb molecular nitrogen at sintering temperatures. Decarburizing to iron powders
Exothermically cracked gas, 17% max H_2. 10% max CO, 4% min CO_2. 1.0% CH_4, bal. N_2. Dew point, 10° F higher than cooling water. Refrigerated or dried to 40° F (4.4° C) point	2.5	Lowest-cost atmosphere. Used for copper, bronze, silver, and iron powders where decarburization is not a factor
		Refrigerated or dried to 40° F (4.4° C) dew point for iron to prevent discoloration. Sulfur must be removed for copper, bronze, and silver if in excess of 8 grains/100 ft³ (0.18 g/m³)
Endothermically cracked gas, 40% H_2, 20% CO, 0-3% CO_2, 0-1.0% CH_4. Dew point 0-70° F. CO and dew point can be adjusted for desired carbon potential	3	Used for medium and high-carbon iron powders to prevent decarburization. Carbon potential adjustable for low or high carbon. Used to obtain more reducing atmosphere than exothermic type. Used for brass sintering. Used for heat-treating and carburizing powdered-iron parts

TOOLING FOR PM PARTS

The design of tooling for sintered metal parts begins with a study of the workpiece drawing. The most important point to consider is whether the part is feasible for the PM process. Can the part be molded? Can it be made within the capability of existing equipment in the fabricating shop? Can it satisfy the basic parameters governing a sound sintered metal part?

An understanding of what happens when powder is compacted between punches in a die is essential to design a good part and the appropriate tools for it (see "Compacting" in this chapter).

The tool engineer should participate in the design of the product as early as possible in its inception and development cycle. This helps to assure that prospective parts are designed in accordance with the capabilities and limits inherent in the PM process.

TOOLING DESIGN FACTORS

The limitations posed by rigid dies are illustrated by the die action shown in Fig. 17-28.[12] A single punch cannot assure uniform density if the part is of varying thickness (actually, varying axial height); therefore, steps are limited to one quarter of height (Fig. 17-28, view a). Much larger steps are allowable with a multiple-sleeve die; however, a very thin sleeve is impractical (view b) and the sleeve should be radiused to prevent excessive wear. Knife-edge punches wear excessively

and should be changed to present a flat face (view c). On withdrawal, a deeply penetrating punch would damage the compact, so it should be tapered (view d). Holes can be made with parallel walls, but should be a minimum of 0.2″ (5 mm) diam to prevent premature core rod failure. The maximum depth-to-diameter ratio range is practically limited to 2-4 (view e). Even under pressure, the powder cannot fill very thin sections (view f).

Diecastings, forgings, extrusions, and plastic parts are made by a process with one common feature. All of these processes rely on plasticity of the component material to flow throughout the cross section of the mold tool to produce the part. Movement of material in the direction transverse to the pressing motion is a natural and necessary phenomenon of these forming techniques. Thin wall sections, or uneven cross sections, can be molded with comparative ease. Multiple levels pose no particular problem. Side coring and curved sections can be made with these molding methods.

Metal powders, on the other hand, do not share the basic characteristic of the other molding and forming methods. Powdered metal does not flow under pressure. This is a basic factor; it imposes restrictions on the tooling design and the manufacturing processing of parts by the PM technique. Since metal powder does not flow under pressure, several other related factors must be considered in tooling design. Some of

CHAPTER 17

TOOLING FOR PM PARTS

the significant tooling design parameters are interrelated and can be grouped based on the following:

1. Metal powder does not flow under pressure. (This factor is fundamental and is repeated for emphasis.) Under vertical axial load, powder can, however, exert a side force. For example, when a simple shape is compacted at 30 tons/in.^{2} (414 MPa), 10 tons/in.^{2} (138 MPa) pressure can be exerted laterally against the die.
2. A compact (unsintered part) has very low tensile strength and ductility. For a given material, these properties are a function of density.
3. A PM part should have uniform density. Structural strength of PM parts is directly related to density. Density is the property that relates to internal transfer of applied loads within the part. To achieve uniform density, tooling design must accommodate the no-flow characteristic of metal powder. Parts with multiple-level cross sections usually require a separate tool member for each level.
4. The finished part should be free of shear planes. Shear planes develop in a sintered metal part when a level of the compact densifies without simultaneous densification of adjacent material. Densification of the adjacent material is necessary to provide support, which prevents angular slippage of the compacted material. Where a shear plane exists (even when the part is ejected as a whole piece), the rupture does not heal during sintering and causes an unsound sintered part to be produced. When the shear plane is at a point of stress concentration, the part may fail in service.
5. The part must be free of cracks. Because compacted material has little green strength, adequate ejection support must be provided for each overhanging level in the mold tooling. Cracking may result if this support is not provided.
6. A compact tends to grow or "pop" as it is ejected from the die. This "pop out" is proportional to the compacting pressure.
7. Tooling must perform reliably. Tool design practices should emphasize the importance of performing effectively, with little maintenance or setup adjustment, for high-volume production runs over a long period of time.

TOOL MATERIAL

Tools used in the production of PM parts perform a variety of operations, such as compacting, coining, sizing, and hot forming. In the early days of the industry, when only bronze powders were compacted, little was required of tooling, other than high wear resistance. With the introduction of iron and steel powders—and, more recently, refractory metal and super-alloy powders—tool materials now require the additional feature of high impact resistance. Additionally, there is an increasing demand for high-density compacts, a requirement that imposes even heavier loads on the compacting tools. And, with recent activity in the hot forming of powdered metal parts, wear resistance at elevated temperatures has been added to the growing list of tooling requirements.

Wear Resistance or Impact Strength

The characteristics of wear resistance and high impact strength are difficult to combine in one material. Tool material selection is determined by the PM part and the powder

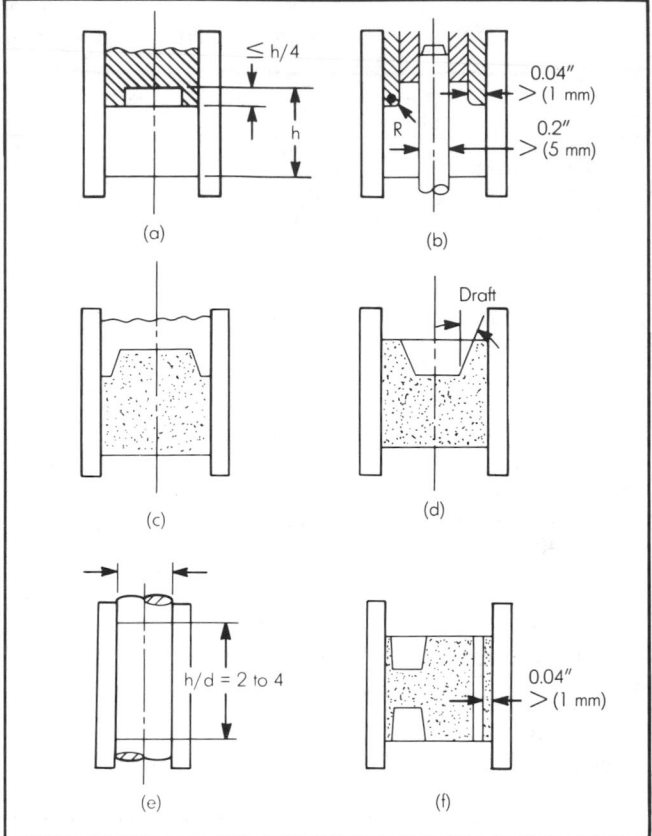

Fig. 17-28 Design and production limitations of PM parts.

material; the method of tool construction; and the PM processes by which the part is to be made or finished. Wear resistance is a key factor in die and core materials. For punch materials, on the other hand, impact resistance or toughness is more important than wear resistance.

Die Materials

The most commonly used die materials are the wear-resistant steels and cemented carbides. The most common steel grades are A2, D2, M2, and SAE No. 6150. Tungsten carbide is used for core rod sleeves. Cemented carbides are used in the form of shrink-fitted linings. Tough steels such as A2 and D2 are recommended for the punches. Cemented-carbide punches are not in common use.

DIE DESIGN

Die cavities and punch faces should be lapped and polished to a very high surface finish, preferably below 10 μ in. (0.25 μ m). Clearances between die walls and punches should not exceed 0.005" (0.13 mm); these clearances should be held between 0.0002-0.0003" (0.005-0.008 mm) for precision parts.

To facilitate ejection and avoid excessive die wear, a slight taper, typically 0.001 in./in. or mm/mm, is machined in the die. Tapers may, however, entrap powder particles and cause fins and burrs; more wear-resistant die materials, such as cemented carbides, may be used to avoid the need for tapers in compacting dies. In coining dies, tapers may be necessary to press oversize sintered pieces into the cavity.

Die Strength

In determining die wall thickness, it is frequently assumed that for reasons of safety, full hydraulic transmission of pressure is obtained, even though this is contrary to the no-side-flow theory.

An exact calculation of the stress on die walls is almost impossible from a practical point of view because of the nature of the work performed. In the first place, stress distribution throughout a compact under pressure, which must be taken into account as part of the structure under consideration, is extremely complicated and includes variables such as part shape, particle-size distribution, and other factors that affect transmission of compressive stress in the lateral direction. The experimental work and stress analysis required for precise calculation of these stresses require far more time than is usually available to the die designer.

Die Dimensions

Simpler empirical methods of calculating die dimensions are usually employed. In one of these, Poisson's ratio of 0.3 for structural steel is employed with a modification of Lame's formula for cylinders of heavy wall thickness subjected to high internal hydrostatic pressures. This is:

$$D = d\sqrt{\frac{s+pu}{s-pu}} \qquad (1)$$

where:

D = outer diameter of die
d = diameter of the compact
S = maximum allowable fiber stress of die material
p = briquetting pressure
u = Poisson's ratio for steel

While the pressure within a cylinder is uniform in the hydrostatic case, it is multiplied by Poisson's ratio for this application.

This formula can be used only as a guide or approximation, since the ratio of die length to compact length, pressure distribution, distribution within the compact, variations in shape, and other important factors are not considered. In many applications, this formula produces safer results than are necessary.

Internal-stress distribution in irregular shapes becomes even more involved; and in sectional dies, the lateral stresses exerted by the compact are transferred from individual inserts to the die ring. As a result, corresponding allowances must be made in calculating stresses. Tool designers invariably allow a high safety factor in such calculations, because the cost of die materials is the least expensive aspect of design and fabrication.

PM TOOLING SYSTEMS

Tooling systems applicable to the various categories of PM parts, as defined in the "Compacting" section of this chapter, include the single-action system, double-action system, floating-die system, and withdrawal system.

Single-Action

Single-action systems, as illustrated in Fig. 17-29, are generally limited to Class I parts. During the pressing portion of the compacting cycle, the die, the core rod, and one of the punches (usually the lower punch) remain stationary. Compacting is performed by the moving punch which is driven by the action of the press. One or more core rods may be used to form any through holes in the part.

During ejection, the upper punch moves away from the formed part and the part is ejected from the die. When the core rod is stationary, the part is ejected from the die and core rod

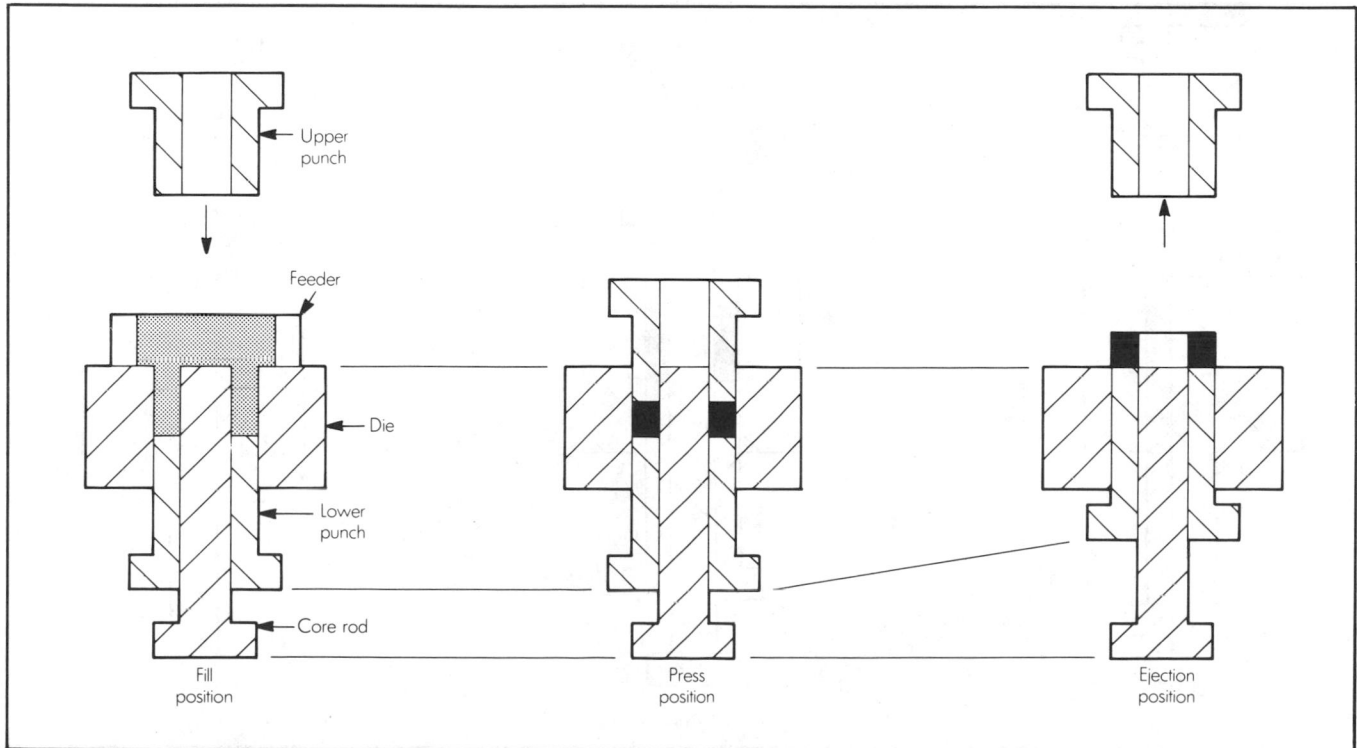

Upper punch

Feeder

Die

Lower punch

Core rod

Fill position

Press position

Ejection position

Fig. 17-29 Single-action press system.

TOOLING FOR PM PARTS

simultaneously. On some presses, the core rod is free to move (float) upward with the part as it is being ejected. Upon final ejection, the compacted part elastically expands slightly. This expansion causes the part to free itself from the core rod. The core is then free to move downward to the fill position. This "floating" core arrangement offers the advantage of reduced ejection forces and reduced core rod wear.

Double-Action

The double-action tooling system shown in Fig. 17-30 is used primarily to produce Class I and Class II parts. Pressure is applied to the top and bottom of the part simultaneously and at the same rate. The die and core rod are stationary. Densification takes place from the top and bottom toward the center with the lowest density region existing near the neutral axis of the part. Although the core rod is shown as being fixed, it can be arranged to function in the same manner as the core rod for single-action pressing, "floating" out with the part during ejection (see earlier section, "Single-Action").

Floating Die

The floating-die tooling system is shown in Fig. 17-31. In principle, it is the same as the double-action system, except that a different means is used to accomplish the same end result. The die is mounted on a yielding mechanism. Springs are used; however, pneumatic or hydraulic cylinders are more often used because they offer an easily adjustable force. As the upper punch enters the die, starting to compact the powder, the friction between the powder and die wall causes the die to float downward. This has the same effect as an upward-moving lower punch. After pressing, the die moves upward to its fill position and the upward-moving lower punch ejects the part. The core rod can be fixed or floating as described earlier.

Withdrawal Tooling System

The withdrawal system uses the floating die principle. The main difference is that the punch forming the bottom level of the part is always stationary. The die and other lower tooling members, including auxiliary lower punches and core rods, move downward from the time pressing begins until ejection is complete. Figure 17-32 shows the sequence of events in a multimotion withdrawal tooling system. During compaction, all elements of the tooling system move downward, except the stationary punch. The die is floating, but is counterbalanced by pneumatic or hydraulic cylinders. The auxiliary punches are mounted on press members which are counterbalanced; in addition, these press members (usually called platens) have positive pressing stops. The positive stop controls the finished length of each of the levels within the compacted part. Before ejection, these stops are released or disengaged so that the lower platens can be moved further downward. During ejection, the upper punch moves upward away from the parts, while the lower punches move downward sequentially until all tool members are level with the top of the stationary punch. The compacted parts are fully supported by the tooling members during ejection. During ejection, the compacted part does not move.

The dieplate and lower coupler then move back into the filling position, and the cycle repeats. The movement of the upper punch and die are shown schematically in the cycle diagram illustrated in Fig. 17-33.[13] Two alternate motions of the die are shown to indicate that the die travel should be adjusted with reference to travel of the upper punch in order to control density distribution along the length of the part.

If the flange thickness does not exceed 20-25% of the total compact thickness, it is possible to compact a part by using only one bottom punch. Punches can be combined with the proper "step." This is accomplished by adding a shoulder in the die

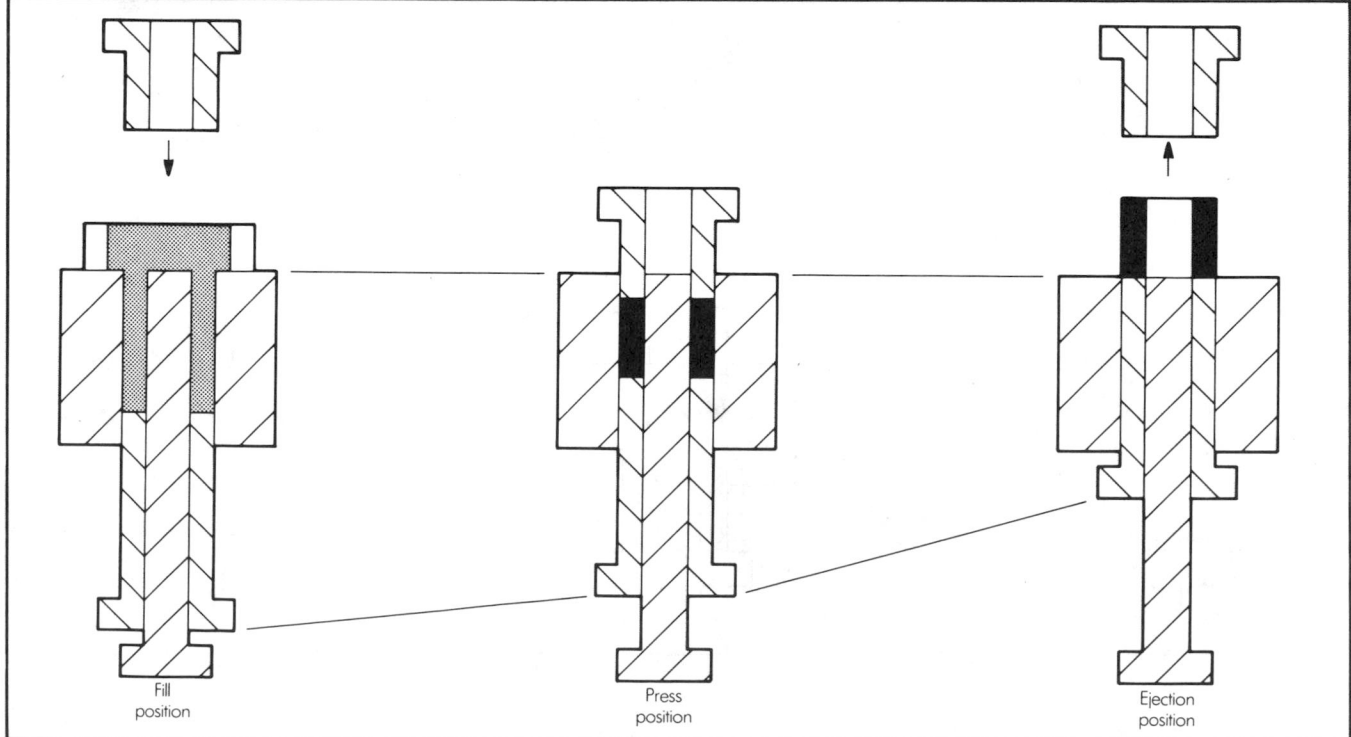

Fig. 17-30 Double-action press system.

Fill position

Press position

Ejection position

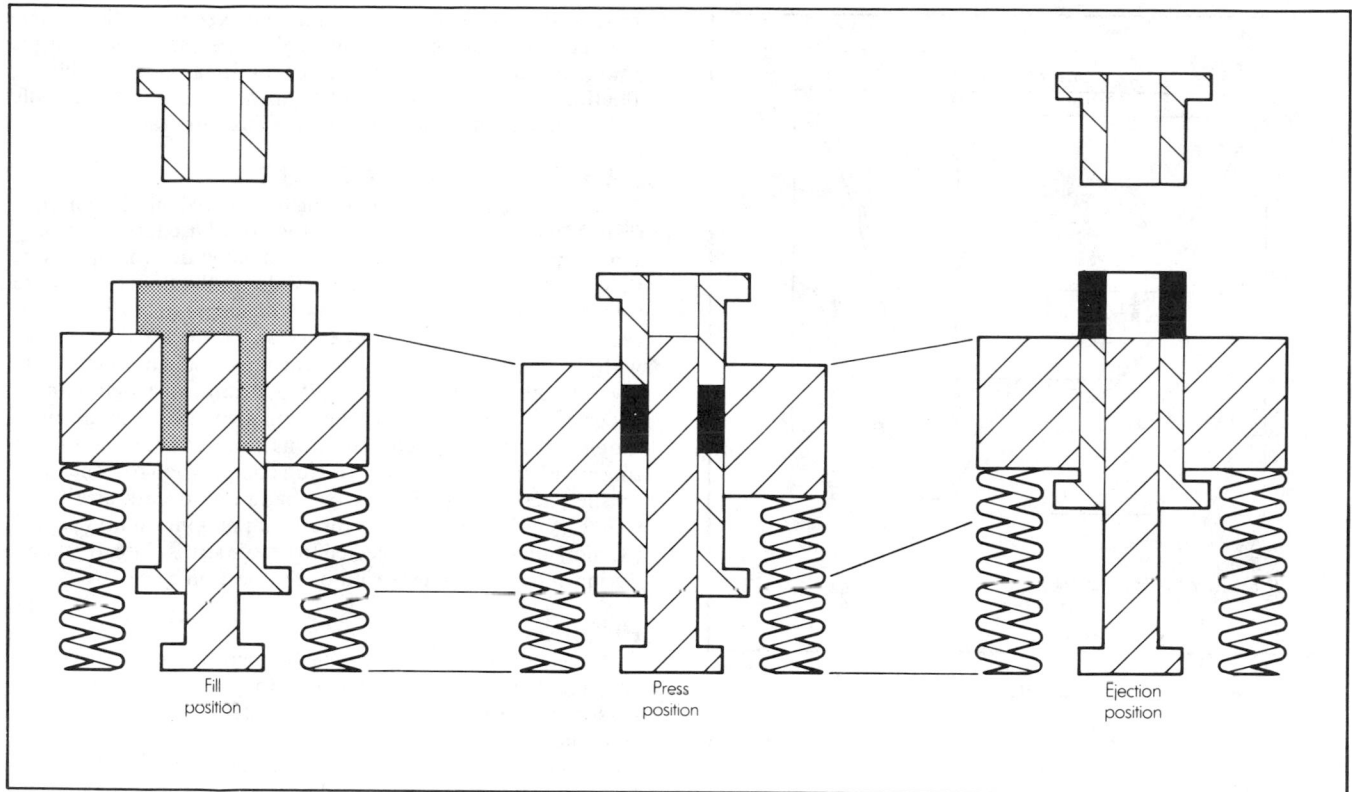

Fig. 17-31 Floating-die press tooling.

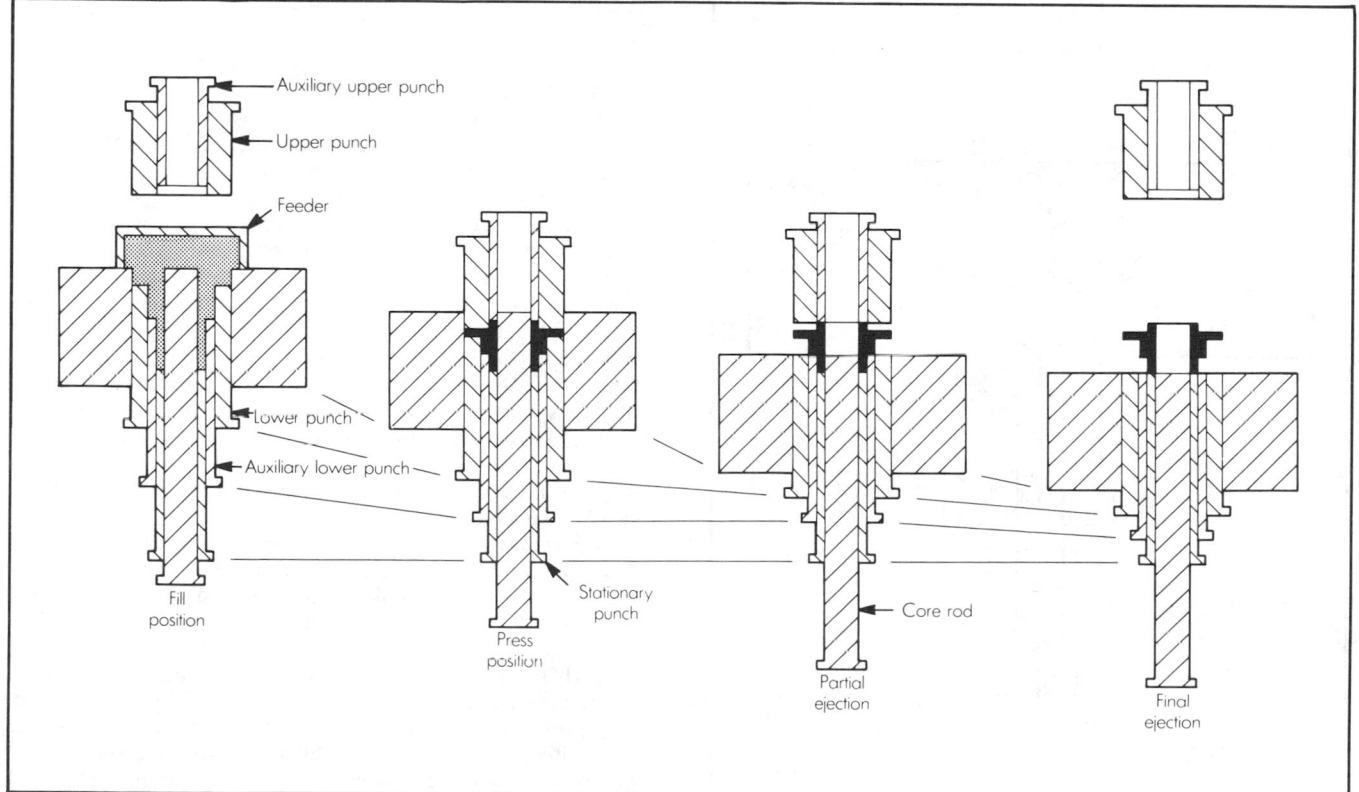

Fig. 17-32 Withdrawal floating-die multiple punches.

TOOLING FOR PM PARTS

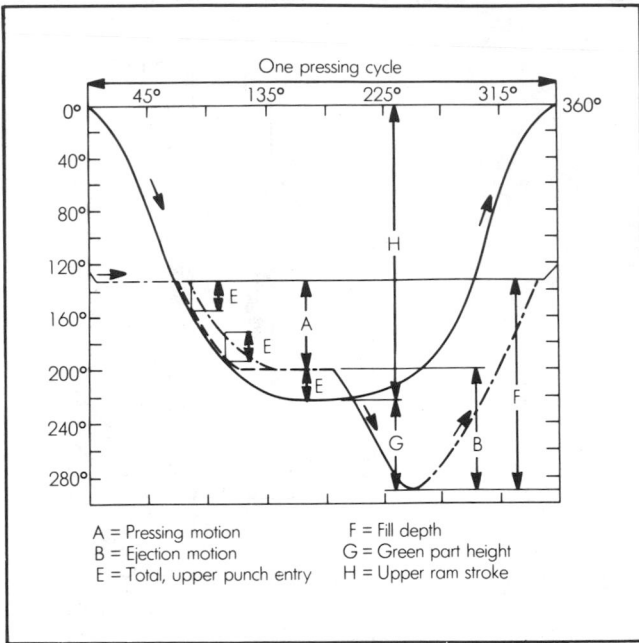

One pressing cycle

A = Pressing motion   F = Fill depth
B = Ejection motion   G = Green part height
E = Total, upper punch entry   H = Upper ram stroke

Fig. 17-33 Cycle diagram shows movement of upper punch and die during compacting with withdrawal system.

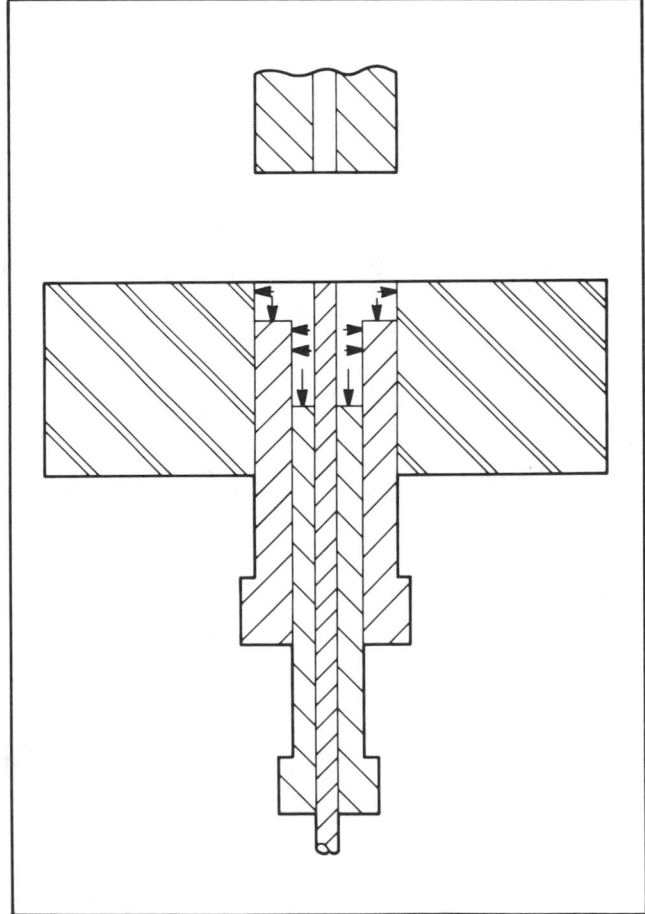

Fig. 17-34 Multilevel part causes side forces on the punches.

bore, as if the outer lower punch were locked in position. Some complex part designs require multiple upper, as well as multiple lower, punches. Core rods may be stationary, retractable, or floating (spring loaded). Split-segment dies are occasionally used, but are not suitable for high production rates.

PRACTICAL OPERATING TIPS

Powder metallurgy compacting forces are high; 50 tons/in.^{2} (690 MPa) is not uncommon for iron-based parts. Long, slender punches may be necessary in some designs; however, they should to be avoided if possible. If the punch walls are thinned to provide relief for powder escape, or for any other reason, column stresses can exceed workable limits. A punch with 1 in.^{2} (645 mm^2) of effective area and anywhere from several inches to over a foot (75-300 mm) in length can be expected to repeatedly lift the equivalent of 50 small automobiles. It can be expected to do this hundreds of thousands of times, with the load cycling from full compression to rather high tensile stress if any binding or "hang-up" occurs on the fill stroke. A core rod of 1/8" (3 mm) diam making an iron part 2" (50 mm) long could be subjected to tensile stress close to its limit during either the compression or the ejection cycle.

Punches

Poorly designed (or improperly operated) punches can be subjected to forces much higher than normal compacting pressures due to thinning of punch areas to provide relief, construction holes, sharp corners, and other stress raisers. Although punches or other tool members may tolerate these high stresses under static conditions, repeated cycling of the load would lead to premature fatigue failure. Any errors in press setup or operation that could cause an overdensity condition could shorten a tool's life expectancy or even destroy it quickly.

Side Forces

Although design concern often focuses on the vertical forces on a punch, a punch used to make a multilevel part may be subjected to heavy side forces as well. For example, in Fig. 17-34 two lower punches are used to make a part that is a combination gear and pinion. The inner lower punch used to compact the pinion would experience only vertical forces; however, the outer lower punch would be subjected not only to vertical forces, but to radial "bursting" forces since it is also acting as the die for the pinion. This means that sufficient wall must be left between the root of the gear and the top of the pinion tooth because this wall, in fact, establishes the working thickness of the die wall for the pinion. If there is not enough wall thickness in relation to the size of the part and the tonnage to be used, the life of the punch is shortened. This type of stress must be taken into consideration whenever the part/tool design causes a punch to act as a die.

A part that uses two lower punches to put even a simple step in the parts causes side forces to act on the punch as shown in Fig. 17-34. In the example of the gear and pinion, these side forces are contained totally within the outer punch; however, in the case of the simple step, the side pressures are transmitted through the punch to the die wall. If these forces are high enough, they can cause galling between the punch and the die. This problem is magnified if the punch is shaped like a wedge where it meets the die. A problem like this can most easily be resolved by close cooperation between the part user and the PM designer.

Pop Out

The expansion or "pop out" of the part as it leaves the die makes it essential that the top edge of the die wall be properly rounded or flared to allow the part to make a smooth transition during ejection. Breaking the top edge of the die with some kind of a shallow chamfer (as is frequently done, especially on gears and parts with sharp corners) may help, but will not do the job properly.

"Pop out" can also cause problems with parts of certain designs; for example, a plate with two hubs which would be formed by the lower punch could create problems during the ejection portion of the cycle. If the hubs were relatively small and far apart and the flange or plate were compacted to a high density, the hubs would tend to shear off as the flange cleared the die. This is illustrated in Fig. 17-35. As the flange tries to expand, the hubs, which are still held captive in the punch system, are not free to follow this expansion, and cracking can result. These problems can be minimized by making the hubs as heavy and short as possible, by decreasing the flange density, and by using one of the various methods of allowing the top punch to maintain some pressure on the part (top-punch hold down). Parts that would require a deep, thin-walled die may be

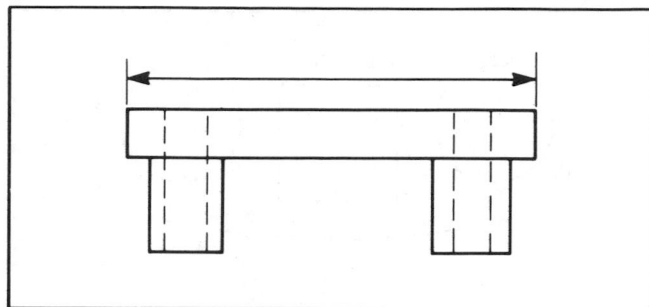

Fig. 17-35 Hub design facilitates part molding and ejection.

difficult to produce, as the die may not fill with consistent uniformity—if it would fill at all. Also, deep, thin dies would require long delicate punches, which could cause problems. Parts that are very thin and flat could have difficulty in uniformly filling the die area, as well as difficulty in filling the die over the very thin sections. Designing in thin sections should be avoided, as the problems inherent in the use of thin sections may more than offset any gain in the material saved.

COMPACTING PRESSES

Both mechanical and hydraulic power presses are used in PM compacting. Each drive has its advantages and limitations. Generally, presses of either type are available for producing a given PM part.

MECHANICAL PRESSES

Mechanical presses most often use an arrangement of gears, a crankshaft, and a connecting rod to provide the necessary pressing and ejection motions and forces to compact and eject the part. This type of drive converts the rotary motion into a linear motion through an eccentric or crankshaft operating the machine slide by means of a connecting rod. Some mechanical presses are cam driven, but these types are generally limited to smaller capacity machines.

Mechanical presses are available in both top and bottom drive configuration. There is no distinct advantage of one over the other. However, maintenance and housekeeping require careful consideration whether a press is above floor level or installed in a pit, so accessibility should be considered.

Mechanical presses are available in a wide pressing tonnage range from 0.75-825 tons (6.7-7339 kN). Production rates range from 900 pieces per hour on the large machines to over 100,000 pieces per hour on the small presses. The depth of fill (depth of loose powder in the die) ranges from 0.040-7" (1.02-178 mm).

Advantages of mechanical presses include high production rates, low connected machine horsepower, and a wide range of pressing tonnages available.

HYDRAULIC PRESSES

Hydraulic presses use one or more cylinders to provide the necessary motion and force to compact and eject the part. Standard hydraulic presses are available in capacities from 60-1250 tons (534-11 120 kN), although presses up to 3000 tons (26 668 kN) are being used in production of PM parts.

Production rates achievable with hydraulic presses are lower than rates for mechanical presses. Usually the hydraulic press has a maximum production of 600 pieces per hour. Greater depth of fill is available in hydraulic presses, with fill depths up to 15" (381 mm).

The advantages of hydraulic presses are overload protection, greater depth of fill available, versatility for complex parts, and lower initial capital investment.

ANVIL PRESSES

Anvil-type single-action presses can compact powder parts that have at least one flat side, are very thin, have holes, and require a high degree of precision and uniformity. These parts can be Class I, II, or III, and can be compacted single or multiple cavity, single or multiple punch. As shown in Fig. 17-36, the tooling consists of a tool set that holds the lower punches, which are moved up and down by the press ram. There are no upper punches. Compacting rates are as high as 350 spm for tiny parts or 40-90 spm for larger parts. In conventional presses, parts are compacted between opposing upper and lower punches. In the anvil-type press, tooling usually is simpler; parts are compacted against an anvil by the upward action of a lower punch.

Anvil presses are available from 0.75-35 tons (6.7-311 kN) pressing capacity, with maximum depth of fill ranging from 0.040-3" (1.02-76 mm). Multiple-cavity pressing is commonly used in anvil presses with possible production rates of over 100,000 pieces per hour.

Some models of anvil presses are arranged to allow double direction pressing, using an upper punch entry system. This type of pressing can produce Class I, II, and III parts, and some Class IV parts. Typical parts that can be made with anvil or upper-punch types of presses are carbide and ceramic inserts with positive rake and chipbreaker, electronic substrates with depressions on both sides, and certain double-flanged parts.

COMPACTING PRESSES

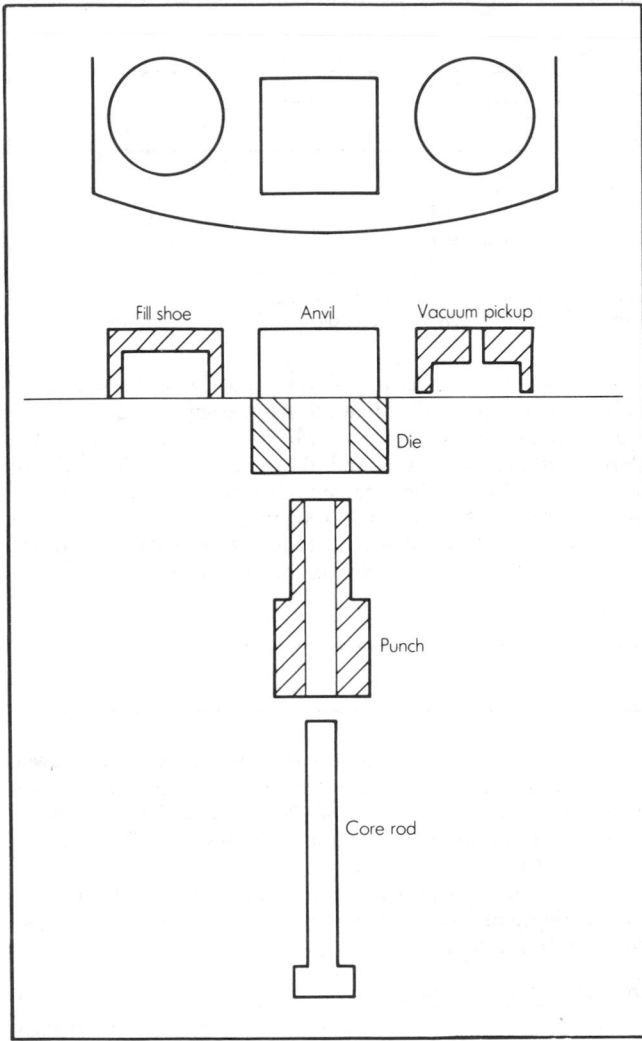

Fig. 17-36 Anvil type operation.

Anvil presses are usually mechanically driven. A schematic of the anvil press operation is shown in Fig. 17-37.

ROTARY PRESSES

These machines generally are limited to single-level Class II types of parts, although some Class III parts such as flanged bushings are produced on rotary machines. Rotary presses are available in capacity ranges from 4-35 tons (36-311 kN) with depth of fill up to 3" (76 mm). Production rates over 1000 pieces per minute are achievable depending on machine size and number of tooling stations. Rotary presses are mechanically driven.

SINGLE LOWER PUNCH, OPPOSED-RAM PRESSES

Like rotary presses, these machines are limited to Class II and some Class III PM parts. These machines are available in both top-drive and bottom-drive models with capacities ranging from 4-110 tons (36-979 kN) with maximum depth of fill up to 4" (102 mm). Production rates up to 50 ppm are possible with single cavity tooling, although production rates of 15-30 ppm

are more common. Ejection of the part is by the lower punch moving upward. Both mechanical and hydraulic presses of this type are available.

SINGLE LOWER PUNCH WITHDRAWAL PRESS

This machine has essentially the same part-making capabilities as described for the single-punch, opposed-ram press, in terms of pressing capacity, depth of fill, and production rate. The major difference is that the floating-die principle is used to achieve top and bottom pressing. The die is moved downward to effect ejection of the part.

MULTIPLE MOTION DIE SET PRESSES

Presses of this type can be arranged to produce the most complex PM parts. Machines of this type all use the floating-die, withdrawal tooling concepts. Machines with both bottom drive and top drive are available. Pressing capacities range from 3-550 tons (27-5000 kN), with maximum depth of fill of 7" (178 mm). Production rates vary from over 100 ppm on the smaller machines to 10 ppm on the 550 ton models. In addition to being able to produce complex parts, the removable die set (toolholder) minimizes press downtime needed to changeover from part to part. This is accomplished by having two or more die sets per press. One of the extra die sets is set up outside the press and is ready for installation into the machine. Pressing position for each level being produced by a separate tooling member is controlled by fixed-height tooling blocks (stop blocks), which are usually ground to the proper height to produce a given dimension on the part. A change in this dimension on the part requires the tooling block to be changed accordingly.

MULTIPLE MOTION ADJUSTABLE STOP PRESSES

Presses of this type have the same part-making capability as die set presses and use the same tooling concepts. Presses available range from 110-825 tons (979-7339 kN), with a maximum depth of fill of 6" (152 mm). The major difference between this type of press and the removable die set press is that the die set is not removable; however, the press stop positions are adjustable and a change of any dimension on the part in the direction of pressing is easily accomplished.

PM PRESS CONTROLS AND GUARDING

Powder metallurgy presses and tooling, especially multi-motion machines, are complex and capital intensive. As a result, the machine must have controls and electrical interlocks that monitor the functions of the machine and tooling as a manufacturing system. Machines of the latest technology are controlled by microprocessors. The microprocessor system has the capability, speed, and reliability to monitor the many machine functions that occur during each cycle of the press, stopping the machine if any malfunction occurs. The microprocessor system can also provide diagnostic information when a malfunction occurs. This facilitates repair of the malfunction and keeps machine downtime to a minimum.

The press guarding must meet all federal, state, and local regulations regarding mechanical and hydraulic-power PM compacting presses. The guarding used to enclose the point of operation should be made of clear, shock-resistant material such as acrylic plastic, rather than expanded metal. The clear

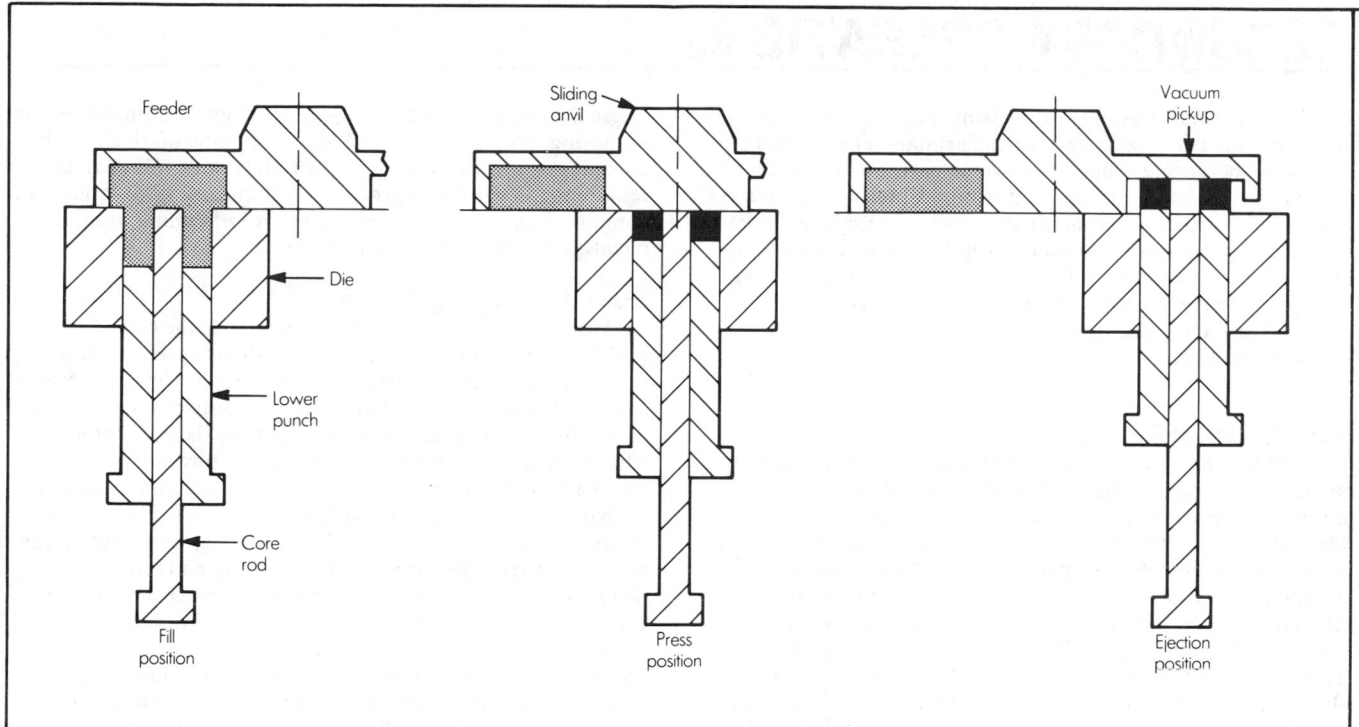

Fig. 17-37 Sliding anvil press tooling system.

plastic materials offer improved visibility and reduce the breathable airborne powder at the operator station.

POWDER FEEDING SYSTEM

Powder metallurgy presses are provided with an automatic powder feeding system. Another function in addition to feeding the powder to the tooling is that the feeder also provides an automatic part removal system. As the feeder or feed shoe approaches the die, the part that has just been compacted and ejected from the tooling is pushed away from the tooling or the point of operation by the feed shoe.

The most common type of feeder has an in-line reciprocating motion. The feed shoe rides on the die table and is spring loaded to provide a clean wiping action. It is connected directly to a press-mounted hopper by means of a flexible hose, and powder is fed to it by gravity. The press-mounted hopper should have a powder level control to maintain a constant head of powder to assure uniform die filling. The feed shoe moves over the die cavity when the tooling is flush and in the ejection mode. The press then moves to its fill position, filling the die cavity volumetrically. With a properly designed powder feeding system, part weight control of +0.75% is easily achievable in a production environment.

On hydraulic presses, the feed shoe is actuated by a hydraulic cylinder that is timed sequentially with the press stroke.

On mechanical presses, the feeder has traditionally been cam driven and timed mechanically with the press stroke. The latest technology in feeder drives is the use of a d-c servomotor driving a ballscrew to actuate the feed shoe. When used in conjunction with a microprocessor, the feeder stroke can be optimized to provide maximum time over the die cavity. The feeder stroke can be varied when using the d-c drive, while a cam-driven feeder has a fixed stroke.

PRESS MAINTENANCE

The most important rule in PM press maintenance is to keep the press clean. Powder particles can be extremely small, as small as 5 microns; and if allowed to accumulate, they will work into critical bearing and guiding surfaces, even though the bearings are protected with wiper, seals or boots. Loose powder on and around the press can be caused by any of the following:

1. Poor bulk powder handling—spillage while loading the press hopper. Automatic bulk loading systems are available and are considered a sound investment. They reduce spillage and improve loading efficiency.
2. Poorly maintained press feed shoes. Feed shoes normally have a replaceable wiper. If they are not properly maintained, a small amount of powder will be lost with each stroke of the press. This can amount to a considerable amount of expensive powder loss during a single shift of operation.
3. Powder loss through tooling clearances. The running clearance in PM tooling is small, generally 0.001 in./in. (0.025 mm/mm) diam. Small amounts of powder sift through this clearance and accumulate. Little can be done to prevent this loss. This is an area that requires frequent cleaning.

A modern PM press should be equipped with an automatic lubrication system with fault monitors. The press manufacturer should include in the operator and maintenance manual a routine maintenance checklist that specifically identifies areas and frequency of critical maintenance items. Some press builders offer, through their service department, a preventative maintenance program in which a service representative visits the customer's plant at intervals to maintain the equipment.

SECONDARY OPERATIONS

Powder metallurgy parts processing and fabrication can be divided into two major categories: primary and secondary. Primary operations, which are covered earlier in this chapter, include powder mixing, compacting, and sintering. Secondary operations, which, if required, are applied selectively to PM structural parts after sintering, include sizing, coining, and repressing (sometimes followed by sintering or annealing); forging; impregnation; infiltration; heat treatment and steam treatment; machining; joining; and plating and other surface finishing.

REPRESSING

Repressing, sometimes called coining or sizing, is used to increase density, provide greater dimensional accuracy, and improve surface smoothness and hardness. In these operations, the sintered structural part is inserted in a confined die and struck by a punch. A principal purpose of "sizing" is to correct distortions that occur during sintering. This operation sometimes is called "coining," although coining actually describes an operation that gives a profile to the part, as in coining a blank to produce a coin. Repressing can be used to produce complex shapes that are not attainable from a single-press operation, or to reshape or emboss a surface. Repressing may be followed by resintering—a second sintering operation to improve mechanical properties and relieve the cold work introduced during repressing.

FORGING

To obtain the same properties in PM parts as in wrought materials, the porosity must be eliminated. This may be done by producing preforms from metal powders and hot forging the preforms to obtain parts of closely controlled dimensions and complete or near complete density.

General Description

The forging of PM preforms permits the production of accurate and complex-shaped parts requiring little or no machining and having properties equal to or exceeding those made from comparable wrought materials. Lower cost compared to the cost of conventional forging, coupled with higher strength compared to the strength of conventional powder metallurgy, are the basic advantages of this technique. Material utilization is often close to 100%. Since the forging is done in a closed die, precisely the proper amount of metal is used; no flash is generated. The powders used are generally more costly than comparable wrought materials. Purity is critical. Powder metallurgy forged parts often cost slightly more than unmachined forgings, but the savings in machining often offset this differential.

Unlike conventional PM which is normally limited to axial deformation, PM forging can create lateral flow to produce shapes not possible with conventional compacting. Surface finish is also better than that possible with conventional forging or casting. The parts are formed accurately in a single blow. This minimizes subsequent machining or the need for multiple dies, as are needed in the case of step forging. The fine grain and homogenous structure produced provide uniform strength in all directions. Intermediate forging steps also are eliminated.

These include shearing or cutting the billets, multihit forming (requiring several dies), and the trimming of flash. Other advantages include precise repeatability and minimal labor requirements when the process is automated. Also, alloys or composite materials can be created by combining immiscible metals, since no melting takes place.

Powder Forging Process

As illustrated schematically in Fig. 17-38, the production of a PM forging consists essentially of making a preform; heating it, usually by induction; placing the preform in a heated die; and forming (forging) it to final shape in a single blow. The die design for hot compaction is such that the flash is eliminated. The design of the preform and the temperature and pressure of the final forging stage ensure complete densification throughout the part. The metal can flow in all directions, thus differentiating it from conventional hot restriking, coining, or densifying, in which the part is already close to final shape and metal flow is primarily in the direction of pressing. The process differs from conventional forging in that lower temperatures are used, only a single hit is required, there is no scaling or flash, close tolerances are maintained, and a longer die life is obtained. Before a preform is forged it must be heated to the forging temperature. For preforms of low alloy steel composition, the forging temperature is in the same range as for conventional forgings, i.e., from 1470-2200°F (800-1200°C).

In conventional forging a fully dense blank is forged. The type of conventional forging closest to powder forging is precision forging in which the blank is forged in a closed die. The weight and geometry of the forging blank as well as the preheating and forging cycle are closely controlled. Nevertheless, even in precision forging, a flash is formed which must be trimmed and the forging must generally be machined. In powder forging, the blank is a more precise preform produced from metal powders by compacting and sintering. As diagrammed in Fig. 17-39, three different approaches are used in forging the preforms.

Hot repressing. The first of these approaches is hot repressing, sometimes called hot densification, in which the shape of the preform is close to that of the final piece except for its length in the forging direction. In this process, the friction

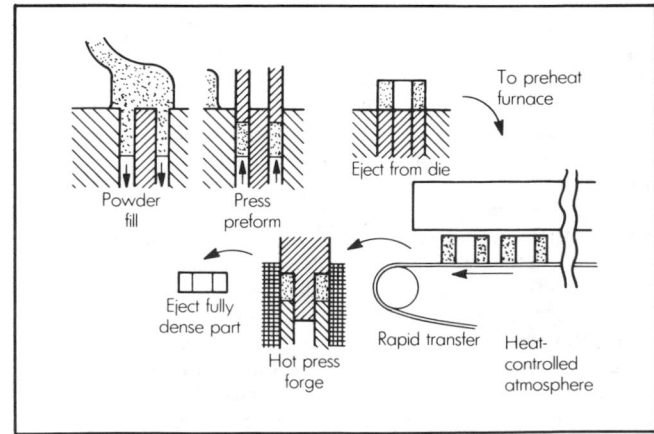

Fig. 17-38 Schematic diagram of powder forging process.

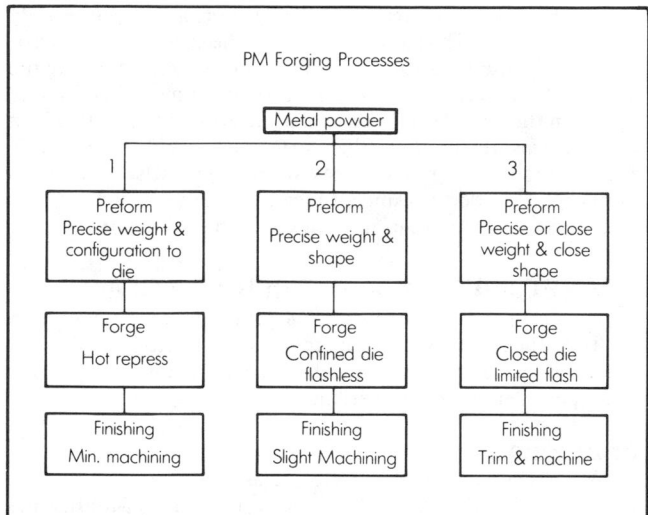

Fig. 17-39 Processes used for PM forging.

between die and preform during hot forging is high and, therefore, the pressure necessary for complete densification also is high. This causes rapid wear of the forging tools. Hot repressing is generally used in applications in which densities on the order of 98% of theoretical are satisfactory.

Flashless. The second approach is the one most widely used industrially. It is a precision forging process without flash. The shape of the preform is simpler than that of the final part, so the desired final shape is produced to closely controlled dimensions in the hot forging step. This is not a hot repressing operation; the preform is upset (and extruded) in hot forging. The advantages of hot forging by upsetting (and extrusion) over hot forging by repressing are attributed to much more lateral flow, especially in the beginning of deformation. This leads to more rapid initial densification and also involves more shear stress at pore surfaces, producing relative motion between opposite sides of the collapsed pore. Mechanical rupturing of any oxide film present at the pore surface exposes the metal and ensures a sound metallurgical bond across collapsed pore surfaces. Upset forging also produces fibering of inclusions in the lateral direction. Toward the end of the forging stroke, by upsetting when the preform has reached the die wall, the mode of deformation becomes the same as in repressing.

Limited flash. A third approach to hot forging of PM preforms involves the process as it pertains to the conventional forge shop. In this situation, the results of the forging step must not necessarily be a product with dimensions as closely or nearly as closely controlled as those of conventional PM structural parts. The forging may even have a flash which must be trimmed after forging.

Materials

Carbon and low alloy steel powders are widely used and some aluminum powders are formed in this way. Oxidation and decarburization can be critical. Nickel and molybdenum are common additions; and copper, cobalt, manganese and chromium are also used. The dies are generally maintained at a temperature between 500-600° F (260-316° C). Forging pressure is normally between 40-75 tons/in.² (552-1034 MPa). Graphite is sprayed on the components as a lubricant prior to forging. Some producers can hold 0.001" (0.03 mm) on outside diameters

and lateral dimensions; however, the parts are costly, because of short die life and close control requirements. A tolerance of ±0.003 or ±0.004" (±0.08 or ±0.10 mm) is realistic and economical for these dimensions. Dimensions in the direction of pressing are more difficult to hold to close tolerance. While ±0.005" can be maintained in some cases, as much as ±0.015" (±0.38 mm) may be necessary, depending on part size, configuration, and density required, as well as the press and tooling used.

PM Forging Machines

Forging machines for powder forging must meet certain requirements:

- The force-displacement characteristics must match deformation characteristics of the preforms.
- Workpiece-tool contact times should be as short as possible.
- The machines should be stiff, and the ram should have effective guidance to obtain desired tolerances in the powder forgings.
- Mechanisms for ejection of the parts are necessary.

Because of these requirements, forging hammers that do not have sufficiently accurate guidance and hydraulic presses that are too slow are inappropriate for powder forging. Mechanical presses, in particular crank presses with short, fast strokes and short contact times, are used. This applies mainly to precision hot forging by upsetting to closely controlled dimensions without a flash.

When the conventional forging approach is applied in forging PM preforms, the same equipment as in conventional forging may be used. Flow stress and the force for forging preforms are initially lower than for conventional forging, but they rise toward the end of the forging stroke as density increases. Tooling for powder forging is quite different from that for conventional forging and closely resembles tooling for powder compacting. On the other hand, the provisions necessary in tooling for powder compacting to obtain uniform density in multilevel parts are not required. An example of a relatively simple tool design for powder forging is shown in Fig. 17-40. The powder preform is upset during forging and ejected after forging.

Only limited data is available on tool life of forging tools for preform forgings. Since the preforms are heated in a protective atmosphere, tool wear due to scale formation is less of a problem than in conventional forging. Also, the flow stress in preform forging is lower and no flash need be formed, which adds to tool life. On the other hand, the dimensional tolerances in preform forging are closer than in conventional forging, which means that tools, or at least those parts of the tooling subjected to wear, must be replaced more often. A tool life of 5000-10,000 forgings for readily replaceable high-wear components of the tooling and of 10,000-20,000 forgings for other components has been attained.

HEAT TREATMENT AND STEAM TREATMENT

Powder metallurgy structural parts can be heat treated by conventional methods that are used for wrought or cast parts. Best results are obtained with dense PM structures. Porosity influences the rate of heat flow through the part, and internal contamination occurs if salt-bath heat-treating chambers are used in the process. For this reason, in heat-treating PM steel

SECONDARY OPERATIONS

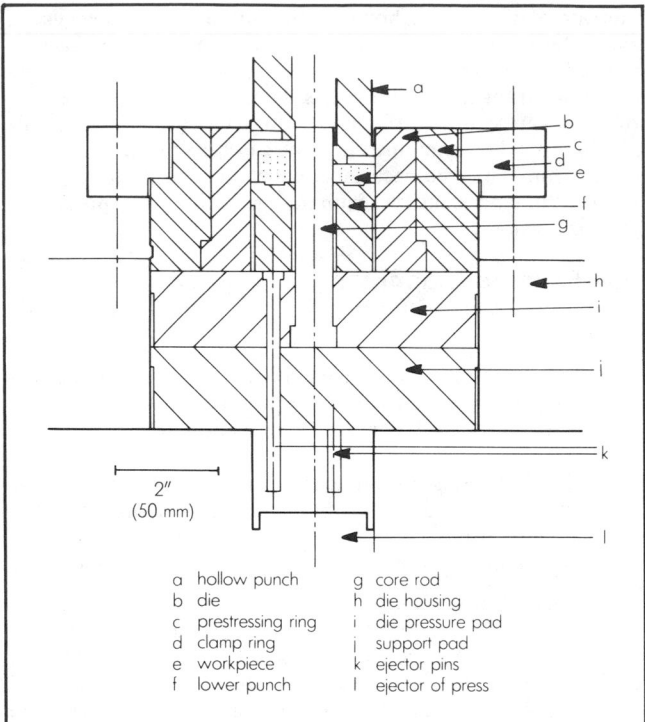

a	hollow punch	g	core rod
b	die	h	die housing
c	prestressing ring	i	die pressure pad
d	clamp ring	j	support pad
e	workpiece	k	ejector pins
f	lower punch	l	ejector of press

Fig. 17-40 Powder forging tooling construction.

parts, austenitizing in salt baths and particularly in cyanide baths is avoided.

Heat Treatment

The surface hardness of PM steel parts may be increased by carburizing and carbonitriding. Ferrous PM parts, containing 0.3% or higher combined carbon, can be quench-hardened for increased strength and wear resistance. The percentages of carbon and other alloying elements combined in the material and density of the part determine the degree of hardening for any given quench condition. Surface hardness of 500-600 Knoop (file hard) is possible with quench hardening.

Ferrous parts without carbon can be carburized by standard methods. Low-density parts carburize throughout, while high-density parts develop a distinct carburized case. Case depth is a function of the part density. Very-high-density parts respond well to fused salt carbonitriding, but density must be high enough to prevent absorption of salt into the pores. Low and medium-density parts absorb brines and salts during salt-bath carbonitriding which can lead to subsequent corrosion. Thus, oil quench hardening is recommended for low and medium-density parts.

The properties of as-sintered aluminum PM parts are improved by a series of thermal treatments. Aluminum PM parts achieve higher strength by solution and precipitation of soluble alloying elements. As-sintered strength is affected by the rate of cooling from sintering temperature. Parts cooled very slowly, about 50° F (10° C) per hr develop the lower strengths of annealed tempers.

Steam Treatment

Steam treating is widely used for PM structural parts. In steam treating, the porosity of PM structural parts is directly

used. The parts are treated in dry steam at approximately 1020° F (550° C). The steam reacts with the surfaces of the part, not only the outer surface, but also the inner surface along the pores connected to the outside. A layer of magnetic black oxide forms on the outside surface, and a skeleton of magnetic black oxide forms throughout the part's interior. This not only provides some corrosion resistance, but also improves mechanical properties, since it increases the density, hardness, wear resistance, and compressive strength of the part.

IMPREGNATION AND INFILTRATION

The controlled porosity of PM parts makes it possible to infiltrate them with another metal or impregnate them with oil or a resin, either to improve mechanical properties or to provide other performance characteristics.

Impregnation

When structural PM parts serve as bearings, they may be impregnated with a lubricant, as is done with self-lubricating bearings. Such bearings are among the most widely used products of powder metallurgy. Porosities ranging from 25-35% generally are used, since higher values result in lower bearing strength. Oil-impregnated bearings hold from 10-30% oil by volume. Impregnation is accomplished either by immersing sintered bearings in heated oil or by means of a vacuum treatment. Most self-lubricating bearings are of porous bronze or iron composition.

When a porous part is to be made impervious to liquids or gases, it is impregnated with a viscous liquid thermosetting polymer or anaerobic resin. The polymer or other impregnating resin is changed to a solid by low temperature or vacuum processes. This treatment is used on PM parts which must be made pressure tight and on parts to which a surface finishing operation, such as plating, is to be applied. During plating operations, the impregnation treatment prevents absorption or entrapment of the plating solution in the pores of the part.

The following are general guidelines for impregnating PM parts:

1. A density range should be planned that is between 80-90% theoretical, or 6.2-7.1 g/cc for iron parts. This is the best range for maximum penetration without bleeding.
2. Parts should be heat treated prior to vacuum sealing. Anaerobic sealants are limited to upper temperatures of 400° F (204.4° C). Also, quenching oils should be removed prior to impregnation by baking, annealing or vapor degreasing.
3. The optimum time for sealing is immediately after sintering. Clean, open pores aid penetration. Tumbling, burnishing, and machining tend to smear surfaces and block the sealant entry. Also, fluids used in these operations can penetrate the pores and inhibit impregnation.
4. PM parts can be coined, sized, and repressed after vacuum sealing. Volume changes of up to 2% can be tolerated without difficulty.
5. Impregnation improves machinability and tool life. Machinability is increased by eliminating the chattering that develops as the tool jumps across pore openings. Although the impregnating resin does not replace machining oil, it does help to lubricate the machining process.

Infiltration

Infiltration is the process of filling the pores of a sintered solid with molten metal or alloy. In this operation, the melting point of the liquid metal must be considerably lower than that of the solid metal. The purpose of infiltration is to obtain a relatively pore-free structure. Liquid metal is infiltrated into the PM part either by allowing it to enter from above or by absorbing it from below. For example, copper placed upon a piece of presintered iron and heated to 2100° F (1150° C) is drawn into the iron by capillarity.

Properties resulting from infiltration with another metal depend upon the metals that constitute the structure of the infiltrated part, together with the manner and the proportions in which they are combined. Infiltration is used to improve mechanical properties, seal pores prior to electroplating, improve machinability, and make parts gas or liquid tight. Advantages of infiltration include:

1. Increased mechanical properties. Higher tensile strength and hardness, greater impact energy and fatigue strength, and other improvements.
2. Uniform density. Parts that contain nonuniform and/or heavy sections can be infiltrated to even out density variations.
3. Higher density. Infiltration increases sintered part weight without changing the size.
4. Removal of porosity for secondary operations. Infiltration may be used in place of impregnation as a method to seal surface porosity. This enables such operations as pickling and plating to be performed without damaging the interior of the part. Infiltration is also a method of sealing a part used for application in which no porosity is desired.
5. Selective property variation. By infiltrating only selected areas of a part, it is possible to obtain a controlled variation of properties such as density, strength, and hardness. This is known as localized infiltration.
6. Assembly of multiple parts. Different sections of the final part, pressed separately, can be assembled by sintering the individual pieces together and bonding them into one part through common infiltration.

MACHINING

Whenever possible, PM structural parts are compacted and sintered to final dimensions, thereby eliminating the need for subsequent machining needed. However, products requiring such features as threads, grooves, undercuts, or side holes cannot be produced directly by powder metallurgy methods and must be finish-machined. Tungsten carbide tools are recommended, although high-speed-steel tools may be used in some low-volume applications.

Machining characteristics of PM parts are similar to those of cast materials. Small amounts of lead, sulfur, copper, or graphite are common additives that improve the machinability of ferrous PM parts. Lead is also used to increase machinability of nonferrous parts. Machining speeds and feeds for high-density parts (above 92% of theoretical density) are similar to those for wrought metals. Lower density parts require adjustment of feed and speed to obtain optimum results. In general, high speeds, light feeds, and very sharp carbide tools are recommended. Lubricants and coolants should be used with caution, especially when porous parts are machined, to avoid

entrapping solutions that could cause corrosion. Grinding of PM parts is similar to grinding of wrought materials; however, when surface porosity is required, it should be remembered that grinding tends to reduce porosity.

FINISHING

Virtually all of the commonly used finishing methods are applicable to PM parts. Some of the more frequently used methods include plating, coating, tumbling, burnishing, and coloring.

Plating

Powder metallurgy parts may be plated by electroplating or other plating processes. To avoid penetration and entrapment of plating solutions in the pores of the part, an impregnation or infiltration treatment is usually applied before plating.

Copper, nickel, chromium, cadmium, and zinc plating may be applied. High-density (7 g/cc) and infiltrated parts can be plated by using methods similar to those used for wrought parts. Lower density parts should be sealed, as noted earlier. Electroless nickel plating can be used as well as electroplating, which is applicable to nonimpregnated ferrous parts in the 6.6-7.2 g/cc density range.

Coating

Parts manufactured by pressing and sintering metal powders are more susceptible to environmental degradation than cast and machined parts. Powder metallurgy parts have interconnected porosity. Internal as well as external surfaces are exposed to the atmosphere. Conventional coatings cannot effectively seal all of the reactive surface. Special protective coatings have been developed for PM parts.

In one coating system an aluminum/ceramic material is used for PM part corrosion protection. The coating eliminates the need for impregnation or plating. The process provides a passivated aluminum coating that serves as a base for application of topcoats that seal the coating and the PM part surface from the atmosphere. Coatings of this type are available as either sacrificial or protective (barrier) coatings.

Tumbling

During tumbling, rust inhibitors should be added to the water. After tumbling, parts should be spun dry and heated to evaporate water from the pores. Tumbling is done after machining to avoid abrasive pickup in the pores, which can cause rapid tool wear.

Burnishing

Burnishing can be used to improve part finish and dimensional accuracy or to work-harden the surfaces. Closer tolerances can be held on PM parts than on wrought parts, because the surface porosity allows metal to be displaced more easily.

Coloring

Ferrous PM parts can be colored by several methods. For indoor corrosion resistance, parts are blackened by heating to the blueing temperature and then cooled. Oil dipping gives a deeper color and slightly more corrosion resistance. Ferrous PM parts also can be blackened chemically, using a salt bath. On parts with density below 7.3 g/cc, care must be taken to avoid entrapment of salt. Nickel and copper-bearing parts are adversely affected by blackening baths.

JOINING

Many of the conventional joining operations for wrought materials can be performed on PM structural parts. Of the various welding techniques, electrical resistance welding is better suited than oxyacetylene welding and arc welding, in which oxidation of the interior porous material is possible. However, argon arc welding is used for stainless steel parts.

Copper brazing is applicable to copper infiltrated parts, and in some instances, copper infiltration and copper brazing may be combined into one operation. Powder metallurgy parts also may be joined by using somewhat different compositions for the components—one that expands slightly during sintering and another that shrinks slightly. The composition that grows is used for the inner portion of the assembly, and the one that shrinks is used for the outer portion. The parts are assembled as compacted; an excellent joint forms during sintering.

SPECIAL PM PROCESSES

In the field of powder metallurgy, die compaction is the most widely used method and is considered the "conventional" technique. It is discontinuous; employs either low pressures (under 10 tons/in.² or 138 MPa) or high pressures (40 tons/in.² or 550 MPa). It applies force only in the axial (vertical) direction to one or both ends of the powder mass, and involves relatively little time (about 1-2 seconds) and a punch movement of about 20 fps (6 m/s). No liquid is used to suspend the powder. The die is a rigid, solid mass with a relatively long lifetime. Both low-density and high-density structural parts with a very broad range of complexities and sizes are made by the conventional die pressing PM techniques. These conventional methods as well as the equipment used in them are covered earlier in this chapter, in the section on "Compacting."

This section presents information on various special PM pressure and pressureless compacting methods. Also included is information on the wrought processes for hot consolidation of metal powders to fully dense compacts, an operation that combines sintering with the application of pressure to the powder at elevated temperature.

PRESSURE COMPACTION METHODS

One of the more frequently used pressure compacting methods is isostatic compaction, either cold or hot; other PM pressure methods include hot pressing, spark sintering, high energy forming, extruding, injection molding, and isothermal PM forging.

ISOSTATIC COMPACTION

In isostatic compaction, pressure is applied simultaneously from all directions on a metal powder compact. Powder is placed in a flexible mold or container that is immersed in a fluid bath within a pressure vessel. The fluid is put under high pressure and exerts hydrostatic pressure on the powder. Isostatically compacted products are characterized by their uniform, high density. With selection of the correct encapsulation technique and knowledge of the influence of the pressure, powder products can be pressed close to their final shape and dimension.

Pressing is done at room temperature in the cold isostatic process. Hot isostatic pressing, on the other hand, involves pressing compacts under high temperature conditions. Powder is contained in a metal or glass mold or can and is placed in an autoclave.

Cold isostatic compacting. Cold isostatic compacting is a "room temperature" process by which pressure is applied uniformly to a deformable container holding the metal powder to be compacted. This technique is especially useful in the manufacturing of parts having a large length-to-diameter ratio.

The system generally includes a pressure vessel designed to contain a fluid under high pressure, a deformable container, and arbors (or cores) if tubes or special shapes are being made. A representative schematic drawing is shown in Fig. 17-41.

Advantages. Variations exist in cold isostatic pressing, and the pressure may not always be completely uniform; however, the friction between powder and die, which is a characteristic of other methods of PM pressing, is absent in cold isostatic pressing. The commercial advantages of cold isostatic over other methods of pressing are:

1. Greater uniformity in density is achieved.
2. Shapes with high ratios of length to diameter which cannot be readily pressed in rigid dies can be cold isostatically pressed.
3. Parts with reentrant angles and undercuts can be pressed.
4. Parts with thinner wall sections can be pressed.
5. The equipment for cold isostatic pressing, dies in particular, is less costly than that for rigid die pressing.
6. Lubricants do not have to be mixed with metal powders.

Disadvantages. On the other hand, cold isostatic pressing has certain disadvantages, including the following:

1. Dimensional control of the green compacts is less precise than in rigid die pressing.
2. The surfaces of cold isostatically pressed compacts are less smooth.
3. The production rate in cold isostatic pressing is considerably lower.
4. The flexible molds used in cold isostatic pressing have shorter lives than rigid steel or carbide dies.

Applications. Cold isostatic pressing is less widely used for metal than for ceramic powders, for which the automatic fabrication of such components as spark plugs is highly mechanized. However, the production of isostatically pressed metal compacts has grown rapidly. Applications include:

• Complex shapes that cannot be pressed in rigid dies. Such shapes are found in powder metallurgy products made from relatively expensive metals such as titanium, for which material savings are important. Examples include an aircraft hydraulic fitting made from a mixture of titanium powder and an aluminum-vanadium alloy,

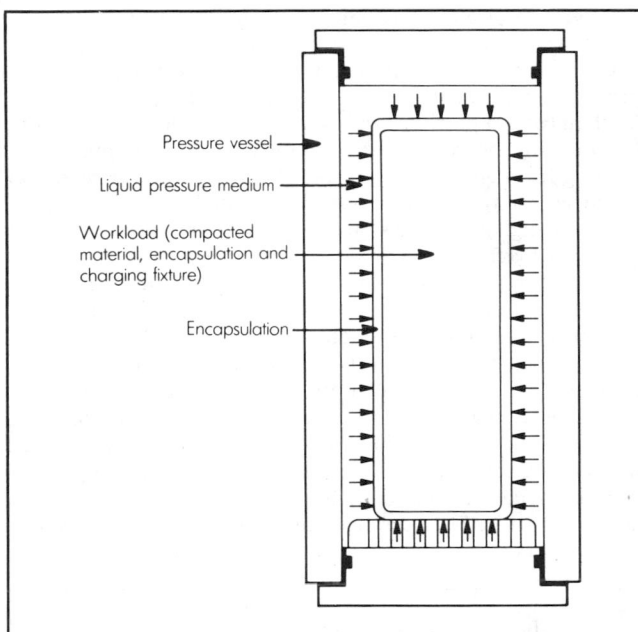

Fig. 17-41 Cold isostatic pressing is performed at room temperature with liquid as the pressure medium. (*ASEA*)

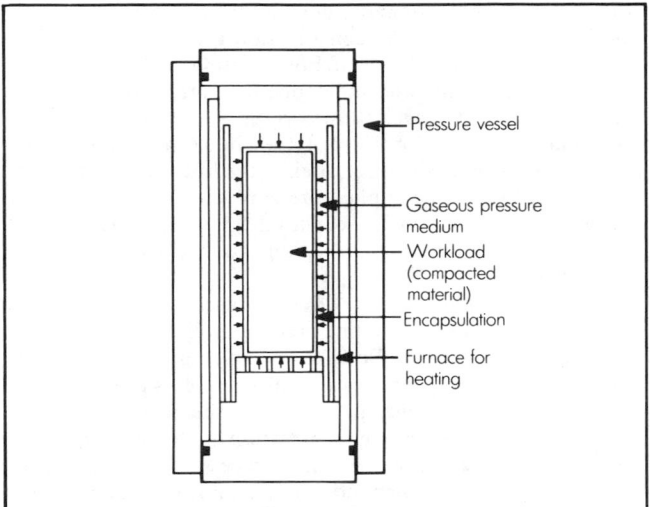

Fig. 17-42 Hot isostatic pressing is performed at elevated temperature with gas as the pressure medium. (*ASEA*)

which is isostatically pressed before being sintered and hot forged; and isostatically pressed titanium ball valves for controlling flow of sea water.

- Shapes such as long, slender, hollow cylinders, which are often used for porous filters because of their large ratio of surface area to volume. Such cylinders generally are isostatically pressed from powder. Stainless steel and titanium powders are commonly used.
- Large shapes, such as rocket nozzles, made from tungsten powder, which are isostatically pressed because production quantities do not justify the cost of building rigid dies. The nozzle shape also is readily producible by the isostatic process.
- The shapes of compacts that are to be fabricated by hot consolidation which are often well suited to cold isostatic pressing as a first step. Examples are compacts from tungsten and molybdenum and their alloys which are to be hot rolled into sheet or hot forged into the shape of dies.

Hot isostatic compacting. Hot isostatic pressing (HIP) is a manufacturing process in which PM parts are compressed by gas at high temperatures and pressure. Commercial HIP systems are typically capable of temperatures to 3632° F (2000° C) and pressure to 30,000 psi (207 MPa).

In forming a part from powder, the powder is placed in a flexible, gas-tight capsule having the shape of the finished part. The capsule is placed in a pressure vessel in which it is heated and subjected to isostatic pressure applied by high-purity argon or helium gas. The part is compressed equally on all sides by the application of heat and pressure. The principle of hot isostatic pressing is illustrated in Fig. 17-42.

Advantages. Hot isostatic pressing provides some important commercial advantages:

- Unique microstructures which substantially improve performance and reliability.

- Alloys and shapes which are impossible to achieve by other means.
- Complex "near net" shapes which require little or no machining.
- Reduced consumption of energy and scarce or expensive materials.
- Reduced overall production costs.

Disadvantages. A significant limitation of HIP processing, even without the mold, is the lengthy cycle time to load, heat, pressurize, hold, cool, and unload. Until recently, cycle times of 12-24 hours were not uncommon. New systems, which incorporate furnaces with forced convection heating and cooling, reduce cycle time to 8 hours or less. The time improvements are at both ends (heating and cooling) of the cycle only. With present technology, parts must be held at a specific temperature and pressure for a predetermined time.

Size of the work chamber is another limiting factor. Autoclaves built for PM parts and billets range from 15-36″ diam (381-914 mm) by 60-108″ (1524-2743 mm) long. Larger HIP units have been built for special aircraft uses and for experimentation.

Applications. Hot isostatic pressing was first commercially used in the aerospace industry. Current applications have grown to encompass the consolidation of high-speed steels and superalloy powders, densification of cemented tungsten carbides and oxides, upgrading of investment castings, and fabrication of high-performance ceramics. With system capabilities expanding and becoming increasingly cost efficient, even the more common metallic and ceramic alloys are being processed commercially using HIP.

While most HIP-processed PM parts have been made directly from powders, another trend is toward eliminating the disposable can. Conventionally pressed and sintered parts (at about 90-95% density) are loaded into the chamber directly for full densification.

Other PM Pressure Compaction Methods

Hot pressing. Hot pressing can produce compacted products with a high level of strength, hardness, accuracy, and density. During hot pressing, the total amount of deformation of the

SPECIAL PM PROCESSES

compact is relatively limited in comparison to hot extrusion and hot forging, but complete densification generally is achieved. Factors that limit the use of hot pressing include die cost, difficulties in heating and atmospheric control, and length of time required for the cycle. Temperatures are too high for steel dies; and a principal problem is the choice of suitable mold material. It must be strong enough at the hot-pressing temperature to withstand the applied pressure without plastic deformation, and it should not react with the powder. A widely used material for hot pressing beryllium and cemented carbides is graphite.

Spark sintering. A method of hot consolidating metal powders closely related to hot pressing is electrical resistance sintering under pressure. Powder or a green powder preform is placed between two punches that also serve as electrodes for conducting a low-voltage, high-amperage current. The powder is heated to the hot-pressing temperature by the electric current and simultaneously pressed. This process is mainly used in pressing beryllium powder and titanium alloy powder compacts in graphite molds, under conditions in which a dense compact is produced in 12-15 seconds.

High-energy-rate forming. In commercial PM practice, limited use is made of high-energy-rate forming techniques for closed die powder compaction. Various methods of energy production have been developed, including pneumatic, mechanical, explosive, and spark discharge. Two unique features are the very short duration of pressure application, ranging from 50 ms to 5 μ s, and the high amounts of energy imparted to the material. Benefits sought are high green densities, high green and sintered strength, and uniform density of the compacts.

One type of high-energy-rate forming uses dies similar to those in conventional compacting, but the upper punch is an impactor that moves at high velocity through a barrel to compact the powder. The impactor may be actuated by an explosive charge or by compressed gas. Another method is explosive compacting, in which the powders are loaded into a steel tube; the tube ends are welded shut; and explosives are taped to the tube and tapered at one end to attach an explosive cap. Available information indicates that explosive compacting activity is limited to experimental investigations and developmental work.

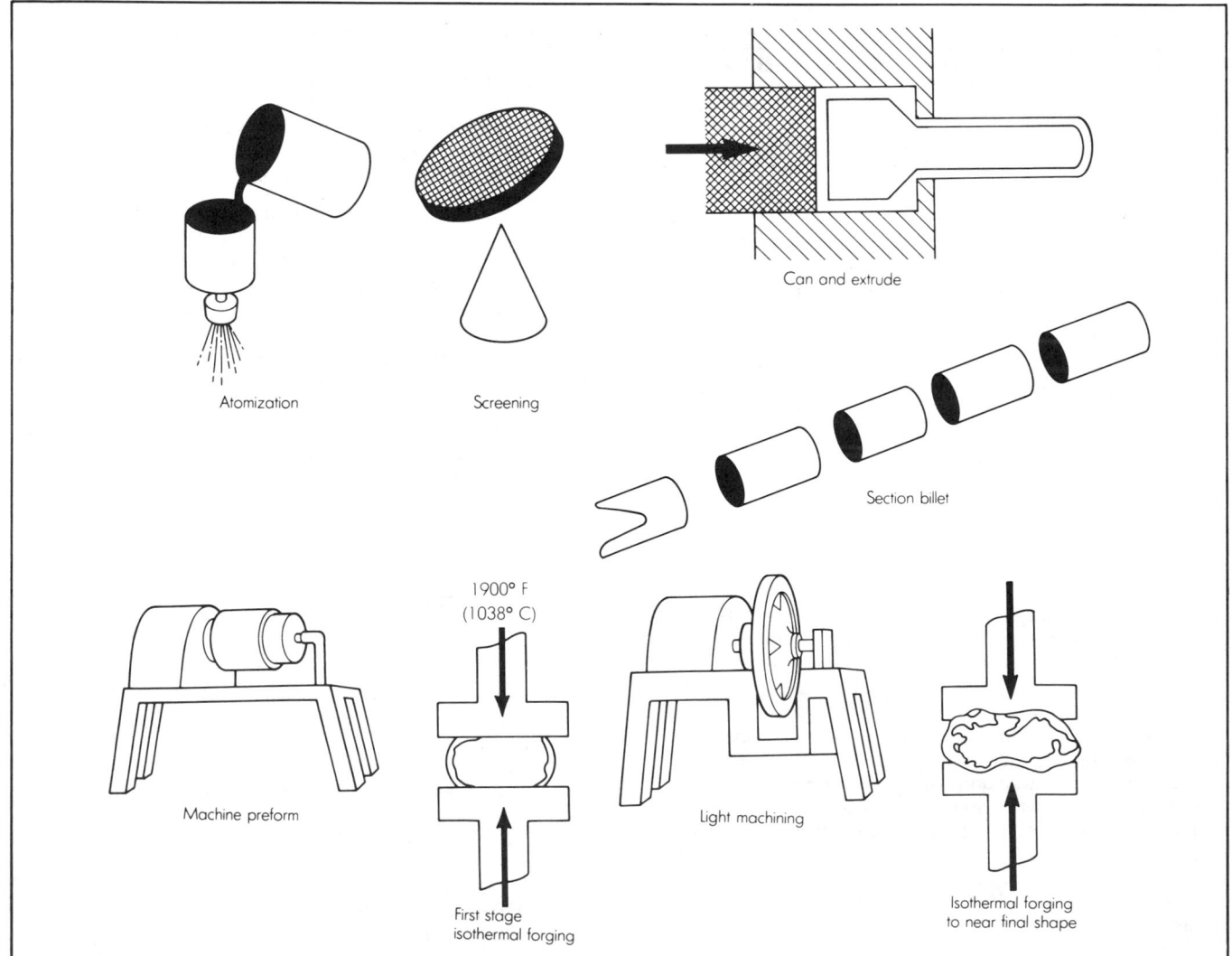

Fig. 17-43 Schematic flow chart shows hot isostatic pressing followed by forging for producing turbine discs.

Extruding. Long shapes produced from metal powders are extruded. Developments in this field make it possible to produce extruded shapes with very high densities and excellent mechanical properties. Methods used for extruding depend upon the characteristics of the powder; some powders are extruded cold with a binder, while others can be heated to a suitable extruding temperature. Hot extrusion combines hot compacting and hot mechanical working, yielding a fully dense product. (General information on extruding is provided in Chapter 13, "Wire Drawing, Extruding and Heading," in this volume.) Generally, the powder is first compressed into a billet and is then heated or sintered in a nonoxidizing atmosphere before being placed in the press. Although various methods are used for PM hot extrusion, in most applications, the metal powders are placed in a metallic capsule or "can," heated, and extruded with the can. Although the greatest use of this process has been to produce nuclear solid fuel elements and other materials for high-temperature applications; aluminum, copper, nickel, beryllium, and other powder metals can be extruded. The process also is used for producing seamless tubing from stainless steel powder.

Injection molding. Complex shapes, with wall thicknesses from 0.2" (5 mm) to 0.023" (0.6 mm), and shapes with cross-cored holes, which are impossible to compact by conventional powder metallurgy processes, can be produced by applying to metal powders (and ceramic powders) the technology of injection molding of plastics.

Injection molding of powder metals is a three-step process, starting with metal powder in a plastic binder. In the first step, part preforms—which are about 20% larger than finished size—are injection molded in a manner similar to that of plastic injection molding. In the second step, the preforms are heated to drive off the plastic binder. In the third step, they are sintered much like traditional powder metal parts. The final parts have a density of 95-98% that of wrought material, are fully annealed, and often require no additional machining.

The principal advantage of powder metal injection molding is its ability to produce complex parts to near net shape, minimizing machining and leading to cost savings in both materials and processing. The batch nature of the process, and the long cycle times, preclude using it in some applications, however. The maximum part size can also be a limitation.

An example of a part produced by injection molding from nickel powder is a 2" (50.8 mm) diam screw seal with a discontinuous internal thread. The seal is used in an aircraft wing flap ballscrew assembly.

Isothermal PM forging. Gatorizing is a Pratt & Whitney patented hot die forging process that uses a powder metal billet as the input material. The process work is performed as a hot isothermal operation in which both the dies and forging stock are heated to the established forging temperature and maintained at that temperature during forging. The billet is made by consolidating the metal powder by either extrusion or hot isostatic pressing into a log that is in a superplastic (low-strength; high-ductility) condition. The reduced forging pressure requirement eliminates the need for a large tonnage press that would be used for conventional forging of the superalloys in high-performance aircraft jet engines. For example, a press with a 3000 ton (27 MN) capacity is used to Gatorize compressor rotor discs, made from IN100 (nickel-base superalloy); whereas, a press with 20,000 ton (178 MN) or larger capacity would be required to produce an equivalent part conventionally. Another advantage of this process is the

fabrication of parts to near net shape. The Gatorizing process is illustrated, schematically, in Fig. 17-43.

PRESSURELESS PM COMPACTION METHODS

The various pressureless PM compaction methods include gravity compaction, continuous compaction, and slip casting.

Gravity Compaction

Gravity compaction refers to filling a die with loose powder and sintering the powder in the die. This method also is called "pressureless molding," "gravity sintering," and "loose sintering." Principal commercial application is for the production of PM filters.

Continuous Compaction

Continuous pressureless compaction is used to produce porous sheet. The process (sometimes referred to as "slurry coating"), consists of preparing a slurry of the metal powder, a liquid, and chemical additives. The slurry then can be coated on a metal screen or solid sheet. It is passed through a set of rolls that apply little pressure, but control slurry thickness. Drying and sintering complete the process. Applications include production of high-porosity sheet for electrodes in rechargeable batteries and the application of porous coatings of various metals to ferrous sheet stock to produce unusual properties.

Slip Casting

Although green compacts for tungsten, molybdenum, and other powders are sometimes made by slip casting, the process is used only to a limited extent for metals; it is more widely used for ceramics. The powder, converted to a slurry mixture, is poured into a plaster-of-paris mold. Since the mold is porous, the liquid drains into the plaster, leaving a solid layer of material deposited on the surface. Upon drying, the green compacts are sintered in the usual manner. The procedure is simple and permits considerable variation in size and complexity; however, it is not suited to high production rates.

WROUGHT PM PROCESSES

Powder metallurgy often is associated with structural parts, or self-lubricating parts of specific shapes produced by rigid die pressing and sintering. However, from its inception, PM also has been applied to wrought materials. These are metal structures that begin as powders; but through processing, they become fully dense, high-performance products that possess unusual metallurgical characteristics. By beginning with metal powders instead of melting and casting the metal, a homogeneous, segregation-free microstructure is achieved, with resulting benefits in uniformity of mechanical properties. This section covers significant commercial processes that use metal powders as a starting point for production of wrought products.

An Early Example

One of the first applications of PM was for a wrought product—the production of tungsten wire for lamp filaments. To produce tungsten wire, specially treated tungsten powder is pressed into bar form using a breakaway die which avoids stress-induced cracking of the very low green strength compact. The green bar is presintered in hydrogen at a relatively low

SPECIAL PM PROCESSES

temperature to impart a degree of interparticle bonding and strength and to remove reducible impurities (primarily oxygen), then it is sintered at a high temperature to full density by a process of electric resistance sintering in hydrogen. Finally, the sintered bar is worked into wire by hot swaging followed by warm and cold wire drawing.

The main rationale for powder processing in this instance is that tungsten, because of its high melting point, cannot be processed readily by other methods. Secondarily, lamp filaments are treated with specialized minor additions to control grain growth, an important process step that is possible only through a PM approach.

Other important driving forces which can lead to the choice of a specialized powder metallurgy process include:

1. Cost reduction through minimizing process steps and through lower requirements for equipment investment. For example, powder rolling of strip, and tube extrusion.
2. Material savings achieved through more efficient use of materials by processing directly to near net shape. For example, HIP for aircraft components of superalloys or titanium.
3. Improved properties for highly alloyed materials through fine dispersion of phases which are a normal part of the alloy microstructure. For example, tool steels and superalloys.
4. Achieving unique combinations of materials not possible by a melting process. For example, tungsten-silver and tungsten-copper materials and oxide dispersion hardened materials.

Powder Processing

The success of the specialized powder processing methods depends upon the powder quality. In an extreme instance, superalloy powders used for aircraft parts such as turbine discs are produced under rigid conditions of exclusion from oxygen and other contaminants. Vacuum-melted metal is argon atomized and then further processed through the point of final consolidation without being exposed to air or any impurity. The cost of such rigorous treatment is offset by savings in the amount of material removed and the cost of removing it using conventional melting, forging, and machining processes.

One method of producing extremely clean powders for a relatively low cost involves vacuum melting metals in the largest available furnaces (five tons) and atomizing them with nitrogen.

Although not requiring such extreme freedom from contamination as powders for aircraft parts, powders for successful powder rolling of specialty metal strip or HIP plus extrusion of tube materials must be quite free of nonmetallic inclusions and consistent in all other properties. Such processes can be adjusted to work well with different powders, but adjustment is difficult if not impractical once the production process conditions have been set.

Powder Rolling

Metal powder can be converted directly into strip by a powder rolling process whereby the powders are consolidated in a rolling mill to form a green strip which is sintered and further rolled to full density. An important purpose in using powder rolling is the elimination of processing steps including melting, ingot casting, homogenizing, conditioning, hot forging, hot rolling, and pickling. Avoiding the capital equipment expense necessary to perform such processing steps also is an important economic consideration.

Cold rolling. One powder rolling approach, illustrated in Fig. 17-44, is characterized by the fact that all working steps are carried out cold (room temperature). The powder is normally fed by a controlled metering system into the roll gap at the top of two horizontally opposed rolls. Such a mill is ordinarily a conventional two-level rolling mill turned on its side. Powder may also be fed to rolls which are vertically aligned as in normal metal rolling using appropriate feed controls. A greater danger of segregation and nonuniform engagement of the two roll surfaces with the powder must be dealt with in the latter case.

Strip monitoring of thickness and density is provided by feedback and by control of the powder feed and roll adjustment to achieve uniformity and desired green strip properties. Green density can vary over a wide range for specific process requirements; but for each specific process and material, it must be controlled within narrow limits. A lower limit would undoubtedly be that which allows strip integrity in the system, and an upper limit should be 90% or less of theoretical density, since a density that is any higher negates the potential benefits of chemical refinement during sintering, and blistering by entrapped gases or reaction products can occur.

The next step in the process is strip sintering to develop metallurgical bonding between the particles. This process is carried out in line with the compacting mill and under a protective atmosphere such as a hydrogen or dissociated ammonia atmosphere. Usually a belt or roller hearth furnace is selected. The belt furnace gives good support to the strip during the sintering operation, but requires heating of the belt, (usually weighing as much or more than the strip). The open mesh belts also drag oxygen into the furnace and result in lower purity for the atmosphere. Roller hearth furnaces are more energy efficient, but provide less support for the strip and must use a specially bricked furnace to achieve good atmosphere purity.

Cold rolling of the sintered strip at densities under 90% theoretical is limited in amount of reduction to no greater than 10-15% because of the low ductility of the sintered porous strip. Greater amounts of cold reduction at this point result in excessive strip cracking. The cold-rolling step at this stage does, in fact, accomplish densification more than strip elongation. If

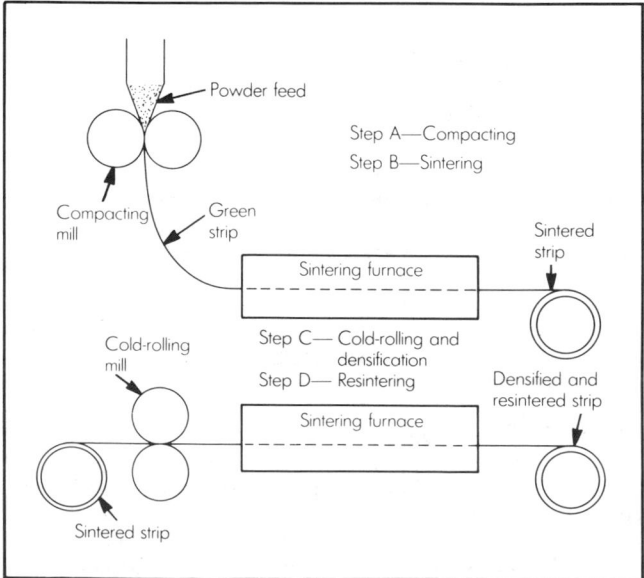

Fig. 17-44 Powder cold-rolling process with in-line sintering.

Powder feed

Step A—Compacting
Step B—Sintering

Compacting mill

Green strip

Sintered strip

Sintering furnace

Cold-rolling mill

Step C— Cold-rolling and densification
Step D— Resintering

Densified and resintered strip

Sintering furnace

Sintered strip

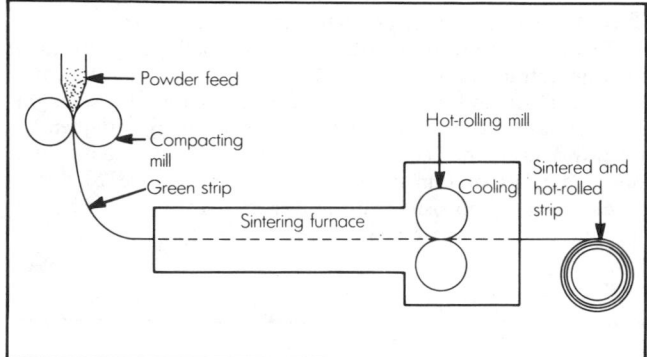

Fig. 17-45 Powder hot-rolling process.

the strip is cold worked after the initial in-line sintering, it must again be sintered in-line since it is at that point too fragile (brittle) to be recoiled. Following a second in-line sintering, however, the strip is close to full density and may be subjected to substantial cold working followed by conventional annealing.

Hot rolling. In-line sintering is limited as to time at temperature by the amount of heating time, line speed, and furnace length. A sufficient degree of sintering allows the strip to be coiled for further processing steps or to be consolidated further by a cold or hot-rolling step in line with the sintering furnace. Such a hot-rolling step is carried out while the strip is still heated from the sintering furnace and under a protective atmosphere as illustrated in Fig. 17-45.

Applications. Metals in strip form made on a commercial scale by powder rolling include nickel and nickel iron alloys for electronic and coinage uses; nickel iron and nickel iron cobalt controlled expansion alloys; cobalt and ductile cobalt alloys for welding applications; and an aluminum-backed, aluminum lead alloy which, after roll bonding to a steel backing, is used widely for automotive bearings.

Tool Steels Production

The manufacture of tool steels by consolidation to full density billets of gas-atomized powders has been a commercial reality since the early 1970's. The fully dense PM billets are worked to finished shapes by conventional hot-forging and hot-rolling methods.

A major advantage of the PM production of tool steels is the ability of this approach to achieve a relatively fine and uniform dispersion of carbide phases compared to the coarse carbide network and heavy segregation usually encountered with normal melting, casting technology. Not only does the PM structure give good product yields, but the end properties are significantly improved, especially for certain applications. It has also been reported that higher alloying levels and, therefore, higher properties can be achieved with PM. Three different approaches are known to be in commercial practice at this time.

Consolidation at Atmospheric Pressure. This process (CAP), developed by Cyclops Corporation, has been used to produce tool steels T-15, M-2, and M-3. Clean, relatively fine, gas-atomized powders are enclosed in glass bottles which are evacuated and sealed and then sintered loose to +99% density preforms or billets which are subsequently forged and rolled. It is reported that a boron-containing addition is used in the powder mix as a sintering activator. For high-speed steels, the metal

powder is produced by air melting and nitrogen atomizing with a resultant nitrogen level of 150 ppm.

This same method is also used to produce high-density preforms or billets of high-temperature nickel-base alloys.

Crucible Particle Metallurgy (CPM). A second method for producing billets and preforms is the Crucible Particle Metallurgy (CPM) process developed by Crucible Specialty Metals Div., Colt Industries. This process consists of pouring gas-atomized alloy powders into a steel can which is evacuated and sealed. The filled and sealed container is hot isostatically pressed to full density and can then be worked to desired shapes by conventional hot forging and rolling while still in the container. Crucible Particle Metallurgy high-alloy steels can be characterized by complete homogeneity in the compact and in the products produced from the compact. The carbide particle size is finer and more uniformly distributed than it is in conventionally produced high-alloy steels.

The Crucible Particle Metallurgy (CPM) process is used to produce conventional tool steel compositions and has also enabled development of higher alloyed grades than are possible with conventional melt-cast technology.

Anti-Segregation Process (ASP). A third and similar method is the Anti-Segregation Process (ASP) developed by NYBY Uddeholm Steel Corp. of Sweden. It includes a cold isostatic pressing (CIP) treatment of the sealed can of powder followed by heating and hot isostatic pressing (HIP). Again, the billet or preform, after hot isostatic pressing to full density is capable of being processed by hot forging and rolling.

Specialty Alloy Tubing

The advances in PM consolidation consisting of gas atomization of powders and powder consolidation to produce high quality tool steel compositions have spurred the development of additional alloys and products along similar lines. One of the noteworthy developments is the production of high-quality specialty alloys in tube form. A process developed and used by NYBY Uddeholm Steel Corp. of Sweden produces seamless tubing from powders in such alloy systems as 304L stainless steel; 316L stainless steel; and various other austenitic, ferritic, and martensitic grades of specialty stainless steels; as well as nonferrous alloys including nickel copper alloy 400.

In the process, a gas-atomized powder is poured into a steel capsule which is vibrated so that the packed density is above 70% of theoretical. After being filled, the capsule is sealed and leak tested. It is then cold isostatically pressed (CIP) under very high pressures (500 MPa, 72,500 psi) to consolidate the powder to a theoretical density of 85-90% and allow it to undergo the extrusion step in a controlled manner. The capsule is heated in two stages to 2200° F (1200° C) and extruded in a conventional extrusion press at an extrusion ratio of 20-30 to 1 based on theoretical density.

Advantages of this process over normal melting, casting, and extruding production methods for seamless tubing are (1) a lower inclusion rate because of the powder cleanliness; (2) closer composition control in the finished tube because of the better control in composition of powders achievable by blending and because of the absence of segregation from the solidification step; (3) and a more homogeneous structure.

Oxide Dispersion Strengthening

Powder metallurgy allows the consolidation of materials which contain fine dispersions of oxide or other insoluble phases that are stable up to the melting point of the base metal.

NONFERROUS PM METALS

Perhaps the most sophisticated approach is the INCO Mechanical Alloying process whereby through intensive ball milling (attriting), the individual powder ingredients of an alloy including oxide phases such as Y_2O_3 are formed into homogeneous powders, each particle having the desired final composition and degree of dispersion. This alloying occurs by a complex dynamic equilibrium of particle fracture and recombination by welding. The alloyed particles are then consolidated by canning and hot extrusion into shapes which can be further worked as desired for aircraft parts.

Tungsten, Tantalum and Molybdenum

In addition to the lamp filaments described earlier, the high melting refractory metals, such as tungsten, tantalum, and molybdenum and their alloys, are fabricated to wrought intermediate shapes by powder metal technology. Frequently, the powders are formed into large green billets by cold isostatic pressing (CIP); vacuum sintered at high temperature to achieve at least a closed porosity state; and then further worked by hot forging, rolling, swaging, etc.

NONFERROUS PM METALS

As in most other metal-oriented fields, powder metallurgy (PM) is linked strongly to the development and use of ferrous materials. It is, however, being increasingly applied in the fabrication of structural (and nonstructural) parts from the light, high strength to weight ratio, nonferrous metals, such as aluminum, magnesium, beryllium, and titanium. When processed by PM, these metals (usually in alloy form), exhibit high levels of mechanical properties that are suited to a wide range of applications—especially in aircraft, aerospace, and nuclear fields. In addition to these metals, structural PM parts make considerable use of copper and copper alloys.

ALUMINUM

The commercial production of precision parts by powder metallurgy techniques is an important development in the fabrication of aluminum alloys. Their high strength, light weight, corrosion resistance, high thermal and electrical conductivity, and response to a variety of finishing processes are utilized in automobiles, appliances, business machines, power tools, and many other applications.

Aluminum PM parts are competitive with many aluminum castings, extrusions, and screw machine products that involve machining operations. They also compete with PM parts manufactured from other metal powders in which some features of aluminum are needed.

Material Characteristics

The commercially available aluminum powder alloys are blends of carefully sized, atomized, aluminum powder mixed with powders of various alloying metals such as copper and magnesium.

Properties and Performance

Properties. Aluminum PM parts can be produced with a wide range of property values. Tensile strength can vary from 16,000-50,000 psi (110-345 MPa) depending on composition, density, sintering practices, thermal treatment, and repressing operations. Figure 17-46 illustrates the general point that aluminum PM parts can be produced with strength levels comparable to the commonly used ferrous PM parts.

Corrosion resistance. Aluminum alloys are widely used in both structural and nonstructural applications because of their resistance to corrosion. The corrosion resistance of aluminum PM alloys can be improved appreciably through the application of chemical conversion coatings or through anodizing treatments. Amorphous chromate coatings are especially useful in providing economical protection to parts exposed to saline environments. When exceptional corrosion resistance is required, anodizing treatments are best.

Light weight. A distinguishing characteristic of aluminum PM parts is their lighter weight in comparison to other common PM materials. Aluminum has a 3 to 1 weight advantage over iron and a 3.3 to 1 advantage over copper.

Conductivity. Another advantage of aluminum is its excellent conductivity, both electrical and thermal, in comparison with most other metals. Aluminum PM parts, therefore, may be utilized as heat sinks or as electrical conductors.

Manufacturing Process

The fabrication of aluminum PM parts involves the same basic manufacturing operations, equipment, and tooling that are employed for other metal powders. There are some differences, however.

Compacting. Aluminum PM premixes exhibit excellent compressibility and yield high-density parts at lower compaction and ejection pressures than are needed for iron powders. Lower compacting pressures permit the use of smaller, faster presses to produce larger parts; or in some cases, multiple-cavity tooling is used for high-production rates. Aluminum powder transfers more readily under pressure in the die than do iron powders. This allows the molding of complex shapes such as slopes and multilevels.

Sintering. Aluminum PM parts can be sintered in various types of furnaces and atmospheres. Sintering time and temperature typically are less than for other materials. Reproducible dimensions can be achieved with proper attention to compact density, sintering, temperature, dew point, and atmosphere. Most parts are sintered in a N_2 atmosphere at 1100° F (593° C) with the dew point controlled to -40° F (-40° C) or better.

The high strength and good ductility of sintered aluminum PM parts are attributable to the sintering process and the liquid-phase sintering that aluminum PM powders undergo. When aluminum premixes are sintered, liquid-phases form as aluminum combines with the added soluble elements—copper, silicon, and magnesium. These liquid constituents migrate along particle boundaries; penetrate the aluminum oxide envelope; and diffuse into the powder particles. This reduces porosity and increases homogeneity.

Secondary operations. Secondary operations performed on aluminum PM parts are similar to those for most other PM materials. These include sizing or coining, heat treatment, machining, finishing, and joining. Cold or hot forming can be added when optimum properties are desired.

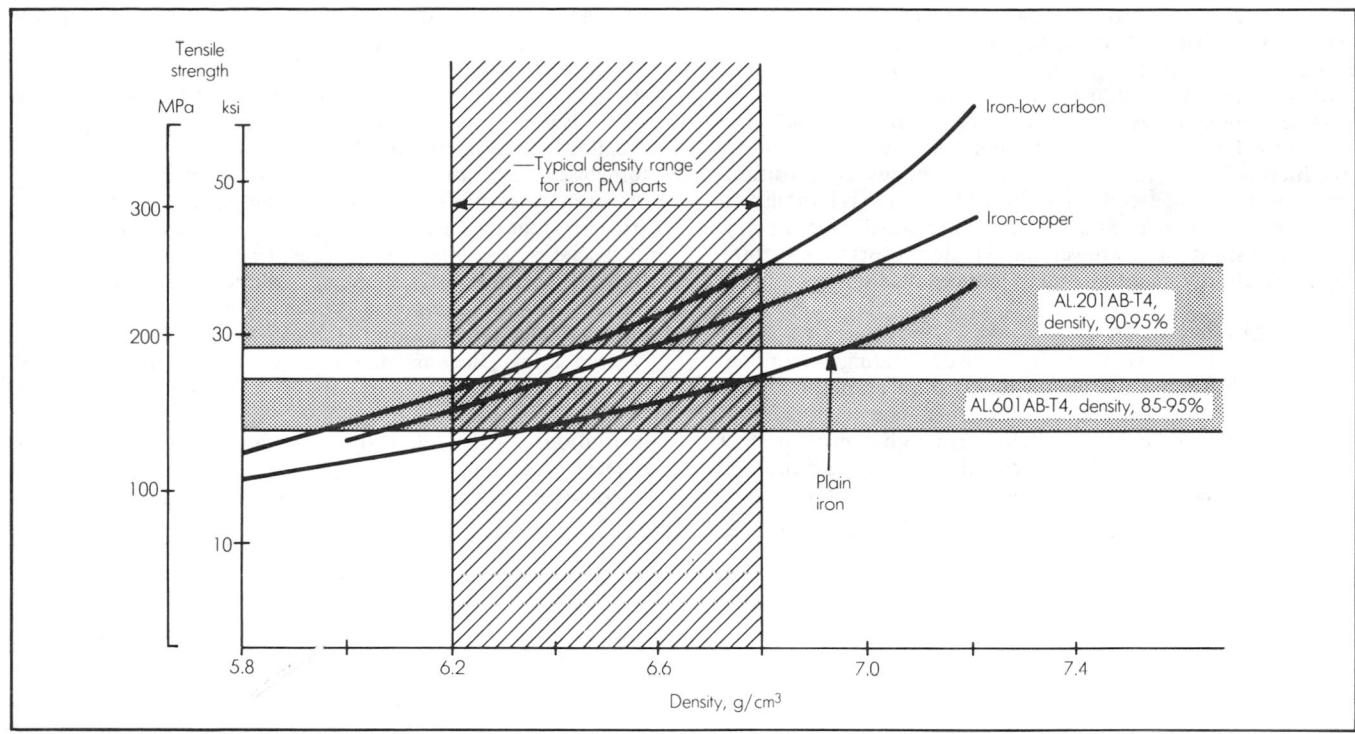

Fig. 17-46 Tensile strength of aluminum and iron PM parts (*American Powder Metals Co.*).

MAGNESIUM

Magnesium alloy powders are processed by a hot-extrusion method in which loose powder is loaded into the heated extrusion chamber and extruded directly through the die. No atmospheric protection is provided, and the heat of the container is used to raise the powder temperature sufficiently to allow for extrusion. The metallurgical structure of magnesium and its alloys is such that coarse-grained alloys have a lower compressive yield strength than tensile yield strength. When magnesium alloys are sufficiently fine grained, they have about the same yield strength in tension and compression.

Fine-grained alloys can be produced from coarse magnesium alloy powders by hot extrusion. Any shape that can be extruded conventionally can be extruded from the magnesium alloy powders or "pellets." These pellet extrusions have a finer grain size than extrusions from chill-cast magnesium alloy ingots—and, therefore, have a ratio of compressive to tensile yield strength near one.

BERYLLIUM

Most beryllium parts are produced by powder metallurgy, because it enables a fine-grained product to be produced. Beryllium powder is consolidated by loose powder sintering. Commercial purity beryllium is produced by vacuum hot pressing in graphite molds. Vacuum hot pressed beryllium, depending on the grade, has yield strengths of 30,000-36,000 psi (200-250 MPa) with 2-4% elongation, or yield strengths of 60,000 psi (410 MPa) with 1-2% elongation.

Better mechanical properties have been obtained from high purity impact attrited powder which is cold isostatically pressed in evacuated bags at 60,000 psi (410 MPa) and then hot isostatically pressed in evacuated and sealed steel cans at 15,000 psi (105 MPa) pressure and peak temperatures of 1679-2120° F (915-1160° C). Typical mechanical properties of this hot isostatically pressed beryllium are:

- Yield strength: 41,000 to 66,000 psi (280 to 460 MPa)
- Tensile strength: 67,000 to 87,000 psi (470 to 600 MPa)
- Elongation: 4 to 6 1/2%

Hot-pressed beryllium can be extruded and rolled. The extrusions have good ductility in the extrusion direction; 10% elongation with 130,000 psi (900 MPa) tensile strength and 80,000 psi (550 MPa) yield strength. Because of this preferred orientation during plastic working, it is also possible by cross rolling to produce beryllium sheet that is relatively ductile in the plane of the sheet, but very brittle in the direction perpendicular to the plane of the sheet.

Beryllium is finding increasing use in aircraft applications, particularly jet engine parts. It is used in gyroscopes and other guidance instruments. Among the aerospace applications of beryllium were heat sinks that were used for the Apollo space capsules. In nuclear applications, the principal advantage of beryllium is its outstanding ability to slow down neutrons to thermal velocities and at the same time not react with the neutrons.

TITANIUM

The high cost of titanium has restricted its use to products that require exceptional corrosion resistance or a high strength to weight ratio. Its chemical reactivity mandates specialized equipment and technology to produce conventional castings or wrought shapes. Furthermore, numerous costly processing steps are involved, as shown in Fig. 17-47.

The powder metallurgy (PM) process has been instrumental in expanding applications for titanium. It is attractive from a raw material cost point of view, since the ore refining process

NONFERROUS PM METALS

produces a sponge product from the magnesium or sodium reduction of TiCl₄. Processing temperatures for PM are a fraction of the melting point of the titanium metal, thus reducing the reactivity problem; and substantially fewer processing steps may be required, as shown in Fig. 17-47. The process offers the generic attributes of powder metallurgy products—fine grain size and homogeneous composition. Perhaps the strongest advantage of PM titanium is its ability to produce near net shape components. This advantage is manifested in a substantially lower initial material cost than that for ingot metallurgy material, and in reduced machining cost.

General Methods

A few applications, primarily those demanding exceptional corrosion resistance, use commercially pure titanium powder consolidated to a near net shape product. The product application may be structural, in which case, a high-density product is required; or it may be nonstructural, in which case, the high specific surface area and/or the permeability of a porous

product is required. Strength can be controlled by varying the oxygen content of the starting material.

More often the applications for titanium relate to the high strength to weight ratio characteristic of its alloys. Two PM methods are routinely used to prepare alloys. In one method, prealloyed ingot metallurgy bar stock is converted to powder form by an atomization process. The resulting product, spherical in form, is of uniform chemical composition and has the strength of the parent alloy. This latter attribute requires the use of special consolidation techniques. In the other PM method, the most economical, elemental alloying constituents are blended with the commercially pure powder to form a mixture having a bulk composition that meets the specifications of the desired alloy. Because the blended elemental powder is composed primarily of soft, commercially pure titanium, it is readily fabricated into shapes by common methods. Homogenization and the full alloy strength are developed in subsequent processing steps.

Fabrication. The chemical reactivity of titanium, especially

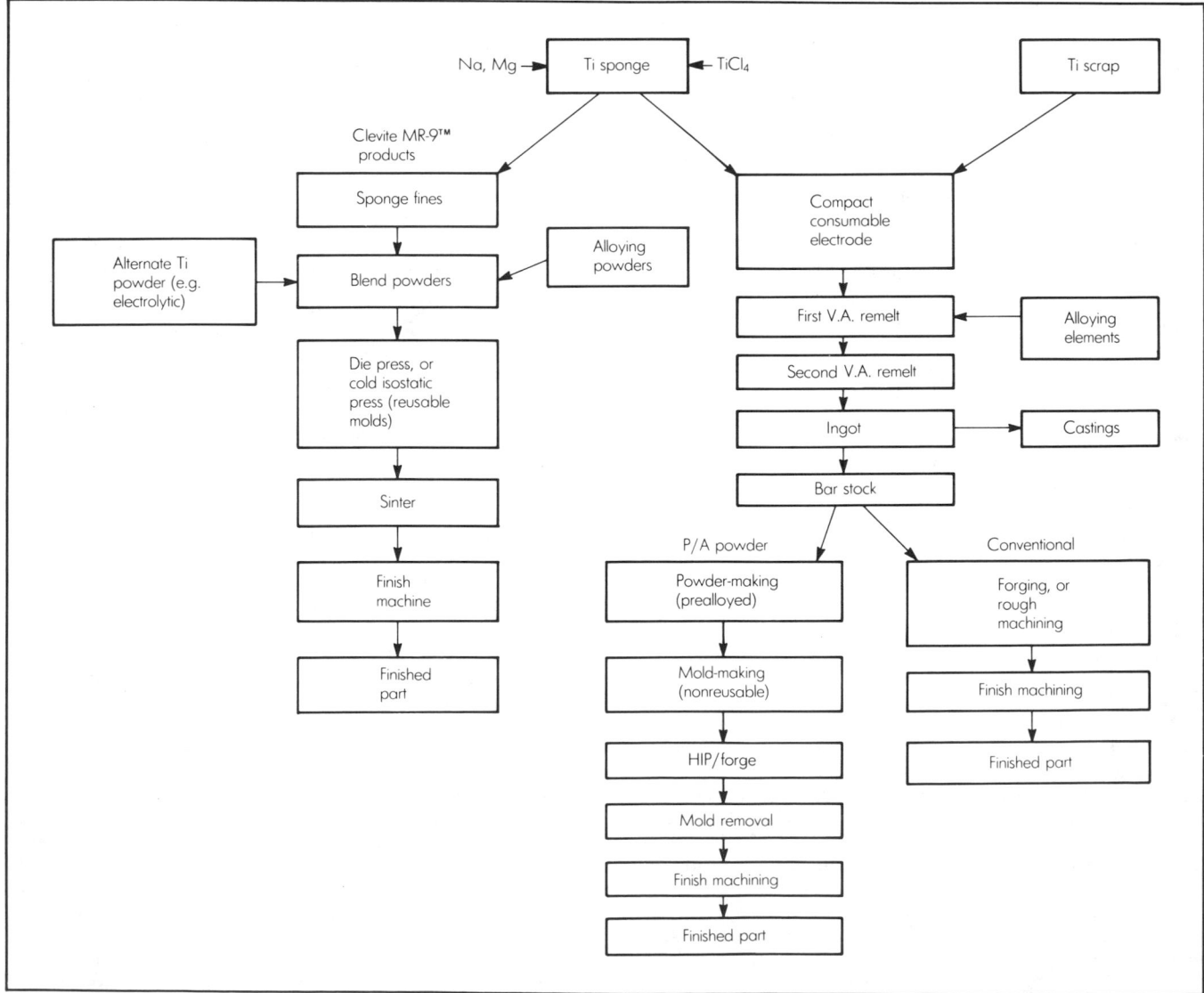

Fig. 17-47 Manufacturing processes for PM and conventional cast and wrought shapes.

in fine powder form dictates that particular care be used in fabrication. Electrical equipment must be explosion proof, and reasonable care must be exercised to preclude fire or explosion. Good housekeeping is mandatory.

In general, the methods used to fabricate titanium PM parts are similar to those for PM fabrication of other metals. Commercially pure powder and blended elemental mixtures can be consolidated inexpensively in rigid dies or cold isostatic pressing (CIP) molds. In the first case, carbide dies are recommended and clearances should be generous. Polyurethane makes a durable CIP mold which, on the average, has a life of 50 parts. Compacting pressures range from 30-50 tons/in.^{2} (415-690 MPa). Blended elemental parts exhibit green densities of 80-85% of theoretical and can be easily handled without breakage. If the product application calls for sheet or foil shapes, the commercially pure or blended elemental powder can be powder rolled directly to these configurations.

Compacting. Prealloyed powder, because of its inherent strength, requires more costly consolidation procedures. The most common process is hot isostatic pressing (HIP). This process requires that the powder be encapsulated in a container and subjected to high temperature. The container is evacuated and sealed for pressing. The pressing cycle is relatively long, and the container must be removed following the HIP cycle. The fluid die process developed for consolidation of high-strength powders eliminates the need for specialized equipment and shortens the production cycle, but still employs an expendable mold for each part. Both processes have the capability of producing fully dense components of intricate shape.

Vacuum hot pressing may be used for either blended elemental or prealloyed powders, with the resulting parts being fully dense. Tooling resembles rigid dies of the reusable type, and special capital equipment is required.

Sintering. Because of its affinity for oxygen, sintering of titanium and its alloys is done in vacuum. It is critically important to control oxygen absorption during processing. Sinter densities range from 95-99.5% for standard parts. In controlled surface area or permeability parts, porosity may vary from 40-80% depending upon design.

Equipment. Fabrication equipment is typically employed throughout the PM industry. Rigid die presses may be either mechanical or hydraulic type. Isostatic compaction chambers, both cold (CIP) and hot (HIP), are commercially available. Vacuum sintering furnaces capable of maintaining pressures below 5 x 10^{-4} Torr are employed and may use inert gas recirculating systems to rapidly cool alloys to obtain the required structure. Finishing equipment parallels equipment that is used universally by the PM industry.

TABLE 17-13
Composition and Density of
Titanium P M Alloys

Alloy	Nominal Composition, %							Density, g/cm^3
	Al	V	Sn	Zr	Mo	O$_2$	Ti	
C.P.	---	---	---	---	---	0.15	99.	4.19
Ti-64	6	4	---	---	---	0.2	Bal.	4.38
Ti-662	6	6	2	---	---	0.2	Bal.	4.47
Ti-6242	6	---	2	4	2	0.2	Bal.	4.47

(Imperial Clevite, Inc.)

TABLE 17-14
Typical Mechanical Properties
of Titanium P M Alloys

Alloy	Yield Strength, (MPa)	Ultimate Tensile Strength, (MPa)	Elong-ation, %	Hardness, R$_A$
C.P.	35	48	13	12
Ti-64 B/E	120	133	12	24
PRE	127	136	17	33
Ti-64 STA	140	155	3	5
Ti-662 B/E	140	150	7	10
Ti-6242 B/E	130	145	12	15

(Imperial Clevite, Inc.)

Properties

Performance of PM alloys is strongly influenced by product integrity. Controlled-porosity parts have lower performance characteristics than fully dense parts. Since the majority of applications for PM titanium are structural, properties given in this section are representative of state-of-the-art materials processed for optimum performance unless otherwise noted.

Nominal composition and typical densities of some commonly used PM alloys are presented in Table 17-13. The density for commercially pure material is based on its use as a structural component. The density of porous parts may be as low as 1.8 g/cm^3. Other physical properties may be estimated from ingot metallurgy data, allowing for a proportional decrease in value depending on the degree of porosity in the final part. Typical mechanical properties are listed in Table 17-14.

Applications

Titanium PM has produced parts for a wide range of applications, and the list is steadily expanding. Commercially pure titanium fasteners have been used by the chemical industry for many years. More recently, this industry has moved toward porous titanium electrodes for conversion cells when high specific surface area is advantageous.

Prealloyed and blended alloys have been used in static applications by the aerospace industry. The near net shape capability accounts for much of the demand for PM titanium. A good example is a missile warhead, for which titanium PM offered material savings of one third of that of the previously used forging. At the other extreme, PM titanium alloys are receiving consideration as prosthetic implants, for which excellent corrosion resistance to body fluids, coupled with high strength and near net shape potential, creates a powerful driving force.

COPPER

Copper has a combination of properties not found in any other metal. It has exceptionally high electrical and thermal conductivity. It has excellent resistance to corrosion, is highly ductile, exhibits good strength, and is nonmagnetic. In addition, it can be welded, brazed, and soldered. It can also be plated. Its pleasing color finds many applications in the decorative field. These factors make copper a useful PM material.

An increasing number of PM manufacturers are producing pure copper parts. Copper parts for electrical and thermal applications, such as wires, contacts, and tubing, are produced by PM. Thin sheet and refrigeration tubing made by PM

NONFERROUS PM METALS

methods allow parts to be produced with properties comparable to those made by conventional methods.

Copper Powder

One of the best known powder metallurgy applications of copper powder is self-lubricating bronze bearings, which are produced from mixtures of elemental copper and tin powders. The grades of copper powder used are free-flowing granular powders with density in the range of 2.5-3.2 g/cm³. Copper powders similar to those for self-lubricating bearings are used:

- As an ingredient in mixes for iron-based structural parts.
- For metallic brushes pressed from mixtures of copper and graphite powder.
- For structural parts with a bronze composition.
- For straight copper powder structural parts for electrical and electronic applications.

A variety of copper powders is available. Their properties are strongly related to the methods by which they are produced. The principal methods for producing copper powder for PM applications are:

- Electrolytic deposition of copper powder.
- Gaseous reduction of copper oxide.
- Atomization.

Copper-Alloy Powders

For producing bronze structural parts, either elemental powders or a prealloyed atomized bronze powder is used. Structural parts from brasses (copper-zinc alloys) and nickel

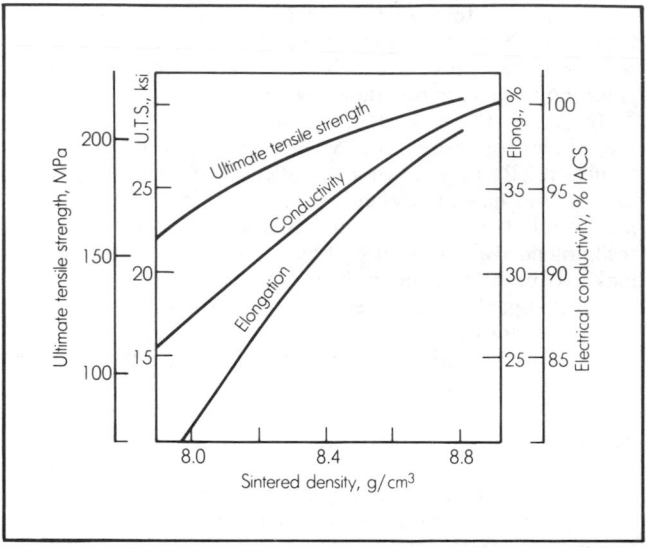

Fig. 17-48 Effect of density on properties of parts made from electrolytic copper powder.

silvers (copper-nickel-zinc alloys) are produced from prealloyed powders. Copper-aluminum alloy powder produced by atomizing the molten alloy with a stream of nitrogen forms the basis for the fabrication of copper that is dispersion strengthened with alumina.

Copper-lead powders are used in the production of bearings that consist of a bearing alloy lining on a steel shell primarily for main and connecting rod bearings. Since copper and lead are not completely miscible even in the liquid state, the alloys from which the powder is produced are melted in electric induction furnaces that have a stirring action to keep the metals finely dispersed. The alloys are then water atomized into powder.

Copper-based metallic filter materials have a copper-tin-bronze composition and are produced from spherical powder. Loose powder sintering of powders with a narrow particle size distribution results in filters having an optimum combination of properties required in filters: retention of fine impurity particles and reasonable fluid permeability.

Properties and Specifications

The data presented in this section relates primarily to compositions that are widely used commercially for structural parts.

TABLE 17-15
Typical Tensile Properties and Electrical Conductivity of Copper P M Parts

Property	Electrical Conductivity	
	Type I	Type II
Density, g/cm³	8.0	8.3
Ultimate tensile strength, psi (MPa)	23,000 (159)	28,000 (193)
Elongation, %	20	30
Electrical conductivity, % of IACS (Ohm⁻¹m⁻¹)	85 (0.493 x 10⁸)	90 (0.522 x 10⁸)

TABLE 17-16
Composition and Properties of P M Bronze

Composition of PM Bronze, MPIF CT-0010: 86.3-90.5% Cu, 9.5-10.5% Sn, 0-1.7% graphite, 0-1.0% Fe. Other elements total 0.5% max. Properties of PM Bronze CT-0010						
Density Range	Ultimate Tensile Strength		Compressive Yield Strength, 0.2% Offset		Elong-ation, %	Comparable Specifications
	psi	MPa	psi	MPa		
N:5.6-6.0g/cm³ AS	8000	55	7000	48	1.0	SAE 840
R:6.4-6.8g/cm³	14,000	97	11,000	76	1.0	SAE 841
S:6.8-7.2g/cm³	18,000	124	17,500	121	2.5	SAE 842 ASTM B255 Type II

TABLE 17-17
Composition and Properties of Sintered Brass and Sintered Leaded Brass

Density Range	Ultimate Tensile Strength		Tensile Yield Strength 0.2% Offset		Elong-ation, %	Hardness
	psi	MPa	psi	MPa		

Composition of PM 90/10 Brass Designation CZ-0010:
88.0-91.0% Cu, 8.3-12.0% Zn, 0-0.3% Fe. Total other elements 0.4% max.
Properties of PM 90/10 Brass CZ-0010

Density Range	psi	MPa	psi	MPa	%	Hardness
T:7.2-7.6g/cm³	20,000	138	9000	62	13	Rockwell H57
U:7.6-8.0g/cm³	27,000	186	10,000	69	18	Rockwell H70

Composition of PM 90/10 Leaded Brass, MPIF Designation CZP-0210:
86.0-90.0% Cu, 7.3-13.0% Zn, 1.0-2.0% Lead, 0-0.3% Fe. Total other elements 0.4% max.
Properties of PM 90/10 Leaded Brass, CZP-0210

Density Range	psi	MPa	psi	MPa	%	Hardness
T:7.2-7.6g/cm³	18,000	124	7000	48	14	Rockwell H46
U:7.6-8.0g/cm³	25,500	176	8000	55	20	Rockwell H60

Structural parts from pure copper. The raw material for PM structural parts from pure copper must be a high-purity copper powder. Green compacts from copper powder pressed to high densities tend to expand during sintering because of gas entrapment in the pores. The usual practice in producing copper parts with high final densities is to compact the powder at moderate pressures of 15-18 tons/in.² (207-248 MPa); sinter the compact at 122-302° F (50-150° C) below the melting point of copper; repress the sintered compact to the desired high density; and then resinter the compact to obtain an annealed structure, if desired. The effect of density on physical properties and on electrical conductivity of copper powder is shown in Fig. 17-48. Typical tensile properties and electrical conductivity of copper PM parts are listed in Table 17-15.

PM bronze structural parts. Powder metallurgy bronze parts usually are produced from mixtures of copper and tin powders by methods similar to those used for self-lubricating bronze bearings. The compositions and properties contained in MPIF Standard 35 are shown in Table 17-16.[14]

PM brass structural parts. In contrast to bronze structural parts, PM parts from brass and leaded brass are produced from prealloyed atomized powder. The purpose of lead in the lead bearing compositions is to make it easier to compact the powder and to facilitate machining of the sintered parts. Adding lithium stearate as a lubricant (instead of zinc stearate as used for iron powder) to the powder improves the mechanical properties of brass. The composition and properties listed in MPIF Standard 35 for a 90/10 brass and 90/10 leaded brass are shown in Table 17-17.

POWDER METALLURGY SUPERALLOYS

The term *superalloy* is applied to alloys of iron, nickel, and cobalt which have high strength at temperatures of 1100° F (600° C) and higher. They are of primary interest for components in jet aircraft engines and for aerospace applications. A large amount of work has gone into the development of superalloys by powder metallurgy. The development work is concerned with nickel-based superalloys having compositions near those of alloys produced by casting or by casting and working, and with dispersion-strengthened alloys.

Nickel Base

The high temperature strength of nickel-based superalloys is attributed to the presence of coherent precipitates, which are nickel-aluminum and nickel-titanium intermetallic compounds produced by solution treatment and aging. In addition to high temperature strength, the alloys must have corrosion resistance, which requires sufficient chromium in the composition. The advanced alloys developed to obtain balanced stress rupture and corrosion resistance exhibit in the cast condition gross segregation and structural inhomogeneity, which is a principal reason why these alloys are produced by powder metallurgy methods.

A principal application of powder metallurgy superalloys is turbine discs in jet engines. In this application, stresses up to 70,000 psi (480 MPa) and temperatures as high as 1400° F (760° C) are encountered. Until this temperature is reached, a relatively fine grained material has better strength than a coarse-grained material. The principal methods of producing superalloy powders are argon atomization, vacuum atomization, and the rotating electrode process. One method for hot consolidating superalloy powders is "Gatorizing" (see Fig. 17-43, which is described earlier under "Special PM Processes").

Dispersion-Strengthened Superalloys

A great amount of research has been done on oxide dispersion strengthened superalloys. The aim in this work is to produce alloys that retain their strength at higher temperatures than the nickel-based superalloys strengthened by precipitation strengthening with the gamma prime phase. The oxides in the fine dispersion in nickel, iron, and cobalt are generally thorium or yttrium oxide. These oxides have been found to be stable, while aluminum oxide is not stable. In addition to work on oxide dispersion strengthened nickel alloys primarily of a fundamental character, three commercial approaches to producing the alloys based on wet methods were developed. Among the well-known methods is "TD-Nickel" (Thoria Dispersed Nickel) developed by the DuPont Company; the so-called "DS-Nickel" of Sherritt Gordon Mines Ltd.; and oxide dispersion strengthened nickel and cobalt-based alloys developed by Sylvania Electric Products, Inc.

QUALITY CONTROL

When parts are produced in large numbers by a high-volume process such as powder metallurgy, 100% inspection is not only slow and costly, but impractical. In addition, reliance on inspection does not assure elimination of all defective parts. Mass inspection tends to be careless; operators become fatigued; and inspection gages become worn or out of adjustment. In relying on inspection, the risk of overlooking defective parts is variable and of unknown magnitude; whereas, in a planned sampling program, the risk can be calculated.

Powder metallurgy technology is well suited to the application of quality control practices based on statistical sampling principles. Using this approach, mathematical concepts underlie the inspection of parts being produced, to determine whether or not the entire stream of production is acceptable. To apply these quality control techniques in inspection, the following steps are implemented:

- Sample the stream of manufactured parts.
- Measure the critical "monitoring" dimensions.
- Calculate deviations of dimensions from the "mean."
- Construct a control chart.
- Plot succeeding data on the control chart.

POWDER TESTS

Standard methods for sampling finished lots of metal powder have been developed by ASTM Committee B-9 and the standards committee of MPIF. A description of these methods can be found in ASTM Standard B215 and in MPIF Standard 1. The two tests which have been standardized by ASTM and MPIF for chemical analysis of metal powders are:

- ASTM Standard E 159, MPIF Standard 2 for the so-called hydrogen loss of copper, tungsten, and iron powder.
- ASTM Standard E 194, MPIF Standard 6 for acid-insoluble content of copper and iron powder.

The following methods are used for determining particle size, particle size distribution, particle shape and structure, and specific surface:

- Sieving.
- Microscopic sizing.
- Methods based on Stokes' Law:
     (c$_1$) The roller air analyzer.
     (c$_2$) The micromerograph.
     (c$_3$) Light and X-ray (sedigraph) turbidimetry.
- Coulter counter and particle analysis by light obscuration.
- Laser light scattering; the microtrac particle analyzer.

For powders with a particle size distribution that includes primarily particle sizes larger than 1732 μ in. (44 μ m), sieving is the most important method. The roller air analyzer, the micromerograph, the Coulter counter, the light obscuration particle analyzer and the microtrac analyzer are used for powders with finer particle sizes, under 1732 μ in. and most commonly in the range from 39-1575 μ in. (1-40 μ m). The turbidimetric methods have been developed for the very fine refractory metal and refractory compound powders with particle sizes from less than 39-390 μ in. (1-10 μ m).

Two methods used for determining the specific surface of metal powders are:

- The Fisher subsieve sizer which is based on permeametry.
- The gas adsorption (BET) method.

QUALITY CONTROL PROGRAM[15]

Following is a representative in-house PM quality control program, as practiced by a manufacturer of approximately 200 different high-density structural PM parts. Most of the parts weigh 6.8 g/cm^3, which is 88% of theoretical density, or higher. Part production runs range from 10,000-100,000 pieces. The metal powder is primarily iron with copper or nickel and some graphite. The quality control system locates unacceptable parts in process, at the operations where they occur—rather than waiting to find them when they have progressed to finished parts.

Powder Quality Control

The initial quality control checks are divided between various departments. When the powder is received, receiving inspection personnel make a visual check of each 2500 lb (1134 kg) bulk pack. They determine if there are any rust balls in the powder, if there is any graphite or lubricant segregation, or if the powder is contaminated with foreign material. Inspection personnel also take a powder sample from each container and forward it to the metallurgical laboratory for testing.

Laboratory personnel check each sample of powder for apparent density and flow rate. If the results do not fall within specifications, the containers are rejectable. These results, if acceptable, are returned to the inspection personnel, who list this information on each container. Depending upon the sampling plan prescribed for each supplier and each specification, physical properties of the incoming blend are determined in the metallurgical laboratory.

In some instances, suppliers may be required to submit a preshipment sample for testing. In all cases, the supplier's in-house test data is sent to the metallurgical engineering quality control section. All suppliers are audited by complete test work on one blend per month. Physical tests performed in the laboratory determine the following:

1. Compressibility—Transverse rupture bars are compacted on a tensile testing machine. Each specification requires that a minimum green density be attained when compacted at a specified tonnage.
2. Green transverse rupture strength—Transverse rupture bars are pressed to a specified density and then broken as per ASTM Standard B312-76.
3. Sintered transverse rupture strength—Transverse rupture bars are pressed to a specified density and sintered in a production furnace. They are then broken as per ASTM Standard B528-76. Transverse rupture bars from a standard lot of powder are pressed and sintered at the

same time as the incoming blend bars. This standard lot is one which has been tested extensively in the metallurgical laboratory and which has known physical properties. This standard is used as a control to ensure sintering conditions are acceptable and to validate the results of incoming lots.

4. Sintered ultimate tensile strength—Tensile bars are pressed to a specified density and sintered in a production furnace. Bars from the standard powder are pressed and sintered at the same time. These are then broken as per MPIF Standard 10-63.
5. Sintered dimensional change—Transverse rupture bars of a specified density are sintered with standard bars of the same density. The difference between the die length and sintered transverse rupture bar length is determined for both the test bars and the standard bars. The incoming powder test bars must be within 0.05% of the standard bars.
6. Sintered hardness—Apparent hardness of sintered tensile and transverse bars is determined.
7. Sintered density—Sintered density is determined by spraying the bars with "krylon" or another appropriate sealer and checking density by weighing wet and dry. For transverse rupture bars, the density may be determined using dry weight, and volume by direct measurement.
8. Composition—C, Mn, Ni, Cr, Mo and Cu content are determined for sintered bars.

After the necessary test work is performed and the results are found to be acceptable, the powder is released for use by production.

Pressing Quality Control

Quality responsibilities during the compaction of the piece parts are divided as follows:

- Manufacturing Responsibilities:

  1. After release from the laboratory, and prior to compaction, all of the powder is screened to remove any rust balls, graphite lumps, or foreign material. Manufacturing personnel are also responsible for cleaning the hoppers before screening, to remove any powder or graphite buildup which may be accumulating.
  2. During the setup, the press operator is responsible for checking all thickness dimensions, overall density, and section densities, as well as for detecting any cracks or shear which may be in the part.
  3. During the production run, the press operator makes visual checks, dimensional checks, overall density and section density checks a minimum of once per hour. These results are entered into an operator's log book. An operator who is having difficulties is required to make as many checks as necessary to ensure that quality is being maintained.

- Inspection Responsibilities:

  1. After a new setup, a line inspector checks all sizes, overall density, and section densities, and makes a visual check for imperfections on the part prior to giving setup approval.
  2. Inspection personnel are required to make visual, size, and density checks two times per shift for each press.

The results are then entered into an inspection log, and notations are made of any problems found.

Sintering Quality Control

As the parts are being sintered or sintered and hardened, quality responsibilities are divided as follows:

- Manufacturing Responsibilities:

  1. During setup, the furnace operator is responsible for setting the belt speed, dew point, and temperatures, and for belt loading. As the first pieces exit the furnace, the operator checks for sizes and hardness and performs any physical testing that may be required.
  2. During the production run, the furnace operator is responsible every hour for measuring critical dimensions and hardness and for any physical testing. He also checks dew point, belt speed, and temperatures every hour. All of this information is entered into the operator's log book.

- Inspection Responsibilities:

  1. After a setup, the line inspector takes some of the first parts out of the furnace, checks dimensions and hardness, performs any necessary physical testing, and visually inspects the parts.
  2. During production sintering, the inspector makes the same checks as the line inspector, two times per shift. This information is entered into the inspection log book.

- Metallurgical Engineering Responsibilities:

  Every week, inspection personnel submit sintered samples to metallurgical engineering personnel as an audit of sintering practices. One sample per furnace per material specification is submitted for microexamination and cross-sectional hardness. If problems with dew point, hardness, or functional tests occur during daily sintering runs, samples are submitted to engineering personnel for disposition.

Steam oxidation quality control. If parts are being steam oxidized for pressure tightness, three pieces from each furnace load are checked for hardness and leak resistance.

Final inspection quality control. As the parts are finished, the line inspector makes a final quality check. Parts from each load are randomly selected, checked for accuracy of all dimensions and hardness, and inspected visually. Any necessary physical tests or pressure tightness checks also are performed. The audit frequency is strictly dependent upon the past quality history of the particular parts, materials, or processing.

NONDESTRUCTIVE EVALUATION

The problems inherent in obtaining accurate and meaningful data useful in quality control have prompted the development and application of nondestructive tests particularly suited for powder metallurgy materials. In one method the specimen is excited by a piezoelectric or electromagnetic transducer. At the fundamental resonant frequency, the amplitude of vibration reaches a maximum. Another technique consists of measuring the ultrasonic velocity by placing transducers on opposite faces of a specimen and measuring the time necessary to transmit a pulse.

QUALITY CONTROL

Nondestructive techniques, such as ultrasonic velocity and resonant frequency measurements, hold considerable promise for evaluating the quality of PM parts. A principal benefit of these techniques is that they can provide nondestructive assessment of pore size, pore shape, and the extent of interparticle bonding, in addition to detecting gross flaws, such as cracks. This is an especially valuable capability with PM materials, which often exhibit wide ranges of strength arising from variations in processing variables and powder characteristics, even when cracks are not present.

Variations in sintering time, temperature, atmosphere, powder type, contaminants, and other variables can produce parts that appear sound but have undesirably low mechanical properties. The ability to rapidly assess the extent of sintering in individual parts is a useful technique for monitoring product quality.

Data Correlation

The ultrasonic velocity through a material is the speed of transmission of a high-frequency (MHz range) sound wave. The velocity is dependent on the interatomic forces in the metal, but microstructural features have an important effect. In recent years it has been found that the microstructural characteristics which control the mechanical strength of some materials, such as PM and cast irons, also control their ultrasonic velocity.

Figure 17-49 compares mechanically measured tensile strengths with nondestructively predicted strengths for specimens sintered for 20 min. Very little deviation existed between the predicted and the actual strength values. Most predicted values differed no more than 1 or 2 ksi from the measured values, and the greatest deviation was 4 ksi. The correlation of velocity and resonant frequency with both yield and tensile strength indicates that these methods provide a useful nondestructive means for assessing quality of PM parts.

Testing of Production Parts

Ultrasonic velocity and resonant frequency measurements have been used to get information on the extent of sintering in PM materials. In practice, differences in the techniques used to take the measurements and differences in part size and shape may affect the choice of equipment and technique to be used. Ultrasonic velocity measurements can be taken by placing a small [approximately 1/2″ (13 mm) diam] transducer on one flat surface and measuring the time required to receive a reflected signal. Alternatively, two transducers can be used on plane parallel surfaces of a part. The shape of the part is not as important as the ability to transmit the sound wave from one

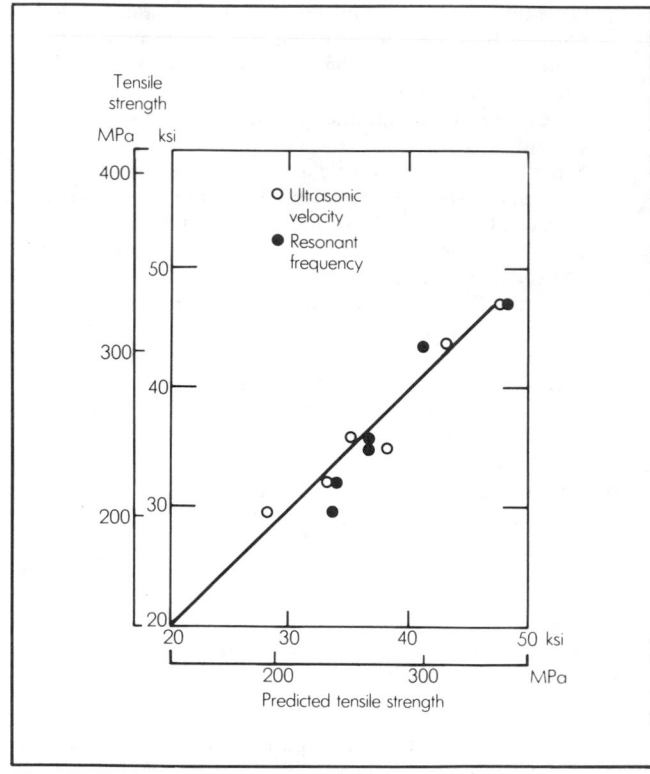

Fig. 17-49 Comparison between measured strength and strength predicted from ultrasonic velocity and resonant frequency.

surface to the other. Curved transducers are available for testing curved parts. The ultrasonic velocity measurement is quick and relatively simple to perform, and a variety of equipment for industrial use is available.

Ultrasonic velocity is influenced to some extent by the length and thickness of the part, and subtle differences in measurement technique can result in different measured values. Measurements of similarly shaped parts by a consistent technique should provide a good comparison of material properties.

Resonant frequency is measured by vibrating an exciter plate adjacent to the part being examined. At the resonant frequency, the part vibrates at an increased amplitude which is detected by a pick-up plate. The frequency of vibration depends on the part shape as well as sintering conditions, but comparison of similar parts eliminates the shape variable and allows evaluation of the extent of sintering.

SAFETY

Until recent years, powder metallurgy has worked with comparatively safe materials such as tungsten carbide, copper, tin, brass, nickel, and iron. Now, aluminum, magnesium, titanium, zirconium, and even uranium are being processed by powder metallurgy and, therefore, special precautions must be taken to avoid the hazards of fire and explosions.

Metal powders of even such active materials as aluminum, magnesium, titanium, and zirconium can be used with complete safety if dust clouds are avoided and proper precautions

are taken in handling them to avoid sources of ignition or chemical reaction. Manufacturers of PM parts should thoroughly review their plant operations and establish the appropriate safety procedures.

For employee/operator protection, various safety procedures and devices are applicable. Among the latest developments are retrofit units that utilize infrared light to provide a safety "curtain" as an invisible protective barrier on PM compacting machines. These devices are connected into the emergency-stop circuit of mechanical clutches and hydraulic compactors. Also included among safety devices are capacitance-type (radio frequency), optical, and ultrasonic presence-sensing devices.

EXPLOSION HAZARDS

The Bureau of Mines' laboratories have investigated dust explosions for over 30 years and have published a number of reports detailing their extensive findings. The summary in Table 17-18 is based on the ignition and explosion characteristics of each metal compared with coal, which is the dividing point between moderate and strong explosions. While this is a useful guide to the relative explosibility hazard, fires and/or explosions have occurred with iron, lead, nickel, and zinc when in extremely fine form (with resulting high surface area). The Bureau of Mines has tested a variety of screen sizes on various metals and found that explosibility increases with the fineness of powders. There are many indications that practically all metal dusts can become explosive if they are fine enough—and powders are continually being made finer.

Fire Hazard Avoidance

A fire or an explosion is a chemical reaction which has three requirements: fuel, a source of ignition, and oxidant. A fire or an explosion can be prevented by removing any one of these factors.

Dust. If no dust cloud is present, there will be no fuel; so metal powder users should avoid the formation of dust clouds. Equipment should be designed to avoid the open dumping of powder. Proper ventilation and dust collection equipment should be used wherever dust clouds may occur. Good housekeeping is also essential, since dust accumulating on high horizontal places, such as rafters and windowsills, can be easily dislodged by drafts, bumps, and other means to create a dust cloud.

Ignition. Open-ignition sources can be prevented in the powder-handling area, and this is sufficient for the less dangerous metal powders. But the active metals such as aluminum, magnesium, titanium, and zirconium require additional care, since static electricity or small sparks can set them off. The following precautions are necessary to eliminate potential sources of ignition throughout the area in which such powders are to be handled:

1. Electrical grounding of all equipment, including all containers should be thorough. Because static cannot be grounded through an oil or grease film in bearings, it is necessary to provide wire "jumpers" around lubricating films.
2. All electric wiring equipment and lighting in the area involved must be explosion proof, conforming to National Electrical Manufacturers Association (NEMA) rating Class II, Group E.
3. All sources of mechanical friction should be eliminated wherever a dust cloud can exist.
4. When tools are required, nonsparking types should be used. It is important to remember that friction, as by hammering, sliding, or rubbing, etc., must be avoided, even with nonsparking-type tools.
5. Sparks caused by metal striking metal must be avoided.
6. Open flames in the area where the powders are being handled must be avoided. No smoking should be permitted.
7. All equipment and the surrounding area should be completely cleaned before repairs are made, particularly if a torch or welding equipment is to be used in the area.

Oxidant. The oxidant can be made ineffective or removed from the mixture, and this should always be done when a dust cloud is being created, as in the blending of metal powders. When possible, it is preferable to use premix powders and let the powder producer assume the responsibility of performing the hazardous blending operation.

Explosive Mix Precautions

To eliminate an explosive mix, it is not generally necessary to remove all the oxygen. The Bureau of Mines has studied the effect of various mixtures of inert gases with air—a process referred to as "inerting." The Bureau has published data for

TABLE 17-18
Explosibility of Metal Powders

Severe	Strong	Moderate	Weak	None
Atomized aluminum	Titanium hydride	Silicon	Aluminum-iron	Aluminum-bronze alloy
Aluminum premixes	Zirconium hydride	Boron	alloy	Beryllium-bronze alloy
Aluminum-magnesium alloy	Aluminum-silicon alloy	Aluminum-nickel alloy	Zinc	Manganese-bronze alloy
Magnesium	Calcium silicide	Aluminum-lithium alloy	Gold bronze	Nickel
Thorium hydride	Iron-carbonyl	Aluminum-cobalt alloy	Ferrosilicon	Selenium
Zirconium	Ferrotitanium	Ferromanganese	Vanadium	Stainless steel
Uranium hydride	Coal	Aluminum-copper alloy	Antimony	
Titanium		Chromium	Cadmium	
Uranium		Manganese	Ferrovanadium	
Thorium		Tantalum	Ferrochromium	
		Tin	Lead	
		Iron-hydrogen reduced	Tellurium	
			Molybdenum	
			Cobalt	
			Tungsten	
			Beryllium	
			Copper	

most reactive metal powders, indicating the maximum amount of oxygen which may be present when inerting with carbon dioxide or nitrogen.

Atmosphere. Great care must be taken in selecting a suitable atmosphere, since many metals react with supposedly inert gases. The limiting percent of oxygen for 100-mesh atomized aluminum ranges from 3% with an air-CO_2 mixture to 9% with air-N_2. Most magnesium, titanium, uranium, and zirconium powders cannot be inerted with CO_2, while the oxygen content must be less than 2-3% with air-N_2 mixtures. Helium is generally recommended for inerting magnesium, and is probably advisable with titanium, uranium, zirconium, etc.

Before inerting, reference should be made to the Bureau of Mines report and the National Fire Protection Association standard, and operations should be conducted well below the minimum oxygen levels indicated. When a mixture of powder is to be inerted, it may be necessary to run special explosibility tests to determine a safe atmosphere, particularly if CO_2 might be the inerting ingredient.

Blending. The blending of metal powders is probably the most hazardous operation undertaken by a powder metallurgy plant. The blending equipment must be filled with the protective atmosphere before powder is charged into it, and any other equipment or container must be similarly purged prior to receiving the product. Care must be exercised to minimize dust clouds when filling or discharging the powder, even with the above precautions; and all sources of ignition must be avoided, as previously discussed. The blender should be operated at the lowest practical speed to avoid abrading the powder particles.

Dust collection. In operating a dust collection system, special precautions are necessary because of the suspension of the finest metal dust in air. The powder should be conveyed in a concentration well below that designated as the "minimum explosive limit." A dry collector, operated where dust is concentrated, will contain an explosive dust cloud and must be located in an isolated area well away from any source of ignition. No personnel should be allowed in the immediate vicinity of the collector while it is operating.

Wet collectors, which collect dust under water, are safer, but the metal powder usually ends up as scrap. Since chemical reactions between water and metal are possible with the evolution of hydrogen and the development of heat, sources of ignition must be avoided in the gas-stream discharge. The sludge containing the metal powder should be brought to a safe area as soon as possible so that the reaction can proceed to its conclusion. When working with metal powders, one should also be careful that combinations of metal powders, together or with other chemicals, are safe. The well-known thermite mixture of aluminum powder and iron oxide is safe under controlled conditions, but could cause trouble under certain circumstances.

Halogenated hydrocarbons. The National Aeronautics and Space Administration (NASA) has investigated the reactions of metal powders with halogenated hydrocarbons and has concluded that great care should be exercised when combining any metal powder with any halogenated hydrocarbon. Aluminum, magnesium, titanium, barium, lithium, and beryllium have been found to explode on impact with various halogenated hydrocarbons including Freon MF, Freon TF, carbon tetrachloride, trichloroethylene, and perchloroethylene. This problem could arise with the use of an aerosol lubricant spray on the compacting press (which would supply the necessary impact).

FIRE FIGHTING

Special fire fighting procedures must be planned for areas containing metal dusts, particularly those of active metals. The local fire department should be advised of the plans, and the plant personnel should be carefully trained.

Drums in a storage area would probably not be subject to a fire, but they should be kept cool. Extreme heat may increase the pressure of the air in the drums to the point at which the drums would burst.

Loose Powder Fire

Loose metal powder is not generally processed or stored in the vicinity of combustible material, so it is unlikely that a metal powder fire will occur. If a fire should develop in the area of loose metal powder, it should be left alone to burn out by itself. Dry sand can be carefully spread on the fire, working from the outside edges to avoid creating a dust cloud. Many of the more dangerous materials from an explosive standpoint, such as atomized aluminum, magnesium, and titanium, require a high temperature before igniting and probably would not ignite. However, uranium ignites spontaneously, and zirconium, gold, bronze, and many hydrides ignite at less than 400°F (204°C).

Streams of water or gas (for instance, from a carbon dioxide extinguisher) should be avoided, since they could stir up a dust cloud that could result in an explosion. It is most important that the fire department be aware of this and of the plant areas requiring special precautions. Plant fire-protection systems should be designed so that automatic sprinklers and CO_2 jets used for building protection do not contact the metal powders in such fashion that they stir up dust.

Fire Fighting Residue

The residues of fires and fire fighting may also be hazardous. For example, the following reactions can occur, resulting in heat and/or dangerous gases:

1. Metal + H_2O $\longrightarrow$ metal oxide + H_2 = heat
2. Metal + CO_2 $\longrightarrow$ metal oxide + C
   Metal + CO_2 $\longrightarrow$ metal oxide + CO
3. Metal + CCl_4 $\longrightarrow$ metal chloride + C + heat

Temperatures above 9000°F (5000°C) are possible from these reactions. Therefore, it is important to be very careful when cleaning up after a fire. If powder is in a container, it can be moved to an isolated location and left until the reaction ceases and the drum cools. If the drum is sealed, the cover should be gently loosened to relieve the pressure and the powder should be left to burn itself out.

References

1. Joel S. Hirschhorn, *Introduction to Powder Metallurgy*, (New York: American Powder Metallurgy Institute, 1969).
2. Fritz V. Lenel, *Powder Metallurgy Principles and Applications*, (Princeton, NJ: Metal Powder Industries Federation, 1980).
3. American Society for Testing and Materials, *Definitions of Terms Used in Powder Metallurgy*, ASTM Standard B243, Philadelphia.

4. B. H. Amstead, Phillip F. Ostwald, Myron L. Begeman, *Manufacturing Processes*, 7th ed., (New York: John Wiley & Sons, 1979).
5. H. W. Blakeslee, *Powder Metallurgy in Aerospace Research*, NASA SP-5098, (Philadelphia: Franklin Institute; and Washington: NASA, 1971).
6. Samuel Bradbury, ed., *Source Book on Powder Metallurgy*, (Metals Park, OH: American Society for Metals, 1979).
7. Hoeganaes Corp., *Creating with Metal Powders*, 5th ed., (Riverton, NJ: Hoeganaes Corp., 1979).
8. American Society for Testing and Materials, *op. cit.*
9. *Ibid.*
10. Lenel, *op. cit.*
11. Powder Metallurgy Equipment Association, *Powder Metallurgy Equipment Directory*, 13th ed., (Princeton, NJ: Metal Powder Industries Federation, 1982).
12. John A. Schey, *Introduction to Manufacturing Processes*, (New York: McGraw-Hill, 1977).
13. Powder Metallurgy Equipment Association, *op. cit.*
14. Schey, *op. cit.*
15. Loren C. Bone, "Quality Control System of P/M at Caterpillar Tractor Co." (technical paper), Metal Powder Industries Federation, Princeton, NJ. 1982.

CASTING

Casting is a manufacturing process in which molten metal is poured or injected and allowed to solidify in a suitably shaped mold cavity. During or after cooling, the cast part is removed from the mold and then processed for delivery.

Casting processes and cast-material technologies vary from simple to highly complex. Material and process selection depends on the part's complexity and function, the product's quality specifications, and the projected cost level. Table 18-1 indicates the range of materials that are feasible for use in parts made by various commonly used casting processes.[1]

CASTING MOLD ELEMENTS

In Fig. 18-1, a typical green-sand mold section is depicted to illustrate the various basic elements that are common to most casting processes. In most casting processes, the term used to describe the molds are the same. Molds are usually, but not always, made in two halves. Exceptions are the investment casting and coreless casting processes, in which one-piece molds are used, and die casting and permanent or semipermanent-mold casting, which may use molds or dies made up of more than two parts for casting complex shapes.

In most processes, the upper half of the mold is called the cope and the lower half is referred to as the drag. Cores made of sand or metal are placed in the mold cavity to form inner surfaces of the casting. The mold requires a gating system to distribute metal in the mold and risers (liquid reservoirs) to feed the casting as it solidifies. The sprue is the channel, usually vertical, through which the metal enters. A runner, usually horizontal, leads the metal into the mold. The metal leaves the runner through a gate to enter the mold cavity or a riser above or adjacent to the cavity. A riser is a reservoir connected to the cavity to provide liquid metal to the casting to offset shrinkage as the casting solidifies.

GENERAL CHARACTERISTICS

In many applications, castings offer cost and performance advantages because their shape, composition, structure, and properties can be tailored for a specific end product. The precision casting processes also offer near-net-shape economic benefits in materials, labor, and energy usage.

Except for certain high-volume production items, such as automotive parts, cast materials usually are produced in batches or melt-lot quantities that are smaller than those obtained from typical wrought-material production runs; hence, castings may more easily be made to accommodate specific application requirements.

Casting Properties

Castings generally exhibit nondirectional properties. Wrought metals, on the other hand, usually are anisotropic—stronger and tougher in one direction than in another. Some casting processes do, however, provide directional strength properties that can be utilized by part designers and manufacturing engineers to increase performance of the finished part.

In some instances, the properties and performance attainable in cast components cannot be obtained readily by other manufacturing methods. For example:

- Cast iron has desirable wear and damping properties for air-conditioner crankshaft and diesel engine cylinder liner applications.
- Compacted graphite (a recent cast iron alloy development) offers the heat and wear-resisting characteristics of gray iron and the strength approaching nodular iron.
- Cast bearing alloys have a controlled dispersion of lubricating materials.
- High rupture strength superalloy airfoils are made possible by the use of nonmachinable cast alloys with creep resistance superior to that of wrought materials.
- Castings allow the manufacture of parts from alloys that are difficult or impossible to machine or forge, and are especially advantageous for cored internal passages.
- Fine equiaxed, directionally solidified, single-crystal, eutectic structures provide a variety of useful properties made possible by modern casting processes and material technology.

For simple shapes, near-net-shape castings often cannot compete economically with forgings. However, the casting processes offer a design flexibility and a capability for size and configuration complexity that are beyond the usual limits for feasible or economic use of the forging techniques. Castings are best used for complex part geometries—components that would require considerable machining and multipiece assembly if made by other processes.

Mold Considerations

Molds are generally made by surrounding a pattern with a mixture of granular refractory and binder. This mixture may be dry or wet, and the composition varies with the mold and casting materials that are used. The choice of mold material depends on casting quality and quantity requirements, as well as on metal temperature and chemical reactivity.

The mold cavity is designed to be oversize to compensate for volume changes due to liquid-to-solid-phase transformations and thermal contraction. The pattern provides the shape and size of the cavity into which the molten metal is poured. Gates and risers may be attached to the pattern or molded in separately. The casting manufacturer generally uses tapered sections, chills, risers, insulation, and hot tops to provide adequate soundness through directional solidification.

Internal surfaces are formed by casting against

GENERAL CHARACTERISTICS

TABLE 18-1
Commercial Capability of Casting Processes

Process	Ductile Iron	Steel	Stainless Steel	Aluminum, Magnesium	Bronze, Brass	Gray Iron	Malleable Iron	Zinc, Lead
Die casting				•	•			•
Continuous	•				•	•		•
Investment	•	•	•	•				
Ceramic cope & drag	•	•	•	•	•	•		•
Permanent mold				•	•	•		•
Plaster mold				•	•			•
Centrifugal	•	•	•		•	•		•
Resin shell	•	•	•	•	•	•	•	
Sand	•	•	•	•	•	•	•	•

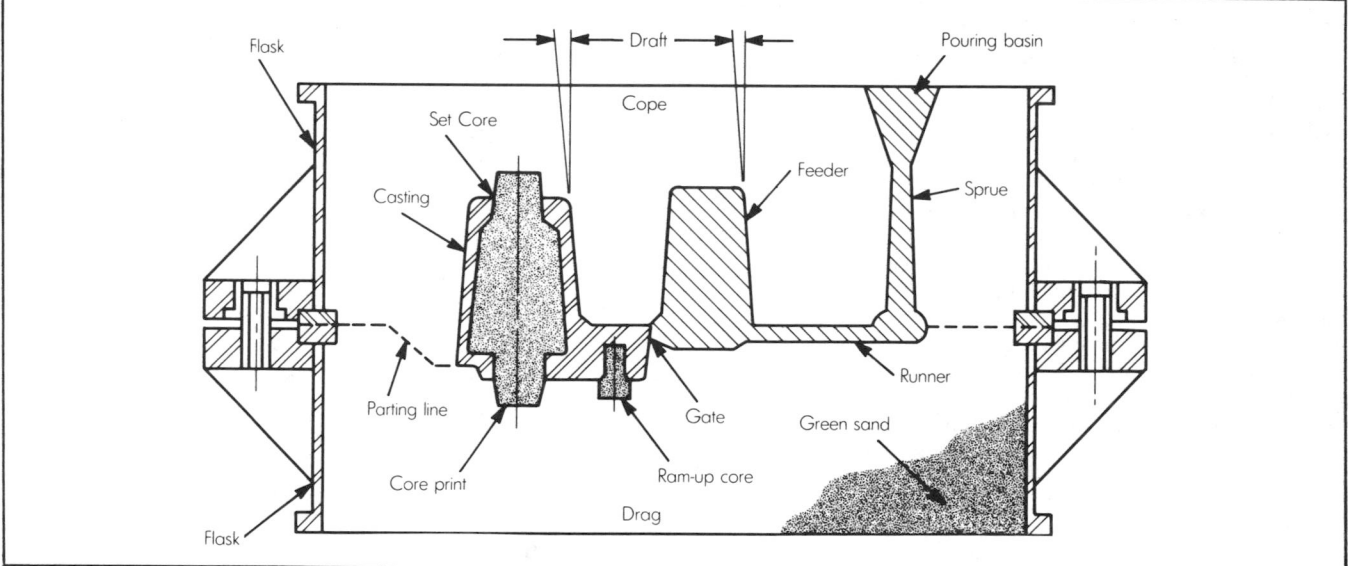

Fig. 18-1 Cross-section view of typical cored casting and the sand mold in which it is produced. (*Iron Castings Society, Inc.*)

cores. Cores are generally made from a similar mold material that offers a greater resistance to the physically harsh and chemically reactive environment in the mold cavity before and during solidification. Hollow parts may also be made by one of the coreless casting techniques, such as centrifugal casting and slush casting.

After the binder hardens sufficiently, the pattern is removed. Sometimes special mold coatings are applied to improve the casting surface finish or reduce cleaning costs. A variation of this practice is found in evaporative-pattern (full-mold) casting, in which a shape made from low-density, expanded polystyrene is left in the sand to evaporate when hot metal is poured into the mold. Another variation is the use of permanent molds that may be reused several thousand times.

The mold is such an important aspect of most casting processes that the name of the molding process and the type of mold media are commonly used to identify the processes used to make castings. Examples include no-bake sand-molded steel

castings, green sand-molded brass castings, and investment-molded nickel-based superalloy castings.

PROCESS SELECTION

The casting processes most often used are identified broadly as sand-mold casting, metal-mold casting, and plaster and ceramic-mold casting. As illustrated by the format used for Table 18-2 (see page 18-4), the major metal casting processes also can be characterized and grouped based on whether a reusable pattern with expendable mold, a reusable mold, or an expendable mold and pattern are employed in the process.

Each casting process has certain inherent advantages and limitations. Size and shape of the casting, dimensional accuracy and tolerance, surface finish, metallurgical properties, choice of alloys, production quantities, and cost all enter into the choice of a molding and casting process. Many sand castings, for example, have low labor and finishing cost; others are cleaned but are not ground or machined. A comparison of the molding processes with respect to these and other factors is given in Table 18-3 (see page 18-6), and a comparative rating of the processes is given in Table 18-4 (see page 18-7). For the highest quality, most cost-effective application of a casting method, advantages of the method must be fully used and its limitations must be recognized.

Effective operation of a foundry requires careful attention to the basics—part geometry, molding, gating, heat transfer, melt and mold materials, metal chemistry, cleanliness, and safety.

Process control is vitally important, because the foundry has more process variables than most other manufacturing operations. A good process control system forces the identification and understanding of key process parameters and their interrelationships. Productivity and consistent casting quality result from knowing and controlling key parameters within critical ranges. Experience indicates that a well-controlled foundry process affords an opportunity to reduce basic material costs by 25-30% while maintaining casting quality at the desired level.

SAND-MOLD CASTING

One of the main advantages of sand-mold casting is the flexibility it permits in shaping the part so that the imposed load is distributed evenly throughout the part for minimum stress concentration. When well-designed castings are used, stress concentrations can be reduced as much as 50%, and in many cases significant increases in service life and strength can be achieved.

DESIGN CONSIDERATIONS

To ensure maximum dispersal of stress, minimum stress concentration, and the most effective configuration for the function of a given design, the following guidelines are applicable to sand-mold castings:

1. External corners should be rounded with radii that are 10-20% of the section thickness (see Fig. 18-2). Rounded corners increase resistance of ductile metals to fatigue rupture, increase static strength of gray iron in bending by 4-7%, and increase gray iron's deflection by 10-20%. Rounding of corners is also the most efficient method of decreasing, or eliminating, chilled edges in gray-iron castings. If a notation to round all external corners is included in the part drawing, the patternmaker must provide for rounded corners at partings and at core prints.

2. Radii equal to the thickness of the smaller section are used when sections of dissimilar size are joined or when L or T junctions are used. This proportioning provides significant increases in resistance to fatigue stresses in all metals and in resistance to static stresses in gray iron (see Figs. 18-3 and 18-4). A radius equal to the section thickness, as shown in Fig. 18-3, b, has a 40-50% higher

endurance limit than a sharp corner, as shown in view a. A further increase in fillet radius to 4t, as shown in view c, increases the endurance limit to 120% more than that of view a. Figure 18-4 shows the average fatigue life of ⅝" (16 mm) thick sections with fillets stressed in tension to a maximum fiber stress of approximately 50,000 psi (345 MPa).

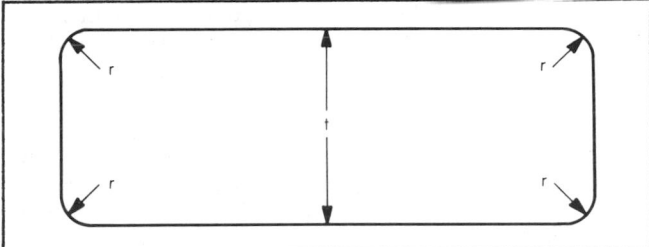

Fig. 18-2 Sand-casting external corner radii guideline: r = 0.10 to 0.20t.

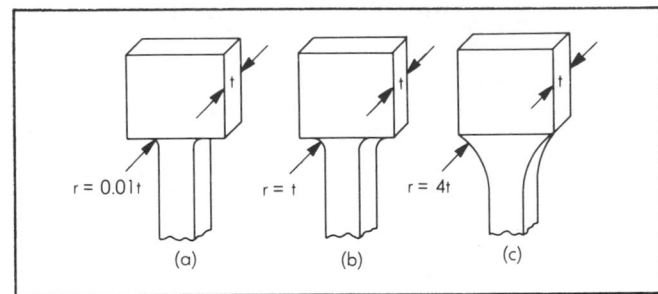

Fig. 18-3 Sand-casting gillet radii comparison for stress endurance and fatigue strength.

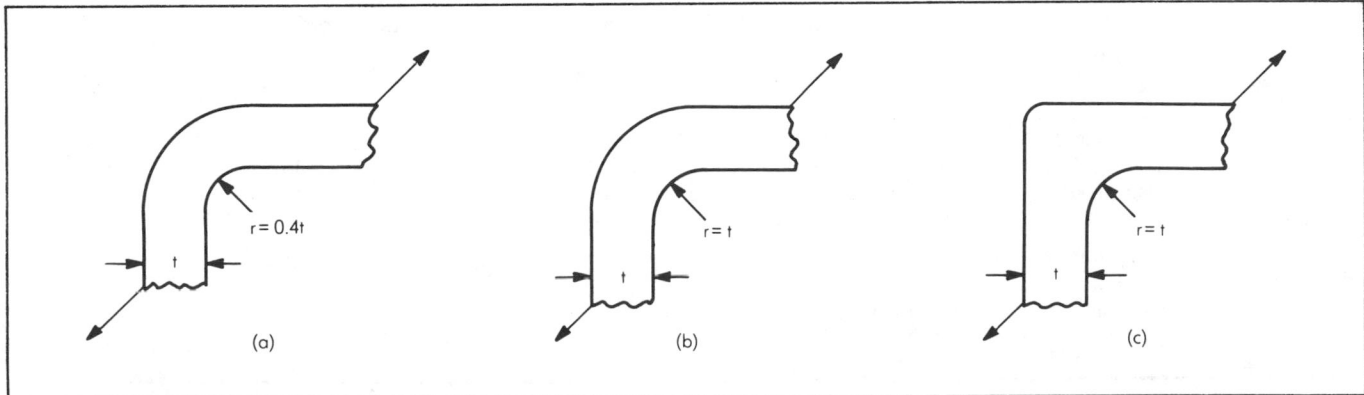

Fig. 18-4 Average fatigue life of cast fillets tension-stressed to 50 ksi (345 MPa): (a) 270,000 cycles; (b) 1,850,000 cycles; (c) 5,900,000 cycles.

SAND-MOLD CASTING

TABLE 18-2

Metal Casting Processes

	Process	Description	Metals Used	Equipment Cost
			Characteristics	
Reusable pattern expendable mold	Sand Mold	Mold made by ramming sand around wood or metal pattern. Sand bonded with clay or chemicals. V-process uses vacuum to attain mechanical bond.	All common metals	Low
	Shell mold	Sand coated with thermosetting resin is poured over heated metal pattern to form a shell. Halves are stripped and assembled.	Primarily ferrous, copper, aluminum	Moderate
	Plaster mold	Molds made by casting plaster around pattern. Molds are baked after pattern removal.	Mainly aluminum, copper	Moderate
	Ceramic mold	Slurry of ceramic aggregate and binder, poured over pattern and chemically set. Resultant mold is stabilized and high-temperature cured. Molds can be poured hot or at room temperature.	All common metals	Moderate
Reusable mold	Die casting (pressure die casting)	Molten metal is forced into metallic die under high pressure. In hot-chamber machines (for zinc), metal is pumped into die. In cold-chamber units (for aluminum), metal is ladled into shot chamber.	Primarily zinc, aluminum, magnesium. Some copper and steel	Very high
	Low-pressure casting	Gas pressure (under 20 psi) is used to inject molten metal into a permanent mold.	Primarily aluminum	High
	Permanent-mold casting	Metal is poured into permanent molds made from metal or graphite.	Primarily nonferrous. Some iron and steel	High
	Centrifugal casting	Permanent or sand-lined mold for a symmetrical part, such as pipe, is rotated rapidly around its longitudinal axis. Centrifugal force distributes molten metal evenly along mold.	Most metals	High
	Squeeze casting	Combines casting and forging in one mold.	Primarily nonferrous	
Expendable pattern and mold	Investment casting (lost-wax process)	A wax pattern is coated with a refractory shell by casting or dipping. Assembly is then heated to melt out the wax pattern. Metal is cast into ceramic mold.	Steels, high-temperature alloys, nonferrous metals	High
	Evaporative pattern (full-mold process)	Pattern is made from foamed polystyrene. Sand is rammed around pattern. When metal is poured into mold, pattern vaporizes.	All metals, mainly iron.	Low

TABLE 18-2—*Continued*

Characteristics				
Tooling Cost	Labor Cost	Tolerances and Surface Finish	Usual Size Range	Status
Low	Low to moderate	Fair	Small to extremely large	Most widely used process for ferrous metals for both small and large-production runs. Various binder systems available.
Moderate	Low to moderate	Fair to good	Small to 100 lb (45 kg)	Used for production of fairly small parts for which closer tolerances are required than are obtainable from sand castings. Widely used for cores.
Moderate	High	Very good	Small to 100 lb (45 kg)	Used for some precision nonferrous castings in moderate quantity. Thin walls can be cast. This casting process is not widely used.
Moderate	Moderate	Excellent	Less than 100 lb (45 kg); sometimes several tons	Unicast and Shaw processes are most common versions. Used for precision casting, particularly for tools and dies. A special-purpose, relatively expensive process.
Very high	Low to moderate	Excellent	Small to over 50 lb (23 kg)	Very widely used for high production of aluminum and zinc castings. An inexpensive way of obtaining precision parts.
High	Low to moderate	Excellent	Under 50 lb (23 kg)	Widely used in Britain; only a few installations in the United States are used for quantities between those produced by die and permanent-mold processes.
High	Moderate	Good	1 to 50 lb (0.5-23 kg)	Used for moderate quantities of semi-precision castings. Is normally less expensive than sand casting for hundreds of parts or a few thousand parts. Limited applicability for ferrous metals.
Moderate	Low to moderate	Fair to good	Large—over 100 lb (45 kg)	Used mainly for producing pipe and large cylinders in large quantities.
High	Low to moderate	Good	Small to 8 lb (4 kg)	Hybrid process, used to obtain design freedom of casting combined with properties and structural integrity of forging. Compatible with wide range of metals.
High	High	Excellent	Very small to 5 lb (2 kg) and over	Used for precision castings, particularly for gas turbine engines. A specialized process usually performed in foundries not used for other processes.
Low to moderate	Low to moderate	Fair	5 lb (2 kg) and larger	Beginning to be used for low-production, complex casting such as machine tool frames. No draft needed in castings since pattern is not removed. Patterns are easy to machine.

(SRI International)

SAND-MOLD CASTING

TABLE 18-3
Summary of Molding and Casting Processes

	Sand	Shell Mold	Permanent Mold	Die Casting
Choice of materials*	1,2,3,4,5,6,7,8,9,10,11	1,2,3,4,5,6,9	1,3,4,5,6,7,8,10,11	4,5,7,8,10,11
Complexity of part	Considerable, limited by pattern drawing. No limit with cores.	Considerable, limited by removal of mold from pattern. Less limited with cores.	Limited, restricted by the rigid molds. Ability to eject casting limits shape.	Moderate, limited by design of movable cores.
Number of castings relative to tool life	Wide range, type of pattern depends upon total castings.	High, metal patterns have a long life.	Moderate to high, casting metal affects life of mold.	High, mold life affected by casting metal.
Casting size or weight	1 oz (28 g) to many tons.	1 oz (28 g) to 100 lb (45 kg) and 60 in.^{2} (0.04 m^2).	Several oz (100 g) to 50 lb (23 kg).	Several oz (100 g) to 75 lb (34 kg) in aluminum, 200 lb (91 kg) in zinc. Usually under 15 lb (7 kg).
Minimum section, in. (mm)	1/8 to 1/4 (3-6) depending upon metal.	1/16 (1.6) for most materials.	3/32 (2.4) for most materials.	0.025 (0.64)
Minimum diameter cored hole, in. (mm)	3/16 to 1/4 (5-6)	1/8 to 1/4 (3-6)	3/16 to 1/4 (5-6)	1/32 to 3/16 (1-5) depending upon metal.
Surface finishes, μ in. (μm)	250-1000 (6.4-25.4)	Somewhat better than sand.	100-250 (2.5-6.4)	40-100 (1-2.5)
Precision tolerances, in. (mm)	1/16 to 11/64 (1.6-4.4) depending upon metal and casting size. Tolerance of ±0.010″ (0.25 mm) possible on some parts.	±0.003 in./in. (mm/mm); 0.003 (0.08) total possible on some dimensions.	±0.015 in./in. (mm/mm) for first in. (25 mm); 0.001-0.002″ (0.03-0.05 mm) for each additional in. (25 mm)	±0.001-0.005 (0.03-0.13) depending upon material.
Tool costs	Low	Low to moderate	Medium	High
Direct labor costs	Wide range, much hand labor required.	Moderate	Moderate	Low to medium
Finishing costs	Wide range, high to low, depends upon cleaning, snagging, and machining required.	Low, often only a minimum required.	Low to moderate	Low, little more than trimming necessary.

* 1. Gray iron	4. Aluminum alloys	7. Zinc alloys	10. Tin alloys
2. Malleable iron	5. Copper alloys	8. Magnesium alloys	11. Lead alloys
3. Steel	6. Nickel alloys	9. Heat and corrosion-resistant alloys	

3. Tapered sections and irregular sections should conform to stress patterns, particularly in bending, as illustrated in Fig. 18-5. The section modulus at the plane of maximum stress *AA* is five times greater with the tapered connecting member (view *b*) than with the straight connecting member (view *a*). This increase in section modulus decreases maximum fiber stress in bending by 60%. The lower stress concentration at *AA* in design *b* decreases maximum stress even more and is particularly important in fatigue loading.

4. Complex sections such as X, V, Y, K, and X-T junctions should be simplified to staggered T junctions and, if possible, to corrugated sections, as illustrated in Fig. 18-6. As shown in view *a*, X junctions should be simplified to staggered T junctions; and as shown in view *b*, V, Y, and K junctions should be streamlined. The X-T junctions should be staggered to T-T junctions as shown in view *c*; and if possible, stiffness should be obtained with corrugated sections such as shown in view *d* rather than with rib-stiffened plates as in *c*.

5. The largest possible radii should be used with L junctions

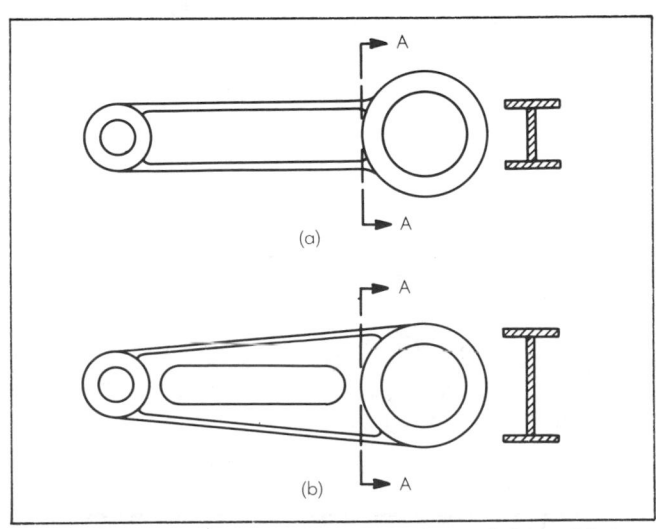

Fig. 18-5 Tapered sections increase the section modulus and fatigue strength of castings.

TABLE 18-3—Continued

Plaster Molding	Investment Casting	Centrifugal Casting	Solid Ceramic Casting
4,5	3,4,5,6,9	1,3,4,5,6,9	1,2,3,4,5,6,7,8,9,10,11
Considerable, possible to make mold of several pieces. Expendable mold.	Considerable, very complex patterns can be assembled from pieces.	Casting of circular periphery most favorable. Almost any shape can be cast.	Unlimited; almost any shape can be cast.
Moderate, depends on pattern material.	Moderate, type of pattern mold depends upon number of castings.	Low to moderate	High
1 oz (28 g) to several hundred lb in most materials.	Under 1 oz (28 g) to 100 lb (45 kg). Best for parts under 2 lb (1 kg).	1 oz (28 g) to many tons.	1 oz (28 g) to many tons.
0.030 (0.76)	0.030 (0.76)	0.030 (0.76)	0.030 (0.76)
1/2 (12.7)	0.020-0.030 (0.51-0.76)	3/16 to 1/4 (5-6)	0.020-0.030 (0.51-0.76)
30-50 (0.8-1.3)	10-85 (0.3-2.2)	100-250 (2.5-6.4) or as in sand.	30-80 (0.8-2.0)
±0.005-0.010 in./in. (mm/mm) or less	±0.005 in./in. (mm/mm)	Same as permanent mold.	±0.003 in./in. (mm/mm) for first in. (25 mm); ±0.001″ (0.03 mm) for each additional in. (25 mm).
Medium	High	Medium	Low
High-skilled operators necessary.	High, many hand operations required.	Moderate	Moderate to high
Low, little machining necessary.	Low, machining usually not necessary.	Low to moderate	Low, machining usually not necessary.

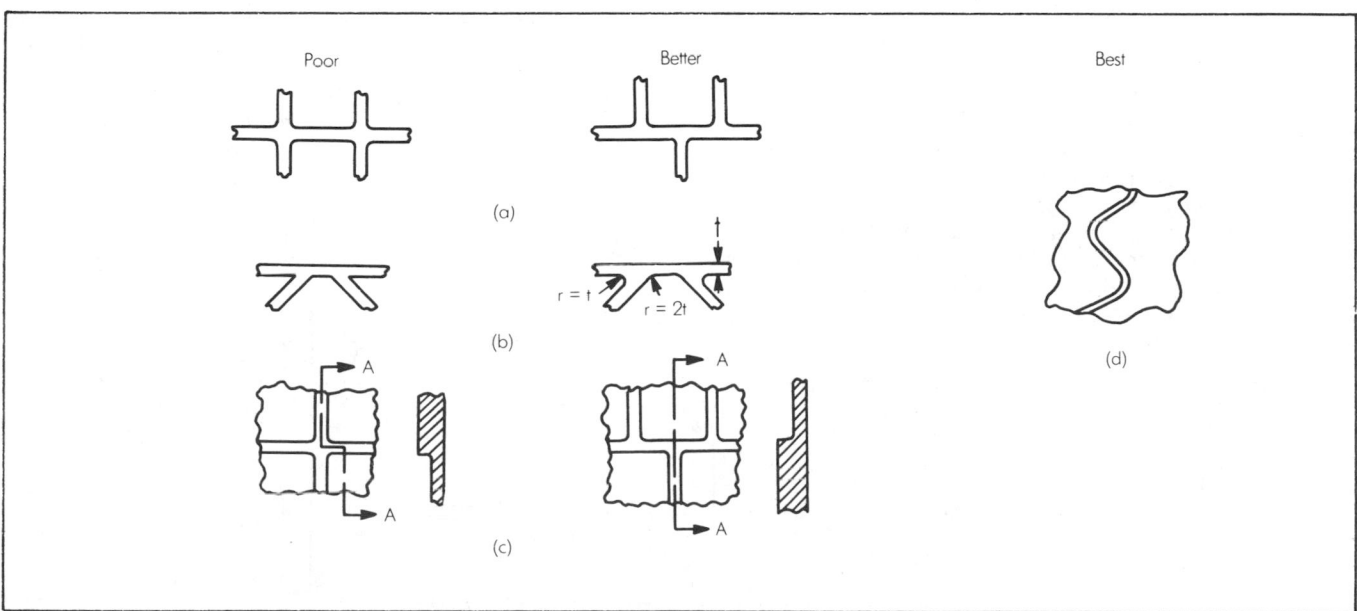

Fig. 18-6 Tubular and reinforced sections are used in castings designed to sustain complex loads.

SAND-MOLD CASTING

TABLE 18-4
Comparative Ratings of Casting Methods*

Production Method	Sand Casting	Plaster-Mold Casting	Centrifugal Casting		Permanent-Mold Casting	Die Casting	Solid Ceramic Casting
Mold material	Sand	Plaster[a]	Sand[a]	Metal[a]	Metal	Metal	Ceramic
Porosity	6	4	2	1	3	4-5 (3-4)[b]	1
Surface	6	1	5	3	4	2 (1-2)[c]	1
Tolerances	6	2	5	3	4	1	1
Strength of solid metal[d]	6	5[e]	3	2	4	1	1
Thick section	6	1	5	3	4	2	1
Speed of production for small runs[f]	1	4	2	3	3	5[g]	3
Speed of production for large runs[f]	6	5	4	2	3	1	4
Possibility to save machining	5	1	4	2	3	1	1
Cost per piece[h]	5	6	4	2	3	1	5
Tool cost	1	3	2	4	4	5	3

* Rating given in order of preference for the particular characteristic: 1 indicates first preference, 2 second preference, etc.

[a] Copper and aluminum-based alloys.

[b] Cold-chamber machines.

[c] On specially finished dies.

[d] To be considered in conjunction with tendency to porosity.

[e] For some aluminum-based alloys lower than in sand.

[f] On basis of most economical setup, as to number of impressions on gate or in mold, for comparative production quantities.

[g] The die-casting process is a high-speed production method for large quantities. If this method is selected to produce a small amount of castings for the initial order, then the choice has been made on expected closer tolerances, less machining, better surface finish, etc.

[h] The cost per piece before machining exclusive of patterns or dies.

or when joining sections with slightly varying sectional moduli. Radii of ten or more times the thickness of the section can be used.

6. For complex loads, tubular and reinforced C sections should be used rather than standard I, H, and channel sections to obtain improved load-bearing capabilities (see Fig. 18-7). For a given weight and overall size, the tubular section has moments of inertia and section moduli about the X axis that are 9-17% greater than those of the standard I section. The tubular section also has design properties about the Y axis that are 140-170% greater than those of the I section. This significant increase in properties makes the tubular section ideal for complex loading. The reinforced C or U section does not have properties about the X axis (70-90% of the I section) that are as good as those of the tubular section, yet shows even better properties about the Y axis than does the tubular section.

7. Ribs should be eliminated entirely, if at all possible, particularly those stressed in tension. Corrugated or U sections should be used instead (see Fig. 18-8).

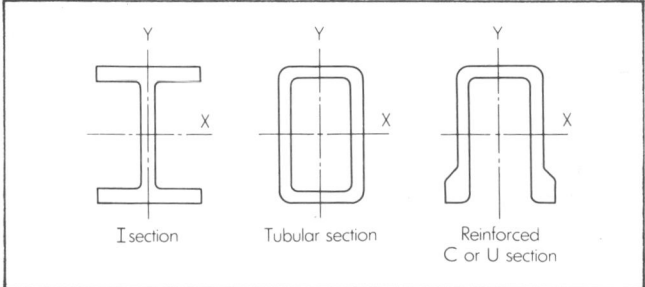

Fig. 18-7 Casting stiffness can be improved by simplifying and streamlining the cross sections.

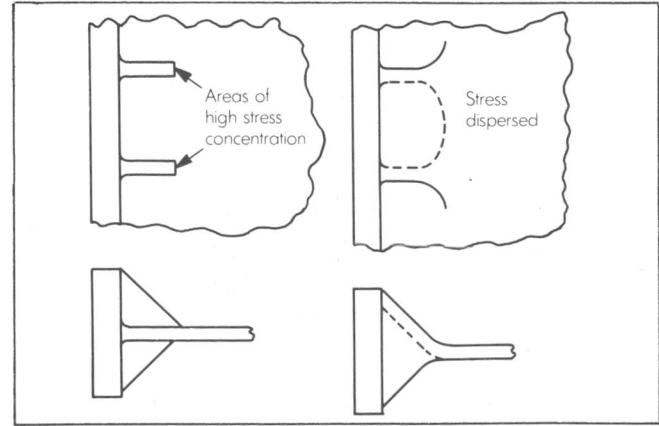

Fig. 18-8 Stress concentrations in tension-loaded castings are avoided by using U-shaped or corrugated sections instead of ribs.

GREEN-SAND MOLDING

More than 20 million product tons of castings are produced annually in the United States, and more than 90% of this foundry product is cast in sand molds, primarily green-sand molds (80%). In green-sand molding, a mold is formed around a pattern with sand-clay-water mixtures which may contain other additives. The molding medium is readily compacted; and when the pattern is removed, the compacted mass retains a reverse of the pattern's shape.

DRY-SAND MOLDING

The term *dry-sand molding* refers to the method of molding in a sand mold that has been dried after the pattern has been removed. This method is used mainly for large castings weighing up to 100 tons (91 metric tons). The drying process increases the strength of the molding sand many times. This additional strength is needed to withstand the higher static pressures of the liquid metal when casting heights are measured in feet (meters). Occasionally, the more rigid walls of dry-sand molds are used in conjunction with precision patterns to obtain more accurate casting dimensions. Generally, the dimensional tolerances and finish stock of clay-bonded, dried-mold castings are smaller than the average tolerances and finish stock for green-sand mold castings.

SHELL MOLDING

The shell molding process is used when extreme dimensional accuracy and precise duplication of intricate shapes are the principal requirements. Basically the method consists of the following steps:

1. A metal pattern (or several patterns) is placed on a metal plate.
2. The pattern is coated with a mixture of fine sand and phenolic resin, 4-6 lb (1.8-2.7 kg) of resin to each 100 lb (45 kg) of sand.
3. The pattern is heated and the resin is allowed to melt to the specified thickness.
4. The resin is cured.
5. The excess sand is dumped.
6. The hardened mold is stripped from the pattern.

The resultant "shell" duplicates the pattern in reverse, with the shape of the pattern forming either a cavity or a projection in the shell.

THE FULL-MOLD PROCESS

The full-mold or cavityless process (also known as the evaporative-pattern process) is a method of making metal castings by the use of expanded polystyrene foam patterns that eliminate the need for traditional mold cavities. Basically, the process consists of embedding the foam patterns in sand and then pouring the casting metal directly into the foam. This vaporizes the polystyrene and leaves a casting that duplicates the orignal pattern.

CEMENT MOLDING

Sand molds using a cement binder are probably the most durable of all the sand-process molds. Cement molding, also called the Randupson process, is used to form large molds for ship stools and other ship parts, and for ingots.

Cement molds are made of washed and graded silica sand to which is added 10% Portland cement mixed with 4-5% (and sometimes more) water. This mixture can be mulled like a green-sand mixture and soon sets to produce an air-dried mold of great strength which may be stored for long periods without deterioration.

Two disadvantages of cement molding are that (1) once the sand-cement mixture is mulled, it must be quickly formed around the pattern before the cement sets and (2) cement is much more expensive than green sand or dry sand for molding. The chief advantage of cement molding, maximum mold-wall rigidity, can also be a disadvantage with some shapes and metals that are subject to hot tearing.

VACUUM MOLDING

The vacuum molding method (V-Process) is a molding process in which the sand is held in place in the mold by vacuum. The mold halves are covered with a thin sheet of plastics to retain the vacuum.

Patterns are made in the usual manner; however, because they are not subject to the jolting and abrasive actions of sand, they do not have to be constructed as strongly as for conventional sand molding. The patterns can be distorted by the negative pressures, so they must be accurately supported in a pattern carrier to withstand the stresses. The pattern carrier is airtight and is evacuated by a connecting line at certain stages in the process.

METAL-MOLD CASTING

In metal-mold casting, molten metal is poured or forced into a mold made entirely of metal or into a mold in which the outer form is made of metal. The principal methods of producing castings in metal molds are high-pressure die casting, permanent and semipermanent-mold casting, low-pressure casting, and centrifugal-mold casting.

A metal-mold casting generally exhibits superior surface finish, close dimensional tolerances, and improved mechanical properties as compared to those of a sand casting. The process can be justified economically when the quantity of castings and the savings in per-piece machining justify the cost of the metal

mold and associated equipment. Refinements in mechanical metal-mold cycling that increase output, reduce machine downtime, and decrease the direct labor content have greatly increased the economic return from these casting methods.

Successful metal-mold casting requires a knowledge of (1) melting, cooling, and handling of alloys; (2) metal flow in metal molds and dies; (3) solidification and shrinkage of alloys; (4) correct gating and venting for sound casting structure; (5) tolerances as they affect mold costs and casting dimensions; and (6) required production rates. In addition, knowledge of sound mechanical concepts of mold design and automation is critical.

METAL-MOLD CASTING

HIGH-PRESSURE DIE CASTING

Die casting has long been recognized as one of the most economical and effective methods of producing moderate to high-volume quantities of near-net-shape components. The primary requirements for producing commercially acceptable high-pressure die castings (referred to hereafter as die castings) are an efficiently operating casting machine; a well-designed and well-constructed die; and a suitable casting alloy. In addition, the product must be designed for production by die casting.

In die casting, molten metal is forced under pressure into metal molds or dies. Necessary equipment consists essentially of the molds and a die-casting machine that holds, opens, and closes the molds or dies. The process is economical for producing castings with complex contours; holes and contours can be cast which would be costly to produce by machining operations. Holes are cast to tolerances that often compare with those of drilled, reamed, or counterbored holes, and surfaces and dimensions of die castings usually require little or no machining or finishing.

Die-Casting Dies

The key to successful die casting is the die. Although close attention must be given to die-casting production variables, such as cycling time, lubrication, and the composition and temperature of the casting metal, closer attention must be given to the variables that determine the surface quality and consistency of the part, which are determined by the die itself. These variables include die design, die material, and the die production method.

A die-casting die must be designed to facilitate ease of ejection of the part from the die. It must also possess the quality of thermal balance (heat input vs. heat extraction) that controls surface quality and soundness of the part and dictates cycling speed. The die must also be designed for optimum mechanical efficiency to attain consistent close tolerances and a fine finish on thousands of parts.

Single-cavity dies. A die for producing a single part consists of four components: (1) the impression blocks containing a cavity or impression identical to the casting's form, (2) the holding blocks, (3) the ejection mechanism, and (4) the die base.

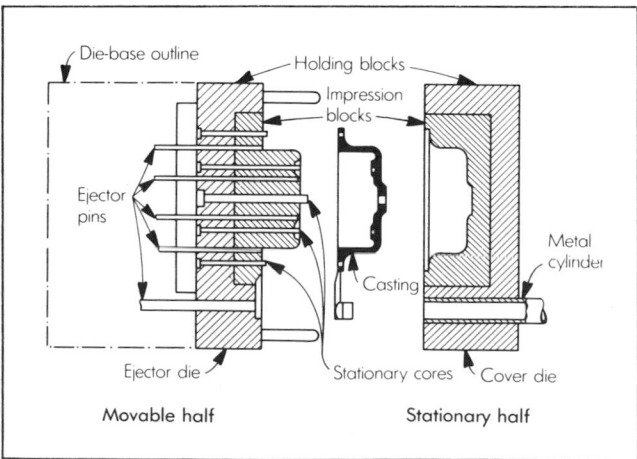

Fig. 18-9 Typical die-casting die.

A single-cavity die is shown in Fig. 18-9. All cast holes in this illustration are formed by stationary cores.

Multiple-cavity dies. Dies can be designed to produce more than one casting at the same time, providing economy if the number of dies and casting machines needed is reduced.

Coring. Cores in die-casting dies may be either stationary or movable. Again, economy and the particular application are the guides to the type of core to be used.

PERMANENT-MOLD CASTING

Permanent-mold castings are produced by forcing molten metal, under pressure of a gravity head or a low-pressure feed system, into a static mold consisting of a clamped metal assembly. In permanent-mold casting, the mold cores are also made of metal. Various metals can be cast in permanent molds, but the process is most common for the lighter nonferrous metals. When ferrous metals are cast in permanent molds, the molds are given refractory coatings to protect the surfaces from the heat and erosive action of the molten metal. It is also necessary to protect the mold when copper-based alloys are cast.

Many pressure-type castings, aircraft and missile castings, automotive pistons, pump bodies, and high-quality castings of any kind (even if the quantities required are small) are produced by the permanent-mold method. Also, the permanent-mold method is used to produce many other commercial castings because of the price advantage, superior as-cast dimensional tolerance and surface finish, and improved mechanical properties obtainable in comparison to the sand casting method. The initial cost of permanent molds is higher than that for sand casting pattern equipment; however, the lower cost of casting results in net savings over other casting methods. Weights of permanent-mold castings may range from a few ounces to 100 lb (45 kg) or more. The more complex the shape of the casting, however, the higher the cost of producing the mold and casting. In such cases, sand castings can sometimes be produced at lower cost.

Slush Casting

Slush-casting procedures are generally the same as those described for gravity permanent-mold casting. The difference between the two casting methods lies in the pouring technique. In slush casting, the mold is constructed so that it can be inverted, either automatically or manually depending on production requirements and ease of operation. The molten metal is poured into the mold and is allowed to solidify for a short time. After a thin shell of metal has solidified on the outside of the casting, the mold is inverted and the liquid metal in the center of the casting is poured out. This molding method leaves a hollow shell casting with a thickness from 1/32" to 1/2" (0.8 to 12.7 mm), depending on the time the metal is allowed to set. Slush casting has an advantage over conventional permanent-mold casting in that hollow castings with roughly defined interior passages can be produced.

Low-Pressure Permanent-Mold Casting

Although gravity is the most common method of pouring permanent-mold castings, forced low-pressure permanent-mold machines are in use. Low-pressure permanent-mold casting resembles die casting in its use of pressure to force molten metal into the mold cavity, but the pressure required is much lower than that of die casting. Usually the quality of castings, the surface finish achieved, and the tolerances attained with low-pressure casting are at least equal to those of conventional gravity permanent-mold casting.

Graphite Permanent-Mold Process

The foundry industry has long recognized the benefits of casting metal into graphite permanent molds. Graphite's superior thermal conductivity promotes rapid solidification, which results in castings that have improved surface finish and good mechanical properties. Graphite is also known for its excellent thermal stability, and it does not warp or distort when used as a die. However, graphite tends to oxidize rapidly at elevated temperatures, and relatively short mold life results when conventional ferrous and nonferrous materials are cast in graphite molds.

Semipermanent-Mold Casting

This method is identical to permanent-mold casting except internal areas of castings are formed by expendable cores.

CENTRIFUGAL CASTING

Centrifugal castings are made by pouring molten metal into a mold that is being rotated or that starts to rotate at a certain point during pouring. The centrifugal force generated by rotation forces the metal under constant pressure against the interior mold wall until it solidifies. Cylindrical parts are usually the most preferred shapes for the centrifugal-casting processes. Tubular castings produced in permanent molds by the true centrifugal-casting method have higher structural strengths and more distinct cast impressions than castings produced by the static permanent-mold or sand-mold processes.

Metals that can be cast by ordinary static casting methods, including carbon and alloy steels, high-alloy corrosion and abrasion-resistant steels, gray iron, brass, and bronze containing up to 30% lead, aluminum, and magnesium, can be cast centrifugally. In addition many other materials, including glass, plastics, and ceramics, may be centrifugally cast.

Either permanent molds or sand molds may be used for centrifugal casting. The selection of the type of mold is determined by the shape of the casting, the quality desired, and the number of castings to be produced.

PLASTER AND CERAMIC-MOLD CASTING

The general term *precision casting* is commonly used to categorize the plaster and ceramic-mold casting processes. These processes are characterized by their use of nonmetallic ceramic and plaster mold materials. The materials may be sand or sandlike materials such as aluminosilicates, materials such as gypsum plaster, or highly refractory, proprietary ceramic powders. The binders used in molding these materials range from sodium silicate to complex, proprietary organic silicate formulations. In the case of plaster, a binder is not necessary since the material is self-supporting.

The material is usually used as a fine powder suspended in the binder as a slurry. Because of the fine particle size of ceramics, molds made from ceramic materials are typified by their extreme accuracy, tolerance, and capability of reproducing extremely fine detail in as-cast parts.

The major precision-casting methods are plaster molding, investment or lost-wax casting, ceramic molding, and ceramic-core molding. Although ceramic-core molding is not really a casting method or process, the production of ceramic cores utilizes similar materials and techniques.

PLASTER MOLDING

Plaster-mold casting employs molds formed with a gypsum-plaster base. This process is basically similar to that of sand casting in that the mold, usually made in two halves corresponding to the cope and drag of sand molding, is assembled for pouring of the metal.

In plaster-mold casting, a permanent pattern is surrounded by a gypsum-based slurry that sets to a solid, self-supporting mold rigid enough to be handled. The mold parts are then stripped from the pattern and baked, or "burned out," to remove moisture. Undercut areas or internal surfaces are formed by separate pieces and cores as in sand casting. The viscosity of the plaster allows it to flow around the pattern to form a uniform mold with excellent detail and finish, using a minimum of skilled labor. The mold material does not have to be heated, rammed, vibrated, or pressed while it is being poured. This increases accuracy over a period of time and allows lightweight pattern construction; in fact, flexible patterns can be used in this process.

Setting time, usually about 20 minutes, is a disadvantage of plaster-mold casting when high production rates are required, but this disadvantage can be offset by using duplicate pattern equipment. Only alloys with casting temperatures below the dissociation temperature of gypsum can be cast by this process.

Plaster-mold castings are applied best where the need for thin walls, accuracy, and good surface finish justifies their cost. The castings may range in size from fractions of an ounce to hundreds of pounds, with the upper limit determined by the capacity of the oven.

Bladed, rotating castings such as pump and impeller parts, which do not usually lend themselves to die casting, are uniquely suitable for production by the plaster-mold method. Applications that require thin casting walls and accuracy can be made by plaster molding. Large numbers of electronic wave-guide components have been cast in plaster because the accuracy and finish required on their internal surfaces are especially difficult to obtain by sheet metal forming, machining, or hand working. All the critical dimensions of a waveguide can be formed on one core or mold part, thus improving accuracy.

INVESTMENT CASTING

Investment casting involves the formation of an expendable pattern in a die or mold and the use of the pattern to form a mold in an investment material. When the mold of investment material (refractory particles and a liquid) has set, the pattern is melted, burned, or dissolved out and the part is cast.

━━━━━━━━━━━━━━━━━━━━━━━━━━━━━━━━

PLASTER AND CERAMIC-MOLD CASTING

This process, sometimes called the lost-wax process because of the loss of the pattern during mold formation, is an ancient one and has been used traditionally to produce fine metal sculpture. In modern industry, the advent of the jet engine provided the impetus to use the investment process to fabricate difficult-to-work alloys into highly complex shapes such as hollow, air-cooled turbine blades. Parts for valves, sewing machines, locks, rifles, golf clubs, aerospace and military equipment components, and burner nozzles are a few of the applications that have demonstrated the versatility and economy of this process.

In comparison with other processes, investment casting has the following advantages:

- Complex-shaped parts can be produced close to final configuration.
- Tighter dimensional tolerances can be achieved.
- Less machining and fewer other finishing operations are usually required.
- Castings are generally sounder, with less porosity, etc.

SOLID-CERAMIC MOLDING

Solid-ceramic molding is a unique foundry process aimed at economically providing a high degree of precision and outstanding metal soundness in the production of cast parts and tooling. The process can be described as filling the gap between conventional sand foundry systems and the plaster-casting or investment-casting methods; it yields the types of tolerances normally associated with the investment process at costs often approaching those of ordinary sand molding. This method of molding has no size limitations, and castings weighing up to several tons are not uncommon. The process is commonly known as the Unicast Process or the Shaw Method and is available under a licensing arrangement.

Because the solid-ceramic process provides a high degree of accuracy and a fine surface finish (generally 65-90 μ in. [1.7-2.3 μ m] or better), castings made in ceramic molds are frequently used without further machining. This suits the process to production of tools, dies, and similar mold forms, particularly those of varied geometry that would otherwise be too time-consuming and costly to machine.

The refractory properties of ceramic molds make them capable of withstanding the high pouring temperatures of almost all castable ferrous and nonferrous alloys, including stainless and tool steels, hard cobalt alloys, high-strength bronzes and beryllium copper, aluminum, Kirksite, and magnesium.

Overall applications of solid-ceramic-mold casting can be divided into two broad categories: (1) component parts, including pump impellers, valves, and aerospace, nuclear, and ordnance castings, and (2) cast-to-size tooling, which is the largest application category.

CERAMIC CORES

Ceramic cores are widely used in the production of precision castings, particularly when the core cannot be formed integrally with the mold. The two types of ceramic cores are molded cores and extruded (injected) cores.

While ceramic cores are intended primarily for use in precision casting processes, they are also becoming more widely used in sand casting and other processes in which the internal sections of the castings formed by the core require greater accuracy and surface finish than would otherwise be obtained.

Molded Ceramic Cores

Molded ceramic cores are most commonly formed by pouring a ceramic molding slurry into a suitable corebox. They can be produced in any suitably equipped foundry. The techniques employed conform generally to the Unicast Process or the Shaw method.

Cores made by this system provide adequate strength for handling and are designed to break down readily under contracting metal pressure. Removal of the core from the finished casting is done by manual or mechanical means. The uniform breakdown properties of the core permit good accuracy with minimal resistance during casting solidification. Since most cores are made by gravity pouring, it is normally possible to use standard coreboxes throughout. Some consideration has to be given to core designs that can entrap air due to the need for filling from a small aperture, and typical in this category are cores for impeller production.

Extruded or Injected Ceramic Cores

Preformed cores are primarily intended for use in the investment-casting industry, particularly for sections that cannot be formed in the normal ceramic shell dipping process. The cores can be assembled with separately made patterns, or they can be inserted into the pattern injection die prior to injection. The cores are strong, and they normally withstand the high pressures of pattern material injection without fracture. Because of their strength and density, core removal after casting is almost invariably by a leaching technique in molten caustic salts. Special leaching techniques have also been developed using pressurized autoclaves and water solutions of caustic materials at temperatures up to 550° F (290° C).

Preformed ceramic cores are normally manufactured by extruding and injecting a specially prepared, dense ceramic paste into a suitable corebox. Because of the pressures of injection, coreboxes are normally machined metal molds. Subsequent processing of the cores requires carefully controlled firing and specialized handling. It is not customary for foundries to be able to produce cores of this type themselves; the cores must usually be purchased from an outside source.

References

1. Timothy L. Coghill, *Investment Castings Widen Applications*, SME Technical Paper MF82-337, 1982.

PRINCIPLES OF METALCUTTING AND MACHINABILITY

The purpose of this chapter is to provide an overview of the various qualitative and quantitative relationships that have been developed in attempts to describe the metalcutting phenomenon. Included in this chapter are discussions of the geometry of chip formation, forces at the cutting tool, surface finish and integrity, machinability, and metalcutting economics. When analyses are presented in metric units, U.S. customary units are omitted to simplify the presentation and to conserve space. When the analyses are presented in U.S. customary units, metric units are added parenthetically.

GEOMETRY OF CHIP FORMATION

The following is a list of symbols and abbreviations used in formulas and discussions of chip formation theory:

Symbol	Definition
B	Depth of cut (in. or mm)
b	Width of work (in. or mm)
b_c	Width of chip (in. or mm)
BUE	Built-up edge
C_s	Side cutting angle
i	Inclination angle
l	Undeformed chip length (in. or mm)
l_c	Corresponding chip length (in. or mm)
n	Angle normal to the cutting edge
r	Cutting ratio or chip length ratio
t	Undeformed chip thickness (in. or mm)
t_c	Chip thickness (in. or mm)
V	Tool velocity or cutting speed (sfm) or m/min)
V_c	Chip speed (fpm or m/min)
V_s	Velocity of chip relative to the work (fpm or m/min)
α	Rake angle
θ	Clearance angle
ϕ	Shear angle
γ	Shear strain
$\dot{\gamma}$	Rate of shear
α_e	Effective rake angle (deg)
α_b	Back rake angle (deg)
α_s	Side rake angle (deg)
α_v	Velocity rake angle (deg)
α_n	Normal rake angle (deg)
η_c	Chip flow angle (deg)

ORTHOGONAL CUTTING MODEL

As with most problems in mechanics, it is advisable to consider a two-dimensional cutting situation before tackling more complex three-dimensional problems. The simplest two-dimensional cutting situation (Fig. 19-1) is obtained under the following conditions:

1. Straight, sharp cutting edge oriented perpendicular to the relative velocity between tool and work.
2. Length of cutting edge greater than width of work, b.
3. Undeformed chip thickness, t, small relative to width of cut, b, (i.e. $t/b < 5$).
4. Medium cutting speed.
5. Homogeneous, highly strain-hardened work material.
6. Low tool face friction.

The chip that forms under these conditions is continuous as shown in Fig. 19-1 where:

α = rake angle (deg)

θ = clearance angle (deg)

Continuous orthogonal chip formation involves concentrated shear. The work material remains elastic until it reaches line AB (Fig. 19-1), then it is sheared abruptly to a large strain. After crossing AB, the material is subjected to no further plastic flow unless the friction stress along contact length AC exceeds the flow stress of the material in the chip in shear.

CUTTING RATIO

The thickness of the chip, t_c, is always greater than the undeformed chip thickness, t, in orthogonal cutting, and the ratio of t to t_c is called the cutting ratio, r.

$$r = \frac{t}{t_c} \qquad (1)$$

In orthogonal cutting, the width of the chip, b_c, equals the width of the work, b, to a good approximation (as long as $b/t < 5$). When any metal is deformed plastically, no change occurs in volume; hence:

$$lbt = l_c b_c t_c \qquad (2)$$

or since the width of the work, b, equals the width of the chip, b_c:

$$r = \frac{t}{t_c} = \frac{l_c}{l} \qquad (3)$$

where:

l = undeformed chip length (in. or mm)

l_c = corresponding chip length (in. or mm)

CHAPTER 19

GEOMETRY OF CHIP FORMATION

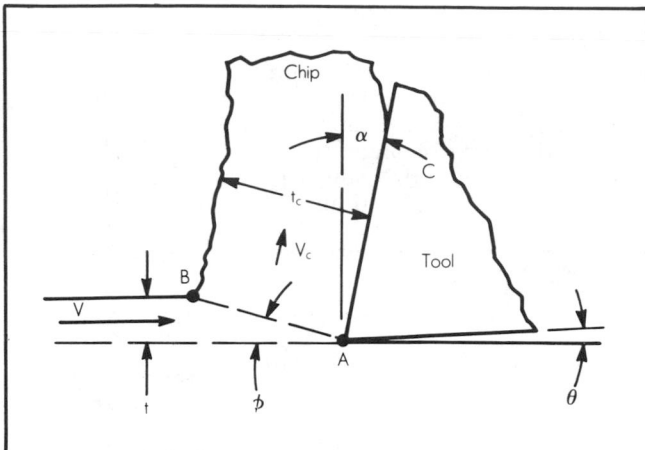

Fig. 19-1 Orthogonal chip formation.

In view of Eq. (3), r is sometimes referred to as the chip length ratio.

The cutting ratio is a convenient measure of cutting efficiency. Figure 19-2 shows material being orthogonally cut with high and low cutting ratios and corresponding shear angles ϕ_1 and ϕ_2. Since most of the energy in orthogonal cutting is associated with the shear plane, less energy is required to form thin chips than thick ones. This is because the shear stress is essentially constant (neglecting strain hardening), while the area sheared is AB_1b for the thin chip, but AB_2b for the thick chip. Thus, the greater the cutting ratio, the more efficient the cutting operation.

The cutting ratio may be measured by use of either Eq. (2) or (3). However, since the back of the chip is usually rough, it is difficult to obtain an accurate measurement of the mean value of t_c; and therefore, when possible, Eq. (3) should be used.

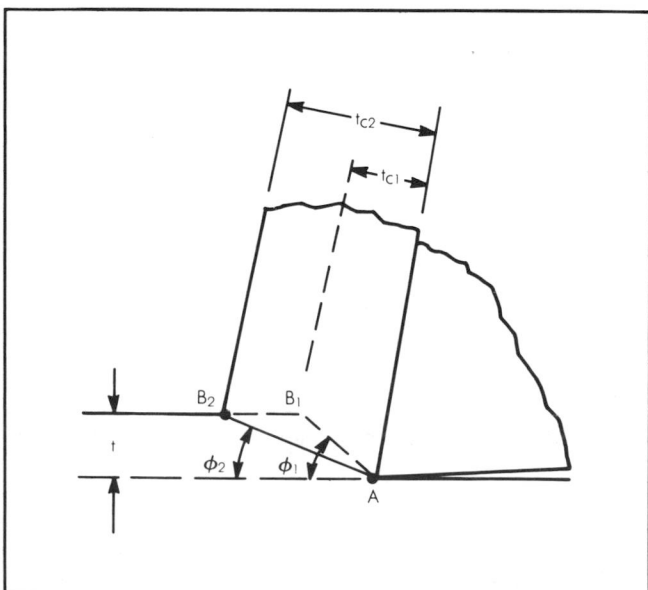

Fig. 19-2 Orthogonal cutting with large and small shear angles, ϕ_1, and ϕ_2.

One of the important uses of the cutting ratio, r, is in estimating the shear angle, ϕ. This may be done by use of the following equation:

$$\tan \phi = \frac{r \cos \alpha}{1 - r \sin \alpha} \qquad (4)$$

STRAIN AND STRAIN RATE

The shear strain, γ, on the shear plane in orthogonal cutting may be obtained as follows:

$$\gamma = \cot \phi + \tan (\phi - \alpha) \qquad (5)$$

As a consequence of r being less than one, the velocity of the chip, V_c, is always less than the cutting speed, V. Figure 19-3 shows the kinematic relationship between the cutting speed, V; the chip speed, V_c; and the velocity of the chip relative to the work, V_s. From this figure, it is evident that:

$$\frac{V_c}{V} = \frac{\cos \alpha}{\cos (\phi - \alpha)} \qquad (6)$$

The rate of shear, $\dot{\gamma}$, is:

$$\dot{\gamma} = \frac{V_s}{\Delta y} = \frac{\cos \alpha}{\cos (\phi - \alpha)} \cdot \frac{V}{\Delta y} \qquad (7)$$

where:

Δy = the thickness of the shear zone along AB in the direction of V_c, which is about 0.001″ (0.03 mm) for a typical orthogonal cut.

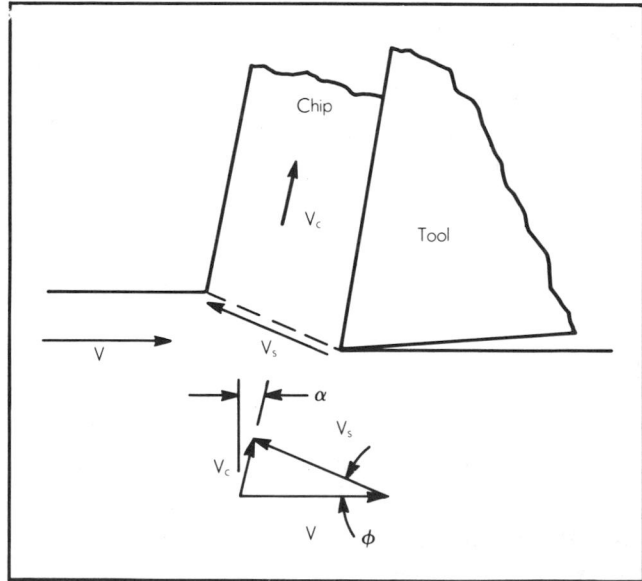

Fig. 19-3 Velocity diagram for orthogonal cutting.

SINGLE POINT TURNING

Figure 19-4 shows a cutting tool of zero side cutting edge angle in a straight turning situation. The depth of cut is B, and the feed rate is t (ipr or mm/rev). There are two cutting edges (of extent B and t respectively). In most cases $B/t \approx 10$; therefore, cutting on the end of the tool is negligible compared with cutting along the main cutting edge of extent B. As a first approximation, therefore, this three-dimensional chip formation situation may be approximated by an equivalent two-dimensional orthogonal case where:

α = side rake angle of tool (deg)
t = feed per revolution (in. or mm)
B = depth of cut (in. or mm)
V = surface speed of work at OD (sfm or m/min)

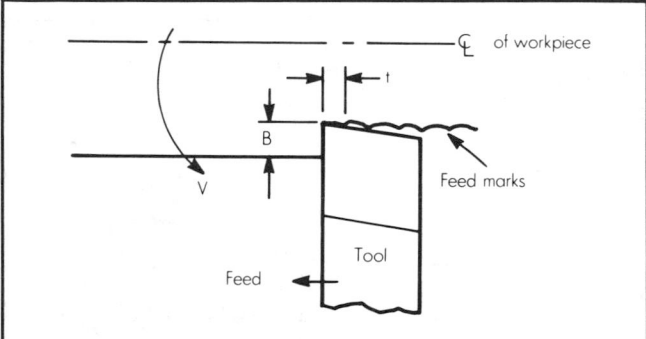

Fig. 19-4 Single point turning operation: B=depth of cut, t=feed per revolution.

The cutting ratio may be obtained by taking a chip of any convenient corresponding chip length, l_c, and calculating the corresponding undeformed length, l, from the weight of the chip, the specific weight of the work material, and the known values of B and t.

PRINCIPAL CHIP TYPES

Up to this point, it has been assumed that the chip produced is a continuous ribbon of uniform thickness, t_c, with a well-defined thin shear plane (Fig. 19-1). However, in practice, this is not always the case.

Discontinuous Chips

At low cutting speeds or when cutting a material containing points of stress concentration (such as the graphite flakes in cast iron or the manganese sulfide inclusions in a free-machining steel), discontinuous chips may form (Fig. 19-5). The result is a

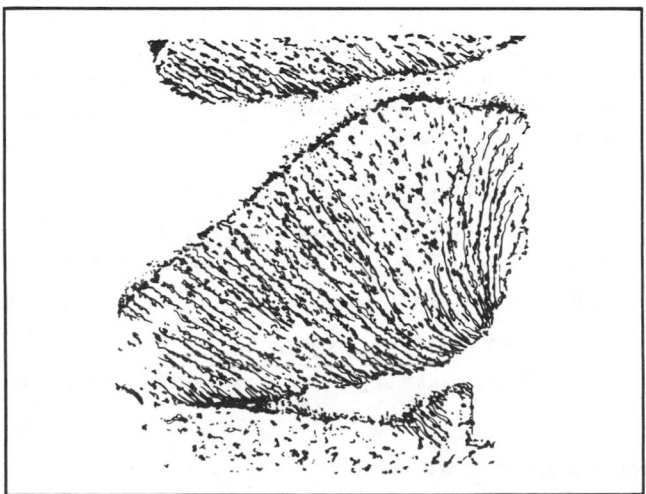

Fig. 19-5 Drawing of a photomicrograph of discontinuous chip.

series of discrete chip segments that have broken at stress concentrations in the workpiece. The orthogonal model and subsequent calculations presented in previous sections represent a very poor approximation for cutting with discontinuous chips.

Continuous Chips with Built-Up Edge

Another deviation from simple orthogonal cutting is continuous chip formation with a built-up edge (BUE). At speeds at which the temperature at the chip/tool interface is relatively low, fracture may occur within the chip, leaving behind a portion of the chip attached to the tool face.

Secondary Shear

Still another deviation from the simple orthogonal model involves secondary shear on the tool face. When the friction stress on the tool face reaches a value equal to the shear flow stress of the chip material, flow occurs internally within the chip adjacent to the tool face. This is called secondary shear flow to distinguish it from shear flow occurring on the shear plane (primary shear).

Extensive Shear Zone

When the material cut is soft and not strain hardened, the shear zone tends to be pie shaped, as shown in Fig. 19-6, instead of being uniformly thin, as in Fig. 19-1. An increase in feed will tend to favor a pie-shaped shear zone. When cutting with a pie-shaped shear zone, there is no definite shear angle. Use of the dotted line in Fig. 19-6 for the equivalent shear angle in the orthogonal analysis represents a good first approximation.

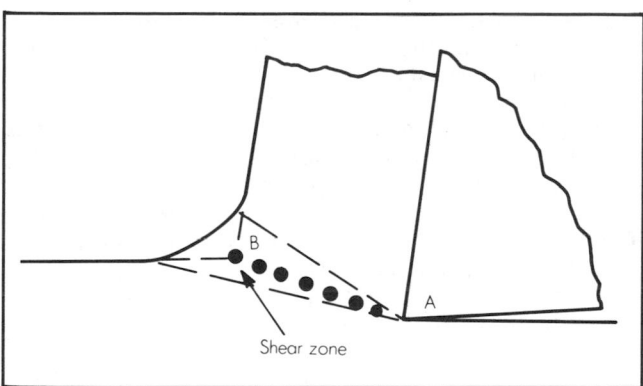

Fig. 19-6 Orthogonal chip formation with extensive shear zone.

Other Variations

Controlled contact cutting (Fig. 19-7, a) and cutting with a small negative rake honed on the cutting edge (Fig. 19-7, b) represent further departures from the ideal orthogonal model. In these cases, a composite rake angle exists and the only reasonable approximation appears to be to use an equivalent rake angle that represents a compromise between the extremes.

INCLINATION ANGLE

Up to this point the cutting edge has been considered to be perpendicular to the direction of relative velocity, V. When the cutting edge deviates from this orthogonal direction, the angle of deviation is called the inclination angle, i. Figure 19-8 shows a tool with an inclination angle, i, other than zero

GEOMETRY OF CHIP FORMATION

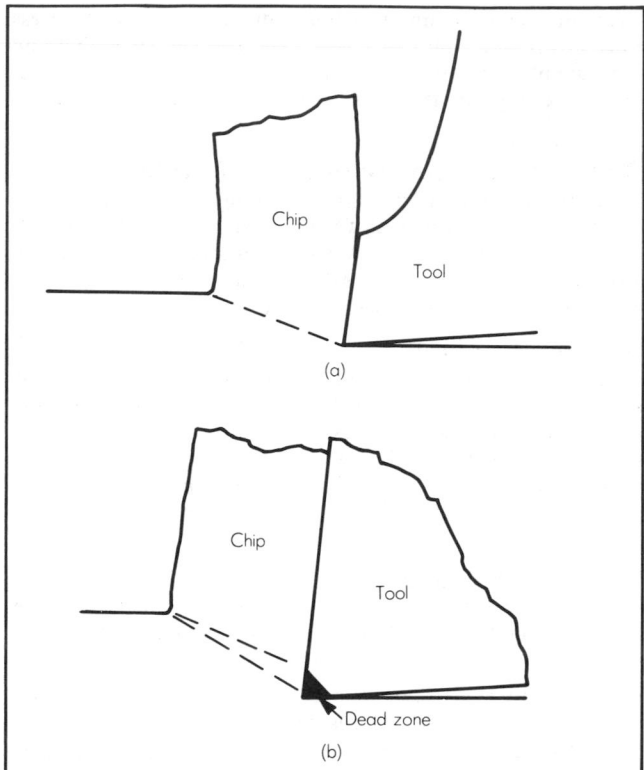

Fig. 19-7 (a) Limited contact tool. (b) Tool with chamfered cutting edge.

degrees. The main effect of this is to cause the chip to flow up the tool face in a direction different from that for orthogonal cutting. In orthogonal cutting (where i is not equal to $0°$), the chip flows up the tool face in the direction of a normal angle to the cutting edge, n. However, when the inclination angle, i, is equal to $0°$, the chip flows at an angle η_c to the normal to the cutting edge measured in the plane of the tool face (Fig. 19-8). Thus, V_c is at an angle η_c to normal, n, when i is not equal to 0. To a reasonably good approximation, the inclination angle, i, measured in the plane of the uncut surface is equal to the chip flow angle, η_c, measured in the plane of the tool face. This is known as Stabler's Rule:

$$\eta_i = i \qquad (8)$$

The effective rake angle, α_e, is measured in the plane of V and V_c and differs from the normal rake angle, α_n, measured in the plane containing V and the angle normal to the cutting edge, n. For the general case when i is not equal to 0, the effective rake angle, α_e, is less than the normal rake angle, α_n.

It may be readily shown that:

$$\sin \alpha_e = \sin^2 i + \cos^2 i \sin \alpha_n \qquad (9)$$

when Stabler's Rule holds. From Eq. (9) it is evident that, only when i is equal to 0, will α_e be equal to α_n.

A rake angle, sometimes referred to as the true rake angle in the literature, should not be confused with the effective rake angle. What is sometimes referred to as the true rake angle is more accurately called the velocity rake angle, α_v, since it is the angle measured from a normal to the finished surface and containing the cutting velocity vector, V. The relation between the effective rake angle, α_e, and the velocity rake angle, α_v, is:

$$\tan \alpha_e = \tan \alpha_v \cos i \qquad (10)$$

The inclination angle, i, is the distinguishing feature between three-dimensional cutting and two-dimensional orthogonal cutting. The simplest three-dimensional case corresponds to a planing situation with i not equal to 0 (Fig. 19-8). When a plane milling cutter has an inclination angle other than $0°$ this inclination angle is referred to as a helix angle.

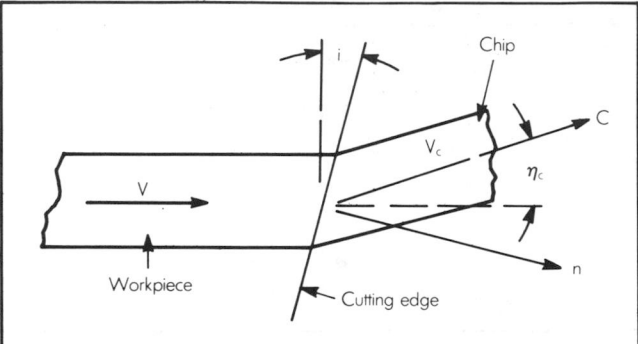

Fig. 19-8 Plan view of tool with nonzero inclination angle.

Two important effects of an inclination angle other than $0°$ are:

1. To give an effective rake angle that is less than the normal rake angle. This in turn gives rise to lower cutting forces, energy, and temperatures for a tool of given wedge angle and hence with a tool tip of given strength and heat absorbing capacity.
2. To cause the chip to flow to the side instead of straight back to produce a spiral with a helix angle. This is illustrated in Fig. 19-9 in which planing chips are shown for cuts of 4″ (102 mm) length made with tools of different inclination angles.

By properly choosing the inclination angle, chips may be caused to flow to that side of the cutter at which they are less likely to become jammed and rub and scratch the finished surface of the workpiece.

From a few of the commonly specified tool dimensions, it is possible to derive the quantities of fundamental importance to the performance of the tool (effective rake angle, α_e, and inclination angle, i). For example, in the case of a single point turning tool, the most significant dimensions are:

1. Back rake angle, α_b.
2. Side rake angle, α_s.
3. Side cutting edge angle, C_s.

For a turning tool, the inclination angle, i, and the normal rake angle, α_n, may be found from the following:

$$\tan (i) = \tan \alpha_b \cos C_s - \tan \alpha_s \sin C_s \qquad (11)$$

$$\tan \alpha_n = (\tan \alpha_s \cos C_s = \tan \alpha_b \sin C_s) \cos (i) \qquad (12)$$

Then, the effective rake angle may be estimated by use of Eq. (9).

INTERACTIONS

The geometry of chip formation interacts with other machining variables to have an important influence on cutting

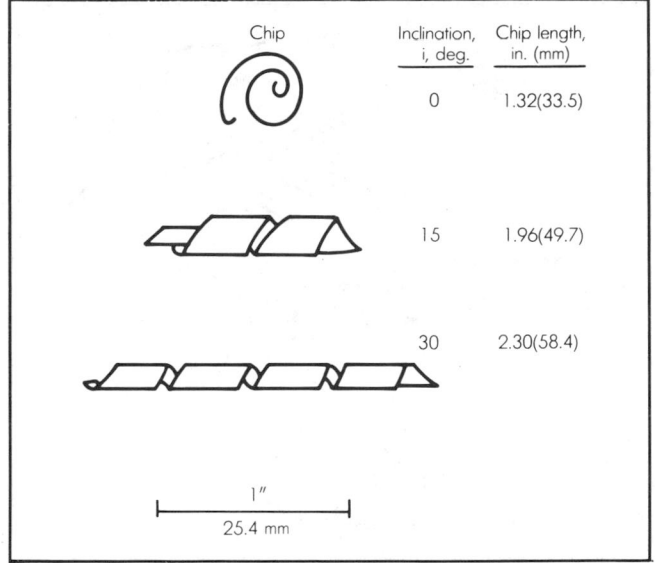

Chip	Inclination, i, deg.	Chip length, in. (mm)
	0	1.32(33.5)
	15	1.96(49.7)
	30	2.30(58.4)

1″
25.4 mm

Fig. 19-9 Chips produced with different inclination angles. Normal rake angle, $\alpha_n = 10°$; length of cut, l: 4″ (102 mm); undeformed chip thickness, 0.005″ (0.13 mm); cutting speed, V: 20 ipm (0.51 m/min); work material, AISI 1015 steel.

forces, surface finish, and chip control.

In general, cutting forces are less with discontinuous chips than with continuous chips and a BUE may decrease (larger effective rake angle) or increase (higher tool face friction) cutting forces. The greater the secondary shear zone on the face of the tool, the greater are the cutting forces. Cutting forces are decreased by a decrease in relative chip thickness (increase in cutting ratio or of shear angle). An increase in inclination angle decreases cutting forces by causing an increase in the effective rake angle of the tool.

The main components of surface roughness are BUE, feed marks associated with a secondary cutting edge, and tool chatter. Cutting with continuous chip formation or with a BUE of variable amplitude gives rise to variable cutting forces which may result in a forced vibration of the cutting tool. Roughness due to feed marks is reduced by a decrease in feed rate and an increase in the nose radius of the tool. The main methods of reducing the size and instability of a BUE include increasing cutting speed, hot or warm machining (heating workpiece by noncutting source of thermal energy), using free-machining additives (MnS, Pb, graphite), increasing the effective rake angle, decreasing the tool face friction, precold-working the work material, and decreasing the tool/chip contact length.

Chip control is an important element of safety and productivity. Long, unbroken, continuous chips are a source of danger to the operator and to the tool and work. Chip curlers, or chip breakers, of different designs are an important means of decreasing the tool/chip contact length and yielding short periodically broken chips that rapidly leave the cutting zone.

CHIP COLOR

The color of a chip is a readily observable characteristic that can be misleading. The color of a chip is due to interference of light reflected from the surface of an oxide coating and from the underlying metal surface. It is thus a measure of the thickness of the oxide coating on the chip and only rather remotely a measure of the cutting temperature involved when the chip is produced.

FORCES AT THE CUTTING TOOL

The following is a list of symbols and abbreviations used in formulas and discussions of forces at the cutting tool:

Symbol	Definition
a	Depth of cut (mm)
A	Area of the undeformed chip section (mm²)
A_c	Area of the chip section (mm²)
A_{shi}	Area of the shear plane (mm²)
b	Width of cut (mm)
C	Capacitance (farads)
C_A	Chip area ratio
C_F	Material constant used in Eq. (48)
E	Apparent efficiency of the machine tool (percent)
E_{sp}	Specific cutting energy (GJ/m³)
F	Resultant cutting force in orthogonal cutting (N)
F_p	Power force in two dimensional cutting (N)
$F_p{'}$	Power force in p′-q′ plane (N)
F_q	Normal force in p′-q′ plane (N)
$F_q{'}$	Normal force at cutting tool (N)
F_r	Resultant cutting force in three dimensional cutting (N)

Symbol	Definition
F_s	Force in the direction of relative tool travel (N)
F_{shi}	Shear force in the shear plane (N)
F_{shin}	Normal force on the shear plane (N)
F_{sn}	Normal force to the direction of relative tool travel (N)
F_x	Power force at cutting tool (N)
F_y	Feed force at cutting tool (N)
F_z	Radial force at cutting tool (N)
F_γ	Shear force on the face (N)
$F_{\gamma n}$	Normal force on the face (N)
GF	Strain gage factor
h	Undeformed chip thickness (mm)
h_c	Chip thickness (mm)
H	Brinell hardness number
i	Inclination angle
$i, j,$ and k	Unit normal vectors in the x, y, z directions
k	Piozoelectric constant
K_n	Metal removal factor, the reciprocal of the specific power consumption
l	Nominal strain (in./in.)
m	Mass of the dynamometer
N	Normalizing magnitude for vector $e_p{'}$ and $e_q{'}$

FORCES AT THE CUTTING TOOL

Symbol	Definition
p'-q'	Orthogonal coordinate system in which cutting is two dimensional
P_g	Gross power developed by a machine tool while cutting
P_n	Net power supplied to a cutting tool to remove metal
P_t	Tare power, equal to P_g-P_h
Q	Electrical charge (coulombs)
R	Electrical resistance (ohms)
R_1, R_2	Coordinate transformation matrices
s	Feed per revolution (mm)
V	Voltage across the capacitor, Eq. (51)
V	Cutting velocity vector
V_1	Local cutting velocity
V_c	Chip velocity vector
ω_n	Undamped natural frequency
W_f	Work done in overcoming friction between chip and tool (GJ/m³)
W_s	Work done in shearing of metal (GJ/m³)
$x, y,$ and z	Orthogonal directions in which cutting forces are measured
μ	Apparent coefficient of friction between chip and tool
τ_{shi}	Shear stress in the shear plane
σ_{shi}	Normal stress on the shear plane
α_n	Normal clearance angle (deg)
β_n	Friction angle (deg)
γ_n	Normal rake angle (deg)
ϕ_i	Imaginary shear angle (deg)
λ_s	Cutting edge inclination angle (deg)
α	Location angle for chip flow direction (deg)
α_b	Tool back rake angle (deg)
α_e	Effective rake angle (deg)
α_s	Modified side rake angle (deg)
η	Location angle for chip flow direction (deg)
η_c	Chip flow angle in the rake face plane (deg)
λ	Normalizing scalar

GENERAL CONSIDERATIONS

In the general case, the force system acting on a cutting tool is three dimensional; i.e., the geometry of the system cannot be represented as lying in a single plane. The resultant force on the tool has three basic components. This situation exists in all cases except that of orthogonal cutting. Cutting-force components are measured by special tool or workholding devices called dynamometers.

In the case of orthogonal cutting, the force geometry is considerably simplified as compared to three-dimensional systems. In orthogonal cutting, the entire force system lies in a single plane, as shown in Fig. 19-10.[1] The resultant force, F, has two basic components, F_s and F_{sn}. The force component in the direction of relative tool travel, F_s, determines the amount of work required to move the cutting tool a given distance. The component F_{sn} does not contribute to the work, but both components produce deflections of the tool relative to the workpiece.

The force system illustrated in Fig. 19-10 is arrived at by assuming that the chip is a body in stable mechanical equilibrium under the action of the forces exerted on it at the face

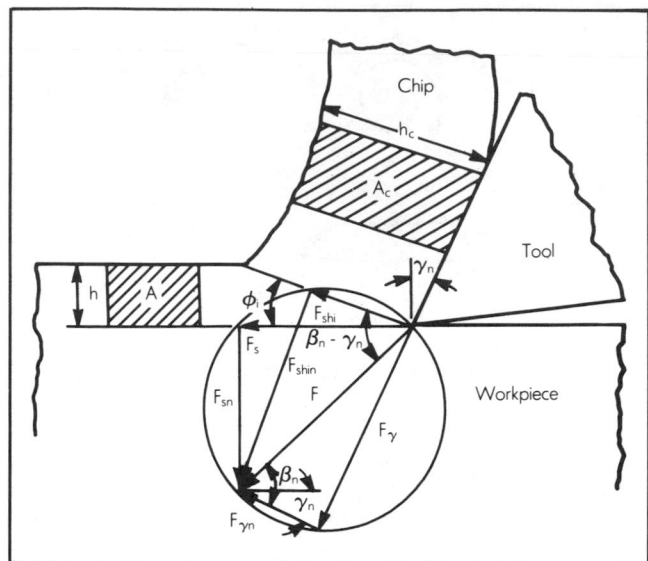

Fig. 19-10 Schematic diagram of force system acting in the case of orthogonal cutting with a continuous-type chip.

and at the shear plane, as shown in Fig. 19-11. At the tool face, the force components F_γ and $F_{\gamma n}$ act on the chip. F_γ, known as the shear force on the face, represents the frictional resistance met by the chip as it slides over the face of the tool. $F_{\gamma n}$ is known as the normal force on the face. The ratio of F_γ to $F_{\gamma n}$ is μ, the apparent coefficient of friction between chip and tool.

The force components acting at the shear plane are F_{shi} and F_{shin}. F_{shi} represents the force required to shear the metal on the plane of shear and is known as the shearing force. F_{shin} acts normal to the plane of shear and results in a compressive stress being applied to the plane of shear. The mean shear stress on the shear plane, which is equal to the mean shear strength of the metal being cut, can be obtained by dividing F_{shi} by the area of the shear plane. Correspondingly, the compressive stress on the shear plane is found by dividing F_{shin} by the area of the shear plane.

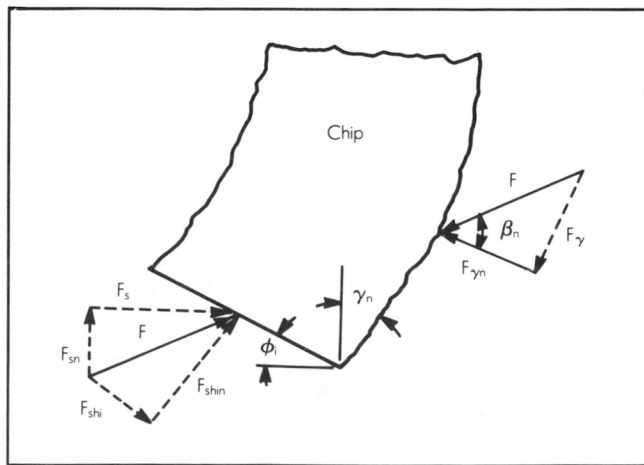

Fig. 19-11 Free body diagram of chip.

ORTHOGONAL CUTTING MODELS

A special case of cutting in which the cutting edge of the tool is arranged to be perpendicular to the direction of relative work/tool motion is known as orthogonal cutting (see Fig. 19-12, *a*). Orthogonal cutting represents a two-dimensional problem rather than a three-dimensional one; therefore, it lends itself to research investigations when the elimination of as many independent variables as possible is desirable. As a consequence, the relatively simple arrangement of orthogonal cutting is widely used in theoretical and experimental work. The other possible top view of Fig. 19-10 is shown as Fig. 19-12,*b*. In this case the cutting action is inclined to the cutting edge and is referred to as oblique cutting. Oblique cutting (drilling, milling, etc.) is far more common in actual practice than orthogonal cutting.

If a free body diagram of a chip is considered, the resultant cutting force exerted by the cutting tool on the work and the reaction of the work on the cutting tool must be equal in magnitude and opposite in direction, as shown in Fig. 19-11. In practice, the chip has a tendency to curl away from the cutting tool. This may be due to noncollinearity in the forces. Ignoring this complication, the resultant force, F, can be divided into three sets of components.

Force Components Parallel and Perpendicular to the Cutting Velocity Vector

These components are generally measured by a cutting tool dynamometer with F_s the component parallel to the cutting velocity vector. It is sometimes called the power component since, when it is multiplied by the cutting speed, the power required for the cut is obtained. From the circular force diagram of Fig. 19-10, it is evident that:

$$F_s = F \cos\ (\beta_n - \gamma_n) \tag{13}$$

$$F_{sn} = F \sin\ (\beta_n - \gamma_n) \tag{14}$$

Force Components Parallel and Perpendicular to the Shear Plane

These force components can be used to estimate the magnitude of the stresses on the shear plane. Again, from the circular force diagram, Fig. 19-10.

$$F_{shi} = F \cos\ (\phi_i + \beta_n - \gamma_n) \tag{15}$$

$$F_{shin} = F \sin\ (\phi_i + \beta_n - \gamma_n) \tag{16}$$

These forces in terms of F_s and F_{sn} (the dynamometer measured components) become:

$$F_{shi} = F_s \cos \phi_i - F_{sn} \sin \phi_i \tag{17}$$

$$F_{shin} = F_s \sin \phi_i + F_{sn} \cos \phi_i \tag{18}$$

Thus, the apparent shear stress of the material in the shear plane, τ_{shi}, is:

$$\tau_{shi} = \frac{F_{shi}}{A_{shi}} = \frac{(F_s \cos \phi_i) - (F_{sn} \sin \phi_i) \sin \phi_i}{A} \tag{19}$$

since the area of the shear plane, A_{shi}, is given by:

$$A_{shi} = \frac{A}{\sin \phi_i} \tag{20}$$

where:

A = the cross-sectional area of the uncut chip.

The area of the shear plane, A_{shi}, and the yield strength of the workpiece material in shear are the two principal factors that determine the magnitude of the force necessary to form the chip. As a result, the shear yield strength in cutting is a frequently calculated parameter in cutting experiments and there is much experimental evidence to show that this parameter varies only slightly over a wide range of cutting conditions. If the area of the shear plane would be constant during metalcutting, the forces in cutting could easily be estimated once the shear yield strength is known. However, the shear plane angle, ϕ_i, and hence the shear plane area, vary widely for different cutting conditions. As a result, the forces needed to shear the metal vary widely and require the analyses of chip formation that are described earlier in this chapter (see "Geometry of Chip Formation").

Force Components Parallel and Perpendicular to the Tool Rake Face

The ratio of the friction to the normal component along the tool rake face gives rise to an apparent coefficient of friction between the cutting tool and chip.

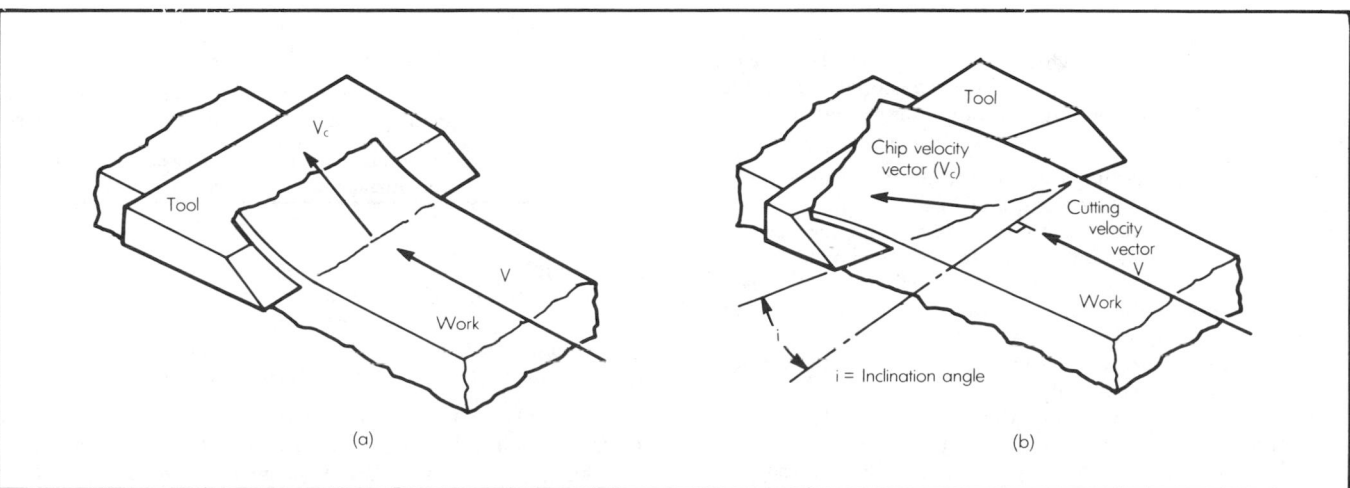

Fig. 19-12 (a)Orthogonal cutting, (b) Nonorthogonal (oblique) cutting.

FORCES AT THE CUTTING TOOL

The friction angle, β_n, is seen in Fig. 19-11 and is given by:

$$\beta_n = \tan^{-1} \mu \qquad (21)$$

The components F_γ and $F_{\gamma n}$ on the tool rake face in terms of F are given by:

$$F_\gamma = F \sin \beta_n \qquad (22)$$

$$F_{\gamma n} = F \cos \beta_n \qquad (23)$$

while in terms of F_s and F_{sn} (the dynamometer measured components), they can be expressed as:

$$F_\gamma = F_s \sin \gamma_n + F_{sn} \cos \gamma_n \qquad (24)$$

$$F_{\gamma n} = F_s \cos \gamma_n - F_{sn} \sin \gamma_n \qquad (25)$$

In reality, the coefficient of friction between the cutting tool and chip in metalcutting is not analogous with coulomb friction (sliding friction) for the following reasons:

1. In coulomb friction, the real area of contact between the two surfaces is only a small fraction of the apparent area of contact; in metalcutting, the real area of contact between tool and chip is significantly larger.

2. In coulomb friction, μ decreases with a reduction in the friction force; in metalcutting, as the friction force decreases, the normal force reduces faster, resulting in an increased μ.

3. In coulomb friction, plastic deformation of the moving body does not occur; in metalcutting, plastic deformation of the chip takes place.

From the force equations and geometry of Fig. 19-10, various mechanical quantities can be calculated if certain quantities are known or readily measurable. These quantities are the shear angle, ϕ_i; the rake angle, γ_n, of the tool; the force components F_s and F_{sn}; the chip cross-sectional area, A; and the cutting speed, V_1. The equations for making such calculations from these known quantities are summarized in Table 19-1.[2]

OBLIQUE CUTTING MODELS

To improve understanding of three-dimensional turning (oblique cutting), as seen in Fig. 19-13, it is useful to have a mathematical model which predicts three-dimensional cutting forces for this process. One method of predicting three-dimensional cutting forces is to apply two-dimensional metalcutting theory on a plane (which must be identified) where the cutting process appears to be two dimensional. The forces which act on the workpiece in the radial, tangential, and axial directions can then be obtained by a coordinate transformation.[3]

In modeling three-dimensional cutting, it is convenient to define a plane (p'-q') which contains both the cutting velocity and chip velocity vectors. In this plane, the methods for predicting two-dimensional cutting forces are applied.

One method of modeling three-dimensional cutting is to analyze the single point turning operation by first predicting the location of the p'-q' plane and then referring the forces acting in this plane to a set of x, y, and z directions in which the forces are experimentally measured.

To reference the position of the tool to the actual turning operation, z is equivalent to the radial direction (depth of cut), y is equivalent to the negative feed direction (chip thickness), and x is equivalent to the tangential direction (power force direction).

TABLE 19-1
Summary of Equations for Calculating Important Mechanical Quantities
(For the case of orthogonal cutting and a continuous chip)

Coefficient of friction	$\mu = \dfrac{F_{sn} + F_s \tan \gamma_n}{F_s - F_{sn} \tan \gamma_n}$	(26)
Friction force	$F_\gamma = F_{sn} \cos \gamma_n + F_s \sin \gamma_n$	(27)
Mean shear strength	$\tau_{shi} = \dfrac{F_s \sin \phi_i \cos \phi_i - F_{sn} \sin^2 \phi_i}{A}$	(28)
Work done in shear	$W_s = \tau_{shi} [\cot \phi_i + \tan (\phi_i - \gamma_n)]$	(29)
Work done in overcoming friction	$W_f = \dfrac{F_\gamma}{A} \cdot \dfrac{\sin \phi_i}{\cos (\phi_i - \gamma_n)}$	(30)
Total work done in cutting	$E_{sp} = \dfrac{F_s}{A}$	(31)

Where:
A = cross-sectional area of chip before removal from workpiece (mm²)

F_γ = shear force in the face; force component acting between tool face and sliding chip (N)

F_s = shear force in the flank; force component acting in direction of tool travel (N)

F_{sn} = normal force on the flank; force component acting in direction perpendicular to surface generated (N)

τ_{shi} = mean shear stress on shear plane; mean shear strength of metal being cut (N/mm²)

W_f = work done in overcoming friction between chip and tool per unit volume of metal removed (GJ/m³)

E_{sp} = specific cutting energy; total work done in cutting per unit volume of metal removed (GJ/m³)

W_s = work done in shearing of metal per unit volume of metal removed (GJ/m³)

γ_n = normal rake angle of tool as measured in a plane perpendicular to its cutting edge (deg)

ϕ_i = imaginary shear angle between shear plane and surface being generated (deg)

To simplify the mathematical analyses, the cutting tool is modeled without a side relief angle, nose radius, or end relief angle. Although these angles are present on a "real cutting tool," their effects are believed to be secondary compared to those of the angles which are included in the analyses.[4]

Figure 19-14 shows a tool cross section perpendicular to the p'-q' plane. The angle α_e in this figure is the effective rake angle. This is the three-dimensional equivalent of the rake in orthogonal cutting. An expression for the effective rake angle is:

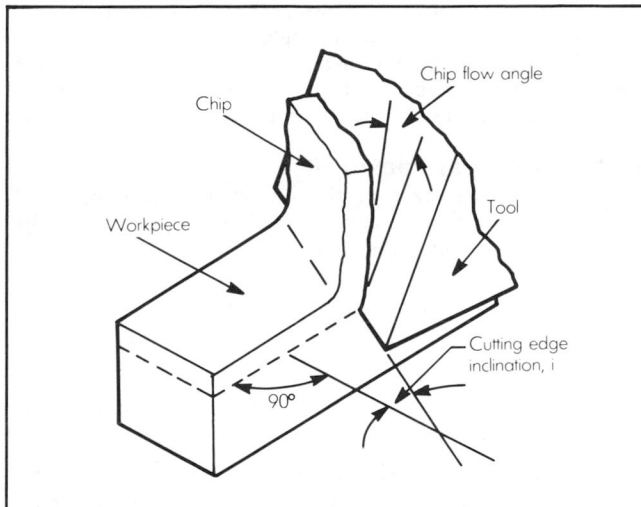

Fig. 19-13 Oblique cutting.

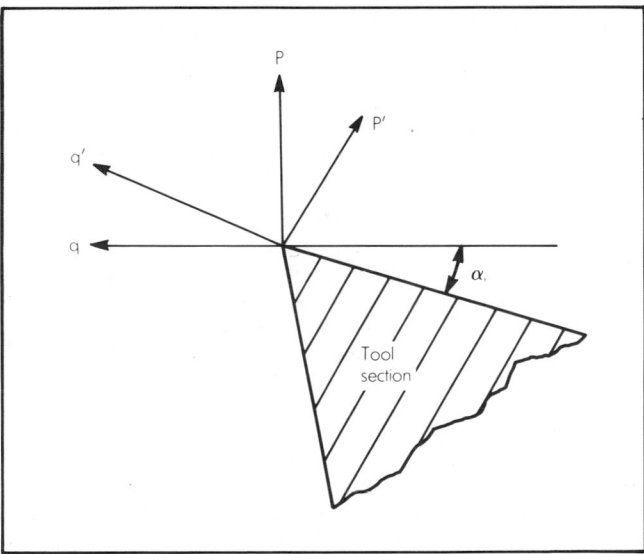

Fig. 19-14 Cross section of cutting tool on plane p'-q'. (On this plane, cutting is two-dimensional.)

$$\sin \alpha_e = \sin \eta_c \cdot \sin \lambda_s + \cos \eta_c \cdot \cos \lambda_s \cdot \cos \gamma_n \qquad (32)$$

where:

γ_n = the normal rake angle

The resultant force, F_r, having components along the x, y, z axes can be expressed by:

$$F_r = F_q' e_q' + F_p' e_p' \qquad (33)$$

$$F_r = F_x i + F_y j + F_z k \qquad (34)$$

Also, F can be written as follows:

$$\begin{bmatrix} F_x \\ F_y \\ F_z \end{bmatrix} = R_2 \begin{bmatrix} F_q' \\ F_p' \end{bmatrix} \qquad (35)$$

The predicted orthogonal forces can be related to q'-p', with the aid of Fig. 19-14, as:

$$\begin{bmatrix} F_q' \\ F_p' \end{bmatrix} = R_1 \begin{bmatrix} F_q \\ F_p \end{bmatrix} \qquad (36)$$

where:

$$R_1 = \begin{bmatrix} \cos \alpha_e & \sin \alpha_e \\ -\sin \alpha_e & \cos \alpha_e \end{bmatrix} \qquad (37)$$

$$R_2 = \begin{bmatrix} -\sin \alpha & (\cos \alpha_s \cos \alpha_b)/N \\ \cos \alpha \cos \eta & (\sin \alpha_s \cos \alpha_b)/N \\ -\cos \alpha \sin \eta & - (\cos \alpha_s \sin \alpha_b)/N \end{bmatrix} \qquad (38)$$

Performing the matrix algebra of Eq. (35), Eq. (36) results in:

$$F_v = F_x = F_{power} = \frac{\tau_{shi} \cdot a \cdot b}{\sin \phi_i \cos (\phi_i + \beta_n - \alpha_e)}$$
$$+ [\sin (\alpha - \alpha_e) \cos (\beta_n - \alpha_e) \cos (\alpha - \alpha_e) \cos (\beta_n - \alpha_e)] \quad (39)$$

$$F_f = F_y = F_{feed} = \frac{\tau_{shi} \cdot a \cdot b \cdot \cos \eta}{\sin \phi_i \cos (\phi_i + \beta_n - \alpha_e)}$$
$$+ [-\cos (\alpha - \alpha_e) \sin (\beta_n - \alpha_e) \sin (\alpha - \alpha_e) \cos (\beta_n - \alpha_e)] \quad (40)$$

$$F_p = F_z = F_{radial} = \frac{\tau_{shi} \cdot a \cdot b \cdot \sin \eta}{\sin \phi_i \cos (\phi_i + \beta_n - \alpha_e)}$$
$$+ [\cos (\alpha - \alpha_e) \sin (\beta_n - \alpha_e) \sin (\alpha - \alpha_e) \cos (\beta_n - \alpha_e)] \quad (41)$$

A matrix model of three-dimensional metalcutting, based on an extension of two-dimensional metalcutting theory, has thus been developed. The matrix model operates by locating a reference plane where cutting is assumed to be two dimensional. Cutting forces are then predicted in this plane, and these forces are rotated to a set of orthogonal axes on the cutting tool.

Experimental results of three-dimensional turning indicate good correlation to the matrix model predictions. The matrix model results are also in good agreement with other models that have been proposed in the literature.[5]

WORK DONE IN CUTTING

The total work done by the cutting tool in removing metal, as determined by the value of the force component F_s, is dissipated in the following forms for a sharp cutting tool: (1) as work done in shear deformation, (2) as work done to overcome chip/tool interfacial friction, (3) as work done to generate the new surfaces in cutting, and (4) as work done due to the change in momentum of the metal as it crosses the shear plane.

The third and fourth forms are of negligible importance for practical cutting conditions and can be ignored. As a result, practically all of the energy generated in metalcutting is dissipated in plastic deformation and friction as heat.

POWER

Various considerations are generally used in specifying the power consumed in machining. These include:

1. Gross power, P_g.
2. Net power, P_n.
3. Specific (or unit) power consumption, E_{sp}.
4. Specific cutting pressure.

FORCES AT THE CUTTING TOOL

5. Metal removal factor, K_n.

Gross Power, P_g

The gross power, or power to the machine, is the power actually developed by the motor (supplied to the machine tool) when the machine is cutting. It can be measured by use of a wattmeter in the electrical line supplying the motor in the case of machine tools powered by individual electric motors (neglecting electrical losses in the motor).

Net Power, P_n

The net power, or power at the tool, is the power actually supplied to the cutting tool and consumed in removing metal in a machining operation. The net power, rather than the gross power, is significant in force and specific power calculations. It is less than the gross power by the amount used in overcoming frictional losses in the machine tool and by the amount used in the feeding system. However, the amount of power consumed in the feeding system is very small compared to the amount consumed in removing metal. For this reason, the power used in feeding is generally combined with the frictional losses in the machine tool; the apparent efficiency of the machine tool is then based on this entire quantity. The relation between the net and gross power is:

$$P_n = P_g \cdot \frac{E}{100} \tag{42}$$

where:

E = apparent efficiency of the machine tool (%).

The Specific (or Unit) Power Consumption, E_{sp}

The specific power consumption is the amount of power (net) required to remove a unit volume of metal in unit time, usually expressed in terms of horsepower per cubic inch per minute or gigajoules per cubic meter. It is related to power consumption and rate of metal removal in the following manner:

$$E_{sp} = \frac{F_s \cdot V_1}{A \cdot V_1} \tag{43}$$

where:

F_s = cutting force
A = area of the undeformed chip section
V_1 = cutting speed

Since the velocity terms in Eq. (43) can be canceled, the specific power consumption can also be expressed as:

$$E_{sp} = \frac{F_s}{A} \tag{44}$$

Specific Cutting Pressure

In Eq. (44) the specific power consumption is expressed as a ratio of a force to an area which is dimensionally (although not physically) a stress; thus, this quantity is also commonly referred to as the specific cutting pressure.

The specific cutting pressure, the specific power consumption, and the unit horsepower are identical terms and can be used to characterize cutting processes. The value of this parameter varies from material to material with the more difficult to machine materials characterized by higher values. The specific cutting pressure also varies considerably for a given material and is affected by a variety of cutting parameters, especially the feed. The value of the parameter tends to be constant at the higher speeds and feeds at which it can be used as a guide to estimate the forces and power required to cut the material.

Metal Removal Factor, K_n

The metal removal factor is the volume of the metal removed per unit of power (net) in a unit of time. It is the reciprocal of the specific power consumption. Thus:

$$K_n = \frac{1}{E_{sp}} \tag{45}$$

where:

K_n = cubic inches of metal removed per minute per horsepower

Both the metal removal factor, or its reciprocal, and the specific power consumption are useful quantities for expressing the power requirements for metal removal in a given machining operation; they remain relatively constant in value for small changes in the cutting conditions and are, therefore, to some extent characteristic of the material being machined.

PRACTICAL MEASUREMENT OF CUTTING FORCES

The cutting forces developed in machining operations may be estimated indirectly by obtaining the power consumed or directly through the use of metalcutting dynamometers.

Desirable Characteristics of Metalcutting Dynamometers

The desirable characteristics of a metalcutting dynamometer can be categorized into two groups: general characteristics and specific characteristics. General characteristics desirable in dynamometers include rigidity, sensitivity, and lack of cross sensitivity and hysteresis. Specific desirable characteristics involve design choices; for example, whether to put the force measuring device on the tool or to put it on the workpiece.

Rigidity and sensitivity. The two primary prerequisites of a cutting tool dynamometer are rigidity and sensitivity. The dynamometer must be rigid to prevent any significant tool deflections affecting the normal cutting operation, yet it must be flexible or sensitive enough to measure force variations with time. To assure the complete transmittibility of the cutting force, the natural frequency of the dynamometer should be at least 4 to 5 times higher than the maximum exciting frequency to which the cutting tool may be subjected.

Cross sensitivity. If the dynamometer is designed to be used to measure two or more cutting force components, considerable care must be exercised to prevent cross sensitivity. Cross sensitivity occurs when the application of a force in one direction causes the dynamometer to record readings of apparent force in other perpendicular directions. If this mutual interference of the force-measuring elements occurs, a set of simultaneous equations must be solved to determine the force components—unnecessarily complicating the data interpretation.

Hysteresis. A cutting force dynamometer should have linear calibration characteristics and not exhibit hysteresis. Hysteresis is an effect that is characterized in dynamometers by a difference that exists in the force vs. displacement curves during loading and unloading. The transfer of forces in dynamometers

FORCES AT THE CUTTING TOOL

should be accomplished by avoiding sliding surfaces with their unknown amounts of friction acting as variable sources of error.

Principles and Examples of Metalcutting Dynamometers

The cutting forces existing in metalcutting operations can be measured directly from a variety of mechanical, hydraulic, or pneumatic dynamometers or from several types of electromechanical dynamometers. In the majority of force-measuring techniques currently employed, the cutting force is applied to an elastic member of the dynamometer and the resulting deflection of the member is measured. If a suitable calibration curve exists between the applied force and the resultant deflection, the cutting force can be determined. As discussed earlier, the dynamometer must be stiff, allowing only small deflections on the order of 10-1000 μ in. (0.25-25.4 μ m). Thus, the measuring devices must be capable of measuring these small deflections.

FRICTION IN METALCUTTING

In metalcutting operations, several factors influence friction. The friction force and coefficient of friction are discussed in this section.

RELATIONSHIPS BETWEEN FORCES, POWER, AND CUTTING VARIABLES

The forces and power in metalcutting are affected by a variety of factors, including cutting speed, dimensions of cut, temperature at the cut, cutting fluids, workpiece and tool material, workpiece hardness, and other variables. Several key factors are discussed in this section.

Cutting Speed

Power consumption in a machining operation is roughly proportional to the cutting speed, since the rate at which metal is removed is proportional to that speed. On the other hand, the specific power consumption, E_{sp}; the metal removal factor, K_n; and the forces on the tool are not greatly dependent on cutting speed at speeds above 10-20 sfm (3.0-6.1 m/min) when positive true rake angle tools are used. The maximum variation of these quantities with cutting speed is on the order of 10-15% over the range of speeds normally used in practice.

The effect of cutting speed on tool forces F_s and F_{sn} depends upon a number of factors including the tool/work combination, tool geometry, speed range involved, feed, depth of cut, and type of machining operation. The frictional characteristics at the tool/chip interface are related to the effect of speed on cutting forces.

In view of the many possible combinations of the foregoing factors, any generalization is hazardous. However, the most reliable criterion is the change in the thickness of the chip with change in speed under otherwise fixed cutting conditions.

The chip thickness ratio is a reliable gage of the amount of shearing strain undergone during chip formation [see Eq. (1) in this chapter]. This shearing action accounts for most of the energy expended in cutting. If a speed change results in little difference in the chip thickness, the forces are substantially constant.

A variety of trends have been observed and may be generalized as follows:

1. In single point turning of steel or cast iron with high-speed steel tools and usual rake angles, cutting speed has

little effect on cutting forces.
2. When employing carbide tools with usual rake angles in single point turning of steel and other metals producing a "continuous" chip [in the range of 200-600 sfm (61-183 m/min)], an increase in speed results in a pronounced decrease in chip thickness and a corresponding decrease in cutting forces. The change is relatively slight above 500-600 sfm (152-183 m/min).
3. In the milling of steel with carbide or high-speed steel cutters, comparatively little effect from speed is noted on either chip thickness or forces. In some instances, the forces increase moderately with an increase in speed.

Dimension of Cut

The size of cut is the variable having the greatest influence on forces and power consumption in the machining of metals. The empirical equations relating cutting force F_s and the metal removal factor, K_n, (or specific power consumption, E_{sp}) to depth of cut, a, and feed per revolution, s, are as follows:

$$F_v = F_s = C_F a^x s^y \qquad (46)$$

$$K_n = \frac{1}{E_{sp}} = \frac{A}{C_F a^x s^y} \qquad (47)$$

where:

C_F = a constant whose value depends on the material being cut and the true rake angle of the tool

x, y = exponents

In average commercial machining practice, in which the nose radius or chamfer is small in relation to the depth, $x = 1$ and $y = 0.8$[6,7] so that Eqs. (46) and (47) become:

$$F_v = F_s = C_F \cdot a \cdot s^{0.8} \qquad (48)$$

and, since $A = a \cdot s$:

$$K_n = \frac{1}{E_{sp}} = \frac{s^{0.2}}{C_F} \qquad (49)$$

Several important conclusions can be drawn from these two equations:

1. A change in feed has less effect on cutting force than does a change in depth.
2. More importantly, the cutting force does not increase in direct proportion to an increase in feed.
3. The metal removal factor, K_n, is to a large extent characteristic of the metal being cut; it is only slightly dependent on the feed and is practically independent of the depth of cut.
4. Most importantly, the metal-removal factor actually increases slightly with increasing feed.

Thus, a general rule may be stated: The use of a high feed and large depth of cut allows metal to be removed most efficiently in machining (i.e., a large volume of metal can be removed per minute per horsepower). The use of the high feed and large depth of cut can be combined with a low cutting speed to give long tool life (as indicated in the general rule stated in the previous discussion of the relation of tool life to the dimensions

FORCES AT THE CUTTING TOOL

of the cut). However, although a high feed and large depth of cut are beneficial to tool life and efficient metal removal, several factors set a limit on the maximum size of cut that can be taken. These are (1) the maximum power available from the machine tool, (2) the maximum forces that the cutter can withstand, (3) the maximum permissible deflections of the machine tool and workpiece consistent with the accuracy required, (4) the tendency to chatter, and (5) the fact that finish grows rougher as the depth of cut is increased.

Workpiece Hardness

As a rough general rule, power consumption and forces increase with increasing workpiece hardness.

In the case of steel and cast iron, empirical relationships between hardness and specific power consumption or cutting force can be stated in terms of the E_{sp} value. Kronenberg[8] has found the following approximate relationships:

For steel:

$$E_{sp} = 4.26 \sqrt{H(85 - \gamma_n)} \tag{50}$$

For cast iron:

$$E_{sp} = 1.07 \sqrt[2.5]{H} \sqrt{85 - \gamma_n} \tag{51}$$

where:

H = Brinell hardness number
γ_n = rake angle

Values of specific power consumption that have been calculated from Eq. (50) for an average case in which $A = 0.001$

in.^{2} (0.64 mm^2) are plotted in Fig. 19-15[9] (for different velocity rake angles). This figure can be used to estimate roughly the power required for machining steel of known hardness. In the special case of good free-machining sulphurized or leaded steels, the power actually required is about 40% less than that estimated from Eq. (50) or Fig. 19-15.

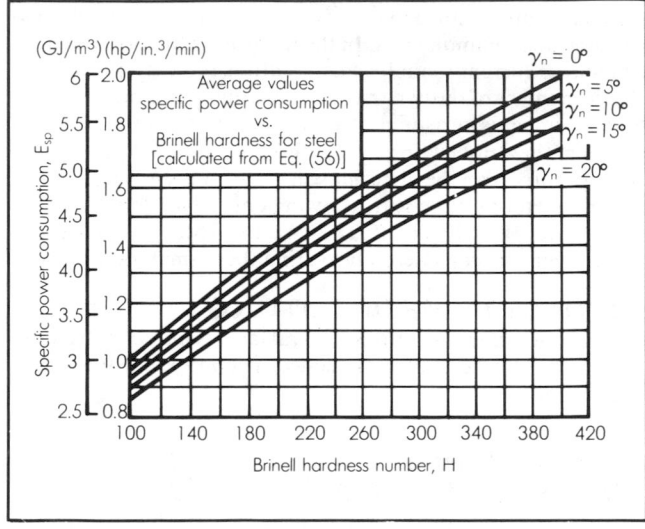

Fig. 19-15 Chart for estimating average power consumption for machining steel of a given hardness with tool of a given velocity rake.

MACHINABILITY

The following is a list of symbols and abbreviations used in formulas and discussions in this section:

Symbol	Definition
C	A constant (dependent on tool/workpiece combination and cutting variables other than speed)
C_A	A constant whose value depends on other machine variables and the work material variables
C_t	A constant equal numerically to the cutting speed that gives a tool life of 1 min (sfm or m/min)
d	Depth of cut (in. or mm)
f	Feed per revolution (ipr or mm/rev)
n	Exponent [see Eq. (53)]
T	Actual cutting time between sharpenings (min)
V	Cutting speed (sfm, m/min)
V_t	Equivalent cutting speed (sfm or m/min)
V_{60}	Cutting speed for tool life of 60 min (sfm or m/min)
x, y	Exponents [see Eq. (54)]
θ_i	Temperature at the tool/chip interface (°F or °C)
θ_s	Temperature rise in the body of the chip due to shear (°F or °C)
θ_f	Temperature rise due to friction of the chip rubbing against the tool face (°F or °C)
θ_0	Workpiece temperature (°F or °C)
α	Rake angle
ϵ	Angle of engagement

The term "machinability" does not lend itself to an exact definition acceptable to all authorities. The ease with which a given material may be worked with a cutting tool changes with the machine variables—the various quantities that define the particular machine setup used in carrying out a given operation on the work material.

MACHINABILITY TEST METHODS[10]

Measurement of machinability is difficult for several reasons. The machinability of a metal is not only a function of the metal's own metallurgical properties, such as hardness, microstructure, and chemical composition, but also a function of the type of machining process, the size and shape of cut, the cutting tool, and the cutting fluid. Variation of any of these environmental conditions may affect the machinability ranking. There does not seem to be any single dependent variable in the metalcutting process that is universally acceptable as an indicator of machinability. Whatever the variable, when it is measured under one set of experimental conditions, the ratings will probably differ from those obtained under a different set of conditions. Also, the rating determined by one test variable may be quite different from the rating obtained by other variables.

These difficulties notwithstanding, a variety of tests have been devised through the years to measure machining performance. These machinability tests include:

1. Tool life or tool wear tests.
2. Surface finish test.
3. Cutting force test.

4. Cutting temperature test.
5. Power consumption test.
6. Cuttability tests (for example, the rate of penetration of a drill under constant feed pressure).
7. Simulated production tests (in which the optimum speed or optimum speed and feed combination are determined while tool life and surface quality are held constant).

Tool Life and Tool Wear Tests

The objective of these tests is not limited to evaluation of work materials; they can also be used to test the performance of the tool or cutting fluid. The tool life test was pioneered by F. W. Taylor, who used it to evaluate the performance of various compositions of tool steels. In Taylor's test, a given work material is machined under given cutting conditions of depth of cut and feed by various tools of different composition but identical geometry. The objective of the test is to determine the cutting speed which will produce a given tool life, which is oftentimes taken to be 60 minutes of tool life. Tool materials are compared on the basis of these speeds. When the test is employed to compare work materials, the tool material is held constant and the work material is varied.

Another test similar to the tool life test is one in which the amount of wear (usually flank land wear) is measured under constant cutting conditions and at a given time of cut. This test is easier to perform, but not quite as reliable due to the irregular nature of the tool wear rates. The wear rate is relatively high at the beginning of the cut, while during the latter portion of the wear process, it is approximately proportional to the time of cut.

Surface Finish

The quality of the machined surface is one of the important criteria by which the success of a machining operation is judged. Unfortunately, the combination of machining conditions that produces a good finish on one work material may produce an unrepresentatively poor finish on another material. For example, in a series of tests conducted to study the effect of several variables on roughness, the following observations were made between two steels, SAE 1035 (ASME Machinability Rating—65%) and SAE 3140 (ASME Machinability Rating—55%): For a light depth of cut (0.010″, 0.25 mm), the SAE 1035 showed a better finish; while for a heavier depth of cut (0.125″, 3.17 mm), the SAE 3140 showed a better finish. For a small nose radius (0 to 1/16″, 1.58 mm), the finish was better on the SAE 3140; but for a larger nose radius (1/8 to 1/4″, 3.17 to 6.35 mm), the surface finish was better on the 1035 steel.[11] These comparisons were made while other cutting variables were held constant.

Tool Force Test

While information about metalcutting forces is most important in the designing of machine tools, it can also be used to evaluate machining performance. The justification for the use of force as an indicator of machinability lies in the logical assumption that the more difficult-to-machine metals require greater cutting force.

A study of tool force tests conducted to appraise the machinability of several steels is documented by Murphy and Aylward in *Machinability of Steel*.[12] The procedure for these tests was to determine for each work material the feed which would produce a given longitudinal or feeding force. The idea

behind this was that the easier-to-machine steels would produce the lower forces. However, the data generated during the study indicates that tool forces are not a good measure of machining quality.

Cutting Temperature Test

The temperature generated during machining has been used to indicate machinability. The justification for the cutting temperature test lies in the close relationship between temperature and tool life. Higher cutting temperatures would have a detrimental effect on tool life. Accordingly, work materials which produce higher temperatures would be expected to be less machinable.

Power Consumption

The power generated in metalcutting has been proposed as an indicator of a metal's machinability. It is obviously related to cutting forces and cutting temperature.

The power consumption in a machining operation can be obtained by attaching a wattmeter or ammeter to the power line coming into the machine tool. However, this gives the total power developed by the machine tool rather than the desired cutting power. The power can also be determined by measuring the heat developed at the tool, since nearly all the energy in cutting is converted into heat. This is done by use of either a calorimeter or a thermocouple. Finally, power can be assessed by measuring the cutting forces on the tool with a dynamometer.

Cuttability Tests

This type of test, also called a ranking test, is adaptable to several different cutting operations. The test measures how much material can be cut in a given length of time and under a given feeding force, other conditions being fixed. It seems reasonable to believe that a larger cut can be taken with the more machinable metals.

Test Standardization

One of the problems of machinability testing, as mentioned in the preceding discussion on test methods, is the variability in results from seemingly minor alterations in test conditions. The logical answer to this problem of test condition changes is standardization. A number of groups[13,14] have worked in past years to develop a standard test procedure which could be used for tool life and machinability testing. Included among these groups is the International Standards Organization (ISO).

SPECIFICATION OF TOOL LIFE

Methods of specifying life of a cutting tool between resharpenings may be specified in various ways:

1. Machine time—elapsed time of operation of machine tool. (Tools may be cutting intermittently during this time.)
2. Actual cutting time—elapsed time during which tools were actually cutting (common definition of tool life).
3. Volume of metal removed.
4. Number of pieces machined.
5. Equivalent cutting speed (often referred to as "Taylor speed"). For example, V_{60} cutting speed, at which a standard value of machine time or actual cutting time, such as 60 min, is obtained under a given set of cutting conditions.
6. Relative cutting speed—a modification of equivalent cutting speed for general practical use. This is the cutting

MACHINABILITY

speed at which the same machine time or actual cutting time is obtained for the test material (or tool) as for standard material (or tools) when cutting is performed under given conditions. This quantity is also called relative machinability or percent machinability. In the latter case, the standard material is assigned a value of 100.

OBSERVING TOOL FAILURE

The actual figure given for tool life in any machining operation or cutting test depends not only on the method used for specifying tool life, but also on the criteria used for judging tool failure. These criteria vary with the type of operation, the tool material used, and other factors. Some of the more common criteria for judging tool failure are:

1. Complete failure—tool completely unable to cut.
2. Preliminary failure—appearance on the finished surface or on the shoulder of a narrow, highly burnished band, indicating rubbing on the flank of the tool.
3. Flank failure—occurrence of a certain size of wear area on the tool flank. (Usually based on either a certain width of wear mark or a certain volume of metal worn away.)
4. Finish failure—occurrence of a sudden, pronounced change in finish on the work surface in the direction of either improvement or deterioration.
5. Size failure—occurrence of a change in dimension(s) of the finished part by a certain amount (for instance, an increase in the diameter of a turned piece, of a specific amount, based on the diameter originally obtained with the sharp tool).
6. Cutting-force (or power) failure—increase of the cutting force (tangential force), or the power consumption, by a certain amount.
7. Thrust-force failure—increase of the thrust on the tool by a certain amount; indicative of end wear.
8. Feeding-force failure—increase in the force needed to feed the tool by a certain amount, indicative of flank wear.

REACTION OF THE WORK MATERIAL ON THE CUTTING TOOL

The primary cause of tool failure under normal cutting conditions is usually gradual wear. Wear, which is a loss of mass or weight of the tool, is caused by five mechanisms:

1. Abrasion.
2. Adhesion.
3. Diffusion.
4. Chemical.
5. Oxidation.

Abrasion

Abrasion wear occurs when hard particles on the surface of the chip slide on the tool faces and remove tool material. These hard particles could be fragments of the built-up edge or abrasive inclusions within the workpiece material.

Adhesion

Adhesion wear occurs when two surfaces are brought together under high pressure and high temperature. The pressures generated are determined by the condition of the workpiece material and the force applied; whereas, the temperature generated is determined by the frictional environment at the tool/chip interface. At sufficiently higher temperatures and pressures, welding occurs between the chip and the tool face; when these welds fracture, minute bits of tool material are carried away with the chip.

Diffusion

Diffusion wear occurs when the atoms of a metallic crystal lattice move from an area of high atomic concentration to an area of low concentration. This process is dependent on (1) the temperature at the interface between the tool and the chip and at the interface between the tool and the workpiece and (2) the atomic bonding affinity of the tool and workpiece material.

Chemical Wear

Chemical wear occurs when the tool and workpiece are used in an environment of suitably active chemicals, which are generally part of the cutting fluid that is present. It is also possible that electrochemical wear is induced through galvanic action. It is this chemical reaction that wears the tool in a corrosive manner. Cratering is believed to be a thermo-chemical reaction.

Oxidation Wear

Oxidation wear of a cutting tool occurs at very high temperatures at the point at which the structure of the cutting tool is weakened. The temperatures are of a magnitude that permits softening of the cutting tool microstructure, which severely weakens the actual cutting edge.

It is significant to note that the temperature at the tool/chip interface is of paramount importance in optimizing tool wear. Substantiated data relative to this phenomenon proves that, as cutting speed increases, temperature increases and, therefore, tool wear also increases.

TEMPERATURE AND TOOL LIFE

The term "cutting temperature" as used in this discussion refers to the temperature at the tool/chip interface and is denoted by the symbol θ_i. It consists of the temperature rise, θ_s, in the body of the chip due to shear, the further rise, θ_f, at the interface as the hot chip rubs on the tool face, and the workpiece temperature, θ_0.

The ratio of θ_s to θ_f varies with cutting speed, generally decreasing with an increase in cutting speed. Most of the mechanical energy expended in metalcutting is transformed into heat. About 75% or more of this heat is carried away by the chip; the remainder is divided between the workpiece and the tool. An increase in speed or feed decreases the proportion of the heat transferred to the tool and workpiece.

The relationship of cutting temperature to cutting speed (in the realm of a continuous chip) is in the form:

$$\theta_i = CV^n \tag{52}$$

where:

θ_i = tool/chip interface temperature
V = cutting speed (sfm or m/min)
C = constant (dependent on tool/workpiece combination and cutting variables other than cutting speed)
n = exponent

TOOL LIFE AND ITS RELATION TO PRACTICAL VARIABLES

Tool life is related to cutting speed, dimensions of the cut, tool angles, tool shape, cutting fluid used, rigidity of the setup, chatter, dimensions of the work, and other variables. Since the largest amount of information on tool life has been obtained from tests on single point tools, many of the relationships and much of the data presented in the following sections are based on them. However, these can be usefully applied to nearly every type of machining operation when the extra factors entering into the particular process are kept in mind.

Cutting Speed

Cutting speed is the variable having by far the greatest influence on tool life. Taylor[15] showed that the relation between tool life and cutting speed ordinarily could be represented approximately by the empirical equation:

$$VT^n = C_t \qquad (53)$$

where:

V = cutting speed (sfm or m/min)
T = actual cutting time between resharpenings (min)
C_t = constant whose value depends on other machine variables and the work material variables. The value of C_t is numerically equal to the cutting speed that gives a tool life of 1 min (sfm or m/min).
n = exponent whose value varies to some extent with other machine variables and work material variables

Equation (53) defines a straight line on log-log graph paper. Figure 19-16 shows the salient features of such a plot.[16] It is evident that tool life decreases as cutting speed is increased. Although there are few exceptions to this general rule, it may fail when cutting speeds are low. Very short tool life can occur when steel is machined with carbides at very low or excessively high cutting speeds.

Equation (53) is commonly known as the cutting speed and tool life relationship. In practice, the exponent n varies in value from about 0.4 to 0.1, depending on the values of the tool variables and material variables.

Dimensions of Cut

The tool life obtained at a given cutting speed is, of course, influenced by the dimensions of the cut. The general empirical relationship between the cutting speed for a chosen tool life (for example, 60 min) and the feed and depth of cut is recognized to be ordinarily in the form:

$$V_t = \frac{C_A}{d^x f^y} \qquad (54)$$

where:

V_t = equivalent cutting speed—cutting speed for a given tool life
C_A = constant whose value depends on machine variables and the work material variables
f = feed per revolution
d = depth of cut
x, y = exponents

Sometimes called the extended tool life relationship, this equation emphasizes two important general facts about the

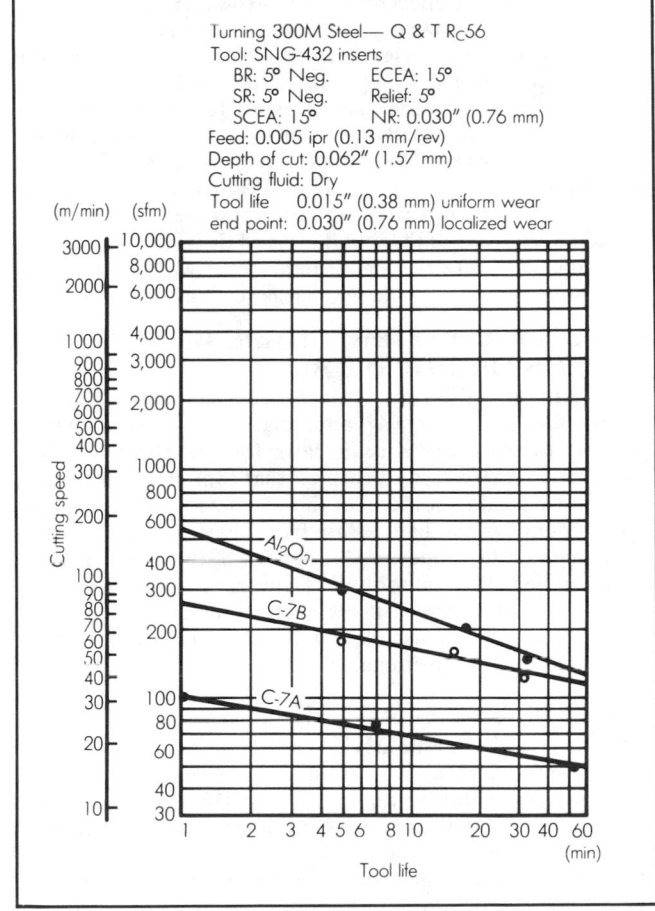

Fig. 19-16 Typical cutting speed versus tool life curves for various cutting tool materials. *(Derivation of Cost Control Criteria for Cutters, SME Technical Paper MR76-996.)*

machining of metals:

1. As feed or depth is increased, the cutting speed must be decreased to keep the tool life constant.
2. However, when this is done, the amount of metal removed by the tool during the same given life is considerably increased. (This is especially true of an increase in the depth of cut, because of its very low exponent.)

Thus, a general rule may be stated: *The combination of a large depth of cut and a high rate of feed with a low cutting speed will allow a large amount of metal to be removed during a given life of the tool.* There are few exceptions to this rule. However, limitations on the extent to which one can proceed in the direction of large cuts and low speeds are set by the increasingly poorer finish and the ability of the tool, workpiece, holding device, and machine tool to resist deflection caused by cutting forces. The greatest benefit from the principle comes in taking roughing cuts on stable workpieces in rigid machines.

Tool Angles and Shape

Tool form, as controlled by such other factors as the amount and type of curvature (nose radius) of the cutting edge(s) and the type of tool (turning, planing, shaping, drilling, etc.), may

MACHINABILITY

have a very marked effect on tool life. However, little numerical correlation of these factors has yet been accomplished.

The purpose of a clearance angle is to avoid physical interference between the tool flank and the workpiece. Clearance angles should be no larger than necessary for a given workpiece material. They are usually between 10 and 12° for machining light alloys and 4 and 6° for the harder steels. In a sharp tool, the amount of clearance, as long as it is sufficient, does not influence the tool forces. As the tool becomes dull, however, actual interference of the tool flank and the workpiece occurs. With smaller clearance angles, flank wear will reach a given width sooner than it would with larger clearance angles.

RIGIDITY, CHATTER, SHAPE AND DIMENSIONS OF WORK

The large effect that any or all of these machine variables can have on tool life is not always appreciated. It has not as yet been possible to work out specific laws for the effects of these quantities. However, it is accepted that tool life is, in general, favored by rigid conditions in the machine and the tool and work mountings and by freedom from chatter.

Changes in the shape and dimensions of the workpiece may have a varied effect on tool life. Generally, in addition to the evident loss of accuracy, if the shape and size are such that excessive deflections take place under the action of the cutting forces, tool life may be impaired.

NATURE OF ENGAGEMENT OF TOOL WITH WORK

If the nature of an operation is such that the tool cuts continuously, as in turning a full cylinder, the tool life will ordinarily be greater than if the cut is interrupted, as in turning a cylindrical piece with slots.

In operations in which the cutting is intermittent in nature, the exact manner in which the tool enters and leaves the cut often has a marked effect on tool life, especially when sintered-carbide tools are used. In this case, it appears that failure will generally be more rapid when the tool angles and position are such that the impact on entering the cut occurs at the sharp cutting edge or the tool point, rather than at a spot on the tool face away from the cutting edge.

In addition, in face milling operations on steel with sintered-carbide cutters, the relative position of the cutter and work can be a factor in tool life. The controlling variable is the angle between a radial plane through the cutter tooth and the plane of the particular face of the workpiece through which the tooth is entering the cut. This is illustrated in Fig. 19-17 in which this angle of engagement is denoted by ϵ. In some cases in the face milling of steel with a carbide cutter, if this angle is less than about 20°, the tool life will be normal; if the angle ϵ is greater than about 35°, the cutter may fail almost immediately after cutting is started.

RELATION OF TOOL LIFE TO WORK MATERIAL VARIABLES

General machinability ratings are expressed in terms of relative values. Rating figures (often called percent machinability or relative machinability) represent the relative speeds to use with each given metal to obtain a given tool life. They are relative cutting speed values. A material with a rating of 50 should be machined at (roughly) half the speed used for a material with a rating of 100 if identical tool life for both is desired.

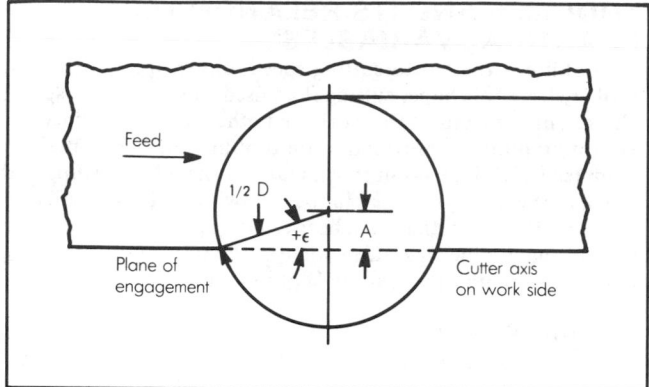

Fig. 19-17 Schematic diagram showing the angle, ϵ, for face milling operations. (Kronenberg[17,18])

Obviously, the primary objective of machinability testing is the development of data which can be used to guide the selection of cutting parameters in production operations. A comparison of machinability information from various sources will show that it does not agree in many cases. However, the recommendations derived from machinability data in this Handbook or other references should serve as a useful starting point—an approach which is considered by many experts to be vastly superior to the use of uninformed judgment. The general consensus of machinability experts is that the use of machinability ratings should be considered with specific speed and feed recommendations to arrive at starting points for production use.

Physical Properties

Sources on machining theory[19] list hardness and strain-hardenability among the most important factors affecting machinability. Other properties are also related to the machining performance of steels.

Workpiece hardness. Brinell hardness has been used as a rough measure of machinability. It is believed that an optimum hardness range for machinability of steel is about 187 to 227 Bhn.[20] As the hardness increases above this range and begins to approach the hardness of the cutting tool, the abrasive action of the chip on the tool causes tool life to be shortened. As the hardness decreases below this range, it is accompanied by an increase in ductility, which is detrimental to good machining because of tearing of the work material and difficulty in chip disposal. Cold drawing is often used on low-carbon and free-cutting steels to make these soft materials more brittle, thus facilitating the breaking up of the chips.

Strength. Research has been reported[21,22] which studies the relationship between the strength properties of a steel and its machinability. It has been concluded that, as the strength of the material increases, an adverse effect on tool life results. However, commercial experience has shown that an optimum condition for machining exists at a tensile strength of approximately 85,000 psi (586 MPa).[23] This corresponds roughly with the optimum Brinell hardness range mentioned earlier.

The U.S. Air Force Machinability Report[24] establishes a more consistent relationship between hardness and strength, on one hand, and machinability as measured by allowable cutting speed, on the other hand. The general trend of their "Guide to the Proper Cutting Speed" is illustrated in Fig. 19-18.[25]

A useful approximate relationship between the Brinell hardness number, *BHN*, and ultimate tensile strength, *UTS*, exists for steel. In U.S. customary units:

$$UTS = BHN \times 500 \qquad (55)$$

In metric:

$$UTS = BHN \times 0.355 \qquad (56)$$

where:

UTS = ultimate tensile strengths (psi or kg/mm²)
BHN = Brinell hardness number

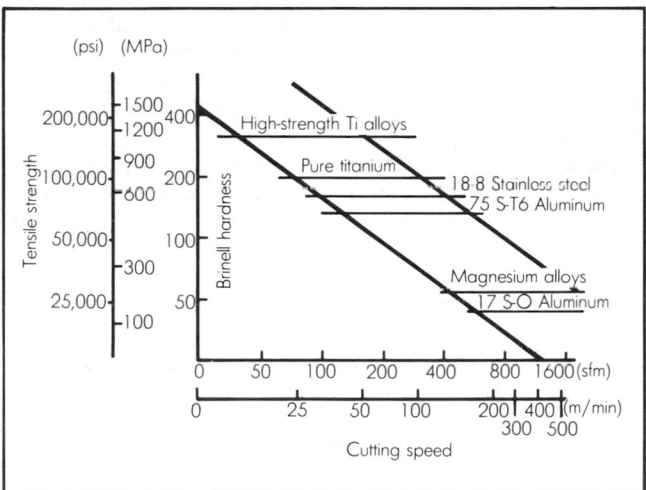

Fig. 19-18 Approximate relationship between Brinell hardness and tensile strength vs. allowable cutting speed. (*United States Air Force Machinability Report*, vol. 3, 1954.)

It should be noted that these formulas apply to steel and, in some cases, certain aluminum alloys. The formulas should not be used for nonferrous alloys and are not sufficiently accurate for use in structural design.

In addition to the hardness and strength of the work material, two additional mechanical factors are strain-hardenability and coefficient of friction between tool and chip.

Strain-hardenability. Strain-hardenability is the capacity of the material for work hardening upon deformation. Because metalcutting is a deformation process, this property is important in the machining of a material. As the strain hardening capacity of the material increases, poorer machinability manifests itself in the form of shorter tool life due to increased hardness of the chip, and poorer surface quality due to the formation of built-up edges.

Coefficient of friction. Another of the important factors influencing tool life, surface quality, and power consumption is the coefficient of friction between the cutting tool and chip. This is not a property of the work material alone, but rather a characteristic of the combination of tool and workpiece. It can be defined as the ratio of the frictional force along the rake face of the tool to the force normal to the tool face. For example, as the coefficient of friction is decreased, through changes in chemistry of either the workpiece material or the tool material, machining performance is improved.

Thermal Properties

Besides the mechanical properties of the workpiece material, the thermal properties have been shown to influence the machinability of metals. In a study of thermal properties and their effect on machinability, Ewel[26,27] found a significant correlation to exist. There appears to be a rather definite relationship between allowable cutting speed, which is used as the measure of machinability, and a characteristic defined as the thermal dispersion. The thermal dispersion of a work material is the ratio of its thermal conductivity to its density. Many of the titanium and superalloys, which have a low value of thermal dispersion are very difficult to machine. On the other hand, many of the aluminum and magnesium alloys, which can be machined at high speeds, possess relatively high values of thermal dispersion.

The attempt to establish a definite and quantitative relationship between a material's physical properties and its machinability is probably best illustrated by the work of Datsko and Henkin.[28,29,30,31]

Microstructure

The literature is replete with results of research testifying to the importance of microstructure in determining the machining qualities of a metal. In one of the most significant studies, Field and Stansbury investigated the effect of structure on the machinability of cast iron.[32] Other sources summarize the results of studies conducted on steels.[33]

For steels of low carbon content (below 0.30% carbon), the structure most desirable for good machinability is lamellar pearlite. This pearlite is a microstructure which contains two phases, ferrite and cementite, in the form of plates or laminates. Ferrite is a soft, ductile phase consisting of iron with a very small amount of carbon (0.007% maximum at room temperature) dissolved in it. Cementite is the hard compound Fe_3C. All things being equal, the proportion of Fe_3C increases as the carbon content increases. At very low carbon contents, the proportion of ferrite present in the steel is too high for good machinability. The consequences of the high ferrite content are built-up edge due to welding of the chip on the tool, poor surface finish, and excessive frictional heat. Ferrite is responsible for these unwanted effects because of its toughness and ductility and its ability to adhere to the cutting edge of the tool.

At carbon contents above about 0.30%, too much of the hard abrasive cementite exists and the result is accelerated tool wear. For these steels, the machinability is improved by spheroidizing the lamellar pearlite.

Between these two carbon levels, good machining is obtained with the pearlitic structure, owing to the combination of brittle carbide plates separating the soft, deformable ferrite layers. This pearlite fractures relatively easily, causing less ductile deformation and therefore less generation of heat. Longer tool life, better surface finish, and better chip removal are the desired results.

Chemical Composition

The chemistry of a metal has a pronounced influence on the metal's mechanical properties and microstructure; through this influence, chemistry affects machinability. It is now well established that significant improvements in machinability can be obtained through proper control of the chemistry and

MACHINING ECONOMICS

microstructure of the workpiece materials.[34] Development of free-machining steels with additions of manganese sulfide and lead inclusions are typical examples.

Carbon. Carbon content greatly affects the properties of steel, including machinability. High-carbon steels, unless spheroidized, are too strong and hard for good machinability. At very low carbon contents, the steels are generally of poor machining quality because of less than optimum hardness. The best carbon range, for the sake of machinability, depends on the steelmaking process. The best carbon content for machinability is about 0.20% for open-hearth steel. Cutting quality decreases rapidly with an increase of carbon to more than 0.30% in open-hearth steel.[35]

Alloying elements. Many alloying elements are added to steel for their beneficial effects on mechanical properties and hardenability. Some of these, such as chromium, molybdenum, vanadium, and tungsten, are carbide-formers and tend to increase abrasion on the tool. Suitable annealing processes reduce the abrasive property of these steels to some extent. Manganese and nickel are ferrite strengtheners which usually reduce machinability by increasing hardness and toughness. The effect of manganese on machinability depends largely on the total content of carbon, manganese, and phosphorus. In free-machining steels, the most favorable manganese content is

about 1.00-1.30% in open-hearth steel.[36]

Other elements which form hard, abrasive inclusions are detrimental to the machining performance of steels. Aluminum and silicon fall into this category.

Free-machining elements. Certain elements are added to steels specifically for the purpose of increasing the machinability of the steels. The advantage of these additives is usually attributed to a reduction in the coefficient of friction between chip and tool face. This reduction has two beneficial effects. First, energy requirements are reduced because a decrease in the coefficient of friction causes a decrease in cutting temperature and cutting forces. Second, surface finish is improved through a reduction in the tendency of a built-up edge to form and, as a consequence, leave behind particles on the work surface and make it rough. The mechanism by which these additives reduce the coefficient of friction is similar to the action of a cutting fluid. Free-machining additives are thought to involve the formation of low-shear-strength contaminating films at points of contact. In this sense, these additives may be referred to as internal lubricants.[37]

The more important elements which have been used as free machining additives in steel are lead, sulphur, phosphorus, nitrogen, selenium and tellurium. Of these, lead and sulphur are the principle additives.[38,39,40,41,42,43]

MACHINING ECONOMICS

The following is a list of symbols and abbreviations used in formulas and discussions in this section:

Symbol	Definition
C	Constant in Taylor's tool life equation [see Eq. (53) in this chapter]
c_d	Cost of direct labor ($)
c_t	Cost of a cutting edge ($)
c_0	Overhead cost per unit time ($/hr)
C_g	Cost per minute to regrind ($/min)
C_I	Initial cost of an insert ($)
C_T	Total cost per part ($)
C_{TMAX}	Cost per part under maximum rate conditions ($)
C_{TMIN}	Cost per part under minimum cost conditions ($)
d	Workpiece diameter (in. or mm)
f	Feed (in. or mm)
k_c	Cost of changing a worn tool ($)
k_m	Machining cost per part ($)
k_r	Cost of raw material per part ($)
k_0	Overhead cost ($)
k_s	Cost of preparing the work station for the actual machining process ($)
k_t	Tool Cost ($)
K	General labor and overhead rate, $c_d + c_0$ ($/hr)
L	Length of cut (in. or mm)
n	Exponent in Taylor's tool life equation [see Eq. (53) in this chapter]
N_e	Number of cutting edges on an insert
N_g	Number of possible regrinds
t_c	Time to change and adjust a cutting tool (min)
t_g	Time required for regrinding (min)
t_m	Machining time (min)
$t_{m(min)}$	Machining time under minimum cost

Symbol	Definition
	conditions (min)
t_s	Time required for setup (min)
T	Tool life (min)
T_{MIN}	Tool life for minimum cost per part (min)
T_{MAX}	Tool life for maximum production rate (min)
T_T	Total time to machine one part (min)
V_{MAX}	Cutting speed for maximum production rate (fpm or m/min)
V_{MIN}	Cutting speed for minimum cost per part (fpm or m/min)

The ultimate purpose of a machining operation is to produce parts which meet all the required specifications (dimensional tolerances, surface characteristics, physical property requirements, etc.) at the lowest possible cost or in the minimum possible time. Due to the high cost of machining operations, careful analysis of the costs and operating conditions are necessary.

DECISION CRITERIA

The first step in the analysis procedure is to decide on the most applicable decision criterion for the operation under consideration. Two basic criteria are commonly used: (1) minimum cost per part and (2) maximum production rate or minimum time per part.

The minimum cost criterion is aimed at producing a part at the lowest cost; whereas, maximum production rate criterion deals with maximizing the number of units produced during a given planning horizon. The choice of criterion to be used is a management decision dependent on numerous factors such as competitive standing, orders waiting to be processed, contractual agreements, number of pieces to be produced, and plant capacity.

COST FACTORS

All machining operations involve at least six basic cost components, described as follows:

1. Material cost, k_r—the cost of raw material per part.
2. Setup cost, k_s—the cost of preparing the work station for the actual machining process. If the cost of direct labor is c_d and the time required for setup is t_s, then the setup cost may be expressed as:

$$k_s = c_d t_s, \tag{57}$$

3. Machining cost, k_m—the cost of actual machining time. If t_m is the machining time required, then the machining cost per part is:

$$k_m = c_d t_m \tag{58}$$

4. Toolchanging cost, k_c—the cost of changing a worn tool. If t_c represents the time necessary to change and adjust a cutting tool, then the toolchanging cost per part is given by:

$$k_c = t_c c_d \left(\frac{t_m}{T} \right) \tag{59}$$

where:

$T =$ tool life
$t_m =$ machining time
$\dfrac{t_m}{T} =$ number of cutting edges needed per workpiece

5. Overhead cost, k_0—indirect cost of producing a part, including factors such as depreciation and general administrative expenses. The overhead cost per part is the production time per part multiplied by the overhead cost per unit time, c_0:

$$k_0 = c_0 T_T \tag{60}$$

where:

$T_T =$ total time needed to machine one part. The total time per part consists of the setup time, t_s; the machining time, t_m; and the toolchanging time, t_c, or:

$$T_T = t_s + t_m + t_c \left(\frac{t_m}{T} \right) \tag{61}$$

Thus, the overhead cost per part becomes:

$$k_0 = c_0 \left(t_s + t_m + t_c \cdot \frac{t_m}{T} \right) \tag{62}$$

6. Tool cost, k_t—the tool cost per part. If c_t represents the cost of a cutting edge, then the tool cost per part is given by:

$$k_t = c_t \left(\frac{t_m}{T} \right) \tag{63}$$

For disposable inserts:

$$c_t = \frac{C_I}{N_e} \tag{64}$$

where:

$C_I =$ initial cost of the insert
$N_e =$ number of cutting edges available on the insert

For regrindable tools:

$$c_t = \frac{C_I + N_g (C_g t_g)}{1 + N_g} \tag{65}$$

where:

$N_g =$ number of possible regrinds
$C_g =$ cost per minute to regrind
$t_g =$ time required for regrinding

The total cost per part, C_T, is the sum of these individual cost components:

$$C_T = k_r + c_d t_s + c_d t_m + c_d t_c \left(\frac{t_m}{T} \right) + c_t \left(\frac{t_m}{T} \right) + \tag{66}$$

$$c_0 \left(t_s + t_m + t_c \cdot \frac{t_m}{T} \right)$$

CUTTING SPEED FOR MINIMUM COST

To determine the cutting speed that will result in minimum cost per part, the total cost equation is expressed in terms of cutting speed and then differentiated with respect to cutting speed, set equal to zero, and solved.

The cutting speed for minimum cost per part, V_{MIN}, is independent of the setup and material costs and is computed from:

$$V_{MIN} = C \left[\frac{K}{(K t_c + c_t) \left(\frac{1}{n} - 1 \right)} \right]^n \tag{67}$$

where:

$C =$ constant in a tool life equation of the form $VT^n = C$
$n =$ exponent in tool life equation
$K =$ general labor and overhead rate, $c_d + c_0$

The tool life for minimum cost per part, T_{MIN}, is found from:

$$T_{MIN} = \left(\frac{C}{V_{MIN}} \right)^{\frac{1}{n}} \tag{68}$$

The total cost per part under minimum cost conditions becomes:

$$C_{TMIN} = K t_s + K t_m + K t_c \left(\frac{t_{m(min)}}{T_{MIN}} \right) + c_t \left(\frac{t_{m(min)}}{T_{MIN}} \right) \tag{69}$$

The value of $t_{m(min)}$, the machining time under minimum cost conditions, depends upon the type of machining operation being performed. For example, for a turning operation:

$$t_{m(min)} = \frac{\pi d L}{12 V_{MIN} f} \tag{70}$$

where:

$d =$ diameter of workpiece
$L =$ length of cut (in. or mm)
$f =$ feed (in./min or mm/min)

In general, t_m is given by:

$$t_m = \frac{Length\ of\ Cut}{Feed\ Rate} \tag{71}$$

CUTTING TOOL MATERIALS

MAXIMUM PRODUCTION RATE

In certain situations, minimizing production time or maximizing production rate may be preferred to cost minimization. As mentioned earlier, the total production time per part, T_T, is given by:

$$T_T = t_s + t_m + t_c \left(\frac{t_m}{T} \right) \tag{72}$$

Expressing the time components in terms of cutting speed and solving for the speed that yields minimum cutting time (maximum rate, independent of the setup timing) result in:

$$V_{MAX} = \frac{C}{\left[t_c \left(\frac{1}{n} - 1 \right) \right]^n} \tag{73}$$

and:

$$T_{MAX} = \left(\frac{C}{V_{MAX}} \right)^{\frac{1}{n}} \tag{74}$$

where:

V_{MAX} = cutting speed for maximum production rate
T_{MAX} = tool life for maximum production rate

CUTTING TOOL MATERIALS

Of the many variables affecting any machining operation, the cutting tool—while small and relatively inexpensive—is one of the most critical. This section is limited to a discussion of the many materials now being used for cutting tools.

MATERIAL SELECTION

Factors affecting the selection of a cutting tool material for a specific application include:

1. Hardness and condition of the workpiece material.
2. Operations to be performed—optimum tool selection may reduce the number of operations required.
3. Amount of stock to be removed.
4. Accuracy and finish requirements.
5. Type, capability, and condition of the machine tool to be used.
6. Rigidity of the tool and workpiece.
7. Production requirements influencing the speeds and feeds selected.
8. Operating conditions such as cutting forces and temperatures.
9. Tool cost per part machined, including initial tool cost, grinding cost, tool life, frequency of regrinding or replacement, and labor cost—the most economical tool is not necessarily the one providing the longest life, or the one having the lowest initial cost.

While highly desirable, no single cutting tool material is available to meet the needs of all machining applications. This is because of the wide range of conditions and requirements encountered. Each tool material has its own combination of properties making it the best for a specific operation.

DESIRABLE PROPERTIES

The most common type of failure in cutting tools is flank wear—abrasion occurring between the flank of the tool and the workpiece. Flank wear is directly related to speed and feed; as they are increase, the rate of wear increases.

Cratering (a combination of abrasion, adhesion, and chemical diffusion) is another common form of tool wear. It occurs on the rake face of the tool, behind the cutting edge where the direction of the chip is abruptly changed and heat and pressure on the tool are at a maximum.

High strength is also critical, especially with high cutting speeds and feed rates. Cutting tools must be tough enough to withstand high mechanical shock loads without chipping or fracturing, and also be resistant to heat deformation.

Toughness has no universally accepted definition, but in the case of cutting tools it is generally considered to be the ability of the material to absorb energy and withstand plastic deformation without fracturing under compressive loading. It can be divided into an elastic component (strength), which increases with increasing hardness, and a plastic component (ductility), which decreases with increasing hardness. In other words, as the hardness of a material increases, it becomes less ductile.

CARBON AND LOW-ALLOY TOOL STEELS

Plain carbon and tool steels having a lower alloy content than high-speed steels (discussed next in this chapter) are seldom used anymore for production metalcutting applications. One reason, in addition to their low hot hardness, is that increasing material and labor costs have resulted in minimal savings over more desirable cutting tool materials. Also, tools made from these materials must be operated at low cutting speeds.

There are, however, limited applications for which such tool steels are still practical. These include less critical and nonproduction applications, specialized operations such as knurling and burnishing, occasional short-run job shop work, and the machining of soft, nonferrous metals such as brass. These tools are also widely employed as woodworking tools and utility tools used in home workshops.

HIGH-SPEED STEELS

Since the beginning of the twentieth century, high-speed steels (HSS's) have been an essential class of cutting tool materials used by the metalworking industry. HSS's are high-alloy steels designed to cut other materials efficiently at high speeds, despite the extreme heat generated at the cutting edges of the tools.

Classification of HSS's

Because of the wide variety of tool steels available, the American Iron and Steel Institute (AISI) has classified HSS's according to their chemical compositions.

All types, whether molybdenum or tungsten, contain about 4% chromium; the carbon and vanadium contents vary. As a general rule, when the vanadium content is increased, the carbon content is usually increased.

Molybdenum types of HSS are identified with the prefix M; the tungsten types, with the prefix T. Molybdenum types M1 through M10 (except M6) contain no cobalt, but most contain some tungsten. The cobalt-bearing, molybdenum-tungsten, premium types are generally classified in the M30 and M40 series. Super HSS's normally range from M40 upward; they are capable of being heat treated to high hardnesses.

The tungsten type T1 does not contain molybdenum or cobalt. Cobalt-bearing tungsten types range from T4 through T15 and contain various amounts of cobalt.

Advantages of HSS Tools

For good cutting tool performance, a material must resist deformation and wear. It must also possess a certain degree of toughness, the ability to absorb shock without catastrophic failure, while maintaining a high hardness at cutting edge temperatures. Also, the material must have the ability to be readily and economically brought to a final desired shape.

HSS's are capable of being heat treated to high hardnesses, within the range of R_C63-68. In fact, the M40 series of HSS's is normally capable of being hardened to R_C70, but a maximum of R_C68 is recommended to avoid brittleness. HSS's are also capable of maintaining a high hardness at cutting temperatures. This hot hardness property of HSS's is related to their composition and to a secondary hardening reaction, which is the precipitation of fine alloy carbides during the tempering operation.

HSS's also possess a high level of wear resistance due to the high hardness of their tempered martensite matrix and the extremely hard refractory carbides distributed within this martensitic structure. The hardness of molybdenum-rich carbide M_6C is approximately R_C75, while the hardness of vanadium-rich carbide MC is about R_C84. Therefore, increasing the amount of MC increases the wear resistance of HSS. Although the higher vanadium HSS's (with up to 5% vanadium) are more wear resistant, they are more difficult to machine or grind.

HSS tools possess an adequate degree of impact toughness and are more capable of taking the shock loading of interrupted cuts than carbide tools. Toughness in HSS's can be increased by adjusting the chemistry to a lower carbon level or by hardening at an austenitizing temperature lower than that usually recommended for the steel, thereby providing a finer grain size. Tempering at a temperature range between 1100-1200° F (593-649° C) will also increase the toughness of HSS. When toughness increases, however, hardness and wear resistance decrease.

When HSS's are in the annealed state, they can be fabricated, hot worked, machined, ground, etc., to produce the cutting tool shape.

Limitations of HSS's

A possible problem with the use of HSS's can result from the tendency of the carbide to agglomerate in the centers of large ingots. This can be minimized by remelting or by adequate hot working. If the agglomeration is not minimized, however, physical properties can be reduced and grinding becomes more difficult. Improved properties and grindability are important advantages of powdered metal HSS's, discussed next in this chapter.

Another limitation of HSS's is that the hardness of these materials falls off rapidly when machining temperatures exceed about 1000-1100° F (538-593° C). This requires the use of lower cutting speeds than those used with carbides, ceramics, and certain other cutting tool materials.

Applications of HSS Tools

Despite the increased use of carbides and other cutting tool materials, HSS's are still employed extensively—some estimates peg their use for about 60% of all metalcutting operations. Most drills, reamers, taps, thread chasers, end mills, and gear cutting tools are made from HSS's. They are also widely used for complexly shaped tools such as form tools, parting (cutoff) tools for which sharp cutting edges are required. Most broaches and many lathe and planer tools are made from HSS's.

HSS tools are usually preferred for operations performed at low cutting speeds; on older, less rigid machine tools with low horsepower; and when good surface finishes are required on workpieces. They are often best for tough, interrupted-cut operations on difficult-to-machine materials, such as heat-treated steels, titanium alloys, and high-temperature materials. Reasons for the continued high usage of HSS tools include their relatively low cost and easy fabrication, good wear resistance and toughness, and versatility (they are suitable for virtually all types of cutting tools).

POWDERED METAL HIGH-SPEED TOOL STEELS

High-speed tool steels made by powder metallurgy processes generally have a uniform structure, with fine carbide particles and no segregation. Powder metallurgy produced HSS's provide many advantages, and tools made from these materials are being increasingly applied.

Material Advantages

While HSS's made by the powder metallurgy process are generally slightly higher in cost, tool manufacturing and performance benefits may rapidly outweigh this premium. In many cases, however, tools made from these materials are lower in cost because of reduced material, labor, and machining costs, compared to those made from wrought materials. Near-net shapes produced often require only a minimum of grinding, and the more complex the tool, the more savings possible. Also, the higher the alloy content of the steel, the greater the savings.

Another important advantage is that the powder metallurgy process permits more design flexibility. This is because complexly shaped tools can be produced economically. Also, the method may allow the use of better grade, higher alloy steels that would be uneconomical to employ for tools with conventional production methods.

Applications

Cutting tools made from steels produced by the powder metallurgy process are recommended for turning, boring, and milling applications in which carbide tools chip, crack, or fail because of interrupted cuts or hard spots, for operations requiring frequent starting and stopping, and for machines with underpowered spindles.

Milling cutters are becoming a major application for these tool steels. Stock removal rates can generally be raised by increasing the cutting speed and/or feed rate. In general, the feed per cutter tooth is increased for roughing operations, and the cutting speed is boosted for finishing.

CUTTING TOOL MATERIALS

CAST COBALT-BASED ALLOYS

Proprietary cutting tool materials are available as cast from cobalt-chromium-tungsten alloys. Molten metal is cast in chill molds made from graphite. Rapid cooling imparts a fine-grained, hard surface of complex carbides with a tough core.

Advantages

High hot hardness and transverse rupture strength, plus good resistance to abrasive wear, thermal and mechanical shock, and impact, as well as a low coefficient of friction against any material, enable cobalt-based alloys to remove large amounts of metal in a limited amount of machining time.

Tools cast from cobalt-based alloys are sometimes referred to as the in-between or intermediate tools—for applications requiring properties between those of high-speed steel tools and carbide tools. For certain applications, however, they combine favorable features of both high-speed steel and cemented carbide tools. They have proven effective for machining operations that are considered too fast for high-speed steel tools and too slow for carbide tools.

Cutting tools cast from cobalt-based alloys are particularly advantageous for machines with multiple tooling setups in which spindle speeds of the machines are restricted and several operations must be performed with widely varying cutting speeds. In such cases, at least one, and often several, of the tools cannot be operated under ideal cutting conditions, since the needs of one dictate the speeds for the rest. Cast cobalt-based alloy tools adapt to such varying conditions as these and allow machining cycles to be shortened.

Cutting tools made from these materials are less apt to fracture or chip than tools made from carbide, and they provide more resistance to heat than high-speed steel tools. They have proven to be especially effective for cutoff and grooving operations. Rough, heavy, and interrupted turning is easily performed, and with proper application, the finishes produced can equal those possible with most other cutting tools. Their high transverse rupture strength permits making interrupted cuts often not possible with carbide tools. Also, the high strength and low coefficient of friction of these tools make them ideal for slow speed, high-pressure operations such as cutoff and grooving.

Applications

Versatility is another important advantage of the cast cobalt-based materials. They are used for a wide variety of tools including solid tool bits, brazed-tip tools, toolholder inserts, cutoff blades, grooving tools, spade drills, milling cutter inserts and blades, and cast-to-form tools and tips. In cast form tools, holes are not practical. Also, dovetails are not generally feasible, because it is more economical to braze the tools to holders.

CEMENTED TUNGSTEN CARBIDES

Cemented carbides include a broad family of hard metals produced by powder metallurgy techniques that provide properties making them suitable for metalcutting tools.

These so-called straight WC-Co carbides are well suited for tools used to machine most cast irons, nonferrous metals, and nonmetallic materials. They provide an increase in cutting speed capability of about five times that possible with tool steels, plus the ability of cutting harder materials with improved efficiency.

Advantages of Cemented Carbides

High hardness at both room and high temperatures makes cemented carbides particularly well suited for metalcutting. The hardness of even the softest carbide used for machining is significantly higher than the hardest tool steel. Hot hardness, the capacity of WC-Co to maintain a high hardness at elevated temperatures, permits the use of higher cutting speeds. Critical loss of hardness does not occur until the cobalt binder has reached a temperature high enough to allow plastic deformation to take place on a microscale at the cutting edge.

Cemented carbides are also characterized by high compressive strength values. The compressive strength is most influenced by Co content, increasing as the Co content is increased to about 4-6%, then decreasing with additional amounts of Co.

Straight Tungsten Carbides

The family of two-phase WC-Co compositions, commonly referred to as the straight tungsten carbide grades, are particularly well suited for tools used to machine materials that cause tool wear primarily due to abrasion. One major class of such materials is cast iron; consequently, these compositions are often referred to as cast iron grades. They are also used, however, for machining many other metals, aluminum, high-temperature alloys, and nonferrous metals.

The straight WC-Co grades are not normally effective in machining steels because of the nature of the wear that develops rapidly on the rake face of the tool—cratering. This is the result of adhesion and diffusion between the tool and the chips because of the affinity of iron in the chips to the cobalt binder in the tool.

Alloyed Tungsten Carbides

Alloying of the two-phase WC-Co system with additional carbides can delay the formation of a crater on the top face of a cutting tool used in the machining operations that form long, continuous chips, as is the case when cutting steels. The alloys can be introduced as single carbides or as solid solutions in combination with part of the WC. After preparation of the carbides, the manufacturing process is essentially the same as for straight WC-Co compositions.

TiC alloyed grades. The most significant contribution of TiC in carbide cutting tools is a reduction in the tendency toward built-up edges on the cutting tools and a reduction in the diffusion wear process. Reduced diffusion between the workpiece and tool at the high temperatures developed during machining delays cratering, which is a common cause of tool failure in cutting steel. Hot hardness is also improved with the addition of TiC.

As the TiC content increases, however, the transverse rupture, compressive, and impact strengths, as well as the elastic modulus, are all reduced for any given Co content. For this reason, it is common practice in producing commercial grades of alloyed carbides to counteract the weakening effect of TiC additions by increasing the amount of Co to maintain the desired strength level.

TaC alloyed grades. The contribution which TaC makes to carbide cutting tool performance is similar to that of TiC in that it prolongs the tool life of tools used to cut materials such as steels that yield long, continuous chips. Small additions of TaC to WC-Co alloys inhibit the recrystallization of the carbide phase, and resulting alloys generally have a finer

CUTTING TOOL MATERIALS

grain size and higher hardness than corresponding TaC-free compositions. Such alloys also permit wider sintering ranges and are therefore less sensitive to oversintering.

Although TaC has lower hardness than TiC at room temperature, the hot hardness is higher. Therefore, TaC may improve wear resistance at cutting temperatures. Also, the coefficient of thermal expansion for TaC more closely matches that for WC-Co, thereby resulting in better resistance to thermal shock.

Micrograin Carbides

So-called micrograin high-strength carbides are actually an extension of conventional WC-Co grades, which are essentially of micrograin structure. The concept is to maintain wear resistance or hardness by producing extremely fine microstructures while increasing binder levels to maximize strength and shock resistance.

The major advantage of micrograin compositions is their higher toughness compared to conventional grades of equal hardness but lower binder content. They are used for machining applications in which their higher transverse rupture strengths and toughness offer an advantage. Such applications include operations requiring severe interrupted cuts, cutoff and form tools that chip or break when made from conventional carbides, and some machining operations on stainless steels, high-temperature alloys, supcralloys, and titanium. Micrograin carbides also have utility for positive-rake tooling in which a free cutting edge is needed but is relatively unsupported. One disadvantage of micrograin carbides, however, is that they have a somewhat greater tendency to fail by cratering than other carbides.

Grade Classifications

The two most popular classification systems for cemented carbide cutting tools are:

1. The unofficial C-classification system initiated in the U.S. automotive industry and more commonly used in the United States (see Table 19-2).

2. The International Organization for Standardization (ISO) system, based on ISO Standard 513-1975(E), which is widely used in Europe and appears to be gaining acceptance in the United States.

Although these two classification systems for identifying carbide cutting tools are widely used, they both share the common fault of being based on application rather than composition, microstructure, and performance characteristics.

Selection and Applications of Carbide Tools

Despite the inroads made by coated carbide inserts, discussed later in this chapter, conventional grades of uncoated carbides are still being used extensively, and they are the most economical and productive for some applications. The wide variety of carbide compositions with different performance characteristics commercially available is necessary because of the many workpiece materials, operations, and production conditions and requirements encountered in industry.

Type of tools available. Four basic types of carbide tools are available: indexable inserts, brazed carbide tools, mechanically-held, regrindable carbide tools, and solid carbide tools. Indexable inserts, mechanically clamped in holders, represent by far the largest percentage of carbide tools used. They provide unlimited grade selection in a wide variety of standard shapes, sizes, and built-in chip-control geometries. Indexable inserts arc uscd in both single-point tools and multiedge cutting heads for combinations of turning, boring, milling, facing, chamfering, and related operations.

Brazed carbide tools, in addition to their use for special applications, have good utility characteristics because of the wide range of shapes and geometries that can be ground with them and because of their relatively low initial cost. Regrindable, mechanically-held tools are well suited for many special applications and are used for heavy-duty turning and planing operations, as well as for certain form tool applications. They are, however, relatively high in maintenance costs and consequently are often replaced with indexable inserts when possible. Solid carbide tools are generally limited to special applications because of their high initial costs and maintenance costs. They are used frequently, however, for applications such as boring of deep holes that require the inherently high stiffness of carbide.

Grade selection factors. Selection of the proper carbide grade is of considerable economic importance because edge wear or breakage and the frequency of tool indexing and replacement are major contributors to production costs.

TITANIUM CARBIDES

Three basic grades of TiC are now being applied in production machining applications. All three grades are manufactured by cold pressing and vacuum sintering, which are standard practices in the carbide industry. Properties of these grades and the areas of application according to the generally accepted U.S. and ISO standard classifications for carbide grades are detailed in Table 19-3.[44]

Advantages

Desirable properties of cemented TiC include high melting point and hardness (TiC is the hardest of all carbides—hardness is retained at high temperatures to resist plastic deformation), good oxidation resistance at temperatures encountered in machining, low density, good crater resistance, and lower thermal conductivity and coefficient of friction than WC, which helps reduce heat in tools. These properties contribute to making TiC a good tooling material for machining steel, as well as certain cast iron applications. Advantages include the following:

- Resistance to edge buildup and cratering is high—superior to that of WC and ceramic materials.
- Keen edge retention because of resistance to wear permits holding close tolerances on long finishing cuts.
- Capability of producing smooth surface finishes exists, often eliminating the need for subsequent grinding.
- The range of possible cutting speeds approaches the range used for ceramic tools, but superior strength permits heavier cuts—resulting in the removal of more metal at the same tool life. Compared with WC tools operating at equivalent speeds, TiC can provide longer tool life or faster cutting speeds at the same tool life.
- TiC tools can tolerate wider variations in cutting speeds than either WC or ceramic tools.
- TiC inserts are less expensive than those made of WC.
- TiC tools require less-strategic raw materials than those made from WC.

Initial wear rates for both TiC-coated WC tools and cemented TiC tools are similar. However, uncoated TiC tools

CUTTING TOOL MATERIALS

TABLE 19-2
Classification of Tungsten Carbides According to Machining Application, per U.S. C-System

Classi-fication Number	Materials to be Machined	Machining Operation	Type of Carbide	Characteristics of Cut	of Carbide	Typical Properties Hardness, R_A	Transverse Rupture Strength, ksi (MPa)
C-1	Cast iron, nonferrous metals, and nonmetallic materials requiring abrasion resistance	Roughing cuts	Wear-resistant grades. Generally, straight WC-Co with varying grain sizes.	Increasing cutting speed ↓	Increasing hardness and wear resistance ↓	89.0	350 (2413)
C-2		General purpose				92.0	250 (1724)
C-3		Finishing				92.5	200 (1379)
C-4		Precision boring and fine finishing		Increasing feed rate	Increasing strength and binder content	93.5	175 (1207)
C-5	Steels and steel alloys requiring crater and deformation resistance	Roughing cuts	Crater-resistant grades. Various WC-Co compositions with TiC and/or TaC alloys.	Increasing cutting speed ↓	Increasing hardness and wear resistance ↓	91.0	300 (2068)
C-6		General purpose				92.0	250 (1724)
C-7		Finishing				93.0	200 (1379)
C-8		Precision boring and fine finishing		Increasing feed rate	Increasing strength and binder content	94.0	150 (1034)

TABLE 19-3
Properties of Titanium Carbide Cutting Tool Grades

Tool Designation U.S.	ISO	Nominal Nickel Content, % (by weight)	Hardness, R_A	Transverse Rupture Strength, ksi (MPa)	Density, lb/in.^{3} (kg/m^3)	Young's Modulus, psi x 10^6 (GPa)
C-7, C-8	P01, P10	12	92.8	200 (1379)	0.200 (5550)	63.9 (440.6)
C-6, C-7	P10, P20	17	92.0	235 (1620)	0.203 (5630)	62.5 (430.9)
C-5, C-6	P20, P30	22	91.0	275 (1896)	0.209 (5800)	59.9 (413.0)

retain the same rate of wear after extended machining, while coated WC tools show an increased wear rate with longer cutting times.[45] Tests under the same conditions have shown that TiC-based grades have 3-4 times as much resistance to flank wear as uncoated WC grades.

Applications

TiC tools are widely used for finishing and precision machining of steels that require high speeds and light-to-moderate feed rates. These were considered the only feasible applications for early available grades; because of this, the material has often been considered usable only in filling a gap between tungsten carbide and ceramic tools.

Now, however, with the improved grades available, tools made from this material are applied to a broader range of applications. These include heavy and semifinish machining of some steels and certain cast irons, particularly the newer modified and malleable types that produce some chip curl, and certain milling operations. They have proven effective for close-tolerance machining with long cuts and for grooving operations in which depth and width dimensions are critical. In some applications involving the replacement of C-7 and C-8 grades of WC tools, improvements in tool life of over 300% have been obtained.

TiC-based tools, however, are not generally used for very heavy cuts or at very slow speeds. Also, they are not recommended for removing heavy, abrasive surface scale or for machining most nonferrous materials, hard cast irons, graphite, or high-temperature alloys. On nonferrous materials, such as aluminum alloys, affinity between the tool and work produces a built-up edge.

COATED CARBIDES

Carbide inserts coated with wear-resistant compounds for increased performance and longer tool life represent the fastest growing segment of the cutting tool materials spectrum. The use of coated carbide inserts has permitted increases in machining rates up to five or more times over machining rates possible with uncoated carbide tools, although in some cases increases are only about 20%. Many consider coated carbide tools the most significant advance in cutting tool materials since the development of WC tooling.

The first coated insert consisted of a thin titanium carbide (TiC) layer on a conventional WC substrate. Since then, various single and multiple coatings of carbides and nitrides of titanium, hafnium, and zirconium, and coatings of oxides of aluminum and zirconium, as well as improved substrates better suited for coating, have been developed to increase the range of applications for coated carbide inserts.

Advantages

A general rule for all carbide tooling is that toughness (impact resistance) decreases as wear resistance (hardness) increases. Conversely, as toughness increases, wear resistance decreases. While it is impossible to alter the general shape of the curve depicting this relationship, it is possible to obtain a more favorable disposition of the curve. A thin layer of a high-temperature, stable, hard material metallurgically bonded to the surface of a proper high-strength, temperature-resistant substrate improves wear resistance and provides longer life for the inserts.

The capability for increased productivity is the most important advantage of using coated carbide inserts. With no loss of tool life, they can be operated at higher cutting speeds than uncoated inserts; longer tool life can be obtained when the tools are operated at the same speed. Higher speed operation, rather than increased tool life, is generally recommended for improved productivity and reduced costs. The feed rate used is generally a function of the insert geometry, not of the coating.

Increased versatility of coated carbide inserts is another major benefit. Fewer grades are required to cover a broader range of machining applications, because the available grades generally overlap several of the C classifications for uncoated carbide tools. This simplifies the selection process and reduces inventory requirements. Most producers of coated carbide inserts offer three grades: one for machining cast iron and nonferrous metals and two for cutting steels. Some, however, offer more grades.

Limitations

Coated carbide inserts are not suitable for all applications. For example, they are generally not suitable for light finishing cuts, including precision boring and turning of thin-walled workpieces, two operations which usually require sharp cutting edges for satisfactory results.

They should not be used in most cases for machining workpieces containing surface sand or scale, inclusions, or other imperfections. Most heavy roughing operations and severely interrupted cuts are not recommended. Also, they are often not as suitable as uncoated carbide inserts or other tooling materials for machining some nonferrous metals and nonmetallic materials.

Coated carbide inserts are slightly higher in cost. However, a cost analysis should be made because the higher cutting speeds possible often increase productivity enough to more than offset their cost premium.

Applications of Coated Carbide Inserts

Most applications for coated carbide inserts are in turning and milling operations for cast irons and steels. Often, these operations can be performed at higher speeds than possible with uncoated inserts. Problems, however, can be encountered with severe interrupted cuts, particularly those with varying depths of cut, which subject the cutting edges to severe mechanical and thermal shocks, as well as fatigue. The greater toughness of uncoated inserts often makes them more desirable for such difficult machining operations.

CERAMICS

Ceramic or aluminum-oxide (Al_2O_3) cutting tools were first proposed for machining operations in Germany as early as 1905—21 years before the introduction of cemented carbides in Germany in 1926. Patents on ceramic tools were issued in England in 1912, and in Germany in 1913. Initial work on ceramic tools began in the United States as early as 1935, but it was not until 1945 that they were considered seriously for use in machining. Ceramic cutting tool inserts became commercially available in the United States during the 1950s.

Initially, these cemented-oxide, nonmetallic tools produced inconsistent and unsatisfactory results. This was partially because of the nonuniformity and weakness of the tools, but primarily because of lack of understanding and misapplication by the users. Ceramic tools were often used on older machines with inadequate rigidity and power.

Since then, many improvements have been made in the mechanical properties of ceramic tools as the result of better control of microstructure (primarily in grain size refinement) and density, improved processing, the use of additives, the development of composite materials, and better grinding and edge preparation methods. Tools made from these materials are now stronger, more uniform, and higher in quality; consequently, resurgence of interest in their application has arisen.

Types of Ceramic Tools

Two basic types of ceramic cutting tools are available:

1. Plain ceramics, which are highly pure (99% or more) Al_2O_3 and contain only minor amounts of secondary oxides. One producer of ceramic cutting tools, however, offers two grades with a higher amount of a secondary oxide—zirconium oxide. One grade contains less than 10% and the other less than 20% of zirconium oxide. Cutting tool inserts made from plain ceramics are often produced by cold pressing fine alumina powder under high pressure, followed by sintering at high temperature, which bonds the particles together. The product, white in color, is then ground to finished dimensions with diamond wheels. Another processing method—hot pressing—simultaneously combines high-pressure compacting and high-temperature sintering in a single operation to pro-

duce inserts that are light gray in color. Hot isostatic pressing, which simplifies the production of chipbreaker geometries, is also used.

2. Composite ceramics, sometimes incorrectly called cermets, are Al_2O_3-based materials containing 15-30% or more titanium carbide (TiC) and/or other alloying ingredients. Cutting tool inserts made from these materials are hot pressed or hot isostatically pressed and are black in color.

Ceramic inserts treated in this way, however, are not commercially available.

Advantages

A major advantage of using ceramic cutting tools is increased productivity for many applications. Ceramic cutting tools are operated at higher cutting speeds than tungsten carbide tools. In many applications, this results in increased metal removal rates. Favorable properties of ceramic tools that promote these benefits include good hot hardness, low coefficient of friction, high wear resistance, chemical inertness, and low coefficient of thermal conductivity. (Most of the heat generated during cutting is carried away in the chips, resulting in less heat buildup in the workpiece, insert, and toolholder.)

Another important advantage is that improved-quality parts can often be produced because of better size control resulting from less tool wear. In addition, smoother surface finishes aid size control. Also, ceramic tools are capable of machining many hard metals, often eliminating the need for subsequent grinding. Machining of hardened steel rolls used in rolling mills is an important application.

Limitations

Despite the many improvements in physical properties and uniformity of ceramic tools, careful application is required because ceramic tools are more brittle than carbides. Mechanical shock must be minimized, and thermal shock must be avoided. Stronger grades now available, however, plus the use of proper tool and holder geometry, help minimize the effects of lower strength and ductility.

While ceramic tools exhibit chemical inertness when used to cut most metals, they tend to develop built-up edges, thereby increasing the wear rate when machining refractory metals, such as titanium and other reactive alloys, and certain aluminum alloys. Tools made from ceramic materials are being used successfully for interrupted cuts of light-to-medium severity, but they are usually not recommended for heavy interrupted cutting.

Another possible limitation of using ceramic tools is that thicker inserts, sometimes required to compensate for the lower transverse rupture strength of the tools, may not be interchangeable in toolholders used for carbide inserts. Some milling cutters and other toolholders are available, however, that permit interchangeability.

Applications

Ceramic cutting tools are used successfully for the high-speed machining of cast irons and steels, particularly those requiring a continuous cutting action. They are generally good replacements for carbide tools that wear rapidly, but not for applications in which carbide tools break. Face milling of steel and iron castings is being done successfully, but heavy interrupted cutting is not recommended. Also, while ceramic cutting tools are useful for machining abrasive materials and most chemically reactive materials, they are not suitable, as previously mentioned, for cutting refractory metals, such as titanium and reactive metal alloys, and certain aluminum alloys. Some examples of improvement in performance obtained with ceramic tools, compared to carbide tools, are presented in Table 19-4.

SINGLE-CRYSTAL DIAMONDS

Increased use of both single-crystal and polycrystalline diamond cutting tools is due primarily to the greater demand for increased precision and smoother finishes in modern manufacturing, the proliferation of lighter weight materials in today's products, and the need to reduce downtime for tool-changing and adjustments to increase productivity. More widespread knowledge of the proper use of these tools and the availability of improved machine tools with greater rigidity, higher speeds, and finer feeds have also contributed to increased usage.

Diamond is the cubic crystalline form of carbon that is produced in various sizes under high heat and pressure. Natural, mined single-crystal stones of the industrial type used for cutting tools are cut (sawed, cleaved, or lapped) to produce the cutting-edge geometry required for the application.

Advantages

Diamond is the hardest known natural substance. Its indentation hardness is about five times that of carbide. Extreme hardness and abrasion resistance can result in single-crystal diamond tools retaining their cutting edges virtually unchanged throughout most of their useful lives. High thermal conductivity and low compressibility and thermal expansion provide dimensional stability, thus assuring the maintenance of close tolerances and the production of smooth finishes.

Although single-crystal diamond tools are much more expensive than those made from other materials, the cost per piece machined is often lower with proper application. Savings result from reduced downtime and scrap, and in most cases, the elimination of subsequent finishing operations. Because of the diamond's chemical inertness, low coefficient of friction, and smoothness, chips do not adhere to its surface or form built-up edges when nonferrous and nonmetallic materials are machined.

Limitations

Selection of industrial single-crystal diamonds is critical. They should be of fine quality, free of cracks or inclusions in the cutting area. Also, skillful orientation is required in the tools for maximum wear. The stone must be mounted so that the tool approaches the workpiece along one of its hard planes—not parallel to soft cleavage planes (which are parallel to the octohedral plane)—or the tool will start to flake and chip at the edge. Orienting the diamond in the soft direction will cause premature wear and possibly flaking or chipping.

Tools with a low impact resistance require careful handling and protection against shock. Such tools should only be used on rigid machines in good condition. Rigid means for holding the tool and workpiece are also essential, and balancing or damping of the workpiece and its driver are often required, especially for turning. Three-jaw chucks are generally not recommended because they cannot be dynamically balanced. If required, they should be provided with dampers. Damping of boring bars is also recommended.

Single-crystal diamond tools are not suitable for cutting ferrous metals, particularly alloys having high tensile strengths, because the high cutting forces required may break the tools.

TABLE 19-4

Comparative Performance of Ceramic vs. Carbide Inserts

Operation	Material	Hard-ness	Cutting Speed, sfm (m/min)		Feed Rate, ipr (mm/rev)		Depth of Cut, in. (mm)	Machining Time, min.	
			Carbide	Ceramic	Carbide	Ceramic		Carbide	Ceramic
Finish turning	AISI 1053 steel forging	R$_C$32	550 (168)	1200 (366)	0.010 (0.25)	0.010 (0.25)	0.020 (0.51)	17	55
Rough turning	Gray iron casting	179-241 Bhn	650 (198)	5000 (1524)	0.025 (0.64)	0.020 (0.51)	0.187 (4.75)	21	18
Rough turning	SAE 4340 steel forging	200 Bhn	700 (213)	1800 (549)	0.018 (0.46)	0.016 (0.41)	0.250 (6.35)	28	15
Rough turning	Gray iron casting	179-241 Bhn	650 (198)	2200 (671)	0.020 (0.51)	0.016 (0.41)	0.187 (4.75)	33	23
Finish turning	SAE 4340 steel forging	R$_C$32	500 (152)	2000 (610)	0.010 (0.25)	0.010 (0.25)	0.020 (0.51)	36	63

The diamond tends to react chemically with such materials, and it will graphitize at temperatures between 1450 and 1800° F (788 and 982° C). Single-crystal diamond tools are also not recommended for interrupted cutting of hard materials or for the removal of scale from rough surfaces.

Applications

Single-crystal diamond cutting tools are generally most efficient when used to machine:

- Nonferrous metals such as aluminum, babbitt, brass, copper, bronze, and other bearing materials.
- Precious metals such as gold, silver, and platinum.
- Nonmetallic and abrasive materials, including hard rubber, phenolic or other plastics or resins, cellulose acetate, compressed graphite and carbon, composites, some carbides and ceramics, fiberglass, and a variety of epoxies and fiberglass-filled resins.

Diamond crystals can be lapped to a fine cutting edge that can produce surface finishes as smooth as 1 μ in. (0.025 μ m) or less. For this reason, single-crystal diamond tools are often used for high-precision machining operations in which a smooth, reflective surface is required. The need for subsequent grinding, polishing, or lapping of workpieces is generally eliminated. One plant is using these tools on a specially built machine tool to produce an optical finish on copper-plated aluminum alloy mirrors.

Other parts machined with single-crystal diamond tools include computer memory discs, printing gravure and photocopy rolls, plastic lenses, lens mounts, guidance system components, ordnance parts, workpieces for which the cost of lapping and polishing can be eliminated, and parts with shapes, or made from materials, that do not lend themselves to lapping or polishing.

POLYCRYSTALLINE DIAMOND CUTTING TOOLS

Polycrystalline diamond blanks, introduced in the United States about 1973, consist of fine diamond crystals that are bonded together under high pressure and temperature. Both natural and synthetic diamond crystals can be sintered in this way, and cutting tool blanks and inserts are currently being produced from both types of crystals.

Various shapes are compacted for cutting tool purposes, and some are made integral with a tungsten or tungsten carbide substrate. Polycrystalline diamond cutting tools are generally recommended only for machining nonferrous metals and nonmetallic materials, and not for cutting ferrous metals.

Advantages

An important advantage of polycrystalline diamond cutting tools is that the crystals are randomly oriented so that the agglomerate does not have the cleavage planes found in single-crystal diamond cutting tools. As a result, hardness and abrasion resistance are uniformly high in all directions. Hardness is about four times that of carbide and nearly equals that of single-crystal natural diamond. When polycrystalline diamond blanks are bonded to a tungsten or tungsten carbide substrate, cutting tools are produced that are not only high in hardness and abrasion resistance, but also greater in strength and shock resistance.

Polycrystalline diamond cutting tools often cost less than single-crystal diamond tools, depending on their design and application; and they have proven superior for most machining applications. They generally show more uniformity, often allowing production results to be predicted more accurately. The compacts are also tougher than single-crystal diamonds and provide increased versatility, permitting the production of a wider variety of cutting tools with more desirable shapes. While smoother surface finishes can be produced with single-crystal diamond tools, polycrystalline diamond tools are competitive in this respect for some applications.

In comparison with carbide cutting tools, cutting tools made from polycrystalline diamond can provide much longer tool life, better size control, improved finishes, increased productivity, reduced scrap and rework, and lower tool cost per machined part for certain applications. The capability of using higher cutting speeds and feeds, plus the reduction in downtime by eliminating many tool changes and adjustments, can result in substantial increases in productivity.

Limitations

One limitation to the use of polycrystalline diamond tools

CUTTING TOOL MATERIALS

which also applies to single-crystal diamond tools is that they are not generally suitable for machining ferrous metals such as steel and cast iron. Diamonds—both natural and synthetic—are carbon, which reacts chemically with ferrous metals at high cutting temperatures and with other materials that are tough and have relatively high tensile strengths that can generate high pressures and induce chipping.

The high cost of polycrystalline diamond tools, as well as single-crystal diamond tools, limits their application to operations in which the specific advantages of the tools are necessary or economically feasible in that increased productivity makes them cost effective. Such applications include the machining of abrasive materials that result in short life with other tool materials and the high-volume production of close-tolerance parts that require good finishes.

Applications

Tools made from polycrystalline diamond are most suitable for cutting very abrasive nonmetallic materials, such as carbon, presintered ceramics, fiberglass and its composites, graphite, reinforced plastics, and hard rubber; nonferrous metals, such as aluminum alloys (particularly those containing silicon), copper, brass, bronze, lead, zinc, and their alloys; and presintered carbides and sintered tungsten carbides having a cobalt content above 6%.

They are being increasingly applied because more nonferrous metals, plastics, and composites are now being used to reduce product weights. Increased demand for parts with closer tolerances and smoother finishes and the availability of improved machines with higher speeds, finer feeds, and greater rigidity have also boosted the use of these tools.

Polycrystalline diamond tools have proven to be superior to natural, single-crystal diamonds for applications in which chipping of the cutting edge rather than wear has caused tool failure. They can better withstand the higher pressures and impact forces of increased speeds, feeds, and depths of cut and are suitable for many interrupted cut applications such as face milling. Sharpness of their cutting edges, however, is limited, and natural, single-crystal diamonds are still preferable for operations in which very smooth surface finishes are required.

Applications exhibiting excessive edge wear with the use of carbide cutting tools generally are good candidates for poly-crystalline diamond tools. Other applications include operations in which materials build up on cutting edges and cause burrs, operations resulting in smeared finishes, and operations that produce out-of-tolerance parts. For certain applications, poly-crystalline diamond tools outlast carbide tools by 50:1 or more.

CUBIC BORON NITRIDE

Cubic boron nitride (CBN), a form of boron nitride (BN), is a superabrasive crystal that is second in hardness and abrasion resistance only to diamond. It is produced by a high-pressure/high-temperature process similar to that used to make synthetic diamonds. CBN crystals are used most commonly in super-abrasive wheels for precision grinding of steels and superalloys. The crystals are also compacted to produce polycrystalline cutting tools.

Advantages

For machining operations, cutting tools compacted from CBN crystals offer the advantage of greater heat resistance than diamond tools. Another important advantage of CBN tools over those made from diamonds is their high level of chemical inertness. This provides greater resistance to oxidation and chemical attack by many workpiece materials machined at high cutting temperatures—including ferrous metals. Compacted CBN tools are suitable, unlike diamond tools, for the high-speed machining of tool and alloy steels with hardnesses to R_C70, steel forgings and Ni-Hard or chilled cast irons with hardnesses from R_C45-68, surface-hardened parts, and nickel or cobalt-based superalloys. They have also been used successfully for machining powdered metals, plastics, and graphite.

The high wear resistance of cutting tools made from compacted CBN has resulted in increased productivity because of the higher cutting speeds that may be utilized and/or the longer tool life possible. Also, in many cases, productivity is substantially improved because the need for grinding is eliminated. The relatively high cost of compacted CBN tools, as well as diamond tools, however, has limited their use to applications, such as difficult-to-machine materials, for which they can be economically justified on a cost-per-piece production basis.

Applications

Applications of cutting tools made from compacted CBN crystals include turning, facing, boring, and milling of various hard materials. Many of the applications eliminate the need for previously required grinding or minimize the amount of grinding needed. With the proper cutting conditions, the same surface finish is often produced as with grinding.

Many successful applications involve interrupted cutting, including the milling of hard ferrous metals. Because of their brittleness, however, CBN cutting tools are not generally recommended for heavy interrupted cutting.

Metal removal rates up to 20 times those of carbide cutting tools have been reported in machining superalloys.

CUTTING FLUIDS

In recent years, water-soluble fluids and cutting fluids comprised of chemicals in water solution have replaced oil-based fluids in many applications. This trend is spurred by dwindling oil supplies and rising costs for petroleum products. Increased costs to clean workpieces and rising costs of cutting fluid disposal have prompted the development and use of synthetic water-based fluids that contain little or no oil.

Increasingly significant in the formulation of both metalcutting fluids and decisions involving application,

maintenance, and disposal of waste cutting fluids is a complex array of government regulations (federal, state, and local). The composition and use of cutting fluids is now more than ever directly affected by human safety considerations, air and water pollution regulations, chemical toxicity registration, waste disposal regulations, shipping regulations, energy policy, etc. The cutting fluid selection process is further complicated by the fact that the cutting fluid is only one component in an integrated metalcutting system. Tools, machines, workpiece material, and operator considerations also play important roles in the decision-making process. Each of these components influence selection, design, application, and operation of the others.

FUNCTIONS OF CUTTING FLUIDS

Cutting fluids typically perform numerous functions simultaneously, including cooling the workpiece/tool interface, lubricating, minimizing the effects of built-up edge (BUE), protecting the workpiece from corrosion, and flushing away chips. The relative significance of these functions of cutting fluids for a particular application is dependent upon a combination of interacting parameters, such as cutting fluid formulation, workpiece material, tool material and tool geometry, surrounding atmosphere, and cutting speed. Machine design is of increasing importance.

Effects of Temperature in Cutting Operations

The energy dissipated through metal deformation and sliding friction processes in a cutting operation appears as thermal energy or heat. About 60% of the heat is generated in the primary deformation zone; the balance is generated in the secondary deformation zone and the friction zones.[46]

High cutting temperatures generated by the processes of shearing, strain hardening, and friction are advantageous only in the sense that they reduce to a limited extent the forces required for deformation of the workpiece during cutting. The disadvantages of high cutting temperatures far outweigh this single advantage in most cases. Characteristic effects of high cutting temperatures often include poor tool life, unacceptable surface finish, and the need to reduce cutting speed.

Temperature vs. tool life. The relationship between tool life and cutting temperature can be described by the following empirical formula:

$$Tt^n = K \qquad (75)$$

where:

T = tool life (minutes)
t = temperature at the chip/tool interface (centigrade)
n = an exponent dependent on the tool (a number usually between 20 and 30)
K = a constant dependent on tool and workpiece materials

This relationship suggests that small reductions in cutting temperature produce marked increases in tool life or permissible cutting speeds. Experience has shown this general relationship to be reasonable in most areas. However, in special cases, such as so-called hot machining, this relationship does not apply.

Hot machining. In hot machining, heat is applied to the workpiece by an external source to raise the temperature of the part just ahead of the cut. In some cases, especially when used with difficult-to-machine alloys, hot machining is reported to increase tool life and provide improved surface finish.[47]

In one application, hot machining was shown to dramatically improve tool life in a turning operation involving 4140 steel (R_C59) workpieces. (Feed: 0.008 ipr (0.20 mm/rev); depth of cut: 0.100" (2.54 mm); tool material: Carboloy 350.) At a cutting speed of 200 fpm (60.9 m/min), tool life increased from about 8 min to about 23 min when the workpiece was heated from 600° F (315° C) to 900° F (482° C). At a cutting speed of 300 fpm (91.4 m/min), tool life increased from about 3 min to about

6 min when the workpieces were heated from 600° F to 900° F. In both cases, tool life determinations were based on 0.015" (0.38 mm) flank wear of the tool.

Cooling Mechanism

The application of a suitable cutting fluid is known to reduce the forces in cutting. This effect is most noticeable at low-to-moderate cutting speeds, the cooling effect of the cutting fluid being more significant at elevated cutting speeds.[48]

In order for a cutting fluid to function effectively as a coolant, two requirements must be met. The fluid must gain access to the sources of heat, and the fluid must have the thermal capability of removing the heat. The factors which effect the accessibility of the fluid, however, are common to both the cooling and lubricating mechanisms.

Fluid accessibility. Fluid accessibility depends on cutting geometry, severity of the operation, properties of the fluid, and to some extent, condition and nature of the workpiece material. It is not completely clear how a cutting fluid actually manages to penetrate to the deformation and friction zones since (1) the relative motions of the chip, tool, and workpiece combine to carry fluid away from the cutting zone and (2) the contact pressures between the tool and the material can be extremely high. Since most materials are believed to undergo extensive plastic deformation at these high contact stresses and temperatures, some authorities suspect that the actual area of contact between the tool and the material closely approaches the geometric interfacial area. This is in sharp contrast to the situations experienced with normal sliding in which the true area of contact can be appreciably less than 1% of the apparent contact area.

Heat removal and cooling properties. Temperature measurements of the cutting zone, although often criticized as not providing a true indication of temperature at the tool/workpiece interface, have repeatedly shown that cutting fluids are effective in reducing cutting temperatures. Estimation of interfacial temperatures has been performed using a variety of methods, including radiation pyrometers, embedded thermocouples, temperature-sensitive paints, and indirect calorimetric techniques.

The properties of a fluid which determine its ability to cool are its thermal conductivity, specific heat, heat of vaporization, and wettability with metal surfaces. Water-based fluids and dilute emulsions have a significant advantage over oil-based fluids in terms of thermal properties, since the specific heat of water is approximately twice that of organic fluids, and since water also has a higher thermal conductivity. Recognition and confirmation of these advantages are demonstrated by the widespread and effective use of aqueous fluids and dilute emulsions in machining operations at higher speeds.

Vaporization is an efficient method of heat removal, since relatively large amounts of thermal energy are required to transform a unit mass of liquid to the gaseous state. The effectiveness of vaporization cooling in a cutting geometry is difficult to establish, however, because the tight clearances may promote the formation of dormant vapor blankets which would actually inhibit further cooling.

Lubricating Mechanism

High pressures and temperatures in most cutting operations suggest that it is highly unlikely that a cutting fluid can sustain a complete liquid film between the cutting tool and workpiece material. Instead, the conditions in a typical metalcutting operation are believed to approach those at which boundary, or extreme-pressure (EP), lubrication can occur. In boundary lubrication, additives in the fluid react chemically with the workpiece material and tool material to form compounds on the metal surfaces. One theory suggests that lubrication in cutting occurs by a reduction in severity of secondary deformation or shear strain.[49] This process is thought to occur by two interrelated mechanisms. First, the lubricant absorbs into the chip surface and restricts the adhesion of chip material to the tool. Second, reactive components of the fluid combine chemically with the freshly generated metal surface of the chip to produce a film of lower shear strength than that of the chip material, thus reducing friction, cutting forces, and temperature. These compounds are protective in that they inhibit welding which would occur with bare metal surfaces in contact. A variety of evidence exists to substantiate the boundary-lubrication mechanism in metalcutting. This includes reduction in cutting forces and tool wear, improvements in surface finish with the use of EP additives, and observation of the expected surface compounds on both tool and chip materials.

Effective boundary lubrication is a matter of achieving proper balances: (1) the fluid additive must be present in sufficient quantities to be effective; (2) the reactive species in the additive must be in the proper form to become available at the metal surface; (3) the temperatures must be high enough to promote surface compound formation, but not so high as to cause compound decomposition or melting; and (4) the sliding speeds must be low enough to permit time for the surface reaction to occur. Increases in cutting speeds, for example, tend to limit fluid accessibility, to decrease reaction times available for compound formation, and to prohibit the use of lower-melting-point compounds. Despite these rather rigid requirements, boundary and EP lubricants are effective in a wide variety of machining operations on many materials over a wide range of speeds.

Corrosion Protection Mechanism

Corrosion protection of the machine tool and workpiece is important when machining operations employ the use of a cutting fluid. One of the first methods used to control corrosion was the addition of soda ash to the cutting fluid, which increased the alkalinity of the fluid and reduced the tendency to cause rust. When the use of mineral oils as cutting fluids increased, it was found that they provided a major deterrent to rust formation—an ability to coat or wet-out on the surfaces of the machine tool and workpiece to form a physical barrier to prevent chemical reaction from taking place. As machining speeds and hardness of metals increased, straight mineral oils were found lacking in that better wetting ability was needed for the oils to penetrate the tool/workpiece interface. This was accomplished by the addition of polar compounds, such as fatty and vegetable oils, to form the so-called emulsifiable oil cutting fluids.

Emulsifiable oils. These cutting fluids combine the cooling properties of water with the lubrication properties of oil. They provide a friction-reducing film between the tool/workpiece interface and conduct heat away from the interface rapidly. This class of fluids, as well as semi-synthetic chemical cutting fluids which contain a small amount of mineral oil, is alkaline in nature to prevent the formation of rust. Components such as alkanolamines, petroleum-sulfonate emulsifiers, wetting agents, and fatty acids are used to enhance the protection of the oily film that remains upon evaporation of the water from the emulsion.

Synthetic coolants. These fluids are defined as water-extendible products that are free of oil. They offer excellent cooling, rust protection, hard-water compatibility, and biological resistance.[50] As with emulsifiable oils, the most important aspect of their rust-preventive characteristics is concentration control. The most common corrosion inhibitor used in this type fluid is a combination alkanolamine/sodium nitrite inhibitor package. This combination results in the formulation of nitrosamines now thought to be harmful.

Chip Removal Mechanism

In machining operations that generate large amounts of metal chips, an important function of a cutting fluid is to flush chips away from the cutting zone. The flushing action removes the chips from the cutting zone and keeps them from scratching the machined surfaces.[51] This action is useful in deep-hole drilling, trepanning, and gundrilling operations, in which fluid is used under pressure and is fed through the cutting tool to force the chips out of the hole. In these operations, when large amounts of fluid are required at high flow rates, proper selection of the cutting fluid is important to avoid excessive foam generation which can interrupt the machining and cutting fluid filtering process.

TYPES OF CUTTING FLUIDS

Although hundreds of cutting fluids and special formulations exist for cooling and lubricating metalcutting operations, all cutting fluids can be classified according to one of four types. Each of the four basic types—straight cutting oils, emulsifiable oils, chemical fluids, and gaseous products—has distinctive features, benefits to the user, and limitations. Often the distinctions are not clearly identifiable, but an understanding of the similarities and differences among the various types of cutting fluids is necessary to obtain optimum cutting fluid performance through proper fluid selection.

Cutting Oils

Cutting oils are made from mineral oil and may be used straight (uncompounded) or compounded—combined with polar additives and/or chemically active additives. Mineral oil based cutting fluids are classified as inactive or active. Applications of compounded cutting oils, whether active or inactive, are generally limited to low-speed, low-feed, chip-crowding conditions on difficult-to-machine metals or in form grinding from the solid. High cost, danger from smoke and fire, and operator health problems generally limit application to those machines not designed to use a water-miscible cutting fluid or to those operations in which water-miscible fluid does not provide satisfactory performance. Compounded cutting oils are generally more expensive than water-miscible fluids.

Inactive cutting oils. These cutting oils are mineral oil compounded with chemically inactive additives. In general, they provide high lubricity and are nonstaining, but exhibit limited antiweld properties.

Active cutting oils. Active cutting oils contain sulfur, chlorine, and/or phosphorus in an active form blended with mineral oil or fatty mineral oil blends. These chemical additives, extreme-pressure lubricants, provide a tough, stable film of lubrication at the tool/chip interface. They are particularly useful in extending tool life in high-temperature and high-pressure applications. Active cutting oils include sulfurized mineral oil, phosphorized mineral oil, sulfa-chlorinated mineral oil, and sulfa-chlorinated fatty oil blends. Many chemical-active cutting oils may stain certain metals.

Emulsifiable Oils

Emulsifiable oils, commonly called soluble oils, water-miscible fluids, or emulsifiable cutting fluids, are oil droplets suspended in water by blending the oil with emulsifying agents and other materials. The addition of polar additives and/or EP additives produces emulsions of greater lubricating value.

Emulsifiable oils form mixtures ranging in appearance from milky to translucent and provide the combined cooling and lubrication required by metal-removal operations conducted at high speeds and low pressures with considerable heat generated. They are available in many forms and variations. The normal emulsified oil contains emulsion particles large enough to reflect incident light and therefore appears milky.

Emulsifiable oils offer the following advantages over straight cutting oil:

1. Greater reduction of heat, allowing higher cutting speeds in some applications.
2. Potentially cleaner working conditions.
3. More economical—dilution with water brings application costs down.
4. Better operator acceptance—cooler, cleaner parts.
5. Improved health and safety benefits—no fire hazard, and reduction of oil misting and fogging (hydrocarbon emissions).

Emulsifiable mineral oils. The most widely used of the emulsifiable oils, emulsifiable mineral oils are light mineral oils made emulsifiable with water through the introduction of petroleum sulfonates, amine fatty acids, etc. For normal cutting applications, emulsifiable mineral oils provide adequate lubricity. Usually oil/water dilutions are about 1:20.

Super-fatted emulsifiable oils are similar to emulsifiable mineral oils except they have added fatty oils. The suppliers of cutting fluids provide emulsifiable oils as concentrates that the user prepares by mixing with water. Oil/water ratios can range from 1:5 to 1:100. Smaller concentrations are used in lighter machining operations and when cooling is the major objective. Higher concentrations are used when increased rust-prevention and lubricating properties are required.

The fatty oils allow the fluid to be used in more demanding applications. Typical oil/water dilution is 1:5 to 1:20.

Extreme-pressure (EP) emulsifiable oils. Sometimes called heavy-duty soluble oils, these oil emulsions contain sulfur, chlorine, or phosphorus and fatty oils to provide lubricity for heavier machining operations. EP emulsifiable oils typically are mixed in an oil/water ratio of 1:5 to 1:20.

In some broaching, gear hobbing, shaving, and shaping operations, EP emulsifiable oils have replaced mineral oil fluids.

Chemical and Semichemical Fluids

Chemical or synthetic fluids are generally defined as cutting fluids containing no petroleum oil. They may form clear solutions, collodial dispersions, or translucent or milky emulsions.

True-solution fluids. Chemical cutting fluids without wetting agents are often called true solutions. They provide excellent rust control, but little or no lubricity. These fluids are usually used at 1:50 to 1:100 ratios; they are generally clear in appearance, but may be dyed to indicate their presence in water. True solutions may leave residue of crystalline or gummy deposits.

Surface-active chemical fluids. These fluids are fine colloidal solutions of organic and inorganic materials dissolved in water. Wetting agents added to the solution provide moderate lubricity. These fluids have low surface-tension and good rust-inhibiting properties and usually leave a powdery residue upon drying. The lubricating qualities of chemical cutting fluids with wetting agents are sufficient to allow machine slides, turrets, and other moving parts to function smoothly. They are typically mixed in ratios of 1:10 to 1:40.

For rougher machining operations, EP surface active chemical fluids are used. These fluids contain sulfur, chlorine, or phosphorus to provide EP properties and are typically mixed at ratios of 1:5 to 1:30. As with true-solution fluids, prior to selecting the surface-active chemical fluid, specific information pertaining to residue should be requested from the supplier or in-plant residue studies should be performed.

Semichemical fluids. Semichemical or semisynthetic fluids, unlike true-solution fluids, contain a small amount of mineral oil (about 5-30% of the base fluid) plus additives to enhance lubricating properties. These products are gaining favor in industry today because they incorporate the best qualities of both chemical fluid and emulsified oils.

Advantages and disadvantages of chemical and semichemical fluids. Both chemical and semichemical fluids are available containing chlorine, sulfur, or other additives which afford extreme-pressure or boundary lubrication effects. Because of these additives, chemical or semichemical fluids can be used on some of the more difficult machining and grinding applications. The concentration of additives may vary from 2-10%.

In general, the chemical and semichemical fluids offer the following advantages:

1. Rapid heat dissipation and good size control.
2. A high degree of cleanliness resulting in clean machine-tool surfaces and clean coolant troughs.
3. Very light residual films that are easy to remove.
4. Ease of mixing, with very little agitation necessary.
5. Relatively easy concentration control, with less interference from tramp oils.

Chemical and semichemical fluids can be formulated to provide very good wet "contact" corrosion control and to exhibit relatively good protection from overall atmospheric corrosion.

The disadvantages sometimes encountered with chemical and semichemical fluids are:

1. Some lack of lubricity (in chemical fluids without wetting agents) that may cause sticking in the moving parts of machine tools.
2. High detergency, which may irritate sensitive hands when operator exposure is continual for long periods of time (may be formulated to minimize this effect).
3. Tendency to foam in high-agitation operations (may be formulated to minimize this effect).
4. Some disposal problems. At this time, no cost-effective technique is available to remove the inorganic and organic, highly soluble, chemical complexes from the water phase of synthetic and semisynthetic compounds.

Gaseous Fluids

Air is the most commonly used gaseous cutting fluid. It is the

CHAPTER 19

CUTTING FLUIDS

sole fluid constituent in dry cutting and is also present, of course, when liquid fluids are used. The cooling and lubricating action of air is taken for granted because it is always present.

Air can also be used as a compressed gas to provide better cooling. A stream of compressed "shop air" directed at the cutting zone removes more heat by forced convection than would be removed by natural convection. In addition, compressed air can be used to blow chips away. (Safety must be considered.)

Other gases such as argon, helium, and nitrogen have been used to prevent the oxidation of workpiece and chip, but their high cost generally makes them uneconomical in production except in very special applications. Gases with boiling points below room temperature, such as carbon dioxide, can be compressed and sprayed at the cutting zone to give evaporative cooling to temperatures well below 0° F (-18° C).

SELECTION OF CUTTING FLUIDS

The proper selection of cutting fluids is a factor that, unfortunately, is sometimes neglected in machining practice. Considerable effort is usually put forth in choosing the correct tooling, workpiece stock, and machining parameters; yet too often, only a cursory review of existing cutting fluid technology is completed in selecting an appropriate cutting fluid.

Realistically, and more practically, cutting fluids should be considered an integral part of the material removal process in that proper selection and use of cutting fluids can significantly affect overall production costs. In addition to the obvious impact on tool life, other factors which cutting fluids can influence include:

1. Machining time per part.
2. Number of rejects resulting from unacceptable surface finish and dimensional out-of-tolerance parts.
3. Machine downtime resulting from tool changes and maintenance.
4. Cutting fluid consumption per part.
5. Cutting fluid batch life.
6. Cutting fluid disposal or recycling costs.

Cutting Fluid Classifications

Although many methods exist for classifying cutting fluids, the following method serves as a practical selection guide, with the fluids classified under two basic types: straight oil cutting fluids and cutting fluids mixed with water.

Straight oil cutting fluids. The four major classifications of straight oil cutting fluids are:

1. General purpose, oil-based, nonstaining (GPO-NS)—some lubricity and antiweld performance. Sulfur additives, if included, are nonstaining to copper and copper alloys.
2. General purpose, oil-based, staining (GPO-S)—similar to GPO-NS, but containing sulfur in active form resulting in staining to copper and copper alloys.
3. Heavy-duty, oil-based, nonstaining (HDO-NS)—high degree of lubricity and antiweld performance. Sulfur, when present, is nonstaining to copper and copper alloys.
4. Heavy-duty, oil-based, staining (HDO-S)—similar to HDO-NS products, but containing sulfur in active form which will stain copper and copper alloys.

Cutting fluids mixed with water. The following major classifications of cutting fluids are mixed with water:

1. General purpose soluble oil (GPS)—emulsifiable oils exhibiting limited lubricity and EP performance.
2. Heavy-duty soluble oil (HDS)—similar to GPS, but providing high levels of lubricity and EP performance. Some of these products may also contain corrosion inhibitors and brocides.
3. General purpose aqueous coolants (GPAC)—chemical fluids generally exhibiting wetting, lubricating, and corrosion-controlling properties.
4. Heavy-duty aqueous coolants (HDAC)—chemical fluids exhibiting enhanced lubricity and EP properties, and semisynthetic fluids having a much lower oil content than soluble oils. These semisynthetic (or preformed chemical emulsion) products exhibit both chemical and physical lubrication properties.

Tool Material/Cutting Fluid Compatibility

To obtain optimum cutting fluid performance, the fluid must be matched with not only the workpiece material, but also the tooling material. The following sections highlight the compatibility of cutting fluids with various tool materials.

High-speed steel tooling. In general, most cutting fluids are compatible with high-speed steel (HSS) tooling. However, tool wear is usually minimized when tool/chip friction is low. A low level of friction can be maintained with the use of oil-based fluids to physically lubricate the area, synthetic-type fluids to chemically lubricate the area, or a combination of the two, depending upon the operation.

Carbide tooling. Carbide and coated carbide tools are also compatible with the various cutting fluids. For a period of time, some question existed as to possible carbide corrosion and reduced tool life resulting from the use of many cutting fluids. Improvements in both carbide and cutting fluid technologies appear to have eliminated this problem.

In general, carbide tooling is operated at higher temperatures than HSS tooling. Fluids that have high cooling rates due to the presence of water are often used in carbide tooling. Carbide is, however, sensitive to thermal shock; rapid thermal cycling can cause early tool failure due to cracking and chipping. This can be minimized by the following actions:

1. Starting full coolant flow before cutting is initiated.
2. Continuing coolant flow for a brief period after cutting is completed.
3. Using oil-based cutting fluids, which have lower heat transfer properties, when intermittent applications of cutting fluid are necessary.

In situations in which mixed tooling (HSS and carbide) is used, overall tool life can generally be maximized by the use of oil or a high-quality synthetic cutting fluid, thus providing the maximum available lubricity required by the high-speed steel tooling.

Ceramic tooling. Just as in carbide tooling, care must be exercised to avoid mechanical and thermal shocks or stresses when using this tooling. Machining with ceramics is usually done without cutting fluids.

Diamond tooling. Diamond tools are used for the machining of carbide, ceramic, and other abrasive or nonferrous material. A cutting fluid, usually a water-soluble type, is used to cool the tool and keep it free of chips.

Metallurgical/Cutting Fluid Compatibility

The effects of residual films of cutting lubricants on the

metallurgical integrity of metallic parts operating under conditions of high stress and temperature have become a highly controversial issue in recent years, especially among producers of aerospace and nuclear products. This concern has been generated primarily as a result of laboratory and service failures of critical components, which have been attributed to stress-corrosion cracking and intergranular corrosion. In general, failure analyses of components and laboratory simulation studies have associated these failures with the presence of chloride (and possibly other ions of the halogen family), as well as sulfide ions and some organic solvents.

Cleaning procedures can be established to remove all traces of metalworking fluids from surfaces of machined parts that do not contain internal recesses or crevices in which fluids can be trapped. For very critical components which cannot be thoroughly cleaned, or when a doubt exists as to the possible effect of residual contamination, or when total procedure compliance may be too uncertain or costly, the only reliable approach is to perform simulated service testing of the part material by subjecting it to fluid being considered for use during processing.

APPLICATION OF CUTTING FLUIDS

It is generally accepted that continuous application of a cutting fluid is preferable to intermittent application. Sporadic fluid applications cause thermal cycling, which leads to the formation and propagation of microcracks in hard and relatively brittle tool materials, such as carbides and high-speed steels. In addition to shortened tool life, intermittent fluid application can also lead to irregular surface finish due to expansion and contraction of the workpiece.

A secondary and sometimes overlooked advantage of proper fluid application is the efficient removal of chips. This can also aid in prolonging tool life, since properly placed fluid nozzles can prevent blockage or packing of the chips in the flutes of milling cutters and drills. Proper fluid flow will also prevent chips from building up in areas of moving machine parts. Proper machine design will allow for fluid flow to continuously wash these sensitive areas.

Manual Application

Cutting fluids, pastes, and solid lubricants are often manually applied in small jobs, or in one-of-a-kind operations, simply because this is the easiest and least expensive method of fluid delivery. The disadvantages of manual application, however, generally preclude its use in larger scale or production operations. These disadvantages include intermittent application of the fluid, poor chip removal, and probably most important, limited accessibility to the cutting zone.

Flood Application

The most common method of fluid application is that of flooding the tool, workpiece, and cutting zone. Flood application of cutting fluids permits a continuous flow of the fluid to the cutting zone and is most efficient in chip removal. A low-pressure pump delivers the cutting fluid through piping and valves to a nozzle situated near the cutting zone. When an operation has its own cutting fluid sump, the used fluid drains over various machine components, collects in the chip pan, and returns by gravity to the sump where it passes through a filtering element. Then the fluid flows into the clean side of the sump where it is pumped back to the metal-removal operation. The volume of the sump must be large enough to allow the cutting fluid to cool and to allow fine swarf to settle before the cutting

fluid is pumped back to the operation. Sumps for individual machines may require capacities ranging from 5 to 50 gal (19 to 190 L) or more depending upon the operation.

Mist Application

In addition to manual application and flooding, cutting fluids may also be applied in the form of an air-carried mist. Mist application is best suited to operations in which the cutting speed is high and the areas of cut are low, as in end milling. Mist application provides better tool life than dry cutting; provides a means of cooling and lubricating in cases in which flood application is impractical; provides a means of applying fluids in otherwise inaccessible areas; and provides better visibility to the cutting zone.

The primary disadvantage of mist application of fluids is the possibility of inhalation of the fluid droplets by the operator and co-workers. The inhalation problem can be minimized by good ventilation, including the use of fans to blow the mist away from personnel. In continuous applications, the problem can be minimized by the use of special mist collectors placed near the cutting zone. Another disadvantage of mist application is that the nozzles are somewhat prone to clogging, necessitating periodic cleaning.

Two types of mist generators are normally used—the aspirator type and the direct-pressure type. The aspirator type consists of a stream of air that is blown over the open end of a tube that is immersed in the fluid. A partial vacuum is created, and the fluid is drawn up the tube to become entrained in the airstream. The direct-pressure type uses either pressurized bottled gas or the shop air line to force the fluid into the airstream.

Special Application Methods

Both chilled cutting fluids and highly pressurized bottled gas have been shown effective in increasing tool life in some applications. These techniques are somewhat more exotic than conventional fluid application methods and, particularly in the case of low-temperature fluids, may not prove economically justifiable. Chilled fluids require, for example, the use of well-insulated piping and specially designed low-temperature pumps and valves. In addition, the operator must be aware of the hazard in handling the cooled workpiece, tool, and fluid plumbing. When pressurized gas is used, the gas is allowed to expand through a nozzle in the region of the cutting zone. The expansion process cools the gas to temperatures below -100° F (-73° C). The same insulation and operator protection required for chilled fluids is required when pressurized gas is used.

FILTRATION OF CUTTING FLUIDS

During machining operations, cutting and grinding fluids can become contaminated rapidly by chips; swarf such as grinding fines, abrasive grains, and bonding material; tramp oil from lubricating and hydraulic systems; and organic wastes such as food particles, rags, paper, gum, and tobacco. If these contaminants are not effectively removed, fluid life decreases, fluid performance diminishes, and costs increase. This section describes the various methods that are used to "clean" cutting fluids and thereby alleviate these problems.[52]

Clarity Requirements

An important factor influencing the selection of cutting fluid cleaning systems is the degree of fluid cleanliness actually required for a specific application, especially since this degree has a major effect on cleaning costs. Other major factors include

CUTTING FLUIDS

the type of fluid; and the fluid's viscosity, temperature, pressure, flow rate, and compatibility with the cleaning medium; the kind, concentration, and size of contaminants; the tramp-oil level; the microbiological content; the type of operation and machine, including chip or swarf and fluid movements; and the material being machined. Other considerations include initial installation, operation, and maintenance costs; floor-space requirements; existing downtime and cost for toolchanging, sump cleaning, coolant dumping; and production losses through rejects.

Determining the minimum amount and size of contaminants that must be removed for satisfactory operation is difficult, yet important, because higher fluid clarity generally means higher cost. Removal of every particle from a fluid is rare and can only be accomplished with costly methods such as microfiltration, ultrafiltration, or reverse osmosis (R/O). Some fluid cleaning techniques may clean the fluid, but produce secondary adverse effects. For most manufacturing operations, removing only a portion of particles of a given size or mass is generally satisfactory.

Cleanliness of fluids can be measured in several ways, including percent-by-weight, percent-by-size, parts-per-million (ppm), and percentage of particles removed. Percent-by-weight is the ratio of the weight of contaminants to the total weight of contaminants and fluid. Percent-by-size is the ratio of removed particles of specific sizes to particles of the same sizes in the fluid. Parts-per-million is a unitless comparative value of weight or volume of particles per weight or volume of fluid. Efficiency of the cleaning system's separation or retention is generally given as a percentage of particles removed. Some manufacturers specify a percentage removal figure and a micron rating. For example, a 90%, 10-micron filter is designed to retain 90% of the particles that are 10 microns or larger in size. One micron (micrometer or μm) equals 0.001 mm or 0.0000394".

No accepted standard is available for such rating systems, and no one measurement can be employed as a reliable means for selecting cleaning equipment to be used with a specific application.

In some cases, the quantity of particles in a fluid may be critical; and in others, the size of particles. For most machining operations filtration to 25 microns (0.001") is sufficient. For more demanding operations, such as grinding, honing, lapping, and deep-hole drilling in which high-quality work is more dependent on the removal of fine swarf and abrasive particles, finer filtration may be required.

General Filtering Considerations

The filtering system for a particular operation may be comprised of numerous components. General considerations regarding these components include straining, sump cleaning, and tramp-oil skimmers.

Straining. Screening or straining is a fundamental requirement for all fluid-handling systems to protect pumps and other equipment from large contaminants and debris, such as rags. It consists of metal screens or woven wire in the form of baskets, drums, cartridges, plates, or flat beds. For water-based fluids that do not contain a rust inhibitor, screens made from stainless steel should be used.

While screens are not generally designed to remove fine contaminants, their efficiency varies according to the size of their openings. Also, some screens can collect chips and contaminants in the form of cakes, thus increasing clarification efficiency. Screens are relatively inexpensive, but operating costs can be high if manual cleaning or frequent replacement is necessary. Screens can sometimes be automatically cleaned by backwashing, or by scraping devices, but exposure of the screen's bare metal to the fluid may not be suitable for certain applications.

Sump cleaning. Periodic cleaning of individual sumps is an important part of an effective program for maintaining cutting fluid performance. Sump cleaning is covered in the section entitled "Maintenance of Cutting Fluids" in this chapter.

Tramp-oil skimmers. In systems in which water-miscible fluid is not recirculated, an overnight delay or a weekend delay can permit tramp oil to float to the surface. It can then be vacuumed or allowed to float off. Oil skimmers can be used to remove tramp oil from operating systems. The typical oil skimmer consists of a slowly rotating disc or continuous belt made from stainless steel or other metal, or materials such as neoprene or polypropylene. The adhesive quality of the tramp oil in the system causes the oil to adhere to the disc or belt as the medium is continuously fed through the fluid. Scraper blades remove the oil from the disc or belt and divert it to a collecting tank or drum.

Rotating disc, belt, and similar-type skimmers only remove free oil on the surface of the fluid; generally, emulsified tramp oil is not removed. Some combination separator-and-skimmer systems for aqueous solutions remove tramp oil, kill bacteria, and aid in recoupling the cutting fluid into a tighter emulsion and in reducing oil particle size. In such systems, a portion of the cutting fluid from a central system is heated to release unemulsified and coarsely emulsified tramp oils to the surface where they are skimmed off. The clean fluid is pumped through a heat exchanger and returned to the central system.

Clarification. Clarification is the cleaning of fluids by the removal of impurities. It is generally accomplished by one of two types of methods: separation or filtration. Separation is accomplished physically without any filtering medium; filtration is accomplished with permanent or disposable filter media consisting of various porous materials through which a fluid is passed to remove contaminants.

Separation methods. Separators are units which remove chips and swarf by gravitational, magnetic, centrifugal, or other attractive forces. Methods of separating include settling, flotation, centrifuges, chip processing, hydrocyclones, and magnetic separators.

MAINTENANCE OF CUTTING FLUIDS

The responsibility for obtaining maximum performance from any cutting fluid rests with both the fluid supplier and user. The supplier must provide a product that, at the time of use, still meets original quality control tests (i.e., has not deteriorated in storage). Equally important are the user's methods of storing the product, his handling and cleaning procedures, and his adherence to a general fluid maintenance program.

Storage of Concentrate

Good storage conditions assure the quality of the cutting fluid at the time of use. Both water-miscible fluids and straight cutting oils are prone to physical changes resulting from high and low temperatures. Therefore, indoor storage of drummed materials at temperatures between 50 and 120° F (10 and 49° C) is best. If outdoor storage is unavoidable, the drums should be covered or set on their sides to avoid water accumulation around the bung.

Bulk storage facilities are best located indoors; however, because of space requirements, they are frequently placed outdoors—aboveground or underground. Tanks located aboveground should have a means of heating and circulating the contents to maintain a constant temperature. In either location, the tanks should have access ports, bottom draft, and drains to facilitate cleaning. Many straight oils and high oil content solubles are sensitive to water contamination. For this reason, it is important to prevent condensation in storage tanks or drums.

Water Quality

The quality of water is extremely important to the performance of aqueous metalcutting fluids. Many cutting fluid experts believe that cutting fluid performance is affected more by the quality of the water with which the concentrate is mixed than by any other single factor. In most cases, water used in cutting fluids represents about 90-99% of the final mixture. Thus, water quality plays a major role in establishing the chemical characteristics of the cutting fluid.

Water hardness. The cleanest of shop water is not pure. Water usually contains minerals or salts or both. The mineral content, or hardness of water, is most conveniently expressed in parts per million (ppm) of carbonates present in the water. Hardness is also measured in grains per gallon (GPG)—17.1 ppm is equal to 1 GPG.

A coolant tank tends to behave much like a still in that, through evaporation, pure water is lost from the system and dissolved minerals stay behind. Fluid "make-up" or additions to the sump usually are about 5-20% per day, depending upon sump capacity, severity of the machining operation, and the magnitude of cutting fluid loss due to splashing. Hence, over a period of a month, the buildup of solids in the fluid mixture can be 3-4 times that of the original water. Therefore, the purer the water used for mixing with cutting fluid concentrate, the longer the fluid can be used before hardness problems diminish the effectiveness of the fluid.

Water hardness is particularly important when cutting fluid concentrate containing wetting agents is used. The fluid concentrate is "used up" in reacting with certain minerals and becomes unavailable for its intended function. This type of reaction places the cutting fluid in a constant state of chemical change, affecting the fluid's performance. The reaction products that are formed between surface-active fluids and certain dissolved minerals tend to cling to parts, and the fluid is carried off or lost from the system more rapidly than would be the case if no such reaction had occurred. The amount of surface-active fluids carried off will usually increase in proportion to the concentration of dissolved minerals.[53]

The buildup of minerals in a cutting fluid can cause a variety of problems, including corrosion, separation, and formation of undesirable residues.

Corrosion. Pure deionized water provides optimum corrosion inhibition at any level of concentration when mixed with most cutting fluids. Chlorides and sulfates in cutting fluids contribute to corrosion, deposits, and staining of ferrous and nonferrous metals.

The use of "softened" water at any given fluid concentration provides a greater tendency for corrosion or staining than the use of untreated hard water. (Water softening is discussed in later sections.) This is true because zeolite softening replaces minerals such as calcium and magnesium with sodium. Sodium chloride and sodium sulfate are more corrosive than the corresponding calcium and magnesium salts.[54]

Iron also promotes corrosive affects of cutting fluids. As the level of iron increases in the cutting fluid, the tendency for iron to be deposited on workpieces and machine tool components increases; thus, staining can occur despite the presence of corrosion inhibitors in the fluid that are effective in reducing other types of corrosion.

Oil particle size. Performance of water-miscible fluids is highly related to the size of emulsion particles in solution.[55] An emulsion comprised of smaller oil particles exhibits a higher surface area per volume of oil emulsified. Because of this, lubricants such as chlorine, sulfur, and phosphorus are more readily available for chemical reaction at the cut. Smaller particles more easily penetrate to the tool/workpiece interface. It is also believed that an emulsion of smaller particles will remove heat more efficiently than an emulsion of larger second-phase particles.

Large particles in soluble-oil emulsions tend to separate from solution and float to the surface of the cutting fluid, causing a dilution of working fluid and formation of residue on workpieces.

Minerals tend to increase the particle size in the cutting fluid. In the case of soluble oils, the emulsified-oil droplets tend to coalesce to form larger particles which promote "creaming" or free-oil separation. Also, soluble-oil concentrates often disperse ineffectively when high concentrations of certain minerals exist in the water used for mixing.

In many cases, these types of reactions caused by water hardness can be avoided through the use of nonionic surface-active additives or formulations that do not react with hardness minerals. However, cutting fluids with nonionic materials sometimes tend to foam, even at low concentrations. Use of nonionic materials adds to the cost of the cutting fluid and may complicate fluid treatment for disposal.

Water treatment. As a general rule, the purest water possible should be used for mixing with cutting fluid concentrate. In most cases, water hardness in excess of 250 ppm may cause problems. Several alternatives are available when water treatment is needed to reduce raw water hardness before mixing.

Water softening. One method of removing hardness is to process the water through an ion-exchange (zeolite) water softener. This method has been used successfully in waters up to 300 ppm in hardness. Generally, water softening can contribute to corrosiveness of the cutting fluid because the process merely replaces hardness minerals with more corrosive sodium chloride or sodium sulfate.

Deionization. Another alternative is to treat the raw water supply with a deionization process. This process can result in a water purity that is often greater than that of distilled water,[56] as shown in Table 19-5. When deionized water is used for mixing with cutting fluid concentrate, the evaporation of water from the cutting fluid concentrate, the evaporation of water fromm the cutting fluid sump does not result in the formationn of salt residue and corrosive effects of the cutting fluid are all but eliminate.

Deionization allows mixing water to be closely held to a predetermined hardness level. If water is supplied at a constant 100 ppm hardness, less-expensive water-miscible cutting fluids can sometimes be used and the fluids can be used longer before bacterial spoilage occurs or gumming and corrosion becomes excessive. In some cases, the use of deionized water allows

CUTTING FLUIDS

TABLE 19-5

**Comparison of Water Purity—
the Best Grade of Commercially Distilled Water and High-Quality Deionized Water**

Element	Distilled Water-ppm	Deionized Water-ppm
Calcium	0.00	0.00
Magnesium	0.00	0.00
Sodium	Less than 0.01	Less than 0.01
Iron	0.02	0.00
Copper	0.01	0.00
Sulfates	0.00	0.00
Chlorides	0.00	0.00
Silica	0.01	0.01
Carbon Dioxide	0.82	0.10
Resistance—ohms	750,000	10,000,000
pH	6.4	7.0

cutting fluids to be used at lower concentrations. Usage of cutting fluid concentrate can be reduced as much as 40% in some instances.[57]

Distilled water. Distilled water from plant boilers is also sometimes used for mixing cutting fluids. This approach may be acceptable if the boiler condensate is not contaminated with materials that might be incompatible with the cutting fluid concentrate—antirust compounds, for example. In general, however, the purchase of distilled water in bulk quantities is less costly than distillation by company-owned facilities, and the quality of purchased water usually is better.

Reverse osmosis. Water purification by reverse osmosis (R/O) is another technique for improving water quality. With this process, high pressure is used to force water through a membrane, leaving behind about 70-90% of the minerals. In general, this process is not considered a satisfactory method of purifying water for water-miscible fluids.[58] Water purity is not sufficient to obtain "infinite" cutting fluid life, and about half of the feed water is waste water adding to the load on plant waste facilities. Sodium salts are not easily rejected by the membranes and therefore can be present in significant amounts in R/O processed water. These sodium salts generally render R/O and softened water unacceptable for use in cutting fluid emulsions.

Rancidity Control

The growth of bacteria and fungi in water-miscible fluids can result in strong offensive odors, staining of workpieces and machines, and interference with filters or fluid clarifiers, which in turn can decrease the effective life of a cutting fluid.

Two types of bacteria are commonly found in cutting fluids: aerobic, which grow in the presence of oxygen, and anaerobic, which grow in the absence of oxygen. However, each type can adjust to the other's environment to some degree. Tramp-oil leakage and other contaminants in the cutting fluid stimulate the growth of bacteria and serve as breeding grounds for both aerobic and anaerobic bacteria.

High concentrations of anaerobic bacteria characteristically produce hydrogen sulfide, which can cause severe dark staining of machines and workpieces and turn the fluid a gray-to-black color.

The odor associated with rancid cutting fluid is most prevalent after a shutdown period because tramp oil rises to the top of the fluid sump and forms a barrier to atmospheric oxygen. This is the ideal environment for Desulfovibrio, an anaerobic bacteria. This bacteria reduces sulfates to hydrogen sulfides. The hydrogen-sulfide gas is trapped under the oil layer until "Monday morning" when the oil barrier is broken by the turbulence created when the machine operator turns on the machine, and the gas escapes.

Concentration Control

Concentration control is needed to obtain optimum tool life, production rates, corrosion control, and resistance to bacterial or other microbial growth. Effective, automatic concentration control can be achieved using variable-ratio, positive-displacement proportioning pumps. These pumps are successfully used for concentration control because the water and fluid concentrate are physically metered and the ability of pumps to provide accurate proportions is unaffected by changes in water pressure, flow rate, or viscosity of the concentrate.

Proportioning pumps can provide initial charge solutions and make-up solutions for individual sumps and/or make-up additions for central systems. Automatic valves are used on central systems to start and stop fluid flow according to the level of the fluid in the system. Automatic fluid concentration control is said to provide savings of 15% in concentrate usage when compared to manual mixing methods.[59]

Machine Cleaning

The need for a complete cleaning of the machine and fluid sump before the addition of fresh fluid is well documented.[60] In some cases, cutting fluid life may be improved 300% merely by following proper cleaning procedures and using a bactericide to wash machine components prior to refilling.

Proper machine cleaning procedures can ensure maximum cutting fluid life. During the cleaning process, the contaminated water-miscible fluid should be pumped out first, and all chips and oil residue cleaned out. Then the sump should be filled with a high-quality cleaner that has been mixed with appropriate quantities of clean water. This cleaning solution should be circulated for several hours and applied directly to machine components not in contact with fluid flow. When the machine and sump are sufficiently clean, the cleaner should be pumped out and the remaining residue and sediment cleaned from the sump. The entire system should then be rinsed by circulating clean water, and all previously cleaned surfaces should be washed down. Rinsing with clean water should be performed as many times as necessary to completely flush all sediment, residue, and cleaning solution. After the machine is completely cleaned and rinsed, it should immediately be recharged with fresh cutting fluid to protect exposed metal surfaces from corrosion.

Testing of Cutting Fluids

Cutting fluids have many chemical and physical properties which influence their performance under machining conditions. Because so many variables are involved in manufacturing operations, including metal differences, cutting tool and machine differences, and the operator's skill, judgment, and experience; any variations in the chemical and physical properties of the cutting fluid can be critical.

Physical tests. The principal physical properties measured in the laboratory are indicated in the following list. ASTM test procedures can be obtained for all listed properties accompanied by an ASTM identifier. Procedures for testing those properties not accompanied by an identifier are detailed in the following text.

1. Viscosity (ASTM D88-57).
2. Flash point (ASTM D92-57).
3. Fire point (ASTM D92-57).
4. Corrosion, copper strip (ASTM D130-56).
5. Stability.
6. Emulsion stability, for water-miscible fluid (ASTM D1479-57T).
7. Residue, for water-miscible fluids.
8. Foaming, for oil (ASTM D892-58T), for water miscibles.

Stability. A typical stability test is as follows:

Place the concentrate in a 4 oz (118 ml) bottle in a cold test chamber at -20° F (-29° C) for a period of 24 hours. After the sample reaches room temperature, examine it for phase separation, flocculation, and sedimentation. If it is a water-miscible type (emulsions, semichemical, or chemical), mix it with distilled or deionized water, and also with typical plant process water, to determine if the concentrate mixes properly after being subjected to this low temperature. The temperature of -20° F may never be reached under normal storage conditions. In this case, determine the lowest temperature that the concentrate could experience, and test it at that temperature to ascertain whether or not its function would be impaired. Repeat this test procedure at 120° F (49° C) to determine high-temperature stability.

Residue, for water-miscible fluids. Nonfluid residues left after water has evaporated from water-miscible fluids can interfere with some machine tools. As machines become more fully automated (e.g., transfer, N/C), it is more necessary than ever that machines operate without impairment. The ideal residue would be one that has high lubricating value and is easily resoluble in the fluid. A typical method for testing is as follows:

Make a solution or emulsion of the cutting fluid at the concentration contemplated for use. Place in a glass petri dish a layer of the solution 1/4" (about 6 mm) thick and allow it to evaporate at room temperature. Examine it for amount, tackiness, fluidity, crystallization, etc.

Ideally, the residue should remain liquid, but under some conditions of operation, a solid residue can be tolerated. In any case, the residue should be readily water soluble or emulsifiable.

Foaming of water-miscible fluids. Excessive foaming can be objectionable. Some fluids that are high in wetting-agent content or have high "wettability" tend to foam more than those that have lower wettability or higher surface tension. Machines that "whip" air into fluids and do not have sufficient sump capacity for foam subsidence will cause even more foam to be generated. Laboratory tests for foaming cannot be used to predict accurately how a fluid will foam in a particular machine tool, but they may give an indication. Some possible foam tests are as follows:

1. Place 100 ml (about 3.5 oz) of fluid (emulsion, chemical, or semichemical) of 1, 2, or 4% concentration in a 200 ml (about 7 oz) glass-stoppered cylinder. Agitate the cylinder vigorously for 1 minute and time the period required for the foam to break. A time interval of up to 30 seconds is usually acceptable.
2. Stir a specific volume of fluid at 1, 2, or 4% in an electric blender or mixer for 5 minutes. Measure the foam heights, sizes of bubbles, and rates of break. Run fluids known to have satisfactory foam characteristics under the conditions of use for comparison.

Chemical tests. The most important chemical tests are those for determining pH for water-miscible fluids and those for determining the chemical or corrosive attack of fluids on metals. Unfortunately laboratory tests cannot always predict production results, but they can be a useful guide.

pH test. Determine the pH of solutions or emulsions of water-miscible fluids at 2 and 4% or at the concentration being used. The measurement of pH of emulsions in use is helpful for controlling the condition of the fluids. A drop in pH of emulsions is almost universal during use. The pH is measured in the laboratory with a pH meter and sometimes in the plant with short-range pH paper. Various test papers for pH cover a range from 2 to 11 or 12. Usually, these papers are accurate to within 1/2 pH, but they should not be used for testing cutting fluids containing dyes. The addition of soda ash or borax will raise the pH. The supplier should be consulted before making such additions.

Corrosion tests. No fluids should corrode metals being machined or ground, nor should they corrode the machine tools. In fact, they should retard the corrosion of metals.

Two examples of typical corrosion tests are as follows:

1. Immerse cleaned and abraded strips of the metals (steel, copper, aluminum, brass, etc.) in a container of the fluid. Close the container and maintain at room temperature, observing reactions daily for 10 days. Particularly observe for gas evolution and discoloration of the fluid as well as the metal. If the fluid being tested is water miscible, test it at several concentrations, such as 2, 4, and 10%. Remove the metal strips, clean them with a suitable solvent, and check for stain and pitting on the surfaces of the strips. Losses or gains in mass and the influence of water quality may also be measured.
2. Abrade and clean flat metal specimens. Place drops about 1/4" (about 6 mm) diam on the metal surface. Maintain at room temperature for a 24-hour period. In the case of water mixtures, a beaker can be placed over the specimen to retard the rate of evaporation. After 24 hours, record the amount and type of stain, corrosion, or pitting.

Ferrous metals are generally not stained or corroded by anhydrous cutting and grinding fluids. If oil-based fluids containing certain types of commonly used sulfur and chlorine additives become contaminated with water, they will stain and sometimes severly corrode ferrous metals.

CUTTING FLUIDS

Microbiological tests. Resistance to microbiological attack is an important property of water-miscible cutting fluids. Microbiological attack may cause annoying odors, a reduction in corrosion protection, emulsion stability, lubrication, and overall cutting efficiency.

Laboratory tests are available to measure the resistance of cutting fluids to microbiological attack;[61] however, the results of the tests do not always correlate satisfactorily with plant experience. This is due to the large variety of organisms and their tendency to undergo mutation, as well as the unavailability of any bactericide or combination of bactericides that can kill all organisms. If an objectionable odor develops the manufacturer of the cutting fluid being used should be contacted.

HEALTH AND SAFETY ASPECTS OF CUTTING FLUIDS

A key element in defining the health and safety aspects of cutting fluids or any type of industrial chemical is that there are two different types of risks associated with their use. The situations in which the risk of harm is immediate or readily apparent are known as acute risks. These include the type of risk that is associated with having a highly active straight cutting oil or highly alkaline synthetic cutting fluid contact the eye of a machine tool operator not wearing safety glasses either through conscious decision or outright forgetfulness. The effect is almost immediately noted by either irritation or encountering a long-term burning sensation and/or nonpermanent vision problems. Other risks are not so obvious or immediate. These are long term in the making and may arise from constant exposure to materials over extremely long periods of time through any of the routes listed previously. These are known as chronic risks and are more recently recognized problems.

In both acute risk and chronic risk cases, attempts to clarify the risks attendant in using cutting fluids of any type have been relegated to the phalanx of animal tests that have been specified under the U.S. Federal Hazardous Substances Acts. These are:

1. Acute Oral Toxicity—16 CFR 1500.3 (c) (1 & 2).
2. Acute Inhalation Toxicity—16 CFR 1500.3 (c) (1 & 2).
3. Acute Dermal Toxicity—16 CFR 1500.40.
4. Primary Skin Irritation—16 CFR 1500.41.
5. Acute Eye Irritation—16 CFR 1500.42.

For acute risks, many of these tests do give some indication of the type of activity that can be expected under fairly narrow conditions should the fluid enter the system in the manner described. In contrast, it has been more difficult and, in fact, the source of great controversy to demonstrate cause and effect with respect to animal testing and chronic health hazards in human beings.

Prudence dictates that contact between the worker and the cutting fluid should be kept to a minimum. This can be accomplished by (1) minimizing misting and (2) imposing physical shielding between the operation and/or the fluid and the operator.

This advice is not based on known or anticipated toxicity. A hazard analysis of metalworking fluids states that exposure to oil mists at current (typical) levels is not harmful to the respiratory tract and, in spite of known carcinogens in some petroleum oils, the level of skin cancer in this work force is not significantly higher than in the general population.[62] However, there are well-known dermatological problems associated with exposure to straight oils (see Table 19-6), although the use of straight oils is not as significant as in past years.

TABLE 19-6
Cutting Fluids: Actions on Metal and Skin

Action/ Effect	Types of Cutting Fluids	
	Straight Oils	Water-Miscible
	Insoluble Oils	Soluble Oils Synthetic Fluids Semisynthetic Fluids
Action on metal	1. Cool the cutting tool, prolonging tool life 2. Lubricate, which minimizes heat due to friction 3. Anti-rust action 4. Flush away metal chips	
Action on Skin	Mechanical blockage of the follicular orifices	Solvent and alkaline actions cause degreasing of skin
Effect on Skin	Oil acne: comedones and folliculitis	Eczematous contact dermatitis: irritant and allergic

METALFORMING LUBRICANTS

Lubrication is vitally important in metalforming operations. Effective lubrication results in controlled friction, with consequential reductions in force and power requirements and in tooling stresses and deflections. Tooling wear can be reduced by proper lubrication, and product quality can be improved by elimination of surface damage and harmful residual stresses.

A lubricant's main function is to minimize surface contact between the tooling and workpiece. If too much surface contact occurs, metal pickup on the tooling can damage the product and cause high maintenance costs from excessive tool wear. If friction is too high, temperature can exceed material limits and reduce production speeds. Workpiece surface quality is directly related to the properties and behavior of lubricants, whether surface contact occurs or not. In general, the lubrication function influences workpiece quality, process productivity, and cost.

In discussing lubrication for metalforming process, it is useful to distinguish between the different modes or "regimes" that can occur. The principal variable to be considered is the thickness of the lubricant film interposed between the surfaces. The four regimes of lubrication are illustrated in Fig. 19-19.[63]

FILM THEORY

For most practical metalforming processes, determining and identifying the lubrication regime is difficult. It is also difficult to assess accurate values of friction for most processes; the use of a constant coefficient of friction is not appropriate. In most processes, lubrication is a combination of all the possible regimes, and thus friction varies during deformation. Lubricant properties must be matched as closely as possible with the properties of the workpiece and with process conditions to direct or to control the lubrication regime that is most likely to produce the desired results.

Thick-Film Lubrication

In thick-film lubrication (Fig. 19-19, *a*), the film minimum thickness is large compared with either the molecular size of the lubrication or the surface roughness of the tooling or workpiece. Thus, the lubricant may be regarded as a continuum (liquid or solid) between smooth surfaces.

The tool and workpiece surfaces are completely separated by the lubrication film. Friction is a function of the viscosity of the lubricant undergoing shear in the contact region. For conventional drawing and extrusion, thick-film lubrication has potential advantages because 30-40% of the total drawing force is expended in overcoming friction. For some applications, possible drawbacks are the matte finish that results and the prospect of producing metallurgical properties that are not desired in the workpiece.

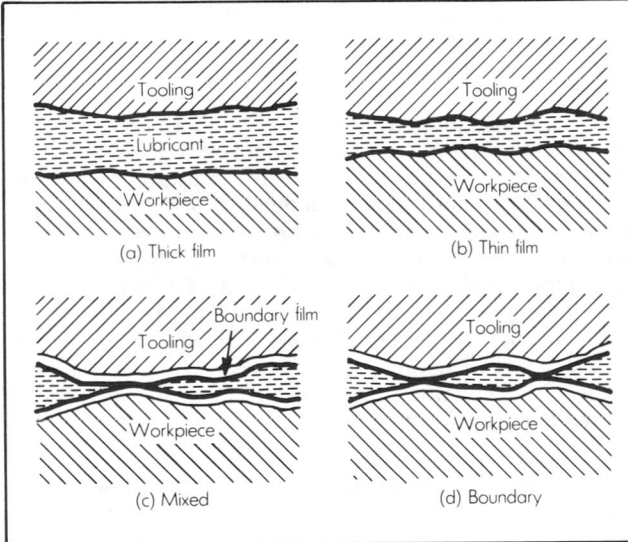

Fig. 19-19 Regimes of lubrication.

Thin-Film Lubrication

If the minimum thickness of lubricant film is reduced or if surface roughness is increased, the system may enter the thin-film lubrication regime (see Fig. 19-19 *b*). In this mode, the minimum film thickness is of the same order as the surface roughness, but it is still much larger than the molecular size of the lubricant. Under these circumstances, the lubricant may be treated as a continuum, but roughness of the surfaces must be considered in the analysis.

The properties of the lubricant—its flow behavior under conditions of pressure, temperature, and shear—are equally important. Lubricant effectiveness is directly dependent on the pressure coefficient of viscosity. Because of their high speed requirements, cold rolling and high-speed wire drawing are among the relatively few metalworking processes for which sustained thin-film lubrication is practicable.

Mixed-Film Lubrication

Further reduction in the minimum film thickness results in potential contact between roughness peaks (asperities). The lubricant, however, contains materials that react chemically with the surfaces, forming tightly adhering boundary films with a thickness on the order of the lubricant molecular size. These films prevent direct metal-to-metal contact between asperities. Part of the load between the surfaces is carried by the thick film in the roughness valleys, and part is carried by the thin boundary films over the peaks. This results in the mixed-film lubrication regimes illustrated in Fig. 19-19, *c*.

Boundary-Film Lubrication

The final lubrication regime of importance in metalforming is shown in Fig. 19-19, *d*. This is purely a boundary-film lubrication regime in which all of the load between the surfaces is carried on thin boundary films on the asperity peaks. The coefficient of friction is usually in the range of 0.1-0.3.

Solid-Film Lubrication

Thick-film lubrication can be produced with lubricating solids as well as with liquids. Solid lubricants vary a great deal in chemical character and in physical properties. In the broadest sense, the products resulting from the interaction of liquid lubricants or semisolid organic boundary lubricants could be described as "solid lubricants," because it is in the solid phase that they become effective. More specifically, however, the term "solid lubrication" describes the reduction of friction and wear through the use of inorganic solids having low shear strengths. Organic materials such as Teflon, powder, and low-shear lamellar pigments also are used. The desired mechanism involves complete separation of surfaces by the solid lubricant (which, in some instances, is soap, wax, or polymer-based, dry film). However, in metal-deformation processes, in which plastic flow of the substrate causes film stretching, solid-film lubrication is often a boundary lubrication process.

OPERATING PARAMETERS

The lubrication regime that occurs in a given metalforming process is dependent on several factors of the process:

- Contact macrogeometry (varies with process and die design).
- Load (contact force, tool to workpiece).
- Speed (surface speed, tool to workpiece).
- Environment (air, moisture, drawing compound, etc.).
- Lubricant properties.
- Contact microgeometry (microtopography or surface finish).

MATERIAL SURFACE PROPERTIES

There is a direct relationship between surface properties of the material worked and the lubricant that is applied to a particular surface. Some materials are more difficult to lubricate than others. Certain surface treatments and coatings require special care. Fabricating problems, such as white rust, staining of nonferrous metals, and peeling and blistering of painted or coated stock, can occur when improper lubricants are used. To facilitate understanding of the interrelationships that are involved, material surfaces can be grouped into four categories: normal, active, inactive, and coated.

METALFORMING LUBRICANTS

Normal Surfaces

Most normal surfaces are material surfaces that have a natural affinity enabling them to retain lubricants readily; they generally do not require special wetting or polarity agents to obtain sufficient lubrication. The material is relatively clean and free of such contaminants as heavy-oxide films and extraneous gases (nitrogen, oxygen, carbon dioxide). Cold-rolled steel, hot-rolled steel, and aluminum-killed steel have surfaces of this type. They tend to hold lubricant that is applied to them.

Active Surfaces

An active material surface is one in which the bond strength between the lubricant additive and metal atom is great. The attractive energy of the metallic surface is high. This tends to encourage desirable chemical reactions. As a result, chemically active additives and wetting agents such as oleic acid, lard oil, and some emulsifiers (such as soaps) are effective in lubricating such materials and coatings as brass, copper, aluminum, terneplate, zincrometal, and tinplate.

Inactive Surfaces

An inactive surface is one in which the strength of the bond between the lubricant additive and the metal atom is low. The attractive energy of the metallic surface also is low. This lessens the tendency for chemical reactions with lubricant chemical additives. When working with inactive surfaces such as stainless steel, titanium, and nickel, the lubricant should have a high film strength. Suitable lubricants contain hydrocarbons, polymers, polar and wetting agents, and extreme-pressure agents. Aluminum metal is a "special case"; since its active surface usually is coated with an inactive oxide film, it needs a high-film strength lubricant.

Coated Surfaces

Nonmetallic surface treatments and coatings include vinyl, paint, lacquer, paper, plastic, and other organic coatings. Lubricants used on these coatings must be compatible and clean and must not cause the surface coating to peel, blister, blush, or stain. Lubricants that work well on coated surfaces are synthetic and chemical solubles and certain natural emulsions.

If the coated surface is electroplated or is a bimetal, it should be treated as an "active surface," for purposes of specifying the lubricant.

TYPES OF LUBRICANTS

The many varied conventional liquid lubricant materials used for lubricating punches and dies can usually be divided into two broad categories: oil based and water dilutable. Both types may use similar additives—sulfurized fats or oils; chlorine, usually in the form of chlorinated paraffin wax ("honey oil"); and phosphorus. Fats are added to improve wetting of the stock with lubricant and also to increase slipperiness or oiliness. In addition, water-dilutable lubricants may contain amine soaps, metallic soaps, and/or other emulsifiers. With the proper amounts of the various additives, as well as the use of inhibitors, they can be used in drawing and stamping compounds.

The new "synthetics" are another broad group of lubricants. They generally contain no mineral oil. Semisynthetics may contain some mineral oil; the remaining ingredients are water-soluble compounds and wetting agents, along with extreme-pressure (EP) additives, corrosion deterrents, and antifoam inhibitors.[64]

Another group of lubricants includes solid films, solid particles (pigments), and eutectic salts.

LUBRICANT PROPERTIES

The difference between success or failure in many metalforming operations can be attributed to properties of lubricants that are formulated to suit a particular operation. Table 19-7 lists properties that characterize metalforming lubricants. As shown, the various physical and chemical properties are broken down into five categories: barrier films, wetting agents, additives, special properties, and dry-film lubricants.

A compound usually can be formulated to provide the properties that are most important for lubricating a specific operation. To formulate and compound a lubricant and tailor it to the requirements, it is necessary to know the material surfaces that are being worked; metal gauge; application techniques; cleaning and removal methods; subsequent operations; and any special considerations that are peculiar to the process, plant, or setup. For example, looking at Table 19-7, it is evident that, if desired, lubricants can be made for easy cleaning, good rust protection, compatibility with welding and heat treating, biodegradability, and no degreasing.

LUBRICANT FORMULATIONS

Lubricant formulations for metalforming differ widely in

TABLE 19-7
Drawing Compound Properties

Barrier Films	Wetting Agents	Additives	Special Properties	Dry Films
Oil	Animal fat	EP Type	Cleaning inducers	Phosphates
Soap	Vegetable	Sulfur	Weld-through	Graphite
Wax	derivatives	Chlorine	Annealing	Oxides
Pigment	Polymers	Phosphorous	Brazing	Teflon
Polymer	Lardates	Friction modifiers	No degreasing	Electrofilm
	(Synthetic)	Rust preventive	Easy painting	Molydisulfide
	Water		Oil base	Ceramic
	Solvent		Water base	Polymer
	Stearates		Adhesives	
	Emulsifiers		Paper clad	
			Biodegradability	
			Long-term storage	
			Outdoor storage	

physical form and chemical composition. The components of the formulations are divided into liquids, solids, and additives and formulation aids.

Liquids

Liquid components include:

- Mineral oils.
- Natural oils (fatty oils).
- Synthetic oils.
- Compounded oils.
- Extreme-pressure oils.
- Emulsions (soluble oils).
- Solutions (mixtures of water with other fluids or additives).
- Eutectic salts (liquids under process conditions).
- Glasses (liquids under process conditions).

Dry-Film Lubricant

Prelubricated stock is suitable for some high-volume jobs in which drawing, blanking, or forming can be performed satisfactorily with a single application of a lubricant. Dry-film lubricants fall into three categories: soaps, waxes, and polymers.

Dry soap films and polymer coatings are applied to sheet or coil stock from an aqueous solution and subsequently allowed to dry before stacking or recoiling of metal.

Use of preheated solution and/or heated oven facilitates drying the film. Wax films are applied from a hot melt using suitable roll coating equipment to deposit a thin film of lubricant.

Soap films are frequently modified by addition of alkali salts. The best known combination is soap borax, which is inexpensive and effective in severe deformation of heavy gauge hot-rolled steel.

Solids

A variety of solids are used as lubricants for metal-deformation processes:

- Dry powdered soaps.
- Lamellar inorganic solids.
- Nonlamellar inorganic solids.
- Organic solids.
- Metallic films.

The term "solid lubricants" covers a wide variety of physical forms and chemical compounds. Physically, the solid lubricant can take the form of a bulk solid, a thin film, or a dispersion in liquid or grease. Chemically, it can be organic or inorganic, reactive or inert.

Additives and Formulation Aids

It is difficult to identify which components in metalworking lubricants should be classified as additives. The lubricants are usually multicomponent formulations, and the functions of some components are often complex and interacting. An additive is a chemical component that favorably influences either the chemical or physical properties of a lubricant. Its concentration usually represents a few percent or less of a solid (usually soluble) or a liquid in an oil-based stock. However, in metalworking lubricants, the additive may be present in up to 50% concentration; in some cases, the liquid major component might be only a vehicle or adjunct-function fluid which does not qualify as a lubricant at all. Therefore, the term *additive* is used to cover liquids employed as vehicles, solvents, and other application aids, as well as the materials that are considered

conventional additives.

Examples of the types of additives used to influence chemical properties of the lubricant are:

- Antioxidants.
- Corrosion inhibitors.
- Oiliness, antiwear, and extreme-pressure agents.
- Metal deactivators or passivators.
- Detergent dispersants.

Additives used to improve physical properties of lubricants are:

- Viscosity-index improvers.
- Pour-point depressants.
- Antifoam agents.
- Emulsifiers.
- Antimicrobial agents.
- Thickeners and tackifiers.
- Solid lubricants.
- Odor-masking agents and dyes.
- Vehicles, solvents, and essentially nonlubricative components.

Of the physical additives, the last seven types listed are most frequently included in metalworking lubricants.

LUBRICANT APPLICATION METHODS

The method of application is an important factor in determining effectiveness of metalforming lubrication. This is apparent when considering how it relates to the way the lubricant performs. Use too little and performance is impaired; use too much and costs go up; misdirect the lubricant and it is not applied at the critical locations. Cleaning, disposal, and housekeeping costs are influenced by application of lubricant.[65]

Some stamping plants use considerably more lubricant than the job requires. The objective in applying a drawing compound or lubricant is to apply the correct compound or lubricant where needed, at the right time, and in the proper amount. In general, lubricant is needed at the punch for punch and pierce operations and form and stretch-form operations; for drawing operations, it is needed at the die radii.

The job requirement is the main factor in selecting the type of lubricant; and the lubricant, in turn, is a key determinant for the application method. Other important considerations include the type of press and the press feed, and the type of die, whether single or multistation. The following are benefits attainable from correct lubricant application:

- Reduced lubricant usage.
- Increased press speed.
- Longer die life.
- Cleaner operations.
- Reduced shop maintenance (cleanup).
- Reduced scrap.
- Reduced lubricant carryoff.
- Simplified waste disposal.

Basic Methods

Five basic methods exist for applying die lubricants, whether they be heavy drawing lubricants or light mineral oils for fast blanking. Selection should be made after considering the advantages and disadvantages of each method, with emphasis

METALFORMING LUBRICANTS

on compatibility with the overall manufacturing operations. In some forming operations, a combination of methods is required to obtain effective lubrication. As illustrated in Fig. 19-20, the commonly used application methods are manual, drip, roller, spraying, and flooding.

Current Practice

Of the five die lubricant application methods available—hand, drip, roller, spray, and flood—the last three are most commonly used in modern metalforming operations. Typically, recirculating roller coating is used for single-point application; and spraying or flooding is used for multipoint application. For best results, the lubricant and application method should be established during the job planning stage, in the early phase of tooling and production engineering. Furthermore, it must be recognized that overall responsibility includes the provision of adequate means for disposal of lubricants after they have performed their function.

CLEANING

Residues of drawing and stamping compounds must be removed from metal surfaces to prepare the parts for in-process storage or subsequent operations. Usually, these surfaces must be cleaned prior to other operations, such as plating, painting, enameling, rustproofing, welding, or adhesive bonding of some other material to the surface of the parts.

The types of cleaners generally used for removing drawing compounds fall in the broad categories of solvent cleaners and alkaline cleaners. Acid cleaners sometimes are used for special applications that require removal of tarnish from metals.

Solvent Cleaners

Certain drawing compounds containing oils, fats, and waxes can be removed by organic solvents, such as:

- Petroleum solvents—kerosene, naptha, or stoddard solvent applied by wiping or immersion.
- Nonflammable solvents—trichlorethylene or perchlore-

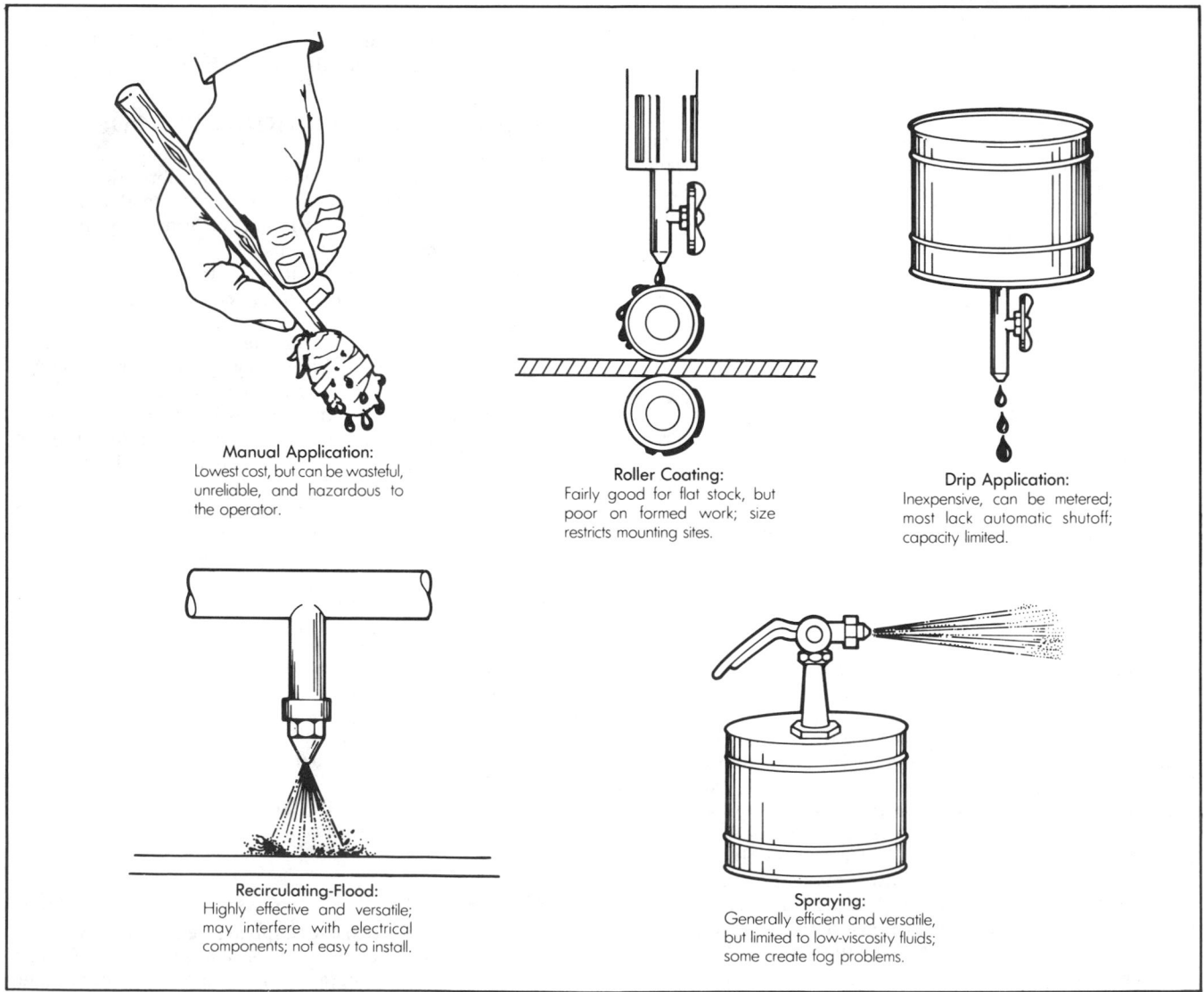

Manual Application:
Lowest cost, but can be wasteful, unreliable, and hazardous to the operator.

Roller Coating:
Fairly good for flat stock, but poor on formed work; size restricts mounting sites.

Drip Application:
Inexpensive, can be metered; most lack automatic shutoff; capacity limited.

Recirculating-Flood:
Highly effective and versatile; may interfere with electrical components; not easy to install.

Spraying:
Generally efficient and versatile, but limited to low-viscosity fluids; some create fog problems.

Fig. 19-20 Methods of applying die lubricants.

thylene, used in vapor degreasers.
- Special formulated solvents—emulsion cleaners, emulsifiable solvents, or diphase cleaners.

Care should be taken because some solvents are flammable and also because some of the organic vapors are toxic.

Alkaline Cleaners

Alkaline cleaners are widely used for removal of drawing compounds in soak cleaning and spray cleaning operations. They are also used for barrel cleaning, electrocleaning, and ultrasonic cleaning. Alkaline cleaners generally are used to remove soils for in-process cleaning and to prepare metals for operations such as painting or plating.

Alkaline cleaners are formulated with alkaline builders, chelating agents, and surfactants. They are formulated to clean by a combination of mechanisms, including saponification, emulsification, dispersion, chelation, wetting, and solvency. Solvents and corrosion inhibitors also are included in formulations for some applications. Specific cleaners are prepared for ferrous and nonferrous metals to avoid undue etch or tarnish.

INDUSTRIAL MACHINE LUBRICANTS

The elements of machines that require lubrication are bearings—plain, rolling elements, guides, and ways; gears; spindles; cylinders; flexible couplings; chains; and cams and cam followers. These elements have fitted or formed surfaces that move with respect to each other by sliding, rolling, approaching and receding or by combinations of these motions. If actual contact between surfaces occurs, high frictional forces leading to high temperatures and wear will result. Therefore, the elements are lubricated in order to prevent or reduce the actual contact between surfaces.

TYPES AND PROPERTIES OF LUBRICATING OILS

Lubricating oils, in a general sense, include all types of lubricating materials that are applied as fluids.[66] Although the greatest percentage of lubricating oils in use today are obtained by refining distillate or residual fractions obtained directly from crude oil, synthetic lubricants in both lubricating oils and greases are growing in use.

Properties of Lubricants

Properties associated with lubricants include: viscosity, the viscosity index, density, flash and fire points, the pour point, and properties dependent upon additives.

Viscosity. The most important property associated with lubricants is that of viscosity. The viscosity of a lubricant has direct impact on heat generation in bearings, gears, etc., and influences the sealing effect of the lubricant and rate of consumption. Viscosity is also the property which determines oil-film thickness between lubricated surfaces. The key is to have viscosity high enough to form the desired film, but not so high that internal fluid friction results in unnecessary heat generation. In selecting a lubricant for a particular application, definition of required viscosity levels at startup and during operating conditions is critically important to ensure optimum lubricant performance.

Viscosity index. Oils of different composition exhibit different rates of change of viscosity with changes in temperature. The viscosity index (VI) is a method of applying a quantitative value to this rate of change. The index is based on a comparison of the relative rates of change of two arbitrarily selected types of oils that differ widely in the characteristic of viscosity vs. temperature. A higher VI means that the oil has a relatively lower rate of change of viscosity with temperature.

Density. The density of a fluid is the mass of a unit volume of the fluid at a standard temperature. The specific gravity (relative density) is the ratio of the mass of a given volume of fluid at a standard temperature to the mass of an equal volume of water at the same temperature. Hydrometers are used to obtain density and gravity measurements.

Flash and fire points. The temperature at which an oil releases sufficient vapor at its surface to ignite when an open flame is applied is called the oil's flash point. The release of vapors at the flash temperature will not sustain combustion, but at an increased temperature, the fire point of the oil will be reached—that temperature at which sufficient vapors are released to sustain combustion.

Pour point. The lowest temperature at which an oil will pour when it is cooled without disturbance is called the oil's pour point. Oils free of wax will thicken due to increases in viscosity as the temperature is lowered. However, most petroleum oils contain some dissolved wax that causes further thickening. As the oil is cooled, the wax crystallizes and traps oil within its structure, thereby thickening the oil.

Other properties. Many of the additional properties of lubricating oils—oxidation resistance, detergency and dispersancy, rust protection, extreme-pressure and antiwear characteristics, emulsibility, antifoaming, and adhesiveness—are functionally dependent on additives (see "Additives for Industrial Lubricants" in this chapter).

Refined Petroleum Oils

Refined petroleum oils fall into two basic categories: paraffinic and naphthenic oils. Paraffinic oils are characterized by pour points, usually 0 to 20° F (-17.8 to -6.7° C), and moderate change in viscosity with increase in temperature. In general VIs will range from 85-100. Paraffinic oils have a lower density than naphthenic oils. Naphthenic oils are characterized by pour points from -60 to +10° F (-50 to -12° C) and larger change in viscosity with increase in temperature. In general, VIs will range from 0-60. Both naphthenic and paraffinic oils have a wide range of flash and fire points.

Paraffinic oils are high in paraffin hydrocarbons and contain some wax. Naphthenic oils are high in napthenic hydrocarbons and contain very little wax. In applications that operate over a wide range of temperatures, a naphthenic oil would generally be less suitable than a paraffinic oil. Naphthenic products are usually used in applications exhibiting a limited range of operating temperatures and when a relatively low pour point is required. Also, naphthenic oils tend to swell seal materials more than most paraffinic oils.

Synthetic Oils

Synthetic lubricants have the potential of satisfying a wide range of requirements, since they can be formulated with nearly

INDUSTRIAL MACHINE LUBRICANTS

any desired range of a specific property. However, certain other properties fixed by the chemical structures must be accepted in many cases. Applications must be considered in terms of all properties associated with the proposed synthetic fluid. Choosing the right synthetic fluid can be tricky because to get special characteristics, the user usually must trade off some other performance feature. Generally, synthetics have good thermal and oxidation stability, but a common weakness is limited lubricity.

The selection of a synthetic lubricating oil is a complex process. Generally, the industrial user is encouraged to seek the technical guidance of the supplier when a synthetic lubricant is under consideration.

LUBRICATING GREASES

A lubricating grease is a lubricating oil to which material has been added to thicken it to a semifluid or solid state. It may also contain additives to enhance specific properties, such as oxidation stability, rust-preventive ability, and extreme-pressure (EP) capability. A more comprehensive definition, which includes the functional requirements of a lubricating grease, is offered by Vold and Vold[67] who state:

A grease is a lubricant which has been thickened in order that it remain in contact with the moving surfaces and not leak out under gravity or centrifugal action, or be squeezed out under pressure. Thus a major practical problem is the provision of a structure [grease formulation] which will stand up under shear, and at all temperatures to which it may be subjected during use. At the same time the grease must be able to flow into the bearing through 'grease guns' from spot to spot in the lubricated machine as needed, and must not of itself add significantly to the power required to operate the machine, particularly at the start. This is an exacting set of rheological requirements.

Lubricating greases are preferred to oil when the application of a continuous supply of oil is impractical. Greases are also preferred when equipment is not readily accessible and when a sufficiently tight enclosure for retaining oil does not exist.

Thickeners

A major factor influencing the properties of a lubricating grease is the thickener employed in it. Thickeners compose 5-17% of a simple grease formulation. Ninety percent of all greases sold in the United States are based on what is termed metallic soap. Soaps utilized in lubricating greases are produced, during grease manufacturing, by saponifying (neutralizing) fats; compounds (neutralizers) most commonly used are the hydroxides of lithium, calcium, sodium, barium, and aluminum. The saponifiable compounds include tallow, lard oil, hydrogenated fats and oils, fish oil, fatty acids, and vegetable oils. The two most commonly used fatty acids are stearic and 12-hydroxystearic.

During the grease manufacturing process, the oil and fatty acids are heated to 275-300° F (135-150° C), at which time the alkaline compound is added and saponification occurs. The water resulting from the chemical reaction is boiled off.

The amount of fatty acid and metal hydroxide added to the oil determines the amount of soap formed. The soap is the thickener. The resultant thickening action is referred to in the grease industry as consistency. Consistency is a measure of the hardness or softness of the grease.

Lubricating Oil

Lubricating oil is the largest single component of a lubricating grease and is the component which provides the grease with its ability to lubricate. Simple greases, only oil and thickener, usually contain 83-95% oil. While the retentive properties of grease, as well as its resistance to heat, water, and extreme loads, depend upon the proportion and type of soap, the frictional characteristics of grease are based on its oil content.[68] The more important oil properties affecting overall grease performance are as follows:

1. Viscosity and viscosity-temperature characteristics, which influence the ability of a grease to form a lubricating film in service. They also influence low-temperature grease behavior.
2. Oxidation resistance and evaporation characteristics, which influence the ability of a grease to lubricate for extended periods, especially at higher temperatures.
3. Characteristics affecting elastomers, which influence the compatibility of a grease with seal materials used in bearings and other devices.

Most greases employ petroleum-based oils as the lubricating oil. Some synthetic fluids are also employed in grease formulating. Diesters, silicones, polyol esters, polyalkylene glycols and fluorosilicones are most commonly used. These fluids offer special characteristics, such as high-temperature performance, chemical resistance, and low-temperature performance, which elude refined petroleum oils. Their cost is substantially higher than that of the refined petroleum oil.

Additives

Lubricating greases are, ever increasingly, required to perform at higher temperature, with heavier loads, and for longer periods of time, or quite simply—under conditions at the extremes of those considered normal. As such, the oils and thickeners are pushed beyond their limits and supplemental materials are required to extend the performance capabilities of the lubricating grease.

Grease properties which may be enhanced by use of soluble (chemical) or insoluble (solid lubricants or fillers) additives are:

1. Oxidation stability.
2. Rust and/or corrosion protection.
3. Water resistance.
4. Extreme-pressure (EP) load-carrying capability.
5. Antiwear.
6. Adhesiveness.
7. Oil separation.
8. Pour point (low temperature properties).

The decision to employ additives is dependent upon the application requirements. The grease formulator is dependent upon a proper and thorough understanding of the application requirements before commencing to mix ingredients.

ADDITIVES FOR INDUSTRIAL LUBRICANTS

Modern industrial lubricants are specialized and sophisticated products with the additive package in them serving as the critical ingredient. Some lubricant experts describe lubricants as primarily carriers of high-technology additives. The selection and matching of the proper additives to a base fluid for a particular application is a complex process. As such, it is carried out by highly trained and skilled formulators who can bring together chemistry, performance, and economics to a successful product application.

Machine Protecting Additives

Antiwear and extreme-pressure (EP) agents. These vital additives increase the load-carrying capacity of the lubricant—be it a metalworking fluid, a hydraulic oil, a gear oil, or a grease. Without such help the lubricant is limited to only the capacity that elastohydrodynamic (EHD) lubrication can carry.

Chemically, antiwear and EP agents are organic phosphates, phosphites, thiophosphites, zinc dithiophosphates and sulfur, or chlorine containing compounds. They work by reacting with the metal surface at high loads and temperatures to form tough, invisible films that prevent metal-to-metal contact between mating metal surfaces. Thus, wear and distress are reduced. The EP film often contains iron sulfide, chloride or phosphate in a semiplastic matrix of organic fragments and reaction products. The difference between antiwear (mild conditions) and EP (severe conditions) is, to a large extent, that of degree and temperature/pressure activation.

Solid lubricants. These are in a sense special types of EP agents that are different from conventional EP agents in that they do not have to react with the metal to form a protective film. Solid lubricants are normally insoluble—they deposit themselves on the metal surface and protect it as long as they stay in place. Solid lubricants include molybdenum disulfide (MoS_2), graphite, borates, phosphates, polyamides, Teflon, and various glasses. They can be applied as a spray, a dispersion (in water or solvent), as a paste, etc. Generally, they are used in high-temperature operations, such as hot extrusion, forging, or rolling, in which a liquid might fail. They are also used in pressing operations for powdered metals, in stamping and drawing operations, in vacuum equipment, and in industrial equipment, as a crutch for marginal equipment design. Solid lubricants work by plating and filling microscopic valleys on the contact surface.

Oiliness agents and friction modifiers (reducers). These additives reduce friction under boundary or near boundary conditions by forming easily sheared, adsorbed or chemisorbed, multimolecular films on metal contact surfaces. Chemically they are long-chain polar compounds of the following types: fatty oils, metal soaps (oiliness agents) or fatty acids, esters, amines, phosphates and derivatives (friction modifiers) of these compound types. Lubricants containing such additives can save energy.

Rust and corrosion inhibitors. These prevent moisture corrosion on ferrous metals and/or corrosive attack on alloy bearings and copper alloys. They function by forming protective films on metal surfaces. Chemically, they are surface active compounds, such as sulfonate salts, amines, fatty acids, half-esters of bicarboxylic acids, and amine salts (for ferrous metals), or complex sulfur and/or nitrogen compounds (for copper alloys).

Lubricant-Protecting and Performance-Extending Additives

Antioxidants. These additives prevent the formation of sludge, varnish, and other deposits, as well as acids due to oxidation. They work by decomposing peroxides and/or chain breaking. Mainly they are hindered phenols, aromatic amines, sulfur and/or phosphorus organic compounds.

Antifoamants. These additives prevent the formation of stable foam by changing the surface tension. They are mostly silicone or acrylate polymers.

Bactericides and fungicides. These additives control the growth of micro-organisms that promote odor, emulsion breaking, and metal staining, as well as skin disorder of workers. Phenols, chlorine compounds, certain amines, alcohols, glycols, and nitrites are among such additives.

Viscosity index improvers (VII) and pour point depressants (PPD). Viscosity index improvers raise the high-temperature viscosity of the oil without an appreciable low-temperature viscosity increase. Some of the VIIs suppress fog or mist formation in metalworking operations. VIIs are olefin copolymers (ethylene/propylene, butylene, alkylated styrene) or polymethacrylates. The PPDs lower the pour point of lubricants by interfering with wax-crystal growth at low temperatures. Examples are styrene maleic anhydride polymer esters, methacrylate polymers, alkylated polystyrene, and naphthalene.

Emulsifiers and demulsifiers. Emulsifiers disperse oil or concentrate in water or make invert emulsions. They are mainly soaps of fatty, sulfonic or naphthenic acids, ashless dispersants (succinimide, ester or Mannich type), polyalcoxylated ester of fatty acids, etc. Demulsifiers lower the emulsion stability and help separate water from oil. Examples are certain polyalcoxylated compounds and metal salts. Both emulsifiers and demulsifiers work by changing the oil/water interface tension.

Tackiness agents. These increase the adhesiveness of the lubricating film on metal surfaces and prevent runoff. Examples are some high-molecular-weight polymers and aluminum soaps of high-molecularweight, unsaturated fatty acids.

APPLICATION OF LUBRICANTS

After the proper lubricant for an application is selected, it must be delivered to the elements that require lubrication. Two categories of lubricant application are prevalent: (1) all-loss methods, in which a relatively small amount of lubricant is applied periodically and allowed to leak or drain away to waste after it is used and (2) reuse methods in which the lubricant leaving the elements is collected and recirculated to lubricate again. Reuse application systems are preferred because they conserve lubricant and minimize waste control and environmental pollution.

HYDRAULIC FLUIDS

Hydraulic fluids can be defined most simply as fluids used to transmit power. Although many different types of fluids are available, ranging from water to combinations of exotic chemicals, the most widely used product by far is petroleum-based hydraulic oil. Other types of fluids are used for specialized applications, such as automotive or aircraft hydraulic systems, or to take advantage of some particular property, such as fire resistance or high-temperature performance. These types of fluids include aqueous-based fluids and a variety of synthetic and nonpetroleum fluids. Because these fluids are special and often call for somewhat different practices in the installation, maintenance, and operation of hydraulic equipment, they have generated a high level of interest for specialized applications.

INDUSTRIAL MACHINE LUBRICANTS

TABLE 19-8
Hydraulic Fluids and Comparative Performance Characteristics*

Type of Hydraulic Fluid	Property or Performance Characteristics						
	Fire Resistant	Viscosity-Temperature Properties	Low-Temperature Properties	Corrosion Resistance	Seal Compatibility	Lubricating Quality	Temperature Range, degrees F (C)
Petroleum Hydraulic Oil:							
R & O	P	G	G	E	G	G	20 to 150 (-7 to 66)
Antiwear	P	G	G	E	G	E	20 to 150 (-7 to 66)
Phosphate Ester	G	F	F	G	F	E	20 to 150 (-7 to 66)
Water-Glycol	E	E	E	F to G	E	F to G	0 to 120 (-18 to 49)
Water-in-Oil Emulsion	F	G	P	F	G	F	40 to 120 (4 to 49)
Oil-Synthetic	F	F to G	F to G	G	F	G	20 to 150 (-7 to 66)

*Ratings: E = excellent, G = good, F = fair, P = poor.
These are broad generalizations. Specific instances will often deviate from indicated performance quality.

One function of hydraulic fluids is that of lubrication. Since hydraulic fluids are used to lubricate the moving parts of hydraulic systems, they almost always serve the dual role of power transmission and lubrication. In most instances, they are lubricants that have been selected to serve as a medium for power transmission. Because of this dual role, much of the information on lubrication and lubricants presented in this chapter is applicable to the consideration of hydraulic fluids. Some significant differences exist pertaining to nonpetroleum products, and these are covered in the following sections.

Hydraulic fluids can be classified by chemical composition (petroleum, synthetic, aqueous, etc.); by application (industrial, automotive, aircraft, marine); and by performance property (fire resistant, high temperature, biodegradable, super-clean, etc.) Table 19-8 indicates various types of fluids and their performance characteristics.

References

1. M. E. Merchant, "Basic Mechanics of the Metal Cutting Process," *Journal of Applied Mechanics*, vol. 11 (1944).
2. *Ibid.*
3. J.A. Kirk, "Matrix Representation and Prediction of Three Dimensional Cutting Forces," *Journal of Engineering for Industry*, *Transactions of ASME* (Nov. 1977), p. 828.
4. *Ibid.*
5. A. B. Husein, M. F. DeVries, and S. M. Wu, "Analysis of Force Components in Bar Turning," *Journal of Engineering for Industry*, *Transactions of ASME*, Series B (1973), p. 960.
6. O. W. Boston, *Metal Processing* (New York: John Wiley & Sons Inc., 1941).
7. M. C. Shaw and C. J. Oxford, Jr., "On the Drilling of Metals, The Torque and Thrust in Drilling," *Transactions of ASME*, Vol. 79 (1957), p. 139.
8. M. Kronenberg, *Grundzuge der Zerspanungslehre*, Vol 1, 2nd ed. (Springer-Verlag, Berlin-Gottingen-Heidelberg, 1954). A book dealing with the analysis of metalcutting investigations in Germany, the United States, and England and derivations of formulas, tabulations, etc., in metric dimensions.
9. *Ibid.*
10. Mikell P. Groover, *A Survey on the Machinability of Metals*, SME Technical Paper MR76-269, 1976, p. 2.
11. American Society of Mechanical Engineers, *Manual on Cutting of Metals* (New York, 1939), (2nd ed., 1952), pp. 135-139.
12. D. W. Murphy and P. T. Aylward, *Machinability of Steel*, Homer Research Laboratories, Bethlehem Steel Corp., Bethlehem, PA.
13. A. W. Chisholm, J. B. Mills, and A. H. Redford, "The Assessment of Machinability," *Manufacturing Engineering Transactions*, Vol. 2 (SME, 1973) pp. 21-26.
14. "New Tool Standards Will Speed NC Programming," An interview with Dr. M. E. Merchant, *Machinery Magazine* (July 1969), pp. 74-77.
15. F. W. Taylor, "On the Art of Cutting Metals," *Transactions of ASME*, Vol. 28 (1907).
16. F. Jack McGee, *Derivation of Cost Control Criteria for Cutters*, SME Technical Paper MR76-996, 1976, p. 22.
17. M. Kronenberg, *op. cit.*
18. "Machining with Single Point Tools," *Transactions of ASM*, (1940); also *Tool Engineer*, vol. 8, nos. 9, 10 (1940). Excerpts of the book mentioned in Reference 14 with formulas, tabulations, etc., converted into U.S. customary dimensions.
19. J.P. Vidosic, *Metal Machining & Forming Technology* (New York, 1964), p. 239; also Michael Field and Norman Zlatin, "Evaluation of Machinability of Rolled Steels, Forgings and Cast Irons," *Machining—Theory and Practice* (Cleveland, 1950), p. 342.
20. American Society of Metals, *Metals Handbook* (Cleveland, 1948), p. 371.
21. M. Field and N. Zlatin, "Evaluation of Machinability of Rolled Steels, Forgings and Cast Irons," *Machining—Theory and Practice*, American Society for Metals (Cleveland, 1950).
22. D. W. Murphy, "Machinability of Steels," *Proceedings of the International Production Engineering Research Conference*, 963, American Society of Mechanical Engineers, pp. 177-187.
23. Murphy and Aylward, *loc. cit.*
24. J. Van Voast, *United States Air Force Machinability Report*, vol. 3 (1954).
25. *Ibid.*
26. J. R. Ewell, "A New Machinability Index," *Metalworking Production* (Jan. 16, 1966), pp. 49-51.
27. J. R. Ewell, *Thermal Coefficients—A Proposed Machinability Index*, ASTME (SME) Technical Paper MR 67-200, 1967.
28. J. Datsko, *Material Properties and Manufacturing Processes* (New York: John Wiley & Sons Inc., 1966), pp. 444-466.

29. J. Datsko, "Thermal Aspects of Machinability," *Tool and Manufacturing Engineer* (August 1968), pp. 63-65.
30. J. Datsko, A. Henkin, and H. Lord, *A Size of Cut Constant for Machinability Equations*, ASTME (SME) Technical Paper MR67-202, 1967.
31. A. Henkin and J. Datsko, "The Influence of Physical Properties on Machinability," *Journal of Engineering for Ind. , Transactions of ASME*, Vol. 85, No. 4 (November 1963), pp. 321-328.
32. M. Field and E. E. Stansbury, "Effect of Microstructure on Machinability of Cast Irons," *Transactions of ASME*, Vol. 69, No. 6 (August 1947), pp.. 665-682.
33. Datsko, *Material Properties and Manufacturing Processes, loc. cit.*
34. J. Hazra, K. Taraman, and R. Jagers, "How Microstructure Influences Tool Life," *Manufacturing Engineering* (December 1976), p. 31.
35. American Society for Metals, *op. cit.* p. 369.
36. American Society for Metals, *op. cit.* p. 369.
37. M. C. Shaw, P. A. Smith, E. G. Loewen, and N. H. Cook, "The Influence of Lead on Metal Cutting Forces and Temperatures," *Transactions of ASME*, Vol. 79 (July 1957), p. 1144.
38. American Society of Mechanical Engineers, *loc. cit.*
39. T. M. Garvey and H. J. Tata, *Machinability and Metallurgy of Resulfurized Low-Carbon Free-Machining Steels*, ASTME (SME) Technical Paper EM66-180, 1966.
40. Murphy, *loc. cit.*
41. Murphy and Aylward, *loc. cit.*
42. D. W. Murphy and P. T. Aylward, "Measurement of Machining Performance in Steels," Paper presented at Annual Meeting, AIME. 1964.
43. Shaw, Smith, Loewen, and Cook, *loc. cit.*
44. "Materials for Metal Cutting," *Proceedings of Materials for Metal Cutting Conference , jointly sponsored by the British Iron and Steel Research Association , the Corporate Laboratories of British Steel Corporation , and The Iron and Steel Institute*, Scarborough, England, April 14-16, 1970.
45. John E. Mayer, Jr., and S. Cowell, *Cemented Titanium Carbide Cutting Tools—Performance of Finishing , Semifinishing , and Roughing Grades*, SME Technical Paper MR71-934, 1971.
46. W. M. Stocker, Jr., and T. Hicks, eds., *Metalcutting: Today's Techniques for Engineers and Shop Personnel* (McGraw-Hill Publications Co., 1979), p. 182.
47. K. C. Tripothi, "Contradictions and Gaps in Present Theory of Lubrication: Main Challenge to Newer Developments," *Proceedings of the International Symposium on Metalworking Lubrication*, 1980, San Francisco, The American Society of Mechanical Engineers, p. 31.
48. J. G. Horne, D. Tabor, and J. A. Williams, "Action of Gaseous and Liquid Lubricants in Metalcutting," *Proceedings of the International Symposium on Metalworking Lubrication*, 1980, San Francisco, The American Society of Mechanical Engineers, p. 193.
49. *Ibid*, p. 195.
50. D. A. Hope, "Cutting Fluids - Pet or Pest," *Tribology International* (February 1977), p. 23.27.
51. W. S. Backer, *Principles of Machining*, Cutting Fluids Section, Metals Engineering Institute Study Course.
52. Charles Wick, "Clean Coolants Cut Costs," *Manufacturing Engineering* (November 1977), p. 34.
53. Joe H. Wright, "Water Quality and the Performance of Water Miscible Cutting and Grinding Fluids," *Cutting Tool Engineering* (March/April 1975), p. 6.
54. *Ibid.*, p.7.
55. Wright, *op. cit.*, p. 5.
56. Herman P. Abel, *High Purity Water for Industrial Processes*, SME Technical Paper MM70-706, 1970, p. 18.
57. Wright, *op. cit.*, p. 8.
58. William A. Sluhan, "Equipment for Control and Maintenance of Water Miscible Cutting and Grinding Fluids," *Cutting Tool Engineering* (May/June 1975), p. 5.
59. *Ibid.*, p. 7.
60. Joseph Tomko, *Cutting Fluid Maintenance*, SME Technical Paper MR71-802, 1971, p. 2.
61. M. R. Roger, A. M. Kaplan, and E. Beaumont, "A Laboratory In-Plant Analysis of a Test Procedure for Biocides in Metalworking Fluids," *Lubrication Engineering* (June 1975), p. 301.
62. U.S. Department of Health, Education, and Welfare, National Institute for Occupational Safety and Health, *Guidelines for the Control of Exposure to Metalworking Fluids*, NIOSH Technical Report, DHEW (NIOSH) Publication No. 78-165 (Washington, DC: U.S. Government Printing Office), February 1978.
63. W. R. D. Wilson, *A Review of Recent Research on the Mechanics of Metal Forming Lubrication*, SME Technical Paper MS77-341, 1977.
64. Joseph Ivaska, Jr., "Synthetic Lubricants in Presswork," *Proceedings of FabTech International*, Society of Manufacturing Engineers and Fabricating Manufacturers Association, Inc., 1981.
65. R. I. Hamilton, *Picking the Right Method for Applying Die Lubricants*, SME Technical Paper MF76-988, 1976.
66. J. George Wills (Mobile Oil Corp.), *Lubrication Fundamentals* (New York: Marcel Dekker, Inc., 1980), p. 9.
67. Marjorie J. and Robert D. Vold, *Journal of the Institute of Petroleum Technology*, vol. 38 (1952), pp. 155-163.
68. E. L. Pilon, "Gear Lubrication-I," *Lubrication*, vol. 66, no. 1 (1980), p. 10.

MACHINE CONTROLS

The evolution of machine tool technology has been paced by dramatic increases in machine control capability, particularly within the past 25 years. In fact, many machine tool experts credit major improvements in manufacturing productivity and enhancements in workpiece quality over the last several decades to the fast-paced growth of capability of machine tool controls. The basic configurations of many machine tools (lathes, for example) have not changed significantly for many years; but, the advent of numerical control, computer numerical control, and related enhancements has spurred important changes and effects in the manufacturing methods and costs.

SEQUENCE CONTROLLERS

Sequence controllers are a class of electromechanical and electronic devices used to control the operation of a machine tool or other equipment in a predetermined step-by-step manner. Characteristic of these devices is the method of establishing the desired control sequence and the manner in which the controller functions. The more common types of sequence controllers available today are electromechanical stepping-drum programmers, perforated wide-paper-tape programmers, and diode-matrix pinboard programmers.

In the drum programmer, the desired control sequence is commonly established by inserting pins into appropriate rows in the surface of a cylinder. Mounted over one row of the cylinder surface are momentary contact switches so that, as each row moves into position under the switches, the pins in that row activate the switches corresponding to the position of the pins present. As the cylinder rotates or steps to the next row, the pins in that row cause the connection of certain input devices, such as pushbuttons, limit switches, and timer contacts, to the logic section of the controller. The logic section, as a result of the inputs, causes the closure of circuits to output devices such as solenoids and motor starters. When the logic section senses that selected inputs in that row are in the proper condition, the controller then advances, or "steps," the cylinder by rotating it to the next row. The pins in the next row then present the next set of input conditions to the controller and cause the closure of the corresponding desired output circuits.

In a perforated wide-paper-tape programmer, the desired control sequence is established by the pattern of holes which are punched into the tape. The operation of this type of device is similar to the operation of the familiar old player piano. In the diode-matrix pinboard programmer, the desired control sequence is established by inserting small plastic pins (each containing a diode) into a plugboard. Alteration of the desired control sequence is accomplished by changing the positions of the plastic plugs, the pattern of holes, or the position of the diode pins. All types of sequence controllers are typically used for applications having a fixed sequence of operation for a large number of repetitions.

PROGRAMMABLE CONTROLLERS

A programmable controller (PC) is a solid-state device used to control machine motion or process operation by means of a stored program. The PC sends output control signals and receives input signals through input/output (I/O) devices. A PC controls outputs in response to stimuli at the inputs according to the logic prescribed by the stored program. The inputs are made up of limit switches, pushbuttons, thumbwheels, switches, pulses, analog signals, ASCII serial data, and binary or BCD data from absolute position encoders. The outputs are voltage or current levels to drive end devices such as solenoids, motor starters, relays, lights, and so on. Other output devices include analog devices, digital BCD displays, ASCII compatible devices, servo variable-speed drives, and even computers.

The processor part of a PC contains a central processing unit and memory. The central processing unit (CPU) is the "traffic director" of the processor; the memory stores information. Coming into the processor are the electrical signals from the input devices, as conditioned by the input module to voltage levels acceptable to processor logic. The processor scans the state of I/O and updates outputs based on instructions stored in the memory of the PC. For example, the processor may be programmed so that if an input connected to a limit switch is true (limit switch closed), then a corresponding output wired to an output module is to be energized. This output might be a solenoid, for example. The processor remembers this command through its memory and compares on each scan to see if that limit switch is, in fact, closed. If it is closed, the processor energizes the solenoid by turning on the output module.

The output device, such as a solenoid or motor starter, is wired to an output module's terminal, and it receives its shift signal from the processor. In effect, the processor is performing a long and complicated series of logic decisions. The PC performs such decisions sequentially and in accordance with the stored program. Similarly, analog I/O allows

CHAPTER 20

PROGRAMMABLE CONTROLLERS

the processor to make decisions based on the magnitude of a signal, rather than just if it is on or off. For example, the processor may be programmed to increase or decrease the steam flow to a boiler (analog output) based on a comparison of the actual temperature in the boiler (analog input) to the desired temperature. This is often performed by utilizing the built-in PID (proportional, integral, derivative) capabilities of the processor.

Because a PC is "software based," its control logic functions can be changed by reprogramming its memory. Keyboard programming devices facilitate entry of the revised program, which can be designed to cause an existing machine or process to operate in a different sequence or to respond to different levels of, or combinations of, stimuli. Hardware modification are needed only if additional, changed, or relocated input/output devices are involved.

PC VS COMPUTER

There are a few key characteristics which make the PC unlike a computer or other types of controllers. First, the PC is designed to communicate with the outside world (the process to be controlled) directly. That is, inputs from the process and controlling outputs to the process are wired directly to the PC system. The PC recognizes these inputs and outputs by means of a unique fixed address assigned to each I/O.

The second difference between PC's and computers or other controllers is the relative ease of programming. The PC uses relatively simple programming techniques that a plant technician or electrician easily can understand with minimal training. Some programmable controllers use a simple relay ladder diagram programming concept. In such cases, knowledge of Fortran, PAL, or any other computer language is not required; nor is the use of Boolean or other logical expressions required, although these can be converted into a relay ladder diagram format when necessary. The programming can be accomplished on-line with a portable programming panel or a CRT programmer in many cases.

An important point to note about PC's is that a good PC can be reprogrammed "on-line"; that is, while the process is running. Such operations are satisfactory and safe if, and only if, complete ladder rungs are operated on by the processor. Furthermore, on-line programming is successful only if the I/O structure is unaffected. An on-line program change could be hazardous for unproven programs. On-line programming capability can be a valuable feature in some process industries when shutting down a production line can be prohibitively expensive. The on-line feature allows certain portions of a program to be changed with minimum disruption of processing. However, the program or changes to a program should be debugged prior to use in a production situation.

The third and perhaps most important difference when PC's are compared to computers is that PC's are designed for an industrial environment. A well-designed PC should allow the user to locate a PC in a relatively high-noise, high-vibration, high-temperature, high-humidity (noncondensing) environment without affecting its operation. The performance of a control system is influenced to a great degree by the environment in which it is expected to operate. Part ICS 1-108 of NEMA Standards Publication ICS[1] provides some guidelines for service and installation conditions of PC's and other industrial controls.

ADVANTAGES OF PROGRAMMABLE CONTROLLERS

Time is saved when PC's are used because reprogramming usually takes less time than changing the wiring of a hardwired control panel. For example, money is saved because the PC can perform multiple jobs for many years and additional equipment may not be required. A PC is built to be easily expandable. Many PC's are computer-compatible, so PC data can be fed to a computer or from a computer to a PC; also, multiple PC's, computers, and peripherals can be tied together in a data network in which each component can communicate with the others. This makes the PC an ideal basis for a system of integrated machine systems.

Furthermore, depending on the application and PC chosen, a considerable space savings can be achieved. Because the PC system is basically modular, the parts of the system which should be close to the machine can be placed closest to the machine and the cable can be run a long distance to the processor. The processor does not need constant attention or close proximity to the function it is controlling. The remote I/O rack can be located near the machine or process it is controlling. Aside from space savings, this replaces a considerable number of wires, which can be both cumbersome and expensive.

Also, no special computer knowledge is needed to operate or maintain a programmable controller. Many PC's are programmed with slightly modified ladder diagrams, the same kind that electrical engineers and technicians employ in relay logic. (However, some PC's are beginning to get more complex and may use different programming languages, each with its own special advantage.) In addition, because PC's are modular, getting them back on-line if a problem develops, is usually just a matter of making a relatively simple hardware replacement. This kind of modularity also makes PC's easily expandable.

APPLICATIONS OF PROGRAMMABLE CONTROLLERS

In general, a PC application should be configured "top-down" according to the following steps:

1. System functional requirements defined.
2. Assembly drawing, bill of materials, schematics and wiring diagrams prepared by appropriate design personnel.
3. Drawings committed to proper format by drafting department.
4. Drawings reviewed and approved for production.
5. Drawings sent to production department for physical assembly and wiring.
6. If necessary, all changes reviewed and approved by appropriate, responsible design function.

Any PC worthy of its name performs logic functions, such as "if input A is on, input B is off, and input C is also off, then turn on output one." They also allow branching of mutiple sets of conditions, any one of which must be true before the output will be activated.

PC's also perform timing and counting functions—how many parts were manufactured, how many pulses from a chain have occurred, how long an interval is desired before an alarm condition is signaled, or what amount of time is needed for a drill to feed and dwell.

The newer generations of PC's can do much more than this, though. They feature, for example, math calculations. A PC can be programmed to add the value at one memory location to that at another location, with the sum used for a subsequent control function and/or displayed on the programming terminal's CRT screen. The capability exists for subtraction, division, and multiplication, though not all PC models can do all four functions.

Report generation is also an attractive attribute of modern day PC's. If the PC is programmed appropriately, on command, an operator can get from the system a record of such information as the number of parts rejected during a shift, the amount of machine downtime, or even the number of times a particular input or output device has cycled. The latest PC's interface to peripheral devices, such as printers, and allow a hard-copy printout of information. This is especially valuable when management information is a requirement.

Data transfer and comparison with PC's allows data to be moved from one memory location to another, either in increments of one "word" at time or in entire blocks. As PC programs become more complex, the ability to shift memory locations can save time for the PC programmer. Coupled with math capabilities, a PC can be programmed, for example, to "get" the value at location 005, put it in location 110, subtract its contents from the value at location 060, and based on that calculation, turn on or off a specified output. An experienced PC programmer can manipulate data in this way for an entire program, affording the application maximum flexibility.

One of the more exciting developments in PC's of late is the data highway concept. This involves tying multiple PC's together, each transferring information back and forth to the other. In such a scheme, each PC is controlling its own machine in an integrated manufacturing system. If machining operations are sequential, the first PC "tells" the second that its work is completed, so the second PC then can begin its functions, and so on for all.

ADVANTAGES OF NUMERICAL CONTROL

Numerical control (NC), computer numerical control (CNC), and direct numerical control (DNC) have given the manufacturing industry the capability to exercise a new and greater degree of freedom in the designing and manufacturing of products. This new freedom is demonstrated by the ability to automatically produce products requiring complex processing with a very high degree of quality and reliability. Furthermore, products which previously were impossible to manufacture economically can now be made with relative ease using NC machines.

The advances in product design and machines have been parallel; each advance in NC machines not only allows designing of products previously not practical, but suggests additional improvements in machines which would permit more complexity in product designing. Thus machine/product designing is a continuing cycle. The complexity of design of the product is reflected in the machine that produces it. Although many basic NC machine tools are currently available from various manufacturers, specialty applications of NC provide a fertile field for new machines. Retrofitting conventional or standard tools for NC has proved practical and popular.

Numerical control is applicable to a wide variety of industrial tasks. In evaluating the applicability of NC to a particular job, the heaviest weight should be given to jobs which include:

1. A long series of operations in which an error in the sequence would destroy the value of the operations.
2. A wide variety of different sequences of operation which must rapidly and frequently be set up on the same piece of equipment.
3. A relatively complex sequence of operations to be performed.
4. An operation in which it is impractical for a human being to operate in the environment required. Some NC machines run unattended by an operator; however, this benefit usually is associated with the use of robots which load and unload NC and non-NC equipment grouped to form a robotized machining cell.

ADVANTAGES OF NC IN MANUFACTURING

Numerical control has been shown to be one of the most significant advances in part manufacturing since the development of methods for interchangeable parts production. Over the past 20 years, NC has demonstrated the ability to improve in dramatic ways such things as:

- Planning, flexibility, and scheduling.
- Setup, lead, and processing time.
- Machine utilization.
- Tooling cost.
- Cutting tool standardization.
- Accuracy, efficiency, and productivity.
- Material flow and workpiece handling time.
- Interchangeability of work, tools, etc.
- Safety.
- Cost estimating.

Planning

Numerically controlled machine tools provide an economic means for manufacturing management to make detailed plans of operation and at the same time retain documentary support for such plans. Where conventional machine tools are employed in job shop manufacturing operations, it is common practice to pre-establish only a general description of the operation sequence content. This broad planning approach makes it necessary for the machine operator to do the more detailed planning at the machine.

Planning-retention capabilities inherent in numerically controlled machine tapes or other storage media provide a means for transferring a substantial degree of planning from the machine operator to specialists who can work without interruption in an environment conducive to concentration. For each part to be machined, the machine programmer prepares a detailed manuscript for the entire operation with respect (1) to sequence of cuts; (2) operating conditions including feed, speed, and auxiliary functions such as coolant application, manual intervention points for inspection, or final tool sizing during the

ADVANTAGES OF NC

operation; (3) a rough sketch of the setup to guide the tool designer in the final shop drawing to be employed; and (4) a complete list of all the cutting and inspection tools required. This documentary base provides a permanent record which can be used by management for repeat runs of the same workpiece. All of this detailed planning data is recorded and is in a format in such a way that the information is understandable to subsequent users.

Flexibility

Because of the advantageous capabilities inherent in NC machine configurations, substantially more individual operations on a workpiece can be completed in a single setup than would be possible if conventional machine tools were employed. This concept is clearly demonstrated on NC machining centers on which a combination of milling, drilling, turning, tapping, boring, and reaming operations can be performed in a single setup on multiple sides of the workpiece.

Scheduling

Acceptance of the complete numerically controlled machining concept means that fewer setups will be performed on a given workpiece with less spindle idle time. Reduced lead time means that management can forecast for a shorter period into the future and thereby realize a proportional increase in accuracy of forecast requirements.

The ability to convert raw materials into finished parts in a relatively short time results in forecasting of raw-material requirements only, rather than in forecasting of completely finished components. When many variations and special customer requirements are involved, better forecasting and scheduling techniques result.

Setup and Lead Time

It is practical to run smaller batch quantities on NC machine tools than would be economical with conventional machine tools performing the same operations. This is because of the minimal setup costs involved with these machines as a result of preset tooling techniques developed to support the machine operation to reduce nonproductive machine time; larger lot sizes (through group technology) can also be handled effectively with NC.

Capabilities of NC machines enable several conventional machining operations to be replaced with a single NC operation. Because of the smaller quantities and fewer operations performed, the work in process for a given volume of output is less than that of equivalent production on conventional machines.

Lead time is a complex factor composed of many individual operational elements—market-forecast accuracy, number of variables involved, lot size, number of operations performed, number of jobs in process, total available machine capacity, and work-force capacity. Because NC machines provide a means for converting raw material to a useable finished part in a minimum number of setups, most of the factors influencing lead time can be reduced. Forecasting accuracy is inversely proportional to the forecasting period. Thus the closed-loop principle applies in that less stock-out and error-forecast protection is required because of faster response to changing sales requirements. Also, ability to quickly convert raw material to finished parts reduces the need to maintain a finished inventory of such parts.

Better Control of Processing and Machining Time

When the human element is removed from the manufacturing process, as is the case on numerically controlled machine tools, manufactured parts are made in the manner prescribed by the manufacturing engineering department. Machining operations are done in the order that has proved to be most economical and desirable from the manufacturing standpoint. This order cannot be altered without the approval of the manufacturing engineering department. The cutting tools and fixtures which are required for the manufacturing of these parts are programmed into the manufacturing process and are the same for all parts. On a machine tool that has automatic toolchanging capabilities and automatic tool selection, the tools which are called for on the original tape or other program control media are those which must be used in order for the machine to operate correctly.

Machine Utilization

Generally, NC machines have a higher unit operating cost per hour than equivalent conventional machines. However, in many cases, reduced cycle time per job offsets much of the increase in operating cost per hour. In situations in which the operating cost per hour is higher than equivalent conventional equipment, multiple-shift operations are advisable. Lack of operator fatigue and minimal operator interference or opportunity to delay the machine result in substantially higher machine-utilization potential.

Tooling Costs

Workpiece-holding devices generally form the most expensive portion of total tooling costs for job shop machining operations. A prime requirement of NC machine workholding devices is maximum accessibility to the workpiece for performing as many operations as possible in a single setup. This suggests considerable simplicity in the configuration of the workholding devices, which in turn means simpler design, manufacturing, and prove-out.

One of the prime advantages of NC machines is their ability to position accurately and repetitively. This capability eliminates the need for almost all cutter-guiding elements, such as bushings and set gages, in the design of the workholding device. This configuration eliminates those tooling elements most prone to deterioration: the cutter-guiding elements which come in contact with the cutter each time the surface is generated. As a result, tool-maintenance time is reduced, less interference with production is encountered, and tool-maintenance labor costs are avoided.

Cutting Tools

With the programmer developing a detailed list of cutting tools required for the complete operation, it follows that standardization of cutting tools will be promoted. Such standardization provides the advantage of familiarity on the part of programmers, tool-crib setup men, and machine operators, thereby reducing the amount of time required in each phase of the work. Standardization by inference would include development of preferred tool sizes and configurations, which in turn influence the engineering-design phase, tool storage, inventory requirements, purchased-quantity prices, and tool-sharpening costs. Over a period of time the inclusion of preferred sizes at the engineering-design phase reduces the need for special cutting tools and virtually eliminates the extended lead time to procure such special items. Also eliminated are the procurement at a high unit cost (with the prove-out problems attendant to every new tool) and the obsolescence of tools caused by engineering modifications.

Accuracy

Numerically controlled machines generally are designed from the ground up with a degree of sophistication that often is not encountered with conventional machine tools. The machine design elements provide inherently higher quality potential because of greater rigidity in the structural members. Closed-loop measuring systems used on many machines make the measuring devices independent of the feed-drive systems. This provides significantly greater accuracy potential than is commonly available on conventional machines.

The programmed sequence of NC operations also contributes significantly to increased accuracy with cutter-workpiece relationships established in response to the instructions on the tape or other media. For NC machines with automatic tool-changing capability, the correct tool is selected, feeds and speeds are changed automatically to the optimum levels for the cutter-workpiece conditions, coolant is provided as required, the number of passes over the workpiece for roughing and finishing cuts is controlled by the machine, the sequence of cuts is optimized, tools are withdrawn to clear chips as required, and complete tool movement to full required travel is accomplished each time. Machining with NC equipment increases repeatability from piece to piece and from run to run as compared with repeatability attainable using conventional machine tools.

Material Flow Time

Many workpieces can be completed in only a few operations on NC machines as compared with three to four times as many setups for accomplishing the same work on conventional machines. Consequently, reduced material-flow time results from the reduced number of operations. This means fewer assignments by the supervisor, fewer tool-kitting operations, and less in-process work in storage in the plant at any one time.

Numerical control machine capabilities make it possible to convert raw material to finished parts in minimum lead time. This capability reduces the need to keep finished parts in inventory. It provides faster response to introduce engineering modifications without the possibility of high obsolescence costs for existing inventory and also permits faster response to customer requests for special designs.

Workpiece Handling

The need to transport parts from operation to operation and internal machine-operator workpiece-handling efforts are both reduced with NC machine manufacturing methods. For example, on an NC machining center, numerous different operations are performed in a single setup. With conventional machines, the workpiece is often scheduled over several different machines to have the same work performed. There are fewer setups and requirements for the operator to load and unload the workholding device. The manual time internal to the machine operating time during the normal NC machining cycle permits the operator to perform work such as deburring, with the result that a separate operation for this purpose can be eliminated, thereby reducing workpiece handling.

Safety

Specialization in planning the details of the operation, in setting up the cutting and workholding tools, and in operating

the machine all contribute to greater operator safety. Under direction of the tape or other program storage media, the machine establishes the cutter-workpiece relationship. The operator is not required to interfere with the operation to adjust measuring devices in hazardous locations. These measuring devices are generally located near the cutter or workpiece on conventional machines for greatest accuracy, but at the same time in the most hazardous location for operator safety.

Transfer of the detailed operation-planning function from the shop environment to an office environment has direct influence on operator safety, since it removes the need for concentration on work for which the operator has no special training, in an environment that is highly distracting. When this detailed planning function is eliminated from the machine operator's scope of responsibility, full attention can be concentrated on doing the job the operator is most familiar with—auditing the machine operation.

Interchangeability

The first time a part is programmed across NC machine tools, manufacturing management is equipped with documentary support in the form of paper tape, magnetic tape, disc, or other storage media. All elements involved in applying the NC machining concept provide a basis for easy interchangeability of work between plants, standardized workholding and cutting tools, standardized NC machines, methods, and programming techniques.

Cost Estimating

In determining the cost of a part, the two major items involved are material cost and cost of labor necessary to machine the part. When using a numerically controlled machine, the time necessary to machine the part, which is a function of slide feed rates and cutter speeds, is predictable. Therefore the estimates of cost of parts can be very accurately determined and the cost of the parts more realistically predicted.

Several other costs are involved in machining operations which are not directly connected with the machine. One of these is inspection cost. Because of the increased reliability of numerically controlled machining, and the fact that it is done on one machine, inspection operations are greatly reduced in number. Usually only final inspection on a selected number of pieces is necessary to prove out the correctness of the tape and to ensure that the quality that is functionally required is being achieved. Often 100% inspection can be accomplished by the operator during periods between loading and unloading. In this way, NC may contribute to improved part quality by allowing the operator more time to concentrate on inspection functions.

Also, the use of numerically controlled machines reduces material-handling costs. Several machining operations can be done in one setup on one machine, and in many cases the only material handling required is bringing raw material to the machine and taking the finished parts from the machine to the stockroom. This is in contrast to the material-handling functions required when parts are milled on one machine, drilled on another, and contoured or form-cut on a third. Again these costs are available immediately and reliably to the cost department so that expenses can be correctly determined.

Another important, but often overlooked, consideration is the depreciation rates which can be established for a numerically controlled machine. On these machines, costs and depreciation rates can be established accurately. This contrasts with several depreciation rates for different machine tools which might be required to produce the same part.

ADVANTAGES OF NC

Productivity

Productivity can be defined as the effective result of the operator in employing machine tools to convert raw materials to useable parts. Numerically controlled machines contribute substantially to increased productivity for a wide variety of reasons. After installation in the reader, the tape or other program storage media is always ready to continue the operation sequence—there is no delay for the operator to implement the operation as is the case in conventional machine operations.

Efficiently programmed operation sequences cause the machine to have a minimum amount of idle time in traversing from one cutting position to another. Where automatic toolchangers are used, toolchanging is performed immediately when desired. The tool is changed in the same amount of time necessary for the operator to change it, yet the automatic changer does not suffer fatigue as would the operator in making manual toolchanges. The toolchanges are performed correctly, and correct feeds and speeds are employed on each cut with coolant applied as required. When tool retractions are required to clear chips, as in the case of deep-hole-drilling operations, they are performed automatically and consistently from part to part.

Combined, these factors all provide for a higher percentage of time devoted to cutting chips during the operation. Since chip cutting is the prime objective in machine tool operation, it follows that increased productivity is a predictable result.

ADVANTAGES OF NC IN DESIGN

The use of NC in the shop dramatically impacts the flexibility of part design. For example, more accurate prototypes can be produced when NC machine tools are employed. When the part is put into production, closer tolerances often can be held if NC equipment is used. In addition, workpieces that were impossible to manufacture using conventional machine tools are now routinely produced using NC equipment.

Numerical control machines which have contouring ability can be economically used to eliminate the cost of special form tools. By the elimination of these special tools, the design flexibility to make engineering changes is greatly simplified. In most cases, an engineering change means a change in the part program and the tape which controls the machine.

When a new design is introduced, it is advantageous to the engineering department to see this design in actual hardware as soon as economically possible. Numerical control has made this lead time short because of the elimination of the need for special tools and fixtures. This allows the designer to review his design and make any necessary engineering and design changes in a short period of time, thus decreasing the time from the drawing board to the finished product.

Accurate Prototypes

A major cost in the manufacturing of a prototype is the expense involved in tooling; this includes both capital tooling expenditures and perishable tooling costs. This use of standard tooling, which is common to many parts, and universal fixtures, which can be used for many parts on numerically controlled machines, has reduced the costs in manufacturing.

Adherence to Specifications

Parts which are manufactured on numerically controlled machine tools often are more representative of the actual engineering design than those made by conventional means. A major reason for this is that the manufacturing of the part and the decisions involved in the manufacturing of the part are removed from the hands of the operator of the machine tool and placed in the hands of the part programmer. The machine operator has little or no control over the sequence of operations or over the tools that are to be used. The tolerances which are designed into the control tape or other program storage media and into the tooling that is used are repetitive on all the parts. These features lead to manufacturing consistency.

Another important benefit available through the use of NC is that, in the future, parts which are manufactured only for service will be the same as parts made during normal production runs at the time the product was originally manufactured. This allows manufacturing specifications to be established which are consistent throughout the life of the part as well as in any parts that are used for service in the future.

Difficult-to-Manufacture Parts

One of the prime advantages of manufacturing with numerically controlled machine tools, from the standpoint of the design engineer, is the ability to design a part which can be quickly and economically manufactured. This is in contrast to the requirements of conventional machine tools which often require form cutters. In many cases, special machines were formerly required to produce parts which today are produced quickly and economically on machines with contouring ability. It is now possible for a tape to be produced for a machine to manufacture a part economically, whereas in the past it may have been impossible to justify the necessary expenditures for the manufacturing of the part. New areas are now open to the design engineer who is aware of the manufacturing abilities available on modern machine tools. Any parts which can be defined mathematically can now be manufactured at nominal costs. Parts which in the past were impossible to manufacture due to economic considerations have now become everyday, commonplace workpieces.

ECONOMIC JUSTIFICATION OF NUMERICAL CONTROL

Evaluating numerically controlled facilities for the first-time buyer is generally encumbered by various fears. The expenditure is large, and the changes on the enterprise are anticipated as being large and disrupting. Frequently, persons evaluating the project are uncomfortable in examining a decision with so many "unknowns" and such large "risks."

The purpose of an economic justification is the evaluation of several proposals under the same set of circumstances to select the one which gives optimum benefit to the enterprise, considering levels of investment and business objectives.

The study of alternatives must include the sources from which economic benefit will issue. Often, in past economic analyses, direct labor savings were so great that they dominated all other benefits, or other benefits were so small that they could be ignored. When NC is being considered, an entirely new range of technology is available, so the areas to consider for economic benefits are much greater.

A report prepared by the University of Michigan's Industrial Development Division based on a survey of 356 users of NC equipment[2] indicated the following ranges of saving attributable to the use of NC: machine setup—20-70%; material handling—20-50%; inspection—30-45%; scrap and rework—30-45%; work in process—20-30%; and part-cycle time—20-75% (see "Advantages of Numerical Control" in this chapter).

Benefits in NC are not common to all types of NC machine tools. For example, the benefits obtained from a simple two-axis NC drill are not the same as expected benefits derived through the use of a toolchanging machining center. Typically, the more operations that can be combined on a single machine, the greater the advantageous impact on the manufacturing organization. An approach to NC justification, then, is to outline each function of the manufacturing organization and estimate the benefits that NC provides for that function, i.e., sales, production control, cost accounting, etc. Each of these benefits must then be quantified.

Many of the benefits of NC will not be realized on a single-machine basis. Therefore, a plan of greater scope than a single machine is necessary. A 5 or 10-year plan is required, comparing the total existing environment with one totally replaced by NC.

GENERAL CONSIDERATIONS

After each alternative has been evaluated based on technical characteristics, each alternative should be assessed based on value to the company as compared to the other alternatives and to the present production method. The present method should be the benchmark against which the alternatives are compared. In the following example, only one alternative is compared to the present method although the same analysis could be performed for each alternative. Usually the one technically best alternative is selected for in-depth economic analysis.

The first step in such an analysis is to develop a sample of the workload to be processed across the new equipment. It must be representative of the work to be performed. From this sample, projections can be made of the effect on the total workload, eliminating the need for a very large, detailed study while preserving statistical accuracy. After the project has been adopted and implemented, this sample forms the basis for a performance audit, a critical but often omitted step.

The categories of benefit and costs should be identified next. Typically savings can be obtained in the following areas.

1. Direct labor.
2. Tool and fixture costs.
3. Consumable tool cost.
4. Inventory carrying cost.
5. Tool setting cost.
6. Programming cost.
7. Inspection cost.
8. In-plant transportation cost.
9. Maintenance cost.

It should be noted that the impact of these factors varies with the project. For example, if workpieces are costly, the inventory considerations may be more of an influence than the direct labor savings. The optimum balance of the costs is what is desired.

DIRECT LABOR SAVINGS

After the NC production analysis (cycle-time, setup-time, and fixture estimates) is obtained, along with the corresponding conventional data, a table such as Table 20-1 can be set up as shown.

At this point, the cycle time of the sample work group for the NC machine tool (column 4 in Table 20-1) is totaled; the same procedure is employed to obtain the conventional total cycle time (column 7 in Table 20-1). These times represent the totals of the machine cycle time plus the pro rata setup time in both cases.

The next question to answer is: what amount or percent of the total available workload (time) does the sample workload represent? What is the sample workload ratio? To obtain this, a table should be established in the form of Table 20-2.

The total hours required per year for the sample workload group is now obtained by totaling the sixth column in Table 20-2—*Hours required Per Year*. This gives an indication of the number of machines required.

The next calculation is to determine the sample workload ratio. First, the number of shifts the NC machine would be operated is determined. Second, this figure is multiplied by the number of hours per shift per year (about 2000) to obtain the total number of NC machine hours available. The total number of hours, however, has to be modified by the NC machine production efficiency. This efficiency represents the amount of time the NC machine is actually making parts. The difference between the NC machine efficiency and 100% represents the

TABLE 20-1
Cycle-Time Comparison

| Part No. | NC Machine Pro Rata Setup | | | Conventional Pro Rata Setup | | |
	Cycle	Rate per Lot Size	Total cycle	Cycle	Rate per Lot Size	Total cycle
0001	0.59	0.50/ 17 = 0.029	0.619	1.86	27.0/100 = 0.27	2.130
0002	0.82	0.50/ 17 = 0.029	0.849	4.46	77.8/100 = 0.78	5.238
0003	0.42	0.25/ 35 = 0.007	0.427	0.85	20.8/140 = 0.15	0.999
0004	0.08	0.25/ 25 = 0.010	0.090	0.35	6.9/150 = 0.05	0.401
0005	0.29	0.25/ 17 = 0.015	0.305	0.88	10.3/100 = 0.10	0.983
		Total =	2.291		Total =	9.751

CHAPTER 20

ECONOMIC JUSTIFICATION OF NC

TABLE 20-2
Sample Workload Ratio*

Part No.	NC Machining Center Cycle Time	Lot Size	Lots per Year	Yearly Requirement	Hours Required per Year	Part Description
0001	0.619	17	12	200	123.88	Housing
0002	0.849	17	12	200	169.88	Gear case
0003	0.427	35	12	420	179.40	Cover
0004	0.090	25	12	300	27.00	Linkage
0005	0.305	17	12	200	60.94	Bracket
				Total hours required per year =	561.11	

* Based on a three-shift operation, one machine would be required.

amount of time the machine is waiting for work, program proveout, maintenance, and general production inefficiencies. The equation is:

$$\frac{NC\ machine\ hours\ available \times \underline{\hspace{1cm}}percent\ efficiency}{NC\ machine\ hours\ required\ per\ year\ for\ sample\ workload} \quad (1)$$

In the example, 6000 hr of NC machine time is available at an assumed 85% efficiency. The sample workload requires 561.11 hr.

6000/561.11 x 0.85 = 9.09 (sample workload ratio)

Thus, the projected sample workload requires 1/9.09, or 11.0%, of the total NC machine availability.

Based on the data in Table 20-1, the productivity ratio can be determined:

$$Productivity\ ratio = \frac{total\ conventional\ cycle\ time\ (sample\ workload)}{total\ NC\ machine\ cycle\ time\ (sample\ workload)} \quad (2)$$

The productivity ratio indicates the number of conventional manufacturing hours NC machine tools will produce in 1 hr. The example below then carries out the calculations to determine direct labor savings. The direct hourly labor rate must include all fringe benefits. The productivity ratio, based on the data in Table 20-1 is:

9.75 hr conventional/2.29 hr NC machine = 4.26

This indicates that every NC machine hour produces 4.26 conventional machine hours.

On the assumption that one NC machine is required, direct labor savings are computed as follows:

2000 hr/shift x 3 shifts x 0.85 efficiency = 5100 available NC machine hours

21,708 conventional machine hours - 6000 NC machine-operator hours = 15,708 hr saved

TOOL AND FIXTURE SAVINGS

Tool and fixture savings occur in two basic forms: (1) new, conventional tooling cost avoided and (2) toolholding costs reduced or eliminated. Table 20-3 on tool and fixture savings considers these items:

1. Part number.
2. NC machine fixture costs. Estimates of the cost of the NC machine fixtures.

3. Conventional fixture cost. The cost of fixtures and tools for the conventional operations replaced by the NC operations. If tools are already built, the historical cost data can be used. However, if these costs are old, they should be increased by at least 5% per year compounded starting from the day of their construction.

The sample group represents fixture savings of $69,812. Thus:

$$Sample\text{-}group\ savings \times the\ sample\ workload \quad (3)$$
$$ratio = total\ fixture\ savings$$

$69,812 x 9.09 = $634,591.08

This savings, of course, exists only in the unlikely case that every part processed for the NC machine would be a new part and would have no existing tooling.

TABLE 20-3
Tool and Fixture Savings

Part No.	NC Machine Fixture Cost	Conventional Fixture Cost
0001	$ 4,440	$27,224
0002	5,840	19,520
0003	5,240	30,920
0004	1,240	1,200
0005	2,440	10,148
Total costs	$19,200	$89,012

Table 20-4 projects five years into the future the anticipated tooling and fixture changeover requirements. By referring to the sample workload, it is possible to determine when these particular parts will require substantial engineering changes or when they will become obsolete and thus be replaced by another workpiece. This will probably require consultation with engineering and marketing departments.

For the purpose of continuing calculations, it should be assumed that 20% of the machine workload will be new parts with no existing tooling and 80% will be old parts. Thus:

0.20 x $634,591.08 (net fixture savings) = $126,918.22

0.80 x $152,301.86 (tool maintenance cost savings) = $121,841.49

Total annual tool and fixture savings = $248,759.71

TABLE 20-4
Tooling and Fixtures Change-Over Requirements

Part No.	Year				
	1	2	3	4	5
0001			●		
0002					●
0003				●	
0004			●		
0005	●				

Step 1*

Year...	1	2	3	4	5
Total % year...	1/5 = 20%	0/5 = 0%	2/5 = 40%	1/5 = 20%	1/5 = 20%

* Step 1: Determine percent of part change-over each year:

$$\frac{\text{Number of parts requiring new tools or retooling}}{\text{Number of parts in sample group}} \qquad (4)$$

= (See Chart) = % of part change-over for specific year

Step 2: Determine average percent change-over for duration of study:

$$\frac{\text{Total of \% change-over of all study years}}{\text{Number of years of study}} \qquad (5)$$

$$= \frac{20\% + 0\% + 40\% + 20\% + 20\%}{5}$$

= 20% average annual part change-over

TOOL CONSUMPTION COST

Several arguments have been advanced on the subject of consumable tool expenditure for conventional versus NC facilities. The heart of the matter is that, per operating hour, the tool cost for NC is higher because more actual metal removal occurs, hence per hour tool usage is increased. However, due to the greater number of hours required to achieve the same value of output, the overall tool consumption for conventional machining exceeds that of NC.

Referring to Fig. 20-1, it can be seen that an average NC facility uses about $4.10 per direct labor hour and a conventional facility $1.75 per direct labor hour. Based on the equivalent hours calculated in an earlier section, the consumable tool costs are:

For a conventional facility:

21,708 hr x $1.75/hr = $37,989

For an NC facility:

6000 hr x $4.10/hr = $24,600

By subtracting the tool costs for the NC facility from those for the conventional facility, it can be seen that use of the NC facility results in a savings of about $13,389.

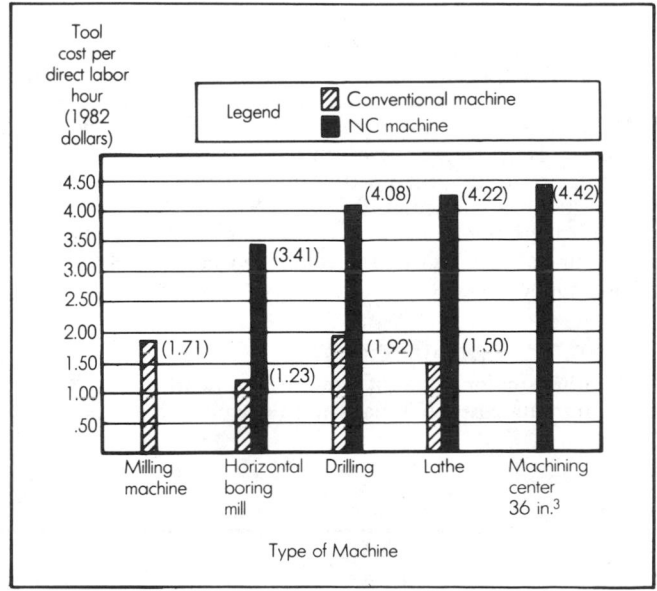

Fig. 20-1 Consumable tool costs—typical, as experienced by one major U.S. manufacturer.

INVENTORY-REDUCTION SAVINGS

Inventory savings take two basic forms. One is the reduction in total in-process inventory; the other is the reduction in inventory holding costs. The data listed on Table 20-5 is required to obtain an average inventory cost using only conventional machine tools. The primary reason for NC's contribution to inventory reduction is its capability to combine operations and, therefore, reduce lead time. Included in Table 20-6 is an analysis of inventory using NC machine tools.

ECONOMIC JUSTIFICATION OF NC

TABLE 20-5
Conventional Average Inventory

Part No.	Lot Size	No. of Lots per Year	Cost Value per Piece	Cost Value of Completed Lot	Average Inventory
0001	100	2	$67.56	$6,756	$ 3,378
0002	100	2	97.96	9,796	4,898
0003	140	3	30.64	4,289	2,144
0004	150	2	10.52	1,578	789
0005	100	2	44.20	4,420	2,210
Total conventional average inventory					$13,419

* This represents the present conventional lot sizes, and in turn, average inventory.

TABLE 20-6
Average Inventory/NC Machine Tool

Part No.	Lot Size	No. of Lots per Year	Cost Value per Piece	Cost Value of Completed Lot	Average Inventory
0001	17	12	$67.56	$1,143.52	$ 574.26
0002	17	12	97.96	1,665.32	832.66
0003	35	12	30.64	1,072.40	536.20
0004	25	12	10.52	263.00	131.50
0005	17	12	44.20	751.40	375.70
Total NC machine tool average inventory					$2,450.32

TOOL-SETTING COST

A concern of manufacturing engineers is the cost of setting tools for NC machine tools that require preset tools. Actually it must be recognized that even with conventional machines, this cost exists in that tool-setting costs are paid for at a machine rate while depth stops are being set, cutters shimmed, etc. With NC, however, tools are preset off the machine and the cost, therefore, is the bench rate of the tool setter.

To determine the cost of setting tools for an NC machine tool, Table 20-7 is presented.

This calculation is based upon resetting the tools completely every time each lot is run. In actual practice many of the tools would not be reset each time. Actual cost could therefore be less than shown.

PROGRAMMING COST

Another major area of concern in justification is NC programming costs. Normally not recognized is the fact that there is such a thing as "conventional programming costs." These costs include the time that process engineering personnel spend setting standards, troubleshooting the conventional machine operations, processing the workpiece, etc., for all the conventional operations. Consider the items of Table 20-8.

If all the workpieces in the sample group workload were already processed conventionally, the cost of programming these workpieces for the first year must be considered as an additional cost for the NC machine tool. These calculations are as follows:

First-year programming would require 91.63 x 9.09 (sample workload ratio) hours programming = 832.81 hr.

For the ensuing years, however, the difference between conventional and NC machine tool process time would have to be considered. At this point it is necessary to consider the new workload percentage that was derived from Table 20-1. From

TABLE 20-7
Toolsetting Cost

Part No.	Lots per Year	Tools per Part	Tools set per Year	Hours per Tool	Total Hours per Year
0001	12	23	276	0.25	69.0
0002	12	46	552	0.25	138.0
0003	12	22	324	0.25	81.0
0004	12	6	72	0.25	18.0
0005	12	27	297	0.25	74.0
				Total =	380.0*

* 380 hr x 9.09 (sample workload ratio) = 3,454 hr. This could be rounded off to 3500 hr.
  3500 hr x 19.28/hr = $67,480 per year.

TABLE 20-8
Programming Cost Calculations

Part No.	NC Machine Cycle	Manual Program Ratio	Total Hours for NC Machine Tool	Conventional Cycle	Conventional Programming Ratio*	Total Hours/ Conventional
0001	0.62	40/1	24.78	1.86	7.5/1	13.95
0002	0.85	40/1	33.98	4.46	7.5/1	33.45
0003	0.43	40/1	17.09	0.85	7.5/1	6.37
0004	0.09	40/1	3.60	0.35	7.5/1	2.66
0005	0.30	40/1	12.19	0.88	7.5/1	6.60
			Total = 91.63			Total = 63.04

* Conventional program ratio is the time required to process, set standards, and troubleshoot the comventional machining process. A ratio of 7.5 hr to a 1-hr cycle time is used in this example.

this data, the difference between conventional and NC programs is:

Percentage of part changeover (0.20) x (91.63 hr - 63.04 hr) x 9.09 = 51.97 hr/year

INSPECTION-COST SAVINGS

Inspection savings are a function of the NC machine's capability to combine operations. Items to be considered are listed in Table 20-9 for NC machines and Table 20-10 for conventional machines.

IN-PLANT TRANSPORTATION COSTS

One method of determining in-plant transportation cost savings is shown in the following listing. The in-plant transportation cost is a function of the number of operations and, in turn, the number of moves. A general rule of thumb is to provide three moves for interdepartmental handlings and two moves for intradepartmental handlings. These would be required for each machine operation. Again, the NC machine that can combine the greatest number of operations contributes the greatest savings.

TABLE 20-9
Inspection-Cost Savings—NC Machine Average Cost*

Part No.	Number of Operations	Parts per Year	Percent Inspected	Number Inspected	Cost per Inspection	Total Cost per Part
0001	2	200	8	32	$8.00	$ 256.00
0002	2	200	8	32	8.00	256.00
0003	1	420	8	33	8.00	264.00
0004	1	300	8	24	8.00	192.00
0005	1	200	8	16	8.00	128.00
					Total =	$1,096.00

* The calculations for conventional manufacturing inspection costs are carried out in the same fashion (see Table 20-10).

TABLE 20-10
Conventional Inspection Cost*

Part No.	Number of Operations	Parts per Year	Percent Inspected	Number Inspected	Cost per Inspection	Total Cost per Part
0001	12	200	30	720	$4.00	$ 2,889.00
0002	15	200	30	900	4.00	3,600.00
0003	10	420	30	1,260	4.00	5,040.00
0004	5	300	30	450	4.00	1,800.00
0005	7	200	30	420	4.00	1,680.00
					Total =	$15,000.00

* Net inspection cost savings equal conventional cost $15,000.00 minus NC machine cost of $1,096.00 times 9.09 (sample workload ratio). Total inspection cost savings = $126,387.36

CNC SYSTEM ELEMENTS

MAINTENANCE COST

There undoubtedly is an increased cost for maintenance of NC. The NC machine itself is more complex, plus the electronic control requires additional skill as compared to conventional facilities. The actual costs vary widely depending on the nature of the equipment being considered and the company's attitude toward machine maintenance and upkeep.

CNC SYSTEM ELEMENTS

The basic elements of a computer numerical control system are shown in Fig. 20-2. The control is the heart of the system. It processes information received from the operator and machine interface. This information is interpreted and manipulated with hardware logic and computer programs (software). Memory provides the means to store programs and manipulate input data. Based on the information received, the control outputs data back to the operator interface and machine.

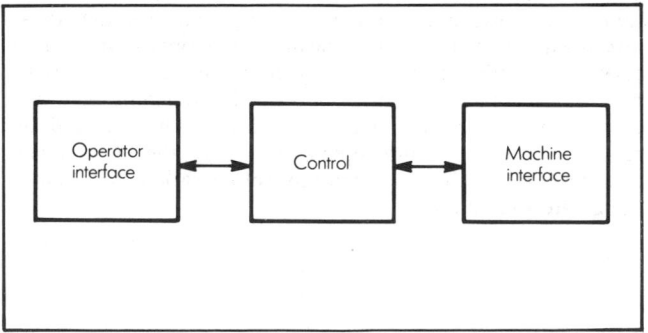

Fig. 20-2 Elements of a computer numerical-control system.

The operator interface consists of devices which send, receive, and interpret information. Since the operations performed by NC systems are defined by the software, interface devices are needed to input the various programs from memory. Paper tape input is the most common. The operator station(s) is the other major operator interface element. It contains all the switches, pushbuttons, displays, etc., required to operate and monitor machine activities.

Machine devices are regulated by the control. Based on information supplied by operator interface devices and feedback from various machine devices, the control turns on and off machine outputs and controls machine motion.

THE CONTROL

The control performs "real-time" decisions on a process that is in operation at the same time. There are several types of control systems; however, each can be broken down into the same functional units. Each unit performs specific functions, and all units function together to execute the programmed instructions. Figure 20-3 shows the five major functional units of a control. The dashed lines with arrows represent the flow of timing and control signals. The solid lines with arrows represent the flow of data.

Input Unit

All instructions and data are fed into the control through the input unit. Software, such as the system operating program, part programs, and diagnostics are input by means of paper tape, magnetic devices, etc., and are stored in memory until

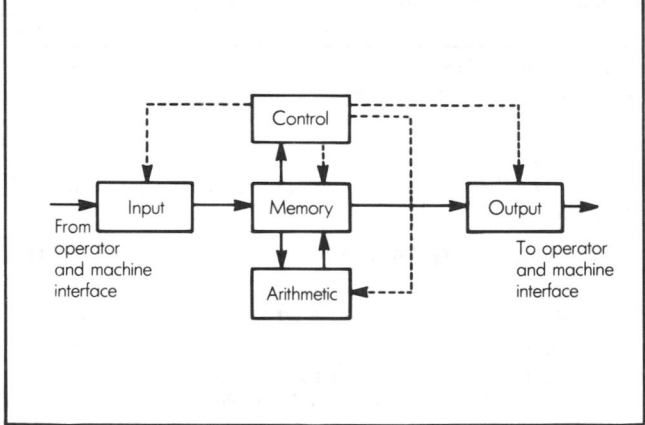

Fig. 20-3 Five major functional units of a computer numerical-control system.

needed. The status of machine and operator station devices are input in the form of a-c, d-c, and analog signals. Analog signals are converted to digital signals (A/D converter) in order to be understood by the control. Input signals are sent to memory, where they are used by the control and arithmetic units to arrive at output decisions.

For systems with many a-c or d-c inputs, a scheme called multiplexing may be used. With this scheme, the state of many devices can be monitored on a single channel. This reduces wiring without restricting real-time operation.

Memory Unit

The memory unit stores instructions and data received from the input. It also stores the results of arithmetic operations and supplies information to the output. The size of the programs and space required to manipulate data determines the amount of memory required. Basically, there are two types of memory—Random Access Memory (RAM) and Read Only Memory (ROM).

RAM. Random Access Memory provides immediate access to any storage location point in memory. Information may be "read" or "written" in the same very fast procedure. Part programs are usually stored in RAM memory to enable editing. While there are many types of RAM, only certain types (i.e., core and bubble) are able to retain data during a power loss. Complementary Metal Oxide Semiconductor (CMOS) memory is retentive if it has battery backup.

ROM. Read Only Memory stores information permanently or semipermanently. Information can be "read," but cannot be altered. Only fixed programs such as the system operating program and diagnostics should be stored on ROM. "Programmable" ROMs are referred to as PROMs, and electrically erased PROMS are called EPROMs.

Arithmetic Unit

The arithmetic unit performs calculations and makes decisions. The results are sent to the memory unit to be stored.

Control Unit

The control unit takes instructions from the memory unit and interprets them one at a time. It then sends appropriate instructions to other units to cause instruction execution.

Output Unit

The output unit takes data from memory when commanded. Outputs are in the form of a-c, d-c, and digital signals. Digital signals used as axis drive commands are first converted to analog (D/A converter). Output signals are used to turn on and off devices, display information, position axes, etc.

OPERATOR INTERFACE

The operator interface consists of all devices, exclusive of the machine, which send and receive control information. Figure 20-4 depicts some of the more common devices.

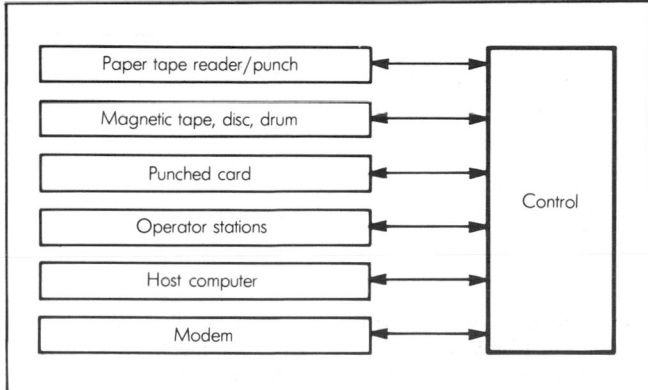

Fig. 20-4 Operator interface devices used in a computer numerical-control system.

Paper Tape Reader/Punch

When punched tape is used, the instructions for a given operation are contained in several rows of information called a block. The tape may be made as long as required in order to contain the entire NC program. A unique feature of tape is that when the beginning and the end of it are joined to form a continuous loop, it is always ready upon completion of one part to start the next part. This feature is used when many parts of a given program are required for a single setup and the tape length is relatively short. The operator merely loads a new part and starts the cycle again. When the length of tape becomes significantly large, it is wound on a takeup reel in belt fashion during the operation; then at the end of the program, the tape is rewound on the first reel and the cycle is started again.

By means of the hole patterns punched in the tape, all the letters of the alphabet as well as the digits 0 through 9 can be coded to form words within a block. Various other symbols useful for controlling machine functions can also be coded. Two types of standard coding are used as described later in this chapter.

Tape readers are usually either electromechanical or photoelectric; both detect the presence or absence of holes and transmit information. Photoelectric tape readers are typically much faster than electromechanical types. Electromechanical tape readers use fingers or other devices to make electrical contact through holes of the tape.

Magnetic Tape, Disc, Drum

Magnetic devices record and read magnetic spots on a moving surface of material. Each of these devices has a thin coating of magnetic material applied to a smooth, nonmagnetic material on plastic tape. Drums are thinly coated metal cylinders. The disk (floppy disk) resembles a phonograph record with magnetic material on both sides.

Magnetic devices have the ability to store large amounts of data on a small amount of surface. Magnetic tape is the most economical of the three. Typically, 1/2" (12.7 mm) wide tape is used which can store 500 characters per inch (20 characters per millimeter) of tape. Both higher and lower densities are available.

A single reel of magnetic tape can store approximately 14 million characters of data. This would be a very long single program, but several programs which might represent all the required programs for a given machine can thus be stored on a single reel of tape.

Punch Cards

In the past, punch cards were used as input to NC systems primarily because of the availability of the equipment on which the programs could be prepared. Because keypunch operators and keypunch departments exist in many businesses for accounting purposes, the same equipment and trained personnel were utilized to assist in NC program preparation. Today, however, punch cards are used as input to relatively few NC machines.

Operator Station(s)

The operator station(s) consists of all the switches, pushbuttons, displays, etc., required to operate the machine (unless the machine has been completely automated with numerical control, in which case the operator's attention is not required). Devices such as switches and pushbuttons are used to command the machine to perform an activity, i.e., machine start and master stop. The commanded actions, machine member position, state of machine devices, etc., are usually displayed for operator reference. Cathode Ray Tubes (CRT), Light Emitting Diodes (LED), and plasma displays are some of the more common methods of displaying information.

The main purpose of the operator station is to initiate automatic operation, to input data, and to monitor activities using display devices.

Host Computer

The direct link of a general-purpose host computer to a machine tool is advantageous for certain applications. (A special-purpose design would be incorporated into the control system of the machine tool itself.) General-purpose computers are normally expensive on either a purchase or rental basis. Recently, lower priced models have become available and have been used for NC. A Direct Numerical Control (DNC) system can have certain characteristics which the computer can handle much more efficiently than an alternative type of system. For instance, computation may be required while running a part to correct for various machine conditions such as tool wear or errors inherent in the machine tool itself. An example of this is a precision leadscrew that has error throughout its length. The error in the screw is measured and stored in the computer memory in the form of a table. When a part is made on this

CNC SYSTEM ELEMENTS

machine, the computer system modifies the part program while it is running by making corrections based on the error table to obtain improved accuracy on the part.

Modem

A MODulator DEModulator (MODEM) converts data from the control into a form compatible with telephone transmission lines. The primary use of the MODEM for NC is diagnostics. For example, some control builders can send and receive data from a customer's control over telephone transmission lines to determine control problems.

MACHINE INTERFACE

The machine interface consists of all devices used to monitor and control the machine tool. Extreme travel limits, miscellaneous position locations, hydraulic and air pressures can be monitored. Additionally, solenoids for hydraulic and air control as well as motor control are provided. Outputs are usually a single d-c and a-c level or a d-c output with remote a-c switching devices.

Several systems employ a multiplexing scheme which greatly reduces hardware requirements. Since multiplex cycles are usually less than 50 μ s, few reliability problems are encountered.

Limit and Proximity Switches

Limit and proximity switches are used to determine the location of a machine member. Proximity switches are located at defined intervals along the machine's travel. The control detects which switch is tripped to determine axis position. This method is no longer in common usage due to limited accuracy.

There are usually two limit switches on each linear axis; one for plus motion, and one for minus motion. When the control detects that a limit switch has been tripped, machine operation is halted until the axis is manually moved off the limit.

Pressure and Temperature Switches

Pressure and temperature switches are used to determine system conditions. Oil and air pressure for the machine and temperatures of the control cabinet and lube may be monitored as needed.

Control Valves

Many machine functions are performed by applying air or oil pressure to devices. Power drawbars, turret indexers, tool-changer magazines, and coolant flow are but a few of the machine mounted devices and functions controlled by the numerical control unit.

Many machine tools use hydraulic or air operated cylinders to control spindle speed and axis feed transmissions. The control of these devices is programmed in the controller and activated by control codes.

Servomechanisms

A servomechanism (often termed a "servo") is a group of elements which convert the NC input into precision mechanical displacements. These elements include motors (hydraulic or electric), gear trains, and transducers (velocity or position).

The drive to spindles and slides in NC tools is usually provided by either hydraulic or electric motors.

Servomechanisms may be either open or closed loop as shown in Fig. 20-5.

Open loop. In the case of the open-loop servo, there is no feedback signal to assure that the machine axis actually moved

the distance programmed. For instance, if the servo is designed to move 0.0001" (0.003 mm) for each input pulse, and 100 pulses are programmed, the servo will move a table 0.010" (0.25 mm). The only assurance that the table actually moved 0.010" in this type of system is the reliability of the system.

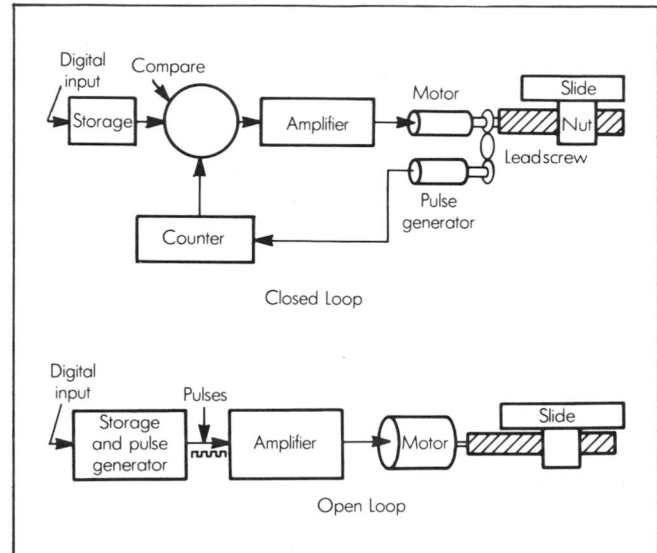

Fig. 20-5 Open and closed-loop servomechanisms.

Closed loop. The closed-loop servo, on the other hand, compares information feedback from the machine slide with programmed information to assure that the motion has actually been performed. The signal to the drive motor is modified by the feedback signal.

Servomechanism elements. The basic or main elements of a numerical control system are shown in Fig. 20-6. The principles here essentially are the same for positioning and contouring, although the principles of contouring are somewhat more complex.

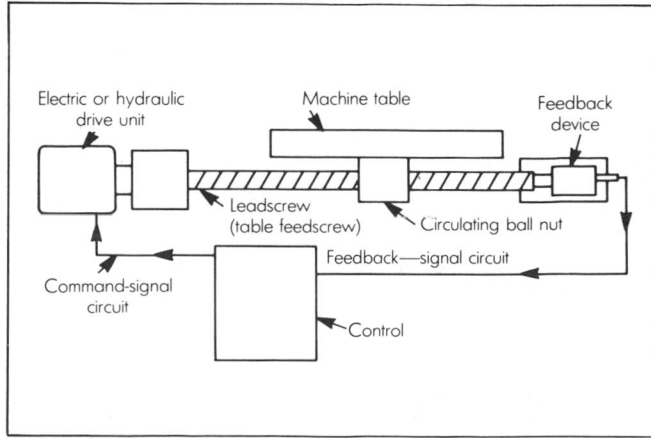

Fig. 20-6 Mechanical elements of a computer numerical-control system.

FUNDAMENTALS OF DIRECT NUMERICAL CONTROL

By EIA definition, direct numerical control (DNC) is a system connecting a group of numerically controlled machines to a common computer memory for part-program storage, with provision for on-demand distribution of machining data. Typically, additional provisions are available for collection, display, or editing of part programs, operator instructions, or data related to the NC process.

In general, two areas of application exist in which DNC has shown specific advantages. First, the DNC concept is often justifiable in applications that have large amounts of control information which must be managed, stored, and distributed—many NC programs or very complex programs. DNC facilitates the management of large numbers of NC programs and helps to sidestep the possibility of using the wrong NC program or using a program that is not the latest version. With DNC, lengthy NC programs can be loaded quickly, eliminating the costly nonproductive time often associated with the loading of complex programs via punched paper tape or other mechanical input media. The payoff is achieved in increased uptime and greater machine tool efficiency.

The DNC concept is also employed as the heart of the control system for so-called flexible production systems in which a number of numerically controlled machine tools are linked by means of electronic data communication and mechanical automation. Often employed to machine families of parts, such systems are equipped with a central computer which directs the flow of parts through the system and operates in a DNC mode, downloading NC programs to the member machine tools when required.

NC MACHINE CONFIGURATIONS

The number of axes or machine motions to which numerical control is applied commonly ranges from two to five. In general, NC machines are grouped into two classes: positioning machines and contouring machines. The functional capabilities of both types of machines are explained in the following sections.

The two axes of a representative point-to-point or positioning system are the straight-line movements of the longitudinal and cross or transverse slides, these two machine motions occurring at 90° to each other. They are respectively X and Y axes, and these motions position the workpiece by positioning the table or surface on which it is mounted according to rectangular coordinates. Two-axis control, if provided with contouring capability, could be used for two-dimensional contouring.

A third axis may be added by applying numerical control to the up and down movement of the spindle of a vertical milling machine or of an upright drill, for example. This becomes the Z axis. These axis designations are diagrammed in Fig. 20-7.

In contouring systems, the third axis provides three-dimensional control—for milling cavities in dies or molds or for milling other contours in three dimensions.

POSITIONING MACHINES AND SYSTEMS

In its simplest form, the positioning machine is provided with NC dimensional control of the slide position only. Slide feed rates and spindle-rotating speeds, for example, may be selected manually. However, most modern NC positioning machines provide tape control of feeds and speeds, coolant on-off, turret indexing, etc. The method of handling these functions varies considerably from one manufacturer to another and cannot be generalized sufficiently to depict in diagrams.

Point-to-Point

A point-to-point machine (sometimes called a positioning machine) is one that moves the slides until a specific point on the workpiece is at the exact position at which the machining operation can begin. In some machines, the table slides move the workpiece to a specific location under the tool so that machining can start. In other machines, the table and workpiece remain stationary and the tool is moved to the desired location in relation to the workpiece. Certain machines can position both part and tool simultaneously.

In the first instance, each slide attempts to move at its maximum traverse rate to the new location, ignoring the status of other slides in the system. Because the slides operate independently of each other, the tool path between operations can be predicted only roughly. The path is affected by the distance between points, acceleration or deceleration, and the maximum traverse rate of each slide. The lack of linearity of the tool path between locations is of little consequence since the tool is not in contact with the workpiece during the traverse sequence.

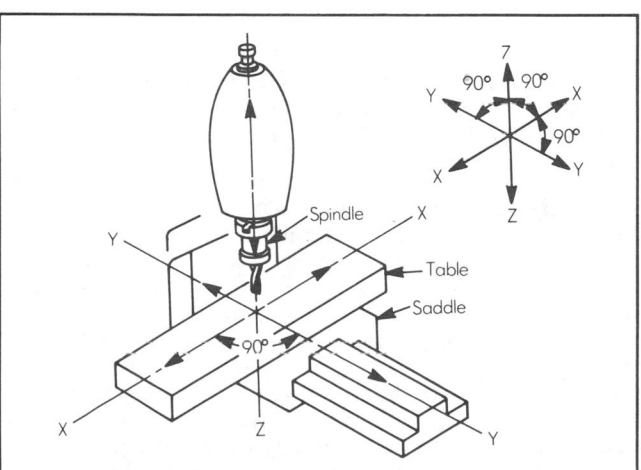

Fig. 20-7 Diagram of a vertical spindle machine tool showing the axes—X, longitudinal; Y, transverse; and Z vertical.

NC MACHINE CONFIGURATIONS

Straight-Cut

The positioning machine operating in the manner described previously would be useful as a "hole-making" machine, that is, drilling, tapping, or boring holes at different locations on a workpiece. Such equipment would be more useful if it could machine (i.e., mill) between adjacent points; however, milling cannot generally be accomplished at maximum traverse rates. Straight-cut systems are capable of moving the cutter at a controlled feed rate along paths parallel to one or more of the machine axes.

Because traverse rate is controlled on a per-axis basis and the path described by the tool between adjacent points in a multiaxis system is unpredictable, the straight-cut-positioning machine is usually limited to milling along a principal axis of the machine. Its path is very predictable because it is as linear as the guide surface (ways) of the machine.

Two-Axis Systems

A two-axis machine capable of drilling, milling, boring, and counterboring is illustrated in Fig. 20-8. In a point-to-point machine of this type, the table and workpiece are moved in both the X and Y axes by NC and positioned beneath the spindle. Spindle feed is controlled manually by the operator because NC of the third (Z-axis) slide is not provided. However, such a machine can be of substantial economic benefit because once it is set up, the operator is concerned only with spindle feeds and speeds and toolchanging.

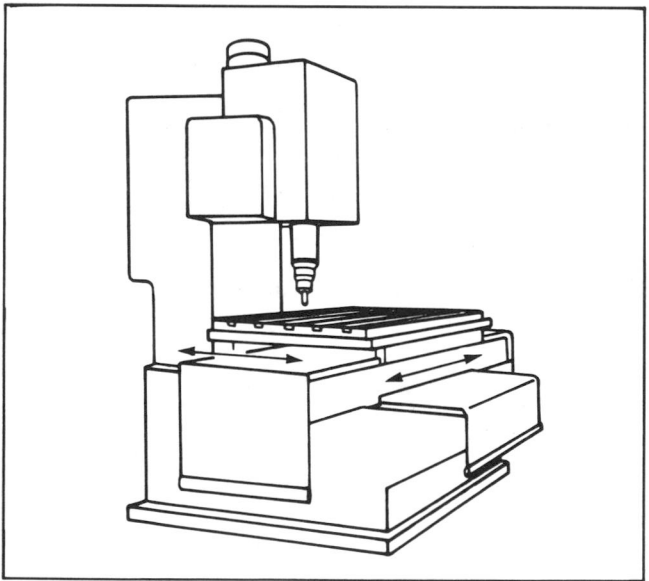

Fig. 20-8 Two-axis, tape-controlled drilling machine.

Three-Axis Systems

A three-axis positioning machine equipped with a tool turret is illustrated in Fig. 20-9. This machine requires an additional servoloop to control the Z-axis machine slides, connected in parallel with the X and Y axes. Since the machine has a turret, which is indexed by tape control, a workpiece requiring as many as eight different tools can be machined without stopping the cycle for a tool change. This type of machine also provides tape control of feeds and speeds, and a tape-controlled dwell cycle.

This three-axis machine may also be equipped with a tool-length compensator. This permits the operator to index to each turret position manually, and advance the turret slide to the workpiece with the rapid-advance control. Using a thickness gage, the operator can then preset each tool to compensate for variances in tool length and the programmer can program actual hole depths. Once a machining cycle is started, the cycle can continue under tape control without interruption.

The rapid-approach-and-retract and the machining-to-depth operations involve movement of the Z-axis slide. Thus the analog principles of the servoloop section of the NC system are applied in the same manner as for a single-slide system.

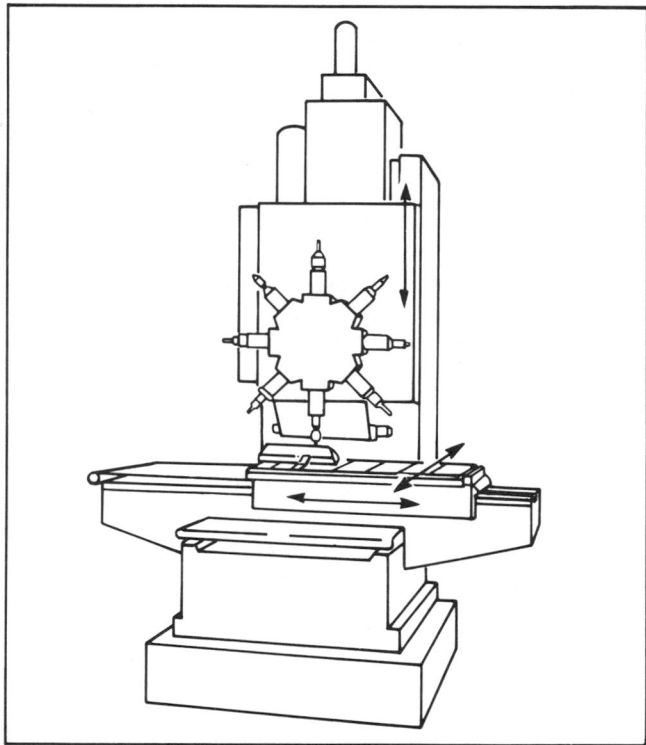

Fig. 20-9 Three-axis, tape-controlled drilling machine with turret.

CONTOURING MACHINES AND SYSTEMS

Milling machines, skin mills, spar mills, lathes, and other machines can cut very complex shapes through the use of NC contouring control systems.

Limited-Contouring Systems

Contouring systems have been built that include interpolation but not buffer storage (see "Buffer Storage" at the end of this section). The development of these systems has been brought about by the need for lower cost contouring systems. One note of caution should be realized, however, with respect to this type of system: there is a significant variation between the programmed feed rate and the actual average feed rate obtained. In the example shown in Fig. 20-10, each span consists of read-time, acceleration, programmed or desired feed rate, and deceleration portions. In averaging the velocity of the slides during these various portions of the span, it is obvious that the average feed rate does not equal the programmed feed rate. However, this is not the important point; the important point is that during the periods of deceleration, read time, and acceleration, there is a greatly reduced chip-per-tooth feed rate in the machining operation. In fact, during the read-time portion of the span, the chip-per-tooth rate is reduced to zero. This results in cutter pressure relief, which in turn may result in undercuts in the workpiece. An even more important point is that when some of the more exotic, work-hardening, space-age materials are machined, this reduction in chip-per-tooth rate results in work hardening prior to the entrance of the next cutter tooth into the workpiece, thereby causing increased cutter wear and damage.

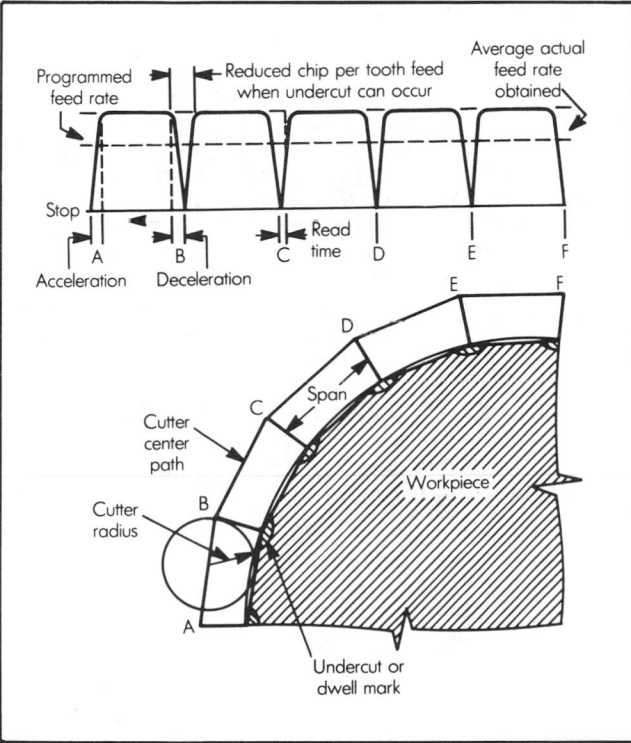

Fig. 20-10 Programmed vs. actual feed rates in a limited-contouring system—a potential source of undercuts.

Full-Contouring Systems

For the purpose of further discussion, the term "full-contouring" or "contouring" connotes a system having both interpolation and buffer storage. A machine with only one slide which, if directed to move, would do so along its assigned axis. Linearity, determined by the built-in tolerance of the slides, could be very accurate. However, to produce an angular movement, a machine must have a minimum of two slides, which must move simultaneously. Figure 20-11 represents the trace of an angular movement which might be produced by the simultaneous movements of the X and Y-axis slides of a positioning machine. The lack of linearity of the path is exaggerated in Fig. 20-11 to emphasize that nothing is built into the control system to assure that the cutter follows a straight path during travel between points.

If cutting operations are to be performed during angular movements of the machine slides, another system (i.e., interpolation) must be employed to assure linearity.

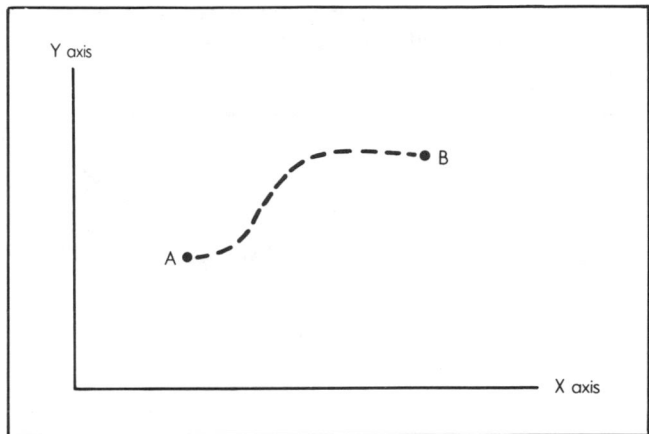

Fig. 20-11 Trace of movement of a positioning machine, illustrating lack of linearity of cutter path.

The slide speed rates required to produce the angular cuts are not feed rates established by the programmer. The programmer selects the feed rate at which the tool is to be fed through the path of the cut consistent with the workpiece, tool, and machine parameters. The NC system then makes the computations required to control the speed of machine slide. These computations are accomplished by the interpolator.

The interpolator may be considered to be a small, fixed-program computer. It receives slide direction and measurement instructions from active storage as well as directions as to how fast the cut of the path is to be made. It then calculates the data and directs the movement of each slide at the correct time/distance constants.

The interpolator assures linearity by constantly "looking ahead." Unless the span—the distance between *A* and *B* (or *A* and *B'*) in Fig. 20-12—is extremely short, the interpolator does not make a single calculation directing the slides to the end of the span. Rather, the interpolator "looks ahead" in a series of tiny segments as shown in Fig. 20-13. The minimum segment depends on the output resolution of the interpolator; thus, a

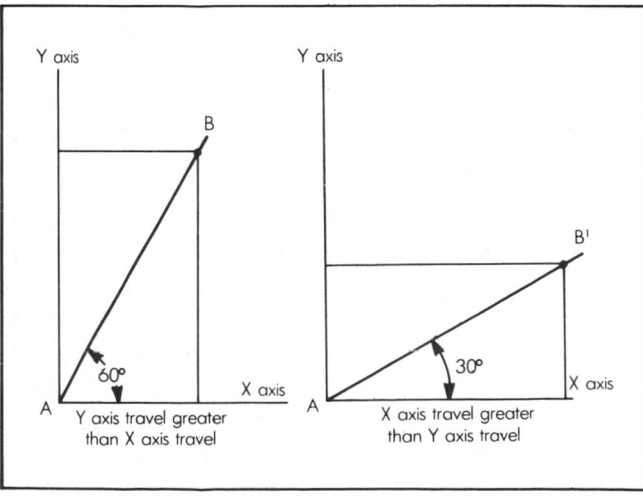

Fig. 20-12 Linear paths of 60° and 30° produced by a contouring machine.

NC MACHINE CONFIGURATIONS

machine having a resolution of 0.0001″ (0.003 mm) can divide the movements of a slide into segments as small as 0.0001″.

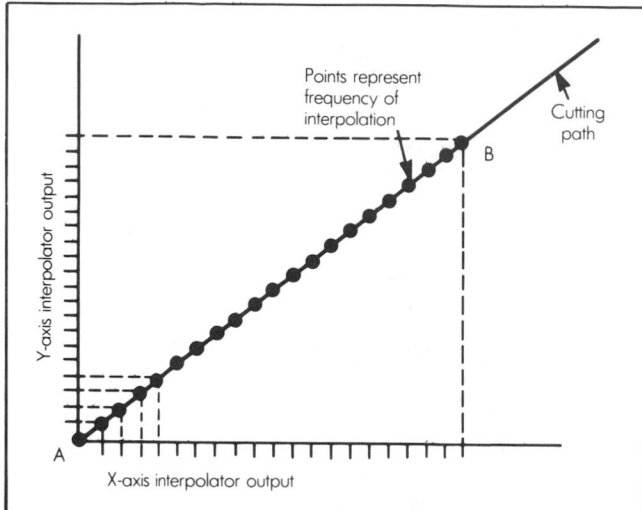

Fig. 20-13 Cutting path segmented by interpolator.

Programming for Contouring

Contouring systems are incremental in that they are not affected by past information, only by the information being received at the present moment. As the system reaches a new span in the programmed path, it interpolates the new span without regard to the previous span.

Span length. When an NC system is equipped with linear, circular, or parabolic interpolation, the programmer must know the maximum span length over which the system can maintain minimum resolution. The length may vary widely among systems from 10″ (254 mm) or less to at least 400″ (10 160 mm). Figure 20-14 illustrates an angular span from A to B of 50″

(1270 mm). If the control system can maintain minimum resolution for a span length greater than 50″ (1270 mm), the programmer can program the coordinates for the angle in one sequence—40″ (1016 mm) for the X axis and 30″ (762 mm) for the Y axis. However, if the system cannot maintain minimum resolution for that long a span, the programmer must break up the span into increments compatible with the system resolution as represented by the subspans in Fig. 20-14.

Linear interpolation. Because, as previously discussed, modern contouring systems can theoretically interpolate linear increments as small as 0.0001″ (0.003 mm), a linear increment can be programmed to be as short as the system tolerances allow. Therefore, by means of linear approximations, slopes, arcs, parabolic curves, and purely free-form surfaces can be machined with precision. A representation of a free-form curve is shown in Fig. 20-15. The amount of tolerance between the desired path and the actual path is represented by the shaded area between A and B. The degree of tolerance varies with the number of XY coordinates programmed between points A and E. With an NC capability of interpolating increments as small as 0.0001″ (0.003 mm), coordinates can theoretically be programmed for 10,000 linear increments for each inch of free-form curves (about 400 linear increments for each millimeter of free-form curves). With manual programming, or even with computer programming, however, the theoretical is impractical because a new block of tape information is needed for each of the increments. Furthermore, the error of approximation of the linear span and the curve does not require such a span length.

When a computer is used as a programming aid, the machining of circular, parabolic, and free-form curves with extremely close tolerances is possible because the programmer needs only to specify the entry and end points of a described path and the computer makes the enormous number of

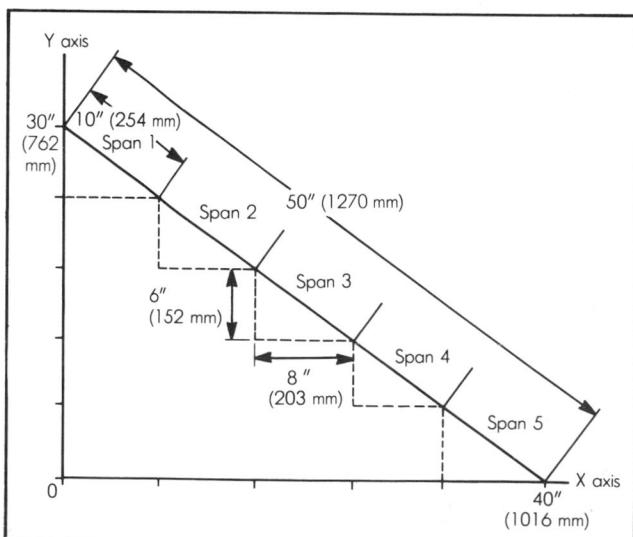

Fig. 20-14 A 50″ (1270 mm) movement executed on an NC system having a maximum span length of 10″ (254 mm).

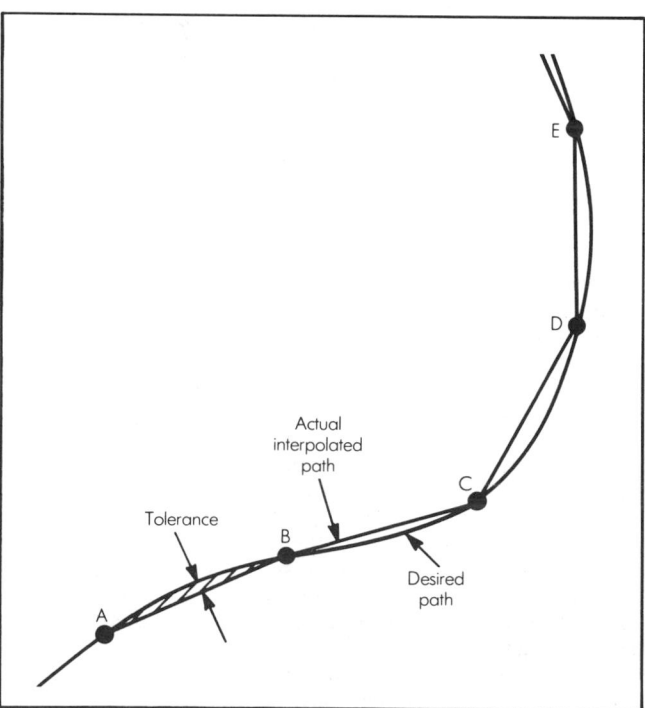

Fig. 20-15 Free-form curve programmed by linear interpolation.

calculations and tape-block information entries required. Such intelligence is now built-in at the machine control itself, in some cases, allowing rather complex workpieces to be machined using so-called manual data input (MDI).

Circular interpolation. In addition to linear interpolation, higher orders of interpolation are built into certain contouring machines. As previously described, the interpolator is a small, fixed-program computer capable of making the many intermediate calculations required along the path of the centerline of a cutter between programmed end points. However, nothing except cost limits this computer merely to subdividing straight lines if given the capability by the builder, the equation or description of the higher order of interpolation required, and the necessary dimensions or locations to describe the specific segment.

Circular interpolation is the most frequently encountered of the higher orders of interpolation. The input required to obtain circular interpolation includes the starting point (from the end point of the previous span), the center point, and the end point of the circle. Using this input, the interpolator calculates the points on the cutter centerline that describe the desired circle and the rates for each axis that provide the necessary feed rate. Circular interpolation is generally limited to one quadrant (90° of arc and no transitions beyond the quadrant change point); if more than a 90° segment is encountered, it must be interpolated in successive spans. Circular interpolation is generally used only to approximate circles and not other second or higher order curves or point-defined curves. It is coplanar in that it can produce a circle only in the principal plane of the machine. It cannot produce tilted circles because a circle tilted into a skewed plane ceases to be circle in a principal plane of the machine and requires another form of interpolation (elliptical) on a per-axis basis. Generally, in many cases, the degree of sophistication in the control system also limits circular interpolation to a principal plane of the machine.

Parabolic interpolation. Parabolic interpolation is another form of higher order interpolation, but it is not as efficient in approximating circles as circular interpolation. Parabolic interpolation has some desirable properties in approximating second and higher order curves as well as point-defined curves in which the portion of the curve between defined points requires a smooth transition. Examples of this type of requirement are often noted on part prints: "fair," "blend," and "smooth transition to. . . ." In general, parabolic interpolation has been well accepted in the production of airframe components, cams, templates, and automotive body dies. Other second or higher orders of interpolation are entirely possible, but their availability depends on the cost to incorporate them into the control system as well as on the ability of the programmer to take advantage of their inherent characteristics.

In many contouring operations the machine is required to switch between modes; i.e., from a linear interpolation path to a circular interpolation of a parabolic path.

Buffer Storage

The addition of buffer or intermediate storage is the element that changes a limited-contouring system to a full-contouring system. During the discussion of the limited-contouring system, it was shown that each span of movement consisted of read-time, acceleration, programmed rate, and deceleration portions. Figure 20-10 shows the trace of velocity during each of these span portions and also the resultant damage to the workpiece caused by stopping to read the next block of information. Figure 20-16 shows the same spans of movement compared on a limited vs. full-contouring system.

On the full-contouring system, while the system is interpolating between points *A* and *B,* the tape reader is reading the information pertaining to the move from point *B* to point *C*. As this information is read, it is stored in a buffer or temporary storage. As soon as the system interpolates to point *B,* the active storage information is dumped and the temporary or buffer information is transferred to active storage. In currently available contouring systems, the time required to transfer this information is measured in microseconds (μ s); the slide of a machine tool does not change velocity during this transfer time. Once the information is cleared from the buffer, the tape reader is commanded to read a new block of information into buffer storage, this time the information concerning the movement from point *C* to point *D*.

Coordinate information is not the only type of information that must be buffered. In fact, the entire block of information is generally buffered—coordinates, feed rate, type of interpolation, need for acceleration or deceleration, and any miscellaneous function that should occur during the next span. From this, it can be deduced that to get from a limited to a full-contouring system is not quite as simple as the addition of the little box labeled "buffer storage." In addition to another storage unit, many circuits for switching and cycling of the data in the unit are required.

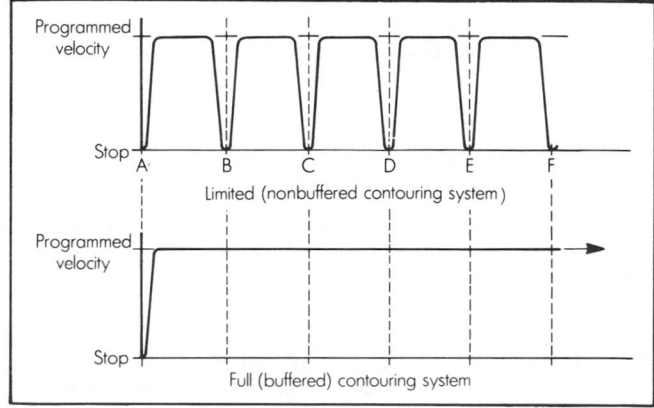

Fig. 20-16 Velocity trace of limited vs. full-contouring systems.

ADAPTIVE CONTROL

In general, adaptive control (AC), sometimes referred to as automatic adaptive control (AAC), is a type of system which automatically and continuously identifies on-line performance of an activity (a process or operation, for example) by measuring one or more variables of the activity; comparing the measured quantities with other measured quantities, calculated

ADAPTIVE CONTROL

quantities, or established values or limits; and modifying the activity by automatically adjusting one or more variables to improve or optimize performance.

ADAPTIVE CONTROL CLASSIFICATIONS

Although much controversy exists relative to the exact definition of AC, particularly as it is applied to control of machining operations, some experts consider it to have two primary classifications—adaptive control for optimization (ACO) and adaptive control for constraint (ACC).

Adaptive Control for Optimization

With ACO, the performance of an operation is optimized according to a prescribed index of performance (IP), sometimes called the figure of merit or performance criterion. The IP or criterion of performance is usually an economic function, such as minimum machining cost or maximum production rate. Part quality is used as the criterion of performance in some investigations. In many cases, the IP is usually a characteristic which is not directly measured, but is calculated from several variables.

Systems which employ ACO require three functions: identification, decision, and modification, as shown schematically in Fig. 20-17.[3] The identification function compares the process performance (output) with the IP value, thus evaluating how well the system is performing. The decision function consists of using this evaluation to determine what should be done to improve the performance of the operation (improve the IP). The modification function involves implementing the changing of process parameters as dictated by the decision function.

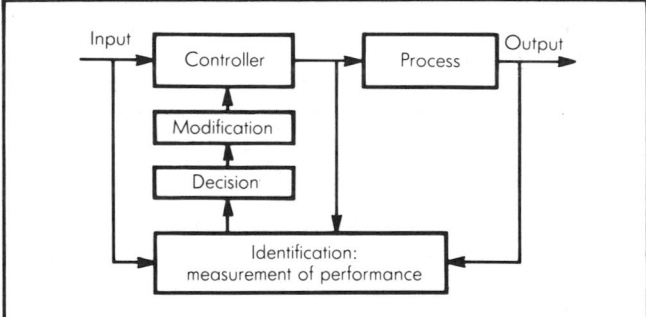

Fig. 20-17 Three functions are required for optimization-type adaptive control: identification (measurement of performance), decision, and modification.

Adaptive Control for Constraint

With ACC, machining conditions such as spindle speed and/or feed rate (usually only feed rate) are maximized within prescribed limits of machine and tool constraints such as maximum horsepower, torque, or force. This type of adaptive control is the most common in metalworking.

TRENDS AND APPLICATIONS

Today, most successful applications of AC continue in the aircraft and aerospace industries, although little if any reliable information is available regarding the number of AC installations. Expertise in CAD/CAM, which is common in these high-technology industries, complements and often parallels the work required to successfully implement an AC system—development of advanced computer techniques and structuring of complex data bases. Additionally, workpieces in the aircraft and aerospace industries are unusually complicated, often requiring a great deal of machining time, long NC programs, and relatively small production runs, thus making conventional methods of optimizing tapes unjustifiable. In some cases, dimensional variations in large forgings used by these industries create variable machining conditions which must be programmed conservatively, thus significantly reducing overall machining productivity. Experience has shown that such workpieces are ideally suited to AC.

In general, it has also been shown that adaptive control is most appropriate for machining operations on complex workpieces of hard-to-cut alloys and operations characterized by significant variations in machining parameters, such as workpiece hardness or machinability, or changes in the dimensions of cut during the machining operation.

ADAPTIVE CONTROL SYSTEMS

Many different types of AC systems are now available, ranging from simple automatic tool compensation systems to sophisticated computer-driven systems which monitor and control a multitude of machining variables. Increasingly, the proven systems are being offered as standard equipment or as options on modern CNC equipment and other machinery.

Automatic Dimensional Control

Automatic tool compensation in the pure sense is generally not considered a form of AC, although many experts consider it somewhat related. Automatic gaging and cutting tool compensation systems are used for turning and boring operations and other processes on many types of machine tools, including transfer equipment. In boring operations, for example, an automatic tool compensation system consists of a gage and feedback circuit that automatically sends a signal to a pneumatically or hydraulically operated tool adjustment mechanism when the tool wear is great enough that the bore size falls out of a set of prescribed "compensate" limits. Upon command, the cutting tool is automatically fed an appropriate amount to bring the bore back to nominal size.

Sensor Technology

Laser and electro-optical methods hold some promise of solving problems related to sensor technology as applied to AC. Simple, low-cost gas lasers can provide a convenient noncontact method of optically measuring a wide range of workpiece dimensions on-line. This method, operating in isolated production applications, requires a well-collimated beam of high intensity light which can give a high signal-to-noise ratio. The originating beam can easily be split into several beams, which is the basis for accurately identifying workpiece edges. The effect of reflected and diffracted light in measuring the diameters of cylindrical surfaces can be eliminated with an adjustable system developed in Japan. The system is shown schematically in Fig. 20-17.[4] The workpiece edge is projected by the optical system and sensed by a position detector.

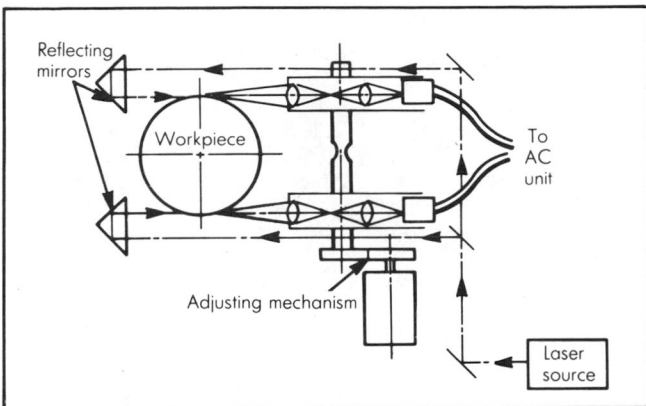

Fig. 20-18 Laser beam can be split and reflected to measure workpiece diameter on this adjustable system for adaptive control.

Tool Wear

Several sensing methods have been developed for both direct and indirect on-line sensing of tool wear. Several indirect methods are being used in production applications of AC, but most direct methods are still confined to the laboratory.

References

1. "NEMA Standards Publications for Industrial Controls," publication number ICS1, part ICS 1-108, National Electrical Manufacturers Association (NEMA), New York, NY, p. 1.
2. Baxter T. Fullterton, *Economic Justification of Numerical Control*, Chapter 14, "Numerical Control in Manufacturing," (NY: McGraw-Hill Book Co., 1963).
3. M. P. Groover, *A Definition and Survey of Adaptive Control Machining*, SME Technical Paper MS70-561, 1970.
4. Arne Novak, "Survey of AC Sensors," State of the Art Briefing on Adaptive Control, June 21, 1977, University of Michigan, Ann Arbor, MI.

SAWING

Sawing is a machining process in which straight, band, or circular blades having a series of small teeth are employed to cut various materials. Practically every manufacturing firm uses wire, shaped bars, tubes, pipes, extrusions, structural shapes, sheets, plates, castings, or forgings. These materials generally must be cut to required lengths for subsequent processing by machining, press forming, or assembly.

In spite of the variety of cutoff methods available, many shops find that sawing slugs for use on chucking-type automatics, as well as for other applications, is preferable because it is often easier, faster, and less costly.

SELECTING A SAWING PROCESS

No single method of sawing is best for all cutoff operations, and the proper choice of power hacksawing, bandsawing, or circular sawing can be difficult to make for certain applications. The advantages and limitations of each sawing process are discussed in detail in subsequent sections of this chapter. Factors that must be considered in selecting a sawing process include the size of the stock and properties of the material to be sawed; accuracy, finish, and production requirements; and the economics of the process.

SIZE OF STOCK TO BE SAWED

Both the size and geometry of the stock to be sawed are important considerations because they determine the machine capacity and affect the type of sawing machine to be used. Hacksaws are available with capacities for handling workpieces of practically any size, as well as any cutoff length. Stock with a large cross section can often be cut more economically on horizontal bandsaws.

MATERIAL TO BE SAWED

Physical properties of the material to be sawed have a major effect on the tooling, feeds and speeds used, and capacity of the sawing machine required; their influence on the type of machine is generally minimal. In general, any reduction in the machinability of the material to be sawed usually requires a corresponding reduction in cutting speed and may necessitate an increase in power requirements and cost of cutting.

ACCURACY, FINISH, AND PRODUCTION REQUIREMENTS

Selection of a sawing method and machine is also influenced by accuracy, finish, and production requirements. The closest dimensional tolerances can generally be maintained and the smoothest surface finish produced, especially on nonferrous metals, with circular sawing. Good results, however, can also be obtained with hacksawing and bandsawing by the proper selection of parameters and careful operation.

High production requirements usually necessitate using more rigid and costly machines, often equipped with automation devices. Hacksawing and bandsawing offer the advantages of lower cost machines, greater versatility, and a large cutting range, which can be important when the sizes and shapes to be cut are widely varied and the production lots are small. Some bandsawing machines provide the additional flexibility of being able to perform contour cutting, friction sawing, and filing operations. Friction sawing can also be done on some circular sawing machines.

ECONOMICS OF SAWING

Maximum economy—the lowest cost per slug or workpiece cut while meeting the specified requirements for production rates and dimensional, surface-finish, and metallurgical quality—is probably the most important consideration in selecting a sawing process. In most cases, cost per cut can be reduced with increased sawing rates; however, there are several factors in addition to the sawing rate that will affect total costs.

Machine Cost

Initial, operating, and maintenance costs of the sawing machine to be used are critical considerations. Larger, more rigid, and higher cost machines are often required to satisfy production and quality requirements. Consistent production of close-tolerance, high-quality slugs can eliminate or minimize the need for secondary operations on the cut surfaces, and provide substantial savings.

Tooling Costs

While the initial cost of a saw blade or band is generally a minimal factor, the cutting rates possible, resharpening capabilities, and tool life are important considerations. These factors can vary widely depending on the sawing method and the material to be cut. A more expensive blade or band often provides longer life, thus decreasing the frequency of tool changing requirements and reducing labor costs—the single most important factor affecting cost per cut.

Long tool life, however, does not in itself mean lower cost per cut. Saw blades and bands should generally be used to their full capabilities with respect to cutting speeds and feed rates, regardless of tool life. Faster cutting rates are more economical because they reduce burden costs per cut drastically, while increasing only slightly the tool cost per cut.

POWER HACKSAWING

Material Utilization

The amount of material lost in the form of chips from the kerf (width of cut) and/or scrap can be an important cost consideration, especially with increasing material costs and when sawing more expensive materials. Bandsawing machines, which use thin cutting bands, produce the smallest kerf. Hacksawing machines require thicker blades, and circular sawing machines generally need the thickest blades of the three sawing methods.

Raw material losses, however, must be balanced against possible increases in productivity and improvement in the accuracy and quality of the slugs or workpieces produced. Eliminating a need for secondary operations to attain the required accuracy and quality can more than offset any increased loss of material in sawing.

POWER HACKSAWING

Power hacksawing is characterized by the reciprocating action of a relatively short, straight, toothed blade that is drawn back and forth over the workpiece in much the same manner as a hand hacksaw. It differs from other sawing methods in that the back-and-forth motion of the blade makes a noncontinuous cut.

The power hacksaw was the first practical cutoff machine. Modern heavy-duty machines provide an economical and efficient means of sawing a wide range of materials and stock sizes. They are used extensively for utility needs and in smaller shops in which production requirements are not high.

ADVANTAGES

A major advantage of power hacksawing is the relatively low capital investment required. The machines themselves are moderate in cost; however, stock feeds, automatic controls, and other accessories and attachments can add substantially to the price.

Hacksawing machines are easy to set up and simple to operate. Unskilled or semiskilled help can be used, and one operator can often attend two or more machines. Tooling costs are low, and the comparatively thin blades used are inexpensive enough to make it economically feasible to throw the blades away when they become worn, rather than resharpen them. Maintenance costs also are low because of the simple design and operation of these machines.

Versatility is another important advantage of power hacksawing. The machines can handle most cutting requirements including practically all materials, a wide range of stock sizes within their capacities, and any cutoff length. Hacksawing is often more practical and economical than bandsawing for cutting large workpieces with thick cross sections, especially when cutting materials that are somewhat difficult to machine.

Accuracies maintained and finishes produced with power hacksawing range from fair to good depending on the material being sawed. Tendency for the hacksaw blades to twist or deflect is minimal. Since power hacksawing machines can provide fairly accurate cuts in hard materials, they are often preferred for cutting tough forgings, hardened tool steels, and similar materials.

LIMITATIONS

A major disadvantage of power hacksawing machines is that they are slower than bandsawing and circular sawing machines. The cutting action is noncontinuous, and only half of each reciprocating stroke is productive. Noncutting time, however, has been reduced on modern machines (discussed next in this chapter) by the development of systems for more rapid return strokes. Bundling of stock for multiple cutting also increases productivity.

The reciprocating action of hacksawing prohibits the use of blade supports close to the area of cutting. This may cause bowing of the blade and some inaccuracy. For this reason, hacksaw blades are made thicker than the bands used on bandsawing machines, thus requiring more power and producing more chips. The kerf (cut width) in hacksawing, however, is less than that in circular sawing. Kerf varies from 0.092-0.183"(2.34-4.65 mm) with regular hacksawing blades. Power hacksawing is essentially a roughing operation, and at least 0.002"(0.05 mm) should be left on cut surfaces for finishing.

Blade wear in power hacksawing is uneven because only part of the blade is used for cutting since the arms holding the blade obstruct use of the blade ends. Also, the necessity for stopping and reversing the direction of blade travel at the end of each stroke causes the cutting speed to vary, thus reducing efficiency.

HACKSAWING MACHINES

Hacksawing machines consist of a supported reciprocating frame and saw blade mounted to a base for supporting the work. They are available in several basic designs. Horizontal machines are the most popular. On column or way-type horizontal machines, as illustrated in Fig.21-1, the supporting member (carrying the reciprocating frame and saw blade) is mounted on one or more vertical columns or uprights with ways. This supporting member is fed downward in a vertical plane on the column(s) to saw the workpiece(s).

On hinge-type horizontal machines (see Fig. 21-2) the supporting member carrying the reciprocating frame and saw blade is mounted on the back of the machine base. Feeding produces a scissor-type motion with the reciprocating blade moving downward in an arc and a vertical plane for sawing. Small portable hacksawing machines with retractable wheels are also available.

Completely automatic power hacksawing machines perform the following steps:

1. Feed stock through the open workholding vise or fixture.
2. Gage length to required dimension.
3. Close and lock clamping vise or fixture.
4. Feed blade through the stock.
5. Raise the blade at the end of the cut.
6. Open the vise or fixture.

This automatic cycle is repeated until the final cut has been made (of a preset number of slugs or at the end of the stock), after which the machine is stopped.

HACKSAW BLADES

Power hacksaw blades made from different materials, in a variety of sizes and pitches and with different tooth geometries, are available. Selecting the best blade for a specific application depends on many factors including the cross-sectional area and hardness of the material to be sawed, cutting speed, blade strength, tooth geometry, and tension. Practically all blades have only one cutting edge, consisting of teeth extending almost the full length of the blade. A pinhole or pinholes are provided near each end of the blade to fit over pins on the saw frame or bow of the machine.

Blades will bow (curve away from the work) under heavy cutting forces. Some bowing is allowable; however, if it results in excessive flexing, the blade tension should be increased or a stronger blade should be used. This problem can be minimized by using blades with pinholes closer to the cutting edge. With this design, the tensioned blade is bowed slightly away from the work when not cutting and straightens during sawing, thus minimizing wandering. Some machines permit the use of backup bars to provide additional support for blades.

Blade Materials

Three types of materials are generally used for power hacksaw blades. The tips of the teeth on all three types typically have a minimum hardness of $R_C 62$. Blades made from through-hardened tool steels are seldom used for production applications, but they are sometimes employed for cutting soft metals, for one-of-a-kind jobs, or for general utility requirements.

Blades made from high-speed steels that have only the tooth area hardened are widely used for sawing many different

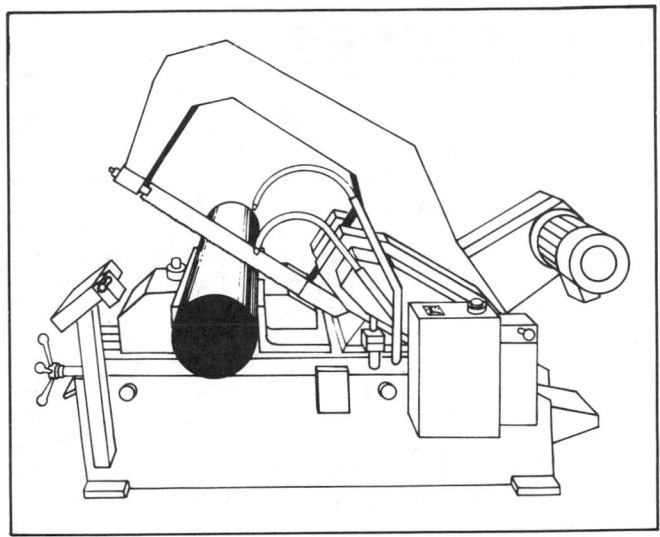

Fig. 21-2   Hinge or scissor-type horizontal hacksawing machine with arc-shaped, push-stroke cutting. (*Kasto-Racine, Inc.*)

materials. They provide good cutting characteristics, but can present a safety hazard in that they have a tendency to shatter if they break under tension.

Composite or bimetal blades, consisting of a HSS cutting edge welded to an alloy steel body or backing, are becoming increasingly popular. This design allows the backing material to be selected for maximum resilience and fatigue resistance. These blades permit safer operation at higher speeds and feed pressures. Like blades made from the other materials, these blades have cutting edges that are hardened to a minimum of $R_C 62$, but the hardness of the body is usually a maximum of $R_C 52$.

OPERATING PARAMETERS

Cutting speeds in strokes per minute are not directly proportional to cutting rates in feet per minute for all hacksawing machines because of different stroke lengths and/or methods of blade reciprocation. The maximum speed—strokes per minute (spm)—at which a machine can be operated is limited by the peak blade speed developed during the cutting stroke. The peak blade speed is limited by the characteristics of the blade. Machines equipped with fast return strokes (previously described) can operate at higher effective spm's without exceeding the peak blade speed and thereby causing blade failure due primarily to excessive heat at the cutting teeth.

Speeds for power hacksawing generally range from 25 to 165 spm, with the maximum speed employed only for cutting some carbon and free-machining steels. When the materials to be cut are hard, heat treated, and/or rough, the use of a lower cutting speed is usually more efficient and economical because blade life will be lengthened. Excessive speeds, too light a feed pressure, or dull blades can cause work hardening of some materials such as austenitic stainless steels, high-temperature materials containing nickel, and some of the soft, ductile, low-carbon steels.

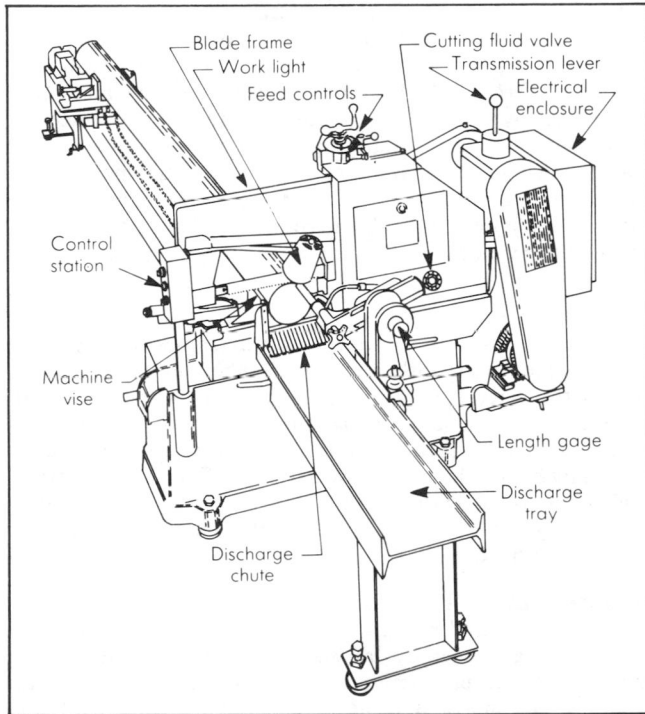

Fig. 21-1   Column-type horizontal hacksawing machine with automatic or manually controlled, power bar feed. (*Armstrong-Blum Mfg. Co.*)

BANDSAWING

Power bandsawing, often called band machining, uses a long endless band with many small teeth traveling over two or more wheels (one is a driven wheel, and the others are idlers) in one direction. The band, with only a portion exposed, produces a continuous and uniform cutting action with evenly distributed, low, individual tooth loads. Bandsawing machines are available in a wide variety of types to suit many different applications.

The cutting action of bandsawing differs from other sawing methods in that its continuous, single-direction cutting action, combined with blade guiding and tensioning, gives it the ability to follow a path that cannot be duplicated with power hacksawing and circular sawing. The bandsaw blade or band can follow the cutting teeth along any path over which it is guided, making radii or contour cuts possible. Band teeth cut with a shearing action and tend to take a full, uniform chip.

ADVANTAGES

Versatility is one of the most important advantages of power bandsawing. The process is not limited to the use of conventional saw bands with cutting teeth; at least nine known methods of band machining exist. These methods are as follows:

1. Conventional sawing, used primarily for cutoff, contour cutting, and slotting.
2. Friction sawing, used for the high-speed cutting of hardened ferrous metals, nonferrous metals, and nonmetallic materials.
3. Diamond-band machining for cutting glass, carbide, semiconductor and graphitic materials, ceramics, and quartz.
4. Electroband (electrical discharge) machining, generally used on aluminum, copper, stainless steel, and titanium honeycomb material, as well as other fragile, cellular structures.
5. Band filing for light stock removal, particularly on internal surfaces, from a wide variety of materials.
6. Band polishing for burr removal and finishing surfaces previously sawed and/or filed.
7. Scallop-edge, wavy-edge, and knife-edge bandsawing, used primarily for cutting soft and fibrous materials that may tear, fray, or otherwise result in poor surface finishes when cut with tooth-type bands.
8. Spiral-edge bandsawing for the omnidirectional (360°) cutting of intricate patterns in thin pieces of metal, plastic, and wood.
9. Abrasive wire bandsawing, used primarily on CNC machines for the omnidirectional cutting of difficult-to-machine materials and for finishing dies, cams, and other complex-shaped parts.

Contour band machining offers several major advantages over other machining methods: rapid cutting to shape, safe and easy operation, raw material savings, and relatively low cost. All these advantages result from the way the bandsawing machine removes unwanted material in sections instead of wasted chips, thus increasing production efficiency. Less time is required to saw around a section than to produce chips, and the resulting unwanted section can sometimes be used to manufacture other products.

This ability to create fewer chips also makes the process the most material and energy efficient of the three basic types of cutoff sawing machines used to produce slugs for further processing. Bandsawing produces a smaller kerf (width of cut) than hacksawing or circular sawing for any given stock size range, thus reducing energy requirements and material losses in the form of chips. Stated another way, more slugs or workpieces can be produced from any given amount of stock. This factor becomes increasingly significant with more expensive materials and as material costs rise.

LIMITATIONS

There are few limitations to the use of power bandsawing. The versatility of the process makes it suitable for a wide variety of applications on many different materials and sizes of workpieces. Machines equipped with bimetallic bands are used to saw materials with hardnesses to 464 Bhn (R_C49). Even harder materials can be cut with friction sawing or abrasive-edge bands.

APPLICATIONS

While bandsawing is most often associated with the cutting of metal or wood, this process is being used for sawing a wide variety of materials ranging from asbestos to zirconium. Although bandsawing is used for operations such as filing, polishing, and others previously listed, by far the largest single application is sawing. The basic bandsawing operations are cutoff, contouring, and slotting.

BANDSAWING MACHINES

Bandsawing machines have evolved from the simple two-wheel vertical machine on which the operator pushed a workpiece through the band into sophisticated machine tools made in many types. They are now available in two, three, or four-wheel versions. Contouring, vertical, horizontal, tilt-frame, angle, cutoff, plate, friction, and universal are some of the names used to designate various types. Some manufacturers offer combination vertical/horizontal bandsawing machines for light to medium-duty cutting of a variety of materials.

Vertical Machines

Vertical contour-type bandsawing machines usually have two or three wheels with a horizontal table mounted between two of the wheels. Workpieces are placed on the table and pushed through the band by hand or some mechanical means.

The table on vertical contouring machines may be fixed or moved by hydraulic or air power. On both fixed and powered-table models, a chain (which may be part of a contouring device) can be wrapped around the workpiece to pull it through the band.

Horizontal Machines

Horizontal bandsawing machines, often known as cutoff or power saws, are generally classified as light-duty, medium-duty, heavy-duty, and production types. They are available in two versions. On one version the stock is advanced manually on rollers; on the other the stock is advanced with powered rollers. Both of these versions require operator manipulation of controls to make each cut. Automatic versions use a powered device to advance the stock to a predetermined setting as close as 0.001″ (0.03 mm) of desired length; they continue automatic cycling until a required number of parts are produced or the stock is exhausted. Machines equipped with two vises on an automatic shuttle table can reduce bar ends or remnants to lengths of 1/2″ (12.7 mm).

Tilt-Frame Universal Machines

While angle sawing can be performed on the types of machines previously described, it is inconvenient; most angle sawing today is done on tilt-frame universal bandsawing machines such as the one shown in Fig. 21-3. On these machines, the frame (sawing head) is mounted with pivot bearings on a moving carriage. Workpieces are held stationary in vises on a machine table structure while the frame guides the band through the stock to be sawed.

With a shuttle vise or automatic indexing system, such as powered rollers and automatic workstop, these machines produce 90° cuts, cuts up to 45° either left or right of vertical, or any angle in between at the discretion of the operator. Automatic machines are available that can be programmed to cut various angular cuts and lengths. The operators can devote most of their time to loading and unloading operations or attending several machines.

Tilt-frame universal saws are often used in conjunction with conveyor systems when material handling time is frequently more of a concern than cutting time. In building and bridge construction work these machines have the versatility to perform the variety of trimming work necessary on long, structural shapes and also maintain the accuracies required.

SAW BANDS

Selecting the proper type of band tool for a specific application is of critical importance. Factors that should be considered in band selection include the following:

1. Type and hardness of material to be cut, which determine the tooth form and composition of the band to be used.
2. Size and variations in cross section of the stock to be cut, which dictate the pitch of the teeth required.
3. Type of cut required—whether straight, contour, or both. The need to cut small radii will limit the width of the band.
4. Type and condition of the machine to be used.
5. Production requirements.
6. Whether a cutting fluid will be used.
7. Overhead costs.

Conventional Sawing

Toothed bands with different tooth geometries and hardnesses for specific applications are used for conventional bandsawing methods.

Tooth geometries. There are three major types of tooth forms, generally classified as standard (regular), skip, and hook teeth. The standard tooth form has a zero rake angle and a full rounded gullet with a smooth radius. Bands with standard teeth are the most versatile and are recommended for intricate contouring and straight cutoff work. They are also widely used to meet smooth finish requirements, to cut thin work, and when small radii are needed.

The skip tooth has the same form as the standard except that the gullet is lengthened by omitting every other tooth to handle larger chip loads. The skip tooth is recommended for acceler-

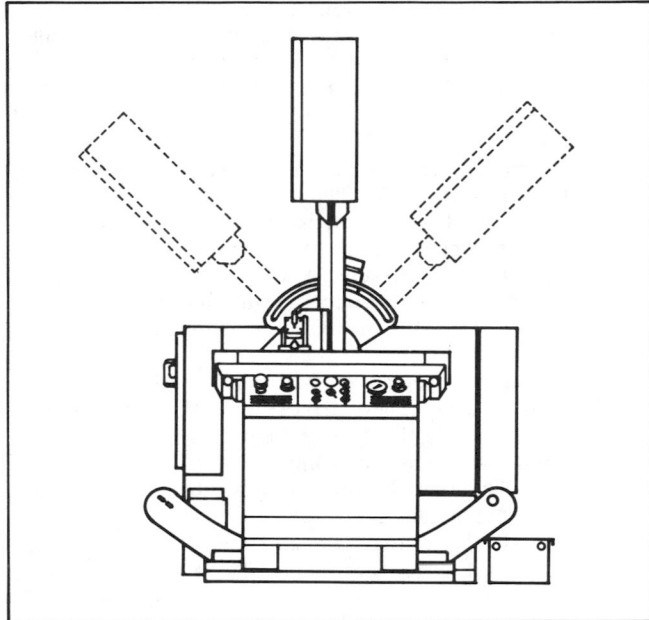

Fig. 21-3   Tilt-frame universal bandsawing machine of the type widely used for angle cutting operations and producing compound miters. (*Armstrong-Blum Mfg. Co.*)

ated cutting of nonferrous metals, plastics, and woods.

The hook tooth has a lengthened gullet, similar to the skip tooth form, and a positive rake angle—up to 10° depending on the manufacturer, type of band, and application. Teeth with positive rake angles tend to pull themselves into the work. As a result, they penetrate the work with less feed pressure than teeth with no rake. Bands with hook teeth permit fast cutting of all metals, plastics, and woods and are generally recommended for sawing hard materials and penetrating work-hardening metals.

Recent variations of the three major tooth forms include one having a standard tooth form except for a 5° positive rake angle instead of none. Other modifications have been introduced in an attempt to reduce the noise level on applications requiring interrupted cuts, such as with structural shapes or tubing. Bands for this purpose use a combination of pitches and/or a combination of set angles and gullet depths to prevent the buildup of sustained resonant conditions by imparting different frequencies that tend to dampen each other.

Band materials. Bands made from a variety of materials are available. Arranged in order from the lowest to highest quality with respect to band life and production capability, they are as follows:

1. Carbon steel bands with hard cutting edges and flexible backs. These bands are sometimes used on hand-fed vertical contouring machines for sawing both ferrous and nonferrous metals, wood, and plastics. They are operated at relatively low band speeds and are generally restricted to light-duty toolroom and maintenance operations.

2. Carbon steel bands with hard cutting edges and hard backs. These bands have almost twice the tensile strength of carbon steel bands with flexible backs and may last up to 10 times longer. Their spring-tempered backs withstand

up to 50% more tension, and a hardness of R_C 45-49 enables them to resist mushrooming of their back edges. A higher cutting rate capability and longer life make them suitable for medium-duty toolroom and maintenance operations, as well as for light production applications.

3. Intermediate alloy steel bands with hard cutting edges and flexible backs. These bands have good shock resistance. They are sometimes used on horizontal cutoff machines for adverse operating conditions such as sawing structural shapes, tubing, and stacks of workpieces. Some band manufacturers have discontinued the production of this type because of the development of bimetallic bands.

4. High-speed steel bands with hard cutting edges and flexible backs. These bands were the original tools instrumental in the development of power bandsawing on horizontal cutoff machines. With the development of bimetallic bands, however, they are being discontinued by most manufacturers.

5. Bimetallic bands that have hardened HSS cutting edges and flexible, alloy steel backs. These bands more than satisfy all the requirements for the single-metal HSS bands used previously. The higher production capabilities and lower cost per piece sawed generally justify the slightly higher cost of these bands. Some producers offer five or six types of bimetallic bands, each tailored for a specific application. A special shock-resistant cutting edge is provided on some, eliminating the need for any break-in period. Others have a very hard cutting edge for sawing exotic metals, and some have a positive rake angle on the teeth for penetrating tough materials. Also available are types having a combination of sets and/or pitches to reduce high resonance when sawing various cross sections such as those encountered with structural shapes, pipe, and tubing.

6. Carbide-tipped alloy steel bands. These bands afford high resistance to heat, abrasion, and fatigue, as well as fast cutting capabilities. They are used to cut materials that cannot be sawed by one of the more conventional types of bands previously discussed. High cost and the possibility of damage precludes their use for general purpose sawing, but cutting rates of 100 in.^{2} (645 cm^2) or more per minute are possible. Development of this type of band is continuing with respect to the selection of carbide grades and methods of bonding the tips to backing materials.

Friction Sawing

In friction sawing, the band teeth do not cut. Instead, they produce friction and scoop out the softened material. For maximum efficiency, selection of a band with the proper pitch is important. It is possible to friction saw with a band having no teeth, but results are generally less than satisfactory.

Diamond Bandsawing

Diamond-edge bands are available in continuous or segmented types for cutting abrasive or friable materials. The straight-line cutting action of these bands gives fast cutting rates, produces smooth finishes, and maintains a high degree of accuracy, parallelism, and flatness.

A recent development is the use of diamond bandsawing for slicing operations that previously required drum-type orifice cutting discs called ID slicers. The thin kerf produced with diamond bands reduces material losses. This can provide a substantial cost savings when cutting semiconductor and other friable materials.

CIRCULAR SAWING

Circular sawing is a process employing a rotating, continuous cutting blade having teeth on its periphery to cut ferrous and nonferrous metals, plastics, and other materials to required lengths. With the workpiece clamped securely, the saw blade is either fed horizontally, vertically, or on an angle into the material. The process is often called cold circular sawing to differentiate it from sawing of hot metal in steel mills and forge shops, which is beyond the scope of this discussion.

Cutting action in circular sawing is essentially the same as in milling, particularly slot milling. Each tooth removes a chip, which curls and is carried away from the cutting area in the tooth gullet, thus allowing continuous cutting. Large circular sawing machines have been used for many years to cut off billets, forgings, extrusions, bars, tubes, and similar stock. Now, smaller machines are being increasingly applied for a wide variety of parts. The process can be used to cut practically any material.

ADVANTAGES

Accuracy is inherent in circular sawing due to the rigidity of the machines and milling-type cutters. Length tolerance for most stock feed systems is ±0.004" (0.10 mm). Accuracy of cut, with respect to combined squareness and parallelism, is generally ±0.001" (0.03 mm) per inch (25.4 mm) of material height or width in the direction of blade travel. One machine builder guarantees 0.00075" (0.0190 mm) per inch. In the plane perpendicular to the direction of blade travel, the tolerance is ±0.0005" (0.013 mm).

Virtually burr-free surface finishes are produced, often eliminating or reducing the need for secondary finishing operations. For blade sizes up to about 16" (406 mm) diam, finishes typically range from 60 to 125 μ in. (1.5 to 3.2 μ m). Usually, surface finishes as smooth as 8 μ in. (0.2 μ m) have been produced in circular sawing aluminum, and finishes as smooth as 32 μ in. (0.8 μ m) in cutting steel. The harder the material being cut, the smoother the finish usually produced.

Tooling costs are relatively low. It has been estimated that the tool cost for circular sawing of mild steels is less than one-half cent per square inch (6.45 cm^2) of material removed, making it one of the least expensive methods of sawing solid metals. Because of its rigidity, there is no tendency for the blade to deflect, which could cause more wear on one side of the blade than on the other. With the resultant uniform wear rate, no loss of accuracy occurs as the blade dulls.

Operating costs are low because the simple operation of circular saws lends itself to the use of unskilled labor. Blade speed selection is normally accomplished by pushbutton. Changeover time for a modern machine to cut different types and sizes of material is only a few seconds. One blade will cut most materials and stock sizes within the capacity of the machine, and blade changing can be done quickly and easily.

Circular saws are relatively safe because of the low rotational speed of their blades. No need exists for the operator to have his hands in the cutting area, and many automatic machines have completely enclosed feeding and sawing areas.

LIMITATIONS

There are no real limitations to the use of circular saws. It is true that the initial capital investment is greater than for a hacksaw or bandsaw because a heavier, higher horsepower machine is required for comparable capacity. Increased productivity and accuracy, however, can result in a rapid write-off of the machine if sufficient work is available to keep it operating efficiently. Circular saw blades are also more expensive initially than bandsaw or hacksaw blades, but they can be resharpened many more times and reground, if necessary, to cut different materials. Long blade life generally results in lower tool cost.

Greater loss of the material being cut, because of the increased kerf (width of cut), is often cited as a disadvantage of circular sawing, but this is often not the case. Circular saw blades as thin as 0.060" (1.52 mm) are available, but such thin tooling cannot withstand the high cutting forces and maintain the close tolerances for which circular sawing is noted. Most bar stock that is slugged into short length is 5" (127 mm) or less in diameter. In this range, circular saw blades normally have a thickness ranging from 0.096-0.118" (2.44-3.00 mm). With the inherent accuracy of circular sawing and the short drop (waste) ends produced, generally 2" (51 mm) or less in length, material loss due to cutting width can be less than with other methods. Even when cutting very short lengths, it is often less expensive to produce a slightly wider kerf with circular sawing than to remove material in a secondary operation to attain the required accuracy.

MACHINES USED

Circular sawing machines, having blades mounted on power-driven rotating spindles, are generally of four basic designs: (1) pivot arm, (2) vertical column, (3) horizontal travel, and (4) plate saws.

Pivot-Arm Machines

Pivot-arm circular saws include table models such as the one shown in Fig. 21-4. Heavy-duty machines of this type are limited to a blade diameter of about 28" (710 mm) in order to maintain an optimum table height. This design is generally considered the most universal within its capacity range. Features include a high degree of safety, the capability of cutting miters and bevels, fast and easy setup, the possibility of fixturing the table top, and easy automation.

Vertical pivot-arm (sometimes called chop-stroke) circular sawing machines are used extensively for high-production slugging operations and cutoff of structural shapes (see Fig. 21-5). Features of these machines include rapid cycle times; rigid construction; fast changeover; and automatic, semiautomatic, or computer numerical controlled (CNC) material handling systems.

Vertical-Column Machines

Vertical-column machines, sometimes called vertical-feed, vertical-stroke, or guillotine-type circular sawing machines (see Fig. 21-6) are also widely used for both high-production

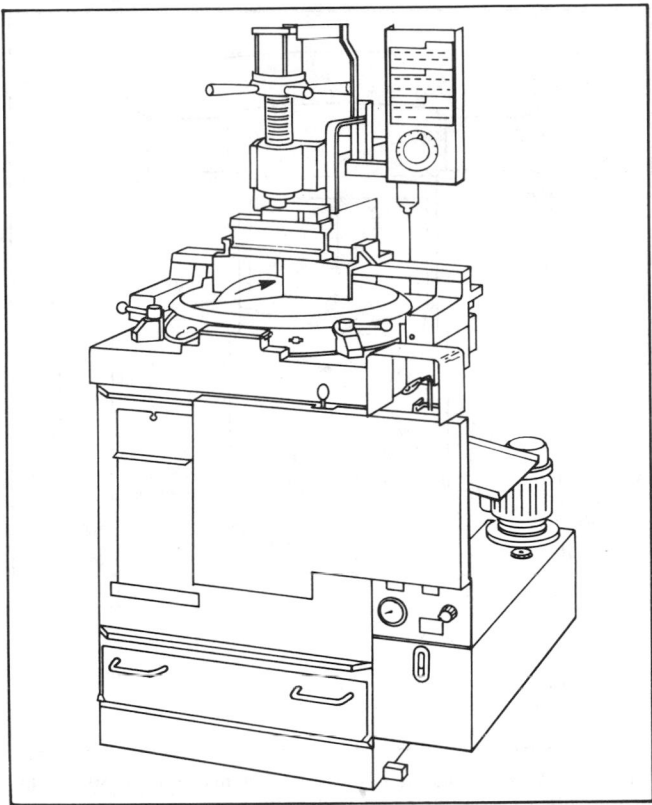

Fig. 21-4 Table-type, pivot-arm circular sawing machine having universal application within its capacity. (*Kaltenbach, Inc.*)

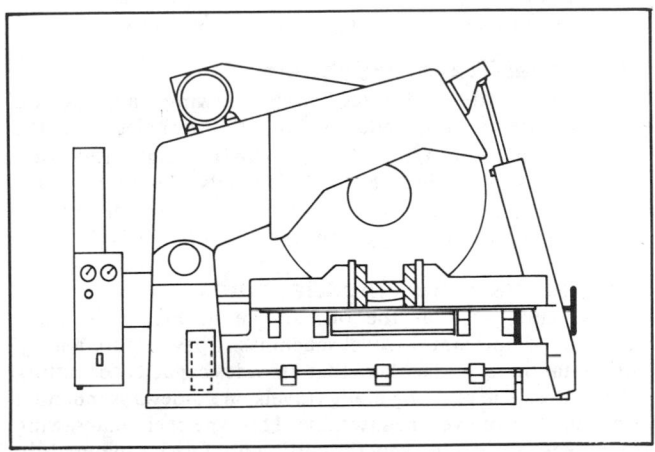

Fig. 21-5 Vertical pivot-arm circular sawing machine used extensively for cutting structural shapes. (*Kaltenbach, Inc.*)

slugging and cutoff of structural shapes. Features of this design include fast changeover and high productivity. With this design, the rotating blade moves down in a straight line to contact the workpiece, with the feed motion of the blade assisted by gravity. Material is centered directly below the centerline of the saw blade and is cut with a high degree of accuracy. Vertical dual-column machines can cut solid or tubular rounds and flat or square stock in multiples with the use of vises. Vertical machines are also available with the saw blade recessed in the

CIRCULAR SAWING

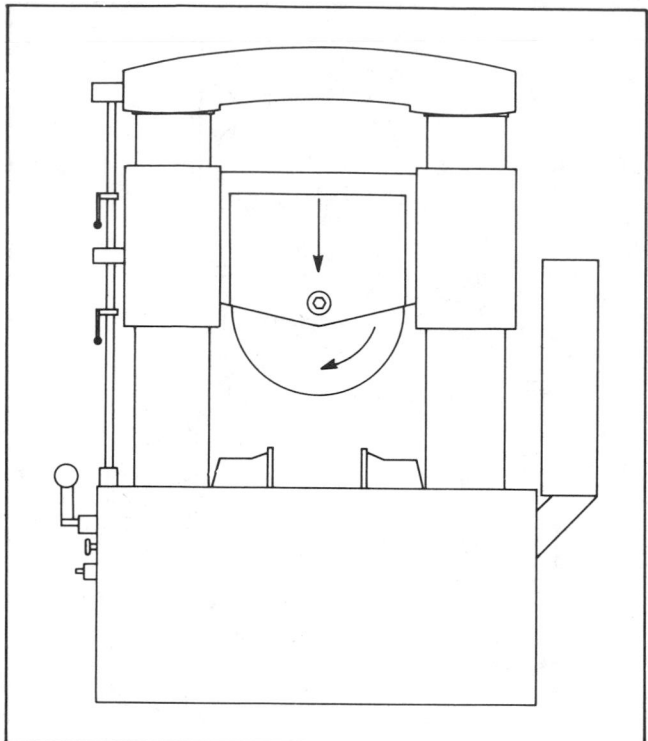

Fig. 21-6 Vertical-column circular sawing machine on which the rotating blade moves down in a straight line.

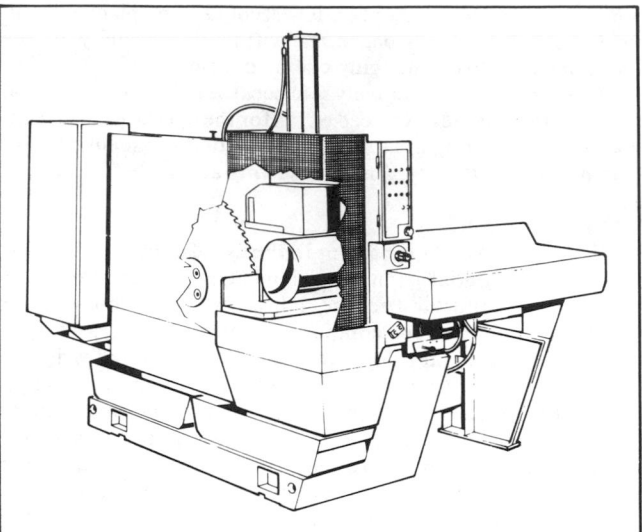

Fig. 21-7 Horizontal-travel circular sawing machine on which the rotating blade is pushed into the work from the side. (*Wagner/Klingehofer Corp.*)

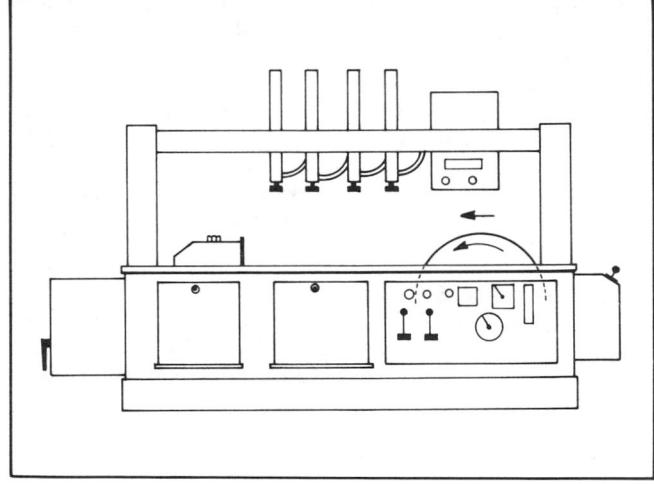

Fig. 21-8 Plate saw providing a long, horizontal travel of the rotating blade for cutting solid plates.

table. The blade is pushed up into the workpiece. This approach is efficient for materials having small cross sections.

Horizontal-Travel Machines

On horizontal-travel or feed circular sawing machines, (see Fig. 21-7), the rotating blade is fed into the workpiece from the side. These machines are used for both low and high-production requirements in cutting off solid materials. Features include rapid cycling, fast changeover, and the availability of a variety of systems for automating the process, including CNC.

Circular Plate-Sawing Machines

Plate saws, such as the one shown in Fig. 21-8, are a variation of horizontal-travel machines. They feature a long, horizontal travel of the blade that provides capacity for cutting solid plates. The rotating blade travels on guideways mounted either beneath or over the saw table. This type of circular sawing machine is used extensively for cutting nonferrous materials in lengths to 20 ft (6 m) or more and up to 6″ (152 mm) thick. For increased productivity, double-headed sawing machines have been built with two horizontally opposed blades. Just before the blades would contact, one blade stops and retracts while the other blade completes the cut.

CIRCULAR SAWING FIXTURES

Workpieces are generally sawed singly since this simplifies material handling. Round bars and tubes are usually held in V-blocks; square, rectangular, or other shaped material can be clamped directly on the bed, table, or supporting plate of the machine. When the stock to be cut is warped or crooked, care is

necessary to assure that it is properly seated and clamped prior to sawing. Many circular sawing machines, however, have the capability of cutting two or more pieces in a single pass, and this is often done to increase productivity. Special fixtures are sometimes required to hold unusual shapes.

SAW BLADES

Three basic types of circular saw blades available are solid, segmental, and carbide tipped. Diameters of the blades used depend on the size of the workpieces to be sawed. Blades should have a diameter sufficient to clear through the maximum thickness of the stock in one pass.

Solid Blades

With solid blades, available from 8 through 16″ (200 through

400 mm) diam, the body and teeth are made from one solid disc of HSS, such as AISI M2 or M7, that is heat treated to a hardness of R_C65. Blade bodies are made slightly concave by hollow grinding on both sides to provide clearance in the cuts. They are used to saw both ferrous and nonferrous materials, and they can be resharpened until they reach a diameter that is no longer practical for use on the machine. Thinner blades can be used for sawing nonferrous materials.

Segmental Blades

Segmental saw blades, available from 12-120" (300-3050 mm) diam, consist of a disc-type body with toothed segments around its periphery. The blade body is produced from a high-strength, low-alloy steel capable of absorbing shock while remaining rigid. The toothed segments, tapered to provide side clearance, are made from HSS with a hardness of R_C65. Segment lengths vary with the blade diameters, ranging from 2 1/2" (63.5 mm) long for a 12" (305 mm) diam blade to 5" (127 mm) for 72" (1829 mm) diam blades.

Most segmental-type, circular saw blades have a tongue machined around the outer periphery of the blade body. Inner surfaces of the segments are grooved to fit over the body tongue. One manufacturer produces segmental blades with grooves in the blade body and tongues on the segments. With both designs, segments are fastened to the blade bodies with rivets. Rivets are also placed outside the blade body, between mating faces of the segments, to provide lateral stability.

Segmental blades are more widely used than solid blades because of their greater ability to absorb shock. Teeth on the segments can be designed to suit specific requirements. Also, when individual segments are worn or broken, they can be removed, resharpened, and replaced a number of times, thus reducing blade costs. However, segmental blades generally have to be thicker than solid blades, and the surface finishes produced are not usually as smooth.

Carbide-Tipped Blades

Carbide tipped circular saw blades, available from 12-72" (305-1829 mm) diam with kerf ranges between 0.157 and 0.430" (4.00 and 10.92 mm), have a high-strength, low-alloy steel body, with carbide brazed to the tooth tips. These blades have been used for many years to saw aluminum, brass, and some plastics. More recently, carbide-tipped blades have been increasingly used in sawing steel, particularly to meet high production requirements and to saw large forged billets. Dramatic improvements in productivity have resulted from the use of carbide-tipped blades for such applications. Because of the critical loading of the carbide in circular sawing, today's state-of-the-art allows economical utilization of this type of blade only for solid shapes. U.S. classification C-5 carbide (ISO P40) is widely used for carbide-tipped blades to saw ferrous metals, and C-2 or C-3 (ISO K20 or K30) carbide for carbide-tipped blades to saw nonferrous materials.

Advantages of sawing large billets with carbide-tipped blades include the elimination of ragged billet ends resulting from the nick-and-break method, shear cracks sometimes caused by cold shearing, and the need for expensive, high-capacity shears required for hot shearing. Also, the flatter, more accurate end surfaces produced by circular sawing reduce rejection rates, save material, and permit easier and more economical billet handling.

BROACHING, PLANING, SHAPING AND SLOTTING

BROACHING

Broaching is a process for internal or external machining of flat, round, or contoured surfaces. Machines of different types are used to push or pull a multitooth cutting tool or the workpiece in relation to each other to remove material. Each tooth on the cutting tool (broach) is generally higher than the preceding tooth (see Fig. 22-1). As a result, the depth of the cut increases as the operation progresses.

Generally, broaching machines differ from other machine tools in that they provide only cutting speed and force—the feed is built into the broach. Infeed, however, is provided by the workholding fixture for some applications. Another exception is helical broaching in which the machine provides rotary motion.

Broaching also differs from other machining processes in that roughing, semifinishing, and finishing teeth are often positioned along the axis of a single tool. This permits completing an operation in a single pass. Several types of broaches are sometimes used in combination to cut different surfaces on the workpiece simultaneously.

Broaching applications are of two major types: external (surface) broaching and internal broaching. Both types are used for machining configurations ranging from flat surfaces to complex contours on or in workpieces varying from small precision components to very large parts made from many different materials. For some applications both external and internal broaching are combined in one operation.

Surface broaching applications are practically unlimited. Any external form can be produced as long as the surfaces are in a straight line and unobstructed. Such forms include slots and keyways, fat and contoured surfaces, rack and gear teeth, and serrations.

An infinite number of forms can also be produced by internal broaching. In addition to machining round, square, rectangular, and other shaped holes, the process is used to cut contoured surfaces, keyways, splines, serrations, and gear teeth. This method is also used to rifle the bores of gun barrels.

ADVANTAGES OF BROACHING

Important advantages of broaching include high productivity, the capability of maintaining close tolerances and producing good finishes, economical operation, and versatility.

Productivity

When the process is properly applied, with the right machines and tools, broaching can remove metal faster than any other machining method. Broaching is competitive with many other machining processes, particularly milling and occasionally grinding, and high production rates are common. The ability to rough and finish machine in one pass increases productivity. Smaller parts are often stacked and broached in multiple in a single pass; larger parts are often produced two at a time. The availability of semiautomatic and automatic loading/ unloading and material handling equipment, as well as improved machine controls, further increases productivity.

Accuracy and Finishes Produced

Broaching is capable of consistently maintaining close tolerances because of its inherent accuracy. Several surfaces on a workpiece can also be held in accurate relationship because the relationship is built into the tooling.

Surfaces finishes produced are smooth compared to many other machining processes, and noncutting burnishing elements can be provided on the finishing end of the broach to further improve the finish obtained. In many applications the need for subsequent grinding has been eliminated.

Economical Operation

While initial tool costs can be high unless standard tooling is employed, cost per workpiece produced is generally low because of long tool life. This is the result of the comparatively low cutting speeds used in broaching and the small portion of total stock removed by each tooth. Long tool life provides the additional benefit of reducing downtime for tool replacement.

Today there is increased availability of standardized, generalpurpose tooling that permits more economical broaching for many applications. The use of automation equipment and automatic machine controls permits employing unskilled or semiskilled operators, which can further reduce operational costs.

Versatility of Broaching

Broaching can be used for a wide range of workpiece sizes— from small screw machine parts; components formed by cold heading or other methods; and stampings to large castings, forgings, and weldments. The process is also suitable for machining many different materials.

External surfaces on several parts can often be

BROACHING

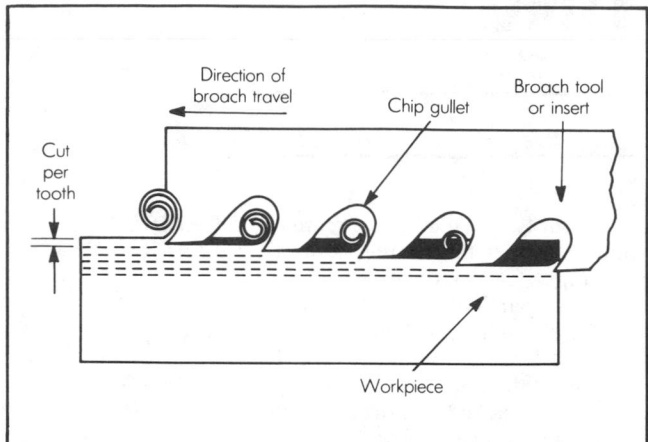

Fig. 22-1 Broach tool on which each successive tooth is generally higher than the preceding tooth. As a result, the cut gets deeper as the operation progresses.

broached simultaneously on wide-ram machines. Universal machines are available to perform a variety of operations, including push and pull broaching and external and internal cutting.

An old misconception that still persists is that broaching is limited to high production requirements necessitating special and costly machines and tools. Instead, broaching is being used for shallow cuts and finishing operations, as well as heavy stock removal in some applications, and even short runs are now often economical. The availability of standard and universal machines plus general-purpose tooling makes small-lot production of families of parts both feasible and economical.

LIMITATIONS OF THE PROCESS

As previously mentioned, workpieces must be suitable for broaching. The surfaces to be broached must be of uniform rotation or parallel to the direction of tool or work travel, and there cannot be any obstructions in the path of the tool. Complex contoured surfaces with curves in two or more planes cannot be formed in a single broaching operation, with the exception of helical surface broaching. In surface broaching, it is not possible to broach to a shoulder if the shoulder is not parallel to the broach axis. Internal broaching requires starting holes in the workpieces. Tapered holes generally cannot be broached, but with some materials, such as aluminum, a tapered swedge can be mounted at the end of a broach. Parts to be broached must also be strong enough to withstand high thrust forces or must be adequately supported.

The high forces produced n broaching require rigid machines and workholding devices which add to capital equipment costs. When special machines and tools are required, production requirements must be sufficient to economically justify the higher costs.

While light burrs are sometimes produced in broaching, they can generally be removed easily by conventional methods such as brushing or tumbling.

MATERIALS BROACHED

Any material that can be machined by other processes can usually be broached. Broachability of materials is essentially the same as machinability; however, because broaching is a high-impact machining process, proper grain structure and hardness are of utmost importance. Broaching has been used to machine most known metal alloys, some plastics, hard rubber, wood, composite materials, and graphite.

BROACHING MACHINES

Broaching machines can be classified by operational characteristics and/or the type of operation performed when the machines are properly tooled. With respect to the direction of cutting stroke, broaching machines are classified as vertical, with the axis of the cutting stroke perpendicular to the floor; horizontal, with the cutting stroke parallel to the floor; and special, which encompasses all other variations or combinations. They can be further classified as surface, internal, and universal or combination broaching machines.

Types of power used to drive the broaching machines are also used to describe them. Machines are powered hydraulically or mechanically, with hydraulic drives in greatest use for vertical and smaller horizontal machines. Some machines, however, such as continuous (chain) types and large, horizontal surface broaching types, are almost exclusively powered electromechanically. With the energy savings possible with electromechanical drives, this type of power is now being used on other broaching machines.

Further classification of broaching machines is based on operational characteristics such as single or dual-ram, pulldown or pullup, pushdown or pushup, rotary, continuous, pot-type, and blind spline. A schematic representation of broaching machine classification according to type of drive, direction of cutting stroke, and operational characteristics is presented in Fig. 22-2.

Important factors in selecting a broaching machine for a specific application include the type of cutting tool needed for the operation and the production requirements. Basic machine features to be considered are the configuration, capacity in terms of tons of ram force, ram stroke and speed, and dimensional capacity for tooling and workpiece. Machine size and capacity are functions of the tool and workpiece sizes, broaching power requirements, and available production space.

Vertical broaching machines offer the advantages of reduced floor-space requirements; having the tools move in a vertical plane, thus avoiding possible sag; generally better cutting fluid dispersement and chip-removal facilities; and easier workpiece loading, clamping, and unloading. Disadvantages of some vertical types of machines, compared to horizontal types, include the need for high ceilings or deep floor pits for long-stroke machines and, generally, more difficult access for toolchanging. Some small, vertical, table-top machines, however, are relatively inexpensive, and feature fast changeover from one setup to the next.

Horizontal broaching machines usually have the advantage of being able to handle larger and heavier workpieces and longer broaches for greater stock removal. They often provide increased versatility in that they can be set up quickly to broach different parts. With the exception of continuous-type machines; special machines; and large, fast, horizontal broaching machines, however, most broaching machines in service and being built today are vertical.

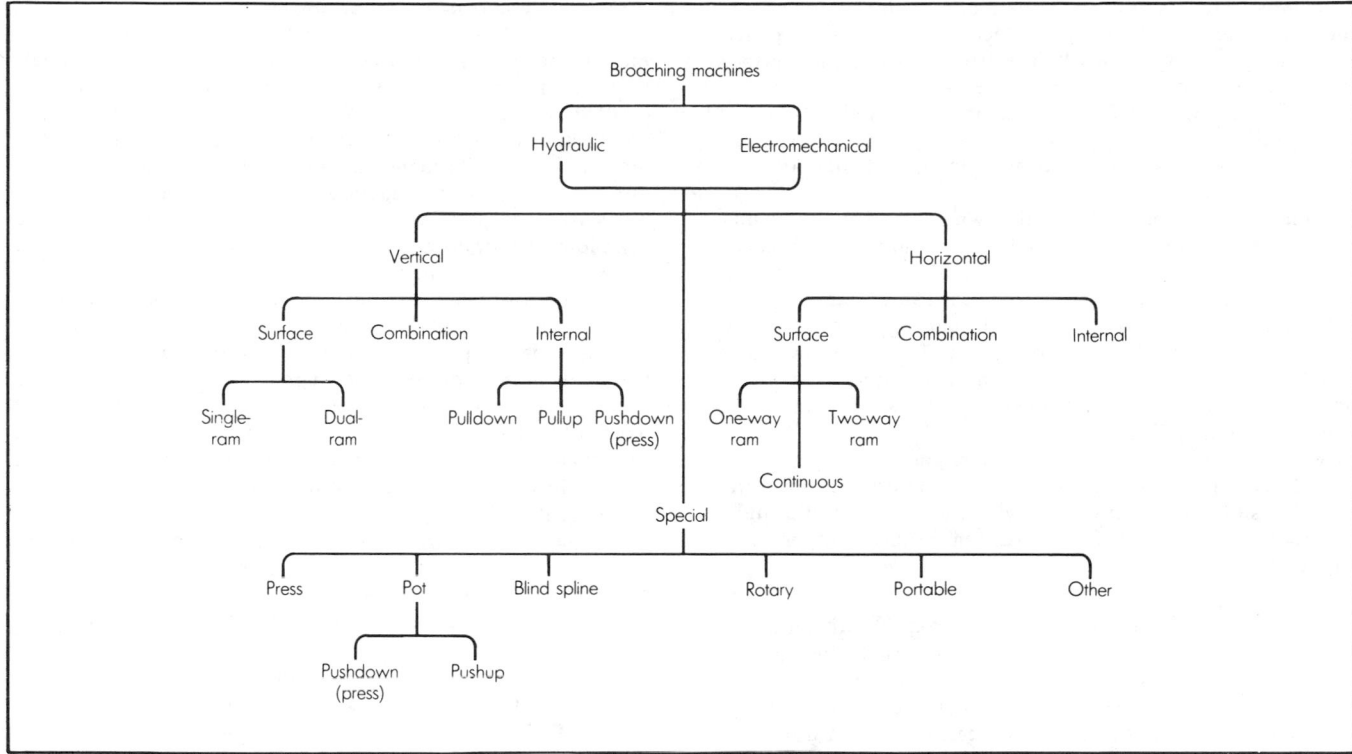

Fig. 22-2 Classification of broaching machines according to type of drive, direction of cutting stroke, and operational characteristics. (*General Broach and Engineering Co.*)

Vertical Surface Broaching Machines

Single-ram broaching machines. Standard vertical surface broaching machines with a single ram and downward cutting stroke are available in sizes from 1 ton (8.9 kN), 18″ (457 mm) stroke to 50 ton (449 kN), 120″ (3048 mm) stroke, and larger size machines are available on special order. Most are equipped with an in-and-out motion shuttle table or a tilting-type table that allows the operator to unload and reload during the return (upward) stroke of the machine ram. Vertical surface broaching machines are usually adaptable to automatic workpiece handling and most have power take-off or an auxiliary power supply for clamping and fixture motion. Machines equipped with wide rams can sometimes hold two or more sets of broaching tools to machine several workpieces simultaneously.

Cutting tools for vertical surface broaching machines are generally mounted in broach holders to form an assembly. An adapter plate is attached to the machine ram and the subholder assembly is bolted and cross-keyed to the main holder. For high-volume production requirements, it is common practice to have three holders, one on the machine, a second preassembled for standby use, and a third in the cutter grinding department.

Dual-ram broaching machines. Dual-ram machines operate like two single-ram vertical surface broaching machines mounted side by side in a common frame, with the two rams moving alternately upward and downward. These machines are preferable to single-ram machines for high production requirements because they permit one operator to load and unload in front of one ram on its return stroke while broaches on the other ram are in the cutting mode.

Production rates on dual-ram machines are not double that of two single-ram machines, however, because the speed of the

return stroke must be the same as the cutting speed of the alternate ram. Usually a 60-70% increase in productivity can be achieved by tooling both rams to perform the same operation as previously done on a single-ram machine. Workpieces requiring multiple broaching passes can often be transferred from one ram to the other with reduced part handling. In such cases, however, the longest cutting stroke required will determine the stroke of each ram.

Vertical Internal Broaching Machines

Pushdown broaching. Vertical internal broaching machines of the pushdown type are basically presses, most of which are of C-frame construction and hydraulically powered. In some cases, the broach is attached to the machine ram and is pushed downward and pulled upward through the workpiece—a process called strip broaching. For most applications, however, the broach drops into a catcher tray after being pushed through the workpiece or a lower powered slide is provided to lift the broach for retrieval.

Pushdown vertical internal broaching is normally used only for low-volume production or for applications requiring manual alignment of the broach with respect to the workpieces. Some high-volume applications exist, however, primarily for burnishing-type jobs. In all cases, stock removal is usually minimal.

Pullup broaching. The pullup method was the original one used on vertical machines for internal broaching. Workpieces are manually or automatically placed in alignment with the broach pull-shank, and the broach is raised through both the workpiece and a thrust plate called a platen until the upper end of the broach engages an automatic broach puller. The upward pulling motion of the broach lifts the workpiece until it contacts

BROACHING

a bushing fixture mounted on the platen. Cutting force holds the workpiece against the bushing face until the broach is pulled through, after which the workpiece drops onto a sloping surface for gravity ejection from the machine.

Problems with chip disposal, cutting fluid application, and the handling of large and heavy workpieces, however, make them undesirable for some applications, and they are now specified less frequently.

Pulldown broaching. The pulldown method of broaching is by far the most commonly used on vertical internal broaching machines. Pulldown broaching is often preferred to the pullup method because large workpieces can be handled more easily and because gravity helps the cutting fluid reach the cutting teeth and facilitates chip removal. Progressive work, in which several broaches are used in succession, is easier to perform, and the machines lend themselves well to automatic loading and unloading.

Machines with a way-type main slide and a movable, upper broach-handling slide are the most common. The broach-handling slide travels in unison with the main slide throughout the cutting stroke for maximum broach support and alignment.

Vertical Combination Broaching Machines

Vertical combination (universal) broaching machines feature a swing-away or detachable toolhandling slide for internal broaching and a machined slide face for surface broach tooling. On three-way machines the broach can be pushed down for broaching external surfaces or pushed or pulled down for cutting internal surfaces.

Horizontal Internal Broaching Machines

At one time, horizontal machines were the predominant type used for internal broaching. Today, however, with the high cost of floor space and a generally lower productivity rate compared to vertical machines, they represent less than 10% of the broaching machines purchased. They are still used where ceiling heights prohibit vertical machines, for large and heavy broaching tools that require in-line pulling, for small tools that require manual handling, for some special low-profile equipment that is adaptable to automated transfer lines, and for short-run job shop applications.

Horizontal internal broaching machines have a box-type framework with a platen on one end. The platen is equipped with a clearance hole to allow the broaches to be pulled through the stationary workpieces in a horizontal direction. A pulling head rides on ways within the machine frame and is aligned with the hole in the platen. Most modern machines have optional outboard and inboard broach supports. They can be supplied with automatic equipment for broach handling and workpiece loading and unloading.

Horizontal Surface Broaching Machines

In a class by themselves, large horizontal machines for broaching external surfaces are used extensively by the automotive industry for heavy stock removal. Surfaces are machined on large parts such as cast engine blocks, cylinder heads, manifolds, and bearing clusters, with stock removals of 1/4" (6.4 mm) or more using carbide broach inserts. Close tolerances are maintained and smooth surface finishes produced, and the machines have proven to be reliable and efficient with little downtime for toolchanging and maintenance.

One-way and two-way broaching machines. These horizontal surface broaching machines are made in single-station, one-way models that cut in one direction only and in two-way models that are capable of cutting in both directions. Workpieces are cradled in swing-up fixtures. On two-way machines for V-type and in-line engine blocks, the pan-rail, half-bore, and bearing-lock surfaces are broached as the machine ram moves in one direction. Then an automatic transfer mechanism moves the block to a rollover fixture that rotates the casting 180°. The head joint face or both bank faces on the block are broached on the return stroke of the ram.

Continuous broaching machines. Continuous chain-type surface broaching machines consist of a horizontal framework having a drive sprocket mounted at one end and an idler sprocket at the opposite end. These sprockets support and power a pair of parallel, continuous chains which move workholding fixture carriers suspended between them. The carriers are guided by a set of ways within the machine frame, and the broaching tools are mounted in a tunnel on top of the machine itself.

Production rates from continuous broaching machines are high, usually from four to ten times that of vertical surface broaching machines. This is because of the continuous cutting action and elimination of the noncutting portion of other broaching machine cycles. Productivity from these machines can also be varied by changing the speed of the chain or increasing or decreasing the number of fixtures used; the maximum number of fixtures is limited by the length and tonnage capacity of the machine.

High production requirements are necessary, however, to justify the high cost of these machines. Their use is also usually restricted to workpieces small enough to pass through the tunnel and sturdy enough to permit gravity ejection without damage. Automatic loading and unloading equipment is available for most workpieces.

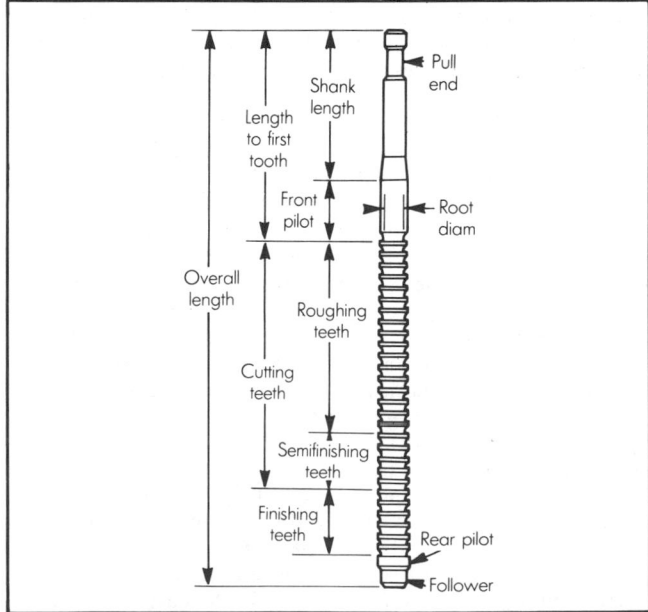

Fig. 22-3   Typical internal round broach of the pull type illustrating standard nomenclature used.

TYPES OF BROACHES AND BROACH DESIGN

Broaches, the cutting tools used for broaching, in their simplest form consist essentially of a slightly tapered round or flat bar with rows of cutting teeth located on one or more surfaces. Because the teeth are stepped, additional stock is removed as each successive tooth contacts the workpiece.

Broaches can be classified according to their purpose or use (internal, external, or combination); method of use (pull, push, helical, or rotary); construction (solid or sectional); and required surface finish (form relieved or generating).

The standard nomenclature used to describe essential parts of most broaches is presented in Fig. 22-3, which illustrates a typical round internal pull-type broach.

PLANING

Planing is a material-removal method for producing flat surfaces that may be horizontal, vertical, or at an angle. With special equipment, planing machines, called planers, can form curved or irregular shapes. Simplicity of operation, cutting tool design, and application make planers versatile machine tools. They are used primarily for medium-to-large size workpieces. Productivity, however, is comparatively low; most of the work previously done on planers is now performed on planer-type milling machines.

THE PLANING PROCESS

In operations performed on planers, the workpiece is reciprocated and a single-point cutting tool is fed into the workpiece. The feed in planing is intermittent and represents the width of the cut. Planers are made with mechanical or hydraulic drives. The mechanical drive consists of a variable speed, reversing drive motor; gear train to the table; and control equipment. The table of a planer with a hydraulic drive is reciprocated by one or more hydraulic cylinders secured to the bed, the piston rods being secured to the table. The speed at which a mechanical-drive planer operates depends on the speed of the driving motor and on the gear ratio. In hydraulic planers, the speed of the table is determined by the effective area of the piston and by the volume of oil pumped against this area in a given time.

While many jobs formerly handled on planers are now being performed on other machine tools, applications still remain for which planing is economical. Workpieces of certain size and shape, and long, narrow, and angular surfaces are often easier to machine on a planer. Planing is often preferred for flat bearing surfaces that have to be hand scraped because, with planing, work hardening of the surfaces is minimized.

Tooling costs are less for planing than milling, which may be important when production quantities are limited. Tool setting and regrinding are easier with single-point planing tools.

Types of Planers

Several types of planers are available; double-housing and open-side planers are the basic types. The heads on the crossrail of some planers are constructed rigidly enough to permit planing across the table.

Double-housing planers. This type of planer has two housings supporting the crossrail, as shown in Fig. 22-4. It is usually equipped with four heads, two on the crossrail and one sidehead on each housing.

Open-side planer. The open-side type shown in Fig. 22-5 has a column on one side of the machine only. The width of the work that can be handled is not limited as it is on a double-housing planer. The work can extend far beyond the left side of the table and may have an additional support on an auxiliary

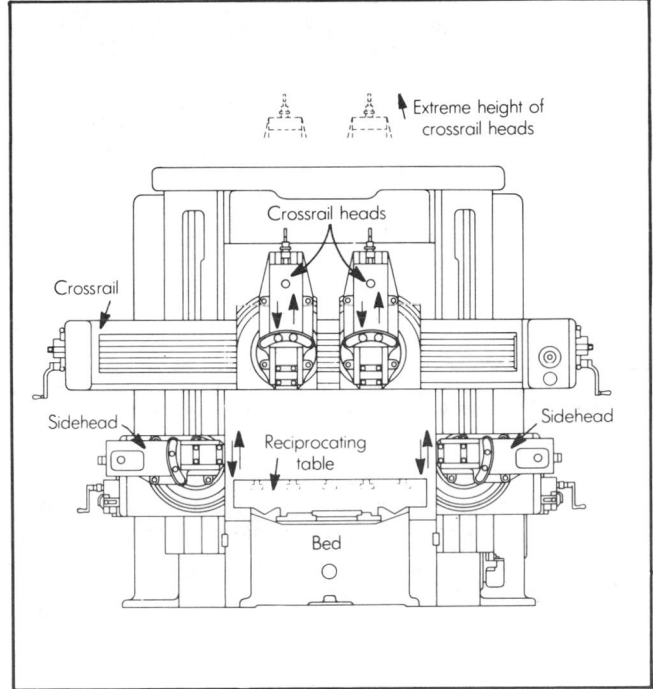

Fig. 22-4   Double-housing planer having two heads on the crossrail and one sidehead on each housing.

rolling table placed to the left of the planer and extending parallel to the bed.

Convertible open-side planers. The convertible open-side planer is an adaptation of the open-side type of planer with a removable housing fastened to the left-hand side of the bed and supporting the outer end of the rail. A sidehead may be mounted on this housing.

Adjustable convertible open-side planers. This type of planer is provided with a removable left-hand housing mounted on a runway perpendicular to the table travel, allowing this housing's position to be adjusted to suit the particular job. The adjustment permits positioning of the left-hand sidehead to the greatest advantage.

Milling planers. These machines are made with various combinations of planing, milling, boring, and drilling heads. They are principally suited for work which requires various types of operations and which can be done to advantage in the same fixturing of the work. In this way, greater accuracy results from eliminating resetting of the work and work handling is

PLANING

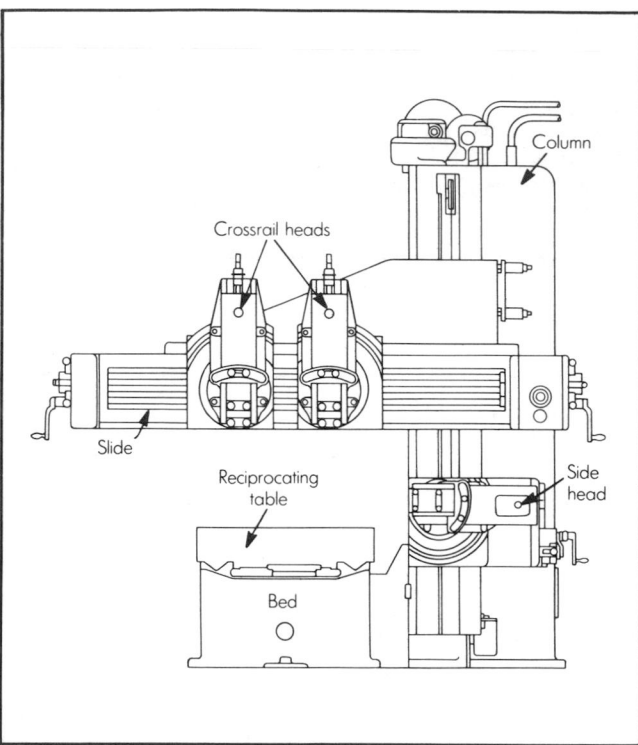

Fig. 22-5 Open-side planer which permits handling work of unlimited width. work supports can be placed at left of machine if needed.

minimized. These machines have found favor for large jig and fixture work. They are made in double-housing, open-side, and convertible types.

Double-cut planers. This type of planer is designed by some manufacturers to incorporate the ability to cut on both the forward and reverse strokes of the table. The head on the planer has a limited rotation spindle, oscillated by a small air cylinder that engages one bit of a double-bit toolholder with the work on the forward stroke of the table and then the other on the table's reverse stroke. This planer is available in both the double-housing and open-side design.

Planer Tools

Cutting tools used on a planer are heavy-duty, single-point tools similar to those used on lathes and shapers. They can be made of forged high-speed steel or they can consist of a heat-treated shank with a high-speed steel, cast-alloy, or carbide tip that is brazed or clamped in place.

CAPACITY OF PLANERS

The width of a planer refers to the maximum width of the work that can be planed on the machine and is slightly less than the distance between the housings. The height refers to the maximum height of the work that can be planed on the machine and is slightly less than the distance between the top of the table and the bottom of the crossrail in its highest position.

The length of a planer refers to the maximum table stroke or to the maximum length of a piece of work that can be planed on the machine and is somewhat less than the distance between the chip pockets of the table. Thus, a 48 x 48″ x 16 ft (1219 x 1219 mm x 4l9 m) planer can plane a piece having a maximum size of 48″ wide, 48″ high, and 16 ft long. The dimensions indicating the size of the planer are always expressed in the order of width, height, and length.

Height and length capacities for an open-side planer are the same as explained previously, but the width capacity is not limited. The maximum distance from the inner side of the column to the tool in the left-hand crossrail head, with the head in a vertical position and at the extreme left-hand end of the rail, is approximately 12″ (300 mm) greater than the nominal width of the planer. For example, on a 48″ (1220 mm) wide open-side planer, this distance is approximately 60″ (1520 mm).

SHAPING AND SLOTTING

Shaping and slotting are material-removal processes in which a single-point cutting tool is reciprocated across or through a stationary workpiece to produce plane or formed surfaces. This mode of operation differentiates shaping from planing. In shaping and slotting, the work is stationary and the tool reciprocates; in planing, the work is reciprocated while the tool is stationary.

Simplicity of operation, flexibility of setup, low-cost tooling, and good accuracy and finish capabilities make shapers and slotting machines desirable for toolroom and die-shop needs and for limited production requirements. The machines, however, are seldom used for medium or high-production applications because of their comparatively low productivity. Possible operations are also limited by the maximum lengths of the ram strokes on these machines.

Several types of shapers and slotting machines are available. Cutting tools used can be of different configurations and can be set at various angles to profile, notch, cut angled slots and grooves, and produce flat surfaces. Both the workpiece and the cutting tool are firmly held in preselected positions, and the toolholder head is reciprocated by a powered ram.

HORIZONTAL SHAPERS

The most common shaper is the horizontal crank-operated push-cut type (Fig. 22-6) with ram movement in the horizontal plane. These shapers range in maximum cutting stroke from 7 or 8″ (178 or 203 mm) in bench models to 36″ (914 mm) in heavy-duty models. They are built with either mechanical or hydraulic drive and with a plain box table or universal table permitting angular tilt in addition to horizontal and vertical adjustments.

A cutting tool is mounted on a shaper head that is attached to the ram, which reciprocates the tool. Workpieces are held in a vise on the shaper table or directly on the table. Power or hand feeding of the table is provided parallel to the table top and perpendicular to the stroke of the ram. The tool cuts on the forward stroke of the ram, and the table feeds the workpiece in a direction perpendicular to the ram motion, for the next cut, on the return stroke of the ram. Many shapers have a rapid traverse for moving the table to various positions along a crossrail fitted to the front of the machine column.

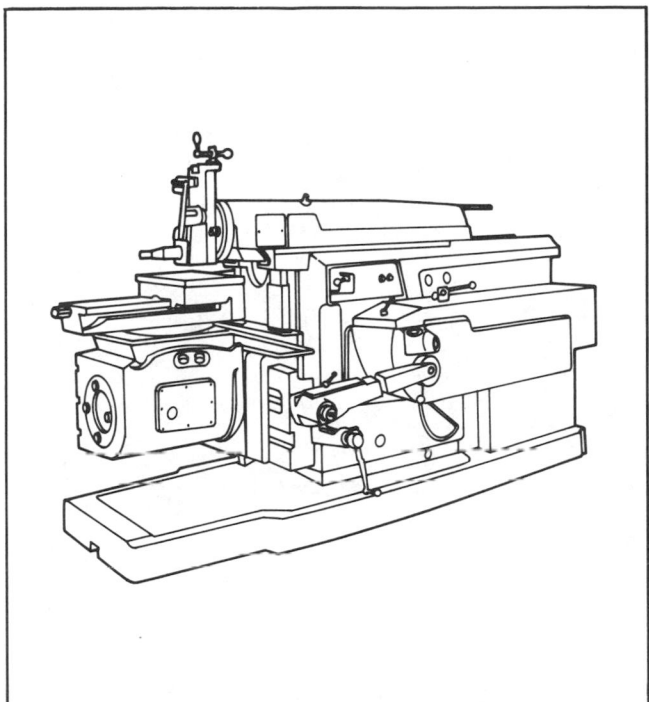

Fig. 22-6   Typical horizontal crank-operated push-cut shaper.

VERTICAL SHAPERS OR SLOTTERS

Vertical shapers, also called slotting machines, operate somewhat like horizontal shapers except that the ram reciprocates vertically rather than horizontally. A typical vertical slotting machine is shown in Fig. 22-7. Most machines of this type have provisions for adjustable inclination of their rams, and rotary tables are practically standard equipment. Standard machines are available with ram strokes ranging from 6-36″ (152-914 mm), with hydraulic or mechanical drives.

Vertical slotting machines are available with five axes—longitudinal and transverse travel of the workpiece in the X and Y axes, vertical movement of the ram in the Z axis, swiveling of the ram in the B axis, and rotating the workpiece in the C axis—to permit a wide variety of operations. Such machines are available for manual operation, numerical control, or tracer control.

Keyseaters are a specialized form of vertical shapers designed specifically for machining internal keyways. They use a tool mounted on a cutter bar above the ram, and it is pulled rather than pushed through the workpiece.

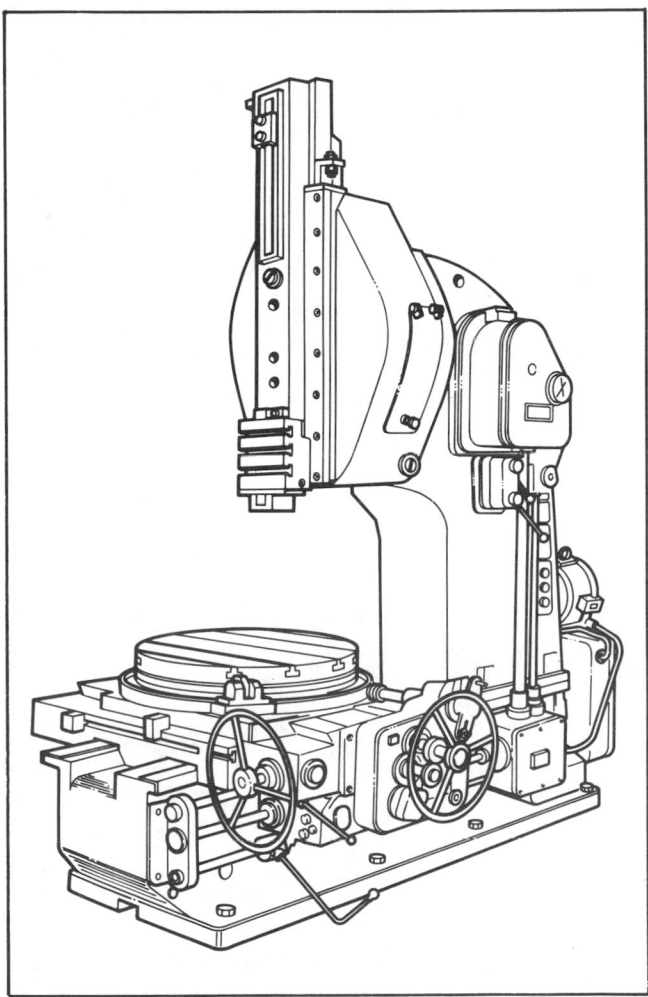

Fig. 22-7   Vertical slotting machine equipped with a compound pivoting ram. (*Cooper Engineering Ltd.*)

TURNING AND BORING

THE TURNING PROCESS

Turning is a machining process in which a workpiece is held and rotated about its longitudinal axis on a machine tool called a lathe. Cutting tools mounted on the lathe are fed into the workpiece to remove material and thus produce the required shape. The principal surfaces machined are concentric with longitudinal axis of the workpiece.

Turning operations are defined as the removal of material from external surfaces on rotating workpieces. Related operations on external surfaces, also performed on lathes, include facing, chamfering, grooving or necking, knurling, skiving, threading, and cutoff (parting).

Operations that can be performed on internal surfaces with a lathe include drilling, reaming, boring, threading, and recessing. Boring operations are also performed on special-purpose machines.

Lathes are one of the most versatile machine tools available. Most lathes have the capability for threading, and with attachments or NC, can cut tapered or contoured surfaces, both external and internal. Other operations that can be performed on some lathes include spinning, honing, polishing, and buffing.

FUNDAMENTALS OF LATHE OPERATION

Many different types of lathes of varying complexity are available to suit specific applications. The basic requirements for any of these lathes are (1) means for holding and rotating the workpieces and (2) a means for holding and moving the cutting tools.

Holding and Rotating the Workpiece

Workpieces are held in a lathe between centers or by a chuck, collet, fixture, or faceplate. Rotation of the workpiece is accomplished by a spindle mounted in the lathe headstock. The spindle is sometimes driven directly by an electric motor, but the drive is usually through belts and/or a gear train.

Chucks or faceplates connected to the headstock spindle are used to hold short, large-diameter workpieces. Collets are used for short, small-diameter workpieces or workpieces machined on the end of a bar or tube that is fed through the spindle and parted from the stock when completed. Between-center holding is used for long workpieces and requires that center holes be previously drilled in each end of the workpiece.

For between-center turning, a center is provided on the spindle and a tailstock is mounted on the outboard end of the bedways. The tailstock is adjustable along the ways for various workpiece lengths and is equipped with a center. The center can be replaced by a drill or reamer when required for chucking operations. Steadyrests or follow rests are sometimes placed against the workpiece at positions between the centers to minimize deflection during machining.

Cutting Tool Movements

The carriage of a basic engine lathe (Fig. 23-1) consists of a carriage, cross slide, compound rest, and apron. The carriage slides longitudinally along ways on the lathe bed, thus guiding the carriage parallel to the lathe and workpiece axis. Movement of the cross slide, actuated by a feedscrew, is across the bedways (perpendicular to the lathe axis) and over slide ways on top of the carriage.

Clamped to the top of the cross slide is a compound rest that can be rotated 360° and secured at any angle with respect to the lathe axis. The compound rest has a T-slot used to clamp a toolpost or toolblock. A slide on the compound rest can be moved along the base by a feedscrew to provide movement of the cutting tool at any desired angle with respect to the workpiece axis.

An apron fastened to the underside of the carriage contains the gears and clutches for longitudinal and cross feeds. It also has a split nut to engage a leadscrew mounted on the lathe bed to drive the carriage when cutting threads.

Operating Variables

Many factors influence any turning operation. The three major ones are cutting speed, feed rate, and depth of cut.

Cutting speed refers to the rotational speed of the lathe spindle and workpiece and can be expressed in revolutions per minute (rpm). For turning and most other machining operations, however, the cutting speed is generally given in surface feet per minute (sfm) or meters per minute (m/min), which is the rate at which the workpiece surface moves past the cutting tool. The surface speed equals the rotary speed (rpm) of the spindle times the circumference of the workpiece (in feet or meters).

Feed rate is the rate at which the tool advances along its cutting path. It is expressed in inches or millimeters per minute (ipm or mm/min), or in inches or millimeters per revolution (ipr or mm/rev).

Depth of cut is the thickness for the layer of material removed from the workpiece surface (the distance from the uncut surface to the cut surface), expressed in inches or millimeters. When turning cylindrical workpieces, the diameter is reduced by twice the depth of cut.

SELECTING A LATHE

Selecting the most appropriate lathe for a specific application can be difficult because of the wide variety of types and sizes available. Size and

TURNING

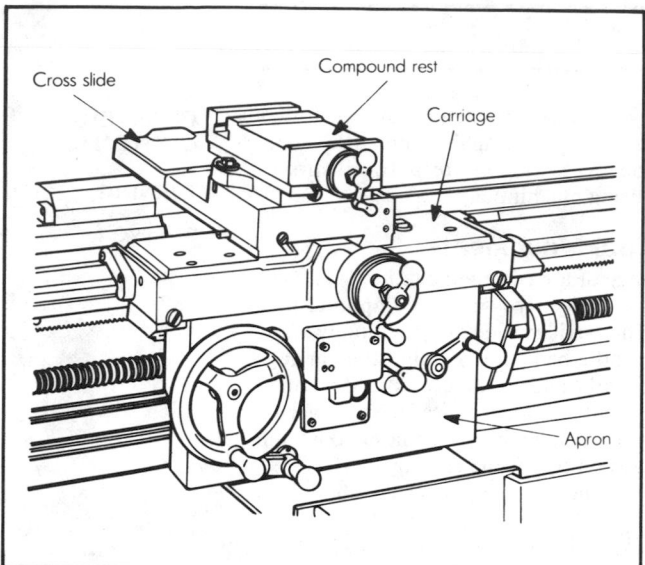

Fig. 23-1 Basic engine lathe carriage consisting of a cross slide, compound rest, and apron. (*LeBlond Makino Machine Tool Co.*)

complexity of the workpieces to be machined; production, accuracy, and surface-finish requirements; operator skills; and economic considerations are major factors in making a selection. With respect to workpiece size, swing over the lathe bed and bed length are important criteria.

Production Requirements

Production requirements for the same or similar parts require a careful analysis with respect to lathe selection, especially for low to medium volume needs. Hand-operated lathes are sometimes preferred for limited requirements of nonrepetitive and relatively simple workpieces.

NC lathes are becoming increasingly popular for producing small to medium, repetitive quantities of both simple and complex workpieces. Large production requirements for identical parts generally dictate the use of single or multiple-spindle automatics or the use of special machines.

Production of metric-dimensioned workpieces poses no serious problems with respect to the operation of lathes. Dual-reading dials and digital readouts are commercially available to permit machining to U.S. Customary or metric dimensions. Lathes are also available equipped with metric feedscrews and nuts. Most NC units have switchable inch/metric operation.

Surface-Finish and Tolerance Requirements

Surface finishes of 20-50 μ in. (0.51-1.27 μ m) are the practical limits that can be expected from turning operations when using well-maintained lathes and tools.[1] Smoother surface finishes, to 1 μ in. (0.025 μ m) or less, however, can be produced, particularly with precision machines and diamond cutting tools (for nonferrous metals), but several cuts are generally required, resulting in increased manufacturing costs.

Dimensional tolerances that can be maintained in turning vary depending upon the machine and operating parameters used, the workpiece, setup rigidity, and other variables. Practical limits for production applications, with machines and tools in

good condition, range from $\pm$0.001" (0.03 mm) for workpieces having diameters of about 1/4" (6.4 mm) or less to $\pm$0.003" (0.08 mm) for diameters of 4" (102 mm) or more. Closer tolerances to $\pm$0.000050" (0.00127 mm) are often maintained, but maintaining these tolerances generally requires the use of more precise machines and results in higher manufacturing costs.

TYPES OF LATHES

A wide variety of lathes and turning machines is available in many sizes to suit specific application requirements. They can be controlled manually, semiautomatically, or automatically. Major classifications of different types include engine lathes, contouring lathes, turret lathes, and NC/CNC turning machines. Each classification is further subdivided into specific kinds.

Engine Lathes

The engine lathe is a basic, general-purpose machine tool that is used primarily to generate forms by removing material with one single-point cutting tool at a time. The tool moves parallel, perpendicular, or at an angle to the axis of rotation of the workpiece.

Through the use of attachments and accessories, a number of different operations can be performed on engine lathes. These operations include single-point threading, thread chasing, tapping, taper turning, duplicating and contouring, drilling, reaming, boring, milling, and grinding. The versatile engine lathe is widely used for producing many different parts in small quantities, as well as for toolroom and maintenance work.

Engine lathes are generally classified as either chucking or center-type machines. On chucking machines, workpieces are held in chucks or collets or on faceplates mounted on the lathe spindles. On center-type machines, workpieces are supported between centers mounted in the spindles and the tailstocks of the lathes.

Lathes are often divided into arbitrary classifications with respect to size, function, and degree of precision. Sizes of lathes are generally specified by their swings over the bed and cross slide and by the distances between centers or bed lengths, which determine the maximum diameters and lengths of workpieces that can be handled.

Every engine lathe provides a means for traversing the cutting tool both along the axis of workpiece revolution and at an angle to that axis. Beyond this similarity, lathes may embody characteristics common to several different classifications.

Accessories and attachments are devices added to lathes to improve their versatility and/or production rate or to perform a particular type of control or function. Some of the more common devices that are applicable to various types of lathes are described in this section, and workholding devices are discussed later in this chapter.

Carriage stops. The carriage stop (Fig. 23-2) is used on the outer way of the lathe bed for accurately spacing grooves, turning multiple diameters and lengths, or cutting off pieces of a required thickness. They can also be applied to the cross slide. Three types of stops are commonly used: (1) positive stops, either single or multiple, (2) dial-indicator stops, and (3) automatic stops, either single or multiple. Positive stops enable the operator to position the carriage manually with accuracy as close as 0.001" (0.03 mm); dial-indicator stops can be positioned manually to 0.0001" (0.003 mm). Automatic stops disengage the feed at the proper location and are accurate to 0.003-0.005" (0.08-0.13 mm). Multiple automatic carriage stops are used on production turning of pieces to desired lengths.

Cross-slide stops. These devices, often referred to as threading stops, operate in the manner indicated for carriage stops but are mounted on the cross slide.

Rapid traverse. Rapid traverse forward is often furnished as a standard accessory and provides a means for rapidly bringing the carriage or cross slide to the starting point when any length of work is being turned or threaded. Rapid traverse reverse is furnished on some machines to provide a means for rapidly bringing the carriage or cross slide to home position.

Taper turning. Tapers may be cut on engine lathes (1) by setting over the tailstock, (2) by use of the cross-slide compound, (3) by power feed to the compound rest, which is available on a number of lathes, (4) by use of a taper attachment (Fig. 23-3), and (5) by use of form tools. Internal as well as external tapers may be cut with all these methods except by setting over the tailstock. Setting over the tailstock throws the dead center out of alignment with the live center, causing improper seating and wear, but it provides a means of producing long slender tapers. When the taper is to be short, or when only one or a few pieces are to be machined, the cross-slide compound can be used to

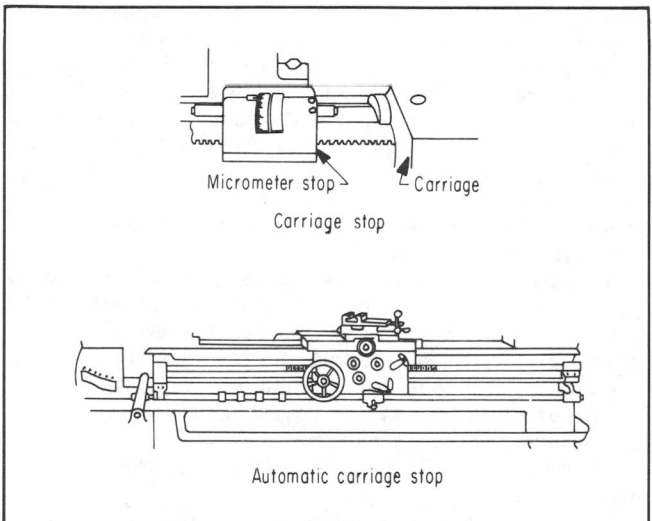

Fig. 23-2 Carriage stops for engine lathes.

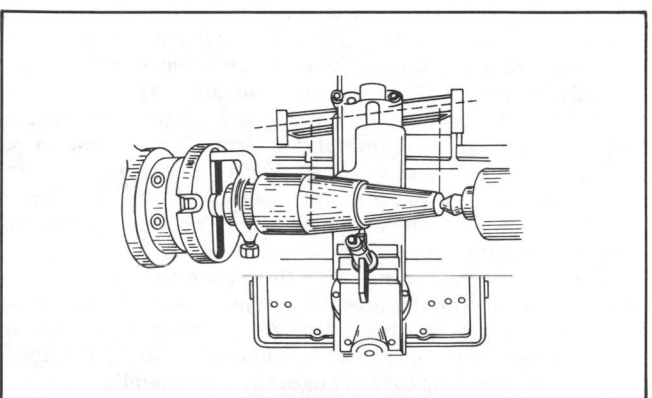

Fig. 23-3 Engine lathe equipped with taper attachment.

advantage. Power angular turning, when available, is advantageous for medium production quantities because it replaces manual movement of the compound top slide.

Taper attachments, which are devices containing a guide to which the cross slide is attached, offer the easiest means to perform such jobs accurately. Attachments are available in bed-mounted and carriage-mounted types; required angles are set by means of graduations on one end of the guide rail. The guide is angularly adjustable from parallel to the spindle centerline to the maximum angle of the device. Either turning or boring of tapers is possible, and two tapered sections diminishing in opposite directions can be produced on the same workpiece. Form tools are generally used only for short tapers on a production basis.

Ball-turning or radius-generating rest. This type of rest replaces the compound rest and is used for turning or boring spherical shapes (Fig. 23-4).

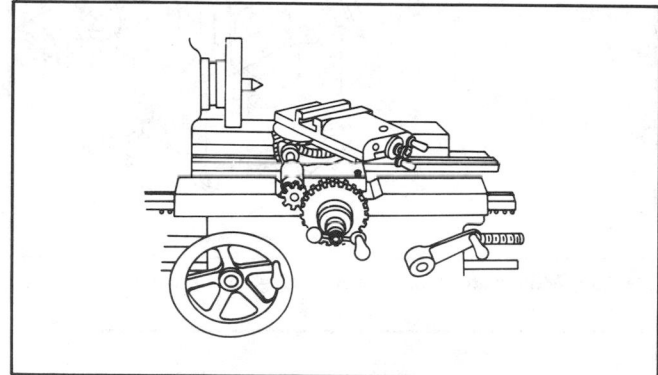

Fig. 23-4 Rest used to turn or bore spherical shapes.

Milling/sawing attachment. This device is attached to the cross slide, replacing the compound. One type is adjustable to hold the workpiece at right angles to the milling cutter or saw blade and at the correct elevation. The cutter is held by the headstock chuck, drill chuck, arbor, or collet. In another type (Fig. 23-5), the milling cutter and driving head are mounted on the compound and the work is held between the lathe centers. In both types three directions of feed are possible, permitting angle milling, dovetailing, T-slotting, keyway cutting, and thread milling.

Grinding attachments. Several types of this attachment are commercially available: one smaller type is mounted on the toolpost; a larger type (Fig. 23-6) is clamped to the compound, replacing the toolpost. A third type replaces the compound and mounts directly on the bottom slide. The grinders have two or three-directional movement and can perform many kinds of grinding operations. They do not have the rigidity of grinding machines, however, so they work best under light cuts.

Gear-cutting attachment. In the use of this attachment, the gear cutter is mounted on a regular arbor held between centers or on a stub arbor. The gear blank is usually clamped on the short arbor in the attachment; cutting is generally done at the bottom of the blank. Indexing of the blank may be performed using a dividing head or a finished indexing gear.

Turret attachments. An engine lathe may be equipped with both a turret toolpost and a ram-type turret attachment to convert it to a hand-screw machine or turret lathe capable of

TURNING

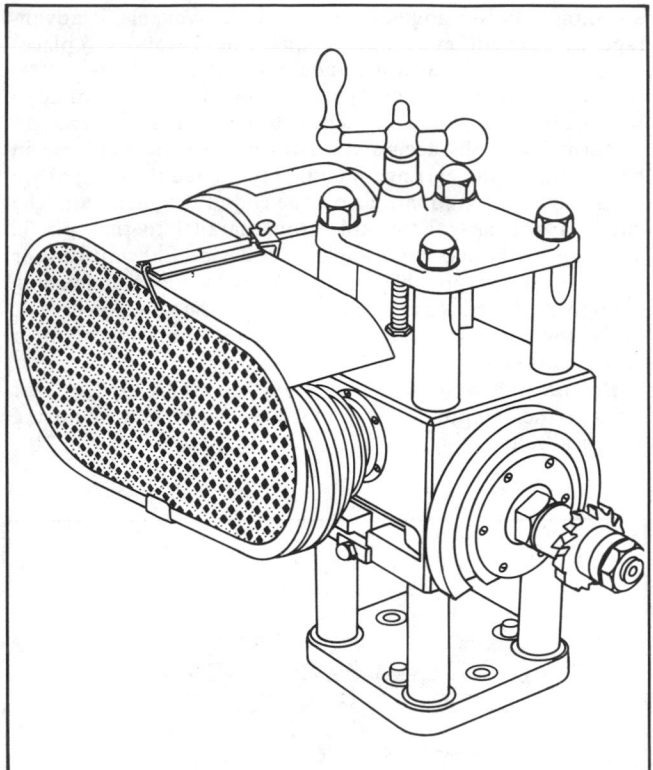

Fig. 23-5 Milling attachment for mounting on compound.

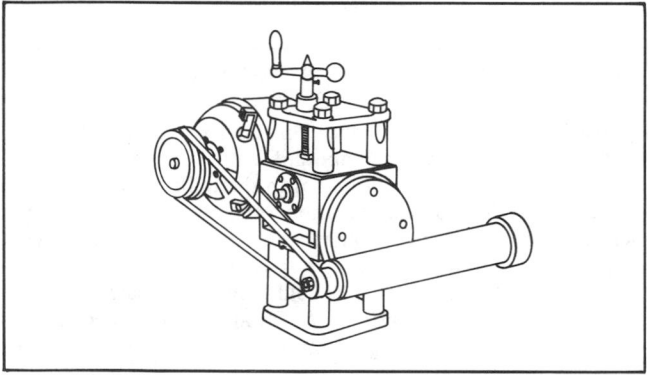

Fig. 23-6 Grinding attachment which replaces lathe toolpost.

efficient quantity production. Ram-type turrets (Fig. 23-7) are usually bed-mounted and are available with or without power feed. In addition, they usually revolve automatically and have an automatic index feed stop for each face of the turret. The ram-type attachment usually has five or six positions; the cross-slide or carriage turret generally holds four tools. Some ram-type turrets are connected with a rear rest for holding a parting or grooving tool.

The two types are advantageously used in combination; i.e., the ram-type turret can be used to countersink, drill, ream, and tap while the cross-slide turret can be used to turn, face, thread, and part. Turret lathes are discussed later in this section.

Cutter-relieving attachment. With this attachment, side or face-milling cutters, straight or spiral-fluted taps, reamers, etc., may be relieved for free-cutting action.

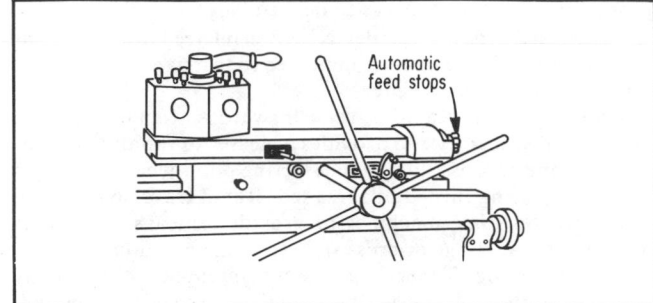

Fig. 23-7 Bed-mounted turret which replaces regular tailstock.

Constant cutting speed. Attachments are available to regulate the speeds of drive motors on engine lathes in direct relation to the diameter being turned. This provides a constant cutting speed, in surface feet per minute (meters per minute), regardless of varying diameters on the workpiece. Constant cutting speed is also a feature of many controls used on NC and CNC lathes, which are discussed later in this chapter.

Boring and drilling. Fig. 23-8 shows the manner in which the workpiece size and shape, as well as the nature of the hole to be bored, affect the method of mounting the workpiece and the type of boring tool or bar to be used. The workpiece should be chucked whenever possible, and if the work is liable to spring, the extended end should be supported by a steadyrest. When a workpiece is to have a hole bored through it, the workpiece must be mounted away from the face of the chuck. When a blind hole is to be bored full depth, a bar should be used that holds the cutting edge of the tool ahead of the bar end. Enough room should be allowed between the tool point and bar end to permit chip curl without crowding.

The smaller the hole, the greater the end clearance must be to prevent the heel of the tool from striking the bored surface. The boring-tool nose should be set level with the centerline of the workpiece and ground with more back rake than a turning tool, in order to reduce tool forces and improve chip formation.

The lathe must always be leveled accurately before any precise boring or drilling is attempted. Any twist in the bed will result in a tapered hole. Jackscrews are usually provided in the base for leveling.

Engine-lathe drilling operations are usually done by rotating the workpiece while the drill is held fixed in the tailstock spindle or by a tailstock chuck. A hole may be drilled in a part having a flat surface by holding the part against a drill pad and advancing it, by the tailstock, against a drill held by a headstock chuck. Holes may be drilled at right angles to the axis of a cylindrical part by locating the part in a V-block mounted on the tailstock spindle. The part may be advanced against the drill in the headstock spindle by revolving the tailstock handwheel. When the workpiece is too large or irregular in shape to be drilled by any of these methods, it may be mounted on the compound rest or on the cross slide with the compound removed. If a relatively large hole is to be drilled, a small lead hole is frequently drilled first.

Thread cutting. Cutting screw threads on an engine lathe is done by connecting the headstock spindle with the leadscrew through a gearbox which provides a number of gearing combinations. This produces the desired ratio of the tool-holding carriage feed to the rpm of the work spindle. With the desired speed-feed ratio established, a thread of the desired pitch may be cut.

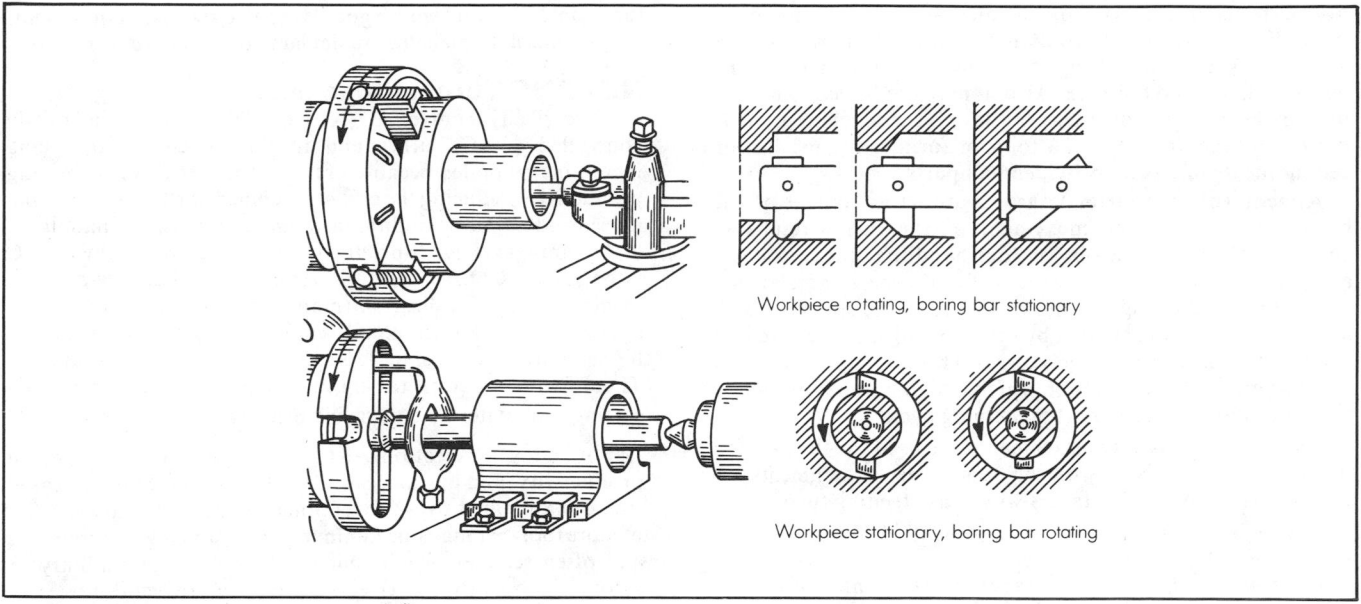

Workpiece rotating, boring bar stationary

Workpiece stationary, boring bar rotating

Fig. 23-8 Different methods of boring on a lathe.

It is possible to cut metric or module-pitch screw threads by using suitable change gears. For example, a setup can be made whereby metric screws of from 0.2 mm lead up to 10 mm lead can be cut by use of a standard four-threads-per-inch leadscrew.

The production cutting of screw threads is often done on single-purpose machines which roll, mill, chase, or grind threads. The decision to cut threads on an engine lathe in production depends upon a number of factors including length, depth, and accuracy of threads; whether threads are single or multiple start, internal or external; workpiece material; accuracy; and surface finish.

Most modern lathes are equipped with a threading dial (Fig. 23-9) which is used to ensure that the leadscrew split nut is engaged with the leadscrew at the proper time so that successive cuts can be taken in the same groove or so that grooves can be spaced properly for cutting multiple threads. Another useful device is a thread-cutting stop, which is a reference stop to the cross slide. It is attached to the cross-slide dovetail.

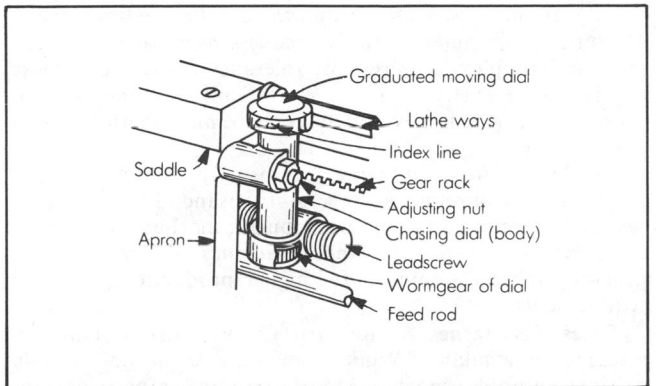

Graduated moving dial
Lathe ways
Index line
Saddle
Gear rack
Adjusting nut
Chasing dial (body)
Apron
Leadscrew
Wormgear of dial
Feed rod

Fig. 23-9 Thread-cutting dial which is standard on most lathes.

Contouring Lathes

Contour turning is the production of three-dimensional forms on workpieces by controlling the path of the cutting tool. Most contour turning is now done on NC lathes, discussed later in this chapter. There is, however, still considerable work of this type being done on standard engine lathes equipped with tracing attachments and on automatic tracer lathes when larger production quantities are required.

Horizontal Turret Lathes

Horizontal turret lathes differ from engine lathes in two basic respects. A square turret is mounted on the cross slide in place of the usual compound rest of the engine lathe and is pivoted about a vertical axis to bring one of four tools into cutting position. On some lathes, a fixed toolholder is mounted on the back end of the cross slide or a separate rear cross slide. The second basic difference is that a multisided turret takes the place of the tailstock on the engine lathe. The turret usually is pivoted about a vertical axis so that, by rotating it, the tool on each side may be brought into cutting position.

Numerically controlled horizontal turret lathes, discussed next in this section, do not always fit the above description because of the numerous turret arrangements available on NC equipment.

Horizontal turret lathes are manufactured as hand-operated, power-fed, automatic, and numerically controlled machines. The hand-operated machines require an operator to manipulate the various controls required for indexing and moving the turrets, changing speeds, etc. On automatic and NC turret lathes the operator places the workpiece in the chuck and starts the machine; all the machine motions are controlled automatically.

A major advantage of turret lathes, compared to engine lathes, is that the availability of more tools permits many parts to be completely machined in one setup at higher production rates. They are particularly well-suited for workpieces requiring

TURNING

both external and internal operations. A possible limitation of turret lathes is the length-to-diameter ratio of the workpieces. Long parts have to be supported by a center in the turret because there is no tailstock. Also, it may not be economical to use power-fed or automatic turret lathes for machining workpieces that require only a few tools or for meeting production requirements of less than 10 identical parts.

Attachments for turret lathes. Automatic control of the headstock through the movement of the turret results in considerable savings on jobs in which handling time constitutes a large part of the total floor-to-floor time. The starting, stopping, speed changing, and reversing of the spindle are all controlled by a unit actuated by the indexing and forward and reverse strokes of the hexagon turret. This attachment finds its best use on small machines on which a high number of spindle changes take place in a short machining cycle.

Cutting tapers. Taper attachments are used for turning and boring angular surfaces with the cross slide. Attachments are also available for cutting tapers with cross-feeding turrets. For steeper tapers, a swivel compound slide can be mounted on the cross slide.

Contouring operations. Tracer attachments, described previously under the discussion of attachments for engine lathes, are also available for turret lathes. They can be mounted on the cross slide, the cross-feeding turret, or one tooling station of the turret for indexing into position as required.

Automatic turret lathes. These lathes, commonly referred to as single-spindle automatic chucking machines, are used basically for the same type of work as the turret lathe fitted with chucking equipment. They generally require hand loading and unloading, but complete the machining cycle automatically.

These machines are used when production requirements are too high for hand or power-fed turret lathes and too low for multiple-spindle automatic machines to produce economically. Setup time is slightly higher than for the hand turret lathe, but operator fatigue and error are considerably reduced. The setup time is much lower than for multiple-spindle automatic machines, and expensive tooling is not usually required. Cost reduction is also an important factor to be considered. The automatic features permit a more constant flow of production, and scrap loss is reduced by eliminating operator error. The machines are designed to permit combined cuts economically and automatically, thereby removing the responsibility from the operator. Also very important is the fact that, during the automatic machining operation, the operator is free to operate another machine or is able to inspect the finished parts completely without loss of time.

Two basic types of automatic turret lathes are available. One has the saddle mounted on the bedways and a turret which rotates around a vertical axis similar to the conventional turret lathe. The other (Fig. 23-10) has a turret mounted on a shaft extending from the headstock. The turret rotates around a horizontal axis parallel to the spindle centerline. It normally consists of four, five, or six tooling stations. Standard holders are available to adapt commonly used turret-lathe tooling. Cross-slide tooling stations are available in the front and rear on one long slide or on independently operated front and rear slides.

Each machine has a control unit which automatically selects the speeds, feeds, lengths of cut, and machine functions. Included under machine functions, as needed, are dwell, cycle stop, index, reverse, cross-slide actuation, and many other

functions. Chip and splash guards are also standard equipment. Other units of the machine are similar to the standard turret lathe.

NC/CNC Turning Machines

Numerically controlled (NC) and computer numerically controlled (CNC) lathes and turning machines are being increasingly applied because of their capabilities for increasing productivity, reducing the cost of machined parts, and providing more production flexibility, including contouring capability.

Advantages. Higher productivity is being obtained with NC lathes because of faster setups, reduced toolchanging requirements, increased utilization (more time spent in cutting), and shorter cycles. Faster metal removal rates are the result of higher horsepower, spindle speeds, and feed rates available. These features permit taking full advantage of the improved cutting tool materials now available.

For many applications, NC lathes have at least doubled productivity, and in some cases, production has been increased four or more times over conventional methods. The availability of more tools per machine minimizes toolchanging requirements and often reduces or eliminates the need for preliminary or secondary operations. Greater accuracy, repeatability, and reliability of these machines has improved the quality of the parts produced and has reduced scrap.

Substantial cost savings can result from reduced operator skill requirements and minimal needs for special tooling, material handling, and inspection. Also, less labor may be needed since it is often possible for one operator to attend two or more NC lathes simultaneously. Shorter leadtimes provide reduced inventory costs and faster delivery of workpieces. Another advantage is that operating variables (cutting speeds, feed rates, depths of cut, tooling, etc.) can be controlled by management and part programmers rather than individual machine operators.

Limitations. A higher capital investment, the need for personnel with programming skills, and requirements for the maintenance of more sophisticated equipment are possible limitations to the use of NC turning equipment. Full-time work flow to these machines and a good preventive maintenance program are essential. The machines are often operated on a multishift basis to justify the higher capital investment.

When to use NC lathes. NC lathes have generally been found to be most economical when lot sizes ranging from about 10 to 200 or more workpieces are required repetitively, when tapes or stored programs can be reused, and/or when families of similar parts are produced. There are exceptions however. Smaller lot sizes, even one-of-a-kind workpieces, can be machined using NC turning equipment with cost reductions in cases when the parts are complex, require close tolerances, would otherwise involve more costly tooling, are difficult or impossible to produce on engine lathes, and/or are to be manufactured again at a later date.

NC lathes are also being increasingly used for higher production requirements—several thousand parts in some cases. Single or multiple-spindle automatic machines, automatic tracer lathes, and special-purpose machines, however, are still generally more economical for higher production, long-run requirements.

Types of NC lathes. A wide variety of NC lathes and turning machines is available. While some have single or multiple vertical spindles, most are of horizontal-spindle design. Horizontal-spindle machines are usually supplied in one of

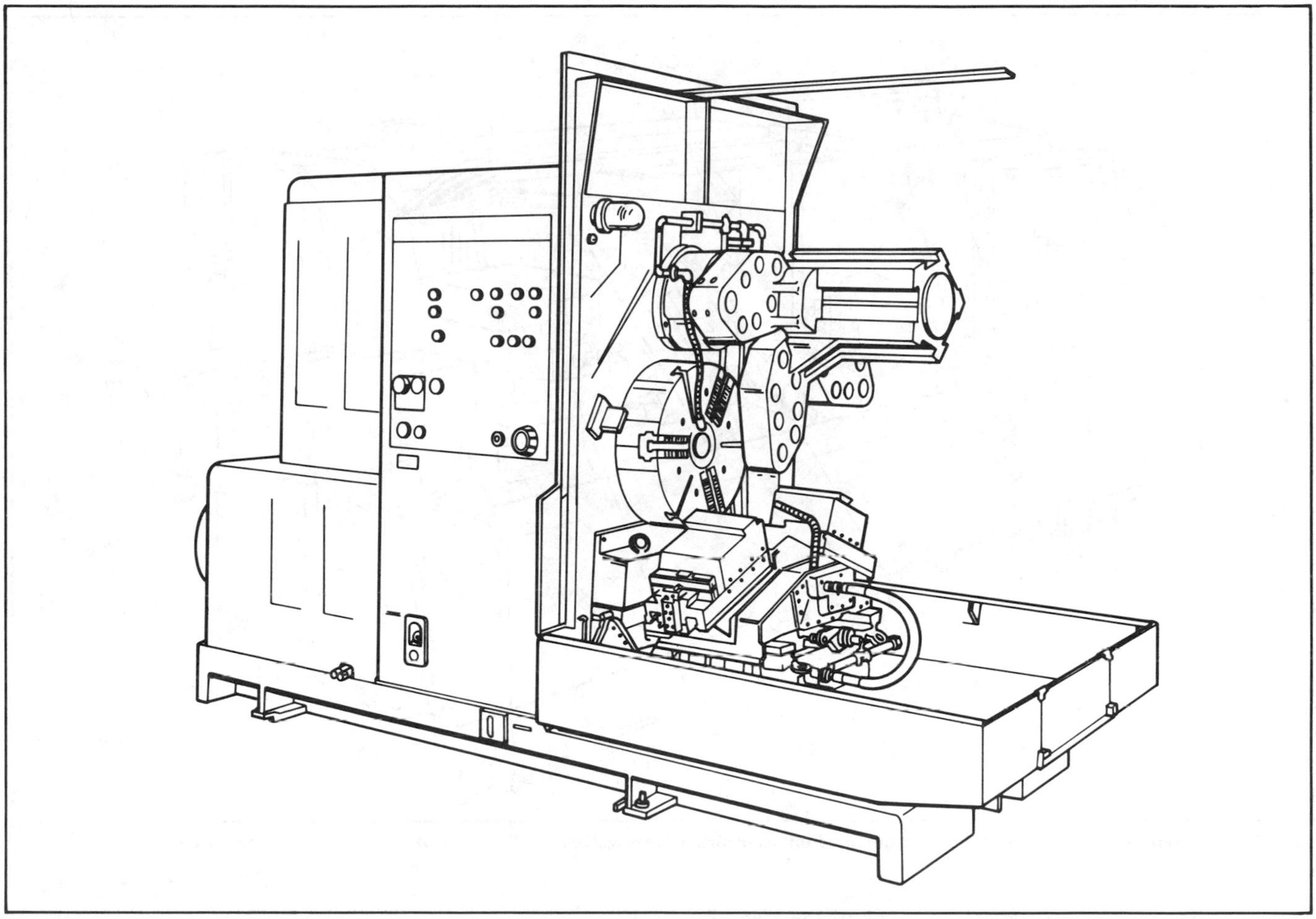

Fig. 23-10 Single-spindle automatic chucking machine. (*Turning Machine Div., Warner & Swasey*)

three basic forms.

1. Center-type machines, often referred to as shaft lathes, are used primarily for between-center work. They are equipped with a tailstock and are available with long bed lengths. High spindle speeds, a single set of slides, and turrets arranged for only OD-type tooling are common characteristics of these machines.

2. Chucking-type machines are characterized by larger and lower speed spindles, wider and heavier slides (sometimes with more than one set), turrets arranged for both OD and ID operations, short bed lengths, and either no tailstocks or optional swing-up style tailstocks for occasional shaft work. A compact, two-axis, CNC, slant-bed chucking center is illustrated in Fig. 23-11. This machine has a single-disc turret which holds both OD and ID tools in combination toolblocks.

3. Universal or combination machines are either basic center-type machines equipped with chucking-type tooling or chucking-type machines provided with tailstocks. A universal lathe with the CNC unit mounted on the headstock is illustrated in Fig. 23-12. This machine is equipped with a round turret for OD operations, an end turret for ID operations, and a tailstock for between-centers work.

On a series of column-type turret lathes offered by one manufacturer, a single 10 or 12-station turret for both turning and end working tools indexes on an axis parallel to the spindle

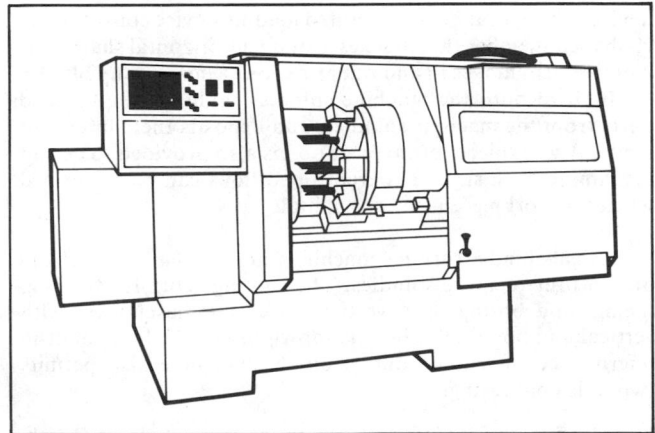

Fig. 23-11 Two-axis, CNC, slant-bed chucking center. (*Cincinnati Milacron*)

TURNING

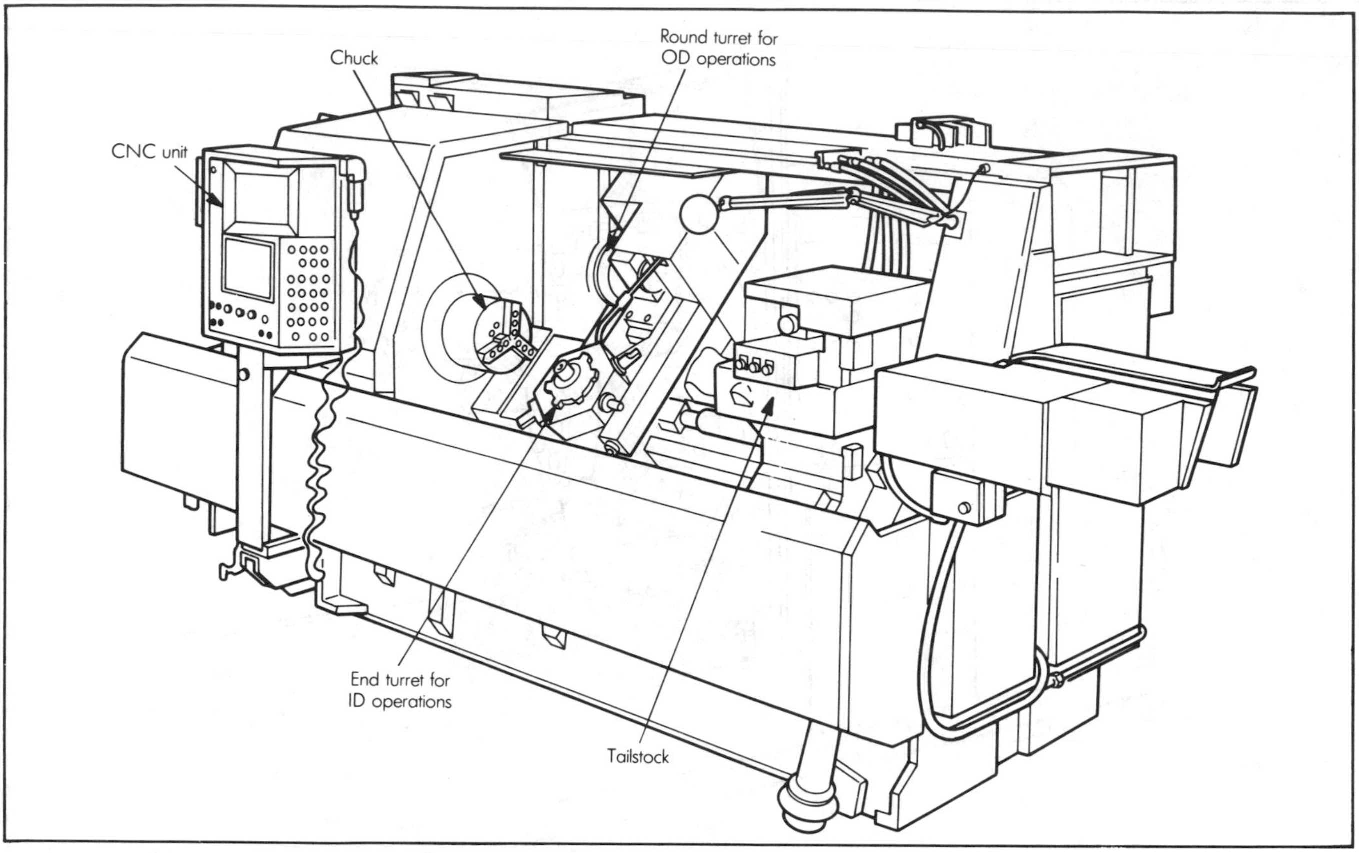

Chuck

Round turret for
OD operations

CNC unit

End turret for
ID operations

Tailstock

Fig. 23-12 Universal-type lathe with CNC unit mounted on headstock. (*Jones & Lamson Products, Waterbury Farrel Div., Textron Inc.*)

axis and also moves on a separate carriage in both the X and Z axes. This arrangement permits setting the points of all cutting tools to a common plane.

Horizontal-spindle turning machines are also available with two or more spindles. Such machines are often equipped with auxiliary equipment such as automatic loading devices since they are more applicable to high production requirements. The CNC chucking-type turning machine with two horizontal spindles shown in Fig. 23-13 features an automatic loading device. The hydraulically-operated loading device consists of an X-shaped member that indexes around a horizontal shaft. This member also moves in and out as its four arms pick up blanks, loads them onto the machine spindles, unloads the finished parts from the machine spindles, and deposits them in an exit chute. A workpiece turnover station is also provided to permit machining both sides. Different operations can be performed when the workpiece is in each spindle.

Vertical-spindle turning machines are available with from one to four or more spindles. The tooling setup for turning, facing, and boring on a vertical three-spindle chucker with vertical and horizontal slides is shown in Fig. 23-14. A built-in microprocessor-based control on this machine also permits two-axis contouring.

Selecting an NC lathe. Selection of a particular NC lathe depends primarily on the application. Factors that must be considered include the variety of workpieces to be produced

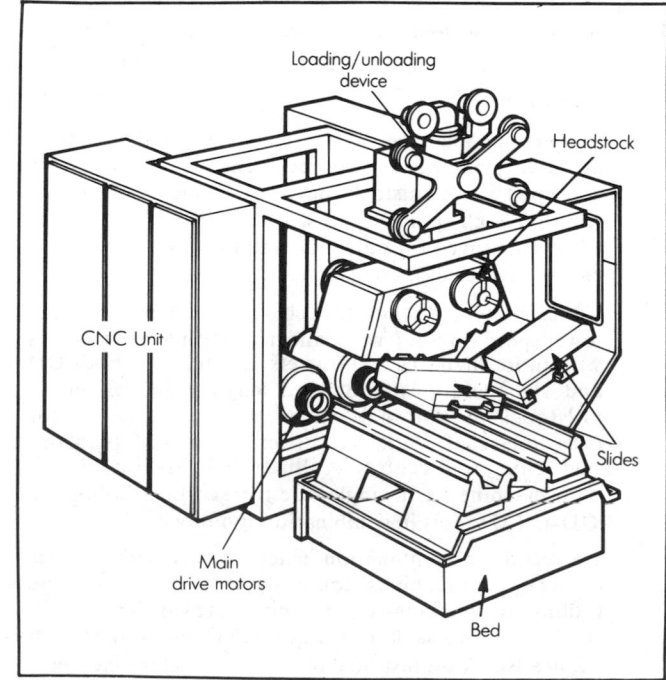

Loading/unloading
device

Headstock

CNC Unit

Slides

Main
drive motors

Bed

Fig. 23-13 Two-spindle, CNC, chucking-type turning machine features automatic loading. (*Turning Machine Div., Warner & Swasey Co.*)

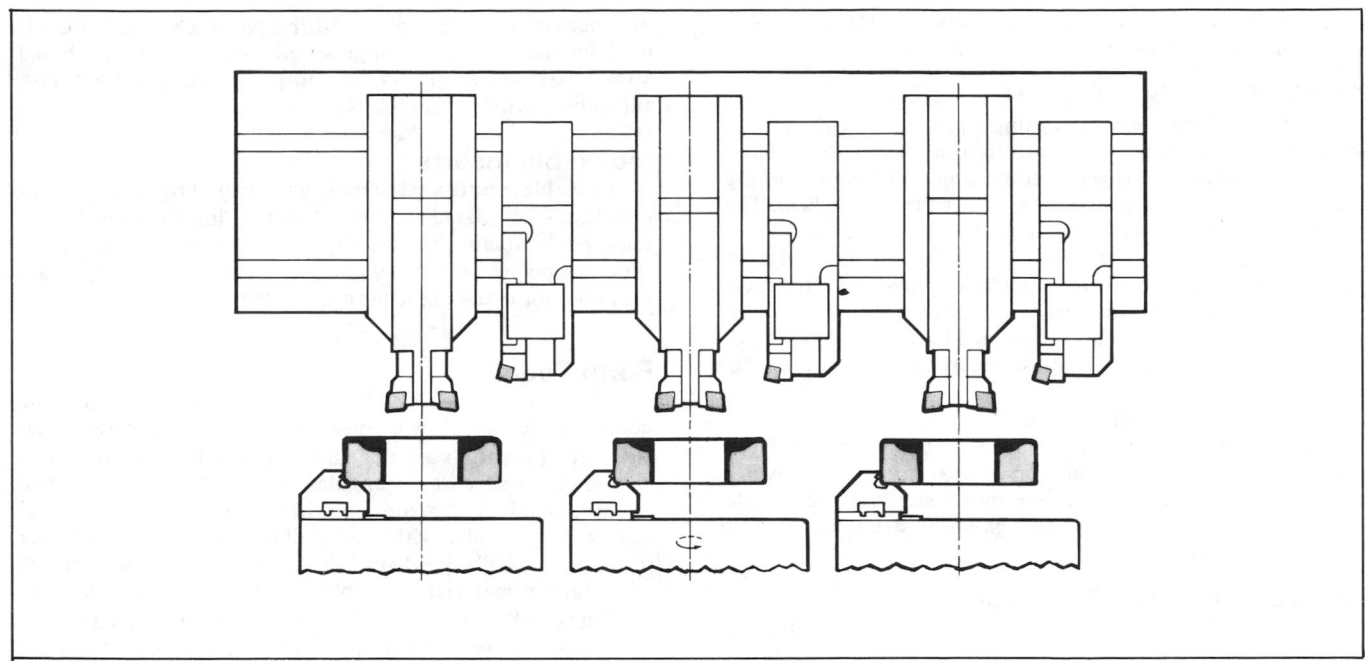

Fig. 23-14 Tooling for turning, facing, and boring on a three-spindle vertical chucker. (*Motch & Merryweather Machinery Co.*)

and their complexity, production lot sizes and repeatability, number and types of tools needed, and tolerance and surface finish requirements.

Machining of long workpieces usually dictates the need for a center-type machine, while short and large-diameter parts are handled better on a chucking-type machine. Requirements for a wide range of different part sizes and shapes indicate the need for a more versatile universal lathe.

Accuracy and repeatability. While no generally accepted standard exists with respect to accuracy for NC turning machines, these machines are usually built to closer accuracy standards than engine lathes. Some builders provide linear resolvers, independent of the feed drives, and guarantee X-axis repeatability to ±0.00015" (0.0038 mm) for diameter control, using the standard plus or minus three sigma definition.

Accuracy and repeatability, as the terms apply to NC machine tools, have been defined by the Numerical Control Committee of the National Machine Tool Builders' Association in the publication "Definition and Evaluation of Accuracy and Repeatability for Numerically Controlled Machine Tools."

Tooling arrangements. The availability of more cutting tools per machine is an important advantage of NC lathes. Up to 20 tools on a single lathe can be presented to a workpiece rapidly and precisely. For many applications, one set of standard tools can be retained on the machine permanently to produce a wide range of workpieces. When tool changes are necessary, only a few generally have to be replaced, thus reducing downtime and increasing productivity.

Turret designs. While turrets have been used for many years to minimize noncutting time on lathes, their design and capabilities have proliferated with the development of NC lathes and turning machines. The wide range of indexable turret designs available include disc, crown, and combination types that carry both ID and OD tools. Some have two sets of bores in concentric circles on a single turret, the bores in the outer circle

being for turning toolholders, and those in the inner circle for end cutting toolholders. Dual-level turrets, with end working tools at one level and turning tools on the other (see Fig. 23-15), are also available on some chuckers.

NC chucking centers made by one machine tool builder have synchronized dual turrets on a single slide, with seven tools on a crown turret and seven on a disc-type ID turret. Both turrets use a common tool point concept to assure interference free machining.

A turret that holds both OD and ID tools, arranged in any

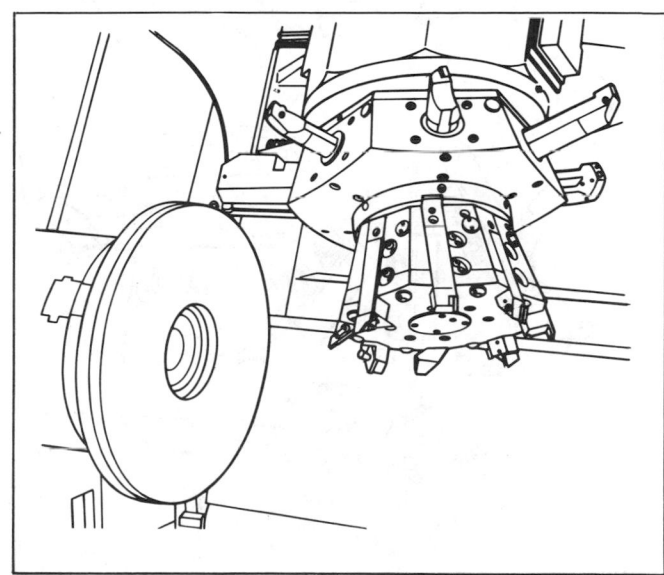

Fig. 23-15 Turret with end-working tools on one level and turning tools on another. (*Giddings & Lewis Machine Tool Co.*)

TURNING

order or combination, is seen in Fig. 23-16. The ID tools can be removed easily for turning shaft-type workpieces.

CUTTING TOOLS FOR TURNING

Most metal removal in turning operations is done with single-point tools. One exception is the use of form tools ground to specific shapes. A single-point cutting tool has one cutting part (tool point) and a shank by which the tool is held. The cutting part consists of the cutting edges, face, and flank.

Single-point tools are available as solid tools produced from bars of tool steel or from carbide blanks with tips brazed to a toolholder. They are also available as indexable inserts made from various cutting tool materials and clamped to holders. Indexable-insert tools have become the most widely used for turning.

Solid Single-Point Tools

Solid single-point tools for turning are produced from castings, forgings, rolled bars, or compacts made by powder metallurgy processes. The cutting tool materials used include carbon and low-alloy tool steels, high-speed steels, cast cobalt-based alloys, and carbides.

Brazed-Tip Single-Point Tools

Single-point tools are available with a body made from a less-costly material and a tip or blank of cutting material brazed or otherwise mounted to the cutting point. Cutting materials used for the tips include high-speed steels, cast cobalt-based alloys, carbides, single-crystal and polycrystalline diamonds, and cubic boron nitride (CBN).

Indexable Inserts

Indexable inserts are the most widely used tools for turning operations. Uncoated and coated carbide inserts are by far the most predominant, but inserts made from high-speed steels, ceramics, polycrystalline diamonds, and cubic boron nitride are also used for many applications.

Form Tools

A form tool is a cutting tool intended to produce a desired contour on a workpiece by means of a turning operation. Flat or circular form tools are available. A flat form tool (Fig. 23-17) embodies a square or rectangular cross section with the form along its end. Flat form tools may be mounted in a conventional tool post or provided with a dovetail to fit a special holder. The tools may be high-speed steel or steel shanks tipped with cast alloy cutting material or carbide. A circular form tool (Fig. 23-17) is round (disc-shaped) with the form or cutting component located on its periphery as a cutout portion. These tools are usually made of high-speed steel, but may be either carbide-tipped or solid carbide. Blanks for circular and flat (dovetailed) form tools, together with their associated mounting and clamping elements, have been standardized in ANSI B94.32-1954 (reaffirmed 1971).

The overall economic considerations of the operation should be the determining factor in deciding whether to use a flat or circular type of form tool in a particular case, but the machine tool and toolholder available for the job usually determine which type will be employed. Original costs of circular form tools are ordinarily high, but the cost per unit produced is less. Flat form tools, particularly those of the end-form kind,

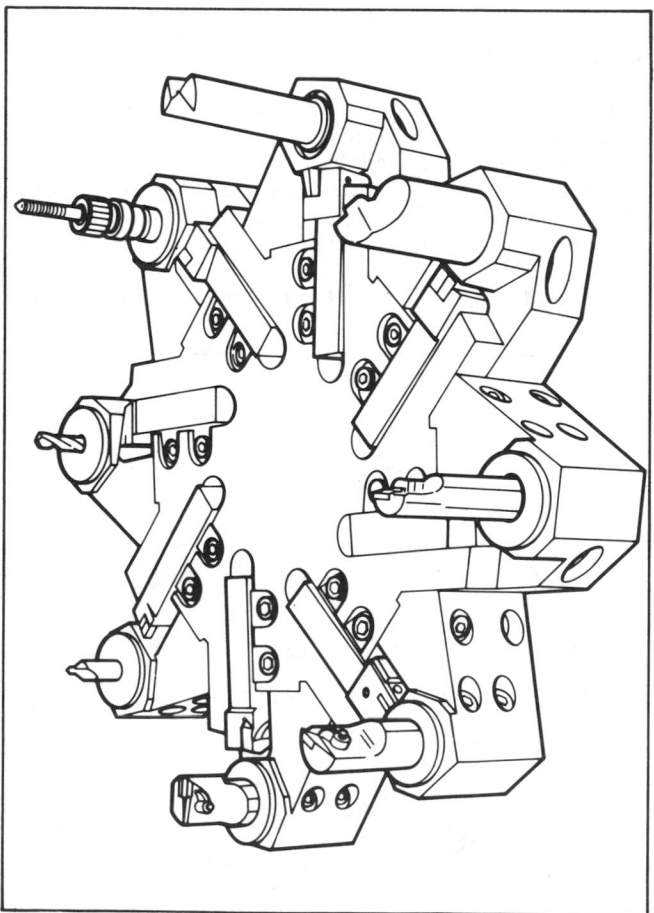

Fig. 23-16 Turret which holds both OD and ID tools. (*Monarch Machine Tool Co.*)

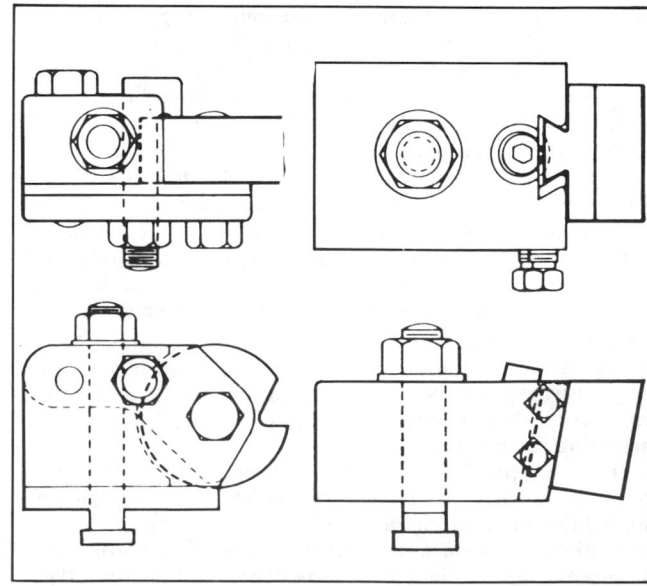

Fig. 23-17 Circular form tool (left) and flat form tool mounted in their holders.

generally cost less, but the cost per unit produced by them frequently is higher because of a shorter tool life. The least expensive form tools to make are the end-form kind made from standard bits with the form ground in the solid.

Knurling Tools

Knurling is most commonly used to obtain decorative surfaces, serrated surfaces when components are locked together in unit assemblies, and hand-grip or nonslip surfaces. These surfaces are obtained by the displacement of the material when the knurl is pressed against the surface of a rotating work blank. Knurls are used for producing straight, diagonal, or diamond knurling, and they have teeth of uniform pitch on cylindrical surfaces. Two general methods of specifying knurls—circular-pitch and diametral-pitch—are now in use. Knurling tools with standardized diametral pitches are covered in ANSI Standard B94.6-1981.

Burnishing Tools

Smooth finishes are produced on turned surfaces by roller burnishing. Roller burnishing tools consist of a series of tapered, hardened, and polished rolls positioned in slots within a retaining cage. As the rolls rotate in a cold-working operation, plastic deformation removes tool marks and surface irregularities. Burnishing can also be accomplished with diamond tools.

Cutoff (Parting) Tools

Cutoff tools are used on bar-type machines to part completed workpieces from the bar stock, pipe, or tube. A straight cutoff blade is a flat piece of tool steel generally having a cross section in the shape of a rectangle, trapezoid, or trapezium when the cross section is taken at right angles to its length. Various shapes, as shown in Fig. 23-18, are provided to fit the different holders and clamping devices in general use. The blade is furnished unsharpened, heat treated, and cut to length. These blades may be used in special holders for grooving and recessing. Dimensions of the straight cutoff blades are presented in ANSI Standard B94.3-1965 (reaffirmed 1972).

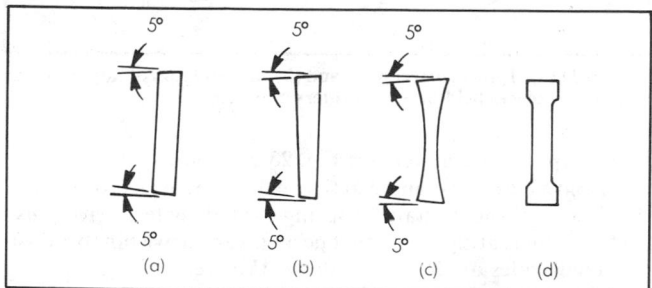

Fig. 23-18 Shapes for straight cutoff blades: (a) without side clearance, (b) with clearance on one side, (c) with concave side clearance, and (d) with channeled sides.

Cutoff tools are also manufactured by using the carbide insert concept. These tools usually consist of a toolholder, length-adjustable support blade, and replaceable insert. The insert can be made with built-in chip control which will produce chips narrower than the slot machined in the part. Some of the geometries for replaceable inserts are shown in Fig. 23-19.

A parting tool with a self-gripped insert is illustrated in Fig. 23-20. The carbide insert fits into a blade type of holder, and a wedging action caused by cutting forces clamps the insert in the blade. V-grooves in the top and bottom surfaces of the insert align the insert and mate with corresponding grooves in the

blade. The insert is removed by an extracting tool with a cam-shaped end. A chipbreaker geometry on the insert forms the chip in two axes for efficient disposal.

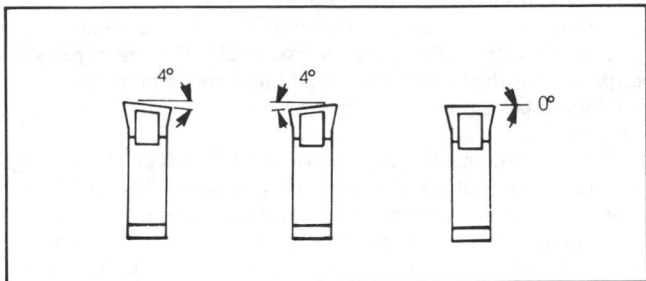

Fig. 23-19 Various geometries for carbide-insert type of cutoff tools. (*Valenite Div., Valeron Corp.*)

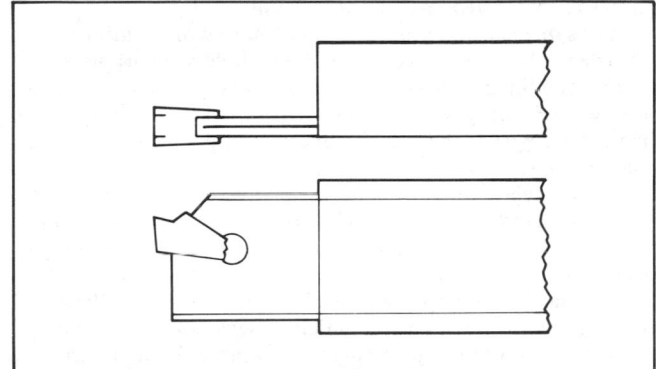

Fig. 23-20 Parting tool with self-gripped insert. (*Iscar Metals, Inc.*)

Qualified and Preset Tooling

Making trial cuts and tool adjustments by means of offsets and compensation systems in the controls of NC lathes can be time consuming and costly, and may cause damage to the workpiece, tools, or the machine. As a result, extensive use is made of qualified or preset tooling.

Qualified tooling. As previously mentioned, qualified (precision) holders for inserts are ground to locate the cutting edges to specified dimensions within a tolerance of ±0.003″ (0.08 mm). Most NC lathes and turning machines are offered with turrets and tool adapter blocks which accept standard qualified toolholders.

The combined accuracy of qualified holders and precision inserts sometimes eliminates the need for using tool offsets provided on the machine control, especially for roughing operations, thus speeding setup. Qualified tooling also facilitates programming and establishing tool positions without the need for presetting, thus reducing costs.

Preset tooling. The presetting of tools before they are brought to the machines offers the advantage of increased flexibility. Compensations can be made for resharpening or the changing of inserts, as well as for slightly altered dimensional requirements. A disadvantage is the cost of presetting equipment. This equipment ranges from relatively inexpensive fixtures or gages with dial indicators to costly precision presetting machines. Presetting machines are available with optical or electronic systems and microscopes, magnifiers, comparator screens, and digital readouts.

TURNING

WORKHOLDING FOR TURNING

Safe, fast, accurate, and rigid means of holding workpieces on lathes are critical requirements for successful turning. All the power required at the cutting tool must be transmitted through the workholding device to the workpiece. As a result, solid gripping of the workpiece is essential. This is especially important with the trend toward higher speed machining and the increased requirements for closer tolerances and smoother finishes.

Force requirements for safe workholding depend on many variables, including the geometry and overhang of the workpieces, workpiece materials and their properties, cutting tools used, speed and feed rates, and whether the workpieces must be kept free of marks and distortion. Formulas have been developed to calculate force requirements as they relate to safety factors, coefficients of friction, and other variables. A formula for force requirements that can be used with jaw-type chucks is presented later in this section.

The safe maximum speed for any rotary workholding device also depends on many factors. These include the workpiece size, shape, and finish; rigidity of the setup; the type and condition of the workholding device; the gripping force available at maximum speed; the type of operations performed; and the cutting tools used.

Major types of workholding devices are faceplates and fixtures, mandrels, jaw-type chucks, step chucks, collets, and, occasionally, magnetic and vacuum chucks. The workpiece, lathe, and tooling used often dictate the type of workholding device that can be employed. In many cases, however, the use of several types is possible and judicious selection is required.

Regardless of the type used, the workpiece should be gripped on the largest diameter practical. This assures a favorable relationship between the gripping and cutting diameters to accommodate torque more easily. Workpieces should also be gripped as close to the faces of chucks as possible.

Between-Center Turning Operations

Many workpieces, particularly shorter parts, are turned on chucking-type lathes without the use of centers. This is done with chucks, collets, or other workholding devices, or by bolting workpieces or fixtures directly to the faceplates of lathes. Some faceplates are equipped with jaws for rotating large-diameter workpieces. Many other workpieces, particularly longer ones, require support on one or two lathe centers with at least one steadyrest in between.

Types of centers. Some of the various centers, both live and dead types, used on lathes are illustrated in Fig. 23-21. Headstock centers always rotate with the lathe spindles and workpieces. Tailstock centers may be of the live type, rotating with the workpiece, or the dead type, stationary.

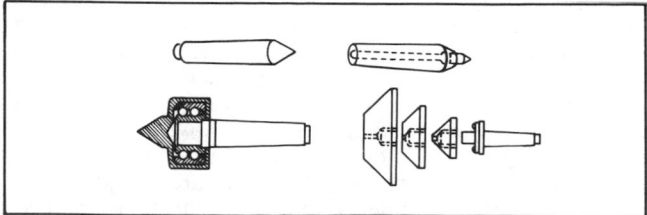

Fig. 23-21 Various types of centers, live and dead, used on lathes.

Rotating the workpiece. Workpiece rotation by means of a headstock-mounted chuck or collet provides a rigid setup and minimizes any chance of chatter during machining. More precise results, however, can often be obtained by supporting the workpiece between two centers.

Rotation of a workpiece held between centers is accomplished with a slotted driver plate, such as the one shown in Fig. 23-22, view a, mounted on the spindle nose of the lathe. A lathe dog, several types of which are shown in Fig. 23-22, view b, is secured to the workpiece, and the bent end (tail) of the dog is positioned in one of the slots in the driver plate. A compensating chuck, with either a solid or spring-loaded center, can also be used to rotate workpieces between centers.

Face drivers. When the design of the workpiece permits, exerting driving power on one face of the workpiece can increase productivity. Face drivers permit machining the entire OD of a part in one clamping, as well as turning at high speeds. A high degree of accuracy is maintained because the position of the workpiece does not have to be changed.

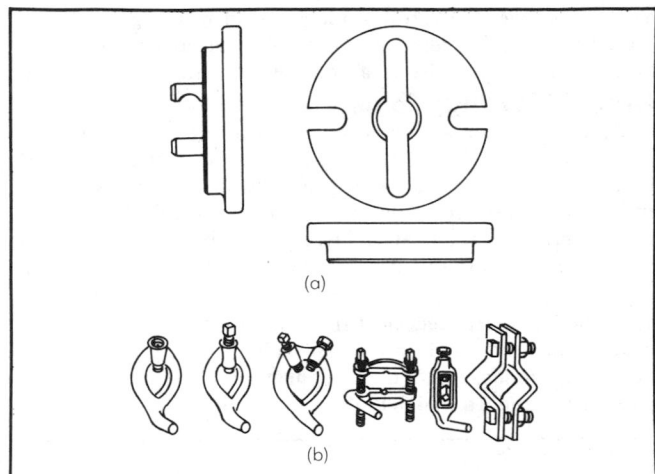

Fig. 23-22 (a) Typical driver plate and (b) various types of dogs used to rotate workpieces held between centers on a lathe.

One type of face driver (see Fig. 23-23) consists of a driving head and a locating shank that fits on the spindle nose of a lathe. The driving head contains a spring-loaded center, drive pins, and a compensating device that permits each drive pin to adjust to irregularities on the face of the workpiece.

As the lathe tailstock applies axial force to the workpiece, the center of the driver retracts slightly against its spring pressure to allow the chisel-edged drive pins to bite into the end face of the workpiece. During cutting, torque is increased and the pins bite deeper into the face for positive clamping. Some workpiece faces have holes and the driving pins enter the holes.

Use of mandrels. Hollow and tubular workpieces are often mounted on mandrels for internal gripping. There is some interchangeability between the terms mandrel and arbor. For the purposes of this discussion, however, the term mandrel is used to describe workholding devices and the term arbor is used to describe devices for holding cutting tools and grinding wheels.

Three types of mandrels for internal gripping are: pin type, expanding type, and threaded type. Pin-type mandrels are used for gripping cast, forged, or rough bores. Three or six pins or

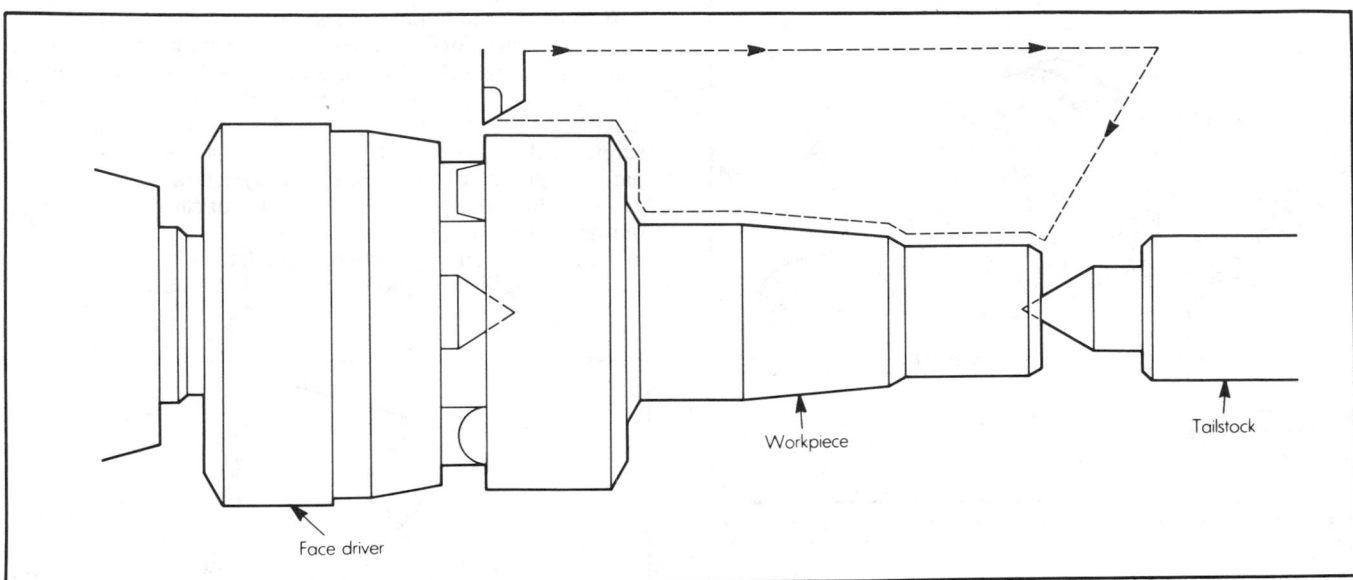

Fig. 23-23 Face driver permits turning entire OD of workpiece mounted between centers in one clamping.

shoes move outward to centralize and grip the parts. These pins are usually power operated through a drawbar that is attached to the mandrel to push the pins, by cam action, through openings in the body of the mandrel. Figure 23-24 illustrates an expanding mandrel with serrated shoes for gripping a 34″ (864 mm) long workpiece.

Expanding bushing type mandrels are generally used in smooth or finished bores. They usually provide better concentricity (end to end) than solid plug mandrels because the bore tolerance does not affect the accuracy as expansion centralizes the workpiece. One type of expanding-bushing mandrel consists of a tapered shaft assembly, threaded on one end, over which various-sized slotted sleeves with a corresponding taper can be fitted to suit a number of workpieces. Rotation of a clamping bolt in the end of the shaft forces the sleeve up the tapered surface on the shaft to grip the workpiece. Drive can be a problem with this type of mandrel, and the use of a drive pin is suggested when possible if heavy cuts are

to be taken.

Mandrels are not limited to workpieces having finished or smooth bores. If the ID is a rough cast surface having a dimensional variation wider than that which can be handled by an expanding sleeve, a segmented sleeve such as the one shown in Fig. 23-25 is used. Segmented sleeves can handle ID variations of 1/8″ (3.2 mm) or more; on large workpieces, variations up to 3/4″ (19 mm) are possible. Segmented sleeves consist of three individual segments held together with spring bands. These sleeves may have serrated segments, or they can be used with end locators.

If the end locating surfaces of workpieces have previously been machined square with the bores to be gripped, locators that are flat and square are used. If not, compensating locators must be used. The locators or end stops are sometimes serrated to increase the driving force.

When the ID is relatively small compared to the OD of a workpiece, expanding mandrels can be used with auxiliary

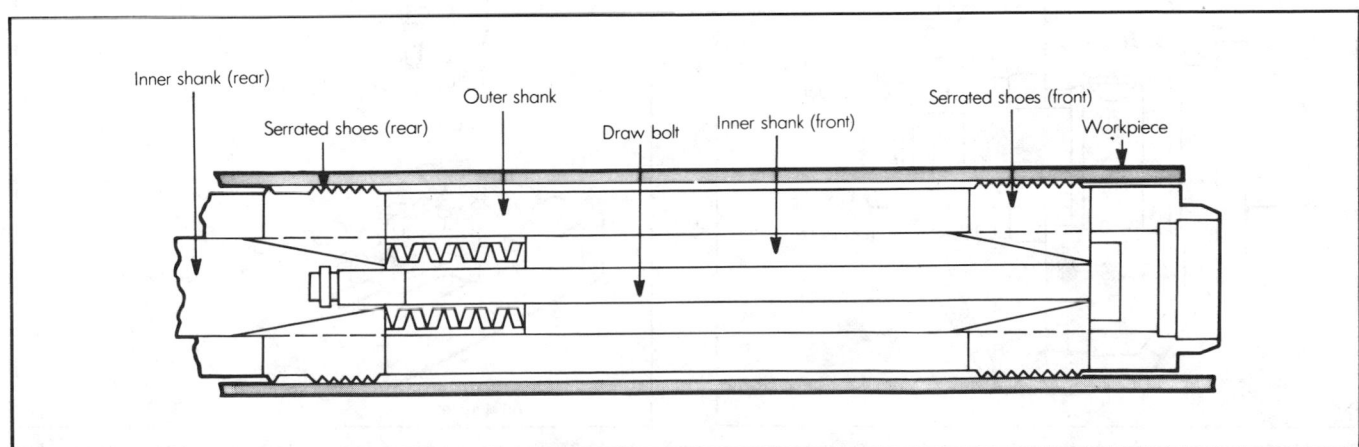

Fig. 23-24 Expanding mandrel and serrated shoes for gripping iong, thin-wall workpieces. (*Erickson Div., Kennametal Inc.*)

TURNING

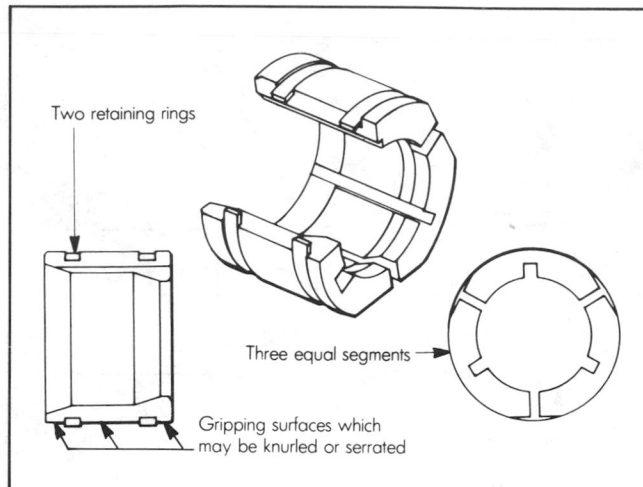

Fig. 23-25 Three-segment sleeve for handling ID variations. (*Erickson Div., Kennametal Inc.*)

clamp supports for increased rigidity. An expanding mandrel and a set of outboard clamps (see Fig. 23-26) is used for rigid holding and positive positioning of gear blanks. In the unit illustrated in Fig. 23-26, an inner threaded locknut forces the expanding sleeve up the mandrel. To simplify removal of the OD support for workpiece mounting, a plate with a swing-out C-clamp is employed. After the workpiece is mounted on the mandrel, the threaded locknut is tightened and locked and the end-clamps are applied.

Threaded mandrels, both ring and plug types, provide means of locating from threads on workpieces. Holding is done by running the workpiece onto the threaded locator and against a stop. The stop can be made retractable to facilitate unloading. Threaded mandrels can be mounted to chuck faces, and the jaw movement used to position and retract the top.

Steadyrests and follower rests. Long, slender workpieces are often supported for between-center turning by steadyrests or follower rests (see Fig. 23-27). When work is mounted between centers, a general rule-of-thumb is that any part having a length-to-diameter ratio of 10:1 or more requires some kind of support. More than one rest is frequently used for very long parts or precision operations. Steadyrests are also used to support the outer ends of chucked workpieces for facing, boring, and other operations.

Steadyrests can be clamped to the lathe bed at any desired position along the workpiece length. Follower rests are attached

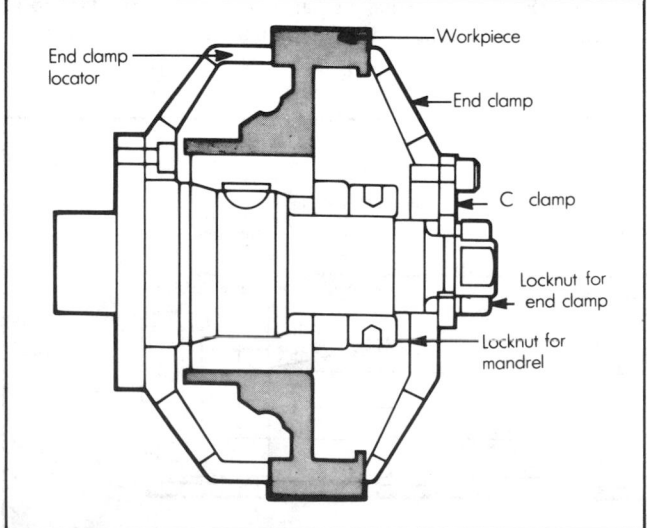

Fig. 23-26 Expanding mandrel and outboard clamps for holding gear blank. (*Erickson Div., Kennametal Inc.*)

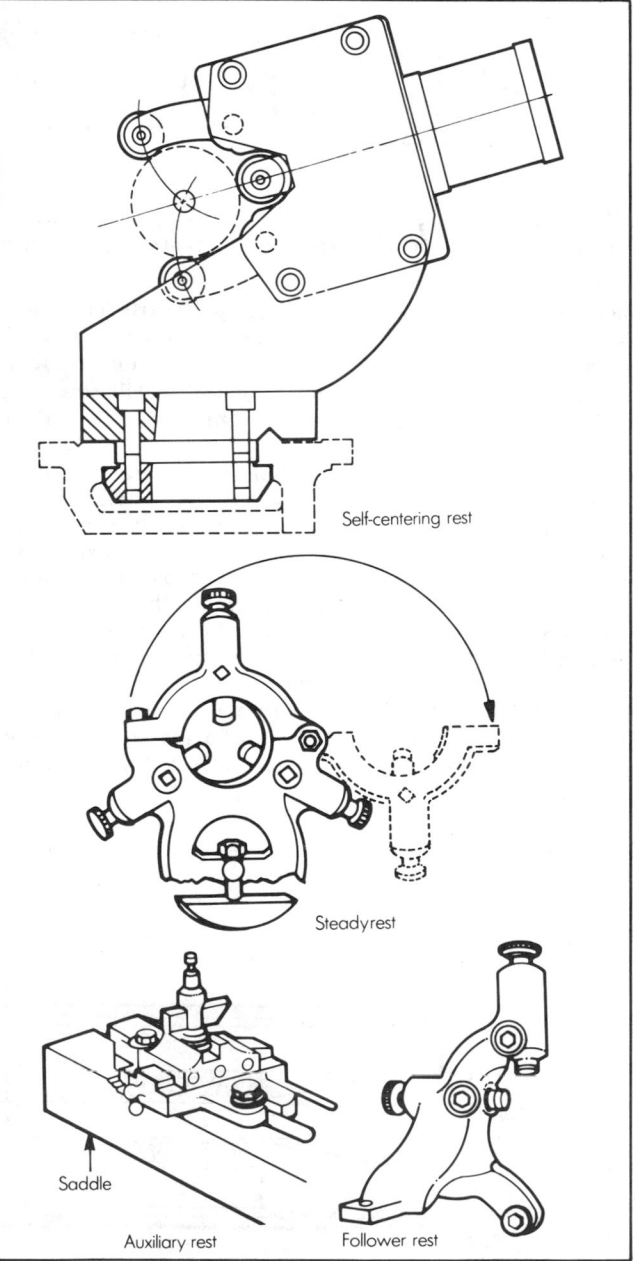

Fig. 23-27 Typical steadyrest, auxiliary rest, and follower rest used to support long workpieces on lathes.

to the carriages of lathes and support the workpieces at points opposite the cutting tools. Auxiliary or full-swing rests mount on the forward wings of lathe saddles for turning to the maximum diameter capacities of the machines.

Steadyrests can be the self-centering or independent-jaw type and can be hand or power operated. They generally consist of a frame containing adjustable or telescoping jaws or rollers to provide three-point bearing. The frame of a steadyrest is usually hinged on one side, allowing the upper half to swing open to facilitate loading and unloading workpieces. Some are designed to automatically open and close, thus permitting turning operations to pass the rest without interference.

Surfaces on which the rests are to ride should be smooth or machined prior to the lathe operation, before the jaws or rolls are brought to bear against the surfaces. On most NC lathes, the steadyrest can be controlled by the NC unit.

Collets for Lathes

Collets, also called collet or bar chucks, are workholding devices used to grip workpieces or stock—including cold-drawn and centerless ground bars having smooth or machined surfaces—on smaller size lathes and other machine tools. Advantages of collets include high holding power because of their large contact area with the stock, the absence of clamping marks normally left by chucks, and relatively low cost. Also, they do not lose their gripping force due to centrifugal effects.

A collet is usually seated directly in the spindle of a lathe. In operation, the collet opens under its own spring tension to allow bar stock to be fed through it or workpieces to be placed in it. The collet is then closed to securely grip the stock or workpiece.

Collets are hollow steel cylinders generally having slots extending along most of their length, with a tapered OD at the closing end and, in some cases, ID threads at one end for mounting stock stops and OD threads at the opposite end for connecting to a draw bar. They are available in fractional, decimal, letter, number, and metric sizes for holding round, square, rectangular, hexagonal, and special-shaped stock. While most collets are made to hold stock on-center, they can be designed to hold stock off-center any desired distance, as is required for eccentric or odd-shaped workpieces.

Serrated, taper hole, step, plug chuck, and extended-nose collets provide additional means to grip stock. So-called emergency collets have a pilot hole that can be drilled or bored to required size. This design is useful for short production runs or when exact collet sizes are not readily available. The three basic collet styles used for metalcutting are stationary, push out, and draw in. These styles are illustrated in Fig. 23-28; the draw-in collet shown has interchangeable serrated pads.

Jaw-Type Chucks

Chucks for use on engine, toolroom, turret, and automatic lathes are designed to fit the spindle noses specified in ANSI Standard B5.9-1967 (reaffirmed 1972). Dimensions of the chucks and jaws are listed, and classifications for different types of duty are specified in ANSI Standard B5.8-1972 (reaffirmed 1979). At present, however, this standard is incomplete in that it does not cover many chuck designs now available.

Chuck selection. In selecting a chuck, a complete analysis of the requirements for the specific application should be made. Factors that must be considered include the size range of the workpieces to be machined, setup and tooling to be used, speed of the operation, production requirements, and jaw forces

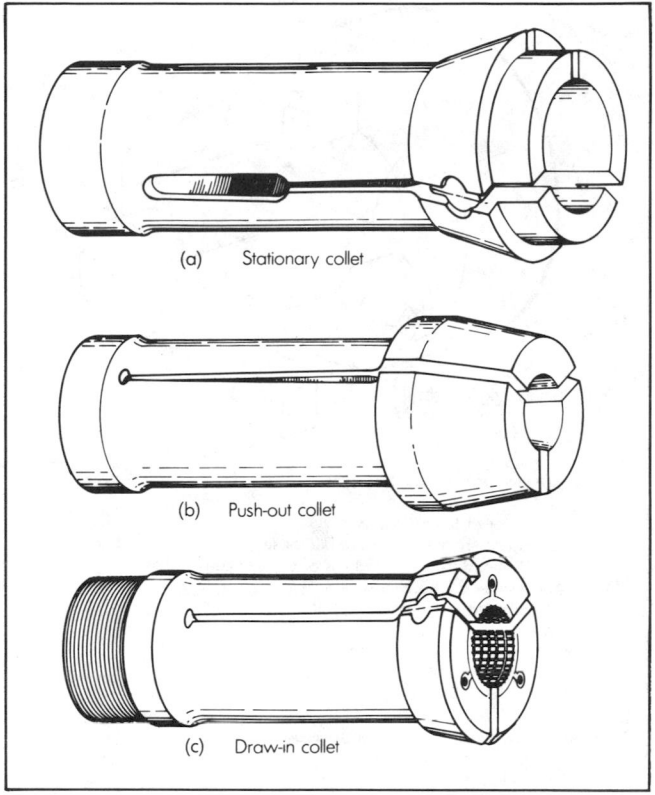

Fig. 23-28 Three basic styles of collets are: (a) stationary, (b) push-out, and (c) draw-in.

necessary to hold the workpieces rigidly.

Jaw forces required to drive a workpiece can be computed from the formula presented in Fig. 23-29. This formula is only recommended for relatively short or tailstock-supported workpieces and when the axial force is absorbed through a workpiece stop. Gripping forces vary widely, depending upon the size and design of the chuck. Typical gripping forces for a 10" (254 mm) diam chuck are 5000-8500 lb (22.2-37.8 kN) per jaw; for a 24" (610 mm) diam chuck, typical gripping forces are 10,000-22,000 lb (44.5-97.9 kN). Chucks are generally guaranteed to maintain from 50-75% of their rated gripping force at maximum speed. Some are provided with internal jaw locks that maintain gripping force in case of power failure or stripped threads on the drawbar or tube. Chucks are available for operation at speeds in the range 4000-6000 rpm or more.

Chucks with improved accuracy are now available to take full advantage of the improved accuracy of NC lathes. Accuracies of 0.001" (0.03 mm) TIR and repeatability of 0.0005" (0.013 mm) are not uncommon for chucks 15" (380 mm) or less in diameter.

Types of chucks. Lathe chucks are available in a wide variety of types and designs, and are either manually or power actuated. Manually operated chucks are generally restricted to toolroom, maintenance, or limited production requirements because the time required for chucking may take longer than for machining. Power chucks cost more, but are faster and more productive. They also permit adjusting the gripping force to suit various requirements. Major types of chucks are independent and self-centering.

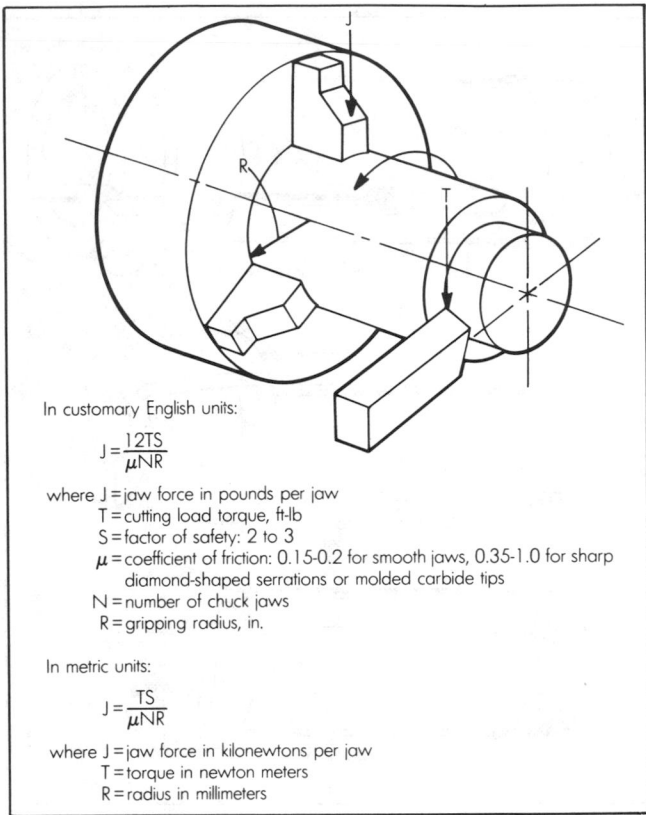

In customary English units:

$$J = \frac{12TS}{\mu NR}$$

where J = jaw force in pounds per jaw
T = cutting load torque, ft-lb
S = factor of safety: 2 to 3
μ = coefficient of friction: 0.15-0.2 for smooth jaws, 0.35-1.0 for sharp diamond-shaped serrations or molded carbide tips
N = number of chuck jaws
R = gripping radius, in.

In metric units:

$$J = \frac{TS}{\mu NR}$$

where J = jaw force in kilonewtons per jaw
T = torque in newton meters
R = radius in millimeters

Fig. 23-29 Formula for computing jaw force requirements to drive a workpiece on a lathe.

Independent chucks. In an independent chuck, each individual workholding jaw can be moved toward or away from the workpiece without influencing the other jaws. They are widely used to grip square or irregular-shaped workpieces. Most independent chucks are constructed with four equally spaced jaws (see Fig. 23-30), but they are also available with two jaws for irregular-shaped castings and forgings that have to be trued up individually before machining.

Independent motion of the jaws on these chucks is accomplished by a screw beneath each jaw which is fixed to the chuck body by a thrust ring. A mating screw thread is machined in the bottom of each jaw. When the operating screw is rotated by a wrench inserted in a socket in the end of the screw, the jaw moves inward or outward, depending upon the direction of screw rotation. With this design, high mechanical advantages are achieved, usually in a ratio of 30-40:1.

Independent chucks require more time to grip workpieces than self-centering and power types; they also require skill and care in setup. The jaws should be indicated to assure that their grip points are a constant distance from the center of rotation. This is necessary to minimize vibration and chatter.

Self-centering chucks. This type of chuck is available in a wide variety of styles and configurations. One is the scroll, or geared-scroll, chuck which is still the most commonly used for general applications in holding round work. These chucks are particularly suitable for short-run requirements of a large variety of workpieces. Combination chucks are also available having both self-centering and independent jaw action.

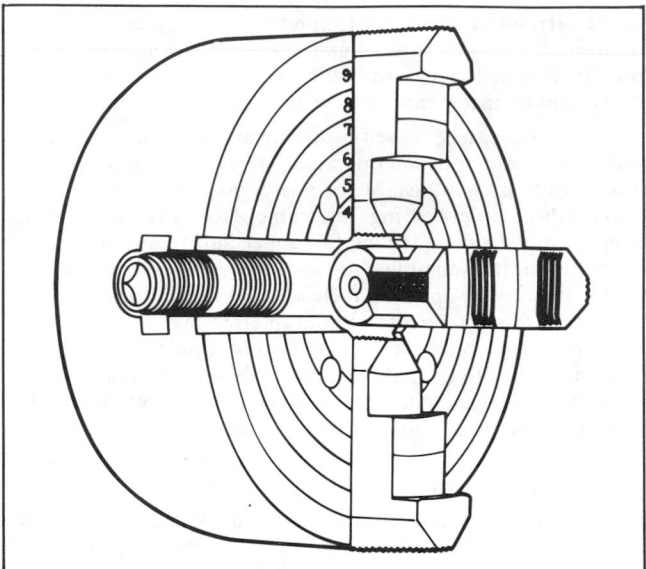

Fig. 23-30 Four-jaw independent chuck (shown with one jaw removed) for gripping irregular-shaped workpieces. (*Cushman Industries, Inc.*)

A three-jaw, self-centering chuck of geared-scroll design is shown in Fig. 23-31. In this design, a pinion is rotated by a manual or power operated driver which, in turn, rotates a gear mounted on a plate. On the reverse side of the gear plate is a face gear commonly referred to as a scroll. Teeth on the scroll engage similar teeth cut in the back of the master jaws.

The set of three jaws on a geared-scroll chuck are matched with the proper offsets so that they move simultaneously toward the chuck center to engage the workpiece and hold it concentric with powerful gripping action. These chucks are made in light, medium, and heavy-duty series to suit various jobs to be performed. It is important that the proper chuck be selected for a specific application to assure accuracy and longevity of the mechanism.

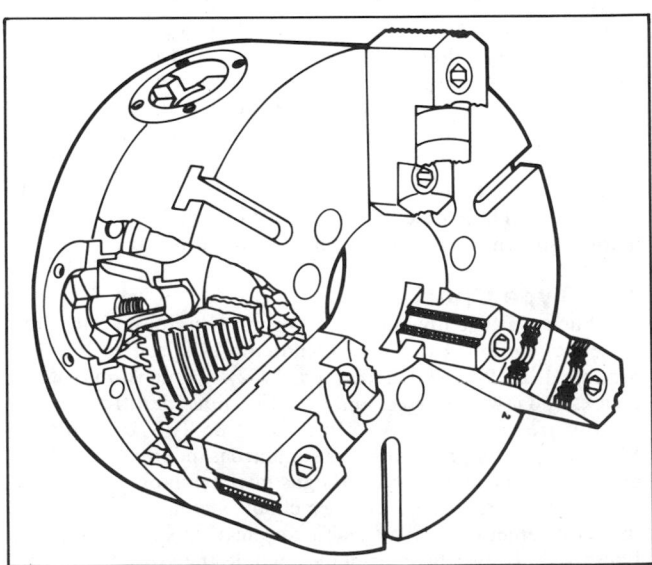

Fig. 23-31 Three-jaw self-centering chuck of geared-scroll design. (*Cushman Industries, Inc.*)

For larger sized lathes, self-centering, geared-scroll chucks can be operated by a wrench powered electrically, hydraulically, or pneumatically. Power-wrench chucks provide a more powerful yet consistent gripping pressure and thereby relieve the operator of a strenuous task.

Power chucks. Power chucks operated by a pneumatically or hydraulically powered drawbar or tube, or having a self-contained power actuating device, are better suited for medium-to-long, repetitive production runs. Many NC lathes are provided with chucks such as these.

Power chucks typically have a shorter jaw stroke than independent or geared-scroll chucks and generally must be equipped with top jaws suited to the workpieces to be machined. Most power chucks have a jaw movement limited to about 3/8 to 1/2″ (9.5 to 12.7 mm) per jaw. This permits a variation of about 1″ (25.4 mm) on the gripping diameter, but the contour of the top jaws does not permit the best gripping condition on all diameters within the range. It is therefore recommended that the variation be limited to about 1/4″ (6.3 mm) on diameters to be gripped with the same set of top jaws. Chuck jaws are discussed later in this section.

Many different designs of power chucks are available from various manufacturers. The higher speed capability of modern NC lathes has necessitated the development of improved power chucks to provide better retention of gripping force under increased centrifugal forces. Most power chucks are either wedge or lever type.

Other Types of Chucks

Many other types of chucks are used on lathes. These include diaphragm, spring-jaw, trunnion-type, indexing, pot, and oval chucks, as well as various proprietary devices.

Chucking Fixtures

Chucking fixtures, used extensively for second-operation work, are generally designed to fit specific workpieces or types of workpieces. Workpieces can be located by using a plug to fit a bore or a ring for an OD. Pins that fit small holes in the workpiece face can also be used for location. When using a solid locating plug or ring, the eccentricity, end to end, will be equal to the diameter tolerance on the gripping diameter plus the tolerance on the locating member and the clearance allowed.

Clamping is done by using power or hand-operated finger clamps or a drawrod and C-washer. Care should be taken that clamping is done through a solid section directly opposite the back stops to prevent distortion of the workpiece. On fragile castings, jackscrews to support sections of the casting may be brought out and locked after the part is located and clamped in the fixture.

Magnetic and Vacuum Chucks

While magnetic and vacuum chucks are more commonly used on machine tables for grinding and milling, they are also employed occasionally for light-duty turning operation. These operations are generally of the precision type and involve shallow cuts. Vacuum or magnetic chucks can be designed to hold many different odd-shaped parts and often eliminate problems of distortion when fragile thin-walled components are to be turned.

THE BORING PROCESS

Boring is a precision machining process for generating internal cylindrical forms by removing metal with single-point tools or tools with multiple cutting edges. This process is most commonly performed with the workpiece held stationary and the cutting tool both rotating and advancing into the work. Boring is also done, however, with the cutting tool stationary and the workpiece rotating.

Common applications for boring include the enlarging or finishing of cored, pierced, or drilled holes and contoured internal surfaces. Related operations sometimes performed simultaneously with boring include turning, facing, chamfering, grooving, and threading.

Applications of boring can be divided into heavy cutting and precision operations. Heavy boring is generally done on large horizontal and vertical boring machines, including vertical turret lathes and boring, drilling, and milling machines. These machines and other machines also used for boring—such as automatic lathes, multispindle bar and chucking machines, machining centers, and transfer machines.

Precision boring is performed on machines specifically designed for this purpose. These machines generally take relatively light cuts, maintain close tolerances, and are often capable of high production rates.

ACCURACY IN PRECISION BORING

Accuracies that can be maintained in precision boring operations depend upon many factors. These include the design and condition of the boring machine and spindles used, proper workholding equipment, the correct cutting tool material and geometry, and optimum cutting speeds and feed rates. The design of the machine tool is one of the most important factors in the economic achievement of desired results.

For very close tolerance requirements, temperature is an important factor. Heat generated during the cutting process may have to be dissipated by the flow of cutting fluid, and the fluid itself may have to be temperature controlled to obtain the necessary tolerances. In some cases, it may be necessary to use thermal-controlled machine components or to install the boring machine in a temperature-controlled room.

PRECISION-BORING MACHINES

Precision-boring machines are available in a wide variety of types to suit many different applications. Configurations include single or multiple spindles arranged horizontally, vertically, or at any required angle. Selection of the type to be used depends primarily upon the size and configuration of the workpieces, operations to be performed, and production requirements.

Cutting tool or workpiece rotation for precision boring depends upon the specific application and the size, shape, and balance of the workpiece. The ability to rotate workpieces or tooling makes it possible to perform many difficult operations simultaneously or in sequence. It also assures concentric diameters and square faces, which are difficult to obtain when a workpiece is relocated for separate operations. Irregularly shaped and/or unbalanced workpieces are generally bored with

BORING

rotating tools. Rotating tools and multiple spindles are also often used when several holes have to be bored in the same workpiece. Rotation of the workpiece is sometimes preferred for more complex operations.

Operational Methods

Methods of operating the slides on precision-boring machines are divided into three major types: hydraulic, cam, and ballscrew.

Hydraulic operation. The most common method of operation for precision-boring machines has been with hydraulic cylinders. This method has the advantage of providing considerable flexibility in slide control. Infinite variation in feed rates is possible by adjusting control orifices, and one or two feed rates can usually be readily set for each direction of travel. Relatively high rapid-traverse rates are also available with hydraulic operation.

Advances in servo controls have virtually eliminated the previous disadvantage of possible erratic feed rates. Independent temperature-controlled hydraulic units, coupled with advanced design, silent-vane, hydraulic pumps help minimize heat generation which could affect accuracy. External mounting of the hydraulic manifolds, valves, and piping also tend to reduce heat. Noise levels have been reduced too. Programmable controllers can provide sequenced cycle capability to suit various requirements.

Cam operation. Cam-operated machines have become increasingly popular because they offer more accurate and consistent control of feed rates. Two cams (one for each axis of motion) are mechanically connected to provide precise timing and cycle control so that operations can be sequenced without complicated controls. Rapid traverse is usually obtained by the operation of pneumatic cylinders.

More recently, the disadvantage of having to change cams to vary the feed rate has been eliminated with the introduction of silicon controlled rectifier (SCR) controlled, variable-speed, d-c feed motors that are directly coupled to the cams.

Ballscrew operation. The operation of slides on precision-boring machines with screws having Acme threads is virtually obsolete. The use of precision ballscrews for slide operation, however, is increasing because of the more widespread use of numerical control for these machines.

Ballscrew operation provides a more reliable and consistent feed than hydraulic cylinders and is particularly advantageous for very low feed rates. Operation with ballscrews, however, tends to be more expensive and is less flexible than hydraulic operation for selecting and changing feed rates unless NC is employed.

Precision Boring Spindles

The success of any precision boring machine depends largely upon the precision characteristics of the spindle. Selection of a spindle requires careful consideration because a wide variety of sizes and types is available to suit specific applications. Spindles may be broadly divided into the following basic types: (1) ball and roller-bearing spindles, (2) high-precision heated or cooled spindles, (3) cluster spindles, (4) motorized spindles, (5) hydrostatic spindles, (6) air-bearing spindles, (7) permanently lubricated bearing spindles, and (8) forced-air or mist-lubricated spindles. Configuration of the spindle nose also varies considerably according to the requirements of the job. The most common flange type has an accurate register diameter and a

number of holes for retaining boring bars, rotating tools, chucks, arbors, or fixtures for rotating parts. Spindles are often hollow to allow for a rod to pass through the spindle to operate chucks, arbors, facing heads, or size-control units. Operation is usually performed by a hydraulically or pneumatically operated cylinder mounted on, and rotating with, the spindle at the rear or drive end.

Spindles are most commonly belt-driven, but for large heavy-duty spindles, worm, helical, or spur gear-boxes may be used to obtain speed reduction. High-speed spindles may be conveniently driven by motors mounted directly on the spindle shaft.

The selection of spindles is influenced by many considerations, including (1) speed of rotation, (2) direction and magnitude of loads, (3) accuracy, (4) surface finish, (5) mounting requirements, (6) drive requirements, and (7) dimensional limitations, such as overhang and center distance.

Special spindle designs may be necessary to suit certain requirements, particularly in the case of multiple-spindle setups in which a cluster of spindles assembled into one housing may be necessary because of a requirement for close centers.

The most recent development in spindles is in the application of hydrostatic and air bearings. These employ a separation of the rotating shafts and, essentially, provide a bearing of high-pressure oil or air film. The bearings have a higher potential for accuracy and for maintaining accuracy over a long period of time. Air-bearing spindles also are ideal for high-speed application, particularly when high accuracies are required because of the relatively low heat generated at the spindle bearings.

Types of Precision Boring Machines

Many types of precision-boring machines are available. Major types include horizontal single and double-end machines, center-drive machines, vertical machines, way-type machines, and NC machines.

Since heat and vibration are major deterrents to the accuracies and finishes required in precision boring, heavy-duty rigid bases are required for the machines to minimize problems of chatter and vibration. Also, to isolate vibrations and avoid heat distortion of machine components, all electrical, hydraulic, and drive equipment is generally located external to the base.

Horizontal single-end machines. A typical horizontal precision-boring machine arranged for single-end operation is illustrated in Fig. 23-32. The single spindle is mounted on a bridge over the table at the left-hand end of this hydraulically operated machine. These single-end machines can be provided with two or more spindles depending upon the size of the workpieces, operation to be performed, and production requirements. Spindle noses and tool shanks for horizontal boring machines are specified in ANSI Standard B5.40-1977.

Single-end boring machines can also be arranged with cross slides to provide either linear motion or feed motions in a direction at a right angle to the direction of slide travel. In addition, the cross slide can be fitted with a manual or automatically operated, indexing or rotary table for mounting workholding fixtures. Tailstocks can also be mounted on the machines for between-center operations.

Additional buildup can be made on this type of boring machine by adding a toolholding turret to an indexing table located on the cross slide. This configuration permits multiple turning and facing-type operations to be performed when the spindle(s) is equipped with a chuck for rotating the workpiece. The machines are also often arranged with automatic loading and unloading equipment to shorten the cycle time.

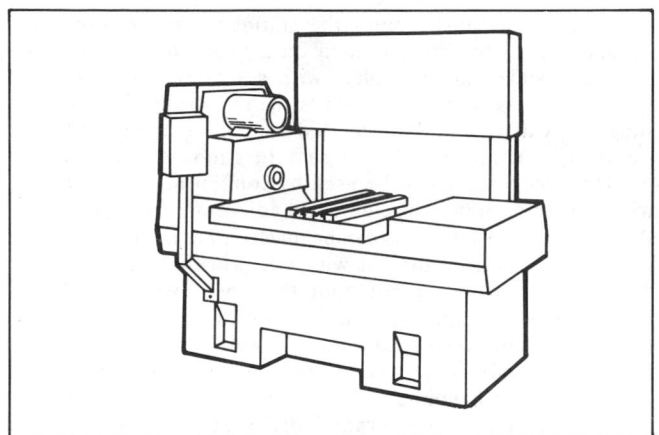

Fig. 23-32 Horizontal, single-spindle, precision-boring machine.

Double-end machines. Horizontal precision-boring machines can also be arranged for double-end operation (see Fig. 23-33). This is accomplished by also mounting a bridge and spindle(s) at the right-hand end of the machine. One or more spindles can be provided at each end; the machine shown in Fig. 23-33 has a total of four spindles.

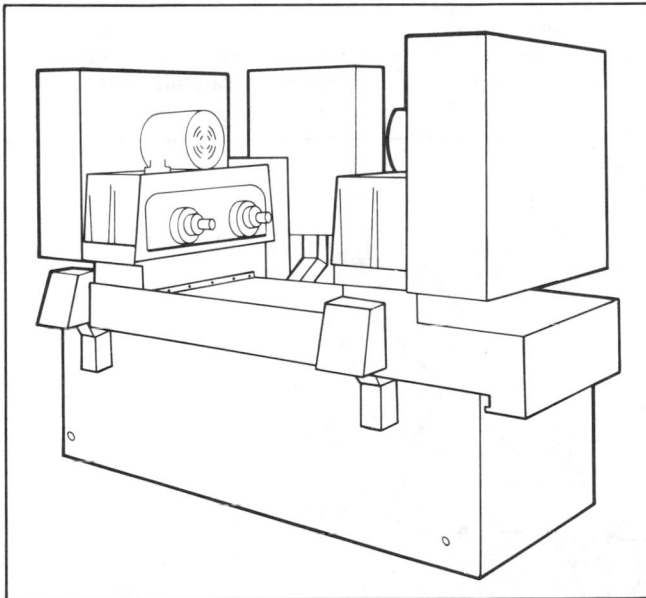

Fig. 23-33 Horizontal, double-end, precision-boring machine with four spindles.

On double-end machines, an operator often loads workpieces on or unloads them from one end while parts on the other end are being machined, thereby saving what otherwise would be downtime for loading and unloading workpieces. As is the case with single-end machines, various attachments are available to improve production.

Workpieces are generally rotated by chucks or fixtures on the spindles for turning-type operations; tools are mounted on the cross slide. For boring, tools are mounted on the spindle

quills and rotated, and the workpieces are mounted on the cross slide. Automatic cycling, tool-wear adjustment, gaging, and workpiece locating and clamping are available.

Center-drive machines. A double-end, cam-controlled, center-drive boring and contouring machine is illustrated in Fig. 23-34. Contouring slides at each end of the center-driven spindles have cam-controlled strokes. Boring, facing, and contouring can be performed on both ends of the workpieces simultaneously, thus assuring concentricity of opposing bores.

On these center-drive machines, workpieces must be held on their outside surfaces by collet or diaphragm chucks mounted within hollow spindle shafts. The angular configuration of the frame on the machine shown in Fig. 23-34 is used to minimize the loading reach to the rear spindle and to provide adequate slope for chip disposal.

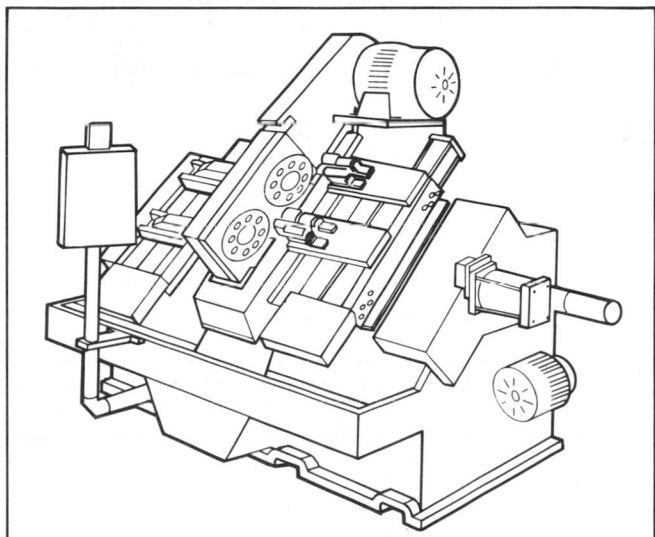

Fig. 23-34 Cam-operated, center-drive, precision-boring machine with two spindles.

Vertical machines. Precision-boring machines with vertical spindles and tools fed from above are often preferred for heavier workpieces. This design facilitates loading and unloading, makes it easier to adjust and change tools, and requires less floor space. Like most other precision-boring machines, these machines can be supplied for completely automatic cycling, controlled by hard-wired relay logic or a programmable controller.

A typical precision-boring machine arranged with two vertical spindles is shown in Fig. 23-35. Turning, facing, contouring, and boring-type operations are performed by means of a compound slide on which the cutting tools are mounted. The machine illustrated is cam operated, but a hydraulic machine would look essentially the same. The cylinder shown in Fig. 23-35 holds the cam followers against the cam and retracts the vertical slide to its uppermost position for easier loading and unloading.

Way-type machines. A way-type precision-boring machine, in its simplest configuration, can be essentially the same as a single-end boring machine, with one exception. Instead of the spindle and motor being stationary on a bridge at one end of the machine, with a hydraulically operated table on a slide in the middle of the machine, the design is reversed. With a way-type

BORING

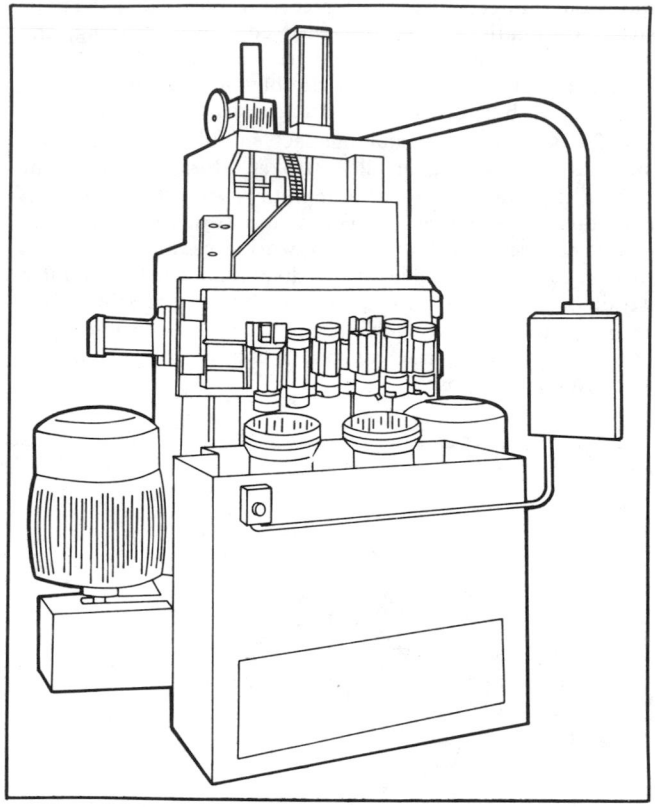

Fig. 23-35 Cam-operated precision-boring machine with two vertical spindles.

machine, the table becomes the stationary section and the spindle and motor are mounted on a hydraulically operated table and slide unit, complete with a self-contained motor-spindle drive system. This permits the self-contained spindle-slide unit, with its spindle-mounted tool, to traverse toward the stationary machine table holding a fixture-mounted workpiece.

This same feature can be used by configuring the machine with two self-contained slide units adjacent to one another. With this design, two parts can be machined at a time when the stationary table is equipped with two workholding fixtures. Another version, depending upon the type of workpieces and production requirements, is an end-loading way-type machine with workholding fixture(s) at that same end and self-contained spindle-slide units traversing toward the operator and fixtures. These way-type machine tools are quite versatile, permitting spindle-slide units to operate individually, simultaneously, and/or sequentially.

Dial-type machines. Precision-boring machines can also be set up as way-type machines. These concepts lead to dial-type configurations in which all the self-contained spindle-slide units are in a circle, mounted on slide wings, and simultaneously traversing toward the center. The center portion of these machines is usually equipped with a large indexing table and subplate containing several workholding chucks or fixtures. The indexing table automatically positions at each station (or wing) having a self-contained spindle-slide unit with its tooling.

Dial-type machines are fully automatic; the operator simply loads and unloads parts as the machine indexes and the slide units traverse in and out (see Fig. 23-36). These machines are usually designed for high production requirements. They can also be equipped with tool-mounted vertical slide units and/or

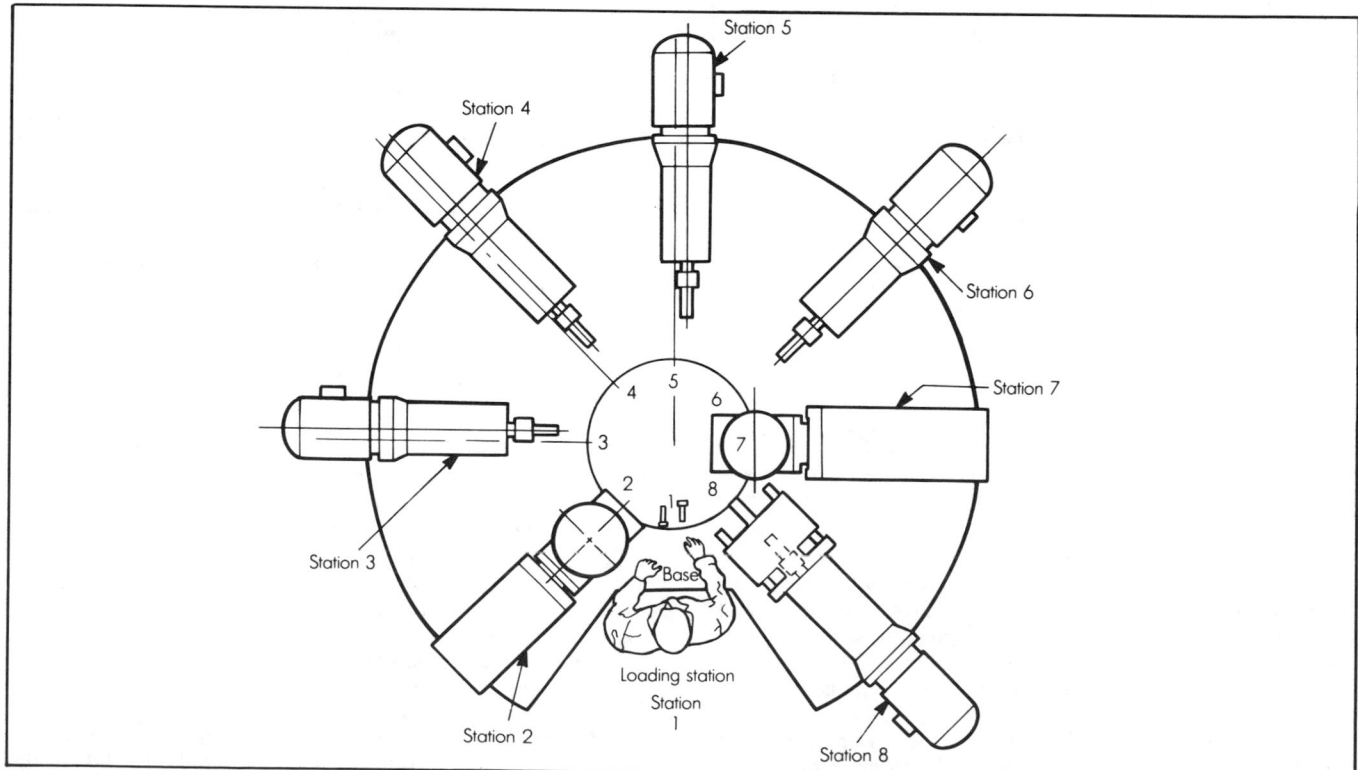

Fig. 23-36 Dial-type precision-boring machine having eight stations. (*Wadell Equipment Co., Inc.*)

hopper feeding for bushing or bearing insertions during the automatic cycle.

NC boring machines. One type of numerically controlled precision-boring machine is illustrated in Fig. 23-37. This horizontal, ballscrew-actuated, CNC machine has three spindles for high-volume production. These machines are also available with one, two, or four spindles and can operate at high metal removal rates with close tolerance capabilities. They also offer the flexibility necessary for high-volume production. Electric servo axes and variable-speed spindle drives allow infinitely programmable variations of spindle speeds, feed rates, and tooling-path control.

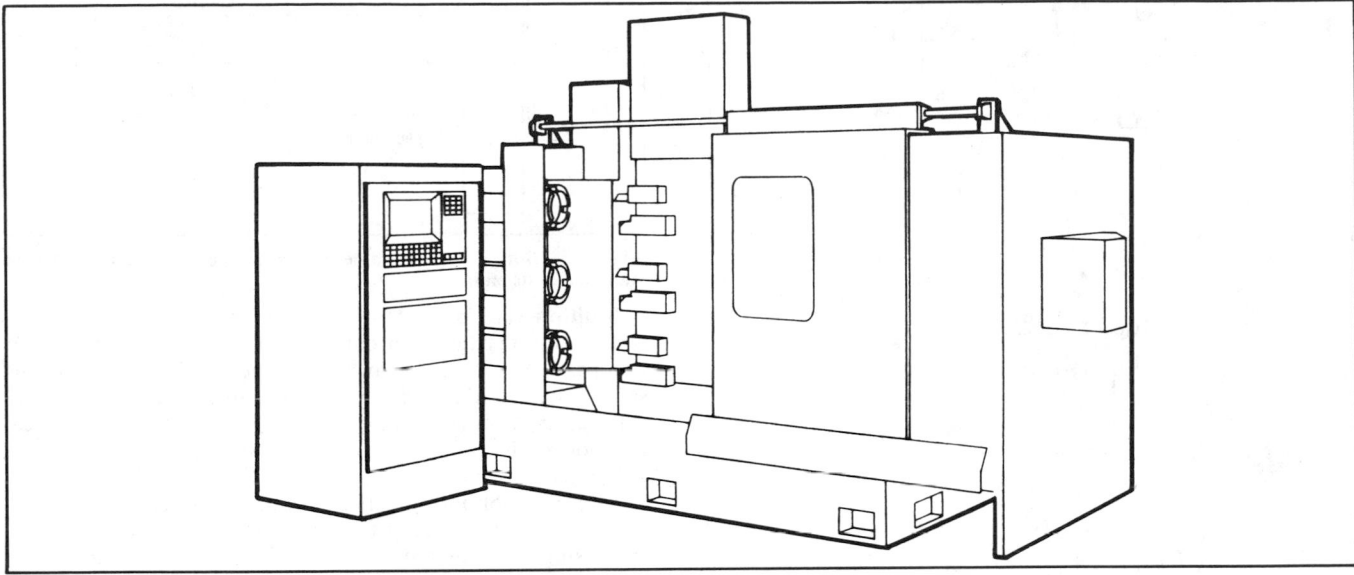

Fig. 23-37 CNC precision-boring machine having three spindles for high production. (*The Olofsson Corp.*)

BORING TOOLS

Boring operations are usually harder on cutting tools than turning operations because of the confined machining area, which can cause chip removal problems, especially from deeper and smaller diameter bores. As a result, the size, strength, and stiffness of boring tools are often limited by hole size and length of cut. If the chips nest or pack, the cutting tools take considerable abuse.

Solid and Tipped Boring Tools

While indexable inserts are used most extensively for boring tools, solid and tipped tools are employed for certain applications. Sometimes, because of the critical nature of the operation, space limitations, or other factors, it is necessary to use solid or tipped tools ground to the exact geometry required instead of indexable inserts.

Solid boring tools are generally made from carbides and occasionally from high-speed steels or cast cobalt-based alloys. Tipped tools are made from these same materials, as well as diamonds (either single-crystal or polycrystalline) and CBN, with carbide-tipped tools being predominant.

Indexable Inserts for Boring

By far the greater number of tools used for precision boring now employ indexable inserts. The use of these inserts affords a reduced cost per cutting edge, and they can normally be obtained as stock items. They eliminate the cost of regrinding, reduce toolchanging time, and assure that tool geometry remains constant.

With proper application, indexable inserts can be used for most boring applications formerly done with solid and tipped tools. Inserts, however, limit to some extent the variations in tool design that can be considered for a specific operation. To use inserts, it is sometimes necessary to forsake the ideal rake or clearance angles in favor of the many advantages of this type of tooling. Once the proper tool geometry has been established for a specific application, it is generally possible to select a standard insert that very closely simulates the desired geometry. When space is limited because of bore size, it may not be possible to use inserts.

TOOLHOLDERS FOR PRECISION BORING

Boring tools can be divided into two main categories: rotating and fixed (nonrotating). Rotating tools are tools mounted in rotating spindles to perform various boring, facing, and related operations with the bore and toolholder on the same centerline. Nonrotating tools are of various arrangements and are mounted to the table or cross slide of the machine to perform operations on rotating workpieces, generally not on the same centerline as the toolholder.

Boring Bars

The most common type of rotating tool is a round boring bar with one cutting edge mounted at the end of the bar to perform a single-diameter boring operation. This type of bar is shown in Fig. 23-38. Table 23-1 gives useful data that can be used as a starting point for boring-bar design. Chip clearance between bar and bore is a very important consideration, but it is also extremely important in many cases to keep the diameter of the bar as large as and the length as short as possible. For fine-finishing operations, it may therefore be desirable to reduce dimension C in order to favor diameter A. Boring bars are usually balanced when they are to operate at high speeds.

BORING

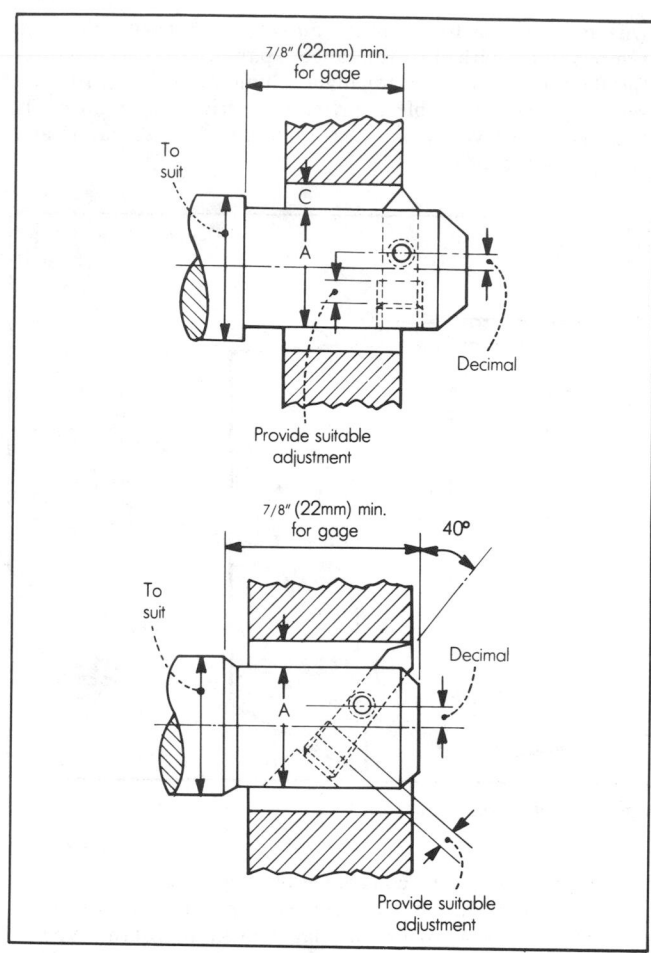

TABLE 23-1
Boring Bar Dimensions Based on Bar Diameter Equaling 0.7071 Times the Bore Diameter

Bore diam, in. (mm)	Bar diam, A, in. (mm)	Chip clearance, C, in. (mm)	Tool diam, in. (mm)
1 1/4 (32)	0.884 (22.45)	0.183 (4.65)	5/16 (8)
1 1/2 (38)	1.061 (26.95)	0.220 (5.59)	5/16 (8)
1 5/8 (41)	1.149 (29.18)	0.238 (6.05)	5/16 (8)
1 3/4 (44)	1.237 (31.42)	0.256 (6.50)	1/2 (13)
1 7/8 (48)	1.326 (33.68)	0.275 (6.98)	1/2 (13)
2 (51)	1.414 (35.92)	0.293 (7.44)	1/2 (13)
2 1/4 (57)	1.591 (40.41)	0.330 (8.38)	1/2 (13)
2 1/2 (63)	1.768 (44.91)	0.366 (9.30)	1/2 (13)
2 3/4 (70)	1.944 (49.38)	0.403 (10.24)	1/2 (13)
3 (76)	2.131 (54.13)	0.439 (11.15)	1/2 (13)
3 1/4 (83)	2.298 (58.37)	0.476 (12.09)	1/2 (13)
3 1/2 (89)	2.475 (62.86)	0.513 (13.03)	1/2 (13)
3 3/4 (95)	2.652 (67.36)	0.549 (13.94)	1/2 (13)
4 (102)	2.828 (71.83)	0.586 (14.88)	1/2 (13)
4 1/2 (114)	3.182 (80.82)	0.659 (16.74)	3/4 (19)
5 (127)	3.536 (89.81)	0.732 (18.59)	3/4 (19)
5 1/2 (140)	3.889 (98.78)	0.805 (20.45)	3/4 (19)
6 (152)	4.243 (107.77)	0.879 (22.33)	3/4 (19)

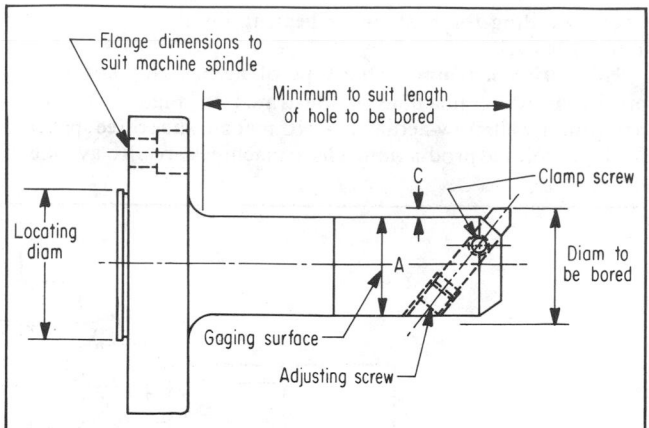

Fig. 23-38 Boring bar of simple design having one single-point tool mounted at its end.

Multiple-tool bars. Many boring bars are designed with several cutting edges to produce bores of various diameters in one pass. Also, a bar may be arranged with a roughing or semifinishing tool ahead of a finishing tool so that a bore can be roughed and finished in one pass. In this case, it is usual to space the tools so that the first tool finishes its cut before the second tool enters the bore.

Multiple-tool boring bars can become very complex, and a great deal of attention must be given to their design. It becomes increasingly important to give consideration to adequate machine power, chip clearances, the strength and proportion of the bar, and proper individual tool adjustments. An adjusting backup screw such as that shown in Fig. 23-38, although still extensively used, is increasingly being replaced by finer and more positive means. Various micrometer-adjustable boring tools are available, such as the one shown in Fig. 23-39. Another method of obtaining fine adjustment in a boring tool is shown in Fig. 23-40. This method employs a boring-bar holder which has a built-in adjusting feature in the main body of the holder. This feature is particularly useful for small-diameter bars for which it may be difficult to provide a fine adjustment at the tool point; however, it is normally applicable only when one diameter is involved because it does not provide individual adjustment to the tools.

Adjustable heads. Rotating toolholders based on the principle of an involute coupling provide a baseplate permanently mounted on the spindle nose of the machine and a mating top plate fitted with a boring bar (see Fig. 23-41). This concept allows several top plates, each with a different boring

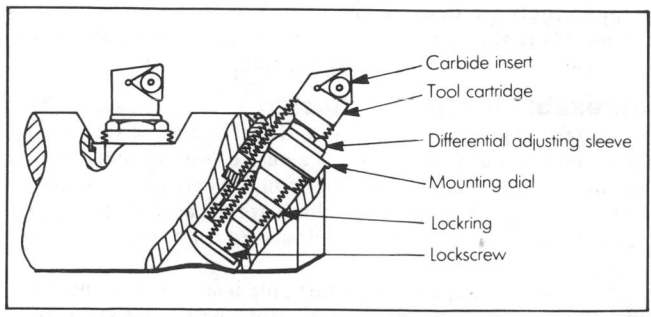

Fig. 23-39 Micrometer-adjustable toolholder for boring operations.

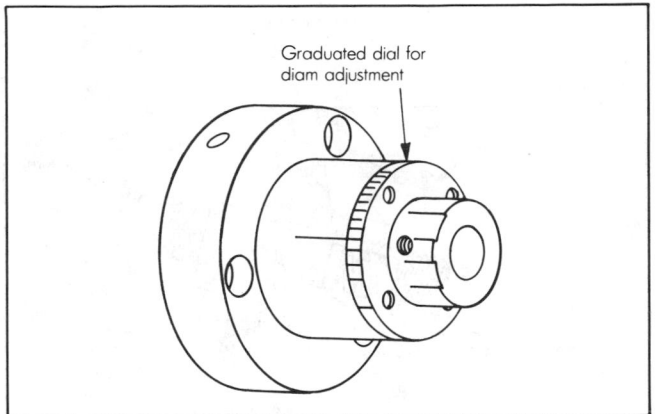

Fig. 23-40 Boring-bar holder with built-in micrometer adjustment.

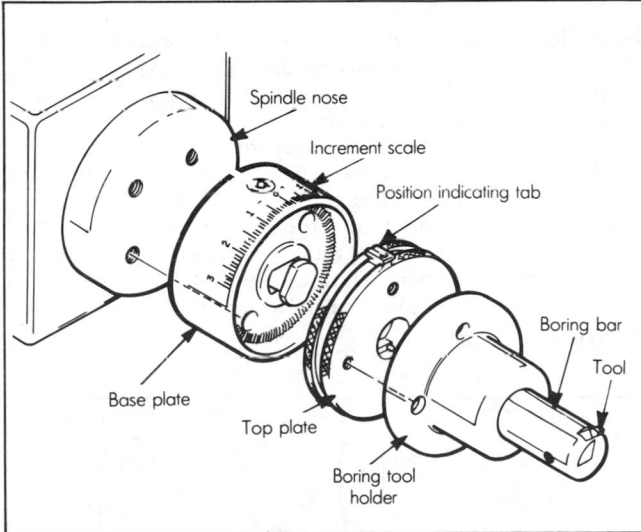

Fig. 23-41 Rotating boring head permits precise adjustments. Top plates can be quickly changed. (*Wadell Equipment Co., Inc.* **)**

bar, to be used with one baseplate. For example, if one had to rough bore, finish bore, and counterbore, the tooling requirements would be one complete unit (baseplate and top plate) and two additional top plates, each with its respective boring bar. Once all adjustments had been made for each of the dimensions involved, the three top plates could be removed and reinstalled repetitively to close tolerances. The tool tips would not be touched, because all precise adjustments are made by rotating the involute-coupling top plate on its baseplate.

Block-type system. With this system, chip load is balanced between two cutters. The opposed cutting action minimizes bar deflection and the effect of tool wear. Tools are available as micrometer-adjustable, single-cutter blocks for short runs; micrometer-adjustable blocks with indexable carbide inserts; solid block cutters for maximum face widths in boring and facing; and multicutter blocks with expandable cutters for combined operations.

Cartridges for Boring Bars

The extensive use of indexable insert tools has brought about the increased application of cartridge-type boring bars (see Fig.

23-42). Instead of pockets being machined into a bar for holding inserts, the bar is provided with one or more slots to mount small insert-holding cartridges. Inserts are mechanically held in place in the cartridges, which can have square, rectangular, or cylindrical-shaped shanks and can be provided with or without adjusting features.

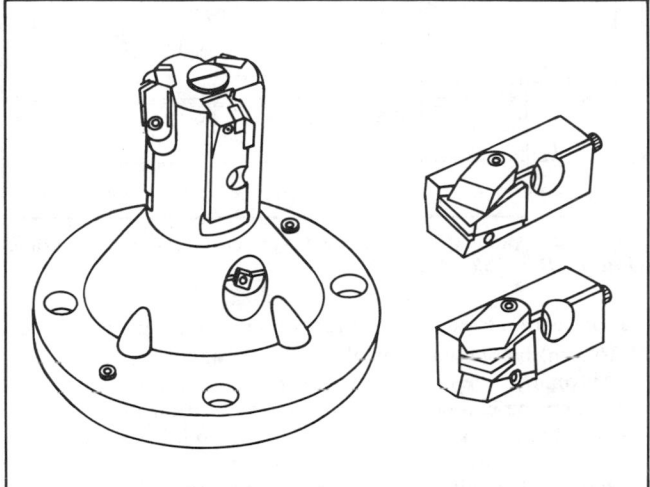

Fig. 23-42 Boring bar with cartridges that hold indexable inserts.

Retracting Boring Tools

Draglines (withdrawal marks) caused by retraction of boring tools at the completion of their cuts can be a troublesome problem in precision boring. A number of methods have been developed to avoid this problem. One method involves the use of a device with a cartridge that contains a cam which adjusts the tool position when it is rotated manually or automatically. Once the cut is complete, axial movement of the cone-shaped cam in the cartridge causes the tool to move away from the workpiece so it can be withdrawn without marring the finished surface.

Another method involves mounting the boring bar on a special retracting head that moves the bar eccentrically or radially for clearance at the end of the cut. Other methods of withdrawing the tool from the bore make use of hydraulic cylinders, slides, and limit switches.

Automatic Boring Tool Adjustment

Automatic size control systems for repositioning the tools are available for precision boring. One such system that can be used on any machine that has a hollow spindle is illustrated schematically in Fig. 23-43. Measuring probes gage the bore, and signals are sent to an amplifier where the dimension is compared to the preset required size. If adjustments are required in the tool position, they can be made manually, semiautomatically, or automatically.

For automatic adjustment, a signal is sent from an electronic compensator panel to a stepper motor. The motor adjusts a micrometer stop assembly which controls the motion of a drawbar. The drawbar extends through the hollow spindle and adjusts the setting of the tool. Outward or inward adjustments of the cutting edges, which can be made while the spindle is rotating or stationary, are made in any increment from 0.000020-0.002″ (0.00051-0.05 mm). When a boring operation

BORING

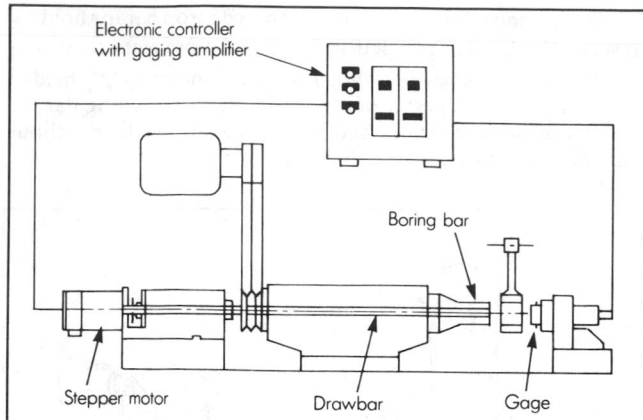

Fig. 23-43 Automatic size-control system for precision boring. (*Valenite Div., Valeron Corp.*)

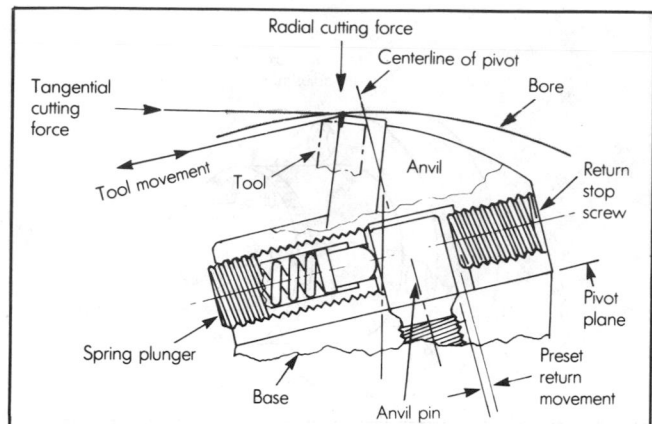

Fig. 23-44 Combined dual-slide crossfeed facing head and bridge-mounted boring head. (*DeVlieg Microbore Tooling Systems Div.*)

has been completed, the cutting tools are retracted about 0.006″ (0.15 mm) before withdrawal to avoid draglines.

Automatic size control of multiple tools can be performed with just one compensator. In one application involving the boring of crankshafts, one compensating module automatically controls two cartridges in a single boring bar independent of each other. In addition to maintaining accurate tolerances, data accumulated by the gages and compensators can be monitored to indicate machining trends such as tool dulling.

Generating-Type Heads

Generating-type heads are used when surfaces other than cylindrical surfaces are to be produced. The most common type is a facing head that produces a surface at right angles to the bore. Special means are provided for operating the facing heads while the spindle is rotating, by means of a drawbar through the spindle and a rotating cylinder at the rear end of the spindle. Control of the cylinder operating speed provides the desired feed rate for the facing slide; facing head stops control the diameter of the surface being generated.

Combining Operations

By effectively combining numerous cutting operations into one head, required machining cycle time can be achieved with conventional cutting speeds and feed rates that are conducive to good tool life. A standard 15″ (381 mm) dual-slide crossfeed facing head was combined with a special bridge-mounted boring head, as shown in Fig. 23-44.

The application involves machining three different bore diameters, a face groove, and a face in one pass. In addition, boring tools for two of the diameters are automatically retracted during the facing operation.

Fixed Toolholders

Fixed toolholders are mounted on the main slide or the cross slide of the boring machine in such a manner as to approach the rotating part and perform a variety of machining operations. Most of the considerations that apply to rotating-type bars also apply to fixed boring bars. One advantage of nonrotating tooling is that it does not have to be balanced. Also, fixed tooling can often be more rigidly constructed and supported. Workpieces requiring boring and facing operations to be performed simultaneously would necessitate complicated

boring bar configurations and cause balancing problems if the tools were rotated. The ability to rotate the workpiece not only simplifies toolholder design, but also allows higher spindle speeds because the tooling is fixed.

Various types of toolblock design are possible, from simple blocks with a single tool to multiple tool designs involving numerous adjusting and gaging features. As with rotating tooling, micrometer-adjustable tools are frequently used, and cartridges for indexable tools with two-way adjustment provide an excellent arrangement. The multiple-toolblock assembly on a vertical two-spindle machine shown in Fig. 23-45 illustrates this type of tooling.

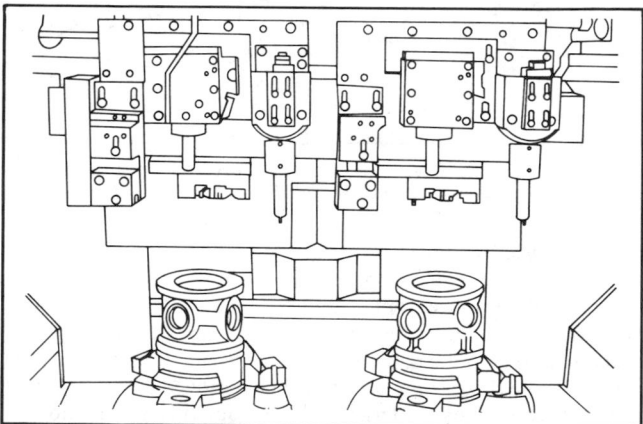

Fig. 23-45 Fixed tooling arrangement on a vertical, two-spindle machine.

Other types of tooling provide for convenient adjustment by means of standard toolblocks that are available. Some give clear indication of tool adjustment amounts by means of graduated dials (see Fig. 23-46) or by means of dial indicator gages (see Fig. 23-47).

Fixed tooling can also be arranged with automatic incremental adjustment. Adjustments can be made by the operator with pushbutton control for size compensation, or they can be automatically performed by suitable feedback from an automatic gage. Tooling can also be arranged with automatic

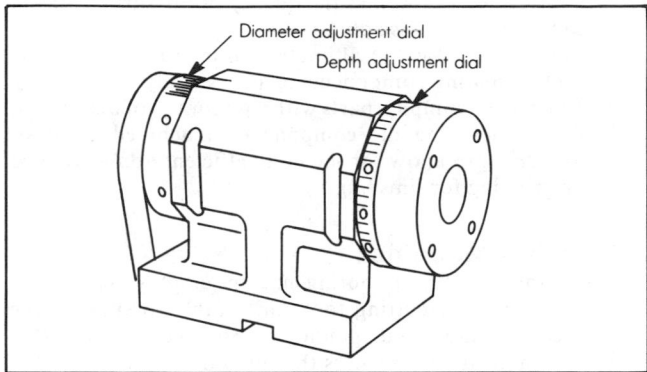

Fig. 23-46 Toolblock with micrometer adjustments for both diameter and depth.

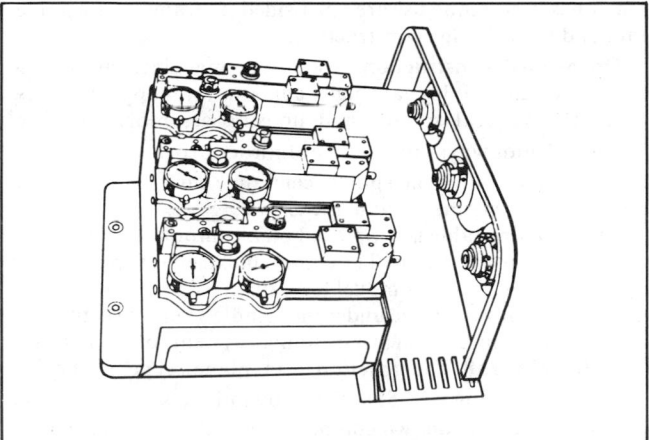

Fig. 23-47 Dial-indicator type of toolholders arranged for multiple operations on workpieces at three stations.

retraction features to avoid drawback lines.

WORKHOLDING FOR BORING

Many of the various types of chucks and collets discussed under turning in a preceding section of this chapter are also used for precision boring, as well as for combination machining operations. Fixtures are also used extensively for precision boring.

Fixturing of workpieces for precision-boring operations is an extremely important and critical matter. When the high degree of accuracy usually demanded of the operation performed by the machine is considered, holding the part during the operation demands careful consideration of the correct locating surfaces and clamping must minimize distortions, which influence accuracy. The compromise between adequate, rigid clamping and small distortions can present a challenge in ingenuity of fixture design.

Design of the part itself can be an extremely important factor. Special provisions for locating and clamping made during part design can often prevent many problems and reduce fixture cost considerably. Adequate preparation of the part in processing prior to precision boring can also help considerably in overcoming problems in fixturing.

Fixtures can be extremely simple or complex, depending upon various factors. Low production requirements may only justify a simple approach with manual clamping. However,

some low-production fixtures may demand power clamping. High production may demand a highly sophisticated, automatic clamping fixture. Regardless, fixtures should be designed with ease of loading in mind, and always with careful attention given to proper clearance for the boring bar and the removal of the chips made by the process.

Boring Tool Setups

All standard boring bars are designed to machine with the cutting point of the tool on the centerline of spindle rotation or slightly above center. If the cutting edge is above the centerline of spindle rotation, the negative rake angle of the tool is increased; if below, the clearance angle is reduced.

On-center tooling is recommended for certain applications, but above centerline positioning of the tool is better than below centerline positioning for most boring operations. With boring operations, insufficient clearance can be a problem; raising the cutting point slightly above the centerline provides additional clearance. Even though a cutting tool is supposed to be on centerline, it may actually be high or low due to machine tool or setting inaccuracies. The tool position should be accurately gaged, especially whenever tool performance is poor.

In use, boring bars are frequently tilted because they are round and easily rotated. If a boring bar is rotated to bring the insert edge on the centerline, the rake and clearance angles will be other than specified. To avoid this, flats, parallel to the workpiece centerline and on the same plane as the tool infeed, are generally provided on boring bars. The use of setscrews aligned with the flats minimizes the problem.

Some boring bars slotted to accept tipped tools are designed so that the slot goes through the center of the bar. This results in the cutting point being considerably above centerline. To compensate for this, the bars should be used with tools having high positive rake angles, or the bars should be positioned below the centerline so that the cutting edge of the tool is on the centerline.

Qualified and Preset Tooling

To achieve the close tolerances required in precision-boring operations, qualified holders and precision inserts are used extensively. Presetting of the tools is also generally recommended to minimize the need for trial cuts and tool adjustments on the machine. Means of presetting can vary from relatively simple, less-costly, dial-indicator gages (see Fig. 23-48) to expensive presetting machines. The setting gage illustrated in Fig. 23-48 requires the use of a master; the V-block locates on the OD of the boring bar, adjacent to the tool. Automatic tool presetting with in-process gaging, as discussed previously, is also used.

JIG BORING

The term jig borer originally pertained to tool (jig and fixture) manufacturing, but the continually increasing demands for accuracy within many branches of metalworking has extended the application possibilities for jig-boring machines.

Applications of Jig Boring

Jig-boring machines are used for a wide range of applications. The locating and measuring features of the machine are employed for establishing the dimensional detail of workpieces, including:

1. Jigs used for the production machining of multiple parts.

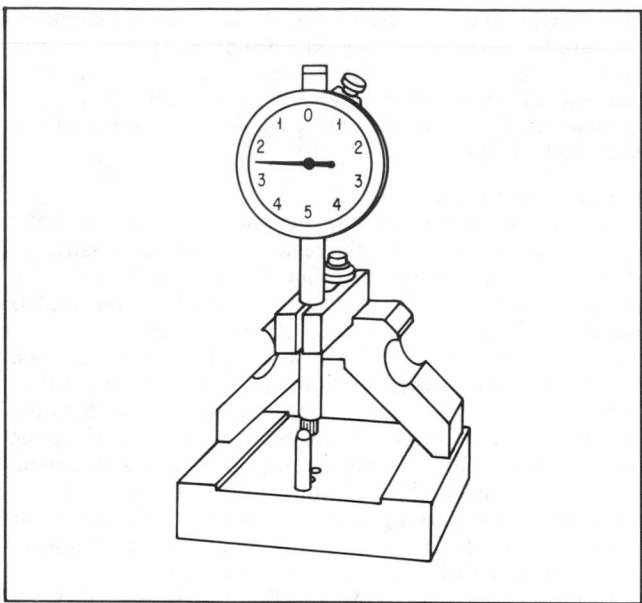

Fig. 23-48 Dial-indicator gage is used with a master to set boring bar diameters.

2. Press tools such as the lamination die seen in Fig. 23-49.
3. Gages used to qualify parts produced on other machines.

These machines are also used for the production of:

1. Prototype parts needed before custom tooling can be designed and manufactured.
2. Parts for which the required accuracy of hole location

and surfaces, as well as the quality of the surface finish, cannot be otherwise obtained.

3. Parts calling for the ultimate in dimensional integrity, such as mating components in an assembly.
4. Delicate or complex parts with a minimum of distortion.
5. Parts, including die components, machined prior to hardening to allow for the more efficient application of jig grinding for finishing.

Jig-Boring Machines

In general terms, the jig-boring machine employs a precision spindle to drive the cutting tool and a table to support the workpiece. The table and spindle are movable and are fitted with built-in measuring devices that provide means for establishing X, Y, Z, and A coordinate positions. The machine is designed to locate and bore holes and to generate surfaces to the highest level of accuracy. Three basic designs of jig-boring machines in common use are open-sided (C-frame), adjustable-rail, and fixed-bridge construction.

Open-sided construction. Jig-boring machines of this C-frame design employ a single column for supporting the machine's vertical spindle and housing assembly (see Fig. 23-50). Guideways in the column control the perpendicular alignment of the spindle centerline throughout the full range of its adjustment along the Z axis.

The machine table is supported on a compound slide and is movable along the X axis. The compound itself is supported on the machine base and is movable along the Y axis. Coordinate settings locating the table under the spindle's vertical centerline are controlled by the linear positioning system for each axis.

Adjustable-rail construction. On planer-type jig-boring machines (see Fig. 23-51), the crossrail is supported and adjusted vertically on two columns. The rail serves to carry the

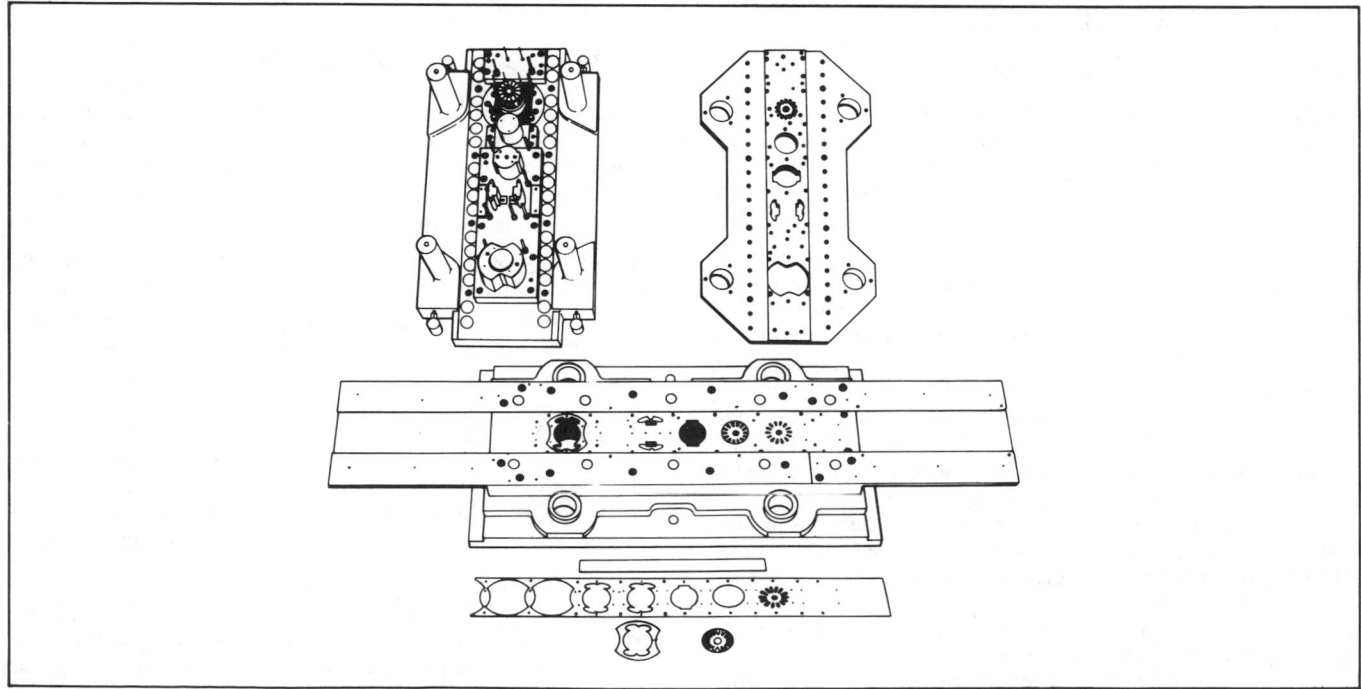

Fig. 23-49 Lamination die illustrates the precise requirements for locational accuracies afforded by the jig borer.

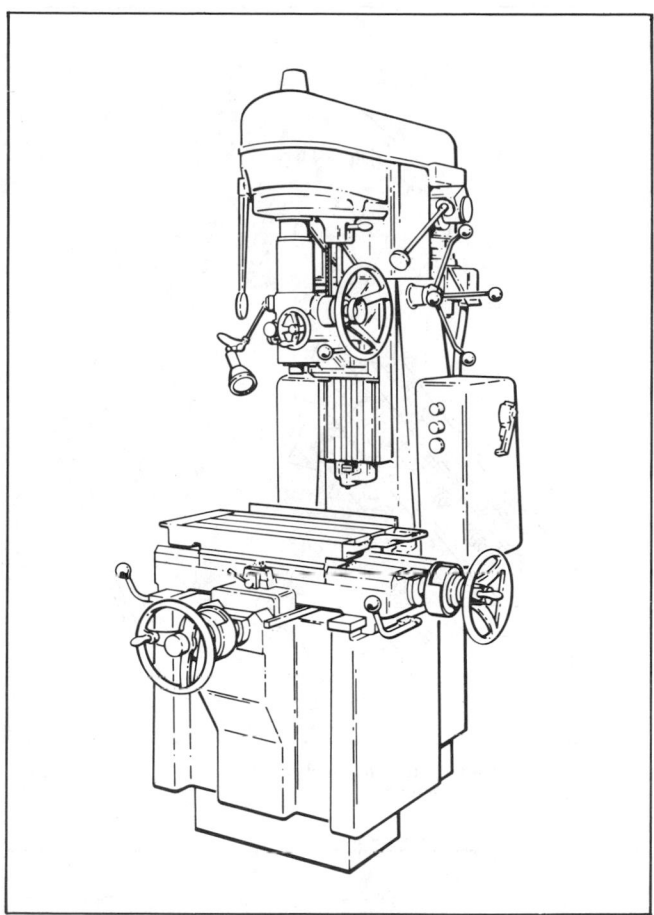

Fig. 23-50 Jig-boring machine of open-sided construction.

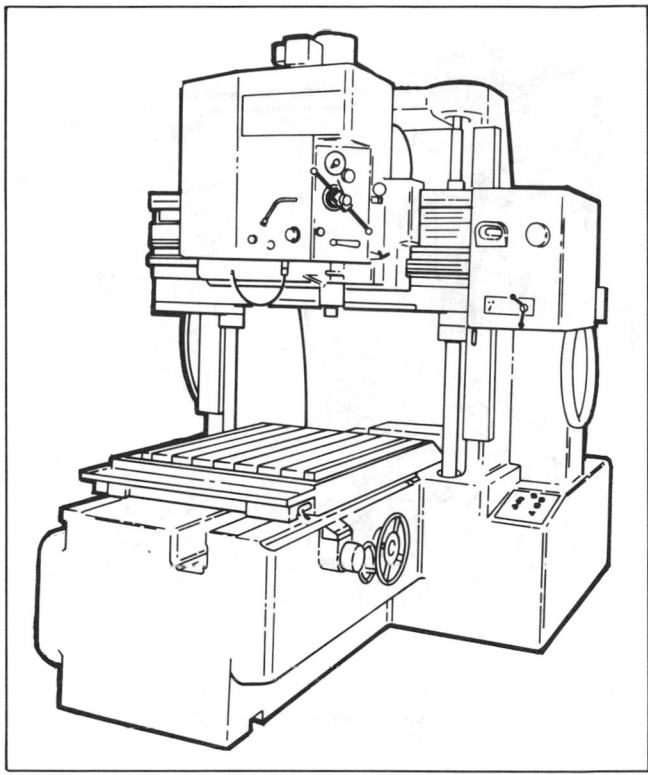

Fig. 23-51 Adjustable-rail or planer-type jig-boring machine equipped with graduated-scale measuring system.

vertical spindle in its housing along the Y axis. The table is supported on the base of the machine and is movable along the Y axis.

Fixed-bridge construction. On jig-boring machines of this design, as illustrated in Fig. 23-52, the worktable is mounted on the base guideways and traverses in the longitudinal (X-axis) direction. The spindle is supported on the cross-slide carriage and travels with it in the transverse (Y-axis) direction on the guideways of the fixed bridge. Vertical guideways, an integral part of the cross-slide carriage, support the spindle housing and guide its vertical adjustment.

NC/CNC jig-boring machines. Jig-boring machines equipped with numerical or computer numerical control systems (see Fig. 23-53) are effectively employed when the job process can be preplanned. Machine functions for coordinate positioning and contouring operations are automatically controlled, thus relieving the operator of the need to attend to the tedious, repetitive setting of machine dials and other control devices.

Production output of NC machines can be predicted with greater certainty since their operation is less dependent upon the operator. The precision machining of curvilinear details in cams, templates, and press tool components can be developed efficiently. Many jobs exist that would be impractical to process on a manually operated jig-boring machine. One job, for example, permits precise, irregularly curved forms to be generated on cams or master templates without operator involvement.

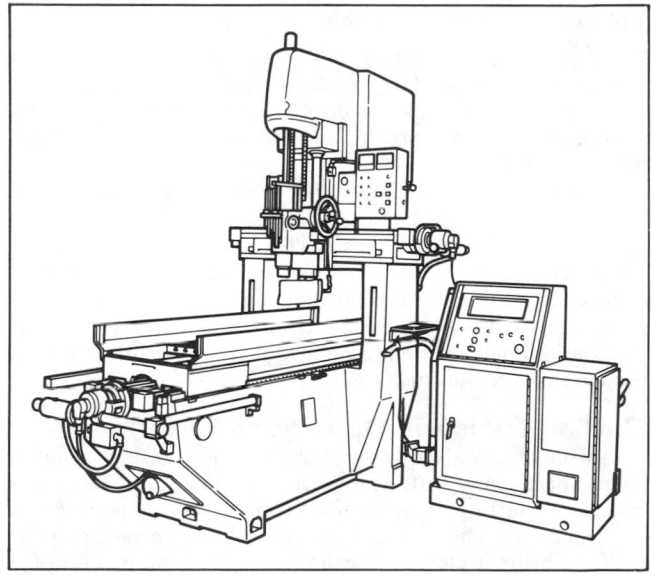

Fig. 23-52 Fixed-bridge design of jig-boring machine on which the worktable traverses in the longitudinal direction.

Workholding Methods

A workpiece must be fixed to the machine table with its datum and geometric features related to the measuring system and the machine spindle centerline. If generating angular features or establishing details having angular dimensions is required, a precision rotary table is used. Angular inclination of

BORING

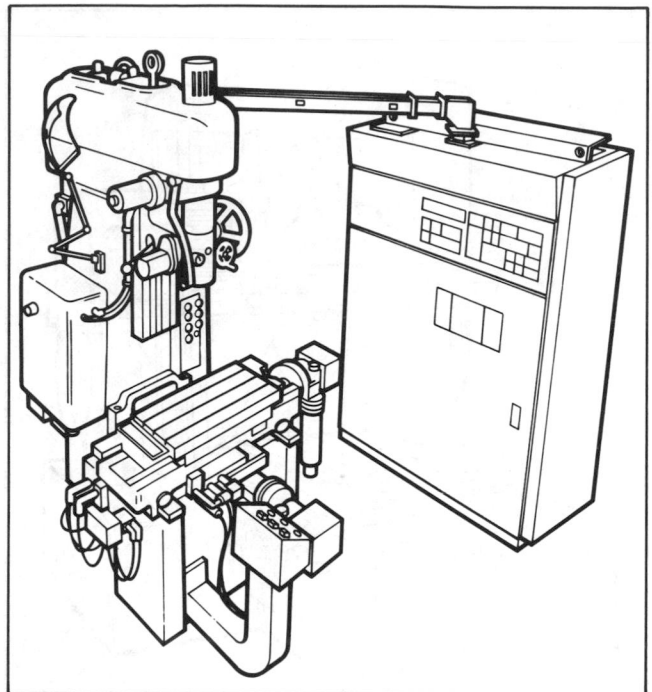

Fig. 23-53 Numerically controlled jig-boring machine of the open-side type.

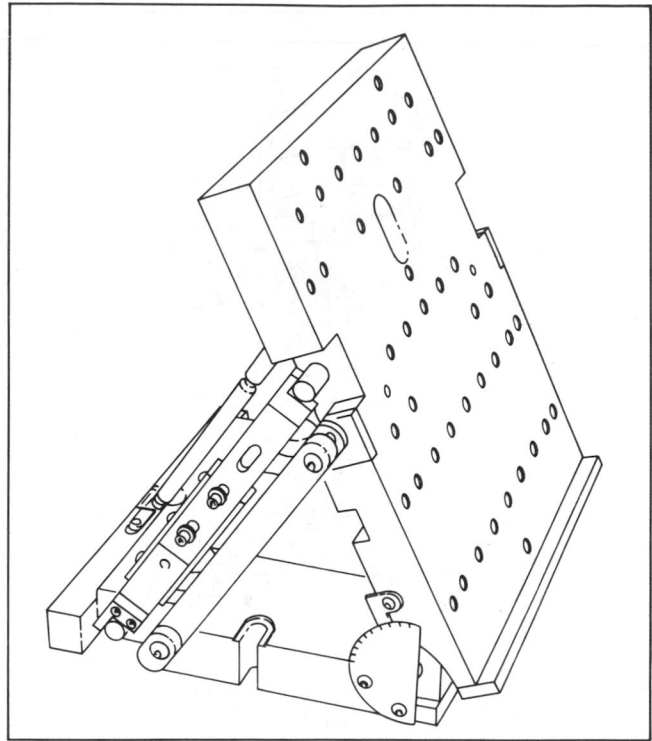

Fig. 23-54 Microsine plate on which angle is set by inserting gage blocks between the gage pins.

the workpiece relative to the horizontal plane of the machine table may be necessary when setting up the workpiece. A microsine table, as shown in Fig. 23-54, or an inclinable rotary table, Fig. 23-55, can be used for this purpose.

To prevent the machine table itself from being cut, the workpiece is supported on parallel setup blocks or in a specially designed fixture. The setup blocks or fixture must be accurately made and arranged to provide adequate and stress-free support for the workpiece.

Preparation of the reference and/or mounting surfaces of the workpiece is critical. Flatness and the geometric relationship of these surfaces must be established to conform to the setup equipment. This should be done before the workpiece is fastened to the machine table so that these surfaces may, in turn, be related to the machine's recitilinear system. It may be necessary to machine, hand scrape, or lap these surfaces even though they are not functional.

Cutting Tools and Operations Performed

A wide variety of cutting tools is used on jig-boring machines to perform many different precision operations. The usual practice in starting a hole (roughing out) is to use a spotting tool or center drill. The hole is then enlarged using a succession of drills to bring it close to finish dimension in preparation for final sizing with a single-point boring tool or reamer.

Intermediate and finish cuts generally account for most of the time required, so it is advisable to rough-cut as close to finish size as practical. Allowances of 0.005-0.010″ (0.13-0.25 mm) for holes under 1/2″ (12.7 mm) diam and 0.015-0.030″ (0.38-0.76 mm) for holes from 1/2″ to the maximum capacity of the machine are generally recommended.

When dealing with close tolerances for size control and locational accuracies, it is important that all workpiece details

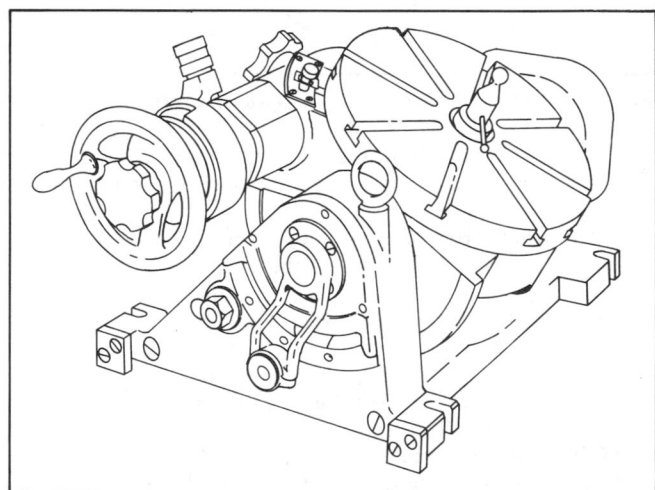

Fig. 23-55 Inclinable rotary table combines angular movement in two planes.

be rough machined first. Then the temperature should be allowed to return to normal, and the workpiece may have to be stress relieved before finish machining.

When working to close tolerances in repeating hole sizes on a number of workpieces, uniform conditions for stock removal in the finish operation must be maintained. Close attention must also be paid to the preparation of the hole before finishing.

The increasing use of NC jig-boring machines has diminished the requirement for the operator to attend to machine functions, while enlarging the requirements for organizing the job process through part programming, tool preparation, and process planning.

Single-point boring. The importance of single-point boring as the most reliable method of attaining locational accuracy with jig-boring machines justifies the wide range of boring tools available for use specifically with these machines. Machine manufacturers have designed the spindle and tool adapter with accuracies and design features consistent with the quality of the machine itself. However, attention to the requirements for care and handling of the tool by the operator, as prescribed by the manufacturer, is of utmost importance.

Solid boring bars. These tools, such as the one illustrated in view *a* of Fig. 23-56, are designed with micrometer-type tool offset adjustment and provide maximum rigidity for the cutting tool. Although the adjustment range with respect to length and diameter for each individual bar is limited, the bars are available in sets sized to cover the full range of the machine's capacity.

Multicutter tools. Tools with two or more cutters (view *b* in Fig. 23-56) can be used for faster machining.

Adjustable offset boring chucks. These tools provide a wider range for adjustment with some compromise in rigidity.

Universal boring and facing head. This tool (see Fig. 23-57) is used to face surfaces perpendicular to the spindle centerline. The boring tool is radially fed, as controlled by the operator. It is effective for operations such as facing, boring, turning outside diameters, recessing, and undercutting.

Finishing holes by reaming. Reamers are also used extensively on jig-boring machines for finishing holes.

Jig-boring and end reamers. These tools (see Fig. 23-58) are used to finish machine holes to size. Held rigid and true with the spindle, they act as multiple-tooth boring tools. They provide a favorable compromise between saving time with only a minor sacrifice in accuracy.

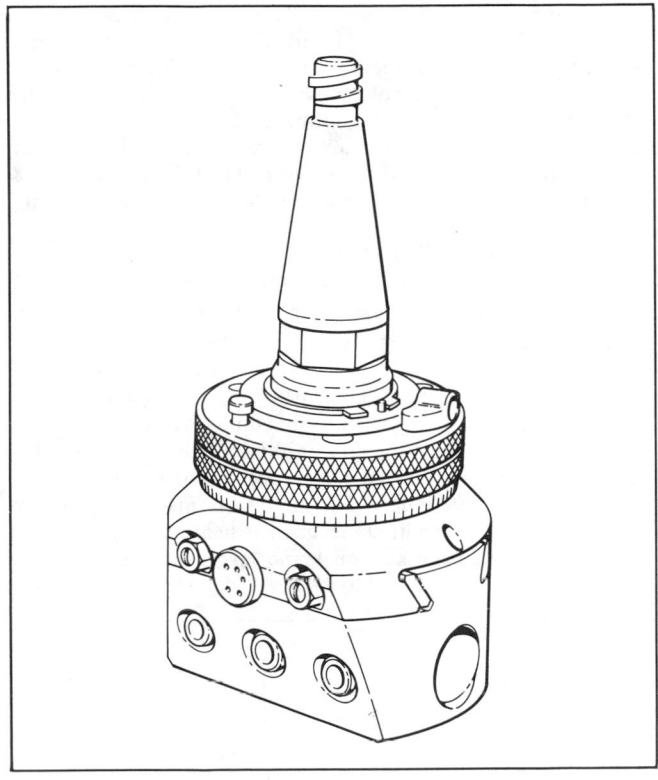

Fig. 23-57 Universal boring and facing head is used to face surfaces perpendicular to the spindle centerline.

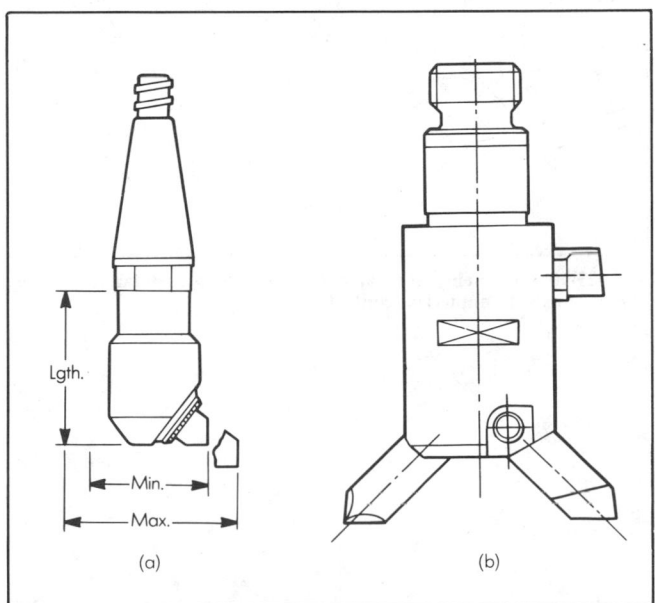

Fig. 23-56 (a) Solid boring bar with micrometer-type tool offset adjustment for diameter cut and (b) multicutter tool.

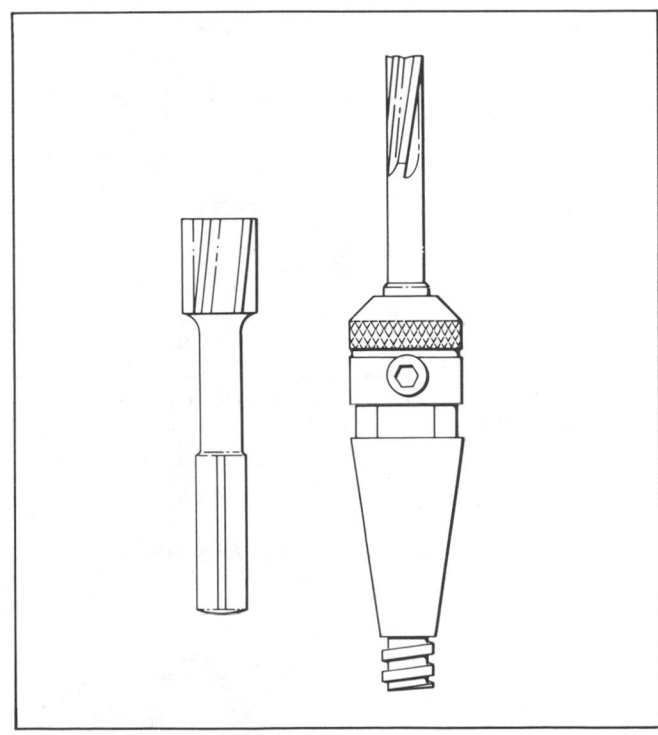

Fig. 23-58 Precision end-cutting reamers used to finish holes to size on jig-boring machines.

BORING

Machine or chucking reamers. These tools may be used for finishing holes if carefully handled. They produce somewhat better diametrical accuracy than the end reamers, but will not serve to locate the hole as well. Machine reamers can be effectively used when a large number of holes are to be finish sized. When used, the hole should be prepared by single-point boring on location, leaving between 0.001-0.003″ (0.03-0.08 mm) for reaming. Their use is particularly effective on NC jig-boring machines.

Flycutting and milling. Plane surfaces parallel to the slide motion can be generated using a single-point tool arranged in a suitable holder, as illustrated in Fig. 23-59. Since a minimum of stress is introduced into the workpiece by single-point machining, the geometric accuracy of the slide motion is faithfully reproduced in the workpiece. Conventional side-cutting end mills may be used to machine vertical surfaces.

The use of fly-cutting and milling cutters on jig-boring machines requires common sense on the part of the operator and the process planner. The precision machining system should not be abused with unnecessarily heavy cuts, but heavier milling cuts can be taken on some larger machines. In the interest of economical machine utilization, large amounts of material should be roughed out on equipment designed for that purpose. Only enough material for finishing to final dimensions should be left for the jig-boring machine. This recommendation applies equally to manually operated or numerically controlled jig-boring machines.

Jobs that would be impractical for machining on a standard jig-boring machine, such as accurate cams and templates, can be handled efficiently on an NC machine. A cam being generated by numerically controlling angular and linear dimensions is illustrated in Fig. 23-60, X and Y-axis or polar coordinates are programmed in very close increments along a path represented by the cutter centerline. The contour is developed automatically and is not dependent upon the operator's making numerous settings manually.

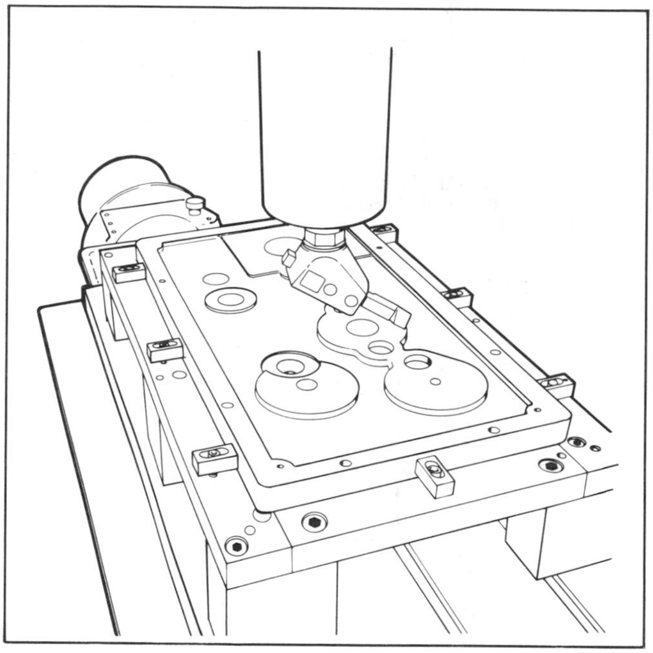

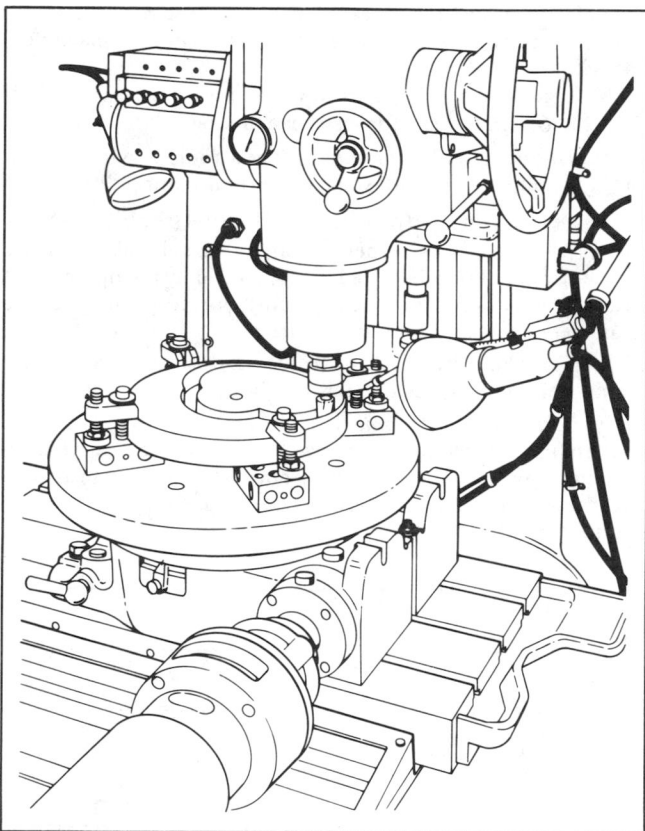

Fig. 23-59 Flycutting a plane surface parallel to the slide motion on a jig-boring machine.

Fig. 23-60 Cam being generated by controlling angular and linear dimensions with numerical control.

References

1. Theodore W. Judson, *Product Design for Turning and Milling,* SME Technical Paper MR76-902, 1976.

DRILLING, REAMING AND RELATED PROCESSES

DRILLING

The production of holes by drilling is one of the oldest and the most widely used methods of all machining processes. Holes are produced by many other processes, including forging, casting, extruding, molding, punching/piercing, and electrical discharge, electrochemical, laser, and electron beam machining. Coverage in this section is confined to the production of holes by drilling.

THE DRILLING PROCESS

Drilling is basically the production or enlarging of holes by the relative motion of a cutting tool and the workpiece, which produces chips. The cutting tool, the workpiece, or both may rotate, with the tool generally being fed. Several different methods of drilling exist, including conventional, deephole, and small-hole drilling. The choice of a method depends upon the size, depth, tolerance, and finish needed; production requirements; and the machines available to perform the operations.

While drilling fast and economical, its cutting action is difficult and inefficient. Cutting speed varies from a maximum at the periphery of the tool to zero at the center of the tool, thus varying the load on the cutting edges. Both chip ejection and flow of the cutting fluid are restricted in drilling. In addition, the production of small, deep holes can create problems with respect to necessary rigidity of the tools.

Cutting tools for drilling—drills—are rotary end-cutting tools having one or more cutting lips, and one or more helical or straight flutes for the passage of chips and the admission of a cutting fluid. They are available in a wide variety of types and geometries, as discussed later in this chapter. The most common are helically fluted twist drills with various shanks and tip geometries. Other types of drills include half-round, coolant-hole, spade, and indexable-insert drills. Gundrills, pressure-coolant drills, and trepanning tools are used extensively for precision and deep-hole operations. So-called pivot drills are used for small holes.

SELECTION AND PERFORMANCE OF DRILLS

Selection of the type of drill to be used for a specific application depends upon many factors. The performance of a drill can be judged on the basis of efficiency (rate of penetration), accuracy maintained, surface finish produced, drill life, and most importantly, the cost per hole produced. These criteria vary with the type of drill used, the workpiece, the machine employed, the rigidity of the setup, the operating parameters, and the cutting fluid used.

Important variables that influence the selection and performance of drills are the material from which they are made and their physical properties, sizes, and geometries. Workpiece criteria include the material from which the workpiece is made, its physical properties and surface condition, the type of holes (diameter, depth, through or blind, etc.) to be drilled, production requirements (lot size, accuracy, and finish), and the rigidity of the setup.

Factors that should be considered with respect to the machine used include its design, condition, and accuracy. The operating parameters of cutting speed and feed rate play a critical part in drill performance. Also important is the cutting fluid employed, including the type, rate of flow, temperature, method of application, and means for chip removal.

Accuracies and Finishes Attainable in Drilling

The accuracy of any hole produced by drilling depends upon many factors, including the type of drilling process, the workpiece, the tool and machine used, operating parameters, and rigidity of the setup. Accuracy is also largely dependent upon the sharpness and geometry of the drill point.

The accuracy of the drill itself, with respect to diameter and runout, is not too critical on machines on which drill bushings are used, but it is extremely important when the drills are to be used on numerically controlled and other precision machines. Standard, off-the shelf drills may need regrinding for precision operations. Inaccurate grinding can produce unbalanced forces that may deflect the drill and result in hole errors.

The surface finishes produced by drilling generally range from about 100-250 μ in. (2.54-6.35 μm) or more. The many variables, similar to those previously discussed for accuracies, make it impractical to predict the actual finish attainable in different applications. The surface finish of many drilled holes is often improved by subsequent reaming, boring, grinding, honing, or roller burnishing.

Effect of Drilling on Workpieces

Drilling has little effect on the physical properties of the workpiece. There is, however, a thin layer of highly stressed material around the drilled hole, which is often removed by subsequent machining. If this material is not removed, the surfaces may be more susceptible to corrosion. Clamping of workpieces for drilling may also result in distortion.

DRILLING MACHINES

Machines designed specifically for drilling are available in many different types, sizes, and capacities. The types include light-duty (sensitive), heavy-duty upright, radial, gang, multispindle, turret, deephole, small-hole, and special purpose machines.

DRILLING

In addition to drilling, many of these machines can also perform related operations, such as reaming, facing, chamfering, counterboring, countersinking, undercutting/recessing, roller burnishing, and tapping. In some cases, depending upon the design and rigidity, the machines are used for boring and milling operations.

Control Systems

Drilling machines are available for manual, semiautomatic, and automatic operation. NC and CNC are used on many drilling machines, and these types of control are particularly suitable for producing patterns of holes in various workpieces. NC or CNC is usually standard on circuit board, tube sheet, and other special-purpose drilling machines. Programmable controllers are also used on some drilling machines and drillheads.

NC/CNC requirements for drilling machines vary, depending upon the application. Simple two-axis (X and Y) positioning systems are used only for table movement on some machines, with the drilling depth (Z axis) controlled manually, electrically, electromechanically, or mechanically. Many drilling machines are equipped with more complex systems that can control table positioning, drilling depths, spindle speeds, feed rates, and other functions. Some systems provide for the compensation of varying tool lengths.

Light-Duty, Sensitive Drilling Machines

Machines of this type are the most common of all drilling machines. These general-purpose machines are most often used for drilling one hole at a time in small workpieces, with hole diameters to about 1″ (25 mm) diam. They are often referred to as drill presses and are employed extensively for many toolroom, machine shop, and maintenance applications, as well as for some production operations.

Upright (Vertical) Drilling Machines

Upright or vertical drilling machines, such as the one illustrated in Fig. 24-1, are similar to the light-duty machines just discussed, but differ in that they are more massive for heavy-duty applications. They permit the production of larger diameter and deeper holes with improved accuracy and quality. Practically all upright drilling machines are equipped with power feed. They are most suitable for workpieces that can be quickly positioned under the tool, require short cycle times, or need only a few holes per part.

Some upright drilling machines have a round column, while others (see Fig. 24-1) have a box column for increased rigidity. Machines with round columns generally have circular tables that can be rotated about the columns and their own centers, as well as raised and lowered. Most box-column machines are equipped with square tables, some of which have knee-type supporting members and one or two screws for positioning the tables vertically. Power elevating systems are available on some machines. Most tables are furnished with T-slots for clamping drilling fixtures or workpieces.

Cross compound tables are also available with scales and/or dials to facilitate drilling holes in various locations. More sophisticated versions, sometimes called layout drilling machines (see Fig. 24-2), are equipped with precision slides for the saddle and table, and digital readout systems. These machines can also be used for precision boring and milling.

Gang Drilling Machines

A gang drilling machine consists of two or more independent, light-duty or upright drilling machines mounted on a common base or table. One machine with six upright spindles is illustrated in Fig. 24-3. The table on this unit is power elevated by two screws.

Gang drilling machines permit higher production rates on workpieces which have multiple holes or require multiple operations by saving time that would be required to change tools on single-spindle machines. Each spindle on a gang drilling machine can hold the same tools for simultaneous operations on a number of workpieces. More often, however, a different size or type of cutting tool is mounted in each spindle for sequential operations. In these cases, the workpieces are manually moved from one spindle to the next. Depending upon the application, one operator can handle operations using several spindles or individual operators can be employed for each spindle.

Radial Drilling Machines

Excellent versatility is an important advantage of radial drilling machines. These machines are used extensively for drilling holes in large and irregularly shaped workpieces that cannot be easily positioned or repositioned. A number of smaller workpieces can also be clamped to the base or floor plate. Flexibility of these machines permits drilling holes in workpiece surfaces that cannot be reached with other drilling

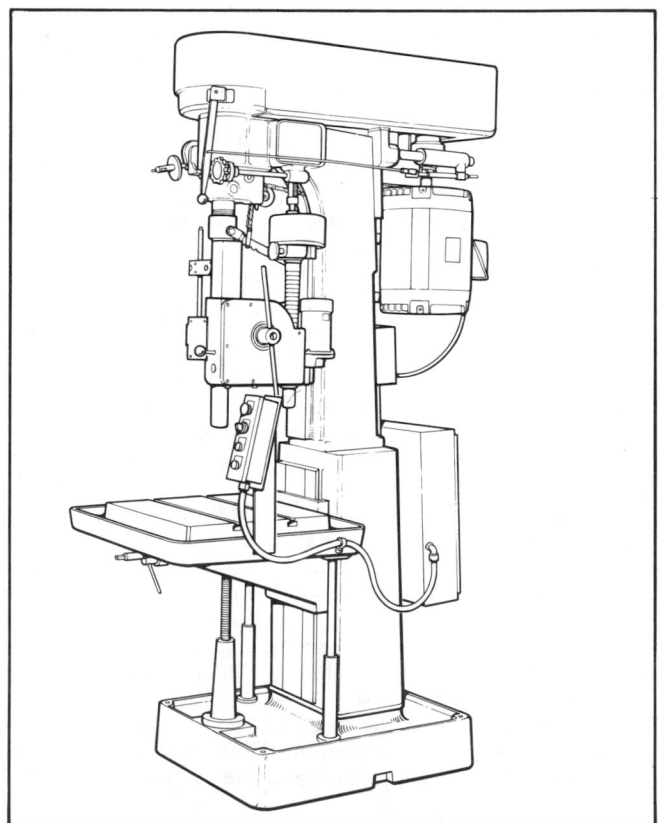

Fig. 24-1 Upright (vertical) drilling and tapping machine with power feed and power traverse. (*Chas. G. Allen Co.*)

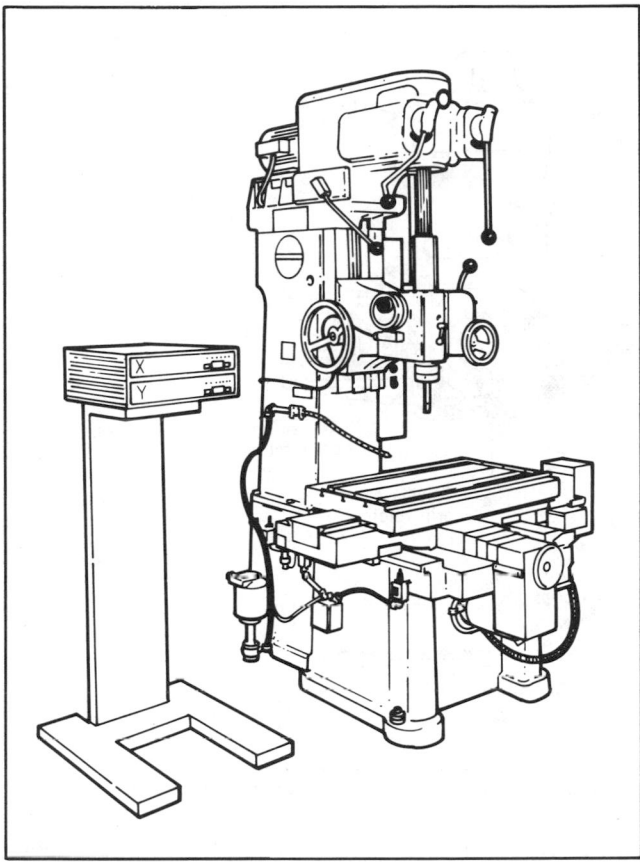

Fig. 24-2 Bed-type layout drilling machine with digital readout system. (*Cleereman Machine Tool Div., Appleton Machine Co.*)

machines. Time is saved by repositioning the drill instead of the workpiece for each operation.

A radial drilling machine (see Fig. 24-4) consists of a horizontal arm, from 2-12 ft (0.6-3.7 m) or more in length, supported by a round, vertical column. The arm can be raised, lowered, and rotated around the column axis. The drillhead mounted on the arm contains the speed-changing and power-feed mechanisms, as well as the spindle, and can be repositioned along the arm and clamped in any desired location. Some machine designs permit tilting the head to produce angular holes.

Multispindle Drilling Machines and Heads

In addition to multispindle drillheads for use on single-spindle machines, multispindle drilling machines are available for high-production requirements. Major time savings can be realized with both heads and machines having multiple spindles by performing a number of machining operations simultaneously and minimizing the need for toolchanging. Multispindle machines are used primarily for three general types of production operations:

1. Multiple operations (drilling, reaming, chamfering, spotfacing, etc.) in a single hole. Machines used for these applications are often equipped with hand-positioned tables, shuttle tables, or rotary indexing tables.
2. One operation in multiple holes which are the same size or different sizes and on the same or different planes.

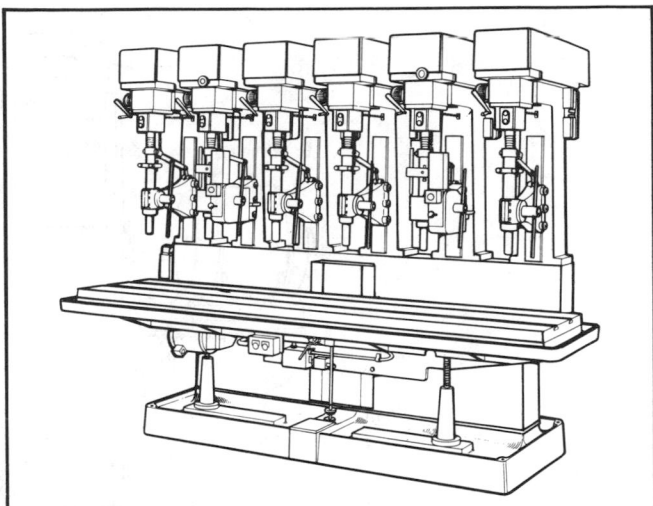

Fig. 24-3 Gang-type, six spindle drilling machine with both hand and power-feed top columns equipped with power elevating table. (*Chas. G. Allen Co.*)

Machines used for these operations may require a rotary indexing table if hole center distances are close. Multiple-plane operations are often performed with multiple-position workholding fixtures.

3. Multiple operations in multiple holes which generally require that the machine be equipped with a rotary indexing table or other type of table, especially when tapping is one of the operations to be performed.

Multispindle machines are made in various types, including an open-side type with way or quill design and a four-post type with vertical, horizontal, and angular construction. An open-side machine with way design is illustrated in Fig. 24-5. Machines of way or four-post design, with drive motors to 100 hp (74.6 kW), are suitable for heavy-duty drilling. The way and four-post machines may have the drillhead movable and the workholding fixture stationary, or they may have the fixture movable and the drillhead stationary. Multispindle drilling generally requires slightly greater hole tolerances than can be obtained with single-spindle machines.

Multispindle drillheads. These units are designed for various applications and have geared or gearless (crank-type) drives. All tools on a head are fed into the workpiece together, but tool lengths are sometimes staggered so that cutting loads are applied progressively.

Turret Drilling Machines

Upright drilling machines, both bench and floor types as well as hand and power-feed types, are available with indexing drums or turrets. The turret typically has six or eight faces, although machines are available with turrets having four and ten faces. Each face has a spindle for holding a drill or other cutting tool. The turrets can be indexed manually or automatically to bring the spindles into operating position with respect to the workpiece. A solid-bed, sliding-head drilling machine with a turret having eight tooling faces and two/three-axis NC is shown in Fig. 24-6.

Turret drilling machines permit performing a number of operations in a hole or group of holes without the need for changing tools. Various tools on the turret are sequenced into

DRILLING

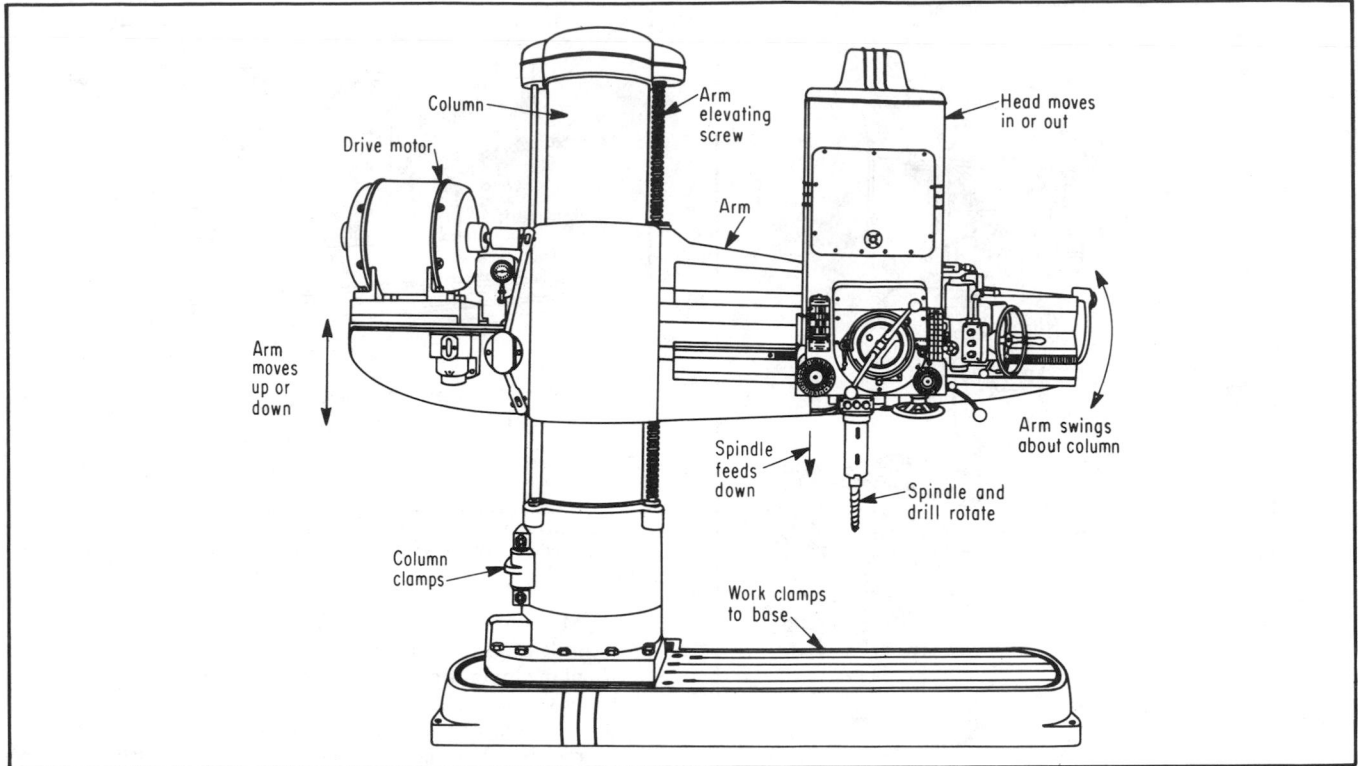

Fig. 24-4 Radial drilling machine. Arm which carries adjustable-position drillhead can be raised, lowered, and pivoted around column.

cutting position with every feed stroke of the machine. Turret drilling machines are suitable for heavier workpieces that can remain stationary, as well as for operations in which quick-change tooling is not practical. The capability of these machines can be expanded by adding indexing, rotating, or shuttling fixtures.

These machines are also made with dual (pancaked) turret heads for small workpieces having many multiple-operation holes. This arrangement reduces the need for toolchanging and two symmetrical workpieces can be machined simultaneously; thus, cycle time is cut in half. Drilling capacity per head, however, is reduced to half that when a single head is used because the spindle drive is not increased.

Deep-Hole Drilling Machines

Deep-hole drilling with gundrilling, gunboring, trepanning, and other self-guided tools using high-pressure cutting fluids is sometimes done by converting conventional machines such as suitably designed lathes and drilling, boring, and milling machines. Most applications, however, are performed on machines specifically designed for deep-hole drilling. These machines are generally horizontal, but some, used for shorter operations on smaller workpieces, have vertical or angular spindles.

Most deep-hole drilling machines have a rotating tool that is fed into a workpiece mounted on a table at one end of the machine (see top view in Fig. 24-7). Some machines, used to drill long slender parts, rotate the workpiece while a nonrotating drill is fed into it (bottom view, Fig. 24-7). For some precision applications, both the workpiece and tool rotate, but in opposite directions.

Deep-hole drilling machines have several basic requirements

which are not necessary on machines used for the more conventional hole-making processes. For optimum tool performance, the machine must:

1. *Be sufficiently rigid* so that moving parts which affect alignment do not deviate from their true path as the machine operates at its designated capabilities and capacity.
2. *Have ample power*, especially in view of the relatively high penetration rates associated with these tools.
3. *Have a system of controls that make precision work feasible.* The most desirable controls include a spindle-load meter, a feed-rate meter, a fluid-pressure gage or pressure switch, and a fluid-flow-control meter.
4. *Have a precision spindle.* The spindle must be designed to operate at the highest speed anticipated in use with an absolute minimum of end play. These machines are available with spindle speeds up to 20,000 rpm. Since very fine feed graduations are characteristic of pressure-coolant tools, spindle end play can result in the tool cutting too deep in one revolution, and then not cutting for the next several revolutions.
5. *Have a feed mechanism that is constant,* finely enough controlled to accommodate the expected range of conditions, and readily adjustable.
6. *Have a start bushing setup that allows near-perfect alignment.*
7. *Be capable of close-tolerance alignment that can be easily set up and then maintained.* Shops doing precise gundrilling may require a maximum of 0.0002″ (0.005 mm) eccentricity per foot, measured from the spindle.
8. *Have a cutting fluid and fine-filtration system.*

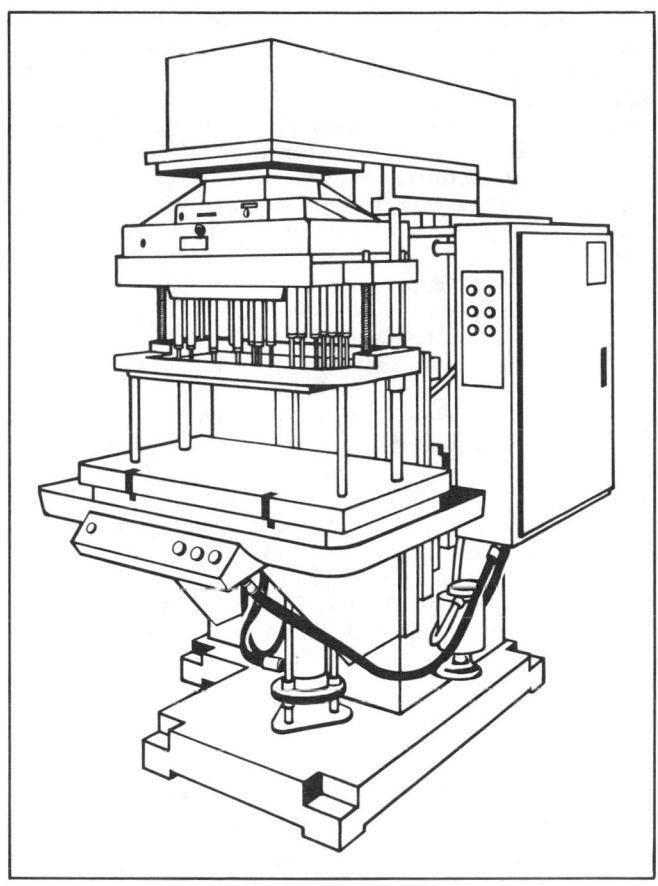

Fig. 24-5 Multispindle drilling machine of the open-side type with way design. (*Zagar, Inc.*)

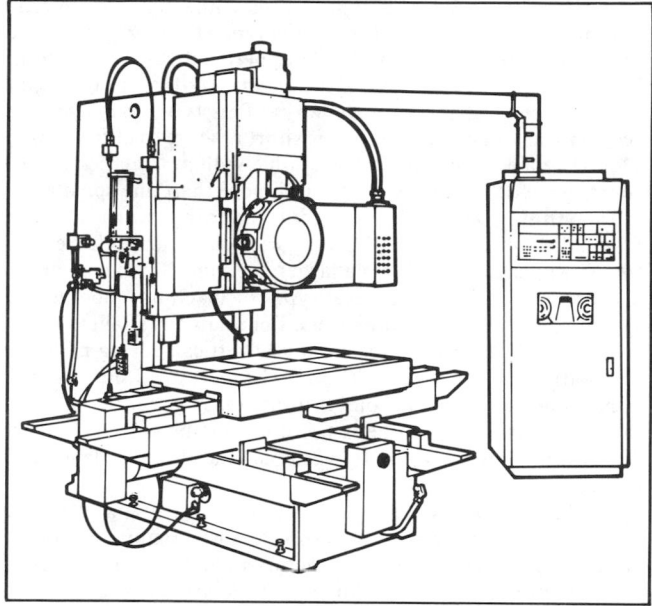

Fig. 24-6 Solid-bed, sliding-head drilling machine with eight-station tooling turret and two/three-axis NC (*Burgmaster Div., Houdaille Industries*)

Machine motions. The simplest type of machine, the fixed-table, advancing-spindle machine (see Fig. 24-8), is generally used for general-purpose applications. The fixed table requires a fixture to hold and position the workpiece.

Advancing-spindle machines are also available with two-axis tables, which travel vertically and horizontally, perpendicular to the tool, and with three-axis tables, which travel vertically and horizontally, both parallel and perpendicular to the tool.

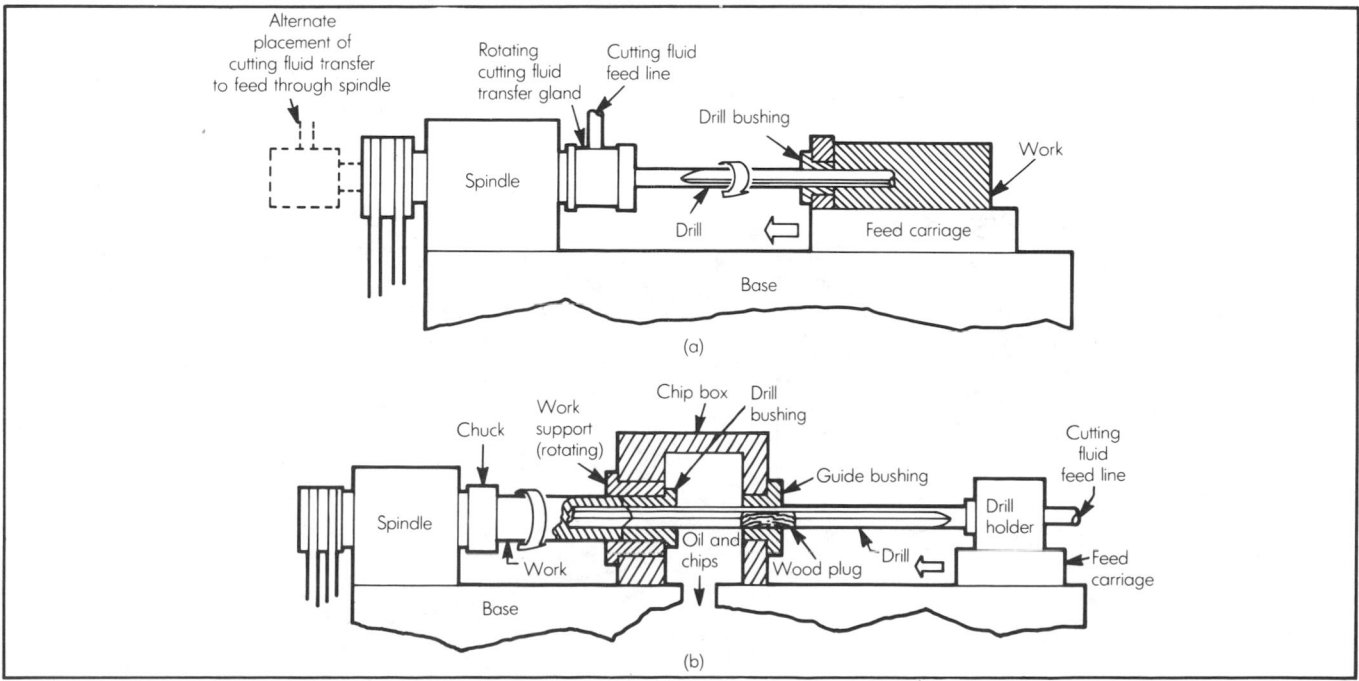

Fig. 24-7 Two methods of gundrilling: (a) tool rotating and workpiece stationary; and (b) workpiece rotating, tool nonrotating. (*Eldorado Tool & Mfg. Corp.*)

DRILLING

The way-type, advancing-spindle machine has the spindle mounted on a column for vertical positioning. The table positions horizontally, parallel, and perpendicular to the tool. Machines are also available with a fixed spindle and a table that advances toward the tool on ways. This type of machine is economical when loading time is short relative to cutting time. The basic machines are also available with automatic-control equipment for high production and more than one spindle.

Trepanning machines. Since trepanning starts at hole diameters where the high-pressure coolant drills leave off, trepanning usually requires a larger machine. Trepanning may be done on any one of several types of machines modified in varying degrees to suit the process. For relatively shallow holes, engine or turret lathes, horizontal or vertical boring mills, or heavy-duty drill presses are used. For deeper holes, engine lathes and some deep-hole drilling machines are suitable. Whatever type of machine is used, it must be extremely rigid and should have infinitely variable and independent feed control.

Coolant systems. Gundrilling, trepanning, and other pressure-coolant tools for deep-hole drilling require a coolant system with the machine which includes a pump, a filtering unit, and sometimes a water chilling or refrigeration system.

Small-Hole Drilling Machines

Major problems in the mechanical drilling of small holes include compensating for the decreased rigidity of the delicate tools required, controlling chip removal, minimizing runout, and maintaining a uniform feed rate. This type of drilling can often be done on conventional machine tools such as lathes, drilling and boring machines, machining and turning centers, and transfer machines. Sensitive drill presses are used extensively for drilling small holes. They are almost always hand fed, with either a sliding quill to advance the rotating drill or an elevating table to force the work into the drill.

Small holes with close tolerances, however, may require special machines with increased rigidity, more accurate spindles,

and sensitive feeding arrangements. Microdrilling machines are available that rotate both the workpiece and the tool and can produce holes of less than 0.001" (0.03 mm) diam. An independently driven, rotating spindle for the drill is mounted in a tailstock on these machines. This rotating, collet-holding spindle assembly is supported on a pair of dovetail slides equipped with micrometer adjustments for precise alignment of the tool centerline with the rotational axis of the workpiece. Sensitive feeding is accomplished by rotating a handwheel on the feedscrew while maintaining pressure on the slide handle.

The ultrasensitive, precision drilling machine illustrated in Fig. 24-9 can be used with various accessories, including a digital readout system and a binocular-type stereoscopic microscope as shown. A pivot-mounted drill-feed mechanism minimizes friction and lost motion and amplifies the operator's sensitivity of touch by 20 times. The spindle is automatically retracted by a calibrated spring when the operator releases the feed lever.

Tool flexing and breakage due to eccentric rotation are minimized on these machines by mounting the drills in mandrels which rotate on two in-line diamond V-bearings. A small collet-type pulley is fitted over the mandrel and connected by an endless belt to the pulley of an isolated vibration-dampened motor. Pull of the belt holds the mandrel firmly against the V-bearings for continuous contact, as shown in the view at the right of Fig. 24-9.

Cam-controlled and CNC models of precision, small-hole drilling machines are also available.

Special-Purpose Drilling Machines

Many drilling machines are built in a wide variety of designs and configurations for special-purpose applications. Special-purpose dedicated machines are often used when large quantities of parts require multiple operations. These include shuttle transfer, dial index, ring index, trunnion index, and in-line transfer machines.

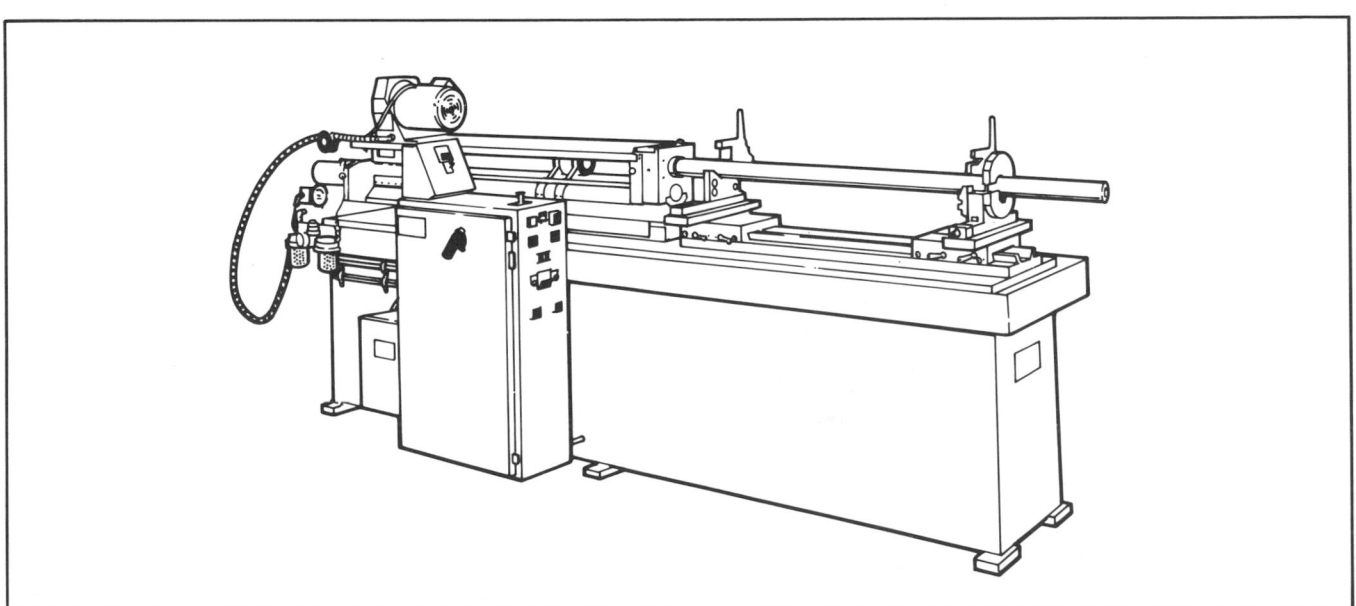

Fig. 24-8 Fixed-table, advancing-spindle machine for deep-hole drilling.

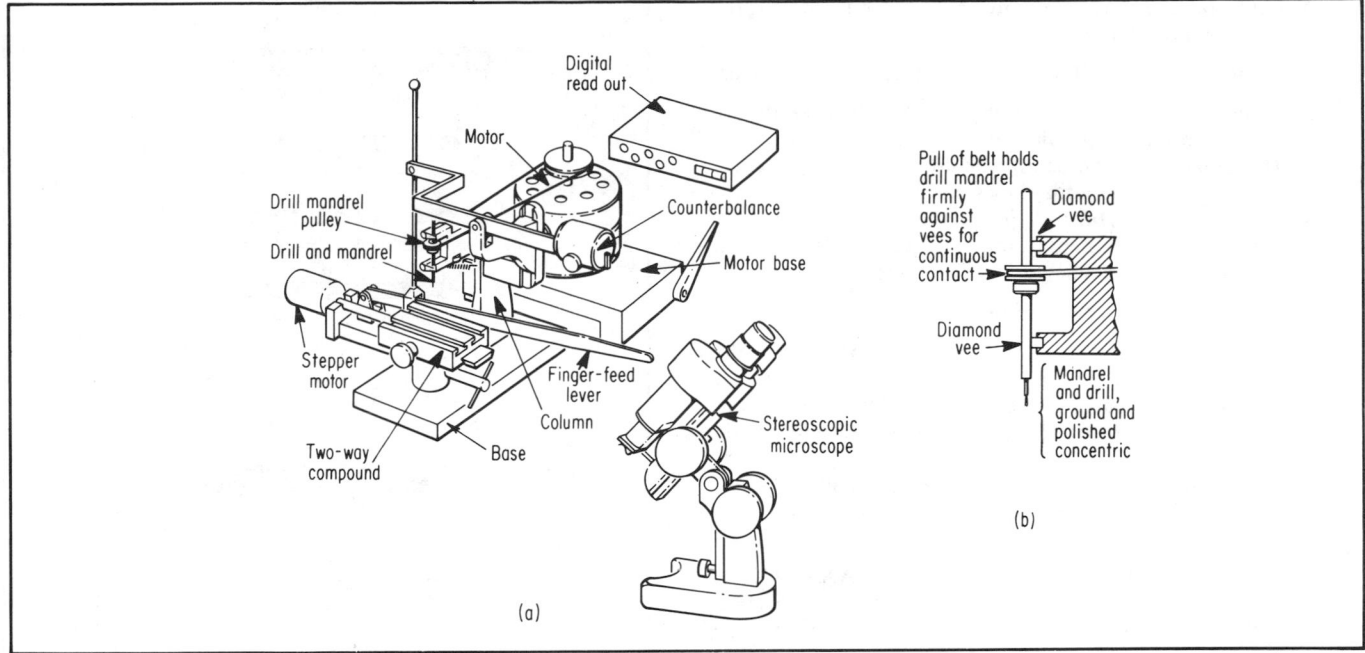

Fig. 24-9 Ultrasensitive drilling machine for producing small holes can be used with digital readout and microscope. Tool breakage is minimized by mounting shown in view at right.

Portable Drilling Units

Considerable drilling is done with portable tools that are powered pneumatically, electrically, or hydraulically. Such tools are used extensively, particularly in the aircraft/aerospace and automotive industries, when workpieces cannot be easily taken to drilling machines. Drilling of fastener holes in airframes with portable tools is probably the most common manufacturing operation required in the aircraft industry, with millions of holes drilled each month.

Some portable tools are available with magnetic bases or other devices for mounting or clamping to the work. In addition to being used for drilling, portable tools are also employed for screwdrivers, nutrunners, impact wrenches, hammers, routers, and grinders, as well as for tapping, nibbling, shearing, sanding, scraping, filing, sawing, and broaching operations.

Portable drills powered by air are the most widely used. Advantages include light weight, smaller size, less vibration, cooler operation, variable speeds, no shock hazard, good torque characteristics, instant reversibility, and in general, lower maintenance costs. Possible limitations include higher initial cost, speed decreasing under load, air exhaust problems, and in some cases, higher operating cost. It is recommended that these tools be operated with clean, dry, and lubricated air, generally at a pressure of about 90 psi (621 kPa), with an air consumption varying from 10-70 cfm (0.3-2m³/min).

Portable electric drills are available for operation on normal (60 Hz) or high-frequency (120, 360, or 400 Hz) current. Advantages of tools that operate on normal frequency current include lower initial cost, readily available power supply, and high efficiency. Disadvantages include a higher weight/power ratio, speed decreasing under load, limited torque characteristics, and possible shock hazard. Many electric drills are now available with electronically controlled, infinitely variable speeds, and tool weights have been reduced. Advantages of tools that operate on high-frequency current include lighter weight, faster speeds, and the ability to maintain speed under load. Disadvantages include the need for a special power source (frequency changer or motor-generator set) and special wiring.

Portable tools with hydraulic motors provide variable speed and feed control. They generally operate at pressures to 1500 psi (10 342 kPa) and require special hydraulic power units.

TWIST DRILLS

Drills are defined as rotary end-cutting tools having one or more cutting lips and one or more helical or straight flutes for the passage of chips and the admission of a cutting fluid. These cutting tools are made in a wide variety of types with many different forms, dimensions, and tolerances.

Twist drills are not considered to be precision cutting tools; rather, they are tools designed to produce holes rapidly and economically. When precision is required, subsequent operations such as boring or reaming are generally required. Drilling, using twist drills having tapered webs, is also generally limited to hole depths of about three to five times the hole diameter unless the woodpeckering technique of periodic tool withdrawal is employed or coolant-fed twist drills (discussed later in this chapter) are used.

Classification of Twist Drills

Twist drills can be classified by the material from which they are made, kinds of shank, number of flutes, hand of cut, length, diameter, and point geometry.

Based on the kind of shank, twist drills can be classified as:

1. *Straight-shank drills.* Those having cylindrical shanks which may be the same or different diameter than the body of the drill. The shanks may be provided with or without driving flats, tangs, grooves, or threads.
2. *Taper-shank drills.* Those having conical shanks suitable for direct fitting into tapered holes in machine spindles, driving sleeves, or sockets. Taper-shank drills generally

DRILLING

have a tang to assist in driving and to permit removing the drill from the spindle or holder.

Based on the number of flutes, twist drills can be classified as:

1. *Single-flute drills.* These tools, having only one flute, are used for originating holes and for drilling plastics.
2. *Two-flute drills.* These are the conventional type drills also used for originating holes.
3. *Three or four-flute drills* (core drills). These are commonly used for enlarging and finishing drilled, cast, or punched holes. They do not produce original holes.

Based on hand of cut, twist drills can be classified as:

1. *Right-hand cut.* As viewed when looking toward the point of these drills, with their shanks extending away, they must be rotated in a counterclockwise direction in order to cut. Most drills are made for right-hand rotation.
2. *Left-hand cut.* When viewed from the cutting point, clockwise rotation is necessary for cutting.

Nomenclature

The following terminology is extracted from ANSI B94.11-M-1979, "Twist Drills—Straight Shank and Taper Shank, Combined Drills and Countersinks," with the permission of the publisher, ASME (see Fig. 24-10). Many of these terms also apply to other types of drills.

Types of Twist Drills

Twist drills are manufactured in a wide variety of types, some of which are illustrated in Fig. 24-11, and in many different sizes. To produce a hole of any given diameter, twist drills are commercially available with variations in length, flute and shank configuration, point geometry, and web thickness. In some cases, a dozen or more drills may be available to produce the same size hole.

Drills are made in many different diameter sizes—fractional, number (wire gage), letter, and metric—ranging from 0.0059" (0.150 mm) to 3 1/2" (89 mm). However, data compiled by National Twist Drill, based on sales of more than 50-million standard twist drills, showed that a median 90% of all sales (5% were for larger sizes, and 5% for smaller) fall between 0.050 and 0.400" (1.27 and 10.16 mm) diam.

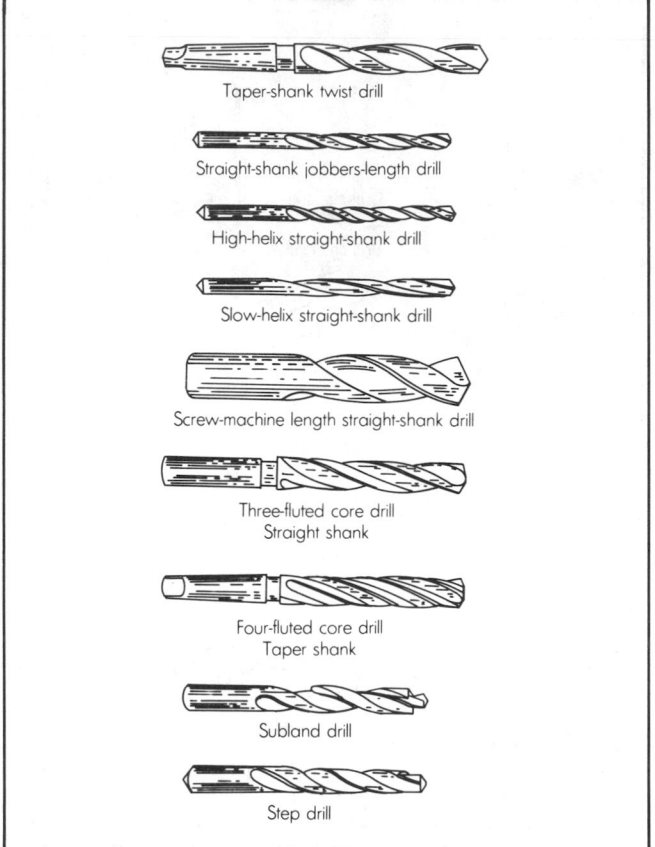

Fig. 24-11 Some conventional and special-purpose twist drills.

For simplification purposes, many styles of drills can be classified separated into general-purpose and heavy-duty categories. General-purpose drills are the most widely used. Slight alterations of the original point angles sometimes improve performance for given speeds and feeds. Heavy-duty drills are designed to provide greater torsional strength and rigidity than general-purpose drills. They can be used to drill steel forgings, hard castings, and high-hardness ferrous alloys.

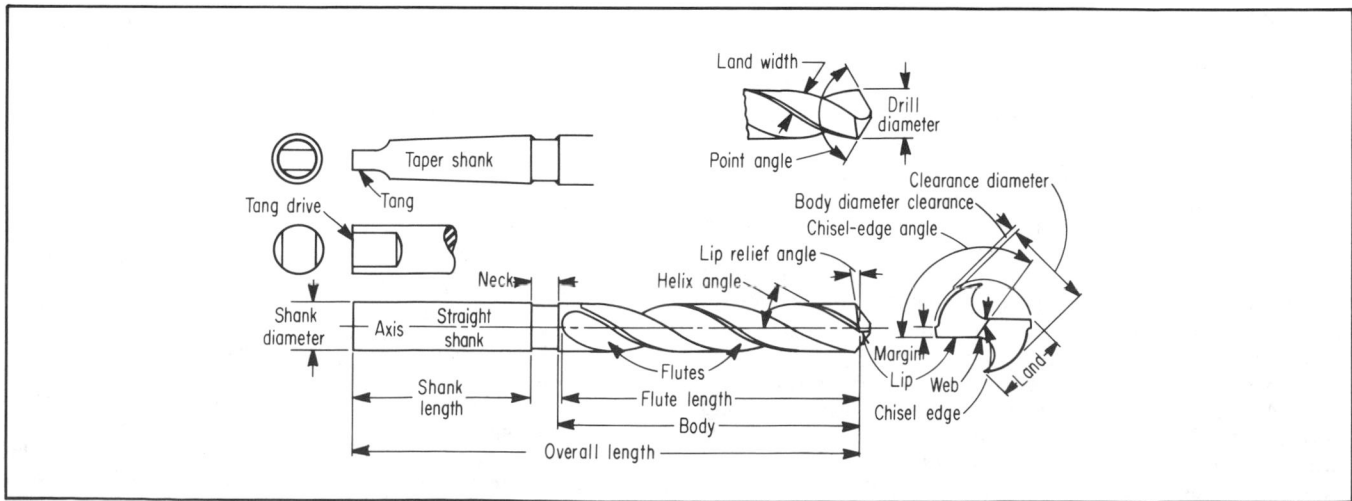

Fig. 24-10 Standard terms used to describe elements of twist drills.

Twist Drill Geometries

Efficient drilling of the wide variety of materials encountered in industry today requires many different drill designs and geometries. Many holes can be drilled satisfactorily with standard off-the-shelf twist drills, but no one drill is best for all applications. Variations in drills being used, while maintaining required strength and sufficient room for easy chip ejection, include different drill points, lip relief and clearance angles, and flute construction (helix angle, web thickness, and web thinning).

Various degrees of included-point angle, with proper lip relief, and specific types of web thinning are used to perform the following:

1. Control the formation of the chips produced.
2. Control the size and shape of the chips.
3. Control chip flow along the flutes.
4. Increase the strength of the cutting lips.
5. Reduce the rate of cutting lip wear.
6. Reduce the thrust required for drilling.
7. Control the hole size and quality.
8. Control the size and amount of burrs produced.
9. Reduce the amount of heat generated.
10. Permit variations in cutting speed and feed rate for more efficient drilling.

Drill points. Since drill points form the cutting edges, their geometries are critical to tool performance. There is a variety of point styles being used today; some of the more common ones are described in this section. Proper selection, control, and use of drill points can result in substantial savings in drilling costs.

Single-angle points. Standard twist drills having conventional points with a 118° included angle are the most commonly used because they provide satisfactory results in drilling a wide variety of materials. The cutting lips on these drills are essentially straight lines, with the heel side of each land a smooth curve (see Fig. 24-12, *a*).

A possible limitation to the use of this conventional point is that its straight chisel edge contributes to wandering of the point, often making it necessary to first use a center drill for improved hole accuracy. Also, the sharp corners tend to break down more rapidly than some other geometries available, and there is more of a tendency to produce burrs on breakthrough.

As a result, drills with this type point are generally best suited for applications for which close tolerances are not required.

As the hardness of the workpiece material decreases, improved drill performance can be achieved by reducing the included angle of the drill point to 60-90°. Drills having these more acute point angles produce thinner chips for a given feed rate and are commonly used, with low-helix flutes, for producing holes in soft plastics and nonferrous materials. Drills having points with a 90° included angle are also used occasionally for drilling soft cast irons and certain woods.

Similarly, as the hardness of the workpiece material or depth of hole increases, the included angle of the drill point is increased to 135-140°. These larger point angles produce thicker and narrower chips for a given feed rate. Drills with these flatter points are generally used to produce holes in harder, tougher materials, and they usually minimize burring. It is especially important to use guide bushings with drill points having higher angles because there is a tendency for the points to skid or walk on the workpiece surfaces when starting holes.

Double-angle points. Twist drills with double-angle points (see Fig. 24-12, *b*) are generated by first grinding a larger included angle (118 or 135°) and then a smaller included angle (typically 90°) on the corners. This provides the effect of chamfers and reduces abrasive wear on the corners.

Initial applications for this style point were in drilling medium and hard cast irons as well as other very abrasive materials to reduce corner wear on the drills. More recent applications include improving hole sizes and finishes and drilling very hard materials to reduce chipping of the corners of the lips. Twist drills with double-angle points are often used for the same applications as drills with rounded-edge (radiused lip) points, discussed later in this section.

Reduced-rake points. A common and easily applied point variation is the flatted cutting lip. Both cutting edges are flatted on their flute faces, called dubbing, from the cutting lip corners to the chisel edge, as illustrated in Fig. 24-12, *c*. This type of point reduces the effective axial rake to 0-5° positive, causing a pushing or plowing of metal rather than a shearing action. Reduced shearing action is an effective method of preventing the tools from digging in when drilling is performed on materials with low tensile strengths such as many types of brass, bronze, and some of the harder acrylic plastics such as

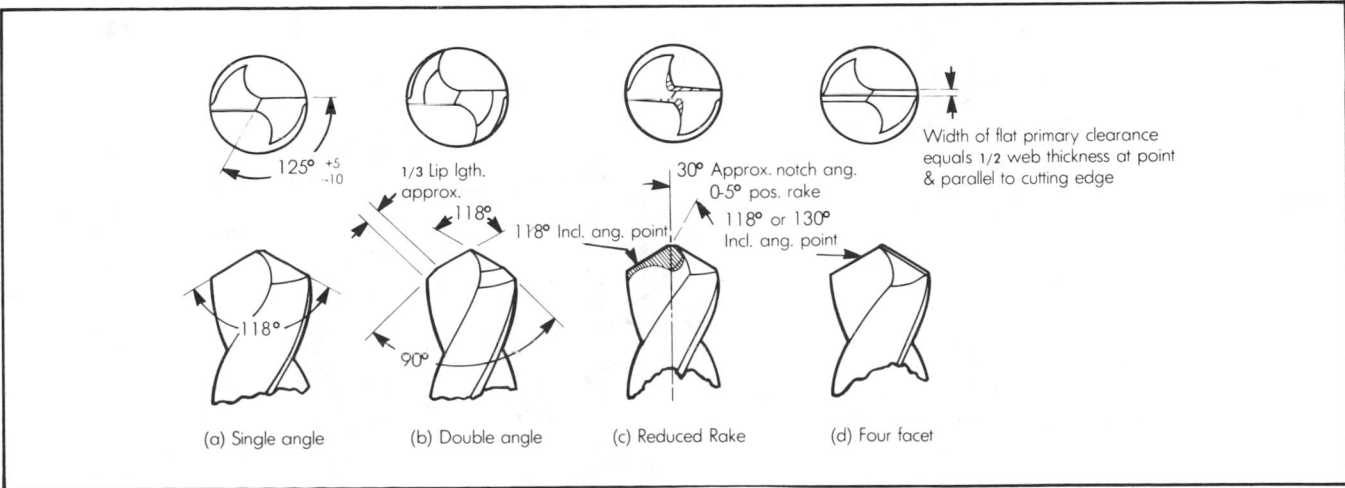

Fig. 24-12 Four types of drill point geometries used for different applications. (*Cleveland Twist Drill Co.*)

DRILLING

Plexiglas. Reducing the rake also strengthens the cutting lips, and this type of point is often used in operations in which chipping of the lips has been a problem.

Four and six-facet points. The geometry of a four-facet point (see Fig. 24-12 *d*) is generated by grinding flat primary relief (10-18°) and secondary clearance angles (25-35°) on the end of each flute. The width of the primary relief flat is equal to one-half the web thickness, resulting in four facets on the end of the drill which subtend at a point on the drill axis and entirely remove the chisel edge. Six-facet points are produced by adding two cutting edges at the web of four-facet points.

Since these points are exactly in the middle of the drills, the tools are self-centering and accurate and straight holes can be produced. They also require less power and thrust and permit increased feed rates. Drills with these points, however, are subject to more wear on their margins, and they cannot be modified to suit drilling of various materials. Another disadvantage is the cost of resharpening with a special machine.

Four and six-facet points have found their greatest use for solid carbide drills used to produce holes in printed circuit board materials such as fiberglass-epoxy. The points may also be used on small-diameter HSS drills that do not lend themselves to normal point-splitting techniques.

Split-points. This type of point, also called a crankshaft point, was originally developed for use on drills designed for producing small-diameter, deep holes in automotive crankshafts. Since then it has gained widespread use for drilling a wide variety of hard and soft materials. Heavy-duty types with thicker webs are used for drilling stainless steels, titanium, tough alloys, and high temperature resistant alloys. Drills with this type of point are also employed extensively for applications in which guide bushings cannot be used, as well as for portable drilling applications.

In generating split points on drills, the clearance face of each cutting edge is given a sharp (55° typical) secondary relief to the center of the chisel edge (see Fig. 24-13), thus creating a secondary cutting lip on the opposite cutting edge. The angle

between these lip segments acts as a chipbreaker when drilling is done on many materials, producing smaller chips that are readily ejected through the flutes. More importantly, however, the additional cutting edges produced and the reduction in width of the original chisel edge reduces thrust requirements (typically 25-30% compared to conventional 118° points) and improves the centering capability. A disadvantage is the need for a point-splitting grinding machine.

Helical (spiral) points. This type of point is generated by reducing the drill point from a chisel edge to a helical (spiral) point, as illustrated in Fig. 24-14. This produces an S-shaped chisel with a radiused crown effect which has its highest point at the center of the drill axis. This S-shaped chisel creates a continuous cutting edge extending from margin to margin across the web.

Advantages of drills with a helical point include a self-centering capability and some reduction of thrust. Their use also results in better hole geometry and improved hole size.

A possible disadvantage of this type of point is that burrs are sometimes produced at hole breakthrough. Also, the S-shaped chisel is weaker than straight chisel points, resulting in faster dulling when hard materials are drilled. Special machines are required to grind these points.

Rounded-edge (radiused-lip) points. These points are generated by grinding a blended, rounded edge (radiused corner or lip) on conventional points (see Fig. 24-15). Points such as these provide a continuously varying point angle, with the lips and margins blended by a smooth curve. Because the drill cuts on long, curved lips, there is less load per unit area and less heat generated. Since the corner is eliminated, margin wear is reduced. Breakthrough burrs are eliminated, and tool life can be lengthened compared to conventionally pointed drills when cast iron is drilled. Feed rates can also be increased because of the improved heat dissipation.

Twist drills with rounded-edge points are used when drill life is most important. Drills with these points are not self-centering and are best applied where guide bushings are used. When used

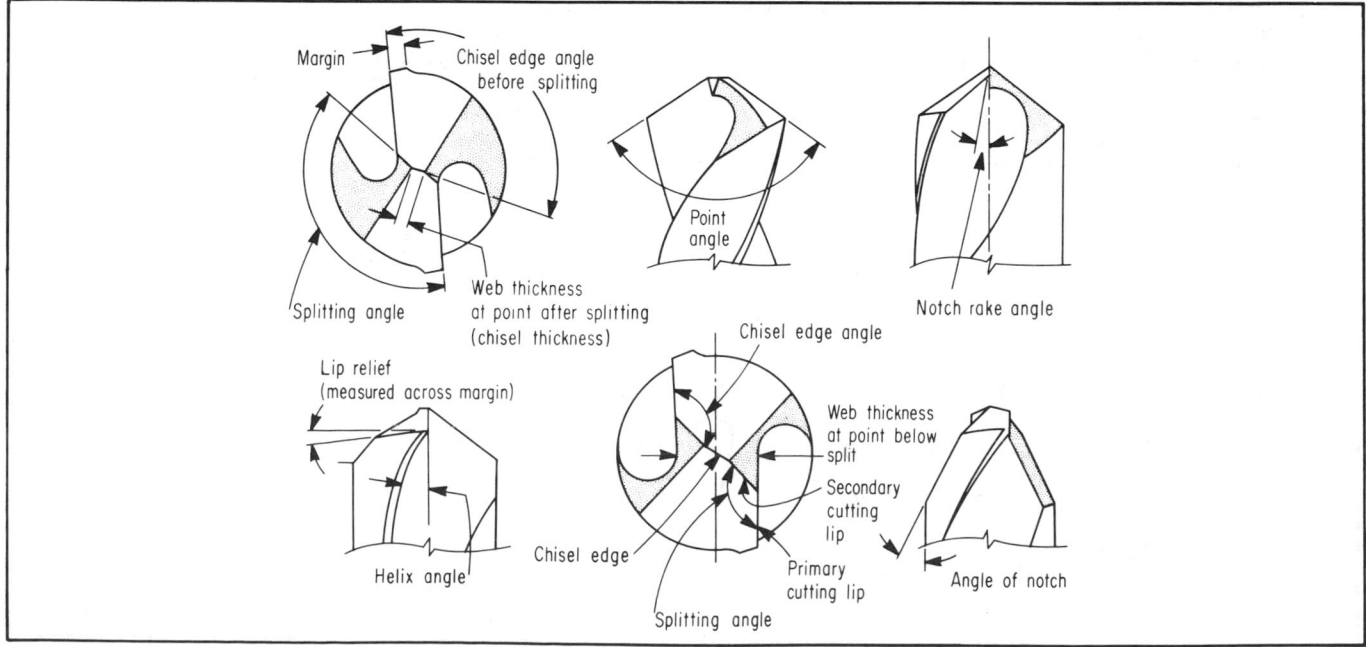

Fig. 24-13 Geometry of split-point twist drill.

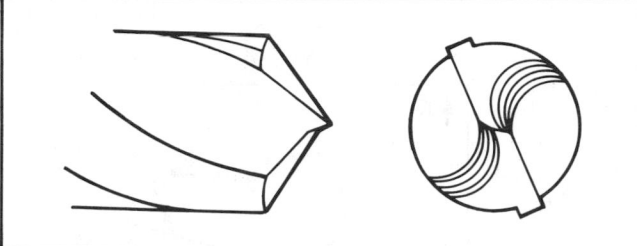

Fig. 24-14 Helical (spiral) point which has an S-shaped point rather than a straight-line chisel edge.

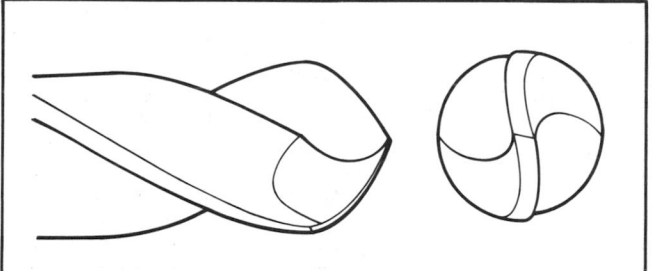

Fig. 24-15 Rounded-edge point which has lips and margins blended by smooth curves.

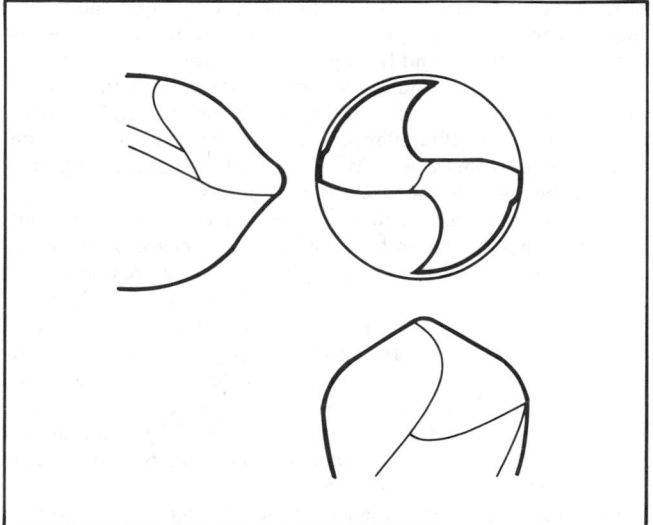

Fig. 24-16 Twist drill point combines features of helical and rounded-edge points. (*Giddings & Lewis-Bickford Machine Co.*)

on NC machines, prior center drilling is required. The time required for center drilling, however, may be more than offset by longer tool life. A possible limitation is that special grinding machines are required to produce these points. Also, when steel is drilled, these points cut closer to size, which may reduce drill life compared to that possible with conventional points because of greater corner and margin wear.

Combined helical/rounded-edge points. Drill grinding machines are available that combine features of both the helical and rounded-edge points. The point produced (see Fig. 24-16) provides the self-centering capability of helical points and the long life, burr-free breakthrough, and higher feed capacity of rounded-edge points. These features make the drills capable of producing accurate holes on NC machines without the need for prior center drilling.

Lip relief. The lip relief angle used on a drill is also important. With inadequate lip relief, a drill will not cut freely; excessive relief will shorten the drill life. It is even more important that the relief angle on each lip be equal and that the relief surfaces be in close axial relationship to each other. The amount of hole oversize produced increases with an increase in relative lip height.

The amount of relief depends primarily upon the drill diameter, cutting edge strength, and the material to be drilled.

Higher relief angles generally provide best results with light feeds and low-strength, nonferrous materials. Some of the plastics and cast irons also require higher relief angles because of their abrasiveness. With heavy feeds, as well as harder workpiece materials, reduced relief angles provide cutting edges with additional support to withstand the higher cutting loads.

Web thickness. Because the chisel edges are noncutting portions of drill points, the webs of twist drills are made as thin as possible, consistent with adequate structural strength. The approximate web thicknesses near the points of standard drills, expressed as a percentage of the drill diameters, are presented in Table 24-1. Heavy-duty drills have thicker webs (about twice the

TABLE 24-1
Approximate Web Thickness of Standard Twist Drills, Percentage of Drill Diameter

Drill Size, Number and Fractional, Inches	Web Thickness Percentage of Drill Diameter
Nos. 80 to 66 (0.0135-0.0330)	30
Nos. 65 to 56 (0.0350-0.0465)	25
No. 55 to 3/16 (0.0520-0.1875)	20
3/16 to 1/4 (0.1875-0.2500)	17
1/4 to 5/8 (0.2500-0.6250)	15
5/8 to 1 3/8 (0.6250-1.3750)	13
1 3/8 to 2 3/8 (1.3750-2.3750)	12
Over 2 3/8 (2.3750)	11

thickness of standard general-purpose drills) and often have narrower flutes to increase torsional stiffness.

Most drills are manufactured with webs which increase in thickness toward their shanks. Resharpening of a worn drill shortens the drill and increases the web thickness and chisel edge length (see Fig. 24-17). This results in increased thrust requirements, additional heat generation, and shorter drill life unless the web is thinned to its original thickness. Heavy-duty drills generally require thinning before they are used. The web thickness on some deep-hole drills, however, does not increase; the thickness is the same at the chisel end as it is at the end of the flutes and is called a parallel web.

Thrust force on a twist drill is more sensitive to changes in web thickness than is the drill torque, as can be seen by comparing the two graphs in Fig. 24-18. These graphs show how drill torque and thrust are influenced by changes in chisel edge length, which is proportional to web thickness. They were calculated from test results with 1/2″ (12.7 mm) diam drills fed at the rate of 0.010 ipr (0.25 mm/rev) in SAE 3245 steel having a

DRILLING

hardness of 200 Brinell. In addition to total torque and thrust requirements, these graphs also show the approximate contributions of drill web and lip regions to the total.

Most of the drill torque results from the outer portions of the drill lips because this is where most of the material removal occurs. For a drill of regular proportions, only about 15% of the torque comes from the web. With a drill of regular design, about 50% of the total thrust force is caused by the web. If the web thickness is doubled, the thrust force is increased by more than 60%; then, about 75% of the total thrust is caused by the web.

Web thinning. Several types of web thinning are commonly used. The type shown in Fig. 24-19, *a*, is perhaps the most common. Length A is usually one-half to three-fourths the length of the cutting lip. In this type of thinning, as well as in all others, it is important that the thinning cut extend far enough up the flute so that an abrupt wedge is not formed at the extreme point. The distance of the thinned cut varies with the amount of thinning required, but an average of one-fourth to one-half the drill diameter is usually satisfactory.

Sometimes it is advisable to extend the thinning out to the extreme edge in order to change the shape of the chip. In this type of thinning (see Fig. 24-19, *b*), a positive effective rake is maintained the full length of the cutting edge. A third type of thinning often used results in the split or crankshaft point described previously.

Some manufacturers offer self-thinned webs on jobbers-length twist drills. These drills have a web which is straight (uniformly thick) for one-third or more of the flute lengths and then tapers toward the shank.

Helix angles. The helix angle on standard twist drills generally ranges from 25-33°. High-helix (fast-spiral) drills with helix angles of 35-40° and low-helix (slow-spiral) drills with helix angles of 15-20° are also commercially available for drilling certain materials and special applications, as discussed previously in the section on types of drills.

Although used in Europe for many years, a relatively recent introduction to the United States is the parabolic flute twist drill

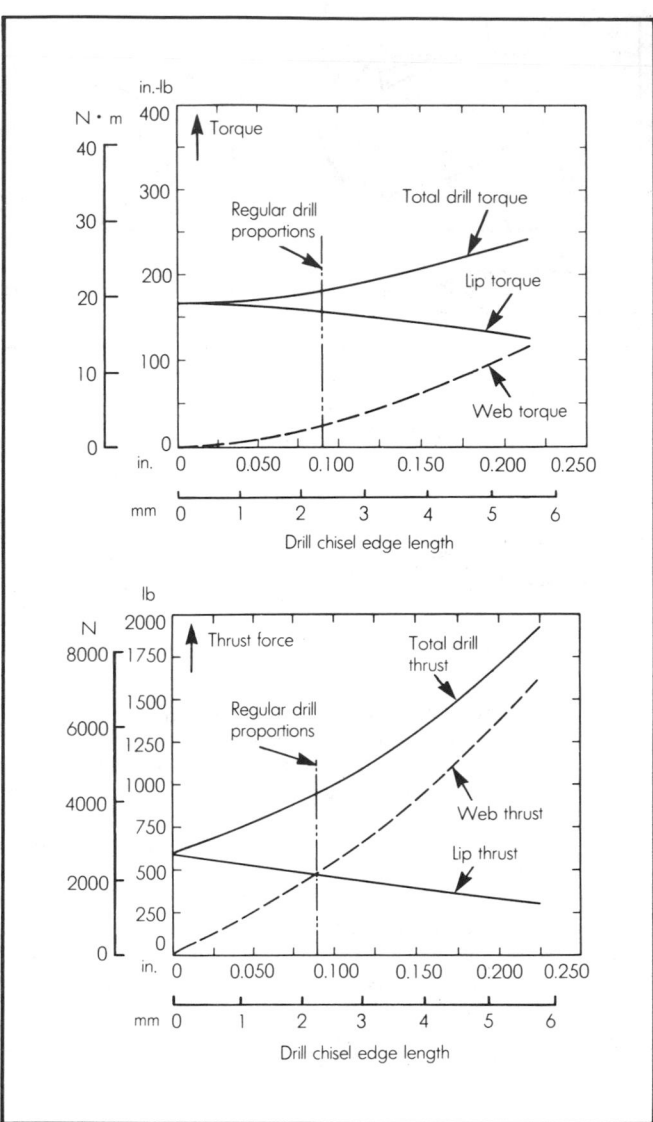

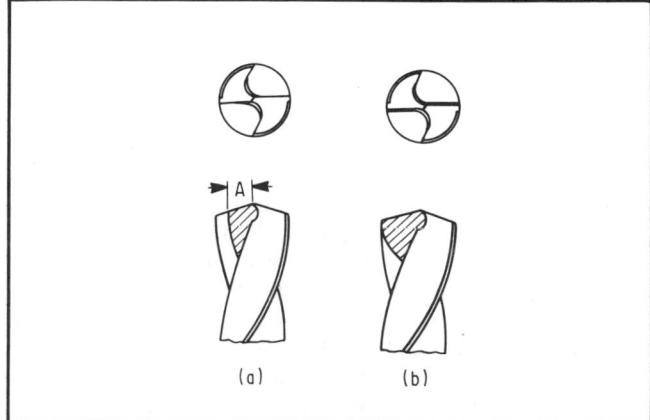

Fig. 24-18 (a) Effect of chisel edge length on torque; (b) thrust force (bottom graph). (*National Twist Drill***)**

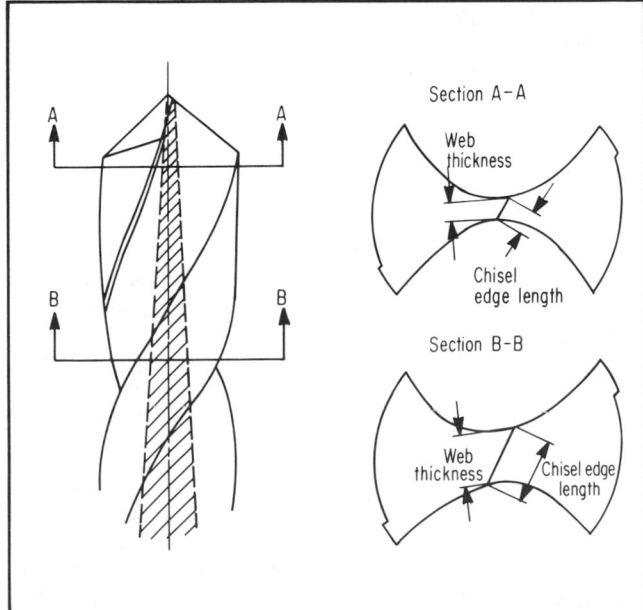

Fig. 24-17 Resharpening of twist drill progressively increased the web thickness and chisel edge length.

Fig. 24-19 Two types of web thinning: (a) at chisel edge and (b) undercut thinned point.

that provides more open flutes for improved chip removal and cutting fluid flow while permitting heavy webs for high torsional strength. Combined with webs of constant thickness, they have proven to be ideal for deep-hole drilling in cast irons, mild steels, and aluminum alloys. A twist drill with parabolic flutes and a split point is illustrated in Fig. 24-20. For some deep-hole applications (with depth-to-diameter ratios to 12:1 or more), speeds and feeds to 100% greater than conventional drills have been reported, often eliminating the need for woodpeckering.

COOLANT-FED TWIST DRILLS

Coolant-fed twist drills having means for directing coolant (fluid, gas, or mist) to the cutting edges offer many advantages for certain drilling applications. Oil-hole drills have been used for many years to produce deep holes. They were originally developed for applications such as horizontal or inverted drilling in which point cooling and/or chip ejection presented problems.

Now, improved types of coolant-fed twist drills are being used increasingly for a wide variety of more common drilling applications, including shallow holes, in which higher penetration rates or longer tool life are desired. They are employed extensively in machining centers, multispindle bar and chucking machines, screw machines, turret lathes, and other machine tools

for producing holes shallower than those that are usually drilled by self-guiding deep-hole drills (discussed later in this chapter). Small-diameter, coolant-fed twist drills are also used extensively for portable drilling applications in the aircraft industry.

Advantages of Coolant-Fed Tooling

In many drilling applications, coolant is misdirected and wasted. As a result, benefits are minimal. With coolant-fed tooling, however, the coolant is directed close to the cutting edge, thereby substantially reducing friction and temperatures at the drill/workpiece interface. This reduces wear and lengthens drill life, resulting in reduced costs per hole drilled because of less downtime for tool changes and regrinds.

Depending upon the application, faster cutting speeds and feed rates can generally be used, thus increasing the metal removal rate and productivity. Results of one drilling study using two solid and two coolant-fed drills showed that the coolant-fed drills were capable of considerably higher penetration rates (see Fig. 24-21). This plot of drill life as a function of penetration rate was made for drilling 4″ (102 mm) deep through holes in SAE 1018 steel, having a hardness of 127 Bhn, for two varieties of solid 7/8″ (22 mm) diam twist drills and two varieties of 7/8″ coolant-fed twist drills. The life of the solid drills for this single test ranged from over 350″ (8890 mm) when

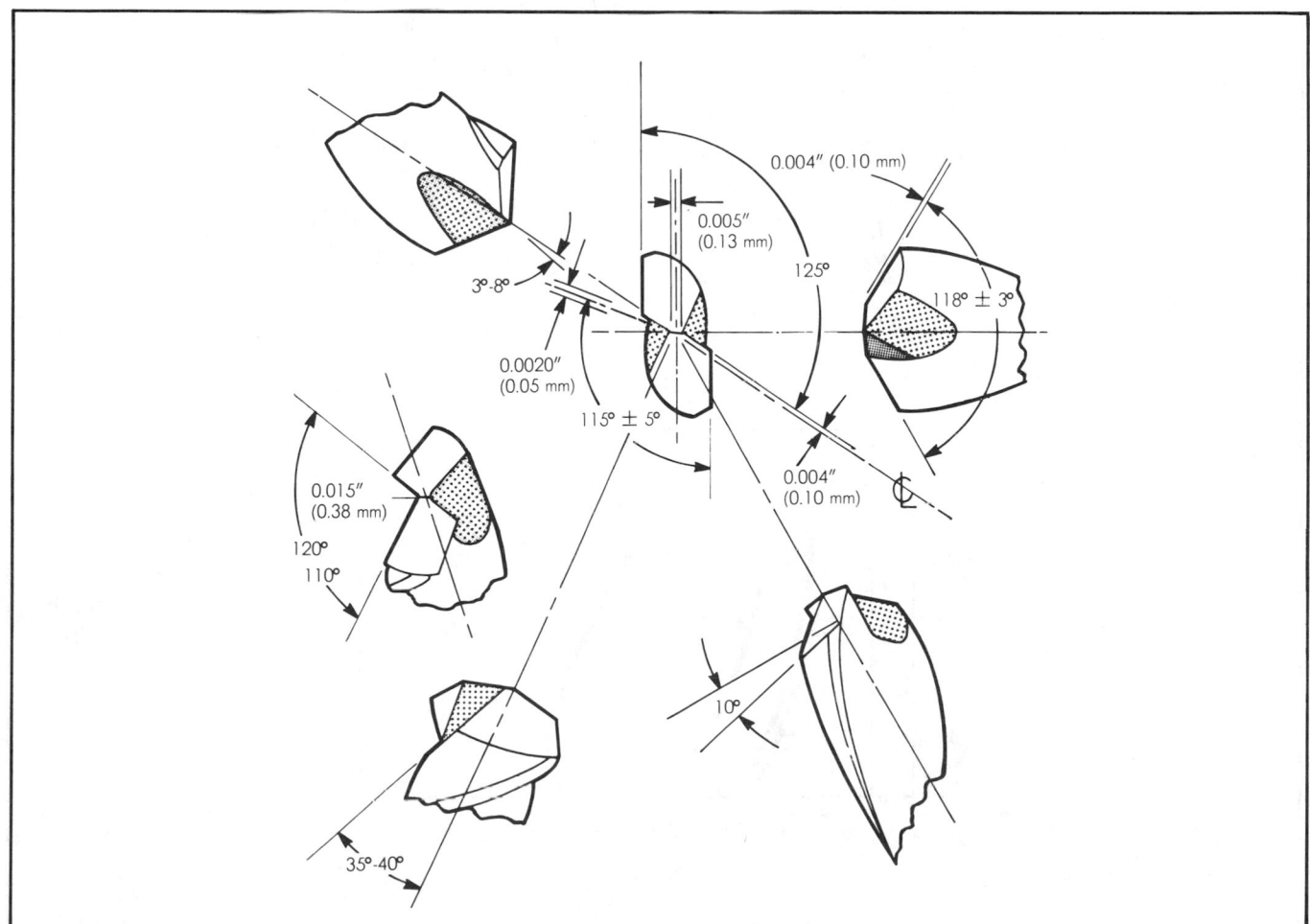

Fig. 24-20 Twist drill with parabolic flutes and a split point. (*Bendix Industrial Tools Div.*)

DRILLING

drilled at a penetration rate of 6 ipm (152 mm/min) to less than 50″ (1270 mm) when drilled at 12 ipm (305 mm/min), using flood coolant. By nature of comparison, coolant-fed drill D produced over 400″ (10 160 mm) at a penetration rate of 11 ipm (279 mm/min), and coolant-fed drill C, more than 400″ at 23 ipm (584 mm/min).

The high-helix, coolant-fed drill, C, is clearly the best style for use in this rather mild, normally stringy chip material and effectively more than triples the penetration rate for this application. A coolant flow of 2.5 gpm (9.5 L/min) was provided through these drills, obtained by using a pressure pump operating at 70 psi (483 kPa). For setting up any coolant-fed drill applications, common practice is to start with speeds 10% higher and feeds 25% higher than those established for solid twist drills.

Productivity is also improved by eliminating the need for interrupting the drilling cycle to withdraw the tool to clear chips (woodpeckering). Coolant-fed drills generally improve chip removal. Consequently, heat transfer to the chips, tool, and workpiece is minimized; buildup on the drill cutting edges is reduced; and holes with improved accuracy and smoother finishes are produced. Air pollution from smoke or mist may also be minimized because of reduced heat and friction.

For some applications in the aircraft, aerospace, and nuclear industries, the use of coolant-fed drills has improved surface integrity by eliminating tearing, checking, and cracking of workpiece materials.

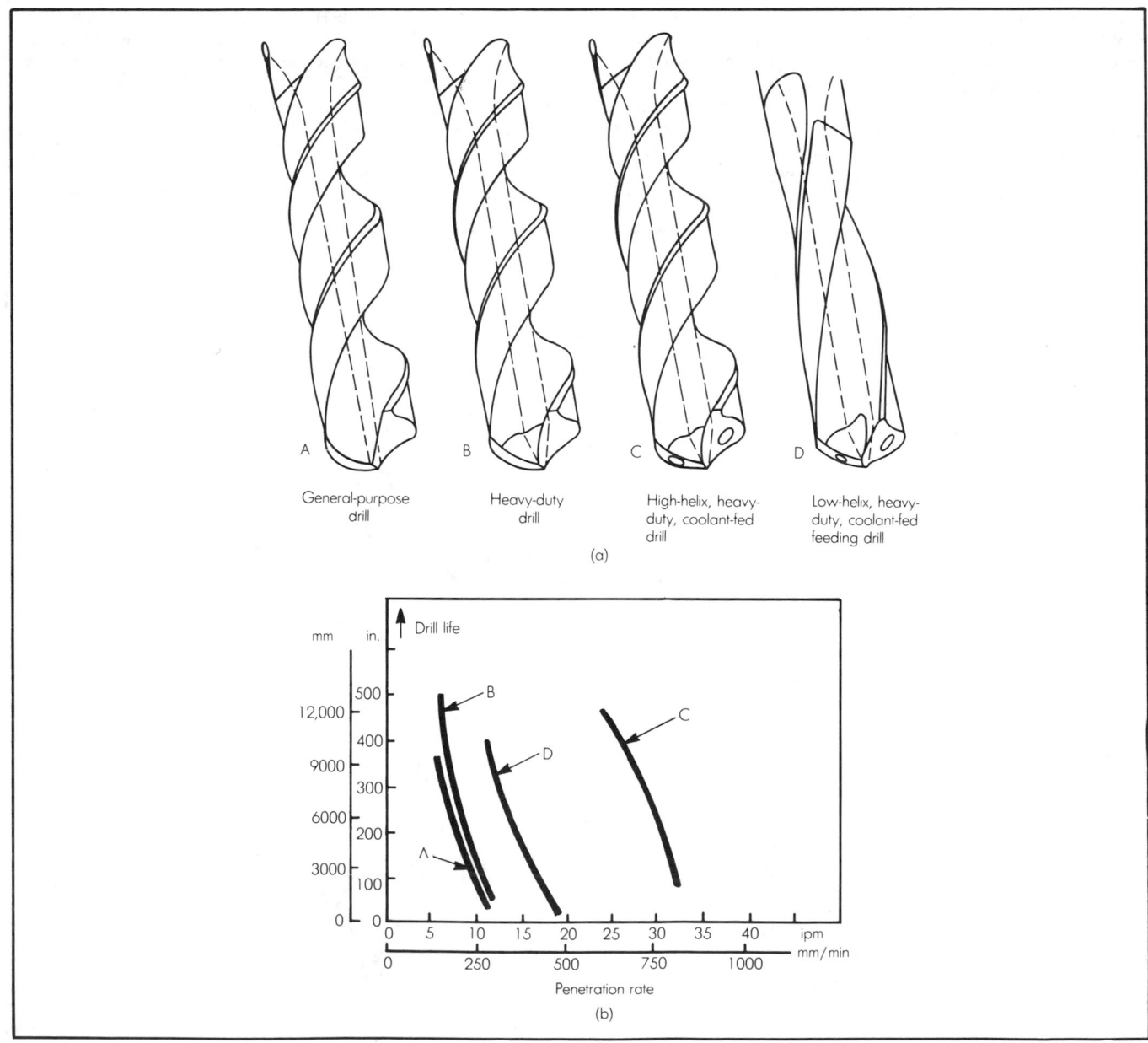

Fig. 24-21 (a) Two solid and two coolant-fed drills used in study to show (b) increased penetration rates possible with coolant-fed drills.

Limitations of Coolant-Fed Twist Drills

The higher initial cost of coolant-fed drills and related equipment is often an unjustified deterrent to the more extensive use of these tools. Comparative studies frequently show that increased productivity, longer tool life, and other advantages often make these tools economically desirable. It is the cost per hole, not the tool cost, that is most important.

Longer setup time may be a problem in justifying coolant-fed tools for some short-run applications. While some machines are equipped with hollow spindles to supply coolant to these tools, other machines may require some alteration to provide coolant piping, splash shielding, and other accessories. Another possible limitation is that the machine to be used may not have adequate power to take advantage of the higher feeds and speeds possible with coolant-fed drills.

Types of Coolant-Fed Drills

There are several styles of coolant-fed twist drills. One style has a tube secured in a groove machined in each land to deliver coolant to the cutting lips. Another, more common, type has holes extending internally through each of the two lands.

Coolant-fed twist drills are available with either straight or taper shanks, in a wide range of sizes, 1/8 to 3″ (3.2 to 76 mm) diam, and in extra-long lengths. Medium to heavy-duty drills with constant (parallel) web construction are generally best for most applications. A fairly heavy web construction, about 30% of the drill diameter, is generally needed for strength because of the increased feed rates often used with these tools.

Drills with a low helix angle of about 14-22° are widely used for stationary tooling, horizontal drilling applications, and cast iron drilling. The low helix angle provides shorter paths for the coolant and chips, but requires higher torque and thrust forces. Drills with a medium-high helix angle of about 30-34° are generally recommended for vertical drilling. They usually outperform low-helix drills in soft materials and in most applications when the tools are rotating.

The points of coolant-fed twist drills, generally having a standard 118° included angle, should be notch thinned to the proper geometry for the material to be drilled so that thrust requirements can be minimized. A web thickness at the chisel point of 5-10% of the drill diameter, depending upon drill size, is generally recommended.

Slight modifications of the point geometry may be necessary in drilling some materials to ensure the formation of short, tightly curled, figure six shaped chips that will flow easily through the drill flutes. Chip width can be reduced and thickness increased by using a higher included-point angle (such as 135°), which produces shorter cutting lips and more desirable chips. A corner chamfer may be helpful for some applications. The shortest possible drill should always be used for the hole depth required to increase rigidity and improve accuracy.

High-speed steel drills are satifactory for most coolant-fed drilling applications. Carbide-tipped drills are generally more economical for producing a large number of holes in cast iron or other abrasive materials and often provide longer life when hard or tough materials are being drilled.

FLAT, HALF-ROUND, AND STRAIGHT-FLUTE DRILLS

All holes produced by the drilling process are not cut with twist drills. For example, the flat, half-round, and straight-flute drills discussed in this section, while not used as extensively as twist drills, have definite advantages for certain applications. Other nontwist drills discussed in subsequent sections of this chapter are indexable-insert, spade, and deep and small-hole drills.

Flat Drills

These tools derive their name from the shape of the drill body, which is flat rather than the normal round configuration (see Fig. 24-22). They are produced by grinding tapered opposite flats on the drill body. The flats are usually not parallel, which creates a web that is thicker at the shank. A slight back taper of 0.001″ (0.03 mm) or less is ground on the body.

Flat drills have a low productive capacity, but because of their simple design and low cost, they are occasionally used for low-volume applications in drilling hard forgings and castings. With spear points, flat drills are also used to produce holes in glass and tile. Standard flat drills, made from high-speed steel or carbide, are available from 3/32 to 1/2″ (2.4 to 13 mm) diam. For small-hole drilling, they are generally made from carbide only in diameters from 0.001 to 3/32″ (0.03 to 2.4 mm).

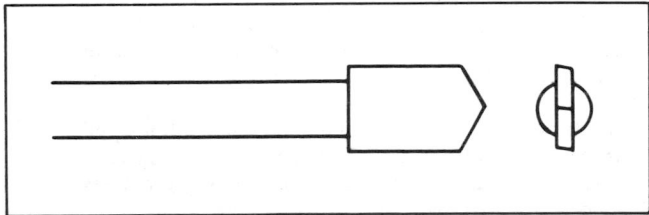

Fig. 24-22 Flat drill of the type sometimes used to produce holes in hardened steel, glass, and tile.

Half-Round Drills

Half-round drills are round rods with about half of their diameters machined or ground away to form the drill bodies (see Fig. 24-23). The drills have a conical point that is offset to provide radial relief for a single cutting lip. The points can be ground either like a conventional twist drill with radial relief or a gundrill (discussed later in this section), depending upon the rigidity of the setup. It is important that the apex of the cone be exactly on the centerline of the drill. Half-round drills are available in fractional, number (wire gage), letter, and metric sizes from about 0.003-1″ (0.08-25.4 mm) diam and are made of high-speed steel, of carbide, or with carbide tips.

Half-round drills with precise conical points can sometimes start holes accurately without the use of guide bushings, especially when the tools are short and rigid, and have little tendency to wander. As a result, they are used extensively for screw machine applications and on some NC machines. For some applications, holes are started with short, rigid center drills and completed with half-round drills. These drills are particularly suitable for use in brass and, in some cases, aluminum alloys and diecast materials. Because of the support they provide in the holes being drilled, they are capable of maintaining close tolerances and producing smooth finishes, sometimes eliminating the need for subsequent reaming. Chip-ejection limitations, however, restrict their deep-hole drilling capabilities.

Straight-Flute Drills

These tools are designed to produce short chips and have limited applications for drilling brass, copper alloys, and other

DRILLING

soft, nonferrous materials, particularly in horizontal drilling applications. The straight flutes eliminate the tendency for the drills to run ahead and grab or pull in the material; because of this, they are desirable for thin sheet metal work. The drills are commercially available in fractional and number sizes with short (jobbers) lengths and straight or taper shanks.

Heavy-duty, carbide-tipped, straight-flute drills are specifically made for drilling steels having a hardness over R_C50 and for producing shallow holes in brittle materials. These tools, sometimes called die drills, have heavy lands and shallow flutes. They are not suitable for drilling soft steels from which long chips are produced.

Coolant-fed, carbide-tipped drills with two straight flutes are also available. Some are made from crimped tubing and others are made from solid HSS bars. Some drill manufacturers offer replaceable tip tools having two straight flutes with HSS or carbide bits being held in place with retaining screws instead of being brazed. Coolant is supplied by tubes brazed into grooves along the lands or through holes in the drill body.

INDEXABLE-INSERT DRILLS

The most important recent advance in drilling technology was the development during the early 1970's of drills with indexable carbide inserts. These tools can produce relatively shallow holes from the solid at faster rates and lower cost than HSS twist drills in many applications.

Studies have shown that about 60% of all drilling applications in industry are considered to be short holes having depths up to about three times their diameters. Many of these holes can be drilled with indexable-insert drills. Others are not practical to produce with these tools because the holes are too small in diameter or because inadequate machines (with respect to speed, power, and rigidity) are employed.

Advantages of Insert Drills

Major advantages of indexable-insert drills are increased productivity, reduced costs, and better versatility.

Increased productivity. The use of carbide inserts brings drilling close to the machining rates possible with turning and milling. The higher cutting speeds possible permit holes to be drilled substantially faster than HSS twist drills and even faster than carbide spade drills (discussed next in this section). The cycle time on transfer machines and other high-production applications is often determined by the capabilities of the HSS

drills used. Now, with the faster penetration rates of indexable-insert drills often matching the rates of other operations, cycle times can generally be reduced. Potential productivity is also increased because the almost flat lead angle of indexable-insert drills results in a shorter feed stroke before cutting, compared to twist or spade drills that have point angles.

Reduced costs. The use of low-cost inserts with multiple cutting edges eliminates regrinding costs. The multiple cutting edges available provide savings from not having to replace the entire tool. Indexing the inserts does not change their positions and the tool length, thus any tool resetting costs are eliminated.

Versatility. Indexable-insert drills can be used as nonrotating tools for applications on lathes or other machines or as rotating tools on drilling machines, machining centers, and other machine tools. The machines used, however, must be rigid, be in good condition, and have ample speed and power capabilities. Some of the tools have the capability, when used on suitable machines, to perform boring as well as drilling operations. For example, mounted on the cross slide of an NC lathe, some tools can be moved radially outward to drill holes larger than the tool diameter or make a boring pass, thus improving the accuracy and finish of the hole.

Limitations of Indexable-Insert Drills

The smallest diameter hole that can be produced with indexable-insert drills now commercially available is 5/8" (16 mm). Maximum drilling depth is generally two to three times the hole diameter; some tools, however, are drilling to four times the diameter, and a few specials to depths over five times the diameter. Indexable-insert drills are not precision hole producing tools, and subsequent operations may be required for improved accuracies and smoother finishes. Small pilot holes are not useful and can be detrimental, and the tools cannot be used to enlarge existing holes.

While indexable-insert drills require less thrust than twist drills because they have no webs or chisel edges, they do require more power because of increased metal removal rates. Rigid machines in good condition, with adequate speed and power capabilities, and cutting fluid under pressure are necessary to take full advantage of the productive capabilities of these tools. Horsepower requirements increase proportionately with the drill diameter. Bench, upright, and radial drilling machines are generally not suitable for use with these tools because they lack sufficient speed, power, or rigidity. Safety guards are required on any machine used for drilling through holes with the workpiece rotating and the drill stationary because slugs produced can be thrown outward at high velocity.

Indexable-insert drills can be used to drill many materials, as is discussed later in this section, but most are not suitable for laminated or stacked materials. This is because the discs or slugs produced would be pressed into or welded to the next layer of material and because increased pressures can damage the inserts and possibly the drill body. The surfaces of workpieces to be drilled should preferably be flat. When using negative-rake inserts, convex surfaces can present problems and concave surfaces are not generally recommended because they might throw the drill out of balance. Angular surfaces rising more than 0.040" (1 mm) in a 2" (51 mm) distance and interrupted cuts are also generally not recommended for use with most of these tools; there are, however, successful applications with angular starting surfaces and interrupted cuts when positive-rake inserts are used.

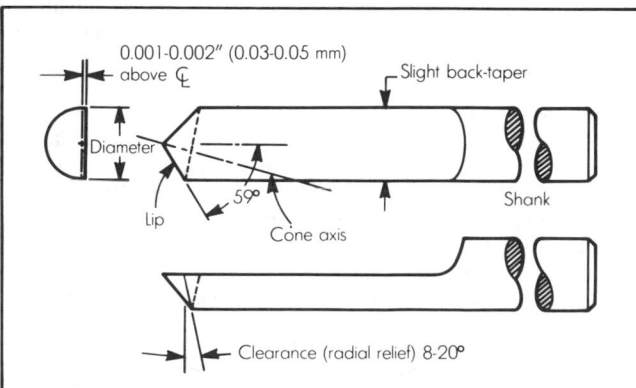

Fig. 24-23 Half-round drill which has a conical point that is offset to provide radial relief for the single cutting lip.[1]

Tool Designs

Indexable-insert drills of slightly different design are available from various tool manufacturers. Most consist of a hardened alloy steel body, with straight or taper shank, which is held by an adapter attached to the machine spindle. Some tools are of one-piece construction and others two-piece, with one of the two pieces being an interchangeable cutting head or nosepiece.

The drills have straight or helical flutes or grooves, and internal coolant holes. Flute or groove design is critical—sufficient space must be provided for the rapid removal of a large volume of chips, but an adequate body cross section must be maintained for strength and rigidity. Coolant enters the tools, usually through tapped openings, and reaches the cutting zones from orifices near the inserts. Chips and coolant exit through the external flutes or grooves on the tools. In applications in which the tool rotates, an inducer or coolant collar (as with other coolant-fed tools) is required unless coolant is supplied through a hollow spindle on the machine.

At the cutting end of each flute or groove, recessed pockets are provided to locate the indexable inserts. Depending upon the drill diameter and design of the tool, one to four inserts are generally used. A few drills, using toolholding cartridges, hold as many as six inserts. Some have a centrally located insert, positioned slightly ahead of the others, for self-centering purposes. The inserts are mounted in positions and at attitudes to counteract each other's lateral cutting forces, thus minimizing side loads. This is necessary because the tools are not guided by the holes being drilled and guide bushings are not used. Several designs of indexable-insert drills are illustrated in Fig. 24-24.

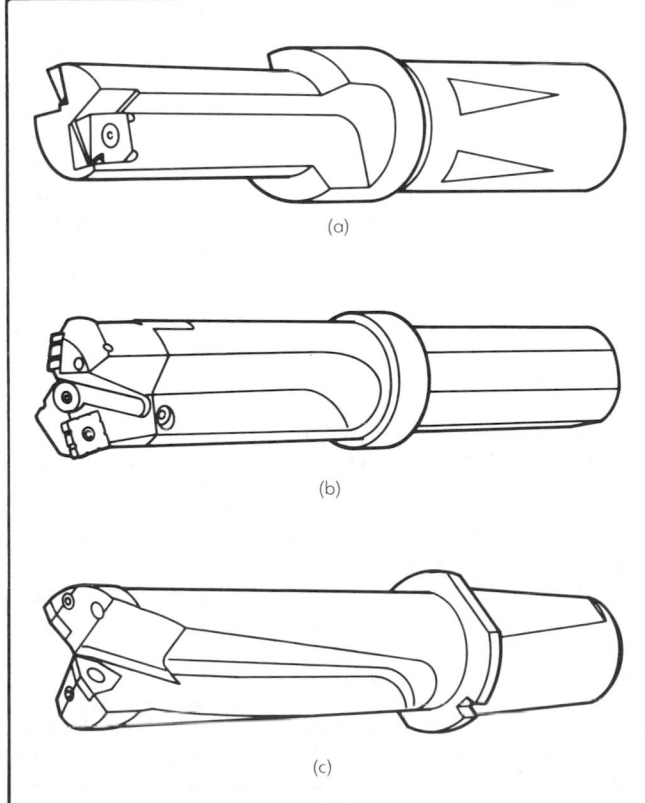

Fig. 24-24 Several designs of indexable-insert drills using carbide inserts: (a) TRW Tools Div.; (b) Valenite Div., Valeron Corp.; (c) Cutting Tool Div., Ingersoll Milling Machine Co.

Materials Drilled and Applications

Indexable-insert drills are being used primarily for producing holes in steels and irons. More ductile materials like aluminum and copper are also drilled with these tools, but chip ejection may be a problem for some applications. When soft, ductile and gummy materials are being drilled, chip control can be a problem. The thicker chips produced with neutral or negative-rake inserts tend to pack in the flutes or grooves. The tools are not suitable for drilling soft materials such as rubber and plastics.

These tools are especially advantageous for medium and high-production applications on NC and transfer machines. They are also being used, however, for many low-production applications on manual machines, lathes, and other machine tools, providing the machines have the required power, speed, and rigidity.

In one low-volume application involving the production of 5" (127 mm) diam x 26" (660 mm) deep holes in large forgings, cycle time was reduced from 2 hours and 10 minutes with HSS twist drills to 18 minutes with indexable-insert drills. This large indexable-insert drill was designed with cartridges holding six inserts.

SPADE DRILLS

Spade drills consist of a toolholder and an interchangeable blade. A dull blade can be replaced on the machine, as on indexable throwaway tools, without the necessity of refinding size, resetting stops, breaking down setups, and increasing or decreasing the length of a drilling setup. Because of this feature, spade drills can easily be preset for use on automatic and NC machine tools. These inserted-blade tools, also now available with indexable double-edge blades, are a type of flat end-cutting drill used to produce large diameter holes. Spade drilling is done with either the tool or workpiece rotating.

Advantages of Spade Drills

The primary advantage of spade drills lies in the diameter range of standard stocked tools. A few manufacturers stock blades below 1" (25 mm) diam, usually down to 5/8" (16 mm), but the standard range of stocked tooling is 1-6" (25-152 mm), with some manufacturers listing standard blades to 15" (381 mm) or more in diameter. When compared with twist drills of comparable diameters, spade drills offer greater rigidity and lower initial cost, but chip removal is more troublesome on vertical applications. Spade drills of large diameters can be used when trepanning is impractical because of a blind hole or lack of high-pressure coolant equipment.

Another advantage is that they are available in larger diameters than twist drills and can drill deeper holes. Depth-to-diameter ratios have exceeded 120:1 in some horizontal applications of spade drills before the drills needed to be reground. For vertical drilling, however, the depth-to-diameter ratio can seldom exceed 10:1 and is even less for smaller diameter tools because of chip ejection problems.

Limitations of the Tools

Spade drills are not precision tools and should not be used for finishing operations requiring tolerances less than about ±0.010" (0.25 mm); subsequent finishing of the holes may be required. Multidiameter blades, however, provide close tolerances with respect to the concentricity of different diameters and radii or chamfers.

DRILLING

Work surfaces that are cylindrical, spherical, or sloping and that have rough surfaces can create problems when spade drills are used, as can be the case with twist drills. Fragile workpieces are also generally difficult to drill with these tools.

Applications of Spade Drills

The majority of spade drills are used for drilling from the solid. Blades for core drilling, counterboring, flat bottoming, and special second-operation work are available for the same holders (see Fig. 24-25). They are generally employed for holes 1" (25 mm) or more in diameter.

Spade drills are popular for toolroom and low-production operations because of the low initial investment required for obtaining a wide range of sizes. For medium or high-production requirements, their primary advantages are the ease with which dull tools can be changed without disturbing the setup, and their rigidity, which permits high feed rates.

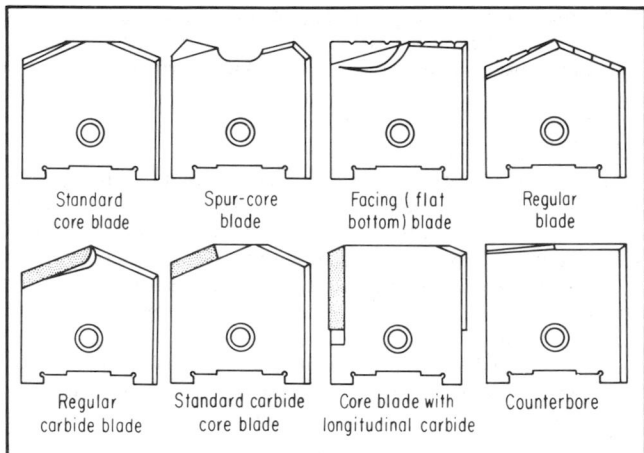

Fig. 24-25 Various blade shapes used on spade drills.

Blades for Spade Drills

Standards for spade drill blades and holders are specified in ANSI Standard B94.49-1975, published by ASME. Nomenclature for spade drill blades is presented in Fig. 24-26. Chip splitters, sometimes called chipbreaker grooves, are notches or grooves on the front lip relief surface for splitting the chips into segments for easier removal from the workpiece. They are always staggered in location from one lip to the other. Locating ears are projections on the back of the spade drill blade, beyond the seating pads, which locate and center the blade in the holder. The locating slot is the space between the locating ears that centralizes the blade in the holder.

Types of blades. Spade drill blades have been accepted by industry manufactured to two different types, the two basically differing from each other with respect to hole location and size. Some suppliers of spade drill blades manufacture them with a keyhole design to encompass both types. Others furnish them with one large hole to encompass both hole locations.

Blade geometry. The geometry of blades for spade drills resemble that of the cutting ends for twist drills with several exceptions.

Point angle. The included angle of points on spade drills generally varies from 118-135°, with 130° being standard. The point angle cannot be changed to any significant degree without losing much of the blade length. As compared with the 118°

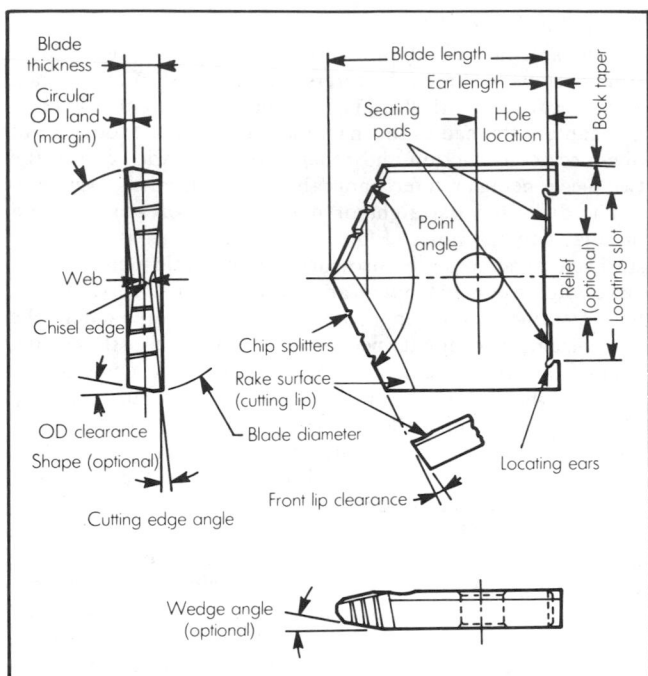

Fig. 24-26 Standard nomenclature for spade drill blades. (*ANSI Standard B94.49-1975, published by ASME*)

point angle of a twist drill, the larger angle shortens the cutting edge, which increases the depth of cut and chip thickness, as well as the cutting force for a given feed. This seeming disadvantage is negated by the lower speeds at which spade drills are operated.

Thicker chips are necessary in spade drilling to create positive curling and breaking. Long stringy chips do not flush from the hole, and they cause packing and breakage. Smaller included angles, 75-90°, however, are sometimes used for drilling certain materials. Split or four-facet points can be ground on the spade drill points to minimize wandering. A secondary point angle or corner chamfer is also used sometimes to lengthen life and permit the use of faster cutting speeds.

Clearance (relief) face. The clearance or relief face, which is generally notched for chip splitting and breaking, is typically ground with a lip relief angle of 6-8°. This angle is increased to 10-12° on core drills, on drills with point angles under 90°, and on drills used for drilling aluminum and other easily machined materials. The thrust requirements on large-diameter drills can also be reduced by increasing the clearance angle and/or by relieving the point. Angles that are more than 12°, however, create a weak cutting edge and should only be used to drill very soft metals. Angles less than 5° generally cause higher thrust requirements and generate excessive heat, thus shortening tool life.

Rake angles. The rake angle on blades ground with a flat top-rake surface is 12°; on those ground with a cylindrical chip curler, it ranges from 12 to nearly 30° at the outer corner and from nearly zero to about 10° adjacent to the chisel edge. Since it is sometimes difficult to duplicate in regrinding, the rake angle must be considered a variable except on blades with a flat top rake surface. With these, rake angles are sometimes reduced for maximum heat dissipation, for abnormally high feed rates, for hard or brittle-abrasive materials, for materials which produce stringy chips, and for carbide blades. Rake angles higher than 12° are sometimes useful for applications with very light feed rates, softer materials, and materials which give a brittle-stiff or tightly curled chip. Higher rake angles reduce cutting forces and produce less heat from chip-tool friction, but the overriding consideration must always be the achieving of a well-curled chip that flushes readily from the hole.

Indexable blades. Double-edge blades of the throwaway type eliminate the need for regrinding. When one edge becomes dull, the blade is indexed 180° so that the second edge can be used. When the second edge becomes dull, the blade is discarded since regrinding it is uneconomical. It is claimed that these blades can be operated with an increase in feed rate of 15-20%, compared to single-edge blades. Cutting-edge geometry is similar to that of conventional spade drill blades except for the two cutting edges (see Fig. 24-27). The V-shape of the two cutting lips serves as a locator for seating the blade.

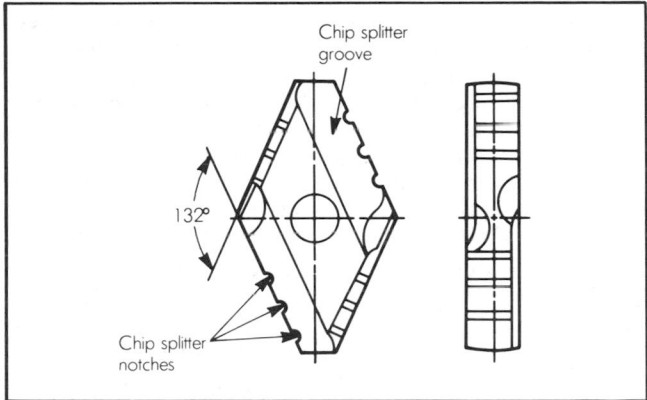

Fig. 24-27 Indexable blade for spade drill which has chip splitter grooves and notches.

Holders for Spade Drills

The nomenclature for spade drill holders is presented in Fig. 24-28. As with the blades, holders have been standardized in two types and grouped into eight series, designated by letters A through H, to accept blades of different widths and diameter ranges. Only eight holders are necessary for the nominal range of 1-6″ (25-152 mm) diam. Other holders are available to hold larger diameter and wider blades.

HIGH-PRESSURE COOLANT DRILLS

High-pressure coolant drills are used to produce deeper and/or more precise holes, as well as shallow holes to close tolerances in one pass. They differ from the coolant-fed drills previously discussed in that they are self-guiding, more costly, operate with higher pressure cutting fluids, and are generally used in specialized machines. They can drill much deeper holes than the high-helix, crankshaft, parabolic flute, coolant-hole, and spade drills already described. The major types of high-pressure coolant drills are gundrills, multiple-lip drills, and trepanning tools.

Gundrills

Gun-type tools, or gundrills and gunbores, are single-lip, self-guiding, pressure-coolant tools. Gun-type tools are classified in two basic categories: (1) external chip removal and (2) internal chip removal.

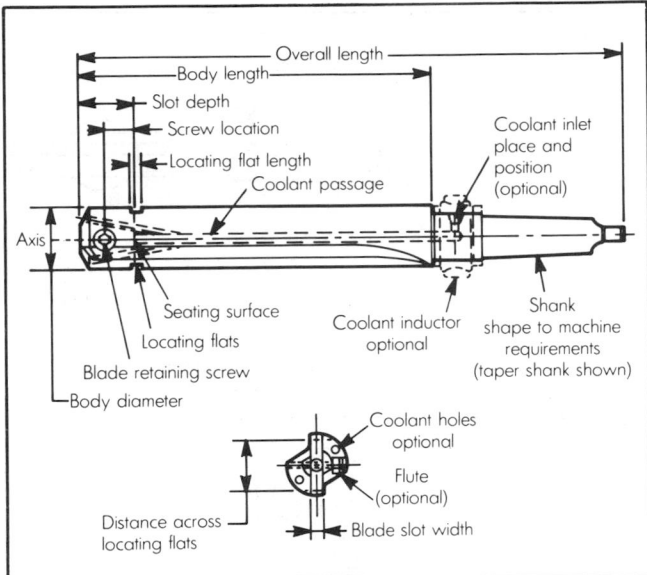

Fig. 24-28 Standard nomenclature for spade drill holders. (*ANSI Standard B94.49-1975, published by ASME*)

External-chip-removal gundrill. An external-chip-removal gundrill (see Fig. 24-29) includes a tip with a single V-shaped cutting edge and a coolant hole, a single-fluted tubular shank, and a driver suitably designed for either a spindle socket or a stationary socket. The cutting edge usually cuts through center on one side of the hole, leaving no material to be extruded as with the web of a twist drill. The seldom-used pin-cutting gundrill does not cut to center, but leaves a central pin. This type is limited to use in through holes because it is difficult to remove the pin from a blind hole.

The tip of a gundrill is solid carbide or a carbide insert in a steel body. Solid carbide tips are preferred to eliminate thermal-expansion differences and possible cracking of carbide, but they are generally available only up to 1.500″ (38.10 mm) diam. The oil hole through the tip is approximately one-fourth the tip diameter. The tip is attached to a steel shank by brazing or by some detachable method. The shank, with the cross section shown in Fig. 24-29, channels high-pressure coolant through the inside, and the chips and coolant exit through the V-flute.

The drill is held in the spindle by a cylindrical driver and is usually retained by setscrews. Other means of retaining the gundrill are used to accomplish quick change and length presetting.

Internal-chip-removal gundrill. Internal-chip-removal gundrills, Fig. 24-30, are single-lip, self-guiding, pressure-coolant tools and are applied for the same purposes as external-chip-removal gundrills. They are sometimes referred to as hollow gundrills or drillheads and are available from 0.24-4.0″ (6.1-102 mm) diam. Depth is limited only by equipment and tools available. The holes produced are round and have good finish with a diametral tolerance from 0.002-0.004″ (0.05-0.10 mm). As with other types of gundrills, runout is low and the hole is straight.

Internal-chip-removal tools (or ID exhaust tools) are mounted on a tubular steel shank. The coolant is introduced between the outside of the boring bar and the ID of the hole being produced. Then, the coolant moves past the cutting edges

DRILLING

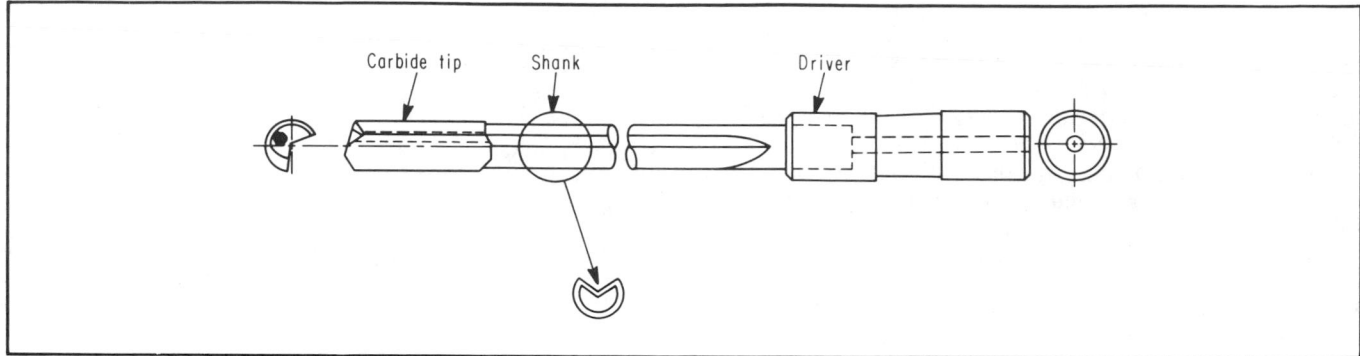

Fig. 24-29 Conventional external-chip removal gundrill.

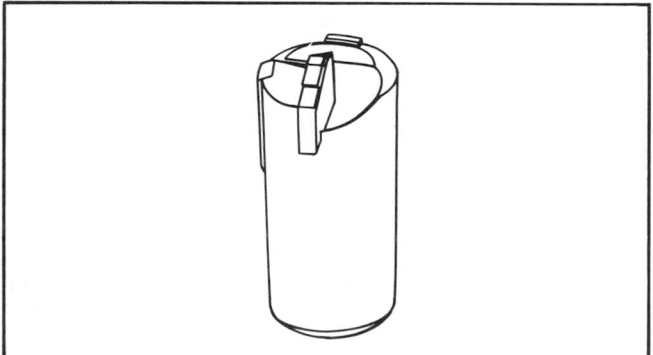

Fig. 24-30 Internal-chip-removal gundrill tip.

of the tool and discharges with the chips through the ID of the tubular shank. This arrangement of drilling can also be used for ID exhaust trepanning and gun-reaming (counterboring).

Multiple-Lip Pressure-Coolant Drills

Multiple-lip pressure-coolant drills are self-piloting tools available as both external and internal-chip-removal types, (see Fig. 24-31). External-chip-removal drills are generally available from 1/4 to 1 3/4″ (6.35 to 44.45 mm) diam, while internal-chip-removal types are generally not available below 5/8″ (16 mm).

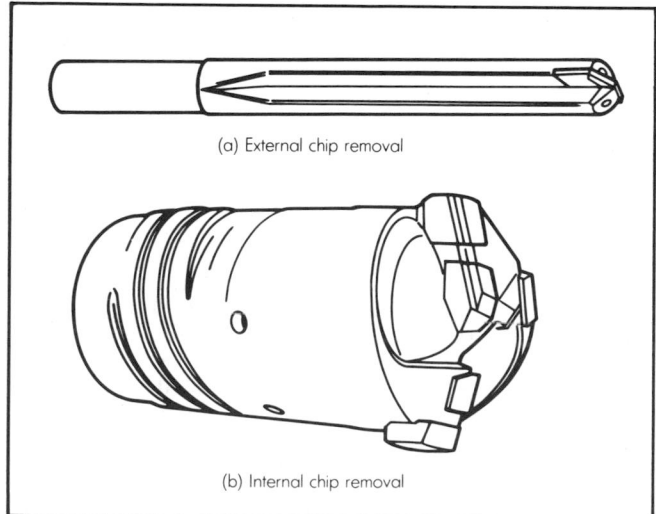

(a) External chip removal

(b) Internal chip removal

Fig. 24-31 (a) External-chip-removal and (b) internal-chip-removal, multiple-lip, pressure-coolant drills.

Trepanning Tools

Trepanning tools are self-guiding pressure-coolant tools available in both internal and external-chip-removal types. They cut an annular groove leaving a central core (see Fig. 24-32). The most important reason for selecting trepanning tools over center-cutting drills is their reduced power requirements. The solid core is also more desirable than chips from the standpoint of salvage value, which can be extremely important for exotic and precious metals. The cores can be used for metallurgical analysis and test specimens, and in large diameters, can be sold or remachined as bar stock for other jobs.

A variety of designs are available in trepanning tools, including brazed and indexable single and multiple-insert styles. Single-insert designs require support pads and starting bushings, while some multiple-insert styles can be used without support pads and starting bushings.

Trepanning tools as small as 1 1/2″ (38 mm) diam are available, although their most common usage is 2″ (51 mm) diam and larger. Trepanning tools which do not have support pads, but depend upon balanced cutting forces provided by multiple inserts, are used for hole depths up to five diameters. Trepanning tools using support pads and bushings can be used successfully for depths up to 100 diameters. Diametral accuracy can be ±0.005″ (0.13 mm) for tools with support pads and ±0.010″ (0.25 mm) for tools without support pads, depending upon tool and machine setup and tool wear.

Trepanning tools are generally applied to through holes because of problems with core removal. Special tools have been designed to cut off the core in large blind holes, but their success depends almost entirely upon operator skill. With few exceptions, they have not proven to be cost effective.

SMALL-HOLE DRILLS

A major problem in drilling small holes mechanically (with the production of chips), as compared to nontraditional methods, is compensating for the decreased rigidity of the delicate tools required. Drill rigidity is roughly inversely proportional to the fourth power of the diameter and the force required to deflect the drill is approximately proportional to the cube of the unsupported drill length. Other problems include chip removal, minimizing runout, impact of the drill with the workpiece, and maintaining a uniform feed rate. Also, machinability of the material does not improve with decreasing hole sizes. In fact, the material can be less homogeneous and machinable in the area being drilled because of unalloyed portions, foreign inclusions, work hardening, or other reasons.

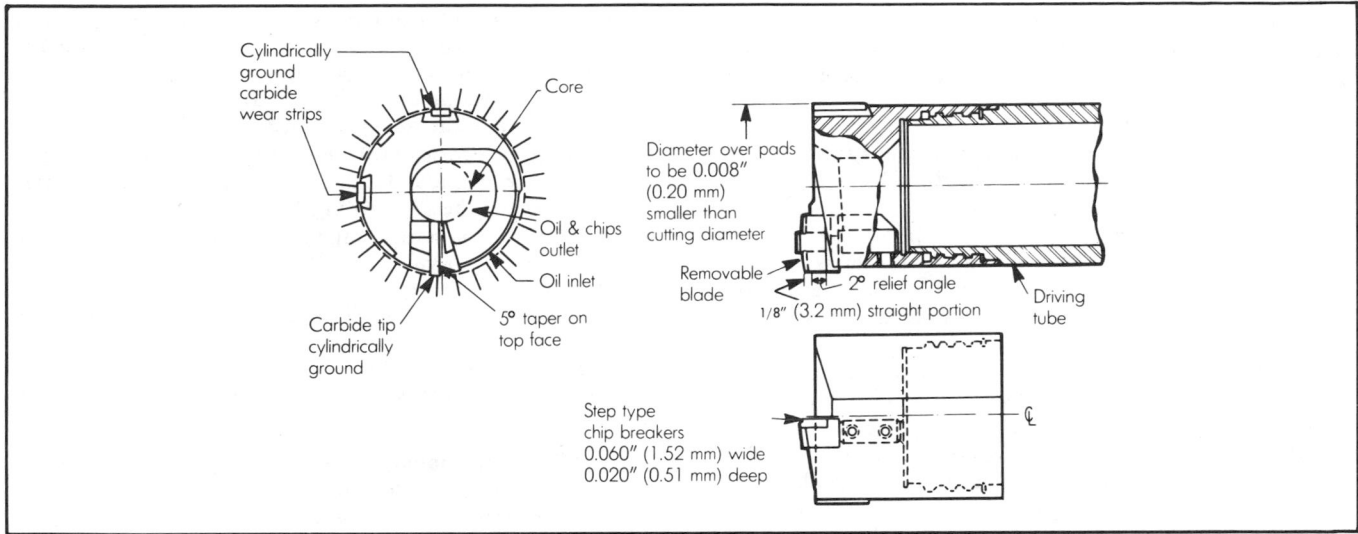

Fig. 24-32 Trepanning tool cuts an annular groove and leaves a central core.

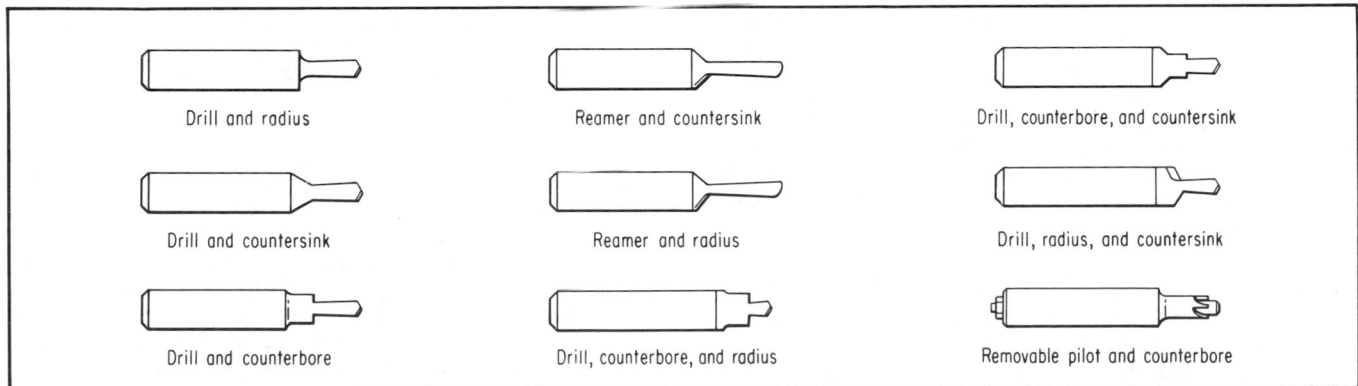

Drill and radius	Reamer and countersink	Drill, counterbore, and countersink
Drill and countersink	Reamer and radius	Drill, radius, and countersink
Drill and counterbore	Drill, counterbore, and radius	Removable pilot and counterbore

Fig. 24-33 Various tools used to produce small holes.

The three types of drills used predominately for producing small holes are center, pivot, and straight-shank drills. Others also used include step drills, drills with long shanks, and drills designed for special applications (see Fig. 24-33).

Center drills are the most rigid in common use because of their short flute lengths (usually about four times the diameter) and oversize shank diameters. They should be used whenever the flute length is adequate or when holes are to be started or centered. When used as a hole starter, the diameter of a center drill should be at least as large as the web thickness of the following drill for guidance and minimum deflection.

Pivot drills are probably the most widely used type for producing small holes. They normally have flute lengths from five to seven times their diameters and shanks larger in diameter than their fluted portions. They are available with spiral flutes having 10°, 20°, or 30° helix angles; in flat (spade) versions; in D-flute (half round) styles; and for both left and right-hand cutting.

Straight-shank drills, with flute lengths of about 12 diameters are available in three flute styles: a spiral flute style with helix angles of 10°, 20°, or 30°; a flat or spade flute, two-lip style with a zero helix angle; and a D-flute or half-round style. Since these tools are less rigid than center or pivot drills, they are used primarily to enlarge and increase the depths of holes started

with other types of drills. They should generally not be used to start holes.

The webs or center sections of small-diameter drills are proportionally thicker than those of larger diameter drills because it is not practical to manufacture them with the same percentage of web. These thicker webs increase the rigidity of the drills, but they also decrease the length of the cutting lips. Also, thicker webs at the points increase the end pressures required to force the drills into the workpieces.

TOOLHOLDERS FOR DRILLING

Many different devices are used to hold drills and provide the driving connection between the machine spindle and the drill. These include sockets, sleeves, chucks, collets, and other arrangements. Selection of the proper device is critical because drills not properly gripped can be pulled from the driver by friction between the drill and workpiece when the drill is retracted.

Taper-Shank Drills

Drills with taper shanks fit directly into the spindles of drilling machines that have the same size taper as the drills. When the hole in the spindle is larger, a reducing socket or

DRILLING

sleeve is used. Short sleeves are preferable to fitted sockets because of the increased rigidity they provide. Drifts are used to remove taper-shank drills from the sockets or sleeves.

Straight-Shank Drills

Drills with straight shanks are held in several ways, including chucks, sleeves, bushings, and collet-type holders.

Chucks. Three-jaw chucks are the most common holders and drivers for small-diameter, straight-shank drills. They are available in wrench, or key-tightening, and wrenchless (keyless) styles. These chucks are made with plain or ball bearing construction, and for taper or threaded mounting.

Sleeves and bushings. Tapered split sleeves are sometimes used to drive small-diameter, straight-shank drills for certain production applications. These sleeves have a taper on their OD to fit the machine spindle or socket and a straight bore to fit the drill shank. Flats or squares on the drill shanks and driving slots in the sleeves are used occasionally, particularly on multispindle machines with close centers.

Collet-type holders. A major advantage of collet-type holders is their capability of gripping drills on their margins or straight shanks. In doing this, the length of the drill projecting from the collet can be varied and kept to a minimum to suit requirements for short-hole, deep-hole, or other drilling applications. Called stubbing, this method increases rigidity by decreasing the length-to-diameter ratios. Resulting benefits can include longer drill life, the capability of using higher feed rates and cutting speeds, reduction in the need for jigs and bushings, possible elimination of center drilling or spotfacing, shorter cycle times, and the ability to use broken drills.

WORKHOLDING DEVICES FOR DRILLING

Jigs and fixtures are precision devices used to accurately machine duplicate parts. As a general rule, jigs and fixtures are designed to hold, support, and locate a workpiece while controlling the position and alignment of the cutting tools. Good jig and fixture design can minimize tool breakage and the production of unsatisfactory workpieces.

The principle difference between a jig and fixture is the method used to position the cutting tool. Jigs securely hold and locate the workpiece while guiding the cutting tool by means of a bushing or similar device. Fixtures securely hold and locate the workpiece while referencing the position of the cutting tool by means of set blocks and feeler gages.

Although both jigs and fixtures are used for a wide variety of machining operations, the jig is by far the most common type of device for drilling, reaming, and related operations. Regardless of the machining operation, the basic construction and function of a jig are the same for drilling and reaming.

Jigs can be divided into two broad categories: open and closed. Open jigs are generally used for machining parts on a single surface, while closed jigs are used for parts that require machining on two or more surfaces. The terms used to identify these jigs are normally directly related to the basic construction of the tool itself.

Locating and Supporting Principles

To ensure the desired precision in any machining operation, the workpiece must be properly located and supported throughout the entire machining cycle. The terms locating and supporting, as used here, refer to the establishment of the proper relationship between the workpiece and the jig. In most cases, locators and supports serve the same purpose: to establish the desired reference location. Supports are simple locators which are positioned beneath the workpiece to establish the reference position on the vertical axis. Locators, likewise, set the position of the workpiece on both horizontal axes.

The most basic form of workpiece location is the six-point or three-two-one method. In this method, the vertical Z-axis position is established by locating the workpiece on three points (Fig. 24-34, *a*). The horizontal axes are then located by three more points, two on one plane (Fig. 24-34, *b*) and one on the other plane (Fig. 24-34, *c*). This method restricts nine of the twelve degrees of freedom. The remaining three degrees are restricted by the clamping device.

When any locating system is designed for a jig, the following points must be considered to prevent inaccuracies and to assure proper location:

1. All locators should contact the workpiece on a machined surface or designated locating area.
2. The reference surfaces, when not specifically indicated on the print, should be those which are used to dimension the part.
3. Locators should always be positioned as far apart as practical to ensure stability and accuracy.
4. Locators should be positioned to avoid chips and foreign matter. When this is not possible the locators should be relieved to prevent interference when the workpiece is loaded or unloaded (see Fig. 24-35).
5. Duplicate locators should always be avoided. Once the reference surface is determined, only that surface should be used to locate the workpiece. Using more than one reference surface to establish the location of the workpiece often results in excessive tolerance stack-up.
6. The location of any workpiece should always be foolproof; that is, the workpiece should only be capable of being loaded into the jig in the correct position. Using a foolproofing pin is one method to prevent improper loading.
7. Locational tolerance should be as liberal as possible. A range of 20-30% of the workpiece tolerance is normally acceptable, and to 50% in some cases. Overly tight tolerance requirements only serve to increase the cost in a disproportionate relationship to the part accuracy.
8. Work supports should always be positioned beneath the area at which the workpiece is to be clamped. Clamping between supports or over an unsupported area can distort or bend the workpiece and may change the location.

Burr Clearance and Part Ejection

Any drilling operation produces burrs. To properly perform its design function, a jig must allow clearance for these burrs to prevent the part from jamming in the jig. Two burrs are formed in a drilling operation—the primary burr on the exit side and the secondary burr on the entry side. The secondary burr is normally taken care of by the bushing clearance. The primary burr, however, can sometimes cause problems. In cases in which the workpiece must slide on or off a locator, or in and out of the jig, there must be a burr clearance groove. A burr clearance groove is simply a milled groove slightly deeper than the height of the burr in the area of the jig in which the burr could jam. Burr interference must always be considered, and clearance planned into the jig design.

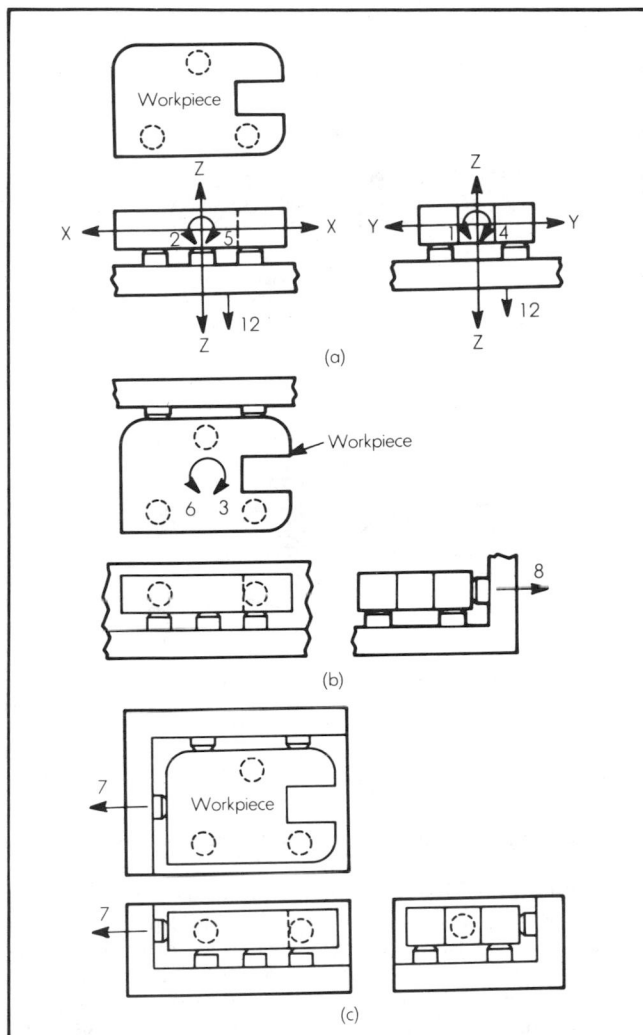

Fig. 24-34 Six-point method of location: (a) 2-axis, (b) horizontal Y-axis, and (c) horizontal X-axis.[2]

Part ejection is also an area which must be considered in the design of a jig. Several very simple methods are commonly used to eject parts. While elaborate power ejection methods can be used, a simple lever or spring ejector often performs as well and costs a fraction of the power system. When designing an ejection system, the only thought should be the removal of the workpiece from the jig. Overly elaborate or complicated ejection systems often cost more and are more likely to malfunction than the simple designs.

Workholding and Clamping Principles

Workholding and clamping devices serve only one purpose in any jig—to hold the workpiece securely against the locators and prevent it from being pulled from the jig by the cutting tool during the machining operation. Many times, the clamps that are selected for a particular jig are actually larger than required. To prevent this, and to help select the proper size and type of clamp, an understanding of the tool forces is important.

Forces are generated by the cutting action of the tool. In drilling, these forces originate at the cutting edge of the drill and

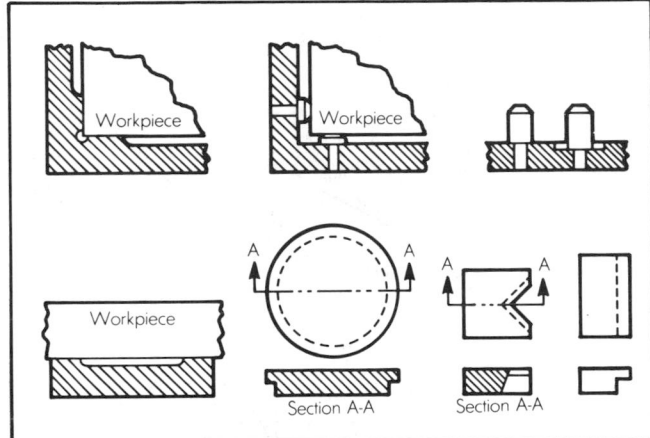

Fig. 24-35 Method of relieving locators to prevent interference.[2]

are dispersed throughout the workpiece in two general directions—downward and radially. In most jig designs, the locators and the tool body resist these forces without any assistance from the clamps. However, once the cutting tool is through the workpiece, another force must be controlled—the natural tendency of the workpiece to climb the flutes of the drill. This is the force that must be restricted or controlled by the clamps. This force represents only a fraction of the force required to drill the hole and should be treated as such when clamping.

Tool Guiding Principles

The principle method used to guide cutting tools in a jig is the drill bushing. These bushings are commonly used to locate and guide drills and reamers to produce or modify a hole.

A few basic rules which should be followed when the proper drill bushings are to be selected are as follows:

1. The length of the drill bushing must be sufficient to support and guide the drill. Too short a bushing permits the drill to bend, producing out-of-line and oversize holes. Too long a bushing reduces the effective length of the drill and may require the use of a more costly extra-length drill. For drills having a normal helix angle, the length of the bushing should be from one and one-half to two and one-half times the diameter of the drill.

2. Sufficient clearance should be provided between the bottom of the bushing and the top surface of the workpiece for the removal of chips and to minimize bushing wear (Fig. 24-36). The recommended clearance for drilling metals such as cast iron, which produce small chips, is one-half the bushing ID. For other metals such as steel, which produce long stringy chips, the clearance should not exceed one and one-half times the bushing ID. An exception to these recommendations is applications requiring maximum precision, in which the bushing is sometimes placed in direct contact with the workpiece. Also, when drilling is performed at an angle relative to the surface of the workpiece, the bushing should be very close to the workpiece. Then, when the drill has penetrated to a depth of about half the drill diameter, the bushing should be retracted to allow chips to escape.

3. The diameters of the bushing bores should provide a

DRILLING

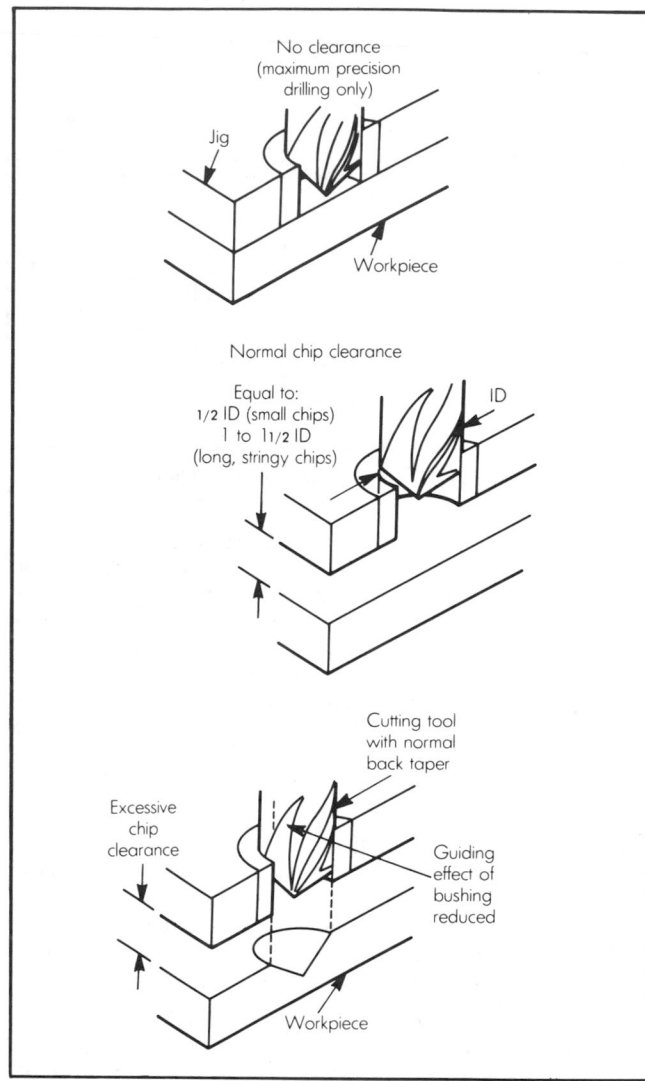

Fig. 24-36 Clearances between bushing and workpiece. Recommended clearance is illustrated in center. (*Welch Drill Bushing Co.*)

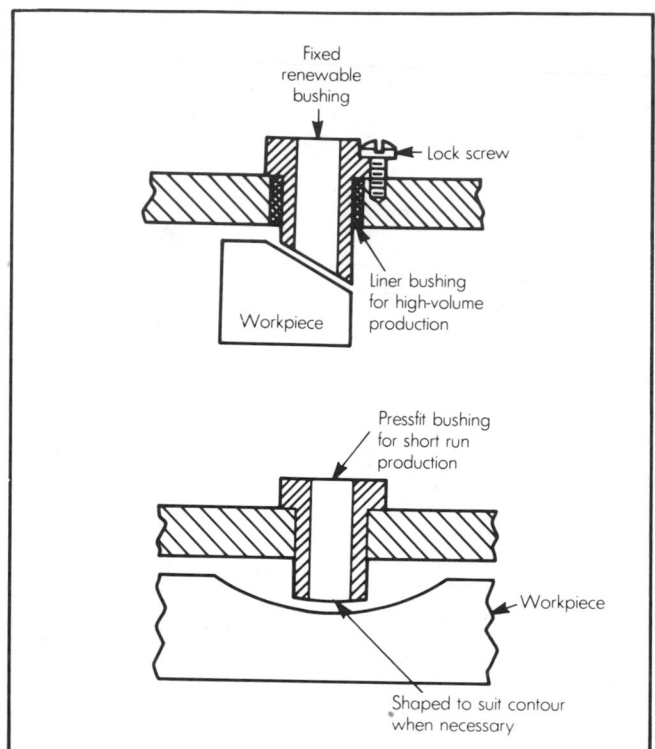

Fig. 24-37 When irregular surfaces are being drilled, the bushing should conform to the surface shape.[2]

minimum clearance of from 0.0005-0.001″ (0.013-0.03 mm) for the drills. The larger the bushing diameter, however, the greater the tolerance on its bore.

4. The jig plate should be thick enough to properly hold and support the bushing. In cases in which a very thin jig plate must be used, template bushings can be used to ensure the proper tool support. In cases in which a very thick plate is used, an extended length bushing should be used. Extended length bushings are relieved to maintain the proper contact length.

5. When irregular surfaces must be drilled with close location tolerances, the bushing should conform to the shape of the surface (see Fig. 24-37).

OPERATING PARAMETERS FOR DRILLING

Obtaining maximum economy in the use of drills requires consideration of many factors. One important factor is selecting the proper drill for a specific application. The wide variety of drills available, many of which have been discussed in the preceding sections of this chapter, makes this selection process difficult.

While a drill of almost any design can be used to produce a hole in almost any material, lower costs for production applications necessitate use of the correct drill. Variables influencing the selection of the proper drill include the composition, hardness, and surface condition of the material to be drilled; the diameter and depth of the holes to be produced; the accuracy, surface finish, and production requirements; the type and condition of the machine to be used; and the rigidity of the setup. Standard drills should be used whenever possible because of reduced costs, interchangeability, better availability, and proven designs.

Once a drill has been selected, many operating parameters must be established. These include power requirements, cutting speeds and feed rates, and the cutting fluid to be used.

DRILLING APPLICATIONS

With the wide variety of materials in which holes must be produced, there are many challenges to the use of drills. There is a practical limit of material hardness and strength beyond which drills are not practical for production applications.

Minimizing Chatter

As with all other machining operations, chatter can cause poor performance in drilling. Excessive chatter causes rapid deterioration of drills and reduces hole accuracy and quality.

Drilling Hard Materials

Holes can be drilled in limited quantities in many hard, high-strength materials with certain procedures. Workpieces must be held rigidly in place and be well supported directly under the drill point. Short drills with their webs not thinned excessively and medium lip clearance angles (7-9°) are recommended. Machines used must have ample power and be in good condition. Cutting speeds should be low (20-30 sfm; 6.1-9.1 m/min or less), with medium to heavy feed rates, preferably using a mechanical power feed unit.

Starting Holes with Carbide Drills

Special care should be given to starting holes in any material when using carbide and carbide-tipped drills. Little difficulty is encountered in starting and getting straight holes with these drills when close-fitting, well-aligned guide bushings are used. If bushings are not used, however, guide holes should be produced first, using stub (screw) length drills having a 135-140°, four-facet or split, self centering point. This allows the OD of the following carbide drill to become secured before cutting starts and can extend tool life.

Drilling Stainless Steels

Most stainless steels, except the free-machining grades, are generally more difficult to drill than carbon steels and most alloy steels. Work-hardening grades in particular should be drilled continuously with a fairly heavy, uniform feed and moderate speed. Accurate sharpening, with an included point angle of 135-140°, a clearance angle of 6-8°, on larger size drills, and smooth finishes on the cutting edges, is recommended.

Drilling Armor Plate

While this material is hard and tough, it can generally be drilled satisfactorily with standard HSS drills. If the material has been flame cut, areas adjoining the cut are hardened and drilling is difficult. Annealing of these areas is recommended, if possible, before drilling. When this is not practical, low cutting speeds may be necessary. A positive power feed at a medium to heavy, uniform rate is recommended for continuous cutting to prevent work hardening.

Drilling Copper

Problems encountered in drilling copper and its alloys are the long, stringy chips produced because of the gummy nature of the material and the tendency for drills to bind or freeze in the workpieces because of the high coefficient of expansion of the material. These problems can be minimized by using drills of proper design, slower cutting speeds, and higher feed rates. Drills with thin webs, narrow margin widths, increased back-taper, and high relief angles on their points reduce the heat generated in drilling.

Drilling Aluminum

Drilling of aluminum and aluminum alloys seldom presents any problems, with the possible exception of some cast alloys and those having a high silicon content. Aluminum alloys having a high silicon content are very abrasive, resulting in rapid tool wear. Soft alloys require drills having polished flutes to prevent chip packaging and material buildup. For deeper holes, twist drills, with high helix angles are recommended to minimize chip packing. Thin webs and high lip relief angles should be provided on the drills, and high penetration rates are possible in drilling these materials.

Drilling Magnesium and Zinc Alloys

Fairly high speeds and heavy feeds should be used to drill magnesium and its alloys. These parameters produce large, thick chips, which reduces the fire hazard. The drills must have ample chip space to accommodate the high penetration rates.

Drilling Titanium

Problems in drilling titanium and titanium alloys can result from the long, thin, curly chips produced. These chips, plus the poor heat conduction of the materials and the heat generated in drilling, tend to cause excessive chip packing and welding to the cutting edges. Successful drilling requires a reduction in the amount of heat generated by using slower speeds, moderate feeds, adequate cutting fluid, sharp and sturdy drills, well-supported workpieces, and rigid machines.

Drilling Plastics

Molded plastics present no drilling problems as long as the drills provide for the good ejection of chips. For drilling small holes, special drills for plastics are available. These drills have wide polished flutes, a thin web, a low helix angle, an included point angle of 60-90°, and a clearance angle at the periphery of about 12°. Drills with high helix angles, however, are better for producing holes in some plastics. For larger holes, a point with a larger included angle (90-120°) can be used and the heel behind the cutting edge may be ground away, leaving a land about 1/16" (1.6 mm) wide, to reduce friction and provide more chip clearance. Drilling of some plastics results in undersize holes, and slightly oversize drills should be used. When a cutting fluid is used, tests should be made to ensure that the plastic will not react with the fluid.

Drilling Composites

Composite materials consisting of high-strength fibers (glass, graphite, etc.) in a plastic matrix are very hard and abrasive, and conventional HSS drills are generally not satisfactory. For small holes, solid carbide drills are being used. For larger holes, diamond-impregnated core drills, operated at high speeds, have been found satisfactory.

Drilling Miniature Holes

Conventional drills and drilling practices, except for slower speeds, are regularly used to produce holes down to 0.015" (0.38 mm) diam or less. When smaller holes are drilled, however, common practice is to start with a center or pivot drill having a flute length not exceeding four times the drill diameter and a diameter at least as large as the web thickness of the following drill. The second tool is usually a pivot drill having a flute length of five to seven times its diameter and a diameter at least equal to the web thickness but somewhat smaller in diameter than the straight-shank drill used to produce the required diameter and depth.

Using Indexable-Insert Drills

Proper toolholders are critical for optimum performance of indexable-insert drills. They should be as short as possible to minimize overhang, and the shank and socket must be clean and free of nicks. Concentricity, straightness, and diameters must be maintained to close tolerances. Loose shanks will create chatter and cause insert damage.

REAMING

REAMING

Reaming is a machining process for enlarging, smoothing, and/or accurately sizing existing holes by means of multiedge fluted cutting tools (reamers). As the reamer and/or workpiece are rotated and advanced relative to each other, chips are produced to remove relatively small amounts of material from the hole wall. Reaming may be performed on the same type of machines used for drilling. The machines used for drilling are discussed earlier in this chapter.

Accuracy of the hole and quality of finish produced by reaming depends primarily upon the condition of the starting hole, rigidity of the machine and fixture, correct speeds and feeds, a suitable and properly applied cutting fluid, and precise resharpening of dull tools.

Since stock removal is small and must be uniform in reaming, the starting holes (drilled or otherwise produced) must have relatively good roundness, straightness, and finish. Reamers tend to follow the existing centerline of the hole being reamed, and in limited instances it may be necessary to bore the holes prior to reaming to maintain required tolerances. With the proper conditions and operating parameters, reaming can produce close tolerances and smooth finishes.

PRODUCT DESIGN FOR REAMING

Better reaming usually results when the product is designed to facilitate that operation. When possible, provision should be made for the reamer to pass through the workpiece (Fig. 24-38, *a*). This eliminates the necessity to ream a blind hole. When reaming a blind hole is unavoidable, the depth of cut should be controlled to prevent bottoming, cutting oversize holes, and possibly damaging the reamer (view *b*). It is advisable to avoid operations requiring multidiameter reamers when the diameters are substantially different because the normally different cutting speeds of the different diameters (view *c*) make it difficult to produce true holes and good surfaces. A reamer should enter a hole at right angles to the work surface to permit all teeth to engage for a good start. This is because reaming at an angle makes it difficult and sometimes impossible to turn out good work (view *d*). Plain reaming should not be depended upon to align a series of holes and center them on a common axis. Concentricity and alignment require line reaming (Fig. 24-38, view *e*), which requires that the holes be of equal or progressively smaller diameters to permit entrance and withdrawal of the reamers. Provision must be made for guiding the reamer bar or arbor at both ends.

STOCK REMOVAL ALLOWANCE

In reaming, the tool normally cuts slightly larger than its own diameter, usually in direct proportion to the amount of stock to be removed. For efficient operation, the amount of stock left in the hole for reaming must be sufficient to permit the reamer to cut at all times rather than to burnish the surface. Variations in the amount of stock to be removed can affect the finish size of the hole reamed.

Removal of too much stock by reaming often causes oversize and rough holes. Oversize holes, walls of holes roughened with grooves at or beyond the finished diameter, bellmouthed holes, or out-of-round holes are common causes of reamer failure. In improperly prepared holes the reamer has a tendency to wedge in the hole rather than machine it. The result can be severe reamer wear and possible breakage.

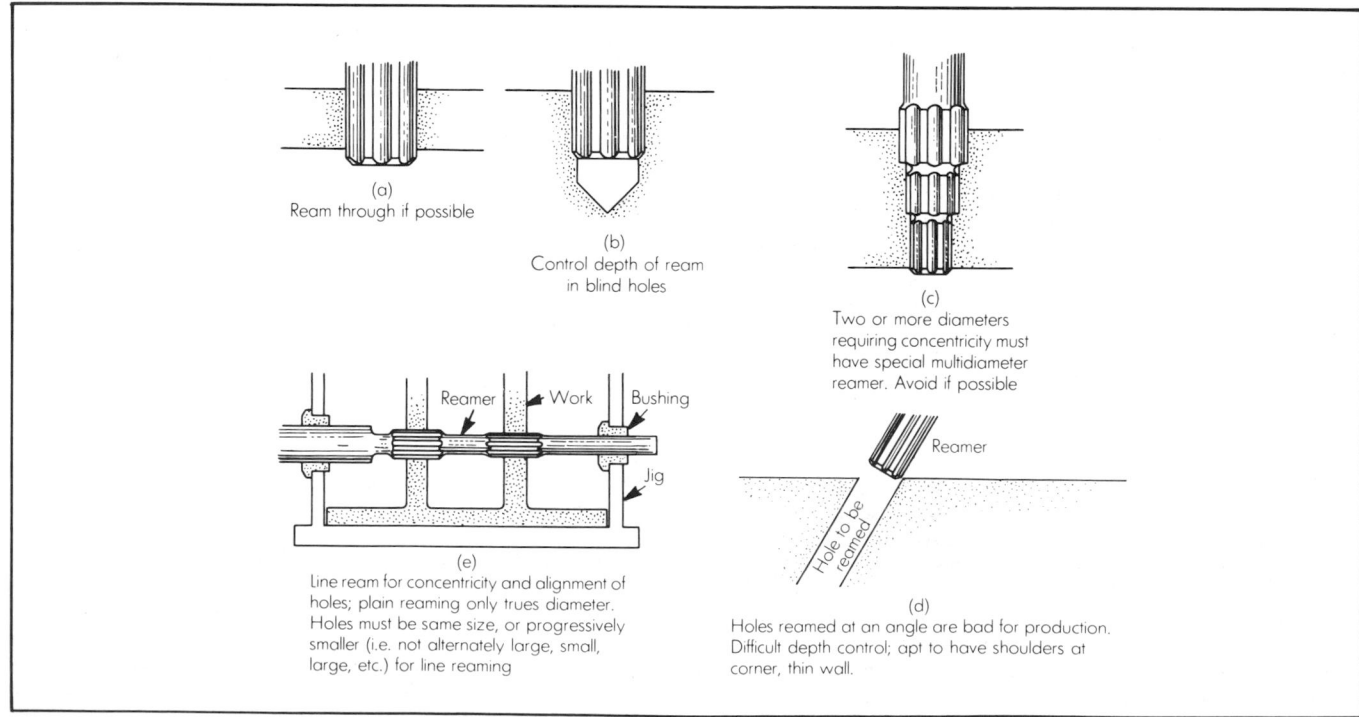

(a)
Ream through if possible

(b)
Control depth of ream in blind holes

(c)
Two or more diameters requiring concentricity must have special multidiameter reamer. Avoid if possible

(e)
Line ream for concentricity and alignment of holes; plain reaming only trues diameter. Holes must be same size, or progressively smaller (i.e. not alternately large, small, large, etc.) for line reaming

(d)
Holes reamed at an angle are bad for production. Difficult depth control; apt to have shoulders at corner, thin wall.

Reamer   Work   Bushing
Jig
Reamer
Hole to be reamed

Fig. 24-38 Product design factors relating to reaming.

REAMERS

A reamer is a rotary cutting tool, generally of cylindrical or conical shape, intended for enlarging and finishing holes to accurate dimensions. It is usually equipped with two or more peripheral channels or flutes, either parallel to its axis or in a right or left-hand helix as required. Those with helical flutes provide smooth shear cutting, are less subject to chatter, and produce a better finish. The flutes form cutting teeth and provide channels for removing the chips.

Clearance and Blade Angles

Cutting done by a reamer (except a hand reamer or taper reamer) is accomplished by the chamfer, which forms a truncated cone on the end of the reamer and carries the cutting edges. The chamfer is shaped so that the reamer will start properly in the hole and the major portion of the cutting is done by the chamfer length. The longitudinal cutting edges should do little or no cutting. The clearance angles in the cutting portions of the reamer are employed to obtain cutting action in the proper places, prevent friction, and clear the chips. Reamers usually embody three types of clearance: chamfer relief, peripheral relief, and longitudinal relief.

Chamfer relief. Chamfer relief is obtained by the clearance angle ground on the cutting ends of the reamer to enable them to penetrate more easily beneath the workpiece surface and produce chips.

Peripheral relief. Peripheral relief is obtained by the clearance angle ground on the lands back of the flute edges to relieve the radial pressure of the reamer flutes against the walls of the hole.

Longitudinal relief. Longitudinal relief or back-taper is the slight taper embodied in standard reamers, which results in a smaller diameter at the shank end than at the cutting end, to prevent the reamer blade from causing side-cutting action due to lack of proper alignment or to dullness of the reamer caused by wear. It is important that reamers used in angular floating holders should embody enough back-taper to prevent interference resulting from improper alignment caused by these types of holders.

Chamfer angle. A chamfer angle usually has a magnitude of about 45°, but it can range from 40-50°. Because most of the dulling of reamer blades occurs at the peripheral corners of the chamfer, the maximum effective cutting action continues only as long as the original sharp chamfer angle is maintained. The chamfer must be uniform and concentric with the cutting diameter of the reamer.

Secondary chamfer. Secondary chamfer (Fig. 24-39) sometimes referred to as starting taper or lead, is provided on some reamers. It consists of a chamfer ranging from 1-10° which may be located immediately behind the first chamfer. Clearance should be provided for this second taper in a manner that enables it to be brought to a sharp edge. It should not be confused either with the primary chamfer-relief angle or with a similar expression that refers to the starting taper or lead of a hand reamer. The secondary chamfer functions to effect a scraping cut that helps to size and smooth the walls of the hole.

Hand of Helix and Hand of Cut

The hand of a reamer cut refers to the direction of rotation (right or left) and may be determined by inspection of the chamfer end of the reamer when mounted to make a cut. If the rotary motion of the reamer is counterclockwise, cut is left-hand; if the rotary motion is clockwise, cut is right-hand.

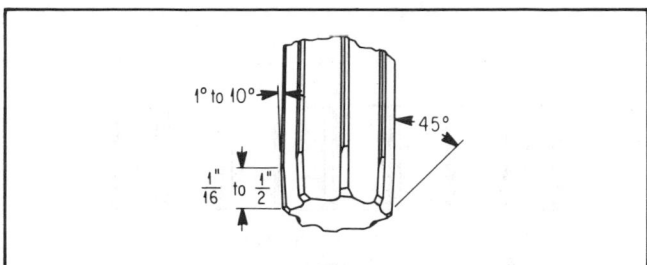

Fig. 24-39 Secondary chamfer is provided on some reamers.

Most reamers (Fig. 24-40) are right-hand cutting and may have straight flutes (a), left-hand helix flutes (b), or right-hand helix flutes (c). Straight flutes cost less originally and are easiest to sharpen or recondition. This type of reamer has proved satisfactory for a great many applications. When reamers are being selected for machine tools with play in the gears or with spindles not in the best of condition, it is usually advisable to choose those with left-hand helical flutes. This type of reamer has a negative axial rake and therefore requires more pressure to feed the tool into the work. The additional pressure and the hand of the helix opposite to the hand of the cut reduce the tendency for the reamer to jump ahead when easier cutting is encountered. For machine tools in very good condition, right-hand fluted reamers are satisfactory. They are inherently free cutting and require less power; however, when used on a worn machine, they tend to dig into the workpiece, cause chatter, and produce a rough hole.

Kinds of Reamers

Reamers are made in many different forms (Fig. 24-41), including solid and inserted-blade types, adjustable and non-adjustable; they are available for either manual operation (hand reamers) or for machine use (chucking reamers). Materials from which cutting elements of most production reamers are made include high-speed steel and cemented carbides.

REAMER HOLDERS/DRIVERS

Reamers are commonly held and driven by three-jaw chucks, straight sleeves and setscrews, and for taper shanks, sleeves or sockets. Reamers with adapters for quick-change chucks are used for production applications.

When reamers must guide themselves into previously made holes, they require floating holders to maintain alignment. There are several types of floating holders. Some permit angular float, others permit a parallel (axial) float, and still others permit both angular and parallel float.

Floating holders have some limitations. If the reamer axis is vertical, floating reamer drives often do a good job of correcting for small amounts of misalignment. When the workpieces rotate, however, as is the case on screw machines, lathes, and some other machine tools, floating holders are sometimes inadequate. This is because relatively large amounts of misalignment are often found on these machines and because the weight of the reamer and holder tend to push the tool into an off-center position.

Some full floating holders, which compensate for both angular and parallel misalignment, are equipped with springs or other components to counterbalance the mass of the holder. A floating holder cannot generally operate both vertically and horizontally and still correct for both angular and parallel

REAMING

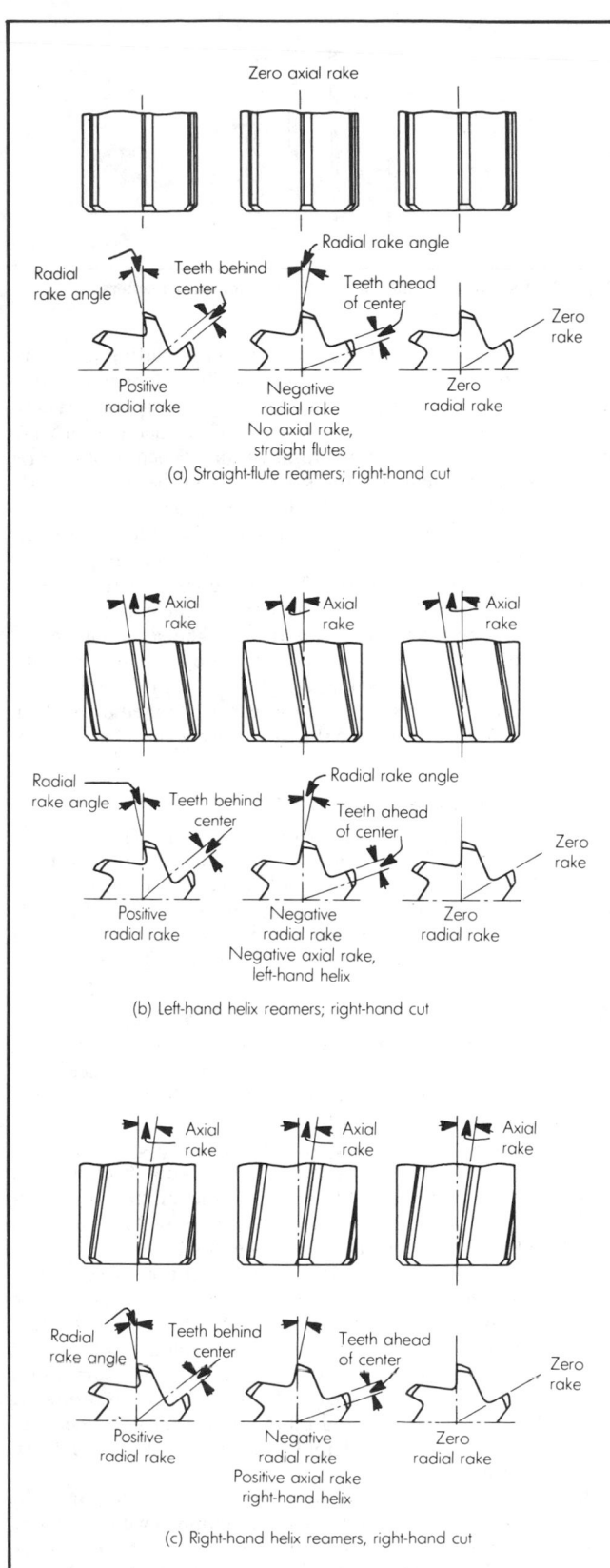

(a) Straight-flute reamers; right-hand cut

Zero axial rake

Radial rake angle · Teeth behind center · Radial rake angle · Teeth ahead of center · Zero rake

Positive radial rake · Negative radial rake No axial rake, straight flutes · Zero radial rake

(b) Left-hand helix reamers; right-hand cut

Axial rake · Axial rake · Axial rake

Radial rake angle · Teeth behind center · Radial rake angle · Teeth ahead of center · Zero rake

Positive radial rake · Negative radial rake Negative axial rake, left-hand helix · Zero radial rake

(c) Right-hand helix reamers, right-hand cut

Axial rake · Axial rake · Axial rake

Radial rake angle · Teeth behind center · Teeth ahead of center · Zero rake

Positive radial rake · Negative radial rake Positive axial rake right-hand helix · Zero radial rake

Fig. 24-40 Reamers for right-hand rotation.

misalignment. Application details (vertical or horizontal operation and rotating or stationary tool) should be specified when a floating holder is ordered.

Various Holder Designs

Holders of many different designs are available, but all have internal mechanisms which are essentially specialized couplings. Each design offers certain advantages over the others.

Plain Oldham coupling. The coupling shown in Fig. 24-42 view *a*, is outstanding in terms of low cost, simplicity, and impact load bearing capacity. Its major drawback is the dead spot which occurs for about 17° around each 90° of rotation. This is caused by steel-on-steel frictional characteristics, which can be modified with lubricants or made neglegible by the addition of balls or rollers. This, however, increases unit loading which decreases impact loading capacity and durability.

Views *b* and *c* of Fig. 24-42 illustrate variations of the basic Oldham coupling which are intended to reduce friction. This is usually accomplished by the inclusion of antifriction elements (not shown) between the load-bearing components.

Another common variation of the basic four-point coupling (see view *d*) works well until the oscillating balls (which travel only half the misalignment capacity of the holder) wear V-grooves in their travel zone. This results in frictional forces greater than those found in Oldham couplings.

Holders of this type are also available with rollers, but they cannot correct both angular and parallel misalignment. They are primarily designed to correct parallel misalignment.

Gear couplings. As illustrated in Fig. 24-42, view *e*, gear coupling systems distribute driving torque over several teeth in any condition of misalignment. Dead spots are eliminated in this design. Driving torque is not as high as with an Oldham coupling of the same size, but high shock loads are readily absorbed. Long life can be expected due to the multitude of driving elements which provide positive lubrication. Clearances between the telescoping tubular elements may be designed to limit the allowable misalignment. The primary disadvantage of this design is its higher cost.

Hexagonal-drive couplings. A somewhat lower cost design utilizes hexagonal driving and driven members in a telescoping package (see view *f*, Fig. 24-42), similar to the gear drive design. Wear life is usually reduced because the greater clearances required by straight hexagonal splines reduce the ability of the coupling to absorb shock loads. If the hexagonal surfaces are curved longitudinally to minimize clearances, the cost of manufacturing is almost as much as for gear couplings.

Holder Types

Full-floating holders are available in collet, bushing, and adjustable-flange types. Quick-change floating holders consist of a holder and a cartridge which holds the reamer. With the spindle stopped, the cartridge is lifted to remove the tool.

WORKHOLDING FOR REAMING

Jig design and the use of bushings for reaming are essentially the same as for drilling, discussed previously in this chapter. Major functions of the jigs and bushings are accurate locating, supporting, and securing of the workpieces, and precise guiding of the tools. A difference for reaming is that closer tolerances are generally required on both the jigs and bushings.

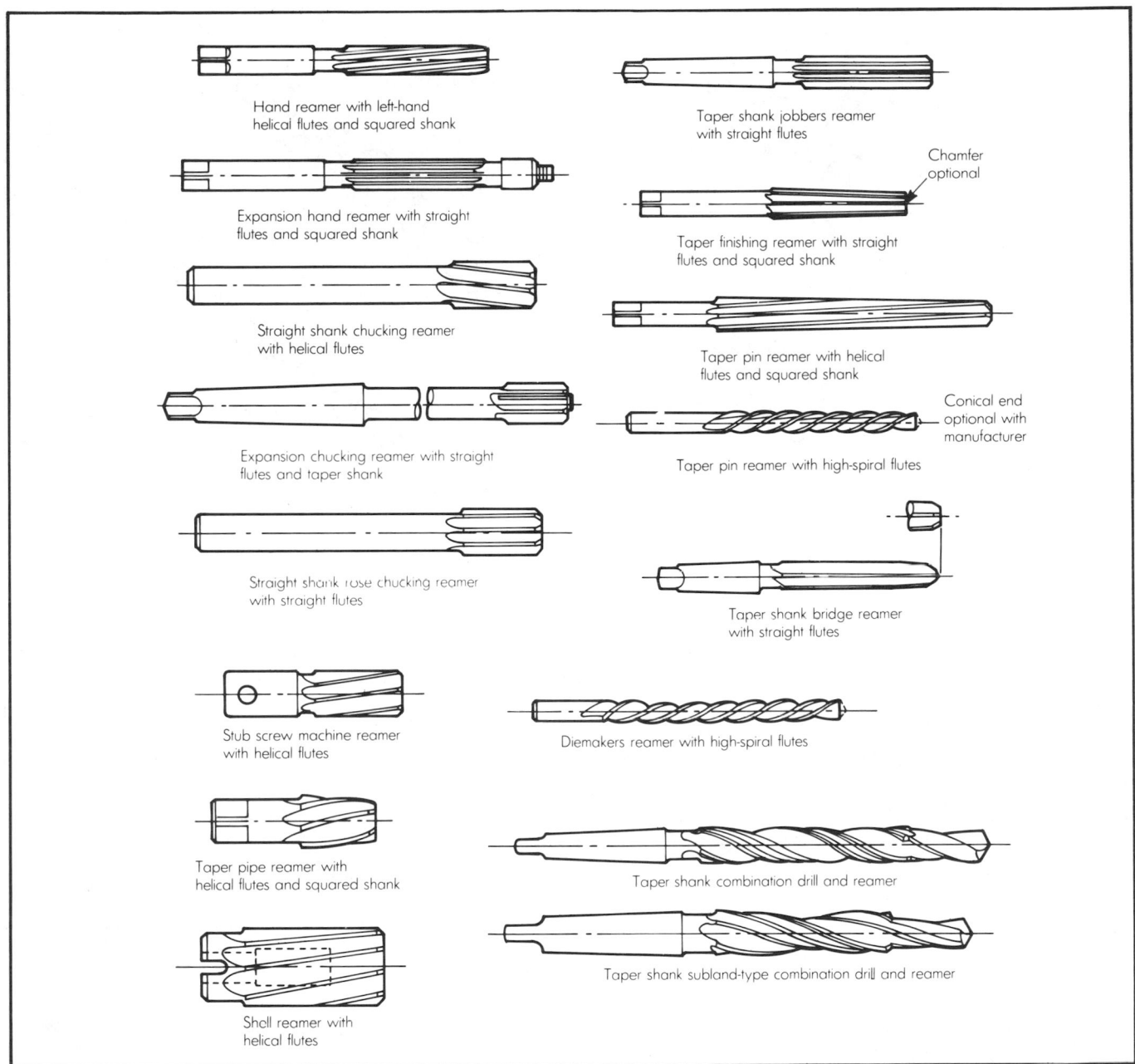

Hand reamer with left-hand
helical flutes and squared shank

Expansion hand reamer with straight
flutes and squared shank

Straight shank chucking reamer
with helical flutes

Expansion chucking reamer with straight
flutes and taper shank

Straight shank rose chucking reamer
with straight flutes

Stub screw machine reamer
with helical flutes

Taper pipe reamer with
helical flutes and squared shank

Shell reamer with
helical flutes

Taper shank jobbers reamer
with straight flutes

Chamfer
optional

Taper finishing reamer with straight
flutes and squared shank

Taper pin reamer with helical
flutes and squared shank

Conical end
optional with
manufacturer

Taper pin reamer with high-spiral flutes

Taper shank bridge reamer
with straight flutes

Diemakers reamer with high-spiral flutes

Taper shank combination drill and reamer

Taper shank subland-type combination drill and reamer

Fig. 24-41 Commercial types of reamers.

Alignment

Close-tolerance reaming requires accurate alignment of the machine spindle with the guide bushing. Using the reamer as a locating device to force the workpiece into alignment is poor practice and can result in excessive wear, chipping, or breakage of the reamer.

When misalignment between the reamer and the hole to be machined amounts to about 30% or more of the stock to be removed, there is often wear on the reamer in the form of a thread. The lead of the thread is equal to the feed rate, and depth is equal to the misalignment. These threads appear to be more readily produced when tough and abrasive materials are reamed. When other materials are reamed, only excessive marginal wear may be noticed.

For precise hole locations, reaming jigs are essential. An ideal arrangement, especially for long holes is to guide the reamer on both sides of the workpiece as illustrated in Fig. 24-43, view *a*. Special piloted reamers are required for this purpose, with the pilots having grooves on their OD's to permit cutting fluid to lubricate the pilots and to assist in chip removal. The jig should be designed so that the pilot enters the bushing before the reamer enters the workpiece, and the reamer should remain piloted until the tool finishes its cut. For short holes, the reamer can be guided only at the entry side of the hole (view *b*), with the bushing made to fit the OD of the reamer flutes.

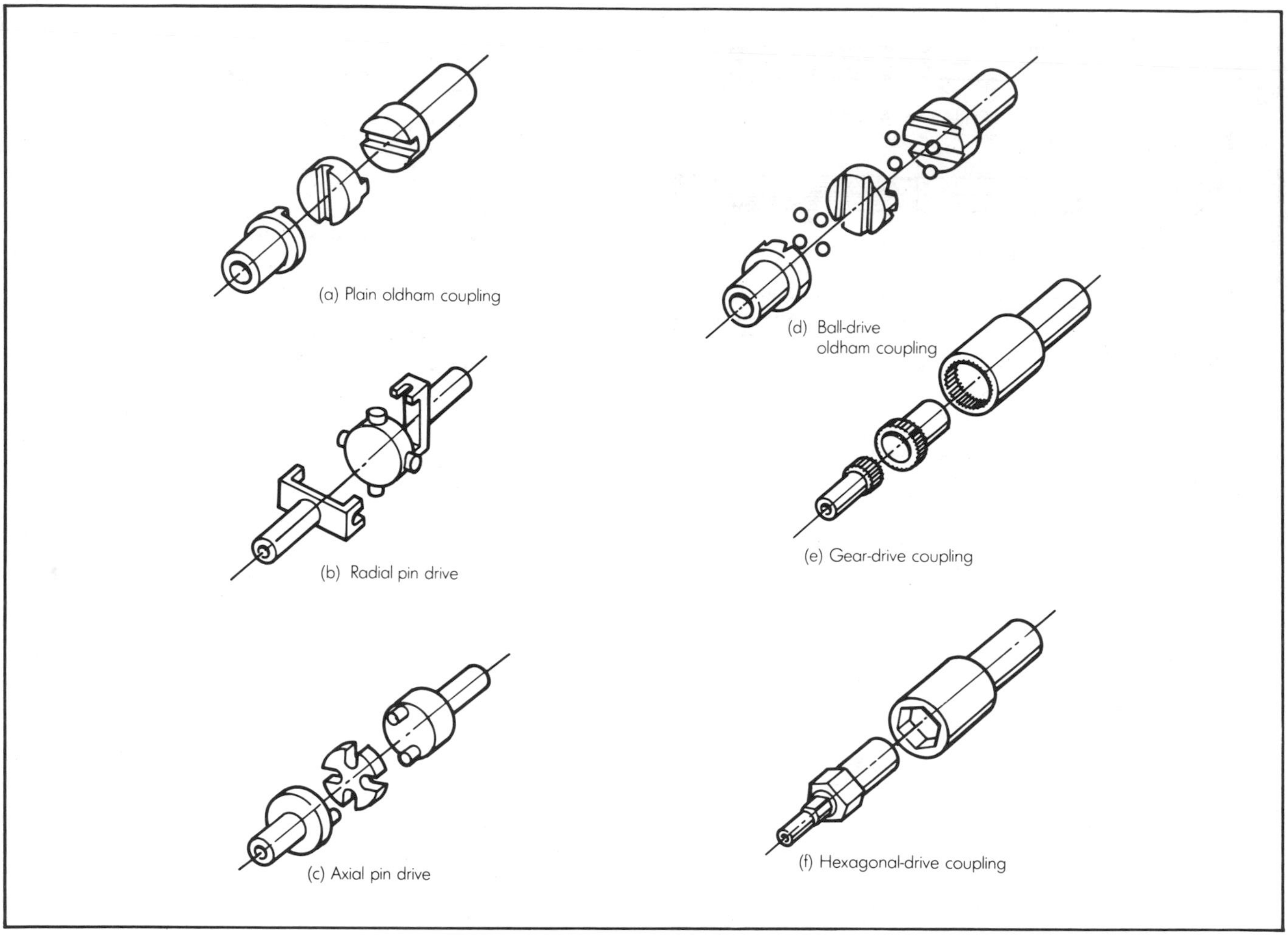

REAMING

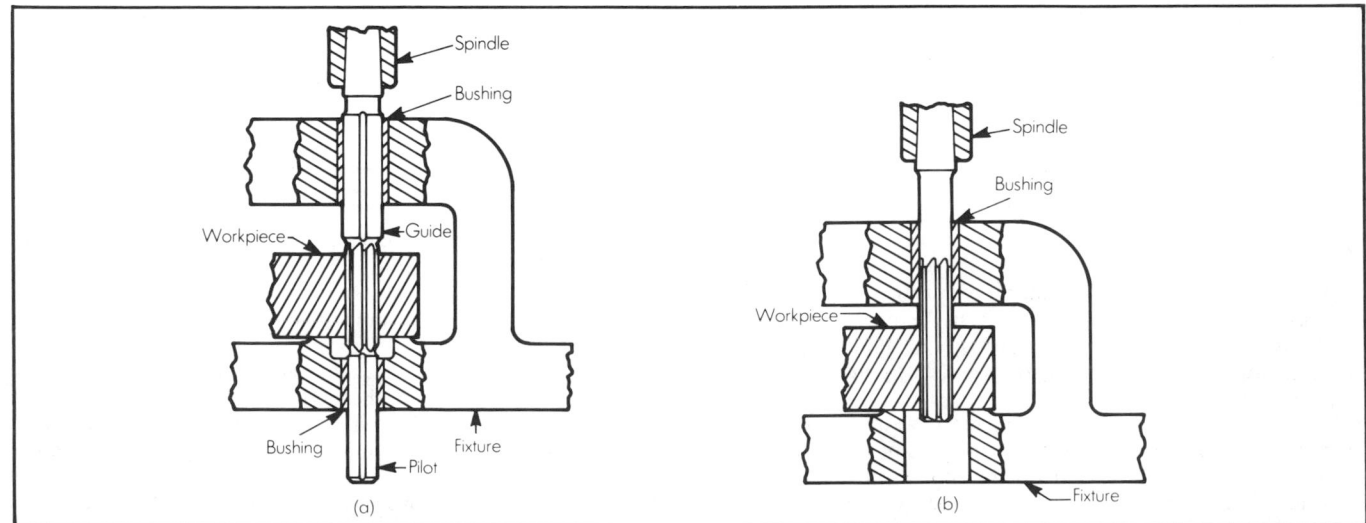

(a) Plain oldham coupling

(b) Radial pin drive

(c) Axial pin drive

(d) Ball-drive oldham coupling

(e) Gear-drive coupling

(f) Hexagonal-drive coupling

Fig. 24-42 Various types of internal coupling mechanisms used for floating holders. (*Industrial Tools Div., Bendix Corp.***)**

Spindle

Bushing

Workpiece

Guide

Bushing

Fixture

Pilot

(a)

Spindle

Bushing

Workpiece

Fixture

(b)

Fig. 24-43 Fixtures for guiding reamers through (a) long holes and (b) short holes.

Bushings for Reaming

Bushings for reaming are generally longer than for drilling, usually having a length equal to 3-4 times the reamer diameter. Chip clearance—the distance from the bottom of the bushing to the top of the workpiece—must be sufficient to permit chip ejection and minimize bushing wear, but it is generally less for reaming than for drilling. Many reaming experts recommend that the clearance distance be limited to one-fourth to one-half

the tool diameter. Others suggest even less clearance—a maximum of 1/8 to 1/4″ (3.2 to 6.3 mm), regardless of the reamer diameter.

Bushing bores must be held to close tolerances for precise reaming. Too small a bushing can result in tool seizure and possible breakage; too large an ID will result in out-of-round or bellmouthed holes. Tolerances that should be maintained on the bushing bores depend upon the tolerances required for the holes to be reamed.

COUNTERBORING, SPOTFACING AND COUNTERSINKING

Counterboring, spotfacing, and countersinking are secondary operations performed with end-cutting tools. Enlarging a hole for a limited depth is called counterboring. If the cut is shallow so that it leaves only a finished face around the original hole, it is called spotfacing. The cutting of an angular opening into the end of a hole is countersinking, sometimes referred to as chamfering. Tools of this type often present difficulty because they are among the most inefficient of cutting tools due to the distance of the cutting edge from the support.

The counterbore is defined as a rotary, pilot-guided, end-cutting tool, having one or more cutting lips and usually having straight or helical flutes for the passage of chips and the admission of cutting fluid. A spotfacer is defined as a rotary, pilot-guided, end-cutting tool, having teeth on one or both ends. Spotfacers are mounted on either straight or taper-shank pilots (drive bars) and are used to produce flat surfaces normal to their axes of rotation. Spotfacers are designed as a variation of the counterbore to reach inaccessible areas. The drive bar acts as the pilot. A countersink is a rotary, end-cutting tool which may or may not be piloted for the purpose of beveling or tapering the work material around the periphery of a hole. The surface cut by the conical tool is concentric with and at an angle of less than 90° to the centerline of the hole.

COUNTERBORES

Six types of counterbores are in general use. They are:

1. *Solid counterbores.* These are made of one piece of tool material, including the pilot (Fig. 24-44, view *a*). One tool manufacturer brazes a pilot sleeve on the solid body (view *b*). The two-lip construction provides good chip space while retaining the advantage of an unbroken surface on the pilot.
2. *Counterbores with interchangeable pilots.* These are counterbores having removable, mechanically held pilots.
3. *Interchangeable counterbores.* These are counterbores having end-cutting portions as well as pilots that are removable and interchangeable so that a series of cutters fit the same holder and a series of pilots fit the same cutter. These types of counterbores are generally available in standard sizes from 1/4 to 5″ (6.3 to 127 mm) diam (Fig. 24-45).
4. *Inserted-blade counterbores.* These are counterbores which have replaceable, mechanically held blades. The blades may be either solid or tipped (Fig. 24-46).

5. *Indexable-insert counterbores.* These are counterbores with indexable-insert tips. They may be used in the same manner as interchangeable counterbores; however, they are more limited in application than other types (Fig. 24-47).
6. *Disposable-insert counterbores.* These counterbores or spotfacers have disposable inserts and removable pilots or pilot drills. The inserts may also be designed to chamfer the holes; depth setting remains constant when the inserts are changed.

Several types of holding mechanisms are available for interchangeable-type counterbores (Fig. 24-48). The holder may have positive stops to control counterboring depth accurately. Figure 24-48, view *b*, illustrates a threaded-stop-nut holder. The ball-bearing stop nut (view *c*) indicates depth of counterboring when the stop nut begins to rotate.

There are many variations of counterbore-type tools used for special applications. Figure 24-49 illustrates a multiple-diameter counterbore, a multiple-diameter subland counterbore, and a port-contour cutter used specifically for hydraulic applications.

Counterbores, as well as spotfaces, can usually be machined with three or four-flute core drills sharpened to an included point angle of 180°. One or two flutes are usually sharpened to center when spotfacing is done without the benefit of a previously drilled hole. The other flutes provide additional support in the bushing, as well as balanced cutting action.

SPOTFACERS

A spotfacer, as its name implies, is designed for shallow machining of a surface for applications such as washers and bolt and nut heads as well as many other special machining purposes. These tools are designed to reach inaccessible spots in castings or similar workpieces. The body of the drive bar acts as a pilot, and the tool is generally run in reverse with the spindle moving toward the machine to produce the desired surface. Because of this, the standard single right-hand cutter actually appears to be a left-hand cutter when viewed in a normal manner. If the cutter is designed to spotface with a spindle feed away from the machine face, a left-hand cutter should be used. Cutters also come in double right-hand or double right-hand and double left-hand types.

Automatic back spotfacing, counterboring, or back chamfering tools are also available. These tools consist of a spindle with a recess into which the cutter, called a wing, folds when the

COUNTERBORING

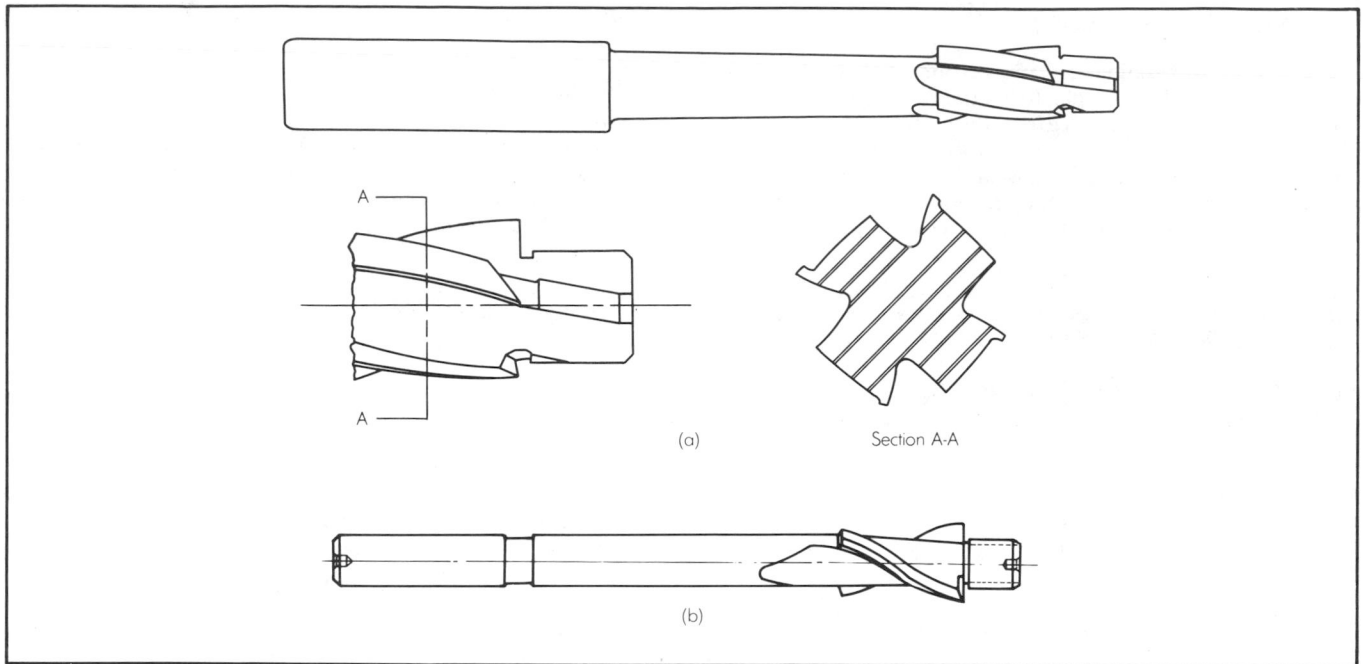

Fig. 24-44 Solid counterbore (a) is of one-piece construction. Counterbore (b) has pilot sleeve brazed to body. (*Weldon Tool Co.*)

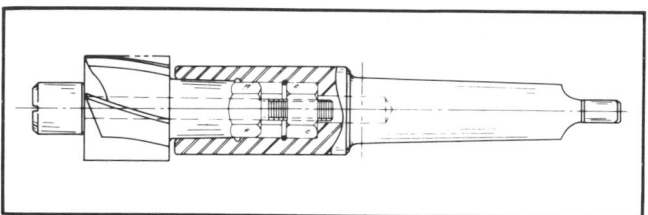

Fig. 24-45 Interchangeable counterbore with removable pilot and end-cutting portion.

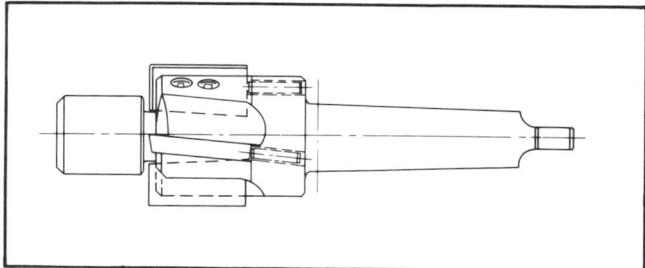

Fig. 24-46 Inserted-blade counterbore.

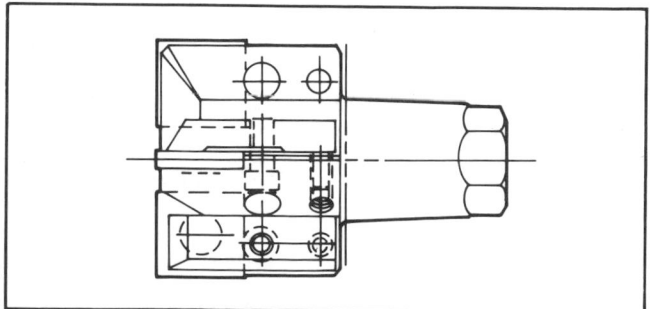

Fig. 24-47 Counterbore equipped with indexable inserts.

spindle enters the hole in the workpiece. When the cutter (wing) leaves the hole, it automatically extends due to centrifugal force. Then when the direction of spindle rotation is reversed and feed applied, the required operation is performed. With the exception of the smallest size tools, which use HSS cutters, the wings are provided with clamped carbide inserts.

The same rules apply for back spotfacing as for counterboring; however, most back spotface cutters are designed without deep flutes on the periphery and therefore are intended only for very shallow work. Designs are also available for deeper work and heavy-duty drives.

COUNTERSINKS

Countersinks are generally classified in two general categories: (1) shank-type countersinks and (2) combined drills and countersinks. Commercially available combined drills and countersinks were discussed previously in this chapter under the subject of types of twist drills.

The types of countersinks shown in Fig. 24-50 may be broadly classified as machine countersinks. These are used mostly to produce countersunk holes for screw and rivet heads, as well as to chamfer and deburr holes. They are available with included point angles of 60°, 72°, 82°, and 90°.

Countersinks are available with tool steel bodies with disposable HSS or carbide inserts. Aircraft-type countersinks normally have an included point angle of 100° and frequently include a cutting radius at the junction of the conical and cylindrical surfaces. These cutters are made to rigid dimensional and quality standards because they must produce fastener holes in aircraft assemblies to close tolerances. They are frequently used in portable tools equipped with precise depth control devices.

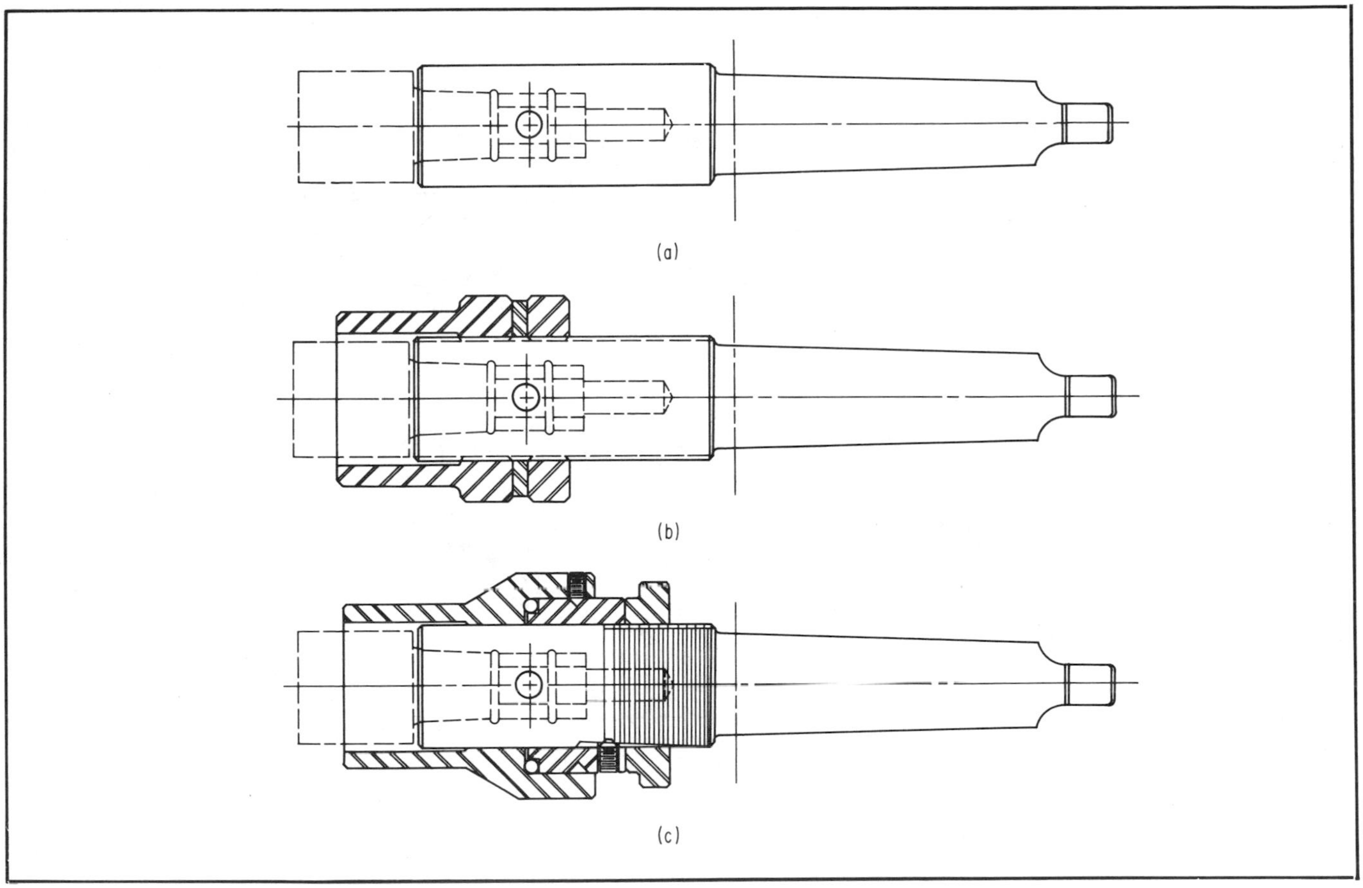

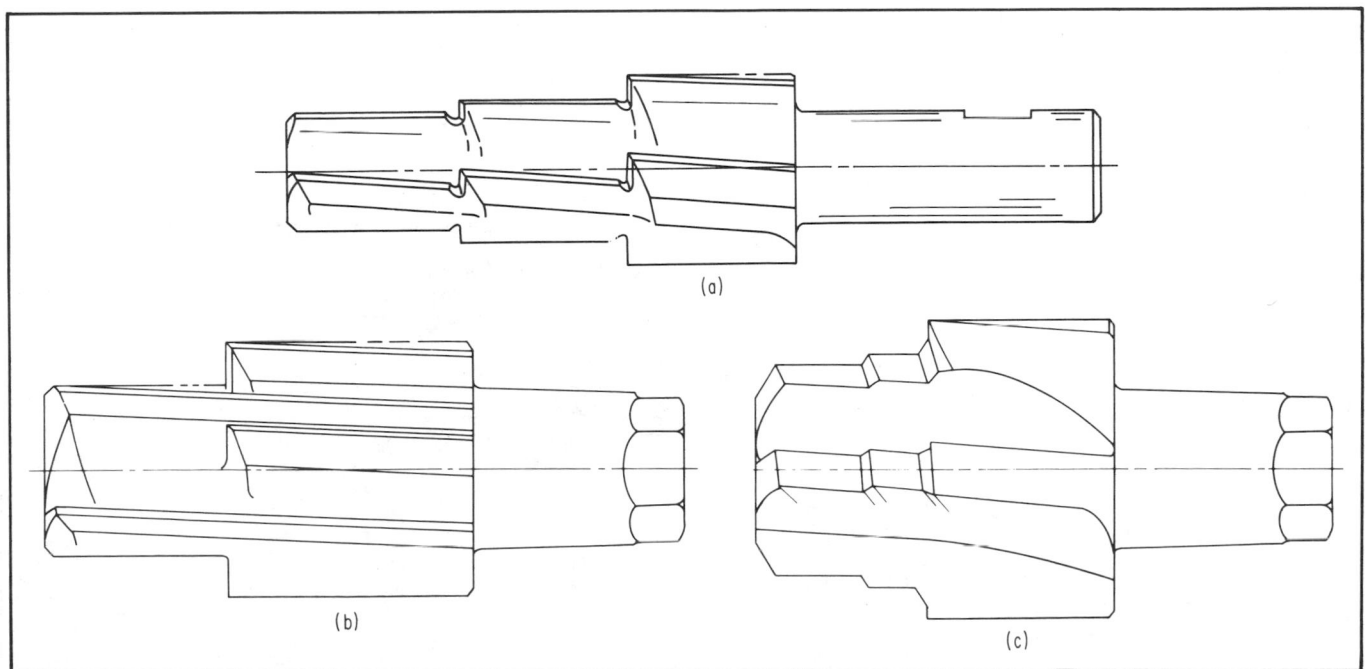

Fig. 24-48 Several types of holders for interchangeable-type counterbores.

(a)

(b)

(c)

(a)

(b)

(c)

Fig. 24-49 Counterbore-type tools for special applications: (a) multidiameter counterbore, (b) multidiameter subland counterfore, and (c) portcontour cutter.

COUNTERBORING

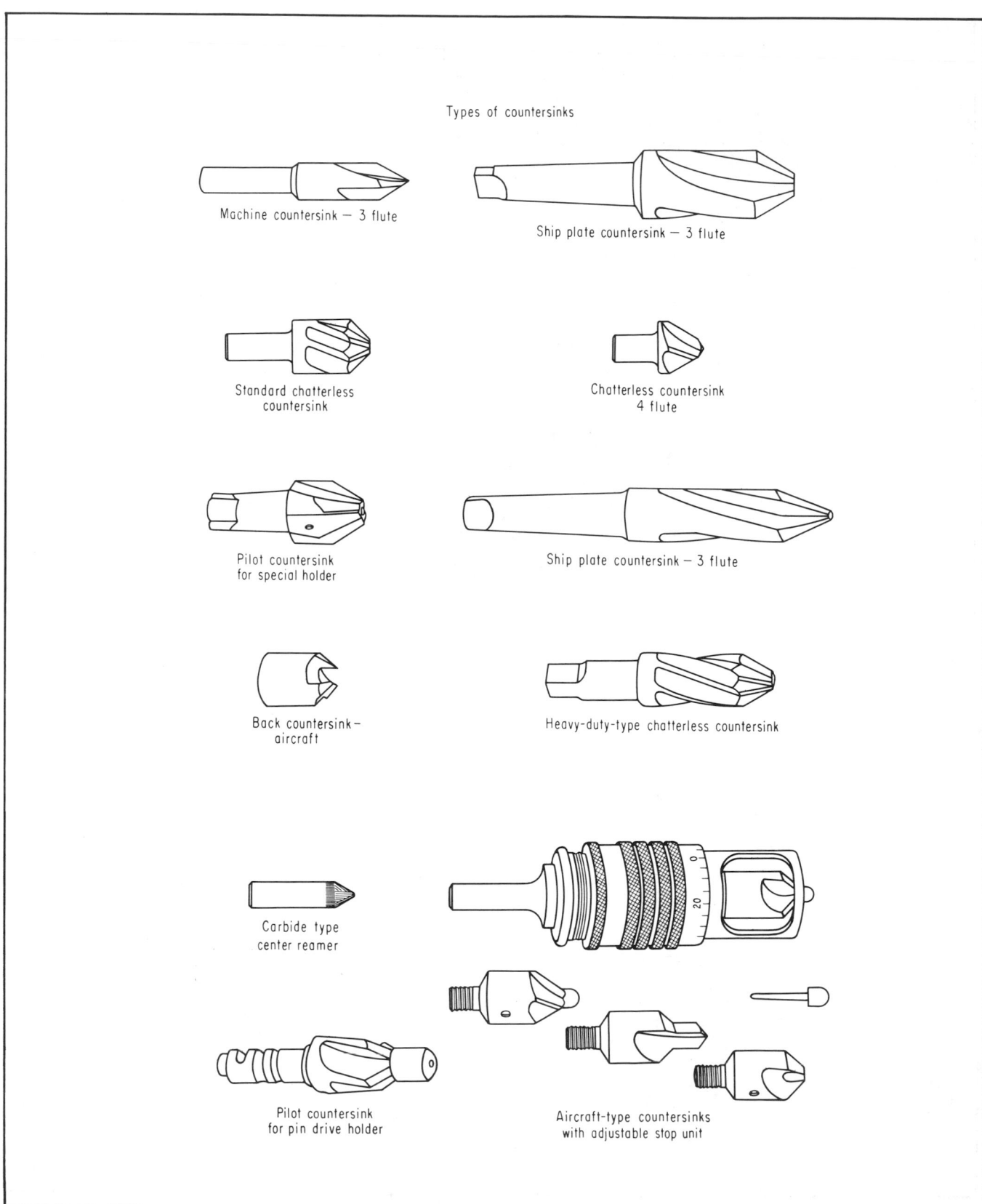

Fig. 24-50 Various types of countersinks broadly classified as machine countersinks.

References

1. R. L. Hatschek. "Fundamentals of Drilling." *American Machinist* (February 1979) pp. 108-130.
2. E. G. Hoffman. *Jig and Fixture Design* (Albany, NY: Delmar Publishers, 1980).

MILLING

Milling is a machining process for removing material by relative motion between a workpiece and a rotating cutter having multiple cutting edges. In some applications, the workpiece is held stationary while the rotating cutter is moved past it at a given feed rate (traversed). In other applications, both the workpiece and cutter are moved in relation to each other and in relation to the milling machine. More frequently, however, the workpiece is advanced at a relatively low rate of movement or feed to a milling cutter rotating at comparatively high speed, with the cutter axis remaining in a fixed position. A characteristic feature of the milling process is that each milling cutter tooth takes its share of the stock in the form of small individual chips. Milling operations are performed on many different machines.

Since both the workpiece and cutter can be moved relative to one another, independently or in combination, a wide variety of operations can be performed by milling. Applications will include the production of flat or contoured surfaces, slots, grooves, recesses, threads, and other such configurations.

MILLING METHODS

The major milling methods are peripheral and face milling; in addition, a number of related methods exist that are variations of these two methods, depending upon the type of workpiece or cutter.

PERIPHERAL MILLING

In peripheral milling, sometimes called slab milling, the milled surface generated by teeth or inserts located on the periphery of the cutter body is generally in a plane parallel to the cutter axis. Milling operations with form-relieved and formed profile cutters are included in this class. The cross section of the milled surface corresponds to the outline or contour of the milling cutter or combination of cutters used.

Peripheral milling operations are usually performed on milling machines with the spindle positioned horizontally; however, they can also be performed with end mills on vertical-spindle machines. The milling cutters are mounted on an arbor which is generally supported at the outer end for increased rigidity, particularly when, because of the conditions of the setup, the cutter or cutters are located at some distance from the nose of the spindle. Peripheral milling should generally not be done if the part can be face milled.

FACE MILLING

Face milling is done on both horizontal and vertical milling machines. The milled surface resulting from the combined action of cutting edges located on the periphery and face of the cutter is generally at right angles to the cutter axis. The milled surface is flat, with no relation to the contour of the teeth, except when milling is done to a shoulder. Generally, face milling should be applied wherever and whenever possible.

Chip thickness in conventional (up) face milling varies from a minimum at the entrance and exit of the cutter tooth to a maximum along the horizontal diameter. The milled surface is characterized by tooth and revolution marks, as in the case of peripheral milling cutters. The prominence of these marks is controlled by the accuracy of grinding the face cutting edge of the teeth, or by the accuracy of the body/insert combination in indexable cutters and of mounting the cutter so that it runs true on the machine spindle. It is also controlled by the rigidity of the machine and workpiece itself. When the length of the face cutting edge is less than the feed per revolution (or the amount the work has moved in one revolution of the cutter), a series of roughly circular grooves or ridges results on the milled surface. Similar marking is produced by the trailing teeth when they drag on the milled surface of the work. This is known as heel drag.

It is considered good practice to tilt the milling machine spindle slightly in a direction so that the trailing part of the face milling cutter does not drag on the finish-milled surface. This angle of tilt should be from 0.001-0.002″ (0.03-0.05 mm) in 12″ (305 mm).

RELATED MILLING METHODS

Many other milling methods can be classified as either peripheral or face milling operations. Because of the type of workpiece being machined and/or the specific type of cutter used, however, these methods are often referred to as end, side, straddle, gang, gear, cam, or other types of milling.

End Milling

End mills have cutting edges on both their end faces and their peripheries. When used in face milling operations, the diameter of the cutter determines the maximum width of cut. In peripheral milling, the axial length of the teeth determines the maximum depth of cut.

Side and Straddle Milling

Side milling consists of machining a plane surface perpendicular to the milling machines arbor with an arbor-mounted tool called a side milling cutter. Straddle milling entails machining two or more parallel surfaces using two or more side milling cutters spaced apart on the machine arbor.

Gang Milling

This method consists of using two or more cutters, mounted on the machine arbor, to mill multiple surfaces simultaneously. The cutters can be of

MILLING METHODS

various types. Care must be exercised in cutter selection to control cutting speeds within an acceptable range. Cutters made from different tool materials are sometimes used to help maintain effective cutting speeds when different diameters are being milled.

Cam Milling

Cams, worm threads, and other helical surfaces are produced on milling machines equipped with universal dividing heads. This is accomplished by rotating the workpiece while it is fed in the direction of the rotational axis.

Thread Milling

With the availability of NC/CNC machines having three-axis contouring capability and advanced controls, thread milling is undergoing a resurgence in popularity. Ease of programming with canned routines, long cutter life, and high-quality threads are among the advantages of this milling method.

Plunge Milling

Plunge milling with multipoint tooling is an alternative to the use of single-point turning tools for facing operations. The rotating multipoint facing head used for this method has a sufficient number of inserts to completely cover the area to be machined. Cutting edges of the inserts are set parallel to the workpiece surface, and as the head is advanced axially, all cutting edges simultaneously engage the face to be milled. Metal removal rates are greater than those possible with single-point tooling.

Crankshaft Milling

Milling of crankshafts, camshafts, and other unbalanced shafts has replaced the traditional turning process in some plants. Advantages of this milling method include faster production, closer tolerances, lower tooling costs, and more rapid change-over. Milling machines for both external and internal cutting of unbalanced shafts are described later in this chapter.

Diesinking

Most diesinking by the milling process is now done on machines with CNC or tracer control. Milling machines for copying are available with tracers operated by mechanical pantograph, air, hydraulic, electric, or combinations of these. At least one machine builder offers a copy mill having both tracer control and CNC.

CHIP FORMATION IN MILLING

Chip formation in milling differs from single-point metal-cutting, however, in several respects. Practically every milling operation consists of an interrupted cut, with each tooth or insert generally in the cut less than half the total machining time per cutter revolution. While the tooth or insert is in the cut, the thickness of the chip being formed constantly changes because of the dual motion—cutter rotation and workpiece feed—which is characteristic of the milling process.

CUTTING CONDITIONS IN MILLING

As each tooth or insert of a milling cutter enters a cut, it is subjected to a mechanical shock load. The magnitude of this load depends upon the workpiece material, cutter position, operating conditions, and cutter geometry. Cutting forces in milling are cyclical, being roughly proportional at any position in the cut to the undeformed chip thickness at that position. Heat generated in the milling operation is also roughly proportional to the undeformed chip thickness and cutting forces. Rapid changes in generated heat place a severe strain upon the cutter material and can lead to thermal cracking.

UP AND DOWN MILLING

If the rotation of the milling cutter is such that the tangential cutting force is generally opposed to the direction of workpiece feed and the axis of the cutter does not intersect the workpiece, the undeformed chip thickness constantly increases during the cut. This is called up milling or sometimes conventional milling (see Fig. 25-1, view a). If the rotation of the cutter is such that the tangential cutting force is generally in the same direction as the workpiece feed and the cutter axis does not intersect the workpiece (view b), the undeformed chip thickness constantly decreases during the cut. This is down milling, also known as climb milling.

Up and down milling exist in their pure form only when the cutter spindle centerline does not intersect the workpiece. This includes all slotting and side milling, and some face milling and end milling. In these operations, either up milling or down milling may be selected by proper selection of the direction of the machine table feed, cutter position, and direction of cutter rotation.

One of the most significant differences between up and down milling is the direction of the cutting forces generated. In up milling, the tangential force opposes the thrust force—the force attempting to push an individual tooth or insert out of the cut. As a result, the feed force must be high for the cut to be made. In down milling, however, tangential and thrust forces generally act in the same direction and the feed force can be low or even negative.

Whenever the cutter axis intersects the workpiece, up and down milling occur sequentially during each cutter revolution (see view c, Fig. 25-1). The switch from up to down milling occurs as each tooth or insert crosses the feed axis of the cutter. Combined up and down milling occurs in most face milling and end milling operations. It generally alters the direction of cutting forces so that feed and tangential cutting force, instead of aiding or opposing each other, act approximately at right angles to each other. When up and down milling are combined, chip thickness, as the teeth or inserts enter and leave the cut, depends upon the tooth or insert entry and exit angles. These angles depend upon the amount that the cutter overhangs the workpiece on the entry and exit sides.

Advantages of Down Milling

Down or climb milling is preferred for several reasons wherever the machine tool and workpiece allow. With up or conventional milling, the undeformed chip thickness at tooth or insert entry is theoretically zero. As a result, the tooth or insert has to work its way gradually into a layer of material that has usually been work hardened by the previous tooth or insert, and tool life may be poor. With down milling, however, chip thickness at entry is at a maximum and any work-hardened layer is avoided. The thicker chips produced by the more efficient cutting action of down milling carry more heat away, which may lengthen cutter life.

In many milling operations, a chip occasionally welds to the

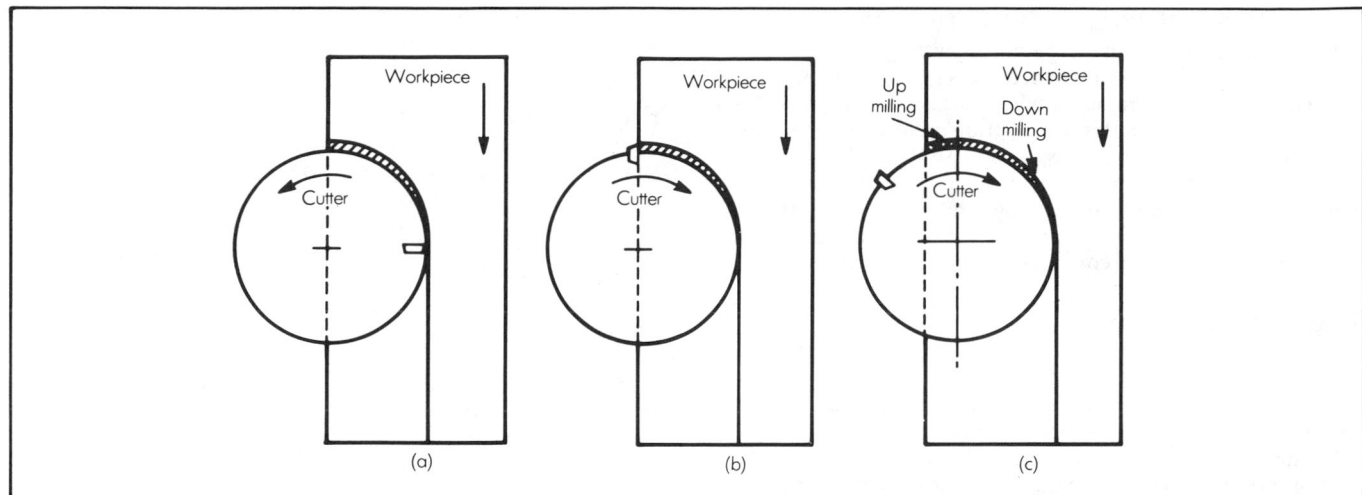

Fig. 25-1 (a) Up or conventional milling, (b) down or climb milling and (c) combined up and down milling.

tooth or insert and is carried around the cutter to the beginning of the cut. When up milling is used, the chip can be easily wedged between the cutting edge and the workpiece (see Fig. 25-2) and may break the tool. When down milling is used, however, such welded chips are generally cut in half and rendered harmless as the tooth or insert enters the cut.

Cutting forces, when down milling is performed on a horizontal spindle machine, press the workpiece down against the fixture, the fixture against the table, and the table against its supports (see Fig. 25-3), thus minimizing the possibility of vibration. When up milling is performed, however, the cutting forces tend to lift the workpiece from the table.

Other advantages of down milling include the following:

1. Feed drive power consumption is much lower, which slightly lowers the total power consumed by the operation.
2. The path described by each tooth or insert in the cut is about 3% shorter than the path in up milling. Since tool life in milling is inversely proportional to the length of cut, tool life when down milling is used is slightly better.
3. With the conventional cutter/workpiece orientation used on horizontal spindle machines, down milling tends to throw the chips downward, thus presenting less hazard to the operator and simplifying chip disposal.
4. Slotting cutters or slitting saws have less tendency to run out or deflect sideways when used for down milling; for many workpiece materials, it is often possible to use higher feed rates, increasing production.

Up Milling Applications

Despite the many advantages of down milling, there are some applications in which it should not be used. For example, on machines on which there is backlash in the spindle or feed drives, the cutter in down milling may bite into the workpiece and pull it further than the intended feed advance. This momentarily increases the undeformed chip thickness and may break the teeth or inserts. Cutting forces in up milling oppose the feed force and tighten less rigid feed systems.

Up milling is generally preferred for machining sandy, scaly, or flame cut surfaces because the cutter enters below the undesirable surfaces and thus avoids their harmful effect on tool life. Up milling may also be desirable if large variations exist in the amount of stock to be removed.

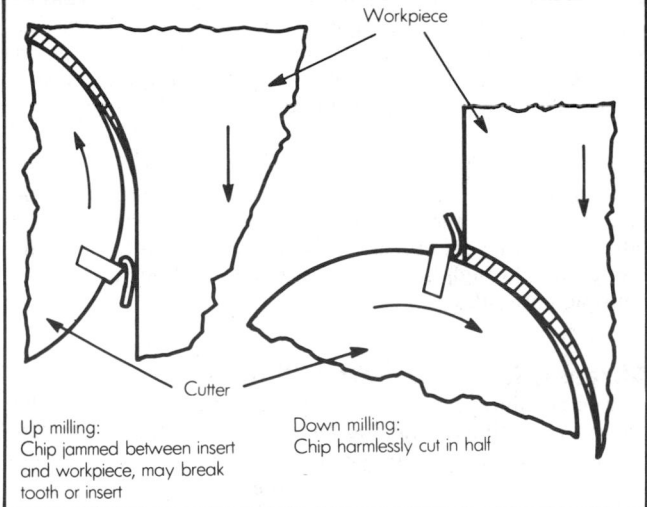

Up milling:
Chip jammed between insert and workpiece, may break tooth or insert

Down milling:
Chip harmlessly cut in half

Fig. 25-2 Chips welded to teeth or inserts are generally cut in half during down milling.

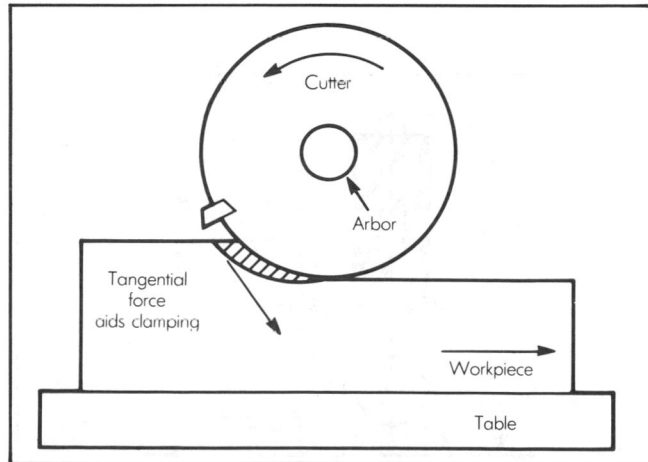

Fig. 25-3 During down milling, cutting forces press workpiece against table.

MILLING METHODS

PRODUCTION MILLING METHODS

Toolroom milling usually requires cutting only a single workpiece at one time. As a result, there is generally no problem with respect to the manner in which the part to be milled is located relative to the cutter. Production milling requirements, however, permit several choices, and these should be analyzed carefully to ensure optimum performance. Some of the more generally used methods of milling are single-piece, string, abreast, progressive, box, reciprocal, transfer-base, index, and rotary milling, as well as combinations of these methods.

Single-Piece Milling

The simplest and most easily applied method of milling is that in which one workpiece is held in a fixture or directly on the machine table and is milled during each machine cycle. This method is known as single-piece milling.

The machine operator places the part in the fixture or on the machine table and clamps it in place. The table is then advanced at a rapid rate to quickly locate the workpiece in position for milling. At this point in the cycle, the rate of table travel is usually changed automatically to the feeding rate by means of trip dogs. When milling is completed, the workpiece is returned to the starting position, where it is removed and a new piece is put in its place. The cycle is then repeated. Hence, loading and unloading of the workpiece are done on the same side of the machine.

String, Multiple-Part Milling

To effect a saving in handling time, two or more parts may be placed in a row in the direction of the feeding movement of the table so that they are milled in consecutive order as the machine is operated through the cycle. This method is known as string, multiple-part milling.

Abreast, Multiple-Part Milling

In some milling applications, savings in the cycle time can be obtained by using the method known as abreast, multiple-part milling. With this method (see Fig. 25-4), two or more pieces are aligned in a row at right angles to the direction of table feed. Thus, the pieces are milled simultaneously rather than consecutively as in string milling. This method offers the advantage of performing either the same or different milling operations on

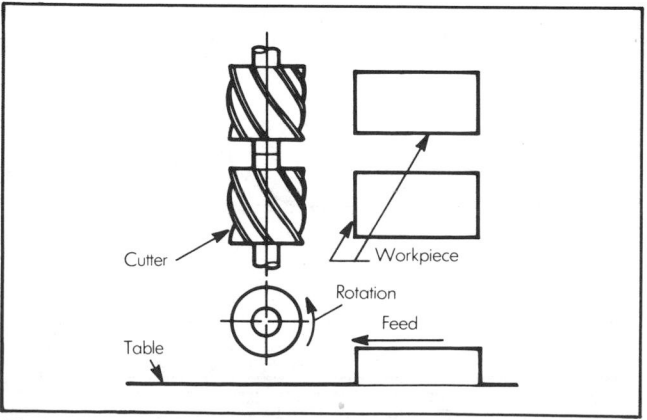

Fig. 25-4 Abreast milling method of machining two parts simultaneously.

the various pieces. The table travel is the same as that required to mill one piece.

Progressive Milling

Progressive milling is a method used when two or more similar or different operations are performed either simultaneously or successively on separate identical parts on the same machine. This method saves costs of equipment and setup time and is especially useful when production runs are short.

In the cycle of operation, a workpiece is milled in the first station and is subsequently placed in the second station so that its opposite end can be milled. The two operations are performed with only one setup rather than the two setups normally required. Substantial savings are obtained not only in the time required for the operation, but also in equipment and cost of the operation.

Box or Frame Milling

Box or frame milling is a method of milling in which the motions of two slides at right angles to each other are automatically coordinated to mill the four sides of a square opening, either internally or externally (see Fig. 25-5).

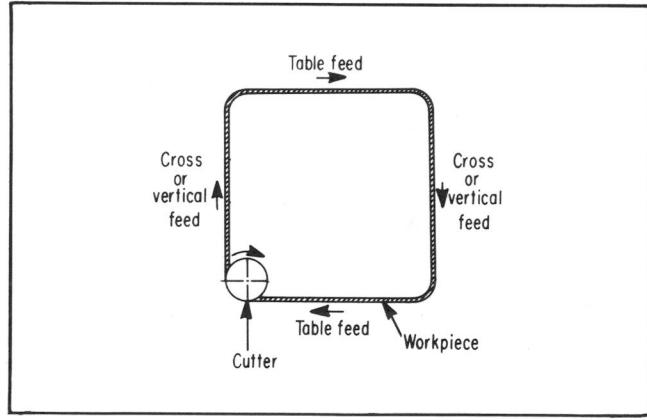

Fig. 25-5 Relationship between the cutter and the square opening in a workpiece during box milling.

Reciprocal Milling

To reduce handling time, a method known as reciprocal milling is sometimes used in production work. In this method, both the right and left-hand ends of the table are equipped with fixtures. While the part in one fixture is being milled, the operator unloads and reloads the other fixture. Thus, loading and unloading time is not charged to the operation, because the machine is productive at all times.

Proper safety precautions are essential when reciprocal milling is used. Length of table travel must be sufficient to place the operator a safe distance from the cutting action while unloading and reloading the second fixture. The milling cycle is often arranged so that the machine table stops after cutting is complete unless the second fixture is fully clamped and limit switch contacts have been made.

Transfer-Base Milling

Transfer-base and index milling include all methods in which the workpiece is either indexed into the next position or transferred from one position to the next in the operation cycle of the machine. A number of different combinations are used in practice.

In one method, two fixtures are located at opposite ends of a two-station index base, which is clamped to one end of the machine table. While a workpiece in one fixture is being milled, the other fixture is unloaded and reloaded. This decreases the loading and unloading time, but adds to the time required to index the base. Loading and unloading of the fixtures are always done at one end of the machine, reducing operator fatigue by eliminating the need for the operator to change his position from one end of the machine to the other.

Index Milling

Index milling is the method used when identical multiple operations are performed on one or more pieces, usually on work mounted between centers or in a chuck-type fixture. Automatic indexing of the work occurs after each cut is made and is followed by a final stop after the last cut is machined.

Rotary Milling

In this method of milling, the parts to be milled are held on a rotary table which either revolves continuously at the feed rate or is set through a cycle of alternate rapid rotation and feeding to bridge the spacing between parts. The principle of operation is shown in Fig. 25-6.

ACCURACIES AND FINISHES ATTAINABLE IN MILLING

Accuracies attainable with the milling process depend on many factors. These include the milling method, workpiece, machine and cutter used, operating parameters, and rigidity of

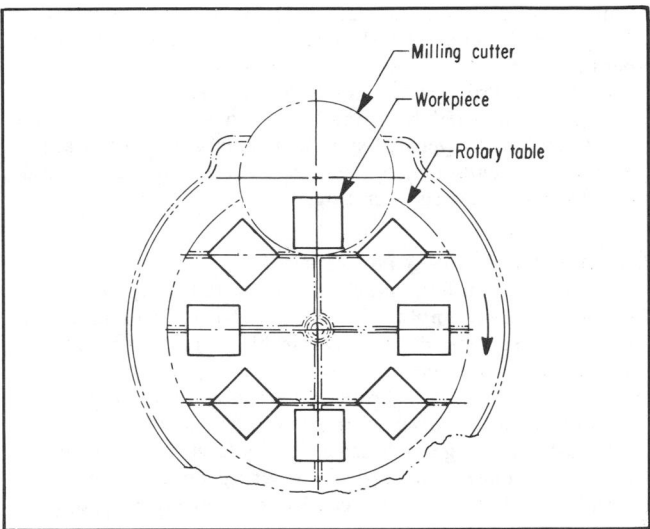

Fig. 25-6 In rotary milling, multiple workpieces are held on a rotary table.

the setup. The influence of these factors on accuracy are discussed in subsequent sections of this chapter. In general, tolerances range from ±0.002″ (0.05 mm) to ±0.005″ (0.13 mm), with ±0.001″ (0.03 mm) usually the best obtainable tolerance.

Surface finishes produced in milling are determined by tooth or insert and revolution marks and by plastic flow of the material removed from the workpiece in the form of chips. The finish varies with the material milled, the milling method, the cutter (size, geometry, and number of cutting edges), the feed rate, whether the cutters have built-up edges, the spindle and cutter runout, and the rigidity of the setup.

MILLING MACHINES

Machines designed specifically for milling are available in many different types, sizes, and capacities to suit specific requirements. Types of milling machines include knee, bed, tracer, programmable, computer numerical control (CNC), and special machines. They range from versatile machines that can perform many different operations to dedicated designs for production applications.

Many operations previously done on milling machines are now being performed on machining centers, as well as on other multifunction machines such as automatics and boring, drilling, and milling machines.

MACHINE REQUIREMENTS

Selection of a milling machine for a specific application depends on many variables. Workpiece size, geometry, and material; production requirements (quantity, accuracy, and finish); and economic factors are major considerations.

Regardless of the type of machine selected, rigidity is of critical importance. Any looseness adversely affects accuracy and finish of the work and shortens cutter life. Accurate, tight bearings and a positive feed mechanism are essential. Power

requirements, discussed in the section on operating parameters later in this chapter, depend primarily upon the material to be milled and the amount of stock to be removed.

MACHINE CONTROL SYSTEMS

Milling machines are available for manual, semiautomatic, and automatic operation. Numerical and computer numerical control (NC and CNC) are used on general-purpose machines for milling dies and molds; on dedicated machines such as skin and spar mills, described later in this section; and even more extensively on horizontal boring mills, machining centers, and other machine tools.

TYPES OF MILLING MACHINES

Because of the wide variety of milling machines available, only the more common types are discussed in this section. These include hand, knee, bed, tracer, programmable, NC/CNC, and special milling machines. Most types are available with horizontal or vertical spindles. The choice between a horizontal or vertical machine depends primarily upon the workpieces to be milled. Relatively flat workpieces are generally milled on vertical-spindle machines. Cubic or odd-shaped parts usually

MILLING MACHINES

require a horizontal-spindle machine. Horizontal machines are also generally used for slotting, side milling, and similar operations.

On horizontal-spindle machines, an arbor holding the cutter(s) is mounted horizontally on an axis parallel to the machine table. On vertical-spindle machines, the cutter axis is normally perpendicular to the machine table, but can often be tilted to perform angular cutting.

Hand-Fed Milling Machines

These small milling machines, mounted on pedestals or benches, are still employed for some toolroom or light-duty operations. Such machines are desirable for milling workpieces having large variations in stock removal requirements because necessary changes in feed rate can be sensed by hand pressure. Their application, however, appears to be declining.

Hand-fed milling machines generally have a rotating cutter mounted on a horizontal spindle. Feed is generally by means of a hand lever, but power feed can be applied to these machines.

Knee-and-Column-Type Milling Machines

Knee-and-column-type machines, in the horizontal version, have the spindle mounted in the column at a fixed height and have the capability of positioning three sliding motions. Vertical motion is obtained by sliding the knee member up and down on the central stationary column. Cross motion is generally obtained by sliding a saddle member in and out across the top of the knee. Longitudinal motion (right or left) is obtained by sliding the workholding table on the saddle at a right angle to the cross motion. Machines with a vertically mounted spindle generally have a fourth sliding motion which is up and down in the same direction as the knee.

Plain machines. On plain machines (see Fig. 25-7), the horizontal spindle is fixed in the column structure and is generally not movable axially. Cutters may be mounted directly on the spindle nose for face mills, on stub arbors for shell-end mills, and on long arbors supported on their outer extremity for slab and gang milling. Plain machines have three movements afforded by the knee, saddle, and table and are the most commonly used type of milling machine.

Universal machines. The universal machine (see Fig. 25-8) is similar to the plain machine, but has one additional movement which permits the table to be swiveled manually with respect to the saddle. Angular surfaces can thus be cut without moving the workpiece. The greatest use for a universal machine is in conjunction with a dividing head to mill helixes in gears, milling cutters, drills, and end mills. Dividing heads and other milling machine attachments are discussed later in this section.

Vertical machines. All the sliding motions used in a plain machine are present in a vertical machine with one addition. The vertical spindle is generally movable toward and away from the table top by manual effort or by power (see Fig. 25-9). No provision is made for support of an arbor-mounted cutter assembly other than at the spindle nose. Vertical machines are grouped as quill head, quill plus swivel head, sliding head, or fixed head.

Other variations. Ram-type or ram-head machines (see Fig. 25-10) have (atop the column) a ram that is movable by hand crank or power in a direction parallel to the saddle movement. At or near the front end of the ram is a single or double-swivel-mounted spindle in fixed or quill mounting. The ram spindle axis can be disposed horizontally, vertically, or angularly.

When the machine is a basic plain machine with a horizontal spindle and the additional ram head is supplied (as either an attachment or an integral part of the machine), two spindles can be used simultaneously.

Bed-Type Milling Machines

The fixed-bed-type milling machine, whether having a horizontal or vertical spindle, has many features that benefit the user. Machine size is usually governed by the horsepower rating of the spindle carrier, which in most cases can be anywhere from 1-50 hp (0.7-37 kW) or more, depending upon the machine type and the manufacturer. The range of machine sizes available permits light to heavy cutting and either up (conventional) or down (climb) milling with high-speed steel, carbide, ceramic, or diamond cutters. Most manufacturers offer wide ranges of spindle speeds and table feed rates that accommodate the majority of cutting requirements and permit correct chip-per-tooth loads for all types of cutters and work materials.

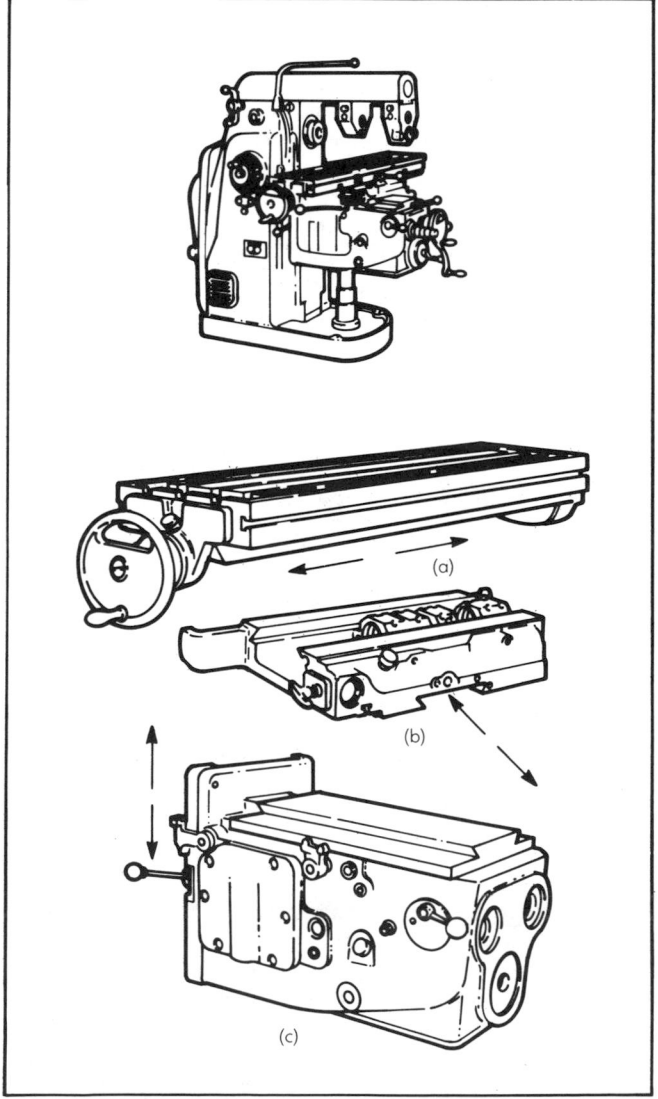

Fig. 25-7 Plain milling machine having three motions provided by the (a) table, (b) saddle, and (c) knee.

Physical size of these machines, along with the available travel for each axis, is also quite varied. Machines and special attachments are made in a wide range of combinations to suit almost any situation or requirement that can be anticipated.

Very close machining tolerances can be obtained on fixed-bed machines, and milling cuts to within 0.0005" (0.013 mm) can be realized in many cases if cutter and workholding devices

are made accordingly. These machines are generally equipped with readout systems to locate the cutters in all directions, and these systems are very useful in increasing machine efficiency and reducing floor-to-floor time to a minimum.

Horizontal machines. The horizontal machine (see Fig. 25-11) consists basically of a headstock or column bolted to or integral with a fixed bed. On this member, a spindle carrier, head, or

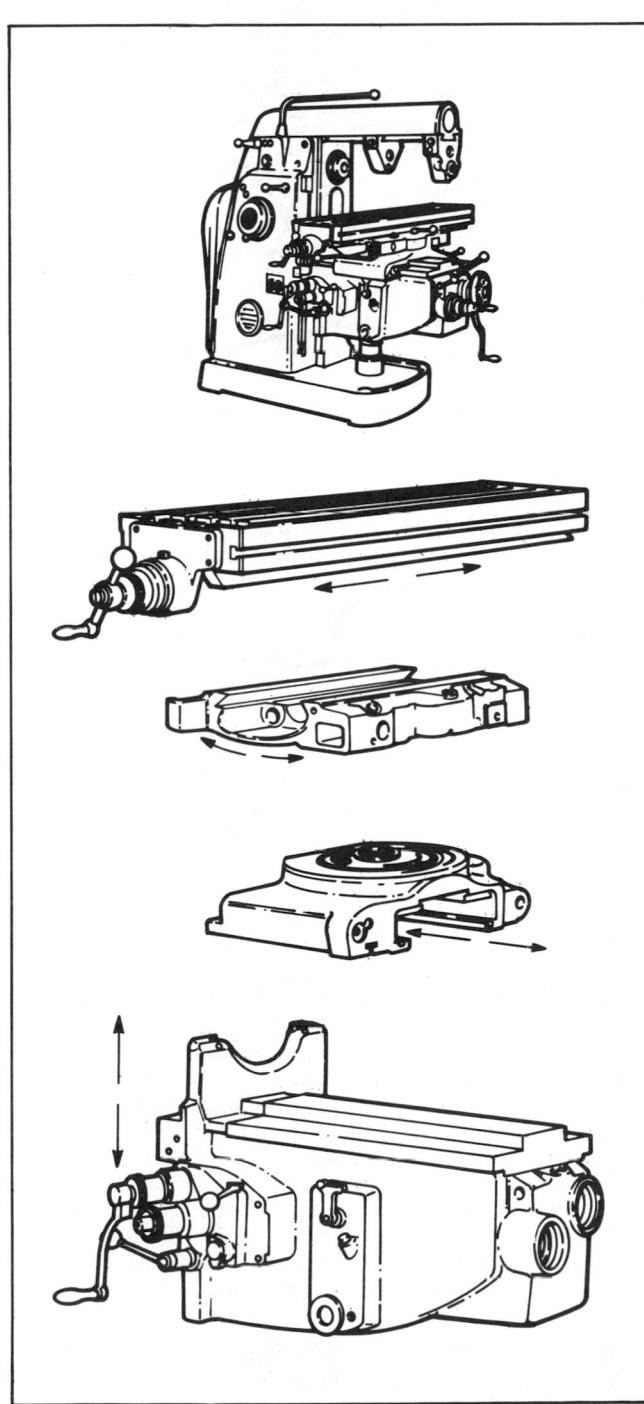

Fig. 25-8 Universal milling machine is similar to the plain type (Fig. 25-7), but has one additional movement which permits the table to be swiveled with respect to the saddle.

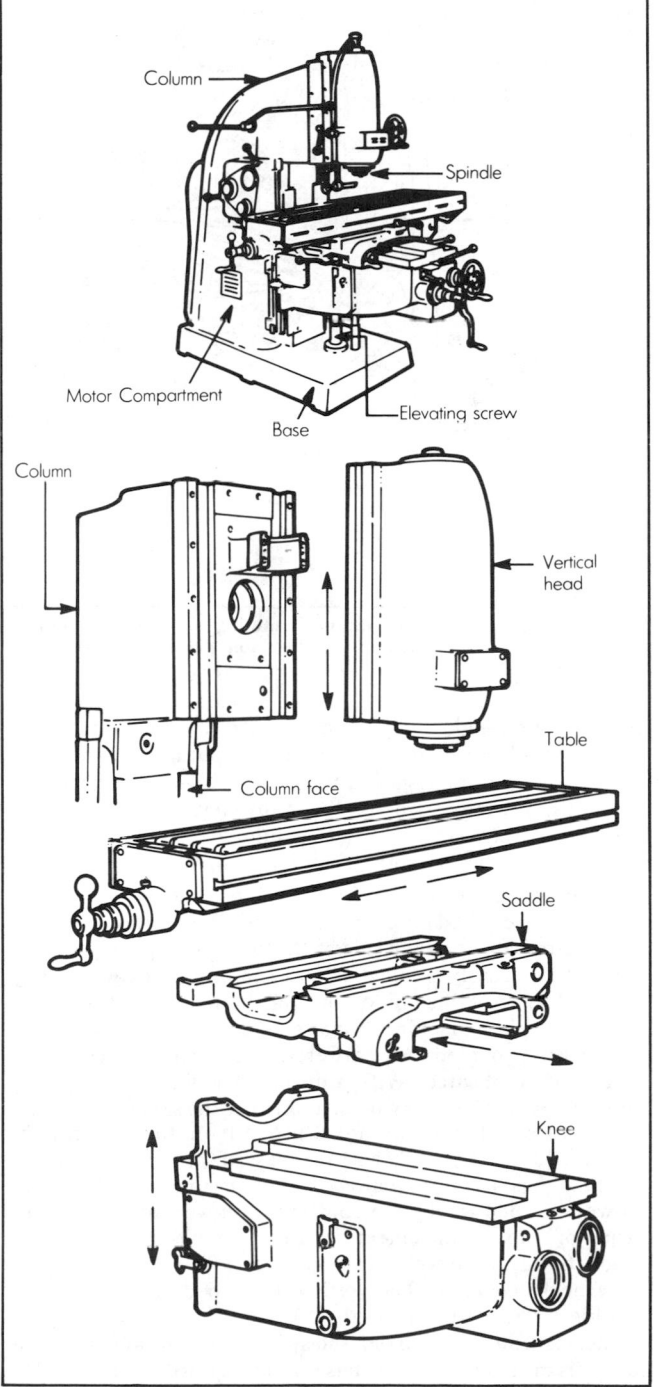

Fig. 25-9 Spindle on vertical milling machine is movable toward and away from the table, either manually or by power.

MILLING MACHINES

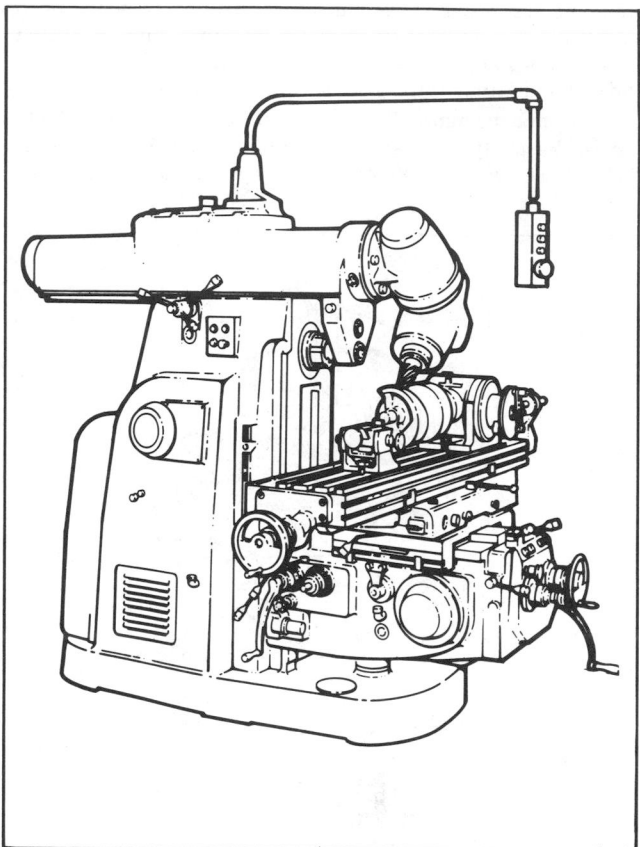

Fig. 25-10 On ram-type or ram-head milling machines, the ram is movable by hand or power in a direction parallel to the saddle movement.

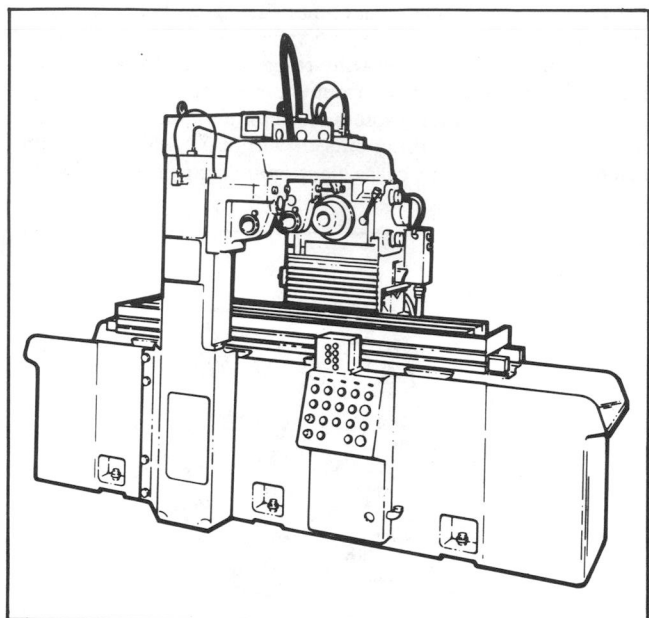

Fig. 25-11 Horizontal milling machine having column bolted to or integral with fixed bed.

block is mounted, carrying a spindle that is horizontally positioned. The axis of this spindle is parallel to the table surface and at right angles to the axis of table movement. The carrier usually moves (manually or automatically) in a vertical direction on the headstock, and the spindle is adjustable axially (in and out) through a spindle quill or ram.

Two-spindle machines. Single-spindle machines (as just described) are called plain or simplex machines. If two spindles are required, one on each side of the table and opposed to each other, the assembly is called a duplex milling machine (see Fig. 25-12). The bed-table unit on the duplex machine is the same as that on the plain machine, but a second headstock and spindle carrier are provided. All carrier features, speeds, feeds, and ranges are duplicated. With a duplex machine, two opposing sides of a workpiece may be machined at the same time or two separate parts that are mounted properly on the table may be machined simultaneously with one pass of the table. The duplex machine has a more limited use than the plain machine. However, when workpiece configuration warrants its use, the value of this arrangement in time savings and increased production is often worth the extra cost.

Vertical machines. The vertical fixed-bed milling machine (see Fig. 25-13) differs from the horizontal machine principally by the position of the carrier and spindle axis. A ram or spindle carrier is mounted on a rear base, which is normally fastened to the fixed bed. This carrier houses the vertical spindle, whose axis is perpendicular to the top of the table and is adjustable

vertically along its own axis through a quill. The carrier assembly is sometimes fixed (with no movement) and in some cases is adjustable manually or by power to travel laterally so that the spindle can be positioned crosswise to the table (forward or to the rear of the table centerline).

This vertical-type machine is well suited to face milling operations and can handle heavy cuts with close tolerance and finish requirements.

Fixed-Bed Saddle-Type Machines

Fixed-bed saddle-type milling machines with vertical spindles (see Fig. 25-14) provide greater rigidity than knee-and-column-type machines. As a result, higher power cuts can be taken with more accuracy for a given size machine. Another advantage of machines of this design is the ability to counterbalance the vertical slide, thus providing sensitive vertical motions.

Tracer-Controlled Milling Machines

Milling machines with tracing capabilities are used to produce parts with complex shapes economically, for either single-piece or mass-production requirements as well as for diesinking operations. One or more types of tracing functions may be used simultaneously to generate the desired complex surfaces. By coordinating the paths of the milling cutter and tracing element, as determined by the master or model, a milling machine which is tracer-controlled may operate under one of the following systems: mechanical, manual hydraulic, manual electric, automatic hydraulic, automatic electric, electric-spark contact, or optical (light-beam, with electric-eye sensor) contact.

Programmable Milling Machines

Programmable milling machines feature pushbutton programming by means of manual data input (MDI). These machines bridge the gap between standard and NC milling machines. They provide the flexibility of many standard

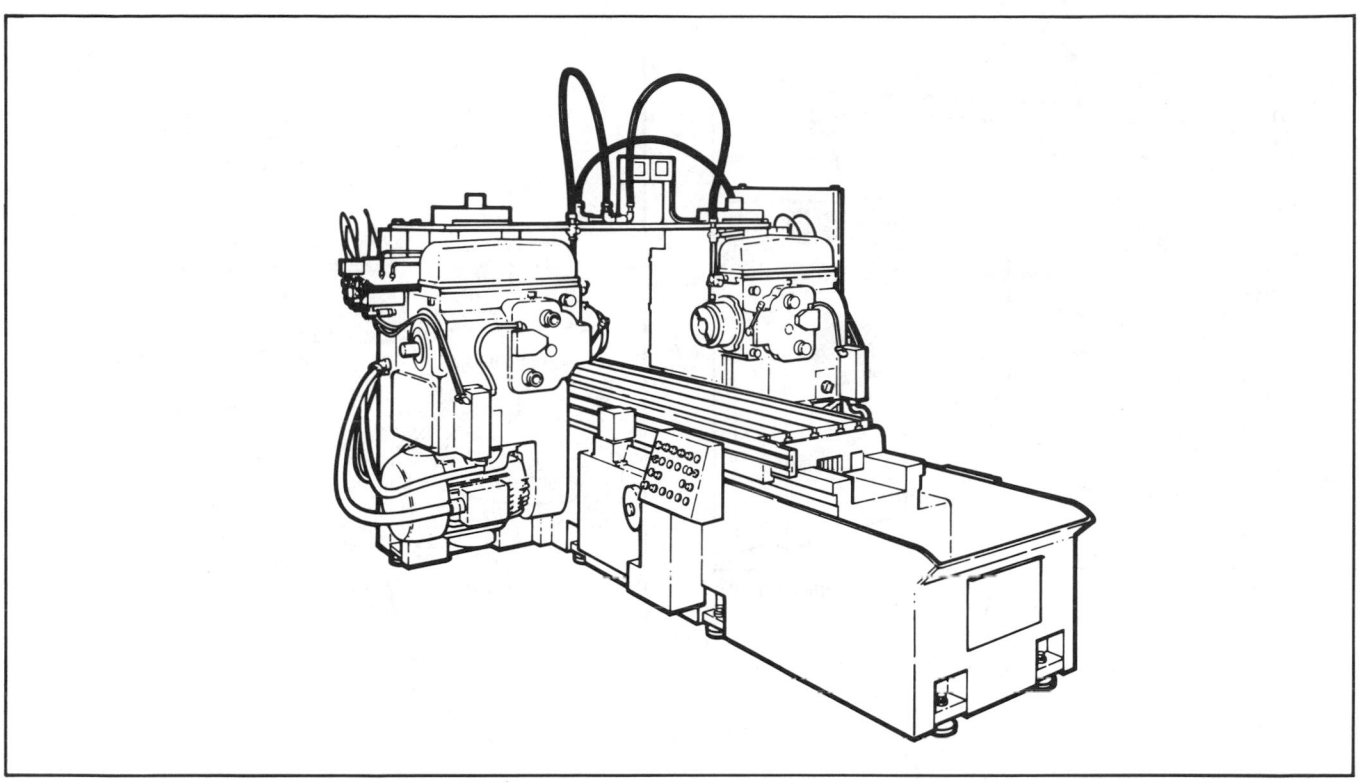

Fig. 25-12 Duplex milling machine has two opposed spindles, one on each side of the table.

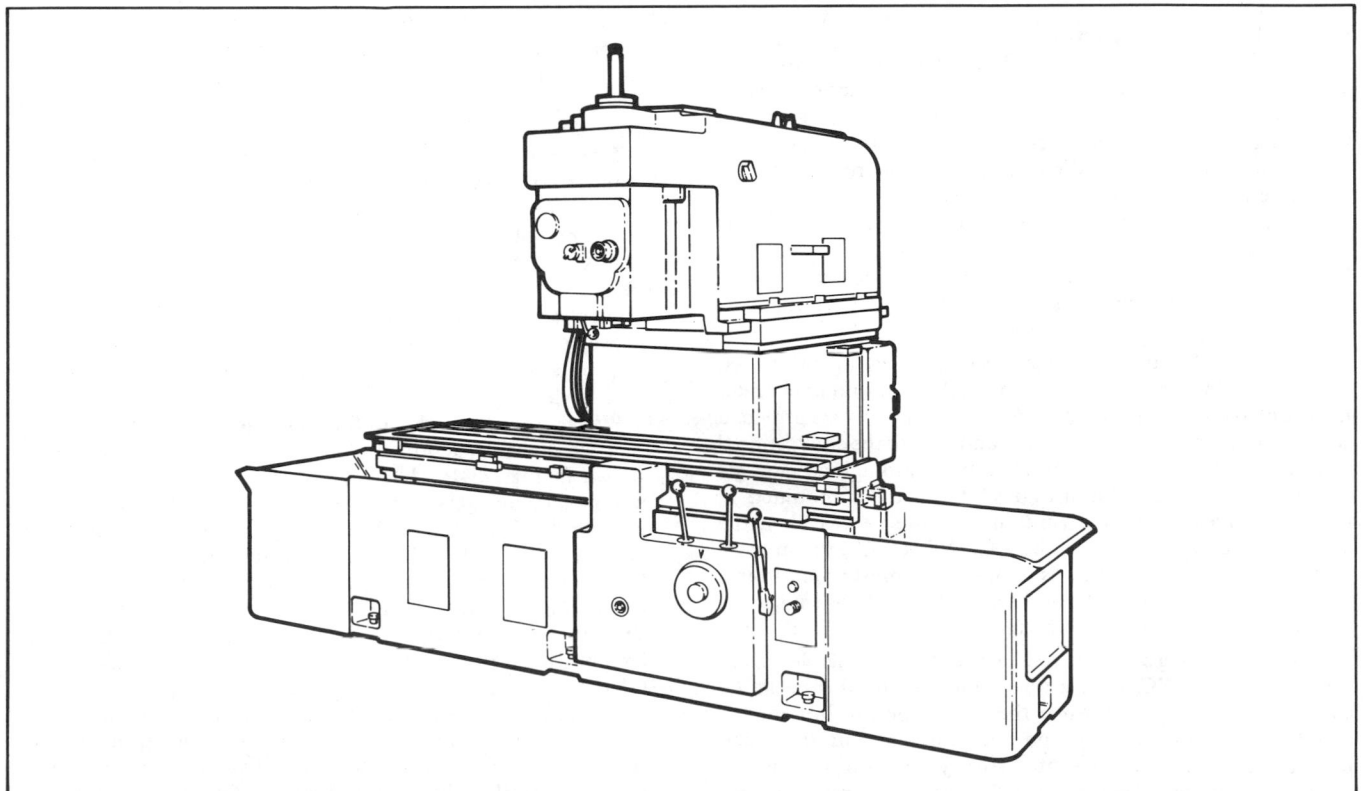

Fig. 25-13 Vertical fixed-bed milling machine has a ram or spindle carrier mounted on a rear base.

MILLING MACHINES

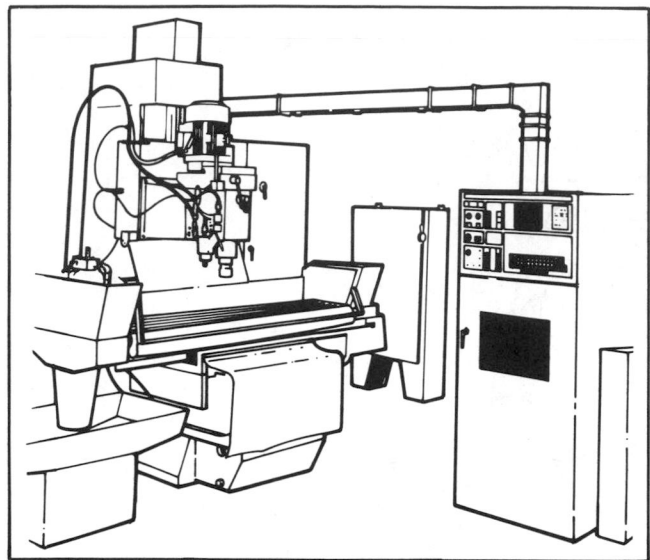

Fig. 25-14 Fixed-bed saddle-type milling machine with vertical spindle and CNC system. (*Boston Digital Corp.*)

machines with the production capabilities of NC machines, without the need for NC coded part programming. Major applications of these machines include tool and die, prototype, and short-run operations, but they are used less frequently in shops that have programming capability for other machines. Programmable milling machines are available in horizontal and vertical-spindle models.

NC/CNC Milling Machines

In addition to mechanical-electrical, mechanical-hydraulic, and mechanical-electrical-hydraulic controls, numerical control and computer numerical control (NC/CNC) are being applied to milling and other machine tools requiring complex cycles. In some cases, both tracer and numerical control are provided on the same machine, and some machines are provided with the option for NC or CNC retrofit at a later date. Automatic toolchangers are also available on some NC machines (particularly machining centers), with a punched tape establishing the programming, selecting cutters from the changer, and determining milling speed and feed.

An NC/CNC milling machine provides control for at least two axes of simultaneous motion, with three or four axes under tape control being quite common. Some machines are provided with five or more axes under NC. In addition to the conventional longitudinal, transverse, and vertical movements, some machines have the column and spindle carrier mounted in circular swivel ways to permit the spindle to swivel in the horizontal and vertical planes. An NC/CNC system with continuous-path capabilities is desirable for most applications, and circular interpolation is frequently used when curved surfaces and contours are to be milled.

Universal milling machines (see Figure 25-15), available with or without NC or CNC, have a vertical milling head that can be swung to a position alongside the ram to permit horizontal-spindle operation. Rotary and tilt tables permit five-sided machining of a workpiece at virtually any angle. Pendant control offers digital readout in all three axes, and programs can be transferred to cassettes for storage.

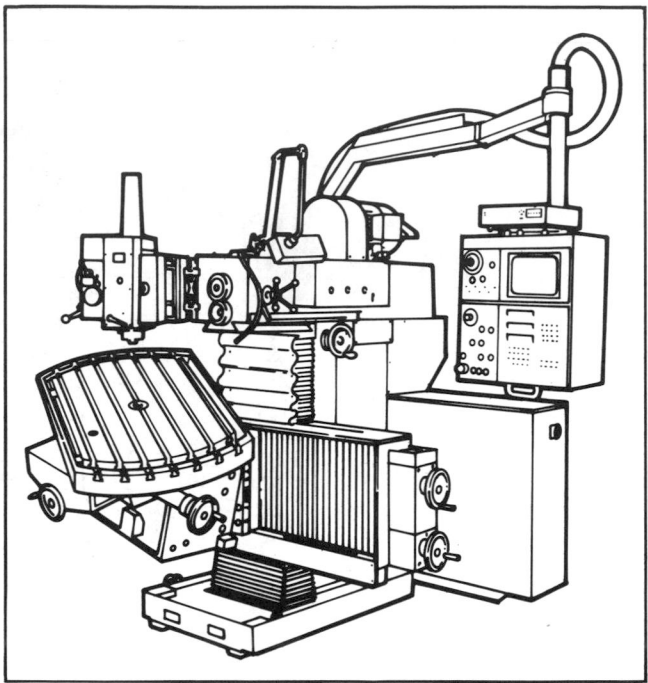

Fig. 25-15 Universal milling machine has horizontal and vertical spindles, and a tilt table. (*Maho Machine Tool Corp.*)

Special Milling Machines

In a general sense, a special milling machine is any milling machine designed and built to machine a specific part or family of parts. Usually a basic standard machine that is specially modified is considered a special milling machine if the modification results in approximately 50% or more change in the basic design.

Special milling machines can take the form of any of the standard milling machines, such as horizontal or vertical spindle, fixed bed, knee type, fixed or moving table, fixed or traveling column, ram type, or almost any other conceivable configuration. The type of machine control can also be highly varied. Controls from straight manual to direct computer control are available for special machines. Although special milling machine configurations can vary considerably, depending upon the job for which the machine was designed, several basic styles are predominant.

Planer, adjustable-rail, or fixed-bridge-type milling machine. The major construction features of this type of machine are shown in Fig. 25-16. These features include a rigid crossrail mounted on uprights that are floor-mounted on each side of the bed-table unit or that are floor-mounted and also attached to the bed. The table, which is the work surface, rides on the bedways and is powered in the longitudinal or X-axis direction by a hydraulic cylinder, screw, or rack-and-pinion drive system. The table usually has a T-slot arrangement for holding work fixtures, but sometimes a bolt-hole pattern is supplied in the tabletop for this purpose.

The spindle carrier or carriers are mounted to a cross saddle and are powered in the Y-axis or cross direction on ways mounted on the crossrail. An alternative to this is driving the entire crossrail in the Y-axis direction. Often, spindle carriers are mounted on both the front and rear faces of the crossrail.

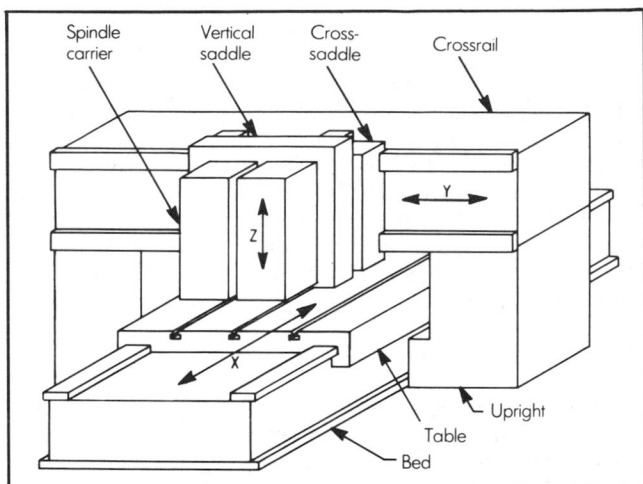

Fig. 25-16 Planer or fixed-bridge type of milling machine.

Moving-bridge or gantry-type machine. The major construction features of this style of machine are shown in Fig. 25-17. Machine configuration is very similar to a planer or bridge-type machine except that the entire gantry, consisting of a crossrail mounted on its uprights and supporting the cross saddle and spindle carriers, moves in the longitudinal or X-axis direction. The work surface is usually integral with the bed and remains stationary. The gantry is driven by a ballscrew or a rack-and-pinion drive system. Except on very narrow machines, the

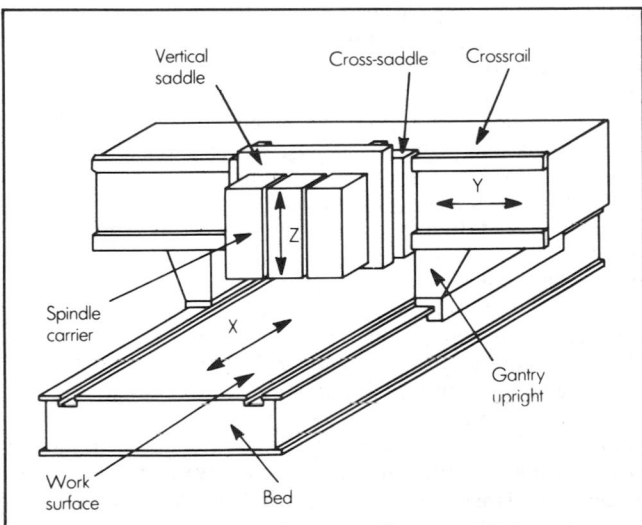

Fig. 25-17 Moving-bridge or gantry-type milling machine.

longitudinal drives act on each gantry upright and are synchronized mechanically, electrically, or by both methods—one being a backup or safety protection for the other. The work surface is usually supplied with T slots or a bolt-hole pattern for holding the work or work fixtures.

The spindle carriers mount to a saddle that travels in the cross or Y-axis direction on a way system. They can also be moved in the Z-axis or vertical direction either independently or by means of a saddle that rides on a set of vertical ways. As is true

with planer or bridge-type machines, the number of spindle carriers is optional and they may be mounted on either side of the crossrail. Additional axes of motions are available if required—one usually being a swivel motion in the YZ plane, and the other a swivel motion in the XZ plane. These motions can be either full contouring or positioning only. The crossrail is usually designed so that it can be raised for additional clearance over the work surface.

Ram-type milling machine. This style of machine (Fig. 25-18) is similar to many standard milling machines. However, special size, ranges, torque rating, number of spindles, or center distances that may be required often place this style of machine in the special-milling-machine category.

Major construction details of ram-type machines include a bed containing a way system on which a table moves in the longitudinal or X-axis direction. A rear base mounts against this bed and contains a way stem on which the ram moves in the cross or Y-axis direction. A vertical saddle mounts on this ram and moves in the Z-axis or vertical direction on a way system. A spindle carrier or carriers are mounted on this vertical saddle. In some designs, the carrier itself contains the vertical ways, thus eliminating the vertical saddle.

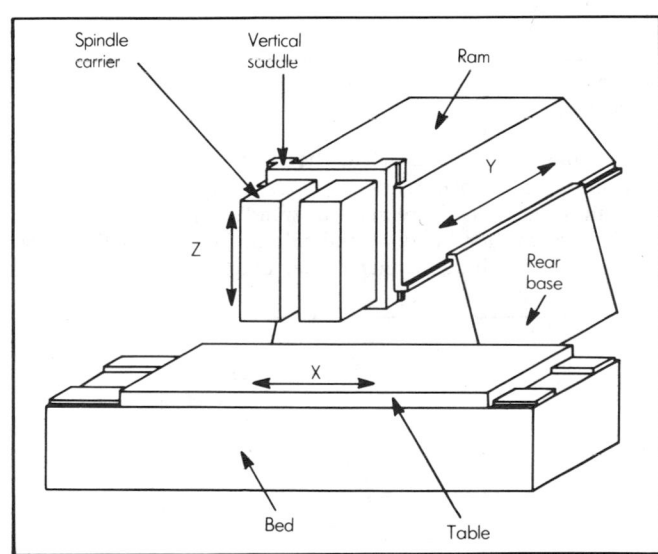

Fig. 25-18 Special ram-type milling machine.

Traveling-column milling machine. Figure 25-19 shows the major design features of one style of traveling-column machine. The column rides on a way system supported by the machine bed. This motion is in the X-axis or longitudinal direction. The column contains a vertical way system on which a vertical saddle travels in the Y-axis direction. A spindle carrier or spindle carriers move in the Z-axis direction on this saddle. The work is held in place on an angle plate that mounts on a work base. Usually this work base has a series of angle-plate locating slots, that allows the angle plate to be positioned farther away or closer to the spindle carrier or carriers.

A common variation of this design is that, instead of the carrier moving in the Z-axis direction, a spindle bar (which may or may not be supported by a quill) extends in the Z-axis direction. This feature allows for deep-pocket milling and gives the machine a boring capability. This configuration is commonly called a bar mill or bar machine.

CHAPTER 25

MILLING MACHINES

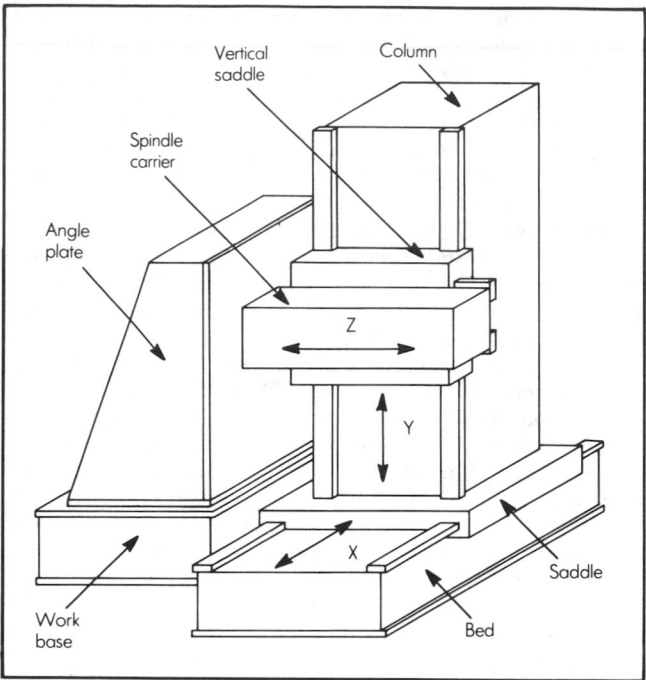

Fig. 25-19 Traveling-column milling machine with X axis under column.

The machine shown schematically in Fig. 25-19 has an advantage over other styles of traveling-column milling machines in that the extended spindle presents the least workpiece interference with the column. However, this very advantage of spindle carrier or bar extension results in less

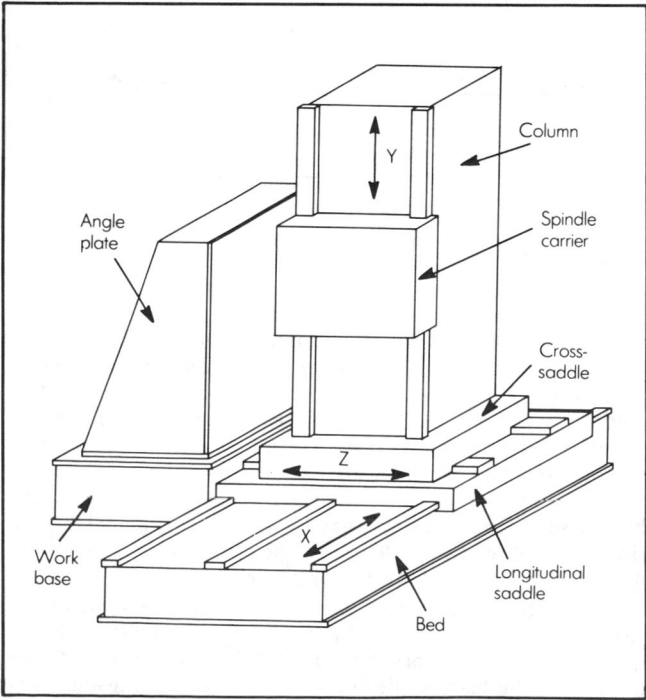

Fig. 25-20 Traveling-column milling machine with both X and Z axes under column.

milling capacity and in spindle droop. This reduced milling capacity is relative, however, and many designs of this nature are extremely rigid and capable of high-torque cuts.

Figure 25-20 shows the major design features of a traveling-column milling machine with both X-axis and Z-axis motions under the column. These motions are accomplished by means of a compound saddle. This design eliminates the reduced cutting capacity and spindle droop of the design shown in Fig. 25-19. However, part geometry may cause interference with the column because of the fixed relationship between the spindle nose and the column wall. To support the column properly, especially if the Z-axis is relatively long, the machine bed is usually much wider than that of other traveling-column designs and usually has three or more longitudinal ways.

Figure 25-21 shows a table-type or traveling-table machine. This design consists of a base on which the column moves in the Z-axis direction. The machine bed supports the angle plate that moves in the X-axis direction. In some designs, a table rides on the bed. Angle plates may not be necessary if the work to be machined is large and boxy.

There are two outstanding advantages to traveling-column milling machines. One advantage is that the cutting fluid and chips fall clear of the work and can easily be carried away by a chip conveyor located between the work base and machine column. The other major advantage is that the operator has an unobstructed view of the cutter and work, even in deep pockets. The greatest disadvantage of these machines is the difficulty of positioning and mounting the work on a vertical surface. Some users reduce this difficulty by removing the entire angle plate or subplate and positioning it horizontally for part loading. Another disadvantage to this type of machine is that the workpiece, when clamped against an angle plate, is generally not set in its natural position.

Crankshaft milling machines. Milling of crankshafts, camshafts, and other unbalanced shafts is replacing the traditional turning process in some plants. Advantages claimed for this process include faster production, closer tolerances, lower tooling costs, and more rapid changeover. Milling machines are available for internal or external cutting.

Milling machines designed for external cutting (see Fig. 25-22) were developed first and are still widely used, depending primarily upon the shaft configuration and production requirements. They are preferred for milling all camshafts because of the lobe configurations of the camshafts; they are also preferred for meeting the high production requirements for large crankshafts and crankshafts having journals with different profiles. As many as seven cutters can be mounted on a single slide to simultaneously mill journals, thus providing short floor-to-floor times. This type of machine is also required to mill square or rectangular surfaces on shafts. Other advantages of milling machines used for external cutting include easier cutter changing and better visibility for the operator.

Planetary milling machines. On these machines, workpieces are held stationary and motion is confined to the cutter. They perform many operations that are normally done on lathes, but for which it is not feasible to rotate the workpieces because of their mass, unbalance, delicateness, or difficulty in machining. Operations performed on these versatile machines include facing; milling circular forms, elongated slots, and radial crankcase bores in aircraft engines; and threading, both internal and external.

One or more cutters may be held in vertical and/or horizontal spindles on planetary milling machines. Operations can be

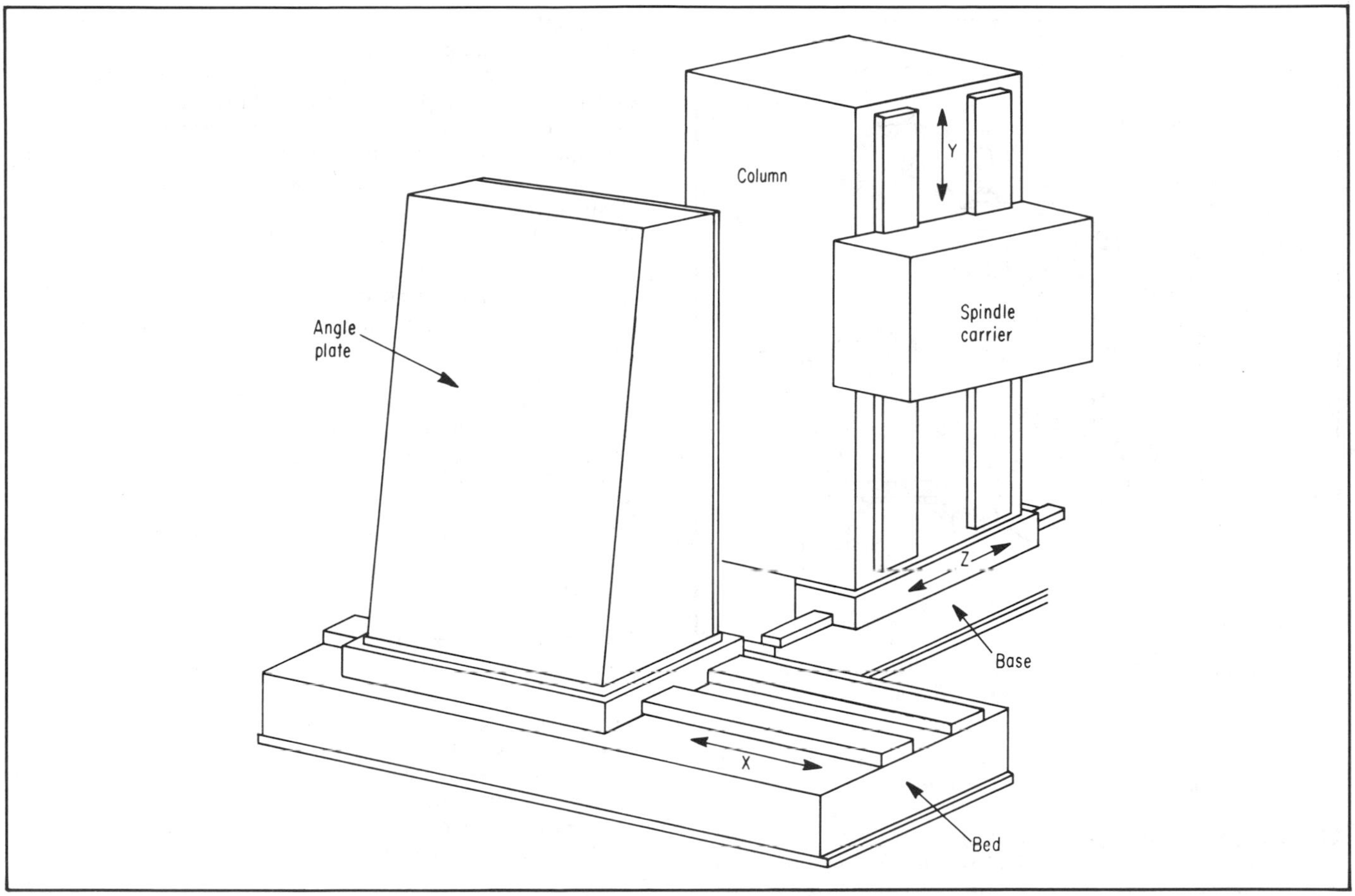

Fig. 25-21 Traveling-table milling machine with Z axis under column.

performed on the ID or OD of a workpiece, or on both internal and external surfaces simultaneously.

Rotary milling machines. On these machines, workpieces are held in fixtures attached to a rotary table that carries the workpieces under facing cutters mounted on one or more vertical spindles. These are considered production machines and are generally used for workpieces such as cylinder heads having large flat surfaces to be milled.

ATTACHMENTS FOR MILLING MACHINES

Many different attachments are available for milling machines. Attachments are standard or special auxiliary devices intended to be fastened to or joined with one or more components of a milling machine to augment the range, versatility, productivity, or accuracy of operation. Some attachments are required to perform certain operations. These accessories may be cutter or workpiece holding and driving mechanisms. Attachments enable the cutting axis or the workpiece to be oriented differently or to be moved along specific geometric paths. Also, they may be precision measuring devices. The cutter holding and driving attachments are usually made to be used on standard horizontal knee-type machines.

Vertical Milling Attachments

These attachments are used to convert horizontal machines to swivel-head vertical types. They permit the cutting-spindle axis to be oriented with reference to a graduated circular base and to be held in any angular position in the vertical plane parallel to the column face. One such attachment (see Fig. 25-23) is mounted against the column face and driven by the machine

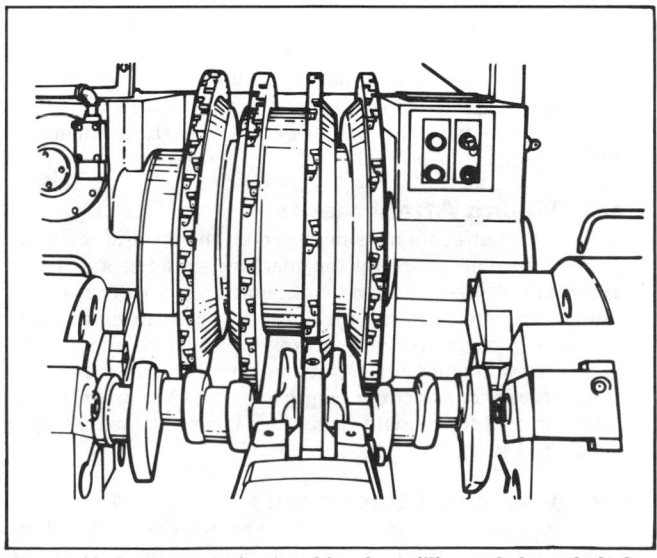

Fig. 25-22 External cutting machine for milling unbalanced shafts. (*American GFM*)

MILLING MACHINES

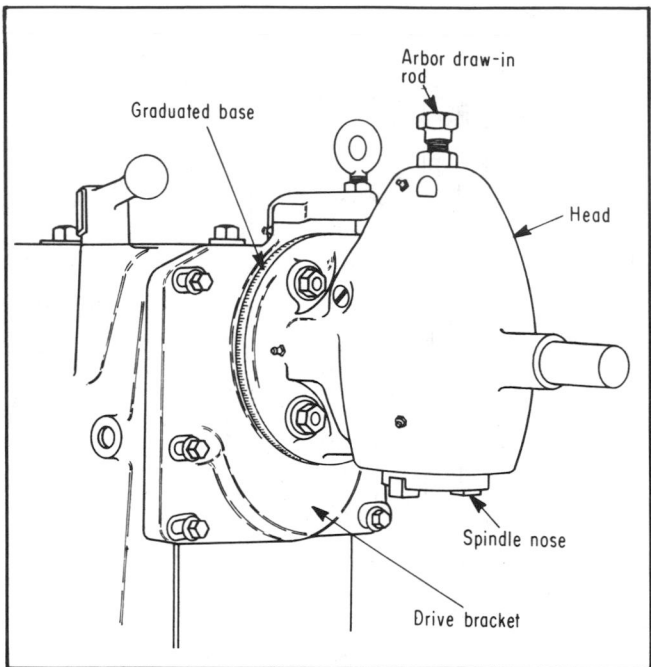

Fig. 25-23 Swivel-head vertical milling attachment.

spindle. Quill-type and fixed spindles are available. Speeds are the same as the machine speeds or at some ratio to them.

Universal Milling Attachments

Similar to a swivel-head vertical attachment but having two swivel axes and associated graduated circular bases at right angles to one another, a universal milling attachment permits the cutting-spindle axis to be held at practically any angle. These attachments are made in a variety of sizes, spindle-speed ratios, spindle-nose tapers, and work capacities, with or without axially adjustable spindle quills.

High-Speed Milling Attachments

Such attachments are driven from the horizontal machine spindle with a speed ratio greater than 1:1, which makes it possible to operate small-diameter cutters at high speeds. Generally, the spindle head is extendable some distance across the table and may contain one or two swivel arrangements for angular milling.

Rack-Milling Attachments

This type of attachment is mounted on the machine column, is driven through gears by the machine spindle, and has a horizontal cutting-spindle axis at right angles to that of the machine. In conjunction with appropriate form cutters and workholding means (usually a rack-milling vise and a rack-indexing attachment), this equipment permits racks or cross-slotted pieces of considerable length to be cut. A plain knee-type machine is used for straight racks, and a universal machine for slanted or skew racks.

Thread-Milling Attachments

This type of mechanism is similar to the rack-milling attachment, but it projects an adjustable distance from the column face so that the cutter is normally directly above the center of the swivel saddle of a universal knee-type machine. It uses thread-milling cutters in conjunction with a dividing head and lead attachment to produce any of the regular forms of external straight, tapered, or worm threads and many special threads, including internal threads when size limitations permit. An adjustable follower rest can be used when necessary on long workpieces. A universal milling attachment having sufficient clearance for this kind of work can also be used for milling threads on a plain knee-type machine.

Slotting Attachments

This equipment, mounted on the machine column and driven by the machine spindle, converts rotary motion into reciprocating motion of adjustable stroke length. The mechanism is mounted on a graduated circular swivel base, permitting reciprocating motion at any angle in the vertical plane parallel to the column face. One end of the sliding ram accepts single-point slotting tools of any practical form. Among other things, this attachment is used for cutting internal or external keyways, splines, serrations, blind holes, cavities, or gears, particularly in inaccessible locations such as those adjacent to large-diameter shoulders.

Crane and Parking Attachments

Much of the previously mentioned equipment is too heavy for a person to lift easily, or it creates a storage problem. To alleviate this situation, various parking attachments, attachment cranes, and parking brackets, which can be fastened to a machine either permanently or temporarily, are available. They facilitate the mounting or dismounting of a heavy attachment; or when the attachment is not in use, they store or park it someplace on the machine.

Rotary Tables

Rotary tables or circular-milling attachments, capable of rotary movement about a vertical axis, are made in a variety of diameters and may be manually or power driven. Manual drive with a handwheel and a graduated dial or an indexing unit enables an operator to position a workpiece for cuts at various angles or to index equal or unequal divisions of a circle in spacing or slotting operations. A rotary table, by virtue of its design, is rigid and can accommodate large workpieces. Power can be applied through a lead attachment in cutting a continuous spiral scroll or through a power-drive unit (which rotates the rotary table at various rates while the machine table remains stationary) in radii milling or continuous rotary milling. On CNC machines these attachments can often be controlled by a fourth axis or a shared third axis drive.

Arbors

Some cutters can be centered on and bolted directly to the spindle nose or if equipped with an integral tapered shank centered in the spindle-nose taper and held in place by a draw-in bolt. Cutter holders are discussed in a subsequent section of this chapter. However, many cutters (especially the peripheral-milling variety) cannot be held in this way and must be mounted on or in intermediate holding, locating, or adapting devices or arbors (see Fig. 25-24). Arbors are available in many diameters, lengths, styles, and standard spindle-nose tapers, the most commonly used being Nos. 40 and 50.

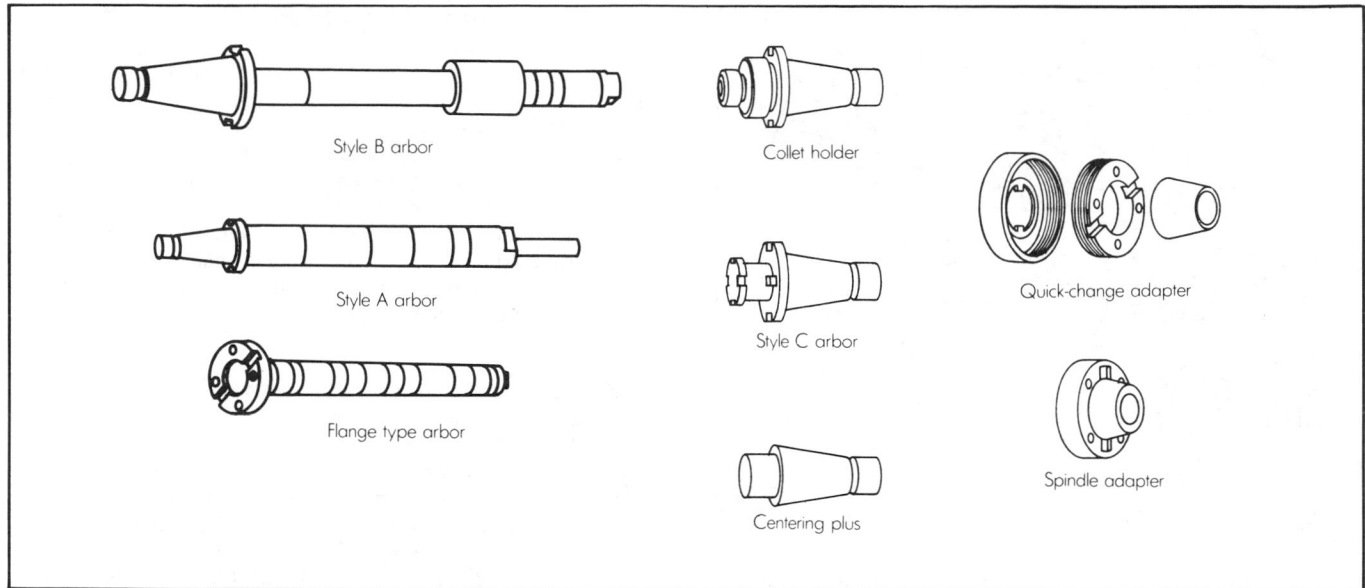

Fig. 25-24 Arbors and adapters used on milling machines.

Vises

Milling-machine vises (Fig. 25-25), keyed and bolted to the table, provide a convenient method of securely holding and accurately orienting a workpiece.

Index Bases

For production milling, an index base placed on the machine table can accommodate duplicate or progressive fixtures at each end. One fixture can be unloaded and reloaded during the cutting cycle. The index table is unclamped, pivoted 180°, and clamped in position by manual means or by power from electric, pneumatic, or hydraulic sources.

Chucks

Chucks in many styles and with various numbers of jaws are used to hold workpieces by gripping either an external or an internal cylindrical surface. They are mounted directly on the machine table, a rotary table, or a dividing head. Chucks also may be mounted with an adapter on a machine-spindle nose, for use in holding and rotating a workpiece which is to be turned or bored with single-point tools that are mounted on the machine table to simulate a chucking lathe. By inserting drills in a spindle-mounted chuck and using saddle travel, drilling and boring operations are possible.

Dividing Heads

Dividing heads (see Fig. 25-26) or index centers are precision measuring devices for accurate workpiece indexing or for positioning from a reference through any desired sector of a circle. They may be manually or power operated, plain with a fixed spindle axis, or universal with a spindle axis that can be located at any angle from horizontal to vertical. They can be equipped with a dog and centers, an arbor or mandrel with or without a center, or a chuck to hold the workpiece.

Lead Attachments

These attachments transmit power through gearing arrangements from a machine-table drive to a dividing head or rotary

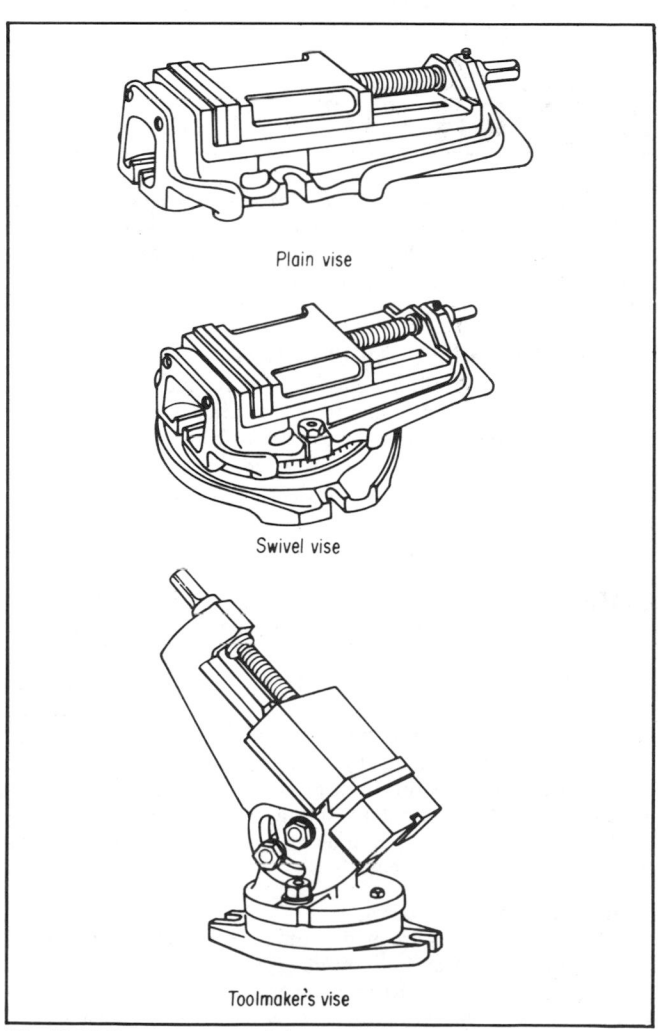

Fig. 25-25 Common types of vises used on milling machines.

MILLING CUTTERS

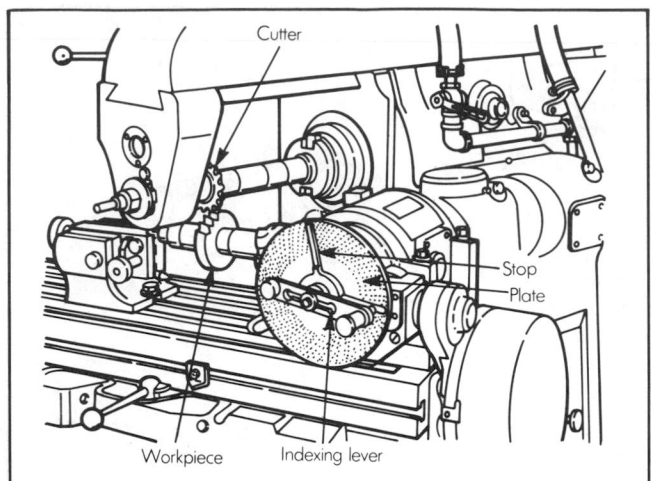

Fig. 25-26 Dividing head mounted on the table of a knee-type milling machine.

table, the rotation of either of these being synchronized with the feed or traverse movement of the machine table. The lead, or ratio of machine-table movement per revolution of the dividing head or rotary table, is varied with change gears.

Precision Measuring and Position Readout

For accurate spacing of milled surfaces, or of drilled and bored holes, a number of methods are available. Equipment used for positioning and measuring includes incremental measuring rods with dial indicators, magnified precision scales, electronic display panels actuated by lead-screw rotation or potentiometer scales between a fixed reader and movable member, and digital readouts. Position indicators are also available ranging from mechanical counters and friction wheels geared to graduated dials, to the aforementioned electronic display panels. Laser beams are also being used for some positioning and measuring.

Multiple-Spindle Attachments

The multiple-spindle attachment mounts to the main spindle-carrier housing. Torque from the main spindle is transmitted through belts or gears to two or more attachment spindles. Primary uses of this attachment are to increase the machine productivity when a number of small identical parts are being milled and to obtain a specific spindle center distance other than the center distances supplied with the machine. As with some other attachments, the original torque rating of the machine must be downgraded because of the added joints, gears, and bearings.

MILLING CUTTERS

A milling cutter is a rotary tool provided with one or more cutting edges which intermittently engage the workpiece and remove material by relative movement of the workpiece and cutter. Milling cutters can be classified by styles or uses, construction characteristics, and methods of mounting.

CUTTER STYLES AND USES

Many different milling cutters are available for various applications. They are sometimes classified or described by terms which refer to their use, purpose for which they are made, shape or position of their cutting edges, or shape of the workpiece produced. Some of the most common types of milling cutters, illustrated in Fig. 25-27, are plain, form, or side milling cutters, shaped profile cutters, and face or end mills.

CONSTRUCTION OF MILLING CUTTERS

Three basic types of construction exist for milling cutters: solid, inserted or brazed blade, and mechanically clamped, indexable insert. Both the solid and blade types can be resharpened and are often referred to as grind-type cutters. While indexable-insert cutters are widely used, grind-type cutters are still required by some companies for certain applications. One advantage of grind-type cutters is that their geometry can be tailored to suit a wide variety of milling applications; in addition, runout can be controlled more closely than with other types of cutters.

Solid Milling Cutters

Solid milling cutters are made from one piece of steel (usually high-speed steel) or carbide by machining the required shape and number of teeth, with the specified cutting and relief angles ground on the teeth. The cutters may be tipped with cast alloy or carbide cutting-tool materials if this is warranted by either the

nature of the work material or the production requirements. Solid cutters are usually the lowest in initial cost, depending upon size, and therefore may be best for short runs or general toolroom use.

Plain and side milling cutters of one-piece HSS construction (see Figs. 25-28, 25-29, and 25-30) are generally classified as light and heavy-duty cutters. The heavy-duty cutters have fewer and stronger teeth than corresponding-diameter, light-duty cutters and are used when a considerable amount of stock is to be removed.

Inserted-Blade Cutters

Many milling operations are performed with cutters that use a HSS or carbide cutting material locked by mechanical means in a steel body. Some cutters have the material brazed to the body. An advantage of cutters that use a mechanically locked cutting material is that the body of the cutter does not have to be replaced every time the cutting material wears out. These cutters are normally higher in initial cost than solid cutters, but generally prove to be lowest in unit cost per piece on production runs.

Indexable-Insert Cutters

A more recently introduced style of construction for milling cutters, which is being used extensively today, is the indexable-insert type (see Fig. 25-31). These cutters use a small cutting insert, normally made of carbide, coated carbide, ceramic, or diamond implanted on a carbide substrate. Cutting tool materials for inserts are discussed at the end of this section on milling cutters. The insert has one or more cutting edges located at various corners and often on both sides of the insert, or around the circumference in the case of round inserts. The inserts are locked into place with mechanical clamping devices

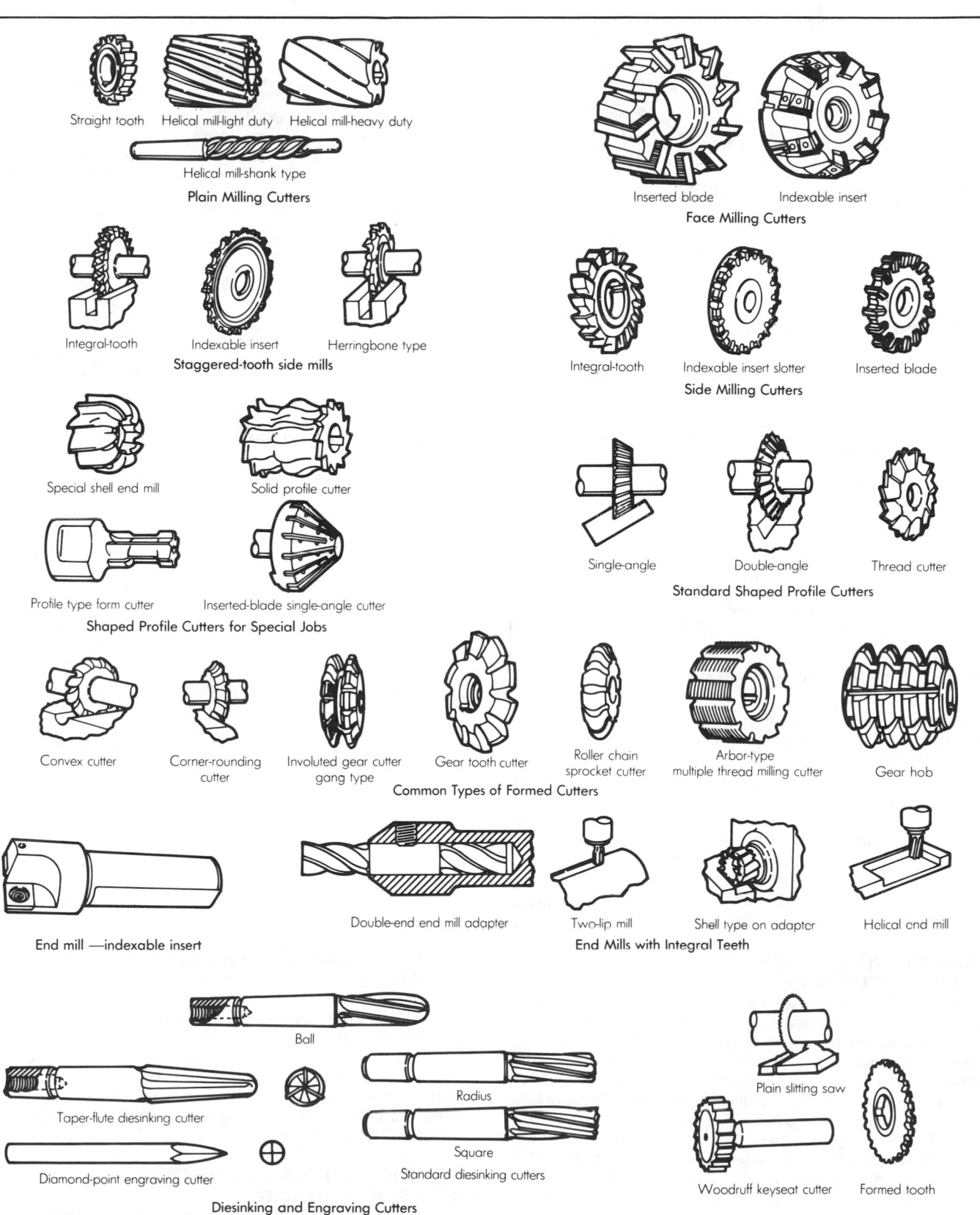

Fig. 25-27 Common types of milling cutters.

MILLING CUTTERS

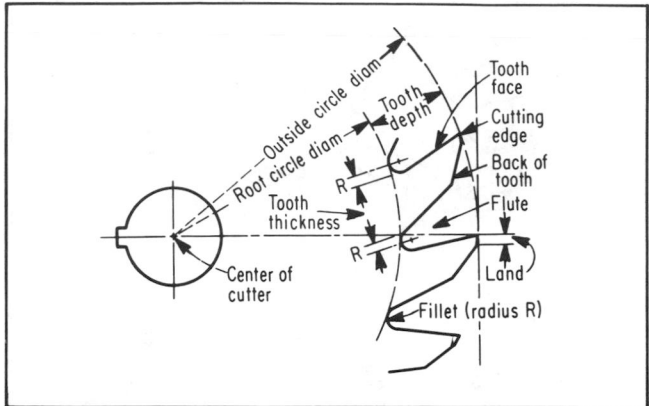

Fig. 25-28 Parts of teeth of a solid plain milling cutter.

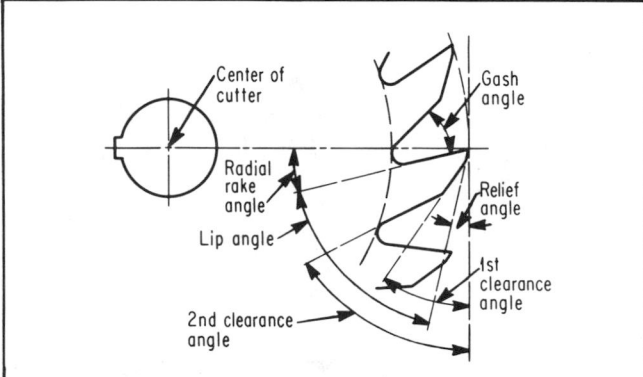

Fig. 25-29 Angles of the teeth on a solid plain milling cutter.

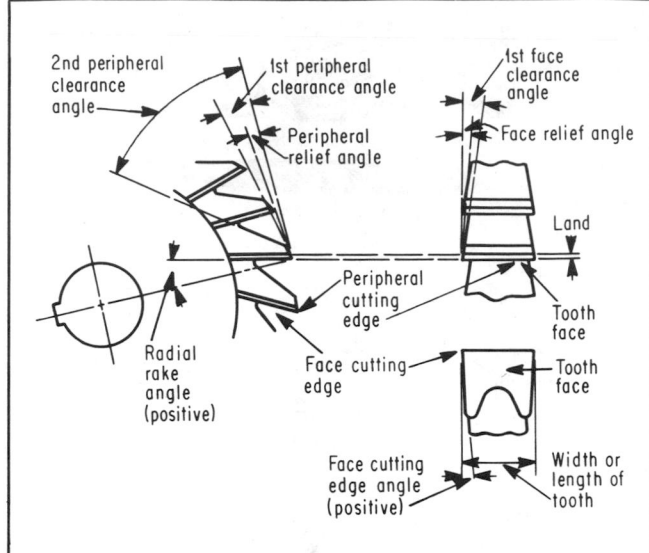

Fig. 25-30 Nomenclature of teeth on solid-type side milling cutter.

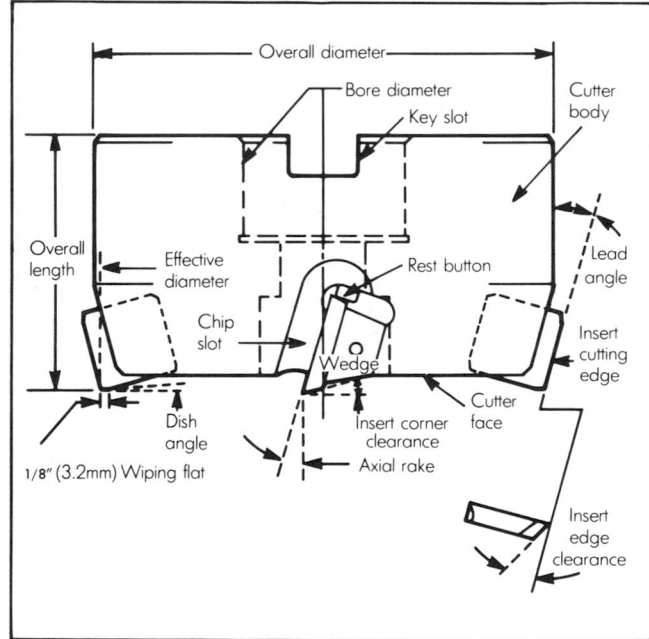

Fig. 25-31 Indexable-insert milling cutter. (*Carboloy Systems Dept., General Electric Co.*)

such as wedges or clamps. When they become dull, the inserts are indexed or repositioned so that new cutting edges contact the workpiece.

Advantages of this style of cutter include elimination of regrinding, low cost per cutting edge, and availability of inserts in a wide variety of cutting materials and geometries. Disadvantages include higher cutting forces and the possibility of rougher surface finishes being produced. Indexable inserts for milling cutters can be held a number of ways. They can be located or clamped by use of nonadjustable insert pockets, adjustable pockets, open slots and rails, and cartridges.

HAND OF ROTATION OF MILLING CUTTERS

Milling cutters are classified as left and right-hand according to their direction of rotation (see Fig. 25-32). To determine if a milling cutter is left or right-hand, the user should hold the cutter from behind with the arm serving as the spindle. If the top of the tool cuts by rotating to the left (counterclockwise), it is a left-hand cutter. If the top of the tool cuts by rotating to the right (clockwise), it is a right-hand cutter.

On horizontal-spindle machines, the direction of rotation should be selected so that the tangential cutting forces press the workpiece down against the table rather than up against the clamp bolts. The same arrangement generally directs chips onto the floor rather than up in the air where they could be hazardous to the machinist. On horizontal duplex (two-opposing spindle)

machines, one right-hand cutter and one left-hand cutter should generally be used.

On vertical-spindle machines, the direction of the cutting forces is often less critical because the part is usually equally supported on either side. If a fixed stop is employed, however, hand and rotation should be selected to direct the tangential force against the fixed stop.

MILLING CUTTER DIAMETERS AND POSITIONING

Two methods exist for measuring the diameter of a face milling cutter. The most important method involves determining

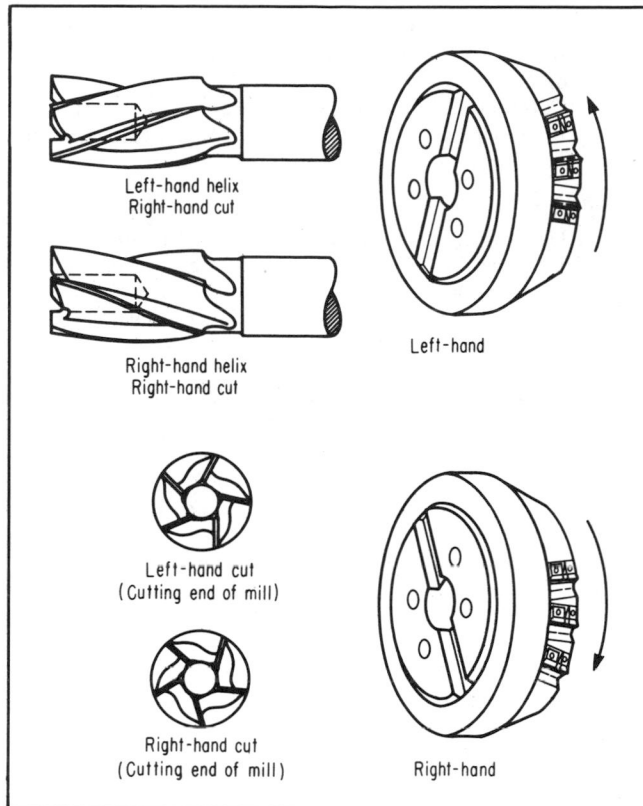

Fig. 25-32 Hand of rotation and helix for milling cutters.

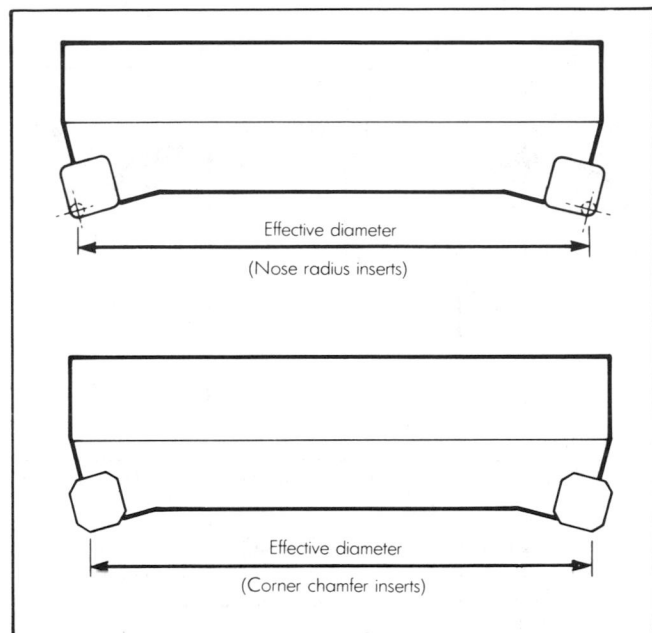

Fig. 25-33 Effective diameters of milling cutters.[1]

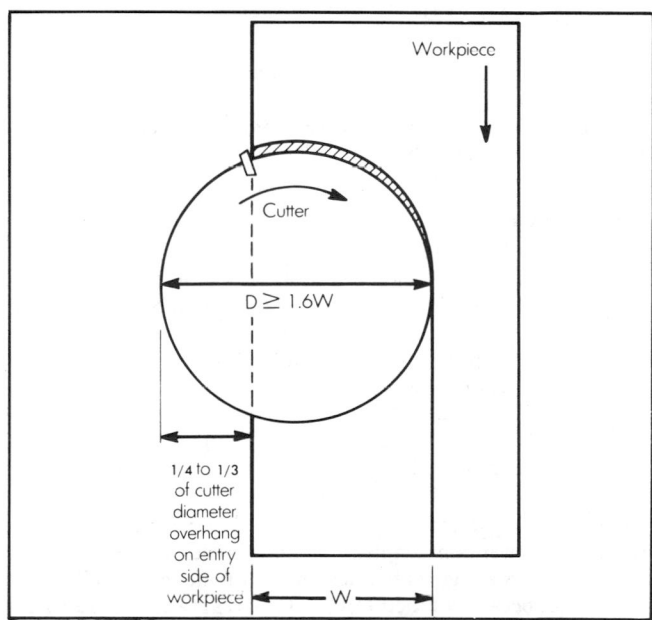

Fig. 25-34 Proper cutter positioning affects insert entry angle.[1]

the effective diameter (see Fig. 25-33). This refers to the maximum width of the flat surface machined by the cutter. It is measured between the points at which the face cutting edges of opposite inserts are tangent to the nose radius or between the highest cutting points of the opposite inserts if inserts with corner chamfers are used.

The other common method of diameter measurement involves determining the maximum diameter. This is the diameter of the cutter body as measured between the parts of the body or inserts on opposite sides that extend furthest in the radial direction.

A good general rule to remember is that the cutter should have an effective diameter at least 1 1/2 times the width of cut and should overhang the part 1/4 to 1/3 of the cutter diameter (see Fig. 25-34). If this rule is followed, chip thickness at insert entry will be equal to or greater than 80% of the feed per insert and the insert will enter the cut away from the vulnerable edge.

Milling cutters having diameters larger than the width of the workpiece or larger than necessary for adequate overhang on the entry side are generally uneconomical and inefficient. Advantages of using smaller diameter cutters when feasible include lower initial cost, the capability of using higher speeds, and reduced torque, deflection, and vibration.

Size and position of the milling cutter are both important factors in achieving optimum tool life. One reason is that these two factors determine undeformed chip thickness at insert entry. Undeformed chip thickness at insert entry should be high enough that the insert avoids the surface layer left by the previous insert because it may be work hardened. High undeformed chip thickness prevents chips from jamming between the insert and workpiece.

Cutter positioning also affects insert entry angle, which helps determine whether the shock of entering the cut is absorbed by a strong or weak section of the insert (see Fig. 25-35). The weakest section of the insert is the cutting edge, so the cutter and workpiece should be arranged so that the initial impact is absorbed on the face of the insert—a much stronger section. Positive entry angles, however, are sometimes required.

When milling cutters are centrally positioned relative to the workpiece, their teeth, blades, or inserts engage the material during a shorter portion of the cycle than if they were positioned toward either side of the workpiece. As a result, centrally located cutters generally provide longer life for a given width of

MILLING CUTTERS

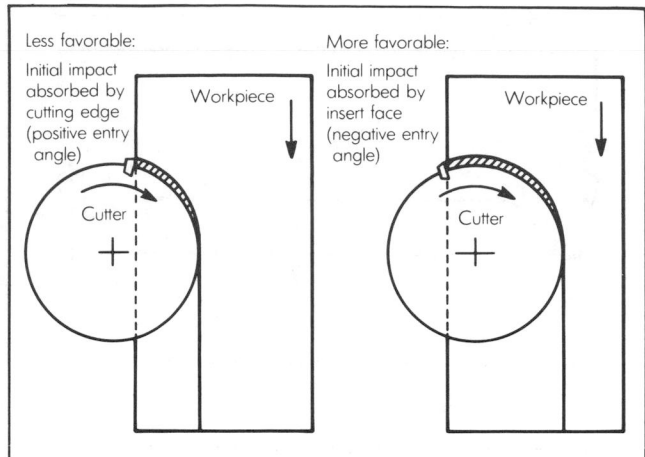

Fig. 25-35 Less favorable and more favorable entry angles for milling cutters.[1]

cut, assuming that at least one tooth, blade, or insert is in the cut at all times. Positioning the cutter directly at the center of the workpiece, however, may cause vibration due to changes in the direction of the cutting forces.

GEOMETRIES OF INDEXABLE INSERT MILLING CUTTERS

The geometry of a milling cutter depends primarily upon the material to be machined, chip disposal, and rigidity of the machine, workpiece, and setup. Important geometrical elements that must be considered in selecting any indexable-insert milling cutter include the rake and lead angles, pitch, and corner geometry of the insert.

Rake Angles

The attitude of the cutting tool, as it is presented to the workpiece, has a significant effect on horsepower consumption, tool life, cost per cutting edge, direction of chip flow, and the manner in which the cutting forces are absorbed. The standard angles used to specify milling cutter geometry are radial rake angle and axial rake angle.

Most HSS milling cutters are made with sharp cutting edges and appreciable positive radial and axial rake angles, which are desirable to separate chips from the workpiece with less effort or force. A high helix angle reduces impact and provides a smooth cutting action, but is not necessarily most efficient with respect to power consumption and heat generation. Cast-alloy milling cutters are generally designed with moderate radial and axial rakes because of their lower edge strength and greater heat resistance as compared with HSS.

Softer workpiece materials permit the use of higher radial rake angles; harder materials require the use of lower radial rake angles. The diameter of the tool also determines the relief angle; small-diameter cutters require higher relief angles than large-diameter cutters. Excessive wear and heat may indicate too small a relief angle, and chatter may indicate too large a relief angle.

Standard milling cutters with indexable inserts are offered in the following four geometries:

1. Cutters with negative radial and negative axial rake angles, as illustrated in Fig. 25-36. These are called double-negative cutters.
2. Cutters with positive radial and positive axial rake angles (see Fig. 25-37). These are called double-positive cutters.
3. Cutters with negative radial and positive axial rake angles (see Fig. 25-38). These are called negative-positive or shear angle cutters.
4. Cutters with high-positive radial and high-positive axial rake angles (see Fig. 25-39). These are called high-positive cutters.

Lead Angles

The lead angle, sometimes called the bevel complementary angle or the cut-entering angle, is the angle formed by the cutting edge and a line parallel to the cutter axis that passes through the theoretical cutting point. This is the cutting point if the insert has a sharp corner.

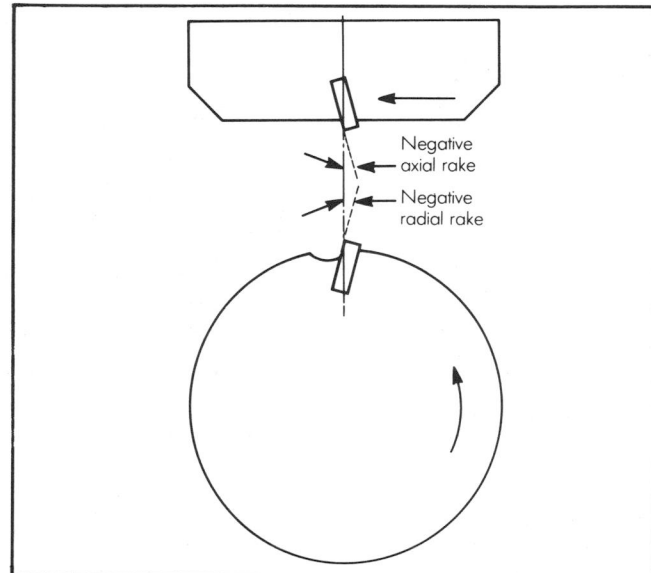

Fig. 25-36 Double-negative milling cutter.[1]

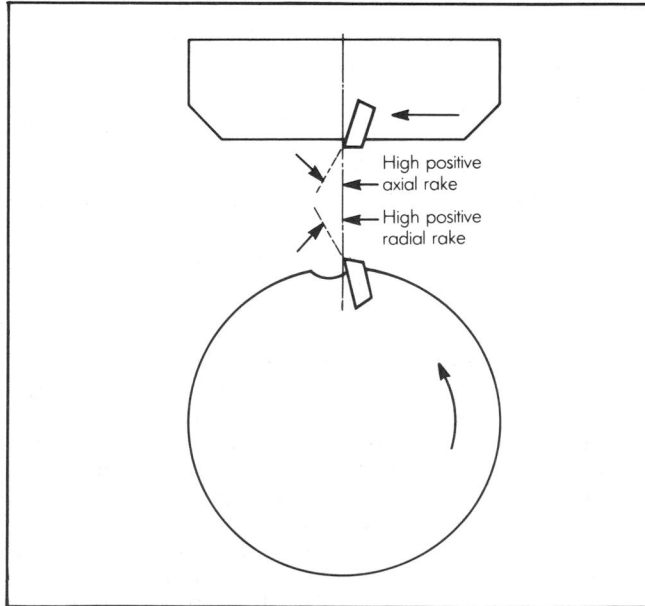

Fig. 25-37 Double-positive milling cutter.[1]

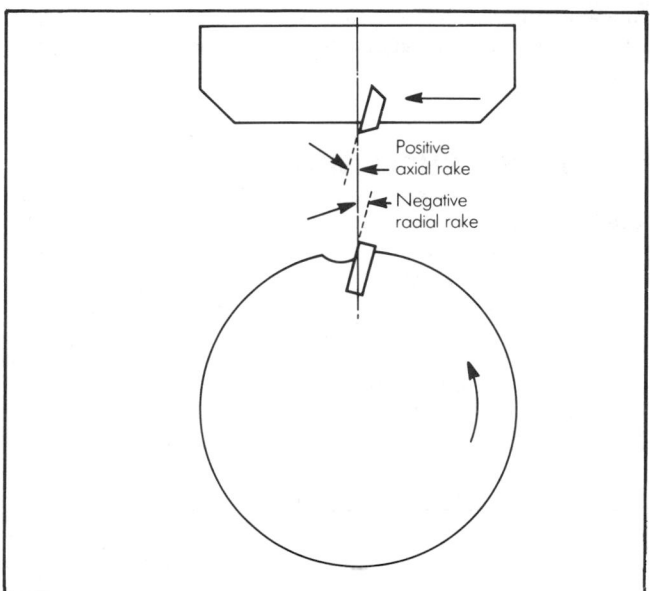

Fig. 25-38 Negative-positive (shear angle) milling cutter.[1]

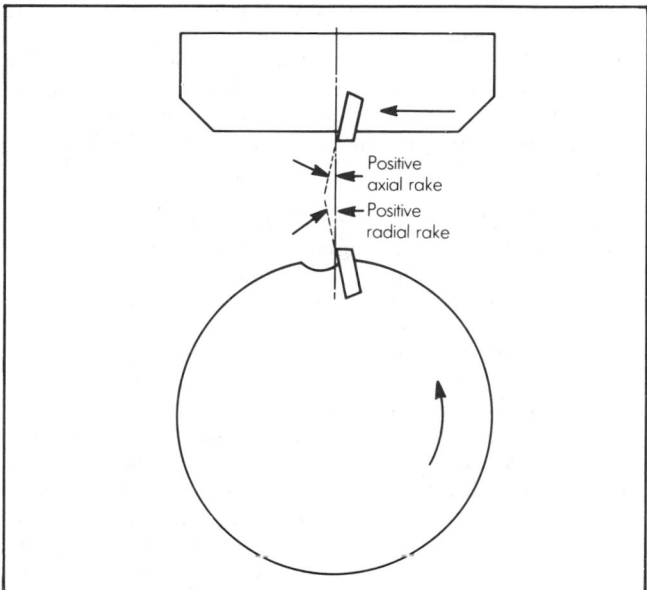

Fig. 25-39 High-positive milling cutter.[1]

Milling Cutter Pitch

Pitch of a milling cutter refers to the distance between cutting edges, or to insert or tooth density—the number of cutting edges in the milling cutter. When a milling cutter with a larger number of cutting edges is used, production rate generally is increased and cost per piece is reduced, assuming the cutting speed, feed per insert, and depth of cut are all maintained at previous levels. When a high feed rate is required, a cutter with a large number of cutting edges should be selected.

Corner Geometries

Selection of the proper corner geometry is one of the most critical elements of insert or inserted blade selection for milling cutters. The types of corner geometry used most frequently are nose radius, chamfer, double chamfer, and wiper.

SELECTING END MILLS

End mills are the most common and widely used type of milling cutter. These versatile tools are also available in more standard styles, shapes, and sizes than any other milling cutter. Major applications include facing (generally for wide cuts of relatively shallow depth), slotting (including keyways, T-slots, dovetails, etc.), profiling (both internal and external), plunge cutting and diesinking, and cavity cutting.

Types of End Mills

End mills are made with both single and double ends, with straight and taper shanks, and in various diameters and lengths (stub, regular, long, and extra long). Single-end tools are usually preferred for general-purpose work that does not entail long production runs, but indexable-insert, single-end tools are used for production applications.

Number of flutes. End mills are available with two, three, four, six, or more flutes. Most end mills have helical flutes, but some have straight flutes. End mills are made with helix angles from 0° (straight-fluted tools) to 50° or more, with 27° to 30° being about average for general-purpose milling. They are also made for either right or left-hand cutting. Straight-fluted end mills are not as common or efficient in cutting, but they are used on tapered tools and for sizing parallel-sided keyways and slots.

Cutting ends. End mills are also made with either ball or square ends. Most square-ended tools, generally having two or three flutes, have their end teeth cutting to the center for axial or plunge cutting. End mills with more flutes are available with or without center-cutting teeth. Tools without center-cutting teeth are made with a counterbore or center hole and are not capable of plunge cutting. Shell-type end mills, available from a few manufacturers as standard in either inch or metric sizes, are used more extensively in Europe than in the United States.

Deflection of end mills. Loss of accuracy and possible chatter resulting from deflection is a common problem with end mills. A tool having the largest diameter and shortest extension length (from the holder) possible should always be used to increase rigidity and minimize deflection. Deflection is directly proportional to the cube of the tool overhang and inversely proportional to the fourth power of the diameter. Deflection is also affected by the number of teeth engaged in the workpiece.

End mills with heavier webs and reduced flute widths can be used to minimize deflection, but they reduce chip space. Some heavy-duty end mills are made with tapered cores.

MOUNTING OF MILLING CUTTERS

Milling cutters are mounted on arbors, in the machine spindle, or on the spindle nose, often with the use of adapters. Regardless of the mounting method, the cutters must be rigidly held to withstand the high interrupted forces of milling and to run true both radially and axially.

To facilitate accurate mounting of cutters, most milling

MOUNTING OF MILLING CUTTERS

machine spindles are provided with a tapered bore, an OD, and a face perpendicular to the spindle axis, all precisely ground. The spindles usually have four threaded holes for holding clamping screws and two keys for driving cutters, adapters, or arbors. Essential spindle dimensions, tool shanks, and draw-in bolt ends for milling machines are presented in ANSI Standard B5.18-1972, published by ASME.

MOUNTING SHANK-TYPE CUTTERS

Small-diameter face milling cutters, generally with a diameter of 2″ (51 mm) or less, and almost all end mills have a straight or tapered integral shank to fit an adapter or the spindle bore. Common styles of integral shanks used on such cutters are illustrated in Fig. 25-40.

Straight-Shank Cutters

These tools are often mounted in an adapter-style holder that fits the spindle bore. The holder has a straight bore with the same diameter as the cutter shank and generally one or more screws that contact flats on the cutter shank for axial retention and radial drive. Holders are also available with cam and bayonet-type locking mechanisms, but the cutter shank must correspond with the holder design.

Because of clearance required between the holder bore and the OD of the cutter shank, the clamping screws can force the cutter off center and result in runout. Runout can be minimized and accuracy improved by using collet-type holders/adapters for straight-shank cutters. With such devices, drive is accomplished by frictional grip on the cutter shank. Some types also have a key that sets axial location and engages the flat on the cutter shank for drive in the case of heavy loads.

Holding straight-shank cutters in a collet is generally feasible only for shanks to 3/4″ (19 mm) diam for roughing cuts and to 1 1/4″ (32 mm) for finishing. Beyond these cutter sizes, adapter-style holders with setscrew clamping are usually recommended for increased resistance to high cutting forces.

Tapered-Shank Cutters

These tools are often made with a self-locking taper. In some cases, however, a steep taper is used, requiring a drawbar or some type of quick locking device. Adapters for tapered-shank cutters have a socket that matches the self-locking taper angle of the cutter shank.

MOUNTING SHELL MILLS

A wide range of small-diameter face milling cutters are available as shell mills. Shell mills are identical in function to face milling cutters, but have hollow bodies. They are mounted on C-style arbor adapters (see Fig. 25-41). The adapter is centered by the internal taper of the machine spindle and is retained by a drawbar. Precision drive keys on the spindle face engage keyslots in the arbor which in turn has drive keys that engage the cutter body. The shell mill is positioned by the pilot diameter on the end of the arbor and held in place by a single lockscrew.

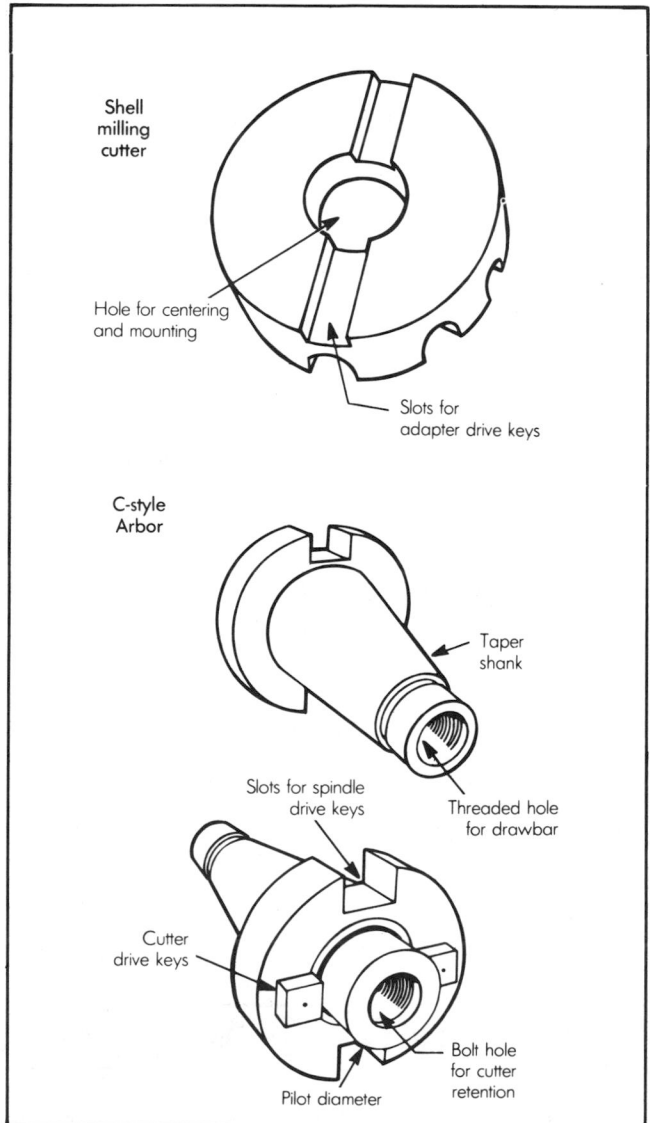

Fig. 25-41 Shell milling cutters 3-6″ diam are mounted on C-style arbors.[1]

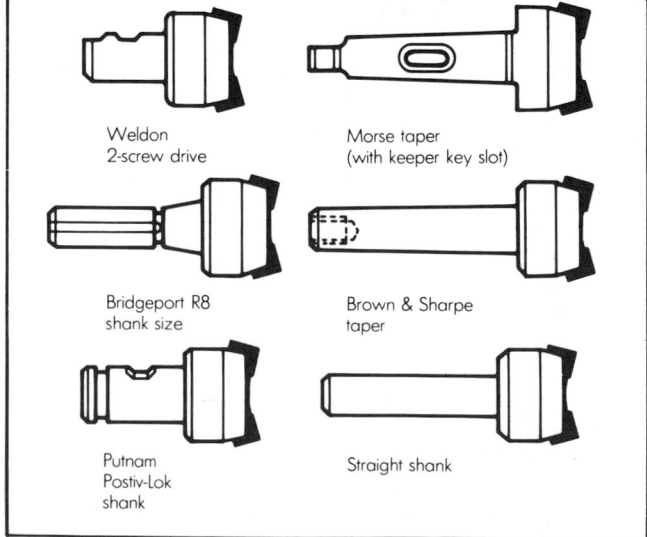

Fig. 25-40 Common shank styles used on end mills.[1]

MOUNTING LARGER FACE MILLS

Face milling cutters larger than about 8" (200 mm) diam are available for either of two popular mounting methods: the flat-back drive and the National Standard drive, also called the National Machine Tool Builders (NMTB) drive.

Flat-Back Drive

With the flat-back drive (see Fig. 25-42), the face milling cutter is located on the pilot diameter of a centering plug that is mounted in the spindle nose of the machine. Drive keys on the spindle nose fit into keyways (slots) in the back face of the cutter body. Four bolts hold the cutter against the spindle face.

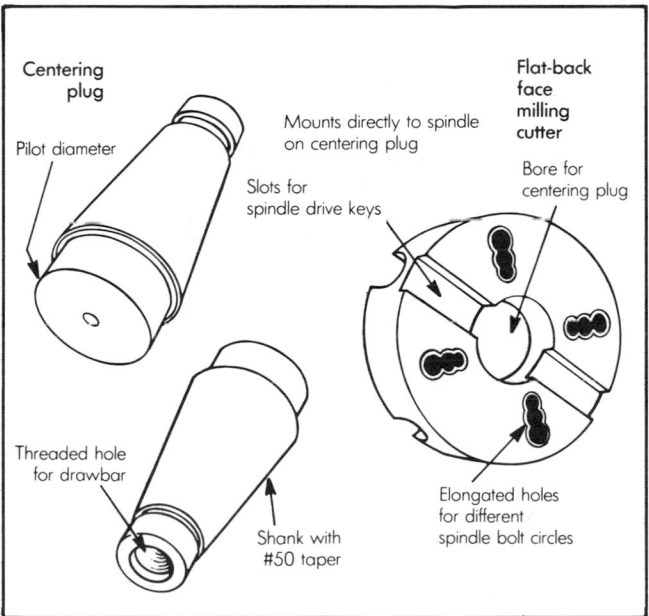

Fig. 25-42 Flat-back mounting for face milling cutters 8" diam or larger.[1]

National Standard Drive

The National Standard (#40, 50, or 60 NMTB) drive (see Fig. 25-43) is similar to the flat-back drive in that the cutter is bolted directly to the spindle face and driven by keys on the spindle nose. The difference between the two lies in the method of centering the cutter. The National Standard mounting does not use a centering plug; instead, there is a precision, counterbored, locating diameter on the back of the cutter body that locates on the OD of the spindle flange.

MOUNTING CUTTERS ON SHAFT-TYPE ARBORS

Plain, side, slotting, and formed milling cutters have keyways in their bores for positive radial drive and have precision-ground center holes for mounting on shaft-type arbors. The keyways extend through the entire lengths of the arbors. One end of each arbor is tapered to fit into the tapered bore of the machine spindle; the opposite end fits into a rotary bearing and is supported by an outboard bracket on the overarm of the milling machine.

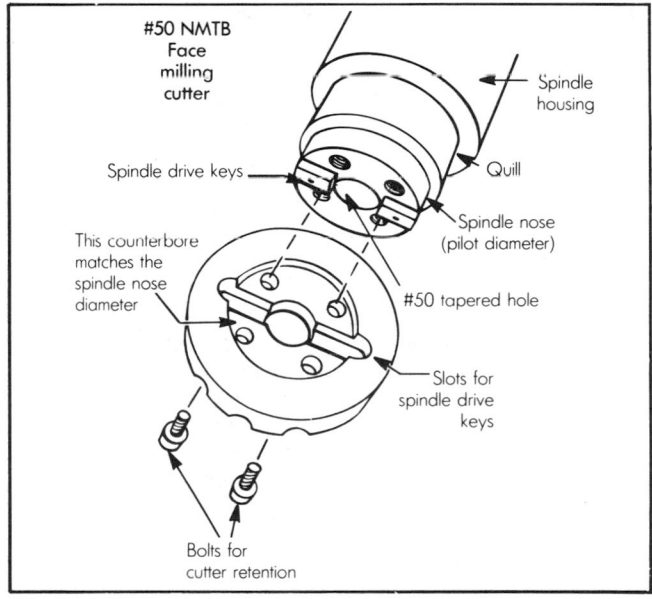

Fig. 25-43 National Standard drive for face milling cutters 8" diam or larger.[1]

WORKHOLDING FOR MILLING

Regardless of how well the milling machine is designed and built or how good the cutting tool is, in most cases proper fixturing determines the success of the milling operation. It can mean the difference between producing good or bad parts or achieving high or low production.

LOCATING WORKPIECES IN FIXTURES

The most important function of any fixture is to locate the workpiece so that the surface to be machined is presented to the cutting tool properly while, at the same time, the surface is kept in a definite dimensional relationship to other surfaces as dictated by the part drawing. In situations in which no previous machining has been done on the workpiece, the location for the first operation can sometimes be difficult.

A workpiece must logically be located in three basic planes or directions. The rest points usually provide the first or vertical plane. Once these are established, the workpiece must then be positioned laterally in the second plane. In this instance, when rough surfaces are the only ones available, two points must be chosen to square the workpiece in this plane. Again, they must be dimensionally related to the surface to be machined. With the workpiece located against these points, it is then located in the third plane. This can be a single point so that it does not conflict with or disturb the locations already obtained.

A simplified rectangular object is illustrated in Fig. 25-44, with six locating points shown. In the absence of machined surfaces or holes that might be used, these six points should be used for locating workpieces of this type.

If the operation to be done is not the first and if previously

WORKHOLDING FOR MILLING

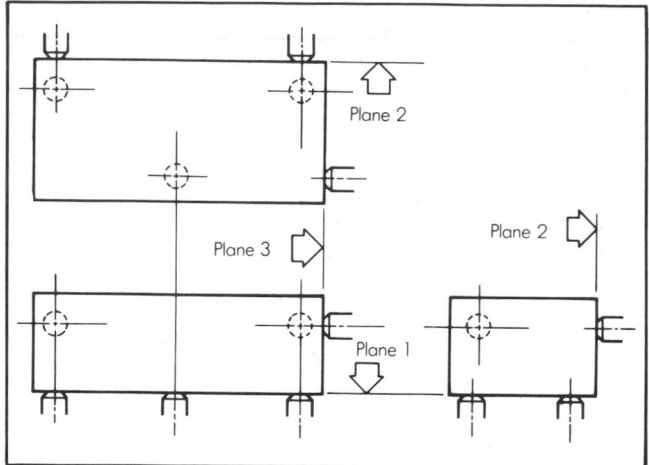

Fig. 25-44 Six points are used for locating this rectangular workpiece. (*Cincinnati Milacron Inc.*)

machined surfaces do exist, location is taken from these surfaces when possible. When accurately machined holes are available, these too are sometimes used with dowels or locating pins. For shafts or parts with turned and ground diameters, when centers and axial centrality are important factors, V-blocks or other types of locators are used that permit orientation of the workpiece to the center line.

TYPES OF CLAMPS

Many different types of clamps are used for fixtures, depending upon the space available and the pressures required. While manually operated clamps are suitable for many applications, quick-acting hydraulic or pneumatic clamping devices facilitate workpiece loading and unloading. Each clamp must be chosen or tailored to suit the existing conditions. Heavy or high-power cuts require stronger clamps and a multiplication of applied force to securely hold the workpiece.

TYPES OF FIXTURES

Milling fixtures can generally be classified in one of five classifications, depending upon their application. These classifications are:

1. Low production fixtures. These are simple manually loaded, hand-clamped fixtures. They are often suitable and most economical for small job-lot quantities of workpieces. A simple fixture for milling the sides and center surface of a workpiece is illustrated in Fig. 25-45. The workpiece is centered on the fixture by hand based on the operator's judgment or on sight locator lines scribed on the mounting surface.

2. Medium to high production fixtures. These are generally manually loaded, with either hand or automatic clamping. Multistation fixtures, used when more than one part is processed at the same time, can be included in this classification. This type of fixture is generally the most popular.

3. High production and transfer machine fixtures. These fixtures are almost always automatically loaded and unloaded and are automatically clamped. They can be made to suit standard milling machines, transfer lines (see Fig. 25-46), or special tailor-made machines for specific operations. Hopper-loaded fixtures for small-part production can be included in this class.

4. Numerical control/computer numerical control machine and machining center fixtures. These are usually manually loaded and clamped. While not complex, these fixtures can be quite a challenge to design because the machining of much of the workpiece must be done in one setup. The space allotted for the placement of clamps and jacks is also generally limited.

5. Pallet-type fixtures. These are used in manufacturing systems for large workpieces in which the pallet (with fixture) must be transported from one machine to another automatically without relocating or reclamping of the workpiece. They usually have to hold large awkward workpieces that must be hoist loaded to and

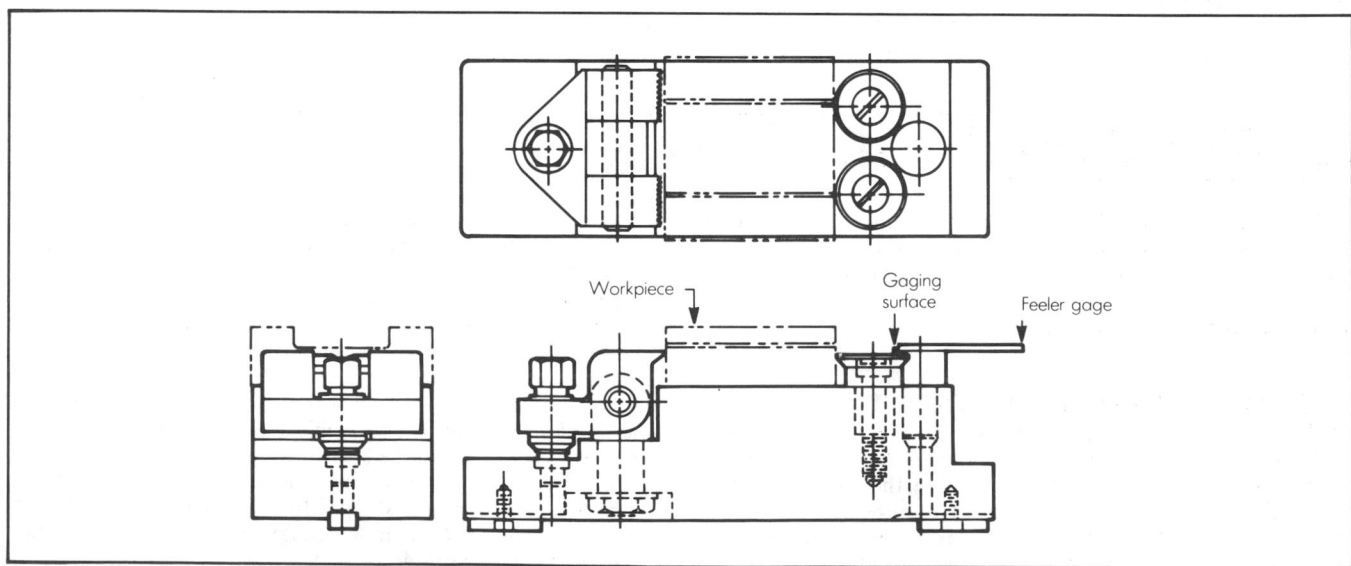

Fig. 25-45 Simple milling fixture in which the workpiece is centered by hand.

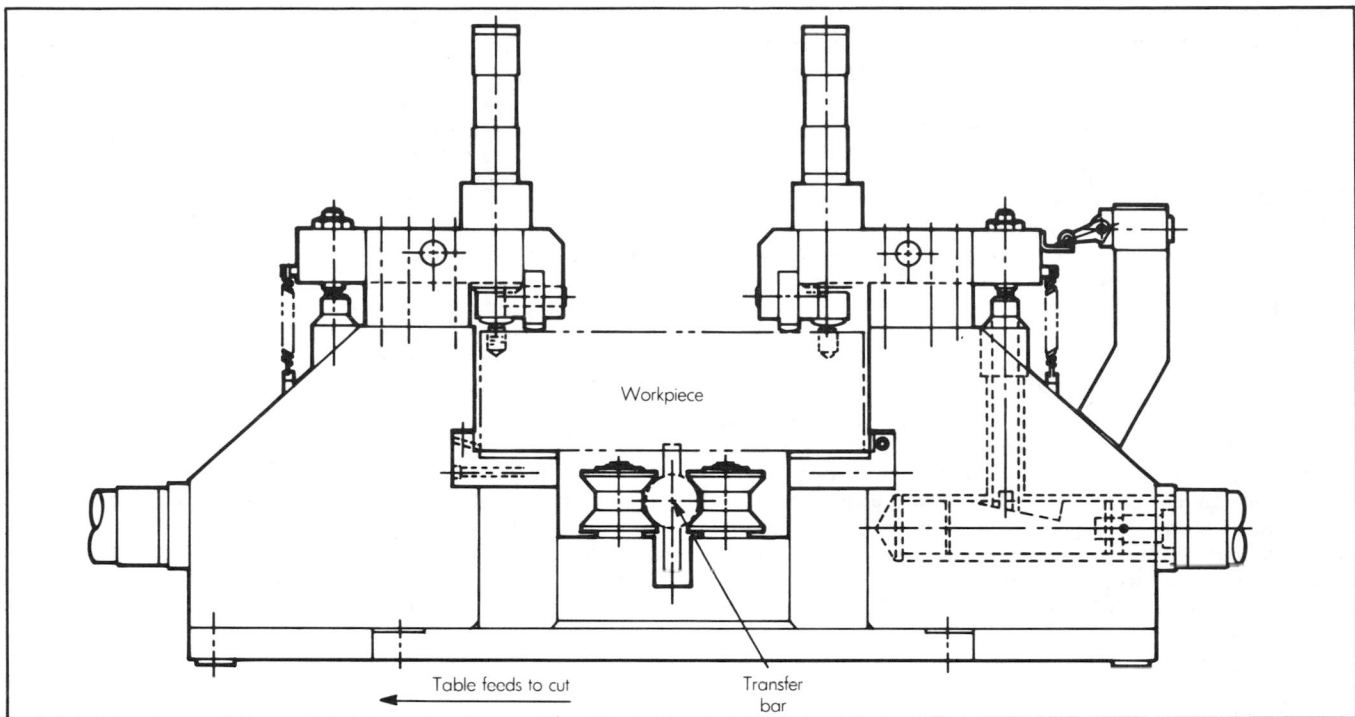

Fig. 25-46 Automatic locating and clamping fixture for transfer line, viewed in the direction of workpiece transfer. (*Cincinnati Milacron Inc.*)

from the fixture, which is permanently attached to the pallet. Clamping can be manual or automatic, and the pallet is designed for transporting and for being located and clamped automatically in any or all of the machining stations. A load/unload area is designated along the route of the system.

MILLING APPLICATIONS

Milling is used for a wide variety of metal removal applications. Because of space limitations, this discussion is limited to some general recommendations for a few of the more common applications.

MILLING VARIOUS MATERIALS

Workpiece material, including its condition and hardness, has a major influence on the cutting tool material, geometry of the cutter, and operating parameters.

Cast Irons

Because of the abrasive nature of cast irons, carbide milling cutters are generally the most economical, especially for production applications, and they may be necessary for milling chilled or very hard cast irons. Diamond milling cutters are being used with good results for cutting very abrasive aluminum alloys, and ceramic cutters are being used for high-speed milling.

Carbon and Alloy Steels

Hardness of the steel is generally the determining factor in selection of a cutting tool material. HSS cutters are often used to mill steels having a hardness less than about 300 Brinell, but carbide cutters are also used for milling these steels. For steels with hardnesses from 300-500 Brinell, cutters made from higher alloy or premium grades of HSS are generally satisfactory, but carbide cutters are usually preferred, especially for production applications. Carbide cutters are generally necessary for milling steels harder than 500 Brinell.

Soft, gummy steels such as SAE 1010 require high cutting speeds. Steels hardened to over 450 Brinell generally require lower speeds. Titanium carbide cutters are being used successfully for lighter milling operations and ceramic cutters for many high-speed milling operations.

Stainless Steels, Heat-Resistant Alloys, and Titanium

HSS cutters are sometimes preferred for milling these materials because the materials tend to weld to the cutting edges of carbide cutters. Good results, however, are being obtained in many applications with carbide cutters. Milling of these materials generally requires using lower speeds and feeds than those used for cutting carbon and other alloy steels. Adequately powered machines are essential because of the greater cutting forces resulting from the high tensile strengths of these materials.

MILLING APPLICATIONS

Nonferrous Materials

When these materials are milled, HSS cutters are generally more economical for short runs and carbide cutters for longer runs. For very abrasive materials, such as some high-silicon aluminum alloys, diamond cutters are being used.

Nonmetallic Materials

Carbide cutters are usually best for milling these materials because most nonmetallic materials are very abrasive. Diamond cutters are also being used to mill some of the more abrasive nonmetallic materials.

SLOTTING OPERATIONS

Cutting of slots is done with both slotting cutters and end mills. The choice between these tools depends primarily upon the width and depth of the slot; workpiece material; and production volume, tolerance, and finish requirements. Slotting cutters are capable of higher metal removal rates and are generally employed for production applications. End mills are easier to set up and change and are used extensively for die and mold making and small-lot production. The deflection of end mills, however, may cause problems and limit production rates if close tolerances must be maintained. Very narrow slots are generally cut with solid HSS cutters. Slots that are deep in relation to their width are also usually machined with slotting cutters rather than end mills.

MILLING HELICAL SURFACES AND CONTOURS

Cams, worm threads, and other helical surfaces are often produced on milling machines by rotating the workpiece with a universal dividing head, which is driven from the table feedscrew through gears. Simultaneously, the workpiece is fed by the machine table in the direction of the axis of rotation.

Contour milling, involving the simultaneous feeding of the cutter in two or more axes of motion, is frequently done on NC/CNC or tracer-controlled machines. For such applications, the feed must be based on the circumference of the milling cutter, not its centerline as is the case in straight-line milling. When contouring is being done, chip thickness for a given depth of cut can vary within the cut and must be calculated differently than it would be for a straight-line cut. Conventional milling (instead of climb milling) with positive-rake cutters usually helps avoid the overloading and chatter often experienced when contour milling is done.

THREAD MILLING

This old process once required special-purpose, manually operated machines, but it is now being done on three-axis NC contouring machines. Threads produced on the NC machines are smooth, accurate, and relatively inexpensive, and the milling cutters used have a long life.

Each tooth of a multiple-thread milling cutter is shaped like the thread form it produces. The teeth are arranged in parallel rows without any spiral lead. The cutter rotates at high speed while its axis slowly moves around the workpiece in a planetary arc of just over 360°. As the spindle axis moves around the workpiece, it advances one pitch in the axial direction.

HIGH-SPEED MILLING

Considerable development work has been performed and is continuing toward the increased use of higher speed milling. Since high-speed machining has not been officially defined, there is a wide range of opinions as to the parameters involved. Many prefer the definition: milling at elevated speeds, feeds, and depths of cut.

Advantages

A major advantage of high-speed milling is increased productivity. Investigations have shown that the rate of temperature increase tends to decrease at higher cutting speeds. There is no detrimental effect on the finishes produced; in fact, in most instances, smoother surfaces finishes are obtained.

Limitations

A possible limitation to high-speed milling is the need for rigid, adequately powered machines with high speed and feed capabilities, strong fixturing, secure workholding, and ample guarding, which add to capital equipment costs. Also, since machining time is only a very small percentage of the total production time for any workpiece, the added cost for high-speed milling may not be economically feasible. Work is being done with gas hydrodynamic, hydrostatic, and active magnetic bearings to increase the high-speed capabilities of milling machines.

Applications

Much of the work in high-speed milling has been done with small end mills for cutting aluminum alloys and honeycomb materials that are easy to machine.

References

1. Carboloy Systems Dept., General Electric Co., *Milling Handbook of High-Efficiency Metal Cutting*, Detroit, 1980.

GRINDING

The fact that abrasive methods in general and grinding, more particularly, occupy a prominent position in modern metalworking is due to the important and, in some respects, unique advantages which these methods of metalworking provide in many areas of industrial production. Every listed advantage does not benefit all the applications of abrasives as means of metalworking. Nevertheless the savings in cost and operation time, the high level of methods'

adaptability, the often superior quality of the produced work surfaces, and several other properties of ground parts have significant positive merit in many applications. The manufacturing engineer should consider abrasive methods as a potentially promising alternative to other methods. This is true even in applications beyond those for which grinding and other abrasive methods are not recognized as the proper or only feasible metalworking procedure.

GRINDING WHEELS AND DISCS

The proper selection of grinding wheels probably is the most important component of planning an efficient and economical grinding operation. The task of selecting the correct wheel or disc is made difficult by the fact that there are thousands of wheels and disc, each with specific characteristics. It is best to work with the grinding wheel supplier for special applications and difficult-to-grind materials.

WHEEL COMPOSITION

Grinding wheels and discs are composed of selectively sized abrasive grains held together by a bonding material. Five distinct elements must be considered when selecting a wheel for a specific application. These elements are:

1. Abrasive—the grinding agent used in the wheel. Chemical composition, physical properties, and particle shape affect performance.
2. Grain size—the particle size of the abrasive grains, which influences stock removal rate and surface finish generated.
3. Bond—the bonding materials that hold the abrasive grains together to form a grinding wheel. Chemical composition affects strength, resilience, and other physical properties of the wheel.
4. Grade—the strength of the grinding wheel, usually controlled by varying amount of bonding material. This is frequently referred to as the hardness of the wheel.
5. Structure—the proportion and arrangement of the abrasive grains and bond. The porosity of the grinding wheel is affected by both the structure and the grade.

WHEEL SPECIFICATION

A standard marking system defined by the American National Standards Institute as ANSI Standard B74.13-1977 is used by all grinding wheel manufacturers.[1] This marking system involves the use of letters or numbers in each of seven positions as indicated in Fig. 26-1.[2] When necessary to show special grain combinations, manufacturers may add an additional symbol to the regular grain-size number. A similar marking system is used by most grinding wheel manufacturers to designate dia-

mond wheels and CBN wheels.[3] This marking system involves the use of letters or numbers in each of seven positions as indicated in Fig. 26-2. Another ANSI standard covers the specifications of shapes and sizes of grinding wheels and mounted wheels.[4]

Types of Grinding Wheels

Figure 26-3 illustrates the various shapes of standard peripheral grinding wheels in use today. Missing numbers in this list of standard shapes pertain to wheel geometries that have been dropped as standards but are usually available as specials. Grinding wheel configurations identified as specials are listed in "Grinding Wheel Specifications for Grinding Machines—1978 Supplement" (Grinding Wheel Institute, Cleveland). Figure 26-4 illustrates the various shapes of standard side or face grinding wheels in use today. Table 26-1 provides a key to letter dimensions and grinding wheel shapes to which the dimensions commonly apply.

Shapes of Grinding Wheel Faces

Figure 26-5 illustrates the various types of standard wheel faces in use today.

WHEEL INSPECTION

All new wheels should be inspected individually for chips, cracks, or other defects before they are put into service. Several methods are available for judging the soundness of a grinding wheel including the ring test and vibration test methods.

Ring Test

The ring test is a method of checking for cracks in a wheel. Small wheels can be suspended from the hole on a peg or the finger, while heavier wheels should be set on edge on a hard floor surface. With the wooden handle of a screwdriver, or a wooden or nylon mallet, the wheel is tapped lightly at a point approximately 45° away from the vertical centerline. A sound, undamaged wheel will give a clear metallic tone, whereas a cracked wheel will give "dead" tone and not ring clear. Wheels bonded with organic materials do not give the same clear metallic sound as do vitrified and silicate wheels. It is often helpful to "ring" several identical wheels for comparison, which will allow rejection of a wheel sounding suspiciously different.

GRINDING WHEELS AND DISCS

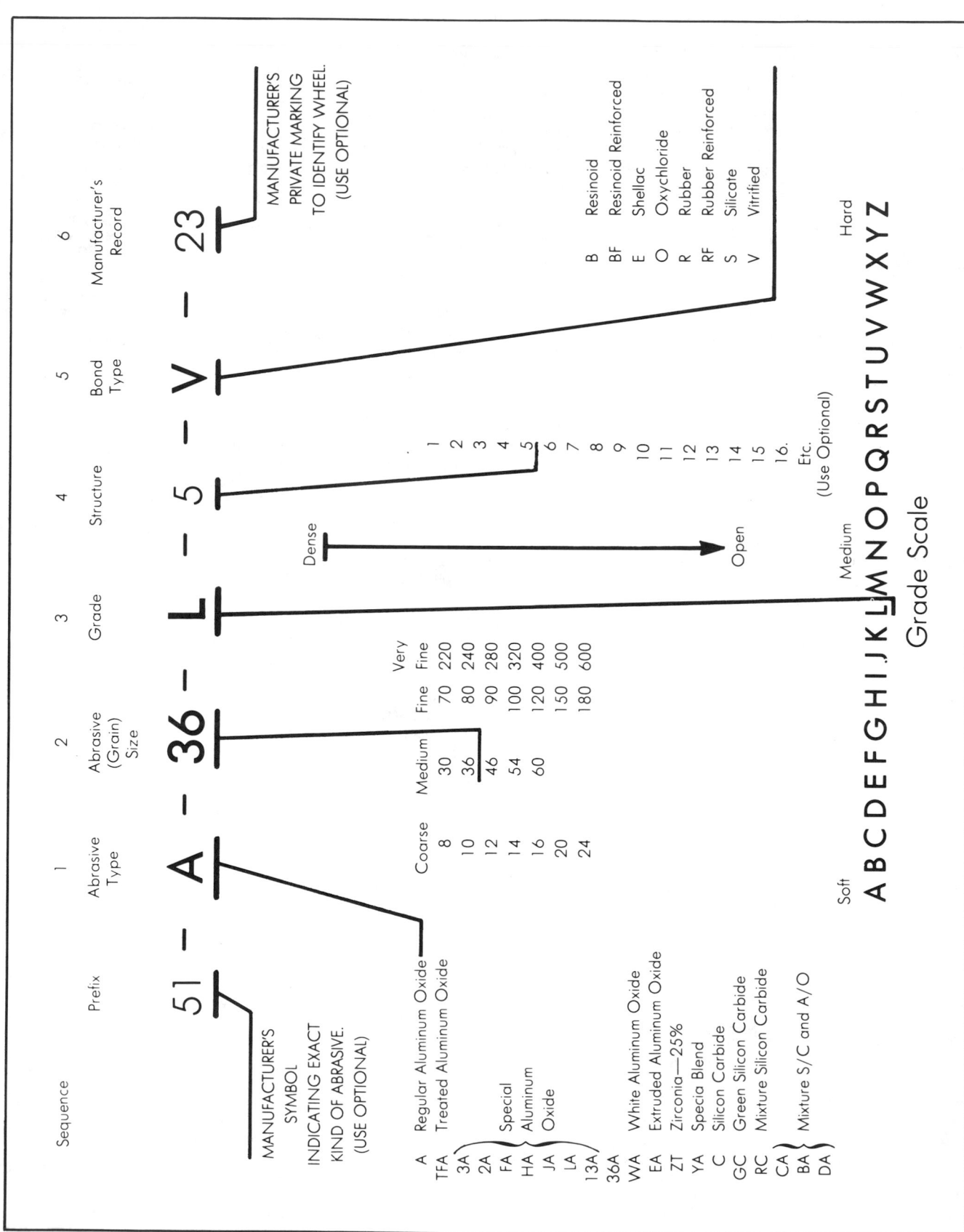

Fig. 26-1 Standard bonded-abrasive wheel-marking system. (*ANSI Standard B74.13-1977*)

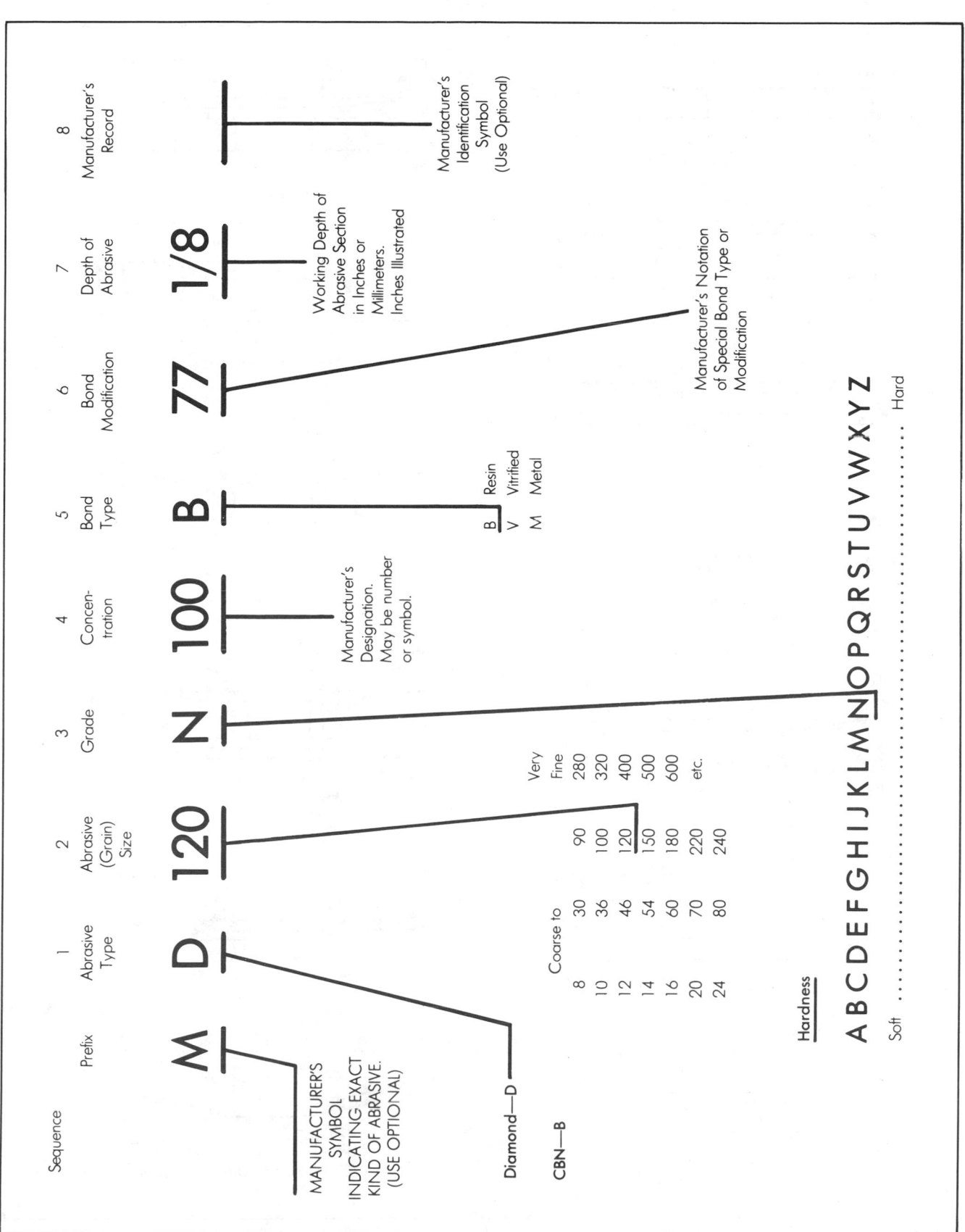

Fig. 26-2 Wheel-marking system for diamond and cubic boron nitride wheels. (*ANSI Standard B74.13-1977*)

GRINDING WHEELS AND DISCS

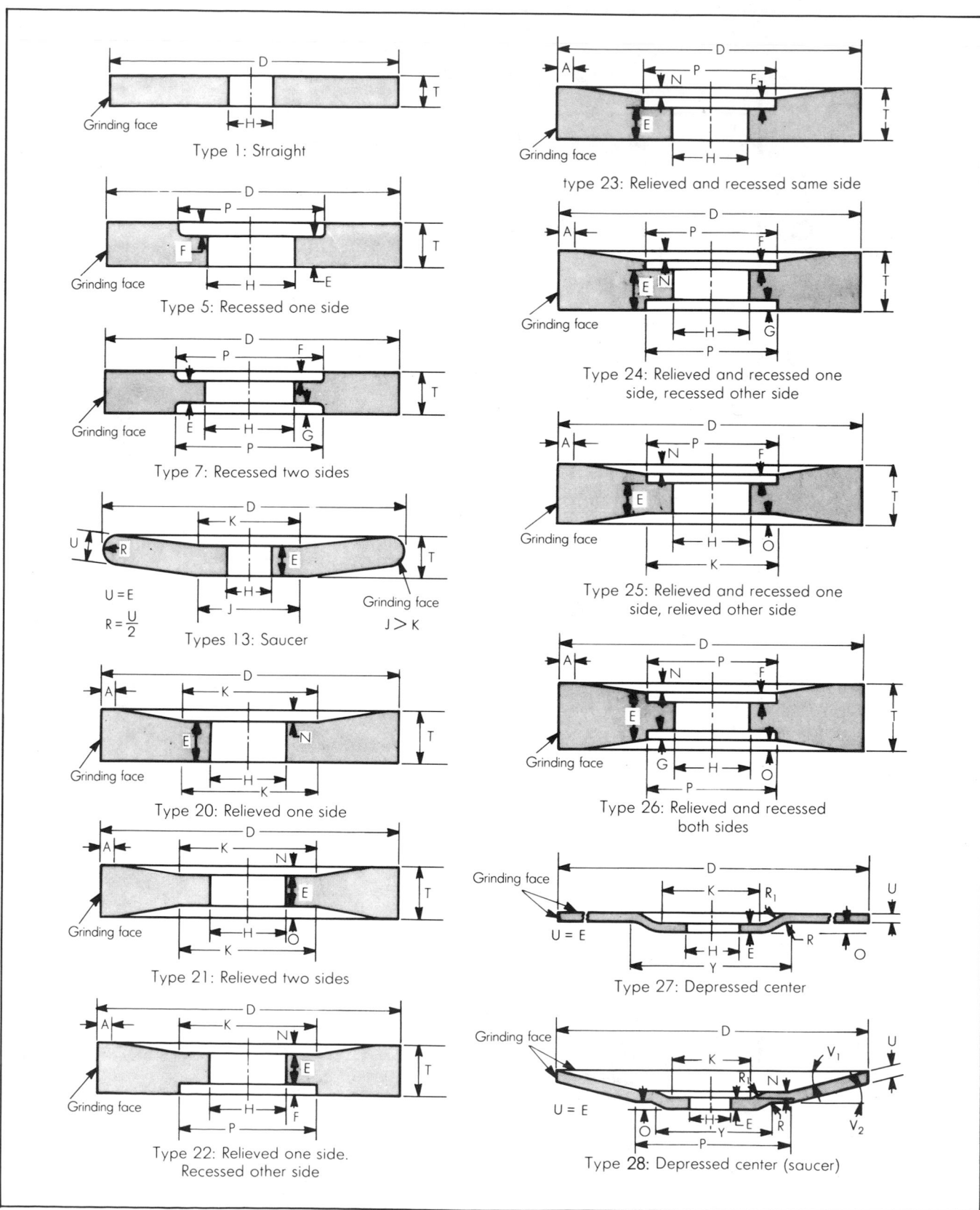

Fig. 26-3 Standard shapes of peripheral grinding wheels. (*Grinding Wheel Institute, ANSI Standard B74.2-1974*)

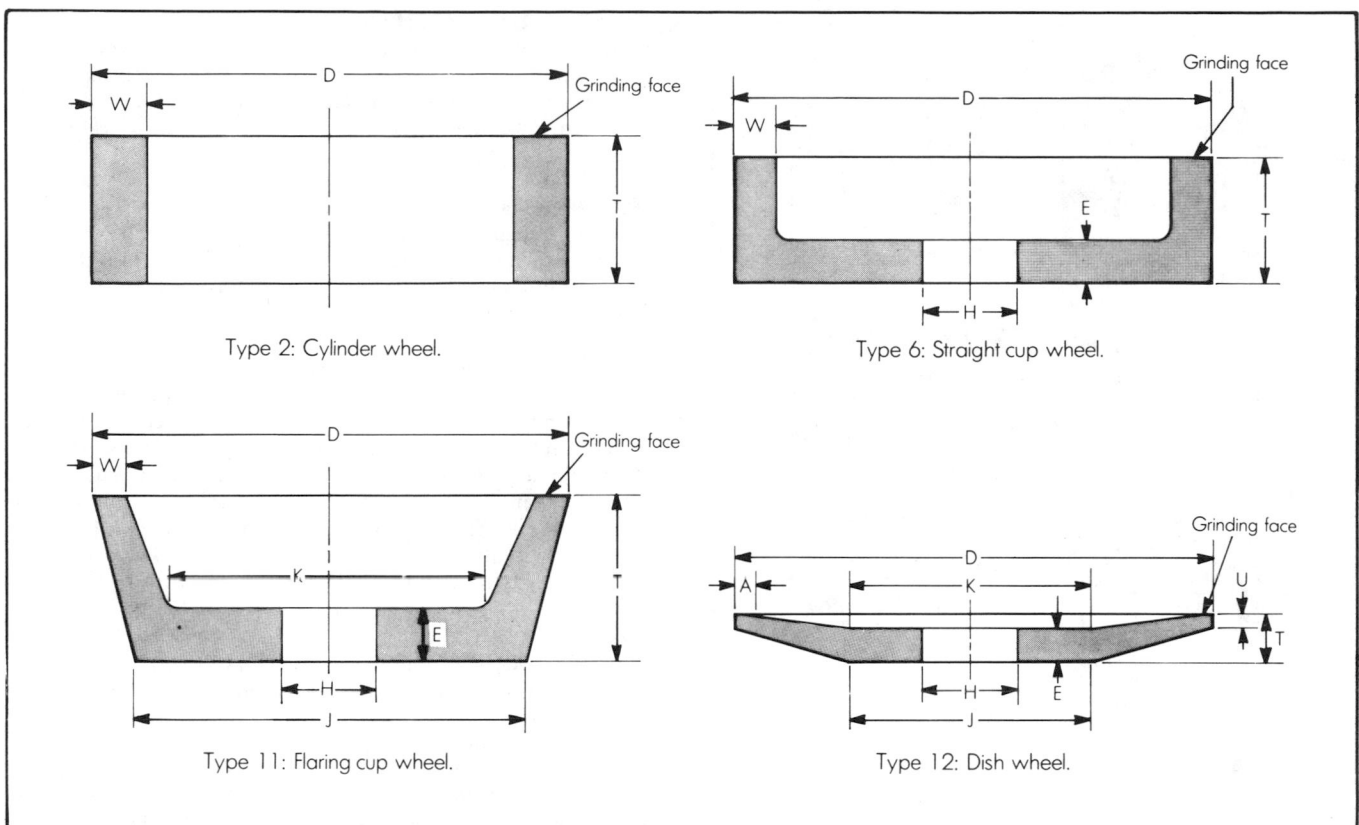

Fig. 26-4 Standard side or face grinding wheels. (*Grinding Wheel Institute, ANSI Standard B74.2-1974*)

TABLE 26-1
Key to Letter Dimensions and Grinding Wheel Types
to Which the Dimensions Commonly Apply*

Letter Dimensions	Grinding Wheel Types
A— Radial width of flat at periphery.	Types 12, 20, 21, 22, 23, 24, 25, 26.
B— Depth of blind hole threaded bushing.	Types 16, 17, 18, 18R, 19.
D— Diameter (overall).	All types.
E— Thickness at hole.	Types 5, 6, 7, 11, 12, 13, 20, 21, 22, 23, 24, 25 26, 27, 28.
F— Depth of recess one side.	Types 5, 7, 22, 23, 24, 25, 26.
G— Depth of recess other side.	Types 7, 24, 26.
H— Hole diameter.	All types except Type 2.
J— Diameter of outside flat.	Types 11, 12, 13, 17, 19.
K— Diameter of inside flat.	Types 11, 12, 13, 20, 21, 22, 25, 27 28.
N— Depth of relief one side.	Types 20, 21, 22, 23, 24, 25, 26.
O— Depth of relief other side.	Types 21, 25, 26, 27, 28.
P— Diameter of recess.	Types 5, 7, 22, 23, 24, 25, 26, 28.
R— Radius.	Types 13, 16, 18R.
S— Length of cylindrical section.	Type 19.
T— Thickness (overall).	All types.
U— Width of edge.	Types 12, 13, 27, 28.
V— Face angle.	Type 1 (Faces B, C, D, E, G, H, I, and N).
V_1—Back angle.	Type 28.
W—Wall (rim) thickness at grinding face.	Types 2, 6, 11.
X— Face dimension.	Type 1 (Face N).
Y— Outside diameter of hub.	Types 27, 28.

(*ANSI Standard B74.2-1974, published by Grinding Wheel Institute*)

GRINDING WHEELS AND DISCS

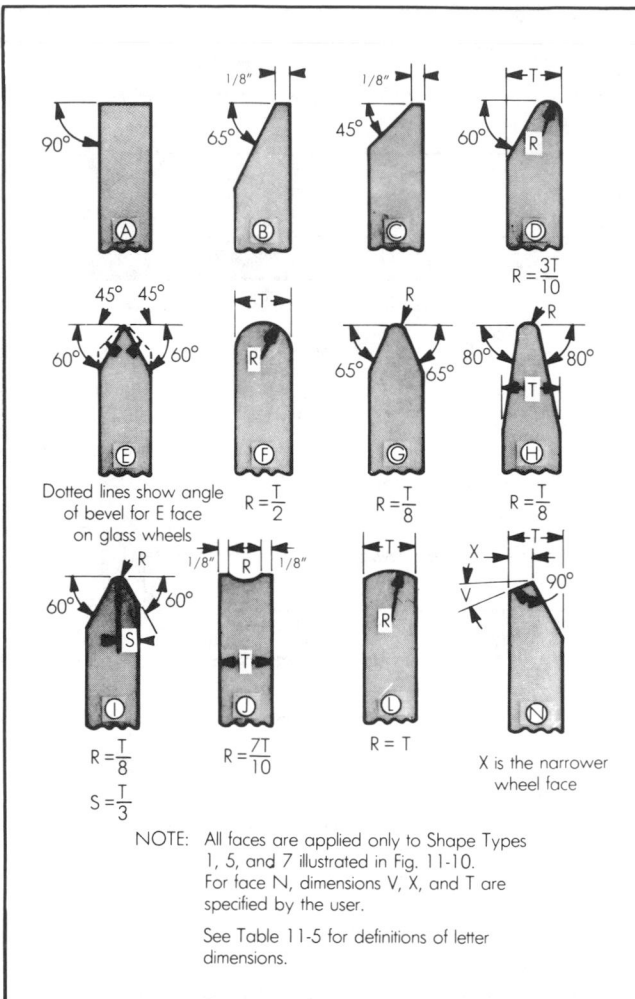

Fig. 26-5 Standard shapes of grinding wheel faces. (*Grinding Wheel Institute, ANSI Standard B74.2-1974*)

Certain grinding wheels cannot be tested using the ring test method because of their size or configuration. These wheels include wheels 4″ (100 mm) diam or smaller, plugs and cones, mounted wheels, segments, plate-mounted wheels, and inserted-nut and projecting-stud disc wheels. In some cases, a vibration test can be used to check for cracks in these grinding wheels.

Vibration Test

As with the ring test, the vibration test should be performed immediately before mounting the grinding wheel (either new or used) because this is the last opportunity to check wheel soundness before using the wheel.

The basis of the vibration test is the way that loose sand or similar material is distributed on the side of a wheel when the wheel is vibrating. As the wheel vibrates, sand granules or other loose material will respond to the vibration energy; the granules will move away from cracks in the wheel. If the wheel is sound, the granules will remain evenly distributed over the surface of the wheel. Both sides of a wheel should be tested by placing, in horizontal position, alternate sides of the wheel on a test vibration fixture and coating the wheel with a thin layer of fine granulated material.

WHEEL SELECTION

Operating conditions that affect the performance of grinding wheels are wheel speed, material removal rates, normal force, material ground, area of contact, grinding fluid, the relationship between wheel and work size, vibration, trueing and dressing, and power.

Abrasive Wear

The mechanism of abrasive wear has been studied by many investigators, and the present information implies that there are three major mechanisms. These mechanisms are: solution of abrasives into the workpiece material (attritious wear), chipping or fracturing of individual abrasive grains, and loss of whole grits through bond post breakage.

All three mechanisms probably occur simultaneously in most operations, but the relative importance of the mechanisms in any given application depends on operating conditions, abrasive type, bond type and amount, and work material. Tough abrasives tend to favor attritious wear and loss of whole grits; friable abrasives favor chipping or fracturing of grains; low bond strength or quality favor loss of whole grains; and abrasives with high solubility in workpiece materials favor attritious wear.

Wheel Speed

Wheel speed in grinding is measured in surface feet per minute (meters per second), rather than revolutions per minute. As wheel speed is increased, each cutting grain is called upon to do less work each time it strikes the workpiece, which results in less wheel wear. Increased wheel speed therefore results in lower abrasive cost. As the wheel speed is reduced, each cutting grain is called upon to do more work each time it strikes the workpiece, and the result is increased wheel wear.

Wheel speed affects the choice of the wheel bond. Vitrified-bond wheels are commonly used for speeds up to and including 8500 sfm (43.2 m/s); but speeds of 12,000 sfm (61 m/s) are also popular; and selected operations now exist in which speeds as high as 16,000 sfm (81.3 m/s) are used. Resinoid-bond grinding wheels generally operate at 9500 sfm (48.3 m/s); however, a speed of 12,500 sfm (63.5 m/s) is common in foundry floorstand grinding and steel conditioning, and speeds of 16,000 sfm (81.3 m/s) are being used for steel conditioning.

Work Speed

Work speed is the speed at which the workpiece traverses across the wheel face or rotates about a center. The main advantage of higher work speed is its ability to retard or prevent thermal damage to the workpiece. Metal removal rate (volume removed/unit time) may be calculated as an area being removed at a rate (in.² x ipm or mm² x mm/s). When an increase in workspeed increases the metal removal rate (in reciprocating surface grinding, for example), higher forces, power, and wheel wear rates occur. When the metal removal rate is unaffected by workspeed (most cylindrical plunge-grinding operations), essentially no change occurs in forces, power, or wheel wear rates, but the surface integrity is improved by higher workspeeds.

Infeed or Downfeed

The rate at which a wheel is fed into the workpiece can cause substantial changes in wheel performance. Higher infeed rates always increase the metal removal rate (area being removed multiplied by infeed rate). This generates higher normal forces, power, and wheel wear rates. A rougher finish, poorer geometry, but higher productivity will occur. If the higher normal force is above the mechanical strength of the wheel, the wheel wear rate may be significantly higher and the new G-ratio (grinding ratio—see following section) may be much lower than the original. Reducing the infeed rate reverses all of these factors.

Traverse or Crossfeed

Traverse or crossfeed is the distance or speed at which the workpiece is moved across the wheel face; it is different from workspeed. In traverse cylindrical grinding, if the crossfeed distance is 25% or less of the wheel width, good surface finishes, but low productivity, will result. Increasing the crossfeed to 50% or more of the wheel width will produce poorer surface finish and higher productivity, but the wheel will wear evenly across its face. The workpiece surface finish depends mainly on the wheel wear rate of the center portion of the wheel (traverse cylindrical) or the exit end of the wheel (in throughfeed centerless grinding).

MATERIAL TO BE GROUND

Materials to be ground can be divided into two types: metallic or nonmetallic. Metallics can further be divided into high or low-tensile materials. The nonmetallic type can be divided into hardness ranges below or above 800 Knoop. To grind metallics, aluminum oxide grinding wheels are primarily used. In selected operations, diamond and cubic boron nitride wheels are also now being used. To grind nonmetallics, silicon carbide wheels are used if the hardness is 800 Knoop or lower; diamond wheels are used to grind the harder nonmetallics. To grind hard materials, soft-grade, fine-grit, friable-abrasive grinding wheels are used. To grind soft materials, hard-grade, coarse-grit, tough-abrasive grinding wheels are used. To grind heat-sensitive materials, soft-grade, friable-abrasive wheels are most commonly used.

AREAS OF CONTACT

Area of contact varies from large, as in vertical spindle/rotary table grinding, to small, as in external cylindrical grinding. Small areas of contact generate high-unit pressures (pressure is normal force divided by contact area) and require hard-grade, fine-grit wheels. Low unit pressures call for soft-grade, coarse-grit wheels. In cylindrical grinding, a parameter called the equivalent diameter, D_e, can be useful. (The relationships between D_e and other grinding process variables are discussed in "Principles of Grinding" in this chapter.) D_e can be obtained by use of the following equation:

$$D_e = \frac{work\ diameter \times wheel\ diameter}{work\ diameter \pm wheel\ diameter} \tag{1}$$

For internal grinding, the - sign is used; for external grinding, the + sign is used. The equivalent diameter, D_e, is the size of the wheel used to grind a flat surface in order to represent the fit of the wheel and work.

WHEEL BALANCE

Particular attention is needed to make sure that a wheel is in balance before it is used for grinding. Balance is not entirely dependent on the wheel itself, but is also affected by the machine spindle and the means of tightening the wheel on the machine. Consequently, the machine/wheel system should be in balance before the wheel is operated.

An out-of-balance wheel sets up excessive vibration, produces faster wheel breakdown, poor finishes, or chatter and can be dangerous. Wheels generally should be statically balanced before putting them on the machine. They then should be dressed into concentricity, taken off, rebalanced, and put on the grinder and operated. Today equipment is available that will balance the wheel while it is running on the machine.

Generally, balancing is done by shifting weights on the wheel mount. Some wheel mounts have two weights, while others have four. The following steps should be taken to balance a wheel:

1. Remove the weights from the mounting, then place the wheel on balancing ways. When the wheel is on the balancing ways, permit the heavy side of the wheel to come to rest. Place a chalk mark at the bottom (the heavy point). Turn the wheel 90°, first to one side and then to the other side, to check the location of this heavy point. If it comes to rest at the same point, the point is properly marked.

2. Draw a line horizontally through the axis on the mount or the wheel. Insert the two weights, placing them above and equidistant from the horizontal line, and repeat the operation of locating the heavy point (Fig. 26-6, a). If it is again at the original mark, move the two weights closer together toward the top; if it is opposite the original mark, move the weights further apart toward the horizontal axis line. At some point between the top and horizontal line, the proper balance should be found. If not, that is, if both weights are opposite the "heavy mark" and touching each other, the wheel is too far out-of-balance for normal corrective measures and a third or fourth balance weight should be added (Fig. 26-6, b).

3. Proceed as before to locate the heavy point of the wheel and draw the horizontal line. Place the four weights in their grooves at approximately 90° apart. Then move the two top weights closer together. If this is not sufficient, move the bottom weights upward toward the horizontal line. Turn the wheel 90° and check the location of the heavy point, which is apt to be in this case 90° away from the bottom. If this is the case, wipe off the original horizontal lines and draw a new line horizontal to the new heavy point and proceed as before to change the weights.

TRUEING AND DRESSING WHEELS

Trueing means removal of abrasive material from the cutting face of the wheel so that the OD will run concentric with the ID. It also means bringing the sides of the wheel parallel to each other and perpendicular to the spindle. Dressing means removing the glaze from a dull wheel, removing loaded material from the face, restoring a wheel to its original geometry, and conditioning the wheel to do a specific job. Grinding wheels can be made to act harder and finer, or softer and coarser, by means of wheel conditioning.

Kinds of wheel dressers available include metal cutters, abrasive sticks, abrasive wheels, single-point diamonds, single-set and matrix diamond dressers, rotary and stationary diamond rolls, and crushing rolls. Each has specific advantages in its field of usage.

GRINDING WHEELS AND DISCS

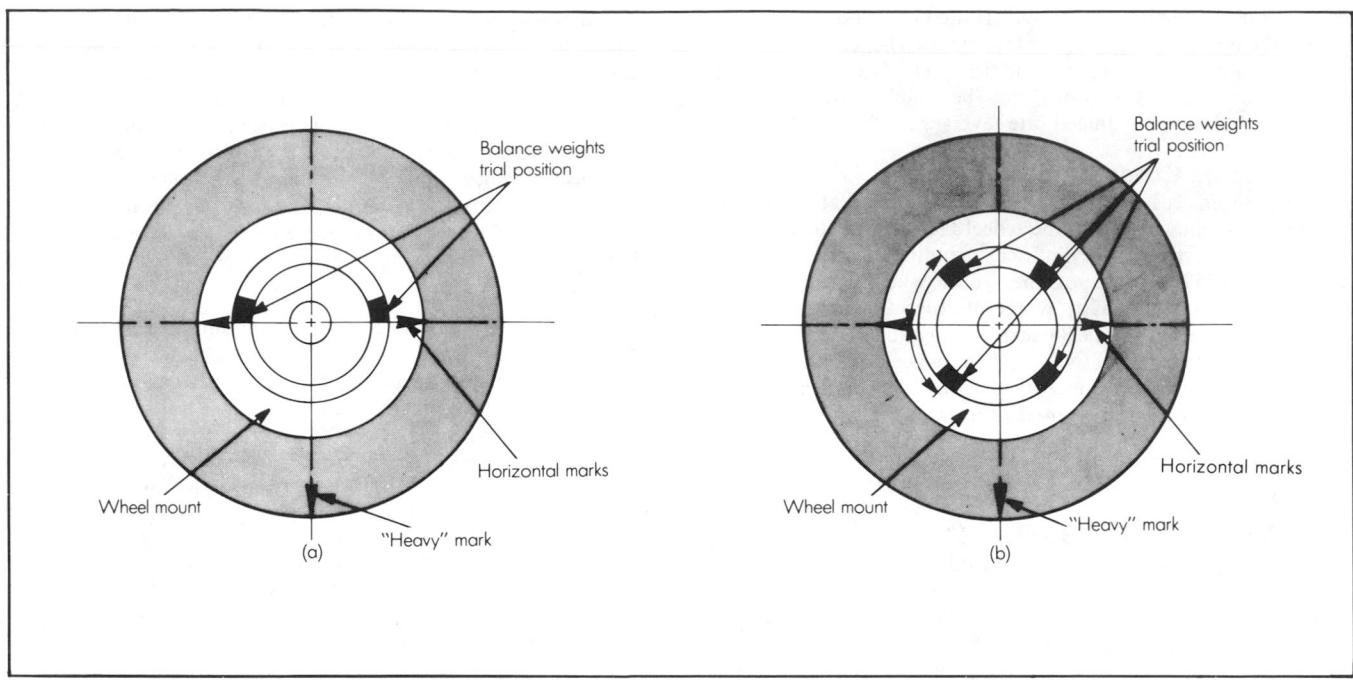

Fig. 26-6 Relative positions of balance weights on a grinding wheel: (a) two weights, (b) four weights.

Method of Dressing

Method of dressing is important in the performance of a grinding wheel. Wheels may be dressed either wet or dry, but the operation should always be carried out under the same condition as the grinding operation. If grinding is to be done wet, then dressing should be done wet. If the dresser is permitted to become dull, the wheel will then be dressed differently than when the dresser is sharp. Consequently, grinding performance varies directly with the condition of the dressing tool. Single-point diamonds, particularly if permitted to become dull, will generate a closed surface on the grinding-wheel face which will result in poor finishes and poor geometry. Single-point diamonds should be rotated frequently about their longitudinal axis to prevent excessive flat development.

Figure 26-7 illustrates the correct positioning of a diamond dressing tool relative to the grinding wheel.

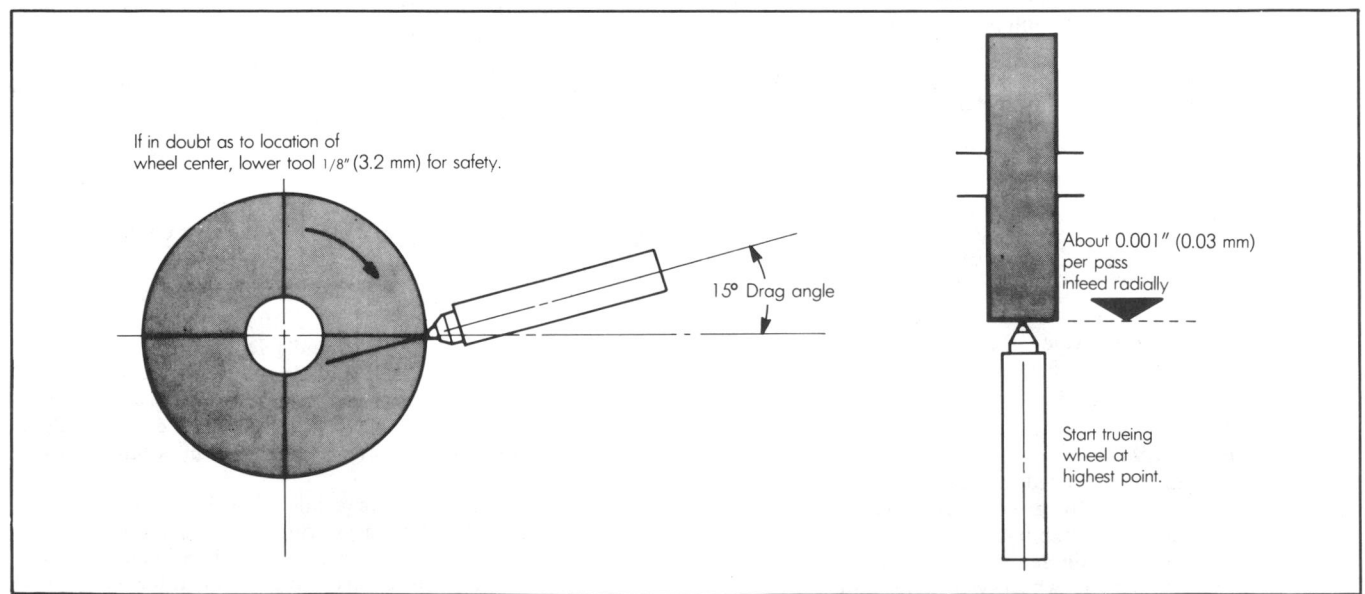

Fig. 26-7 Position of a diamond tool dresser relative to the grinding wheel.

Dressing for Form Grinding

Forming of a wheel to the reverse shape of the part to be ground can be done in a number of ways: mechanically crushing the form into the wheel by means of a roll, dressing the form using a single-point diamond with a pantograph system and template, grinding the form into the wheel using a rotary-diamond formed dresser roll, or grinding the form with a stationary-diamond formed dresser.

In crush forming, the profile desired on the workpiece is ground or machined on a metal roll having a diameter between one-third and one-fourth that of the grinding wheel and a length generally slightly greater than the width of the wheel face. This roll is rigidly mounted and placed so that the roll can be brought into contact with the grinding wheel.

GRINDING WHEEL SAFETY

Grinding wheels and machines should always be used in accordance with guidelines and mandatory regulations of the Occupational Safety and Health Act of 1970. Grinding operations, which are covered in Section 1910 Subparts O and P of the act, are based on ANSI Standards B7.1-1978[5] and B11.9-1975.[6] These standards should be consulted for detailed recommendations not covered specifically in the act. (Grinding

Wheel Guarding

State and federal safety regulations mandate that with few exceptions, safety guards must be used on grinding machines. Surveys show unguarded grinding wheels to be the most violated safety regulation and one of OSHA's top 20 citations. Unfortunately, the numerous grinding wheel injuries that have occurred could have been prevented had the wheel been properly guarded.

Abrasive wheels, 2" (50 mm) diam and smaller, attached to steel mandrels do not require guarding. Since the abrasive portion of the mounted wheel is basically a solid mass (except for the shallow recess in one side to accept the mandrel), the ultimate centrifugal bursting strength of the abrasive is quite high and usually exceeds the critical speed of a steel mandrel. ANSI B7.1 lists the standard mounted wheel maximum speed at 10,000 sfm (51 m/s), provided the strength of the steel shank and overhang are adequate. (See tables detailing maximum operating speed for mounted wheels presented in Section 10 of ANSI B7.1.)

Wheel Speeds

Maximum operating speeds are indicated in rpm (revolutions per minute) on all grinding wheels or the cartons in which they are packed. This maximum is not the recommended speed for most efficient grinding, but rather the approved maximum safe speed dependent upon the wheel shape and strength.

Centrifugal force from rotational speed is the primary source of stress in the wheel body. It is important to recognize the relationship of these forces to the ultimate strength of the wheel being used. Centrifugal force increases as the square of the velocity; therefore, this force, which works to pull the wheel apart, is four times greater with a wheel operating at 3,600 rpm, for example, than with the same wheel operating at 1,800 rpm.

Occasional failures of mounted abrasive wheels and points occur primarily as bending or rupturing of the steel mandrels. This is caused by deflection and whip of the mandrel due to excessive speed for the mounting conditions. For complete safety, an adequate safety factor considerably below the critical mandrel speed is desirable. Generally, a maximum recommended operating speed approximately 25% below the critical speed is

followed in ANSI safety code recommendations. Factors governing maximum allowed speed are size, shape, and weight of the abrasive portion; diameter of the mandrel; and amount of overhang distance between the machine collet or chuck and the abrasive portion (exposed mandrel).

Before mounting a wheel, the spindle speed of the machine should always be checked to ensure that it does not exceed the maximum speed marked on the wheel. It should be noted, however, that the number of revolutions (rpm) may be increased as the diameter of the wheel wears smaller provided the original peripheral speed in surface feet per minute (sfm), or meters per second (m/s), is not exceeded.

Special Higher Speeds

In recent years, it has been demonstrated in certain types of high-production cylindrical and form-grinding applications that definite advantages are realized at surface speeds higher than standard. Very recently, speeds from 12,000-18,000 sfm have been successful on these applications with specially constructed vitrified-bond wheels on equipment specifically designed and guarded for such usage. Similar advances have also been made with special reinforced organic-bond wheels on high-speed, floor-stand types of snagging machines in the foundry and with special high-strength, resinoid-bonded wheels on mechanical slab and billet grinders in the basic steel industry. Safety of such higher-speed operations is so dependent upon the proper combination of conditions that only wheels and machines designed and marked for such usage by the manufacturer should be used.

ABRASIVE DISCS

Discs used for disc grinding are available in a wide variety of abrasive types, grain sizes, grades, structures, bonds, mounting methods, and designs up to 53" (1346 mm) diam. Selection of the proper disc is generally more critical than for most other types of grinding because usually more area is in contact with the work.

Abrasives

Aluminum oxide and silicon carbide are the most common abrasives for disc grinding, with aluminum oxide being used more extensively. Most disc manufacturers make several types of both abrasives; the types vary in toughness, friability, and sharpness. Some discs made from cubic boron nitride are being used to grind tool steels, and some diamond-impregnated discs are being used for carbide.

Grain Size

Grain sizes generally range from 8 (coarse) for heavy stock removal and rough surface finishes to 320 extra fine for light stock removal and finer finishes. Grades range from soft for light stock removal on hard materials to hard for heavy stock removal on soft materials. Because the surface speed of the abrasive discs and the rate of stock removal changes as the workpieces move between the discs, discs are available with harder abrasives in their outer sections and softer near their centers.

Structures

Structures range from dense for heavy-duty operations to open for lighter stock removal, smoother finishes, and grinding of harder materials. Resinoid (phenolic plastic) bond is used almost exclusively for abrasive discs, but it is sometimes modified by the addition of fillers to control breakdown and maintain sharp cutting surfaces.

COATED ABRASIVES

Discs are available with perforations and/or slots molded into their faces. This helps supply an ample flow of coolant to the grinding zone, remove swarf, dissipate heat, and decrease the contact area, increasing grain penetration. The results are freer and cooler cutting, and flatter disc surfaces.

Grinding Speeds

About 5500 sfm (27.9 m/s)—at the periphery of the disc—is generally recommended as best for all disc grinding operations. Higher speeds have not been found to increase productivity appreciably. Somewhat higher speeds, with a maximum of about 6000 sfm (30.5 m/s), may be required for some materials, while lower speeds may be necessary for grinding hard, brittle materials such as carbide. When grinding bimetallic parts having a different material at each end, different speeds are generally used for the two abrasive discs. There are also other parts, some with different surface areas on opposite ends, that may require different disc speeds. Discs should never be rotated at speeds exceeding the manufacturers' recommendations.

Dressing and Trueing

While there are some successful applications of discs that are self sharpening, others are uneconomical because of a short life resulting from high abrasive usage. Most discs which are highly efficient for a specific application will not break down at a steady rate during grinding. As a result, it is usually necessary to periodically dress discs to sharpen their faces and restore their cutting efficiencies, as well as to true them to restore their flatness.

Types of dressing tools include star-type steel cutters with sharp or flat teeth, single-point diamond nibs, cluster-type diamond nibs, and power-driven diamond rolls.

COATED ABRASIVES

Coated abrasives are versatile, multiple-point cutting tools available in sheet, disc, roll, belt, and other forms, which perform heavy-to-light stock removal, dimensioning, shaping, fitting, blending, finishing, and polishing operations.

ELEMENTS

Modern coated abrasives are the products of an extremely technical process developed through many years of research and development. They remain, however, a product comprised of three basic elements—a flexible or semirigid backing to which abrasive grains are bonded by an adhesive. Hence, it is the selection and manufacturing of the most suitable components from the numerous elements available that produces a coated-abrasive product designed to provide the most efficient results in a particular application. Therefore, many combinations of backing, adhesive bond, and abrasive grain are required to satisfy the countless variables encountered in industry. The backings used include cloth, paper, vulcanized fiber, or a combination. Adhesives include glue and/or resin. The most common abrasives are zirconia alumina, aluminum oxide, silicon carbide, garnet, flint, emery, and crocus.

In the manufacturing process, the backing serves as the base upon which a coating of adhesive known as the "maker" coat is uniformly applied to anchor a single layer of abrasive particles (see Fig. 26-8). Individual abrasive particles are applied uniformly to the maker coat and oriented in an electrostatic field or with a mechanical process to maximize the probability that a particle will be positioned with its major, or longitudinal, axis perpendicular to the backing. The maker coat is solidified, and a second coating of adhesive known as the "sizer" coat is applied. In coated-abrasive terminology, the maker and sizer coats are often considered as a unit and are commonly referred to as an adhesive bond.

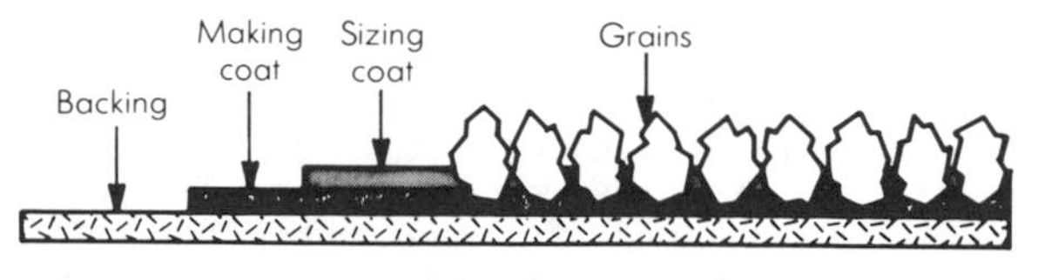

Coated abrasives are generally manufactured in two levels of abrasive grain surface density—open and closed. A closed coated abrasive is one whose backing is fully covered with mineral particles to maximize the number of cutting points available and to produce a high cutting rate in a grinding operation. However, grinding operations on softer materials frequently clog or load the space between particles, rendering the coated abrasive ineffective. To combat loading, manufacturers of coated abrasives produce an open-coat construction (wider area between particles) which produces a self-cleaning action during grinding. In coated-abrasive terminology, an open-coat construction has 50-70% of its backing surface covered with mineral. Open-coat abrasives are often used to abrade softer materials such as plastics, aluminum, copper, wood, and painted surfaces.

ABRASIVE GRAIN SIZE

After the crude abrasives have been crushed, the grains are separated into standard particle sizes (grades) using screens carefully made from silk threads of exact size and number per square inch to insure extreme accuracy. The grit number (mesh number) appearing on the coated abrasive backing represents the approximate number of openings per linear inch in the final screen. Grits 240 and finer, called flours, are graded by hydraulic separators, air classifiers, and levigating tanks. These grades are regularly checked against industry standards (ANSI Standard B74.18) by testing on a series of standardized laboratory sieves and sedimentation devices.

All domestic coated abrasive manufacturers produce products that adhere to the Coated Abrasive Manufacturers Institute

Fig. 26-8 Elements of a coated abrasive. (*Norton Co.*)

grading specifications, called "CAMI grades." Accurate abrasive grading practices are of vital importance in insuring absolutely uniform performance of the finished product and in eliminating random oversized grains which could damage the item being abraded.

COATED-ABRASIVE FORMS

The final step in the manufacturing process, prior to packaging, is the conversion of the coated-abrasive product into one of the shapes or forms designed for use on specific grinding, sanding or polishing equipment. Several basic categories of coated-abrasive shapes exist, including sheets, belts, discs, and specialties. The latter category consists of a number of special shapes tailored to meet industry's countless requirements.

Sheets

Sheets of coated abrasives are produced in a wide variety of sizes for use in manual operations (by hand or hand block) or on machines with straight-line or orbital action. Precut sheets are also used on a number of drum machines.

Discs

Discs are circular coated-abrasive products of varying diameters produced with or without center holes for attaching to air or electric-powered tools. Disc abrasives are used for grinding and finishing operations, particularly in difficult-to-work areas requiring portable tools. Coated abrasives converted into rolls are most commonly 50 yds (45.7 m) in length, but vary in width depending on ultimate use. Usage of rollstock varies from precision-slit abrasives used in crankshaft and bearing-polishing operations to wide rolls used on drum machines.

Belts

Abrasive belts are fabricated from lengths of roll goods made endless when joined by splices. Belts vary in width from 1/4" to over 100" (6.3-2540 mm) and can be almost any practical length.

GRINDING FLUIDS

Many fluid formulations used to cool and lubricate cutting operations are also used to perform similar functions in grinding operations. However, the grinding process by its nature, exhibits several unique characteristics which make it significantly different from conventional cutting processes. For this reason, special considerations must be given to the functions, selection, and use of grinding fluids. The following sections highlight several topics in fluid technology peculiar to the grinding process.

FUNCTIONS OF GRINDING FLUIDS

In metalcutting the energy necessary to deform metal to form a chip is approximately twice that required to overcome friction between the tool/workpiece and the chip/workpiece interfaces. In grinding, the force necessary to overcome friction is approximately the same as that necessary for chip formation. Consequently, friction forces are much more important in grinding than in cutting, making lubrication in grinding critical, not only from the standpoint of power, wheel life, and surface finish, but also in relation to heat development and possible damage to the ground surface.

In single point turning it has been shown that approximately 97% of the energy required to remove metal comes "out of the system" in the form of heat, with approximately 3% of the energy left behind in the cut surface. In comparing cutting to grinding, only about 4% of the energy required to grind "leaves the system" with chips; about 12% is absorbed by the grinding grit; and the remainder, about 84%, is left behind in the ground surface. This high energy retention in the workpiece in grinding is further evidence of the need for relatively high lubrication in grinding to prevent heat generation and of the need for only enough cooling to prevent heat buildup in the part.

SELECTION OF GRINDING FLUIDS

Table 26-2 provides general recommendations for selecting a grinding fluid for specific workpiece materials.

A current trend in manufacturing is to attempt to minimize the number of fluids in use in a plant. This is normally done by selecting heavy-duty fluids which have broad-range capabilities; i.e., they are compatible with many work materials. When used at low concentrations (2-4%), they function as light-duty fluids; at medium concentrations (4-8%), the same fluids function as general-purpose fluids; and at high concentrations (10-20%), they function as heavy-duty fluids. The advantages of using one or two fluids in this manner is obvious: fewer materials need to be purchased and fewer inventory, control, and waste-treatment disposal procedures need to be developed.

TABLE 26-2
Grinding Fluid Recommendations*

Work Materials	Thread, Gear, Form Grind	Centerless, Cylindrical	Internal	Surface	Abrasive Cutoff	Hone**
Free-Machining Steel (low-medium carbon)	MD oil, HD water	LD oil, M-HD water miscible	GP water miscible	LD-GP water miscible	Water miscible	LD oil, spec. fluids
Low-Alloy Structural Steel (martensitic)	HD oil, HD water miscible	HE oil, HD water miscible	LD oil, water miscible	GP water miscible	Water miscible	LD oil, spec. fluids

GRINDING FLUIDS

TABLE 26-2—*Continued*
Grinding Fluid Recommendations*

Work Materials	Thread, Gear, Form Grind	Centerless, Cylindrical	Internal	Surface	Abrasive Cutoff	Hone**
Hot-Work Die Steels (martensitic) Stainless Steels (austenitic, martensitic, precipitation hardening) maraging steels nickel & cobalt alloys	HD oil, HD water miscible	HD water miscible	GP oil, GP water miscible	HD water miscible	Water miscible	LD oil, spec. fluids
Cast Iron	HD water miscible	GP water miscible	GP water miscible	GP water miscible	Water miscible	LD oil, spec. fluids
Magnesium & Alloys	LD oil, spec. fluids	LD oil, spec. fluids	LD oil, spec. fluids	LD oil, spec. fluids	LD oil, spec. fluids	LD oil, spec. fluids
Aluminum & Alloys	HD water miscible	HD water miscible	HD water miscible	HD water miscible	HD water miscible	LD oil, spec. fluids
Copper & Alloys	HD water, miscible	LD oil, HD water miscible	LD oil, HD water miscible	LD oil, HD water miscible	HD water miscible	LD oil, spec. fluids
Titanium & Alloys	HD water miscible	HD water miscible	HD water miscible	HD water miscible	HD water miscible	LD oil, spec. fluids
Beryllium & Alloys	HD water miscible	HD water miscible, spec. fluids	HD water miscible, spec. fluids	HD water miscible, spec. fluids	Water miscible	LD oil, spec. fluids
Refractories	HD oil	HD oil, HD water miscible	HD oil, HD water miscible	HD oil, HD water miscible	HD oil, HD water miscible	LD oil

* HD = Heavy-duty; GP = General-purpose; LD = Light-duty; MD = Medium-duty.
** Some honing is now being successfully done using heavy-duty, water-miscible fluids and honing stones specifically designed for use with water which incorporate cubic boron nitride abrasives. This application is so sufficiently new that general recommendations can not yet be made.

GRINDING MACHINES AND FIXTURES

A major factor in the metal removal performance of the latest generation of grinders is the trend toward increased grinding wheel peripheral speeds. This development has made possible significant improvements in productivity, with reductions in machining costs.

Over the past decade, grinding machine builders have introduced a wide variety of new machine control features aimed at boosting the operating performance and overall productivity of new grinders. These new control features are generally classified as one of two different types: (1) machine controls designed to control grinding process variables, such as speed, infeed pressure or workspeed, in response to changes in the grinding operation and (2) machine controls designed to control positioning or "tool path."

The latest generation of electronically controlled grinders feature "canned cycles" to assist in programming—a convenience that speeds programming and helps eliminate costly programming errors.

In the future, grinding machines will feature increased capability due to still more sophisticated controls. Advances are expected to be made in both tool positioning and the controlling of the physical process of grinding. It is expected that control capabilities now found only on NC lathes, machining centers, and sophisticated milling machines will carry over and be available on grinders as well. This phenomenon is evidenced by the fact that some machine builders are now offering equivalent grinding machines that closely resemble, with respect to controls, certain machining centers and turning machines in their product line.

SURFACE GRINDING

Surface grinders are used to produce high-quality flat surfaces on workpieces. Peripheral surface grinders with horizontal spindles use the periphery of the grinding wheel to impart a flat surface to the workpiece. Vertical-spindle grinders use the face of cup, cylinder, disc, or segmental wheels to produce a flat surface. Workpiece motion relative to the grinding wheel during the grinding process on horizontal-spindle (peripheral) surface grinders and vertical-spindle (wheel-face) grinders can be either traverse or rotary, as illustrated in Fig. 26-9.

Disc grinding is often thought of as a special type of wheel-face grinding that utilizes a broad contact of the face area of the wheel during grinding. As illustrated in Fig. 26-10, in disc grinding, the contact area between the grinding disc and workpiece is relatively large in comparison with conventional wheel-face grinding in which the contact area is significantly less.

In general, peripheral grinders are used in high-precision operations in which control of size and geometry is more important than heavy stock removal. The fine, straight-line pattern produced by peripheral grinding is desirable for certain products, such as sliding bearing parts. Some newer peripheral grinders equipped with grinding wheels from 32-36" (810-915 mm) diam and drive motors up to 125 hp (93 kW) can be used to effect stock removal rates comparable to those of high-performance wheel-face grinders.

Horizontal-Spindle Surface Grinders (Peripheral)

Typical applications for horizontal-spindle surface grinders include:

- Plain, flat surfaces—continuous or interrupted.
- Taper grinding—workpiece supported at an angle to produce an inclined flat surface.
- Angular grinding—parallel flat surfaces at different angles of inclination.
- Slots in a common plane.
- Flat surfaces next to a shoulder.
- Flat surfaces positioned around the periphery of a workpiece.
- Flat, recessed surfaces in different orientations on the face of the part.
- Straight surfaces with several cross-sectional elements of regular form.
- Straight, flat surfaces with special profiles.
- Single-plane, flat surfaces in controlled locations.
- Flat surfaces in several parallel or related planes.

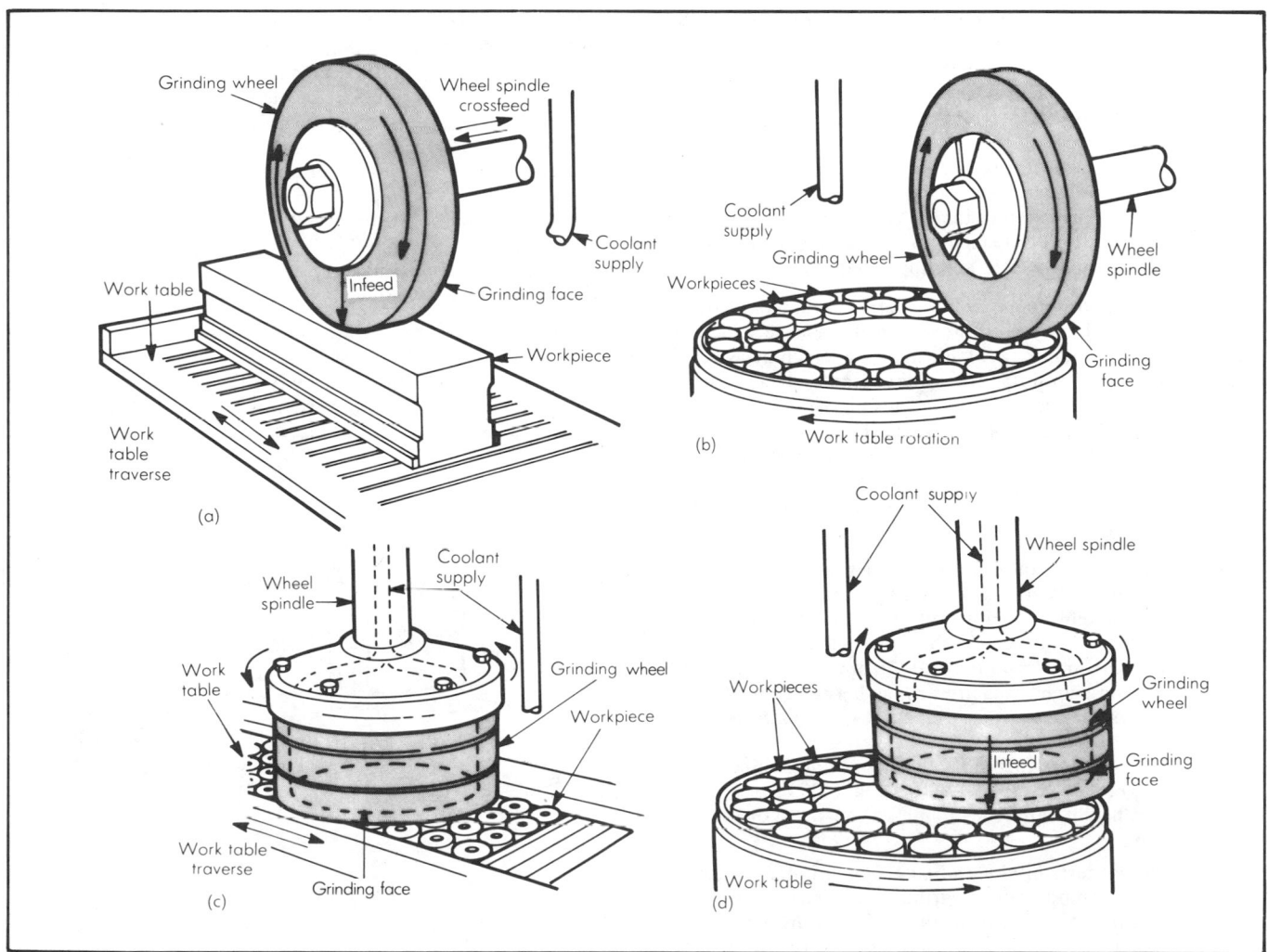

Fig. 26-9 (a) Periphery grinding—traverse workpiece motion, (b) Periphery grinding—rotary workpiece motion, (c) Wheel-face grinding—traverse workpiece motion, (d) Wheel-face grinding—rotary workpiece motion.

GRINDING MACHINES AND FIXTURES

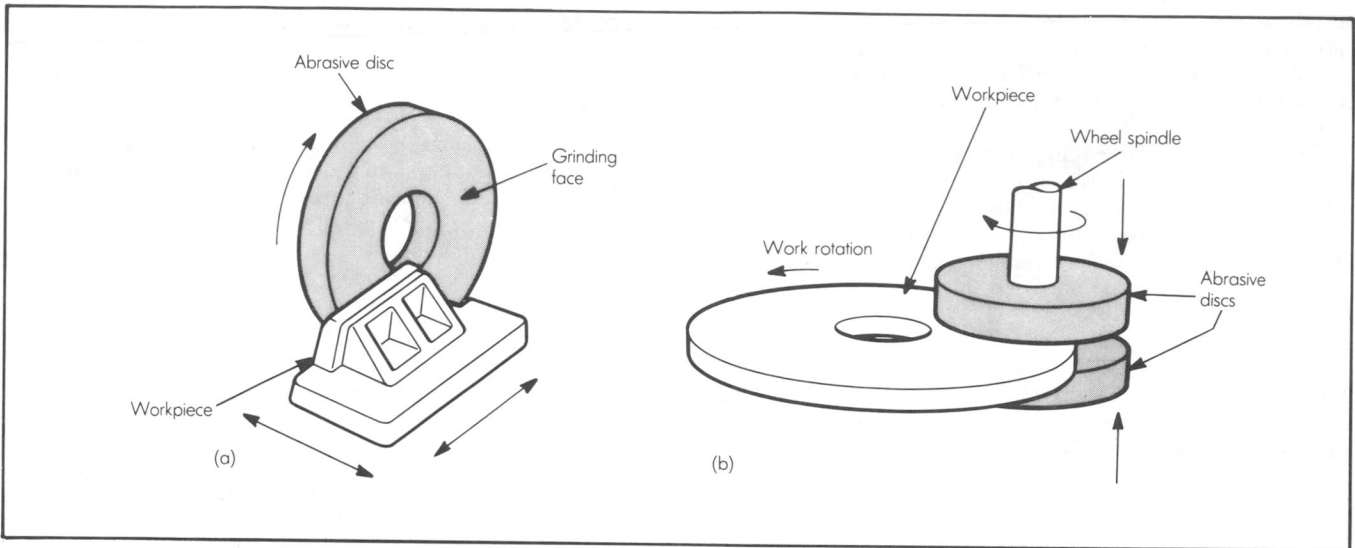

Fig. 26-10 (a) Single-disc grinding, (b) Double-disc grinding.

Light-duty, horizontal-spindle surface grinders. Many light-duty horizontal-spindle surface grinders are well suited for both toolroom and production applications. Within this class of grinders, numerous accessories are available to provide increased versatility required for toolroom and production jobs.

Light-duty, horizontal-spindle surface grinders are available in a variety of configurations, including hand feed, single axis with powered longitudinal table, two axis with powered longitudinal table and crossfeed, and three axis with powered longitudinal table, crossfeed, and downfeed.

Medium-duty, horizontal-spindle surface grinders. Production grinders of this class are used to grind a wide variety of workpiece sizes. Figure 26-11 illustrates a machine which is typical of the medium-duty, horizontal-spindle surface grinder in use today for production applications.

Within this class of grinders, worktable capacities usually range between 12-24" (300-610 mm) in width, 40-170" (1.02-4.31 m) in length, and 16-36" (400-910 mm) in table height. Grinding wheels up to about 20" (510 mm) diam, varying in widths from 3-6" (75-150 mm), are used on these machines.

Heavy-duty, horizontal-spindle surface grinders. Peripheral surface grinders within this class are used to grind large workpieces that require significant stock removal with high accuracy and good surface finish. Table capacities of these machines range from 24 x 60"(610 x 1520 mm) to 36 x 120" (910 x 3050 mm), and height capacities range between 25-36" (630-910 mm). Horsepower of these machines is usually between 30-50 hp (22-37 kW).

The largest horizontal-spindle surface grinders in common use are equipped with tables up to 42 x 240" (1 x 6 m) in capacity, and height capacities to 40" (about 1 m) or more in some cases.

Rotary-table, horizontal-spindle surface grinders. Rotary-table, horizontal-spindle surface grinders are generally used for precision grinding of small to medium-sized workpieces. The grinding wheel rotates about a horizontal axis while the workpiece(s) is revolved about a vertical axis. The grinding wheel spindle is on a wheel slide which is traversed across the work. Metal removal rate is established by the amount of downfeed of the wheel per revolution of the table. Some machines can be set up to change downfeed increments automatically from rough to fine feed at a point between 0.001-0.005" (0.03-0.13 mm) from finish size.

Wide-angle corner or concave-conical surfaces can be generated on rotary-table, horizontal-spindle surface grinders by swiveling the workpiece chuck about a horizontal axis which is tangent to the table. Figure 26-12 shows how these surfaces are generated.

Rotary-table surface grinding is used in a variety of applications including:

- Round thin parts with flat surfaces.
- Round thin parts, such as saw blades, that must be ground with slight concavity to relieve the center of the tool from the cutting periphery.

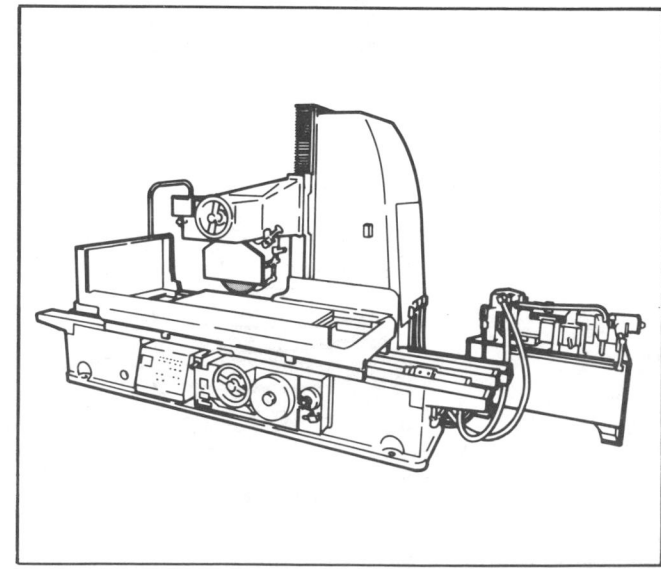

Fig. 26-11 Medium-duty, horizontal-spindle surface grinder for production. (*Hill Acme Co.*)

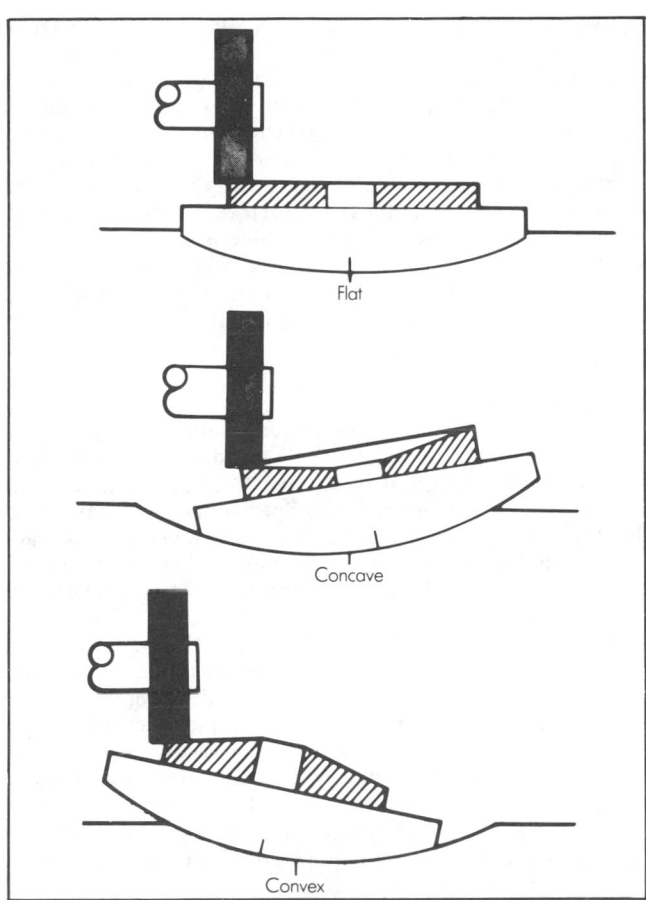

Fig. 26-12 Flat, concave, or corner surfaces generated on a rotary-table, horizontal-spindle surface grinder by tilting the workpiece fixture relative to the table. (*Heald Machine Div., Cincinnati Milacron, Inc.*)

- Annular shoulders around an extending hub.
- Medium-sized workpieces in batched production.

Vertical-Spindle Surface Grinders (Wheel Face)

Surface grinding on a vertical-spindle machine (wheel-face grinding) is accomplished by grinding with the face of a cup, cylinder, or segmental-shaped wheel. Grinding machines of this type are available in a wide range of sizes and configurations to suit surface grinding requirements of nearly any small to moderately large workpiece. The following sections discuss some of the more common types of wheel-face surface grinders.

Vertical-spindle surface grinders with reciprocating tables. The self-dressing characteristics inherent in vertical-spindle grinding, coupled with the consistent cross-hatch pattern produced by the grinder, make this method of grinding desirable for flat grinding certain high-precision workpieces. Although highly accurate size control and high-quality surface finish are not usually the primary objective of most vertical-spindle surface grinders, some are designed for unusually close-tolerance work for which surface finish and flatness are highly critical. These high-precision surface grinders are normally employed in the processing of relatively small workpieces and may be equipped with either a rotary table or reciprocating table.

Rotary-table, vertical-spindle surface grinders. Normally, grinding machines of this class are used in production applications involving significant stock removal. Some large machines can remove 0.25-0.5" (6.3-12.7 mm) of metal from castings in a single pass. The machines are available in a wide range of sizes and are equipped with cylinder or segmental wheels. Flatness and parallelism is obtainable to 0.0002" (0.005 mm) depending upon the size and rigidity of the machine. Size-holding capability is usually on the order of 0.0005-0.001" (0.013-0.03 mm).

Multiple-head, rotary-table, vertical-spindle surface grinders. Machines of this class are similar to machines discussed in the previous section except that they are equipped with two, three, four, or five vertical spindles. On most two-spindle models, the spindles are mounted on peripheral columns; three, four, and five-spindle models usually are equipped with the spindle mounted on a center column. Sequential rough grinding, intermediate grinding, and finish grinding operations can be performed on a single machine equipped with wheels of various sizes and grades operating at various speeds. Figure 26-13 illustrates an example of this class of grinder—a five-spindle, rotary-table surface grinder for the processing of small to moderate-sized workpieces.

Multiple-head, index-table surface grinders. In contrast to rotary-table grinders which operate with continuous rotating table motion, index-table grinders feature multiple indexing positions, usually four positions 90° apart, that allow one station to be loaded and unloaded while the remaining stations are used to perform various sequential grinding operations. This machine design is particularly effective for production grinding of parts which require more unloading and loading time than available with continuous rotary-table machines.

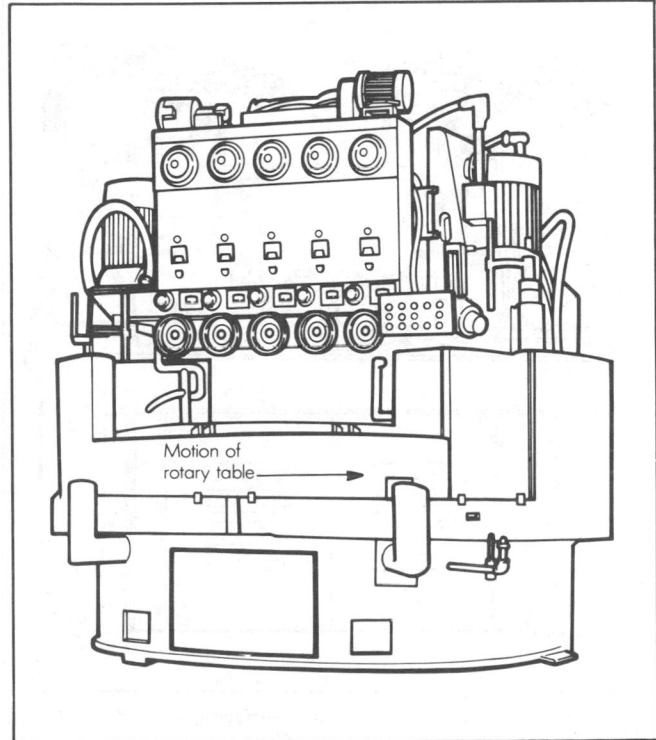

Fig. 26-13 Five-spindle, rotary-table, surface grinder.

GRINDING MACHINES AND FIXTURES

The machine illustrated in Fig. 26-14 is typical of the indexing-type, rotary-table, vertical-spindle surface grinder in use today. The index table is available with either four or eight workholding spindles that can handle small or medium-sized workpieces. Spindles are mounted on either two or three columns, usually with one or two spindles per column. Turning, boring, or honing can be performed by substituting special tool heads for grinding heads at one or more stations.

Oscillating-wheel surface grinders. A variation of the vertical-spindle surface grinder, somewhat like a reciprocating-table grinder in function, is the oscillating-wheel surface grinder. Machines of this class differ from reciprocating-table, vertical-spindle grinders in that relative motion between the grinding wheel and workpiece is along a circular arc instead of a straight line and relative motion between the grinding wheel and workpiece is brought about by the oscillation of the wheelhead column about a fixed vertical axis. In this way, the work remains stationary while the grinding wheel is traversed across the workpiece along a circular path.

Horizontal-spindle, wheel-face surface grinders. Machines of this type are similar to horizontal-spindle milling machines in the way in which the wheel is traversed across the workpiece. These machines use either a reciprocating table or a traveling wheelhead configuration to effect relative motion between the wheel and workpiece. Horizontal-spindle machines are used to grind workpieces that are more easily handled and are less prone to deflection when fixtured on a vertical table. Often very large, difficult-to-handle workpieces are ground in this way.

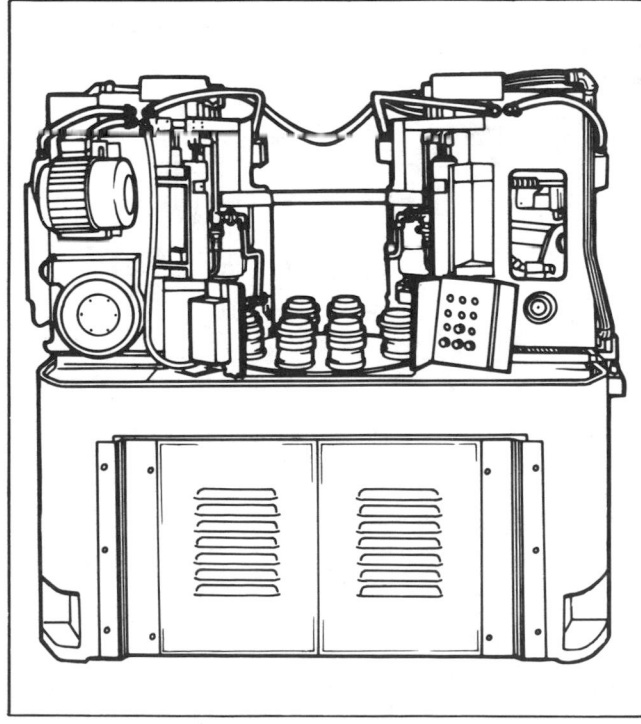

Fig. 26-14 Multiple-head, index-table surface grinder. (*New Britain Machine Div., Litton Industries*)

Throughfeed wheel-face grinders. A relatively new variation of wheel-face grinders, throughfeed grinders use continuous conveyor feed in the surface grinding of relatively small workpieces. As shown in Fig. 26-15, the typical throughfeed grinding system consists of a vertical-spindle grinding wheel mounted over a continuous-feeding conveyor belt. A variable-power, electromagnetic table serves as the machine table, magnetic chuck, and locating surface. A conveyor belt supported by the electromagnetic table is used to transport workpieces under the grinding wheel. Adjustable guide rails position parts on the conveyor and absorb the horizontal force, or side thrust, created by the grinding action. Air gages compensate for wheel wear.

Disc Grinders

A simple description of disc surface grinding is grinding with the face of an abrasive disc. Single-spindle disc grinders and double-spindle disc grinders (see Fig. 26-10) are manufactured in vertical and horizontal types. Special machines have been built with three or four spindles. Some machines are manufactured with the head and related disc mounted on an adjustment device, enabling the head attitude to be varied to meet special requirements.

Modern disc grinders are among the most efficient machines available for generating flat surfaces to close tolerances and fine finishes at high production rates. Thousands of abrasive grains contact the work simultaneously, thus rapidly developing the entire surface to the size and finish required. Flat surfaces generated by disc grinding are generally flatter than those produced by the periphery of a wheel and often eliminate or minimize the need for subsequent lapping. Many surfaces ground in this way do not require gaskets or sealants between mating surfaces to prevent leaks.

For parts with opposed flat surfaces, double-disc grinders provide the best and most economical method of grinding flat, smooth surfaces to precise tolerances with respect to parallelism and overall size (thickness or length). Grinding two sides of a part simultaneously also results in profitable production because of the low cost per part.

Vertical-spindle, single-disc grinders. Currently the indexing, rotating fixture is used exclusively on vertical-spindle, single-disc machines. This tooling concept has proved extremely successful on applications in which relatively high production is involved and optimum flatness on the surface being ground is an important criteria.

Double-disc grinders. A simple description of double-disc grinding is the grinding of two surfaces at the same time in one machine. On double-spindle machines, the two abrasive discs are opposed and the workpieces are fed between the discs to grind parallel surfaces simultaneously. Double-disc grinders are manufactured in both vertical and horizontal types. As in the case of single-disc machines, double-disc machines are also manufactured with the heads either set at a prescribed angle or mounted on adjustable devices allowing them to be inclined as required (see Fig. 26-16). Double-disc grinders are also provided with the heads offset. The degree of offset involved varies according to the type of work being delivered to the machine. In general, the majority of double-disc grinders are involved with workpieces for which equal or semiequal metal removal is required on two parallel, external surfaces.

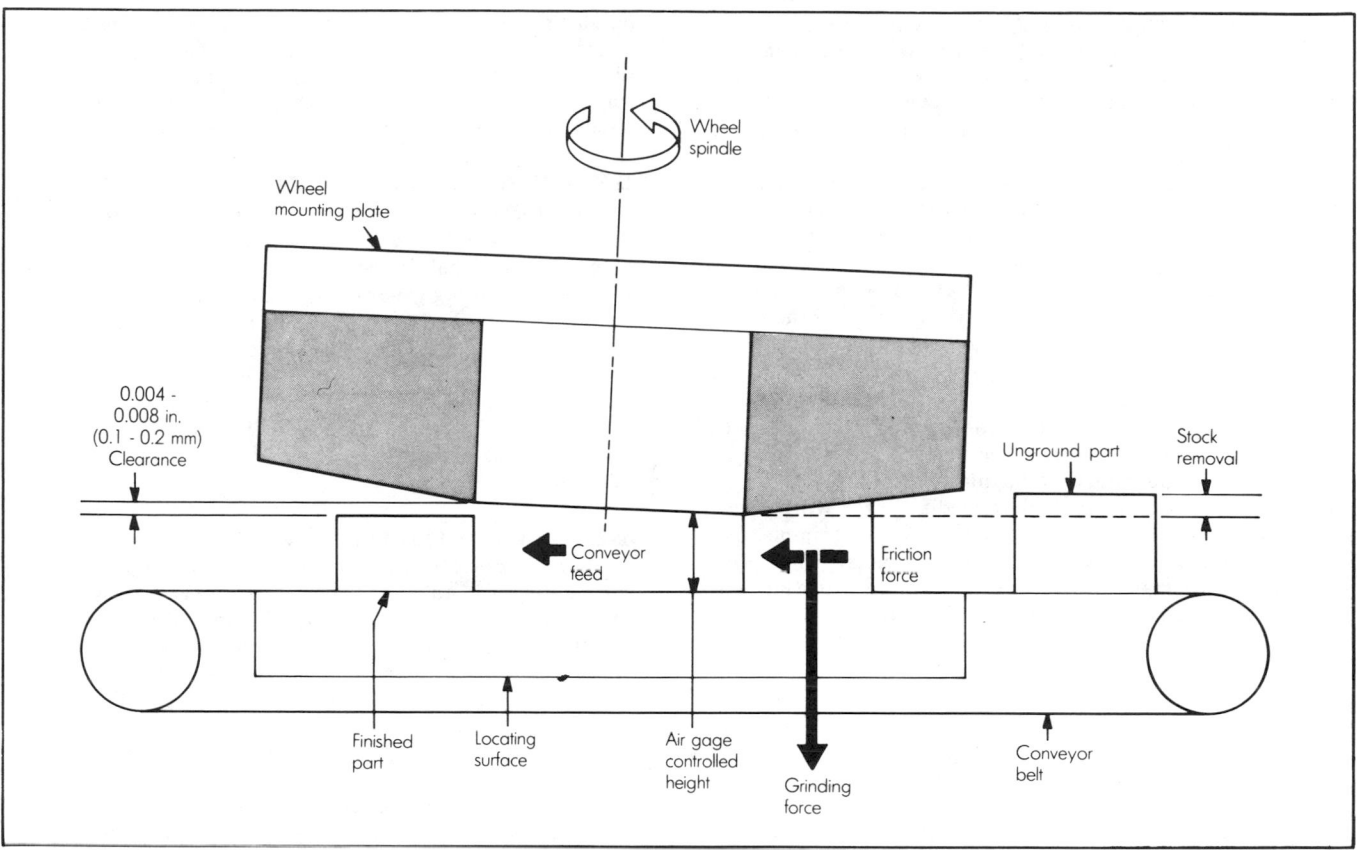

Fig. 26-15 The concept of throughfeed grinding. (*Speedfam*)

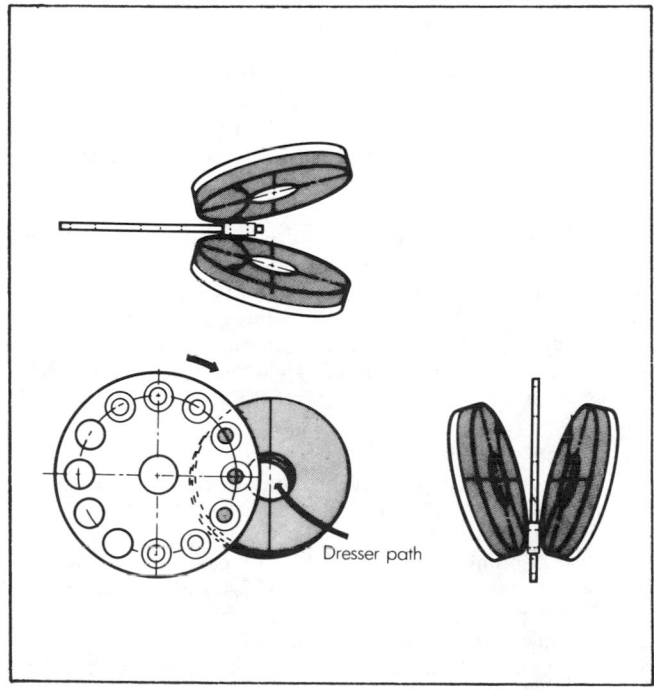

Fig. 26-16 Compound head setting for progressive grinding with a rotary carrier consisting of tilting discs together at their front and bottom edges. (*Gardner Machine Co.*)

WORKHOLDING METHODS IN SURFACE GRINDING

Magnetic chucks, vacuum chucks, and vises are commonly used workholding devices for surface grinding operations. In addition, special surface grinding fixtures which may or may not include a magnetic chuck or vacuum chuck as a major component are sometimes used to hold nonmagnetic workpieces or irregularly shaped parts. Many high-speed, high-production operations require specially designed surface grinding fixtures such as these.

Magnetic Chucks

For horizontal-spindle surface grinders and some vertical-spindle surface grinders, magnetic chucks are usually rectangular in configuration and are available in a wide variety of standard and special sizes up to about 3.5 x 8 ft (1 x 2.5 m). Circular magnetic chucks are used on many rotary-table, vertical and horizontal surface grinders. V-block chucks and other magnetic chucks with special shapes are used in some applications.

Types of magnetic chucks. There are three basic types of magnetic chucks: electromagnetic, permanent magnet, and electrically energized permanent magnet chucks.

Electromagnetic chucks. Most magnetic chucks are electromagnetic. Electric power, usually d-c, is supplied to the chuck during the grinding operation, then switched off to release the workpiece for unloading.

GRINDING MACHINES AND FIXTURES

Permanent magnet chucks. Magnetic chucks of permanent magnet design are heavily used and are available in small and medium sizes. Available as a solid base or swivel design, these chucks operate without electric supply and are turned "off" and "on" through use of a manually operated mechanical switching device.

Electrically energized permanent magnet chucks. A variation of magnetic chucks combines the electromagnet and permanent magnet. This hybrid design requires an initial pulse of current to activate the permanent magnet and a current impulse of opposite polarity to deactivate the chuck. The advantage of this type of chuck is that a loss of electrical power to the chuck during grinding will not cause loss of holding power.

Vacuum Chucks

A vacuum chuck is similar in configuration to a magnetic chuck except that the holding force is developed by a vacuum instead of magnetic attraction. Vacuum chucks are used to hold magnetic or nonmagnetic, small to medium-sized workpieces.

The principle operation of a vacuum chuck is simple. The face of the chuck is constructed with multiple air-entry ports (holes or porous material), and a vacuum pump is used to suck air through these ports. When a workpiece is placed on the face of the chuck, atmospheric pressure on the workpiece holds the part firmly against the chuck face.

Pin-hole chucks. These vacuum chucks are the simplest in design—a metal box with a pattern of small drilled holes in the top plate.

Grooved-plate chucks. Usually used for round vacuum chucks, this design employs a series of concentric grooves on the face of the chuck. Each groove features at least one porthole to the vacuum chamber.

Porous-plate chucks. Some very thin or extremely fragile workpieces tend to deform when held on a conventional pin-hole vacuum chuck; the workpiece material is pulled into the portholes. Also, some very small workpieces may cock or be otherwise dislocated by grooves or portholes in the face of a conventional vacuum chuck. In these cases, a vacuum chuck equipped with a porous ceramic chuck face can be used. However, experience has shown that some special masking problems can develop when using porous-plate chucks.

Rotary chucks. Rotary vacuum chucks are used for workholding in both rotary-table surface grinding and cylindrical grinding applications. These chucks may be designed with pin-hole plates, porous plates, grooved plates, or other configurations. (In cylindrical grinding, these chucks are used as faceplate holding fixtures.) In horizontal surface grinding, rotary chucks are used on Blanchard-type machines for multiple part grinding.

Special vacuum chucks. When extremely thin workpieces are to be ground, vacuum chucks with specially designed faceplates are used. The faceplate of the chuck usually features recessed areas that fit exactly the contour of the workpieces. Often, these special vacuum chucks use porous ceramic inserts in the counterbores to provide the vacuum surface for holding. Parts as thin as 0.007" (0.18 mm) have been ground in this way. These special vacuum chucks are mounted on reciprocating-table and rotary-table, horizontal and vertical surface grinders.

Precision Grinding Vises

Special vises used for workholding of relatively small workpieces feature accuracy to about 0.0002" (0.005 mm) in parallelism and squareness of the holding surfaces. These special vises, called grinding vises, may feature a swivel base or tilt adjustment. Some special fixtures used for surface grinding employ modified standard vises as components. These are discussed later in this chapter.

CYLINDRICAL GRINDING

Cylindrical grinding is performed to remove stock, create precise geometry, and obtain desired surface finishes on external or internal surfaces of round workpieces. The term cylindrical grinding generally refers to outside diameter (OD) grinding. Internal grinding generally is the term used to refer to the grinding of the internal surfaces, or internal diameter (ID), of workpieces. These surfaces (OD or ID) are usually cylinders, shoulders, or tapers, but they may include fillets, grooves, or other formed surfaces of revolution. This section describes the various types of internal and external cylindrical grinders used in metalworking today.

Manual vs. Automatic Grinding

Manually operated machines will not move or perform their various functions unless the operator moves each machine unit. Even if some type of mechanical or hydraulic servomechanism is supplied for the wheelhead infeed or power-table traverse, the machine is still considered a manual machine.

Semiautomatic machines will perform one complete cycle of operation automatically and then stop. This means that the machine must still be operator attended, with the operator responsible for each cycle of operation. However, in order for the machine to cycle independently, it must be equipped with some type of automatic infeed mechanism. Single or multiple rates of infeed can be obtained. When units such as these are supplied, the wheelhead will also rapidly traverse to and from the workpiece.

Automatic machines are similar to semiautomatic machines with a few exceptions. To be fully automatic, the machine must have some type of automatic device to load the workpiece, and if gage sizing is used, then an automatic jump-on gage must replace the hand-caliper gage. Limit switches and detection devices are used on automatic machine setups to determine the location of parts to be ground in relation to the grinding wheel area.

Fully automatic machines require no permanent operator attendance. They are capable of handling parts as they come to the machining area, orienting these parts if necessary, automatically loading them into the machine, grinding them to size, and unloading them. Machines such as these also stop cycling if no parts are present in the loading chutes, or if the unloading chutes are jammed.

Traverse vs. Plunge Grinding

In cylindrical grinding, the grinding wheel can feed into the workpiece using one of several techniques. A comparison of plunge and traverse grinding is illustrated in Fig. 26-17. Traverse grinding up to a shoulder or other obstruction, as shown in views *a* and *b*, produces a series of reverse arcs or cross-hatch patterns, as in view *c*, which could be objectionable, for example, on a thrust-bearing surface. An improvement would be to use a dished wheel or a wheelhead set at an angle, as shown in view *d*. A still better method is to plunge grind the journal and face simultaneously, as shown in view *e*, having the wheel set at an angle of 20-30°.

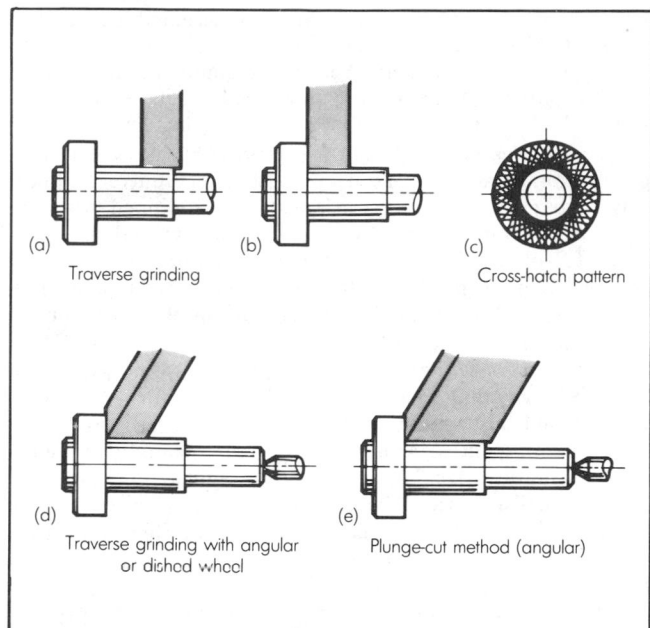

Fig. 26-17 Comparison of traverse and plunge grinding.

External Cylindrical Grinders (OD Grinders)

There are three principal external cylindrical-grinding techniques. In the first technique, the part is captured between two centers as the grinding wheel removes stock. This technique is called center-type cylindrical or OD grinding. In the second technique, the workpiece is held securely in a fixture mounted on a rotating spindle in a workhead; this technique is called chuck grinding. In the third technique, the work is ground while it is supported on shoes or a fixed blade and regulating wheel. Since no centers are required in this process, it is called centerless grinding.

The three techniques cited are distinguished by the method in which the workpiece is constrained. In operational parameters, such as wheel speed, work speed, feed rates, and fluid application, the methods are quite similar. Conceptual views of the various types of external cylindrical-grinding methods are presented in Fig. 26-18. Table 26-3 lists general tolerance-holding capabilities of cylindrical grinders.

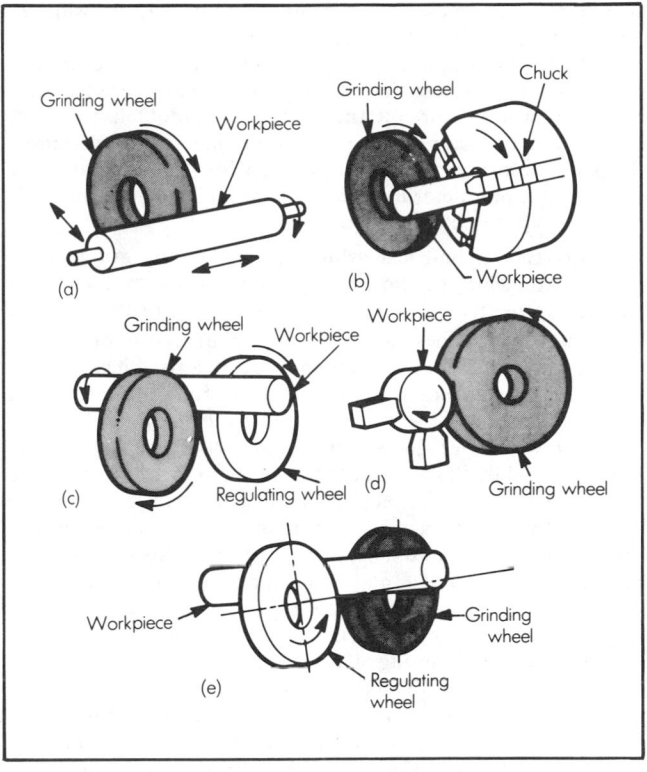

Fig. 26-18 Cylindrical grinding: (a) between centers, (b) chucking type, (c) centerless, (d) shoe-type centerless, (e) throughfeed centerless (Reprinted with modifications from *Metalcutting: Today's Techniques for Engineers and Shop Personnel*, **McGraw-Hill Publications Co., 1979, p.164.)**

Selecting center-type or centerless grinding. The several different methods of center-type and centerless grinding must be considered in choosing between the two. Center-type grinding methods include plunge and traverse grinding, while centerless grinding methods include infeed and throughfeed grinding. Throughfeed grinding on a centerless machine is not quite the same as traverse grinding on a center-type machine. In throughfeed grinding on a centerless machine, the length of

TABLE 26-3
Capabilities of Cylindrical Grinding

Dimensional Characteristics	Optimum Tolerance Limits, μ in. (μ m)		
	Regular Cylindrical Grinding	Precision Cylindrical Grinding	High-Precision Cylindrical Grinding
Size holding (diameter)	50 (1.27)	25 (0.635)	10 (0.25)
Geometric accuracy (straightness, roundness, etc.)	75 (1.9)	25 (0.635)	6-10 (0.15-0.25)
Surface finish, AA (R_A)	8 (0.2)	2-4 (0.05-0.1)	1-2 (0.025-0.05)

Source: Francis T. Farago, *Abrasive Engineering Methods,* Vol. I, (New York: Industrial Press Inc., 1976).

GRINDING MACHINES AND FIXTURES

surface to be ground can be shorter or longer than the width of the grinding wheel on the machine.

There are advantages to both center-type and centerless grinding. The first decision in the selection of either method is based on whether or not the workpiece should have center holes. To the process engineer or the engineer who is designing the part, this may be a rather costly decision. In many cases, the design of the part determines whether or not it can be ground on a center-type or centerless machine.

Center-type cylindrical grinders. Center-type grinders are machines on which the workpiece is rotated between centers, on backrests, steadyrests, or journal rests, or held in some type of clamping device. These machines consist primarily of a bed, a wheelhead (which may or may not swivel), a workhead (which also may or may not swivel), and a tailstock mounted on a swivel table which in turn is mounted on a sliding table.

As shown in Fig. 26-19, center-type grinding machines are characterized by the workpiece being held between centers. On these machines, externally ground work can be no more accurate than the location and geometry of the work centers of both the workpiece and the machine. Stress in the machine and machine alignment also play important roles in accuracy.

Roll grinders. Roll grinders are a special class of extra-heavy, plain, center-type cylindrical grinding machines used for accurate external grinding of large workpieces such as steel mill rolls which require crowning.

Types of roll-grinding machines. To meet the many procedures and wide range of roll lengths and diameters, roll-grinding machines are made in several types. One type has a traveling table and a stationary, single-wheel, grinding head. The table carries the roll and the roll-driving and supporting equipment. This type of machine is generally used for small-diameter and short-length rolls and is somewhat similar to a conventional cylindrical grinder.

A second type of machine, the most commonly used, has a traveling single wheel, with the roll and roll-driving and supporting equipment on a stationary bed. The grinding wheel is supported on a carriage that travels on a separate bed, usually attached to the roll bed. This type of grinding machine is

classified by the maximum-diameter roll accepted, usually 24-60″ (610-1520 mm) and larger.

A third type, which has been used almost exclusively to regrind paper-mill rolls, is a single-bed machine with two opposed wheels mounted on a traveling carriage.

Workhead and drive. With the exception of two-wheel, roll-grinding machines (which use a retractable or a universal-joint driving bar), roll-turning workheads are equipped with an equalizing wobbler mounted on the faceplate and used for accurate roll driving and to minimize minor errors in roll settings. To prevent lifting, the wobbler (with the two driving rollers) should be pulled by the pivots in the direction of roll rotation.

Tailstocks for roll grinders. With the exception of the two-wheel roll-grinding machine, a tailstock is furnished with longitudinal adjustment on the roll bed to accommodate a range of roll lengths. Adjustment is made manually or by an optional motor drive. When in position, rigid locking prevents slippage. Tailstocks are usually made in two sections so that the upper section can be transversely adjusted for alignment of its center with the workhead center. The spindle-mounted center may be either a dead or a live center.

Roll supports. Roll-supporting equipment is of two types. Two-wheel, paper-mill, roll-grinding machines use two cradle-type neck rests or journal supports, one under each roll neck. Each of these supports uses either two or three bearing blocks, two at equal angles below the horizontal centerline and, when three are used, the third one at the bottom of the vertical centerline. Supports are located on the centerline of the single bed and are manually adjusted longitudinally to accommodate various roll lengths. Journals and necks cannot be ground with this supporting equipment.

Crowning mechanism. Equipment for crowning or concaving roll bodies is, with few exceptions, built into the roll-grinding machine. This equipment is adjustable for both magnitude and contour of the crown.

Multiple-wheel grinding. High-production, OD, cylindrical grinding is normally done in a plunge-grinding cycle. Frequently, more than one surface on the workpiece must be ground at a time. Multiple-wheel mounts are used on both center-type and centerless plunge grinders for this purpose. On longer shafts with wide spreads of cylindrical surfaces that require finishing, a machine specifically designed for multiple-wheel mounting is desirable. Center-type cylindrical grinders of this type are now available with up to about 30″ (762 mm) of wheel span. Figure 26-20 illustrates a typical multiple-wheel machine. One operation that requires a multiple-wheel machine, and is common to both crankshafts and camshafts, is the grinding of main bearings.

Because the multiple-wheel grinder is a specialized machine for high production, it includes in its standard equipment an automatic wheel-trueing mechanism. This may include a trueing head for each wheel, or it may be arranged with a single trueing head that traverses the entire span of wheels. In the latter case, the trueing device is typically a roll with inset diamonds. As the trueing head traverses the wheels, it may be called upon to dress radii on the wheel corners as well as the straight faces. This requires a complex form bar which must have accurate contour, steps, and spacing for the wheels.

Chucking-type cylindrical grinders. Chucking grinders hold workpieces in a fixture (usually a chuck) mounted on a rotating spindle in a workhead. This type of cylindrical grinder is almost

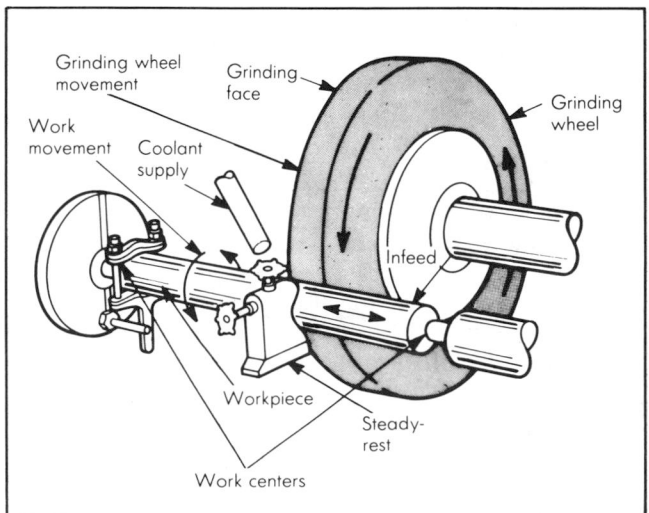

Fig. 26-19 Machine and work movements in OD, center-type cylindrical grinding.

GRINDING MACHINES AND FIXTURES

exactly the same as the shoe-type centerless machine (discussed later in this chapter) except that a collet, diaphragm, gear chuck, or other workholding device is mounted on the workhead instead of a magnetic chuck, drive-plate adapter, and shoe-support assembly. This basic difference makes the chucking grinder more versatile since it can accommodate a wide variety of part configurations. However, both chucking and shoe-type centerless work can be done on the same machine provided both sets of tooling are supplied.

General-purpose chucking-type grinders. Chucking grinders are widely used to finish external cylindrical surfaces on relatively short parts having no convenient surface for driving. They are also widely used when providing center holes in the part is impractical or impossible. When the machine is provided with automatic chucks and loaders, it becomes an extremely productive cylindrical grinder ideally suited to the finishing of screw machine parts as well as to the grinding of automobile engine valve seats.

Special chucking-type external cylindrical grinders—crankpin grinders. A major finishing operation on crankshafts is the external cylindrical grinding of crankpins. Pins on crankshafts are a series of short cylindrical bearing surfaces which are eccentric from the centerline of the shaft. They are angularly displaced from each other to create a series of throws for the attachment of connecting rods, which are pinned to the pistons in a reciprocating engine or compressor. Crankpins, therefore, are bearing surfaces which must have precisely controlled geometry in order to operate with a long life, at high speeds, and under rapidly fluctuating heavy loads.

Centerless cylindrical grinders. Centerless grinding is different from center-type grinding in that the workpiece is not held physically in place while it is being ground. Instead, it rests on a workrest blade and is backed up by a regulating wheel. Machines such as these consist primarily of a bed, a wheelhead, upper and lower slides, and a regulating wheel

housing. Centerless machines are built in various sizes; however, unlike the center-type machines, they all operate the same way. Also, they all can be used for either toolroom or high-production grinding.

Centerless grinding eliminates the need for workpiece center holes, drivers, or workhead fixtures that are required in the other two cylindrical-grinding methods—center-type and chucking-type. Much of the tooling for the job is acomplished in the trueing of the grinding and regulating wheels, and some capability exists for additional fixturing in the steadyrest geometry and the work stops and supports.

In centerless grinding, the grinding wheel drives the workpiece while the regulating wheel controls the work speed. The regulating wheel must have sufficient friction to prevent the workpiece from running away with the grinding wheel. The grinding wheel, regulating wheel, and work rest are placed in a way so that the workpiece is constrained at all times. In the axial direction, the work is held by special stops, by an adjacent workpiece, or by friction in the axial direction produced by the regulating wheel. This makes centerless grinding amenable to both long bars and short cylindrical pieces which can be stacked next to each other. Examples of the former are ground bar stock and tubing; examples of the latter are ball-bearing races and automobile engine piston pins.

Theory of centerless grinding. The three elements of a centerless grinder—the grinding wheel, regulating wheel, and workrest are illustrated in Fig. 26-21.

The work lies between the two wheels—a grinding wheel of the correct size to fit the machine and of specifications appropriate to the material and nature of the work and a regulating wheel. The regulating wheel serves as both a driving wheel and a brake, rotating the work at a constant surface speed equal to that of the regulating wheel.

The workrest blade, which supports the work between the two wheels, is adjustable to raise or lower the center of the work in relation to the centerline of the grinding wheel and the regulating wheel. When the work is to be ground cylindrically, the workrest blade height is usually adjusted to raise the center of the work above the centerline of the wheels an amount equal to 50% of the work diameter on small-diameter parts and to

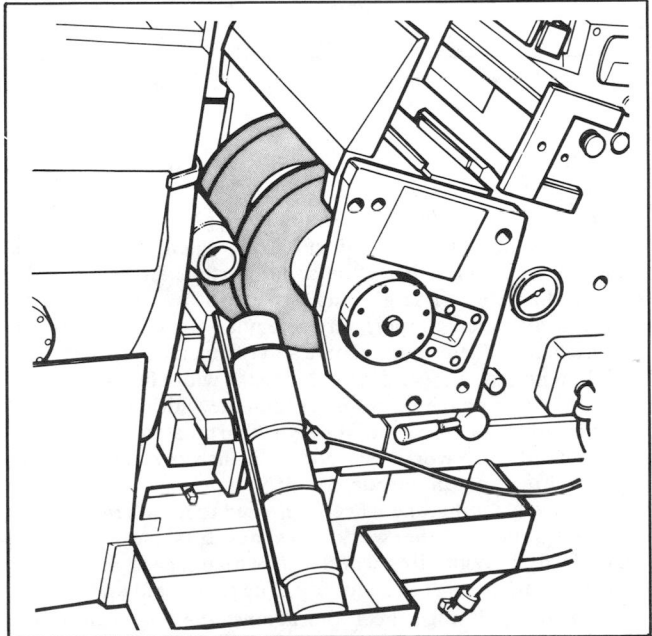

Fig. 26-20 Typical OD, multiple-wheel grinding machine. (*Bryant*)

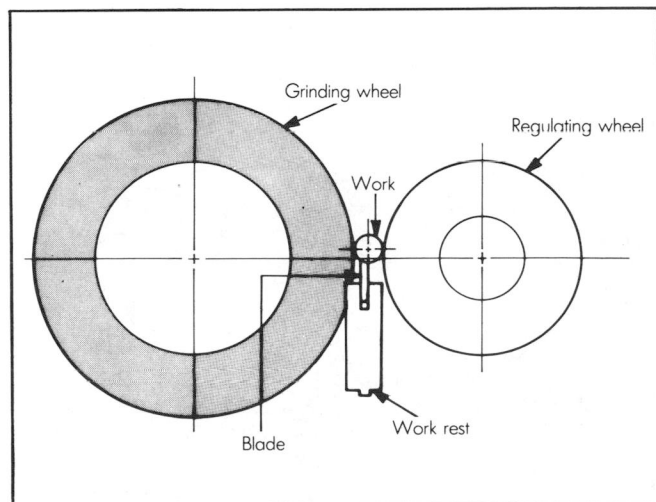

Fig. 26-21 Wheel and work movements in centerless cylindrical grinding.

GRINDING MACHINES AND FIXTURES

1/2" (12.7 mm) maximum for work over 1" (25.4 mm) diam. The distance between the grinding wheel and the regulating wheel controls the diameter of the work; the height of the center of the work in relation to the centerline of the wheels controls the roundness of the work.

When the center of the work is raised above the centerline of the wheels by raising the workrest blade; any high spot on the work coming in contact with the regulating wheel pushes the work into the grinding wheel, creating a low, but not diametrically opposite, spot. As the work is rotated, the high and low spots do not occur opposite each other as they do when the center of the work is on the centerline of the wheels. Instead, a gradual rounding takes place. Maximum rounding action occurs when an angled blade is used, as shown in Fig. 26-22.

Most centerless grinding is done with an angled-top blade. The angle of the blade should be varied to match the diameter of the work. The larger the work diameter or the longer the blade, the flatter the blade angle. Smaller diameter work requires a steeper blade angle. By using the steeper blade angle, more pressure is put on the regulating wheel, giving it more control of the rotating speed of the work. This prevents the work from picking up the speed of the grinding wheel. However, this also increases the side pressure on the workrest blade, and especially on narrow workrest blades. Too steep an angle can cause the blade to deflect under the pressure, thus developing chatter. For work 1/2" (13 mm) diam or larger, a blade angle of 20-30° is generally satisfactory.

Throughfeed grinding. Throughfeed grinding is performed by passing the workpiece between the grinding wheel and the regulating wheel, with a lateral or axial movement of the work past the grinding wheel as shown in Fig. 26-23. The speed, diameter, and angle of inclination of the regulating wheel determine the work traverse rate. This traverse rate can be approximated by multiplying the diameter of the regulating wheel by 3.14 times the rpm of the feed wheel, times the sine of the angle of inclination of the feed wheel (angle α in Fig. 26-24). For the fastest and smoothest roughing, a slow regulating-wheel speed with a large angle of inclination is used. In finish grinding, the angle of inclination should be reduced and the regulating wheel speeded up to give the wheel

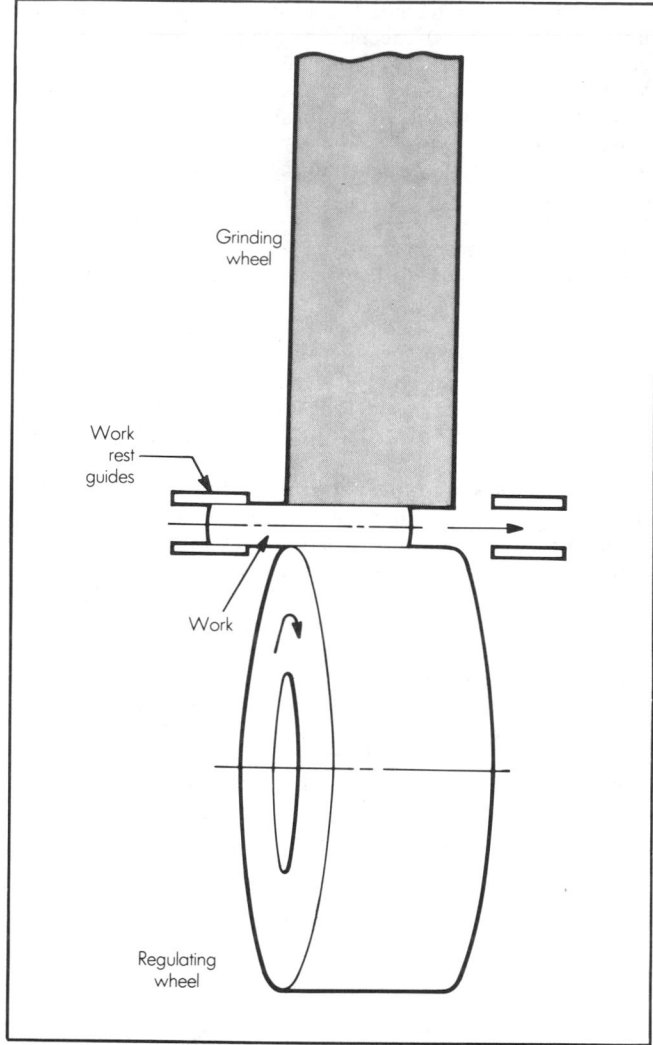

Fig. 26-23 Top view of throughfeed centerless grinding setup.

more time to cut the material and longer sparkout time to produce better finishes.

Infeed grinding. This method, similar to plunge grinding on a center-type grinder, is usually employed when grinding work that has a shoulder, head, or some portion larger than the ground diameter. It is also used when grinding work with multiple diameters, taper, any irregular profile, or groove requirements. There is no relative axial movement of the work, and the length of the grind is limited to the width of the grinding wheel. If the grind length is longer than the width of the wheels and the work must be ground only a short distance from each end, one end of the work is supported by the workrest blade; the other end rests on an outboard roller support.

In infeed grinding, the wheel is dressed to match the form of the part. Because the work does not traverse across the wheel face, the regulating wheel is set with only a slight angle to keep the work against the end stop. The part is laid on the work blade and regulating wheel and against the end stop, either manually or mechanically, and advanced into the grinding wheel (see Fig. 26-25).

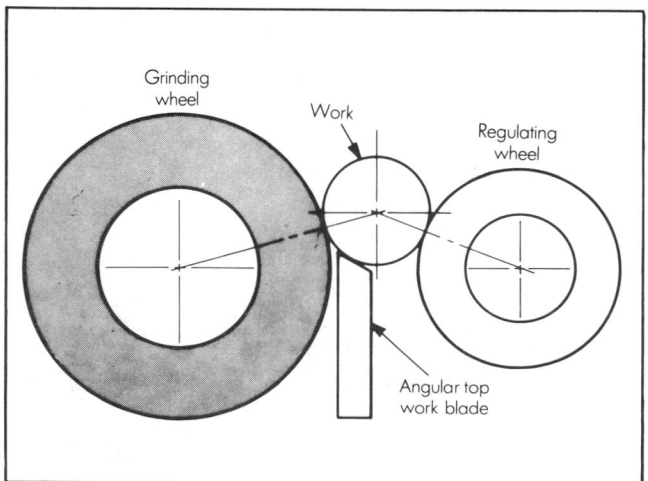

Fig. 26-22 Centerless grinding setup that produces maximum corrective rounding action.

GRINDING MACHINES AND FIXTURES

When the work is ground to size, the regulating wheel is moved back away from the grinding wheel; either a manual or automatic ejector kicks the work out from between the wheels. Then the operator or an automated loading device places another piece in position.

End feed grinding. This method is used on tapered or straight work. The grinding wheel, regulating wheel, and workrest blade are set in fixed relation to each other, and the work is fed from the front, either manually or mechanically, to a fixed end stop. The grinding wheel or the regulating wheel, or both, must be trued to the proper taper (see Fig. 26-26).

Combination infeed and throughfeed grinding. In some applications, the infeed and throughfeed grinding methods can be combined to achieve increased production efficiency. This relatively special technique is sometimes used for:

1. Parts that are more conveniently ground in a single pass, but require too large a stock removal for conventional throughfeed grinding.
2. Parts that have two diameters. Combination grinding is used to process the smaller diameter on such parts, where the portion to be ground exceeds the width of the grinding wheel (see Fig. 26-27).
3. Parts that are warped, in cases where the warpage or bow does not exceed the total stock removal, and the length of the part is less than the width of the wheels.

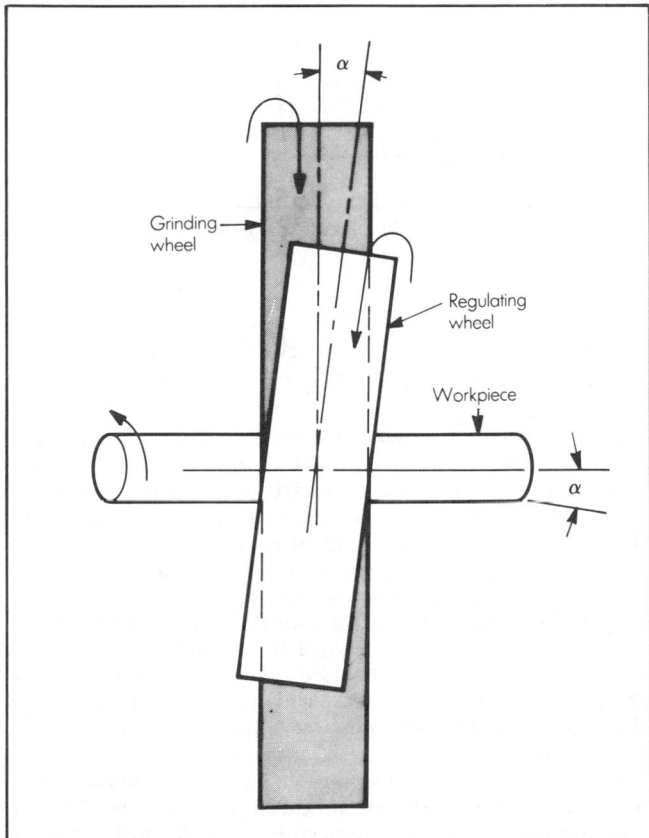

Fig. 26-24 The angle of inclination,, the speed, and the diameter of the regulating wheel determine the traverse rate of the workpiece in throughfeed centerless grinding.

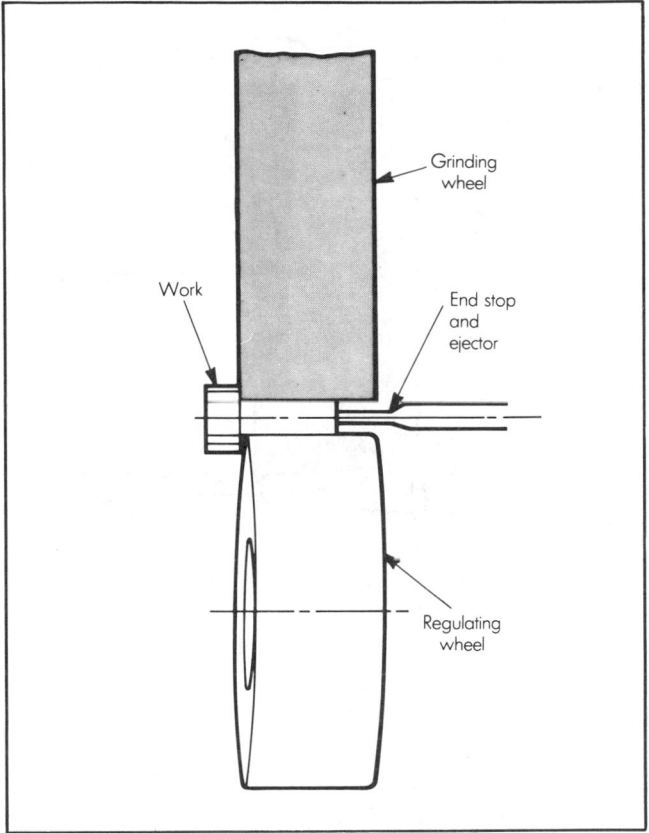

Fig. 26-25 Top view of infeed centerless grinding.

Internal Grinders

Internal grinding is generally used to produce precision holes in workpieces. Straight or tapered, blind or through holes are produced by the process. Also, internal grinders are used to produce holes with multiple IDs, internal shapes, contours, and flat sections. Often, internal grinding is applied to bring holes to final shape and surface finish, correcting variations in geometry caused by previous operations.

Stock removal. Amount of stock left in a hole for grinding is a function of several variables including the size, length, and out-of-roundness of the unground holes, distortion from heat treatment, and depth of decarburization. To minimize grinding costs, the amount of stock is selected just large enough to ensure a clean grind.

Surface finish. In most production-type internal-grinding applications, surface finishes of 8-15 μ in. (0.20 to 0.38 μ m) rms are commonly obtained. Surface finishes as fine as 2-3 μ in. (0.05-0.08 μ m) rms can be obtained.

Although internal grinding traditionally has been considered a precision operation, newer internal grinders are characterized by the ability to achieve required close surface finishes in shorter cycle times.

Types of internal grinders. Conventional internal grinders have a horizontal workhead spindle located on the left side of the machine (viewed by the operator) and a wheelhead, which

GRINDING MACHINES AND FIXTURES

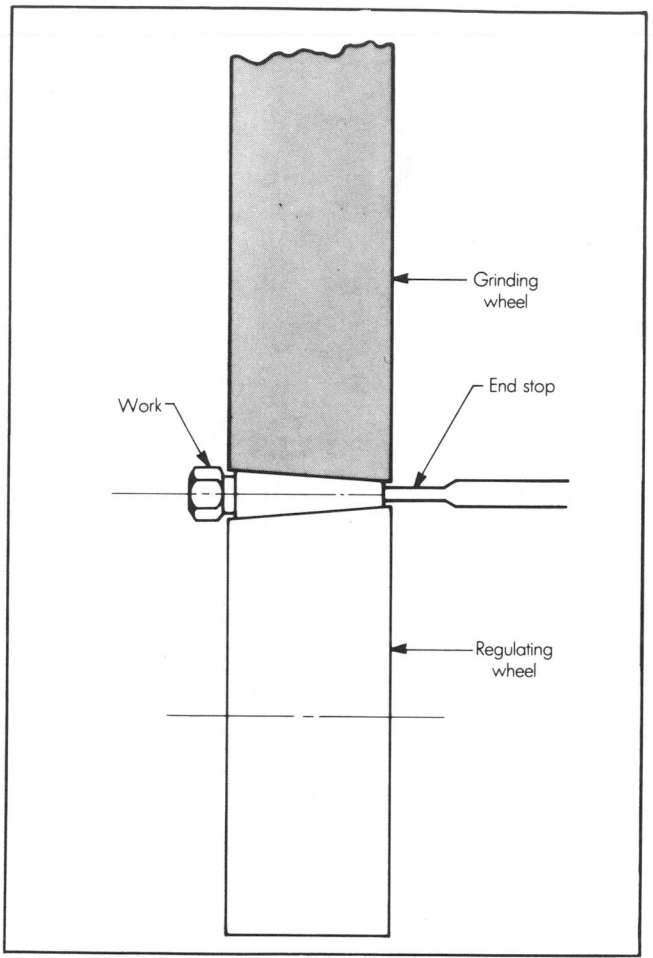

Fig. 26-26 Top view of end feed centerless grinding.

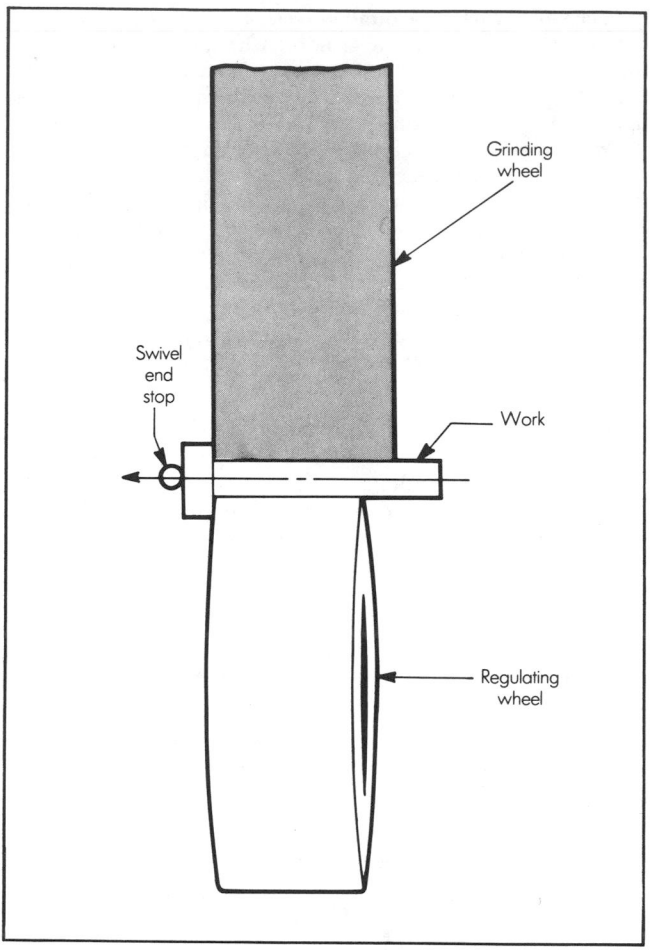

Fig. 26-27 Top view of combination infeed and throughfeed grinding.

accepts and drives the grinding wheel, on the right side of the machine. On universal-type internal grinders, a longitudinal slide generally moves the wheel axially and a cross slide moves the wheel radially with respect to the work. Both slides are mounted under the wheelhead. Other internal-grinding machines, especially production-type units, may have the longitudinal slide (table) or the cross slide (feed slide) under the workhead.

The universal internal grinder is used for toolroom and high-production applications in which quick setup and large machine capacity covering a wide range of workpiece types and sizes is required. Machines of this type can grind straight and tapered bores, external diameters, and internal and external faces. In addition, rotary face grinding can also be accomplished. Figure 26-28 illustrates the many configurations available in a line of universal grinders featuring CNC.

Vertical internal grinders. The primary advantage of the vertical internal grinder is that it is capable of grinding contoured bores with simple, cam-operated fixtures. Large swing (above 24", 610 mm) and heavy workpiece capabilities are additional advantages for grinding cam rings and crown gears. Loading and positioning of unwieldy parts is easier on this type of machine, and the weight of the work adds to the holding force

on the rotary table or magnetic chuck. Vertical internal grinders can also be set up to perform taper, face, OD, and contour grinding.

Planetary internal grinders. Internal grinders of the planetary type are generally used for operations in which it is impractical to rotate the workpiece and for jig grinding. On these machines, the wheel describes a planetary motion and is fed radially into the work. An eccentric mechanism increases the orbiting diameter of the wheel to grind the hole to finish size.

Chucking-type vs. centerless internal grinding. Types of devices used for locating, orienting, holding, and driving workpieces are normally dictated by the job. There are two basic workholding principles used in internal grinding. One is the chucking type, in which the workpiece is held rigidly in a fixture on the spindle and is rotated against the grinding wheel. This is called conventional internal grinding (Fig. 26-29). The other is the centerless type, in which the work center is not coincident with the workhead spindle axis. On this type the work center is determined by the V-block effect of the shoes or rolls which support the part on its OD; work direction is the same as that of the wheel. This is called climb grinding (Fig. 26-30).

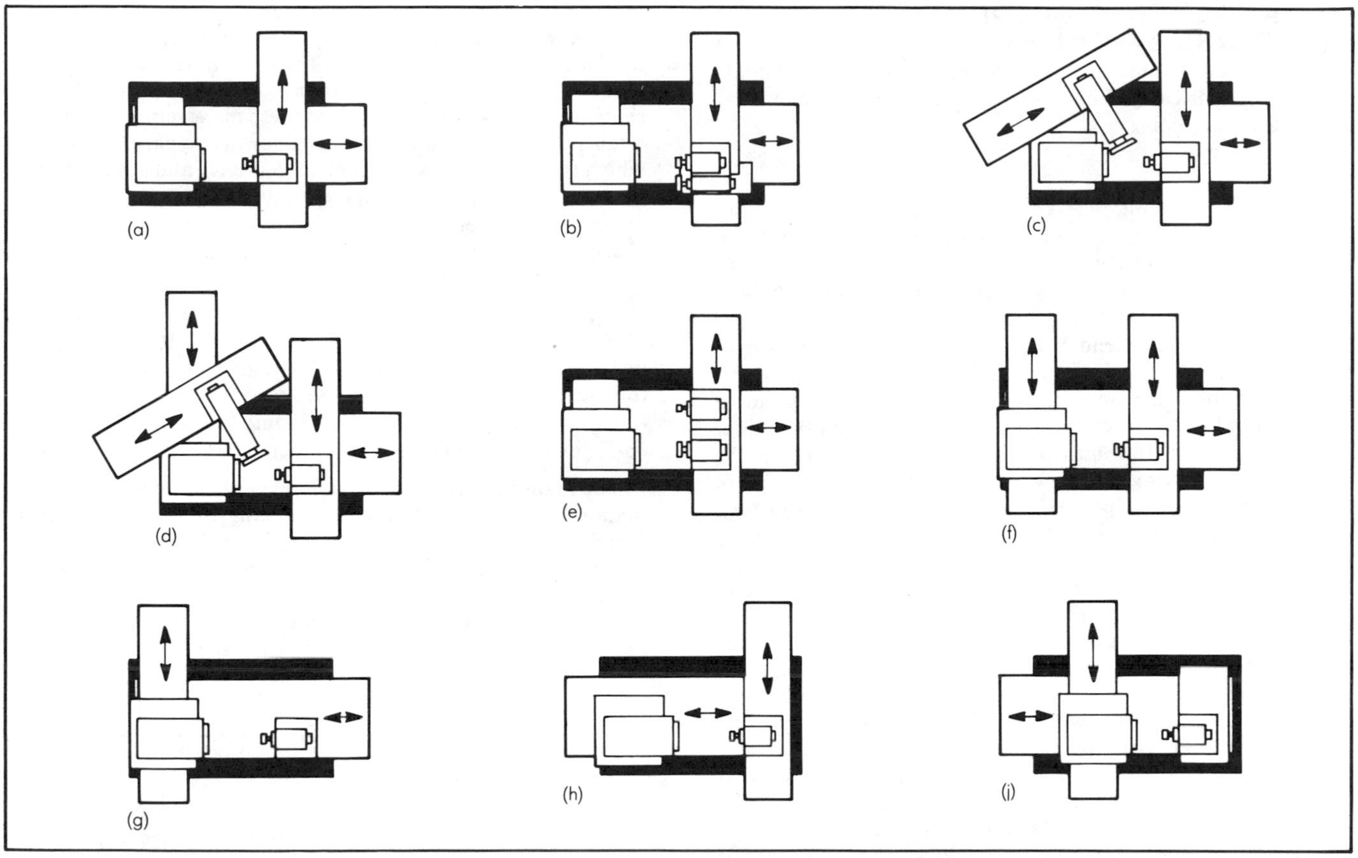

(a)   (b)   (c)

(d)   (e)   (f)

(g)   (h)   (j)

Fig. 26-28 Universal CN grinders are available in a wide variety of configurations. One model featuring modular components can provide (a) compound slide under wheel, (b) compound slide under wheel with front facing attachment, (c) compound slide under wheel with rear facing attachment, (d) compound slide under both bore and facing wheels (4 axes), (e) compound slide under two-spindle arrangement, (f) compound slide under wheel with workhead cross slide (3 axes), (g) longitudinal slide under wheel and cross slide under work, (h) cross slide under wheel and longitudinal slide under work or, (j) compound slide under work. (*Bryant*)

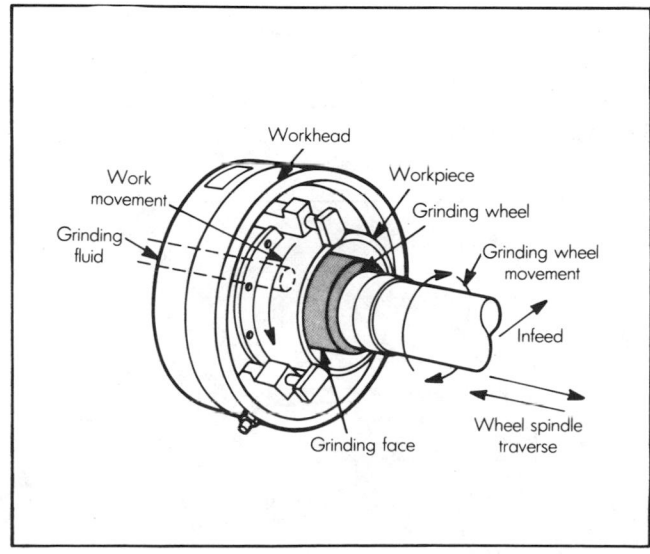

Fig. 26-29 Motions of wheel and work in conventional internal grinding.

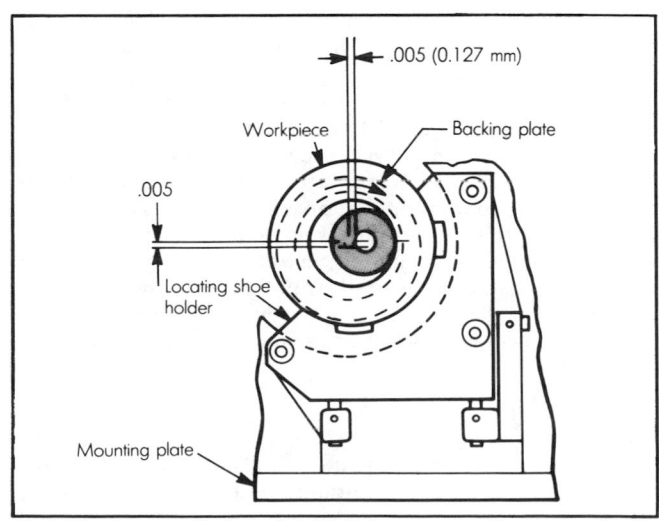

Fig. 26-30 Centerless internal climb grinding in which work center (in relation to workhead spindle) is determined by V-block effect of work-supporting shoes.

GRINDING MACHINES AND FIXTURES

WORKHOLDING METHODS IN CYLINDRICAL GRINDING

The most commonly used workholding devices for general-purpose cylindrical grinding are centers, chucks, mandrels, collets, and faceplates.

Centers

The most common type of workholding device used on cylindrical grinding machines is the center. In practice, the work is actually mounted between centers on the center points (see "Special Grinding Machines and Processes" in this chapter). Centers generally have a 60° point on the workholding end and a taper on the other end which goes into the footstock or headstock. Points on these centers may be either high-speed steel or tungsten carbide. High-speed steel or carbide grinding centers should have some type of lubricant between the center and the workpiece. In some cases, special centers are used in the headstock for driving the workpiece as well as for holding it in position. This can be done only when a live-spindle headstock has been supplied with the machine. This technique eliminates the need for driving dogs or pins.

On all center-type grinding machines, the workpiece and wheel have a negative contact between one another. Viewing the workpiece and grinding wheel from the headstock end of the machine, both the workpiece and wheel would be revolving in a clockwise direction. At the point of contact between the workpiece and wheel, the workpiece would be traveling in one direction and the grinding wheel in the opposite direction. These directions of rotation are maintained to provide solid contact between the dog clamped on the workpiece and the driving pin which sticks out of the headstock. If the headstock rotates in the opposite direction, it would act as a brake to stop the workpiece from rotating. These directions of rotation are useful when grinding is done between centers, since the work is simply supported by the centers (without being actually clamped in place). They are all that gives the work positive drive with the headstock.

Chucks, Collets and Faceplates

Chucks, collets, and faceplates are workholding devices which are sometimes used for fixturing parts that must be cylindrically ground.

Before chucks can be used in grinding, a live-spindle headstock (workhead) is needed. This means that chucks can be used only on universal center-type grinders or plain grinders with live-spindle headstocks. A four-jaw independent chuck is useful when odd-shaped work must be ground and there are no center holes. When this type of chuck is used, the work must be indicated and each jaw adjusted separately so that the surface to be ground rotates concentrically with the axis of rotation of the headstock spindle. When using a chuck to grind work, the runout in the headstock spindle must also be taken into consideration.

Mandrels

Mandrels are commonly used for locating and driving workpieces in grinding operations. In addition to providing excellent fixturing, mandrels also provide an accurate method to ensure concentricity between the OD and ID of the workpiece. The principle variations of mandrels commonly used for fixturing are: solid mandrels, expansion mandrels, nut mandrels, and special-purpose mandrels.

Solid mandrels. Solid mandrels are generally used for close tolerance concentric grinding. These mandrels are normally made of tool steel and are hardened and ground with lapped center holes. The gripping area of these mandrels generally has a taper ground to match the tolerance of the part. In cases in which the OD must be concentric to the ID and square to the sides, a fixture such as the that shown in Fig. 26-31 can be used. Here the mandrel is used to mount and drive the part. The sliding sleeve is used to ensure the squareness of the part on the mandrel.

Expansion mandrels. Expansion mandrels are normally used for parts that have a larger tolerance on the ID of the workpiece or for parts that do not have an extremely close concentricity tolerance. Expansion mandrels are capable of tolerances in the range of 0.0003-0.001" (0.008-0.03 mm) TIR. As shown in Fig. 26-32, expansion mandrels are rather simple in design.

Nut mandrels. Nut mandrels are similar in design to solid mandrels, the principle difference being the method used to secure the part. Nut mandrels use pressure from either a screw or nut rather than wedge action of a taper, to secure the part to the mandrel. As shown in Fig. 26-33, the basic nut mandrel holds a workpiece by simply applying force to one end of the part and binding it against the opposite side of the mandrel.

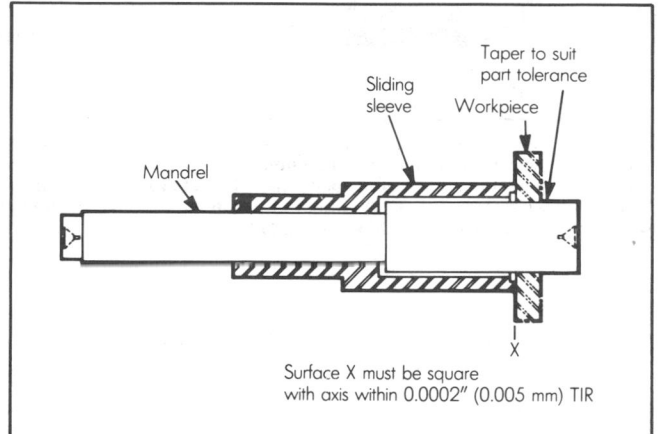

Fig. 26-31 Solid mandrel.

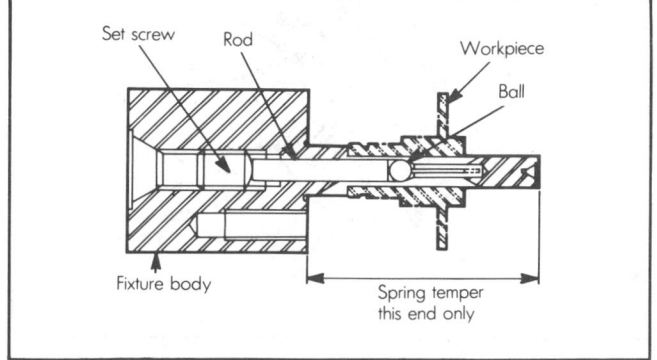

Fig. 26-32 Expanding mandrel.

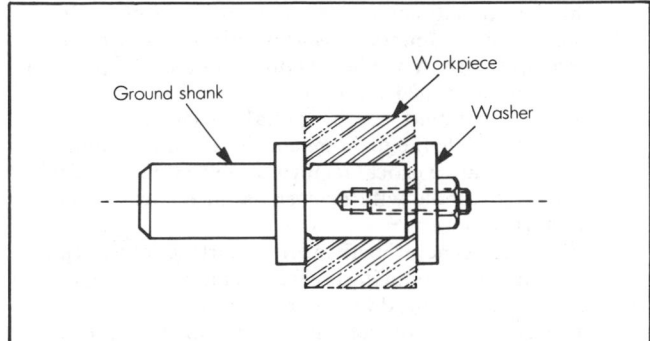

Fig. 26-33 Nut mandrel.

Special mandrels. Special mandrels are those that are not easily classified by any standard term. These mandrels include those designed to hold parts with odd, or irregular, internal details or those that combine features of the standard form of mandrels. The mandrel shown in Fig. 26-34 is specially designed to hold the part shown. With this mandrel, the bearing surface has a pentagonal shaped form to match the internal detail of the die insert.

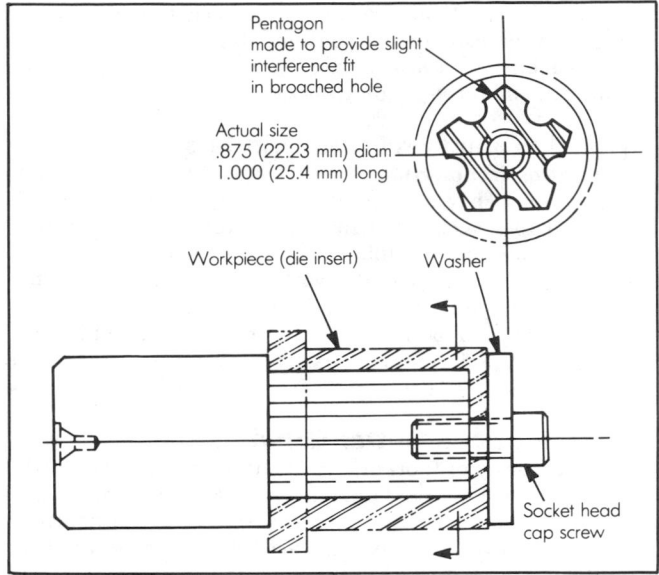

Fig. 26-34 Special mandrel for grinding of die insert.

SPECIAL GRINDING PROCESSES

Grinding, as a class of metalworking operation, includes many processes, methods, and techniques not easily classified by conventional means.

CENTER HOLE GRINDING

The accuracy of center-type turning and grinding operations is heavily dependent upon the accuracy of the workpiece centers themselves.

Properly ground centers must be round and ground at the precise angle. A true conical form must be generated, and the surfaces of the center hole must be free of ridges for proper location. In addition, concentricity is an important consideration.

Common Errors in Center Holes

Figure 26-35 illustrates common errors found in center holes. These errors must be avoided because no amount of lapping or polishing can correct these geometric variances.

Center Hole Grinders

Precision center holes can be ground using several grinding techniques, including plunge grinding and generation. Simple plunge grinding is effective for many applications, but when particularly close control of roundness and concentricity is required, center holes may be ground with a generation-type process, as illustrated in Fig. 26-36.

TOOL GRINDING

The sharpening of tools and cutters covers a wide range of styles and types of tools; consequently, the purchase of a single machine to achieve the desired reconditioning is impossible. As an example, a tool and cutter grinder can grind many cutting tools, but it is not a satisfactory machine for repointing of twist

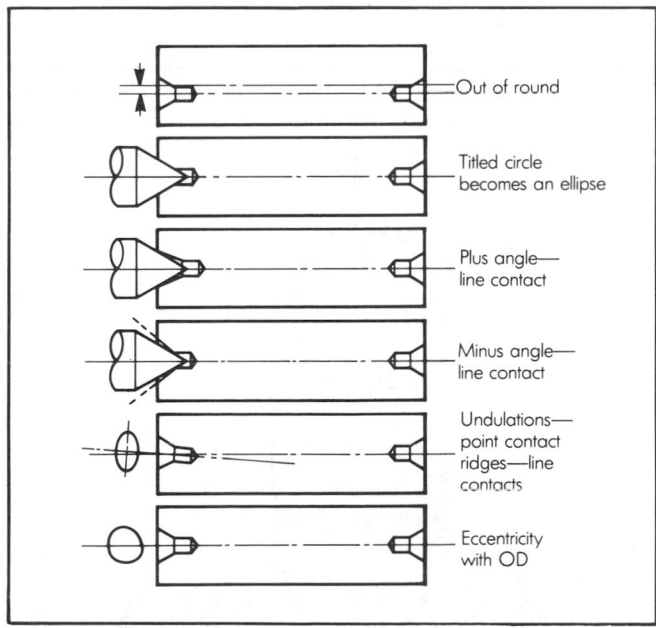

Fig. 26-35 Common errors in center holes which effect accuracy of finished workpieces.

drills. The types of machines to be considered must be consistent with the volume of tools to be sharpened and any special manufacturing conditions that exist.

Standard Tool and Cutter Grinders

The general-purpose tool and cutter grinder is the most popular of all the tool-grinding machines because of its capacity

SPECIAL GRINDING PROCESSES

and capabilities. Using various attachments, this class of grinder can be used to sharpen most types of cutting tools. These machines can also be used to perform most internal, cylindrical, and form-grinding operations.

Optical Projection Form Grinders

Optical-projection grinders are machines with built-in optical comparators. They are used for accurate grinding of small profiled shapes, such as flat and circular form tools, templates, carbide cutter tips, profiling masters, lamination dies, and similar parts. An image of the work being ground is projected from 5-100 magnifications onto a glass screen on which the desired form has been drawn at an equal magnification. Alternatively, a large-scale master drawing can be placed behind the viewing screen.

Single-Purpose Cutter Grinders

If the quantity of tools of a particular type is large enough, specialized single-purpose grinding machines can be purchased to give superior results for tool life, surface finish, production rates, etc. Machine tools of this type are hob sharpeners, face mill grinders, broach sharpeners, gear cutter grinding machines, and so on.

JIG GRINDING

Jig grinding machines differ from jig borers in that the machine spindle is replaced by a more complex unit offering the following capabilities:

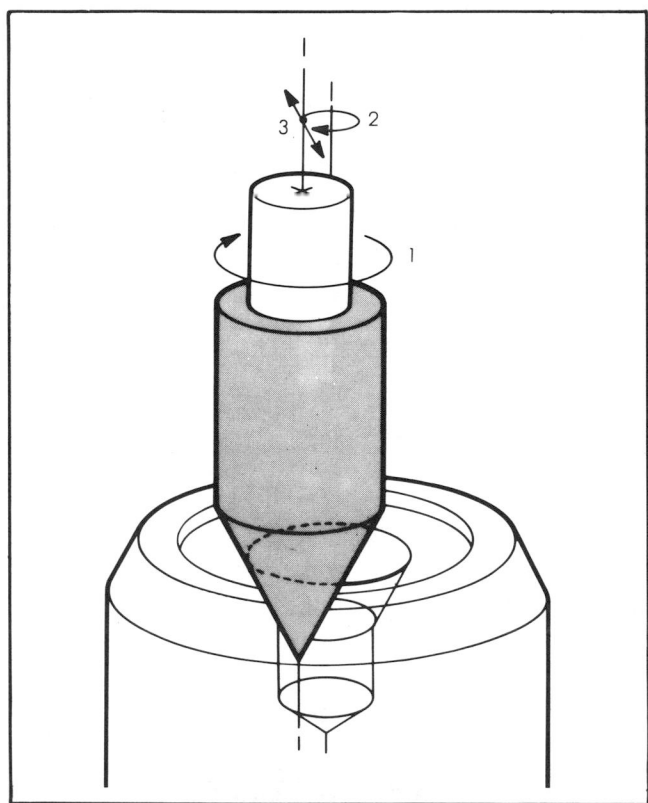

Fig. 26-36 Center holes ground on generation-type grinders are produced with three simultaneous grinding motions.

1. Means for adjusting the radial offset of the grinding spindle to accommodate various diameters or radii.
2. Provisions to drive the grinding spindle in a planetary orbit at controlled speeds.
3. Fine adjustment of the radial offset engineered to function while the main machine spindle is operating.
4. An automatic vertical reciprocating feed motion for the grinding spindle with provisions for control of its rate and traverse range.
5. Means for generating the vertical surfaces of workpieces at set angles, producing tapered diameters and contoured surfaces as required for clearance in press tools.
6. Provisions for controlling the angular direction of the planetary offset for the grinding spindle relative to the machine's slide motion.
7. An engineered system for transmitting and controlling power to the machine spindle and the grinding wheel, both simultaneously and independently.
8. Provisions for interchanging a variety of grinding spindles as required for universal application.

Jig Grinder Applications

The jig grinder is essential to the tool and die industry for the manufacturing of press tools. The functional details of die components are ground to specifications after hardening, thus eliminating inaccuracies resulting from distortion produced by heat-treating. The integrity of wear surfaces and the precise control of clearance between punch and die is assured. Precise dimensional control allows the fabrication of interchangeable die components. Die parts can be stocked for quick replacement in press tools. Hand fitting and adjustment of matching die components is eliminated.

The application of the jig grinder is extended into other areas of manufacturing. Examples are found in the machine-tool, aerospace, and instrument-manufacturing industries. These include gearboxes or bearing plates having hardened inserts requiring precise location, parts that are too large or asymmetrical for conventional internal grinding, keyslots or other rectilinear details, and curvilinear forms in cams used for mechanical control of instruments or other devices. Numerically controlled jig grinders effectively accommodate the complex dimensional detail of these parts.

Accessories for the Jig Grinder

Spindle accessories, specifically designed for use on the jig grinder, include the following:

1. Vertical-axis grinding spindles designed for interchangeable mounting on the main spindle of the machine. These grinding spindles, or heads, provide appropriate speed and power for wheels from 0.020″ (0.5 mm) to approximately 3.0″ (76.2 mm) diam.
2. Horizontal-axis spindle (slot grinder) unit with interchangeable spindles for wheels from approximately 0.75″ (19.0 mm) to 3.0″ (76.2 mm) diam.
3. Adapters for the grinding spindles extending the range of diameters and depths for grinding.
4. A 45° angle spindle-mounting adapter used when generating concave spherical forms.
5. A wheel dresser (Fig. 26-37) used for dressing grinding wheels that require frequent dressing or conditioning to restore their cutting properties and geometry which

normally deteriorate with use. This reconditioning is commonly done using a diamond-tipped dressing tool supported on the machine table.

Flexibility and low-cost jig grinding capability can be added to the tool spindle of any precision machine, such as a jig borer, boring machine, or milling machine, with the use of an air-operated jig grinding attachment. The result is a dual-purpose machine capable of precision jig grinding hole sizes from 0.020-8.000" (0.51-203 mm) diam.

Wheels for Jig Grinding

Grinding wheels used in the jig grinder include the following types:

1. Mounted wheels with abrasive material bonded to steel or tungsten carbide shanks.
2. Wheels designed for mounting in arbors or directly on the spindle end of the grinding head.
3. Wheels designed for use in the horizontal-axis spindle of the slot grinder.

HIGH-SPEED GRINDING

The theory of high-speed grinding, a relative newcomer to metalworking, suggests that, under certain conditions, grinding wheel speeds can be increased significantly beyond normal wheel speeds to effect proportional increases in material removal rates without significant changes in chip geometry, grinding forces, energy required per unit volume of material removed, surface finish, or residual stresses in the workpiece. The theory of high-speed grinding dictates that dressing the grinding wheel can be used to control normal grinding force, surface finish, and wheel wear.

DEEP AND CREEP-FEED GRINDING

Creep-feed grinding originated in Europe in about 1958, when the first prototype creep-feed grinder was developed by ELB-Schliff of West Germany.[7] Within five years, several production-type creep-feed grinding applications surfaced. Today, several machine tool builders, both domestic and overseas, offer special creep-feed grinding machines. Particular interest recently has been centered around creep-feed machines which feature both conventional grinding and creep-feed capabilities.

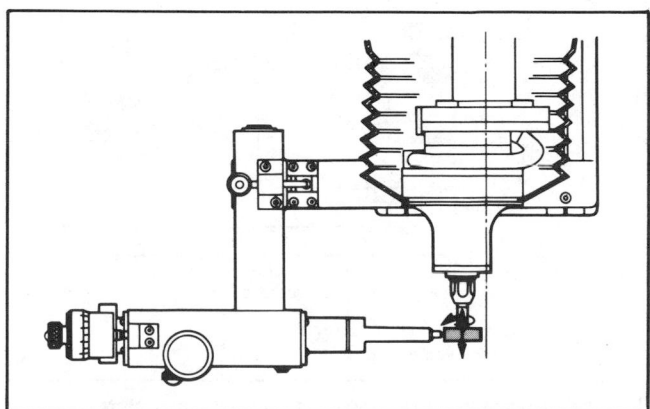

Fig. 26-37 Wheel dresser for the jig grinder. (*Moore Special Tool Co., Inc.*)

Process Characteristics

Creep-feed grinding is generally used to describe a surface grinding operation performed in a single pass with an unusually large depth of cut. The term deep grinding is used in Europe to describe creep-feed operations in external cylindrical grinding such as tool, thread, and gear grinding.

Generally, the creep-feed grinding process is marked by a special mode of operation. As illustrated in Fig. 26-38, in contrast to the conventional grinding technique, the depth of cut per pass or revolution is increased 1000-10,000 times and the work speed is decreased in the same proportion. Thus, it is possible to grind profiles with a depth of 1.0-30.0 mm (0.04-1.2") or more in one pass, using work speeds from 0.25-0.75 m/min (9.8-30 ipm), and to reduce machining times 50-80%. Figure 26-38 illustrates the difference between the two modes of operation in surface grinding. At creep-feed conditions, the multiple initial wheel/work contacts, typical for conventional operation, are avoided. As a consequence, the profile stability of the grinding wheel is improved considerably. On the other hand, the stroke length is increased at creep-feed conditions due to the extended contact length of the wheel and workpiece.

Compared with conventional grinding processes at the same metal removal rates, deep or creep-feed operations are characterized by the following technological features.[8]

- Increased total grinding forces.
- Reduced average force per individual grit.
- Increased temperature in the wheel/work contact zone.
- Reduced temperatures in the newly generated work surface.

To make full use of the economic and technological advantages of this high-efficiency, high-precision manufacturing process, the application of specially developed and

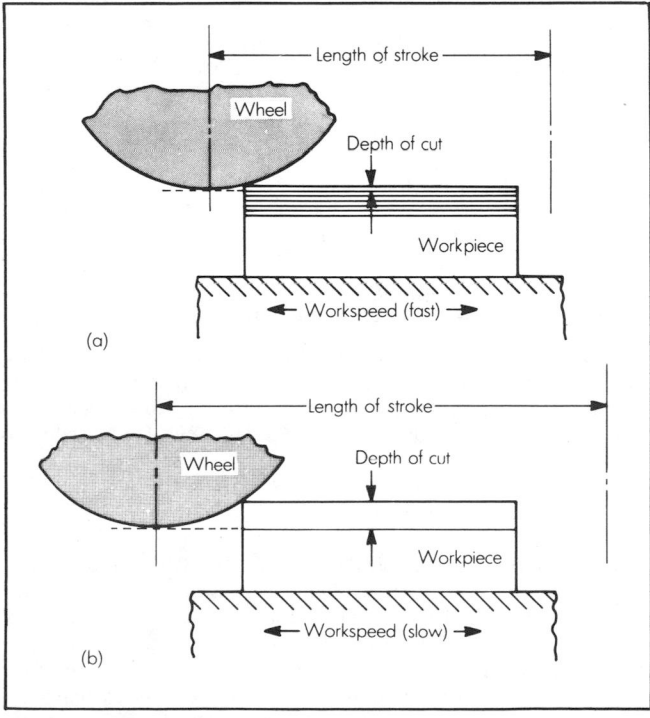

Fig. 26-38 Feed, length of stroke, and depth of cut for (a) conventional surface grinding and (b) creep-feed grinding.

SPECIAL GRINDING PROCESSES

constructed machine tools, grinding wheels, dressing methods, and controlling techniques is essential. A manufacturing system such as this should provide the following features:[9]

- High static and dynamic stability of the machine tool.
- High-accuracy, stick-slip free slides with favorable damping characteristics.
- Considerably increased spindle power (2-3 times higher than in conventional surface grinding).
- Infinitely variable spindle speed.
- Highly balanced and directly connected motor-spindle system with high-accuracy/high-performance ball bearings.
- Nonhydraulic, single-unit, table drive covering the whole area from the creep-feed to the conventional region, with infinitely variable speed.
- Consistent table speed, especially in the lower speed range.
- High-pressure cooling and cleaning system.
- Integrated dressing devices.
- Integrated controlling systems.
- Pertinent grinding wheels.
- Updated process know-how.

Surface Grinding Applications

Generally, two classes of applications exist for creep-feed surface grinding. The first class is the grinding of deep slots with parallel sides; the second class is the grinding of profiles, including especially those applications featuring high depth to width ratios and those with profiles to be ground in difficult-to-grind materials.

The following workpieces, representing the first class of application, have been successfully processed using creep-feed grinding:

- Racks of chuck jaws.
- Locating slots in connecting rods.
- Cavities in mould inserts.
- Slot-type ways in chucks.
- Cutting teeth on straight jaws.
- Complete profiles of small racks.
- Keyseats in rotors of hydraulic motors.
- Gear elements on automobile steering parts.
- Keyseats in gear bodies.
- Profiles in coupling parts.
- Slot-type ways in textile machine parts.

Turbine blades made of superalloys are an important application of creep-feed grinding of profiles. Usually profiles (blade roots, for example) are ground in one or two roughing passes and a single finishing pass, using creep-feed conditions throughout.

Cylindrical Deep-Grinding Applications

An advantage of cylindrical deep grinding is that the contact zone in deep grinding is significantly less than in creep-feed surface grinding. This results in grinding forces up to three times smaller than creep-feed surface grinding at the same removal rate. A disadvantage exists, however, in external deep grinding. The process involves the grind wheel plunging down into the workpiece first, then performing the creep-feed operation by a full revolution of the workpiece, and finally retracting the wheel without leaving a mark on the ground work surface.

The most impressive example of the potential of the creep-feed method in general is the deep grinding of twist drill flutes with a maximum depth of cut of 0.68" (17.3 mm) and with wheel speeds up to 20,000 sfm (100 m/s).

LOW-STRESS GRINDING

Low-stress grinding, a somewhat nontraditional use of the conventional surface grinding process, leaves a low-magnitude, residual stress in the workpiece surface, thus increasing fatigue strength and improving end product durability and reliability.[10] Typically, low-stress grinding is used on workpieces that will be subjected to high stress or stress corrosion environments. Usually, the process is applied as a finishing operation, with conventional grinding techniques used for roughing and semifinishing operations.

Typical applications for low-stress grinding are found in the processing of turbine blades and in the preparation of test specimens for evaluation of material properties.

Effects of Stress

The effect of high-stress, conventional, and low-stress grinding on the fatigue-endurance limit of various materials, including steel, titanium, and nickel-based alloys, is shown in Fig. 26-39. High-stress grinding refers to an inadvert

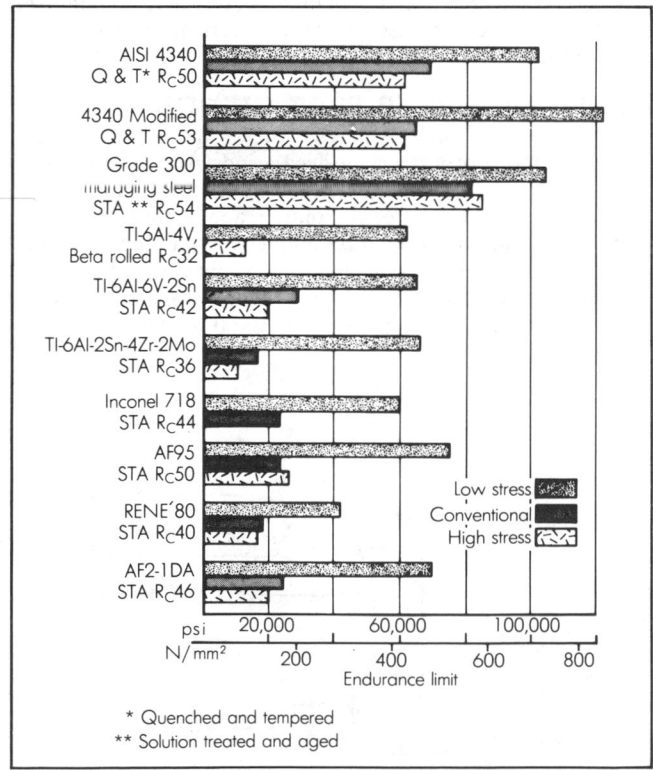

Fig. 26-39 High cycle fatigue response of various materials created with low-stress, conventional, and high-stress grinding.

"accident" during grinding—for example, grinding dry due to a plugged lubricant nozzle or grinding with an excessively hard wheel that was not changed from a previous operation.

Control of residual stress is critical in areas requiring close dimensional control for mating parts or in critical stress areas. A high-stress pattern, tensile or compression, can result in distortion of the part. The curves in Fig. 26-40 show that conventional grinding can produce a relatively shallow but rather high tensile stress. The low-stress technique produces a surface with a low-level stress pattern which is generally compressive in nature.

Low-Stress Grinding Parameters

Conventional surface grinding typically involves wheel speeds of about 6000 sfm (30 m/s), an infeed of about 0.001-0.003″ (0.03-0.08 mm) per pass, and a water-based fluid.

In low-stress grinding, the wheel is soft and is run at a much slower speed, which tends to make the wheel act as if it were softer. Infeed is very light, usually about 0.0002″ (0.005 mm) per pass. It is decreased progressively as grinding approaches the finished dimension. Typical statistics are 0.0005″ (0.013 mm) per pass for the first 0.009″ (0.23 mm) and 0.0002″ (0.005 mm) per pass for the last 0.001″ (0.025 mm).

Low-stress grinding does not require the use of special equipment, but rather adjustments or modifications of various grinding parameters. Infeed rate and wheel speed are normally limited by the grinding machine. If the proper levels of the other parameters are selected, a ground surface of acceptable quality can be obtained on almost any traditional grinder.

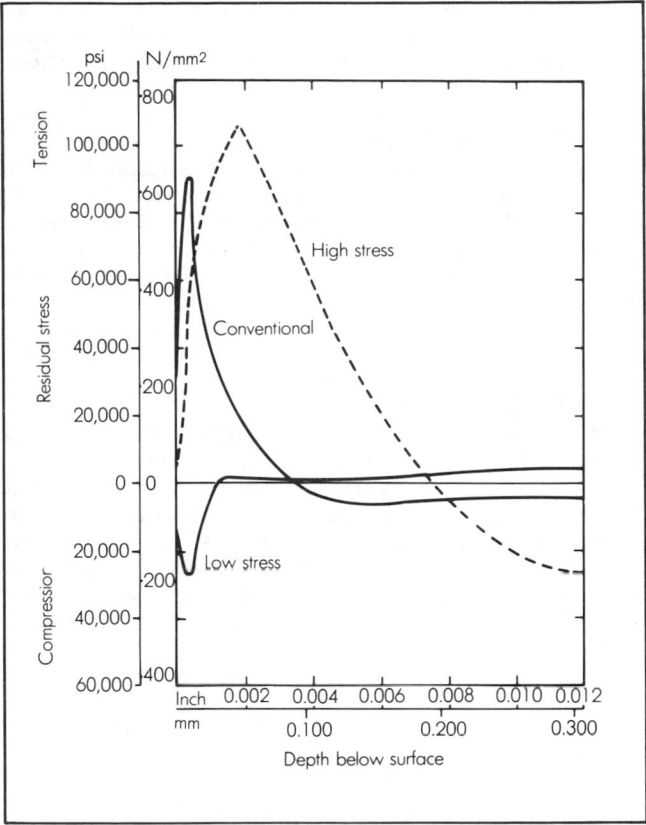

Fig. 26-40 The nature of high-stress, conventional, and low-stress at various depths below the surface of a workpiece.

CONTROL GAGING FOR GRINDING OPERATIONS

There are four categories that control gaging systems fall into when applied to abrasive operations. These are referred to as pre-process gaging, in-process gaging, post-process gaging, and match gaging. The first three are widely used, with each having its own distinct advantages and disadvantages that should be given proper attention when a decision is made as to which type would best suit a particular grinding process. The fourth, match gaging, is more specialized and only used in limited applications.

PRE-PROCESS GAGING

Pre-process gaging is used when overall work size must be consistent before entering a manufacturing process. It is commonly used when finishing parts on throughfeed centerless grinders or lappers. Better tolerances on size and surface finish can be maintained on these machines when the parts entering them are consistent.

IN-PROCESS GAGING

In-process gaging is the most common type of machine control and can be applied to most grinding operations. This technique monitors the part size while machining is being performed.

TREND GAGING

Trend gaging is a form of in-process gaging that is normally used for continuous applications such as throughfeed centerless grinding. On this type of operation, the part size remains fairly consistent from one piece to the next. They are so consistent, in fact, that some systems are unable to detect any differences at all. This enables the gage to maintain tolerance requirements without having to check every piece. Circuit designs let the gage overlook sporadic readings that may be caused by dirt or sludge.

POST-PROCESS GAGING

Post-process gaging is used to measure part size after machining has been completed and parts have left the machine. The gaging area can be located some distance from the operation; however, for best results as a machine control, the part should be gaged as quickly as possible. This enables size corrections to be made on the machine before the desired tolerance is exceeded.

This type of gaging interfaces well with CNC equipment, such as the type used to grind multiple diameters with a single

CONTROL GAGING

grinding wheel. After being ground, the part goes to an inspection station, which analyzes all dimensions and sends information back to the controller so that any size corrections can be made on the next piece.

MATCH GAGING

Match gaging is a system which enables an operator to grind pieces to size, using a previously manufactured part as the gaging standard. Clearances between the mating parts can be set in the gaging system and maintained regardless of the variations in the previously machined part. This type of gaging is most frequently used in applications in which a cylindrical part is inserted in a bore, such as a valve body and spool configuration.

CONTACT GAGING

All types of control gaging must sense the size of the parts either directly or indirectly. Gaging systems that make mechanical contact with the workpiece tend to be the most accurate and are used when tight tolerance requirements are to be maintained. Gage contacts must be made of high wear-resistant material, such as diamond or carbide, and arms and holders must be rigid enough not to deflect or distort when part contact is made. Thermal deflection of gage elements is an important consideration.

NONCONTACT GAGING

Noncontacting or open-orifice gages have no wear characteristics to speak of. There are no moving parts; therefore, dirt is of no major concern to their reliability. Also, they cannot cause chatter or burnish marks on the workpiece, because of the absence of physical contact. However, large stock removal cannot be tolerated because of the fixed gap between the gage orifice and finished workpieces.

The limitation caused by excessive stock removal can be overcome by spring loading the orifices against a fixed stop. When an oversized piece comes between the orifices, they are opened to allow the piece through and then closed against the fixed stops. By using an air-to-electronic pressure transducer and the proper electronic circuit, air gaging can be used to check parts that have interrupted surfaces.

If the metallic structure of the parts being ground remains constant and tolerance requirements are not excessively tight, systems using capacitance or inductive pick-up heads can be used.

Other forms of noncontact gaging incorporate electronic proximity sensors, and still others use scanning lasers against photosensitive backgrounds.

GAGE CONTROL UNITS

There are three different ways a control system can interpret information from a sensing unit. It can interpret using all electronics, all pneumatics, or a combination of the two. The all electronics and combination types are by far the most widely used in industry today.

In the combination of an air and electronic gage system, the back pressure from the air orifice being used is changed to an analog electronic signal before it reaches the control console. This signal is then processed electronically and displayed on a meter. With this system, one achieves the advantages of a self-cleaning air gage and the accuracy, versatility, and dependability of an electronic control console.

An all-electronic gage system is the most accurate and simplest type to use and maintain. As with the air-electronic system, the control console is all solid state and can be made without any moving or mechanical parts. This is done through the use of LED displays and solid state relay outputs.

SELECTING A GAGING SYSTEM

Overall stability in any type of gaging system is essential. Gage fixtures must be well designed and free from mechanical hysteresis or twist; electronic controls must be accurate and consistent. Rapid heat buildup can adversely affect the performance of a gaging system. A brief warm-up period of the machine may be necessary in order for the process to thermally stabilize.

Every good machine control gaging system should come complete with protection circuitry to shut down gage function in the event of failure. For example, when a machine is dependent upon a signal from a gage before executing a different function and that signal never arrives, extensive machine damage could result.

Fail-safe features should also be designed into the mechanical tooling of the gage fixtures themselves. For instance, as a machine process begins and a gage is improperly adjusted, it would be more economical to shear off a gage contact than to freeze up a precision machine slide.

GAGING FOR INTERNAL GRINDING

For the toolroom or for low-production internal operations, holes are generally gaged manually. This is done by manually interrupting the finish grind or spark-out cycle and checking the hole with a go-no-go plug, dial-bore, gage, air gage, or electronic gage. On high-production internal grinders, gaging is generally automatic. The most common and least costly approach is the diamond sizing method shown in Fig. 26-41. Here the dressing tool (diamond) serves as a reference point. After the wheel is dressed, it is fed a constant amount (0.001", 0.03 mm is typical). The bore radius will be equal to the fixed distance, D, that the diamond is set from the center of the work, plus the amount, F, that the wheel is fed after dressing. With this method, sizing accuracy is 0.001-0.003" (0.003-0.076 mm), depending upon variation in wheel wear after dressing, diamond wear, slide repeatability, system deflection, and thermal drift.

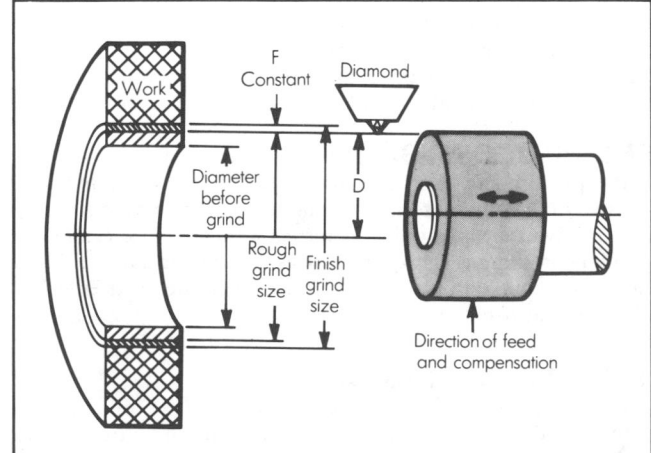

Fig. 26-41 Most common and least costly method of automatically gaging internal grinding operations is diamond sizing.

ABRASIVE-BELT MACHINING

The capability of abrasive-belt machining to remove metal at high stock removal rates is the result of availability of stronger, tougher, and sharper grains; better bonds; and stronger backings, as well as the development of machines for optimum use of the improved belts (see "Coated Abrasives" in this chapter). Versatility is a major advantage, since machines can be quickly converted from heavy stock removal to finishing operations, or for grinding different materials or parts, by simply changing the belts, and/or contact wheels. Most materials can be ground with abrasive belts, but the harder the material, the more difficult the operation.

STOCK REMOVAL RATES

Stock removal rates are proportional to pressure applied, depending upon the coated abrasive, cutting fluid, surface finish required, and workpiece material. A stock removal rate as high as 30 in.³/min/in. (322 mm³/s/mm) of belt width is practical with standard belts. By gradually increasing the pressure, it is possible to obtain a nearly constant cutting rate for the life of the belt. When using contact wheels, grinding pressure is often expressed as the horsepower (watts) available per inch (millimeter) of belt width for driving the contact wheel. This can vary from 1/2 hp/in. (14.7 W/mm) for light stock removal to 30 hp/in. (881 W/mm) of belt width for heavy stock removal.

BELT SPEEDS

Belt speeds of 5000-9000 sfm (25.4-45.7 m/s) are generally the most satisfactory for grinding ferrous and nonferrous metals. Toughness of the material to be ground is more critical than hardness, and some materials such as titanium are best ground at belt speeds in the 1500-3000 sfm (7.6-15.2 m/s) range.

CONTACT WHEELS, ROLLS AND PLATENS

Contact wheels, rolls, or platens are necessary as a backup support behind the abrasive belt when pressure is applied for most grinding operations. Contact wheels are usually made of cloth or rubber, but special compositions or metal are sometimes used. Hardness or density of the contact wheel affects stock removal and the finish produced. The harder the wheel, the greater the stock removal and the coarser the finish.

TYPES OF ABRASIVE-BELT MACHINES

Abrasive-belt machines are available in a wide variety of types to suit specific applications, as shown in Fig. 26-42. Most of them can be arranged for manual, semiautomatic, or fully automatic operation.

Backstand Grinders

Backstand grinders are some of the simplest, lowest cost, and most versatile abrasive-belt machines (see Fig. 26-42, a). They are basically conversions of polishing lathes to abrasive-belt use by the addition of backstand idlers. Workpieces can be held against the belt manually or with semiautomatic workholding devices, as shown, for faster production. Longer belts can be used without sacrificing floor space by using two idler pulleys, or the idler can be mounted above the contact wheel or on the wall to conserve floor space.

Arm attachments with the belt spring loaded between a contact wheel and an idler pulley are also available for installation on polishing or buffing lathes to permit abrasive-belt grinding operations on existing equipment. Backstand grinders or lathes with abrasive-belt arm attachments can be arranged along work-indexing or conveying semiautomatic machines to perform any number of operations, including, through the use of different belts on successive heads, roughing and finishing operations in a single pass. Figure 26-42, b, shows a straight-line machine with two backstand grinders for finishing two opposed sides of workpieces. Contact wheels can be contoured or straight depending upon the surfaces required. Such machines are made in a wide variety of sizes and configurations, including straight-line, rectangular, and rotary. A semiautomatic rotary-type abrasive-belt grinder is shown schematically in Fig. 26-42, c.

Swing-Frame Grinders

Swing-frame abrasive-belt grinders (Fig. 26-42, d) are generally used on large and heavy parts when tolerance is not critical. They can be suspended from overhead for removing weld beads, mounted on wheels for cleaning large plates, or rigidly mounted to a carriage for grinding odd-shaped parts.

Free Belt Roll Grinders

In finish grinding or polishing, the work need not necessarily be applied to the belt at the wheel. It may be "strapped" against the unsupported belt or against a belt made firmer by a parallel backup or saddle belt of leather, rubber, or canvas, as shown in Fig. 26-42, e. Machining of this sort, which forces the belt to conform to the workpiece, requires a guide yoke or deeply flanged pulley to keep the belt tracking properly. Abrasive-belt attachments such as these are available for cylindrical grinding on center-type machines such as roll grinders and lathes. Some are bolted to the cross slides of lathes.

With stroke-type finishing machines, workpiece contact is made by stroking the back of a moving abrasive belt with hand blocks, a hand lever with pressure pad, or an automatic traveling head. These machines usually have two or more pulleys over which the belt travels and a movable workholding table. Another stroke machine is an automatic-gantry type on which the machine rides on crane rails and traverses stationary workpieces and a contact roll head strokes the belt against the work.

Vertical Grinders

Vertical abrasive-belt grinders are used in several ways, with workpieces generally being supported on tables. Work can be applied against a section of unsupported belt, a platen (Fig. 26-42, f) or contact wheel behind the belt, or a section of belt between two rollers (Fig. 26-42, g). The roller arrangement is useful for grinding radii on the edges of workpieces. Belts can be arranged to operate vertically, horizontally, or at an angle, and the worktable can be adjusted to various angular settings on most machines. Oscillation of the work across the face of the

ABRASIVE-BELT MACHINING

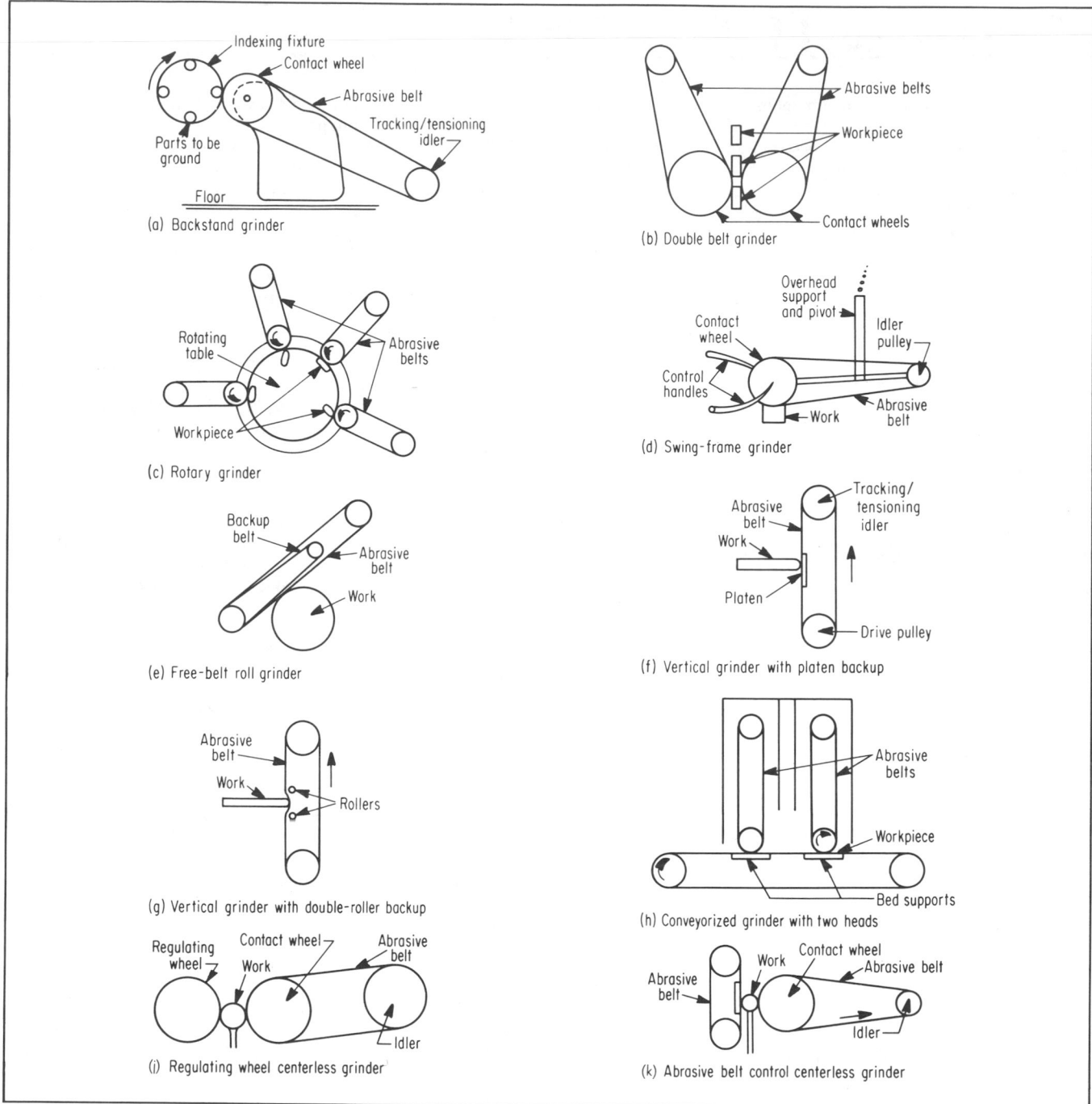

Fig. 26-42 Typical configurations and applications of abrasive-belt machining.

belt is desirable for uniform belt wear and surface finish. Cutting rates can be controlled by hand, air, mechanical means, or hydraulic power.

Vertical-head contact-wheel surface grinders can be of either the reciprocating-bed (or table) type or the continuous-throughfeed type with workholding conveyor. Many continuous-feed contact-wheel surface grinders are made with two or more belt heads (Fig. 26-42, *h*) and a common conveyor belt to carry workpieces under the belts. By varying the grit sizes on

successive belts, parts can be rough and finish-ground in a single pass. Close tolerances can be held on flatness, parallelism, and thickness with these machines.

Multiple floating-type abrasive-belt heads can be used to rough and finish-grind contoured parts in one pass. Each head floats independently, with rise and fall controlled by the workpiece contour, a cam, or a template. Continuous or reciprocating conveyors can be used to move parts beneath the heads.

Centerless Grinders

Abrasive-belt machines are also available for centerless grinding cylindrical-shaped parts, tubing, rod, and bar stock. These machines are widely used for throughfeeding of parts requiring grinding of only one external diametral surface. Parts are fed across a steadyrest between an abrasive belt (running over an idler and contact wheel) and a regulating wheel (Fig. 26-42, *j*) or another abrasive belt (Fig. 26-42, *k*).

Existing centerless grinding machines can be converted for the use of abrasive belts by providing a contact wheel, idler, and belt. Some machines are equipped for reciprocating feed for heavier stock removal. Reciprocating feed can be done automatically by reversing the rotating direction of the regulating wheel (abrasive regulating belt) or repositioning the wheel of the feed belt at the end of each stroke.

ABRASIVE CUTOFF

Abrasive cutoff differs from most conventional grinding operations (in which flat, cylindrical, or contoured surfaces are finished) in that abrasive cutoff uses thin, bonded abrasive wheels to sever billets, bars, castings, forgings, extrusions, or other shapes for subsequent processing.

Cost per cut in abrasive cutoff can be relatively high because of high power requirements, limited wheel life, and material losses in the kerf, but in many cases it is more economical than other cutoff methods, especially for materials having higher strengths, temperature resistance, and hardness.

ABRASIVE CUTOFF WHEELS

Cutoff operations are performed either wet or dry, depending upon the workpiece material, cutoff machine setup, and other parameters. Specific recommendations to be used in initial selection of wheels for cutting different materials are given in Table 26-4. In the table, soft, medium, and hard designations are used instead of letter grades.

Dry Cutting

Dry cutting is the simplest and fastest method of abrasive cutting. It is generally used when quality of the surface finish produced is not of primary importance. Dry-abrasive cutoff is usually done with a resinoid-bonded wheel of rather coarse grit size and with relatively hard grades for soft materials and soft grades for hard materials. Aluminum oxide abrasive is generally used to cut most metals, and silicon carbide for nonmetallics.

Wet Cutting

Wet cutting was previously performed almost exclusively with calendered rubber wheels. These wheels minimize burning, burr formation, and possible workpiece damage and produce smooth surface finishes. High-speed wet cutting is now possible with so-called rubber-resin or pressed-rubber bonds. These wheels have high strength and can be easily reinforced with fiberglass materials.

Wheel Speed and Feed Rates

If the feed rate, d, at which a wheel is fed radially into the work is increased with the wheel peripheral speed, V, so that the ratio, d/V, is held constant, the efficiency of cutting increases. In other words, the rate of cutting will increase while wheel wear remains substantially the same.

Increased wheel speed without a corresponding increase in feed rate will make the wheel act harder. Also, if the feed rate is increased while the wheel speed is held constant, the wheel will act softer. If the feed rate is increased too much, the wheel will break. With the ratio, d/V, held constant, the same wheel grade range used for cutting at lower rates can be used for fast cutting. Since higher wheel speeds induce higher strains, however, stiffer wheels are required.

Normally, in wet cutting, rubber-bonded wheels should be operated at speeds ranging from 7500-9500 sfm (38.1-48.3 m/s). However, slower speeds in most wet cutoff operations will yield better quality without significant reduction of cutting rates.

In dry cutting, a fast rate of cutoff is essential for efficient operation. When cutting dry, wheel speed is generally higher than that used in wet cutting; speeds from 12,000-16,000 sfm (60.9-81.3 m/s) are suggested.

Inspection of Cutting Edge

Observation of wheel edges after cutting can give an indication of whether the proper wheel has been selected and whether the proper fluid is being used in wet cutoff operations. Figure 26-43 illustrates the most common cutting edge geometries after cutting. The significance of these geometries to the cutoff operation is detailed in the caption of Fig. 26-43.

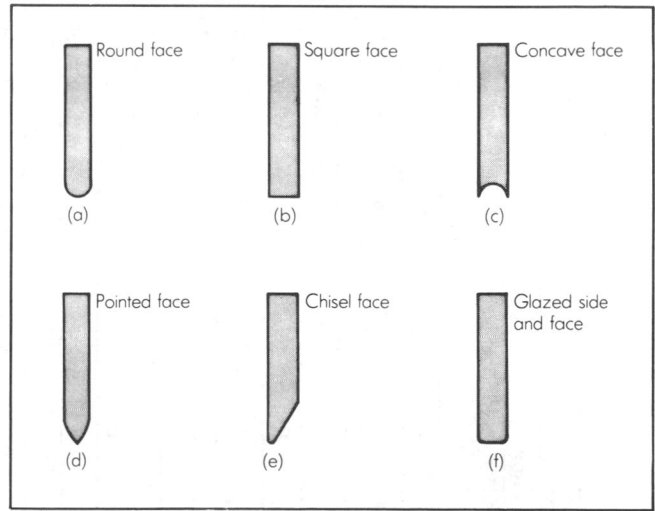

Fig. 26-43 Common cutoff wheel geometries: (a) Round face—normal when using proper wheel to cut large solids. (b) Square face—normal when using proper wheel to cut small solids, structurals, medium-wall pipe and tubing. (c) Concave face—normal when using proper wheel to cut tubing and thin wall sections. (d) Pointed face—means wall is too hard. May cause binding, breakage, and excessive burns on the cut. (e) Chisel face—wet cutting problem. Normally indicates wrong applications of fluid. May cause breakage and crooked cuts. (f) Glazed side and face—means wheel is too hard or cutting too slowly. Requires excessive pressure and power to cut. Causes breakage, excessive burr, and burn. (*Continental Machine Tool Co.*)

ABRASIVE CUTOFF

TABLE 26-4
Selection of Abrasive Cutting Wheels*

Material to be Cut	Wet — Soft — Size of Grain	Wet — Soft — Type of Bond	Wet — Medium — Size of Grain	Wet — Medium — Type of Bond	Wet — Hard — Size of Grain	Wet — Hard — Type of Bond	Dry — Soft — Size of Grain	Dry — Soft — Type of Bond	Dry — Medium — Size of Grain	Dry — Medium — Type of Bond	Dry — Hard — Size of Grain	Dry — Hard — Type of Bond
Alnico	A120	R	A80	R	A80	R	A60	B	A46	B	A36	B
Aluminum (hard): Bar	A46	R	A46	RB	A24	RB	A46	B	A36	B	A36	B
Tubing	A120	R	A90	R	A80	R	A90	R	A90	RB	A90	B
Asbestos products (molded)			C24	B			C36	B	C30	B	C24	B
Beryllium	C120	R	C90	R	C60	R						
Bits (mine or drill)			A46	R	A46	RB	A46	B	A36	B	A30	B
Brass and bronze (hard): Bar	A90	R	A46	R	A46	R	A60	B	A46	B	A36	B
Tubing	A120	R	A90	R	A80	R	A90	R	A90	RB	A90	B
Brick: Common			C24	B			C20	B	C20	B	C20	B
Face							C24	B	C20	B	C20	B
Cable (steel)	A120	R	A90	R	A46	RB	A90	R	A46	B	A30	B
Carbon							C60	B	C46	B	C36	B
Cast-iron pipe			A46	R	A24	RB	A36	B	A36	B	A30	B
Channel Iron	A90	R	A46	R	A24	RB	A36	B	A30	B	A24	B
Concrete and cinder block			C24	B	C24	B	C20	B	C20	B	C20	B
Copper (hard): Bar	A90	R	A46	R	A46	R	A60	B	A46	B	A36	B
Tubing	A120	R	A90	R	A80	R	A90	R	A90	RB	A90	B
Drill rod	A80	R	A46	R	A46	R	A60	B	A46	B	A36	B
Drills, twist	A60	R	A46	R	A46	R	A46	B	A36	B	A36	B
Fiber: Tubing	C60	R	C60	R	C60	R	C46	B	C46	B	C36	B
Solids	C60	R	C60	R			C46	B	C46	B	C36	B
Gates and risers: Steel									A30	B	A24	B
Brass and bronze									A30	B	A24	B
Germanium: Large sections	C120	R	C120	R	C120	R						
Small sections			C240	R	C180	R						
Glass: Solids and heavy wall	C120	R	C90	R	C120	R						
Tubing and thin wall			C120	R	C120	R						
Pyrex and Vycor			C120	R								
High-temperature alloys	A46	R	A60	R	A46	R			A30	B	A24	B
Investment castings									A46	B	A30	B
Knives (machine)	A60	R	A80	R	A60	R	A46	B	A36	B	A30	B

TABLE 26-4—Continued

Material to be Cut	Wet Cutting Soft — Size of Grain	Type of Bond	Medium — Size of Grain	Type of Bond	Hard — Size of Grain	Type of Bond	Dry Cutting Soft — Size of Grain	Type of Bond	Medium — Size of Grain	Type of Bond	Hard — Size of Grain	Type of Bond
Metallographic specimens:												
Large sections	A60	RB	A90	R	A60	R			A60	B		
Small sections	A120	R	A90	R	A80	R						
Molybdenum	A90	R	A46	R	A46	R						
Nickel alloys	A46	R	A46	R	A36	R			A36	B	A30	B
Nickel anodes	A46	R	A46	R	A36	R	A36		A30	B	A24	B
Pen points	A320	R	A240	R	A220	R			A240	R		
Pipe (steel)	A46	RB	A46	RB	A24	RB	A36	RB	A30	B	A24	B
Plastics (thermosetting)			C80	R	C60	R	C46	B	C36	B	C30	B
Porcelain			C90	R	C60	R	C60	B	C46	B	C36	B
Refractory brick			C24	B			C20	B	C20	B	C20	B
Rubber (hard)	C60	R	C60	R	C46	R	C36	B	C30	B	C24	B
Steel: Carbon bars	A46	R	A46	R	A46	RB	A36	B	A30	B	A24	B
Alloys and tool bars	A60	R	A46	R	A46	R	A46	B	A36	B	A30	B
Plate	A46	RB	A46	RB	A46	RB	A24	RB	A24	RB	A24	B
Tubing (including flexible)	A120	R	A90	R	A60	R	A90	B	A60	B	A46	B
Tubing (capillary)									A240	R	A180	R
Stainless steel: Bars	A46	R	A46	R	A36	R	A36	B	A30	B	A24	B
Tubing (including flexible)	A120	R	A90	R	A60	R	A120	B	A90	B	A60	B
Stellite	A60	R	A46	RB	A46	RB			A30	B	A24	B
Tile	C24	B	C24	B			C24	B	C24	B	C24	B
Titanium: Large sections	C120	R	C60	R	C46	RB						
Small sections	C240	R	C120	R	C120	R						
Tools (salvage)	A90	R	A60	R	A60	R			A36	B	A36	B
Transformer cores	A60	R	A46	R	A46	R						
Tungsten: Rod	A180	R	A180	R	A120	R						
Large sections (high density)	C120	R	C120	R	C120	R						
Uranium	C120	R	C90	R	C46	RB						
Valve stems	A46	R	A46	R	A46	R			A36	B	A30	B
Zirconium	C120	R	C60	R	C46	RB						B

* Find the material you wish to cut, read to the left if it is to be cut wet, to the right if dry. The selection from the three columns on either side should be based on the following general rules: (1) Soft wheels give highest quality, fastest cutting, and may be required to cut the harder varieties of some materials. (2) Medium wheels are for the average job, giving a good compromise of quality, speed of cut, and economy. (3) Hard wheels give longer wheel life where quality requirements are less exacting and will give excellent results on the softer variations of some materials. Code: Abrasive type: A, aluminum oxide; C, silicon carbide. Bond type: R, rubber; B, resinoid; RB, rubber-resin.

ABRASIVE CUTOFF

ABRASIVE CUTOFF MACHINES

There are four basic types of abrasive cutoff machines: chopstroke, oscillating, horizontal, and rotary, as shown in Fig. 26-44. Each type is available for manual, semiautomatic, or fully automatic operation. All machines must be rigidly designed to minimize vibration and must have sufficient horsepower for fast wheel speeds and fast cutting rates. Large cylinders are needed to feed the wheels at fast rates into the work.

An adaptive control unit is available on some abrasive cutoff machines to show total cost per cut. A computer is used to automatically control the feed rate at which the machine operates to obtain the conditions for the lowest cost per cut. Programmed into the computer are direct labor costs, variable and fixed costs related to the machine, and cost of the wheel. Cost of each cut is computed and reflected in both a visual and a printed readout. This information is stored in the computer memory and compared with subsequent cuts made with different feed rates. The computer then makes a decision to either increase or decrease the feed rate as it seeks the optimum feed rate that will give minimum cost per cut.

Chopstroke Machines

Chopstroke machines are the simplest and generally are used for cutting bars or tubes from 2-4″ (51-102 mm) diam. Workpieces are held in a fixed position, and a pivoted wheel, up to about 26″ (660 mm) diam, cuts down through the work. Workpiece capacity is dependent upon the wheel diameter and horsepower of the wheel drive motor. The longest cross-sectional dimension of the work should be placed parallel to the direction in which the wheel is fed to minimize the length of chip produced. Fast feeds minimize burning of the work. Coarse, hard wheels are more efficient. Fine, soft wheels minimize burrs, but wear faster.

Oscillating Machines

Oscillating abrasive cutoff machines simulate a sawing action and can handle larger sections up to 12″ (305 mm) round or square. Newer machines of this type are designed so that the amplitude of oscillation of the wheel remains the same over the entire vertical distance it travels, thus increasing cutting efficiency. Most modern machines are also equipped so that

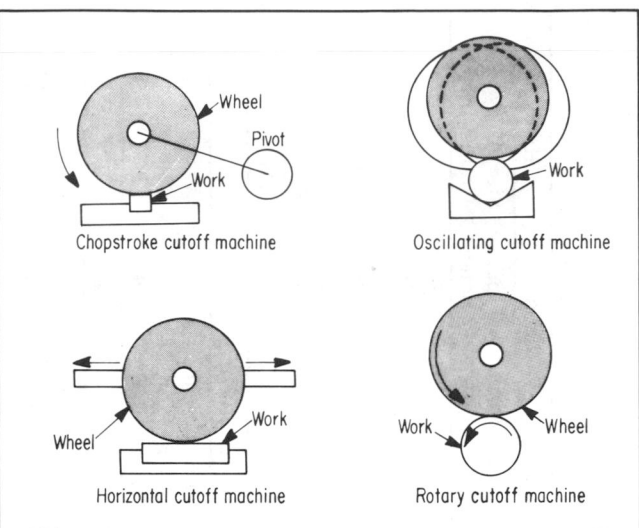

Fig. 26-44 Four basic types of abrasive cutoff machines. Each type is available for manual, semiautomatic, or fully automatic operation. operation.

both amplitude and frequency of oscillation may be varied over a wide range.

Horizontal-Traverse Machines

Horizontal-traverse machines have either a wheel that moves horizontally across the work (traversing wheel) or a fixed wheel against which the work is moved (fixed spindle). Traversing-wheel machines are used for cutting medium or large plates and slabs several inches (about 75 mm) thick, while fixed-spindle machines are employed to cut glass and nonmetallic materials such as brick, tile, and refractories.

Rotary Machines

Rotary machines have both the wheel and work rotating, making it possible to cut solid round stock of twice the diameter that could be cut if the work were stationary. This method is recommended for cutting bars over 8″ (203 mm) diam. Wheels can be worn to a smaller diameter, thus reducing cost per cut.

HONING FOR HEAVY STOCK REMOVAL

Honing is an abrasive machining operation in which heavy stock can be removed from the wall of a bore by the shearing action of abrasive grains.

The honing operation is actually the only production stock removal process that can be used on any length of bore without loss of accuracy. The accuracy of the honing operation is not dependent upon the alignment or rigidity of the honing tool. Inaccuracies of previous operations are overcome. Axial straightness is generated through the length of the stones. This extra length assures stock removal on the high spots first. Diametric roundness is generated by the rotary motion of the tool and its freedom to center itself with the neutral axis of the bore. Diametric straightness (freedom of taper) is generated by the reciprocation of the tool and the maintenance of a constant

pressure throughout the stone area. Cutting pressure is equal at all points of the stone surface since the honing stones stabilize the center of rotation on the neutral axis of the bore.

HEAVY STOCK REMOVAL

Since the honing operation is the only type of machining that is suitable for certain types of parts, it must also be used for heavy stock removal operations. The term heavy stock removal is sometimes a little misleading since an automotive cylinder bore with 0.006-0.008″ (0.15-0.20 mm) stock would be heavy while a steel cylinder tube with this amount of stock would be rather light.

Honing is the only machining operation that can successfully remove the stock and generate the bore accuracy and still maintain an economical production operation. The following require-

HONING FOR HEAVY STOCK REMOVAL

ments are necessary for a heavy stock removal application:

- The honing machine must be of the most rugged spindle and head construction available.
- The horsepower of both the spindle and the hydraulic reciprocation must be greater than the horsepower of standard machines.
- Monitors should be employed on motors to check power consumption.
- A heavy-duty hone expansion system must be used to give the maximum cutting action to the stones.
- The fixtures must be of an extremely rigid construction to resist both the up and down thrust of the tool, hold the torque, and at the same time prevent distortion of the part.
- Sufficient honing fluid must be supplied at all times to flush away the metal and grit. Traditionally, the honing fluid is cooled to control heat buildup in the workpiece. However, tests have shown that heated honing oil sometimes contributes to faster cutting action.
- The basic honing tool carrying the stones must be of a heavy-duty type including both the upper and lower universal joints.

BORE FINISH CONTROL

The important factor in heavy stock removal honing operations is that it is impossible to hone large amounts of stock from the bore at a good production rate and at the same time obtain a good surface finish. Heavy stock removal applications require the use of relatively coarse grits in the honing stones, and these stones must operate under extreme force against the wall of the bore; they thereby inherently cause the finish to be rough. From this point, if a fine finish is required, fine-grit stones must be used and a second honing operation applied. On this type of operation, small amounts of stock are removed at a slower rate and the proper finish is obtained.

HONING FLUIDS

The fluid in honing operations has two major roles: (1) it keeps abrasive elements clean and lubricated and (2) it carries away the heat and sludge generated by the cutting action. Fluid cleanliness will result in fewer rejects, and increased efficiency is realized in that the honing stones do not become loaded with waste particles. The load-free fluid flush minimizes abrasive deposits on the machine surfaces, fixtures, tables, and critical working parts of the honing machine.

The primary function of refrigerated honing fluid is to remove the heat energy created by the work being done. Heavy stock removal applications in which high removal rates are employed will produce temperatures in excess of 150° F (65° C).

Most materials can be honed with either the mixtures as noted in Table 26-5 or some slight variation. If a fine finish is required, the chemical activity of the honing fluid should be increased by the addition of the sulfur-based oil; however, in some cases, the cutting will be somewhat retarded. Conversely, a low-activity fluid (kerosene) is very aggressive in the honing of soft steel and, in some instances, will tend to tear the bore, so the fluid must always be dampened with some sulfur-based oil.

Fluids for the honing of aluminum are also somewhat critical since aluminum tends to load the stones and retard the cutting. Because aluminum is rather soft, an aggressive stone and fluid

will tear the bore, so both the fluid and the grit and grade of the stones are somewhat more critical.

TABLE 26-5
Honing Fluid Formulations for Various Materials

Material	Honing Fluid Formulation
Cast iron	100% kerosene or mineral seal oil, or 90% kerosene or mineral seal with 10% sulphur base oil.
Soft steel	75-80% kerosene or mineral seal with 20-25% sulphur base oil.
Hard steel	100% kerosene or mineral seal oil, or 95% kerosene or mineral seal with 5% sulphur base oil.

References

1. "Markings for Identifying Grinding Wheels and Other Bonded Abrasives," ANSI Standard B74.13-1977, American National Standards Institute, New York, p. 6.
2. *Ibid.*
3. *Ibid.*, p. 7.
4. "Specifications for Shapes and Sizes of Grinding Wheels, and Identification of Mounted Wheels," ANSI Standard B74.2-1974, American National Standards Institute, New York.
5. "Safety Requirements for the Use, Care and Protection of Abrasive Wheels," ANSI Standard B7.1-1978, American National Standards Institute, New York.
6. "Safety Requirements for the Construction Care and Use of Grinding Machines," ANSI Standard B11.9-1975, American National Standards Institute, New York.
7. P. Guenther Werner, "Application and Technological Fundamentals of Deep and Creep Feed Grinding," SME Technical Paper MR79-319, 1979.
8. P. Guenther Werner, "Technological Fundamentals and Practical Feasibility of Creep Feed Grinding," Research Project, Laboratory for Manufacturing and Productivity, MIT, Cambridge, MA, 1979.
9. "Development and Application of Creep-Feed Surface Grinding," ELB Grinders Corp., 1978.
10. John B. Kohls and Guy Bellows, "Low Stress Grinding: Its Parameters and Potential," *Manufacturing Engineering* (October 1976) p. 38.

THREADING

Threads are used extensively on many different components. The two basic types of threads are as follows:

1. Threads used on fasteners, such as screws, bolts, studs, nuts, and inserts, to hold compo-

nents together. Some fasteners, such as tapping screws, cut or form a mating thread when driven into holes.

2. Threads used on components, such as lead-screws, to transmit power and motion.

THREAD MANUFACTURING

Threads are produced on workpieces by a number of different tools and processes. Tools used are single-point tools, chasers, taps, or dies. Processes employed include turning, boring, milling, grinding, or rolling. The method selected depends primarily upon the workpiece size, shape, and material; whether internal or external threads are to be cut; equipment available; and the required production rate, accuracy, and surface finish.

SINGLE-POINT THREADING

Many threads are produced on both external and internal surfaces of workpieces with single-point tools using a wide variety of machines. The tool moves longitudinally in constant relation to rotation of the workpiece, thus determining the lead of the thread. To cut right-hand threads, the tool is moved from right to left; for left-hand threads, the tool must be moved from left to right. External threads can be cut with the workpiece mounted either between centers or held in a chuck; internal thread cutting requires that the workpiece be held in a chuck, collet, or fixture. Threads are produced by taking a series of cuts until desired thread depth is reached.

Single-Point Tools for Threading

Thread cutting with single-point tools is one of the most difficult machining operations. The small, tapered nose of the tool is buried in the workpiece, making it susceptible to breakage from the cutting forces and deformation from heat concentrated at the weakest part of the tool. High feed rates required for threading necessitate large clearance angles on the tools, making them weaker and less able to dissipate heat.

High-speed steel tools. Single-point threading tools made from HSS are generally limited to low-volume requirements because they cannot be operated at cutting speeds as high as those for carbide or ceramic tools.

Brazed carbide tools. The initial cost of a brazed-tip carbide tool is usually less than that of an indexable carbide insert tool, but the cost per cutting edge is higher. As a result, brazed carbide tools are generally used only for low-volume applications or special threading applications when indexable tooling would be more expensive.

Indexable carbide inserts. Mechanically held indexable carbide inserts are the most extensively used tools for single-point threading. Their advantages include assurance of correct thread profiles,

efficient geometries for fast production, and eliminating the need for tool regrinding.

Various types of inserts and holders are available for threading. One popular combination for cutting vee or modified vee threads consists of an unground triangular insert having either negative or neutral-rake geometry and a suitable toolholder (see Fig. 27-1, view c). Such standard turning inserts cost less than threading inserts and are available with pressed-in chip control grooves. Negative rake inserts have a 90° included angle between their rake and flank faces and are therefore stronger than most other threading inserts. When an insert with a 60° included angle is used in a toolholder that positions it at a negative-rake angle, the thread profile produced has an included angle slightly more than 60°. For this reason, such tools are generally restricted to rough threading that does not require precise tolerances. When neutral-rake toolholders are used, however, exact 60° vee threads are produced.

Laydown insert tooling (Fig. 27-1, view b) is also used extensively for threading, especially internal threading as it allows indexable tools to be used for threading smaller bores. It consists of a triangular insert, with the thread form profile ground on its face, set down flat in a toolholder or boring bar. The tooling is available with negative or neutral-rake angles. Negative-rake inserts are available unground at less cost, but they are less accurate than precision-ground, neutral-rake inserts. The negative-rake inserts can be used for either internal or external threading, and can be turned over for the opposite thread form, thus providing six cutting edges per insert.

On-edge tooling (Fig. 27-1, view c) consists of a triangular insert, with the thread form profile ground across its width, set on edge in a toolholder or boring bar. Such tooling is more expensive than laydown tooling, but is more versatile and allows a single toolholder to perform both threading and grooving operations. Three cutting edges are available on each insert. Some on-edge threading inserts are available with positive-rake angles. They can be used in neutral-rake tool-holders and are recommended for very gummy materials when built-up edges are a problem.

Vee bottom tooling uses a so-called dogbone insert (Fig. 27-1, view d) that has the thread form profile ground across its width. This tooling is generally more expensive than the other types of indexable tooling discussed, but it requires less

SINGLE-POINT THREADING

space and is well suited for internal threading of small holes. Two cutting edges are available on each insert.

Figure 27-2 shows several different inserts for single-point threading. View *a* illustrates nontopping, lead topping, follow topping, and full topping inserts. To use nontopping inserts, the OD or ID of the workpieces must be finish turned or bored before threading because the inserts perform no topping. The other three inserts require that a small amount of stock be left on the workpiece before threading, with the stock being removed on the final threading pass. A typical lead and follow topping, indexable insert is illustrated in Fig. 27-2, view *b*.

The insert and bar shown in Fig. 27-2, view *c*, is used to thread both ends of small pipe couplings on low-powered machines with feed in only one direction. During cutting of the front thread in the coupling, the insert is lead topping; in cutting the back thread, the insert is follow topping.

Many internal threads are generated in small-diameter bores with taps (discussed later in this chapter). An increasing number of thread cutting operations in small bores, however, are being performed with carbide inserts, especially when frequent changeovers in thread sizes are needed. One type of tooling, consisting of inserts and boring bars for threading bores as small as 0.440″ (11.18 mm) diam is illustrated in Fig. 27-3. Inserts made from several grades of carbide are available for threading various materials. A four-way locking system pulls the insert down and back into a pocket in the bar for accurate positioning and secure holding through the combination of a clamp and lockscrew. Inserts are also available for internal grooving operations.

Helix angles of the tools are important in single-point threading to create the correct side clearances, especially when coarse pitch, small diameter, multiple-lead, or square threads are to be produced.

Operating Parameters for Single-Point Threading

Three methods of cutting vee or modified vee threads with single-point tools are as follows:

1. The single-point tool can be compound fed at just under half the thread angle (normally 29°) so that the leading edge of the insert removes almost all the metal (see Fig. 27-4, view *a*). This compound feed method is generally used only for roughing cuts. Tool life is slightly better than with other types of feed motions.
2. Plunge feed of the tool (Fig. 27-4, view *b*) can be used for both roughing and finishing. The thread form produced is usually an exact duplicate of the insert form.
3. Very large threads are sometimes machined a third way. The threading tool is plunge fed on one side of the form, incremented, plunge fed again, and so on until the full width of the form is machined (Fig. 27-4, view *c*).

When threads must be cut close to shoulders with single-point tools, relief grooves are often machined directly adjacent to the shoulders prior to cutting the threads. This allows the noses of the threading tools to clear the workpieces before they are withdrawn, thus avoiding possible tool damage. Thread relief grooves are not needed when threading is done on NC/CNC or cam-operated threading machines which withdraw the tools at exactly the same point each pass.

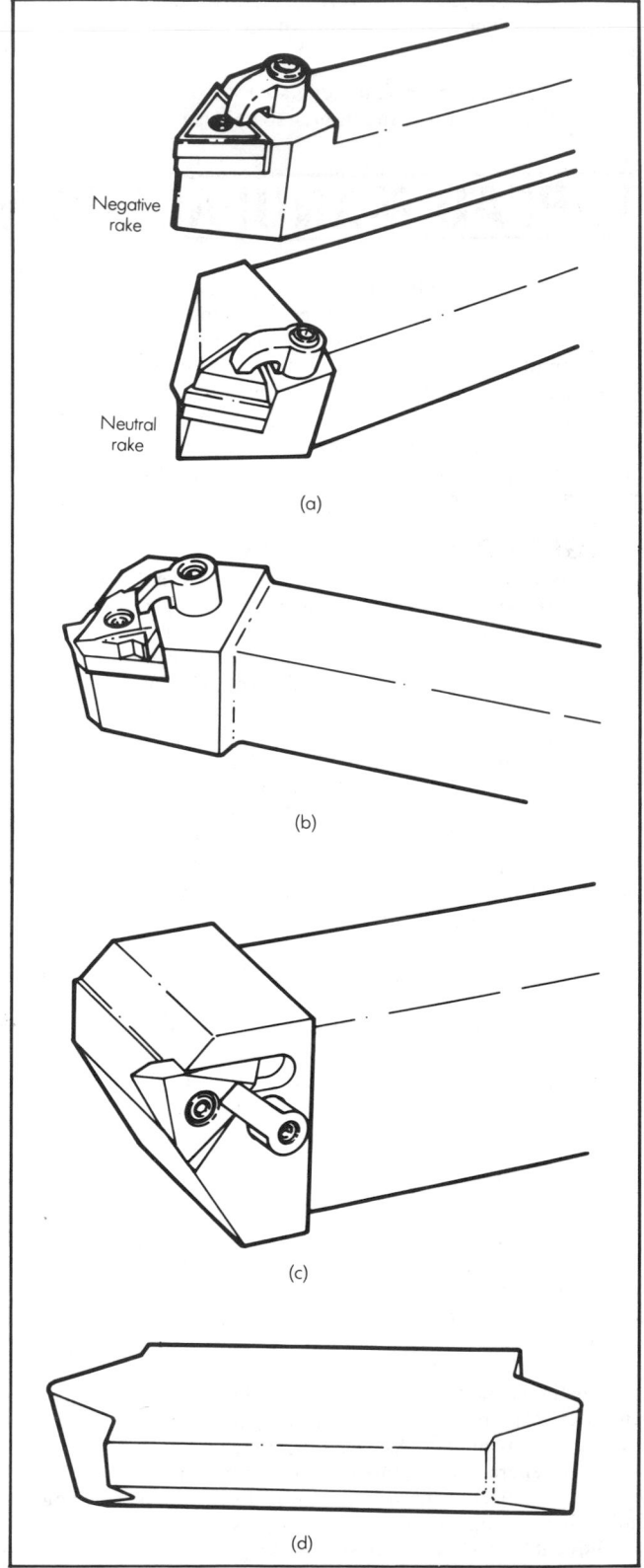

Negative rake

Neutral rake

(a)

(b)

(c)

(d)

Fig. 27-1 Various types of insert tooling for single-point threading: (a) unground triangular insert with either negative or neutral rake geometry, (b) laydown triangular insert, (c) on-edge tooling, and (d) vee bottom tooling. (*Carboloy Systems Dept., General Electric Co.*)

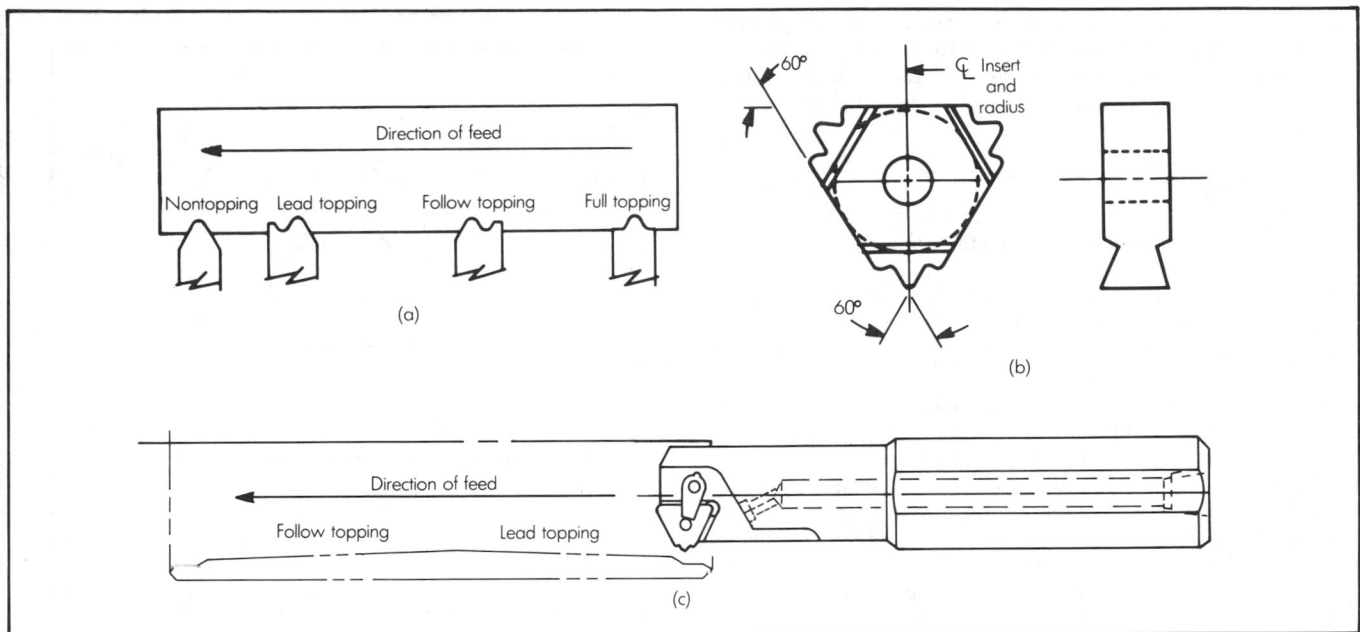

Fig. 27-2 Single-point threading tools: (a) various inserts, (b) an indexable insert, and (c) insert and bar. (*Valenite Div., Valeron Corp.*)

THREAD CHASING

Chasing is a widely used, high-production method of producing uniform helical threads on external or internal surfaces of workpieces. All common thread forms, including close-tolerance straight or taper pipe threads, are produced by chasing.

Process Fundamentals

Self-opening die heads and collapsible taps are assembled tools incorporating clusters of multipoint, inserted cutting components called chasers. The cutting edges are not integral with the tool body, as is the case with solid dies and taps discussed later in this chapter.

The tools continually cut while traversing the length of the thread, parallel to the axis of the workpiece. Traverse rate of the tool is governed by the lead of the thread required. When a thread is completed, the individual cutting components are automatically pulled clear of the workpiece, thus permitting withdrawal of the tool head without the need for reversing the spindle.

Advantages of Chasing

Since self-opening mechanisms are used in chasing, time is saved because it is not necessary to backtrack the tool to clear the work; time is also saved and tool life is lengthened appreciably because the individual sets of chasers (cutters) are readily adjustable for pitch diameter and may be reground or replaced when dulled or worn. The quality of thread is improved, since limits may be more closely maintained and, because the necessity for backtracking is eliminated, there is less danger of damage to threads in copper and other soft materials, particularly with fine-pitch threads.

Thread Chasing Applications

Nonrotating types of self-opening die heads and collapsible taps are used when the tool is held stationary and the work is

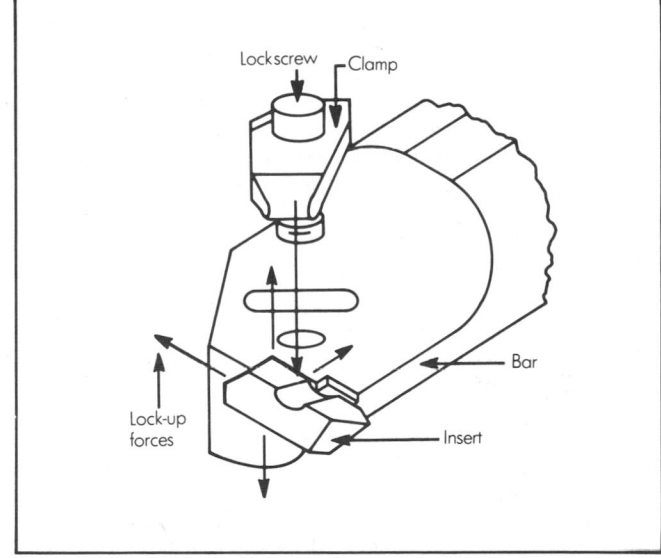

Fig. 27-3 Clamping system for threading small bores with a carbide insert. (*Kennametal Inc.*)

rotated. Applications of each type are found on bolt threading and special threading machines, hand and automatic screw machines, engine and turret lathes, and different types of drilling machines.

Self-Opening Die Heads

Both stationary and rotary types of self-opening die heads are external thread-cutting tools in which the chasers automatically withdraw from the work at the completion of the thread, making reversal of the machine unnecessary. Tools of this description, in addition to saving considerable time, have many other advantages over solid threading dies. Chasers, made in

THREAD CHASING

sets of four or more, can be easily removed for resharpening and can be quickly and accurately adjusted to size. These tools, with suitable chasers, cut either right or left-hand threads, straight or taper, in a range of diameters within the rated capacity of the tool.

Collapsing Taps

Collapsing taps are internal thread cutting tools in which the chasers automatically withdraw from the work at the completion of the thread, making reversal of the machine unnecessary. These tools save the reversal time of solid taps. The chasers, made in sets of three or more, can be easily removed for resharpening and can also be quickly and accurately adjusted to size. These taps, with suitable chasers, cut either right or left-hand threads, straight or tapered, in a range of diameters within the rated capacity of the tool.

There are two methods of producing taper threads with a collapsible tap. Taps that are primarily intended for cutting straight threads can be used to produce taper threads by employing appropriate chaser sets which have the rate of the thread incorporated into the chasers. With this method, the chasers cut across their full length and the thread is jam cut. This generally restricts the taper thread which can be produced to the National Pipe Thread (NPT) form.

Fully receding chaser-type taps are available to produce NPT and similar forms when more exacting tolerance and quality standards must be met, or to cut the longer-length precision threads dictated by American Petroleum Institute (API) standards. With these taps, the thread is produced by the throat section and first full thread of the chaser, and the rate of taper is realized through the use of a cam mechanism. Provision is made to change the cam mechanism to produce different taper rates. The full receding tap must be used with leadscrew or positive feed.

All collapsible-type taps, including stationary and rotary taps, can be supplied for either nonrotating or revolving type applications.

Solid Adjustable Taps

The chasers of solid adjustable taps do not automatically withdraw from the work at the conclusion of the threading operation. They can be easily removed for resharpening and accurately adjusted for size, giving this tool a definite advantage over solid taps.

Solid adjustable taps are used on multiple-spindle automatics, automatic screw machines, and other similar applications where tool space is limited and collapsing taps cannot be used. Means must be provided on the machine for reversing the tap or reducing the spindle speed with respect to the workpiece. The type of shank varies with the application. It is not uncommon to use solid adjustable taps for sizing purposes in cases in which, for various reasons, it is desirable to finish a thread by hand.

Special Taps

Included in the special tap classification are modifications of standard tools which can be designed to meet a wide variety of unusual requirements. Pilots in lengths to meet specific requirements can be added to the front end of the tap in place of the usual cap to ensure concentricity with previously bored holes. Guides can be placed on the body of the tap behind the chasers for alignment with a previously finished hole in the work or a guide bushing in the jig or fixture.

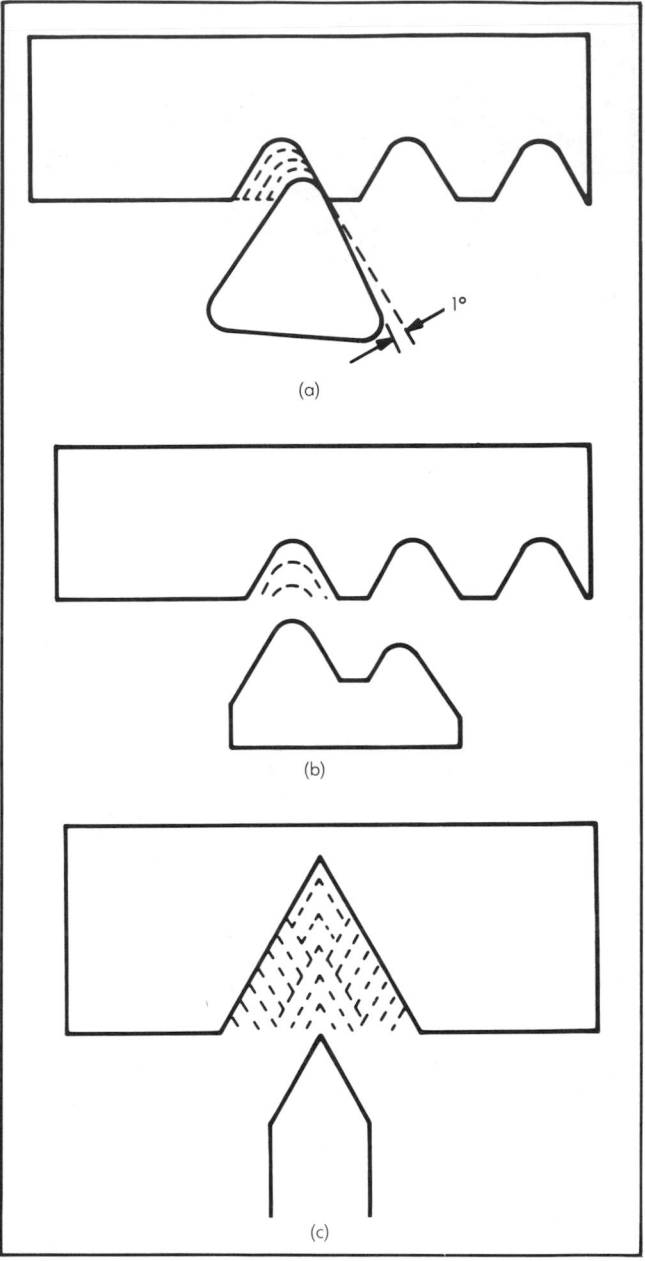

Fig. 27-4 Three methods of cutting vee or modified vee threads with inserts; (a) compound feed, (b) plunge feed, and (c) incremental feed. (*Carboloy Systems Dept., General Electric Co.*)

Tap Chasers

Three types of tap chasers are in use: regular, overhanging, and circular.

Regular chasers. Regular chasers (see Fig. 27-5, view *a*) do not extend through the front cap of the tap body and are furnished when tapping is not close to a shoulder or bottom. They can be resharpened on both the chamfer and the cutting face.

Overhanging chasers. Overhanging chasers (Fig. 27-5, view *b*) extend through the front cap of the tap and are required for bottoming and close-to-shoulder work. Practically all the resharpening is done on the cutting face. Occasionally they are lightly reground on the chamfer.

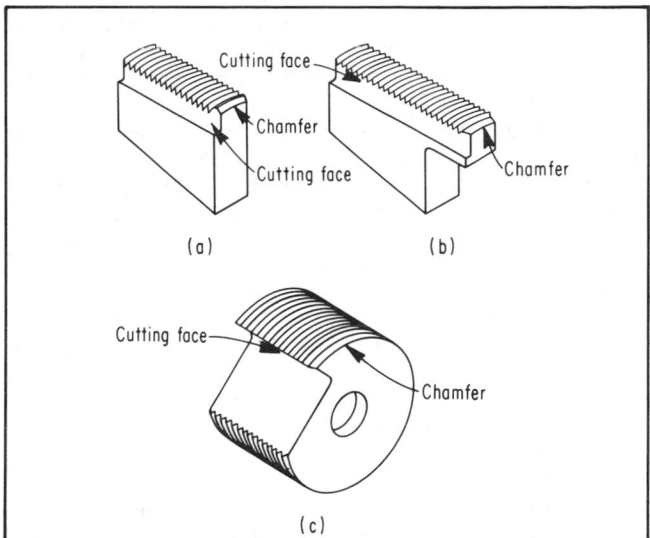

Fig. 27-5 Types of tap chasers: (a) regular, (b) overhanging, and (c) circular.

Circular chasers. Circular chaser (Fig. 27-5, view *c*) have a single flute which provides the cutting edge and also the necessary chip space. These chasers are resharpened on the cutting face only.

Metric threads. Both collapsible and solid adjustable taps can be converted for use in metric threading operations by inserting sets of metric chasers in existing taps that have the proper range capability.

INTERNAL THREADING WITH SOLID TAPS

Tapping is a process for producing internal helical threads using a tool, called a tap, that has threads on its periphery to cut or form the required threads in existing holes by a combination of axial and rotary motions. A solid tap is basically a precise screw which has been fluted to provide multiple cutting surfaces and spaces for cutting fluid and chips. Cutting edges are created by radially relieved chamfers at the working ends of the taps, which are made from hard cutting tool materials.

Tapping involves relative axial and rotational motions between the tap and the workpiece. In most cases, the tap is rotated and fed into the workpiece, but sometimes the workpiece is rotated and either the workpiece or tap is fed. The feed per revolution must be the same as the pitch of the required thread.

Accuracy of Tapped Threads

The main function of a tap is to produce internal threads. It is usually required that the threads have a reasonable degree of accuracy with respect to size and form. Primary accuracy requirements apply to the size or pitch diameter of the threads. Thread form is generally easy to control and is seldom a problem. The size of the threaded holes, however, can be affected by the hole size before tapping, operating conditions, and properties of the material being threaded.

The most important requirements for precision tapping are true-running spindles and taps. A tap may not run true even if the machine spindle does; tap shanks and holders must be equally accurate. Holes cannot be uniformly tapped to close tolerance unless the pitch diameter, lead, and angle of the tap thread are all carefully held to specifications.

It is of utmost importance that the chamfer on the tap be accurately ground on every land. Even though the tap runs true, if the chamfer is not accurately ground, there will be considerable variation in tapped holes.

A tap mounted in a machine having a worn spindle will not consistently produce accurately tapped holes. When pressure is applied to a loose spindle during a tapping operation, the tap is forced out of alignment with the hole and strain is placed on the tap. As the tap enters the hole and starts to cut, there is a tendency for the tap to wobble and shave a slight amount of metal off the side of the thread. When the tap is reversing, the tapped hole, being larger than the tap itself, gives no support to the tap and the tap cuts while running backward. This may cause dulling, oversized holes, and galling of the thread flanks.

A comparison is shown in Fig. 27-6 between the quality of threaded connections obtained under various conditions of tap trueness and pitch tolerances on a nut and bolt. These conditions are summarized in the following list. A condition somewhere between conditions 2 and 3 is best.

1. *Poor condition.* A bellmouthed tapped hole condition (see Fig. 27-6, view *a*) results when the tap does not run true, when too much pressure is applied to the tap, or when the tap is used in some floating chucks.
2. *Acceptable condition.* This results when the hole is tapped to a maximum nut pitch diameter limit (see Fig. 27-6, view *b*); no lead or thread-angle errors exist. Metal-to-metal contact on one flank is obtained over the entire length of engagement, but the nut is at its weakest acceptable condition.
3. *Good condition.* This results when the hole is tapped to a minimum nut pitch diameter limit (see Fig. 27-6, view *c*); no lead or thread-angle errors exist. Metal-to-metal contact is maximum over the entire length of engagement, but assembly would be difficult with a maximum bolt.

Percentage of Thread in Tapped Holes

The percentage of depth of thread being tapped is important to efficient and economical tapping. Too great a percentage throws a strain on the teeth of the tap and serves no useful purpose. The greater the percentage, the more power required to tap, the more difficult to hold size, and the greater the amount of tap breakage, because more metal must be removed in a given time. Many difficulties in tapping are direct results of attempting to tap too great a percentage of thread.

Even the generally accepted 70-75% depth of thread is rather difficult to produce with certain small-sized taps of the UNC standard, since the smaller taps in the coarse pitches have to remove too great a percentage of metal in relation to their dimensions and strength.

As a general rule, the tougher the material, the lower should be the percentage of thread. It is difficult to tap even 60% depth of thread into stainless steel, Monel, copper, and some of the heat-treated alloy steels. Manufacturers who have studied this problem have reduced the percentage of thread in these materials, in many cases without sacrificing the usefulness of the tapped hole. The minor diameter of the tapped hole should fall within the limits specified for the class of thread required.

If small-diameter taps of coarse pitches are closely examined, it can be found that, after the amount of metal removed to form the flute of the tap and the amount of metal removed to form the thread are deducted, more than 50% of the total cross-sectional

INTERNAL THREADING

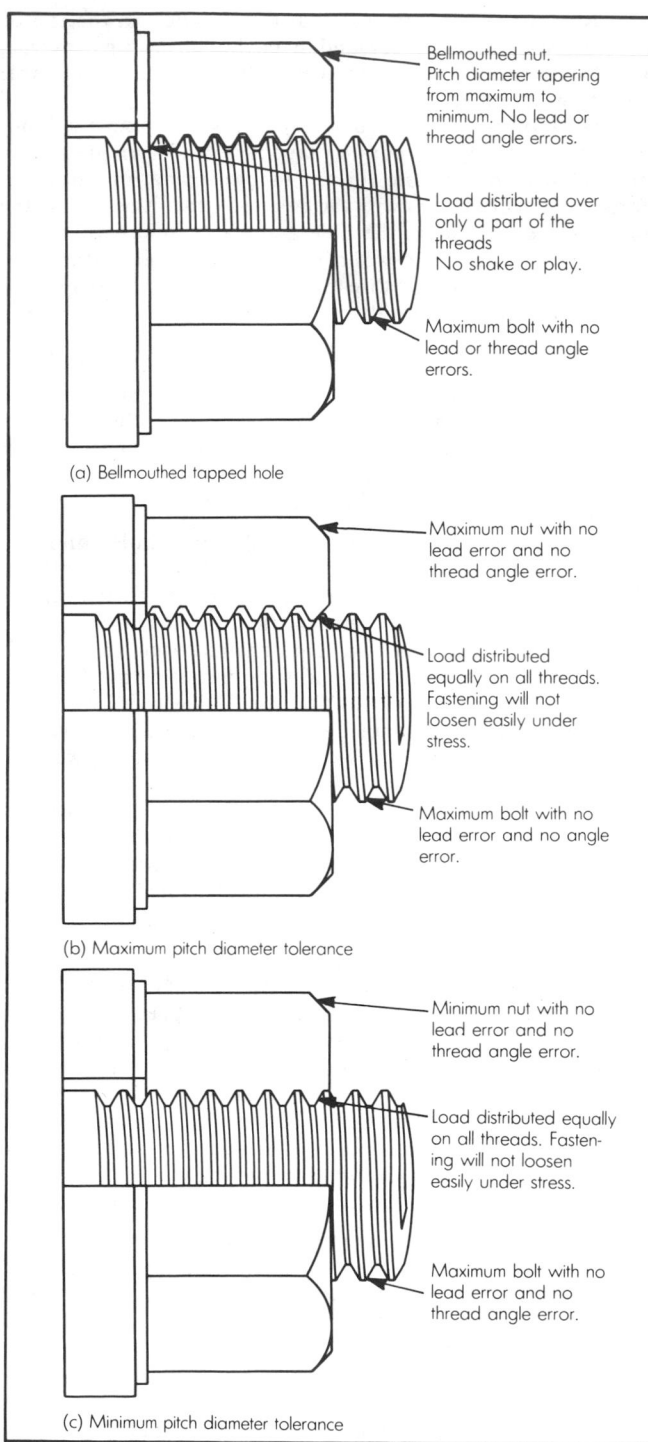

(a) Bellmouthed tapped hole

- Bellmouthed nut. Pitch diameter tapering from maximum to minimum. No lead or thread angle errors.
- Load distributed over only a part of the threads No shake or play.
- Maximum bolt with no lead or thread angle errors.

(b) Maximum pitch diameter tolerance

- Maximum nut with no lead error and no thread angle error.
- Load distributed equally on all threads. Fastening will not loosen easily under stress.
- Maximum bolt with no lead error and no angle error.

(c) Minimum pitch diameter tolerance

- Minimum nut with no lead error and no thread angle error.
- Load distributed equally on all threads. Fastening will not loosen easily under stress.
- Maximum bolt with no lead error and no thread angle error.

Fig. 27-6 Quality of tapped-hole threaded connections.

area of the tap has been cut away. This is one of the reasons why it is difficult to remove a greater percentage of thread in a **tapped hole.** The core diameter of such a tap is very small in relation to its outside diameter, and the tap is weakened to such an extent that, if an attempt is made to tap 70-90% depth of thread, the tap might break. On the larger sizes an entirely

different condition exists, since the amount of metal cut away for the flute and thread provides sufficient core diameter so that the tap is capable of producing a large percentage of thread without breaking.

Definite limits for the minor diameters of tapped holes have been set for both the UNC and the UNF series in ANSI Standard B1.1 and other standards, assuming a certain minimum length of engagement. For the most commonly used classes of thread fit, 1B and 2B, the maximum minor diameter corresponds to the percentage of thread height as given in Table 27-1. For the closer fitting class 3B threads, the maximum minor diameter is reduced to ensure a larger area of engagement. The thread height percentages in Table 27-1 provide ample strength to ensure that a screw or bolt of the same material and hardness as the tapped part will break before stripping of threads occurs when the length of engagement is 67% of nominal diameter or more.

When the length of engagement is less than 67%, the thread height percentage should be increased. With such shallow tapped holes, there is less difficulty in tapping increased thread heights. When the length of engagement is more than 150% of nominal diameter, the hole is considered deep and the thread height percentage may be further reduced, thus easing the problem of tapping such holes without reducing the strength of the threaded joint.

TABLE 27-1
Thread Height Percentages for
Classes 1B and 2B Thread Fits

Thread Size	Thread Height, %
#0 to #12	53 to 65
1/4 to 1/2″	64 to 66.5
1/2 to 1″	64 to 67
1 to 2″	66 to 71

Effect of tap diameter and pitch. The percentage of thread in a tapped hole should be governed by, in order of importance, (1) the diameter and pitch of the tap, (2) the hardness and toughness of the material being tapped, (3) the depth of tapped hole, and (4) the kind of hole, whether blind or through. As an example, the factor of tap diameter and pitch would make it difficult to tap a No. 8—32 thread in a hole in tool steel with 70% depth of thread, since a No. 8—32 thread has a small diameter in proportion to its pitch. Yet, the same pitch on a 1/4″ tap would be entirely practical, since a 1/4—32 tap has sufficient strength to tap even 100% depth of thread. It can therefore be seen that the smaller the diameter and the coarser the pitch of the tap, the lower the percentage of thread that should be required. This is dependent upon the material, but in no case should it ever exceed 83 1/3%.

Effect of material hardness and toughness. The hardness and toughness of the material to a great extent govern the amount of material that a tap is able to remove. Generally, the harder and tougher the material, the lower the percentage of thread that should be required. For example, on 3140 nickel-chromium steel, it is difficult to tap 70% depth of thread commercially; yet on a high-grade free-cutting screw stock, it would be entirely practical. There are many other tough metals, such as copper, Monel, nickel, bronze, and the various grades of alloy steels, in which it is difficult to tap a large percentage of thread. The minimum percentage should be adopted whenever possible.

Effect of tapped-hole depth. The depth of the tapped hole is the third important factor governing the percentage of thread. Calculations should be based on the length of engagement, i.e., the length of contact between a screw and a tapped hole measured axially; this length of engagement should equal the basic major diameter. It would be possible to tap greater percentages of threads if the depth of the tapped holes were less than their basic major diameter; therefore, the percentage of thread should be reduced whenever the tapped hole exceeds the basic major diameter. This is particularly true in tapping blind holes, especially with the smaller taps and the coarser pitches where there is difficulty in finding room for the chips.

With the proper percentage of thread, very little pressure is required to start a tap. When too much pressure is applied in feeding or retracting, the tap lacks support in the thread and cuts away each succeeding thread as the tap revolves. This quite frequently happens in automatic screw machines when the cams are not correct for the lead of the tap. Tension-type tap holders are recommended for cam feed tapping, with the cam designed to have a lead slightly less than that of the tap. This gives the tap a positive start in the hole and allows it to establish its own lead.

Solid Taps

A solid (nonadjustable, noncollapsing) tap is a tool for producing a screw thread in an existing hole. Cutting edges are created by radially relieved chamfers at the nose ends of the fluted tools.

Tap Holders

In any tapping operation, some kind of a tap holder is required to make an appropriate connection between the spindle of the tapping machine or head and the tap. Such a holder can be as simple as a split-sleeve driver, or tap chuck, or it can be a sophisticated device that provides radial float, tension, compression, and torque control.

Split-sleeve driver. The split-sleeve tap driver (also known as a style A tap chuck) is possibly the most commonly used tap holding means for general-purpose machine tapping. This tool has a tap shank pilot hole that is machined concentric to a standard external Morse taper (see Fig. 27-7). The bottom of the tap shank hole is machined with a square opening to accommodate the standard tap shank drive square. Four splits are provided to effect a centrally closing collet action when the sleeve and tap assembly is tightly seated into any matching internal Morse taper socket.

This type of holder provides a simple means for making a solid, direct-drive connection for taps. A split-sleeve driver can be applied directly (or with Morse taper reducing sockets) to the spindle of a leadscrew tapping machine or a reversible spindle

drill press. Alignment of hole and spindle centerlines must be accomplished by the skill of the machinist. Lead control in the case of the drill press may be accomplished through the skill of the machinist by allowing the spindle quill to float so that the tap lead can provide a self-feeding action.

Solid holders and extensions. Solid, heavy-duty holders (see Fig. 27-8) are used for large taps (sizes commonly range from 3/4 to 3"). Shanks cover the range from 0.590-2.625". The tap shank is piloted in this holder through a pilot hole that is concentric to the Morse taper shank. A square drive is provided, and setscrews are employed for retention. As with the split-sleeve driver just described, this type of holder provides a solid, direct-drive connection for a tap in similar applications.

Solid extensions may often be required when tapping is performed close to a shoulder, hub, or fixture wall. Several commonly used approaches for providing a relatively accurate and positively driven, extended tap holder are illustrated in Fig. 27-9. One important factor is that the A diameter may be sized to allow piloting in a standard slip, renewable, drill-bushing liner. This allows piloted tap drilling through such a bushing and then subsequent piloted tapping through the same bushing liner.

As shown in the spit-sleeve style (Fig. 27-9), a standard Morse taper extension socket and split-sleeve drive (style A tap chuck) may be used. Some commercially available extensions of this type, however, are available with a special taper of 0.500"/ft. This slower taper allows a smaller A diameter to be made and produces a tighter grip on the tap shank.

Extensions of the styles shown in Fig. 27-9 are commonly available in tap sizes through 3/4". The use of these extensions with standard hand taps may provide a viable cost alternative to special-length, solid pulley taps or to one-piece, extension-length taps.

Collet-type holders. Taps may be accurately gripped and driven simply by the use of a collet holder and collet sized to match the tap shank being used (see Fig. 27-10). The development of antifriction collet nut systems and extended-range, collet slotting techniques has resulted in greater collet gripping efficiency. Many manufacturers of collet chucks provide extended range systems that accept shank sizes varying 1/64" (0.4 mm) in diam. One system allows shank variations of 0.020-1" (0.51-25.4 mm) diam. These factors allow the direct use of taps with a collet chuck in many machine tapping applications.

The extended-range gripping feature is of importance because tap shanks are not made to match standard fractional diameters. As an example, a standard 3/8" tap has a shank diameter of 0.381". This shank may be readily chucked with a common, extended-range collet that is available with an effective locking

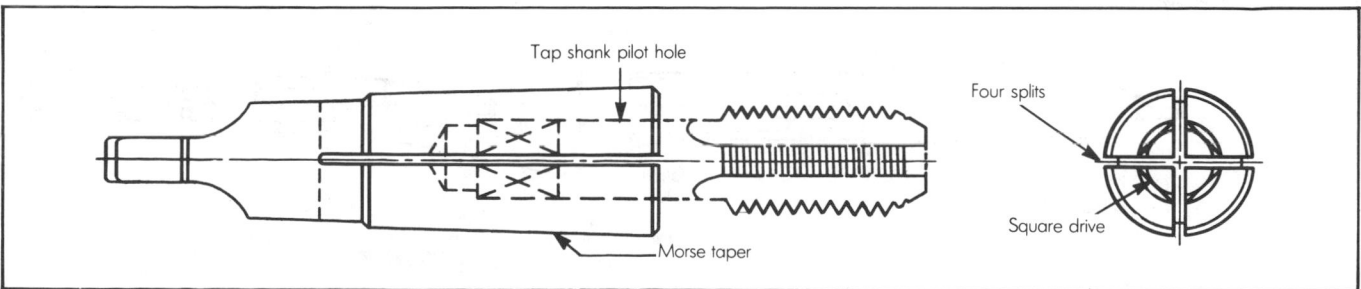

Fig. 27-7 Split sleeve tap driver, also known as a style A tap chuck. (*Universal Engineering Div., Houdaille Industries, Inc.*)

Tap shank pilot hole
Square drive
Set screws
Morse taper

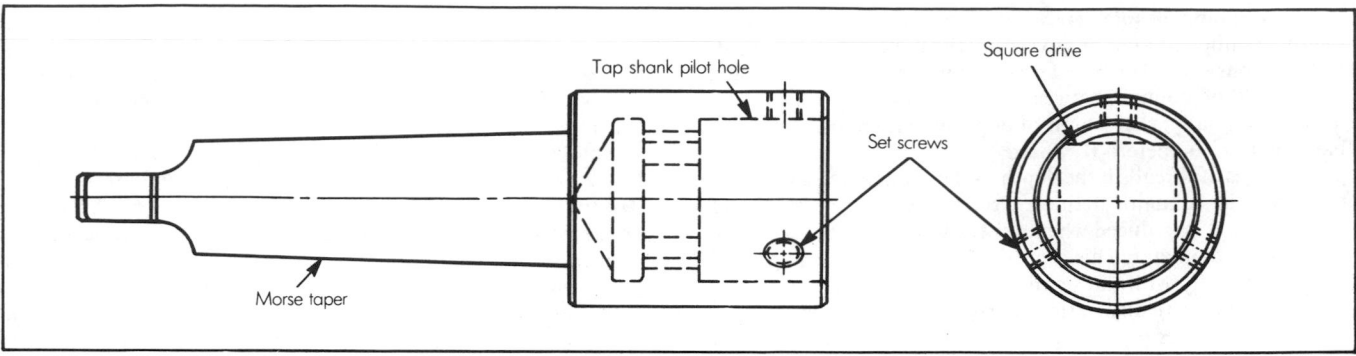

Fig. 27-8 Solid, heavy-duty holder for large taps (¾ to 3″). (*Universal Engineering Div., Houdaille Industries, Inc.*)

Setscrew style with morse taper shank:
Morse taper shank
Setscrew
A
Pilot hole
Square drive
Setscrew style with straight tap shank:
A
Straight shank
A
Optional through drive slot
Optional setscrew drive against tap shank square
Back taper modification for setscrew seat
Tap shank
A
Split-sleeve style extension:
Morse taper shank
A
Drive tang
Square drive
Drive slot
Matching taper
Note: may be a standard morse taper or a special slow taper to permit minimum A diameter (one common taper used today is 0.500″/ft)
Pilot hole
Taper Shank Extension Socket
Split Sleeve Tap Chuck
Tap

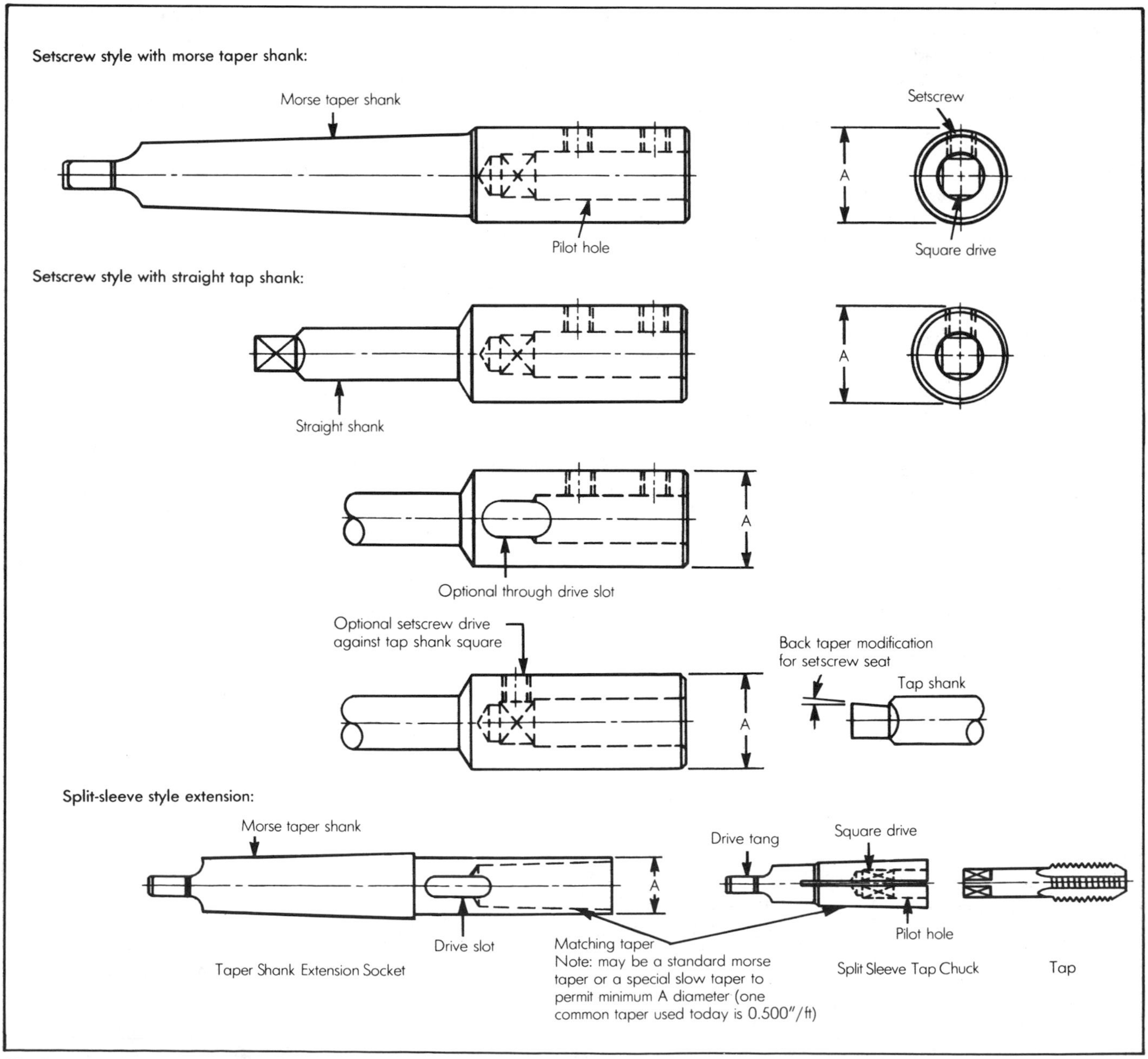

Fig. 27-9 Common varieties of extension holders for solid taps. (*Universal Engineering Div., Houdaille Industries, Inc.*)

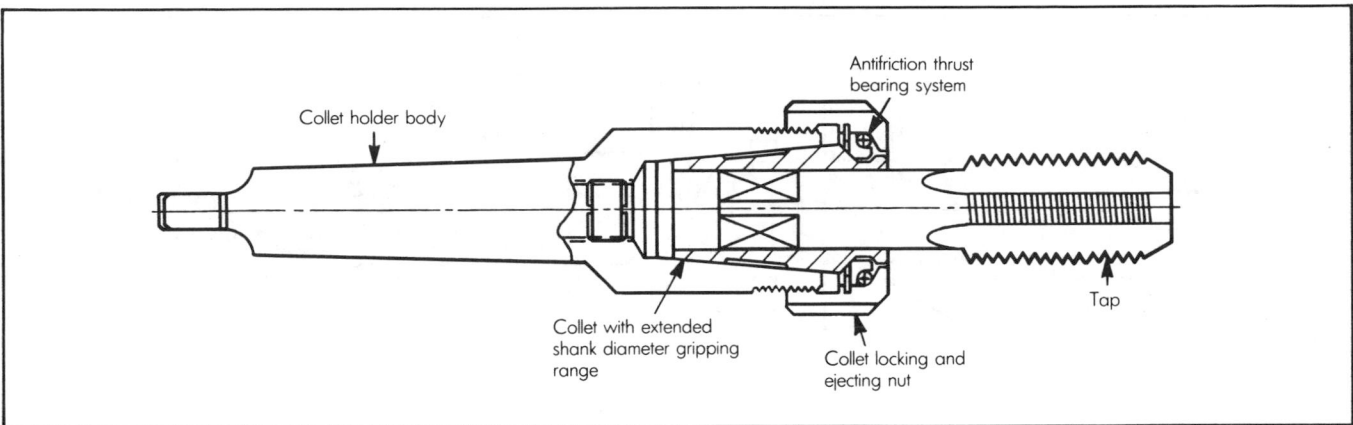

Fig. 27-10 Collet-type holder for taps. (*Universal Engineering Div., Houdaille Industries, Inc.*)

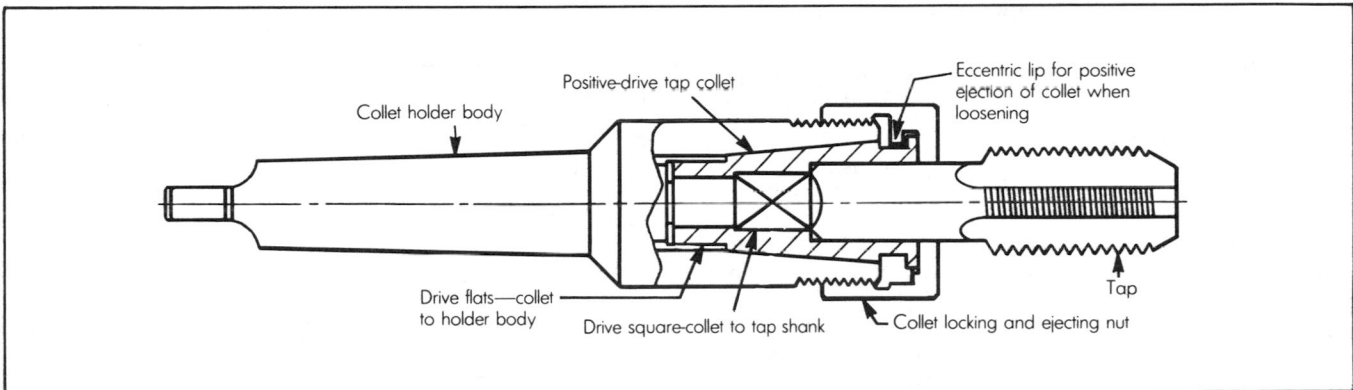

Fig. 27-11 Positive-drive collet holder for taps. (*Universal Engineering Div., Houdaille Industries, Inc.*)

range from 3/8 to 25/64" (0.375 to 0.391").

Positive-drive collet holders. While the use of a conventional collet holder provides a practical tap driving means, many users feel more comfortable when the driving holder takes advantage of the positive torsional driving feature provided by the square end on the standard tap shank. To accommodate this, collet chucks are available that provide a broached square hole in the collet and drive flats on the outer end surface of the collet (see Fig. 27-11). In this design, the square hole in the collet mates with the tap shank drive square and the drive flats on the outer end of the collet cooperate with a similar drive pocket in the collet chuck body.

Floating holders. One of the design objectives of all the tap holders that have been discussed is to hold the tap centerline coincident to the centerline of the holder. Use of these holders, however, requires accurate setups to ensure that the centerlines of the machine spindle and hole in the workpiece are coincident with those of the tap and holder.

Accurate setups are generally not difficult when skilled operators are using manually operated machines or tapping is being done on NC/CNC machines. Precise centerline control often cannot be maintained, however, when automatic production tapping is done on certain machines such as transfer-line or dial-type machines on which workpieces are transferred and relocated automatically for each operation. In such cases, tap holders with radial float are required.

A tap holder with radial float is shown schematically in Fig. 27-12. The holder nose is separated from the shank by a bearing that allows a small amount of radial sliding to occur between the nose and shank. A flexible drive coupling connects the nose and shank to transmit and absorb the torque generated by tapping. A fastening nut is provided for adjusting and retaining the shank and nose through the bearing elements.

While Fig. 27-12 illustrates the basic principles of floating holder construction, many variations exist with respect to specific design elements in commercially available holders. For example, the holder nose can have a Morse taper (as shown) or it can be made to accommodate a collet or many other tap shank mountings. The bearing elements can be hardened steel, bronze, plastic, or ball thrust bearings. The drive coupling can be of the Oldham design (as shown) or a gear-type coupling.

Other holders. Tension, compression, and tension/compression tap holders compensate for infeed variables such as feed/lead mismatch and no-hole conditions. Other tap holders available provide torque control and quick-change features. These holders are similar in design to the tapping spindles and attachments discussed previously in this section.

DIES FOR EXTERNAL THREADING

Most external threads are produced with single-point tools or die-head chasers, as discussed earlier in this chapter, or by milling, grinding, or rolling, to be discussed later. Some

EXTERNAL THREADING

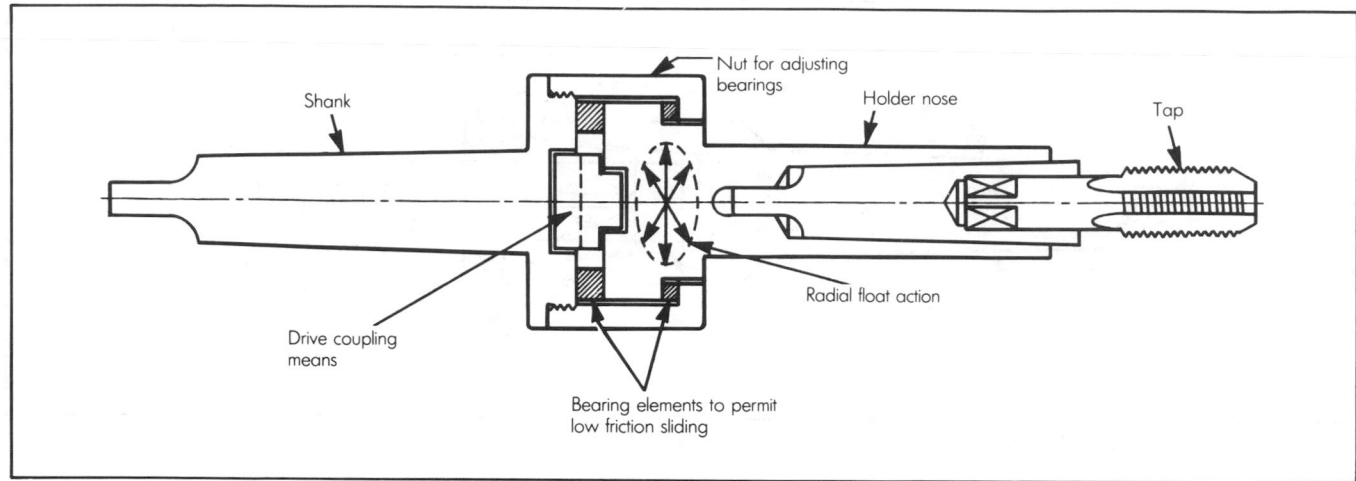

Fig. 27-12 Schematic of a tap holder with radial float. (*Universal Engineering Div., Houdaille Industries, Inc.*)

external threads, however, are produced with multiedged, internally-threaded cutting tools often called solid dies.

Types of Solid Dies

Solid threading dies are of one or two-piece construction with integral cutting edges and are available in either adjustable or nonadjustable types.

Nonadjustable dies. These are one-piece threading dies with internal threads, holes to divide the threads into sections, and square or hexagonal-shaped peripheries. They are basically a form of nut with chamfers on the faces of the threads that create multiple cutting edges. The holes serve to relieve the cutting pressures and give the cutting teeth an effective rake.

A typical nonadjustable, solid, square die is illustrated in Fig. 27-13. Such dies can be used in stocks or wrenches for hand threading or in die holders for machine threading.

Adjustable dies. These threading dies are available in several constructions: two piece; round, with open or screw adjusting means; and spring or acorn-type.

Two-piece adjustable dies. These tools are made in halves for adjustability and in several styles.

Round adjustable dies. These tools are similar to nonadjustable dies, except their bodies are slotted for either open adjusting or screw adjusting (see Fig. 27-14). Both means of adjustment are limited and are available primarily to compensate for wear and to maintain accuracy.

Spring adjustable dies. These are adjustable, thread-cutting dies of spring-tempered construction. Adjustability is provided by the design of the body and holder (see Fig. 27-15), which function like a collet chuck. As the outer nut or cap on the holder is tightened, pressure is applied to the tapered nose of the die, causing the threaded sections to move inward.

Applications of Solid Dies

Solid dies are not used as extensively as other tools for producing external threads. A major disadvantage for production threading is that the dies must be retracted from the workpieces after the threads are cut. This slows production, limits the equipment that can be used, causes die wear, and can damage the threads produced.

Applications of solid dies include small-quantity requirements in toolroom, maintenance, and repair operations. They are also used for hand or machine threading of bolts and pipe, and for

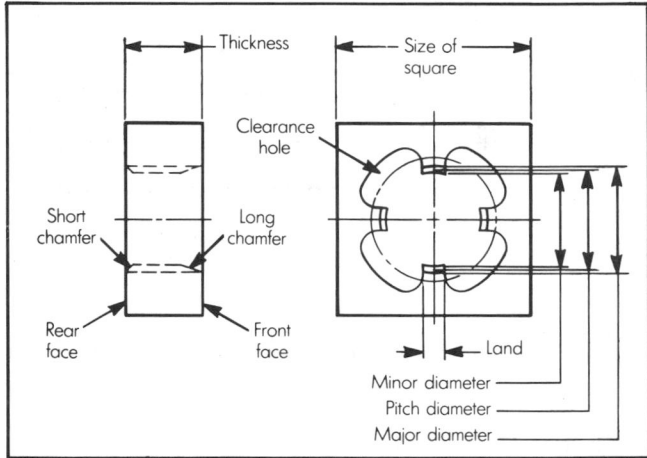

Fig. 27-13 Nonadjustable, solid, square die for use in hand stock or machine die holder.[1]

some applications on threading machines, multiple-spindle automatics, and screw machines. They are advantageous for machines that do not have sufficient space for thread chasing with self-opening die heads. Another advantage for some applications is their increased strength.

THREAD MILLING

Thread milling is an established method of producing accurate threads in both small and large quantities. With proper work preparation and rigid workholding and supporting means, accurate threads can be economically produced in true relation to a specified surface on the work.

Accurate threads can be produced and pitch diameters held closely with a surface finish of about 55 μin. (1.4 μm). Lead errors can be held to 0.001 in./in. (mm/mm), and spacing errors on multiple-start work can be held within 0.0003-0.0004" (0.008-0.010 mm). Long screws and multiple-start work may require rough and finish cuts, with a stress-relieving period between cuts, to overcome distortion. The threads are produced by conventional thread milling and planetary thread milling.

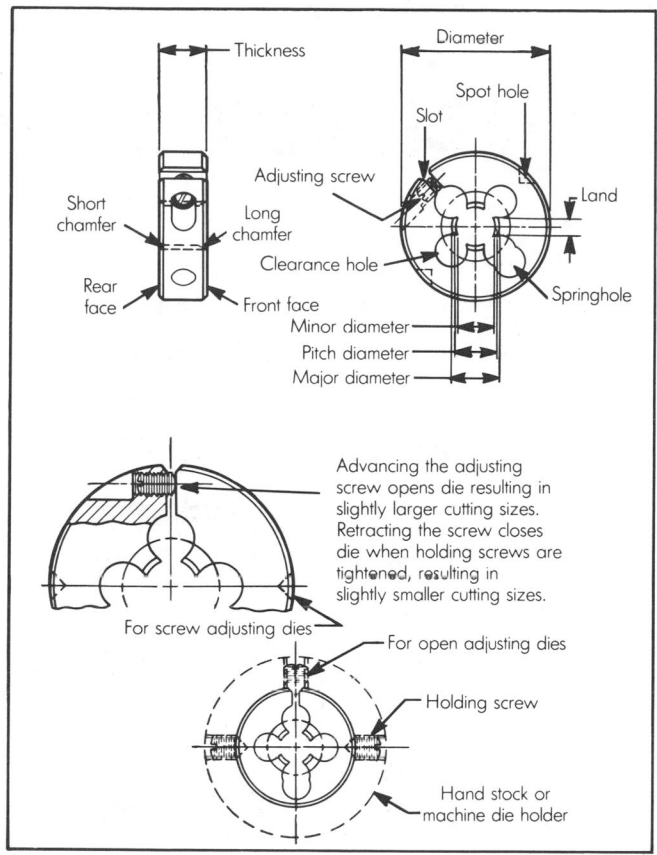

Fig. 27-14 Round adjusting die is available with screw or open adjustment.[1]

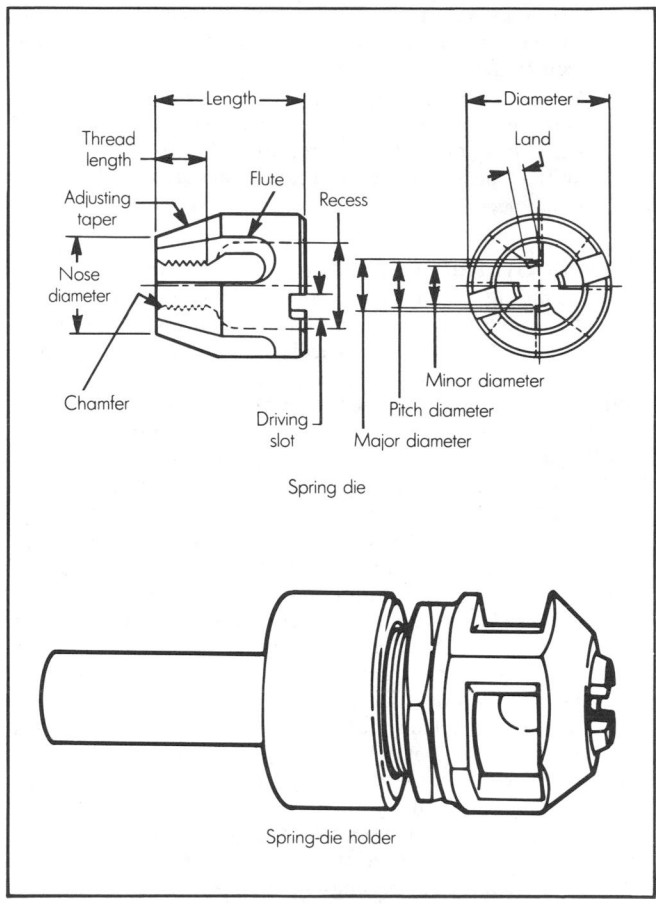

Fig. 27-15 Spring die and die holder for producing external threads.[1]

THREAD GRINDING

Threads are ground by cutting contact between a rotating workpiece and a rotating, suitably formed grinding wheel, with relative axial transverse motion between the two equal to the lead per revolution of the thread being ground. The procedures may be applied to the grinding of helical peripheries, external or internal, of any form or for any purpose.

When the hardness of the material makes it difficult or impractical to thread with normal thread-cutting or rolling tools, or when the accuracy required is not attainable by using such methods, thread grinding is not only practical but economical. On precision work, such as taps and thread gages, thread grinding is essential.

Ordinarily it is advantageous to grind threads in materials harder than $R_C 27$. Other methods for producing threads in materials harder than $R_C 36$ are usually impractical. No commonly used work material is known to exist in a state so hard (or so soft) that it cannot be threaded by grinding. Certain materials softer than $R_C 17$, however, do not machine well and may best be threaded by grinding.

Grinding of threads frequently is specified in highly stressed parts subject to failure by fatigue, such as aircraft, tank, gun, and motor parts. Threading such parts by grinding avoids the minute torn areas which usually exist at the root of cut threads and cause these threads to become the focus of stress concentrations contributing to progressive rupture by fatigue.

Thread Grinding Machines

Thread grinding machines are distinguished from other machines for grinding surfaces of rotation (either external or internal) by inclusion of the following structural features:

1. Means for imparting a precise traverse (pitch or lead) of the work for each revolution of helical periphery being ground. Devices of this type usually employ a leadscrew and change gears.
2. Suitable means for trueing or dressing the cutting periphery of the grinding wheel to generate in the rotating workpiece the precise form required when the rotating grinding wheel traces the required helical path in the work.
3. Means for inclining the plane of rotation of the grinding wheel in accordance with the helix angle to be ground in the work, thus tending to cause the wheel to cut in the workpiece a form which is precisely complementary to the form dressed on the wheel. For tap grinding, a predetermined plane of rotation may be fixed for the grinding wheel.

Thread grinding machines are basically differentiated in four ways:

1. With respect to the cutting periphery of the grinding wheel used; these are either single-rib or multirib.

THREAD GRINDING

2. The manner in which the work is supported: (a) on centers; (b) on rolls, which may also cooperate in axial feed of the work as in centerless grinders.
3. With respect to the method of forming the cutting periphery of the grinding wheel: (a) diamond-dressed (trued); (b) crush-trued (dressed).
4. With respect to relieving or nonrelieving capability of the machine.

Thread-Grinding Wheels

The grinding of threads requires a grinding wheel with a cutting periphery of such form that it will transfer the desired thread form to the work. The wheel may be of the single-rib type (see Fig. 27-16, view *a*) in which the rib of the wheel must completely traverse the length of the thread, or it may be of the multirib type (view *b*) which is especially convenient for grinding a thread that is approximately one pitch longer than the face width of the wheel. In the latter instance the grinding wheel may be plunged to within a few thousandths of an inch (about 0.07 mm) of its entire depth before rotation of the work is started, the remaining infeeding of the wheel being completed in the first fractional rotation of the work. The work rotates only one complete revolution while traversing one thread pitch to generate the complete length of thread, as in thread milling. In practice, however, a fractional overtravel is allowed at both ends to avoid leaving a flat at one or both ends of the cut.

The multirib wheel may be used in complete traverse grinding (see Fig. 27-16, view *c*). This, however, is not recommended, because the leading few ribs of the wheel suffer the greatest wear. The threads cut by these ribs become oversized and incorrect in form. Correction of this condition requires redressing of the entire wheel, regardless of whether the trailing ribs may be in need of dressing.

A multirib wheel having a rib pitch that is a multiple (here twice) of the thread pitch is more easily diamond dressed. Two revolutions of the work and a traverse of two pitches are required to form a complete thread. Figure 27-16, view *d* 1, shows such an arrangement at the end of the first work revolution; view *d* 2 shows the work completed at the end of the second work revolution. Another advantage in using a rib pitch that is a multiple of the thread pitch is the increased amount of grinding fluid that may be brought into proximity of the areas of cutting contact between the wheel and the work.

Wheel-Dressing Devices

Wheel-dressing devices form the effective cutting surface of the wheel to a contour which, when operated in contact with the work under predetermined conditions of work rotation and helix angle, depth of wheel engagement, etc., generates the desired thread form on the work. The thread form generated on the work can be no more precise than the form that is dressed on the grinding wheel.

In most instances, suitably mounted diamond points are the cutting tools used to impart the desired form to the grinding-wheel surface. It is the function of the dressing device to give to diamond dressing points the predetermined path of movement for generating the desired wheel form.

In the relatively simpler instances in which the form to be dressed on the wheel is bounded by straight lines, separate diamond tools are either pivotally mounted or slide mounted so that the several tools may traverse the respective surfaces of the

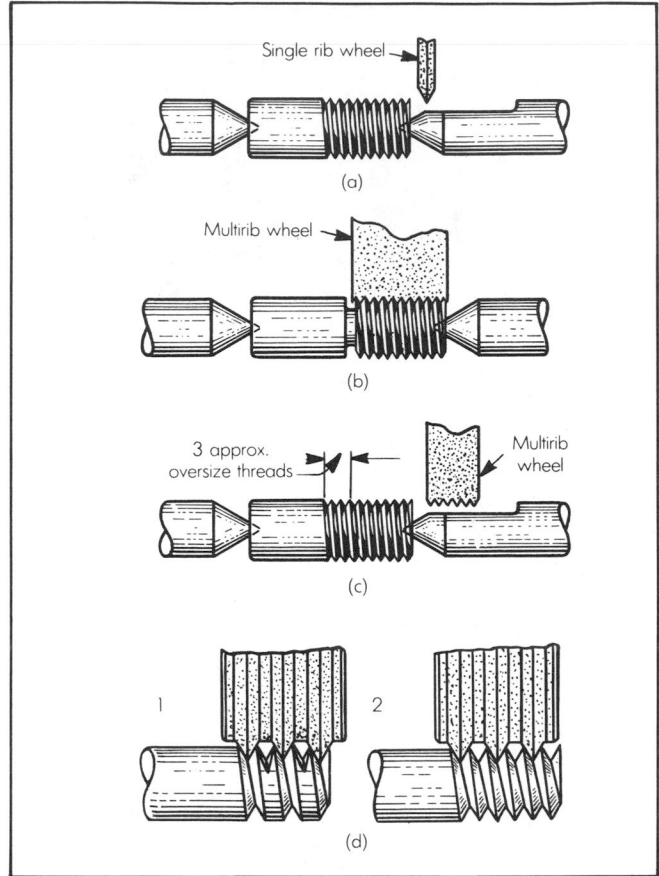

Fig. 27-16 Use of ribbed wheels: (a) complete traverse grinding with single-rib wheels: (b) partial traverse grinding with multirib wheel: (c) complete traverse grinding with multirib wheel; (d) multirib wheel with nib pitch twice the thread pitch—(1) at end of first revolution of the work; (2) at end of second revolution of the work.

wheel. These separate diamond points may be moved in a straight line when supported on respective slides, or they may be pivotally mounted (see Fig. 27-17) to traverse accurately the wheel surfaces to be dressed by them.

Universal dressers (see Fig. 27-17) are capable of dressing any form which may be dressed by straight-line dressers; additionally, they are capable of dressing forms bounded by curves or including curves together with straight or broken lines in their boundaries. Such dressers usually include a formed template with or without pantographic reduction of scale, or they include a cam-controlled mechanism for altering the approach and the retraction of the diamond tool while a leadscrew traverses the dressing point across the face of the wheel in a plane that includes the wheel axis.

For mechanical reasons and to avoid the necessity for using a diamond point so small that it would have prohibitively short life, it is preferable that separate diamonds be provided for dressing opposite flanks of the wheel rib. To avoid chipping of the wheel rib in dressing, it is desirable that the diamond points be in cutting contact only while traversing the rib from the apex toward its base and return out of contact with the wheel.

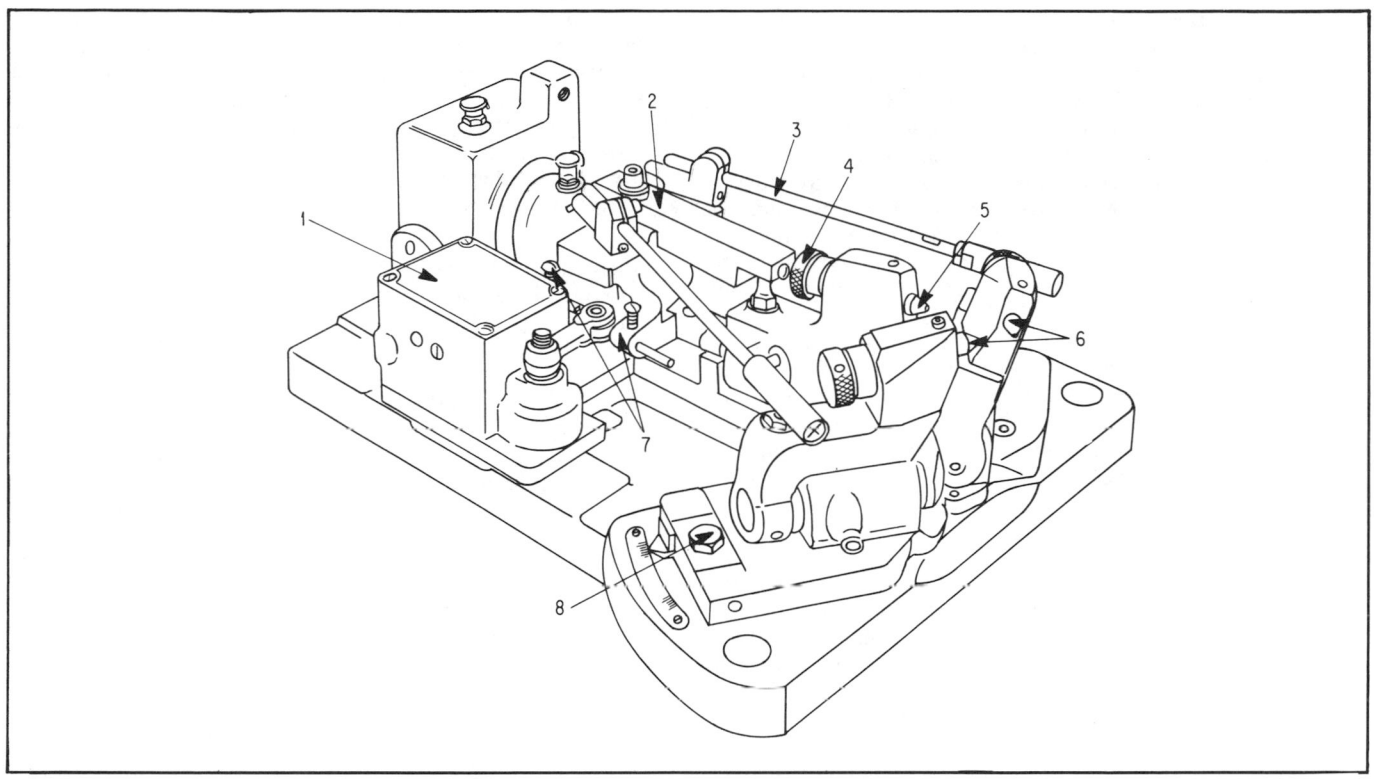

Fig. 27-17 Three-way diamond wheel dresser: (1) control switch, (2) diamond oscillating slide, (3) flank diamond oscillating rod, (4) diamond-adjusting screw, (5) apex of diamond, (6) flank diamonds, (7) stops to limit stroke, (8) flank-angle lock.

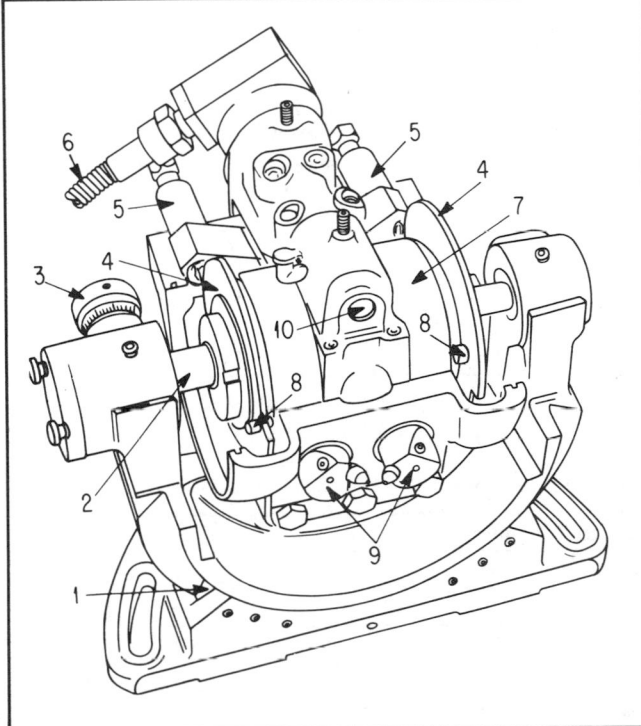

Fig. 27-18 Universal dresser: (1) helix-angle gib, (2) leadscrew shaft, (3) rib-width adjustment, (4) control cams, (5) cam-follower diamond-positioning adjustment, (6) flexible drive shaft, (7) longitudinal moving lead-nut carriage, (8) limit-switch actuators, (9) traversely moving cam-controlled diamond carriers, (10) worm-wheel driving shaft.

Centerless Thread Grinding

Centerless thread grinding basically bears close relation to centerless plain cylindrical grinding.

The productivity of this method far exceeds that of any other method for grinding screw threads, and it has been applied to the production of many commercial items that are made in large quantities, including headless setscrews, high-strength continuously threaded studs, adjusting worms, valve-clearance adjusting screws, self-tapping threading inserts, and similar components. Classes 2, 2A, 3, 3A, and 7 thread tolerances are maintained at high-production speeds; classes 4 and 5 threads are produced at slower rates of production.

Thread-Grinding Applications

Determining the most economical conditions for a long-run production job usually involves considerable experimentation in which the following are factors:

1. Wheel grit, grain, and bond.
2. Wheel surface speed.
3. Hardness and material of the workpiece.
4. Work peripheral speed.
5. Amount of material removed per pass.
6. Complexity of the form to be ground.
7. Tolerances and finish required on the workpiece.
8. Kind, amount, and manner of delivery of the cutting fluid to the cutting zone.

Shorter production runs usually do not permit extensive experimental determinations; consequently, the skill and

CHAPTER 27

THREAD ROLLING

experience of the operator ordinarily are relied upon for choice of the conditions for doing such jobs.

The number of roughing and finishing cuts that are necessary depends upon the workpiece material and the nature and precision requirements of the job. The approximate depth of the ordinary roughing cut is from 0.020-0.040″ (0.51-1.02 mm). When two or more cuts are taken, it is generally advisable to take from a minimum of 0.0015″ (0.038 mm) to a maximum of 0.004″ (0.10 mm) depth of cut for the last finish cut. In some cases, two or even more light finishing cuts are advisable, even on the shallow threads, where extreme accuracy in lead, diameter, and finish is required.

On large production runs, especially of close-tolerance work or work that is difficult to grind because of severe machinability conditions, it is economical to rough and finish grind in separate operations. This allows the use of a coarser, freer cutting wheel for the rough-grinding operation and limits the temperature conditions during finish grinding.

THREAD ROLLING

Thread rolling is a simple cold forging process for producing threads on cylindrical or conical workpieces. The helical threads are produced by displacing or rearranging the blank material rather than by removing material as in thread cutting or grinding. Production rates for rolling are generally higher than the rates for cutting or grinding; the threads produced have improved strength and fatigue properties, the surface finish produced is good, and the work-hardened surface often provides additional advantages. Most rolling is performed with the blanks at room temperature, although heat may be applied to facilitate metal displacement, most often in the case of high-hardness materials.

In addition to forming threads, this process is also used to produce other helical or annular forms. This discussion is confined primarily to thread rolling.

Many types of equipment are used for thread rolling, ranging from machines which can thread small-diameter fasteners at rates of 1000 pieces per minute to equipment capable of rolling 15″ (381 mm) diam heat-treated studs. Machines are available which can produce continuous threads to any length required or helical fins, either intermittent or continuous, on heat-exchanger tubing in lengths of 50 ft (15.2 m). Thread-rolling attachments are used on automatic screw machines or lathes which produce threads at rates compatible with other operations being performed and in locations not accessible to die heads.

Threads or other forms are produced on ductile workpieces by rotating the cylindrical or conical workpiece between hardened-steel dies so that the form on the die faces is impressed into the blank. The blank is smaller than the finished outside diameter so that the material displaced at the root can flow outward to form the thread crests as shown in Fig. 27-19. The die may be either flat or cylindrical as required by the rolling equipment to be used.

Advantages and Limitations of Rolled Threads

Rolled threads have improved physical properties and surface finish compared with those provided by other production methods; in addition they provide material savings and in many cases lower production costs. Tables 27-2 and 27-3 show the material savings at the threaded portion and also comparative surface finishes produced by the various methods.

The cold working which takes place in roll forming produces a work-hardened surface with an increase of up to 10% in tensile strength. In addition, because of the surface hardness and excellent finish, wear characteristics and antigalling properties are greatly improved.

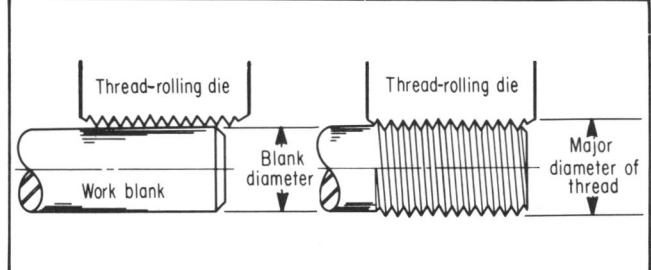

Fig. 27-19 Material displacement in thread rolling.

TABLE 27-2
Percentage of Material Saved by Thread Rolling

Thread Size	Material Saving, %	Thread Size	Material Saving, %
8—32	24	¾—10	16
¼—20	25	1—8	18
⅜—16	27	1¼—7	16
½—13	19	1½—6	16
⅝—11	19	2—4½	15

TABLE 27-3
Comparison of Typical Thread Surface Finishes

Type of Thread	250 / 4	125 / 2	63 / 1	32 / 0.5	16	8 / 0.1	4	2 / μ in. μ m
Screw machine chased threads	■	■						
Milled threads		■	■					
Ground threads				■				
Rolled threads				■	■	■		

THREAD ROLLING

Rolled threads also provide improved shear strength, since the material fibers are reformed into lines following the thread contour as shown in Fig. 27-20, view *a*. Such threads resist stripping because a shear failure can occur only across the grain, while in cut or ground threads, the shear failure would occur parallel to the grain (see view *b*).

An important effect of thread rolling is an improvement in fatigue life of up to ten times that provided by cut or ground threads. The fatigue resistance is provided by the residual compressive stresses induced in the screw during rolling. Because any subsequent heat treatment would relieve the stresses, it is absolutely necessary to thread roll after heat treating in order to obtain full advantage of this feature.

The use of such hard-rolled fasteners has been common in aircraft and other aerospace applications for many years; however, with increased emphasis on product reliability, and particularly highway safety, the use of these fasteners is expanding rapidly in areas such as automotive and machine-tool and related automation equipment.

Fasteners of extremely high hardness may be rolled warm. The blanks are heated prior to rolling to a temperature less than the tempering temperature, so that the rolling stresses and therefore the fatigue resistance are maintained. Dies for this type of rolling are generally made with an expanded thread pitch so that the lead of the threaded part is correct after cooling to room temperature. Special die steels may also be used to withstand the higher than normal operating temperatures. On materials over $R_C 35$, considerable improvement in die life is obtained compared to that possible with cold rolling; and on materials of $R_C 45$ or higher, cold rolling is generally not practical. Warm-rolled fasteners are in use which have a room-temperature Rockwell C in the middle fifties. Even when the material permits rolling at 900 to 1000° F (480-540° C), the die life is extremely low, and rolling in this hardness range is done only when strength requirements make a rolled thread absolutely necessary.

The rolling of hard materials requires greater care on the part of the operator in the matter of adjustment and matching of the dies and in the use of blanks of proper diameter and uniformity of size. Matching of the dies is determined by viewing the initial impressions produced by one die relative to the impressions produced by the other die. Some thread rolling machines require the use of shims; machines of later design usually provide a simple means of adjusting for proper die matching.

Rollability

The ability to roll a specific part depends upon the type of thread to be produced and the method of rolling, as well as the ductility and cold-flow properties of the blank material.

The type of form, that is, the shape, to be produced affects the rollability of a part to a great extent. Fortunately the Unified and similar 60° thread forms, which represent a majority of the threads produced, are very suitable for rolling. Dies for rolling these forms have comparatively sharp crests, usually with a radius contour rather than sharp corners, and penetrate most materials easily. The 30° flank angles provide force components which cause the blank material to flow axially and radially in a satisfactory manner.

Flat-crested forms such as Acme or worm threads produce high pressures at the wide crests, and the displaced material must flow a great distance. Therefore, flakes may be produced on the rolled surface, as well as checked crests or rough crests, and in some cases an exaggerated crest seam. The rollability of Acme and similar threads is improved by modifying the root contour to permit a full radius or a chamfered crest on the dies as shown in Fig. 27-21. Some firms that roll threads find that a vee shape in the bottom or root of Acme threads works better in many cases than the radius shown. The vee provides a parting line in the center of the root. Flank angles of less than 10° should also be avoided when possible.

To produce good results when threads with poor rollability, such as the unmodified Acme, are rolled, a material with extremely good rollability must be used; a standard 60° thread may be rolled satisfactorily with a material of poor rollability.

A crest seam as illustrated in Fig. 27-22 is typical in most thread-rolling applications and, except in unusual circumstances, is not considered detrimental. If a thread is rolled full so that the die root is completely filled, the seam may be hidden and can be seen only by grinding away the thread crest. Since the seam is restricted to a limited depth at the crest, it can have no appreciable influence on the strength of the fastener. In the

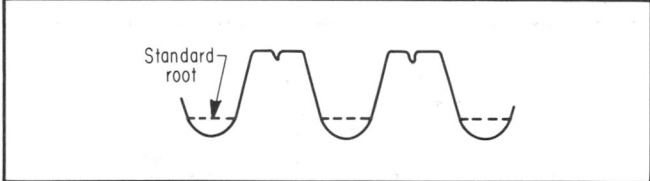
Fig. 27-21 Acme thread with modified root for improved rollability.

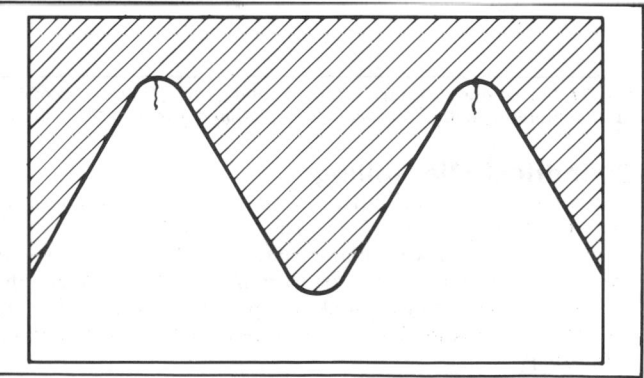
Fig. 27-22 Typical crest seam in a thread rolled with a full crest.

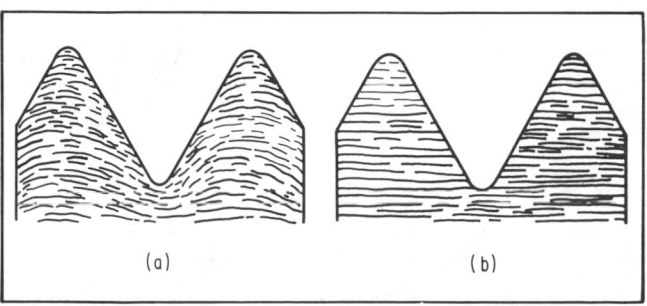
Fig. 27-20 Typical grain flow: (a) in a rolled thread and (b) in a machined or ground thread.

THREAD ROLLING

interest of die life, it is desirable to roll an unfilled or open-seam crest as shown in Fig. 27-23. The exact nature and depth of the seam depends upon the rolling method used, in some cases the die design used, and to a very great extent the blank diameter and material used. The amount or depth of seam is reduced when harder materials are rolled and also when those materials which work-harden considerably during rolling are rolled.

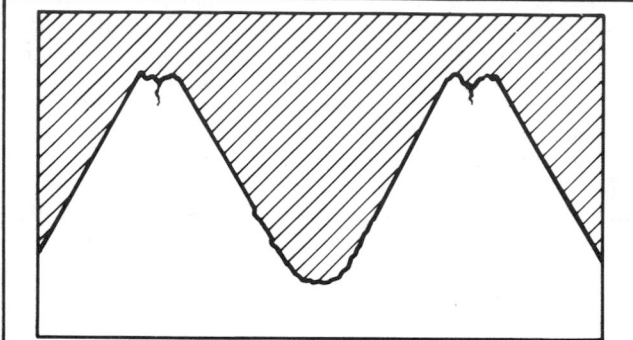

Fig. 27-23 Threads rolled with unfilled crests.

Flat-Die Rolling

The threads on many screws and bolts are rolled on flat-die machines. These machines operate by rolling the blank across the face of a stationary die with a traversing stroke of the moving die, as illustrated in Fig. 27-24. A mechanical or pneumatically operated starting finger positions the blank in the dies. The blank then rolls between the die faces and is penetrated progressively so that final size is reached prior to the blank's rolling off the finish end of the dies. In this type of rolling the penetration rate is established by the total number of blank revolutions provided by the available die length. Each machine size has a maximum die length which establishes the number of work revolutions and therefore the diameter of thread which can be rolled satisfactorily.

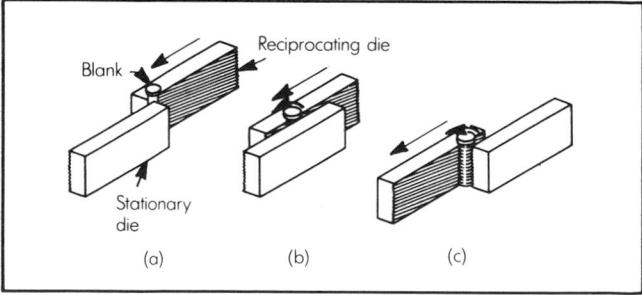

Fig. 27-24 Flat dies: (a) start of thread-rolling cycle, (b) relation of dies after completing half of stroke, (c) completion of thread-rolling stroke.

Cylindrical-Die Rolling

Common types of cylindrical-die machines have two or three dies, as shown in Fig. 27-25. They produce threads by the infeed process. The work blank rotates with the rotating dies as they close in to impress the die form into the blank. When the dies have penetrated the blank to a preset dimension, they are retracted, the threaded workpiece is removed, and a new blank is inserted.

Machines of this type are versatile by virtue of the infinite die length and number of work revolutions available, so relatively

small machines are capable of rolling large-diameter threads in hard materials. A medium-sized two-die machine, for example, rolls diameters from 0.060-3″ (1.52-76 mm). Two-die machines normally provide a greater die-load capacity than comparable three-die machines because they can use large-diameter dies regardless of work diameter, permitting heavy bearings and supporting members.

The maximum die diameter on three-die machines is five to six times the work diameter, so spindle-bearing sizes are restricted. For this reason such machines are not commonly used for thread sizes below 1/4″ (6 mm), and they also have limited thread lengths and blank-hardness capacity in the smaller sizes.

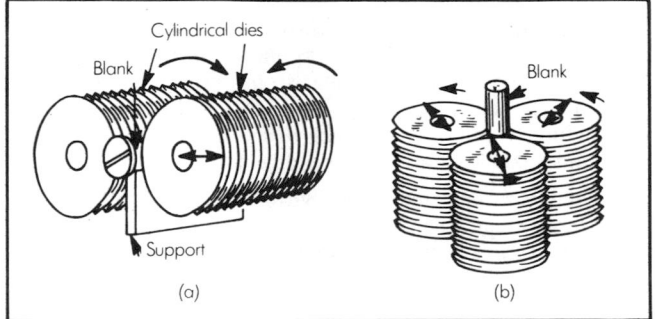

Fig. 27-25 Types of cylindrical-die thread rolling machines: (a) two die and (b) three die.

Planetary Rolling

Planetary thread rolling machines have a cylindrical die rotating on a fixed axis and one or more stationary concave die segments located a spaced distance from the periphery of the rotary die as shown in Fig. 27-26. The blanks are inserted between the rotary and segment dies at the proper instant by a starting finger, and the blank then rolls between the two dies and progresses to the finish end of the segment. Starting mechanisms can insert more than one blank per die revolution, generally 3-8, so that high production rates are possible on small diameters, typically 300 pieces per minute on 1/2″ workpieces. Actual feed rates are often determined by the feeding characteristic of the blank itself. Planetary machines are

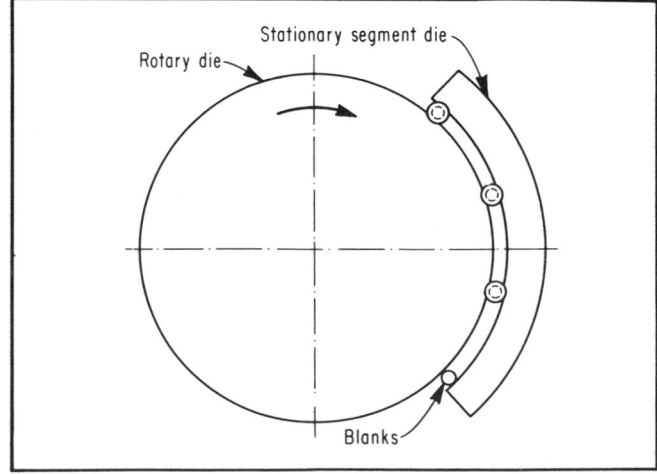

Fig. 27-26 Planetary thread-rolling principle.

used extensively for the high-production rolling of threads on machine screws, as well as for nails.

In flat-die rolling, the size capacity is determined by the available number of work revolutions as determined by die length, in this case the length of the segment die.

References

1. *Metal Cutting Tool Handbook*, Metal Cutting Tool Institute, Cleveland, 1969.

GEAR AND SPLINE PRODUCTION

Gears and splines are important drive elements used in a wide variety of machines and mechanical devices. The engaging teeth of gears provide positive driving action for the accurate transmission of rotary motion and power. Splines are commonly used to fasten together two members to prevent relative rotation.

GEARS

Gears are available in various types (spur, helical, bevel, etc.), each type having individual advantages for specific applications. The many applications for gears range from transmitting motion at high or low speeds under heavy or light loads to holding some elements in a fixed position.

The meshing teeth of practically all gears are based on the involute form. Gear-tooth forms simulate conjugate cams, one acting against its mate to produce the required action, which is generally uniform rotary motion.

GEARS AS RELATED TO AXIS POSITIONS

Gears used to transmit uniform rotary motion have definite pitch surfaces (see Fig. 28-1), the forms of which depend upon the types of the tooth elements and the position relation of the axes of the two gears.

Parallel axes are associated with pitch surfaces that consist of two tangent pitch cylinders with spur or helical gear-tooth forms. Intersecting axes are associated with pitch surfaces that are cones with straight or curved bevel gear teeth. Axes that are not parallel and do not intersect each other may be associated with any one of several types of gears, as follows:

1. Crossed helical gears with pitch surfaces consisting of two cylinders and two planes, both with helical teeth.
2. Wormgears with pitch surfaces consisting of a plane for the worm and a cylinder for the wormgear, with helical threads or teeth on the worm and enveloping teeth on the gear.
3. Hypoid gears with pitch surfaces in the form of hyperboloids of revolution with conjugate teeth which generally are of Formate form (gear form selected arbitrarily and the pinion made conjugate with it).
4. Hourglass worms of many types, usually with indeterminate pitch surfaces; the hourglass worm being a barrel cam with a multiple-tooth follower.

Gear on Parallel Axes

Spur gears. For any spur-gear tooth-form system there is a basic rack form. The rack is a gear of infinite pitch diameter with a plane pitch surface. Its basic form is that of a rack that meshes with the given tooth form. The simplest and most effective way to specify the tooth forms for any given gear-tooth system is in terms of the basic rack form. The four standard forms and two Fellows systems for spur gears are as follows:

1. The 14 ½° composite system.
2. The 14 ½° full-depth involute system.
3. The 20° or 25° full-depth involute system.
4. The 20° stub-tooth involute system.
5. The Fellows 20° stub-tooth system.
6. The Fellows 20° full-depth involute system.

The 14 ½° composite tooth system. This form was developed to be cut with formed milling cutters, to operate on standard centers with mating gears having equal addendums, and to permit a 12-tooth pinion to operate with anything from an equal 12-tooth pinion to a rack. The gears are conjugate to the basic rack of Fig. 28-2.

The 14 ½° full-depth involute system. This form (see Fig. 28-3) is used for gears produced by gear hobs and generating (pinion-type) shaping cutters. The tooth proportions of this basic rack form are the same as those for the 14 ½° composite system. The conventional design of gears of this system is also the same as for the 14 ½° composite system.

The 20° and 25° full-depth involute system. The basic rack (see Fig. 28-4) is used for specifying tooth proportions in designing spur gearing with 20° and 25° pressure angle, full-depth tooth forms so that cutting tools can be designed to closely approximate this form regardless of the generating method used in manufacturing. For 20° pressure angle, equal-addendum teeth are used where the number of teeth are equal to or exceed 18 in the pinion or 36 in the pair. For 25° pressure angle, equal-addendum teeth are used where the number of teeth are equal to or exceed 12 in the pinion or 24 in the pair. Long and short-addendum teeth are used with pinions having number of teeth as specified in AGMA Standards 201.02 and 207.06. However, the use of long-addendum pinions and short-addendum gears as specified in these standards should be limited to speed-reducing drives only.

The 20° stub-tooth involute system. This form was developed to obtain a stronger tooth for heavy loading, mostly at low speeds, and also to avoid undercutting of the smaller gears. These are several different designs of this stub-tooth form with slightly different tooth proportions. The basic rack form (see Fig. 28-5) meshes with all of them; the

GEARS

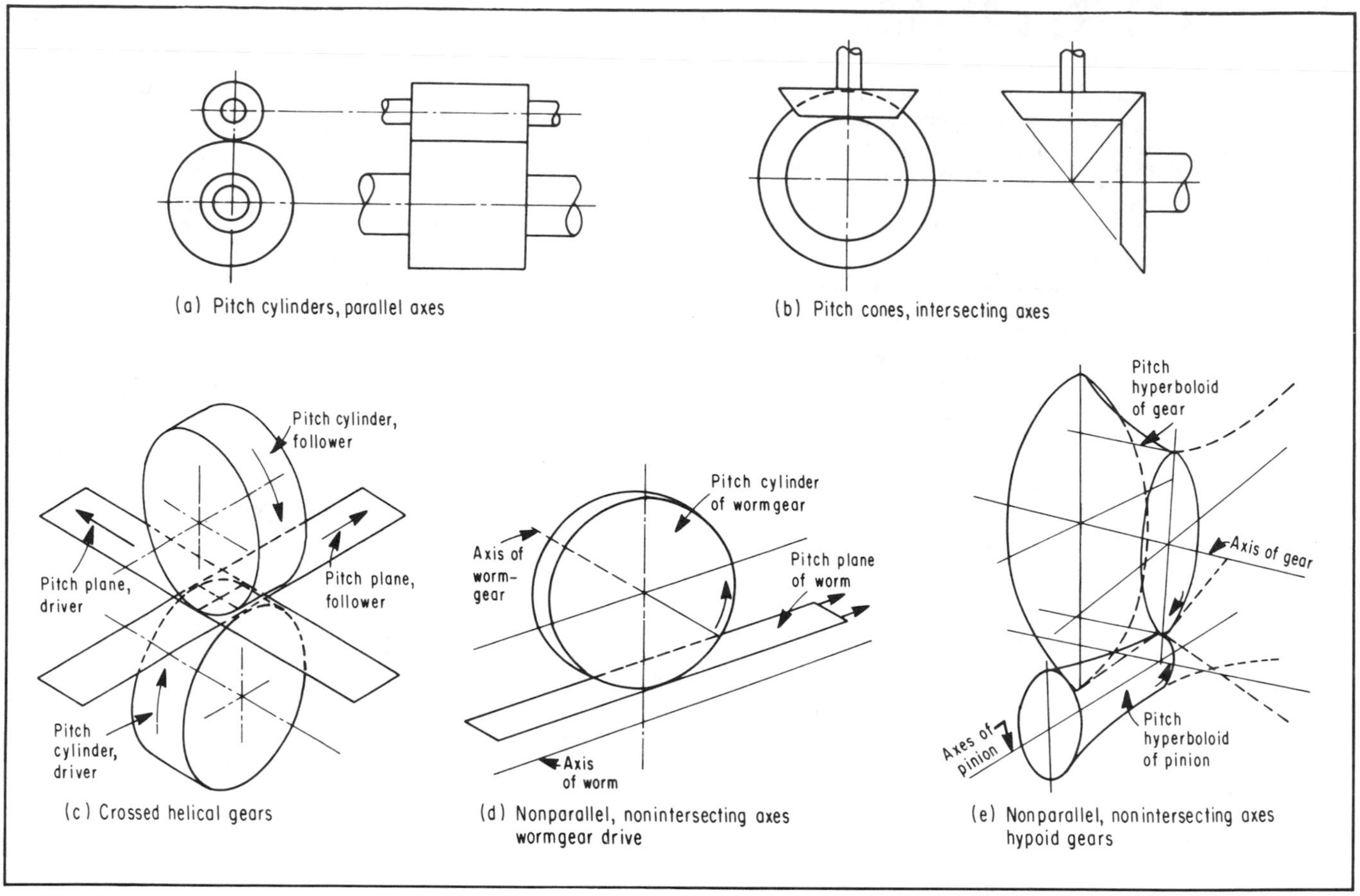

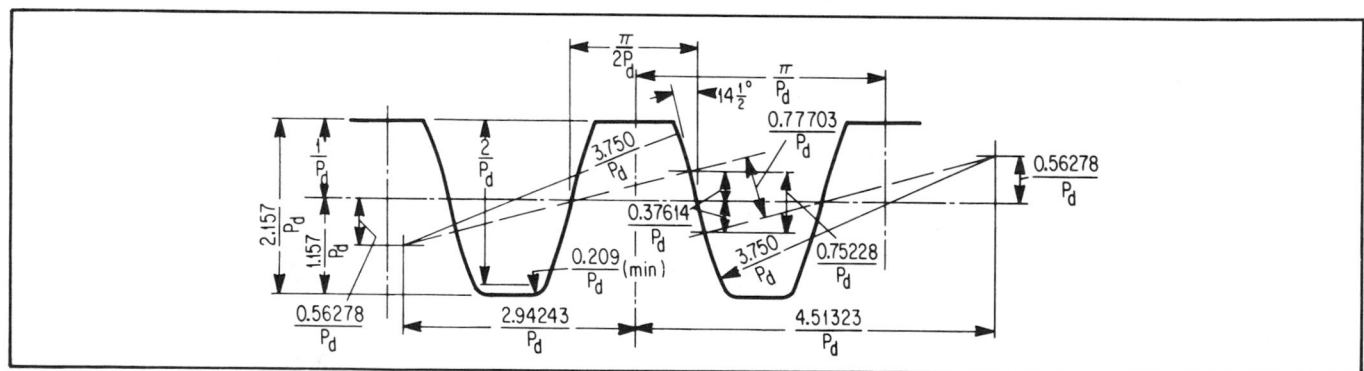

Fig. 28-1 Pitch cylinders for various types of gears.

(a) Pitch cylinders, parallel axes

(b) Pitch cones, intersecting axes

(c) Crossed helical gears

(d) Nonparallel, nonintersecting axes wormgear drive

(e) Nonparallel, nonintersecting axes hypoid gears

Fig. 28-2 Basic rack form, 14 ½° composite tooth form.

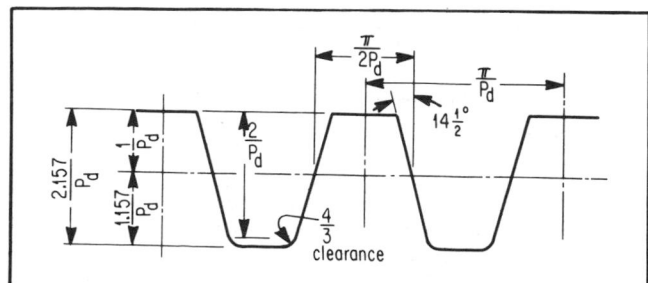

Fig. 28-3 Basic rack form, 14 ½° full-depth involute system.

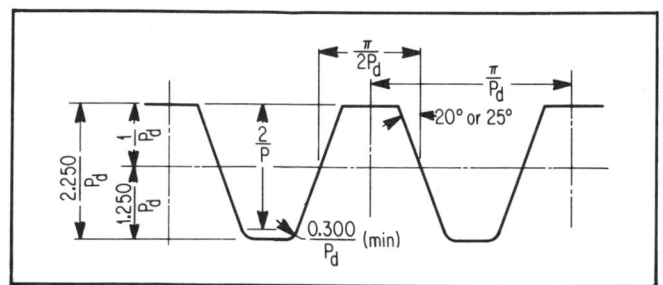

Fig. 28-4 Basic rack form, 20° or 25° full-depth involute system, when P_d is less than 20.

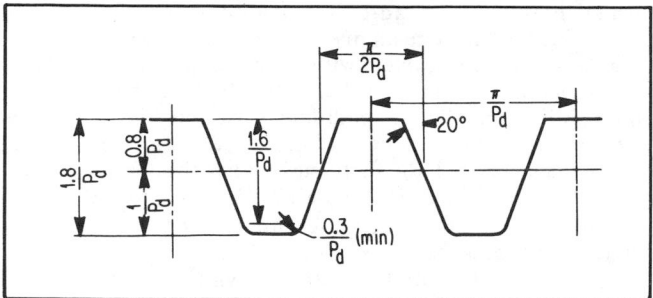

Fig. 28-5 Basic rack form, 20° stub-tooth involute system.

different tooth proportions make only a slight change in the amount of the clearance at the roots of the teeth.

Helical gears. The teeth of helical gears are cut along a helix on the pitch cylinder; otherwise, they are similar to spur gears and the action on any given plane of rotation is exactly the same as for spur gears. All other factors being equal, helical gears run more smoothly and quietly. The helical teeth introduce an end thrust, which must be met in the design of the mounting or must be neutralized within the gear itself by the use of herringbone or double-helical teeth.

The same basic rack forms are used for helical gears as for spur gears. When these gears are milled, hobbed, or shaped, this form is the normal basic rack form; in these cases, the diameters of the gears are larger than the equivalent spur gears. Hobs can be swiveled to cut any helix angle; Fellows and Sykes cutters are limited to the helix angles of the cutters and guides; Maag-type machines using rack-type cutters may be swiveled to any angle. Mating external helical gears on parallel shafts have helixes of opposite hand. Helical gears are readily designed to operate on any specified center distance by varying the helix angle.

Gears on Intersecting Axes

Gears on intersecting axes may have straight bevel, spiral bevel, or Zerol bevel teeth. The pitch surfaces of these gears are cones, and the point where the apexes of the two pitch cones meet (cone apex) is the intersection point of the two axes.

Bevel gears. The crown gear for bevel gears corresponds to the basic rack for spur gears. Its pitch surface is a plane. The elements of its tooth form converge and meet at the cone apex. The form of the teeth on the crown gear determines the form of the teeth of all bevel gears of the system. Almost universally, external bevel gears should be used and internal bevel gear drives should be avoided. For bevel gear nomenclature see Fig. 28-6.

Bevel gear tooth proportions are based on the tooth depth along the back cone. The teeth are tapered to the cone apex. The length of the back cone element from its apex to the pitch circle is used as the pitch and radius of the equivalent spur gear. The tooth proportions along the back cone are translated into their angular values in relation to the pitch cone of the bevel gear.

Gleason 20° straight bevel-gear system. This system for the design of straight bevel gears is a development from a system originated by Gleason Works and adopted by the AGMA as Standard 208.03.

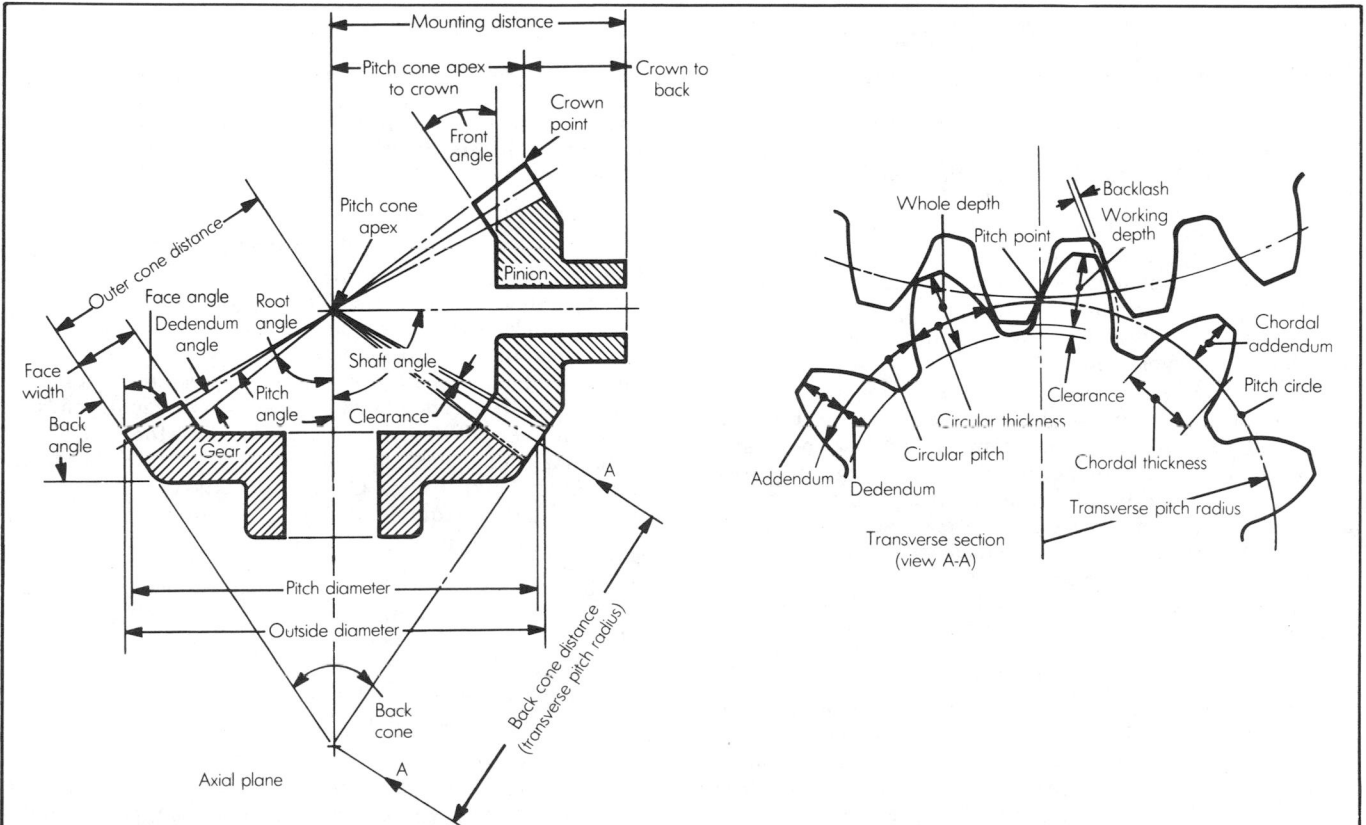

Fig. 28-6 Bevel gear nomenclature.

GEARS

Straight bevel gears that are cut on modern bevel gear generators have a localized tooth contact pattern and are known as Coniflex gears. The superiority of the Coniflex gears over straight bevels cut with full-length tooth contact lies in the control of the tooth contact length. This localization of contact permits some adjustment of the gears in assembly and compensates for small displacement due to deflection under operating loads without concentrating the load on the ends of the teeth.

Ratios. The system is designed to include ratios in common use. Ratios outside the system can be designed according to the same general principles used in determining the system. The basic pressure angle is 20°.

Gleason spiral bevel gear system. This system for the design of spiral bevel gears is a revision of the original Gleason system adopted by the AGMA in 1922 and most recently revised in 1964 and reaffirmed in 1972 (AGMA Standard 209.03). Changes have been made that affect ratios, depth, angles, and other factors.

Gears on Nonparallel, Nonintersecting Axes

When helical gears are used to drive on nonparallel non-intersecting axes, they are called spiral (crossed helical) gears. Drives for such axes are also accomplished with worms and wormgears.

Crossed helical gears. The driving gear is called the driver and the driven gear, the follower. The action between these gears is a sliding action. In effect, the teeth act as wedges, the one driving its mate ahead. The contact between these teeth is point contact, which limits their load-carrying ability. Tooth sizes are determined in the same manner as tooth sizes for helical gears. The most difficult problem with them is determining the helix angles that will match a specified center distance and a specified ratio. Minimum sliding conditions exist and maximum efficiency is attained when both gears have the same helix angle, which is also one half the shaft angle. When the helix angles are different, the larger one should always be on the driver.

Worms and wormgears. A common conception of a wormgear drive is that of a screw driving a nut. A better analogy would be that of a spiral gear drive in which one member has been made to envelop the other partly to obtain line contact between the mating teeth. A wormgear drive consists of two members: one with a uniform axial lead and a constant thread form, and the other with a member partly enveloping the first one. Generally, the smaller member (usually the driving member) embodies the uniform axial lead. Most wormgear drives are used to drive shafts that are at right angles to each other, but they can be made to drive shafts that are at other angles.

OTHER TYPES OF GEARS

In addition to the conventional types of gear drives, several special types exist. These special types meet needs the conventional types cannot meet because they are larger than desired or are otherwise inadequate. All these other types of gears are of the proprietary type, and the designs are necessarily made by the manufacturer of the units. Any engineering data needed should be secured directly from the manufacturer.

INVOLUTE SPLINES

A common problem encountered in engineering practice is the fastening together of two members to prevent relative rotation. Splines, keys, pins, multiple keys, and keys cut integral with the shaft and hub have served to solve this problem. Because involute splines are stronger than parallel-sided splines and straight-sided serrations, the latter have been superseded by the involute form. The term "involute serration," formerly applied to involute splines with 45° pressure angle, has been superseded by the term "involute spline," which applies to all splines with involute forms.

The involute form as generated with a straight-sided hob remains constant, even though the hob position is varied to a considerable extent. A hob of any diametral pitch can be used to cut any number of teeth of the same pitch. Hobbing is discussed in a subsequent section of this chapter. In most cases of spline use, one or both of the members are hardened and tooth thickness has to be changed to compensate for the movement due to heat treatment. The ease of controlling fits has led to the extended use of the involute-spline form, and standards have been adopted for general use.

TYPES AND CLASSES OF FIT

The ANSI Standard B92.1 deals with two types of fit, side fit and major-diameter fit for 30° pressure angle splines; and only one type of fit, the side fit for 37.5° and 45° pressure angle splines. For side fit, the mating members contact on the side of the teeth only; major and minor diameters are clearance dimensions. For major-diameter fit, the mating members contact at the major diameter for centralizing; the sides of the teeth act as drivers; and the minor diameters are the clearance dimensions.

SPLINE DESIGN

The involute splines in ANSI Standard B92.1 are straight (nonhelical) along their axes. The term "spline" is defined as the entire configuration of the component, which includes all teeth, and is bounded by the major circle and minor circle of the teeth. This standard is based on a stub pitch design and includes involute splines with 30°, 37.5°, and 45° pressure angles.

Press fits are not tabulated because their design depends on the degree of tightness desired and must allow for factors such as the shape of the blank, wall thickness, material, hardness, and thermal expansion. Close tolerances or selective size grouping may be required to limit fit variations.

Pitches

For both 30° and 37.5° pressure angle splines, a range from 2.5/5 to 48/96 pitch and a range from 6-60 teeth are covered with basic dimensions and equations; for 45° pressure angle splines, the full range from 6-100 teeth for the 10/20, 16/32, and 24/48 pitches, and a more limited range of teeth in the 32/64, 40/80, 48/96, 64/128, 80/160 and 128/256 pitches are covered.

Eccentricity

Eccentricity of major and minor diameters, in relation to the effective diameter of side-fit splines, should not cause contact beyond the form diameters of the mating splines, even under conditions of maximum effective clearance. The standard does not establish specific tolerances.

Eccentricity of major diameters in relation to the effective diameters of major-diameter-fit splines should be absorbed within the maximum material limits established by the tolerances on major diameter and effective space width or tooth thickness.

If the alignment of mating splines is affected by eccentricity of locating surfaces relative to each other and/or the splines, it may be necessary to decrease the effective and actual tooth thickness of the external splines in order to maintain the desired fit condition. The standard does not include allowances for eccentric location.

SPLINE APPLICATIONS

Terms and symbols for 30° pressure angle, flat root, side-fit and major-diameter-fit splines are shown in Fig. 28-7. Side-fit splines of this type are used in restricted areas (such as with tubular parts having a wall thickness too small to permit the use of fillet roots, to allow hobbing closer to shoulders), and for economy when hobbing, shaping, etc. Side-fit splines permit using shorter broaches for the internal member.

Splines with 30° pressure angle, flat root, and major-diameter fit are used for assemblies in which runout of the member having the internal spline must be held to a minimum, such as a gear on a shaft. With a major-diameter fit, eccentricity

This is usually effected by providing a chamfer on the top corners of the external member. This method may not be possible or feasible for the following reasons:

1. If the external member is roll formed by plastic deformation, a chamfer cannot be provided by the process.
2. A semitopping cutter may not be available.
3. When cutting external splines with small numbers of teeth, a semitopping cutter may reduce the width of the top land a prohibitive amount.

In such cases, the corner clearance can be provided on the internal spline as shown in Fig. 28-8. When this option is used, the form diameter may fall in the protuberant area.

Terms and symbols for fillet root, side-fit splines with 30°, 37.5°, and 45° pressure angles are shown in Fig. 28-9. The fillet radius permits heavier loading and effects greater fatigue resistance through the absence of stress raisers. The 37.5° pressure angle and proportions of the spline shown in the center of this drawing are a direct compromise between the 30° (top) and 45° (bottom) pressure angle splines. They are often used on couplings where the external spline is to be cold formed, especially where a 45° pressure angle spline does not satisfy functional requirements and the shaft material is above the hardness limitation for 30° pressure angle, cold-forming tools. Involute splines with a 45° pressure angle are used where the toothed member delivers torque only (does not slide under

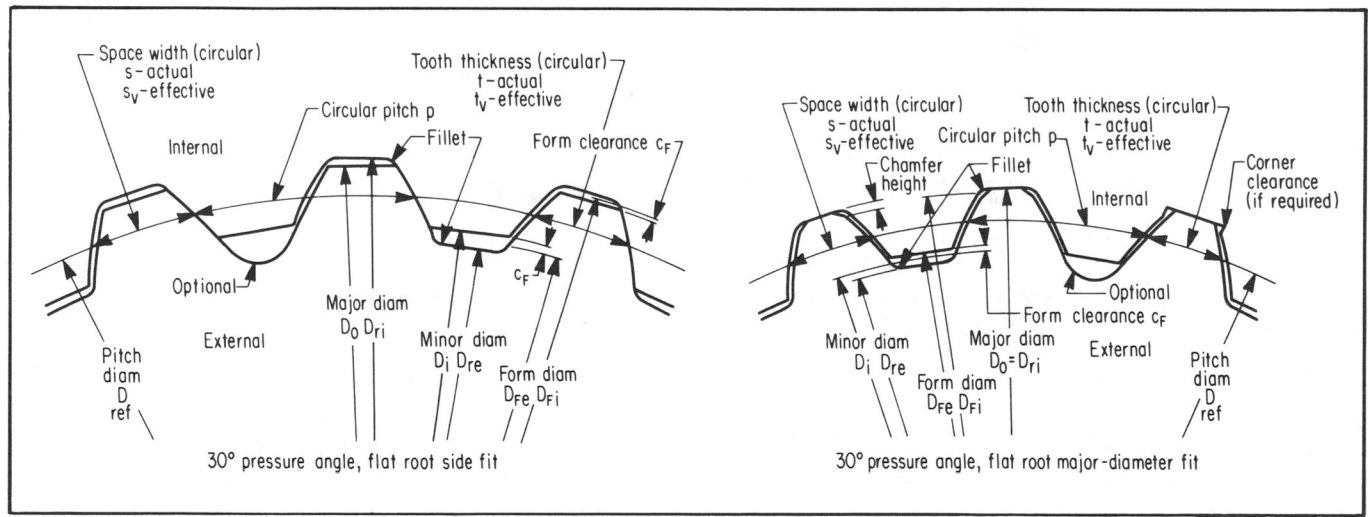

Fig. 28-7 Spline terms and symbols for 30° pressure angle, flat root, side and major-diameter fits.

between mating members is limited by the radial major-diameter clearance.

Caution should be used in considering a major-diameter fit, because when eccentricity does not occur between the major circle and the effective spline, excessive effective clearance may be present. Also, when eccentricity does occur, torque load is borne by only a few teeth.

In addition, caution should be used with finer pitches and smaller numbers of teeth to make sure that the major-diameter chamfer is not so great that the remaining top land would be too small for the fit to be ineffective.

With major-diameter fits, it is always necessary to provide corner clearance at the major diameter of the spline coupling.

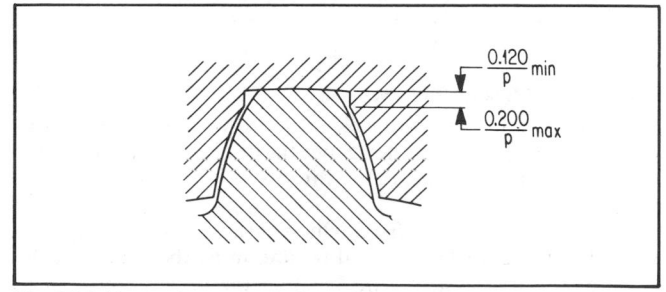

Fig. 28-8 Alternative method of providing corner clearance on internal spline when chamfering top corners of external member is not possible or feasible.

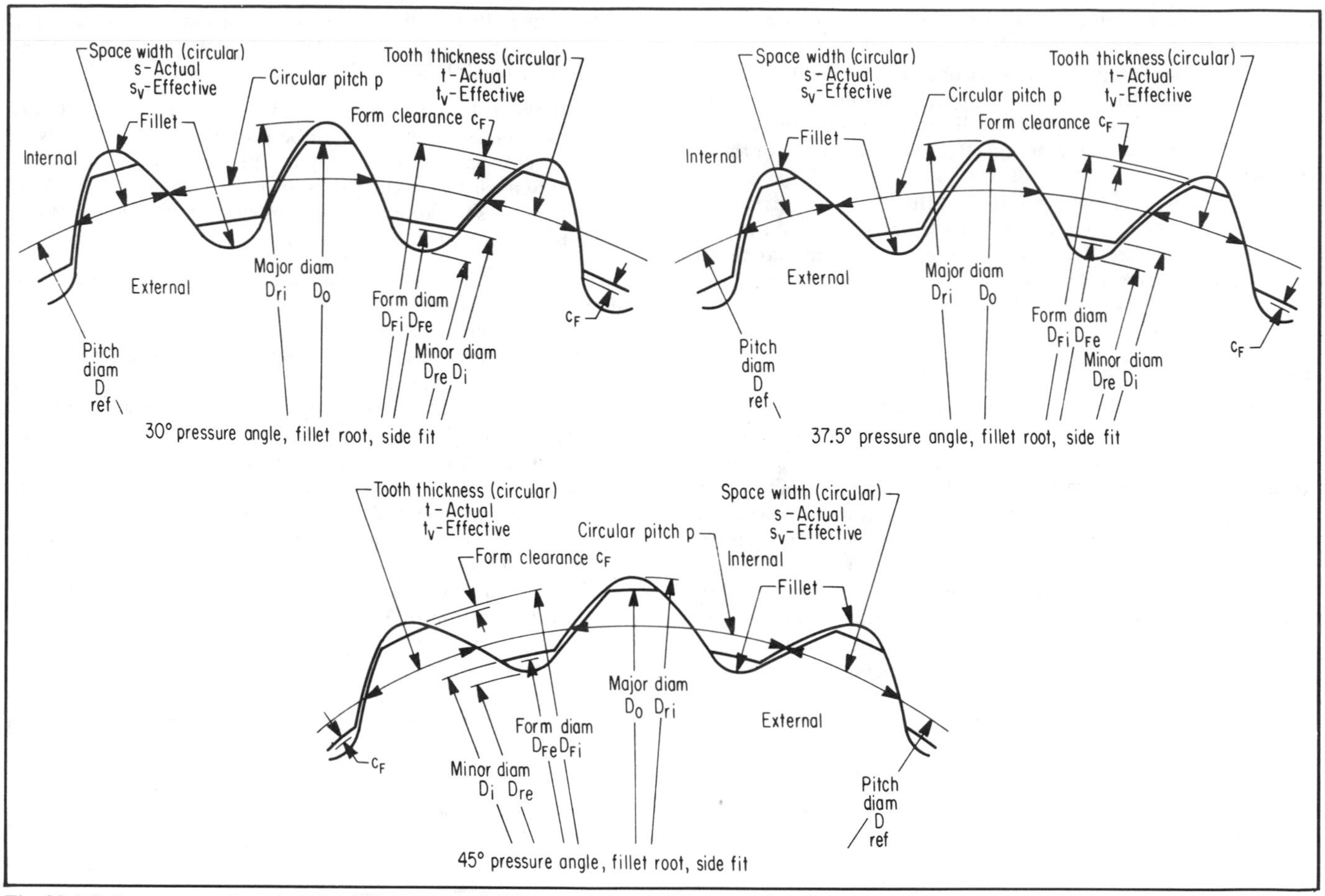

INVOLUTE SPLINES

Fig. 28-9 Spline terms and symbols for 30°, 37.5°, and 45° pressure angel, fillet root, side-fit splines.

load) and where the wall thickness is great enough to resist bursting tendencies. The 45° pressure angle spline is highly suitable for cold forming.

On internal, 45° pressure angle splines, straight-sided profiles may be specified as optional for involute profiles if the deviation of the straight side from the involute is compatible with design requirements. External splines are always designed with involute profiles. Straight-sided profiles on internal splines localize the tooth contacts.

The *internal form angle* for 45° pressure angle, internal splines with a straight-sided profile is that angle with legs tangent at the pitch line to the involute profiles which bound the basic space (see Fig. 28-10).

SPLINE VARIATIONS

Index variations cause the clearance to vary from one set of mating-tooth sides to another. Since the fit depends on the areas with minimum clearance, index variations reduce looseness or increase tightness.

The reference profile, from which variations occur, passes, through the point which is used to determine the actual space width or tooth thickness. This is either the pitch point or the contact point of standard measuring pins. Profile variation is positive in the direction of the space and negative in the direc-

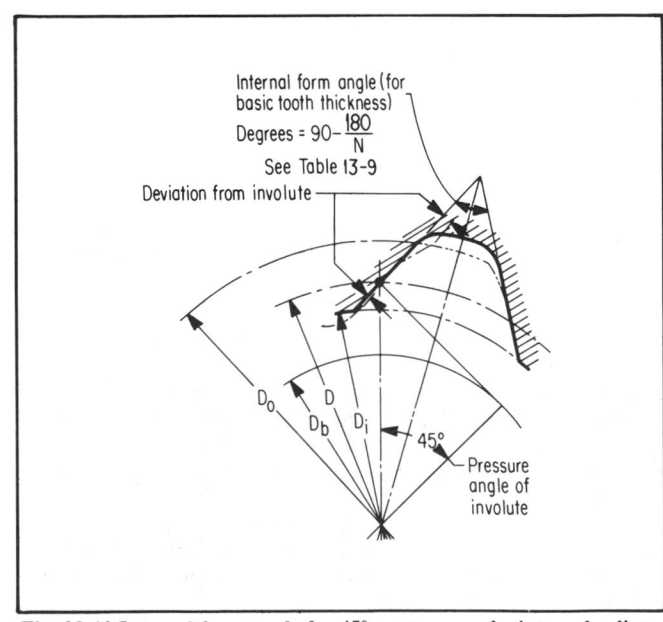

Fig. 28-10 Internal form angle for 45° pressure angle, internal splines with straight profiles.

tion of the tooth. Positive profile variation affect the fit by reducing effective clearance or increasing the interference; negative profile errors do not affect the fit but they reduce the contact area.

The variation of parallelism of a single spline tooth with respect to any other single spline tooth is seen in Fig. 28-11.

Lead variation is the variation of the direction of the spline tooth from its intended direction parallel to the reference axis; this variation includes parallelism and alignment variations (see Fig. 28-11).

The effect of individual spline variations on the fit (effective variation) is less than the total spline variations, because areas of more than minimum clearance can be altered without changing the fit. The variation allowance is 60% of the sum of twice the positive profile variation, the total index variation, and the lead variation for the length of engagement.

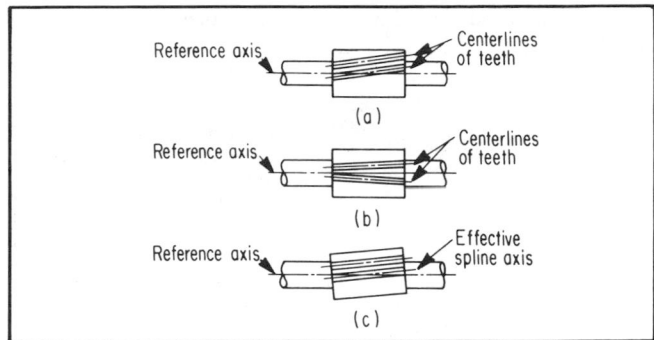

Fig. 28-11 Spline variations: (a) lead, (b) parallelism, and (c) alignment.

MANUFACTURING GEARS AND SPLINES

Gears and splines are produced by a variety of methods, including nonmachining (forming) and machining processes. Selection of a method to manufacture a specific workpiece requires consideration of a number of factors. These include the design of the gear or spline; type, hardness, and condition of the workpiece material; amount of stock to be removed or formed; accuracy and finish requirements; type, capability, and condition of the machine tool to be used; rigidity of the setup; production requirements; operating conditions; and tooling costs per part produced.

FORMING OF GEARS AND SPLINES

Forming (nonmachining) processes for manufacturing gears and splines include stamping, extruding, heading, forging, casting, powder metallurgy, and plastics molding. Another nonmachining process, gear rolling, is discussed later in this chapter.

A major advantage of forming is material savings by the elimination of chips. The forging and rolling processes also generally produce stronger gears and splines. While many external splines are manufactured by rolling, this process is usually limited to the production of finer pitch gears or the finishing of gears that have been previously machined.

Diecast Gears

Zinc diecasting is an economical forming process for the high-volume production of small gears subjected to light or moderate loading.[1] Process improvements now permit tolerances of ±0.001" (0.03 mm) on all critical tooth dimensions and ±0.0005" (0.013 mm) on as-cast center holes; flash-free castings and the elimination of any visible gate; and center holes with smooth finishes and no taper. Gears having a pitch diameter to 1 3/4" (44.5 mm) x 1/16" (1.6 mm) face width and pinions with face widths to 3/8" (9.5 mm) can be produced in this way. Shafts, keyways, face details, and other features can be incorporated into the castings, thus reducing costs.

Plastic Molding

Similar gear tolerances and sizes are obtainable in molding thermoplastic resins such as nylon, acetal, polycarbonate, and polyester, as well as low durometer elastomeric materials. For some applications, the self-lubricating properties of plastic gears are an important advantage.

Stamping and Extruding

Stamping and extruding impose design limitations and are generally restricted to the production of flat face (single dimension) details from ductile materials.

Gears from Powdered Metal

Sintered gears produced by powder metallurgy processes are widely used for high-production requirements of small gears and pump rotors. Predictability of performance of such gears has been significantly improved by advances in the processes. Some limitations with respect to strength, however, generally prevent the use of this method for larger size gears and for gears that must carry appreciable loads.

MACHINING OF GEARS AND SPLINES[2]

While the forming methods just discussed are used extensively to produce gears and splines, machining is the predominant method for manufacturing these components. The various machining processes used for gears and splines can be classified as form cutting or generating methods, discussed in detail later in this chapter.

Form-cutting processes include milling, broaching, gashing, grinding, and template-controlled shaping. These methods use a formed-tooth cutter (a tool preformed into the mirror image of the required shape) or a single-point tool following a template.

Generating methods of gear cutting involve relative motion between a rotating cutting tool and the rotation (generating motion) of the workpiece. These processes include hobbing and shaping, as well as some forms of bevel gear cutting.

Machining Splines

External splines are machined by form cutting (milling and broaching) or by generating with a shaper cutter or hob. Internal splines, especially those of smaller size, are usually produced by broaching, by other form-cutting methods, or by generating with a shaper cutter. Splines in blind holes are generally shaped.

MANUFACTURING GEARS AND SPLINES

Figure 28-12 shows the tooth shapes for shaper cutters, hobs, broaches, and racks used in producing splines.

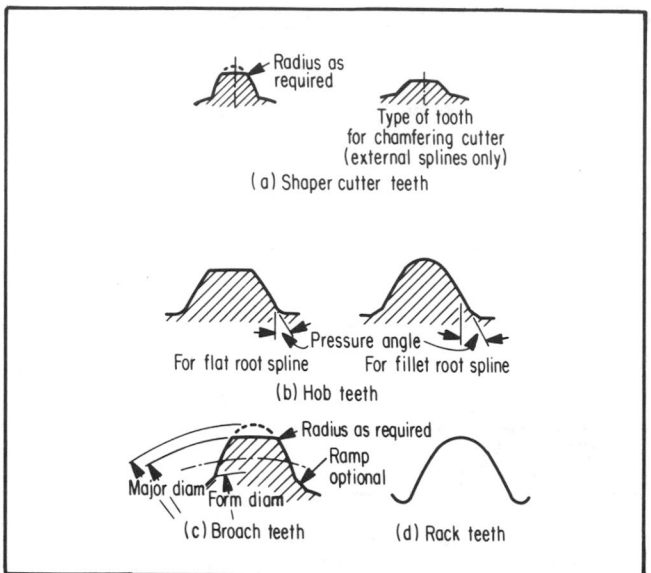

Fig. 28-12 Tooth shapes fo shaper cutters, hobs, broaches, and racks used in producing splines.

Machining Gears

Gears are most commonly machined by the shaping or hobbing generating methods, discussed in detail later in this chapter. Many gears, however, are also machined by broaching, and some by other form-cutting processes.

Photochemical machining. The teeth on gears of complex geometry, such as noncircular gears, can be milled or shaped, but small, thin, and flat gears are sometimes manufactured by photochemical machining when production quantities are small.[3] Photochemical machining is an etching process that uses shaped masks to produce parts from thin metal sheets. Metal removal rates with this process are slow, and tolerances increase with metal thickness. Thicker gears can be produced by laminating thinner components.

Milling of gears and splines. This form-cutting method of producing spline and gear teeth, discussed later in this chapter, offers the advantage of permitting the convenient production of small quantities of gears without the need for special gear cutting machines. Another advantage is that milling cutters cost less than hobs, especially for coarse pitches.

A disadvantage of milling has been slow production rates because the tooth spaces are machined one at a time. Modern gear gashing machines (discussed later in this chapter), however, permit the rapid production of large, coarse-pitch gears. Another limitation is that milling produces only an approximation of involute tooth forms unless the milling cutter is specifically designed for the exact number of teeth required. Coarse-pitch gears are sometimes rough cut with milling cutters and then finished by hobbing.

Milling is used primarily for limited production requirements of coarse-pitch spur gears, large internal gears, racks, gear segments, worms, and other toothed parts such as sprockets and ratchets.

Broaching gears and splines. Broaching is the fastest of all gear machining methods. Conventional broaching is used primarily for machining of internal gears, and pot broaching is employed to produce external gears. Both methods are generally limited to high-production applications because machine and tooling costs are high. With sufficient production requirements, however, cost per part produced is generally favorable. A possible limitation of broaching is that accurate profiles are not as easy to maintain as they are with generating methods.

Hobbing or shaping. These two generating methods, discussed in detail later in this chapter, are the most common ways of producing gears. Hobbing is the most widely used method for making spur and helical gears, and the only method available for machining wormgears.

Accuracy. While universal agreement does not exist, the consensus is that hobbing usually has the advantage with respect to tooth spacing and runout accuracy because continuous indexing is inherent in this machining method. Shaping, however, is generally better when it comes to accuracy of tooth form (profile). Both methods are about equal with regard to lead accuracy. Selection of either method necessitates consideration of many factors, including production, accuracy, and finish requirements.

Production rates. Productivity with hobbing and shaping depends on the specific job. Hobbing is generally faster, particularly when gears can be stacked in multiple. One exception is a recently developed shaper (described later in this chapter) that can operate at speeds to 1300 spm and can handle a stack of gears up to 8" (203 mm) thick and 50" (1270) diam. Shapers built by another manufacturer permit speeds to 2000 spm.

Surface finish. Both hobbers and shapers produce good finishes, but there are differences. Hobbing generally leaves a series of slight, radial tooth marks, with the width of the marks depending on the rate at which the hob is fed across the workpiece. For some applications, it may be necessary to remove these marks by a secondary operation such as shaving or grinding. Shaping usually leaves a series of straight lines parallel to the axis of the gear. With some newer gear shapers, a light finishing stroke at high stroking speeds minimizes these lines and generally reduces the need for secondary finishing operations.

Versatility. Gear shapers are inherently more versatile and can handle internal gears, shoulder gears, and other jobs that cannot be done on a hobbing machine. Hobbers are limited to external spur or helical open gears and other external shapes. Shapers can produce a variety of noninvolute shapes, either by themselves or in conjunction with gears. For example, a cam and a gear on the same shaft are frequently produced on shaping machines in a single setup. Shaping of helical gears, however, requires a guide for each helix and hand, whereas hobbers use differential gearing and can cut either right or left-hand helixes. In modern CNC hobbers and shapers, however, the gear train, including differential gearing, is no longer required.

Gear finishing. Methods used as secondary operations to improve the accuracy or surface quality of gear teeth include shaving, lapping, honing, grinding, and rolling, all discussed at the end of this chapter. Shaving is still a widely used process, but the excellent finishes now being obtained with some modern gear generating machines have reduced the need for shaving.

Grinding is used as a primary production process for some applications to produce gear teeth from the solid. It is used more extensively to finish teeth accurately after hardening.

MANUFACTURING GEARS AND SPLINES

Another method available for finishing hardened gears is skive hobbing with carbide hobs. Modern methods of hardening by induction heating or laser beam, however, minimize distortion and the need for subsequent finishing. Finish grinding is now generally limited to the production of gears for aircraft, aerospace, and similar maximum performance applications, or where hardened gears with weak support webs subject to large variations after heat treatment are required.

ROLLING OF SPLINES, GEARS AND WORMS

Many external splines and some gears are produced by rolling (cold forming). Gear rolling is used more extensively as a secondary finishing operation on previously machined gears, discussed at the end of this chapter.

Advantages of rolling include high production rates, material savings by eliminating chips, stronger teeth and shafts, smoother surface finishes, and in most cases, longer tool life. Increased strength results from the denser grain structure with improved flow, work hardening, and reduced stress concentrations of the rolled components. This often provides increased fatigue life and higher torque ratings. In some cases, secondary operations such as heat treating and/or grinding may be eliminated or a lower cost steel may be substituted for the original material.

Spline Rolling

Cylindrical die rolling. Both straight and helical splines and serrations, as well as other forms, are produced on thread and form rolling machines equipped with two cylindrical dies. On machines made by one manufacturer, the two cylindrical dies are held at a fixed center distance and the workpiece (blank) is throughfed between the dies (see Fig. 28-13).

A center-type fixture holding the workpiece on a hydraulically driven slide carries the blank through the rolling zone. After the proper spline or serration length has been formed, the right-hand die is automatically retracted and the slide returns to the loading position.

The minimum number of teeth that can be rolled by this method is 18, and the spline must be of the fillet root, side-fit

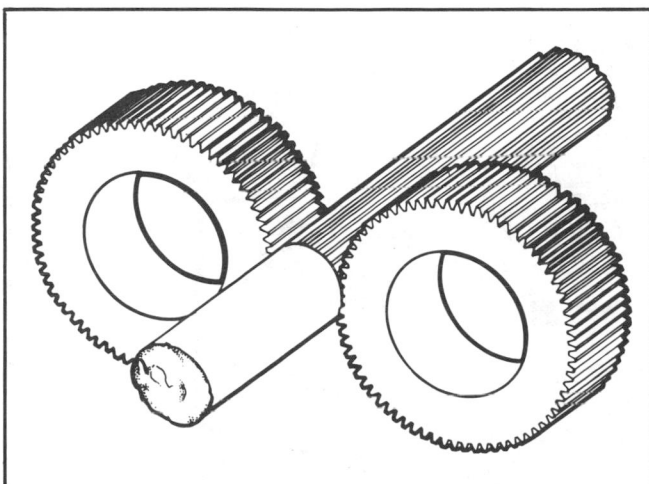

Fig. 28-13 Splines are roll formed by throughfeeding shaft between two cylindrical dies mounted at a fixed center distance. (*Teledyne Landis Machine*)

type. The largest spline that can be rolled depends upon the spline specifications, workpiece material, and power and capacity of the machine.

Reciprocating rack process. In this method, straight, helical, and taper splines, as well as serrations, grooves, threads, and similar forms, are produced on shafts, axles, formed sheet metal blanks, and other cylindrical parts with reciprocating rack-type forming tools. Forms can be produced at any desired position lengthwise on the workpieces and right up to shoulders. Splines or threads of the same or different diameter can be rolled on a single machine in one continuous cycle, and in some cases, marking or grooving can be done at the same time. More than one spline can be rolled on the same workpiece by placing two or more machines in line.

Worm Rolling[4]

The cold forming of helical grooves in worms to engage with wormwheels or wormgears is done by rolling. Worm rolling is generally more economical than milling or grinding and can be up to 50 times faster. The grooves are produced by penetration of a blank (workpiece) by hardened cylindrical dies to displace material in the blank both axially and radially.

Worm rolling is done by both the infeed and throughfeed methods, as well as by modifications of both processes, with infeed rolling being more common. The coarsest worm that has been rolled by the infeed method is 4 *DP*; with the throughfeed method, the coarsest worm is 8 *DP*.

Close control of blank diameter, straightness, and roundness is important for successful worm rolling. The blank surfaces should also be free of scale and oxide. Blanks for short worm shafts that can be contained within the threaded section of the die should be chamfered.

Worms designed with a full root radius or slight angle and large crest radii facilitate material flow in rolling. While it is practical to roll worms having 14 1/2° pressure angles, higher pressure angles are preferable for easier rolling, lower force requirements, better control, and longer die life.

Forces required for rolling vary with the workpiece material; number of revolutions required; and worm diameter, pitch, depth, and length. Materials rolled in worm production are generally limited to carbon and alloy steels, with only fine-pitch worms being rolled in stainless steels, aluminum, brass, and bronze. Steels used for successful worm rolling include AISI 1117, 1120, 1132, 1137 and the AISI 1300, 3100, 4000, 4100, 4300, and 8600 series. The additions of sulfur and lead to steels, which improves machinability, are detrimental in rolling.

MILLING SPLINES AND GEARS

Splines and gears are milled using multitooth formed cutters. The cutters for milling gears are usually flat discs with teeth on their peripheries; for some applications, they are of the end-mill type (see Fig. 28-14). Gears can be milled on gear cutting machines or on hobbing machines with milling attachments, and less efficiently on plain or universal milling machines.

Advantages and Limitations of Milling

Milling permits the convenient production of small quantities of gears without the need for special gear-cutting machines, and the cutters cost less than hobs, especially for coarse-pitch gears. A major disadvantage of milling is the slow production rates resulting from the tooth spaces being machined one at a time, with cutter retraction and blank indexing required

MANUFACTURING GEARS AND SPLINES

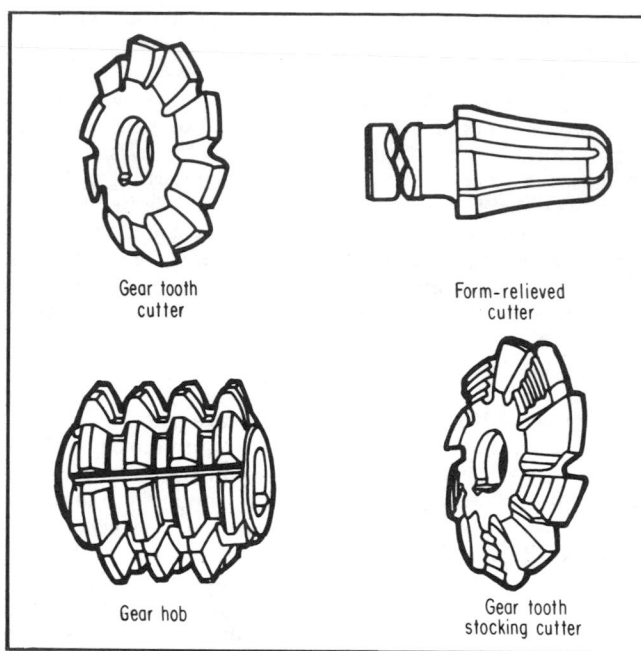

Gear tooth cutter

Form-relieved cutter

Gear hob

Gear tooth stocking cutter

Fig. 28-14 Typical gear milling cutters and a hob.

between cutting operations. Another limitation for some applications is that the involute tooth forms produced are approximations unless the cutters are specifically designed for the exact number of teeth required.

As a result of its limitations, milling is generally restricted primarily to small production requirements for coarse-pitch spur gears, large gears, racks, gear segments, worms, and other toothed parts such as sprockets and ratchets. Sometimes, gear teeth are roughed by milling (usually with carbide cutters) and finished by hobbing.

Milling Cutters

For milled gears that operate together, which is the usual case, it is well to use cutters of the American Standard 14.5° composite tooth form which is partly cycloidal and partly involute. This compromise shape makes it possible to utilize a set of eight numbered range cutters and, optionally, seven half-number intermediate cutters.

Gear Gashing

Many large, coarse-pitch ($4DP$ and coarser), external and internal gears are now being produced rapidly on heavy-duty, rigid milling machines called gashers (see Fig. 28-15). These powerful gear-cutting machines have horizontal and vertical slideways, precise indexing, large-diameter ballscrews, and d-c spindle drive motors to 100 hp (75kW) for fast metal removal. They are available with CNC and microprocessor-based controls and can be used to produce spur, bevel, and helical gears, as well as racks and sprockets. Rough cutting is most efficient, but these machines are sometimes used for roughing and finishing. For some applications, the gashed gears are finished by hobbing, shaping, or shaving.

In gashing, the blank is mounted on the index table of the machine. The rotating milling cutter is positioned properly with

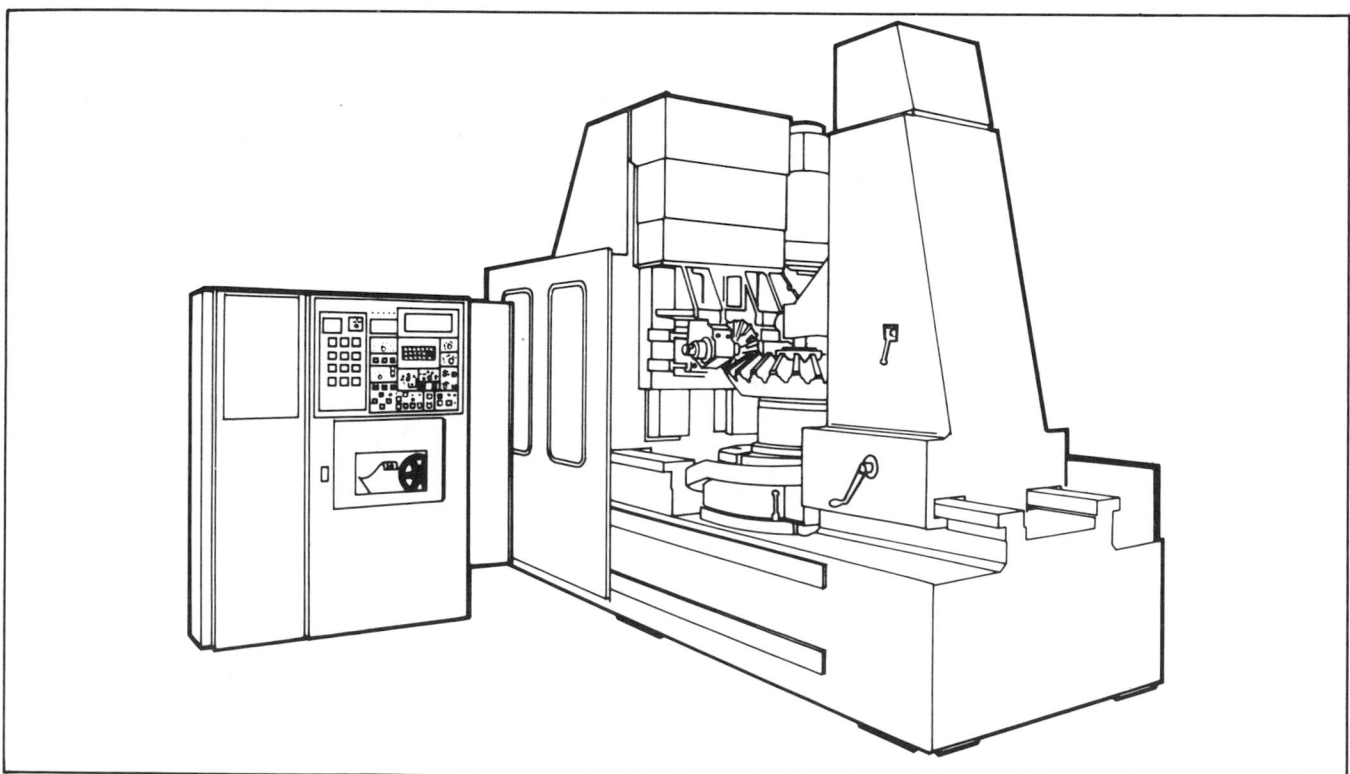

Fig. 28-15 Gashing machine with CNC for milling spur, bevel, and helical gears, as well as racks and sprockets. (*Gould & Eberhardt Gear Machinery Corp.*)

respect to the blank; the cutting action can be conventional or up (climb) cutting. In many applications the cutter is axially fed or plunged into the blank to reduce the hammering effect of entering the cut.

Standard form-relieved milling cutters, solid or inserted blade, with tooth profiles that are mirror images of the required shape, are used for gashing. Cutters with indexable carbide inserts, however, are being increasingly applied for such operations. Indexable inserts permit faster metal removal rates, provide longer tool life, and in many cases, reduce cost. The inserts can be designed to produce straight sides on the teeth or a rough shape approximating that of an involute profile. Carbide form cutters are also available for producing the finished profile on roller-chain sprockets.

BROACHING SPLINES AND GEARS

Many splines and gears are produced by broaching. As previously mentioned, broaching is the fastest of all gear machining methods. The process, however, is generally limited to high-production application because machine and tooling costs are high. With sufficient production requirements, cost per part produced is low.

Spline Broaching

Before splined holes are broached, it should first be determined what splined portion of the spline fits its mating member. Most involute-spline fits are on the sides (pitch diameter) of the teeth, but others may locate on the major or minor diameters of the spline teeth. If the spline in the gear is a side-bearing fit with its mating part and the part is processed from the ID, the spline inside diameter must be broached or otherwise machined concentric with the sides of the teeth. If it is a major-diameter fit and the part is processed from the ID, the spline minor diameter must be machined concentric with the major diameter and the sides of the teeth.

Broaching Internal Gears

Internal spur and helical gears are being economically and accurately produced in high production by a single pass of a full-form finishing broaching-tool assembly. Such assemblies consist of a one-operation, two-piece broach comprising a roughing section and a finish broaching tool. The roughing section is of the nibbling type that produces the desired involute form by a generating process as it moves through the work. Each tooth is of increasing height. This roughing section is followed by a floating, side-shaving shell which removes stock along the entire tooth thickness. The amount of stock removed by the full-form finishing shell is usually about 0.010" (0.25 mm) on the tooth thickness, 0.005" (0.13 mm) per surface on helical parts, and half that amount on spur applications.

Broaching External Gears

External gears, splines, and parts with specially formed teeth can be produced rapidly and economically in medium and high-production lots by pot broaching, utilizing tools having internal cutting teeth. External helical gears are produced by using special pot-broaching machines equipped with lead bars, but this process is limited by gear size, helix angle, and material.

A relatively new process called push-up pot broaching uses a machine in which the part is pushed upward through a fixed pot-broaching tool of either stick, ring, or combination design to produce external teeth. Ring-type broaching tools are used where tooth form and spacing are critical, and the lower cost stick type is used where accuracy permits and where the length of the cut is very short. Machines have the pot broach securely mounted in a stationary position on the front, directly above a hydraulic cylinder with a nonrotating piston rod. The rod has a splined push plate which forces the workpiece up through the pot broach. This method ensures quick and complete chip removal from the broach teeth, with coolant being flushed into the tool area. Smooth finishes and precise tooth form, size, and spacing can be obtained. Tool life varies from 500,000 parts on steel applications to 1,250,000 on cast-iron and pearlitic malleable parts.

The process is ideally adapted to full automation. Finished parts can be ejected at the top of the pot broach, where gravity can help move them to the next operation. One such setup is illustrated in Fig. 28-16. Incoming parts from a roller conveyor are fed into a loading chute through a gage that prevents oversized parts from entering. A pivoting-arm moves each part from this chute to a position above the nosepiece on the end of the push-up cylinder rod. An unloader above the pot broach holder is a mechanical, spring-loaded linkage that pushes the finished part into a gravity chute. As the part slides down this chute, it trips a switch that permits the cylinder rod to retract for the next broaching sequence.

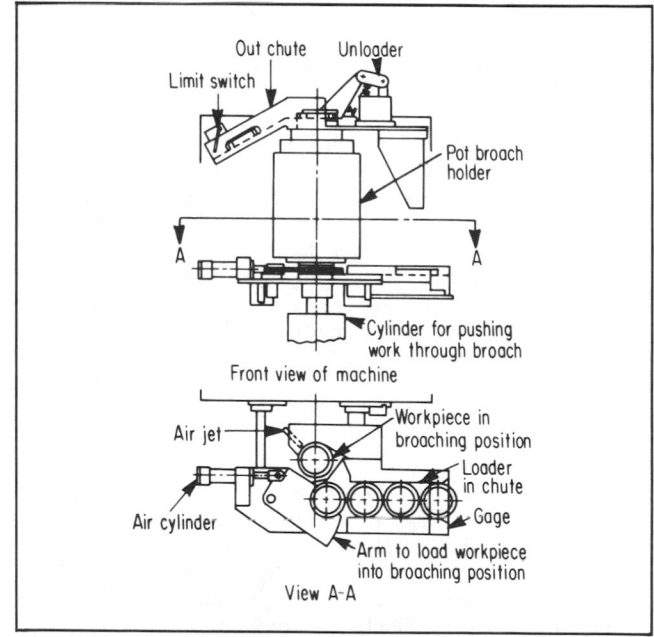

Fig. 28-16 Automatic loading and unloading arrangement for pot-broaching gears. (*National Broach & Machine Div., Lear Siegler, Inc.*)

HOBBING SPLINES AND GEARS

The hobbing method produces gears by means of a hardened cutter called a hob. A hob is cylindrical and resembles a worm in appearance; the teeth on its periphery follow a helical path like a worm thread (see Fig. 28-14). In the hobbing method, both the hob and gear blank revolve continuously in timed relationship, the teeth being generated by the hob as it gradually feeds across or into the blank. The word *generate*, when used in gearing, indicates that the cutter produces tooth profiles differing from the form of the cutter itself.

MANUFACTURING GEARS AND SPLINES

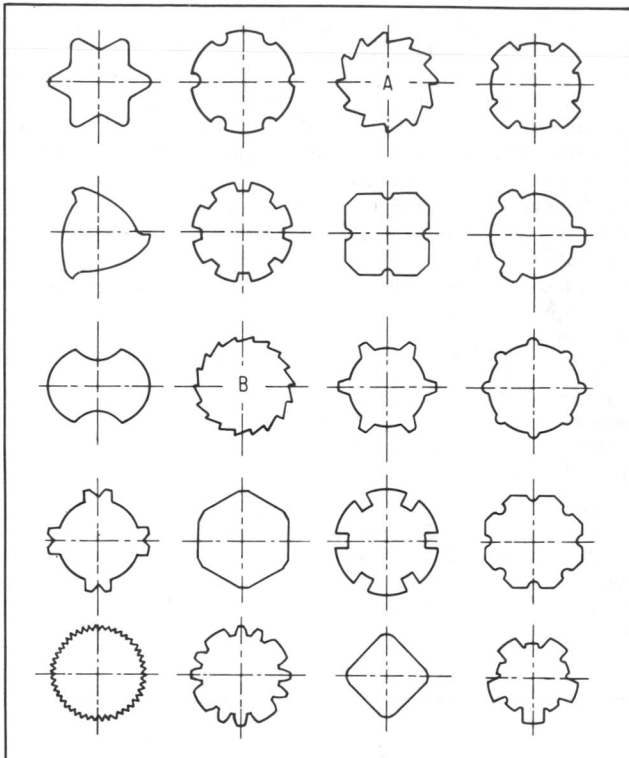

Fig. 28-17 Typical forms generated by special hobs.

Hobbing can be used for production of not only spur gears, helical gears, wormgears, and splines, but also most forms that are uniformly spaced around an axis. Sprockets for both silent and roller chains are common examples. Chamfering the ends of gear teeth by means of special hobs has long been practiced. Other forms produced by hobbing are shown in Fig. 28-17. Forms marked *A* and *B* are typically cut with single-position semigenerating hobs, permitting the last engaged tooth in the hob to produce the radial face on the work. The projections or indentations need not necessarily be symmetrical about an axis that intersects the center of the work, nor does the form need to be of any special curvature. The only limiting factor is that the indentations or projections must be of sufficient width in proportion to height to roll in and out of the hob without interference. A single-position hob for cutting ratchet teeth must be accurately centralized with respect to the blank and cannot be shifted to a new position when the teeth commence to dull. A new centralizing position must be determined after each resharpening of such a single-position hob.

Hobbing is the most widely used gear-cutting process for spur and helical gears. It is applicable when large numbers of identical gears are to be manufactured, as well as for single gears or small lots. The process permits a wide latitude in gear design. Involute-form hobs with ground or EDM finish, made to very close accuracy, are readily obtainable, and their use on suitable gear-hobbing machines results in excellent uniformity of tooth spacing and correctness of gear-tooth profiles. A single hob can cut any number of interchangeable involute gear teeth up to, but not including, a rack, either equal-addendum or long and short-addendum design, and either spur or with almost any helix angle; however, this is seldom, if ever, done in actual practice. The pitch range of hobbing is from 3/4 to 250 P_d.

Single or multiple fly tools offer advantages for generating multiple-thread wormgears. A process called skive hobbing for finishing hardened gears is discussed later in this chapter under the subject of gear finishing.

Hobbing Machines

Typical hobbing machines are illustrated in Fig. 28-18 and 28-19. As previously mentioned, hobbing is a continuous

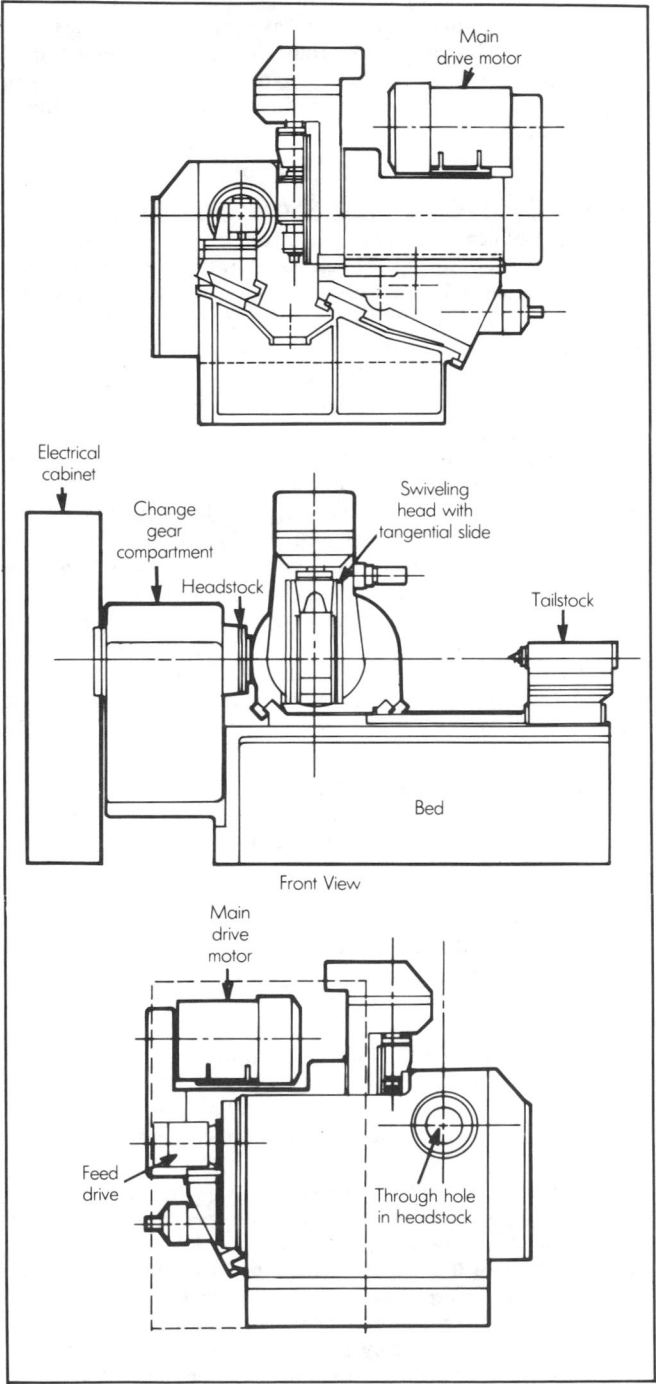

Fig. 28-18 Horizontal hobbing machine with guards removed. (*American Pfauter Corp.*)

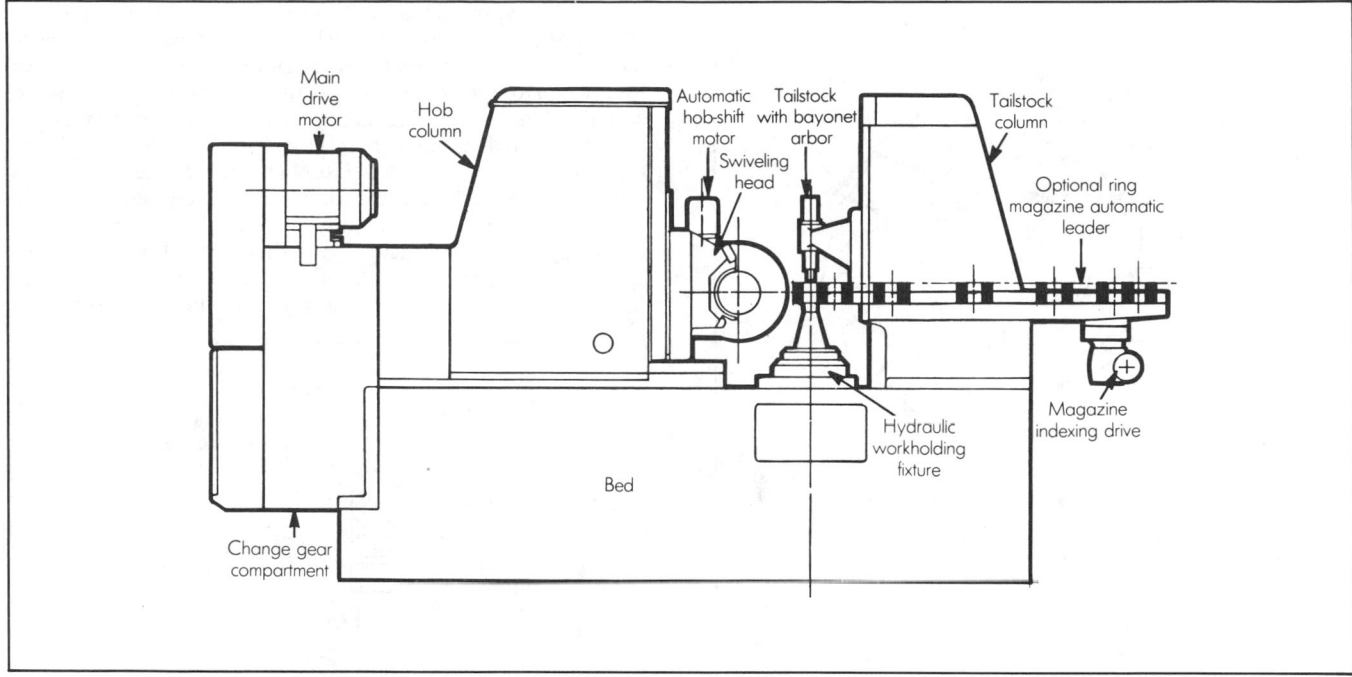

Fig. 28-19 Vertical hobbing machine with guards removed. (*American Pfauter Corp.*)

process in which the hob and blank both rotate in timed relationship with each other. In addition to the rotary motion, the hob and gear blank are fed relative to each other to produce the spur gear, helical gear, or wormgear. In the hobbing process, the cutting action is continuous in one direction until the gear is completed.

Programmable control. Hobbing machines with electronic control are available, using programmable controllers or CNC. Some machines with programmable controllers feature electronic lead control, set with digital thumbwheels, eliminating the need for lead-change gears. Other features include digital selector switches for setting travel limits and cutting cycles, infinitely variable feeds and speeds, automatic feed and speed changing, power tailstock positioning, and inch/metric digital readouts.

Computer numerical control. On CNC hobbing machines, the microprocessor and software control all movable axes. The number of teeth; helix angle; swivel angle for the hob head; amount and sequence of hob shifting increments; radial, axial, and tangential motions of the slides; crowning and taper cutting; and cutting parameters (hob speed and feed) can all be preset.

Hobs

In gear hobbing the cutting tool is called a hob. Most hobs are cylindrical in form and greater in length than in diameter (see Fig. 28-14). With only one hob, it is possible to cut interchangeable gears with a given pitch of any number of teeth within the range of the hobbing machine. There is a trend toward the use of longer and larger diameter hobs; the reasons: newer machines have the capacity to handle them, longer hobs extend tool life, and larger hobs provide more teeth to perform the cutting and generation of the profiles. They also accommodate larger bores and permit more rigid operations.

A hob resembles a worm in appearance, with its cutting teeth on the outside of a cylindrical body following a helical path corresponding to the thread of either a left or right-hand worm. It is not strictly correct to say that an axial section of a hob is a rack, but it is useful to think of a hob as a cylinder with a series of racks fastened on its periphery, each rack being parallel to the hob axis, or nearly so, and each one slightly displaced axially with respect to the preceding rack. As the hob rotates in timed relationship with the blank, each row of teeth successively cuts the next portion of the gear-tooth spaces.

Hob terminology and symbols. Conventional hob terminology is presented in Fig. 28-20.

Hobbing Fixtures

Adequate fixtures for supporting gear blanks during hobbing are most important, and fixtures are related to the equally important matter of accuracy of blanks. An adequate fixture must support the blanks very rigidly; otherwise, chatter and vibration and poor finish result. The fixture must accurately position the blanks with respect to radial runout and side runout or wobble, and it must not distort the blanks. At times a fixture must provide positive driving means such as a key or pin to lock the blank against rotation or to register it with respect to tooth location. The fixture design must take into account ease of loading and may involve automatic loading and unloading in the case of fully automated machine setups.

Hardened mandrels and certain fixture parts are preferred over soft ones, especially if the quantity of gears warrants the expense of hardening. These must be carefully finished to run true within close tolerances. Clamping collars must have parallel faces and should be hard. They need not fit the mandrels tightly; in fact, they can be slightly larger for ease in loading and unloading.

Figure 28-21 shows a gear-hobbing fixture of the mandrel type. It is intended for a vertical-spindle hobbing machine, but

MANUFACTURING GEARS AND SPLINES

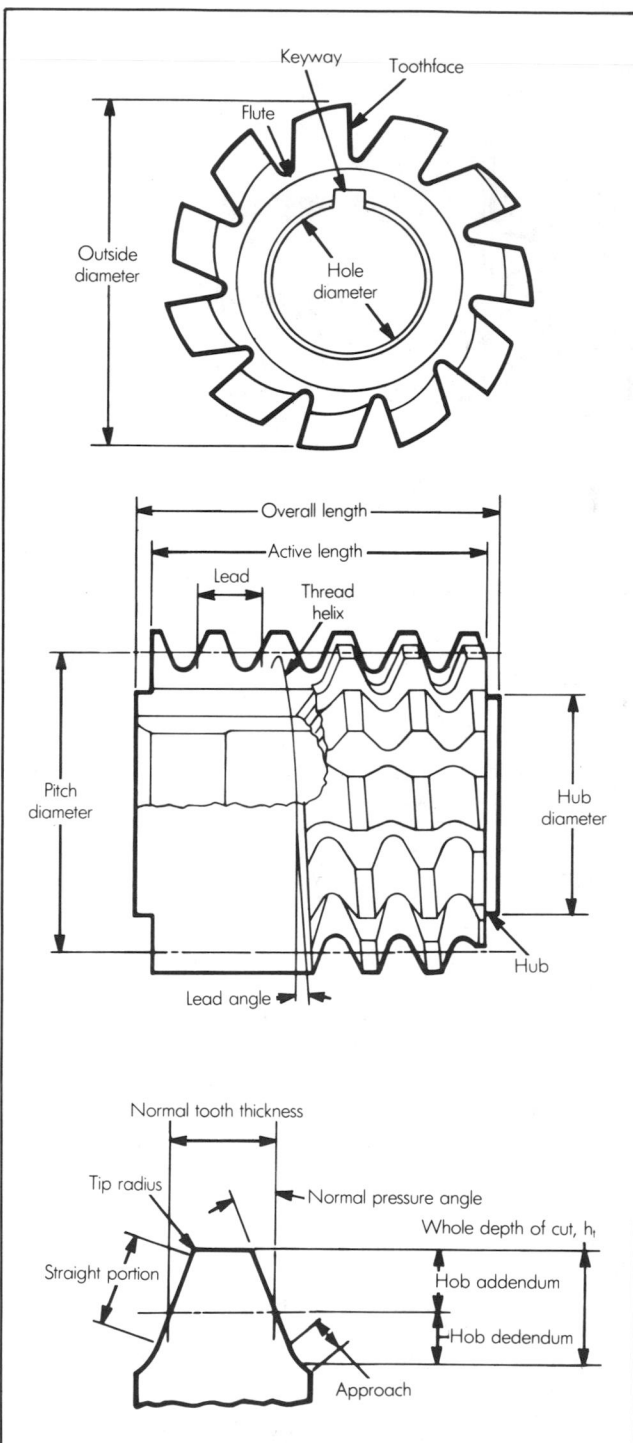

Fig. 28-20 Nomenclature of hob terms.

D is the hob approach or overtravel, at the start or end of cut. This allowance is greater for helical gears, especially for those having high helix angles for which more approach is required for the hob to start the cut and greater overtravel is necessary to complete the generating action. The pilot diameter, E, is commonly made smaller than the hole in the table, permitting tapping the loosely clamped fixture until it indicates true within the required accuracy, after which it is securely clamped.

Typical hobbing fixtures are illustrated in Fig. 28-22, all being applicable in principle for either vertical or horizontal-spindle hobbing machines. A common mandrel-type fixture for flat-face gears is shown in view a. Incorporated in the fixture

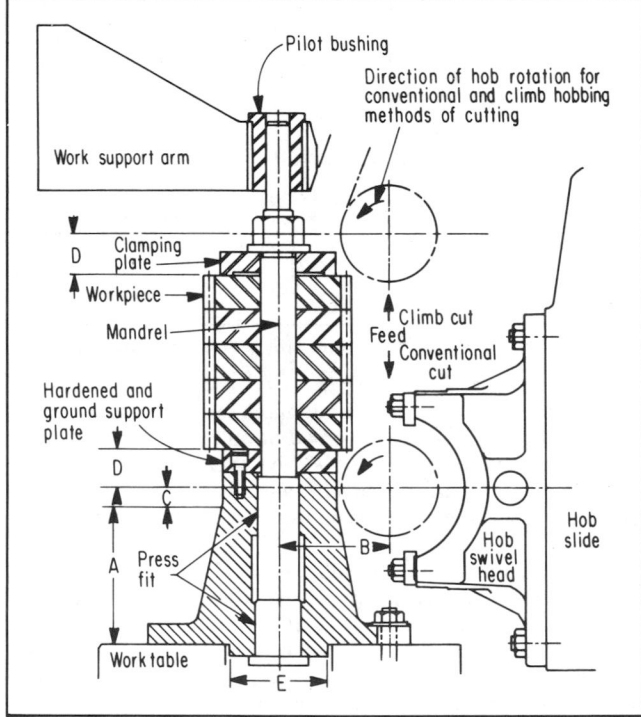

Fig. 28-21 Nomenclature and important dimensions of fixture used for hobbing. (*Gould & Eberhardt Gear Machinery Corp.*)

the same principles are applicable to horizontal-type hobbers. Dimension A is the minimum distance between the center of the hob and face of worktable or spindle, obtainable from the hobbing machine manufacturer or by measuring the machine. It may vary according to the center distance, B, between the hob and work axis. Dimension C is the safety clearance. Dimension

may be reversible or interchangeable bottom plates to utilize one fixture for various-size gears. Interchangeable mandrels or mandrels with light interference-fit bushings can be used. The clamp plate should be as large as possible and relieved to concentrate clamping action near the outer edge of the blank. View b shows a mandrel-type fixture with spacing collars between gear blanks having hubs wider than the face width of the gear teeth. A mandrel-type fixture with an auxiliary support ring and clamping straps is shown in view c. Light interference-fit bushings are used on the mandrel to accommodate the hole size. This fixture may be used without the auxiliary support ring. The use of an adjustable tail center in conjunction with a collet-type chuck is illustrated in view d. An intermediate steadyrest may be used to support long shafts on which gear teeth are to be hobbed. A plate-type driving dog can be fastened to one end of a long pinion shaft mounted between centers (see view e). Ring gears can be hobbed in the drum-type fixture shown in view f. The fixture is positioned on the base by the center pilot and held in place with the drawbolt. If production

MANUFACTURING GEARS AND SPLINES

justifies the use of two drums, one can be unloaded and loaded by the operator off the machine while the other is in use.

It is essential that the axis about which gear teeth are generated be concentric with the axis of the bore or the axis of the bearing surfaces. Therefore, it is desirable to locate the gear blank from these surfaces during the hobbing process. If this is impractical and it is necessary to clamp the gear blanks on a rim face or some other surface, then that rim face or surface must be accurately positioned with respect to bore or bearing surfaces. The accuracy of blanks must be planned with these factors in mind, and fixture design is a closely related problem.

Inaccurate blanks generally impair the quality of the product. There are some surfaces on blanks which are of little importance. An example is the outside cylinder of a spur gear, unless it is needed for trueing up the blank prior to the cut or for sizing of the gear teeth, in which case it would have to be accurately machined with respect to the hole or bearing surfaces.

Hobbing Applications

Hobbing is used for many different applications, including producing splines and cutting different gears such as spur, helical, and worm.

Spur-gear hobbing. For producing spur gears only, a hobbing machine does not require a differential. Index-change gears are selected from a chart or are calculated so that the number of revolutions made by the hob for one revolution of the worktable is exactly the number of teeth being cut divided by the number of hob threads.

Spline hobbing. In spline hobbing, the teeth are generated in one pass of the hob except when they are relatively coarse, in which case it is more economical first to take a roughing cut with a roughing hob. The hobs used may be of top or side-bearing type, depending upon the type of spline. A great majority of splines are of the American Standard involute type and are hobbed the same as pinions. A single hob can generate any number of involute splines of a given pitch. The only major differences between such involute splines and gear teeth are their shallow depth and high pressure angles.

Nondifferential helical-gear hobbing. The same machine used for hobbing spur gears can be used for nondifferential cutting of helical gears, as long as the design is such that feed-change gears and a feedscrew cause the feed motion, rather than a hydraulic cylinder, for example. The cutting of a helix requires tilting the hob to the helix angle plus or minus the lead angle of the hob and introducing a slight angular creepage of the work with respect to any integral number of hob revolutions. Thus as the hob feeds across the face of the blank, the desired helix angle is produced by the advancing or retarding of the blank rotation as governed by specially calculated index and feed-change gearing.

Differential helical-gear hobbing. The differential mechanism permits the slight increment or decrement motion of the worktable to be independent of the index and feed-change gearing. In the differential method, index gearing is selected directly from a chart furnished by the hobbing machine builder, the same method as used for spur gears. Ordinarily, no index-change gearing calculations are required. The feed-change gearing is also selected directly from a chart, without any calculating, and may be approximate.

Double-helical gear hobbing. Double-helical or herringbone gears are widely produced by the hobbing process, particularly

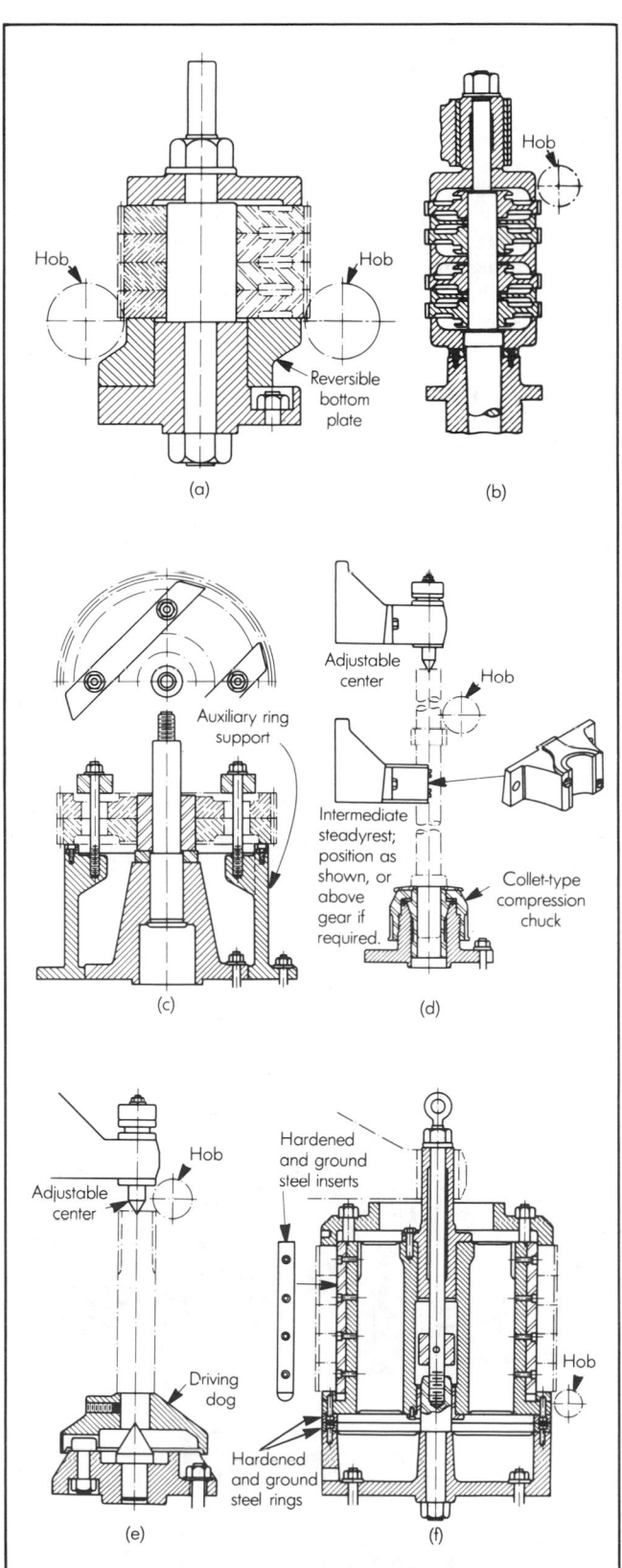

Fig. 28-22 Basic types of hobbing fixture. (*Gould & Eberhardt Gear Machinery Corp.*)

in large sizes such as those for ship-propulsion gears. The two halves are identical, except opposite in hand. Right and left-hand hobs are used for cutting their respective right and left-hand helixes of the blank.

Fine-pitch hobbing. Both the AGMA and ANSI define pitch as 20 P_d and finer. Standard hobs are available for hobbing fine pitches between 20 and 120 P_d and, in general, are available to a high degree of accuracy. Ground hobs have been made as fine as 200 P_d, and unground hobs as fine as 250 P_d. At about 120 P_d some limitations occur in the accuracy of hobs and other cutters, partly because of problems in measurement. For example, the tolerance on profiles should logically be proportionally smaller on fine-pitch hobs and gears than those on coarse-pitch hobs and gears, but the tolerances for very fine pitch profiles cannot be held closer than about 0.0002″ (0.005 mm) at best. The situation is particularly aggravated because many fine-pitch gear tolerances involve eight-tooth pinions, and with such low numbers of teeth, profile accuracy is critical. The limitations of fine-pitch hobbing, therefore, are caused by limitations of tooling, rather than of hobbing machines.

Crown and taper hobbing. Spur and helical gears are sometimes given a slight crown during the hobbing operation to avoid the possibility of edge contact which is objectionable from the standpoint of noise as well as failure from uneven tooth loading. If the crown is very slight, a few ten thousandths or thousandths of an inch (about 0.005-0.05 mm) across the face of the gear, it can usually be produced economically by a subsequent finishing operation. However, with special attachments on the hobbing machine, crown hobbing is possible. The feed of the hob across the spur or helical gear is first given a slight outfeed motion for one half the face, then a slight infeed motion for the rest of the face, in addition to the axial feed, thus obtaining the crown effect. A large amount of crown is necessary for spur gears used in gear-type couplings, in which the mating internal gear has straight teeth, and the external hobbed gear is actually convex on the outside diameter as well as along the tooth profiles, to accommodate shaft misalignment.

Taper hobbing is employed to allow for deflection and for backlash adjustment. This also requires a special mechanism on the hobbing machine to permit slight infeeding or outfeeding simultaneously with regular axial feeding. Crowning and tapering can be performed on NC/CNC hobbing machines by programming.

THE G-TRAC PROCESS

A relatively new method for rapidly generating spur and helical gears is the G-TRAC process developed by Gleason Machine Div., Gleason Works, Rochester, NY. This method has been referred to as gear cutting with an infinite-diameter hob, chain broaching, and a process that produces chips and generating flats resembling those produced by shaping. Production rates, however, can be 3-10 times those possible on hobbing and shaping machines.

The process uses a chain concept of cutting. Rack-type cutters are fastened in holders mounted on links joined together to form an endless driven chain guided by a track. The gear-tooth generating cycle consists of feeding the cutters radially into a stack of blanks while the blanks rotate in timed relation to the tools. This design allows a stack of gears to be cut in the same time that it takes to cut one gear.

Applications

This process is especially suitable for high-production requirements of stackable gears having flat, parallel faces, large bores, and no hubs. Spurs or helical gears up to 14″ (356 mm) diam in stacks to 7 1/2″ (190 mm) high can be produced. Helical gears with helix angles to 45° are produced by tilting the cutter housing.

Pitches of 6 *DP* and finer can be cut in either spur or helical gears; coarser pitches can be cut under certain conditions. Besides cutting spur and helical gears, the process can be used to cut slots in other parts. Sprockets, external splines (straight side or involute form), steering racks, and other similar shaped parts can be cut.

Machines Used

On the G-TRAC gear generator (see Fig. 28-23), a chain-like assembly of cutting tools is driven along a straight line through the cutting zone. The cutters are fed radially into the stack of gears to be cut while the gears are rotating in timed relationship to the cutters. Upon reaching full depth, the cutters and gears continue to rotate in timed relationship for a 360° rotation of the gears. Another cycle that may be selected consists of an additional small feed and one more 360° rotation if improved finish and geometry are desired.

Gear blanks are stacked on a hydraulically actuated arbor carried by a spindle extension that can be changed for different sizes of gears. The arbor centers and clamps the gears by expanding into their bores or clamping on their faces. A tailstock having a live center also provides support.

A programmable controller regulates all machine functions and facilitates troubleshooting. Machine functions are controlled with pushbuttons, and operating cycles are fully automatic with manual interrupt. The machines can be equipped with chutes and swing arms as shown in Fig. 28-23 for automatic loading and unloading.

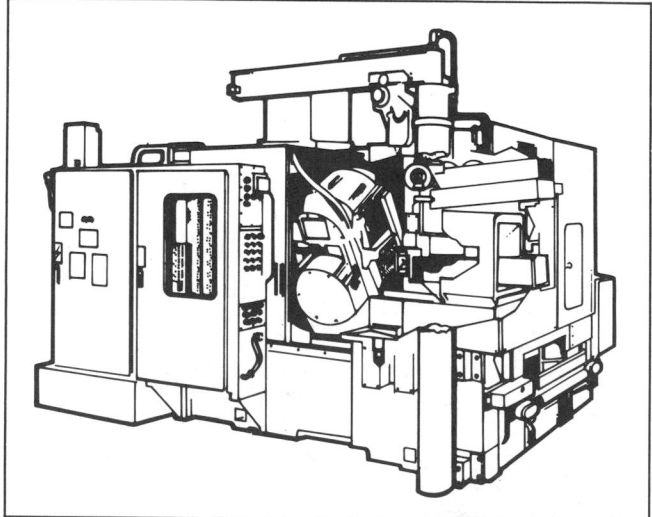

Fig. 28-23 G-TRAC gear generator with swing-arm automatic loader. (*Gleason Machine Div., Gleason Works*)

Cutting Tools Employed

Cutters are mounted to 14 articulated links (see Fig. 28-24) joined together to form an endless driven track. Six rack-type cutters are fastened to a toolholder mounted on each link. Normally, half the cutters are made to cut gear-tooth profiles only; the other half cut only in the roots and at the tops of the teeth. This arrangement serves to break up the chips produced. If preshave undercut is desired, it is produced by the side cutting blades. Other cutter arrangements can be accommodated.

GEAR SHAPING

Gear teeth are shaped in several ways. Unlike hobbing and milling, which involve rotary tool motion, shaping involves reciprocation of the tool.

The Gear-Shaper Method

Gear-shaper cutters generate a tooth form by a process known as molding-generating. The gear-like cutter, having suitable relief to provide cutting edges and cutting clearances, rotates in timed relationship with the workpiece. The cutter rotates and reciprocates to provide the cutting function, and the work rotates only. The rate of stroking and the length of stroke

of the cutter determine the cutting speed. The rate of work rotation determines the feed. These increments are illustrated in Fig. 28-25. It should be noted that the work is generated by these successive strokes of the cutter through the workpiece as they rotate together. Since the shaper cuts only in one direction, a relief is provided for the return stroke. This is usually done by separating the cutter and work. The amount of this separation is slight and can be accomplished by moving either the cutter or work spindle. On most modern shaping machines relief on the return stroke is accomplished by moving the cutter rather than the workslide. This design permits higher stroking speeds because less mass has to be moved.

The gear shaper with its associated tooling accurately produces both external and internal spur and helical gears as well as splines. Gears may be cut not only on conventional blanks but against flanges and in blanks where only narrow recesses are provided for cutting clearances. Thus, certain types of gears can be generated by the gear-shaper method only. Crown and taper can be produced easily and economically on some gear shapers. There are some applications in which multiple gears or other shapes can be produced simultaneously.

The new heavy-duty machines, while not to be considered primarily as roughing machines, remove stock with ease and rapidity. Some overtravel is necessary above and below the workpiece; however, this amount of overtravel is very small and obviously is much less than that required by a hob or a milling cutter.

Gear Shaping Machines

A general-purpose machine for cutting internal or external spur or helical gears is shown in Fig. 28-26. This machine features infinitely variable speeds and feeds, automatic speed and feed changing, and automatic high lift of the cutter.

Gear shapers are used principally in the production of gears. They are also extensively used for generating racks, cams, latches, ratchets, clutches, and many other irregular shapes, and can also be used for slotting and forming operations when equipped with the proper fixtures and attachments. A typical attachment for cutting racks is shown in Fig. 28-27. Gear shapers are available for a wide range of gear diameters. Pinions of 1/16″ pitch diameter to gears of 120″ pitch diameter are produced on these machines.

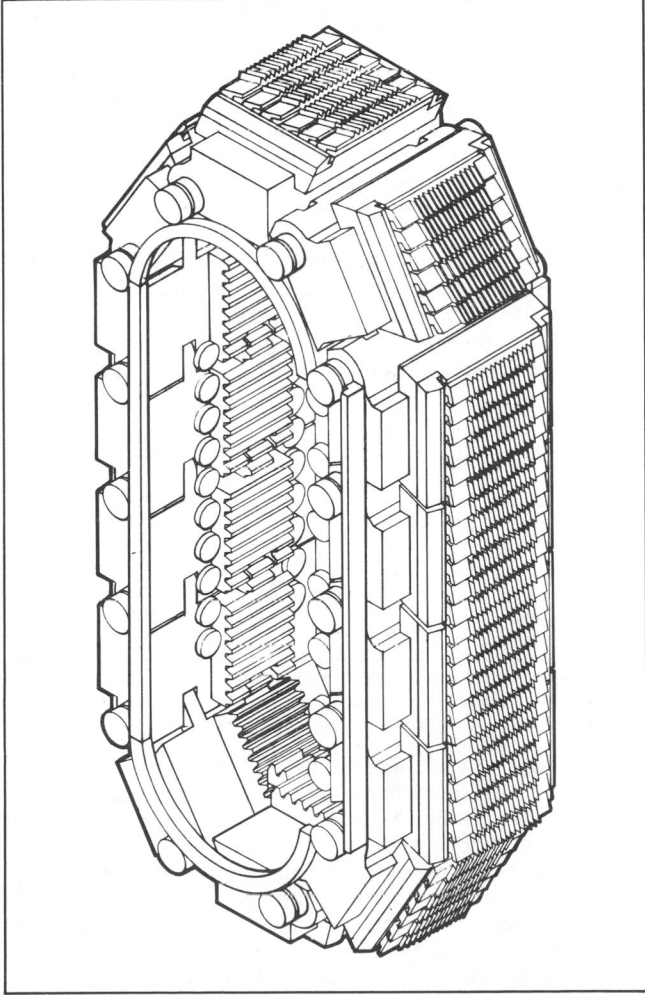

Fig. 28-24 Rack-style cutters are fastened to toolholders mounted on articulated links of endless driven track. (*Gleason Machine Div., Gleason Works***)**

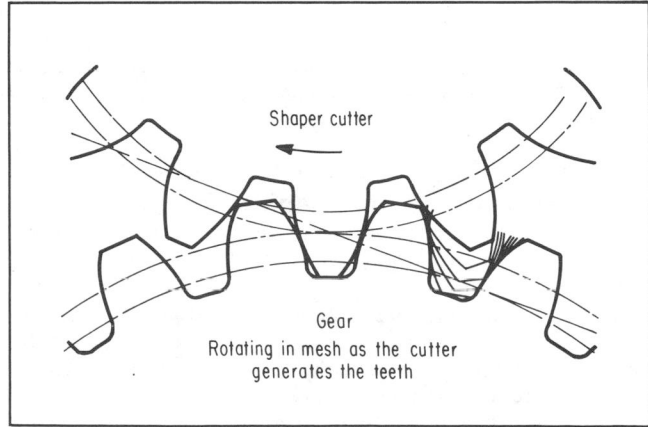

Fig. 28-25 Molding-generation action of a gear-shaper cutter.

MANUFACTURING GEARS AND SPLINES

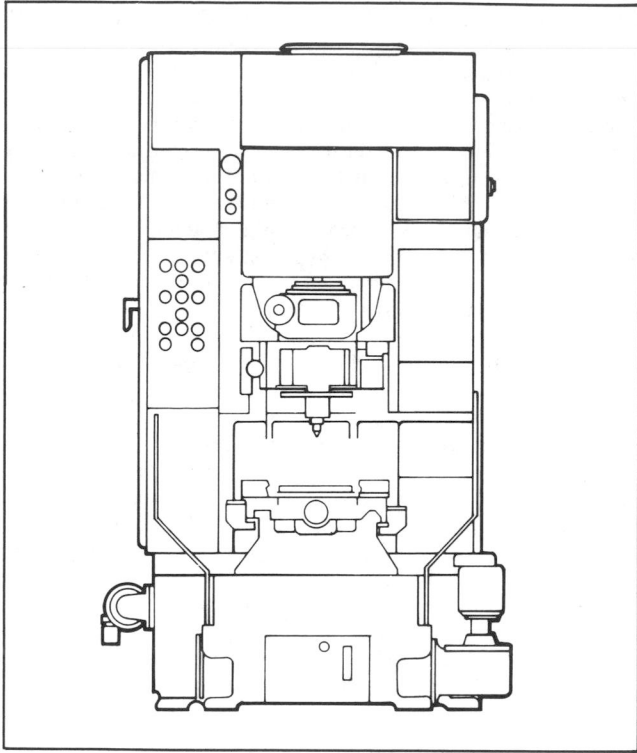

Fig. 28-26 Universal gear shaper for generating internal or external forms. (*Barber-Colman Co.*)

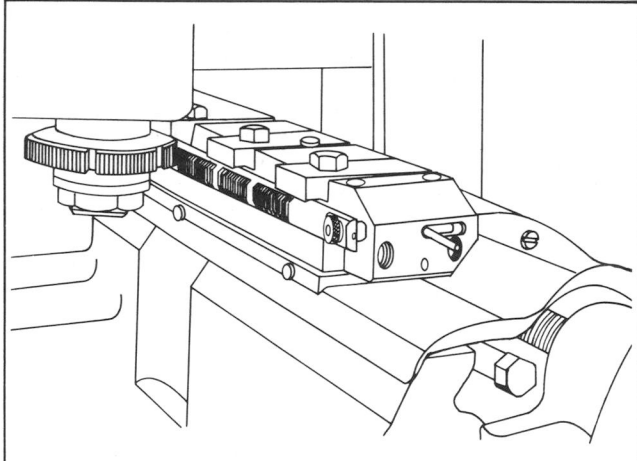

Fig. 28-27 Attachment for cutting racks on a gear shaper. (*Fellows Corp.*)

Applications of Gear Shaping

Much of the success in producing accurate gears comes from care in manufacturing blanks and in planning proper work-holding fixtures.

Shaping of internal gears. Internal gears are produced as readily as external gears, especially where gear teeth are to be shrouded by an inner flange, with a resultant blind hole through which a cutter cannot pass.

Cutter clearance. In cutting internal or external gears where the path of the cutter is restricted by a shoulder or other obstruction, a groove or recess of adequate width to allow sufficient overstroke and chip clearance must be provided. The groove width varies with gear pitch, face width, and helix angle if the cutter is helical sharpened. The face sharpening angle must also be considered on coarse-pitch cutters, in addition to the material being cut. In general, the total stroke of the cutter must be increased by 10-12% of the face width of the gear, shared equally at the top and bottom for spur gears. Additional stroke must be provided to compensate for helix angle and tool sharpening.

Cutting internal-clutch gears. When an internal-clutch gear having a small number of teeth is to be cut, its inside diameter should be increased to the base-circle diameter of the gear or larger. This does not affect the positive action or strength of the clutch. Since the involute form cannot extend to a diameter smaller than the base-circle diameter, no part of the tooth surface below this diameter contacts the mating external-clutch member. Furthermore, the clutch gear is, from its inherent design, so much stronger than gears that run in action that the clutch teeth could be extremely short without seriously affecting the gear's strength or positive action.

Figure 28-28 illustrates the preceding remarks with respect to the base-circle diameter. Line *A* represents a cord wound around a cylinder identified as the base circle. Point *B* on line *A* traces the involute curve of the tooth. It is evident that the tracing point cannot travel below the cylinder upon which it is wound without giving a reverse curve and causing interference. The involute curve then ends at point *C*, and there is no tooth contact below this point. Metal *S* is therefore useless. This useless metal makes tooth cutting more difficult; hence, it is advisable to bore the internal gear to the base-circle diameter or even slightly larger.

Special gear shaper applications. Both external and internal involute splines are produced in much the same manner as has been described for gear production. External and internal serrations can be cut in a manner similar to involute splines if suitable cutters are provided.

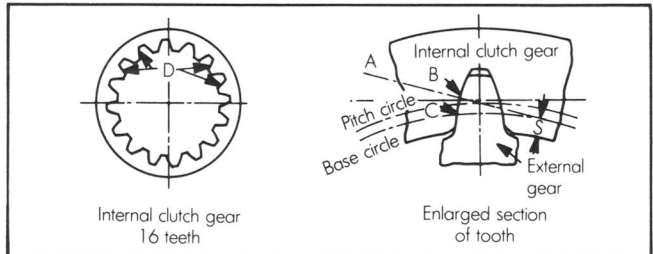

Fig. 28-28 Interference is avoided by trimming the teeth of internal gears and increasing the inside diameter.

Both external and internal parallel-sided splines can be produced on the gear shaper with suitable tooling. In some cases, the external members can be generated. The generating action automatically produces a fillet as indicated in Fig. 28-29, view *a*. The height of this fillet can be reduced by providing projections at the tip corners of the cutter teeth (view *b*). When generating action is not feasible and in all internal parallel-sided splines, the spaces are slotted with either a single-tooth cutter or a straddle-tooth cutter (views *c* and *d*). In such cases, several teeth are provided in a cutter; and when one is dulled, the cutter is indexed to the next tooth and so forth until all are dull, at which time the tool is removed for sharpening.

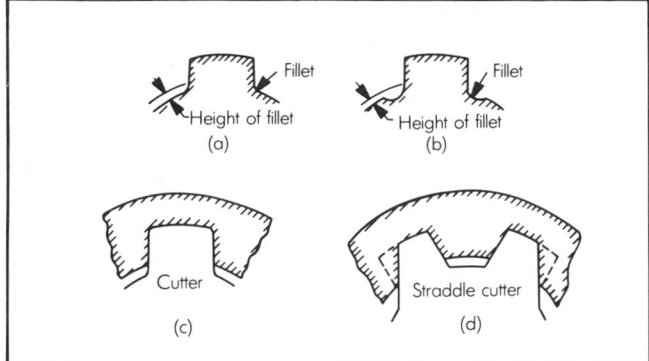

Fig. 28-29 Splines: external—a and b; internal—c and d.

Single-tooth slotting cutters must, of necessity, have clearance on the sides of the teeth. Thus, as they are sharpened, the space cut becomes narrower. The amount this width can be allowed to vary controls the amount of sharpening life in the cutter. The straddle-type cutter is preferred since the thickness of the spline teeth can be maintained as the cutter is sharpened by increasing the center distance between the cutter and the work. The depth is maintained by a proper outside angle on the cutter.

Noncircular type gears, namely elliptical, oval, and special-contour gears, can be cut easily and accurately on the gear shaper if suitable cutters and attachments or tooling are provided. Numerically controlled gear shapers are best for producing such parts. Forms such as ratchets, cams, and others are also easily produced on the gear shaper with proper tooling.

Shaping of face gears. The face gear is that gear form which is produced on the face of a ring by the generating action of the gear-shaper cutter. The axes of the cutter and the work during the process of cutting are located at an angle to each other (see Fig. 28-30), usually, but not necessarily, a right angle. The inclination of the sides of the teeth on the face gear increases from the inside to the outside extremities. The sides of the teeth are for the most part, straight. Inside and outside diameters are restricted by the ratio of the number of teeth in the face gear to the number of teeth in the pinion.

Face gears may be cut so that the axis of the pinion lies in the same plane as the axis of the gear. It is then commonly termed an on-center face gear, and the sides of the teeth are symmetrical (see Fig. 28-25, view *a*). The face gear may also be cut so that the centerline of the pinion is offset from the centerline of the face gear. It is then termed an off-center face gear, and the sides of the teeth are not symmetrical (see Fig. 28-25, view *c*). A special universal attachment is required to produce this type of gear. The cutter will always have the same number of teeth as the pinion or one tooth more than the pinion.

Shaping face clutches. Face clutches can be readily produced with the same equipment required to produce face gears. One type of face clutch is merely two face gears meshing tightly together. To ensure a tight mesh at the outside diameter, the face-gear fixture is tipped slightly from its right-angle position. Face clutches that have helicoidal surfaces can also be easily produced on this same equipment (see Fig. 28-31). In this case, a single tool cutter is used. Its infeed is timed in relation to the work rotation to produce the desired form. This process is known as the describing-generating process.

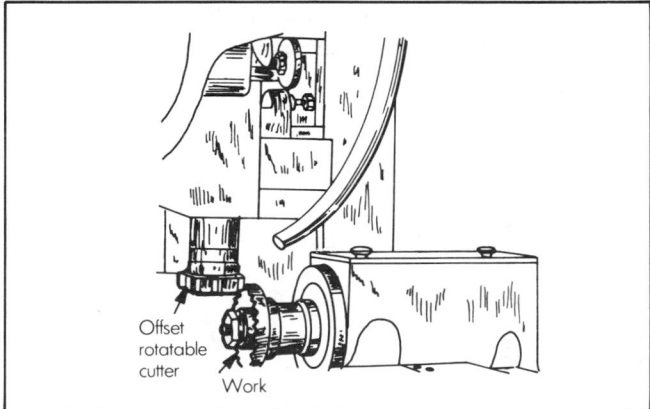

Fig. 28-31 Offset shaping of face-clutch teeth by the describing-generating process.

Gear-Shaper Cutters

A gear-shaper cutter is basically a gear with teeth relieved to provide suitable cutting edges and clearances. The stroking, together with the related rotation of the cutter and workpiece, results in what is known as the molding-generating process.

Practically all involute gear-shaper cutters have ground tooth profiles with clearances on the sides of the teeth, and a rake angle on the face. The types of cutters in general use fall in three main categories: disc, deep counterbore, and shank (see Fig. 28-32).

Standard gear-shaper cutters. A standard cutter is theoretically designed to produce a gear of standard tooth proportions. In other words, such a cutter, when used to produce a gear the outside diameter of which is equal to $(N + 2)/P_d$, would produce an arc tooth thickness of $0.5p$ at approximately standard depth of cut.

Special gear-shaper cutters. The blank design of special disc-type cutters has been standard as far as possible and falls into two general groups. One design is for use when there is no danger of the cutter clamping nut hitting any part of the workpiece or its holding fixture. The second design, known as the deep-counterbore cutter, is for use when the cutter clamping

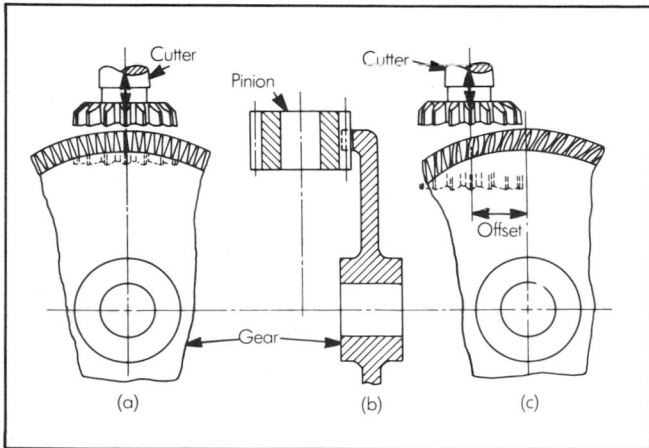

Fig. 28-30 Methods of cutting face ears: on center—a and b; offset—c.

MANUFACTURING GEARS AND SPLINES

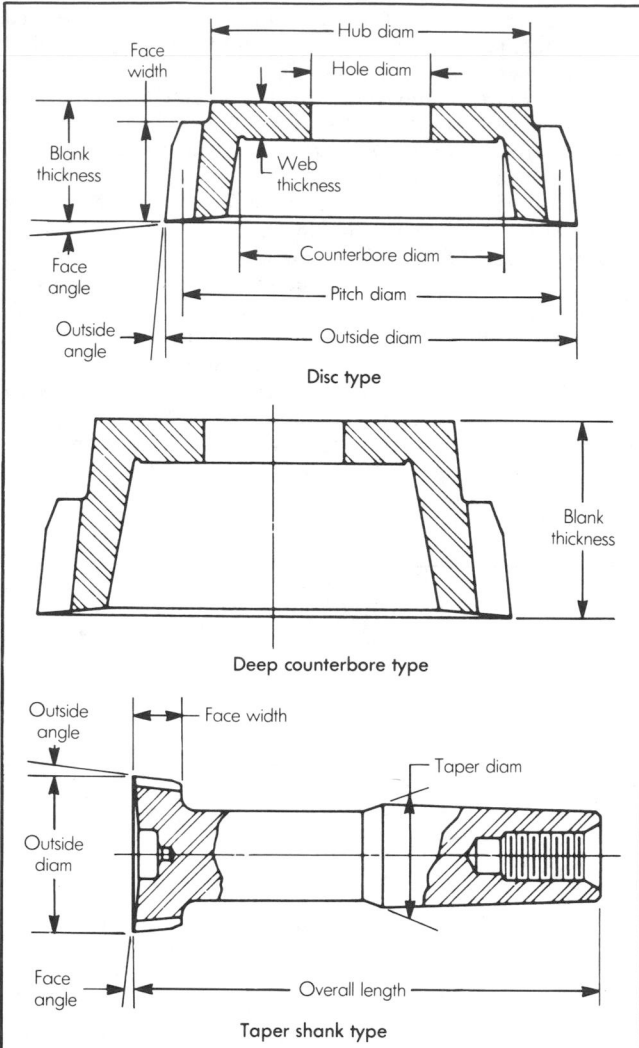

Fig. 28-32 Styles of gear-shaper cutter.

that its junction with the involute profile is at a constant distance from the centerline of the cutter. Consequently, when the cutter is sharpened and the center distance between the cutter and the workpiece decreases by reason of this sharpening, the amount of modification obviously increases. With the *H*-type flank, the cutter is ground so that the amount of modification remains substantially the same throughout the useful life of the cutter. The straight-flank feature can be

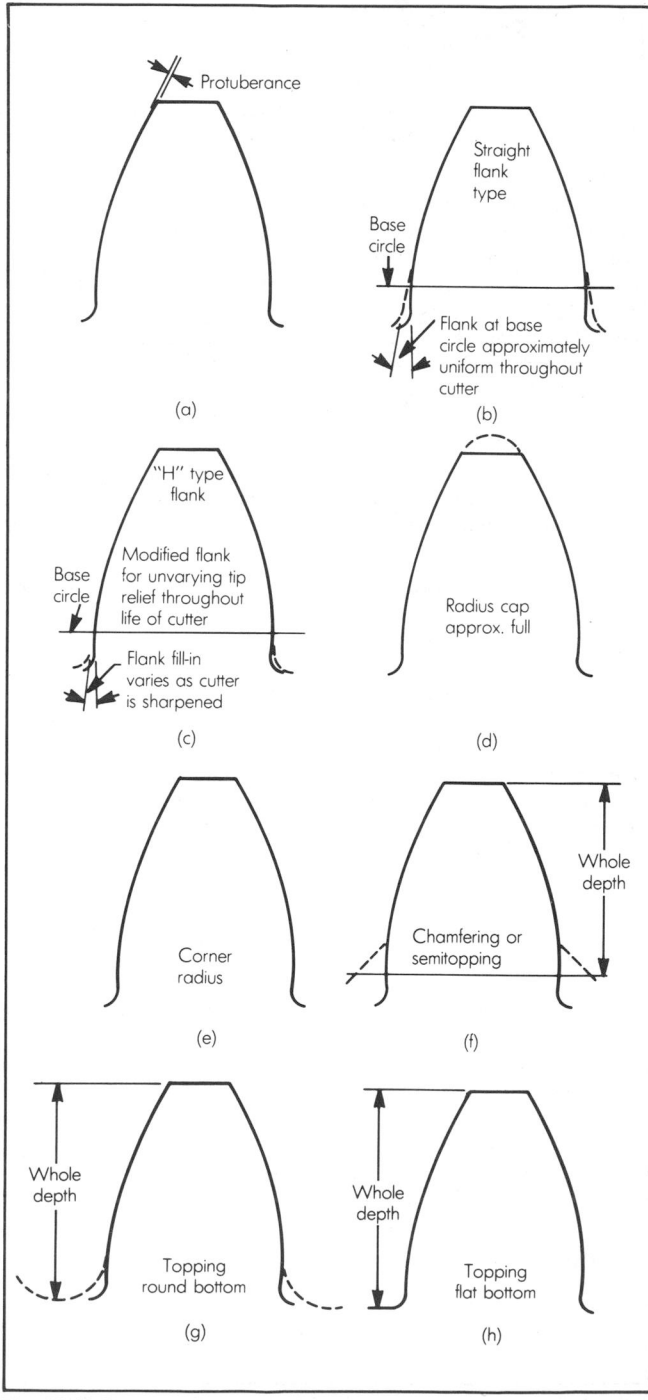

Fig. 28-33 Common forms of gear-shaper cutter teeth.

nut must be recessed far enough so that it does not project beyond the cutting edge even at the discard thickness. This is done to avoid interference with some portion of the workholding fixture or with a web or flange on the workpiece. These cutters are thicker, thus requiring more material, and are somewhat higher in price.

Gear-shaper-cutter tooth forms. It is desirable, whenever possible, to use true involute tooth-form cutters. Design and production considerations, however, sometimes make modifying features necessary. Gears that are to be finished by the shaving operation, with the exception of small pinions, are usually cut with extra depth and with a relief in the root to accommodate the shaving tool. This means the cutter has an extra length of addendum and a protuberance to provide the relief in the root of the gear tooth (see Fig. 28-33, view *a*). If a modification of the involute at the tip of the gear teeth is required, a flank or fullness near the bottom of the cutter space is necessary. This is commonly termed flank. Two types of flank are in common use, one known as the straight flank (view *b*), the other known as *H* type (view *c*). The straight flank is ground so obtained in cutters of approximately 16 pitch and coarser. The *H*-type flank can be obtained in cutters of approximately 5-9 pitch, inclusive.

In most cases, it is important to have practically a full radius or a radius corner in the roots of the gear spaces. This requires a radius modification on the tips of the cutter teeth (see Fig. 28-33, views *d* and *e*). It is sometimes necessary to combine this radius feature with protuberance in the case of a cutter for cutting a gear previous to the shaving operation. A chamfer is sometimes required on the corners at the tips of the gear teeth. This requires a different type of flank in the cutter known as chamfering or semitopping (view *f*). All these special features are available in gear-shaper cutters, as in other gear-cutting tools, but they result in increased cost.

Certain gears are well suited to the use of a topping cutter (see Fig. 28-33, view *g* and *h*). This type of cutter has a root diameter held to a close tolerance in relation to the tooth thickness. The object of this design is to size the OD of the gear at the same time that the teeth are generated.

Many gear-shaper cutters are not manufactured to exact diametral pitch, but are modified for load, noise, or other gear design considerations. Considerable time is being saved by some cutter manufacturers with the use of computers to design the cutters.[5]

The Shear-Speed Process

The Shear-Speed gear shaper, developed by Ex-Cell-O Corp., is designed for rough, semifinish, and finish cuts in high-volume production. The process is distinguished from other methods of gear-shaping in that all the gear teeth are form-cut simultaneously, the cutter teeth being of the same shape as the gear-tooth spaces. This process is adapted for cutting internal and external gears and involute and noninvolute tooth forms such as serrations, ratchets, sprockets, cam lobes, and interrupted tooth forms. Shoulders or flanges adjacent to the tooth forms do not restrict the use of the equipment if adequate necking is provided so that the cutter can clear the work before the blades are relieved for the return stroke. Additional forms that can be cut on these machines are shown in Fig. 28-34.

The machine base supports the ram assembly and the work fixture; columns support the cutter head slide and related assemblies. The ram carrying the work is reciprocated vertically, and the length of travel in both its upstroke and downstroke can be controlled to suit the face width of the gear to be cut. The cutter-head slide is moved downward to the cutting position and upward to the loading position. In the cutting position, the cutter-head slide is locked against positive stops. The upstroke of the work ram is the cutting stroke, and the downstroke is the relief stroke.

The cutting blades are mounted in a radially slotted cutter head (see Fig. 28-35). There is a projection on each blade which contacts feed cones, effecting a radial motion of the blades. An outer cone causes the blades to feed toward the center prior to each cutting stroke, and an inner cone retracts the blades to effect a relief on the return stroke. Blade holders are designed for a specific gear, and the blades are furnished in sets. Blades are sharpened in sets by grinding the cutting faces, and it is essential that the correct hook angle and blade height be maintained.

Many combinations of work adapters can be furnished depending upon the nature of the part to be cut. The accuracy that can be obtained is affected by the accuracy of the blanks,

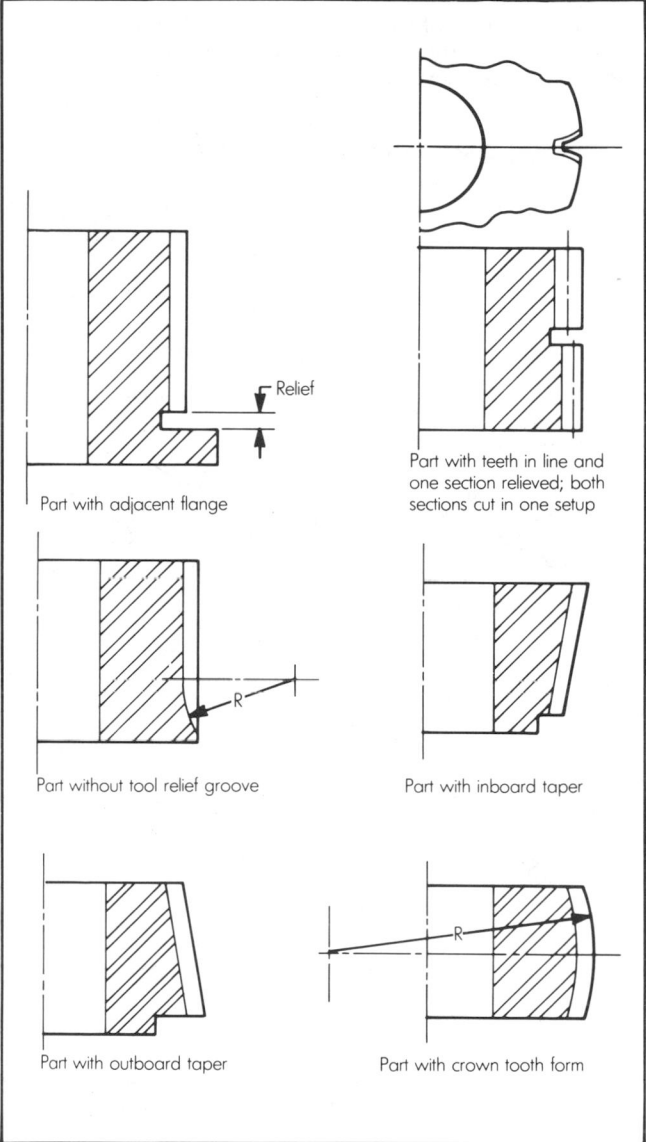

Fig. 28-34 Various forms produced on the Shear-Speed machine. (*Process Systems Operations, Ex-Cell-O Corp.*)

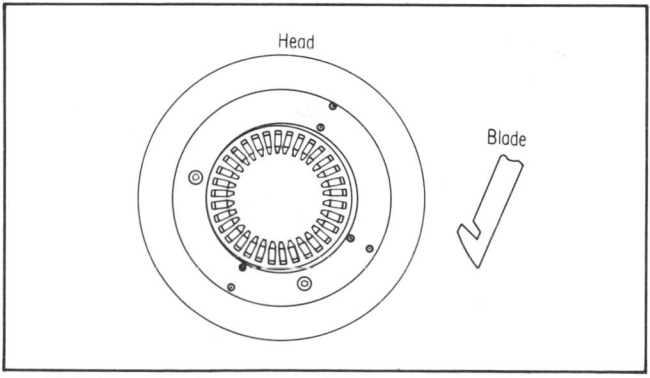

Fig. 28-35 Cutter head used in Shear-Speed process. Head shown is for a 33-tooth gear. Individual form-ground tool blades are removable and replaceable as a unit. (*Process Systems Operations, Ex-Cell-O Corp.*)

MANUFACTURING GEARS AND SPLINES

feed rate, number of finishing strokes, and condition of the cutters. It is important that the faces of the blanks be parallel and square with the bore or controlling diameter.

BEVEL GEAR MANUFACTURING

Bevel gears are conical in shape. Figure 28-36 reflects this concept, illustrating bevel gear nomenclature in the axial plane. The transverse plane of a pair of bevel gears is illustrated in Fig.

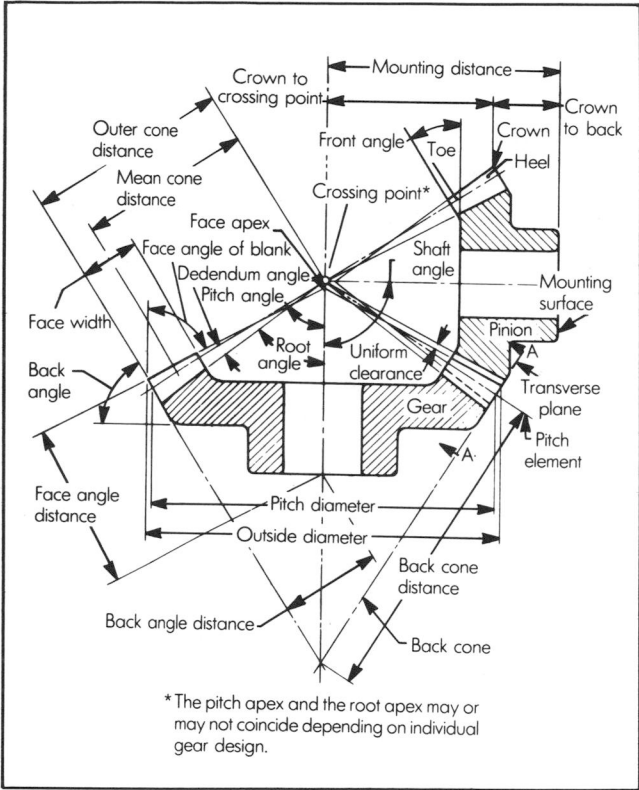

Fig. 28-36 Nomenclature of bevel gears in the axial plane.

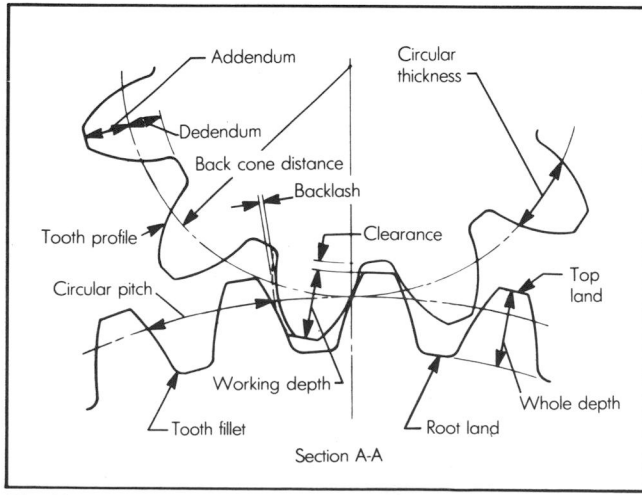

Fig. 28-37 Nomenclature of bevel gears in the transverse plane.

28-37. In the transverse plane, the nomenclature is generally consistent with that for spur or helical gear nomenclature. The pitch plane of bevel gears (see Fig. 28-38) is often used in visualizing a bevel gear tooth.

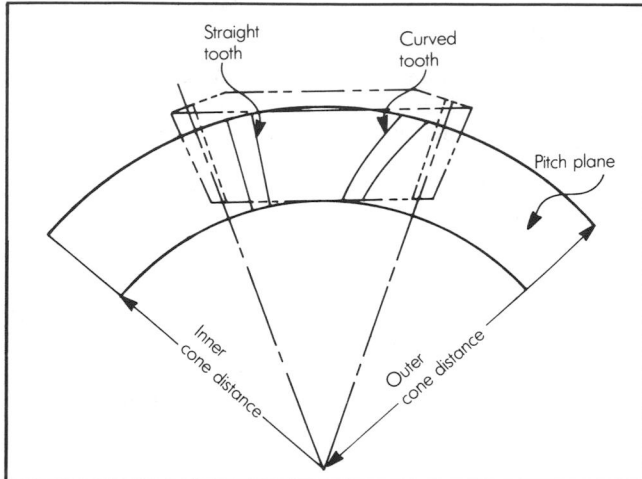

Fig. 28-38 Pitch plane of the bevel gear.

Types of Bevel Gears

Bevel gears fall into two general groups when viewed in the pitch plane: straight-tooth gears or curved-tooth gears. When viewed in the transverse plane, bevel gears fall into two other groups: generated gears or nongenerated gears.

Straight teeth. Straight bevel gears (see Fig. 28-39) are the simplest of all bevel gears. The tooth centerline is straight; and if it were extended inward, it would intersect the axis of the workpiece. The centerline is a section of the pitch cone element.

Curved teeth. Curved teeth have lengthwise curvature. This type of tooth appears on three types of gears: spiral bevel, Zerol bevel, and hypoid gears.

Spiral bevel gears. The teeth on a spiral bevel gear (see Fig. 28-40) are curved and at an angle to the pitch cone elements (the centerline of a straight bevel tooth). This oblique inclination of the teeth permits a gradual engagement with the mating tooth along the length of the tooth, thus assuring continual contact. Before one pair of teeth leaves engagement, the adjacent pair comes into engagement, i.e., the tooth action overlaps.

Zerol Gears. These gears (see Fig. 28-41) have curved teeth with the centerline tangent to the pitch cone element at midface. They are essentially spiral bevel gears with a 0° spiral angle. They have the same operating characteristics as straight bevel gears and may be used in the same mountings. They can be cut on the same machines used to produce spiral bevel or hypoid gears.

Hypoid gears. These gears (see Fig. 28-42) are similar in appearance to spiral bevel gears, but are unique in that the pinion axis is offset from the gear axis. Their geometry is complex, and several factors, including the radius of the lengthwise tooth curve, affect the final tooth and blank design. The geometry is such that the pinion spiral angle is larger than that of the gear. Similarly, the diameter of the pinion is larger

MANUFACTURING GEARS AND SPLINES

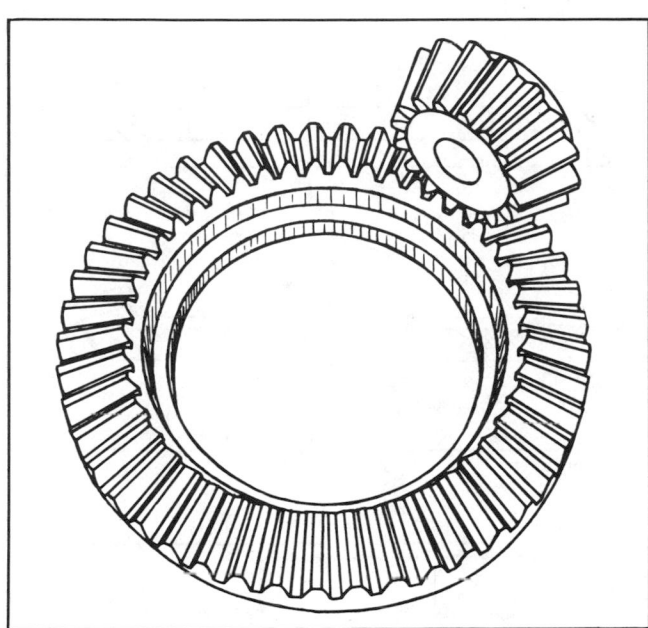

Fig. 28-39 Straight bevel gears.

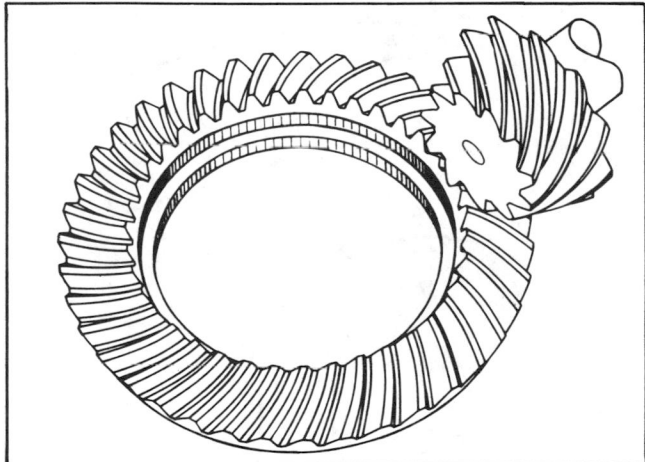

Fig. 28-40 Spiral bevel gears.

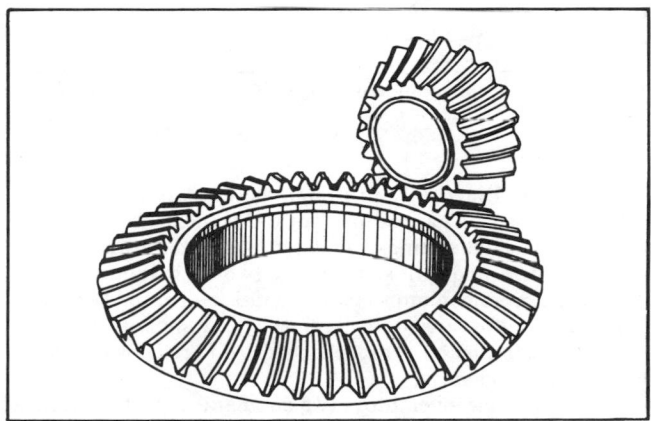

Fig. 28-41 Zerol gears.

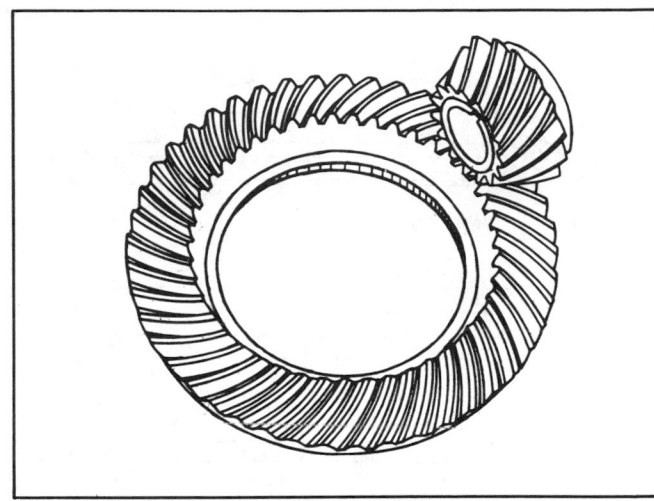

Fig. 28-42 Hypoid gears.

than that of the comparable spiral bevel pinion mating with the same size gear of the same gear ratio. Both the pinion spiral angle and the pinion diameter increase directly with the offset.

Blanks for Bevel Gears

Machine and product designers are responsible for assuring that gears run true and are stable under specified operating conditions. However, since the quality of the finished gear is primarily dependent upon the design and accuracy of the blank, the manufacturing process must be considered as well. The blank shape should provide for ease of machining, rigidity during processing, proper positioning and stability when the teeth are cut, and minimum distortion during hardening. The surfaces which are used to position the gear during assembly should be the same as those used to position the gear for cutting and testing. Close control of the position of the crown point with reference to the mounting surface and the axis is essential.

To ensure rigidity, the bores, hubs, and other locating surfaces of the blanks must be in proportion to the gear diameters and their diametral pitches. Unusually small bores, thin webs, or short hubs, or any condition that permits excessive overhang during cutting, should be avoided. In general, the accumulation of tolerances affecting eccentricity during assembly should be restricted. Thus, it is frequently desirable to make the gear and its shaft or hub integral. When doing so, a preliminary check should be made to determine if the part fits properly in the cutting and testing machine.

Ring gears. Gears which are relatively large [8″ (203 mm) diam or more] in reference to their shafts are usually made as rings. These gears are mounted on centering hubs. Ring gears can be more effectively hardened in simple quenching dies. This design is also more economical because the hubs need not be hardened and can be made of lower cost material than the rings.

The most common ring gear designs are the webless, the web, and the counterbored types (see Fig. 28-43). The webless type is generally preferred because of its more compact cross section. If little heat-treatment distortion is anticipated, such as with flame hardening, large gears [40-50″ (1016-1270 mm) or more diam] may be made integral with the hub.

MANUFACTURING GEARS AND SPLINES

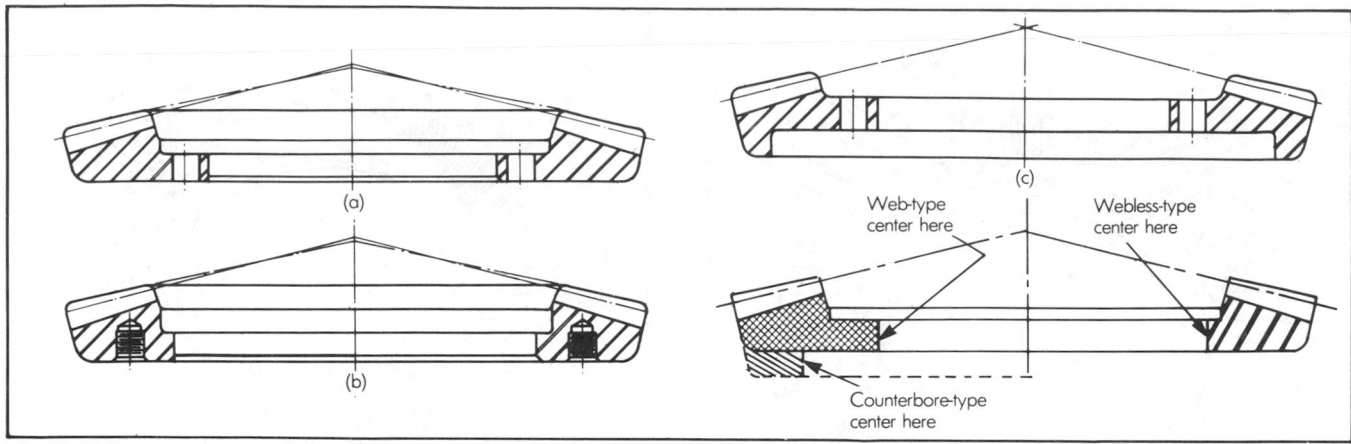

Fig. 28-43 Common ring gear designs: (a) web type, (b) webless type, and (c) counterbore type.

Shank-type gears. These gears are held for cutting and testing by means of an internal or external thread at the end of the shank. If no thread exists on the designed part, one must be provided for holding purposes. When production quantities justify special equipment, contracting collet equipment can be used and the holding threads are unnecessary. Similarly, bored members may be held with expanding collets or arbors.

A front hub which projects beyond the root line of the teeth should be avoided. Such a hub interferes with a circular cutter, causing it to mutilate the hub and resulting in increased cutter wear. On straight bevel machines utilizing reciprocating tools, special tools or toolholders may permit the use of front hubs, but rigidity is sacrificed and loading of the blank into the machine may be complicated.

Blanks for gears that are to be cut and ground to high precision (AGMA Class 12 or better) should be machined with radial and axial proof spots near their OD and ends of their teeth. These indicator tracks can then be used in trueing the part for all operations.

Cutting Bevel Gears

All curved-tooth gear generating machines are designed to the basic configuration illustrated in Fig. 28-44. The cutting tools are held by the cradle mechanism of the machine, and the blank is mounted to the workhead. Machine adjustments permit proper positioning of the cutter and blank in reference to each other.

Generating, the basic process, is achieved with straight-sided tools which simulate an imaginary crown gear. This is a basic flat gear that has straight-sided tooth profiles, with its pitch plane in the plane of rotation. During generation, the cutter is revolved about the axis of the cradle. The cradle is rotated at the proper rate of roll relative to the blank, which is simultaneously rotated about its axis. This rolling motion combined with the movement of the cutter along the length of the tooth produces the desired profile shape.

Cutting Straight Bevel Gears

The straight, bevel-gear tooth form is the simplest form of bevel tooth. Theoretically, the sides converge if extended inward to the axis of the gear. Actually, the sides are machined with end relief to provide a localized tooth contact. Such teeth are identified as Coniflex.

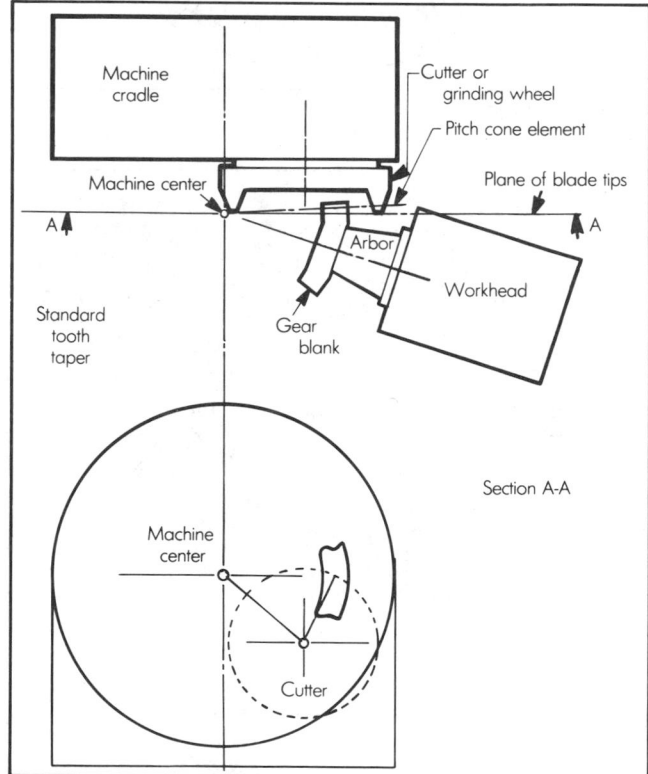

Fig. 28-44 Basic configuration of machine for generating curved-tooth bevel gears.

Tools used. Practically all straight bevel gears are generated with two tools. Changes in tooth thickness are made by adjusting machine settings, and a set of tools covers a range of tooth numbers and ratios. There are two basic tool concepts. The older, more common method consists of using two tools (see Fig. 28-45) carried on reciprocating slides. The tools straddle the tooth and cut on each side. End relief is produced by the slide mechanism.

The newer concept employs two circular interlocking cutters which cut on either side of the tooth space (see Fig. 28-46). End

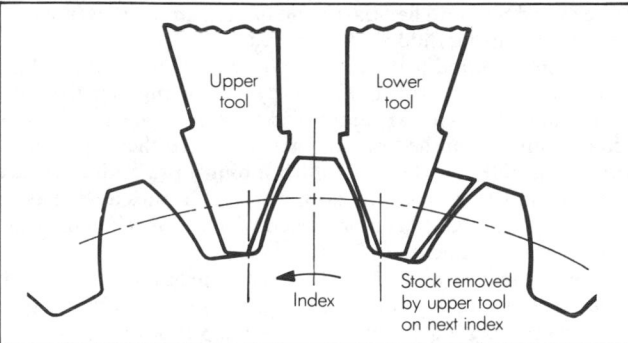

Fig. 28-45 Straight bevel tools.

relief results from the geometry of the cutter, and the cutters are not moved along the root line. The cutters thus produce a curved root which is slightly deeper than standard at the center of the face width.

Revacycle gears. A special process is used for the high-volume production of straight bevel gears which operate at low speeds. The primary application is automotive and truck/tractor differential gearing. Machinery used is completely automatic. Teeth are completed in one revolution of a circular broach-type cutter (see Fig. 28-47). The cutter shown contains three types of blades: roughing, semifinishing, and finishing. It is rotated in the counterclockwise direction and is given a lateral motion along the line *AC*. The work is held stationary during cutting

and is positioned so that the root line is essentially parallel to the line *AC*. Indexing takes place in the gap between the last finishing blade and the first roughing blade.

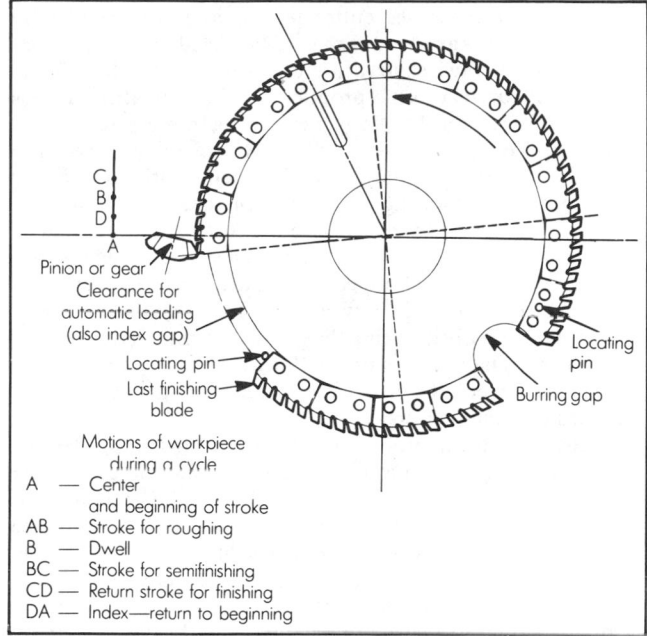

Fig. 28-47 Revacycle cutter and cutting action for producing straight bevel gears.

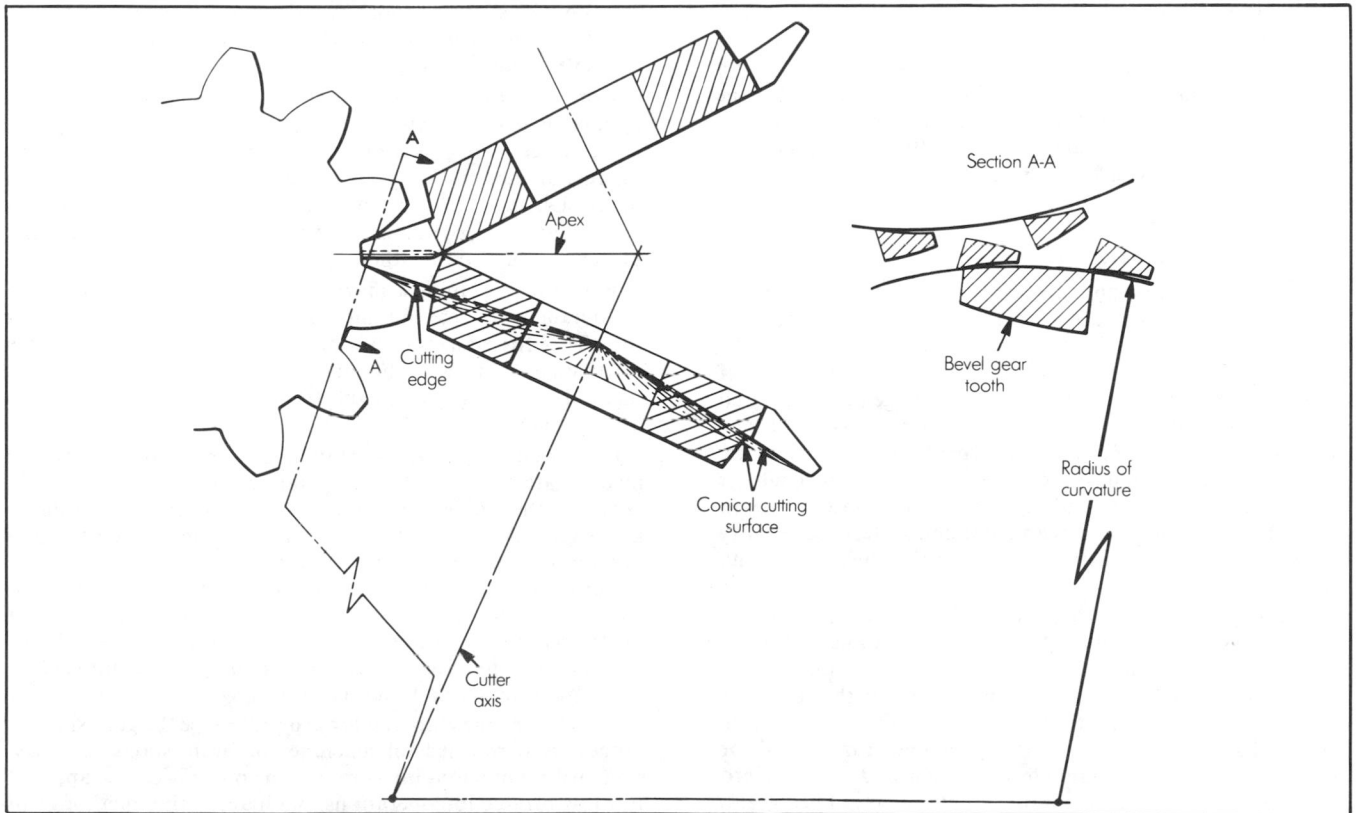

Fig. 28-46 Circular interlocking cutters cut on either side of tooth space

MANUFACTURING GEARS AND SPLINES

Cutting Curved-Tooth Bevel Gears

Teeth with lengthwise curvature encompass spiral bevel, Zerol, and hypoid gears. While these gears differ in design and performance, the cutting process is essentially the same for all of them. The same machines, cutter designs, and cutting cycles are used. All the gears are produced with localized tooth contact by varying the lengthwise curvature of the mating tooth surfaces.

The basic curved tooth is produced by the generating process as discussed previously. Nongenerated teeth are produced by either the Formate process or the Helixform process. The Formate process produces straight-sided tooth profiles by plunge feeding a rotating cutter into the gear held in a fixed position or by feeding the gear into the cutter. Finishing can be done with a Single Cycle cutter in which successive blades are set radially beyond each preceding blade, forming, in effect, a circular broach. A gap between the first and last blade is provided for rapidly indexing the gear at the completion of each tooth space. The cutter is not withdrawn until all teeth in the gear have been cut. The Formate completing process employs standard face-mill cutters.

In the Helixform process for finish cutting nongenerated gears, the cutter is advanced into the work axially as each cutter blade passes through the face of the gear. The combined motions of rotation and axial advance of the cutter produce gear tooth surfaces which are close to true mathematical conjugacy with the mating generated pinion. The width of the gear tooth space is controlled by the diameters of the last two blades in the cutter. The cutter has successive blades set radially beyond each preceding blade. A gap is provided between the first and last blades for rapidly indexing the gear at the completion of each tooth space. The cutter is withdrawn only after all teeth have been cut.

If both parts are to be generated, both sides of the tooth slots of the gear member are usually cut at the same time, using a cutter with inside and outside cutting blades. Here, too, the tooth slot width is controlled by the difference between the inside and outside diameters of the cutter. This process is identified as the Spread Blade process.

GEAR FINISHING

Gear-finishing operations are distinguished from gear-cutting operations in that they are used for improving the accuracy and/or uniformity of the various gear-tooth elements. The functional requirements of gears determine the degree of accuracy. Greater accuracy is necessary if the gears are required to operate quietly and at high speeds and/or to transmit heavy loads. The velocity change resulting from base-pitch errors can, when repeated at high speeds, result in dynamic loads of sufficient intensity to destroy the teeth. To operate within an established range of quietness and maximum life, it is necessary to control errors of eccentricity, pitch, profile, helix angle, and tooth spacing.

Methods used to finish gears include shaving, lapping, honing, grinding, and rolling. Each of these methods, discussed in detail in this section, has a variety of applications. Good results are being obtained in some applications with a relatively new process called hard finishing. With this method, large generated gears are finish cut after hardening, using carbide or other hard tooling to eliminate distortion and errors. Hard finishing, however, which is most adaptable to hobbed gears, requires the use of rigid gear-cutting machines in good condition

(free of end play and backlash) and having ample power; a high volume of cutting fluid is also needed.

Another method, called skive hobbing, is used to machine gears after heat treatment. Carbide hobs having negative rake angles of -15° to -30° are employed for this process. A skiving effect results from the draw-cut action due to the negative top rake angle of the hob teeth. Climb hobbing is preferable because it results in less wear of the hob. Surface finishes as fine as 15 μ in. (0.38 μ m) have been produced with this method on gears having case hardnesses to R_C 65.

The general use of the several corrective processes mentioned, other than the continuous-indexing, involute-generating type of gear grinding, may require that the depth of tooth space be increased or that the teeth be generated with protuberance tools to avoid stresses at the tip of the finishing tool. The corrective tools should extend into the space of the work gear a distance of about half the clearance more than that of the mating gear without encountering fillet interference.

Shaving of Gears

Shaving is a widely used method of finishing spur and helical gear teeth following the gear-cutting operation, but prior to hardening. As a result, the process is frequently referred to as soft finishing. It is strictly a cutting and not a cold-working process; small amounts of metal are removed from the gear-tooth profiles by a cutter resembling a gear or a rack. Each tooth of the cutting tool is serrated to provide a series of cutting edges. Gears ranging from a fraction of an inch to many feet in diameter are successfully finished by shaving. The forms of the cutter identify the method of shaving as either rotary or linear (rack). The rotary method employs a gearlike cutter; the rack method uses a cutting tool having the general shape of a rack. There are several cutter-to-work relations that are indicative of the development of the process to meet production conditions.

Rotary crossed-axes shaving. Rotary crossed-axes shaving is applicable to either external or internal spur and helical gears. The gear teeth are finished by rotating the gear and cutter in the manner of intermeshing gears with their axes at an angle to each other. During the rotation, either the gear or the cutter is reciprocated to move the crossed-axes pivot point from one end of the gear face to the other.

Rack shaving. In rack shaving, the gear teeth are finished by rolling the work gear in tight mesh with a rack-shaped cutting tool. The crossed-axes or finishing angle is dependent upon the relative helix angles of the rack teeth and the work gear. This method of shaving is applicable to spur or helical external gears under 6" (150 mm).

Crown shaving. Crown shaving is a process that can be incorporated in the shaving operation. It consists of slightly crowning the gear teeth by shaving them so that they are thinner at the ends than they are at the center of the gear face or any point along the teeth where maximum tooth thickness may be required. The primary purpose of crown shaving is to prevent concentrated loading at the ends of the gear teeth. The amount of crown required is dependent upon the circumstances relative to a particular job. However, 0.0003 in./in. (or mm/mm) of face width per side is usually sufficient.

Automating the gear-shaving process. Since the gear-shaving process is performed on machines of basic standard types, standard production-line automation concepts can be applied. For low-production operations, manual loading methods can be used. For higher production schedules, semiautomatic loaders can be economically utilized to ensure more consistent production efficiency and uniform accuracy. In the semi-automatic loading methods, the work gear is placed on an approximate locator and then the cycle button is pressed. When the shaving operation is completed, the gear is manually removed from the locator.

Both semiautomatic and fully automatic loaders of more specialized types are utilized on standard internal gear-shaving machines. Fully automatic loaders for gear-shaving machines can have magazines that are manually loaded, or they can operate in conjunction with a variety of types of feeding and part-storage devices.

Lapping of Gears

Lapping of spur and helical gears is generally no longer recommended and has been replaced in many applications by honing, grinding, or other finishing processes. Lapping is usually done by running a set of gears in mesh or by running one gear with a gear-shaped master lapping tool. It may correct small errors in involute profile, helix angle, tooth spacing, and concentricity and can improve surface finish, refine tooth contact, and produce quieter operation in service. In some cases, however, lapping may produce less desirable tooth contact and, when overdone, may result in scrap gears.

Honing Gear Teeth

Gear-tooth honing is a finishing method for hardened gears that is intended to correct gear geometry and/or improve the finish of spur or helical gears. The process can correct errors in profile, lead, and eccentricity, as well as oversize conditions resulting from heat treatment, but it cannot correct tooth spacing errors. Nicks and burrs are removed, and the noise generated in gear operation is generally reduced. It can be economically adapted to both high and low-production requirements. Basically, gear honing consists of rotating a hardened gear at high speed in mesh with an abrasive-impregnated or diamond or carbide-coated, gear-shaped, precision honing tool. The honing process is utilized in conjunction with conventional methods for producing accurate gears. The gear teeth are often hobbed or shaped, then shaved, and then honed after heat treating.

The honing process is carried out on high-speed honing machines of standard design. The work gear is meshed in crossed-axes relationship with the honing tool. The work gear is traversed back and forth across the honing tool in a path parallel to the work-gear axis. The gear is run in both directions during the process. The process can be carried out under either controlled backlash or zero backlash conditions, depending upon the amount of tooth correction desired. Manual, semi-automatic, or fully automatic loading arrangements can be utilized on gear-tooth honing machines. Crown-honed gear teeth can be produced by rocking the machine table during the honing process, as is done in crown shaving.

Gear-tooth hones are essentially abrasive-impregnated plastic or diamond or carbide-coated steel gear-shaped tools. Plastic tools must be reshaped as they wear; coated tools are stripped and recoated when worn. Hones shaped like a worm pinion or an Acme-thread screw, made from a urethane/epoxy matrix loaded with abrasive grit, are also being used. These hones are resharpened when they become worn.

Gear Grinding

Gear grinding is one of the earliest methods of finishing gears; it is also used occasionally to produce gear teeth from the solid. It is especially adapted to finishing hardened gears to obtain a predetermined quality.

Since grinding is the most accurate way of finishing gears, this method is used for producing gears of the highest precision to be used for accurate positioning or for transmitting power at high speeds or under heavy loads. Gear grinding machines can basically be classified into two groups: form grinders and the involute-generation types of gear grinding machines.

Formed-wheel grinding. Form grinders are always of the intermittent-indexing type. This method of grinding gear teeth follows, in principle, the cutting of gears with a rotary formed-milling cutter used in conjunction with an index head on a milling machine. The contour of the grinding wheel is formed by single-point diamond, crush dressing, or profile dressing with diamond-coated tapes. A variation of tooth forms can be produced by changing the contour of the templates, crusher roll, or profile dresser used in the dressing mechanisms. To obtain consistent tooth profile when involute gears are form ground, it is imperative to control accurately the distance between the head setting for dressing the wheel and the head setting for finish grinding of the gear.

Involute-generation grinding. This type of gear grinding machine is being built in both intermittent-indexing and continuous-indexing types. Both types use the standard rack-tooth profile to generate the involute form. Intermittent-type machines, however, use the rack-tooth profile dressed on one or two single-rib wheels, while continuous-type machines use a rack profile dressed on the OD of a grinding wheel in the form of a thread.

Bevel-gear grinding. Grinding the teeth of Zerol bevel, spiral bevel, and hypoid gears is the most economical method of finishing such gears to meet the requirements of accuracy and strength for many applications. It is often the most practical solution to the problems inherent in the manufacturing of gears of such size and such thin cross section that the control of errors during heat-treatment and subsequent operations is difficult. In addition, grinding results in a smooth finish and accurate blending of the root radius into the bottom of the tooth space, thereby avoiding the stress concentration that exists when pronounced surface interruptions occur.

Roll Finishing

While the teeth on some gears are formed by full-depth rolling from the solid, as discussed previously in this chapter, rolling is being used more extensively for the finishing of gear teeth. Roll finishing of gear teeth is being done primarily in high-production applications, in many cases replacing rotary gear shaving. Significant production economies result from shorter work cycles and long roll-forming die life. More than one million gears have been roll finished by a set of dies before regrinding.

Smooth surface finishes, improved tooth strength, and consistent dimensional uniformity are other advantages obtained with roll finishing. Surface finishes of 6-8 μ in. (0.15-0.20 μ m) measured axially and 15-20 μ in. (0.38-0.51 μ m) measured along the profile are achieved.

Double-die gear rolling. In this process, the work gear is meshed between two hardened-steel rolling dies (see Fig.

MANUFACTURING GEARS AND SPLINES

28-48). The center distance between the dies is reduced during the work cycle to cold flow metal and to produce tooth forms of high accuracy.

Gear rolling is different from gear shaving in that a flow of material is involved, rather than a removal of material. In Fig. 28-49, it can be seen that as a gear-rolling die tooth engages the approach side of a workpiece tooth, sliding action occurs along the line of action in the arc of approach up to the pitch point, where instantaneous rolling action is achieved. As soon as the contact leaves the pitch point, sliding action occurs again in the opposite direction in the arc of recession. On the trail side (see Fig. 28-50), the flow path is entirely different from that on the approach side. The result is that the material is being compressed toward the pitch point on the approach side and extended away from the pitch point to the trail side (see Fig. 28-51). Thus,

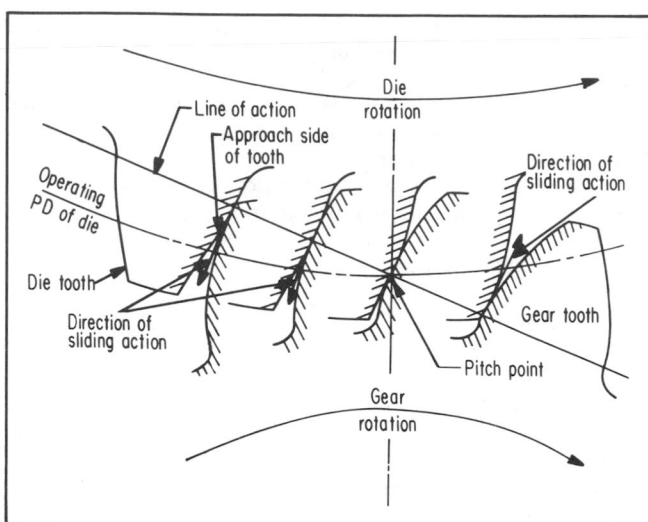

Fig. 28-49 Rolling action in cold-flow finishing of gear teeth. (*National Broach & Machine Div., Lear Siegler, Inc.*)

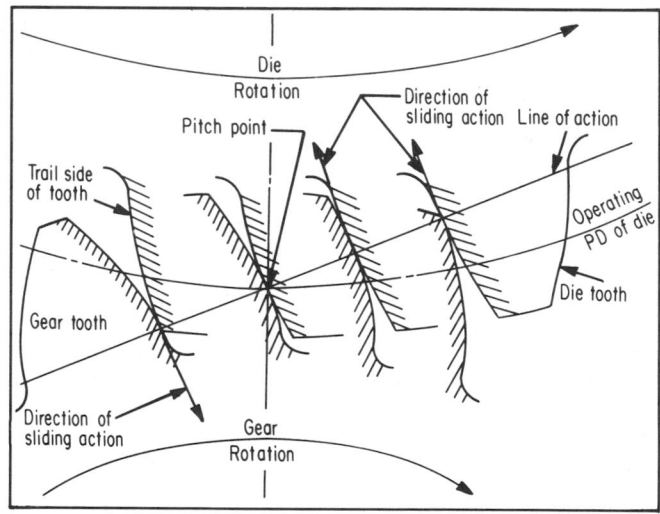

Fig. 28-50 Flow path of metal on the trail side of the teeth during gear rolling. (*National Broach & Machine Div., Lear Siegler, Inc.*)

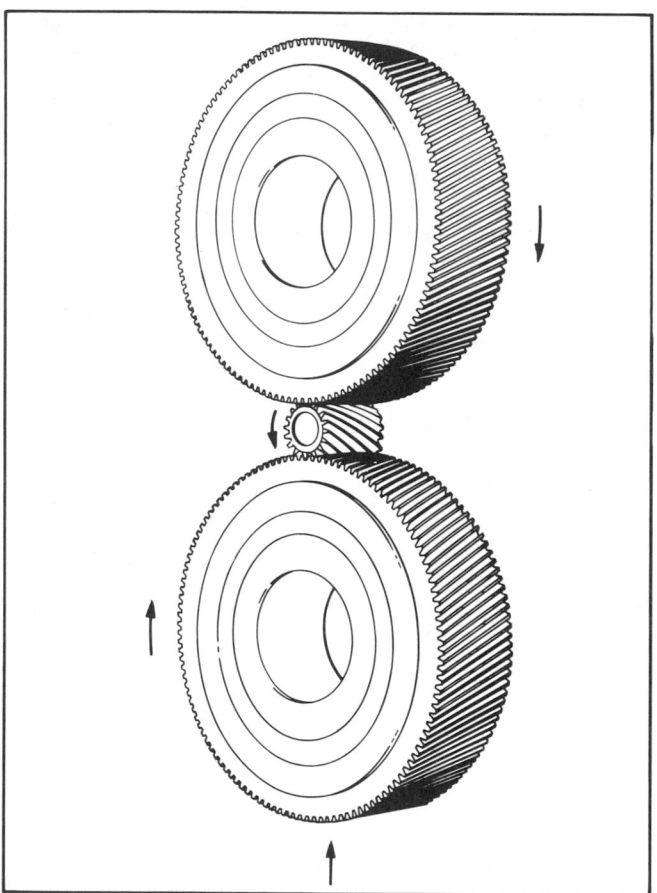

Fig. 28-48 Roll finishing of gear teeth between two hardened-steel dies. (*National Broach & Machine Div., Lear Siegler, Inc.*)

completely unlike a metal-removal process such as gear shaving, the amount of material to be flowed during the rolling process has a significant effect on the accuracy of the resultant form produced.

Since roll forming involves material flow rather than metal removal, the tooth form on the die is not faithfully reproduced on the workpiece tooth because of minute material springback and material-flow conditions. With gear shaving, it is necessary

to modify the shaving cutter-tooth profiles somewhat to produce a desired form on the work gear teeth. A much greater amount of tooth-form modification is required for gear-rolling dies.

Single-die gear rolling. Roll finishing of gears is also being done with single-die machines. With a single-die application, the hobbed blank is positioned on an arbor which is normally supported with backup support rolls (see Fig. 28-52). A controlled feeding mechanism is used to advance the die to mesh with the gear blank under sufficient force to cause material displacement. Single-die applications have a time savings advantage in that a reduced amount of set-up time is required, no die matching procedure is necessary, and tooling cost is less than that for two-die rolling. The single-die approach is generally more suitable for lower production requirements.

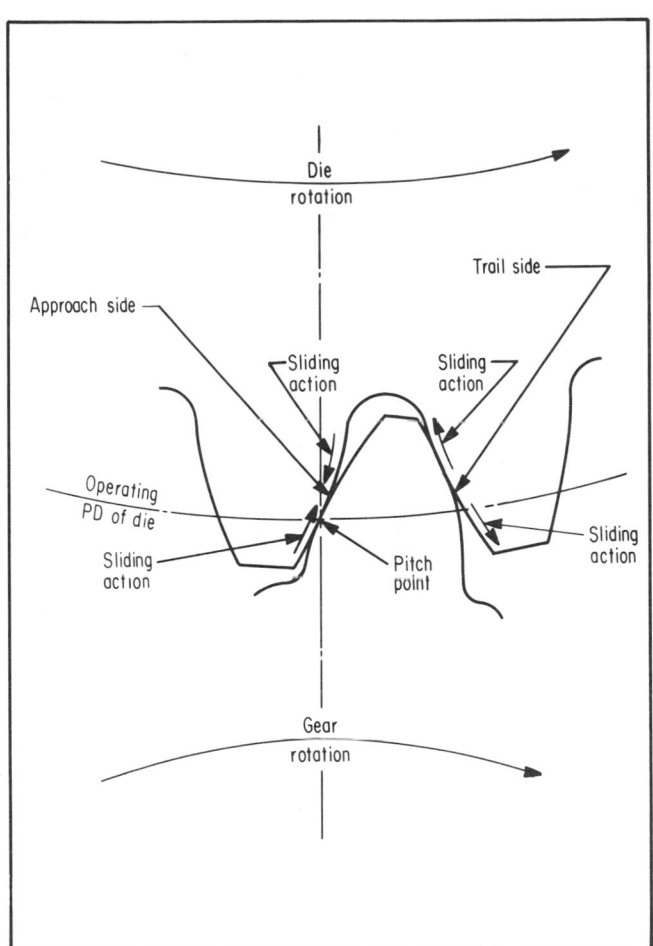

Fig. 28-51 Material flow paths are different on approach and trail sides of teeth gear rolling. (*National Broach & Machine Div., Lear Siegler, Inc.*)

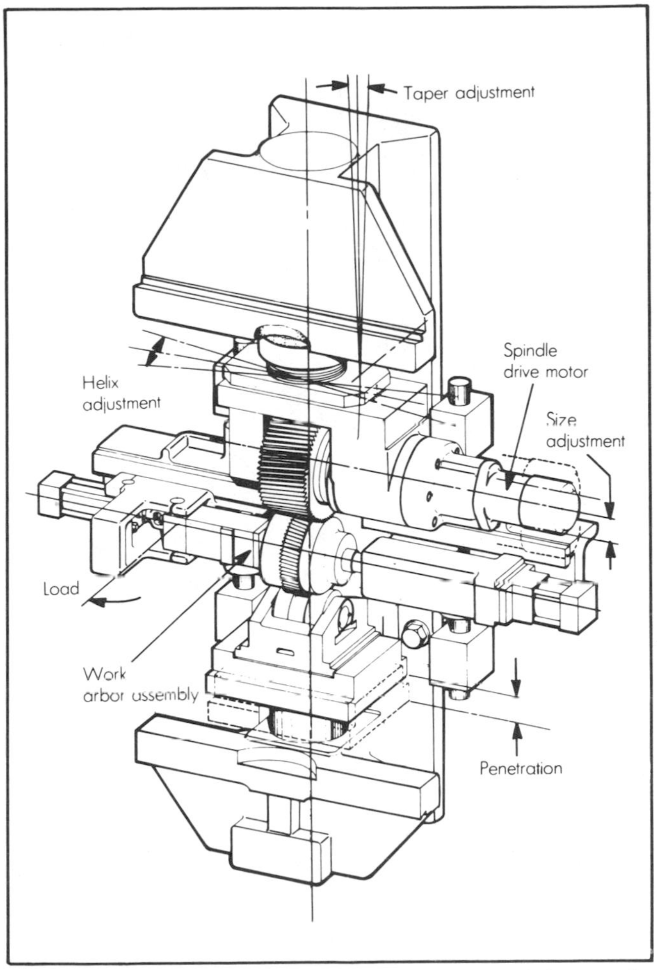

Fig. 28-52 Single-die machine for roll finishing gears. (*Teledyne Landis Machine*)

References

1. Jack McDermott, "Diecasting Precision Gears," *Manufacturing Engineering* (August 1977), pp. 42-44.
2. Carl S. Rice, "Gear Production Update," *Manufacturing Engineering* (April 1979), pp. 83-85.
3. James T. Sharpsteen, "Photo Chemical Machining of Gears," *Machine Design* (March 12, 1981), pp. 107-111.
4. Russel A. Brezler, Jr., "Making Sense of Worm Rolling," *American Machinist* (December 1980), pp. 129-140.
5. Louis Belisle, "Custom Gear Cutter Design in Minutes—by Computer," *Manufacturing Engineering* (December 1979), pp. 64-67.

NONTRADITIONAL MACHINING

Nontraditional machining, as a classification of manufacturing operations, includes literally scores of processes; some are applied on a large scale, while others are not much more than laboratory curiosities. The purpose of this chapter is to present a discussion of the more commonly used nontraditional machining processes as well as a discussion of those processes which hold the most promise of increased usage.

In general, nontraditional machining processes are characterized by higher power consumption as a function of material removal rate as compared with traditional machining processes. Although notable exceptions exist, the stock removal rate of nontraditional machining processes is usually less than that attainable with conventional machining techniques. In most nontraditional machining processes, however, increased throughput is of secondary concern. Rather, users select a unique machining approach to overcome the problems that an unusual part configuration might present to traditional methods. In addition, experience has shown that many nontraditional processes can successfully contribute to special surface integrity in the areas of surface roughness, maximum depth of plastic deformation, hardness alteration, cracks, residual stress, recrystallization, metallurgical transformations, heat-affected zones, etc.

MECHANICAL PROCESSES

There are several nontraditional machining processes which use mechanical energy as their primary source of energy for processing.

HYDRODYNAMIC MACHINING (HDM)

Hydrodynamic machining removes workpiece material and produces a narrow kerf by the cutting action of a fine, high-pressure (usually up to 60 ksi, 414 MPa), high-velocity stream of water or water-based fluid with additives. A lower pressure (usually about 250 psi, 1.7 MPa) version of the process called water jet machining (WJM) is used primarily as a deburring or finishing process.

In HDM, the water used for cutting is pressurized by a hydraulically powered intensifier. An accumulator is used to eliminate pulsation as shown in Fig. 29-1. The relationship between nozzle and workpiece in hydrodynamic machining is illustrated in Fig. 29-2. View *a* defines the standoff distance, penetration depth, and rake angle. View *b* shows the configuration of positive rake in relation to nozzle feed.

Applications

HDM is effective in slitting and contour cutting many nonmetallic materials, such as wood and paper, asbestos, plastics, gypsum, leather, felt, rubber, nylon, fiberglass, and fiberglass-reinforced plastics. Some very thin workpieces of soft metal can be cut effectively by the process; steel sheet (0.005″, 0.13 mm thick) and aluminum sheet (0.020″, 0.51 mm thick) are processed, but water pressure in excess of 100 ksi (690 MPa) is usually required.

Equipment

Generally, HDM equipment is specially built to suit the needs of the particular user. Equipment available today develops about 60,000 psi (415 MPa) water pressure, although higher pressures are obtainable for special applications.

Both optical tracing systems and NC systems are available. Each has distinct advantages and disadvantages.

Optical tracing systems. The simplest control system used in HDM equipment is the optical tracing system which features an optical scanner that is used to trace a line drawing and produce electronic signals for control of the X-Y coordinate axes. Cutting speed is limited by the drawing complexity. Typically, machines of this type are designed so that the tracing head and jet nozzle are fixed and only the table moves according to the signals received from the tracing head photo cell.

The template for cutting used by an optical tracing system is usually a simple line drawing which often may be done in pencil. A change in shape is easily accomplished by erasing part of the drawing and redrawing it to incorporate the changes. In this way, no programming is required to make changes in part configuration.

NC systems. With NC, any desired shape can be cut on a continuous, repetitive basis with high precision, so NC systems for HDM operations are ideally suited for mass production. Also, maximum cutting speed is not limited by the complexity of workpieces to the extent that cutting speed is limited by optical tracing systems.

In some applications NC systems with three-axis capability offer an important advantage over other systems. By the use of three-dimensional control, it is possible to maintain a constant height of the cutting nozzle above a nonflat workpiece surface and thereby maintain a uniform finish of the cut edge.

With NC systems, the programmed tape can also control the timing of loading and unloading of workpieces as well as the cutting sequence.

ULTRASONIC MACHINING (USM)

Ultrasonic machining, sometimes called ultrasonic abrasive machining or impact machining, is a mechanical nontraditional machining process by which workpiece material is removed and an exact shape is imparted to the workpiece surface via the cutting action of an abrasive slurry that is driven by a tool vibrating at high frequency in line with its longitudinal axis. As shown in Fig. 29-3, the cut-

MECHANICAL PROCESSES

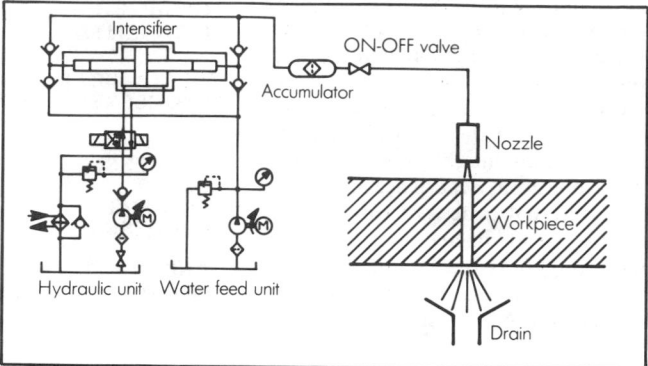

Fig. 29-1 Schematic of hydrodynamic machining (HDM) operation.

ting tool is attached to a vibrating horn. The tool is shaped in the exact configuration to be ground in the workpiece. In this way, the vibration of the tool forces the cutting action of the abrasive grits in the slurry. The slurry is recirculated in the space between the tool and workpiece. In most applications, the slurry is automatically cooled in the recirculation cycle.

Workpiece Materials

USM employs a "chipping" mechanism to remove material.[1] For this reason, materials which succumb to brittle fracture are the best candidates for USM. However, the process is effective on both hard and soft materials. Harder materials are cut by brittle fracture due to the action of the abrasive and the vibrating tool. Softer materials are cut effectively because of a tendency of the abrasive grit to become imbedded in the material by plastic deformation. Experiments have shown that, in cases in which abrasive grit becomes imbedded in the material, work hardening occurs and, upon successive vibrations, material is chipped away due to the contracted brittleness.[2] Practical experience has shown the process to be most effective on materials harder than $R_C 40$, although USM is applicable to nearly any material, whether conductive or nonconductive, metallic, ceramic, or composite.

Applications

USM is used to produce blind and through holes, slots, and irregular shapes, limited in complexity only by the configuration of the tooling. However, in some applications, tool wear and/or taper in the cut may discount the process's effectiveness. Depth-to-width ratio of the cut is usually less than about 3:1. Current practice is limited to 3.5" (89 mm) diam tools machining cavities up to about 2.5" (64 mm) deep.

Tools

In USM, mild steel is usually used as the tool material, although 303 stainless steel, Monel, 52100 steel, and molybdenum are also used. Tough, ductile materials are preferred.

The mass of the tool used in USM is important because too large a mass will absorb ultrasonic energy and reduce machining efficiency. Tools that are too long may whip. Generally, a slenderness ratio of less than 20:1 is recommended. For tools with equal contact areas, there is an increase in penetration rates for tools with larger perimeters. This is because the slurry does not travel far from the tool periphery to cover the entire work surface. Stubby tools are more apt to experience slurry starvation at their centers.

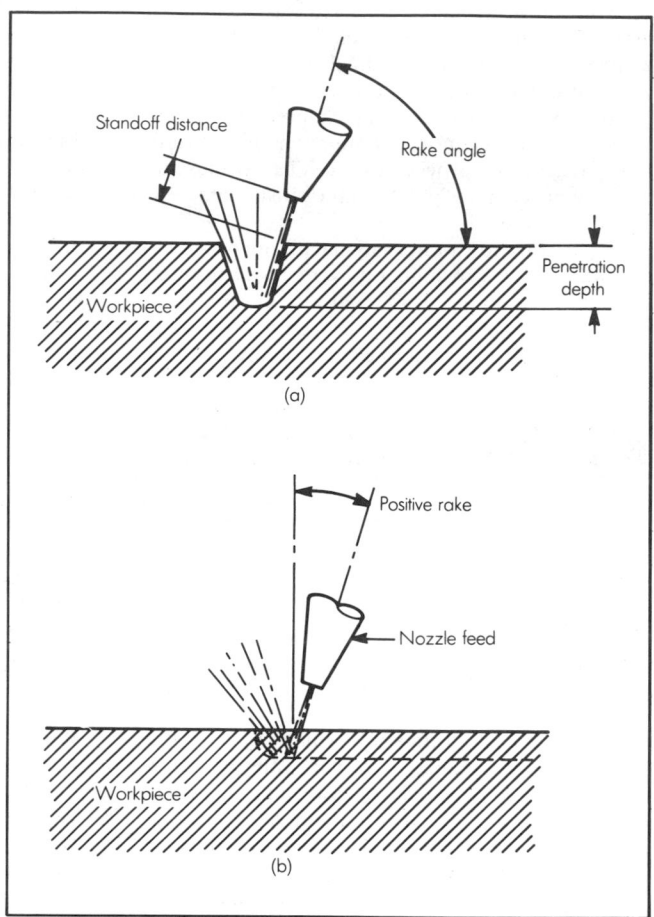

Fig. 29-2 (a) Definition of standoff distance, penetration depth, and rake angle in hydrodynamic machining (HDM). (b) Relationship between nozzle and workpiece under positive-rake conditions.

Abrasives

Several different types of abrasives are used in the USM process including diamond (knoop hardness: 6500-7000), cubic boron nitride (CBN, knoop hardness: 4700), boron carbide (B_4C, knoop hardness: 2800), silicon carbide (SiC, knoop hardness: 2480-2500), and aluminum oxide (Al_2O_3, knoop hardness: 2000-2100). Boron carbide is the most widely used abrasive in USM operations. The abrasive is used most often for processing materials such as tungsten carbide, metals, high-density ceramics, minerals, and semiprecious and precious stones. Silicon carbide is used primarily for low-density ceramics, glass silicon, germanium, and mineral stones. Aluminum oxide is used for glass, low-density, sintered or hard powder compounds.

Equipment

Ultrasonic machining units are available as cutting heads for installation on other machine tools, as bench units, and as self-contained machine tools. USM equipment for sinking cavities or piercing is available with power ratings ranging from 200 to 2400 watts. Special machines can be built up to 4000 watts. The power rating of a machine is important because it determines the area of the tool that can be accommodated and influences the maximum material removal rate obtainable.

The source of vibration in USM equipment, sometimes called the electronic oscillator or generator, converts low-frequency power (60 Hz) to high-frequency power (20,000 Hz). The transducer operates by magnetostriction; its main elements are an electromagnet and a stack of nickel plates, the length of which varies in response to the alternating field of the magnet.

ROTARY ULTRASONIC MACHINING (RUM)

Rotary ultrasonic machining consists of several similar types of nontraditional machining processes in which tools rotating at high speeds (up to about 5000 rpm) and vibrating axially at high frequency (about 20 kHz) are used to affect drilling, cutting, milling, or threading operations on difficult-to-work materials. There are three primary differences between rotary ultrasonic machining (RUM) and ultrasonic machining (USM): (1) RUM drives the tool with a dual motion—axial, high-frequency vibration and axial rotation (in some RUM operations the workpiece is revolved to affect the rotary motion)— while USM employs only high-frequency vibration at the tool; (2) RUM uses diamond tools while USM employs tools made of tough, ductile materials such as steel or Monel; and (3) RUM uses the abrasive properties of the diamond tool to remove stock while USM uses the tool to drive an abrasive slurry which actually performs the cutting; in this way, the tools used for cutting in RUM actually contact the workpiece while the tools used in USM only drive the slurry—no actual tool/workpiece contact is made.

Workpiece Materials

Materials such as aluminum, glass, ferrite, quartz, zirconium, ruby, sapphire, beryllium oxide, boron composites, and laminates are successfully machined using RUM.

Applications

The applications of RUM are currently limited by tool size. The horn/tool assembly must have a resonant (natural) frequency of about 20 kHz, so tool size is limited. Any variance in tool weight changes the natural frequency of the horn/tool assembly; too heavy a tool increases horn/tool assembly frequency beyond the resonant frequency of the transducer and power supply causing the tool not to vibrate.

RUM is used widely in prototype work as well as production applications. The process is effective in producing prototypes because it can make precise parts which can be used to make molds for large-volume production runs.

The process is particularly effective in the machining of sintered materials such as ceramic and ferrites. Conventionally, these materials are machined and drilled in the "green" state—prior to firing. When fired, the materials experience as much as 16% shrinkage which destroys the accuracy created during machining. RUM is used to machine materials such as these after firing and close tolerance relationships are maintained. Some applications include the machining of precision ceramic components, drilling small holes in ceramic printed circuit boards, and drilling small-diameter, deep, intersecting holes in quartz for laser development.

Other applications of RUM include machining precision glass components, nuclear reactor materials, laboratory glassware, ferrite computer parts, plasma-sprayed coatings, and drilling composite aircraft skins. In the electronics field, RUM is used to successfully drill aluminum substrates for microelectronic circuits.

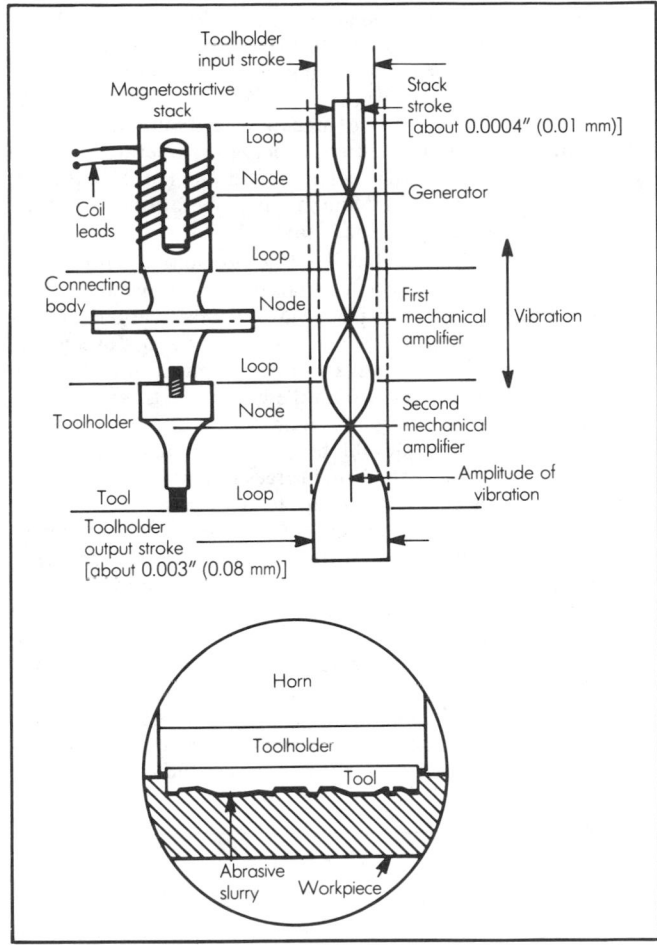

Fig. 29-3 Workpiece/tool configuration in ultrasonic machining (USM). (*Branson Sonic Power Co. and Vought Corp.*)

Drilling. RUM is used in drilling small-diameter, deep holes in extremely hard materials. With traditional tooling used on these materials, the drill sometimes wanders making it difficult to closely control hole straightness. In addition, traditional drilling of hard materials often requires backoff of the tool to allow cutting fluid, which is fed through the tool's center, to flush away chips. This procedure is eliminated through the use of RUM; consequently, RUM can significantly improve accuracy and eliminate the time required for tool backoff. The axial ultrasonic vibrations of the diamond drill reduce the friction between the tool and workpiece to provide faster and smoother cutting, eliminate binding, and enable cutting at lighter tool pressures. The combination of reduced friction and lower tool pressure increases tool life and permits machining of delicate components without cracking. Also, shelling at the points of tool entry and breakthrough are minimized.

Core drilling. Hard materials can also be core drilled to attain deep holes using RUM. With traditional core-drilling methods, cores sometimes jam in the base of the tool, especially in deep-hole drilling operations. If this occurs, the machine must be stopped and the tool must be extracted so that the core can be removed. This is less of a problem with RUM because the diamond tool is ultrasonically vibrated, and even in extremely deep holes, the core is generally left loose in the hole after the drill is withdrawn. It has been reported that the use of RUM in core drilling operations produces an increase in cutting efficiency, allowing hard materials to be cut faster than is possible by conventional means.[3]

Milling. RUM is used to machine hard materials using special diamond milling cutters. Successful operations have been performed on both vertical and horizontal-spindle machines. The use of RUM in milling operations is not as prevalent as drilling operations, however.

Internal threading. As shown in Fig. 29-4, internal threading using RUM is performed on materials of extreme hardness. For internal threading, the workpiece must be rotated about an axis eccentric to the tool axis. The tool remains stationary except for axial vibration and rotation. For these applications, the tool must be smaller in diameter than the bore to be threaded. The diamond tool must be larger in diameter than the tool shank. Generally, the shank should be greater than about 3/32″ (2.4 mm) diam to withstand side forces during cutting and to withstand stresses generated by ultrasonic vibration.

External threading. When RUM is used for external threading, the horn/tool assembly is rotated about 2000-5000 rpm and is vibrated at high frequency—about 20kHz, as shown in Fig. 29-5. The tool remains stationary except for these motions. The workpiece is mounted on an X-Y machine table and is rotated at up to 4 rpm. In this way, the movements of the table are used to effect the generation process for thread formation. The workpiece is raised or lowered one thread width for each revolution of the chuck motor. Thread depth is controlled by adjusting the distance between the tool axis and chuck axis.

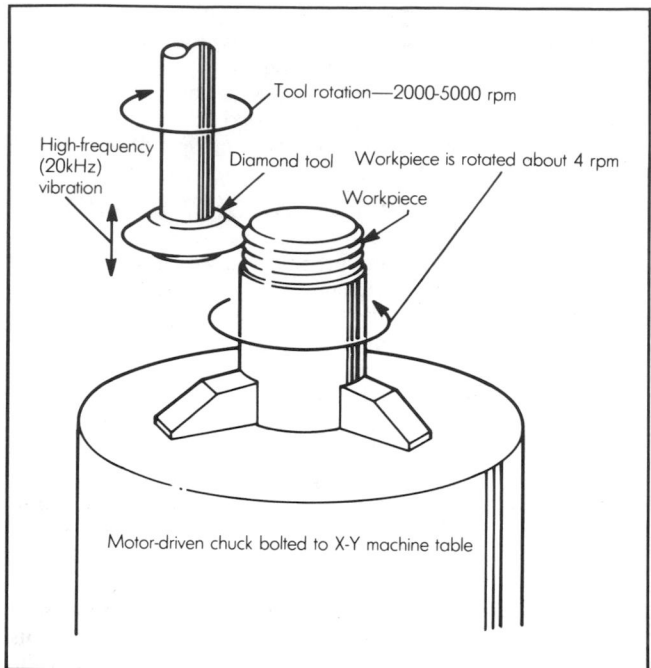

Fig. 29-5 External threading using rotary ultrasonic machining (RUM).

Equipment

RUM equipment is similar to the equipment used for USM except that no slurry recirculation system is required, and with RUM, means must be provided for rotary tool motion. Equipment is available in a range of sizes, and many accessories can be used. Some manufacturers of equipment offer portable units.

ULTRASONICALLY ASSISTED MACHINING (UAM)

Ultrasonically assisted machining consists of coupling an outside source of vibrating energy to the standard drills or toolholders and insert assemblies that are used in traditional machining processes such as drilling and turning. UAM has evolved over the last several years in response to the need for increased cutting quality and speed in the processing of hard, tough materials.[4]

Ultrasonic Lathe Turning

Under certain conditions, ultrasonic lathe turning (Fig. 29-6) has been shown to increase cutting rates by factors of four in aluminum, two to three in 9310, 4340, 17-4 PH steel and in 6A1-4V and Ti-3A1 titanium alloys, and five in cutting ESR 4340 steel. Nonmetallic materials have also shown marked increases in cutting rates when UAM is used. Alumina can be machined two times faster, and magnesium silicate can be machined up to four times faster in some cases, according to manufacturers of UAM equipment.

Some materials that are too brittle to machine traditionally can be machined effectively with UAM. For example, in one test, low-porosity mullite was machined with a good cut by applying ultrasonic vibrations to the tool post and carbide-tipped tool, but when ultrasonic power was turned off, the workpiece immediately shattered.

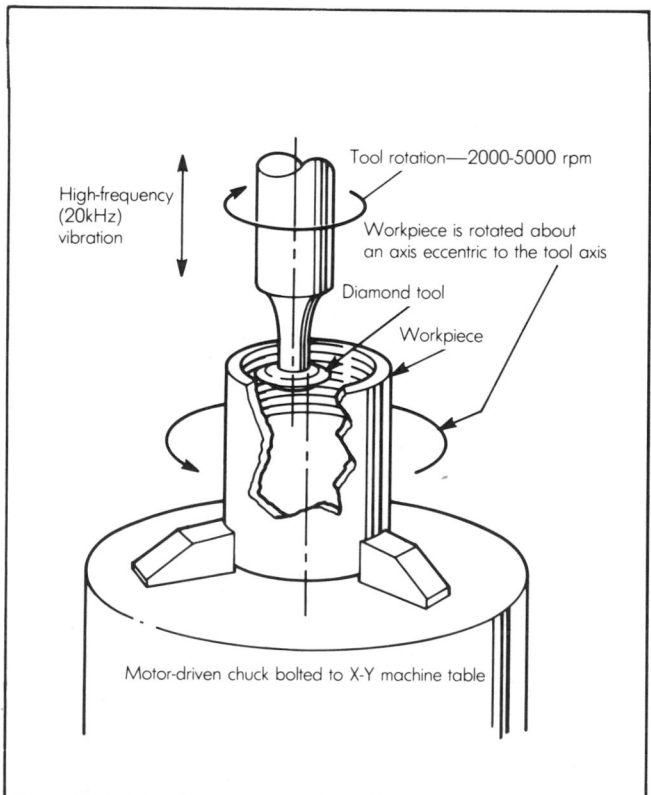

Fig. 29-4 Internal threading using rotary ultrasonic machining (RUM).

30% were experienced when copper and cast iron were drilled, and 54% when titanium was drilled. Torque reductions of 25% were experienced for mild steel, 50% for titanium, and 65% for aluminum alloys.

Chip packing is said to be less of a problem when UAM is used in twist drilling applications. For this reason, periodic retraction of the drill is not required as frequently as in traditional drilling. For example, drill depth in titanium is normally limited to two to four times the drill diameter; with UAM, depths up to eight times the diameter have been successfully obtained without drill retraction. Depths of 20 times the drill diameter have been achieved before drill retraction when aluminum was drilled using UAM techniques [1/8″ (3.2 mm) holes drilled to a depth of 2.5″ (63 mm)].

Experiments indicate that the tool wear on ultrasonically assisted drill bits exhibit a different wear pattern than on conventionally powered drill bits. After equivalent periods of ultrasonic and nonultrasonic cutting, traditionally applied bits were worn at the outer periphery while drills applied with ultrasonics were worn evenly along the cutting edge.

ELECTROMECHANICAL MACHINING (EMM)

Electromechanical machining is an experimental nontraditional process that enhances the capabilities of traditional machining operations such as drilling and turning. Metal removal is effected in a conventional manner using standard equipment and tooling except that the workpiece is electrochemically polarized. A controlled voltage is applied across the interface of the workpiece and an electrolyte. In drilling operations, the workpiece is submerged in a bath of electrolyte; in turning operations, the surface of the workpiece is flooded with electrolyte.

The principle of EMM is that when the applied voltage is closely controlled and the electrolytic solution is matched to the workpiece material, the surface of the workpiece can be changed to achieve favorable characteristics which will enhance machining performance. When the variables in the process are controlled, the workpiece surface can be changed from passive (oxide film on the surface) to active dissolution (surface being slowly dissolved) to hydrogen reduction (surface is discharging hydrogen ions).

The theory behind EMM is that relatively soft and work-hardenable materials are more easily cut when the work surface is passive. In this state, the workpiece surface is hardened by the presence of oxide film which also minimizes cutting friction. On the other hand, hard materials are more easily cut when the workpiece surface is in the active dissolution region in which the material is softened.

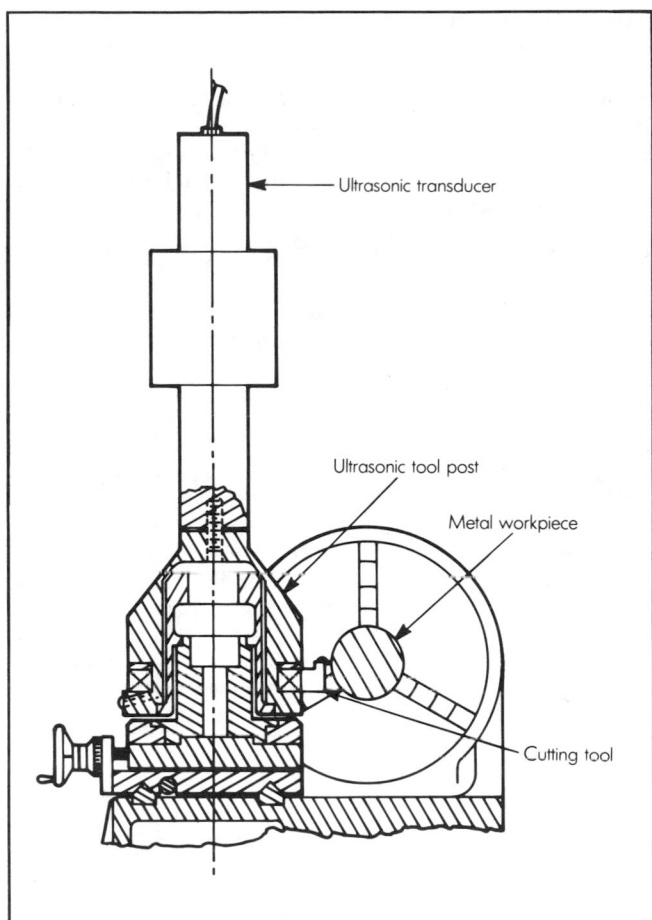

Fig. 29-6 Typical setup for ultrasonically assisted lathe turning. (*Sonobond Corp.*)

Some tests have shown that UAM reduces turning forces in some materials as much as 30-50% as compared to traditional turning methods.[5] In the same tests, it was shown that surfaces produced by UAM exhibited a matte finish, evidence of more complete shearing of the chips from the workpiece. This phenomenon is in sharp contrast to traditional machining which often produces a glossy surface as a result of tearing, material enfoldment, and burnishing. Subsurface tearing and plastic flow are reported to be all but eliminated by UAM.

Ultrasonic Twist Drilling

In twist drilling applications, UAM has been shown to reduce thrust and torque in some cases.[6] Thrust reductions of

ELECTRICAL PROCESSES

The purpose of this section is to provide an overview of the various nontraditional machining processes that use electrical energy as the primary source of energy for material removal. These electrical processes are sometimes called electrochemical or electrolytic processes because chemical fluids (electrolytes) are used in combination with electrical energy to effect a "cutting" action.

ELECTRICAL PROCESSES

ELECTROCHEMICAL DISCHARGE GRINDING (ECDG)

Electrochemical discharge grinding, sometimes called electrochemical discharge machining (ECDM), is a combination of two processes: electrochemical grinding (ECG), discussed in the next section of this chapter, and electrical discharge grinding (EDG), discussed in a later section of this chapter.

In ECDG, a-c or pulsating d-c is passed from a conductive "wheel" made of bonded graphite to a positively charged workpiece. Electrolyte is pumped between the gap. No mechanical contact is made between the workpiece and wheel, although some separation force is developed as a result of the electrolyte being compressed in the gap between the wheel and workpiece. With ECDG, most of the workpiece material is removed by the action of ECG: The oxides that form as a result of this process are removed effectively by the intermittent random-spark discharges of EDG (see Fig. 29-7). Relatively high amperage, low voltage current is employed in the process.[7]

Applications

The production uses of ECDG are somewhat limited although certain applications exist that are routinely performed, mostly in the grinding and sharpening of carbide tooling. Nearly any electrically conductive material can be processed, but careful comparison of the relative advantages and disadvantages of ECDG versus processes such as ECG and EDG should be made before specifying the process. For example, ECDG can remove material five times faster than EDG, but uses up to 15 times the current used in EDG. Typical production tolerances of $\pm$ 0.001" (0.03 mm) are achieved with ECDG.

Current successful applications of the process include grinding and sharpening of carbide inserts, generation of delicate profiles using form grinding, grinding of honeycomb materials, and grinding of carbide thread chasers.

Equipment

Machines used for ECDG operations are usually purchased on special order from machine tool builders. Available equipment is usually in the range of 20-1000 A and is normally built to suit the specific requirements of the user. Like all electrolytic processes, ECDG equipment is provided with stainless steel and/or plastic fixturing to minimize corrosive damage caused by the electrolyte.

ELECTROCHEMICAL GRINDING (ECG)

A special form of electrochemical machining, electrochemical grinding employs the combined actions of electrochemical attack and abrasion to rapidly remove material from electrically conductive workpieces, usually hard, tough materials.

The operating principles of ECG are the same as those of ECM except that ECG employs a rotating grinding wheel. Direct current is passed through an electrolyte which is pumped in a small gap, about 0.001" (0.03 mm), between the wheel (cathode) and workpiece (anode). In ECG, the majority (95-98%) of the material is removed by electrochemical attack; significantly less (2-5%) of the workpiece material is removed by the abrasive action of the wheel. The protruding abrasive particles in the wheel serve to remove electrochemical oxidation on the workpiece surface (see Fig. 29-8).

ECG can be compared to electroplating, but with major differences. ECG deplates material from the work and deposits it in the electrolyte; however, it does not plate material from the work onto the wheel.

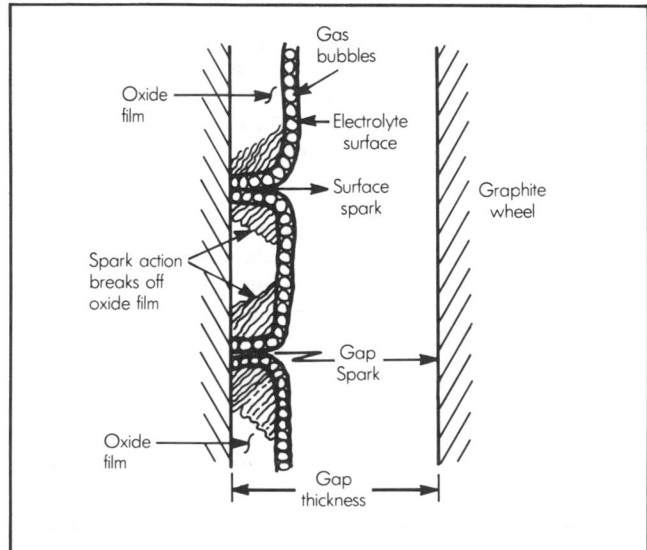

Fig. 29-7 In electrochemical discharge grinding (ECDG), most of the workpiece material is removed by the action of electrochemical grinding (ECG); the oxides that form as a result of this process are removed by the intermittent random-spark discharges of electrical discharge grinding (EDG).

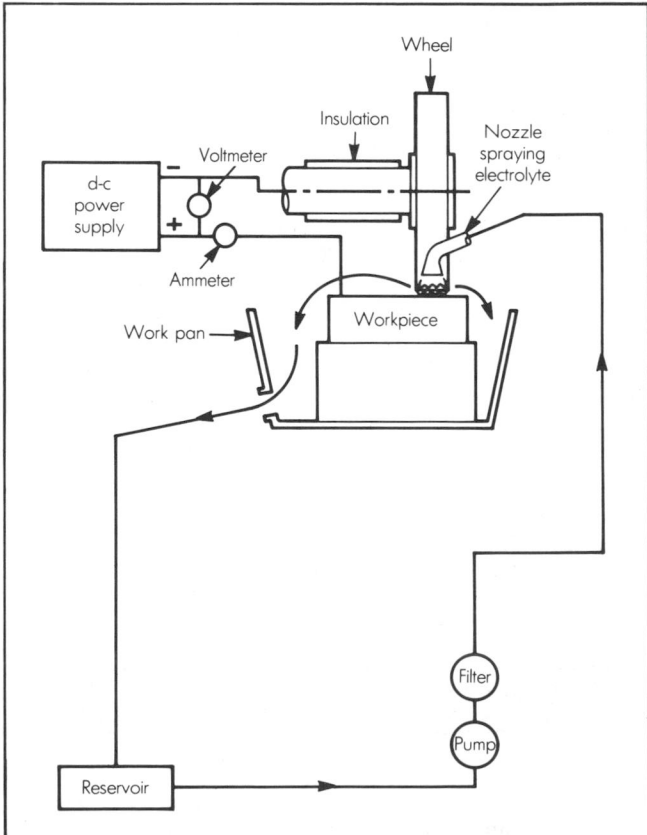

Fig. 29-8 Typical setup for electrochemical grinding (ECG) using wheel periphery. The process is also used for face grinding applications.

Wheels for ECG

During ECG, the abrasive wheel functions as follows:

1. The abrasive in the wheel continuously removes an electrically resistant film from the face of the work. If this dielectric film were allowed to remain, the flow of direct current would stop and there would be no electrochemical action.
2. The abrasive provides an electrically insulated gap between the cathodic wheel and the anodic work. Without this there would be a direct electrical short and resultant damage to both the wheel and the work. For optimum or maximum stock removal, the gap must be less than 0.001″ (0.03 mm).
3. The wheel carries the electrolyte in the spaces between the abrasive grains across the face of the work. Without the electrolyte between the wheel and the work, there would be no electrochemical action.

Several types of current-carrying abrasive wheels are used for ECG grinding. These include diamond wheels, peripheral wheels, nondiamond-face wheels, and nondiamond wheels.

Electrolytes for ECG

For years, a variety of electrolytes have been developed and tested for use with both carbides and various steels. Some electrolytes appear to perform well by visual observation; however, the only true test of an electrolyte is to measure both stock removal and wheel wear against known standards. This is most important in the grinding of carbide, which requires the use of an expensive diamond wheel for maximum stock removal.

The most efficient electrolyte for ferrous, nickel, and cobalt alloys is sodium chloride, but this salt solution is not necessarily the best overall because corrosion problems can be quite severe and tolerance control can be troublesome. For most alloys and for tungsten carbide, the best electrolyte formulations contain sodium nitrate as the active ingredient, with rust inhibitor and chelating-agent additives. Sodium chloride formulations are recommended only for titanium, zirconium, and columbium. Alkaline formulas, such as sodium carbonate-sodium hydroxide are recommended for tungsten and molybdenum. Electrochemically reactive metals, such as copper or silver, are best ground with weaker electrolytes such as sodium nitrite.

Applications

In operations in which ECG can be applied, it produces results far beyond those that conventional grinding methods can provide. In many cases it can reduce abrasive costs up to 90%. This reduction is most easily observed in connection with diamond wheels and carbide grinding. However, it is also significant with respect to steel and alloy steel grinding with nondiamond wheels.

Also, because it is a cool process, ECG can be used to grind any electrically conductive material without damage to it from heat. Therefore, ECG can simplify fracture-inspection procedures or entirely eliminate scrap due to grinding-heat fractures. In addition, this process can grind steel or alloy steel parts without generating any burr. Thus, the costly operation of subsequent deburring is automatically eliminated.

ECG has found many applications in the aerospace, automotive instrumentation, textile, and medical manufacturing industries, among others. The process is most frequently used to grind hard, tough materials. Because ECG is performed with significantly less wheel wear than conventional grinding, the process is sometimes more desirable than conventional grinding, or even milling. The process has proved effective in grinding turbine blade "Z" notches, in grinding honeycomb seal rings and in slotting piston rings. Surgical needles and thin-wall tubing are cut effectively due to the low forces generated in the ECG process.

Equipment and Tools

Many types of ECG machines are now available including surface grinders, vertical-spindle cylindrical grinders, burr-free cutoff machines, and many special machines including automatic parts transfer types. Machines are now available with both manual digital input (MDI) and with DNC and CNC. The various components of a simple ECG machine are shown in Fig. 29-9.

ECG tooling for carbide is relatively simple. While there is a large variety of sizes of carbide tools, there is not a large variety of shapes. In most cases, standard tooling is available for these applications.

Tooling is different for steel and alloy steel parts because of the large variety of workpiece shapes. Fortunately, standard basic fixtures are available with d-c power pickups and designs that have been optimized, particularly to resist corrosion by the electrolyte. These fixtures are mainly rotary mechanisms which are loaded at the point where the operator faces them. They are then either manually or automatically rotated, after which the work is fed to the wheel by an automatic table mechanism.

ELECTROCHEMICAL HONING (ECH)

Electrochemical honing is similar to electrochemical grinding (ECG) in that both processes combine electrolytic metal removal with abrasive cutting action. With ECH, metal is removed by introducing an electrolyte into a gap between a cathodic honing tool body and an anodic workpiece, as illustrated in Fig. 29-10.[8] The honing stones are nonconductive; the difference in potential is developed across the gap between the tool body and the workpiece. Direct current is passed across the gap, and the tool is stroked through the bore with the same generating motions of conventional honing. Several rows of small holes in the tool body enable electrolyte to be introduced directly between the tool and work surface. Conventional flooding is also used.

Bonded-abrasive honing stones are inserted in slots in the tool. These stones are forced out radially by the wedging action of the cone in the tool. This expansion is controlled by an adjusting head or fluid power cylinder in the spindle of the machine. The stones, which must be nonconductive, assist in the material-removal action and generate a round, straight cylinder. They are fed out with equal pressure in all directions so that their cutting faces are in constant contact with the cylinder's stones cut most aggressively on the high or tight areas and remove the geometric errors. The removal of approximately 90% of the metal in ECH operations is accomplished via electrolytic action; the honing stones maintain size and surface finish and continuously expose clean workpiece metal to the electrolytic process.

Applications

To be processed by ECH, workpieces must be conductive. The process is most effective when used to hone hard, tough metals and is well suited for the processing of parts that are

ELECTRICAL PROCESSES

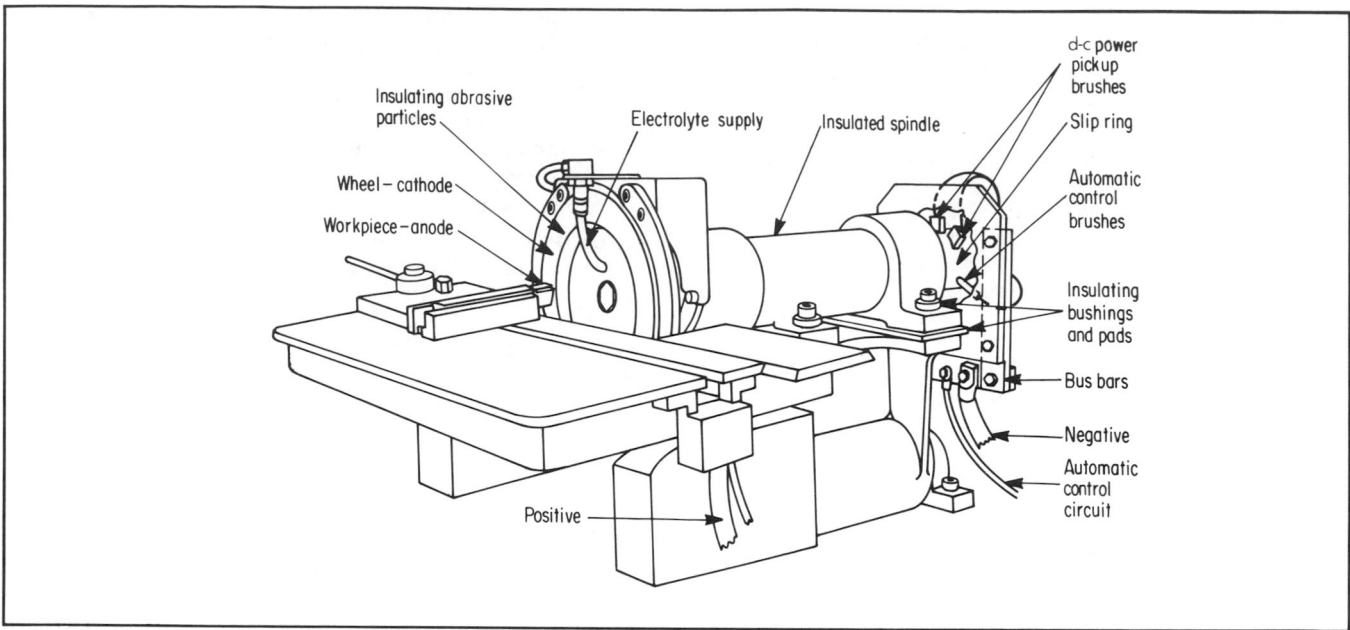

Fig. 29-9 Components of a simple electrochemical grinding (ECG) machine.

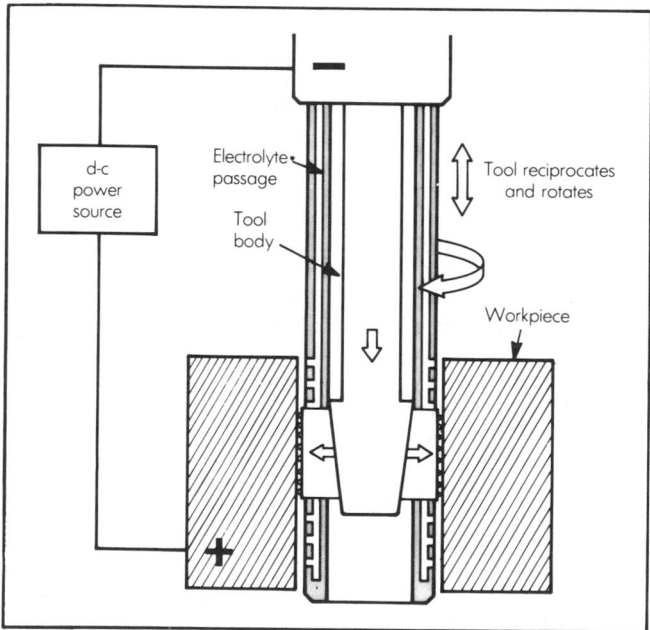

Fig. 29-10 Schematic of electrochemical honing (ECH).

susceptible to heat distortion. Electrochemical honing causes little heat buildup and no significant stresses, and automatically deburrs the workpiece. The process is particularly effective for parts that require fast stock removal with good surface finish control.

The size of cylinder that can be processed using ECH is limited only by the amount of current and electrolyte that can be supplied to the workpiece and by practical limits on honing tool size. With currently available equipment, bores from 3/8 to 6" (9.5 to 150 mm) diam can be elctrochemically honed.

Equipment

Electrochemical honing equipment for internal cylindrical honing applications closely resembles conventional honing machines with respect to general configuration. However, like any electrochemical process, ECH equipment is enclosed to contain electrolyte splashes and is ventilated to remove salt-laden vapors and gases that formulate as a result of the electrolytic process. Stainless steel or plastic is used for tools and fixtures.

Current is delivered to the tool and spindle through a brush assembly, as is done on electrolytic grinding equipment.

Electrolyte is pumped through a rotating seal assembly through the tool to the work gap. Filtration is usually accomplished with coarse cartridge filtration and settling. A magnetic separator can be used as well as a centrifugal filter if the metal removal rates increase to ECM proportions.

Automatic gaging devices are often built into ECH equipment. With this type of system, the cycle is automatically terminated when final size is reached.

HONE-FORMING™ (HF)

A reversed modification of the electrochemical honing (ECH) process, Hone-Forming is a trade name used to describe a combination honing and electroplating process developed in the early 1970's by Micromatic Industries, Inc.

With Hone-Forming, controlled abrading (honing) generates accurate dimensional tolerances, shape, and surface finish characteristics, and simultaneous electroforming adds metal to produce surfaces with specific metallurgical characteristics such as hardness, wear resistance, and density (see Fig. 29-11). The tool motions involved in the Hone-Forming process are the same as required in conventional honing or electrochemical honing (ECH)—rotation and reciprocation of a honing tool body through the workpiece. Metal is deposited at rates up to 50 times those achievable with conventional plating methods. Since metal is deposited only on the surface that is honed, it is

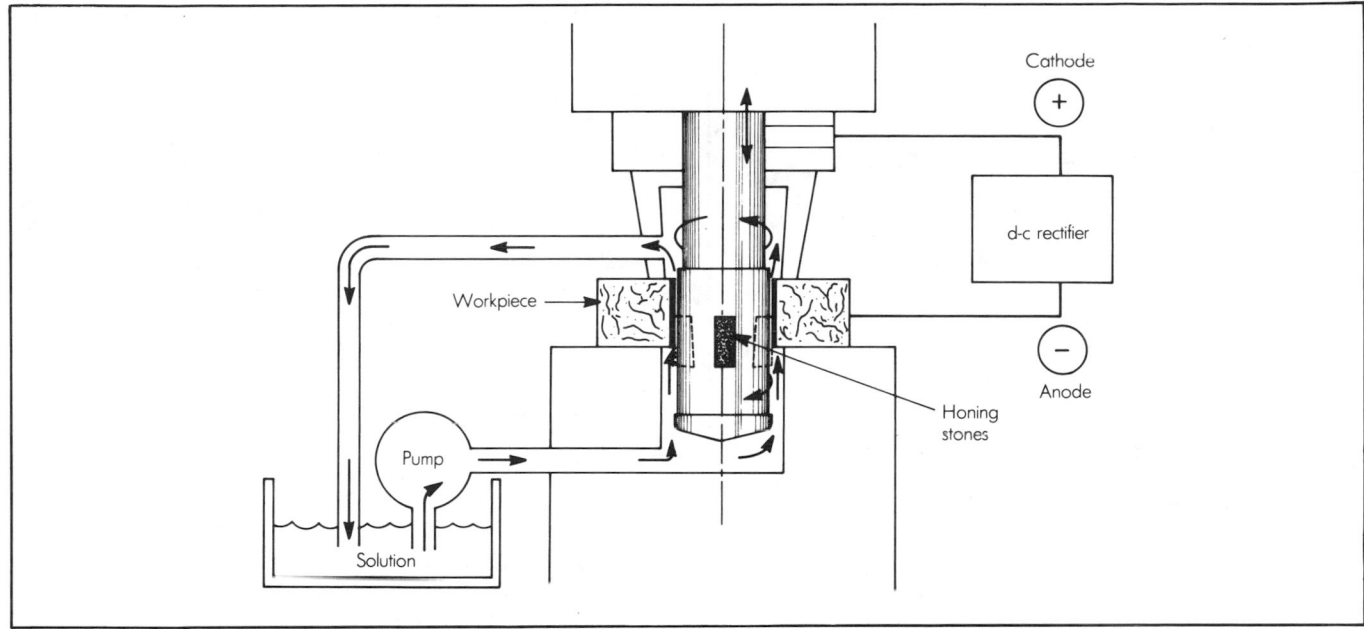

Fig. 29-11 Schematic of Hone-Forming (HF).

unnecessary to mask surfaces that are not to be plated. Preparation of the surface by acid etching and associated washing operations are eliminated. Also eliminated is the need to put a "strike" of one metal (such as copper) on the workpiece surface prior to the HF operation.

Applications

In HF applications, the workpiece must be conductive. To date, most materials used in HF are copper, bronze, tin, nickel, cobalt, or chromium-plated and are hone-formed on workpiece materials such as iron, steel, stainless steel, and bronze. Theoretically, any surface that can be honed can be processed with HF. Potential applications of the process include salvaging out-of-tolerance parts, reconditioning worn surfaces, and production manufacturing operations.

Equipment

As shown in Fig. 29-11, the equipment used in HF processes is comprised of a mechanism to support the workholding fixture and actuate the tool, a rectifier to supply direct current, a solution tank, and a circulating system. An insoluble anode connected to the positive side of the rectifier is part of the honing tool. A sealed-solution system is used, with the workpiece sealed at both ends to prevent wasting solution and to keep fumes from escaping. As in conventional honing, the tool rotates and reciprocates and the abrasive stones are forced outward to contact the work surface.

Stock is removed by abrading action of the stones in from 3-15 s (depending on workpiece material) at the beginning of the cycle. Then, current is applied to deposit metal, while pressure on the honing stones is reduced and only enough abrading is done to keep the work surface clean. Depositing of metal is stopped by either a timer or an automatic gaging unit. Abrading is then continued for a few seconds to produce the desired surface finish.

ELECTROCHEMICAL MACHINING (ECM)

Electrochemical machining is a widely employed method of removing metal without the use of mechanical or thermal energy. Electric energy is combined with a chemical to form a reaction of reverse plating. Direct current at relatively high amperage and low voltage is continuously passed between the anodic workpiece and cathodic tool (electrode) through a conductive electrolyte. At the anode surface, electrons are removed by the current flow, and the metallic bonds of the molecular structure of the surface are broken. These surface atoms go into solution as metal ions. Simultaneously, positive hydrogen ions are attracted to the negatively charged surface and emitted at the cathode surface to form hydrogen atoms, which combine to form hydrogen molecules. Dissolved material is removed from the gap between the work and tool by the flow of electrolyte, which also aids in carrying away the heat and hydrogen formed. Exposure of the workpiece to hydrogen is thus reduced. As shown schematically in Fig. 29-12, ECM operations require:

1. A cathode tool prepared with an approximate mirror image of the configuration to be machined into the workpiece (with compensation for overcut).
2. A workpiece and means to hold and locate it in close proximity to the tool. (In the case of ECM sinking operations, a means of feeding the tool into the workpiece while maintaining a proper gap is required.)
3. A means of supplying the gap between the tool and workpiece with pressurized, flowing, conductive liquid (electrolyte).
4. A carefully controlled source of d-c electrical power of sufficient capacity to maintain a current density between the tool and workpiece.

Electrolytes

An effective and efficient ECM electrolyte should have good

ELECTRICAL PROCESSES

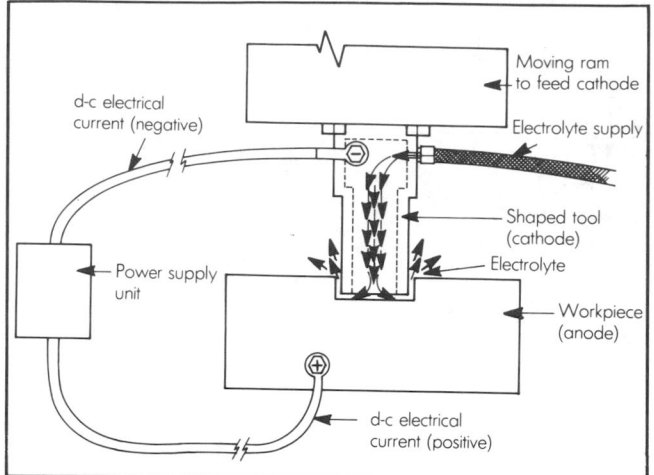

Fig. 29-12 Schematic of electrochemical machining (ECM).

electrical conductivity and should be inexpensive, readily available, nontoxic and safe to use, and as noncorrosive as possible.

Sodium chloride in water solution at various concentrations is used in about 80% of current ECM applications. Sodium nitrate in water solution at various concentrations is used in about 18% of current ECM applications. Other electrolytes, including special mixtures and proprietory solutions, are used about 2% of the time, although development of low-corrosivity electrolytes in recent years has spurred increasing interest in special mixtures.

Applications

ECM is used in a wide variety of industries to machine many different metals. Typically, the process is used to machine hard metals, but theoretically it can be used on any electrically conductive metal. Experience has shown, however, that not all materials can be machined successfully (to acceptable metal removal rates and surface finish) using the ECM process. For example, some high-silicon aluminum alloys, such as cast alloys with a substantial silicon content, sometimes cannot be machined with acceptable surface finish. Some troublesome experiences have been documented with SAE 332 aluminum pistons with 10% silicon, for example.

Equipment and Tools

Machine tools. The machine tool itself is one of the prime factors influencing the tolerances obtainable with ECM. Tolerances are affected by both the accuracy of movement and the rigidity of the machine tool. ECM machines are available in many different sizes and configurations, with different means for loading, setup, tooling, alignment between work and tool, and methods for control.

ECM cathodes. Cathode accuracy directly affects product accuracy in ECM because the product cannot be more accurate than the cathode tool which produced it. The accuracy of the basic cathode form is one, but not the only, consideration. The surface finish of the cathode is also reproduced in the surface of the machined part; therefore, poor cathode surface finish produces a poor surface finish in the part. Part accuracy is also affected by irregularities in electrolyte flow or current flow.

Tool design for ECM. The initial cost of ECM tooling can be

high (the tools may have a long life), but because the tools are made from soft metals such as brass, copper, or bronze, they usually require continuous refurbishing. Their design must incorporate practical ways of transmitting the high current required to the tool and workpiece, as well as ways to protect metal portions of the tooling from attack. A knowledge of hydrodynamics is helpful in obtaining uniform flow of the electrolyte. Tools are often modified during development and tryout to improve electrolyte distribution to all areas of the machining gap.

The design of ECM tools for drilling, trepanning, deburring, and similar operations is not difficult, but tools for sinking complex cavities or machining external contours can be complicated and costly. In contouring, the gap varies with the slope and curvature of the tool surface. The resulting variation in current densities and metal removal rates makes contouring-tool design difficult. Geometrical, graphical, and empirical methods, as well as computer programs, have been developed to assist in design.

ELECTROCHEMICAL TURNING (ECT)

Electrochemical turning is a special application of electrochemical machining (ECM). The principles of ECM are applied in the process to electrolytically machine rotating workpieces. Peripheral cuts and face cuts are accomplished as illustrated in Fig. 29-13.

Electrochemical turning is distinguished from a related process, electromechanical machining (EMM), in that ECT employs a noncontacting tool and all metal removal is accomplished via electrolytic action.

Applications

Large disc forgings are machined using ECT. In some cases, full-face electrodes are plunged into a rotating disc. Bearing races have been finished, with close tolerances and with surface roughness held to less than 5 μ in. (0.13 μ m) R_a. Another application, AISI 316 stainless steel workpieces (2.5″, 6.35 mm diam) are electrochemically turned, using an electrolyte of NaCl and NaNo$_3$(2:3), to a surface finish of less than 10 μ in. (0.25 μ m) R_a with out-of-roundness of less than 0.0002″ (0.005 mm) TIR.

Equipment

Peripheral and face ECT machines are available on special order. Capacities are provided up to about 20,000 A. One horizontal electrochemical lathe is equipped with 5000 A power supply. The lathe is used to hold 0.0003″ (0.008 mm) tolerances.

SHAPED TUBE ELECTROLYTIC MACHINING (STEM™)

Shaped Tube Electrolytic Machining, a "drilling" process developed by General Electric Company's Aircraft Engine Group, is a variation of electrochemical machining (ECM). The process is used to drill small shaped or round roles (0.025-0.250″, 0.64-6.35 mm diam) in electrically conductive materials, usually difficult-to-machine alloys.

Like conventional ECM, the STEM process employs a negatively charged tool, electrolyte, and a positively charged workpiece. A major difference between STEM and conventional ECM, however, is that STEM uses an acid electrolyte. Workpiece material is dissolved into solution in the electrolyte

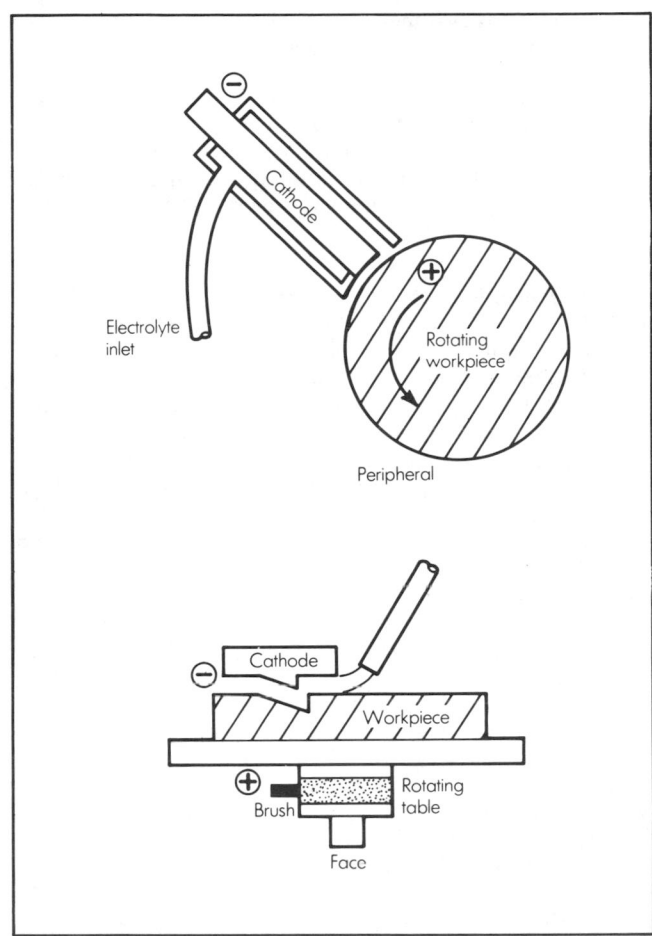

Fig. 29-13 Configurations for peripheral and face cuts using electrochemical turning (ECT). (*Courtesy: Modern Machine Shop*)

insulation permits only the exposed end to perform frontal cutting. The electrolyte is pumped through the electrode tubes and exits via the narrow gap between the electrode tube and ID of the hole being drilled.

Multiple electrodes with various diameters and shapes can be used simultaneously. The electrodes are plunge fed into the workpiece at a constant rate consistent with the metal removal rate. In this way, a constant gap thickness is maintained. The electrodes are guided by a guide plate which functions similarly to a bushing plate used to guide multiple conventional drills.

STEM is used to drill small holes in hard, tough materials such as 300 and 400 series stainless steels, alloy and tool steels, nickel, Inconel, Incoloy, tungsten, and Hastelloy alloys. Although holes up to 24″ (610 mm) deep with length-to-diameter ratios of up to about 300:1 can be produced using STEM, the process has not been widely applied since its introduction in the late 1960's. Experience has shown that irregular-shaped holes should have a minimum width of about 0.020″ (0.51 mm). Oval-shaped holes and holes that are similar to them should have a major-to-minor axis ratio of no more than 3:1. Up to 100 holes can be drilled per cycle.

ELECTRO-STREAM™ (ES)

Extremely small holes (0.008-0.040″, 0.20-1.02 mm) are "drilled" using the Electro-Stream process, an electrolytic operation developed by General Electric Co.'s Aircraft Engine Group. A stream of acid electrolyte flows through a glass insulated nozzle containing a metallic cathode and is ejected against the workpiece to transform the positively charged workpiece into solution at the point of acid impingement. High voltages are used to produce holes up to 0.75″ (19.0 mm) deep. The use of an acid electrolyte eliminates the formation of sludge that occurs when using salt-based electrolytes.

In general, any electrically conductive material can be processed with ES, although the operation is usually used to produce holes in hardened or tough materials such as 300 series stainless steels, Rene, Inconel, Incoloy, and Hastelloy alloys. The process has been used successfully in the drilling of holes in the leading edge of a superalloy gas turbine vane.

Holes can be drilled effectively at angles as low as 10°, and up to 100 holes can be drilled simultaneously. Depth-to-diameter ratios of drilled holes are usually less than 50:1.

instead of forming a sludge which could clog small drilled holes during processing.

Small-diameter, acid-resistant, metal tubes coated with an enamel-type film are used as electrodes in STEM. This

THERMAL PROCESSES

Nontraditional thermal machining processes use thermal energy as the primary source of energy for metal removal. These processes include electron beam machining (EBM), electrical discharge machining (EDM) and related processes, laser beam machining (LBM), and plasma beam machining (PBM).

Nontraditional thermal machining processes are characterized by high temperatures and high thermal energy densities. These processes typically produce significantly different physical and metallurgical effects as compared to traditional and other nontraditional processes. Much study in recent years has been aimed at attaining a better understanding of how the effects of the nontraditional thermal processes influence workpiece metallurgy and/or functional performance.

ELECTRON BEAM MACHINING (EBM)

Electron beam machining uses electrical energy to generate thermal energy for removing material. A pulsating stream of high-speed electrons produced by a generator is focused by electrostatic and electromagnetic fields to concentrate energy on a very small area of work. High-power beams are used with electron velocities exceeding half the speed of light. As the electrons impinge on the work, their kinetic energy is transformed into thermal energy and melts or evaporates the material locally.

Electron beams are concentrated on spots as small as 0.0002″ (0.05 mm) diam. The process is usually performed in a vacuum, as shown schematically in Fig. 29-14. A vacuum is used both to

THERMAL PROCESSES

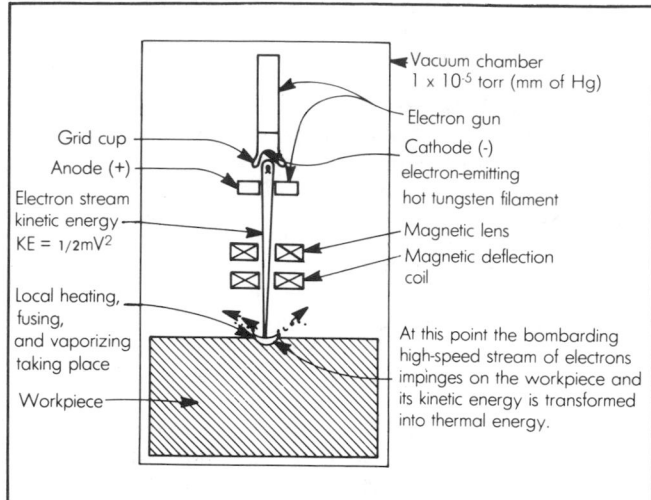

Fig. 29-14 Elements of an electron beam machine.

prevent collisions of electrons with gas molecules, which would scatter or diffuse the beam, and to protect the workpiece from oxidation and other atmospheric contamination. Lead shielding is required to protect the operator from X-ray radiation produced by the electron beam.

Principles of Operation

When electrons impinge upon a solid material at a certain speed, their kinetic energy is immediately translated into thermal energy.[9] What happens within the workpiece after this initial effect depends not only on electron beam parameters, such as total power, power density, and duration of impact, but also on the thermal properties of the workpiece, such as heat capacity, level of melting and vaporizing points, heat conductivity, heat of fusion, and vaporization. The material can be heated, melted or vaporized.

In removing material by electron beam machining, one of two different mechanisms is employed: The material is either totally evaporated, or it is simply melted. Then the liquid phase is taken away by additional forces such as centrifugal forces.

If achieving the desired size and shape of the hole is not possible with a single pulse, a multipulse drilling technique is applied. At pulse frequencies of between 50-1000 Hz, the beam spot is manipulated (moved by means of electromagnetic deflection or size change by means of focus adjustment) according to the operation desired. To obtain the machined shape required, sequences of hundreds to thousands of pulses are necessary. Reproducibility of the machining operations is normally ensured by suitable computer control.

Applications

Any known material, metal or nonmetal, that will exist in high vacuum can be cut, although experience has shown that diamonds do not cut well. Holes with depth-to-diameter ratios up to 100:1 can be cut. Limitations include high equipment costs and the need for a vacuum, which usually necessitates batch processing and restricts workpiece size. The process is generally economical only for small cuts in thin parts.

Typical applications of EBM include:

1. Drilling gas orifices for pressure-differential devices, in

which closely dimensioned holes must be drilled through the part. These holes regulate the amount of gas that flows in a given amount of time.
2. Producing wire-drawing dies, light-ray orifices, and spinnerets to produce synthetic fibers.
3. Producing metering holes, either round or profile shaped, to be used as flow holes on sleeve valves, rocket-fuel injectors, or injection nozzles on diesel engines.

Equipment

Beam generation. The electron beam is formed by a triode-style electron gun consisting of (1) a cathode—a heated emitter of electrons which is maintained at a filament emitting high negative potential; (2) a grid cup—an electrode negatively biased with respect to the filament; and (3) an anode—a ground potential electrode through which the accelerated electrons pass. Electrons are randomly emitted from the surface of the hot cathode and are accelerated toward the anode by the high accelerating potential applied between the anode and the cathode. The degree of negative bias applied to the grid cup controls this flow of electrons, the magnitude of the beam current produced, and is used as a highly responsive means for turning the beam on and off. Because of the shape of the electrostatic field formed by the anode grid cup configuration employed, the emitted electrons are electrostatically shaped into a slightly diverging beam that passes through a hole in the center of the anode. As soon as the electrons have passed through the anode, they attain the maximum velocity available from the applied accelerating voltage and maintain this velocity, when the process takes place in a vacuum environment, until they collide with the workpiece.

Beam control. The electron beam column assembly has a built-in optical system which enables the operator to accurately position the beam impact point and observe the drilling, cutting, or milling operation taking place. Through the use of visual optics, the operator can simultaneously view the workpiece and impingement spot at up to 40 times magnification on some equipment.

EBM machines. Electron beam machines used for drilling and for related processes are available in a wide range of chamber sizes. On special order, machines have been built with chamber sizes up to 20 x 27 ft (6 x 8 m).

NC Systems. The specific behavior of an electron beam, which is a beam of charged particles with very low mass but very high velocity, offers ideal conditions for the application of numerical control. The low-inertia beam can simply be controlled by electromagnetic fields, thus giving the possibility to economically adapt this extremely fast process to intricate machining geometries. A simultaneous control of the beam and of the workpiece movement is required in some cases.

ELECTRICAL DISCHARGE MACHINING (EDM)

Electrical discharge machining, sometimes referred to as spark machining, is a nontraditional method of removing metal by a series of rapidly recurring electrical discharges between an electrode (the cutting tool) and the workpiece in the presence of a dielectric fluid. Minute particles of metal or chips, generally in the form of hollow spheres, are removed by melting and vaporization, and are washed from the gap by the dielectric fluid which is continuously flushed between the tool and workpiece.

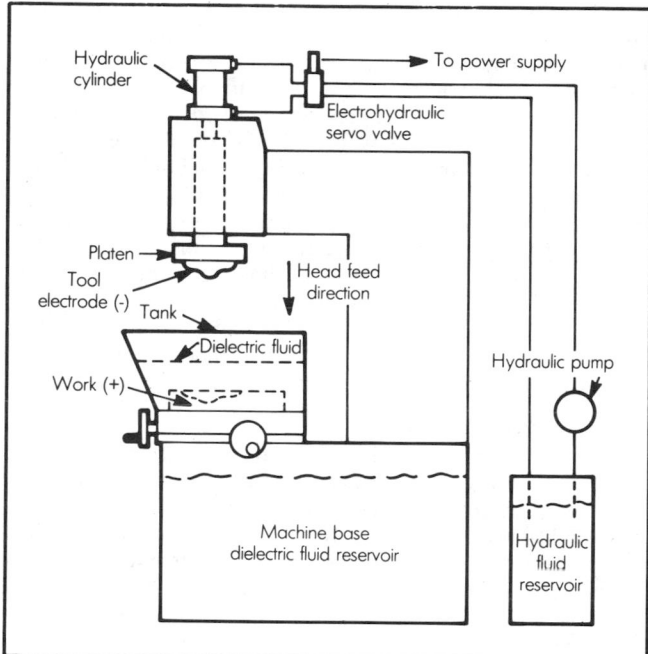

Fig. 29-15 Components of an electrical discharge machine (EDM).

Use of electric sparks for cutting imposes several special requirements, shown schematically in Fig. 29-15, not normally associated with more conventional machine tools. The workpiece, which constitutes one of the electrodes between which the sparks occur, must be of electrically conductive material. The other electrode (tool), which also must be made of electrically conductive material, is located in close proximity to, but not in contact with, the workpiece during cutting. In cavity-type EDM, shaped electrodes are mounted on a machine ram and are fed into the workpiece to achieve three-dimensional machining. This section describes cavity-type EDM; other sections of this chapter are dedicated to electrical discharge grinding (EDG), electrical discharge wire cutting (EDWC), and electrical discharge machining using orbital electrodes.

Principles of Operation

The removal of material in electrical discharge machining is based upon the erosion effect of electric sparks occurring between two electrodes. Several theories have been forwarded in attempts to explain the complex phenomenon known as "erosive spark."

The theory best supported by experimental evidence suggests that metal removal in EDM operations takes place as a result of the generation of extremely high temperature generated by the high intensity of the discharge current. Although well supported, this theory cannot be considered as definite and complete because of difficulties in interpretation.

Applications

The application of EDM is limited to the machining of electrically conductive workpiece materials, but the process has the capability of cutting these materials regardless of their hardness or toughness. Nonconductors such as glass, ceramics, or plastics cannot be machined using EDM techniques. Machining of hardened steel using EDM eliminates the need for subsequent heat treatment with possible distortion. Complex shapes can be cut in hardened steel or carbide without costly sectional construction being necessary.

The EDM process is most widely used by the mold-making tool and die industries, but it is increasingly applied to make prototype and production parts, especially in the aerospace and electronics industries in which production requirements are relatively low. Production of stamping dies is a major application of this process because of the favorable economics afforded by using EDM to match one portion of the die made conventionally. Extruding, heading, drawing, forging, and die casting dies, as well as molds for plastics, are also made using EDM techniques.

Electrical discharge machining is particularly well suited for parts which are made from materials that are difficult to machine and/or contain small or odd-shaped holes, a large number of holes, holes having shallow entrance angles, intricate cavities, or intricate contours. Miniature parts and parts made from material too thin or fragile to withstand conventional, mechanical cutting forces are also good applications. Round or irregular-shaped holes as small as 0.002" (0.05 mm) diam can be produced with length-to-diameter ratios of about 20:1. Narrow slots as small as 0.002-0.012" (0.05-0.30 mm) wide are cut routinely.

Burr-free cutting is characteristic of EDM. Many features of modern EDM equipment, such as multiple electrodes, automated dressing, and NC motion control, contribute to broaden process applicability. The scope of EDM applications range from tool and die and cavity work to automated transfer line operations.

Dielectric Fluids

A dielectric fluid must meet the following three requirements to ensure optimum performance in an EDM operation:[10]

1. The fluid must insulate until the required conditions are achieved between the electrode and workpiece, and then it must act as a conductor.
2. The fluid must cool the workpiece, electrode, and "chips."
3. The fluid must flush the particles out of the spark gap.

Equipment and Tools

Electrode materials. The EDM tool electrode is the means by which electric current is transported to the workpiece. The shape of the electrode establishes a pattern whereby sparks occur between the tool and workpiece and the desired shape is machined. Shapes machined are the opposite of the electrode shapes. A requirement for any material used for an EDM electrode is that it be a conductor of electricity. Insulating materials are not useable. A wide variety of materials are used in the manufacturing of electrodes. The most used materials are graphite and copper for machining steel and copper tungsten for machining carbide. Other materials used for electrodes are brass, tungsten, and carbide. Each material is available in different grades or alloys that can be used for specific needs.

Machining electrodes. In most cases, machining electrodes is a primary concern. This is approached in the same manner as producing the part, except the electrode material is usually easier to machine than the part material. Electrodes may be sectioned and inserted if this is the most economical approach

THERMAL PROCESSES

for fabrication. It is best not to mix electrode materials when building an electrode assembly.

Electrodes are produced on equipment available in most shops. Lathes, milling machines, and grinders are widely used. When three-dimensional electrodes are required, manual and automatic duplicators are used. When possible, multiple-spindle duplicators should be used if many electrodes are required. Undersized roughing electrodes can be produced at the same time as the full-sized finishers, from the same size of duplicating master, by using oversized cutting tools.

Wafer-type electrodes, having the required size only on their ends and a smaller diameter shank, are sometimes used to minimize deflection, produce straight walls, and closely control overcut. Wafer-type electrodes minimize electrode material costs.

Equipment. Electrical discharge machining requires a machine to hold the electrode tool and workpiece, and a power supply to provide the spark energy for the cut. In addition, the power supply contains electronic circuits for automatically advancing the electrode toward the workpiece, by means of the machine-tool servosystem, as material is removed. The power supply may be separate from the machine tool and connected through electrical cables, or it may be mounted directly on the machine.

Electrical discharge machining tools are generally of C-frame design, consisting of a base, column, and head. The machine base normally serves as a reservoir for the dielectric fluid. The column supports the critical head assembly over the work area. A coordinate X-Y-axis table is usually mounted on the machine base for holding and positioning the workpiece.

An antifriction-way system is generally used for the machine head, with the head being advanced or retracted from the cut by means of a servosystem. The servo is generally a hydraulic cylinder operated by an electrohydraulic valve. On some machines, the servo may also be an electric motor. In either event, it is most important that the system used be of the "zero-backlash" type, so that there is instantaneous response on any retraction signal of the servosystem. Any backlash will cause erratic cutting action; therefore, it is especially important that no backlash occur during smooth-surface-finish cuts, where a small amount of stock is removed and the spark gap is about 0.0005" (0.013 mm).

ELECTRODE ROTATING AND ORBITING EDM

The need for improved flushing techniques in certain EDM applications contributed to the development of electrode rotating and electrode orbiting devices. Flushing conditions are particularly poor when working at the low power levels required for fine finishing or necessary for small-hole work. Electrode rotating was the first of the two processes to be developed, and although it is effective, it is limited in its applicability. Electrode orbiting is a relatively new development which, along with improved flushing, has several important functions in EDM.

Electrode rotating is generally used for small-hole work while electrode orbiting is most useful for contoured cavities and for fine finishing.

Electrode Rotating

Electrode rotating devices consist of a precision spindle, a drive mechanism, and a speed control. Most spindles are designed with built-in seals to effect flushing through the electrode. The spindle drive is usually either electrical or pneumatic; the pneumatic drive devices are designed to operate even when immersed in dielectric oil. Spindle rotation speed is set manually and is generally low, with speeds of about 200 rpm maximum.

Electrode rotating helps to solve some of the flushing difficulty encountered when machining small holes with EDM. The relative motion between the electrode and the workpiece circulates dielectric oil through the gap improving flushing and increasing cutting speed. In addition to the increase in cutting speed, the quality of the hole produced is superior to that obtained using a stationary electrode. Holes machined by rotating electrodes tend to be rounder and straighter and tend to have a finer finish. The better finish is obtained because the effect of irregularities on the electrode surface is minimized.

Electrode Orbiting

Electrode orbiting differs significantly from electrode rotating both in operating principle and in actual application. In orbiting, the electrode normally does not rotate, rather it revolves in a prescribed orbit (see Fig. 29-16).[11] Orbiting produces holes the shape of the electrode, whereas rotating is inherently limited to round holes. The size of the holes produced by orbiting is determined by the size of the electrode and the radius of the orbit. The maximum radius for most orbiters is about 0.100" (2.5 mm). Electrodes with external square corners will leave a radius in each corner of the hole they produce which is equal to the radius of the orbit plus the overcut.

The relative motion that takes place between the electrode and the workpiece during orbiting results in improved flushing. The flushing benefits in two ways: First, the average space between the electrode and the workpiece is larger than the gap in the standard EDM process because of the radius of the orbit; second, the nature of the electrode movement creates a pumping effect of dielectric oil through the gap. These improvements in flushing become increasingly important for finishing work, since in fine cuts the gap is small. In addition to flushing benefits, electrode orbiting has several other desirable results compared to stationary electrode machining.

NO-WEAR ELECTRICAL DISCHARGE MACHINING (EDM)

"No-wear" EDM is a mode of operation in which electrode wear is reduced to such a small amount that it is virtually eliminated. The term is generally applied to cases in which the electrode-to-workpiece wear ratio is 1% or less. Users of EDM have continuously sought ways to control electrode wear, but most efforts, until the development of pulse-type power supplies, were either unsuccessful or impractical. The development of pulse-type power supplies provided greater control over the arc discharge and led to the discovery of the no-wear process.

In controlled-pulse power supplies, energy is delivered to the gap in the form of rectangular pulses of variable widths. The ability to control the pulse width (arc duration) is one requirement for the occurrence of no-wear. Another requirement is that the power supply be capable of operating in reverse polarity; i.e., with the electrode positive and the workpiece negative. Power supplies in which the pulse height (peak current) is also variable are better suited for the no-wear process since variable peak current allows control over the finish of the workpiece. In addition to power supply requirements, the choice of electrode and workpiece materials affects the ability to achieve no-wear.

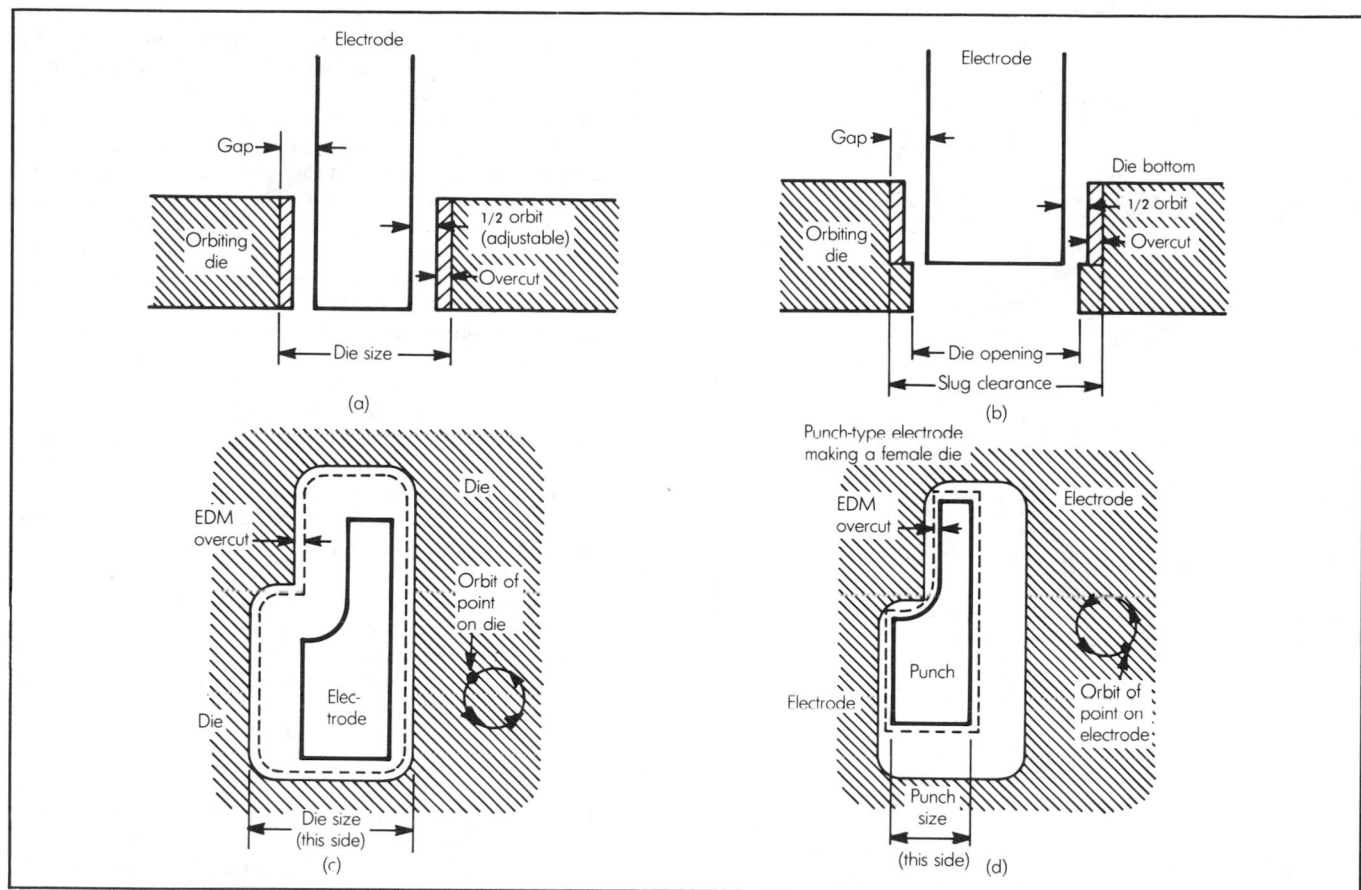

Fig. 29-16 Various configurations in orbiting electrical discharge machining (EDM); (a) relationship between electrode size, die size, orbit, and overcut; (b) a single, punch-type electrode machine both slug clearance and die opening with EDM; (c) punch-type electrode machining a female die; (d) female electrode machining a male punch. (*Courtesy: American Machinist*)

Several combinations of materials are known to be suitable for no-wear EDM. The most common combination is that of copper or graphite as the electrode and steel as the workpiece. Silver is also a suitable electrode material for steel workpieces, but is rarely used due to its high cost. Copper and graphite electrodes also demonstrate no-wear with aluminum workpieces, but these combinations are less common. Unfortunately, brass and copper tungsten, which are widely used in many EDM applications, are not capable of operating in the no-wear mode.

No-wear has several important applications in EDM today. The largest single user of the process is probably the tool and die industry, in which the process is widely used to make coining dies and molds. No-wear is also applicable to jobs requiring complicated or costly electrodes. In general, the conventional EDM mode is capable of higher metal removal rates than the no-wear mode, but this is often offset by the decrease in electrode life. For the same reason, no-wear has found some limited use in high-production, multiple-electrode jobs. In certain jobs it is more cost effective than conventional EDM, when the time spent redressing and replacing the electrodes is taken into account.

Two common misconceptions exist concerning the use of no-wear: first, that the process is strictly a roughing operation, and second, that it is only suitable for large work. There is no

basis for these limitations in no-wear theory. In practice, finishes in the 50-100 μ in. (1.27-2.54 μ m) range have been produced and no-wear has been performed with electrodes as small as 0.005 in.^{2} (3.2 mm^2) of surface area.

ELECTRICAL DISCHARGE WIRE CUTTING (EDWC)

Sometimes called traveling wire EDM, electrical discharge wire cutting is a process that is similar in configuration to bandsawing, except in the case of EDWC, the "saw" is a wire electrode of small diameter. Material removal is effected as a result of spark erosion as the wire electrode is fed (from a spool) through the workpiece. In most cases, horizontal movement of the worktable, controlled by CNC on modern machines, determines the path of cut, as illustrated in Fig. 29-17. However, some EDWC machines move the wire horizontally to define the path of cut, leaving the part stationary. On both types of machine configurations, the wire electrode moves vertically over sapphire or diamond wire guides, one above and one below the workpiece. The electrode wire is used only once, then discarded because the wire becomes misshapened after one pass through the workpiece. A steady stream of deionized water or other fluid is used to cool the workpiece and electrode wire and to flush the cut area.

THERMAL PROCESSES

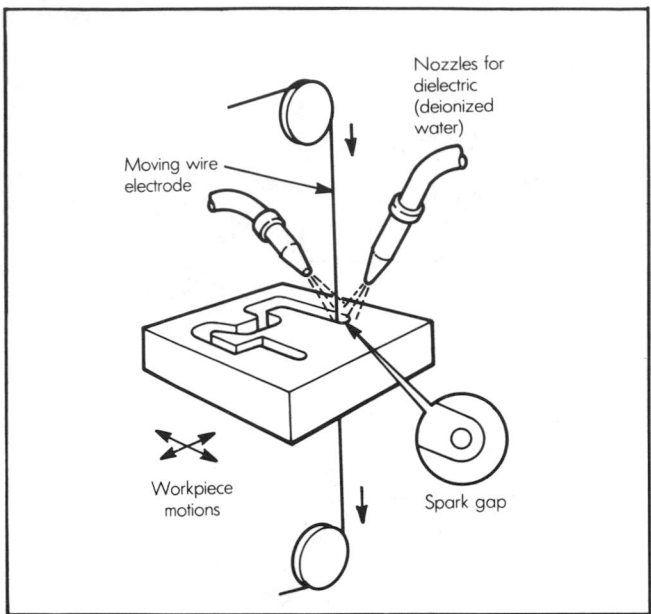

Fig. 29-17 Electrical Discharge Wire Cutting (EDWC). (*Charmilles*)

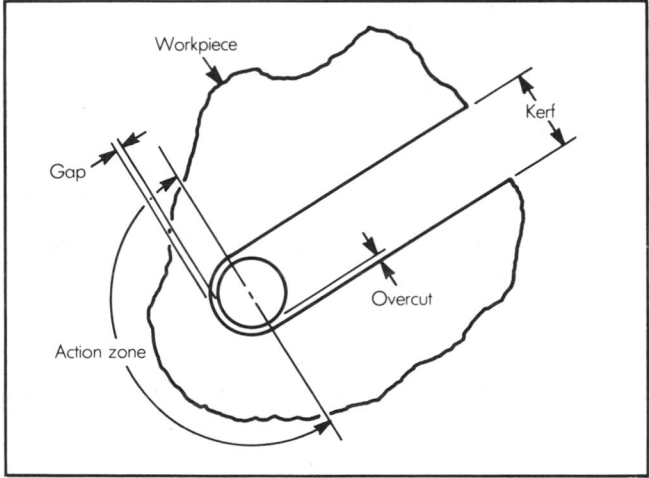

Fig. 29-18 Definition of kerf in electrical discharge wire cutting (EDWC). (*Charmilles*)

Viewed from above, the electrode wire cuts a slot or "kerf." The width of the kerf is the wire diameter plus EDM overcut, as illustrated in Fig. 29-18.

Starter or threading holes are required. In steel or other material, a drilled hole suffices; for carbide, the hole may have to be produced by EDM.

Applications

As is the case with any electrical discharge process, EDWC requires that the workpiece be electrically conductive. The cut produced by the process is free of bellmouth or flaring and is controllable to produce small radii. Workpieces up to about 6" (152 mm) in thickness can be processed using standard equipment; workpiece stacking effects greater productivity.

Stamping dies. Normally produced from hardened metals such as tool steel, stamping dies are routinely cut using EDWC. The process facilitates cutting after heat treatment, thereby eliminating distortion. The use of EDWC in the manufacturing of dies affords significant savings. By conventional methods, dies are sometimes split into two or more sections to facilitate grinding with an optical projection form grinder. Usually, after the contour has been ground in the split sections, the sections are fitted in a holder or adapter. This time-consuming and costly process is eliminated when EDWC is employed to produce the dies. Some experts claim that tool components such as dies can be produced in less than one third the time required by conventional methods.[12]

Prototype manufacturing. Using the EDWC process, complex-shaped blanks can be cut quickly and easily and, as mentioned earlier, layers of sheet metal can be stacked and gang-cut to produce dozens or hundreds of parts in a single pass. A distinct advantage of EDWC in prototype work is that NC programming used to produce the prototype can be used for production parts, often with only minor modifications. The flexibility afforded by the use of NC in the process greatly speeds the production of blanks for test forming in blank development work.

Molds. Manufacturing of molds of all types is most often accomplished using EDM cavity-type sinking units. Expensive electrodes for these machines normally employ slight tapers and extremely accurate size requirements and provide an excellent application for EDWC. Mold work demands exceptional electrode surface finish quality, which is usually obtainable using the EDWC process. Mold inserts, as well as two-piece molds, can be cut with the process. This "step backward" in construction technique can provide significant savings when sections are complex and cavity-type EDM is difficult.

Lathe tools. The OD plunge and grooving-form types of lathe tools are normally manufactured in a grinding operation. In recent years, however, EDWC has made significant inroads in these areas. The ability of EDWC to cut an accurate tapered form is critical to these applications as tapered front and side relief keeps the tools from dragging during cutting operations. The EDWC process eliminates many costly, tedious hours of optical or form grinding—one set up produces the tool.

Equipment

Machine tools used for EDWC are very precise. High-strength construction ensures stability. Materials such as tool steel, meehanite, and granite are used extensively.

Ways and leadscrews are usually the antifriction, recirculating ball type with compensation for leadscrew error provided through the memory of the control using stored calibration information. Temperature control of the deionized water (or other dielectric fluid), an option offered by some manufacturers, helps to maintain accuracy of lengthy cuts. Some models of wire machines are offered with an automatic wire threading feature. This feature is particularly useful when openings are to be cut in progressive dies.

Controllers (see Fig. 29-19) are capable of resolving highly complex tasks. The most demanding task required of the controller is to control interfacing with the power supply. The controller monitors positions and keeps the wire in a constant relationship to the work, thereby preserving accuracy. Changes in part contour produce different cutting conditions requiring the controller to modify the speed of cutting "on the fly." This requires sophistication within the controller and the computer/power supply interface.

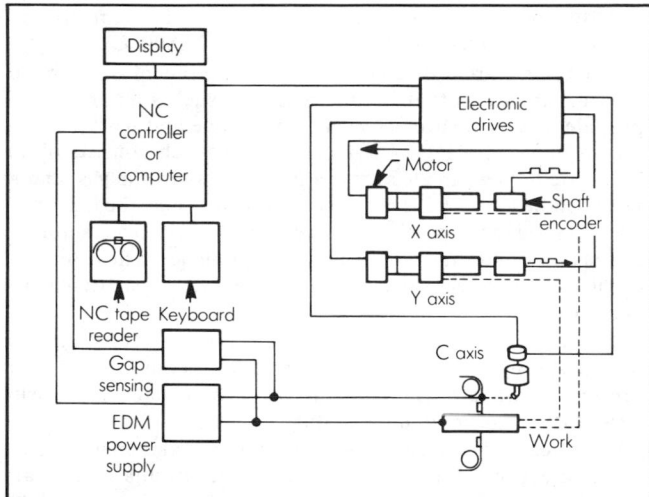

Fig. 29-19 Schematic of electrical discharge wire cutting (EDWC) system. (*Charmilles*)

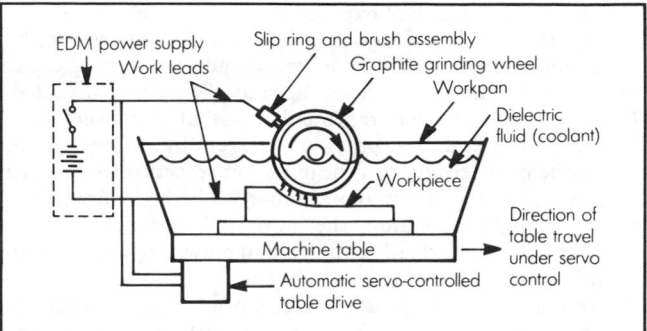

Fig. 29-20 Components of an electrical discharge grinding (EDG) machine.

ELECTRICAL DISCHARGE GRINDING (EDG)

Electrical discharge grinding is similar to electrical discharge machining (EDM), which is covered in a previous section of this chapter, except that the electrode is a rotating wheel, generally graphite but sometimes brass. Positively charged workpieces are immersed in or flooded by a dielectric fluid and fed past the negatively charged wheel by a servo-controlled machine table, as shown schematically in Fig. 29-20. Metal is removed by intermittent high-frequency electrical discharges passing through the gap between the wheel and work. The reverse of the form on the wheel face is transferred to the workpiece surface. Chips are flushed away by fluid carried through the cutting area by the wheel rotation. The wheel never comes closer to the workpiece than the preset length of spark (usually 0.0005-0.003″, 0.013-0.08 mm).

Applications

Electrical discharge grinding is generally used for operations such as the following:

1. Grinding steel and carbide at the same time without wheel loading.
2. Grinding thin sections on which abrasive-wheel pressures might cause distortion.
3. Grinding brittle materials or fragile parts on which abrasive materials might cause fracturing.
4. Grinding through forms for which diamond-wheel costs would be excessive.
5. Grinding circular forms in direct competition with abrasive-wheel methods.

Electrical discharge grinding is used to grind hard materials such as carbide form tools, hardened steel gear racks, or tungsten carbide inserts. The process is also used to grind hardened lamination dies. Cast iron workpieces are usually not processed using EDG because sand inclusions can damage the graphite grinding wheel.

Equipment

Standard EDG machines are available, and conventional horizontal-spindle milling or surface-grinding machines can be converted to the process. A pan or tank is mounted on the machine table to hold the dielectric fluid. Sometimes the EDG operation is performed on an EDM machine with the wheel mounted and rotated on the vertical spindle and the machine modified for servo feed of the table instead of the tool. In the past, brass wheels used to be common for this process and are still employed sometimes for thin-section workpieces, but graphite is now widely used because it is more economical and easier to form and dress. The negative lead from the d-c power supply is connected to the wheel (the hub of which is insulated from the rest of the machine), and the positive lead to the workpiece is mounted on the machine table.

LASER BEAM MACHINING (LBM)

The use of lasers in part manufacturing for cutting, drilling, slotting, welding, scribing, and heat treating operations has increased dramatically in recent years. The purpose of this section is to provide an overview of the use of lasers for machining operations such as drilling and cutting.

Applications

Any industrial application of the laser should be based on one of three criteria: (1) It can perform a superior job in terms of quality and cost over existing methods, (2) it is the only tool capable or available for the specific job, or (3) it allows restructuring of the manufacturing process, resulting in lower total cost.

Limitations may include low efficiency, low repetition rate, limited durability and reliability, and the necessity for careful control and effective safety procedures. Also, the process is generally limited to thin sheet or wire fabrication, holes machined are not always round or straight, and control is difficult in some cases.

Because of the laser's ability to melt or vaporize any known metal and operate in any desired atmospheric environment, it is sometimes preferred over EBM (electronic beam machining) which requires a vacuum chamber for certain applications. Other advantages include (1) the ability to machine areas not readily accessible and extremely small holes, (2) the fact that no direct contact exists between the tool (laser) and the workpiece, (3) small heat-affected zones, and (4) easy control of beam configuration and size of exposed area.

Cutting. Cutting a material with a laser generally is done by initiating a hole through the material and then moving either the focused beam or the workpiece as the laser is operated. Pulsed lasers are fired repeatedly so that each successive focused spot overlaps the previous one, resulting in the speed of cutting being determined by the maximum repetition rate of the laser. Continuous or CW (continuous wave) lasers are simply turned on and moved along the cut path. When metal is being cut, a jet of gas is normally employed to blow the partly melted, partly vaporized material out of the cut.

Drilling. One of the most attractive production applications of LBM has been the drilling of cooling holes in jet engine components. Here, the laser must compete with the electrical discharge machining and electrochemical machining processes. Most jet engine manufacturers are using pulsed lasers for production or engineering development activities.

Drilling with LBM can be accomplished in a relatively short time. For example, a 0.020" (0.51 mm) diam hole can be drilled through 0.100" (2.5 mm) thick superalloy materials in 1-3 s. Small-diameter holes (several microns) can normally be drilled with an approximate 20:1 length-to-diameter ratio.

The noncontact aspect of the process eliminates drill-breakage costs and minimizes the requirements for hold-down clamps. However, it is difficult to reliably control diameter tolerances any greater than ±5%, and considerations must be made to minimize or eliminate microcracking and recasting. Also, special techniques are necessary to facilitate drilling blind holes.

Other laser machining applications. Pulsed lasers are also being used to balance parts dynamically as they rotate at their designed operating speeds; this affords faster balancing and increased accuracy. In this application, the part need not be stopped prior to removing the material. Conventional sensing equipment is integrated with the laser system, and the laser's output pulse is synchronized with the sensing equipment.

Lasers are also being used in a service function to vaporize electron-microscope apertures that are clogged with foreign material. Two techniques are used to accomplish this task: (1) A spot larger than the aperture is used to clean out the foreign particles and (2) on large apertures, a small spot is focused directly onto a specific spot to vaporize it.

Equipment

Only a few of the many types of lasers are practical for metal-working applications. Ruby lasers produce the highest energy and peak power outputs, but they are more costly. Ruby lasers are generally used when a large amount of material must be removed with a single pulse. Nd:YAG lasers are less efficient electrically (1-3%), but have smaller laser heads because of the Nd:YAG rod. Nd:YAG and Nd:glass lasers have shorter wavelengths and can be focused to smaller spot sizes. This can be advantageous for drilling holes smaller than 0.002" (0.05 mm) diam.

CO_2 lasers are the most efficient (5-15% for industrial units) with respect to converting electrical energy to laser-light energy.

PLASMA ARC MACHINING (PAM)

Plasma is defined as a gas that has been heated to a sufficiently high temperature to become partially ionized and therefore electrically conductive. The term plasma, as employed in physics, means ionized particles. This phenomenon may be likened to a streak of lightning which ionizes the gases of the

atmosphere and heats them to incandescence. The temperature of plasma may reach as high as 50,000° F (27,800° C).

The plasma arc produced by modern equipment is generated by a plasma torch that is constructed in such a manner as to provide an electric arc between an electrode and workpiece as shown in Fig. 29-21.[13] A typical plasma torch consists of an electrode holder, an electrode, a device to swirl the gas, and a water-cooled nozzle. The "swirler" which may be ceramic, encircles the lower portion of the electrode, serving to stabilize the gas flow and thus preventing gas turbulence. The geometry of the torch nozzle is such that the hot gases are constricted in a narrow column.

Primary gases, such as nitrogen, argon-hydrogen, or air, are forced through the nozzle and arc and become heated and ionized. Secondary gases or water flow are often used to help clean the kerf of molten metal during cutting.

The stream of ionized particles from the nozzle can be used to perform a variety of industrial jobs. The plasma arc, as an industrial tool, is most heavily employed in sheet and plate cutting operations as an alternative to more conventional oxy-fuel torches or other cutting tools. Plasma arc is routinely used as an integral component of some modern punching machines.

Plasma arc methods are also employed in special applications to replace conventional machining operations such as lathe turning, and to a much lesser extent, milling and planing. The purpose of this section is to provide an overview of plasma arc machining and cutting.

Principles of Operation

In PAM, the basic plasma jet is generated by constricting an electric arc through a nozzle, as shown in Fig. 29-21. Instead of diverging into an open arc, the nozzle constricts the arc into a small cross section. This action greatly increases the power of the arc so that both temperature and voltage are raised. After passing through the nozzle, the arc exists in the form of a high-velocity, well-columnated, intensely hot plasma jet.

The basic heating phenomenon that takes place at the workpiece is a combination of heating due to energy transfer of electrons, recombination of dissociated molecules on the work-pieces, and convective heating from the high-temperature plasma that accompanies the arc. In some cases, it is desirable to achieve a third source of heating by injecting oxygen into the work area and taking advantage of the exothermic oxidation reaction. Once the material has been raised to the molten point, the high-velocity gas stream effectively blows the material away. For an optimized PAM cutting or machining operation, up to 45% of the electrical power delivered to the torch is used to remove metal from the workpiece. Of the remaining power, approximately 10% goes into the cooling water in the plasma generator and the rest is wasted in the hot gas and in heating the workpiece.

A major improvement in mechanized plasma arc cutting occurred in recent years with the development of so-called "water injection." When the water injection technique is employed, the arc is constricted by a flow of water around the arc. This injection of water has many advantages, including:

1. A square cut can be made.
2. Arc stability is increased.
3. Cutting speed can be increased.
4. Workpieces are heated less.
5. Less smoke and fumes are generated.

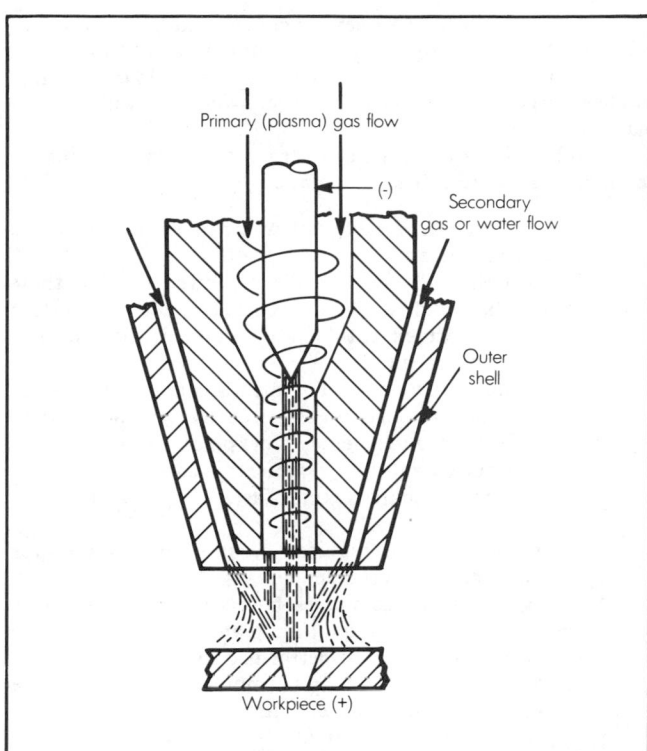

Fig. 29-21 Basic configuration of a plasma arc torch. Electrode is negatively charged; the workpiece is positively charged. Primary gas flow is ionized and heated to high temperatures; secondary gas flow cleans the cut of molten metal.

6. Nozzle life is increased.

Figure 29-22 illustrates the principle of water swirl injection.

Applications

Cutting. With appropriate equipment and techniques, the plasma arc can be employed to make cuts in electrically conductive metals. Table 29-1 lists some materials that are successfully cut using plasma arc techniques. The process is employed in a variety of cutting operations including straight line, circle, shape, level grooving, gouging, and stack cutting. Plasma arc techniques are also used for ripping, squaring, plate piercing, trimming, and plate edge preparation for welding. Figure 29-23 illustrates the general setup for cutting using a plasma arc torch.

Hole piercing. Reproducible, high-quality holes are made rapidly in a variety of materials with the plasma arc. The size and quality of the pierced holes are determined by arc current, arc duration, gas flow rate, gas composition, nozzle shape, and nozzle standoff. Holes can be pierced much faster than they can be drilled.

Stack cutting. Plasma can effectively stack-cut stainless steel and aluminum. Plasma stack-cutting of thin carbon steel tends to weld the layers making them difficult to separate after cutting.

During cutting, the layers should be clamped firmly enough to minimize gaps, but loose enough to permit slippage between layers due to differential expansion. The upper layer may buckle if clamping does not allow slippage.

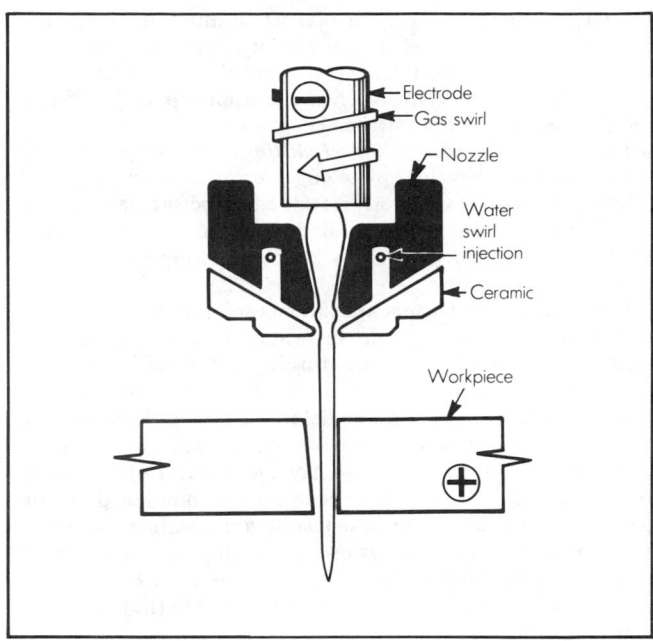

Fig. 29-22 Principle of water swirl injection in plasma arc machining (PAM). (*Linde Div., Union Carbide Corp.*)

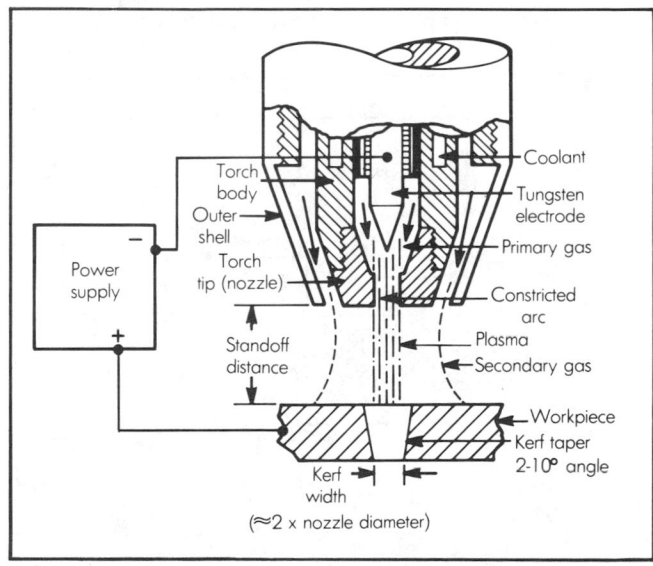

Fig. 29-23 Configuration of plasma arc torch for cutting operations.

TABLE 29-1
**Some Materials Cut
Using Plasma Arc Methods**

Brass	Alloy steel	Molybdenum
Bronze	Carbon steel	Monel
Nickel	Stainless steel	Inconel
Tungsten	Copper	Magnesium
Aluminum	Cast Iron	Titanium
Mild steel		

THERMAL PROCESSES

Gouging and grooving. The plasma cutting torch is suitable for machine gouging and grooving. Gouging is accomplished by using lower power or faster speed than that required for full penetration cuts, with the torch angled approximately 45° into the direction the torch is traversed.

Plate edge preparation (bevel cutting). Plasma arc cutting can be used for beveling plate edges prior to welding. Metal plates have been beveled on all four edges before being rolled into shape for welding into cylinders. Edges have been prepared by plasma arc cutting for welding in longitudinal and circumferential joints.

Machining. The plasma arc can be used for "machining" or removing the metal from the surface of a rotating cylinder to simulate a conventional lathe or turning operation. The process is shown schematically in Fig. 29-24. As the workpiece is turned, the torch is moved parallel to the axis of the work. The torch is positioned so the arc will impinge tangentially on the workpiece and remove the outer layer of metal. Cutting can be accomplished with the workpiece rotating in either direction relative to the torch, but best results are obtained when the direction of rotation permits use of the shortest arc length for cutting. The flow of molten metal being removed must be in such a direction that it does not tend to adhere to the hot surface that has just been machined.

Equipment

Cutting. Much of the equipment featuring plasma arc cutting today is similar in configuration to oxy-fuel, shape-cutting machines except that plasma torches are employed rather than conventional torches. Most new machines used for cutting are NC or CNC and/or employ optical tracing systems. Table sizes range to 44 x 82 ft (13.4 x 25 m). Portable, hand-held plasma arc torches and compact, portable power consoles are available for manual operation.

The following is a summary of features available in many modern plasma arc cutting machines:

- Square cuts can be made with water-injection plasma arc cutting equipment.
- High-quality cuts can be made at a lower cost than these same cuts would cost with oxy-gas fuel cutting. Cutting can be performed with relative ease in all positions, including overhead.
- Most electrically conductive metals can be cut. Plasma cutting is faster than oxy-gas fuel cutting depending upon the quality requirements, workpiece thickness, and materials being cut; for example, thin carbon steel plates can be cut more than five times faster if high quality is not a requirement.
- No preheat time is required because "preheating" for starting a cut is instantaneous.
- Straight lines, circles, shapes, bevels, grooves, and stacks can be cut. Ripping, squaring, plate piercing, and plate edge preparation can be performed for welding.
- A conical torch nozzle tip permits getting close to the workpiece, making bevel cuts easier and providing maximum operator visibility of the working arc. The conical nozzle tip also permits the shortest air gap and arc length in beveling.
- New torch designs are lightweight and compact, requiring minimum mounting space and providing maximum maneuverability.
- Connecting cables required for the torch are protected and insulated. Minimum interconnecting cables contribute to the total lightness and improve torch maneuverability for beveling and other special operations.
- Electrodes are easy to remove when replacement is necessary. Electrode adjustment and alignment operations are required for some types of torches.
- Only one electrode size is required for all general-purpose cutting. At least two electrode sizes may be required for high-quality cutting.
- Electrode centering may be accomplished either automatically or mechanically, depending upon equipment design.
- Torches can be easily mounted with a suitable torchholder adapter in any standard holder used on any conventional cutting machine capable of plasma cutting speeds.
- Some torches require only one gas plenum size for general-purpose cutting. At least two may be required for high-quality cutting.
- Plasma gas swirlers are designed either as a separate part that is usually replaced only when damaged or as an integral part of the nozzle.
- Some torches require only the change of nozzle size for different (power level) work thicknesses.
- Choice can be made from a wide variety of nozzle sizes.
- Some torch systems require only one torch head size for all work regardless of nozzle size.

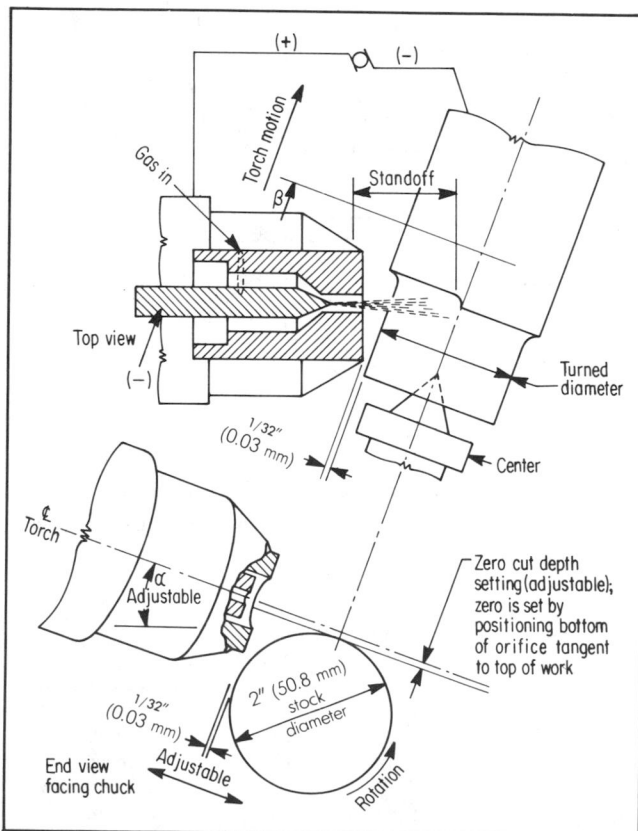

Fig. 29-24 Torch-to-work geometry in plasma arc machining (PAM).

Machining. Items required for a PAM setup (turning) include a plasma torch, a motion control for the torch, a rotational device for the workpiece, an exhaust hood for venting the area, a control console d-c rectifier power supply, and a supply of appropriate gases for the plasma torch. A cooling water loop is required to maintain proper operating temperature of the plasma generator electrodes. A standard shop lathe can be adapted for plasma arc application.

CHEMICAL PROCESSES

FUNDAMENTALS OF CHEMICAL PROCESSES

The common tie among the various chemical material-removal processes is the use of acid or alkaline solutions to dissolve unwanted material, leaving the final desired pattern or part configuration. However, significant differences exist among the various chemical techniques which make up the family of chemical material-removal processes. The similarities and differences between chemical milling and photochemical machining or blanking are covered in the following sections.

Maskants and Resists

Maskants and resists are workpiece coatings used to protect areas of the workpiece which are not to be exposed to the etchant and to define exposed areas for etchant attack.

The three classifications of maskants and resists in general use today are cut-and-peel maskants, photographic resists, and screen resists.

Cut-and-peel maskants. Cut-and-peel maskants, which are used almost exclusively for chemical milling of aircraft, missile, and structural parts, are applied by flowing, dipping, or spraying a coating to thicknesses of 0.008-0.015" (0.20-0.38 mm) in dry-film form. The materials are removed from areas to be etched by cutting and hand peeling away the unwanted areas, generally with a template to aid accuracy. Etching depths of 0.5" (12.7 mm) or more can be attained, and after a certain area has been etched, additional maskant may be removed so that step etching is possible.

Photographic resists. Photographic resists are materials which produce etchant-resistant images by means of photographic techniques. When exposed through a high-contrast negative and then developed, these materials produce an image of the negative itself. Both positive and negative-working resists are available, but they are used for different purposes. Positive resists are used in the manufacturing of mesh screens, gratings, and semiconductors, as well as in other applications.

Photoresists are generally characterized as extremely thin coatings which produce high detail, are sensitive to light, require careful handling and a clean environment, and have more complicated processing steps than required by other resists.

Screen resists. Screen resists are applied through a polyester or stainless steel mesh which has an image stencil on it. Although the stencils are generally made photographically, printing accuracy does not approach that of photographic printing. The image accuracies are, however, better than can generally be achieved by the cutting and peeling of maskants. The chemical resistance of screen resists is higher than that of photographic resists, but lower than that of cut-and-peel maskants. Screen printing is a rapid method of producing a large number of parts to moderate accuracies.

Etchants and their Selection

Selection of an etchant is dependent upon numerous factors, some of which are: (1) material to be etched, (2) type of maskant or resist used, (3) depth of etch, (4) surface finish required, (5) potential damage to or alteration of metallurgical properties of the material, (6) speed of material removal, (7) permissible operating environment, (8) economics of material removal, and (9) heat-treated condition of material.

CHEMICAL MILLING

Chemical milling is the process used to shape metals to an exacting tolerance by the chemical removal of metal, or deep etching of parts, rather than by conventional mechanical milling machining operations. The amount of metal removed, or depth of etch, is controlled by the amount of immersion time in the etching solution. Location of the unetched or unmilled areas on a part is controlled by masking or protecting these areas from the action of the etchant solution. The process consists of five main steps: cleaning, masking, scribing, etching, and demasking.

In general, chemical milling is used to:

- Remove metal from a portion or the entire surface of formed or irregularly shaped parts such as forgings, castings, extrusions, or formed wrought stock.
- Reduce web thicknesses below practical machining, forging, casting, or forming limits.
- Taper sheets and preformed shapes.
- Produce stepped webs, resulting in consolidation of several details into one integral piece.
- Remove the decarburized layer from low-alloy steel forgings.
- Remove up to 0.125" (3.2 mm) per surface of metal to remove decarb and also create finished dimensions of die forgings.
- Improve surface finish.
- Remove surface cracks, laps, and other defects of forgings.
- Remove alpha case from titanium forgings.
- Improve surface finish and control dimensions of aluminum forgings.

PHOTOCHEMICAL MACHINING

Photochemical machining or chemical blanking is the process of producing metallic and nonmetallic parts by chemical action. Basically, the process consists of placing a chemical-resistant image of the part on a sheet of metal and exposing the sheet to chemical action which dissolves all the metal except the desired part. Most parts produced in this way are similar to thin-gage stampings and are generally flat and of complex design.

CHEMICAL PROCESSES

Applications

Photochemical machining has a number of applications wherein it provides unique advantages. Some of these include:

1. Working on extremely thin materials when handling difficulties and die accuracies preclude the use of normal mechanical methods.
2. Working on hardened or brittle materials when mechanical action would cause breakage or stress-concentration points. Chemical blanking works well on spring materials and hardened materials which are relatively difficult to punch.
3. Production of parts which must be absolutely burr free.
4. Production of extremely complex parts for which die costs would be prohibitive.
5. Producing short-run parts for which the relatively low setup costs and short time from print to production offer advantages. This is especially important in research and development projects and in model shops.

The use of photochemical machining is generally limited to relatively thin materials, from 0.0001-0.050" (0.003-1.27 mm) thick. The limit on material thickness is generally a function of the tolerance desired on finished parts.

Photographic-Resist Processing Fundamentals

The photographic-resist process of photochemical machining is by far the most common one in use today. Figure 29-25 shows the process steps involved.

Cleaning. Metal can be chemically cleaned in numerous ways including degreasing, pumice scrubbing, electrocleaning, or chemical cleaning.

Coating. The cleaned metal is coated with photographic material which, when exposed to light of the proper wavelength, will polymerize and remain on the panel as it goes through a developing stage. This polymerized layer then acts as the barrier to the etching solution applied to the metal. Methods of coating the metal with the photoresist are dipping, spraying, flow coating, roller coating, or laminating. The type of resist used and the part's physical form determine which method is most applicable.

Prebake. After being coated with resist, the panel must usually be baked prior to being exposed. This "prebake," as it is called, is used to remove all solvents from the resist in a simple drying operation. Care must be taken not to over-bake the photoresists, since most of them are sensitive to heat prior to exposure.

Exposure. Artwork that has been drawn and photographically reduced is used to expose the photographic resist. The negatives are generally used in matched pairs so that a minimum amount of undercut is achieved and so that the final part has straight sidewalls. The metallic-coated panel is placed between sets of negatives (either film or glass) and is clamped by either vacuum or pressure. Exposure times depend upon light intensity, the type of resist being used, and the amount of sensitizers present in the resist. Typical exposure times of from 10-30 s are generally required.

Equipment used for printing ranges from very simple, single-sided, graphic-arts types of vacuum frames (such as those used by photoengravers) to extremely complex automatic equipment for printing on continuous strips. The exposed image can be developed by a number of methods. Each photoresist has its own developing solution, which may be water, alkaline solution,

hydrocarbons, solvents, or proprietary developers. In most cases the image is developed either by immersion followed by subsequent wash off or by spray equipment. Developing is always followed by a washing operation to ensure that no residual resist is left on the panels in the areas to be etched away.

Postbake. Certain resists require an additional baking operation following development. This "postbake" is necessary to drive out residual solvents or cause further polymerization, which improves the chemical resistance of the resist image. Postbaking is not as critical as prebaking in regard to time and temperature, but it is generally tailored to the specific resist used and the depth of etching to be obtained. Infrared lamps, conveyorized infrared ovens, or circulating air ovens are used for postbaking. In isolated instances, induction heating equipment has been used on ferrous materials. Following postbaking, it is generally advisable to cool the resist prior to etching.

Processing. The next step is etching to remove the unwanted metal that is not protected by the photoresists. A large number of etchants are available for different materials. Many materials can be attacked by a number of etchants, with the deciding factors being cost, quality, and speed of material removal.

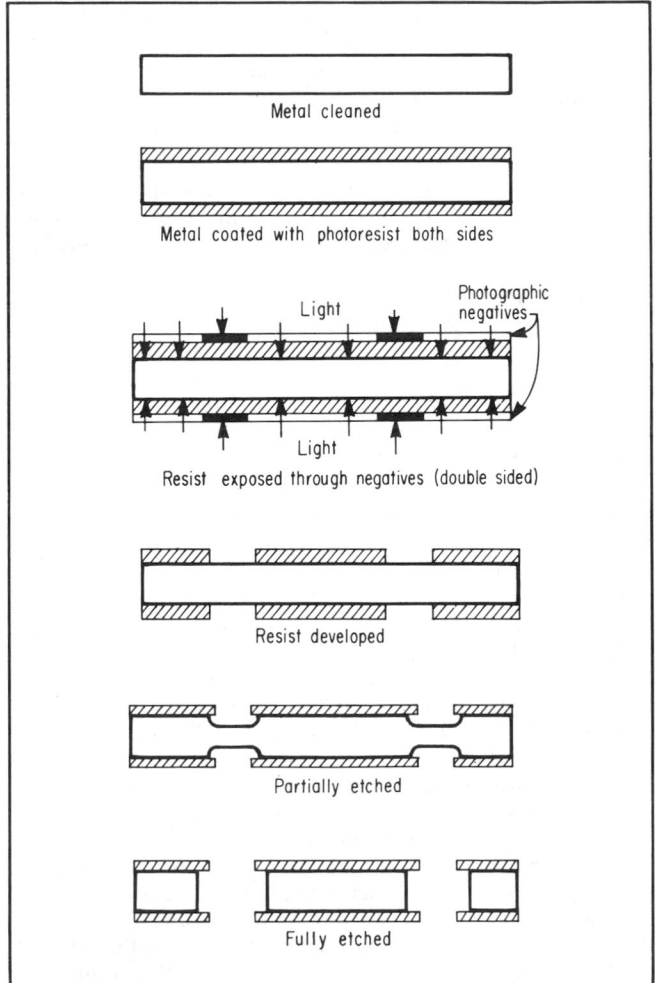

Fig. 29-25 Process steps involved in the photographic-resist process of photochemical machining.

Etchant may be applied to the workpiece by immersion, splash, or spray. Less commonly used techniques are air-driven mists or fogs, and gaseous-medium etching. Following etching, the workpiece is generally washed and dried if resist removal is not required. When removing the resist is necessary, the removal can be accomplished manually or by machines either with spray-on removal compounds or with the use of mechanical action in addition to chemical action.

Screen-Printed Resist
Processing Fundamentals

Most of the steps involved are identical when using a screen-printed resist rather than a photographically printed resist. Cleaning for screen resists is generally not as critical as it is for photographic resists because the screen resists have better adhesion and their adhesion is less dependent upon the surface cleanliness of the material on which they are printed. The clean panel is placed in either a manual or automatic screen printer, and acid-resistant ink is screened onto the part. Following printing, the resist must be dried and quite often it is necessary to print the reverse side of the panel if higher accuracy or thicker materials are to be chemically blanked.

After printing is complete and the acid resist has been properly dried or baked, the part is etched in the normal manner. Following etching, the screen resists are generally removed by either chemical action or a combination of chemical and mechanical action. Because of the inherent limitations of screen printing, high-tolerance work cannot be done with currently available screen-printing equipment. However, the cost of screen printing is so much lower than the cost of photographic printing that, when tolerances permit, the former technique should be used. Generally, the cost of screen printing is only 20% of the cost of photographic printing on a per-unit-area basis.

References

1. M. P. Wojchiechowski and K. S. Taraman, *Ultrasonic Machining; Past, Present, and Future*, SME Technical Paper MR72-188, p. 1.
2. G. Miller, "Special Theory of Ultrasonic Machining," *Journal of Applied Physics* (February 1951), pp. 149-156.
3. Paul D. Larson, "Ultrasonics—Machining the Unmachinable," *Automation* (now *Production Engineering*) (February 1975), p. 62.
4. Janet Devine, "Ultrasonically Assisted Machining," *The Carbide and Tool Journal* (September-October 1980), p. 26.
5. *Ibid.*
6. *Ibid.*, p. 28.
7. W. G. Voorhees, *Electrochemical Discharge Machining*, SME Technical Paper MR67-165, 1967, p. 1.
8. E. A. Randlett, Jr., and Myron P. Ellis, *Electrochemical Honing-ECH*, SME Technical Paper MR68-815, 1968, p. 9.
9. W. W. Closs and J. Drew, *Electron Beam Drilling*, SME Technical Paper MR78-597, 1978, p. 2.
10. Charles Vollaro, Jr., *Specification of EDM Dielectric Fluids*, SME Technical Paper MR77-546, 1977, p. 1.
11. J. T. Winship, "EDM Operations Go Into Orbit," *American Machinist* (March 1977), p. 115.
12. R. Snoeys and F. Van Dijck "Physico-Mathematical Analysis of the E.D.M. Process," *North American Metalworking Research Conference Proceedings*, McMaster University, Hamilton Ontario, 1973, pp. 181-202.
13. John E. Barger, *Plasma Arc Cutting*, SME Technical Paper, MR76-712, 1976, p. 2.

MULTIFUNCTION MACHINES

SINGLE-SPINDLE AUTOMATIC LATHES

A major advantage of single-spindle automatic lathes is high-speed production, resulting from having a number of tools cutting simultaneously, with no time lost for tool indexing or positioning. Customarily, as many tools as possible are used without exceeding the machine's power and staying within the rigidity constraints of the workpiece.

Single-spindle automatic lathes generally are best suited for high production requirements in turning and facing multiple-diameter or long workpieces. The more complex the setup, the longer the production run should be for minimum cost because setup and changeover is time consuming.

When these machines are used for shorter production runs, consideration should be given to reducing the number of tools, thereby increasing the cycle time and decreasing the setup time. Setup time can also be reduced by sequentially scheduling the production of families of parts, thus minimizing changeover time. Lathes and turning centers equipped with NC/CNC, are being used extensively for short production runs and increased flexibility.

MACHINE DESIGN

Most single-spindle automatic lathes are arranged to turn workpieces held between centers, but some are designed for chucking work, with the workpiece held in a chuck, collet, or special workholding fixture. Most machines are of horizontal configuration, but some are built with vertical spindles. Depending upon the manufacturer, feed of the slides is accomplished with hydraulics, air/hydraulics, leadscrews, or cams. Figure 30-1, view *a* illustrates a machine with cam feed for the front slide; view *b* shows a machine with a leadscrew fed front slide.

The basic machine consists of headstock, a bed with front and rear ways mounted on a suitable base, a tailstock, a carriage with both longitudinal and crossfeed mounted on the front ways, and a squaring attachment clamped to the rear ways that provides crossfeed only.

ATTACHMENTS

Many attachments are available to tailor single-spindle automatic lathes for requirements of specific applications. These include modifications of the front turning carriage, rear and overhead squaring attachments, a headstock turning attachment, various tailstocks, double-end and center drives, steadyrest, and automatic loaders.

WORKHOLDING

Any type of workdriving means appropriate for the job can be used, but manual actuation is not recommended. The problem with manual chucking is that it wastes time. (It may take longer to chuck the part than it takes to machine it). Also, no assurance exists that the operator has tightened the chuck properly. When power chucks are used, their actuation can be monitored and interlocked with the spindle-start circuit.

Collets, both external and internal, can be used on machined or cold-finished surfaces. When an internal collet is long in relation to its diameter, it is usually necessary to support the outer end with a relieving tailstock. Expanding-jaw drivers can be used on as-forged or as-cast cylindrical workpieces.

Two-jaw equalizing drivers with cam-shaped jaws (see Fig. 30-2) can be used on shafts mounted between centers for manually loaded operations. These are much less expensive than a power chuck and cylinder. Face drivers are useful when the entire length of a shaft must be turned in one operation.

Slotted and lug-type drivers are used extensively for workpieces held between centers when there is a suitable projection or indentation against which the driver can exert the required torque. When possible, it is best to drive against two symmetrical surfaces to eliminate the tendency of the applied torque to push the workpiece off center. When using such a two-point drive, it is necessary that the driver nose be floating to compensate for minor variations in symmetry of the driven surfaces. Such driving surfaces are often incorporated into the design of the workpiece.

TOOLHOLDERS

Toolblocks serve to hold the cutting tools on the various attachments. The tool is clamped in a slot, and the block is clamped to the slide. Single toolblocks, containing one tool, are more flexible because the spacing between the blocks on a slide can be varied. Multiple toolblocks containing two or more tools are used when the tools must be spaced close together.

Another use for multiple toolblocks is when the machine is to be employed for a number of setups. A separate multiple toolblock can be provided for each setup. By leaving the tools in the block, all that is required to change from one tooling setup to another is to interchange blocks. When required by close tolerance requirements, micrometer or dial-indicator adjustment can be provided.

The magazine toolblock is a variation of the multiple toolblock. Tools are mounted within a precision block (the magazine) which is mounted in a precision cavity in a block which attaches to the slide. This design is normally used with brazed tools when indexable inserts cannot be applied. Three magazines are generally provided for each block: one in use in the machine, the second ready for use, and the third in the toolroom for tool resharpening and adjustment.

SINGLE-SPINDLE AUTOMATIC LATHES

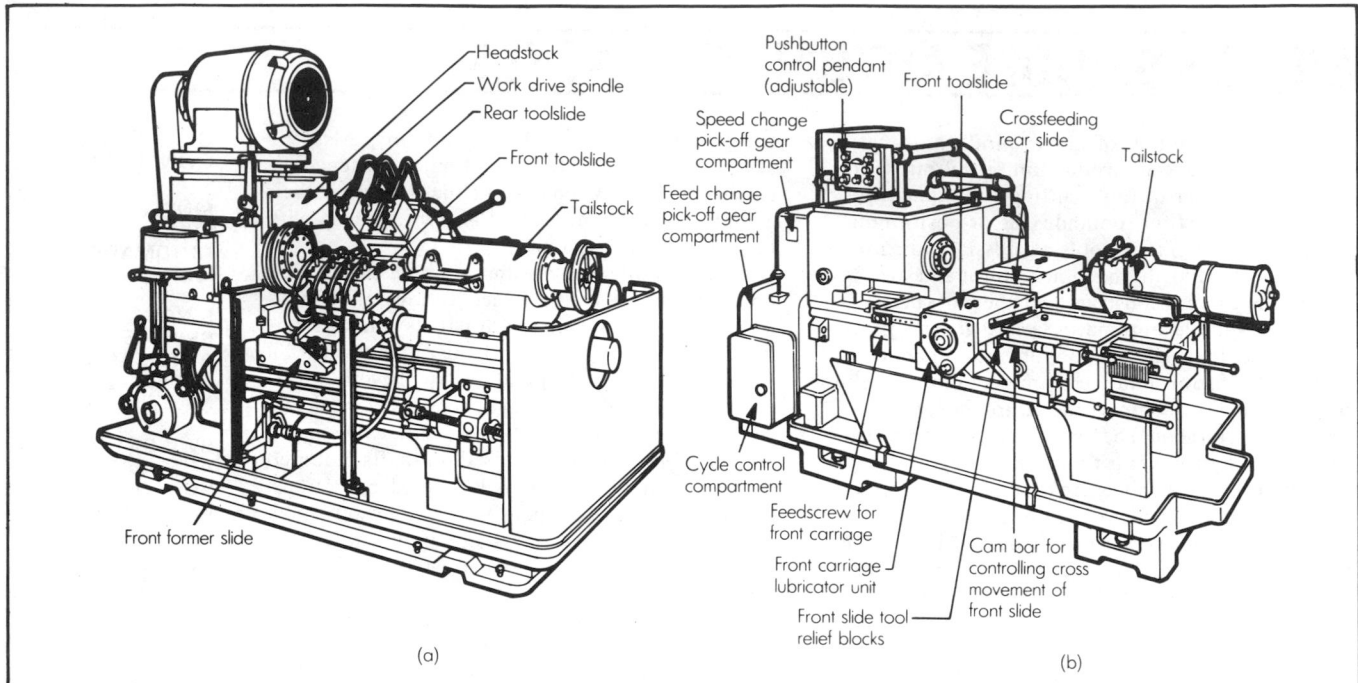

Fig. 30-1 Single-spindle automatic lathes: (a) cam feed for front slide, and (b) leadscrew-fed front slide.

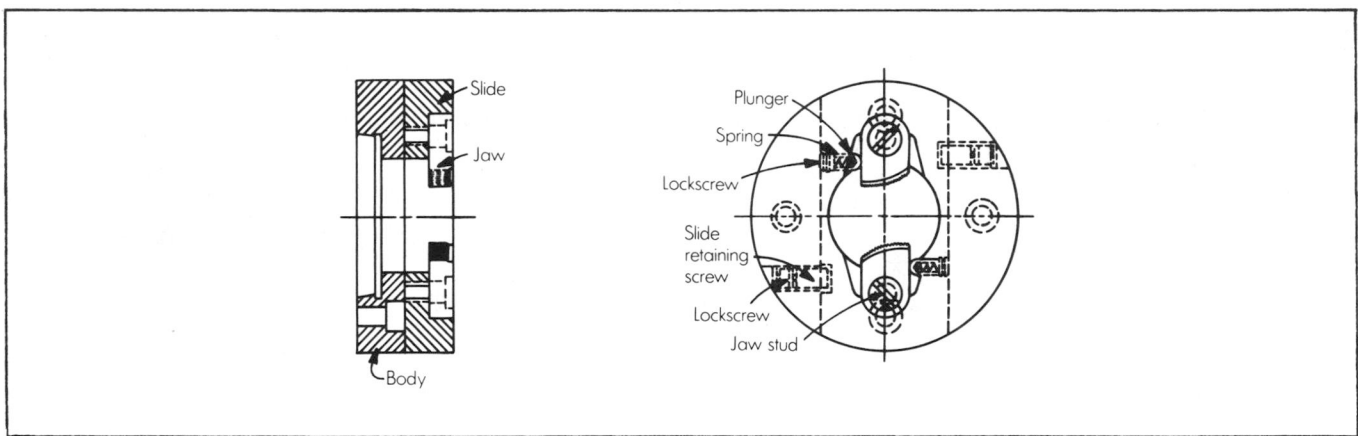

Fig. 30-2 Two-jaw equalizing driver with cam-shaped jaws.

SINGLE-SPINDLE AUTOMATIC SCREW MACHINES

Automatic screw machines are designed to produce parts from bar or coil stock. With automatic operations taking place successively or simultaneously, using tools mounted on a turret and cross slides, these machines can complete workpieces at high production rates. Machines of this type having many tooling and operating principles similar to those used for horizontal turret lathes.

Two major classifications for single-spindle automatic screw machines are cam-controlled and programmable (camless) machines. Cam-controlled automatics, requiring cams and speed-change gears for specific applications, are used more extensively for the high-production requirements of a single

part or family of parts. Camless automatics, programmed by toggle switches, pegboards, or NC/CNC units, provide simpler setup, faster changeover, and increased flexibility for shorter run production.

CAM-CONTROLLED AUTOMATICS

Design elements of a cam-controlled, single-spindle automatic screw machine are illustrated in Fig. 30-3. A bar of stock is held firmly in the spindle by a spring collet and rotated. Two sprockets on the spindle are driven by roller chains from driveshafts in the base. These sprockets run free and either one or the other is engaged to drive the spindle by means of a friction clutch

SINGLE-SPINDLE AUTOMATIC SCREW MACHINES

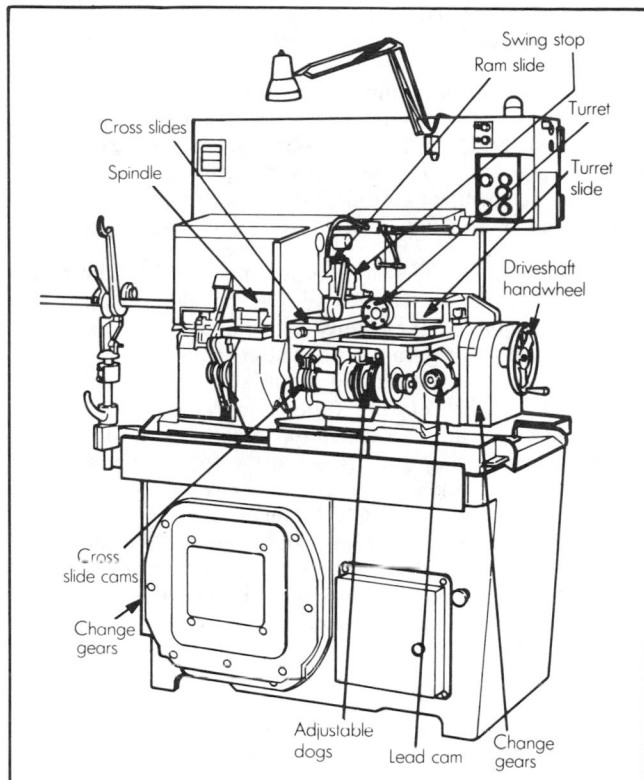

Fig. 30-3 Single-spindle automatic screw machine with cam control. (*Brown & Sharpe Manufacturing Co.*)

between the sprockets. This type of drive allows direction of rotation to be reversed.

Cutting operations are performed on the bar of stock by cutting tools held in a turret and on the cross slides. The regular turret has six or eight tool positions and is automatically indexed to bring each tool into position. The cross slides are two independent slides at right angles to the spindle. Both turret and cross slides are moved to the work through levers actuated by plate cams designed to give the proper feed to each tool. The slides are withdrawn from the work by springs. Adjustable stops for the cross slides permit accurate repetition of formed diameters within close tolerances. Cutting off the completed workpiece is done by the cross slides or one of the upper slides actuated by a plate cam and lever.

The holder for the cutoff blade is constructed so that the position of the blade can be reversed to permit cutting off by either direction of spindle rotation. The basic attachments are mounted on a ledge at the front of the spindle (to the left of the front cross slide) for the performance of overlapping operations such as slotting and drilling of holes in the cutoff end of a given part. The bracket supporting the arm for transferring the workpiece from the spindle to the attachment is mounted to the right of the front cross slide.

The bar of stock is automatically fed forward to the new cutting position after each piece has been completed. It is located by being butted up against a swing stop or turret stop. Coupled driving shafts, at the rear of the machine, are driven at constant speed through transposing gears, the positioning of which determines the direction of rotation and driveshaft speed.

Timing of idle movements of the machine such as indexing,

feeding stock, and reversing the spindle is governed by clutches mounted on the driving shaft. These clutches are actuated by trip levers and trip dogs which are adjustable on the dog carriers that rotate with the camshafts.

The main driveshaft supplies power through feed change gears to the lead wormshaft (in the machine bed), which operates the two front camshafts through separate worms and adjustable wormwheels. The turret is indexed from the driveshaft through an intermediate gear and a sliding gear, then through a simple Geneva movement to index the turret.

ATTACHMENTS FOR AUTOMATIC SCREW MACHINES

A number of standard and special attachments are available for use with these machines. The most frequently used standard attachments are the upper front slide, screw-slotting attachment, deburring attachment, turret drilling attachment, bar feed magazine, and thread-chasing attachment. In addition to these, many attachments are available that are designed to meet the particular requirements of the work to be produced. Examples of these attachments are cross milling, offset drilling, and combination cross-drill and turret milling attachments.

Magazine feeding attachments can also be applied for handling small parts and second-operation work. Second-operation magazines may be of circular type, chute type, trough type, hopper type, or other styles, as required by the work to be done.

Special milling attachments are frequently used. These may be mounted on the cross slide or held in the turret. A suitable motor-drive arrangement is provided for these special attachments. If a milling operation is required in exact relation to some other dimension of the blanks, it is possible to stop the spindle in a fixed relationship to a flat on hexagonal or square stock, drill a crosshole or mill, then index the spindle a fixed number of degrees, and repeat the cross-slide operation.

Special attachments have been designed for numerous operations such as broaching, splining, back countersinking, and assembling.

PROGRAMMABLE AUTOMATICS

Camless single-spindle automatics are programmed by toggle switches, pegboards, control drums, punched cards, or NC/CNC units. They are simple to set up, permit faster changeover, and provide considerable flexibility. As a result, they are being used more extensively than cam-controlled automatics for shorter run production requirements.

Toggle Switch Programming

Camless automatics made by one machine tool builder are called Programmed Turning Centers (PTC). Cycling is controlled by solid-state electronic logic with plug-in circuits and a built-in diagnostic system. Programming is done by simply flipping toggle switches on a sequence controller, with verification accomplished visually. Data can be added, deleted, or modified immediately. Automatic program loading, which permits the storage of a program in a tape cassette, is available as an option. Complete manual control for fast set up is standard.

Universal spindles on the hydraulically operated PTC machines accommodate either bar or chucking equipment. A fast-indexing, eight-tool turret with tool relief can be fed at any rate between 0.250-100 ipm (6.35-2540 mm/min) for any turret station. The turret slide, with a feed stroke of 7 1/2″ (190 mm), is rapid traversed at 300 ipm (7620 mm/min) and retracted at 600 ipm (15 240 mm/min).

Positions for up to four hydraulically fed cross slides are provided on each PTC machine. A forming and cutoff slide can be mounted in any of the four positions. A single-point, longitudinal turning slide can be installed in three of the positions. An electronic single-point threading unit can be mounted in two of the four positions, and a hydraulic tracing device on one slide. Cross-slide operations may be overlapped together and can be performed with any operation or successive operations of the turret slide.

Control Drum Programming

On a camless automatic made by another machine tool builder, the entire program is placed into a main control drum. Trip dogs positioned on this drum activate hydraulic control blocks and electrical switches which control the functions of the turret and cross slides. An additional control drum that can be preset out of the machine to further reduce setup time is offered as an option.

These drum-controlled automatics feature the ability to offset the turret. When single-point turning or boring from the turret, use of the offset eliminates withdrawal marks on the workpiece. The offset can also be used to control size. Once the turning or boring tool is clamped in its holder, all diametral size adjustments can be accomplished with the offset.

The turret slide on these drum-controlled machines carries an exchangeable turret with six or eight tool holes, and an exchangeable stop carrier for limiting the lengths of travel. Four hydraulically fed cross slides can be independently adjusted for travel and rate.

CNC Programming

Several machine tool builders offer camless single-spindle automatics with CNC units. One machine with a two-axis CNC unit features a turret mounted in a plane perpendicular to the bar stock that rotates on its axis to provide the X-axis cutting action normally achieved with cross slides. Longitudinal motion of the turret slide actuates the end-working tools. The eight-tool turret, an independent cutoff slide, and a retractable tailstock provide up to 11 tool functions. Pretooled turrets can be quickly interchanged.

Another builder offers a camless single-spindle automatic with a microcomputer control system that permits up to 94 different machining operations. A simple card data entry system is used for programming. The machines are equipped with four radial tool slides and an interchangeable eight-tool turret that accepts rotating tools in any station. A front compound cross slide can be equipped with a two-tool turret and hydraulic tracing unit. A d-c drive for optimum speed selection is also available.

With the microprocessor CNC offered on one single-spindle automatic, many part programs can be fed into the computer memory by means of previously punched tapes, by manual data input (MDI) or by means of a time-sharing terminal. Changeover from one program to another can be done in a few seconds by MDI commands. Programming is simplified by numerous subprograms that can be stored in the computer memory. These include rough and finish turning, thread chasing, and deep-hole drilling. Necessary geometric calculations for tool nose radii are carried out automatically, and the control can calculate the most economical position for turret indexing. Indexing logic of the machine (selecting the shortest route for turret indexing) permits the use of standard tool sets.

SWISS-TYPE AUTOMATIC SCREW MACHINES

The Swiss-type single-spindle automatic screw machine is not, strictly speaking, a screw machine, since it does not perform the ordinary screw jobs with the same facility as the conventional type of screw machine. Owing to the method by which the stock is fed, while rotating, by a sliding headstock through an adjustable carbide-lined guide bushing into the cutting tools, it should probably be known as a Swiss bushing-type or precision sliding-headstock automatic lathe. The Swiss-type automatic differs from the traditional automatic screw machine, which employs form tools, indexing turrets, and box tools, in that it uses single-point tools.

Machines commonly in use for instrument work have a range of 1/32 to 3/8" (0.8 to 9.5 mm) diam stock capacity and 1/32" to 2 3/4" (0.8 to 70 mm) turning lengths. Watch manufacturers employ smaller machines with a maximum stock capacity of 5/32" (4 mm) diam and a maximum length of 1 9/16" (40 mm). Other Swiss-type automatics are available with a maximum stock capacity of 1 1/4" (32 mm) diam and a maximum turning length of 9" (229 mm).

The Swiss-type automatic has distinct advantages over the conventional type of screw machine in that it is capable of producing long, slender, and complexly contoured parts with a high degree of accuracy. In the hands of a skilled operator, Swiss-type automatics have been known to repeat, over long periods of time, a total tolerance on diameters as close as 0.0002" (0.005 mm). Shoulder lengths have been held to a tolerance of 0.0005" (0.013 mm); however, a tolerance of 0.0008" (0.020 mm) is more practical.

A high quality of finish can be turned to a degree comparable to that of a ground finish using Swiss-type automatics. Therefore, the machines are invaluable when high-finish close-tolerance bearing surfaces are required on small shafts, such as those used in electric meters, watches, clocks, and other parts necessary for the instrument trade.

In addition to providing close tolerances and a high quality of finish, this class of machine is able to produce long, slender parts of extremely small diameters—down to about 0.005" (0.13 mm) diam. This is possible because the guide bushing, through which the bar to be turned must pass while rotating, can be adjusted to practically eliminate all radial movement. Best results are obtained by using centerless-ground stock as round as possible and uniform in its diameter throughout each bar length, although drawn wire to a total tolerance of 0.0003" (0.008 mm) is usually sufficient for critical applications.

CAM-CONTROLLED MACHINES

Movements on a typical cam-controlled Swiss-type automatic are shown diagrammatically in Fig. 30-4. A toolframe

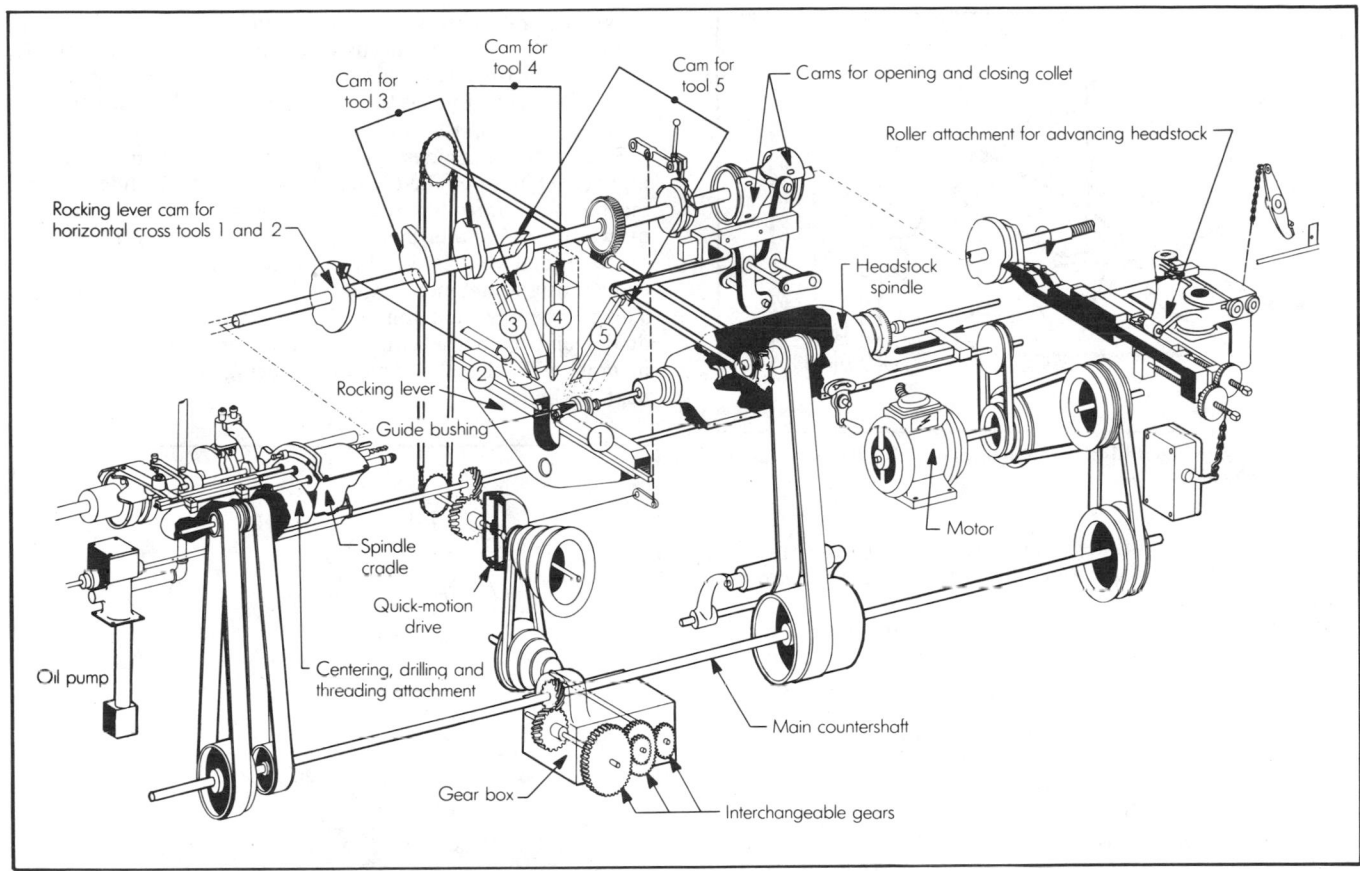

Fig. 30-4 Diagram of movements on a cam-controlled Swiss-type automatic.

mounted vertically on the machine bed carries five toolslides that are arranged like a fan and directed toward a common center and the work area. Tools 1 and 2, mounted on a cam-actuated rocking lever, are used for turning most surfaces. Tools 3, 4, and 5, each actuated by an individual cam, are generally used for chamfering, undercutting, cutting off, spotting, boring, back and front recessing, and knurling. A stationary or rotating guide bushing is the common device used to support the bar stock properly at this point. Movements of the tools are only toward the center.

All actual motion or feeding for turning operations is provided by the moving headstock. The headstock, with the material-gripping device, is located behind the toolframe, with the headstock spindle perfectly aligned with the guide bushing, and slides on a bed. Tools mounted in the frame have minimum overhang from the guide bushing at all times, regardless of the length to be turned. The use of a ground bushing and centerless-ground workpiece material permits the relationship between the cutting edge of the tool and the centerline of the bar to be maintained within 0.0002" (0.005 mm), thus ensuring close tolerances on workpieces.

Straight turning of a cylindrical shape is accomplished by presenting a tool at a given diameter and feeding the headstock forward, thus feeding the stock past the tool for the length to be turned. Tapers, spheres, or any other shapes can be generated by combining movements of the tool and headstock.

CNC MACHINES

Swiss-type automatics with CNC eliminate the need for cams, minimize setup times and necessary operator skill, and are being used extensively for lower volume production requirements. Another important advantage of machines equipped with CNC is that the restriction to 360° layouts on cam-controlled machines is eliminated. This permits operations to be performed that are difficult or impossible to perform on cam-controlled machines. These operations include certain deep-hole drilling, single-point threading (both left and right-hand), taper cutting, and contouring.

Swiss-type automatics with CNC made by one machine tool builder have simultaneous two-axis control for the X-axis toolholder and the Z-axis headstock. This permits straight, taper, and circular turning, as well as threading. Five toolholders, arranged in a radial configuration on these machines, are controlled by a servodisc (see Fig. 30-5) that comes with the machines and does not have to be designed and built. Programmed signals from the CNC unit command the disc to select the predetermined toolholders, which travel the required distances by rotation of the disc.

The sliding headstock on these machines has a hydraulic chucking device that carries the bar stock longitudinally. Advancement and retraction of the headstock is controlled by a servomotor which rotates a ballscrew for travel in increments of 0.00004" (0.0010 mm). The machine spindle is driven by an a-c

SWISS TYPE AUTOMATIC SCREW MACHINES

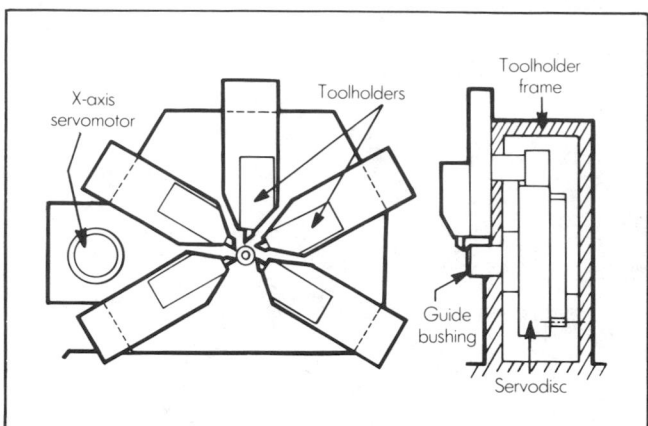

Fig. 30-5 Servodisc controls five toolholders on this CNC Swiss automatic (*Hirschmann Corp.*)

motor and provides infinitely variable, programmable speeds. A standard self-diagnostic function in the CNC unit permits fast troubleshooting.

Attachments similar to those described for the cam-controlled automatics are available for the CNC machines. These include cross milling and drilling attachments, rotary guide bushings, and automatic bar feeders. Also available is a sliding attachment with four dead (nonrotating) spindles that moves laterally (front to back) and provides single-spindle back-drilling capability. Each spindle is positioned by hydraulic cylinder and locator screw.

Different designs of Swiss-type automatics are offered by other machine tool builders. With one design (see Fig. 30-6), movements of the toolslides are individually controlled by ballscrews. This permits repeatability of toolslide positioning within 0.00005″ (0.0013 mm).

On another machine, there are no radial slides. Tooling is mounted on two five-tool turrets, one turret being indexed while tools on the other turret are cutting. On this machine, the headstock is fixed, but the guide bushing is mounted on a slanted carriage and moves with the tools.

Another builder offers a machine with a 12 station, 30° slanted, universal turret with servocontrolled movement in the X axis. The Z-axis movement is derived from a servocontrolled sliding headstock. The headstock spindle provides for the C axis which permits (in conjunction with the turret tools) cross-machining operations. A four-position endworking attachment with lateral tool positioning is also provided.

Some CNC machines permit programming by manual data input (MDI) or punched tape. The six radial toolslides on one machine are controlled by two axes, allowing simultaneous use of two tools. Another machine allows independent movement of six radial toolslides, the headstock, and a four-spindle endworking attachment. Any five of the eight programmable axes can be operated simultaneously at varying feed rates. A dual memory in the control permits production from one memory while the second memory is being programmed for the next workpiece.

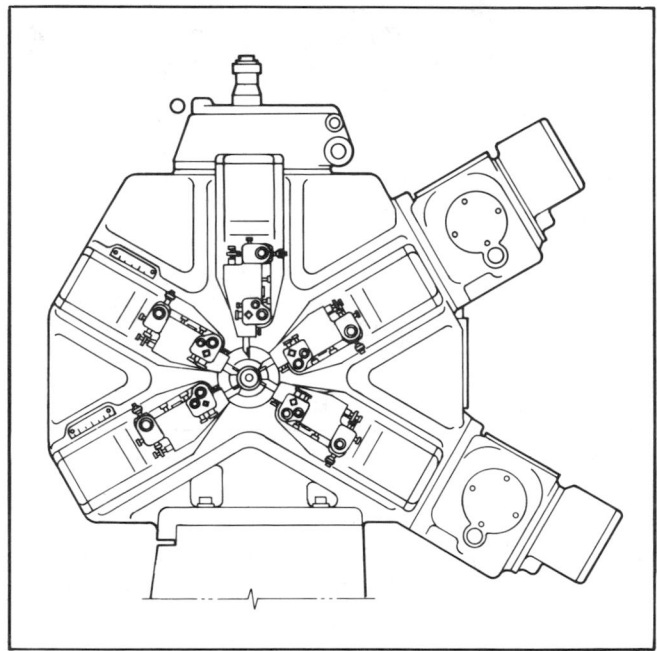

Fig. 30-6 Individual ballscrews permit precise positioning of toolslides. (*Nomura, Inc.*)

MULTIPLE-SPINDLE AUTOMATIC BAR AND CHUCKING MACHINES

The principal advantage of the multiple-spindle automatic over the single-spindle machine is the reduction in time required per piece. In contrast to the single-spindle machine, on which one turret face at a time is working on one spindle, the multiple-spindle machine has each turret or end-slide tool working on its respective spindle at the same time. While on the single-spindle machine the time required to complete one piece is a total of the time needed for each turret operation plus the times necessary to index the turret; on the multiple-spindle machine, the time necessary for one cycle is the time required only for the longest single cut plus idle time.

The range of work produced by the multiple-spindle machine is comparable to that produced by lathes, single-spindle bar machines, and turret lathes. Because of its longer setup time and increased tooling cost, the multiple-spindle machine is generally less economical than the other three on short runs; however, it is more economical on long runs. Changeover time has been reduced on modern multiple-spindle automatics by features such as preset tooling, master collets and pushers which accept different stock sizes, magazine-fed bar feeders which feed stock into the reel tubes without stopping the machine, quadrant mechanisms which permit changing tooling strokes by adjustments instead of changing cams, and machine sequencing by programmable controller. Multiple-spindle machines lend them-

MULTIPLE-SPINDLE AUTOMATIC BAR AND CHUCKING MACHINES

selves well to the application of special fixtures and attachments that may eliminate secondary operations on the work.

CLASSIFICATION OF MACHINES

There are five general features by which multiple-spindle automatic bar and chucking machines are classified. To identify any machine properly, all five must be used. The five classifications are as follows:

1. Method of chucking.
2. Capacity.
3. Arrangement of spindles.
4. Number of spindles.
5. Method of indexing.

Method of Chucking

The method of chucking distinguishes bar-type machines and chucking machines from each other. Bar-type machines employ collets—push, draw, or stationary types. Although the collet actuation is usually automatic, the machines may be arranged to permit manual actuation in the case of second-operation work. Chucking machines may be equipped with any type of workholding fixture within the machine capacity. Hydraulic chucking or automated mechanical chucking frequently allows the use of automatic loading and unloading devices. Manual or hydraulic chucking may be employed when the operator loads and unloads the machine.

Capacity

The capacity of a bar-type machine is the maximum diameter of stock that can be fed through the spindle, limited by the capacity of the feed fingers. It is possible to run over-capacity, round bar stock by using a roller feed mechanism, which eliminates the need for feed fingers. Square, hexagonal, and other extruded-shape bars can also be run, providing they fit within the cross-section of the round stock.

On second-operation (chucking type) work for which the feed fingers are not used, the collet-type machine usually chucks a slightly larger diameter than the rated capacity and the portion of the work extending from the collet into the tooling zone may be larger still. The capacity of the multiple-spindle chucking machine is limited by the center distance between spindles.

Other capacities are the maximum length of stock feed and the maximum length that can be turned. The maximum length of stock feed is the longest piece of work that the bar-type machine can automatically feed out and cut off. The maximum length that can be turned is generally governed by the stroke of the endworking toolslide that must make the turning cut, withdraw, and clear the work before the machine indexes for the next cycle. Extra length can be turned, however, with the use of auxiliary spindles.

Arrangment of Spindles

On indexing-type machines, spindles are arranged radially about the endworking toolslide (see Fig. 30-7). One type of machine, with the spindles arranged vertically, is used primarily for simpler work. Each spindle on vertical-spindle machines has one end working position and two cross slides, one of which must be used for cutting off. The endworking slide can be tooled for drilling, boring, or turning; and one cross slide can be tooled for light forming or chamfering. If two pieces can be made per spindle, both cross slides are tooled for cutting off. The advantage of this machine is the added production. Each cycle

Fig. 30-7 Cross slides, end slide, and spindle arrangements for multiple-spindle machines. (*National Acme Co.*)

MULTIPLE-SPINDLE AUTOMATIC BAR AND CHUCKING MACHINES

of the machine produces four pieces.

Number of Spindles

The number of spindles on a multispindle machine is ordinarily four, five, six, or eight, varying with the manufacturer. An eight-spindle machine produces the average part faster than a four or six-spindle machine, within certain limitations. The advantages of a machine with the greater number of spindles are the greater variety of work that can be produced, the possibility of producing more than one piece per cycle, and a better quality of work obtainable by using roughing and finishing cuts on all surfaces to be machined.

Method of Indexing

The method of indexing on bar machines is usually one position per cycle, with work being performed on each spindle in every position. Chucking machines are similarly indexed one position per cycle with one position being an idle station for loading and unloading. With automatic loading and unloading, it is often beneficial to load and unload in separate stations when possible since this simplifies the mechanisms required.

Double indexing (indexing the spindle two positions per cycle) is often employed on six and eight-spindle chucking machines. Double-index chucking machines require two idle spindle positions equipped with chuck-operating mechanisms that serve as the load and unload positions. Position 1 is the load and unload station when the workpiece is being machined in the odd-numbered positions. The part is unloaded from position 1, inverted, and loaded into position 2 so that machining may be performed on the other end of the workpiece in the even-numbered positions. Bar machines can utilize feed-out in two positions as well as double index.

Multiple-spindle bar or chucking machines may also have the work or tool rotating, but the usual type has only the work rotating. The advantage of tool rotation is the ability to control the surface speed of the individual tool when the work has a large differential in diameters being turned.

CONSTRUCTION FEATURES OF MACHINES

Shown in Fig. 30-8 is a side view of a six-spindle bar machine, the principal operating features and general construction of which are common to all multiple-spindle bar machines. Chucking machines have much the same design, with the exception of the spindles and elimination of the stock feed mechanism.

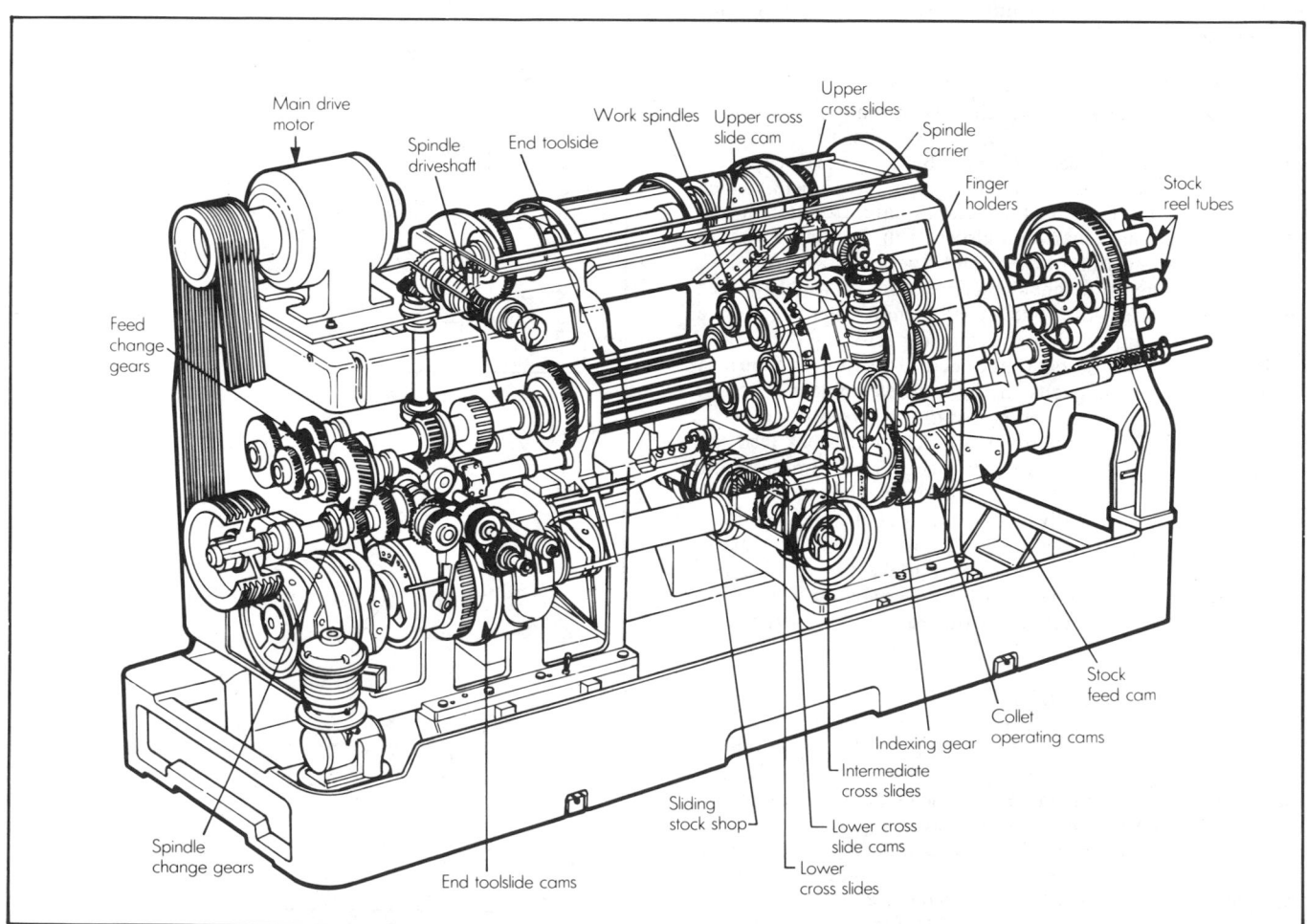

Fig. 30-8 Six-spindle automatic bar machine. (*National Acme Co.*)

TOOLS AND ATTACHMENTS

The actual cutting tools applied to workpieces on multiple-spindle machines are the same as those used on single-spindle automatics and turret lathes. Single-point and forming tools may be used; in fact, most setups show a combination of both. The cutting tools on one make of automatic may generally be used on any other, provided the machine capacities are the same.

The design of the multiple-spindle automatic permits the use of a number of special attachments that may increase production, eliminate secondary operations, or improve machine performance. Operations such as threading, tapping, eccentric drilling, contour turning, thread chasing, thread milling, thread rolling, knurling, spiral grooving, burnishing, stenciling, stamping, broaching, polygon milling, and many others may be performed on the automatic by the use of special attachments.

Identifying part numbers, trademarks, etc., may be impressed onto the outer diameter of the work by the use of a stencil roll and holder mounted on the cross slide and advanced into the work so that the stamping tool makes one revolution in contact with the work. Stamping may also be performed from the endworking slide by a stamp held in a spindle rotating at the same speed as the work spindle.

CENTER DRILLING AND FACING MACHINES

The center drilling and facing machine is a multifunction machine now used extensively for shaft-type workpieces. The importance of center drilling is often overlooked, probably because the centers usually have no function once the workpieces are completed. Accuracy of the centers, however, has a major effect on tolerances that can be maintained in subsequent operations, such as turning, grinding, and hobbing, where the centers must be used for location.

CENTER DRILLING

Most workpieces which require centering are repositioned, end-for-end on centers when they are manufactured. For the features machined on both ends of the workpieces to be in proper relationship, the distance between centers must be maintained accurately. This dictates the use of a machine that drills both ends at once and that consistently and accurately repeats the end-cutting operations.

Axes of the centers must be coincident, and the centers must be round and have a reasonably good finish. Failure to achieve these conditions results in imperfect contact between the countersunk holes and the machine centers.

PLUNGE FACING AND CENTERING MACHINES

These machines consist of a fixed main head and a bed, both mounted on a base. Mounted on the bed is another head that is adjustable along the length of the bed and a workholding device. Each head has a spindle mounted in a quill which feeds out of the head by mechanical, electrical, or hydraulic means.

Each spindle is rotated by its own motor-driven gear train, which includes change gears for speed changes. Standard automatic machines are available with 18-240" (457-6096 mm) length capacities and 5-25 hp (3.7-18.6 kW) motors per head. Two independent feed-cycle cams are provided: one for rapid traverse that operates at the end of the cutting cycle, and one for feed that is set by a graduated dial for proper depth of cut.

Workholding devices usually consist of a pair of self-centering vises, but special fixtures are employed for non-cylindrical and other workpieces.

MILLING AND CENTERING MACHINES

These machines consist of a base having ways on which two cross-sliding heads and a workholding means (usually two heavy-duty self-centering vises) are mounted. Both heads have two quill-mounted spindles, one for drilling and the other for milling.

The drilling quills are power fed in and out. The milling quills are manually adjustable for cutter position. They may incorporate cutter relief at the end of the face-milling strokes and/or offer provision for cutter advance to furnish rough and finish-milling capability. Both heads are mounted on ways that are transverse to the bedways. Fixed stops position the drilling spindles central with the workpiece, while variable stops are set to return the milling cutters at the conclusion of the operation.

Standard milling and centering machines are available with milling cutter capacities to 15" (381 mm), length capacities to 240" (6096 mm), and milling-spindle drive motors of 10-40 hp (7.5-29.8 kW) per head. The machine illustrated in Fig. 15-35 is equipped with 8" (203 mm) diam milling cutters and 25 hp (18.6 kW) drive motors.

HORIZONTAL BORING MACHINES

Boring, the machining process for removing metal from internal cylindrical surfaces, is performed on many different machine tools.

CHARACTERISTIC MACHINE FEATURES

Horizontal boring machines (HBM's) usually do many other operations besides boring, especially milling. As a result, they are often called horizontal boring mills or horizontal boring, milling, drilling, and tapping machines. These heavy-duty machines are employed extensively for large, complex castings, forgings, weldments, and similar workpieces. They perform different operations at various locations on the workpieces without the need for changing the basic setup, and they can maintain accurate relationships between the machined surfaces. These machines are not, however, high-production machines and are generally limited to low to medium size runs.

Characteristic features of HBM's include the following:

1. Horizontal spindles that rotate the cutting tools.
2. Horizontal surfaces on which workpieces are mounted.
3. Power feed of the spindle to advance cutting tools into the workpieces.
4. Power-fed relative motion between the spindle and workpiece in at least two axes perpendicular to the

HORIZONTAL BORING MACHINES

spindle axis.
5. Power saddle feed parallel to the spindle axis.
6. Outboard supports, on some machines, for the ends of line boring bars and arbor-mounted slotting cutters.

Horizontal boring machines are available in a wide range of capacities. The size of a machine is often identified by the diameter of its spindle, which generally varies from 3-10″ (76-254 mm). Spindle rigidity is directly related to the fourth power of its diameter. As a result, considerable additional cutting power is obtainable with larger spindle diameters. Main drive motors range from 15-75 hp (11.2-56 kW) or more.

TYPES OF HBM's

Various designs of horizontal boring machines are available. Three major designs are table, planer, and floor-type machines. They are also available in traveling-bar and traveling-head types. With respect to boring only (excluding milling and other operations), they can be classified as stub boring or line boring machines. Stub boring is done with a bar supported only by the spindle. Line boring is done with a bar that extends through the workpiece and is supported at one or more points in addition to the machine spindle. Cross-feed column machines are also available, providing the column with two axes of travel: one perpendicular to the spindle travel and the other parallel to the spindle travel.

Table-Type Machines

In table-type machines (see Fig. 30-9), the table feeds horizontally on saddle ways both parallel and at right angles to the spindle axis. On machines having a long table travel perpendicular to the spindle support, additional outboard supports on runways are often provided. The headstock moves

vertically on the column, and the spindle has a horizontal feed motion. This type of machine is well suited to general-purpose work for which other machining operations are required in addition to boring.

Planer-Type Machines

These horizontal boring machines are similar to the table-type design except that they have no table-supporting saddle. The table travel is at right angles to the spindle along the base ways. Feed perpendicular to the table (parallel to the spindle) is obtained by feed motion of the spindle. Feed motion of the column along the base ways is used when exceptional rigidity is required to maintain accuracy in machining long and heavy work. A horizontal-spindle planer-type boring machine equipped with CNC and a rotary table is shown in Fig. 30-10.

Floor-Type, Traveling-Column Machines

These machines (see Fig. 30-11) use a stationary floor plate equipped with T-slots instead of a table to hold the work. They are ordinarily used to handle large workpieces of a weight, size, or shape that would make it impractical to employ a reciprocating table. Horizontal feeds perpendicular to the spindle axis are obtained by movement of the column along the base ways rather than by table movement. The headstock moves vertically on the column, and the spindle has a horizontal feed motion. On some machines of this type, the column is mounted on a saddle providing an additional motion parallel to the spindle axis.

Portable Machines

This type of machine is used when it is more convenient to move the machine to the workpiece. Such machines are used inside large vessels and/or to repair assembled components of large mechanisms in place.

Traveling-Bar Machines

Traveling-bar, heavy-duty horizontal boring machines consist essentially of a headstock containing a motor and gear reduction unit giving rotary motion to the bar or spindle. A transmission unit is also included giving feed and rapid traverse

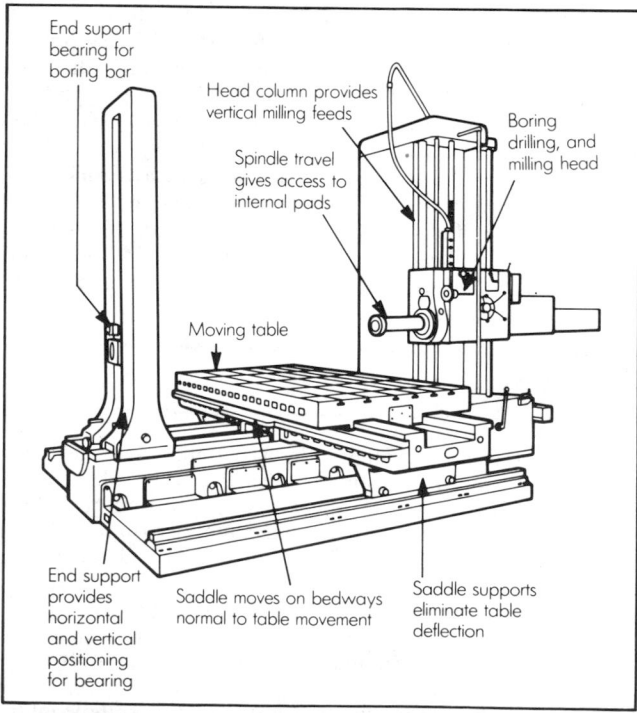

Fig. 30-9 Table-type horizontal boring, drilling, and milling machine with end support for line boring operations.

End suport bearing for boring bar

Head column provides vertical milling feeds

Spindle travel gives access to internal pads

Boring drilling, and milling head

Moving table

End support provides horizontal and vertical positioning for bearing

Saddle moves on bedways normal to table movement

Saddle supports eliminate table deflection

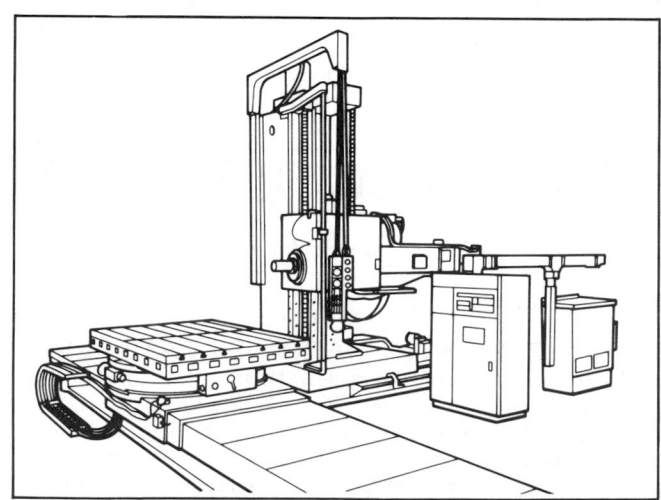

Fig. 30-10 Planer-type horizontal boring machine equipped with rotary table. (*Cincinnati Gilbert Machine Tool Co.*)

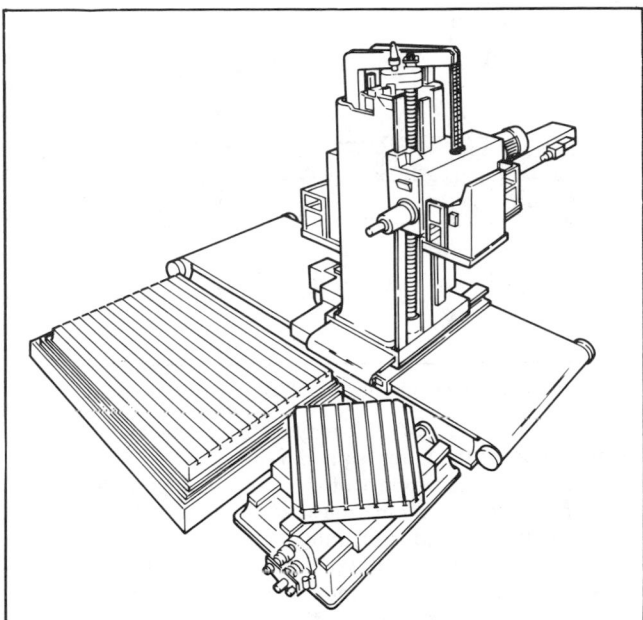

Fig. 30-11 Floor-type horizontal boring machine. (*Gray Div., Warner & Swasey Co.*)

motion, in and out, to the bar. An outboard support is used to support the bar after the bar has been positioned through the bore of the workpiece. A boring head is added and clamped securely to the bar; feeding motion is then given to the bar through means in the headstock. This type of heavy-duty horizontal boring machine has one disadvantage in that it must occupy floor space almost three times its own length because of the length of the boring bar.

Traveling-Head Machines

Traveling-head machines are essentially the same as traveling-bar machines except that the boring bar contains a screw attached by a nut to the boring head and derives its feed motion from a planetary-type gearbox attached to the outboard or inboard end of the boring bar. The headstock supplies power to rotate the bar while the feed mechanism on the bar imparts feed and rapid traverse to the boring head. For loading and unloading the workpiece, the boring head may be locked securely to the outboard support. An air motor is attached to a coupling on the outboard end of the screw; and with a rolling dolly to support the boring bar, the bar is traversed to a loading position and returned to operating position after work loading is completed.

When split workpieces such as some housings and casings are machined, the lower half of the workpiece is positioned on supports under the boring bar. The bar is then lowered onto pedestal supports and the upper half of the workpiece is bolted to its lower half, with the boring bar inside the workpiece.

This machine requires floor space twice its own length and then only when loading and unloading a workpiece. Constant sag is maintained in the boring bar between two supports because the boring head feeds over the bar. A traveling-support head may be used when long holes are to be bored to fairly close tolerances.

Toolchanging HBM's

Many builders of horizontal boring machines offer automatic toolchangers as an option. This places the machines in the class of machining centers, discussed subsequently in this chapter.

MACHINE CONTROLS

Horizontal boring machines are still built for manual operation, but most are now supplied with manual data input (MDI) or CNC for relative positioning between the cutting tool and workpiece. Digital readout units are used extensively on manually controlled machines.

MDI Controls

Manual data input controllers provide a simple and more economical alternative to CNC for small-lot production. With these controllers, the machine operator places required dimensional, feed, and speed data into the control by means of dials or switches. Once the command data is entered, the operator pushes a button and the machine automatically moves to the commanded position in the prescribed manner. The next data is then entered, the button is pushed again, and so on until the workpiece is completed.

Controllers with MDI are now available with electronic, integrated memory systems. The control/memory unit automatically records each operating sequence instructed by the machine operator. Sequence numbers are automatically assigned to each operation. Program instructions can also be entered manually, viewed, and/or edited. In most cases, in order to retain maximum operator control, feed rates and spindle speeds are not stored.

In the automatic mode, a stored program operates the controller and machine. The controller operates block by block, stopping at the completion of each block. Information for the next block is displayed, so the operator can change feed rates and spindle speeds as required. Displayed programs can be modified without changing the stored programs. The stored programs can be transferred to any compatible storage medium, such as tape cassettes, punched paper tape, or hard copy. Prerecorded program tapes can be loaded into storage.

CNC Units

Horizontal boring machines equipped with CNC can produce slopes, circles, arcs, and complex shapes. Most HBM's have four motions under CNC. On table-type machines, the spindle, head, table, and saddle are controlled; on planer-type machines, the spindle, head, table, and column are controlled; and on floor-type machines, the spindle, head, column, and on certain machines, the saddle.

Slide motions on horizontal boring machines with CNC are generally identified as follows:

- X axis ..... Table, horizontal.
- Y axis ..... Head, vertical.
- Z axis ..... Spindle.
- W axis .... Saddle, column, or rotary table on slide.
- A axis ..... Rotary table tilt.
- B axis ..... Rotary table, horizontal.
- C axis ..... Rotary table, vertical.

SETUP AND OPERATION OF HBM's

Rigid setups, with adequate bar support and proper fixtures, are critical to performing successful operations on horizontal boring machines. The most successful boring operations are

HORIZONTAL BORING MACHINES

performed when there is adequate rigidity in all elements, including the machine.

Bar Support

In horizontal boring machines, the workpieces are normally stationary during machining operations, but the workpieces are sometimes moved on rotary index tables. Cutting tools are mounted on various types of boring bars that transmit motion, and power is imparted to them from the machine spindle. The method of bar support varies to suit the length of bar required to reach the surface to be machined, the accessibility of the bore, and the degree of precision or finish required.

Stub bars are supported only at the spindle end and are used to bore holes that may be positioned comparatively close to the headstock. Blind holes do not permit extension of a line bar through the work to an end support, and ordinarily a stub bar must be employed. Line bars extend through the workpiece and require some form of support external to the spindle. Generally, an end support (see Fig. 30-12, view *a*) is used for this purpose, since it may be readily brought into alignment by a simple adjustment of its bearing block.

The use of the workpiece for bar support (Fig. 30-13, view *b*) may sometimes be preferable or necessary. In certain types of blind holes with lateral holes that permit inspection of the cutter, the finished bore behind the cutter may be bushed to bar size. This procedure is also used when some form of support between the machine spindle and the end column is required and when the workpiece obstructs the use of fixture bearings at points of necessary support. Although the use of the workpiece for bar support usually consumes more machining time and in

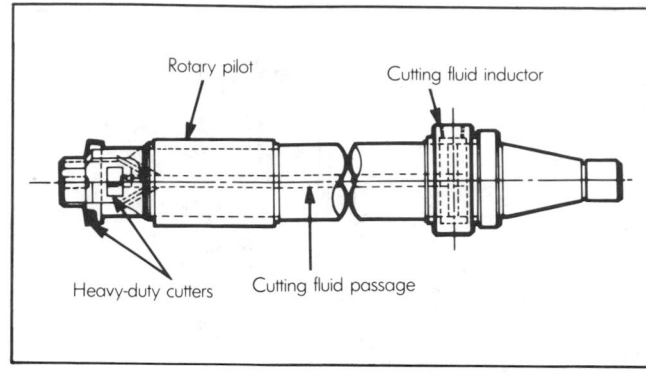

Fig. 30-13 Rotary-piloted boring bar. (*Muskegon Tool Industries*)

most cases is not desirable, it may be preferable over a fixture when the cost of the latter is prohibitive.

When workpiece support of the bar is not possible, a back rotary-pilot support is sometimes used, especially for deep-hole boring. A stub tool can be employed to bore the starting hole and then replaced with a piloted boring bar. A better method is to use a stationary bushing, mounted on a machine underarm support or in its own support on the machine table, to guide the piloted boring tool.

Back-piloted boring bars (see Fig. 30-13) have a rotary pilot behind the cutting tools. The bars hold at least one rough-boring cutter, followed by a finishing cutter. The pilot is designed to remain stationary in relation to the workpiece, with the bar revolving in the pilot. Proper clearance between the pilot and workpiece is essential to prevent jamming. A supply of cutting fluid through the tool is necessary for extended tool life.

Back-piloted bars for operation in blind holes are designed to permit chips to escape through the centers of the hollow bars. If the hole is large enough, this can be accomplished by providing a bronze roller pilot on which wear strips are mounted. Otherwise, wear pads are mounted directly on the bar and rotate on the ID of the bore instead of remaining stationary. High-pressure cutting fluid, forced over the bar, flushes chips back through the center of the hollow bar.

Boring Fixtures

When the need arises, boring fixtures are used to support and at the same time align the bar at the proper position preparatory to a boring operation. In general, they are used to increase the productivity of the machine when large quantities are involved. Best applications of fixtures simplify the setup and facilitate any subsequent shifting of the work on the table to a new position during the machining. Boring fixtures are of distinct advantage in producing work involving the duplication of center distances.

Most applications favor two bearing supports for every bar position in the fixture. Thus, the fixture is responsible for bar alignment and eliminates the need for close adjustments of the headstock. A floating adapter connection between bar and spindle is generally used to compensate for small differences in alignment between the axis of the fixture bearings and the spindle. The fixture bearings are usually the sleeve type, made of cast iron, hardened steel, bronze, or bearing alloy to suit the hardness of the bar and the probable length of service of the fixture. Antifriction bearings are to be preferred when center distances and first costs allow for this more expensive construction, or when high surface speeds tend to cause heat resulting from friction which may cause the bar to seize and score.

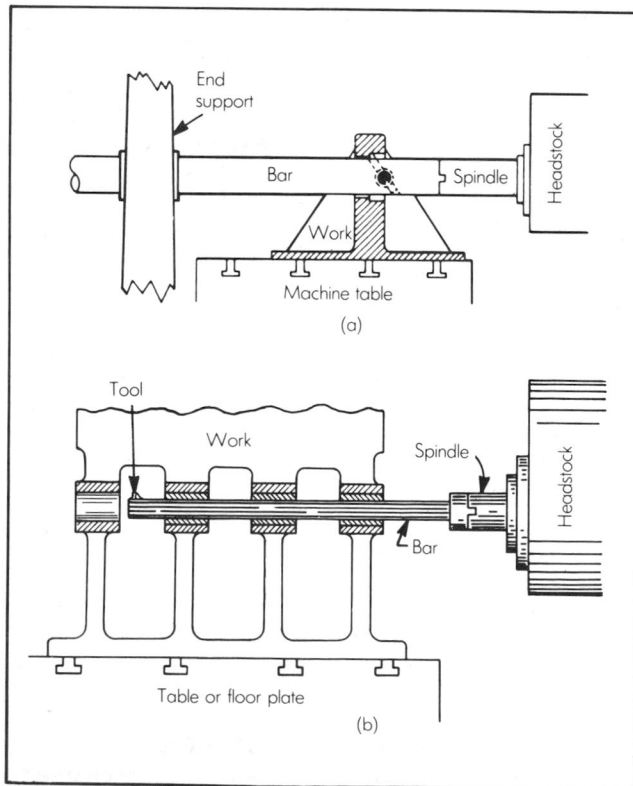

Fig. 30-12 Support of boring bar by: (a) end-support column and (b) workpiece.

VERTICAL BORING MACHINES AND TURRET LATHES

With NC machines, many line-boring operations are being performed by saddle feeding of the workpiece. This reduces the need for line bars or fixtures.

Combined Operations

Combined machining operations are typical on horizontal boring machine. Figure 30-14 shows the application of two continuous-feed facing and boring heads set up on a line bar, one head at each end of a workpiece. The use of two heads eliminates the need to turn the work after one end is machined and gives a common center. Such a tooling arrangement is warranted when large quantities are involved, since the machining time is approximately half that required when only one head is used. This is a good example of boring, counterboring, and facing operations being performed in one setup.

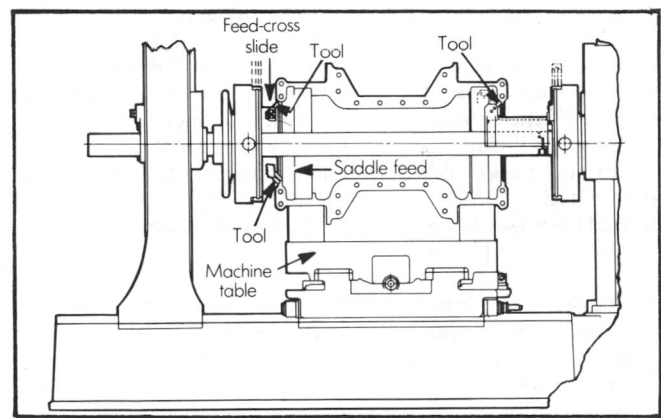

Fig. 30-14 Boring and facing both ends of axle housings using two continuous-feed heads.

VERTICAL BORING MACHINES AND TURRET LATHES

Vertical boring machines (VBM's), such as the one shown in Fig. 30-15, and vertical turret lathes (VTL's) (Fig. 30-16) are turning machines that in many ways are similar to conventional lathes turned on end. Workpieces are mounted on a horizontal table or chuck rotating about a vertical axis. Cutting tools, which are generally nonrotating, are fed horizontally or vertically into the workpieces.

Operations performed on a VBM or VTL are similar to those done on conventional lathes. They include turning, facing, boring, grooving, generating threads, and contouring. These machines are commonly used to make round parts having short lengths in relation to their diameters and to make large, heavy, and cumbersome parts.

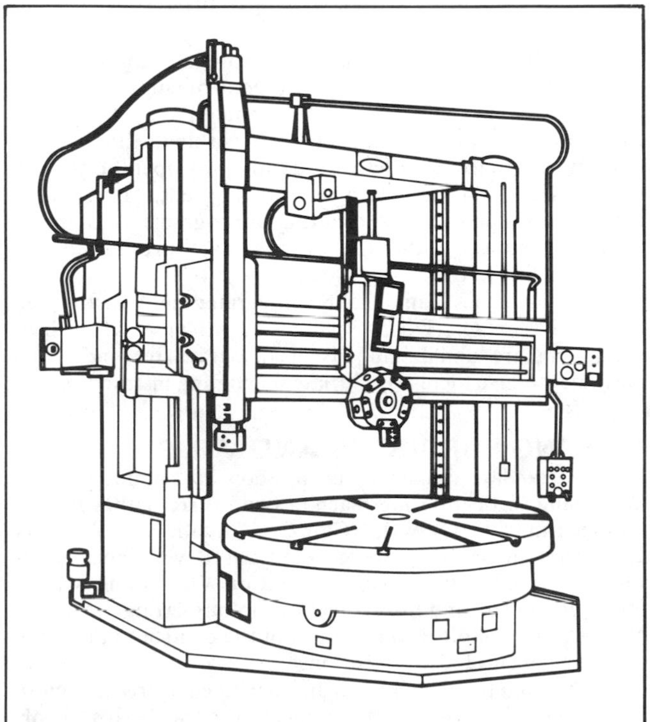

DIFFERENCES BETWEEN VBM'S AND VTL'S

Vertical boring machines (or mills) originally had one or two ram-type heads, while VTL's had a turret-type head. Since modern machines frequently combine the two types of heads and many ram heads now have indexable turrets, the historical distinction between the two machines has less validity than before. Also, the basic construction, tooling, workholding, controls, and operation of the machines are essentially the

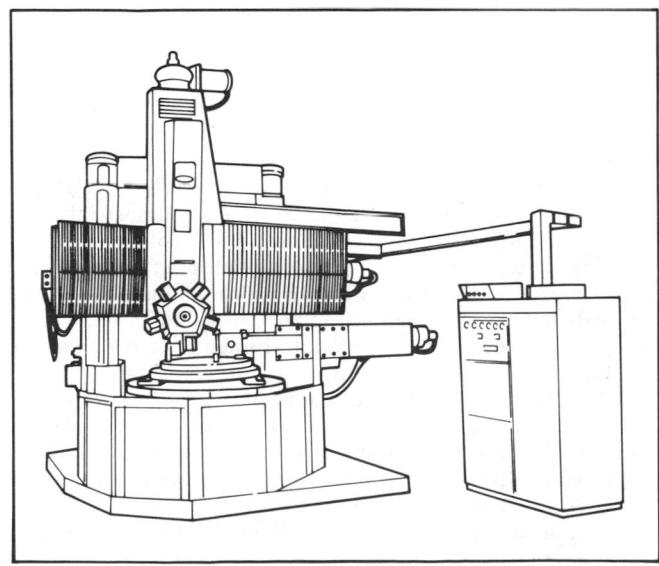

Fig. 30-15 Vertical boring machine. (*Bullard Co.*)

Fig. 30-16 Vertical turret lathe with CNC. (*Bullard Co.*)

VERTICAL BORING MACHINES AND TURRET LATHES

same. To avoid confusion, the term "vertical turning machine" is sometimes used for both machine types.

Some machine builders and users distinguish between a VBM and VTL based on machine size and, to a lesser extent, the volume of the production run. Loosely defined, a machine is called a VTL if it handles workpiece sizes to 100″ (2540 mm) diam; for workpieces above that diameter, the machine is designated a VBM. To some extent, VBM's are often characterized by one-of-a-kind and small-lot production requirements; but they can be tooled for long production runs.

ADVANTAGES OF THE MACHINES

An important advantage of VBM's and VTL's is the ease with which large or heavy workpieces can be set up and held. Gravity is the key to the relative ease of work handling with these machines. It is easier to place workpieces on the horizontal table top than it is to mount them on horizontal-spindle machines. The weight of heavy workpieces is distributed uniformly downward through the bearings and absorbed in the massive bases of the machines. This ensures accurate machining, even at relatively high cutting speeds; reduces chatter; and permits high metal-removal rates.

Another advantage of these machines involves applications that require indicating for quality assurance during job setup. The horizontal table presents workers with a surface on which parts may be set up, adjusted, and leveled without preliminary strapping.

Vertical boring machines and turret lathes provide increased workpiece accessibility and reduced floor-space requirements compared to horizontal-spindle lathes of similar machining capability. Through the use of counterbalances applied to the top of the worktable, they have the ability to easily balance irregular or off-center workloads and to eliminate excessive centrifugal force or radial thrust load.

CONTROLS FOR VBM'S AND VTL'S

Vertical boring machines and turret lathes can be operated in a number of modes, including manual, automatic, and numerically controlled. Manual operation is really semiautomatic, typically involving a worker using a swing-away pendant control to direct basic machine movements or a worker directing the same motions from a floor-mounted control. Handwheels can also be provided on these machines, although axis feeds generally operate under power even in a manual machine.

Automatic Controls

Machines equipped with automatic controls or cycling devices for each head can be set up for an almost infinite number of different production jobs. Most control devices permit the automatic cycle to be interrupted at any point, so the machine can be manually operated without disturbing the automatic setup. The machine can be returned to its automatic cycle at the point at which it was interrupted or at any point in the cycle desired by the operator.

Automatic controls consist of a memory device which is set up for a predetermined sequence of operations. These include machine functions such as feed and traverse rates, dwell, feed and traverse direction, speed changes, start/stop, and turret index. A function drum with locating holes filled by pins arranged in various sequences is an example of such a device.

Automatic controls also incorporate detectors for the horizontal and vertical movements of the heads. These detectors

work in cooperation with the memory unit to control the exact limit of head travel and to initiate the next function required for the job.

In operation, the memory or function device is preset for the job and the detectors are set during the actual machining of the first piece (or a finished piece is used as a master gage). At the completion of the first machining operations, heads return to their start position by the shortest path and the control mechanism automatically indexes to a zero or neutral position, ready for the next cycle.

Tracer Controls

Tracer controls are also available for vertical boring machines and turret lathes. This mode of control drives both vertical and horizontal feed motions to accurately follow a stylus tracing a template, providing a means to machine complicated shapes without using form tools or NC/CNC units.

NC/CNC Units

Point-to-point NC is a digital electronic system which directs the motions of the machine from coded signals on punched tape. It may also control various auxiliary operations, such as selecting tools, feed rates, spindle speeds, and the flow of cutting fluid.

This form of control moves the cutting tool(s) to prescribed points at preset feed rates, thus permitting orthogonal machining only. Accuracy of the motions depends on the resolution (least permissible increment) of the electronic system and the accuracy of the position feedback devices on each axis.

Most NC units have digital switches through which commands to the control may be entered manually, instead of being inserted by tape. Point-to-point NC has been used less extensively on VBM's and VTL's than contouring, computerized numerical control (CNC), which permits greater machine flexibility and control.

CNC offers continuous-path contouring capability by providing velocity and displacement control continuously for all machine motions. As a result, tool(s) may be moved continuously along any prescribed path within the limits of the machine. CNC also handles various auxiliary operations, such as the selection of tools, feed rates, and speeds. Manual data input features permit on-site editing of programs in computer memory and the punching of new part program tapes corresponding to the changes.

These machines can also be integrated into distributed numerical control (DNC) systems in which a larger host computer stores and downloads part programs into individual machines to give them appropriate machining instructions.

TOOLING FOR VBM'S AND VTL'S

Basic, standard classes of cutting tools are commonly used for tooling vertical boring machines and turret lathes for the average run of parts. With NC or CNC, qualified toolholders and preset inserts that are generally used with horizontal-spindle NC/CNC lathes can be used on VBM's and VTL's. Such toolholders and inserts reduce tool presetting downtime by using the tool offset capabilities of the control to make the final adjustments for tool position.

As the quantity of parts to be machined increases, more attention should be paid to multiple tooling setups. Tools should be laid out for optimum use of each turret face. Step, gang, form, multiple, or magazine-type tooling significantly

VERTICAL BORING MACHINES AND TURRET LATHES

decreases cutting time per workpiece.

Automatic Toolchanging

Many builders of VBM's offer automatic toolchangers. One design (see Fig. 30-17) consists of a 12-tool storage drum with pockets coded for tool location. The spindle nose on the machine has two hardened, ground pins for radial location. Toolblocks are retained on the ram by a hydraulic-mechanical bayonet type of clamping system.

With such devices, cutting could take place with a single toolblock, carrying only one tool, to take advantage of the ram head's deep reach and relatively slim envelope. With another design, the toolblock changer draws from a library of toolblocks mounted in an adjacent carousel holding fixture similar to the automatic toolchangers on machining centers, discussed later in this chapter.

When a cut is completed, the entire block is interchanged in the ram. A typical system involves a transporter mechanism, which positions the next toolblock to be called beside the ram head. At the end of the cut, the ram retracts, toolblocks are automatically exchanged, and the ram returns to the workpiece for the next cut.

Another toolblock changing technique involves ram head traverse to the carousel for direct exchange of the blocks. This design is generally more economical with smaller machines. For larger machines and workpieces above 50-60" diam (1270-1524 mm), the time lost while the ram traverses the distance to the carousel would probably make the toolblock transporter a more viable alternative. Workpiece size, general economic considerations, and the number of toolchanges per part are among the factors to be considered in making this application decision.

Benefits to be gained from the toolblock changer include no loss of maximum swing capacity from tooling constraints, general minimization of tool interference, faster tool exchange for more in-the-cut time, and tooling flexibility.

Rotating Tooling

Special attachments are available from machine manufacturers that permit rotating tooling operations, such as milling, drilling, and grinding, to be performed on workpieces. These can be temporary or permanent attachments.

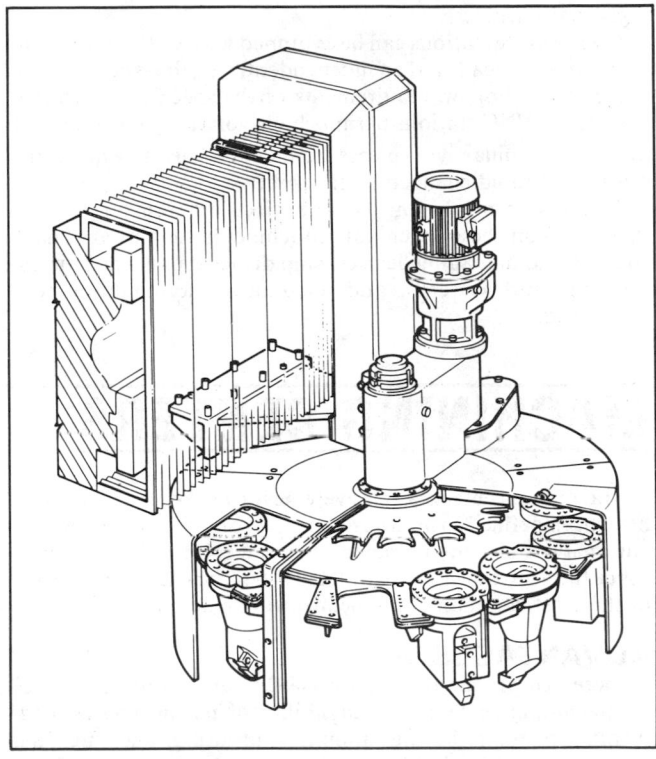

Fig. 30-17 Automatic toolchanger for CNC vertical turning and boring machine. (*Monarch Sidney*)

MULTIPLE-SPINDLE VERTICAL, AUTOMATIC CHUCKING MACHINES

Various types of multiple-spindle vertical, automatic chucking machines are available, similar to the one shown in Fig. 30-18. The machines embody a carrier with six or eight equally spaced, vertical columns encircling a stationary column. On the column over each spindle, except at the loading station, are combination or multiple-tool heads.

Each spindle and head comprises a station or machining unit having independent feed and speed controls for maximum flexibility and efficiency. Each station is set up to perform specific operations in sequence with the next station, so that one carrier cycle around the column produces a finished workpiece. Since all stations of the machine are working simultaneously on various operations, each spindle successively transfers a finished workpiece as it indexes through the loading station.

For continuous or long production jobs, the standard design of the machine can be varied to suit the specific application. Dual spindles and heads can be used at each station, permitting duplicate or first and second chucking operations at each station. Production is also increased on simpler jobs that can be completely machined in half the cycle by arranging two loading stations. Double indexing the spindle carrier has been used extensively where two chuckings or two sets of identical operations can be accomplished on the one machine.

Multiple-spindle vertical chucking machines have minimum floor-space requirements and are easy to relocate to suit production-line manufacturing techniques.

TOOLING

The type of head at each station is usually selected from a group of standard heads and is affixed when the machine is built. Standard power-operated chucks, top jaws, fixtures, and tooling are used extensively. For ease and speed of loading and unloading, some chucks and fixtures are equipped with power-operated work-lifting or ejector mechanisms.

Available standard heads include a plain vertical type for vertical motion only, a universal (swiveling) type for angular motion, and a double-purpose type for combination vertical and horizontal motion.

MULTIPLE-SPINDLE VERTICAL, AUTOMATIC CHUCKING MACHINES

ATTACHMENTS

Attachments are available to increase production rates for specific jobs. These include drilling or tapping heads (either single or multiple), boring and precision boring heads, inside or outside spherical turning heads, elliptical facing heads, CNC heads for contouring, and many other special heads and spindle registry devices.

One or more stations can be equipped with CNC; a universal tool-carrying head; and an independent, variable-speed spindle drive, depending on requirements of the specific application. The use of CNC stations permits high-volume production of a variety of similar workpieces in small to medium quantities because of rapid changeover capabilities.

For faster machining by the circular transfer method employed on these machines, attachments such as automatic loading and unloading devices, chip disposal units, pressurized cutting fluid systems, and automatic gaging have been developed.

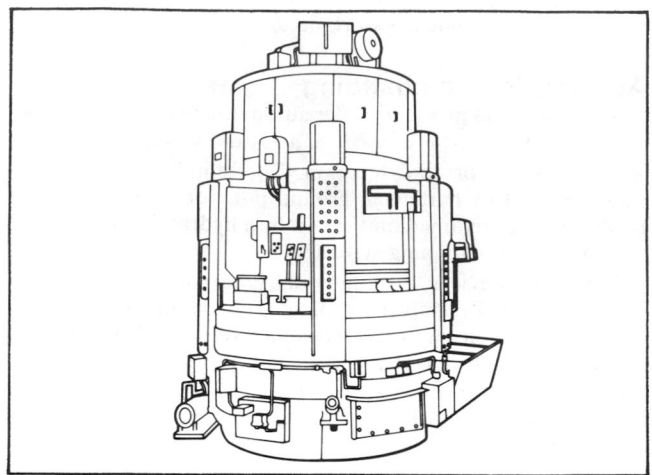

Fig. 30-18 Multiple-spindle automatic chucker. (*Bullard Co.*)

MACHINING CENTERS

Machining centers, a relatively new class of machine tools, have been defined as multifunction, NC or CNC machines with automatic toolchanging capabilities and rotating cutting tools. Since their introduction in the late 1950's, they have become one of the most common of all metalcutting machines.

ADVANTAGES

Increased productivity and versatility are major advantages of machining centers. The capability of performing drilling, turning, reaming, boring, milling, contouring, and threading operations on a single machine eliminates the need for a number of individual machine tools, thus reducing capital equipment and labor requirements. One relatively unskilled operator can often attend two machining centers and sometimes more. Most workpieces can be completed on a single machining center, often with one setup.

Additional savings result from reduced material handling, fixture costs, and floor space requirements. Substantial time conventionally spent moving work from machine to machine is saved, and throughput is much faster. Also, in-process inventory, represented by skids of workpieces normally seen at several machines, is replaced by work at only one machine.

Most machining centers maintain close, consistently repetitive tolerances, resulting in higher quality parts, as well as reduced inspection costs and scrap. In particular, the relationship of machined features on the several faces of a workpiece are more easily held within tolerances. Changeover from the production of one workpiece to another can be done quickly.

Actual machining time on machining centers can be two or more times that of single-purpose, manually operated machine tools. Estimates of increases in productivity per man-hour range from 300 to 500% or more, especially on applications requiring many tools and frequent changeover.

While machining centers have a higher initial cost than many other machine tools, annual return on investment has been conservatively estimated to be about 30%. Smaller, compact models now available make these machines affordable even to small job shops. Accuracies that can be maintained and the reliability of the machines and their controls have been continuously improved.

APPLICATIONS

Machining centers have traditionally been employed primarily for automating the manufacturing of small lots of a wide variety of workpiece shapes and sizes requiring multiple operations. Now, however, they are being increasingly used for medium-lot requirements and some have been tooled for long production runs of a single workpiece.

Careful work scheduling is necessary to keep machining centers operating and thus more fully realize the profit potential of these machines. Most shops try to operate their machining centers, as well as other NC machines, at least two shifts per day to obtain a more rapid return on investment.

Another application becoming increasingly popular for machining centers is the integration of these centers with other NC machines to form flexible machining systems, discussed later in this chapter.

TYPES OF MACHINING CENTERS

Machining centers are available in a wide variety of types, configurations, capabilities, sizes, and costs. Machines with manual toolchanging are still available and being used, but most users do not consider such machines to be machining centers. Machining centers with automatic toolchangers are much more popular. Most machining centers can be categorized as horizontal or vertical-spindle types and traveling-table or column types.

The two major types of machining centers are vertical and horizontal-spindle models. Some are available with two spindles (one horizontal and the other vertical), others have more than two spindles, and another has a single spindle that can be swiveled to either a horizontal or a vertical position. One model has a full contouring head with a 150° sweep from 30° above the horizontal to 30° beyond the vertical.

Selection of a specific type of machining center depends primarily upon the application—the size, complexity, and variety of the workpieces to be machined; production requirements; the number and types of tools needed; tolerances that have to be maintained; and other factors. Group technology, the classification of workpieces into families on the basis of commonality of size, shape, and/or part features, aids in selecting the proper type and size of machine, required tooling, and desirable options.

Vertical Spindle Models

Machining centers with vertical spindles (see Fig. 30-19) provide clear work areas for easy setup and loading/unloading. They are usually preferred for plate-type workpieces if the X-axis travel is sufficient to clear the spindle from over the table. A wide variety of work positioning and indexing equipment available for processing small, multisided parts increases the versatility of these machines. Figure 30-20 illustrates a dual setup on a vertical machining center for performing operations on large diesel engine blocks and heads.

Many vertical-spindle machining centers provide X and Y-axis motions with a traveling table and saddle. Machines are also available with traveling columns for X-axis movements to handle larger workpieces, and sliding heads or rail types for Y-axis motions. Z-axis movements are provided by quill-type spindles, sliding heads, or knees under the machine tables.

Horizontal-Spindle Models

Machining centers with horizontal spindles are generally more flexible than vertical-spindle models and are available in a wider range of sizes. Horizontal-spindle machining centers with numerical control of three, four, and five axes are illustrated in Fig. 30-21. These machines are usually preferred for large, multisided parts because they have no restrictions on workpiece height.

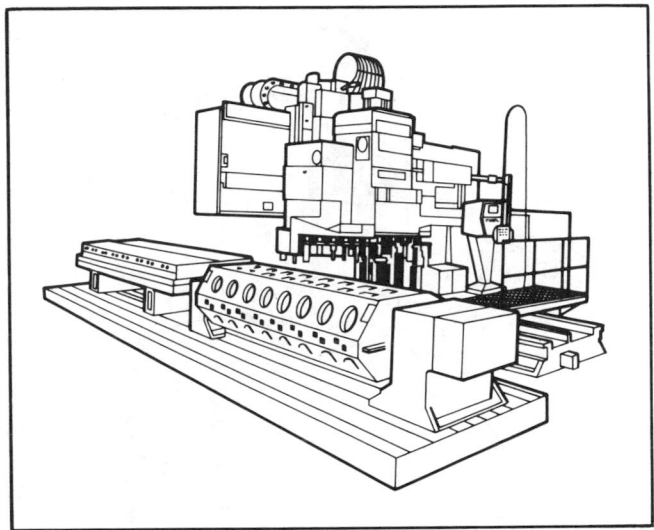

Fig. 30-20 Dual setup for diesel engine blocks and heads on a vertical-spindle machining center. (*Giddings & Lewis Machine Tool Co.*)

Horizontal-spindle bar-type machining centers (see Fig. 30-22) are direct descendants of horizontal bar-type boring mills discussed previously in this chapter. The addition of automatic toolchangers, numerical control, and pallet loading has resulted in accurate, large-capacity machining centers having four linear and one or two rotary axes.

Many horizontal-spindle machining centers provide X-axis motions with a traveling table, sometimes in combination with a saddle to furnish W-axis movements. Motions in the Y axis on some traveling-table machines are provided by a vertical column or spindle carrier mounted on a ram, both located on a rear base.

AUTOMATIC TOOLCHANGERS

A variety of toolchangers are available on machining centers offered by different builders. Most toolchangers consist essentially of a chain, drum, or dial-type magazine or matrix for idle tool storage and a device for interchanging these tools with one in the machine spindle (see Fig. 30-23). With the design shown in Fig. 30-24, tools are stored in an inverted position. The work area is clear, permitting the changing arm to be positioned close to the workpiece for rigidity. The swinging motion during toolchanging requires minimum clearance above the workpiece, resulting in minimum quill extension as the tool moves to the workpiece.

Some machines do not require an intermediate exchange mechanism such as a transfer arm. On one machining center, tools are loaded directly from a rotary drum to the spindle (and from the spindle to the drum) without an interchange device by axial motion of the quill (see Fig. 30-25). Grippers at each tool storage pocket around the drum periphery clamp and unclamp the tools at appropriate times.

Most builders offer a bidirectional rotation, random selection toolchanger system that automatically selects the shortest route to the next tool, thus reducing change time. A few machining centers, however, are available with lower cost, sequential tool selectors. Most toolchangers are an integral part of the machining centers, but some are free-standing, with a shuttle transfer system from storage to spindle.

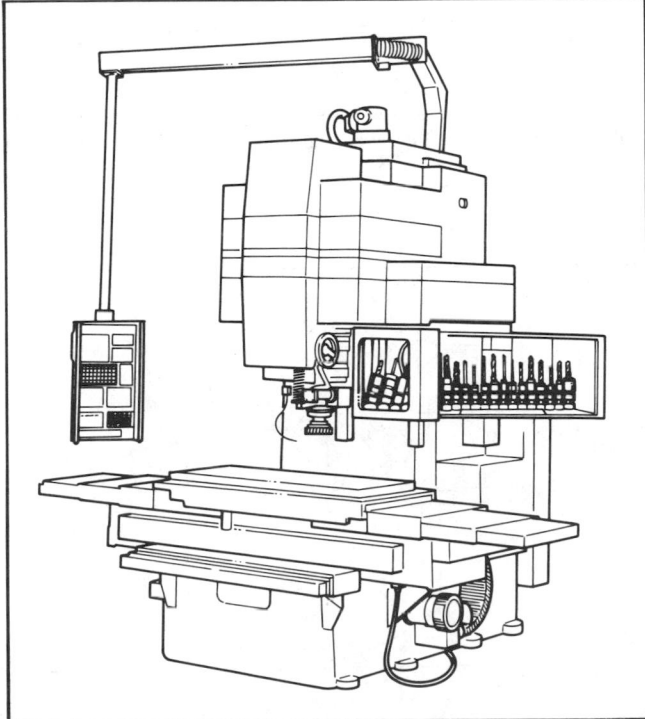

Fig. 30-19 Vertical-spindle machining center with pendant CNC. (*Monarch Cortland*)

MACHINING CENTERS

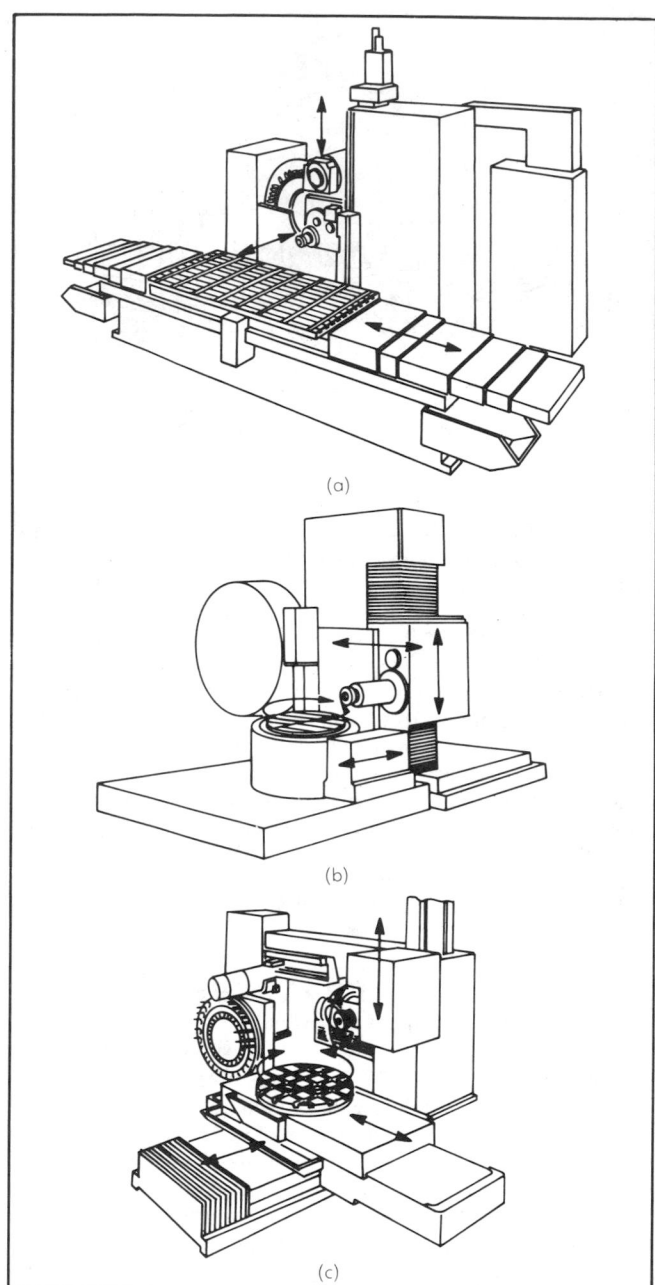

(a)

(b)

(c)

Fig. 30-21 Horizontal-spindle machining centers with numerical control of: (a) three axes, (b) four axes, and (c) five axes.

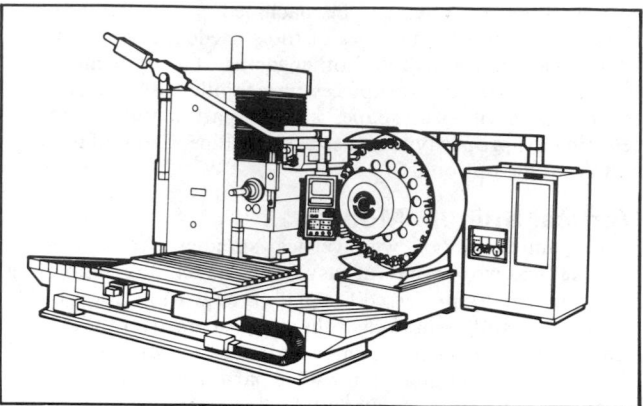

Fig. 30-22 Horizontal-spindle bar-type machining center. (DeVlieg Machine Co.)

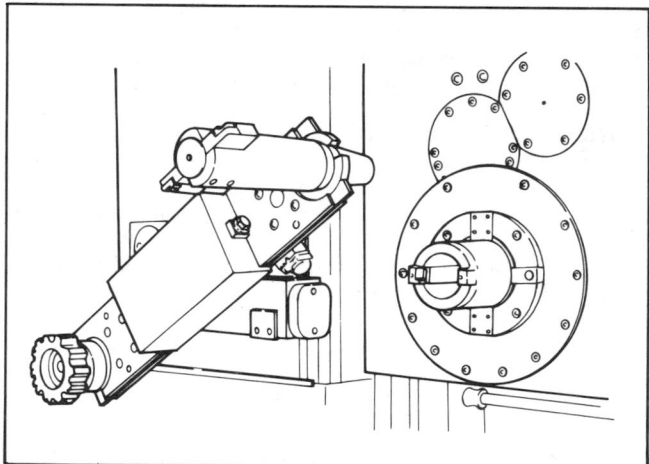

Fig. 30-23 Device for interchanging tool from storage with one in machine spindle. (*Giddings & Lewis Machine Tool Co.*)

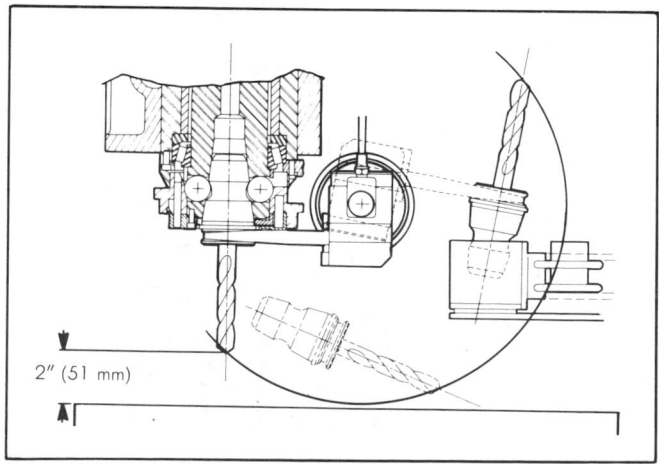

2" (51 mm)

Fig. 30-24 Toolchanger with tools stored in an inverted position and swinging motion of changer arm. (*Monarch Cortland*)

Capacities of the different storage units vary from 3 to 120 tools or more. Some builders offer optional or expandable tool storage capacities. One vertical-spindle machining center has two tool storage magazines, each holding 15 tools and each serviced by its own toolchanger arm. On some multispindle machines, the tools are changed in all spindles simultaneously. Chip-to-chip toolchanging time varies according to design of the changer, with a minimum time of about 4 seconds.

Large-diameter tools and cluster (multispindle) heads can be accommodated in the storage magazines of some machining centers if the adjacent pockets contain smaller diameter tools or

- Program editing capability at the machine.
- Display, readout, or cathode ray tube (CRT) for position and block data.
- Linear and circular interpolation.
- Direct spindle speed and feed rate programming.
- Speed and feed overrides.

Other features (standard or optional) that can be useful include tool and fixture offsets, inch/metric switching, and cutter diameter, tool length, and backlash compensation. Manual data input (MDI) is essential for program editing at the machine, and an alphanumeric keyboard is desirable for this purpose.

Adaptive control systems to make automatic adjustments of spindle speeds and/or feed rates to compensate for changing workpiece/tool conditions are offered by some builders. Computer-based, analytic diagnostic systems are also available to quickly detect and isolate faults, problems, or malfunctions, thus reducing downtime.

TOOLING AND TOOLHOLDERS

Standard cutting tools can be used on most machining centers, but slight modifications may be required for use on some machines. High-speed steel drills and reamers and carbide cutting tools, both coated and uncoated, are used most extensively on machining centers, with ceramic and diamond tools employed to a lesser degree for certain applications.

The increasing use of machining centers has led to the availability of tooling systems (packages of modular tool components) from some cutting tool manufacturers which reduce inventory requirements and costs. Typical systems consist of a shank-end holder, an intermediate component (such as a boring bar or milling cutter body), and indexable inserts. Collet chucks, extensions, adapters for taper shank tools, and bushings of various sizes for different diameter tool shanks are available.

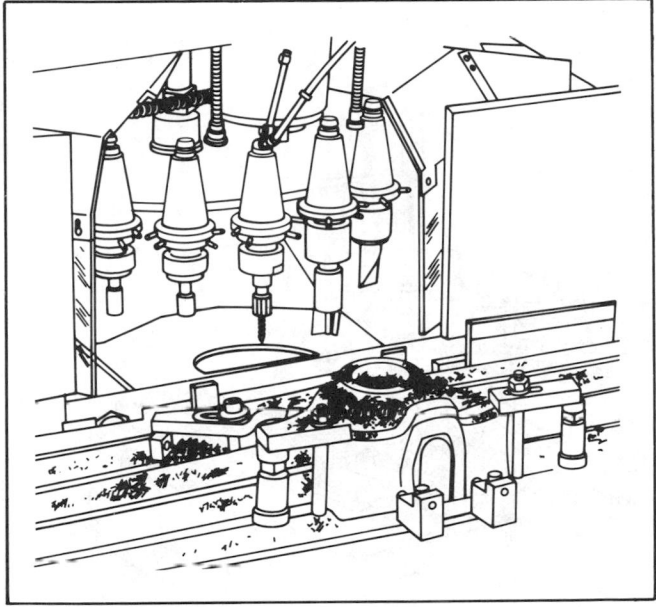

Fig. 30-25 Device for loading tools directly from rotary drum without an interchange arm. (*Kearney & Trecker Corp.*)

are left empty. Some machines provide means for heavy tools to be mounted in cradles, away from the storage matrix, and located conveniently for engagement by the machine spindle.

CONTROLS FOR MACHINING CENTERS

Features generally desirable on controls for machining centers include the following:

- Sufficient memory storage for multiple part programs.
- Canned cycles and subroutines that reduce programming times.

HEADCHANGING MACHINES

Headchanging machines, like machining centers discussed in the preceding section of this chapter, are also a relatively new class of multifunction, numerically controlled machine tools. They differ from machining centers in that single or multiple-spindle heads, rather than tools, are transferred to a single work station in proper sequence to perform the required series of operations. The single work station is equipped with a spindle drive and slide feed unit; the workpiece remains in a fixed or indexable position. Additional work stations can be added on some machines if required.

Advantages of headchanging machines are similar to those of machining centers: increased productivity and versatility, reduced capital equipment and labor costs, and less material handling. Headchanging machines are generally used for larger lots of similar workpieces and for faster production requirements than are usually obtainable with machining centers. The use of modular heads and pallets on headchanging machines, however, permits quick changeover to suit various workpiece requirements. These machines are also being integrated with other NC machines in flexible machining systems, discussed later in this chapter.

On the machine shown in Fig. 30-26, standard size, cubical machining heads, with single or multiple preset tools, are stored on a multilevel carousel alongside the traveling-column machine. On command of the machine controller, the proper head is automatically transferred, positioned, and clamped on the machine spindle. Multitooth couplings ensure accurate registration of toolheads and work pallets. The shuttle pallets on the machine table permit loading and unloading one workpiece while another is being machined. Programs and tooling can be stored in this system for a variety of workpieces. Some toolheads can be dedicated to operations performed on a specific workpiece, while others can be used for one or more operations common to several workpieces.

A CNC headchanging machine made by another builder (see Fig. 30-27) is equipped with four multiple-spindle heads in an overhead indexing unit that rotates in either direction. With a workpiece loaded in the fixture, the required head is automatically indexed over the feed unit, lowered into position on ways on the column face, and located and clamped. The drive quill in the feed unit then automatically advances and engages the driver in the multispindle head.

HEADCHANGING MACHINES

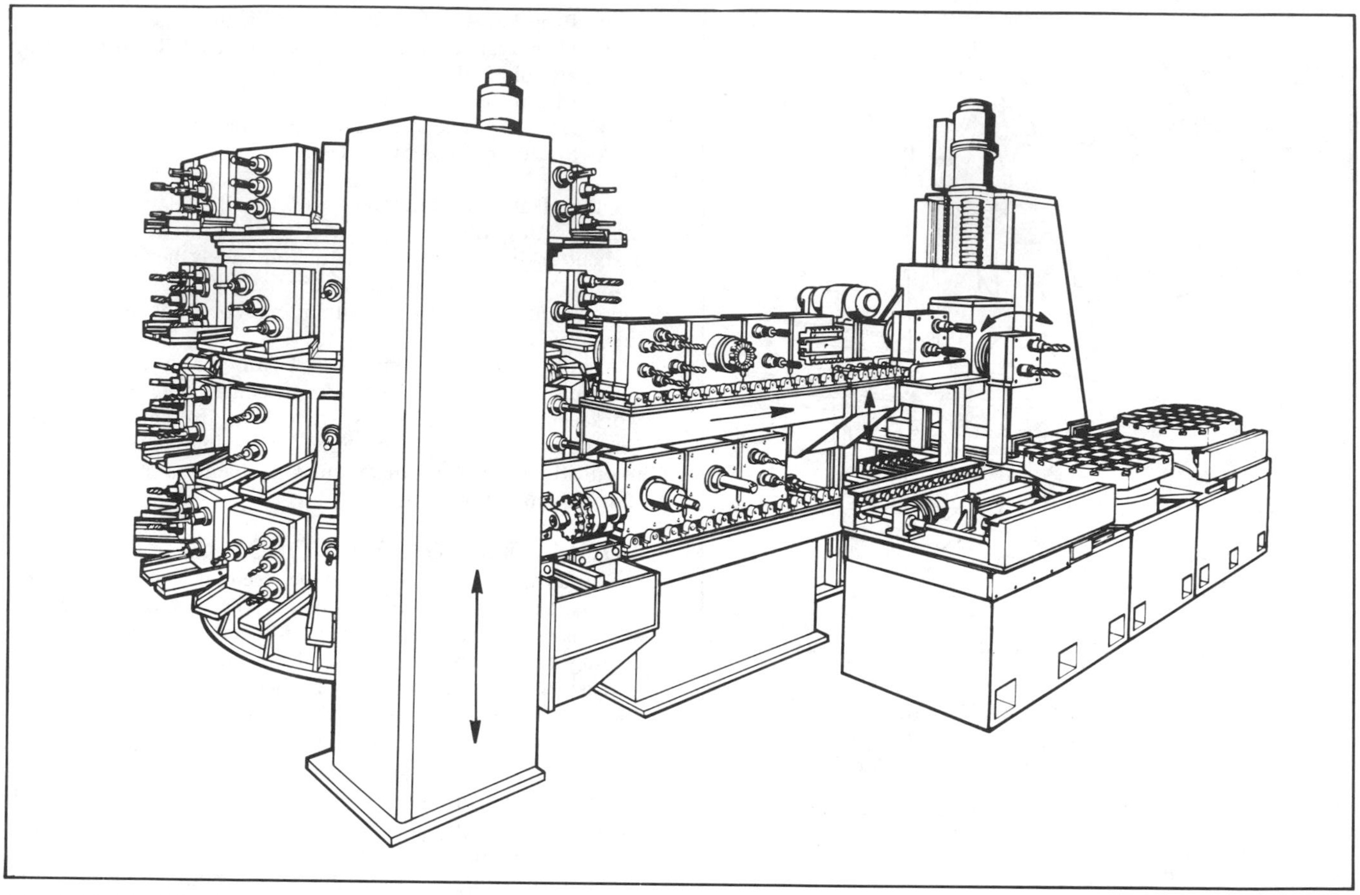

Fig. 30-26 Machining heads, stored on a multilevel carousel, are automatically transferred to spindle of traveling-column machine.

When machining is completed, the feed unit returns, the head is raised, the index unit brings the next head into position, and the process is repeated. The complete headchanging sequence is accomplished in 25 seconds. The machine can be equipped with T-slot mounted fixtures, indexing fixtures, or shuttle fixtures.

Programs can be loaded into the CNC unit by punched tape, magnetic tape cassette, or manual data input (MDI). With MDI, the control can be programmed by the operator when the first workpiece is being machined or during dry-run cycling. Programming normally only involves the Z axis with cutting tools preset to the required length in each head.

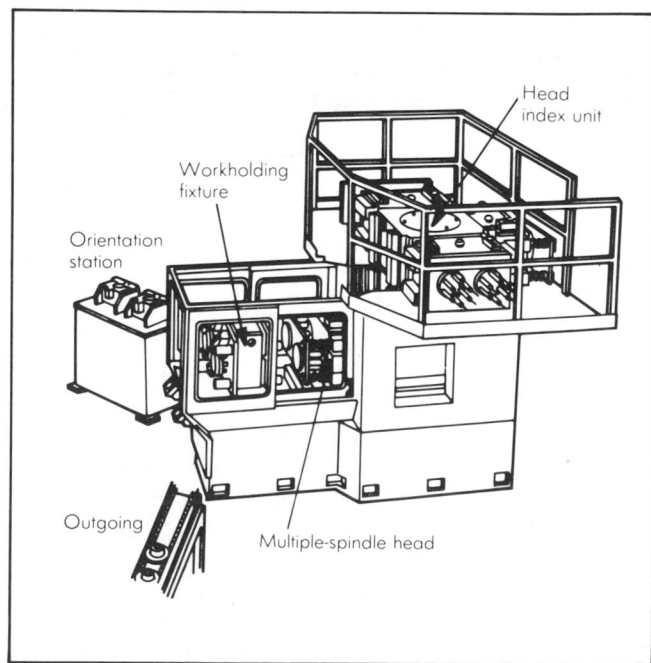

Fig. 30-27 Headchanging machine with four multiple-spindle heads in an overhead indexing unit. (*Olofsson Corp.*)

AUTOMATED AND SPECIAL-PURPOSE MACHINES

Many of the standard machine tools already discussed in this volume are partially automated. In many cases, the addition of automatic feeding, loading/unloading, and gaging equipment can completely automate these standard machines, providing substantial production economies.

Standard machines and equipment should generally be used whenever possible because of their lower cost, quicker availability, and usually, proven performance. A possible disadvantage is that the use of such machines is usually a compromise of the ideal answer to specific automation requirements. The degree of compromise determines whether it is more economical to develop special-purpose machines and equipment that would better suit present and future automation requirements than to use standard machines.

When it is impractical, impossible, or uneconomical to use standard machines for automation, special-purpose machines and equipment must be designed and built or purchased. Special machine tools often provide production economies because of built-in automation concepts that provide maximum efficiency in a minimum of floor space. Although they may not provide the inherent flexibility of standard machine tools, specials can have sufficient flexibility built in to produce a variety of related parts for medium or lower production if requirements are carefully planned in the design stages. If possible, continuous production should replace batch manufacturing methods. When quantities of identical parts are not sufficient for continuous production, the use of more flexible automation equipment to handle families of parts (similar in size or shape) or similar operations should be considered.

When special-purpose equipment is considered, the possibility of combining several operations normally done on a number of individual machines should be investigated. As many operations as possible should be performed while the part is still located and clamped in the special machine. Cost savings resulting from eliminating the need for moving, relocating, and reclamping the workpieces can pay part of the development costs for the special machine.

A variety of special-purpose machines have been developed for automation, some of which are discussed in this section. These machines actually represent various degrees of automation refinement for parts having different machining and production requirements. Selection of a specific type depends on many factors, including the design of the workpiece, number and type of operations to be performed, accuracy specfications, floor space available, production requirements, and need for flexibility.

LINK LINES

A flexible and relatively inexpensive automation concept is the link line in which individual and independent, standard or special machine tools and other production equipment are connected by conveyors or other automatic materials-handling units to move workpieces from operation to operation (see Fig. 30-28 and Fig. 30-29). One operator can handle more than one machine and still provide a certain amount of visual control of the operations, keep hoppers full, change dull tools, etc. The conveyors, hoppers, storage elevators, etc., also serve as banks for in-process parts. Each machine in the line can cycle at its own predetermined rate as long as a part is available and room

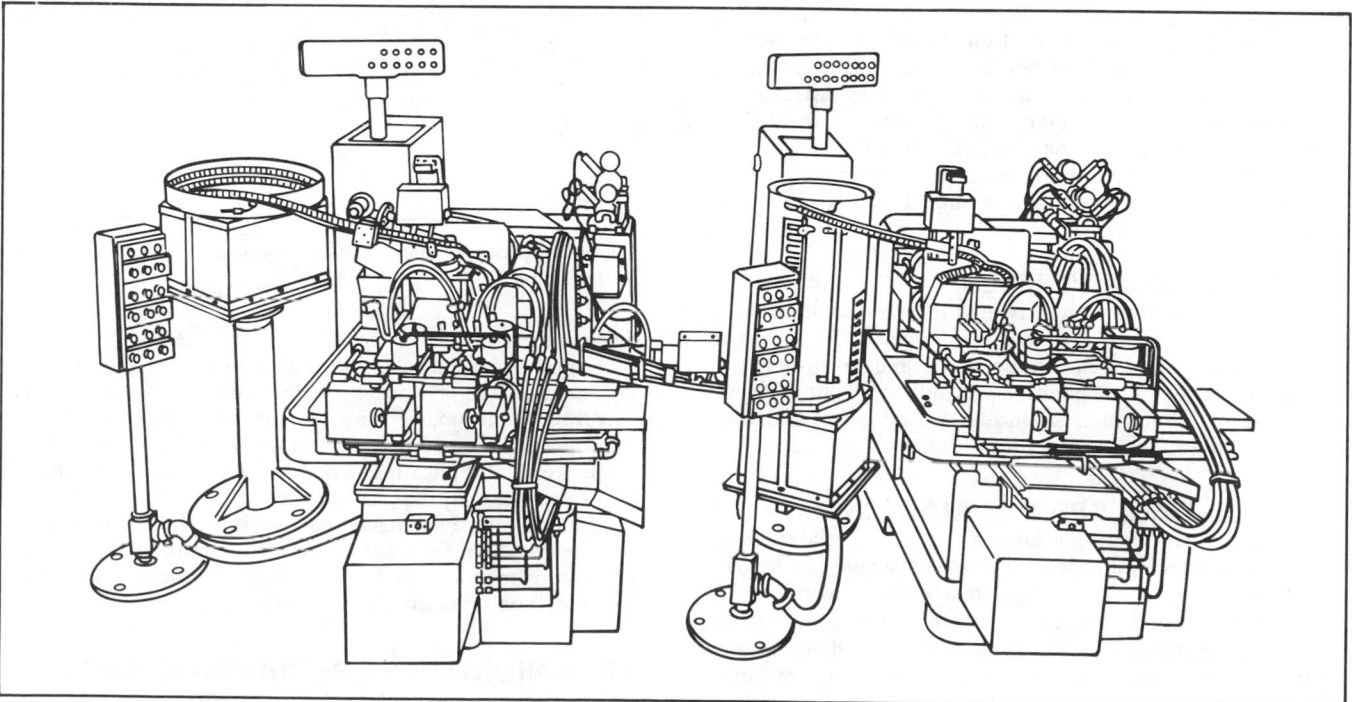

Fig. 30-28 Machine tools interconnected by material-handling and workpiece storage units.

AUTOMATED AND SPECIAL-PURPOSE MACHINES

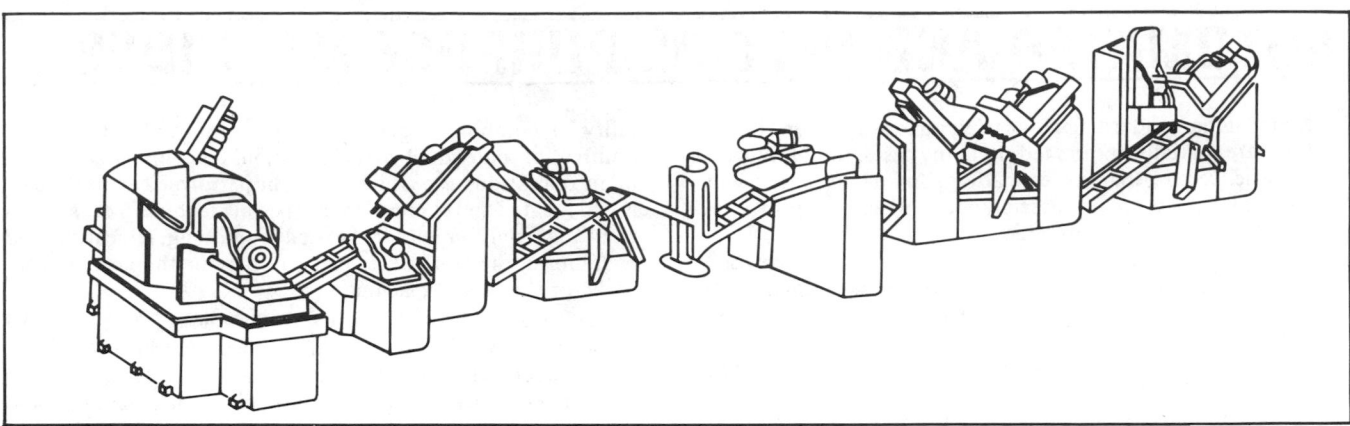

Fig. 30-29 Schematic drawing of link line. Workpieces are transferred from machine to machine by elevating mechanisms, each including a storage magazine.

exists in the subsequent bank for a finished part. In-process gaging is desirable with such setups to prevent producing too much scrap before operations can be corrected. Industrial robots are being used in some applications to transfer workpieces from machine to machine.

COMBINATION-OPERATION MACHINES

Substantial savings in floor space can be achieved in relatively low production applications by clamping the workpiece in a fixed fixture and then feeding machine heads on slides from various directions into the part, as shown in Fig. 30-30. The machines can be two, three, or four way, depending on how many sides of the workpiece are to be machined. Such machines permit one or more of the basic metalworking operations on each part face, including milling, drilling, tapping, and spotfacing, which do not require the movement or rotation of the workpiece during the process. Automatic loading or unloading features are not usually provided on special machine tools of this type, although it is often feasible to clamp the part in the fixture outside the machining area and slide it on rails into the machining position for clamping. Flexibility in such a combined-operation machine is limited, but can be provided by using indexing or shuttle-type heads. Such machines also are capable of being readapted for new-model or part changes at the end of a production run.

DOUBLE-END MACHINES

The double-end or two-way type of machine combines two machining units to perform production operations. A part is chucked between two machining units, and both ends are machined. Such single operations as milling, drilling, chamfering, facing, centering, or boring can be performed economically on double-end machines.

SHUTTLE-TYPE SPECIAL MACHINES

A higher degree of automation refinement of special machine tools is achieved with shuttle or line-index machines, such as the one shown in Fig. 30-31. On these machines, the workpiece is loaded in a fixture, indexed in a straight line to one or more machining positions between single or opposed machining heads, machined, indexed to subsequent machining positions, and then indexed back to the unloading position. The number of machining stations is controlled by the number and type of

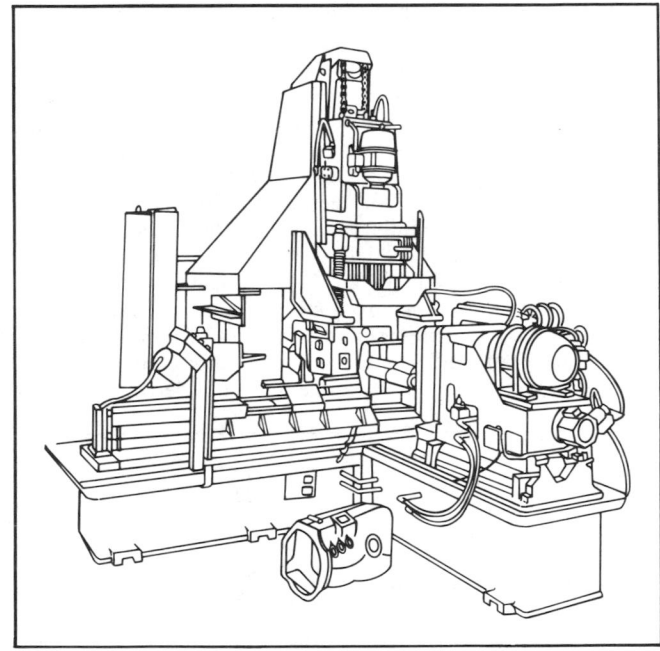

Fig. 30-30 Special combined-operation machine used for the production of tractor transmission cases. (*Snyder Corp.*)

operations, the required production, and the size of the part. This type of special machine tool is in the medium to low-production category but provides some of the automated features of automatic transfer machines (discussed in a subsequent section of this chapter). Heavy parts or parts of odd shape are ideal applications for shuttle or line-index machines. Some flexibility in production can be achieved by providing for head and fixture changes, but such machines should be considered mainly for the efficient production of a single part in the low to medium-production range. Numerical control is being used on some shuttle machines.

TRUNNION-TYPE SPECIAL MACHINES

The simultaneous operation at two or more machining stations is the next-highest degree of special-machine-tool

AUTOMATED AND SPECIAL-PURPOSE MACHINES

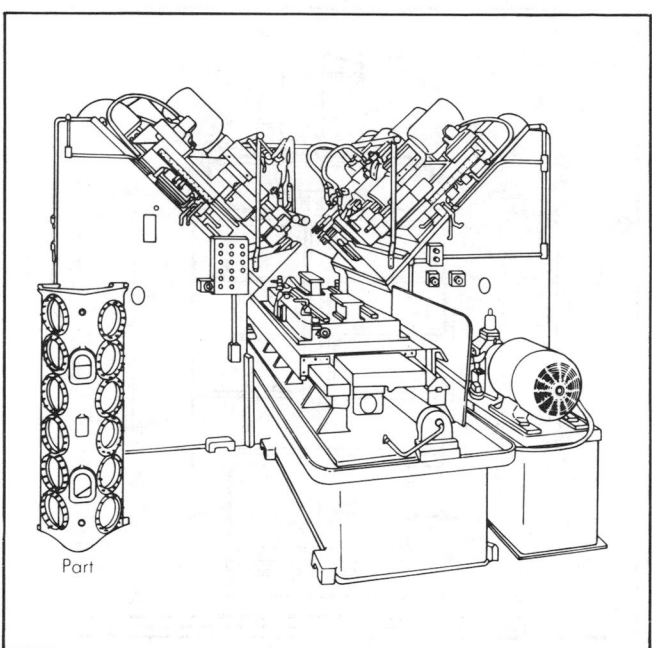

Fig. 30-31 Special line-index machine for drilling and tapping large V-12 engine blocks. (*Snyder Corp.*)

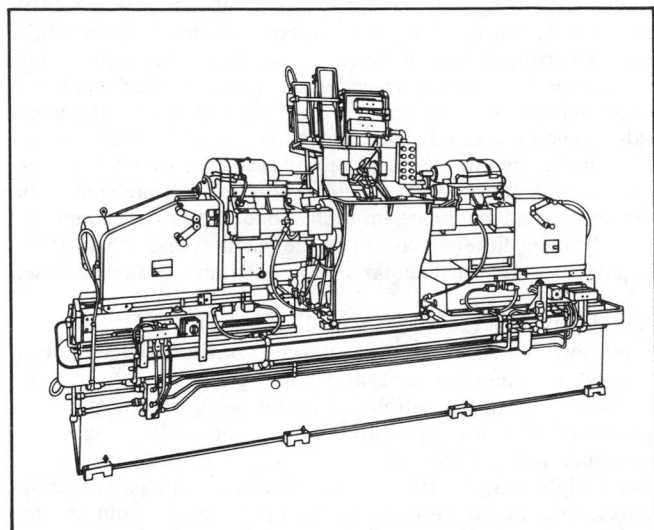

Fig. 30-32 Trunnion-type machine for drilling and milling grooves in a variety of differential spiders. (*Snyder Corp.*)

automation. This is sometimes done in the higher production ranges on trunnion-type machines. In these machines (see Fig. 30-32), several fixtures are mounted on a vertical table or trunnion between opposed machining heads and indexed from one machining station to the next. All machining operations are performed simultaneously, and a finished part is produced with each index of the trunnion. It is possible to perform machining operations on five sides of each workpiece and from the periphery of the trunnion housing if desired.

The part is loaded and unloaded at one station. Some part-production flexibility can be had on trunnion-type machines by providing interchangeable heads and fixtures or fixture details for similar parts which require milling, drilling, boring, reaming, countersinking, and related operations on both ends. Maximum accuracy in trunnion-type machines demands rugged design and provision of individual bushing plates for each station, each of which picks up its own locating pins in fixture bushings. For many applications, dial-type machines have replaced trunnion-type machines.

DIAL-TYPE MACHINES

Higher production rates in a more compact floor space are achieved in automated special machines so designed that the parts are mounted in fixtures on a horizontal-index table and indexed from one station to the next in front of radial, horizontal, or vertical machining units (see Fig. 30-33). With one part in each fixture, two part faces are generally machined. Additional operations can be performed in a machine of this type by clamping two or more parts in each fixture in different positions to present more part areas for machining. One or more finished parts are produced with each machine index.

With modular construction, these dial-type (rotary-index) machines permit tailoring to specific requirements. Workpieces can be loaded and unloaded manually or automatically, and robots are being used for handling in some applications. Rotary

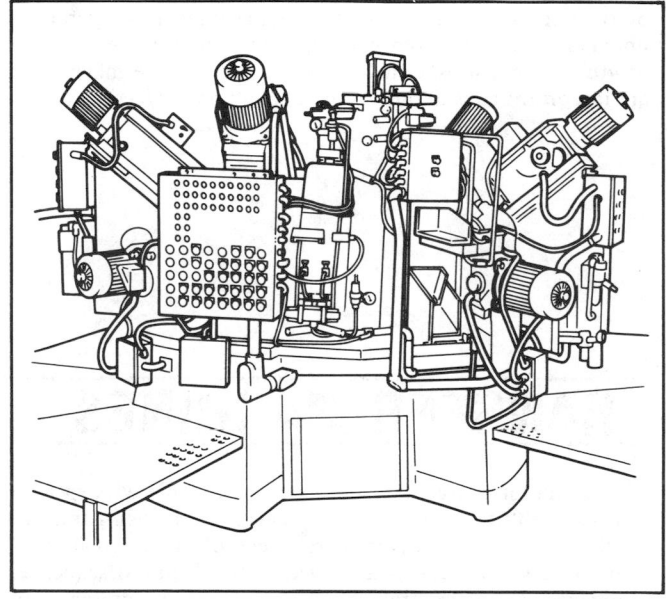

Fig. 30-33 Dial-type (rotary-index) machine with horizontal and angular-spindle heads. (*Kingsbury Machine Tool Corp.*)

index dials are available in various diameters to accommodate different sizes of workpieces and a number of operations. In some cases, rotating workholding fixtures are employed to allow the tools to reach different surfaces. Multiple-spindle heads are common on dial-type machines.

CENTER-COLUMN MACHINES

One limitation of the dial-type machine is that the number of vertical units limits the number of horizontal units that can be placed around the index table. The maximum number of workpiece faces and machining operations in a machine requiring minimum floor space is provided by the automated

AUTOMATED AND SPECIAL-PURPOSE MACHINES

center-column special machine (see Fig. 30-34). Here, the parts are mounted in fixtures on a horizontal-index table which is indexed from station to station. The vertical machining slide units are mounted on a center column, and the radial horizontal or angular units are mounted around the periphery of the index table. The parts are loaded and unloaded at one station. All machining operations occur simultaneously, thus permitting one or more finished parts to be produced with each index. In center-column machines, more than one part can be clamped in each fixture, either to complete the machining of a part or to produce several finished parts with each index of the machine.

MODULAR CONSTRUCTION UNITS

Almost any configuration of special-purpose machines can be made with modular units and building-block construction to perform various operations in proper sequence on different products. Various types and sizes of power feeding units, equipped with tooling devices such as milling heads and single or multiple-spindle drilling heads, can be mounted on standard bases, columns, and angular risers. The bases and columns can be arranged around a central base containing an index table (as on a dial machine), or along a shuttle-type or in-line transfer machine, and equipped with the required number of work-holding fixtures.

Power feeding units can be either way or quill type, depending on the operation to be performed; actuation can be hydraulic, pneumatic, or electromechanical. The hole pattern to be produced, hole sizes, and tolerances that must be maintained are important considerations in selecting power feeding units.

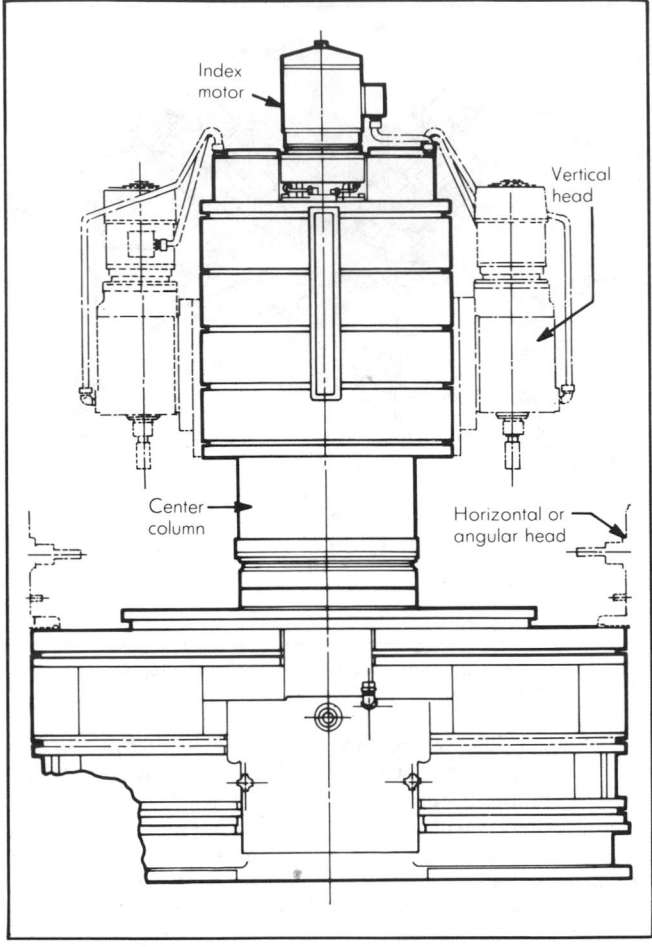

Fig. 30-34 Center column supports vertical heads on dial-type machine. (*Kingsbury Machine Tool Corp.*)

TRANSFER MACHINES

The highest degree of automation obtainable with special-purpose, multifunction machines is achieved by using transfer machines. Transfer machines are essentially a combination of individual work stations arranged in the required sequence, connected by work transfer devices, and integrated with interlocked controls. Workpieces are automatically transferred between the stations, which are equipped with horizontal, vertical, or angular units to perform machining, gaging, workpiece repositioning, assembling, washing, or other operations. The two major classes of transfer machines are rotary and in-line types.

An important advantage of transfer machines is that they permit the maximum number of operations to be performed simultaneously. There is relatively no limitation on the number of workpiece surfaces or planes that can be machined, since devices can be interposed in transfer machines at practically any point for inverting or rotating the workpiece, or orienting it, so as to complete the machining operations. Work repositioning also minimizes the need for angular machining heads and allows operations to be performed in optimum sequence.

Complete processing from rough castings or forgings to finished parts is often possible.

One or more finished parts are produced on a transfer machine with each index of the transfer system that moves the parts from station to station. Production efficiencies of such machines generally range from 50% for a machine producing a variety of different parts to 85% for a machine producing one part in high production, depending upon the workpiece and how the machine is operated (material handling method, maintenance procedures, etc.).

All types of machining operations, such as drilling, tapping, reaming, boring, and milling, are economically combined on transfer machines. Lathe-type operations such as turning and facing are also being performed on in-line transfer machines, with the workpieces being rotated in selected machining stations. Turning operations are performed in lathe-type segments in which multiple toolholders are fed on slides mounted on tunnel-type bridge units. Workpieces are located on centers and rotated by chucks at each turning station. Turning stations with CNC are available for use on in-line transfer machines. The CNC units allow the machine cycles to be easily altered to accommodate changes in workpiece design and can also be used for automatic tool adjustments.

ROTARY TRANSFER MACHINES

Rotary transfer machines (see Fig. 30-35) are a relatively new development. They combine many of the desirable features of dial-type machines (discussed previously in this chapter) with those of in-line, pallet-type transfer machines (described next), while eliminating some of the disadvantages of each. While rotary transfer machines are similar in appearance to dial-type machines, there are major differences between the two. For example, rotary transfer machines have no dial or table and no center column.

On rotary transfer machines, workpieces are located and clamped in floating, pallet-type fixtures that are indexed in a circular path. This eliminates the need for pallet-return conveyor systems (required on palletized, in-line transfer machines) and substantially reduces floor space and installation requirements. The centers of the machines are open, permitting horizontal, vertical, and angular machining units to be mounted inside as well as outside the pallet-carrying rails. The number and positions of the machining units can be easily changed to suit production requirements.

Pallets are accurately located independently at each station with pins and wedges. They are clamped to a fixed bed, rather than to a movable table, as is the case in dial-type machines, thus providing increased rigidity. Indexing fixtures or fixtures that hold multiple workpieces are mounted on the pallets when required. Programmable controllers are used on most rotary transfer machines and many of the other machines discussed in this chapter to direct and monitor all machine functions.

While rotary transfer machines are lower in cost and require less floor space than in-line, pallet-type transfer machines, they are generally limited to smaller workpieces and fewer stations.

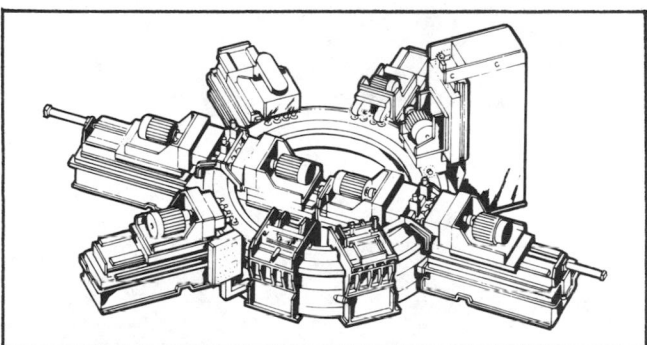

Fig. 30-35 Rotary transfer machine on which workholding pallets are transferred in a circular path. (*Greenlee Manufacturing Systems Div., Ex-Cell-O Corp.*)

IN-LINE TRANSFER MACHINES

With in-line, sometimes called straight-line, transfer machines, workpieces always move in a straight line. These machines are generally suitable for operations involving larger workpieces and for those in which more work stations are required.

Major types of in-line transfer machines are sliding or free transfer, walking-beam (lift-and-carry) transfer, and palletized transfer. The type of transfer used for moving workpieces from station to station is usually dictated by the shape, size, and rigidity of the workpieces, as well as their locating surfaces or points.

CONTROL OF TRANSFER MACHINES

Electrical interlocks are provided on transfer machines to show that a workpiece has been loaded at the first station and another part unloaded from the last station before transfer takes place. At each station, electrical interlocks also assure that workpieces or pallets are properly located and securely clamped before the machining units perform their operations. All machining, inspecting, ejecting, repositioning, and orienting units, as well as the lubrication and cutting fluid systems, are also electrically interlocked to show their operating status and ensure proper cycling. Pressure switches and solenoid-operated valves are often provided to prevent damage or stop the machine in case of hydraulic, air, or electrical power failure. In addition to full controls on a conveniently located operator's console, pushbuttons with selector switches are generally provided at each operating unit so that the units can be operated independently during setup or changeover.

On some versatile transfer machines, electrical interlocking assures proper setup when different parts are being produced. The operator simply selects the part to be produced by means of a switch on the console; the machine cannot be cycled until the required heads and slides for that particular part are in their required positions. In some cases certain heads are automatically made inoperative when specific parts are being produced.

Some means, such as pilot lights on the control console, are provided to quickly locate improperly operating units or other functions, thus minimizing downtime. A disconnect switch or circuit breaker should be provided. Limit switches must be kept away or sealed from the cutting fluid, hydraulic fluid, and other wet areas.

Conventional electromechanical relay sequence-control panels, long the standard on transfer and other machines, are being superseded by programmable controllers and microprocessors. Reasons for this change include increased versatility (easy reprogramming), greater reliability, floor-space savings, fast setups, diagnostic capability for fast troubleshooting, reduced downtime and maintenance, and easy interfacing with computers.

Interfacing of transfer-machine controls for future connection to computers is now common practice. Computers are being used to control some transfer machines. Functions performed by the computer include making necessary logic determinations, signaling for each action in the operating sequence, and supplying data for management information systems (production counts, downtime, comparing actual and planned cycle times, etc.) In general, however, computers have been found more valuable for monitoring transfer machines, including a rapid means of diagnostic troubleshooting. Diagnostic systems are resulting in increased productivity from transfer machines.

References

1. Kenneth Fox, *Variable Mission Manufacturing Systems*, SME Technical Paper MS81-158, p. 1.
2. Raymond J. Larsen, "Flexible Manufacturing: More Companies Make Competition Intense," *Iron Age* (September 28, 1981), p. 85.
3. Robert F. Huber, "Flexible Machining Systems," Manufacturing Planbook Supplement, *Production* (August 1981), p. 5-68.
4. *Ibid.*, p. 5-65.
5. Melvin Blumberg and Antone Alber, "The Human Element: Its Impact on the Productivity of Advanced Manufacturing Systems," *Journal of Manufacturing Systems*, vol. 1, no. 1 (1982).

SHEET METAL FORMABILITY

From a manufacturing viewpoint, the main requirement for most applications of sheet metal is good formability. Formability is generally understood to mean the capability of being extensively deformed into intricate shapes without fracture or defects in the finished part. The manufacturing operation by which this is done is called press forming, deep drawing, or stamping. Figure 31-1 is a generalized representation of forming operations performed in producing a sheet metal stamping.

Press forming is the most common sheet metal forming method. In this process, a flat blank is formed into a finished shape between a pair of matched dies. Other forming methods exist, but in all of them two principal kinds of deformation, drawing and stretching, are involved.

The properties of the sheet metal required for good drawability are not the same as those required for good stretchability. The relative severity of a process in terms of drawing and stretching depends on the shape of the part being formed. It also depends on mechanical factors of the forming operation, such as die design, lubrication, and press speed. As a consequence, the formability of a sheet metal cannot be expressed by a single property; instead, it is a combination of several properties and formability differs from one part or operation to the next. Table 31-1 lists some important variables and their effects on the forming process.[1] Analysis of the mechanics of forming operations highlights the properties of the sheet that are of major importance to drawability and stretchability.

SHEET METAL FORMING

Sheet metal formability is undergoing a transition from an art to a science. Formability—within each forming mode—can be related to specific metal formability parameters. These parameters may or may not decrease as the yield strength of a high-strength steel increases. The important point to bear in mind is that they change gradually and predictably as the yield strength of the steel increases. No discontinuous drop in formability is experienced. In fact, certain formability modes are insensitive to yield strength. Therefore, knowing the change in formability parameters expected, compensation can be made in part design, tool design, lubricant selection, and press parameters.

A complex forming operation is usually composed of several primary forming modes, each of which is dependent on a different mechanical property. Therefore, the suitability of a sheet steel for an operation has to be decided on the basis of its formability in each of these several modes.[2]

FORMING MODES
The three most common primary forming modes are cup drawing, bending and straightening, and stretching, illustrated in Fig. 31-2. Blanking, punching, flanging, and trimming are considered secondary forming operations.

Cup Drawing Mode
In cup drawing, also referred to as radial drawing, a circular blank is usually drawn into a circular die by a flat-bottom, cylindrical punch (see Fig. 31-2, view a). As the flange is pulled toward the die opening, the decrease in blank circumference causes a circumferential compression of the metal. Unless controlled by blankholder pressure, this circumferential compression can easily generate radial buckles in the flange.

Bending and Straightening Mode
The bending and straightening mode is often

confused with the cup drawing mode. In both cases, metal is pulled from a flange, bent over a die radius, and then restraightened. However, in bending and straightening (see Fig. 31-2, view b), the die line is straight, the flange length does not change, and no circumferential compression or buckles are generated.

During deformation, the outer fiber (convex side of the bend) is first elongated as it bends over the die radius. It is then compressed as the sheet is straightened. The inner fiber (concave side) undergoes the reverse sequence of compression followed by tension. Thus, no radial elongation or sheet thinning is observed in a pure bending and straightening operation.

Stretching Mode
In stretching (see Fig. 31-2, view c), a blank is clamped at the die ring by hold-down pressure or lock beads. A domed punch is pushed into the blank, causing tensile elongation of the metal in all directions of the dome. The thickness of the sheet must therefore decrease. This deformation is called biaxial stretch forming.

If the punch is long compared to its width (for a rectangular die opening), tensile elongation of the clamped blank occurs only in one direction—across the small punch radius. This tensile elongation is offset by a reduction in sheet thickness. This very common type of deformation is called plane strain stretching.

One important problem which develops when a formed edge is elongated or stretched is that any damage in the blanking or shearing operation, as evidenced by a burr or rounding of the edge, reduces the formability of the edge.

Complex Stampings
The complex stamping shown in Fig. 31-3 should help to place the individual forming modes in perspective. The flange can be divided into four

SHEET METAL FORMING

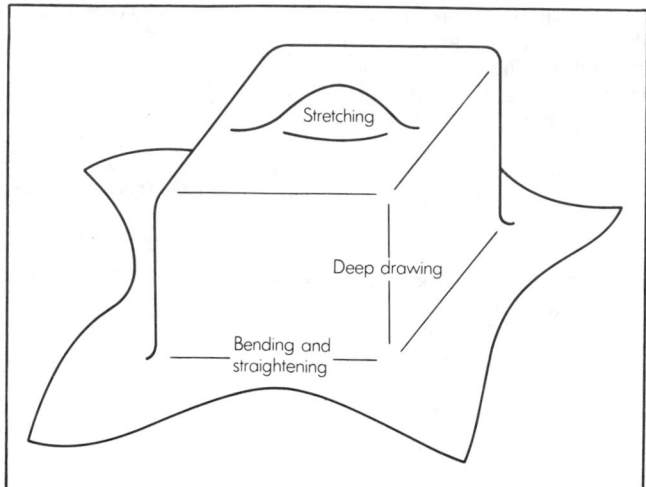

Fig. 31-1 A complex stamping embodies several modes of forming.

TABLE 31-1
Variables in the Press Forming Process

MAJOR VARIABLES:

Sheet material
— n-value (ability to strain harden, a measure of stretchability of material)
— r-value (resistance to thinning, a measure of deep drawability of material)
— anisotropy in the plane of the sheet (r_0, r_{45}, r_{90} values, a measured tendency to earing)
— uniformity of thickness

Lubricant
— pressure sensitivity
— temperature sensitivity
— stability
— thickness and position of application

Blank
— size
— shape

Tooling
— stiffness of die and blankholder plates (use of shims to flex blankholder plate)
— surface roughness
— die radius (may sometimes be alterable)

MINOR VARIABLES:

Sheet material
— strain rate sensitivity of yield stress
— surface roughness (affects lubrication)

Blank
— edge condition (burred, heavily worked)
— location on die plate

Press
— ram speed
— method of blankholding
— stiffness of frame, accuracy of movement in guides

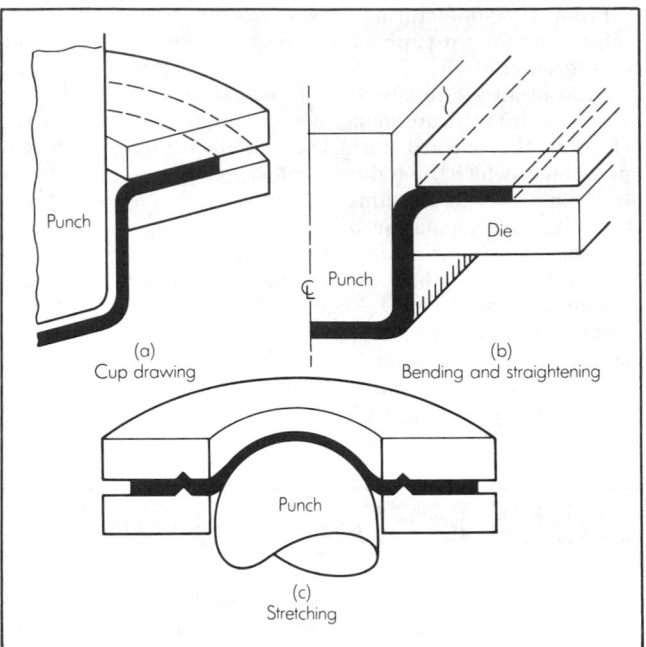

Fig. 31-2 Primary forming modes in a complex stamping. Each mode is dependent on a different metal property.

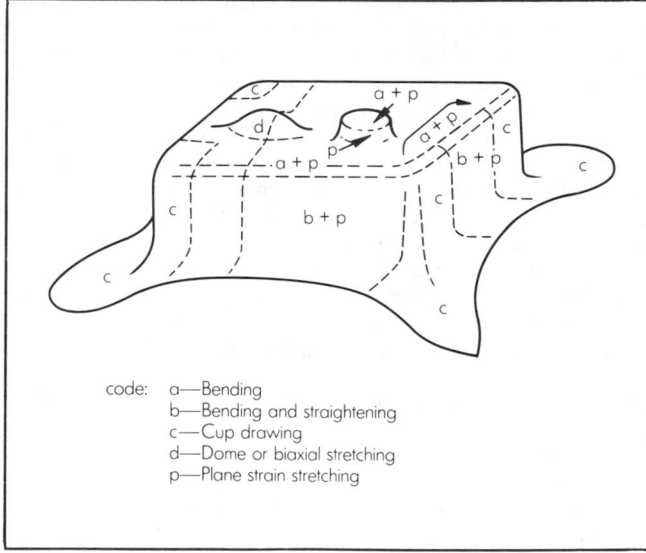

code: a—Bending
       b—Bending and straightening
       c—Cup drawing
       d—Dome or biaxial stretching
       p—Plane strain stretching

Fig. 31-3 Breakdown of a stamping into its component forming modes. Dotted line shows typical length of line generated to fulfill design requirement.

corners connected by four straight segments. The four corners are created by cup drawing, and each represents one-quarter of a cylindrical cup. The straight line segments joining the corners are created by bending and straightening. However, if hold-down pressure or draw beads create a high radial tensile stress over the die radius, plane strain stretching is added to the bending and straightening action. The bottom radii are a combination of bending (one-half of the bending and straightening operation) plus plane strain stretching. The dome on the bottom of the pan is formed by biaxial stretching, while the embossment and character line are formed by plane strain stretching and bending.

FORMING LIMITS

For a particular stamping, the limiting factors can be grouped according to the specific forming mode—cup drawing, bending and straightening, or stretching—and the applicable process parameters and metal physical properties.

Cup Drawing Limits

In cup drawing, the punch button is pushed against the cup bottom to pull the flange into the cup wall. The cup wall must be able to carry the load required to deform the flange and overcome friction. If the cup wall can carry a larger force without necking down, a larger blank can then be drawn into a deeper cup. One method of characterizing this resistance of the cup wall to necking down is by the normal anisotropy of the metal, or the $\bar{r}$. The higher the $\bar{r}$, the greater the deep drawability of the metal.

Typical $\bar{r}$ values for steel are indicated in the following table:

Type of Steel	$\bar{r}$ Value
Hot-rolled 1008	0.8-1.0
Cold-rolled 1008, rimmed	1.0-1.4
Cold-rolled 1008, aluminum killed (AK)	1.3-1.9
Hot-rolled, high-strength, low-alloy (HSLA)	0.8-1.0
Cold-rolled HSLA	1.0-1.4

Based on the $\bar{r}$ values, hot-rolled HSLA steels, whether 50 or 80 ksi (345 or 552 MPa) yield strength, can be drawn to a cup depth equivalent to hot-rolled 1008 steels. Cold-rolled HSLA steels have cup drawability equivalent to cold-rolled 1008 rimmed steels. A more direct measure of cup drawability is the limiting drawing ratio, LDR, which equals D_b/D_p where D_b is the maximum blank diameter that can be successfully drawn with a punch of diameter, D_p. A comparison between an 80 ksi (552 MPa) yield strength, cold-rolled HSLA steel with a low $\bar{r}$ of 1.0, and a 27 ksi (186 MPa) yield, cold-rolled AK steel with a high $\bar{r}$ of 1.8 shows only a 25% reduction in the LDR, but a 300% increase in yield strength. Dramatic increases in yield strength can be achieved with only small reductions in cup drawability.

Bending and Straightening Limits

The limiting factor in the bending and straightening mode is the ability of the inner fiber of the metal to withstand the tensile strain in straightening after being cold worked in compression during bending. In the case of bending only, the outer fiber element must withstand the required tensile strain. In both cases, the ability of the metal to withstand the bending and straightening deformation mode can be correlated to the total elongation of the metal as measured by a tensile test. The higher the total elongation, the sharper the bend radius that can be formed. Typical percentages of total elongation in a 2" (51 mm) gage length are indicated in the following table:

Yield Strength	Percentage of Longitudinal Elongation	Percentage of Transverse Elongation
30 ksi (207 MPa)	48	46
50 ksi (345 MPa)	35	30
80 ksi (552 MPa)	20	20

These measurements are important in three ways. First, the gain in yield strength is accompanied by a loss in total elongation. Thus, an increase in yield strength requires an increase in bend radius for equal thickness. As a result, formability in this mode is inversely proportional to yield strength.

Second, the longitudinal total elongation of the 50 ksi (345 MPa) yield strength steel is greater than the transverse total elongation. Thus, the preferred bending and straightening axis is across the rolling direction of the fiber. Blank orientation can significantly improve formability in this mode.

Third, inclusion shape control of the 80 ksi (552 MPa) yield strength steel is important in elevating the level of the transverse total elongation to that of the longitudinal direction. Inclusion shape control can improve the transverse bending and straightening capacity of HSLA steels.

Stretching Limits

Stretching capacity of a metal is related to its ability to delay or resist the onset of a tensile instability or necking. One measure of this resistance to necking is the work-hardening exponent, or n value (from $\sigma = K\epsilon^n$). The higher the n value, the larger the uniform elongation, the greater the resistance to necking.

This relationship between yield strength of steel and the n value is shown in Fig. 31-4. The n value influences stretchability in two ways. First, a higher n value improves ability of the metal to resist localization of strain in the presence of a stress gradient. This generates a more uniform distribution of strain and permits more effective utilization of available metal.

Second, the biaxial stretching portion of the forming limit diagram (FLD) is dependent on the n value. (See "Analytical Methods," later in this chapter.) The FLD (see Fig. 31-5) specifies the maximum strain that sheet metal can withstand

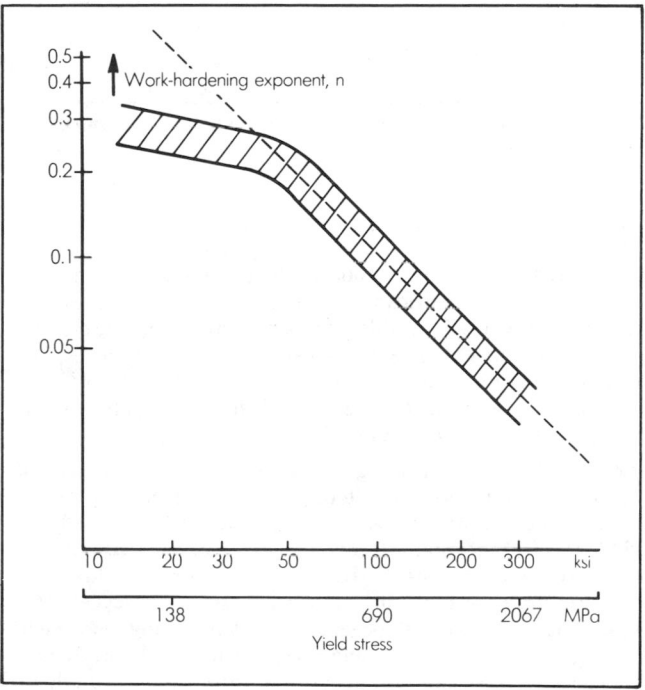

Fig. 31-4 Relationship of work-hardening exponent, n, to yield strength.

SHEET METAL FORMING

without necking for a wide combination of strain states. The level of this standard shaped curve for low-carbon steel is fixed by the intercept of the $e_2 = 0$ axis; this point is labeled the FLD_0. The dependence of the FLD_0 on the n value for different thicknesses is shown in Fig. 31-6

It can be noted in Fig. 31-4 that the n values of a 30 ksi (207 MPa) and a 50 ksi (345 MPa) yield strength steel are approximately equal (within the scatter band). In addition, the FLD's for these two steels are quite close (see Fig. 31-5). Forming experience has confirmed that stretchability of 30 and 50 ksi (207 and 345 MPa) yield strength steels is approximately equal.

A reduction in stretchability is observed for an 80 ksi (552 MPa) yield strength steel because of the lower n value.

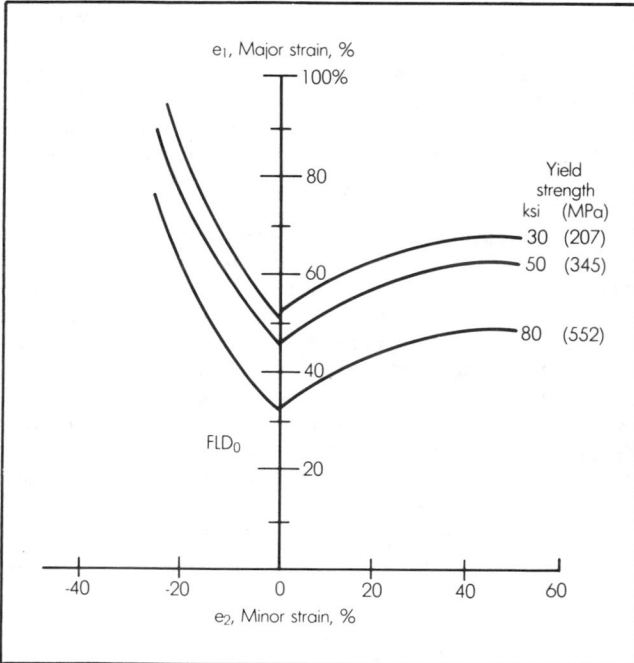

Fig. 31-5 Forming limit diagram for three 0.08" (2 mm) thick low-carbon steels.

Influencing Factors

In the previous section the formability of high-strength steels is compared with ordinary 1008 steels, assuming the influence of design, tooling, lubricant, and press adjustments does not change. However, all variables in the forming system are closely interrelated, and a change in one variable (steel properties, for example) requires modifications in the other variables. A number of these interactions can be illustrated with the aid of the schematic drawing in Fig. 31-3.

Part design. The part design requires that a specific length of line be generated, whether it originates by stretching or by bending and straightening. The stretchability of an 80 ksi (552 MPa) yield strength steel is reduced in comparison to that of an ordinary 1008 steel. However, if die radii, hold-down pressure, draw bead radii, etc., are carefully selected, the required length of line can be generated by replacing the stretch forming component by pulling metal from the flange. Thus, proper tool design can optimize the forming modes for which high-strength steels are most suited.

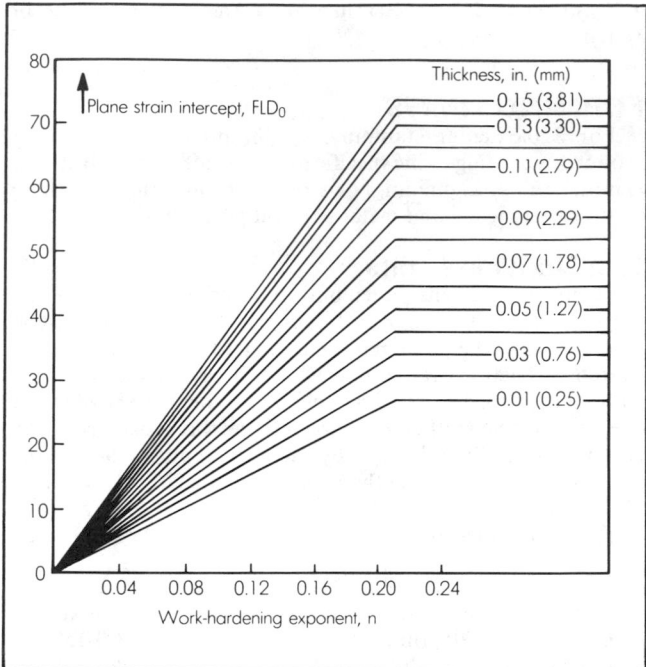

Fig. 31-6 Graphic relationship among work-hardening exponent, n: sheet thickness; and the plane strain intercept of the forming limit diagram, FLD_0.

The four flange corners are more susceptible to wrinkling or buckling if the yield strength of the metal is increased or if the sheet thickness is reduced. This greater tendency of a high-strength steel to wrinkle can be compensated for by increased hold-down pressures. However, increased hold-down pressures result in increased binder (flange) forces unless the lubricant coefficient of friction is reduced to offset the increased pressures.

Deformation parameter. The increased forces required to deform the higher strength steels generate higher interface pressures. Lubricants may have to be upgraded to withstand these increased interface pressures without lubricant break-down. Furthermore, careful lubricant selection is required to avoid increased tool wear.

The reduced work-hardening exponent, n, of the high-strength steel indicates a reduced ability to resist localization of strain in the presence of a stress gradient. Therefore, part and tool designs should compensate by reducing stress gradients. Included in a long list of possible modifications are increasing punch and die radii, selecting lubricants to encourage uniform distribution of deformation, avoiding plane strain stretching, reducing flange loads, reducing depths of embossments, bringing in more metal from the flange, etc. Proper part and die design changes can help compensate for reduced stretchability of the new higher strength-to-weight ratio metals.

Other deformation parameters are less well defined. One example is springback. In bending, springback increases with increased yield strength. This can be corrected by appropriate overbending, overcrowning, or subsequent restriking. In stretch forming, however, the interaction of deformation with metal properties is very complex and predictions of springback are difficult.

Some other considerations which must also be taken into account in the secondary forming operations include increased press loads to blank, punch, and shear; blanking clearances; and edge cracking during flanging.

THE ROLE OF LUBRICATION

Friction and lubrication are of vital importance in most metalforming operations. Effective lubrication systems result in low friction levels which reduce the loads imposed on tooling and workpieces. This can eliminate problems with tooling or workpiece failures or permit a reduction in the number of steps required to form a part. Lower force levels also reduce tooling deflection and can improve the dimensional accuracy of the product.

Lubrication is an important process variable in sheet metal forming since it controls the friction between the die and the sheet. Lubricants are chosen to minimize metallic transfer (galling) and wear, to regulate surface finish, and to control the force that draws the sheet into the die cavity. Even though friction is a relatively small part of the force required to form sheet metal, it directly influences formability by affecting the ratio of draw to stretch and the strain distribution in various regions in a stamping. The friction component may often be critical in the stamping of materials with reduced formability due to cost or weight restraints.

Metal Flow

A primary function of lubrication in sheet metal forming is to permit metal flow in a controlled manner. Metal flow requirements vary from point to point on a particular stamping and also vary from one stamping to another. A given lubricant can cause a different response in each set of dies. Each individual application should be considered in terms of its specific conditions and requirements.

In current practice, lubricant requirements and effectiveness are considered in conjunction with drawbeads, which control the flow of sheet metal into the die cavity to prevent either splitting or wrinkling. A drawbead consists of a semicylindrical, raised rod on one binder surface and a matching groove on the opposing binder surface.

Surface Roughness

Sheet metal surface roughness and material properties interact with lubricant viscosity in a complex way to change friction. Effects similar to those of lubrication are obtained by varying the surface roughness of the blank. Like poor lubrication, rough surfaces may retard metal being drawn in from the flange and thereby force higher strains in the punch stretching region. Conversely, rough surfaces can also entrap and carry more lubrication into the deformation zone, thereby reducing the friction and nonuniformity of the strain distribution. At the other extreme, a blank that is too smooth may "run in" too fast, resulting in either a lack of material for trimming or buckles which lock the metal. Each apparent lubrication problem, therefore, must be investigated separately.

Lubrication Regimes

The type of lubrication regime that occurs in a metalforming operation has a strong influence on frictional conditions, as well as on important factors such as product surface finish and tooling wear rates. Four main lubrication regimes occur in sheet metal forming with liquid or solid lubricants: the thick-film regime; the thin-film regime; the mixed regime; and the boundary regime.

The majority of metalforming operations are characterized by high pressures and low speeds. Under such conditions, the metal surfaces are separated by an extremely thin lubricant film of molecular thickness. Analysis on lubrication of sheet metal forming operations indicates that the lubricant's mechanical properties and boundary lubricity, as well as workpiece surface roughness and deformation speed, have important influences on lubrication. Thus, it seems likely that while thick-film or boundary lubrication may occur under unusual circumstances, significant regions in most processes operate in a thin-film or mixed regime. It is, therefore, desirable to be able to estimate the lubricant film thickness in different parts of the interface between workpiece and tooling. This permits selection of important lubrication parameters on a logical basis and estimation of resultant frictional conditions.

The term *sheet metal forming* covers a wide variety of operations. Some of these operations, such as bending, are usually unlubricated, while others, such as shallow drawing, do not place stringent requirements on the lubricant.

SHEET STEEL MATERIALS

In recent years, sheet steel and other sheet metals with higher strength and better formability have become available. Formable and weldable high-strength steels in the 50-80 ksi (345-552 MPa) yield strength range are being specified in product design. For a broad comparison, steels can be arranged in a general formability classification system according to their yield strength and tensile characteristics, as shown in Table 31-2.

Low-Carbon Sheet Steel

Regular low-carbon sheet steel, a type commonly used in the automotive industry, has a typical yield strength in the 25-35 ksi range (172-241 MPa). These materials are easily formed and welded with high-volume, mass-production techniques. Their combination of strength, modulus, and fabricability means that the design of even low-cost components can meet all the performance requirements.

Low-carbon sheet steels are available in products cold rolled to as thin as 0.014" (0.36 mm) and hot rolled to as thick as 0.50" (12.7 mm) and thicker. Specific availability of hot and cold-rolled products as well as maximum widths at various thicknesses vary. In searching these products, it is best to consult the producers.

TABLE 31-2
Formability Classification of Steels

Material	Tensile Strength,		Yield Strength,		Formability Factor
	ksi	MPa	ksi	MPa	
Mild steel	55	379	35	241	1
	65	448	45	310	
High-tensile, low-yield steel	80	552	30	207	1.2
	90	621	40	276	
Medium-tensile, medium-yield steel	60	414	45	310	1.7
	75	517	55	379	
High-tensile, high-yield steel	105	724	90	621	3.1
	135	931	100	690	

SHEET METAL FORMING

High-Strength Sheet Steels

Low-carbon sheet steels provide an effective balance of strength and modulus for many components. However, many components can be designed more effectively by using higher strength steels at reduced thicknesses.

A range of high-strength steels is available in strength levels from 35-80 ksi (241-552 MPa). These steels offer many of the same advantages as the low-carbon steels. Because of this, they are compatible with existing manufacturing equipment. They can be formed, joined, and painted at high production rates.

The wide range of qualities of high-strength steels permits optimization of selection in terms of cost, formability, and weldability. At the same time, these steels meet part performance requirements of strength, fatigue, and toughness.

Carbon-manganese steel. Although carbon and manganese are added to increase the strength of steel, they impair its ductility and weldability.

Nitrogenized steel. In addition to carbon and manganese, nitrogen is added to these steels to increase strength and hardness. The addition of nitrogen enables the producer to use slightly lower carbon and/or manganese levels than are used in the carbon-manganese grades, thus improving formability.

Nitrogenized steels are also characterized by accelerated strain aging properties. This characteristic enables the steel to attain yield strength increases of as much as 25% in the finished part over the as-received condition. The increase in yield strength is accompanied by a loss of ductility and toughness.

Phosphorized steel. Like nitrogenized steels, the phosphorized steels are characterized by the addition of a strengthening element—phosphorus. The carbon and/or manganese content of the metal may be reduced slightly from the carbon-manganese grades. Stretchability, weldability, and toughness are comparable to that of carbon-manganese and nitrogenized steels, and drawability is somewhat better than that of nitrogenized and carbon-manganese steels.

High-Strength, Low-Alloy Steel

The HSLA steels are strengthened by the addition of microalloying elements such as columbium, vanadium, titanium, and zirconium, or by having low levels of alloying elements such as silicon, chromium, molybdenum, copper, and nickel. The use of these elements enables producers to significantly reduce the carbon and/or manganese levels to improve formability, toughness, and weldability when compared to structural quality steels. Figure 31-7 shows elongation vs. yield strength for plain carbon steels and HSLA steels.

The principal differences between these types of steel, and among the grades within them, are the deoxidation practices and the spread between yield point and tensile strength.

The major element affecting tensile strength is carbon. High-strength steels with higher carbon levels generally have a greater yield strength to tensile strength spread (20 ksi; 138 MPa). Thus, for steel specified to a minimum yield strength, a higher tensile strength and improved fatigue characteristics are attainable with the higher carbon levels. The greater yield strength to tensile strength spread also coincides with better formability. Lower carbon steels with other alloying elements for strength properties do, however, merit consideration for applications in which weldability and other fabricating and performance factors are primary considerations in material selection.

Deoxidation practices can significantly affect the quality of steel. Semikilled steels, like capped and rimmed steels, are less homogeneous than killed steels. As a result, they are not as formable nor are they as tough. Killed steels are more homogeneous with improved toughness and formability.

Sulfide inclusion control can be obtained in killed steels through the addition of small amounts of zirconium, titanium, or rare earth elements. This results in a steel with optimum formability in both the longitudinal and transverse directions. The deoxidation practices increase the cost of producing the steel.

The formability properties of HSLA steels can be summarized as follows:

- Their performance is comparable to mild steels in simple bending areas as well as in straight line areas of draw dies.
- In stretching, performance is similar to mild steels except for reduced elongation to the point of fracture and poor strain distribution. Stretched shapes must, therefore, be less demanding for the high-strength steels.
- Regarding drawing, areas of radial cup shaped deep draws are borderline. Abnormal tonnages are required to avoid wrinkles, and the tendency is toward fractures and laminations.
- With regard to springback, although HSLA steels generally have a greater degree of springback than mild steels, problems are manageable within normal part design and die practices.

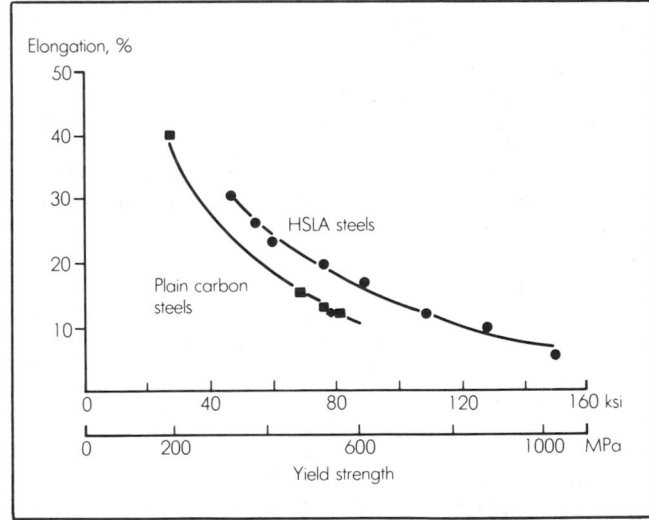

Fig. 31-7 Elongation (formability) versus yield strength for plain carbon steels and high-strength, low-alloy steels.

Ultrahigh-Strength Steels

These steels should be considered when part strength is critical. They are characterized by good weldability and formability that, while limited, is adequate for roll-forming or press-brake operations.

At the lower yield range, specially processed low-carbon steels can be produced in a cold-rolled condition to minimum yield points of 85 ksi (586 MPa).

Titanium, vanadium, or columbium-bearing, low-carbon steels can be produced in a cold-rolled, annealed condition at yield point minimums of 100 ksi (689 MPa), 120 ksi (827 MPa), and 140 ksi (965 MPa). Low-carbon martensitic steels are available in strengths up to 200 ksi (1379 MPa) yield strength.

Strength in Finished Part

All steels are characterized by an ability to work harden and strengthen from strain induced during part forming. In addition, many steels age harden at ambient temperatures or at elevated temperatures such as those incurred during painting-baking cycles. These two properties are important in imparting additional strength to the finished part and should be taken into consideration when steel is being compared to other materials. Strength increases in the finished part due to straining and aging of 20-30 ksi (138-207 MPa) are not uncommon. Most steels have individual strain aging characteristics, and the purchaser should consult with the steel producer for specifics.

A new family of dual-phase steels is characterized by very rapid work-hardening characteristics. Increases of 20,000 psi (138 MPa) in yield point can be obtained in areas of a part which have less than 3% strain. This characteristic enables relatively low strength steel to be used in producing high-strength parts that require complex forming.

Strain Rate Sensitivity

One of the characteristics of some metals is that common tensile test properties change with the speed of testing. This important property is called strain rate sensitivity. A common and simple measure of strain rate sensitivity is the change of yield strength as the speed of deformation is changed.[3]

Equations. While there are a number of equations which can describe this behavior, the following are most widely used:

$$\sigma_T = K\dot{\epsilon}^m \tag{1}$$

where:

σ_T = true stress
K = constant defined as the stress at a strain rate of $\dot{\epsilon} = 1$
$\dot{\epsilon}$ = true strain rate
m = strain rate hardening exponent

and:

$$\sigma_T = K\epsilon^n \tag{2}$$

where:

ϵ = true strain
n = strain-hardening (work-hardening) exponent

The strain-hardening and strain rate hardening effects usually are combined into one equation:

$$\sigma_T = K\epsilon^n\dot{\epsilon}^m \tag{3}$$

Energy absorption. Of increasing importance to the design engineer are the effects of impact loading, controlled crush, and energy absorption on vehicle components. A knowledge of the change in mechanical properties of a material with changes in strain rate (strain rate sensitivity) is paramount in understanding and designing for vehicle crash protection. Studies show that for both low-carbon steels and high-strength, low-alloy steels, yield and tensile strengths increase with increasing strain rate. The total elongations remain constant.

Absorbed energy tends to increase with increasing strain rate. Figure 31-8 shows examples of relative increases in yield strength with strain rate for a number of steels and for an aluminum alloy. In a practical sense, ferrous alloys are stronger at high loading rates than expected from ordinary mechanical property measurements. This provides dent resistance, impact loading resistance, and energy absorption.

NONFERROUS SHEET METAL FORMABILITY

The formability parameters and methods of analysis for nonferrous sheet metal are similar to those used for steel. The correlation of physical and mechanical properties to formability, however, differs from one material to another. Expert knowledge and careful treatment of data are required to achieve valid formability comparisons among different groups of materials.

Sheet Aluminum Alloy Formability

Aluminum and its alloys are among the most readily formable of the commonly fabricated metals. Aluminum alloys for sheet metal forming applications are available in various combinations of strength and formability. There are, of course, differences between aluminum alloys and other metals in the deformation that is attainable, as well as differences in some aspects of tool design and in operation procedural details. These differences are caused primarily by the lower tensile and yield strengths of aluminum alloys and by their comparatively low rate of work hardening and low strain rate sensitivity. The compositions and tempers also affect aluminum alloy formability.

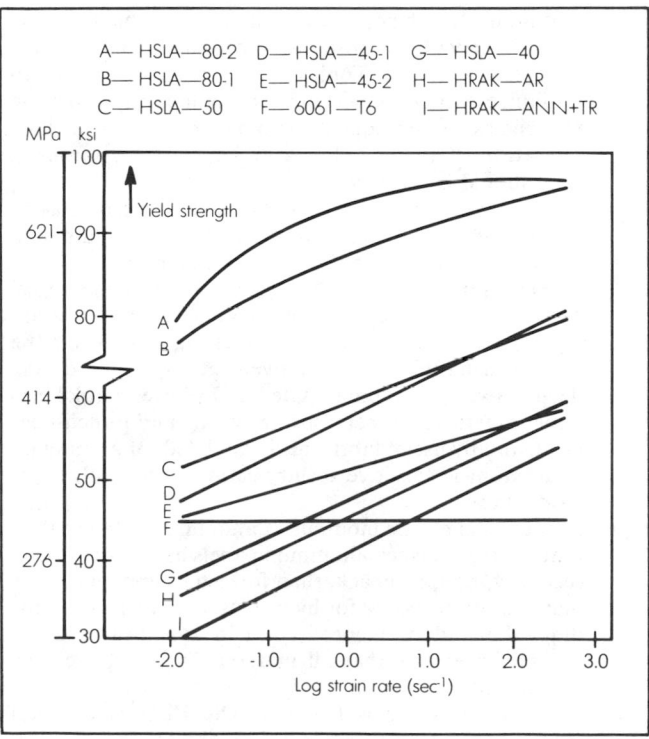

Fig. 31-8 Effect of strain rate on yield strength.

SHEET METAL FORMING

The strain-hardening alloys of the 5xxx series have excellent formability in the annealed temper. However, in the conventional "0" temper, they are susceptible to formation of Luder lines during deformation. Use of such materials generally is restricted to interior or nonvisible panels. This limitation does not apply to the Lüders' line resistant variations of the "0" temper. The heat-treatable alloys have good to excellent formability, with formability generally varying inversely in relation to strength of the alloy.

High-Volume Production. Aluminum sheet has recently begun to be specified in applications that require high-volume forming techniques, such as mechanical stamping with hard tooling. High strength-to-weight ratio and excellent corrosion resistance are the primary engineering advantages of aluminum over low-carbon steel in such applications.[4]

In evaluating the ease with which a particular stamping can be formed from aluminum sheet, three basic forming parameters—the shape of the part, the specific alloy and the tooling (or process)—should be considered.

Aluminum forming characteristics. Aluminum stampings often are considered replacements for stampings of low-carbon steel. Choosing between an aluminum alloy and a low-carbon steel for a particular application requires detailed analysis and should take into consideration the following general comments:

- Formability of medium-strength aluminum alloys in deep draw and biaxial stretch cup type forming operations is about two-thirds that of low-carbon steel.
- Minimum bend radii are approximately three times those for steel. The lower bendability is related to aluminum's characteristically low reduction in area. Aluminum cannot be severely strained in local areas that have sharp formations.
- Aluminum's high notch sensitivity requires that blanking tools—particularly those with sharp edges—be designed for close tolerances. Tools must be sharp and precise to minimize formation of burrs and reduce edge-splitting tendencies in subsequent bending or flange-stretching operations. Lancing of blanks to improve interior metal flow should be avoided.
- Yield strengths of steels generally increase with increasing strain rate, while yield strengths of typical aluminum alloys are relatively unaffected by strain rate.
- In mechanical presses, the highest speed in the stroke cycle occurs during workpiece contact. The low strain rate sensitivity of aluminum creates high stresses in the metal during initial metal movement, especially during deep drawing. It is compensated for by lower blank hold-down pressure, by increased draw-ring and punch-nose radii, and by use of lubricants formulated for aluminum. Aluminum is sensitive to lubrication as a result of its oxide layer.
- Because the elastic modulus of aluminum is lower than that of steel, formed aluminum panels have more elastic recovery, or springback, than formed steel panels. This must be compensated for by increasing overcrown in the draw die and/or incorporating locking beads in the binder, to ensure that all material has been "set" by plastic deformation.

Forming limit diagrams (FLD's). The FLD is a useful representation of aluminum sheet formability. Basically, it depicts the biaxial combinations of strain that can occur without failure. A variety of FLD shapes are found for aluminum alloys. However, a number of aluminum alloys have FLD's with shapes similar to that of low-carbon steel. This similarity is illustrated in Fig. 31-9.

Wrought Zinc Alloy Formability

The material properties used to characterize the formability of steel do not correlate with the properties that characterize the formability of the various zinc alloy series. When drawing is being considered, the plastic strain ratio at 0° to the rolling direction is a better indicator of the alloy's performance than the normal anisotropy coefficient used with other materials. In assessing the stretch forming characteristics of zinc alloys, the strain-hardening exponent, n_{90}, does not accurately predict behavior. Because of the high strain rate sensitivity of zinc alloys, the m value, as well as the total elongation, should be considered. More work is needed in this area to develop a reliable correlation. Therefore, caution should be used in attempting to compare the formability of zinc alloys to different types of materials based strictly on mechanical property test data. The absolute data may not correlate directly with the ability of the material to withstand certain forming operations, and/or it may not fully describe the material's capability. The latter is especially true for zinc alloys.

The forming limit diagrams for the various zinc alloy series can be used to evaluate any forming process in conjunction with circular grid strain analyses in the same way that the FLD for steel is used. Forming limit diagrams for representative steel and zinc alloys are shown in Fig. 31-10.[5]

Nonferrous Formability Data

Punch stretching accompanied by flange draw-in is called "combined stretching." The combined stretching depends on

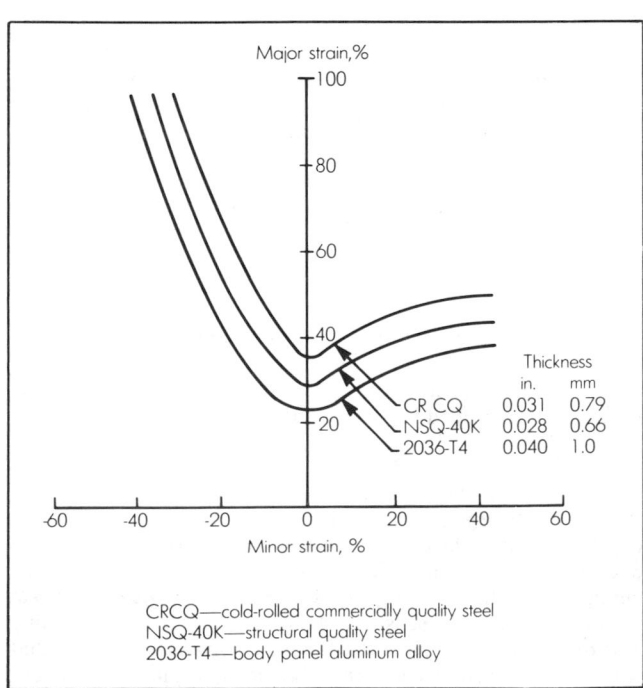

Fig. 31-9 Forming limit diagrams for selected steel and aluminum sheet materials.

the pure stretchability and deep drawability, that is, mainly on the n and r values. Figure 31-11 illustrates some typical relationships between the forming limit (as measured by stretching depth, h_{max}) and n or r value for shells of different geometry.[6] The relationship between h_{max} and r in sheet steels is strong, although it exhibits effects varying from forming geometry. In nonferrous materials that have virtually the same r value, the forming limit, h_{max}, is closely related to the n value for all the different geometries of forming (in this particular set of tests). The stress-strain relationship characterized by the n value is very important and also quite complex.

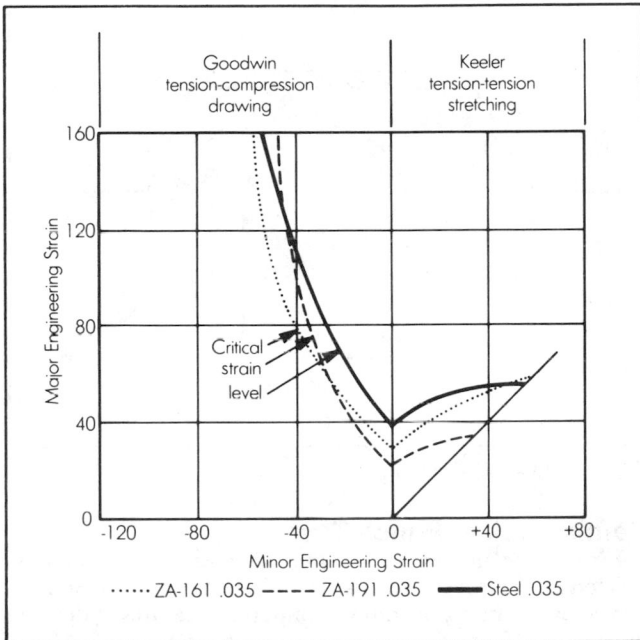

Fig. 31-10 Forming limit diagrams for representative steel and zinc alloys.

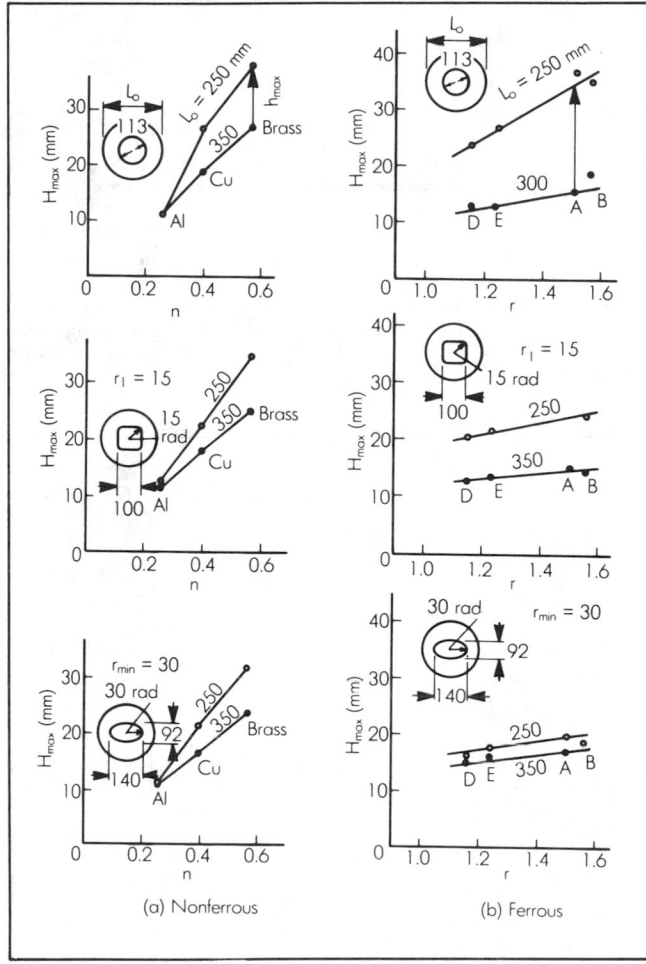

Fig. 31-11 Relationship between stretching depth and n or r value for different forming geometry. (Dimensions are in mm.)

SIMULATIVE FORMABILITY TESTS

When complex stampings are broken down into their component operations, each operation can be simulated and studied in the laboratory. Tests that subject sheet metal to the same types of deformation found in stamping are used to evaluate formability. These simulative tests enable the effects of surface textures of materials, lubrication, anisotropy, and large surface areas to be evaluated. Figure 31-12 shows, schematically, the interrelationship between forming operations, material properties, and simulative tests. In addition to the tests discussed here, the simulative tests also include a number of other cup/dome, bend, and hole-expansion tests.

Olsen and Erichsen Tests

The Erichsen (Europe) and Olsen (North America) tests are similar in that they are both ball-punch deformation tests that simulate stretch forming. The principal difference is in the size of the ball, 0.875" (22.23 mm) for the Olsen and approximately 0.8" (20 mm) for the Erichsen tests. In both tests, a ball-punch penetrator is pressed into a metal sheet clamped over a cup. The end point of the test is indicated by a drop in load, indicating

necking in the specimen. Maximum cup height is measured when necking occurs. The cup-test value is reported as the ratio of cup height to cup diameter. A typical cupping test is shown in Fig. 31-13. The procedures for conducting Olsen and Erichsen tests are described in ASTM Specification E643.78.

The Swift test is commonly used to simulate deep drawing. The test consists of drawing a circular blank specimen into a cylindrical cup. It has not been entirely standardized because results are affected by many factors: die opening, die approach radius, surface finish, thickness, blank lubrication, hold-down pressure, and material properties. The Swift index or limiting draw ratio, LDR, is obtained with a 2" (51 mm) diam flat-bottom punch and draw die appropriate for thickness of the specimen. A circular blank is cut to a diameter smaller than the expected draw limit. The blank is drawn to maximum punch load, which occurs before the cup is fully formed. Successively larger blanks are drawn until one fractures before being drawn completely through the die. The diameter of the largest blank that can be drawn without fracturing, divided by cup diameter, determines the limiting draw ratio, LDR.

Correlation of Results

Results of simulative forming tests correlate well with results

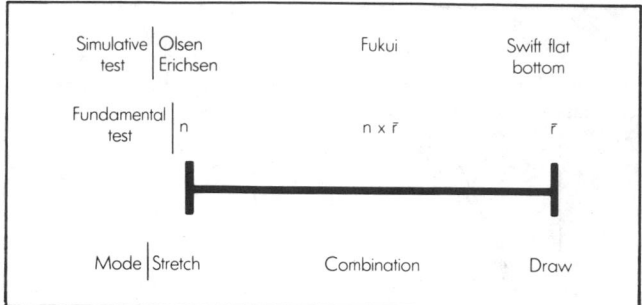

Fig. 31-12 Forming classification. Certain material properties and simulative tests can be correlated between the two extremes (stretching and drawing).

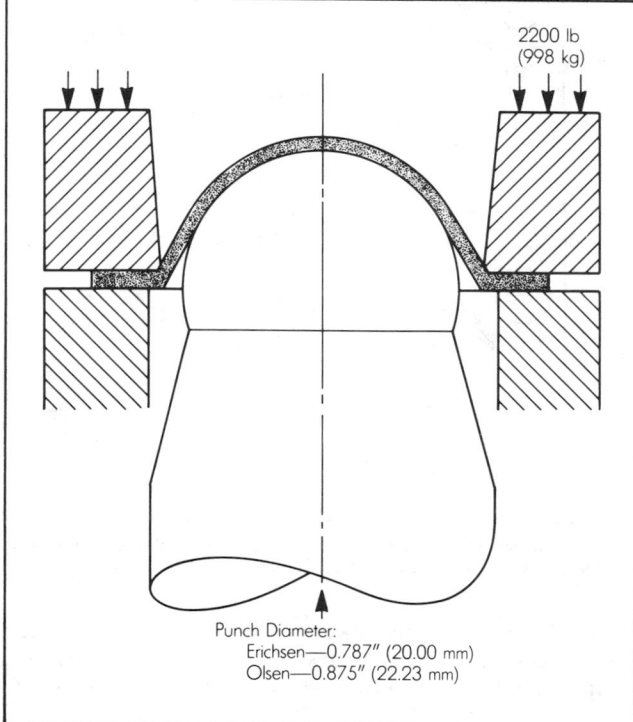

Fig. 31-13 Erichsen or Olsen Cup test.

of tension tests. Specifically, results of cup ductility tests, such as the Olsen and Swift tests, show good correlation with values of tensile elongation, the strain-hardening exponent, and the plastic strain ratio. In production forming, the material properties that apply to flange stretching are tensile elongation and plastic strain ratio. Ease of forming ribs and troughs in parts is related to the plastic strain ratio and can best be predicted from tests that produce conditions of plane strain. The formability test must be matched to a particular stamping for valid correlation with press performance data.

Fukui Test

Combined stretching and drawing are simulated in the Fukui Conical Cup test (see Fig. 31-14). Since a majority of stampings are complex combinations of many separate operations, including stretching, drawing, bending, etc., the Fukui test often is more meaningful than the Olsen test.

The Fukui Conical Cup test is based on forcing a disc of sheet steel into a cone with a hemispherical punch. A 60° conical die is used so that no clamping force is required to hold the blank. The apparatus and procedure are derived from the need for a test that combines biaxial stretching over a punch and drawing-in over a radius as occurs in most press forming operations.

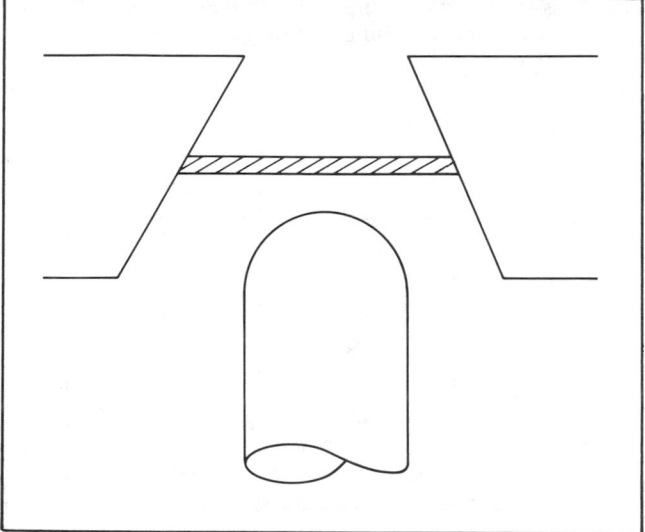

Fig. 31-14 Fukui Conical Cup test.

Hemispherical Punch Test

Limitations inherent in the Olsen Cup test led to efforts to develop an improved dome stretching test for evaluation of pure stretch forming operations. Important features of the test (see Fig. 31-15) include a common punch diameter of 4" (102 mm) and a locking bead to insure pure metal stretch.

Usefulness of Test Results

Simulative tests, such as mechanical property tests, are limited in value for the evaluation of sheet metal formability. This is because the exact placement of a stamping on the classification spectrum varies or is unknown. Several combinations of forming operations may be found in various

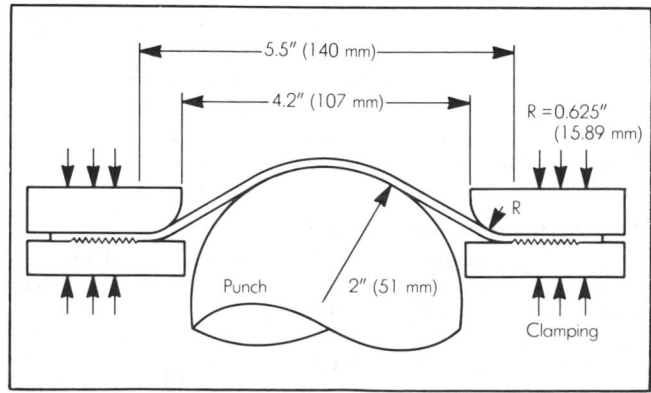

Fig. 31-15 Hemispherical punch test.

locations of the part. The relative amounts of stretching and drawing vary with material properties, lubrication, die conditions, time, and the depth of the stamping. The fundamental and simulative tests are limited to comparing various materials.

SUPERPLASTIC METALFORMING

In metalforming, one of the significant emerging technologies is based on superplasticity—the property that permits the forming of metal as if it were a polymer or glass. The basic definition of a superplastic metal is that it can develop extremely high tensile elongations at elevated temperatures and under controlled rates of deformation.[7] As shown in Fig. 31-16, a conventional metal or alloy would develop perhaps 10-30% tensile elongation in an ordinary tensile test. This ductility is normally unchanged even though the temperatures may be increased. However, a superplastic material develops extremely high tensile elongations characteristically exceeding 300% elongation and not infrequently achieving as high as 2000-3000% tensile elongation. This is achieved at elevated temperatures and controlled strain rates. The other characteristic normally observed concurrently with the high tensile deformation is a substantial reduction in the flow stress of the material. That is, the forces and stresses required to cause this deformation can be as little as 1/2 to 1/20th that of the conventional alloy under the same conditions. It is these two factors (high tensile elongation and low flow stress) that provide the exceptional potential available through superplastic forming.

A characteristic of a superplastic alloy is the strong sensitivity of flow stress to strain rate. This characteristic is quantified by the following relationship:

$$\sigma = K\epsilon^m \qquad (4)$$

where:

σ = flow stress
K = material constant
ϵ = strain rate
m = strain rate sensitivity exponent

The value of m for a superplastic material is not a constant function of strain rate. It normally follows a bell curve.

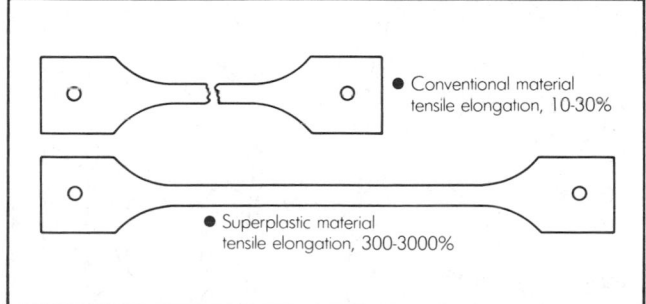

- Conventional material tensile elongation, 10-30%
- Superplastic material tensile elongation, 300-3000%

Fig. 31-16 Specimens illustrating superplasticity, which is the capability of certain alloys to develop extremely high tensile elongations at elevated temperatures and controlled strain rates.

Superplasticity Requirements

The most fundamental requirements for superplasticity are (1) grain size must be fine and stable and normally less than about 10 microns, although the grain size requirement may vary with material and other conditions; (2) the temperature at which the deformation proceeds is usually in excess of one-half the absolute melting point; and (3) the rate of straining must be controlled since superplasticity is observed only within a specified strain rate range. As the strain rate increases beyond the superplastic region, the ductility drops dramatically; and if the strain rate is decreased below the superplastic strain rate, the ductility likewise drops dramatically.

Materials

While most ferrous and nonferrous metal and alloy systems have the potential for being superplastically formed, titanium alloys and high-strength aluminum alloys are regarded as having outstanding potential for application of this technology. Several alloy systems, such as zinc-aluminum (Zn-Al) and aluminum-copper-zinc (Al-Cu-Zn), have been developed specifically for their superplastic properties, and most titanium-based alloys exhibit superplasticity as conventionally produced sheet material.

Advantages

Superplastic forming offers a number of advantages. First, because of the very high tensile elongation and resistance of superplastic material to localized necking and rupture, complex parts are readily formed. Since the forming typically is caused by gas pressure, it is necessary to use only a single configurational tool; that is, a tool designed to provide the shape of the part required. This results in both low cost of die fabrication and reduced lead time, since it is not necessary to fabricate a mating die and impose the costly hand-work operations necessary to cause the dies to mate accurately. The gas pressures normally used for superplastic forming are quite low, typically less than 300 psi (2 MPa). This permits the use of inexpensive die materials and can permit the forming of large complex parts with low press load capacity.

Perhaps the most important benefit of the superplastic forming process is related to the design of structural components. Because it is capable of forming complex parts, superplastic forming greatly increases the design flexibility. This can result in reduced part and fastener counts, thereby resulting in more efficient structural designs and systems that are lighter in weight.

The other area of keen importance is that of fabrication costs. The fabrication labor costs are greatly reduced since there are fewer parts; consequently, less time is expended in fabrication assembly. Both of these factors result in lower costs for the component. It is noted that the greatest benefits of this technology depends on a coupling of the design and manufacturing functions to result in the most efficient structure with the lowest cost.

Limitations

Superplastic materials do not offer advantages in conventional deep drawing processes under isothermal conditions. The reason is that to draw in the flange, the material in contact with the punch nose as well as the cup walls must first work harden. At temperatures necessary for superplastic forming, no significant work hardening occurs; thus, if the friction between punch and blank is high, the punch typically pierces the blank or fails in the cup walls. The most significant disadvantage of superplastic forming is its inherently low forming rate (particularly for sheet structural parts), which is measured in terms of

ANALYTICAL METHODS

several inches per minute or less. This limitation disqualifies the superplastic alloys for high-production parts.

Process Selection

In general, superplastic forming merits consideration when the part design requires complex, relatively deep shapes with compound curves or when redesigning of built-up, multiple-piece structures can reduce the part and fastener count and simplify assembly operations. The process would not be specified for easy-to-fabricate parts that require little tooling.

ANALYTICAL METHODS

Sheet metal forming is an experience-oriented technology. Throughout the years, a great deal of know-how and experience have been accumulated in this field, largely by trial-and-error methods. The complex physical phenomena describing a metal-forming process are difficult to express mathematically. The metal flow, the friction at the tool-workpiece interface, the heat generation and transfer during plastic deformation, and the behavior and properties of the material are difficult to predict and analyze.

The development of analytical methods to study and describe mechanisms in metalforming has been active since 1940. Although considerable progress has been made, the techniques currently available are limited in their quantitative applicability. They have, however, become useful as qualitative guides.

Grid strain analysis involves etching a pattern of fine circles onto the sheet steel before pressing. During pressing, the circles are deformed into ellipses which can be measured to determine major and minor strains produced in the component. An estimate of how close the metal is to failure can be obtained by reference to the forming limit diagram (FLD), which is a plot of the major and minor strains at fracture over a wide range of conditions, from deep drawing (tension-compression) to stretch forming (tension-tension). A knowledge of how close the metal is to failure enables an estimate to be made of the criticality of the press forming operation. The strain values and the ratio of major to minor strain give information on the type of deformation in various areas of the press-formed part; for example, whether the metal has been drawn or stretched. This information provides insight into the press forming operation that can be used to solve problems in die development work and part design.

CIRCULAR GRID SYSTEM

The circular grid system is widely used to evaluate sheet metal formability. It permits immediate and direct measurement of the maximum elongation of the sheet at any location. The grid consists of a pattern of small circles, typically 0.1" (2.5 mm) diam, electrochemically etched into the surface of the blank prior to forming. Analysis of the deformed circles after forming (see Fig. 31-17) indicates the level of mechanical properties required in the sheet to form the part without breakage. Alternatively, it suggests the type and amount of rework to be performed on dies so that the part may be formed from a given grade of sheet metal.

Imprinting the Pattern

Electrochemical marking is commonly used to etch the circular grid pattern onto the test metal sheet. This process eliminates the problems encountered with techniques such as scribing, printing, and photoprinting.

In this process, an "electrical stencil" is placed on the cleaned blank. A felt pad, soaked with electrolyte, is then placed on top of the blank, and an electrode—which may be either flat or "rocking"—is placed above the felt pad. The type of electrolyte used depends on the material to be gridded. Leads from a 14-volt power source are attached to the electrode and the blank. Current varies from 15-200 A, depending on stencil size and line density.

Application time ranges from 15 seconds for a flat electrode to under one minute for a rocker or roller type of electrode. The depth of the etched mark is 0.0005" (0.013 mm) or less and is controlled by the application time. After etching, the solution on the blank is neutralized and a polarized oil is applied to prevent rusting.

Several hundred grids can be obtained from each stencil. For large areas, the stencil is stepped along the sheet until the desired area is covered; however, this is usually not necessary since only one or two potentially critical areas need be gridded on each panel. Once the pattern is etched into the sheet, the grid is not removed by rubbing the part over the die nor is it removed by applications of oil or chemicals.

The marked sheet is placed in a tryout press and formed, approaching as nearly as possible the conditions under which the part is to be formed in production. This is important because such variables as the type of lubricant used, the rate at which deformation occurs, and the force exerted on the hold-down ring have a substantial effect on the distribution of stresses in the blank and on the resulting deformation or strain.

Measuring Strain

Strain is a measurement of linear deformation; that is, the amount by which a unit length of metal is stretched. Each type

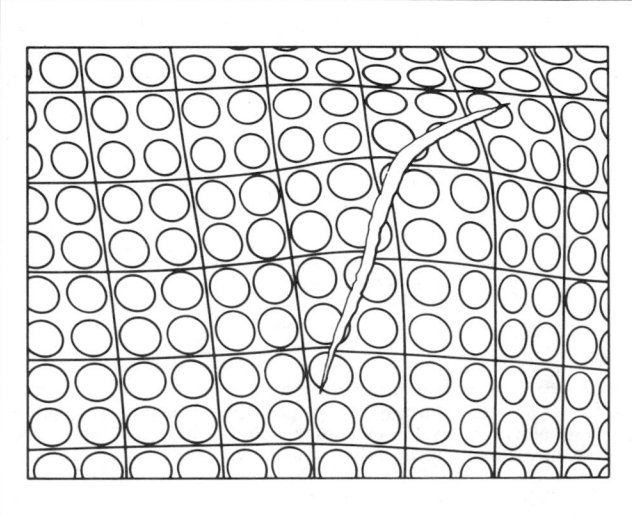

Fig. 31-17 Strain patterns in a formed sheet metal part are made visible by deformation of circles. Analysis enables failure cause to be identified and eliminated.

of material has an allowable strain also called the critical strain level. If the critical strain level is exceeded, the metal fails, usually by tearing. To evaluate how well the metal responds to a given set of forming conditions, the actual strain must be measured at each potential failure location. Strain is identified with the standard symbol ϵ and is measured in percentages:

$$\epsilon = \frac{l_f - l_o \times 100}{l_o} = \frac{\Delta l \times 100}{l_o} \tag{5}$$

where:

l_o = original length
l_f = final length
Δl = difference between final and original length

Depending on the accuracy desired, a selection can be made from several grid measuring techniques. For relatively small volume, routine measuring ($\pm 5\%$ accuracy is sufficient), simple flexible rulers or calibrated strips are satisfactory. For high-volume operations, measurement of the outcome of circle-grid testing is done most effectively either by use of stereo binoculars fitted with a calibrated reticle or by use of a specially marked mylar tape on which diverging lines are marked to allow a direct reading of the strain (elongation of circles in one or both axes). A computerized measuring system is also gaining acceptance.

When the material is strained, a circle becomes an ellipse (see Fig. 31-18). The largest surface strain is along the major axis of the ellipse. The formula for calculating strain is:

$$\epsilon = \frac{l_a - d_o \times 100}{d_o} \tag{6}$$

where:

ϵ = strain
l_a = length, major axis
d_o = diameter of original circle

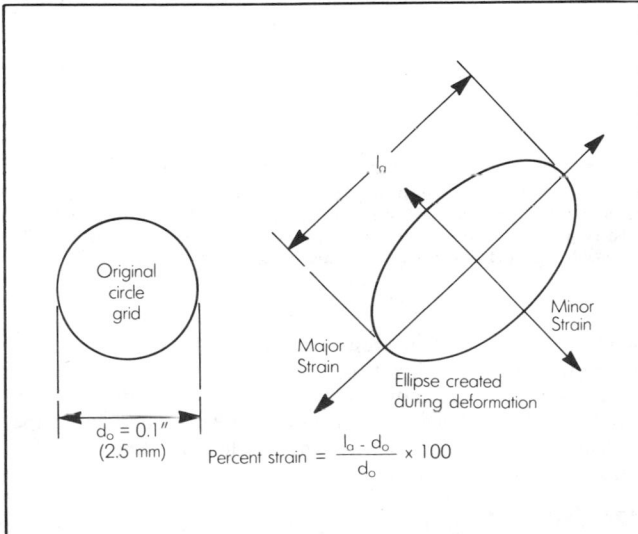

Fig. 31-18 Circles stretch into ellipses as a result of strain. Maximum strain is along major axis.

A similar calculation is made to determine the cross strain or the strain along the minor axis of the ellipse.

The grid spacing must be small enough to detect point-to-point variations in the strain distribution. For this reason, the circle diameters range from 0.1-0.2" (2.5-5 mm). In research experiments, diameters 0.05" (1.3 mm) and smaller may be used.

One important safety factor to be kept in mind is that when a stamping tears during forming, the tear is a visible indication that the metal has been worked beyond its formability limit. A more formable material, different lubricants, or reworked tools are needed. Modification of the tools is often more economical than paying the increased cost of premium materials or lubricants during the life of a product model.

Many stampings are close to failure, but yet not to the point at which they tear. These are called "critical" stampings. During die tryout, conditions may permit critical stampings to be formed successfully. The conditions include the use of slow speeds, careful blanking, spot lubrication, carefully adjusted tools, and selected blanks. In production, conditions less than optimum may prevail and breakage may result. Breakage during production runs is costly. Modifications then are time consuming when time is at a premium. The ability to predict failure—to identify critical stampings—is very desirable, and the circular grid system provides at least a partial solution to this problem.

The goal in measuring strain is to find the safety factor for each combination of material, lubricant, die set, and press. This safety factor indicates how close to failure a particular area of the finished part is. It is defined as the percent strain difference between the critical strain and the peak strain found in the stamping.

FORMING LIMIT DIAGRAM

The forming limit diagram (FLD) is sometimes referred to as a "formability map." The FLD shows, for different strain rates, the maximum strain that a sheet metal can sustain before onset of localized thinning. For steel, the FLD is dependent upon sheet gage and the strain-hardening exponent, n.

Formability Map

In the forming limit diagram (see Fig. 31-19) the bands indicating the critical strain level separate failure and nonfailure conditions for annealed and lightly rolled low-carbon sheet steel. The portion of the graph on the right represents tension-tension strains. These most commonly occur over the head of the punch or under conditions of stretching in which the blank is clamped and the punch is pushed into the sheet. The major and minor axes of the ellipse are both larger than the diameter of the original grid circle.

The portion of the graph on the left is for conditions encountered in deep drawing, or the tension-compression strain states. Here the major axis of the ellipse is greater than the original diameter of the circle, while the minor axis is shortened or compressed to less than the circle diameter. The curve apparently continues as a straight line to very high strain levels (such as 225% tension and 85% compression). These very high strains are possible because compressing the metal from the sides contributes to material elongation in the other direction.

The critical strain level drops to lower values as the material is cold worked. It is relatively insensitive to variations in cleanliness, gage, direction in the sheet, and other properties.

ANALYTICAL METHODS

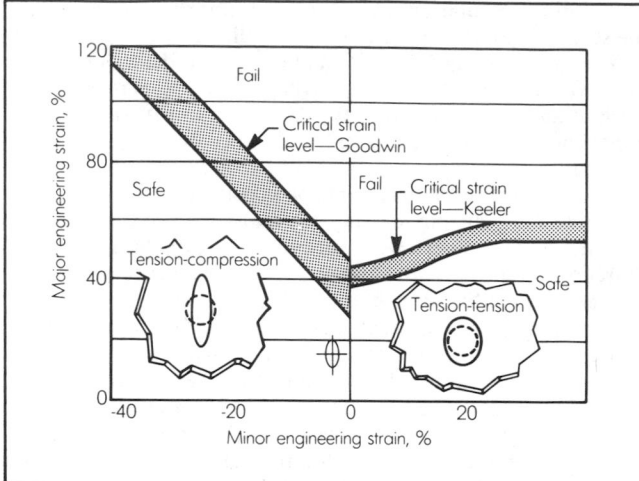

Fig. 31-19 Basic forming limit diagram. Critical strain band separates failure from nonfailure conditions. Vertical axis is for maximum strain (major axis of ellipse). Horizontal axis is for strain along minor axis of ellipse.

Strain Distribution

The requirement for a satisfactory stamping is to obtain as uniform a strain distribution as possible, under the critical level (see Fig. 31-20). The more uniformly the strain is distributed, the lower the peak strain is and the higher the safety factor is for equal depths of the stamping.

The important criterion is how uniformly a particular steel distributes the strain in the presence of a stress gradient. It must be emphasized, however, that material properties—and corresponding grades of steel—are not the only variables that influence strain distribution. Small changes in other factors—lubrication, die design, etc.—can overshadow large variations in material properties.

COMPUTER SYSTEM

The sequence of operations for General Motors Corporation's grid-circle analyzer (GCA), a computerized system for optically transforming the results of a grid-circle experiment into an FLD is shown in Fig. 31-21. The system uses a solid-state camera and computer to convert formed metal distortions directly into major and minor strains, which can be plotted as an FLD. Time to measure one ellipse by GCA is 15 seconds.

SHAPE ANALYSIS

Shape analysis is a method for determining the forming severity of a stamped part. Forming severity indicates, through a numerical value, how near the part is to fracture failure. Shape analysis is based on stretching and deep drawing actions in sheet metal forming. These actions occur when a blank is stretched over a punch nose and drawn into a die cavity. They influence each other and react with the tooling to affect the onset and character of failure. The shape analysis concept is extendable to any sheet metal undergoing similar kinds of strain. Determining the forming severity permits reduction in strain and improvement in material economy and process efficiency by changes in material, forming process, or part shape. The method can also be applied to parts of various designs, parts made of different

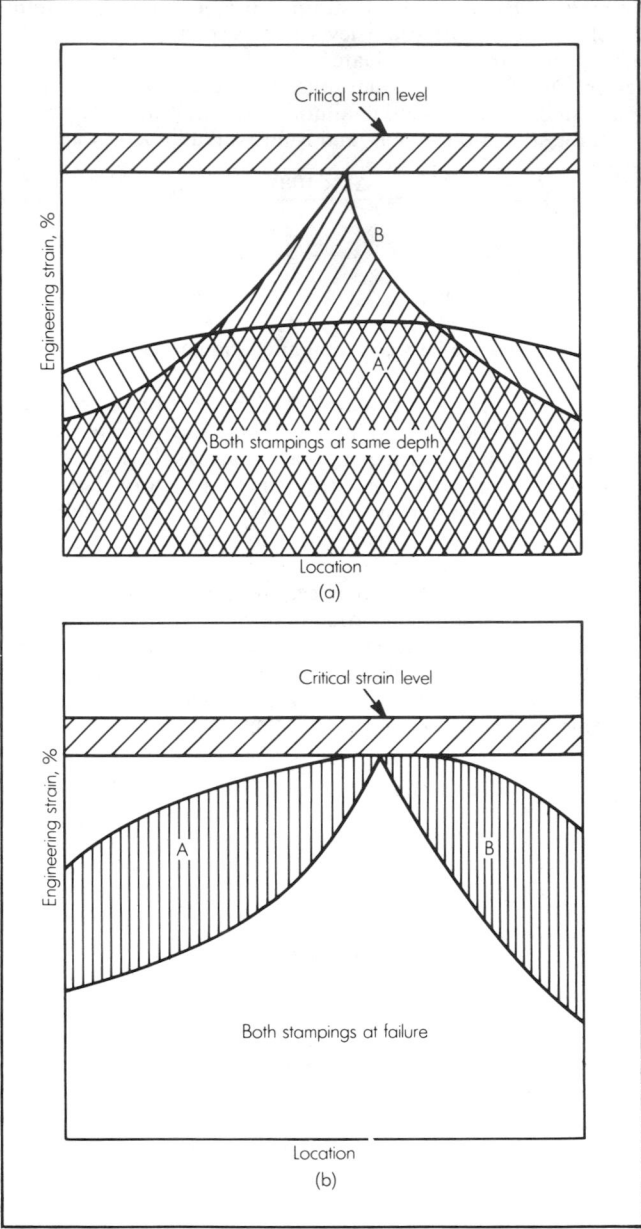

Fig. 31-20 Schematic strain distribution of two materials formed over the same punch. Because it distributes the same total strain more uniformly, (a) material A does not fail, while material B does and (b) material A absorbs much more strain before it fails.

materials and with different tooling, and parts on which different drawing lubricants are used.

Areas, lines, and points used in shape analysis are shown in Fig. 31-22. Symbols are identified in Table 31-3. The basic shape analysis procedure consists of part selection, line analysis, measuring, and calculating.

Part Selection

A portion of the part featuring a section of a cup shape should be selected. This can be the corner of a rectangular pan or the end of an elliptical or trough shape. Among these areas, the

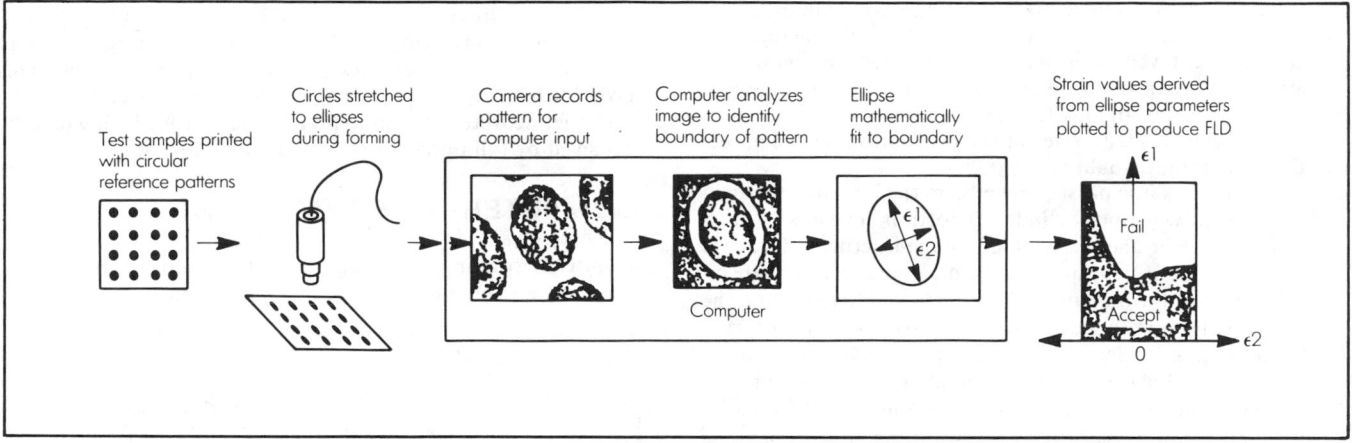

Fig. 31-21 Computer analysis of circle deformation in circle-grid technique. Computerized measurements use solid-state camera focused on a formed dome. Cathode ray tube in foreground shows two of the ellipses magnified for measurements.

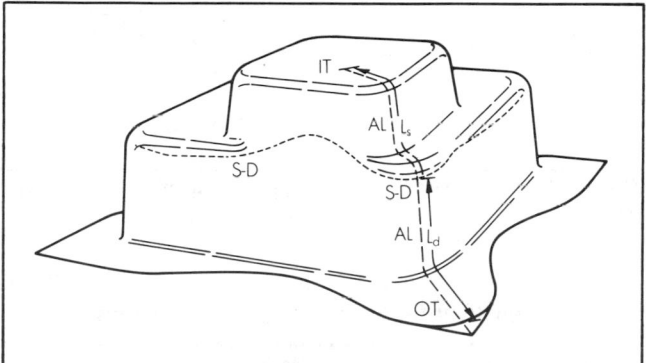

Fig. 31-22 Deep-drawn pan illustrating analysis line locations for measurements using shape analysis technique.

deepest and steepest formation is usually the most critical. Localized necking or incipient fracturing may be present. When such critical strains are elsewhere on a part, they may be traceable to efforts by press operators to compensate for the deeper formation.

The selected portion of the part is divided into two areas. The bottom area resembles a dome shape over the punch nose where the metal undergoes biaxial strain. This contour resembles various laboratory cups, such as the Olsen, Erichsen, and Dome Height Stretch cups. The principal factor affecting formability of these cups is the strain-hardening exponent, n. In the wall or cylindrical area, strain relates to such draw cups as the Swift, Engelhardt, and Single Blank Limiting Draw Ratio cups. The principle factor affecting formability of these draw cups is average anisotropy, $\bar{r}$.

These two groups of cups establish forming parameter limits of the material which appear in the calculations. Small shop presses can make these tests. A test part for analysis is formed with the blank gridded by circle strain patterns. The marked pattern should extend from the center of the part bottom outward to the corner or edge of the part.

Line Analysis

The analysis line, AL, represents the profile cross section of the cup-shaped area, a half cup from bottom center to its outer

TABLE 31-3
Identification of Symbols for Shape Analysis

Symbol	Identification
AL	Analysis line
IT	Inner terminal of analysis line
OT	Outer terminal of analysis line
$S\text{-}D$	Stretch-draw boundary between biaxial stretch and deep draw forming
L_s	Final length biaxial stretch portion of analysis line
L_d	Final length deep draw portion of analysis line
L_{os}	Original length biaxial stretch portion of analysis line
L_{od}	Original length deep draw portion of analysis line
L_{ds}	Final total analysis line length
L_o	Original total analysis line length
C_{hs}	Part stretch cup height
C_{hd}	Part draw cup height
C_{ws}	Biaxial stretch cup width at stretch-draw boundary
C_{wd}	Draw cup width at die ring
E_{bw}	Effective blank width derived from L_o ($2 \times L_o$)
STR	Amount of forming contributed to analysis line by biaxial stretch
$DRAW$	Amount of forming contributed to analysis line by deep draw
R_s	Stretch cup height to width ratio of the part
R_d	Draw cup blank to cup width ratio of the part
$*O_d$	Biaxial stretch material cup forming parameter
$**LDR$	Deep draw material cup forming parameter
SEV	Forming severity value obtained from shape analysis calculations

* O_d is the value of a 1" (25.4 mm) Olsen laboratory cup height in inches (millimeters) formed using oiled polyethylene lubrication on the punch. Dome height test cup ratio, h/w, is equally valid when using oiled polyethylene on punch.

** Limited Draw Ratio, *LDR,* the value of critical blank size/cup size from a Swift Cup Test or from a Single Blank Draw Cup Test, polyethylene and oil.

ANALYTICAL METHODS

limit. The location and ends of this line are important in obtaining useful measurements. The line is marked on the part as if a vertical cut were being made from the dome center out to the edge. It passes through the failure area. The center of the cup dome, the inner terminal, *IT*, is marked. This is not the part center but the projected center of the cup bottom at which the cup dome midpoint would be located.

As the analysis line passes down from the biaxially strained dome to the draw formed cylindrical portion, it passes through the stretch-draw boundary, *S-D*. Often the fracture failures are found near it. Identification is by the die impact mark made on the workpiece by the die ring as the sheet began to move into the die cavity. This mark in the metal is easily seen when the die ring has a tight radius edge. Circle-grid strain markings show a transition from biaxial stretch to elongation in draw in this area. Other identifying marks in the metal may be the start of scratches and sliding marks due to its movement on the die ring.

The outer terminal, *OT*, is marked at the outer limit in which material has effectively contributed to the cup formation. Although the outer terminal is frequently at the outer edge, the metal in the corner flanges does not draw into the die and is not strained by the forming action. This unstrained area can be observed by unaltered circle-grid marks. A draw bead can also prevent metal movement toward the cup.

Measuring

Two groups of measurements are taken. From the first group, the added length of the analysis line from blank to final shape for each kind of forming is measured. To do this, the circle-grid pattern is required. The distance, L_s, along the part surface from the inner terminal, *IT* to the stretch-draw boundary, *S-D*, is measured. For stretching, the original distance, L_{os}, of this line is obtained by counting grid circles and multiplying the number obtained by the unit fraction. Then the distance, L_d, from the stretch-draw boundary, *S-D*, to the outer terminal, *OT*, is measured along the part surface. Similarly, for drawing, the original distance, L_{od}, is determined by grid circle counting.

The second group of measurements (see Fig. 31-23) is used to determine the stretch cup and draw cup dimensions of the part. Toolmaker measuring devices are helpful in taking these measurements. Vertical height, C_{hs}, from the level of the inner terminal down to the stretch-draw boundary is measured. The horizontal distance from inner terminal to stretch-draw boundary is measured. This is equal to half the stretch cup width, C_{ws}. These measurements describe the stretch cup portion of the analysis line. For the draw cup portion, the vertical height, C_{hd}, from stretch-draw boundary to the outer terminal is measured. The horizontal distance from the inner terminal to the base of the draw cup is measured. This is equal to half the draw cup width, C_{wd}. The base of the draw cup is at the bend from cup wall to the outer flange which has not been drawn into the cup.

Calculating

The ratio of analysis line lengthening due to stretching can be obtained by calculating Eq. (7) in Table 31-4. The ratio of line lengthening due to draw can be found by calculating Eq. (8). When compared, these ratio values show the relative amount of stretching and drawing used to obtain the shape. This information is used in applying analysis results to indicate process changes or material specifications. Stretch and draw cup proportions can be obtained by calculating Eq. (9) and Eq. (10).

The final equation, Eq. (11), compares cup shape ratios and line lengthening ratios to the theoretical material forming parameters from the cup tests, a three-way comparison. This gives the forming severity, *SEV*, which shows how close the part is to the theoretical forming limit value of 1.0 which would be achieved by full utilization of the analysis line.

COMPUTER-AIDED MODELING

Research activity is aimed at enabling the computer to have a significant role in evaluating alternatives and optimizing the designing and manufacturing of sheet metal parts. In approach-

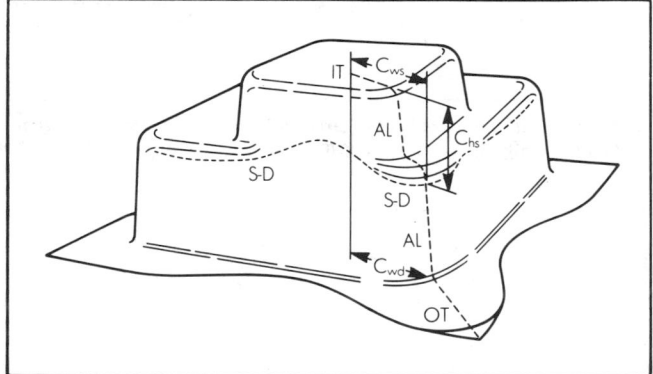

Fig. 31-23 Deep-drawn pan illustrating measurements taken for shape analysis.

TABLE 31-4
Equations for Shape Analysis Calculations

Analysis Line Lengthening:

$$STR = \frac{L_s - L_{os}}{L_{ds} - L_o} \qquad \text{where } L_{ds} = L_d + L_s \qquad (7)$$

$$DRAW = \frac{L_d - L_{od}}{L_{dx} - L_o} \qquad \text{where } L_o = L_{od} + L_{os} \qquad (8)$$

Cup Forming Ratios:

$$R_s = \frac{C_{hs}}{C_{ws}}$$

NOTE
C_{ws} should approximate 2 x L_{os}, since the analysis line profile accounts for half cup. $\qquad (9)$

$$R_d = \frac{E_{bw}}{C_{wd}} \qquad \text{where } E_{bw} = 2 \times L_o \qquad (10)$$

Forming Severity:

$$SEV = \frac{(R_s \times STR) + (R_d \times DRAW) - DRAW}{DRAW(LDR - O_d) + O_d - DRAW} \qquad (11)$$

NOTE
Substitution of *LDR* and O_d values in the Forming Severity equation with *LDR* and O_d values for other materials gives *SEV* values for those materials under identical forming conditions.

ing an understanding of the application of mathematical modeling and computers to sheet metal forming analysis and prediction, one begins by recognizing that the familiar formability parameters and relationships are the main ingredients for constructing a numerical model.

The sheet metal is described by its n, r, and m values; its yield and tensile strengths; and the forming limit diagram. The lubricant affects the punch-sheet interaction, and draw beads determine the conditions on the binder surface. To these factors are added a geometrical description of the punch and die and the equations of sheet metal plasticity. The output is the strain in the finished part and a prediction of any failure mode (necking, fracturing, wrinkling, etc.). Computer modeling of draw dies is in its infancy, and the general mathematical problem has not yet been solved. Hence, it is important to note that the computer models are presently used (1) as research tools and (2) for analysis of certain critical areas of stampings.

It is expected that, eventually, the computer will aid in making forming decisions on a broad basis. It will select material based not only on mechanical properties but also on overall part cost. Die dimensions will be worked out; dies will be constructed; and parts will be finished and delivered to final inspection—all with the aid of a computer.

The objective is to eliminate the "cut-and-try" aspect of sheet metal designing and fabrication, a fine-tuning process that can take as long as two years from initial die design to startup on the production line.

In predicting the success or failure of an automobile body stamping for a given die design, the computer is playing a significant role. In the technique represented by the graph shown in Fig. 31-24, experimental data and computer calculations combine to determine the feasibility of forming the part from a particular sheet metal material.

The data is presented as a forming limit diagram (FLD). Above a maximum combination of major and minor strain, the sheet metal will fail. The FLD is determined experimentally for each material.

A model based on the mathematical theory of plasticity is then used to calculate the strains that would occur in the metal during the stamping of a particular shape. Using parameters such as forces generated by the tool, material properties, and

panel geometry, the computer calculates strain paths such as the one shown in Fig. 31-24 for various locations on the sheet. The most critical strain path is then isolated.

To determine this critical path, calculated strains at various punch depths are compared with the maximum allowable strain on the FLD. In this example of an automobile body stamping, the maximum attainable punch depth is reached when the maximum calculated strain intercepts the FLD. Since this depth is less than the design depth, the part would develop a split and would fail.

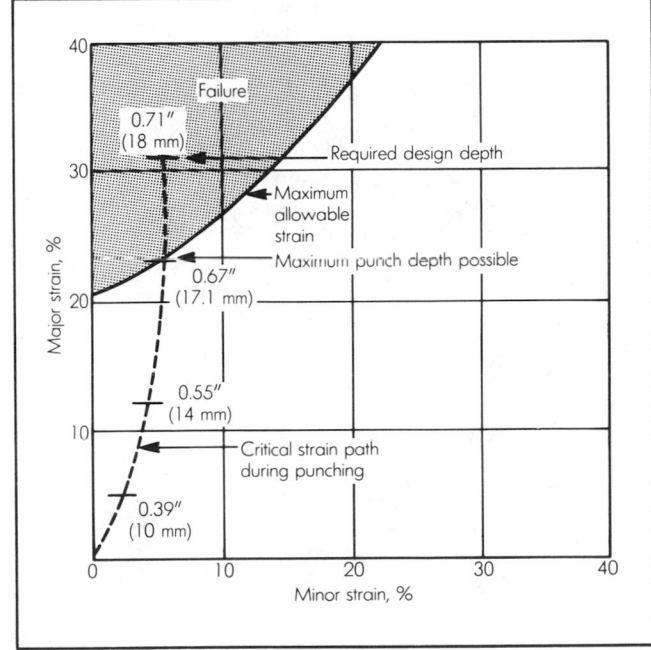

Fig. 31-24 Graph developed for predicting part formability. Experimental data and computer calculations are combined to assess feasibility of forming the part from a particular sheet metal material. This forming limit diagram delineates the failure zone, above a maximum feasible combination of major and minor strain.

FORMABILITY PREDICTION AND EVALUATION

It is recognized that fractures which occur during forming can be due to part design, tooling irregularities, steel quality, lubrication, or various press or shop conditions. Steel quality has been measured for many years by standard tests for determining yield strength, uniform elongation, total elongation, tensile strength, and resistance to thinning (plastic strain ratio). Lubricants have been characterized using various tests to obtain the coefficient of friction.

Until recently, the weak link in the analysis system has been the inability to quantitatively determine whether failures are attributable to a difficult design or to tooling irregularities. Now, however, by using both the forming limit diagram and shape analysis concepts in the analysis of parts from prototype through production, this weak link can be eliminated. At the General Electric Co. an ongoing forming analysis procedure

exemplifies this approach in a sophisticated application that combines the circle grid, forming limit diagram, and shape analysis systems.

The use of accepted analysis techniques to separate a design problem from a tooling problem is desirable because it permits quick identification of the true cause of a problem, which allows rapid implementation of corrective action. It also permits any improvement achieved by corrective action to be quantitatively measured.

SURFACE PATTERN FOR ANALYSES

Electrochemical etching is used to apply the circular-grid pattern on sheet metals that will be formed on prototype or production dies. A recommended pattern consists of four 0.1" (2.5 mm) diam circles within any number of 0.25" (6.4 mm)

FORMABILITY PREDICTION AND EVALUATION

squares (see Fig. 31-25, view *a*). The circles and squares are distorted during the forming process. Measurement of this distortion allows both the forming limit diagram and shape analysis techniques to be carried out. Electrochemical etching equipment is available from various manufacturers.

FORMING LIMIT DIAGRAM (FLD) CONCEPT

The FLD, originally developed by G. M. Goodwin and S. P. Keeler, allows forming severity to be obtained from the strains that occur during sheet metal forming. Measurement of the

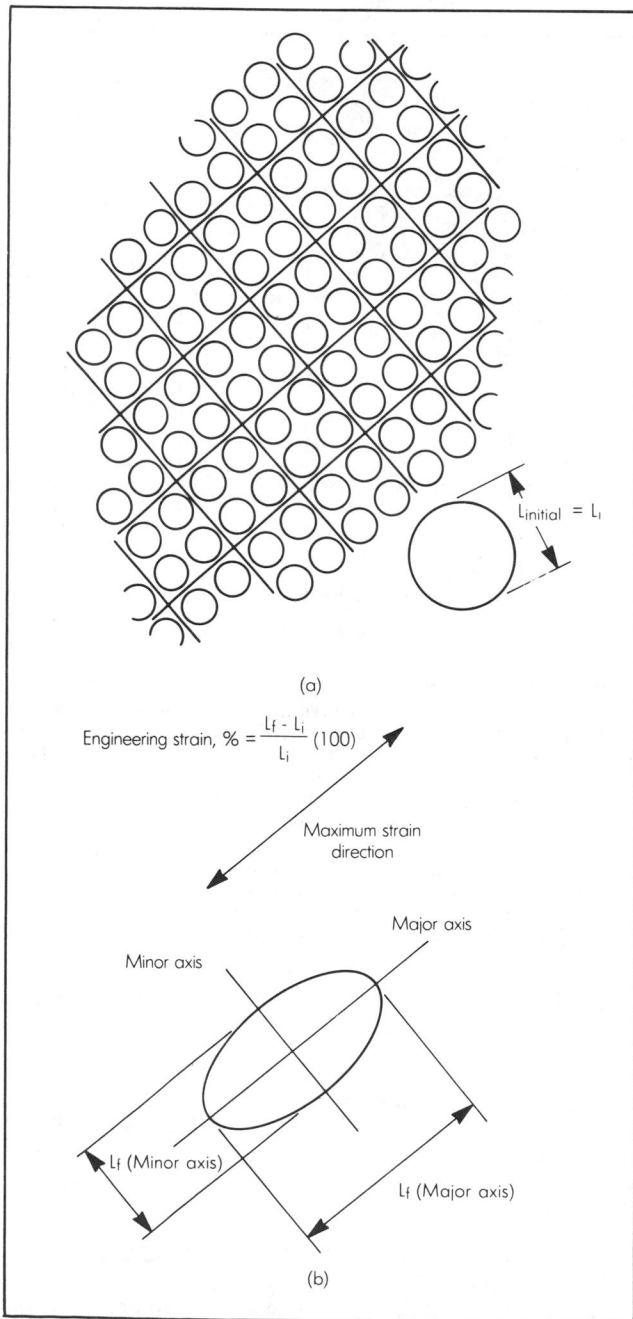

Fig. 31-25 Typical grid pattern: (a) undeformed and (b) deformed; and elongation equation.

critical strains on many production and laboratory parts formed from 0.035″ (0.89 mm) cold-rolled steel resulted in the compilation of the original Keeler-Goodwin diagram (see Fig. 31-26).

Critical strains are those strains measured after local thinning has started. The critical strain level for a given material is obtained by measuring the final major and minor ellipse diameters (see Fig. 31-25, view *b*) in the severely deformed region of the part and converting them into engineering strain. This major-minor strain combination defines one point on the critical strain level curve of the FLD.

Forming limit diagrams have been developed for many materials and material thicknesses since the original FLD was published. These FLD's are available in the literature or from steel and aluminum suppliers. By using them, part evaluation can be simplified, because it is only necessary to measure the critical part strains and then plot them on an FLD that is readily available.

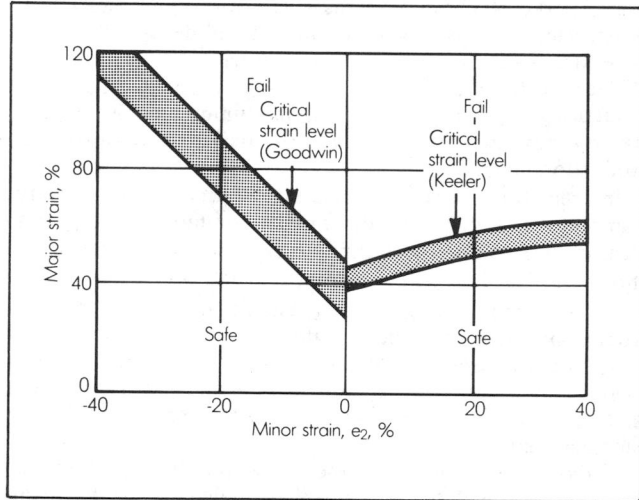

Fig. 31-26 Forming limit diagram illustrates tension-compression strain rate (left) and tension-tension strain (right).

SHAPE ANALYSIS (SA)

Shape analysis was initially conceived by A. S. Kasper. It is a line analysis technique that breaks the critical portion of the part as identified by the FLD into stretch and draw. This technique, since it is a line analysis, extends beyond the localized strains and therefore determines the average design severity.

Material Capability

In using the stretch-draw chart, the first parameter, the forming line, determines the material's capabilities. The end points of the forming line are most easily obtained from the material properties (total elongation and plastic anisotropy) and the equation shown in Fig. 31-27. These material properties are obtainable from a standard tensile test. It has been proven that these end points can be joined by a straight line.

Percent Draw

The second parameter of the stretch-draw chart, the percent draw, is obtained from the circle grid on the formed part. The

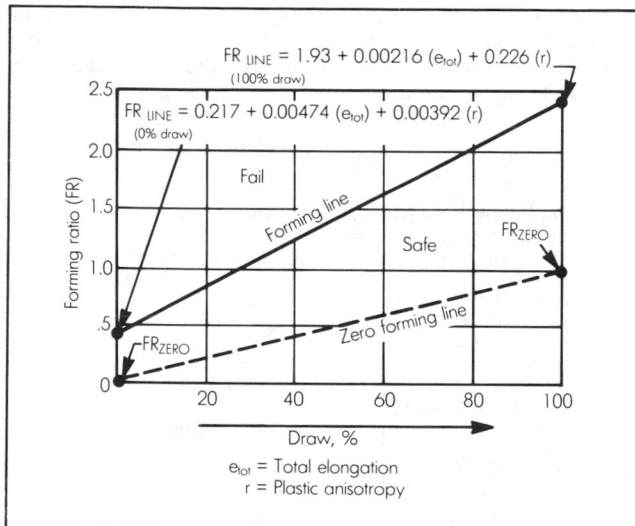

Fig. 31-27 Shape analysis stretch-draw chart.

portion of the material deformed to produce the critical region of the part must be identified and split into stretch and draw areas before the calculations can be performed.

Stretch/draw separation. To separate into stretch and draw areas, an analysis line is drawn on the part (see Fig. 31-28). The die impact line that is visible on the part is identified as the boundary between stretch and draw areas. It is now necessary to determine the portion of material formed by drawing. This determination is done on a part with the recommended electroetched grid pattern of four 0.1″ (2.5 mm) diam circles within a 0.25″ (6.4 mm) square by setting dividers at 0.1″ (2.5 mm), and traversing down the sidewall and into the flange along the analysis line, until the dividers match the major diameter of the grid pattern. This location identifies the outer draw boundary. The inner stretch boundary is obtained in the same fashion, except in this case one traverses up the sidewall and toward the blank center along the analysis line until the material is no longer affected by the critically formed region.

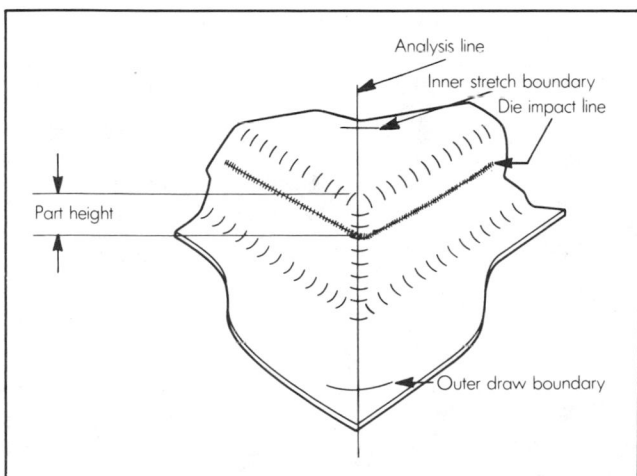

Fig. 31-28 Boundary identification used to calculate percent draw.

Percent draw calculations. After all three boundaries have been determined, it is possible to measure or calculate the formed lengths required to obtain the percent draw. The final stretch length, S_F, is the distance between the die impact line and the inner stretch boundary. The final draw length, D_F, is the distance between the outer draw boundary and the die impact line. These lengths can be conveniently measured with a flexible scale. The original stretch, S_I, and draw, D_I, lengths can be obtained by counting the number of squares between the die impact and the appropriate boundary. To obtain the initial lengths, the number of squares is multiplied by 0.25 if the analysis line runs parallel to the sides of the squares and by 0.3535 if the analysis line runs parallel to the square diagonals. The percent draw is then calculated:

$$\% \ draw = \left[\frac{(D_F - D_I)}{(F - I)} \right] 100 \qquad (12)$$

where:

D_F = distance between outer draw boundary and die impact line
D_I = initial or original draw length
S_I = initial stretch length
$F = S_F + D_F$
$I = S_I + D_I$

Forming Ratio

The forming ratio is the third parameter on the stretch-draw chart. Prior to calculating this ratio, the part height, P_h, must be measured from the die impact line to the closed end of the gridded part (see Fig. 31-28). The part width stretch, PW_s, is twice the distance from the inner stretch boundary to the inner surface of the part. The final required length is the part width draw, PW_D. The PW_D is equal to twice the distance from the inner stretch boundary to the outer surface of the part. It is known that the percent stretch equals 100 minus percent draw and that the effective blank width, BW, equals $2I$. It is now possible to calculate the stretch forming ratio and draw forming ratio as follows:

$$(FR_S) = \left(\frac{P_h}{PW_s} \right) \times \left(\frac{percent \ stretch}{100} \right) \qquad (13)$$

where:

FR_S = stretch forming ratio
P_h = part height
PW_s = part width stretch

and:

$$(FR_D) = \left(\frac{BW}{PW_D} \right) \times \left(\frac{percent \ draw}{100} \right) \qquad (14)$$

where:

FR_D = draw forming ratio
BW = blank width
PW_D = part width draw

The total forming ratio, FR, that is plotted in Fig. 31-27 is obtained by adding the FR_S and FR_D. This describes shape analysis.

FORMABILITY PREDICTION AND EVALUATION

Application Technique

The shape analysis technique has been further refined to allow a direct comparison between it and the combined FLD. This refinement was achieved using Kasper's definition for severity, *SEV*:

$$SEV = \frac{(FR_{calc} - FR_{zero})}{(FR_{line} - FR_{zero})} \qquad (15)$$

where:

SEV = 0.8 at bottom of FLD marginal regions and 1.3 at top of necking failure region

FR_{calc} = the "unknown," the forming ratio that is calculated by solving the severity equation

FR_{zero} = 1 at 100% draw

FR_{line} = quantity defined in Fig. 31-27

Information in the literature defines the severity as 0.8 at the bottom of the combined FLD marginal region and as 1.3 at the top of the necking failure region. Solving the severity equation for FR_{calc} at 0% and 100% draw for these severity values defines the marginal and necking failure regions on the stretch-draw chart. All forming ratios, *FR*, except FR_{calc} are defined in Fig. 31-27.

The result is a modified stretch-draw chart that allows a direct comparison between the FLD and SA results (see Fig. 31-29).

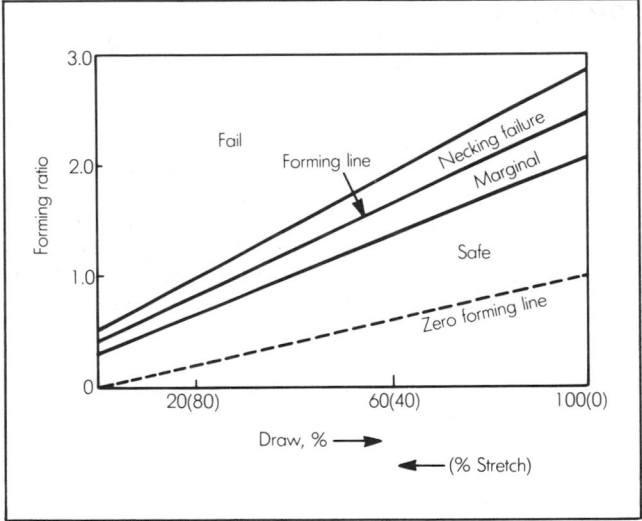

Fig. 31-29 Modified stretch-draw chart: shape analysis diagram for determining severity of design. Percent draw is read from left to right; percent stretch (in brackets) is read from right to left.

COMPARING FLD AND SA RESULTS

The use of forming limit diagram and shape analysis techniques together proves to be a powerful tool, because it allows one to determine if fractures are caused by the design or by tooling irregularities. This separation of design and tooling problems is very important, because once the real cause of metal splitting is determined, everyone can work together to implement the necessary corrective action. Thus, accepted techniques (not opinion) can be used to determine the true cause of the problem.

A severe design is the cause of fractures when equivalent high severities are observed on both the FLD and SA charts; and tooling irregularities are the cause of the problem when SA

indicates a "safe" design yet very high strains are observed on the FLD. These techniques allow the benefit of corrective action to be quantitatively measured and compared with previous forming conditions.

References

1. R. M. Hobbs, *Source Book on Forming of Steel Sheet*, Metals Park, OH: American Society for Metals, 1976.
2. American Iron and Steel Institute, "Modern Sheet Steels—What They Are and How They're Worked," *Manufacturing Engineering* (October 1977), p. 22.
3. National Steel Corporation, *The Importance of Strain Rate Hardening*, Automotive Technical Bulletin GI-3D9.
4. "Properties and Selection: Nonferrous Alloys and Pure Metals," *Metals Handbook*, 9th ed., Vol. 2, Metals Park, OH: American Society for Metals, 1979.
5. D. L. Dollar *Formability of Wrought Zinc Alloys*, SME Technical Paper MF77-588, 1977.
6. Donald P. Koistinen and Neng-Ming Wang, *Mechanics of Sheet Forming*, NY: Plenum Press, 1978.
7. C. H. Hamilton, "Superplastic Forming of Aluminum," Paper presented at Toulouse International Show of Technologies and Energies of the Future, Toulouse, France, 1981.

DIE AND MOLD MATERIALS

Essential requirements for any die or mold, with respect to optimum performance and economy, include the following:

1. Proper design.
2. Proper materials.
3. Accurate manufacture.
4. Correct heat treatment.
5. Proper setup, use, and maintenance.

MATERIAL SELECTION

A wide variety of materials are used for dies and molds, and many dies and molds contain several materials.

Factors affecting the selection of a proper die or mold material for a specific application include:

1. The operations to be performed, including their severity, forces applied, temperature encountered, and lubricants used.
2. The workpiece material, including its hardness, thickness, and condition, as well as the size of the workpiece.
3. The production rate and quantity, accuracy, and finish requirements.
4. The press or machine to be used, including its type and condition.
5. The design of the die or mold.
6. The accuracy and rigidity of the setup.
7. The cost per part produced, based upon the material, manufacturing, heat treatment, and maintenance costs, as well as the life of the die or mold.
8. The current availability of the die or mold material.
9. The properties of the material, including resistance to wear, heat, and deformation, and the ease with which it can be machined, heat treated, and ground.

Different applications require specific characteristics and properties for the material to be used, as discussed later in this chapter. For many materials, the chemical analyses and heat treatments can be adjusted to change the properties. The relative evaluation of properties for various materials, however, is of necessity qualitative, and the proper choice for a specific application cannot always be made with assurance. Consultation with the material supplier, die or mold producer, and heat treater is recommended, to advise them of the specifics of the application.

In many instances, the choice is not limited to a single material that can be used for an application. It is desirable, however, to select the one material that provides the most economical overall performance, based on the factors just discussed. A continuing evaluation of the materials used is important, employing accumulated performance data.

CARBON AND LOW-ALLOY STEELS

Wrought plain-carbon and low-alloy steels, in the form of plates, rounds, and shapes, are often used in the fabrication of auxiliary die components, as well as some die parts. Applications for dies are mainly those in which strength and weldability, rather than wear resistance, are the primary requirements.

HOT-ROLLED STEELS

Hot-rolled low-carbon steels are relatively inexpensive and they are used extensively for die components for which machining and/or welding are required. These materials can be purchased in standard-size bars and plates from stock. Large plates may be cut to required sizes and contours with torches and templates, thus substantially reducing machining costs during die construction. These materials can be case hardened to provide limited hardness and toughness for short-run dies.

Hot-rolled steels hold their shape well when machined and welded. This is because of the minimal surface stresses caused by hot rolling at the steel mill. A limitation of hot-rolled steels is their poor wear resistance. When used for die components, these materials gall and cause scoring of the workpiece surfaces in applications subjecting the dies to wear.

COLD-ROLLED STEELS

Cold-rolled low-carbon steels have smoother surface finishes, closer dimensional tolerances, and higher strengths than hot-rolled low-carbon steels because of their cold-roll processing at the steel mill. They are generally used for die components for which hardening is not required, but wear surfaces are often cyanided.

The major advantage of cold-rolled steels is that they can often be used without machining, thus reducing costs. Such cost reductions frequently exceed the initial high price of the materials—about 50% more than hot-rolled steels. Cold-rolled steels, however, have internal stresses which are relieved by machining or welding. This can cause sufficient bowing, warping, or twisting to require additional costly operations, which often negates the use of cold-rolled steels for die components needing machining or welding.

CAST IRONS AND STEELS

CAST IRONS AND STEELS

Wrought irons are used only occasionally for dies, one example being bases for welded composite tool-steel cutting sections for trim dies. Castings of iron or steel, however, are used extensively for large dies to form, draw, or trim sheet metal. While such dies are sometimes made in one piece, they are often of composite construction. Composite dies have inserts made from carbon, alloy, or tool steel or other materials, or liners placed at sections most subject to wear or breakage.

CAST IRONS FOR DIES

Irons are comparatively low in cost and are easily cast and machined. For uniform properties and improved machinability, they should be free of excessively large flake graphite, large primary carbides, and excessive phosphates. Another advantage of irons is their ability to resist galling. These materials, however, have relatively poor weldability.

Unalloyed Cast Irons

Castings of unalloyed irons are used for many die applications in which no actual operations are performed on the irons themselves. These applications include upper and lower die shoes, upper die holding pads, slides, slide adapters, and slide drivers (with tool steel inserts).

Alloyed Cast Irons

A major limitation of alloyed cast irons, like unalloyed cast irons, is their lack of structural strength. The brittle nature of these materials requires careful consideration when designing die sections that must have high strength. For some applications, stronger materials, such as ductile irons or cast steels, or Meehanite, must be used. High-strength, wear-resistant iron castings produced by the Meehanite licensed process have only limited use for dies.

Ductile Cast Irons

Ductile irons, sometimes called nodular irons, have most of the desirable properties of unalloyed and alloyed cast irons, with the added features of higher structural strength and toughness levels approaching those of steel because of their spheroidal free graphite. These materials are available in two grades: unalloyed and alloyed.

Unalloyed ductile irons are used where added strength—to 80,000 psi (552 MPa)—is required. Applications include die shoes having thin sections, slides, and slide adapters.

Alloyed ductile irons are used where even higher strength—to 90,000 psi (621 MPa)—and more wear resistance are needed. Applications include punches, thin-section die pads, cams for dies, blankholder rings, and lower die posts for collapsible cam dies. Flame hardened, alloyed ductile iron dies have replaced more expensive cast iron dies with steel inserts.

A limitation of the use of ductile iron castings is that they must be stress relieved, which increases their cost. Castings of these materials also cost about 30% more than unalloyed iron castings, and weldability is poor. Steel castings should be considered for high strength requirements if repair welds are anticipated.

STEEL CASTINGS FOR DIES

Steel castings used for dies include medium-carbon, high-carbon, and alloy steels. Some of the more commonly used steels are listed in Table 32-1.

Medium-Carbon Steels

Steel castings having a medium carbon content, such as the medium-carbon mild steel casting (Table 32-1), are used for die components that require higher structural strengths and toughness than can be obtained with cast irons. They have the lowest cost and best machinability of the various steel castings used for dies, but their cost is about twice that of unalloyed cast irons.

High-Carbon Steels

Castings made from high-carbon steels are used for punches, inserts, and other die components in which savings in material and machining costs are realized in comparison to the use of tool steels. They are usually flame hardened in localized areas, but are sometimes hardened by annealing or normalizing and tempering. Such castings are not recommended for applications in which there is a tendency toward galling, seizing, or metal pickup, and they should not be used for delicate dies which might break or distort during heat treatment.

Alloy Steel Castings

Castings made from alloy steels, such as one in Table 32-1, have good machinability and wear resistance, very good toughness, high strength, and excellent flame hardening properties. These characteristics, together with good weldability for repairs, makes them versatile die materials.

Applications for alloy steel castings include punches, die inserts, collapsible slides, and 45° clinching dies requiring the toughness of steels which can be flame hardened in critical areas. Flame hardening only the critical working areas provides tougher, unhardened material in the more fragile, thin sections of the die components. These materials can be fully flame hardened with air cooling.

High-Alloy Steel Castings

High-alloy steel castings, such as the high-carbon, high-chromium type in Table 32-1, are also used for die components. Excellent wear resistance is the primary advantage of these materials, resulting in little or no maintenance under high-production conditions.

Uses for high-alloy steel castings include inserts for blanking, trimming, forming, and drawing dies in high-production applications in which galling or wear are problems. A possible limitation is high initial cost of the materials. The need for heat treatment before and after machining and the need for rework after hardening to remove scale and any distortion add to the cost.

CAST IRONS AND STEELS

TABLE 32-1
Composition and Properties of Steel Castings Commonly Used for Dies

	Type of Steel Castings			
	Medium-Carbon Mild Steel	High-Carbon Mild Steel	Alloy Steel	High-Carbon, High-Chromium Steel
Composition, %				
C	0.25-0.40	0.65-0.80	0.40-0.60	1.5-1.8
Mn	0.50-0.85	0.50-0.80	0.90-1.20	0.5-0.8
Cr			0.90-1.25	11.5-14.0
Mo			0.35-0.50	0.5-1.0
V			Optional	0.2-1.0
Cu			Optional	
Co				Optional
Ni			Optional	Optional
P	0.05 max	0.05 max	0.045 max	0.025 max
S	0.06 max	0.06 max	0.05 max	0.025 max
Si				0.4-0.6
Brinell hardness before machining	120-180	185-250	185-250	269 max
Heat treatment	Full anneal or normalize and temper, not less than 900 °F (482°C), to required hardness.	Full anneal or normalize and temper to required hardness. Flame harden to R_C58-60.	Flame harden and air cool to R_C50-56.	R_C59-61 after machining or die tryout.
Comparative characteristics:				
Cost	Lowest, but twice that of unalloyed cast iron.	About 225% of unalloyed cast iron.	About 225% of unalloyed cast iron.	About 650% of unalloyed cast iron.
Machinability	Best	Good	Good	Poor
Wear resistance	Fair	Good	Good	Excellent
Toughness	Very good	Fair	Very good	Poor
Flame hardening properties	Poor	Very good	Excellent	Very poor
Strength	Good	Good	Very good	Fair

STAINLESS AND MARAGING STEELS

Martensitic stainless steels and maraging steels are being used for some dies and molds, especially those of intricate design and requiring long life. While these materials have a high initial cost, the cost per part formed or molded in long production runs is often lower than with dies or molds made from other materials.

STAINLESS STEELS

Stainless steels of martensitic, hardenable metallurgical structure are used for dies and molds. These materials have a ferritic structure in the annealed conditions; but when they are cooled quickly from above the critical temperature range, which is about 1600°F (870°C), they develop a martensitic structure.

MARAGING STEELS

Maraging steels, generally containing 18% nickel, are used for aluminum die-casting dies and core pins, intricate plastic molds, hot-forging and extrusion dies, punches, and blanking and cold-forming dies. Applications to plastic molds are most common for compression molds requiring high pressures. A major advantage of maraging steels, especially for intricate dies and molds with close tolerance requirements, is the simple precipitation-hardening (aging) treatment. Steels supplied in the solution-annealed condition are relatively soft (R_C 30-35) and readily machinable. Depending upon the specific type of steel, hardnesses to R_C60 can be produced after machining.

TOOL STEELS

Tool steels are special grades of carbon, alloy, or high-speed steels capable of being hardened and tempered, and are the most widely used materials for dies and molds. They are usually melted in electric furnaces and produced under high-quality, tool steel practice to meet special requirements. Tool steels are produced in the form of hot and cold-finished bars, special shapes, forgings, hollow bar, hot extrusions, wire, drill rod, plate, sheets, strip, tool bits, powdered metal products, and castings. They are made in small quantities compared to the high-volume production of carbon and alloy steels.

Tool steels are used for a wide variety of applications, including those in many nontooling areas, in which strength, toughness, resistance to wear, and other properties are selected for optimum performance.

SELECTING TOOL STEELS

Selecting the proper tool steel for a specific application requires careful consideration of many factors. One approach is to use a material that has proved successful in the past for a certain die or mold and operation. It is essential, however, to have an understanding of the reasoning behind using different tool steels for various applications, thus permitting some judgment in the selection process.

Desirable Properties

Many different properties are desirable for tool steels used to make dies and molds for various operations. These properties can be separated into the following two groups:

1. Primary or surface properties. These are inherent performance characteristics which pertain directly to the properties the steel possesses to perform the required operation.
2. Secondary or fabricating properties. These are material characteristics which affect the manufacture of the die or mold.

Primary properties. These include wear resistance, toughness, and heat resistance. An additional primary property required for hot-work tool steel applications is resistance to heat checking or thermal fatigue cracking. Heat checking is characterized by a network of fine cracks that appear on the working surfaces of tooling as a result of stresses associated with alternate rapid heating and cooling during service.

Although hardness is a property developed in heat treatment, rather than an inherent property, it is still very important. Without adequate hardness, the steel would not be able to withstand the loads imposed upon the die or mold.

Secondary properties. These include the many characteristics that influence the ability to make a die or mold, as well as the cost of manufacturing. Some of these are machinability, grindability, polishability, hardenability, and distortion and safety in heat treatment. Availability and cost of the tool steels are also important considerations.

SURFACE TREATMENTS FOR DIES AND MOLDS

Various surface treatments of tool steels have been used to improve the performance of dies and molds, principally with respect to wear resistance. The most popular surface treatments used in industry for tool steels have been nitriding, oxidizing, and chromium plating. Carburizing is also a popular surface-hardening method, used primarily for steels with low to medium carbon contents. Because of their high carbon content, most tool steels are not normally carburized.

Nitriding of Tool Steels

The nitriding process imparts a hard surface to the die or mold by the penetration of nitrogen atoms into the material and the formation of hard nitrides. Nitriding can prevent or minimize galling, but the nitrided surface can spall from small radii.

A nitrided case has a hardness of R_C 70-74. Depth of the nitride case varies considerably, depending upon the nitriding process and the time/temperature parameters employed. Case depth must be adjusted to avoid brittleness. Nitriding is accomplished either in a molten salt bath, in gaseous ammonia, or by the glow discharge method (ion implantation).

Oxidizing Treatment

Some dies and molds are produced with a black oxide film which extends tool life. The oxide film reduces direct metal-to-metal contact between tool and workpiece and retains cutting lubricant, thus promoting improved tool life. The oxide film can be developed by a steam treatment or by immersion in a molten oxidizing salt.

Chromium Plating

Chromium plating is employed to advantage for some dies or molds on which friction is a critical factor in tool life. A chromium-plated surface has a reduced coefficient of friction as compared to a machined steel surface. It is also useful in minimizing or preventing galling for some severe applications, but the plating may spall from small radii. This method can also be used to build up worn areas of a die or mold. A typical chrome plate thickness used for antifriction purposes is 0.001-0.005" (0.03-0.13 mm) and has a hardness of R_C 65-75.

Vapor Deposition Coatings

Among the most promising of new coating methods are those based on vapor deposition. Extensive testing of tools coated with titanium nitride shows promising results for metal-forming tools such as punches, dies, and rolls. Increased tool life is attributed to the lubricous hard quantities of titanium nitride which resists galling and metal pickup.

Physical vapor deposition. In the process termed physical vapor deposition (PVD), the finished die or mold is placed in a chamber where it is bombarded with titanium ions in the presence of nitrogen, producing a thin layer of titanium nitride. The PVD process is conducted at temperatures below the tempering temperature.

Chemical vapor deposition. The chemical vapor deposition (CVD) process requires a high temperature and therefore

CEMENTED TUNGSTEN CARBIDE

necessitates subsequent vacuum reheat treating after coating. In CVD, the die or mold is heated to approximately 1900° F (1038° C) in the presence of titanium tetrachloride gas and methane or nitrogen. Two separate layers of first titanium carbide and then titanium nitride are deposited on the tool.

Coating thickness and materials. A deposited layer thickness of 0.0002-0.0003" (0.005-0.008 mm) is typical for the vapor deposition processes. Both the PVD and CVD processes can be adapted to a variety of coating materials, such as hafnium nitride, aluminum oxide, tungsten carbide, and nickel borides.

STEEL-BONDED CARBIDES

Advantages of steel-bonded carbides for dies and molds include machinability in the annealed condition, hardenability, good wear resistance, minimum friction, and the ability to withstand heavy compressive loads at high temperatures. Annealing of these materials to hardness levels of R_C 43-46 permits machining (discussed later in this section) with conventional steel-cutting tools.

The wear resistance of steel-bonded carbides is much better than that of most tool steels and approaches that of some cemented tungsten carbides with cobalt binder. This is the result of the titanium carbide particles, about 0.0002-0.0003" (0.005-0.008 mm) diam and having a Vickers hardness of 3300,

embedded in the hardened matrix. These materials are less brittle than cemented tungsten carbides, thus reducing the possibility of chipping.

Steel-bonded carbides are being used primarily for single-station and progressive dies employed in severe stamping operations, such as forming, drawing, notching, and blanking, including the production of laminations. Rigid presses with good parallelism between moving and stationary members are essential for the use of these die materials. Excessive deflection reduces the productivity and life of the dies. The applications of steel-bonded carbides for plastic molds include gate and mold inserts, and nozzles.

CEMENTED TUNGSTEN CARBIDE

Tungsten carbides cemented with cobalt have replaced steels for many tools used in metalforming operations, primarily because of their high abrasion (wear) resistance and compressive strengths. These materials are normally used for long production runs in which their higher initial cost can be economically justified as the result of longer tool life, reduced downtime, and decreased cost per part produced. Some stamping operations, such as the production of small holes in hard and tough materials, can only be done with tungsten carbide punches. Precise tolerances are maintained for long periods, thus improving product quality and reducing rejects.

The high elastic modulus (stiffness under bending loads) of cemented tungsten carbides permits their use for punches with length-to-diameter ratios exceeding 4:1. These materials also reduce the severity of galling, which is a problem common with punches and dies made from tool steels.

APPLICATIONS

Cemented tungsten carbide dies are being used extensively for drawing wire, bars, and tubes; extruding steels and non-ferrous alloys; cold and hot heading dies; swaging hammers and mandrels; and powder compacting punches and dies. Tungsten carbide is also used to make dies to draw sheet metal parts. Other important applications include punching, coining, sizing, and ironing tools for beverage and food cans and the production of a variety of laminations and other stamped metal parts.

Typical products produced by tungsten-carbide forming tools include automotive parts such as piston pins, bearing cups for universal joints, spark plug shells, bearing races for front-wheel drives, air pump rotors, transmission gear blanks, and valves. In the construction and farm equipment industries, tungsten carbide is used to form hitch pins, track link bushings, hydraulic hose fittings, diesel piston pins, and a variety of gear

blanks. Tungsten carbide is also used in manufacturing fasteners, drawn and ironed beverage cans, cartridge cases, wrench sockets, bicycle drive cups, motor laminations, electronic terminals, and many other stamped parts.

CEMENTED CARBIDE PROPERTIES

The cemented carbide materials used most extensively for forming operations are the so-called straight tungsten carbides with cobalt binder, a family of two-phase WC-Co compositions. Occasionally, tantalum carbide is added for lubricity, for increased hot strength, or for inhibited grain growth, but other additives are normally avoided for die materials.

Tungsten carbide grains in these materials range from less than 1 micron (0.00004") to 10 microns (0.0004"), and cobalt contents vary from 3-25%.

Desirable properties of the straight tungsten carbides used for forming-die applications include high hardness at room and elevated temperatures, high abrasion or wear resistance, high modulus of elasticity, high compressive strength (much higher than its tensile strength), and low rate of thermal expansion.

GRADE SELECTION

Past experience in using tungsten carbides is most helpful in selecting the proper grade or composition for a specific application. Good production records should be maintained so that the experience can be used as a guide for new applications, as well as to improve current applications. Such records should include the exact grade of carbide used; the workpiece material and condition; the type of lubricant and/or coolant used and method of application; the press speed and forces and press condition; the details of any tool failures and suspected causes; and the number of pieces produced.

For new applications, the supplier of the material should be contacted for technical help. When either cemented carbide or a tool steel are being considered, selection must be based upon the number of parts to be produced and the relevant need for wear resistance vs. strength. Consideration must also be given to the difference in cost between carbide and steel. The initial cost of carbide is significantly higher, and subsequent finishing can add substantially to the cost. Each application must be evaluated individually, comparing total cost of the tool with its expected life and overall maintenance costs. The number of parts produced per dressing (sharpening and/or polishing) should always be considered.

DESIGN CONSIDERATIONS

Special design techniques are required for the successful application of tungsten carbide materials. Sharp edges, notches, or abrupt changes in cross section are stress risers and should be avoided. Dies should be designed to keep the carbides in compression because the compressive strengths of these materials are much higher than their tensile strengths. Draw radii or approach angles, punch and die clearances, and reliefs are similar to those for steel dies.

NONFERROUS METALS

Several nonferrous metals, including aluminum bronzes, beryllium coppers, zinc-based alloys, antimonial lead, and bismuth alloys, are used for dies and molds, generally for specific applications.

ALUMINUM BRONZES

The major advantage of aluminum bronzes is their excellent resistance to scratching, scoring, and galling of the workpiece materials. They also have good resistance to impact and deformation because of their high compressive strengths, which results in long life. A low coefficient of friction, about 0.08 compared to 0.11 for many tool steels, allows easier, smoother metal flow. Easy repair is another important advantage.

Aluminum bronze dies and molds are usually employed in applications in which smooth surface finishes are required on the workpieces. They are also employed in applications in which materials must be formed that are difficult to produce with steel dies. Aluminum bronzes are not recommended for blanking or forging dies. Materials formed include low-carbon and stainless steels; aluminum, magnesium, and titanium alloys; and prefinished materials. The aluminum bronzes are sometimes used as inserts for cast-iron and cast-steel dies employed for high production requirements. The higher cost of these materials is generally offset by savings in finishing the workpieces. For large cast-iron or steel dies, for which aluminum bronze would be uneconomical, the radii of the dies are often overlaid using aluminum bronze welding rods.

One common application is deep-drawing dies, especially when forming the tougher grades of stainless steels. In addition to the improved quality of parts produced, smaller blanks can be used because draw beads are not necessary. Higher pressure-pad pressures, however, are necessary.

BERYLLIUM COPPERS

Cast alloys of beryllium, cobalt, and copper have characteristics comparable to those of the proprietary aluminum bronzes just discussed. These alloys are sometimes used for molds to form plastics, plunger tips for die-casting dies, and other components. Ample exhaust ventilation is essential in making such components to minimize concentrations of beryllium in the air, which can cause a health hazard.

ZINC-BASED ALLOYS

Zinc alloys provide a low cost and fast method of making punches, dies, and molds having a dense, smooth working surface. These materials are easy to melt, cast, machine, grind, polish, weld, remelt, and recast. Casting provides sharp definition of contours because of the fluidity of the alloys, and accuracy of the castings minimizes the need for costly finishing.

Other important advantages of these alloys include no scratching of the workpiece material, good abrasion resistance, inherent self-lubricating properties, and high impact and compressive strengths. Their low melting temperatures reduce energy costs, and the tools can be remelted and recast a number of times without loss of mechanical properties. Care must be taken, however, to ensure that contaminants, such as iron or lead, are minimized and that excessive casting temperatures, which might cause de-alloying and immoderate grain growth, are avoided.

ANTIMONIAL LEAD

Punches made of antimonial lead are sometimes used with dies made of zinc alloy, especially for drop hammer operations on soft metals. Lead-antimony alloys are available with various percentages of antimony to suit specific requirements. The balance of the contents of these alloys is lead, but from 0.25-0.75% tin is often added to improve the casting properties. The alloys generally best suited for forming operations contain 6-7% antimony, which provides the best combination of mechanical properties, including adequate ductility, hardness, and tensile strength. These alloys have a melting range of 539-552° F (282-289° C), a Brinell hardness of about 12, a tensile strength of approximately 7000 psi (48.3 MPa), and a density of 0.39 lb/in.^{3} (10.8 g/cm^3).

Antimonial-lead punches are made by casting into the cavity of zinc alloy dies. The antimonial lead is sufficiently ductile to accurately assume the dimensions of the zinc alloy die under impact. These alloys, like zinc alloys, can be remelted and recast.

BISMUTH ALLOYS

The alloys of bismuth, often called low-melting-point alloys, are used chiefly as matrix material for securing punch and die parts in small die sets, and as-cast punches and dies for short-run forming and drawing operations.

PLASTICS FOR DIES AND MOLDS

ADVANTAGES OF USING PLASTICS

A major advantage of using plastics for dies and molds is the short lead time needed with them. If patterns, prototype parts, or models are available for casting or for layup of the resins, plastics can be molded to complex contours quickly, in a fraction of the time required to produce metal dies or molds. Other advantages include their low initial cost, minimum finishing requirements, light weight, and toughness and flexibility.

LIMITATIONS OF PLASTICS

The strengths, 10-40 ksi (69-276 MPa), and hardnesses of plastics are lower than those of metallic die materials. As a result, the requirements of the application must be considered and the die or mold carefully designed. Low edge strength, reduced wear resistance, and limited resistance to elevated temperatures must be given careful consideration.

The normal life of dies and molds made of plastics is the production of about 20,000 parts. Surface coating or casting, however, can generally restore the tools to their initial conditions. The use of metallic inserts at areas of highest stress extends the life of such tools.

Smooth workpiece blanks are essential for the successful use of dies made from plastics. The low tensile strengths and soft surfaces of plastics do not withstand the shearing action of burrs or rough edges.

TYPICAL APPLICATIONS

Plastics are used extensively for dies, primarily for forming aluminum alloys and other light metals, but also for forming low-carbon and stainless steels. For blanking and trimming operations, the dies are generally provided with metal inserts. Ironing of wall sections is not recommended since a sufficient compressive force cannot be obtained to perform the required sizing. Spanking or bottoming in dies made of plastics is of little value for the removal of wrinkles formed in metal stampings.

Many molds for forming parts are now being made from plastics. Other applications include stretch forming dies (form blocks), snakes for bending, and dies for stretch forming operations.

PLASTICS USED

The plastics originally used for dies and molds were predominantly polyesters and phenolics. Instability of these materials, however, caused dimensional changes that required frequent checking and modification of the tools. Now, the harder epoxies and improved polyurethane resins available are being used practically exclusively for dies and molds. Graphite fibers and fabrics are being employed to produce heat-resistant molds of plastics for forming parts made from composite materials.

OTHER NONMETALLIC DIE MATERIALS

In addition to plastics, just discussed, several other non-metallic materials are used for forming dies, chucks, mandrels, and other components. Their applications, however, are generally limited to forming prototype or experimental parts from aluminum alloys and other light metals, or for short production runs.

HARDWOODS

Dies are sometimes made of hardwoods, such as maple or beech, for blanking, forming, or shallow drawing of light metals, but applications are limited. Such woods are hard, dense, and close grained, and do not have a tendency to splinter. The woods used, however, must be carefully selected, cured, and kiln dried. For more severe operations, wood dies are faced with metal or plastic, or provided with steel inserts at areas of highest stress.

HARDBOARDS

Hardboards are high-density panels of compressed wood fiber and lignin (a natural binder). These materials are used for forming and drawing dies, plastic molds, spinning mandrels, and stretch forming dies, as well as jigs, fixtures, templates, and patterns. Advantages of hardboards include good dimensional stability, light weight, smooth surfaces, uniform density, and abrasion resistance.

DENSIFIED WOOD

Densified wood is used for punches and dies to form and draw aluminum alloys and other light metals. In drawing operations, scoring of the workpieces is minimized because of the low coefficient of friction of densified wood when properly finished. Dies made from these materials can be used for short to moderate production runs, depending upon the operation and its severity. Service life is often extended by the use of metal inserts.

RUBBER

Molded rubber dies and rubber covered punches are used for some difficult forming operations, such as deep fluting and bulging. Rubber pads or diaphragms are also used for flexible-die forming processes.

CORK

Soft, medium, and hard cork layers, compressed into sheet form, are sometimes used with, or in place of, rubber pads. Cork deforms only slightly in any direction other than that of the applied load, while rubber flows in all directions.

SHEET METAL BLANKING AND FORMING

Metal stampings are an indispensable, pervasive part of the contemporary industrialized society. An examination of most machines and products would disclose metal stampings in the assembly. Currently, stampings are widely used in machines, tools, vehicles of all kinds, household appliances, hardware, office equipment, electrical and electronic equipment, containers, buildings, clothing, and most manufactured products.

STAMPING PRESS OPERATIONS

In this chapter, stamping is used as a general term to cover all pressworking operations on sheet metal; it is not confined to forming and drawing processes. The stamping of parts from sheet metal is a straightforward operation in which the metal is shaped or cut through deformation by shearing, punching, drawing, stretching, bending, coining, etc. Production rates are high and secondary machining is generally not required to produce finished parts within tolerances.

A stamped part may be produced by one or a combination of three fundamental press operations applied to a given material. These include:

1. Cutting (blanking, punching, perforating, or lancing) to a predetermined configuration by exceeding the shear strength of the material.
2. Drawing (bending or forming) whereby the desired part shape is achieved by overcoming the tensile resistance of the material.
3. Coining (compression, squeezing, or forging) accomplishes surface displacement by overcoming the material's compressive strength.

Whether applied to blanking or forming, the underlying principles of the stamping process may be described as the use of force and pressure to cut or form a piece of sheet metal into the desired shape. Part shape is produced by the punch and die, which are positioned in the stamping press as shown schematically in Fig. 33-1. In most production operations, the sheet metal is placed over the die and the descending punch is forced into the workpiece by the press.

Inherent characteristics of the stamping process make it versatile and foster wide usage. Costs tend to be low, since complex parts can be made in a few operations at high production rates. Sheet metal has a high strength-to-weight factor, enabling production of parts that are lightweight and strong. Part interchangeability is assured because virtually identical parts are produced by the dies. Stamped parts can be made from a large number of different metals and alloys.

MATERIALS USED FOR STAMPINGS

Most metal stampings are made from steel in sheet form. The following are the principal characteristics and requirements needed in raw materials to be used for stampings in press work:

- Comparatively low cost.
- High strength.
- Good surface finish.
- Uniform crystalline metal structure.
- Uniformity of dimensions.
- Workability.

A variety of raw materials can be used for metal stamping production. In most applications, the strength of the material is an important consideration. However, other characteristics such as formability, appearance, and predictable performance often are contributing factors in the selection of materials and production methods. In general all materials that are available in the form of sheets or strips and that do not shatter under impact can be worked with press tools. Materials used for stampings can be grouped in three categories; ferrous metals, nonferrous metals, and nonmetallic.

Ferrous Metals

This group contains alloys in which the principal element is iron. If a special functional requirement does not dictate material selection, the first choice for stamping usually is low-carbon (0.05-0.20%), cold-rolled or hot-rolled steel. Cold-rolled steel (CRS) is available in gages up to 1/16" (1.6 mm) in the United States and up to 3/16" (4.76 mm) in Canada, while hot-rolled steel (HRS) is supplied in heavier gages. Low-carbon steels are the predominant material used for stampings, although there is a trend toward increasing use of high-strength, low alloy (HSLA) steels.

In some applications, special specifications or considerations must be fulfilled to increase the material's strength and resistance to unusually rigorous adverse conditions (oxidation, corrosion, temperature, etc.). In these instances, alloy steels such as high-carbon steels, silicon steels, stainless steels, and heat-resistant steels often are used in stampings. These alloys, however, typically are

STAMPING PRESS OPERATIONS

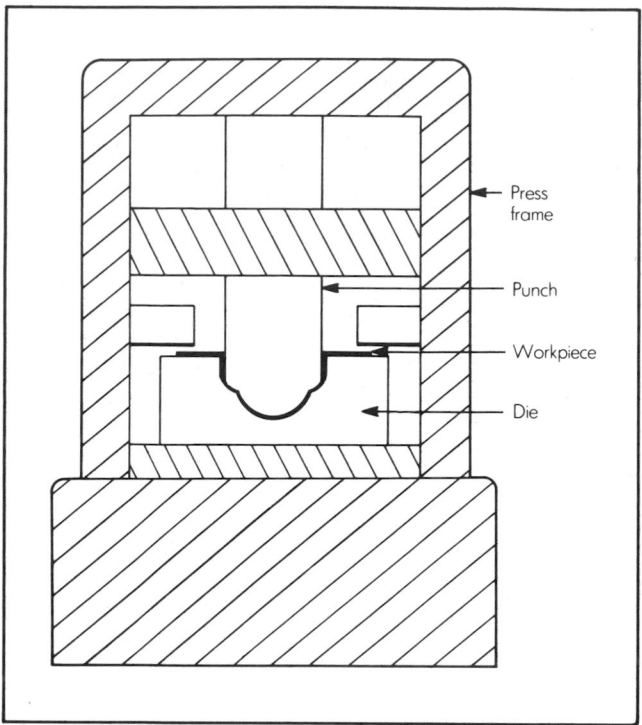

Fig. 33-1 Basic production setup for stamping operation. Pressure is applied by the press. The sheet metal is formed into the shape determined by the punch and die.

more difficult to work in dies and presses, especially during forming operations.

Nonferrous Metals

Aluminum in a range of alloys and tempers is used extensively for stampings. Copper and its alloys of brass, beryllium copper, phosphor bronze, cupronickel, and nickel silver also are used. Alloys based on magnesium, zinc, titanium, and nickel also are widely used for stampings. Alloys of other nonferrous metals, including zirconium, tantalum, niobium, tungsten, molybdenum, and vanadium, and precious metals, including gold, silver, platinum, and palladium, are used for special applications.

Nonmetallic Materials

Some nonmetallic materials have sufficient hardness and consistency to permit stamping with standard dies. The so-called dinking, hollow, or steel rule dies (similar to cookie cutters) are used for softer materials.

Thickness

The thickness of sheet metal used for stampings varies widely from that of foil as thin as 0.003" (0.08 mm) to that of metal as thick as 1/2" (12.7 mm) or more. The majority of stampings, however, are made from metal having a thickness in the range of 0.020-0.080" (0.51-2.03 mm). No rigid standard exists for defining the expressions *light*, *medium*, and *heavy* which are used in describing the gages of sheet metal. In general, sheets up to 0.031" (0.79 mm) are considered light gage; sheets from 0.031-0.109" (2.77 mm) are considered medium gage; and those above 0.109" are considered heavy gage. The term *plate* (rather than sheet) is usually applied to metals having a thickness greater than 1/4" (6.3 mm).

BLANKING AND FORMING OVERVIEW

Blanking (cutting) and forming operations are the primary stamping or pressworking operations. Manufacturing of sheet metal components involves a combination of these two operations, which are carried out for mass production using power shears, slitters and presses.

Cutting operations are classified by either the purpose of the cutting action or the shape it produces. Shearing, cutoff, parting, and blanking operations are employed to produce blanks; punching, slotting, and perforating operations are employed to cut holes; notching, seminotching, lancing, parting, and cutoff are used for progressive working; and trimming, slitting, and shaving are used for size control. Fine blanking, high-speed blanking, and roll blanking are nonconventional cutting operations developed to meet special requirements.

Forming operations include bending, drawing, spinning, embossing, and miscellaneous operations such as coining, ironing, bulging, crimping, dimpling, necking, and swaging. Bending and drawing operations are further classified and identified in industry based on the functions performed and appearance of the formed product. Most of these pressworking operations are listed, illustrated, and briefly described in Table 33-1. Basic theory of the primary operations and their characteristic metal flow are described in fundamental terms in this chapter.

TABLE 33-1
Pressworking Operations

SHEARING

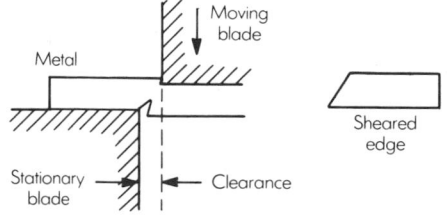

Shearing is the cutting action along a straight line to separate metal by two moving blades. Machines used for shearing are called squaring shears. In shearing, a narrow strip of metal is plastically deformed to the point where it fractures at the sur-

faces in contact with the blades. The fracture then propagates inward to provide complete separation. It is used for producing blanks.

CUTOFF:

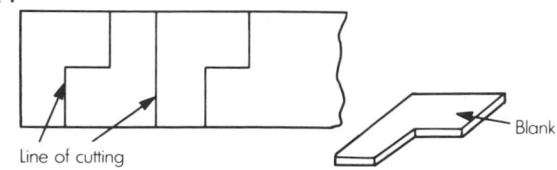

Cutoff is the cutting action along a line. It may involve one or more cuts where the line of cutting is straight, angular,

STAMPING PRESS OPERATIONS

TABLE 33-1—Continued

jogged, or curved. It is performed in a die operated by a press, similar to blades in shears. The use of cutoff operations is limited to blank shapes that nest readily. However, it is more versatile because it is not limited to straight-line cuts, as is shearing. A small amount of scrap or waste sheet metal may be produced at the start or finish of the strip or coil of sheet metal.

PARTING:

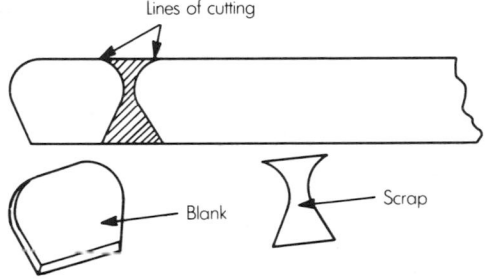

Parting is an operation that involves two cutoff operations to produce blanks from the strip as shown in the figure. During parting, some scrap is produced. Therefore, parting is the next best method (after cutoff) for cutting blanks. It is used when the blanks do not nest perfectly. Parting is carried out in presses using a die.

BLANKING:

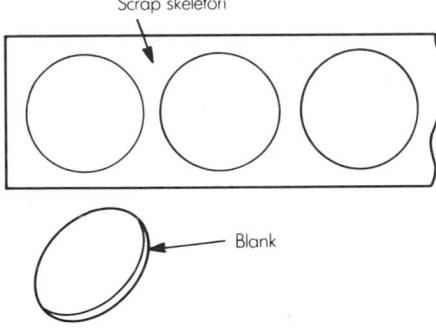

Blanking involves shearing a piece out of stock (strip of sheet metal) to a predetermined contour. It results in excessive waste of metal compared to cutoff and parting. However, the blank shape makes the use of blanking a necessity in most cases. It is performed in a die operated by a press.

PUNCHING (PIERCING):

Punching involves the cutting of clean holes with resulting scrap slugs. This operation is often called piercing, although piercing is properly used to identify the operation for producing holes by tearing action, which is not typical of cutting

operations. In general, the term *punching* is widely used to describe die-cut holes regardless of size and shape. Punching is performed in a press with a die.

SLOTTING:

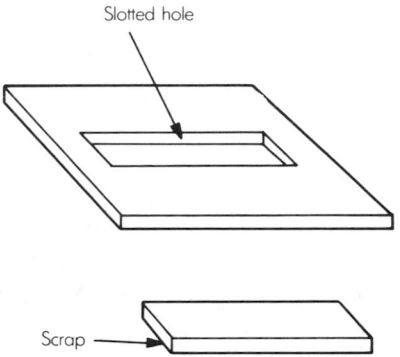

Slotting is a punching operation in which elongated and rectangular holes are cut.

PERFORATING:

Perforating is also a punching operation. It is used to punch many holes in a product with a specific pattern for decorative purposes or to permit the passage of light, gas, or liquid.

NOTCHING AND SEMINOTCHING:

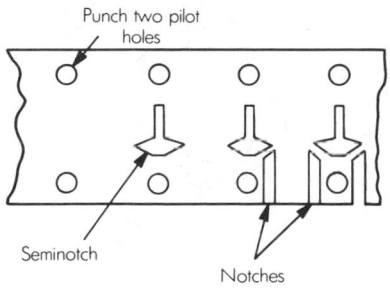

STAMPING PRESS OPERATIONS

TABLE 33-1—*Continued*

Notching is a cutting operation used for removing a piece of metal from the edge of a strip to a required blank. By making several notches, notching gradually produces a blank contour before the blank is detached. In some cases notching is done on the product itself. Generally, progressive dies are used for notching. The term *seminotching* represents the same cutting operation if it is done at the central portion of the strip.

Trimming is the operation of cutting scrap off a fully or partially formed product to an established trim line. It is comparatively easier to trim the flanges of a drawn cup than the wall of the cup. For some irregular panels, trimming is done in a series of dies with notchlike cutting. The edge of a cup is sometimes trimmed by pinching or pushing the flange or lip of the cup over the cutting edge of a stationary punch.

LANCING:

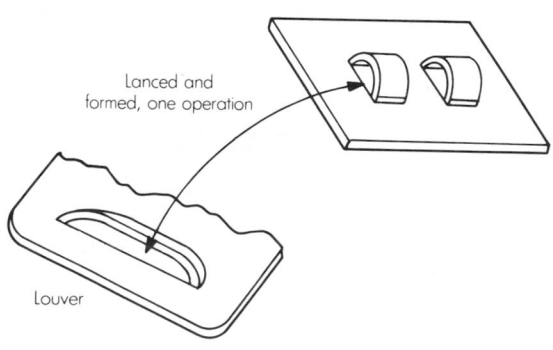

Lancing is cutting along a line in the product without freeing the scrap from the product. It is performed using a progressive die operated on a press. Lancing cuts are necessary to create louvers, which are formed in sheet metal for venting functions.

TRIMMING:

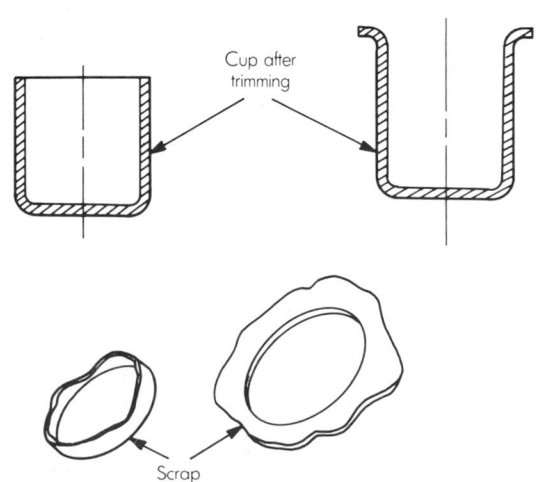

SHAVING:

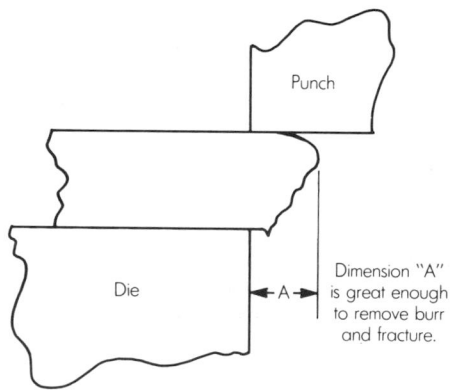

Shaving involves cutting off metal in a chip fashion to obtain accurate dimensions and also to remove the rough fractured edge of the sheet metal. Shaving is performed using dies with a very small clearance, as shown in the figure. It is considered to be a secondary shearing operation.

SLITTING:

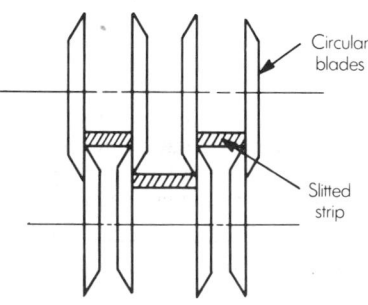

Slitting is cutting along single lines. A gang of circular blades cuts strips from a sheet. This operation is also used to cut along lines of given length or contour in a sheet or in products.

TABLE 33-1—*Continued*

BENDING:

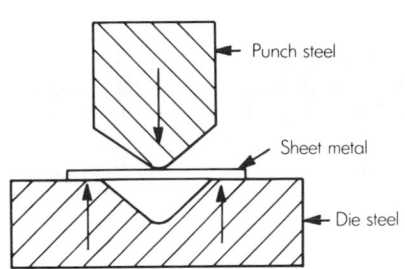

Bending is a process by which a straight length of sheet metal is plastically deformed to a required curved length, as illustrated in the figure. It is common forming operation for changing sheet and plate into channel, drums, tanks, etc. In addition, it is part of the deformation in many other forming operations.

STRAIGHT FLANGING:

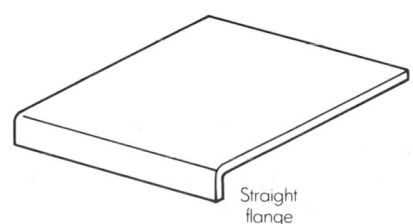

Straight flanging is a bending operation in which the line of bending is straight. It is the easiest operation to perform, and there are few restrictions on the flange width.

STRETCH FLANGING:

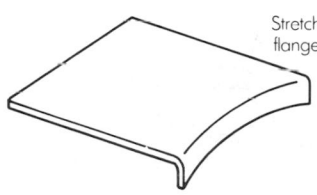

Stretch flanging is also a bending operation, but the line of bending is not straight. It is a concave curvature, as shown in the figure. The flange is known as a stretch flange and the process is called stretch flanging because the material undergoes tension when the flange is being formed. Tearing or breaking of the edge is common. To reduce the possibility of tensile tears, the width of stretch flanges must be limited.

SHRINK FLANGING:

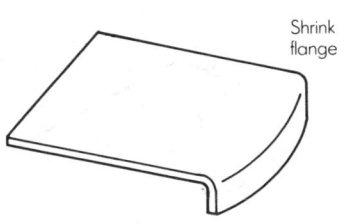

During shrink flanging, the line of bending is a convex curve and the metal is under severe compressive stress, so wrinkles are likely to occur. Therefore, the flange width must be limited. An alternative is the design of preplanned offsets in the flange to take up excess metal.

JOGGLING:

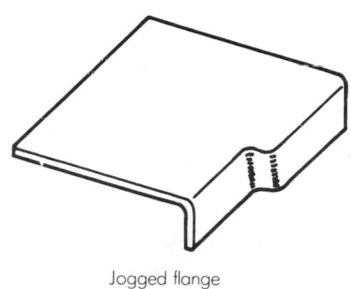

Joggling is a flanging operation by which an offset is produced at a desired place in the flange, as shown in the figure. A joggle consists of two adjacent, continuous or nearly continuous, short radius bends of opposite curvature.

REVERSE FLANGING:

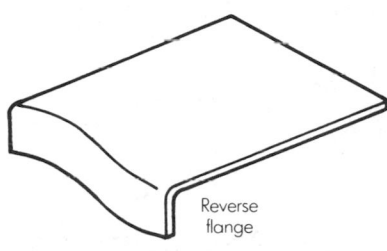

Reverse flanging is similar to joggling. In this case the product has at least one shrink flange and one stretch flange which are connected by a joggle.

STAMPING PRESS OPERATIONS

TABLE 33-1—*Continued*

HOLE FLANGING:

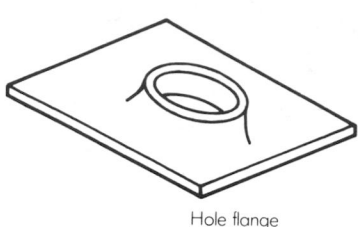

Hole flange

Hole flanging involves stretch flanging of a hole in the product. Higher hole flanges require a smaller punched hole diameter to provide the additional metal.

STRETCH FORMING:

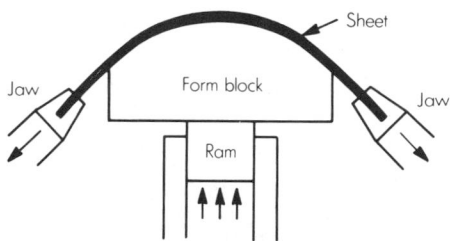

Stretch forming is the process of forming by the application of primarily tensile forces to stretch the sheet metal over a tool or formblock as shown in the figure. The process is an outgrowth of the stretcher leveling of rolled sheet. This operation is used most extensively in the aircraft industry to produce parts of large radius of curvature, frequently with double curvature.

SHALLOW AND DEEP DRAWING:

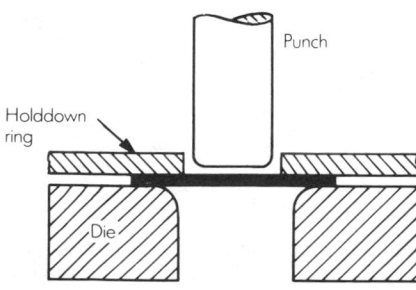

Drawing is used for shaping flat sheets into cup-shaped workpieces. If the depth of the cup formed is equal to or more than the radius of the cup, the process is known as deep drawing. Otherwise, it is considered shallow drawing. Drawing is performed by placing a blank of appropriate size over a shaped die and pressing the metal into the die with a punch. It requires blankholder pressure to press the blank against the die to prevent wrinkling.

IRONING:

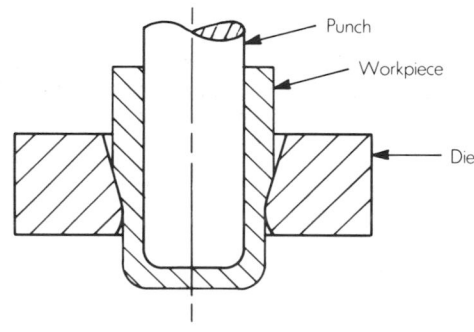

Ironing is the process of smoothing and thinning the wall of a shell or cup by forcing the shell or cup through a die with a punch, as shown in the figure. The working of the metal is severe, and annealing of parts is often necessary between ironing processes.

EMBOSSING:

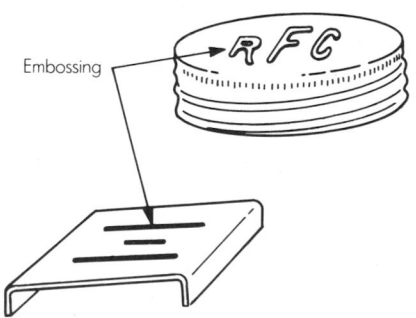

Embossing is the process that produces relatively shallow indentation or raised designs with theoretically no change in metal thickness. This group of operations is used to deform sheet metal away from the blank or product edge or in the central region. The common characteristic of all embossments is well-defined localized stretching of sheet metal into crisp contours. Forming of beads, ribs, and letters on sheet metal is done with embossing operations.

TABLE 33-1—*Continued*

COINING:

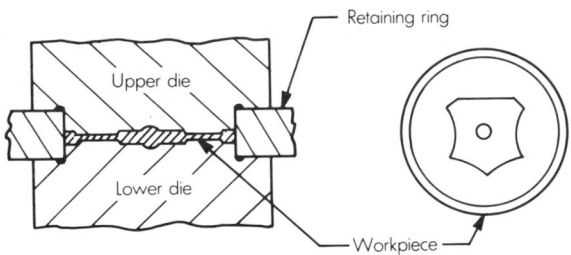

Coining is used for sheet metal working as well as for bulk forming. During this operation, metal is intentionally thinned or thickened to achieve the required indentations or raised designs. Coining is widely used for lettering on sheet metal or components such as coins. It is done in a closed die in which all surfaces of the sheet metal are confined or restricted, resulting in a well-defined imprint of the die on the workpiece.

SPINNING:

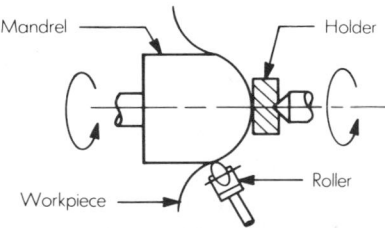

Spinning is a method of forming sheet metal or tubing into seamless hollow cylinders, cones, hemispheres, or other circular shapes by the combined forces of rotation and pressure. It does not result in any change in thickness. The operation is usually done in a lathe by pressing a tool against a circular metal blank that is rotated by a headstock.

SHEAR FORMING:

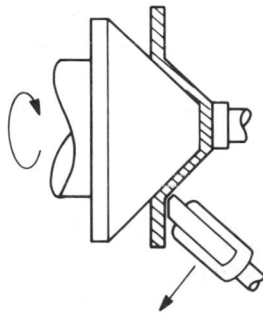

Shear forming, also known as flow turning, is similar to spinning, but during flow turning the metal is intentionally thinned by shear forces. This is also known as power spinning. It is sometimes done at hot-working condition because the metal undergoes severe shear deformation which demands high ductility. This process is done in a lathe.

BULGING:

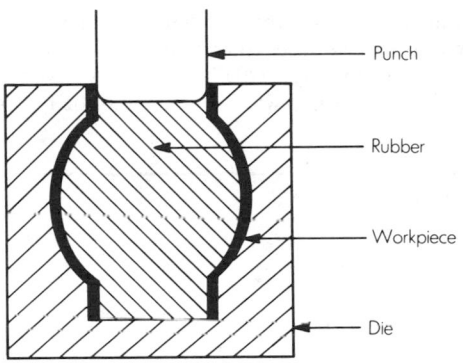

In bulging, an internal pressure is applied to form a tube to the desired shape. The internal pressure can be delivered by expanding a segmented punch through a fluid, or by using an elastomer, as illustrated.

NECKING AND SWAGING:

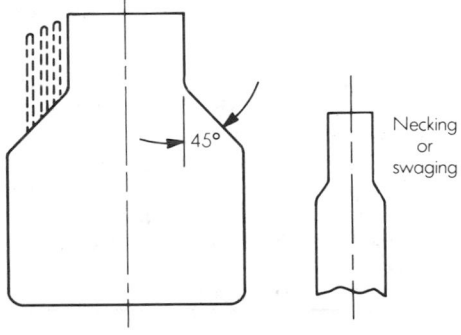

Necking and swaging reduce the diameter on the tube or drawn cup. Necking is accomplished between dies in a manner similar to other drawing operations. It can also be performed by spinning and swaging. Swaging is primarily used to reduce diameter, and it represents the squeezing operation in which part of the metal under compression plastically flows into contours of the die; the remaining metal is unconfined and flows generally at an angle to the direction of applied pressure.

STAMPING PRESS OPERATIONS

TABLE 33-1—*Continued*

CORRUGATING:

Corrugating involves making parallel bends across either the length or width of the sheet to increase the section modules of the sheet. The bends may be "U", "V" or any desired shape. Corrugating is performed with a punch and die in brake press.

CURLING AND WIRING:

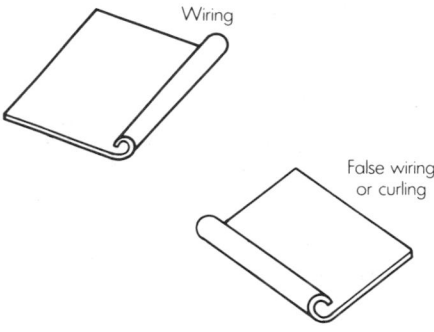

During wiring, the metal is curled up and over a length of wire to strengthen the edge of sheet metal. When the wire is not used, the operation is known as curling. Curling and wiring are used on flat parts or on round parts such as cams or drums. On round parts, curling is done in a lathe (like spinning) and also is done using a die operated on a press. Generally, it is combined with flanging operations in press working.

HEMMING AND SEAMING:

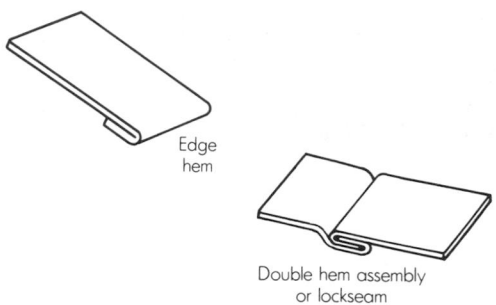

Hemming and seaming are the processes of joining two edges of sheet metal by multiple bending, as shown in the figure. A hem is folded at the edge of the sheet metal to remove the burred edge and improve the appearance of the edge. As used in the clothing industry, the term *seam* applies to an area in which two edges have been joined.

DIMPLING:

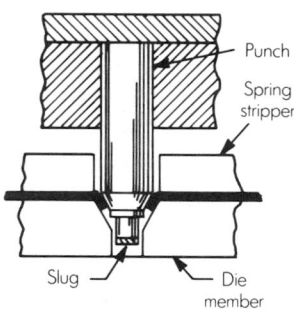

Dimpling is a process for producing a small conical flange around a hole in sheet metal parts that are to be assembled with flush or flat-headed rivets. Dimpling is commonly applied to sheets that are too thin for countersinking.

BLANKING

Preparing a sheet metal blank or workpiece from coils, strips, or sheets by a cutting operation is the first step in the production of most sheet metal parts. When the piece of sheet metal cut from stock is to become the manufactured part, the piece is called the blank or workpiece (see Fig. 33-2) and the process is known as blanking. The blank sometimes is the finished product and requires no further working; in most cases, however, it is formed or drawn to make the desired product.

Additional cutting operations often are performed on the blank to complete the product. Blanks that are to be formed or drawn are usually referred to as developed blanks. Blanks may be simple round discs, squares, rectangles, or cylinders, or they may be more complex shapes.

High-volume production cutting of sheet metal using slitters, power shears, and dies in presses can be classified by shape or purpose of the cutting action into operations for producing blanks, for cutting holes, for progressive working, or for size control.[1] Operations for producing blanks are subdivided into shearing, cutoff, parting, and blanking (see Table 33-1).

TERMINOLOGY

The terminology dealing with the processes of sheet metal cutting or separation can sometimes be confusing. Several words may be used to describe one process; or, conversely, one word may have several different meanings. For example, the term *shear* can refer to a specific process by which straight cuts are made on metal or it can refer to a machine. Some people refer to the overall process of cutting as shearing. Metal has shear strength and resists shear force. (These terms are explained later in this chapter.) Finally, shear refers to the relief angle or shear angle on a punch or die or shear blade to provide efficient cutting.

Shearing

Shearing is a cutting process performed between two cutting edges; it does not form a chip. It may be a straight cut on a machine called a squaring shear, or it may be done between a punch and die.

Blanking

Any part cut from a sheet of metal that is not scrap is called a blank. Blanking, however, is a specific operation of cutting by which a part is cut from a sheet or strip of metal by a punch and die with the cut touching no edge of the sheet or strip.

Punching

As shown in Fig. 33-2, the opposite of blanking is punching. Although the punching process is identical to that of blanking, the difference between the two operations lies in which part is used and which part is scrapped. In blanking, the part cut from the original metal is saved; in punching, the part that is cut out (called a slug) is scrapped and the original metal is saved.

Piercing

Piercing is a process that is often confused with punching. It consists of cutting (or tearing) a hole in metal; however, it does not generate a slug. Instead, the metal is pushed back to form a jagged flange on the back side of the hole. A pierced hole looks somewhat like a bullet hole in a sheet of metal.

Extruding

A process similar to piercing is extruding. Extruding is another word with several meanings in the metals area. Pertaining to metal separation, it refers not only to punching a slug from a piece of metal (as in punching), but also to forming a flange on the backside of the hole (as in piercing).

Notching

Notching is another process by which a slug is removed from a blank. The cutting line of the slug must touch one edge of the blank or strip (as opposed to punching). A notch can be made in any shape and is generally cut to release metal for bending or fitting up.

Parting

Parting is a process similar to notching, except that the cut-out part is kept and the original strip is scrapped. The cut must touch the edge of the metal and may extend over part or all of the metal surface. Some scrap is always generated in this process.

Cutoff

Shearing is both a generic term and one used to describe a cutting process by which a straight cut is made across metal using a squaring shear. When a similar cut is made using a punch and die, the process is called cutoff.

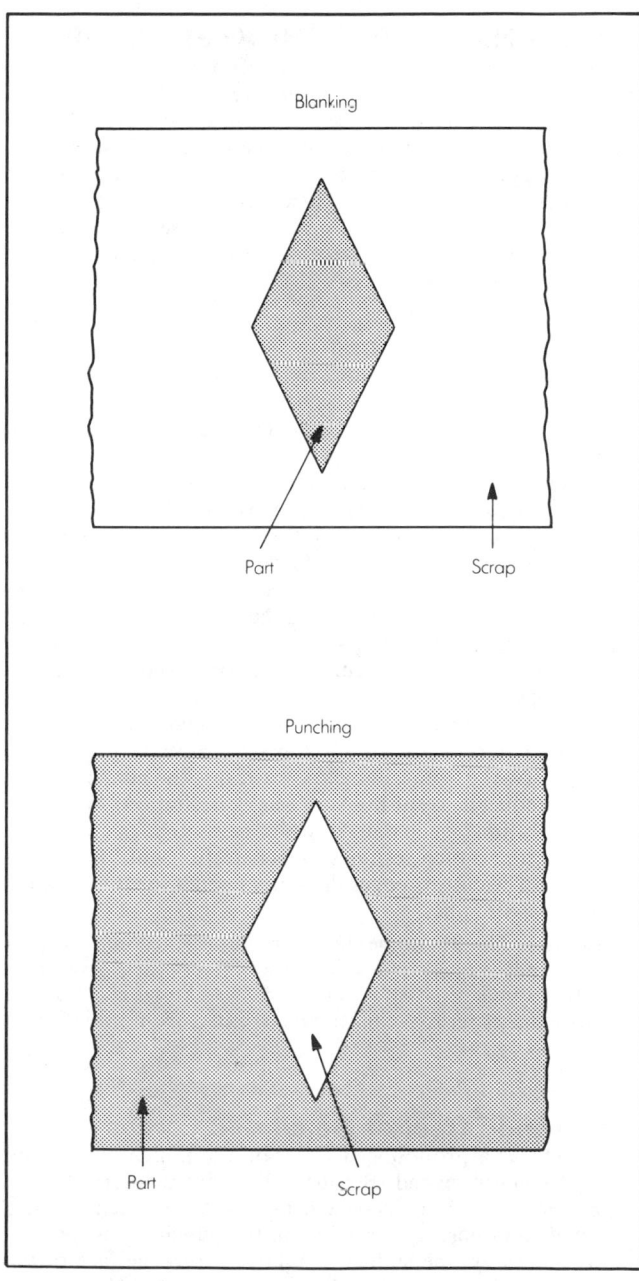

Fig. 33-2 Comparison of basic stamping operations. In punching, the metal inside the part is removed; in blanking, the metal around the part is removed.

BLANKING

Nibbling

Nibbling is a variation of notching, with overlapping notches being cut into the metal. This process may be used to cut almost any desired shape; it is also effective for cutting flanges, collars, etc., from heavier thicknesses of metal.

Perforating

Perforating is the process of punching a number of uniformly spaced holes in a piece of metal. The holes may be any shape, and they usually cover the entire sheet of metal. During the punching operation, care must be taken to avoid warping the perforated workpiece.

THE BLANKING/PUNCHING PROCESS

The blanking/punching process is a complex operation. The shear cutting, blanking, or punching action results from material being placed between two sharp, closely adjoined edges that have a closing motion. The material is stressed in shear to the point of fracture while going through three phases: elastic deformation (impact), penetration, and fracture (see Fig. 33-3). For analysis and discussion purposes, it is useful to divide the process into the operational sequence and the cause and effect of generated forces.

Operational Sequence

Punching a hole or producing a blank requires the same sequence of events: impact, penetration, and fracture. Contrary to appearances, the entire sequence is not a smoothly integrated series of events.[2]

Impact. The initial contact between the punch and the stock involves impact and deformation. As the stock begins to resist the penetration of the punch, sufficient force is developed to overcome the weight of the slide ram system and the punch stops moving. When the clearances in the ram, the pitman connection, the crank bearing, and the main bearings are taken up, the punch again impacts the stock. As the cutting edges close on the material, deformation occurs on both sides, near the cutting edge.

Penetration. The punch continues to penetrate the stock until sufficient resistance is developed to cause the press frame to stretch. As the frame elongates vertically, the punch velocity must be reduced, resulting in a slight hesitation. When the frame deflection is such that the stored energy can overcome the resistance, the punch resumes its penetration until fracture is imminent. The cutting edges then cut or penetrate the material, causing fracture lines.

Fracture. The phenomenon of fracture is accomplished in three distinct stages—crack initiation, slow crack extension, and rapid crack extension. The sketches shown in Fig. 33-4 illustrate the progressive nature of fracture, from initiation to completion.

Cause and Effect of Generated Forces

Impact has a pronounced effect on the punch and on the material being punched. Because solids are theoretically not compressible, material displacement must occur when a solid is subjected to opposing forces. When the punch slams into the material initially, the sudden resistance stops the face of the punch while the opposite end continues to move downward. Since the loaded punch is shortened and the volume remains the same, lateral displacement or bulging must occur.

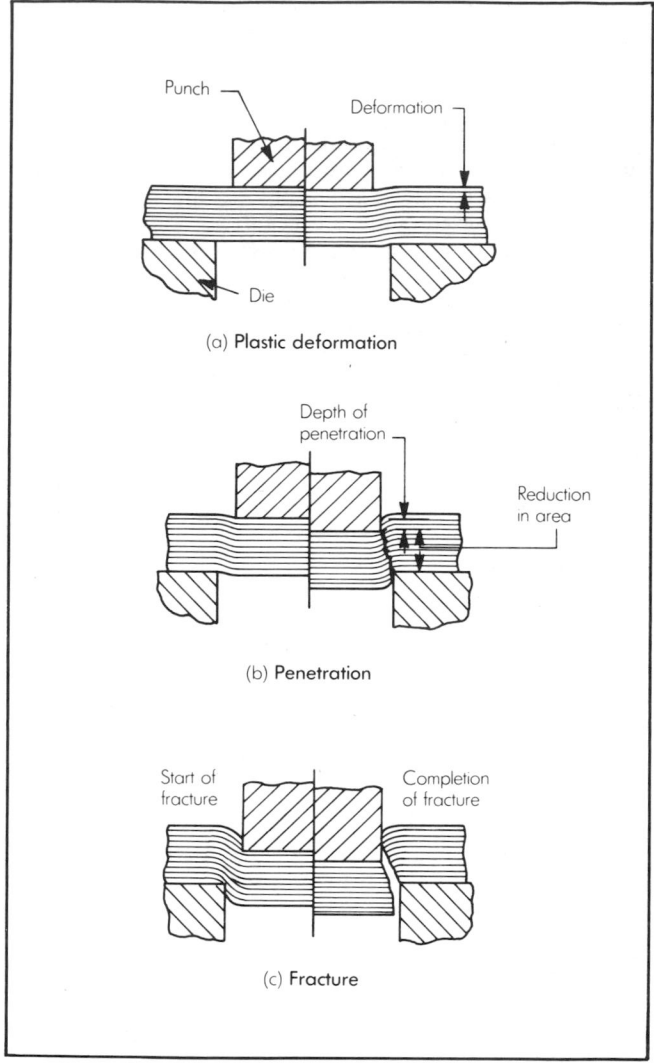

(a) Plastic deformation

(b) Penetration

(c) Fracture

Fig. 33-3 Three phases of shear cutting, as performed in blanking and punching.

Bulging. Bulging of the punch point causes a lateral thrust on the material being punched. The direction of least resistance to displacement is vertical, and a bulge develops around the periphery of the punch point.

Reaction. The reaction force of the material is generated by the die cavity. Consequently, the reaction is concentrated at a locus of points near the edge periphery of the punch. This permits the center of the punch face to project beyond the edges. As the press clearances are taken up, the time element permits the loads to be equalized. Suddenly, the press delivers another blow and the original displacement is intensified.

As punch penetration continues, frame elongation provides another time period during which the punch attempts to equalize the load distribution. Again the power builds up, the punch is confined between two extremely heavy loads, and further displacement occurs. During this total time period, shock waves travel upward along the length of the punch. The shock waves are attenuated as they travel through the punched material, and a major dissipation occurs when the waves are absorbed by the mass of the punch retainer. As each hesitation

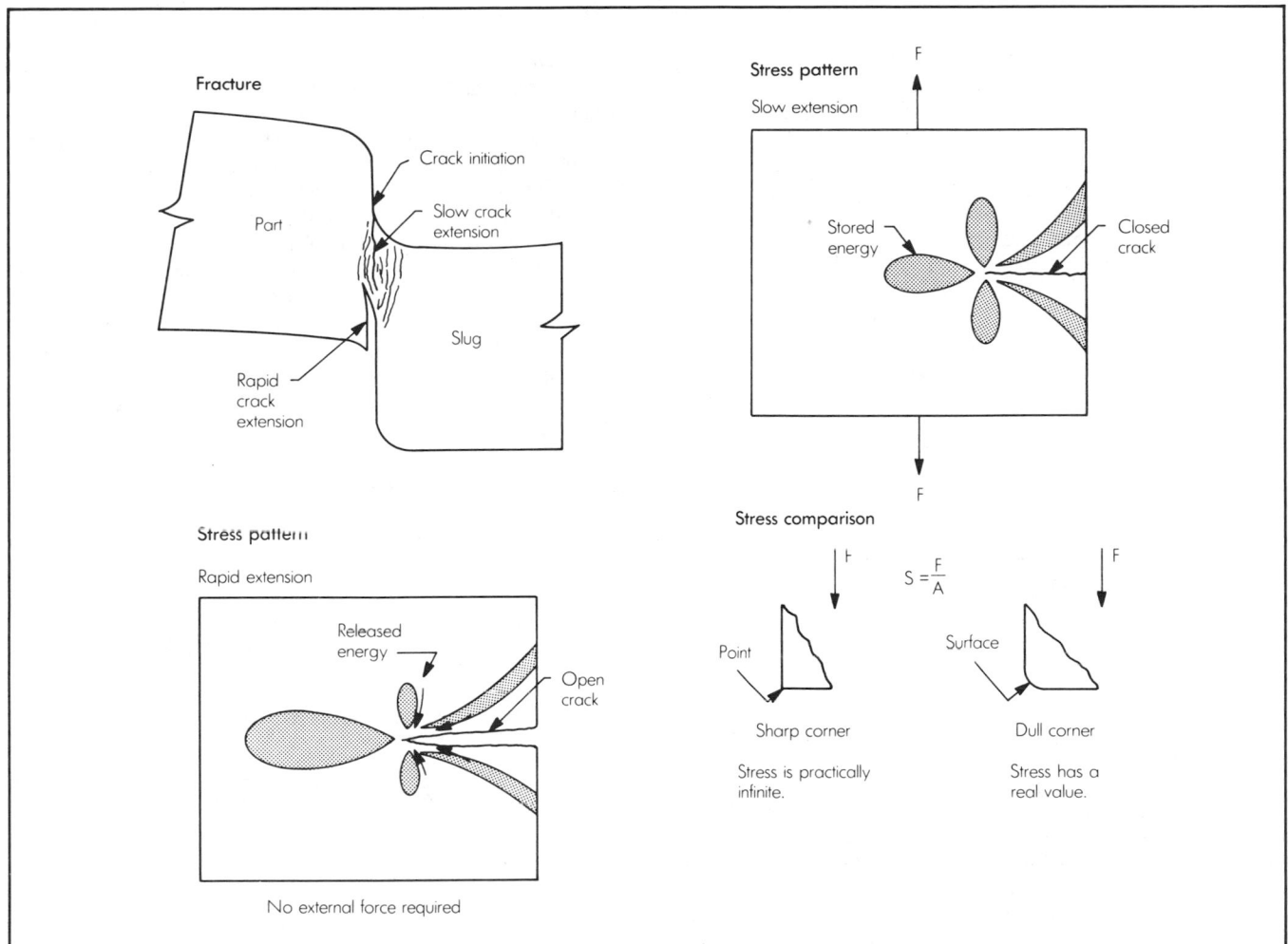

Fig. 33-4 Illustration of fracture, from initiation to completion. (*Danly Machine Co.*)

occurs, however, another series of waves starts to travel upward.

Fracture. When ultimate fracture takes place, a violent reaction is generated within the punch. The load at the face of the punch is abruptly removed, and the punch immediately tries to regain its original dimensional stability. The stored energy drives the punch face downward and generates a series of alternations during which the punch is either too long or too short. Gradually, the amplitude of the oscillations is reduced to zero and the punch is in equilibrium.

Meanwhile, the direction of shock wave travel through the punch is reversed. Instead of encountering increasing diameters, the shock waves now meet decreasing diameters. Head breakage or breakage at the blend-radius tangent points often results from this type of stress concentration. On rare occasions, the shock wave moving downward joins an upward-traveling wave; both waves then move in phase and snap the shank within its retainer.

As the punch load is removed abruptly, the sudden extension of the point reduces its cross-sectional dimensions. The residual energy stored in the stock strip and the suddenly acquired space between the punch and the hole cause a fluttering action that tends to polish or burnish the land. A similar combination of stored energy and space for movement causes the slug to undergo rather violent gyrations.

ZONES OF A SHEARED PART

A part edge which has been cut usually has four major zones (see Fig. 33-5). Perhaps the most obvious portion is the burr. With proper punch or die clearance adjustment the burr should be small enough so that in most cases it will not require removal. If clearance between the punch and die is too great, the burr may be sufficiently large to cause problems. If the clearance is too small, a phenomenon called secondary shear takes place. This is caused by the fracture lines' missing each other and actually producing two fracture areas.

As the upper blade or punch descends and makes contact with the workpiece, the metal becomes elastically deformed. If the force is removed during this stage, no deformation or cutting takes place. Of course, the blade or punch usually continues to descend and plastic deformation begins to take place at the lower die. This is the second zone—the zone of plastic deformation, which is the flattened area along the bottom of the cut. This deformation is localized because of the

BLANKING

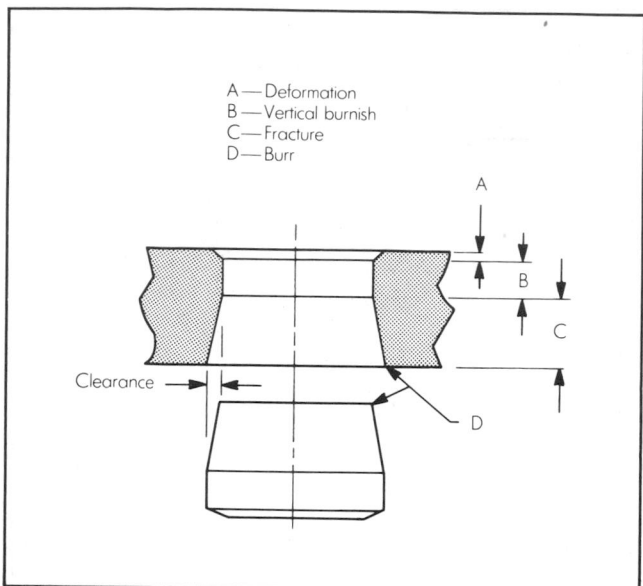

Fig. 33-5 Four zones of a shear cut.

small amount of clearance between the shear blades or between the punch and die.

As the force continues, the descending blade or punch penetrates the metal. This depth of penetration is the shiny area seen on the edge of the cut part. After shearing occurs, the blade slides over this area and burnishes it; hence, it is called the burnish or the burnished zone.

When a sheared part is viewed, the burnished zone stands out in shiny contrast to the rough area adjoining it. This rough area is called the fracture zone and is the result of sudden failure as the penetration increases from 15 to 60% of the metal thickness. This percentage varies depending upon the metal's strength, ductility, and thickness. As the shear forces exceed the shear strength, the metal fails and fracture is completed. This fracture creates the rough area (burr zone) on the edge of the cut part.

BLANK DESIGN

Blanks can be cut from either flat or preformed stock. The flat blank usually requires subsequent operations. The development of the shape of the blank is determined by the end product. For example, circular blanks are used for round products such as drum heads and drawn cylindrical shells. Rectangular and irregularly shaped blanks are used to provide material for further working such as bending, flanging, or bulging. In addition to the material required for a finished part, the blank normally contains additional stock to permit holding during working and final trimming. Typical blanked semifinished parts are laminations for motors, transformers, and padlock cases made from stacked stampings.

FINE BLANKING

Fine blanking and piercing is a process developed in Switzerland for producing blanks and holes with smoother edges and closer tolerances than are possible with conventional stamping practice.

Advantages

Conventional blanking or stamping operations produce

parts with sheared surfaces that are only partially—generally one third—cleanly sheared, the remaining two thirds showing a rough break as illustrated in Fig. 33-6. When functional demands are made on these sheared/break surfaces concerning tolerances or quality of surface finish, the piece parts must be reworked by such methods as shaving, milling, reaming, broaching or grinding. For the production of precision devices, it is often necessary that at least two, but generally more, secondary operations be performed per piece-part.[3]

Using fine blanking, precise finished components with inner and outer forms cleanly sheared over the whole material thickness are produced in one operation (see Fig. 33-6), thereby effecting significant production cost savings. To achieve these benefits, a triple action press and a specially constructed tool are required.

Another major advantage of fine blanking is that hole diameters, slot widths, and wall thicknesses can be made

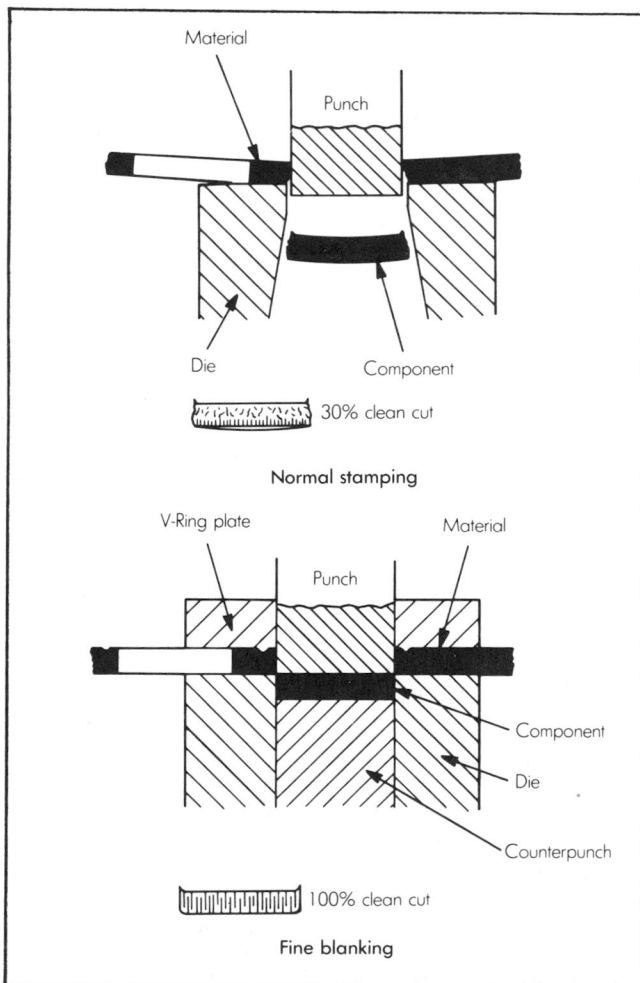

Fig. 33-6 Elements of conventional stamping compared with fine blanking. Before the material is fine blanked, it is firmly clamped so that it can flow only in the cutting direction. On the outside of the component's cutting line, the material is sandwiched by the die and the V-ring plate (stinger); inside of the cutting line, the punch and the counter-punch locate and control the material. The clearance between punch and die measures only a few 100ths of a millimeter (1/1000 of an inch) and the cutting speed is relatively slow. (*Schmid Corp. of America*)

smaller than with conventional stampings—as small as 50% of material thickness in low-carbon steels. Also, other operations such as bending, embossing, and coining can be combined in the same operation, and the press can be used for conventional stamping dies when not required for fine blanking.

Materials Handled

Many different materials are being fine blanked. These include ferrous materials such as low and medium-carbon steels and some alloy and stainless steels, as well as nonferrous materials such as brass, copper, and aluminum alloys. In fact, any material suitable for cold forming can be fine blanked.

Fine blanking is best for applications in which manufacturing costs can be reduced by minimizing or eliminating secondary operations in producing smooth, accurate functional edges, or for improving product edge quality. When the edges produced in conventional stamping are satisfactory for a specific application, fine blanking can seldom be justified economically.

Applications

Fine blanking is an accepted process in many fields of production. The potential cost savings depend on the number and complexity of secondary operations that can be eliminated. The use of progressive tools is expanding the range of new applications of fine blanked parts involving forming operations. Figure 33-7 shows various forming operations that are feasible for fine blanking.

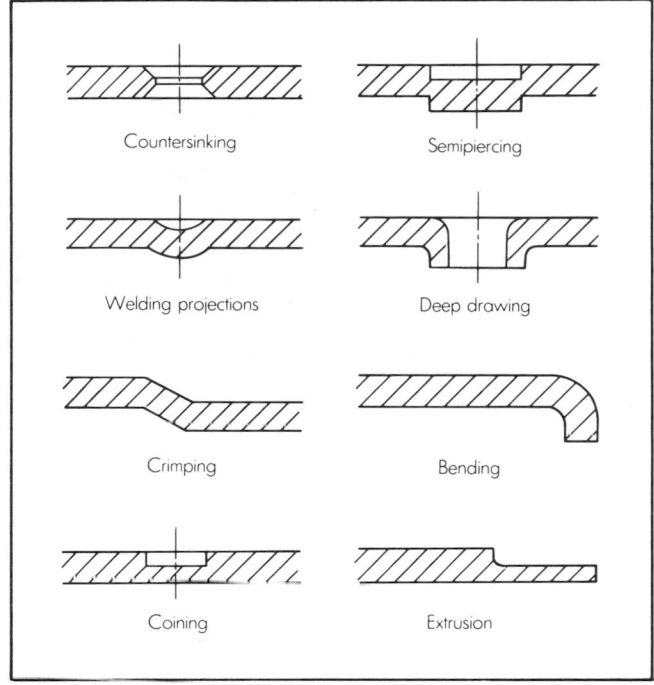

Fig. 33-7 Various forming operations are feasible with fine blanking.

FORMING

Forming is a broad term for the metalworking processes in which the shape of a punch and die is reproduced directly in the metal. Bending, drawing, ironing, bulging, and various compression processes are included here as general subclasses under forming.

BENDING AND FLANGING

Bending and flanging are methods of forming shapes by stressing metal beyond its yield strength but below the ultimate strength. Flanging is similar to the bending of sheet metal, except that during flanging, the bent down metal is short compared to overall part size. There is no well-defined bent-over length that distinguishes bending from flanging. As explained later in this chapter, however, flanges and bends have distinctly different functions.

Bending

Bends are made in sheet metal to gain rigidity and to produce a part of desired shape to perform a particular function. Bending is commonly used to produce structural stampings such as braces, brackets, supports, hinges, angles, and channels. Bending in several directions can produce parts that otherwise would require a drawing operation. Bending is usually done to a 90° angle, but other angles are sometimes produced.

Flanging

Flanging is a forming operation in which a narrow strip at the edge of a sheet is bent down along a straight or curved line. Flanges can be open, at 90°, or at an acute angle—all of which are shown in Fig. 33-8. A flange is used for appearance, rigidity,

edge strengthening, and removal of a sheared edge, as well as for an accurately positioned fastening surface.

The three major types of flanges are the straight, stretch, and skrink flanges, shown in Fig. 33-9. The joggled flange in Fig. 33-9, view *f*, is a combination of all three major types. The reverse flange, Fig. 33-9, view *g*, is a combination of the stretch and skrink flanges; and the hole flange, Fig. 33-9, view *h*, is a special case of the stretch flange.

Hemming

A hem is a flange that has been bent more than 180°. Hems are primarily used for appearance and for the attachment of one sheet metal part to another. They are not as rigid or accurate as a flange; but they very effectively remove a dangerous sheared edge. They are used extensively in automobiles to join inner and outer door and trunk lid stampings.

Four different types of hems are shown in Fig. 33-10. The tear drop hem is used for materials that do not have the ductility required to form the flattened hem. The open hem and rope hem are used for attachment to other sheet metal parts. The rope hem is used for materials that do not have sufficient ductility to form the open hem.

DRAWING

Drawing is a process of cold forming a flat precut metal blank into a hollow vessel without excessive wrinkling, thinning, or fracturing. The various forms produced may be cylindrical or box shaped, with straight or tapered sides or a combination of straight, tapered, and curved sides. The parts may vary from 1/4″ (6 mm) diam parts or smaller to aircraft or automotive

FORMING

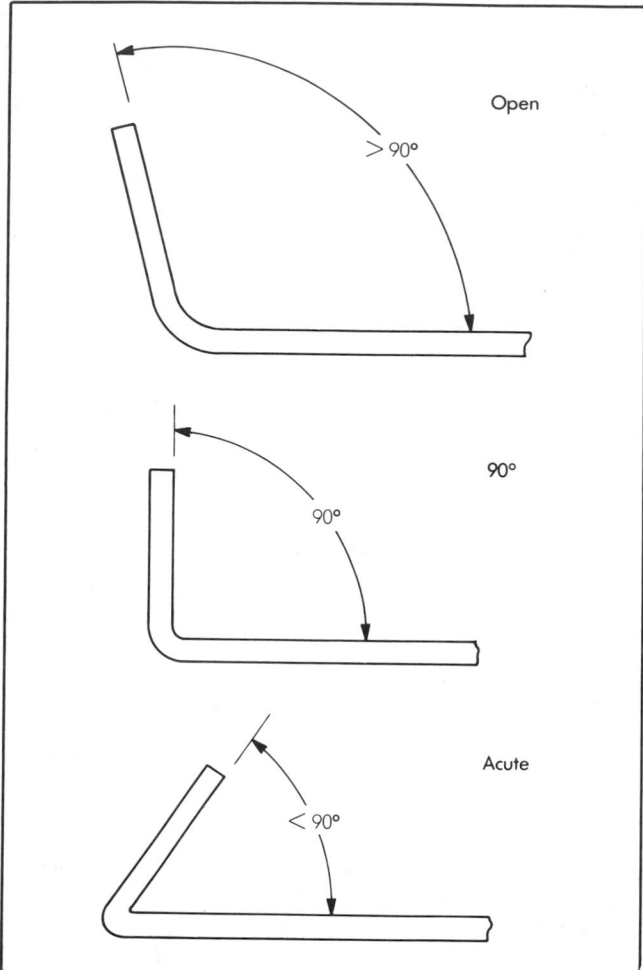

Fig. 33-8 Flange angles of bend.

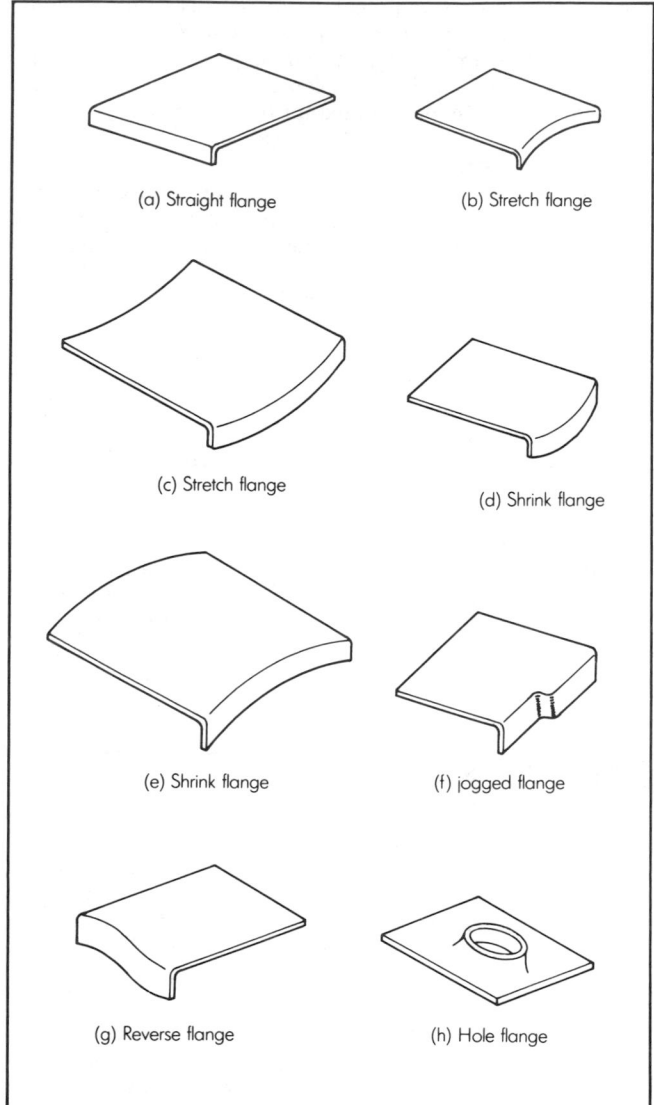

(a) Straight flange   (b) Stretch flange

(c) Stretch flange   (d) Shrink flange

(e) Shrink flange   (f) jogged flange

(g) Reverse flange   (h) Hole flange

Fig. 33-9 The major types of flanges are straight, stretch, and shrink.

parts large enough to require mechanical handling equipment.

The process of drawing basically involves forcing the flat sheet of metal into a die cavity with a punch. The force exerted by the punch must be sufficient to draw the metal over the edge of the die opening and into the die. The metal flow is similar to that of a viscous fluid.

The metal being drawn must have a combination of strength and ductility, to avoid rupture in the critical area where metal blends from the punch face to the vertical portion of the punch. This area is subjected to the stress that occurs when the metal is pulled from the flat blank into the die. The blank must have sufficient ductility to permit metal flow toward the die opening by the combination of compressive and tensile forces that are applied.

Redrawing

The term *redrawing* is used for a variety of operations in which a part is reduced in its lateral dimensions by means of single or double-action dies without reducing the wall thickness. Regular redrawing is done by positioning the part under the punch, which forces the cup into the die, reducing the bottom dimensions, and increasing the side-wall height. Reverse or inside-out redrawing is done by positioning the cup over a die

ring; the punch contacts the outside of the bottom, turning the part inside-out into the die opening.

Number of operations. When the height of the cup drawn from the blank is larger than the diameter of the required part, the cup must be redrawn, according to recommended percentages, until the required diameter is obtained. Knowing the blank diameter, the number of operations needed to reduce the blank diameter to the required part diameter can be determined. General practice is to make a 40-45% reduction of blank diameter for the first draw. For the second draw, the reduction is 30%; and for the third draw, the reduction is 16%. These percentages are given only as a general guide.

Reductions in drawing. One important factor in the success or failure of a drawing operation is the thickness-diameter ratio, or the relationship of the metal thickness to the blank or previous shell diameter; this ratio is expressed as t/d. As this ratio decreases, the tendency to wrinkle increases and necessitates more blankholding pressure to control the flow properly

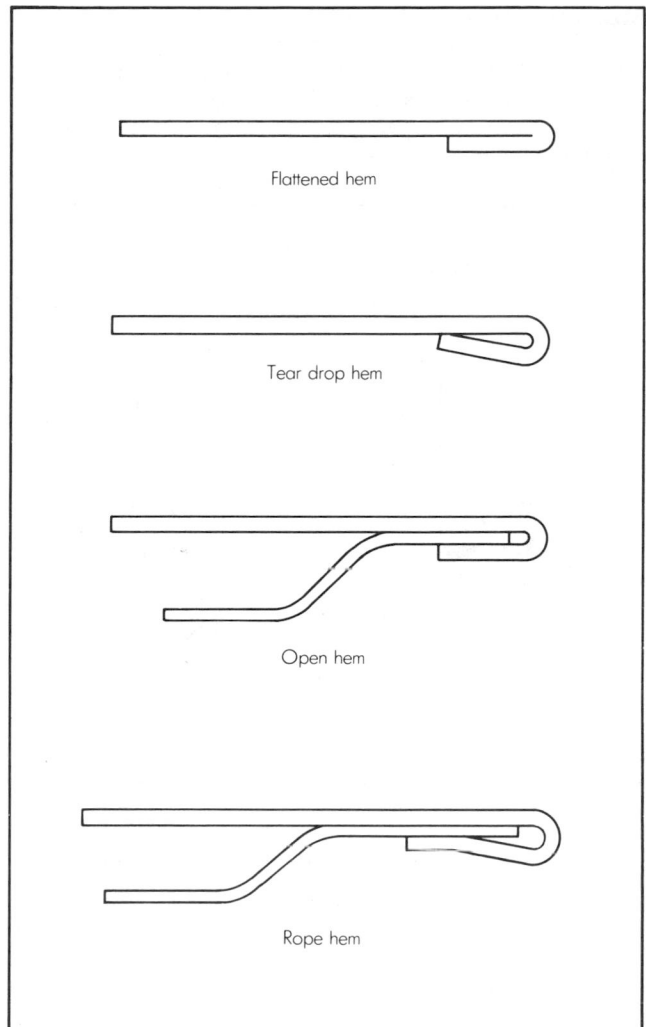

Fig. 33-10 Four types of hems.

and prevent wrinkles from starting.

Metal Flow

Deep-drawing cylindrical cup. When the punch of a drawing press forces a portion of a metal blank through the bore of the draw ring, a number of different forces interact (see Fig. 33-11) to cause plastic flow of the material. Volume and thickness of the metal remain essentially constant, and the final shape of the cup is similar to the contour of the punch.

The progressive stages of cupping are shown schematically in Fig. 33-12. After a small stroke of the punch (cupping stage A), the metal volume element (2) of the blank is bent and wrapped around the punch nose. Simultaneously and subsequently, the outer portions of the blank (depicted by 3, 4, and 5) move radially toward the center of the blank, as shown in cupping stages B and C. The various volume elements decrease in circumferential length (not shown) and correspondingly increase in radial length until they reach the bore of the draw ring. They then bend over, conforming to the edge of the die. After becoming part of the shell wall, the elements are straight. During drawing, Area 1 (for the specific example illustrated) is

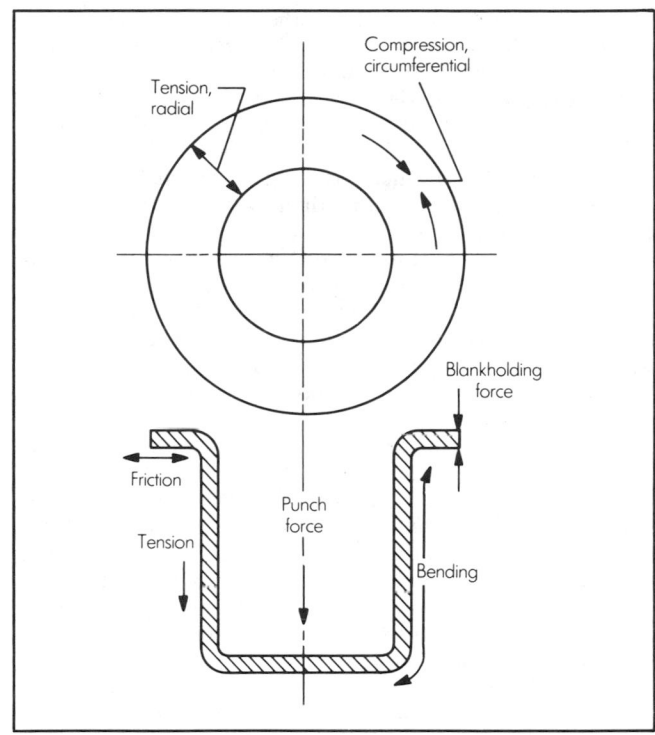

Fig. 33-11 Forces involved in metal flow during cupping.

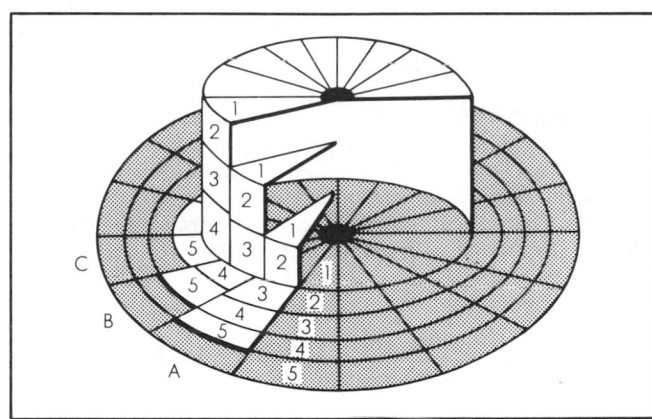

Fig. 33-12 Sequential flow of metal shows progressive stages of cupping.

unchanged in the bottom of the cup. The areas that become the side wall of the shell (2, 3, and 4) change in shape from angular segments to longer parallel-sided shapes as they are drawn over the inner edge of the draw ring; from this point on, no further metal flow takes place.

Metal flow in rectangular shells. The drawing of a rectangular shell involves varying degrees of flow severity. Some parts of the shell may require severe cold working; and others, simple bending. In contrast to circular shells in which pressure is uniform on all diameters, some areas of rectangular and irregular shells may require more pressure than others. True drawing occurs at the corners only; at the sides and ends, metal movement is more closely allied to bending. The stresses at the corner of the shell are compressive on the metal moving toward

FORMING

the die radius and are tensile on the metal that has already moved over the radius. The metal between the corners is in tension only on the side wall and in the flange areas.

Wrinkling and puckering. The shaping of a shell necessitates severe cold working and involves plastic flow of the metal; therefore, any condition retarding the flow must be avoided to minimize the stress to which the metal is subjected.

The metal may buckle rather than shrink in any location of the blank, if it is very thin and if a sufficiently wide area is free to move away from the tools. The buckles produced by this buckling are called "wrinkles" when they occur at the edge of the blank and "puckers" when they appear in any other part of the blank. The formation of wrinkles in the flange area is to be expected, since the stress direction is circumferential. This wrinkling must be controlled because it may adversely affect the normal metal flow.

Since relatively thin metals have a high wrinkling tendency, blankholding pressures required for such draws are higher than for draws with relatively thick metals. When the thickness-diameter ratio of the blank is low, high blankholding pressure is required; when this ratio is high, little or no blankholding pressure is required. Also, in general, as the thickness-diameter ratio of the blank decreases, the amount of drawing that is feasible decreases correspondingly, and the tools for these draws must be finished with greater care.

The shape of the shell section governs, to some extent, whether wrinkles or puckers will be more prevalent under conditions of poor control. Straight-sided shells are typical shapes in which wrinkles often occur; whereas puckers are most likely to appear in domed or tapered shells. If the die radius and/or the punch radius is too large, even though the sides are straight, the conditions approach those of domed shapes and both wrinkles and puckers tend to occur.

Drawing Limits

The work that can be done in a single pass is limited and depends on metal conditions, die design, lubrication, blank diameter to blank thickness ratio, etc.

The work done can be expressed as the drawing reduction, which is the reduction in diameter from blank to inside cup.

Percentage reduction

$$= \frac{Blank\ diam - inside\ cup\ diam}{Inside\ cup\ diam} \times 100\% \qquad (1)$$

The limiting draw ratio, LDR, is used to show the maximum drawing reduction possible:

$$LDR = \frac{Max\ blank\ diam}{Cup\ inside\ diam} \qquad (2)$$

The maximum draw reduction with ordinary tooling is about 48% for aluminum; but with steel or tin plate, 52-56% reductions are possible.

It can be seen that a 50% reduction means an LDR of 2 and, therefore, the LDR for aluminum should be less than 2 (1.92 for 48%) and the LDR for tin plate should be higher than 2 (for example, 2.17 for 54% reduction). The greater the blank diameter/stock thickness ratio, the smaller the possible reduction or LDR. Limiting draw ratio is related mathematically to material properties, and the strain ratio, r, and work-hardening exponent, n, are primary determinants of LDR.

Multiple Draws

If required cup diameter is smaller than can be obtained with a maximum reduction in one pass, multiple draws are needed. These can be done with a straight redraw (see Fig. 33-13) or with a reverse redraw (see Fig. 33-14) whereby the cup is actually turned inside-out.

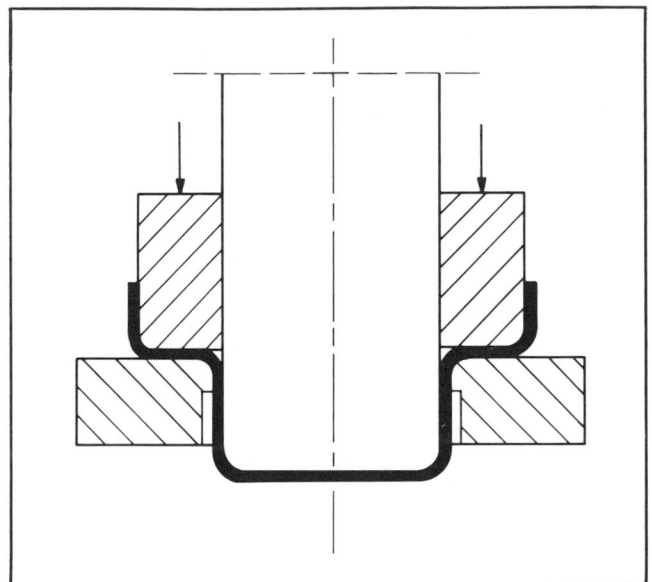

Fig. 33-13 Straight redraw operation.

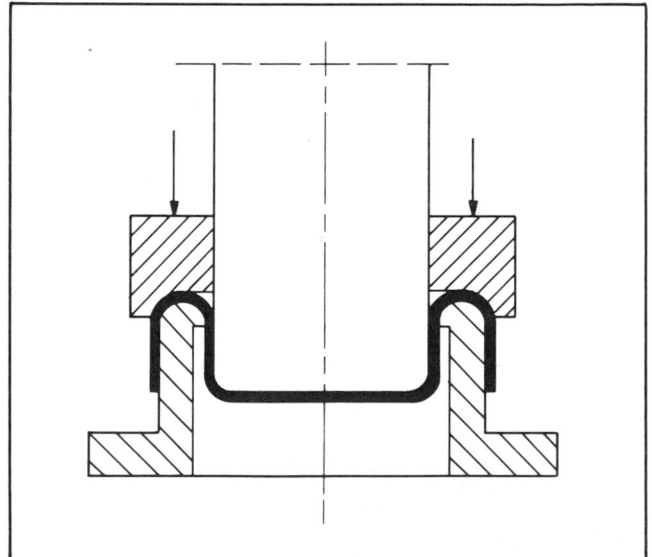

Fig. 33-14 Reverse redraw operation.

Earing

The earing characteristic (shown in Fig. 33-15) is frequently noted on drawn cups with and without flanges.

During the drawing process, material in the flange of the cup between draw pad and blankholder must move from a large diameter (blank size) to a much smaller size, that is, the cup diameter. As shown in Fig. 33-16, the metal is subjected to a

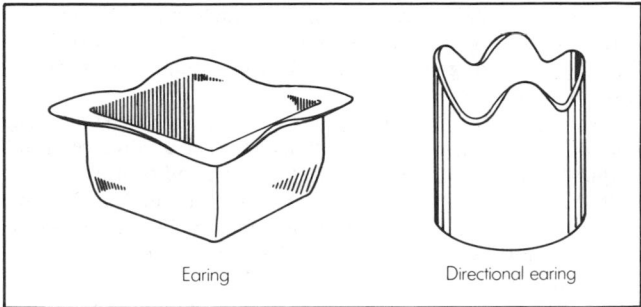

Earing   Directional earing

Fig. 33-15 Typical earing.

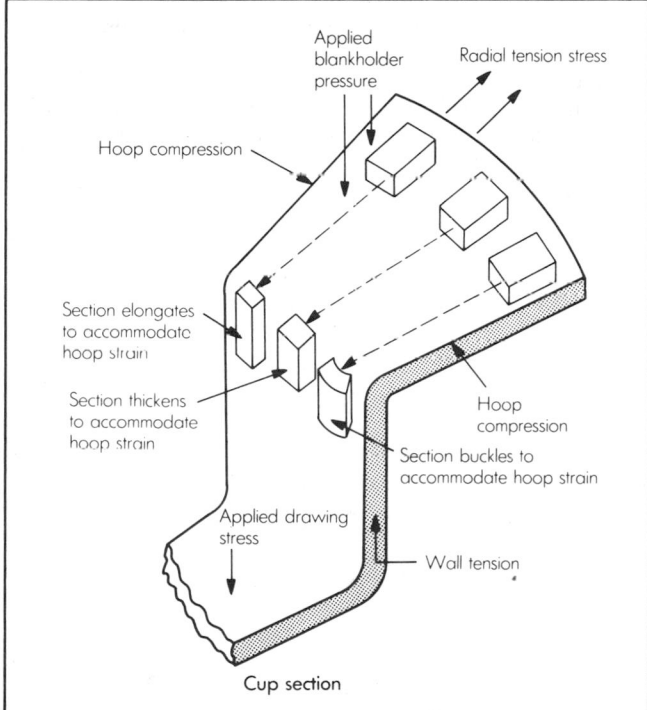

Applied blankholder pressure

Radial tension stress

Hoop compression

Section elongates to accommodate hoop strain

Section thickens to accommodate hoop strain

Hoop compression

Section buckles to accommodate hoop strain

Applied drawing stress

Wall tension

Cup section

Fig. 33-16 Schematic drawing of a cup section shows stresses and types of deformation that occur during the drawing process.

compressive hoop stress as well as a radial tensile stress and can deform by buckling, elongating, or thickening. Buckling is avoided by proper tool design, sufficient blankholder pressure, and the correct draw reduction.

A good drawing material should exhibit less than 4% earing. Earing is very undesirable. It can lead to pinching or clipping in the draw dies because at the end of the draw, the full blankholder load is concentrated on the tips of the ears. These ear tips can be pinched off due to the high unit load, and an accumulation of the clippings in the dies can be a serious problem.

Various means can be used to prevent ear pinching. On some presses the dies can be designed in such a way that the blankholder lifts off the blank at the precise end of the draw. This requires precise setting and shimming of the dies after regrinding to maintain the original die height.

In double-action presses with a cam-actuated blanking ram, the dies can be designed so that the blankholder always stays away from the draw pad by about 80% of the stock thickness

and cannot snap shut at the end of the draw.

Drawing Parameters

The most common failure of a drawing operation is rupturing of metal in a critical area because of insufficient strength to withstand the force required to draw the metal from the blank area into the die. Many factors determine whether this area has sufficient strength: (1) the relationship of the diameter of the blank to the diameter of the cup, (2) the contour of the punch edge and the contour of the die edge, (3) the type of lubricant being used to minimize friction between the metal being drawn and the surfaces of the blankholder and the die, (4) the ductility of the metal being drawn, and (5) the speed of the press.

IRONING

In blanking, metal is fractured in shear; in drawing, it is worked primarily by application of a tensile load on the side walls. Ironing is distinguished from blanking and drawing by the fact that the primary working stress is compressive. (Other compression processes, such as coining and swaging, are described later in this chapter.)

The Ironing Process

Ironing, which (as stated previously) is the reduction in thickness of drawn shell walls by pulling them through tight dies, is related to both shell drawing and wire drawing. It is done to obtain a wall that is thin compared with the shell bottom; to obtain a uniform wall; to obtain a tapered wall, such as those in cartridge cases; or merely to correct the natural wall thickening toward the top edge of a drawn shell.

The theoretical maximum reduction in wall thickness per operation due to ironing is approximately 50%. In such a case, the cross-section area of the (unstrained) metal before ironing is about double the cross-section area after ironing.

Typical Tooling

Basically, in the ironing process, a drawn cup is placed on a punch or ram and is pushed through a die that has a smaller inside diameter than the outside diameter of the cup (see Fig. 33-17, view *a*). The wall thickness is thereby reduced, and the wall elongated and given a smooth, uniform surface. This is done by providing clearance space between the punch and the die wall. When the walls of the shell must be thinner at the top than toward the bottom, the punch is given a taper corresponding to the desired variation in wall thickness. Unless the material being worked is especially ductile, reductions should be limited to 10-12% of the thickness of the shell wall in one operation. The bottom of the shell is unaffected by ironing operations and retains the original metal thickness. Two-step ironing dies (see Fig. 33-17, view *b*) permit a second reduction of up to 75% of the first, depending upon the spacing of the dies.

BULGING

Bulging is a metalforming process used to expand a tubular or cylindrical blank or part. The forming may be limited to a portion of a part, as in the expanding of pipe ends and the forming of rolling or stiffening beads in steel drums or washer tubs (see Fig. 33-18), or the entire part may be formed, as in the production of missile venturi sections. The two principal methods of bulge forming are mechanical bulging and hydrostatic bulging.

FORMING

Mechanical Bulging

Relatively symmetrical shapes may be produced by segmented bulging dies in which the various segments, held together by springs, are pushed apart by the punch to expand a superimposed shell. The main disadvantage of this method is that the resulting surface is marred by slight flats; however, if this slight marring is not objectionable, segmented dies are easily operated and maintained.

Bulging by mechanical methods that utilize a segmented, radially expanding mandrel or die set has been used successfully for parts as small as 2″ (51 mm) diam when conditions of length, wall thickness, physical properties, and amount of bulging required are favorable. There is no inherent limitation to the maximum diameter bulged by mechanical expanding.

Another method of mechanical bulging involves inserting steel balls and grease, to make up a volume equal to that of the cubic content of the finished piece, into the shell that has been placed in a split die, and subsequently using the punch to compress the filler to form or bend the shell.

It is advisable to use annealed shells for bulging. If the expansion must be considerable, the work may best be accomplished in two, three, or even more steps. It may be necessary to anneal between operations. The more ductile metals such as aluminum, copper, soft brass, silver, and low-

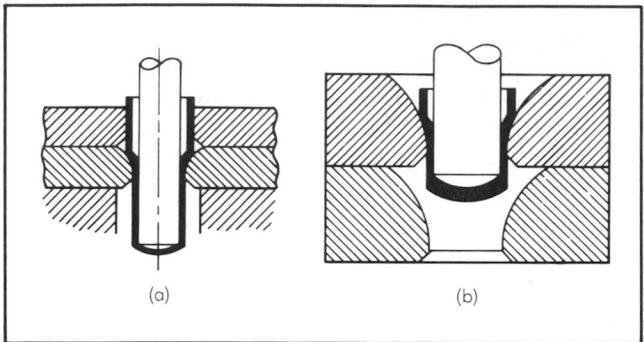

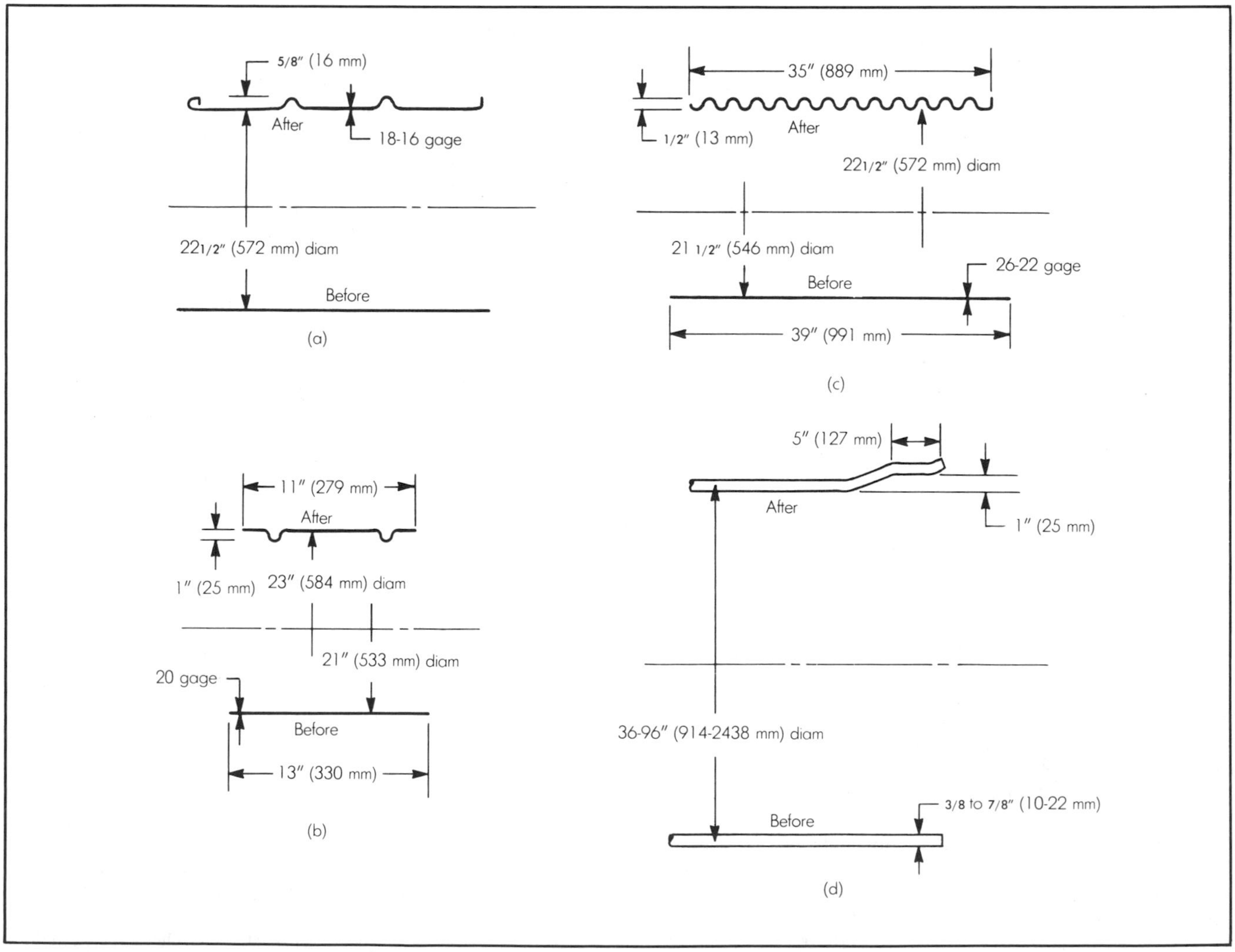

Fig. 33-17 Basic principle of ironing: (a) operation partially completed; (b) two-step die. Ironing often is the final operation in a series of draws.

Fig. 33-18 Typical bulge-formed parts before and after bulging: (a) standard 55 gallon (208 L) drum body; (b) drier drum; (c) lightweight 55 gallon drum body; and (d) large-bore pipe.

carbon steel may be enlarged about 30% of the blank diameter in one operation.

Hydrostatic Bulging

The hydrostatic method of bulge forming uses a fluid or rubber, usually polyurethane, to apply internal pressure to the inside of the workpiece as the die is closed.

The comparative advantages of hydrostatic bulging include:

1. There is no inherent limitation of the minimum diameter or length of a part that may be formed.
2. There is no marking of the workpiece by the internal pressure medium.
3. The reduction of workpiece wall thickness is minimized by freedom of the workpiece to shorten during the bulging operation.

COMPRESSION OPERATIONS

Coining, swaging, and sizing are metal-compression processes employed to impart a pattern, configuration, or decoration to parts produced from flat-rolled material.

Coining

Coining is the most severe of the metal-squeezing operations in the amount of pressure applied to each square inch of material. In this process, the metal thickness is changed, as is the internal structure of the workpiece. Because a closed die is generally used to confine the metal, the workpiece becomes an accurate reproduction of the die cavity.

Materials. Materials that can be successfully coined are gold, silver, mild steels of the low-carbon type, brass, bronze, and copper. High-carbon steels, as well as those of the sulfur type, commonly fracture during coining.

Advantages and limitations. The advantages of parts produced by coining include dimensional accuracy, polished surfaces, increased strength, and economy both in material and manufacturing. The limitations of coining processes are that die steels must be used that can withstand the high unit pressures generated and that metal movement of die components must be held to a minimum.

Sizing

Sizing operations are closely related to coining in that sizing, like coining, changes the metal thickness and configuration by squeezing and working metal beyond the yield point.

Most sizing operations are performed in open dies; therefore, the entire workpiece is not confined in the die and the only contact between the workpiece and the die occurs in the section in which the sizing takes place. There is usually no restriction to metal flow. Sizing is used to sharpen corners on stampings, flatten areas around pierced holes, etc. Some malleable-iron castings and drop forgings are sized in this manner.

Swaging

Swaging is also closely related to coining in the family of compression operations. In swaging, which is somewhat more severe than sizing, the shape of the blank or slug is considerably altered as part of it flows into the contours of the die. The swaging process differs from coining, however, in that the remaining metal is unconfined and generally flows at an angle to the direction of applied force. Compared with sizing, there is greater restriction to metal flow, although more metal is moved.

Swaging is applied to the production of parts such as small gears or cams or other small parts of irregular contour.

Embossing

In the manufacturing of metal parts with a die set and press, embossing is the process used to create shallow designs theoretically without changing the metal thickness.

Embossing differs from coining in that with embossing the same design is created on both sides of the workpiece, one side being depressed and the other raised, whereas with coining a different design is created on each side. During embossing, therefore, the metal is bent along the lines of the design. Some stretching and compressing takes place along the design lines, the amount depending on the extent to which the design height is changed.

Beading

Beading is a process used to form shallow, round troughs of uniform width (either recessed or raised) in a straight, curved, or circular form. Pressures required to form strengthening or ornamental beads in sheet metal parts are approximately the same as those required for embossing operations and are considerably less than those required for coining. Beads increase overall rigidity without increasing material thickness. They can be produced in either single or progressive operations.

Beading is applied to round can or container bodies in a rolling operation between male and female roll forms. Both semiautomatic and automatic machines are available for this operation, and occasionally trimming and flanging are combined with beading.

CREEP FORMING

Creep forming is the deformation of metal at a stress level below its yield point and the application of heat to the metal for a time sufficient to permit metallurgical creep to cause relaxation of the induced elastic stresses to such a level that plastic deformation to the desired shape is achieved.

This process is used almost exclusively by the aerospace industry. Applications range from jet engine parts to large, comparatively thin, and relatively shallow-contour components for which one-piece construction and the resultant product life-cycle costs or payload benefits offset the unit costs of creep forming. The materals that are predominately creep formed are aluminum and titanium alloys for skins in missiles and airplanes. One of the production applications is the forming of airplane wing skins.

RUBBER PAD FORMING

The principle of rubber pad forming is that when the underlying rubber is placed in a cylinder and pressure is brought to bear upon it by applying a force to a ram of a press, the force causes a resultant reaction on every surface with which the rubber comes in contact. This resultant reaction is used for forming sheet metals to a required shape using form blocks or punches and dies.

Guerin Process

The Guerin process employs a rubber pad on the ram of the press and a form block that is placed on the lower platen mounted on the press bed. This process is the oldest and most widely used, but it is limited to the forming of relatively shallow parts of light materials, normally not exceeding 1.2-1.5″ (30-

FORMING

38 mm) deep.

Marforming Process

This method was developed to form shrink flanges and deep draw shells. Figure 33-19 shows that the process uses a deep rubber pad on the ram of the press with a stationary punch fixed on the press bed. A steel pressure plate cut to fit the container and to slip freely over the punch provides the bottom support for the rubber pad in the container. As the ram is lowered, the blank is clamped between the rubber pad and the blankholder before forming begins. As the ram continues to descend, the blank is drawn over the punch. The pressure in the pneumatic cushion must be controlled. Such constant control of pressure on the blankholder provides smooth forming and eliminates wrinkling. The variable draw radii in a rubber pad permit the material to draw more easily than the fixed radius of a steel die. It is also possible to draw square and rectangular boxes and hemispherical and tapered stampings with this process.

Rubber-Die Process

This process is used to draw shallow-recessed parts. In this process, a die is used instead of a punch. The die is mounted on the press bed and fits in the container exactly. A sheet is placed on the die, and the ram is brought down. As it descends, the rubber pad in the container pushes the sheet into the cavity. Initially, the rubber pressure acts uniformly over the entire surface, but when the rubber pushes the sheet into the die cavity, the pressure is increased in that region because the rubber is squeezed into a smaller area. Therefore, due to difference in pressures on the flange and the die cavity, the sheet is drawn. The blankholder plate is not necessary for this process.

Dieless Process

In this process, a draw ring is used instead of a die with the external contour of the component. The material is pushed inside a circular hole in an annular ring. Since the rubber flows in hemispherical form when it is pushed against a hole, hemispherical components can be produced without difficulty.

Fluid Cell Process

The fluid cell process was developed from the Guerin process. It uses higher pressure and is designed primarily for forming slightly deeper parts, using a rubber pad as either the die or punch. A flexible hydraulic fluid cell forces an auxiliary

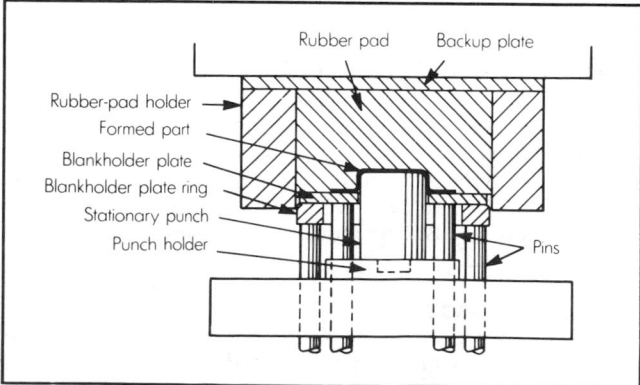

Fig. 33-19 Tooling and setup for rubber-pad forming by the Marform process.

rubber pad to follow the contour of the form block and exert a nearly uniform pressure at all points.

The distribution of pressure on the sides of the form block permits forming of wider flanges than are possible with the Guerin process. Also, shrink flanges, joggles, and beads and ribs in flanges and web surfaces can be formed in one operation to sharp detail in aluminum, low-carbon steel, stainless steel, heat-resisting alloys, and titanium.

Fluid Forming

This process differs from those previously described in that the die cavity is not completely filled with rubber, but with hydraulic fluid retained by a cup-shaped rubber diaphragm. This cavity is called the pressure dome. A replaceable wear sheet is cemented to the lower surface of the diaphragm.

More severe draws can be made with this process than with processes using conventional draw dies, because oil pressure against the diaphragm causes the metal to be held tightly against the sides as well as against the tip of the punch.

Demarest Process

Cylindrical and conical parts can also be formed by a modified rubber bulging punch. The punch, equipped with a hydraulic cell, is placed inside the workpiece, which in turn is placed inside the die. Hydraulic pressure expands the punch. Figure 33-20 shows a fuel tank section made by the Demarest process.

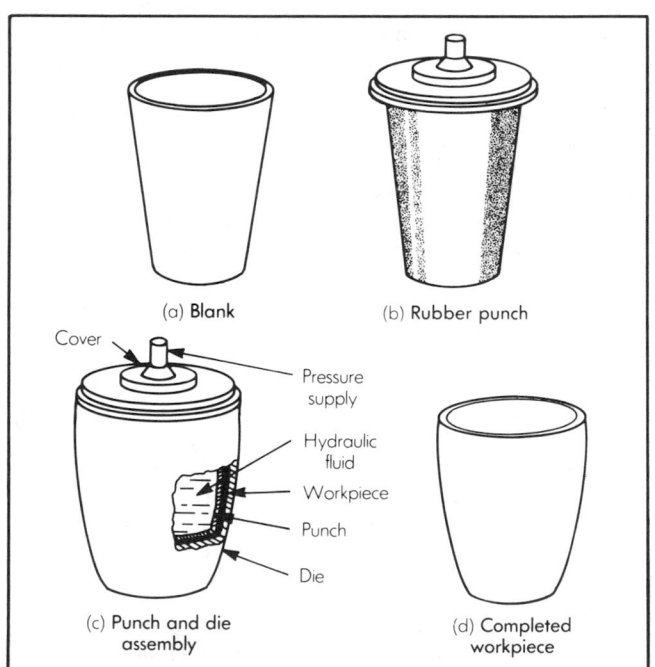

Fig. 33-20 Forming a fuel tank section by the Demarest process.

SUPERPLASTIC FORMING

Materials that can be stretched to unusually large strains (approaching 500%) without localized necking are said to be superplastic. In general, superplastic materials can be formed into more complex shapes using lower loads and can attain higher strains without fracturing than materials with conventional stress-strain characteristics.

Key Factors

A key factor in superplasticity is the capability of certain metal alloys to develop extremely high tensile elongations at elevated temperatures and under controlled deformation rates. The other characteristic that is normally observed is a substantial reduction in the flow stress of the material. This means that the forces and stresses required to cause deformation can be as much or as little as 1/2 to 1/20th that of the conventional alloy under the same conditions. It is these two factors (high tensile elongation and low flow stress) that provide the exceptional potential that is anticipated for superplastic forming.

Typical Process

The typical process that utilizes this unique characteristic of superplasticity is called superplastic forming and is illustrated in Fig. 33-21. In this process, the superplastic blank is inserted between two die elements or tools, one of which is configured to the part required. In this case the lower die is the configuration die. The upper die piece is utilized to provide application of the gas pressure which is introduced to cause forming.

The tooling and the superplastic blank are then placed between heated elements, as shown, and heated to a temperature suitable for superplastic forming. A clamping pressure is applied to this sandwich of heated platens and tooling to contain the gas pressure, and the gas pressure is then imposed over the top of the sheet causing it to blow form or stretch form into the die cavity. The rate of pressure application must be controlled, since it translates directly into the strain rate imposed on the material—a critical factor in achieving superplasticity and superplastic forming. Once the forming has been achieved, the die assembly is opened, the formed part is removed, and then trimming and subsequent processing operations are performed similarly to those of parts formed by conventional forming.

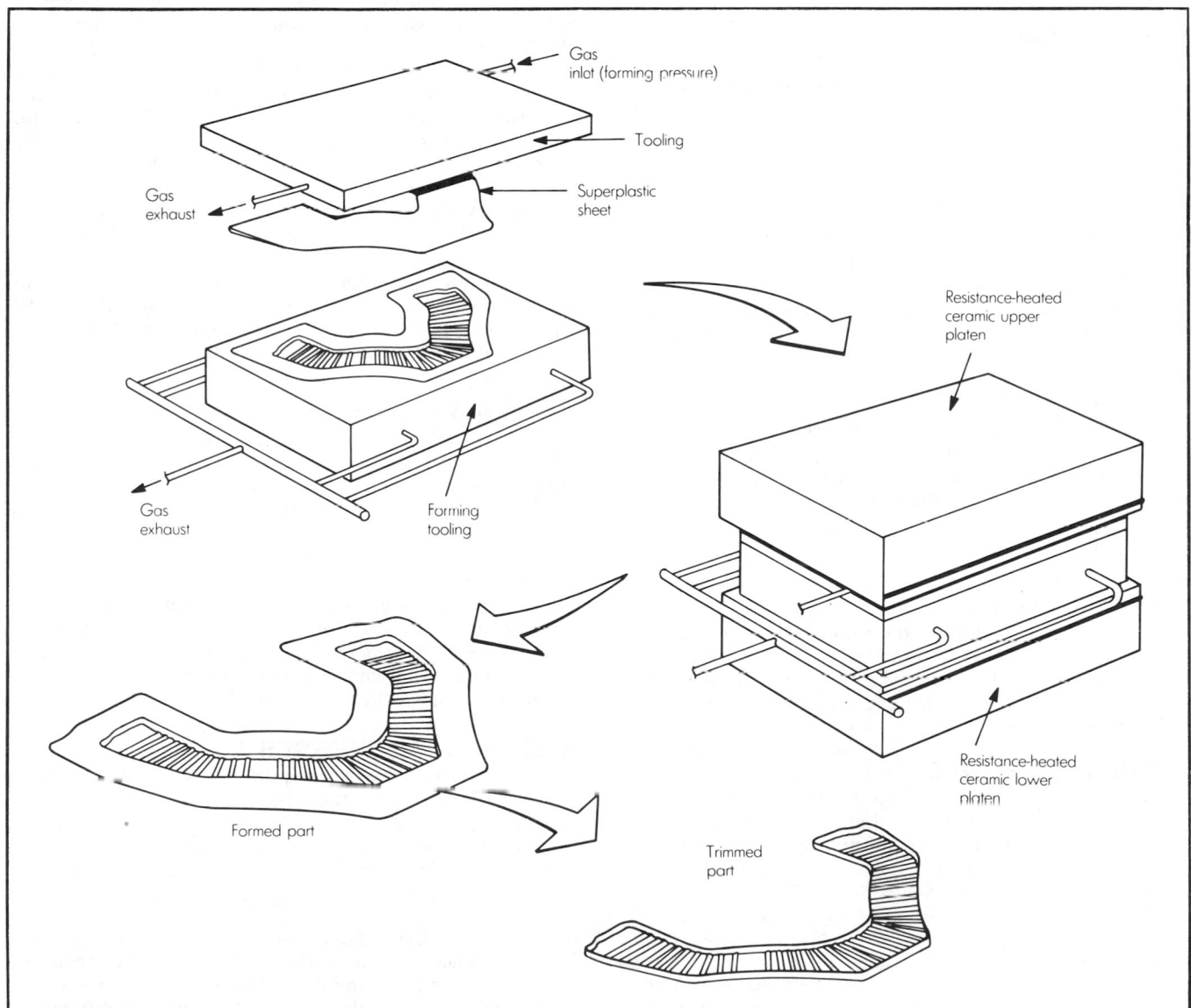

Fig. 33-21 Superplastic forming process, schematic view of sequence.

PRESSES FOR SHEET METAL FORMING

PRESSES FOR SHEET METAL FORMING

Presses are powered machines having stationary beds and slides (rams) which have controlled reciprocating motions toward and away from the beds, guided by their frames. They supply energy to press-mounted dies that form and cut materials. Presses discussed in this chapter are used to form and cut (blank, trim, punch, etc.) sheet metal, and in some cases, thicker materials such as plates.

TYPES OF PRESSES

Presses are classified by one or a combination of characteristics which include the source of power and the number of slides. Other classification methods, discussed in subsequent sections of this chapter, are the types of frames and construction, types of drive, and intended applications.

Manual Presses

Manual presses are either hand or foot powered through levers, screws, or gears. The most common press of this type is the arbor press used for various assembly operations. These presses are often converted to power operation by the addition of air or hydraulic cylinders.

Mechanical Presses

Mechanical presses utilize flywheel energy which is transferred to the workpiece by gears, cranks, eccentrics, or levers. As discussed in detail in a subsequent section of this chapter, mechanical presses can be nongeared or geared, with single or multiple-reduction gear drives, depending upon the press size and force requirements.

Hydraulic Presses

Hydraulic presses provide working force through the application of fluid pressure on a piston by means of pumps, valves, intensifiers, and accumulators. While mechanical presses are still the predominant type in use, hydraulic presses are being increasingly applied because of their improved performance and reliability.

Pneumatic Presses

Using air cylinders to exert the required force, pneumatic presses are usually smaller in size and capacity than mechanical or hydraulic presses. They are generally employed for lighter duty operations. Advantages include low cost, high speed, and minimum maintenance.

NUMBER OF SLIDES

With respect to function, presses may be classified by the number of slides incorporated and are referred to as single, double, and triple-action presses. On multislide machines, each slide may use a common energy source or each may have a separate, independent power source.

Single-Action Presses

A single-action press has one reciprocating slide (tool carrier) acting against a fixed bed. Presses of this type, which are the most widely used, can be employed for many different metal stamping operations, including blanking, embossing, coining, and drawing. Depending upon the depth of draw, single-action presses often require the use of a die cushion for blankholding. In such applications, a blankholder ring is depressed by the slide (through pins) against the die cushion, usually mounted in the bed of the press.

Double-Action Presses

A double-action press has two slides moving in the same direction against a fixed bed. These slides are generally referred to as the outer blankholder slide and the inner draw slide. The blankholder slide is a hollow rectangle, while the inner slide is a solid rectangle that reciprocates within the blankholder.

Double-action presses are more suitable for drawing operations, especially deep drawing, than single-action presses. In single-action presses, force is required to depress the cushion. In double-action presses, the blankholder slide has a shorter stroke and dwells at the bottom of its stroke, before the punch mounted on the inner slide contacts the work. As a result, practically the entire capacity of the press is available for drawing. Another advantage is that the four corners of the blankholder are individually adjustable so that nonuniform forces can be exerted on the work when required. A double-action press equipped with a die having an open bottom permits pushing the stamping through the die to perform other operations, such as ironing, after drawing.

Deep-draw operations and irregular-shaped stampings generally require the use of a double-action press. Most operations performed on double-action presses require a cushion either for liftout or reverse drawing of the stamping.

Triple-Action Presses

A triple-action press has three moving slides, two slides moving in the same direction as in a double-action press and a third or lower slide moving upward through the fixed bed in a direction opposite to the blankholder and inner slides. This action permits reverse-drawing, forming, or beading operations against the inner slide while both upper actions are dwelling.

Cycle time for a triple-action press is necessarily longer than for a double-action press because of the time required for the third action. Since most drawn stampings require subsequent restriking and/or trimming operations, which are done in faster, single-action presses, most stamping manufacturers consider the triple-action press too slow.

MECHANICAL PRESSES

Press frames are made of cast iron, cast steel, or welded or bolted-steel construction. Some frames are made from machined posts or pillars. Many press builders are now using computers for frame design to optimize material utilization and ensure maximum stiffness, strength, and performance. The five most common types of construction are as follows:

1. One-piece frame of cast iron, cast steel, or steel weldments.
2. Four-piece, steel, tie-rod frame. This construction consists of the bed, two uprights, and the crown held together by steel tie rods (usually four) which are preshrunk in excess of the rated force. The tie rods can be heated to obtain the

proper expanded length, the nuts are tightened, and the rods are allowed to cool to produce the required tension, with the frame parts in compression. Pretensioning of tie rods by heating is becoming obsolete with the availability of hydraulically actuated tie-rod nuts and hydraulic tensioning devices. As load is applied to the press, the tension stresses in the tie rods increase while the compressive prestresses in the frame parts decrease in direct proportion to the load. This type of construction is employed on most large, straight-side presses.

3. Bolted frame. This construction consists of the bed, two side members, and the crown keyed and held together by bolts. This type of construction is used frequently for single and double-crank, gap-frame presses.

4. Modified tie-rod frame. This construction combines the tie-rod and bolted types of frames.

5. Solid frame with tie rods. With this type of construction, steel tie rods are shrunk into the solid frame.

Gap-Frame Presses

The housings of a gap frame (also called C-frame) press are cut back below the gibs to form the shape of a letter C. Presses of this type are the most versatile and common in use and are lower in cost than straight-side presses. They provide unobstructed access to the dies from three sides, and their backs are usually open for the ejection of stampings and/or scrap. Press feeding, discussed later in this chapter, can be done conveniently from the side or front (on open-back presses). Gap-frame presses generally have a lower overall height than straight-side presses of the same capacity, which is important when overhead clearance is limited.

Gap-frame presses are available in several different designs, some of which are shown in Fig. 33-22. The types include permanently upright presses, such as the adjustable-bed stationary (ABS) and open-back stationary (OBS) presses illustrated; permanently inclined presses; and open-back inclinable (OBI) presses, which are the most common. The inclined presses often facilitate feeding and permit finished stampings to fall out by gravity or to be blown out by air at the rear of the press.

Straight-Side Presses

Presses with straight-side frames consist of a crown, two uprights, a bed which supports the bolster, and a slide which reciprocates between the two straight sides or housings. The crown and bed are connected with the uprights by tie rods or by bolting and keying together, or all members can be cast or welded into one piece. Fabricated construction of members made by one press builder is shown in Fig. 33-23. Continuous, welded, box-type construction is commonly used to minimize twisting, especially when the press is to be subjected to off-center loading. Each construction method has certain advantages and limitations. Solid-frame, straight-side presses are generally less expensive than tie-rod presses, but their size is limited because they must be transported from builder to user in one piece.

Round-Column Presses

Column-type presses are similar to straight-side presses, but they have round columns, pillars, or posts instead of the side uprights. Most column-type presses have four columns, but some have two or three columns. Bushings of the bronze-sleeve or ball-type surround the columns for good guidance. Column

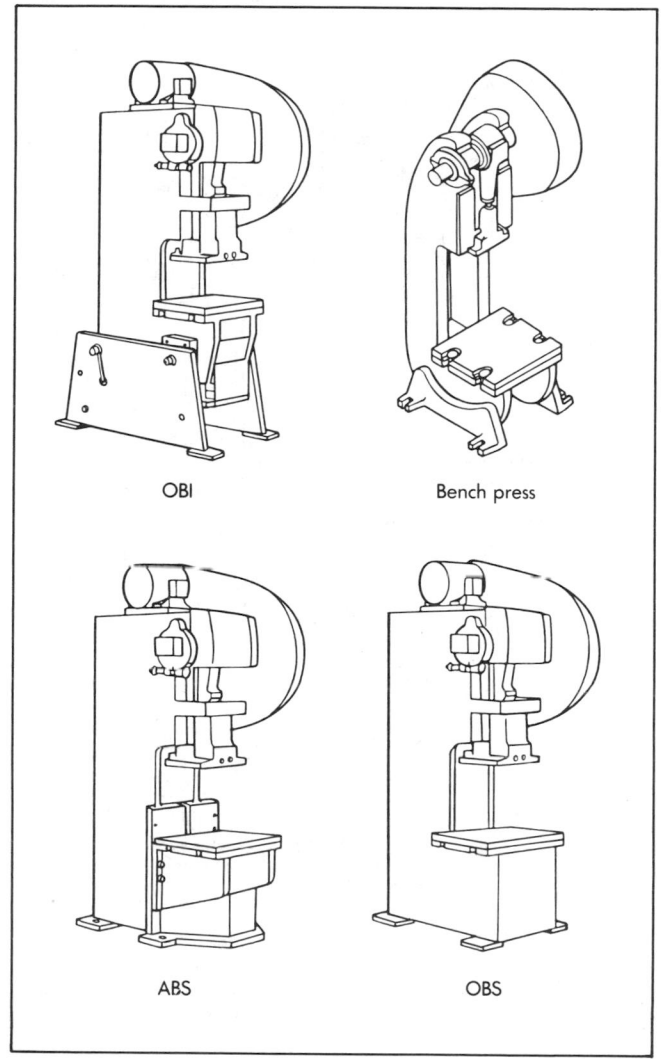

OBI

Bench press

ABS

OBS

Fig. 33-22 Several types of gap-frame presses: OBI—open-back inclinable, ABS—adjustable-bed stationary, OBS—open-back stationary; and bench press.[4]

presses are available for horizontal operation, permitting gravity ejection of stampings and/or scrap.

Press Feeding and Unloading

A wide variety of equipment is available to transfer blanks, stampings, or material to, from, and between presses. Such equipment includes feed units for blanks, workpieces, or strip or coil stock; coil processing lines; and unloading, conveying, and transfer units. Equipment selection depends upon many factors, including the size and shape of the material or workpiece, type of press, die design, safety considerations, production volume and accuracy requirements, cost, and scrap collection and removal.

Manual feeding. Feeding of blanks or stampings by hand is still a common practice, but this method is generally limited to low-production requirements which do not warrant the cost of semiautomatic or automatic feeds. Manual feeding, however, requires the use of a guard or, if a guard is impossible, hand feeding tools and a point-of-operation safety device. The use of

PRESSES FOR SHEET METAL FORMING

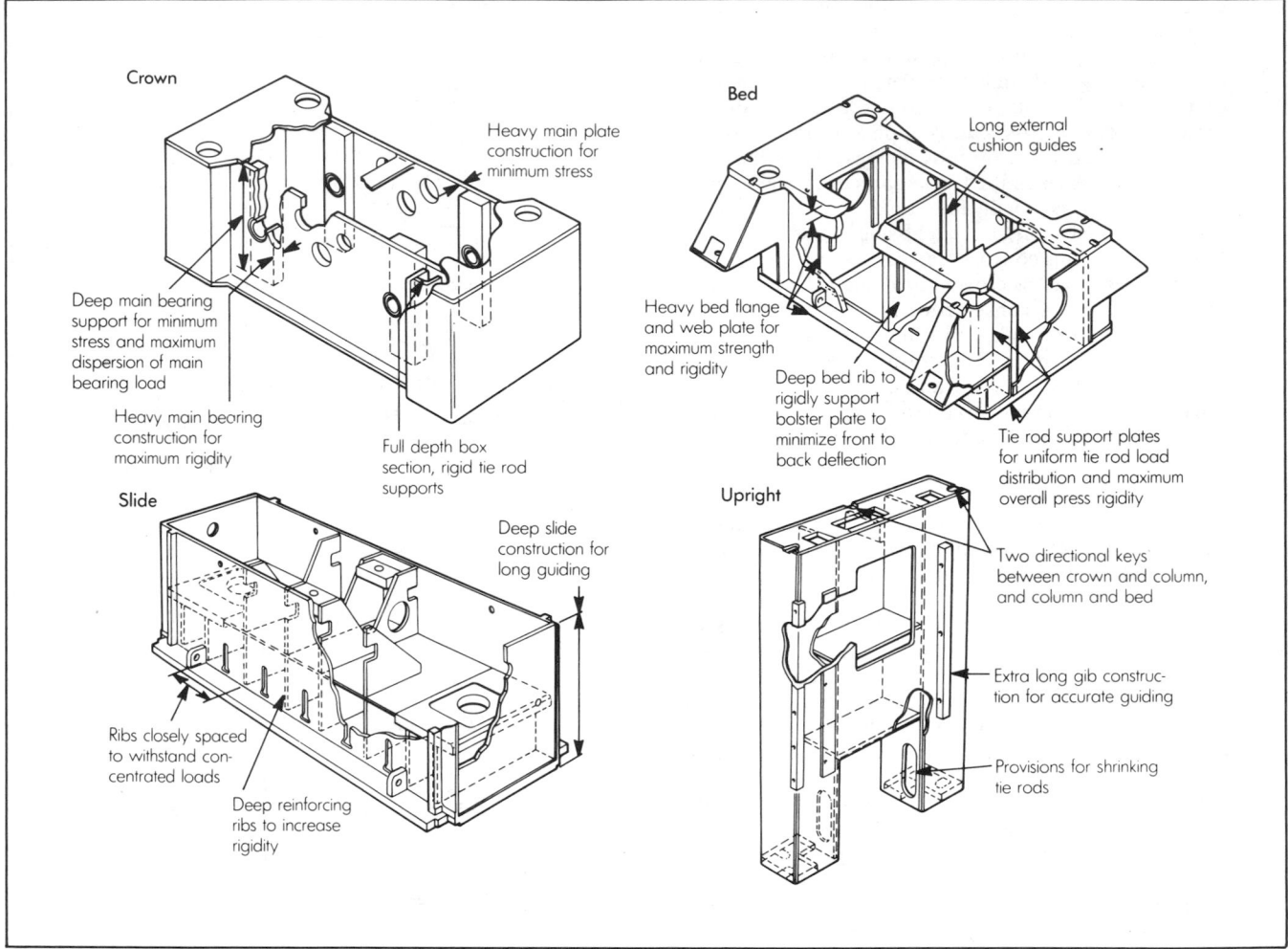

Fig. 33-23 Fabricated members for a straight-side press. (*Verson Allsteel Press Co.*)

tools and a safety device eliminates the need for the operator to place hands or fingers within the point of operation and safeguards the operator who inadvertently reaches into the point of operation, as discussed previously in this chapter under the subject of mechanical press safety.

A variety of hand-held feeding tools are available for loading and unloading dies. These include special pliers, tongs, tweezers, vacuum lifters, magnetic pickups, hooks, and other tools in a variety of sizes and types. Most are made from aluminum or other light, ductile material. Some are spring loaded and provided with finger-guarding loops.

Chute feeds. Simple, low-cost chutes are often used for feeding small parts, with the blanks or stampings generally sliding by gravity along skid rails in the bottoms of the chutes. Side members guide the workpieces, and rollers are sometimes added to facilitate sliding of the parts. A typical gravity chute feed for loading press dies is shown in Fig. 33-24. Production rates to 1800 parts per hour are not uncommon with such feeds.

Slide chutes are designed for a specific die and blank or stamping and are generally attached permanently to the die, thus reducing setup time. To provide a proper slide angle, usually 20-30°, the dies are often operated in OBI presses. With

the die set at an angle in the press, unloading is facilitated.

Push feeds. These feeds (see Fig. 33-25) are used when blanks must be oriented in specific relation to the die, or when irregularly shaped parts are fed that do not slide down a chute and orient themselves properly in the die nest. Workpieces can be manually placed in a nest in a slide, one at a time, and the slide pushed until the piece falls into the die nest. An interlock is generally provided so that the press cannot be operated until the slide has correctly located the part in the die. Slide length should be sufficient to allow placement of workpieces in the pusher slide nest outside a barrier guard enclosure. Strippers, knock-outs, or air can be used to eject finished parts from the die. In some cases, holes can be provided in the bottom plates of the slides through which finished pieces fall on the return stroke of the pusher.

Another type of push feed, called a follow feed (see Fig. 33-26), is used when the shape of blanks or stampings permits pushing similar workpieces and precise orientation by nesting is not required. Such feeds generally consist of a flat plate, on which parts are pushed one behind the other, and of side plates, which serve as guides. One or more parts may be pushed into the die area simultaneously, depending on the operation and

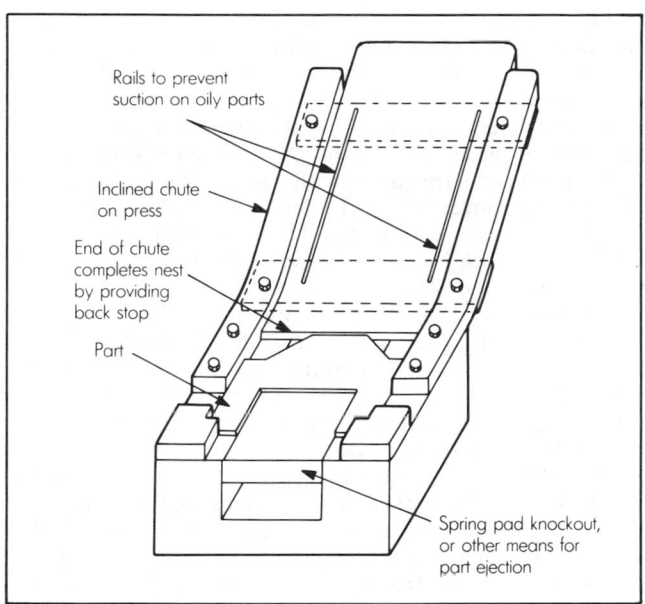

Fig. 33-24 Gravity chute feed for loading press dies.

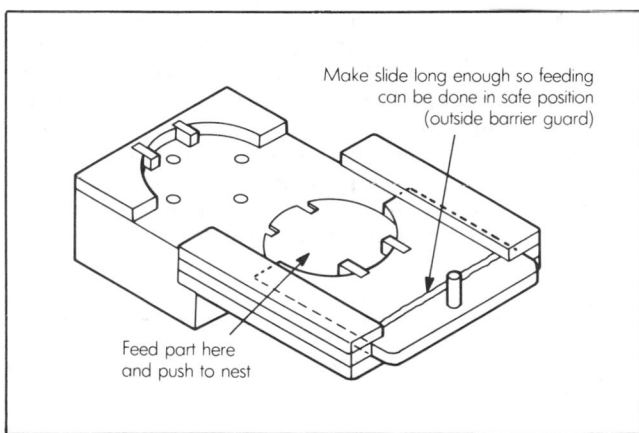

Fig. 33-25 Push feed is used when blanks must be oriented in relation to the die.

workpieces. In some applications, completed parts can be pushed from the back of the die by incoming parts. In other cases, air or other ejection means may be required.

Sliding dies. Partially formed parts that cannot be fed to secondary operations by means of gravity chute or push or follow feeds can be fed automatically or semiautomatically by other means. One semiautomatic method uses sliding dies or bolsters, in which the lower die slides forward from under the punch and outside the danger zone during each feeding operation and then returns to operating position for the downward ram stroke. The die can be reciprocated by hand, by foot treadle, or by automatic means in synchronization with the press slide. Operator protection must also be assured by the use of safety guards or devices. Die or bolster slides are incorporated as original equipment on some presses.

Lift-and-transfer devices. In some automated installations, blanks are lifted one at a time from stacks by vacuum or suction cups and moved to the die by transfer units. Separation of the

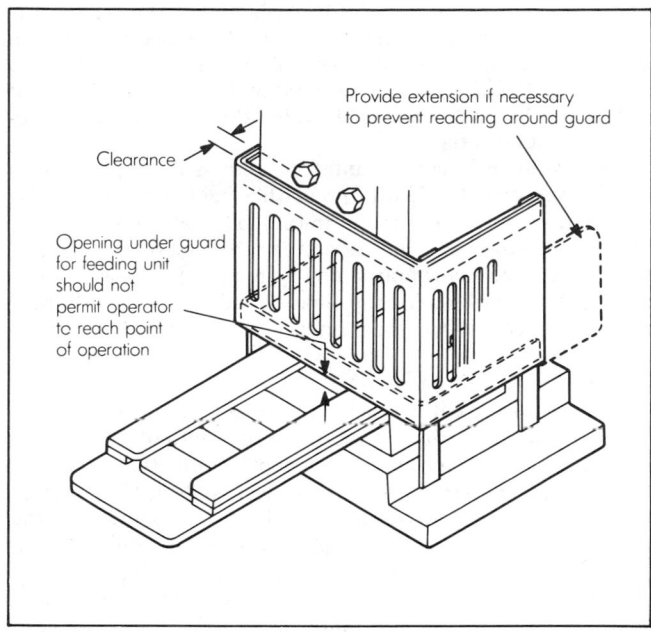

Fig. 33-26 Follow feed is often used when shape of blanks or stamping permits pushing similar workpieces and orientation is not required. (*Liberty Mutual*)

top blank from a stack is usually done magnetically, pneumatically, or mechanically. The top level of a stack can be controlled by a height-detection system that regulates a stack elevating cylinder. Two or more stacks can be arranged to be automatically moved into the elevating station when the previous stack has been used. Blank feeds for transfer presses are discussed later in this chapter under the subject of transfer presses.

Dial feeds. Another method of feeding secondary operations that is being increasingly applied because of greater safety and increased productivity is the dial feed. Such feeds consist of rotary indexing tables having nests or fixtures for holding workpieces as they are carried to the press tooling. Parts can be placed in the nests or fixtures at the loading station (away from the point of operation) manually or by the use of hoppers, chutes, magazines, vibratory feeders, robots, or other means. Dial feeds can be built into or added to presses.

Dial feeds can be actuated several ways. Ratchet drives, which are generally used for low-speed operations, have a reciprocating index slide and pawl for driving and are positioned by a cam-operated, positive-locking pawl. Friction drives use a reciprocating band to move the dial and index ring into position on the forward stroke. Then a spring-loaded stop pawl engages the index ring and holds it stationary while the band returns to its starting position. Geneva-wheel drives are also used to provide positive intermittent motion from a continuous rotary drive. Roller gear drives, which are generally smoother acting and more versatile than Geneva drives, use a worm having a dwell provided in its lead. Air or hydraulic drives, independent of the press operation, are also used for dial feeds.

Robots. Industrial robots are being used extensively for press loading (see Fig. 33-27) and other industrial applications. These mechanical arms, manipulators, or universal transfer and positioning units are descendants of the iron hands or swinging arms (discussed next in this section) long used for press loading

PRESSES FOR SHEET METAL FORMING

and unloading. The big difference between them and true robots is that true robots can be programmed to perform different operations. Various types of tooling can be attached to the arms to handle different sizes and shapes of workpieces. Not only do such units increase safety, but they also boost production rates substantially.

Robots are particularly suitable for low-volume production requirements and for operations in which large differences exist in size and geometry of the workpieces to be handled. Two basic types available are servo and nonservo robots. Servo robots have good accuracy and programmability, but are more costly. Nonservo robots, with fixed stops, have good positional accuracy and are less costly, but programming is limited and slower.

Press Feeds for Coil Stock

Two major classifications of automatic press feeds for coil stock are slide (or gripper) and roll feeds. Both of these can be further subdivided into press or independently driven types.

Mechanical slide feeds. Press-driven slide feeds (see Fig. 33-28) have a gripper arrangement which clamps and feeds the stock during its forward movement and releases it on the return stroke. Material is prevented from backing up during the return stroke of the gripper by a drag unit (frictional brake) or roller checks (rolls with a one-way clutch that allows stock to move in one direction only).

Grippers reciprocate on rods or slides between adjustable positive stops to ensure accuracy. Some feeds have sufficient power to pull stock through a nonpowered straightener when required, thus reducing the cost of the installation. Marring of material supplied by slide feeds can be minimized by using special gripping fingers or inserts or by gripping the stock on its scrap portions.

Hitch-type feed. These units, sometimes called Dickerman feed units because of the originator, differ from press-driven, mechanical slide feeds in that actuation is by a simple, flat cam attached to the ram or punch holder (Fig. 33-29), instead of by the press crankshaft. On the downstroke of the press, one or more springs are compressed by the cam action; then on the upstroke, the springs provide the force to feed stock into the die. Different models are made with gripper plates, blades, or cylinders to move the stock. On the cylinder grip types, overriding clutches permit the cylinders to rotate in only one direction for stock feeding. This type permits feeding polished material without marring.

Air slide feeds. These feeds are providing a rapidly growing method of feeding coil stock, particularly for short-run job shops, because of their low initial cost and versatility. Like mechanical slide feeds, most have grippers or clamps that reciprocate on guide rails or slides between adjustable positive stops to push and/or pull stock into a die.

They differ in that they are powered by an air cylinder instead of the press crankshaft or cams and springs, with actuation and timing of valves by cam-operated limit switches or by an adjustable rod or screw on the press ram or punch.

Coil stock is controlled throughout the cycle by two clamps—one gripping the material during feeding and the other holding it while the feed head returns for the next cycle. The clamps can be air actuated or mechanical. If mechanical holding clamps, such as one-way clutches or cam checks, are used, the material is free to be moved forward by pilots in the die during the backstroke of the feed. With an air-operated holding clamp, a stock release device must be employed with dies having pilots.

Hydraulic slide feeds. These feeds are usually made to special order only. They cost more than air feeds, but can handle thicker stock. They operate similarly to air slide feeds, with gripper heads reciprocating between positive stops, but they are powered by a hydraulic cylinder instead of air.

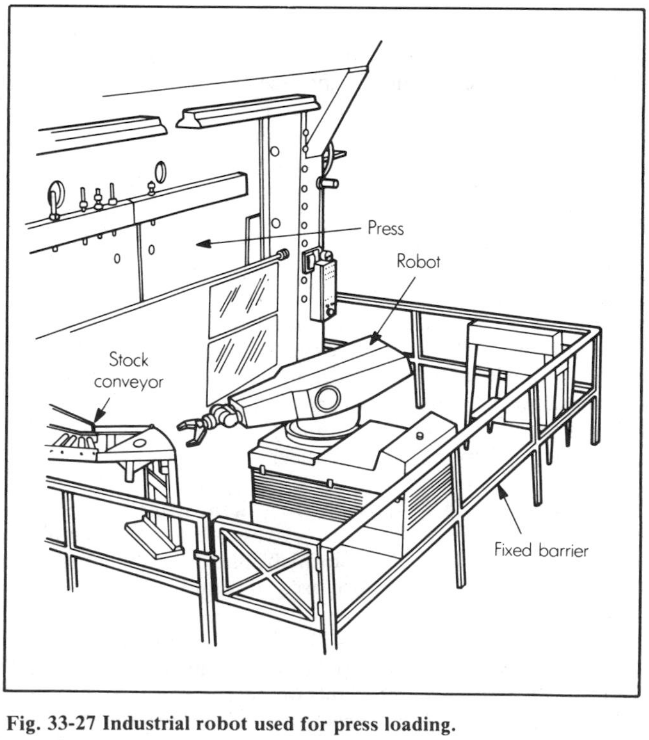

Fig. 33-27 Industrial robot used for press loading.

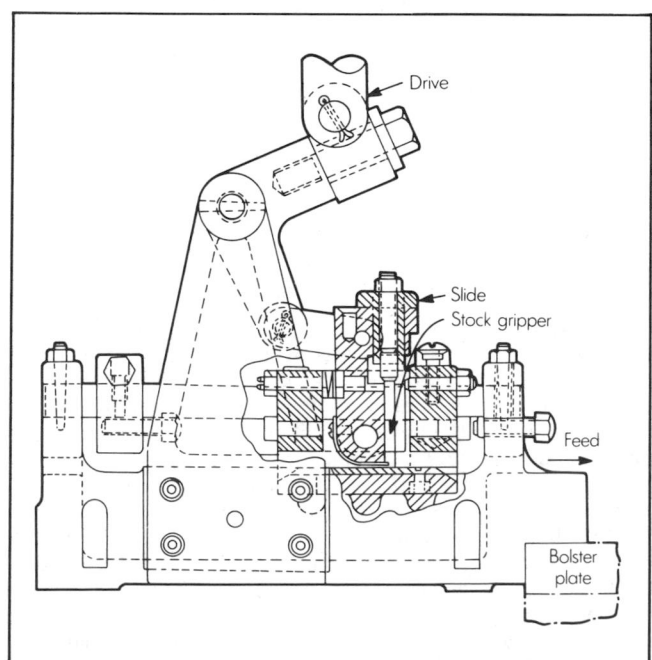

Fig. 33-28 Press-driven slide feed. (*U.S. Baird Co.*)

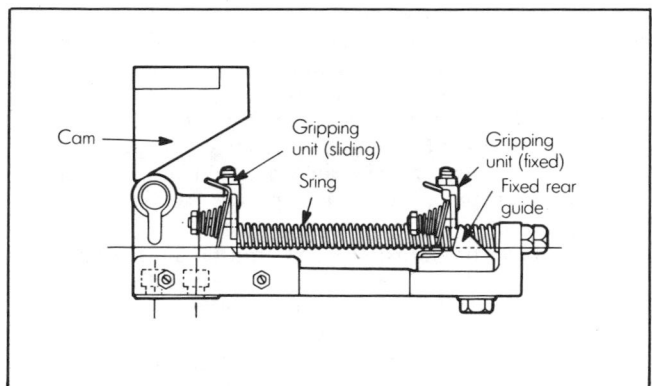

Fig. 33-29 Hitch feed is actuated by a cam attached to press ram or punch holder. (*Dickerman Div., Reed National Corp.*)

Gripping pressure can be adjusted to suit the material being fed. Valve actuation can be from the press crankshaft or ram.

Motor-driven slide feeds. Slide feeds with independent motor drives are sometimes employed when the feed units are to be used on different presses. Feed lengths are adjustable, timing can be varied for different portions of the press cycle, and independent units can be mounted to feed in any direction. Eccentric feed-block motion and feed-blade gripping are generally used on small models, and air grippers are provided on some large models.

Roll feeds. These feeds advance coil stock by pressure exerted between intermittently driven, opposed rolls which allow the stock to dwell during the working part of the press stroke. They are available in several types and in a wide variety of sizes suitable for almost any width and thickness of stock. While their design and construction often entail a higher cost than slide feeds, they are often more economical to operate, depending on the application.

Increased durability, minimum maintenance and material marking, and long life are important advantages accounting for the extensive use of roll feeds. They can feed narrow or wide, thin or thick material in short or long lengths, with high speeds for short increments.

Press Unloading

Gravity and air ejection. Gravity is the simplest and least expensive method of unloading presses, but it is not applicable for many operations. In some cases, dies can be designed so that the stampings fall through a hole in the press bed. The use of OBI presses facilitates unloading by means of gravity when there are no holes in the beds; stampings fall out the open backs of the presses. When press inclination is not practical, chutes are sometimes provided to carry the stampings away. Air ejection is still common for lightweight parts, but this method is expensive and noisy.

Kickers, lifters, and shuttle extractors. Kickers consist of pivoted levers, generally air actuated, that are mounted in the dies and throw stampings out of the dies when the dies open. Lifters are similar, but simply move vertically and require other means for stamping ejection. Pan shuttle-type extractors (see Fig. 33-30) swing to and from the die area, catching stampings as they are stripped from the punches or upper dies and dropping them outside the presses. Actuation of the pans can be from either the press rams or the independent drives.

Mechanical hands. Mechanical hands, often called iron hands, are air or electrically actuated mechanisms commonly used to remove stampings from presses. Gripping fingers or jaws are mounted on arms which swing (see Fig. 33-31) or reciprocate into the die area to lift the stampings and place them on a mechanism for transfer to the next press or operation. Standard units are available as swing-arm or straight-path types.

Robots. Industrial robots, discussed previously in this section, are also used for press unloading. An important

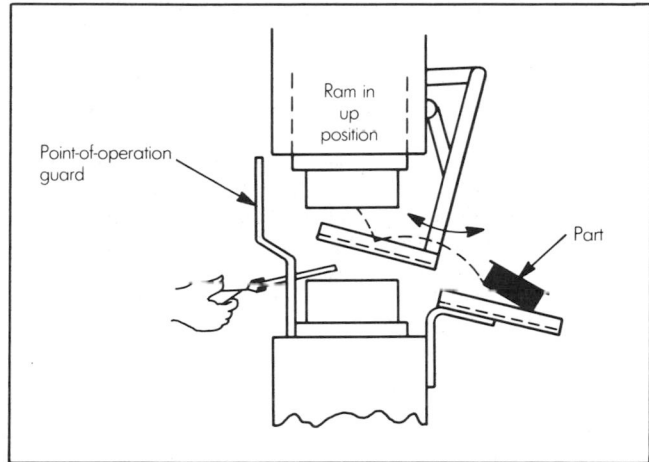

Fig. 33-30 Pan, shuttle-type extractor swings to and from the die area.

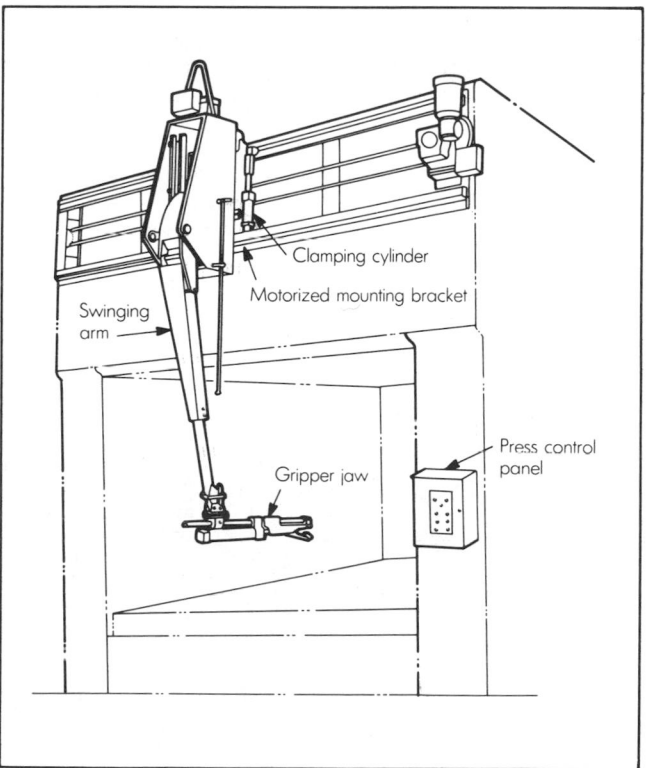

Fig. 33-31 Gripping jaw is mounted on swinging arm of mechanical hand.

PRESSES FOR SHEET METAL FORMING

advantage of robots is their programmability to suit various workpieces and requirements.

Strip recoiling. Some workpieces, such as small terminals, produced from coil stock, are left in the strip which is recoiled for subsequent separation of the parts at assembly.

Work Transfer Between Presses

Several methods are used to automatically transfer stampings from press to press for high-production requirements. When applicable, the use of chutes, on which the stampings slide, provide the lowest cost method. Power-driven, slat or belt conveyors are commonly employed. Adjustable-speed drives for the conveyors are often desirable to suit various cycle times.

Shuttle-type transfer devices. These units are used extensively. With some units, the stampings are pushed by reciprocating fingers that extend and retract as required; others use the lift-and-carry (walking-beam) method. Shuttle units are driven by hydraulic, pneumatic, or electric power, or they are driven mechanically from the press. Adjustable side rails are often provided to accommodate workpieces having different widths.

Lift-and-carry devices. One lift-and-carry device, which employs a parallelogram motion, is shown in Fig. 33-32. Two rails move into slots milled in a die, rise vertically to lift a stamping from the die, retract and lower to deposit the stamping on a set of idle rails, and return to pick up the next stamping. Each time the presses cycle, the stampings are progressively moved from one press to the next. This type of transfer unit maintains full control of the stampings from unloading them from one die through loading them into the next die.

Turnover and/or turnaround devices. These devices are sometimes added to transfer systems to change the positions of the stampings as they pass from one press to another. Turnaround devices generally consist of turntables that lift the stampings, rotate them the required amount, and lower them onto the transfer system. Turnover devices often have one arm and use one or more vacuum cups.

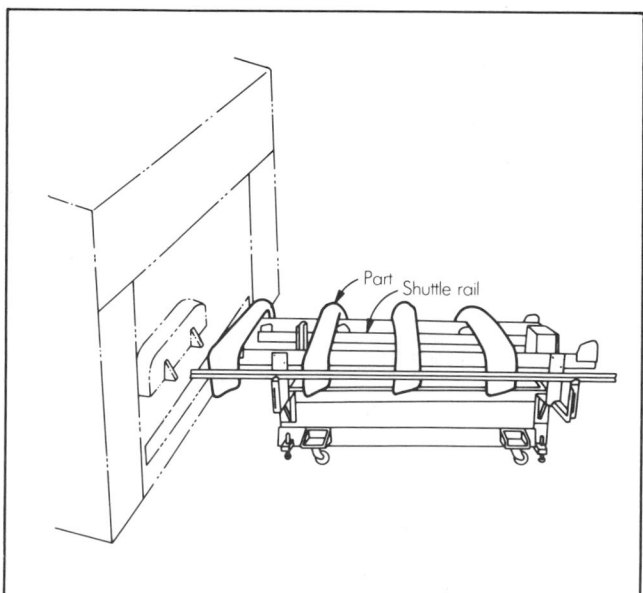

Fig. 33-32 Lift-and-carry transfer device for stampings. (*Press Automation Systems, Inc.*)

Robots. Industrial robots, electrically interlocked to two or more presses, are also being used for the automatic unloading, transferring, and loading of stampings. Advantages include increased flexibility, with programmability permitting different stampings to be produced over the same press line.

Transfer with CNC. Transfer systems controlled by programmable CNC units are available for automating press lines. Such systems are independent of the presses, can be adapted to stampings of all sizes, and are easily reset.

Modular construction of the CNC transfer units permits use with conveyor belts, buffer storage devices, and turnover or turnaround units. Manual data input (MDI) is employed to enter information directly into the control memory, or cassettes can be used to enter programs. Pushbuttons are provided to call up stored programs.

Stackers/loaders. Stackers or conveyor loaders are often provided at the ends of the lines to stack or remove finished stampings that are unloaded from the last press. Low-profile, under-the-die conveyors are used for some applications.

HYDRAULIC PRESSES

Hydraulic presses are machines that use one or more cylinders and pressurized fluid to provide the required motion and force to form or blank workpieces. While mechanical presses are still the predominant type, hydraulic presses are being increasingly applied. About one out of every four presses in U.S. industry today is hydraulic, and the use of hydraulic presses is even more extensive in Europe.

Major reasons for the increased use of hydraulic presses in recent years are their improved performance and reliability. Improved hydraulic circuits and new valves with higher flow capacities and faster response times are major factors.

Advantages of Hydraulic Presses

The greatest advantage of a hydraulic press is its adjustability, which increases the versatility of the machine. With a nonfixed cycle and full force availability at any point in the stroke, a hydraulic press is compatible with various dies and operations. Hydraulic presses have been built with stroke lengths of 100" (2540 mm) and more. To obtain the long-stroke capabilities of hydraulic presses, mechanical presses require taller and more massive frames.

The force exerted by a hydraulic press is infinitely adjustable from about 20% of its maximum rated capacity by simply varying the pressure relief valve setting. This is important in protecting dies designed for limited capacities and for various operations on different workpiece materials. The preset force is relatively constant throughout the stroke. It is practically impossible to overload a hydraulic press because the press only operates to the preset force, regardless of variations in stock thickness, inaccurate dies, doubleheaders, or other factors.

Full force capacities of hydraulic presses can be applied at any point in their strokes, regardless of stroke lengths, thus permitting their use for both short and long-stroke applications. This capability allows the use of a hydraulic press with a lower force rating than that needed for a mechanical press on which the operation requires the application of force high above bottom of stroke. For example, on a 500 ton (4.4 MN) mechanical press, only 175 tons (1.6 MN) are available for an operation requiring the application of force 5" (127 mm) up on the stroke. A mechanical press comparable to a 500 ton hydraulic press for this operation would require a 1350 ton

PRESSES FOR SHEET METAL FORMING

(12 MN) force capacity.

Compared to the fixed stroke of a mechanical press, the stroke of a hydraulic press can be easily adjusted to stop and reverse the slide at any position in the stroke. The speed of hydraulic presses is also variable; slide speed can be slowed from rapid advance to pressing speed just prior to contacting the workpiece. This can lengthen die life by reducing shock loads. Variable speed also permits selecting the optimum speed for each operation and workpiece material, thus ensuring high-quality parts and reducing setup time.

Variable capacity is another feature of hydraulic presses. Bed size, stroke length, press speed, and force capacity are not necessarily interdependent. Hydraulic presses are available with large beds and low force ratings, small beds and high force ratings, and a wide variety of stroke lengths. While standard-size hydraulic presses are available, many are purchased especially designed to suit user requirements. Hydraulic presses are more compact than mechanical presses of comparable capacity.

Since hydraulic presses have fewer moving parts than mechanical presses, there is generally less downtime and maintenance required. Hydraulic presses are essentially self-lubricating; the only additional lubrication required is that needed for the slide gibbing or column bearings. With properly designed and mounted hydraulic systems, the presses provide quiet operation.

Press Limitations

Hydraulic presses still have slower speeds than mechanical presses. The speed, however, depends upon stroke length, and many applications exist in which hydraulic presses can outperform mechanical presses. There are small, automatic-cycling hydraulic presses operating at 900 spm for short-stroke applications. Pressing speeds range to about 600 ipm (15 240 mm/min), with approach and return speeds as high as 2000 ipm (50 800 mm/min).

Even with slower speeds, hydraulic presses are ideally suited for many applications, particularly hand-fed operations and small lot sizes. Automatic feeds require the use of an external or auxiliary power unit, integrated with the press control system.

Shock loads resulting from the sudden acceleration of press slides at the bottom of their strokes when metal has been sheared in blanking and piercing operations are particularly critical. Most builders of hydraulic presses have developed systems to relieve the downward force on the slide at the moment of die breakthrough, and some of these systems are described later in this section.

Frame Construction

Straight-Side Presses. Straight-side hydraulic presses (Fig. 33-33) are available with single or two-point (connection) suspensions, having one or two cylinders, and may be single, double, or triple acting. Force capacities generally range from 50-5000 tons (0.4-44.5 MN) for conventional metalforming and blanking operations to 85,000 tons (756.5 MN) for hot forging.

Round-Column Presses. Column-type hydraulic presses are similar to straight-side presses, but they have round columns or posts instead of side frames. Column presses are popular when various applications are required, when production runs are short, and when initial cost is a factor. An important advantage is good accessibility to the dies from all sides.

C-Frame Presses. Hydraulic presses with C frames (Fig.

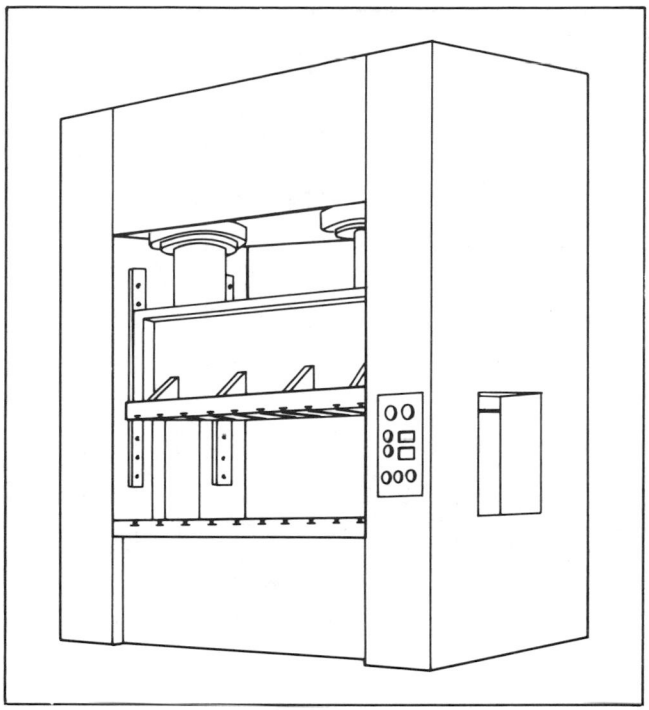

Fig. 33-33 Straight-side hydraulic press with dual cylinder. (*Pacific Press & Shear Co.*)

33-34), also called gap-frame presses, are a more recent development. The two solid steel housings on each press are cut back below the gibs to form the shape of a letter C, similar to the gap-frame mechanical presses discussed earlier in this chapter. The ample throat and open sides of these presses provide easy access to the die area from three sides and permit loading/unloading wide or irregular-shaped workpieces.

OBI and OBS Presses. Hydraulic presses with C frames are also available in open-back inclinable (OBI) and open-back stationary (OBS) designs. A typical OBS press is shown in Fig. 33-35. These presses are designed to have stroking speeds comparable to mechanical presses of similar design. Force ratings

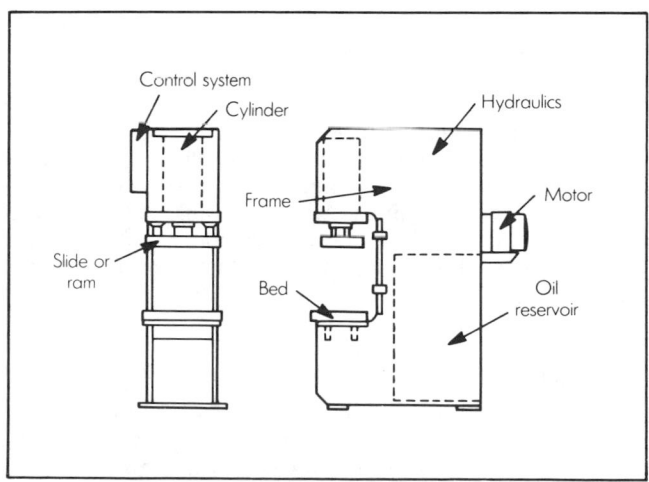

Fig. 33-34 Hydraulic press with C (gap) frame. (*Greenerd Press & Machine Co.*)

PRESSES FOR SHEET METAL FORMING

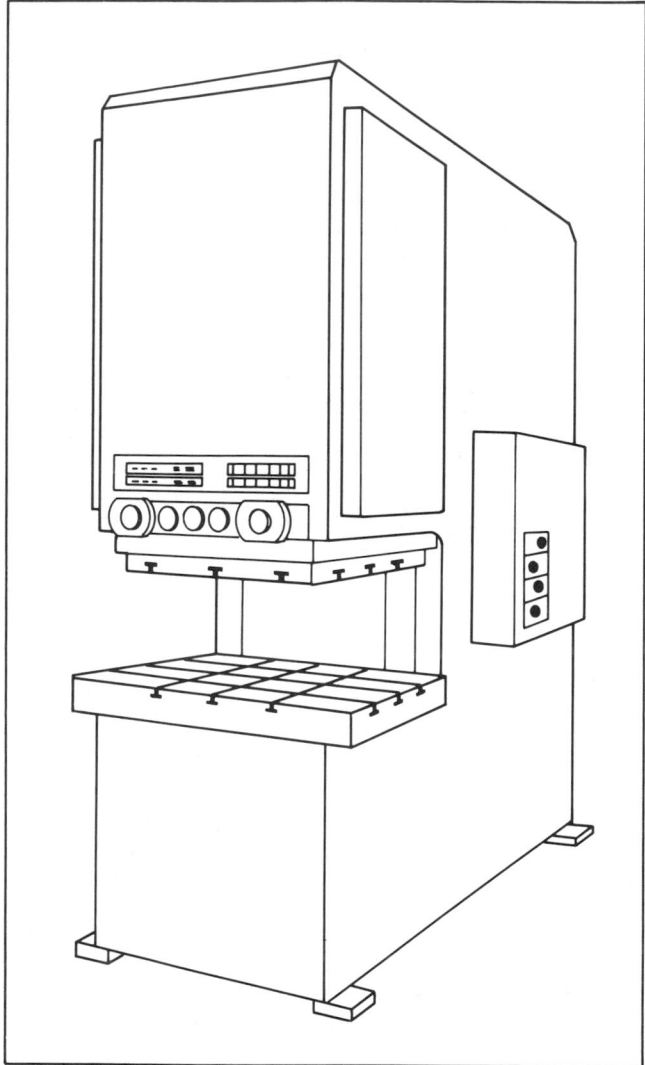

Fig. 33-35 Typical C-frame hydraulic press of open-back stationary (OBS) design. (*Pacific Press & Shear Co.*)

generally range from 6-250 tons (53-2224 kN). Advantages include the ability to feed from front to back of the press, as well as from either side, and the ability to eject workpieces from the rear of the press.

These single-cylinder presses have compact frames; integral, box-type slides; and full-length gibbing. A self-contained, high-speed power unit is mounted within the upper area of the frame. The presses can be equipped with removable bolsters, a die cushion in the bed for deep-drawing operations, and automatic feeding or material-handling systems for high-speed production applications.

PNEUMATIC PRESSES

Pneumatic presses use pressurized air to exert the required force. They are smaller in size and capacity than most mechanical and hydraulic presses and are generally employed for light-duty operations. Some pneumatic presses, however, are used for heavy-duty cutting, punching, and notching operations.

Important advantages of pneumatic presses include low cost, minimum maintenance, and high ram velocities. These presses eliminate the need for crankshafts, motors, clutches, brakes, and other components required on mechanical presses. As a result, there is less downtime for adjustments, repairs, and replacements. Installation of pneumatic presses is simple, requiring only connection to an adequate air supply; and the presses are fast cycling, with quick response.

Another major advantage of pneumatic presses is their adjustability with respect to force, speed, stroke, and shutheight. The preset pressure is essentially constant throughout the stroke, with a slight reduction for the compression of return springs on presses of single-acting design. Pneumatic presses are of compact design, generally being rectangular assemblies having low profiles. They can be mounted for operation in any position.

Limited capacities and short strokes of pneumatic presses may present problems, depending upon the application. The impact forces of these presses are most effective when the energies of the rapidly moving rams can be absorbed with short tool penetrations. As a result, the presses are generally best suited for coining, shallow embossing, blanking of thin materials, and similar operations. Pneumatic presses of high capacity require a considerable volume of air, which should be an economic consideration in press selection.

Applications of Pneumatic Presses

Pneumatic presses are being used extensively on roll forming lines for both preforming and postforming operations such as punching, notching, lancing, and cutoff of formed parts to required lengths. Other applications include production stamping operations such as blanking, piercing, cutting, trimming, forming, embossing, and coining, as well as assembly operations. The presses are especially well suited for use with steel-rule dies and unitized tooling.

Types of Pneumatic Presses

Pneumatic presses are available in several types, with a wide range of die areas. Some are actually air-operated, precision die sets consisting of upper and lower shoes on which punches and dies are mounted and having guide or leader pins and bushings for proper alignment.

Pneumatic presses are made with one, two, four, or more posts or columns, or they are of gap-frame design. They have single or multiple air-actuated cylinders and are arranged for bench or floor mounting. On most presses, except those of larger size, the rams are returned to their upper positions by springs. Presses are available, however, with double-acting cylinders to provide power on their return strokes for lifting, positive stripping, and other functions.

Standard equipment generally includes air and electric controls, pressure regulators, and air filters and lubricators. Controls and safety guards are similar to those used for mechanical and hydraulic presses. Some pneumatic presses have air logic controls, eliminating the need for electrical connections, but response time is generally slower. Control equipment using air, however, must be protected against foreign material and water entering the system, as discussed previously under the section on controls for mechanical presses. Many optional items are available, including index tables, air reserve tanks, and mufflers for exhaust parts.

PRESSES FOR SHEET METAL FORMING

SPECIAL-PURPOSE PRESSES

There are a number of special types of presses available to suit specific application requirements. Some of the more common of these special-purpose presses are discussed in this section.

Die-Setting Presses

Presses used for final finishing of dies to indicate inaccuracies, and also to test mating and functioning of parts, are called die-setting, spotting, die-development, or tryout presses. They are often used in toolrooms for die construction, with hand grinders being employed to remove cutter marks. Then, punches are spotted to dies (and vice versa), using red lead or blueing, and necessary corrections are made.

The presses are also used to determine the size and shape of blanks, lengths of bends, shape and depth of draws, and other development work which must be done before a die or a set of dies can be completed.

Dieing Machines

Dieing machines, sometimes called die presses, are used for high-speed precision stamping operation on small workpieces, often with progressive dies and coil feeds. These machines are actually inverted mechanical presses with their drive mechanisms located under the beds (Fig. 33-36). Advantages include accurate die alignment and a low center of gravity. No floor pits

are required, and the machines can be installed in rooms with low ceilings.

Lamination Presses

So-called "lamination presses" are high-speed, automatic, mechanical presses frequently used for stamping laminations, but also employed for shallow-drawing operations, progressive-die operations, and other operations. The short-stroke presses are generally of straight-side, tie-rod construction, but C-frame types are also used. Variable speed drives are standard. Coil-stock reels, straighteners, and feeders are offered as optional equipment.

Presses for Fluid Forming

Special hydraulic presses used for fluid forming have a forming chamber (pressure dome) attached to their slides. The cavities are filled with hydraulic fluid, which is retained by a flexible diaphragm made from rubber. The diaphragm serves both as a blankholder and as a universal die for producing various-shaped parts. A single tool (generally a punch, but in some cases, a cavity die) is mounted on the ram of a hydraulic cylinder in the press bed, and a pressure pad surrounds the tool.

Adjustability and precise control of the pressure in fluid forming permits deeper draws than with conventional dies, the handling of materials that cannot be formed by deep drawing,

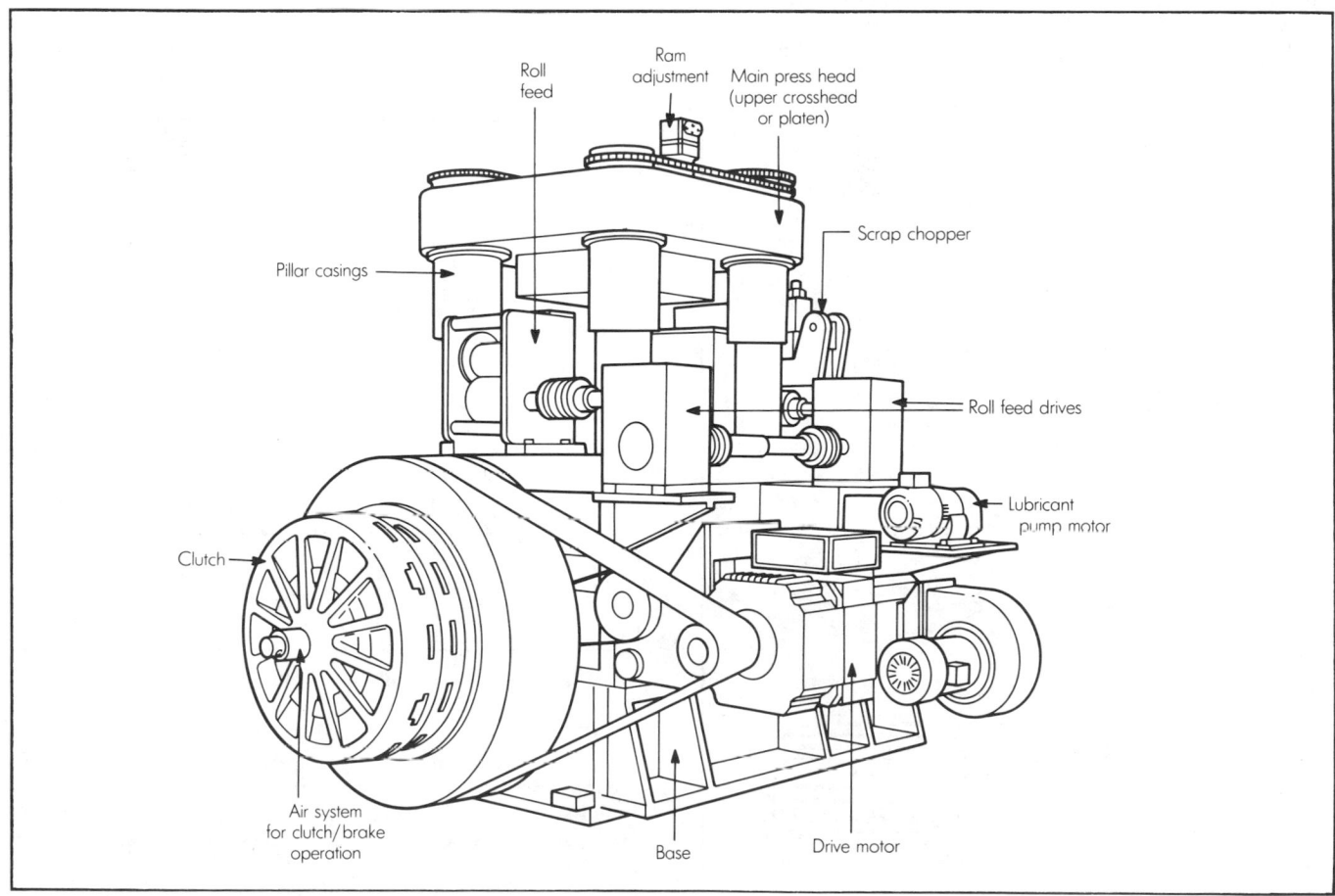

Fig. 33-36 Dieing machine provides accurate alignment and low center of gravity. (*Metform International Ltd.*)

DIE DESIGN FOR SHEET METAL FORMING

one operation. Controlled metal flow minimizes localized stress concentrations and buckling of workpiece sidewalls, and the wrapping action of the process results in less thinning of the material. Parts produced are as accurate as the single punch or die used.

DIE DESIGN FOR SHEET METAL FORMING

Die design is a specialized profession that combines the elements of craft, art, and science. The objective is to prepare drawings that can be translated into stamping dies by skilled craftsmen known as diemakers. The stamping dies, in turn, are mounted in presses in which they blank, bend, form, draw, extrude, trim, pierce, and coin sheet metal into finished parts or into components which may be assembled with other parts (which may or may not be stampings) to form finished products.

DIE COMPONENTS

Typical die sets (see Fig. 33-37) range in size from extremely small sets, such as those used to produce watch parts, to extremely large sets, such as those used to produce automotive stampings. Standard die sets are specified in ANSI Standards B5.25 and B5.25M (metric). Steel, cast iron, and cast steel are typical materials used in die sets. Large, special-design die sets are cast to order from custom-made patterns.

Alignment between the upper and lower members of a die set is maintained by pins with matched or ball bushings. Large sets also use heel blocks on two or more sides or corners as aids in maintaining alignment of the die shoes before the pins and bushings are engaged. Purchased die sets can be obtained in

three grades: commercial, precision, and superprecision. Superprecision die sets are not standard and specifications must be negotiated between the customer and the die set manufacturer.

Types of die set pins and bushings available are shown in Figs. 33-38 and 33-39. A hole-punching unit that requires a separate die set or other means for alignment is shown in Fig. 33-40, view *a*, while view *b* depicts a self-enclosing hole-punching unit requiring no die set because of its self-contained alignment.

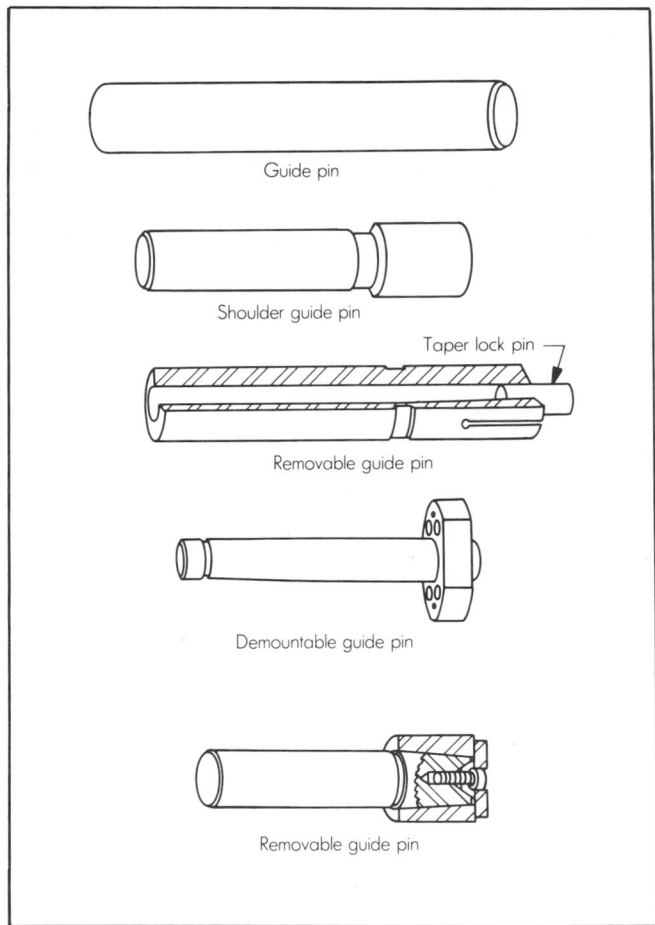

Fig. 33-38 Commercial standard guide pins.

Strippers

Two types of strippers are generally used—the fixed type and the movable type (with pressure from air, nitrogen, or springs). Fixed strippers are permanently attached to the die and may also guide the stock. Stock clearances are critical. Movable types strip the stock from tools, but may also apply hold-down pressure to prevent distortion of part or web while force is being applied to the material.

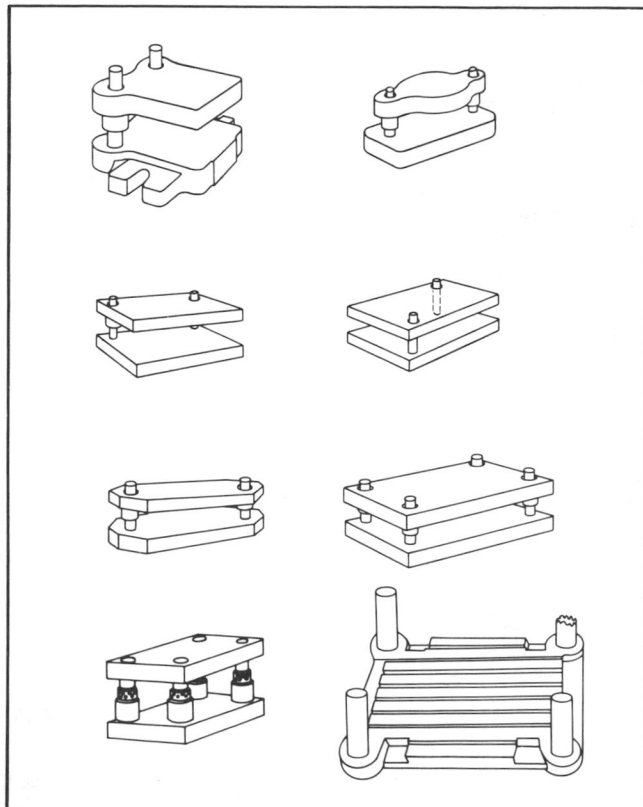

Fig. 33-37 Typical commercially available die sets.

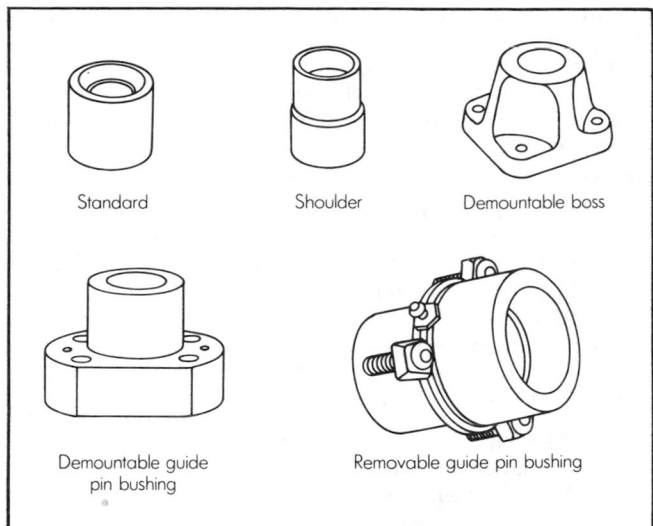

Fig. 33-39 Commercial standard guide-pin bushings.

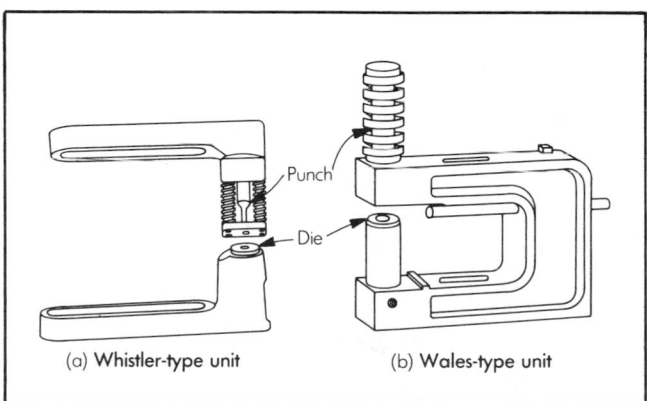

Fig. 33-40 Hole-punching units.

Methods for retaining strippers are shown in Fig. 33-41. Practical designs allow the removal of strippers from large dies while they are in the press and from the working side of small dies to facilitate repairs without complete disassembly of the dies. Pressure strippers may guide punches or do some forming. For such applications, the strippers must be well guided for accurate alignment and positioning. The lower edge of a draw-die ring may be undercut to catch the edge of a drawn shell and to strip it from the draw punch (see Fig. 33-42).

Knockouts

Knockouts usually push or lift parts from die cavities. A commonly used positive knockout for stripping parts from an inverted compound die is illustrated in Fig. 33-43. A knockout rod forces the knockout plate to strip the part from the die. The part is prevented from adhering to the plate by an oil-seal breaker pin.

Blanked parts may be shed just before the top of the stroke in an inclined press so that they drop away from the working area of the die. Cam-actuated knockouts may shed heavy blanks, 2 lb (0.9 kg) or heavier, in a straight-sided press at a preset position below the top of the stroke to prevent damage to die surfaces or injury to the operator.

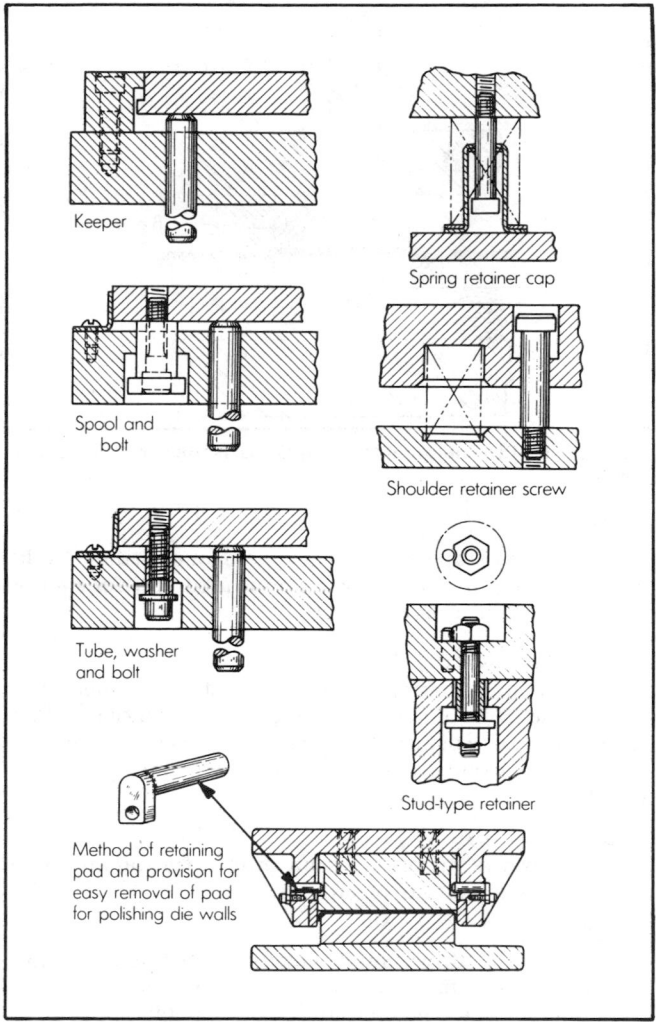

Fig. 33-41 Methods for retaining stripper plates.

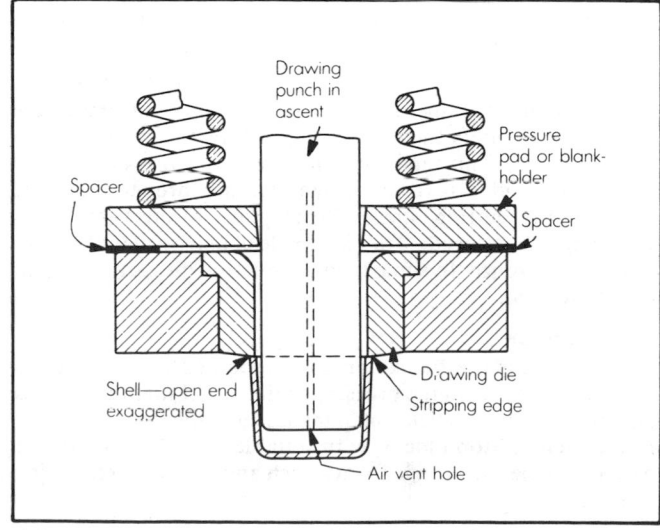

Fig. 33-42 Lower edge of a draw ring performing the function of a stripper.

DIE DESIGN FOR SHEET METAL FORMING

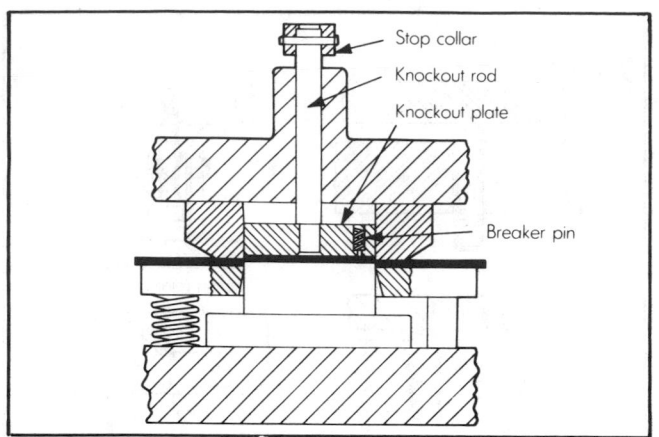

Fig. 33-43 Positive knockout for stripping parts from an inverted compound die.

Stops

One or more stops (gages) are required for most dies. A solid registering stop or a temporary stop is used only for starting stock through a progressive die.

Kicker (Shedder) Pins

Kicker pins are spring-actuated pins extending from dies to prevent the stamped part from adhering to a working surface, generally because of an oil-film seal. They are usually built into strippers, knockouts, blank punches, formed tool surfaces, and the like.

Stock Pushers

Stock pushers are used to ensure proper registration of part or strip to gaging surface or surfaces.

Guides

Stock guides direct stock material along suitable slots or grooves. In some progressive dies in which deep draws are produced, a combination stock guide and lifter is used.

Heel and Wear Plates

Heels are incorporated in dies to hold punches, dies, and the blankholder in alignment and to prevent damage to dies if the press ram has too much play. A typical large-die, heel-block installation is shown in Fig. 33-44, view *a*. Notching punches or punches that cut along the edge of stock (french cuts) may have a heel which enters the die opening before any cutting action starts (view *b*). This tends to minimize punch breakage due to side loads and also ensures maintaining proper clearance between the cutting steels. Wear plates protect die parts receiving greatest wear. They are made of hardened tool steel or aluminum bronze. In some high-production dies. carbide wear strips are used.

Stop Blocks

Stop blocks are blocks or posts mounted to die shoes to assist the diesetter in the proper positioning of mating punches and dies or the entering of punches into die cavities to the proper depth. Stop blocks, with suitable spacers, also prevent damage to dies in storage from punch and die members hitting together.

Perforators (Punches)

Specifications for variable, press-fit, punch-guide bushings

are presented in ANSI Standard B94.23. Perforators are made of a good grade of tool steel properly hardened and ground. After grinding, vertical lapping of the cutting portion of the punch is recommended, particularly for operations in which thin stock is cut, shaving operations, or operations in which die clearances are less than normal.

Pilots

Pilots accurately register stock in progressive dies. To be effective, a pilot must be strong enough to align the stock without bending. For this reason, a pilot with the largest possible diameter is preferred. Typical pilots are shown in Fig. 33-45. Pilots should be made of a good grade of tool steel, heat treated to maximum toughness and a hardness of R_C 56-60. Pilot holes should extend through the dieholder to clear slugs produced during misfeeds.

Pilot Holders

A pilot holder is usually a block of steel which can be fastened to the punch shoe. Some commercial holders, such as

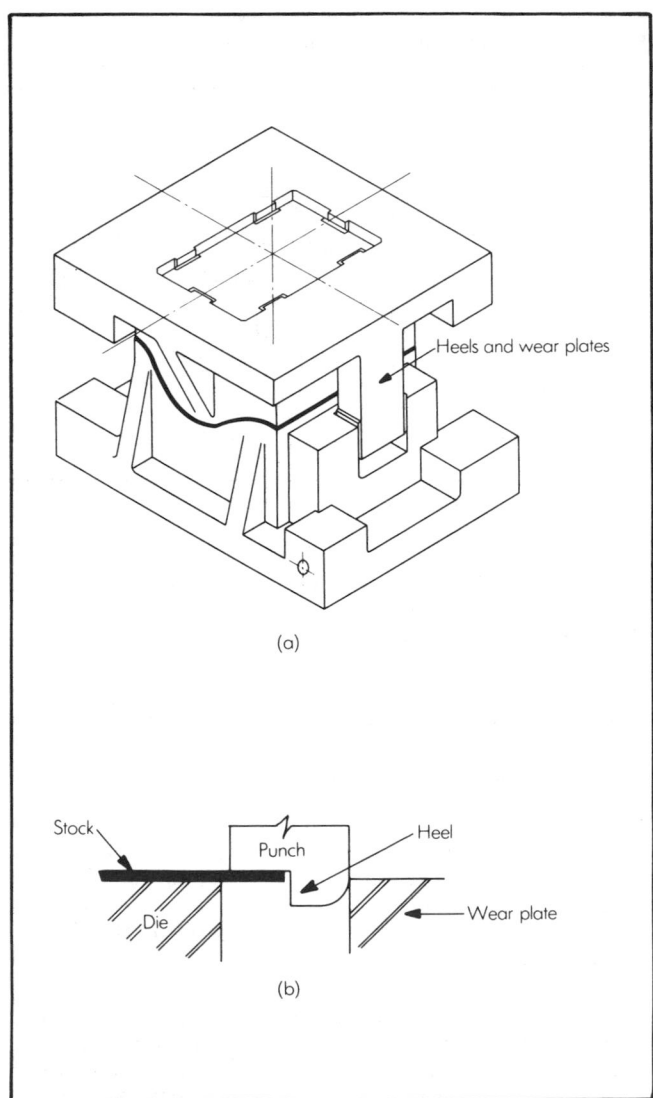

Fig. 33-44 Heel and wear plates: (a) on a large die and (b) heel that enters die opening before cutting starts.

the ball-lock type of holder (see Fig. 33-45), can be used. Holders for press fit of the pilots are also used.

Misfeed Detectors

Misfeed detectors are devices to stop the presses in case of misfeeds (see Fig. 33-46). Detectors should ensure that the stock is in proper position for the pilots to enter. They generally incorporate a spring-loaded detector to actuate a limit switch and are commonly employed in progressive dies. Designed like a perforator, the point is smaller in diameter than the pilot hole by the amount of over or under-feeding allowed.

Die Buttons

Small die steels called die buttons are available in the same shapes and general size range as perforators and punches. The button opening is always larger than the punch point size, generally by a percentage of the thickness of the material being pierced.

Retainers

Punch and die button retainers are provided in several shapes, depending on the die space or mounting method used (see Fig. 33-47). Specifications for basic ball-lock, punch and die-button retainers, both light and heavy duty, are presented in ANSI Standards B94.16 and B94.16.1 (metric). When close spacing of two or three punches is required, end retainers are useful although they are generally used only for pilots. For very

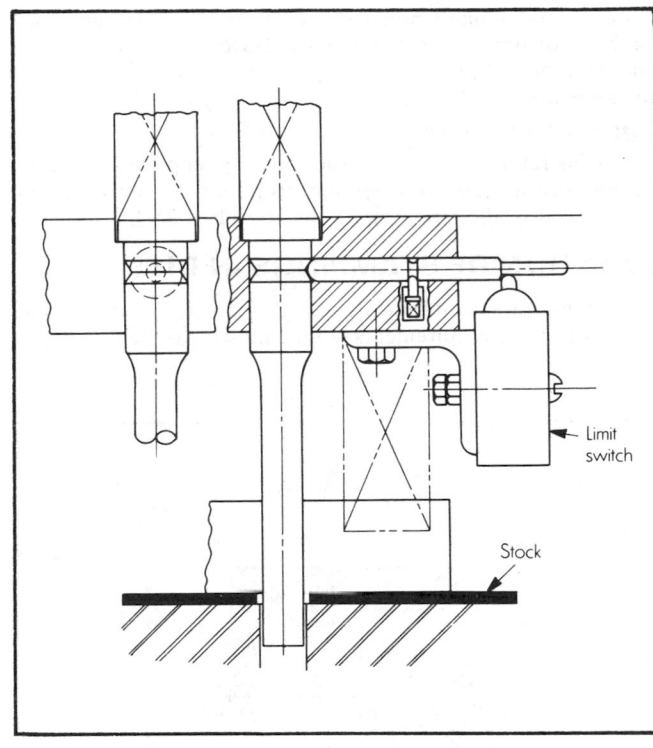

Fig. 33-46 Automatic limit-switch press top for misfeeds.

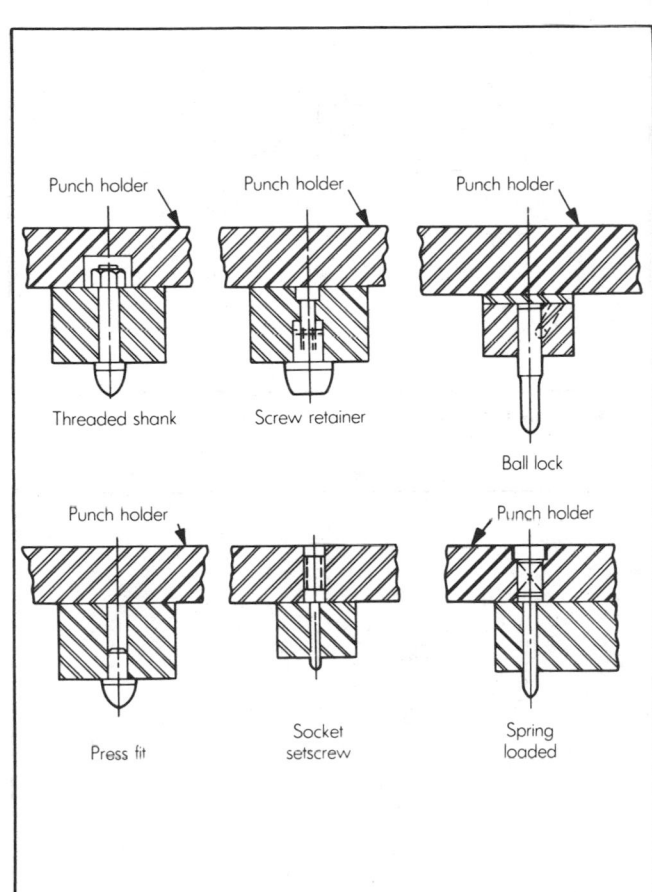

Fig. 33-45 Various pilots and methods of retaining them.

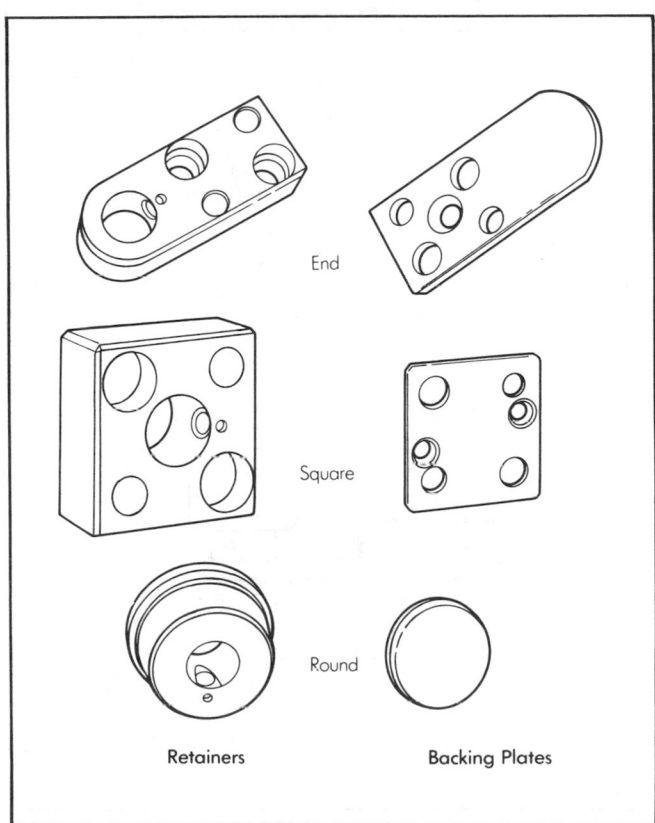

Fig. 33-47 Retainers and backing plates. (*Richard Brothers Punch Co.*)

DIE DESIGN FOR SHEET METAL FORMING

close spacing of many punches, special one-piece retainers can be made or obtained commercially. Hardened backing plates may be required to back up the punches, but improved design retainers now available require no backup plate.

Spring Retainers

Spring retainers are used to permit stripper plates or pads to be removed without loose springs dropping out. Two types of commercial spring retainers are shown in Fig. 33-48.

LOCATION OF STAMPINGS IN DIES

Qualified areas for locating stampings in dies are those areas which fulfill the requirements of the following three main types of tests:

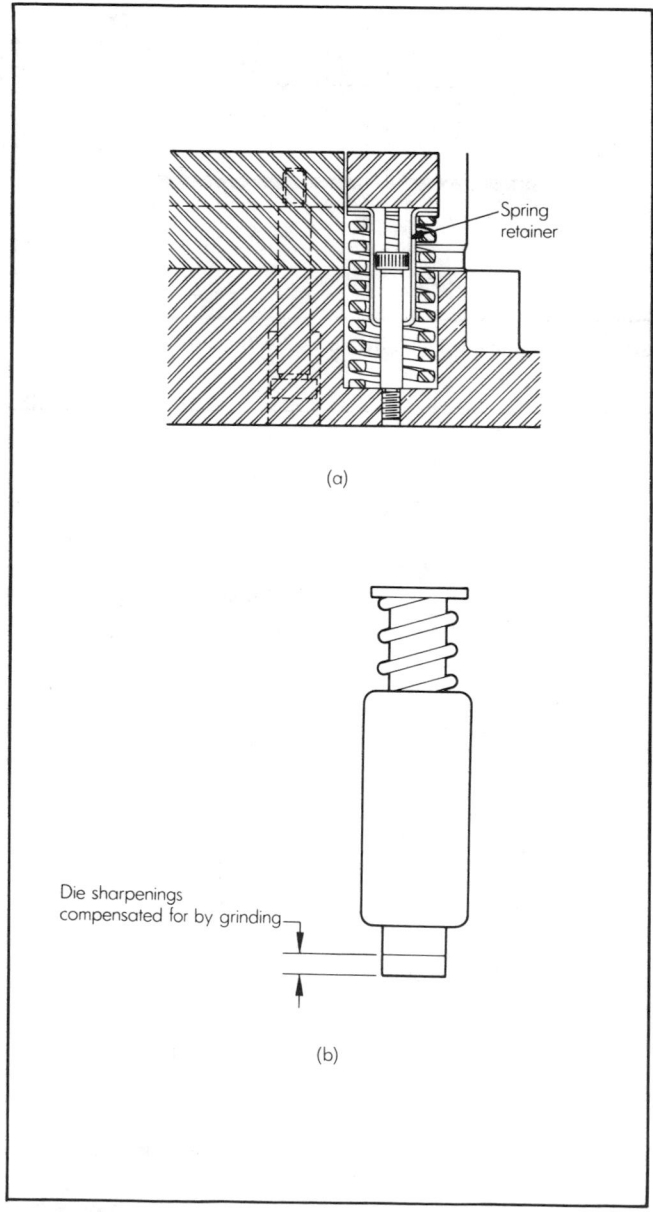

(a)

(b)

Die sharpenings compensated for by grinding

Fig. 33-48 Spring retainers: (a) with external spring and (b) with self-contained, preloaded spring.

1. Arithmetical test. The selected surface of registry must not cause a limit stack with respect to allowable tolerances. If the surfaces cannot be selected, they must be qualified; that is, they must be produced to tolerances closer than those required and specified by the product engineer.

2. Mechanical test. The size, shape, and finish of the selected surfaces of registry must withstand the operating forces exerted and also the necessary holding forces.

3. Geometrical test. This test pertains to the distribution of the surfaces of registry so that the workpiece is positionally stable. If surfaces of registry are not thus qualified, the process planner must consider suitable redesign with the product engineer.

In a 3-2-1 locating system (see Fig. 33-49), six points are the minimum number required to fix a square or rectangular shape in space. Three points establish a plane; two points define a straight line; and one point designates a point in space. Combined, they total six points. A small pyramid symbol is used to designate a locating point. In Fig. 33-50, this symbol is

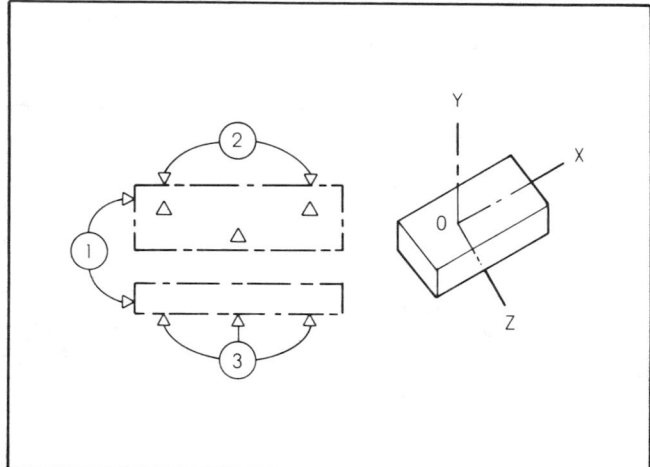

Fig. 33-49 The 3-2-1 locating system.

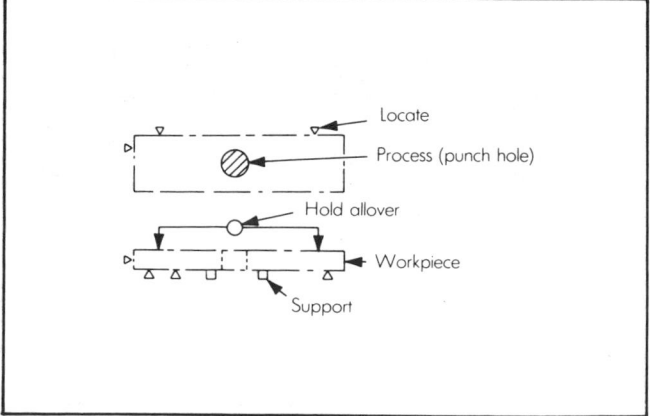

Fig. 33-50 Application of process symbols.

used to illustrate a locating system for a rectangular solid. Variations of the illustrated system can be used to fix location of a cylinder, cone, disc, or other geometric shapes.

The surface of the device used by the die designer to establish the locating points specified by the process planner is known as a seat of registry. The corresponding area on the workpiece is known as a surface of registry.

Process planning symbols can be used to avoid lengthy writing in the preliminary stages of planning the utilization of critical areas for primary and secondary manufacturing operations. Figure 33-50 illustrates use of such symbols.

CUTTING DIES

The various types of die cutting that may be performed include (1) blanking, (2) punching, (3) perforating, (4) slotting, (5) notching and seminotching, (6) lancing, (7) trimming, (8) slugging, (9) piercing, and (10) parting or cutoff.

Clearance

Die cutting requires a certain amount of clearance between the punch and the die. Figure 33-51 shows a cross section of a punch and die illustrating the characteristics of blanks or slugs formed by normal and abnormal clearances. As a punch begins to penetrate the stock, the edges of the punch and the die first deform and then cut into the material. As the stock is stressed further by the punch, a fracture begins to form in the material. Proper clearance between the cutting edges enables the fracture to form a clean edge. Proper clearance is a function of the kind, thickness, and temper of the work material, as well as the size of the hole or blank being produced. A small ratio of hole or blank size to stock thickness requires greater clearance than a larger ratio.

Characteristics of the cut edges on both the stock and the blank are shown in Fig. 33-51. The upper corner, A, of the cut edge of the stock and the lower corner, A', of the blank will have rounded corners where the punch and die edges, respectively, make contact with the material. This rounded edge is due to the plastic deformation that first takes place and is more pronounced when soft metals are being cut. Excessive clearance will also cause a large radius at these corners, as well as a burr on opposite corners (view a).

In an ideal die-cutting operation, the punch penetrates the material to a depth equal to about one third of material thickness before fracture occurs, and it forces an equal part of the material into the die opening. The portion of the material penetrated will be highly burnished, appearing as a bright cut band around the entire contour of the cut adjacent to the edge radius, as indicated at B and B'1 in Fig. 33-51. When clearance is not sufficient, additional banks of metal must be cut before complete separation is accomplished, as shown in view b. With correct clearance, the angle of fracture permits a clean break below the cut bank because the upper and lower fractures extend toward one another. Excessive clearance results in a tapered cut edge, since for any cutting operation the opposite side of the material that the punch enters will, after cutting, be the same size as the die opening.

The width of the cut band is an indication of the hardness of the material. Provided that the die clearance and material thickness are constant, the wider the cut band, the softer the material. The harder metals permit less penetration by the punch than do ductile metals; dull tools create the effect of too

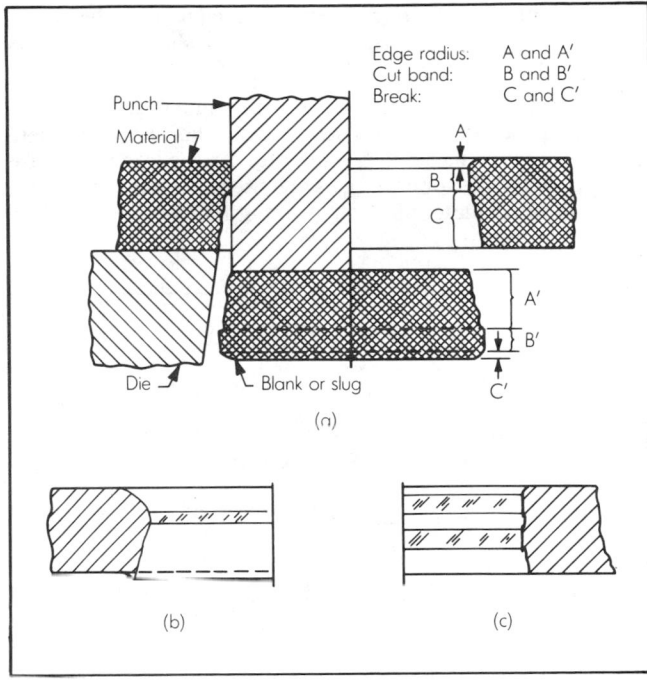

Fig. 33-51 Die-cut edge characteristics: (a) normal clearance, (b) excessive clearance and (c) insufficient clearance.

small a clearance as well as a burr on the die side of the stock. Clearances are universally expressed as a percentage of stock thickness and, for clarity, should apply to one side only; that is, the clearance for a round hole is one-half the difference between punch and die diameters.

Types of die-cut edges that are representative of the types that can be obtained and used by varying punch/die clearances (see Fig. 33-52) include the following:

1. Type I edges—These edges are obtained at the upper limits of clearance for usable die cutting. This type of hole or blank has a large edge radius, a large angle on the side, and a large tensile burr. Type I edge clearances are generally used on structural metalworking machines to punch a wide range of thicknesses; they are also generally used when the main purpose of the operation is to produce holes. If blanks are to be produced, Type I edges may be used if the large edge radius and burr are not important.
2. Type II edges—These have a large edge radius, a normal tensile burr, and a medium edge angle. Such edge clearances enable maximum die life to be obtained, as well as a hole or blank that is acceptable for general purposes.
3. Type III edges—Generally suitable for most purposes, these edges have a normal edge radius and show only a shallow edge angle. They are desirable for work-hardenable material that is to undergo severe forming. These clean, stress-free edges reduce the possibility of edge forming to a minimum.
4. Type IV edges—These edges are desirable for parts that require edge finishing, such as polishing. Type IV edges have a minimum edge radius, are nearly perpendicular to the face of the stock, and have heavy compressive and

DIE DESIGN FOR SHEET METAL FORMING

normal tensile burrs. Such an edge may be easily recognized by the spotty secondary shear areas on its break.

5. Type V edges—These have a minimum edge radius, are perpendicular to the stock face, and show complete secondary shear. Clearances for such edges may cause poor die life for cutting hard material, but may be useful on softer materials such as brass, lead, soft copper, and aluminum.

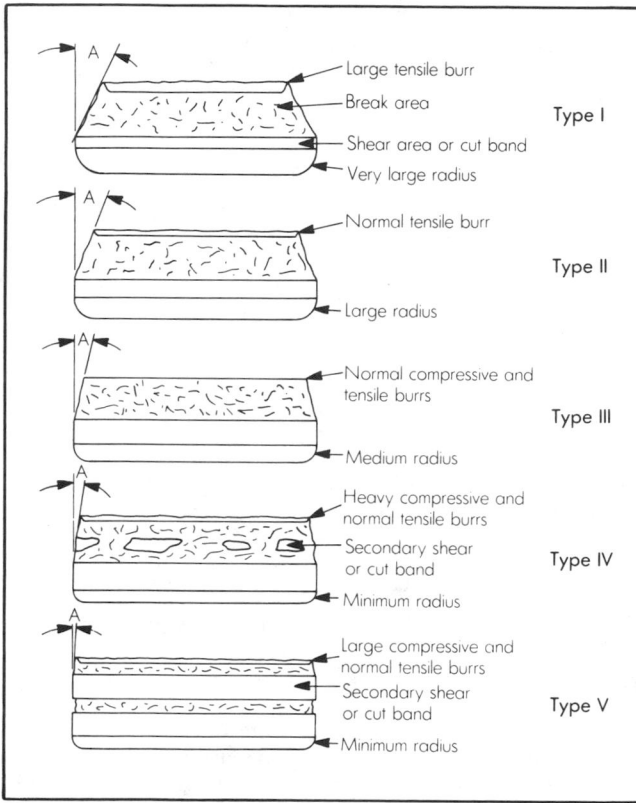

Fig. 33-52 Five basic types of die-cut edges as variations of punch-to-die clearance.

Die Design

A blanking die is generally cheaper to make and faster in operation than a trim die. Depending upon the tolerances of a part, it may be better to blank before forming than to trim all around the edges after forming. A single blanking die can produce either a right-hand or a left-hand part, while two trim dies (right and left-handed) are needed for trimming around the edges of the two parts.

A flat blank sheared by a blank-through type of blanking die (see Fig. 33-53) drops through the die block (lower shoe) and onto the bolster plate, often provided with an unloading chute, or drops through a hole in both die block and bolster plate. In a return-blank die (see Fig. 33-54), the blank is pushed up into the die cavity, after which it is ejected by a spring-loaded knockout. Different spring pressures are important for various applications. The stripper removes the stock from the punch as the press slide rises and the die opens. Return-blank die designs frequently incorporate positive knockouts actuated through linkages in the press ram instead of through spring pressure. A

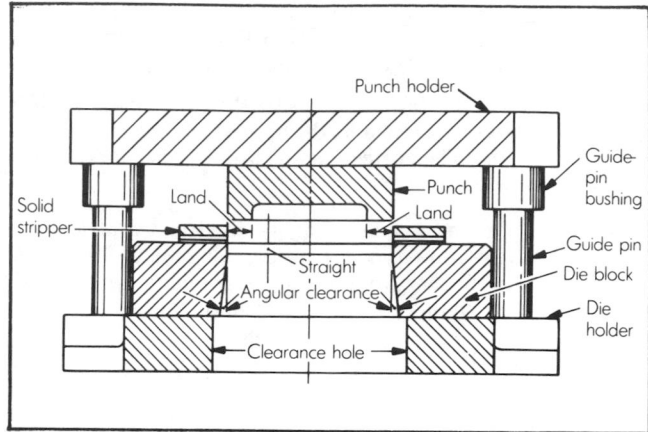

Fig. 33-53 Drop-through blanking die showing straight, land, and angular clearance.

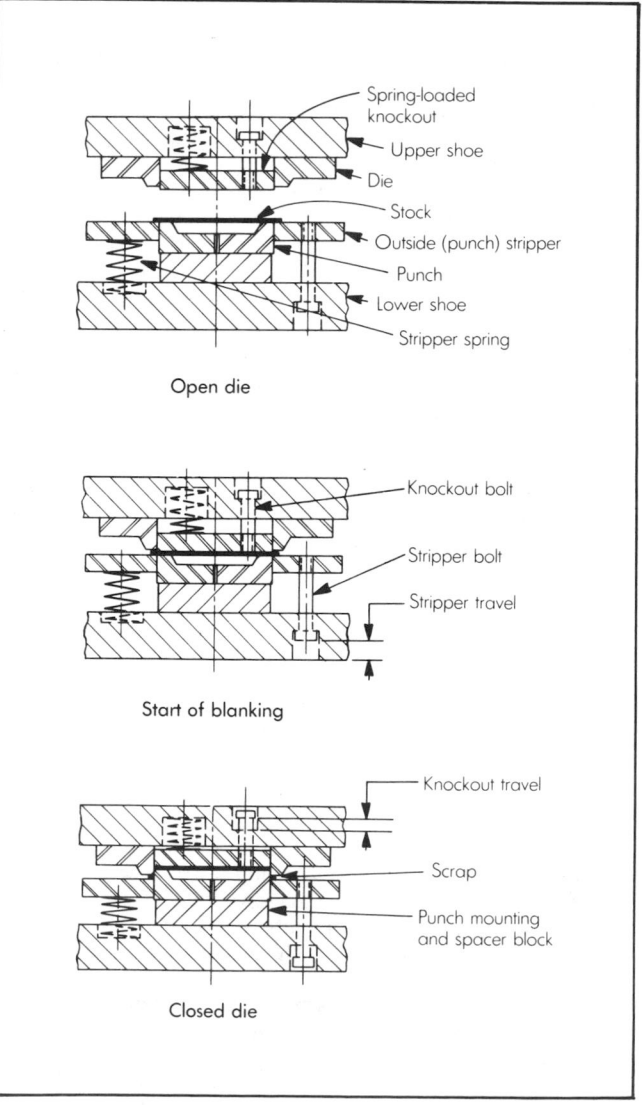

Fig. 33-54 Return-blank blanking die.

return-blank die is slower in operation due to the need for blank removal and costs more to build than a drop-through die because of the additional die sections required.

The perforating die shown in Fig. 33-55 is a typical single-station design for producing holes in flat stock that is manually or mechanically fed and is kept on a straight path through the die by the stock guides. The amount of stock travel is controlled by the method of feeding, by stops of various designs, or by direct or indirect piloting. The spring-loaded stripper clamps and helps position the stock during the punching of the three holes.

The die shown in Fig. 33-56 vertically punches a central hole in the bottom of a copper bowl and, by cam action, a hole in the side of the bowl. The stripper plate guides the vertical punch and prevents distortion in the flat bottom of the bowl as the punch is withdrawn. It also positions and holds the bottom

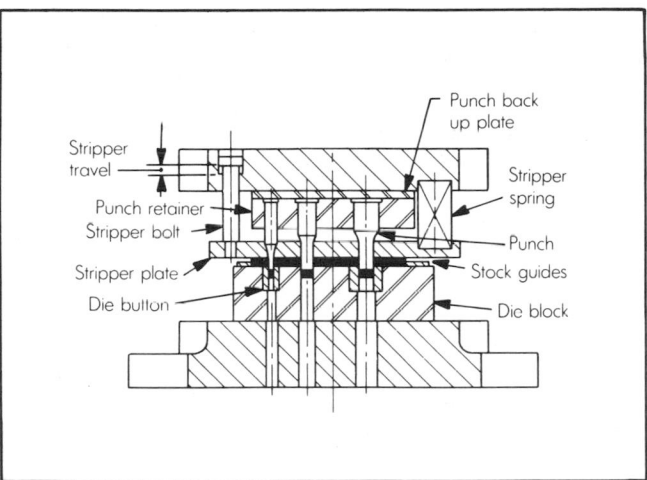

Fig. 33-55 Perforating die.

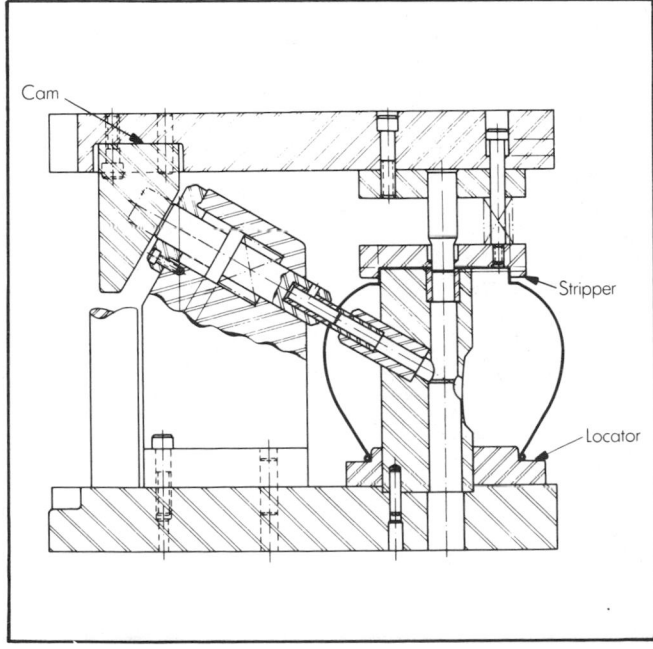

Fig. 33-56 Vertical and angular punching. (*Knapp-Monarch Co.* **)**

while the open end fits around the locator. The side punch sleeve allows punch removal. Slugs from both holes drop through a clearance hole in the lower shoe. Deep parts of this type must be handled manually, and tongs are generally used to meet safety requirements for loading and unloading. It should be noted that the side punch is returned by spring action as the cam withdraws with the slide.

FORMING DIES

Dies are used for many sheet metal forming operations. The more common forming operations accomplished with press-mounted dies include bending and flanging, embossing, beading, drawing, ironing, bulging, and compression operations.

The forming die shown in Fig. 33-57, used in a conventional press, was designed to form a part to close limits (see Fig. 33-58). All punches and the heel blocks incorporate carbide inserts. The vertical form punch limits the height of the bent ear to 0.185″ (4.70 mm) ±0.005″ (0.13 mm). A flattening punch holds the radius of the bend to 1/64″ (0.4 mm) and is backed up by the heel block. The sliding punch swages a 1.210″ (30.73 mm) radius on the bent ear through the action of the free cam. A locating pin is provided on the lower form punch. The contour of the part is machined in the face of the flattening punch. The 90° bend is formed between the sliding punch and the flattening punch. This is a triple-action die, with one action accomplished through pressure pins which force the lower form punch 1/2″ (12.7 mm) upward.

While various cam designs are often incorporated in dies for cutting operations, they are also frequently used in forming at an angle to the press ram. The dogleg cam driver (see Fig. 33-59) reciprocates through a slot in the cam slide and ensures positive cam-slide travel in both directions. The heel block resists the return and forming thrusts of the vertical portion of the driver. More commonly used are spring-returned designs such as that shown in Fig. 33-60, having a protective housing around the projecting members of the assembly. Spring returns are the most inexpensive cam-return methods; but if the spring fails, the dies and the parts may be damaged. A positive return method to replace the spring return is shown in Fig. 33-61. In this positive method, the cam slide is driven and returned by a tabbed gib which slides freely in slots in both the cam slide and the driver.

Punch and Die Contours

One of the most significant factors in obtaining the reduction of the blank diameter is the contour of the area at which the face of the punch is radiused into the side of the punch and the contour of the area at which the wall of the die is radiused into the face of the die. If these transition contours are too abrupt, the critical area in the bottom of the cup will be so severely stressed that the strength left to overcome the flow resistance of the metal on the die face will be insufficient and the bottom of the part will tear. If these contours are too sweeping, a puckering will occur in the length of unsupported metal at the point at which, in the beginning of the draw, the metal is tangent to the transition contour of the die.

Usual practice is to specify a punch edge radius of approximately five times the metal thickness. The punch radius, however, is often determined by part design and often varies from four to ten times the metal thickness. The surface of the radius and the sides of the punch should also be polished in the direction of metal flow to minimize friction. Because the die

DIE DESIGN FOR SHEET METAL FORMING

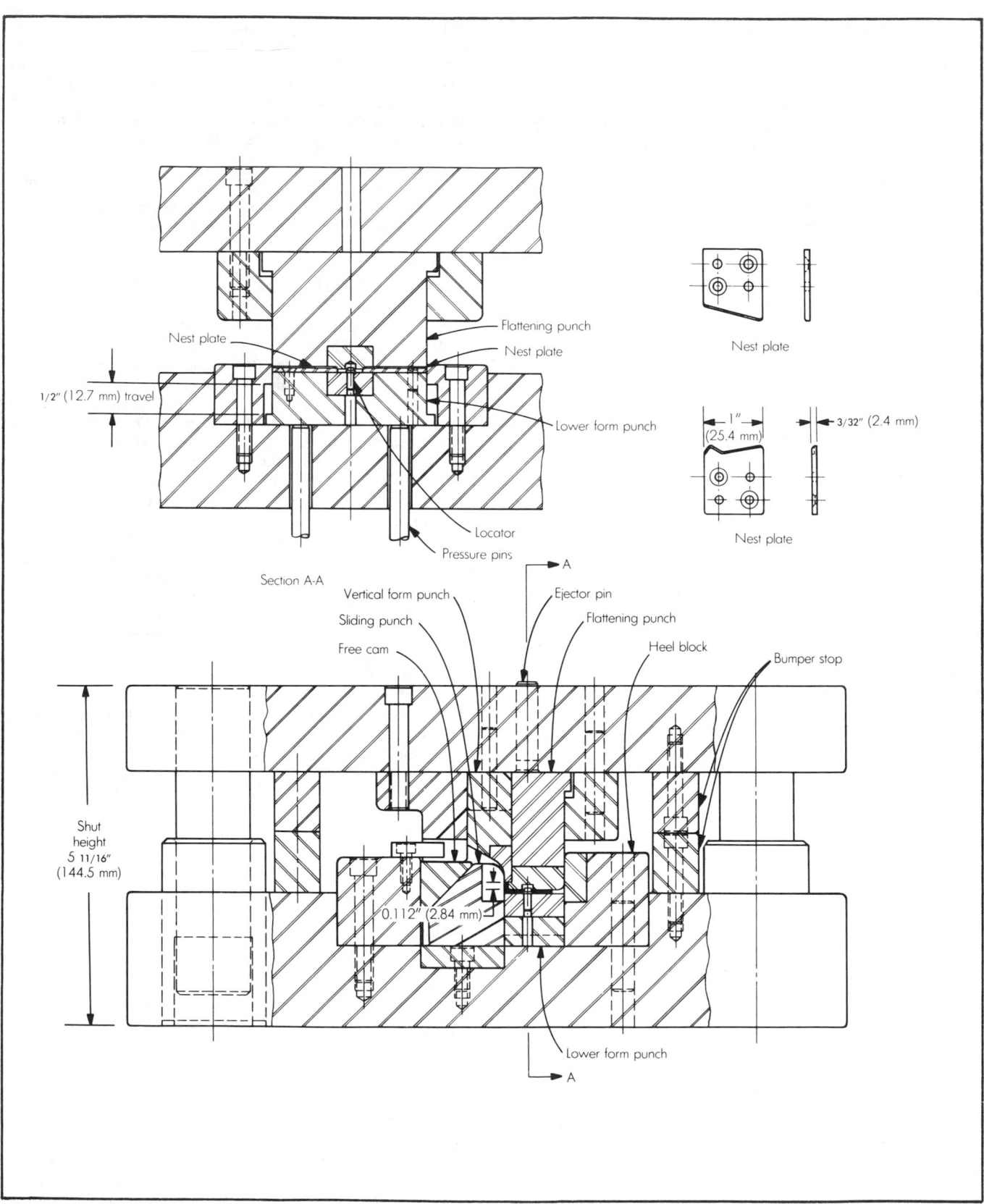

Fig. 33-57 Forming die with carbide inserts. (*National Cash Register Co.*)

DIE DESIGN FOR SHEET METAL FORMING

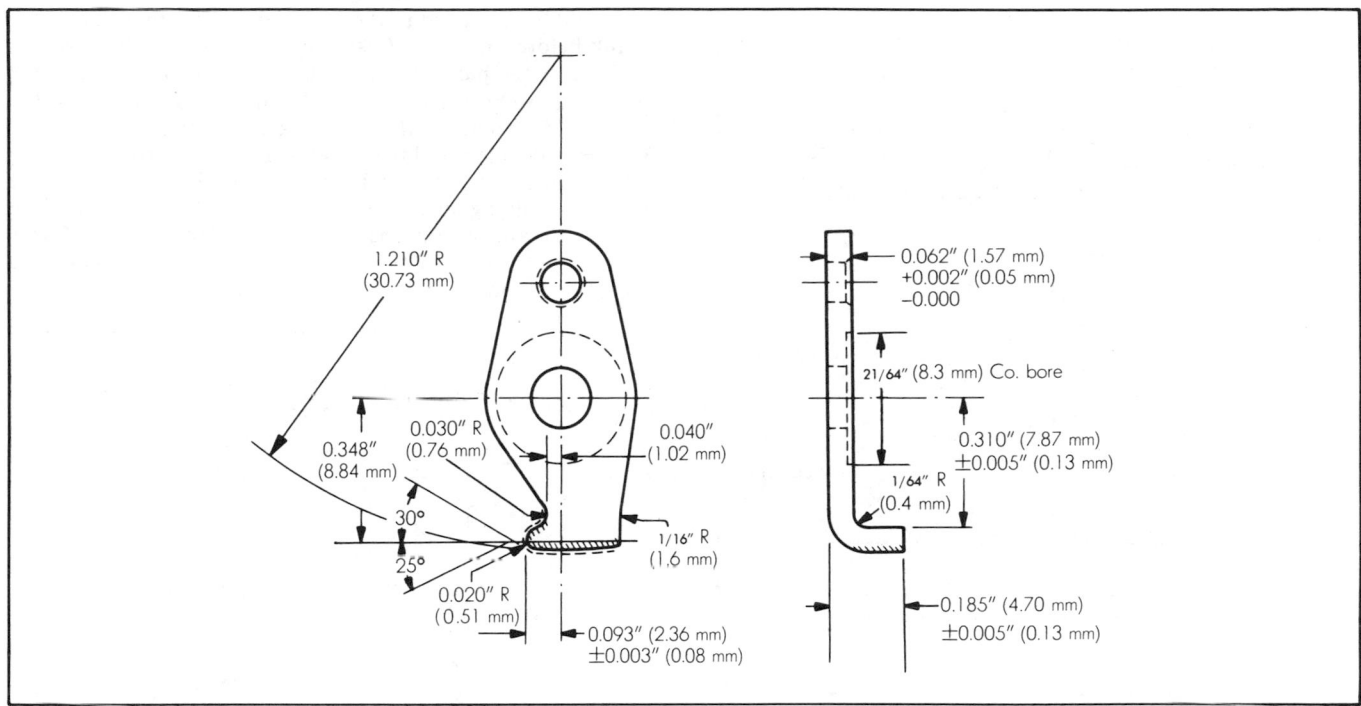

Fig. 33-58 Part formed in die illustrated in Fig. 33-57.

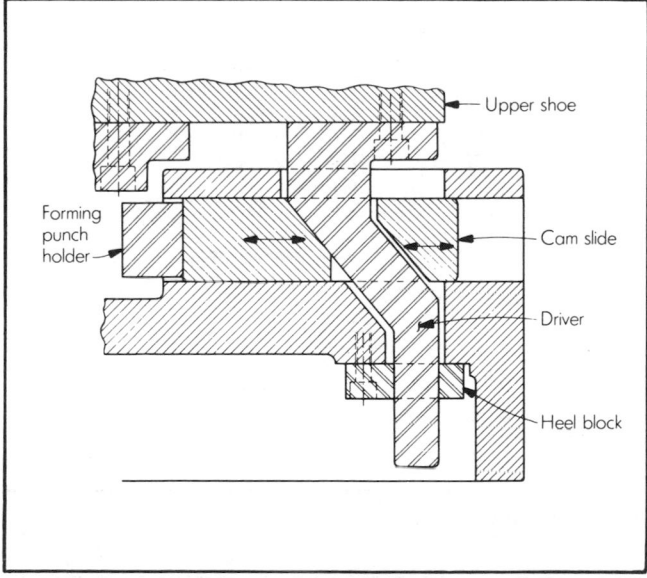

Fig. 33-59 Forming die with positive dogleg cam drive and return.

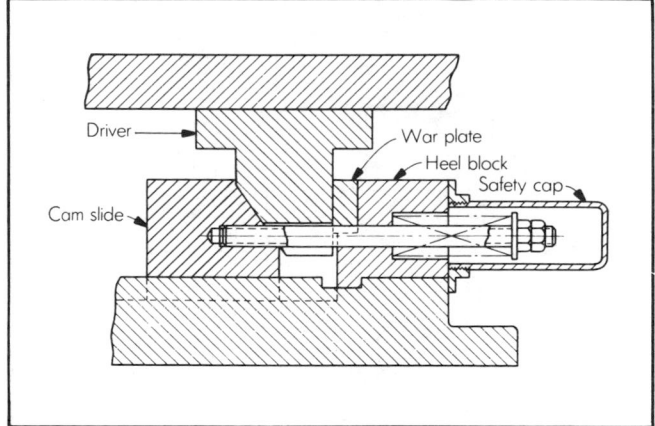

Fig. 33-60 Forming die with spring-returned cam slide.

edge is subjected to high sliding pressures, it is particularly important that this area be polished to provide a smooth surface on the drawn part and to provide maximum die life.

The curved working surface of a draw die or draw ring, for best practice, should have a radius of four times the stock thickness for stock 1/64 to 1/8" (0.4 to 3.2 mm) thick, although a radius of six to eight times stock thickness is required for drawing heavy-gage metals without a blankholder.

The die space usually allowed for drawing any metal should be proportional to the metal thickness plus clearance to reduce wall friction. This allowance ranges from 7-20% of the metal thickness depending on the type of material and the operation. As the shearing strength of the stock decreases, the allowance must be increased.

Draw Dies

The die shown in Fig. 33-62 is designed to be used in a single-action press with an air cushion that supplies the blankholding pressure. This type of setup can be used for shallow draws, deep draws such as those used in making washer and drier tubs, and draws used to make shapes such as engine oil pans. When cushion size is a limiting factor, hydropneumatic cushions can be used on mechanical presses or hydraulic presses.

A typical double-action die (see Fig. 33-63) incorporates a

DIE DESIGN FOR SHEET METAL FORMING

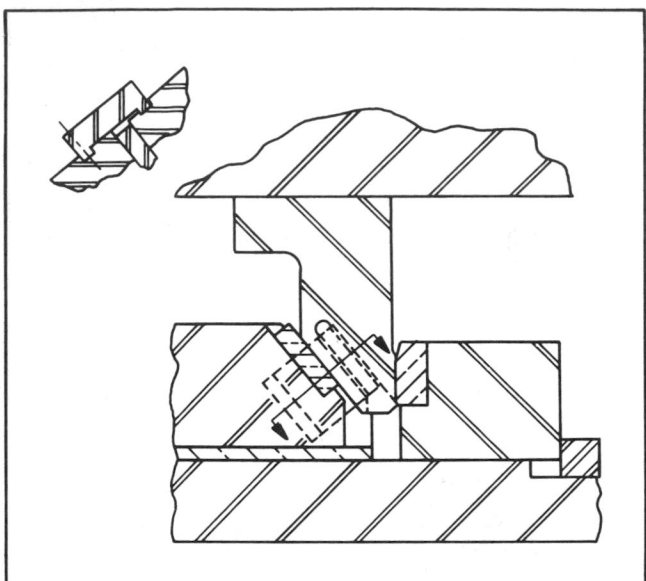

Fig. 33-61 Forming die cam slide with positive tabbed-gib drive and return. (*Livernois Automation Co.*)

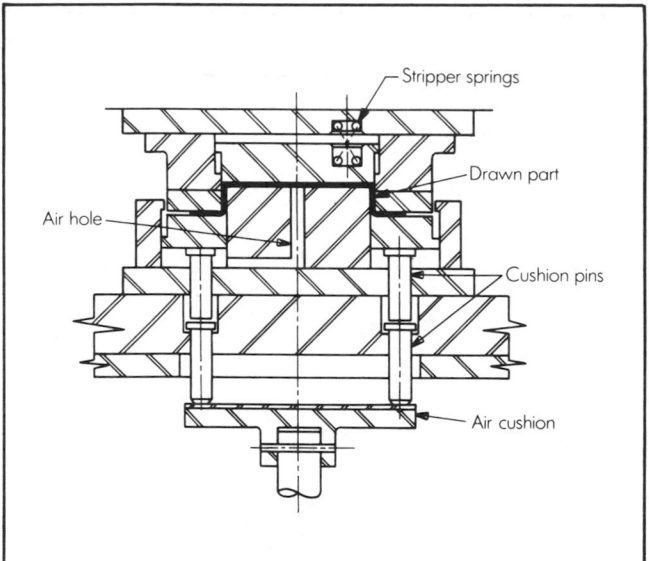

Fig. 33-62 Drawing die with air-cushion blankholding.

blankholder, attached to the outer press slide, that clamps the blank before the punch (fastened to the inner slide) descends and draws the part. While pushing the part into the die, the punch assembly also forces down the air cushion, which lifts the part out of the die after the slide retracts. On the return stroke of the press, the blankholder prevents the drawn part from being carried up by the punch and it dwells in its down position until the blankholding slide starts on its upstroke. If a controlled delay of the air cushion is necessary to avoid the opposing forces of the blankholder and the air cushion, which could buckle the part, timing pins or other devices must be provided.

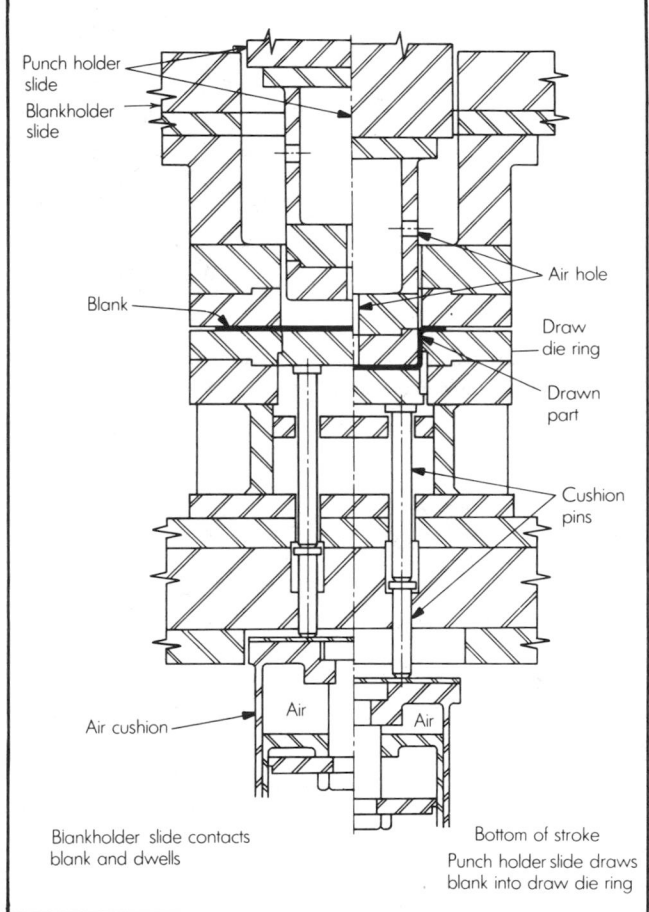

Fig. 33-63 Typical double-action cylindrical drawing die.

EXPANDING

Radial stretch forming on cone-type expanding machines has proven to be an accurate, versatile, and economic means of producing parts in a wide range of sizes from many different materials. The circumferences of workpieces can be increased in localized areas or along their entire lengths. A variety of tapers, spherical sections beads, offsets, and contours can be formed.

On cone-type expanding machines, the part to be formed or sized is placed around a cluster of retracted, internal forming shoes. These shoes are either jaw dies or are attached to master

segments or jaws that are keyed to a slotted table (see Fig. 33-64). As a multisided cone (driver) is moved axially by a drawbar, a cam action (created by the wedge surfaces on the cone sliding along mating wedges on the inner surfaces of the master segments) forces the forming shoes radially outward against the workpiece at a constant and controlled rate. The shoes are supported and guided by a table having locating slots and retainer gibs.

Hollow cylindrical shapes such as sheet metal sleeves com-

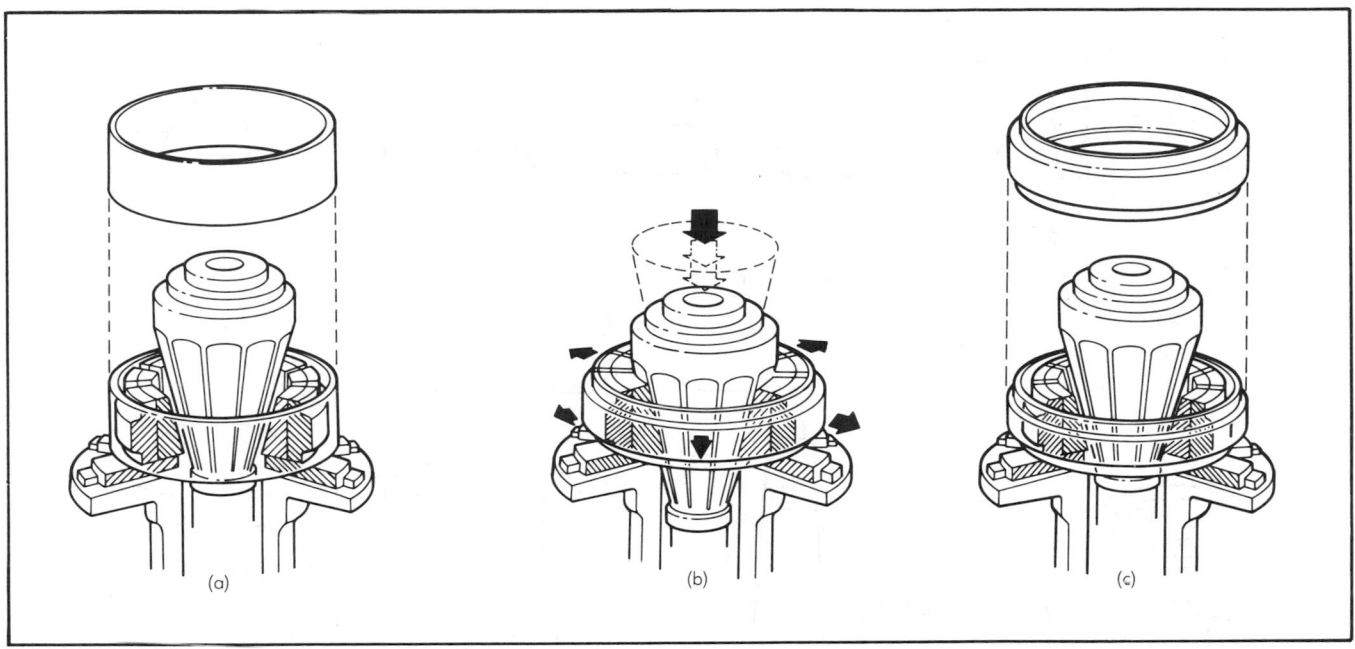

Fig. 33-64 Successive steps in forming a workpiece on a cone-type expanding machine: (a) workpiece is positioned around collapsed tools; (b) as drawbar pulls cone down, inclined surfaces force tools outward to expand part; then (c) tools return to starting position and formed part is unloaded. (*Grotnes Metalforming Systems, Inc.*)

prise the majority of applications for this type of expanding. The process, however, is also well suited to forming other hollow shapes such as ovals, triangles, rectangles, squares, irregular polygons, and many other kinds of closed sections. Heavy sections, such as lengths of tubes, pipes, and forged or welded rings, are expanded in this way. Parts must be fabricated with high-quality welds, and their seams should be planished smooth prior to expanding.

ADVANTAGES OF EXPANDING

Expanding produces high-quality parts having good strength. Improved strength results from stretching the metal over the entire blank surface, with uniform elongation and work hardening and the permanent deformation which takes place during expanding. There is no localized thinning, weakening, wrinkling, or distortion. Intricate contours and sharp details are easily formed.

Other important advantages include reduced material requirements and machining costs. By eliminating the binder material required for draw dies and the resultant scrap, material savings are considerable.

MATERIALS EXPANDED

Any material with sufficient ductility can be expanded. The materials most commonly expanded include aluminum alloys and carbon, alloy, and stainless steels. Superalloys, such as the Hastelloys and René alloys, are successfully formed by expanding. Brittle materials such as cast iron cannot be expanded.

Materials in a soft annealed condition are easiest to expand. Hard metals, including heat-treated steels, can be formed by expanding, but with less elongation. Most high-alloy materials must be normalized or stress-relieved expanding.

For parts requiring considerable forming, several expanding operations are sometimes performed. When work hardening

interferes with subsequent forming, the parts are annealed between operations. Hot forming and sizing are performed on some materials, such as titanium and high-strength alloys.

Expanding machines can elongate materials beyond the limits possible with drawing and stretching processes because metal is available from the entire blank without the restriction of binders or grippers. Elongation in expanding varies from a few percent in sizing operations to 40% or more in some forming applications.

Experience has shown that it is generally advisable to limit material elongations to about 75% of the limits determined by conventional tensile testing. When forming localized bosses, beads, or offsets by expanding, it is generally best to exceed by 10-50% the minimum bend radii recommended for the material being formed.

The amount of springback (elastic recovery) of expanded parts, which determines the accuracy that can be obtained, depends upon the dimensions of the parts, the maximum yield stress present in the material, and the modulus of elasticity.

EXPANDING APPLICATIONS

Beads, threads, flanges, bosses, flutes, and practically any contour can be formed by expanding. Square and conical parts can be produced from cylindrical blanks. A few of the many different shapes formed or sized by expanding are illustrated in Fig. 33-65. Configurations of the expanded parts need not be geometrically symmetrical. Double-end configurations are formed by placing the workpiece between two expander heads which move together to form both ends of the workpiece simultaneously.

The appliance industry is a major user of the expanding process, with one-piece cabinets, liners, tubs, baskets, and similar components for kitchen and laundry equipment formed in this way. Expanding of refrigerator liners provides material savings

EXPANDING

Fig. 33-65 Typical shapes formed or sized on cone-type expanding machines. (*Arrowsmith Industries, Inc.*)

of about 30%. In producing dishwasher housings, one expanding operation has replaced 20 die operations previously required.

Expanding is also used extensively in the aircraft and aerospace industry for forming fuel tanks, missile cases, rocket motor cases and thrust chambers, jet engine rings, nozzles, shrouds, and other components. There are also many applications in the automotive industry. One example is forming and sizing wheel rims for automobiles and trucks. Multiple-panel expansion applications are discussed subsequently in this section.

Other expanding applications include ring-shaped weldments or forgings for generator and motor frames, transmission gear blanks, and pulleys. Expanding is also used for many operations requiring the assembly of two or more parts. Some subassemblies are expanded to eliminate distortion from the assembly operation. In some applications, expanding is performed specifically to achieve an improvement in material strength.

TOOLING FOR EXPANDING

Forming shoes are clamped or bolted to the master segments; or in some cases, they are simply rested on the segment tails. One quick-change method consists of attaching the forming shoes to the master segments by means of keyhole-shaped locking lugs on the inner bearing surfaces (Fig. 33-66). Wear plates are often provided on the master segments to extend segment life.

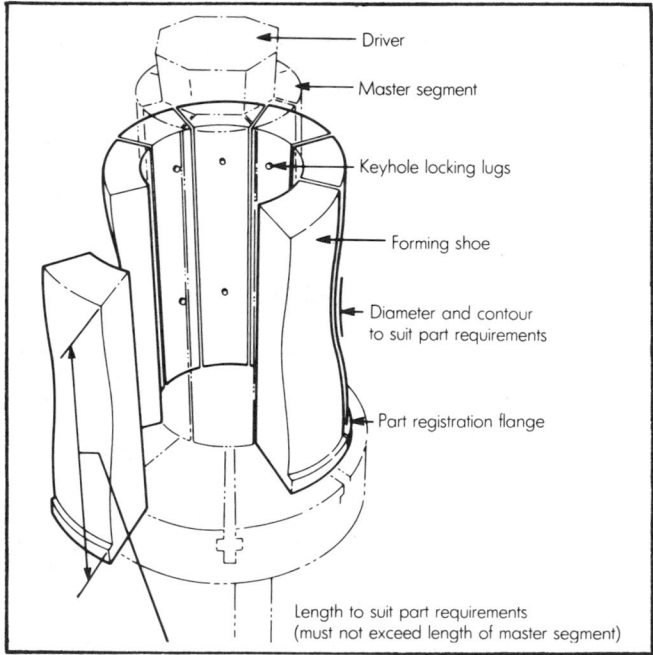

Driver

Master segment

Keyhole locking lugs

Forming shoe

Diameter and contour to suit part requirements

Part registration flange

Length to suit part requirements (must not exceed length of master segment)

Fig. 33-66 Keyhole-shaped locking lugs permit quick changing of forming shoes. (*Arrowsmith Industries, Inc.*)

FLUID EXPANDING

Fluid or hydrostatic expansion is similar to the mechanical expanding process just discussed, with the exception that the inner tooling cluster is replaced with a pressurized fluid (water or oil). Since there is no inner tooling in contact with the workpiece during forming, the inside of the part is devoid of die marks.

Three types of fluid expanding now being used for commercial production applications are (1) expanding with conventional blank slippage, (2) expanding with 100% stretch, and (3) expanding with column compression and fluid expansion. All three types are similar in that an outer die surrounds the blank and injected fluid provides the forming medium. The selection of the type to be used is based upon the geometry of the workpiece.

SHRINKING

Shrinking is the opposite of expanding, with the metal workpiece being formed or sized by exceeding the material yield stress in compression rather than in tension to decrease diameters. Forces act radially inward toward the machine centerline rather than outward. The force required to form parts by shrinking can vary from the same as that required to expand an equivalent mass of material to four or five times as much. The use of fewer segments increases the shrinkability and reduces the force requirements. Parts can be accurately sized by shrinking about 0.5%, compared to the approximately 2% needed to expand to accurate size.

A typical shrinker is shown in Fig. 33-67. Principle elements include an outer reaction or pressure ring and a group of wedges. When the pressure ring and wedges are moved axially, the wedges force a set of mating jaws radially inward at a uniform rate toward a common center. The jaws have suitable die or shoe mounting provisions and are supported and guided by a table.

MATERIALS AND SHAPES

Radial compression by shrinking is applied to a wide variety of materials and workpieces having a wide range of sizes and wall thicknesses. Typical hollow cylindrical blanks include lengths of tubing, pipe, or fabricated parts made from flat stock that is cut to length, coiled, welded, and trimmed.

Circumferences of workpieces can be reduced either in localized areas or along their entire lengths. The process is well suited to forming a variety of tapers, spherical sections, inward beads, offsets, and contours. Forming of localized bosses or depressions requires inner restraint tooling. Localized details can be formed in unsymmetrical locations around the peripheries of the workpieces.

Diameter tolerances of 0.001-0.005" (0.03-0.13 mm) can generally be maintained, and shrinking is generally preferred over other methods of forming when the area of reduced diameter is relatively small and accuracy of the finished part is critical. In many cases, the need for subsequent forming or machining operations is eliminated and the amount of material, labor, and production time is reduced, thus cutting costs. Workpiece strength is increased by cold working of the material. There is no inherent limitation to the minimum diameter, the length-to-diameter ratio, or the maximum wall thickness that may be formed by shrinking.

SHRINKING APPLICATIONS

Shrinking machines are widely applied in the automotive industry. One large machine, open at both ends, forms and sizes axle housings having wall thicknesses to ⅝" (16 mm). It is part of an automated system for producing several sizes of truck and trailer axle housings. The feed system, an integral part of the machine, receives pieces from the preceding operation, positions them for two shrinking cycles on one end, repositions them for two cycles on the opposite end, and then moves them to the next

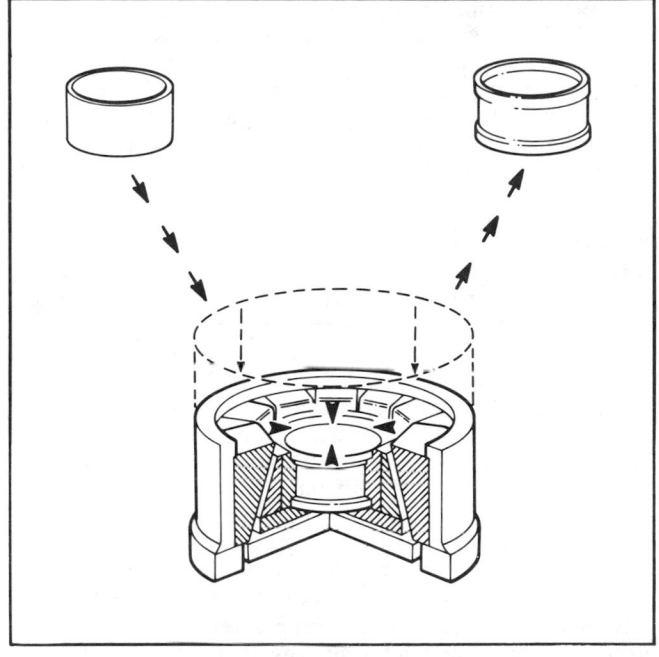

Fig. 33-67 Shrinking consists of compressing hollow cylindrical blanks to decrease their diameters. (*Grotnes Metalforming Systems, Inc.*)

operation. Shrinking provides higher production rates, closer tolerances, longer tool life, and lower costs than the hot swaging operation it replaces.

Other automotive applications include shrinking wheel rims, coining brake shoes, and forming steering linkage. Applications in the aircraft industry include forming and sizing jet engine rings. One 265 ton (2357 kN) shrinker accepts different dies to accommodate ring outside diameters ranging from 10-52" (254-1321 mm) with wall thicknesses to 3" (76 mm).

Shrinking is used extensively for assembly operations and is particularly effective for assembling dissimilar materials. One application consists of shrinking metal rings around rubber sleeves for use in shock absorbers. Other assembly operations include attaching connection fittings to rubber or plastic hose, shrinking the outer races of self-aligning bearings around the inner races, and locking copper rotating bands to artillery shells.

COMBINED EXPANDING AND SHRINKING

For some applications, the principles of both expanding and shrinking are combined in a single machine. The center of such machines is an expander, while the outside elements include the pressure ring and compression tools. The machines are used for expanding applications requiring the formation of localized embossments, beads, offsets, or other contoured transitional areas along the surface of the workpiece.

The outer ring and tool assembly on combination expanding/shrinking machines is used as a locking or locating ring and has the required shapes into which the metal is expanded. Machine controls provide the capability of combining motions so that the workpiece can be initially expanded and then shrunk. The cycle sequence can be reversed to provide shrinking first and then expanding.

STRETCH FORMING

Stretch forming is a method that combines controlled stretching and bending of sheet metal blanks, roll-formed sections, and extrusions around form blocks (dies) to produce accurately contoured parts without wrinkles. Usually, two opposite ends of the workpiece are gripped in jaws and pulled or wrapped around the die (form block). This is accomplished in several ways, one of which is shown schematically in Fig. 33-68.

ADVANTAGES OF STRETCH FORMING

In most cases, there is practically no springback or tendency to buckle with stretch formed parts because the stresses imposed on the metal are primarily tensile and the amount of stretch is carefully controlled. As a result, accurate parts that hold their shape are produced.

Stretch formed parts have a uniform increase in tensile strength up to 10% and an increase in hardness of about 2%. Increase in strength is approximately equal to the percentage of stretch multiplied by the difference between the yield and ultimate tensile strengths of the material being formed. The workpieces are generally free of residual stresses, and stress relieving is seldom required. Warpage or distortion is seldom experienced as the result of subsequent machining or welding.

Substantial savings result from reduced material requirements. Blanks for stretch forming are about 15% smaller than those needed for drawing on presses. The material for blank restraint is required on only two opposed edges, while for press drawing, the blank must be large enough for restraint around the entire periphery. Scrap losses for subsequent trimming operations are reduced as much as 50%.

Pressure requirements for stretch forming are from 30-70% less than that for press forming because of the increased formability of the stretched material. This reduces capital equipment costs and floor space requirements. Stretch forming machines are less expensive than presses of comparable capacity.

Tooling costs are also lower since usually only one die is required. (The exception is in stretch-draw forming between mating punch and die.) The dies for stretch forming are usually smaller and can be made of lighter, less costly materials because of lower pressure requirements, which also lengthens die life. Stretch forming dies do not generally require modification for springback allowance; thus, they reduce development, machining, and tryout times. The same dies can often be used to stretch form various materials by adjusting the tension exerted. Labor costs are sometimes lower because of fast, easy setup, loading, and unloading.

STRETCH FORMED MATERIALS

Practically any metal can be stretch formed providing a suitable range exists between the yield point and ultimate strength of the metal. The metals most commonly stretch formed are aluminum alloys, stainless steels, low-carbon steels, and commercially pure titanium. Metals that are less commonly

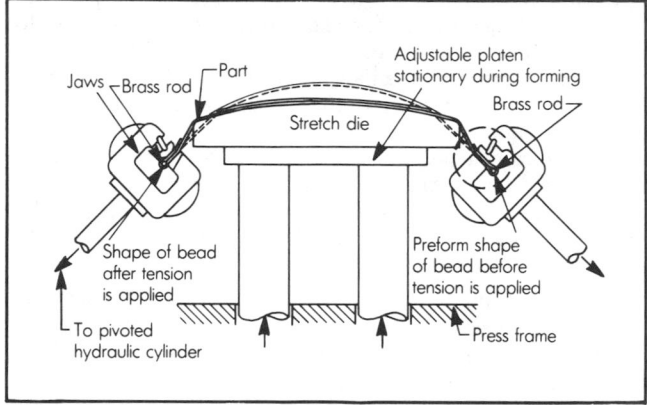

Fig. 33-68 One method of stretch forming, with part gripped in movable jaws. (*The Cyril Bath Co.*)

formed in this way include titanium, alloys, heat-resistant alloys, and magnesium alloys. Alloys difficult to form in press operations can often be contoured easily because of the increased formability of the stretched metal.

APPLICATIONS OF STRETCH FORMING

Stretch forming is being used extensively by the aircraft and aerospace industries. Large machines have been built for forming wing members, tail structures, fuselage segments, and engine components. The process permits tolerances to be held as close as ±0.005″ (0.13 mm) for the leading edges of wings used on large jet aircraft. Other airplane parts stretch formed from 2024, 2219, and 7075 aluminum alloys include ribs, pylons, fairings, wing attachment tees, and skins.

Helicopter blades with lengths to 312″ (7925 mm) have their leading edges stretch formed from Type 301 stainless steel to a tolerance of ±0.005″. External fuel tanks for the space shuttles have several of their outer ogive skins and dome gores stretch formed from sheets of 2219 aluminum alloy. These compound-contoured skins range in size from 87 x 144″ (2210 x 3658 mm) to 97 x 204″ (2464 x 5182 mm), with thicknesses to ½″ (12.7 mm). T-shaped chords, made from 311″ (7899 mm) long, 2219 aluminum alloy extrusions, are stretched 3% and formed to a radius of 165.5″ (4204 mm) for supporting the skins on the external fuel tanks of the space shuttles.

Stretch forming is not limited to aircraft and aerospace manufacturing. Other applications include the production of truck bumpers, structural frames for buses and recreational vehicles, monorail guide beams, window frames for mobile homes, structural building members, telecommunication antennas, and many appliance components. The outer skins covering the corner segments of school bus frames are stretch formed from 1010 steel because other methods could not produce the complex contours required. One such skin is 4 x 8 ft (1219 x 2438 mm) in size and 0.080″ (2.03 mm) thick.

TOOLING FOR STRETCH FORMING

Tooling requirements for stretch forming include the gripping jaws and the dies (form blocks), which vary depending upon whether sheets, plates, or sections are to be formed. Accessories often needed include blocks to form depressions (joggles) in the workpiece at desired locations, drill jigs for uniform hole positions with relation to the contour, scribe blocks to produce trim lines on the workpieces, and snakes (flexible filler pieces) to prevent the collapse or deformation of light extrusions during forming.

ANDROFORMING

The patented Androform process is a method used to form sheet or plate stock into shallow, compound-curved parts. Among the major advantages of Androforming over stretch forming is that without having to make any dies, flat blanks can be elongated differentially to produce a variety of convex shapes. Forming extends to the side edges of the blanks without changing their lengths and without necking, even when the blanks are triangular or trapezium shaped.

Most production applications of Androforming consist of zero elongation at the blank edges or elongation only at the edges. A few applications, however, consist of elongation at the central area of the blanks and shrinkage along the edges. Materials can be formed at room temperature in the hard-rolled or heat-treated condition, thus eliminating the need for heat treating after forming. Flatness of the blanks is not critical because the machine that is used irons out wrinkles and warps during forming.

Androforming is being used to form compound-curved surfaces for aircraft skins and petals for parabolic antennas employed in radio telescope systems, which require precise tolerances and consistent repeatability. It can also be applied to the forming of panels for automobile bodies, appliances, and ship hulls.

The process is not suitable for producing deep drawn shapes. Limitations with respect to the depth of draw depend upon the properties, widths, and thicknesses of the materials to be formed. Maximum depths of draw are generally limited to a minimum spherical radius of about 1 ½ times the blank width.

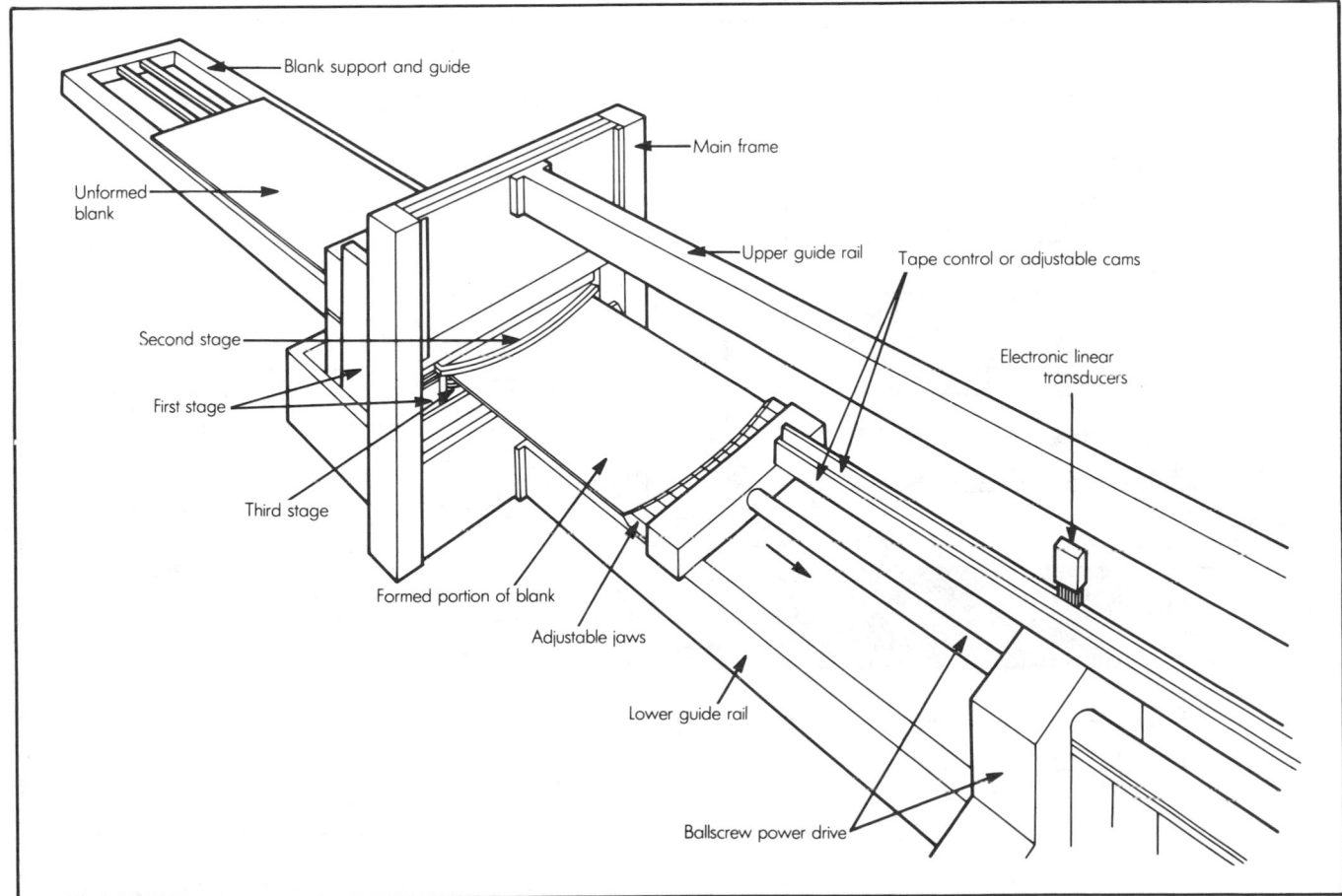

Fig. 33-69 Androform machine for forming sheets into shallow curved parts. (*Anderson Industries, Inc.*)

ANDROFORMING

FORMING PRINCIPLE

The Androform process operates on the principle of selective differential elongation of metal blanks by drawing them through a series of dynamically controlled forming elements. With jaws pulling one end of the blank through the forming elements, the blank traverses a path consisting of a series of reverse bends and variable differential steps.

The path traversed is adjustably different for each increment of the blank width and is also variable along its length. With this variable pattern of individual paths, the blank is differentially stressed according to a predetermined program. The program is selected to localize the strain pattern at the low portion of the plastic range of the material.

ANDROFORMING MACHINES

A typical machine is shown schematically in Fig. 33-69. It consists essentially of a support and guide for feeding blanks, a frame for holding the programmable forming elements, guide rails, a tape control or adjustable cams, and a power drive and adjustable jaws for pulling one end of the blank. The tensile load at the jaws is only about 12% of the yield point of the material.

Machines have been built to form blanks to 9/16" (14.3 mm) thick x 8 ft (2.4 m) wide x 36 ft (11 m) long. Tolerances of 0.001"/ft (0.08 mm/m) are held, and production rates of 150-180 parts per hour have been attained. Setup time for producing new parts varies from a few minutes to several hours. By proper selection of the forming elements, the largest machines have formed stainless steel as thin as 0.008" (0.20 mm).

As the blank travels over and under certain beads of the forming elements, it is subjected to simultaneous bending and tensile loads. This results in severe gradients of stress throughout the thickness and full width of the material, with the greatest tensile stress at the outer layers of the bends. The degree of the stress gradient is controlled by the dynamic actions and positioning of the forming element stages, relative to each other and their geometric differential.

Almost all the differential elongation of the blank surface takes place between the last bead of the first stage and the single bead in the second stage, where the bend is reversed. The tangent portion of the blank between the first and second-stage beads is not elongated since the tensile load is below the yield point of the material. The third-stage tooling co-acts with the second-stage bead and the horizontal lands of the second stage to control the final differential elongation throughout the material thickness; this tooling is programmed to produce the desired longitudinal curvature of the part.

TOOLING FOR ANDROFORMING

Universally adjustable forming elements (see Fig. 33-70) eliminate the need for dies. The elements are preadjusted to shape according to formulas, calculations, and measurements taken from form-checking fixtures used for inspection.

Distances that the elements are apart and above or below

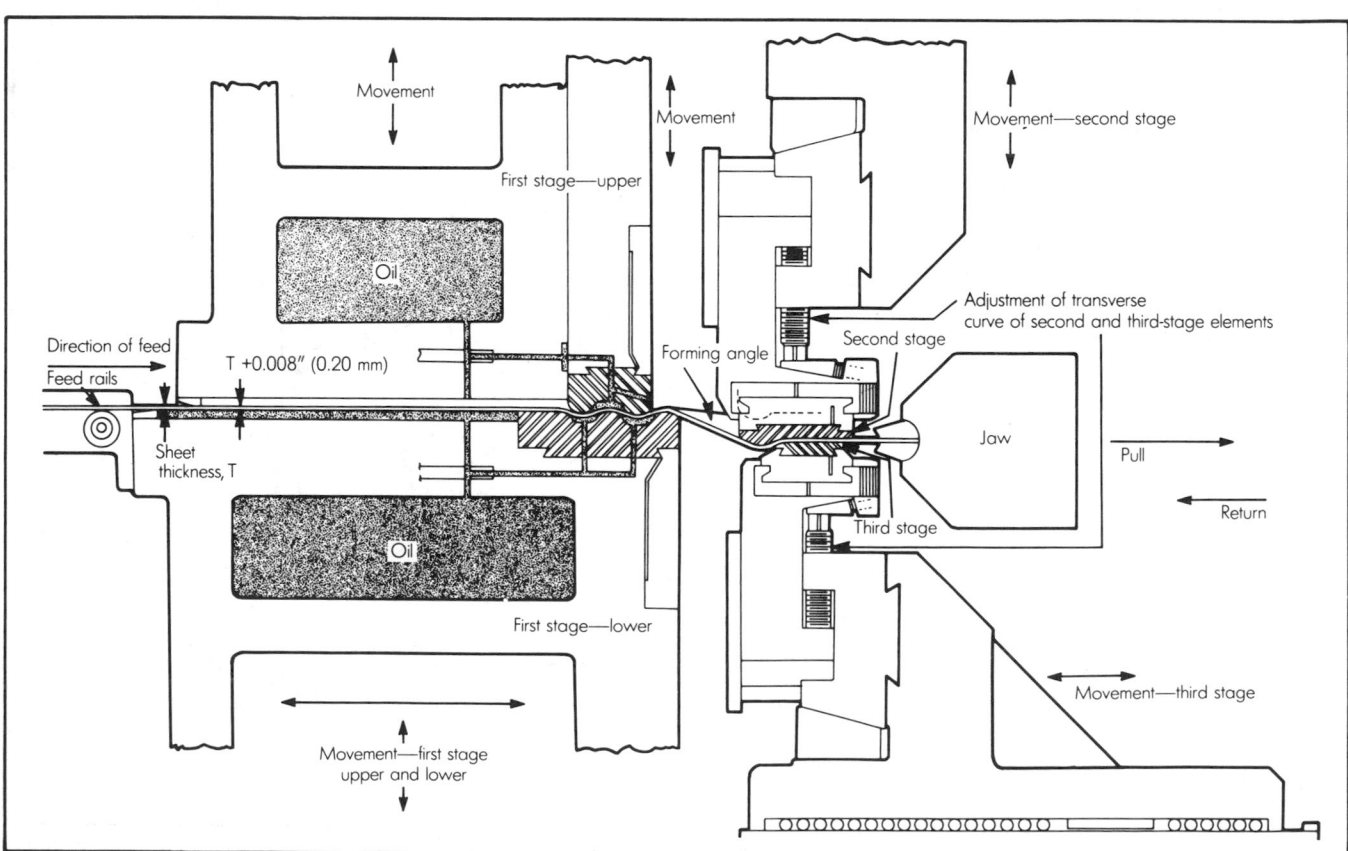

Fig. 33-70 Forming elements for Androforming are arranged in three stages. (*Anderson Industries, Inc.*)

each other, combined with the contours of the elements in the second and third stages, determine the shape produced. Automatic positioning of the elements to produce the desired curvature is controlled by punched tapes or a series of adjustable cams and linear transducers.

Working surfaces of the forming elements are interchangeable inserts which are selected according to the metal thickness to be formed. Profiles of these element inserts perform best when the bead radius is eight times the metal thickness. They have highly polished, hardened surfaces. Element inserts for the first stage are rigid; those for the second and third stages are adjustable to a curve proportional to the transverse curve of the part to be formed.

Before the blank enters the first-stage elements, it passes between two rigid flat plates. The plates are lined with flat hardened tool-steel sections arranged in a zig-zag pattern to provide grooves for the passage of oil. The oil lubricant is automatically forced under pressure against both faces of the blank. In addition, when titanium is being formed, a plastic coating is applied to both sides of the sheet and dried before forming. This coating, which prevents galling, is easily peeled from the sheet after forming.

References

1. Donald F. Eary and Edward A. Reed, *Techniques of Pressworking Sheet Metal*, 2nd ed., Englewood Cliffs, NJ: Prentice-Hall Inc., 1974.
2. Harding R. Hugo, *How to Improve Stamping Die Performance*, Cleveland: Society of Manufacturing Engineers, 1979.
3. *Fine-Blanking Practical Handbook*, Hallwag AG, Bern, Switzerland: Feintool AG, Lyss.

ROLL FORMING

Roll forming is a continuous process for forming metal from sheet, strip, or coiled stock into shapes of essentially uniform cross section. The material is fed between successive pairs of rolls, which progressively shape it until the desired cross section is produced. During the process, only bending takes place; the material thickness is not changed except for a slight thinning at bend radii.

ROLL FORMING METHODS

The two methods used when shaped parts are roll formed are the precut or cut-to-length method and the post-cut method. Method selection is based on the complexity of the cross section and the production length specification.

Precut Method

In precut operations, the material is cut to length prior to entering the roll forming machine. This process usually incorporates a stacking and feeding system to move the blanks into the roll forming machine, a roll forming machine running at a fixed speed of about 50-250 fpm (15-76 m/min), and an exit conveyor and stacking system. The cut-to-length process is used primarily for lower volume parts and whenever notching cannot be easily accomplished in a post-cut line as in miter cuts in vertical legs. Often, the material is run from coil into a shear or blanking press and then mechanically fed into the roll former.

Tooling cost is inexpensive with this method because cutting requires only a flat shear die or end notch die. However, end flare is more pronounced and side roll tooling is required to obtain a good finished shape.

Post-Cut Method

Even though some configurations require the cut-to-length method, the most efficient, most productive, most consistent, and least troublesome is the post-cut method. This method requires an uncoiler, a roll forming machine, a cutoff machine, and runout table. In most segments of the industry, this is the most widely used method. It can be augmented by various auxiliary operations, including prenotching, punching, embossing, marking, trimming, welding, curving, coiling, and die forming. Any or all of these procedures can be combined to eliminate the need for secondary operations, resulting in a complete or net shape product. However, the cost of tooling and the tooling changeover time for this method are greater than the tooling cost and changeover time for the precut method.

DESIGN CONSIDERATIONS

The cross section or shape to be roll formed can be as varied as the materials used. The most effective and trouble-free operations involve shapes that are designed (or modified) with the roll forming process in mind. Many sections that traditionally have been produced by press braking, extruding, or stamping can be successfully converted to roll forming by keeping a few simple rules in mind.

Symmetry

Many nonsymmetrical sections are roll formed without difficulty, but the section that is symmetrical about its vertical centerline when formed results in an equal amount of forming being done on each edge of the metal as it passes through the form rolls. When this condition is achieved, the stresses imparted by the forming process are equalized.

Cross Section Depth

Extreme depth in a cross section should be avoided. The stresses produced in roll forming are much more complex than those in other types of bending. In deep sections, the metal movement around the arc of the bend is much greater—and so is the resulting edge stress.

Bend Radii

The minimum bend radius is largely determined by the ductility of the material to be formed. Generally, sharper radii can be obtained by roll forming than by other forming methods. Given a material of sufficient ductility, bend radii should be equal to or greater than the material thickness (see Fig. 34-1). To form a radius smaller than the metal thickness, grooving or beading of the metal must be done (see Fig. 34-2). However, this practice, combined with the inherent thinning that occurs during bending, can result in fracturing of the metal at the bends (see Fig. 34-3).

Blind Corners

A blind corner is a bend or area of a bend that cannot be controlled by direct contact of the rolls (see Fig. 34-4). Whenever a blind corner is present, sectional dimensions cannot be controlled accurately unless the corner is accessible by slides or side idler forming rolls.

Leg Length

The minimum practical leg length is three times the material thickness (see Fig. 34-1). A leg length shorter than this does not allow the rolls to properly form the leg. In fact, attempting to form short legs results in nipping the edge of the material. This nipping can cause edge stretch and can result in a wave along the edge of the finished part.

Section Width

Sections with wide flat areas that are exposed when the sections are assembled into the end product should be viewed with caution. The stresses developed during roll forming can cause these areas to lose their flatness. Longitudinal ribs, based on material thickness, can be evenly spaced across the flat area to mask or hide coil imperfections such as wavy edges or lack of flatness in the center (oil canning). Roll forming cannot remove coil imperfections in wide flat areas; it can only try to hide or bury them in the cross section.

DESIGN CONSIDERATIONS

Notches and Punched Holes

Whenever possible, prepunched holes and notches should be kept away from bend lines or edges. Generally, holes are placed three to five times material thickness beyond bend radius (see Fig. 34-1). Slight distortions in their size and shape during forming is highly possible and should be expected. To minimize distortion, the number of forming passes should be increased.

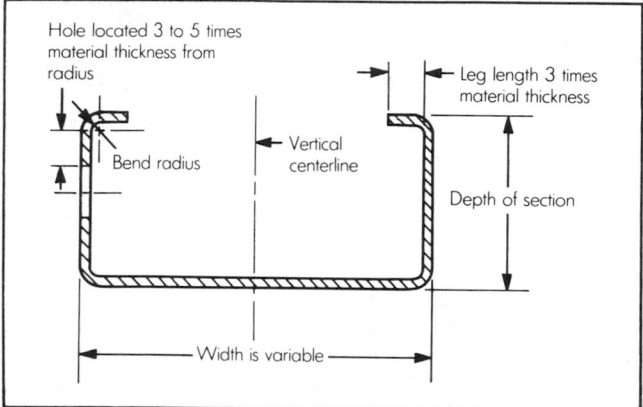

Fig 34-1 Several rules must be taken into consideration when designing a part to be produced on a roll forming machine. (*Contour Roll Co.*)

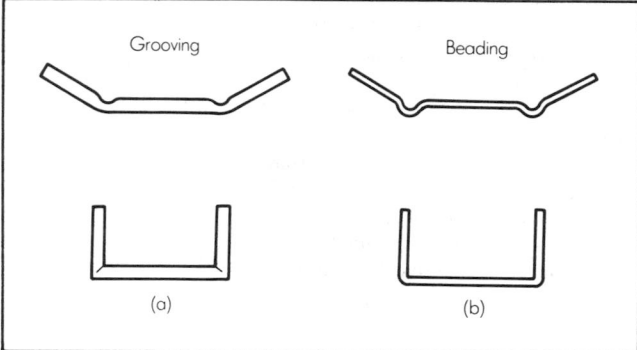

Fig 34-2 Grooving or beading the metal enables a smaller radius to be formed, but may result in fracturing the metal. (*Lockformer Co.*)

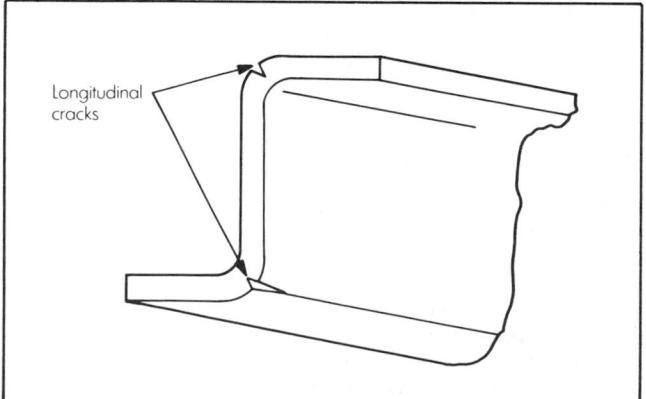

Fig 34-3 A bend radius that is too small results in longitudinal cracks at the bend. (*Lockformer Co.*)

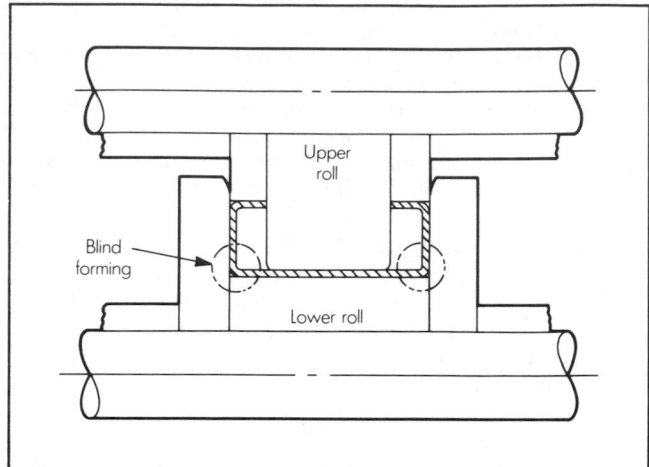

Fig 34-4 Blind corners cannot be controlled by direct contact of the rolls. (*Lockformer Co.*)

Part Length

Cutting the roll-formed cross section to length is accomplished using the precut or the post-cut method. To minimize post cutoff distortion, it is recommended that the shape be designed or roll formed in such a way as to facilitate cutoff. The shortest length for precut parts is twice the horizontal center distance between roll forming stations.

ADVANTAGES AND LIMITATIONS

Roll forming is a high-volume process of producing uniform, accurately dimensioned parts. Production speeds of approximately 50-600 fpm (15-185 m/min) are obtained, with 100-180 fpm (30-55 m/min) an average. Parts are produced with a minimum of handling, requiring only the loading of coils at the starting end of the machine and removal of finished parts at the exit end, generally accomplished by a minimum of operators. Roll forming can also be used for low-volume production because setup or changeover time from one cross section to another rarely takes more than a few hours, and length changes generally take only a few minutes on simple shapes. However, considerable time is required for more complex shapes.

The process is readily adaptable for combination with other operations and processes to form automatically a broad variety of metal parts. The initial cost of a roll forming line can be compared quite favorably with the cost of a standard stamping line or progressive die operation.

Maintenance costs are generally low. With proper roll design, the right tooling materials, good forming material, and proper lubricant, the form rolls can produce several million feet (900 000 m) of product before shape and tolerance problems develop. If through-hardened steel rolls are used, they can be recut or retrofitted, at a fraction of replacement cost, to produce for many more years.

The designing of rolls for complicated shapes must be done by experienced roll engineers. Complicated tubular or closed shapes sometimes require mandrels to form the shape properly, and delicate breakable parts require frequent replacement when high-production runs are made.

MATERIALS ROLL FORMED

Any material known today that can withstand bending to a desired radius can be roll formed. The material can be ferrous or nonferrous, cold rolled, hot rolled, polished, prepainted, or plated. Thicknesses of 0.005 to 3/4" (0.13 to 19 mm) and material widths of 1/8 to 72" (3 to 1830 mm) or more can be used in roll forming. Length of the finished part is limited only by the length that can be conveniently handled after it leaves the roll forming machine.

In some instances, multiple sections can be formed from a single strip or several strips can be fed simultaneously and combined to produce one composite section. The only absolute requirement for a material, whatever the type, coating, thickness, or width, is that it be capable of being formed at room temperature to the specified radii. Some materials, such as certain titanium alloys, have poor forming characteristics at room temperature. Therefore, the material must be heated and then formed on specially designed roll forming machines.

QUALITY AND ACCURACY

Two areas that can affect the quality and accuracy of a roll-formed section are springback and end flare.

Springback

Springback is a phenomenon that occurs when the material being formed has not been stressed beyond its elastic limit. This distortion becomes evident after the straining of the part has been discontinued. The amount of springback varies with different metal properties such as yield and elastic modulus. Springback can be compensated for in the tool design by overforming. Overforming forms the material past its expected final shape.

End Flare

End flare is the distortion that appears at the ends of a roll-formed part. The internal stresses incurred in roll forming are much more complex than in other types of bending. These stresses usually are higher in the edges of the material being formed and are released when the part is cut off. End flare can be minimized by using proper tool design. For example, extra roll passes, avoidance of prepunched edges at the cutoff zone, and more ductile materials help to reduce end flare.

ROLL FORMING APPLICATIONS

Roll forming as a metal fabricating process is used in many diverse industries to produce a variety of shapes and products. Figure 34-5 illustrates several complicated shapes that can be produced on a roll forming machine. Roll forming is also used for parts that were manufactured by extrusion processes. This is limited, however, to parts that can be redesigned to have a constant wall thickness. Some industries that use roll-formed products are the automotive, building, office furniture, home appliances and products, medical, rail car, aircraft, and heating ventilation and air conditioning (HVAC) industries.

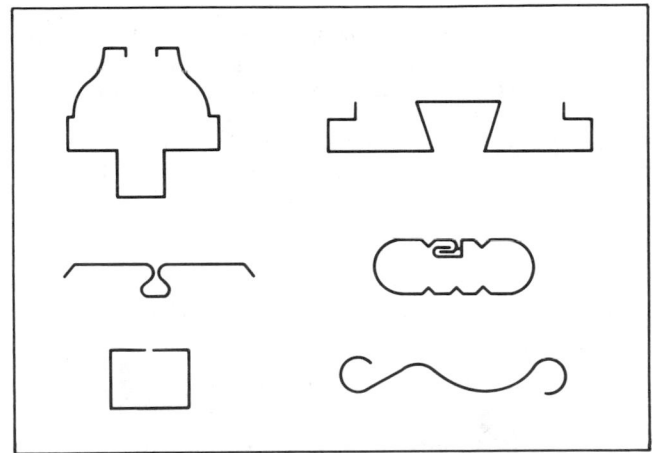

Fig 34-5 complicated profiles are attainable with roll forming.

ROLL FORMING MACHINES

The roll forming machine (roll former) most commonly used has a number of individual units, each of which is actually a dual-spindle roll forming machine, mounted on a suitable baseplate to make a multiple-unit machine (see Fig. 34-6). The flexibility of this construction permits the user to purchase enough units for immediate needs only. By purchasing additional length of baseplate on the machine, units can be added at any time for future needs. Some of these machines are provided with machined ends on the baseplates, making it possible to couple several machines together, in tandem, to provide additional units as required.

Adjusting screws, for making vertical adjustment of the top rolls, are designed with dials and scales to provide micrometer adjustment and a means of recording the position of the top shaft for each roll pass and each shape being formed. The shaft diameter of most machines is from 1-4" (25-90 mm).

SPINDLE SUPPORTED MACHINES

Roll forming machines can be classified according to the method by which the spindles are supported in the unit. Generally, two types exist: (1) inboard or over-hung spindle machines and (2) outboard machines.

Inboard Machines

Inboard-type machines have spindle shafts supported on one end which are 1 to 1 1/2" (25 to 38 mm) in diameter and up to 4" (100 mm) in length. They are used for forming light-gage moldings, weather strips, and other simple shapes. The material thickness is limited to about 0.040" (1.0 mm), and the top roll shaft is generally geared directly to the bottom shaft. This direct-mesh gearing permits only a small amount of roll redressing (no more than the thickness of the material being formed) on top and bottom rolls. Tooling changeover is faster on this machine than on the outboard type of machine.

Outboard Machines

Outboard machines have housings supporting both ends of the spindle shafts (see Fig. 34-7). The outboard housing is generally adjustable along the spindles, permitting shortening of the distance between the supports to accommodate small shapes of heavy gage material. This adjustment also permits the

ROLL FORMING MACHINES

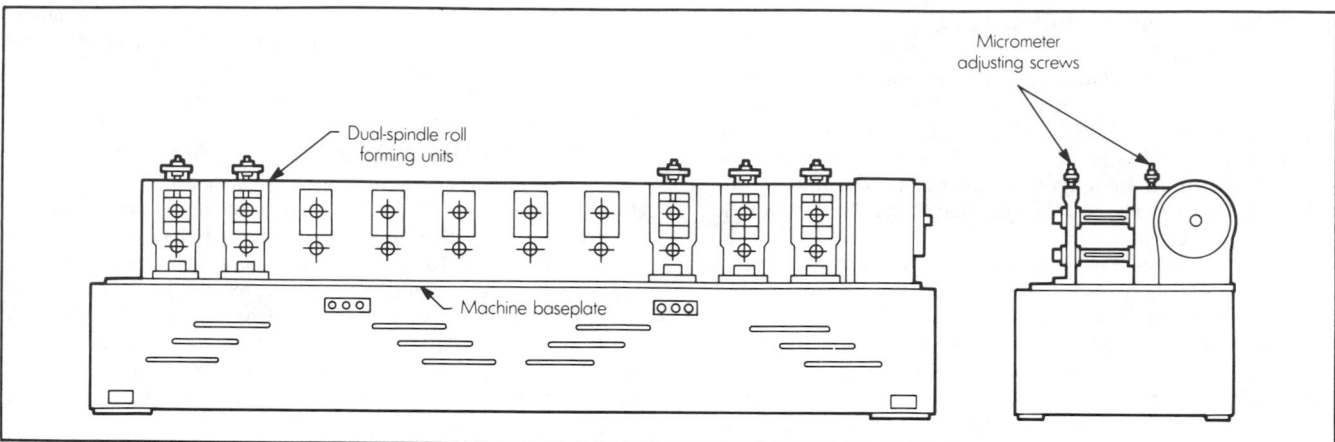

Fig 34-6 A roll former consists of several forming units mounted on a common baseplate. (*Lockformer Co.*)

machine to be used as an inboard type of machine when desired. Outboard machines can be readily designed to accommodate any width of material by making the spindle lengths to suit the material width and then mounting the individual units and spindles on a baseplate of suitable width. This type of machine is built with spindle sizes from 1 ½ to 4″ (38 to 100 mm) diam and width capacities up to 72″ (1830 mm).

STATION CONFIGURED MACHINES

As was previously mentioned, a typical roll forming machine consists of several individual roll forming units mounted on a common baseplate. The manner in which they are mounted determines to a great extent the type of shapes that are formed on the machine.

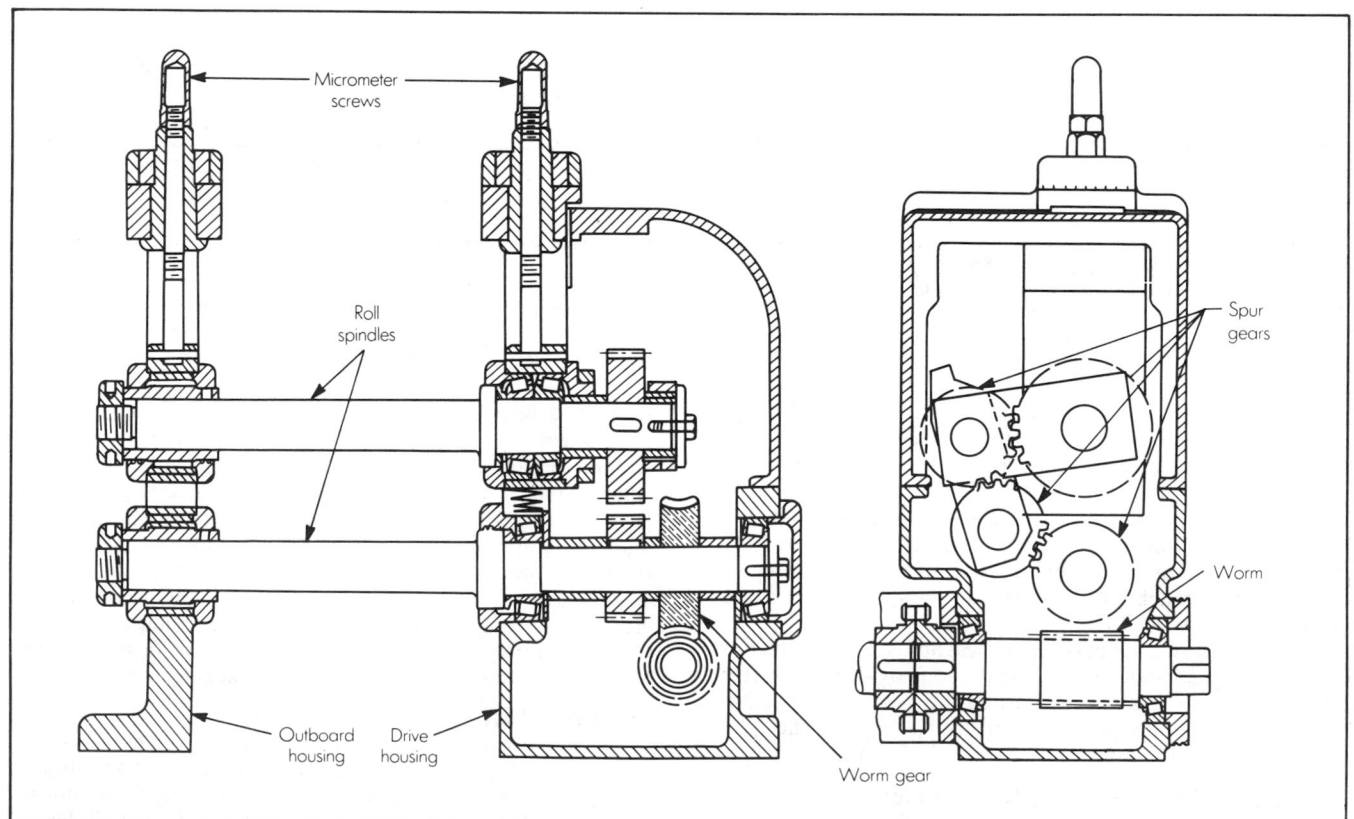

Fig 34-7 Cross section of an outboard roll stand with square gearing.

Single-Duty Machines

This type of machine is built and designed for a one-purpose profile or for one particular set of roll tooling and is not normally designed for convenient roll changing. The cost of this machine is low in comparison to the other styles and is generally used for long production runs.

Conventional or Standard Machines

This particular type of machine is more versatile than the single-duty machine because the outboard supports are easily removed. This permits the roll tooling to be interchanged with other profiles to make it more suitable for a variety of production requirements.

Side-by-Side Machine

This machine is designed for multiple profiled tooling and provides the flexibility of having more than one set of roll tooling mounted on the spindle shaft at the same time (see Fig. 34-8). Generally, this type of machine is limited to two sets of rolls at a given time, but there can be up to three or four sets of rolls when small profiles are being run in production. Changeover from one production profile to another is accomplished by shifting the machine bed to the desired profile. The main advantages of the side-by-side configuration are low initial investments, fast tooling change, and reduced floor space requirement. Roll wear, however, can create problems because one set cannot be reground without regrinding the others at the same time. Adjusting for material variations can also be a problem.

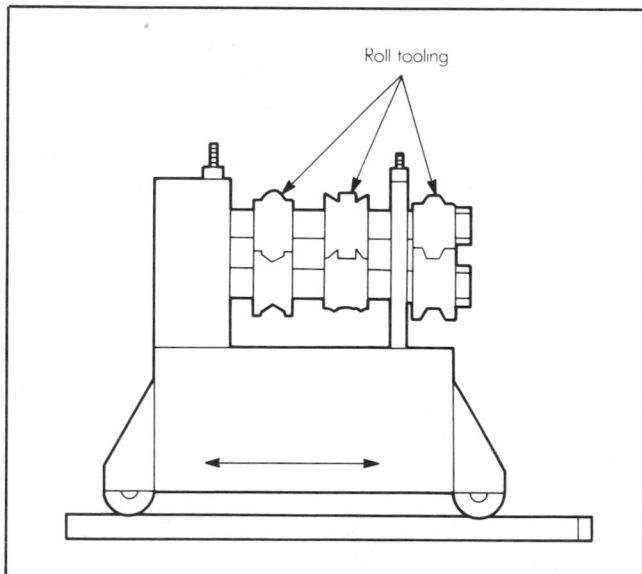

Fig 34-8 The side-by-side configuration permits roll forming of several different profiles on the same machine.

Double-High Machines

The double-high configuration consists of one set of roll tooling mounted on its own roll shafts and housings at one level on the bed frame, and a second complete set of roll tooling and housings mounted at a different level on the same common frame (see Fig. 34-9). This particular type of machine is used in the metal building industry for forming building panels up to 60" (1520 mm) wide.

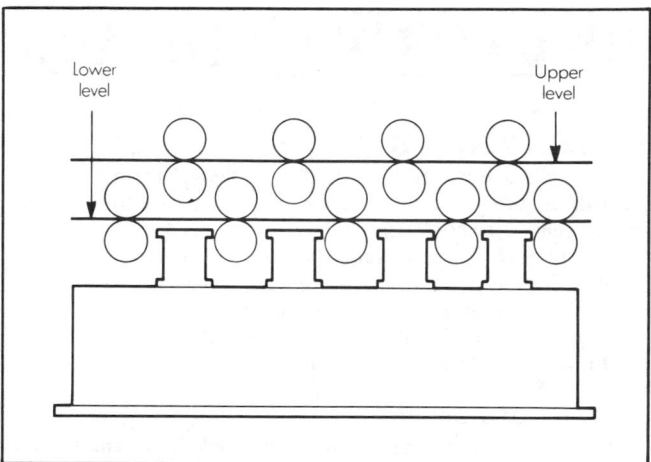

Fig 34-9 The double-high configuration consists of two independent sets of roll forming stations, one mounted above the other.

Rafted Machines

The rafted configuration resembles the single-duty and conventional configurations since each configuration has housings and spindle shafts with one particular set of roll tooling mounted on it. However, the rafted configuration has several roll forming units mounted on rafts or subplates that are removable from the roll former base (see Fig. 34-10). During tool changeover, the individual rafts are removed from the base and the replacement rafts with the roll forming units and tooling are installed. On a typical 16-stand roll forming machine there are four sets of rafts containing four forming units each.

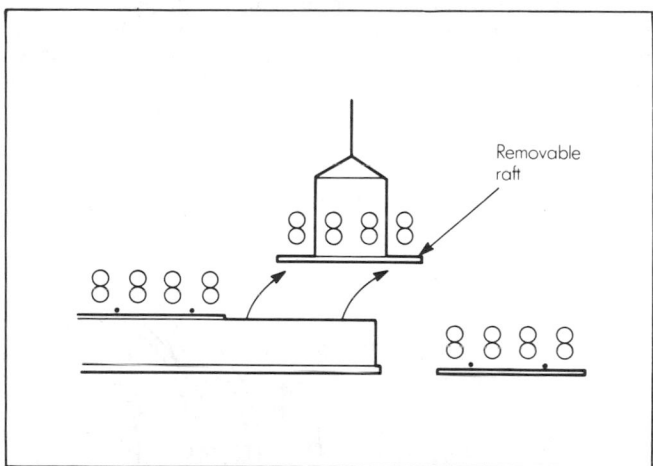

Fig 34-10 The rafted configuration permits quick roll tooling changeover and flexibility in tooling profile.

Double-Head Machine

This type of machine is designed and constructed with two separate sets of housings and roll shafts mounted so that they face one another. Each housing is mounted on an adjustable plate mechanism to allow the housing to be shifted for a change in overall width while at the same time maintaining the same profile for the edge formation.

ROLL FORMING TOOLING

ROLL FORMING TOOLING

FORMING ROLLS

The rolls are the tools that do the actual forming of the material as it moves through the roll forming machine. Several factors need to be considered when designing the rolls to form a particular part. These include the number of required passes, the material width, the flower design, the roll design parameters, and the roll material. "Flower" is the name given to the progressive section contours starting with the flat material and ending with the desired section profile.

Number of Passes

Roll forming material into a desired final shape is a progressive operation in which small amounts of forming are performed at each pass or pair of rolls. The amount of change of shape or contour in each pass must be restricted so that the required bends can be formed without elongating the material. Too few passes can cause distortion and loss of tolerances; too many passes increase the initial tooling cost.

Generally, the number of passes depends upon the properties of the material and the complexity of the shape. Other areas to consider are part width, horizontal center distance between the individual stations, and part tolerances. The number of passes must be increased as the tolerances of the shape become tighter.

Strip Width

The width of the flat material needed to produce the shape can be determined by making an enlarged layout of the part and dividing it into its component curved and straight sections. The bend allowance for the curved sections must be calculated. The width of material required for producing the shape is obtained by totaling the individual lengths of these sections. This width is theoretical only and usually must be modified slightly when the part is run.

Flower Design

The development of the flower is the initial step in the design of roll tooling. This is the station-by-station overlay of progressive section contours starting with the flat strip width before forming, and ending with the final desired section profile (see Fig. 34-11). The flower can also be obtained by starting with the finished profile and unfolding it into a flat strip. The intermediate profiles between flat material and finished profile are graduated at a rate that enables the section to be completed in the fewest number of stations or passes without compromising general roll forming parameters. The flower shows graphically the number of passes required to roll form the given profile.

The two prime considerations in designing the flower are (1) a smooth flow of material from first to last pass and (2) maximum control over fixed dimensions while roll forming. Getting the smoothest flow of material might be visualized by considering a roll of paper rolled out long enough to crimp the end of the roll into the shape of the desired cross section. By holding both the roll and cross section taut, the flow of material will be smooth and natural. If cross sections were taken at equally spaced intervals between beginning and end, a flower would be generated, perfect in flow, but lacking in dimensional control. Most corners formed in this manner would be air formed rather than positively formed by direct roll contact. The distance from flat material to finished profile is critical; forming too fast would be unnatural to the flat strip and would create problems in a number of ways. Forming usually starts near the center and works toward the edges. This avoids tearing which might occur if the edges were formed and acted as a lock against material flow toward the center.

The second consideration, dimensional control, would best be achieved by forming each corner to its completed angle with total or maximum roll contact before proceeding to form the

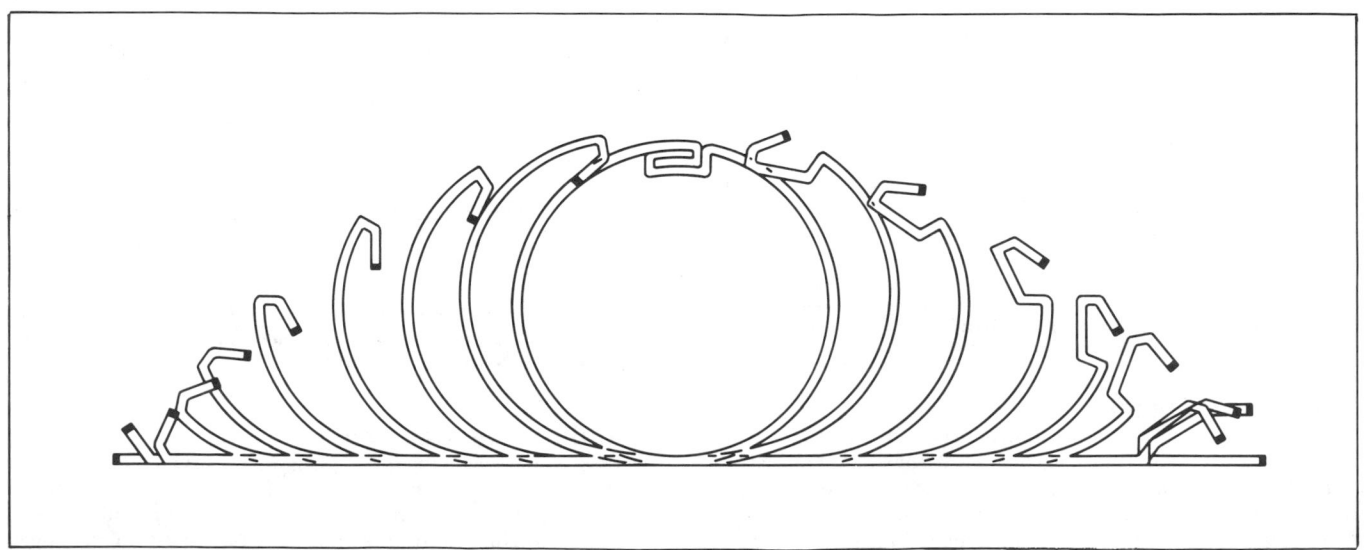

Fig 34-11 Flower development of a lock-seamed tube showing the progressive section contours starting with the flat strip and ending with the final section. (*Roll Design Service*)

---

next corner. The object being to eliminate air forming or blind corners. This approach would require more passes to complete the section, and the flower would show a jerky, step-to-step motion rather than a flowing motion. This deviation from a smooth flow in the flower shows itself as stress in the forming process and results in forming problems.

Computer Application

Computers are becoming an important aid in the design of roll forming tooling. Consistency, accuracy, and speed enable the designer to determine the optimum design for each roll pass in less time than is required when the calculations are performed by hand. The capability to display the profile of the part enables the designer to see how the material flows through each pass. This profile enables the designer to determine whether too much work is being performed at a particular pass.

The numerical information compiled by the computer can be employed to produce punched tapes used by numerically controlled machines. These tapes ensure that the rolls are accurately produced. The computer also aids in the setup of the rolls on the machine by specifying the size and locations of the required shims and spacers. All this information and data can be stored for future use and reproduced whenever necessary.

To design the rolls, information about the roll forming machine, the cross section of the final shape, and the initial forming sequence are entered in the computer program. The computer defines the coordinates of each corner numerically and displays the profile of the part at each pass and various perspectives of the flower diagram on the computer terminal. Input changes can be made to vary the material flow through the roll forming machine so that the optimum flow is achieved. Computer output includes flower diagrams, drawings of the cross-sectional shape (see Fig. 34-12), drawings of the rolls, and the tabular data defining the material and rolls. The computer can also produce the tapes used in the manufacturing of the rolls on numerically controlled machines.

FLYING CUTOFF DIES

Although there are many variations, generally only two basic types of flying cutoff dies are used. They are most commonly referred to as the slug-type die and the slugless-type die. The decision as to which type of die to use in each case is determined by the contour of the shape to be cut, the gage of the material to be cut, the maintenance involved when cutting certain materials, the line speed to be achieved, the available press stroke, the ability to match prepunched areas, and whether other operations must be performed in the cutoff die.

TUBE AND PIPE ROLLING

Tube mills produce welded tube and pipe in a range of sizes from 1/4 to 24" (6 to 600 mm) diam and with wall thicknesses from several thousandths of an inch to 3/4" (19 mm) thick. The mill generally consists of a machine for forming the strip of material into a tubular shape, a welder to weld the seam, a cooling unit, a sizing and straightening machine for cutting the tube to the required lengths. The tooling for a given size of tube for these mills consist of forming tools, welder tooling, weld-flash-removing devices, sizing rolls, and cutoff tooling.

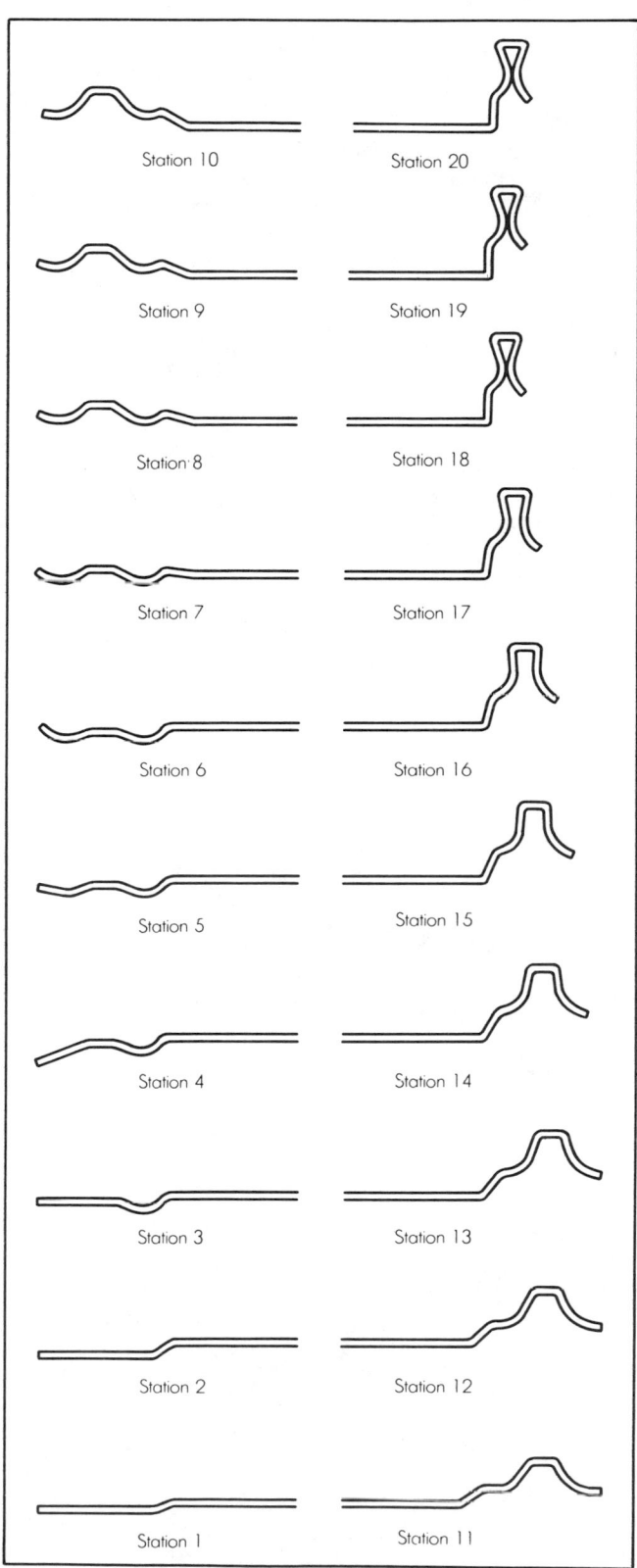

Fig 34-12 Using the computer for roll design provides the designer with drawings of the cross-sectional shape of the part at each station. This is the output for a part requiring 20 passes. (Only half of the cross section is shown here since the part is symmetrical.)

SPINNING

Spinning is a chipless production method of forming axially symmetrical metal shapes. It is a point deformation process by which a metal disc, cylindrical workpiece, or preform is plastically deformed into contact with a rotating chuck (mandrel) by axial or axial-radial motions of a tool or rollers. Shapes produced include cones, hemispheres, tubes, cylinders, and other radially symmetrical, hollow parts in a wide variety of sizes and contours.

TYPES OF METAL SPINNING

The spinning process can be classified into four basic types: manual (hand) spinning, power spinning, shear forming, and tube spinning, as illustrated in Fig. 35-1. These types can be further subdivided into other categories, some of which are discussed in this section.

MANUAL SPINNING

Manual spinning is one of the oldest known methods of metalforming. It is generally done on lathe-type machines with no mechanical assistance to increase the force. A large mechanical advantage is achieved, however, when using tools of scissor design. Normally, a circular disc of metal, called the blank, is clamped between a rotating mandrel (chuck) and a follower on the tailstock of the machine. Manual pressure is applied to a levered tool to progressively bend or flare the metal over the mandrel, practically always with multiple passes of the tool.

POWER SPINNING

Power spinning is commonly used to describe shear forming (discussed next in this section), but the two processes differ greatly. With both manual and power-assisted spinning, the starting blank diameters must be considerably larger than the diameters of the finished workpieces; there is no appreciable or intentional thinning of the material and less working of the metal during spinning than during shear forming. The blank size depends upon the surface area of the spun part. With shear forming, starting blank diameters are approximately the same as the diameter of the finished parts, and there is a controlled reduction in blank thickness.

SHEAR FORMING

Shear forming is a rotary-point extrusion process for spinning conical or hemispherical shapes. One axial-radial pass of the roller(s) produces a significant reduction in blank thickness. This produces high compressive shear stresses in the transverse (material thickness) direction, resulting in a thickness reduction that obeys the sine law equation (see Fig. 35-2).

The process is a variation of power spinning that is sometimes referred to as shear spinning, Hydrospinning, Flo-turning, flow turning, spin forging, compression spinning, Rotoforming, and rotary extrusion. Required shapes are spirally generated by the metal as it is progressively displaced axially between the rotating mandrels and the power-fed rolls. Metal required for forming is obtained from the blank or preform thickness, and starting diameters are approximately the same as those of the finished parts. The final shape can be conical, parabolic, hemispherical, or any other surface of revolution within reason.

TUBE SPINNING

Tube spinning is used to reduce the wall thickness and increase the length of tubes or preformed shapes (cast, roll formed and welded, forged, machined, pressed, or spun) without changing their inside diameters. Reductions in wall thicknesses of 90% and increases in length of 800% have been accomplished in this way without annealing between passes. This method follows a purely volumetric rule, and the sine law does not apply because there is no included angle. Limitations depend upon the amount of reduction the specific metal can withstand without the need for annealing; the percentage reduction necessary to make the metal flow, usually about 15-25%; and the force capacity of the machine.

In addition to reducing wall thicknesses and increasing lengths, with resultant improvements in strength due to plastic deformation, this process is often used to form shaped parts from tubing or preforms, such as parts with flanges at various locations. Varying wall thicknesses can also be produced by employing a tracing attachment on the machine or by using a CNC machine.

ELEVATED TEMPERATURE SPINNING

When the workpiece material, thickness, configuration, or size dictates, the starting blanks and/or mandrels are often heated to facilitate metal movement. Applications requiring multipass spinning at room temperature, with intermediate annealing between passes, can often be done in a single pass, or fewer passes, by raising the temperature of the blank or preform. Heating also decreases the force requirements of the machine used.

The application of heat for spinning increases the forming limits for most materials. Materials that generally require heating are those with low ductility at room temperature. These include titanium alloys, tungsten, beryllium, high-strength and temperature-resistant alloys, refractory metals, and most of the superalloys.

Overheating must be avoided. When shear forming is accomplished below the recrystallization temperature of the material, mechanical working occurs, with a substantial increase in the

TYPES OF METAL SPINNING

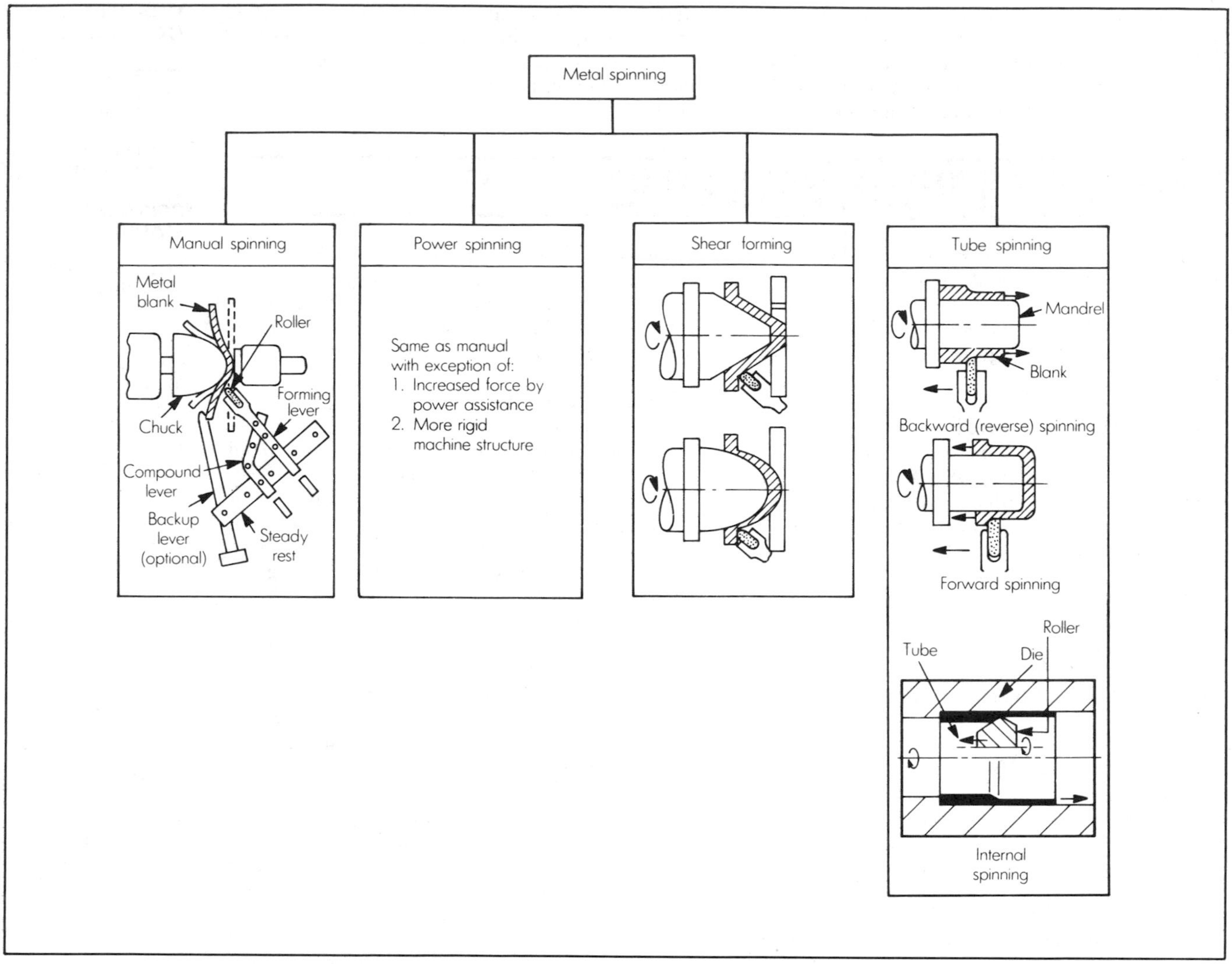

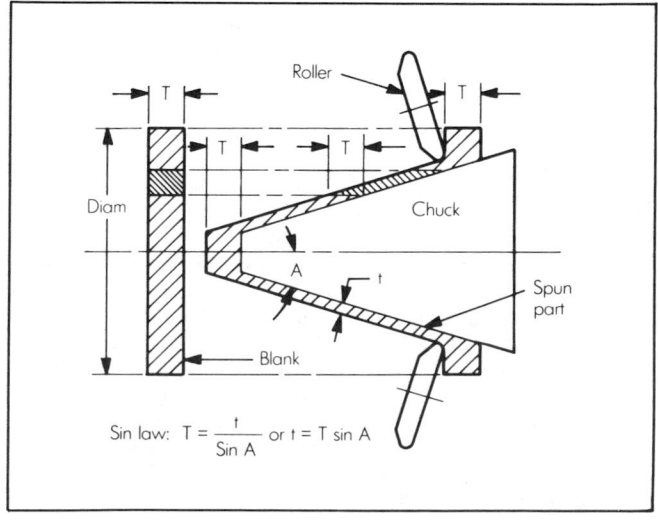

Fig. 35-1 Types of metal spinning processes.

mechanical properties of the spun part.

COMBINED AND SUPPLEMENTARY OPERATIONS

Other processes often used to produce preforms for spinning include casting, forging, and deep drawing. Operations sometimes performed in the same spinning setup include turning, facing, beading, crimping, flanging, trimming, and cutoff, thus eliminating the need to transfer workpieces to another machine. A multiposition, swiveling toolpost is mounted on the machine for such operations.

Necking-in (shrinking) operations are performed on the open ends of cylindrical preforms with a number of spinning passes, thus controlling shape and material thickness in the necked-in area. Hollow cylindrical parts are also expanded by having the roller apply force to the inside of the part.

Sin law: $T = \dfrac{t}{\text{Sin } A}$ or $t = T \sin A$

Fig. 35-2 Sine law relationship in shear forming straight-sided conical parts from flat blanks.

SPINNING CAPABILITIES

Properly applied, spinning has many advantages, but it also has some limitations. A wide variety of materials can be spun and shapes produced, and numerous successful applications exist.

PROCESS ADVANTAGES

Major advantages of spinning include lower production costs for many applications, reduced tooling costs, close tolerances and smooth finishes, and improved mechanical properties.

LIMITATIONS OF SPINNING

Manual or hand spinning is limited with respect to the workpiece material and thickness, and the size and shape of part that can be spun. Skilled operators are required. A common problem with manual spinning is wrinkling of the flanges, the amount of wrinkling depending upon the skill of the operator.

Power spinning and shear forming are also limited with respect to the shape and size of the parts produced, as well as the workpiece material and thickness, as discussed later in this section.

SHAPES PRODUCED

Spinning is employed to produce hollow parts in a wide variety of contours (see Fig. 35-3), including multidiameter shapes. While most parts that are spun are circular in cross section and radially symmetrical about their axes, it is possible to spin nonconcentric and elliptical parts with special tooling (discussed later in this chapter). Spun parts are sometimes cut apart and used in various assemblies.

Conical parts, which are generally difficult to draw in press operations, are the easiest and most economical parts to produce by spinning. The angle at which the metal meets the mandrel is small, allowing good control of the metal during spinning. Also, the metal is not subjected to severe strain.

Hemispherical shapes are more difficult to spin than cones, but are still ideally suited for the spinning process. Initial spinning is relatively easy because of the small angles between the metal and mandrel; however, as the angles become larger, spinning becomes more difficult.

Straight-sided cylinders with sharp corners are not as easily produced by metal spinning as cones or hemispheres. Spinning the sharp corner angles exposes the metal to high strain and requires more time and skill. In many cases, press-drawn cylindrical shapes are used as preforms for spinning. For some applications, lower production costs can be attained by using welded cylinders as the preforms for spinning operations.

Corner radii should be as generous as possible because sharp corners cause the metal to thin during spinning. Minimum recommended radii are about 1 1/2 times the metal thickness. Smaller radii or sharp corners generally require subsequent machining. Angles between the metal and the mandrel should be as small as possible, with a gradual transition from one angle

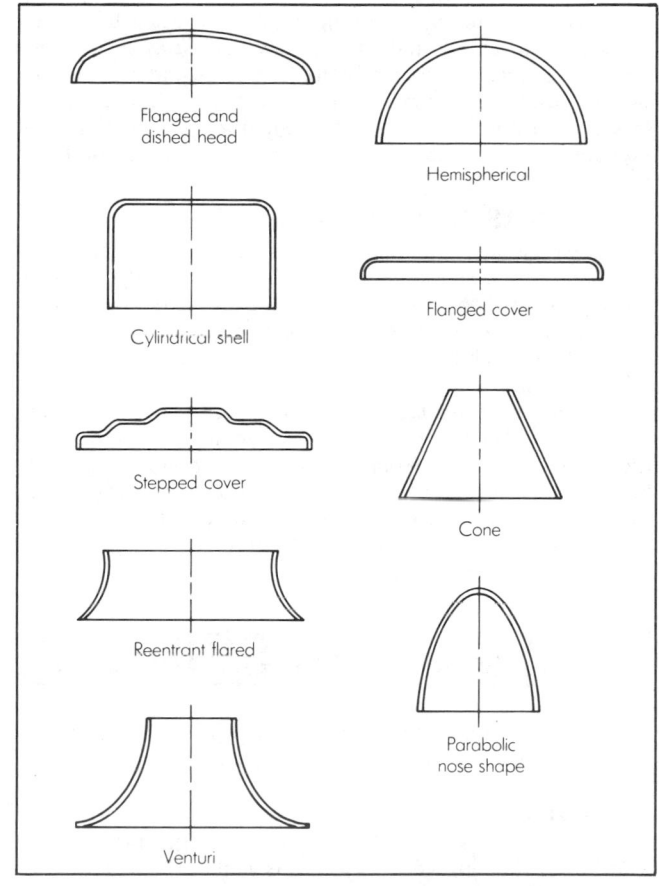

Fig. 35-3 Variety of basic metal shapes that can be spun. (*Metal Spinners, Inc.*)

to another. Workpieces with smooth flowing contours generally result in greater rigidity and lower spinning costs.

Reentrant shapes are more costly to spin because additional tooling is required, but they are difficult or impossible to produce by stamping. While outside beads and flanges can generally be formed on a single spinning mandrel, secondary operations and tools are needed to form inside beads or flanges.

APPLICATIONS OF SPINNING

Spun parts are used extensively by the automotive, appliance, air handling, aircraft and aerospace, machinery, ordnance, power generation, and petroleum industries. The wide variety of parts produced include tank heads, pressure vessels, air diffusers and deflectors, housings, cooking utensils, light fixtures, cylinders, holloware, milk cans, television picture tubes, cream-separator centrifuge discs, turbine engine components, nose cones, missile cases, and weapon components.

SPINNING MACHINES

Machines used for spinning are available in a wide variety of types and capacities. Major types include manual, powered,

and automatic machines. Standard spinning machines are available, but many are specifically designed to produce a

TOOLING FOR SPINNING

particular part or family of parts.

MANUAL SPINNING LATHES

Machines used for manual or hand spinning are similar to lathes and are often called spinning lathes, but they do not have leadscrews or compound slides. They consist essentially of a headstock and a tailstock mounted on a bed and are equipped with an adjustable toolrest. Some machines have handwheels or levers on a compound slide for longitudinal and transverse movements of the tools, eliminating the need to use hand-held tools.

POWER-ASSISTED MACHINES

Power-assisted spinning machines also resemble lathes, but are equipped with mechanical, hydraulic, or air-actuated slides. They have headstocks with power trains, tailstocks, and main slides that move the cross slides, which support the forming rollers. One machine has been built that can spin parts to 26 ft (7.9 m) diam.

Machines are available with horizontal or vertical-spindle structures and can be equipped with tracing systems to control the paths of the rollers. Some machines have hollow spindles for handling long tubes and pipes. The forming rollers are generally free wheeling (rotated by frictional contact with the workpiece); but on some machines, they are brought to operating speed by a hydraulic motor with a slip clutch.

Semiautomatic or fully automatic spinning, requiring even less operator skill than tracer control, is being used to attain higher production rates and to maintain closer tolerances. For semiautomatic operation, automatic positioning of the saddles, cross slides, and tailstocks during the cycle can be controlled by limit switches. Fully automatic spinning is attained by electrical sequential programming, NC, or CNC.

SHEAR FORMING MACHINES

Shear forming machines are available in horizontal and vertical models, with various capacities and one to three forming rollers. In many cases, shear forming machines are also suitable or adaptable for power-assisted spinning; and for some applications, power-assisted spinning and shear forming are combined in one continuous cycle. While these machines also resemble metalcutting lathes, they generally exert higher forces in both the longitudinal and transverse directions and provide higher feed rates.

Most shear forming machines are hydraulically operated and can be fitted with tracer control or CNC. They generally have variable speed drives and variable feed mechanisms. More sophisticated models incorporate electronic and hydraulic controls to integrate the spindle speed and roller feed rate, thus producing constant feed per revolution and constant surface speed for varying workpiece diameters.

TOOLING FOR SPINNING

Major tooling requirements for spinning are the chucks (mandrels) and the forming tools or rollers.

CHUCKS

Spinning chucks, or mandrels, determine the internal shape and size of the finished workpiece, as well as the surface finish produced in the bore of the part. These tools are often referred to as spinning forms, arbors, blocks, or patterns.

Makeup of the chuck is governed by the following factors:

1. Tolerance requirements on the part to be spun.
2. Quantity of parts to be spun.
3. Type of metal to be spun, which may require hot spinning.
4. Thickness of the metal.
5. Workpiece size.
6. Desired life for the chuck or mandrel.

Many spun items can be produced on a single chuck turned to the inside shape of the part, but it is frequently necessary for the sake of economy or metal-thickness control to spin through several progressions or breakdown operations similar to those of deep drawing (see Fig. 35-4). Fewer operations are generally required when spinning thinner materials. Reentrant shapes can generally be made on segmented or split chucks, such as that illustrated in Fig. 35-5, or on internal rollers, as shown in Fig. 35-6, when the part has a smaller open-end diameter than its largest diameter. There are other methods to achieve this forming that are not so commonly used, such as spinning over semihard rubber balloons; over a low-melting-temperature bismuth alloy chuck; or when making just one piece, over wood which is then chipped or burned out.

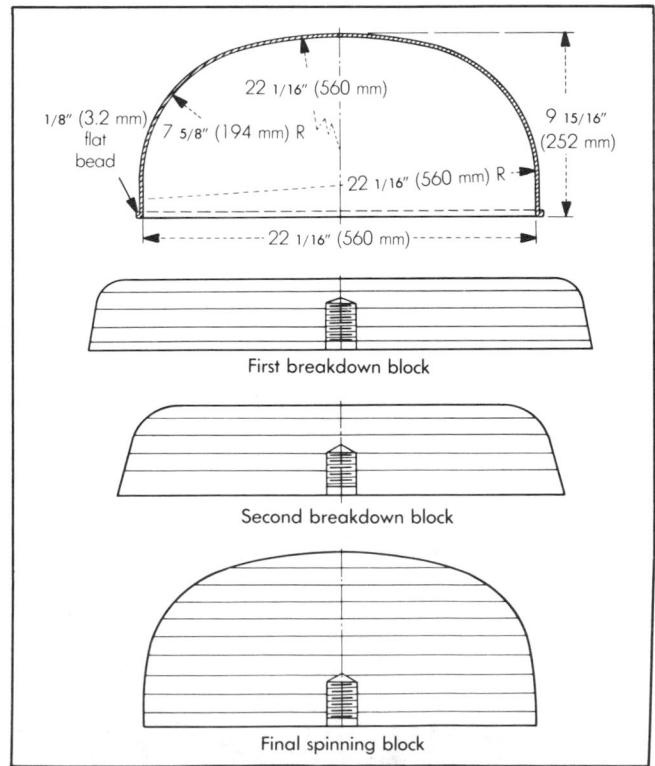

First breakdown block

Second breakdown block

Final spinning block

Fig. 35-4 Progressive chucks or breakdown blocks for producing the spun part shown in the top view. Fewer operations can generally be employed for thinner materials.

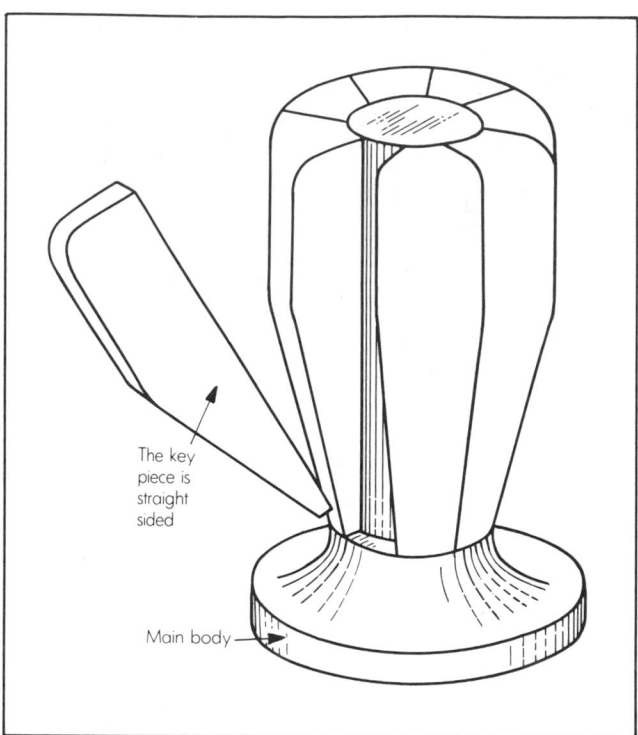

Fig. 35-5 Collapsible sectional chuck used for spinning a vase or pitcher. After part is formed, the split tool ring is removed, starting with the key piece having parallel sides.

ROLLERS FOR SHEAR FORMING AND TUBE SPINNING

Most shear forming machines are equipped with two rollers, sometimes called tool rings, but some machines have three or more rollers. With multiple rollers, they can be set opposite

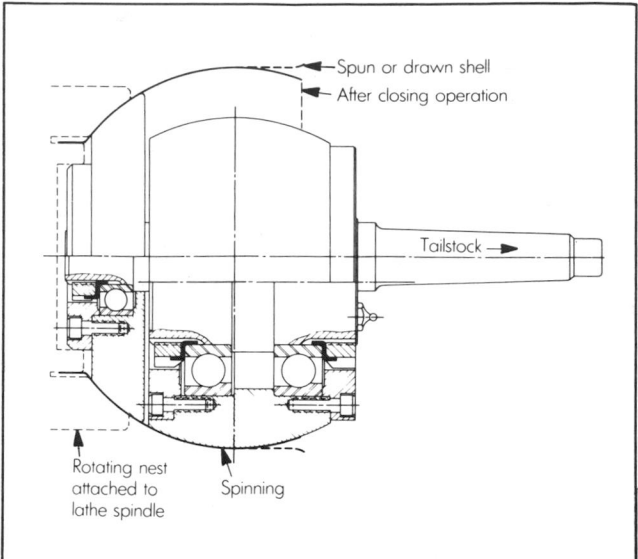

Fig. 35-6 Off-center chuck for spinning reentrant shapes. (*Spincraft*)

each other or offset from each other. The rollers are interchangeable to handle various applications.

On machines with two rollers, stepped cones and compound conical parts having two or more progressively smaller included angles can be shear formed in several passes, using one or both rollers to form each conical wall on stepped or separate mandrels. Alternatively, one roller is set to spin the first cone and, in the same setup, the second roller is used to spin the second cone. This method, however, requires a stepped mandrel. With a third method, one or both rollers are tracer controlled to traverse the entire length of the part, using a stepped mandrel. For thicker materials, however, problems may be encountered in using the same rollers to form different included angles.

BENDING AND STRAIGHTENING

Bending is a method of producing shapes by stressing metal beyond its yield strength, but not past its ultimate tensile strength. The forces applied during bending are in opposite directions, just as in the cutting of sheet metal. Bending forces, however, are spread farther apart, resulting in plastic distortion of metal without failure.

This chapter covers processes, equipment, and operations for sheet and plate metal, tube, pipe, and rod bending.

The general term *straightening* is applicable to the straightening of metal stock prior to processing and also to the straightening of workpieces and manufactured parts. Information in this chapter deals with applications, equipment, and operations for the various straightening methods.

SHEET AND PLATE BENDING

The bending process appears to be simple; yet, in reality, it is a rather complex process involving a number of technical factors. Included are characteristics of the workpiece material, the material flow and reactions during various stages of deformation, the effect of tooling design on force required to form the bend, and the type of equipment used.

The principal kinds of equipment used to bend sheet metal and plate can be grouped in the following categories:

- Mechanical press brakes—elongated presses with numerous tooling options. Work is performed by means of energy released from a motor-driven flywheel. These machines normally have a 3″ or 4″ stroke length.
- Hydraulic press brakes—stretched C-frame presses that are likewise compatible with a wide range and diversity of tooling. High-pressure oil in hydraulic cylinders supplies the force, which is directed downward in most models. The stroking length usually exceeds 6″.
- Hydraulic-mechanical press brakes—presses with drives that combine hydraulic and mechanical principles. In operation, oil forces a piston to move arms that push the ram toward the bed.
- Pneumatic press brakes—low-tonnage bending machines that are available with suitable tooling options.
- Bending brakes—powered or manual brakes commonly used for bending light-gage sheet metal.
- Special equipment—custom-built benders and panel formers designed for specific forming applications.

TYPES OF BENDING

The basic types of bending applicable to sheet metal forming are straight bending, flange bending, and contour bending. Examples of these three types of bending are shown in Fig. 36-1.

Straight Bending

The terminology for a straight bend is shown in Fig. 36-2. During the forming of a straight bend, the inner grains are compressed and the outer grains are elongated in the bend zone. Tensile strain builds up in the outer grains and increases with the decreasing bend radius. Therefore, the minimum bend radius is an important quantity in straight bending since it determines the limit of bending beyond which splitting occurs.

A second factor to be considered in straight bending is springback. As the forming pressure is released from the part, the part tends to regain its original shape through elastic recovery. Normally, in room-temperature forming the metal is overformed to allow for springback; that is, it is formed to a smaller bend angle. The amount of overform is found through experimentation and may vary between heat applications for a given sheet metal because of slight variation in mechanical and physical properties. A second method for springback control is to maintain a low residual-stress level in the formed part. Springback is a function of the residual-stress level in the formed part, and the application of heat during bending tends to reduce residual stress.

Flange Bending

Flange bend forming consists of forming shrink and stretch flanges as illustrated by views *d* and *e* in Fig. 36-1.

Parts requiring very little handwork are produced if the flange height and free-form-radius requirements are not severe. However, forming metals with low modulus of elasticity to yield strength ratios, such as magnesium and titanium, may result in undesirable buckling and springback.

Contour Bending

Contour bending is illustrated by the single-contoured part in Fig. 36-1, *f*, and the reverse-contoured part in Fig. 36-1, *g*. Single-contour bending is performed on a 3-roll bender, or by using special feeding devices with a conventional press brake. Higher production rates are attained using a three-roll bending machine, as described later in this chapter. Contour radii are generally quite large; forming limits are not a factor. However, springback is a factor because of the residual-stress buildup in the part; therefore, overforming is necessary to produce a part within tolerance.

BENDING WITH PRESS BRAKES

Press brake bending is a process by which a piece of metal is placed between upper and lower

SHEET AND PLATE BENDING

dies and formed through the force and pressure exerted by lowering the ram. The press brake is a specialized type of press consisting of a long, narrow ram and bed. Almost any type of straight bend can be produced using a press brake. This versatility has led to wide use of press brake bending in the metal fabricating industry. The press brake can be used for prototype and short-run custom work, as well as for more lengthy production runs.

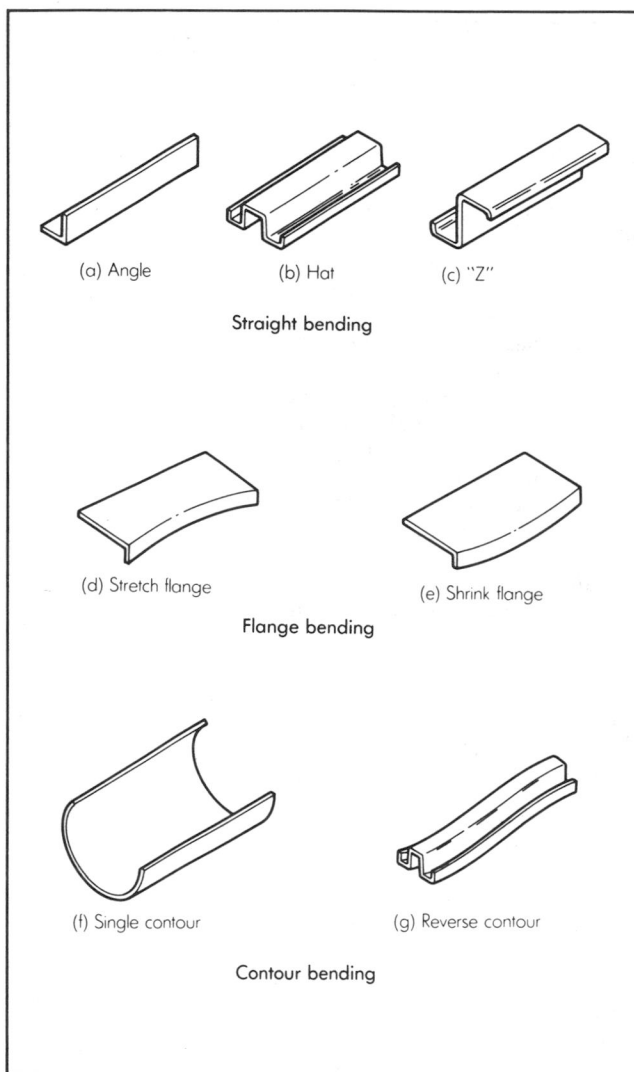

Fig. 36-1 Types of bend forming.

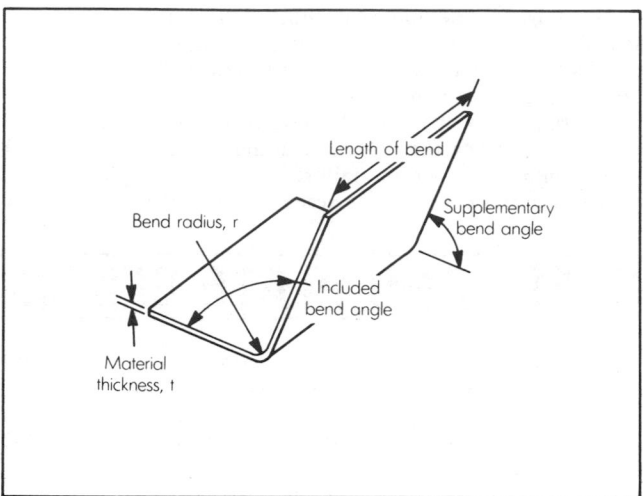

Fig. 36-2 Terminology for a straight bend.

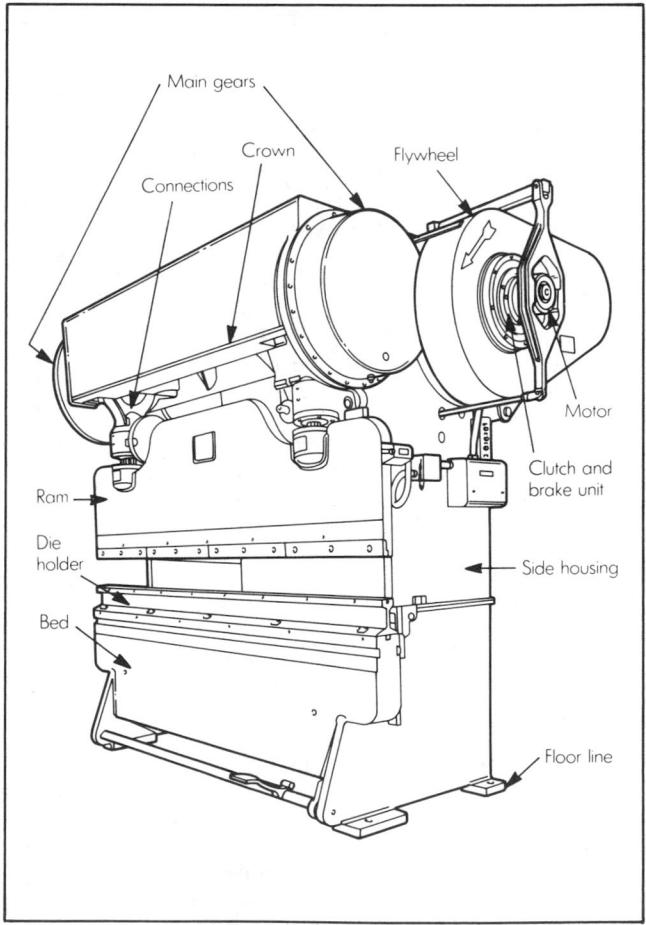

Fig. 36-3 Typical mechanical press brake. (*Verson Allsteel Press Co.*)

Basic Construction

As shown in Fig. 36-3, a press brake is a rather simple machine tool consisting of the following basic components or subsystems: housings, bed, ram, and a drive that activates the ram.

The housings are the side frames and serve as basic supports for the bed (and the lower die), as well as for ram guides and ram drive mechanisms. Housings also serve as mounting surfaces for control system elements and for gaging systems. Steel weldments are generally used for various press brake components that are assembled by bolting or welding them together.

Types of Press Brakes

Generally, press brakes can be divided into two categories—mechanical and hydraulic—depending on the type of ram drive that is used. An additional category (or sub-group) is the hybrid type, which incorporates both hydraulic and mechanical design elements for ram actuation. Schematic drawings of the three types of press brakes are shown in Fig. 36-4.

PRESS BRAKE DIES

In addition to bending, other types of work, such as punching, countersinking, dimpling, and embossing, can be done on press brakes. Press brakes can perform virtually any forming job that can be accomplished with a relatively short stroke of the ram under power. However, although the press brake is a highly versatile machine, bending dies comprise the bulk of press brake tooling. These dies are the focus of information presented in the following section.

V-Type Dies

The most extensive family of punches and dies for bending are the V-type dies. In every case, the lower dies are available with different die openings to accommodate various material thicknesses. Dies for air bending have included angles of 85°, while dies for bottom bending normally have 90° angles. V-type tooling can be ordered with various material capacities and with acute-angle dies that permit forming angles as small as 30°.

Rotary Bending

The rotary bending design eliminates the need for any type of hold-down pad or device. It provides its own inherent holding action at the same time the bending operation is proceeding.

The rotary bender is comprised of three components: the saddle (punch), the adjustable rocker, and the die anvil. The rocker is cylindrical in shape with an 88° V-notch cut out along the length. The edges of the rocker jaws are flatted and radiused to minimize marking. Three stages of a rotary bender operation are illustrated in Fig. 36-5. In view *a*, the material is clamped and the rocker rotation has begun; view *b* shows that humping is controlled and limited to space between edges of the rocker; and view *c* shows how the rocker clamps the workpiece in position and overbends it sufficiently to allow for springback.

The primary application for rotary benders is in progressive dies. Z-bends and short leg bends can be made in a single operation; and where needed, dart stiffeners can be rolled into the workpiece at the same time it is being bent.[1]

Diversity of Tooling

As stated previously, the press brake is a highly versatile machine, capable of performing a variety of operations, including a considerable range and diversity of bending jobs. The demarcation between a pure bending operation and a pure forming operation is not clear cut; hence, a stamping operation sometimes classified as either bending or forming may include both. Since bending and flanging basically produce straight-line shapes, most of the tools do not require contouring and can be produced by shaping, milling, and planing. Representative sets of commonly used tooling are illustrated in Fig. 36-6.

Plastic Tooling[2]

Urethanes and other plastic materials are used for tooling that embodies deformable dies. A key characteristic is the inherent property of changing shape while retaining a constant volume. When used as a female die, the urethane material forces the work material around the tip of the punch to conform to the

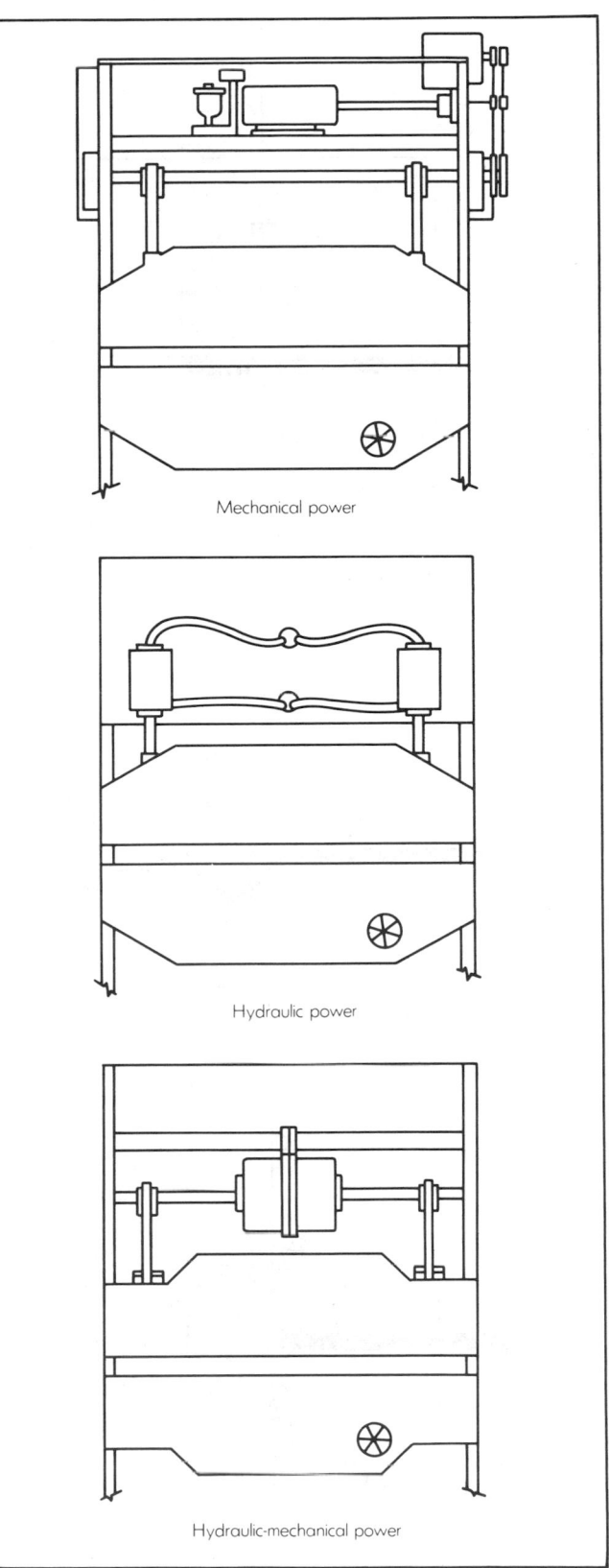

Mechanical power

Hydraulic power

Hydraulic-mechanical power

Fig. 36-4 Press brake ram drive methods. (*Di-Acro Div., Houdaille Industries, Inc.*)

SHEET AND PLATE BENDING

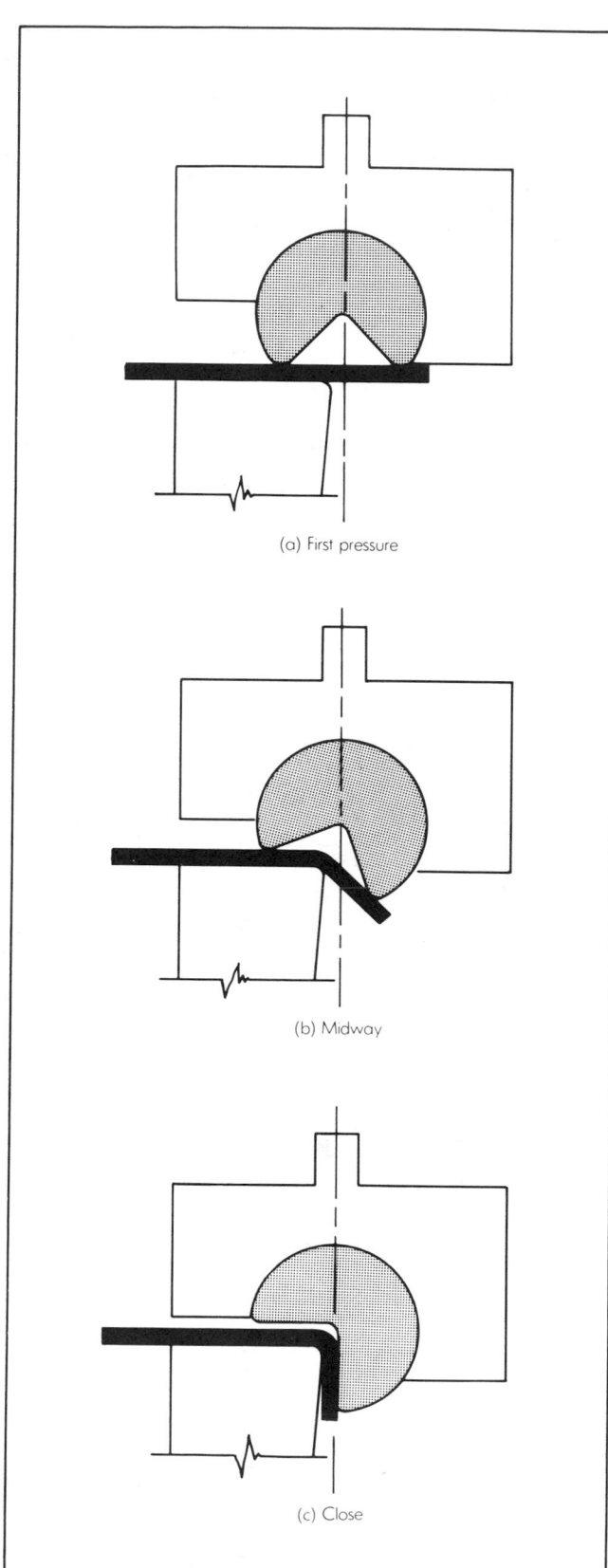

Fig. 36-5 Sequence of operations for press brake rotary bending.

(a) First pressure

(b) Midway

(c) Close

punch contour as illustrated in Fig. 36-7.

ROLL BENDING

Rolling or curving metal into cylinders or cylindrical segments is carried out on machines which use two or more rolls that rotate and bend the metal as it passes between them. Flattened cylinders and elliptical cylinders can also be formed. One type of machine using three rolls, as well as a special version of a two-roll machine, can be employed to form truncated cones. These shapes find application as hoppers, bins, vertical storage tanks, appliance parts, and ordnance parts.

Any metal that can be conventionally formed can also be formed by these machines. Thicknesses of metals commonly used range from 16-gage (0.061"; 1.56 mm) to 10" (254 mm) plate, although many parts are thicker or thinner. Maximum thickness that can be curved depends upon the type, size, and power of machine. Minimum thickness usually is determined by the ability of the metal to be curved without damage.

Cylinder rolling machines for sheet metal are made in a wide variety of models and sizes; however, they can be classified according to the number of rolls. The three-roll machines can be further classified into pyramid or pinch types.

Three-Roll Machines

Conventional pinch-type, three-roll machines have rolls arranged as shown in Fig. 36-8. All three rolls are power driven on most models. The top roll on this type of machine is fixed, while the lower roll can be adjusted vertically for blank thickness. The rear roll can be adjusted angularly for the diameter of the cylinder to be formed.

Pyramid-type, three-roll machines (Fig. 36-9) have the top roll mounted between the two bottom rolls. The bottom rolls, which in larger models are supported by two smaller rolls, usually cannot be adjusted. The top roll is adjustable vertically to control the diameter of the cylinder to be formed. The two bottom rolls are gear driven, while the top roll rotates through contact with the blank.

Two-Roll Machines

The two-roll machine, as shown in Fig. 36-8, has a steel roll located directly above a urethane roll. The top roll is fixed, while the lower roll can be adjusted vertically for metal and slip-on-tube thicknesses. The lower roll is driven, while the top roll rotates through contact with the blank.

In operation, the rolls are set so that the top roll penetrates the lower urethane roll. Bending is accomplished under very high pressure, the urethane roll literally wrapping the blank around the top roll. The diameter of the workpiece is governed by the diameter of the top roll, the inner diameter of the part being equal to the outer diameter of the top roll plus springback of the metal.

PLATE BENDING

A variety of machines are used for bending metal plate in thicknesses from 1/4 to 10" (6.4 to 250 mm) or more. Included among machines for plate bending and curving are press brakes; initial (single)-pinch, pinch-pyramid, and pyramid,

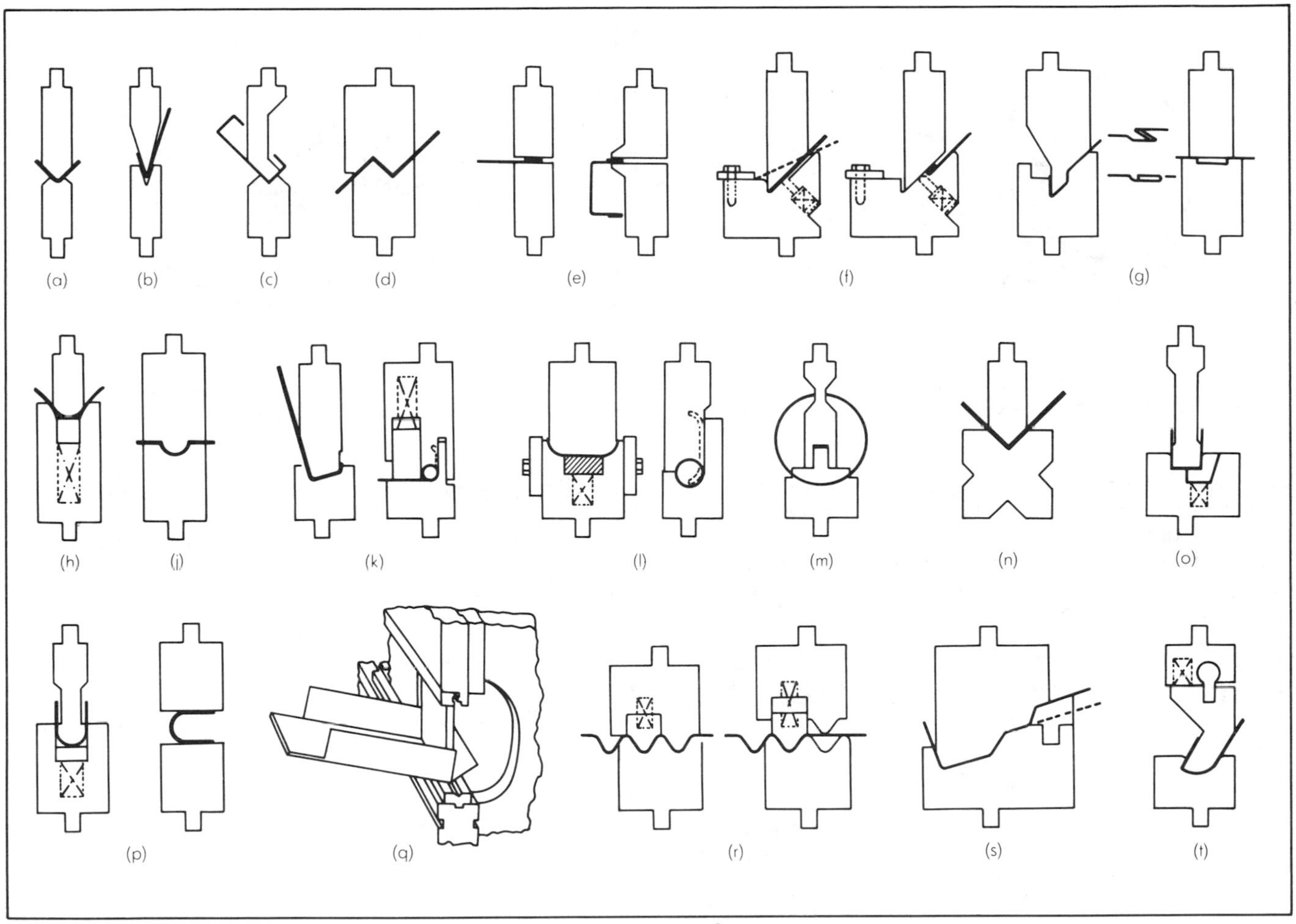

Fig. 36-6 Typical press brake bending and forming dies. (*Cincinnati Incorporated***)**

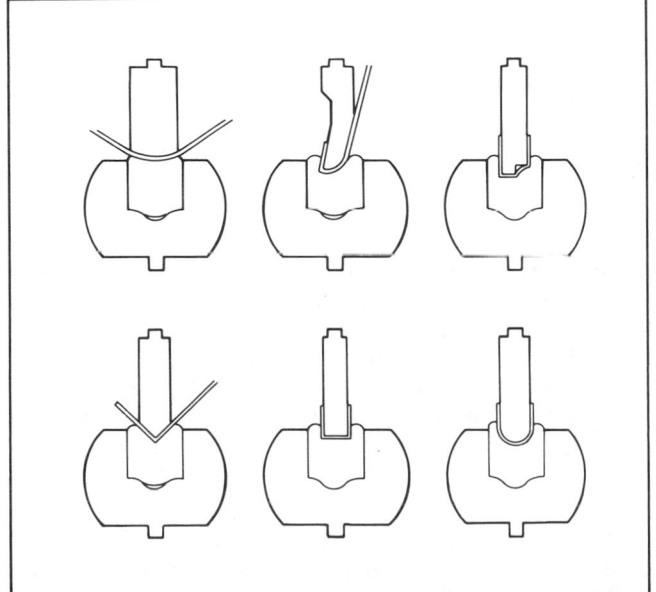

Fig. 36-7 Urethane pads are used as dies in some power press brake operations. (*Di-Acro Div., Houdaille Industries, Inc.***)**

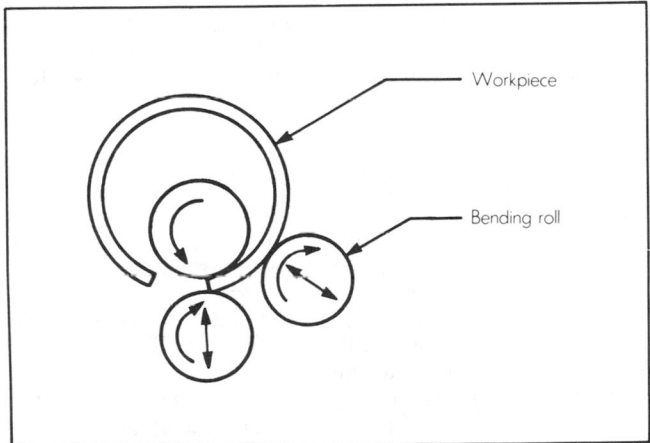

Fig. 36-8 Roll arrangement for a three-roll, pinch-type roll bending machine.

three-roll benders; double-pinch, four-roll machines; and vertical (roll) presses that bend heavy plate up to 10" (250 mm) thick. Most machines that roll thick plate material have a slip clutch to compensate for the separate inside diameter (ID) and outside diameter (OD) dimensions of the material being rolled.

TUBE, PIPE, AND BAR BENDING

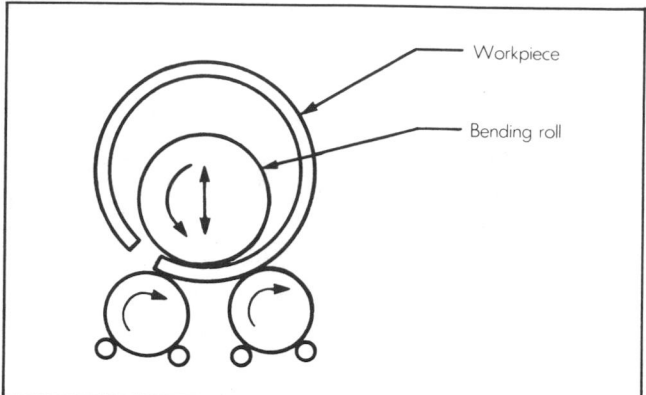

Fig. 36-9 Roll arrangement for a three-roll, pyramid-type roll bending machine.

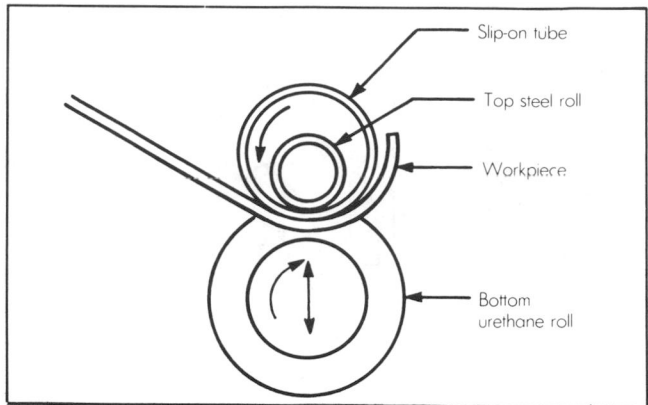

Fig. 36-10 Roll arrangement for a two-roll bending machine.

Sheet metal machines for bending stock of up to 1/4" (6.4 mm) thick are usually of lighter construction and are less complex than plate bending machines. Rolls can be made of bar stock, without crowning, and the ID/OD speed variation is less significant. Plate bending machines, on the other hand, normally include a higher degree of sophistication, because the com- pression and stretch factors, torque requirements, speed varia- tions, and metal thicknesses vastly increase the number of variables involved in the bending operation. Sheets that are more than 10' (3 m) wide also require a sophisticated machine, because of the potential deflection that is inherent in long bending machines.

TUBE, PIPE, AND BAR BENDING

The latest techniques and machines permit bending almost any ductile material ranging from small-diameter tubing to thin-wall, large-diameter tubing, and from large-diameter pipe to massive, structural iron beams. The ductile materials cover a wide range of ferrous and nonferrous metals, including carbon steel, stainless steel, aluminum, copper, and titanium.

The current state-of-the-art offers a greatly expanded range in using the strength-weight advantages of the tubular section in various engineering applications. In bending tubular sections, the radius and angular degree of bend can be precisely controlled and outer wall thickness can be reduced uniformly without collapsing. Repetitive accuracy is excellent, and close dimensional tolerances can be maintained.

BENDING THEORY AND PROCESS

Practically all methods of pipe and tube bending are based on the theory of applying a bending force great enough to stress the material beyond its elastic limit, but not so great as to cause stresses exceeding the materials ultimate strength, to the point at which the structure would fail and rupture.

As illustrated in Fig. 36-11, under the influence of an applied force, the material is made to flow, resulting in plastic deformation that thins the outside and thickens the inside wall of the bend throughout its length. This thinning, and hence the decrease in strength of the outer wall, together with a cor- responding thickening and strength increase in the inner wall, causes a shift of the tube's neutral axis. The neutral axis, which originally was located in the center of the tube, shifts toward the compression side, resulting in a relatively larger displacement of metal in the outer portion of the bend.

Whenever the likelihood exists that this metal flow would weaken the outer wall or flatten the bend excessively (especially in the case of thin-wall tubes), the metal flow must be held within well-defined limits.

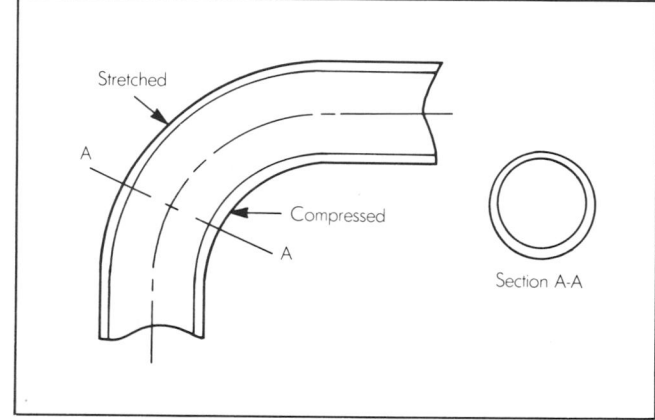

Fig. 36-11 Stretching and compression and ovality in bent tube. (*H & H Tool Division, Teledyne Pines*)

TUBE AND BAR BENDING

Regardless of the method used, most tube-bending processes involve the same principle and use similar fundamental tools, although hand-operated, manual benders and the powered bending machines on the market vary widely in appearance, construction, output capability, and field of application.

In bending, the material is stressed beyond its yield strength, but below its ultimate strength. This is done by holding (clamping) the part with tooling while applying a force sufficient to surpass the yield strength of the material. If the applied force is below the proportional elastic limit of the material, the material returns to its original shape when the force is relaxed.

When the applied force exceeds the yield strength, however, stretching of the material under tension is suddenly increased along the outside radius of the workpiece and the material is compressed along the inside radius. Under these conditions, the material enters the plastic range and the part is permanently formed to the desired shape. The boundary line between tensile and compressive stresses is known as the neutral axis (see Fig. 36-12).

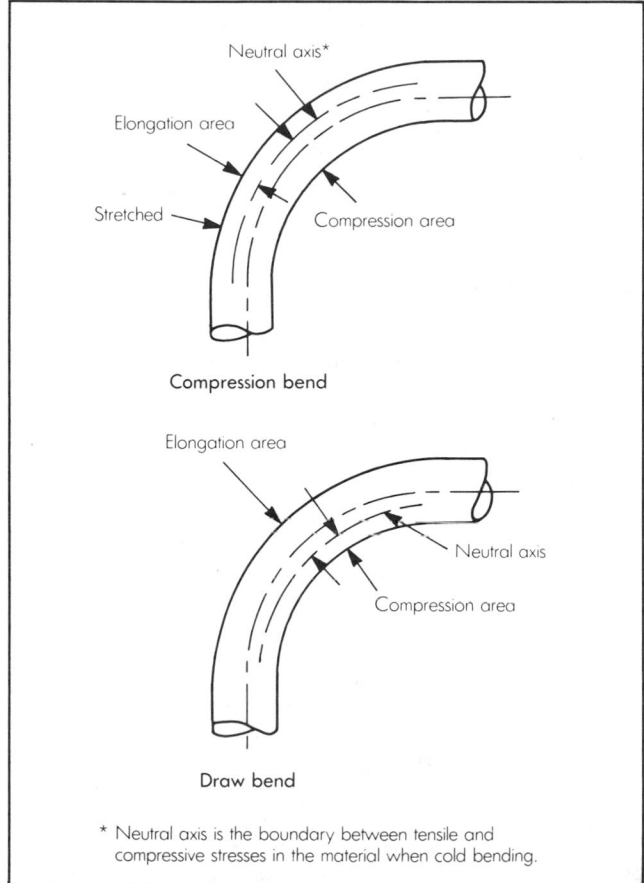

Fig. 36-12 Characteristic neutral-axis shift for tube compression and draw bending.

The tendency of a part to return to its original shape, even after the material is formed in its plastic range, is known as springback. This can be overcome by slight overbending, accompanied, in some instances, by bending to a smaller radius.

BENDING METHODS

Several different methods are commonly used for bending tube, pipe, and extruded metal shapes. Key factors in making a bending operation economically productive are the method, tooling, and bending technique used. The operator is, of course, a factor, but the equipment should minimize the degree of skill or artisanship required. The various methods of bending embodied in manual benders, powered bending machines, and automatic bending machines can be divided basically into draw, compression, roll, and stretch bending.

Draw Bending

The method generally considered to be the most versatile and accurate for bending tubing is draw bending, illustrated schematically in Fig. 36-13. With the workpiece clamped against the bending die and locked in position, the die and

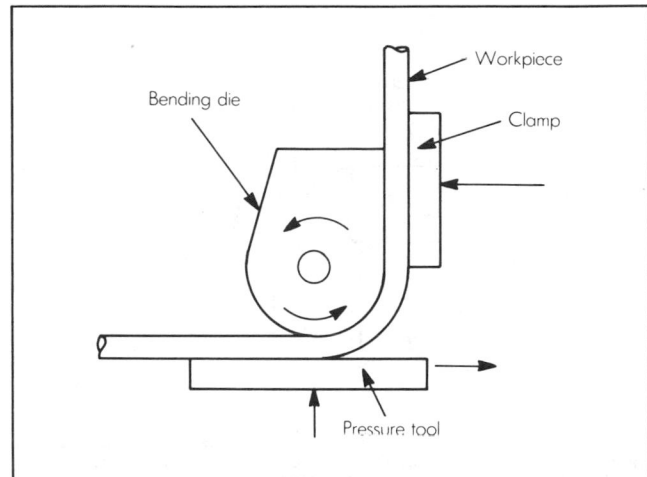

Fig. 36-13 In draw bending, the bending form and clamp rotate to pull the workpiece and the pressure die. This method is accurate and versatile.

clamp are rotated, moving the workpiece through a pressure tool. The pressure tool can be a roller, sliding shoe, or static shoe. The mandrel remains stationary, and the tube is drawn over the mandrel during the bending operation; hence, the term *draw bending* is used.

Draw bending is the most suitable method for tight radius bending or any bending that requires a mandrel or mandrel-and-wiper-die combination. Main applications for this method are the bending of pipe, thin-wall tubing, and extrusions. The basic limitation of draw bending is that the workpiece must have a straight length to permit it to be clamped to the bending form. The straight length keeps the material from slipping as it is drawn against the force applied by the pressure tool.

Compression Bending

The compression-bending method is used primarily to bend pipe, tube, rod, bar, and various other extruded shapes. As shown in Fig. 36-14, the workpiece is clamped to a stationary bending form and wrapped around it. A variety of pressure tools can be used—a static wiper shoe, a follower block, or a roller. This method works well for applications in which little clamping distance is available between bends.

Compression bending requires much less clamping area than draw bending, because the pressure tool forces the material to flow and become wrapped around the bending form. This method is capable of producing bends in various planes with practically no straight sections between the bends. Since the flow of metal in compression bending is not controlled as well as it is in draw bending, however, some distortion should be expected when bending tubing. Mandrels cannot be used in compression bending, because they would have to move with the workpieces as they are wrapped around the bending form.

Press Bending

An extension of compression bending, known as press, or ram, bending (see Fig. 36-15), is a means of obtaining two simultaneous compression bends. Each of the two bends is equal to one-half of the total desired included angle. In press bending, the bending form is mounted on the ram of a press and two wiping or pressure shoes pivot to wipe the material around

TUBE, PIPE AND BAR BENDING

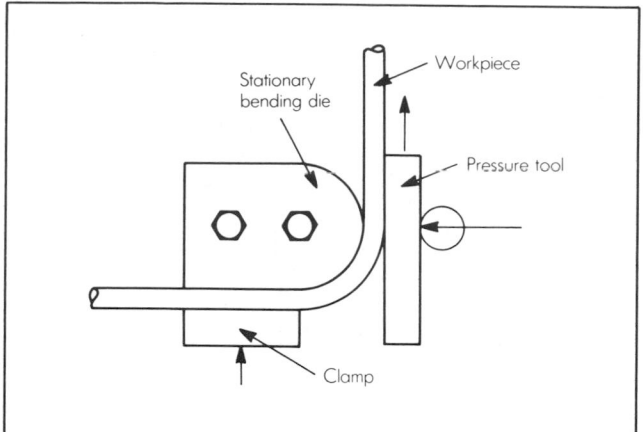

Fig. 36-14 In compression bending, the bending form is stationary. This technique works well when little clamping distance is available between bends on the workpiece.

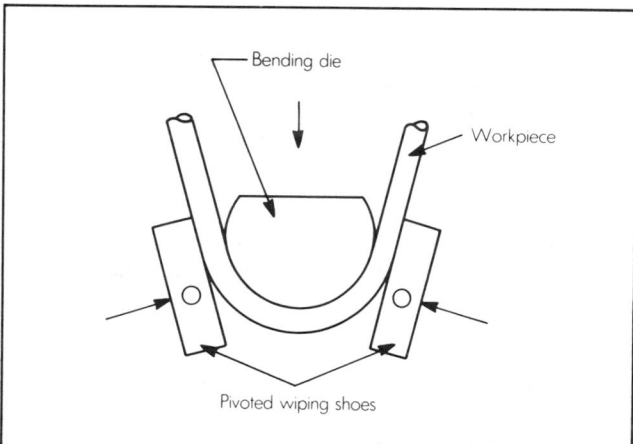

Fig. 36-15 Press (ram) bending is performed with a bending form mounted on a press ram. This is a high-speed method for producing two simultaneous compression bends.

the bending form. This method is used primarily for high-volume production bending of tube, bar, and pipe, typically when wall thickness and bending radius are relatively large.

Roll Bending

This method, shown schematically in Fig. 36-16, is similar to the basic process employed for rolling sheet metal and plates. It is possible to adjust the rolls to give a wide range for the radius selection. For bending tubing, the roll method is limited to heavy-wall material, because it produces a high degree of wall thinning. This method can be practical in bending solid shapes into circular parts. It is also used to produce full circles, to produce helical coils, and to bend pipe, heavy tube, and solid bars.

Stretch Bending

Stretch bending (see Fig. 36-17) is probably the most sophisticated bending method, and requires expensive tooling and machines. Furthermore, stretch bending requires lengths of material beyond the desired shape to permit gripping and pulling. The material is stretched longitudinally, past its elastic limit, by pulling both ends and then wrapping around the

bending form. This method is used primarily for bending irregular shapes; it is generally not used for high production.

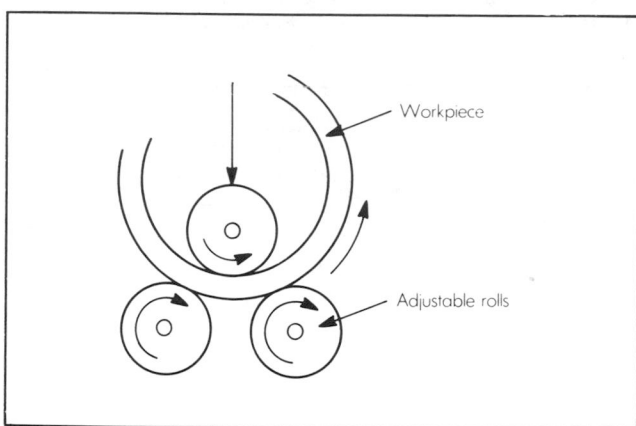

Fig. 36-16 Roll bending is useful for forming solid bars, rods, special shapes, and heavy tubing into circular parts.

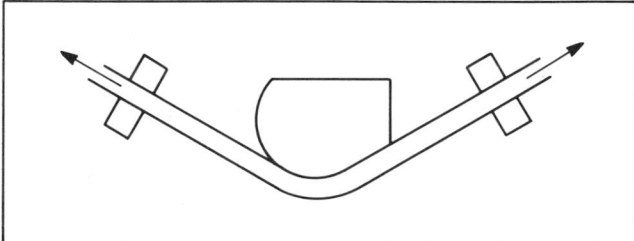

Fig. 36-17 Stretch bending is a sophisticated method that requires costly tooling and machines, as well as extra material for gripping and pulling.

BENDING EQUIPMENT

The different types of bends can be made on a variety of commercially available bending machines—small and large capacity, manually operated and power driven, and general and special purpose. For specialized operations, such as bending thin-wall tubing at high production rates, an automatic draw bender would be best. If the bending operation requires high production rates, but close tolerances are not necessary and the "D" of bend and wall factor permit; some type of press bender should probably be used. However, if the requirements are for bending a wide variety of materials and shapes, then a universal, general-purpose bender—most likely a draw type—should be used.

Types of Production Machines

Three basic types of machines are used in production tube bending: (1) ram benders, including specialized, hydraulic ram benders as well as mechanical power presses; (2) roll benders; and (3) rotary benders, including rotary-compression, rotary-draw, and stretch-forming machines.

Ram benders. Most types of ram benders are hydraulically operated. They are commonly used for bending tubular parts, but can bend solid sections as well. They embody a moving ram that forces the workpiece between two relatively fixed dies. These dies may be completely fixed, or they may be allowed to pivot in such a way that they accommodate the part moving through the die, as in the high-volume production vertical ram bender shown in Fig. 36-18. In this way, it is possible to make a 180° bend in a single pass. With fixed-radius tooling, the angle of bend can be controlled by the final ram position. Appropriate set fixtures on the machine allow bending relative to stock ends or previous bends. Thus, by using the machine's "positive stops," a multiple-bend part can be produced with minimum tool cost.

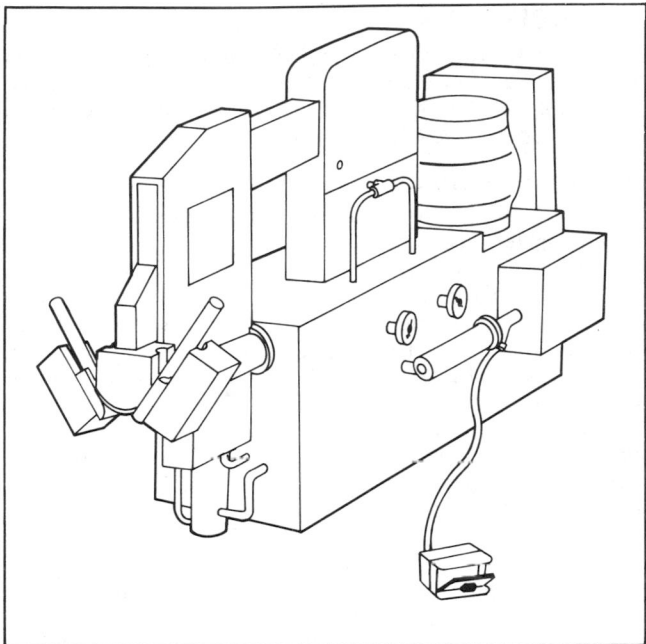

Fig. 36-18 General view of a hydraulic-ram vertical bending machine. (*Teledyne Pines*)

Power presses. Press bending is probably the most common type of bending because of the wide variety of techniques and tooling that can be used. It is normally desirable to use two or four-post die sets to maintain better accuracy. Tolerances from ±0.02 to ±0.06" (0.5 to 1.5 mm) can be held depending upon tools, material, and equipment. Reasonable accuracy can be maintained, but care should be taken to allow for springback and pulling or stretching.

Ram-mounted cams may be employed to actuate drivers, turn rotating drivers, and even bend the part directly. Accuracy is primarily a function of the type of tooling.

Roll benders. Roll benders (see Fig. 36-19) consist of three rolls set in a pyramid arrangement in either a horizontal or vertical plane. The piece to be rolled is laid across the two bottom rolls, which are power driven, and the top roll is brought into contact with the piece to be bent by means of a leadscrew or hydraulic-cylinder arrangement.

Roll benders are particularly adapted to the production of rings and coils. Spirals and multiturn coils are easily produced by the addition of deflectors to offset the emerging end of the part. One disadvantage of roll benders is that a short, straight section at each end of the stock is left unbent. If this is objectionable, it may either be cut off or be bent in a press as a separate operation. The tools are simple, consisting of rolls suitably grooved to match the stock. These are often made adjustable by spacers, especially for the bending of structural shapes and bars. Work produced on these machines is quite accurate, and very little flattening of tubes takes place.

Rotary bending. Rotary-bending machines wrap the workpiece around a tool called the bend die or form block. The basic rotary processes are rotary-compression bending and rotary-

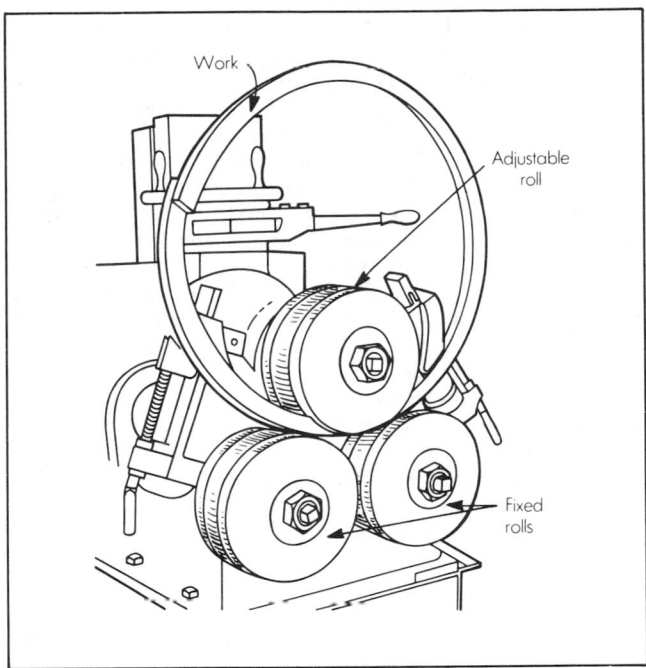

Fig. 36-19 Typical elements and application of a three-roll bending machine. (*Buffalo Forge Co.*)

draw bending. Stretch forming is a form of rotary-draw bending with an additional preload on the part; it is especially useful for bending special-shaped workpieces, such as angles, through their deepest leg.

Bending Tools

As shown in Fig. 36-20, five basic tools are associated with rotary-draw bending: (1) radius block or bend die, (2) clamp die, (3) pressure die, (4) mandrel, and (5) wiper die. The first three are always required; the last two are support tools employed in tube and pipe bending when the tube lacks sufficient strength for self-support.

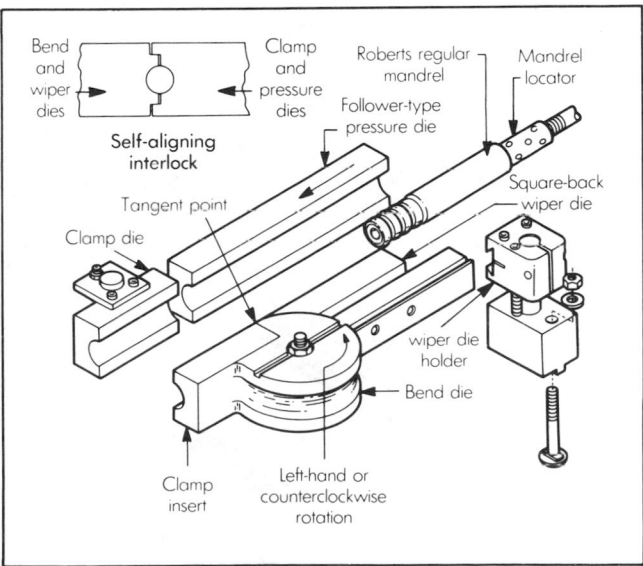

Fig. 36-20 Basic tooling elements for rotary-draw tube bending. (*Tools for Bending, Inc.*)

TUBE, PIPE AND BAR BENDING

Automated Tube Bending[3]

The use of computers in the fabrication of tube assemblies began in the early 1960's. The subsequent development of microcomputers and large, computer-aided-design systems has dramatically accelerated the growth in automated tube fabrication technology. The following text summarizes current automated bending technology, beginning with the concept of automated tube bending and the bend accuracy and setup problems that first brought the computer into the tube shop.

The concept. Tube bend contours are defined in terms of intersecting vectors that define the straight portions of the tube in relation to a static reference point. This information is converted to lengths, rotations, and angles and entered into a programmable bending machine. The machine automatically uses the information to precisely control its operation.

Bend accuracy considerations. In the rotary-bending process, material, setup, and machine variables change from job to job. This means that the machine feed and rotation commands that worked well on one job may not work on another. Each setup usually requires modifications in the program for producing a part.

In addition, the machine precision on the feeds and rotations that form the tube does not relate directly to the "goodness of fit" tolerances. An accurate frame of reference is essential in the tube shop to objectively evaluate goodness of fit and to make the frequent bend-data corrections. In the past this absolute reference was either a master tube or a hard fixture. By positioning the tube in the fixture or comparing it to a master tube, the operator could estimate the required corrections and could eventually produce a good part.

Many companies are now using computer-controlled tube-measurement systems that inspect the tube against an absolute framework of XYZ coordinates and make corrections on the bend data based on the centerline "tunnel" tolerances. The inspection consists of digitizing the part shape and mathematically converging the best fit to the XYZ coordinates specified in the master shape.

PIPE BENDING

The relatively simple, basic, hydraulically operated draw-bending machine of the late 1940's with manual controls, static pressure die, and plug mandrel for generous radius bends has now evolved into the CNC machine.

Induction Bending

The new induction benders were designed specifically for large-diameter pipe in wall thicknesses of up to 4″ (102 mm); however, they had the capability of achieving bends of less than 5 times the diameter and, in fact, could in many instances go as low as 1 1/2 times the diameter—well below the limits of hot-slab bending. Furthermore, the process was much quicker, was far less labor intensive, and achieved better wall-thinning and ovality tolerances.

The principle of hot bending by the induction process is a significant departure from other methods. The pipe is contained in the body of the machine and clamped at the front end, beyond the tangent or starting point of the bend, by means of a swing arm extended from a fixed pivot point. The distance from the pivot point to the centerline of the pipe in the clamp and along its length determines the radius of the bend. This radius distance is infinitely adjustable to as small as 0.10″ (2.5 mm). Thus, within the minimum and maximum radius limits of the machine, almost any desired radius is possible, taking into consideration such factors as material type, diameter, and wall thickness. A general view of an induction bender for large-diameter (32″; 813 mm) pipe is shown in Fig. 36-21.

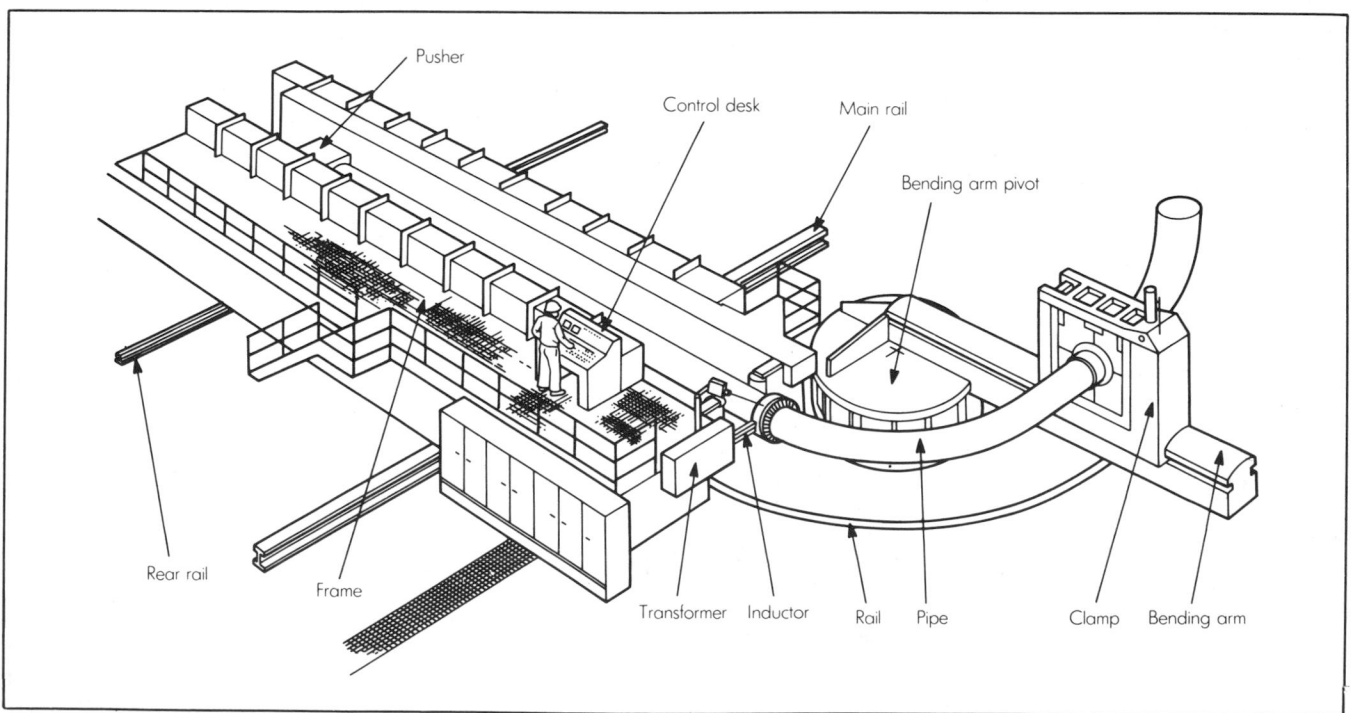

Fig. 36-21 Induction-bending machine for large-diameter pipe (32″; 813 mm). Example of operational data: 16″ (406 mm) pipe, 3.6″ (91 mm) wall thickness, 48″ (1.2 m) bending radius, 1.4% ovality, and 11.5% wall thinning. (*Inkamaf Corp., Cojafex B.V., Pipebending Div.*)

Hydraulic Pipe Benders[4]

Rotary-draw pipe benders have attained a state of development that enables them to meet pipe wall thickness and ovality specifications when cold bending pipe on small radii down to 1 1/2 times the diameter. The state-of-the-art in this type of equipment is represented by the microprocessor-controlled, pipe-bending machine shown in Fig. 36-22.

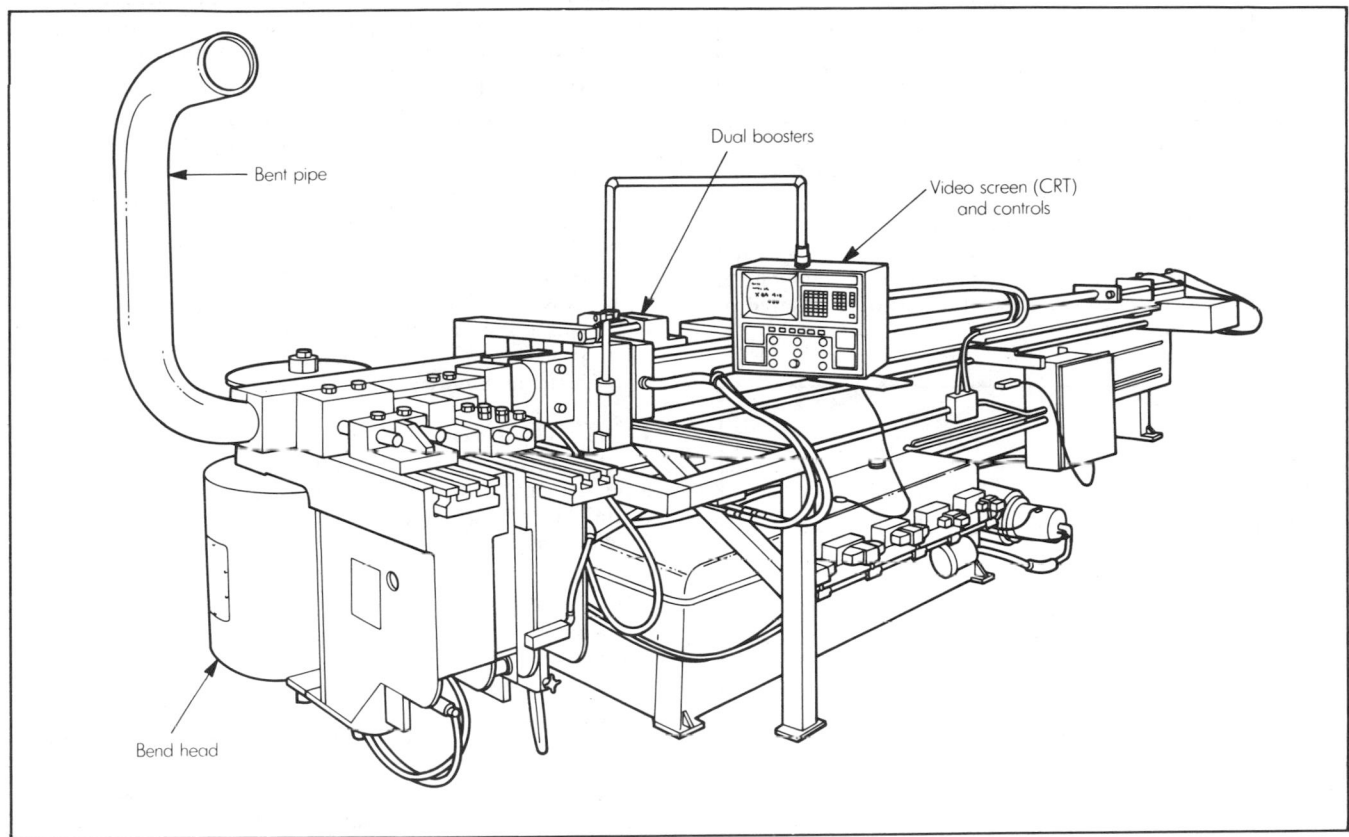

Fig. 36-22 A modern, rotary-draw, microprocessor-controlled automatic bending machine that is capable of fulfilling pipe wall thickness and ovality specifications. (*Conrac Machine Tool Div.*)

STRAIGHTENING

Cold or hot metal forming processes can cause residual stresses in rod, bar, sheet, wire, or tubing—and in components made from these materials—as a result of nonuniform plastic flow of the material. Metallurgically, residual stress occurs because of many conditions inherent in the structure and properties of the metal, including molecular disorientation, and the presence of this stress can cause part deformation in shape and size. Such stresses are often induced in the cold or hot working of stock material and later cause deformations when the stock is cut or formed into components or shapes.

In rods or tubes, residual stresses usually take the form of bows or snakes (a series of bows) in the part (see Fig. 36-23). In flat rectangular or irregularly shaped parts, deviation from a straight line is generally in the form of camber (see Fig. 36-24). Another out-of-straight condition that can occur in all parts is twist, in which the face of the part is out-of-plane (see Fig. 36-25). Stock materials and piece parts can have any or a combination of all of these conditions.

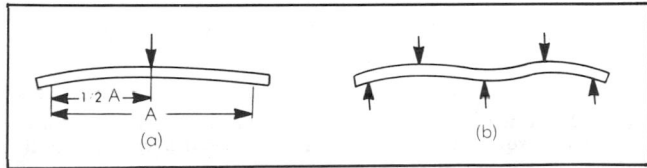

Fig. 36-23 Types of stress deformation in rods and tubes: (a) simple bow and (b) snaking or multiple bows.

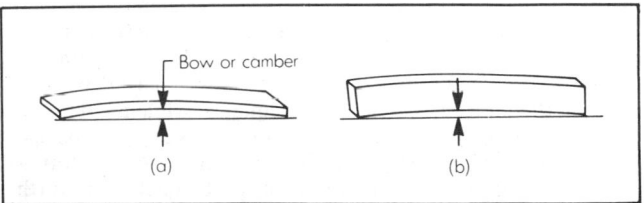

Fig. 36-24 Types of stress deformation in rectangular bars: (a) face bow or camber and (b) edge camber.

STRAIGHTENING

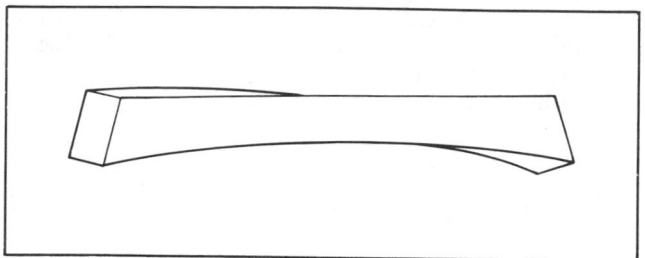

Fig. 36-25 Stress deformation-twist. (*Bertolette Machines, Inc.*)

PRINCIPLES OF STRAIGHTENING

The general principle of straightening deformations in stock or component parts is to move the material beyond its elastic limit. Figure 36-26 illustrates the application of the general beam-bending formula to the calculation of force required in the straightening process.

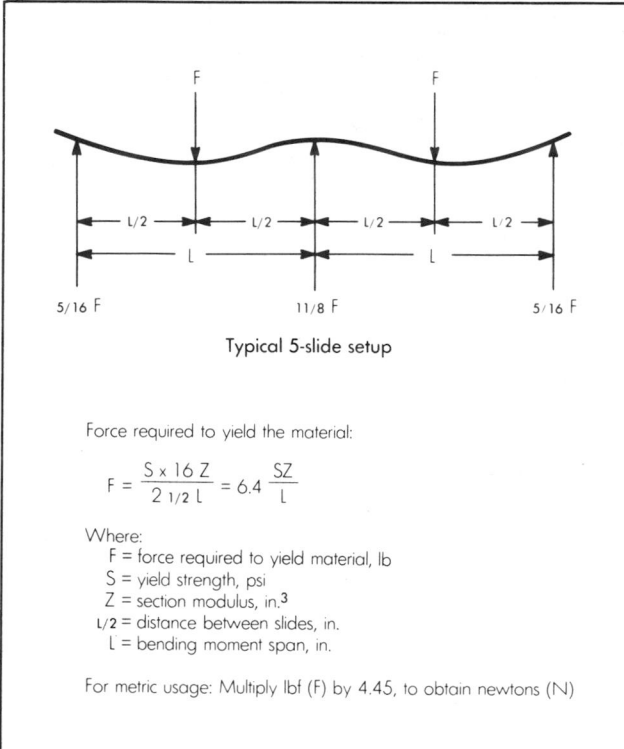

Typical 5-slide setup

Force required to yield the material:

$$F = \frac{S \times 16\,Z}{2\,1/2\,L} = 6.4\,\frac{SZ}{L}$$

Where:
F = force required to yield material, lb
S = yield strength, psi
Z = section modulus, in.^{3}
L/2 = distance between slides, in.
L = bending moment span, in.

For metric usage: Multiply lbf (F) by 4.45, to obtain newtons (N)

Fig. 36-26 Principal elements of basic formula for force required to straighten a workpiece by deforming the material beyond its elastic limit. (*Bertolette Machines, Inc.*)

At normal room temperatures, straightening can be done by locating a deformation and moving the material in the opposite direction, so that when pressure is removed, the deformation is equalized. Stock or parts can also be heated to high temperatures and placed under continuous pressure for a period of time, allowing the molecular structure to equalize while the material cools. Stretching or drawing of stock materials through dies can equalize molecular surface tensions and overcome deformations. Flexing stock or component parts back and forth, returning them to a straight line, can stress relieve them and bring them to a straight condition.

ADVANTAGES

Straightness is important in stock materials, since component parts manufactured from straight stock tend to remain straight. Straightness is obviously necessary for component parts that are used in assembly with other parts, since proper functioning of the assembly depends upon the correct relationship of one part to another. Other advantages of straightness include:

- Parts can be consistently held to close dimensions.
- Relief of residual stresses enhances part stability.
- Straight parts can be machined at greater production rates.
- Less labor and skill are required in subsequent machining operations.
- Part life is increased, since stability of a part provides better resistance to fatigue and improved yield strength.
- Less material is needed when allowances are made for cuts as a means of obtaining straightness.
- Parts which are used alone (that is, hand tools) have a better and more salable appearance.

LIMITATIONS

Straightening does not always overcome all stresses; and after machining or heat treatment, a part may need to be restraightened. Straightening does not correct out-of-round conditions such as those caused by mismatch in forgings or ovality.

TOOLING

Tooling requirements for straightening vary with the type of equipment used. Tools range from hammers, mallets, grooved blocks, vises, and levers for the simplest types of manual straightening to hardened-steel rolls of various contours, including concave, grooved, and flat, required for the parallel and rotary-roll straightening equipment. For the automatic press roll straighteners, tooling consists of crowned rolls, hardened and ground, and hardened-steel chuck jaw inserts or hardened-steel lug drivers. The tooling for eipcyclic straighteners consists of interchangeable inserts for the fixed arm and movable arm clamps to accommodate various sizes and shapes of parts. For parallel-rail straightening, a series of hardened and ground rails are used. Moving-insert straightening requires individual sets of tools, or parts of them, for different sizes and shapes of components.

References

1. Gary S. Vasilash, "A New Approach to Bending," *Manufacturing Engineering* (March 1982), pp. 87-89.
2. Patrick E. Oldenburg, *The Art of Forming*, Di-Acro Division, Houdaille Industries, Inc.
3. Joseph J. Kirby, "Automated Tube Bending—A Technology Update," Presentation at AFIT/FMA Conference, 1982.
4. Alan Williamson, "Meeting Wall Thinning and Ovality Specifications When Bending Pipe," Conrac Machine Tool Co., Pipe wall thinning tutorial paper.

SHEARING AND PUNCHING

Shearing is a process by which large sheets of material are cut into pieces of smaller length and width. These pieces are often used in subsequent operations such as punching and forming. Shearing is also used to produce blanks or slugs to be used in subsequent forming and machining processes. Because shearing is often the initial step in a series of processes, it is essential that the operating procedures result in an accurate workpiece.

Shearing offers several advantages over most metalcutting operations. Since shearing is a chipless operation, waste scrap is reduced. The shearing process is a much faster process because the blades do not have to cut through the full thickness of the material, as is required in some of the typical metalcutting processes. Instead, the blades penetrate only slightly into the material, causing a slip plane to develop which then severs the material.

Shears are used to cut mild, high-strength alloy, and other steels, as well as nonferrous and nonmetallic materials of all kinds. In general, materials should be no harder than R_C30.

The workpiece capacity of shears generally ranges from very light gages to 1 ½" (1.5 to 38 mm) in thickness and from 12 to 240" (305 to mm) in width. The capacity in alloy and high-strength steels generally is 2/3 to ¾ the mild steel capacity of the shear. For aluminum, the capacity is generally 1 ¼ to 1 ½ times the mild steel capacity.

Punching involves the cutting of holes and results in scrap slugs. It can be performed with punching presses specifically designed to hold the tooling or with stamping presses equipped with unitized tooling.

Punching on a punch press is fast and economical. A variety of shapes and sizes can be punched with standard tooling. Many presses are capable of nibbling large cutouts and contours in workpieces that would generally be produced with other, more costly metalcutting techniques. Plasma and laser cutting attachments permit small internal angles, scrolls, spirals, etc., to be cut on the punch press.

SHEARING PRINCIPLES

The principle of shearing is simply that as the blades come together and contact the material being sheared, the blades penetrate the material until the tensile strength is overcome and a crack or tear, called the slip plane, develops from both sides (see Fig. 37-1, a). Blade clearance has a considerable effect on the quality of the sheared edge. If the planes match, a clean cut is produced. If they do not match, a tear occurs if the gap is too great; if the gap is too small, a tongue develops and is recut as the blade passes (see Fig. 37-1, b). Insufficient blade clearance results in a poor edge condition; and recutting the tongue is commonly called secondary shear.

During the shearing process, as the knife continues down, freeing the sheared piece from the original metal, the wall of the knife rubs against the metal to cause an area of burnish that extends along the length of the metal where the knife makes contact with it. The sheared piece of metal rubs against the wall of the lower knife, causing a second burnish area on the metal. A burr occurs on the sheared piece because the fracture starts just above the cutting edge of the knife, not at the exact corner of the knife edge. Another burr is formed on the original metal piece by the fracture starting just off the exact corner of the knife edge.

On most shears, the upper knife is slanted at an angle (see Fig. 37-2). Generally, this angle is set between ½ and 2 ½°. An angle of 2 ½° reduces the shear load by as much as 25%, but the squareness of cut and edge quality are affected. This inclination causes the knife to move down and to back away from the lower knife. This action ensures that the sheared piece will not become wedged between the two knife blades, and it helps to concentrate the shearing force in the exact area of blade engagement between the two knives. This action also causes the fractures to start on a straight line approximately parallel to the surface of the knife.

SHEAR CONSTRUCTION

The elements of a typical shear are illustrated in Fig. 37-3. The upper knife is mounted at an angle or slope with respect to the horizontal lower knife. The lower knife is rigidly supported by the table and bed for accurate alignment and knife clearance. The frame can be constructed with or without a gap depending upon the work that is to be performed on the shear.

A workholding device is as important in shearing as it is in precision machining. Hold-down feet clamp the sheet or plate to the table to prevent movement during the shearing operation. Hold-downs can be either mechanically or hydraulically actuated. Mechanical hold-downs utilize springs whose pressure is automatically determined by the spring deflection. Hydraulic hold-down use hydraulic pressure to clamp the material to the table; the pressure can be adjusted so that soft or highly polished surfaces are not damaged or marred. With either method, the hold down feet can be furnished with mar-resistant caps to prevent surface damage or marring. Some hold-down feet can be offset, decreasing the distance between the shear knife edge and the hold-down, to facilitate the shearing

SHEAR CONSTRUCTION

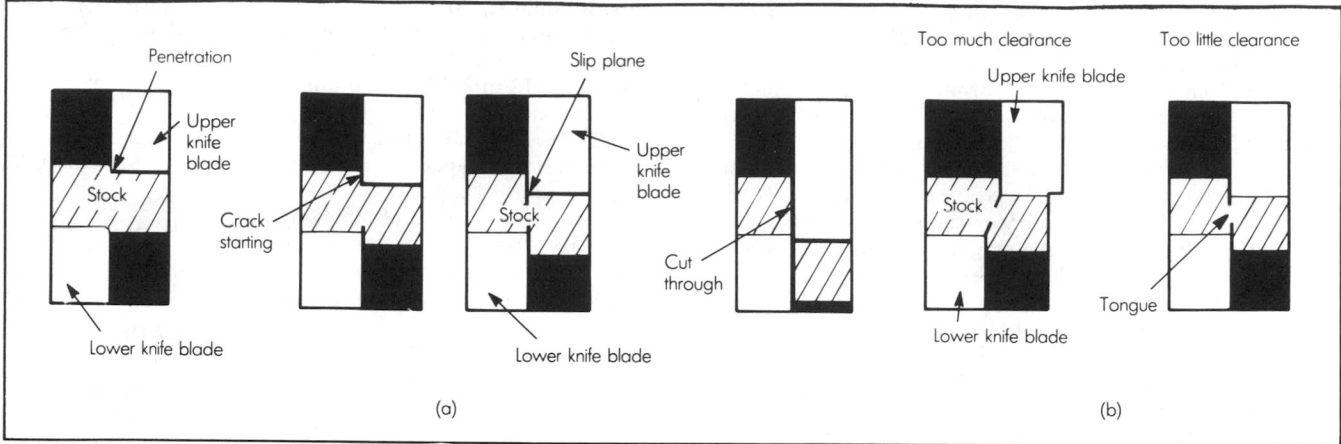

Fig. 37-1 Sequence of steps in shearing action: (a) with proper blade clearance and (b) with improper blade clearance. (*Di-Arco Division, Houdaille Industries, Inc.*)

of narrow sheets.

The three basic shear design configurations for crosshead action are (1) overdriven, (2) underdriven, (3) swing beam.

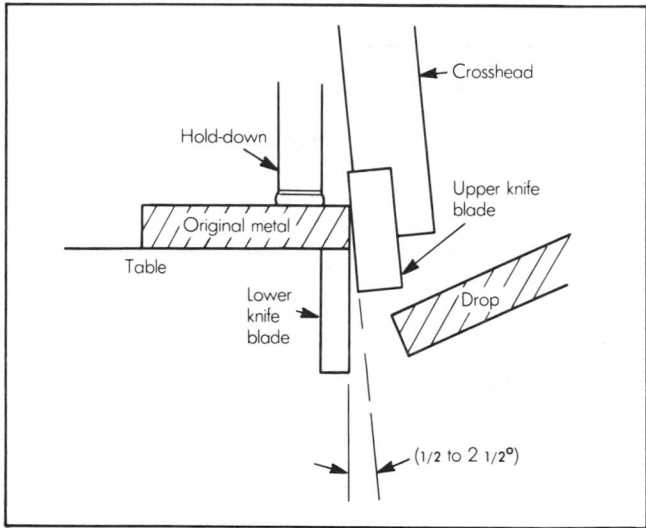

Fig. 37-2 Alignment of upper knife with respect to the vertical plane. (*Edward A. Lynch Machinery Co.*)

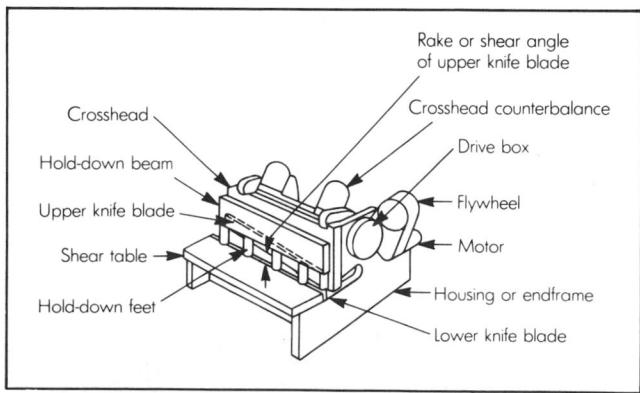

Fig. 37-3 Components of a typical shear.

OVERDRIVEN SHEARS

Overdriven shears (see Fig. 37-4) were formerly quite popular and still offer several advantages. These include the capability of slitting or notching by moving the sheet through the machine. If the machine uses a swing beam design, it will offer an easy adjustment of the blade clearance. Since the machine has nothing in back of it, a clear area exists for the drop to fall and for sheared parts to be stacked.

UNDERDRIVEN SHEARS

Underdriven shears (see Fig. 37-5) offer lower silhouette, lower weight, and lower cost than overdriven shears. Since generally no gap exists (the side plates completely enclosed the ends), the frame is basically highly stable without being unduly heavy. Obviously, an underdriven shear cannot slit or notch.

SWINGING BEAM SHEARS

Swing beam shears (see Fig. 37-6) offer the advantage of a blade clearance adjustment that is quick and easy. Also, there is no need to incline the crosshead, so another variable can be eliminated from the operating parameters of the shear. However, this type of shear requires a special spirally ground top blade to compensate for the combination of the radius and the rake of the top blade. The upper blade holder must also be spirally ground.

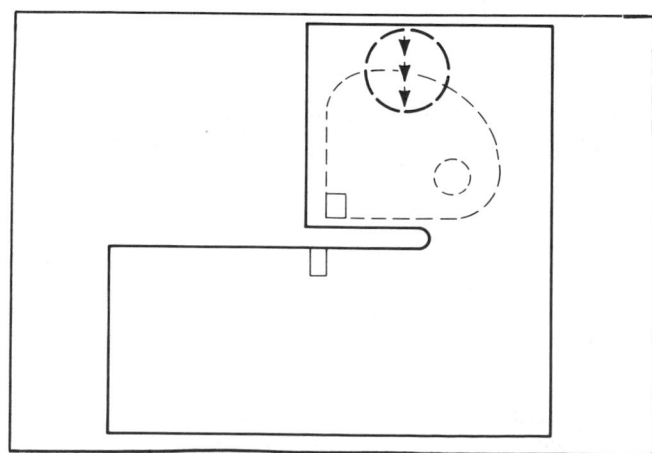

Fig. 37-4 Overdriven ram design with gap frame. (*Di-Acro Division, Houdaille Industries, Inc.*)

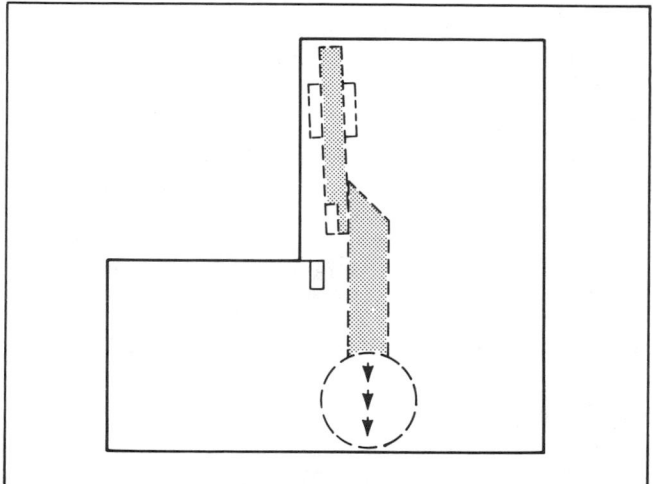

Fig. 37-5 Underdriven ram design. (*Di-Acro Division, Houdaille Industries, Inc.*)

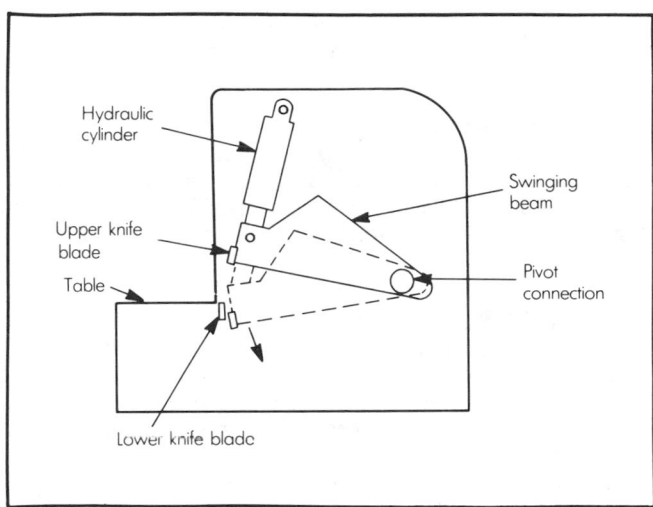

Fig. 37-6 Swinging-beam ram design. (*Pacific Press and Shear Company*)

TYPES OF SHEARS

Although shears are made in a wide variety of sizes and styles to satisfy the needs of the metal fabricator, they can be classified according to either (1) the means by which the crosshead is driven or (2) the type of work that the shear was designed to perform. Some shears are capable of performing more than one type of work but can still be classified under these general categories.

CROSSHEAD DRIVE

Crosshead drive is the means by which the crosshead is powered. It can be (1) manual, (2) mechanical, (3) hydraulic, or (4) pneumatic.

SHEAR DESIGN

Design of the shear determines to a large extent the type of work that can be performed. Some of the more common designs are (1) gapless shears, (2) gap shears, (3) alligator or pivot shears, (4) ironworkers, (5) cutoff machines, (6) bar-billet shears, (7) computer numerical control (CNC) shears, and (8) rotary shears.

Gapless Shears

Gapless shears follow the same concept found in modern press brakes. Two side frames support the power unit and are joined together by the bed and crosshead.

Gapless shears are normally used for the production of large and small straight-sided blanks from sheet and plate. They can also be used for cutting accurate blanks which are used in subsequent metal forming operations.

Gap Shears

The principle of the gap shear frame is the same as in a gap press. A driving mechanism is located on top of a basically C-type side frame and forces the blade down. Since the frame must support the weight of the power unit as well as the shearing forces, the frame tends to be heavier than a frame used for a gapless shear.

Gap shears are used for squaring sheets and producing blanks; because of the gap in the frame, they can be used to slit long sheets. Notching can also be performed on a gap shear.

Alligator or Pivot Shears

Alligator shears have a shearing action similar to that of scissors. The pivoting blade is actuated either mechanically or hydraulically. This type of shear is generally used to shear bar stock, rods, and narrow plates and to cut metal into scrap.

Some of the accessories that can increase accuracy and productivity are automatic feed rolls, length gages, automatic hold-downs, bar supports for long cuts, and blades that enable shearing of more than one bar at a time.

Ironworkers

Ironworkers (see Fig. 37-7) are machines which utilize the shearing principle and enable the operator to perform several different operations on the same machine. Some of these

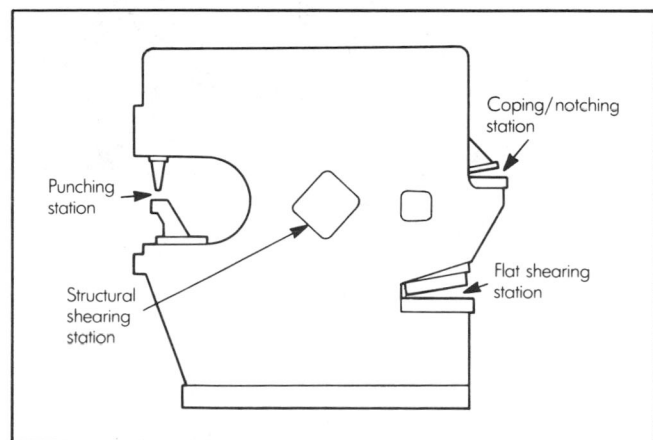

Fig. 37-7 Ironworker showing typical work stations. (*American National Standards Institute Inc.*)

TYPES OF SHEARS

operations include punching, shearing, notching, coping, and forming. These operations can be performed simultaneously or singly.

Cutoff Machines

Cutoff-type shearing machines are used for cutting round, square, flat, or special-shaped bars into blanks or slugs. This process can be performed on a machine specifically designed for slug cutoff, or it can be performed using a box-type shearing die in conjunction with a press.

Bar-Billet Shears

Bar-billet shears usually form part of a completely automated system to produce blanks that are used in subsequent metal-forming and machining operations. The shear is designed to incorporate either a nutcracker (pivot) or a guillotine type of cutting action.

The cutting action of a pivot-type shear is the same as that of scissors closing. With the guillotine action, the upper blade descends toward the lower blade; this is the same action that is used with the conventional underdriven or overdriven shear.

CNC Shears

Computer numerical control (CNC) technology applied to shearing is generally limited to a single-axis positioning table attached to a conventional hydraulic or mechanically driven shear. A sheet to be sheared is placed in the workholders of a direct-current servo driven carriage and positioned in the shear for each cut. The CNC unit can be programmed so that a variety of lengths can be sheared from a single sheet, as well as a variety of initial trimming cuts.

All the advantages of CNC machining apply to CNC shearing, including accuracy, repeatability, increased production, hands-off safe operation, and predictable production rates. When prepunched parts are sheared, errors are not cumulative, as could be the case when back-gaging is used with manually operated shears. Accuracy and repeatability are generally good.

Rotary Shear

Rotary shearing is used to produce circular and irregular shapes from steel plate. It can also be used for straight-line cutting. It is practical for shearing applications up to a maximum plate thickness of 1" (25.4 mm). Two revolving, tapered, circular cutters or knives cut the material. Because the blades are round, no restrictions need be made to the movement of the workpiece right or left. This permits circles, irregular shapes with small radii, and straight lines to be cut. Bevel cuts can also be made.

SLITTING

A slitting line is a group of machines designed to reduce a single-width coil into multiple narrower width coils (see Fig. 37-8). The slitting process shears the coiled strip in the lengthwise direction. A basic slitting line consists of an uncoiler or pay-off reel, a slitter, and a recoiler. Other equipment can be added for scrap disposal, coil handling and packaging, leveling, and edge conditioning.

Process Description

The coil of material to be slit is held on a mandrel of the pay-off reel. The mandrel expands to tightly grip the inside diameter of the coil. The coil is unwound by rotating the mandrel and using auxiliary equipment to thread the material to the slitter arbors. The work and equipment required to unwind or unbend the material varies greatly with the width, thickness, and yield strength.

The material to be slit passes between two parallel shafts containing the rotary cutting knives (see Fig. 37-9). These knives

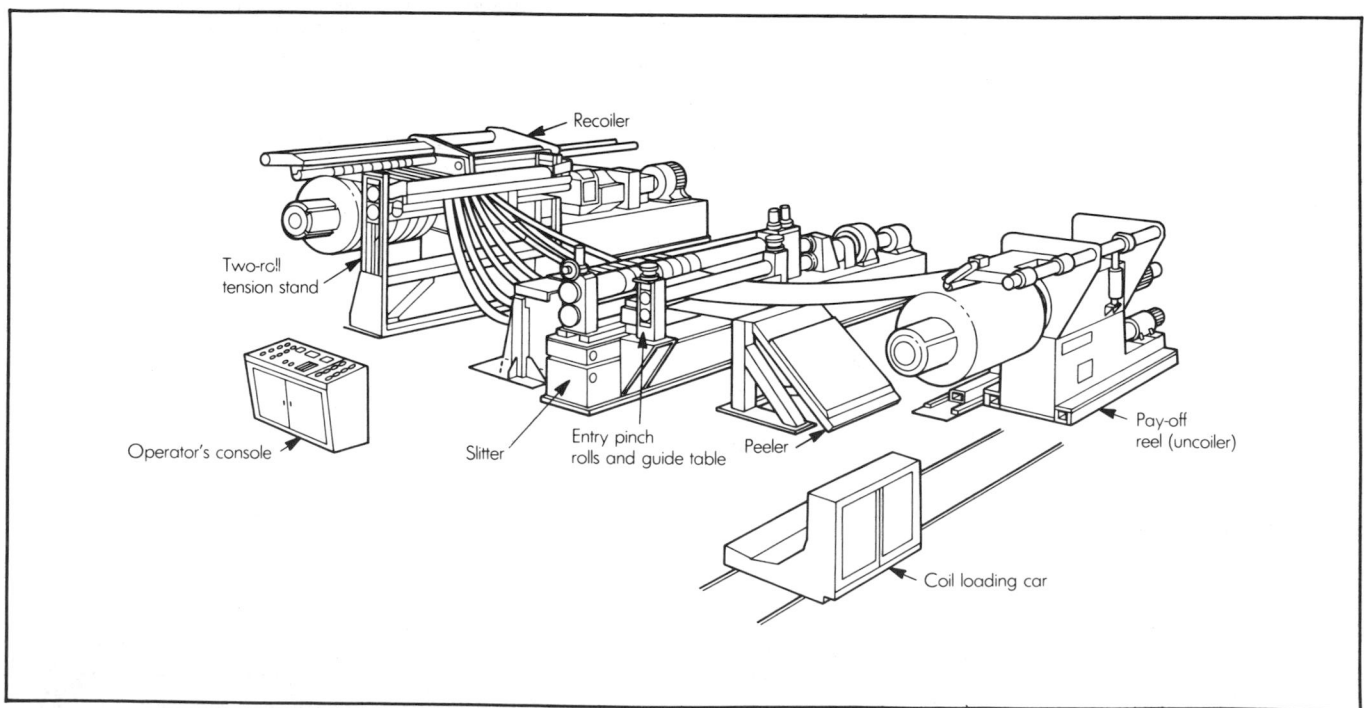

Fig. 37-8 Slitting line incorporating pay-off reel, slitter, tensioner, and recoiler. (*Paxson Machine Co.*)

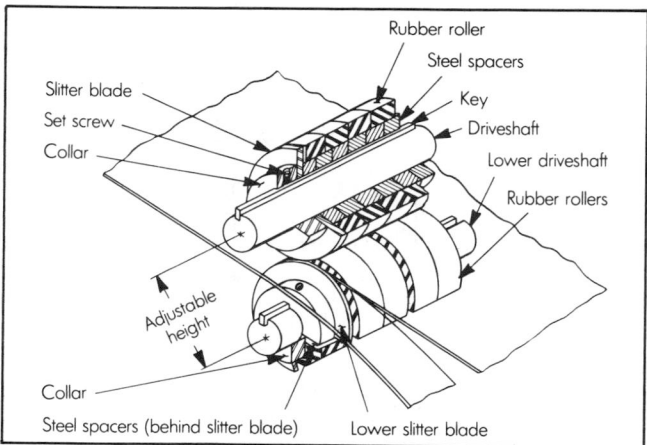

Fig. 37-9 Rotary knives used to slit material.

shear the material on a continuous basis in much the same manner as a conventional shear. The force required to maintain the two shafts parallel, and therefore maintain the vertical clearance of the rotary knives, is directed through the end housings of the machine. The horizontal knife clearance is adjusted using tool steel spacers and shims during the tooling setup.

Types of Slitting Lines

Three basic types of slitting lines exist: pull through, single loop, and double loop slitting. Each type of slitting has its own particular application depending on material, yield strength, thickness, and other requirements such as tightness of the coil.

The single and double-loop slitting lines are primarily used on light-gage material or where pulling tension on the strip can change the grain structure of the material. The pull-through slitting line is the more common type in general use.

SHEAR KNIVES

Shear knives are precision cutting tools that are usually rectangular in cross section. In general, each knife has four cutting edges. Special applications call for either the upper or lower knife to be specially shaped to cut corrugated material, wire mesh, and other items of unusual geometry. Bow knives have no advantage in standard shears except for special applications.

Shear knives come in many grades and hardnesses, but three grades are used most often. These grades are: (1) Grade I, (2) Grade II, and (3) Grade III.

Grade I is a tool steel that is normally used in low-production, general-purpose applications. This grade is relatively inexpensive and is satisfactory for intermittent shearing of mild steel, brass, and aluminum.

Grade II is an intermediate alloy that is shock resistant and is used for shearing plate 5/16" (8 mm) and thicker. It can also be used for light-gage shearing with reasonable life. This alloy is more durable than Grade I, and the added cost is usually well justified.

Grade III is a high-carbon, high-chrome alloy that is used for shearing mild steel up to 1/4" (6.3 mm) thick. It is usually recommended for continuous shearing of steels up to 1/4" (6.3 mm) in thickness. It is also used for shearing aluminum, brass, and stainless steel up to 3/16" (4.8 mm) thick. Because this grade is hard and somewhat brittle, it is not recommended for shearing mild steel greater than 1/4" (6.3 mm) thick since edge chipping and spalling can result. Grade III can, however, give excellent results on certain materials over 1/4" (6.3 mm) in thickness.

PUNCH PRESSES

Punch presses are used to punch holes of different shapes and sizes in various type of materials. Some of the applications for punch presses are in the production of electronic metal work, electrical boxes, appliances, construction equipment, farm machinery, trucks, office furniture, and vending machines. Figure 37-10 shows a few of the many products that are produced with modern punch presses.

Other operations that can be performed on the punch press include notching, forming, tapping, nibbling, and louvering.

Punch presses are made with different force capabilities, frame configurations, tool-mounting capabilities, and controls, but the mode of operation for all punch presses is the same.

The workpiece is generally positioned and firmly held down on the worktable prior to punching. When the controls are actuated, the ram descends and the punch knocks out the material as determined by the size of the punch and die (see Fig. 37-11). The stripper holds the material firmly in place until the punch has fully withdrawn. If the press numerically controlled, the workpiece is then automatically moved to the next punching location. On certain presses, lifting devices in the die block prevent burrs created during punching from holding the work-

piece on the die.

Power to the ram is derived manually, mechanically, or hydraulically. Manual punch presses are equipped with a long lever that converts the pull of a human hand to the forces necessary to punch the workpiece. Hydraulic punch presses develop the punching force through the application of fluid pressure on a piston using pumps, valves, intensifiers, and accumulators. Hydraulic presses are capable of maintaining full punching force throughout their entire stroke lengths.

TYPES OF PUNCH PRESSES

The two types of punch presses built are the single-station press and the multiple-station press. Multiple-station punch presses are generally referred to as turret presses. However, some multiple-station presses are built that contain two or three punching stations. The tooling is mounted individually in the toolholder. These presses fall into a classification between single-station presses and turret presses and are generally used when heavy plate, angles, or beams are being punched for structural steel fabrication.

PUNCH PRESSES

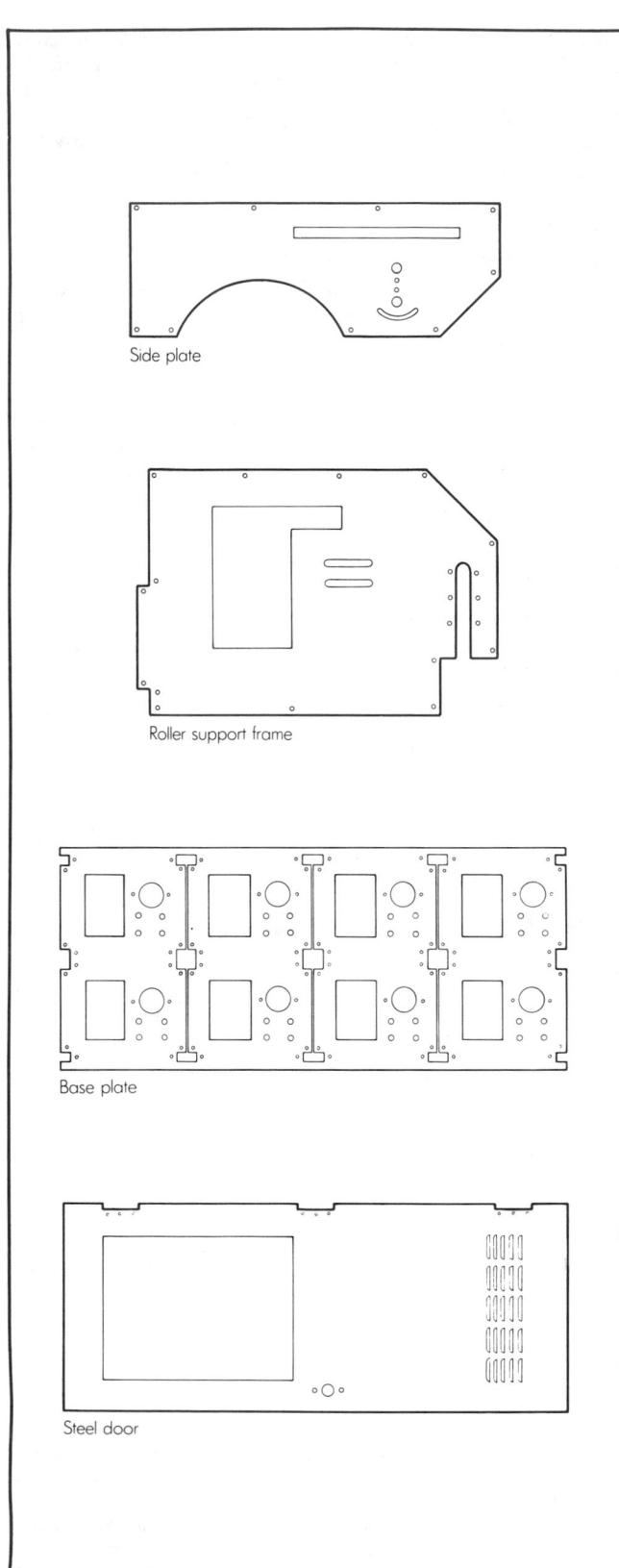

Side plate

Roller support frame

Base plate

Steel door

Fig. 37-10 A few of the many different products fabricated on a punch press. (*Wiedemann Div., Warner & Swasey Co.*)

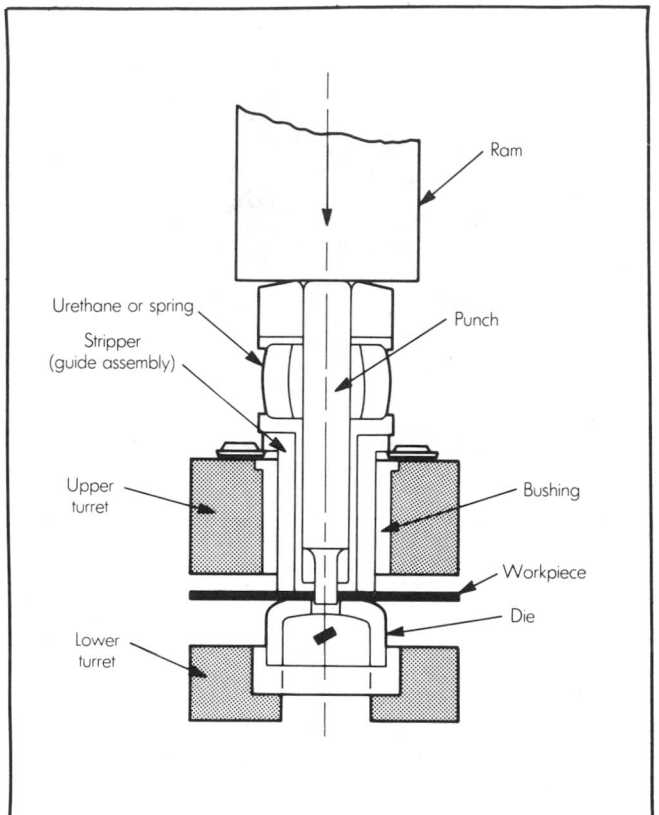

Fig. 37-11 The punch knocks out the material as the ram descends. (*Raskin, Datason Corp.*)

Another type of multiple-station press contains two punching stations, but incorporates removable cartridges to mount the tooling. The cartridges are capable of holding up to 12 different styles of punches and are positioned under the punching head with servo-drive motors. The advantage of this type over the turret press is that the tooling can be mounted in the cartridges for another workpiece while the press is in operation. This type of press is particularly useful when two identical workpieces are being punched simultaneously.

PRESS CONTROL

Three methods are used to control the operation of the press: manual, semiautomatic (manual data input), and automatic control.

PUNCH PRESS ACCESSORIES

Several accessories, when incorporated with the punch press, enable the press to perform a greater variety of work with a minimum of special tooling. These accessories also provide the means by which the press can operate automatically and thus reduce the number of operators needed for production. Some of these accessories include a plasma cutting torch, a laser cutting attachment, and material loading and unloading equipment. A useful feature is the capability of repositioning the workpiece during punch press operation.

NOTCHING MACHINES

A notching machine is a stand-alone unit with dedicated tooling capable of cutting 90° corners and V-notches in sheet metal. The basic unit generally includes a base, ram, hydraulic power pack and cylinder for actuation of the ram, tooling, a worktable, and positioning guides for supporting and locating the workpiece (see Fig. 37-12). The cutting action is initiated by either a foot switch or microswitches in the positioning guides.

The setup of a notching machine involves the relocation of the positioning guides for the desired notch depth and the adjustment of the blade clearance to the setting required for the material thickness being cut. Insufficient blade clearance causes secondary shearing and too much blade clearance generates excessive burrs on the underside of the workpiece. Each of these conditions causes premature blade wear due to excessive forces on the cutting edges.

Accuracy of the 90° cut angle is ensured because the fixed relation of the blades is controlled by the machining of their seats. The accuracy of the cut lengths is controlled by setting the positioning to the scales that are fixed to the tabletop. Micrometer adjusters are normally available for closer tolerance work.

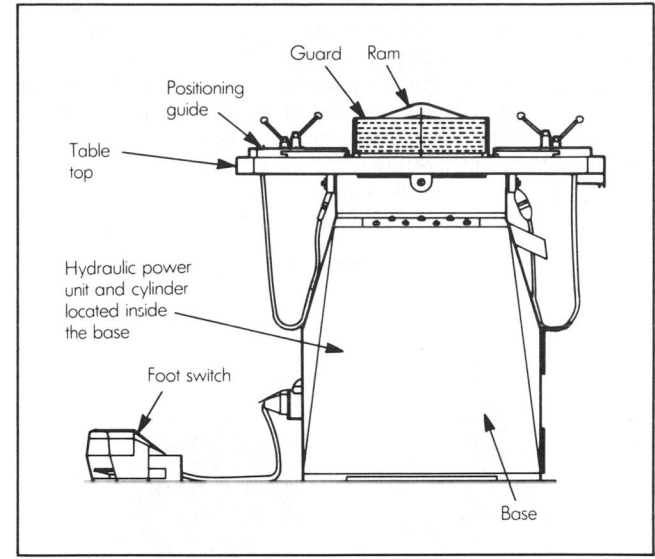

Fig. 37-12 Typical components on a sheet metal notching machine. (*Strippit Div. of Houdaille Industries Inc.*)

TOOLING FOR PUNCH PRESSES

Tooling for a punch press consists of a punch, a die, and a stripper. The size of the punched hole is determined by the punch size, while the die size (opening) affects the condition of the hole and tool life. The clearance between the die and punch is based on the type and thickness of material. Some manufacturers use a punch holder with the punch and a dieholder with the die. Generally, tooling is interchangeable between presses of the same manufacturer, but not presses of other manufacturers.

The punch is stripped from the metal using either a positive stripping method or a self-stripping method. The force necessary for positive stripping is derived from the press. Positive stripper plates and urethane strippers are used with the positive stripping plate to reduce workpiece distortion as the punch is being stripped. The positive stripper plates are mounted on the bottom of the turret or toolholder and can be set at a fixed distance from the workpiece or adjusted to contact the workpiece. The force for the self-stripping method is achieved from stripper springs incorporated in the tooling. The stripper or guide assembly is in contact with the workpiece during punching and until the punch is stripped from the workpiece.

PUNCH SELECTION

Punches for a punch press generally are selected based on the size and contour of the hole to be punched in a given material and the material thickness. Tip configuration also affects punch selection. The two most common configurations are the flat tip and the shear ground tip. Shear ground punches reduce the required punching force and the punching noise. Figure 37-13 illustrates the different types of shear ground on a punch tip.

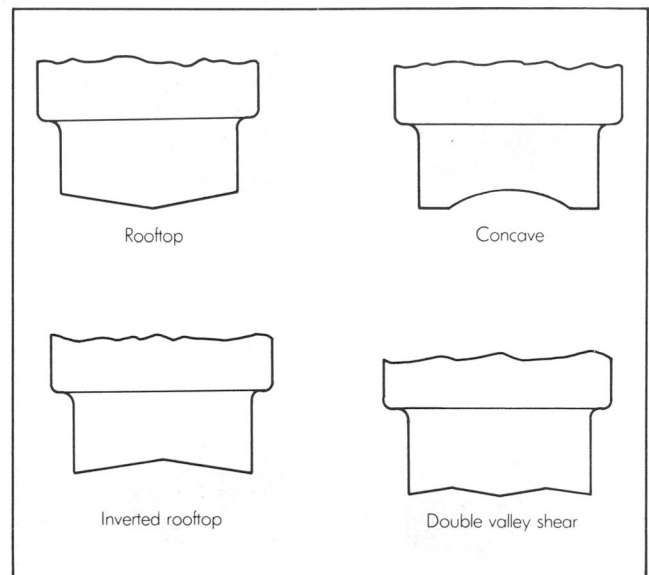

Fig. 37-13 Punches with different types of shear ground on them. (*Wilson Tool*)

Punches are available in many styles to accommodate the various contours that must be punched with the punch press. Figure 37-14 shows the shapes of the standard types of punches. Special shapes are also available to enable the fabricator to punch holes for specific applications. Some of these punches are employed in the formation of louvers, electrical knockouts,

TOOLING FOR PUNCH PRESSES

multiple holes, and tap extrusions. Figure 37-15 illustrates the shapes of some of these special punches.

FORMING ON A PUNCH PRESS

The NC punch press is one of the most productive machine tools in the modern sheet metal fabricating industry. The machines are universally accepted for their ability to rapidly and precisely punch parts in runs of 1-100,000 and more. In addition to simple hole punching, they can be used to perform forming operations, including forming the interior of a work-piece with the proper tooling. Figure 37-16 illustrates the basic forms produced on an NC punch press.

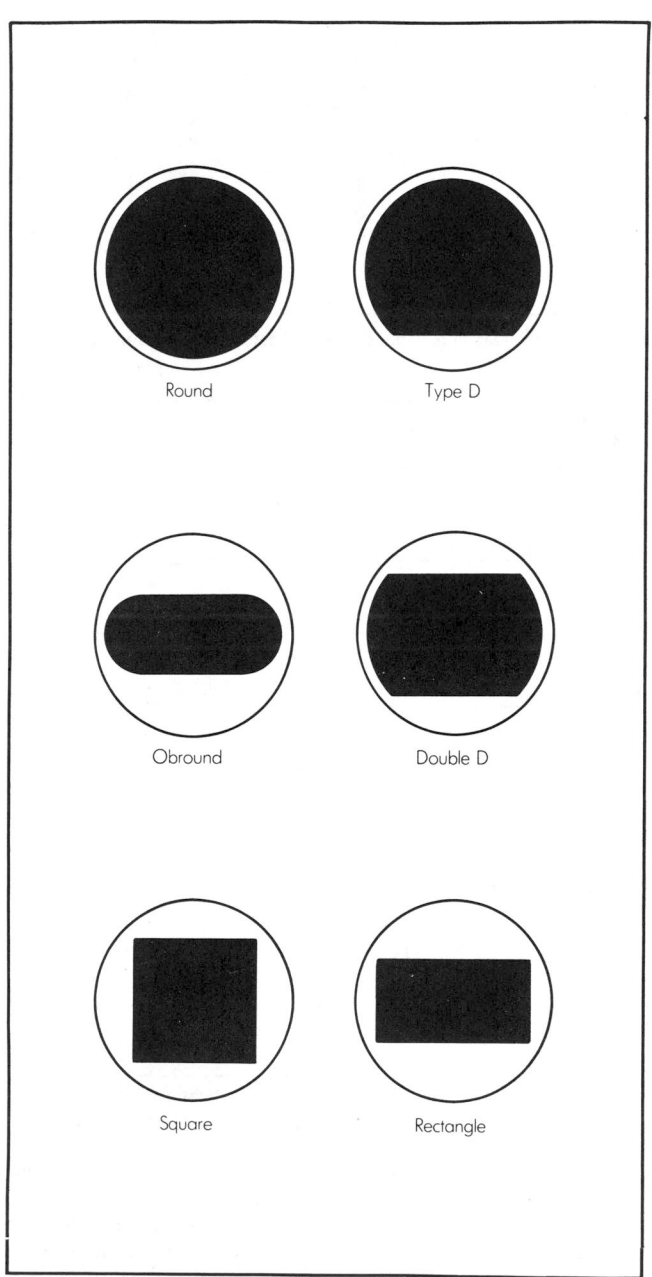

Fig. 37-14 Shapes of punches commonly used on punch presses.

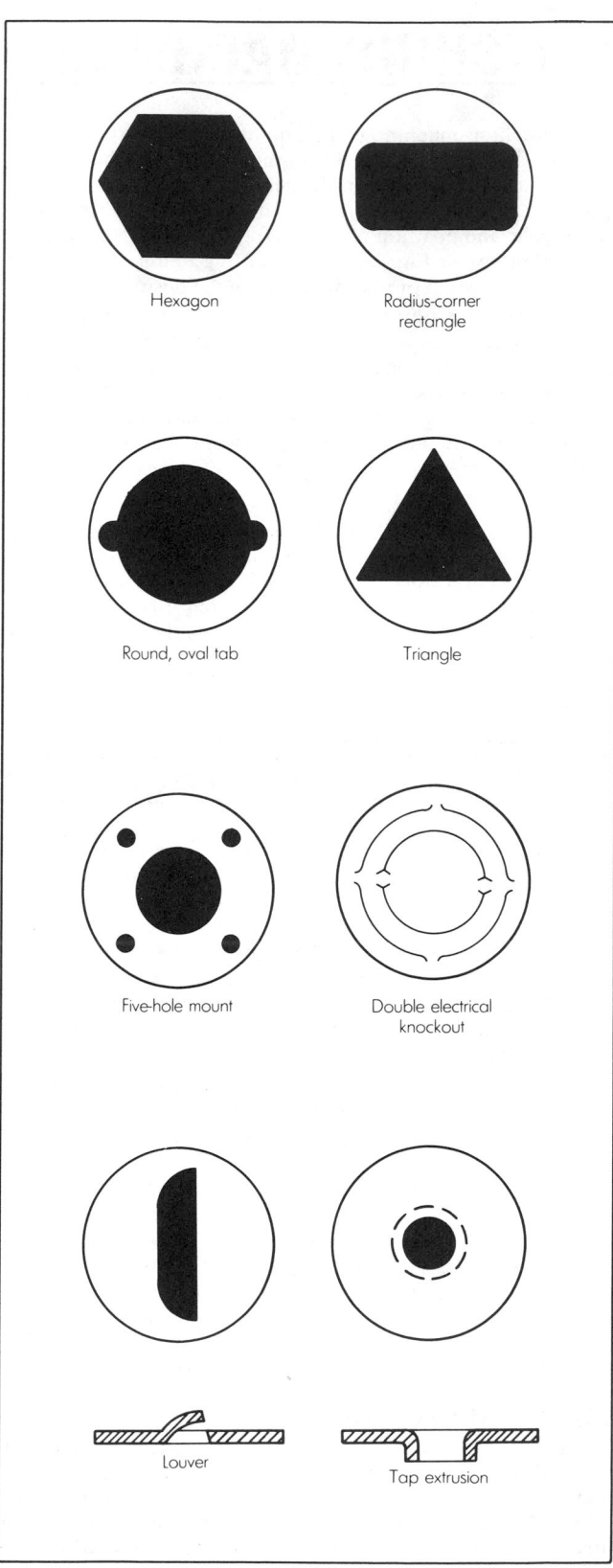

Fig. 37-15 Special-shaped punches permit the fabricator to punch holes for special applications with only one punch.

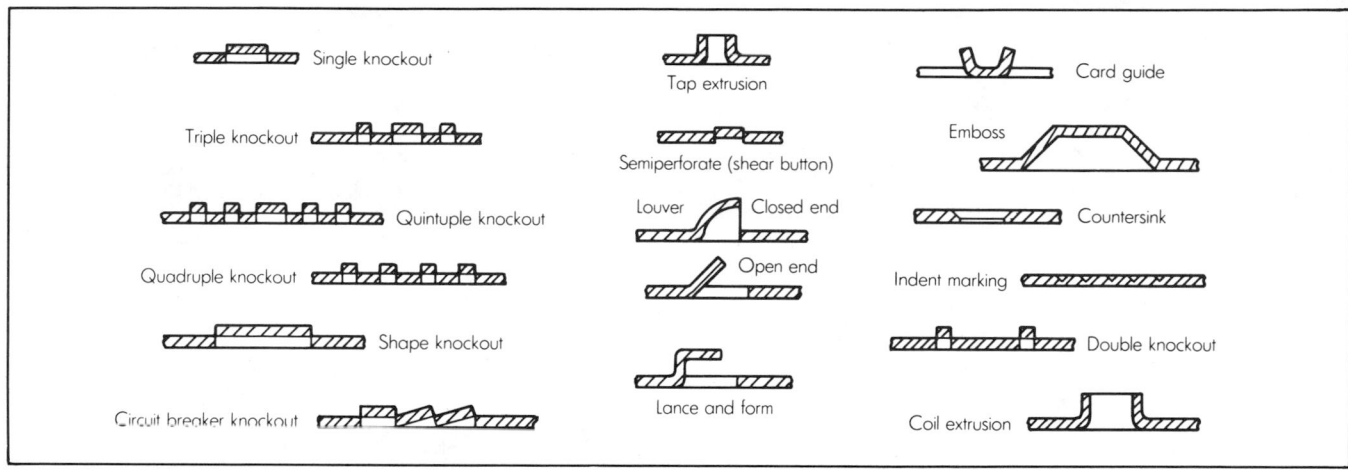

Fig. 37-16 Numerically controlled punch presses are capable of producing these typical forms with upward forming tools. (*Mate Punch and Die Co. and NC Shop Owner*)

DRAWING, EXTRUDING AND UPSETTING

COLD DRAWING OF BAR, WIRE AND TUBE

The cold drawing of a metal bar, rod, or wire consists essentially of pulling the part through a die of similar shape but smaller size (see Fig. 38-1). For a tubular part, an internal bar or mandrel can be introduced for simultaneous working of the interior surface (see Fig. 38-2). As the name implies, cold drawing is usually performed with the bar, rod, or wire at room temperature.

Drawing can also be done with the material preheated to temperatures up to the metal's recrystallization temperature. Called warm drawing, this technique can make drawing easier or impart special mechanical properties to the workpiece. For example, brittle materials generally require drawing at an elevated temperature at which the material remains ductile; prior processing of the material by rolling, extruding, or other compression deformation processes to improve the ductility of the material; or a combination of these techniques.

In addition to the production of bar, wire, and tube, many special sections are also cold drawn, thus reducing subsequent processing requirements. Parts produced are generally steel bars having the same cross-sectional shape throughout their length. Individual components are obtained by cutting pieces from the bars. Shapes possible are virtually unlimited and include intricate, nonsymmetrical shapes. Starting stock can be flat, square, round, or hexagonal bars, bars of other shape, or coils. Flat stock, however, is the most common starting material for drawing.

DRAFT, REDUCTION AND ELONGATION

Cold-drawing applications range from the production of fine wire that is substantially less than 0.001" (0.03 mm) diam to tubes 12" (305 mm) or more in diameter. Regardless of size, however, several unifying relationships are maintained. These relationships are the draft, reduction in area, and elongation.

Draft and Area Reduction

In the cold drawing of bar, rod, and large-diameter wire, especially for upsetting, draft is generally referred to as the difference between the original and final diameters:

$$\text{Draft} = D_o - D_f \qquad (1)$$

where:

D_o = original diam, in. or mm
D_f = final diam, in. or mm

In cold drawing small-diameter wire, draft is referred to as the percentage of area reduction and is calculated as follows:

$$\text{Percent area reduction} = \frac{A_o - A_f}{A_o} \times 100 \qquad (2)$$

where:

A_o = original cross-sectional area ($0.7854\,D_o^2$), in.^{2} or mm^2
A_f = final cross-sectional area ($0.7854\,D_f^2$), in.^{2} or mm^2

Die Pull

Approximate die pull—the force which is required to pull stock through the die and which determines the machine capacity needed—can be calculated as follows:

$$F = T \times C = (A_o - A_f) \qquad (3)$$

where:

F = die pull—force required to pull stock through die, lb
T = tensile strength of material before drawing, psi
C = constant varying with percent area reduction
$A_o - A_f$ = difference between original and final cross-sectional areas, in.^{2}

Values obtained for die pull with this formula are approximate; lubrication and die design influence the pull required. For metric usage, the die pull, F (lb), should be multiplied by 4.448 to obtain newtons (N).

Percentage of Elongation

Another unifying relationship which holds for any cold-drawing pass, regardless of size, is the percentage of elongation. To compute the percentage of elongation, the equation is:

$$\text{Percent elongation} = \frac{L_f - L_o}{L_o} \times 100 \qquad (4)$$

where:

L_o = original length, in. or mm
L_f = final length, in. or mm

COLD DRAWING OF BAR, WIRE AND TUBE

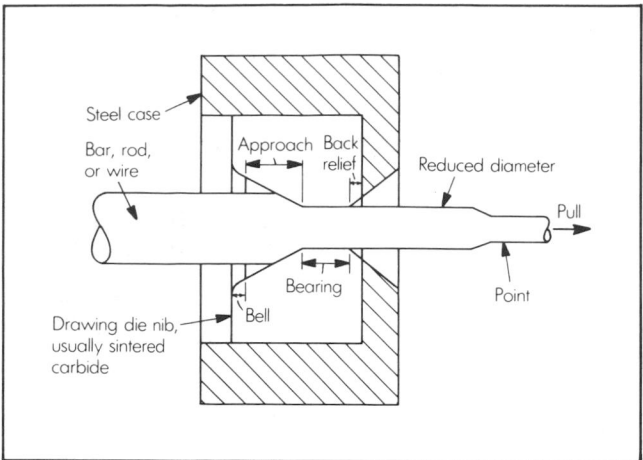

Fig. 38-1 Die for drawing bar, rod, or wire.

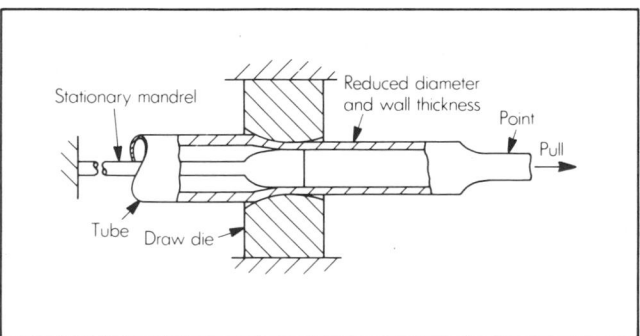

Fig. 38-2 Die and internal mandrel for drawing tube.

This formula can be simplified for solid round shapes, using the same terms already used to find the percentage of area reduction, as follows:

$$\text{Percent elongation} = (\text{Percent area reduction}) \div \left(\frac{D_f}{D_o} \right) \quad (5)$$

From this form of the percentage-of-elongation formula, it can be seen that a given percentage of area reduction always produces a larger percentage of elongation, a fact also true for cold drawing of nonround workpieces.

PREPARING FOR COLD DRAWING

One or more of three basic preparation steps are usually required prior to successful cold drawing. These three steps, naturally dependent on the state of the part before drawing and on the desired drawing results, are heat treatment, surface preparation, and pointing.

DRAWING ROD AND WIRE

Methods and equipment used for cold drawing of rod and wire, as well as small-diameter tubing, are generally designed so that the products can be uncoiled and then recoiled after drawing. On multiple-die continuous machines, uncoiling, drawing, and recoiling are repeated at successive stations. Rod coils, when ready for processing, are usually butt welded together for continuous drawing.

In the drawing process, cleaned and coated coils of rod or wire are first placed on a payoff tray, stand, or reel (see Fig.

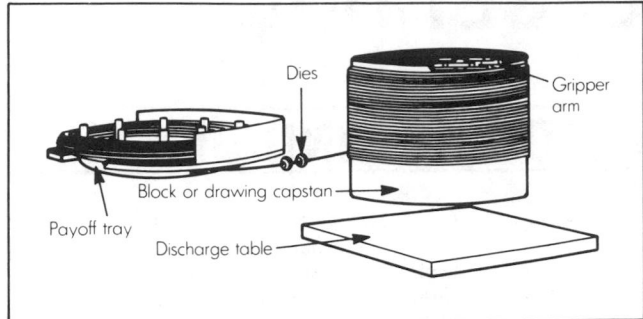

Fig. 38-3 Payoff tray and capstan for drawing coil stock. (*Vaughn Div., Wean United*)

38-3), which permits free unwinding of the stock. The leading end of the rod or wire, after being pointed, is then inserted through the drawing die and seized by a gripper attached to a powered cylindrical block or capstan. On so-called dry machines, the die is mounted in an adapter within a box. This die box contains, if necessary, grease, dry soap, oil, or other lubricants through which the stock must pass before reaching the die.

Bull Blocks

Bull blocks are single-die drawing machines with individual drive systems. They are used extensively for breakdown, finishing, or sizing operations on large diameter rod and wire, made from both ferrous and nonferrous metals, by firms with production requirements that do not warrant more sophisticated, continuous machines (discussed next in this section).

Dry-Drawing, Nonslip Continuous Machines

For the dry drawing of ferrous metals, four types of nonslip continuous machines are in general use: accumulating-type machines; double-block, accumulating-type machines; controlled-speed machines; and straight-through machines.

Accumulating type. The simplest continuous machine for dry drawing is the accumulating-type, or storage, machine.

Modern versions of accumulating machines, with individual direct-current drives for each block, permit more precise regulation and efficient operation. The geometry of these machines, however, imparts a twist to the wire with each revolution of the flyer (a sheave that revolves around the block), which for certain products is undesirable.

Double-block accumulating machines. Another of the nonslip continuous machines is the double-block accumulating machine with individually driven blocks. With this arrangement, wire is transferred from the first drawing block by means of an intermediate flyer sheave which reverses the direction of the wire (without twisting it) onto a coiling block mounted immediately above the first drawing block. Here, the wire is held temporarily in storage until demanded by the second drawing block.

Controlled-speed machines. A third type of nonslip continuous machine for drawing ferrous wires is the controlled-speed machine. On such machines, the wire follows an essentially flat path from block to block with a constant, unvarying amount of wire storage, without twisting and slipping. A tension arm between blocks, activated by a loop of the wire being drawn, regulates the speed of the adjustable-speed, direct-current motor on the preceding block.

COLD DRAWING OF BAR, WIRE AND TUBE

Straight-through machines. Straight-through, dry-drawing, nonslip continuous machines, without tension arms, are also available. In many instances, particularly those in which large-size workpieces are required, the spindles are canted from the vertical axis to accommodate wire buildup on the blocks and to provide unimpeded, straight entry into the succeeding die.

Wet-Drawing, Slip-Type Continuous Machines

The continuous drawing of nonferrous rod and wire, as well as some intermediate and fine sizes of ferrous wire, is generally done on wet-drawing, slip-type machines. On these machines, the surface speed of the capstans, except for the final (pull-out) capstans, exceeds the speed of the wire being drawn, thus creating slip of the wire on the capstans. Brighter surface finishes are generally produced with these machines, but the machines are limited to smaller reductions per pass than with dry-drawing nonslip continuous machines.

DRAWING BARS

The continuous machine illustrated in Fig. 38-4 has a fixed die box with a recirculating wet-die lubricating system. Drawing is accomplished with three moving grip slides: one slide for push pointing before the die box and two opposed-motion drawing slides after the die box. The push-pointing grip runs twice as fast as the drawing grips to minimize production loss when push pointing. This machine also has one set each of vertical and horizontal straightening rollers, and a set of feed-out rolls. Most cold-drawn bars are produced from hot-rolled or extruded

bars up to 55 ft (16.8 m) long x 6″ (150 mm) diam, with seldom more than one cold-drawing pass performed.

DRAWING TUBES

Tubes, particularly those having small diameters and requiring working only of their outer surfaces, are produced from cold-drawn coils on machines that straighten the stock and cut it to required lengths. As with bars, however, most tubes are produced from straight lengths rather than coiled stock. With four exceptions, the methods and equipment used for cold drawing tubes in straight lengths are basically identical to those used for bar drawing. The four exceptions are:

1. There are tubes that require more than one drawing pass.
2. Tubes are usually longer than bars. Drawbenches for tubes are usually correspondingly longer, some permitting drawn lengths of over 100 ft (30.5 m).
3. Tube diameters are generally larger than bar diameters, ranging to about 12″ (305 mm). The bigger tube drawbenches have larger components than do bar drawbenches.
4. Tubes require internal mandrels or bars for simultaneous working or support of the interior surface during drawing.

DIES FOR DRAWING

Proper design of the dies is critical for optimum cold drawing. The dies are basically conical, with a bell-shaped mouth and a cylindrical land. Drawing starts in the conical section and is completed at the intersection of the conical approach section and the bearing. The die land helps to maintain size as the conical approach section wears.

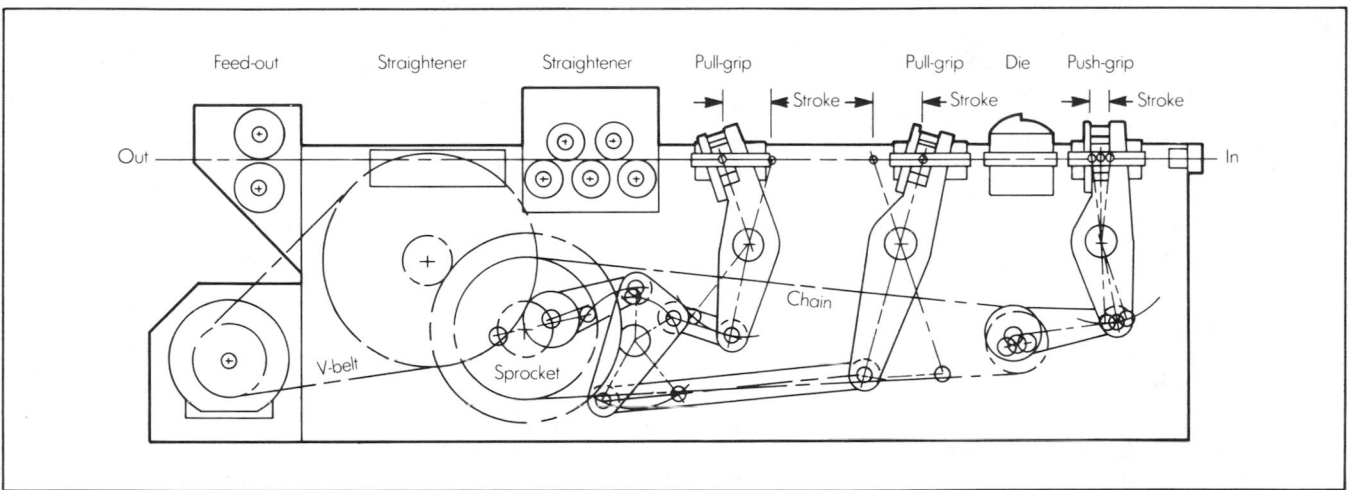

Fig. 38-4 In-line drawing and straightening machine for producing cold-drawn bars from hot-rolled steel coils or bars. (*Ajax Manufacturing Co.*)

HOT EXTRUSION

Extrusion is a plastic deformation process in which material is forced under pressure to flow through one or more die orifices to produce products of the desired configuration. In hot extrusion, heated billets are reduced in size and forced to flow

through dies to form products of uniform cross section along their continuous lengths. With special tooling, stepped and tapered extrusions are produced.

HOT EXTRUSION

ADVANTAGES OF EXTRUSION

The extrusion process provides a practical forming method for producing a limitless variety of parallel-surfaced shapes to meet almost any design requirement. Other advantages include improving the microstructure and physical properties of the material, maintaining close tolerances, material conservation, economical production, and increased design flexibility.

Shapes and Sizes Produced

Extruded sections can be hollow or solid, thick or thin, of simple or intricate shape, and of any size within the capacity of the press. A few examples of aluminum extrusions are illustrated in 38-5. Gears, airfoils, and many other shapes are produced.

Some shapes which cannot be rolled because of their geometry (such as those with reentrant angles) can be readily extruded. Also, some alloys which cannot be hot rolled because of a severe decrease in temperature during rolling can sometimes be extruded. Other alloys which break up when deformed unless they are contained on all sides can be extruded more readily than they can be rolled.

Improved Properties

The rapid and severe reduction of the material under high pressure in hot extrusion refines the grain structure, minimizes decarburization or coating, and usually imparts improved and uniform properties to the extruded product. For many applications, the products are used as extruded, after stretch straightening. For other applications, the properties of the extrusions are further improved by subsequent heat-treating or cold-working processes, such as drawing.

POSSIBLE LIMITATIONS

Because of limitations with respect to the diameter and length relationship of the starting billets, production rates from extrusion presses may be lower than for some other metal-forming processes. For example, about 95% of all carbon-steel tubing produced is made on tube mills rather than extrusion presses because tube mills permit faster production rates. The concentricity of tubing can generally be held to closer tolerances with tube mills than with extrusion presses. The initial investment required for an extrusion plant, however, is far less than for a tube mill. Also, when the cross sections of required shapes embody elements of various thicknesses, miscellaneous appendages, heavy sections, or voids, extruding is more economical and may be the only method of forming possible.

METHODS OF EXTRUDING

The extrusion process can be classified into two main groups: direct and indirect extrusion, with direct extrusion being more common. Another method of extrusion is the hydrostatic process, which is used with both heated and unheated billets.

Direct Extrusion

In direct, or forward, extrusion (see Fig. 38-6), a billet of metal (No. 4) is placed in a heavy-walled container (Nos. 7 and 8) and the extruded product (No. 1) exits through a die (No. 3) secured in a holder. The force for extruding is applied by a pressing stem or ram (No. 6), with an intermediate, reusable dummy block (No. 5). Metal flow from the die is in the same

Fig. 38-5 Examples of aluminum extrusions. (*Aluminum Extruders Council, Aluminum Assn.*)

direction as the forward movement of the stem.

The direct method is by far the most common method of extrusion, but it does have some disadvantages. The surface of the entire length of the billet must slide along the container wall. The ease with which this is done depends upon the material being extruded and whether a lubricating film is present. In all cases, part of the extrusion load (the amount depending upon the length of the billet) is expended in overcoming the friction between the billet and the container, or in shearing inner billet material from the slower moving, peripheral layer of billet material adjacent to the container wall.

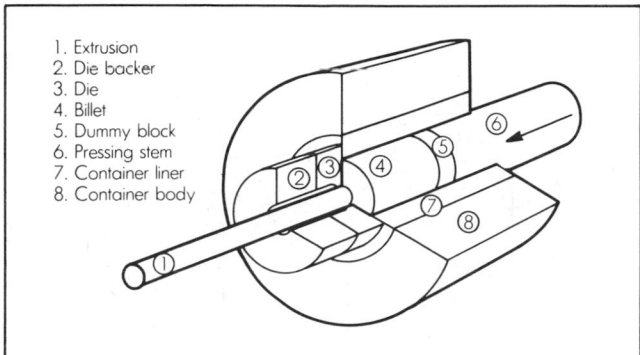

1. Extrusion
2. Die backer
3. Die
4. Billet
5. Dummy block
6. Pressing stem
7. Container liner
8. Container body

Fig. 38-6 Direct method of hot extrusion. (*Wean United*)

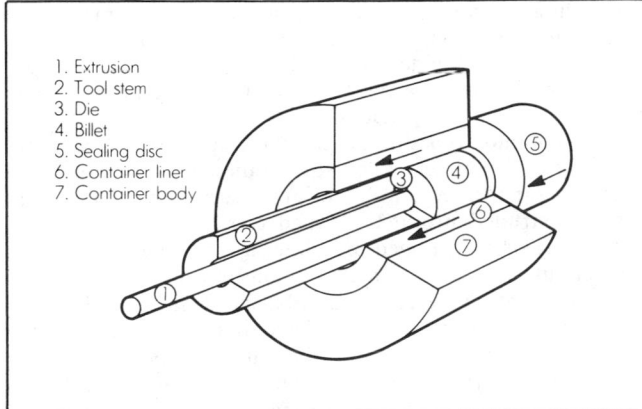

1. Extrusion
2. Tool stem
3. Die
4. Billet
5. Sealing disc
6. Container liner
7. Container body

Fig. 38-7 Indirect method of hot extrusion. (*Wean United*)

Indirect Extrusion

In indirect, or backward, extrusion, the billet remains stationary relative to the container wall while the die is pushed into the billet by a hollow stem (ram); or the container and billet are pushed over the stationary stem and stem-mounted die (see Fig. 38-7). The die is loosely attached to the end of the stem, and the extrusion exits through the hollow stem. Lengths of the billets used in indirect extrusion are limited only by the column strengths of the stems. Since there is no relative motion between the outer surface of the billet and the bore of the container, friction between these two surfaces is eliminated and the force necessary is decreased.

Advantages. The advantages of indirect extrusion are the results obtained through both decreased force requirements and a more uniform flow pattern of the material being extruded.

Disadvantages. A major disadvantage of indirect extrusion is that impurities or defects on the surfaces of the billets affect the surfaces of the extrusions. Impurities or defects on the extrusion surfaces preclude the use of the extrusions for architectural purposes and make them unacceptable for anodizing.

Hydrostatic Extrusion

In hydrostatic extrusion, the billet is surrounded by a pressurized liquid acting on all surfaces of the billet except that at which the billet contacts the die opening. As with indirect extrusion, virtually no friction exists between the billet and the container wall. Hydrostatic extrusion is not exclusively a hot process; it is frequently performed with the billets at room temperature or with the billets only warmed. In fact, the billet temperature is limited by the stability of the fluid medium used.

Advantages. Many materials subjected to high hydrostatic pressures generally have increased ductility. As a result, hydrostatic extrusion is suitable for both brittle and ductile metals.

Other advantages of hydrostatic extrusion include an even flow of material, the absence of a residue of extruded material on the container wall, the ability to extrude large-diameter and long billets, and the freedom for the billets to rotate during extrusion. An even flow of material facilitates the manufacturing of clad products. The pressurized medium used also helps lubricate the surfaces between the billet and the die.

Disadvantages. One disadvantage of hydrostatic extrusion is the prior preparation required for the billets. Every billet has

to be tapered at one end to match the die entry angle. This is necessary to form a seal at the start of the extrusion cycle. Also, the entire surface of the billet generally has to be machined, particularly if cast billets are being used, to remove surface defects. Containing the fluid medium under the high pressures employed can present problems and necessitates special design considerations.

MATERIALS EXTRUDED AND APPLICATIONS

The uses to which extrusions are applied appear endless and are expanding constantly. A large proportion of metal consumption is in the form of extrusions. Depending upon the material used, extrusions serve the transportation, construction, mechanical, and electrical sectors of the economy. They are used for durable goods, for industrial equipment, and for heating and air conditioning applications, as well as in deep-well drilling and in the production of nuclear power.

Practically all metals can be extruded, but their extrudability varies with their deformation properties. Soft metals are easier to extrude, while hard metals require higher billet temperatures and extruding pressures and sturdier presses and dies.

PRESSES FOR HOT EXTRUSION

Both horizontal and vertical presses are available for hot extrusion, with the horizontal type being predominant. Hot extrusion is also done on hydrostatic presses, discussed later in this section, and on high-energy-rate forming (HERF) machines.

Hydrostatic extrusion presses have been built for production applications with pressure capacities to 200 ksi (1379 MPa), using an intensifier in a 6500 psi (44.8 MPa) hydraulic system. Speeds in excess of 2.8 ips (70.6 mm/s) have been attained. Castor oil is generally used as the pressure medium because of its good lubricity and high-pressure properties.

TOOLING FOR HOT EXTRUSION

Successful and economical hot extrusion requires careful consideration with respect to the design of the tooling components, selection of the materials from which they are made, and method by which they are manufactured and heat treated. High-quality materials are essential because the tooling must operate under high pressures and high temperatures, and is subjected to severe strain and abrasive wear.

HOT EXTRUSION

Tooling for hot extrusion consists of many components, including containers, container liners, stems (rams), dummy blocks, mandrels, spider or bridge dies for producing hollow extrusions, and flat or feeder plate dies. Complete die assemblies are often called tooling stacks.

Two common types of dies are flat faced and shaped. Flat-faced dies, sometimes called square dies, have one or more openings (apertures) similar in cross section to that of the desired extruded product. Shaped dies, also referred to as converging or streamlined dies, have a smooth entry opening with circular cross section that changes progressively to the final extruded shape required. Flat-faced dies are easier to design and manufacture than shaped dies, and are commonly used for the hot extrusion of aluminum, copper, brass, and magnesium alloys. Shaped dies, which are more difficult and costly to design and manufacture, are used for the hot extrusion of steels, titanium alloys, and other metals.

Dies For Solid Shapes

A typical die-slide tooling arrangement for the direct extrusion of solid shapes is shown in Fig. 38-8. Stepped extrusions having two or more cross-sectional dimensions are produced by using two or more separate dies. The die with the smallest opening is used first. This die is then removed and progressively larger dies are employed.

Dies for Hollow Shapes

Hollow or semihollow shapes are extruded from hollow or solid billets. Fixed or floating mandrels, separate from the dies, are used to extrude hollow billets. Mandrels fixed to the ends of

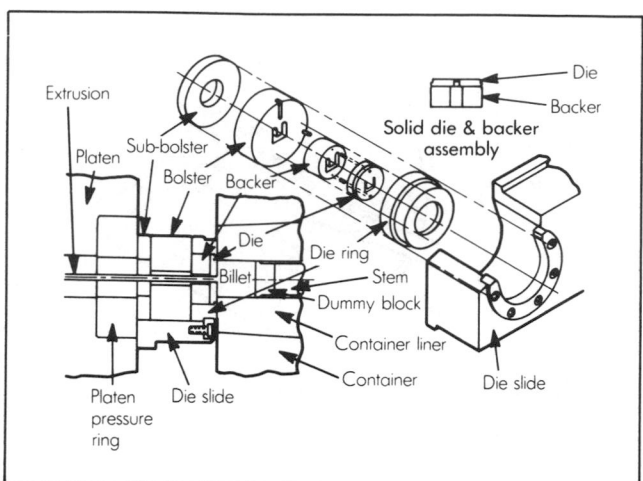

Fig. 38-8 Typical die-slide tooling arrangement for hot, direct extrusion of solid shapes. (*Wean United*)

the stem are referred to as German types. Floating mandrels, called French types, are generally set in slots in the dummy blocks and center themselves in the dies as the metal is extruded.

For solid billets, hollow dies classified as spider, porthole, or bridge types are used. These dies have stub mandrels as integral parts of the dies. The extrusions produced have one or more seams (longitudinal weld lines) resulting from the metal's dividing to flow around the mandrel supports and welding together before passing through the die.

COLD AND WARM EXTRUSION

Cold and warm extrusion differ from hot extrusion, discussed previously in this chapter, in that the starting workpieces (often called slugs) are cold (at room temperature) or warm (heated to below the critical temperature of the metal). Metal is forced to flow by plastic deformation under compression around punches and into or through shape-forming dies to produce parts of the desired configuration. Since the temperatures of the slugs are always below the recrystallization temperatures of the metals to be formed, the process is essentially one of cold working. Most steels, nonferrous metals, and superalloys can be extruded cold or at low deformation temperatures, with stresses in the tooling being the primary limiting factor.

ADVANTAGES OF THE PROCESS

Important advantages of cold and warm extrusion include substantial cost savings in many applications, fast production rates, improved physical properties, close tolerances, energy conservation, and elimination of pollution problems.

LIMITATIONS OF COLD EXTRUSION

One disadvantage of cold extrusion is its limitations with respect to the shapes, length-to-diameter ratios, and maximum size to which parts can be produced.

SHAPES AND SIZES PRODUCED

The most economical applications of cold extrusion are generally limited to the forming of symmetrical parts with solid or hollow cross sections. Parts with other geometries, including noncircular and complex-shaped components, are formed, but at a higher cost. When cross-sectional shapes are highly unsymmetrical, unequalized pressures are exerted on the tools and can cause breakage.

The length of cold-extruded parts is generally several times the diameter. In fact, shaft-type shapes account for about 80% of the total cold-extruded output. Upsetting (heading), discussed later in this chapter, is often combined with extrusion, as in the production of flanged parts. While cylindrical parts are most common, other shapes extruded include internal or external splines, squares, flats, hexagons, ovals, and tapers. Hollow parts having bottoms thicker than the sidewalls are also common.

The bases of closed-end parts can be flat, conical, hemispherical, or other shapes, and projections or depressions can be formed in one or both faces. Inner and/or outer surfaces of the side walls can be provided with beads, flutes, grooves, ribs, splines, teeth, or any other longitudinal projections or depressions. Axial holes can be produced if they are not too small in diameter or too long. Figure 38-9 illustrates a part cold extruded from AISI 4140 steel in a single hit.

COLD AND WARM EXTRUSION

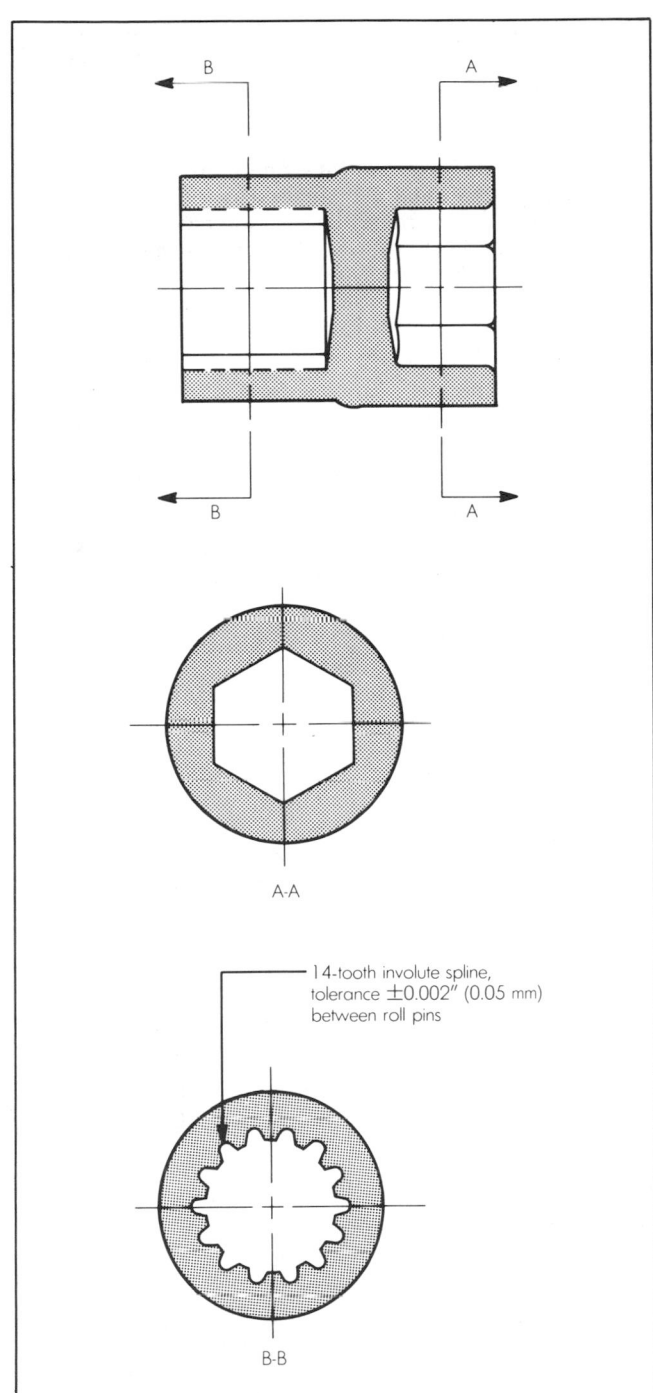

B   A

A-A

14-tooth involute spline,
tolerance ±0.002″ (0.05 mm)
between roll pins

B-B

Fig. 38-9 Part cold extruded from AISI 4140 steel in a single hit. (*Imerman Industries, Inc.*)

MATERIALS EXTRUDED

Most metals can be cold extruded, providing enough pressure can be applied to exceed the yield strengths of the materials and tooling of sufficient strength is available. Material selection depends primarily upon the desired properties in the extruded product, a sufficient spread between yield and ultimate strengths of the material, a fair degree of ductility, and the availability of a press and of tooling capable of withstanding the required pressure and produce the cold extrusions economically.

With respect to steels, cold extruders predominantly use the softer, lower carbon grades. However, the use of alloy steels is increasing because of the need for higher strength in smaller, more lightweight components. Carbon steels employed include the AISI 1005 to 1070 types, some of the resulfurized 1100 series, and the higher manganese 1500 series. Popular alloy steels for cold extruding include AISI 4023, 4037, 4130, 4140, 4820, and the 5100 and 8600 series.

Many stainless steels are cold extruded. Nonferrous metals that are cold extruded include aluminum, lead, magnesium, and copper alloys.

APPLICATIONS

Cold extrusion is now being used for producing more economically a wide variety of parts that were previously cast, forged, or machined by metal-removal processes. Some large, hollow extrusions, such as wheel spindles and axles, are replacing parts formerly shaped from tubing by hot swaging. Industries using cold-extruded products include automotive, aircraft and aerospace, appliance, ordnance, hardware, farm and construction equipment, electrical equipment, and air conditioning. Typical parts produced by cold extrusion include bearing races, a variety of fasteners, piston pins, spark plug shells, socket wrenches, track link bushings, transmission and axle shafts, pinions and gear blanks, ball joint sockets, switch housings, and steering and suspension components.

METHODS OF EXTRUDING

Cold and warm extrusion are performed in several ways. Methods employed include backward, forward, radial, combination, impact, and continuous extrusion.

Backward Extrusion

In backward (indirect or reverse) extrusion, metal is forced to flow in the opposite direction to the travel of the punch (see Fig. 38-10). Backward extrusion is most commonly employed for the production of hollow parts, but metal can also be forced to flow into recesses in the punch to form splines and other shapes. The outside diameters of the parts formed take on the shapes of the dies and/or recesses in the punches, and the inside diameters of hollow parts are controlled by the punches.

Forward Extrusion

In forward (direct) extrusion, metal is forced to flow ahead of the punch through an orifice in the die (see Fig. 38-11). Forward extrusion is most commonly employed to produce shaft-type components, but is also used to form other shapes.

Radial Extrusion

Radial extrusion, sometimes called cross, lateral, or transverse extrusion, is an adaptation of forward extrusion in which the die orifices allow the metal to flow radially, usually at an angle of 90° to the direction of punch travel.

Combination Extrusion

Backward, forward, and radial extrusion are sometimes performed simultaneously with a single press stroke, permitting the forming of more-complex-shaped parts. Examples of simultaneous backward and forward extrusion are illustrated in

COLD AND WARM EXTRUSION

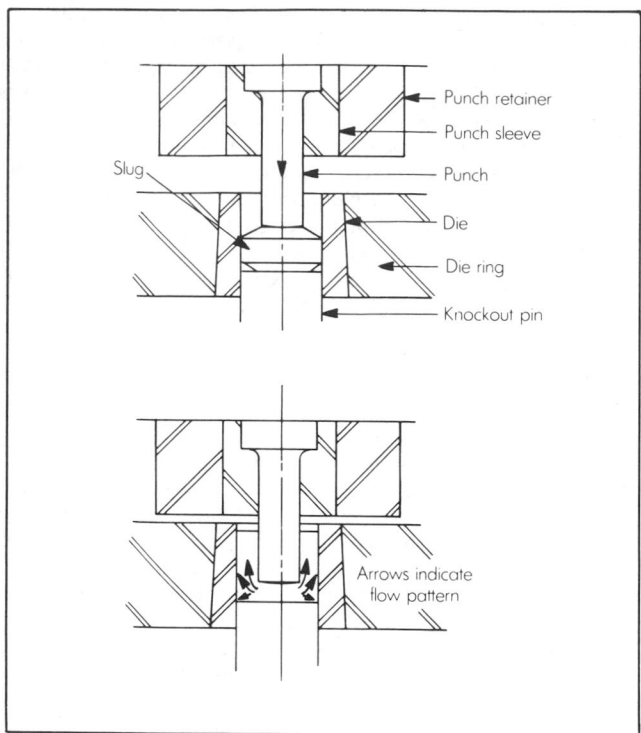

Fig. 38-10 Backward extrusion.

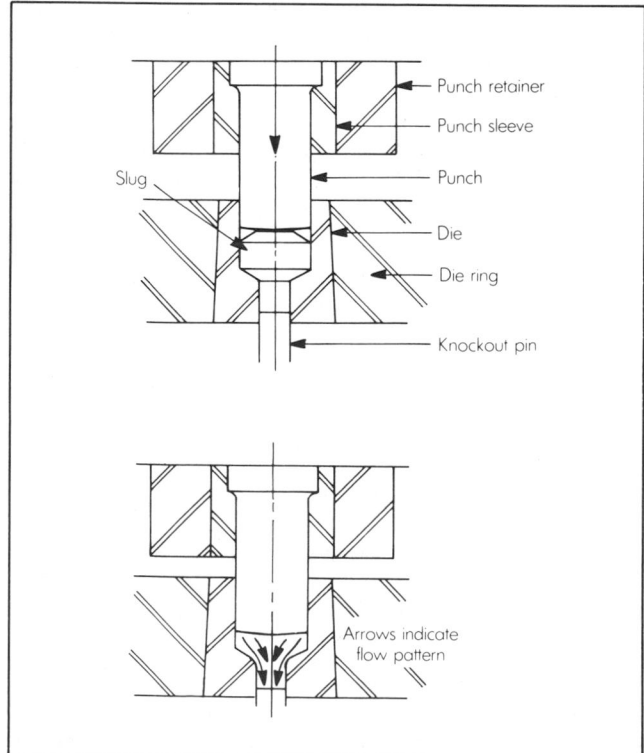

Fig. 38-11 Forward extrusion.

Fig. 38-12. Upsetting (heading), discussed later in this chapter, is also often combined with extrusion to enlarge the diameters of parts at desired sections.

Impact Extrusion

Impact extrusion, often called simply impacting, is similar to backward, forward, and combination extrusion except that faster speeds, shorter strokes, and shallower dies are employed. Impact of the punch causes the metal to move upward, downward, or both upward and downward.

PRESSES FOR COLD AND WARM EXTRUSION

Cold and warm extrusion are performed on both mechanical and hydraulic presses, as well as on upsetting (heading) machines and multistation, automatic forming machines, discussed later in this chapter. Major factors influencing press selection include the size and shape of the part to be extruded, material from which it is made, reduction in area required, production rate and total number of parts needed, tolerances to be held, initial cost, and maintenance costs.

Mechanical Presses

A major advantage of mechanical presses is their high-speed capability. The slide speed is highest at midstroke and can be variable. Possible limitations include a variable force (depending upon slide position) and a maximum practical force capacity of about 6000 tons (53 MN). To establish the drive capacity for mechanical presses, the force required must be determined for a specific distance up on the stroke.

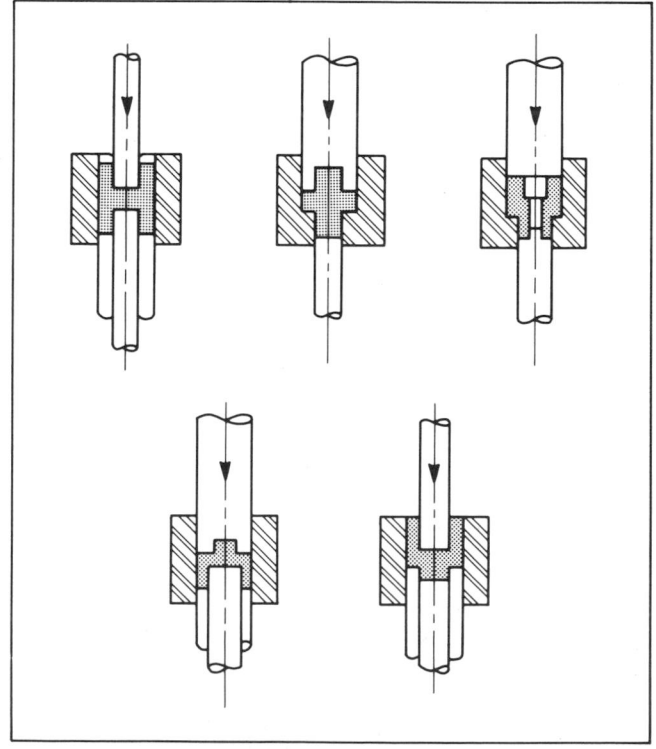

Fig. 38-12 Simultaneous backward and forward extrusion can produce complex-shaped parts. (*Verson Allsteel Press Co.*)

COLD AND WARM EXTRUSION

Most mechanical presses used for cold or warm extrusion are the straight-side type, with slide actuation by crankshaft, eccentric gear, knuckle joint, or drag links. Presses with crankshaft actuation of the slides are frequently used for long extrusions because of their positive action. Crankshafts are most common for presses to about 600 tons (5338 kN), but are available on presses with capacities to 3000 tons (26.7 MN) and stroke lengths to 48″ (1219 mm).

Hydraulic Presses

Important advantages of hydraulic presses include relatively constant force throughout the stroke; long stroke capabilities, 100″ (2540 mm) or more; and high force capacities, 50,000 tons (445 MN) or more. A possible limitation is lower speeds, as determined by the hydraulic pump capabilities.

Horizontal hydraulic presses with multiple die stations and work transfer devices are used extensively for the cold extrusion of shaft-type parts. For the extrusion of automotive control arms, three-action hydraulic presses have been built with two opposed horizontal platens, one vertical platen, multiple die stations, and automatic work transfer.

TOOLING FOR COLD AND WARM EXTRUSION

Tool design and tool material selection are critical to successful cold extrusion. The punch profile must be such that the tool properly meters the lubricant, allowing the tools to last for a sufficient number of blows and making the process economically feasible. Typically, punches and dies are encased in retainers and shrink rings so that they are under compressive stresses at all times. Surface finish of the tools in contact with the workpiece should be 5 μ in. (0.13 μ m) or less.

A typical backward-extrusion die is shown in Fig. 38-13. A carbide die insert and its ring are tapered in the holder, which consists of two members shrunk or pressed together. The carbide insert and die ring are supported by toughened steel plates that enable the high local loads to be distributed. The extruding punch is guided by a spring-loaded guideplate which must clear the punch nose and is positioned by being piloted in a ring on the lower die. Ejection of the part from the die is by means of a delayed-action stripper which lifts the bottom portion of the die cavity. Figure 38-14 illustrates one design of a forward-extrusion die.

PRODUCING SLUGS FOR EXTRUDING

The production of slugs for cold or warm extrusion is a costly part of the complete processing. Slugs must have accurate dimensions, smooth surfaces, and uniform volumes, especially if closed dies are used. Tolerances that must be maintained on the size and shape of slugs depend primarily upon the accuracy required in the extruded parts. Slugs that fit closely into the die are particularly important for backward-extruding operations, but preformed slugs need not conform closely to the contour of the die, except at locating surfaces.

Shapes and dimensions of slugs should generally conform as closely as possible to those of the extrusions. When a part can be extruded in a single operation, the slug diameter is usually made equal to the maximum diameter of the extruded part. When several extrusions are required, however, slug diameters are often smaller than the maximum diameter of the required part.

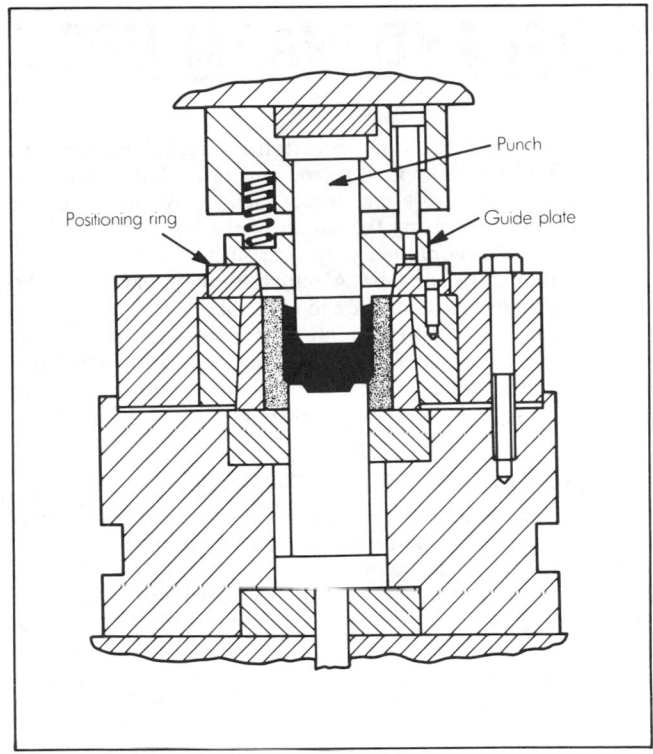

Fig. 38-13 Typical backward-extrusion die with a carbide insert.

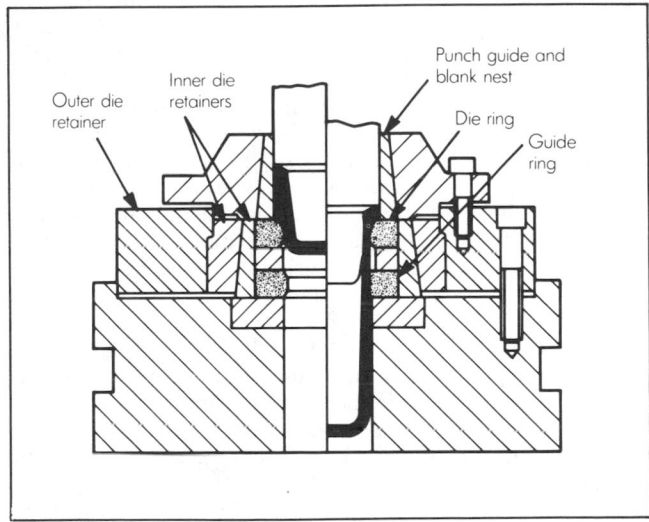

Fig. 38-14 One design of a forward-extrusion die with carbide inserts in a compression ring.

Controlling only the lengths of slugs is not generally sufficient because of volume variations that can result from differences in diameters of the slugs. It is usually best to control the weights of the slugs, which are a direct indication of their volumes. Slug weights are often controlled within 1% or less. Flat, parallel ends; perpendicularity of the ends to the sides; and clean, smooth surfaces are also important.

COLD AND WARM UPSETTING

COLD AND WARM UPSETTING (HEADING)

Upsetting is a forming operation for reshaping metal by plastic flow. Force applied to the end of a blank, contained between a punch and a die, causes metal flow, increasing the diameter and decreasing the length of the blank.

Upsetting is accomplished by inserting a blank of a specific length into a stationary die. A punch, moving parallel to the axis of the blank, contacts the end of the blank protruding from the die and compresses the metal. Impressions in the punch or die, or both, determine the upset shape produced. Some parts are upset in the punch, some in the die, some in both, and some in an open space between the punch and the die (see Fig. 38-15).

ADVANTAGES OF UPSETTING

Major advantages of upsetting are economical production, the forming of high-quality parts, increased part strength, and versatility in product design.

Cold working during upsetting increases tensile, yield, and shear strengths of the metal, as well as its fatigue life. The uninterrupted grain flow pattern produced follows the part contour. For some applications, the upset parts can be made smaller without sacrificing strength, or lower cost metals can be substituted for more expensive raw materials.

Upsetting produces smooth surface finishes. The exact finish obtained depends upon the condition of the raw material, the surface coating and/or lubricant employed, the finish on the tools, and other factors. Surface finishes from 10-100 μin. (0.25-2.54 μm) are common. Cold-drawn raw material is used extensively for upsetting, and the smooth surfaces produced in drawing are retained in upsetting.

The tolerances that can be maintained in upsetting depend upon many variables, including the style of the upset, the length-to-diameter ratio of the blank, the severity of the operation, the type of workpiece material and size of workpiece, and the quality of the tooling and machine. Dimensional tolerances as close as 0.0005" (0.013 mm) on shank diameter and 0.005" (0.13 mm) on overall length are held in some applications, but such close tolerances increase production costs.

LIMITATIONS OF UPSETTING

Possible limitations of upsetting include the need for substantial production requirements and the limit to the maximum size of parts that can be formed, which depends upon the capacity of the machine with respect to force, energy, and cutoff capability.

MATERIALS UPSET

A wide variety of ferrous and nonferrous metals are formed by cold and warm upsetting. The degree of upsetting possible varies for different metals. Desirable chemical compositions, melting practices, and properties, as well as undesirable defects, of metals to be upset are essentially the same as those discussed previously in this chapter for cold and warm extrusion.

APPLICATIONS OF UPSETTING

Upsetting, often combined with extruding, trimming, thread rolling, and other operations, has long been employed for the production of nails, bolts, screws, nuts, rivets, and other fasteners. More recently, the process has been applied to the low-cost, mass production of many other components. Parts being manufactured in this way include pipe fittings and plugs, spark-plug shells, ball studs, shafts, bearing pins and spacers, and wrist pins.

Other components being produced by upsetting include cams, gears, worms, ratchets, hose clamps, electrical terminals, ordnance parts, balls and rollers, and shifter forks. The process is also being used extensively to form slugs to required size and shape for subsequent extruding, forming, or machining. Upsetting tests the quality of the starting material, opening any surface seams and eliminating the need for further processing.

Upsetting can also be used to bend or flatten metal on specific parts of the blanks. However, this is usually done on only one end of each blank unless double-end machines are employed. To form shanks having cross sections other than round, wire or rod of the required cross section is sometimes used. In other cases, shanks are shaped by pressing round stock into dies of the desired shape.

METHODS OF UPSETTING

Most upsetting is done on horizontal mechanically powered machines, often called headers or formers, described later in this section. The process is also performed on conventional vertical presses and special machines, powered either mechanically or hydraulically, with the starting metal unheated (cold

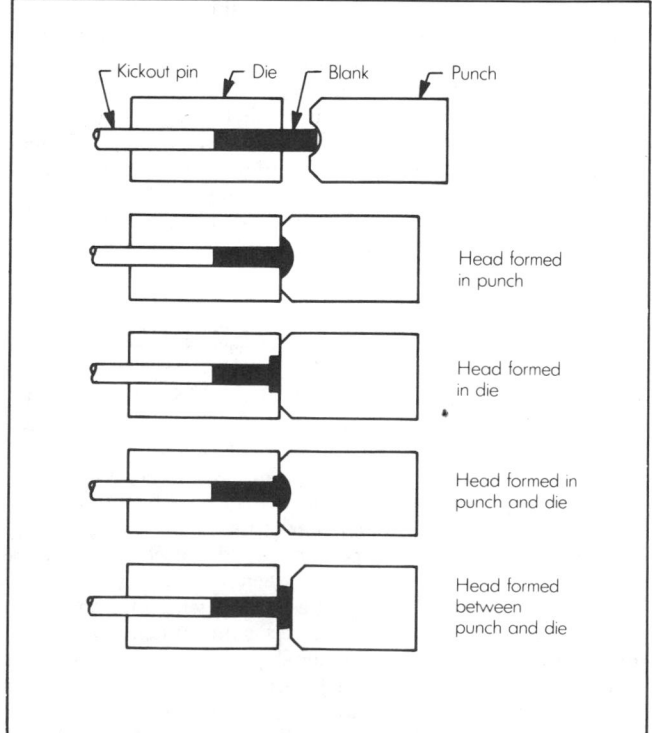

Fig. 38-15 Various types of upsetting.

upsetting) or heated (warm upsetting). Mechanical presses are generally preferred for forming because of their higher production capability, but they cost more than hydraulic presses of comparable force capacity. Hydraulic presses generally provide longer tool life when cold forming; for warm forming, the longer contact time between the tools and the workpieces tends to shorten punch life.

Warm Upsetting

Heating the metal to a temperature below its recrystallization temperature adds to the capabilities of upsetting. Most metals undergo a drastic reduction in tensile strength and increase in formability when heated to a temperature range of about 1100-1300°F (600-700°C). This is especially important in forming alloy steels, some stainless steels, and other metals having high tensile strengths, or in making parts that require considerable deformation.

Controlled-Flow Heading

In controlled-flow heading, slugs are upset after they are guided in a die. A typical die stack is seen in Fig. 38-16. In this application, slugs 3/4" (19 mm) diam x 3" (76 mm) long, sheared from AISI 5120 steel bar stock, are upset into pancake shaped slugs 2 1/8" (54 mm) diam x 3/8" (9.5 mm) thick in a single press stroke. Sheared slugs are inserted through the top of a restraining guide bushing and fall through the bushing bore against an anvil. The guide bushing is supported within its

retainer at a predetermined height by a cushion mounted under the press bolster.

Cold-Flow Forming

Gleason Machine Div. has developed a patented G-Flow machine for cold-flow forming. The machine has three working elements: a ram punch, an anvil, and a power pad, each hydraulically driven and activated independently by an electronic solid-state control system. All three elements are programmable for velocity, displacement, and force. In cold-flow forming, the slug is subjected to pressure by the ram and anvil punches until it reaches a plastic state. The material then flows until the part is fully formed. The metal may flow backward, forward, or radially under this steady, uniformly controlled pressure.

Orbital Forming

Orbital forming, a relatively new process of cold forging, is a method for producing shapes by lateral upsetting or vertical displacement, or by a combination of these operations. An upset ratio of 4:1 can be obtained. Metal is plastically deformed progressively between a lower die moved vertically by a hydraulic ram and an orbiting upper die having a conical working face (see Fig. 38-17). Since there is no impact between

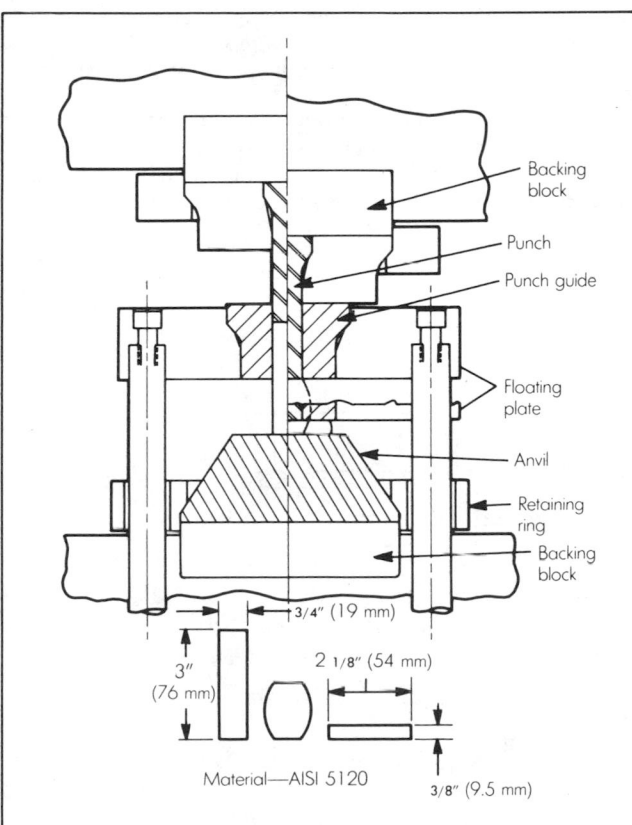

Fig. 38-16 Typical die stack for controlled-flow heading. (*Verson All-steel Press Co.*)

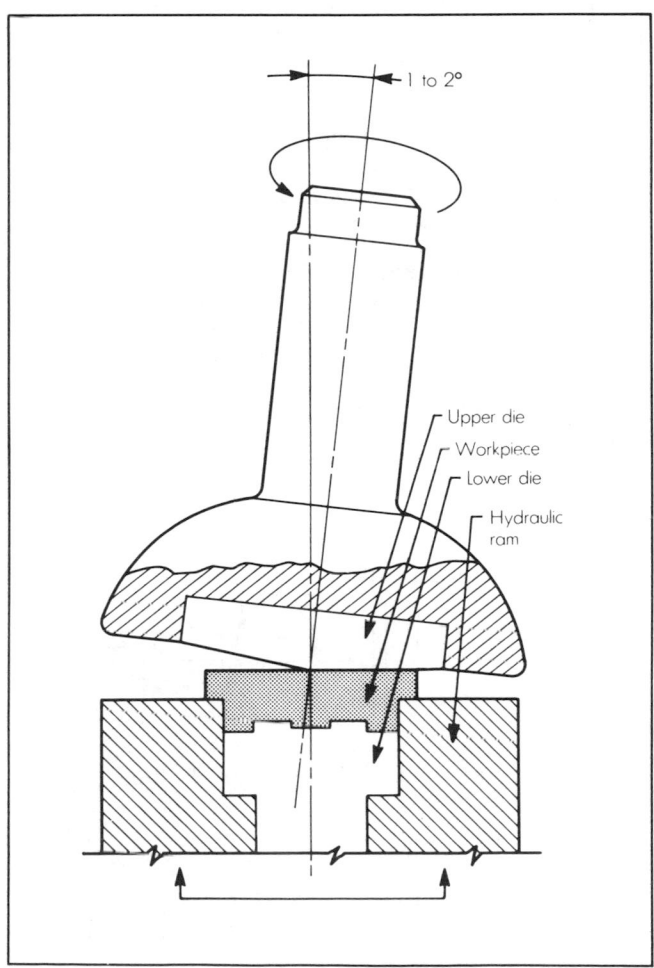

Fig. 38-17 In orbital forming, the upper die has a conical working face. (*VSI Automation*)

COLD AND WARM UPSETTING

the tooling and workpiece, the process is quiet; and because only a small area is formed at a time, pressure requirements are low (about one-fourth of normal forging pressures). The axis of the upper die is inclined, usually at an angle of 1-2°.

MACHINES FOR UPSETTING

Horizontal machines (presses) for upsetting are generally called headers or formers. They are available in small to large sizes, with varying degrees of capability. With a blank held in a stationary die on a horizontal press, the end protruding from the face of the die is struck axially by an upsetting tool. Since only so much metal can be formed in one blow, the number of dies, blows, and wire-size capacities usually describe specific machines. Most machines have automatic wire feeding, cutoff, transferring, and kickout capabilities.

Single-Stroke Headers

These machines have one die and one punch. They make simple parts that can be formed on one blow. Ball headers are a variation of this type of machine. Speeds range up to 900 parts per minute. Double-stroke headers have one die and two punches. Cone and finish punches change position between blows. This is the most popular machine for producing screw blanks and other fasteners.

Three-blow, two-die headers have two dies and three punches. Of basic double-stroke header design, these headers offer the added advantage of allowing extruding or upsetting to be performed in the first die before double-blow heading or heading and trimming are performed in the second die. They produce large-headed, small-shanked, special parts by combining trapped extrusion and upsetting in one simple machine. They are also suitable for stepped parts when transfer between dies would be difficult.

Progressive or Transfer Headers

These upsetters are multistation machines with two, three, four, five, or more dies and a like number of tools. A transfer unit moves workpieces from the cutter through a succession of dies, either straight through, with end-for-end turnaround between stations, or a combination of the two. Multiple upsetting blows combined with extrusion, piercing, and trimming make these versatile machines ideal for producing long-shank or complex-shaped parts.

TOOLING FOR UPSETTING

Design and material selection for tooling are critical for successful and economical upsetting. Various tooling components required include those for cutoff, coning, and kickout.

Cutoff Tooling

Good cutoff quality is important to accurate upsetting. Ends with a minimum of distortion are easier on tooling, provide better control of metal flow, and give good ends on the finished parts. Quality of the cutoff blank is determined by the type of wire used (its material and hardness), the type of cutoff tooling, and the type of cutoff quill (or stationary cutter) in the die block and by the movement of a cutter insert in a plate mounted on a slide or lever.

Cone Tool Design

The importance of the cone operation cannot be overstressed. Just as the preparation of the wire is of prime importance, the cone operation is the foundation upon which the final upset is to be built. The function of a coning operation in two-blow heading is to reduce the amount of unsupported length to less than 2 1/4 times the average cone diameter for the finish blow. As shown in Fig. 38-18, $(E + F) - J = 2 1/4$ or less. This amount of unsupported length upsets satisfactorily in the second blow.

Figure 38-18 also shows the detail of the cone tool design and cone upset. Cone tool design is very specific; in attempting a two-blow upset, some bending takes place in the first blow and the cone tool holds this bending to acceptable limits.

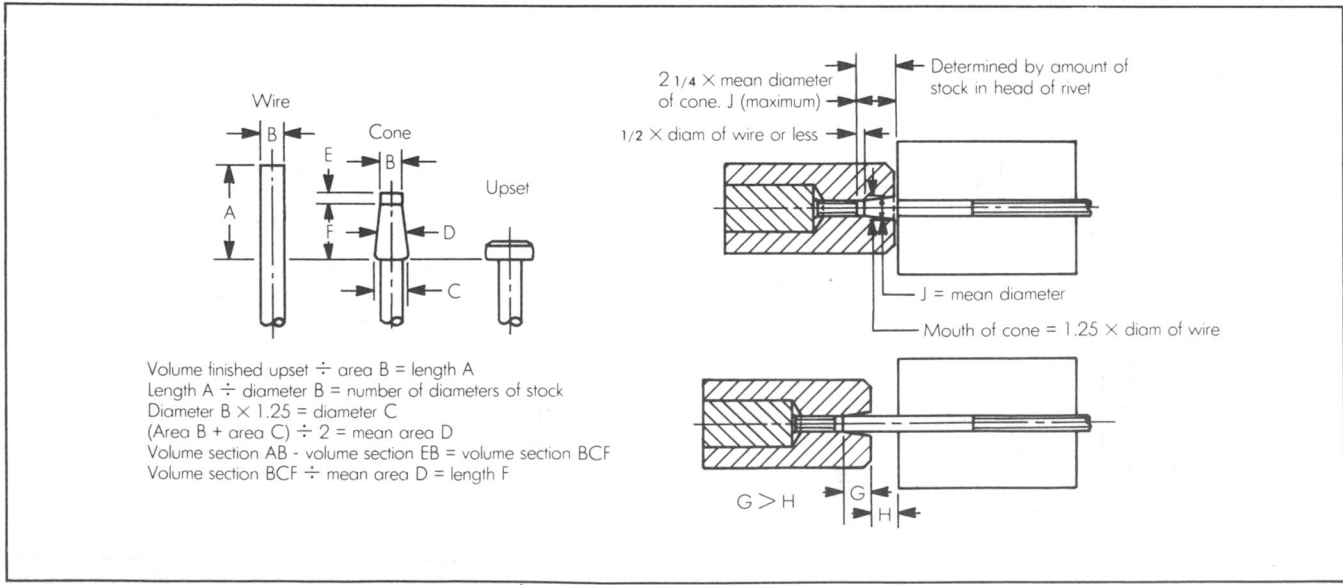

Volume finished upset ÷ area B = length A
Length A ÷ diameter B = number of diameters of stock
Diameter B × 1.25 = diameter C
(Area B + area C) ÷ 2 = mean area D
Volume section AB - volume section EB = volume section BCF
Volume section BCF ÷ mean area D = length F

Fig. 38-18 Two-blow upsetting sequence showing the relationship of the cone dimensions.

AUTOMATIC COLD AND WARM FORMING

Kickout Pins

When the workpiece has been headed, it must be ejected by a kickout pin to clear the die for the next blank. At the start of the operation, the blank enters the die until the kickout pin stops it and upsetting begins. Therefore, the kickout pin must support some of the upsetting pressure as seen in Fig. 38-19, *a*. If the unsupported length of the kickout pin is more than 10-12 diameters, it tends to bend or break under upsetting pressure or kickout load. However, the second function of the kickout pin is to eject the part from the die, and pin length is even more critical (and apparent) when the blank is die-pointed, as shown in view *b*. Even though the part diameter and length are unchanged, the kickout pin is smaller in diameter and therefore weaker. In such a case, the die supports some of the upsetting load, but the pin would probably fail quickly from kickout loads.

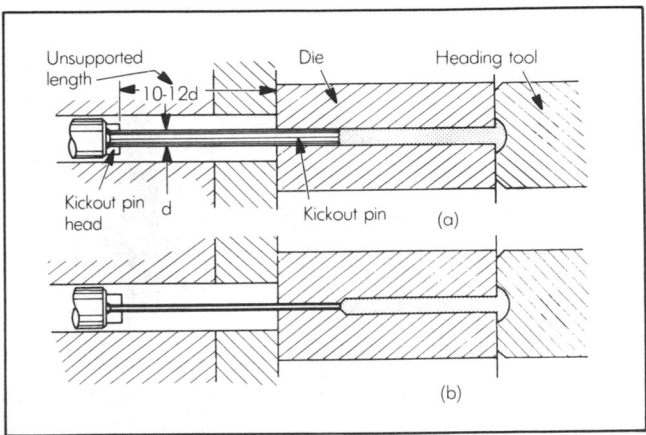

Fig. 38-19 Unsupported kickout pins.

AUTOMATIC COLD AND WARM FORMING

Automatic cold and warm forming is done on completely automated, multistation machines equipped with a high-speed device for automatically transferring parts through a series of punch and die setups. Operations commonly performed on these machines include extruding and upsetting (discussed previously in this chapter), shearing (cutoff), coining, piercing, trimming, threading, and knurling.

ADVANTAGES AND LIMITATIONS

Advantages and limitations of automatic forming are similar to those given earlier in this chapter for extruding and upsetting. A major advantage is cost savings resulting from reduced material requirements and handling, the elimination or reduction of subsequent machining, and high production rates. Other benefits include improved physical properties, smooth surface finishes, and close tolerances of the parts formed.

An additional advantage of automatic forming, compared to extruding and heading, is the capability of performing more operations in the same setup. Production rates on automatic forming machines vary from about 35 to as many as 120 parts per minute, depending upon the size and shape of the parts, and the material being formed.

Possible limitations of automatic forming are the size and shape of the parts that can be produced (discussed next in this section) and the need for substantial production requirements to make the process economical. The substantial cost of automatic forming machines and necessary tooling makes high production requirements essential. However, advances in machine design and controls have reduced the time required for changeover, thus making shorter production runs feasible.

APPLICATIONS OF AUTOMATIC FORMING

Parts produced on automatic forming machines are used by many different industries for a wide variety of applications. They have replaced many components which were previously cast, forged, machined, or produced by other processes. The versatility of automatic forming machines has led to their being referred to as parts makers. Considerable savings can be realized by forming different parts of similar size and shape. This minimizes tooling costs and changeover time, and makes the production of smaller lot sizes more economical.

MACHINES FOR AUTOMATIC FORMING

Machines used for automatic cold and warm forming are available in various sizes and capacities to handle stock to 2"(51 mm) diam or larger. The machines are usually special, built to specific customer requirements, and are often sold fully tooled. They are all equipped with high-speed transfer units that automatically move the workpieces from station to station.

Most automatic forming machines are designed with the stations arranged and work transfer accomplished in a horizontal plane. Figure 38-20 shows a cross section of the tooling area on a four-die horizontal machine. Some machines, however, have the stations arranged vertically, with the workpieces being transferred from the top of the machine to the bottom as they progress through the forming sequence.

Automatic forming machines, supported with an uncoiler, are generally equipped with a wire straightener, a roll-feed unit, and a cutoff station to shear blanks of the required length. When equipped with a cutoff station, the machines are identified by the number of stations and number of dies; for example, a six-station, five-die forming machine. The starting coil stock is usually phosphatized and lubricated, and sometimes annealed. In-line cold-drawing machines are occasionally employed to size and smooth the stock.

Practically all automatic forming machines are mechanically operated. A motor-driven flywheel drives an eccentric shaft that is connected to the machine slide by a pitman. The reciprocating slide carries a punch at each station to force metal into the stationary dies mounted on the machine opposite the punches. Normally, a forming operation is completed with each stroke of the slide, with the partially formed part being removed from the die by a kickout mechanism. At the final station, a completely formed part is removed from the die.

AUTOMATIC COLD AND WARM FORMING

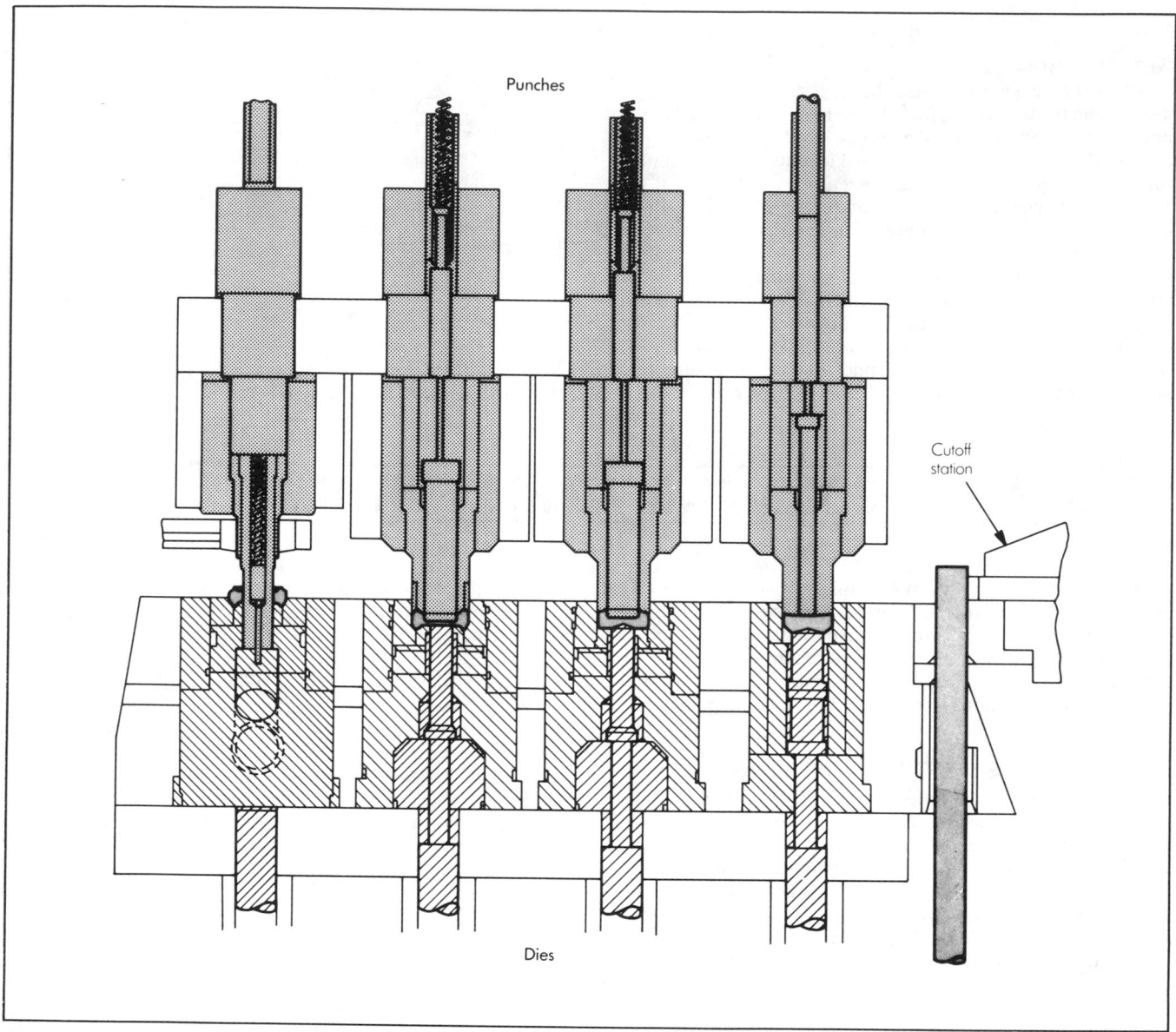

Fig. 38-20 A four-die automatic forming machine tooled to produce gear blanks.

SWAGING

Swaging is a metalforming process in which a rapid series of impact blows is delivered radially to either solid or tubular work. This causes a reduction in cross-sectional area and/or a change in geometric shape. The method is basically a forging process, especially similar to radial forging.

THE SWAGING PROCESS

In swaging, impact blows are transferred to the work in rapid succession by dies in the machine. The contour built into the dies controls the cross section formed.

METAL FLOW

Under normal operating conditions, each swaging blow to a solid bar produces a flow of metal, as shown in Fig. 39-1. It is often assumed that the metal moves entirely in the direction of the feed, but this is not the case. Flow takes place in all directions in amounts dependent upon conditions surrounding the metal in question. Pressure in an ordinary swaging die is exerted across a single axis. Free flow of the metal is resisted by high surface friction within the die. If this friction is overly large, no longitudinal flow takes place and excessive localized stresses in the groove of the die spall or break out the hardened surface. This stressing takes place when the length of the work under compression exceeds ten times the diameter.

WORK ROTATION

Another action which takes place in swaging is slow rotation of the work. This rotation appears to be a steady motion; and for practical purposes it may be considered so, although actually it is intermittent, with intervals so close together that they cannot be seen or felt. The dies intermittently compress the work and rotate around it, and it is during the compression that the dies grip the piece, causing it to rotate at approximately spindle speed. After the swaging blow, the dies release the work, which continues to rotate at a slower rate from its own inertia. Repeated at very rapid intervals, it gives the impression that the work rotates steadily.

EFFECTS ON MATERIAL PROPERTIES

Whether or not the physical effects of swaging actually penetrate the bar depends upon whether the machine is heavy enough for the job. A light machine on a heavy piece has only a surface effect, and the tensile strength is not increased in proportion to the apparent surface hardness. On the other hand, if the machine is heavier than the job actually requires, both the hardness and strength are increased. The effects of these two conditions are visible on a swaged piece. A rod that is cold worked only on the surface is concave on the end, while a bar that is thoroughly cold worked has a definite convex bulge at the same point.

ADVANTAGES AND LIMITATIONS OF SWAGING

Economy, versatility, and improved workpiece quality are considered important advantages of the swaging process.

ECONOMY OF SWAGING

Swaging is one of the most economical processes available for forming cylindrical parts required in medium to large production quantities. Machines used are relatively inexpensive, and they are simple to set up, operate, and maintain. Skilled operators are not required; for machines having automatic feeds, one operator can attend several machines, thus reducing labor costs. Since no metal is removed in swaging, material savings add to the economy of the process. A variety of shaped sections (square, hexagonal, etc.) can be formed from low-cost round stock. Assemblies made by swaging eliminate the cost of fastening devices or joining operations.

VERSATILITY OF SWAGING

For some applications, swaging can produce parts that cannot be economically made in any other way. One example is the forming of copper welding tips having angular holes that are drilled before the tips are reduced, tapered, and elongated by swaging. Wire mandrels are inserted to prevent deformation of the holes during swaging.

IMPROVEMENTS IN QUALITY

Swaging refines, rearranges, and improves the grain structure of the metal, resulting in increases in surface hardness, elastic limit, and tensile strengthen of both ferrous and nonferrous materials. Stainless and alloy steels exhibit such increases to a greater extent than other metals. Carbon steels show an increase in tensile strength of about 1000 psi (6.9 MPa) for each 10% of area reduction.

Close dimensional tolerances can be consistently maintained in swaging, depending upon the condition and size of the machine and dies. New dies, properly designed and made, can sometimes swage initial parts to tolerances of 0.0001" (0.003 mm) or less. Die wear, however, generally makes such tolerances impractical for production applications. The dies are usually manufactured to pro-

METHODS OF SWAGING

duce parts at the low limit of required tolerance, and they gradually wear to the high tolerance limit in a straight line variation over a period of time.

LIMITATIONS OF SWAGING

Limitations of swaging include the need for workpieces of symmetrical cross section and restrictions on the angles and lengths of taper that can be formed in one operation. If more than one pass is used, lines of demarcation may be visible where one die overlaps the other. Forming of sharp tapers or swaging close to shoulders is difficult.

Swaging is a noisy operation, which can be objectionable. The noise level, however, can be reduced by proper mounting of the machine and the use of baffles and/or enclosures. For many applications, the use of ear protectors is required.

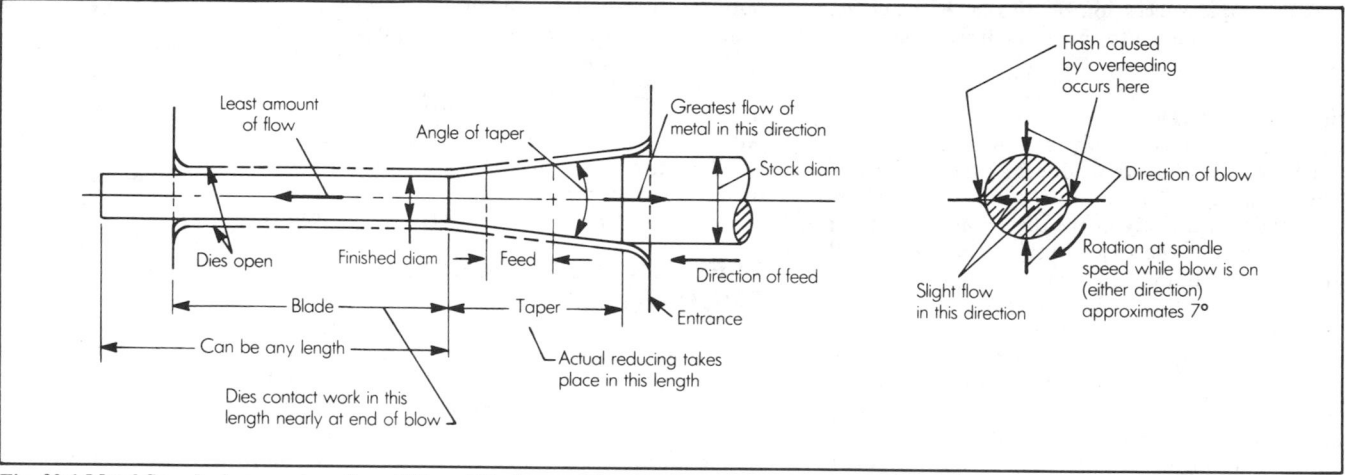

Fig. 39-1 Metal flow during swaging of a solid bar. (*Machinery Div., The Torrington Co.*)

MATERIALS SWAGED

Any metal having a reasonable amount of ductility and elongation can be swaged. Hot-rolled steel is usually more ductile and can be swaged more easily than cold-rolled or drawn stock because cold working can reduce the deformation properties.

Among the ferrous metals, the low-carbon steels, such as 1010, 1015, or 1020 steel, are the easiest to swage and normally can be reduced 40% or more in cross-sectional area in one operation. Multiple operations are necessary to secure greater area reductions. As the metal's carbon content or alloy content is increased, its capability of being cold formed by swaging is decreased. Alloys such as manganese, nickel, and chromium increase metal strength and thereby decrease the cold-forming

capabilities of the metal.

Depending upon the alloy, nonferrous metals such as copper, brass, and aluminum usually adapt readily to swaging. It is possible to obtain taper reductions of as much as 70% in cross-sectional area, because of the high ductility of these metals. Leaded brass is generally not recommended for swaging, since it usually fractures under the stress of cold working. With proper die design, however, leaded brass can sometimes be swaged to area reductions of about 10%.

Materials such as tungsten and molybdenum, which have low ductility, are formed better with hot-swaging techniques. Many materials that are brittle at room temperature must be preheated before insertion into a swaging machine.

METHODS OF SWAGING

The various methods of swaging include solid, tube, mandrel, cold (room temperature), hot, and internal methods. Swagers can be through-fed to reduce an entire bar or tube, or the workpiece can simply be fed in and out to reduce only the end. Multiple passes may be necessary to make long tapers. In central reductions, the part is advanced into the swager for a given distance, the diameter is reduced for a specified length, and the entire part is removed from the machine. It is possible to produce regular or irregular internal shapes. Stationary-spindle machines can swage external shapes.

TUBE SWAGING

The swaging of tubing involves somewhat different factors from those involved in swaging solid material. Each time a blow is struck, part of the action is used to increase the thickness of the tube wall. The movement of metal longitudinally also occurs; the amount of this movement, or lengthening, as well as the amount of wall thickening, depends on the original proportion of wall thickness to outer diameter, amount of reduction, angle of taper, and other factors.

Figure 39-2 shows the inner cone surface being compressed not as a straight line but as the curved surface, *A*. As this surface approaches a point, compression lines, *B*, build up to roughen the surface increasingly. Ordinarily this roughening is of no consequence. When tube diameters become theoretically solid, the material is not completely or actually solid, but contains laps and seams resulting from the collapse of the original inner surface, *C*. In aluminum or other soft materials, a cold weld sometimes takes place and the seams disappear.

MANDREL SWAGING

For certain applications it is desirable to maintain or reduce the wall thickness of a tube or to meet a specific inner diameter. In such cases, a mandrel is used. Mandrels are also used to support thin-wall tubes during reduction and to form internal shapes. When extended through the front of the dies, the mandrel can be used as a pilot to support the first part of an assembly to be swaged.

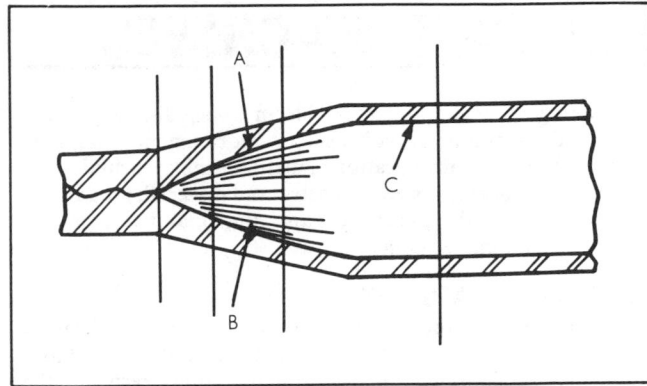

Fig. 39-2 Reduction flow pattern during tube swaging. (*Machinery Div. The Torrington Co.*)

SWAGING APPLICATIONS

Swaging is used for a wide variety of applications, including tapering, pointing, reducing, external and internal forming, compacting, sizing, and assembling. A few typical examples are illustrated in Fig. 39-3. Typical cross sections of internal shapes produced by swaging tubular stock over shaped mandrels are shown in Fig. 39-4.

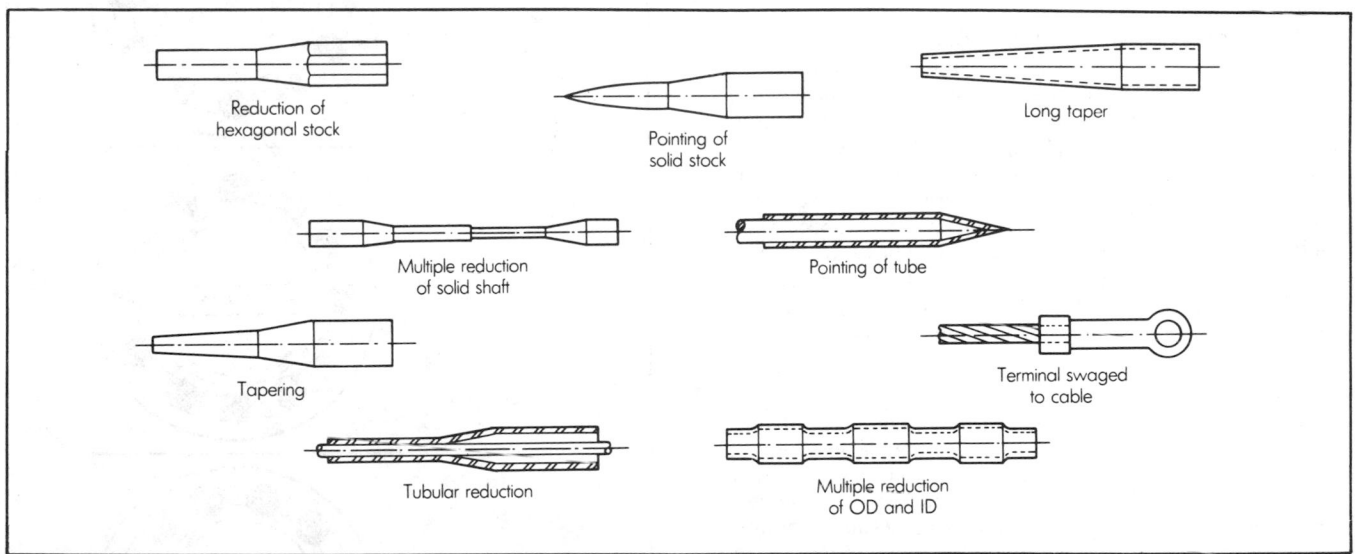

Reduction of
hexagonal stock

Pointing of
solid stock

Long taper

Multiple reduction
of solid shaft

Pointing of tube

Tapering

Terminal swaged
to cable

Tubular reduction

Multiple reduction
of OD and ID

Fig. 39-3 Examples of typical swaging applications. (*Machinery Div., The Torrington Co.*)

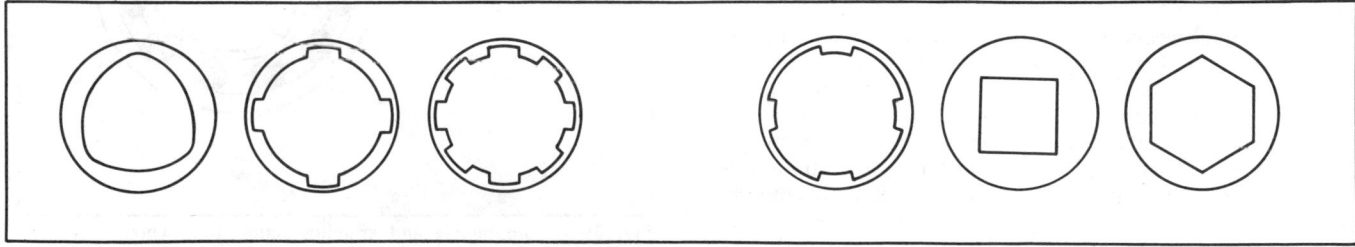

Fig. 39-4 Various cross sections produced by swaging tubes over shaped mandrels. (*Abbey Etna Machine Co.*)

SWAGING MACHINES

SWAGING MACHINES

Swaging machines are available in many different types, sizes, and capacities to suit specific requirements. Machine selection requires consideration of many variables including the application; workpiece size, geometry, and material; production requirements (quality, accuracy, and finish); and cost (initial, operating, and maintenance).

MACHINE CAPACITY

The proper machine size for a particular swaging application depends primarily upon the strength of the head designed into the machine. The load on the head is a direct result of the projected area of material under compression and the tensile strength of the material being swaged.

The rated diameter of solid stock that can be swaged on a machine can be calculated from the following formula:

$$D = \frac{C}{L \times S} \tag{1}$$

where:

D = rated diameter of solid stock, in.
C = capacity (safe working load), lb
L = die length, in.
S = tensile strength of workpiece material, psi

ROTARY SWAGING MACHINES

The action of a rotary swager is illustrated in Fig. 39-5, which shows the interior of the machine after the faceplate is removed. As the spindle is rotated, the backers strike opposing rolls and are driven inward, giving a blow to the work. As the spindle continues to revolve, centrifugal force causes the dies to separate. The number of blows delivered to the work is a function of the number of rolls and the revolution speed of the spindle, which varies from about 100 rpm in large machines to 1000 rpm or more in small machines. The amount of die movement varies from 0.005-0.375″ (0.13-9.52 mm), depending on the type of machine and the work being performed.

DIE-CLOSING SWAGERS

Die-closing swagers are used whenever it is necessary to open the die faces a greater amount for loading than is possible with rotary machines. A cross-sectional view of such a machine is shown in Fig. 39-6. The general construction is the same as that of the rotary swager in that both machines have common parts such as backers, rolls, an inside ring, and shims, but the die-closing swager differs in the addition of a wedge mechanism. The back of the die is ground at an angle, and a wedge is inserted between the angular die and the backer.

The use of the wedge permits a large opening between the die faces with the wedge retracted. Therefore, work of a larger diameter can be inserted in the machine for swaging. As the wedges are advanced to the forward position, the machine functions exactly like a rotary swager. The die-closing swager can be used for center reductions and fastening operations. It is versatile to the extent that it may be used as a rotary machine by simply removing the wedges and installing the proper tooling. Reductions are limited to 25% of the diameter of the work. The angle of the wedges generally varies between 4 and 7 1/2°.

STATIONARY-SPINDLE SWAGING MACHINES

Stationary-spindle swagers are rotary machines in reverse. As the name implies, the spindle is fixed so that the dies reciprocate in a vertical or horizontal plane; the head of the machine rotates about the spindle, thus giving the blow to the backers and dies.

These machines are used to manufacture shapes that are not round. They are available in two, three, and four-die configurations to handle various applications. One limitation is the need for a transition region between changes in cross-sectional shapes when workpieces are fed into and out of the dies; 90° shoulders cannot be formed.

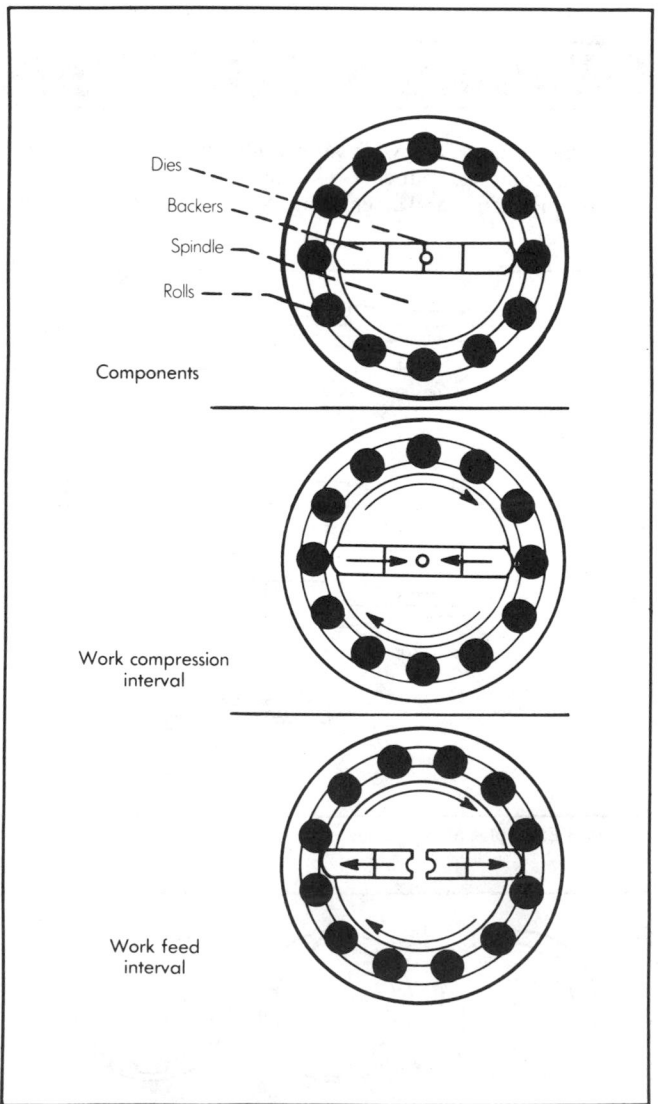

Fig. 39-5 Components and swaging action in a rotary machine. (*Machinery Div., The Torrington Co.*)

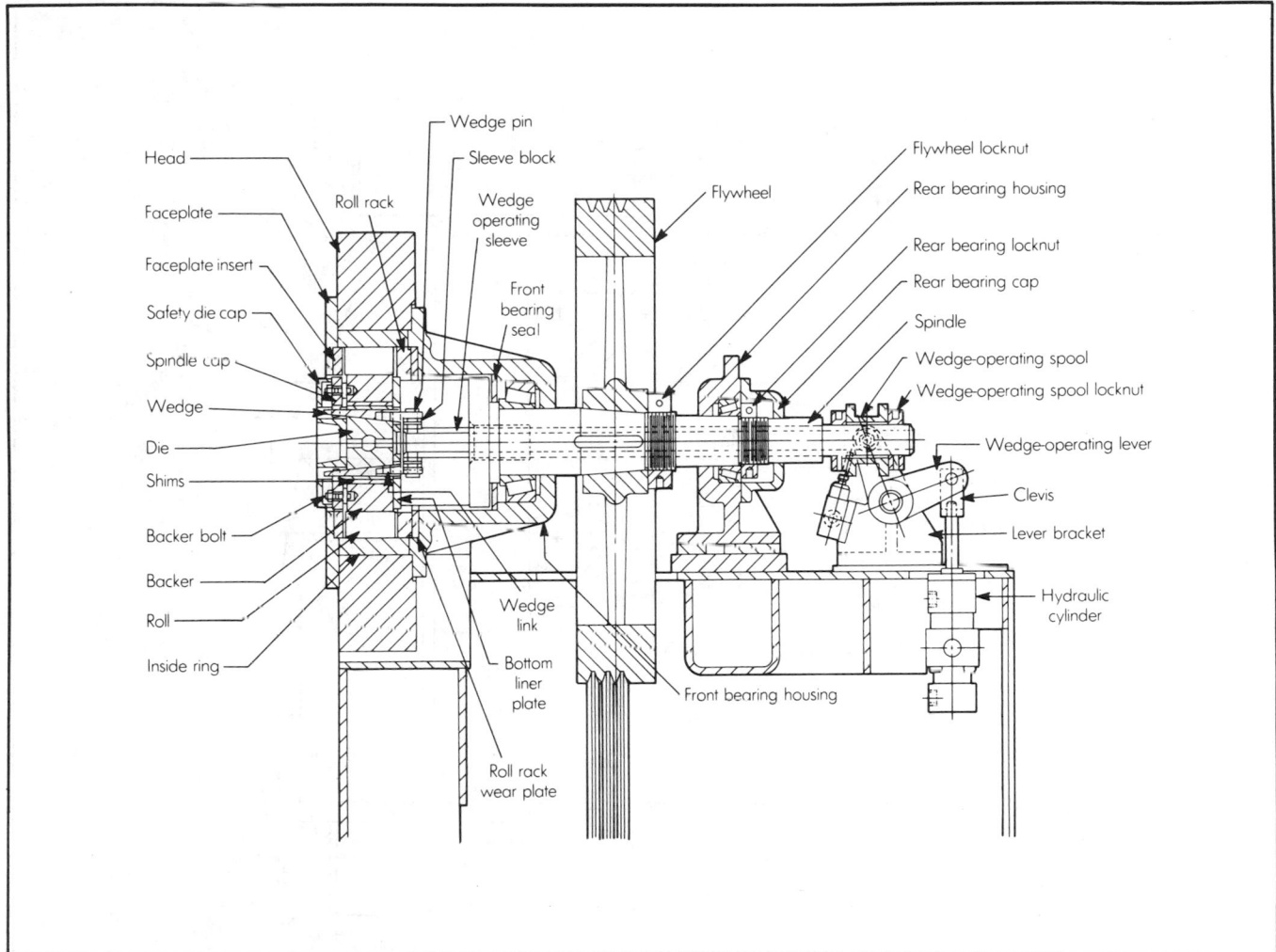

Fig. 39-6 Cross section of a die-closing swaging machine. (*Machinery Div., The Torrington Co.***)**

CREEPING-SPINDLE SWAGERS

Creeping-spindle swaging machines employ the principles of both stationary-spindle and rotary swagers. On these machines, the spindle head is mounted on a slowly rotating shaft which is driven by a reduction gear and variable-speed motor. The spindle head, containing the hammers and dies, revolves slowly within a rapidly rotating roller cage.

One advantage of creeping-spindle swaging is more accurate control of die reciprocation. These machines are used for swaging applications that are not suitable for stationary-spindle machines, such as forming rods or tubes into coils or forming workpieces that cannot be easily oscillated. Advantages include minimum flash on the workpieces and reduced possibility of the workpieces whipping.

SIMULTANEOUS-BLOW SWAGING MACHINES

In simultaneous-blow swaging, performed with four-die stationary-spindle machines, all four dies contact the work simultaneously. This method is used to form fluted shapes and other circular cross sections.

ALTERNATE-BLOW SWAGING MACHINES

Alternate-blow swaging (see Fig. 39-7) is effective for swaging shapes in a four-die stationary-spindle machine. It is accomplished by having alternate rolls recessed. With this arrangement, when two opposing rolls hammer the dies, the rolls 90° away do not (see Fig. 39-8), thus eliminating forming fins on the workpieces. Applications include swaging chisels, screwdrivers, file tangs, tapered leaf springs, and similar products.

HOT SWAGING MACHINES

Machines used for hot swaging are commonly water cooled. A channel is machined into the head of the swager to permit the circulation of water for extracting heat from the machine.

The method of heating workpieces for hot swaging should be one that keeps oxidation and resulting scale to a minimum. Because of its abrasiveness, scale is detrimental to the life of the internal components of the machine.

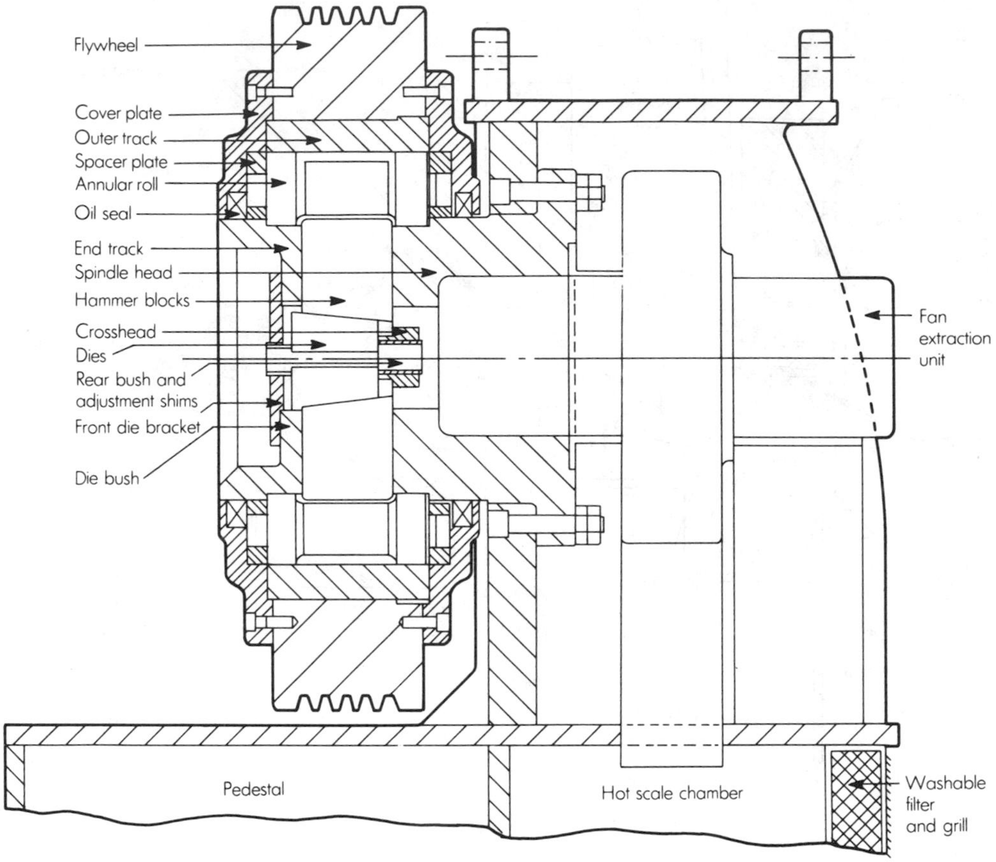

SWAGING MACHINES

Flywheel

Cover plate
Outer track
Spacer plate
Annular roll
Oil seal

End track
Spindle head
Hammer blocks
Crosshead
Dies
Rear bush and
adjustment shims
Front die bracket

Die bush

Fan
extraction
unit

Pedestal

Hot scale chamber

Washable
filter
and grill

Fig. 39-7 A four-die stationary-spindle machine equipped with rolls for alternate-blow swaging. (*Abbey Etna Machine Co.*)

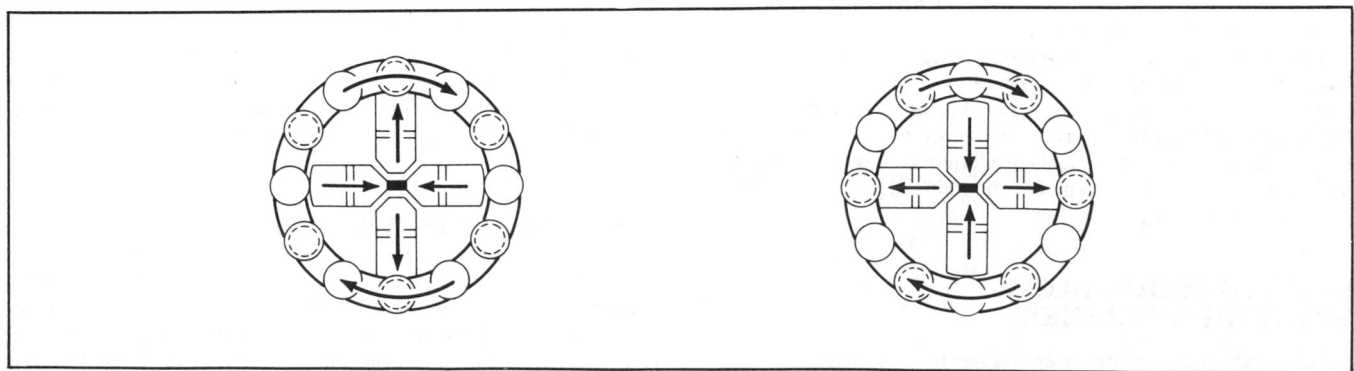

Fig. 39-8 With alternate recessed rolls, two opposing rolls hammer two dies while the rolls 90° away do not. (*Abbey Etna Machine Co.*)

SWAGING DIES

Good swaging performance depends primarily upon the dies. Therefore, it is imperative that the dies be properly designed and carefully manufactured. Improper design can lead to feeding problems and poor surface quality such as finning, wrinkling, and rippling.

Basically, swaging dies are constructed for three types of operations: (1) solid reduction, (2) tubular reduction, and (3) fastening and mandrel swaging. The difference in the dies used for these operations lies in the geometry of the die cavity. Because of the volume of metal being formed, dies for solid workpieces must have more clearance than those used for tubing. The function of the clearance is to prevent metal from being trapped and consequently overloading the dies and breaking them. Two types of construction, for solid reduction and tubular reduction, are illustrated in Figs. 39-9 and 39-10.

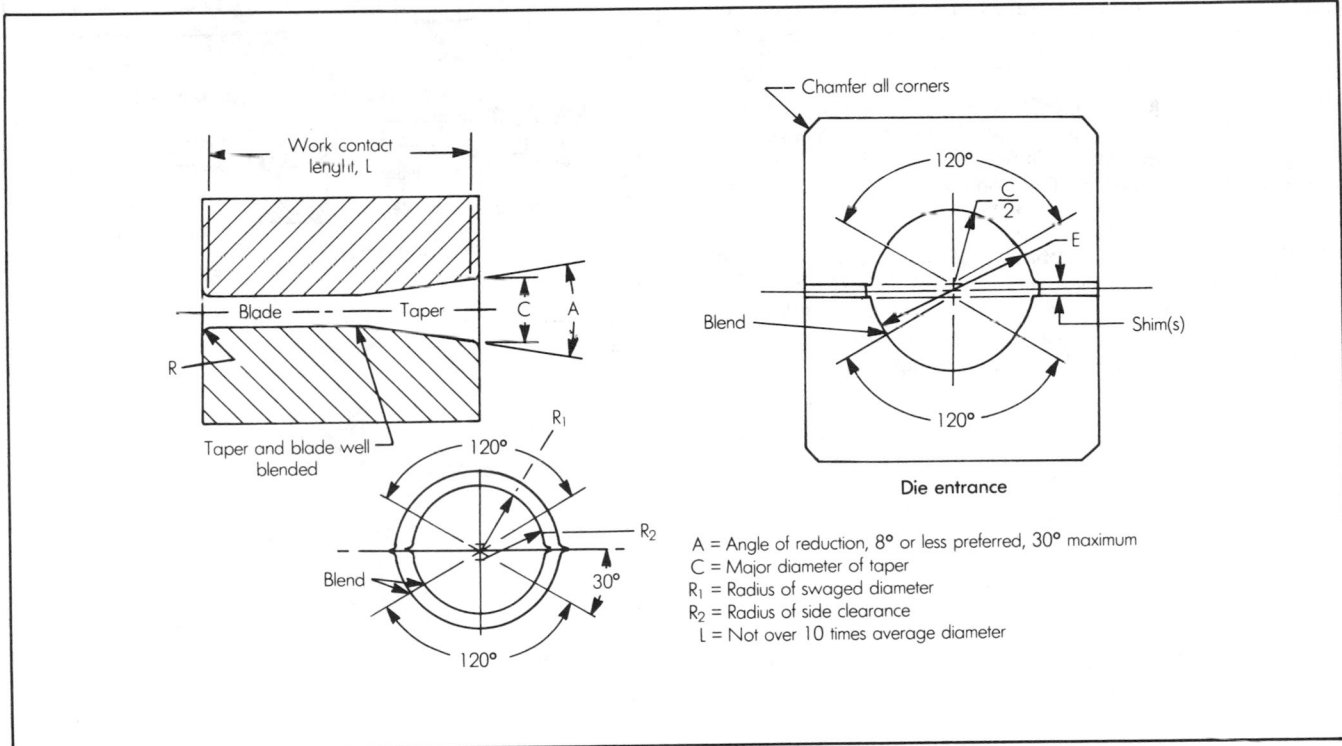

A = Angle of reduction, 8° or less preferred, 30° maximum
C = Major diameter of taper
R_1 = Radius of swaged diameter
R_2 = Radius of side clearance
L = Not over 10 times average diameter

Fig. 39-9 Swaging die for solid reduction. (*Machinery Div., The Torrington Co.*)

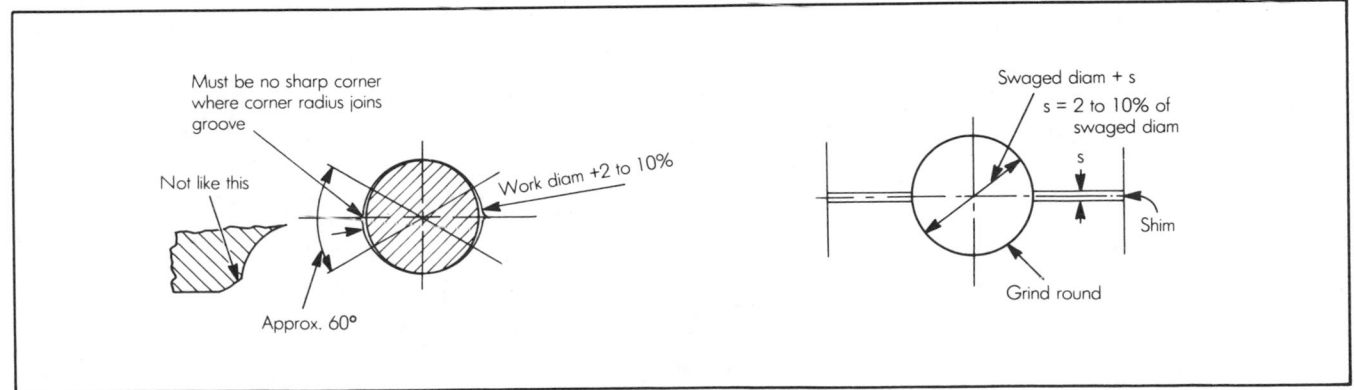

Fig. 39-10 Swaging die for tubular reduction. (*Machinery Div., The Torrington Co.*)

SWAGING MANDRELS

Several types of mandrels are used for swaging, depending upon the job to be performed (see Fig. 39-11). Most mandrels, however, can be classified into the following three basic types: (1) hand mandrels, (2) floating or plug-type mandrels, and (3) built-in mandrels. A slight taper on the mandrels, if not objectionable, facilitates removal of the swaged parts.

Hand mandrels are used on workpieces that are fairly simple and that can be easily handled along with the mandrel. Hand mandrels are generally used when thin-wall tubing is swaged to avoid any wrinkling of the unswaged part and to give support to the swaged area. They are usually not employed when close control of wall thickness is required.

Floating or plug-type mandrels are used when the bead in welded tubing is ironed or the inside diameter of seamless tubing is sized. The mandrel is positioned in the die, and the work is fed by means of roll feeds on the front and exit ends of the swager.

Built-in mandrels are probably the most commonly used type of mandrel. They are used basically to size the inside diameter of a tube within the confines of the die length itself. Built-in mandrels are also used to gage lengths when mandrels and stops are manufactured as integral units.

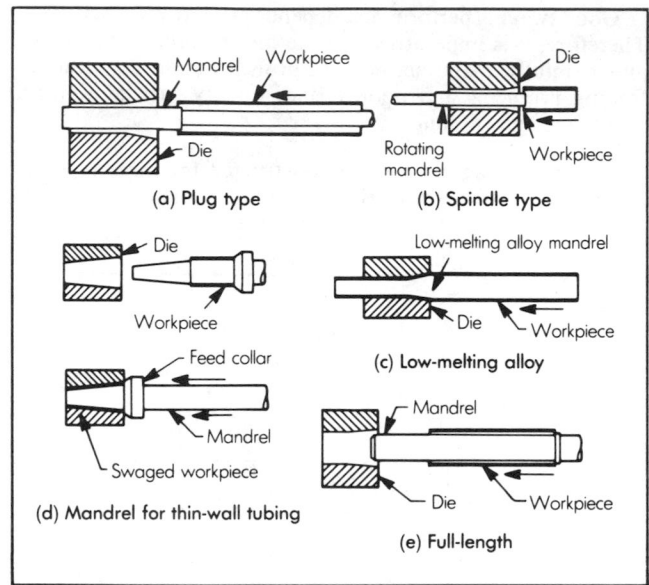

Fig. 39-11 Various types of swaging mandrels. (*Abbey Etna Machine Co.*)

HOT FORGING

Hot forging is defined as the controlled, plastic deformation or working of metals into predetermined shapes by means of pressure or impact blows, or a combination of both. In hot forging, this plastic deformation is performed above the recrystallization temperature to prevent strain hardening of the metal.

During the deformation process, the crystalline structure of the base metal is refined and any nonmetallic or alloy segregation is properly oriented. In bar stock, the grain flow is only in one direction. When the contour of the part is changed, the grain flow lines are cut, rendering the metal more sus-ceptible to fatigue and stress corrosion. Hot forging develops the grain flow so that it follows the outline of the part being formed as seen in Fig. 40-1. The directional alignment of the grains or fibers helps increase strength, ductility, and resistance to impact and fatigue in the metal.

Deformation is affected by the stress inherent in the metal, the microstructural characteristics of the starting material, the temperature at which the deformation occurs, the rate at which the deformation occurs, and the frictional restraint between the material being forged and the die surface.

FORGING PROCESSES

Metal flow during the forging process normally falls into two categories: upsetting and extrusion. Upsetting occurs when the metal is compressed parallel to the longitudinal axis of the workpiece. This action enables the metal to flow freely in one direction as in open-die forging, or it can be restrained as in impression-die forging. Extrusion occurs when the metal is compressed parallel to the longitudinal axis of the workpiece and allowed to flow through an orifice in the die cavity.

OPEN-DIE FORGING

Open-die forging, also referred to as smith forging, blacksmith forging, hand forging, and flat-die forging, is generally performed without special tooling. The forms obtained and the dimensions maintained are usually dependent upon the skill of the operator and the type of equipment used. However, with the addition of computer control to the equipment, more complex forgings can be produced and better dimensional control is maintained. This equipment may range from the simple anvil and hammer of the blacksmith to giant, computer-controlled, hydraulic presses capable of delivering up to 75,000 tons (667 MN) of force and producing single forgings weighing several thousand pounds. Most open-die forgings are simple geometric shapes such as discs, rings, or shafts. Open-die forging is also used in the steelmaking industry to cog ingots or to draw down billets from one size to a smaller one.

IMPRESSION-DIE FORGING

In impression-die forging, the workpiece is placed between two dies containing the impression of the forging shape to be produced. The dies are brought together and the workpiece is plastically deformed until the sides come in contact with the walls of the die (see Fig. 40-2). As the deformation continues, a small amount of material begins to flow outside the die impression, forming flash. The thin flash cools rapidly, creating a pressure increase inside the workpiece. The increased pressure assists the flow of material into the unfilled portion of the impression. The majority of the forgings produced are done using impression-die forging.

Closed-die forging or flashless forging, which is a special form of impression-die forging, does not depend on the flash to achieve complete die filling. Generally, the material is deformed in a cavity that does not allow excess material to flow outside the impression. Therefore, die design and workpiece volume are more critical than in impression-die forging so that complete die filling is achieved without generating excess pressures due to overfilling.

Currently, closed-die forging is moving more and more toward near-net-shaped and net-shaped forging. Near-net-shaped parts are those parts that require minor metal removal before assembly. Net-shaped parts have finished functional surfaces that do not require additional metal removal. Gears, airfoils, and high-temperature jet engine disc forgings are being produced using this process.

RELATED PROCESSES

Several other processes are employed when workpieces are forged for a particular application. These processes incorporate principles from both open and closed-die forging. Two of the more common processes are radial forging and ring rolling. Orbital forging, isothermal forging, Gatorizing (a process developed by Pratt and Whitney Aircraft), and incremental forging are special processes frequently employed in the aircraft and aerospace industries.

Radial Forging

Radial forging is a process used to reduce the cross-sectional area of billets, bars, and tubes. Normally four different types of operations are performed by radial forging: (1) axial feed into tapered dies (see Fig. 40-3), (2) infeed of dies (see Fig. 40-4), (3) axial feed into tapered dies while simultaneously upsetting (see Fig. 40-5), (4) combination of axial feed and infeed of dies (see Fig. 40-6). A mandrel can be attached to the backstop to control internal material flow when hollow work-

FORGING PROCESSES

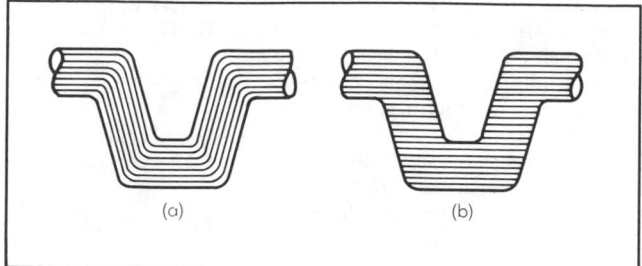

Fig. 40-1 (a) Grain flow in hot forging follows the outline of the component. (b) During machining, the grain flow is broken. (*Forging Industry Association*)

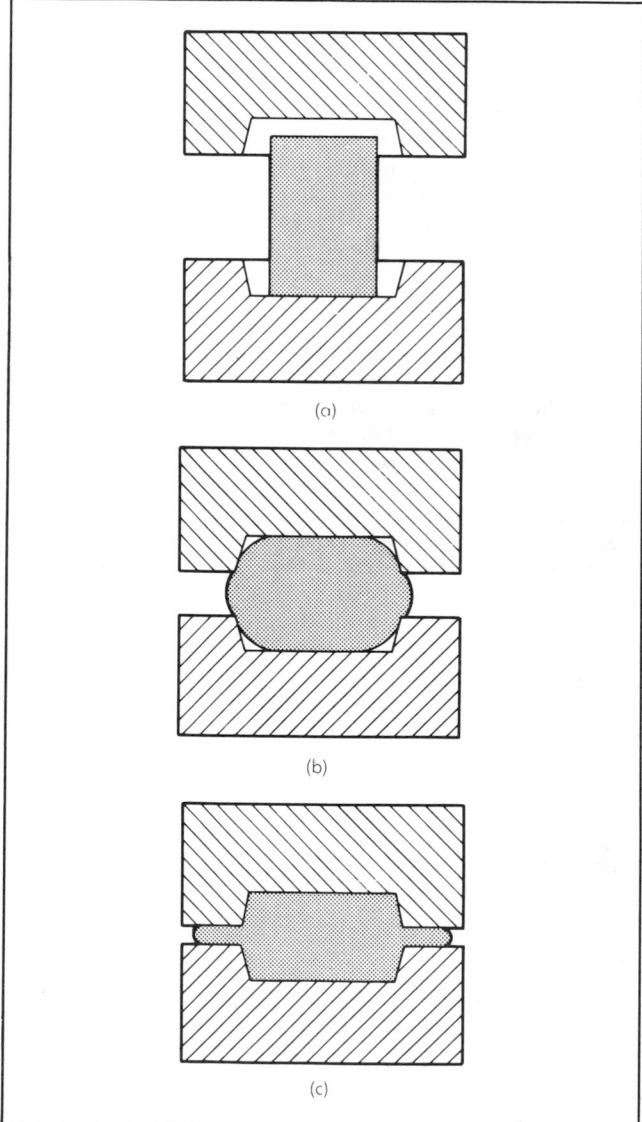

Fig. 40-2 In impression-die forging: (a) the workpiece is inserted between the dies; (b) the dies are brought together deforming the workpiece until the sides come in contact with the walls; and (c) the thin flash assists the flow of material and completes die filling. (*Forging Industry Association*)

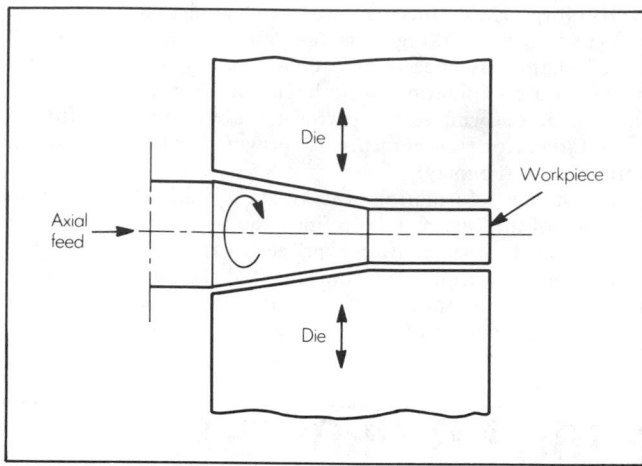

Fig. 40-3 Reductions in cross section are achieved by axially feeding the workpiece through tapered dies. (*Fenn Manufacturing Co.*)

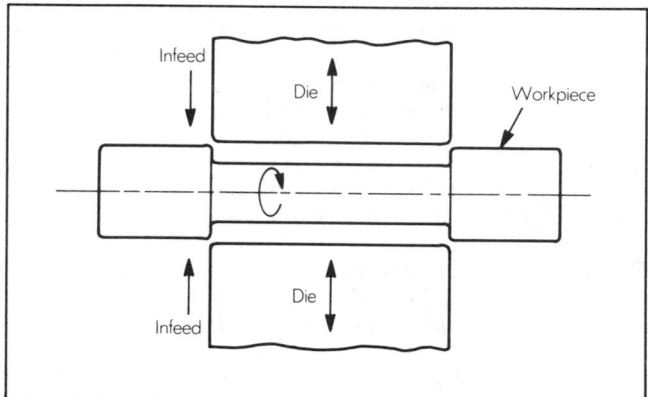

Fig. 40-4 Reductions in cross section are also obtainable in the middle of the workpiece by controlling the die feed. (*Fenn Manufacturing Co.*)

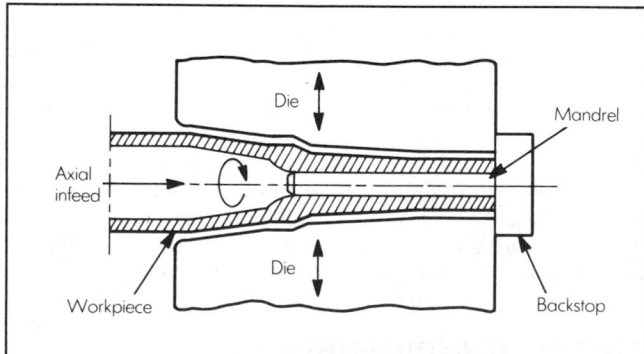

Fig. 40-5 Radial forging machines can simultaneously upset the workpiece and reduce its cross section. (*Fenn Manufacturing Co.*)

pieces are being upset.

Radial forging permits a wide variety of shapes to be produced with a minimum amount of tooling. The process lends itself to automation. Accuracy and repeatability are dependent on the design of the dies rather than operator skill.

Radial forging is being used in several diverse industries including the railroad, power utility, construction equipment, automotive, steel, aircraft, and defense industries.

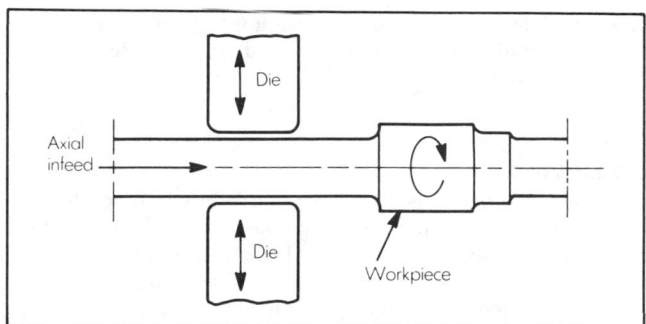

Fig. 40-6 Cross sections can be varied on the workpiece by regulating the infeed of the dies and axial feed of the workpiece. (*Fenn Manufacturing Co.***)**

Ring Rolling

Ring rolling is a process used to produce seamless rings having rectangular or contoured cross sections and specified diameters. Figure 40-7 illustrates a few of the contoured cross sections that can be produced on a ring-rolling machine. Radial

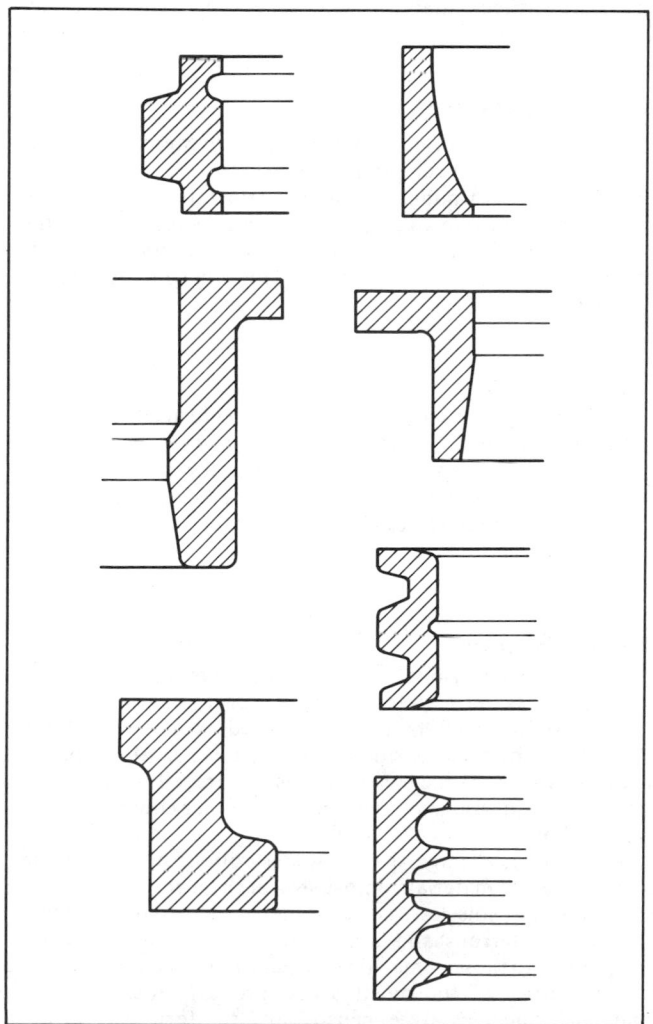

Fig. 40-7 A few of the many different ring cross sections obtainable on a ring rolling machine.

ring rolling decreases the wall thickness while increasing the ring diameter. Radial-axial ring rolling decreases both the wall thickness and height of the ring while increasing the ring diameter.

Ring rolling is less expensive than closed-die forging because less waste material results and the ring is much closer to a finished shape. The metallurgical structure and physical properties are also improved. Ring rolling is used in a variety of industries to produce products of diverse applications. Some of these industries include the automotive, agricultural, machine tool, mining, aircraft, aerospace, and defense industries.

Orbital Forging

In orbital forging, the workpiece is subjected to a combined rolling and pressing action between a flat bottom platen and a swiveling upper die with a conical working face instead of a direct pressing action between two flat platens (see Fig. 40-8). The cone axis is inclined so that the narrow sector in contact with the workpiece is parallel to the lower platen. As the cone rotates about the cone apex, the contact zone also rotates. At the same time, the platens are pressed toward each other so that the workpiece is progressively compressed by the rolling action. Press loading is appreciably less than that of conventional upsetting because of the relatively small area of instantaneous contact.

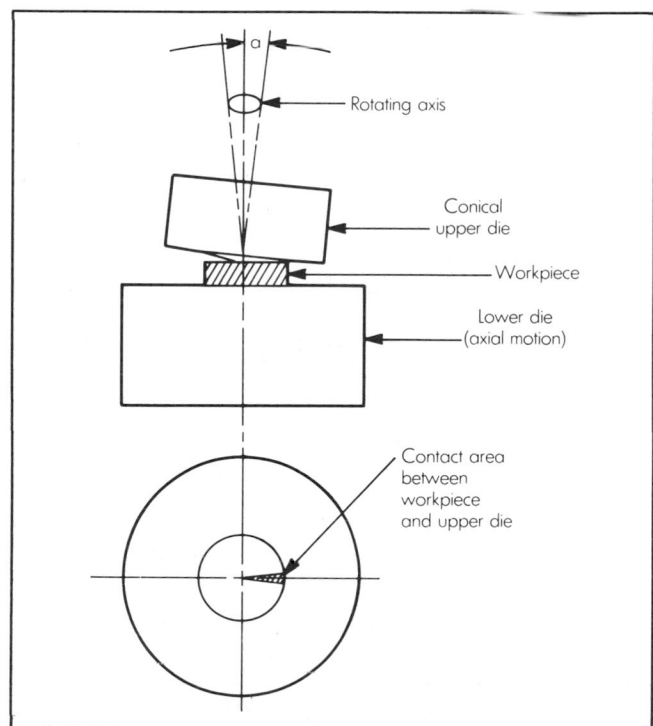

Fig. 40-8 Orbital forging combines a rolling action and a pressing action to forge the workpiece.

Isothermal Forging

Isothermal forging is a process in which the preform or billet is forged at one temperature and does not experience the die chill, surface cooling, or thermal gradients that are associated with conventional forging. This is accomplished by surrounding the billet with surfaces that are at the same temperature as the

FORGING PROCESSES

billet. Preheated tooling maintains the temperature of the billet ends or preform faces, and a die-billet heater maintains the billet temperature at the billet periphery. The deformation occurs at a speed relatively slow enough to produce a part with greater complexity using a minimum of force. In effect, time substitutes for a portion of the forging load that would normally be required. Isothermal forging has been beneficial for forging the more expensive or difficult-to-forge materials, such as titanium and superalloys.

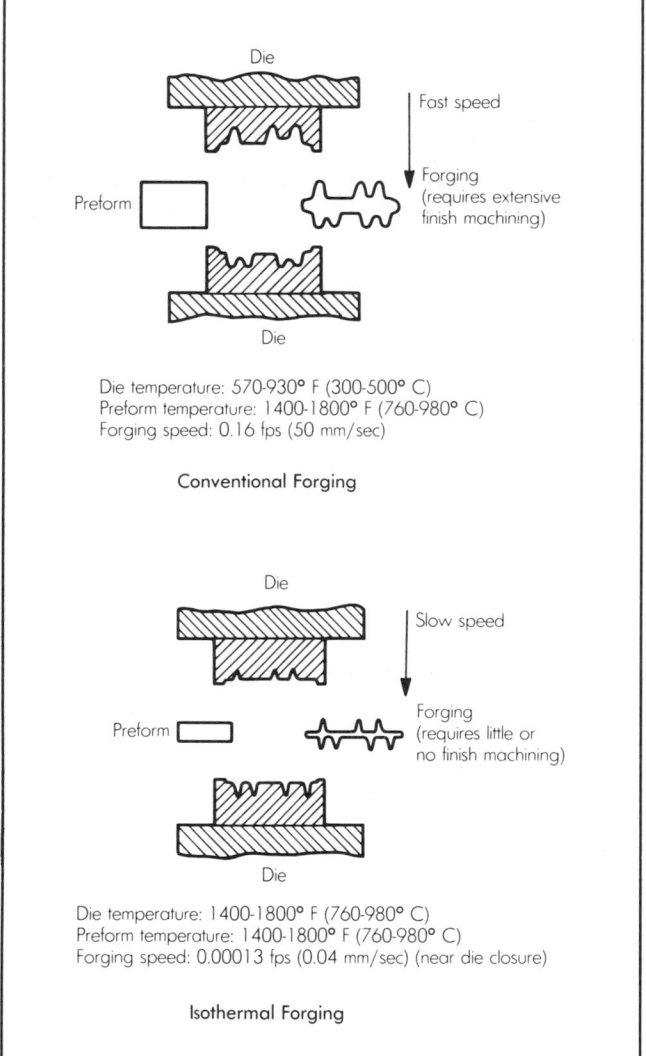

Die temperature: 570-930° F (300-500° C)
Preform temperature: 1400-1800° F (760-980° C)
Forging speed: 0.16 fps (50 mm/sec)

Conventional Forging

Die temperature: 1400-1800° F (760-980° C)
Preform temperature: 1400-1800° F (760-980° C)
Forging speed: 0.00013 fps (0.04 mm/sec) (near die closure)

Isothermal Forging

Fig. 40-9 The isothermal process is compared to the conventional impression-die process.

The main advantages of isothermal forging are the ability to produce complex profiles having a near-net shape; lower forging pressures, thereby permitting the use of existing equipment to forge larger components; reduced initial material weight and secondary machining; and lower part costs. Figure 40-9 compares the conventional forging process with isothermal forging. However, the advantages of increased material utili-

zation and decreased machining cost must offset the increased cost of the dies and equipment used and the decrease in production output.

Gatorizing

Gatorizing (developed by Pratt and Whitney Aircraft) is a forging process that includes isothermal forging as a step in the normal application of the process. The material is first preconditioned to develop a fine grain size and superplastic structure, and then forged isothermally in an atmosphere containing nitrogen or argon gas, or a vacuum. This process is often used when powder metals and superalloys are being forged.

Incremental Forging

Incremental forging is a recently developed process in which only part of the workpiece is deformed at one time. This process is similar to cogging, fullering, or drawing out and can be employed to produce rib and web-type blocker preforms that are finish formed in a closed die or machined to final dimensions. Steel, titanium, and superalloys can be forged using incremental forging.

PREFORMING

Preforming is a forging operation used to preform, descale, and properly orient the grain flow prior to the main forging operation. In preforming, the number of operations is increased, which results in improved productivity and reduced tooling costs. Some of the machines used in preforming include hammers, presses, forging machines, forging rolls, and wedge rolling machines.

Roll Forging

Roll forging is employed to produce a preformed blank to be finish formed in a hammer or press, or to produce parts requiring a long, tapered, symmetrical section. Crankshafts, connecting rods, and other automotive-related components are frequently roll forged prior to being finish formed. Roll forging is performed on forging rolls.

Wedge Rolling

Wedge rolling, also referred to as transverse roll forming or cross rolling, is a process for accurately forming various shapes on the peripheries of shafts or preformed parts. Figure 40-10 illustrates some of the various shapes suitable for this process. The process is performed on machines that are self-contained or are designed for use in conjunction with other equipment in a forging shop.

A major advantage of the wedge-rolling process is the complete use of material; almost 98% of the metal is used. The process is fast, noiseless, and automatic and can form almost any type of ferrous and nonferrous metal. Tolerances are comparable to those of machining operations, and the mechanical properties of the metal are improved. However, self-contained machines are expensive and the forming dies are difficult to design. This process is also limited to external surfaces and axisymmetric part geometries.

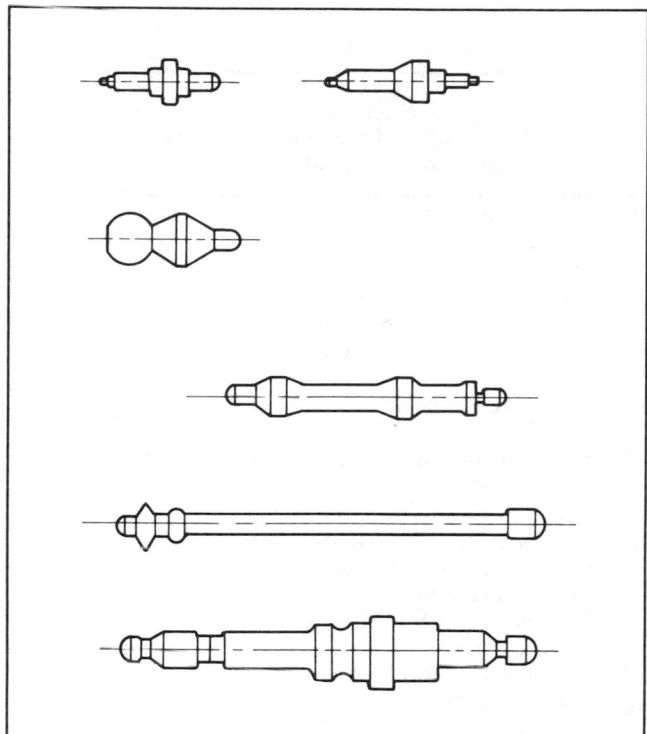

Fig. 40-10 Wedge rolling is capable of forming various cross sections on the peripheries of shafts.

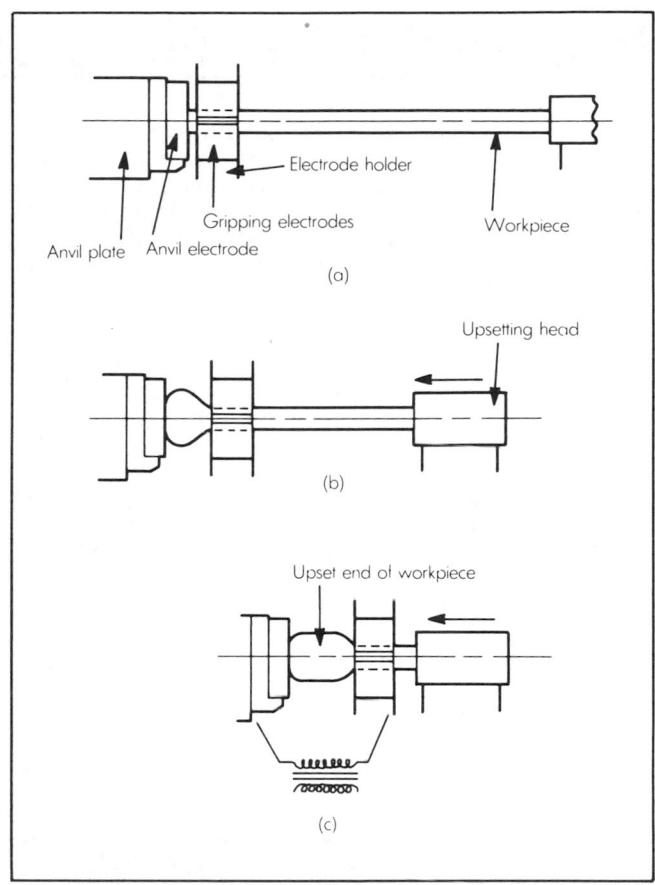

Fig. 40-11 Electric upsetting is commonly used in preforming operations to gather a large amount of material at one end of a bar.

Electric Upsetting

Electric upsetting is used mostly in preforming operations to gather a large amount of material at one end of a round bar. The principle of operation is illustrated in Fig. 40-11. A bar of circular cross section is gripped between the tools of the electrode and is pushed by the hydraulically or pneumatically operated upsetting head against the anvil plate on which the other electrode is secured (see view *a*). When the current is switched on, the rod section contained between the electrodes heats rapidly and the formation of the head begins (see view *b*). The cold bar is continuously fed between the gripping electrodes; thus, the metal accumulates continuously in the head (see view *c*). The anvil electrode is gradually retracted to give enough space for the formation of the head. As soon as a sufficient quantity of metal is gathered, the machine switches off and the product can be removed by its cold end. Normally, the head is formed to final shape in a mechanical or screw-type press in the same heat. The process is suitable for preforming components like valves, or steam turbine blades.

ADVANTAGES

Forging orients the grain flow to follow the contour of the part. This orientation provides the highest strength in the direction of the greatest stress. The higher strength-to-weight ratio permits the use of smaller, more lightweight components without the reduction of strength or toughness. Forgings can be made from a wide range of materials. Materials that are difficult to machine have been successfully forged into the desired shape. Gas pockets or voids usually found in other metal fabricating methods are eliminated, and the material's structural integrity and mechanical properties are improved. Parts can be economically produced in sizes ranging from less than 1 to 300" (25-7600 mm) in length. Forgings are also readily adaptable to secondary operations such as heat treating, machining, welding, and surface conditioning.

APPLICATIONS

Forging of almost all forged components begins with open-die forging to achieve the initial material characteristics. Impression-die or closed-die forging is used to obtain a variety of shapes, sizes, and properties.

Forgings are used in a variety of industries to obtain the required component properties. In the automotive industry, forgings are used in the production of engine components, transmission components, and suspension components. High strength-to-weight ratios and reliability of forgings satisfy the stringent requirements in the aircraft and aerospace industry when airframe components, landing gear components, and other structural components are being produced. Forgings made from materials that are able to withstand elevated temperatures while maintaining strength are used in turbine engines. Other industries that use forgings include off-highway equipment, ordnance, oil field, metalworking, plumbing, railroad, and refrigeration.

MATERIALS FOR FORGING

An important consideration when selecting a material to be forged is its forgeability. Other considerations would be based on the mechanical properties that are inherent in the material or that can be obtained as a result of forging and heat treatment. These properties include elastic modulus, density, and strength; resistance to wear, fatigue, shock, or bending; response to heat treatment; machining characteristics; and durability or economy.

Forgeability denotes a combination of resistance to deformation and the ability to deform without fracture and can be defined as the capability of the material to deform without failure regardless of the pressure and load applied. Table 40-1 is a list of the different metals and alloys in increasing order of forging difficulty. The forgeability of a particular material is based on metallurgical and mechanical factors. The temperature range over which a material can be forged also contributes to a material's forgeability. Materials with a narrow range of forging temperatures are more difficult to forge because they can only be forged for a short time. The need to obtain a fine grain structure and certain mechanical properties may further restrict the temperature and deformation range in forging.

TABLE 40-1
Forgeability of Materials in Order of Increasing Forging Difficulty[1]

Highest forgeability
- Aluminum alloys
- Magnesium alloys
- Copper alloys
- Carbon and low-alloy steels
- Martensitic stainless steels
- Maraging steels
- Austenitic stainless steels
- Nickel alloys
- Semiaustenitic precipitation hardening (PH) stainless steels
- Titanium alloys
- Iron-based superalloys
- Cobalt-based superalloys
- Columbium alloys
- Tantalum alloys
- Molybdenum alloys
- Nickel-based superalloys
- Tungsten alloys
- Beryllium

Lowest forgeability

FORGING EQUIPMENT

Many different types of machines and equipment are used for the forging process. These include various machines for the actual forging and auxiliary equipment for heating, loading, and unloading the stock, as well as other machines to produce a completed part.

Forging machines are generally classified with respect to their principle of operation. Hammers and high energy rate forming (HERF) machines are classified as *energy-restricted* machines because the deformation results from the kinetic energy of the hammer ram. Mechanical presses are referred to as *stroke-restricted* machines because their ability to deform the material is determined by the length of the press stroke and the available force at the various stroke positions. Hydraulic presses are called *force-restricted* machines because their ability to deform the material depends on the maximum force rating of the press. Screw-type presses are other examples of *energy-restricted* machines even though they are similar in construction to mechanical and hydraulic presses.

FORGING HAMMERS

Forging hammers are energy-restricted machines and are the most inexpensive and versatile types of machines used in forging. This is due to the hammer's capability of developing large forces and the short die contact time. The main components are a ram, frame assembly, anvil, and anvil cap. The anvil is connected directly to the frame assembly, the upper die is attached to the ram, and the lower die is attached to the anvil cap.

In operation, the workpiece is placed on the lower die. The ram moves downward, exerting a force on the anvil and causing the workpiece to deform.

Forging hammers are classified by the method used to drive the ram downward. The two common methods are by gravity or by an external power source. Another type of forging hammer is the counterblow type. Hammers used in open-die forging are slightly different from those used in closed-die forging.

HIGH ENERGY RATE FORMING MACHINES

High energy rate forming (HERF) machines are classified as load-restricted machines since the amount of deformation obtainable is determined by the kinetic energy of the ram. These machines use the sudden release of high-pressure inert gases to accelerate opposing rams at a high velocity. Since the ram velocity is from two to ten times faster than the ram of a forging hammer, the mass of the HERF machine ram is considerably less than that of the forging hammer ram. The high velocity of the ram induces metal flow at a rate greater than in other types of forging equipment. However, these high speeds often result in increased die wear and limited die life.

MECHANICAL PRESSES

Basically, mechanical forging presses are characterized by a ram that is moved in a vertical direction. Energy to move the ram vertically is generated by a large rotating flywheel powered by an electric motor. A mechanical drive translates the rotary motion into reciprocating linear motion. All the components are contained in a heavy, rigid frame that is generally made from cast steel. Smaller presses use one-piece construction whereas larger presses use multiple-piece construction and tie rods.

During its stroke, the ram is guided at all four corners by full-length guides that are adjustable and contain replaceable liners to compensate for wear. The guides can be of the box-type or diagonal-type design.

A clutch to disengage the flywheel and a brake to stop the eccentric shaft at the end of the stroke are important components on a mechanical forging press. Small and medium-sized presses use positive-type or friction-type clutches. Large presses use air-operated clutches.

The controls are usually set to operate through a single stroke but can be adjusted to operate on a continuing, repetitive cycle. Lubrication to the various bearing points is accomplished by a pressurized central lubrication system. Part ejectors, designed into the press table or press ram, are used for removing parts from the die cavity. These ejectors are actuated by cams or levers that are operated from the main eccentric shaft.

In comparison to drop or hammer forging, mechanical press forging results in accurate, close tolerance parts. Mechanical presses permit automatic feed and transfer mechanisms to feed, pick up, and move the part from one die to the next. The dies used with these presses are lighter and less expensive than dies for forging hammers. Since the dies are subject to squeezing forces instead of impact forces, harder die materials can be used to extend die life.

One limitation of mechanical presses is that they cost approximately three times as much as forging hammers which can do the same amount of work. They are also not capable of performing as many preliminary operations as hammers. Generally, mechanical presses forge the preform and final shape in one, two, or three blows while hammers are capable of delivering up to ten or more blows.

HYDRAULIC PRESSES

Hydraulic presses are essentially force-restricted machines, and metal forming results from a squeezing action rather than from impact. The capability of hydraulic presses to carry out the forging operation is determined mainly by the maximum force available. The maximum force can be limited to protect the tooling and the machine through pressure relief valves that limit the fluid pressure acting upon the ram.

A basic hydraulic press consists of a frame, piston and cylinder, power ram, and electric motor driven hydraulic pumps. The electric motor driven hydraulic pumps are usually an integral part of the press. The hydraulic pumps may also be in a central location and provide hydraulic pressure for several presses within the shop. Hydraulic presses have been built with several pistons. These pistons may act independently and in different directions to hold split dies and the workpiece during forging. The pistons may also actuate side rams which permit multiram forging of hollow components.

Press Frame

The frame of the press must be capable of resisting the force imposed on the press bed by the hydraulic cylinder. This is accomplished by employing cast or welded frames that have been prestressed with tie rods, or it is accomplished by assembling laminated plates together with large transverse pins. Hydraulic presses are also built using two or four-column

construction (see Fig. 40-12). Four-column presses are employed for both open and closed-die forging, and two-column presses are usually employed only for open-die forging.

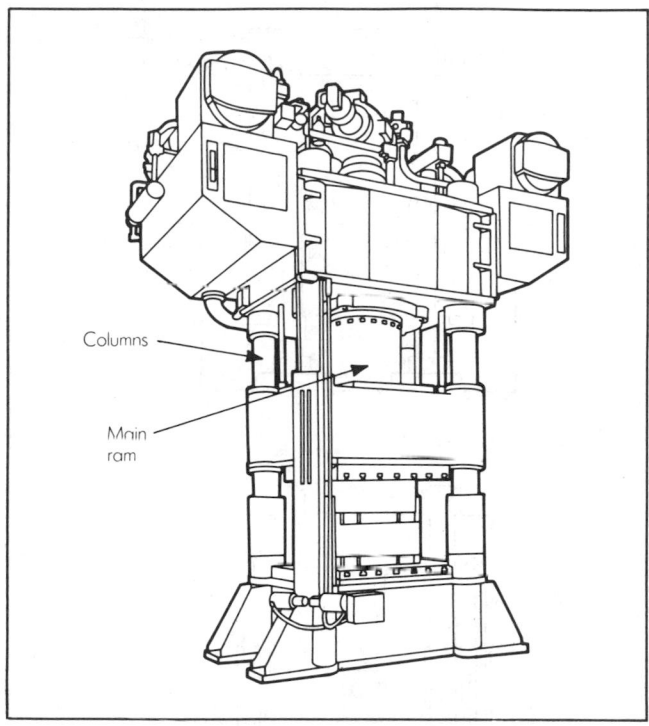

Columns

Main ram

Fig. 40-12 Typical four-column hydraulic press. (*Erie Press Systems*)

Press Operation

The operation of a hydraulic press is determined by the design of the drive configuration and the type of drive system that is utilized.

The two main drive configurations for hydraulic presses are the push-down design and the pull-down design.

Push-down design. In the push-down drive configuration (see Fig. 40-13, *a*), the stationary cylinder and crosshead are located above the work. The cylinder crosshead and the stationary press bed are connected by four columns. These columns are designed to take up the press load and simultaneously guide the moving piston-ram assembly. During operation, the piston-ram assembly is pushed down by the cylinder in the crosshead. Bushings in the piston-ram assembly guide the assembly as it moves. Return cylinders push the piston-ram assembly back to the proper starting position.

The push-down drive design is the least expensive drive configuration to build and does not require expensive press foundations. Since the press components are exposed, maintenance is simplified and existing problems are easily detected. However, presses utilizing the push-down drive design require greater ceiling heights than do pull-down drive presses. Since all the hydraulic system is located above the workpiece, there is a possibility of fluid leakage resulting in a fire and safety hazard. The push-down drive press exhibits elastic deflections during

FORGING EQUIPMENT

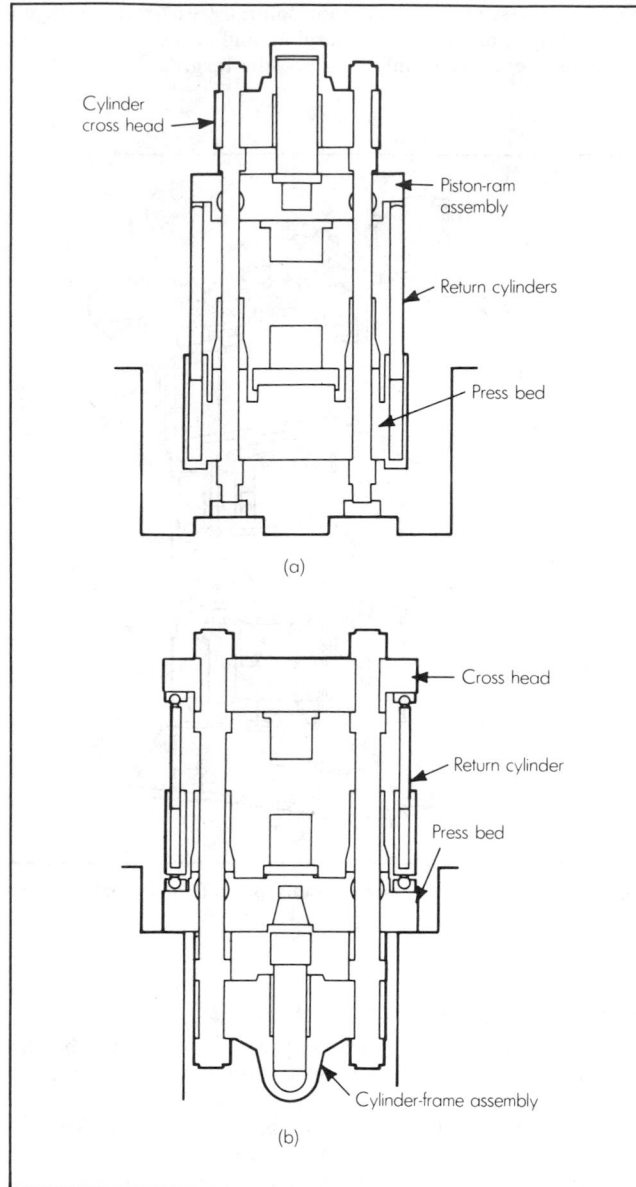

(a)

(b)

Fig. 40-13 Hydraulic presses can incorporate either (a) a push-down drive design or (b) a pull-down drive design.

off-center loading and does not lend itself to two-column construction because of insufficient stability.

Pull-down design. In the pull-down drive design (see Fig. 40-13, *b*), the movable cylinder frame assembly is located below the press bed in the foundation pit. The movable crosshead and cylinder frame assembly are connected together with either two or four columns that slide in bushings located in the press bed. During operation, the crosshead is pulled down by the columns. Return cylinders push the crosshead back to the proper starting position.

Pull-down drive presses require the minimum amount of height above the floor, which results in a lower center of gravity and increased static and dynamic stiffness. Most of the hydraulic and auxiliary equipment can be located beneath the

floor level. Fire hazards due to leaking hydraulic fluid are eliminated, and the length of hydraulic piping is shortened. However, the foundation for pull-down drive presses is more expensive than for push-down drive presses. Since more than half of the press weight is moving, heavy column guides are required. Maintenance generally requires working in the pit, and problems are not as easily detected as on push-down drive presses.

Advantages and Limitations

Hydraulic presses are employed for open and closed-die forging operations. The force applied by the hydraulic press can be varied throughout the stroke by adjusting the control valve. The ram speed can also be continuously adjusted during the cycle when materials that are susceptible to rupturing under high deformation rates are being forged. Hydraulic presses are ideally suited for extrusion-type forging operations that require a fairly constant load over a long stroke and relatively large amounts of energy for the deformation.

Because hydraulic presses are relatively slow, the workpiece is in contact with the dies for a longer period of time than it is on mechanical presses, resulting in a transfer of heat from the workpiece to the dies. The heat transfer reduces the number of times that the workpiece can be forged between reheats and causes abnormal die wear. For these reasons, hydraulic presses for closed-die forging are best suited for materials that have low forging temperatures, such as aluminum and magnesium. The heat-transfer problem can be minimized by heating the dies to approximately the same temperature as the workpiece.

SCREW PRESSES

Screw presses are energy-restricted machines and use energy stored in a flywheel to provide the force for forging. The rotating energy or inertia of the flywheel is converted to linear motion by a threaded screw attached on one end to the flywheel and on the other end to the ram.

Drive Systems

The three main types of drive systems used on screw presses are friction drive, direct electric drive, and hydraulic drive. A fourth drive system has a flywheel that rotates constantly and a controllable clutch.

Advantages and Limitations

Screw presses are used for open and closed-die forging operations. They usually have more energy available per stroke than mechanical presses, permitting them to accomplish more work per stroke. When the energy has been dissipated, the ram comes to a halt, even though the dies have not closed. Stopping the ram permits multiple blows to be made to the workpiece in the same die impression. The die height adjustment is not critical, and the press is not capable of jamming. Die stresses are minimized and are not affected by the temperature or height of the workpiece, resulting in good die life. The impact speed is much greater than with mechanical presses, ensuring the filling of deep die cavities. However, most screw presses permit full force operation only near the center of the bed and ram bolsters.

FORGING MACHINES

Forging machines (see Fig. 40-14) are basically double-acting mechanical presses operating in a horizontal plane and are often called horizontal upsetters or heading machines. The

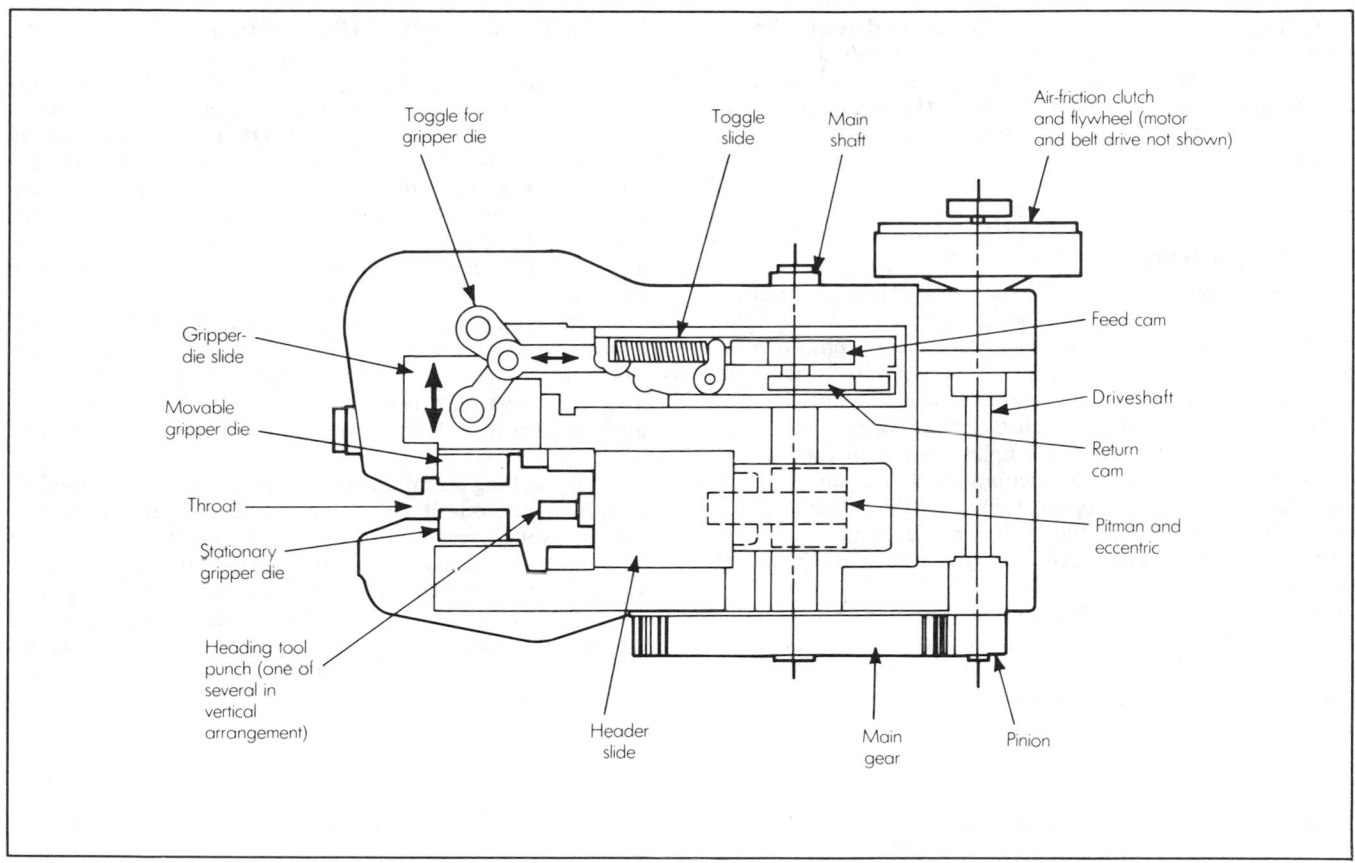

Fig. 40-14 Top view of a vertical forging machine. (*American Machinist*)

forging is accomplished between closed dies and is referred to as upset forging.

Energy stored in a flywheel driven by an electric motor powers a main shaft which drives the header slide in a horizontal direction through a pitman arm or an eccentric. This is similar to the action of a ram in a mechanical press. The total length that the header slide travels forward is the stroke length. The advance is the distance that the header slide travels forward before contacting the stock, and the stock gather is the working portion of the stroke. The header slide is long and supported by wide bearing surfaces to ensure accurate alignment and guidance during forging. Attached to the header slide is a set of punches or forming tools that force the stock into the die cavities.

The die area consists of a die block split vertically or horizontally into two parts. The two die halves contain matching cavities or passes in which the stock is gripped and formed during forging. The fixed half is referred to as the stationary die, and the other half is referred to as the movable die. The movable die is attached to the gripper slide, which is driven in a direction perpendicular to the header slide by means of a toggle mechanism and a toggle slide. The length of travel of the movable die is the die opening. A flywheel clutch and brake mechanism controls single-stroke and nonrepeat operations as well as machine stop motion. A bed frame and crown surround the die area to provide support and rigidity during forging.

Forging machines can upset, deep-pierce, split, bend, and extrude simple or intricate shapes to close tolerances, usually with a savings in material. The tolerances obtained are based on the configuration of the forging and the accuracy of the die design. Machining the part after forging permits looser tolerances, but tighter tolerances often eliminate secondary operations. Tolerances of 0 to +1/16" (1.6 mm) on the diameter are

HOT FORMERS

Hot formers are self-contained feeding, shearing, and forging machines. They are similar to forging machines in design since they are mechanically operated, horizontal forging machines. However, the forging takes place in closed dies on hot formers, whereas on forging machines, the forging takes place in split dies.

A typical hot former installation consists of a bar rack, an in-line induction heater, and a hot former machine that usually incorporates a shear and three or four forming stations.

The hot former obtains its energy from the momentum of a motor-driven flywheel which drives an eccentric shaft. The eccentric shaft is connected to a heading slide through a pitman connection. The heading slide moves back and forth with the throw of the eccentric. Attached to the front of the heading slide is a set of three or four tools (punches) that force the metal into the die cavities during part forming. An operation is performed in each die on each stroke. At the final die, the formed part is removed from the die by a kickout mechanism, thus making a finished forging with each stroke.

Parts forged on a hot former are typically round or square, are symmetrical in shape, and have a hole pierced through

FORGING EQUIPMENT

them. The part lengths are usually less than the diameter. Some typical parts include transmission gear blanks, side gears, drive flanges, and bearing races. More complex parts with irregular shapes such as trunnions, tripods, hubs and spindles, connecting rod caps, and drive yokes are also feasible with the appropriate tooling.

FORGING ROLLS

Forging rolls are highly productive machines designed to preform blanks in a variety of shapes, lengths, and sizes for finish forging on presses or hammers. Forging rolls are also referred to as reducer rolls, back rolls, or gap rolls. In addition to shaping parts or preforms, forging rolls also descale the stock, an operation normally performed in the press or forging machines.

A motor-driven driveshaft supplies power for turning the lower roll shaft through reduction gears. An air-operated diaphragm clutch transmits the torque from the reduction gears to the lower roll shaft, and a disc brake ensures accurate stopping. The roll shafts are geared together to maintain timing between the rolls.

Forging rolls are available in several sizes for rolling blanks up to 5" (127 mm) thick and 40" (1016 mm) long. Typical parts preformed are automobile crankshafts, axle shafts, connecting rods, wheel spindles, and wrenches.

WEDGE ROLLING MACHINES

Wedge rolling machines are designed to preform balls, tapers, undercuts, 90° shoulders, or a combination of these on one shaft. The self-contained machines consist of a welded frame in which two rolls are rotated in the same direction by an electric motor (see Fig. 40-15); however, some manufacturers build the machine with three rolls. Wedge-shaped dies are bolted to T-slots in the periphery of the rolls. A feeder loads the bar into rolls, and an induction heater heats the material to the desired forging temperature. Portable machines consist of a frame and electrically driven rolls.

The rolls on two-roll machines are as large as 48" (1220 mm) diam x 42" (1065 mm) wide. These machines can accept bar stock from 1/4 to 5" (6 to 127 mm) diam and up to 36" (915 mm) long. The rolls on three-roll machines are smaller and can preform parts from 1/2 to 1" (12 to 25 mm) diam and from 6 to 8" (152 to 200 mm) long.

Wedge rolling machines are capable of producing 600-1200 preforms per hour if only single parts are being run. The quantity would increase proportionally in multiple-pass runs. Tolerances can be maintained at +0.004" (0.10 mm) diam and approximately ±0.004 to ±0.006" (0.10-0.15 mm) in length.

Wedge rolling machines are currently being used to preform transmission output shafts, cluster gears, chassis idler arms, pitman arms, ball joints, front wheel spindles, connecting rods, stem pinions, and mining tools.

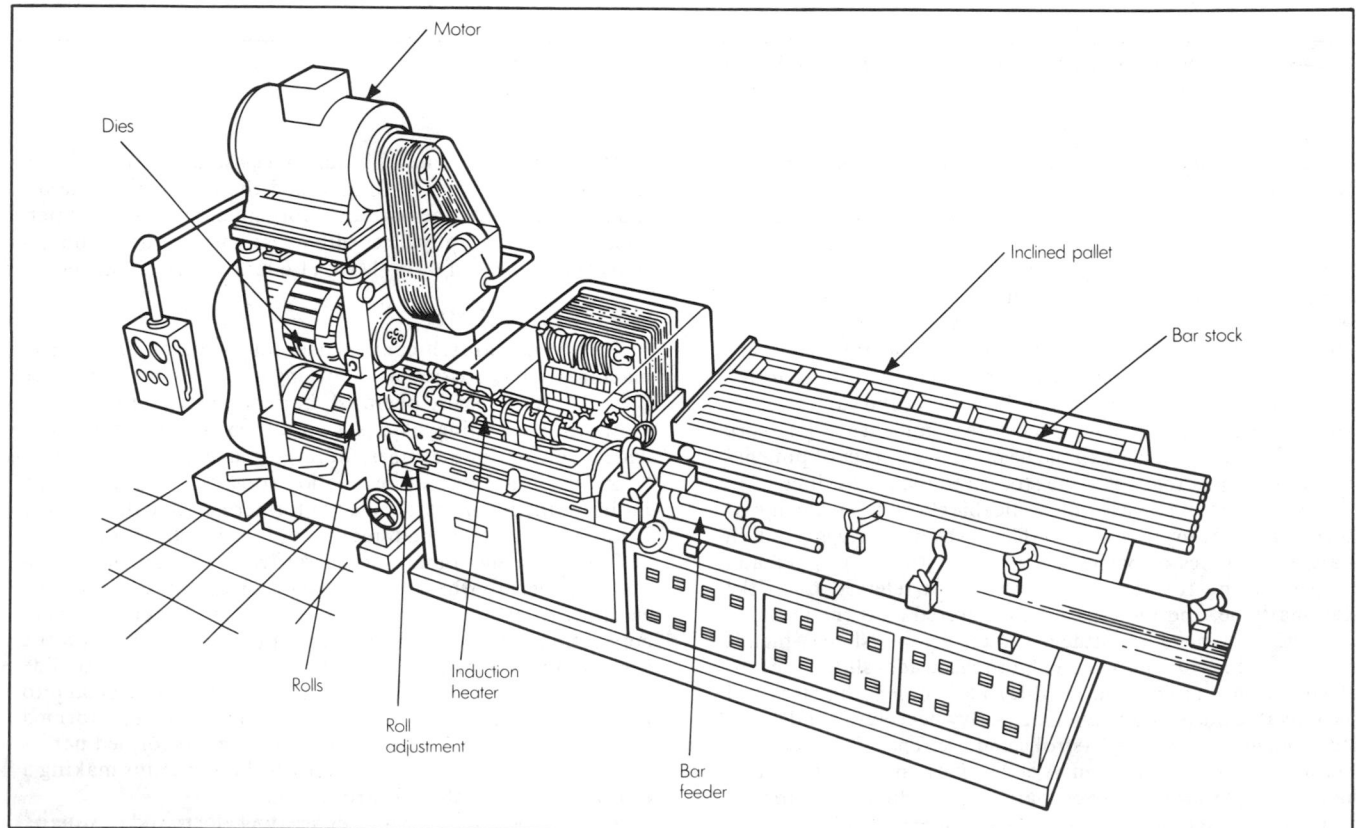

Fig. 40-15 An automated wedge rolling machine incorporates a bar feeder, an induction heater, and the rolling machine.

RADIAL FORGING MACHINES

The radial forging machine deforms the workpiece between two or four opposed dies that deliver a series of short, rapid strokes. The dies are mounted in levers driven by a main driveshaft through eccentrics (see Fig. 40-16). The die holders

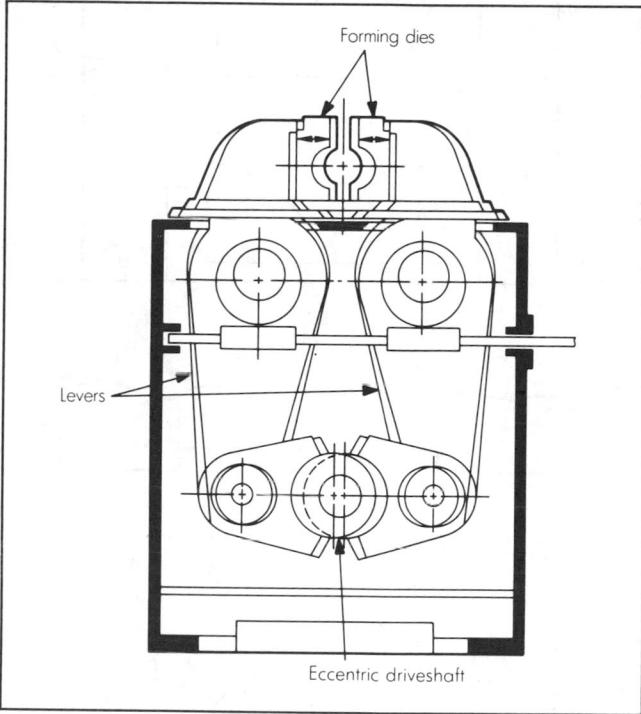

Fig. 40-16 Side view of radial forging machine. (*Battelle Columbus Laboratories*)

are water cooled to maintain temperature control. The distance between the dies is controlled manually by adjusting the eccentrics or automatically by an infeed control. The workpiece is held at the proper location and is fed into the dies using either one or two chuck heads mounted on the machine bed. Two chuck heads, mounted on each side of the forging dies, are used when long parts are being forged.

Radial forging machines that are currently being constructed are capable of forging steel bars to 6" (150 mm) diam and tubes having a 1" (25 mm) wall thickness to 13" (330 mm) diam. These machines range in capacity from 60-250 tons (534-2244 kN) per die. Dies can be made to 20" (510 mm) in length.

Radial forging machines are widely used for precision forging of bars with round, square, and rectangular cross sections. These machines are also used for producing profiled parts, such as solid or hollow-stepped shafts, and for finishing tubes with cylindrical and conical profiles.

RING ROLLING MACHINES

Seamless rings are predominantly produced on ring rolling machines. The preform required for ring rolling is produced by upsetting and piercing a heated block or billet having correct volume into a donut-shaped forging.

In operation, the blank forging is placed over the inner mandrel of the ring rolling machine. The wall thickness of the blank is reduced between the mandrel and an outer roll by moving the two rolls against each other while driving the blank with the outer roll. As the wall thickness is reduced, the diameter increases. Shaping the cross section can be performed at the same time.

The three basic types of ring rolling machines generally used are table ring mills, radial machines, and radial-axial machines.

TOOLING

Tooling used in the forging process consists mainly of the dies in which the workpieces are forged. Forging may be accomplished with open or impression-type dies, or a combination of both.

OPEN DIES

Dies employed in open-die forging are relatively simple compared with those used for closed-die forging. The types of dies normally employed are flat dies, swage dies, and V-dies. Each die set is composed of a top and bottom half. The top half is attached to the ram, and the bottom half is attached to the hammer or press bed. Auxiliary tools are also employed to cut forged bars, control final forging size, and initiate setdowns or changes in sections on the forged parts. Piercing, punching, or trepanning tools may be used to remove the center slug when manufacturing rings from upset discs.

Flat Dies

Flat dies, as illustrated in Fig. 40-17, are used for the majority of open-die forgings. The flat surfaces are parallel to

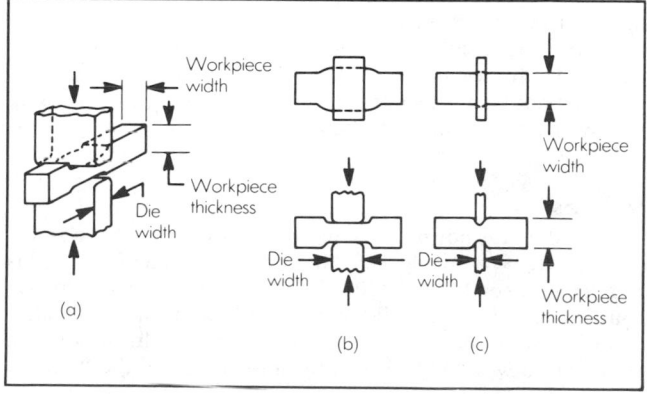

Fig. 40-17 Typical flat dies as used in open-die forging. (*Forging Industry Association*)

avoid tapering the workpiece. Flat dies range from 12-20" (300-500 mm) in width, but normally are 16-18" (400-450 mm) wide. The edges are rounded to prevent the workpiece from being

TOOLING

pinched or torn during the forging operation and to prevent the formation of laps.

Flat dies are used to forge bars, flat forgings, and other parts, either round or shaped. Wide dies are employed when transverse flow (side movement) is desired (see Fig. 40-17, view *b*) or when the workpiece is drawn out by using repeated blows. Narrow dies are employed for cutting off or for necking down various cross sections (see view *c*). Flat dies are also used in combination with other types of dies. The flat die is usually on top, and the shaped die is on the bottom.

Swage Dies

Swage dies are basically flat dies with a V shape cut in their centers (see Fig. 40-18). The V shape usually has a 120° included

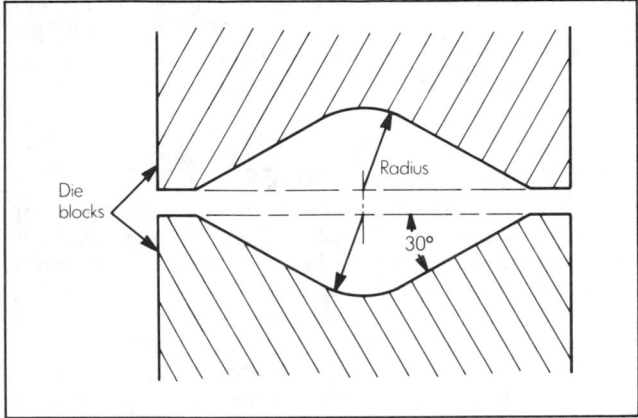

Fig. 40-18 Cross section of swaging dies used in open-die forging. (*Battelle Columbus Laboratories*)

angle, and the center of the V contains a radius corresponding to the minimum diameter shaft that can be produced.

When round shafts are being manufactured, swage dies can be used to round off the polygonal surfaces produced by a flat die; or if properly designed, they can be used to produce the complete shaft.

The advantages of swage dies over flat dies for forging round bars include minimal side bulging, longitudinal movement of all metal, faster operation, and greater deformation in the center of the bar. The disadvantage is that swage dies are normally designed to forge a single-size bar. Another disadvantage is that parts cannot be marked or cut off when swaging dies are used; the swaging dies must be removed and replaced with flat dies first.

V-Dies

In V-dies, the bottom die contains a V form and the top die is always flat (see Fig. 40-19). The optimum angle for the V is usually between 90 and 120°. V-dies can be used to produce round parts, but are usually employed to forge hollow cylinders from a hollow billet. A hollow or solid mandrel is used in conjunction with the V-dies to form the inside of the cylinder.

IMPRESSION DIES

Impression-die forging (sometimes called closed-die forging) is performed on hammers and presses with dies attached to the ram and to the sow block or the bolster plate. The dies for use on

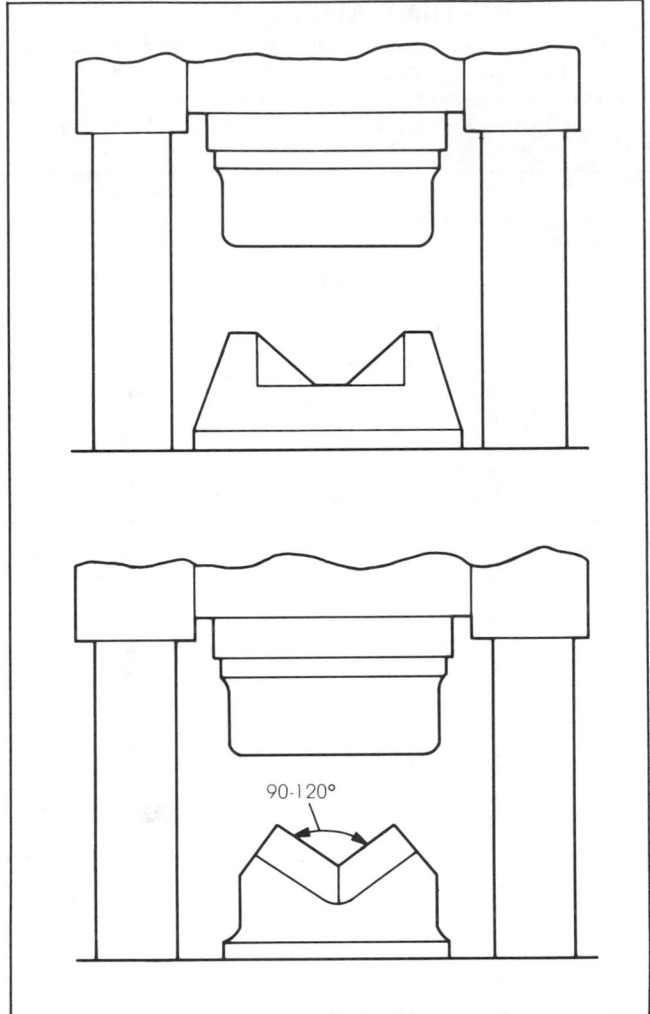

Fig. 40-19 V-dies contain an included angle of 90-120° for the bottom die; the top die is always flat. (*Battelle Columbus Laboratories*)

presses are often designed to forge the part in one blow, and knock-out pins are often incorporated to mechanically eject the forging from the impression. Dies may contain impressions for several parts.

Hammer forgings are normally made with several blows in successive die impressions. A typical die for hammer forgings is shown in Fig. 40-20. The edger or roller impression is used to preform the workpiece so that the metal is distributed along its length for subsequent steps. If a portion of the bar stock is being reduced, the impression is referred to as a fullering impression. The bending impression bends the workpiece so that it fits the shape of the blocking impression. The blocking impression is used as an intermediate step to impart the general shape to the part. The final shape is formed in the finishing impression. Excess material flows into the gutter surrounding the finishing impression as the die halves are brought together. The excess material or flash is removed in a subsequent operation. When several forgings are produced sequentially from bar stock, a cutoff impression is machined into one corner of the die to sever the finished forging from the bar.

Since mechanical presses operate with a fixed stroke, the

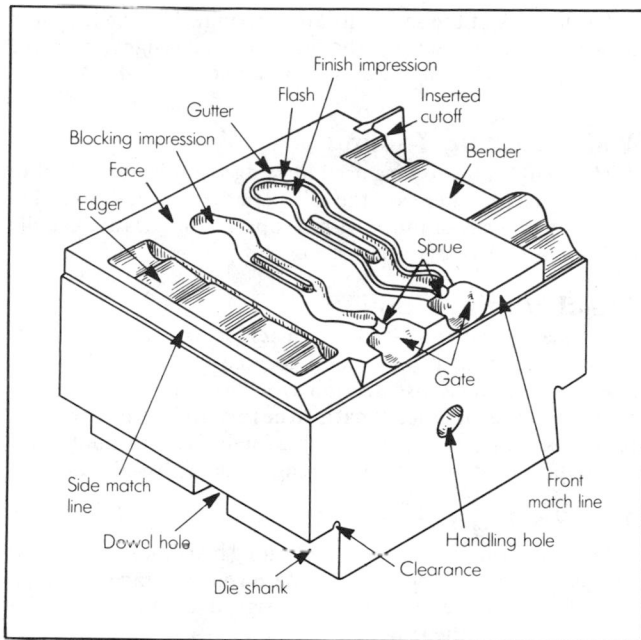

Fig. 40-20 Elements of a die block for drop forging.

dies used on these presses are designed so that die filling occurs without the two die halves making contact. Contact of the die halves can cause the press to lock or could possibly cause serious damage to the dies or press. Dies used on hammers and hydraulic presses are designed to have sufficient bearing area so that the dies can make contact lightly without incurring damage.

FORGING MACHINE DIES

Forging machines are capable of upsetting, deep-piercing, splitting, bending, and extruding simple or intricate shapes. The workpiece is gripped in the cavities or passes contained in the die halves, and the header tool forces the heated material into the die cavity. Figure 40-21 illustrates a typical three-pass operation to produce gear blanks.

TRIMMING AND PUNCHING DIES

Trimming is the removal of flash that is produced on the part during the forging operation. Trimming may also be used to

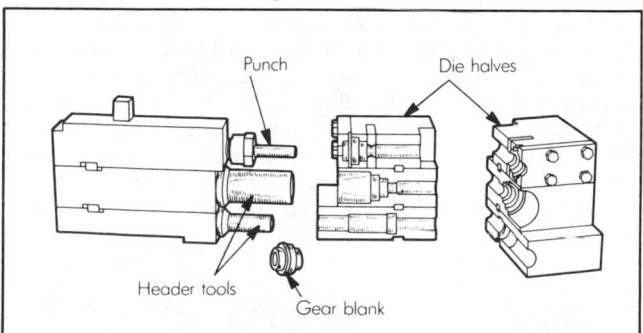

Fig. 40-21 Set of dies used in a vertical-type forging machine. Gathering takes place in the top die; upsetting to final dimensions takes place in the center die; and separating from the bar takes place in the top die.

remove some of the draft material thereby producing straight side walls on the part. It is usually performed by a top die and bottom die that are shaped to the contour of the part. The top die acts as a punch to push the part through the lower die containing the cutting edge. If the top die does not follow the contour of the part, the part may be deformed during the trimming operation. Figure 40-22 illustrates typical tools for trimming impression-die forgings.

An operation similar to trimming is punching in which excess material on an internal surface is removed (see Fig. 40-23). To ensure accurate cuts, punching and trimming operations are often performed simultaneously (see Fig. 40-24).

Materials for trimming and punching dies are selected based on the type of material to be trimmed and whether the part is to

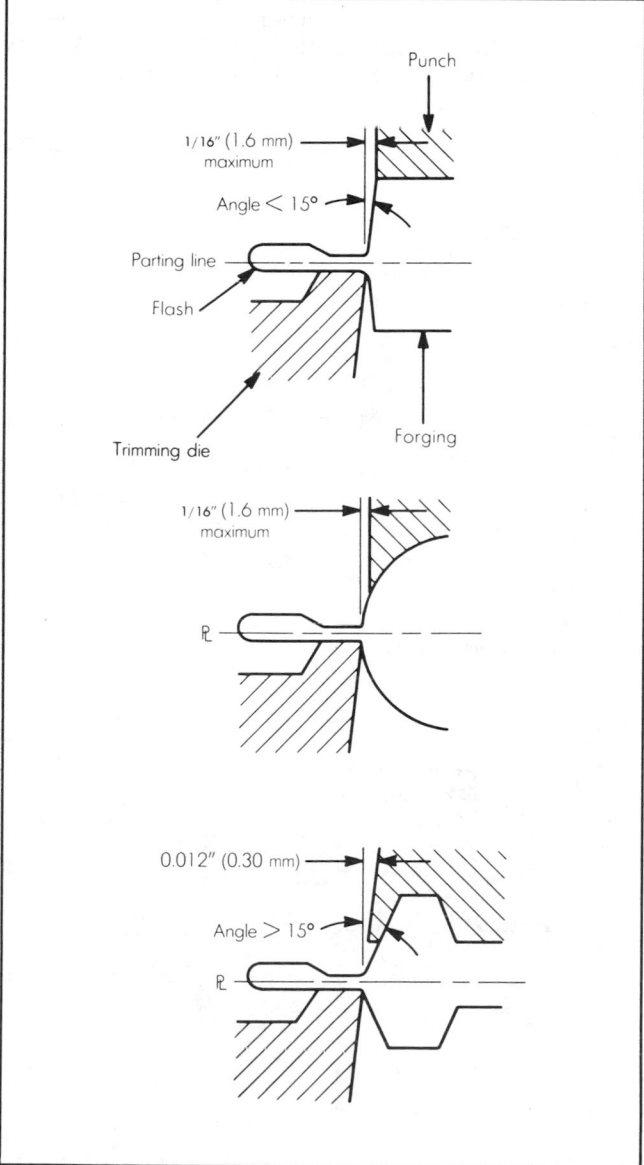

Fig. 40-22 Typical trimming tools for removing flash from impression-die forgings. (*Forging Industry Association*)

TOOLING

be trimmed hot or cold. Punches are normally made from proprietary tool steels when carbon and stainless steels are to be trimmed, and from 1020 steel that has been hard faced when nonferrous alloys are to be trimmed. The trimming die, or bottom die, can be made from D2 or A2 alloys. It can also be made from cold-rolled steel that has a high strength alloy hard facing applied to the cutting edge.

OTHER TOOLING

Other types of tooling employed in forging include dies used in roll forging, wedge rolling, radial forging, and ring rolling.

Roll Forging Tooling

The tools used in roll forging consist of a pair of ring segments, or dies, for each forming pass. The segments can be mounted on the rolls individually for single-pass operation or with other pairs of ring segments for use in multiple-pass operation. An undercut step maintains the rings in the proper location, and thrust bolts fasten the segments to the rolls. Keys are designed in the rolls to absorb the tangential thrust.

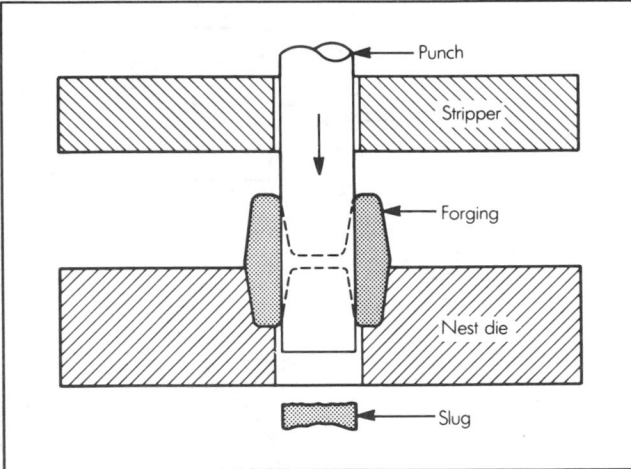

Fig. 40-23 Schematic diagram of typical punching operation on an impression-die forging. (*Forging Industry Association*)

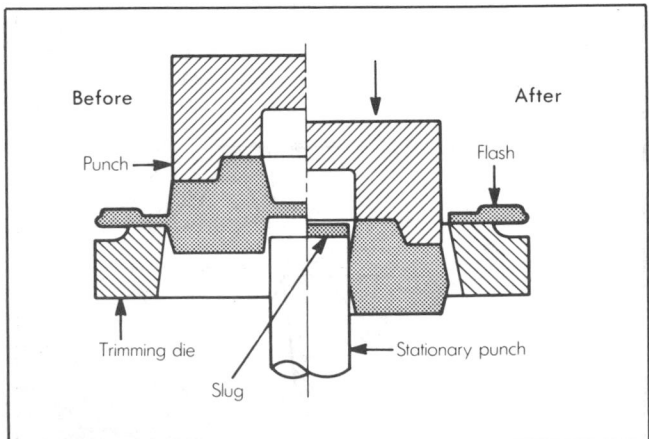

Fig. 40-24 Schematic diagram of combined trimming and punching operation. (*Forging Industry Association*)

The lengths of the segments are determined by the length of the workpieces. Generally, the segments are designed to forge the workpiece up to half the roll circumference.

Wedge Rolling Tooling

The wedge-shaped dies used in wedge rolling are bolted to T-slots in the peripheries of the rolls. The dies can be designed to permit single-pass or multiple-pass operation. Dies are usually made from H11 or H13 tool steel.

Radial Forging Tooling

The dies used on radial forging machines contain two or four segments mounted in dieholders located on top of the drive housing. The die cross section can be designed to permit circular, square, or tapered parts to be forged. Dies can be made from nickel-chromium steel with a high strength alloy hard facing applied or from a high-strength, nickel-based alloy.

Ring Rolling Tooling

Deformation of rings on a ring rolling machine is performed between an inner mandrel and a main roll. The inner mandrel and main roll can be cylindrical or designed to form a particular finished shape in the ring.

COMPUTER APPLICATIONS

Computer aided design and manufacturing (CAD/CAM) techniques are being increasingly applied in forging technology. Using the three-dimensional description of a machined part, which may have been computer designed, it is possible to generate the geometry of the associated forging. For this purpose, it is best to use a CAD/CAM system with software for handling geometry, drafting, dimensioning, and numerical control (NC) machining. Thus, the forging sections can be obtained from a common database.

Using well-proven analyses based on the slab method or other techniques, the forging load and stresses can be obtained and flash dimensions can be selected for each section, permitting metal flow to be regarded as approximately two-dimensional (plane strain or axisymmetric). In some relatively simple section geometries, a computer simulation can be conducted to evaluate initial estimates on blocker or preform sections. Once the blocker and finisher sections are obtained to the designer's satisfaction, this geometric database can be utilized to write NC part programs and thereby obtain NC tapes or discs for cutting the forging die (or the die used for electrodischarge machining of the forging die).

This CAD/CAM procedure is still in a stage of development. In the near future, this technology can be expected to evolve in two main directions: (1) handling the geometry of complex forgings, for example, three-dimensional description, automatic drafting and sectioning, and NC machining, and (2) utilizing design analysis, for example, calculation of stresses in the forging and stress concentrations in the dies, prediction of elastic deflections in the dies, metal flow analysis, and blocker/preform design.

References

1. *Open Die Forging Manual*, 3rd ed. (Ohio: Forging Industry Association, 1982), p.91.

HEAT AND SURFACE TREATMENT OF METALS

Heat treatment is an operation or combination of operations involving the controlled heating and cooling of solid metals and alloys to obtain a required microstructure with resultant desired properties. These properties vary widely, depending upon the applications for the metals. With current technology, heat treatment is very versatile and can provide many different and predictable properties or combinations of properties.

Most heat treating operations can be classified into the two following types of processes:

1. Processes such as through hardening and surface (case) hardening that increase the strength, hardness, and toughness of metals.
2. Processes such as annealing and normalizing that decrease the hardness of metals in order to improve their homogeneity, machinability, and formability, or to relieve stresses.

Proper heat treatment of any metal requires the combined input of design engineers, metallurgists, and manufacturing engineers. Essential information required for optimum heat treatment includes the following:

1. The composition and condition of the metal to be heat treated, and the intended applications.
2. The critical time-temperature transformation relationship for the specific metal to be heat treated.
3. The response of the metal to quenching and the method of cooling or quenching to be used.
4. The desired hardness and/or strength.

HEAT TREATMENT OF STEEL

The three major operations performed in the hardening of steel by heat treatment are: austenitizing, equalizing, and cooling.

AUSTENITIZING

As steel is heated and cooled, its structure changes in certain predictable steps that must be recognized for each alloy. Initially, steel that has not been previously heat treated is usually composed of a mixture of ferrite and carbides, often present in a lamellar microstructure known as pearlite.

When steel with this ferrite-pearlite structure is heated, it reaches a temperature at which the carbides in the lamellar pearlite begin to dissolve into the iron. As the temperature is raised, more of the carbides are dissolved until the steel reaches a point at which all the carbides are dissolved and the steel consists completely of a solid solution of carbon in iron called austenite. The temperature at which pearlite begins to transform into austenite is identified as the lower critical temperature, Ac_1, the temperature at which the steel becomes composed completely of austenite is called the upper critical temperature, Ac_3, and the temperature range between is the critical range or transformation range for the particular alloy.

The lower critical temperature is shown by the line A_1 in the iron-carbon equilibrium diagram (see Fig. 41-1). In actual practice, this temperature varies slightly depending upon whether the pearlite is beginning to be transformed to austenite or the austenite has completed transformation to pearlite—in other words, whether the steel is being heated or cooled. This difference is designated by the letters Ac_1 upon heating and Ar_1 upon cooling.

These temperatures vary with the chemical composition of the steel.

The upper critical temperature varies in the same way. Shown as A_3 in the equilibrium diagram, it is known as Ac_3 upon heating and Ar_3 upon cooling. It is also designated as A_{cm} when the carbon content of the steel is above 0.80%. The temperature at which the steel is completely converted to austenite or at which pearlite just begins to form is partially dependent upon the alloying element content of the steel but primarily upon the carbon content.

As shown in Fig. 41-1, a plain carbon steel of 0.80% carbon will have the lowest full transformation temperature because, at this composition, the upper critical temperature A_3 is the same as the lower critical temperature A_1. This 0.80% carbon composition is called eutectoid steel; it is 100% pearlite below the transformation temperature and is characterized by the complete change from pearlite to austenite (and back to pearlite) at a single temperature. All other compositions of various percentages will transform over a range of temperatures.

Hypoeutectoid Steels

Steels containing less than 0.80% carbon are called hypoeutectoid steels. Upon heating, the pearlite in such steels begins to transform to austenite at A_1; but because of the excess ferrite (alpha iron) in the composition, the transformation is not completed until the temperature reaches A_3. Holding at temperatures above the upper critical temperature increases the rate at which carbon and other alloying elements go into solution, but it also increases the austenitic grain size. Although large-

HEAT TREATMENT OF STEELS

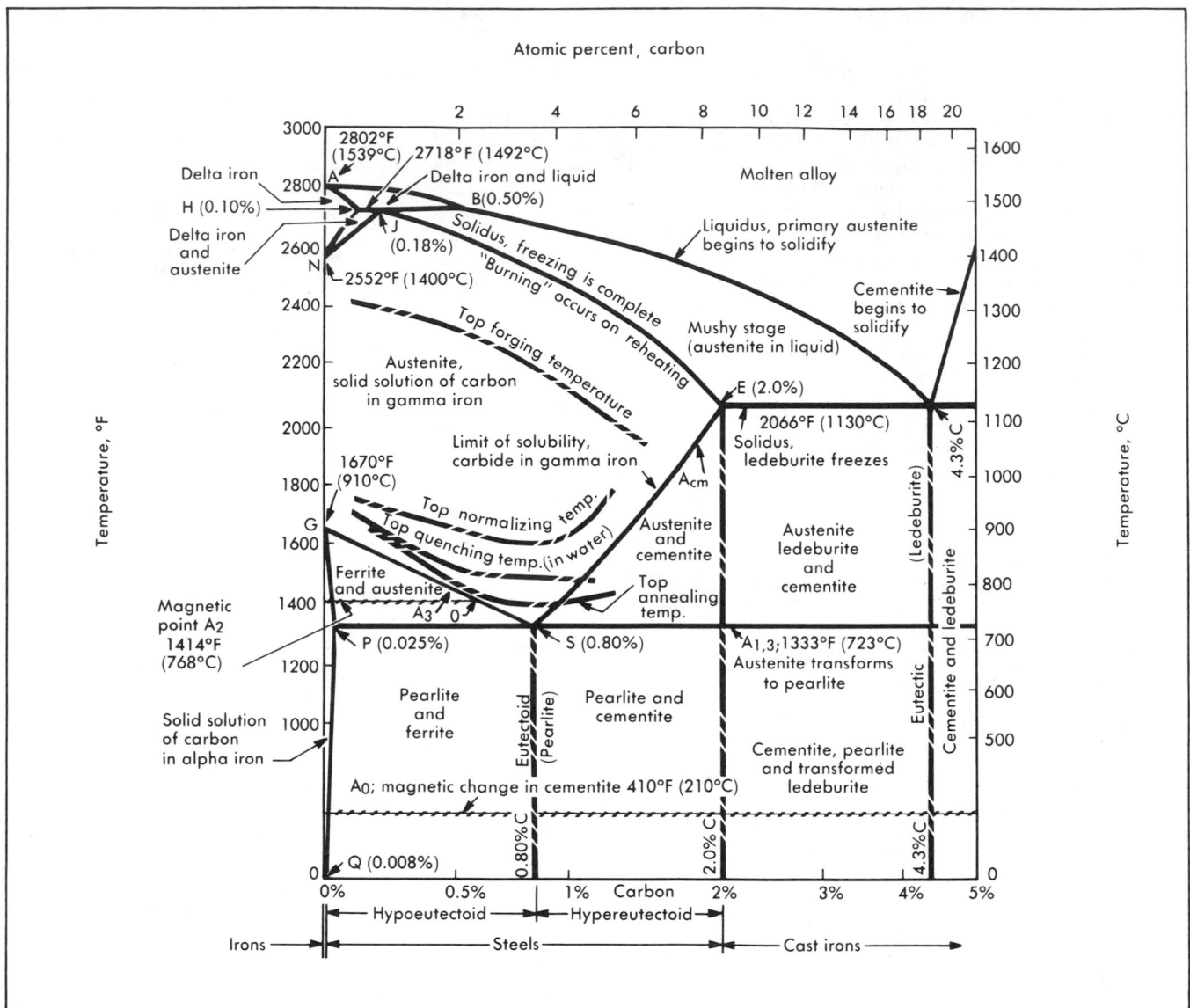

Fig. 41-1 The iron-carbon phase diagram. The critical temperature lines A_1, A_2, and A_{cm} represent transformation upon both heating and cooling. Because of the hysteresis of steel transformation and the effects of elements other than carbon, the transformations upon heating and cooling actually occur at different temperatures.

grained steels harden to a greater depth, large grains decrease the steel's fatigue and rupture strengths. If the steel is held below A_3, some of the ferrite will not go into solution. Because the undissolved ferrite contains only a minimal amount of carbon, it does not harden when cooled, and the steel cannot reach its maximum hardness.

Hypereutectoid Steels

Reaching a full solution is not as great a problem with hypereutectoid steels (steels with a carbon content greater than 0.80%) because the undissolved materials form cementite (iron carbides and other carbides), which is harder than ferrite. However, to achieve maximum depth of hardening, the steel must be held above the upper critical temperature. (A_{cm}). The steepness of the A_{cm} line means that, for steels of 1.00% carbon or more,

rapid growth of large grains will occur. Therefore, a compromise temperature between the upper and lower critical temperatures is generally chosen in order to leave some carbides to retard austenite grain growth and to serve as sites at which phase changes can initiate during cooling.

EQUALIZING

The rate of heating is usually not significant unless the steel is highly stressed initially, and then it should be heated slowly. Preheating in another furnace is often necessary during production when a furnace temperature cannot be altered because other parts are being processed at the same time or because productivity would decline. For equalizing or soaking (the operation that holds the steel at Ac_3, the upper critical temperature, until all sections are uniformly at heat), an adequate soak time is generally about ½-1 hour for each inch (25 mm) of the thickest cross section.

QUENCHING

Quenching, or the rate of cooing, is important in heat treating operations because it dictates the structure and properties of the steel. This present discussion is limited to the microstructural transformations during cooling; details of the various processes and media for quenching various steels are presented later in this chapter.

Pearlite Formations

Upon very slow cooling, ferrite begins to form at the austenite grain boundaries when the temperature reaches the A_3 line in the equilibrium diagram (Fig. 41-1) and continues to grow in amount until the temperature reaches the A_1 line. While the temperature is changing and ferrite is forming, the carbon content of the austenite increases from its nominal value to about 0.80%. The A_{cm} line also represents the saturation limit of carbon in the austenite. Therefore, in steels having a carbon content greater than 0.80%, cementite will precipitate on cooling, and the carbon content of the austenite will again approach 0.80% as the temperature approaches 1333° F (723° C).

Bainite Formation

The procutectoid line joins the beginning of the pearlite transformation line at approximately 1000° F (540° C). This means that only pearlite would be present when fully transformed at this temperature, regardless of the carbon content of the steel. The transformation of austenite by isothermal decomposition below the knee of the diagram, 1000° F, results in the formation of bainite, a microstructure containing ferrite and carbide phases that looks distinctly different from pearlite. The structure of bainite is said to be acicular and like pearlite; the degree of fineness of the bainite structure increases as the temperature of formation is lowered from 1000° F. Pearlite is thought to be nucleated by cementite and bainite is thought to be nucleated by ferrite. Like pearlite, as the fineness of the bainite structure increases, so does the strength of the bainite.

Martensite Formation

As the temperature of the quenching bath is lowered, a temperature level is reached at which austenite will undergo a spontaneous transformation to martensite—a single-phase, body-centered, tetragonal structure. Martensite continues to form as the temperature is lowered, forming athermally; and it will not form isothermally. The temperature at which martensite first begins to form from austenite is termed the M_s point, and the temperature at which the austenite is fully transformed to martensite is called the martensite finish or the M_f point.

HARDENABILITY OF STEELS

Hardenability is the relative ability of ferrous metals to harden. It is the property that determines the depth and distribution of hardness induced by quenching or the size of a workpiece that can be hardened under given cooling conditions. It does not refer to the maximum hardness that can be attained in a given steel.

Hardenability is commonly measured as the distance below a quenched surface where the metal has a specific hardness or a specific percentage of martensite in the microstructure, as discussed later in this section.

MEASURING HARDENABILITY

The most commonly used method of determining hardenability is the Jominy end-quench test. This test consists of heating a standard specimen, a 1" (25 mm) diam x 4" (102 mm) long round bar, above the upper critical temperature of the metal. The hot specimen is supported vertically in a fixture, and its lower end is quenched with a stream of cold water. After the specimen has cooled to room temperature, flat surfaces are ground on opposite sides and hardnesses are measured at 1/16" (1.6 mm) increments along the length of the specimen. Details of this laboratory test procedure are presented in SAE Standard J406c, "Method of Determining Hardenability of Steels," and ANSI/ASTM Standard A255, "End-Quench Test for Hardenability of Steel."

Data from these tests is plotted as hardness versus distance from the quenched end, the hardness decreasing as the distance from the quenched end increases. Published data, called hardenability bands (H-bands), is used to predict the hardening characteristics of various grades of steels, parts of different shapes, and parts having various cross-sectional shapes.

H STEELS AND HARDENABILITY BANDS

For the identification of steels specified to hardenability limits, the suffix letter H is added to the conventional series number. In the unified numbering system (UNS), the H appears as a prefix. To permit steel producers to meet the standards for hardenability limits, the chemical compositions of some steels have been modified somewhat from the same grades of steels that do not have a specified hardenability band.

Hardenability bands for carbon and alloy H steels are specified in SAE Standard J1268. The band graphs and tabular values show maximum and minimum hardenability limits, in Rockwell C-scale values, for various steels, based on standard end-quench tests. Steels are available with narrower (about one third) bands than standard hardenability bands. Such steels are sometimes used to help control distortion when heat treating certain parts, such as gears.

PROBLEMS IN HARDENING

Many problems can occur in hardening, most of which are the result of improper heat treatment specifications or poor heat treating practices. Some of the more common problems are due to decarburization, scaling, quench cracking, residual stresses, retained austenite, and dimensional changes.

Decarburization

Steel parts are often decarburized to some extent during heating for hot forming operations, such as rolling, extruding, and forging. The loss of surface carbon may prevent attaining full hardness in the finished parts. This situation may necessitate the removal of the softer surfaces of the parts by grinding or other means, preferably before heat treatment.

HARDENABILITY OF STEELS

Decarburization during heating can be eliminated by using protective atmospheres in the furnaces. Decarburization can also be corrected by carbon restoration (carburizing), but it is better prevented than corrected.

Scaling

The formation of surface layers of oxidation products, called scaling, is another undesirable result of hardening. Such a condition often requires machining, grinding, cleaning, or other methods of descaling. Scaling can be minimized by using protective atmospheres in the heating furnaces.

Quench Cracking

The formation of cracks when quenching heated steels is a major problem. As the carbon content of a steel increases, the tendency to crack increases. Higher austenitizing temperatures also increase the tendency toward quench cracking. Steels with coarser grain size are more susceptible to cracks than fine-grained steels because the latter have more grain boundary area to block the movement of cracks, and grain boundaries help to absorb and redistribute residual stresses, as discussed next in this section. Nicks, scratches, too small a radius between section changes, and impurities on the surfaces of workpieces to be hardened are also possible sources of cracks. Careful machining, grinding, and cleaning prior to heat treatment is generally advisable.

Residual Stresses

Residual stresses (stresses that exist in a part that is free of external forces or thermal gradients) can cause distortion, warpage, cracking, or breakage, especially after quenching and before tempering. Major reasons for the formation of residual stresses are the nonuniform contraction of heated parts during cooling, expansion during transformation, or a combination of the two, as well as variations in heating and cooling rates.

Fast quenching produces higher stresses, and therefore the slowest cooling rate for producing the desired microstructure and hardness should be used. Subsequent tempering reduces the hardness and tensile strength, but minimizes stresses and improves ductility and toughness.

Retained Austenite

Austenite that is not transformed during the heat treating cycle is soft and weak, and lowers the overall hardness of the steel if excessive in amount. It may also cause dimensional instability because of the possible transformation of the austenite at room temperature over a long period of time. In addition, retained austenite will often transform to martensite with the application of stresses.

The amount of retained austenite is affected by the alloy content of the steel, the austenitizing temperature, the cooling rate, and, in some cases, the amount and distribution of the stresses in the quenched parts. The effect of alloy content is so strong that some steels are entirely austenitic at room temperature. High austenitizing temperatures can result in increased amounts of retained austenite. Slow cooling rates also increase the tendency to retain austenite.

HEAT TREATMENT OF OTHER METALS

Many other metals beside steels are heat treated. The heat treatment of carbon and alloy steels is discussed in other portions of this chapter. This section provides information on the heat treatment of some of the other more common metals: cast irons; cast steels; stainless and maraging steels; titanium alloys; heat-resisting, high-strength alloys; and aluminum, magnesium, and copper alloys.

CAST IRONS

In general, heat treatment of cast irons is performed for one or more of the following reasons:

1. To relieve residual stresses.
2. To reduce hardness, which improves machinability but reduces strength.
3. To produce the necessary microstructure for desired mechanical or physical properties.
4. To harden the entire casting and change the mechanical properties.
5. To increase surface hardness.

Hardening of cast irons is accomplished by quenching the castings in a liquid medium that can be oil, water, brine, or a water-soluble polymer, after they have been held at a high enough temperature to austenitize the structure. The higher the temperature of austenitizing, the higher the hardness after quenching, but the greater the tendency to crack. After quenching, tempering is required to reduce residual stresses, reduce the amount of retained austenite, and lessen the possibility of cracking. Tempering temperatures range from 450° F (230° C) for maximum hardness to 1050° F (565° C) for maximum machinability.

While normalizing or air quenching produces a pearlitic microstructure in cast irons, liquid quenching should produce a martensitic microstructure. Alloy cast irons, both gray and ductile, require higher tempering temperatures than unalloyed irons for obtaining equivalent hardnesses. It is recommended that time-temperature transformation (TTT) diagrams be used as a means to predict the microstructure and hardness that can be obtained for cast irons having a given chemical composition. Such diagrams define the time and temperature before transformation will occur. Cast irons of differing chemical composition each have their own individual TTT diagram.

Varying the austenitizing temperatures affects the hardness of both unalloyed and alloyed gray irons. Low hardnesses are generally the result of failure to heat above the critical temperature, usually 1450 to 1500° F (790 to 815° C). Subsequent tempering increases the strength and toughness, but reduces the hardness. The higher the tempering temperature, the greater the decrease in hardness. The presence of alloys in the material, however, reduces the decrease in hardness. There are specialized hardening treatments for attaining specific microstructures and properties, the most common of which are austempering and martempering.

HEAT TREATMENT OF OTHER METALS

CAST STEELS

Most steel castings,[1] are heat treated for one or more of the following reasons:

1. To improve the as-cast structure and attain the desired mechanical properties.
2. To relieve stresses in the castings.
3. To improve machinability, facilitate processing, and avoid difficulties during finishing of the castings.
4. To produce optimum corrosion resistance of high-alloy steels and austenitic stainless steels.

This discussion is a general overview of the heat treatment of steel castings. Specific data with respect to heating rate, temperature, time at temperature, and cooling rate for a specific material should be obtained from the material supplier or the casting producer.

For increased productivity and maximum economy, steel castings are generally placed in a hot furnace, allowed to soak until their centers reach the temperature in the furnace, maintained at this temperature for 15 minutes or more (as required by the specifications), and then furnace cooled, liquid quenched, or air cooled. This type of short heating procedure will not usually cause distortion or cracking except in infrequent cases with some casting designs or highly alloyed steels, such as some tool steels.

Controlled-atmosphere or molten-salt-bath furnaces are used when it is desirable to prevent oxidation scaling or other surface reactions during heat treating. Such furnaces are also used when it is necessary to produce a compositional change on the surfaces of the castings, such as in carburization. Some steels that are investment cast are heat treated in vacuum furnaces.

STAINLESS AND MARAGING STEELS

The five main types of stainless steel are austenitic, ferritic, martensitic, duplex (austenitic-ferritic), and precipitation hardening (PH).

Austenitic Stainless Steels

The austenitic stainless steels are not hardenable by heat treatment but can be moderately hardened by cold working. These alloys, however, are often annealed, heat treated to eliminate sensitization, or stress relieved.

Ferritic Alloys

The ferritic family of stainless steels cannot be hardened by heat treatment, except for a partial hardening that can take place in certain modifications of 430 and 434 grades. Therefore, annealing is the only heat treating process commonly used.

Martensitic Stainless Steels

As a result of their high carbon content, the hardenability of the martensitic stainless steels is high. Drastic quenching is not required.

Hardening treatments for the martensitic stainless steels are listed in Table 41-1. Preheating is frequently used prior to austenitizing these alloys and is almost mandatory for the higher carbon grades (Types 420 and 440 series). Cracking or warpage of parts can occur if preheating is not used. Preheating is accomplished by heating slowly and holding for about one

TABLE 41-1
Hardening Treatments for Martensitic Stainless Steels

Grade		Austenitizing Temperature,*	Typical Hardness,
UNS	AISI/SAE	°F (°C)	Bhn
S40300	403	1700-1850 (925-1010)	410
S41000	410	1700-1850 (925-1010)	410
S41400	414	1800-1900 (980-1040)	420
S41600	416	1700-1850 (925-1010)	410
S42000	420	1800-1950 (980-1065)	500
S43100	431	1800-1950 (980-1065)	430
S44002	440A	1850-1950 (1010-1065)	560
S44003	440B	1850-1950 (1010-1065)	580
S44004	440C	1850-1950 (1010-1065)	610

(AL Tech Specialty Steel Corp.)
* Time at temperature: 15-60 minutes
Air or oil quench.

hour at 1400 to 1450° F (760 to 790° C) prior to austenitizing. Extremely large parts must be held at temperature until all portions of the part have reached the preheat temperature. After hardening, martensitic stainless steels must be either stress relieved or tempered, discussed subsequently in this section.

In order to obtain optimum toughness in martensitic stainless steels, the hardening temperature should be selected based upon the subsequent heat treatment. A hardening temperature on the high side of the allowable range should be used if the material will be subsequently stress relieved. Conversely, a hardening temperature on the low side of the range should be used if the metal will be tempered.

Precipitation-Hardening Alloys

Generally, the martensitic, precipitation-hardening alloys are not recommended for use in the unaged condition. In this condition they have lower ductility than material in the aged condition. Because of the complexity of these alloys, it is recommended that the user consult published standards or the producer of the material for detailed heat treatment recommendations.

Maraging Steels

Maraging steels are strengthened by the precipitation of intermetallic compounds produced by age hardening a matrix of low-carbon martensite. Because of the low-carbon, iron-nickel, martensitic matrix, these alloys possess excellent toughness and ductility, both in the solution-annealed and aged conditions. Aging develops high strength and hardness. At the present time, only maraging steels containing 18% nickel are being produced.

Duplex Stainless Steels

These alloys have two phases present in their microstructure, austenite and ferrite. Depending upon their composition, the alloys can be predominantly ferrite, predominantly austenite,

HEAT TREATMENT OF OTHER METALS

or have approximately equal amounts of each phase present. These grades are not hardenable by heat treatment, but can be moderately hardened by cold working. The only heat treatment commonly used is annealing. Annealing treatments are very similar to those used for austenitic stainless steels. Temperatures of 1850 to 1950° F (1010 to 1065° C) are often used, followed by water quenching. However, it is recommended that the user contact the producer for exact annealing recommendations.

TITANIUM AND ITS ALLOYS

The grain size of titanium and its alloys cannot be refined by heat treatment alone. Either hot or cold working of the metal is necessary for grain refinement. The degree of cold working performed on single-phase alloys also affects the recrystallization temperature and time of heating required. Mixed-phase alloys are recrystallized during hot working and are generally not cold rollable to a degree sufficient to cause grain refinement during recrystallization. The final properties of the heat-treated materials thus reflect the variables introduced during prior cold or hot working.

Many types of heat treatment are performed on titanium and titanium alloys to suit specific requirements. The more common treatments include stress relieving, annealing, stabilizing, beta-tizing, solution treating, and age hardening. Solution treating and age hardening are usually combined in a two-stage thermal treatment to provide high strength. Another heat treatment, recrystallizing, is done at intermediate-to-high temperatures to produce a uniform, dislocation-free microstructure. Recrystallizing may or may not induce grain refinement or a new texture, depending upon prior working of the metal.

HEAT-RESISTING, HIGH-STRENGTH ALLOYS

Heat-resisting, high-strength alloys are used extensively in the aircraft and aerospace industries, chemical and petrochemical processing equipment, industrial furnaces and related heat treating equipment, and a variety of other applications involving strenuous service conditions imposed by oxidizing and corrosive atmospheres over a wide range of temperatures. These materials consist essentially of iron, nickel, and cobalt-based alloys, and are available in many special, proprietary compositions.

Heat treatment of these alloys varies with their compositions, the size and shape of the products, and the applications.

Some heat-resisting alloys are strengthened by means of aging treatments designed to promote precipitation hardening, using second phases; these are usually referred to as precipitation-strengthened alloys. Other alloys are normally used in the annealed or solution heat-treated condition and develop strength from in-service precipitation of carbides or from solid-solution strengthening. These alloys are usually called solution-strengthened or carbide-strengthened alloys. Still a third group of alloys are oxide dispersion strengthened (ODS) alloys, which derive their strength from a fine dispersion of inert oxide particles. These alloys are also typically used in the annealed condition.

Examples of wrought, iron-based, solution-strengthened alloys include iron-nickel-chromium alloys such as alloys 800H and 330, and Type 310 stainless steel. Also included are materials of the more complex iron-nickel-chromium-cobalt family, such as alloy N-155. Precipitation-strengthened, iron-based, heat-resisting alloys usually contain some amount of titanium (to

3%) and sometimes aluminum. Examples are alloys A-286 and 901, both of which also contain molybdenum. Inco Co.'s Incoloy alloy MA 956, which contains a dispersion of yttrium oxide particles, is a good example of an iron-based ODS alloy.

ALUMINUM ALLOYS

In high-purity form, aluminum is soft and ductile. Most commercial uses, however, require greater strength than pure aluminum affords. Strengthening of aluminum is achieved first by the addition of other elements to produce various alloys,[2] which singly or in combination impart strength to the metal. Further strengthening is possible by means that classify the alloys roughly into two categories, nonheat-treatable and heat-treatable.

Nonheat-Treatable Alloys

The initial strength of alloys in this group depends upon the hardening effect of elements such as manganese, silicon, iron and magnesium, singly or in various combinations.

Heat-Treatable Alloys

The initial strength of heat-treatable aluminum alloys is enhanced by the addition of alloying elements such as copper, magnesium, zinc, and silicon. Since these elements singly or in various combinations show increasing solid solubility in aluminum with increasing temperature, it is possible to subject them to thermal treatments that will impart pronounced strengthening.

MAGNESIUM ALLOYS

Like many other metals, magnesium alloys are heat treated to improve their mechanical properties or to facilitate fabrication. The type of heat treatment used depends upon the specific alloy, the form of the product (wrought or cast), and the service requirements. Die castings are not usually heat treated; but sand, investment, and permanent-mold castings are generally heat treated to improve their properties.

Reheat treatment of magnesium alloys is not usually necessary. However, if the parts have been overaged or the compound ratings of the castings are too high, reheat treating can usually be accomplished without any detrimental effects. An exception to this may be with the AZ and thorium-containing (HK and HM) alloys, which are subject to grain coarsening. Products made from these alloys should be carefully examined after reheat treatments for possible coarse grain structures.

COPPERS AND COPPER ALLOYS

The wrought coppers and many copper alloys, are single-phase metals. As a result, heat treatment is limited to the annealing of cold worked metal for recrystallization or stress relieving. Castings are also sometimes annealed to soften them and increase their ductility and/or toughness. Annealing may be carried out in roller-hearth, batch-type, and strip or strand-annealing furnaces.

Castings and billets of copper alloys are sometimes given a homogenizing heat treatment to reduce chemical segregation and to attain the required hardness, ductility, or toughness. Homogenizing consists of heating to temperatures above the upper annealing range and soaking at temperature for up to 10 hours. Temperatures and times vary with the alloy, the size of the cast grains, and the desired results.

Brasses

Copper-zinc alloys, in general, are called brasses, although each has a commonly used trade name. When these alloys are annealed after cold working, they are annealed to meet a specific grain size or tensile strength requirement. Grain size is the average diameter in millimeters of the grains observed. For sheet and strip stock, grain size is measured on a plane parallel to the surface of the metal.

Copper-Nickel Alloys

The two most popular copper-nickel alloys are C70600 and C71500. They are used extensively in applications requiring resistance to corrosion in both fresh and salt water. In tubular form, they are used in power plant condensers where the coolant may be salt, brackish, or fresh water. They contain iron, and it is important that the iron be in solution in the copper-nickel alloy matrix. Annealing temperatures are high, in the range of 1100 to 1500° F (595 to 815° C), in order to put the iron into solution. Rapid cooling by quenching is desirable to keep the iron in solution.

Nickel-Silver Alloys

The nickel silvers are copper-nickel-zinc alloys, also called nickel brasses. Their nickel contents vary from 8 to 18%, and zinc contents from 10 to 27%. Their name is derived from their silvery color. They are used in the fabrication of silver-plated holloware and flatware, and also as relay springs, connectors, and terminals in electronic and communication devices. The grades used to make holloware are frequently supplied in annealed tempers. The high-zinc, high-strength grades are used in cold rolled tempers and seldom annealed during parts fabrication. Annealing, when done, is used to meet grain size requirements.

Heat Treatment of Beryllium Copper Alloys

A major advantage of beryllium copper alloys is their ability to be strengthened by a low-temperature thermal treatment—called aging, age hardening, or precipitation hardening—after workpieces have been cast or formed. The properties of beryllium copper alloys are enhanced by cold working prior to age hardening. Another thermal treatment for these materials is solution heat treatment, frequently called annealing, which results in softening and in dissolving alloy constituents that cause precipitation hardening during subsequent aging. The thermal treatments vary for wrought and casting alloys.

HARDENING PROCEDURES

Optimum heat treatment requires the use of proper furnaces, accurate use of the time-temperature transformation relationships, and the right quenchant and cooling method. For many applications, controlled atmospheres in the furnaces are essential.

Heat treating procedures—with respect to temperatures, times, quenchants, and cooling methods—vary with the composition and condition of the metal, and the microstructure and properties desired.

CONTROLLED ATMOSPHERES

The use of controlled atmospheres in heat treating processes is often for protection of the metal surfaces from oxidation. Suitable atmospheres for this purpose are those that do not discolor the surface of the metal and that allow the surface chemistry to retain its original composition. Surface oxides are also reduced, if present, to produce bright surfaces. The most notable use of controlled atmospheres for other purposes occurs in special heat treatments of ferrous alloys, such as in carburizing, nitriding, and carbonitriding.

Atmospheres Used

Controlled atmospheres are usually a mixture of a number of gases. Most furnace atmospheres are prepared by the reaction of a fuel gas with air in generators, although specially prepared cylinder or bulk-storage gases are also commonly used. The more common gases are:

N_2 — Nitrogen
O_2 — Oxygen
H_2O — Water vapor
CO_2 — Carbon dioxide

CO — Carbon monoxide
H_2 — Hydrogen
CH_4 — Methane (natural gas)

Classification of Prepared Atmospheres

Mixtures of gases commonly used as protective atmospheres in the heat treatment of metals have been classified by the American Gas Association. The gases generated for furnace atmospheres are divided into six categories, as follows:

Class 100—Exothermic Base: An atmosphere composed of products of partial or complete combustion of an air-fuel mixture. The base may be modified by various degrees and methods of moisture removal, and the use of various air-fuel ratios.

Class 200—Prepared Nitrogen Base: An exothermic base (Class 100) with most of the carbon dioxide and water vapor removed.

Class 300—Endothermic Base: Formed by partial reaction of a gaseous fuel and air mixture in an externally heated catalyst-filled chamber.

Class 400—Charcoal Base: Formed by passing air through incandescent charcoal in an externally heated vertical retort. Popularity and acceptance of other atmosphere systems have made this class essentially obsolete.

Class 500—Exothermic-Endothermic Base: Formed by complete combustion of a mixture of fuel gas and air, removing most of the water vapor, and reforming most of the carbon dioxide to carbon monoxide by reaction with fuel gas in an externally heated catalyst reactor.

Class 600—Ammonia Base: Any atmosphere produced using ammonia as the feed stock, including raw ammonia,

HARDENING PROCEDURES

dissociated ammonia, or partially or completely combusted ammonia with most of the water vapor removed.

Class 100, 200, 300, and 500 atmospheres are prepared by the controlled reaction of a fuel gas with air. These atmospheres are normally used to produce an environment that is void of free oxygen. For example, fuel plus air produces CO_2, CO, H_2, H_2O, and N_2. Class 600 atmospheres are prepared by dissociating anhydrous ammonia to produce a gas consisting of H_2 and N_2. The six broad areas of atmosphere classification are subclassified by three-digit designations to indicate variations in the method by which they are prepared.

Nitrogen-Based Atmospheres

Gas mixtures equivalent to those produced from fuel gases and ammonia can be produced by blending bottled or bulk-storage gases and enriching nitrogen with a fuel gas (usually methane) or liquid alcohol (usually methanol). These are simple to apply as they basically require only regulation of the flow of component gases. Both the composition and flow rate of the atmospheres can be independently controlled. Safety purging with inert nitrogen can eliminate dangers associated with handling combustible gases at elevated temperatures. Industrially supplied nitrogen is most commonly produced through air separation (liquefaction and fractional distillation). The air is filtered, purified, compressed to drive it through the system, and cooled to remove the water and carbon dioxide. After being liquefied, it is distilled into its major constituents, the most abundant being nitrogen.

Hydrogen is also frequently blended with nitrogen, producing an atmosphere used as a replacement for either the exothermic base or dissociated ammonia atmospheres. Users of dissociated ammonia often do not require high hydrogen levels and can use a replacement nitrogen-based system with low hydrogen additions.

QUENCHING

The optimum combination of strength and ductility in a given steel is generally achieved by heat treatments that yield a homogeneous microstructure. One of the most effective means of accomplishing homogeneity is by first quenching to a martensitic structure and then tempering to obtain the desired hardness and ductility.

Effective heat treatment involves not only critical heating rates and temperatures, but also critical quenching rates and temperatures. These critical factors depend primarily upon the carbon and alloy content of the material to be heat treated, and the section size and shape of the workpiece. For optimum results in quenching, it is necessary that the quenching medium provide heat extraction fast enough to avoid pearlite transformation, but slow enough to ensure uniformity of heat extraction throughout the workpiece.

Quenching Media

A wide variety of quenchants are used for various heat treating processes. Those most readily satisfying the requirements discussed include air, water, oils, aqueous polymer solutions, brine, caustic solutions, and molten-salt and lead baths.

Cooling in air. Air is used preferably whenever the degree of distortion by oil quenching is objectionable or whenever the high alloy content of the workpiece material will permit full hardening by air. Both direct and indirect costs are low when the desired structure can be achieved by air cooling.

Water. Plain water is probably the most widely used of all quenchants except air and fully meets the requirements of low cost and availability. It is easily handled and safe, but its cooling characteristics change more with agitation and variations in temperature than do those of many oils and polymer solutions. The high cooling rate of water may result in excessive distortion or cracking of some workpieces.

With vigorous circulation and with maintenance of substantially constant bath temperatures, water may be considered a satisfactory quenchant for many applications. However, whenever the flow of water is slow and there is no provision for keeping it cool, water may prove wholly unsatisfactory. Also, its use is limited to parts of simple configuration made from water-hardening steels and certain nonferrous compositions.

Water quenching is effective for breaking scale from the surfaces of steel parts that are heated in furnaces without protective atmospheres. The water is generally maintained at a temperature of about 65° F (18° C) for most applications. As the temperature increases and/or agitation decreases, there is a tendency for an envelope of steam to form around the workpiece, thus reducing the cooling rate.

Quenching in oil. Oils comprise one of the most important groups of quenching liquids. In addition to straight mineral oils, many different types of oils are available in a wide variety of blends compounded to accelerate cooling rates by shortening the vapor-blanket stage. Heavier oils are available that have flash and fire points in excess of 500° F (260° C). These oils are used for quenching at elevated temperatures, such as 300-400° F (150-205° C) in modified martempering (marquenching), discussed subsequently in this section.

Most quenching oils have good stability and chemical inactivity with hot steel, plus little change in the cooling rate with minor variations in temperature. Cooling coils are sometimes used to control the temperature of the oil.

Polymer quenchants. Water-based polymer quenchants, sometimes called synthetics, are being used increasingly because they offer quenching characteristics intermediate between water and oil and, in some cases, very similar to oil. Because aqueous solutions are used, these quenchants are nonflammable, clean to use, offer fewer ecological problems, and are often more economical. On the other hand, they require more careful selection of quenching conditions, control, and maintenance. The principal types of polymer quenchants are polyglycols (PAG's), which are most widely used because they've been available longer, the newer polyvinylpyrrolidones (PVP's), and sodium polyacrylates (SPA's). These water-soluble polymers work by somewhat different mechanisms than other quenchants, but all act to some degree to slow down both the vapor transport and liquid cooling stages, compared with water. Polymer type, concentration, quenchant temperature, and agitation all strongly influence their cooling rates. Agitation is particularly important in comparison with quenching with oil.

Quenching in brine. Some brine quenchants include aqueous, sodium chloride solutions. Proprietary brines, which eliminate rusting and prevent corrosion, are also widely used in place of water when more uniform and faster cooling in the vapor blanket/vapor transport stages are desired. Control of agitation and temperature are important as with water. Disadvantages of brines include higher cost than plain water, possible corrosiveness, and the need for fume vent hoods in some applications.

Caustic solutions. Caustic solutions, such as sodium hydroxide, with strengths of about 5% are sometimes used to give a brine-like quench. These quenchants, however, are losing favor because of their corrosivity and handling problems, plus their tendency to pick up carbon dioxide. Carbon dioxide changes quench characteristics gradually and makes control difficult. High alkalinity of the solutions also make them harmful to the skin.

Molten salt. Baths of molten salt are used predominantly for quenching high-speed steels and for the interrupted quenching methods discussed subsequently in this section. Because of the high thermal conductivity of molten salts and the high temperatures at which they can be maintained, to 950-1050° F (510-565° C), these quenchants provide rapid initial cooling with low distortion and cracking. For interrupted quenching operations, molten-salt baths can also be used at temperatures ranging from 300 to 1000° F (150 to 540° C).

Lead baths. Lead baths are the only metal baths that have proved suitable as quenching media for heat treating. Lead has a working temperature range of 650 to 1700° F (345 to 925° C) and a high level of heat conductivity; thus, its quenching rates are high. However, the extreme toxicity of lead has greatly reduced its use in recent years.

Gas quenching. Quenching with pressurized gas provides cooling rates more rapid than with still air, but slower than with oil. Gas quenching is done in gas-tight chambers or zones of furnaces. Relatively cold gases are directed onto the workpiece surfaces, and after absorbing heat they are cooled and recirculated. Pressurized gases used include air, nitrogen, and mixtures of various gases. Cooling rates can be adjusted by varying the type, pressure, and velocity of the gas.

Fog quenching. In this process, streams of gas containing droplets of water are used to increase the cooling rate with minimal distortion.

Interrupted Quenching

Interrupted quenching is used to improve the ductility and toughness of steel, while retaining high hardness levels with minimum distortion and residual stresses. In interrupted quenching, the rapid cooling of the metal is stopped and held at points above the M_s temperature for specified lengths of time,

followed by cooling in air. Three types of interrupted quenching are: austempering, marquenching (martempering), and isothermal quenching. For each of these methods, the temperature at which the quenching is interrupted, the length of time the steel is held at temperature, and the rate of air cooling are varied for different types of steels and workpiece sizes.

Austempering. The process known as austempering consists of a rapid quench through the pearlite formation range down to a temperature of about 450 to 750° F (230 to 400° C), depending upon the transformation characteristics of the particular steel involved; a hold at temperature for a length of time sufficient for isothermal transformation; and air cooling. Subsequent tempering is not required.

Marquenching (martempering). This process is similar to austempering in that the work is quenched rapidly from the austenitizing range into an agitated salt bath or similar medium held near the M_s temperature. It differs from austempering in that the work is allowed to remain at temperature only long enough for the temperature to be equalized throughout all sections of the workpiece. The process takes advantage of the time allowed in the temperature range just above M_s, where the beginning of transformation is quite sluggish. When the temperature has become equalized, but before the beginning of any transformation, the work is removed from the salt bath and allowed to cool in air to room temperature. During this time, martensite forms at a reasonably uniform rate throughout all sections.

Isothermal quenching. Isothermal quenching is similar to austempering and, as such, is often not classified as a different type of quenching. The steel is rapidly quenched through the pearlite formation range to a temperature just above M_s where bainite is formed. However, isothermal quenching differs from austempering in that a two-bath quench is employed. After the first quench, and before transformation has time to begin, the work is quenched in another bath at a somewhat higher temperature. It is allowed to transform isothermally, after which it is allowed to cool in air. This method of quenching must be tailored for each specific application and must be closely controlled. As a result, it is not used extensively.

SOLUTION TREATING AND AGING

Solution treating and aging are processes employed to harden and strengthen many nonferrous alloys and some steels. The procedure generally requires the following two consecutive operations:

1. Solution heat treatment to produce a homogeneous solid solution that is retained by rapid quenching to room temperature.
2. Aging to produce fine precipitates in the solid solution.

SOLUTION HEAT TREATMENT

In solution heat treatment, an alloy is heated to a suitable temperature, held at this temperature for sufficient time to allow a desired constituent to enter into solid solution, and then rapidly cooled to hold the constituent in solution. Most of these solid solutions are comparatively soft and ductile. They are also

structurally unstable and have a tendency to return to the form of an aggregate with aging. Solution annealing is discussed in a subsequent section of this chapter under the subject of annealing.

Metals with solid solutions that age harden at room temperature can be prevented from doing so by cooling below the freezing temperature after quenching and holding at a subzero temperature for as long as required. Such a delay in precipitation facilitates forming or other operations prior to aging. For example, rivets made from heat-treatable aluminum alloys are often refrigerated after solution treating, removed from low-temperature storage for assembly, and then allowed to age at room temperature.

AGING

Aging, also called age hardening or precipitation hardening, is a time-temperature dependent change in the properties of certain metals (higher strength and hardness) occurring at room

TEMPERING

or elevated temperatures. Aging at room temperature is called natural aging; aging above room temperature, which requires less time, is termed artificial aging. Quench aging is aging by rapid cooling after solution heat treatment.

Interrupted aging is aging at two or more different temperatures, with cooling to room temperature after each heating; step aging is also aging at two or more different temperatures, but without cooling to room temperature after each step. Double aging refers to a solution annealing followed by reheating, a second quenching, and a second reheating. Some alloys will precipitation harden after a double-aging cycle with no prior solution annealing.

TEMPERING

In its hardened, as-quenched, fully martensitic form, steel is hard and brittle, thus restricting its usefulness. Hardened steel must be subsequently tempered to relieve quenching stresses and to provide a limited but necessary degree of toughness and ductility, protecting the part from cracking in storage, installation, and use. Impact resistance and improved elongation and area reduction qualities are afforded by tempering, but are brought about by a sacrifice in hardness, tensile strength, and wear resistance. Tempering consists of reheating previously hardened metal to a relatively low temperature (below the transformation range), generally followed by slow cooling. During this treatment, the martensite phase transforms to the more stable, two-phase mixture of ferrite and carbide. Certain steel parts, tempered in the temperature range of 400 to 700° F (205 to 370° C) may be water quenched to increase their impact strength.

Machinability is a function of hardness and toughness and is seldom changed appreciably by hardening and tempering at low temperatures. With tempering at low temperatures, grinding is often the only machining possible on some tempered steels. After tempering operations at 900 to 1200° F (480 to 650° C), turning or milling of medium-carbon steels is possible.

The higher the tempering temperature, or the longer the time at that temperature, the softer and more ductile the steel. Alloy steels containing carbide-forming elements show greater resistance to softening during tempering than do plain carbon steels. Therefore, higher temperatures and longer times should be used in tempering the higher alloy steels, as shown in Fig. 41-2.

Tempering may be performed to give almost any desired combination of properties by correct selection of the time-temperature cycle, because the strength of steel is proportional to its hardness, as shown in Fig. 41-3. The composition of the steel, its condition before quenching, and the effectiveness of the quench all affect the tempering temperature required to produce a specified hardness.

Media for tempering are usually simple baths or furnace atmospheres. The four most commonly used are:

1. *Hydrogen-nitrogen*. Hydrogen-nitrogen atmospheres for tempering are prepared by the dissociation of ammonia. Such atmospheres can leave bright surface finishes when the work is allowed to cool in a low dew-point hydrogen atmosphere.
2. *Air*. Air is a slightly oxidizing tempering medium and may produce scaling at temperatures above 1000° F (540° C).
3. *Molten nitrite/nitrate salts*. These media produce oxidizing effects very similar to those of air.
4. *Steam*. Dry steam is used to purge tempering furnaces heated to 700° F (370° C). The addition of steam is continued at the tempering temperature, and then the work is cooled in sulfonated, emulsified oil to enhance the resulting lustrous black finish.

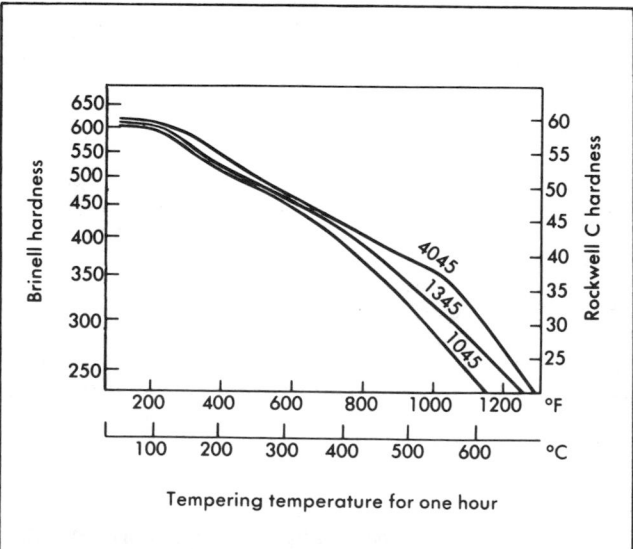

Fig. 41-2 Tempered hardness as affected by alloy content.

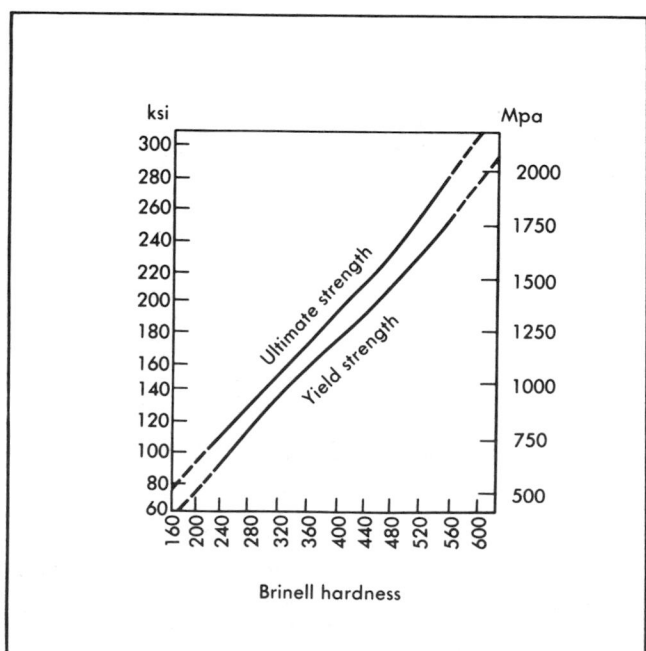

Fig. 41-3 Increase in strength of steel with increased hardness.

Multiple tempers may be obtained in the following ways:

1. *Selective tempering.* Localized areas of the steel can be heated to tempering temperature by a torch, salt bath, or induction heater to produce special localized impact or tensile properties without affecting the properties of the part as a whole.
2. *Cold treatment.* Tempered steel with over 10% austenite retained after quenching can be cooled to -120° F (-84° C) and then retempered to convert the remaining austenite to martensite, thereby reducing brittleness. Cold treatment is also useful for stabilizing closely toleranced parts. Additional information on cold treatment is presented in a subsequent section of this chapter.
3. *Nitriding.* Nitriding in dissociated ammonia or in molten cyanide salt provides wear-resistant nitride cases.

ANNEALING

Annealing is a heat treatment process that consists of heating metal to a suitable temperature, followed by slow cooling. The purposes of annealing include one or more of the following:

1. To reduce hardness or brittleness.
2. To relieve stresses.
3. To improve machinability or facilitate cold working.
4. To produce desired microstructure or properties.
5. To remove gases.
6. To alter the electrical or magnetic properties.

STRESS RELIEVING

Stress relieving by heat treatment is a method of reducing the stresses that may be introduced with such operations as cold working, machining, welding, drawing, heading, and extrusion, without resorting to complete annealing or normalizing and without greatly affecting other properties. The reduction of such stress is important to avoid excessive distortion during hardening and to avoid cracking, which could result from the addition of the residual stress to the thermal stress produced in heating to the hardening temperature.

Stress relieving of steel basically involves the heating of the part to a subcritical temperature below Ac_1, holding at that temperature long enough to assure uniformity, and slow cooling to room temperature, usually in air, which will prevent the reintroduction of stresses. Microstructures are essentially unchanged. The temperatures most commonly used range from about 1100 to 1300° F (595 to 705° C). Stress relieving is commonly performed on structures where usual annealing or normalizing methods would be prohibitive because of part size or shape, warpage, or scale.

Stress relieving is not as effective as annealing in reducing residual stresses. However, annealing is a more costly and time-consuming operation; and because of the higher temperatures in annealing, decarburization, scaling, and grain growth are more of a problem. Because of the relatively low temperature involved in stress relieving, surface protection against scale or decarburization is usually not required. The temperature used is always below the transformation range of the steel. Therefore, the cooling rate is unimportant except that it must not be such as to cause thermal stress. Rapid cooling produces higher stresses than slow cooling.

FULL ANNEALING

Full annealing involves heating steel to above the upper critical temperature, Ac_3, for hypoeutectoid steels and just above the lower critical temperature, Ac_1, for hypereutectoid steels, followed by sufficient slow cooling through the transformation range to under 1000° F (540° C). This operation results in the softest pearlitic structure. Steel may be annealed to reduce hardness, to improve machinability, to improve cold working characteristics, to produce a desired microstructure, or to obtain desired physical properties. Ordinarily, full annealing is carried out in a batch-type furnace rather than a continuous furnace, and usually the work is cooled in the furnace. Slower rates of cooling may be obtained by progressively lowering the furnace controls to regulate the cooling at preselected rates. More recently, programmed heating and cooling is being accomplished accurately by the use of microprocessor-based temperature controls.

ISOTHERMAL (CYCLE) ANNEALING

Isothermal annealing may be defined as the austenitizing of a steel by heating it above its critical temperature Ac_3, followed by cooling it to and holding it for 4 to 8 hours at a preselected temperature, usually in the range of 1050 to 1300° F (565 to 705° C). In this temperature range, the austenite transforms to a relatively soft ferrite-carbide aggregate in accordance with the transformation diagram of the steel.

Isothermal annealing takes less time and is less costly than conventional full annealing with continuous cooling. In addition, the uniformity of hardness and structure is better with isothermal annealing. However, very close temperature control must be maintained. The equipment for isothermal annealing consists of a continuous furnace that includes one zone for austenitizing and another zone for holding and transformation. Salt baths can be ideal for isothermal annealing, depending upon cost. Properly rectified baths will protect steel from decarburization, surface attack, and scale formation. Salt baths permit close control of temperature for austenitization as well as for transformation, which is more important in cycle annealing than in full annealing.

SPHEROIDIZING

Spheroidize annealing is a modified annealing process that results in a spheroidized, rather than lamellar, microstructure. This microstructure consists essentially of small globules or spheroidized cementite particles in a ferrite mixture, which is the softest condition for steels.

Spheroidized structures are generally preferred for cold heading, wire drawing, and cold forming operations where greater resistance to work hardening and cracking is desired. They are also generally preferred for subsequent hardening of tool and die steels. Low and medium-carbon steels that have thoroughly spheroidized structures, however, are slow to

ANNEALING

austenitize for hardening, and a blocky ferrite/pearlite structure is preferred. For best results, the spheroidized carbides should be small and uniformly distributed.

LOW-TEMPERATURE ANNEALING

Heating of a severely cold worked ferrous alloy in the 200 to 500° F (95 to 260° C) range results in a 10 to 20% increase in the alloy's yield strength due to the segregation of carbon atoms to defects in the structure. In production, this effect will be masked by variations in processing and composition from lot to lot.

RECRYSTALLIZATION ANNEALING

At a temperature determined by the purity of the metal, its cold worked grain size, and the amount of cold work done on it, recrystallization will begin with nuclei of strain-free (defect-free) metal forming at regions of high stress. These nuclei grow at a rate that increases to a maximum and then decreases as the cold worked material is eliminated. This rearrangement is not a phase change but an atomic rearrangement in which the defects (dislocations) generated during cold work are eliminated. The rate of recrystallization increases with an increase in temperature.

RECOVERY ANNEALING

There is a region between room temperature and the recrystallization temperature wherein a large portion of residual stress is relieved, but no grains start to grow. In the low end of this range, the stresses decrease because of rearrangement of point defects (vacancies and solute atoms dissolved in the grain structure) into more stable configurations. At higher temperatures in the recovery range, the line defects (dislocations) introduced during cold working are free to move to more stable rearrangements in which small strain-free subgrains are formed. This rearrangement of crystal defects to form more perfect subgrains is called polygonization. While recovery decreases the residual stresses of cold work, it does not appreciably decrease the tensile strength. Likewise, hardness and magnetic susceptibility are not decreased. However, electrical resistivity and springback are sensitive functions of the distribution of point and line defects, and they decrease with decreasing stress level. Thus, for situations where it is desirable to retain most of the benefits of cold working, but the residual stress level is not wanted, recovery annealing is used.

PROCESS ANNEALING

In *nonferrous* metal production, process annealing refers to a quick annealing—heating without regard to rate, holding for a short period at temperature, and cooling without regard to rate—in the temperature range from the high end of the stress-relieving range through the top of the full-annealing range. In the lower end of the range, recovery, recrystallization, and grain growth take place without solution of impurities or secondary phases. As the temperatures come up into the full-annealing range, impurities and secondary phases begin to dissolve in the base metal or alloy. At these temperatures, the alloy elements rejected into the interdentritic volumes of a billet or casting during slow solidification can be taken back into solution.

In *ferrous* metal technology, process annealing refers both to quick annealing in the transformation temperature range and to subcritical annealing. The quick annealing involves heating without regard to rate into the full-annealing temperature range, holding for a short time (15 to 60 minutes) at temperature, and cooling at a moderate rate. Subcritical annealing involves heating at a moderate rate to just below the lower critical temperature, holding for a reasonable time [for example, two hours plus one hour for each inch (25 mm) of section thickness in plain carbon steel], and cooling at a moderate rate (such as still-air cooling for a plain carbon steel).

All the process annealing methods are used as intermediate softening treatments during a series of forming operations, such as in the multiple deformations of deep drawing, to allow forming without tearing or splitting. As the temperature increases, the hardness and tensile strength are decreased. A balance of physical properties must be determined experimentally to fit the part specifications. Alloy producers can generally supply guidelines to aid in pinpointing the time and temperature necessary to produce the desired result. Process annealing is suitable for either batch or continuous furnace equipment, and production is limited only by the furnace capacity.

HOMOGENIZATION ANNEALING

In castings, especially those of copper and copper alloys, coring and severe segregation of certain alloying elements and different melting temperature phases can take place. In hot rolled alloy shapes, moderate or rapid cooling may result in segregation of a constituent or phase at the grain boundaries. Subsequent cold or hot rolling of a segregated material can result in a laminated structure, as shown in Fig. 41-4. If the pressures and temperatures are high enough, the segregated material may soften and smear or even melt, allowing the various matrix layers to tear, wrinkle, or pull apart. Heating from 100 to 300° F (55 to 165° C) above the maximum annealing temperature for an extended period of time reduces segregation by diffusion of the segregated species into the matrix, a process called homogenization. The disadvantage of the process is the resulting large grain size. However, the homogenized structure can be cold worked to refine the grain.

SOLUTION ANNEALING

Solution annealing is the heating of a multiple-phase alloy into a temperature range in which only one homogeneous phase exists at equilibrium, holding at this temperature until the desired degree of homogeneity is achieved, and then rapidly cooling to freeze the atoms in their fixed positions. The atoms are not allowed time enough at the intermediate temperatures to reform the separate phases, which would be in equilibrium at room temperature. The trapped solute atoms in the frozen

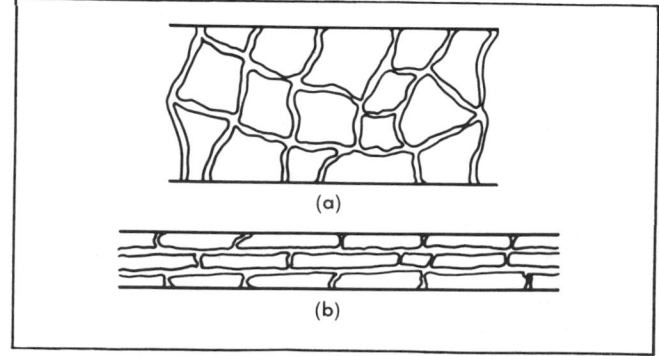

Fig. 41-4 Material segregated at grain boundaries: (a) forms seams that separate laminar, elongated grains after rolling; (b) high temperature can diffuse segregated layers into matrix.

solution create a situation that provides a source of energy that tends to rearrange the atoms into separate phases when atom mobility is increased by reheating into an intermediate temperature range. Depending on the relative solid solubilities of the

phases, this rearrangement can be a hardening and strengthening mechanism. Other alloys are solution annealed to obtain a uniform microstructure that will respond uniformly to subsequent cold work.

NORMALIZING

Normalizing involves the heating of steel to above the critical temperature Ac3, followed by still-air cooling to room temperature to obtain a uniform, fine-grained pearlitic structure. Normalizing differs from stress relieving, annealing, and quenching in that it is carried out from temperatures of about 1600 to 1700°F (870 to 925°C)—approximately 100-200°F (55-110°C) higher than the regular hardening temperature and as much as 200-250°F (110-140°C) over the regular annealing temperature (fully air-hardened steels are exceptions, however)—and in that the cooling rate is neither restricted nor accelerated.

Normalizing was originally applied to forgings of medium-carbon steels to refine their coarse grain structure. Normalizing results in finer grained, harder, more homogeneous structures

than annealed structures because of the more rapid air cooling involved in the process. This finer microstructure (usually pearlitic) often coincides with higher mechanical properties for the normalized steels. In fact, normalized materials sometimes provide the specified properties without further heat treatment. Ferrous castings are frequently normalized to remove the strains of solidification and improve toughness or impact strength.

Higher alloy, medium-carbon steels may be given good strength and ductility by normalizing them and then tempering at 1200 to 1250°F (650 to 675°C). High alloyed, air-hardening steels, however, are never treated by other than a stress-relieving process at approximately 1200°F. A true normalizing would cause these steels to reaustenitize and then harden fully, thus defeating the primary purpose of the operation.

COLD TREATMENT

Cold (cryogenic) treatment consists of exposing metal parts or tools to subzero temperatures for the purposes of obtaining desired conditions or properties. Such treatment can provide improved strength, dimensional or microstructural stability, greater resistance to wear, stress relieving, and retarded aging.

For steels, proper cold treatment ensures a more uniform and completely transformed microstructure. Primarily, soft, retained austenite is transformed into hard, more stable martensite, which can be subsequently tempered.

RETAINED AUSTENITE

Depending upon the intended applications for heat-treated steel parts, it is often necessary to subject them to cold treatment in order to reduce or eliminate retained austenite. Some metals, especially nickel-containing alloy steels or steels having carbon contents above about 0.60%, have a tendency to retain austenite after hardening. In these instances, the M_f temperature is below room temperature, and the resulting retained austenite yields a reduced hardness. The higher carbon content in the surfaces of carburized parts can have as much as 30% or more of the soft, retained austenite, which greatly reduces the wear and fatigue resistance.

STRESS RELIEVING AND AGING PREVENTION

Cold treatment is also used for stress relieving of castings and machined parts made from steels and aluminum alloys. This process is accomplished by alternately cooling and heating the parts a number of times to achieve dimensional stability.

Cold treatment also prevents or retards the aging of some metals. For example, rivets made from aluminum alloy are solution treated, quenched, cold treated, and held at the subzero temperature until ready for riveting. After the cold working during riveting, the rivets naturally age harden at room temperature to the required strength over a period of a few hours.

WEAR RESISTANCE

The improved wear resistance and longer life sometimes resulting from cold treatment are the major reasons for many of its applications. Many cutting tools and punches made from high-speed steels, cast alloys, and carbides are cold treated for longer life. The treatment stabilizes structures and dimensions and forces transformations closer to completion.

When copper welding electrodes are cold treated, electrical conductivity is improved and wear of the tools is reduced. Other cold-treated components include ball and roller bearings, gears, splines, springs, and powder metallurgy parts.

THE COLD TREATMENT PROCESS

Cold treatment immediately after heat treatment is generally the best procedure. However, care must be taken to prevent cracking. Workpieces especially susceptible to cracking may require tempering prior to cold treatment. Some firms specializing in cold treatment recommend controlled soaking for longer times at lower temperatures.

EQUIPMENT USED

A variety of equipment is used for the cold treatment of metals. For some applications, a simple freezer, which produces a temperature of about 0°F (-18°C), is satisfactory. Dry ice (solid CO_2) placed on workpieces in an insulated container produces a temperature of about -75°F (-60°C). Some firms use a liquid bath, such as alcohol, plus dry ice to reduce the temperature to -110°F (-79°C). Mechanical refrigeration systems are available to achieve a temperature of -140°F (-96°C) or lower. Liquid nitrogen, with a temperature of -320°F (-196°C), is also used, but less frequently because of the cost and danger of thermal shock.

CARBURIZING

CARBURIZING

Surface-hardening thermochemical processes are used extensively for low-to-medium carbon steel parts requiring high hardness or fatigue strength primarily at their surfaces, as in wear-resistant applications. The processes also provide sufficient core strength and toughness to withstand tensile or impact stresses and fatigue.

Carburizing is a heat treating process for increasing the carbon content of exposed surfaces on steel parts, usually low-carbon grades with carbon contents below 0.30%. This procedure is accomplished by heating the steel above its upper critical temperature under controlled conditions and in contact with a suitable carbonaceous medium. Carburizing is normally done in the temperature range of 1600 to 1800°F (870 to 980°C). With proper conditions, an enriched carbon case is produced to the desired depth.

The basis for any carburizing operation is the equilibrium of the system. Given the proper conditions, the carbon content of the steel and the carbon potential of the surrounding gases—in the case of gas carburizing—will try to equalize. If the atmosphere has a higher potential than the steel, the steel will absorb the carbon. With atmospheres having extremely high carbon potential, iron carbides may form on the surface of the steel. If the carbon potential of the atmosphere is too low, the steel may yield carbon to the atmosphere and become decarburized.

Being a diffusion process, carburizing is affected by the amount of alloying elements in the steel. The case depth produced is temperature and time dependent, as shown in Fig. 41-5.

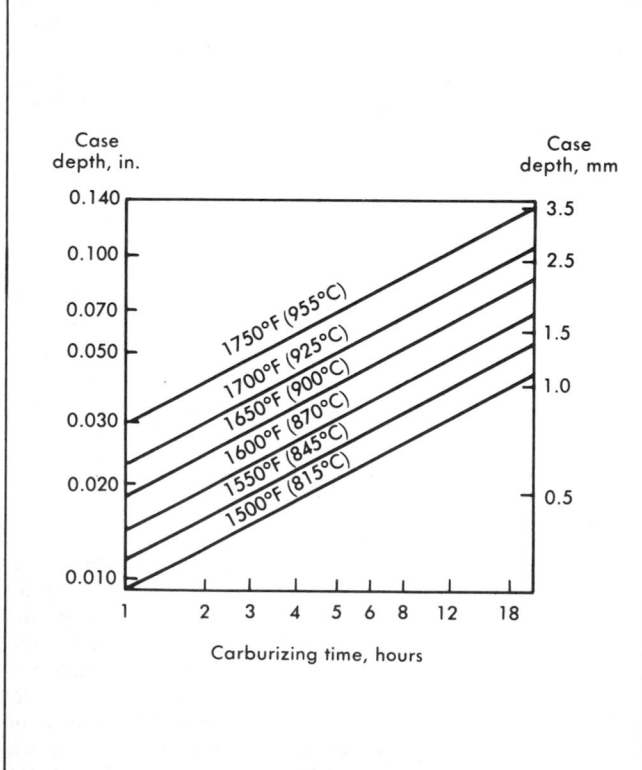

Fig. 41-5 Relation of case depth to carburizing time.

LIQUID CARBURIZING

Liquid carburizing uses a molten salt primarily consisting of controlled percentages of sodium cyanide (8-12%), barium chloride, and small percentages of other salts. This method of surface hardening is used to produce case depths of 0.020-0.062" (0.51-1.57 mm), although it can be used for deeper cases, to 0.250" (6.35 mm). For general use, the most economical operating temperature for liquid carburizing is 1650-1700°F (900-925°C). Temperatures to 1750°F (955°C) provide more rapid penetration, but at some added expense for increased material loss (due to oxidation of the salt) and a slight increase in equipment deterioration.

Liquid carburizing is generally done in batches, but continuous installations may be justified where production requirements are high. The liquid carburizing process has the flexibility to handle a wide range of parts of varied design and to produce different case depths simultaneously by removing parts at specified times. It is relatively rapid because of the short time required for the work to heat to the carburizing temperature. It also has the advantage of producing clean work, after a rinse in a molten-cyanide bath to remove carbonates.

CYANIDING

Cyaniding, sometimes referred to as liquid carbonitriding, is similar to the liquid carburizing process in that it employs a molten-sodium-cyanide bath to provide the hardening elements. However, cyaniding differs from carburizing in both its operating principles and its effects. In cyaniding, 20% or more of the salt bath is composed of sodium cyanide, and the balance, sodium carbonate and sodium chloride in specific percentages. This mixture, when used at temperatures ranging from 1450 to 1650°F (790 to 900°C), decomposes to free carbon and nitrogen, which are then absorbed into the steel to form a hardened carbide-nitride case. Thus, the resulting case is similar to that produced by carbonitriding, discussed later in this chapter. In fact, the term gas cyaniding is a misnomer for carbonitriding.

Cases produced by cyaniding are usually held to 0.001-0.015" (0.03-0.38 mm) in depth. Small stampings and screw machine parts made from carbon or free-machining steels are commonly cyanided. The addition of nitrogen and carbon to the surface provides sufficient hardenability that the surface will harden, even in an oil quench, to full file-hard condition. The superficial nitrided case, referred to as hot hardness, is harder than a carbon case and resists tempering, thus providing an advantage for parts operating without lubrication.

NONCYANIDE LIQUID CARBURIZING

Liquid carburizing in a molten-salt bath containing a special grade of carbon has been growing in commercial use. In this bath, carbon particles are dispersed in the molten salt by mechanical agitation, which is achieved by means of one or more simple propeller agitators that occupy a small fraction of the bath.

The chemical reaction involved is not fully understood but is thought to involve adsorption of carbon monoxide on carbon particles. The carbon monoxide is generated by reaction between the carbon and carbonates and the air. Then the adsorbed carbon monoxide is presumed to react with steel surfaces, similar to gas or pack carburizing.

Operating temperatures for this type of bath are generally higher than those in cyanide-type baths. A range of about 1650 to 1750°F (900 to 955°C) is most commonly used. Temperatures below about 1600°F (870°C) are not recommended and may even lead to decarburization of the steel. The case depths and carbon gradients produced are in the same range as for high-temperature cyanide-type baths, but there is no nitrogen in the case.

Because of the lack of nitrogen, slowly cooled noncyanide carburized parts are more easily machined than cyanide carburized parts. Also, retained austenite is less likely to be present in quenched cases that contain no nitrogen.

The noncyanide carburizing process is limited to applications where the parts to be carburized are individually spaced or suspended. Success of the process depends on free circulation of the mechanically agitated salt around all surfaces to be carburized. Shallow basket loading may be used if the geometry of the parts allows free flow of the salt through the load. Control of the carbon potential is also difficult with noncyanide carburizing.

PACK CARBURIZING

Pack carburizing is the carburizing process that requires the least specialized equipment and techniques. It requires a source of carbon that will be diffused into the surface of the heated low-carbon steel to form a carburized case.

Commercially available packing compounds include a catalyst or activator that permeates the compound. This activator deteriorates with use, so additions of at least 10% to as much as 50% of new compound should be made after each cycle of heating

Applications

Pack carburizing is normally not used for light case work, less than 0.050" (1.27 mm) deep, but is more often used for deep cases, such as 0.100" (2.54 mm) or more. With pack carburizing, little control over the surface carbon content is possible as saturated austenite is produced at the carburizing temperature.

Limitations

Pack carburizing is a labor intensive, low production, deep case process used for such items as rolling mill rolls, earth drilling bits, and large-diameter wear pins. Some of the disadvantages of pack carburizing are:

1. The compound is dirty and difficult to handle when hot.
2. It is difficult to remove parts from the pack for quenching.
3. Case depths may be uneven because of the insulating qualities of the compound. This factor causes the edges and thin sections of the work to heat first and carburize deeper than the slower heating heavy sections.
4. The compound is becoming more expensive and difficult to obtain because the process to produce it is more expensive as environmental standards are raised.

GAS CARBURIZING

Most carburizing is performed with gaseous atmospheres in sealed furnaces where the products of combustion and air do not come in contact with the work. The gaseous atmosphere used can vary from natural gas to endothermic to nitrogen (plus additives), and each, when controlled, can be used successfully.

With gas carburizing, the atmosphere can be controlled by monitoring the moisture (dew point), carbon dioxide, methane, oxygen, or a combination of these, and adjusting the entering gases to provide the carbon potential desired. Instrumentation is available to program the time, temperature, and carbon potential to produce the desired case properties and to duplicate the process from batch to batch.

Vacuum Carburizing

Vacuum carburizing, sometimes called partial-pressure carburizing, is a form of gas carburizing. The requirements of temperature, time, and carbon potential are essentially the same as in gas carburizing to produce a given case depth. Normally, nonoxygen-bearing gases are used in vacuum carburizing to provide the carbon, at a pressure of 300 to 400 torr (760 torr equals 1 atmosphere). The advantages of vacuum carburizing include versatility, closely controllable operations, and shorter cycle times if carburizing temperatures are raised.

Ion (Plasma) Carburizing

In ion carburizing, carbon is imparted to steel surfaces by the impingement of carbon ions escaping from an ionized gas (plasma). The process is performed in vacuum furnaces equipped with a high-voltage power supply and conventional radiant heating elements. Energy for the absorption reaction is achieved by a high-voltage glow discharge between the cathodic workpiece and an anodic electrode in the furnace. Carbon ions accelerate from the ionized hydrocarbon gas toward the workpiece and impinge on the surfaces.

The advantages of ion carburizing include energy conservation and reduced requirements for gas, compared to atmosphere and vacuum carburizing. Processing time is shorter as well. This method produces more uniform case depths, especially on irregular surfaces. It can also provide deeper cases in blind holes and cavities. Equipment and maintenance costs, however, are high compared to conventional methods of carburizing.

High-Temperature Carburizing

If higher temperature carburizing can be used, the time required to produce a given case is reduced substantially. The risks involved include greater furnace maintenance, increased usage of alloy trays and fixtures, less load weight per tray, possibly more warpage, and, sometimes, increased grain size. Careful consideration must be given to these factors before the advantages of higher temperature carburizing can be realized.

Carbon Correction

Carbon correction or restoration is the process of increasing or decreasing the surface carbon content of steel parts, generally to restore carbon content to a decarburized case equal to that of the core of the part. For example, if an SAE 4140 steel were being heat treated and simultaneously carbon corrected, a hardening temperature of 1600°F (870°C) would be used. A furnace dew point of 52°F (11°C) would be in equilibrium with the carbon content of the core.

If steel bolts were soaked at 1600°F (870°C), the surface carbon would be restored to 0.50%. There would be no danger of exceeding this amount regardless of time and temperature. Usually a soak time of about twice that required for normal

NITRIDING

hardening is used, but this time also depends upon the depth and degree of decarburization.

Selective Carburizing

If it is necessary to prevent carburization on certain areas of a part, stopoff compounds or copper plating may be used. Preventing carburization requires attention to cleanliness and handling to achieve the desired stopoff. Copper plate thicknesses of 0.001″ (0.03 mm) minimum are required. Stopoff compounds are proprietary, and instructions should be closely followed as it is difficult to achieve 100% stopoff. Carburization prevention may be necessary on areas to be further machined after heat treating or to prevent a thin area from being carburized all the way through its section and thereby becoming brittle.

NITRIDING

Nitriding is a surface hardening process in which nitrogen is diffused into the surfaces of ferrous alloys at subcritical temperatures to produce a shallow case of nitrides without requiring quenching. The purposes of nitriding include the following:

1. To increase the surface hardness.
2. To improve wear resistance.
3. To increase fatigue life.
4. To possibly increase corrosion resistance slightly, except in the case of stainless steels.

The low temperatures employed and the lack of quenching in nitriding minimize distortion, but the process may require considerable time, especially for producing deep cases with gas nitriding.

STEELS NITRIDED

Steels that are to be nitrided should contain at least one of the following alloying elements: aluminum, chromium, vanadium, tungsten, or molybdenum. These elements form the nitride precipitates that are necessary for diffused cases. Commercial alloy steels contain varying amounts of these elements, with aluminum, chromium, and molybdenum being the most desirable. Steels that are commonly nitrided include AISI 4140 and 4340.

PRIOR TREATMENT

Unlike some other surface hardening processes, most parts must be hardened and tempered before being successfully nitrided. The final tempering temperature before nitriding should be at least 50° F (28° C) above the nitriding temperature. This treatment produces the proper metallurgical structure for nitriding and minimizes dimensional distortion during the nitriding process.

LIQUID NITRIDING

Advantages of liquid nitriding include precise uniformity of temperature throughout the bath, minimal distortion of the workpieces due to the buoyancy effect, and the capability of nitriding plain carbon steels. The principal disadvantage is in the use of salts containing cyanides and cyanates, requiring precautions discussed previously in this chapter under the heading of liquid carburizing. The availability of nontoxic salts containing no cyanides, however, has minimized this problem.

The treatment of cutting tools and forming dies is a major application for nitriding because of the significant improvement in performance attained. Nitrides that are formed improve properties, including high surface hardness, and provide excellent lubricity, with resulting increases in tool and die life ranging from 200 to 1000%.

GAS NITRIDING

Most nitriding is done with gaseous atmospheres in retort furnaces where the products of combustion and air do not contact the workpieces. Both single and double-stage processes are employed. Nitriding is also done in fluidized-bed and vacuum furnaces and by the ion (plasma) process.

In gas nitriding, the term "dissociation rate" is commonly used to describe the percentage of gas volume in the furnace that is not molecular ammonia. However, dissociated ammonia cannot nitride steel. It is the availability of usable nitrogen in undissociated ammonia (NH_3) that controls the nitriding process.

Single-Stage Nitriding

In the single-stage nitriding process, ammonia with a dissociation rate of 15 to 30% is added to the chamber of the furnace and the load is heated to the temperature range of 950 to 1000° F (510 to 540° C). A byproduct of this process is a brittle white layer that forms on the surface of steel. This layer is made up of iron nitrides, and its thickness ranges from 0.0001-0.002″ (0.003-0.05 mm), depending upon the temperature, the time at processing temperature, and the nitriding potential employed. This layer is sometimes removed by chemical or mechanical means to prevent it from spalling when the part is used. In most cases, the thickness of the white nitride layer is simply controlled to a reasonable level, about 0.0005″ (0.013 mm) by use of the two-stage process.

Vacuum Nitriding

Controlled case depths can be produced on critical parts with energy and time savings by nitriding in vacuum furnaces. After the heating chamber is evacuated, the workpieces are heated radiantly, and the furnace is back-filled with a controlled amount of ammonia and natural gas or propane. After a predetermined time, the gas flow is stopped and diffusion begins. This process has had limited application.

Ion (Plasma) Nitriding

Ion nitriding is similar to ion carburizing, discussed previously in this chapter, with two important differences:

1. The gas mixture used is a mixture of nitrogen and hydrogen to which a small amount of methane is sometimes added.
2. Radiant heating elements are not generally required in the vacuum vessels because the energy from the glow discharge and current passing through the workpieces is sufficient for heating. However, radiant elements are sometimes provided for faster heating and better temperature uniformity.

CARBONITRIDING

Carbonitriding is similar to cyaniding, discussed previously in this chapter under the subject of carburizing, except that the simultaneous absorption of carbon and nitrogen into the steel surfaces is accomplished by heating in a gaseous atmosphere. The process is sometimes referred to as dry cyaniding or gas cyaniding. The composition of the case produced depends upon the atmosphere, temperature, time, and steel composition. While carbonitriding is done above the phase-transformation temperatures, the process called nitrocarburizing is performed at temperatures below phase transformation. However, both processes are performed at temperatures higher than required for nitriding.

ADVANTAGES

An important advantage of carbonitriding over carburizing is the effect of nitrogen in improving the hardenability of the case. This process makes possible the use of low-carbon steel to achieve surface hardness equivalent to high-alloy carburized steel without the need for drastic quenching, resulting in less distortion and reduced danger of cracking the work.

Carbonitriding is sometimes combined with carburizing. A thin carbonitrided case is added to the surface of a previously carburized part to provide high surface hardness. Such surfaces can be highly polished to give better frictional properties and longer wear life than the original carburized surfaces.

ATMOSPHERES USED

Atmospheres required for carbonitriding are similar to those used for carburizing except for the addition of ammonia. Hydrocarbon-gas additions to the atmosphere are generally maintained between 2 and 10%. Ammonia additions vary from 0.5 to 25%, the lower percentages being recommended when liquid quenching is used. The higher percentages of ammonia are necessary to produce a nitrogen case for full hardening without benefit of quenching.

CHROMIZING

Chromizing is a high-temperature process in which chromium is transported to and diffused into the surface of metals to provide a chromium-enriched alloy layer with high corrosion, heat, and wear-resistance properties. Current commercial techniques that provide for the simultaneous transportation and diffusion of chromium are:

1. Powder-pack cementation process. In this process, parts to be chromized are placed in a retort in direct contact with a powder mixture of a chromium source, chromium halide salts, and inert refractory oxides. The retort may be sealed, or it may be designed so that a reducing or inert atmosphere can be maintained in it. It may also be placed under a vacuum.
2. Fused salt-bath process. In this process, parts are placed in a salt bath containing chromium halide salts and elemental chromium, and the bath is protected by an inert atmosphere such as argon. The process may be carried out with or without the use of an external current that, if used, deposits chromium on the base part, which serves as the cathode. Faster deposition is possible with the fused salt-bath technique, but its major disadvantages include the need for increased facilities for production and the need for special handling fixtures.
3. Granular-pack process. The granular-pack process uses only porous granules of chromium containing halides within the pores; no inert refractories are used. Workpieces may be either in direct contact with the granules or out of contact if a smoother finish is required. Parts and granules are packed in a retort; and upon heating, the chromium halides vaporize and pass to the parts, where chromium is deposited and diffused into the surfaces. The gaseous reaction products are then transported back to the chromium-source granules to generate more chromium halides. Upon completion of the diffusion, the retort is cooled, and the halides are reabsorbed into the granules, thereby providing primed granules for the next chromizing heat.
4. Gas convection process. In this method, also called chemical vapor deposition (CVD), the parts are placed apart from the chromium sources. Gaseous halogens or halogen acids are then made to react with the chromium to form a gas that is conveyed by forced circulation to the parts. The gaseous reaction products are then exhausted or returned to the source, where a reverse reaction generates additional chromium halides. More detailed information about the CVD process is presented in Chapter 24, "Vapor Deposition Processes," of this volume.

Differences among these processes are chromizing potential, heating and cooling rates, surface finish, transporting power, and economy.

Chromizing offers a variety of advantages. It purifies the steel by removing carbon and nitrogen, causes coarsening of the ferrite grain, removes the stresses and strains of fabrication, provides air-gap stability in electrical components, and increases wear and corrosion resistance. Because chromizing entails high temperatures and relatively long processing times, however, possible distortion and dimensional change of workpieces that have thin cross sections or those containing residual stresses must be considered. Excessive decarburization because of chromizing can occur in thin cross sections, since carbon diffuses outward from the base steel to the surface to combine with the chromium. Bulky parts with large surface area to weight ratios are sometimes costly to chromize because of the volume they occupy in the furnace.

HIGH-FREQUENCY RESISTANCE HARDENING

BORONIZING

Boronizing is another diffusion process for the surface hardening of steels. Compatible materials for this process include mild steels, tool steels, cast irons, nickel-based alloys, and cobalt-based alloys. When a boride layer is applied to the appropriate substrate, the layer will provide additional wear and abrasion resistance, often comparable to that of sintered carbide.

Boronizing can be carried out in a variety of media: gases, molten-salt mixtures or powders, and by plasma processes. The temperature at which the boron is diffused depends upon the material and case depth required. Usually the temperature is between 1550 and 1850° F (845 and 1010°C).

The case depth that can be achieved with boronizing depends primarily upon the material being processed. For example, case depths of 0.005" (0.13 mm) can be produced on low-alloy and carbon steels. Usually, case depths greater than 0.002" (0.05 mm) are not economical for high-alloyed materials, such as stainless steels and tool steels. The most common case depths are 0.001-0.002" (0.03-0.05 mm) for low-alloy and carbon steels, and 0.0005" (0.013 mm) for high-alloyed materials.

HIGH-FREQUENCY RESISTANCE HARDENING

High-frequency (400 kHz) resistance heating is used to selectively harden specified areas on the surfaces of workpieces, rather than entire surfaces. In this way, only those areas most subject to wear are hardened, thus considerably reducing energy requirements and distortion of the workpieces. The fast heating cycles make this process especially suitable for high-production applications.

An advantage of resistance heating with high-frequency current is that a closed loop of current is not required, as is the case with high-frequency induction heating, discussed previously in this chapter. A line or stripe of almost any reasonable shape can be heated between two points. The basic principle is illustrated in Fig. 41-6 where a block of hardenable steel is arranged with a pair of contacts on its outer edges. A water-cooled proximity conductor is placed close to the surface to be heated and connected to the contacts. The source of 400 kHz power for heating is typically 50-300 kW, depending upon the area to be hardened.

When 400 kHz current is applied, a shallow line of heat is rapidly generated on the surface of the workpiece, immediately underneath the proximity conductor. In hardening steel, the metal is heated to about 1600° F (870° C), and the power is then turned off. The high power densities generated by this process heat very rapidly (typically in ½ second or less), thus resulting in hardening through self-quenching by the cold steel surrounding the hot stripe.

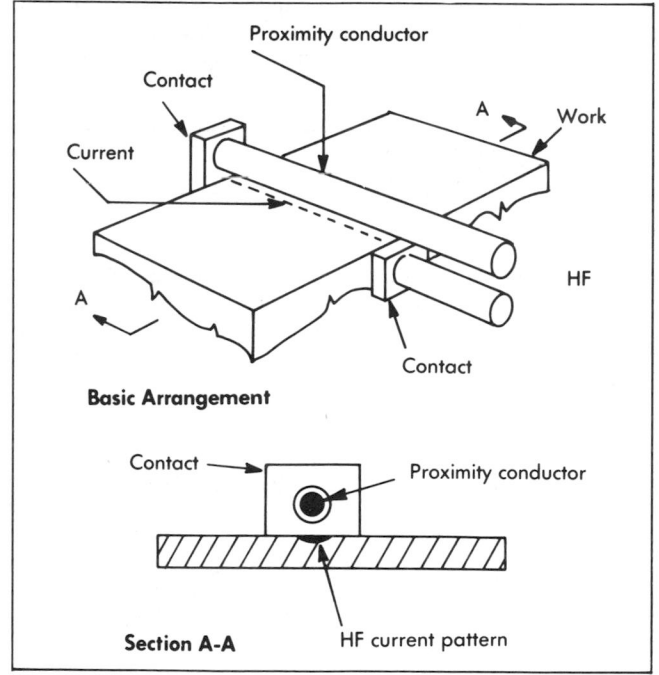

Fig. 41-6 Basic principle of high-frequency resistance hardening. (*Thermatool Corp.*)

INDUCTION HARDENING

Induction systems provide a fast, efficient, and economical method of heating any electrically conductive material to a precise temperature. The equipment uses readily available electric power to heat the entire surface of the workpiece or selected areas. Heat depth can be limited to just the surfaces or can include the entire cross section.

Induction heating can be equally efficient for job shops or high-production operations. The same basic equipment can be used to heat a wide range of sizes and shapes of parts, as well as different materials. Since radiated and secondary heating is eliminated, process heating can be installed directly in a production line or general work area. The equipment is compatible with existing in-plant material handling systems and can be automated to meet specific production requirements.

Important advantages of induction heating include increased production, reduced costs, and improved products. Cycle times are a matter of seconds, and machines can be completely automated. Precise controls reduce or eliminate scrap, distortion is minimized, and the need for more costly alloy steels is sometimes eliminated. Floorspace requirements are reduced, and working conditions improved.

Hardened areas can be accurately controlled with respect to depth, width, location, and hardness. The original ductility of the cores is retained, and the rapid heating reduces scale formation. Compressive residual stresses generated in selective, localized hardening enhance fatigue life.

An induction heating system consists essentially of a power supply, a workstation, a heating coil or inductor, controls, workpiece handling units, and ancillary equipment. After the required frequency has been determined, equipment selection should be dictated by an evaluation of the cost of the equipment, operating and maintenance costs, and, where applicable, flexibility of the equipment for job changeover.

FLAME HARDENING

Flame hardening of steels and cast irons is a practical method of developing general or local surface hardness to increase resistance to wear under abrasive conditions and to increase resistance to surface breakdown under concentrated unit loading. Basically, the hardening of structural carbon and alloy steels, tool steels, and cast irons is accomplished by rapid heating of surface areas followed by suitable quenching. Flame-heating equipment may be a single torch with a specially designed head or an elaborate apparatus that automatically indexes, heats, and quenches parts.

Flame hardening has become a standard method of surface hardening as a result of the development of equipment and techniques that have refined the process. Large parts such as gears and machine-tool ways, with sizes or shapes that would make furnace heat treatment impractical, are easily flame hardened. With improvements in gas-mixing equipment, infrared temperature measurement and control, and burner design, flame hardening has been accepted as a reliable heat treating process that is adaptable to many varied applications.

APPLICATIONS

This method of surface hardening is suitable for small, odd-lot quantities, as well as for medium-to-high production requirements. Its initial cost is low, it has flexibility for complex shapes, and it can be adapted to automatic control. Flame hardening competes favorably with the other surface hardening methods for most applications, and is generally preferable for the surface treatment of massive parts that would be beyond the capacity of induction hardening equipment. The original equipment cost and setup costs are also lower for flame hardening than for the other methods, and the price differential

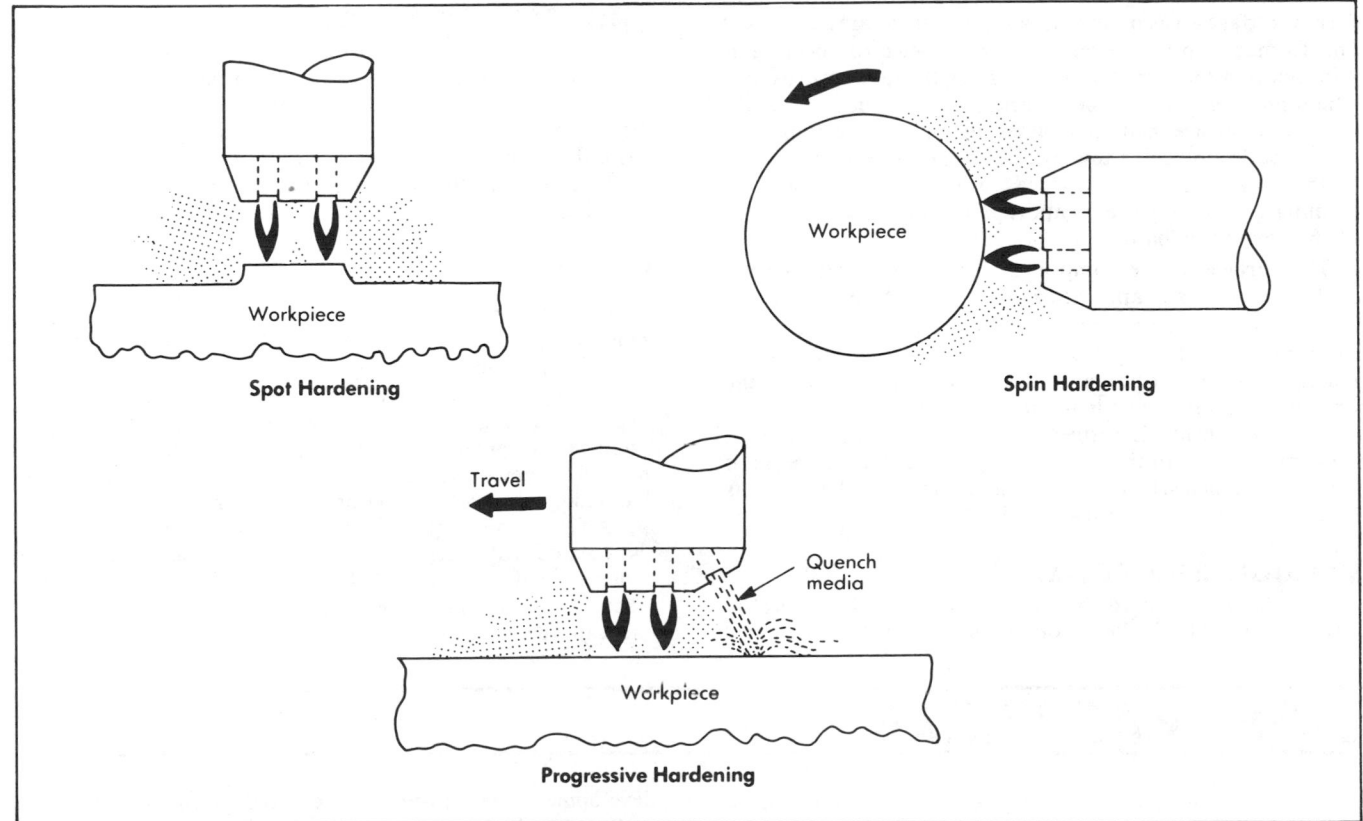

Spot Hardening

Spin Hardening

Progressive Hardening

Fig. 41-7 Three basic methods of flame hardening. (*MAPP Products*)

ELECTRON-BEAM HARDENING

increases with part size.

Material intended for flame hardening may or may not have had previous heat treatment. As a rule, parts requiring high-strength applications are first heat treated conventionally to obtain the desired core properties. The surface areas are then heated as rapidly as possible to the desired temperature and are quenched, either by immersion or by a spray quench trailing the flame head or burner.

METHODS

The three methods of flame hardening (see Fig. 41-7) are:

1. Spot hardening. Spot or stationary flame hardening is accomplished by positioning a flame or group of flames over a given area of the part and applying heat until the part's surface is above the critical temperature. The part is then quenched.
2. Spin hardening. In spin hardening, a torch or group of torches is arranged around the periphery of the work-piece. The part is then revolved at approximately 100 sfm (30.5 m/min) while flames are applied. After the surface is heated above the critical point, it is quenched.
3. Progressive hardening. Progressive flame hardening may be applied to either flat surfaces or cylindrical parts. In this method, the torch is passed over the work surface, and the quench is applied immediately after the last flames have passed. The heat input and the motion must be coordinated so that the work surface is above the critical temperature when the quench is applied. The quench most frequently used is water; but soluble oil, air, and polymer quenches are also used, especially for alloy steels having a high susceptibility to cracking.

ELECTRON-BEAM HARDENING

Recent technological advancements have accelerated the use of electron-beam (EB) heat treating (transformation hardening), a relatively new process for localized surface hardening of components made from carbon and alloy steels.

THE PROCESS

The EB heat treating process uses a concentrated beam of high-velocity electrons as an energy source to selectively heat desired surface areas of ferrous parts. Electrons are accelerated and formed into a directed beam by an electron-beam gun. After exiting the gun, the beam passes through a focus coil, which precisely controls beam density levels (spot size) at the workpiece surface, and then passes through a deflection coil.

The deflection coil allows the beam spot to be moved about on the workpiece surface at speeds to 400,000 ips (10 160 m/s), forming geometric patterns appropriate for the configuration of the zone to be hardened.

The surface of the component being bombarded by the electron beam heats rapidly to a high temperature, confined to the target area of the beam; the rest of the component remains relatively cold. This rapid and precise buildup of heat, which austenitizes the surface and metal immediately under the surface, normally occurs in 0.5 to 3.0 seconds.

When the beam is turned off, heat flows from the high temperature zone to the region that is still cold. The result of this flow is called self-quenching and is more rapid and just as effective as immersion into a liquid.

VACUUM ENVIRONMENT

To produce an electron beam, a high vacuum of 10^{-5} torr (1.3 x 10^{-3} Pa) is needed in the region where the electrons are emitted and accelerated. This vacuum environment protects the emitter from oxidizing and avoids scattering of the electrons while they are still traveling at a relatively low velocity.

Surfaces to be heat treated, however, can be located in any of three different environments, as follows: high vacuum, partial vacuum, and nonvacuum.

PROCESS ADVANTAGES

Surface hardening with the EB process offers many advantages, including eliminating the need for quenchants. Processing in a vacuum eliminates oxidation and scaling; and there is only minimum, if any, distortion of the workpieces. Also, the process does not disturb the surface finishes on the workpieces, and extensive testing has shown that no cracks are produced.

LIMITATIONS

Workpiece materials to be heat treated by the EB process must contain sufficient carbon, alloying elements, and hardenability to produce the required hardness. Areas on the workpieces requiring heat treatment must be capable of being exposed to a beam of electrons, with a minimum beam impingement angle of 25°. Workpieces that have been magnetized in previous processing must be demagnetized prior to hardening to prevent deflection of the beam.

An important requirement for successful EB heat treatment is that the workpiece mass must be sufficient to permit self-quenching of the heat-treated areas. A mass of up to eight times that of the volume to be hardened is required around and beneath the heated surfaces.

LASER HARDENING

Surface-transformation hardening with lasers (*laser* is an acronym for "light amplification by stimulated emission of radiation") is a relatively new process made possible by the development of high-power industrial lasers. As in other surface-transformation hardening processes, a relatively thin surface layer is generated in which the material has undergone transformation to martensite. The process is limited to materials, such as hardenable cast irons and steels, that are capable of undergoing such a transformation. A carbon content of at least 0.30% is generally necessary to attain any significant hardness in steels.

In surface hardening, only the surfaces of the workpieces need to be heated to the austenitizing temperature, and it is desirable that the surface heating be as rapid as possible. This requirement makes the laser an ideal heat source because it can easily produce the energy fluxes (power densities) needed. In fact, lasers are capable of heating surfaces so rapidly that the required, subsequent quenching occurs by fast heat conduction to the still-cold interiors of the workpieces. This so-called self-quenching is a major advantage of laser surface hardening.

For surface-transformation hardening with lasers, the required power density is much lower than for laser welding and cutting, but the exposure time is longer. The power densities for laser hardening generally range from 15.5 to 1550 W/in.^{2} (2.4 to 240 W/cm^2). Laser output power is spread uniformly over a relatively large area (spot), typically 0.4" (1 cm) square, depending upon the area to be hardened.

Hardening is performed by moving the spot over the workpiece surface at a controlled speed. With the proper power density and speed, the desired hardened strip is produced. Output power of the laser can be shaped or raster scanned into

other forms to cover broad-area spots, but the principle is the same. When more than one path is required to cover an area, consideration must be given to overlap of the paths. Insufficient overlap produces a thinning of the case. Overlap may also cause a tempered zone in the previous path.

Major advantages of laser hardening include:

- Easy and accurate control of power input to the workpiece.
- Rapid heating and self-quenching, with reduced distortion.
- Ability to case harden specific areas to controlled depths.
- High power flux reduces total energy input.
- Ability to harden normally inaccessible areas on workpiece surfaces.
- Ability to harden specific areas on large and irregularly shaped workpieces because no protective atmosphere is required and the distance from the last optical element can be long.

Possible limitations of laser hardening include:

- High cost of capital equipment.
- Maximum depth of case obtainable is limited.
- Need for absorption coatings, entailing costs for application and removal.

HEAT TREATING FURNACES

Furnaces are either fuel fired, with gas or oil, or electrically heated. The advantages and disadvantages of each type are summarized in Table 41-2. The metal to be heated and the type of treatment to be performed are important considerations in selecting the method of heat application. Surfaces of metals absorb heat transmitted by radiation, convection, or conduction, or a combination of these; and the heat is transferred through the metals by conduction.

DIRECT-FIRED FURNACES

In direct-fired furnaces, the work being processed is directly exposed to the products of combustion, normally referred to as flue products. The analysis of the flue products can be varied to minimize scaling (oxidation) of the work. This control is accomplished by adjusting the fuel-air ratio of the combustion system. Adjustment can be manual or, for a more precise analysis, can be controlled automatically by a variety of fuel-air ratio control systems available.

When direct-fired burner equipment is used in a heat treat furnace, the parts being processed are generally in some primary or intermediate stage of manufacture. As a result, the oxide formed is not usually detrimental to the part and is generally removed subsequently in the manufacturing process. Such is the case in the annealing of cold formed parts between successive drawing operations and in the annealing of rough castings prior to machining operations.

ELECTRICALLY HEATED FURNACES

Electrically heated furnaces are used for practically all temperature ranges, from low-temperature tempering to high forging temperatures. A basic consideration in the use of electric

furnaces is selecting the type of heating element. Elements available include the open type, which are exposed to the furnace's environment, and the indirect type, which are protected from the furnace's internal environment by some means, such as a radiant tube, muffle, or retort.

Factors affecting the selection of the type of heating element include the furnace atmosphere, the need for protection, and the available space.

RADIANT-TUBE FURNACES

With fuel-fired, radiant-tube heated furnaces, the work chamber is protected from the products of combustion. Normally, the work chamber contains a manufactured controlled atmosphere as dictated by the process. There are, however, cases where the chamber remains filled with air, and the only purpose of the radiant tubes is to protect the work from the high dew point and/or corrosive flue products. Electrically heated radiant tubes are normally used to protect the heating element material from attack by the furnace atmosphere.

TYPES OF FURNACES

Heat treating furnaces are heat-holding enclosures that can be classified as either batch or continuous types. There are many variations in design and construction within each type. Selection of a specific furnace depends primarily upon the size, weight, and shape of the parts to be heat treated; the type of heat treatment to be performed; production rates required; and the initial and operating costs. The productivity of furnaces can be rated in pounds-per-hour production per dollar of capital expenditure (including installation), per dollar of energy cost,

HEAT-TREATING FURNACES

TABLE 41-2
Advantages and Disadvantages of Fuel-Fired and
Electrically Heated Furnaces

Fuel-Fired Furnaces		Electrically Heated Furnaces	
Advantages	Disadvantages	Advantages	Disadvantages
1. Easy adjustment. Input can be easily varied, normally with a simple orifice change.	1. Requires extensive ventilation system.	1. Systems are clean and free of pollution.	1. System is inflexible with respect to changing heating capacity.
2. Recuperator-type heat-saving devices can be added.	2. Potential hazards of fire or explosion.	2. Cooler plant environment, without need for exhaust hoods and stacks.	2. Higher initial, operating, and maintenance costs.
3. Easily controlled cooling in furnace, with properly designed combustion system.	3. Requires more labor for startup and shutdown.	3. Quieter operation—no blower or combustion noise.	3. Longer cooldown times.
4. Generally faster heatup.	4. Easier to get out of adjustment, resulting in excessive fuel use.	4. More uniform heat pattern.	
5. Lower operating and maintenance costs.		5. No exhaust or makeup air systems required.	
		6. Purge and flame safety systems not required.	
		7. Availability of electric power.	

and per dollar of labor costs (including maintenance).

Direct-fired, batch-type furnaces are the simplest kind. Continuous furnaces, with automatic control for high-production requirements, are much more sophisticated. Many furnaces are equipped for controlling the atmospheres in their work chambers. While standard furnaces are available in a wide variety of sizes, many are of special design to suit a specific application.

SALT-BATH FURNACES

Salt-bath furnaces are basically ceramic or metal containers with molten salt in which workpieces are immersed for either heating or cooling within a temperature range of 300 to 2400° F (150 to 1315° C). The molten media generally consists of one or more salts, such as nitrates, chlorides, carbonates, cyanides, or hydroxides. The furnaces are heated by gas, oil, or electricity.

A major advantage of salt-bath furnaces is rapid heating of the workpieces. The conduction method of heating with molten salts is up to six times faster than convection or radiation methods of heating. The heating rate is limited only by the thermal conductivity of the metal being heated and the ability of the furnace to supply energy at a rate fast enough to maintain the bath temperature. Rapid heating permits increased production rates and/or the use of a smaller furnace.

Protection of the workpiece surfaces from the atmosphere during heating is another important advantage of salt-bath furnaces. Decarburization of steel parts and oxidation and scaling are generally eliminated. While these advantages are also obtained with controlled atmosphere and vacuum furnaces, capital expenditure requirements for salt-bath furnaces of similar production capacities are lower.

Another advantage of salt-bath furnaces is the uniformity of heating. The temperature throughout any size of internally heated bath averages ±5° F (3° C) of the preset temperature, thus heating all surfaces and sections simultaneously. For high-temperature applications, temperature conformity of ±1 1/2° F (0.8° C) is not unusual. The uniformity of workpiece heating and precise control of temperature minimize distortion, prevent cracking, and ensure consistently high-quality results. The density of the molten bath helps support the workpieces, thus minimizing sagging, bending, or distortion. Salt-bath furnaces can also be used for selective hardening by using fixtures to immerse only the portions of the workpieces to be hardened. Parts of different sizes and shapes may be treated simultaneously if desired.

Salt-bath furnaces are best suited for production work requiring daily or continuous operation. Applications requiring intermittent use are best served with externally heated pot furnaces.

Buoyant workpieces are difficult to handle in salt baths, and it is desirable to avoid such applications by redesign of the workpieces if possible. Blind cavities, which can trap air or salt, present problems in handling and salt removal. These problems can sometimes be solved by redesigning the parts or repositioning them for satisfactory drainage.

Salt-bath furnaces are being used for a wide variety of heat treating operations. These include austenitizing, solution treating, age hardening, tempering, annealing, normalizing, liquid carburizing, cyaniding, liquid nitriding, carbonitriding, quenching, and dip brazing. The furnaces are used extensively for heat treating ferrous and nonferrous alloys; ceramics, such as optical glass; and for curing some polymers.

One major application of salt-bath furnaces is the hardening of high-speed steel tools that require maximum surface protection and uniformity. Reasons for the predominant use of salt-bath furnaces for this application include simplicity and versatility, uniform and rapid heating, precise control, and freedom from scaling.

VACUUM FURNACES

Vacuum furnaces basically consist of a container that is evacuated to create a vacuum in which workpieces are thermally treated by electric radiant heat. Substantial advances have been made during recent years in the design, operation, control, and versatility of vacuum furnaces. As a result, they are being used extensively as an alternative to atmosphere-controlled and salt-bath furnaces.

A major advantage of vacuum furnaces for many heat treating applications is in eliminating the need for costly protective atmospheres, controls, and venting systems. The use of a vacuum prevents unwanted gases from contaminating or oxidizing the metal being treated. By eliminating oxygen, workpieces are kept bright and scale-free, and chemistry of the metal, including carbon content, remains unchanged. Dissolved gases, such as hydrogen, water vapor, and air, are evaporated from the workpieces; and other surface contaminants, such as films, solvents, and lubricants, are removed. In many cases, superior surface properties are attained with vacuum heat treatment.

Precise control of vacuum and temperature ensures consistently high quality of heat-treated parts. Versatility is another important benefit of vacuum furnaces. The furnaces are used for many different heat treating processes, discussed later in this section. Energy efficiency of vacuum furnaces is high. Also, energy is only required when the furnace is in use; the furnace can be completely shut down when not needed.

The initial cost of vacuum furnaces is a possible limitation to their use. However, the operating savings possible for many applications permit rapid write-off of the investment. In some cases, the cost of operating a vacuum furnace is much less than for a controlled-atmosphere furnace.

Vacuum furnaces were originally used primarily for the high-temperature processing of highly reactive and refractory metals, such as columbium, tantalum, tungsten, molybdenum, and titanium alloys. With advances in design and control, these furnaces are no longer limited to special heat treating operations on small, expensive parts, but are now used extensively for hardening and annealing many alloys previously heat treated in atmosphere or salt-bath furnaces.

FLUIDIZED-BED FURNACES

Fluidized-bed heat processing is performed in a retort containing mobile, inert particles of uniform size that are suspended in a flowing stream of gas. When properly fluidized, the bed attains liquid-like properties, and products are heated by direct immersion. A variety of materials may be used for the bed media, such as aluminum oxide, silicon carbide, or zirconia sand. The primary requirements of the medium are that it be uniform in size and remain inert at operating temperature.

The general nature of fluidized-bed heat transfer is illustrated in Fig. 41-8 with a graph of the heat transfer coefficient versus fluidizing-gas velocity. Heat transfer characteristics of a fluidized bed fall into three distinct areas. In Section 1, the bed is in a static state, with the gas velocity insufficient for fluidization. The heat transfer coefficient rises only slightly with relation to gas velocity and is at a low value.

The minimum velocity for the start of fluidization is indicated by V_1 (Fig. 41-8). Across Section 2, the heat transfer coefficient rises rapidly until the optimal velocity V is reached. Beyond this velocity, the bed becomes separated and attains gas-like properties. Thus, in Section 2, the heat transfer coefficient decreases with increasing velocity.

Pressure drop across the bed increases linearly with gas flow in Section 1 (Fig. 41-8), attaining a maximum at velocity V_1. The pressure then quickly drops slightly to a value that remains constant across Section 2. For media commonly in use, this pressure value is approximately two inches of water column per inch of bed depth (0.5 kPa per cm of bed depth). In Section 3, the pressure drop decreases with increasing gas velocity.

In general, the majority of heat treating is done using calcined, aluminum-oxide media of 99% purity, with a size range of 46 to 100 mesh. This type of medium remains inert to a temperature of 3300° F (1815° C). Operating velocities are in a range of 0.3 to 2 fps (0.09 to 0.61 m/s), approximately double V_1 for the particles being used.

Furnace Design

Modern fluidized-bed furnaces are used in three configurations. Two types are fuel fired, using products of combustion as the fluidizing gas, and are known as internally and externally fired types. The third type is indirectly fuel fired or electrically heated, independent of the source of fluidization, and may use any fluidizing gas desired.

Process Capabilities

Fluidized-bed furnaces are being used for many different heat treating operations. Common applications include neutral hardening, carburizing, carbonitriding, nitriding, nitrocarburizing, and steam tempering. When using generated atmospheres, however, care has to be exercised to ensure that the pressure and flow rate of the atmosphere generated is consistent with the fluidization requirements of the bed.

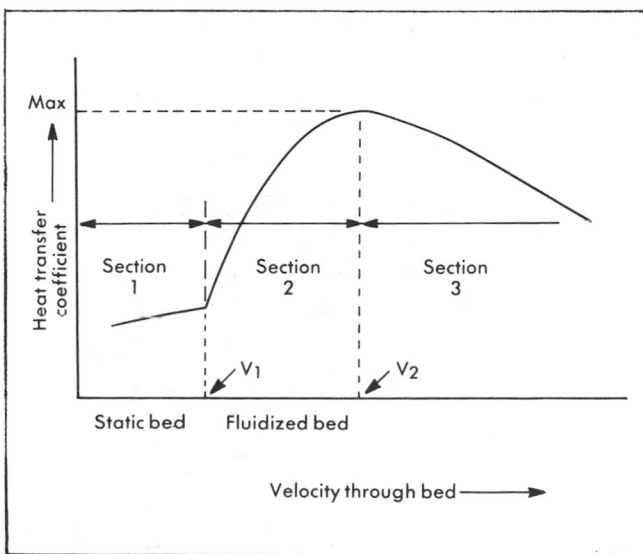

Fig. 41-8 Heat transfer coefficient versus gas velocity in fluidized-bed furnace.

HEAT-TREATING FURNACES

FURNACE CONTROLS

The control of a process variable requires a sensor, a controller, and a final control element or actuator connected to the process in a control loop. This basic control loop is used for both on-off and proportioning or modulating types of control. The basic control loop for a heat treating process concerned with temperature control is illustrated schematically in Fig. 41-9. A temperature sensor detects the process temperature and generates a signal proportional to this temperature, which is transmitted to the controller. The controller set-point (the desired temperature) is compared to this signal (the actual temperature).

The difference or error signal between the actual and desired temperature determines the controller's action. In heating processes using on-off control, the energy source is turned off when the actual temperature is above the set-point and turned on when it is below the set-point. Consequently, the process temperature varies above and below the desired set-point. A common misconception is that this temperature cycling arises because such controllers exhibit a dead-band between the power-off and power-on switching points, and therefore cycling can be reduced or eliminated by reducing the dead-band. In fact, cycling is caused by process dynamics and only in exceptional cases will changing the dead-band have any effect.

Continuous control systems adjust the process energy input as required to maintain process temperature. Proportional controllers, which produce an output proportional to the current error, are easy to adjust, but allow some offsets to exist. Adding integral and derivative terms to the error-signal computation results in the popular proportional-integral-derivative (PID) controller. Although more expensive and more difficult to adjust, PID controllers are generally preferred when very close control is required.

The basic control loop is frequently provided with auxiliary devices, such as recording instruments and set-point programmers. The measurement instruments may be recorders or indicators, showing the process temperature for guidance to the process operator and to maintain process records. Computer-based data acquisition and microcomputer control systems are advanced methods, which use printers or typewriters to log the process temperature.

With some applications of multiple devices, the temperature sensor signal will be measured by a temperature transmitter, which amplifies the signal. This amplification helps to avoid interaction between the measurement and controlling instruments, and minimizes pickup of electrical noise when these signals are transmitted long distances. The set-point programmer automatically varies the controller set-point to provide a temperature versus time cycle, which is called a recipe or program. The rate of heating or cooling and the time at specific temperatures can be automatically maintained as required by the process. Many modern controllers combine the set-point programmer and controller in a single unit, in both single and multiple-loop forms. Temperature controllers also often use directly connected thermocouples and provide a process signal for recording instruments.

Sensors and transmitters used to determine process variables must be accurate, reliable, and properly installed and maintained. As part of the basic control loop, these sensors and transmitters may represent only 1% of the instrumentation cost, but their performance is vital to the operation of the control loop.

Major atmosphere-controlled heat treating applications include carburizing, hardening, carbonitriding, and nitriding. Carburizing and hardening using carbonaceous atmospheres are the largest volume applications. In hardening, the metal has the desired carbon concentration, and the objective is to maintain it while the part is brought to temperature prior to quenching. In carburizing, the objective is to increase the carbon content of the metal at its surface. Consequently, carbon-rich atmospheres (atmospheres with a high carbon potential) are used for carburizing, and atmospheres with a lower carbon potential are used for hardening. Carbonitriding involves the additions of nitrogen to a carbonaceous atmosphere, while nitriding involves only nitrogen. This discussion is limited to carburizing and hardening applications.

Atmospheres produced by generators and furnace atmospheres are controlled. A variety of components exist in a carboneacous atmosphere, and their concentration, with allowance for temperature, may be related to carbon potential. Oxygen measured with a zirconia probe and carbon dioxide measured with an infrared gas analyzer are the most common measurements for continuous control. Water measured with a dew point analyzer is the most common basis for manual control.

References

1. Peter F. Weiser, *Steel Castings Handbook* (Des Plaines, IL: Steel Founders' Society of America, 1980), pp. 21-15 to 21-23.
2. The Aluminum Association, *Aluminum Standards and Data*, 7th ed. (Washington, DC: 1982).

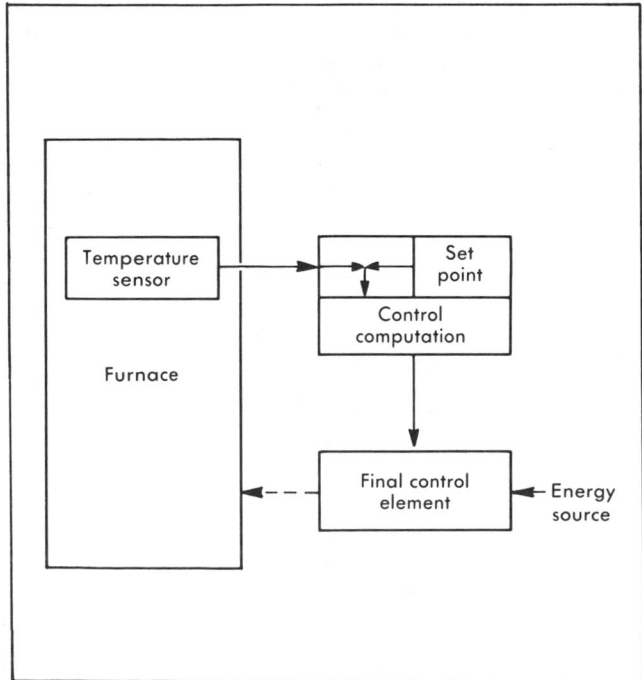

Fig. 41-9 Basic control loop for temperature control of a heat treating furnace.

FASTENING AND BONDING

Assembly in manufacturing often involves some type of mechanical fastening of a part to itself, or two or more parts or subassemblies together, to form a functional product or a higher level subassembly.

While standard mechanical fasteners are available in many types and sizes, there are numerous requirements and an increasing demand for special fasteners. For some applications, fastener manufacturers can meet special requirements with only slight alterations to existing fasteners, thus reducing costs compared to designing an entirely new special fastener.

Selection of a specific mechanical fastener or fastening method depends primarily on the materials to be joined, the function of the joint, strength and reliability requirements, weight limitations, dimensions of the components, and environmental conditions. Other important factors that must be carefully considered include costs, available installation equipment, appearance, and whether the assembly has to be dismantled. Value analysis in the product design stage can often make assembly easier and more economical by reducing the number of components in the assembly or by modifying the design or processing to facilitate assembly.

INTEGRAL FASTENERS

Integral fasteners are formed areas of the component part or parts that function by interfering or interlocking with other areas of the assembly. This type of fastening is most commonly applied to formed sheet metal products and is generally performed by lanced or shear-formed tabs, extruded hole flanges, embossed protrusions, edge seams, and crimps. In all these methods, the joint is made by some method of metal shearing and/or forming.

LANCED OR SHEAR-FORMED TABS

Tabs, also called ears, flaps, lugs, and prongs, are a versatile construction element for lightweight products made from sheet metal components. The economic advantages of tabs for assembly are reduced material use, lower labor costs, reduced weight, and reduced tooling costs. Lanced tabs are used most widely for permanent assembly but rarely for temporary or even semipermanent assembly.

A common use of a tab bent or curved around a shaft, wire, or cable to locate and hold the parts firmly is shown in Fig. 42-1, view *a*. A similar design is the lanced bridge, view *b*, in which both ends of the lanced area remain attached.

Tabs that are shear formed in one part may be introduced into matching slots or holes in a second part and then folded over, as shown in Fig. 42-2. According to the best bending techniques, the tab should always be bent so that its burred edge is located on the inside of the bend. The finish bend of the tab should always be in the same direction as the primary bend. In some cases, auxiliary parts are included in the tab fastening design, as shown in Fig. 42-3.

EXTRUDED HOLES

A simple, inexpensive method of increasing the length of a hole in sheet metal is to form an integral, extended collar around the hole. The hole is then called an extruded, flanged, collared, embossed, or drifted hole. Extruded holes are widely used as integral fasteners, not only on flat surfaces but also on curved, bent, or drawn surfaces.

In the majority of cases, extruded holes are used for joining two components, one of which is the sheet metal part with the hole. The extruded collar is often used as an integral hollow rivet for joining two thin sheet metal components. The free end of the flange is simply flared or swaged out, creating a heat that forms a firm joint (see Fig. 42-4), view *a*). Common eyelets belong to this type of fastening method. If the length of the flange with respect to the thickness of the second part is favorable, the end of the flange may be curled to form the head.

Tubing may be joined with an extruded hole by means of a bead in the tubing, which acts as a stop, and by flaring or half curling the end of the tube. Tubing may also be fastened by interference fitting of its inner diameter to the flange (see Fig. 42-4, view *b*). A proper guide for shaft riveting may be provided by an extruded hole (view *c*); but often, for limited-strength joints, the shaft may simply be press fit in the flange, with knurling for increased joint strength and torsional resistance. The shaft may also be fastened by beading the flange.

Perhaps the most common use of extruded holes for fastening is in conjunction with discrete fasteners. As shown in Fig. 42-4, view *d*, the flange is tapped and acts as an integral nut with a separate screw or bolt. The nut is twice or more the sheet metal thickness, and the strength of the joint is considerably increased.

EMBOSSED PROTRUSIONS

Embossed protrusions, also referred to as partial extrusions, lugs, and extruded dowels, are bosses forced out from the surface of a metal sheet or part on one side of the material. Such protrusions may be used as integral rivets to form permanent joints, as shown in Fig. 42-5. However, this fastening method has limitations. The bosses must be formed on comparatively thick stock, not less than 0.10" (2.5 mm) thick, and the part to be fastened must never be more than half the thickness of the embossed part because the length of the boss is generally limited to a fraction of stock thickness

INTEGRAL FASTENERS

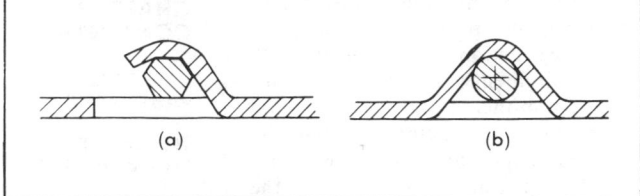

Fig. 42-1 Methods of fastening shafts, wires, or cables to metal plates: (a) lanced tab and (b) lanced bridge.

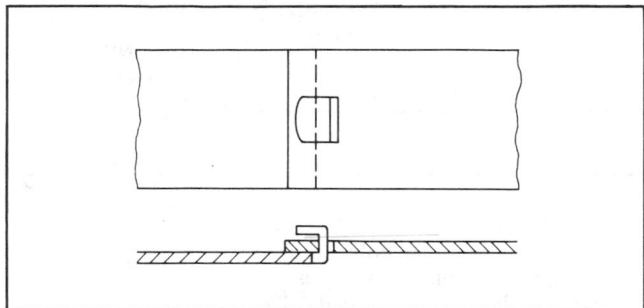

Fig. 42-2 Shear-formed tab folded through a slot for fastening.

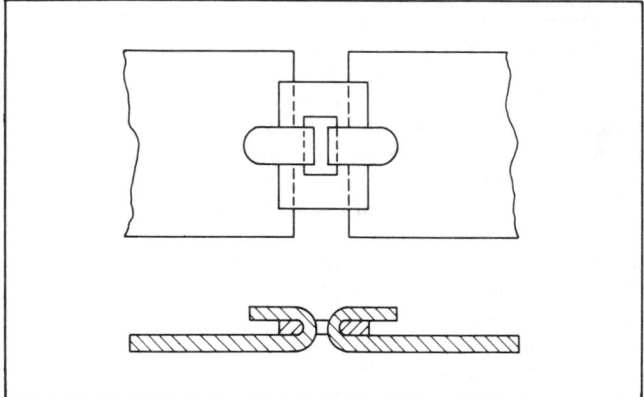

Fig. 42-3 Auxiliary part included in a tab fastening design.

and is not sufficient to make a regular rivet head. For this same reason, joint strength is usually low.

SEAMS

Seaming is often used to interlock the edges of two separate sheet metal parts or the opposite edges of a given curved or bent part. While the chief purpose of seaming is assembly, seams also reinforce the assembly and eliminate sharp edges. Seams are used when other mechanical assembly methods would be impractical or uneconomical and when welding would cause excessive distortion. Seaming also often provides greater strength and tightness under high temperature conditions than do other joining methods. Seams are normally used on metal sheets 0.011-0.050″ (0.28-1.27 mm) thick; heavier gage sheets require too much force for the seaming operation.

Seams may be classified as follows according to the shape of the workpiece to be joined:

- *Jacket or longitudinal seams.* Straight seams for the bodies of tubular workpieces or simple formed parts.
- *Circumferential seams.* Closed seams such as those used for joining a top or a bottom to the tubular body of a can or for joining two tubular parts.

The most common seam for light-gage sheets is the simple or single-lock seam, also known as the standard seam or folded-pipe seam. The edges to be seamed are first bent to acute angles; then they are fitted together, and the seam is flattened closed. In most cases the two joined areas must be flush, as shown in Fig. 42-6. The seam may be located inside or outside the workpiece.

For higher strength, a double-lock seam is formed in the following steps: the two edges are bent square, with one edge bent longer than the other; the longer leg is bent over the shorter one; a standing seam is formed; and the seam is bent down and flattened against the joined parts (see Fig. 42-7).

The seams just described are direct seams; that is, they are formed directly on the parts. In special cases, and indirect seam using an intermediate connector strap or plate may be formed to fasten parts; such as a seam is shown in Fig. 42-8.

CRIMPS

Crimps are permanent interlocking joints in sheet metal assemblies created by deforming the thin wall of one or both of the fitted components. Crimped fastening methods may be classified roughly into the following five groups:

1. Matching beads (formed inward or outward).
2. Matching dimples (formed inward or outward).
3. Formed ribs or flanged unions.
4. Holding beads.
5. Special shapes.

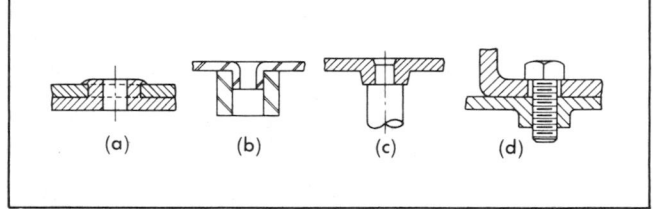

Fig. 42-4 Uses of an extruded hole for joining: (a) as a rivet with end flared or swaged, (b) as an interference fitting, (c) with a riveted shaft, and (d) with a bolt fastener.

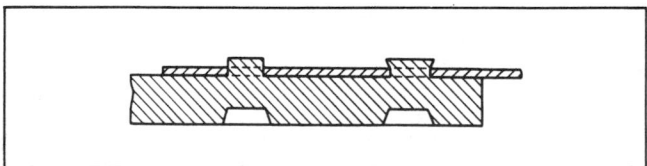

Fig. 42-5 Embossed protrusions before and after flattening to form an integral rivet.

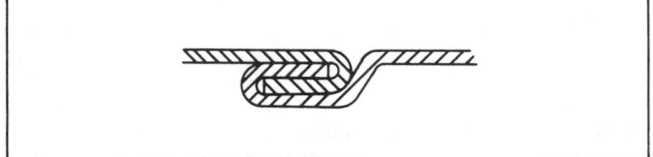

Fig. 42-6 Simple or single-lock seam flattened flush with joined areas.

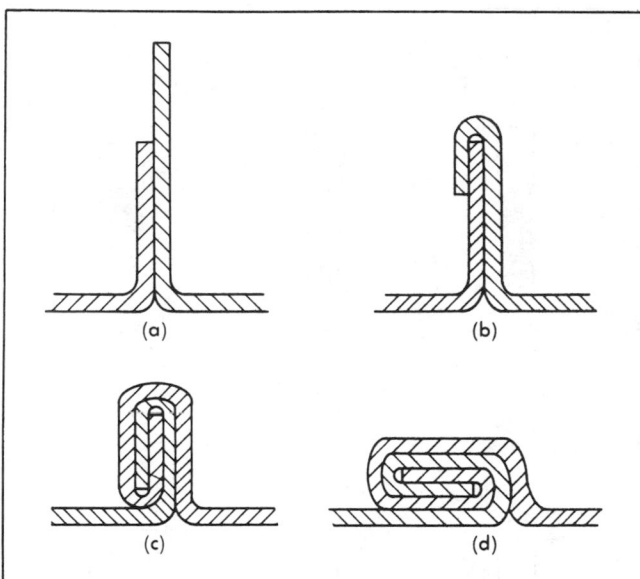

Fig. 42-7 Steps in forming a double-lock seam.

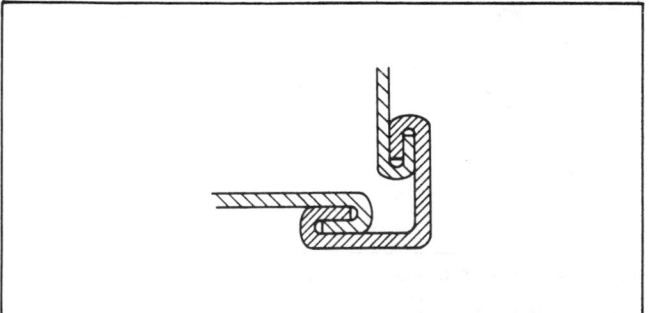

Fig. 42-8 Indirect seam with an intermediate connector plate.

Crimping cannot be employed without limitations. The sheet metal of the deformed components should be thin, preferably less than 0.030″ (0.76 mm). The stock must also be naturally ductile or softened by an annealing process. Copper, tin, brass, aluminum, and low-carbon steel have the proper yield characteristics and are often fastened by crimping.

Beading

Matching beads are used for crimping pipe and tubing together when the outer diameter of one component matches the inner diameter of the other, as shown in Fig. 42-9. The two beads are formed together in light-walled ductile tubing; but to

avoid overstress in heavier gages and harder metals, it is customary to form the inner bead first, with the outer bead formed against the inner one after assembly.

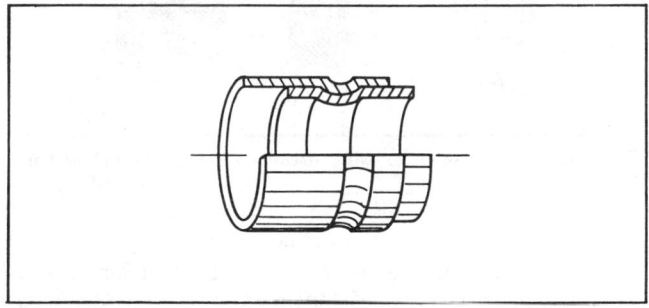

Fig. 42-9 Use of matching beads for crimp fastening of pipe or tubing.

Dimpling

Matching dimples often serve well for fastening when joint tightness requirements are not too severe. The holding strength of dimples is usually low. The simplest dimples are round, although dimples may be formed rather deeply and assume the shape of double-slit bridges. For increased strength, several dimples may be formed (see Fig. 42-10, view *a*), although only a single dimple is required for very simple cases. As in beading, thin, soft materials allow both inner and outer dimples to be formed simultaneously; but in harder, thicker materials, the internal component must be spot drilled or grooved before assembly (view *b*).

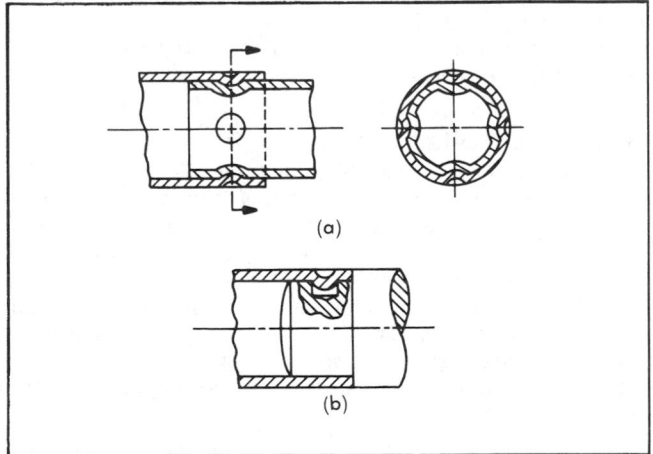

Fig. 42-10 Crimped dimple fastening of tubular parts: (a) with several dimples for increased strength and (b) with internal components spot drilled before assembly.

THREADED FASTENERS

Threaded fasteners are separate components having internal or external threads for mechanically joining parts. The most common types of threaded fasteners include bolts, studs, nuts, and screws, all discussed subsequently in this section.

A primary application of threaded fasteners is for joining

and holding parts together for load-carrying requirements, especially when disassembly and reassembly may be required. Typical assemblies for several types of threaded fasteners are illustrated in Fig. 42-11. Threaded fasteners are also used extensively for assemblies subject to environmental conditions

THREADED FASTENERS

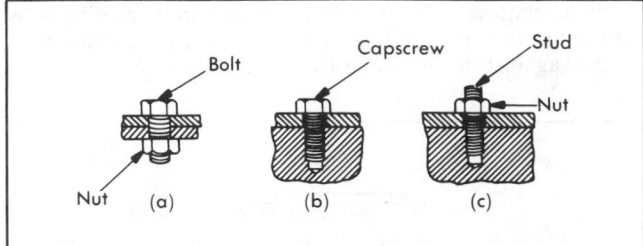

Fig. 42-11 Typical assemblies using threaded fasteners: (a) bolt and nut, (b) capscrew, and (c) stud.

such as elevated temperatures and corrosion.

Advantages of threaded fasteners include their commercial availability in a wide range of standard and special types, sizes, materials, and strengths. Extensive standardization efforts have made most threaded fasteners interchangeable. Most of these fasteners are easy to install, remove, and replace, thus providing a low-cost method of assembly. They are capable of joining identical or different materials and workpieces of various configurations.

BOLTS AND STUDS

Bolts are externally threaded fasteners generally assembled with nuts (refer to Fig. 42-11, view *a*). While most bolts are headed, some are not. The means of distinguishing between bolts and screws are discussed in ANSI Standard B18.2.1, "Square and Hexagonal Bolts and Screws, Inch Series," and in the introduction to this section on threaded fasteners. Studs are cylindrical rods threaded on one or both ends or throughout their lengths (refer to Fig. 42-11, view *c*).

Bolts are available in a wide variety of types and sizes, a few of which are shown in Fig. 42-12.

Hex-Head Bolts

Bolts with hexagonal heads (commonly called hex heads, the term that will be used throughout this section) are the most commonly used. These heads have a flat or indented top surface, six flat sides, and a flat bearing surface. The flat sides facilitate tightening the bolts with wrenches. Hex heads are often used on high-strength bolts and are easier to tighten than bolts with square heads. They are generally available in standard strength grades as specified by ASTM, SAE, and other organizations and to special strength requirements for specific applications.

Round-Head Bolts

Round-head bolts have thin circular heads with rounded or flat top surfaces and flat bearing surfaces. When provided with an underhead configuration that locks into the joint material, round-head bolts resist rotation and are tightened by turning their mating nuts. Included in this classification, even though the configurations differ, are countersunk and T-head bolts.

Variations of round-head bolts include those with square, ribbed, or finned necks on the shanks below the heads to prevent the fasteners from rotating in their holes. Specifications for round-head and countersunk bolts are included in ANSI Standard B18.5. Data for metric sized, round-head, square-neck bolts are presented in ANSI/ASME Standard B18.5.2.2M,

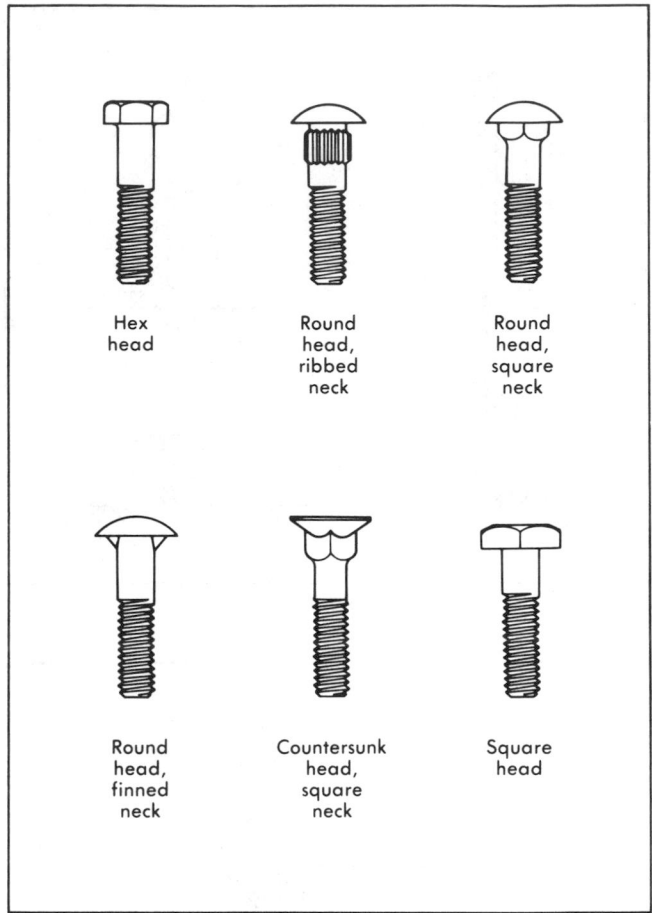

Hex head

Round head, ribbed neck

Round head, square neck

Round head, finned neck

Countersunk head, square neck

Square head

Fig. 42-12 A few of the many types of bolt available.

and short, square-neck bolts are covered in Standard B18.5.2.1M.

Square-Head Bolts

These bolts have square-shaped, external wrenching heads. Dimensional specifications are presented in ANSI Standard B18.2.1, and they are available in two strength grades. Lag bolts, sometimes called lag screws, usually have square or hex heads, gimlet or cone points, and thin, sharp, coarse-pitch threads. They produce mating threads in wood or other resilient materials and are used in masonry with expanding anchors.

Battery bolts have square heads and are generally stainless steel or lead or tin coated for clamping onto battery terminals. Fitting-up bolts have square heads and coarse-pitch, 60° stub threads. They are used for the preliminary assembly of structural steel components. T-bolts are square-head bolts used in the T-slots of machine tools.

Bent Bolts

Bent bolts are cylindrical rods having one end threaded and the other end bent to various configurations. These include eyebolts, hook bolts, and J-bolts. Other bent bolts, such as U-bolts, have both ends threaded. The ends of bent bolts are usually square (as sheared).

Studs

Studs are unheaded, externally threaded fasteners. They are available with threads on one or both ends or continuously threaded. Studs with collars and threaded on one or both ends are also available (see Fig. 42-13). Heat-treated and/or plated studs are available to suit specific requirements. They are also made with chamfered or dog-point ends.

An advantage of studs for some applications, such as the assembly of large and heavy components, is that they can serve as pilots to facilitate mating of the components. These fasteners also facilitate the automatic assembly of various components. For many applications, studs provide fixed external threads and nuts are the only components that have to be assembled.

NUTS

Nuts are internally threaded fasteners that fit on bolts, studs, screws, or other externally threaded fasteners for mechanically joining parts. They also serve for adjusting, transmitting motion, or transmitting power in some applications, but generally require special thread forms. Nuts are available in a wide range of standard and special types (see Fig. 42-14), sizes, materials, and strengths to suit specific requirements.

Hex and square nuts, sometimes referred to as full nuts, are the most common. Hex nuts are used for most general-purpose applications. Square machine screw nuts are usually limited to light-duty and special assemblies. Regular and heavy square nuts are often used for bolted flange connections.

Single-Thread Nuts

Single-thread nuts, sometimes called spring nuts, are formed by stamping a thread-engaging impression (arched prongs) in a flat piece of metal (see Fig. 42-15). These nuts are generally made from high-carbon spring steel (SAE 1050-1064), but are also

available in corrosion-resistant steel, beryllium copper, and other metals.

Single-thread nuts are made in many shapes and styles, but all depend on spring action for their holding power and resistance to vibration. Flat, circular, and round types are common, and some have spanner holes for driving. They are also available in J and U-types that snap over the edges of panels or into hole locations, holding themselves in place for blind assemblies. Angle nuts having a single thread impression on each leg are used to join perpendicular components.

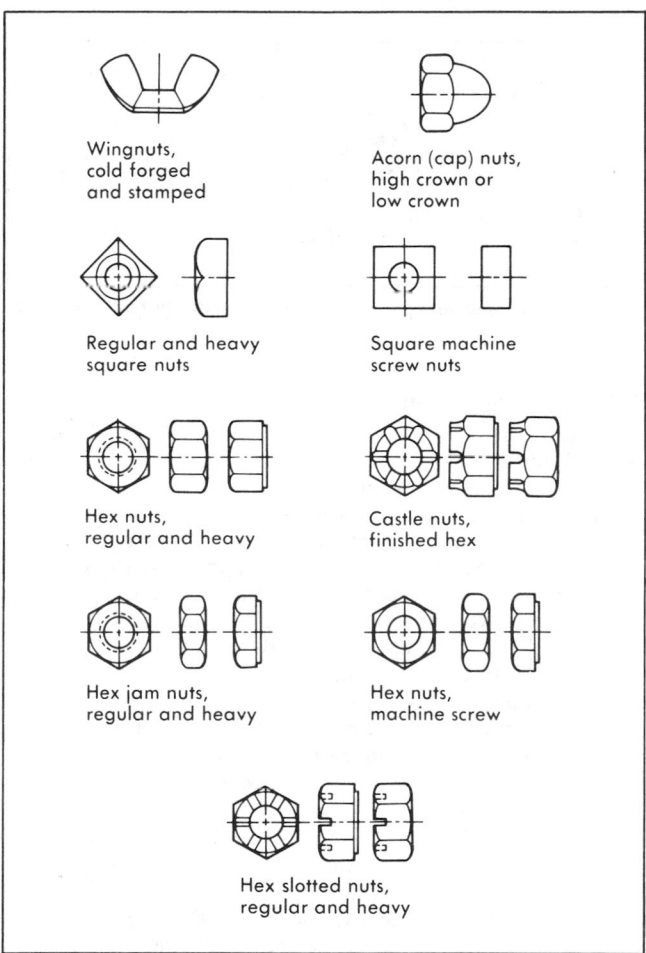

Fig. 42-14 **Various types of nuts.** (*Tri-West Products Inc.*)

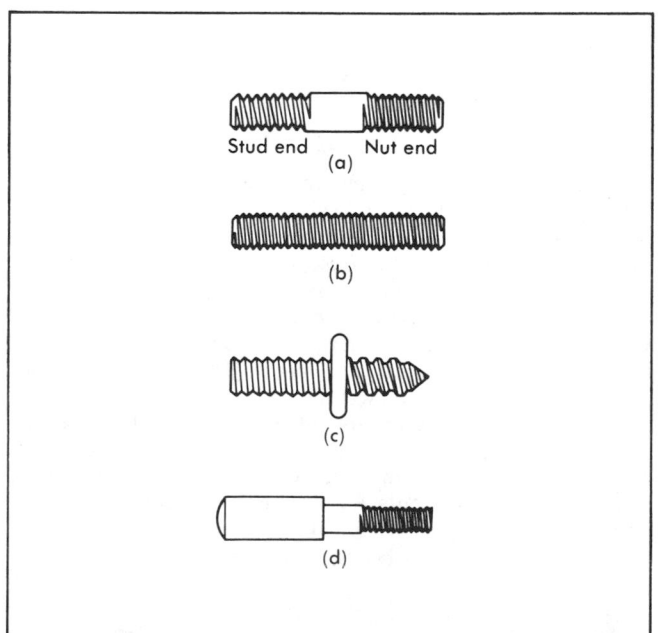

Fig. 42-13 **Studies of various types: (a) double-end stud of interference thread type, (b) continuous-thread stud, (c) collared stud with machine screw thread on left end and thread for plastics on right end, and (d) shouldered stud.** (*Tri-West Products Inc.*)

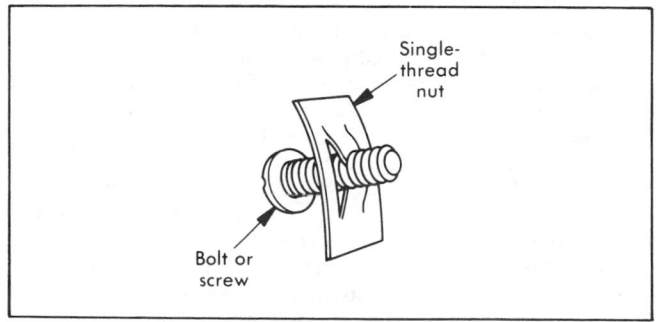

Fig. 42-15 **Single-thread nut.**

THREADED FASTENERS

Stamped Nuts

Stamped nuts are hex fasteners stamped from spring steel or other metals, with prongs formed to engage mating threads. They are similar to single-thread nuts in that they rely on spring action for clamping and resistance to loosening, but they have more prongs to engage the threads on the mating fastener. Applications include replacements for full nuts in low-stress uses and as retaining nuts against full nuts (see Fig. 42-16). Stamped nuts are made with integral washers, in closed top or bottom styles, and as wingnuts.

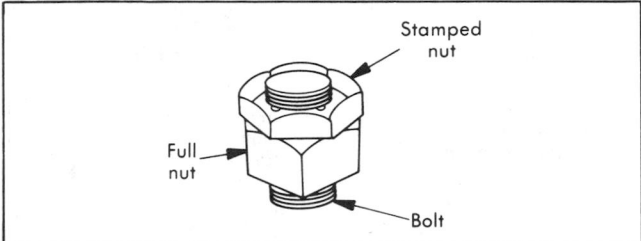

Fig. 42-16 Stamped nut applied and tightened after full nut is in place.

Other Types of Nuts

There are many other types of nuts available, most designed for the requirements of specific applications. A few of the more common types are described in this section.

Crown nuts. These nuts, also called acorn or cap nuts, are hex fasteners having an acorn-shaped top and a blind threaded hole. They are available with high or low crowns. Their closed tops protect the projecting ends of mating, externally threaded fasteners and provide a pleasing appearance. They are commonly used when the projecting ends of externally threaded fasteners may be hazardous, as in toys.

Track-bolt nuts. These square nuts were originally designed for use with track bolts in joining railroad track rails. They are available with 45 or 60° chamfers. Dimensional specifications for track-bolt nuts are presented in ANSI Standard B18.10.

Coupling and conduit nuts. Coupling nuts, generally thin and round, are used to connect pipes or tubes. They are generally stamped and are available in square, hexagonal, or octagonal shapes. Conduit nuts are used to connect electrical pipe or fittings to boxes. Most conduit nuts are round and have ears that provide wrenching surfaces, locking action, and electrical grounding. These nuts normally have one to two threads that are either tapped or formed. Most conduit nuts are made from steel, but they are also available as zinc die castings.

Panel nuts. These thin nuts, normally hexagonal, are similar to conduit nuts but are used to assemble externally threaded fasteners to panels. They typically have fine or extrafine threads and are available made from steel, brass, or zinc alloy.

T-nuts. These square nuts having T-shapes are designed to fit into the T-slots on machine tools.

Barrel and sleeve nuts. These nuts are made in two types. Type 1 is a blind, internally threaded fastener having an external shape like a machine screw (see Fig. 42-17). Type 2 is a cylindrical nut having its internal thread at a right angle to the axis of the cylinder. Sleeve nuts are essentially the same as Type 1 barrel nuts except that their threads extend throughout their entire lengths.

Aircraft nuts. These nuts, usually of high strength and light weight, conform to material and dimensional standards promulgated by the aerospace industry and other organizations.

Round nuts. These nuts have plain cylindrical peripheries with no provisions for wrenching onto mating threads. They are usually applied by hand tightening. Round nuts having part(s) of their cylindrical peripheries knurled to facilitate hand tightening are called knurled nuts.

Spline nuts. These internally threaded cylindrical fasteners have external splines or serrations that hold them in place when the nuts are forced into holes that are slightly smaller in diameter. They are also cast in place in plastics and low-strength, die cast alloys.

Internal wrenching nuts. These cylindrical nuts have sockets in their ends for wrenching (see Fig. 42-18).

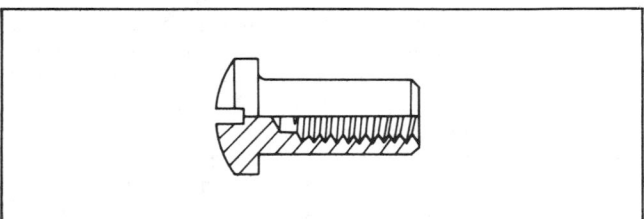

Fig. 42-17 Type 1 barrel nut with a fillister head.

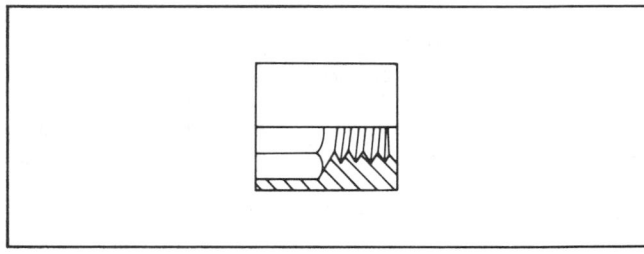

Fig. 42-18 Internal wrenching nut.

SCREWS

Screws are externally threaded fasteners capable of being inserted into holes in assembled parts, of mating with preformed internal threads, or of cutting or forming their own threads. They are generally tightened or released by rotating the screwheads. Because of their basic design, it is possible to use some screws, which are sometimes called bolts, in combination with nuts. Criteria for distinguishing between such screws and bolts are delineated in ANSI Standard B18.2.1, "Square and Hexagonal Bolts and Screws, Inch Series." ISO terminology identifies screws as having threads extending to their heads, with bolts having unthreaded portions under their heads.

Screws are available in a wide variety of types and sizes to suit specific requirements for different applications. Major types discussed in this section include machine screws, capscrews, setscrews, sems (screw and washer assemblies), and tapping screws.

Machine Screws

Machine screws are usually inserted into tapped holes, but are sometimes used with nuts. They are generally supplied with plain (as sheared) points, but for some special applications they are made with various types of points. Machine screws have slotted, recessed, or wrenching heads in a variety of styles and are usually made from steel, stainless steel, brass, or aluminum. Many machine screws are made from unhardened materials, but hardened screws are available.

Capscrews

Capscrews are manufactured to close dimensional tolerances and are designed for applications requiring high tensile strengths. Heat-treated, alloy steel capscrews have tensile strengths to 180 ksi (1240 MPa). Metric socket-head capscrews have tensile strengths varying from 830 to 1220 MPa. They are available in standard sizes from 1/4 to 3″ diam.

The shanks of capscrews are generally not fully threaded to their heads, but some are, and the ends are as specified in ANSI Standard B18.2.1. They are made with hex, socket, or fillister slotted heads (see Fig. 42-19). Low-head capscrews are available for applications having head clearance problems. Most capscrews are made from steels, stainless steels, brasses, bronzes, and aluminum alloys.

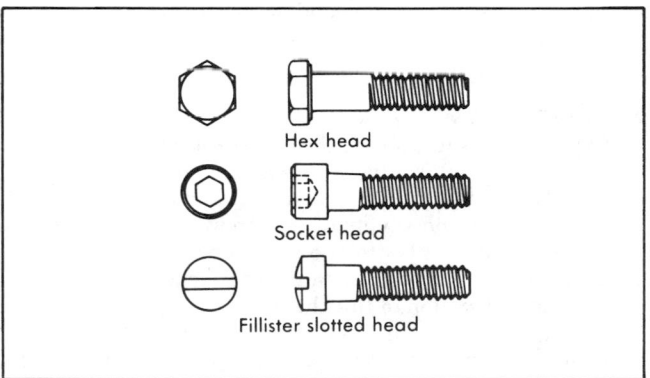

Fig. 42-19 Capscrews with various heads.

Setscrews

Setscrews (see Fig. 42-20) are hardened fasteners generally used to hold pulleys, gears, and other components on shafts. Hardness of the shaft is an important consideration in selecting a proper setscrew. They are available in various styles, with square-head, headless-slotted, hex-socket, and splined (fluted) socket styles being the most common. Holding power is provided by compressive forces, with some setscrews providing additional resistance to rotation by penetration of their points into the shaft material.

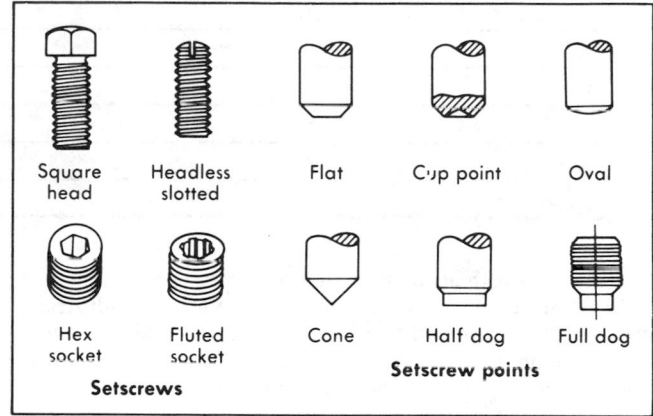

Fig. 42-20 Common types of setscrews and setscrew points.

Sems—Screw and Washer Assemblies

Sems is a generic word for a preassembled screw and washer fastener. The washer is placed on the screw blank prior to roll threading and becomes a permanent part of the assembly after roll threading, but is free to rotate. Sems are available in various combinations of head styles and washer types (see Fig. 42-21 and Table 42-1). Washers commonly used include flat (plain), conical, spring, and toothed lock washers. Some manufacturers

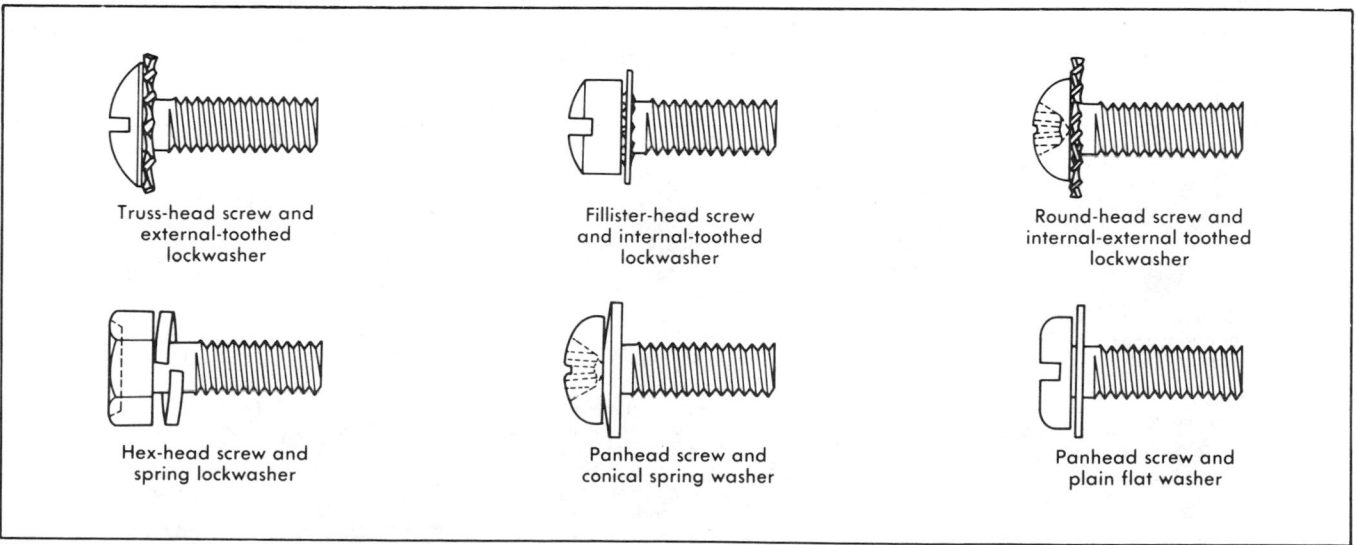

Fig. 42-21 Various screw and washer assemblies.[1]

THREADED FASTENERS

TABLE 42-1
Screw and Washer Assembly Combinations[2]

Screw Head Style	Toothed Lockwasher External	Internal	Internal-External	Spring Lockwasher	Conical Spring Washer	Plain Washer
Fillister		X	X	X	X	X
Flat	X					
Hex	X	X	X	X	X	X
Hex washer	X	X	X	X	X	
Oval	X					
Pan	X	X	X	X	X	X
Round	X	X	X	X	X	X
Truss	X	X	X	X	X	X
Hex socket	X	X	X	X		X

produce sems with as many as four washers per assembly.

Sems are used extensively in mass production industries, such as automotive and appliance, and are suitable for automatic assembly operations. These fasteners permit more convenient and rapid assembly by eliminating the need for a separate washer assembly operation, ensure the presence of the proper washer in each assembly, and prevent the loss of washers during maintenance.

Tapping Screws

Tapping screws (see Fig. 42-22) cut or form mating threads when driven into holes. Self-drilling, self-piercing, and special tapping screws are also available. They are made with slotted, recessed, or wrenching heads in various head styles and with spaced (coarse) inch or metric threads. Tapping screws are generally used in thin materials, but some can be driven through materials to 1/2" (12.7 mm) thick.

Advantages of tapping screws include rapid installation because nuts are not needed and access is required from only one side. Mating threads fit the screw threads closely, with no clearances necessary. Underhead serrations or nibs on some screws increase locking action and minimize thread stripout.

Captive Screws

Captive screws remain attached to panels or assembly components after they have been disengaged from their mating parts. Advantages include fast assembly and disassembly and elimination of the possibility of the screws coming loose and damaging other assembly components or becoming lost. Other types of captive (self-retained) threaded fasteners are discussed in a subsequent section of this chapter.

Various methods are used to attach the screws. Figure 42-23 illustrates a snap-in captive screw assembly. Retaining rings and nut retainers are used in some designs to captivate the screws, and split washers can be added after the screws have been inserted. Other designs use a ferrule or sleeve that is pressed, swaged, or flared to the assembly component. Captive screws are available with various head styles and drives, single or multiple-lead threads, and spring loading for partial or full retraction.

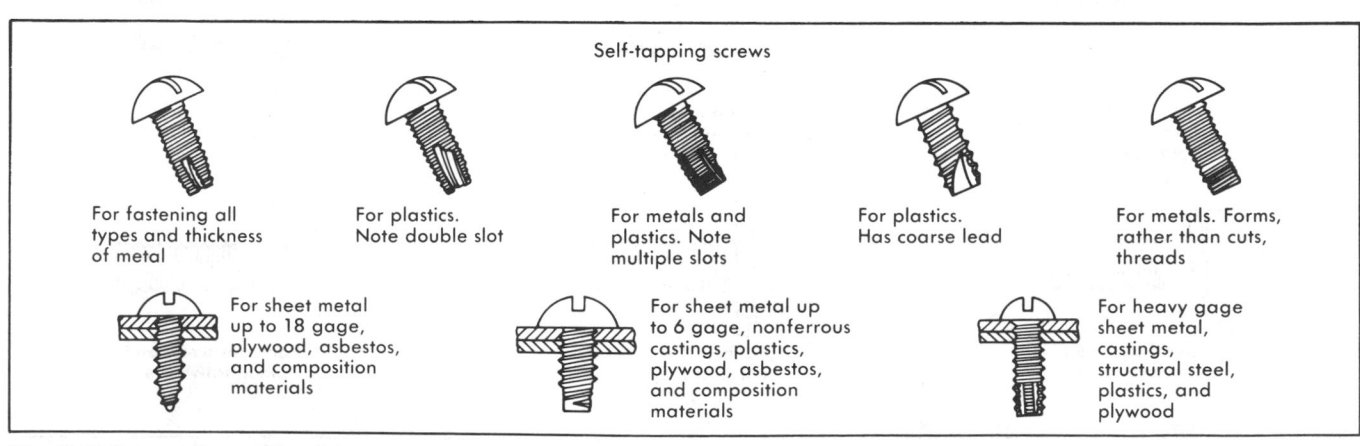

Fig. 42-22 Common types of tapping screws.

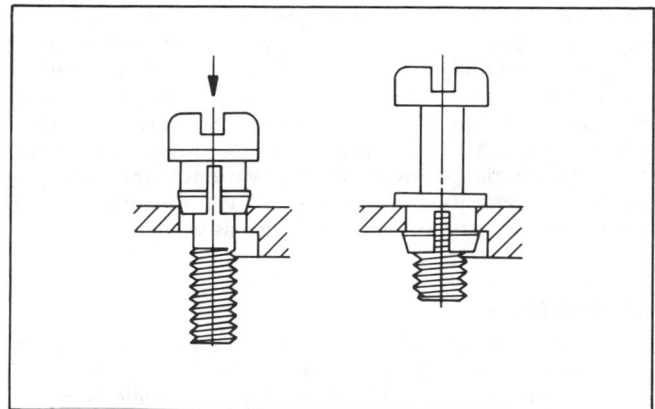

Fig. 42-23 Snap-in captive screw assembly. (*Specialty Fasteners Div., Rexnord*)

SCREW THREAD INSERTS

Screw thread inserts are threaded plugs or spiral coils that serve as tapped holes for bolts, studs, and screws. They provide strong threads, allowing frequent assembly and disassembly of externally threaded fasteners.

Applications

The major application for screw thread inserts is to provide strong threads in lightweight materials, such as plastics, aluminum, magnesium, and wood. Such lightweight materials are weaker and less resistant to wear than iron or steel, and the disadvantages of having to tap them can be avoided by using threaded inserts. Inserts are also used sometimes in hard materials to provide wear-resistant threads, thread-locking features, and to permit the repair of damaged assemblies by replacing the inserts. Certain floating types of inserts can be used to allow nuts to align themselves radially.

Assembly Design

It is important to design threaded assemblies to ensure the correct loading of mating parts. When designing clearance diameters of component parts, the insert and not the parent material should carry the load (see Fig. 42-24). The correct assembly is referred to as a "clamping condition" and the incorrect assembly as a "jackout" (torque tension) condition. However, with externally threaded inserts, the external thread transmits load to the parent material.

The insert length and external thread (on externally threaded inserts) allow selection so that the tensile strength of the assembly exceeds the tensile strength of the bolt or screw. The length of thread engagement required depends on the shear strength of the parent material. From a repairability standpoint, if the assembly is overloaded, the bolt should fail, not the insert assembly.

Types of Inserts

A wide selection of screw thread inserts, some of which are illustrated in Fig. 42-25, is available to suit various applications. Some, such as wire thread, solid bushing, thread-cutting, and thread-forming inserts, have both external threads (to hold the

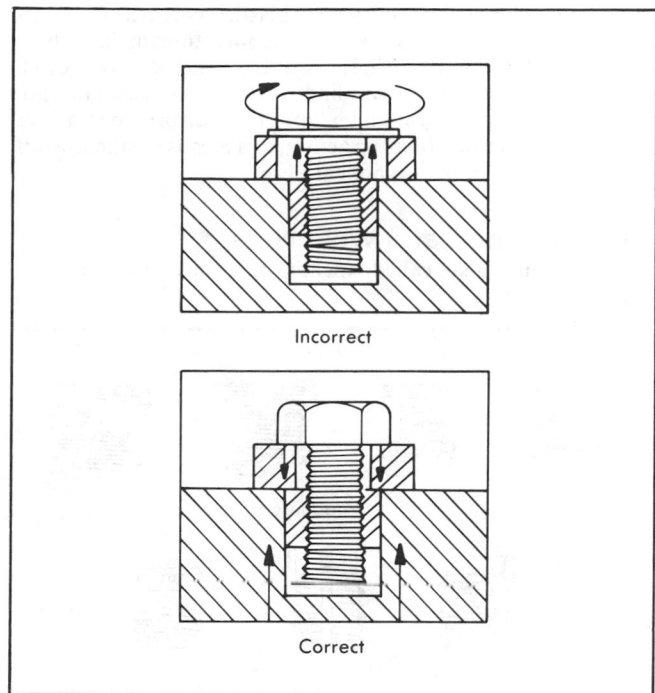

Fig. 42-24 Incorrect and correct methods of designing assemblies with screw thread inserts.

inserts in place) and internal threads (to accommodate the fasteners). Others, such as ultrasonic, expansion, mold-in, cast-in, potted-in, and press-in inserts, have only internal threads and are used in drilled or cored holes and solid or sandwich-panel or honeycomb materials.

CAPTIVE (SELF-RETAINED) THREADED FASTENERS

Captive threaded fasteners are preassembled to and become an integral part of assembly components (panels, brackets, and chassis). They are captivated fasteners used for the subsequent acceptance of mating fasteners, such as bolts, studs, nuts, or screws. The fasteners are captivated by various means, including riveting, welding, pressing, caging, clinching, and swaging.

Advantages of Captive Fasteners

Captive fasteners can provide strong threads in thin materials, permitting repeated assembly and disassembly of their mating fasteners. For some applications, they permit the use of thinner materials in assemblies. Captive fasteners permit fastening from one side of assemblies in blind locations, resist loosening, ensure the positive positioning of mating fasteners, and minimize the possible loss of fasteners. Versatility is another advantage of captive fasteners: they can be installed during fabrication of a product, many can be installed after components have been coated or painted, or they can be finished as part of the assembly.

Typical Applications

Captive fasteners are used in many different consumer, industrial, and military products. They are commonly used in

THREADED FASTENERS

sheet metal, die castings, or molded plastics where the materials are too soft or thin to permit tapping threads or where additional thread strength is required. They are also often necessary for inaccessible or blind locations. As inserts for thin components or printed circuit boards, they can provide features of prevailing torque, floating action, or a means of standing off a secondary panel or component.

Plate, Anchor, and Weld Nuts

Plate nuts, also called anchor nuts, have one or more mounting lugs projecting from the bases of their threaded bodies or a flange (see Fig. 42-26) for permanent attachment by riveting or welding to the surface of the part to be assembled. When multiple nuts are required, channel assemblies consisting of a number of nuts in a long mounting carrier are used. Some forms of plate nuts are called T-nuts. Mounting lugs on the baseplate and flanges are available in various shapes and sizes to suit requirements. Prong-type nuts have straight or twisted projections that grip soft materials such as wood.

Caged Nuts

In caged nuts, a standard nut, usually square, is retained in a spring-steel box or cage (see Fig. 42-27). The nuts can be staked to the retainers or assembled loosely to provide float for possible misalignment. Lugs on the retainers can be snapped into square holes, slipped over panel edges, or locked behind panels. On some designs, the lugs engage and lock the threads of the mating fastener. Advantages of caged nuts include eliminating the need for riveting, welding, clinching, or staking, but they are usually hand installed. These nuts also permit easy replacement in case of thread damage during assembly or while in service.

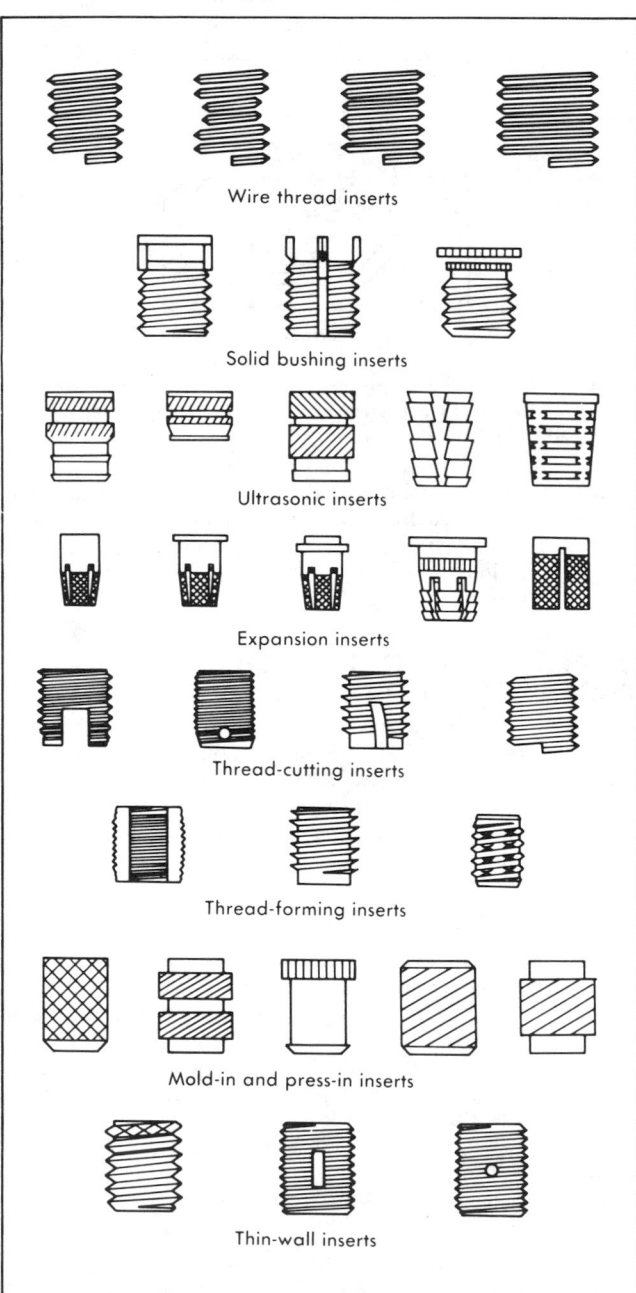

Fig. 42-25 Some of the many types of screw thread inserts. (*Heli-Coil Products, Div. of Mite Corp.*)

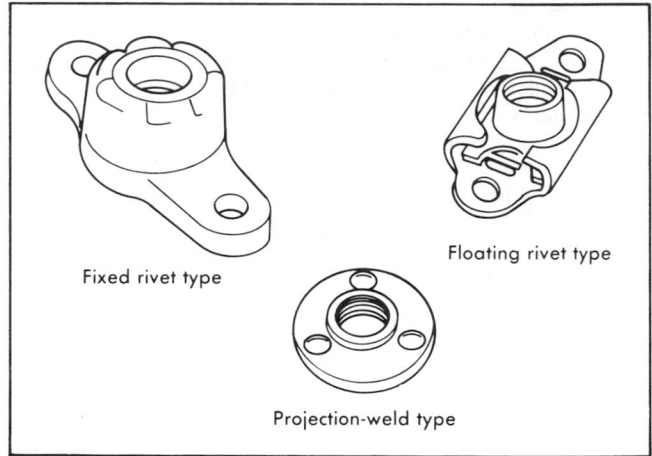

Fig. 42-26 Several types of plate, anchor, and weld nuts.

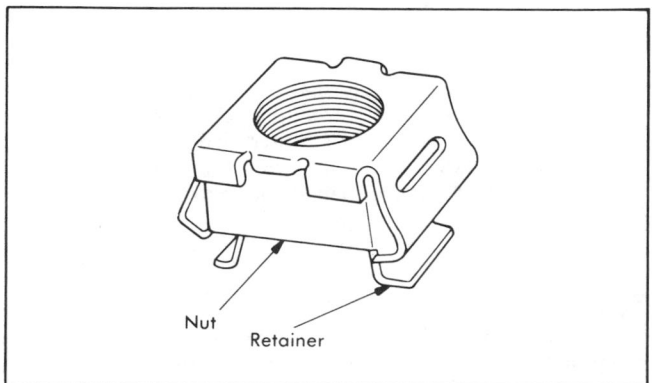

Fig. 42-27 Caged nut.

Other Push or Snap-In Fasteners

Nuts similar to plate or anchor nuts, having internally threaded bushings and baseplates, are available for pushing or snapping into assembly components. These fasteners, sometimes called clip nuts, eliminate the need for riveting or welding, but are generally limited to lighter duty applications.

A push-in type, panel-retained fastener is illustrated in Fig. 42-28. Two spring-resilient loop legs extend from a flat plate in which there is a single helical thread for accepting a tapping screw. When the fastener is pushed into a hole in a panel, the two loops compress together and then snap back, with the shoulder tops pressing firmly against the back of the panel for retention. When the screw is applied, it experiences prevailing-torque resistance from the helical-form thread. Removal is prevented by the blocking of the shoulder sections of the loops, thus keeping them from deflecting inward. The fastener can be used in both sheet metal and plastics.

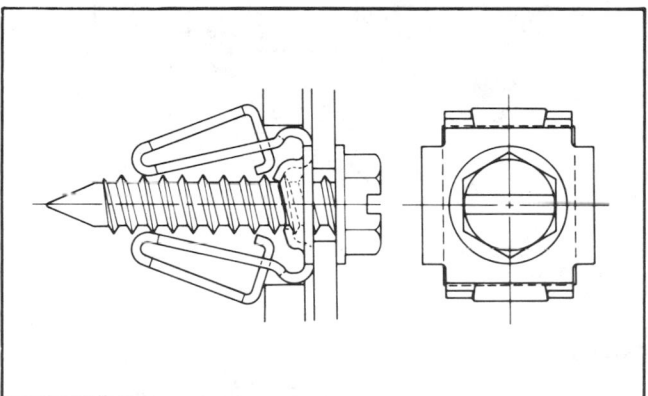

Fig. 42-28 Push-in type, panel-retained fastener. (*Fasteners Div., TRW Assemblies & Fasteners Group***)**

Clinched Nuts

These captive fasteners are solid nuts having pilot collars projecting from one end. The collar is inserted into a hole in the assembly component and spread, flared, or rolled over to produce a "clinch" (see Fig. 42-29). Possible limitations are that special tooling is required for clinching, and the nut collars must be soft enough to permit plastic flow. Also, hole diameters must be held to close tolerances, generally a total of 0.003-0.004″ (0.08-0.10 mm).

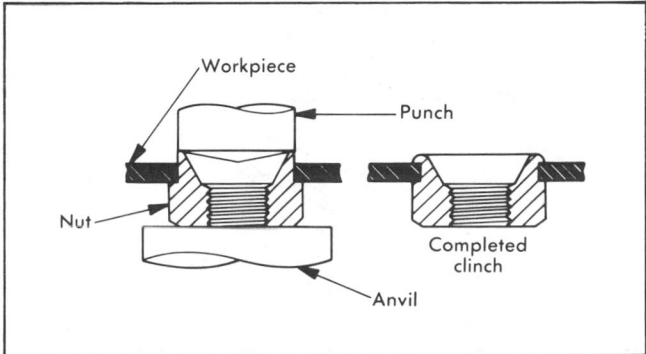

Fig. 42-29 Installation of clinch nut.

Self-Clinching Fasteners

Self-clinching nuts, sometimes called press nuts, have a pilot shank containing knurls or ribs and an undercut, recess, or groove (see Fig. 42-30). They are installed simply by pressing into holes in the sheet materials. All self-clinching fasteners must be harder than the materials into which they are inserted to effect cold flow of the materials instead of distortion of the fasteners. For this reason, most are heat treated.

Various designs of self-clinching fasteners (see Fig. 42-31) include blind, floating, self-locking, floating self-locking, prevailing-torque, and removable nut features. Broaching-type self-clinching fasteners are used extensively in printed circuit boards made of plastics. Specially formed axial grooves around the fastener shank broach (cut) into the boards, creating a firm interference fit. In addition to nuts, self-clinching fasteners are available as

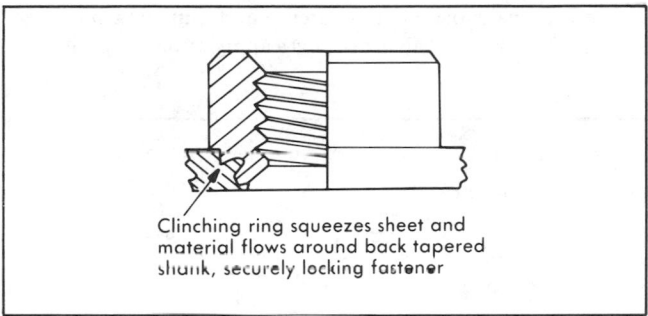

Fig. 42-30 Self-clinching nut. (*Penn Engineering & Mfg. Corp.***)**

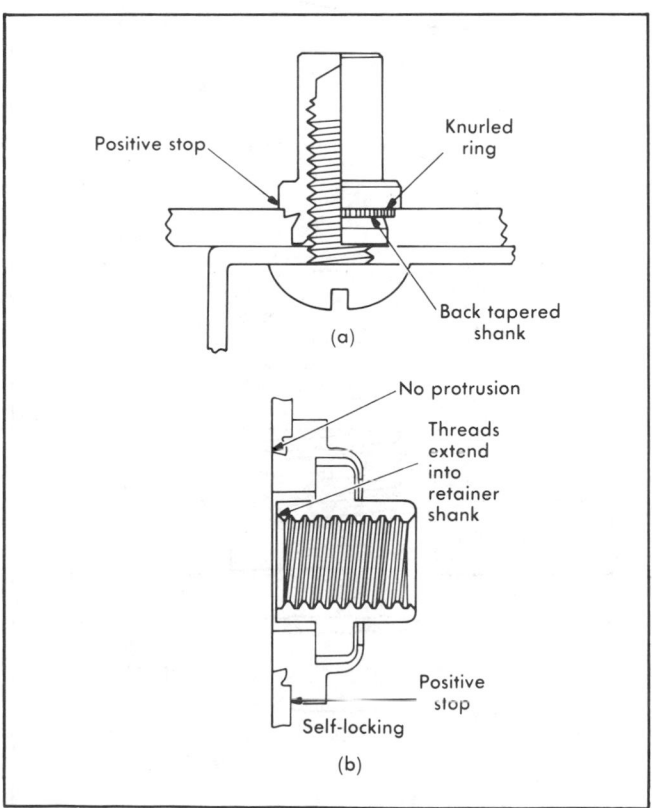

Fig. 42-31 Self-clinching fasteners: (a) blind and (b) floating. (*Penn Engineering & Mfg. Corp.***)**

THREADED FASTENERS

inserts (flush on both sides), studs, nonthreaded pins (used as guides), and spacers and standoffs to hold assembly components apart from each other .

Self-Piercing Fasteners

Self-piercing and clinching nuts for thin sheet materials generally have a piloted body, an undercut or back tapered pilot, and a shoulder or embossment feature (see Fig. 42-32, view *a*). When pressed into an assembly component, they pierce their own mounting holes, and material from the component flows into the undercuts or around the back tapered pilots for secure fastening. They are available in strip form for feeding under a press ram or in loose bulk form for hopper feeding. The assembly components must be fixtured or automatically located to ensure proper fastener location.

Another category of self-piercing and clinching nuts (see Fig. 42-32, view *b*) for higher strength applications is specifically designed for use in structural bracket components formed from thicker sheet and plate materials.

Nut Retainers

Nut retainers (see Fig. 42-33) are clinched in position by the controlled collapse of the portions that extend through the attachment holes. They are used extensively for blind-side installations and are available made from steel, aluminum, and various other metals, and in different styles. Flush mounting with countersunk heads and closed ends for watertight installations are two of the more common types, in addition to the flanged-head style shown. For additional antirotation protection, keyed or hex styles are available.

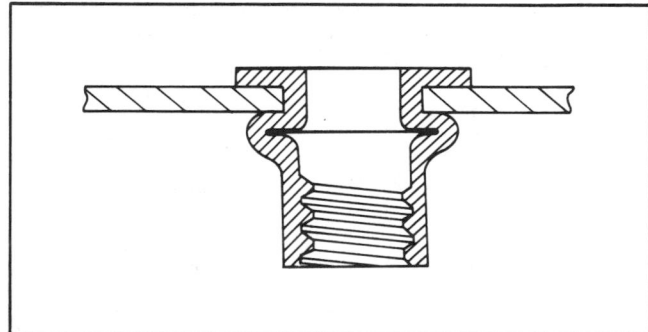

Fig. 42-33 Nut retainer.

Studs

Studs and other externally threaded fasteners are available in self-clinching designs (see Fig. 42-34, view *a*). Weld studs and screws (view *b*) are also available. For capacitor-discharge

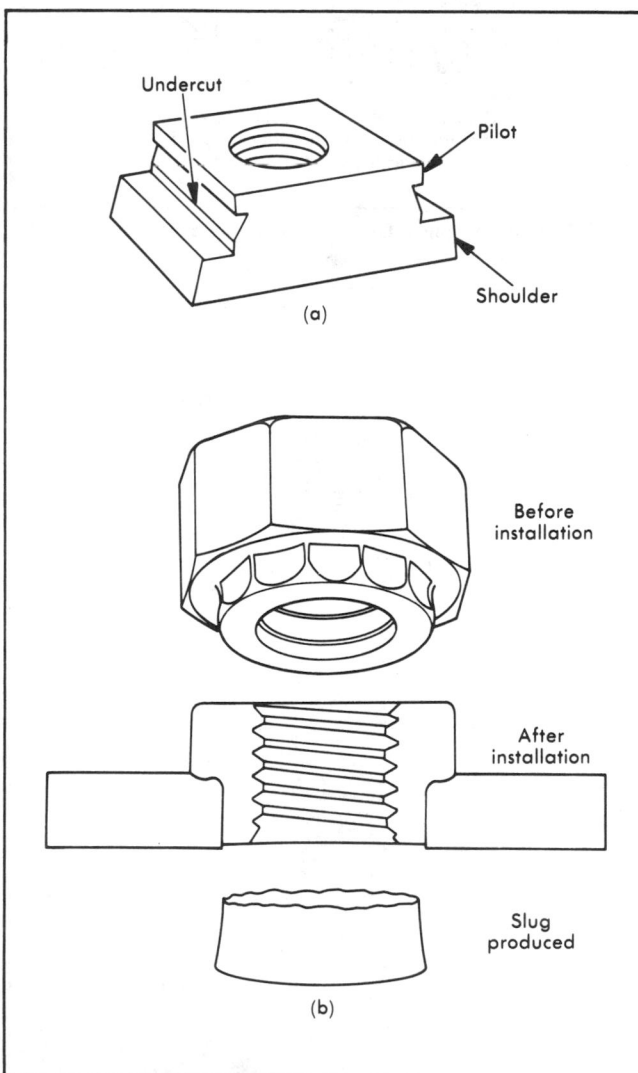

Fig. 42-32 Self-piercing and clinching nuts. (*Russell, Burdsall & Ward Corp.*)

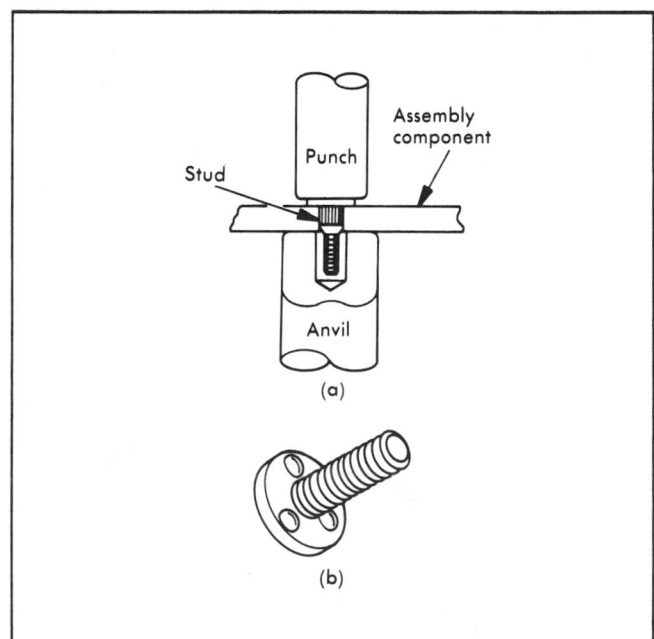

Fig. 42-34 Captive fasteners: (a) stud with knurled shank and (b) weld screw with projection-weld projections under head.)

welding, weld studs and screws are made with a single, small projection in the center of their heads. Projection welding by capacitor discharge permits attaching studs to thin metal with minimum distortion or discoloration. However, some large studs must be arc welded in place.

Self-clinching studs are supplied for flush head mounting, with thin heads for mounting to thin sheet, and as structural studs, with heads stronger in tension than the threads. All are simply pressed into thin sheet metal and become self-retained with a simple punch and anvil. Broaching studs can be used for pressing into brittle materials, such as printed circuit boards.

Bolt-Nut Combination

A self-retaining, positive-locking bolt-nut combination is shown in Fig. 42-35. The fastener consists of a retained receptacle assembly attached to the blind surface (inside) of a structure and a sleevebolt that passes through and is retained in the attachment or panel. Self-locking is provided by the configuration of the internal threads in the sleevebolt.

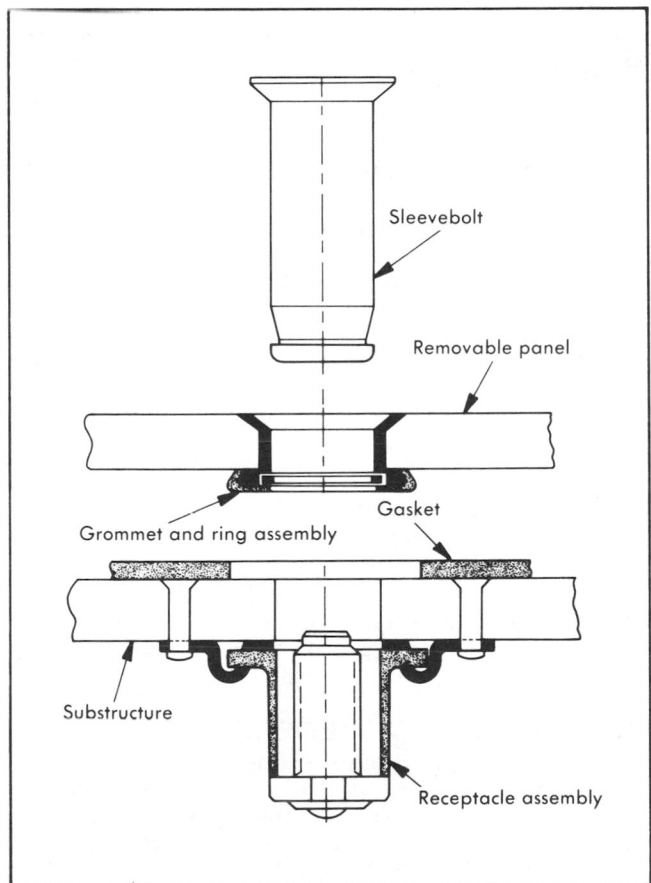

Fig. 42-35 Self-retaining, positive-locking bolt-nut combination. (*SPS Technologies*)

SELF-LOCKING
THREADED FASTENERS

There are many different types of self-locking fasteners available, each having some advantages and disadvantages. Most of these fasteners are satisfactory for some applications,

but no one type is suitable for all applications. The three basic types of self-locking fasteners are: free-spinning, prevailing-torque, and chemical locking. Locknuts are more common than locking bolts or screws. Self-locking types of screw thread inserts are discussed previously in this chapter.

Free-Spinning Fasteners

Captive toothed washers. Free-spinning devices for self-locking are provided on bolts, nuts, or screws, usually in the form of toothed captive washers that facilitate assembly but increase cost. However, while fastener costs are higher, assembled costs are generally lower.

Integral teeth. Self-locking fasteners having integral teeth or serrations (see Fig. 42-36) use the preloaded tension of the fasteners for part of the locking action, but add mechanical engagement between bolt or screwhead, or nut, and the bearing surface. This provides an additional amount that the pretension must relax before fastener disengagement.

Spring washers. Spring washers, of cylindrically curved, waveform, conical, Belleville, or helical design (all discussed later in this chapter), add some slight additional tension to the amount applied in preloading. While there are many different designs of these so-called self-locking fasteners with spring washers, most should be tightened sufficiently to flatten the washers. Performance varies with different designs.

Self-locking threads. Special or modified taps are also used to produce self-locking threads in locknuts (see Fig. 42-37). At the bottom of the nut thread, the thread is angled to form a wedge ramp. Wider clearances thus provided permit easy rotation of the nut for assembly, making it a free-spinning

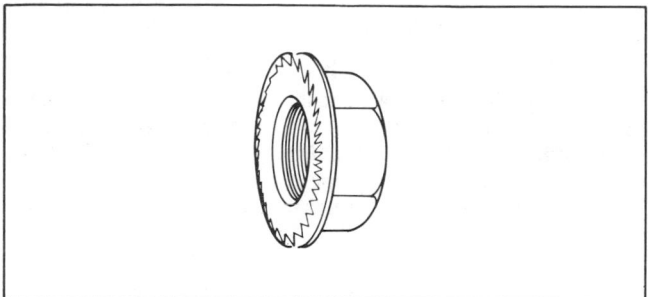

Fig. 42-36 Ratchet-shaped serrated teeth on flange of locknut embed into bearing surface for locking action.

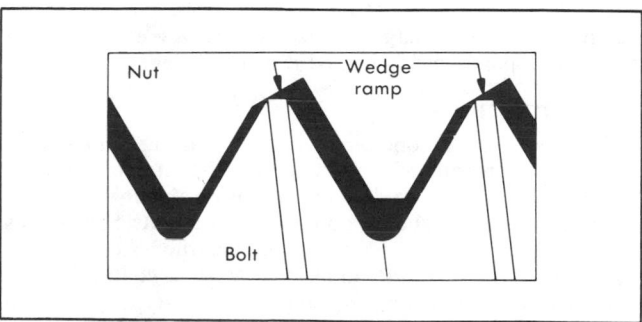

Fig. 42-37 Special or modified taps produce self-locking threads in locknuts. Wedge ramps force bolt threads into locking position. (*Spralock Nut, Microdot*)

SPECIAL-PURPOSE FASTENERS

fastener. However, when the nut is seated, tightening pulls the bolt threads along the wedge ramps for metal-to-metal thread mating and self-locking. A clamp load is essential for optimum performance of this type of self-locking thread.

Prevailing-Torque Fasteners

Prevailing-torque fasteners are based on an interference fit between the mating threads. Unlike free-spinning fasteners, they require continuous tightening during installation. However, prevailing-torque fasteners do not require contact with seating surfaces; they stay in whatever position where tightening stops as the result of their built-in self-locking action. The locking torque is generally retained independent of the clamping load. The two major kinds of prevailing-torque fasteners are the plastic additive types and all-metal fasteners with distorted or deflected thread types.

Chemical Locking

Chemical locking as a method of minimizing the loosening of threaded fasteners is accomplished by coating the fasteners with an adhesive. Adhesives commonly used and methods of applying include using strips of two-component epoxies, applying a single-component anaerobic at assembly, and preapplying microencapsulated epoxies or anaerobics. Certain types of cyanoacrylate adhesives are also being used. All of the adhesives are available in different strengths to suit application requirements.

Advantages of using adhesives for locking include simple and easy application and curing, and good performance under severe service conditions. Adhesives provide a fluid seal and prevent corrosion of the threads. Anaerobic adhesives remain liquid while exposed to air, but when oxygen is excluded by the mating threads, they cure rapidly. Curing produces a thermoset bond, providing a solid plastic, zero-clearance fit between the mating threads, regardless of the thread tolerances.

Limitations of using adhesives for locking are that the shelf life of most adhesives is about one to four years, not all metals or plastics can be bonded with equal strength, and their use is restricted by temperature and other environmental conditions.

SPECIAL-PURPOSE FASTENERS

Special fasteners, including threaded and nonthreaded types, sometimes perform several functions and often reduce assembly costs or the number of parts required for an assembly. In some cases, they permit the use of thinner and less expensive panel materials by using the strength of the fasteners to meet requirements. Some special fasteners may cost more than standard fasteners, and their use should therefore be based on reduced assembly costs and/or improved product quality.

QUICK-OPERATING FASTENERS

Many quick-operating fasteners, also called quick-release fasteners, are now being used so extensively that they are no longer considered to be special-purpose fasteners. They are used most commonly when repetitive access to components is required. Major types of quick-operating fasteners include turn-operated, lever-actuated, lift-and-turn (a combination of turn-operated and lever-actuated), slide-action, push or pull, magnetic-action, and various designs of hose clamps. The types include turn-operated, stud-receptacle fasteners with fast-lead threads; fasteners that operate with push-action draw latches that pull edge-mating panels together; slide latches that retain edge-mating panels perpendicular to their surface planes; and detent latches using magnetic attraction or a specially shaped stud that expands spring-loaded receptacle blades.

SPRING CLIPS

Spring clips are one-piece stamped fasteners or simple assemblies, generally self-retaining, that slip into holes or onto panel edges. They are held by spring tension and do not require secondary fasteners, such as bolts, screws, or rivets. Spring clips are usually made from hardened, high-carbon steel, but are available in other metals and plastics. Various coatings can be applied to suit application requirements. Dart-type spring clips have dart-shaped retainers to engage the holes or panels. Spring clips are made in many different shapes to hold various assembly components.

TAMPER-RESISTANT FASTENERS

Tamper-resistant fasteners, such as screws, bolts, quick-operating types, and other fasteners, are designed to be difficult to disassemble, thus minimizing unauthorized entry, vandalism, or theft. This is often accomplished by providing the fasteners with unusual heads, such as special sockets or recesses, standard sockets with integral pins or inserts, heads with one-way slots or nonstandard shapes, and breakoff (breakaway) heads. Such fasteners generally require the use of special tools for disassembly. Fasteners can be made permanent by riveting, welding, or adhesive bonding.

EXPANDING FASTENERS

Fasteners that expand radially when an axial load is applied remove clearances between the holes and the fasteners, thus ensuring rigid joints. Typical applications include linkage and structural joints, and as rod-end bearing pins. Assemblies with expanding fasteners permit periodic adjustments to compensate for wear or to vary the fit as desired.

SELF-SEALING FASTENERS

When required to retain gases or liquids, fasteners are available with preassembled or built-in seals. The choice of sealing material, such as rubber, neoprene, silicone, nylon, or polyethylene, depends on the pressure and temperature to which the seal will be exposed, possible reaction of the material to the gas or liquid, environmental factors such as corrosion, and cost. Some thread-locking materials and interference fits, discussed previously in this chapter, serve as seals for some applications.

FASTENERS MADE OF PLASTICS

The increasing use of fasteners made of plastics makes them no longer special-purpose assembly components. Threaded fasteners being made of plastics include bolts, studs, nuts, and screws; nonthreaded fasteners include rivets, washers, retaining rings, and pins.

Advantages of plastic fasteners include low cost, light weight, corrosion and chemical resistance, and electric insulation. Versatility is another advantage; fasteners can be produced in various colors, with molded-in inserts, and in special shapes. Dimensional standards for fasteners made of plastics are the same as for metal fasteners. A possible limitation is lower load-carrying capacity than metal fasteners.

MECHANICAL FASTENERS FOR PLASTICS

The more extensive use of plastics in various products and the many types of plastics available have increased the demand for special fasteners. Advantages of such fasteners over standard types often include lower torque requirements for driving the fasteners into assemblies, higher shear strengths because of the special threads used, and the capability of withstanding higher torque loads before the fastener threads begin to strip the plastics. Screw thread inserts, discussed previously in this chapter, are used extensively to hold fasteners in plastics.

Many types of special fasteners are available because requirements vary with the plastics used in the assemblies. The plastics must be sufficiently strong to withstand the strain of fastener insertion, and the fasteners must distribute the loads and stresses properly. General requirements for special fasteners used in plastics include large flank areas on their threads, wide thread spacing, and sharp threads.

Special fasteners of the thread-forming type, which eliminate the need for tapping and inserts, thus resulting in lower costs, are used most extensively for softer plastics. Thread-cutting fasteners are more common for harder plastics. Metal inserts are sometimes provided in the plastics components, especially if the fasteners must be removed periodically. Most fasteners are available with a variety of head and point styles.

FASTENERS FOR COMPOSITE MATERIALS

The advent of advanced composite materials, which are finding increased use in the aircraft and aerospace industries because of their strength and light weight, has posed some fastening problems. Many metallic fasteners are fairly incompatible with composite materials because of corrosion. Stainless steel and titanium fasteners work relatively well for composites, but stainless steel introduces some weight penalties, and titanium results in increased costs.

One design for a sleeve-and-pin type fastener made of glass-reinforced epoxy is illustrated in Fig. 42-38. When these fasteners are made from thermosetting plastics, they are installed with an adhesive. When made from thermoplastic materials, they swell on installation, thus eliminating the need for close hole tolerances.

BOLT-NUT COMBINATION

A self-retaining, positive-locking bolt-nut combination is shown in Fig. 42-39. The locking feature of this special-purpose fastener consists of a spring-loaded plunger pin loaded and two hardened steel balls positioned within the shank of the bolt. Spring force maintains the plunger in an extended position, securely maintaining the balls in an expanded position. This expansion provides a mechanical lock with mating axial grooves or splines in the nut. To unlock the fastener, it is necessary to depress the plunger pin, which allows the balls to retract and permits the nut to rotate freely on the bolt. Because of the hollow design of the bolt, tension applications should be avoided. Shear applications, such as clevis joints, where the bolt-nut is free to turn with the joint, are the primary uses for this type of fastener.

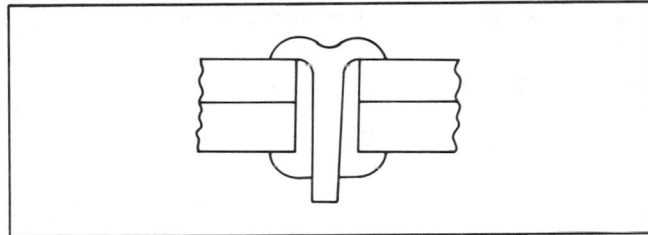

Fig. 42-38 Glass-reinforced epoxy fastener for use with composite materials.

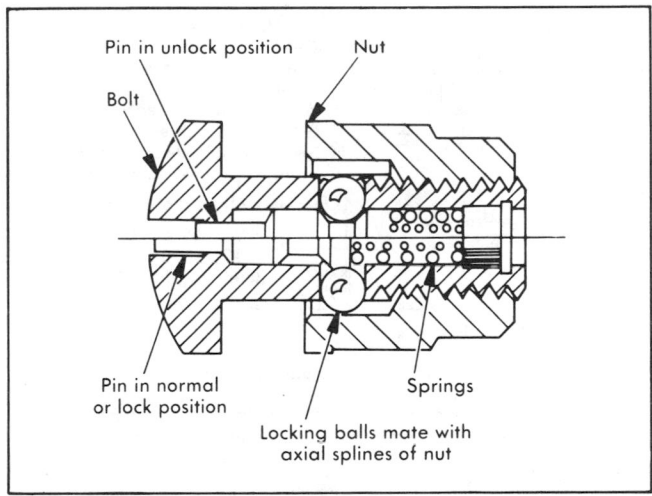

Fig. 42-39 Self-retaining, positive-locking bolt-nut combination. (*Specialty Fastener Div., Rexnord*)

RIVETS

A rivet is a one-piece, unthreaded, permanent fastener consisting of a head and a body. It is used for fastening two or more pieces together by passing the body through a hole in each piece and then clinching or forming a second head on the body end. Once set in place, a rivet cannot be removed except by chipping off the head or clinched end. The terminology for a rivet and riveted joint is illustrated in Fig. 42-40.

A major advantage of rivets is that they can be installed economically and rapidly and are suitable for automatic assembly operations. Other advantages include low cost and the

RIVETS

fact that rivets are good for joining dissimilar materials of different hardnesses or thicknesses. A possible limitation is that the impact required for clinching can deform thin sheets. Rivets with large heads or washers can be used to spread the stresses. Rivets are usually less expensive than threaded fasteners, but their strength in shear or tension may be lower, especially when compared with heat-treated bolts.

Riveting is the primary fastening method used by the aircraft and aerospace industries for joining together members such as skins, channels, spars, and other structural components and subassemblies. The process is also used in many other industries for a wide variety of assemblies. In addition to their use as fasteners, rivets also serve as electrical contacts, inserts, spacers, and pivot shafts.

RIVET TYPES

There are six basic types of small rivets: solid, semitubular, tubular, bifurcated (split), compression, and special solid types as shown in Fig. 42-41. Structural rivets are large-diameter solid rivets (1/2″ diam and over). Blind rivets and eyelets are discussed in subsequent sections of this chapter.

Rivet Caps

Caps are often used in combination with full-tubular and split rivets to conceal the clinch. Functioning as a washer, the cap prevents the clinch from tearing through the material, adds strength, and gives the appearance of a second head.

Structural Rivets

Large rivets, 1/2″ diam and larger, commonly called structural rivets, are cold squeezed or compressed, depending on the application. For structural steel work, rivet diameters range from 1.2 to 1.4 times the square root of the thickness of the thickest of the riveted plates. Smaller sizes are usually preferred for multiple-riveted joints. For aluminum, the rivet diameter usually ranges from one to three times the thickness of the thickest plate that it holds, depending on the anticipated stresses.

Metal Piercing Rivets

Thin metals can be pierced by semitubular, tubular, split, and pointed rivets. With semitubular and tubular rivets, piercing is done by the tubular walls of the rivets; with split rivets, piercing is accomplished with the legs or prongs of the rivets. The walls and legs are sometimes hardened to facilitate piercing. Metals pierced with such rivets include low-carbon steels and aluminum alloys, generally having a hardness less than $R_B 50$.

Pointed rivets do not pass through both parts to be joined and do not require clinching. They generally have a groove behind their pointed end into which material from the assembly

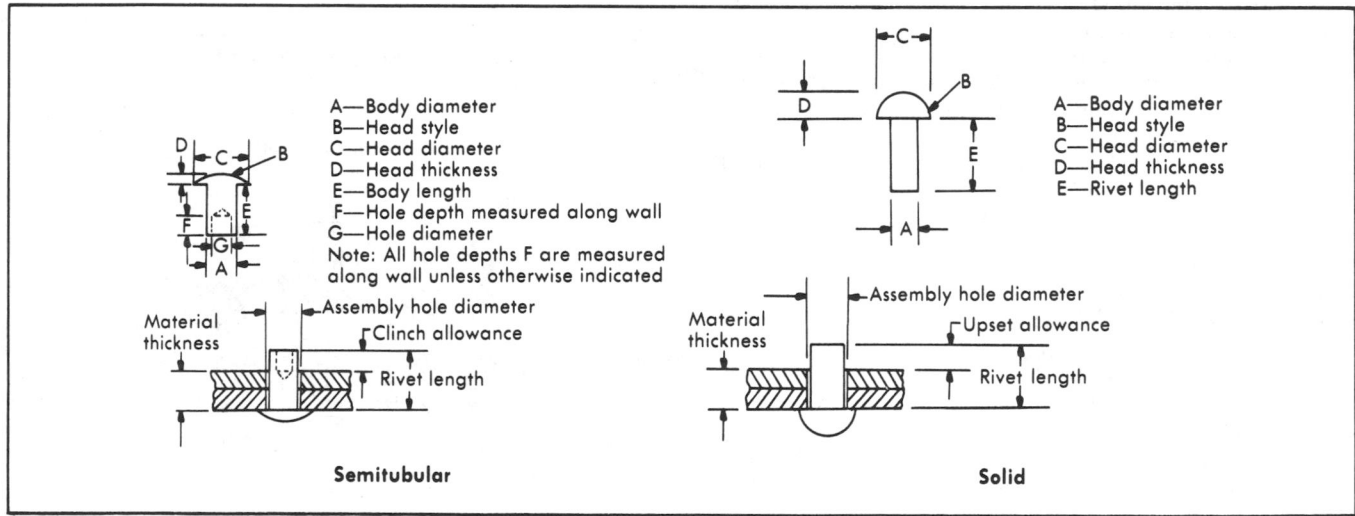

Fig. 42-40 Rivet and riveted joint terminology. (*Brainard Rivet Co.*)

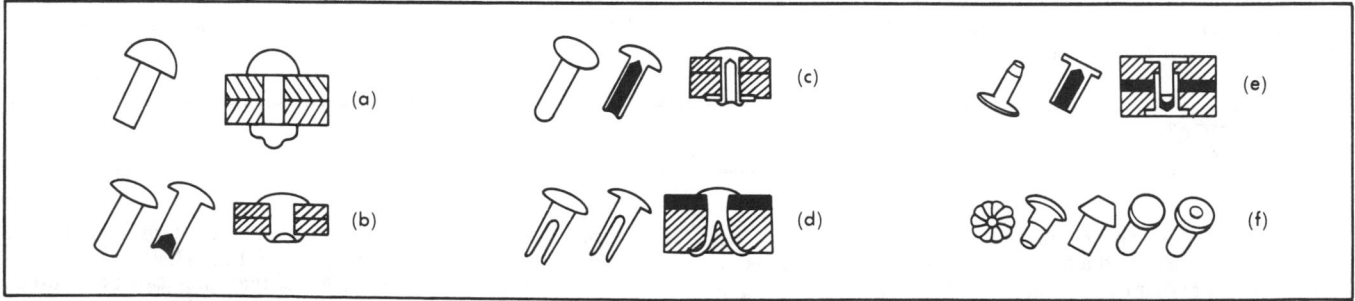

Fig. 42-41 Types of small rivets: (a) solid, (b) semitubular, (c) tubular, (d) bifurcated (split), (e) compressions, and (f) special rivets with decorative heads and various shoulders.

component flows for locking purposes. Pointed rivets are generally limited to light-duty applications such as attaching nameplates.

PORTABLE RIVETING TOOLS

It is important that the correct shape and size of riveting tool be used and that excessive driving pressures be avoided. Excessive pressure in driving may result in bulging of the edge of the piece being riveted; buckling or other distortion, particularly if thin material is used; and weakening or fracturing of metal adjacent to the hole.

Pneumatic Hammers

Portable pneumatic hammers are used extensively for riveting. These tools operate with compressed air that accelerates a mass and transfers force through a rivet, the force stopping on impact with a bucking bar and forming a head on the rivet. They may be of the one-shot, slow-hitting, or fast-hitting type. One-shot pneumatic hammers are the easiest to control because the rivet is driven with a single blow. However, one-shot hammers cannot be used to rivet thin sheets because of the danger of damaging the sheet, and they are limited as to size and alloy of rivet that can be driven.

Squeeze Riveters

The best control in riveting is obtained by using a squeeze (compression-type) riveter. A squeeze riveter differs from a pneumatic hammer in that the set and the buck (called dollies) are integral parts, and the upset is produced by a slow squeezing action. After this type of riveter is set up, it is relatively easy to produce properly upset shanks with well-centered heads. However, squeeze riveters are slower than hammers and their use is limited by the structural design of the assembly. Because of the latter factor, squeeze riveters are used primarily for subassembly work.

RIVETING MACHINES

Manual or automatic riveting machines, bench or floor-mounted (see Fig. 42-42), use the same principle of operation as portable riveting tools. The rivet is fed from the hopper to a track that deposits it, shank down, in the center of the upper jaws (see Fig. 42-43). As the cycle proceeds, a driver descends and contacts the rivet head, forcing it downward past the point where the jaws come to a stop. This action pushes the rivet through the jaws and onto a spring-mounted plunger on the lower arm of the machine. With continued downward motion, the plunger pin retracts and guides the rivet through the work until it bottoms against the lower die and is clinched. When the driver and the jaws retract, the plunger pushes the rivet and work off the die.

AUTOMATIC DRILLING AND RIVETING MACHINES

The high cost, low production rates, and inconsistent results associated with manual riveting, especially for joining aluminum components in the aircraft industry, has led to the extensive use of automation in fastening. Machines are available that automatically position and clamp the assembly, drill and/or countersink the required holes, feed and insert the proper rivets, head the rivets by upsetting, and unclamp the assembly.

In addition to extensive use by the commercial aircraft industry, automatic fastening is being applied in a growing number of

other industries. Materials joined include aluminum, titanium, and other metal alloys, as well as composite materials. The automatic machines are also being used for the application of threaded fasteners, nut plates, and blind fasteners, in addition to rivets.

Applications include the assembly of helicopter tail sections, cargo-bay doors for the space shuttle, dish-shaped antennas, and components for military vehicles. The technology is also being used in the primary assembly line for the all-aluminum

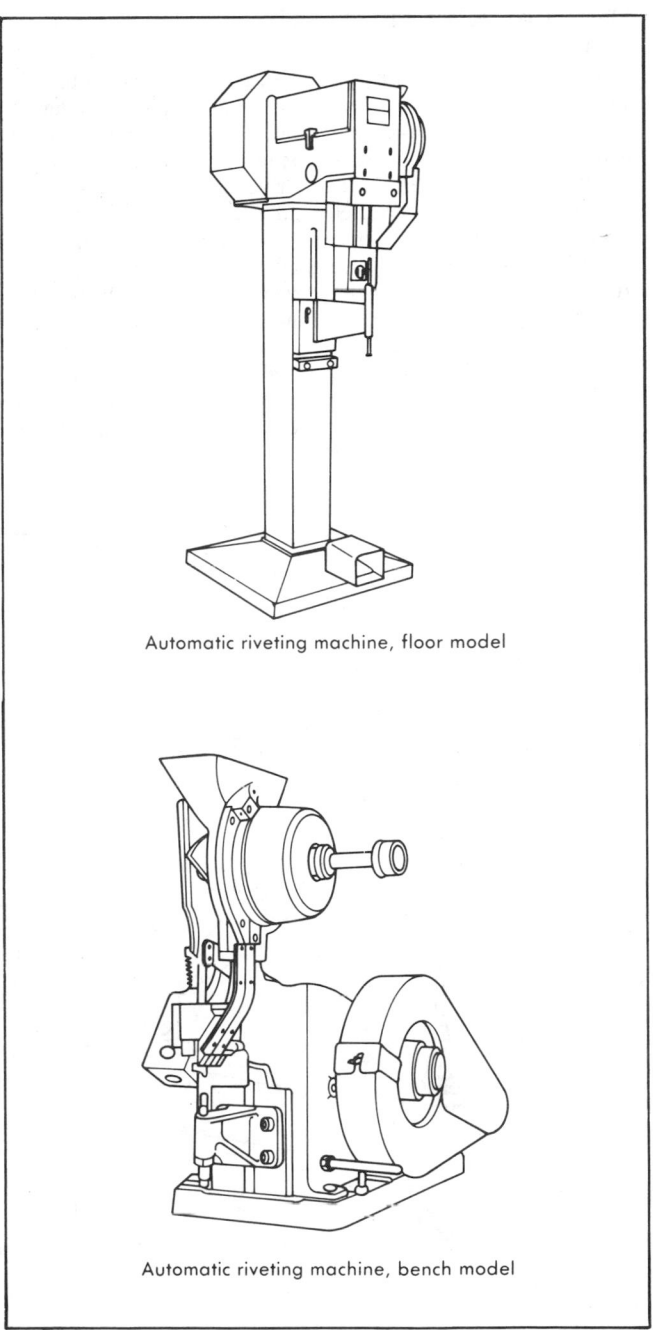

Automatic riveting machine, floor model

Automatic riveting machine, bench model

Fig. 42-42 Floor and bench models of automatic riveting machines.

RIVETS

Hummer vehicle, which is now being produced to replace the U.S. Army jeep.

Automatic drilling and riveting machines are also being used for the application of slug rivets—low-cost, headless slugs of aluminum alloy. The slugs are hydraulically squeezed from both ends, forming leakproof interference fits. This technique has eliminated the need for fuel tanks previously built into the wings of large aircraft. By making fuel storage integral with the wings (called wet wings), fuel-carrying capacity has been increased and weight and complexity of the wings decreased.

ORBITAL RIVETING

Orbital riveting (see Fig. 42-44) is a low-pressure, line-of-contact (T), cold forming process. The riveting tool, mounted in a rotating spindle, is inclined at a slight angle (3-6°) so that the tool axis intersects the centerline, P, of the spindle at the working end of the tool. As the orbiting tool is fed toward the work, material at the end of the rivet shank is incrementally displaced to form the required head. Machines are available for pneumatic or hydraulic operation and in bench, floor, and opposed-head models. Modular heads that fit most machines are also available with one or more spindles. Multispindle systems with center distances ranging from 3/16 to 20" (5 to 508 mm) and multilevel assembly systems are being used.

An important advantage of orbital riveting is the consistently high-quality results attained, with close tolerances and smooth finishes. Because there is no impact between the tooling and the workpiece, the process is quiet.

RADIAL RIVETING

Radial riveting is similar to orbital riveting except that the tools move in a planetary or rosette motion instead of being mounted in rotating spindles. In the rosette forming pattern, R, shown in Fig. 42-45, each loop of the rosette path is guided through center Z. The longitudinal axis of the riveting tool always overlaps the center of rivet point N. A cycloidal movement guides the tool through the rosette pattern. The rivet material is spread radially outward and inward, with some tangential overlapping, to form the required head.

Advantages of radial riveting are the same as those just discussed for orbital riveting. However, radial riveting is said to impart improved conductivity to the materials because of the kneading action. As a result, it is used extensively in the production of electrical contact points.

ELECTROMAGNETIC RIVETING

Electromagnetic riveting (EMR) allows fast semi to fully automatic, single-impact riveting with the advantages of built-in repeatability and quality assurance. Systems used for electromagnetic riveting are capable of installing up to 20 rivets per minute. They can also install rivets made from various materials up to 3/4" diam and allow rapid changes of conventional rivet dies to easily adapt to varying end uses. With EMR, rivets can be installed to precision interference profiles for fluidtight and fatigue-critical applications.

BLIND RIVETS/FASTENERS

Blind rivets are mechanical fasteners having self-contained mechanical, chemical, or other features that form upsets on their blind ends and expand their shanks to join parts of

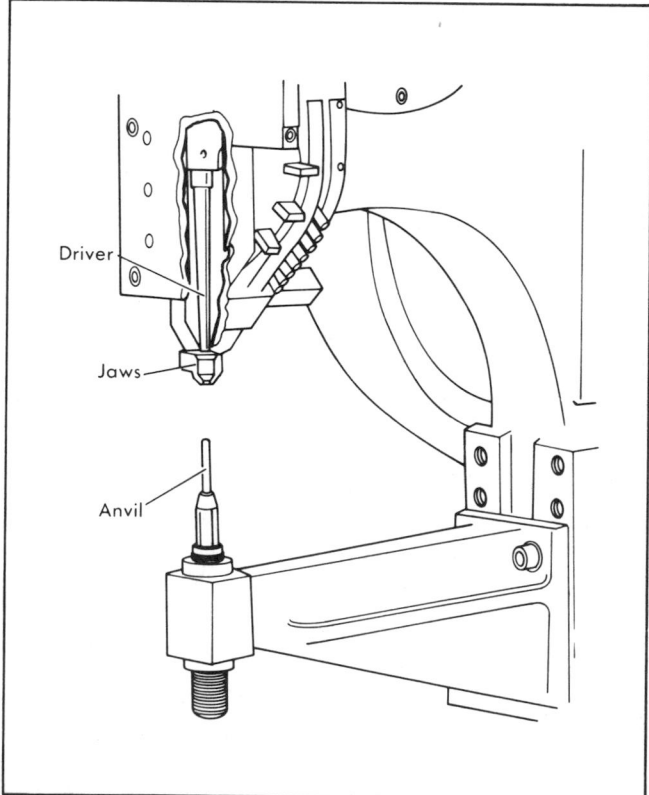

Fig. 42-43 Driver, jaws, and anvil mounted on a riveting machine.

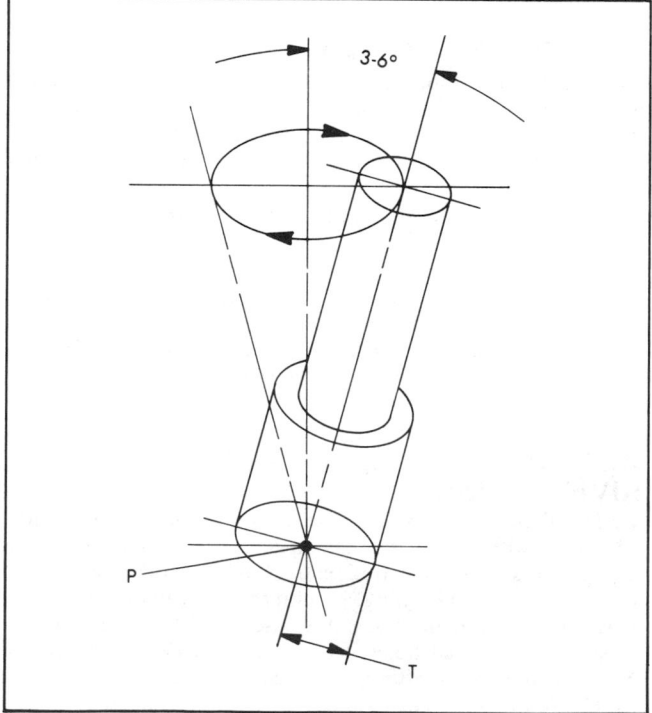

Fig. 42-44 Orbital riveting. (*VSI Automation Assembly*)

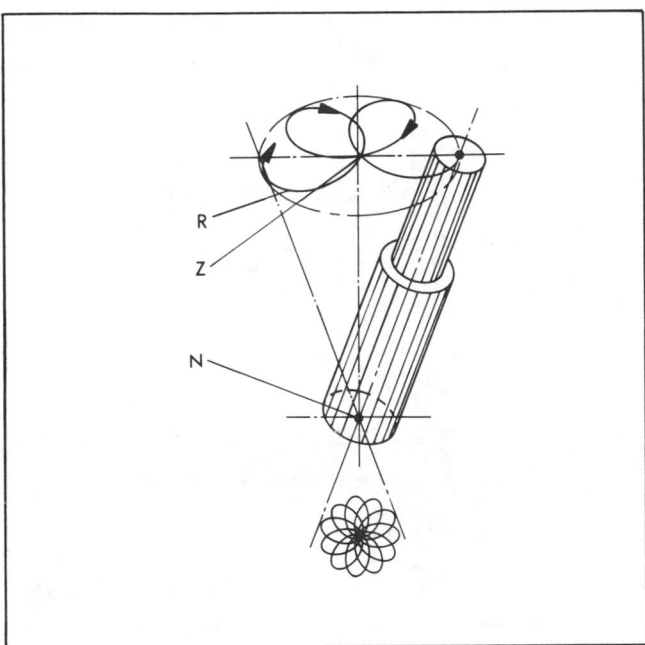

Fig. 42-45 Radial riveting. (*Bracker Corp.*)

assemblies. This design permits the fasteners to be installed in the holes of joints that are accessible from only one side.

Advantages and Limitations

In addition to their use in joints that are accessible from only one side, blind rivets are increasingly being applied where both sides of joints are accessible. The reasons include lower installed costs, faster and easier assembly, and/or improved appearance. Another important advantage of blind rivets is that the operators have no negative effect on the consistently uniform and reliable tightening of the joint.

Blind rivets are suitable for fastening many materials, including plastics, and they are resistant to vibration and tampering. These rivets are suitable for semiautomatic and automatic assembly, with feed rates to 3000 per hour. In addition to fastening, the rivets can serve as pivot shafts, spacers, electrical contacts, nut plates, and stops. Some blind rivets have a mechanical lock between the mandrel and the stem, providing high fatigue resistance.

A possible limitation is that some blind rivets require special installation tools. Also, ample clearance is required for the pulling heads and setting tools used with some types of blind rivets.

Classification of Blind Rivets

Blind rivets can be made from any material that can be cold formed. The metals most commonly used include steels, stainless steels, aluminum alloys, brasses, bronzes, other copper alloys, and titanium. Blind rivets are also available made from plastics. The rivets are generally available with shank diameters from 3/32 to 1/4″ and 2.4 to 6.3 mm, but special rivets have been made with shank diameters to 3/4″. The major types of blind rivets are pull-mandrel, drive-pin, threaded, and chemically expanded.

Pull-mandrel. Blind rivets of this type generally consist of a rivet body and a mandrel or, sometimes, a locking collar. In

setting, the rivet is inserted into holes in the parts to be joined, the mandrel is gripped and pulled axially, and its head upsets the rivet body to form a blind head. These rivets are further classified into pull-through mandrel, break-mandrel, non-break-mandrel, and flush-break, self-plugging multigrip types.

Threaded. Threaded blind rivets have internally threaded rivet bodies. A rivet is threaded onto the mandrel of an installation tool and inserted into holes in the assembly components (see Fig. 42-46, view *a*). When the tool mandrel is pulled or rotated, the walls of the rivet body are bulged outward to form a blind head (view *b*). If upset by rotating, the mandrel may be left in the rivet body or replaced to provide sealing or increased shear and tensile properties.

Figure 42-47 illustrates a compression-type blind fastener consisting of a threaded machine screw, made from carbon or stainless steel, which is mechanically joined to a slotted aluminum rivet sleeve. A neoprene composition washer provides a positive seal. The fastener is inserted into a hole and installed with a power driver equipped with a holding sleeve. As the screw turns, the sleeve is pulled into four clamping tines that provide the holding power. These fasteners are available with clamping sleeves made from plastics to provide increased corrosion resistance.

Chemically expanded. Chemically expanded blind rivets, often called explosive rivets, have hollowed ends filled with an explosive chemical. In setting, the rivet is inserted into holes in the assembly components and either heat or an electrical current is applied to the rivet head.

Body Styles

Blind rivets are available with various body styles. These styles include open, closed, and split ends; slotted shanks; and special designs, such as soft-set rivets.

Head Styles

A variety of heads, both protruding and flush, are provided on blind rivets. Common protruding heads are the dome and large-flanged types. Countersunk heads are the most common flush type.

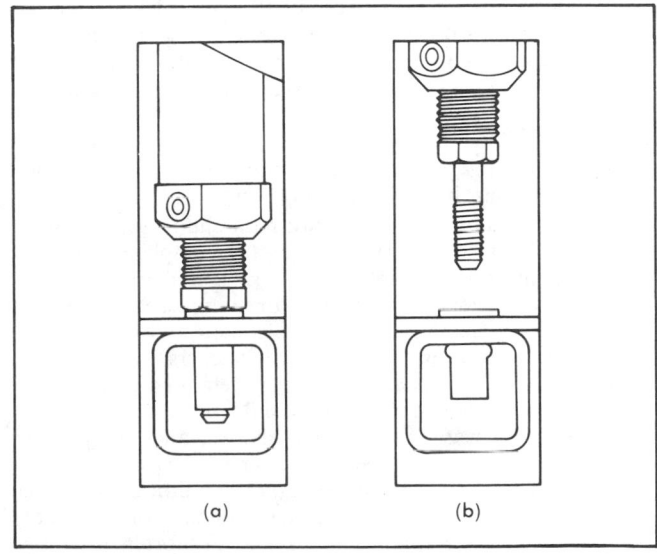

(a) (b)

Fig. 42-46 Threaded blind rivet: (a) before setting and (b) after setting. (*Aerospace and Defense Div., The BFGoodrich Co.*)

RIVETS

EYELETS

Eyelets are thin-walled tubular fasteners having a flange or formed head on one end. Most are formed from metal strip, but some are machined, and are set during assembly by forcing their small diameter ends against dies that curl or funnel the edges and clinch the eyelets against the workpieces. The assembly of eyelets, called setting or eyeleting, requires access to both sides of the parts to be assembled.

Eyelets differ from rivets in that their bores extend completely through the fasteners. Grommets, not discussed in this section, are large eyelet-type fasteners designed for securing by curling their tubular ends over formed washers to provide strength in holes through resilient materials.

Applications

Eyeleting is used extensively in the metalworking industry as a fastening method for the assembly of many different types of light-gage parts. Typical applications include the assembly of automotive components, electrical and electronic components (including use as terminals), hardware, toys, paper products, shoes, textiles, and garments.

Advantages

Eyelets can be inserted at high rates of production, and the process is easily adaptable to automatic assembly. From an economic standpoint, eyelets are one of the lowest cost fasteners

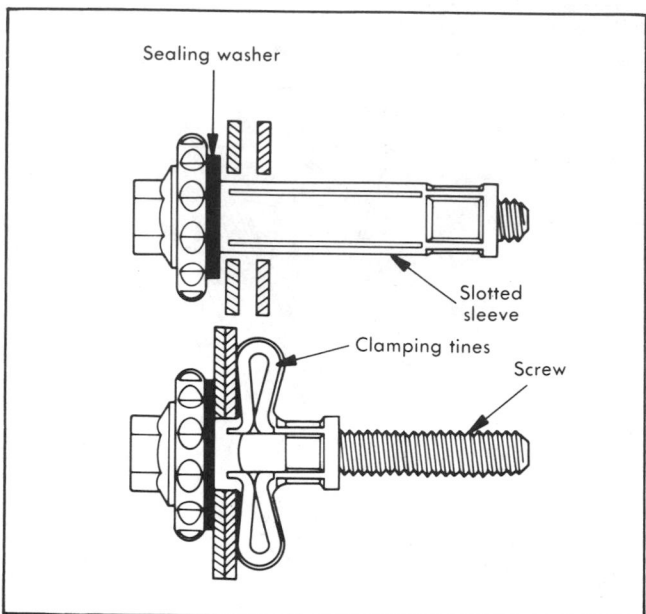

Fig. 42-47 Compression-type blind fastener before (top view) and after installation. (*Fabco Fastening Systems, Townsend Div., Textron Inc.*)

available. They can be obtained in a wide variety of materials, sizes, and styles. Also, they can be set by relatively unskilled labor.

RETAINING RINGS

Retaining rings, sometimes called snap rings, are fastening devices that provide shoulders and/or bearing surfaces for locating or limiting the movement of parts on shafts or in bores or housings. They are designed to exert a radial clamping force. For most applications, the rings provide a removable means of fastening. Some are designed to take up end play caused by accumulated tolerances or wear of the parts being retained. Retaining rings are usually made from spring steel or other materials having good spring properties to allow deformation during assembly and a return to original ring shape for use.

ADVANTAGES

Retaining rings provide a number of advantages over other fastening systems, including the following:

- *Product simplification.* With retaining rings, it is often possible to reduce the number and complexity of components in an assembly. A single ring, used in conjunction with a flat cover or face plate, for example, can replace an expensive custom-designed cover plate and four or more screws, bolts, or other threaded fasteners.
- *Savings on parts and materials.* Retaining rings can be used to eliminate machined shoulders, set collars, cotter pins and washers, threaded sleeves, and many other bulkier and more expensive fastening devices.
- *Reductions in size and weight.* In addition to being smaller and lighter than the fasteners they replace, retaining rings often can be used with shorter shafts and thinner housings, with substantial savings on materials as well as size and weight.

- *Elimination of expensive machining.* Retaining rings often eliminate the need for drilling, tapping, threading, facing, turning, and other costly machining operations. Ring grooves can usually be cut simultaneously, at no extra cost, during shaft cutoff and chamfering or bore drilling operations.
- *Faster assembly.* Retaining rings can be assembled quickly and economically, even by unskilled labor, with pliers, applicators, dispensers, and other hand tools, or with semiautomatic or automatic assembly equipment for high-volume mass production.

TYPICAL APPLICATIONS

Retaining rings are specified for a wide variety of consumer, industrial, and military products. In one application for garden hose reels (see Fig. 42-48), retaining rings have replaced formed and welded stops for positioning the hose connector sleeves, resulting in a reduction in assembly costs of 50% per unit. For tapping attachments (see Fig. 42-49), retaining rings have been found to be 10 times more cost efficient than threaded fasteners to lock collet assemblies and other components in housings and to position and secure clutch bearings and sleeves.

For industrial pumps, self-locking retaining rings are used to hold plastic rollers on shafts; the rings are pushed over the ends of the shafts and no grooves or other machining operations are needed. In the original design, the shafts were drilled and tapped, and the rollers secured by washers and screws. Savings with retaining rings amount to 74 cents per assembly.

TYPES OF RETAINING RINGS

The three major types of retaining rings are:

1. Stamped, tapered-section retaining rings. These rings have a tapered radial width that decreases symmetrically from their center sections to their free ends.
2. Spiral-wound retaining rings. These rings have one or more turns of rectangular, rounded-edge material that is wound on edge to provide a continuous coil. Rings with a single turn have a gap; those with two or more turns are of gapless design.
3. Wire-formed (wire-wound or bent-wire) retaining rings. These rings have a uniform cross-sectional area.

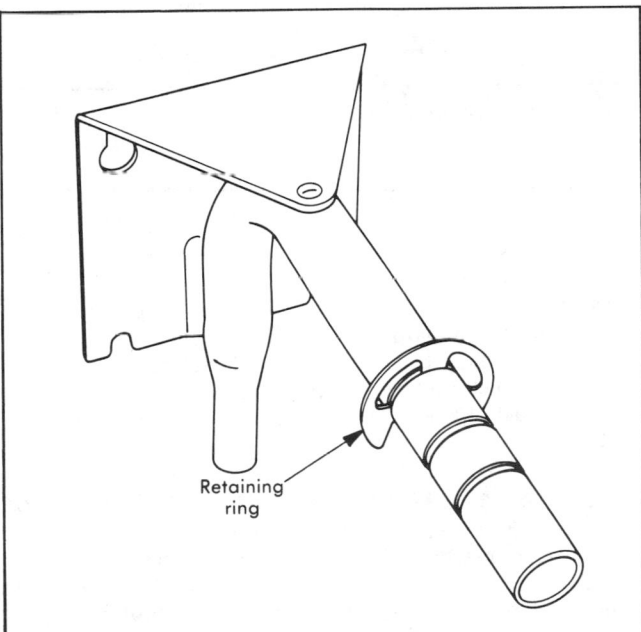

Fig. 42-48 Retaining ring replaces formed and welded stop for positioning the connector sleeve on a garden hose reel. (*Waldes Kohinoor, Inc.*)

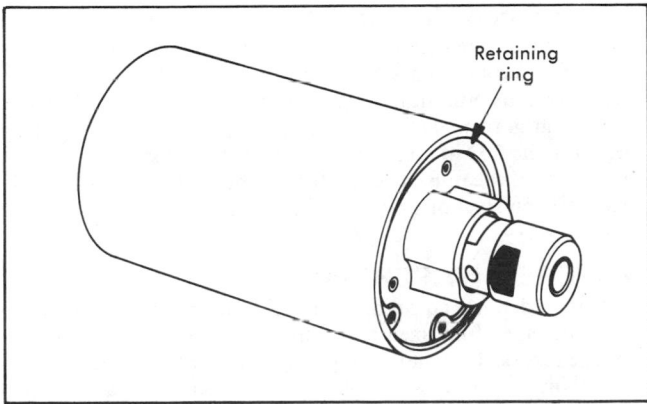

Fig. 42-49 Internal retaining ring locks collet assembly and other components in housing of tapping attachment. (*Waldes Kohinoor, Inc.*)

TAPERED-SECTION RETAINING RINGS

There are more than 50 functionally different types of tapered-section retaining rings manufactured. They are available in about 1200 standard inch and metric sizes for shafts and bores from 0.040 to 10″ (1 to 250 mm) diam. Rings as large as 40″ (1000 mm) in diameter have been produced for special applications.

SPIRAL-WOUND RETAINING RINGS

Spiral-wound retaining rings having two or more turns offer the advantage of providing a 360° retaining shoulder because they are of gapless design. These rings are also available with single turns; with this design they have gaps. Spiral-wound retaining rings can be made without incurring tooling costs for applications requiring special sizes.

The use of spiral-wound retaining rings is widespread in industries making everything from small electrical appliances to the space shuttle. While most applications are for the retention of components of assemblies, there are many other uses, including the following:

- *Vibration dampers.* Spiral-wound, statically balanced rings function well as dampening devices when balance of the assembly is critical.
- *Oil dams.* Spiral-wound rings are used to form an oil reservoir for spline gears in mechanical couplings and other applications.
- *Backup rings.* Spiral-wound rings are used as backup rings for packings in cylinders because of the 360° shoulders they provide.
- *Oil or grease slingers.* Spiral-wound rings have been employed successfully as slinger rings in many applications; however, if high rotary speeds are involved, it might be necessary to use a self-locking ring.
- *Spacer or shim stock.* Spiral-wound rings are used as spacers or shims for positive tolerance take-up.
- *Location stops.* Spiral-wound rings are used successfully as location stops in a number of applications, but if impact loads are involved, care must be taken to use a properly designed ring.
- *Spring-loading components.* Dished spiral-wound rings can function as spring components in assemblies to exert a controlled load on other components.

WIRE-FORMED RETAINING RINGS

Wire-formed retaining rings, also called wire-wound or bent-wire rings, are split rings formed and cut from spring wire of uniform cross-sectional size and shape. The grain flow follows the contours of these rings for equalized distribution of stresses. The rings can be formed to ensure full peripheral contact on shafts or in housings.

Standard, wire-formed retaining rings are made in sizes ranging from 1/8 to 30″ (3.2 to 762 mm) diam, with larger sizes available by special order. The rings are made in a variety of cross-sectional shapes (see Fig. 42-50), with rectangular, square, or round being the most popular, depending on the ring function and requirements. Round-section rings, used in rounded grooves, have less load-bearing capacity than rectangular or square-section rings. Tapered-section rings help to take up end play caused by tolerances on ring thicknesses, groove locations, and the retained components.

PINS

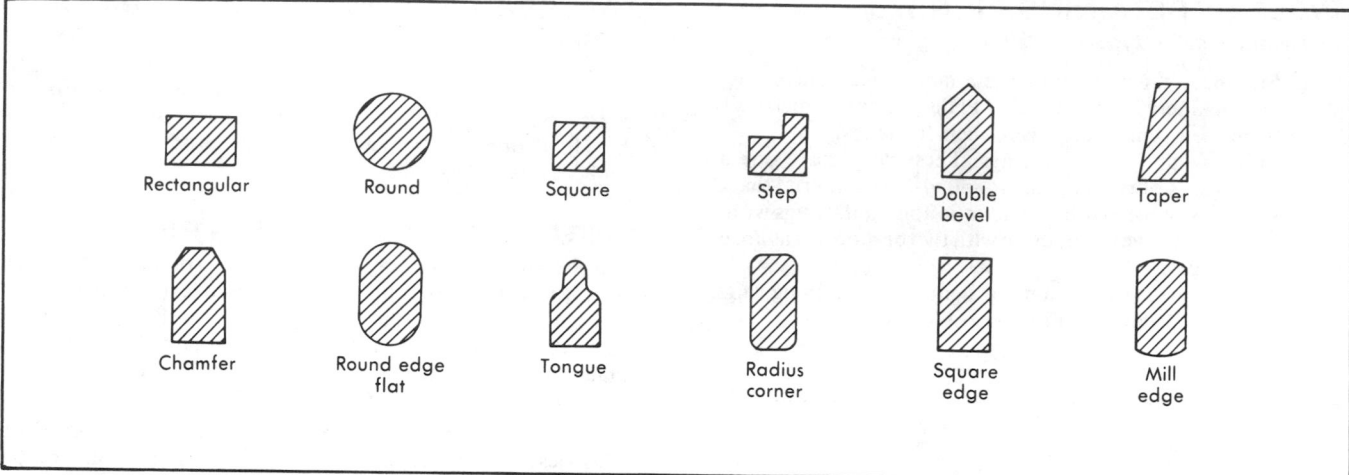

Fig. 42-50 Cross-sectional shapes of wire-formed retaining rings. (*Engineered Fasteners Div., Easton Corp.*)

PINS

Pins provide a simple and low-cost method of mechanical fastening. They are available in straight-cylindrical or tapered designs, with or without heads, and generally rely on elastic compression for their gripping power. Applications of pins are common in industrial machines and in commercial products.

Pins are used as locking devices, locating elements, pivots, and bearing faces. They often secure the positions of two or more parts relative to each other. Applications are primarily for shear loading where there is not a high amount of end loading. Most pins are hardened for maximum strength and permanent assembly, but some are used soft so that they will shear before the assembly or mechanism is damaged.

An advantage of pins, in addition to their low cost and effectiveness, is that many of them can be inserted in simple drilled or cored holes. However, some press-fit pins require varying degrees of hole preparation for proper insertion. Application methods vary from the simple use of hammers to automated assembly machines for high-volume requirements.

A wide variety of standard types and sizes of pins are available, and special designs are made for specific applications.

STRAIGHT PINS

Solid, straight-cylindrical pins are usually cut from wire or bar stock and have unground surfaces. They are available in chamfered or square-end designs. Square-end straight pins can have the corners on both ends broken with small radii.

DOWEL PINS

Dowel pins are precision, straight-cylindrical pins available in hardened and ground types and in unhardened and ground types. They are used extensively in the production of machines, tools, dies, jigs, and fixtures to retain parts in fixed positions or to preserve alignments.

Hardened and Ground Machine Dowel Pins

These pins are available in standard and oversize series,
ranging from 1/16 to 1″ diam and 3/16 to 6″ long, as well as in metric sizes. Standard inch-size pins, intended for initial installations, have basic diameters 0.0002″ more than their nominal diameters. Oversize pins, intended for replacement use, have basic diameters 0.001″ more than nominal diameters. Both series are made from carbon or alloy steels.

Hardened and Ground Production Dowel Pins

These pins are similar to the standard-size series of hardened and ground machine dowel pins. Differences include that standard inch sizes only range from 1/16 to 3/8″ diam, with lengths from 3/16 to 3″; the corners at both ends of the pins are rounded; and the pins are made from a carbon steel that is case hardened to produce a minimum surface hardness of R_C58. These pins are generally employed for volume production applications, using automated installation equipment.

Unhardened Ground Dowel Pins

These pins are often used where strength, shock, and wear resistance requirements do not warrant the additional cost of hardened pins. Standard inch sizes range from 1/16 to 1″ diam, with lengths from 1/4 to 4″. They are generally produced by grinding the OD of commercial wire or rod to size. Corners at both ends of the pins are chamfered. The pins are usually made from carbon steel or brass.

TAPERED (TAPER) PINS

Tapered pins, commonly called taper pins, inserted by a drive fit, are often used to position parts or to transmit low torque forces. They have a taper of 1/4″ per foot, measured on the diameter, and both ends are crowned with a spherical radius. Tapered pins are available in commercial and precision classes, with the precision pins having closer tolerances. The pins are generally made from AISI 1211 steel or cold-drawn AISI 1212 or 1213 steel.

CLEVIS PINS

Clevis pins are solid pins having cylindrical heads at one end and a drilled hole for a cotter pin at the other end (see Fig. 42-51). They are commonly used as pivots in many mechanisms and for use with clevices and rod-end eyes in industrial applications.

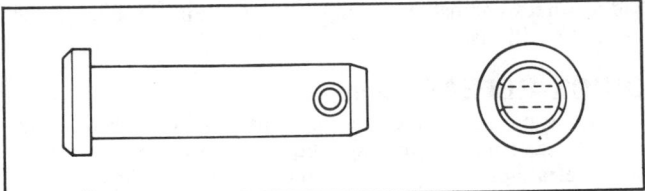

Fig. 42-51 Clevis pin.[3]

COTTER PINS

Cotter (split) pins are double-bodied pins formed from half-round wire. A loop at one end of each pin provides a head and various point styles are available (see Fig. 42-52). They are used in clevis pins and other pinned assemblies. The pins are driven into holes, the loop heads limiting travel, and their legs are split for locking. Cotter pins have been standardized into 18 sizes with nominal sizes (basic pin diameters) ranging from 1/32 to 3/4″. They are generally made from AISI 1015 steel but are also available in brass, bronze, stainless steel, and aluminum.

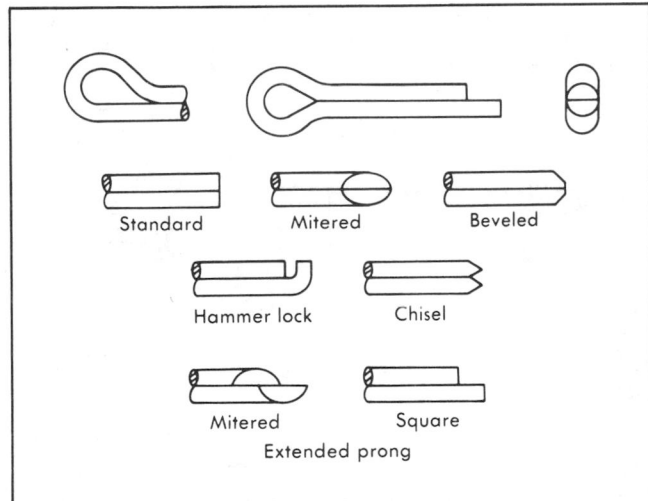

Fig. 42-52 Cotter pins and various point styles.[4]

WIRE PINS

Formed spring-wire pins or clips are of two-legged design, similar to cotter pins. However, unlike a cotter pin, only one leg of a wire pin is inserted in the hole, and the pin holds itself in place by elastic compression.

GROOVED PINS

Grooved pins are solid, unground, straight-cylindrical pins having three longitudinal grooves equally spaced around their peripheries. No metal is removed during manufacture of the pins. Instead, the grooves are formed by a swaging operation in which three tools penetrate the nominal diameter of the pin to a predetermined depth. Metal displaced by the tools forms a raised portion or flute along each side of each groove.

The crests of the formed flutes produce an expanded diameter, shown as D_x in Fig. 42-53. Amount of expansion varies with the size of the pin and the material from which it is made, but the expanded diameter can be precisely controlled. Holes into which grooved pins are to be inserted are drilled slightly larger than the nominal diameters of the pins, but never smaller. When the expanded portions of a pin are compressed in a hole, the displaced metal is forced back into the grooves, thus developing radial holding forces. The locking action is a function of the expanded diameter and the effective length of engagement.

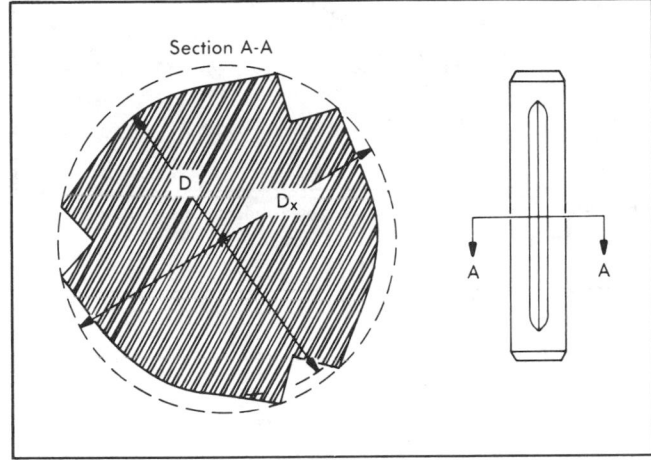

Fig. 42-53 Grooved pin having a nominal diameter, D, and an expanded diameter, D_x. (*Driv-Lok, Inc.*)

KNURLED PINS

Knurled pins are similar to grooved pins in that there are serrations around the nominal diameter of the pin that, when compressed, result in radial holding forces that retain the fastener in place. However, whereas a grooved pin has only six raised portions, knurled pins have many smaller raised sections around the nominal diameter. A knurled section may either be a straight, helical, or diamond configuration.

KNURLED DRIVE STUDS

Knurled (ribbed), hardened studs (see Fig. 42-54) are designed for applications in materials subject to plastic deformation. Such materials include cold and hot-rolled steels, zinc die castings, and sand or die castings made from aluminum or magnesium alloys. They are recommended to ensure secure fastening in applications subject to vibration.

The two sets of longitudinal ribs on these studs are offset one from the other by one-half pitch. The lower set of ribs, first engaged during insertion, forces the hole wall material into the valleys between ribs. The flow of displaced material is then deflected to follow the offset path when the upper ribbed section engages and the stud is securely locked in the work material.

BARBED PINS

Barbed pins and studs (see Fig. 42-55) provide positive fastening for plastics, wood, and other soft materials. Standard

PINS

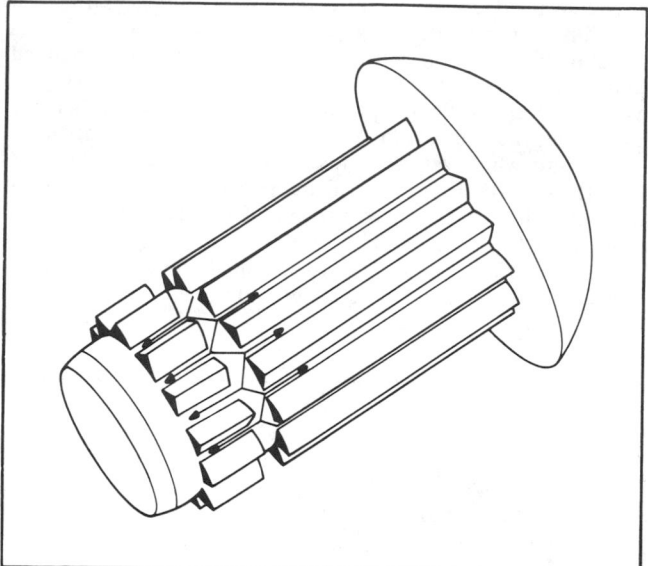

Fig. 42-54 Knurled drive stud. Arrows indicate flow of workpiece material. (*Groov-Pin Corp.*)

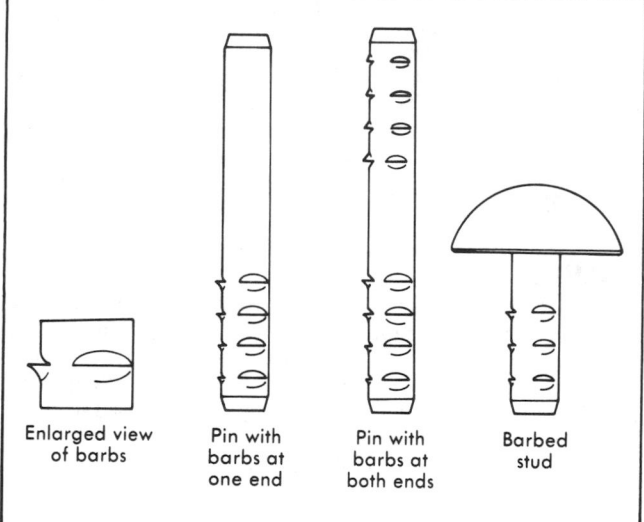

Fig. 42-55 Pins barbed at one and both ends, and a barbed stud. (*Driv-Lok, Inc.*)

pins are available in diameters of 3/16, 1/4, 5/16, and 3/8", with lengths from 1 to 2" in 1/4" increments. Pins with barbs at both ends provide holding power in both directions. The pins and studs are made from low-carbon steel, aluminum, and brass. Sets of three barbs are located at 120° positions around the peripheries of the pins and studs. The impressed barbs displace a predetermined amount of material, with the crests of the barbs creating an expanded diameter for locking.

SPRING PINS

Spring pins are made in slotted (split) tubular and coiled (spirally wrapped) designs. Pins of both designs have smaller cross-sectional areas than solid pins of the same diameter, sometimes resulting in lower shear strengths. However, some heat-treated spring pins have higher shear strengths than low-carbon solid pins. Also, spring pins provide good shock and vibration absorption, and stresses are distributed equally. Also, their inherent springiness makes insertion in holes easier.

When manufactured, spring pins are made oversized with respect to the diameters of the holes in which they will be inserted. When inserted, the pins are compressed, resulting in radial forces against the hole walls to retain the pins in the desired positions.

QUICK-RELEASE PINS

Special-purpose, quick-release pins are used where rapid assembly and disassembly are required. Two major types of quick-release pins are push-pull and positive locking.

Push-Pull Pins

The shanks of these pins contain detents consisting of buttons or balls backed by resilient plugs or springs (see Fig. 42-56). When the pins are inserted into holes, the buttons or balls exert a locking action. In pin withdrawal, the buttons or balls are automatically depressed.

Positive-Locking Pins

Several designs of positive-locking pins are available. One design uses a plunger-actuated mechanism. When the plunger is moved in one direction, a locking element projects from the pin; movement in the other direction retracts the locking element. A double-acting, ball-lock, positive-acting pin is illustrated in Fig. 42-57. Release is achieved by pulling or pushing the handle. Another design uses a cammed core in the pin to expand a ramped sleeve against the hole bore.

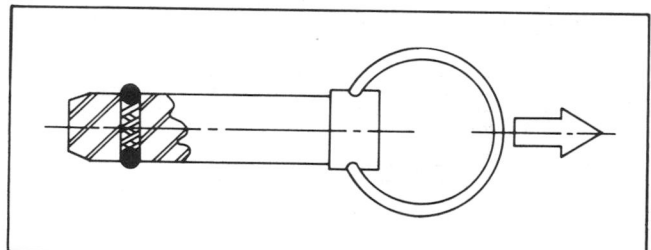

Fig. 42-56 Push-pull detent pin for quick-release locating. (*Carr Lane Mfg. Co.*)

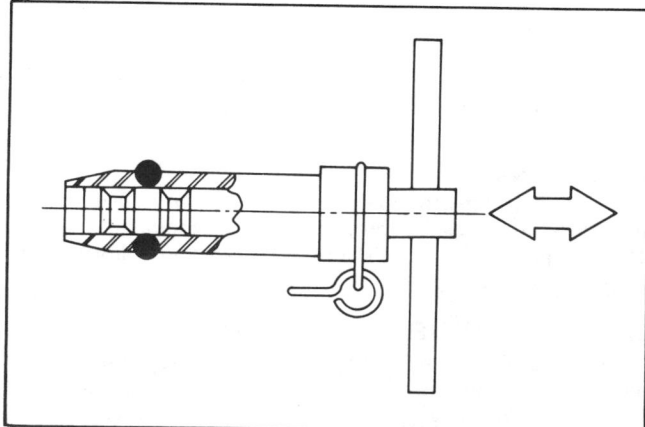

Fig. 42-57 Double-acting, ball-lock, positive-acting pin. (*Carr Lane Mfg. Co.*)

WASHERS

Washers are simple fastener components, often consisting of cylindrical slugs of metal with holes in their centers. They are available in numerous types and sizes, and proper selection can be critical to the successful and economical operation of many assemblies.

Washers serve many functions, depending on the specific application. A primary use is to serve as seats under bolt heads and nuts to distribute stresses and loads. In such applications they also provide surfaces for uniform torque control in tightening bolt-nut assemblies. Other uses for washers include compensating for oversize bolt holes, adjusting for proper grip length, providing spring tension, protecting assembly surfaces, sealing the assembly, and providing electrical connections. In some cases, washers serve as insulators or corrosion barriers.

Major types of washers include flat (plain), spring, and special-purpose. They are available in many sizes and are made from a variety of materials, including steel, stainless steel, brass, copper, bronze, aluminum, lead, zinc, and nonmetallics such as plastics and paper. For some applications, washers are plated or coated to help resist corrosion.

FLAT (PLAIN) WASHERS

Flat (plain) washers are circular or square, relatively thin components having central holes that fit around bolts or screws and under heads or nuts (see Fig. 42-58) to provide bearing surfaces. These washers are made from steel, brass, copper, silicon bronze, stainless steel, and nonmetallic materials.

SPRING WASHERS

A spring washer is a single fastener component that replaces a separate spring and washer, thus reducing costs and space requirements and decreasing assembly weight. Applications include minimizing vibration in mechanically fastened joints, compensating for wear or expansion, and helping to keep mating parts together. Various spring washers can withstand a wide range of pressures, but they have limited deflections; larger deflections can be obtained by stacking them. The possibility of hydrogen embrittlement in hardened spring washers can be minimized by proper plating and baking after plating. Major types of spring washers include cylindrically curved, waveform, conical design, Belleville, toothed lockwashers, and helical spring lockwashers.

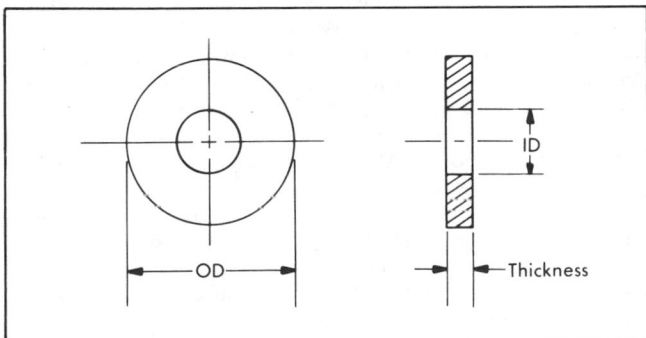

Fig. 42-58 Flat (plain) washer having an ID that fits around a bolt or screw.

OTHER WASHER TYPES

Many other washers are available to suit specific requirements. Typical examples are slotted Belleville, cup, and flanged cup washers illustrated in Fig. 42-59. Some washers are specially designed to provide more or less deflection, unusual locking arrangements, increased surface contact, or for other reasons. Some spring washers are spherically curved to provide an extra stiffening effect, resulting in slightly higher spring rates than comparable conical washers.

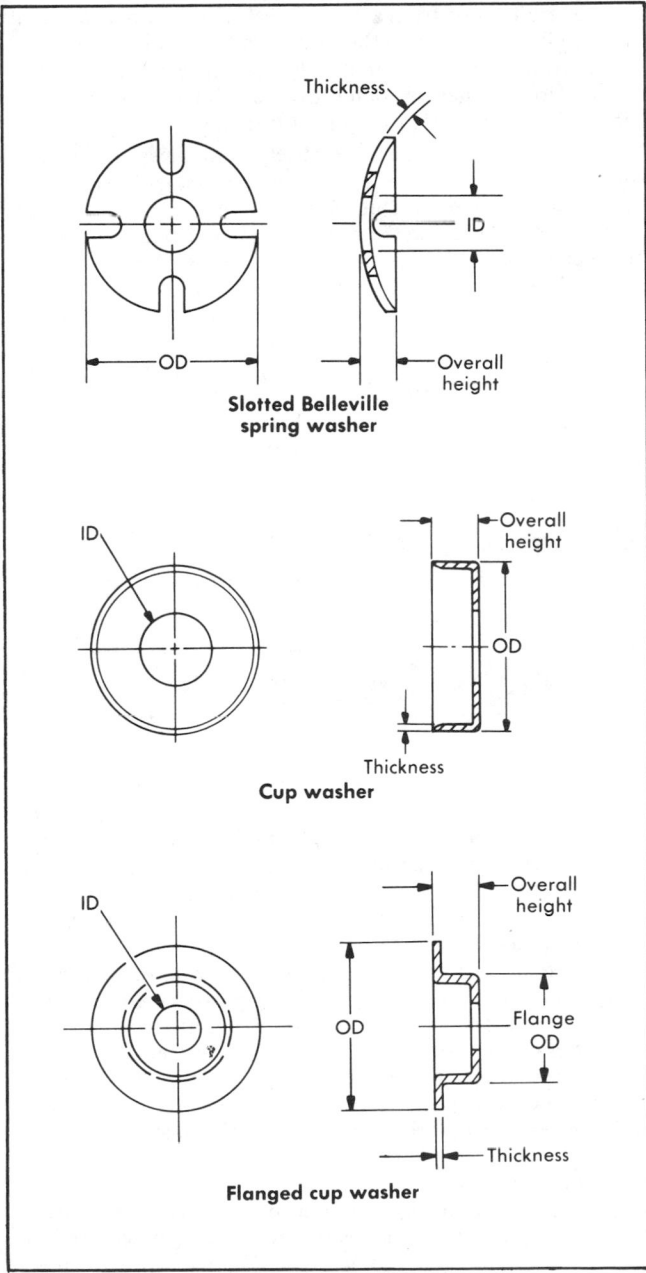

Fig. 42-59 Slotted Belleville, cup, and flanged cup washer. (*H. K. Metalcraft Mfg. Corp.*)

INDUSTRIAL STITCHING AND STAPLING

Stitching and stapling are similar processes in that they both use U-shaped fasteners for product assembly. They differ, however, in how the fasteners are made and applied. Stitches are formed on machines that also apply them, while staples are individually preformed and applied from strips, generally with portable pneumatic tools.

WIRE STITCHING

Wire stitching is a fastening method in which U-shaped stitches are formed from a coil of steel wire by a machine that also applies the stitch to the materials being joined together. When the method is used to fasten together two or more pieces of metal, or to fasten one or more pieces of metal to nonmetallic materials, it is referred to as metal stitching.

Stitching is used for a wide variety of applications in many different industries. The process is used extensively in the graphic arts field for binding pamphlets, magazines, and books. Another major use is in the production of corrugated boxes. In the electronics industry, stitches are used to form soldering terminals, jumpers, or other type connections.

There are many applications of stitching for joining two or more metals, or metals to nonmetallic materials. Typical applications include joining door hinges to frames, assembling washer and dryer drums, applying metal hinges to plastic housings, mounting rubber gaskets onto plastic or metal surfaces, and joining lining material to metal for brake assemblies.

INDUSTRIAL STAPLING

Conventional U-shaped staples, cohered into convenient, easy-to-handle strips, are becoming increasingly popular for industry to use in product fastening applications. Staples are available made from wire ranging from 0.026 to 0.072″ (0.66 to 1.83 mm) diam and 1/8 to 2 1/2″ (3.2 to 63.5 mm) long. Staples are normally available made from aluminum, bronze, Monel, stainless steel, and low, medium, and high-carbon steel wire, with a galvanized, tin, or liquor protective finish. They are also available with their crowns painted to blend with the materials with which they are to be used.

Staples are also available in many different crown sizes and types, and with various leg lengths and types of points. For example, one manufacturer offers staples with 20 different crown sizes and wire cross sections. Each size is made for optimum performance for different fastening applications.

Tooling Used

Staples used by industry for fastening applications are normally applied with pneumatic portable tools. The size of the tool is proportional to the size of the staple to be driven. Because stapling tools are relatively small in size, they are easy to work with and easy to mount side by side in a fixtured arrangement.

Stapling Applications

There are many applications for joining materials together where staples are the lowest cost fastener to use. However, there are two situations where staples should not be used: (1) when repetitive, fast, and easy removal of the fastener is required, and (2) when the shear and tension force requirements of the assembly exceeds the strength of the wire.

SHRINK AND EXPANSION FITS

A shrink fit is composed of two normally interfering parts in which the interference has been eliminated during assembly by dimensional change in one or both of the parts by heating one part only or by heating one part and cooling the other. An expansion fit is one that is achieved by cooling only the male or internal member of an assembly. This discussion embraces both concepts under the term *shrink fits*.

Because of its high joint strength, the shrink fit is useful in heavy construction where high holding power is required. It is effective in assembling parts whose materials have different properties or corrosion resistance, such as a steel shell over an aluminum or copper liner. It can sometimes permit a rather weak, low-cost material to be used in a prestressed condition and thus replace a more costly high-strength material.

ADVANTAGES

The advantages of expansion fits over ordinary press fitting are the greater allowances possible with nitrogen cooling and freedom from longitudinal scratches on the work by press fitting. Subzero temperatures can facilitate removal of some assembled parts. In the case of large bushings, a tight-fitting, cup-type container filled with a subzero convection fluid can be inserted, and the bushing will be able to be fairly easily removed after shrinking.

Cooling of an internal member of an assembly provides, in the case of liquid nitrogen, a 390° F (215° C) differential from room temperature. Such a differential obtained by heating the external member would bring its temperature to 460° F (240° C). This can be disadvantageous for most aluminum alloys and certain steels, particularly where the parts are massive, whereas subzero refrigeration does not distort, warp, or otherwise have an effect on the parts.

Cooling below the dew point, however, causes condensation and moisture trapped in the joint may cause subsequent corrosion. Also, cooling below 32° F (0° C) may cause icing, which can cause a dimensional change, a different fit, and a bad joint. If these problems are significant, as with precision bearing fits, a low-humidity environment should be used.

METHODS OF CHANGING DIMENSIONS

Dimensional change can be obtained by heating the hub or cooling the shaft, or by combining the two methods. The optimum method is dependent on a large number of factors, some of which are:

1. Dimensional change required to ensure success in assembly.
2. Effect of shrinking process on physical properties of parts.
3. Effect of shrinking process on surface condition of parts.
4. Susceptibility of the parts to be damaged in any other way by the method being considered.
5. Size and shape of parts.
6. Quantity of assemblies.
7. Available equipment.
8. Availability of materials required.
9. Relative cost.

INJECTED METAL ASSEMBLY

Injected metal assembly (IMA) is a parts assembly process created by injecting molten metal into a die cavity to form a hub or other shaped joint. Surface contact is 100% between the components forming the assembly and the joint. The joint is achieved by the injection under pressure of the molten metal. During the rapid solidification and cooling of the molten metal, it shrinks minutely, permanently locking the components together. The joint, if properly designed, is stronger than the parts being joined.

THE PROCESS

The molten metal injection process is basically simple. Once the components to be assembled are located within the assembly tool, the operating head containing the tool is advanced by a moving mechanism onto an injection nozzle. Molten metal injection occurs through the actuation of an injection unit by means of an external pneumatic cylinder that pumps the metal through the nozzle into the tool. The tool contains the cavity that forms the hub or joint and the components being assembled.

Injecting molten metal into a die cavity holding premanufactured parts, to assemble such parts accurately and securely, is not a new process. It originated in the United States more than a century ago with a nationally known clockmaker. Little used until the mid-1940s, the concept has since grown in development and application.

ADVANTAGES AND LIMITATIONS

Primary advantages of assembly by injecting molten metal are cost savings, improved product quality, and the versatility of the process. Up to 80% savings in assembly costs have been reported by users of the process.

Cost Savings

Reduced part requirements. Parts of an assembly can often be eliminated by combining several components—injecting and forming them as an integral part of the hub or joint. Cams, ratchets, pinions, keys, spacers, shims, and other parts are not required for many injected metal assemblies. Cost savings result by eliminating the need to manufacture, stock, and handle such parts. Reductions in the diameters and types of stock required, as well as the amount of machining needed, for shafts also reduces costs.

Relaxed tolerances. More liberal tolerances can be specified for the locations and diameters of holes in the parts to be assembled, thus reducing the cost to manufacture them, without affecting the accuracy and repeatability of the assemblies. This is permissible because the pressurized molten metal fills all voids and compensates for inaccuracies.

Reduced preprocessing costs. Preassembly cleaning or chemical preparation of the metal surfaces is not required. This is possible because the joints are mechanically locked rather than joined by adhesion between the metal surfaces.

Low cost of the process. Except for the molten metal injection machine and tooling, no other special equipment, such as ovens, jigs, and presses, is required. Also, alloys injected in the process are low in cost. Machines needed for the process can be incorporated into production lines, thus reducing material handling costs. While the components to be assembled are usually loaded and unloaded manually, the process can be completely automated, eliminating the need for any manual operations. Operators can be quickly trained to achieve high production rates.

Reduced inspection costs. Assembly tools in the injection machines are often used as checking fixtures, thus minimizing or eliminating the need for postprocess inspection. This is possible because the assembly tool locates and holds the parts by their functional surfaces.

Reduced postprocessing costs. Because injected metal assembly leaves no sprues, gates, runners, or flash, subsequent trimming and cleaning operations are not required. Other secondary operations are rarely needed.

Improved Product Quality

Overall consistency and repeatability of assemblies made with the injected metal process are excellent. Rejects and the need for rework are minimal. The process is clean and odorless, and assemblies are ready for any subsequent processing required or installation into end products.

Versatility

Flexibility permitted in the design of assemblies is a major advantage of the injected metal process. Dissimilar materials can be easily joined, mainly because of the rapid dissipation of heat through the water-cooled tooling. Materials joined by the process include most metals, plastics, elastomers, ceramics, glass, and even paper products.

Limitations

One possible limitation to use of the injected metal process is that the joints are permanent. Disassembly cannot be accom-

INJECTED METAL ASSEMBLY

plished without destroying the injected metal hubs. Another limitation to the process is the production of assemblies for high-load applications where locking configurations must be designed into the parts.

Typical Applications

Cable terminations. Zinc alloy terminations are being injected onto the ends of wires and cables. Because of the rapid heat conduction from molded zinc, plastic-covered wires and cables can be safely terminated without damage to the plastic. The terminations are as strong as those produced by swaging and provide substantial savings in both time and cost.

Abrasive points. When assembling abrasive points (small grinding wheels), the abrasive material and the steel mandrel are held in the required relationship in the assembly tooling during injection. The molten zinc alloy enters the voids between the abrasive material and the knurled mandrel ends. The zinc alloy penetrates the grains and solidifies, thus securing the abrasive to the mandrel. Assemblies can be handled immediately after ejection from the tool. Assembly costs have been greatly reduced due to the high production rates, the low cost of the zinc alloy, and elimination of the curing time involved in the previous cementing method.

Riveting. Another useful variation of injected metal assembly is its use to "rivet" similar or dissimilar materials by injecting molten zinc alloy into what would normally be rivet holes. The rivet heads are formed by a cavity within the tooling that holds the parts in their correct relationship. An advantage over conventional riveting is that the rivet holes do not need to be accurate or even in alignment. Compensation for misaligned holes can be made even if they vary in size or shape.

Electric motor rotors. Injected metal assembly is particularly efficient when two or more components need to be assembled into one complete subassembly, as is the case with the rotors of small induction or stepper motors. One nominal size of center hole can accommodate several shaft diameters. An annular gap between the rotor and shaft of 0.030" (0.76 mm) or more is filled by the injected molten metal. This eliminates the stocking or manufacture of different rotors for each size shaft.

Locking tubes to plates. A conventional method of securing a tube to a plate normally requires a bushing with precise diameters and tight tolerances on the diameter of the hole in the plate. With the IMA method, close tolerances are not necessary because the injected molten metal forms a ring. As the ring cools, it shrinks into premade grooves in the tube and into peripheral holes in the plate (see Fig. 42-60). This permanently locks the two components together, and no secondary operations are necessary.

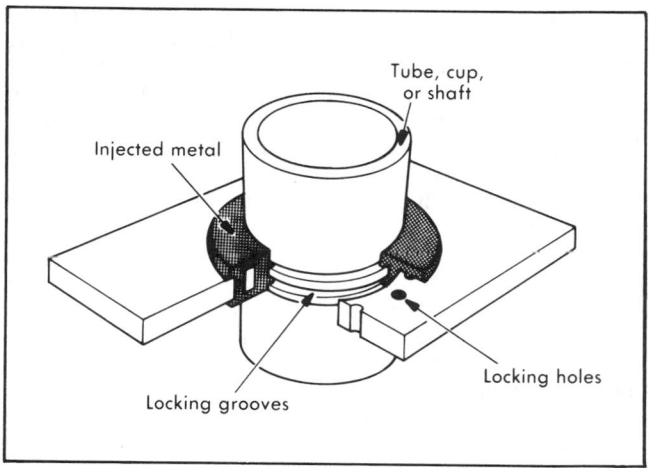

Fig. 42-60 In assembling a tube to a plate, the injected metal forms a ring, thus eliminating the need for close tolerance components. (*Fisher Gauge Ltd.*)

ADHESIVE JOINING

While no universal theory of adhesion exists, the following definition explains the bonding or joining process: "The molecular force exerted across a surface of contact between unlike liquids or solids that resists interfacial separation. One surface is the adhesive while the other is the adherend.[5] The adhesive is a substance capable of holding materials together by surface attachment. The adherend is a body that is held to another body by an adhesive. Structural (engineering) adhesives are bonding agents used for transferring required loads between adherends exposed to service environments. Additional definitions are presented in ASTM D 907, "Standard Definitions of Terms Relating to Adhesives."

Curing is the changing of the physical properties of an adhesive by chemical reaction, which may be condensation, polymerization, or vulcanization. It is often accomplished by the action of heat and/or a catalyst and with or without pressure. Setting is the conversion of an adhesive into a fixed or hardened state by chemical or physical action.

ADVANTAGES OF ADHESIVE JOINING

Advantages with respect to the use of adhesive joining include the following:

1. Stresses are distributed uniformly over a large area, significantly reducing stress concentrations that cause fatigue and failure.
2. A wide variety of similar and dissimilar materials, as well as combinations of materials, can be joined, including those with vastly different thermal coefficients of expansion.
3. Very thin and fragile materials not suitable for mechanical fasteners or welding, as well as thick parts, can be fastened.
4. Components of all sizes and shapes can be joined.
5. Joints with smooth surfaces and contours can be produced.

ADHESIVE JOINING

6. Joints can be sealed against a variety of environments, heat transfer may be slowed, and electrolytic corrosion may be reduced.
7. Fatigue life is improved, vibration is damped, and thermal shock and impact are resisted.
8. Cures are effected at relatively low temperatures, avoiding the need for the high temperatures required for some other joining processes.
9. Costs are frequently less than for other fastening methods.
10. The weight of assemblies can be significantly reduced.
11. Joint design is simplified.
12. Some adhesives form flexible bonds that are tolerant of repeated cycling, resulting in improved fatigue life.
13. Special properties can be produced. Adhesive formulations are available to provide electrical insulation, conduction, or semiconduction between members.

PROCESS LIMITATIONS

Possible limitations with respect to the use of adhesive joining include the following:

1. Careful adhesive selection is required to resist a specific environment. This may necessitate carefully planned testing with respect to the anticipated service of the assembly.
2. Rigid attention is demanded with respect to surface preparation and cleanliness prior to adhesive joining.
3. Heat and pressure or a relatively long cure period are sometimes required.
4. Jigs and fixtures are often necessary for good location of the parts to be assembled.
5. Maximum service temperatures of organic adhesives are low compared to the temperatures that can be withstood by many metals.
6. Nondestructive inspection of adhesive-bonded joints is difficult but desirable.
7. Many adhesive-bonded joints are not readily able to be disassembled.
8. Rigid process control is sometimes necessary.

TYPICAL APPLICATIONS

Adhesives have been used for thousands of years to join various materials. Their use for bonding metals in structural (load-bearing) applications, however, did not begin until World War II. Structural adhesives were first used in the aircraft industry, but are now being applied in a variety of industries.

Now, the major users of adhesive bonding are the automotive, aircraft, building products, and packaging industries. These four groups consume a major portion of the adhesive raw materials sold today. Other industries using adhesives include the shoe, apparel, furniture, bookbinding, electrical, railroad, shipbuilding, and medical industries. The following few specific examples serve to illustrate the importance of the adhesive joining process as an assembly technique.

Automotive Uses

Beginning in 1960, automobile companies began to use heat-curing plastisol mastic adhesive to bond the inner and outer panels of hood and trunk compartment lids. This system eliminated the flutter and rattle of hood and trunk lid components over rough roads or at high speeds and reduced the weight of the lid assemblies. The adhesive is oil tolerant and can be dispensed from automated applicators in an assembly line operation.[6] Because the adhesive may be applied in conjunction with spot welding on the same part, it can be applied in a parts stamping operation and then heat cured later in the paint ovens.[7] The joining method combining structural adhesives and resistance spot welding, called weldbonding, is discussed later in this section.

Mastic adhesive is also used for bonding interior reinforcements to door panels and framing members to the inside of van-type vehicles. The automotive industry also uses adhesives for joining metal to fabric for interior trim, vinyl-to-metal exterior trim, improved performance of tire cords, adhering brake linings, and general fastening. For adhering the textured vinyl coverings to metal roof surfaces, the contact neoprene-phenolic cements have shown excellent resistance to exterior weathering conditions. Hot-melt adhesives are used to bond various carpet materials for floor mats and interior kick panels.

Food Packaging

In the food packaging industry, hot-melt adhesives are used for a large number of applications such as carton, can, and bag sealing, and the lamination of films, papers, and foils. The advantages of hot melts for such applications include rapid setup on cooling, which permits the use of high-speed fabrication machinery, and no volatile byproducts during the joining process, which permits their use on nonporous materials such as plastic film and metal foil. As a result, a number of rapid coating techniques have become feasible for manufacturing. In the heat sealing of plastic bags and containers, the plastic itself acts as the adhesive by sticking to itself in the melted state.

Structural Applications

Other major uses for adhesives include veneer and plywood laminated structures. In making wood particle boards, the adhesive is mixed uniformly with the particulate wood so it becomes the matrix holding the whole structure together. Similarly, epoxy adhesive is used as the binder material holding fiberglass, carbon, or boron fibers in composite structures. In the building construction industry, contact adhesives often replace nails and screws for attachment of paneling to studs.[8]

The sidewall construction for over-the-road trailers and motor homes is often a sandwich panel construction in which the exterior metal and interior metal, wood, or plastic facings are adhesively bonded directly to insulating plastic foam slabs. Similarly, the wall panels for commercial buildings and schools may consist of metal, wood, or plastic facings adhered directly to a wide variety of insulating foam core materials.[9]

Weldbonding

Weldbonding is a joining method that combines structural adhesives and resistance spot welding. Advantages over spot welding alone include improved fatigue life and durability and better resistance to peel forces. Also, the adhesive can act as a sealant to provide better corrosion resistance. Possible problems include making good welds through an adhesive and preventing contamination of visible metal surfaces and the electrodes by the adhesive. Applications include aircraft construction, aluminum truck cabs and van body sidewalls, and aluminum body sheets for automobiles.

ADHESIVE JOINING

The predominant weldbonding method consists of applying a paste adhesive to the area to be joined, followed by spot welding through the adhesive. In another method, a tape or film adhesive is applied to the area to be joined, holes are cut in the adhesive where the spot welds are required, and then conventional spot welding is performed. Yet another method consists of spot welding the parts together, applying adhesive to the edges of the joint, and then heating to cause the adhesive to flow between the joined surfaces by capillary action.

Bonded Sandwich Construction

One of the lightest and strongest constructions is the laminated or bonded sandwich consisting of thin, high-density facing members adhesively joined to a relatively thick, lightweight core. Both the facing and core materials can vary from metals like aluminum and steel to nonmetals such as wood, paper, and plastics. The basic elements of a bonded sandwich are shown in Fig. 42-61. Many structural honeycomb panels are made with reticulating adhesive where surface tension causes the adhesive to move up or down the walls of the honeycomb and form a fillet of adhesive. Applications of adhesively bonded sandwich structures are ever increasing in number; some examples are listed in Table 42-2.

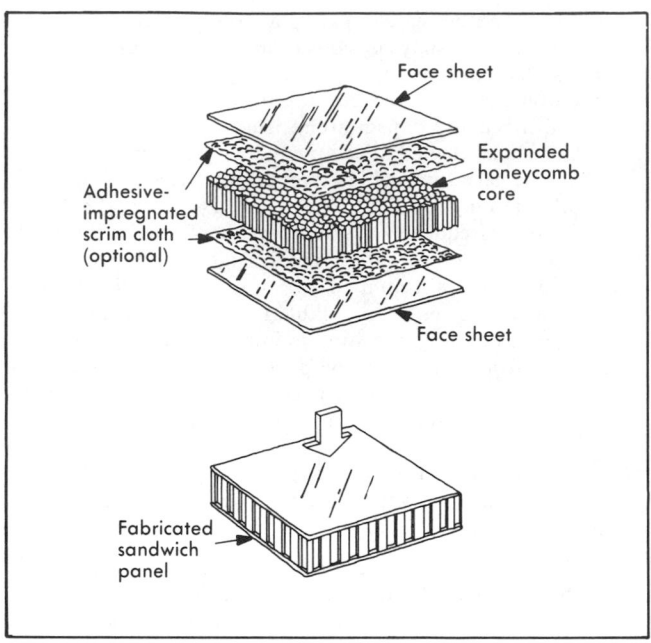

Fig. 42-61 Elements of a bonded sandwich.

TYPES OF ADHESIVES

Just as a variety of materials can be bonded with adhesives, there are thousands of adhesive formulations available for bonding these materials.[10] Adhesives are available as liquids (pastes, solutions, and emulsions) and solids (films, tapes, rods, pellets, and powders). Formulations are often identified by brand name, but it is important to the user to be able to identify the chemical type as well. Suppliers are usually willing to provide such information, as well as pertinent data on the properties of the adhesive and test results on its performance in joints.

The three main adhesive material categories are: (1) natural product raw materials, (2) inorganic raw materials, and (3) synthetic organic materials.

TABLE 42-2
Applications of Bonded Sandwich Construction

Aircraft:	
Control surfaces	Doors (structural access, and entry)
Control tabs	Engine cowling
Bulkheads	Wing panels
Helicopter blades	Fairings
Flooring (cargo and passenger compartment)	Fan air ducts
Missile and spacecraft electronics and communications:	
Fins and control surfaces	Radomes
Structural shells	Shipping containers
Antenna reflectors	Intertank structures
Tankage	Electronic packaging
Heat shields	
Buildings:	
Prefab shelters	Partitions and doors
Curtain walls	
Miscellaneous:	House-trailer flooring
Desk tops	Boats
Scaffolding	Cargo containers

Natural Adhesives

Examples of natural product materials are gums and resins, starch, dextrin, casein, soya flour, and animal products such as blood and collagen. Adhesives made from these natural materials are most applicable to products where lower stresses are permissible. They are usually too weak for metal joints that may need to resist intermittent or steady stressing conditions. In many product applications, however, relatively large areas can be used so that the unit load is small. The number of such applications is large enough that natural-product-based adhesives still constitute the major poundage of adhesives used.

Inorganic Adhesives

The principal inorganic adhesives are sodium silicate and magnesium oxychloride. They have the advantage of low cost, but have serious shortcomings in their low strength, negligible flexibility, and, in some cases, sensitivity to moisture.

Synthetic Adhesives

The synthetic organic adhesives are of primary interest to the manufacturing engineer. These adhesives have been developed in the laboratory to give high-strength bonds to wood, glass, plastics, and metals. Technical assistance is usually available from the adhesive manufacturers to fit one of these adhesives to a given assembly process. The synthetic organic adhesives fall into the raw material classes of elastomers and resins.

Resins may be further subdivided into thermoplastic and thermoset types. The most common individual members of these classes are styrene block copolymers; acrylic, polyolefin, nylon, and vinyl thermoplastic resins; and acrylic (anaerobics), epoxy, phenolic, polyurethane, and silicone thermosets. New technology also includes many hybrid types, which are alloys of the older classic types.

Chemically Reactive Adhesives (Class I)

The chemically reactive adhesives all undergo a curing or crosslinking reaction within the adhesive. Most reactive adhesives provide high lap-shear strengths, to 7000 psi (48.3 MPa) or more, at room temperature. When crosslinked (thermoset), these adhesives retain properties well. Because many of these thermoset resins are relatively brittle, the peel strengths are frequently low. To improve the peel strengths, polymer alloys are commonly prepared from chemically reactive adhesives and various flexible thermoplastics and elastomers.

Plural Components (Class IA). In this type of adhesive, the chemical reaction is initiated by mixing a reactive component or catalyst with the adhesive before application. The reaction then proceeds at some rate, depending on the particular curing agent or catalyst, until an inert thermoset, chemically resistant resin develops. Heating will usually accelerate the cure rate as well as improve initial fluidity for better substrate wetting, resulting in improved bond durability. Epoxies are probably the most common resin bases for this class of adhesives, although polyester, polysulfide, polyurethane, and silicone resins are available in two-part mix formulations.

Heat-Activated Adhesives (Class IB)—Epoxies, Urethanes and Phenolics. This class of adhesives is often referred to as the one-part, heat-curing type. All of the necessary ingredients have been premixed by the adhesive supplier, but heating is required to initiate the chemical reaction. Because they are premixed, shelf life, even at room temperature may be limited to a few months. Such adhesives can be stored at subambient temperatures to improve shelf life. Every manufacturer of this type of adhesive tries to optimize shelf life, yet permit as rapid a cure as possible in the 180-350° F (82-177° C) temperature range.

One-Part Specially Catalyzed Adhesives (Class IC)— Cyanoacrylates and Anaerobics. There are several types of adhesives that need neither on-site mixing nor heat to cure, including cyanoacrylates, anaerobics, and acrylics with surface activators.

Cyanoacrylics. One of these types of adhesives that has attracted considerable attention because of ease of use is a cyanoacrylate.[11] The picture of an elephant being supported by the strength developed by one drop of adhesive is familiar. It seems incredible that a tensile strength of 5000 psi (34.5 MPa) is developed without the benefit of adding a separate catalyst or heat. This high strength is developed within a minute after the bondline is closed. Polymerization of the cyanoacrylate only occurs rapidly in the presence of a weakly basic compound, such as an amine, an alcohol, or trace amounts of water on the surface. For this latter reason, some describe the cure as moisture induced.

Anaerobics. Also prominent in this one-part class are the anaerobic adhesives that achieve cure at room temperature only in the absence of oxygen.[12] As long as oxygen is available, the curing mechanism cannot proceed, which is why these adhesives are stored in oxygen-permeable containers. When oxygen is excluded, such as by confinement between surfaces to be joined, polymerization can start, and the adhesive becomes a thermoset plastic. These adhesives have important properties, including rapid cure at ambient temperature, no need for metering and mixing prior to application, and resistance to a wide variety of solvents and industrial fluids. From a purely chemical point of view, these properties are not always achieved optimally and simultaneously. Ingenuity in chemistry, however, has permitted remarkable tradeoff compromises in such properties.

Radiation-curing adhesives (Class ID). Radiation curing of adhesives permits rapid curing, conserves energy, allows easy automation, and avoids air pollution by eliminating volatile products. Energy sources used for radiation curing are ultraviolet (UV) light, visible light, electron beam (EB), and gamma radiation. Gamma radiation has limited application, being restricted to a few specialized and electronic uses.

Ultraviolet light curing adhesives. Modified acrylics, anaerobics, and epoxies can be cured with UV light at 365 nm (3650 angstrom units) wavelength and 10,000 to 100,000 μW/cm^2 (64 500 to 645 000 μW/in.^{2}) intensity. They are prepared with photoinitiator chemicals that become active in the presence of the light. At the higher light intensities, cure takes place in 3-15 seconds, and air-exposed anaerobic material can be cured dry to touch. Obviously, the bondline must be visible to the light from at least one substrate to have direct activation.

ADHESIVE JOINING

Electron beam curing. Electron beam (EB) curing adhesives are being used with flocking, metallized paper, plastics, and foil laminates. Applications include the manufacture of magnetic discs and tapes with thermoplastic hot-melt or polyurethane adhesives.

Moisture-curing adhesives (Class IE)—Polysufides, Polyurethanes and Polysiloxanes (Silicones). These are liquid or paste adhesives that react on exposure to atmospheric moisture. Moisture-curing polysulfides[13] are primarily used as adhesive/sealants, but polyurethanes[14] can be applicable for either true structural bonding or as adhesive/sealants. The silicones are also available in moisture-curing room-temperature-vulcanizing (RTV) formulations that are structural or adhesive/sealant in nature.[15]

Evaporative Adhesives (Class II)

With evaporative adhesives, curing or setting occurs through the loss of solvent or water. Therefore, at least one of the adherends must be porous enough to absorb the solvent or water, or sufficient drying time must be allowed before assembly. Both thermoplastic and thermoset systems can be applied by this method. Soluble, nonreactive materials include rubber, vinyl resins, thermoplastic urethanes, acrylics, phenoxy resin, and natural materials such as cellulose esters, asphalt, starch, and casein. Many reactive resins, such as phenolics and urethanes, are also used in solvents. Some of these adhesives are flexible and have good peel strengths, some up to 100 lb/in. (17.5 N/mm) of width. Adhesion in shear or tension will generally be low and susceptible to more creep than the chemically reactive types. Latex (emulsion) adhesives are being used to bond impermeable surfaces when the required longer drying time can be tolerated or if forced drying is used.

Hot-Melt Adhesives (Class III)

Hot-melt adhesive[16] must be formulated with thermoplastic resins because by definition a thermoset resin will not form a melt condition upon reheating. Synthetic polymers used in hot-melt adhesives include ethylene vinyl acetate (EVA), polyethylene, styrene block copolymer, butyl rubber, polyamide, polyurethane, and polyester. Hot-melt adhesives must be applied in the molten state and depend on a rapid solidification for the development of bondline strength. Thus, polymer properties such as melting point, hot tack, melt viscosity, and heat stability are most important in determining the usefulness of resins in hot melts.[17] The apparent simplistic manner of applying and developing fast bond strength using hot melts would lead to the conclusion that they might be the perfect adhesive product, but there are both advantages and disadvantages that should also be recognized. Hot-melt adhesives are used extensively in the packaging industry and for product assembly applications to bond a variety of substrates, including metals, plastics, glass, fabrics, wood, and paper-related products.

Delayed-Tack Adhesives (Class IV)

Delayed-tack adhesives are nontacky solids that are heat-activated to produce a state of tackiness that is retained upon cooling for periods of up to several days. Blends of a resin such as polyvinyl acetate, polystyrene, or polyamide, with a solid plasticizer give this characteristic.

Film Adhesives (Class V)

Film adhesives[18] are related to the one-part heat activated, chemically reactive adhesives (Class IB) discussed previously in that similar adhesives are used and similar bond properties are obtained. They may also be similar to Class III or Class VI adhesives. The advantage of film adhesives include: (1) controlled glue-line thickness, (2) ease of application, (3) freedom from solvents, and (4) the opportunity to prepare two-sided films, each side with different adhesive properties to bond dissimilar surfaces. Also, film adhesives may be supplied on a flexible carrier, such as cloth or paper, in sheet or tape form. The most serious disadvantage for the curing type is the requirement for precise heating of the parts for an extended length of time. The difficulty of automating the tape feeding and cutting limits the application of these adhesives to hand operations.

In aerospace and aircraft applications, much of the adhesive is used in honeycomb construction, producing very lightweight assemblies with high peel strength, high impact strength, and cleavage and fatigue strength hitherto impossible. The interlayer in automotive safety glass is also based on a film adhesive made from polyvinyl butyral resin. Many other laminated structures are made with thermoplastic film adhesives. Thermoplastic films based on polyolefins are heat-laminated; films having pressure-sensitive adhesive on both sides are used to assemble without heat.

Pressure-Sensitive Adhesives (Class VI)

A pressure-sensitive adhesive[19] may be defined as a material capable of bond formation by the brief application of pressure on a coated adherend at room temperature. The adhesive is applied to one surface from solution, emulsion, or hot melt, and then the adhesive is dried to a permanently tacky state. The coated surface is then brought into contact with a second adherend, and light pressure is applied to flow the adhesive on to the surface.

Masking tape, surgical tape, and labels are the major uses for pressure-sensitive adhesives, which are collectively called PSAs in the trade. A variety of other products using PSAs include wall and shelf coverings, imitation wood grain coverings, ceiling and floor tile, disposable diaper tabs, medical and sanitary products, graphic artwork, and protective maskings.

PRODUCT AND PROCESS SELECTION

The four basic requirements that should be considered when analyzing an adhesive application are as follows:

1. The type of material to be bonded is important, whether the adherends are metal, wood, paper, fabric, leather, plastic, elastomer, or ceramic. Are they bondable? Are they able to support the load under all conditions? Physical properties of the adherend such as size, flexibility, porosity, and heat distortion temperature should be considered. The design of the joint should be engineered around the weakest member of the system. Because the quality of the final assembly may be structural, the strength of the adherend itself is important.
2. All service conditions must be considered. A stress analysis is necessary to determine if the bond is within the stress limits for life expectancy. The stress cycle is important. Whether the type of loading is continuous or intermittent should be considered. Adhesive bonds should be downrated for conditions such as heat and heat aging, cold,

water, humidity, chemicals, oil, and solvents. Test data should be found or developed to substantiate the suitability of any strength assumptions.

3. All possible process or bonding procedures should be thoroughly investigated. The most simple process that will satisfy the final requirements should be selected. All assembly steps, such as surface preparation, adhesive application, and curing or setting methods, should be reviewed with the performance requirements as a guide. Keep the procedure as simple as possible. Special equipment such as fixtures, ovens (drying and bonding), and applicators should be included in the evaluation.

4. As a final requirement, evaluate the economics of the system. The cost of the adhesive itself per unit usually is minor compared to the cost of the process. The cost of labor may prohibit the purchase of cheap but hard-to-apply adhesives. Automated equipment will reduce the cost of assembly.

APPLICATION METHODS

Before choosing a method of applying the adhesive, the user should consider the following:[20]

1. Various methods for the best filling of the bondline and wetting of the adherends.
2. Economy of the application.
3. Production rate for the piece being fabricated.
4. Method of application from the viewpoint of simplicity.

The testing of the adherend should be initiated at the beginning of the investigation. The tests will likely reveal several suitable ways to apply the adhesive. Adhesives may be applied manually by roller, brush, extrusion and flow, and trowel. They can be applied semiautomatically with spray guns or high-pressure extrusion guns, or they can be applied automatically by machine methods that are usually geared for mass production of a particular part. Industrial robots are also being used for the application of adhesives and sealants.

Manual Roller Application

Rollers for manual application can be constructed from wood, paper, cork, metal mesh, rubber, or synthetic fibers. The length of nap on a roller determines the amount of material left on the coated surface.

Screen or Stencil Printing

Anaerobics are uniquely suited for screen or stencil application because of their stable nature in the presence of air. Accurate control of quantity is possible, and intricate patterns are applied in a second or two.

Brushing

Brush bristles for applying adhesives are made of various types of hair, synthetic fibers, wood, and metal. Compatibility with the adhesive may be important. The anaerobics, in particular, may require the use of all synthetic fibers so that the material does not cure in the bristles. Brushing is usually a manual operation, although sometimes the adhesive is fed to the brushes under pressure.

Extrusion and Flow

Extrusion and flow are general methods of applications used by operators equipped with caulking guns. Extrusion applica-

tion is also used in curtain coaters, flow coaters, and high-pressure air-powered extrusion units. Rotary extrusion is a method similar to screen printing for applying precise patterns of hot-melt adhesive to continuous webs of various substrates. A rotating print cylinder and doctor-blade assembly forces adhesive from heated supply units through the patterned mesh opening of the cylinder onto the substrate. Hot-melt adhesives are also being applied with extruders having capillary rheometers that permit rapid measurement of melt viscosity.

Troweling

A toothed trowel normally leaves a fairly constant amount of adhesive on the work surface. Small cutouts or teeth along one margin of the trowel allow a predictable amount of material to pass through and remain on the surface.

Spraying

The selection of spray equipment over other methods of application is usually predicated by economic considerations. This is particularly true when the products are large or of a complex shape. Spraying is fast and provides a means of reaching inaccessible areas easily. Furthermore, the drying time of the coating usually is reduced when it is sprayed because of the fine distribution of solvent into the airspace above the workpiece. When automated spray equipment is employed, particularly for long runs of identical objects, the optimum advantages of spray equipment are realized. Spray equipment can be classified by method: air spray or airless spray, depending on the technique used to project the liquid.

Vacuum Impregnation

Vacuum impregnation is commonly used, especially in applying anaerobic adhesives to powder metal, laminated, and die cast parts. Adhesive is pushed into microscopic pores after air has been excluded by a vacuum cycle. This is done in a large mesh basket in a vacuum vat with the parts immersed. Excess adhesive is spun off, leaving a relatively clean surface.

Manual Applicators

Adhesive applicators can be handheld or machine (or fixture) mounted. Handheld applicators include heavy-duty diaphragm-valve handguns and light-duty pinch-tube pencil applicators with fingertip lever actuators. With the actuator depressed, adhesive flows out of the nozzle; when released, flow stops. Pencil applicators are also available with poppet valves in the nozzles—when the nozzle is pushed against a surface, the valve opens and adhesive flows; when lifted, flow stops.

Roll Coaters

More adhesives are applied with roll coaters than by any other single method. Roll coaters are very efficient, with waste as low as 2%. They may be used to coat webs or individual flat sheets or panels of materials such as paper, paperboard, plastics, synthetic rubbers, cloth, wood composition materials, and metals. Bench-type roll coaters are available in widths from 4 to 26" (102 to 660 mm). Some models have open-end rollers that permit material larger than the rollers to be fed through the machine. Floor-mounted roll coaters are available in various types, including kiss-roll, pressure-roll, and reverse-roll coaters.

Robotic Applicators

Industrial robots are being used for the application of adhesives and sealants. The robots are generally used to manipulate

ADHESIVE JOINING

the dispensing gun, but occasionally the parts to be joined are manipulated by the robots. Advantages of using robots for such applications include reduced labor requirements and costs, faster production, consistently high quality, and reduced adhesive usage. Adhesives can be applied to a number of parts simultaneously by using multiple guns on a single robot. A possible limitation is that high volumes are generally necessary for cost-effectiveness. However, the flexibility of robots permits handling a variety of different parts in small batches.

References

1. "Glossary of Terms for Mechanical Fasteners," ANSI B18.12 (New York: American Society of Mechanical Engineers).
2. *Ibid.*
3. *Ibid.*
4. *Ibid.*
5. D. H. Kaelble, *Physical Chemistry of Adhesion* (New York: Wiley & Sons, 1971).
6. J. D. Minford and E. M. Vader, *Adhesive Bonding of Aluminum Automotive Body Sheet*, Paper No. 740078, SAE Congress and Exposition, held February 1974, Detroit (Warrendale, PA: Society of Automotive Engineers, 1974).
7. J. D. Minford, F. R. Hoch, and E. M. Vader, *Weldbond and Its Performance in Aluminum Automotive Body Sheet*, Paper No. 750462, SAE Congress and Exposition, held February 1975, Detroit (Warrendale, PA: Society of Automotive Engineers, 1974).
8. C. C. Booth, "A Guide to Building Construction Adhesives," *Adhesives Age* (February 1979), p. 31-37.
9. J. D. Minford and E. M. Vader, "Aluminum Faced Sandwich Panels and Laminates," *Adhesvies Age* (February 1975), p. 30.
10. I. Skeist, *Handbook of Adhesives*, 2nd ed. (New York: Van Nostrand Reinhold, 1977).
11. William F. Thomsen, *Adhesives in Manufacturing*, ed. G. L. Schneberger (New York: Marcel Dekker, 1983), chap. 12, pp. 305-323.
12. M. Hauser and G. S. Haviland, *Adhesives in Manufacturing*, ed. G.L. Schneberger (New York: Marcel Dekker, 1983), chap. 11, pp. 269-303.
13. M. E. Kimball, "Polyurethane Adhesives: Properties and Bonding Procedures," *Adhesives Age* (June 1981), pp. 21-26.
14. J. D. Minford, *Durability of Structural Adhesives*, ed. A. J. Kinloch (London: Applied Science Publishers, 1983), chap. 4, pp. 197-198.
15. J. V. Lindyberg, *Adhesives in Manufacturing*, ed. G. L. Schneberger (New York: Marcel Dekker, 1983), chap. 15, pp. 387-406.
16. R. D. Dexheimer and L. R. Vertnik, *Adhesives in Manufacturing*, ed. G. L. Schneberger (New York: Marcel Dekker, 1983), chap. 13, pp. 325-352.
17. D. J. Hines, "Testing and Performance of Hot-Melt Adhesives," *Adhesives Age* (June 1980), pp. 27-32.
18. J. C. Bolger, *Treatise of Adhesion and Adhesives*, ed. R. L. Patrick (New York: Marcel Dekker, 1973), vol. 3, chap. 1, pp. 31-50.
19. J. W. Hagan and K. C. Steuben, *Adhesives in Manufacturing*, ed. G. L. Schneberger (New York: Marcel Dekker, 1983), chap. 14, pp. 353-386.
20. "What's New in Machinery and Equipment," *Adhesives Age* (May 1979), pp. 38-43; (May 1980), pp. 16-22; (May 1981), pp. 24-29; (May 1982), pp. 23-29.

WELDING, CUTTING, BRAZING AND SOLDERING

Welding is a materials joining process in which localized coalescence (joining) is produced along the faying surfaces of the workpieces. Coalescence is produced either by heating the materials to suitable temperatures, with or without the application of pressure, or it is produced by the application of pressure alone. With some welding processes, filler material is added during welding.

There are more then 50 different welding processes, some of which are listed in Table 43-1. Most of these are discussed in detail in this chapter. The processes can be classified as either fusion or solid-state (nonfusion) methods.

Fusion welding processes, in which the workpieces are melted together at their faying surfaces, are the most commonly used processes. Arc, resistance, and oxyfuel gas welding are the pre-dominant fusion processes. Filler metals often used with the arc and oxyfuel gas welding methods have melting points about the same as or just below those of the metals being joined.

In solid-state welding, the workpieces are joined by the application of heat and usually pressure, or by the application of pressure only. However, with these processes, the welding temperature is essentially below the melting point of the materials being joined or if any liquid metal is present it is squeezed out of the joint. No filler metal is added during welding.

Brazing and soldering are joining processes that use heat and filler metals to produce metallurgical bonds. Unlike most of the fusion welding processes discussed earlier, brazing and soldering do not involve any melting of the base metals being joined. As a result, the mechanical and physical properties of the base metals are not generally duplicated at the joints. However, diffusion brazing can produce a strength equal to the base metal.

OXYFUEL GAS WELDING AND CUTTING

Oxyfuel gas welding (OFW) is a group of welding processes that produces coalescence by heating materials with an oxyfuel gas flame or flames, with or without the application of pressure, and with or without the use of filler metal. In these processes, the base metal, as well as filler metal, if used, is melted by the flame from the tip of a welding torch.

Oxyfuel gas cutting is a group of cutting processes used to sever or remove metals by means of the chemical reaction of oxygen with the base metal at elevated temperatures. In the case of oxidation-resistant metals, the reaction is facilitated by the use of a chemical flux or metal powder.

OXYFUEL GAS WELDING

The three most commonly used oxyfuel gas welding processes are:

- Oxyacetylene welding (OAW). In this process, heating is done with a gas flame or flames obtained from the combustion of acetylene with oxygen. The process may be used with or without the application of pressure and with or without the use of filler metal.
- Oxyhydrogen welding (OHW). In this process, heating is done with a gas flame or flames obtained from the combustion of hydrogen with oxygen. The process is used without the application of pressure and with or without the use of filler metal.
- Pressure gas welding (PGW). In this process, coalescence is produced simultaneously over the entire area of abutting surfaces by heating them with flames obtained from the combustion of a fuel gas with oxygen. The process entails the application of pressure, but without the use of filler metal.

A fourth oxyfuel gas welding process, air-acetylene welding (AAW), uses heating obtained from the combustion of acetylene with air, without the application of pressure and with or without the use of filler metal. However, by using air instead of oxygen, the resulting available heat is lower. As a result, the air-acetylene welding process is obsolete or seldom used.

Advantages and Applications

Oxyfuel gas welding offers considerable flexibility because the operator can control the rate of heat input, the temperature in the weld zone, the rate of filler metal deposition, and speed, making it suitable for joining most metals. Other advantages are that no power source is required, and the equipment can so be used for related operations such as bending and straightening, preheating and postheating, and torch brazing. A limitation is that the process is slower than most other welding methods on thicker metals.

The equipment required for oxyfuel gas welding is comparatively simple, compact, usually portable, and inexpensive, making it especially useful for maintenance and repairs, odd job-shop work, and certain types of tube and pipe welding. It is the preferred process for welding of lead, and it is also preferred in many cases for cast iron when a joint defect of any considerable magnitude is to be repaired. Oxyhydrogen welding is generally re-

OXYFUEL GAS WELDING AND CUTTING

TABLE 43-1
Welding Processes

Fusion Methods	
Arc welding (AW):	Resistance welding (RW):
shielded metal arc welding (SMAW)	resistance spot welding (RSW)
submerged arc welding (SAW)	resistance projection welding (RPW)
gas metal arc welding (GMAW)	resistance seam welding (RSEW)
flux-cored arc welding (FCAW)	upset welding (UW)
gas tungsten arc welding (GTAW)	flash welding (FW)
plasma arc welding (PAW)	percussion welding (PEW)
electrogas welding (EGW)	high-frequency resistance welding (HFRW)
carbon arc welding (CAW)	
gas carbon arc welding (CAW-G)*	Electroslag welding (ESW)
shielded carbon arc welding (CAW-S)	
bare metal arc welding (BMAW)*	Electron beam welding (EBW)
atomic hydrogen welding (AHW)*	
stud arc welding (SW)	Laser beam welding (LBW)
Oxyfuel gas welding (OFW):	Thermit welding (TW)
oxyacetylene welding (OAW)	
oxyhydrogen welding (OHW)	
air-acetylene welding (AAW)*	
pressure gas welding (PGW)	

Solid-State Methods	
Diffusion welding (DFW)	Cold welding (CW)
Friction welding (FRW)	Forge welding (FOW)
Ultrasonic welding (USW)	Coextrusion welding (CEW)
Explosion welding (EXW)	Hot pressure welding (HPW)

* Obsolete or seldom used processes.

stricted to aluminum or lead alloys. Pressure gas welding has been used for uniting links of rail and pipe, for making rings, and for similar applications where bar or pipe sections of essentially similar cross sections are to be joined. Although it has some highly specialized favorable applications, its use is generally on the decline.

Methods of Welding

Oxyfuel gas welding may be performed by one of two methods: forehand welding or backhand welding. These designations are derived from the direction of the welding.

Forehand welding. In this technique (see Fig. 43-1, view *a*), the torch and the welding rod are disposed in the joint so that the torch points ahead in the direction of welding, and the rod precedes the torch. Distribution of the heat and molten metal is secured by imparting to the torch and rod opposite oscillating motions in semicircular paths on large weldments.

In backhand welding (see Fig. 43-1, view *b*), the torch and the welding rod are disposed in the joint so that the torch points back at the completed weld, and the rod is interposed between the torch and the weld puddle. This arrangement permits a simpler distribution of the heat and molten metal. It has the further advantage that the flame playing back on the molten puddle, and the completed weld protects them from the atmosphere. Backhand welding commonly progresses at faster speeds than forehand welding. In addition, backhand welds are of higher quality. Moderately faster speeds can be achieved with a slightly reducing flame, which can increase the carbon content

and thus reduce the melting point.

Braze welding. Braze welding is a method whereby a groove, fillet, or slot weld is made with a nonferrous filler metal having a melting point below that of the base metal, but above 800° F (425° C). The filler metal is not distributed in the joint by capillary attraction as in brazing. Braze welding, as generally practiced, employs a brass filler rod composed of 60% copper and 40% zinc, with small additions of tin, manganese, iron, or silicon.

Hard facing (surfacing). Hard facing is a process by means of which hard, wear-resistant alloys are applied to the surfaces of softer metals, thereby prolonging their service life. Standard oxyfuel gas welding techniques are employed except that melting of the base metal is avoided, and a strongly reducing or carburizing flame is used. Melting the base metal tends to dilute the alloying ingredients in the deposit with resultant loss of hardness. Consequently, only surface fusion (sometimes called "sweating") is used. Varying degrees of hardness and toughness are obtainable, thus providing wear-resistant metal to suit a variety of conditions.

THERMAL CUTTING PROCESSES

Oxygen cutting, sometimes called flame cutting, is a group of processes used to sever or remove metals by means of the chemical reaction of oxygen with the base metal at elevated temperatures. The most commonly used oxygen cutting process is oxyfuel gas cutting (OFC) in which the necessary temperatures for cutting are maintained by means of gas flames

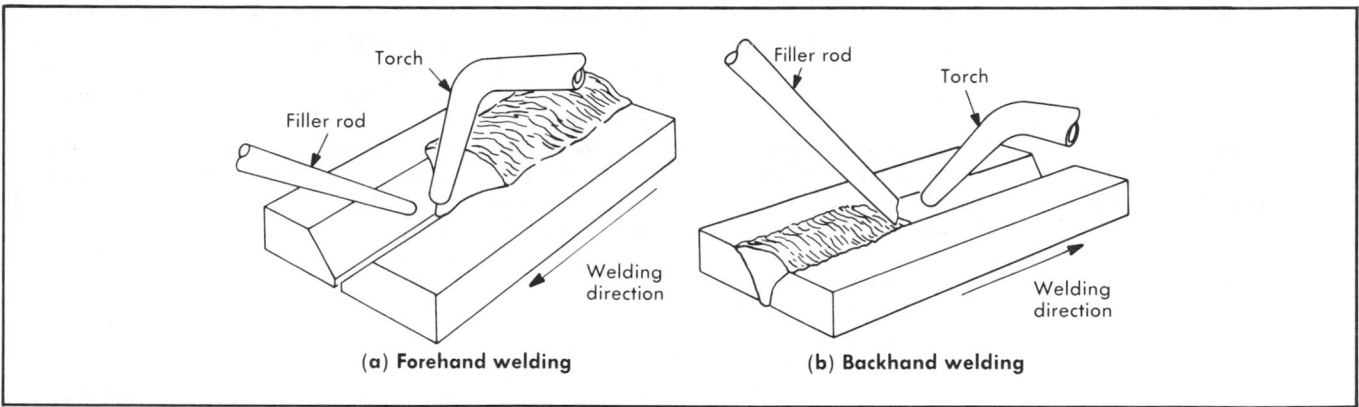

Fig. 43-1 Fundamental methods of oxyfuel gas welding.

obtained from the combustion that takes place between a specified fuel gas and oxygen.

Oxyfuel gas cutting is used most extensively to cut low and medium-carbon steels. Other readily oxidizable materials such as titanium can also be cut by this process. Oxidation-resistant materials such as stainless steel are cut by adding metal powder, such as iron, or chemical flux to the cutting oxygen stream. These processes are known respectively as metal powder cutting (POC) and chemical flux cutting (FOC).

OXYFUEL GAS CUTTING

Oxyfuel gas cutting is the most widely used thermal cutting process. It has been given many names, such as burning, flame cutting, oxygen cutting, and flame machining. The process can be performed with equipment ranging from lightweight, inexpensive, handheld cutting torches to costly, computer-controlled, multitorch cutting machines. Although the process has

been used to cut steel up to 8' (2.4 m) thick, the majority of material cut is under 2" (51 mm) in thickness.

Oxyfuel gas cutting is a versatile process that can be used to cut straight lines or continual change of direction lines because the cutting oxygen stream acts as a tool with a 360° cutting edge. Cuts can be started at the edges of workpieces or piercing can be used to start a cut at any point on the work surface. With proper conditions, edge quality is good. Two or more pieces can be cut simultaneously by stack cutting, and edges can be bevel-cut for weld joint preparation. In addition, the process can operate in any axis with equal facility.

The process is fast compared to machining and slow compared to plasma arc cutting, but the speed can be increased by the use of multiple torches, cutting machines, and stack cutting. Heat-affected zones can be large with oxyfuel gas cutting, and workpieces can be distorted, especially if they are made from thin metals.

ARC WELDING AND CUTTING

Arc welding (AW) involves a group of fusion welding processes that produces coalescence (joining) of metals by heating them with an electric arc, with or without the application of pressure and with or without the use of filler metal. Most of these processes, listed in Table 43-1, are discussed in this chapter. Gas-shielded arc welding is a general term used to describe gas metal arc welding, gas tungsten arc welding, and flux-cored arc welding when gas shielding is used.

Arc cutting is a group of cutting processes that melts the metal to be cut with the heat of an electric arc between an electrode and the metal. The processes used extensively in industry are plasma arc cutting and air-carbon arc cutting, discussed subsequently. Other arc cutting processes that are not used extensively or are used only for special applications are described briefly at the end of this section.

FUNDAMENTALS OF ARC WELDING

By the application of intense heat during arc welding, the base metals at the joint are melted and caused to intermix either directly or, more commonly, with a molten filler metal. Upon cooling and solidification, a metallurgical bond results. Because

the joining takes place by melting together one part with the other part, with or without a filler metal of suitable composition, the welded joint may have strength properties similar to those of the base metals. This is in contrast to nonfusion processes of joining that use a separate filler, such as soldering, brazing, or adhesive bonding, in which the mechanical and physical properties of the base materials cannot be duplicated at the joint.

In arc welding, the intense heat needed to melt metals is produced by an electric arc. The arc is generally formed between the work to be welded and an electrode that is manually or mechanically moved along the joint, or the work may be moved under a stationary electrode. The electrode may be a carbon or tungsten rod that conducts the welding current to the electric arc between the hot electrode tip and the workpiece. Also, it may be a specially prepared rod or wire that not only conducts the welding current and sustains the arc, but also melts and provides filler metal to the joint.

If a carbon or tungsten electrode is used and the joint requires added filler metal, that metal is added from a separate filler metal rod or wire. Most welding in the manufacture of steel products where filler metal is required, however, is accomplished with consumable electrodes—those that supply filler metal as well as conduct the welding current.

ARC WELDING AND CUTTING

Use of the heat of an electric arc to join metals, however, requires more than the moving of the electrode with respect to the weld joint. Metals at high temperatures react chemically with the main constituents of air, oxygen, and nitrogen to form oxides and nitrides. Upon solidification of the molten weld pool, the oxides and nitrides reduce the strength and ductility properties of the welded joint. For this reason, the various arc welding processes provide some means for covering the arc, electrode tip, the arc, and the molten weld pool with a protective shield of gas or slag. This is referred to as arc shielding.

Arc shielding is accomplished by various techniques, such as the use of (1) a vapor-generating covering on consumable electrodes, (2) an inert gas or a granular flux covering the arc and molten pool, and (3) fluxing materials within the core of tubular electrodes that generate shielding vapors. Whatever the shielding method, the intent is to provide a blanket of gas or slag, or both, that prevents or minimizes contact of hot weld metal with air.

The shielding method also affects the stability and the energy of the arc. When the shielding is produced by an electrode covering, by electrode core substances, or by separately applied granular flux, a fluxing or alloying function, or both, are usually provided. Thus, the core materials in a flux-cored electrode may supply deoxidizing and alloying functions as well as a shielding function. In submerged arc welding, the granular flux applied to the joint ahead of the arc has a similar effect.

Figure 43-2 illustrates the shielding of the welding arc and molten weld pool with a covered electrode. The extruded covering on the filler metal rod, under the heat of the arc, generates a gaseous shield that displaces the surrounding air from the molten weld metal. It also supplies ingredients that react with deleterious substances on or in the metals, such as oxides and other compounds, and ties these substances up chemically in a slag. The slag, being lighter than the weld metal, rises to the surface of the molten weld pool and solidifies with the weld metal. This slag, after solidification, has a protective function; it protects the hot solidified metal from air.

of the inherent cost advantage of welding can be lost through poor design, as well as through poor procedure control. Factors to be considered in designing for welding include performance requirements, location of welds, stress distribution, and joint placement.

Types of joints are illustrated in Fig. 43-3. Groove and fillet welds (see Fig. 43-4) are the common types produced by arc welding. Major factors in the selection of the types of joints and welds are application requirements and costs. Combinations of fillet and groove welds are used for some joints, depending on the loading conditions.

Fillet Welds

Fillet welds are more economical than groove welds but they sometimes require more weld metal. Simple or no edge preparation is necessary, but some surface cleaning may be required. Fillet welds are generally preferred when stresses are low, when designs permit, and when required weld sizes are less than about 5/8" (16 mm).

When feasible from the strength standpoint, intermittent fillet welding is used instead of continuous welding for greater economy and distortion control. Fillet weld size should be limited to that required; doubling the size of a fillet requires four times as much weld metal and increases the amount of distortion.

Groove Welds

Groove welds are of several types (see Fig. 43-5). A general classification is according to groove preparation: square, V, bevel, J, and U-shaped grooves. All groove welds should be designed for minimum cross-sectional area and most economical edge preparation. Shearing and flame cutting of the groove faces are common; machining of the faces is generally the most expensive method, but can result in the highest quality joints.

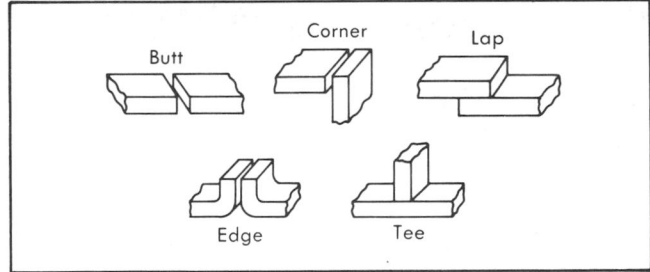

Fig. 43-3 Types of joints. (*Hobart Brothers Co.*)

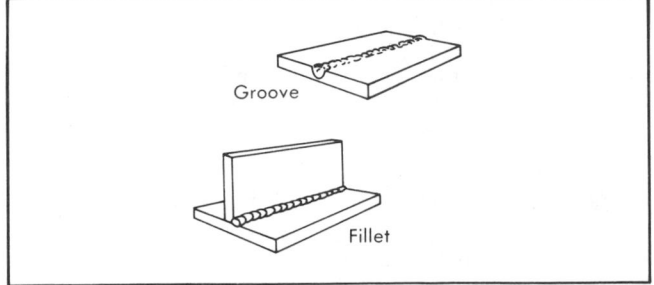

Fig. 43-4 Groove and fillet welds. (*Hobart Brothers Co.*)

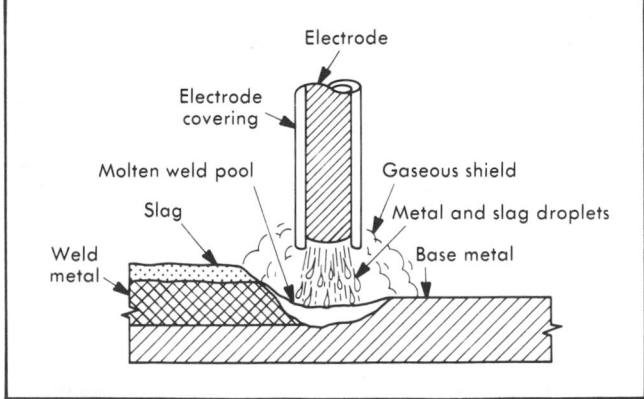

Fig. 43-2 Arc and molten pool are shielded by a gaseous blanket. Slag forms over hot solidified metal. (*Lincoln Electric Co.*)

JOINTS, WELDS AND GROOVES

The relationship between joint design and the production welding process is significant when arc welding is used. Much

Savings can often be realized by using simulated grooves. These consist of consumable backing materials, such as square or round rods, placed between the straight edges of the weldment components. The use of simulated grooves eliminates the need and cost for machining or cutting the component edges. For joining thick sections, double-groove welds require considerably less weld metal, but they require welding from both sides.

ARC WELDING DEFECTS

Defects commonly occurring as the result of arc welding include spatter, undercut, incomplete fusion, cracks, porosity, slag inclusions, inadequate joint penetration, and overlap. Distortion, common to other welding processes in addition to arc welding, is discussed in the introductory section of this chapter. Some of the discontinuities and corrective measures are summarized in Table 43-2.

SHIELDED METAL ARC WELDING

Shielded metal arc welding (SMAW) is an arc welding process that produces coalescence (joining) of metals by heating them with an arc between a covered (or coated) metal electrode and the work (see Fig. 43-6). Shielding is provided by decomposition of the electrode covering. Pressure is not used, and filler metal is obtained from the electrode. The SMAW process is commonly called stick-electrode or manual welding.

Applications

The shielded metal arc method is one of the oldest and the most widely used of the various arc welding processes. It is basically a manual process used by small welding shops, home mechanics, and farmers for the repair of equipment. The process also has extensive application in industrial fabrication, structural steel erection, weldment manufacture, and other commercial metals joining operations.

Advantages

Major advantages of shielded metal arc welding include application versatility and flexibility and the simplicity, portability, and low cost of the equipment required. The process is capable of welding thin and thick steels and some nonferrous metals in all positions.

Limitations

Required periodic changing of the electrode is one of the major disadvantages of shielded metal arc welding for production applications. This decreases the percentage of time actually spent in welding. Another disadvantage is the limitation placed on the current that can be used. High amperages, such as those used with semiautomatic guns or automatic welding heads, are impractical because of the long and varying length of electrode between the arc and the point of electrical contact in the jaws of the electrode holder.

Welding current is limited by the resistance heating of the electrode. The electrode temperature must not exceed the breakdown temperature of the covering. If the temperature is too high, the covering chemicals react with each other or with

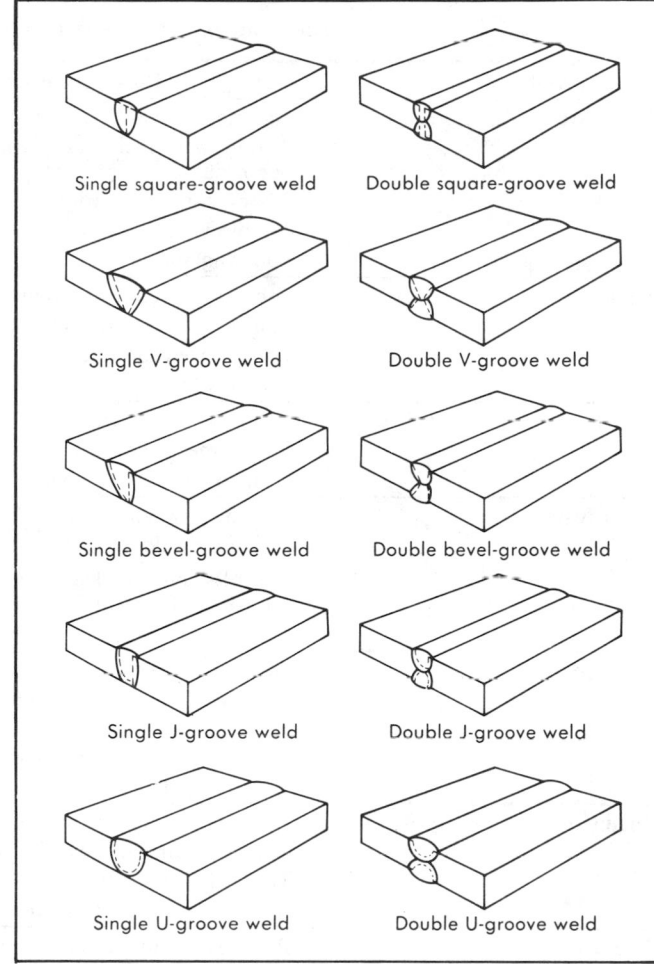

Fig. 43-5 Various types of groove welds. (*Reprinted from the AWS Welding Handbook with permission.*)

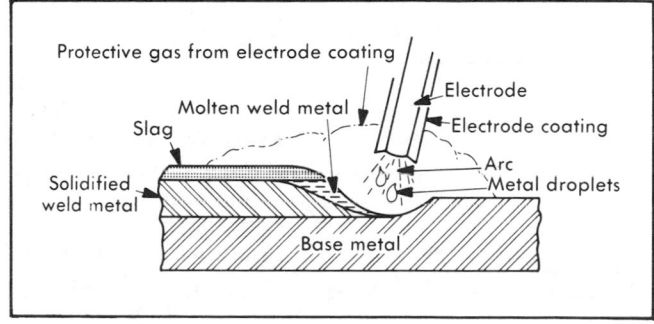

Fig. 43-6 Shielded metal arc welding. (*Hobart Brothers Co.*)

air and therefore do not function properly at the arc. As a result of limited temperatures, deposition rates and efficiency are low.

With the development of processes, such as semiautomatic, self-shielded, flux-cored arc welding, having similar or even superior versatility and flexibility, there is less justification for using shielded metal arc welding in applications requiring substantial amounts of weld metal.

ARC WELDING AND CUTTING

TABLE 43-2
Possible Causes and Suggested Solutions for Common Welding Problems

Problems	Possible Causes	Suggested Solutions
Excessive weld spatter	Too high a welding current	Use proper current setting
	Wrong, wet, unclean, or damaged electrode	Use proper electrode
	Wrong current polarity	Use correct polarity
	Arc blow	Reduce effect of arc blow
	Too long an arc	Use minimum arc length
Undercut	Too high a welding current	Use proper current setting
	Improper electrode manipulation	Correct welding procedure
	Travel speed too fast	Reduce speed
	Arc blow	Reduce effect of arc blow
Overlap	Too large an electrode	Reduce electrode size
	Travel speed too slow	Increase speed
	Improper electrode angle	Use correct angle
Poor fusion	Too low a welding current	Use proper current setting
	Improper welding technique	Correct welding procedure
	Improper joint preparation	Prepare joint correctly
	Improper electrode size	Use proper electrode
	Arc blow	Reduce effect of arc blow
Poor penetration	Too long an arc	Use minimum arc length
	Improper joint preparation	Prepare joint correctly
	Too low a welding current	Use proper current setting
	Improper size or type electrode	Use proper electrode
	Travel speed too fast	Reduce speed
Inclusions	Incomplete slag removal between passes	Completely remove slag
	Too large an electrode	Reduce size of electrode
	Travel speed erratic	Use uniform speed
	Improper welding technique	Correct welding procedure
Cracks	Base metal not weldable or clean	Use weldable metal and clean
	Improper joint preparation	Prepare joint correctly
	Improper welding technique	Correct welding procedure
	Joint restraint too rigid	Reduce restraint
	Welds too small or incorrect shape	Increase weld size; correct shape
	Cooling rate too rapid	Preheat before welding
	Defective electrode	Change electrode
Porosity	Improper or dirty base metal	Change base metal and clean
	Improper welding technique	Correct welding procedure
	Excessively long or short arc	Use proper arc length
	Welding current and travel speed too high	Reduce current and travel speed
	Wrong, wet, unclean, or damaged electrode	Use proper electrode
	Insufficient or improper shielding gas	Increase flow and check gas
Arc blow	Unbalanced magnetic field	Switch to a-c if possible and reduce welding current
	Excessive magnetism in parts or fixture	Reduce welding current and arc length. Move work connection as far from weld as possible. Weld toward a heavy tack weld or toward a completed weld
Distortion	Overwelding	Keep weld metal to a minimum
	Improper edge preparation	Keep bevel below 30°
	Improper tack welding	Tack-weld with allowance for distortion
	Excessive weld size	Make welds to specified size
	Improper setup and fixturing	Tack-weld or clamp parts securely

GAS TUNGSTEN ARC WELDING

Gas tungsten arc welding (GTAW) is an arc welding process that produces coalescence (joining) of metals by heating them with an arc between a tungsten (nonconsumable) electrode and the work (see Fig. 43-7). Shielding is obtained by an envelope of an inert gas or gas mixture. Pressure and filler metal may or may not be used. The GTAW process is also known as TIG (tungsten inert gas), Heliarc, argon arc, and tungsten arc welding.

Applications

While a wide range of metal thicknesses can be welded, the gas tungsten arc method is especially adapted for welding thin metals where the requirements for quality and finish are exacting. It is one of the few arc welding processes that is satisfactory for welding such tiny and thin-walled objects as transistor cases, instrument diaphragms, and delicate expansion bellows. Gas tungsten arc welding is also used to join various combinations of dissimilar metals and for applying hard-facing and surfacing materials to steel. The process is performed manually, semiautomatically, or automatically.

Advantages

An important advantage of the gas tungsten arc process is that it is suitable for welding most metals, both ferrous and nonferrous, and producing high-quality joints. It is generally not used, however, for metals that melt at low temperatures, such as tin and lead. Materials weldable by the process include most grades of carbon, alloy, and stainless steels; aluminum and most of its alloys; magnesium and most of its alloys; copper and various brasses and bronzes; high-temperature alloys of various types; numerous hard-surfacing alloys; and such metals as titanium, zirconium, gold, and silver.

Another advantage is that this process does not produce weld spatter because no filler metal crosses the arc. Also, because no fluxing agents are used, cleaning after welding is seldom required. Welding is possible in all positions.

Limitations

A possible limitation to the use of the gas tungsten arc process is that it is slower than consumable-electrode arc welding processes. Also, this method requires an externally supplied inert shielding gas or a gas mixture, adding to the cost of welding. Any transfer of tungsten particles from the electrode to the weld causes hard, brittle contamination.

GAS METAL ARC WELDING

Gas metal arc welding (GMAW) is an arc welding process that produces coalescence (joining) of metals by heating them with an arc between a continuous, solid (consumable) electrode for filler metal and the work (see Fig. 43-8). Shielding is provided by an externally supplied gas or gas mixture. The GMAW process is also known as MIG (metal inert gas), MAG (metal active gas), CO_2, short-circuit arc, dip transfer, and wire welding.

Applications

Gas metal arc welding is performed using either a handheld gun or mechanical welding head or torch to which the electrode is fed automatically. The process is used extensively for high-production welding operations.

Advantages

The major features of gas metal arc welding are (1) the capability of obtaining high-quality welds in almost any metal, (2) the small amount of postweld cleaning it requires, (3) the

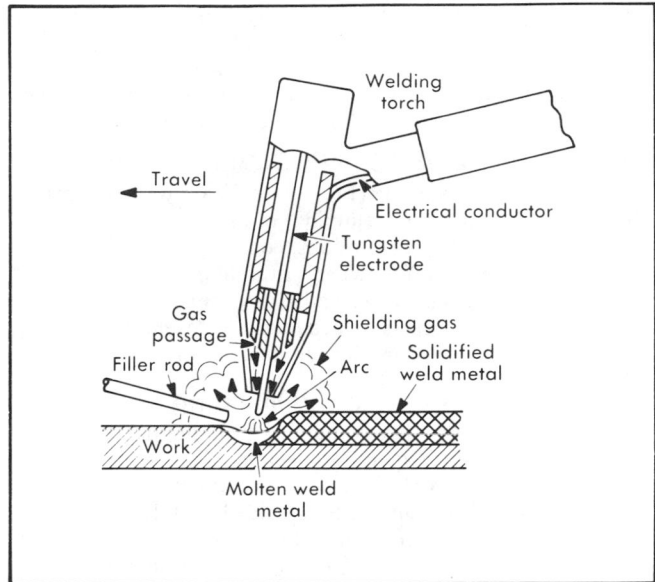

Fig. 43-7 Gas tungsten arc welding. When filler metal is required, it is fed into the pool from a separate rod. (*Lincoln Electric Co.*)

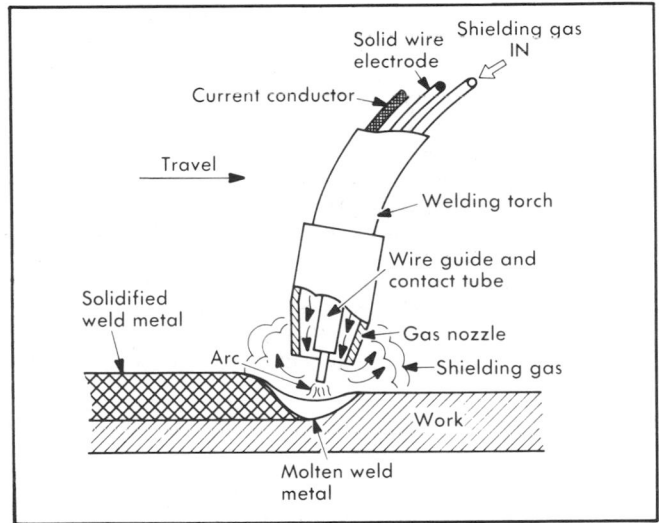

Fig. 43-8 Gas metal arc welding. (*Lincoln Electric Co.*)

visibility of its arc and weld pool to the welder, (4) its all-position capability, (5) its relatively high speed and economy, and (6) its elimination of slag entrapment in the weld. In addition, variations of the process have special advantages.

The gas metal arc process may be used to weld all of the major commercial metals, including carbon, alloy, and stainless steels, as well as aluminum, magnesium, copper, iron, titanium, and zirconium. It is a preferred process for the welding of aluminum, magnesium, copper, and many of the alloys of these reactive metals. Most of the irons and steels can be satisfactorily joined by this process, including the carbon-free irons; the low-carbon and low-alloy steels; the high-strength, quenched and tempered steels; the chromium irons and steels; the high-nickel steels; and some of the so-called superalloys.

Limitations

As with the gas tungsten arc process previously discussed, gas

ARC WELDING AND CUTTING

metal arc welding requires an externally supplied inert shielding gas or a gas mixture, adding to welding costs. Equipment required is complex and costly, and not readily portable. The welding gun must be kept close to the work to ensure adequate shielding, making it difficult for hard-to-reach joints.

FLUX-CORED ARC WELDING

Flux-cored arc welding (FCAW) is an arc welding process that produces coalescence (joining) of metals by heating them with an arc between a continuous, consumable, tubular filler-metal electrode and the work. In self-shielded flux-cored welding, shielding is provided entirely by the constituents of the tubular electrode. In gas-shielded flux-cored welding, shielding is provided from an externally supplied gas or gas mixture.

Self-Shielded Flux-Cored Welding

The self-shielded flux-cored arc welding process is an outgrowth of shielded metal arc welding. The versatility and maneuverability of stick electrodes in manual welding stimulated efforts to mechanize the shielded metal arc process. Developments consisted of making an electrode with self-shielding characteristics in coil form and feeding it mechanically to the arc (see Fig. 43-9), thus eliminating welding tie lost in changing electrodes and the material lost as electrode stubs. The result of these efforts was the development of the semiautomatic and fully automatic processes for welding with continuous, flux-cored, tubular electrode "wires." Such fabricated wires contain in their cores the ingredients for fluxing and deoxidizing molten metal and for generating shielding gases and vapors and slag coverings.

One of the advantages of the self-shielded fluxcored arc welding process is the high deposition rates possible with hand-held semiautomatic guns. High deposition rates, automatic electrode feed, and elimination of lost time for changing electrodes have resulted in substantial production economies wherever the semiautomatic process has been used to replace stick-electrode welding. Decreases in welding costs as great as 50% have been common, and in some production welding, deposition rates have been increased as much as 400%. The process permits the use of long electrode extensions (the lengths of the unmelted electrodes extending beyond the ends of the contact tube during welding), which increase the deposition rate for a given voltage and current.

Another advantage of the process is its tolerance for poor fitup, which often reduces rework and repair without affecting final product quality. The tolerance of the semiautomatic process to poor fitup has expanded the use of tubular steel members in structures by making possible sound connections where perfect fitup would be too difficult or costly to achieve.

Gas-Shielded Flux-Cored Welding

The gas-shielded flux-cored process is a hybrid of self-shielded flux-cored arc welding and gas metal arc welding. Tubular electrode wire is used, as in the self-shielded process (refer to Fig. 43-9), but the ingredients in its core are for fluxing, deoxidizing, scavenging, and, sometimes, alloying additions, rather than for these functions plus the generation of protective vapors. The process is similar to gas metal arc welding (refer to Fig. 43-8) in that a gas is separately applied to act as an arc shield.

Applications and advantages. The gas-shielded flux-cored process is used primarily for welding mild and low-alloy steels, as well as some stainless steels. It gives high deposition rates, high deposition efficiencies, and high operating factors. Radiographic-quality welds are easily produced, and the weld metal, with mild and low-alloy steels, has good ductility and toughness. The process is adaptable to a wide variety of joints and gives the capability for all-position welding.

Shielding gases. The supplementary external shielding gas normally used is carbon dioxide, although for stainless and certain alloy steels argon-carbon dioxide or argon-oxygen mixtures are used, depending on the base metal and the electrode type. Gas flow rate is dependent on the type of gas used, the base metal, the welding position, and the welding current.

ELECTROGAS WELDING

Electrogas welding (EGW) is an arc welding process that produces coalescence (joining) of metals by heating them with an arc between a continuous filler-metal (consumable) electrode and the work. Molding shoes span the gap between parts being

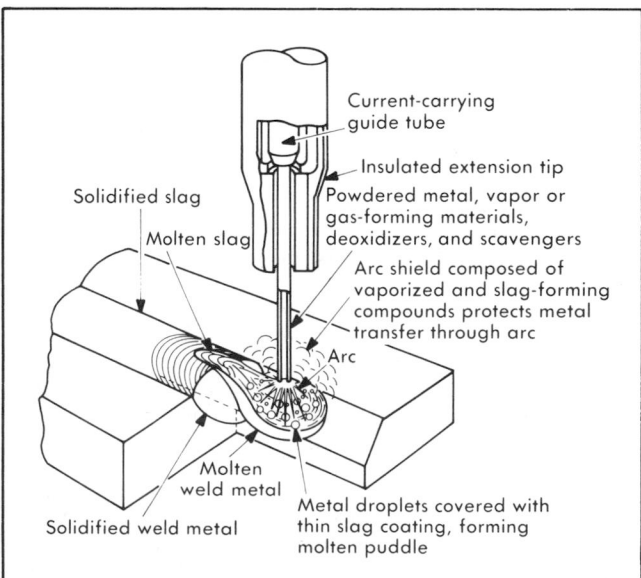

Current-carrying guide tube
Insulated extension tip
Powdered metal, vapor or gas-forming materials, deoxidizers, and scavengers
Arc shield composed of vaporized and slag-forming compounds protects metal transfer through arc
Arc
Solidified slag
Molten slag
Molten weld metal
Solidified weld metal
Metal droplets covered with thin slag coating, forming molten puddle

Fig. 43-9 Self-shielded, flux-cored welding. (*Lincoln Electric Co.*)

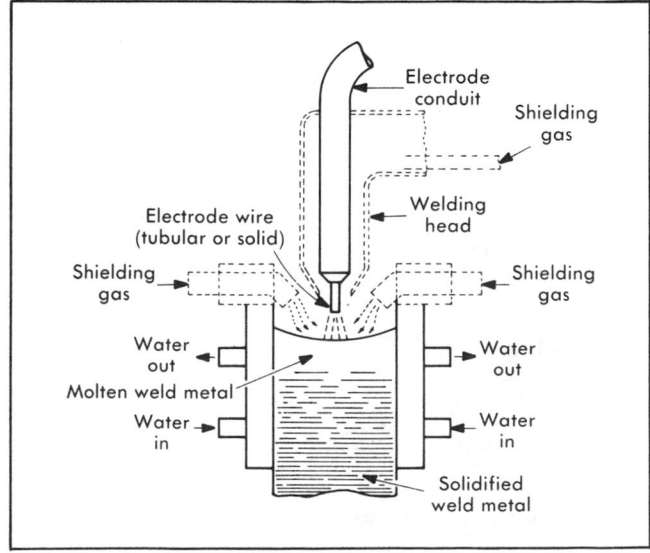

Electrode conduit
Shielding gas
Electrode wire (tubular or solid)
Welding head
Shielding gas
Shielding gas
Water out
Water out
Molten weld metal
Water in
Water in
Solidified weld metal

Fig. 43-10 Electrogas welding process. (*Hobart Brothers Co.*)

joined and confine the molten weld metal for vertical position welding. The electrodes may be either flux-cored or solid, and shielding may or may not be obtained from an externally supplied gas or gas mixture. There are two basic variations: one uses the solid consumable electrode wire and externally supplied shielding gas, normally CO_2 (see Fig. 43-10), and the second utilizes flux-cored electrode wire and does not ordinarily use an external shielding gas because shielding gases are formed as the flux-cored electrode wire is consumed in the arc.

Applications and Advantages

Metals welded by the electrogas process include low-carbon steels, low-alloy high-strength steels, medium-carbon steels, and certain stainless steels. The process can also be used for welding quenched and tempered steels providing that the correct heat input is maintained for the type of steel being welded. The major use of electrogas welding has been for the field erection of storage tanks for oil, water, and other liquids. Another use is in the shipbuilding industry for joining shell plates.

Weld sizes. Under normal conditions, the minimum thickness of metal welded with electrogas is 3/8″ (9.5 mm). The maximum thickness, utilizing one electrode, is 3/4″ (19 mm). The height (or length) of the joint is practically unlimited. The process can be used for joints as short as 4″ (100 mm) and/or as long or high as 50′ (15 m).

Deposition rates and weld quality. The deposition rates for electrogas welding are relatively high. Deposition rates with flux-cored wires vary with wire types and manufacturer because the ratio of fill to metal varies.

Electrogas welding is considered a low-hydrogen type of process because hydrogen is not present in any of the materials involved in making a weld. The cooling rate of the deposit weld metal is somewhat slower than for gas metal arc or flux-cored arc welding and, hence, impurities are more likely to be removed.

Electrogas welds possess properties and characteristics surpassing welds made with the shielded metal arc process. The higher than normal heat input of electrogas welding reduces the cooling rate. This in turn allows larger grain growth of the weld metal and also in the heat-affected zone of the base metal. Large grain growth, however, can be detrimental because strength is reduced substantially, especially if proper weld procedures are not used. The lower cooling rate minimizes the risk of cracking and reduces the high hardness zones in the weld and heat-affected zone that are sometimes found with shielded metal arc welding. The hardness of the weld is normally uniform across the cross section of the weld and is very similar to the unaffected base metal.

Weld metal produced by electrogas welding will qualify under most codes and specifications. Ductility of the weld metal or electrogas weld is relatively high, in the range of 25% elongation. Impact requirements for electrogas welds will meet those required by the AWS Structural Welding Code. V-notch Charpy impact specimens producing 5-30 ft-lbf (6.8-40.7 N·m) at 0°F (-18°C) are normal and expected.

Limitations

The major limitation of the electrogas process is with respect to welding position, which is generally vertical. The process should not be used if the joint is at an angle in excess of 15° from the vertical. Also, the length (height) of the weld produced is limited by the length of the elevating mechanism for moving the weld head vertically.

SUBMERGED ARC WELDING

Submerged arc welding (SAW) differs from other arc welding processes in that a blanket of fusible, granular material—commonly called flux—is used for shielding the arc and the molten metal (see Fig. 43-11). The arc is struck between the workpiece and a bare, consumable wire electrode, the tip of which is submerged in the flux. Because the arc is completely covered by the flux, it is not visible, and the weld is produced without the flash, spatter, and sparks that characterize open arc processes. Pressure is not used. The nature of the flux is such that very little smoke or visible fumes are developed.

The process is either semiautomatic or fully automatic, with the electrode(s) fed mechanically to the welding gun, head, or heads. In semiautomatic welding, the welder moves the gun, usually equipped with a flux-feeding device, along the joint. Flux feed may be by gravity flow through a nozzle concentric with the electrode, from a small hopper atop the gun, or it may be through a concentric nozzle tube connected to an air-pressurized flux tank.

Flux may also be applied in advance of the welding operation or ahead of the arc from a hopper run along the joint. In fully automatic submerged arc welding, flux is fed continuously to the joint ahead of or concentric to the arc. Fully automatic installations are commonly equipped with vacuum systems to pick up the unfused flux left by the welding head or heads for cleaning and reuse.

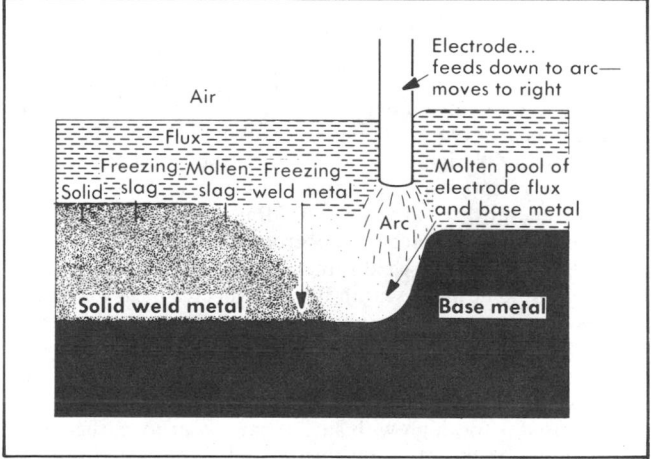

Fig. 43-11 Submerged arc process: enlarged cross sectional view of arc welding under a blanket of flux. (*Lincoln Electric Co.*)

Applications

With the proper selection of equipment, the submerged arc process is applicable to a wide variety of welding requirements by industry. It can be used with all types of joints and permits welding a full range of carbon and low-alloy steels, from 16-gage [0.063″ (1.69 mm)] sheet to the thickest plate. It is also applicable to some high-alloy and heat-treated steels, as well as stainless steels, and is a favored process for rebuilding and hard-surfacing. Any degree of mechanization can be used, from handheld semiautomatic guns to boom or track-carried and fixture-held multiple welding heads. The submerged arc process is used extensively in ship and barge building, railroad car building, pipe manufacture, and in fabricating structural beams, girders, and columns where long welds are required. Automatic

ARC WELDING AND CUTTING

submerged arc installations are also key features of the welding areas of plants turning out mass-produced assemblies joined with repetitive short welds.

Advantages

The high quality of submerged arc welds, high deposition rates, deep penetration, adaptability of the process to full mechanization, and the comfort characteristics (no glare, sparks, spatter, smoke, or excessive heat radiation) make it a preferred process in steel fabrication. The high deposition rates attained by the use of high currents are chiefly responsible for the economies achieved with the process. Cost reductions when changing from the manual shielded metal arc process to submerged arc are frequently dramatic. For example, a hand-held submerged arc gun with mechanized travel may reduce welding costs more than 50%. With fully automatic multiarc equipment, it is not unusual for the costs to be only 10% of those with stick-electrode welding.

Welds made under the protective layer of flux have good ductility and impact resistance, and uniformity in bead appearance. Mechanical properties at least equal to those of the base metal are consistently obtained. In single-pass welds, the fused base metal may greatly influence the chemical and mechanical properties of the weld. For this reason, it is sometimes unnecessary to use electrodes of the same composition as the base metal for welding many of the low-alloy steels.

Limitations

Except for special applications, the submerged arc process is limited to welding in the flat and horizontal positions. As a result, workpieces must be flat or nearly flat. Flux, flux handling equipment, and workholding fixtures are required. Many joints also require the use of backing plates.

Because of its high penetration, the submerged arc process requires less deposited metal and, therefore, a change in joint design. Generally, for automatic welding, V-grooves should be wider than they are deep. The groove is used primarily to prevent buildup of the weld rather than to secure penetration. The vee should be made within 10% of expected bead width and only as deep as required to eliminate unnecessary buildup.

If a deep, narrow groove, such as that designed for hand welding, is used, internal bead cracking may result from internal shrinkage unless low currents are used. If the arc voltage used is too high with such a narrow groove, there will also be a possibility of slag inclusion and incomplete fusion at the bottom of the vee. With low voltage, an undercut may appear at the edge of the bead. The arc being deep in the groove, there may also be a tendency to wander to one side, resulting in a weld being off the seam. A good rule to follow is to have the weld 1 1/2 times as wide as it is deep, as seen in Fig. 43-12.

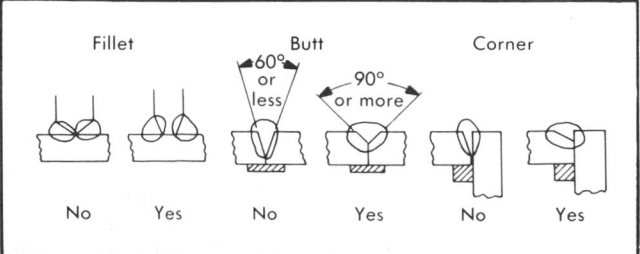

Fig. 43-12 V-grooves for submerged arc welds.

STUD WELDING

Stud welding (SW) is an arc welding process that produces coalescence (joining) by heating with an arc between a metal stud or other fastener and base metal. When the abutting surfaces to be joined are heated to the proper temperature, they are brought together under pressure for solidification to take place. Shielding gas may or may not be used.

Applications

Studs are attached to only one side of workpieces, thus eliminating the need to have access to the reverse sides of assemblies. Stud-welded fasteners are used in place of rivets, drilled and tapped holes, and manually arc-welded fasteners.

Applications for stud welding include the attaching of insulation to ductwork, truck cabs, and bulkheads. Other applications include attachment of handles to cookware, heat transfer studs in boilers, heat radiation fins in motors, assembling electronic panels, securing electrical and hydraulic lines, and the attachment of panels in the automotive industry. Stud welding is being used extensively in shipbuilding, in the automotive industry, in both large and small appliance industries, and other industries where fasteners must be attached.

Stud and base materials are the same as those joined by other arc welding processes. Metals most frequently stud welded are low-carbon steels, ferritic and austenitic stainless steels, low-alloy steels, titanium, nickel alloys, aluminum, and copper alloys. In addition, zinc die castings, magnesium alloys, and zirconium alloys are stud welded.

Advantages

Stud welding is a rapid process. Up to 20 studs per minute can be welded by handheld equipment, while up to 50 studs or more can be welded utilizing automatic, capacitor-discharge stud welding equipment. Robotic systems with automatic feeds have been developed for stud welding.

Base plates can be as thin as 0.015" (0.38 mm) when using the capacitor-discharge process, while the base plate thickness for arc stud welding should normally be no less than one-third of the stud diameter to achieve maximum strength.

Studs of various cross-sectional shapes, such as round, square, rectangular, and hexagonal shapes, are commonly welded. Stud welds are generally made to plane surfaces, but with appropriate accessories, studs can be welded to curved surfaces such as tubes and pipes.

Stud welding eliminates the need for drilling and tapping and provides a neat appearance. There is no need for cleaning or polishing after welding. Full fastener strength is developed—the weld is as strong as the fastener and parent metal. The fasteners cannot vibrate loose or drop off. The studs can be precisely positioned at any desired location. Recommended practices for stud welding are presented in ANSI/AWS Standard C5.4.

Limitations

Studs, fasteners, or other similar parts must be of a size and shape that permit chucking. Areas to be welded must be clean and free from rust, grease, oil, dirt, or plated materials. Studs or fasteners to be joined must be made of a weldable material, and one end must be designed for welding.

PLASMA ARC WELDING

Plasma arc welding (PAW) is an arc welding process that employs a high-temperature constricted or nonconstricted plasma column to obtain the melting and coalescence of most metals. The term *plasma* refers to a gas that has been sufficiently ionized to conduct an electrical current. The plasma is produced by forcing an inert gas and an electrical current from a tungsten electrode through a constricting orifice (nozzle). As a result, the plasma arc takes on a narrow columnar shape with properties that can enhance welding.

Applications

Plasma welding is not a new process, but only in the past few years has it gained significant acceptance. It has now proven its value in the area of repetitious automated welds and is being used most frequently as an alternative to the gas tungsten arc welding (GTAW) process.

Plasma welding is being used extensively in the automotive industry for the production of various subassemblies, such as alternator, transmission, drivetrain, and engine components. Other applications include formed sheet metal boxes, filing cabinets, computer cabinets, door and window frames, battery and capacitor canisters, and home appliances. The process is also being used in the production of pipe and tubing and for joining coils and other cylindrical components made from flat plate stock.

Advantages

For most applications, the plasma arc process offers increased electrode life, reliable arc starting, improved arc stability, better penetration control, and reduced current levels. In some cases, it permits increased travel speeds and improved weld quality. Also, the plasma arc process is less sensitive to operating variables.

Electrode protection. In the plasma arc process, the tungsten electrode, which is secured inside the plasma torch and behind the orifice, is protected from outside impurities that would normally attack a hot surface. With this protection, the electrode is not exposed to base material contaminants such as forming and stamping oils, degreasers, and surface oxides. These contaminants, under intense arc temperatures, can constantly attack a tungsten electrode, causing contamination and erosion. The tungsten electrode in plasma welding can operate many hours before requiring a change.

Reliable arc starting. Arc initiation for the plasma arc process is provided by a pilot arc (see Fig. 43-13, view *a*) that resides in the orifice area of the torch. The pilot arc is an arc that exists between the tungsten electrode and the orifice. It is started by imposing high frequency (from a small high-frequency generator inside the control console) on a low direct current for a short duration of time to start the ionization of the gas. Once the pilot arc has been established, the requirements for high frequency are no longer needed. The pilot arc now remains on to assist the starting of the main transferred welding arc (view *b*).

Limitations

Possible limitations of the plasma welding process include the high initial cost of the equipment, size of the torches, and the reduced accessibility to certain weld joint configurations. Plasma welding is also limited to metal thicknesses of approximately 3/8″ (9.5 mm) on stainless steel and 1/2″ (12.7 mm) on

titanium. The process is generally limited to flat, horizontal, or vertical-up welding when performing single-pass welds in the keyhole mode.

Keyhole Fusion Welding

Keyhole fusion welds are generally produced by using a stiff, more constricted arc. In the keyhole mode, penetration is obtained by the combination of plasma and gas momentum with thermal conduction. With increased plasma gas flow rates and electrode setback, a hole known as the *keyhole* is pierced through the entire metal thickness at the leading edge of the weld puddle, where the forces of the plasma jet (column) displace the molten metal. As the torch travel progresses constantly, the molten metal, supported by surface tension, flows behind the keyhole to form the weld bead.

Keyhole welding is almost exclusively performed in the automated mode. Manual keyhole welding is not generally recommended because of difficulties in maintaining consistent travel speeds, torch position, or filler material additions. The keyhole mode is typically used to produce square butt welds.

Advantages. Advantages of the keyhole mode of plasma arc welding include minimum preparation requirements for welding

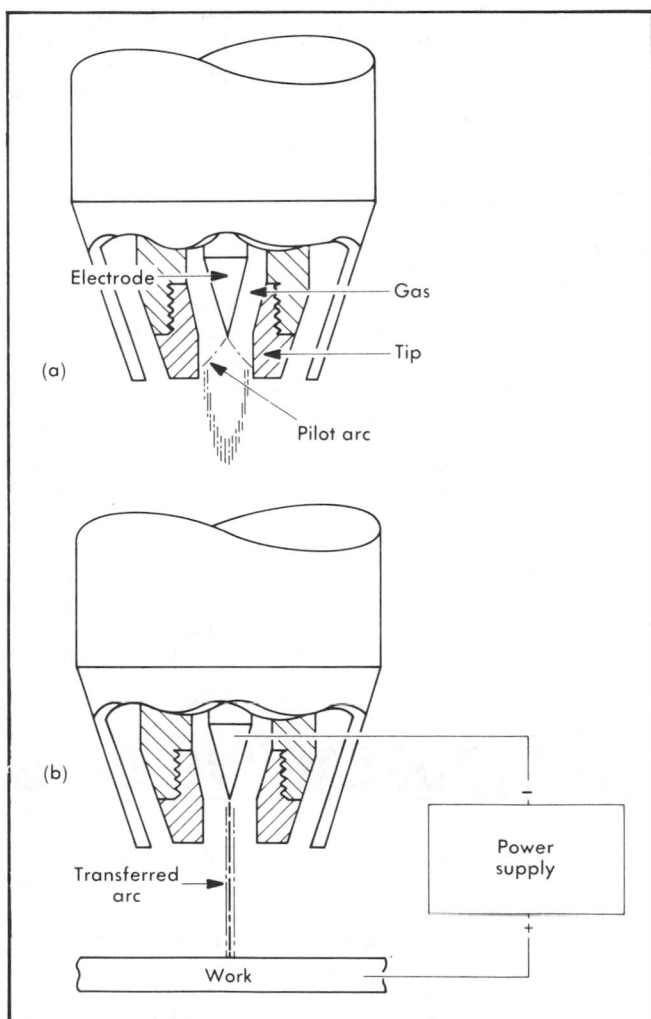

Fig. 43-13 Current flows in pilot arc (view *a*) and arc (view *b*). (*Thermal Dynamics Corp.*)

ARC WELDING AND CUTTING

and the capabilities for producing single-pass welds with narrow beads at reduced current levels. Also, less filler metal is required, and visual proof is provided of 100% weld penetration.

Limitations. A possible limitation to use of the keyhole mode is that it should only be employed for automated operations. The process is also limited to the flat, horizontal, and vertical-up welding positions and is more sensitive to changes in operating variables.

PLASMA ARC CUTTING

Plasma arc cutting (PAC) is an arc cutting process that severs metal by melting a localized area with the heat of a constricted arc. Molten metal is removed with a high-velocity jet of hot, ionized gas issuing from the orifice. The arc penetrates the workpiece as in keyhole welding with a plasma arc, previously discussed in this section. The voltage used for plasma arc cutting, however, is much higher, and the nozzle is designed to create a higher velocity arc to blow away the molten metal.

Applications

While originally developed for severing nonferrous metals, such as aluminum, and stainless steels, modifications of the plasma arc process and equipment now make it possible to cut any metal that conducts electricity. The method is being used extensively to cut carbon steel, generally from about 0.038 to 1 1/2″ (0.95 to 38 mm) thick. Operations performed include stack cutting, plate and pipe edge beveling, shape cutting, and piercing. Plasma cutting torches are being mounted integrally on CNC punch presses for making contours, slots, and large cutouts in sheet metal.

Advantages

A major advantage of the plasma arc process is the fast cutting speeds possible. Low-carbon steel, 1/2″ (12.7 mm) thick, can be cut at 100 ipm (2540 mm/min). Speed and cost advantages compared to oxyfuel cutting decrease, however, with increasing workpiece thicknesses.

The fast speeds possible with plasma arc cutting minimize thermal distortion and result in a narrow heat-affected zone. No preheating is required, and parts cut in this way can be handled immediately after the operation. More precise cuts can generally be made at lower costs than with air-carbon arc cutting.

Limitations

A possible limitation to the use of plasma arc cutting is that the top edges of the cuts are generally rounded, and the cuts are beveled (wider at the top than the bottom). Smoothness of the cut surfaces is generally satisfactory for most applications.

Another possible limitation is that capital equipment costs for plasma arc cutting are higher than for oxyfuel cutting. Also, power demands are high. Depending on the material and thickness to be cut, the power supply may have to provide up to 250 V at 1000 A.

OTHER ARC CUTTING PROCESSES

In addition to air-carbon arc cutting and plasma arc cutting, discussed previously, there are several other arc cutting processes, but they are not used extensively or only for special applications. These include oxygen arc cutting, gas metal arc cutting, gas tungsten arc cutting, shielded metal arc cutting, and carbon arc cutting.

Oxygen Arc Cutting

In oxygen arc cutting, oxygen passes through a tubular electrode made from a ferrous metal and covered with a flux. An electric arc between the electrode and the workpiece provides the heat required for an oxidation reaction. Cuts produced in this way are not of high quality, but are satisfactory for some applications. The method is used primarily for underwater applications.

Gas Metal Arc Cutting

In gas metal arc cutting, an electric arc between a continuously fed wire electrode and the workpiece, with inert gas shielding, produces the required heat. Force from a pressure gradient in the gas ejects molten metal to form the kerf.

Gas Tungsten Arc Cutting

Gas tungsten arc cutting is similar to gas tungsten arc welding (GTAW) except that higher currents and shielding gas flows are used. Molten metal is blown away by the gas jet to form the kerf.

Shielded Metal Arc Cutting

In shielded metal arc cutting, standard covered electrodes are used without any compressed gas. Molten metal is removed by gravity.

Carbon Arc Cutting

In carbon arc cutting, heat is provided by an electric arc between a carbon electrode and the workpiece. Molten metal is removed by forces from the arc and by gravity.

ELECTROSLAG WELDING

Electroslag welding (ESW) is a process in which coalescence of metals is produced by molten slag that melts the filler metal and the surfaces of the work to be welded. The molten weld pool is shielded by this slag, which moves along the full cross section of the joint as welding progresses.

Electroslag welding is not an arc welding process, but it is initiated by an arc that heats the slag. Also, it uses the same basic equipment as the other consumable-electrode arc welding processes and is most similar to electrogas welding, previously discussed in this chapter. When the arc is extinguished, the conductive slag is maintained molten by its resistance to electric current passing between the electrode and the work. In consumable-guide electroslag welding, the most commonly used variation of electroslag welding, filler metal is supplied by an electrode and its guiding member (see Fig. 43-14). Consumables used for electroslag welding of carbon and high-strength, low-alloy steels are specified in ANSI/AWS Standard A5.25.

APPLICATIONS

The major user of electroslag welding has been the heavy-plate fabrication industry, which includes manufacturers of frames, bases, and metalworking machinery. A frequent use of the process is the splicing of rolled steel plates to obtain a larger piece for a specific application.

Another major user of electroslag welding is the structural steel industry, for making subassemblies for steel buildings. It has also been used for field erection at building sites. A common application is the welding of continuity plates inside box columns. The continuity plate carries the load from one side of the column to the other side at the point of beam-to-column connections. Continuity plates must be welded with complete-penetration welds to the two sides of the box column. The electrical machinery industry also utilizes electroslag welding for producing electric motor housings.

PROCESS ADVANTAGES

The electroslag welding process is one of the most productive welding processes when it can be applied. Some of its advantages are:

1. Extremely high metal deposition rates. Electroslag has a deposition rate of 35-45 lb/hr (15.9-20.4 kg/hr) per electrode.
2. Ability to weld thick materials in one pass. Because there is only one pass, only one setup is required, and interpass cleaning is not necessary.
3. High-quality weld deposits. Weld metal stays molten longer, allowing gases to esape.
4. Minimized joint preparation and fitup requirements. Mill edges and square flame-cut edges are normally employed.
5. It is a mechanized process: once started, it continues to completion. There is little operator fatigue because manipulative skill is not involved.
6. Minimized material handling. The equipment may be moved to the work, rather than the work moved to the equipment.
7. High filler-metal utilization. All of the welding electrode is melted into the joint. In addition, the amount of flux consumed is small.
8. Minimum distortion. There is no angular distortion in the horizontal plane. There is minimum distortion (shrinkage) in the vertical plane.
9. Minimal time. It is the fastest welding process for large, thick materials.
10. There is no weld spatter, and finishing of the weld is minimal.

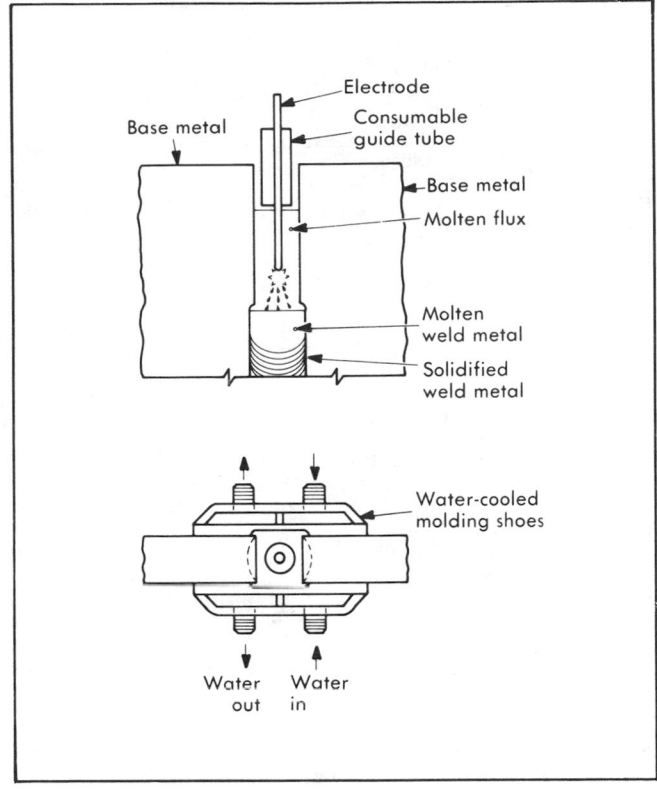

Fig. 43-14 Consumable-guide electroslag welding. (*Hobart Brothers Co.*)

11. There is no arc flash, so a welding helmet is not required.

LIMITATIONS

The major limitation of electroslag welding is that of welding position. The process can be used only when the axis of the weld is vertical. A tilt of up to 15° is permitted, but beyond this the process may not function correctly. A second limitation is that the process can be used only for welding steels. Also, the long thermal cycle of the process may result in low toughness of the weld metal and the heat-affected zone. High heat input and slow cooling can also produce coarse grain size.

A possible problem is lack of fusion at the sidewall on one surface if the electrode is incorrectly placed. Also, there may be lack of fusion if the weld stops and has to be restarted. These problems are rarely encountered, however, with the use of good welding practices.

RESISTANCE WELDING

Resistance welding (RW) is a group of welding processes that produces coalescence of metals with the heat obtained from the resistance of the work to electric current flowing in a circuit of which the work is a part, and by the application of pressure. There is no external heat source, and pressure is applied by the welding machine through electrodes. No flux, filler metal, or shielding is used, but in welding reactive metals, the process is sometimes performed in a vacuum or inert-gas environment.

The major types of resistance welding, all discussed in this section, are spot, seam, projection, flash, upset, percussion, and induction. Some of these processes are illustrated schematically in Fig. 43-15. Essential elements for resistance welding include a low-voltage, high-current welding transformer; electrodes for contacting the work; conductors connecting the electrodes with the welding transformer; means for exerting the electrode force (pressure) on the work; means to regulate current by changing the

RESISTANCE WELDING

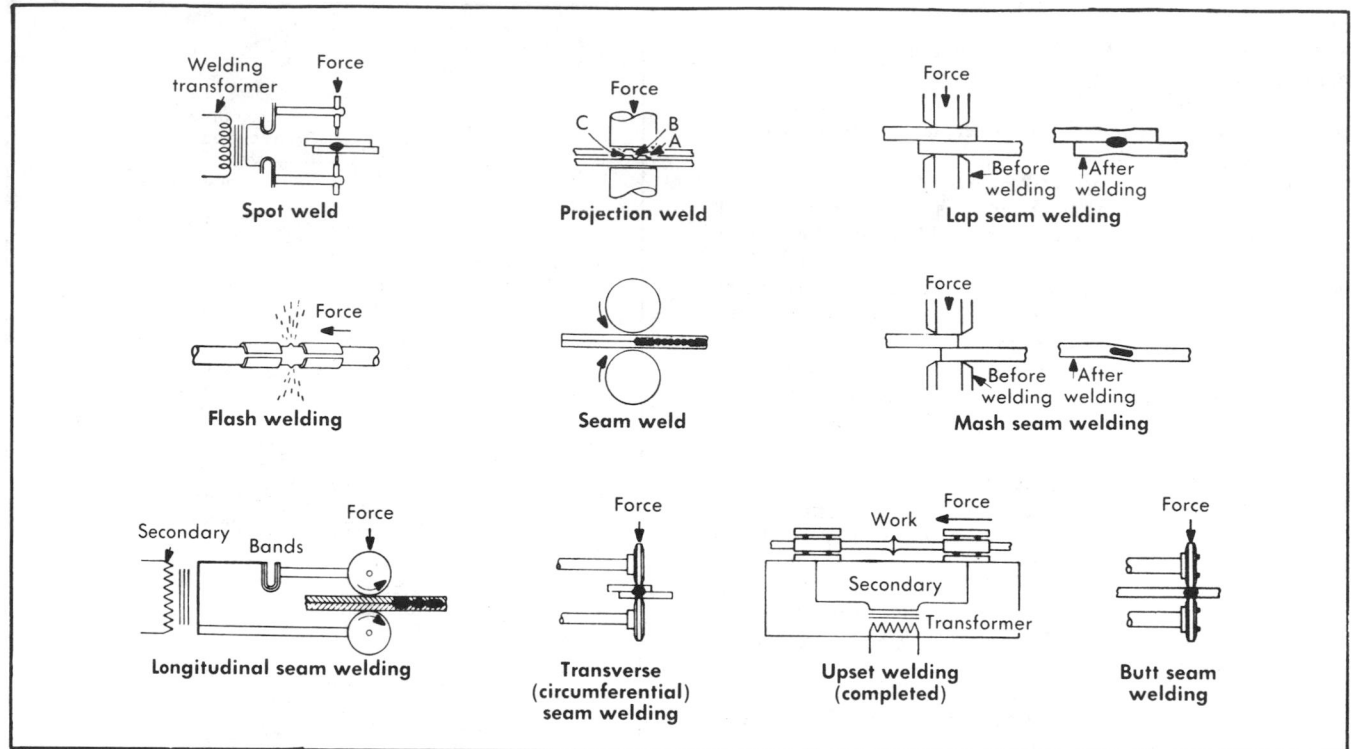

Fig. 43-15 Some of the basic methods of resistance welding.

transformer turns ratio or by electronic phase-shift heat-control unit; a power contactor to open and close the circuit to the welding transformer; and a welding timer to control energization and deenergization of the power contactor (see Fig. 43-16).

RESISTANCE SPOT WELDING

Resistance spot welding (RSW) produces coalescence at the faying surfaces in one spot. The size and shape of the individually formed welds (nuggets) are influenced primarily by the size and contour of the electrodes. Most spot welding is done by clamping the workpieces between a pair of electrodes and passing a low-voltage, high-amperage current through the electrodes and workpieces for a short cycle. Resistance heating at the joint contacting surfaces forms a fused nugget of weld material. The heat developed in spot welding depends on several variables, including the magnitude of the current, electrical resistance of the workpieces, time of current flow, conduction losses, and electrode force.

Applications

Spot-welded lap joints are used extensively to join sheet steels up to about 1/8″ (3.2 mm) thick when gas or liquid-tight joints are not required. Sometimes, steel thicknesses to 1/4″ (6.4 mm) are joined. With special equipment, 1″ (25.4 mm) thicknesses or more can be welded, although these thicknesses are more suited for other joining processes.

Applications include the fabrication of containers and the attachment of braces, brackets, and similar components. The process is commonly used by mass production industries such as automotive, appliance, and furniture. The ease and speed of the welding operation also make the process suitable for the assembly of components that are to be subsequently brazed or bonded.

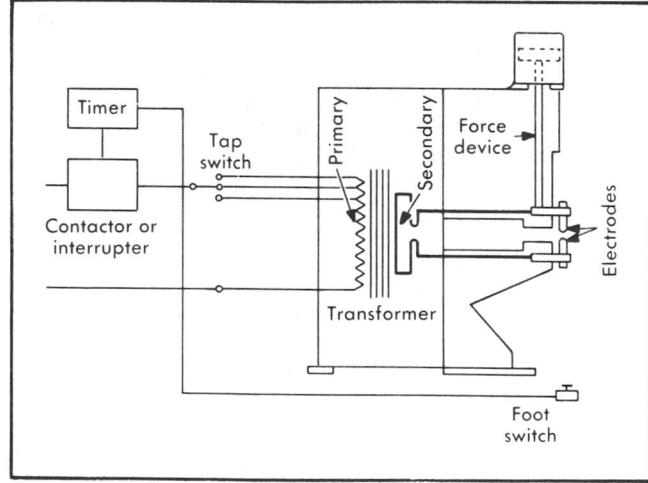

Fig. 43-16 Essential elements for resistance welding.

Advantages

A major advantage of resistance welding is its high speed. Also, the process is adaptable to mass production requirements, and equipment can be made an integral part of production lines. However, the process is also used for many job shop operations because it is faster than arc welding and can be performed with less skilled operators.

Because no flux, filler metal, or shielding gas are used with resistance welding, the composition of the base metal is not altered. Also, the application of electrode force refines the grain structure and makes it more uniform. With proper controls, the process produces consistently sound, high-quality welds at high production rates and with low labor costs.

Other advantages include no limitations with respect to welding position; localized heating, which minimizes the possibility of distortion; and applicability to practically all steels and aluminum and copper alloys. The process is often more economical than using mechanical fasteners for assemblies that do not require gas or liquid-tight joints and where disassembly is not required.

Limitations

Equipment costs for resistance welding are generally higher than for arc welding, and the spot welds have lower strength. Because workpiece clamping is required, access to both sides of the joint is necessary. Special fixtures and material handling equipment are required for mass production applications. Another possible limitation is the high power demands of resistance welding, even though the duration of current flow per weld is short.

Process Variations

Spot welding is done by either the direct or indirect method. Parallel and series variations are used for multiple spot welding. Other variations include roll spot welding and weldbonding.

Direct welding. In this method, both the welding current and the pressure are applied by the electrodes (see Fig. 43-17, view *a*). All of the secondary current passes through the weld nugget(s). This results in indentations in both components of the assembly unless special provisions are made in electrode design.

Indirect welding. In this method, the welding current is applied to one of the workpieces through a contact located next to the electrode that applies pressure (see Fig. 43-17, view *b*). Indirect welding with two transformers, sometimes called push-pull welding, produces a higher voltage for welding metals having high electrical resistance (see view *c*).

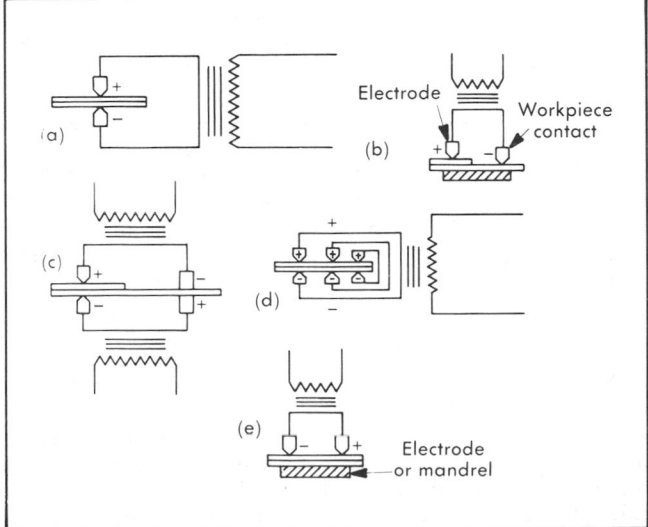

Fig. 43-17 Spot welding variations: (a) direct welding, (b) indirect welding, (c) indirect welding with two transformers, (d) parallel welding, and (e) series welding.

Parallel welding. In this method, two or more spot welds are made simultaneously with current flowing parallel from a single transformer (see Fig. 43-17, view *d*).

Series welding. In this method, current flows from one electrode into a third electrode or mandrel and then to the second electrode producing two spot welds (see Fig. 43-17, view *e*).

Roll spot welding. In this method, a row of separate and spaced spot welds are made with a seam welding machine (discussed later in this section). The rotating electrode wheel is not retracted, and electrode force is continued between welds.

Weldbonding. This method is a combination of resistance spot or seam welding and adhesive bonding. The procedure used most commonly is to apply a structural adhesive to the area to be joined, followed by spot welding through the adhesive. Another method consists of applying tape or film adhesive, with holes cut in the adhesive where welds are required.

Advantages of weldbonding over spot welding or adhesive bonding alone include improved fatigue life and durability, and better resistance to peel forces. Also, the adhesive acts as a seal in the joints to provide better corrosion protection and a generally tighter construction.

Robotic Spot Welding

Spot welding of metal components in the automotive industry represents the largest use of industrial robots. Robotics have also been successfully integrated into the manufacturing process for welding appliances, cabinets, truck assemblies, and other sheet metal assemblies. Major reasons for these applications are the increased flexibility and cost savings obtained. Even though a robotic system is expensive, it is not susceptible to obsolescence. Another important advantage is improved product quality. Robotic systems ensure uniform weld placement, accuracy in following welding procedures, and, if required, a feedback printout of every weld produced.

Robotic spot welding is done by two different methods. In one method, the robot holds the workpiece and passes it through a stationary welding gun. In the second method, which is more prevalent, the welding gun is attached to the robot and moves to the component to be spot welded.

In the automotive sector of robotic spot welding, there are two major categories of applications: respot line welding and subassembly buildup. In respot line welding, the body or subassembly is passed through special framing fixtures to locate the parts to one another and tack weld them together with stationary welding guns. The component is then passed downstream via a conveyor system or transfer bars to an area where the robots add the additional structural load-carrying spot welds. Typical component buildups that are done in this fashion are final body framing, front structure, underbody, and body sides. A typical assembly line for right and left-hand body sides is shown schematically in Fig. 43-18.

The other area of subassembly buildup generally uses smaller off-line groups of automation employing indexing lines, turntables, and stationary fixtures for part presentation. Typical components built up with this method are inner rails and package tray subassemblies, instrument panels, torque boxes, front apron assemblies, and bumper buildups.

RESISTANCE WELDING

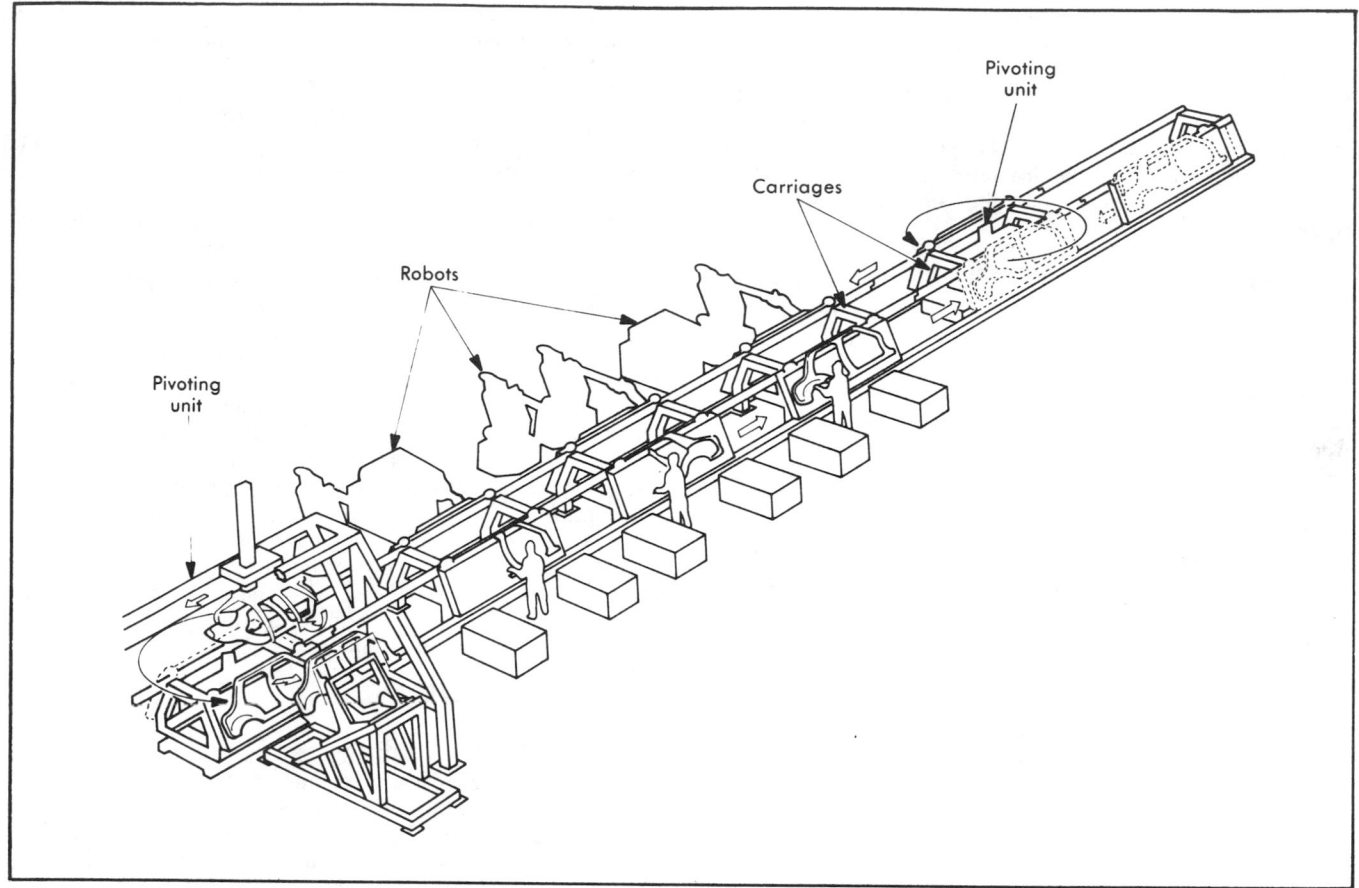

Fig. 43-18 Assembly line for robotic spot welding of right and lefthand automotive body sides. (*Sciaky Bros., Inc.*)

RESISTANCE SEAM WELDING

Resistance seam welding (RSEW) produces coalescence at the faying surfaces by a series of overlapping spot welds made progressively along a joint by rotating wheel-like or roller electrodes. Seam welding has much in common with spot welding, discussed in the preceding section. Welds produced may be direct or indirect, similar to spot welding. The major difference is that seam welding uses rotating electrode wheels that maintain contact force during a succession of welds along a seam.

Applications

Seam welding is used for a variety of workpiece shapes. Applications include longitudinal welds and encircling welds on round, square, or rectangular parts. A major application is producing gas or liquid-tight joints on sheet metal tanks. Other applications include the welding of mufflers, cans, and other containers.

Advantages

Seam welding offers similar advantages to spot welding, previously discussed, with the additional benefit of being capable of producing continuous, leaktight welds. Also, overlaps can be less than for spot or projection welding, and seam widths can be less than the diameters of spot welds. Seam welding is generally practical for metal thicknesses ranging from 0.001 to 0.187" (0.03 to 4.75 mm).

Limitations

In addition to the same limitations discussed previously for spot welding, an additional limitation is that seam welds generally have to be in a straight or uniformly curved line, with no obstructions or sharp corners. The lengths of longitudinal seam joints are limited by the throat depths of the welding machines available.

Warpage of workpieces is a factor that must be considered in seam welding, but several techniques are used to minimize distortion. Metal thicknesses more than about 1/8" (3.2 mm) are more difficult to weld than with the spot or projection methods. Seam welding is not ordinarily used for joining large sheets because of the high amounts of electrical energy that are required.

Process Variations

Seam welding is performed in several ways, primarily depending on travel speed and timing of the welding current. In *continuous-motion welding*, the electrodes (or workpieces) are driven at a constant speed, and welding current is either interrupted or flows continuously. In either case, a continuous, leaktight seam is produced. This method is generally used for metals less than about 3/16" (4.8 mm) thick.

In *intermittent-motion welding*, rotation of the electrode wheels is automatically stopped to make a spot weld, then the

RESISTANCE WELDING

electrodes are rotated to move the workpiece the required distance for the next weld. This method is often used for aluminum and steel alloys less than 3/16" (4.8 mm) thick and some metals more than 3/16" thick.

Seam welding. In this process (refer to Fig. 43-15), sometimes called stitch or roll spot welding, the on and off times of the current with continuously rotating electrodes determines the weld spacing. The minimum joint overlap is the same as for spot welding. There is generally no forging (mash-down) with lap seam welding.

Mash seam welding. In this process (refer to Fig. 43-15), the overlap is generally less than for lap seam welding, and there is more mash-down (electrode force) with continuous current. Joint thickness after welding usually varies from 120 to 150% of the sheet thickness. Continuous seams having a good appearance are produced in this way, but rigid workholding fixtures are required to minimize distortion.

Finish seam welding. In this process, mash-down is done on only one side of the joint, using an electrode wheel that is beveled on one side, to produce smooth surface finishes. Overlap is more than for mash seam welding, and higher current amperages and electrode forces are required

Foil butt seam welding. In this process, metal foil is placed on one or both sides of a butt joint prior to seam welding. The foil distributes current to the edges of the sheet, provides additional electrical resistance, helps contain molten metal, and serves as a filler.

RESISTANCE PROJECTION WELDING

Projection welding is a resistance welding process wherein coalescence is produced by the heat obtained from the resistance to the flow of current through the work parts held together under pressure by electrodes. The resulting welds are localized at predetermined points by the design of the parts to be welded. Localization is accomplished by projections, embossments, or intersections that direct the flow of current from one workpiece to the other. The projected metal embossment is heated to a temperature sufficient to fuse the parts together. Force is always applied before, during, and after the application of current.

Applications

Projection welding is used principally to assemble blanked, stamped, formed, and machined parts. The process is especially useful for producing several welds simultaneously between two parts. Mechanical fasteners, brackets, pins, handles, clips, and similar components are attached to many products in this way. Cross-wire welding, discussed subsequently in this section, is used extensively for producing stove and refrigerator parts, fence wire, electronic connections, and grills. The process is generally used to join metal thicknesses ranging from 0.020 to 0.125" (0.51 to 3.18 mm).

Advantages

An important advantage of projection welding is that a number of welds can be made in a single cycle. Also, the welds require less overlap, can be spaced closer, and can be produced with narrower flanges than spot welds. Weld locations are more accurate, and nugget diameters and thicknesses are generally more consistent than those produced in spot welding.

Another advantage of projection welding is that thicker materials can be joined than with spot welding, including thickness ratios of six or more to one. Projection welding also

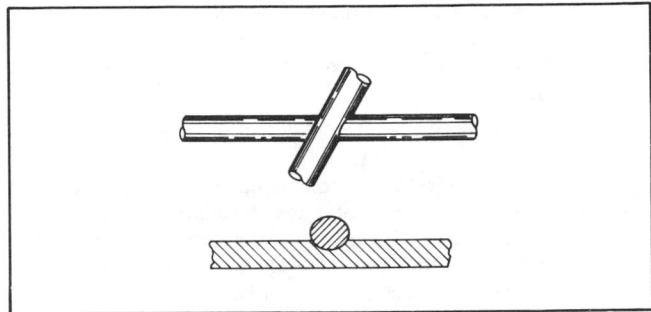

Fig. 43-19 General arrangement for cross-wire welding.

uses larger diameter electrodes than spot welding, thus reducing the current density and maintenance requirements. Projections can be placed to minimize marking of critical surfaces.

Limitations

Projection welding is limited to joining two thicknesses in one operation, and the nugget sizes produced are limited by the sizes of the projections. In some applications, the projections have to be produced in a separate operation, thus adding to the cost. When several welds are made at once, the dimensional tolerances and alignment of the workpieces must be closely controlled.

Cross-Wire Welding

Cross-wire welding (see Fig. 43-19) is variation of projection welding used extensively to produce wire products. The curved surfaces of two intersecting wires serves the function of a projection. The process is generally performed by welding a number of parallel wires perpendicular to one or more other wires. Any combination of wire sizes in a variety of metals can be joined. If the wires are closely spaced, a seam welding machine can be used.

FLASH, UPSET, AND PERCUSSION WELDING

Flash welding (FW), upset welding (UW), and percussion welding (PEW) are related resistance welding processes. All three processes produce coalescence of metals by the application of electrical heating and pressure. They differ in the method of heating and the timing of the pressure application.

In flash welding, which is limited to the production of butt and miter welds, the abutting surfaces of the workpieces are heated prior to the application of pressure to forge the surfaces together. In upset welding, pressure is applied before the application of current and is maintained throughout the heating period to produce butt or seam welds. In percussion welding, coalescence of abutting surfaces is produced by heat from an arc established by the rapid discharge of electrical energy and pressure applied percussively during or immediately following the electrical discharge.

Similar equipment is used for flash and for upset welding. Flash welding is preferred in many industries because the resulting weld exhibits greater weld strength and a smaller upset. Power demand is less, more heat is evident at the welded surface and less in the body of the work, and less preparation of weld surface by machining is required. Dissimilar metals of widely varying fusion temperatures may be flash welded together because flashing (arcing) may be continued until the

RESISTANCE WELDING

fusion temperature of each metal is reached. Successful flash welding of workpieces formed from relatively light gages of sheet aluminum is accomplished on a production basis.

Flash Welding

In flash welding, the parts are loaded in the machine in very light contact with each other or slightly separated. After clamping by the electrodes (dies), current is applied and movement of the traveling platen is initiated practically simultaneously. Heating results from resistance of the workpiece contact surfaces to the flow of electric current and by arcs between the faying surfaces. Force applied by the platen expels molten metal from the joint and upsets the base metal. The flow of current is usually stopped during upsetting.

Applications. Flash welds are most commonly employed in joining two pieces of metal end to end or in welding one piece of metal to a projecting part of another piece. Some examples are the welding of strips end to end in steelmaking and processing to form a continuous strip; the welding of circled strips or bars to form rings for automobile wheel rims and ring gears; the welding of tubular sections end to end; the production of electrical motor and generator frames; and joining airframe and jet engine structural members.

Advantages. Flash welding is a fast and economical process for producing uniform, high-quality welds in many ferrous and nonferrous metals. A variety of shapes, including sheet, plate, rings, pipe, tubes, wire, and extrusions, can be joined. Little or no joint preparation is necessary and ejection of metal during upsetting helps remove impurities from the interface of the joint.

Limitations. Safety precautions are necessary when using flash welding because of the hot, molten metal particles ejected. Another possible limitation is that the parts to be joined must have cross sections that are practically identical. Also, for some applications, the upset material must be removed, thus adding to production costs.

Upset Welding

Upset welding is a resistance welding process that produces coalescence simultaneously over the entire areas of abutting surfaces or progressively along a joint. Heating to welding temperature results from the resistance to electric current through the area where the surfaces are in contact. Pressure is applied before heating starts, is maintained throughout heating, and increases to upset the workpieces when the welding temperature is reached. Upset welding differs from flash welding, discussed previously, in that the heating results entirely from the resistance to current at the contact surfaces, and there is no flashing or arcing.

Applications. Upset welding is used extensively in the manufacture of continuously welded pipe and tubing and to join wire coils for continuous operations. The process is also employed to make many different products from wire, bar, strip, and tubing.

Advantages and limitations. Upset welding has advantages and limitations similar to flash welding except that safety precautions for flashing and arcing are not required. Upset welds are generally characterized by large symmetrical upsets. Capabilities of the process include joining wire and rod ranging from 0.05 to 1.25" (1.3 to 31.8 mm) diam.

Process variations. The two major variations of upset welding are for making butt and seam joints. For butt joints, two sections having the same cross section are joined end to end. The seams of roll-formed products such as pipe and tubing are continuously welded with this process.

Percussion Welding

Percussion welding is a resistance welding process that produces coalescence over the entire areas of abutting surfaces. Heat is supplied by a high-current arc produced by the rapid discharge of electrical energy between the two workpieces to be joined. Force is applied percussively during or immediately following the short pulse of electrical energy. The impact of one workpiece against the other extinguishes the arc, expels molten metal, and completes the weld. There are two major variations of the process: capacitor-discharge and magnetic-force percussion welding.

Applications. The use of percussion welding for butt joints (joining wires, rods, or tubes of equal cross section end to end) is generally limited to dissimilar metals and/or where minimum upsetting is required. This is because similar metals can be butt welded more economically by other processes. Major applications include the production of electrical and electronic connections and contact devices, and joining small components to other or larger parts.

Advantages. An important advantage of percussion welding is that the short time the arc exists limits melting of the base metal to a thin surface layer. This results in a shallow heat-affected zone and minimum upsetting, oxidation of the abutting surfaces, and alloying of dissimilar metals. Heat-treated and cold-worked metals can generally be welded without any softening, and prefinished metals are usually unaffected. Wires as small as 0.005" (0.13 mm) diam can be joined with the capacitor-discharge process. The magnetic-force method can join flat workpieces with weld areas from 0.04 to 0.70 in.^{2} (25.8 to 452 mm^2).

Limitations. Flat parts have to be joined to flat surfaces and butt joints require parts of similar sections. As previously mentioned, butt welds of similar metals can be made more economically by other processes. Percussion welding requires two pieces to be joined; the ends of a single workpiece cannot be joined to produce a ring.

HIGH-FREQUENCY WELDING

With the high-frequency welding processes, the coalescence of metals is produced with the heat generated from the resistance of the workpieces to a high-frequency alternating current. In high-frequency resistance welding (HFRW), called the contact method, current is introduced to the workpieces by actual physical contact (see Fig. 43-20). An upsetting force is rapidly applied after heating is substantially completed.

In high-frequency induction welding (HFIW), called the induction method, current is induced in the workpieces by an external induction coil (see Fig. 43-21). There is no contact between the workpieces and the current.

Applications

The most common application for the high-frequency welding processes is the continuous seam welding of the edges of a single piece of metal in the production of metal pipe and tubing. Another application is the welding of butt joints between two parts, such as joining coil ends or sections and producing large strip and sheet blanks for forming. The processes are also used to produce structural shapes, spiral pipe and tubing, and helically and longitudinally finned tubing.

Satisfactory welds are normally produced in air, and the welds can be made with water or soluble-oil cutting fluids present. For some applications, such as the welding of titanium

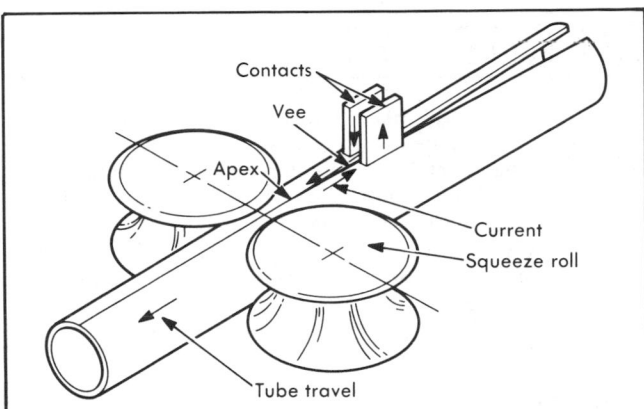

Fig. 43-20 High-frequency resistance welding. (*Fabricating Manufacturers Assn. and Thermatool Corp.*)

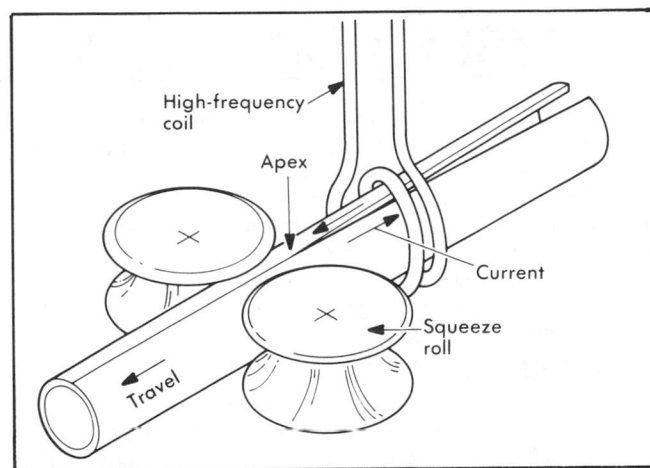

Fig. 43-21 High-frequency induction welding. (*Fabricating Manufacturers Assn. and Thermatool Corp.*)

alloys, inert gas shielding is used. Flux is not generally required, but is helpful in welding some copper alloys.

Advantages

An important advantage of high-frequency welding is the narrow heat-affected zone produced. This limits oxidation and distortion and generally results in stronger joints. Concentration of the heating current at the work surfaces (shallow heating) permits welding temperatures to be reached with less power consumption than other resistance welding processes. High speeds make the processes suitable for high-production applications. Some pipes and tubes can be welded at rates to 1000 fpm (305 m/min).

Limitations

High-frequency induction welding requires a closed-loop path or a complete circuit for the flow of current entirely within the workpieces. This limits applications to flat, coiled, or tubular stock having a constant joint symmetry throughout the workpiece lengths. Equipment required is generally built into fully automated mills or production lines, necessitating a high capital investment.

Special precautions are necessary to protect personnel from the hazards of high-frequency current. Also, because the equipment operates near the radio-frequency range, care is necessary to avoid radiation interference and to meet regulations of the Federal Communications Commission.

High-Frequency Resistance Welding

The HFRW contact process differs from conventional resistance seam welding (discussed previously), which produces a series of overlapped nuggets, by producing a continuous weld without nuggets and at much faster speeds. There are three major variations of the HFRW process: continuous seam, finite length, and melt welding.

Continuous seam welding. This variation of the HFRW process is used to produce pipe and tubing to more than 50″ (1270 mm) diam, with wall thicknesses from 0.005 to 1″ (0.13 to 25 mm). Sliding contacts are placed on either side of an open vee (4 to 7°) formed by the converging edges of strip stock, and pressure is applied by squeeze rolls (refer to Fig. 43-20). Coalescence of the metal is produced with the heat generated from the resistance of the workpiece to the flow of current, and the upsetting force completes the weld.

Finite length welding. In this variation of the HFRW process, usually limited to carbon steels and ferritic stainless

steels, butt joints are welded between two parts, such as the joining of coil ends and producing large strip and sheet blanks for subsequent forming. Heating is produced along a seam already closed under light pressure. When the edges have been heated to fusion temperature, the pressure is increased to complete the weld.

Melt welding. In this variation of the HFRW process, high-frequency current melts a small volume of metal between electrodes that contact parts adjacent to each other. The molten metal flows together to produce a cast welded joint. One application consists of welding stacks of motor or transformer laminations together.

High-Frequency Induction Welding

In the HFIW process, high-frequency current flowing through an induction coil surrounding the work establishes a concentrated magnetic field. This field induces an electric potential causing a flow of current in the closed circuit provided by the workpiece. The resistance of the workpiece material to the flow of current provides the heat necessary for welding. Three major variations of the HFIW process are: continuous seam, butt end, and magnetic pulse welding.

Continuous seam welding. This variation of HFIW is used to produce longitudinal butt-seam tubing to 6″ (152 mm) diam, with wall thicknesses to 0.375″ (9.52 mm). An induction coil surrounds the tube at the open portion of the vee, some distance from the pressure (squeeze) rolls (refer to Fig. 43-21).

Butt end welding. Induction heating is used to provide welds between tubular-shaped pieces. Typically, the ends of the workpieces are prepared so that reasonably smooth surfaces are provided, and the tube ends are aligned end to end. An induction coil is placed around the joint, and, after a heat time of up to 60 seconds, pressure is applied to produce the weld. The process is used for tubes from 1 to 12″ (25 to 305 mm) diam having wall thicknesses to 3/8″ (9.5 mm).

Magnetic pulse welding. In this variation of HFIW, lap or sleeve joints between two tubes or pipes are welded. After the joint reaches welding temperature, a pulse of current from a capacitor bank is discharged through the inductor surrounding the joint. The current induced in the outer tube or pipe of the joint flows in a direction opposite to that in the coil. Magnetic forces thus produced repel each other and drive the heated outer component against the heated inner component, forging them together.

ELECTRON BEAM WELDING AND CUTTING

ELECTRON BEAM WELDING AND CUTTING

Electron beam welding (EBW) is a fusion joining process accomplished by impinging a high intensity beam of electrons on the joint to be welded. This results in precise melting and coalescence of the joint interface surfaces. This accurately controllable process provides a direct means of delivering high-energy densities.

In addition to their use for welding, electron beams are also employed for other processing operations, including machining, heat treating, and curing.

PROCESS OVERVIEW

An electron beam welder operates in basically the same manner as do most EB devices commonly in use today, the best known of which is the cathode ray tube (CRT or picture tube) used in television sets and other video display units. In principle, some form of hot emitter is employed as a continuous source of thermal electrons. These emitted electrons are accelerated to speeds between 30 and 70% that of light, shaped into a collimated stream, and finally focused into a beam spot at a target.

In a CRT, the target is a screen coated with luminescent material. A relatively low-intensity beam spot is repetitively scanned over the entire screen area to produce visible images. In EBW, the target is a workpiece joint, and a relatively high-intensity beam spot is impinged on the joint to produce fusion welding. The fusion welding produced results from the kinetic energy of the beam electrons converting to heat when they impact with and penetrate into the workpiece.

This method of direct energy transferral provides a rapid, localized temperature rise, causing an instantaneous melting and vaporization of the workpiece material that results in the formation of a "keyhole" (a vapor channel with molten sides). When this keyhole is advanced along the joint, the molten material at the leading edge continuously flows around the sides, to the trailing edge, and solidifies to form a welded seam having a high depth-to-width ratio. Welds that are 10-40 times as deep as they are wide are not unusual in EBW. The keyhole formation process is a necessary and critical element for deep penetration welding. Without it, energy is only delivered to the top surface of the workpiece, and the heat must progress inward by thermal conduction, as in arc welding. There are several applications, however, in welding thin sections or delicate components where the electron beam is used to produce fine welds with depth-to-width ratios of 1:1.

APPLICATIONS

Electron beam welding is employed in a variety of precision and production applications. In the automotive industry, semiautomated and fully automated partial vacuum and non-vacuum EBW systems are being used to hermetically assemble die cast aluminum manifolds, steel torque converters, and catalytic converters, and for the fabrication welding of a large number of transmission components of varying materials. Other products joined by electron beam welding include solenoid valves, transducers, sealed bearings, diesel engine valves and injectors, and medical implants.

In the aerospace and nuclear industries, high-vacuum and partial-vacuum manual, semiautomated, and fully automated systems are used to perform a broad range of production assembly and repair procedure tasks on a wide variety of materials. In the saw blade industry, air-to-air mode, high-vacuum semiautomated and fully automated systems are used to produce the bimetallic (dissimilar metal) strip employed in making improved hack and bandsaw blades. Fast production of thin-walled tubing is another major application.

The various applications of electron beam welding cover a wide range of production rates, ranging from tens to hundreds of parts per hour. They involve making weld penetrations ranging from less than 0.050" (1.27 mm) to greater than 6" (150 mm) deep in a single weld pass.

ADVANTAGES

An important advantage of the EBW process is its capability for making high-quality welds that are deeper and narrower than arc welds and that are made with lower heat input. Very shallow welds with almost parallel sides can also be produced. Thick sections can be welded in a single pass, and the heat-affected zones (HAZs) are narrow, thus minimizing distortion. Welding speeds are fast, typically 30-100 ipm (762-2540 mm/min).

By projecting the electron beams, welds can be made in locations that are normally inaccessible. The beams can also be deflected to produce various shapes of welds and oscillated to improve quality and penetration. No filler metal, flux, or shielding gas are normally required, and welding can be done in any position. With the high-vacuum mode of operation, contamination of the metals being joined is minimized.

LIMITATIONS

Capital equipment costs for electron beam welding equipment are higher than for other welding processes, but operating costs are lower for many applications. Workpiece sizes that can be welded are limited by available vacuum chamber capacities. Many applications require precise edge preparation and alignment, and good fitup, which adds to costs.

When using the vacuum mode of EBW, production rates are limited by the time required to pump down the work chamber. With nonvacuum EBW, the distance that workpieces can be placed from the electron gun is limited. Electron beam welding also requires safety precautions for protection from X-ray and visible radiation.

OPERATIONAL MODES

Modern electron beam technology offers users of the process a variety of operational modes and provides a high degree of application versatility. Technology available allows EBW to be accomplished in or out of vacuum, at a high or low beam voltage, with a fixed or moving gun, and other possibilities.

High-Vacuum Welding

When EBW was first employed as a means for joining materials, welding was accomplished in the same vacuum environment as that required for beam generation, 1×10^{-4} mm of Hg (1×10^{-2} Pa) or less. This mode of operation, sometimes identified as high-vacuum electron beam welding (EBW-HV), produces the extremely high-quality welds for which EBW was initially developed.

A disadvantage of high-vacuum systems, however, is the time needed to evacuate the work chamber to the high-vacuum level required, which is unproductive time. The part geometry

ELECTRON BEAM WELDING AND CUTTING

to be welded dictates the work chamber size and thus affects the time required to reach the high-vacuum level necessary for welding. Because the pumpdown time required depends on both work chamber size and the pumping system employed, this time can range anywhere from 15 seconds to as long as 1 hour.

Medium (Partial) Vacuum Welding

One solution for reducing the time needed to reach an acceptable weld-vacuum level has been the development of medium-vacuum electron beam welding (EBW-MV). In this mode of operation, commonly referred to as soft or partial-vacuum EBW, the welding is accomplished in a vacuum environment that is several orders of magnitude higher in pressure than that required for beam generation, generally somewhere in the range of 2×10^{-2} to 2×10^{-1} mm of Hg (2.6 to 26 Pa).

This method of EBW requires that the beam generation and work chamber regions be separated from each other by use of a vacuum divider. This is an aperture sized to impede gas flow without restricting beam passage. The two individual vacuum zones provided by employing such a device must each be evacuated by its own pumping system. Operating in this fashion, the beam can still be generated in a high-vacuum environment, while the workpiece surroundings need never be pumped to a vacuum level of any lower than 2×10^{-2} mm of Hg (2.6 Pa).

With partial-vacuum systems, the weld chamber can be custom designed to closely encompass the workpiece and any part fixturing involved. When this is done, it allows for the construction of a high-production repetitive-type system, where the cyclic pumpdown time required is typically in the range of only 3 to 30 seconds.

Nonvacuum Welding

The ultimate solution for reducing the time required to reach an acceptable vacuum level for welding has been the development of nonvacuum electron beam welding (EBW-NV). In this mode, welding is accomplished at or near atmospheric pressure.

This method of EBW requires that the beam generation and workpiece regions be separated by more than one vacuum divider. Also, the series of individual vacuum zones provided by employing several such apertures must each be evacuated by its own pumping system. Operating in this fashion, a graded pressure path is produced for the beam passage, ranging in value from a high vacuum level (where the beam is generated) to atmospheric pressure (where the welding is performed). With this arrangement, the workpiece need never be exposed to a vacuum environment of any level, and a required time for achieving an acceptable weld-vacuum level is entirely eliminated. The nonvacuum system is limited, however, in that welding performed in air must be done within 3/4" (19 mm) and preferably 1/2" (12.7 mm) of the gun orifice.

Effect of Mode on Penetration

When either the partial-vacuum or nonvacuum mode of operation is employed, some loss in penetration capability will be incurred, compared to that attainable in the high-vacuum mode under similar operating conditions. The magnitude of this loss in penetration capability can vary from as low as a few percent to as high as nearly 100%.

Loss in penetration is caused by the fact that as the pressure surrounding the workpiece is increased above a high-vacuum level, the collision frequency between electrons in the beam and residual gas molecules also increases. This results in a beam dispersion action that causes both the beam and the focused beam spot to become larger, thereby reducing the effective beam power density being delivered to the workpiece.

Figure 43-22 gives a representative plot of how penetration can decrease with increasing pressure. This data is normalized to that achievable under high-vacuum conditions. The spread shown in this representative plot is because operating parameters other than pressure, such as beam voltage, distance traveled, residual gas composition, and other parameters, will also affect the beam penetration achievable at various pressure levels.

At pressures on the order of 5×10^{-2} mm Hg (6.5 Pa), both high and low-voltage electron beams can travel relatively long distances, 5-10" (127-254 mm), with only a minor reduction in penetration capability. At atmospheric pressure, even high-voltage electron beams will incur a drastic reduction in penetration capability over extremely short distances, 0.5-1" (12.7-25.4 mm).

Fusion Zone Profile

A representative comparison of the fusion zone profiles produced by the high-vacuum electron beam, laser beam, nonvacuum electron beam, and gas tungsten arc welding processes is presented in Table 43-3. The drawings also help to illustrate the degree to which beam scattering can affect final weld profile. They also indicate how much narrower the fusion zone of an energy beam process is when compared to an arc process. In addition, the operational data listed for the four processes, which are nominal values for penetration of an aluminum alloy of roughly 15/64" (6 mm) thickness, illustrates that the electron beam process is the most energy efficient.

ELECTRON BEAM CUTTING

In electron beam cutting (EBC), an electron beam is focused to a beam spot intensity of approximately 10^{10} W/in.^{2} (1.55 x 10^{13} W/m^2). This intensity is several orders of magnitude greater than that employed for electron beam welding. When impinged on a workpiece, the electrons produce complete vaporization of material in the beam spot's path. The EBC process provides an effective method for severing (cutting or slitting) refractory-type materials with accurate control.

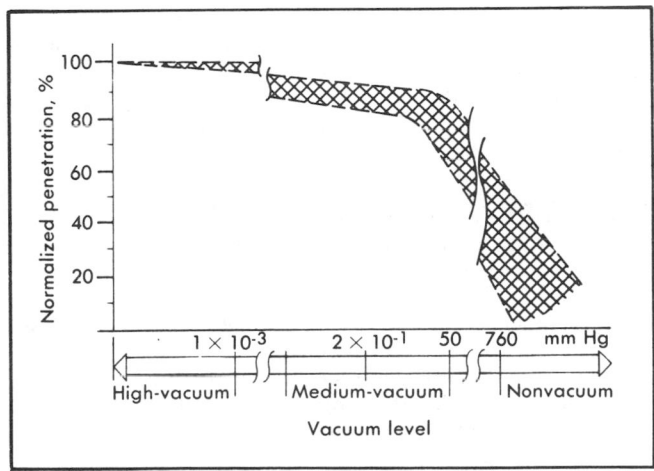

Fig. 43-22 Effect of operating pressure on penetrating capability with various operational modes of electron beam welding. (*Leybold-Heraeus Vacuum Systems*)

ELECTRON BEAM WELDING AND CUTTING

TABLE 43-3
Comparison of Various Fusion Processes

	Process			
	High-Vacuum Electron Beam Welding	Laser Beam Welding	Nonvacuum Electron Beam Welding	Gas Tungsten Arc Welding
Fusion zone profile				
Operating power, kW*	3.0	3.7	3.5	3.5
Speed, ipm (mm/min)*	100 (2540)	50 (1270)	75 (1905)	20 (508)
Power density, W/in.² (W/m²)*	10^7 (155×10^8)	10^6 (155×10^7)	10^5 (155×10^6)	10^4 (155×10^5)
Rate of energy input, kJ/in. (kJ/mm)*	1.8 (0.07)	4.4 (0.17)	2.8 (0.11)	10.3 (0.41)
Total energy consumption rate, kJ/in. (kJ/mm)*	6 (0.24)	45 (1.77)	10 (0.39)	18 (0.71)

* Approximate values.   (*Leybold-Heraeus Vacuum Systems*)

The EBC process is normally accomplished under fairly high-vacuum conditions. This mode of operation requires an optimum degree of beam focusing capability and beam control versatility to be achieved. Precisely contoured slitting or cutting of thin materials can be performed with minimal kerf and maximum processing speed. The beam is usually operated in a relatively high-frequency pulsed mode for this type of operation.

Electron beam cutting, however, is used to only a limited extent. More recently, laser beam cutting (LBC), discussed next in this chapter, has become a major competitor of EBC.

LASER BEAM WELDING AND CUTTING

Laser beam welding and laser beam cutting are both being used extensively for industrial applications. The word laser is an acronym for "light amplification by stimulated emission of radiation."

In addition to their use for welding, laser beams are also employed for other processing operations, including machining, marking, and the heat treatment of metals.

LASER BEAM WELDING

Laser beam welding (LBW) is a fusion joining process that produces coalescence of metals with the heat generated by the absorption of a concentrated, coherent light beam impinging on the components to be joined. In the LBW process, the laser beam is focused to a small spot for high power density and directed by optical elements such as mirrors or lenses. It is a noncontact process, with no pressure being applied. Inert gas shielding is generally employed to reduce oxidation, but filler metal is rarely used.

While laser beam welding is similar to electron beam welding, discussed in the preceding section, there are important differences. Unlike electron beam welding, which often requires a vacuum, laser beam welding can be performed in air or in a controlled atmosphere. Laser beams do not penetrate sections much thicker than 3/4" (19 mm); electron beams can penetrate metal thicknesses of 2" (51 mm) or more in a single pass.

Applications

Most applications of laser beam welding can be grouped into one of four major categories: structural, assembly, sealing, and conduction welds. Structural welds are generally butt and fillet welds with metal thicknesses ranging from about 1/32 to 1/2" (0.8 to 12.7 mm) where maximum load-carrying efficiency is required per unit of joint length.

Assembly welds are usually lap, spot, or seam welds in thin metals, to about 1/8" (3.2 mm) thick, where strength is not a major consideration. Partial-penetration assembly welds, however, are made in thicker metals. Sealing welds are a special class of assembly welds for joining two parts (usually a cover to a container) and providing the joint with a specified level of hermeticity. Sealing welds are often made in a chamber filled with a special atmosphere that is contained in the product after sealing to improve component life or to permit detection of leaks in service.

Conduction welds are another special class of assembly welds for joining electrical wires or connectors. The main requirement is the establishment of sufficient joint area to pass the required amount of electricity with minimum disturbance to current flow.

Laser beam welding is being used for an extensive variety of applications. A number of welds are being made in the production of automotive transmissions and air-conditioner clutch assemblies. In the latter application, laser welding permits the use of a design that could not otherwise be manufactured. The process is also being used in the production of relays and relay containers and for sealing electronic devices and heart pacemaker cases. Other applications include the continuous welding of aluminum tubing for thermal windows and for refrigerator doors.

Advantages

Major advantages of laser beam welding include the following:

1. Heat input is close to the minimum required to fuse the weld metal; thus, metallurgical effects in adjacent material (heat-affected zones) are reduced, and heat-induced workpiece distortion is minimized. Materials that would be damaged by heat can be assembled close to laser welds.
2. Single-pass laser welding procedures have been qualified in materials more than 1/2" (12.7 mm) thick, reducing the time required to weld thick sections and reducing or eliminating the need for filler wire and elaborate joint preparation.
3. No electrodes are required; welding is performed with freedom from electrode contamination, indentation, or damage from high-resistance welding currents. Because LBW is a noncontact process, distortion is minimized and tool wear eliminated.
4. The laser can be located a convenient distance from the workpiece and redirected around tooling and obstacles in the workpiece, permitting welding in areas not otherwise accessible. Laser beams are readily focused, aligned, and redirected by optical elements.
5. The workpiece can be located and hermetically welded in an enclosure that is evacuated or that contains a controlled atmosphere.
6. The laser beam can be focused on a small area, permitting the joining of small, closely spaced components with tiny welds.
7. A wide variety of materials can be welded, including some combinations formerly considered "unweldable."
8. The laser can be readily mechanized for highly automated, high-speed welding techniques, including numerical and computer control.
9. Surface contaminants such as oxides, organic materials, and dirt from handling are evaporated when the beam is used at maximum intensity and thus may not cause unacceptable defects in some noncritical welds.
10. Welds in thin material and small diameter wires are less susceptible to burn-back than is the case with arc welding.
11. Laser welds are not influenced by the presence of magnetic fields, as are arc and electron beam welds.
12. Laser welds are somewhat more tolerant of poor joint fitup than are electron beam welds, but fitup should be as tight as possible.
13. The laser beam tends to follow the weld joint through to the root of the workpiece, even when not exactly aligned with it. Electron beams tend to penetrate straight through a part, regardless of alignment.
14. Although lasers generate a beam at low efficiency (about 10%), narrow, deep welds can usually be produced at an energy saving when compared to arc welds.
15. Metals with dissimilar physical properties, such as resistance, can be welded.
16. No vacuum or X-ray shielding are required.
17. Aspect (depth-to-width) ratios—up to 5:1—are attainable when the weld is made by forming a cavity in the metal.

TABLE 43-4
Advantages of Laser Beam Welds with Relation to Application Categories

Principal Advantages of Laser Welds	Weld Application Categories			
	Structural Welds	Sealing Welds	Assembly Welds	Conduction Welds
Minimum heat input to heating thermally sensitive materials		X		
Minimum heat input to metal	X	X	X	
Rapid single pass	X		X	
No filler wire	X			
Noncontact weld			X	X
No electrodes			X	X
Workpiece in enclosure		X		X
Small welds in foils or thin wires				X
Wide variety of metals				X
Simple automation		X		

CHAPTER 43

LASER BEAM WELDING AND CUTTING

Some advantages are more important to one major application category than another. Table 43-4 relates the advantages of laser beam welding to the four major application categories.

Assembly welds exhibit the advantages of low heat input, minimum distortion, elimination of electrodes, and high speed offered by laser beam welding. Laser sealing welds take advantage of the fact that welding can be accomplished under conditions where the interior of the container is filled with a special atmosphere at or near ambient pressure. Advantages of laser beam welding for conductors include the ability to weld in crowded areas where electrodes would not fit, avoidance of marking or deformation of delicate conductors, and reliability for high-volume production.

Limitations

Laser beam welding has several limitations when compared to electron beam and conventional arc welding methods. These limitations include the following:

1. Joints must be accurately positioned laterally under the beam and at a controlled position with respect to the focal point of the beam. With short focal length lenses, the focus limits can be more critical than for electron beams; for long focal length lenses, the focus lengths can be comparable to limitations for electron beams.
2. If surfaces to be welded must be forced together mechanically, the clamping mechanisms must ensure that the final position of the joint is correct with respect to limitation 1, compared to resistance welding, which can clamp and weld in one action.
3. Laser weld depth is generally less than that produced by electron beam welders. Laser beam welding is also limited with respect to the maximum metal thicknesses that can be joined.
4. Laser welds have lower depth-to-width ratios than electron beam welders operating above 100 kV.
5. Materials such as magnesium tend to evaporate, producing voids. Rimmed steels, when welded at high speeds, also exhibit voids. Killed or semikilled steels may have to be substituted when high-speed welding is required. The reflectivity and high heat conductivity of some materials, such as aluminum and copper alloys, reduces weldability.

Wire Feed

Most laser welds, even structural types, are made without filler metal. However, as the thicknesses of butt welds increase from sheet metal to plate, the tendency for undercut increases. The surface tension of the pool causes the surface of the weld to pull the pool into a high crown, leaving a depression at the edge of the weld bead. Wire feed can be used in conjunction with a second pass to fill excessive undercut.

The focus of the second pass may be broadened. A ratio of one unit of wire to one unit of travel is typical. Wire diameter should not exceed focal spot diameter. Large diameter wire may be split by the beam if a fine spot is used. Otherwise, the large molten zone on the end of such wires acts as a variable reflector. This molten reflector makes control of the beam-weld interaction difficult.

Wire feed is rarely encountered in assembly welds because they do not usually involve sheet or plate thickness, where wire would be beneficial in overcoming undercut. Wire may be added when assembling tubes or rods. Braze material has been used as filler when joining cold drawn rods or wires. In such applications, lasers are employed to minimize annealing of the work-hardened material.

Because of reflection problems with wire feed, powder injection into the weld pool is being used for many applications.

LASER BEAM CUTTING

Laser beam cutting (LBC), like laser beam welding just discussed, uses a concentrated, coherent light beam impinging on the workpieces. The heat produced generally results in melting and vaporization of the material to be cut. However, with some materials, such as carbon, material removal is entirely by vaporization. For most applications, an externally supplied, pressurized gas is used.

Applications

Laser beam cutting is being used for both straight and contour cutting of sheet and plate stock, as well as formed components, in a wide variety of materials. Complex contour cutting of cylindrical surfaces is being done by a combination of laser beam movement and workpiece rotation, using NC or CNC for control. Many lasers are being used as an integral part of or as attachments for CNC punch presses.

Advantages

Important advantages of laser beam cutting are that it produces a narrower kerf and a smaller heat-affected zone than other thermal cutting processes. This permits cutting fragile and intricate parts with minimum distortion and provides material savings. Other major advantages include fast speeds, the ability to cut a wide range of materials, and the capability of cutting in locations having limited accessibility. Being a noncontact process, there are no mechanical forces applied to the workpieces and no wear, as with mechanical cutting tools.

Generally, no special surface preparation is required for laser beam cutting, but heavily scaled or rusted metals may prevent cutting. Subsequent finishing of the cut surfaces is generally not required. The process is easily automated, and the use of CNC provides low tooling costs and flexibility in workpiece design.

Limitations

Equipment costs for laser beam cutting are high compared to oxyfuel gas and plasma arc cutting. However, the process is cost effective for many applications, especially if the same equipment can also be used for welding requirements. The process is also limited with respect to material thicknesses that can be cut. While 2" (51 mm) thick steel has been cut in this way, most metal applications are for thicknesses of 1/2" (13 mm) or less. Thickness capability depends on speed requirements and the quality of cut desired.

Most applications of laser cutting require the use of a high-velocity gas jet. Cutting speeds possible vary with the power density of the laser, the thickness of the cut, and the thermal properties of the workpiece material. Partial-depth operations, such as countersinking and pocketing, cannot be performed because the process cuts through the entire material thickness.

Cutting Various Materials

Lasers are being used to cut a wide variety of metals, ceramics, and many other materials. The process is especially useful for severing materials that are difficult to cut, such as titanium, tungsten, tantalum, and natural diamond. Plastics, fabrics, leather, and paper are cut faster and more cleanly than with other cutting methods. Rubber, wood, and composite materials are also cut in this way.

Stainless and alloy steels are easily cut, but at slower speeds than carbon steels. Most tool steels, except tungsten high-speed and hot-work grades, can be cut satisfactorily. Aluminum,

copper, and other reflective metals are more difficult to cut. Aluminum alloys require more laser energy than steel because of their reflectivity and thermal dissipation. Pure copper is generally not cut with laser beams, but some copper alloys having lower electrical conductivities, such as brasses, can be cut. Beryllium copper and thin copper foil can be cut.

THERMIT WELDING

Thermit, a term commonly used to identify aluminothermic welding processes, is a registered trademark of Th. Goldschmidt, AG, Essen, West Germany. In Thermit welding, coalescence (joining) of metals is produced by heating them with superheated molten metal from a reaction between a metal oxide and aluminum. Although termed a welding process, Thermit welding by definition actually more closely resembles metal casting.

The process offers advantages for certain specialized applications, especially for joining heavy and/or complex cross sections that very often are not weldable with conventional gas or electric arc processes. The most common application is welding rail sections into continuous lengths. Other applications include welding and splicing concrete-reinforcing steel bars together, welding electrical connections, and repairing large components.

DIFFUSION WELDING

Diffusion welding (DFW) is one of several solid-state welding processes discussed in the remainder of this chapter. As mentioned in the introduction to this chapter, with solid-state welding, workpieces are joined by the application of heat and usually pressure, or by the application of pressure only.

Temperatures produced in the solid-state welding processes are generally below the melting points of the materials being joined. As a result, there is usually no melting, and any liquid metal present is squeezed from the joint by the pressure exerted.

In diffusion welding, the surfaces to be joined are brought together under moderate pressure at an elevated temperature, generally in a controlled atmosphere. There is no melting of the materials being joined, and there is only minimum deformation of the workpieces. The primary mechanism for joint formation is solid-state diffusion.

APPLICATIONS

Diffusion welding is being used in the aircraft, aerospace, and nuclear industries to join high-strength materials. Applications include joining similar and dissimilar metals, often with a thin layer of a different metal (a diffusion aid) between them. In some applications, diffusion welding is being combined with superplastic forming to produce complex components, thus reducing the number of parts required and assembly costs. The process is generally most economical when close dimensional tolerances or special material properties are required.

ADVANTAGES

Advantages of diffusion welding include the following:

1. High-quality welds can be produced that have essentially the same physical, chemical, and mechanical properties as the base metal, with no impairment of the base material's properties.
2. Welds can be produced below the recrystallization temperature of nearly all metals, thus minimizing distortion and metallurgical damage and often requiring no subsequent operations.

3. Weldability is largely independent of material thickness.
4. Many dissimilar metals, not weldable by fusion processes, can be joined.
5. Continuous, leaktight welds can be produced.
6. Numerous welds in an assembly can be made simultaneously.
7. Joints with limited access can be welded.

LIMITATIONS

Diffusion welding is only capable of low production rates because weld cycles are longer than other processes. Equipment costs are high, and consumable material costs are also high if precious-metal fillers and/or inert gases are used. If the diffusion rate of one metal is considerably higher than the other metal, there is a possibility of porosity in the weld. Also, if the metals being joined have a large difference in thermal expansion, failure may occur during cooling of the weldment.

PROCESS VARIATIONS

Diffusion welding may be considered to be a two-stage process, even though the two stages may occur simultaneously. The two stages are: (1) microscopic plastic deformation resulting in intimate metal-to-metal contact and (2) diffusion and grain growth to complete the weld. There are several variations of the process, the most common being combined forming and welding, and continuous-seam diffusion welding.

Combined Forming and Welding

Forming and welding of superplastic metals and alloys are being combined to produce complex shapes in the aircraft and aerospace industries. Two versions of this method are creep isostatic pressing and superplastic-forming diffusion welding.

Creep isostatic pressing. In this two-step process, creep forming of superplastic sheets is combined with hot isostatic pressing to produce one-piece, diffusion-welded structures. One sheet is creep-formed to the contour of a die, shaped inserts are placed on this sheet, and then a second sheet is creep-formed over the first sheet and the inserts. Diffusion welding of the formed sheets and inserts is then performed by hot isostatic pressing in an autoclave.

Superplastic-forming diffusion welding. In this process, superplastic forming and diffusion welding are combined in a single cycle, using identical process temperatures. Welding is done under low pressure conditions. Forming can be done first, followed by welding, or the steps can be reversed.

Continuous-Seam Diffusion Welding

In this process, workpieces positioned by tooling are fed through a machine having four rollers. Upper and lower rollers function like resistance seam-welding rollers. The side rollers maintain the shape of the workpieces. Rollers and workpieces are heated by electrical resistance, and the rollers apply pressure on the seam.

FRICTION WELDING

Friction welding (FRW) is a solid-state joining process that produces coalescence in metals or nonmetals using the heat developed between two surfaces by a combination of mechanically induced rubbing motion and applied load. Mechanical energy is directly converted to thermal energy at the joint interface. Under normal conditions, the faying surfaces do not melt. Filler metal, flux, and shielding gas are not required with this process, but shielding gas is sometimes used for welding reactive metals.

APPLICATIONS

Friction welding has been established in all areas of metalworking. Typical applications include the following:

- Automotive industry:
    Engine valves, driveshafts, steering shafts, transmission shafts, gears, clutch components, turbochargers, fan-clutch shafts, air conditioning clutch housings, and struts.
- Truck and agricultural industries:
    Track rollers, hydraulic piston rods, pin assemblies, cluster gears, axle housings, and power takeoff shafts.
- Aerospace and aircraft industries:
    Compressor rotors, fan shafts, cluster gears, rivets, driveshafts, propeller hub extensions, drag braces for landing gears, rocket-engine injector posts, helicopter main-rotor shafts, and fuel cell ports.
- Oil and gas industries:
    Drill pipe-to-tool joints, sucker rods, pump shafts, manifold or surface pipe to connections, and high-pressure valve flanges.
- Miscellaneous:
    Copper-aluminum electrical connectors, bimetallic electric motor shafts, bimetallic outboard motor shafts, drills, reamers, hubs to pulleys, socket wrenches, bomb fuse housings, hydraulic pump pistons, bicycle forks, aluminum-steel anodes, steel-steel anodes, and printing press rollers.

ADVANTAGES

Important advantages of friction welding include the suitability of the process for joining a wide variety of dissimilar metal combinations, short cycle times, and adaptability to automation for mass production applications. Joints produced are generally as strong as the base metals, and, because the heat is localized at the interface, only a narrow heat-affected zone results. Surface preparation and cleanliness are less critical than for other solid-state welding processes, and power requirements are less than for flash welding.

Friction welding can sometimes be performed on finish machined parts, maintaining common manufacturing tolerances. The process is being used to replace large, long, costly forgings with bar stock welded to smaller forgings, thus reducing costs.

LIMITATIONS

A possible limitation to the use of rotational friction welding is that one of the components must be capable of being rotated about its axis, and the weld interface should generally be axially symmetric (circular). It is not necessary that both pieces be of the same cross-sectional shape throughout; for example, small diameter shafts can be welded to large square or rectangular plates or irregular-shaped forgings. Initial equipment costs for friction welders are generally higher than for flash or upset welders, but return on investment can be rapid. Also, alignment of workpieces after welding (axial displacement) can cause a problem if finished parts are to be welded.

PROCESS VARIATIONS

The friction welding process can be classified into two main energy variations and five motion variations (see Fig. 43-23). Historically, the most widely used system in the United States has been the inertia friction welding or flywheel friction welding process, while the direct-drive friction welding process has been used primarily in Europe, the USSR, and Japan; however, the direct-drive process is gaining in popularity in the U.S. Any energy system may be used with any motion system.

About 99% of all friction welding machines employ the rotational method. With this method, one component is rotated relative to and in contact with the mating face of the other component to generate heat. The other relative motion variations of friction welding are as follows:

- Radial. A method in which one component is rotated relative to and in contact with one or more other components. The contact faces or faying surfaces are the OD of one component(s) and the ID of the other component(s).
- Orbital. A method in which one component is moved in a small circular motion relative to and in contact with the mating face of another component. Either both components rotate about their own axis, with their axes displaced, or neither component rotates about its own axis, and the components move in an orbital motion to each other. This method allows the joining of nonround components and the radially oriented joining of round or nonround components.
- Angular oscillating. A method in which one component is moved in an angular oscillating motion about its own axis and in relative contact with the mating face of another component.

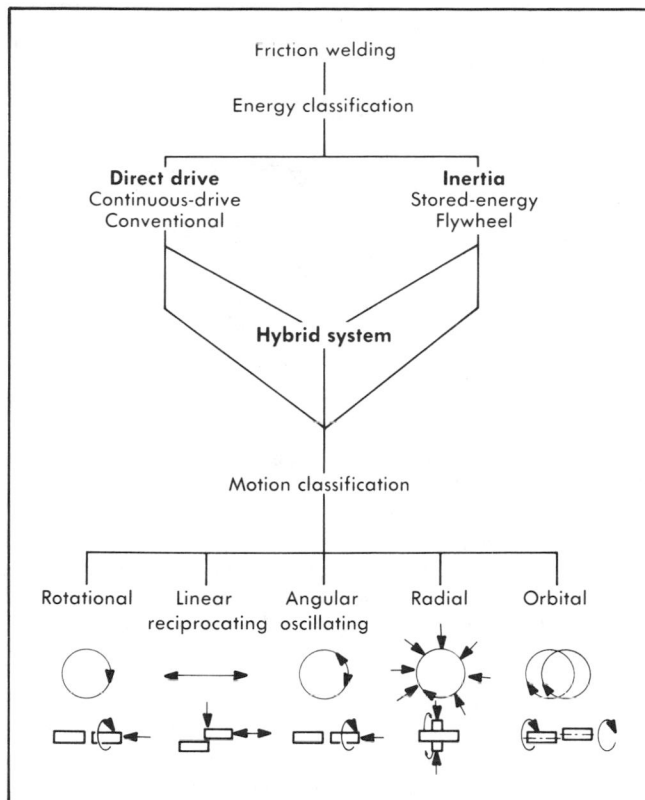

Fig. 43-23 Classification of friction welding process variations. (*Manufacturing Technology, Inc.*)

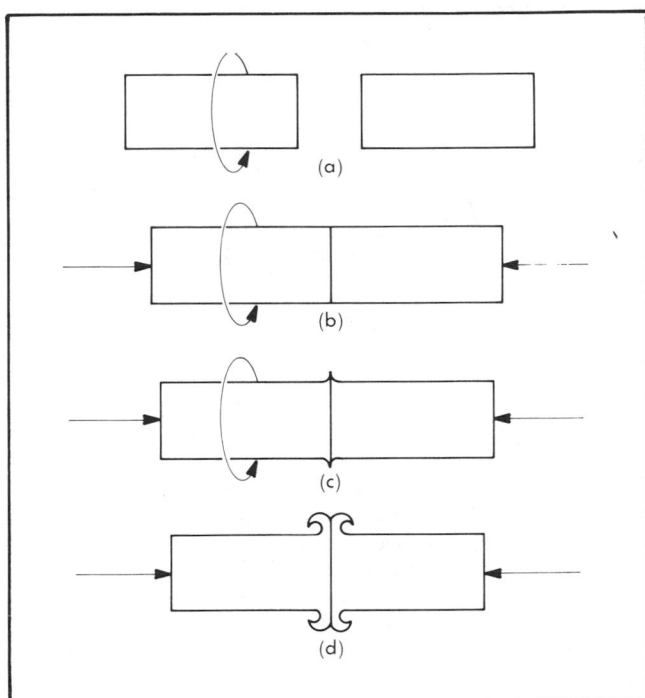

Fig. 43-24 Basic steps in rotational friction welding.

- Linear reciprocating. A method in which one component is moved linearly in a reciprocating motion relative to and in contact with the mating face of the other part.

Rotational Friction Welding

Friction welding in production is normally an automatic welding process. The basic steps in rotational friction welding are illustrated in Fig. 43-24. First, one workpiece is rotated, and the other is held stationary (view *a*). The two workpieces are then brought together under an axial compressive force (friction welding force), as shown in view *b*.

Rubbing of the faying surfaces heats the workpieces locally, and upsetting (change in length) begins (Fig. 43-24, view *c*). Then, once the proper interface temperature is reached, the rotating piece is abruptly stopped to complete the process by forging the two pieces together. The forging phase is responsible for most of the upsetting of the material (view *d*). The weld produced is characterized by the absence of a fusion zone, the narrow heat-affected zone, and the presence of plastically deformed material around the weld (flash). Weld quality is dependent on the proper selection of the material, joint design, welding variables, and postweld processes.

Inertia Friction Welding

In the inertia friction welding variation, one of the workpieces is connected to a flywheel, and the other is restrained from rotating. The flywheel is accelerated to a predetermined rotational speed, storing the energy required for welding. The drive motor is disengaged, and the workpieces are forced

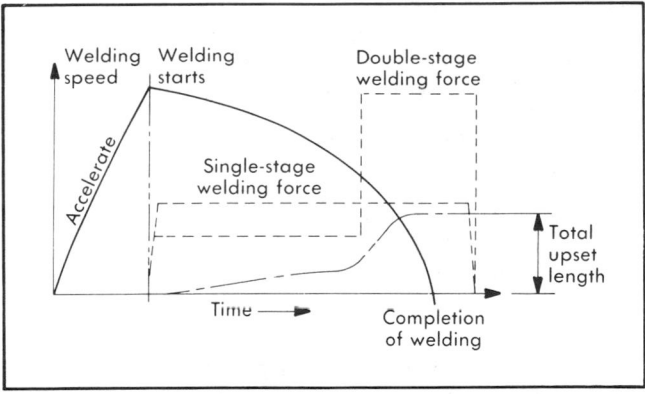

Fig. 43-25 Inertia friction welding using single or double-stage welding force.

together by the friction welding force. This causes the faying surfaces to rub together under pressure.

Kinetic energy stored in the rotating flywheel is dissipated as heat, through friction at the weld interface, causing the flywheel speed to decrease. An increase in friction welding force (forge force) may be applied before rotation stops. The forge force is maintained for a predetermined time after rotation ceases. The relationship between the inertia friction welding parameter characteristics appears in Fig. 43-25.

Direct-Drive Friction Welding

In the direct-drive variation of friction welding, one of the workpieces is attached to a motor-driven unit, while the other is restrained from rotation. The motor-driven workpiece is generally rotated at a predetermined constant speed, and the workpieces to be welded are forced together by a friction

FRICTION WELDING

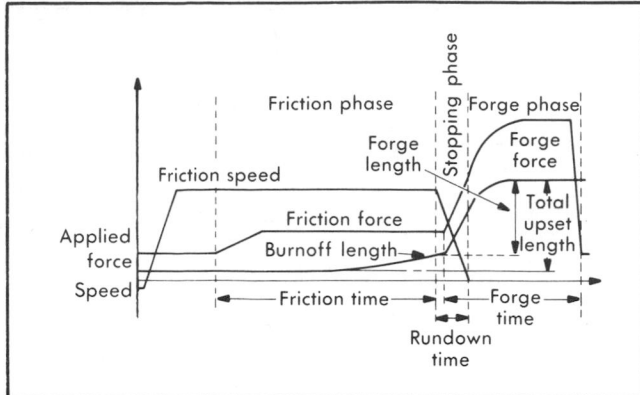

Fig. 43-26 Direct-drive friction welding consists of friction, stopping, and forge phases.

welding force. For some applications, it is beneficial to vary the speed during welding. Heat is generated as the faying surfaces (weld interfaces) rub together. This continues for a predetermined time or until a preset amount of upset takes place.

The rotational driving torque is then discontinued, and the rotating workpiece is stopped by the application of a braking force. The welding force is maintained or increased to a forging force for a predetermined time after rotation ceases. The relationship between parameter characteristics for direct-drive friction welding is shown in Fig. 43-26.

Hybrid Systems

Hybrid systems combine some features from both inertia and direct-drive welding processes. One method for a direct-drive friction welder is to vary the braking point or not to brake the spindle to zero before applying the forge force. In this way the rotating spindle chuck assembly dissipates its kinetic energy during the forge cycle in a similar fashion as an inertia friction welder. This rotating forging action can be increased by adding flywheels to the chuck assembly. Another method is to use a d-c drive system for a direct-drive friction welder and simulate, with a speed and power program, the inertia or power input during the forge phase.

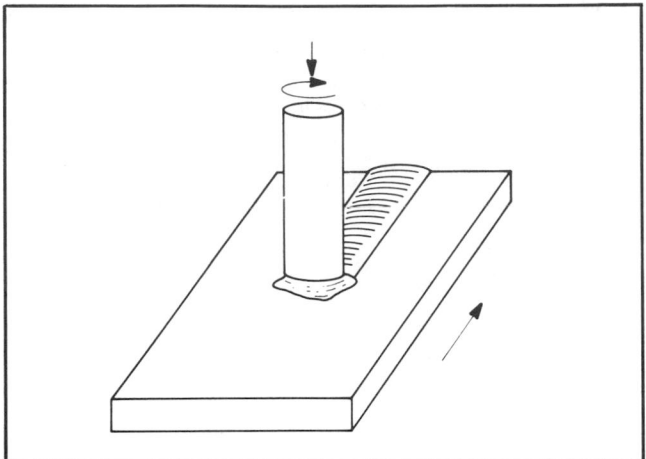

Fig. 43-27 Friction surfacing.

Friction surfacing is a method in which a rod is rotated relative to and in contact with another component (see Fig. 43-27). Both components also move relative to each other in linear motion. As a result, a plasticized layer of rod material is deposited on the surface of the second component.

WELDING VARIOUS MATERIALS

Most of the metals and alloys that can be friction welded are listed in Table 43-5. Many more combinations can be welded with various degrees of success. As a general rule, materials that are good, dry bearing materials or that exhibit hot shortness cannot be friction welded. Cast iron, for example, cannot be friction welded because any incipient bonding that occurs is so brittle that it has no commercial value. Also, materials with high directional properties will produce poor welds.

Generally, at least one of the weld members must be forgeable at the welding temperature if it is to be successfully friction welded. Weld interface temperatures usually reach a value within a few hundred degrees of the melting temperature of the lower-melting metal. Some plastics are joined by the friction welding process.

ULTRASONIC WELDING

Ultrasonic welding (USW) is the joining of materials induced by clamping the components together under a modest static force normal to their interface and applying oscillating shear stresses of ultrasonic frequencies approximately parallel to the plane of the interface. The combined static and vibratory forces cause oscillating, interfacial shear stresses between the workpieces, dispersing surface films and other foreign matter so that intimate contact and bonding of the component surfaces occurs. The solid-state ultrasonic welding process does not involve melting of metals nor does it involve the high pressures and large deformations characteristic of deformation welding; the process is accomplished in much shorter times and at lower pressures than those that are required for diffusion bonding.

APPLICATIONS

Although many metals can be ultrasonically bonded, the easiest to weld are aluminum and copper alloys. Typical applications include foil welding in aluminum and copper mills, wire-to-wire wire terminations, tube-to-sheet welding for solar panels, power transformer wire terminations, field coils, motor armatures, and brush-wire terminal attachments.

Wire Termination and Splicing[1]

Both single and stranded wires are welded to terminals, providing a high-strength, low ohmic resistance joint and eliminating the need for crimping and soldering. Stranded or braided wires joined by ultrasonic welding provide substantial savings in both assembly time and materials and better conductivity than crimped, soldered, or resistance-welded joints. Many wire-to-wire splices and wire-to-terminal joints are made in assembling wire harnesses for automotive use.

Contact buttons for relays and circuit breakers, such as silver-tungsten or silver-cadmium oxide, can be welded to

TABLE 43-5
Metals Joined by Friction Welding

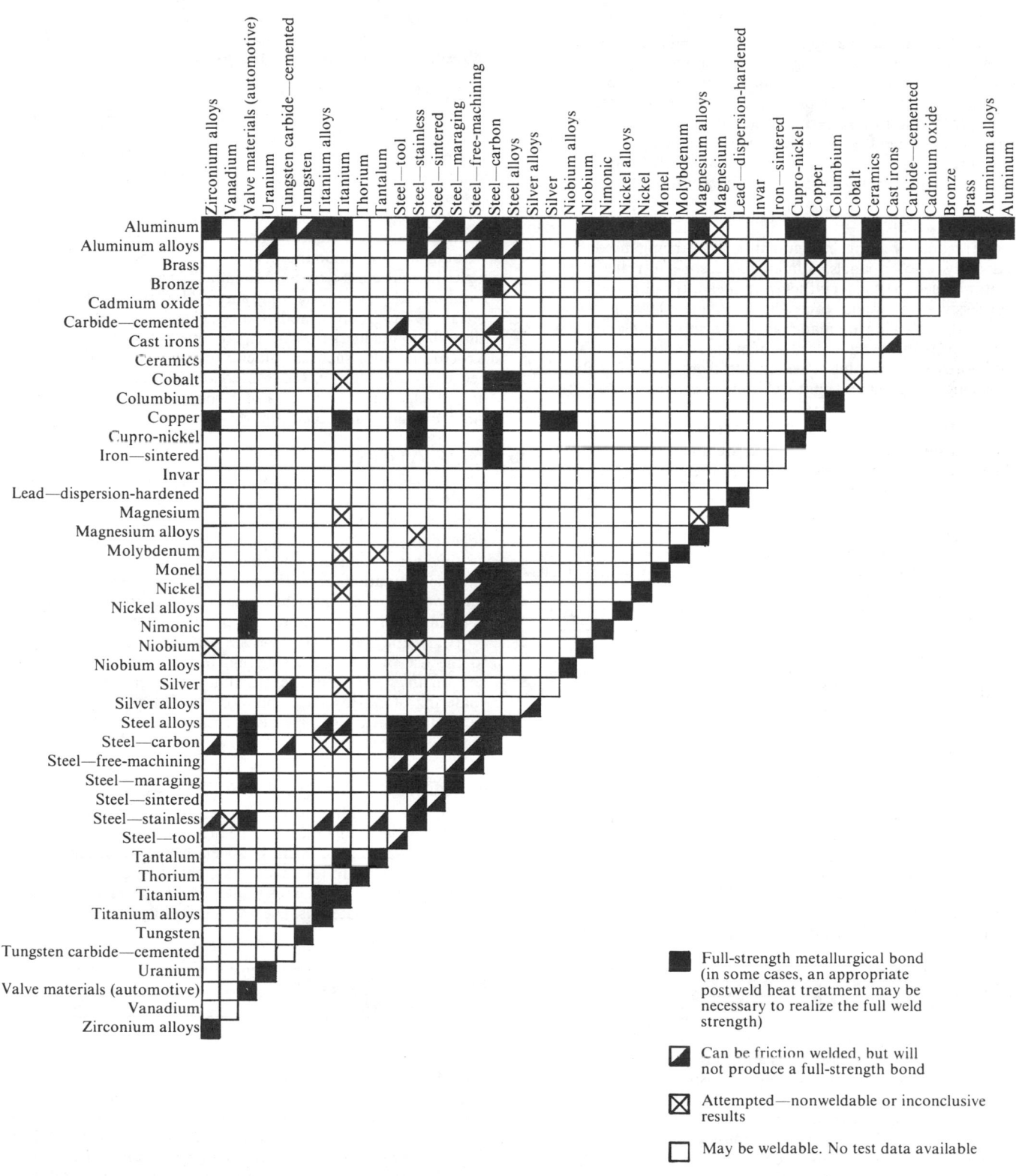

Full-strength metallurgical bond (in some cases, an appropriate postweld heat treatment may be necessary to realize the full weld strength)

Can be friction welded, but will not produce a full-strength bond

Attempted—nonweldable or inconclusive results

May be weldable. No test data available

ULTRASONIC WELDING

copper or brass arms. If a full area weld is necessary, the button size should be limited to about 9.5 mm (0.374″) diam or equivalent area.

Panel Assembly[2]

Successive ultrasonic spot welds are being used to assemble aluminum panels, replacing adhesive bonding, riveting, or resistance welding. The advantages of ultrasonic welding include minimum surface preparation, no added materials, no complex tooling or fixturing, and low energy requirements. Present equipment is available for ultrasonic spot welding of aluminum sheet up to about 2 mm (0.079″) thick. This limitation applies only to the sheet adjacent to the vibrating tip.

Solar Panels[3]

Ultrasonic welding equipment is now being used in the assembly of solar panels. A microprocessor-controlled stepper motor is used to transfer either the panel or the ultrasonic head. Successive spot welds, each about 23 mm (0.906″) long and 2 mm (0.079″) wide are made between a copper fin and copper tube. Ultrasonic welding is also being used in the manufacture of photovoltaic modules, where ultrasonic seam welding is replacing soldering and spot welding operations.

Transformers, Coils, and Armatures

Ultrasonics is being used for the welding of magnet wire to the terminals of power transformers. Magnet wires that can be ultrasonically bonded without prestripping include polyamid, polyester, and polyamid-imide. Field coil assembly involves joints between stranded copper wire and aluminum ribbon, and joints between aluminum ribbon to itself and to copper ribbon. All these joints are being made ultrasonically, providing high strength and conductivity.

Automotive starter motor armatures are assembled using automated ultrasonic welding equipment.[4] The commutator has a slotted riser into which pairs of copper wire are inserted. The wires are welded to each other and to the sides and bottom of the slot in a single short (0.35 second) weld pulse. Each automated system permits a production rate of up to 180 armatures per hour.

Ultrasonic Weldbonding

A recent development is ultrasonic weldbonding (a combination of ultrasonic welding and adhesive bonding) used by the U.S. Air Force on aluminum panels for ground support aircraft.[5] Fatigue strength tests of ultrasonically weldbonded panels were superior to those produced by other methods, and the cost savings were considerable.[6] Weldbonding is preferred to either adhesive bonding or spot welding alone where structural strength is critical or watertight sealing is required.

An ultrasonic metal spot welder incorporating power and force programming is required for successful weldbonding. The major advantage of this machine is the potential for significant cost and weight reductions for use in aircraft assembly.[7] Consideration of relative factors such as weight, cost, and utility generates an overall comparison favorable to the use of ultrasonic weldbonding for panel assembly.

ADVANTAGES

In addition to the advantages cited in the applications just discussed, there are other benefits from the use of ultrasonic welding. Low heat input and no melting of the metals being joined results in minimum distortion, and there are no weak cast nuggets or brittle intermetallics formed, as with resistance spot welding.

Power requirements are considerably less than for resistance welding in joining aluminum, copper, and other metals having high thermal conductivity. Minimum surface preparation is required for ultrasonic welding, and welds can be made through certain surface coatings and platings. The absence of an arc and air pollution reduces the safety precautions that are necessary. No consumables such as solder and flux are required, and, because no cooling water is needed, the equipment can be lightweight and portable. Long tool life and consistently uniform quality are other important advantages.

LIMITATIONS

One possible limitation to the use of ultrasonic welding is that the workpiece next to the tip must be relatively thin. A thickness of 1/8″ (3.2 mm) or less is generally preferred, depending on the material and application. However, there is no thickness limitation on the other workpiece being joined. Another limitation is that the process is restricted to lap joints. Butt welds are not possible because there are no means of applying clamping forces and supporting the workpieces.

High capital equipment costs is another possible limitation to the use of ultrasonic welding, but the negligible cost of consumables and welding cycles that are faster than brazing or soldering often offset the initial costs. Ultrasonic welding is generally limited to soft metals; with ultrasonic welding of hard metals, tip wear is faster.

WELDING VARIOUS MATERIALS

Ultrasonic welding has been used for many years to join thermoplastics. More recently, the process is being successfully applied to welding soft metals, especially nonferrous metals. It is also being used to join dissimilar metals, such as copper to aluminum and aluminum to stainless steel, as well as metals to nonconductive materials, such as the joining of aluminum to ceramics or glass.

EXPLOSIVE WELDING AND CLADDING

Explosive welding (EXW) is a joining process in which the controlled energy of a detonating explosive is used to create a metallurgical bond between two or more similar or dissimilar metals. No diffusion occurs during bonding, no intermediate filler metal is needed to promote bonding, and no external heat is applied. The solid-state process is also commonly termed explosion or explosive cladding and explosive bonding.

APPLICATIONS

Explosive welding is being used for a wide variety of industrial applications. These include the production of chemical process vessels, conversion rolled billets, and transition joints. Other uses include electrical, marine, tube and pipe, and specialty applications, as well as buildup and repair operations.

EXPLOSIVE WELDING AND CLADDING

Chemical Process Vessels

Explosion-bonded products are used in the manufacture of process equipment for the chemical, petrochemical, and petroleum industries, where corrosion resistance of an expensive metal is combined with the strength and economy of another metal. Typical applications include explosively clad titanium to Monel tube sheets and titanium to carbon-steel clad vessels for use in making chemical intermediates for man-made fibers.

Conversion-Rolled Billets

Large amounts of clad plate and strip have been made by hot and cold rolling of explosion-bonded slabs and billets. Explosion bonding is economically attractive for such conversion rolling because the capital investment for plating and welding equipment for conventional bonding methods is avoided. Highly alloyed stainless steels and some copper alloys that are difficult to clad by roll bonding are practical candidates for plate made by converting explosion-bonded slabs and billets.

Conventional hot rolling and heat treating practices are used when stainless steels and nickel and copper alloys are converted. Hot rolling of explosion-bonded titanium, however, must be restricted below about 1550° F (845° C) to avoid diffusion and the attendant formation of undesirable intermetallic compounds at the bond interface. Hot rolling of titanium also requires a stiff rolling mill because of the large separation forces required to accomplish reduction.

The most notable application of conversion-rolled, explosion-bonded clad material was in the production of United States coinage during the mid-1960s. After explosion bonding of triclad composites, consisting of 70 Cu-30 Ni bonded to copper and to 70 Cu-30 Ni, conventional hot and cold rolling methods were used to convert the clad billets to strip from which 10 and 25-cent coins were minted.

Transition Joints

Use of explosion-clad transition joints avoids the limitations involved in joining two incompatible materials by bolting or riveting. Many transition joints can be cut from a single large-area clad flat plate. Conventional fusion welding processes then can be used to attach the members of the transition joint to their respective similar-metal components.

Electrical Applications

Aluminum, copper, and steel are the most common metals used in high-current, low-voltage conductor systems. Use of these metals in dissimilar metal systems often maximizes the effects of the special properties of each material. However, joints between incompatible metals must be electrically efficient to minimize power losses. Mechanical connections involving aluminum offer high resistance because of the presence of the self-healing oxide skin on the aluminum member. Because this oxide layer is removed from the interface in an explosion-clad assembly, there is essentially no resistance to the current.

Welded transition joints cut from thick composite plates of aluminum to carbon steel or aluminum to copper permit highly efficient electrical conduction between dissimilar metal conductors. Sections can be added by fusion welding the aluminum side of the transition joint to the adjoining aluminum member. This concept is routinely employed by the primary aluminum reduction industry in anode rod fabrication.

Usually, copper surfaces are mated when joints must be periodically disconnected because copper offers low resistance and good wear. Joints between copper and aluminum bus bars are improved by using a copper-to-aluminum transition joint that is welded to the aluminum member. Deterioration of aluminum shunt connections by arcing is eliminated when a transition joint is welded to both the primary bar and the shunting bar.

Marine Applications

The use of aluminum as a superstructure material in the shipbuilding industry has highlighted the shortcomings of bolted or riveted dissimilar-metal combinations. In the presence of an electrolyte such as seawater, aluminum and steel form a galvanic cell, and corrosion takes place at the interface. When the aluminum superstructure is bolted to the steel bulkhead in a lap joint, crevice corrosion is masked and may go unnoticed until replacement is required. By using a transition joint cut from explosion-welded clad materials, corrosion can be eliminated. Because the transition joint is metallurgically bonded, there is no crevice in which the electrolyte can act, and galvanic action cannot take place. Steel corrosion is confined to external surfaces, where it can easily be detected and corrected by simple wire brushing and painting.

Tube and Pipe Applications

Explosion welding is a practical method for joining dissimilar-metal tubes and pipes, such as aluminum, titanium, or zirconium, to steel or stainless steel using standard welding equipment and techniques. The process provides a strong metallurgical bond that is maintenance-free throughout years of thermal and pressure-vacuum cycling. Explosion-welded tubular transition joints are used in many diverse applications in the aerospace, nuclear, and cryogenic industries.

Explosion-welded joints operate reliably through the full range of temperatures, pressures, and stresses normally encountered in piping systems. Tubular transition joints in various configurations can be cut and machined from explosion-welded plate, or they can be made by joining tubes by overlap cladding. Standard welding practices are used to make the final joints.

Tube welding and plugging. Explosion bonding is used to bond tubes and tube plugs to tube sheets in heat exchanger fabrication. The commercial process resembles the cladding of internal surfaces of thick-walled cylinders or pressure vessel nozzles. Countersinking of the tube entrance provides an angled surface of 10-20° at a depth of 0.5-0.6″ (12.7-15.2 mm). The exploding detonator propels the tube or tube plug against the face of the tube sheet to form the proper collision angle, which in turn provides the required metallurgical bond.

Pipeline welding. Explosion welding methods have been developed to join sections of large-diameter pipe of the kind used in the construction of high-volume oil and gas pipelines. In one method, internal and external-band charges of welding explosive are simultaneously detonated adjacent to overlapped, telescoped pipe ends (see Fig. 43-28).[8] The welding charges are detonated simultaneously by high-detonation velocity initiation explosive charges placed along a leading edge of each welding explosive charge. The initiating explosive charges are each set off by a single detonator.

Specialty Applications

The inside walls of hollow forgings that are used for connections to heavy-walled pressure vessels are metallurgically bonded with stainless steel. These bonded forgings, or nozzles,

EXPLOSIVE WELDING AND CLADDING

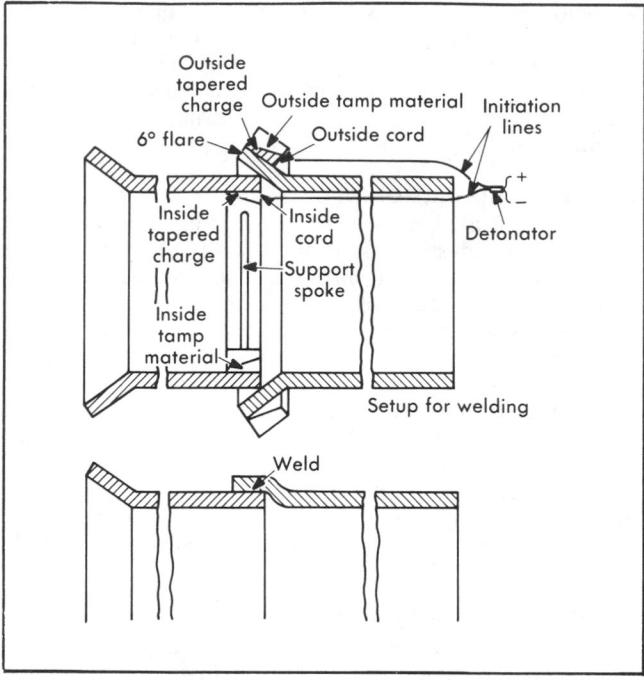

Fig. 43-28 Explosion welding of large-diameter pipe sections. (*V.D. Linse and H. E. Pattee, Canadian Industries, Ltd., U.S. Patent 4,248,373, February 3, 1981*)

range from 2 to 24" (51 to 610 mm) ID and up to 3' (0.9 m) long. Large clad cylinders and internally clad heavy-walled tubes are being extruded using conventional equipment. Figure 43-29 shows other explosive welding applications.

Buildup and Repair Operations

Explosion welding is also used for the repair and buildup of worn flat and cylindrical components. The worn area is clad with an appropriate thickness of metal and subsequently

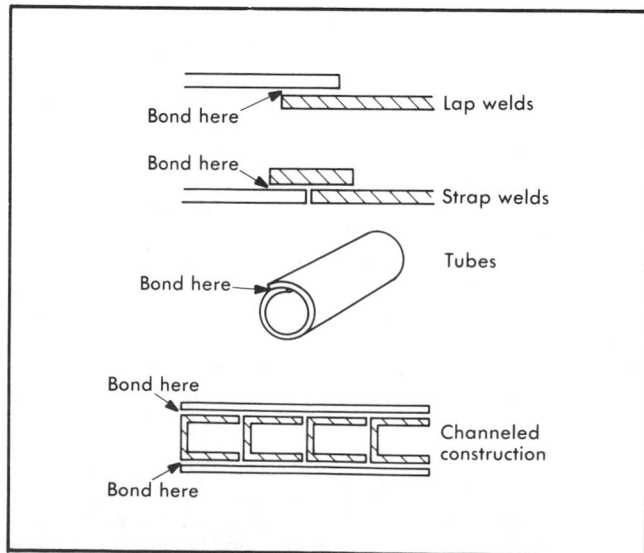

Fig. 43-29 Explosive welding applications.

machined to the proper dimensions. In some cases, the repair can be made with a material that exhibits superior strength or abrasion and corrosion resistance in comparison with the original material. Explosion bonding to repair turbine-shaft bearing surfaces is one example of these operations.

Process Versatility

With explosive welding, high-quality metallurgical bonds can be formed not only between similar metals but also between those dissimilar metals classified as incompatible when fusion or diffusion joining methods are used. Brittle, intermetallic compounds that are formed in an undesirable continuous layer at the interface during bonding by conventional methods are minimized. More importantly, the compounds are isolated and surrounded by ductile metal in explosion clads. Titanium clad to steel is an example of such a system.

Metals with widely different properties, such as copper and maraging steel, can be joined explosively. Also, metals having widely different melting points, such as aluminum with a melting point of 1220° F (660° C) and tantalum with a melting point of 5425° F (2995° C), can be clad in this way. Metals having tenacious surface films that make roll bonding difficult, such as joining stainless steel to chromium-molybdenum steel, can be explosively welded.

High-quality wrought metals are clad without altering the chemical composition of the metals. Various clad metals can also be bonded to rolled plate that is strand-cast, annealed, normalized, or quenched and tempered.

Multiple-layered composite sheets and plates can be bonded in a single explosion. Cladding of both sides of a backing metal can be achieved simultaneously. When two sides are clad, the two prime or clad metals need not be of the same thickness or of the same metal or clad. A common tube-sheet composite contains titanium on one side, stainless steel on the other side, and carbon steel in the center.

Size Capabilities

Large clad-to-backer ratio limits can be achieved by explosion cladding. Stainless-steel clad components as thin as 0.001" (0.03 mm) and as thick as 1 1/4" (32 mm) have been explosion-clad. The thickness of the backing plate in explosion cladding is essentially unlimited. Backers more than 20" (508 mm) thick and weighing 50 tons (45 t) have been commercially clad. Explosive cladding can be achieved over areas limited only by the size of the available cladding plate and the size of the explosion that can be tolerated. Areas as small as 0.02 in.^{2} (12.9 mm^2) and as large as 300 ft^2 (28 m^2) have been bonded.

LIMITATIONS

Possible limitations with respect to the use of explosive welding and cladding include the following:

- Problems with explosive welding and cladding include the inherent hazards of storing and handling explosives; the ability to obtain explosives with the proper energy, form, and detonation velocity; and the undesirable noise and blast effects.
- Metals to be explosively bonded must possess some ductility and resistance to impact. Brittle metals and metal alloys cannot be used because they fracture during bonding.
- In certain metal systems in which one or more metals to be explosion-clad has a high initial yield strength or a high strain-hardening rate, a high-quality bond may be

EXPLOSIVE WELDING AND CLADDING

difficult to achieve. This phenomenon is magnified when there is also a large density difference between the metals. Such combinations are often improved by using a thin, low-yield-strength interlayer between the metals.

- In general, the process is best suited to the bonding of flat and cylindrical surfaces that allow straight-line egression of the high-velocity jet emanating from between the metals during bonding.
- Backer thinness rather than thickness is a limiting factor. Thin backers must be supported, thus adding to manufacturing cost.
- The preparation and assembly of clads are not amenable to automated production techniques. Each assembly requires considerable manual labor.

METALS WELDED AND CLAD

More than 300 dissimilar combinations of metals have been explosion welded, as well as numerous similar combinations. Many of these combinations were only in small sample configurations to demonstrate that a metallurgical bond could be achieved. The industrially useful combinations that are available in commercial sizes are shown in Table 43-6. The chart does not include triclads or combinations that corrosion or materials engineers or equipment designers may yet envision. The combinations that explosion cladding can provide are virtually limitless.

TABLE 43-6
Commercially Available Explosion-Clad Metal Combinations

	Zirconium	Magnesium	Stellite 6B	Platinum	Gold	Silver	Columbium	Tantalum	Hastelloy	Titanium	Nickel alloys	Copper alloys	Aluminum	Stainless steels	Alloy steels	Carbon steels
Carbon steels	•	•			•	•	•	•	•	•	•	•	•	•	•	•
Alloy steels	•	•	•					•	•	•	•	•	•	•	•	
Stainless steels			•		•	•	•	•	•	•	•	•	•	•		
Aluminum		•			•	•	•	•			•	•	•			
Copper alloys					•	•	•	•	•	•	•	•				
Nickel alloys		•		•	•			•	•	•	•					
Titanium	•	•				•	•			•						
Hastelloy								•	•							
Tantalum					•		•	•								
Columbium			•				•									
Silver						•										
Gold																
Platinum					•											
Stellite 6B																
Magnesium		•														
Zirconium	•															

(*Detaclad Operations, E. I. du Pont de Nemours and Co.*)

OTHER SOLID-STATE WELDING PROCESSES

In addition to the solid-state welding processes discussed previously—diffusion, friction, ultrasonic, and explosive welding—there are several others of industrial significance that are mentioned briefly in the remainder of this chapter.

COLD WELDING

Cold welding (CW) is defined as a solid-state welding process in which coalescence is produced by the external application of mechanical force alone. A characteristic of the process is minimum heat. No heat is applied externally, and little is generated by the welding process itself. With extensive plastic deformation, however, some heat is generated, but this heat is not required to complete the weld and is not generally sufficient to cause any problems.

The welding operation is done at or near room temperature, and there is substantial deformation. A fundamental requirement

OTHER SOLID-STATE WELDING PROCESSES

for satisfactory cold welding is that at least one and preferably both of the metals to be joined be highly ductile and not exhibit extreme work hardening. As a result, the process is generally used for nonferrous materials.

Soft tempers of metals such as aluminum and copper are most easily cold welded. It is more difficult to use the process on cold-worked or heat-treated alloys of these metals because work hardening at the interface becomes pronounced, and ductility may become exhausted. The joining of copper to aluminum by cold welding is a common application of the process, especially when aluminum tubing or electrical conductor-grade aluminum is joined to short sections of copper to facilitate interconnection by soldering or brazing.

To make a cold weld, two pieces of metal are placed between a pair of dies or rolls, and force is applied to deform the metal. In sheet materials, a weld will be formed when a thickness reduction of about 50% has been reached, provided that the surfaces were reasonably clean at the start of the process.

Very simple tools may be designed for cold welding. For example, joints between wires may be formed manually with a pair of special pliers. Hydraulic and mechanical presses are also used for cold welding.

Although the welds are made at room temperature, the service temperatures of the welds must be considered, because mutually soluble materials may cause a brittle joint in service. This embrittlement is usually not a problem when cold welds are made between dissimilar metals that are not mutually soluble.

Clean metal faces on the workpieces are essential for strong cold welds. Dirt, oils, or oxide films must be removed to ensure metal-to-metal contact. Degreasing and wire brushing are commonly used for this purpose.

Butt Joints

Cold welding is used to produce butt joints in the ends of wire, rod, tubing, and extruded shapes. The workpieces are held securely in dies, with sufficient metal extending beyond the dies to permit upsetting during welding as the workpieces are pushed against each other. Distance between the dies should not be greater than four times the diameter or thickness of the workpieces. Multiple upsets are sometimes required, depending on the workpiece material and size.

Lap Joints

Cold welding is used to produce lap joints in ductile sheet or foil stock. Dies generally indent the metal and apply pressure to cause plastic flow at the interface. Pressures applied depend on the compressive yield strengths of the metals being joined and vary up to 500 ksi (3447 MPa) for some aluminum alloys.

Slide Welding

Slide welding is a less common form of cold welding in which the surfaces to be joined slide relative to each other, thus minimizing deformation during upsetting. Upsetting forces are less than for butt welding.

FORGE WELDING

Forge welding (FOW) is one of the earliest solid-state welding processes and was used extensively by blacksmiths to mount rims on wagon wheels. In this process, the components to be joined are heated to high temperatures below their melting points and are then forged together by dies, hammers, or rollers to cause permanent deformation at the interface. These processes are limited to special uses and have been largely replaced by the other welding processes described in this chapter.

COEXTRUSION WELDING

In this solid-state welding process, two or more metal parts are coextruded by heating and forcing the metals through an extrusion die. Some cold coextrusion welding has been done, but the metal parts are generally heated to reduce pressure requirements and improve the welding process.

Workpieces to be welded are generally placed in a tapered retort to facilitate extrusion. For reactive metals, the retort is usually evacuated. Coextrusion welding is used to join a variety of metals, including low-carbon steels, aluminum and copper alloys, nickel-based alloys, and reactive metals, such as titanium and zirconium.

PULSED MAGNETIC WELDING

Pulsed magnetic welding is a solid-state process similar in concept to explosive welding, previously discussed, but without the hazards of using explosives. Metallurgical bonding is produced by impacting metal parts against each other at high velocities using high-frequency, high-intensity pulsed magnetic fields. The process is used to join stainless steels, Inconel, and other metals. Dissimilar and crack-susceptible metals can be joined. Bond lengths of 5-10 times the cladding thickness can be produced.

VIBRATION WELDING

Vibration welding differs from ultrasonic welding, discussed previously, in that frictional heat from a small reciprocating linear motion is used to join thermoplastic and rubber parts. Frictional heat is generated by clamping two workpieces together under pressure and vibrating one workpiece at a preset amplitude and frequency (see Fig. 43-30). A continuous weld line is produced along the entire contact surface.

Bonds produced by vibration welding are strong and structurally sound, and operating costs are low. The process is being used to produce pressuretight joints in both small and large parts of circular, rectangular, or irregular shape. Total cycle times, including loading and unloading, average 6-15 seconds, and multicavity fixtures can be used.

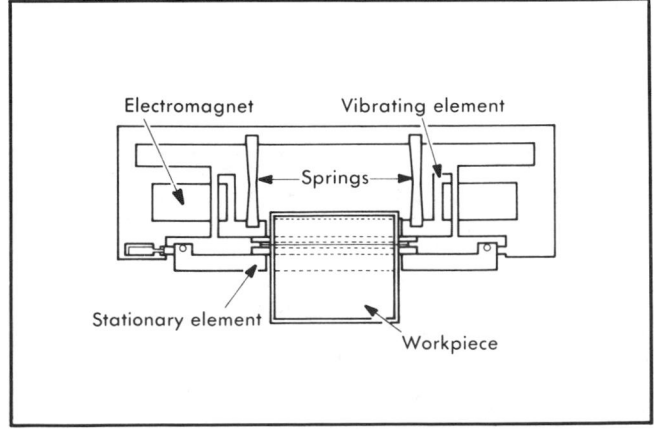

Fig. 43-30 Major components of vibratory welding equipment. (*Branson Sonic Power Co.*)

BRAZING

Brazing is defined by the American Welding Society (AWS) as: "A group of welding processes which produces coalescence of materials by heating them in the presence of a filler metal having a liquidus above 840° F (450° C) and below the solidus of the base metal. The filler metal is distributed between the closely fitted faying surfaces of the joint by capillary action." Braze welding differs from brazing in that the filler metal is not distributed in the joint by capillary action.

APPLICATIONS

Applications for brazing are widely varied, and the process is used in practically every industry, from jewelry to aerospace. High-vacuum, refrigeration, and air-conditioning equipment manufacturers use the process extensively in making leaktight joints. Applications in the automotive industry include the production of accessories and steering wheels and in joining tubing. Aircraft and aerospace uses include making honeycomb structures, engine nozzles, tubing joints, and many other brazements.

Heating and plumbing manufacturers and contractors use brazing for joining pipe, tubing, and headers. Seams and spud connections for water heaters and tanks are made by brazing. Pasteurizers, separators, and tanks for dairy equipment are also brazed. Electrical wire, cables, and bus bars are joined by brazing, and the chemical industry uses the process for producing tanks, vats, and piping.

The selection of brazing versus welding or other joining processes depends primarily on the sizes of the components and the materials to be joined, configurations of the joints, thicknesses of the sections, the number of joints to be made, and service requirements. Brazing is generally more suitable for joining smaller parts because of the difficulty in applying the required heat to larger components. However, parts as large as 70″ (1780 mm) diam and 15′ (4.6 m) long are brazed. The process is also usually preferred for joining thin sections to thick sections because reduced heat requirements minimize distortion.

Brazing is used extensively for joining many dissimilar material combinations and is often better for joints having interfaces with complex contours. When designed properly, applications satisfy requirements for permanent, strong joints. The process is generally not used for nonpermanent joints that require disassembly or for permanent, low-strength joints where other joining processes are generally more economical.

ADVANTAGES

Brazing is selected as a fastening process over other joining methods, such as welding, mechanical fastening, soldering, or adhesive bonding, because of the following characteristics:

1. Inaccessible joint areas that could not be made by gas metal arc, gas tungsten arc, and spot or seam welding can be joined by brazing.
2. Thin-walled tubes and light-gage sheet metal assemblies not joinable by welding can be joined by brazing.
3. Brazing can join dissimilar materials such as copper to stainless steels, brass to carbon steel, and ceramics to nickel alloys.
4. Leaktight joints for pressurized and vacuum systems are readily joined by brazing.
5. The joining of materials with filler metals at temperatures below 1300° F (705° C) can be performed.
6. The nickel-brazed joints in steel and the nickel alloy brazed joints in stainless steels are made for high-temperature service.
7. Multiple joints can be made at one time, as in furnace brazing, with potentially high production rates. Brazements produced in furnaces with protective atmospheres do not require cleaning or stress relieving after brazing.
8. Corrosion resistance can be provided for food-service equipment that employs silver or nickel filler metals for joining stainless steels. The chemical industry uses nickel filler metals for brazing stainless steels subject to corrosive service.
9. Less-skilled operators are required for high-production brazing.
10. Diffusion brazing can be used to join heat-resistant base metals for service temperatures far above the solidus temperature of the nickel filler metal.
11. Braze joints are ductile.
12. Brazing is readily automated, and high production rates are possible.

LIMITATIONS

Size limitation of the parts to be brazed is of major importance. Extremely large assemblies, although brazable, may often be made economically by welding, particularly if the linear distances to be joined are small, because of the cost and availability of large equipment such as brazing furnaces. By definition, brazing requires closely mating parts to ensure capillary flow of the filler metal. The cost of machining to attain the desired fit may rule out brazing as a joining process.

The general availability of equipment for either torch, induction, or furnace brazing in a plant or by a vendor may be a determining factor in selecting the process. The true worth of the process and determining factor in its use must be decided from its cost and desired joint characteristics on any particular joining operation. In such a case, a value analysis must be made to compare brazing accurately with any other joining process under consideration.

BRAZING PROCESSES

There are many brazing processes currently being used. They are generally classified by the method used to heat the assembly. In some applications, however, several methods of heating are used to produce brazed joints. Selection of a process depends primarily on the parts to be brazed, equipment available, and costs. Some brazing filler metals and base metals can be brazed by only one of the heating methods.

The most common brazing processes are torch, induction, dip, infrared, and furnace brazing. Other processes used less commonly include arc, diffusion, electron beam, exothermic, laser beam, resistance, block, blanket, and flow brazing.

Torch Brazing

A torch is the most common process of heating for brazing. Heat for the torch brazing operation is supplied by burning gas combinations such as air and natural gas, oxygen and acetylene, air and propane, and other mixtures, depending on heat requirements.

BRAZING

Induction Brazing

Induction heating, applied widely in other operations such as heat treating, is ideally suited as a heat source for brazing, especially where rapid heating is required. In contrast to torch brazing, the immediate limitations are the necessity of locating the inductor precisely close to the workpiece and the selection of fixture materials for holding parts during brazing. The fixtures should be kept out of the induction field as much as possible to avoid excessive heating of fixtures or should be constructed of nonmagnetic materials such as ceramics.

Induction heating has a distinct advantage in that once properly set up, a very closely controlled heating area (generally smaller than that possible with torch brazing) can be obtained. In this manner, brazing can often be accomplished close to previously heat-treated areas without seriously lowering their hardness. Typical joint and coil designs used in induction brazing are shown in Fig. 43-31.

Dip Brazing

In dip brazing, the heat required is furnished by a molten chemical or metal bath. When a molten chemical bath is used,

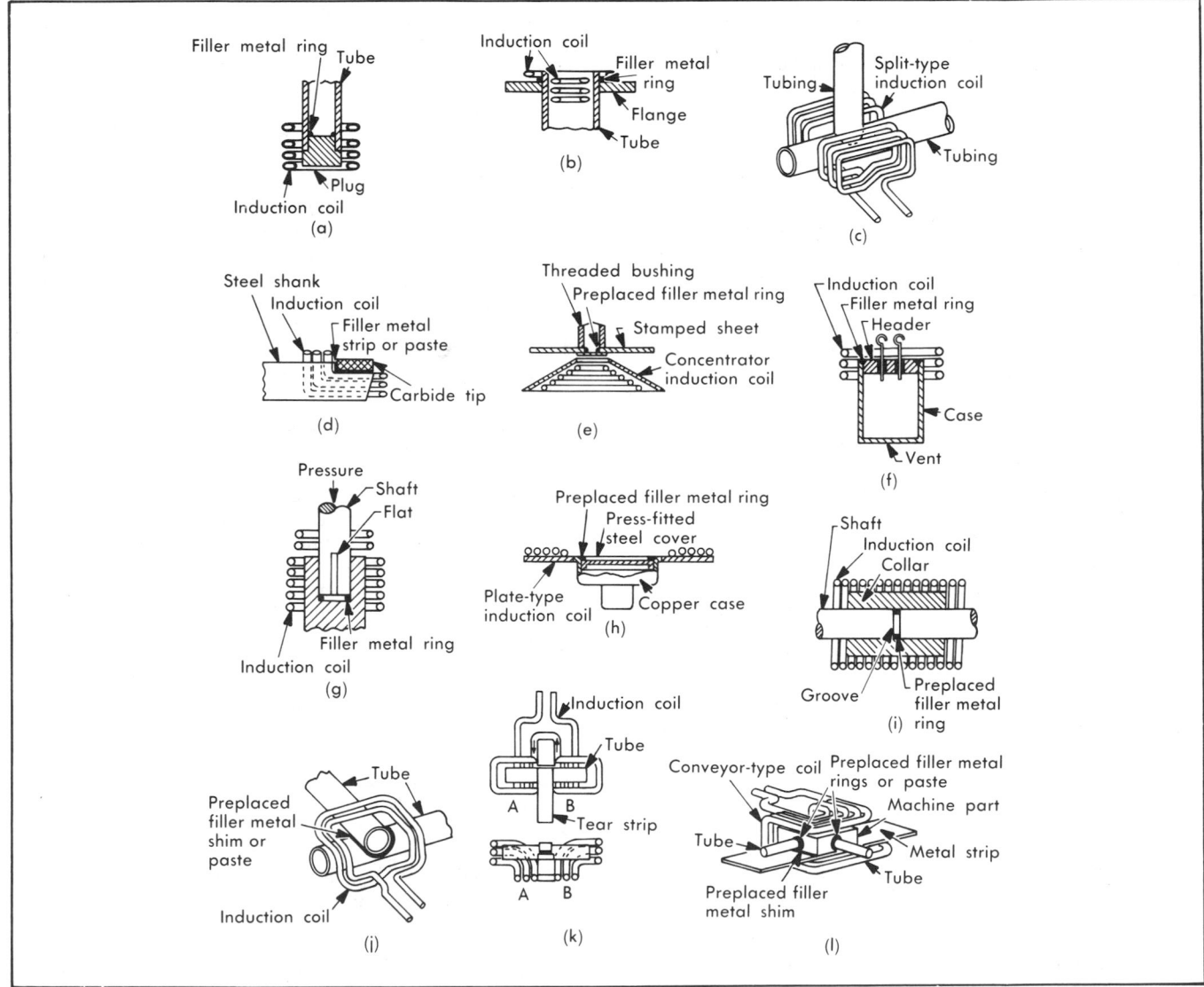

Fig. 43-31 Induction brazing coil and joint design: (a) Plug-to-tube. Turns of inductor coil may be spaced for suitable heat pattern depending on materials being joined; minimum air gap between the inductor coil and workpiece is desirable for maximum energy transfer. (b) Flange-to-tube. Internal-external coil; flange chamfered to hold preplaced filler metal. (c) Tube-to-tube. T-split coil; filler metal ring preplaced internally to provide uniform fillet without excess joining filler metal along the sides of the tube. (d) Carbide tip-to-shank. Open-end coil; filler metal strip preplaced as shown. (e) Threaded bushing-to-stamping. Concentrator coil localizes heat; filler metal preplaced at base of bushing. (f) Header-to-case seal. Simple inductor coil for uniform heating; preplaced filler metal recessed; vent permits escape of expanded air to avoid leaky joint. (g) Shaft-to-fitting. Inductor coil with varying diameter; filler metal preplaced internally at base of recess; pressure used to seat shaft; small flat permits escape of gases. (h) Formed-shape assembly. Plate coil for localized heating; filler metal preform partially shielded from electromagnetic field by case. (i) Shaft-to-collar. Inductor coil; filler metal ring preplaced in machined groove. (j) Tube-to-tube. L-shaped pancake coil. (k) Tear strip-to-tube with current reversal between A and B to prevent overheating strip. Filler metal preplaced beneath strip. (l) Component assembly. Conveyor-type coil; filler metal shim preplaced between machine part and metal strip; filler metal rings preplaced on tubes.

BRAZING

the bath may act as a flux. When a molten metal bath is used, the bath provides the filler metal. A cover of flux is provided over molten (filler) metal baths.

The principal use of dip brazing is in joining aluminum and its alloys using a molten bath of fluoride and chloride salts with melting points in the range of 660 to 9500°F (350 to 510°C). Essential features of the process include the following:

1. Precleaning is performed prior to brazing, usually in a chemical bath, to reduce aluminum oxide and prepare the surfaces.
2. Components are assembled, and the filler metal is placed in the joint area, often in the form of a paste or wire preform. Many assemblies incorporate sheet aluminum clad with the braze filler metal, a design used especially for dip brazing.
3. Because brazing operation takes place at temperatures in the range of 1040 to 1160°F (560 to 625°C), very close to the melting point of the parent metals, a means must be provided for supporting the assembly at these temperatures to prevent sagging or collapse of components.
4. Any convenient means of preheating parts can be employed, but an air furnace is best suited. The assemblies or fixtured parts are preheated to about 1000°F and then transferred to the molten-salt bath for brazing.
5. The preheated parts rapidly attain the temperature of the salt bath. It is seldom necessary to have the parts in the molten salt more than 1-6 minutes, depending on the size of the work. The filler metal melts and rapidly fills the joint areas. After brazing, the load is raised from the bath, and the excess flux is drained back into the bath. Joints should be designed properly to facilitate drainage of the flux.
6. As soon as the filler metal has solidified and while the parts are still hot—500°F (260°C)—the parts are immediately lowered into a hot water rinse. This rinse cracks and loosens the bulk of the flux residues. Subsequent warm and cold rinses remove the remaining flux and salt.

Salt-bath dip brazing of carbon and alloy steels, tool steels, and other metals is being successfully carried out on a production basis. Copper, brass, silver, and nickel are some of the suitable filler metals. Molten-metal dip brazing is also used for small applications, such as the brazing of twisted electrical wire to ensure good conductivity.

Infrared Brazing

Infrared brazing primarily uses quartz-iodine incandescent lamps as a source of heat energy. The special lamps are tubular and can easily be focused to concentrate the heat at the area to be brazed. With this technique, it is not uncommon to obtain heat from ten 1000 W lamps (10 kW) concentrated at a joint area of less than 10 in.^{2} (64.5 cm^2) or wattage density of about 1000 W/in.^{2} (155 W/cm^2).

Gas infrared heat sources are used to preheat assemblies for brazing to a temperature somewhat below the actual flow point of the filler metal, as in silver brazing. The final braze then can be performed easily and rapidly with torch heating. The preheating part of the cycle is particularly effective when large sections must be heated to brazing temperature.

Furnace Brazing

Furnace brazing is the process most suited to mass-production brazing and for critical applications. This is particularly true in brazing small to medium-sized components of up to 3-4 lb (1.4-1.8 kg) each. This process probably accounts for the largest share of brazed hardware in the United States today. The following features distinguish furnace brazing:

1. The filler metal must be preplaced so that it will flow into the joints with no operator assistance after the parts have reached brazing temperature.
2. Fixturing of the parts must be kept at a minimum and best design makes the brazement self-fixturing. Large quantities of fixtures increase process cost and lower furnace productivity by adding deadweight.
3. An atmosphere protects the parts from oxidation at brazing temperatures, reduces trace oxides, and aids in the wetting of the filler metal on the parent metal.

Furnace types. Furnace brazing may be performed as either a batch or a continuous operation. Batch operations use retorts or cold-wall vacuum furnaces in which the load is stacked in rows on trays of nickel-chromium alloy. The entire load is then brought to brazing temperature, and all the parts braze at the same time. Vacuum furnaces are hermetically sealed, and the air is pumped out to produce a protective atmosphere. Semicontinuous vacuum furnaces are used for brazing aluminum automotive components such as radiators and air-conditioner heat exchangers. Continuous furnace brazing uses a conveyor mechanism that carries the parts through the heat zone and into a cooling zone on a mesh belt or on rolls driven by a chain and sprocket arrangement. The latter design is known as a roller-hearth furnace.

Atmospheres. To meet the requirements of all the various metals that can and are furnace brazed, a further classification of furnace brazing is often made by the atmosphere used. Exothermic and endothermic atmospheres are produced in a separate generator by the controlled combustion of natural gas. They are suitable for brazing carbon steel, brass, copper, and other metals. The most common use of these atmospheres in industry is the brazing of appliance and automotive components made from steel, using copper as the filler metal—the so-called copper brazing process. Brass and copper are usually brazed with lower melting point, silver-bearing filler metals.

Resistance Brazing

Resistance brazing involves the use of low-voltage, high alternating-current power applied between two electrodes. The workpiece to be brazed is held between the electrodes under light pressure, and the heat developed in the workpiece from the resistance to the flow of electric current causes the filler metal to melt and flow into the joint. Two typical examples are brazing of electrical contacts and copper transformer leads. In the first case, the contact is clad on the back face with the filler metal, usually one of the BAg silver brazing filler metals. Heat is usually applied through the power supply of a resistance spot welder, with pressure adjusted carefully so that only enough pressure is applied to secure the position of the contact at brazing heat. The tips of the welder are generally shaped to the contour of the electrode. In some cases, it is advisable to use one of the lower conductivity electrode materials and let the electrode act as a heat source as it heats itself. Flux is employed and heating time is generally short.

Filler metals may be preplaced in the form of shims, washers, rings, or paste. In some cases, particularly when using the incandescent carbon-block tongs for heating copper and copper alloys to which the BCuP series are applied, it is possible to

BRAZING

face-feed the filler metal. Fluxes are generally necessary with all the filler metals except the BCuP alloys, which when used on copper to copper are considered to be self-fluxing. Because dry fluxes are nonconductors of electricity, the fluxes should be moist when brazing is started.

Laser Brazing

The use of lasers as a source of heat for brazing and soldering is a relatively recent development. A major advantage of using lasers is the capability of selectively applying heating energy to small areas without heating the entire component. Another advantage is close control of heat input and the ability to locate or position the heat accurately. The use of lasers also controls grain structure and intermetallic formations.

Because of their advantages, lasers are being used for the production of miniature and thin precision parts, to make joints near thermally sensitive connections, and for connections inside evacuated or pressurized vessels or containers. However, because of the high costs of laser equipment, the method is generally only being used when other brazing methods are not found to be adequate.

Diffusion Brazing

Diffusion brazing differs from other brazing methods in that a distinct layer of brazing filler metal is diffused into and with the base metal to change the physical properties of the joint. During diffusion brazing, the filler metal melts or a eutectic liquid forms from alloying between the two higher melting metals or alloys such as copper and silver-plated copper. Diffusion at the interface continues, and a layer of a new alloy may remain or the filler metal may disappear. As a result, the joint properties are nearly the same as those of the base metal. A limitation is that the cycles for diffusion brazing are longer than for other brazing processes. Depending on the variables of temperature, quantity of filler metal, and mutual solubility, the time at the brazing temperature can range from 10 minutes to many hours.

Electron Beam Brazing

Electron beam welding equipment, discussed in Chapter 9, is only being used to a limited extent for brazing. Applications are generally restricted to small assemblies or the encapsulating of packaged devices. High vacuums in the work chambers permit the brazing of clean joints without the need for a flux or an atmosphere. The electron beams are defocused to reduce the power density and heating effect.

Exothermic Brazing

In exothermic brazing, the heat required is generated by the reaction of several chemical compounds. Solid-state or nearly solid-state metal-metal oxide reactions are used. Ignition of the exothermic mixture is by a flame, a hot spark, or a resistance heater. The preparation of the brazement, filler metal, flux, or atmosphere are similar to other brazing processes.

Other Brazing Processes

There are several other brazing processes, generally less commonly used than the methods that have been described.

Arc brazing. In this process, the heat required for brazing is obtained from an electric arc. In twin carbon arc brazing, the electric arc is established between two carbon electrodes.

Block brazing. In this process, the heat required for brazing is obtained from heated blocks applied to the parts to be joined.

Flow brazing. In this process, a molten nonferrous metal is poured over the joint until brazing temperature is attained.

Blanket brazing. In this process, a resistance-heated blanket is placed over the parts to be joined, generally using ceramic dies. Heat is transferred to the parts by conduction and radiation. This process is used frequently for brazed honeycomb fabrication.

Step brazing. In this method, which can be used with many of the brazing processes discussed, brazing of successive joints on an assembly is done with filler metals of successively lower melting temperatures. In this way, joining is accomplished without disturbing the joints previously brazed.

BRAZING FILLER METALS

The AWS defines brazing filler metals as those to be added in making a braze. They are metals or alloys with liquidus temperature above 840° F (450° C). By the definition of brazing, the filler metal must melt below the melting point of the parts joined and must be capable of distribution in the closely fitted joint by capillary action. These filler metals were formerly identified as hard solders, silver solder, and brazing alloys, but these terms are now considered obsolete and, in their place, the term *brazing filler metal* is preferred.

The AWS *Brazing Manual* lists the following four properties as essential for brazing filler metal:[9]

1. Ability to wet the base metals on which it is used in order to make a strong, sound bond.
2. Proper melting temperature and flow properties that permit distribution in properly prepared joints by capillary action.
3. A composition of sufficient homogeneity and stability to minimize separation by liquation under the brazing conditions to be encountered, and free of excessively volatile constituents.
4. Desirable mechanical and physical properties in the joint, such as strength and ductility.

Brazing filler metal melting does not occur at one distinct temperature (except for pure metals and those of eutectic composition), but rather over a range. The lower temperature of the range is known as the *solidus*; the upper temperature of the range is known as the *liquidus*. The definitions of these points given in the AWS *Brazing Manual* are as follows: "Solidus is the highest temperature at which a metal or alloy is completely solid...Liquidus is the lowest temperature at which a metal or alloy is completely liquid." Brazing usually takes place at a temperature above the liquidus. However, certain alloys exhibit the peculiar property of being essentially molten below the true liquidus and, in consequence, brazing with these alloys may be performed at a temperature below the liquidus. To identify these points for a given alloy and not create confusion, each alloy is identified by its solidus and liquidus. A brazing temperature range is also provided that indicates the range of temperatures at which brazing is best performed.

BRAZING FLUX

The purpose of a brazing flux is to prevent oxidation of the joint and to promote wetting, flow, and the formation of a soundly brazed joint. A brazing flux, which is a mixture of chemical compounds, performs this function by combining with, excluding, or otherwise rendering harmless those products on the base metal surface that would retard or prevent the formation of a sound brazed joint. A brazing atmosphere provides a similar function as a flux and surrounds the part with an atmosphere that will generally prevent the formation of deleterious substances or that, as with an active gas such as hydrogen, may reduce the substances and render them harmless.

SOLDERING

Soldering is defined by the American Welding Society (AWS) as:

"A group of welding processes which produce coalescence of materials by heating them to a suitable temperature and by using a filler metal having a liquidus not exceeding 840° F (450° C) and below the solidus of the base material. The filler metal is distributed between the closely fitted surfaces by capillary attraction."

Soldering is one of the oldest methods of joining metals and still finds varied and extensive use in industry. Most soldering operations produce a metallurgical intermetallic-type bond between the filler metal and the base material. Joints can be made to surfaces without this bond as in glass-to-metal joining, where surface activity and adhesion are the main mechanisms of joining.

Selection of soldering as a joining method over mechanical fastening, welding, brazing, or adhesive bonding depends primarily on end-use requirements with respect to joint strength, application, and operating temperature and environment, as well as production costs.

APPLICATIONS

Application areas of soldering vary widely. They include copper plumbing systems, automotive copper and brass radiators, aluminum refrigeration components, and electrical and electronic connections. The most sophisticated computers contain many thousands of soldered joints.

The methods of producing the soldered joints and the availability of a wide range of soldering alloys facilitates these uses. The technology is still changing, and new joining materials in the soldering group continue to appear and find application.

Electrical and electronic applications, including printed circuit boards, represent the major use for soldering. Common products produced by soldering include television and radio sets, car radiators, light bulbs, telephones, typewriters, and automotive fuel and ignition systems.

ADVANTAGES

Soldering offers many advantages for joining operations, including the following:

1. *Versatility.* The wide variety of solders, fluxes, and heating methods available make the process suitable for numerous applications. Multiple joints can be soldered simultaneously or sequentially.
2. *Reliability.* Reliable joints, impermeable to gases and liquids, can be produced consistently. The quality of most soldered joints can be evaluated by visual inspection, and unsatisfactory joints can be easily repaired and reworked. Low temperatures employed for soldering minimize distortion and heat damage to components being joined.
3. *Precise control.* The amount of solder and flux used, as well as the amount of heat applied, can be controlled accurately, thus ensuring consistent quality.
4. *Fast production.* The process is easily automated to attain high production rates.
5. *Low cost.* Soldering is generally an economical joining process, with minimal energy requirements.

LIMITATIONS

A possible drawback to the use of soldering is the limited mechanical strengths attained. However, joints strong enough for many applications can be made with proper joint designs, filler metals, and soldering procedures.

SOLDERING METHODS

Soldering methods are generally classified by the method of heat application. Typical methods are conduction, convection, radiation, resistance, and induction. Ultrasonic energy may also be used as an aid to soldering. Selection of a heating method depends primarily on the cost and efficiency of the method, production requirements, and the sensitivity of the assembly to heat.

Conduction Heating

Conduction is the transmission of heat through, or by means of, a thermal conductor that is in physical contact with a body without appreciable displacement of the molecules of the material. In this type of heating, a soldering tip is heated, and the heat is transferred to the area to be soldered by direct contact. For example, a simple handheld soldering iron is a type of conduction heater. Consequently, it is of primary importance that the heat transmission area be kept clean and free from any insulating layers such as oxides that may be formed at elevated temperatures.

Convection Heating

Convection is the transfer of heat by moving masses of fluids or gases. With convection equipment, heat can be applied to the work by a stream of hot gases that may be either reducing or inert in nature. The heat-transfer medium is not limited to gases. Many liquids, such as oils, may be used to raise the work to the soldering temperature.

Radiation Heating

Radiation is the total effect of emittance, transmittance, and absorptance of energy. Thermal radiation is electromagnetic energy in transport. Soldering is concerned mainly with the radiation of heat. In practice, the three methods of heat transfer—convection, conduction, and radiation—are difficult to separate into the various types of equipment.

SOLDERING

Resistance Soldering

An electric current generates heat as it flows through a circuit. Contact soldering uses resistance heating elements to apply a preset amount of pressure to the feet of surface-mounted components. The current is programmed through the elements to reflow solder the components to printed circuit boards.

Electrodes vary from 0.078″ (1.98 mm) diam metal probes to large carbon blocks. Resistance soldering has the advantage of high joint production, no warmup requirements, and instant, controlled heat. Joints can be made in from 0.5 to 2 seconds, depending on wire size and materials involved. Another advantage is the degree of miniaturization possible; tiny electrodes can be used to connect modular circuitry components or other closely spaced components.

Induction Soldering

Electromagnetic induction soldering uses the part to be soldered as the heating element. Current induced in the part by an induction coil heats the joint to a depth that depends on current frequency. Because of skin effects, the higher the frequency, the more heat will be confined to the material surfaces—an extremely useful phenomenon in soldering because it minimizes distortion and oxidation of the base metal. Flux and solder are applied to the joints prior to joining, and preformed solder shapes can be used. A requirement for induction soldering is that the base metal be electrically conductive.

Ultrasonic Soldering

Cavitation induced by ultrasonic excitation of molten solder removes oxides from submerged metal surfaces to allow alloying of the molten solder with the base metal. Implosion of the cavitation bubbles creates a scrubbing action that fractures and dislodges oxides from the metal surfaces, and the oxides float to the surface of the molten solder.

This method eliminates the need for flux in many soldering operations and is used to join hard-to-solder metals such as aluminum. However, the ultrasonic action does not enhance wetting of the metal surfaces, as do fluxing agents, and there is no capillary flow of the molten solder. As a result, it is sometimes necessary to pretin one or both surfaces to be joined or place preformed or solid wire solder directly into the joint before or during ultrasonic excitation. However, it is not necessary nor desirable to pretin aluminum surfaces to be joined by ultrasonic soldering because this requires an extra operation and accelerates the rate of aluminum dissolution into the solder bath.

Other Soldering Processes

There are several soldering processes in addition to those already discussed, most of which are used for specific applications.

Abrasion soldering. In this variation of soldering, sometimes called friction soldering, the faying surfaces of the base metals are mechanically abraded with the solder or other instrument during soldering.

Screen printing. Solder pastes (blends of powdered filler metals, fluxes, and paste binders) are being used with automatic applicators and screens, generally 60-80 mesh, to provide precise placement of solder dots, each containing a premeasured amount. The pastes provide tack retention for several hours, acting as temporary adhesives to hold components in place until they are reflow soldered. Heat for melting the solder is applied by electric hot plates, convection ovens, infrared, lasers, or vapor-phase systems.

Spray gun soldering. Gas-fired and electrically heated guns are being used to spray molten or semimolten solder from a continuously fed wire onto joints.

Step soldering. This process consists of soldering successive joints on an assembly with solders of successively lower melting temperatures to obtain joining without disturbing the joints previously soldered.

Sweat soldering. A process in which two or more parts that have been precoated with solder are reheated and assembled into a joint without the use of additional solder.

References

1. J. Devine, "Joining Electric Contacts," *Welding Design and Fabrication*, vol. 53, no. 3 (1980), pp. 112-115.
2. J. Devine, "Ultrasonic Welding Helps Lighten Aircraft," *Welding Design and Fabrication*, vol. 51, no. 8 (1978), pp. 74-76.
3. T. J. Kelly, "Ultrasonic Welding of Cu-Ni to Steel," *Welding Journal*, vol. 60, no. 4 (1981), pp. 29-31.
4. F. R. Meyer, "Ultrasonic Produces Strong Oxide-Free Welds," *Assembly Engineering*, vol. 20, no. 5 (1977), pp. 26-29.
5. T. Renshaw, J. Curatola, and A. Sarrantonio, "Developments in Ultrasonic Welding for Aircraft," *SAMPE 11th National Technical Conference Proceedings* (Boston: 1979), pp. 681-693.
6. T. Renshaw, K. Wongwiwat, and A. Sarrantonio, "A Comparison of Properties of Single Overlap Tension Joints Prepared by Ultrasonic Welding and Other Means," *AIAA/ASME/ASCE 23rd Conference Proceedings* (New Orleans: 1983), pp. 1-8.
7. T. Renshaw and A. Sarrantonio, "Properties of Large Multispot Ultrasonically Welded Joints," *Journal of Aircraft*, vol. 18 (September 1981), pp. 761-765.
8. M. A. Cook, *The Science of High Explosives* (New York: Reinhold Publishing Corp., 1966), p. 274.
9. *Brazing Manual* (Miami: American Welding Society, 1976).

AUTOMATED ASSEMBLY

Assembly in the manufacturing process consists of putting together all the component parts and subassemblies of a given product, fastening, performing inspections and functional tests, labeling, separating good assemblies from bad, and packaging and/or preparing them for final use. Assembly is unique compared to the methods of manufacturing such as machining, grinding, and welding in that most of these processes involve only a few disciplines and possibly only one. Most of these nonassembly operations cannot be performed without the aid of equipment, thus the development of automatic methods has been necessary rather than optional. Assembly, on the other hand, may involve in one machine many of the fastening methods, such as riveting, welding, screwdriving, and adhesive application, as well as automatic parts selection, probing, gaging, functional testing, labeling, and packaging. The state of the art in assembly operations has not reached the level of standardization; much manual work is still being performed in this area.

Assembly has traditionally been one of the highest areas of direct labor costs. In some cases, assembly accounts for 50% or more of manufacturing costs and typically 20-50%. However, closer cooperation between design and manufacturing engineers has resulted in reducing and in a few cases eliminating altogether the need for assembly. When assembly is required, improved design or redesign of products has simplified automated (semiautomatic or automatic) assembly.

PRACTICALITY OF AUTOMATION

Determining the practicality of automated assembly requires careful evaluation of the following:

- The number of parts in the assembly.
- Design of the parts with respect to producibility, assemblability, automatic handling, and testability (materials, forms, sizes, dimensional tolerances, and weights).
- Quality of parts to be assembled. Out-of-tolerances or defective parts can cause production losses and increased costs because of stoppages.
- Availability of qualified, technically competent personnel to be responsible for equipment operation.
- Total production and production-rate requirements.
- Product variations and frequency of design changes.
- Joining methods required.
- Assembly times and costs.
- Assembly line or system configuration, using simulation, including material handling.

The best candidates for successful and economical automated assembly are generally simple, small products having a fairly stable design life. Such products are usually required in relatively large volumes and have a high labor content and/or a high reject rate because of their manual assembly. However, the development of flexible, programmable, and robotic assembly systems (discussed subsequently in this chapter) can decrease production and product-life requirements.

POTENTIAL ADVANTAGES
Potential advantages resulting from assembly automation include the following:

1. Improved product quality, consistent product repeatability with fewer rejects, and a high degree of production reliability as a result of reducing or eliminating human errors. Component inspection and part testing during assembly prevents defective parts from being used. The consistently high-quality products obtained reduce liability and warranty costs.
2. Reduced manufacturing costs resulting from decreased labor requirements and increased productivity. Savings result from reductions in both direct and indirect labor.
3. Improved safety and better working conditions by removing operators from hazardous operations.
4. More efficient production scheduling (such as just-in-time techniques) and reduced inventory requirements because of the ability of automated assembly systems to respond immediately to production demands.
5. Reduced floor space requirements.

POSSIBLE LIMITATIONS
The high initial cost of automated assembly machines, systems, and equipment has been a deterrent to increased use, especially for smaller factories producing limited quantities of various products. However, the development of flexible manufacturing systems are expected to make automated assembly more economically justifiable.

Automatic assembly cannot be divorced from preceding operations because clean, consistently uniform, and high-quality parts are required for its success. The parts do not necessarily have to be held to closer tolerances, but uniformity from part to part is essential. Complete inspection of components on assembly machines is generally not practical or economical. It is usually better to inspect the parts prior to assembly; only their critical dimensions, locations, and presence on assembly machines need be checked.

In addition to problems caused by excessive

variations in parts, random machine failures (occasional misfeeds or incomplete assemblies) may be due to the presence of chips or foreign material, poor hopper construction, misadjusted or worn transfer units, or erratic operation of tooling. When assembly is combined with machining operations, care must be taken to prevent chips from entering the assemblies. Burrs, flash, or distorted parts, as well as thin or fragile parts, can be troublesome because they might interfere with tracking or escapement. In some cases, trouble may be avoided by prestacking the parts on mandrels, inserting them in magazines on the assembly machine, and using a shuttle mechanism to transfer parts (one at a time) from the top or bottom of the stack.

TYPICAL APPLICATIONS

The predominant users of automated assembly systems are the automotive industry, appliance manufacturers, producers of electrical and electronic hardware, farm equipment builders, consumer product makers, the defense industry, and the pharmaceutical industry.

In one automotive application, needle bearings are being automatically assembled in automatic transmission pinions at a production rate of 1200 assemblies per hour. Cycle time per assembly is 3 seconds, an automatic greasing operation is performed on each assembly, and the machine handles 45,600 individual parts each hour. The machine can be modified to single or double-row bearings.

In another automotive application, a 98-station synchronous system assembles any of 64 pump configurations, consisting of as many as 37 different components, at the rate of 1000 assemblies per hour. The pumps are for automotive hydraulic steering units. The assembly system consists of two main lines and two auxiliary off-line dial machines, with all four components equipped with chain-driven workholding pallets. A data-code entry system is used to program the system for various pump configurations.

PRODUCT DESIGN FOR AUTOMATED ASSEMBLY

Optimum design or redesign of a product and its components is essential for successful, efficient, and economical automatic assembly. Considerable amounts of money are often spent to automate the assembly of existing product designs when it would be much more economical to redesign the products to facilitate automatic assembly. Design for assembly (DFA) is being increasingly practiced because of the realization of potential production savings and better quality and improved reliability in the product.

Close cooperation is required between design and manufacturing engineers in evaluating a product design for improved assembly. The inherent capabilities and limitations of assembly operations should be considered during the early design or redesign stages. At the earliest possible design stages, it is also best to assess the parts for the ease with which they can be supplied and oriented. Assembly of various designs should be evaluated and compared.

DESIGN FOR SIMPLIFICATION

The optimum product design is one that eliminates the need for assembly or reduces the number of parts to be assembled to a minimum. One simple example is shown in Fig. 44-1, where a single stamping replaces a two-part assembly.

When single-component products are impossible or uneconomical, the number of parts required should generally be kept as low as possible, and their complexity should be minimized. There are rare occasions, however, where it may be more economical to manufacture two or more pieces to replace one. The reason for minimizing the number of parts is to improve the remaining, more functional parts and to eliminate nonfunctional ones. To determine if a part can be eliminated, the following three questions should be answered:

1. Does the part move with respect to other parts?
2. Is the part made from a different material than the other parts?
3. Will the part require removal for product servicing?

An affirmative answer to any of these questions generally indicates that the part is required. Negative answers to all three questions indicate that the part may not be necessary and any function it performs may be able to be transferred to a more essential component.

DESIGN FOR EASE OF AUTOMATIC ASSEMBLY

Parts to be assembled automatically should be designed for ease of handling, feeding, orienting, positioning, and joining.

Part configurations that can be easily oriented include the following:

1. Completely symmetrical parts such as spheres, cylinders, pins, and rods. Figure 44-2 illustrates some examples of how parts can be made symmetrical. In general, the lengths of cylindrical parts should be at least 25% longer or shorter than their diameters to facilitate feeding.
2. Substantially disproportionate parts, either with respect to weight or with respect to dimensions, such as headed screws, bolts, and rivets. The center of gravity should be near one end of each part to produce a tendency to naturally feed in one specific orientation. If this natural orientation is not the desired position, it is relatively easy to rotate the parts to the proper position.

Parts that are nearly symmetrical generally present the greatest number of problems in feeding and orienting. Parts having features such as off-center holes or cavities are also difficult to orient and may require tooling outside the hopper or other storage device for orientation. Sometimes external features can be added to the parts (see Fig. 44-3) to permit easier orienting in the hopper. Such features should allow the feed tracks from the hopper to maintain orientation.

Weight distribution is an important consideration in part

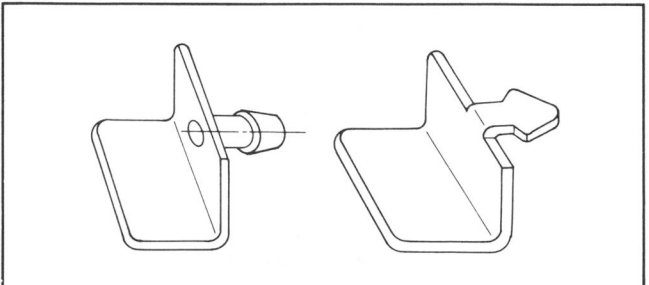

Fig. 44-1 Two-part assembly (left) is replaced by a single stamping.

PRODUCT DESIGN FOR AUTOMATED ASSEMBLY

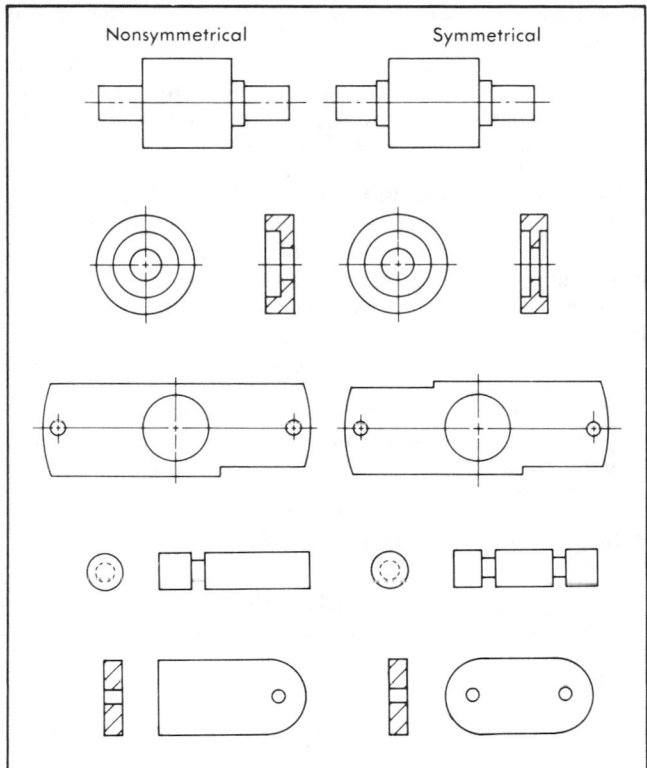

Fig. 44-2 Parts made symmetrical for easier orientation.

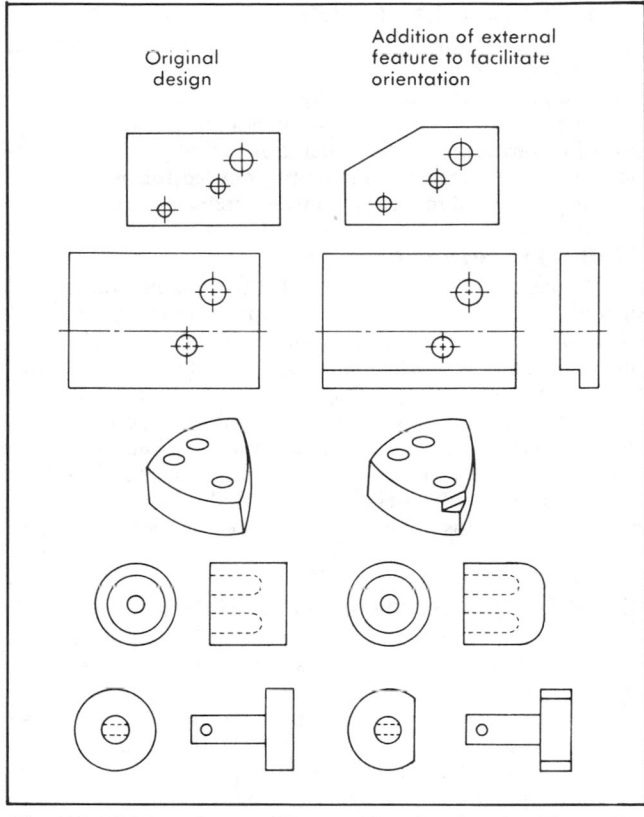

Fig. 44-3 Addition of external feature (chamfer, slot, shoulder, radius, or flat) can facilitate orientation.

design because gravity is used extensively in feeding systems for automatic assembly. Designers should try to avoid instability in part feeding by providing the part with a low center of gravity. Unstable parts having a high center of gravity with relation to the tracking surface tend to topple. Increasing the size of the tracking surface may help in some cases. In some applications, it is effective to feed the part in an inverted position to that desired. By providing a twist in the feed track, the part can subsequently be brought into correct orientation.

ASSEMBLY MACHINES AND SYSTEMS

SELECTION FACTORS

Selection of the optimum assembly system often depends on careful consideration of many factors, including the following:[1]

1. Production rate requirements.
2. Size and weight of parts to be assembled.
3. Manual operations required, if any.
4. Number of automated operations.
5. Complexity of the operations performed.
6. Material handling and supply logistics.

The possibility of product and/or component design changes is another important factor to be considered.

Production Rate Requirements

Approximate production rates for various assembly system arrangements having single tooling are shown in Fig. 44-4. Higher production rates can be realized with systems having multiple tooling. Physical size and weight of the parts to be assembled and the complexity and number of operations must be considered in determining the most efficient system.

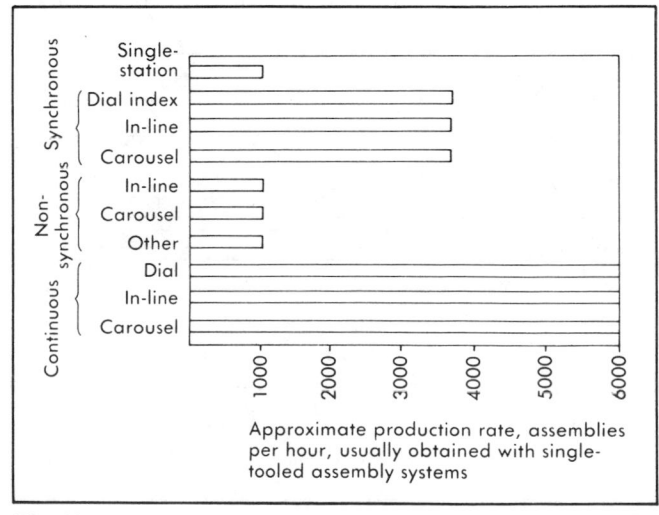

Fig. 44-4 Approximate production rates with single-tooled assembly systems.

ASSEMBLY MACHINES AND SYSTEMS

Size and Weight of Parts

The size and weight of the parts to be assembled can present several problems, including difficulty with positioning accuracy and equipment necessary to physically move the parts if the parts are large. Single-station machines are generally best for precision location where few operations are required. Synchronous and nonsynchronous systems are used for more operations and/or when manual operations are necessary.

Manual Operations

Although it is generally desirable to eliminate all manual operations, this is not always possible. Dial-type (rotary) assembly machines are usually limited to one or two manual operations, in-line machines have space for a number of operators, and carousel systems allow even more manual operations. A number of manual operations can also be performed on synchronous and nonsynchronous systems. Continuous systems are generally almost fully automatic for the high-speed production of small assemblies and usually have many or all manual operations for the low-volume production of large assemblies.

Number of Automated Operations

The suggested number of automated operations for various assembly machine configurations is presented in Fig. 44-5. As the number of automated operations increases, the efficiency of the individual stations must be higher to maintain an acceptable machine efficiency because the overall machine efficiency is the product of individual station efficiencies. Combining too many assembly operations in one machine or system can sometimes be inefficient; it may be better to divide the operations among several machines.

Complexity of Operations

The complexity of the individual operations to be performed must be carefully considered along with the efficiencies of the various assembly configurations possible in determining which type of automation arrangement is most suitable for the assembly task.

Material Handling and Supply Logistics

Floor space and additional equipment required for material handling and storage may possibly be greater than that needed for assembly itself. Synchronous and nonsynchronous in-line assembly systems permit spreading out equipment for the orderly handling of material and accessibility for operators and maintenance personnel. Concepts such as just-in-time inventory help minimize space requirements.

BASIC EQUIPMENT REQUIREMENTS

Most assembly machines and systems are specially designed for a special product or a family of products. They can be of continuous or intermittent operation, with intermittent transfer being the most common for automated assembly. Basic assembly machine components include workholding devices, transfer and/or indexing mechanisms, parts feeding, and orienting devices.

All assembly machines and systems must provide means for easy and rapid removal of jammed parts or defective assemblies. Safety interlocks, noise control devices, and environmental protection are also essential.

SINGLE-STATION ASSEMBLY

Machines having a single workstation are used most extensively when a specific operation has to be performed many times on one or a few parts. Assembling many parts into a single unit, like inserting blades or buckets into turbine or compressor wheels, is a common application. These machines may also be used when a number of different operations have to be performed, if the required tooling is not too complicated. These machines are also incorporated into multistation assembly systems.

SYNCHRONOUS ASSEMBLY SYSTEMS

Synchronous (indexing) assembly systems are available in dial (rotary), in-line, and carousel varieties. With these systems, all pallets or workpieces are moved at the same time and for the same distance. Because indexing intervals are determined by the slowest operation to be performed at any of the stations, operation time is the determining factor affecting production rate. Operators cannot vary the production rate, and a breakdown at any station causes the whole line to stop. By proper consideration to line balancing and parallel assembly operations, such downtime problems can be minimized.

Synchronous systems are used primarily for high-speed and high-volume applications on small, lightweight assemblies where the various operations required have relatively equal cycle times. They are also generally used for fully or substantially automated operations because manual operations are not usually compatible with these systems. However, manual stations, both semiautomatic and completely manual, can be used on synchronous lines.

NONSYNCHRONOUS ASSEMBLY SYSTEMS

Nonsynchronous transfer (accumulative or power-and-free type) assembly systems, with free or floating pallets or workpieces and independently operated individual stations, are being widely used where the times required to perform different operations vary greatly and for larger products having many components. Such machines have slower cycle rates than synchronous machines, but slower stations can be double or triple tooled to boost production. One major advantage of these so-called power-and-free systems is increased versatility.

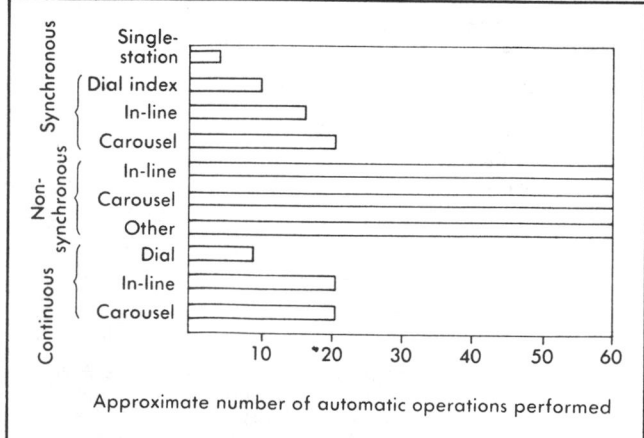

Fig. 44-5 Approximate number of automated operations that can be performed with various assembly systems.

ASSEMBLY MACHINES AND SYSTEMS

CONTINUOUS-MOTION SYSTEMS

With continuous-motion systems, assembly operations are performed while the workpieces or pallets move at a constant speed and the workheads reciprocate. High production rates are possible because indexing time is eliminated. However, the cost and complexity of these systems are high because the workheads have to synchronize and move with the product being assembled. Applications for continuous-motion automated assembly are limited except for high-production uses in the packaging and bottling industries. The systems are, however, used for the manual assembly of large and heavy products, such as automobiles and refrigerators, with the operators moving with the products while performing their functions.

DIAL (ROTARY) ASSEMBLY

Dial or rotary index machines of synchronous design, one of the first types used for assembly, are still used for many applications. Workstations and tooling can be mounted on a central column or around the periphery of the indexing table. These machines are generally limited to small and medium-sized lightweight assemblies requiring a relatively low number of operations that are not too complex; as the table diameter increases, its mass and complexity can become impractical. Another possible disadvantage is limited accessibility to the workheads and tooling. Also, servicing the indexing table and mechanism, as well as the controls, is difficult with center-column designs.

Advantages and Limitations

Advantages of dial machines include minimum floor space requirements because of their compact designs, high production rates—up to 3600 or more assemblies per hour, and the ease with which standard modules and tooling can be used. Cycle time, however, is limited by the slowest operation required. Dial machines are often tied together with transfer devices to other machines and systems. Limitations include practical physical size and space available for loading, unloading, tooling, maintenance, and repairs.

Versatility

Tables for rotary indexing machines are available in various sizes, with a maximum practical diameter of about 200" (5080 mm). Fixtures or nests are equally spaced around the tables, and standard tables usually have from 4 to 32 stations. The stations can be single or double tooled, depending on production requirements.

Double indexing is possible when it is desired to have a workpiece pass a manual operating station twice during assembly. Lift-and-carry devices can be provided to transport parts from station to station where they must be placed down into nests or fixtures.

IN-LINE SYSTEMS

In-line assembly machines are used in synchronous (indexing), nonsynchronous (accumulative or power-and-free), and continuous designs. In-line indexing assembly machines can be of a wraparound (circumferential) or over-and-under type (see Fig. 44-6) or of a conventional transfer-machine type.

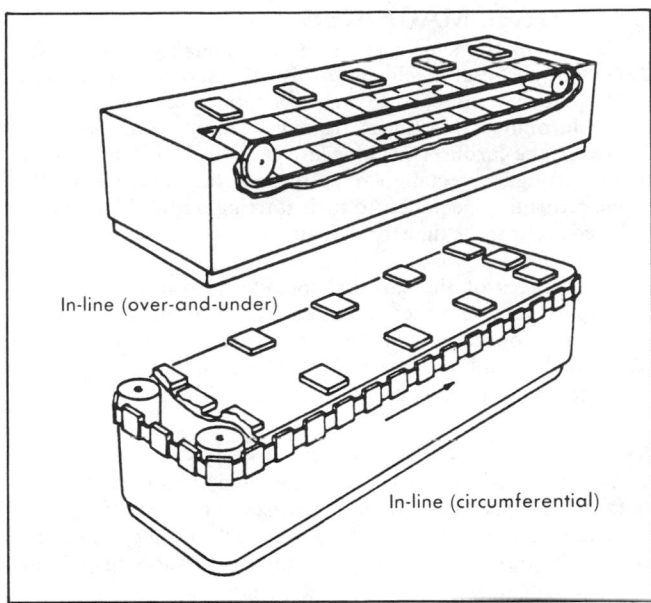

Fig. 44-6 In-line indexing assembly machine bases of the over-and-under and circumferential (wraparound) types.

Various methods of moving the workpieces from station to station are used on different assembly machines. On one over-and-under type, the platens are rolled over in two 90° rotations when they reach the end of the machine and are returned on a lower track to the starting end. In another type, for assembling smaller components, the platens are indexed along two sets of parallel tracks, with automatic operations performed as the platens are transferred along the back row and manual operations (if required) performed as the platens return along the front row. On one in-line wraparound type, a single indexing unit is provided at one end of the machine, with a flexible steel band that is driven by a drum wheel and rides around the edge of a built-up table to support the pallets for moving from station to station. The workholder pallets are attached to and indexed by the steel-band drive, with locator pins preventing shifting of the band on the drive drum. Another type of assembly machine is equipped with self-propelled pallets.

Advantages

In-line indexing systems allow more operations and provide more accessibility than dial machines. They can also be used for heavier and more complex assemblies. Manual operations and automatic stations can be added anywhere along the line, and repair and storage loops can be provided as required. Virtually any number of operations can be tied together, subject only to mechanical limitations. Modular construction is possible because of the availability of standard transfer mechanisms, workstations, tooling, and other components.

Limitations

The inefficiency of in-line assembly systems becomes increasingly cumulative as additional stations are added. The slowest operation limits the production rate, but the use of multiple tooling increases the output. Nonsynchronous systems are more costly and have lower production rates than dial machines and synchronous systems and require more floor space.

ASSEMBLY MACHINES AND SYSTEMS

CAROUSEL MACHINES

Similar to the synchronous in-line assembly systems just discussed, carousel machines consist of a series of fixtures or holding devices attached to a roller chain, precision chain, or steel belts or moved by fingers from one workstation to another. However, the carousel machine moves the work in a horizontal plane through a rectangular path, or some variation of the same, returning the pallets to their starting point. All parts are indexed at the same time for the same distance on either a timed or an on-demand basis.

Advantages of the carousel include utilization of all the fixtures in the system because none are returned below, possibility of more operations in the same space, operations can be performed on all sides of the machine, and workpieces are returned to the starting point.

FLEXIBLE ASSEMBLY SYSTEMS

Greater flexibility from automated assembly systems is essential because of continuing increases in product differences resulting from market demands and reductions in product lifecycles. Requirements for high-volume, long-running production are decreasing.

Considerable development work has been done and is continuing with respect to more flexible assembly systems for handling smaller lot sizes and a wider variety of products. The objectives of such systems include increased cost effectiveness and reduced obsolescence of capital equipment expenditures.

One developing concept is the use of automatic guided vehicles (AGVs), which are currently being applied to low-volume large assemblies such as automotive and appliance products. The vehicles are usually self-powered electrically or by compressed air. They electrically follow cables buried in the floor and are computer controlled for any required paths to various assembly stations. The cost of AGVs and their control systems limit their application to large assemblies required in low volumes. Combining AGVs with programmable workstations offers considerable flexibility.

Dedicated, special-purpose assembly systems are designed to assemble specific products with few or no modifications. They generally require high-volume production for economic justification. Flexible assembly systems are capable of assembling more than one product model or models. Truly flexible systems can assemble on demand from an ensemble of different but similar products without tooling changeovers. Other systems may require only extra fixtures or different pallets, changes in tooling, and, for some applications, extra stations. These systems can be economically justified with lower production requirements.

Adaptable systems that are totally automated and capable of assembling any variety of products are difficult to implement and are rare today, but they are expected to become more common in the future. They require both passive controls for programming and active controls (sensors) capable of decision and control tasks. A mixture of manual, dedicated, and flexible methods seems to be one promising solution for adaptable assembly systems.

ROBOTIC ASSEMBLY SYSTEMS

Industrial robots are programmable manipulators that perform a variety of tasks. An effective robotic assembly system requires careful consideration of the delivery of components to the workstations, component feeding and orienting, robot end effectors, sensing requirements, and system controls.

Robot characteristics that are especially suited for assembly applications include the following:

- High accuracy and repeatability in both point-to-point and path conformance.
- Reliability, flexibility, and dexterity.
- Capability for a large number of inputs and outputs.
- Sensory communications and system communications capability.
- Off-line programmability with adaptability to a high-level language.
- Memory capacity for program storage.

Advantages

Robots now available for assembly operations have more specialized features than general-purpose robots, including increased precision (better repeatability), faster speeds, better controls and operating systems, improved capability for interacting with other equipment, and more flexible and convenient programming. Major advantages of robotic assembly systems include the following:

- Consistently repeatable quality and predictable output.
- Flexibility—the ability to assemble multiple products on a single system and to reconfigure the system to perform a variety of tasks.
- Reduced costs per product assembled.
- Minimum obsolescence of capital equipment.
- Modular construction of systems permits adding capacity in required increments.

Possible Limitations

For successful and economical robotic assembly, the products may have to be designed or redesigned for compatibility with the process. Components to be assembled must be held to close tolerances and properly oriented. It is desirable to take advantage of gravity and assemble components vertically. Grippers and part presentation devices for these systems can sometimes cost as much or more than the robots. In many cases, retooling is required at additional expense to assemble a different product with the robot.

Robotic assembly is generally slower than with fixed, dedicated, or hard automated systems. Robotic systems are generally best suited for low to medium volume requirements. The robotic assembly of small products required in high volumes and large parts in low volumes is often not economically justifiable. Also, robots may sometimes be too costly for simple pick-and-place, three-axis transfer functions unless they are justifiable for other considerations such as unhealthy or unsafe working environments.

Typical Applications

Most current applications of robotic assembly systems involve small products in medium volume requirements, families of products, and products or production mixes that are likely to change significantly. Predominant users of such systems include the automotive, electronic, electromechanical, and precision mechanical industries.

ASSEMBLY MACHINES AND SYSTEMS

CONTROLS FOR AUTOMATED ASSEMBLY

A variety of control products are being used for the automation of assembly operations. Primary objectives of the controls include maintaining or improving product quality, increasing output, reducing inventories and scrap, and creating and processing production information (database). Specific requirements of the controls for integrated automation include the following:

- Determine where (and what) each part to be assembled is, track the part from station to station, and know the specific operation to be performed at each station.
- Evaluate the overall quality of the parts, subassemblies, or assembled products at each station, with provisions for rejecting them if necessary.
- Verify the operations performed and product quality attained at each station.
- Prepare for and accommodate operational and/or product changes on-line.

Hierarchical Control Systems

Depending on the degree of sophistication needed or desired, automated control systems can be provided in a hierarchy of interactive levels. Cam-actuated assembly machines generally require a minimum of control sophistication. Power-and-free machines having independent stations need more extensive control systems. Flexible assembly systems require programmable controls. Integrated automation systems involve the coordinated operation of multiple microprocessor-based controls and rely on computer-based production scheduling and data management linked by interactive communication networks.

Modern hierarchical control systems, exclusive of the actual mechanical elements, can include the following:

1. *Programmable logic controllers.* These microprocessor-based controllers, discussed in Volume I, *Machining*, of this Handbook series, are linked by discrete, analog, and intelligent input/output (I/O) devices to the actual physical operations (see Fig. 44-7). They can also be linked by proprietary networks to other intelligent devices such as computerized numerical control (CNC) units and robots. Although they were originally designed for sequential control, they are sometimes used to perform batch process operations, mathematical computations for selective assembly, or data gathering for maintenance, production quality, or management information systems.
2. *Motion or robot controls.* These controls cause drive systems, robots, precision metalcutting units, and other devices to perform one or more linear or rotary motions according to a prescribed pattern.
3. *Computers.* Minicomputers and mainframe computers are electronic devices used for all levels of supervisory functions and information processing. Personal computers have recently begun to be used for the control of manufacturing processes. They can perform the same type of I/O functions as programmable controllers, but usually at a slower processing rate. The personal computers have good data accumulation and reporting capabilities, and network communications are easily incorporated. The time required for software development for

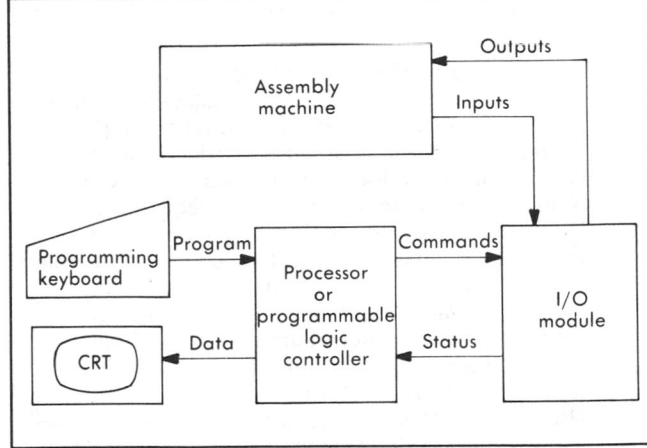

Fig. 44-7 Block diagram of a programmable logic controller used for an assembly machine.

personal computers can vary widely depending on the complexity of the application.
4. *Communication systems.* These systems are integrated networks that permit the sharing of both proprietary (control-oriented, real-time) information and broadband (wide-based, data-oriented) information.

Machine Controls

Essential to any automated assembly machine and forming the base for hierarchical control systems are real-time control devices that interface to programmable controllers and other control devices. These devices are generally connected via I/O modules that interface limit switches, pushbuttons, proximity switches, solenoids, motor starters, pilot lights, and other sensing and drive devices. The devices typically involve digital I/O points or on/off controls.

A more sophisticated category of I/O modules offers not only interface to real-time devices but also some conversion and communication capabilities. An analog input module in which a varying voltage or current is converted to a digital number is an example. New developments in analog I/O devices include modules that read, convert, and forward signals dealing with level, temperature, speed, light intensity, position, and wire faults and offer high levels of common-mode isolation. With the use of a concept called Block Transfer and a minimum of programming, large amounts of information can be quickly and efficiently transferred between I/O modules and the processors of programmable controllers.

Station Controls

Also essential to any automated assembly machine and forming a next higher level for hierarchical control systems are devices for real-time control at the station level. This is a more complex level and generally involves the use of intelligent I/O modules, real-time, logic-solving programmable controllers, and various motion control systems.

Intelligent I/O modules. These modules are called intelligent because they preprocess information—looking at input status, providing control algorithms and solutions, and directly controlling outputs, all as an integral part of a programmable controller system. Developments have increased the capabili-

ASSEMBLY MACHINES AND SYSTEMS

ties of intelligent I/O modules. These capabilities include the following:

- Motion control offering closed-loop servocontrol, open-loop stepper-motor positioning, and even specialized control of clutches and brakes for mechanical presses.
- Proportional-integral-derivative (PID) control implementation. Closed-loop controls can be executed independently of the programmable controller scans.
- High-speed logic control, providing high-speed throughput, reading inputs, making decisions, and controlling outputs independent of the scan.
- Direct communication capability. An intelligent I/O module can divide control among one or a number of processors on small programmable controllers that report to a larger (supervisory) controller.
- User-written BASIC programs can be run on specially designed intelligent I/O modules and implemented independent of processor memory.

Programmable logic controllers. Operation at the station level involves single or multiple programmable controllers performing real-time decisionmaking based on input from I/O modules. These devices are available in small, medium, and large sizes.

Even the smallest programmable controllers are now considered cost-effective replacements for many electromechanical relays, timers, hard-wired logic, and drum controllers. Advantages include the superiority of solid-state configuration, reduced wiring and panel space requirements, and increased flexibility and cost savings. In addition to ladder logic for machine control, they offer additional capabilities such as floating-point mathematics, interactive report generation, data manipulation instructions, and other features for performing computation and data acquisition functions. The devices also have peripheral interfaces such as CRTs and color graphics systems that allow interaction with the machine or process under the control of the programmable controller.

New capabilities are continually being incorporated into programmable controllers for station control. With controllers that often occupy only a single slot in an I/O rack, specific features can include the following:

- Sequential function chart programming. This supplement to ladder logic programming reduces scan times by partitioning a program into blocks, each with its own ladder logic rungs. Only those blocks specifically required at any point in the program are executed.
- Built-in communications interface for peer-to-peer communications, program uploading and downloading, remote programming, and networking functions, without the expense of additional external modules.
- Built-in remote I/O scanner/adapter capabilities that allow the programmable controllers to control the I/O points in either local or remote racks or to act as remote I/O adapters for use on remote I/O links.

Motion controls. Numerous developments in microprocessor-based motion controls allow many improvements in productivity, including reduced inventories, smaller lot sizes, and higher product quality. Some of the motion control systems used primarily for assembly stations include the following:

1. *One to three-axis motion controllers for velocity and position control.* These devices can be operated in a nonintegrated environment and are usually matched to stand-alone machines. Programming of these devices is typically done through keyboards integral with the units.
2. *Stepper or servopositioning modules.* These devices are integral parts of many programmable controller-based systems. They provide distributed control for point-to-point positioning applications. The units are typically located in the remote I/O racks of systems for distribution of a wide range of motion control functionality within the systems.
3. *Synchronized axis controllers.* This classification covers a large group of sophisticated velocity/position controllers with synchronized axis and multiaxis capabilities, often controlling several axes simultaneously. They include devices that can follow complex paths generated by either a host computer or taught to them by teach pendants; examples include CNCs and robot controls. They offer from 2 to 17 axes of control and generally feature color graphics displays of motion paths and a variety of operator interface functions. In addition to interfacing with power amplifiers and feedback devices, they communicate with programmable controllers, other control devices, and/or host computers via local area networks such as the Data Highway.
4. *Power amplifiers.* These controllers provide the power to drive servomotors for actual process motions. They are available in a wide range based on modularity, power conversion types, and ratings.
5. *Integrated controllers.* Integrated velocity/position controllers with power amplifiers are a combination of technologies for use on motors integrated into a system. These systems tend to be more application specific; a typical example is a single-axis slide position controller used for transfer functions.

Cell Controls

At the cell level, control emphasis shifts to the coordination of multiple stations, with the level of control moving upward from real-time operations to supervisory tasks. High-capability supervisory programmable controllers or computers use either Data Highway or peer-to-peer communications to direct the operations of station-level programmable controllers or computers. This is the basis for the concept of distributed control and computer-integrated manufacturing (CIM).

Distributed control. With distributed control, supervisory programmable controllers or computers oversee networks of smaller controllers located close to the actual operation over which they are exerting real-time control. Such a system reduces the severity of a particular station becoming inoperative and increases both system flexibility and fault-isolation time.

Beginning with the supervisory functions of the cell level, greater importance becomes placed on information generation and operator interface. Documentation of the program and I/O wiring, for example, is extremely critical. At the top of the cell level, the focus turns toward linking the databases that support plant management with the real-time activities that occur on the plant floor. This task represents the foundation of the concept called area management.

Area management. Area controllers are the tools through which the database-to-real-time link can be implemented. Cell-level industrial management systems are interfaced with station-level controllers. Designed to operate in industrial environments, area controllers gather data for transmission over local area networks (LANs) such as a Data Highway. They then interpret the collected data and communicate it, both horizontally to other area controllers and upward to assembly center and plant computers over a broad-band communications network. Information requirements and production directions are then sent back down from these computers to the appropriate controllers on the plant floor.

Communications

A final requirement for a hierarchy of automation control (MAP) is a system of integrated communications. The basis for a system of communication networks is the integration of control automation functions both horizontally and vertically. Horizontal integration covers single-level communications between like and unlike devices such as programmable controllers, CNCs, robots, and computers. Vertical integration, using one or more networks, ties together the various levels of control. An integrated system of communication networks provides the link to and from the real-time, plant-floor level through multiple-station (supervisory) control and up to database management, scheduling, and administration.

At lower control levels, proprietary master-slave systems of local and remote I/O communications are most effective. Such a system can transfer information between a central processor and an I/O subsystem. For the next level of control, low-cost, general-purpose networks, often referred to as Data Highways, communicate through the station and cell levels. This is the ideal communications medium for moving blocks of data between stations (production profiles).

The next higher level of communications is a flexible, service-oriented system called mini-MAP. This network differs from the Data Highway in that it is more optimized for cell subnetwork applications. Demands placed on this network include fast, predictable response times and current or eventual compatibility with the industry's evolving communications standards. For the highest control level, the cell-level controllers communicate with the computers through a broad-band system. A broad-band system carries communications capability from the cell level to the top of the automation control hierarchy.

References

1. Jack D. Lane, *Automated Assembly*, 2nd ed. (Dearborn, MI: Society of Manufacturing Engineers, 1986), pp. 157-174.

MECHANICAL DEBURRING AND FINISHING

There are many different reasons why surface, edge, and corner preparation, conditioning, cleaning, or finishing are required. Most of these reasons can be classified with respect to functional or appearance requirements.

Improving the appearance of a product for purely aesthetic reasons can be important because it often increases the salability of the product, with appearance reflecting a concern for quality by the producer. The increased product performance and safety provided by proper edge and surface finishing is also important. The removal of burrs and shape edges improves safety for both the worker and product user by eliminating the possibility of cuts and making parts easier to handle. For critical components, the surface condition and edge geometry can be a major influence on component performance and durability.

FUNCTIONAL REQUIREMENTS

Many functional requirements necessitate surface and edge preparation. These requirements include improved surface finishes and better surfaces for subsequent coating, easier assembly, improved operating performance, and increased strength.

IMPROVED SURFACE FINISHES

Improved surface finishes are often required for increased wear resistance, lubricant retention, and corrosion resistance. The efficiency of gears and other power transmission components is improved by smooth surfaces finishes. Proper finishing can eliminate surface defects, such as nicks, scratches, or tool marks, that can act as stress risers. Smooth, blended internal passages, as well as some external surfaces, reduce turbulence and increase the flow rates of gases or fluids.

HIGH-QUALITY COATINGS

Requirements for surface and edge conditioning are often dictated by subsequent processing, such as plating, painting, anodizing, or other coating, or by the intended applications for the components. For the subsequent application of organic and inorganic coatings, specifications with respect to surface finish and cleanliness vary with the specific coating method.

Surface finish and cleanliness affect the adhesion, appearance, quality, and performance of the coating. Any boundary layer, chemical or physical, between the coating and the substrate can interfere with proper bonding. Rough surfaces and the presence of flash or burrs can ruin the coating. High-quality coatings require proper preparation of surfaces and edges, as well as mechanical and/or chemical cleaning. The type of coating dictates the types of finishing and cleaning processes used prior to coating.

FACILITATING ASSEMBLY

Proper surface and edge finishing facilitates assembly, thus reducing costs, and is required for automatic assembly. By preventing interferences and damage to mating parts, the possibility of mechanisms jamming or assemblies failing is minimized.

IMPROVED PERFORMANCE

Proper conditioning often improves operating performance and lengthens product life. Burrs and flash not removed can break off during service and may cut wires or seals, or cause electrical shorts. The reduction of stress concentrations also helps lengthen product life.

INCREASED FATIGUE STRENGTH

Producing specified chamfers or radii on edges and corners can increase the resistance to fatigue failure of highly stressed components. With some finishing processes, surface integrity can be improved by reducing or removing tensile stresses, or by imparting compressive stresses to the surfaces, thus improving fatigue strength.

BURR FORMATION

Burrs, flash, and related protrusions are formed by the six physical principles listed in Table 45-1. Burrs formed by one of the first three principles listed in this table involve plastic deformation of the workpiece material. Solidification of material on the working edges, the fourth principle of formation, forms a burr-like projection. The fifth type of burr occurs when the workpiece is allowed to fall from the part before the cut is completed. Flash forms whenever the pressure on molten material is sufficient to force the material between the two halves of a die or mold.

Common Characteristic

The Poisson burr, the rollover burr, and the tear burr all have one common characteristic: a radius occurs on the back side of these burrs (see Fig. 45-1). The total shape of the burr cross section can be expressed by height and radius. When all of the burr must be removed, the burr thickness should be specified.

FUNCTIONAL REQUIREMENTS

TABLE 45-1
Physical Principles in Forming Burrs, Flash, and Related Protrusions

Physical Principle of Formation	Name of Protrusion
Lateral flow of material	Poisson burr
Bending of material (such as chip rollover)	Rollover burr
Tearing of chip from workpiece*	Tear burr
Redeposition of material	Recast bead
Incomplete cutoff	Cutoff projection
Flow of material into cracks	Flash

* A tear burr also forms in stamping operations when the punch tears the part from the stock.

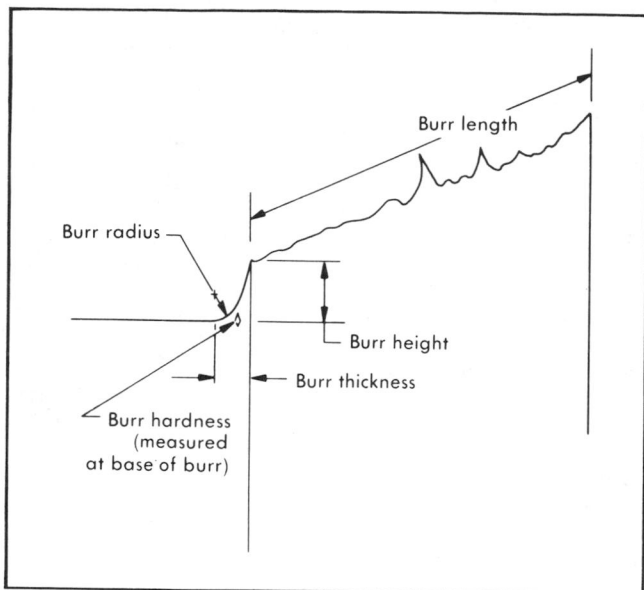

Fig. 45-1 Definitions of burr characteristics. (*Bendix Corp.*)

Recast Material

Recast material is formed when molten metal resolidifies on an edge of a workpiece. The most common occurrence of this type of burr is found on electrical discharge machined (EDM) features. The amount of recast material is a function of polarity, workpiece material, and frequency and amperage of the current.

Cutoff Projections

Cutoff projections (see Fig. 45-2) occur when workpieces are severed from barstock. In such cases, the workpiece is allowed to fall from the stock before the parting tool completely severs the material. Projections can occur in any parting operation, although they are most common in turning operations.

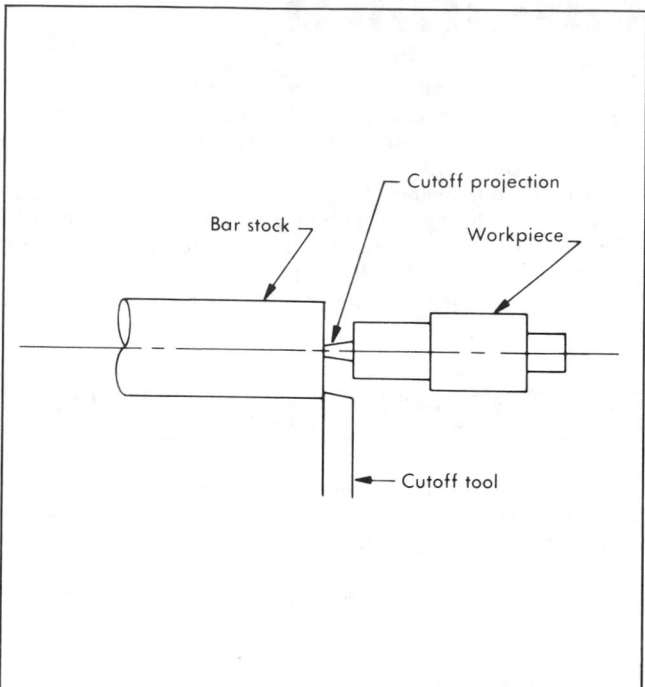

Fig. 45-2 Projection left on workpiece after cutoff operation.

Flash

Provided the clamping pressure between dies or molds is adequate, flash will only occur when die or mold halves are not perfectly matched. In such cases, flash thickness is equal to the thickness of the voids between die or mold halves, and flash height is equal to or shorter than the length of these voids. The hardness of the flash is approximately the same as the workpiece.

BURR PROPERTIES

The difficulty in removing a burr varies with each situation, but the following list, in approximately the correct order of significance, is typical with respect to difficulty in removal:

- Burr thickness.
- Burr location.
- Burr toughness.
- Burr height (length).
- Workpiece tolerances.
- Burr radius.

In the past, measuring burrs meant measuring burr height, but burr thickness is the single most important size consideration for burr removal. In most situations, the combination of thickness and height, or thickness and location, rather than just a single measurement, is important. Burr properties depend on which metalcutting mechanism produced the burr.

It is burr thickness at the root of the burr, not burr height, that makes a burr difficult to remove. From a theoretical standpoint, burr height is directly related to burr thickness; but from a practical standpoint, the relationship is not readily evident.

Burrs assume many shapes. They can be triangular or rectangular in cross section: and they can be uniform or ragged (irregular), or featherlike in height. Each of these shapes indicates a different metalcutting phenomenon.

SURFACE AND EDGE FINISHING METHODS

There are many different processes employed for surface, edge, and corner preparation, conditioning, cleaning, and finishing. In recent years, there has been dynamic growth in the development and improvement of these processes, as well as the equipment, tooling, media, and compounds used.

Lack of knowledge about many of these processes and the improvements that have been made has limited their application. There is currently no formal undergraduate program available in the United States to train mechanical finishing engineers, nor is there any requirement for students of mechanical or manufacturing engineering to take any courses in these

processes. Much has been accomplished in educating industry about these advances, however, by conferences, technical papers, and books prepared by the Burr, Edge and Surface Conditioning Technology (BEST) Division of SME.

Of the many different processes used for finishing, some simply clean contaminants from surfaces. Others remove or form the surface material to produce the desired results. The finishing processes can be broadly classified into mechanical, abrasive, thermal, chemical, and electrochemical methods, but some combine several methods.

HAND (MANUAL) DEBURRING

Hand deburring, also called hand or bench work, benching, or manual deburring, is any operation in which a handheld deburring tool is used or in which a handheld part is placed against a fixtured tool. The process employs various cutters and motorized tools.

WHY HAND DEBURRING IS USED

Hand deburring is still used extensively, even though it is slow, labor intensive, and costly, and often provides less consistent results than desired. Advantages of hand deburring include the versatility of the process and minimal capital investment.

Precision edge breaks are difficult to maintain consistently with hand deburring, especially when the workpieces have a number of edges that require breaking. It is almost impossible to produce breaks of 0.002 to 0.003″ (0.05 to 0.08 mm) on all portions of every edge of intricate workpieces. Larger breaks, typically 0.005 to 0.010″ (0.13 to 0.25 mm), generally have to be specified to ensure that most parts will be acceptable. In the aerospace industry, edge radii to 0.062″ (1.57 mm) are sometimes specified. Hand deburring, however, is very time consuming when edge breaks or radii greater than 0.015″ (0.38 mm) are required.

DEBURRING TOOLS

There are basically 19 types of tools with 59 subcategories of these tools in everyday use for hand deburring. These tools include knives, files, rotary burs, brushes, abrasive products, and various other items.

Knives

A wide variety of knives are used for hand deburring. While knives are inherently dangerous, they do not generally present a safety problem in normal use. Most knives are of special design for a specific application. They are typically made from American Iron and Steel Institute (AISI) Type M2 high-speed steel and generally have a hardness of R_C61.

Triangular knives are typically used to cut or scrape burrs from straight edges. Oval knives are normally used for hole edges or hard-to-reach areas. Specially shaped knives are designed to remove burrs from specific workpieces, but are often useful for other applications as well. Scalpel blades are

used extensively to trim flash from parts made of plastics, but they are rarely successful for removing metal burrs.

Files

More than 2700 different files in a variety of sizes are available commercially. Common types include Swiss escapement, parallel machine, needle, and riffler. The files, in a variety of miniature sizes, are rectangular, triangular, round, curved, or bent. Some are made from high-speed steels, and others have carbide or diamond particles bonded onto steel shanks.

Most files can be used on any workpiece, although it is easy to exceed 0.003″ (0.08 mm) edge breaks with many of these tools. Needle files have almost sharp points, generally with a radius of about 0.030″ (0.76 mm). The narrowest rectangular file is about 0.015″ (0.38 mm) thick. Some triangular files have knife-like edges thinner than 0.015″. All files can be further thinned if required.

Rotary Burs

Rotary burs, bur balls, and related tools, sometimes called rotary files, are available in a variety of diameters, shapes, tooth coarseness, and materials. Shapes include round, oval, cone, inverted cone, cup, barrel, cylinder, wheel, tree, flame, knife edge, and round edge. Although these tools are sometimes called burrs, it is preferable to refer to them as *burs* or *rotary burs* to eliminate confusion between the tools and the material being removed.

For hand deburring of most miniature parts, a bur tool is placed in pin vises and rotated by hand. The tools, however, are also inserted in bench-mounted electric motors, air motors, and dental motors for faster action. They are also used on various machine tools.

Brushes

The seven basic types of brushes used for hand deburring are radial, cup, end, tube, crosshole, side action, and toothbrush.

Radial brushes. These brushes, which resemble wheels with spokes extending from them, are the most commonly used for deburring. They are generally used in a bench motor but are also employed by hand. They should never be used with high-

HAND DEBURRING

speed air motors because fibers will be thrown from the brushes and small-diameter shanks may bend.

Cup brushes. Inverted cup brushes are useful for deburring the edges of relatively large gears, parts having short shafts extending from them, and difficult-to-reach areas where a soft action is required. They are also handy for deburring parts that can be held in the hand, and for larger parts or features 1/2″ (13 mm) or more in diameter. Figure 45-3 illustrates several applications of these brushes.

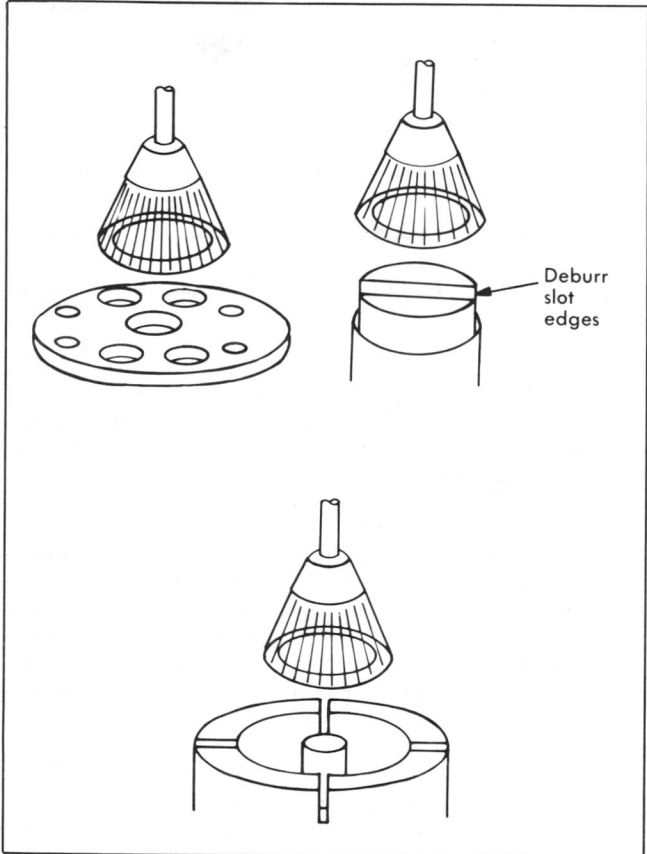

Fig. 45-3 Typical applications for cup brushes. (*Bendix Corp.*)

End brushes. On these tools, the fibers all extend axially outward from the ends of the brushes. These brushes are relatively stiff and, because of this, are often used in hard-to-reach places. A typical application is shown in Fig. 45-4. End brushes are also used to remove recast metal from EDM operations, as well as to clean the workpieces.

Tube brushes. These tools are often used to deburr the insides of tubes, through holes, or relatively deep blind holes. They are available in a variety of stiffnesses and materials, as well as different diameters.

Crosshole brushes. These tools have their stainless steel or nylon fibers extending outward in a helical path around the shanks of the brushes. They are available in sizes as small as 0.024″ (0.61 mm) diam, and can be made smaller. While these tools are visually the same as tube brushes, they are classified as a separate entity because of their minute sizes.

Side-action and related brushes. Side-action (butterfly) brushes are similar to sibot (square trim) brushes. An advantage of side-action brushes is that they can be obtained in sizes as small as 1/4″ (6.4 mm) diam. These brushes are very aggressive and are typically used to deburr plain or threaded holes.

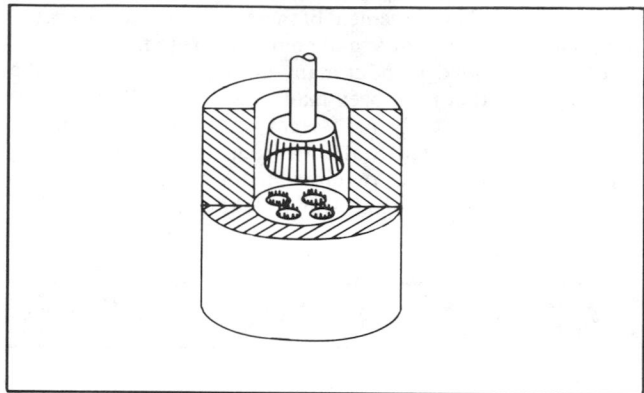

Fig. 45-4 An application of end brushing. (*Bendix Corp.*)

Abrasive Tools

A variety of abrasive tools are used for deburring. The more common include abrasive-filled rubber, cotton, and cork products, abrasive paper, and hand stones.

Abrasive-filled rubber products. For deburring small holes, bullet-shaped rubber tools are used extensively. They are available in four different levels of aggressiveness, the degree of aggressiveness being determined by the size and number of silicon carbide particles molded into the rubber. To facilitate identification, the degree of aggressiveness is indicated by colors, the color codes varying with different manufacturers of the products.

Abrasive-filled cotton products. When more aggressive cutting is required than provided by abrasive-filled rubber, abrasive-filled cotton or muslin tools are often used. By varying abrasive size and the type of bonding agent, it is possible to produce smooth radii and fast burr removal with these tools. While these tools are relatively unknown in the general metalworking industry, they are used extensively by aircraft firms.

Abrasive-filled cork products. Cork and abrasive particles, bonded together with special glues or resins, are also used for fast cutting with smooth radiusing.

Abrasive paper products. A variety of sandpaper-like products are used for deburring and finishing. Miniature discs, with adhesive backs for holding them to mandrels, are used for small workpieces. The smallest commercially available disc is 0.5″ (12.7 mm) diam, but smaller sizes can be fabricated. Abrasive belts for deburring and finishing are discussed later in this chapter.

Hand stones. A wide variety of handheld abrasive stones are used to remove burrs and improve finishes. They are available in sizes as small as 0.010″ (0.2 mm) thick or less.

Mounted points. Miniature grinding wheels, known as mounted points, are used for edge finishing by many firms. They are available in a wide variety of sizes, shapes, and materials. Mounted points, however, are too aggressive for many applications and often tend to chatter in operation.

BRUSHING, POLISHING AND BUFFING

Brushing, polishing, and buffing are related but different processes. Brushing is used for both deburring and/or finishing, including hand deburring, discussed in the preceding section of this chapter. Polishing is an abrading operation using abrasives on resilient wheels, belts, or buffs, with the amount of stock removed dependent primarily upon the grit size and abrasive used, as well as on the pressure exerted. It is more aggressive on surfaces than brushing and leaves a defined pattern on workpiece surfaces. Chemical polishing and electropolishing do not leave lines on the surfaces. Buffing is a final surface finishing process that produces smooth, lustrous surface finishes with less-defined line effects and slower stock removal than polishing. All three processes can be used for descaling, deflashing, deburring, radius generating, surface improving, and stress-relieving operations.

POWER BRUSHING

Power-driven, rotary industrial brushes are widely used for deburring, cleaning, and finishing because they result in time and cost savings for many applications. Being flexible tools and available in an extensive range of types, sizes, and materials, industrial brushes are employed for many different purposes. Applications include edge blending, deburring, controlled surface roughening or refinement, cleaning, and finishing.

Stock removal with brushes varies from a minimum to substantial amounts. Fine finishes are produced on miniature components, and scale is removed from large parts. Depending upon brush filament size and speed, wire-wheel brushes can affect workpiece dimensions; being flexible, they are not suitable tools for achieving final dimensional size. Equipment used to rotate wheel brushes includes bench-mounted electric or air motors, flexible shaft tools, bench and pedestal grinders, portable tools, polishing and buffing lathes, and other machine tools. When improperly used, wire wheels can displace material rather than removing it.

Potential limitations to the use of power brushing include the possibility of contaminating the workpieces, changing the color or surface finish of the workpieces, the generation or turning over of burrs, and hardening of the workpiece surfaces.

The primary types of power brushes are radial or wheel, both standard and centerless; cup; end; tube; strip; wide-face or cylinder; and miniature (see Fig. 45-5). In addition, elastomer-bonded brushes in most of these types are in common use. Each of these basic types varies in design and composition, and is otherwise modified to provide the versatility required in thousands of complex and sophisticated industrial applications.

POLISHING

Wheels and coated-abrasive belts can generally perform many polishing operations equally well. Some of their special features and advantages are summarized in Table 45-2. Precoated-abrasive belts are available in various grain sizes that are ready for polishing without the need for a setup room. The softness or stiffness of belts depends upon the type of cloth backing and the type of adhesive used to bond the abrasive to the belt surface. Belts are often best for polishing flat surfaces, and wheels best for concave and contoured surfaces.

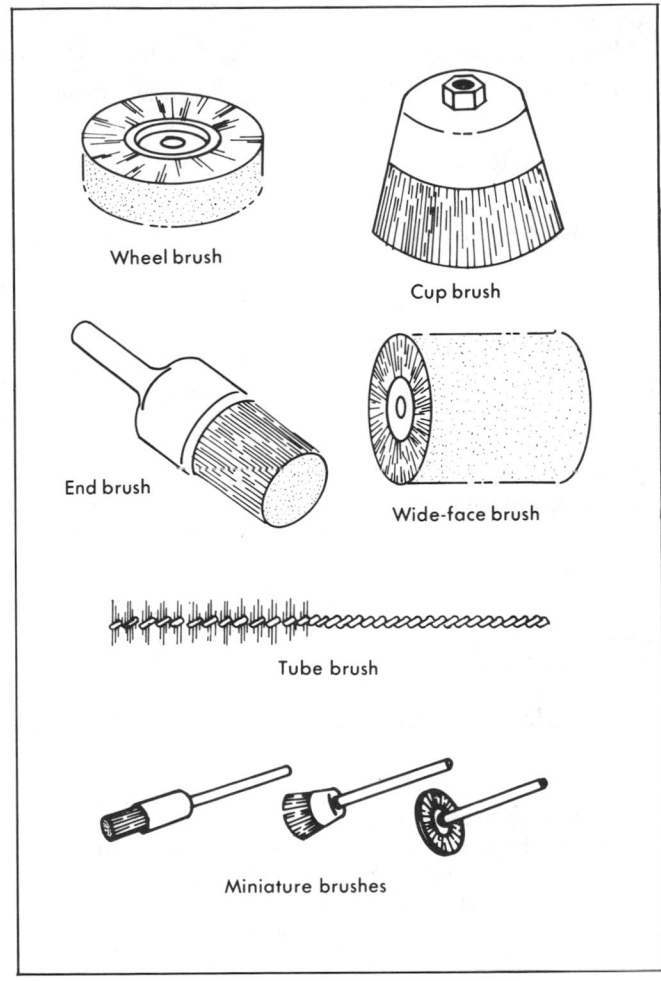

Wheel brush

Cup brush

End brush

Wide-face brush

Tube brush

Miniature brushes

Fig. 45-5 Primary types of power brushes. (*Weiler Brush Co.*)

Polishing Wheels

Polishing wheels, also called setup wheels or headed wheels, are usually made of circular plies of cloth or felt. The type of cloth, the number of plies, the number of stitches per linear unit of length, the design of the stitching, and the type of adhesive bond and compression all control the density of the wheel. Leather wheels were once used extensively, but they are now less common, generally being confined to the fine polishing required in cutlery and gun work. Brushes and coated-abrasive flap wheels are also used for polishing. The different materials and methods of construction allow great flexibility and wide variations in hardness to meet various requirements for specific applications.

In general, more rigid polishing wheels are used when there is a requirement for fast stock removal or when the workpieces have flat surfaces. Softer wheels are employed when workpiece surfaces have contours or irregularities and rapid stock removal is not necessary.

BRUSHING, POLISHING AND BUFFING

TABLE 45-2
Polishing with Wheels and Belts

Criterion	Wheels	Belts
Adaptability		
Wide flat surfaces	Limited to a few inches per pass.	Available in widths of several feet.
Contours	Yes, by forming faces. No scuffing adjacent surfaces.	Mild contours only without special equipment.
Use in hand tools	Yes.	Requires idler wheel—sometimes awkward.
Automatic operations	Limited by factors of wheel wear and more frequent changes.	Yes.
Inner or closed surfaces	Yes.	Not generally.
Work on flat or side of wheel	Yes.	No, but can be used with platen.
Grit sizes available	Any.	Any.
Densities available	Any.	Softness limited by tension and body of belt. No limit on hardness.
Special equipment required	Setup room with drying facilities, wheel dresser, balancer, etc.	Back stand; idler wheel arrangement for deep work.
Convenience	Wheel changes plus reheading.	High; belt changes only on run of same work.
Uniformity of finish throughout life of abrasive	Good.	Tend to cut finer as the grains dull.
Quality of finish obtainable	Probably little difference when each is used within its proper limits.	

Polishing Abrasives

Natural abrasives such as emery and corundum are used occasionally in specialized operations that require the finest quality finishes. Turkish emery was once used as the standard natural abrasive, and its fast smoothing action still makes it valuable for fine polishing. Artificial abrasives, however, chiefly aluminum oxide and silicon carbide, will handle practically any polishing problem. Aluminum oxide is easier to bond to the wheel than silicon carbide. Aluminum oxide, which is tough and hard, is used on most carbon, alloy, and high-speed steels; wrought and malleable iron; and nonferrous metals except aluminum. Silicon carbide, which is sharp and hard but brittle, is recommended for finishing low-tensile-strength materials such as brass, copper, cast iron, and aluminum; it is also the preferred abrasive for polishing marble, granite, glass, and other ceramic products. Any abrasive used on stainless steel should be iron-free to prevent contamination and possible rust.

BUFFING

Buffing is a surface finishing process that can produce smooth, lustrous finishes, with minimal pronounced line effects. The process is accomplished with rotating wheels, called buffs, to which abrasives and compounds are applied. The buffing wheels by themselves do little work; they are designed to be carriers for the abrasives and compounds. However, the density and construction of the buff, type of abrasive and compound, pressure exerted, and rotary speed of the buff all affect the aggressiveness (ability to do work) of the process.

Buffing may be considered a two-stage operation: (1) cutting down and (2) coloring. Cutting down is done with the workpiece moving against the motion of the buff using medium-to-hard pressure. It is performed to refine a surface by removing scratch lines from polishing, stretch marks from forming, die marks, or other surface imperfections. It can make a relatively smooth surface smoother. Buffing can also deburr, blend edges, generate radii, and stress relieve. Coloring, with the workpiece traveling with the motion of the buff using medium-to-light pressure, refines the cut-down surface and brings out maximum luster or a mirror finish.

Buff Construction

Buff construction controls the action of the buff by making it harder or softer, or more or less aggressive. The construction itself may be of more importance in determining final results on a particular job than the thread count (see Fig. 45-6).

Buffing Abrasives

Tripoli. This abrasive is often considered to be an amorphous silica that occurs in nature. Too soft and fragile for use on the ferrous metals, it is highly suitable for buffing aluminum, copper, brass, and die castings. Soft or amorphous silica also occurs in the natural state, but, unlike tripoli, is iron-free and white in color. It may be used alone for coloring nonferrous metals, or it may be mixed with tripoli to give added coloring ability to so-called cut-and-color compounds.

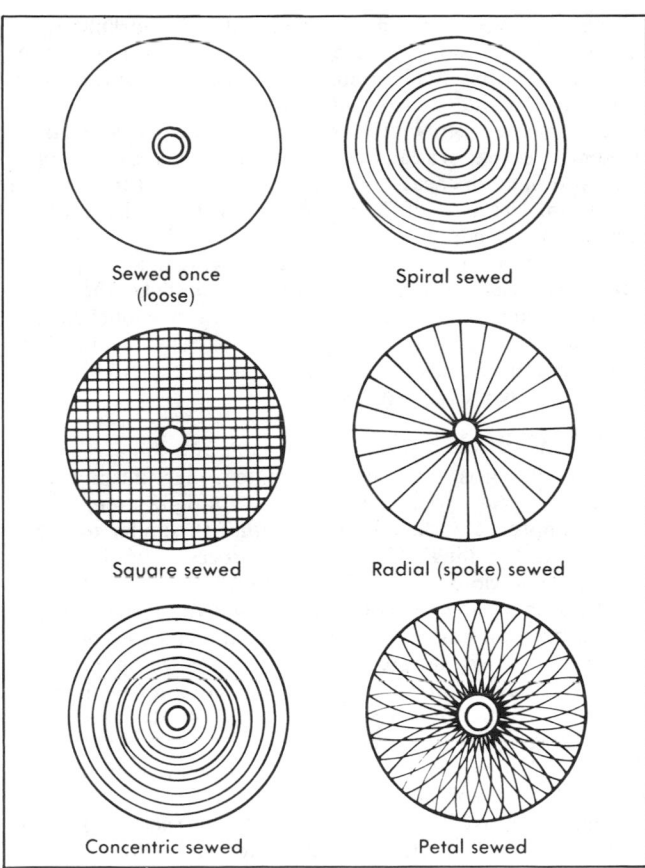

Fig. 45-6 Various types of sewing used for full-disc buffs. (*Divine Brother Co.*)

Aluminum oxide and other powders. Aluminum oxide powders, fused and unfused, are the abrasives in most compounds for buffing hard metals. Chromium oxide is used for highest color buffing of stainless steel, chromium, and nickel plate. Rouge is the preferred compound for color buffing on copper, brass, gold, and silver.

Pumice. This is a natural product used with tampico brushes for scratch finishes, in compounds for buffing plastics, and with water for wet-ashing operations on plastics and glass that cannot tolerate the heat generated by normal buffing.

Buffing Compounds

Buffing compounds are supplied in either solid bar or liquid form. Both forms use the same abrasive agents, only the vehicles differ.

Solid bars. Bar compounds get their shape from the binder, consisting usually of a blend of tallow, stearic acid, waxes, or petroleum greases. These binders vary widely in their effect on the buffing operation and in their ease of cleaning from the work prior to plating. Greaseless compounds are also used, mainly for satin finishing. These compounds combine fast-cutting abrasives with glue binders, and they are generally used at speeds of 5000 to 6000 sfm (1525 to 1830 m/min).

Liquid compounds. Spray-type buffing compounds use the same abrasives as the bar compounds, but they are used in oils or water emulsions that remain fluid at ordinary temperatures. These mixtures are sprayed onto the buffing wheel under air pressure. Liquid compounds are more easily cleaned from workpieces than solid compounds and are highly suitable for machine or automatic buffing. Automatic spray guns are often a part of buffing equipment.

ROLLER AND BALL FINISHING/BURNISHING

Finishing or burnishing with rollers or balls is a surface finishing technique based on the cold forming of metal. The high forces generated in the contact zone between the tools and the workpieces results in plastic deformation of the work surfaces. Although the degree of metal flow in these finishing processes is low compared to more severe cold forming operations, such as extruding, heading, and swaging, they also result in the characteristic cold forming advantages of increased strength, improved size accuracy, and low manufacturing costs.

Roller finishing and roller burnishing are similar processes, and the terms are often used interchangeably. For the purposes of discussion in this section, however, roller finishing, including deep rolling, is considered a heavy-duty operation. Roller burnishing, discussed later in this section, employs multiroll tools for lighter duty applications. Ball burnishing, also called ballizing, produces dimensionally precise, smooth holes by forcing balls through the holes.

ROLLER FINISHING

Roller finishing, together with size rolling and deep rolling, is a process employed for cylindrical components. It has been used for many years by railroad car manufacturers for finishing sleeve-bearing seats on railcar axles.

Advantages and Limitations

Besides providing the desired surface finish and improvements in geometrical accuracy, roller finishing also has the following advantages:

- Improved surface finish and roundness will result in noise level reductions for shafts, such as motor armatures, that run in sintered-metal sleeve bearings with only microscopic, noncushioning oil films.
- Direct cost savings may be realized by the elimination of some and the replacement of other finishing methods, such as grinding, polishing, lapping, and honing.
- Direct cost savings may also result from the possible elimination of surface heat treating operations such as induction hardening.
- Other cost savings may be achieved by reductions in tool costs, possible changes to lower grade materials, the elimination of grinding wheels, and the relaxation of quality control.

The major limitation of roller finishing is the initial hardness of the workpiece; however, roller finishing can still be performed on materials with hardnesses of R_C 40 to 45, which are slightly

ROLLER AND BALL FINISHING/BURNISHING

above the general limits for machinability. Some processing bypasses the hardness specification. For example, particular parts may be induction hardened after roller finishing and then passed through a chemical wash to remove the resultant oxides before chrome plating. Many applications, such as for shock absorber rods, permit the roller finishing of materials at hardnesses of approximately R_C 40, which will still provide hard enough surfaces to avoid scratching during handling or assembly.

Effects of Roller Finishing

Surface hardness. The characteristic of steel to work harden under plastic deformation explains the fact that roller-finished components show an increase in surface hardness. Because of stress distribution, the greatest hardness increases actually occur below the surface. Conventional hardness tests cannot measure these increases because the testing tools break through the hardness scale under normal preloads. However, micro-hardness techniques, such as the Knoop test with 50 or 100 gram preloads, indicate a hardness increase of 2 to 8 points on the Rockwell C scale, with the lesser increases on materials with higher hardnesses before rolling.

Surface finishing. Roller finishing results primarily in a desired surface finish. When properly employed, the process will produce surface finishes between 1 and 5 μin. (0.025 and 0.127 μm) from a turned surface of 125 to 150 μin. (3.2 to 3.8 μm); thus, the best finishes for improved wear resistance can easily be obtained. The degree of finish depends upon the application. For example, the bearing diameter for a seal should not be roller finished below a surface value of approximately 15 μin. (0.38 μm); on the other hand, the stem of an engine valve could be roller finished to a surface value of 8 μin. (0.20 μm), provided the accompanying valve guide is manufactured with a surface roughness capable of retaining lubricating oil.

Diameter reduction. Roller finishing reduces workpiece diameter in proportion to the surface finishes before and after rolling. The diameter reduction will average approximately four times the difference in rms values before and after rolling, measured in μin. If the surface roughness before rolling and the rolling force are kept within a permissible limit of variation, the diameter reduction will remain constant.

The most accurate way to determine the diameter reduction is to make rolling tests after the machine is set up or the finishing has been done. However, workpieces that require close dimensional accuracy must be machined to a size that takes into consideration the change in diameter; and even though a finish-grinding operation to obtain the required dimensional accuracy may be necessary, roller finishing still offers considerable advantages. Another means of obtaining high dimensional accuracy is to premachine the workpiece to approximately 150 to 200 μin. (3.8 to 5.1 μm) and then roller finish it with a multiple-roller attachment. In this case, however, dimensional deviations resulting from previous operations will lead to a varying surface finish and bearing-contact area.

Product quality. The surface quality of the part is determined not only by the surface finish prior to rolling and the hardness of the material, but also by the form accuracy. Excessive roller finishing forces could result in undesirable geometry changes such as elongation, end tapering, and metal flow into grooves or small crossholes.

The plastic deformation that takes place during roller finishing creates compressive stress layers in the surface of the workpiece. These stresses are symmetrical to the workpiece axis and should not result in macrogeometric changes. Experience, however, indicates that long components can bend during roller finishing. Bending, at first interpreted as a deficiency in the process, has been shown to occur only if the workpiece has an unequal stress pattern caused by such operations as machining, cold forming, or heat treating before the roller finishing operation. The relief of these unbalanced stresses by finishing results in the bending.

Similarly, a certain type of surface flaking in a line pattern parallel to the part axis has been falsely attributed to the rolling process. Actually, such flaking is the result of minute surface cracks created during previous operations. Thus, roller finishing reveals manufacturing faults that, in the past, were probably never properly recognized.

DEEP ROLLING

Deep rolling is a process related to roller finishing that results in increased bending or torsional fatigue strengths, as well as improved surface finishes. Although similar to roller finishing, deep rolling differs from that process in its objectives, results, applications, and tooling designs.

The primary objective of deep rolling is to impart a deeply penetrating compressive stress layer into highly stressed portions of workpieces. Any failure of a highly stressed component can be analyzed as a failure in tension. The compressive stresses provided by deep rolling oppose the tension stresses that occur during part operation. Deep rolling shows increased stress levels to a depth of more than 0.125" (3.18 mm) from the part surface. The average values of these stresses, measured by X-ray diffraction, are as high as 60,000 psi (414 MPa) near the surface of parts deep rolled with an average specific rolling force of 500,000 psi (3448 MPa). Sectional dimension changes of as much as 5 to 20% may occur under these pressures.

Higher specific rolling forces and the pressure control required demand a much more sophisticated machine tool design for deep rolling than for roller finishing. Deep-rolled workpieces are rotated positively in the machines and, in turn, rotate the tooling. Feed rates are generated by a feed screw or hydraulic feed cylinder, and rolling pressure is varied according to the tool position relative to the workpiece.

Deep rolling compares favorably with most processes commonly employed for increasing fatigue strength, such as nitriding, shot peening, and induction hardening. Further distinct advantages are the cleanliness of the process, its reliability, and its low cost.

Manufacturing cost savings are obtainable directly by eliminating grinding, polishing, or heat treating operations. Further savings are possible through savings on grinding wheels, changes to less costly or lower quality materials, and higher production line efficiency or increased tool life. Another advantage of deep rolling is the possibility of combining roller finishing and deep rolling.

Like roller finishing, deep rolling is most applicable to materials that have a percentage elongation of over 6%. Common candidates are plain carbon steel, alloy steel, stainless steel, and nodular cast iron. Materials such as low-grade steels or cast iron, bronze, aluminum, and brass may be finished by roller finishing, but they will not withstand the high specific rolling forces applied during deep rolling.

Another limitation concerns the hardness of the material to be deep rolled. Hardness values of R_C 40 are the top limit and require extremely high rolling forces, resulting in excessive bearing and tool wear. The high rolling pressures also endanger the form accuracy of the component. A practical value for surface hardness limits is R_C 35.

ROLLER BURNISHING

Roller burnishing is a plastic deformation process employing a variety of rotary tools containing caged rollers. The process is used to improve the surface finish, tolerance control, surface hardness, and fatigue life of metal components. It is applied to the inside diameters of holes, outside diameters of shafts, flat surfaces of revolution, tapered and spherical surfaces, and fillets (radii at shoulders). Special tools burnish multiple surfaces simultaneously.

Process Advantages

There are four predominant reasons for roller burnishing parts: (1) improved surface finish, (2) improved tolerance control, (3) increased surface hardness, and (4) improved fatigue life.

Surface finish. Surface finishes typically obtained from various metalworking processes on steel and aluminum are compared in Fig. 45-7. Roller burnishing would normally follow a turning or reaming operation, where the preburnished finish would typically be in the 60 to 120 μin. (1.5 to 3 μm) range.

Tolerance control. Consider a steel part in which it is required to machine a 1.000" (25.4 mm) diam hole with a tolerance of ±0.0005" (0.013 mm). This requirement would normally present a difficult problem, but one that is commonly encountered in wristpin holes in pistons or connecting rods, as well as in hydraulic valves and other components. If the hole is drilled and then reamed or bored slightly undersized, say to 0.9995" (25.387 mm), ±0.001" (0.25 mm), with a surface finish of 250 μin. (6.35 μm), it can be roller burnished to the required size and tolerance.

Increased surface hardness. Roller burnishing can be applied to any ductile or malleable material having a hardness to R_C40, although harder parts have been burnished on occasion. Since the metal is compressed past its yield point, the grain structure is

changed, and the part becomes strain hardened. Through this granular dislocation and deformation, the grain size is decreased and the boundary area is increased after the cold working during roller burnishing.

Roller burnishing can increase hardness from 5 to 10%, with a surface penetration of 0.010 to 0.030" (0.25 to 0.76 mm). Bearingizing can increase hardness to 30%, with less surface penetration.

Improved fatigue life. The fact that fatigue life can be improved through the elimination of surface imperfections, such as machining marks, is well known. In addition to improved surface finish, however, roller burnishing plastically deforms the material near the surface, leaving a compressive residual stress that extends into the material. This compressive stress has the effect of minimizing the maximum tensile stress that the material experiences through the stress reversal cycles during its lifetime.

In general, no matter in which direction the original machine marks are (parallel or perpendicular to the applied stress), about a 300% improvement in fatigue life, as a rule of thumb, can be expected in roller burnishing aluminum or steel. Some relatively new applications have taken a unique approach. For example, holes in aluminum plates are drilled and reamed undersized. The holes are then burnished well beyond what is required for a good finish, to the point that the metal surface fatigues and surface flaking occurs. Finally, the holes are reamed again, thus removing the surface imperfections. Fatigue life is reported to be improved up to 500%.

Other Applications

In addition to the many applications of roller burnishing due to the four major benefits already discussed, the process is also employed for other reasons, such as the reduction of noise and/or vibration. Roller burnishing the shafts of windshield wiper motors mounted inside a car's passenger compartment eliminated a noise problem. Burnishing the platter shaft and bushings for a high-fidelity turntable reduces vibration that can be transmitted to the tone arm and pickup unit.

Roller burnishing two diameters simultaneously on a previously ground stepped shaft provides a smoother finish that has doubled the life of sliding O-rings. Centerless grinding of motor shafts for small appliances sometimes produces a three-lobed diameter; this condition is eliminated by roller burnishing. Electric motor shafts are also roller burnished to reduce friction up to 35%, thus improving efficiency. Shafts to be chromium plated are roller burnished to improve the finish; this step reduces chromium requirements and lessens the need for polishing.

Additional applications for roller burnishing include the surfaces of disc-brake rotors to eliminate undesirable tool marks, brazed faucet assemblies to eliminate distortion, and holes for gear shafts in planetary carriers (consisting of two stampings welded together) to ensure axial alignment.

BALL BURNISHING

Dimensionally precise holes with smooth, high-density surfaces are produced by a process called ball burnishing or ballizing. In this process, an oversized, tungsten carbide ball is forced through an undersized hole. High pressure is used to force the ball through the hole at high speed. A lubricant is applied to prevent galling, seizing, or distortion of either the ball or the workpiece.

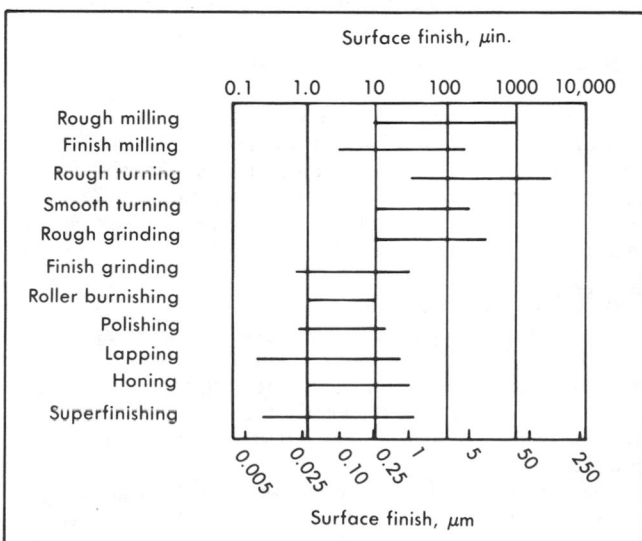

Fig. 45-7 Typical surface finishes produced by various metalworking processes.

ROLLER AND BALL FINISHING/BURNISHING

Unlike abrasive finishing methods, ballizing does not remove any metal or leave any residue. The process is similar to roller burnishing, discussed previously in this section, in that the workpiece surface is compressed by the tooling. However, roller burnishing involves cold working of the metal, while ballizing entails hot working.

Ball burnishing also differs from other types of burnishing in that a narrow, peripheral line on the ball creates a concentrated radial force that pushes the workpiece material into the surface of the hole. This narrow contact line between the ball and the wall of the hole work hardens the surface. There is no flaking of the material, and no ringlets are formed through overlapping the peaks and valleys of the machined surface.

Process Advantages

Hot working of the metal during ball burnishing refines the molecular structure of the hole surfaces. The refined structure increases bearing surface density and strength, and provides improved resistance to friction and/or heat stress. Also, to a limited degree, the process stabilizes the molecules so that workpiece distortion during subsequent heat treatment is minimized. If more precise tolerances are required after heat treating, the workpieces can be ball burnished first, then heat treated, and finally ball burnished again to correct any minor distortion that may occur during heat treatment.

Surfaces and Materials Burnished

Ballizing is used to produce smooth surfaces in blind, through, cross, and elliptical holes. It is also used to finish surfaces in elbows, S-bends, interrupted segments, and undercuts. A typical setup for ball burnishing a blind hole is illustrated in Fig. 45-8. Blind holes are also ballized by the step method, as depicted in Fig. 45-9.

Ball burnishing has been used successfully on a wide variety of metals, both soft and hard. These metals include the full range of low and high-carbon steels, tool steels, stainless steels and other nickel-bearing alloys, and superalloys. The process is also employed on sintered metal parts and many nonferrous materials, including aluminum, magnesium, and copper alloys. Cadmium and copper-plated parts and soft tungsten carbide are also finished by ball burnishing.

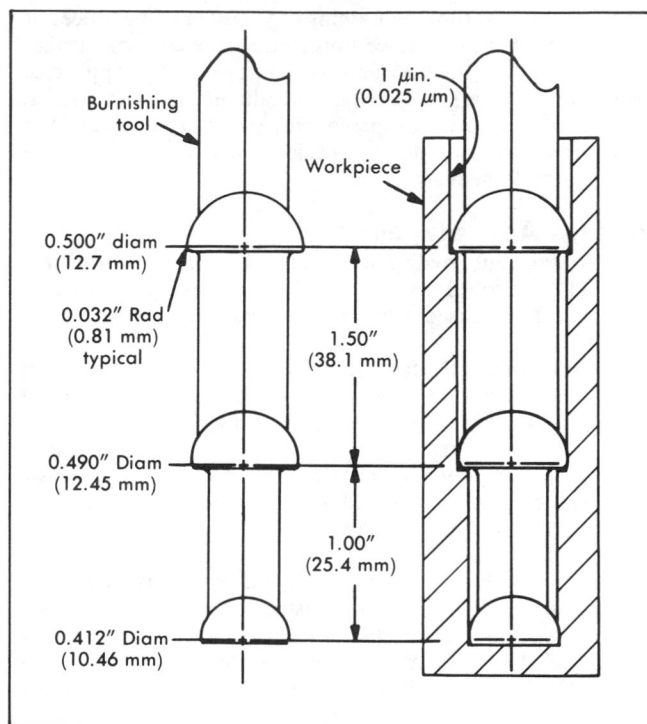

Fig. 45-9 Step ballizing of a blind hole. (*French Enterprises*)

Limitations

There are certain limitations to the ball burnishing process. If, for example, specifications require parts to be case hardened to R_C 62, with a case depth of 0.010 to 0.020″ (0.25 to 0.51 mm), the parts can be ballized after heat treating, but only for size. Through-hardened parts with the same hardness must be ballized for both size and finish prior to heat treating.

In some cases, especially with improper burnishing speeds, pressures, and lubricants, ballizing can produce small chips and burrs. Another possible limitation is that ball burnishing will generally improve out-of-round or tapered conditions by only about 50%. Workpieces must also be clean and dry before ballizing.

Typical Applications

Ball burnishing is an efficient method of forming, sizing, finishing, and deburring bores, all in one operation. Other applications include coining or staking parts together, expanding, and changing wall thickness. Figure 45-10 illustrates a swaging operation that eliminated the need for brazing in producing pressure vessels.

Deburring operations in which size or finish are generally of no concern are a common application for the ballizing process. For example, when a hole is drilled from both ends of a workpiece to maintain a sharp entry edge at both ends of the hole, there is often a mismatch and burr produced near the

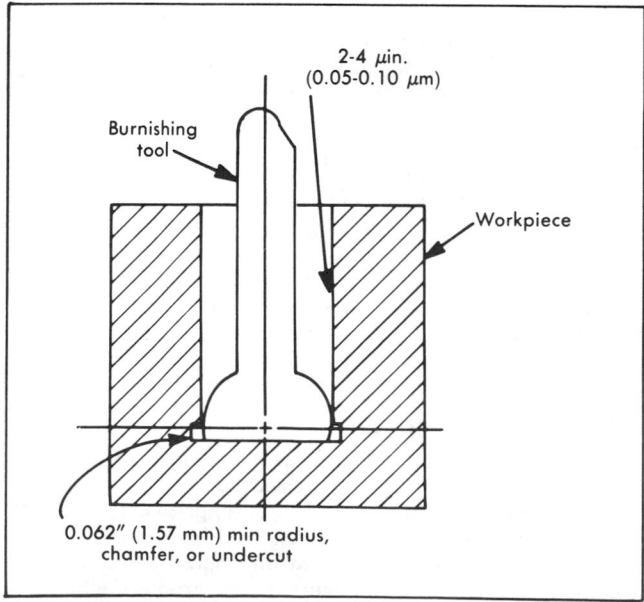

Fig. 45-8 Ball burnishing of a blind hole. (*French Enterprises*)

center of the hole (see Fig. 45-11, view *a*). Such burrs can interfere with the flow of liquids or gases in operation. Ballizing irons out such burrs (see view *b*), producing a small radius at the mismatch area but without significantly changing the sharp edges at the ends of the hole.

In many cases, ballizing eliminates the need for finishing operations such as precision boring, honing, lapping, or other burnishing methods. With proper machines and precision balls, many jobs can be done faster, more precisely, and more economically.

Successful applications include parts for electric motors, grinders, precision machine tools, and automotive and aircraft assemblies. Other high-precision components finished by ballizing include parts for missiles, electrical and electronic instruments, medical and dental devices, air and hydraulic valves, fuel injection nozzles, carburetor jets, robot components, and computer linkages.

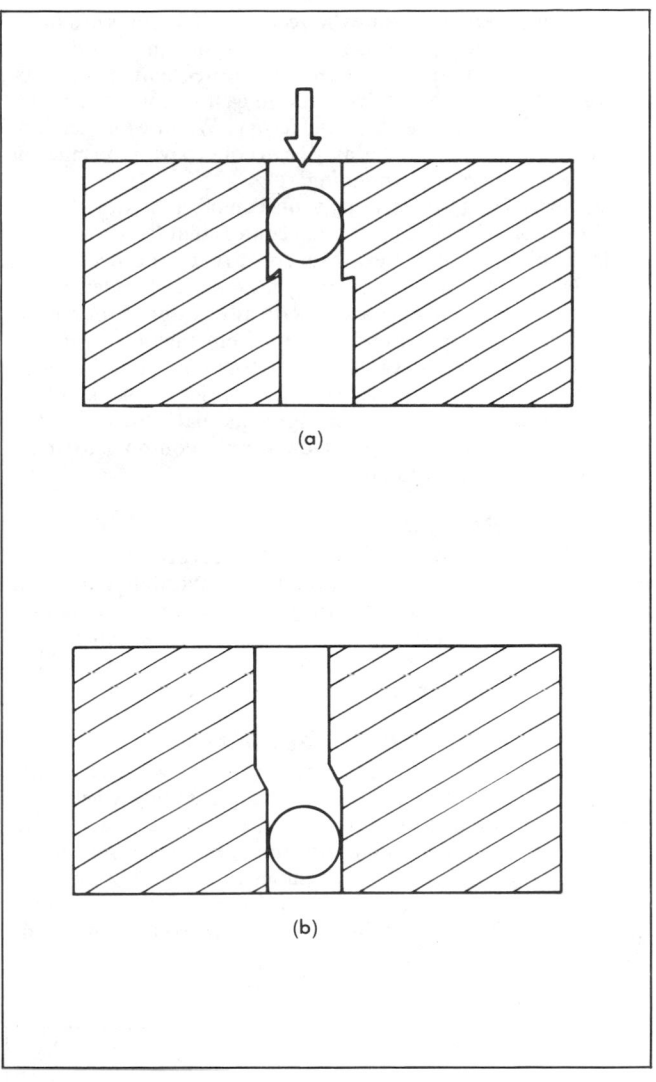

(a)

(b)

Fig. 45-11 Deburring by ballizing: (a) burrs near midpoint of hole produced by drilling from both ends and (b) burrs ironed out by pressing ball through hole.

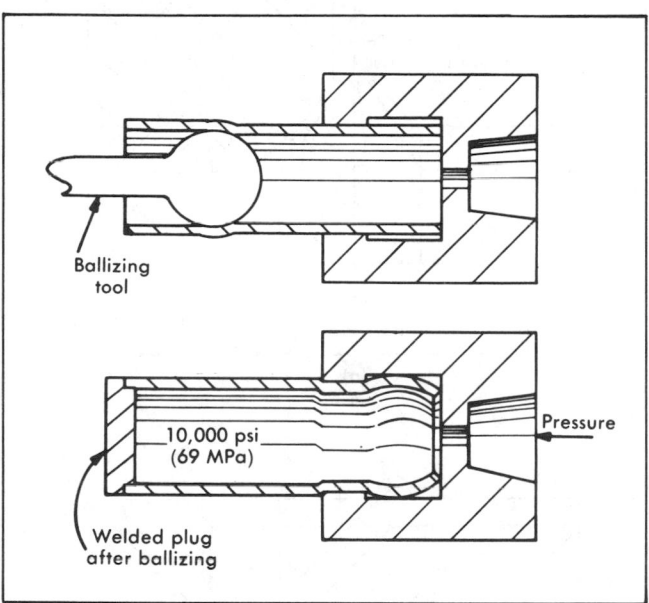

Fig. 45-10 Swaging by ballizing eliminates the need for brazing. (*French Enterprises*)

SPECIAL-PURPOSE MACHINES AND ROBOTIC DEBURRING

Specialized machines are being used extensively to remove burrs and finish parts when production requirements are high or families of similar parts are processed. Various machines available are manually, semiautomatically, or automatically operated, depending upon production needs.

Tools employed on the different machines include trimming dies, rotary cutters or pinch rolls, grinding wheels, brushes, and honing stones. Typical parts processed on such machines include stampings, castings, forgings, and extrusions; sheet and plate stock; many different types of workpieces; tubes and bars; gears; and cutting tool inserts.

TYPES OF SPECIALIZED MACHINES

Specialized machines for deburring and finishing include trimming presses, edgers, end finishers, gear tooth deburring/chamfering machines, and cutting-tool-insert finishing machines. Also, when feasible, industrial robots and NC machining centers are used. Robotic deburring is discussed later in this section.

Use of NC/CNC Machines

The NC/CNC machines that produce parts can often effectively deburr or finish the parts, or many features of the

SPECIAL PURPOSE MACHINES AND ROBOTIC DEBURRING

parts. These machines ensure the accuracy of features produced in the machining operations and can result in considerable savings by eliminating the need for subsequent operations. Because of more liberal tolerances on cast or forged surfaces, these machines may not be satisfactory. When wall locations vary from part to part, edges may be produced with too much or too little chamfering or rounding.

Deburring and/or finishing tools can often be stored in the magazines of NC/CNC machining centers that have automatic toolchanging capabilities. Macros are available for the NC/CNC units to remove burrs by automatic chamfering.

Several CNC machines are specifically designed for removing sprues, risers, gates, and runners from castings, a process called *fettling*. These are rigid, single-tool machines that often employ touch sensors to define surface orientations and then rotate the part to provide a straight-line path for the cutter. Such CNC machines are used on simple contours for non-precision edge requirements.

Trimming Presses

Mechanical, hydraulic, or pneumatic presses are used extensively to remove excess material from stampings or drawn parts, or to remove flash from forgings, castings, or moldings. This method requires the use of cutting dies, such as pinch-trim, Brehm (shimmy), or notching dies. Shaving dies or broaching tools are employed for more precise requirements.

Edging Machines for Sheet Metal

Sheet metal edgers use either small grinding wheels or pinch rolls to remove burrs. Those employing grinding wheels are generally adjustable to vary the chamfer produced, and some will deburr both the top and bottom edges on one side of the sheet (see Fig. 45-12). Such machines are available for sheet stock ranging from 0.023 to 0.250" (0.58 to 6.35 mm) thick and in widths of 1/2" (12.7 mm) or more. Linear feed rates of 60 fpm (18.3 m/min) are possible.

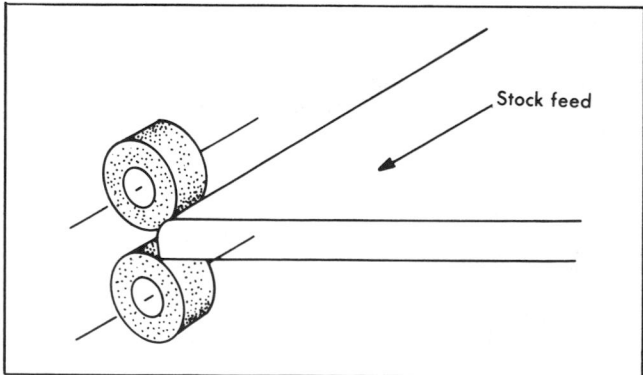

Fig. 45-12 Small grinding wheels deburr and chamfer top and bottom edges of sheet stock at feed rates to 60 fpm (18.3 m/min). (*Bendix Corp.*)

Workpiece Edgers

Two basic approaches are used for general-purpose workpiece edging. With one approach, rectangular workpieces are placed in an angle-iron trough and hand fed over a small grinding wheel, providing a small, adjustable chamfer. The second approach is to use a piloted chamfering tool extending upward through the flat table of a machine (see Fig. 45-13, view *a*). Workpieces are moved into contact with the pilot on the cutter and then fed across the cutter, using the pilot as a guide or stop. Chamfer depth is controlled by adjusting the cutter upward or downward. Another approach is to install a permanent stop (view *b* of Fig. 45-13) or a magnetic device and use a standard chamfering tool. Straight and contoured edges are deburred with such machines.

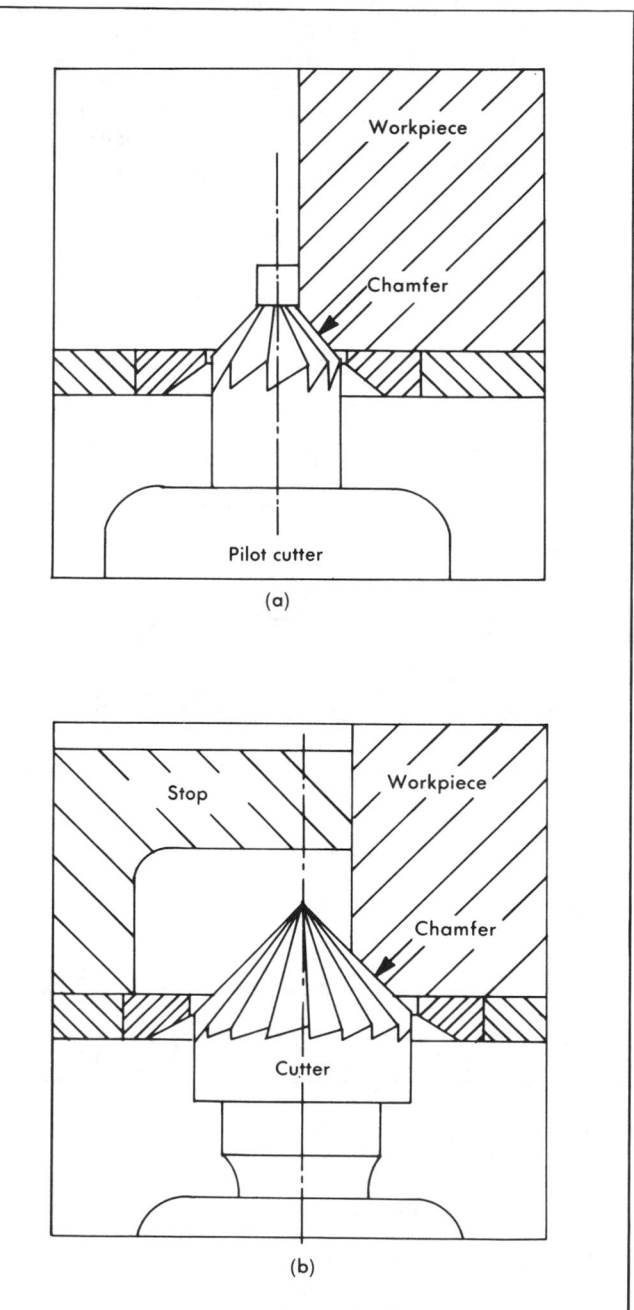

Fig. 45-13 Two concepts for locating edges on a general-purpose workpiece edger: (a) piloted chamfering tool and (b) permanent stop. (*Reishauer Corp.*)

SPECIAL PURPOSE MACHINES AND ROBOTIC DEBURRING

End-Finishing Machines

Finishing machines for the ends of tubes and bars are available in various degrees of sophistication and automation. A manually operated machine capable of finishing up to 1500 ends per hour is illustrated in Fig. 45-14. Simultaneous inside-outside deburring, chamfering, and facing are possible on this machine. The operator places the workpiece through the self-centering chuck jaws, against an adjustable stop, and pulls the starting lever. This action closes the chuck jaws, pivots the stop clear, and feeds the work to the rotating cutters.

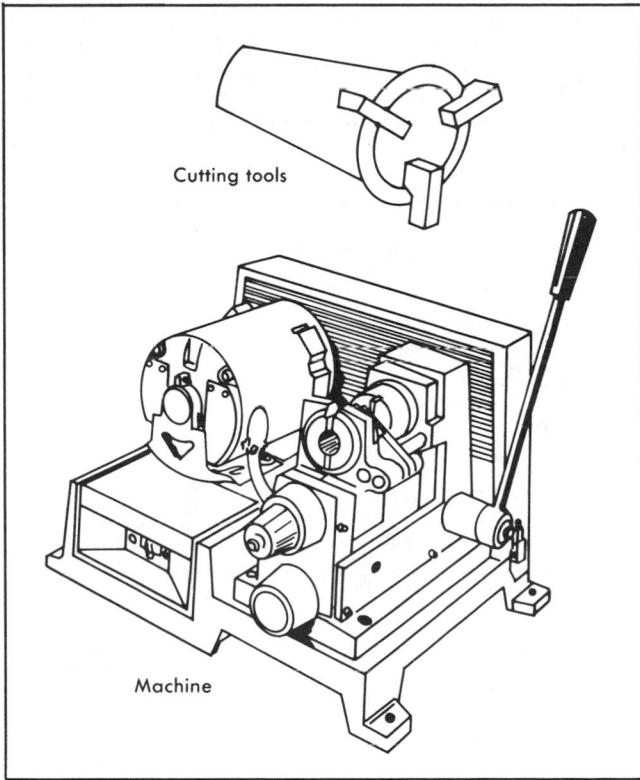

Fig. 45-14 Tube and rod end-finishing machine. (*Teledyne Pines*)

Gear Deburring Machines

In gear hobbing or shaping, burrs are formed on the end faces of the teeth. Such burrs can seriously impair smooth and reliable gear operation. A wide variety of methods are used to deburr and chamfer gear teeth. These methods include using a rotating tool or small grinding wheel to traverse all tooth edges, brushes, a skiving tool and subsequent brushing, an abrasive-belt grinder (sometimes followed by brushing), and blasting with steel shot.

For heavy burrs, it is possible to combine a milling operation with tooth chamfering. Many gears, particularly those used by the watch industry, are being deburred on gear hobbing machines, thus eliminating a secondary operation. Small pinions are deburred by automatically holding a lathe tool against the hob exit side of the workpiece, the tool shearing the burrs. Some machines retract the burr cutting tools several rotations prior to the end of the hobbing cycle. This action allows the hob to remove the remaining burrs between the gear teeth produced by the tool. Rotating milling cutters are used on larger gears.

Gear Burnishing Machines

Machines are available to remove nicks and burrs from the tooth surfaces of gears. One machine is of the centerless type and uses three hardened or abrasive-impregnated burnishing gears to finish the workpiece with adjustable burnishing pressure. Gears are automatically fed into the workstation, where they are engaged by the burnishing gears. The workpiece gear is constrained by pads supported by a series of leaf springs that are driven by an eccentric shaft. This motion causes the workpiece gear to oscillate as the burnishing gears revolve. Production rates are as high as 900 gears per hour.

Edge Honing of Cutting Tool Inserts

Machines are available for deburring and honing the edges of carbide or ceramic inserts for cutting tools. In addition, the machines are used for deburring flat and cylindrical components, and can also produce sharp corners with no burrs.

ROBOTIC DEBURRING, FETTLING AND FINISHING

For many companies, the use of industrial robots for deburring, fettling, and finishing has considerably reduced costs and improved quality. Robots can operate three shifts a day, virtually untended; they reproduce the same motions accurately; they can process parts faster than humans; they can use heavier, higher powered tools for faster finishing; and they can work in dusty, noisy environments that are unsuitable and/or hazardous for humans. Robotic deburring, fettling, and finishing are not actually processes in themselves, but are simply automation added to mechanical cutting, grinding, brushing, blasting, and other operations.

Robotic deburring, fettling, and finishing are typically used for parts that have production rates falling between job shop quantities and automotive industry requirements. Robotic methods are not normally economical for one-time runs of very low quantities because the engineering and programming time exceed savings. Unlike many off-hand processes, the use of robotic systems requires considerable planning to ensure optimum results.

Typical Applications

Industrial robots are being used for many different deburring and finishing operations. Most applications are for large parts and are dedicated to a specific part or close geometric family of parts. Some precision and intricate parts are being deburred by robots, but they are the exception because many robots are not technically capable of performing precision deburring.

The foundry industry is a major robot user, with the robots handling the castings or tools, depending upon the size, weight, and configuration of the casting; the material from which the casting is made; the amount of stock to be removed; the type of operation; and production requirements. Operations performed include deburring and chamfering internal edges, and removing sprues, flash, risers, gates, parting lines, and runners—a process called *fettling*.

Because fettling requires cutting through thick sections of cast metal and smoothening wide sections of flash, high-powered tools are required and large forces occur, necessitating more powerful robots.

SPECIAL PURPOSE MACHINES AND ROBOTIC DEBURRING

Robot Accuracies

Positioning accuracy. Few manufacturers of industrial robots state the accuracy of their products. Many robots cannot go to a predefined point or location, such as x = 1 mm, y = 2 mm, and z = 0.00 mm. Because of this limitation, the traditional NC machine concept of programming to a point and then measuring how close the machine came to that point is not directly transferable to robots. Even when robot controls allow this predefinition of destination, precision robots may miss their targets. This limitation is not acceptable for deburring when a tolerance of ±0.005″ (0.13 mm) is required on parts. While compliance overcomes some of the accuracy limitations, it is desirable to have a robot with high accuracy for deburring. Less accuracy is acceptable for fettling operations.

Repeatability. The repeatability of an industrial robot in deburring applications depends upon a combination of the following factors:

- The accuracy and positioning repeatability of the robot mechanism.
- Consistency in positioning the edges of the workpiece to a reference surface (clamping forces can significantly deflect some parts).
- Nature of the edge before deburring (burr uniformity, thickness, and location consistency).
- Repeatability of the deburring tool in the robot holder.
- Repeatability and accuracy of the cutting tool geometry.

Robot Capabilities

It is important to understand robot capabilities before selecting one for deburring. With the radial robot arm shown in Fig. 45-15, whenever the end of the arm is moved in an X or Y direction, the tool remains in the same angular orientation with respect to the arm, but changes significantly with respect to the workpiece. As a result, every movement (other than a radial motion into the horizontal plane) requires a reorientation of the tool to provide perpendicularity to the workpiece edges. Because off-line programming is not yet available for many robots, thousands of manual reorientations are required with such robots for deburring most parts.

Similarly, some robot wrists roll automatically with up-and-down movements of one of the principal axes. Some robots can take data for a feature in one position and then automatically provide the data for any other position, but most robot software does not allow this. An example is entering the data for deburring a 0.625″ (15.88 mm) diam hole in one horizontal plane and then translating that data to deburr the same size hole on a higher surface. Those robots that cannot automatically perform the translation and rotation require data reentry for each feature. Each of these limitations is a software restriction. Software may be developed to eliminate these restraints, but users should know that they exist.

Most deburring robots currently rely on an operator manually teaching the robot how to move to perform deburring. Such programming is the most convenient approach for many workpieces. For complex parts that already have an NC database, however, the ability to use off-line programming is desirable.

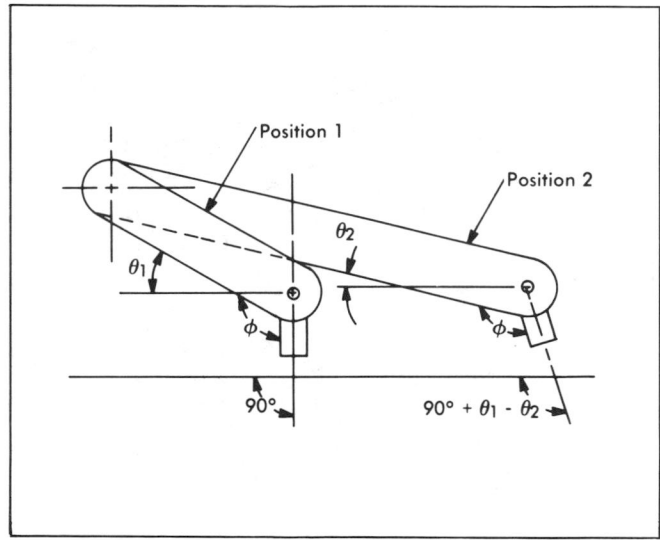

Fig. 45-15 When robot arm is moved from position 1 to position 2, the tool is no longer perpendicular to the workpiece. (*Bendix Corp.*)

MASS FINISHING

Mass finishing refers to several processes for cleaning, deburring, deflashing, edge and corner radiusing, and surface finishing. In general, mass finishing means handling a quantity of workpieces in bulk. A more precise definition is: the edge and surface conditioning of workpieces in a mass of media, normally, but not necessarily, involving a mass of workpieces.

All mass finishing processes are based on loading parts into a container, usually holding abrasive or nonabrasive media, water, and a compound. While mass finishing commonly refers to workpieces loosely loaded into a container, equipment is available in which the workpieces are either fixtured or located in individual compartments within the container.

Action of the container causes the media to rub against the workpieces or the workpieces to rub against one another, thus producing the desired results. The major mass finishing processes are rotary barrel (tumbling), vibratory, centrifugal barrel, centrifugal disc, and spindle finishing.

For most mass finishing applications, workpieces are loaded into a container with some form of media. Most processes are also performed wet, using a solution of water and a compound within the container or flowing through the container. The different media and compounds used are discussed subsequently in this section.

PROCESS ADVANTAGES

Mass finishing is a simple, versatile, and low-cost means of conditioning the edges and surfaces of various components. Normally, individual handling or fixturing of workpieces is not required, thus eliminating costs associated with manual and most other mechanized finishing processes. With proper control, consistent results can be attained from workpiece to workpiece and batch to batch.

All metals and many nonmetals, as well as most sizes and shapes of workpieces, can be processed by mass finishing. Surface finishes smoother than 1 μin. (0.025 μm) are produced in some cases. In addition, the process can be highly automated for increased productivity.

The texture (surface irregularities) of machined or ground parts has a directional pattern characteristic of the specific cutting operation used. When surfaces are mass finished, this directional pattern is changed to a random one that has been found to be particularly advantageous for parts requiring lubrication because lubricants are more readily trapped by the random, nondirectional surface pattern. Also, product break-in periods can be substantially reduced when functional parts are mass finished prior to operation.

LIMITATIONS

A limitation to the use of mass finishing is that its action is generally effective on *all* surfaces, edges, and corners of workpieces that contact the media. It is not normally possible to give preferential treatment to specific areas; however, masking specific areas has been successfully used for some applications. The action is greater on the edges of workpieces than on equally exposed surfaces. The action in holes and recesses is significantly less than on exposed areas; and in small, deep recesses, it is unusual to be able to do any finishing unless the workpiece is fixtured.

APPLICATIONS OF MASS FINISHING

Mass finishing processes are being used for many different purposes. Major uses include deburring, deflashing, edge and corner radiusing, improving surface finish, and cleaning (removing rust, scale, and other surface contaminants). Other applications involve changing surface profiles, generating suitable surface textures for coating or painting, modifying surface stresses (normally to develop compressive stresses), inhibiting corrosion, removing discoloration, drying workpieces, and applying coatings, such as lubricants and wax.

BARREL FINISHING/TUMBLING

Conventional rotary barrel tumbling was the original mass finishing technique. Ancient Chinese and Egyptians used tumbling barrels with natural stones as media to achieve smooth finishes on weapons and jewelry. The process was known as barreling, rattling, or tubbing.

Barrel finishing is now a vastly improved process compared to the old-time tumbling operations, but it is generally slow. As a result, the more sophisticated mass finishing processes discussed next in this section are making the barrel obsolete for most applications. However, barrel finishing is a versatile means of edge and surface conditioning, equipment costs are generally low, operation is simple, and there are still applications where this process offers economies.

Barrel finishing machines are simple in design, relatively low in cost, and available in a wide variety of sizes and types (see Fig. 45-16). Open-ended and horizontal types are the most popular. Horizontal units generally provide faster action, but open-ended units offer the advantages of inspection and making additions while in operation, plus easier unloading. Barrels are generally of multisided construction, with octagonal or hexagonal-shaped interiors being common. Most modern machines have flexible, wear-resistant, and replaceable linings in the barrels. Such linings, frequently polyurethane, extend barrel life, offer some protection to workpieces, and reduce noise levels. Machines are also available with individual compartments that allow workpieces to be processed singly.

VIBRATORY FINISHING

Vibratory finishing is now the most popular type of mass finishing and, next to hand deburring, the most common surface conditioning method used by industry. This versatile process is used for cleaning, deburring, deflashing, descaling, edge and corner radiusing, surface finishing, and stress relieving. Workpieces in a wide variety of sizes and shapes are handled, and all metals and many nonmetallic materials are processed. Large quantities of parts can be run in batch or continuous process setups without handling or fixturing, thus minimizing costs.

Vibratory equipment is made in two basic configurations: rectangular tub and round bowl types. The first tub-type vibratory finishing machine was introduced commercially in 1957, and the bowl type about five years later. Both types use an open-top work chamber containing an aggregate of media, compound, water, and the workpieces. While the chamber is vibrated, work is performed by the scrubbing or peening action of the media and compound on the workpieces.

Tub-Type Vibratory Equipment

With tub-type machines, workpieces are loaded into the open top of a container holding the media, compound, and water. The tub (container) is rectangular, generally has a U-shaped cross section with flat parallel ends, and is usually mounted on coil or rubber springs (see Fig. 45-17). On some machines, the containers are suspended on air bags, and certain small units employ composite or metal strips for suspension. Processing containers other than U-shaped, such as keyhole shapes, and enclosed tubular units are sometimes used to improve unrestricted mass movement. Tub liners, generally polyurethane, are used to prevent wear, reduce noise, and resist chemical attack; they also transmit energy to the media. Removable separators can be installed to divide the rectangular tub into a number of compartments, thus permitting workpieces to be processed individually or the use of different media to finish various parts at the same time.

Round Bowls

Round bowl, or toroidal, vibratory finishing machines have a doughnut-shaped chamber (see Fig. 45-18) that permits a continuous circular flow of media and workpieces. The bowls may have either flat or spiral bottoms. As with tub-type machines, the chambers are provided with liners.

Vibration of the bowl is accomplished either by a vibratory motor or by an eccentric weight system mounted vertically in the center tube of the bowl. With either method, the amount of weight placed on the top and bottom of the eccentric system and the angular displacement between the two weights control the following:

- The finishing action (the amount of media vibration against the workpieces).
- The speed at which the mass rolls over within the bowl.
- The speed at which the mass rotates around the bowl.

MASS FINISHING

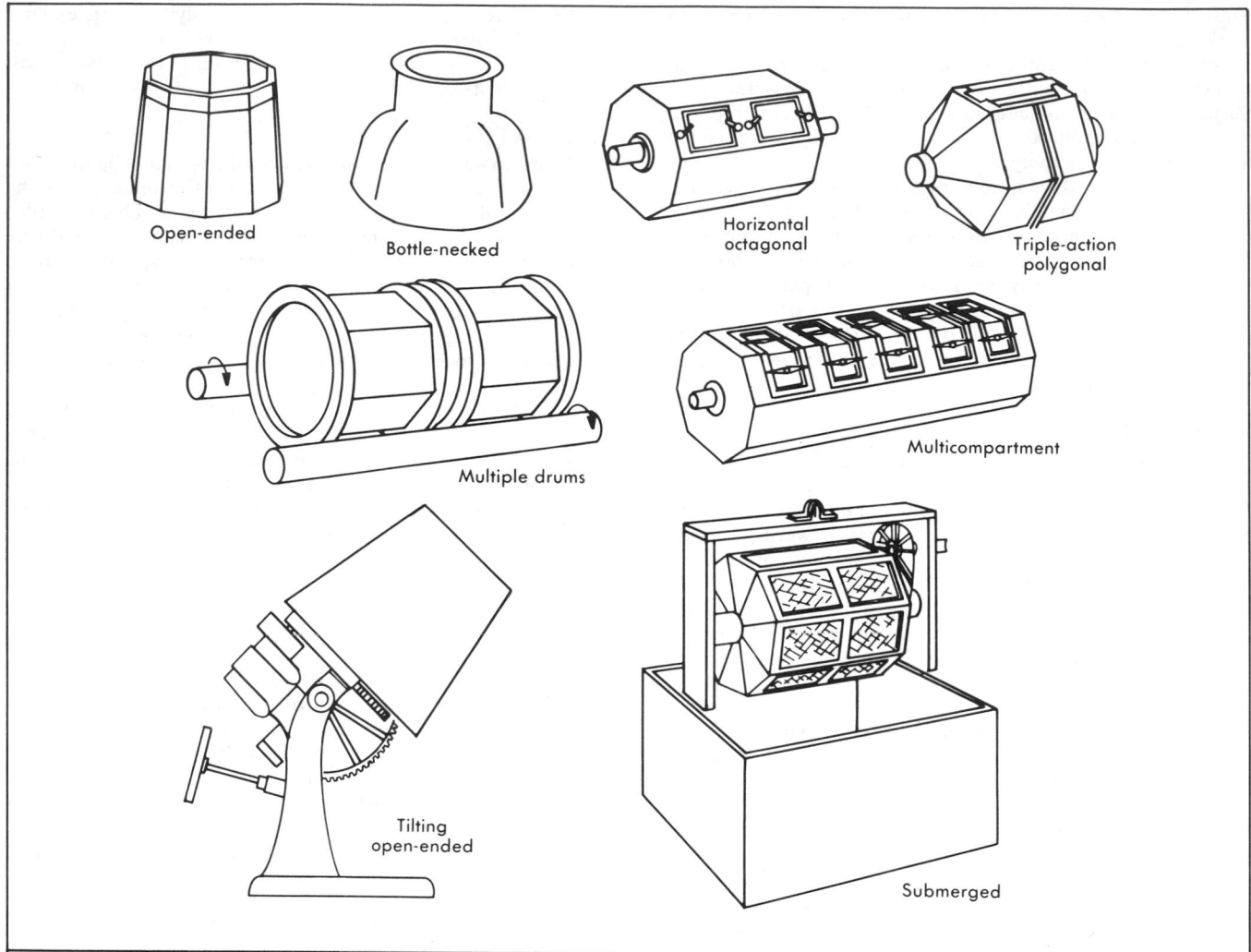

Fig. 45-16 Various types of barrel finishing machines. (*Harper Co.*)

Advantages of Vibratory Finishing

The basic merit of vibratory machines, both tub and bowl types, is that they offer a more convenient and faster means of finishing than do barrels. They are also more versatile, more easily automated, and provide cleaner operation. Processing cycles generally range from 20 minutes to several hours, but many applications are being done in 3 to 20 minutes with continuous processing.

Bowl vibratory equipment may be 5-10% slower than tub vibrators. However, the convenience and economy of integral separation of workpieces and media, along with the gentle-to-aggressive action, ease of adjustment, and versatility of the equipment make bowl vibrator machines desirable for finishing a wide range of products. Floor space requirements, capital investment, and noise are also minimized with internal media/parts separation. For all these reasons, bowl vibratory equipment is being used extensively for finishing.

HIGH-ENERGY MASS FINISHING

High-energy mass finishing encompasses processes in which the energy created within the mass in a container is greater than that obtained with standard vibratory methods. One advantage of the high-energy method is shorter processing cycles. Some high-energy systems permit easy adjustment of the energy level. Maximum energy can be used for fast deburring, edge radiusing, and metal removal, and reduced energy for gentler action to refine edges and surfaces. With some systems there is no workpiece impingement. High-energy mass finishing methods include centrifugal barrel, centrifugal disc, and spindle finishing, as well as chemically and electrochemically accelerated standard processes.

Centrifugal Barrel Finishing

Centrifugal barrel finishing, like other mass finishing processes, uses media, compound, and water to deburr and surface finish components. The difference between this and other processes is that centrifugal action results in a very fast, highly controllable operation. The process, sometimes called orbital barrel finishing, maintains a smooth rubbing action with no workpiece impingement, making it possible to produce fine finishes on precision and fragile parts. Another important

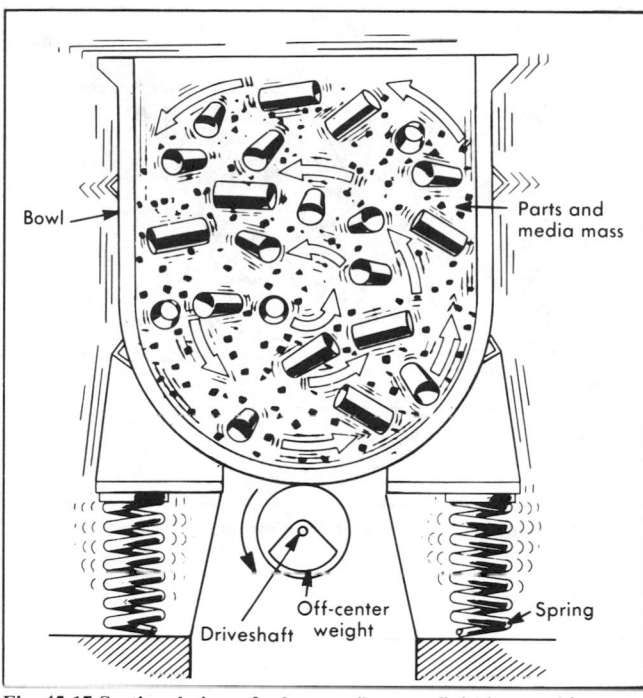

Fig. 45-17 Sectional view of tub-type vibratory finishing machine.

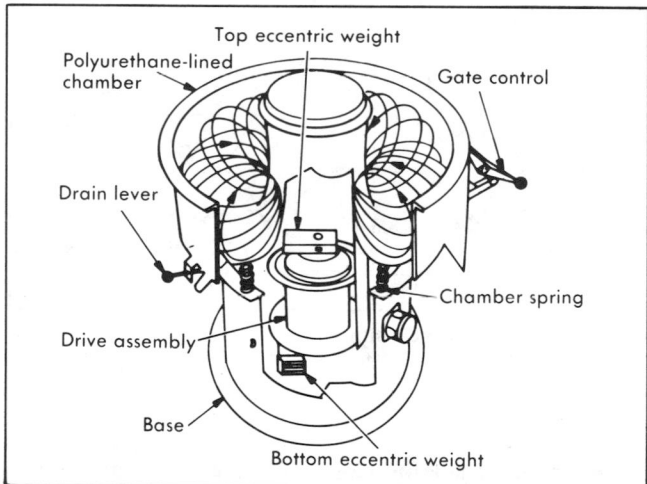

Fig. 45-18 Basic configuration of a round bowl vibratory finishing machine. (*Sweco, Inc.*)

advantage is the capability of imparting high compressive stresses in the surfaces of workpieces.

Process advantages. The abrading action under high centrifugal forces results in short processing cycles—20 to 50 times faster than conventional vibratory finishing. Another important advantage is that counter-rotation of the drums produces a smooth sliding action of media against workpieces, with no possibility of one workpiece impacting against another. As a result, consistent and reproducible results can be obtained; close tolerances can be maintained, even with fragile and precision components; and very smooth surface finishes can be produced.

Small-sized media can be used with centrifugal barrel finishing, thus ensuring uniformity of radii and edges, and permitting greater action in holes and recesses. Small parts can be handled as well. All equipment is quiet in operation and requires no special noise-abatement measures.

Applications. Originally, centrifugal barrel equipment was developed for finishing small, light components and workpieces having critical tolerances that could not be handled in other types of mass finishing machines. With the development of large machines, up to 100 ft³ (2.8 m³), and automation, the process is now being used for a broader range of applications.

Figure 45-19 illustrates one type of automatic centrifugal barrel machine. Automatic centrifugal barrel machines still involve batch operation, but they provide automatic loading, unloading, and separation of workpieces from the media. The equipment may be used for heavy stock removal and edge radiusing operations for both high and low-volume applications, as well as for precision finishing. Standard deburring and finishing operations seldom require more than 15 minutes.

Another important application for centrifugal barrel equipment involves imparting compressive stresses into the workpiece surfaces. This procedure improves resistance to fatigue failure and is being used for bearings, aircraft engine parts, springs, bearings, and pump components. Edge radiusing and surface finishing can be performed simultaneously, thus further enhancing the fatigue strength. This method generally costs less and is more effective than a combination of another finishing operation followed by shot peening.

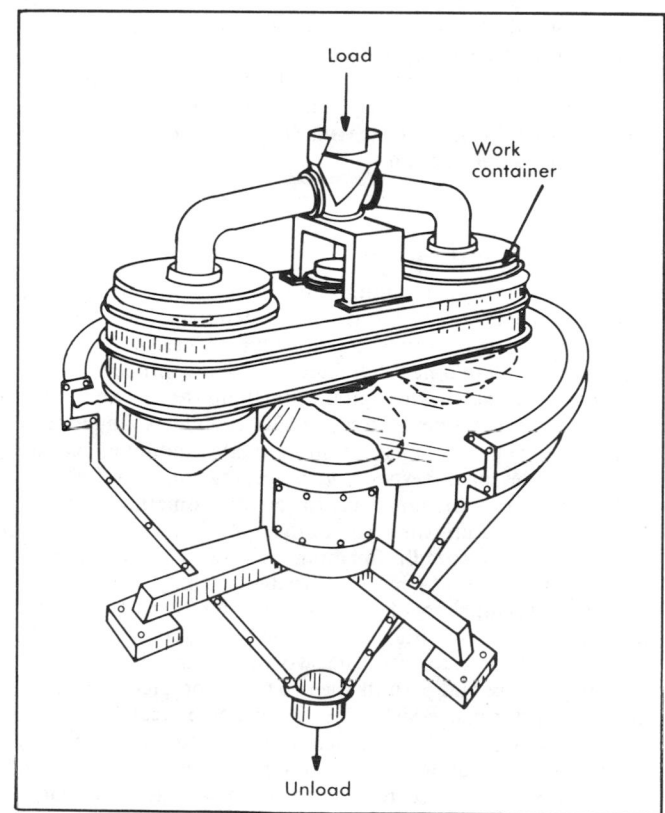

Fig. 45-19 Automatic centrifugal barrel finishing machine. (*The Harper Co.*)

Centrifugal Disc Finishing

The centrifugal disc process is the newest of the high-energy mass finishing methods. Machines consist of an open-top bowl having stationary sidewalls and a rotary disc for a base (see Fig. 45-20). Media, compound, and workpieces are combined in the bowl.

Process advantages. The action in centrifugal disc machines is substantially faster than in vibratory equipment. Centrifugal force developed is as much as 10 times the earth's gravity, which presses the media against the workpieces. Processing cycles typically vary between one tenth and one twentieth those possible with vibratory finishing.

Short process cycles result in decreased costs, reduced floor space requirements, and less work in process and inventory. Centrifugal disc finishing is a fairly versatile process and easily adapted to batch automation. As with vibratory finishing equipment, workpieces can be readily inspected during the process cycle. With variable-speed equipment, it is frequently possible to combine heavy deburring and edge radiusing with a final, more gentle surface refinement operation.

Centrifugal disc equipment provides a smooth action. While centrifugal disc machines cost about five times that of vibratory equipment, processing cycles are typically one-tenth less, thus making them economically justifiable for many applications. The cost of media and compounds per part processed is comparable to their cost in vibratory finishing.

Limitations. The centrifugal disc process complements the barrel, vibratory, and centrifugal barrel processes. It is capable of producing very fine finishes, but cannot yet handle as wide a variety of parts as barrel, vibratory, and centrifugal barrel processes. Machines currently available cannot handle parts much larger than about 6 in.^{3} (98 cm^3), although parts to 12" (305 mm) long are being processed. Very small parts or media cannot be handled easily because there must be some gap, generally less than 0.010" (0.25 mm), between the disc and the cylinder walls. Also, centrifugal disc machines are not adaptable to continuous automation.

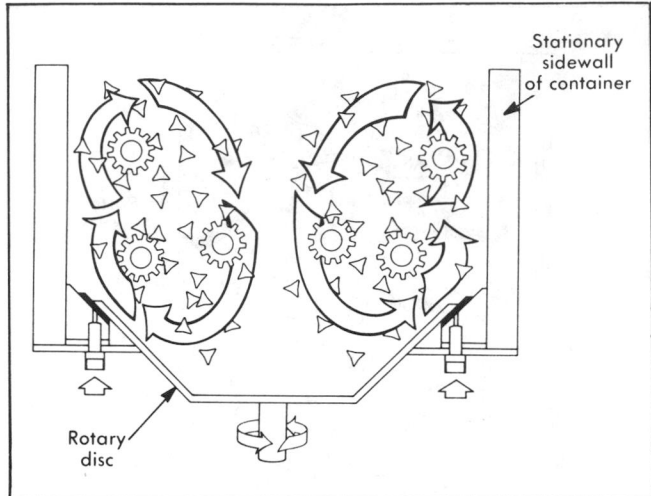

Fig. 45-20 Principle of centrifugal disc finishing. (*The Harper Co.*)

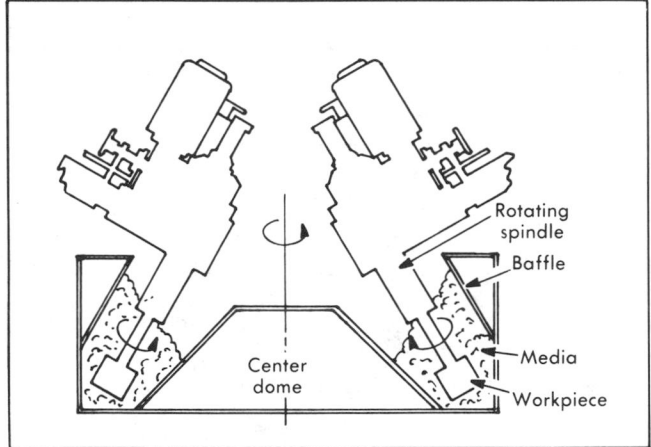

Fig. 45-21 Tub is equipped with a baffle and center dome for high-pressure spindle finishing. (*Almco Industrial Finishing Systems*)

Spindle Finishing

Spindle finishing is another high-energy, mass finishing process that features fast and precise deburring or finishing. Good control, smooth finishes, and a high degree of reliability and uniformity are other characteristics of this process.

Processing cycles with spindle finishing rarely exceed five minutes and are frequently less than 30 seconds. A limitation is that the workpieces must be individually mounted on the spindles of the machines with workholding collets or fixtures. Mechanical arms or industrial robots are sometimes used to automate the loading and unloading.

High-pressure spindle finishing. Higher velocity and confinement of the media generates greater finishing forces. These requirements can be met by fitting a standard tub with a baffle and center dome (see Fig. 45-21). The baffle tends to force the media downward toward the workpiece as the result of centrifugal force and permits the tub to be operated at a higher speed for faster processing. The center dome creates a pocket effect that does not allow the media to flow into the center area of the tub. For small workpieces, the dome allows the media to recover faster and creates a dense, solid mass. For large workpieces, the confinement generates high finishing forces, resulting in short cycling times.

Continuous spindle finishing. To eliminate the unproductive time spent removing spindles from the tubs and unloading/ reloading workpieces, continuous machines, such as the one illustrated in Fig. 45-22, have been developed. With this continuous machine, a head holding six rotating spindles indexes the workpieces into and out of the media in a continuously rotating tub. Unloading and reloading of the workpieces can be done manually or with a robot (as shown in Fig. 45-22) to increase productivity.

Typical applications. Spindle machines are well suited for deburring and finishing uniformly shaped cylindrical components, such as gears, sprockets, and bearing cages. Such components are easily fixtured, and the action of the media is uniform over all significant surfaces. Because the parts are fixtured, there is no possibility of impingement of one against another. Workpieces can often be stacked on a spindle so that several parts can be deburred or finished simultaneously.

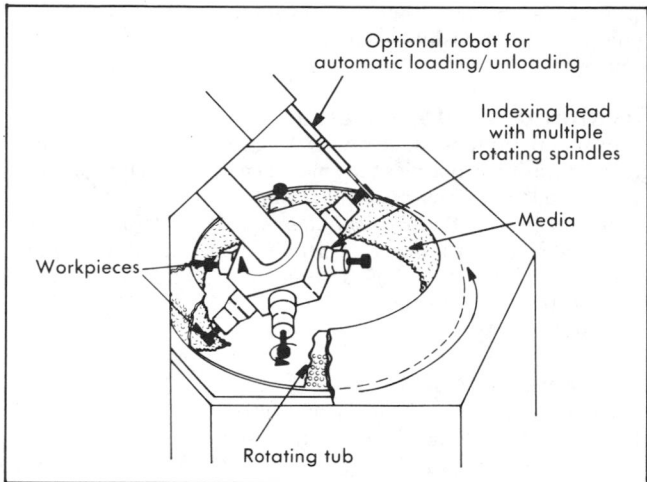

Fig. 45-22 Continuous spindle finishing with indexing multispindle head and robot for loading/unloading.

OTHER MASS FINISHING PROCESSES

There are many other mass finishing processes that have been developed. Some, such as resonant energy, chemically accelerated, electrochemically accelerated, and cryogenic finishing, are being employed and show promise for many applications. Other mass finishing methods having only limited, if any, commercial application are discussed briefly later in this section.

Use of Resonant Energy

Cleaning, deburring, and radiusing of intricate internal passages and recesses is being done with resonant power. Essentially, the process consists of submerging vibrating workpieces, fixtured at the ends of a resonating beam, in abrasive media for a predetermined time (see Fig. 45-23). The combination of resonant motion of the workpieces and orbital movement of the abrasive grains cleans and finishes the surfaces.

One or more workpieces are clamped in fixtures secured to both ends of a steel beam. High energy levels are produced by

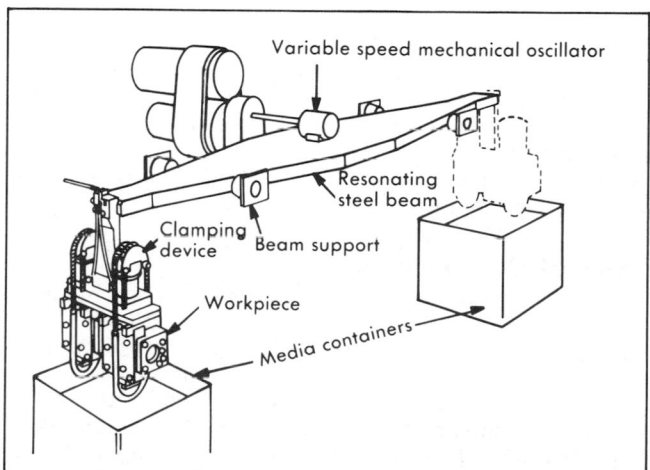

Fig. 45-23 Machine for internal finishing and cleaning of precision castings, which are vibrated at high frequencies by means of a resonant beam. (*Wheelabrator-Frye, Inc.*)

resonating the elastic beam near its natural frequency, using a mechanical oscillator with a counterweighted shaft, connected to a variable-speed drive motor. Processing is generally done at 75 to 100 Hz (4500 to 6000 vibrations per minute), depending upon the weight of the workpieces. Typical cycle times for cast iron workpieces range from 2 to 3 minutes.

Use of Chemical Accelerators

When chemical accelerators are added to abrasive media in a vibratory machine, the chemicals react with the metal workpieces to remove metal. The vibrating media wipes away any passivating films that form and provides additional, mechanical cutting and burnishing action. Conventional vibratory finishing media and machines can be used, although linings in the tubs or bowls may be affected by the chemical solutions.

While accelerators are used for finishing steel and brass parts, they are also employed for zinc die castings. The chemical accelerators are most useful for vibratory deburring if the die castings have been trimmed closely to leave only small burrs; the large, jagged burrs left on many trimmed castings require the use of abrasive belts before vibratory finishing.

Cryogenic Deflashing

Cryogenic deflashing of molded rubber or plastics products and aluminum or zinc die castings is being done in barrels and vibratory machines by freezing the workpieces with liquid nitrogen or carbon dioxide. Flash on the workpiece becomes embrittled when its temperature is reduced, and mechanical means are used to remove the flash. When using liquid nitrogen, proper ventilation is essential, and care is required in handling the cold parts and media. The cost of liquid nitrogen may be a limitation to the use of this process.

Barrels and vibratory machines used for cryogenic deflashing require special double-walled, insulated work chambers to conserve the liquid nitrogen. The chambers are fitted with multiple nozzles for spraying the nitrogen. It is general practice to cool the media in the work chamber prior to adding the workpieces, which must then also be cooled prior to starting the machine. Temperature control during processing is essential. Temperatures as low as -320° F (-196° C) are used for some parts.

Electrochemical Mass Finishing

In this process, workpieces are placed in an electrically insulated drum filled with electrolyte and media, which may be graphite spheres. British patents, filed in 1968, indicate that phosphoric acid is used as the electrolyte and that either silicon carbide or copper-coated aluminum oxide can also be used as the deburring media. Electrodes, connected to an external power source, are also placed in the drum. When the drum is vibrated, the media acts as extensions of the electrodes to remove the burrs electrolytically. The action is similar to nonvibratory electrochemical deburring. The media also abrades the passivating surface oxides formed on the workpieces, thus exposing fresh surfaces to the electrolytic action.

The major advantage of this process is fast cycling; but the equipment required is comparatively expensive, and the process is limited to workpiece materials that conduct electricity.

Limited Application Methods

There are several other mass finishing methods that have only limited or no commercial application. Consequently, they are only discussed briefly in this section.

MASS FINISHING

Vibratory rotary barrel finishing. Conventional rotary barrels that vibrate as they rotate have been developed for specific applications when problems are encountered with workpieces migrating out of the media in vibratory machines.

Reciprocal finishing. In this process, workpieces are moved back and forth in a stationary tub containing media. It is similar to spindle finishing in that the workpieces must be attached to a holding device, but the workpieces are oscillated rather than being rotated. The process permits handling parts too large or odd shaped for spindle finishing equipment. Finishing action can be concentrated on certain areas while shielding other areas. Processing cycles are normally much longer than with spindle finishing machines.

Reciprocal finishing can be fully automated. One design incorporates a traverse unit that reciprocates on rails fixed to an upper frame, fixture clamping arms pivoted to the traverse unit, a loading apparatus, and a transfer mechanism for loading and unloading. Several modifications of these machines are in use, including one type that employs spindle rotation.

Magnetic-abrasive mass finishing. Workpieces are placed in a container of magnetic, loose abrasive media, and an oscillating magnetic field is produced to vibrate the media. While the workpieces can be stationary, more effective finishing is obtained by tumbling or otherwise moving the parts.

When magnetic media is used, the workpieces must be nonmagnetic to obtain relative motion. However, it is conceivable that a magnetic field could oscillate miniature magnetic parts through nonmagnetic media. Magnetic media can be coated with ceramics or other metals to minimize contamination of the workpieces. Most iron-based components will not react well to high-frequency changes in a magnetic field.

In an experimental method of magnetic-abrasive finishing, cylindrical parts are vibrated, rotated, and fed axially in a magnetic field between two poles. Abrasive grains are combined magnetically between the poles and the workpiece to perform the cutting action. This process is also being used for non-cylindrical parts.

MEDIA FOR MASS FINISHING

Media refers to the abrasive or nonabrasive, consumable elements used in mass finishing processes. The main function of media is to abrade or burnish the edges and surfaces of components to the desired finish. Media also helps keep the workpieces from impinging on each other and serves as a carrier for any compounds used.

The most important types of mass finishing media, from the standpoint of most common usage, include natural abrasives, agricultural products, synthetic random media, preformed ceramic and resin-bonded media, and metallic media.

Natural Abrasives

Quarried, crushed, and graded stones were the original mass finishing media. They have, however, been largely replaced by synthetic materials primarily because natural stones are softer, wear more rapidly, are less consistent, and occur only in random shapes. Synthetic materials are harder, provide longer life, and have more consistent cutting action, wear rate, and dimensions.

Agricultural and Wood Products

Ground corncobs and walnut or other nut shells, as well as hardwood sawdust, are used in tumbling barrels and heated barrels for drying parts. These materials produce a good luster on some workpieces. When mixed with fine abrasives, they are suitable for fine polishing operations, particularly in the jewelry industry.

Synthetic Random Media

Fused aluminum oxide (Al_2O_3), crushed and graded, has greater abrasion properties than natural materials. Other advantages include good wear resistance and consistency of size and quality. However, the physical characteristics of fused aluminum oxide vary with different producers. Sintered aluminum oxide is the longest lasting random-shaped abrasive material available for mass finishing. It is used extensively for fine deburring and finishing.

Preformed Media

The development of media of controlled shape, size, and abrasion and finishing characteristics has been largely responsible for making mass finishing a precision process. Preformed media is available in ceramic, resin-bonded, and metallic types, all of which are used extensively. The abrasives used in preformed ceramic and resin-bonded media are often aluminum oxide, silica, or silicon carbide.

COMPOUND SOLUTIONS FOR MASS FINISHING

Compounds are combinations of chemicals that dissolve in water and form solutions to maintain consistency or to modify the action of media against the workpieces in mass finishing. The use of too little, too much, or an improper compound can adversely affect the cycle time and/or ability of the media to perform as intended.

There are some finishing applications where no compound solutions are used. For example, loads of workpieces are sometimes finished dry, perhaps with sawdust, ground corncobs, wood pegs, or other media, for burnishing purposes. Media for dry finishing is often treated with an oil, grease, or wax-based formulation with finely powdered abrasives to produce smooth surface finishes; cycle times are much longer than for wet operations. There are other applications where the desired results are achieved with a suitable compound solution and no media; the workpieces themselves act as the media, tumbling against each other for the required action.

Functions of Solutions

There are many different functions served by various compound solutions. Major functions include cleaning of the workpieces and media, and control of the process. In some applications, the solution modifies the luster or color of the workpieces. The use of corrosion-inhibiting compounds is especially important when any metal is used.

Types of Compounds

Compound types may be classified basically according to function, as follows: (1) abrasive, (2) descaling or bleaching, (3) cleaning, (4) deburring and edge radiusing, and (5) burnishing and coloring. Many different compounds are available for specific functions. Selection depends upon numerous factors, including workpiece material, media type, the finishing process being used, water hardness, and cycle times. Compounds are available in liquid and powder forms. When a finishing application requires free abrasives to influence the cutting action of the media, the compounds containing free abrasives must necessarily be powders. Requirements for free abrasives, however, are limited; and liquid compounds are preferred for most mass finishing applications because they are easier to handle and to consistently use with precise results.

Most compounds contain several types of ingredients, such as chemicals to perform a certain function and other ingredients to facilitate finishing. Water conditioners minimize the deposit of hard salts on the media and workpieces by reducing the water hardness. If the available water has an exceptionally high mineral content (over 200 ppm), it may be necessary to use demineralized or preconditioned water. Detergents help keep the workload clean. Corrosion inhibitors minimize rusting. In general, the compound used must be tailored to the workpiece material and condition, and to the results required.

ABRASIVE-FLOW MACHINING

Abrasive-flow machining (AFM) is a process in which a semisolid abrasive media is forced, or extruded, through a workpiece passage. The three major elements required for the AFM process are the machine, the workpiece fixture (tooling), and the media.

Machines used (see Fig. 45-24) hydraulically clamp the workholding fixtures between two vertically opposed media cylinders. These cylinders extrude the media back and forth through the workpiece(s). Two strokes, one from the lower and one from the upper cylinder, comprise one process cycle, as illustrated in Fig. 45-25.

The AFM process can be thought of as the use of a self-forming abrasive tool that precisely removes workpiece material from those areas in which media flow is purposely restricted. In general, the media used determines the kind of abrasion that occurs, the fixture determines where the abrasion occurs, and the machine determines how much abrasion occurs.

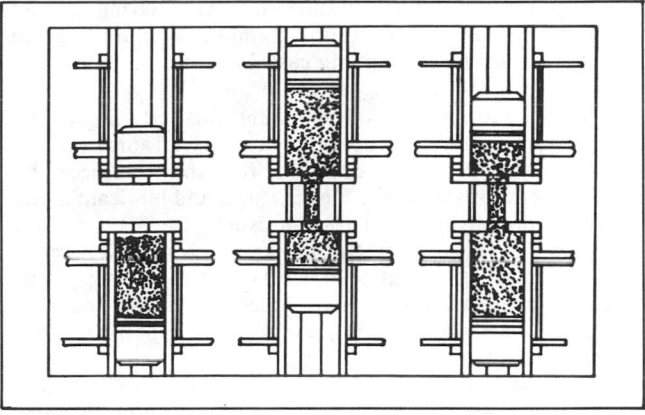

Fig. 45-25 One AFM process cycle consists of two cylinder strokes that extrude the media through the workpiece twice. (*Extrude Hone Corp.*)

PROCESS ADVANTAGES

By proper control of parameters and abrasive flow, the AFM process can perform a wide range of precision machining and finishing operations. These operations include deburring, edge radiusing, honing, polishing, and the removal of recast layers from workpiece surfaces. Important features of the process include selectivity, the capability of finishing inaccessible areas, and versatility.

Selectivity and Finishing Inaccessible Areas

Abrasion in the AFM process occurs only in areas where media flow is restricted; other areas are unaffected. Inaccessible areas and any restricted places through which the media can be forced to flow can be finished, including complex internal passages.

Versatility of the Process

The AFM process is being used on a wide range of workpiece and passage sizes. It can also process many selected areas on a workpiece simultaneously. Several to hundreds of holes, slots, or edges can be deburred, radiused, and/or polished in one operation.

A number of workpieces can also be processed simultaneously. Depending upon workpiece and machine sizes, several or even dozens of parts can be processed in one fixture load, resulting in production rates to hundreds of parts per hour.

Both small and large production quantities can be handled economically with the AFM process. Changeover from one job to another, including replacing the tooling and media, can normally be done in minutes.

LIMITATIONS OF THE PROCESS

Abrasive-flow machining is a versatile and controllable finishing process because the workpiece is held stationary and

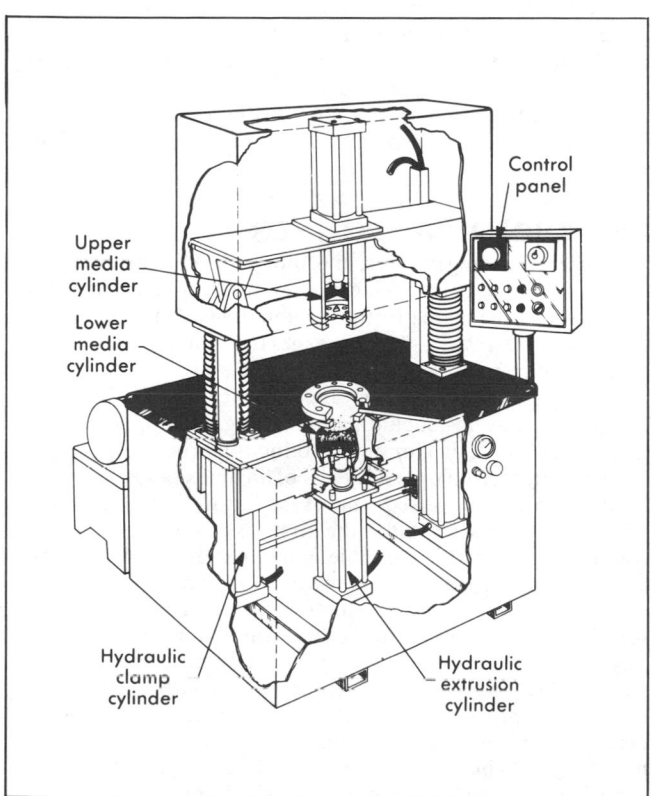

Control panel

Upper media cylinder

Lower media cylinder

Hydraulic clamp cylinder

Hydraulic extrusion cylinder

Fig. 45-24 Cutaway view of high-production machine for abrasive-flow machining (AFM). (*Extrude Hone Corp.*)

ABRASIVE-FLOW MACHINING

the abrasive media is directed to and often through the passages to be finished by the tooling. These characteristics, however, also impose some limitations on the process. One limitation is that most workpieces require a fixture, which involves some expense. Also, the workpieces must be loaded and oriented in the fixture, and then removed from the fixture after processing.

After processing, the abrasive media normally remains both within the part's interior and surrounding its exterior, making fully automated processing and handling difficult. Some recent, fully automated systems incorporate a machine with sufficient capacity to completely process a fixture load of workpieces in one stroke. Flowing only from the interior of the workpieces, the abrasive media exits freely and falls into a receiving cylinder or collection hopper. This approach makes both tooling and automatic unloading/reloading easier because the outside of the workpieces are relatively free of media.

Removal and retrieval of media and final cleaning of the finished workpieces is another task required with abrasive-flow machining. Media can be removed from the workpieces by blowing it out with shop air. Fine particles and lubricant in the media are normally removed in an ultrasonic cleaning operation using commercial solvents. Such cleaning is essential because fine, loose particles left after blowoff can cause plug gages or mating components to seize in the holes. The careful choice of abrasive size and tooling will prevent abrasive particles from lodging in small holes.

The removal and retrieval of media and final cleaning of parts has recently been made more convenient for automated systems by using vacuum and water-based solvents. The solvents dissolve the media carrier and can be used as a spray or pulsed flush, without special venting.

TYPICAL APPLICATIONS

The AFM process is being used on workpiece sizes ranging from as small as 0.060" (1.52 mm) diam to turbine discs nearly 4 ft (1.2 m) diam. Passages in the workpieces range from orifices as small as 0.004" (0.10 mm) diam to splines 2" (51 mm) or more across. The process can generate edge radii from less than 0.001" (0.03 mm) to more than 0.060" (1.52 mm).

For a given set of deburring conditions, the edge radius produced after removing the burr is a function of burr size. Thick, tall burrs reduce the radiusing action. With standard tooling, removing 0.005" (0.13 mm) thick x 0.002" (0.05 mm) high burrs in stainless steel results in a radius of about 0.005". The same conditions in aluminum result in a radius of about 0.0075" (0.19 mm). It is not possible with standard tooling to remove large burrs and produce small edge radii of 0.005" or less.

Polishing with AFM can improve surface finishes of 30 to 300 μin. (0.76 to 7.6 μm) to one tenth or less of the original finishes. Material removal by the abrasion results in a dimensional change of about 25 to 35% more than the total roughness of the surface. For example, in reducing a surface finish of 100 μin. (2.54 μm) produced by EDM to a finish of 10 μin. (0.25 μm) requires the removal of about 0.001" (0.03 mm) of stock. In most cases, stock removal can be held uniform throughout a passage within $\pm 20\%$.

The finishing of dies (extruding, compacting, cold heading, upsetting, and others) is a major application of the AFM process. Advantages include reduced costs and longer die life. Costs are reduced by eliminating or minimizing the need for time-consuming hand polishing of the dies. Longer die life results from the directional finish produced by AFM and the improved uniformity and quality of the finished surfaces.

Other components commonly finished by the AFM process include gears, bearing races and cages, and splined parts. The manufacturers of jet engines and turbines use the process extensively for finishing components such as fuel swirlers, combustion liners, turbine discs and blades, and compressor wheels and vanes. Finishing by AFM is also used for critical components made by the aerospace, medical, and other industries in which demanding performance is essential.

MACHINES USED

Machines used for the AFM process primarily control extrusion pressure, a crucial parameter for determining the amount of abrasion that will eventually be produced. Within the range of machines available, pressures from 100 to 3200 psi (690 to 22 060 kPa) can be produced, and at flow rates of up to 100 gpm (378 L/min) and higher. The ideal media flow rate depends upon the size and number of passages to be processed and the kind of flow characteristics desired. Flow rate is affected by media viscosity and extrusion pressure, and is generally not a crucial variable.

The dominant factors in controlling the amount of work done by a specific media composition are flow volume and extrusion pressure. These variables are controlled at the machine by presetting the displacement of each media cylinder stroke, the number of two-stroke cycles for the job, and the hydraulic extrusion pressure. Low-cost, low-production machines have media cylinder diameters ranging from 3 to 6" (76 to 152 mm). Machines for larger components or higher production rates have cylinders from 6 to 24" (152 to 610 mm) diam.

Microprocessor controllers can monitor and modify additional process parameters at the machine, such as media temperature, media viscosity, media wear, and flow speed. Accessories such as part cleaning stations, unload/reload stations, media refeed devices, and media heat exchangers are frequently included in installations for production applications.

WORKHOLDING FIXTURES

The workholding fixtures, or tooling, for AFM are primarily designed to hold the workpiece(s) in position on the machine and to direct the media to the desired areas. If necessary, the fixture can also restrict those passages that must be abraded but that do not restrict the media flow sufficiently.

High-production fixtures are designed to facilitate part handling operations, including unloading, loading, and cleaning. A common design for high-production processing uses two fixtures mounted on opposite ends of an index table. While one fixture is being processed, the other fixture is unloaded and reloaded with parts. After the first fixture-load of parts is completely processed, the table is indexed 180°, swinging the second fixture into position between the media cylinders. These and other types of high-production fixture arrangements are sometimes designed in conjunction with automated part handling systems to further increase production efficiency.

One of the more recent developments in AFM fixturing has enabled the process to accurately machine an external workpiece surface to a specific close-tolerance shape while also polishing or finishing it. Although large amounts of stock cannot be efficiently removed by AFM, precise forms and shapes can be produced on workpieces by placing specially shaped restrictors over the workpiece areas to be abraded.

BLAST FINISHING

The two major methods of modern blast finishing are dry and wet. Dry blasting is done with pressurized air or by airless processes. In air blasting, the media is propelled by a stream of pressurized air. In airless or mechanical blasting, the media is thrown against the work surfaces by centrifugal force, using a rotating bladed wheel. In wet blasting, the media is generally suspended in water that is forced by compressed air through nozzles to clean or finish the workpieces.

PROCESS ADVANTAGES AND LIMITATIONS

Blast finishing is generally an economical process, often requiring less labor than many other cleaning and finishing methods. The equipment can be used for many different operations and a wide variety of workpieces. The media is generally reused, thus reducing costs. Most blasting processes are suitable for low or high-volume production requirements.

APPLICATIONS OF BLAST FINISHING

Blast finishing is used extensively for cleaning operations. These include the removal of sand from castings, scale from forgings and heat treated parts, mill scale and rust, paint and other coatings, various soils, and other surface contaminants. Soils or dirt to be removed must be dry and workpiece surfaces free of grease or oil when using dry blasting.

Finishing applications of media blasting generally include either roughening or smoothening workpiece surfaces. Surface roughening (conditioning) is often required prior to the application of adhesives, paints, or other coatings. Smoothening operations include the removal of burrs, flash, directional machining or grinding lines, and other surface irregularities; the rounding of edges; and improvement in surface finishes. The use of media such as plastic pellets permits the removal of burrs and flash without affecting the surface finish.

DRY BLASTING

There are two commonly used methods of dry blasting. In the air-blast system, the media is propelled by a stream of pressurized air. In the airless system, the media is fed into the center of a rotating vaned wheel, which hurls the media by centrifugal force. Although the air-blast system is the most versatile, it has the limitations of requiring a source of high-pressure air and being more energy intensive. However, air-blast systems accelerate the media to higher velocities, permitting the effective use of smaller media particles to produce smooth finishes.

Abrasive-Jet Machining

Abrasive-jet machining (AJM) is a specialized form of blasting for removing material by a high-speed stream of media particles carried from a nozzle by a gas, usually air. It is used to cut, deburr, and clean hard, brittle materials such as germanium, silicon, mica, glass, ceramics, titanium, and tantalum without heating or cracking. Cutting rates are generally low. However, since the tool does not contact the workpiece, the process is inherently free from chatter and vibration problems. Also, the cutting action is cool because the carrier gas serves as a coolant. This cool action makes the method ideal for cutting materials

that are sensitive to heat damage, as well as thin sections of hard materials that might chip easily.

Airless Blast Systems

Centrifugal wheel (airless) blasting is a mechanical method by which media is propelled by centrifugal force from a rotating vaned wheel (slinger). The media forms an elongated, cone-shaped pattern, and the operator remains outside the machine during blasting. The economy of this type of equipment is apparent from the fact that a single wheel, with a 100 hp (75 kW) drive motor, can discharge up to about 2600 lb (1180 kg) of steel shot or grit per minute at velocities reaching 14,000 fpm (4267 m/min). In comparison, a single air nozzle is limited to about 100 lb (45 kg) of media per minute.

Airless blasting is used most commonly in batch and continuous equipment, especially when a large volume of media is required over a fairly large work area. The kind and size of unit will depend on the size, shape, and fragility of the metal parts to be cleaned. The mechanical wheels on single or multiple units are positioned on the equipment to expose the desired areas of the work to the proper volume of abrasive at the proper angle and velocity. The equipment must turn or roll the workpieces continuously to expose their surfaces completely.

Mechanical blast cleaning will effectively remove molding sands from iron or steel castings and iron oxide scale from forgings and heat-treated parts. Descaling of structural steel and plate is more readily performed with airless blasting than with an air-blast system. Removal of the carbonaceous film accumulated in oil quenches on heat-treated parts is another ideal application. Some of the more popular airless systems include barrels, tables, hanging machines, axial-flow units, rooms, cabinets, and special-purpose machines.

WET BLASTING

Wet blasting, sometimes called vapor or hydraulic blasting, is a process using fine media particles in a slurry form. The process does not require a dust collector or ventilation equipment and, with the use of rust-inhibiting compounds, prevents immediate oxidation. Finer media, down to a particle size of 0.0001" (0.003 mm), can be used. The process is generally considered a precision finishing operation. It can be controlled to produce or avoid metal removal and permits maintaining dimensional tolerances to within 0.0001".

Advantages and Limitations

The advantages of wet blasting as a cleaning and finishing method are useful in many industries. In the preparation of metals for plating, it can be used instead of pickling. Hydrogen embrittlement is avoided, and a metallurgically clean surface is produced, with various matte finishes obtainable by the selection of finer or coarser media. If polishing is required, the time is reduced for polishing prior to plating, and also for polishing on many types of dies such as those for molding, drawing, stamping, forging, forming, die casting, and rubber and glass molding.

Wet blasting also provides a good surface for paint adhesion. The surfaces generated by wet blasting generally have a lower rms value than those generated by dry blasting, although laboratory tests indicate that stainless steel and titanium are

SHOT PEENING

exceptions to this statement. However, the surface generated on *any* metal by wet blasting will appear to have a smoother finish than that resulting from dry blasting.

Another advantage of the wet blast process is its suitability for use in toolrooms and tool grinding departments. A slurry of very fine particles is used to remove feather burrs from multitooth cutting tools such as milling cutters, hobs, broaches, and taps, thus eliminating hours of hand honing time.

Wet blasting also deburrs intersecting hole junctions in precision parts that are inaccessible by any other method. The use of glass beads for close-tolerance peening of relatively thin-walled parts has become a successful application of the wet blasting process. Other advantages of wet blasting include the ability to blast wet parts, the capability of removing oily or wet contaminants, and the beneficial cushioning or buffering effect of the liquid used, resulting in less wear of the equipment and longer media life. However, media reclamation is difficult.

Wet blasting does have certain limitations and is particularly not recommended for heavy work that can withstand sand-blasting or shot peening, such as the preparation of castings and forgings for machining. Wet blasting is also not ordinarily used for the removal of heavy burrs adjacent to smooth finished areas or machined configurations on which close fits or tolerances must be held. Wet blasting is not considered to be a high-production process because it requires more time than dry blasting. It is also not as clean a process as dry blasting, and precautions must be taken against oxidation of the workpieces. In addition, wet media may pack into cavities, holes, and crevices, causing removal problems.

Equipment Used

Many types and sizes of wet blasting equipment are available. Machines do not require special rooms and can be placed in production lines. Whether a machine is a simple hand-operated cabinet, just large enough to handle the product, or a complicated multigun, automated machine, a properly designed unit based on the experience of the manufacturer is required. The lowest priced unit may be the most expensive in the long run. Because of the specific gravity of even the finest particles, these must be kept in suspension in a hopper, usually accomplished by air agitation, mechanical movement, or pump recirculation.

SHOT PEENING

Shot peening is the cold working of a metal surface with a stream of spherical shot particles applied to the surface at high velocity under carefully controlled conditions.

EFFECTS OF SHOT PEENING

Shot peening is described as a process that provides the major advantage of inducing residual compressive stresses or work hardening. While stress relief may occur provided stresses are present, and while work hardening may also occur if the material is susceptible and the peening application is heavy enough and of long enough duration, shot peening is not generally used for either of these purposes. Its primary benefits are the generation of a uniform compressive stress pattern and the effective elimination of microscopic defects in the thin surface shell of the part.

Shot peening is most effective in reducing fatigue failures in parts subject to cyclic loading. Failures originate in surface areas under repeated tensile loading, and cracks will propagate from a surface defect or other stress riser. Shot peening prevents these failures by creating compressive stress layers in the surfaces of parts. As a part is loaded, its critical surface area will not develop tensile stresses until the shot-peen-induced compressive stresses are first overcome, thus permitting an increase in the allowable stress level and hence in the service life of the part. The effect of shot peening in improving the surface integrity of the part is also important. No matter how carefully a part is manufactured, it will exhibit some surface imperfections. These flaws may be localized areas of tensile stresses or phase transformations from machining or grinding, as well as pits, scratches, and other surface defects. As peening cold works the part surface, it blends these surface imperfections and effectively eliminates them as stress concentration points.

As each individual particle of shot strikes the metal surface, it produces a slightly rounded depression. Plastic flow and radial stretching of the surface metal occur at the instant of contact, and the edges of the depression may rise slightly above the original surface. In a completely worked part, the residual compressive stress layer usually extends to about 0.005 to 0.040″ (0.13 to 1.02 mm) below the surface. Below this depth, a tensile stress layer will develop to achieve equilibrium. This tensile stress will be much lower than the surface compressive stress because it is distributed in a comparatively thicker core.

In thin materials peened on one side, a convex curve will develop with the peened surface on the outside. In this condition, the permanent compressive stress is low because the thin, undisturbed layer countering the compressive stress is too thin to completely resist the elongation of the peened side and curving results. This ability of shot peening to curve relatively thin materials is the basis of the standard test-strip method used for control of the peening process.

SHOT PEENING APPLICATIONS

Peening has long been used to improve the fatigue characteristics of leaf and coil springs. Increases in fatigue life up to 800% are often obtained. The process is also used extensively on gears, driveshafts, crankshafts, torsion bars, axles, ball studs, high-strength fasteners, railroad wheels, and oil well drilling equipment. Often it is applied only at a critical area, such as a fillet radius. Overspray of shot is often permitted. If not, simple masking techniques can be used.

Peening will reduce the notch sensitivity of hard steels. Applied to highly stressed parts prior to chrome and electroless nickel plating, peening acts to prevent any cracks or imperfections in the chrome deposit from spreading into the parent part, and is required by federal specification QQC-320 for plated parts subject to dynamic loading.

The automotive industry uses peening extensively since the moving parts of the drivetrain are subject to cyclical loading. As the industry shifts to lighter weight cars, shot peening can give the industry lighter weight parts with excellent fatigue characteristics. Some special uses of shot peening include building high-performance racing engines from specially shot peened parts and peening aluminum die-cast transmission housings or gearboxes to prevent "leakers" or loss of lubricant through porous wall areas. Bearing surfaces of engine crankshafts are peened to retain lubricants, with the shot indentations acting as minute reservoirs. Fillet radii are also peened on most crankshafts.

The aerospace industry has long used shot peening for the improvement of the fatigue life of landing gear and other structural members. It is used extensively on jet engine parts, such as compressor and turbine blades. Wing and stabilizer skins are formed by peening and then saturation peened for fatigue resistance. Some of this work is done with glass beads, ceramic shot, cast steel shot, and shot produced from conditioned cut wire made of carbon or stainless steel.

Stress-corrosion cracking is a problem that has become critical in recent years as a result of the use of higher strength materials. Failures resulting from such cracks are caused by the complex interaction of corrosive (environmental) attack and sustained tensile stress (residual or applied) at the surface of a metal. Sustained static loadings are present in any thin-walled tank under a constant internal pressure. For example, the hydraulic reservoirs in aircraft landing gear are stressed by internal hydraulic pressure while at rest on the ground. Shot peening is highly effective in helping to prevent stress-corrosion cracking. Since most materials are susceptible to stress-corrosion cracking under specific conditions, parts should be designed for a stress level below the stress-corrosion threshold if possible. Shot peening is also effective in reducing fretting corrosion. It is widely used on bolt and fastener holes in aerospace structures when diameters permit.

Peening is sometimes used to straighten parts that may have become distorted in heat treatment or other operations. Rings that are out of round can sometimes be corrected by peening. Highly machined bulkheads and other large structural shapes that twist or deform as a result of machining operations can sometimes be straightened by judicious peening. The technique used in such cases is to select and peen a critical area that if expanded or elongated will straighten the part. Shot peening is also used to rework shafting to make diameters slightly larger and holes slightly smaller in diameter.

Shot peening is generally performed using cast steel shot, conditioned cut wire shot, or glass beads. Most controlled shot peening is done with cast steel shot.

Conditioned cut wire shot, also allowable under the military specification, is a wrought material that breaks down more slowly than cast steel shot and may produce better surface finishes for some applications; it is also more expensive than cast steel shot.

Selection of the shot size depends upon the thickness of the work, the appearance desired, the size of fillets, and the intensity desired. At a given velocity, smaller shot will provide a lower intensity, and larger shot, a higher intensity. Also, smaller shot, having more particles per pound, provides coverage more rapidly and is therefore more economical. Peen forming of heavy sections may employ steel balls up to 1/4" (6.4 mm) in diameter or larger. The use of the larger balls provides a smoother finish.

The use of glass beads as a media has good application for peening thin sections requiring low intensities. Steel shot will leave a ferric contamination on aluminum, which can be removed by acid dipping and, in some cases, by overpeening with glass beads; however, this overpeening is not as effective as acid dipping. Because glass beads are inert, they will not contaminate the aluminum. Glass is also effective in peening stainless steel and titanium, provided effective equipment is available to remove broken particles. Consideration should also be given to ceramic shot. Tests indicate ceramic shot can produce acceptable intensities without as much breakdown as glass beads.

SHOT PROPULSION

Peening media is propelled by two methods: compressed air or centrifugal force. For a discussion of the mechanics of these methods, refer to the preceding dry and wet blasting sections in this chapter.

GRINDING WITH BONDED ABRASIVES

Methods using bonded abrasives to finish parts include grinding with bonded wheels, coated-abrasive grinding, honing, and superfinishing.

GRINDING WITH BONDED WHEELS

Grinding with bonded wheels is a common process for both substantial stock removal and the fine finishing of flat, round, or curved surfaces to close tolerances and desired requirements. This process removes material by means of abrasive grains bonded into solid bodies that are referred to as wheels.

Advantages of grinding with bonded wheels include superior size control and the capability of varying the finish and lay of the surface produced. Since only a minimum force is exerted on the workpieces in finish grinding, there is little if any distortion. The process is easily automated, and rough and finish grinding can often be combined in a single operation.

COATED-ABRASIVE GRINDING

Coated abrasives are multipoint cutting tools available in sheet, disc, roll, belt, and other forms. They are used extensively for both heavy and light stock removal. Finishing operations performed include deburring, deflashing, blending, surface finishing, and polishing. Polishing operations with coated-abrasive belts and flap wheels are discussed in a preceding section of this chapter.

The versatility of coated-abrasive products results from their wide range in flexibility, sizes available, and adaptability to manual, semiautomatic, or automatic operation.

Coated-abrasive products, especially belts, are being used for a wide variety of finishing applications. New abrasives, backings, and bonds, as well as improved machines, are continuously expanding the use of coated-abrasive products. Materials finished with coated abrasives include practically all

GRINDING WITH BONDED ABRASIVES

metals (both ferrous and nonferrous), glass, stone, concrete, wood, leather, ceramics, and plastics. Abrasives of finer grit size are used for finishing; but for maximum efficiency and economy, the coarsest grit that will produce the required finish should be used.

HONING

Honing is a controlled, low-velocity abrasive process using bonded-abrasive stones, sometimes called sticks, to remove stock and improve surface finishes. The process is used for both heavy and light stock removal.

In addition to removing stock, honing serves the important purpose of generating specified functional characteristics for surfaces and involves the correction of errors resulting from previous operations. Functional characteristics generated by honing include geometric accuracy (diametric roundness and straightness, and axial straightness), dimensional accuracy, and surface character (roughness, lay pattern, and integrity). Ten common bore errors caused by machining, heat treating, or workholding are illustrated in Fig. 45-26. Honing can correct all of these conditions with the least possible amount of material removal.

The most common application of honing is on internal cylindrical surfaces. For simplicity, such surfaces will be used throughout most of this section to explain the process. However, honing is also used to generate functional characteristics on external cylindrical surfaces, flat surfaces, truncated spherical surfaces, and toroidal surfaces (both internal and external). A characteristic common to all these shapes is that they can be generated by a simple combination of motions.

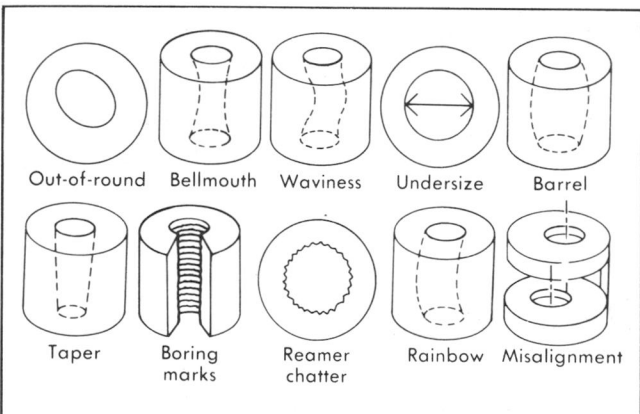

Fig. 45-26 Ten common bore errors that can be corrected by honing. (*Sunnen Products Co.*)

Materials and Parts Honed

Any metallic material can be honed including cast iron, all types of steel and carbides, brass, bronze, aluminum, chromium, and silver, as well as many nonmetallic materials such as glass, ceramic, and plastics. Hardness of the material does not limit the honing process, it only affects the rate at which the stock may be removed.

With fixtured honing equipment, the smallest part believed to have been honed to date is 0.060″ (1.52 mm) diam. The maximum bore size honed to date is 60″ (1524 mm) diam and 52 ft (15.8 m) long. The only honing limitation for part size is the

machine on which the tool is mounted. On manual or power-stroked honing equipment, the diameter range is about 0.060 to 6.000″ (1.52 to 152.4 mm).

Any amount of material can be removed by honing. However, if roughing operations used to locate the bore prior to honing can remove stock more economically, then a minimum of material should be left for honing. For parts such as long steel tubing, 4 to 30 ft (1.2 to 9.1 m) in length, honing is often the only practical and economical method of machining the bore.

Related Processes

There are several processes that are similar to yet different than conventional honing.

Plateau honing. This honing process is a method of producing a special plateau finish, having the surface peaks removed, but retaining the deep valleys. Such a finish has been found desirable in engine performance because the valleys act as oil reservoirs for improved lubrication, especially during engine break-in.

A plateau finish is produced by first rough honing to final size. Then the surface is finished with a finer grit stone for about 45 seconds, depending upon the amount of plateauing desired. The plateauing operation, with a 600 grit stone, removes so little stock that the bore diameter is not measurably increased.

Single-stroke process. This process is a fast and accurate method of sizing certain bores to final size. The tool used is an expandable, diamond-plated or CBN sleeve mounted on a tapered arbor. The sleeve is expanded only during setup, and no adjustments are necessary during honing. The rotating tool is pushed through the bore only one time, with the workpiece being removed after the return stroke.

This process is limited with respect to the types and volumes of material that can be removed. The size and volume of the chips produced must be no more than the spaces between the diamond grits on the sleeve; otherwise, the tool will seize in the bore of the workpiece. The process is best suited for interrupted or short bores that produce a low volume of chips, and is most successful for honing cast iron.

External honing. This process is used to polish and improve the surface finish on the outside diameters of cylindrical workpieces. Instead of using reciprocating tools, as in conventional inside-diameter honing, cup or flat abrasive wheels or stock hones arranged in opposed vees are used. While surfaces can be finished faster with cylindrical or centerless grinding, honing is often preferred because of the desirable surface character (smoothness and lay pattern) obtained and the elimination of damage to surfaces through the use of lower speeds and gentler action.

Flat honing. This process produces burr-free, smooth, flat surfaces with multidirectional patterns. Workpieces are allowed to float while being guided over or between honing wheel faces. On two-wheel machines (see Fig. 45-27), both sides of the workpieces can be finished simultaneously, while maintaining precise tolerances with respect to flatness, parallelism, and thickness. Machines used differ from disc grinders (face grinding machines) in that the wheels move at a slower speed and the abrading action is more gentle, resulting in little if any surface damage.

Edge honing, rounding, and deburring. Machines are available to hone the edges of carbide and ceramic cutting tool inserts without chipping them. Inserts can be rounded on one side or, with a two-wheel machine, on both sides. The rounded edges produced are multiple-radius, compound curves that

GRINDING WITH BONDED ABRASIVES

Fig. 45-27 Two-wheel flat honing machine. (*Peter Wolters of America*)

produce good results and long life in machining operations.

The machines used are similar to those for external and flat honing. On two-wheel machines, three independent drives are provided to operate the lower wheel, upper wheel, and work-holder. Each insert is held and guided in a separate aperture of the workpiece carrier. Wheels used are generally fine-grit silicon carbide in a rubberlike, resilient bond. Pressure is applied through an adjustable pneumatic device.

Gear-tooth honing. This process is performed to correct the geometry and improve the surface finish of hardened spur or helical gears. Honing can correct errors in profile, lead, and eccentricity, as well as oversize conditions resulting from heat treating, but cannot correct tooth spacing errors. The process also removes nicks and burrs, and generally reduces the noise generated in the operation of the gears.

SUPERFINISHING

Superfinishing, also referred to as microfinishing, microstoning, superfinish honing, short-stroke honing, and microhoning, is a low-temperature abrading process, closely related to honing, for producing smooth, long-wearing surfaces. The process uses bonded-abrasive, stick-type stones for cylindrical work or cup wheels for flat and spherical work, with finer grit sizes (320 to 6000) than honing generally being used. When using cup wheels, the process is practically the same as flat honing, discussed in the preceding section of this chapter.

Superfinishing produces controlled surface conditions involving size, finish, geometry, and metallurgical structure. The resulting optically smooth surfaces are metallurgically free of any fragmented, amorphous, or smeared metal from previous operations. The process also corrects inequalities in workpiece geometries, such as grinding flats, and restores surface integrity by eliminating surface stresses and burns. Surface finishes of 0.5 μin. (0.013 μm) or less are being produced, with roundness held to 0.000040" (0.00102 mm) and sphericity to 0.000010" (0.00025 mm).

Superfinishing is efficient in the surface refinement of cylindrical, flat, spherical, and cone-shaped parts. Although it is not primarily a dimension-changing process, stock averaging 0.0002 to 0.001" (0.005 to 0.03 mm) on diameter is removed. With multistage operation and synthetic diamond or cubic boron nitride (CBN) abrasives, stock removal to 0.004"(0.10 mm) is being achieved.

Almost any reasonable depth of scratch pattern can be produced, from practically none at all (mirror finish) to 30 μin. (0.76 μm) or more. The smoother finishes do not have sufficient scratches to exhibit any directional effect; they react the same to every direction of movement. When an intentional scratch pattern is produced, it will be a crosshatch at an angle or almost perpendicular to any normal direction of motion. Such patterns are desirable from the standpoint of reduction in friction or galling when surfaces rub together, as in bearing applications, or for better retention of lubricant.

Both general-purpose and high-production superfinishing machines are available for application of the process to almost any reasonably symmetrical surface. Multistep machines are also available for successive roughing and finishing. The high degree of surface improvement by superfinishing is often achieved at a lower overall cost than with other methods because only a short time is required to obtain the finish, there is a smaller percentage of rejection for reworking or complete loss, and the process usually offers a more reliable operation.

Cylindrical Superfinishing

In grinding, only a line contact is in effect; while in superfinishing, a large area of abrasive contact is employed (see Fig. 45-28). For example, on small cylindrical work, the usual superfinishing method uses a stone that is 25 to 60% of the part diameter in width, and often the same length as that of the surface to be refined. With such a large area of contact, grinding imperfections, such as chatter and feed lines, are completely removed, together with any smearing or burning.

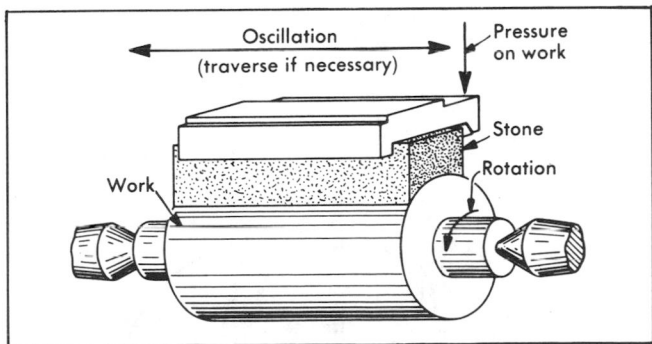

Fig. 45-28 Motions in superfinishing.

Centerless Short-Stroke Honing

With centerless through-feed machines (see Fig. 45-29), one or more fine-grit stones contact about 60 to 70° of the total workpiece circumference. Stone pressure varies from 15 to 175 psi (103 to 1207 kPa), workpiece rotation from 500 to 6000 rpm, feed rates to 280 ipm (7 m/min), oscillation frequency from 500 to 3000 double strokes per minute, and stroke length from 0.039 to 0.315" (0.99 to 8.00 mm). These machines can be

GRINDING WITH BONDED ABRASIVES

computer controlled and equipped with automatic preprocess and postprocess gaging.

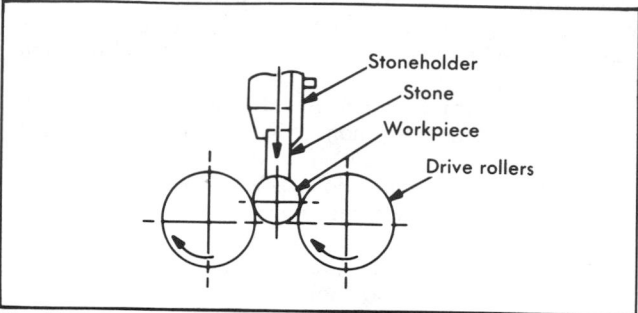

Fig. 45-29 Centerless short-stroke honing.

Finishing Bearing Races

One common method of finishing bearing raceways uses the centerless shoe principle. Two carbide shoes are applied on the ID of an inner race (see Fig. 45-30, view *a*) or on the OD of an outer race (view *b*). The shoes have a highly polished surface to avoid cold working the races. The races may be driven by friction clamp or magnetic drivers. The centerline of the drive spindle is offset slightly from the centerline of the bearing race, preventing any eccentricity or runout of the driven spindle from being transmitted to the bearing race. This design also forces the race downward for more positive seating against the shoes.

In another method of superfinishing the ball and roller paths of bearing races, the races are held in hydrocentric chucks, where they rotate on a film of pressurized oil (see Fig. 45-31). For ball bearing races, the stone is pivoted; for roller bearing races, the stone is reciprocated. These operations are generally performed in two steps, first with a roughing stone and then with a finer polishing stone. During the last few revolutions of the races in the finishing step, stone motion is slowed. This slowing of the stone motion eliminates crosshatched surfaces, leaving only annular lines invisible to the naked eye and resulting in quiet bearing operation.

Flat and Spherical Superfinishing

Both flat and spherical superfinishing, similar to flat honing (discussed previously in this chapter), are performed with a

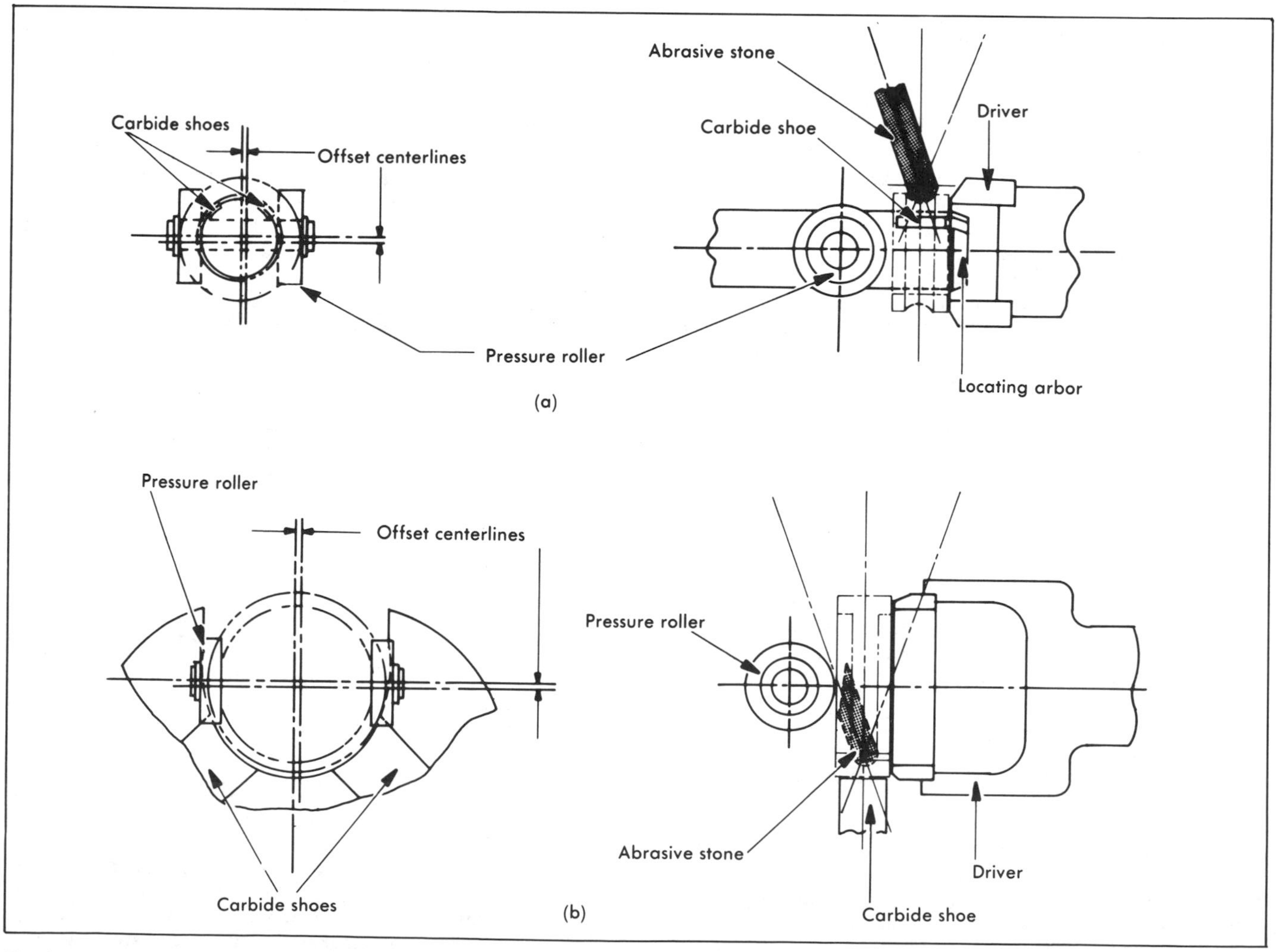

Fig. 45-30 Centerless shoe method of finishing bearing raceways. (*Ex-Cell-O Corp., Micromatic Operations*)

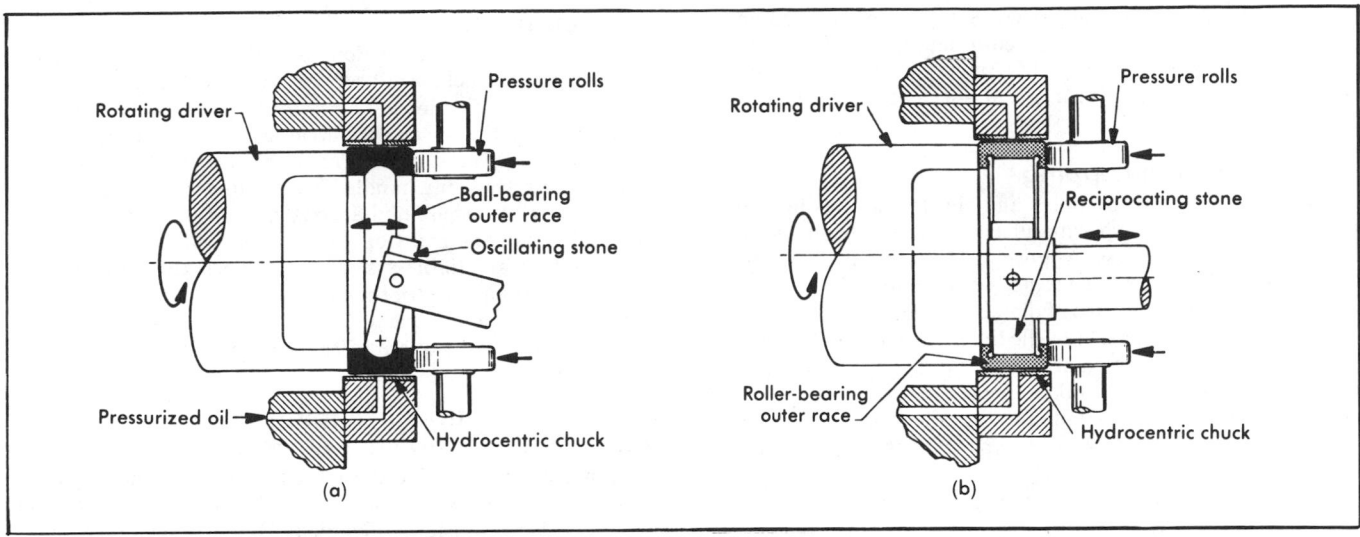

Fig. 45-31 Superfinishing of (a) ball bearing races and (b) roller bearing races. (*Thielenhaus Microfinishing Corp.*)

machine (see Fig. 45-32) containing an upper and a lower vertical, rotating spindle. The upper spindle has a spring or hydraulically loaded quill on which the cup-shaped stone is located, while the lower spindle carries the work. Positions of work and stone can be reversed. As the work revolves, the end face of the cup is brought into contact with the work. Some degree of offset is given the cup with relation to the work position so that the path of any grit is not repeated.

When the two spindles are exactly parallel, the combined effect of both stone and work revolution results in the generation of flatness. If the upper spindle is adjusted to some angularity with the lower, a spherical shape is generated. As in cylindrical work, the stone automatically wears to the most desirable shape.

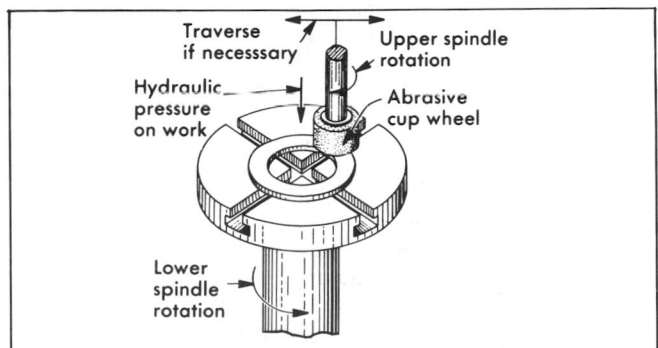

Fig. 45-32 Basic features of a flat superfinishing machine.

FINISHING WITH LOOSE ROLLING ABRASIVES

Lapping is a low-velocity abrading process that removes controlled, very small amounts of material. It is accomplished with loose abrasive grains (usually retained in a viscous or liquid media, called the vehicle) between a tooling plate or wheel, called the lap, and the work surface to be finished.

Lapping and free-abrasive machining use the same basic techniques, but there are several different designs of machines employed for the processes. Some manufacturing personnel feel that the distinction between the two processes is as follows: with lapping, material is removed by abrasive grains that have been embedded in the lap; with free-abrasive machining, material is removed by rolling abrasive grains. However, this distinction is not always the case. For example, abrasive grains do not become embedded in hardened steel laps.

Basic lapping machines are usually of open-face design with pressure between the lap and work surfaces applied by hand or weights; these machines can be equipped with liquid cooling of the lap. Other lapping and free-abrasive machines are equipped for applying pneumatic pressure and with pumps to constantly replenish the laps with abrasive.

LAPPING

Lapping is generally a final finishing operation that results in four major refinements in the workpiece: (1) extreme accuracy of dimension, (2) correction of minor imperfections of shape, (3) refinement of surface finish, and (4) close fit between mating surfaces. The life of moving parts that are subject to wear can be greatly increased by eliminating the hills and valleys on workpiece surfaces and creating a maximum percentage of bearing area. Besides developing a workpiece that meets the surface finish requirements and is correct for geometrical and dimensional accuracy, there is no distortion, as lapping procedures do not require the use of magnetic chucks or other holding or clamping devices.

In normal lapping operations, less heat is generated than in most other finishing operations, thus minimizing the possibility of rehardened and decarburized areas on hardened or heat-treated parts. When both sides of a flat piece are lapped in the same operation, extreme accuracy in flatness and parallelism can be accomplished; and by removing the same amount of stock from both sides of the part simultaneously, any inherent

FINISHING WITH LOOSE ROLLING ABRASIVES

stresses in the piece are equally relieved. In both manual lapping operations and semiautomatic machine lapping operations, the end results depend on many factors, chief of which are: type of lap material, type of lapping medium, speed of lapping motion, and material to be lapped.

Internal or Hole Lapping

Long holes with small bores and short holes having large bores are difficult to lap without encountering bellmouthing and errors in straightness. A loosely fitted lap will cause both these defects. There are two methods of lapping holes. The first calls for a series of solid laps of diameters ranging from the size of the unlapped hole to that of the finished product. The series must be in small increments, depending upon the size of the product, and care must be taken to use each size only until the next larger lap in the series will enter the hole. The other method utilizes an adjustable lap. When size permits, this latter method is quite satisfactory.

Cylindrical Lapping

Vertical lapping machines typically carry one rotating lap and one stationary lap. The lower lap rotates at a speed of not over 300 sfm (90 m/min). The upper lap does not rotate and is free to float and rest upon the work, while the latter rides upon the face of the lower lapping plate. The laps are of heavy ring-type construction, and the lapping pressure is provided by gravity or pneumatically.

Lapping machines of the type shown in Fig. 45-33 can handle both cylindrical and flat lapping operations with the same arrangement of the lapping plates. In flat lapping, a quantity of similar pieces are drawn between the parallel surfaces of the laps, with resulting parallelism imparted to the products.

The principle of lapping multiple parts at one setting results in remarkable size control because the rate of stock removal decreases as more and more of the pieces are finished. It is therefore possible to hold the final size to very close tolerance limits. The resultant accuracy can be as close as 0.00001″ (0.0003 mm) on gage work and 0.000025″ (0.00064 mm) on regular production.

Flat Lapping

Flat machine lapping is done on the same general type of vertical spindle machine as used for cylindrical lapping, except for certain modifications. The motion given to flat work is comparable to that given an individual piece when one face is being lapped by hand. However, because a large quantity of similar parts are being handled at one time and both sides of each piece are surfaced simultaneously, the resultant parallelism and uniformity of dimension are finer than can be obtained by hand lapping, and flatness is equal to the best that can be done by hand. Lapping time for the entire load is little more than that required for lapping one side of one piece. Therefore, the efficiency is proportionate to the quantity of parts that can be handled.

Flat and Cylindrical Lapping with Bonded-Abrasive Wheels

In machines similar to those used for flat honing (see Fig. 45-27), two bonded-abrasive lapping wheels rotate on precision spindles having adjustable alignment. Hydraulic cylinders raise and lower the upper lap and actuate the diamond trueing device, which trues the laps while they are both rotating. Lapping pressure can be regulated to suit the product. Two-wheel lapping machines are available with electronically controlled hydraulic pressure systems, permitting infinitely variable working pressures during the preload portion of the cycle.

Centerless Lapping with Bonded-Abrasive Wheels

Machines of the type shown in Fig. 45-34 are a refinement of centerless grinding to provide higher surface finish on straight cylindrical objects. An extra-long grinding wheel and regulating wheel are provided to allow the work to remain in abrading contact longer than is necessary for regular centerless grinding. The wheel spindles are swiveled so that, when trued, they form a mild hourglass shape. This shape results in a line of contact at an angle with the axis of the work, with a wraparound effect upon the latter.

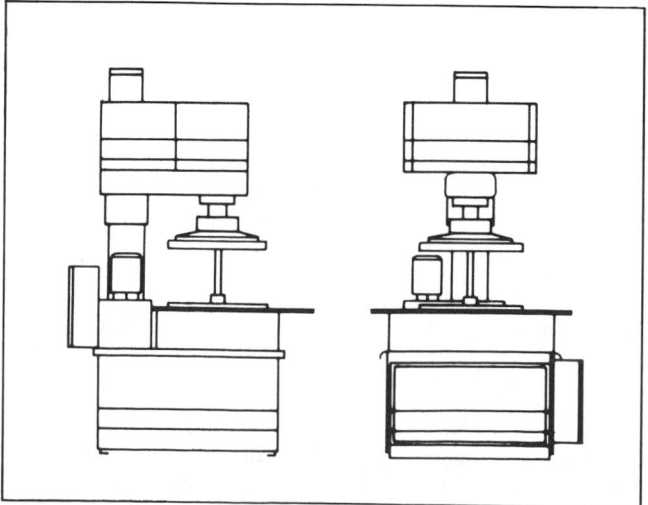

Fig. 45-33 Double-wheel lapping machine. (*Spitfire Tool and Machine Co.*)

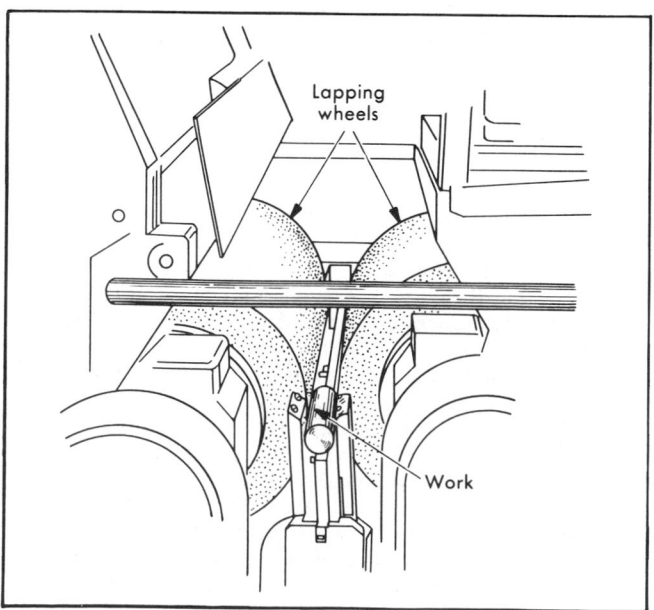

Fig. 45-34 Setup for centerless lapping.

Spherical Lapping

The lapping of spherical surfaces other than balls, shown diagrammatically in Fig. 45-35, view *a*, uses a lap that is the counterpart of the surface to be finished. When used for lapping hardened steel, the lap may be of cast iron of suitable proportions, cut with a concave or convex surface to suit the work. The lap is carried in a machine similar to a drill press. A crank of suitable throw is held in the chuck. The crankpin is furnished with a ball end that enters freely into a blind hole in the back of the lap, on the centerline of the curved surface. With the workpiece in line with the drill spindle, the latter is rotated, thus gyrating the lap. The lap itself must be heavy enough to provide the lapping pressure.

Another method of lapping convex spherical surfaces, shown in Fig. 45-35, view *b*, consists of having a pair of rotatable spindles at an angle to each other. The lap is rigidly attached to one spindle, and the work to the other. Axial alignment must be accurate in order to generate a true radius. One spindle must be free to slide, to take up wear and apply the necessary pressure. The lap in this instance can be of ring formation, with only the rim concave. This method is used for generating spherical surfaces in the manufacture of lenses and makes use of diamond wheels as the abrading medium.

FREE-ABRASIVE MACHINING

Free-abrasive machining, also called lapping, is a process for removing hard material by the action of abrasive grains, suspended in oil or water, that are interposed between a rotating wheel and the workpieces. As the wheel rotates, carrying the loose abrasive across the face of the work, it removes stock from the work—often as effectively and efficiently as a conventional grinding wheel. The process is frequently considered competitive with conventional grinding, especially for stock removal from flat surfaces. It is also used extensively for applications that are impractical for conventional grinding and machining. Typical application examples include the machining of solid materials, extremely thin work, and parts that might distort if clamped or magnetized. Plastics, glass, ceramics, and nonmagnetic material are also surface ground by free-abrasive machining.

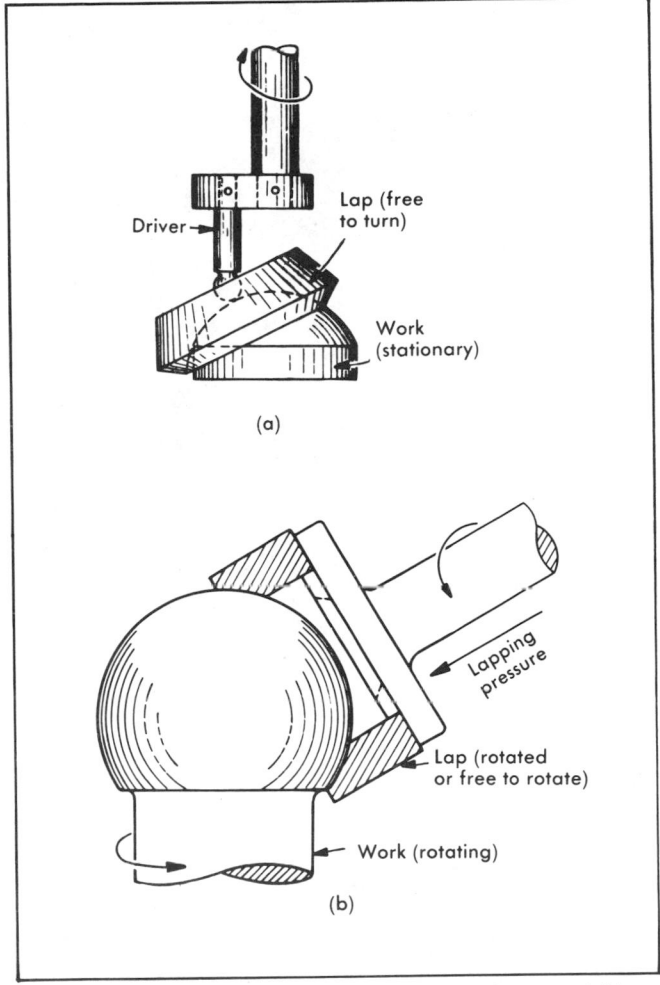

Fig. 45-35 Spherical lapping motions: (a) work stationary and (b) work rotating.

CHEMICAL CLEANING AND FINISHING

Cleaning is the process of removing objectionable matter from the surfaces of manufactured products. Drawing and stamping lubricants, cutting fluids, heat treatment scale and oxides, and fingerprints are typical of soils that must be removed.

Important reasons for adequate cleaning of components and products are as follows:

- As an intermediate step to facilitate manufacturing operations, like inspection and assembly.

- To prepare surfaces for subsequent operations such as coating.

- As a final finish, to improve performance, appearance, and salability.

SELECTING A CLEANING PROCESS

No one cleaner or cleaning method is best for all applications because of the many variables, including the workpiece, the contaminants, and the requirements. Successful surface preparation for subsequent coating operations often requires the use of more than one type of cleaner and operation. For example, a solvent or alkaline cleaner may be used to remove oil, and then an acid cleaner used to provide an oxide-free surface.

Important considerations in selecting a cleaning material and/or method include the following:

- Workpiece material, size, and shape.
- Contaminants to be removed and their adherence to the surfaces.

- Degree of cleanliness required.
- Subsequent operations to be performed, including the type of coating to be applied.
- Quality and hardness of the water to be used for cleaning.
- Production requirements.
- Floor space available.
- Efficiency and economy of the cleaning method and material.
- Environmental and safety considerations, including the disposal of spent solutions.

Table 46-1 presents some metal cleaning processes used for various purposes.

CHEMICAL CLEANING

Chemical cleaning is the most widely used method of providing a suitable surface for subsequent finishing by phosphating, electroplating, organic coating, or other coating processes. Chemical cleaning usually depends upon the use of solvents or a chemical action between the cleaning material and the contaminant.

SOLVENT CLEANERS

Solvents are derived from coal or petroleum and vary in naphthenic and aromatic content. Glycol derivatives are water soluble and may be used to add solvency to water-based cleaners. While aromatic solvents are primarily used directly as solvent cleaners, some are also used in alkaline and acid cleaners.

Certain soils containing oils, fats, and waxes can be removed with organic solvents by the mechanism of solvency. The solvents used for this purpose are of three types:

1. Petroleum solvents such as kerosene, naphtha, or stoddard solvent, applied by wiping or immersion.
2. Nonflammable solvents, generally chlorinated, such as trichloroethane or perchlorethylene, used in vapor degreasers, discussed later in this chapter.
3. Specially formulated solvents, such as emulsion cleaners, emulsifiable solvents, or di-phase cleaners, which allow the use of water-solvent mixtures.

ALKALINE CLEANERS

Alkaline cleaners are most widely used for the removal of metalworking compound soils in soak cleaning and spray cleaning operations. They are also used for barrel cleaning, electrocleaning, and ultrasonic cleaning (discussed later in this chapter). They are generally used to remove soils for in-process cleaning and to prepare metals for operations such as painting or plating.

Alkaline cleaners have the advantage of being economical. They can remove insoluble solid soils, water-soluble soils, and oily soils, and they can be rinsed with water. Alkaline cleaners can be formulated to operate at room or elevated temperature, depending upon the soil conditions. They can also be formulated for immersion or spray applications and for minimal or no attack on metals. Accurate

CHEMICAL CLEANING

TABLE 46-1

**Metal Cleaning Processes Typically Used for
Various Purposes (Listed in Order of Decreasing Preference)**[1]

Types of Production	In-Process Cleaning	Preparation for Painting	Preparation for Phosphating	Preparation for Plating
Removal of pigmented drawing compounds:[a]				
Occasional or intermittent	Hot-emulsion hand slush, spray emulsion in single stage, vapor slush degrease.[b]	Boiling alkaline, blow off, hand wipe. Vapor slush degrease, hand wipe. Acid clean.[c]	Hot-emulsion hand slush, spray emulsion in single stage, hot rinse, hand wipe.	Hot alkaline soak, hot rinse (hand wipe, if possible), electrolytic alkaline, cold water rinse.
Continuous high production	Conveyorized spray-emulsion washer.	Alkaline soak, hot rinse, alkaline spray, hot rinse.	Alkaline or acid[d] soak, rinse, alkaline or acid[d] spray, rinse.	Hot emulsion or alkaline soak, rinse, electrolytic alkaline, rinse.
Removal of unpigmented oil and grease:				
Occasional or intermittent	Solvent wipe. Emulsion dip or spray. Vapor degrease. Cold solvent dip. Alkaline dip, rinse, dry or dip in rust preventive.	Solvent wipe. Vapor degrease or phosphoric acid clean.[d]	Solvent wipe. Emulsion dip or spray, rinse. Vapor degrease. Alkaline soak or spray.	Solvent wipe. Emulsion soak, barrel rinse, electrolytic alkaline rinse, hydrochloric acid dip, rinse.
Continuous high production	Automatic vapor degrease. Emulsion, tumble, spray, rinse, dry.	Automatic vapor degrease.	Emulsion power spray, rinse. Vapor degrease. Acid clean.[c]	Alkaline soak, electrolytic alkaline rinse, hydrochloric acid dip, rinse, alkaline soak, rinse.
Removal of chips and cutting fluid:				
Occasional or intermittent	Solvent wipe. Alkaline dip and emulsion surfactant. Stoddard solvent or trichlo-rethylene. Steam.	Solvent wipe. Alkaline dip and emulsion surfactant. Solvent or vapor.	Solvent wipe. Alkaline dip and emulsion surfactant.[f] Solvent or vapor.	Solvent wipe. Alkaline dip, rinse, electrolytic alkaline,[g] rinse, acid dip, rinse.[h]
Continuous high production	Alkaline (dip or spray) and emulsion surfactant.	Alkaline (dip or spray) and emulsion surfactant.	Alkaline (dip or spray) and emulsion surfactant.	Alkaline soak, rinse, electrolytic alkaline,[g] rinse, acid dip and rinse.[h]
Removal of polishing and buffing compounds:				
Occasional or intermittent	Seldom required.	Solvent wipe. Surfactant alkaline (agitated soak), rinse. Emulsion soak, rinse.	Solvent wipe. Surfactant alkaline (agitated soak), rinse. Emulsion soak, rinse.	Solvent wipe. Surfactant alkaline (agitated soak), rinse, electroclean.[i]
Continuous high production	Seldom required.	Surfactant alkaline spray, spray rinse. Agitated soak or spray, rinse.[j]	Surfactant alkaline spray, spray rinse. Emulsion spray, rinse.	Surfactant alkaline soak and spray, alkaline soak, spray and rinse, electrolytic alkaline,[i] rinse, mild acid pickle, rinse.

[a] For complete removal of pigment, parts should be cleaned immediately after the forming operation, and all rinses should be spray when practical.

^b Used only when pigment residue can be tolerated in subsequent operations.
^c Phosphoric acid cleaner-coaters are often sprayed on the parts to clean the surface and leave a thin phosphate coating.
^d Phosphoric acid for cleaning and iron phosphating. Proprietary products for high and low-temperature application are available.
^e Some plating processes may require additional cleaning dips.
^f Neutral emulsion or solvent should be used before manganese phosphating.
^g Reverse-current cleaning may be necessary to remove chips from parts having deep recesses.
^h For cyanide plating, acid dip and water rinse are followed by alkaline and water rinses.
ⁱ Other preferences: stable or diphase emulsion spray or soak, rinse, alkaline spray or soak, rinse, electroclean; or solvent presoak, alkaline soak or spray, electroclean.
^j Third preference: emulsion spray rinse.

control of the effective alkali concentration in the solution is essential for effective cleaning. This control is usually accomplished by simple titration of the alkali content.

The alkali cleaners available differ in composition depending upon the metal to be processed and the method by which they are applied. So-called "heavy duty," uninhibited, highly alkaline cleaners are not suitable for brass, zinc, and aluminum. Cleaners used in spray washers or electrocleaning tanks require special detergents, emulsifying agents, and low-foaming surfactants. These requirements are necessary to prevent excessive foaming caused by aeration in spray washers or the absorption of gases in electrocleaning. For cleaning steel, the cleaner may have a pH value of 9 to 14, depending primarily upon the type of soil.

Alkaline cleaners are formulated for optimum performance and economy. They usually contain alkaline builders, sequestering and chelating agents, and surfactants. They may also contain solvents and corrosion inhibitors for some applications. They are formulated to clean by a combination of mechanisms, including saponification, emulsification, dispersion, chelation, wetting, and solvency.

Low-Temperature Cleaners

The availability of heating can have a profound effect on cleaning. In general, the speed of the chemical reactions in cleaning about doubles with each 20°F (11°C) rise in temperature. This temperature effect is more pronounced in removing buffing compounds, heavy greases, and lubricant residues. In such instances, a temperature above the softening point of the soil should be maintained for effective removal. Lower temperatures can be more easily compensated for in spray cleaning applications owing to the impingement energy of the spray compensating for some loss of chemical cleaning activity. Low-temperature spray cleaners and soak cleaners are readily available.

Electrolytic Cleaning

Another form of alkaline cleaning, electrolytic cleaning or electrocleaning, involves the use of electric current to release gas bubbles on the work surface. These bubbles produce a scrubbing action that, when combined with the selected electrocleaning detergent, results in a high degree of cleaning. The parts to be cleaned are immersed in a hot alkaline solution, 140 to 180°F (60 to 80°C), and current is applied. Basically there are three methods of electrocleaning: cathodic or direct current cleaning, anodic or reverse current cleaning, and periodic reverse current cleaning.

Alkaline Descaling

Alkaline descaling is a cleaning method in which soil, paints, oil, scale, and oxides can be removed from aluminum, zinc, steel, and tin in one operation, eliminating the need for acid descaling, which may introduce hydrogen embrittlement into the metals. This method is normally not recommended for stainless steel, magnesium, copper, brass, and certain other metals. Alkaline descaling operations may be accomplished in tanks or barrels, or with spray equipment or electric current; but they are most effective when used with periodic reverse current electrocleaning. Alkaline descalers (derusters) are often used to remove light rust from steel parts prior to plating. The solutions sometimes contain surfactants to aid in removing light soils or soak cleaner films. Periodic reverse current is required to remove rust.

ACIDIC CLEANERS

Acidic cleaners are designed to remove oxides, rust, flux residues, corrosion products, tarnish films, perspiration stains, and heat scales resulting from forging, heat treating, extruding, welding, soldering, and brazing. Phosphoric acid is the most frequently used acid for cleaning and painting preparation; sulfuric and hydrochloric acids for rust and scale removal; and chromic acid for cleaning zinc, aluminum, and magnesium alloys. In preparing metals for plating, chromic acid is avoided in the pretreatment steps, unless the work is to be chromium plated directly (without intermediate plates of other metals). If plating is not done directly, precautions are required to remove any traces of chromic acid residues from the surface before subsequent activation and plating operations.

Nitric acid alone and/or with hydrofluoric acid is used to deoxidize and remove smuts from aluminum alloys. These two acids are also used to remove scale from stainless steels. Other acids such as gluconic, sulfamic, citric, oxalic, and acetic have specific applications. These acids may be compounded with surface-active agents to increase wetting and detergency, with solvents to permit one-step cleaning and oxide removal, and with inhibitors to prevent attack on base metals. While organic inhibitors are beneficial, they can cause problems in subsequent operations, especially in plating lines, if improperly controlled or inadequately rinsed.

RINSING

Factors that determine whether a rinse is necessary after cleaning include: the type of cleaning materials used, the next processing step, and the destination of the workpieces. If the next step is painting and the cleaning has been done with an alkaline solution, then rinsing and a neutralizing dip are necessary. If the parts are to be stored and have been cleaned in a solvent material, then rinsing is normally not required.

Most rinsing operations consist of water only, although proprietary rinse aids are available that may be used in conjunction with the water. Most water contains varying

CHEMICAL CLEANING

quantities of chlorides, sulfates, and carbonates of such metals as calcium, magnesium, and iron. These materials may cause spotting or contamination of plating solutions used in subsequent finishing. Water-softening equipment is suitable for preparing hard water for use as rinse water; but deionized water, although it is more expensive, may be desirable for rinses preceding bright plating, chromium plating, and anodizing solutions. Wetting agents or antispotting additives can be used to prevent spotting or rusting in recesses and blind holes during subsequent drying. Reclamation of used rinse water is often necessary for maximum economy of water use, as well as for compliance with waste disposal regulations.

DRYING

As previously mentioned, heating of the rinse water facilitates drying. For parts that do not readily dry upon removal from the final rinse stage, a dryoff station is often required. The two most common drying methods are a forced blowoff with room temperature air or a heated, recirculating air dryer. Heated air is generally preferable because it permits faster drying and reduces air and floor space requirements. The temperature of heated air for drying is usually limited to a maximum of 170° F (75° C).

PROCESSES AND EQUIPMENT

The primary methods of cleaning workpieces are by hand, by immersion (dipping or soaking), by spraying, or by a combination of immersion and spraying. Automated process lines incorporating cleaning, rinsing, and drying are often used for high-production requirements. Selection of the type of chemical cleaner to be used depends upon the method of application.

Hand Cleaning

Chemical cleaning by hand wiping or scrubbing is less commonly used than other methods because of high labor costs, but it has advantages for some applications. It requires only simple, low-cost equipment, such as common mops, sponges, brushes, and cloths; but it is labor intensive and restricted by OSHA regulations. When strongly acidic or caustic cleaners are used, resistant pails and protective clothing for workers are required.

Immersion Cleaning

Chemical cleaning by workpiece immersion (dipping or soaking) is a simple and efficient process that is used extensively. It is performed in tanks, barrels, or drums, with heated or unheated chemical solutions. Tanks are the predominant means for chemical cleaning, with barrels and drums being more commonly used in plating operations. Installations vary from a single, unheated tank to multistage systems (see Fig. 46-1) having heated and agitated solutions.

Advantages. When immersion tanks, barrels, and drums are constructed of proper materials, they can be used for emulsion, alkaline, electrolytic, and acidic cleaning, as well as for pickling. The immersion process is well suited to cleaning castings, weldments, machined parts, and some sheet metal components. Workpieces in a wide variety of shapes, sizes, and weights can be processed.

Limitations. Drag-out losses of chemical solution from immersion equipment can be high, contaminating the water used for subsequent rinsing and increasing the cost of treating the effluent for disposal. Immersion cleaning often requires higher solution concentrations, higher operating temperatures,

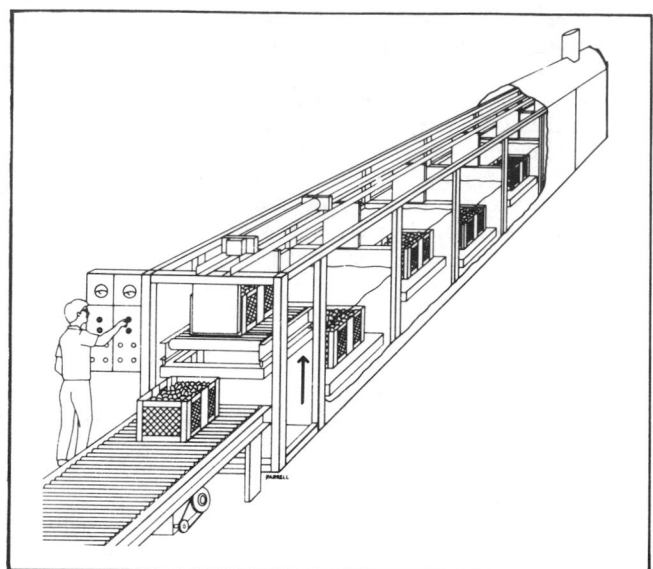

Fig. 46-1 Multistage processing line for chemical cleaning. (*Automated Chemical Systems Corp.*)

and longer cycle times than spray cleaning.

Spray Cleaning

Spray cleaning consists of impinging the spray of a cleaning solution upon the workpieces to remove unwanted soil. Machines used for spray cleaning, called spray washers, have a pump to pressurize the solution, a reservoir tank, connecting piping, spray nozzles, and, generally, some means for moving the workpieces or nozzles and for heating the solution. Multistage washers often have zones for cleaning, rinsing, and drying the parts. Drainage corridors should be provided between stations to facilitate drainage and reduce drag-out.

Advantages. An important advantage of spray cleaning is that high-production rates are possible, especially with similarly shaped workpieces. Clean solution is directed onto the work surfaces, and impingement of the pressurized solution assists in the cleaning operation.

Cleaner consumption is less than with immersion methods because the solution can be recirculated many times and solution concentration can often be lower. With proper draining time, drag-out losses of solution are minimal; and with proper workholding, uniform cleaning results are obtained. Spray cleaning is also ideal for light sheet metal parts that tend to float in immersion tanks.

Limitations. Equipment costs for spray washers are higher than for immersion tanks, and hence high-production requirements are generally necessary for economic justification. Also, more floor space and maintenance are generally required, and energy costs are usually higher. In addition, safety considerations limit the use of combustible petroleum solvents in spray washers.

Spray washers require regular maintenance. The nozzles must be free of all obstructions and properly aligned at all times. Pumps should be kept in good repair and provided with double screens between the cleaning solution and the pump intake to reduce plugging of the nozzles and to prolong pump life. Since foaming can be a problem with spray cleaning, the cleaners used should be specially formulated for low foaming.

STEAM AND FLAME CLEANING

Steam and flame cleaning are less commonly used than the conventional chemical cleaning methods previously described. However, these processes are desirable for certain applications; for example, they are used to clean large and heavy parts that are difficult to move or that cannot be conveniently accommodated in immersion tanks or spray washers. These methods are also used to preclean some parts that are especially difficult to clean. Both steam and flame cleaning are faster than manual cleaning, and the portability of the equipment used is advantageous for some applications.

STEAM CLEANING

Steam cleaning, a variation of spray cleaning, is the application of a hot blast of steam and cleaning solution on parts to remove soil. The live, pressurized steam moves through an eductor, thereby creating a vacuum that picks up the cleaning solution. This type of cleaning offers several advantages over manual and immersion methods by combining three effective cleaning agents: heat, pressure, and chemical action. Heat speeds up and generally increases the cleaning action of any operation. Pressure provides force at the point of impact to loosen soils, making them easier to remove. Chemical action is provided by a material that chemically attacks soils, by either saponification or emulsification, also easing and speeding their removal.

FLAME CLEANING

In flame cleaning, flames from an oxyacetylene torch are used to remove loose mill scale and rust. The flames are played over the metal surface, and the sudden temperature increase causes the scale to expand and flake away. Flame cleaning may also be used to burn off oils that will not leave heavy smut and to dry water from the metal surface. Any residue, loosened scale, or rust left after flame cleaning is usually removed by wire brushing. Flame cleaning must be closely controlled to prevent overheating of the metal surface with consequent surface hardening or changes in metallurgical properties. The flames used should be adjusted to have a neutral characteristic. Traverse of the flame on work surfaces should be fast enough to prevent fusing of the scale and foreign matter to the surfaces; however, a slow traverse is often necessary to clean heavily scaled or rusted surfaces. Flame cleaning is not generally applicable to thin sections that are subject to warping. The process is an alternative to blast cleaning, but results obtained are not usually as good.

VAPOR DEGREASING

Vapor degreasing is a method of dissolving solvent-soluble and other soils, such as oils and greases, from the surfaces, crevices, and capillaries of metal, porcelain, and plastics products. Parts at ambient temperatures are brought into contact with hot solvent vapors, causing the vapors to condense on the parts. This condensation results in a liquid flow over the surface and throughout the part. The high rate of condensation results in an erosion effect that helps remove some nonsoluble soils like carbon black and lint. The solvents cannot dissolve inorganics such as oxides, salts, or smut.

PROCESS ADVANTAGES

With the proper degreasing equipment and solvent, vapor degreasing is a proven, economical, and reliable method for cleaning many manufactured components. It produces a dry surface free of organic contamination and is often the preferred method for most finishing operations, without further treatment.

The vapor degreasing process can be used to clean all common industrial metals, including all types of cast iron, steels, copper, brass, bronze, zinc, aluminum, magnesium, nickel, lead, tin, titanium, and their alloys. As the process is primarily a physical rather than a chemical method, there is no detrimental chemical attack or etching of highly polished surfaces or delicate metal parts. Vapor degreasing also has the advantage of being able to clean assemblies and workloads containing parts of different metals. With the proper choice of solvents, many other materials, such as glass and plastics, can be cleaned as individual components or in assemblies.

Solvent vapor degreasing is often the most economical method of cleaning because of the low initial cost, minimum floor space requirements, and ease of installing the equipment. Degreasers used according to the equipment manufacturer's recommendations can provide low unit cleaning costs. The major cost of vapor degreasing is the solvent. The major costs of aqueous cleaning include utilities, equipment, and waste water treatment.

LIMITATIONS OF THE PROCESS

Vapor degreasing may not be effective in removing contaminants that are not soluble in solvent or that do not contain a sufficient portion of solvent-soluble material. These contaminants are materials such as metallic salts, oxides, heat treatment and welding scale, graphite or carbonaceous deposits, and certain inorganic soldering, welding, and brazing fluxes.

METHODS OF CLEANING

Basically, there are three variations of vapor degreasing: (1) vapor only, (2) vapor-spray-vapor, and (3) liquid-immersion vapor.

Vapor Only

The simplest vapor degreasing machine uses the straight vapor cycle. The work to be cleaned is lowered into the vapor zone (see Fig. 46-2). When the solvent ceases to drip from the parts, the workload is drawn into the freeboard area. Freeboard is the distance from the established vapor zone to the degreaser lip, where substantially all of the escaping vapors are confined before the cleaned parts are moved to the unloading area.

VAPOR DEGREASING

Vapor-Spray-Vapor

When the workload contains a large surface area, recessed cavities, or blind holes, or when the solid portion of the soil is heavy and not readily removed by the vapors, a more thorough cleaning can be obtained by augmenting the vapor cycle with a forceful spray of clean liquid solvent, referred to as the vapor-spray-vapor cycle. Parts can be sprayed by a hand spray lance in an open-top degreaser (see Fig. 46-3, view *a*), or by fixed banks of multispray nozzles in conveyorized equipment such as a monorail (view *b*).

Liquid-Immersion Vapor

To clean either work of large dimensions—such as tubing, piping, or large heat treatment trays—or small items nested in work baskets, the parts can be immersed in warm solvent, followed by a vapor rinse and dry (see Fig. 46-4). This commonly used cycle produces satisfactory results, especially when the major portion of the soil to be removed is solvent soluble. Ultrasonic devices can also be incorporated in the degreaser, particularly in the clean dip tank, to aid in soil removal.

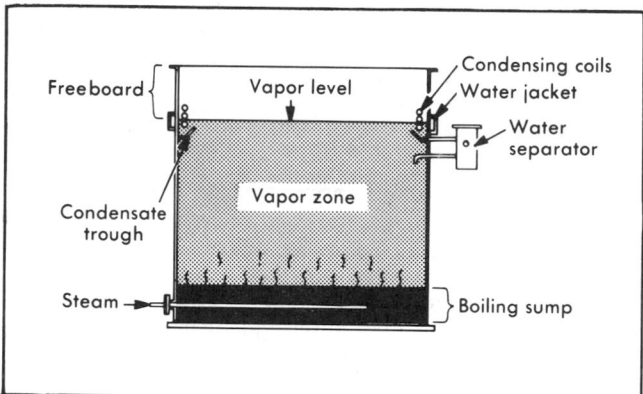

Fig. 46-2 Vapor-only degreaser.

VAPOR DEGREASING SOLVENTS

There are four types of vapor degreasing solvents available and in use today:

1. Trichloroethylene
2. Perchloroethylene
3. 1, 1, 1 - Trichloroethane
4. Methylene Chloride

Trichloroethylene

Trichloroethylene had been the most commonly used solvent for vapor degreasing. Its boiling point of 188° F (87° C) makes vapor hot enough to dissolve most soils. However, this liquid is now regulated as a volatile organic compound (VOC) under the EPA's Clean Air Act and is therefore a nonexempt solvent.

Perchloroethylene

Perchloroethylene is used when a hot vapor, 250° F (121° C), is required, as is the case in removing waxes and tar having high melting temperatures. It is the most costly solvent to heat, requiring steam at 50 to 60 psi (345 to 444 kPa). Any moisture trapped in the workpieces is vaporized, resulting in completely

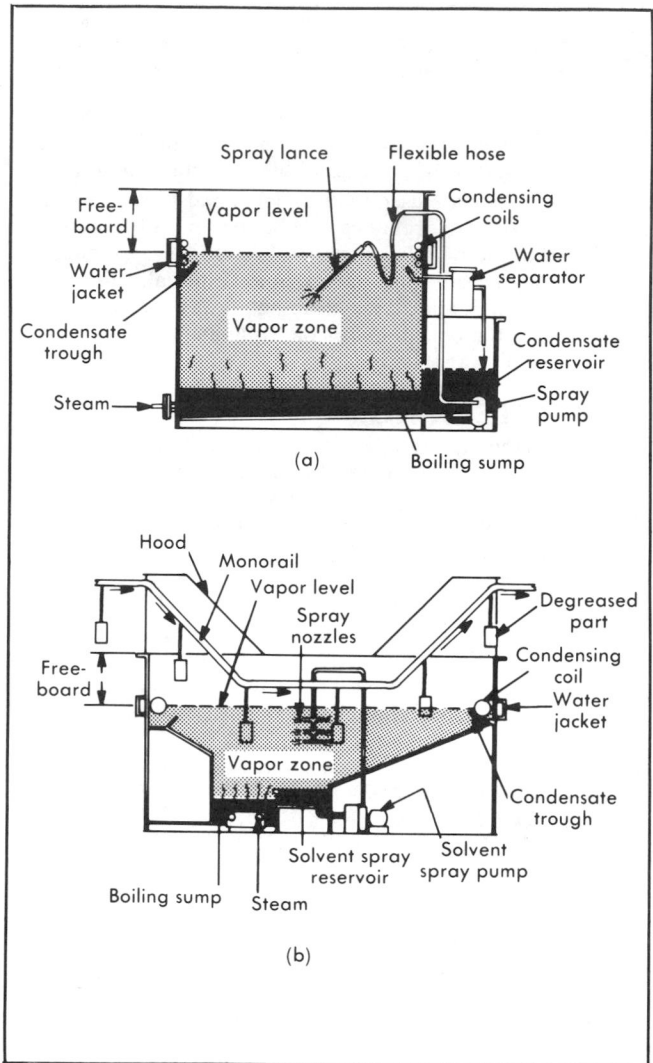

Fig. 46-3 Vapor-spray-vapor degreasers: (a) vertical loading/unloading and (b) equipped with monorail work carrier.

dry parts. However, use of this solvent is also limited by air pollution controls.

1,1,1-Trichloroethane

This solvent has become a replacement for trichloroethylene and perchloroethylene because it is exempt from current (1982) federal Clean Air Act regulations. It can be used to clean such metals as aluminum, magnesium, and zinc, as well as ferrous metals. This solvent is also appropriate when ultrasonic devices are used for vapor degreasing because it has low surface tension, vapor pressure, and specific gravity. For most applications, a frequency of 20 to 25 kHz is used.

Methylene Chloride

The comparatively cool vapors, 104° F (40° C), of methylene chloride solvent make it ideal for cleaning temperature-sensitive parts and lightly soiled components.

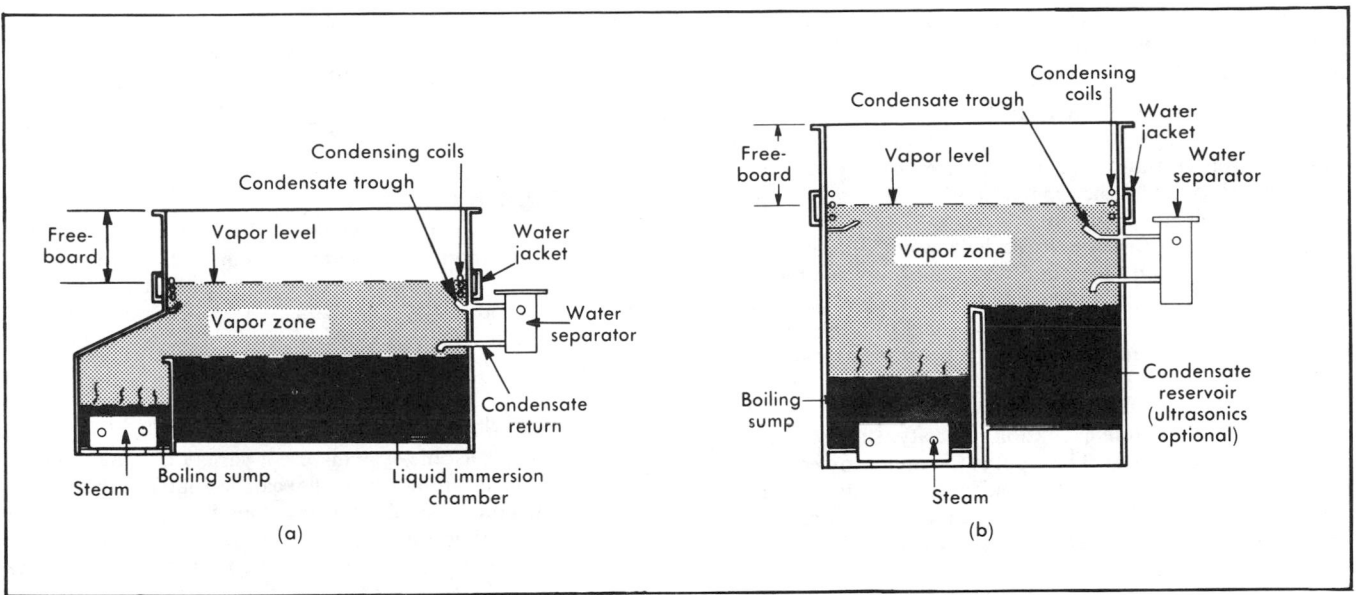

Fig. 46-4 (a) Warm-solvent immersion degreaser; (b) boiling-solvent vapor degreaser.

ULTRASONIC CLEANING

Ultrasonic cleaning uses high-frequency vibrations in a cleaning system. In the process, a cleaning solution is subjected to the rapid oscillation of longitudinal waves, identical to audible sound waves but of higher frequency.

Before ultrasonics can be used effectively, it is important to realize the following:

- Parts to be cleaned must be immersed in a liquid.
- Generally, with a few exceptions, the entire volume of liquid must be supplied with ultrasonic energy.
- The use of ultrasonics does not eliminate the need for cleaning chemicals.

Workpieces to be cleaned are placed in the solution, and the rapid oscillation of the solution resulting from the high-frequency sound waves creates minute vapor voids in the solution that implode against the workpiece and effectively clean its surfaces. Mechanically held contamination is released from the surfaces, soluble materials are rapidly dissolved, and oil and similar contaminants are easily emulsified.

CAVITATION PRINCIPLES

The effect created by the action of ultrasound waves in a liquid cleaning agent is a phenomenon known as cavitation. It consists of the formation and collapse of countless tiny cavities, or vapor voids, in the liquid. These voids occur throughout the liquid, even in recesses, cavities, and holes in the workpieces that the liquid penetrates.

Cavitation is produced by the alternating patterns of compression and rarefaction—high and low pressure points—generated during sound wave half-cycles. During rarefaction, the liquid is stretched beyond its tensile strength, and the pressure is lowered to allow instantaneous vaporization. The cavities formed grow from microscopic nuclei. During the subsequent compression phase, they implode violently. This phenomenon occurs at a rate proportional to the applied ultrasonic frequency, which can range from the ultrasonic threshold up to a practical limit of about 90 kHz.

Although cavitation vacuities are extremely small and release only minute amounts of energy individually, the cumulative effect of millions of implosions per second is intense. Theoretical localized temperatures of 20,000° F (11 093° C) and pressures of 10,000 psi (69 MPa) are created, providing a strong scouring action that can dislodge tenacious soils. Intimate mixing of the cleaning media with the contaminants speeds the rate at which soil is dissolved or dispersed. Cavitation prevents the formation of a neutral film on workpiece surfaces that could impede cleaning and raises the temperature of the liquid, thereby increasing the rate of chemical activity.

The point at which cavitation starts is called the cavitation threshold. It is reached when the applied energy is sufficient to drop the pressure within the liquid below its vapor pressure during rarefaction. The initial quantity of energy required to attain this point varies with different cleaning solutions. Frequency also plays a significant role in the onset of cavitation.

Physical properties of a cleaning agent affect not only its ability to achieve a cavitation threshold, but the intensity of the cavitation process as well. Thus, different cleaning media will cavitate at different levels according to their density, viscosity, surface tension, vapor pressure, and temperature.

SYSTEM COMPONENTS

Industrial ultrasonic cleaning systems are composed of three basic components: (1) a generator, (2) a transducer, and (3) a tank containing the cleaning solution. The generator transforms standard line current of 50 or 60 Hz into a desired higher frequency. This high-frequency current, in turn, is converted into sound waves (mechanical energy) of a corresponding frequency via a transducer, which radiates the waves into a cleaning solution in the tank.

Generator (Power Supply)

Generators differ in the wave forms they emit and in their power output ratings. The best choice for a given system depends primarily on the type, number, and frequency of the transducer elements involved.

Three wave forms are used: half wave, full wave, and continuous wave. Of these, half-wave and full-wave forms are most common. For a full-wave unit, peak power is twice the average power output; for a half-wave generator, four times the average. In a continuous-wave system, peak and average power are the same.

Progressively increasing the power for ultrasonic cleaning tends first to accelerate cavitation intensity, then to quell the process if carried too far. The input of too much power creates a superagitated state in which the liquid near the radiating surface becomes elastic. This phenomenon, called surface cavitation, actually blocks sound wave transmission by preventing coupling.

Transducers

Like tuning forks, transducers are fashioned to generate sound waves of specific frequencies. Different frequencies produce distinct variations in the character and intensity of cavitation. Within the effective cleaning range of ultrasonics, the higher the frequency, the greater the volume of cavitation voids created and the smaller their size. The lower the frequency, the more intense the implosion. For industrial cleaning, frequencies are usually 20 to 40 kHz.

Cleaning Units

There are two major types of ultrasonic cleaning units: integrated and modular. Integrated units have all components, including the tank for the cleaning solution, in a single enclosure. Modular systems consist of a separate generator linked to either tanks equipped with transducers or immersible transducers.

Cleaning Media

Aqueous ultrasonic systems use a variety of water-soluble detergents and cleaning agents that can be diluted with water to the concentration desired. The most common aqueous cleaning media are alkaline detergents, discussed previously in this chapter. Acidic solutions are seldom used in ultrasonic cleaning systems, but there are certain exceptions. One proprietary, mildly acidic cleaner, formulated especially for ultrasonic cleaning, attacks soil combinations such as oxides and light oil residues.

THERMAL ENERGY FINISHING

Burrs and flash, both internal and external, are rapidly burned away by the thermal energy method (TEM), also called thermal energy deburring (TED). Parts to be deburred or deflashed are placed in the chamber (pressure vessel) of a machine in which a gas mixture is ignited to create intense heat.

While the equipment required is more expensive than for more traditional deburring systems, the thermal energy method is the fastest known means of deburring most parts. Burning of the burrs takes less than 20 milliseconds. The usual cycle times for a high-production machine, including loading and unloading, is about 25 seconds. Results achieved are of consistent quality, reducing the need for inspection and subsequent part rejection or rework; and treated parts are free of contaminants.

The process is ideal for metal parts through which fluids or gases must flow. It has the unique ability of deburring blind and intersecting holes, while simultaneously deburring the outside surfaces of parts. Since the process does not use any abrasive media, there is no change in the dimensions of surfaces adjoining the burrs; also, these surfaces are not generally affected by heat. The bodies of most parts processed rarely exceed a temperature of 300°F (150°C). With a watercooled chamber and the fast cycling, only thin parts, such as some stampings, get hot enough to disturb the parent metal. A recast layer that forms at the workpiece-burr interface is usually of negligible thickness—0.00008 to 0.001″ (0.0020 to 0.03 mm); however, this layer may cause cracks in previously hardened steels.

Burrs or flash of uniform thickness, but limited size, are removed completely, down to their roots. With parting lines, however, which generally have a thicker root than a burr, a rounded rise is left on the surface of the part. When designing parts to be thermally deburred, the thinnest sections that have useful functions should be at least 15 times thicker than the burrs. This design limitation is beneficial in that the process will not remove threads, but only slightly round their extreme edges. For most stamped parts, however, which typically have triangular-shaped burrs, the process removes only the tips of the burrs.

Parts to be deburred by the thermal energy method must be free of oil. If oil remains on the parts, it will be burned into the surfaces, leaving a carbon smut that is difficult to remove. Also, blind and tapped holes must be free of compacted chips. If the gas cannot surround each chip, they will not be removed by the process. Another possible limitation is that it is not always possible to achieve specific radii on individual edges. Some edge radiusing is possible on steel and cast iron parts, but is seldom achieved on aluminum or stainless steel workpieces. In many cases, it is possible to remove burrs, but keep edges sharp.

Safety has been no problem with hundreds of machines in use for many years. Nevertheless, local and federal safety regulations require that these machines meet stringent safety codes.

APPLICATIONS

The thermal energy method is being used to deburr and deflash many different parts. Impact of the process on costs, production rates, and suitability of the parts varies with the specific applications. All metals can be treated by TED, but certain metals are more difficult to process. The oxidation resistance of stainless steels, for example, makes them less adaptable to the method. Metals with low thermal conductivity, such as steels and zinc alloys, however, give excellent results.

Iron and Steel Castings

Deburring and deflashing of iron and steel castings are major applications of the thermal energy method. The process is particularly suitable for and offers the most substantial savings with castings having internal intersections of recesses and bores that are difficult to reach. Hydraulic and pneumatic valve bodies are typical castings that are deburred and deflashed by TED.

Zinc Die Castings

A wide variety of zinc die castings are being deburred, deflashed, and cleaned by the thermal energy method. Carburetor components, automotive-lock cylinders, and many other automotive parts are being treated in this way. A major benefit is the consistently high quality obtained. Substantial savings also result because no tooling is necessary and no change in setup is required to handle parts of different shapes or sizes.

Machined Steel Components

Stainless steel valve spools and steel gears are just two of many machined components treated by the thermal energy method. Ring grooves and slots on the valve spools are deburred at the rate of 720 spools per hour, with six spools being handled per cycle. For the gears, burrs are removed from the teeth and from tapped and through holes at the rate of 120 gears per hour.

Plastics

Deflashing and cleaning of plastics parts is a recent development for the thermal energy method. Machines used for such parts operate at lower pressures and temperatures, and gases are monitored more precisely. The chamber is generally evacuated of air before gases are introduced to maintain precise mixtures and to minimize contamination. Temperatures are held to about 2000° F (1095° C); and because of the short duration of the heat, workpiece temperatures rise only approximately 30° F (15° C), with a maximum increase of 100° F (55° C).

Aluminum

Heat sinks used to dissipate heat from electronic modules are one of many aluminum components being deburred by the thermal energy method. Cycle time has been reduced from 15 minutes to 1 minute per unit, and the quality of the heat sinks has been improved.

MACHINES USED

Machines for thermal energy deburring are available with C frames (see Fig. 46-5) or three posts to hold the water-cooled chamber halves together. A mechanical toggle mechanism is provided to clamp and lock the chamber. Machines are now available to handle parts up to 10″ (254 mm) in diameter and 30″ (762 mm) long.

A dial-type indexing table permits unloading and reloading a lower closure (bottom half of the chamber) while parts on another closure are being processed. The number of closure stations on the table depends upon the size of the workpieces and the production requirements.

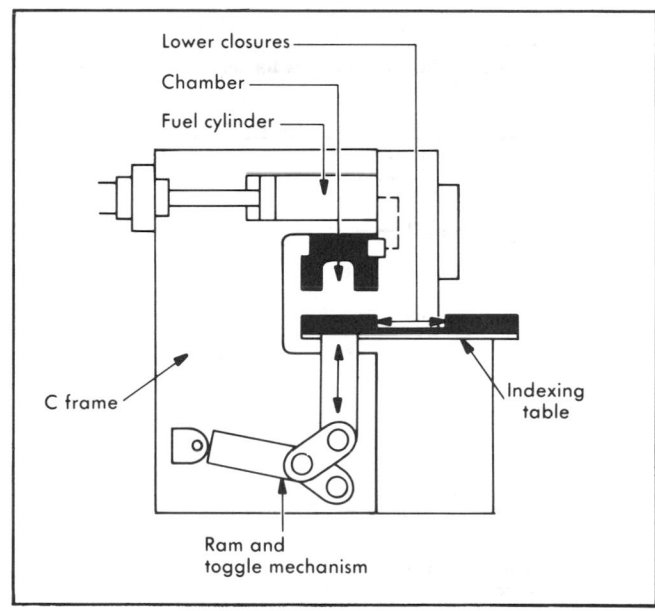

Fig. 46-5 C-frame type machine for thermal energy deburring. (*SurfTran*)

OTHER THERMAL FINISHING METHODS

In addition to the thermal energy method discussed in the preceding section of this chapter, there are several other, less commonly used methods employing heat to deburr and finish parts. These processes include hot wire deflashing, and resistance heat, flame, electrical discharge, plasma, chlorine gas, and laser deburring. Most of these processes are used in very limited applications but are of interest for special requirements.

HOT WIRE DEFLASHING

External edges and the surfaces of large cutouts of thermoplastic parts can be deflashed with an electrically heated thin wire that is moved parallel to the edges and surfaces. The heat in the thin wire melts and removes the flash. Cycle time is proportional to the lineal distance to be trimmed. With some plastics, it should be possible to deflash at a rate of 24 ipm (610 mm/min) or more.

For this process, the heated wire passes over tensioning and drive pulleys (see Fig. 46-6). On most parts, a radius will not be produced on the edges. Typically, a small projection of flash is left. It is possible, however, to produce a chamfer if required.

RESISTANCE HEATING

Heat generated by current passing through a burr can be sufficient to burn away the burr. Workpieces are attached to a power supply (see Fig. 46-7) that provides low-voltage, high-amperage current. The workpiece is attached to the negative side of the electrical source, and a positively charged electrode is placed in contact with the burr. The process can be used for any shape of part, provided electrical current connections can be made. In one application of this process, burrs are removed from gear teeth by using a meshing gear electrode.

Possible limitations of the resistance heating process include the need for the workpieces to be electrically conductive and for the electrode to be movable as the burrs shorten. In addition,

OTHER THERMAL FINISHING METHODS

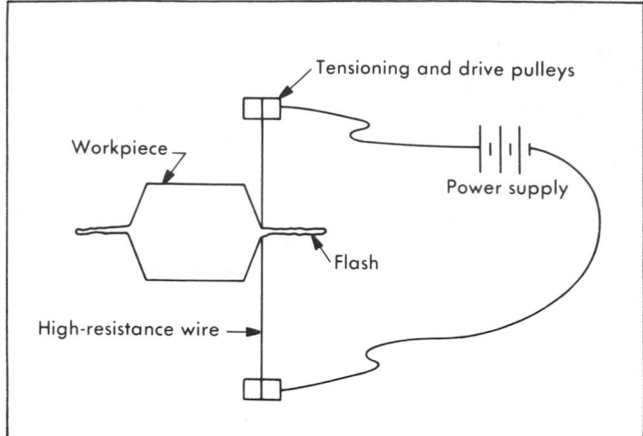

Fig. 46-6 Schematic of hot wire process for deflashing thermoplastic parts.

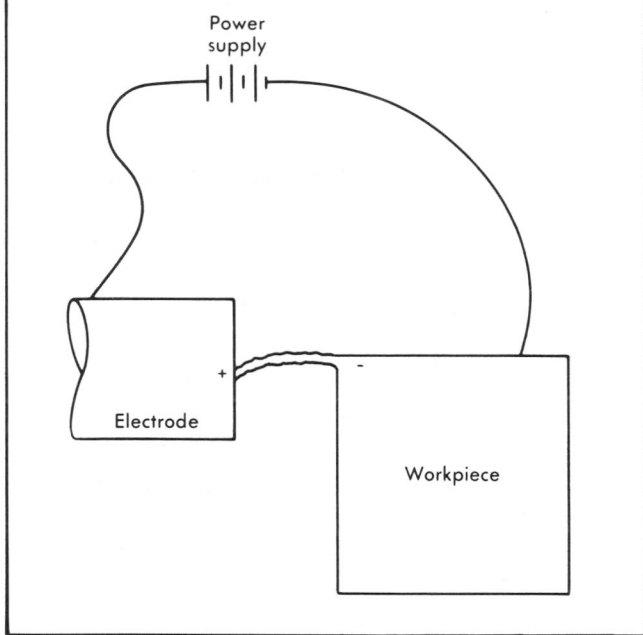

Fig. 46-7 Schematic of resistance heating method of deburring.

the larger the burrs, the higher the current required.

TORCH FLAME DEBURRING

The flames from oxyacetylene or similar torches can be used to melt burrs and the edges of parts. This process has been used to trim flash, sprues, and gates from large castings. Torch traverse rates of 20 to 40 ipm (508 to 1016 mm/min) are possible. Most edges exposed to this process will have a radius of 0.005″ (0.13 mm) or more, but smaller radii are possible. Possible limitations of torch flame deburring include a heat-affected zone and possibly resolidified droplets around the edges, plus the need for workholding fixtures and some means for traversing the torches. In some cases, electric arcs are being used rather than flames. Robots are currently being applied to automate this process in foundries.

ELECTRICAL DISCHARGE DEBURRING

Burrs can be removed by the electrical discharge machining (EDM) process. An electrode and the workpiece are submerged in an electrolyte, and the electrode is advanced to within 0.001 to 0.003″ (0.03 to 0.08 mm) of the burr-laden edge. With power on, sparks melt the burrs, and the electrode continues to advance until it is below the burred edge. For circular parts with burrs projecting from their diameters, rod or tube electrodes can be used.

This process removes heavy burrs fairly quickly, but it leaves a recast surface at the edges having a roughness that is normally 30 to 100 μin. (0.76 to 2.54 μm). The recast surfaces must be removed if the parts are to be used for highly stressed, fatigue-prone applications. Most edges treated by this process will have a small radius, about 0.003″ (0.03 mm), but larger radii can be produced with special tooling.

PLASMA AND LASER DEBURRING

Burrs can be removed by placing the edges of parts in a plasma flame. Thermal energy from the flame is concentrated at the corners and edges of the parts, and the high temperature quickly melts the burrs. This process is limited in that both small and thin precision parts may be distorted. Loose fiber ends resulting from machining fiberglass-reinforced products are being removed by laser beams and glow-discharge plasma deburring.

ELECTROPOLISHING

Electropolishing or, more correctly, electrochemical polishing has been used since the early 1930s, originally for metallography. The process is similar to electroplating with respect to processing, except that, in electropolishing, metal is selectively removed rather than deposited. Under proper conditions, metal is removed uniformly, thus causing smoothening and/or brightening. With proper techniques, the process can also be made burr selective—the burr being removed faster than adjacent stock. However, electropolishing cannot be confined to burr removal without stock removal unless the adjacent metal is electrically insulated or masked.

When the current is applied in electropolishing, a polarized

film forms on the surface of the metal. The nature of this film is responsible for both the brightening and leveling actions. Film strength and viscosity of the electrolyte are responsible for the nature of this anodic film. The metal ions are converted to metallic salts and must diffuse through this film. The film is thinner over the projections and thicker over the depressions of the metal, allowing the projections to be more exposed to electrolytic action and to have lower electrical resistance than the depressions. The thinner film results in the projections being more rapidly dissolved by electrolysis than the depressions, which are more protected by the thicker film.

Atoms of the metal being removed in electropolishing pass

through the polarized anodic film as metal salts and enter the electrolyte, either to be dissolved therein, deposited on the cathode, or to precipitate as sludge. Electropolishing solutions are therefore considered full sludging, semisludging, or non-sludging solutions.

APPLICATIONS

A number of specialized electrochemical processes have evolved over the years, all based on the mechanisms of electropolishing. Some of these processes are:

- Electrochemical brightening. In this process, surfaces are brightened, but not smoothened or leveled as in conventional electropolishing. A smoother surface is required initially for electrochemical brightening.
- Electrochemical deburring, discussed later in this chapter.
- Electrochemical machining (ECM).

In addition to smoothening and brightening operations, electropolishing is used for many other applications. These include the reduction of friction, fatigue, and out-gassing. Electropolishing can eliminate the gases, vapors, and volatiles absorbed on surfaces, which would be released during pump-down for high-vacuum service. The process provides superior results in antistick and release properties, wear and corrosion resistance, and passivity. Electropolishing is also used as a means of inspecting metal surfaces and welds, and as a means of controlling size and/or weight. Electropolishing is applicable to a great variety of metals and alloys, the most popular being: aluminum and aluminum alloys, copper and copper alloys, iron, steel, and stainless steels.

EQUIPMENT USED

The electropolishing tank may either be made of austenitic stainless steel or mild steel lined with polyvinyl chloride, polyethylene, polypropylene, fiberglass, or special types of rubber. For some applications, either lead-lined or plain steel tanks are used. However, steel tanks are electrically conductive, which may create problems and be undesirable. Selection of materials for tank construction depends mainly on the electropolishing solution, composition, and operating temperature.

Electropolishing tanks are usually rectangular, greater in length than width.

The electropolishing tank is fitted with tank rods or bars, and the pieces to be electropolished are hung on the work (anode) rods, which carries positive current. On a single work-rod tank (see Fig. 46-8), the rod is centered with respect to the width of the tank and is parallel to the longer tank sides. The cathode rods are parallel to and equidistant from the anode or work rod, and are charged with negative current.

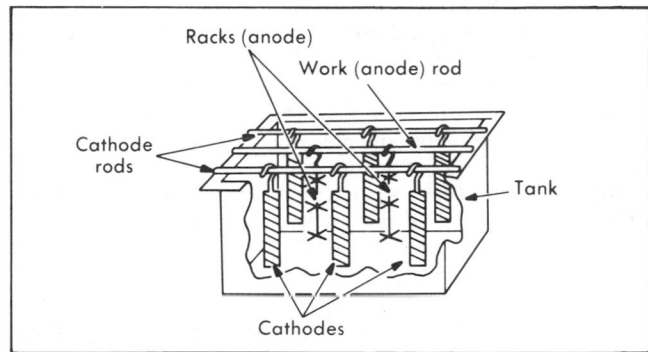

Fig. 46-8 Typical electropolishing tank with single work rod. (*Electro Glo Co.*)

ELECTROPOLISHING SOLUTIONS

There is no one electropolishing solution that can successfully electropolish all metals and alloys well; therefore, many specific types of electropolishing solutions exist. One supplier makes electrolytes (solutions) for over 55 different metals and alloys.

Electropolishing solutions are most often acid-based for the more commonly electropolished alloys; however, other electrolytes may be alkaline, cyanide, or metal salt systems. The characteristics of these various electrolytes are not only different in composition, but also in operating conditions—mainly operating temperatures and current densities. Temperatures may range from ambient to near their boiling points, and current densities range from 2.70 to 27.00 A/dm^2 (25 to 250 A/ft^2), depending upon the specific solution.

CHEMICAL POLISHING AND BRIGHT DIPPING

Over the years, the progression of various chemical surface treatments for metals evolved into what has become known as chemical polishing. During the industrial revolution, the pickling, or acid dipping, of ferrous metals became important as a means of removing oxide and scale. At the same time, an etch or open structure resulted in the surfaces of the metals, which provided better bonding or adhesion for galvanizing and enameling.

Copper and copper alloys, such as brass and bronze, required a pickle for similar reasons. The pickle most generally used was a mixture of sulfuric and nitric acids with various additives. It was found (accidently) that, under the proper conditions, a brightening of the surface was attainable; hence, "bright dipping" became the accepted term.

PROCESS DIFFERENCES

Chemical polishing and bright dipping are incorrectly used

interchangeably. Bright dipping evolved from pickling in much the same way that chemical polishing followed bright dipping. While bright dipping is still in wide use, mainly due to its lower cost, it is less sophisticated and generally does not have the surface leveling, or microdeburring effect, that is achieved by chemical polishing. Chemical polishing is selective stock removal, somewhat like electropolishing (discussed in the preceding section of this chapter), whereas bright dipping is not.

As the name implies, bright dips are generally used after electroplating, such as on zinc or cadmium for improved corrosion resistance, and also on solid, nonplated metal surfaces for visual improvement or brightening. The process is also used for improved electroplate adhesion.

Chemical polishing will also brighten the surface of metals, but is more selective in nature than bright dipping. It is thus able, to some extent, to smooth or level the surface and also cause a deburring effect. Chemical polishing is somewhat

CHEMICAL POLISHING AND BRIGHT DIPPING

electrochemical in nature because of the oxidizing agent in the solution; an electrochemical potential thus exists.

Of the various metals and alloys that are bright dipped or chemically polished, aluminum is by far the most popular, followed by copper and its alloys. The brightening of zinc and cadmium on plated articles accounts for the greatest tonnage of bright-dip chemical consumption. Nickel and its alloys, carbon steels, and stainless steels are also applicable, but to a much lesser extent.

EQUIPMENT USED

Because most bright-dipping and chemical polishing solutions are acidic, they require corrosion-resistant equipment. Solution and rinse tanks are usually constructed of austenitic stainless steel, fiberglass, rubber, and plastics such as polyethylene, polypropylene, and polyvinyl chloride. Because of the variety of solution compositions and temperatures used, the various materials of construction must be evaluated to determine which are best suited for the particular application.

Parts may be processed in several different ways, depending upon their size and shape. Parts with flat surfaces or large workpieces are usually racked individually. Small parts that do not tangle or nest and that are not fragile can be processed in bulk in either a dipping basket or a tumbling barrel. When parts cannot be bulk processed and when individual hand racking is expensive, a compromise is the use of compartmentalized or partitioned baskets or containers.

SOLUTIONS FOR VARIOUS METALS

Typical solutions for the chemical polishing and bright dipping of various metals are presented in Table 46-2. Operation and control of these solutions, which have been used for many years, is entirely dependent on the proficiency of the operator and is still more of an art than a science. Recent improvements in proprietary formulations for both bright dipping and chemical polishing have reduced many of the shortcomings inherent in these earlier solutions and provide a more scientific means of control and analysis.

TABLE 46-2
Typical Chemical Polishing and Bright Dipping Solutions

Workpiece Material	Solution Components	Component Amounts	Temperature, °F (°C)
Aluminum	Phosphoric acid Nitric acid Acetic acid Water	80% (by vol.) 5% (by vol.) 5% (by vol.) 10% (by vol.)	220 (105)
	Phosphoric acid Hydrogen peroxide Water	75% (by wt.) 3.5% (by wt.) 21.5% (by wt.)	195 (90)
Cadmium	Chromic acid Sulfuric acid	13.4 oz/gal (100 g/L) 1/8 to 1/4 oz/gal (0.9 to 1.9 g/L)	Room
	Hydrogen peroxide (30%) Sulfuric acid	7% (by vol.) 0.3% (by vol.)	Room
Copper and alloys	Sulfuric acid Nitric acid Water Hydrochloric acid	45% (by vol.) 22% (by vol.) 33% (by vol.) 1/2 oz/gal (3.7 g/L)	Room
Iron and steel	Oxalic acid Hydrogen peroxide Sulfuric acid	3.3 oz/gal (24.7 g/L) 1.7 oz/gal (12.7 g/L) 0.01 oz/gal (0.07 g/L)	Room
Stainless steel	Nitric acid Muriatic acid Phosphoric acid Acetic acid (First depassivated by immersion in hot 5% sulfuric acid)	36% (by vol.) 9% (by vol.) 9% (by vol.) 46% (by vol.)	160 (70)
Zinc and alloys	Chromic acid Sodium sulfate (5 to 30 s followed by cold water rinse)	30 to 40 oz/gal (225 to 300 g/L) 2 to 4 oz/gal (15 to 30 g/L)	Room

ELECTROCHEMICAL DEBURRING

In electrochemical deburring (ECD), burrs are dissolved from metallic workpieces electrochemically and are flushed away by pressurized electrolyte. In addition to deburring, edge and corner radii are generated. The process is a specialized,

ELECTROCHEMICAL DEBURRING

static adaptation of electrochemical machining.

With the ECD process, electrolyte flows through a gap between a tool (cathode) and the workpiece (anode), thus completing the electrical circuit needed for the d-c power to dissolve the burrs (see Fig. 46-9). The tool and workpiece do not contact each other, and the workpiece is not exposed to any mechanical or thermal stresses. As a result, there are no changes in the physical or chemical properties of the metal.

Special workholding fixtures and tools are used to ensure that the conductive surfaces of the tools conform to the areas or edges of the workpieces to be deburred. Proper insulation of the tools and protective shielding or masking of the workpieces limit the electrochemical action to the desired surfaces. Multiple tooling stations are commonly used for high-production requirements.

Optimum use of the ECD process for consistently uniform results requires control of the tool design, current density, electrolyte, and cycle time. Variables with respect to the electrolyte that must be controlled include its type, concentration, pH, temperature, clarification, pressure, and velocity.

ADVANTAGES OF THE PROCESS

Fast production and consistent results are major advantages of the ECD process. Electrochemical deburring is ideal for selective (controlled) deburring and the removal of burrs that are inaccessible with most other processes. For parts having surfaces that cannot be altered or scratched, ECD is often the only possible method of deburring. The process is used extensively to deburr cross, threaded, and intersecting holes, and parts made from metals that would work harden.

It has been estimated that electrochemical deburring is from 5 to 40 times faster than hand deburring, with cycle times generally ranging from 5 to 60 seconds, depending upon burr size. Smooth edge breaks of from 0.001 to 0.020" (0.03 to 0.51 mm) are consistently produced. Large or small workpieces of various shapes and materials can be handled on the same machine. Holes as small as 0.034" (0.86 mm) diam can be deburred. The absence of mechanical forces permits the deburring of thin sections and fragile parts without distortion or damage.

The process does not effect workpiece dimensions, except at the edges being deburred. It can be used as a manual or fully automatic operation, and ECD stations can be incorporated in transfer machines or other automated production systems.

PROCESS LIMITATIONS

One obvious limitation to the use of ECD is that parts made from nonconductive materials cannot be deburred in this way. Conductive parts to be deburred must be clean; and, in most cases, loose chips clinging to the workpieces from preceding operations should be removed to prevent short circuits during the ECD process. In addition, relatively close tolerances are required for the workpieces because of the small clearance required between the burrs and the tool, and orientation of the burrs must be consistent from part to part to prevent short circuits and ensure uniform burr removal.

The capability for close-tolerance edge radiusing is limited to small radii, typically not larger than 0.020" (0.51 mm). Another possible limitation is that the process may produce slight etching effects on areas immediately adjacent to edges being deburred. Etching is evidenced by some discoloration

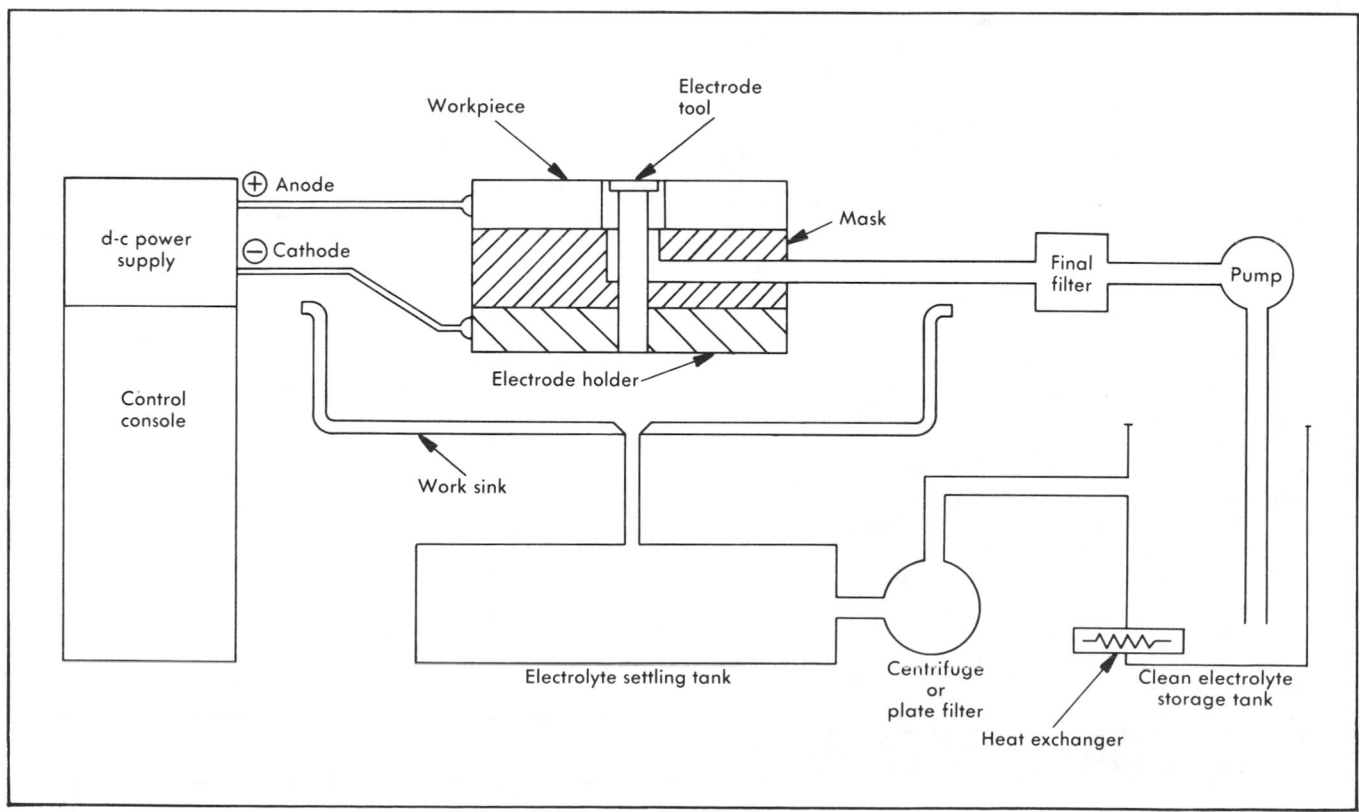

Fig. 46-9 Schematic drawing of the electrochemical deburring process. (*Chemtool, Inc.*)

ELECTROCHEMICAL DEBURRING

(slight darkening) but can be controlled by providing insulating masks in the tooling or eliminated by bright dipping the parts. Smut is the word commonly used to describe the darkened surfaces around deburred edges produced by the ECD process on steel components.

Another limitation of the ECD process is lack of versatility. Workholding fixtures and tooling are generally required for each workpiece to be deburred.

TYPICAL APPLICATIONS

The ECD process is primarily used for removing specific burrs. It is also used extensively to remove recast (remelt) surfaces resulting from electrical discharge machining (EDM) and laser and electron beam machining (LBM and EBM). The process for polishing or finishing surfaces is referred to as static electrochemical machining, with no motion between the cathode and workpiece, and is usually done on a deburring bench.

Electrochemical deburring can be used for parts of any size or shape that are made from practically any conductive metal. The process is used extensively on parts made from most steels, stainless steels, aluminum, aluminum alloys, and exotic materials. Aluminum alloys with high silicon contents, however, result in a textured rather than a smooth surface. Nonuniform and possibly unsatisfactory results are obtained with some titanium alloys unless special additives are mixed in the electrolyte. Deburring of sintered tungsten requires the use of special chemicals, and zinc die castings often present processing problems.

There are many applications for the ECD process in automotive manufacturing, with many machines having multiple tooling. Deburring of pistons, connecting rods, and crankshafts is commonplace. Wristpin holes, snap-ring grooves, and oil-return slots are all deburred on pistons. Bearing lock slots, bolt holes, thrust faces, snap-ring grooves, and weight control bosses on connecting rods are deburred simultaneously.

Deburring the edges of pump gears is another major application. Many hydraulic and pneumatic components, including valve bodies, with interconnecting and crosshole passages are deburred with the ECD process to improve fluid and gas flow. The ECD process is also being used to deburr the cooling holes in turbine blades, as well as for many other aircraft engine components.

TOOL DESIGN

Based on considerable experience and extensive testing, recent improvements have been made in the ECD process with respect to the positioning of the tool in relation to the burr on the workpiece. For many years, this gap was maintained between 0.010 and 0.015" (0.25 and 0.38 mm). Such small gaps, however, created problems, including shorts when burrs touched the tools and frequent overcutting on critical parts. Variations in the tools because of manufacturing tolerances caused some parts of the gap to be only 0.002 to 0.005" (0.05 to 0.13 mm). Variations in the gap change the velocity of the electrolyte and cause irregular flow, and, in some cases, create air bubbles. Air acts as an insulator and thereby stops the deburring action.

Pulsating d-c power supplies and gaps of 0.025 to 0.040" (0.64 to 1.02 mm) are being used for some applications. Advantages of the larger gaps include fewer shorting problems, longer tool life, and better finishes, but cycle times are generally longer. An even flow and uniform velocity of the electrolyte flushes the metal hydroxides away faster, which reduces smutting of the workpiece surfaces. Cathode wear can also be minimized by using spark-detection protection systems.

Practically all tooling for the ECD process is designed so that the tools have a corner-to-corner relationship to the burred edges of the workpieces (see Fig. 46-10), resulting in removal of the burrs and rounding of the edges. The gap, established by the X and Y dimensions shown, is varied to suit the application and to provide the desired corner break. The electrolyte flow path safely removes any particles of metal cut away during the process.

Modifications of the working gap, by increasing or decreasing the X and Y dimensions, will affect the type of corner break produced. However, both dimensions must be sufficient to allow for the maximum variations in workpiece geometry permitted by production tolerances. Even under the most adverse conditions of dimensional tolerance stacking, a gap must still be provided to prevent electrical contact and to permit sufficient electrolyte flow. The corner-to-corner relationship can be designed in different ways to accommodate workpieces of various configurations.

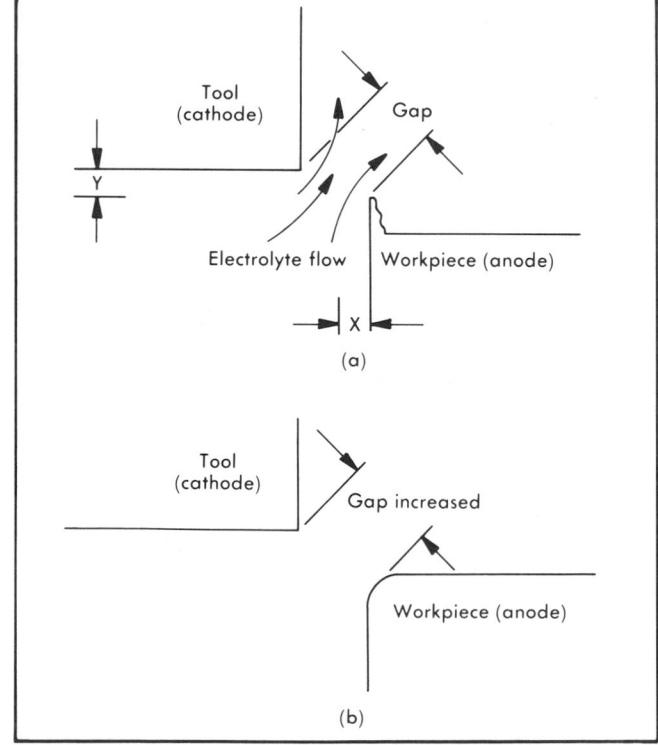

Fig. 46-10 Corner-to-corner relationship for the ECD process, (a) before and (b) after deburring. (*Chemform, Inc.*)

ULTRASONIC DEBURRING

Ultrasonic deburring uses ultrasonic cavitation and a specially compounded acid slurry. The slurry consists of weak etching solutions and small quantities of abrasive particles. Ultrasound provides high-energy shock waves that cause the abrasives to remain suspended and to constantly bombard the workpiece; the shock waves also increase the etching action. Edges of the workpieces are attacked more than the surfaces because of strain-hardening microstructural changes in the areas of the burrs. Finishes produced are bright and oxide-free.

Little information is available on the ultrasonic deburring process, primarily because the contents of the slurries are considered secret. Apparently, fine-grained abrasives, such as silicon carbide, 0.0012 to 0.0079" (0.030 to 0.200 mm) diam, are used. Other slurry constituents that have been identified include calcinated soda, stearic acid, sulfuric acid, and glycerin, but the amounts are not known. Vibration frequencies to 30 kHz have been used. Because of the use of acids, tank linings are required.

Ultrasonic deburring is used primarily for thin burrs, those having a thickness of about 0.0005" (0.013 mm). It can only generate small edge radii, normally not larger than 0.005" (0.13 mm). The process can be used on a number of different materials, but is generally limited to small parts. Cavitation is directly proportional to the size of the transducer. Large parts require large tanks and powerful, costly transducers. Cycle times are directly proportional to burr sizes and have been reported to range from 10 to 25 minutes. Workpieces should be rinsed with water after ultrasonic deburring.

When workpieces are racked, allowing the slurry flow more penetration, the results are often more desirable. Racking increases production costs, but close-tolerance workpieces requiring this type of finish generally have to be handled delicately.

Applications include the removal of flash from complexly shaped parts having through or blind holes. The process is especially suitable for reaching inaccessible areas of workpieces. Other applications include deburring the teeth of precision gears, the ends of needles, and small precision stampings.

References

1. William G. Wood, coordinator, *Metals Handbook*, vol. 5, *Surface Cleaning, Finishing, and Coating*, 9th ed. (Metals Park, OH: American Society for Metals, 1982), p. 5.

PLATING

ELECTROPLATING

Electroplating is an electrolytic process whereby a metal is cathodically deposited onto another metal or a surface that has been made conductive. Thus, a part made of metal, plastics, or other materials may be coated with a thin metal deposit to impart certain desirable properties while avoiding the prohibitive cost of fabricating the part entirely from the metal used as a coating. Plating provides desirable characteristics such as protection of the basis metal (substrate) from corrosion, improvement of the appearance of the substrate, and improved solderability, wear resistance, electrical conductivity, contact resistance, and lubricity. Depending on their use, electroplated coatings may be classified as either decorative or engineering, with some falling into both classifications.

THEORY

In electroplating, the workpiece is made cathodic in a solution containing the ions of the metal being deposited. Direct current is passed between the anode and the workpiece (cathode). The anode is usually constructed of the same material as the metal being plated, although some plating processes use insoluble anodes. As the current flows, the metal ions gain electrons at the cathodic workpiece and transform into a metal coating.

Proprietary additives (brighteners) are usually incorporated in the plating solution to alter the deposit in a desirable fashion. These additives brighten or level the deposit as well as improve the uniformity of the deposit's thickness over the entire workpiece. The additives may also be used to alter physical properties such as hardness, ductility, internal stress, and corrosion resistance.

METAL ELECTROPLATED

Many different metals can be successfully electroplated onto other materials. Each metal possesses unique properties and characteristics that can improve the usefulness of the basis metal. Some of the more common electroplating metals are nickel, copper, chromium, zinc, tin, cadmium, and lead. Alloys and precious metals are also deposited.

Nickel Plating

Solutions. Nickel plating is documented as early as 1842, but modern nickel plating really began in 1916 with the introduction of the Watts bath. The Watts formulation, consisting of nickel sulfate, nickel chloride, and boric acid, is by far the most widely used electrolyte. Modern-day organic additives produce brilliant, level, low-stress deposits. These additives revolutionized conventional nickel plating in that they have virtually eliminated the laborious process of mechanical buffing. The more corrosion-resistant, sulfur-free, semibright nickel deposits have also become important as undercoatings for bright nickel.

A nickel sulfamate bath is used for engineering (usually nondecorative) applications to produce low-stress deposits. This bath is also useful in electroforming and for plating parts that are susceptible to fatigue failure. An all-chloride Woods nickel formulation is useful as a strike bath for treating passivated nickel and difficult-to-plate substrates such as stainless steel. There is also limited use of the nickel fluoborate bath for electroforming and other engineering applications.

Applications. Nickel plating is widely used for decorative purposes. Bright nickel plate—especially in combination with a lower layer of sulfur-free, semibright nickel and a much thinner upper layer of chromium—is very widely used over steel, brass, zinc die castings, aluminum, and chemically metallized plastics to provide a bright and corrosion-resistant finish with a nontarnishing and wear-resistant surface. Typical applications are decorative trim for automotive and consumer products. For best corrosion resistance, the chromium deposit should be microdiscontinuous (microcracked or microporous).

Nickel deposits are also used for nondecorative purposes to improve or modify surface properties such as corrosion resistance, hardness, wear, and magnetic characteristics.

Copper Plating

Solutions. Copper is deposited from two main types of plating baths, the alkaline cyanide copper and acid sulfate copper baths. Among the alkaline baths, the pyrophosphate copper bath is used to some extent for electronic applications; among acid baths, the fluoborate bath is also used for electronic applications.

Despite waste disposal problems, the cyanide copper bath continues to be widely used owing to its superior throwing power and ability to satisfactorily plate steel and zinc die castings or zincate or stannate-treated aluminum substrates before nickel plating. For these applications, copper is generally first deposited from a cyanide copper strike, followed by a high-speed cyanide copper or an acid copper bath.

The acid copper bath is primarily used for decorative applications, especially for plating on plastics. Proprietary additives help achieve good microthrowing power (leveling) and brightness. Additional uses of the copper sulfate and sometimes the fluoborate bath include pattern plating of printed circuit boards, electroforming, and plating of rotogravure printing plates.

Applications. Copper plating is commonly used:

- As a decorative and corrosion-resistant deposit under nickel and chromium.
- As a base deposit for nickel and/or chromi-

CHAPTER 47

ELECTROPLATING

um-plated plastics and zinc die castings.
- For electroforming applications (records and wave-guides).
- As a decorative final finish (usually lacquered).
- For through-hole plating of printed circuit boards.

Chromium Plating

Solutions. Most chromium plating is done from hexavalent (CrO_3) baths, but trivalent systems are gaining in popularity. There has also been a fair amount of microdiscontinuous, either microcracked or microporous, chromium deposits used to improve corrosion resistance. In the galvanic couple, the underlying nickel acts as the anode, and the chromium behaves as the cathode. By exposing a greater surface area of nickel through the use of microdiscontinuous chromium, the corrosion current is spread over a large area; consequently, corrosion proceeds uniformly. As a result, corrosion protection in outdoor environments has been improved fivefold.

Hexavalent chromium plating baths consist of chromic acid and small amounts of a catalyst ($SO_4^=$). Recently, mixed catalyst baths containing flouride compounds in addition to chromic acid and sulfate have been employed. Proprietary self-regulating baths control the concentration of the catalyst automatically.

Applications. Chromium plating is divided into decorative and hard coatings. Decorative coatings are applied over a base deposit of nickel or copper plus nickel to provide color and tarnish resistance as well as a hard, protective finish. Coating thicknesses are usually less than 0.03 mil (0.75 μm). Decorative chromium coatings are most often found on automobiles, furniture, and kitchen appliances.

Hard chromium coatings are generally deposited directly on the base material without a nickel undercoat in thicknesses ranging from 0.1 to 20 mils (2.5 to 500 μm). Hard coatings provide resistance to wear, heat, abrasion, and/or corrosion. Typical applications for hard coatings include hydraulic pistons and cylinders, piston rings, wearing parts in business machines, aircraft engine parts, yarn and thread guides for textiles, plastics molds, and various parts of nuclear reactors where galling is a particular concern.

Zinc Plating

Solutions. Commercially, zinc is deposited from three different baths: the conventional cyanide bath, the acid chloride bath, and the alkaline noncyanide (or zincate) bath. Cyanide baths offer ease of control and normally trouble-free plating. However, the cost of cyanide destruction and the toxicity of the bath have prompted platers to install low-cyanide solutions or cyanide-free baths.

Chloride zinc baths have been available since the late 1960s. The original baths were chelated or based on complexing agents such as ammonium chloride. Today, state-of-the-art chloride baths use potassium or ammonium chloride. The advantages of the chloride systems include brilliant deposits, high cathode efficiency, low electric power consumption, and nontoxic, easily treated electrolyte. The disadvantages are poor throwing power, a higher initial equipment investment, and higher brightener costs compared to the alkaline processes.

Alkaline noncyanidic electrolytes consist of zinc and sodium hydroxide. In the absence of cyanide, proprietary sequestering agents are sometimes used to yield grain refinement. Alkaline noncyanide electrolytes are simple and low cost. The solutions and rinse waters are easily treated, and metal hydroxide sludges

are reduced owing to low zinc content in the bath. These baths, however, offer the lowest cathode efficiency, and the deposits may be yellowish in color. Blistering is common at higher thicknesses and may be related to the greater hydrogen occlusion.

Applications. Zinc is plated over iron and steel on a wide variety of parts where sacrificial corrosion resistance is required. The conventional zinc coating is dull gray in color with a matte finish, but whiter and more lustrous deposits can be produced by the use of proprietary addition agents. Zinc plate is almost always passivated with a chromate coating for added corrosion protection. Coating thickness ranges from 0.2 to 2.0 mils (5 to 50 μm) after chromate coating, depending on the particular application.

The formation of white corrosion products in marine environments makes zinc less desirable than cadmium; but because it is less toxic and less expensive and its electrolytes are more easily waste treated, zinc has replaced cadmium in many applications. Zinc coatings are also superior to cadmium coatings in industrial environments. Common applications for zinc plating include fasteners, wire goods, tools, and sheet metal parts.

Tin Plating

Tin deposit finishes may be bright as plated or matte. Matte deposits may be reflowed, a practice which is almost universally applied to continuously plated steel strip for can manufacturing and is referred to as tinplate or electrotinplate. In tinplating, the reflowing is accomplished by induction or resistance heating of the continuously moving strip. Small articles are often reflowed in hot oil or fat; however, many tin-plated articles are used without reflowing. Tin plating is covered by ASTM Specification B 545.

Solutions. Tin may be plated from either alkaline electrolytes (stannate) or acid electrolytes (sulfate, fluorborate). A special Halogen tin electrolyte containing stannous chloride, sodium fluoride, potassium bifluoride, sodium chloride, plus other additives is also used for tinplating rapidly moving strip at high current densities. Typical operating conditions are a temperature of 150°F (65°C), pH of 2.7, and current density of 4.8 A/ft² (45 A/dm²). The factors influencing the choice of electrolytes are coating appearance, operation, equipment, anodes, and power requirements.

Coating appearance. Alkaline baths provide a matte coating that is sensitive to fingerprints. Acid baths can be used with proprietary brighteners to produce a bright coating that is less sensitive to fingerprinting.

Operation. Alkaline baths are easier to operate than acid baths. The preplate cycles are also simpler and require fewer steps than acid baths.

Equipment. Tanks for alkaline baths can be made from unlined steel, while acid baths require lined tanks. Alkaline baths need to be heated to 170 to 190°F (77 to 88°C), while bright acid baths need to be cooled to 60 to 80°F (16 to 27°C).

Anodes. Alkaline baths can be operated with inert anodes for plating internal threads or steel couplings, as well as soluble tin anodes or tin anodes alloyed with 1% aluminum (high-speed anodes). Acid baths cannot be operated with inert anodes.

Power requirements. The metal deposition rate at the same current density is at least twice as high in acid baths as in alkaline baths because the electrochemical equivalent of Sn^{2+} (acid baths) is twice as high as Sn^{4+} (alkaline baths), and because acid baths have a higher current efficiency. Operating temperatures and bath voltages are lower in the acid baths.

47-2

Applications. Tin, as a metal, displays some very desirable properties. Tin is compatible with foods, is nontoxic, has a relatively low melting point [450°F (232°C)], and is readily soldered. Consequently, tin electroplate finds use in a multitude of products, including tinplate (tin-plated steel strip) for use in consumer food containers, buttons, gas-tank hardware, semiconductors, copper wire, electronic devices, and printed circuit boards.

Advantages and limitations. Tin provides sacrificial protection for copper, nickel, and other nonferrous metals; it does not provide similar protection to steel. A drawback with tin is the possibility of whisker growth, which is the formation of fine metal slivers that can short-circuit electronic devices. Tin is also a relatively expensive metal.

Cadmium Plating

Cadmium is a soft, silver-white metal with unique engineering properties that is obtained as a by-product of zinc smelting. Some of these properties include good conductivity, solderability, lubricity, ductility, and adhesive retention; excellent corrosion resistance and porous surface coverage; and minimal hydrogen embrittlement. Chromating after plating provides additional corrosion resistance. However, cadmium is extremely toxic and costly and is consequently being replaced by zinc wherever possible. About one third of the cadmium produced today is used in electroplating.

Solutions. Cadmium is primarily plated from a cyanide electrolyte. Acid cadmium baths are also used to a limited extent, and are fluoborate, sulfate, or chloride in nature. The acid-type baths are more desirable if hydrogen embrittlement is a problem, and their waste treatment is simplified. However, the cyanide baths are easier to control than the acid baths.

Applications. Cadmium is used as a protective coating over steel, cast iron, and malleable iron. It also provides galvanic protection on iron and steel. The government is by far the largest specifier of cadmium, for military applications. Deposit thicknesses range from 0.2 to 1 mil (5 to 25 μm), depending on the degree of exposure to corrosives and wear. Typical applications include springs, lock washers, fasteners, electronic and electrical parts, washing machine parts, and military hardware. Cadmium plating should never be used on parts that will come in contact with food or beverages.

Lead

Lead is electroplated to a limited extent to provide corrosion resistance or a good bearing surface, and is more apt to be plated as an alloy than as a pure metal. Lead baths may be fluoborate, fluosilicate, perchlorate, or sulfamate. The fluoborate is the most often used for storage battery parts and the linings of tanks and chemical apparatus.

Alloy Electroplating

Although hundreds of alloys have been successfully electroplated in the laboratory, few have been commercially used. The more important processes are described subsequently.

Brass. The main brass alloy consists of approximately 70% copper and 30% zinc, and has been plated for many years for decorative purposes as a substitute for solid brass. Most deposits are rather thin, from a mere flash up to 1 mil (25 μm) thick, and are generally protected by a clear lacquer coating. Brass is often plated over bright nickel to improve the luster of the nickel coating.

Brass has been plated over steel to promote rubber adhesion and to provide lubricating characteristics. White brass, containing 30% copper and 70% zinc, is also used as a substitute for bright nickel on toys, tubular furniture, and automotive interior trim and hardware; this practice is decreasing, however, because of the superior performance of decorative nickel/chromium coatings. The main brass plating bath is cyanide.

Bronze. The main electroplating alloy in this group contains from 8 to 15% tin, with the remainder copper. Bronze may be deposited from a potassium stannate and copper cyanide bath that contains potassium hydroxide and potassium cyanide. Relatively little bronze plating is done, but bronze plating has been used as an undercoating in the preparation of aluminum alloys for plating with nickel-chromium coatings.

Tin alloy deposits. Tin-lead alloy plating is used to protect steel from corrosion and for etch resistance. However, the major purpose for its use in the plating of wire, electronic devices, and printed circuit boards is to facilitate solderability. The most widely used tin alloy electrolyte is the fluoborate bath. The deposit normally has a matte appearance as plated, but the deposit can be reflowed, as in tin plating, to improve the appearance. Recently, proprietary organic additives have been developed to produce brilliant deposits. Proprietary, fluoborate-free electrolytes have also been introduced and appear to offer advantages such as ease of waste disposal and reduction in the rate of tin oxidation.

Nickel alloys. Nickel-iron alloys, containing 10-40% iron, have been deposited for over 10 years as a substitute for decorative bright nickel, including those demanding high corrosion protection. Deposit appearance is identical to bright nickel, and reasonable improvements in ductility, adhesion, and chromium receptivity are achieved.

Nickel-cobalt alloys have improved high-temperature properties, are harder than pure nickel deposits, and are also available commercially; however, they are not extensively used.

Plating with Precious Metals

The electrodeposition of precious metals for decorative and engineering purposes is an important part of the metal finishing industry. The high cost of each gallon of solution requires exceptionally good housekeeping. Metal recovery, security, personnel capability, and accounting are critical when operating a precious metal plating facility.

Silver. Commercial silver electroplating has been practiced since the middle of the nineteenth century. The plating bath contains silver in the form of potassium-silver cyanide, $KAg(CN)_2$, and free-potassium cyanide. Sodium cyanide may be used, but the potassium cyanide formulation is preferred. Usually a small amount of potassium carbonate and/or potassium hydroxide is also added. Silver baths are generally operated at room temperature, although high-speed plating has been done at temperatures as high as 120°F (50°C).

When hard, bright silver deposits are desired, proprietary additives containing metals or organic brighteners are generally used. Some additive combinations increase the tarnish resistance of the silver deposit. As with all bright solutions, the metal content of the bath must be closely controlled. The free cyanide is also monitored regularly.

Gold. There are four types of gold plating solutions: alkaline, neutral, acid, and noncyanide baths. The alkaline cyanide baths were used for over a century. Because of the complexing action of cyanide, however, it was difficult to

ELECTROPLATING

obtain consistent codeposition of other metals with the gold, except at high current densities and temperatures; as a result, deposits were limited to flash deposits.

Until recently, gold plating was primarily used for decorative purposes in jewelry, flatware, holloware, and similar items. In the last 20 years, however, the use of gold plating has widely expanded in the electronics industry because of its good electrical contact properties and corrosion and oxidation resistance. Typical applications include printed circuit boards, contacts, connectors, transistor bases, and integrated circuit components. Gold plating is also used in the chemical industry for reactors and heat exchangers. The high cost of gold in recent years has made conservation critical and has led to a search for substitutes.

Rhodium. Rhodium is plated from sulfate (rhodium sulfate plus sulfuric acid), phosphate (rhodium phosphate plus phosphoric acid), and phosphate-sulfate (rhodium phosphate plus sulfuric acid) baths. Low-stressed deposits are obtained from sulfate baths containing proprietary stress-reducing agents. The bright bath (phosphate or phosphate-sulfate) deposits are highly stressed and cracked, but have an attractive color that sets off diamonds well. The rhodium sulfate baths yield relatively heavy deposits that are hard and wear resistant. The low-stressed deposits are used when heavy plate [up to 10 mils (254 μm)] is required for good wear resistance with no cracks. Low-stressed deposits are not bright.

Platinum. A number of platinum plating solutions are available. Titanium anodes plated with platinum are used as auxiliary anodes for gold and other precious metal plating baths when plating plastics, die castings, and steel parts with complex shapes. However, an anode of mechanically clad tantalum and titanium is generally preferred. Platinum can be plated to very heavy thicknesses, but the cost is so high that there is little demand for these deposits. Heavy platinum deposits are not bright, although thin deposits can be.

Palladium. Palladium plating is more common in Europe than in the United States. Palladium baths are of the pH 9.0 to 10.0 variety and based upon palladium P salt (a palladium diamino dinitrite). Palladium coatings are not used for decorative finishes because they are dark in color and tarnish. They have been used as an undercoating for rhodium. Two common applications are watch cases and moving watch parts. The use of palladium and palladium-nickel alloy deposits appears to be growing in the electronics industry.

Ruthenium. Processes for electrodeposition of ruthenium are available. This relatively low-cost precious metal is finding use in switching devices and other electronics-related applications.

METAL SUBSTRATES

The three most common basis metals are steel, brass, and zinc (die castings). The physical properties and composition of these metals have a major influence on the platability of the part or selection of the specific finish. Adherent coatings can be deposited upon hard-to-plate surfaces by using specially developed preplating cycles or intermediate coatings differing from the final coating specified.

DESIGN CONSIDERATIONS

Some of the more important design considerations affecting plating are illustrated in Fig. 47-1. Although the illustration is primarily concerned with die castings, the same principles apply to other types of parts. The plating of assembled parts can also present the problem of proper distribution of deposited metal. Often the individual parts can be more economically plated prior to assembly, especially if the individual pieces could

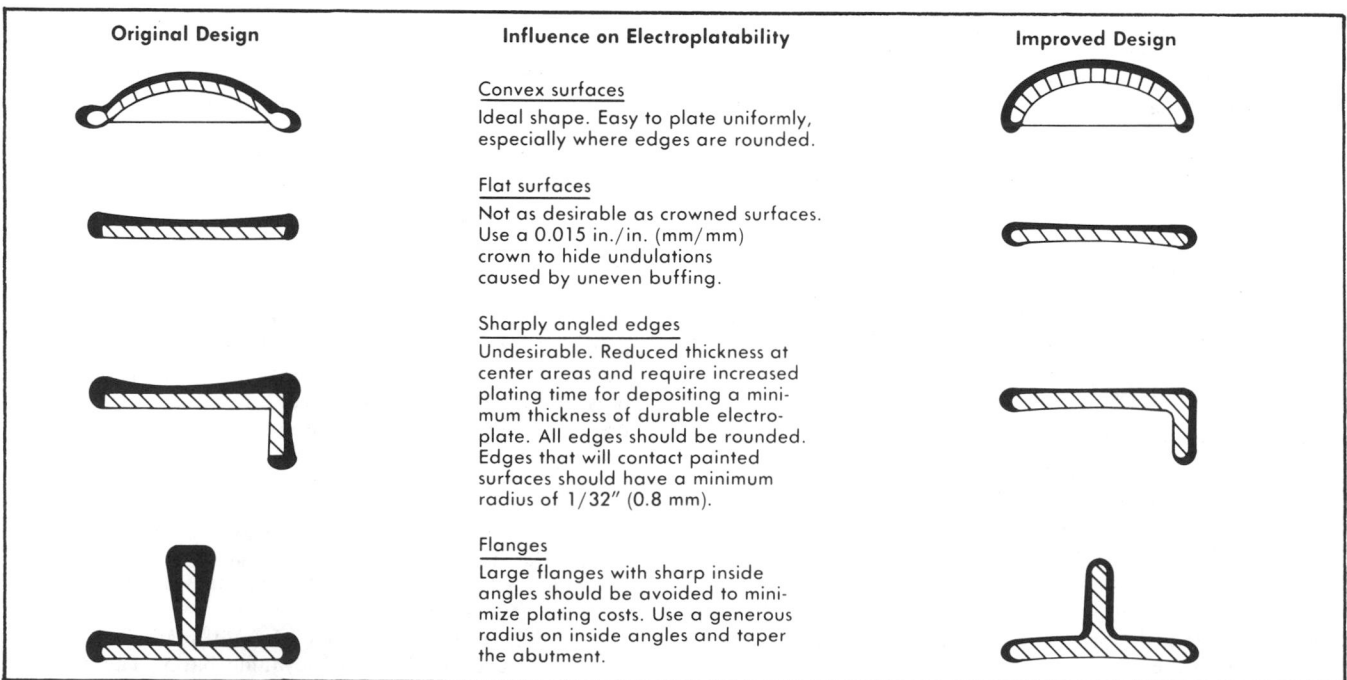

Original Design	Influence on Electroplatability	Improved Design
	Convex surfaces Ideal shape. Easy to plate uniformly, especially where edges are rounded.	
	Flat surfaces Not as desirable as crowned surfaces. Use a 0.015 in./in. (mm/mm) crown to hide undulations caused by uneven buffing.	
	Sharply angled edges Undesirable. Reduced thickness at center areas and require increased plating time for depositing a minimum thickness of durable electroplate. All edges should be rounded. Edges that will contact painted surfaces should have a minimum radius of 1/32" (0.8 mm).	
	Flanges Large flanges with sharp inside angles should be avoided to minimize plating costs. Use a generous radius on inside angles and taper the abutment.	

Fig. 47-1 Improved part design permits better electroplating.

(continued)

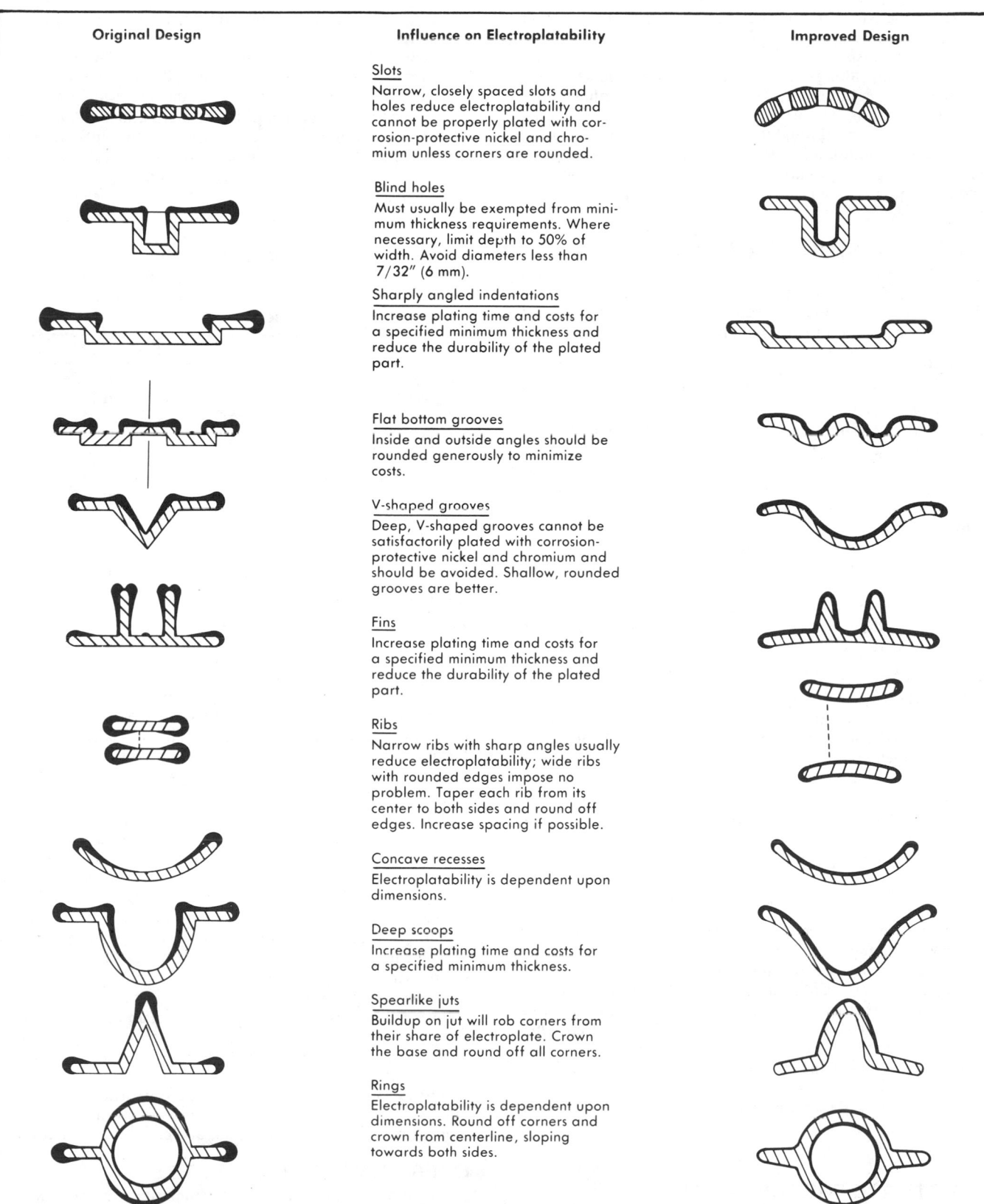

Original Design	Influence on Electroplatability	Improved Design

Slots
Narrow, closely spaced slots and holes reduce electroplatability and cannot be properly plated with corrosion-protective nickel and chromium unless corners are rounded.

Blind holes
Must usually be exempted from minimum thickness requirements. Where necessary, limit depth to 50% of width. Avoid diameters less than 7/32" (6 mm).

Sharply angled indentations
Increase plating time and costs for a specified minimum thickness and reduce the durability of the plated part.

Flat bottom grooves
Inside and outside angles should be rounded generously to minimize costs.

V-shaped grooves
Deep, V-shaped grooves cannot be satisfactorily plated with corrosion-protective nickel and chromium and should be avoided. Shallow, rounded grooves are better.

Fins
Increase plating time and costs for a specified minimum thickness and reduce the durability of the plated part.

Ribs
Narrow ribs with sharp angles usually reduce electroplatability; wide ribs with rounded edges impose no problem. Taper each rib from its center to both sides and round off edges. Increase spacing if possible.

Concave recesses
Electroplatability is dependent upon dimensions.

Deep scoops
Increase plating time and costs for a specified minimum thickness.

Spearlike juts
Buildup on jut will rob corners from their share of electroplate. Crown the base and round off all corners.

Rings
Electroplatability is dependent upon dimensions. Round off corners and crown from centerline, sloping towards both sides.

Fig. 47-1 —*Continued* **Improved part design permits better electroplating.** (*Zinc Institute, Inc. and Metal Finishing Suppliers' Association, Inc.*)

ELECTROPLATING

be barrel plated while the assembled part would have to be rack plated.

Crimped or spotwelded assemblies usually have crevices under the crimp, along the weld line, or between spots that trap the processing solutions. The solution is almost impossible to rinse away because of the very small opening and may cause a number of problems throughout the processing sequence. After final rinse, the solution bleeds out and stains the finished piece. The unrinsed plating solution is also a source of contamination and may cause problems in post-treatment baths.

PLATING METHODS AND EQUIPMENT

Electroplating may be divided into barrel, rack, and strip (continuous reel-to-reel) plating. Barrel plating is used for plating smaller parts in some electrolytes. Rack plating is used for larger parts and for chromium plating.

Barrel Plating

Barrel plating is usually performed in either horizontal or oblique barrels constructed of polypropylene or other suitable plastics. The walls of the barrels are perforated, and the barrel is rotated during plating. Electrical contact is obtained via a flexible conductor known as a dangler. Some barrels are not perforated, but contain the plating solution and an anode.

Rack Plating

Rack plating is usually employed in the processing of parts that are too heavy, too large, or too complex in shape to be barrel plated. The parts can vary from a small knob that is to be nickel-chromium plated, to a large roller, weighing a ton or more, for hard chromium plating. Rack plating is used with manual, semiautomatic, and fully automatic machines.

Strip Plating

Strip plating is a plating process whereby the workpiece is a continuous strip being pulled through each process station (tank) by a take-up roll. Wire and lead frames are commonly strip plated with tin, tin lead, nickel, and precious metals. Steel sheet may be continuously zinc, tin, chromium, copper, brass, nickel-iron, or nickel-zinc plated. The strip may be plated at specific points as it goes through the cycle; such selective plating is very common with precious metals.

Automated Control

Electroplating is subject to a wide variety of variables that frequently change. Automatic controllers add stability and consistency to the operation and should be used wherever possible. Automatic ampere hour feeders monitor the plating time and may be used to approximate thickness as well as automatically feed addition agents. Solution pH may be controlled automatically with a relatively inexpensive piece of equipment; such control is especially useful in electrolytes where the pH tends to rise due to generation of the hydroxyl ion, such as in nickel and chloride zinc solutions. Rinse waters may be controlled by automatic conductivity meters connected to solenoid valves; these ensure good rinsing with reduced water consumption.

SUBSTRATE PREPARATION

In preparing the substrate for plating, it is important to properly select the correct pretreatment method. Pretreatment

influences the adhesion, appearance, composition, and corrosion resistance of the deposit.

Some of the factors that should be considered when selecting the pretreatment cycle are type of substrate, nature of the contamination, how the part is used, and part geometry.[1] Each basis metal may require a different pretreatment. Aluminum, for example, cannot be properly processed in solutions formulated for steel. Even variations in alloy may cause the finisher to change pretreatments. Table 47-1 identifies the various pretreatment practices published by the American Society for Testing and Materials (ASTM).

TABLE 47-1
American Society for Testing and Materials'
Recommended Practices for Preparation of Substrates
to be Electroplated

Metal Substrate	Standard Number
Low-carbon steel	B 183
High-carbon steel	B 242
Zinc alloy die castings	B 252
Aluminum alloys	B 253
Stainless steel	B 254
Copper and copper-based alloys	B 281
Lead and lead alloys	B 319
Iron castings	B 320
Nickel	B 343
Magnesium and magnesium alloys	B 480
Titanium and titanium alloys	B 481
Tungsten and tungsten alloys	B 482
Nickel alloys	B 558

Several stages are generally required to provide adequate cleaning of the substrate and activation: precleaning, intermediate alkaline cleaning, and electrocleaning.[2] Precleaning is designed to remove a large excess of soil, especially deposits of buffing compound or grease. It is also useful in reducing the viscosity of waxes and heavy oils to enable later cleaning stages to be more effective, or to surround fingerprints and dry dust with an oily matrix to facilitate removal by alkaline cleaners.

Intermediate alkaline cleaning removes solvent residues and residual soil that has been softened or conditioned by precleaning. Spray or soak alkaline cleaning may also be used as a precleaning stage, followed by additional alkaline cleaning, if the soil and metal lend themselves to this treatment. Electrocleaning is soak cleaning with agitation provided by the upward movement of bubbles of hydrogen or oxygen formed by the electrolytic decomposition of water in the solution.

Some parts cannot be etched because surface finish must be maintained, just as parts used in structural applications should not be subjected to pretreatments that may cause hydrogen embrittlement. The design of the work may require special handling and surface treatment. For example, a large part may require external manual finishing or parts with deep recesses or blind holes may require special handling and drainage techniques to avoid excessive drag-out and cross-contamination.

OPERATING PARAMETERS

The four main concerns in electroplating are temperature, pH, and chemistry of the plating bath as well as current density. Most plating solutions have an optimum temperature range for producing best results, and close control of temperature is important for proper current control. As the temperature of the solution increases, conductivity increases, and therefore the current increases for a fixed applied voltage; the converse is also true. Overplating or underplating occurs if the temperature is not maintained properly.

The pH control of plating solutions is necessary to maintain the acidity or alkalinity that has been determined to produce the best results. Appearance, stress, leveling, electrode efficiency, and coating hardness are influenced by the pH of the solution.[3] Current density is a very important variable in all electroplating operations. The character of the deposit, its distribution, the current efficiency, and perhaps whether a deposit forms at all may depend on the current density employed.[4]

PLATING PLASTICS

Plating can be successfully performed on many plastics, including ABS, polypropylene, polysulfone, modified polyphenylene oxide, polycarbonate, polyester, and nylon, to provide a decorative finish or a hard surface for wear and corrosion resistance. Plating can improve physical properties of the plastics part, such as tensile and flexural strength and the heat deflection temperature. Because of their light weight and ease of design, plastics have been used in many applications to replace zinc die castings, brass, and steel. The total cost to plate plastics is competitive with metals.

Various specifications and tests have been standardized by the American Society for Testing and Materials (ASTM) and the International Organization for Standardization (ISO). These standards help facilitate world trade, improve productivity, make mass production techniques possible, and lead to

TABLE 47-2
American Society for Testing and Materials' Standards for Electroplated Plastics

Standard Number	Title
ASTM B 532	Specification for the Appearance of Electroplated Plastics Surfaces
ASTM B 533	Test Method for Peel Strength of Metal Electroplated Plastics
ASTM B 553	Test Method for thermal Cycling of Electroplated Plastics
ASTM B 554	Measurement of Thickness of Metallic Coatings on Nonmetallic Surfaces
ASTM B 604	Specification for Decorative Electroplated Coatings of Copper/Nickel/Chromium on Plastics
ASTM B 727	Preparation of Plastics Materials for Electroplating

consumer satisfaction. Table 47-2 lists the standards published by the ASTM for electroplated plastics.

Preplate Cycle

Since plastics are nonconductive, they must first be processed through a preplate cycle, during which a metallic coating is deposited by an electroless plating process to make the plastics part conductive. The preplate cycle consists of etching, neutralizing, catalyzing, accelerating, and electroless plating. A typical cycle for plating ABS plastics is shown in Fig. 47-2. The actual cycle is dependent on the type of plastics being processed and the end application.

Depending on their condition, parts may require alkaline cleaning and/or conditioning before etching. If these two preliminary steps are performed, multiple rinses are recommended between each step.

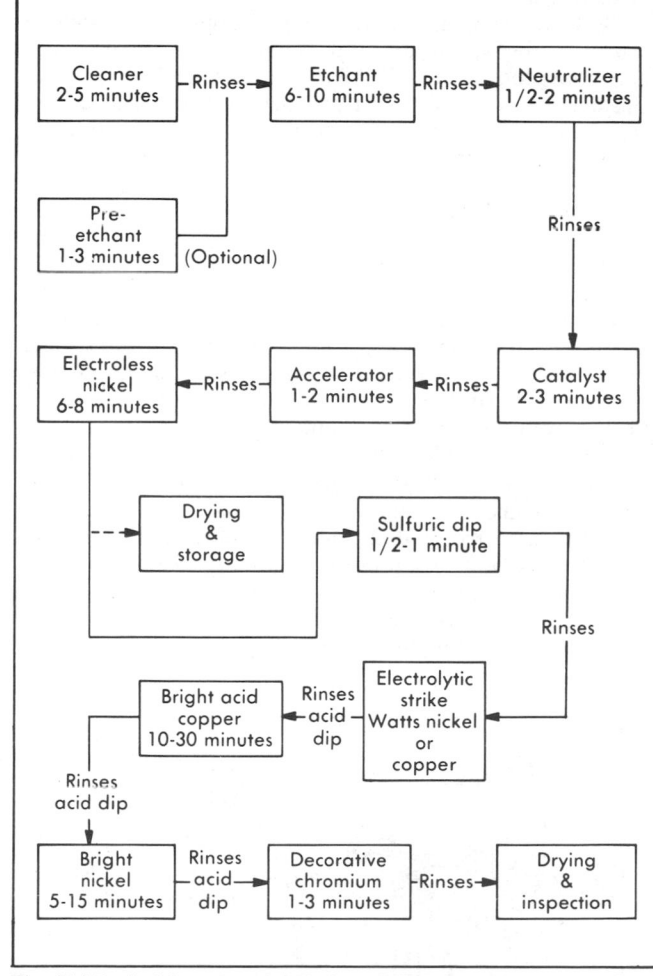

Fig. 47-2 Typical flow chart for plating ABS plastics. (*McGean-Rohco, Inc.*)

ELECTROFORMING

Electroforming[10] is a special type of electroplating in which a part is fabricated by the deposition of the desired metal on a form called a mandrel or matrix. The electrodeposited metal is built up to the desired thickness on the mandrel, and then the

ELECTROFORMING

two are separated (see Fig. 47-3). Much of the equipment and many of the techniques that are employed in electroforming are the same as those used in the production of electrodeposited coatings. Electroforms differ from electrodeposited coatings, however, in that they are used as separate structures and are therefore usually substantially thicker than plated coatings. Electrodeposited coatings for decorative use are normally less than 2 mils (50 μm) thick. Requirements for some electroforms dictate that the thickness exceeds 1/4″ (6 mm).

New techniques of electroforming make it possible to duplicate complex forms at lower costs by using high-quality, precision mass-production methods. In many applications, electroforming eliminates machining and joining, producing one-piece forms of continuous, uniform, nonporous, stress-free metal. The most intricate surface detail and the most irregular internal designs can be reproduced with tolerances as small as 0.0001″ (2.5 μm). The quality of the surfaces is limited only by the quality of the mandrel.

Electroforming offers a wide range of control over strength, density, porosity, and purity of the deposited metal to meet individual product needs. While electroforming in the past was considered to be a high-cost production method, its current costs compare favorably with mechanical reproduction in many applications and are often lower.

APPLICATIONS

Extremely fine molds and dies can be electroformed from a variety of metals. The virtually perfect surface reproducibility offered by electroforming processes make them ideal for such dimensionally critical applications as lens molds, phonograph record stampers, embossing plates, fine printing plates, and, most recently, high-resolution video disk and optical disk molds. The video disk, read by a pinpoint laser beam, is the greatest testimony to the accuracy of electroforming as a process that provides virtually absolute replicability and accuracy. Information bits encoded on the average optically read disk consist of impressions having an average mean diameter of 0.000008″ (0.2 μm), a tolerance well within the range of electroforming process accuracy. Nickel stampers for replicating holograms have also been produced by electroforming. Like optical disks, these holograms have microsurfaces with tolerances in the submicronic range.

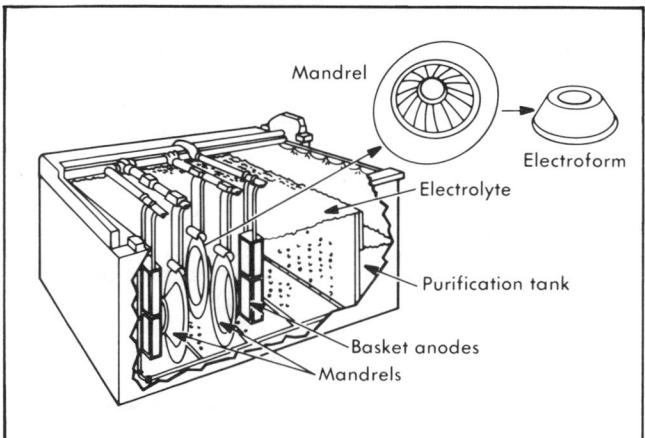

Fig. 47-3 Typical electroforming operation. (*The International Nickel Co., Inc.*)

ELECTROFORMED METALS

A variety of metals are available having properties suitable for thin metal-mold electroforming. Since many of the molding processes that use thin metal molds involve heat transfer through the mold to a thermoplastic or heat-setting material, the thermal conductivity of the metal selected is important. The metal's durability and abrasion and scratch resistance are also important when considering the quantity and quality of the moldings being manufactured. The metals most commonly used in electroforming are copper, nickel, and iron.

ELECTROFORMING BATHS

Plating solutions for electroforming do not differ in principle from ordinary plating baths for decorative and protective purposes. But because the physical properties of electroforms are usually of much more concern than those of ordinary electroplates, the composition and operating conditions of electroforming solutions tend to be more critical than those for the thinner deposits used in standard electroplating. Many agents, added for brightness, leveling, and other purposes, are not allowable in electroforming solutions because they introduce trace contaminants into the deposits that have deleterious effects on the properties of the electroforms. Also, because thicker deposits are involved, speed of plating is of greater importance; plating times, which are normally long, should be minimized.[6]

MANDRELS

By the proper selection of mandrels, it is possible to electroform complicated shapes in one piece with extreme accuracy. The design of mandrels and the choice of materials from which to make them involve several considerations. They should be impervious to various types of cleaning and plating solutions, and should be dimensionally stable. They should also have the proper surface finish required for the applications and be capable of being separated or dissolved from the electrodeposited metal.

Types of Mandrels

Mandrels used in electroforming can be completely reusable or completely destroyed in the process, depending on the particular applications.

Permanent mandrels. Permanent mandrels, also known as matrices, are used to produce many electroformed parts and are usually machined, cast, or electroformed. A permanent mandrel must be treated to form a parting film on its surface to ensure separation from the electroform. Common methods used to form this film include passivation in dichromate solutions, anodic treatment, or by applying an absorbed film from a colloidal material. A part intended for production on permanent mandrels must be designed with sufficient draft (1 to 3°) to permit removal of the mandrel from the part without damage. If the design is such that these conditions cannot be met, expendable mandrels will probably be required. Common substrates for permanent mandrels are stainless steels, electroplated metals, copper, brass, nickel, and rigid plastics.

Expendable mandrels. Expendable mandrels are completely destroyed during separation from the electroform and are usually made of nonmetallic, nonconductive materials that generally require metallizing after preparation in order to accept the electrodeposit. Some common materials used in producing expendable mandrels include aluminum alloys (2024, 6061, and 7075), plastics, fusible metals, waxes, glass, wood, and plaster.

Mandrel Design

Mandrels for electroforming are designed to produce the desired pattern and texture on either the inside or the outside surface of the part. When the outside surface of a part is the significant area, the internal surface of the mandrel upon which it is formed must be carefully designed. When the inside surface of a part is important, the external surface of the mandrel requires special care. In the former case, the mandrel is called a negative mandrel; in the latter, a positive mandrel.

Negative mandrels. The following suggestions apply only to mandrels in which the internal surfaces are significant:

- Sharp internal angles must be avoided to prevent weak corners.
- Fillets should be used if acute angles are necessary.
- Grooves should be made as shallow as possible; the width should exceed the depth.
- Corners should have a 1/32″ (0.8 mm) radius.

Positive mandrels. The suggestions for negative mandrels also apply to positive mandrels, but to a lesser degree because external surfaces are easier to prepare than internal ones.

EQUIPMENT

Certain features are commonly included in electroforming equipment systems that differ from conventional plating equipment. Electroforming tanks are usually designed to accommodate the particular shape and size of electroforms being produced. Agitation systems are generally included to enhance the high-speed deposition. Power supplies must have output ripple characteristics consistent with the mechanical properties desired on the formed deposit. Special rectifier controls that automatically raise the plating current from an initially low starting current to high-speed levels are desirable in most production applications where close monitoring of plating conditions is essential. Microprocessor controls have been integrated into electroforming systems used in the manufacture of disks and holograms. These controls allow a wide range of process variations to be programmed into a system, adding flexibility, stability, and reproducibility when manufacturing specialized electroforms.

SELECTIVE PLATING

The principle of selective plating is the same as that of tank electroplating—metal ions in a liquid electrolyte are chemically reduced by an electric current and deposited as a metal at the cathode (workpiece). The main difference is that a large electrolytic bath is not used. Rather, the selective plating electrolyte is carried in an absorbent anode covering and applied directly to the area of the workpiece to be plated. As with tank plating, the workpiece must be electrically conductive, either intrinsically (e.g., a metal workpiece) or artificially (e.g., covered with a conductive paint).

PROCESS

In operation, the cathode (electrically negative) lead from the direct current power supply is connected to the workpiece being plated, and the anode (electrically positive) lead is connected to an insulated plating tool handle. An anode, covered by absorbent material, is attached to the insulating handle to complete the basic equipment (see Fig. 47-4). The actual plating is a hand operation accomplished by alternately dipping the covered anode into a plating solution and then rubbing it over the area to be plated. When the plating solution comes into contact with the workpiece, the electrical circuit is completed, a low-voltage current flows, and metal ions begin depositing on the workpiece as described by Faraday's law.

ADVANTAGES AND LIMITATIONS

The equipment for selective plating is portable and hence permits the plating or repair to be performed at the work location. Parts may also be plated without having to be extensively masked or disassembled; however, since liquids are used, the ability to completely clean and dry the workpiece will dictate the amount of masking and disassembly required. The selective plating process is simple and does not require nearly the same degree of control over electric current and solution chemistry as does tank plating. Yet, selective plating can

provide greater deposition rates than tank plating. The basic equipment configuration provides fast and simple plating for applications that do not require close tolerances for thickness or flatness; for applications having close tolerances or requirements to minimize mechanical finishing (grinding, lapping, etc.), more complex equipment with current control, electrolyte pumps, and mechanically controlled anode movement is available. With frequent anode dipping or adequate electrolyte flow, atomic hydrogen deposition can be minimized to reduce the danger of hydrogen embrittlement to high-strength workpieces. Finally, workpieces that are large and of complex shape can be successfully selectively plated.

Selective plating is generally a labor-intensive process, and the plating solutions can be more costly than equal quantities of tank plating solutions because of their complex formulations and higher metal content. However, since smaller quantities of solutions are used in selective plating, the capital investment is not prohibitive. Industrial use is usually limited to low-production rates because the parts are plated one at a time. In general, high-production volumes can be more efficiently tank plated, unless the workpieces are large and the areas to be plated relatively small, making tank plating impractical.

APPLICATIONS

Selective plating has diverse uses and should be considered any time that a surface requires modification to improve appearance, dimension, or chemical and mechanical properties. Mismachined or worn parts can often be salvaged with a buildup plating of nickel, while contact resistance on copper busbar joint areas can be reduced with a plating of silver. Steel parts can be protected from corrosion with a zinc or cadmium plating, while printed circuit board contact fingers can be plated (originally or as a repair) with gold. Bearing surfaces can be repaired with tin or babbitt metal, while steel parts can be brass plated to improve appearance. A plating thickness of 2 mils (50

SELECTIVE PLATING

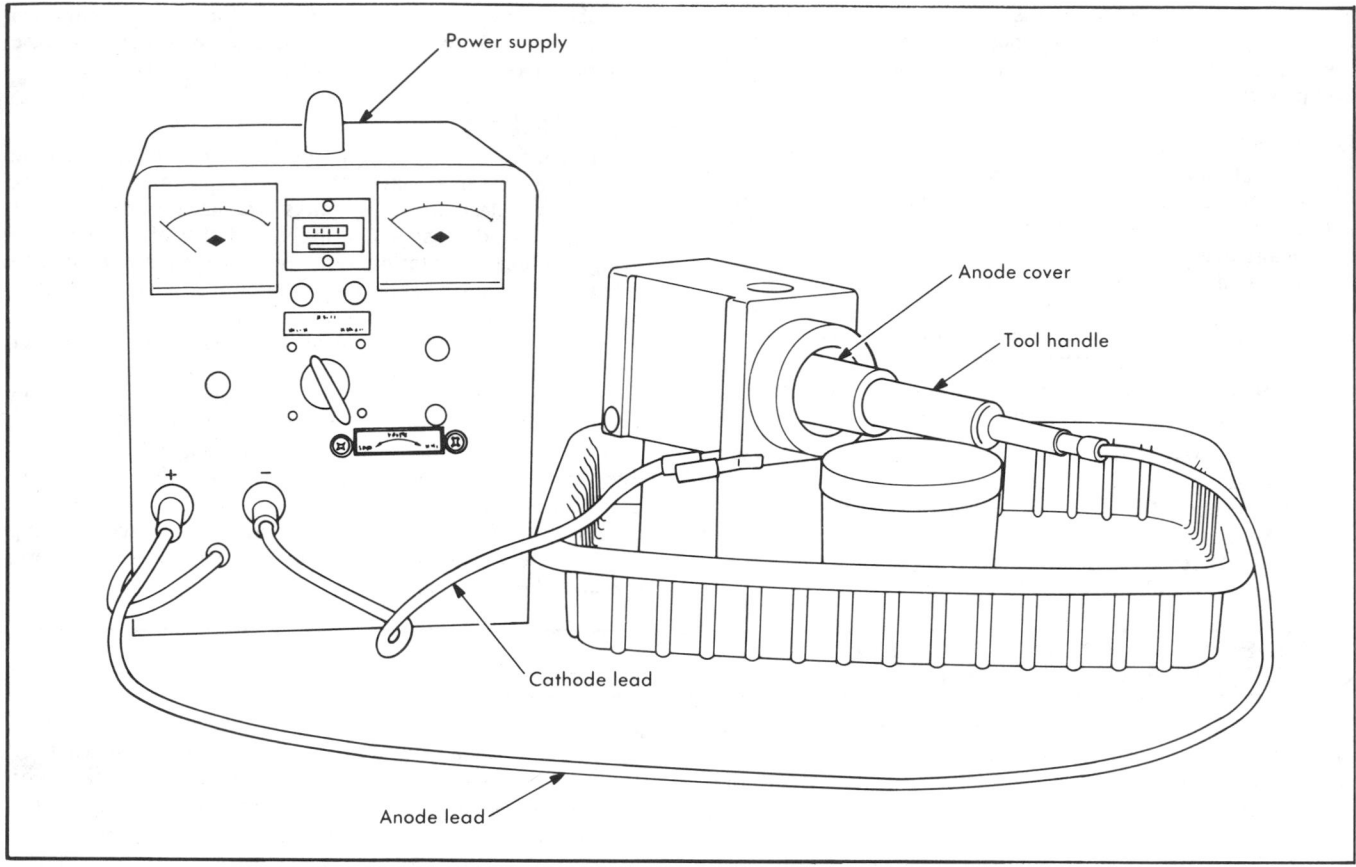

Fig. 47-4 Selective plating the inside diameter of a mismachined workpiece. (*SIFCO Selective Plating*)

μm) can routinely be applied; and with proper technique and solution flow, 10-70 mils (250-1780 μm) can be applied.[7] The application of selective plating is limited only by the imagination, availability of a particular plating solution, and labor considerations.

In general, conflicting requirements for surface and bulk properties can be resolved with the proper selection of a plating solution. Limitations on the area to be plated, disassembly, or transportation problems that would make conventional tank plating impractical can usually be overcome by the selective nature and portability of selective plating.

EQUIPMENT

In addition to the solutions already discussed, the equipment used in selective plating includes a variable, direct current power supply, a plating tool with anodes, and auxiliary materials such as anode covers and masking material. Equipment variations include semiautomated to fully automated configurations involving pumps to feed electrolyte to the anode, and actuators to apply the anode and replace workpieces in an assembly line operation.

MECHANICAL PLATING

Mechanical plating is a process used to deposit malleable metals onto the surface of metallic parts. Mechanical plating has also been referred to as peen plating and impact plating. The term *mechanical galvanizing* is used in reference to deposits of zinc thicker than 2 mils (50 μm).

Mechanical plating is a room temperature process in which metal coatings are applied to parts without electricity, which is used in electroplating, and without high heat, as used in hot-dip galvanizing. The parts to be coated are tumbled in a lined barrel with water, metal powder, special promoters or accelerators, and glass impact beads. Most metal powders are approximately 0.0002" (5 μm) in size. The promoter or accelerator provides the proper chemical environment for the plating process to take place. The glass beads or media are usually spherical in shape with a diameter of 0.006 to 0.25" (0.15 to 6.4 mm). The media may also be made from ceramic materials and may be angular in shape. The mechanical energy generated from the barrel's rotation is transmitted through the media and causes the metal particles to be peened flat into a metallurgical bond.

PROCESS DESCRIPTION

The process sequence for mechanical plating and galvanizing is a straightforward sequence of soil and/or scale removal, surface preparation, addition of promoters or accelerators, and addition of metal powders. Descaling and/or soil removal can be accomplished in either the plating barrel or in an off-line cleaning system. After cleaning, the parts, glass beads, water, and surface conditioners are added to the rotating barrel. The surface conditioners remove residual traces of metal scale and oxides, producing a lightly coppered workpiece. The slurry of glass beads exerts a scrubbing action that facilitates oxide removal during surface preparation and provides a cushion between heavy parts, which minimizes damage to edges and sharp corners. Flat parts are also kept from clinging together owing to surface tension created by the slurry mixture. Finally, the slurry carries the plating material into the holes and recesses of the parts providing the mechanical energy necessary for plating. After the accelerator and metal powder are added, the metal particles are cold welded onto the parts by the many impingements of the small glass beads.

Advantages and Limitations

Mechanical plating eliminates the hydrogen embrittlement of steel parts, commonly associated with electroplating, since no electric current is required in the plating process. Thicker coatings can be deposited at little increased cost; and corners, recesses, threads, and the inside of tubular parts can be successfully plated. Using just one barrel, coatings of different metals (sandwich coatings) can be applied merely by adding powders of different metals in the proper sequence. Composite coatings can be deposited by using mixtures of two or more metal powders.

The chemical environments encountered in both surface preparation and plating are relatively mild. The materials are sold as concentrates; however, in use, the concentration of alkaline or acid surface preparation solutions is approximately 5%. Plating environments are even milder. The chemicals used are depleted and discarded after the cycle. Hazardous materials, such as fulminates, are not used, nor are highly toxic materials, such as cyanides, employed. Consequently, personnel safety problems are minimized, and waste disposal is simple when required. In addition, the relatively mild nature of the chemical system makes it possible to plate most powdered metal parts without initially filling or sealing the parts with organic materials.

Applications

The parts to be mechanically plated are most commonly made from ferrous metals (including highly alloyed and heat-treated steels), brass, bronze, and copper. Powdered metals can also be successfully plated.

The size and shape of the part determines how suitable it is for plating or galvanizing. Generally, parts range in size from 3/8 to 8″ (9.5 to 200 mm) and weigh less than 1 lb (0.5 kg). Threaded rods in excess of 40″ (1000 mm) long have been plated, but the cost is usually prohibitive for parts of that size.

Mechanical plating and galvanizing are performed on parts that are normally handled in batches. Parts that are normally rack plated electrolytically cannot be mechanically plated.

Typical parts that are mechanically plated include screws, bolts, nuts, washers, J-nuts, U-clips, self-tapping screws, nails, and chain links. Parts that are frequently mechanically galvanized include those previously mentioned, as well as parts used by the construction and highway maintenance industries. Through sandwich or composite procedures, the coatings can be tailored to meet special requirements such as enhanced corrosion protection for the base metal, improved surface appearance, resistance to tarnish, and improved lubricity of the surface.

Metals Deposited

The plating metals used, in order of current volumes, are zinc, cadmium, tin, lead, and their alloys. Copper, silver, and gold have also been deposited by this process. Corrosion resistance imparted by a mechanical zinc or cadmium plate is essentially the same, thickness for thickness, as that applied by other methods.

The surfaces of mechanically plated parts exhibit a bright nonspecular appearance. The mirror-bright surface possible with electroplate is not achieved, but the appearance is much brighter and smoother than is produced by hot-dip galvanizing. In addition, postplating treatments such as dichromating can be applied.

The thickness of the metals deposited by mechanical plating is usually thinner than by mechanical galvanizing. Coating thickness for mechanically plated parts varies from 0.2 to 1 mil (5 to 25 μm), and for mechanically galvanized parts the coating thickness ranges from 1 to 3 mil (25 to 75 μm).

MECHANICAL PLATING EQUIPMENT

The equipment used in mechanical plating and galvanizing

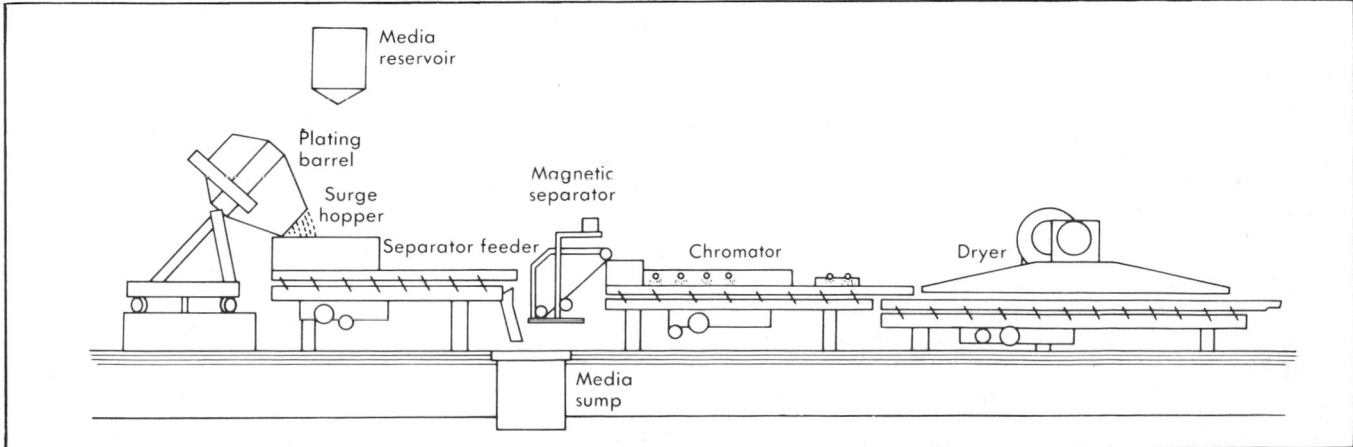

Fig. 47-5 Components used in a typical mechanical plating system. (*Renold, Inc.*)

consists of several individual components. The main component is a rotating barrel having a metal parts capacity of 1 to 20 ft^3 (0.003 to 0.6 m^3); the actual barrel volume is approximately 4.5 times greater than the metal parts capacity. The barrel may be of the open-ended inclined or closed horizontal types, and is made from stainless or mild steel with a rubber or polypropylene liner. The depth to diameter ratio is approximately 1.4:1. Barrel actuation is achieved either hydraulically or electrically, with hydraulic actuation being the most popular. The speed of the barrel is usually adjustable from 70 to 200 sfm (20 to 60 m/min) to permit plating of both heavy and light parts.

Other components include a media supply hopper, media separator, and a dryer, all of which may be used as separate units or integrated and mechanized together. Figure 47-5 shows an integrated mechanical plating system incorporating a plating barrel, surge hopper, feeder and media separator, chromator, and dryer. Weighing, loading, media handling, and chemical feeding systems are also included to complete the plating system. The surge hopper/separator feeder receives the load of plated parts from the barrel and then separates the parts from the glass media with a vibrating screen separator or magnetic belt, or a combination of these components. The media is pumped back to an overhead reservoir to be used in the next coating run. After separation, the parts are either dried or chromated and dried.

ELECTROLESS PLATING

The electroless plating process, also called autocatalytic deposition, deposits a uniform coating onto catalytic surfaces, regardless of the shape of the part. Once a primary layer of metal has formed on the substrate, that layer, as well as each subsequent layer, becomes the catalyst that causes the reaction to continue. Electroless plating, in contrast to conventional plating, does not use external electric current to produce a deposit. Deposition occurs in an aqueous solution containing metal ions, a reducing agent, and a catalyst (part). Chemical reactions on the surface of the catalytic part being plated cause deposition of the metal or alloy.

Electroless plating provides several unique characteristics superior to electrodeposition processes:

- The process produces a uniformly thick coating on both simple and complexly shaped workpieces.
- The process may be applicable to a variety of substrates ranging from metals and semiconductors to nonconductors.
- The use of an auxiliary power supply and the need for electrical contact is eliminated, except for precleaning and surface activation purposes.
- Some electroless deposits have unique and controlled chemical, mechanical, and magnetic properties.

Electroless plating processes are used by industry to alter the surface of a part, providing a uniform, conductive metallic coating. Nickel, copper, cobalt, and gold are the most commonly deposited metals. The commercially produced electroless alloys are listed in Table 47-3.

Composite coatings have also been successfully deposited. These coatings consist of particles of such materials as synthetic diamonds, silicon carbide, aluminum oxide, and polytetrafluorethylene (PTFE), codeposited with nickel or cobalt. Composite coatings enhance the wear and friction characteristics of the metal deposit.

PROPERTIES

The properties of electroless coatings are varied and are determined by the specific metal and process employed. In the case of electroless nickel, the corrosion and wear resistance, conductivity, solderability, and magnetic properties of the deposit find useful application.

Producing specific properties in the deposit from a particular plating process requires careful control. For example, the hardness of the base metal determines which heat treatments are required to prevent hydrogen embrittlement caused by the pretreatment processes. It may be necessary to control the surface finish, elongation, structure of the deposit, reflectivity, conductivity, melting point, composition, coefficient of thermal expansion, density, internal stress, and elasticity to achieve specified properties. The producer must therefore have a working knowledge of how the process parameters affect the deposit.

APPLICATIONS

The applications of electroless metal deposits are many and diverse. Each metal has specific applications for which it can be used. Typical metal deposits include copper, gold, nickel, and nickel alloys.

TABLE 47-3

Commercially Produced Electroless Alloys

Electroless Process	Au	Cu	Ni	Co	P	B	Tl	Trace
Copper		99.9						0.1
Gold	99.98							0.02
Nickel phosphorus low			98		2			0.3
Nickel phosphorus medium			94		6			0.3
Nickel phosphorus high			89		11			0.1
Nickel cobalt phosphorus			75	20	5			0.3
Nickel cobalt phosphorus			16	78	6			0.3
Nickel boron			99.5			0.5		0.1
Nickel thallium boron			92			3.5	4.5	0.3

(Stapleton Company)

ELECTROLESS PLATING PROCESS

Electroless plating processes depend on chemical reduction reactions to deposit uniform metallic coatings on parts, eliminating the need for external current. The coating is uniform on all wetted surfaces. Thickness is determined by the length of time the article or part is kept immersed in the solution. The entire process involves several different steps as discussed in this section.

Precleaning

Precleaning removes heavy soils and scales on the surface and exposes the bare base material. The precleaning can be accomplished by wet or dry blasting, vapor degreasing, mechanical cleaning, and descaling, among other methods. In almost all cases, the base material will not be clean enough after precleaning to achieve adequate adhesion. The surface will still have oxides and oils present.

Cleaning

Cleaning removes the oils and organic material on the surface of the parts and is first accomplished by soaking in a solubilizing solution at an elevated temperature. Some base materials require electrocleaning as a second step to remove carbon or grinding material. The last step is to completely remove the oxides in an acidic solution.

The cleaning of metals prior to electroplating is discussed in American Society for Testing and Materials (ASTM) Standard B 322. Most of the information in that standard is applicable to the preparation of metals for electroless deposition. Additional information can be obtained in those standards that deal with specific metals and alloys.[8]

Initiating Deposition

Autocatalytic nickel will usually deposit on clean, wetted surfaces. Aluminum, beryllium, platinum metals, iron, cobalt, nickel, titanium, and their alloys can be plated directly. Certain base metals cannot be plated directly; these include zinc, lead, cadmium, tin, bismuth, arsenic, antimony, and alloys containing large proportions of these metals. The metals that cannot be plated directly should be electroplated with a thin copper or nickel strike prior to being immersed in the electroless plating solution.

Preliminary electrolysis or contact with a catalytic metal like iron or nickel is required for deposition on copper, silver, gold, carbon, vanadium, molybdenum, tungsten, chromium, selenium, and uranium. In some cases, immersion deposition processes may be used to initiate electroless deposition. Special heat treatments may be required on aluminum, beryllium, titanium, and other metals to obtain maximum adhesion.[9]

Plating

When a properly prepared material is placed into the electroless plating solution, the surface potential reaches a value where metal deposition is possible. The deposition potential is dependent on the pH, temperature, ionic concentration, and chemical composition of the solution.

As the potential changes, a charge between the solution and the base material is created. The charge causes the cations in the solution to organize themselves and produce what is called the matrix. This matrix is like a blanket that covers the surface and controls the deposition process. The reducing agents in the solution provide electrons at the interface. Through several sequential reactions within the matrix, the metal ions in solution are reduced, producing the coating.

Each electroless plating process uses unique chemistry to achieve this reduction reaction. Powerful reducing agents like sodium borohydride and titanium trichloride are used to plate out thallium and gold, while sodium hypophosphite and formaldehyde will reduce nickel and copper, respectively. The concentrations of these reducing agents and the metal salts change as the plating process proceeds and by-products are produced. To sustain the reduction reactions, additions of fresh chemicals must be made. In addition, the special additives used to provide brightness, stability, wetting, controlled cloud points, and controlled transition temperatures must be monitored and kept at optimum levels.

Proprietary electroless processes are available, and suppliers of these processes provide instructions for maintaining and controlling individual processes. Electroless processes can be maintained by performing simple chemical analyses from which chemicals required to replenish the solution can be determined.

EQUIPMENT

The choice of electroless plating equipment influences the life of the plating bath and the quality of the deposits. Plating tanks are generally rectangular in shape and may be made from a variety of materials. Alternating the plating operation between two tanks minimizes downtime and allows more time for stripping the tank not being used.

Most electroless baths operate at approximately 200° F (90° C) and require heaters and temperature controllers for proper control; the maximum temperature variation is ±5.0° F (3.0° C). Equipment should be checked frequently to ensure accuracy. Steam heat exchangers are the most efficient for tanks having a capacity of greater than 200 gal (760 L), while electric immersion heaters work well in smaller tanks. Electric heaters should have a safety interlock that would prevent a fire in case the heater elements are exposed.

Pumps are required for solution transfer and filtration. Vertical centrifugal pumps are most commonly used and are usually made from CPVC plastic or stainless steel. Cartridge filters and filter bags are used to filter out particles larger than 0.2 mils (5 μm) in size. Filter bags are less expensive than cartridges and minimize the restriction at the discharge side of the pump. Mechanical or low-pressure air agitators are used to provide a fresh supply of solution to the part and to remove the hydrogen produced during deposition.

Rectifiers are used for some pretreatments, such as electrocleaning, and are also used when the activation process cannot employ immersion techniques. Rectifiers must be sized to achieve the specified current density of the electrocleaner. Typically their size range is between 50 and 300 A/ft² (5.4 and 32 A/dm²).

References

1. Carmine P. Nargi, "Preparing Metals for Plating," *Products Finishing Directory* (1984), pp. 87-89.
2. American Society for Testing and Materials, *Cleaning Metals Prior to Electroplating*, ASTM Standard B 322 (Philadelphia, PA: 1979).
3. Frederick A. Lowenheim, *Electroplating* (New York: McGraw-Hill Inc., 1978), p. 516.
4. *Ibid.*, p. 14.

CHAPTER 47

REFERENCES

5. Carl M. Rodia and J. L. Lester, "Electroforming," *Metal Finishing—Guidebook Directory Issue* (1984), pp. 379-387.
6. Lowenheim, *op.cit.*, p. 436.
7. Joe C. Norris, "New Developments in Brush Plating," *Products Finishing* (May 1983), p. 65.
8. American Society for Testing and Materials, *1984 Annual Book of ASTM Standards*, vol. 02.05 (Philadelphia, PA: 1984).
9. *Ibid.*

INORGANIC COATINGS

CONVERSION COATINGS

Conversion coating, sometimes referred to as chemical reaction priming, is the formation of a coating on a ferrous or nonferrous metal surface as a result of controlled chemical or electrochemical attack. The converted surface is not superimposed on the underlying metal, such as a paint coating, but is rather a strongly adherent chemical entity formed at the interface by interaction between the chemical coating solution and the ions formed from the metallic surface immersed in the solution. The two most common methods of applying conversion coatings are spraying and immersion.

CONVERSION COATING TYPES

Conversion coatings may be classified as either natural or man-made depending on the environment that was used to cause the interaction. Manmade conversion coatings can be further broken into chemical and electrochemical processes.

Natural Conversion Coatings

Coatings, usually oxides, form on many metals in their natural environment. In the presence of moisture, anodic and cathodic areas develop all over a metal surface providing a corrosion mechanism. The process of converting outer metal atoms into soluble or nonadherent chemical compounds continues until all, or almost all, of the metal is consumed or combined with oxygen, as in the rusting of iron. However, if the corrosion products form an invisible, adherent film on the metal, as occurs naturally in the formation of an oxide on aluminum or copper, further attack is stopped or greatly retarded. The chemical reactions and thermodynamic relationships inherent in destructive corrosion are basically the same as those that result in beneficial surface layers.

Chemical Conversion Coatings

Chemical conversion coatings are produced by contacting the metallic surface with a chemical solution. The most common are phosphate, chromate, and oxide coatings.

Phosphate conversion coatings. Phosphate conversion coatings are produced from chemicals containing phosphoric acid and its salts. The coatings formed from heavy metal phosphates are crystalline in nature and consist of layers of water insoluble phosphorus compounds of iron, zinc, manganese, calcium, or a combination of these. Phosphate coatings formed from alkali metals of Group I elements in the periodic table and phosphoric acid are known as iron phosphates and are amorphous (noncrystalline) in nature. Crystalline phosphate coatings are usually different shades of gray; however, pretreatments or post-treatments may be performed to produce various colors including black, red, or green. Iron phosphates are light blue to red iridescent.

Chromate conversion coatings. Chromate conversion coatings are produced from compounds of chromium in combination with other water-soluble inorganic materials. During the conversion process, the base metal (aluminum, cadmium, or zinc) is converted on its southside surface to a complex chemical entity constituting salts to hexavalent chromium and trivalent chromium. Chromate conversion coatings are amorphorus and gelatinous when applied to the parts, but harden and become hydrophobic after they are dried. These coatings can be produced in shades of bright clear, yellow, bronze, green olive drab, or black. Some chromate conversion coatings can absorb certain organic dyes (similar to anodized aluminum coatings) to produce a spectrum of hues.

Oxide conversion coatings. Two types of oxide coatings are currently being used. The first is a black or bluish oxide coating produced on iron or steel when they are treated with hot caustic soda solutions containing accelerators. The second oxide coating is produced on cadmium, copper, iron, steel, and zinc alloys from acidic compositions at moderate temperatures. Unlike other conversion coatings, oxide conversion coatings contribute little corrosion protection to the part; they are generally produced for abrasion resistance, aesthetic, or identification purposes only. The colors range from gray to blue to black.

Electrochemical Conversion Coatings

Electrochemical conversion coatings are produced on the surfaces of aluminum, magnesium, and titanium alloys by the anodizing process. This type of conversion coating can also be applied to zinc and zinc alloys using proprietary chemical formulations. Electrochemical conversion coatings provide good corrosion and abrasion resistance. The color of the coatings ranges from clear to yellow to green to black. In some cases, it is necessary to seal the coating to obtain maximum benefit.

APPLICATIONS

Some of the purposes of conversion coating can be illustrated by the following objectives for which coating provides economic value:

1. Corrosion protection.
2. Prepainting treatment.
3. Cold forming; lubrication carrier.
4. Wear reduction/resistance.
5. Electrical-resistance coating.
6. Decorative final finish.
7. Identification.

In analyzing the economics of a treatment, not only must the cost of application per unit area be considered, but also what this cost may bring about

CONVERSION COATINGS

in possible savings. Savings may be related to reductions in material costs, changes in complexity of manufacturing procedures, and elimination of costly service failures.

Corrosion Protection

Conversion coatings provide resistance to corrosive environments in their own right; but when coupled with a rust-preventive oil or wax, they may greatly enhance the resistance to corrosion. The coating may act as a blotter to absorb the oil and increase the protection of articles that are not to be painted.

Prepaint Treatments

Paint adhesion and life are usually improved by conversion coatings because they (1) provide mechanical bonds such as capillary pores and cavities for the paint, (2) provide increased surface area on which the molecular forces contributing to adhesion can act, (3) minimize or inhibit the spread of corrosion if the organic finish is damaged, (4) result in a nonalkaline surface that is not harmful to paint or to sensitive metals, (5) ensure a clean surface before painting, and (6) in the case of zinc and other sensitive metal surfaces, prevent reaction between the paint and the metal surface.

Cold Forming Lubrication

Some deep draws would be virtually impossible without the use of zinc phosphate coatings. These coatings are capable of reacting with or absorbing oil and soap-type lubricants and, in some cases, an insoluble lubricant film. The inherent heat-resistant characteristics of the conversion coatings permit their use in such applications that might otherwise destroy other types of drawing compounds or lubricants.

Wear Reduction/Resistance

Certain phosphate coatings, through their ability to produce parting layers and promote continuous oil films that are not subject to rupture, are used to reduce wear on bearing surfaces and permit uniform break-in of new parts. Most of the coatings used for this purpose are manganese phosphate coatings. However, zinc phosphate coatings are receiving increasing interest.

In metalforming, the coating acts in conjunction with the lubricant to form a separating layer. However, when used to aid wear resistance, the coating is rapidly removed by the interaction of the two surfaces rubbing together. Small, uniform pits produced in the base metal during the formation of the coating act as reservoirs to maintain a uniform oil film between the two surfaces and to prevent seizing of the surfaces.

Phosphate coatings that reduce wear have been used extensively in automotive engines and in refrigerator compressors. Typical parts treated include pinion gears, camshafts, pistons and rings, rocker arms, worm gears, tappets, and oil-distribution rods. However, coatings have not been successful in reducing wear in roller or ball bearings.

Electrical-Resistance Coating

These coatings are formed from baths of chromium, iron, alumina, and silica, with or without mica, and are applied by the roll-on technique. The coatings produced must: (1) prevent the adhesion of steel surfaces during gas-fired annealing for two hours at 1550° F (845° C); (2) have an electrical-resistance value before and after annealing no greater than 5/10 as measured by the Franklin tester (a lower measurement preferred); (3) not add

more than 1% to the thickness of stacked laminates (although more is permissible in some instances); (4) not hold dust during handling; (5) not cause wear on stamping dies; and (6) upgrade low-carbon steel to a performance equal to low-silicon steel.

METALS TREATED

The four metals of major industrial importance in the automotive, electrical appliance, office equipment, housing, and related fields are steel, zinc, galvanized steel, and aluminum. Most metal products are painted to add decorative value, decrease corrosion, and increase service life. In addition, many are cold formed and/or subject to wear in use. However, almost any metal may be conversion coated for a useful purpose. The fabrication of quality metal products generally presupposes the use of conversion processes to serve one or more purposes.

Conversion coatings are applied to cleaned articles by immersion or by spraying on solutions at the required temperature for the required length of time. Coating weights depend upon the manner in which the articles are cleaned, the composition of the processing immersion bath or spray, and the type and surface condition of the metal.

PHOSPHATE CONVERSION COATINGS

Phosphate conversion coatings bring about transformations of metal substrates into new surfaces having nonmetallic and nonconducting properties. The transformations occur in phosphating solutions containing divalent metal phosphates and, in some instances, in solutions containing monovalent metal phosphates. Generally, the solutions are prepared from liquid concentrates containing one or more divalent metals (zinc, magnesium, calcium, etc., phosphates), free phosphoric acid, and an accelerator.

Three types of phosphate conversion coatings are currently being used: zinc, iron, and manganese. Zinc phosphating is often used as a pretreatment for painted parts. It is also used to impart corrosion resistance and to aid in cold forming operations. Zinc coating weights are usually 200-500 mg/ft^2 (2.2-5.4 g/m^2). Iron phosphate coatings are primarily used to form a passive substrate under paint and have coating weights of 50 to 100 mg/ft^2 (0.5 to 1.0 g/m^2). Manganese phosphate coatings are used primarily on machined parts such as gears and internal combustion engine components as an antiscuff film for break-in wear. Coating weights are usually 1000-3000 mg/ft^2 (10.8-32.2 g/m^2).

Since the seventies, a trend to reduce heating costs, improve working conditions, prolong equipment life, reduce sludge, and reduce processing steps has resulted in low-temperature iron and zinc phosphate coatings and, to a limited degree, solvent phosphating solutions.

The addition of heavy metal ions, such as cupric ions, to a conversion bath greatly reduces the coating formation time and the size and nonuniformity of the coating crystals. Copper, which is cathodic to the dissolving metals, deposits on the base metal to form many local cells, thus increasing the potential difference between the local anode and cathode areas. Hence, the rate of dissolution of the metal is greatly increased, with a proportionate reduction in hydrogen ion concentration in the solution layer next to the metal, resulting in faster coating precipitation.

Nickel salts behave differently than cupric ions, and their benefit may result from a catalytic action connected with the release of molecular hydrogen or from the control of certain reactions with other accelerators present in the bath. Nickel additions are frequently used when hardened materials are treated and when the activity of the metal surface being treated is low. Nickel is also used to improve a zinc phosphate coating on galvanized steel surfaces.

Besides copper and nickel, other heavy metal compounds act as promoters, catalysts, accelerators, or coating supplements. These accelerators include molybdenum, tungsten, vanadium, zirconium, and cerium compounds. However, adding most of these compounds to phosphate coating baths has been generally discarded because of the difficulty of maintaining the proper concentration in the processing solution and because of the reduced corrosion resistance of the coatings obtained. Some solution manufacturers have used molybdenum compounds as an integral part of proprietary iron phosphate compounds.

CHROMATE CONVERSION COATINGS

Chromate conversion coatings, often referred to as chromate coatings, are produced by chemically converting certain metal surfaces with aqueous solutions of chromic acid, chromates, dichromates, and certain other organic and inorganic chemicals. The treating bath compositions are generally proprietary, but all contain two basic ingredients—hexavalent chromium ions and enough acid to produce a desired pH. A few recent formulations, however, are based on trivalent chromium ions that are used to produce clear coatings on electroplated zinc and cadmium. Chromate-phosphate mixtures are also used to form combination conversion coatings on aluminum.

One of the oldest and still popular chromating processes for cadmium and zinc is based on a solution containing sodium dichromate slightly acidified with sulfuric acid. One chromating process for aluminum uses a bath of chromic, phosphoric, and hydrofluoric acids in well-defined proportions. Several chromating processes for magnesium have been developed by Dow Chemical Company.

Metals commonly treated include aluminum, cadmium, copper, magnesium, silver, zinc, and their alloys. The coatings are generally applied by immersion, although spraying, brushing, swabbing, or electrolytic methods are also used.

Chemical Reaction

The films in most common use are formed by the chemical reaction of hexavalent chromium with a metal surface in the presence of other components, or activators, in an acid solution. The hexavalent chromium is partially reduced to trivalent chromium during the reaction, with a concurrent rise in pH, forming a complex mixture consisting largely of hydrated chromium chromate and hydrous oxides of both chromium and the basis metal. The composition of the film is rather indefinite since it contains varying quantities of the reactants, reaction products, and water of hydration, as well as the associated ions of the particular systems.[1]

Regulated concentrations of activators are added to the many proprietary formulations to promote the formation of the chromate film on the metal surface. Some of the common activators added include acetate, formate, sulfate, chloride, ferricyanide, fluoride, nitrate, phosphate, and sulfamate ions. Selection, separation, and control of the activator in a given formulation are performed by the chemical supplier.

Coating Characteristics

Chromate coatings are generally amorphous, nonporous, and gel-like when initially formed. As the coating dries, it slowly hardens or ages and becomes hydrophobic, less soluble, and more abrasion resistant. The coatings formed from solutions containing both hexavalent and trivalent chromium provide maximum protection by creating a mechanical barrier against corrosion and by allowing hexavalent chromium to leach out and resist corrosion.

The film formation begins at the interface between the chromate coating and the material surface and then grows outward. The amount of coating deposited is generally expressed in grams per unit of surface area, which is referred to as coating weight. Typical coating weights range from 15 to 150 mg/ft^2 (0.16 to 1.6 g/m^2). Generally, the coating weight or thickness increases in proportion to the immersion time and solution temperature.

Chromate coatings are available in a wide range of colors such as olive drab, bronze, iridescent yellow, blue bright, and clear. The actual color attained depends on the type of chromating solution used, the pH of the solution, and the thickness of the coating. For example, thinner coatings are usually lighter in color.

Applications

Chromate conversion coatings were widely used during World War II for the protection of cadmium and zinc-plated steel parts in tropical service. Since then they have been used in a variety of applications for decorative and functional purposes. Decorative chromate coatings are usually very thin and colorless, and are used as sealants over phosphate, oxide, or metallic coatings. The functional coatings are thicker, usually complete in themselves, and provide good corrosion resistance for the base metal that is exposed to an oxidizing environment. The degree of protection is proportional to the coating or film thickness. Chromate coatings can also be used as a nonporous bond for all paints that have good molecular adhesion.

Chromate coatings are used over zinc and cadmium to simulate the appearance of bright nickel and chromium. They are also used to prevent the formation of white rust on zinc or cadmium-plated parts.

OXIDE CONVERSION COATINGS

Oxide-type conversion coatings are chemically produced on iron, steel, stainless steel, aluminum, copper and copper alloy, zinc, and cadmium surfaces. These coatings may be used to provide color corrosion protection or abrasion resistance to the base metal.

The processes used to produce these coatings are referred to as blackening, nitriding, carbonitriding, sulfidizing, and QPQ™. The abbreviation QPQ™ stands for quench-polish-quench, which is a process licensed by Kolene Corporation.

QPQ™ Process

The QPQ™ process is based on a salt-bath nitriding process that also incorporates an oxidizing salt-bath quench and mechanical polishing. A typical cycle consists of heating the parts to 750° F (400° C) and then immersing them in an aerated nitriding salt bath at 1000 to 1075° F (540 to 580° C) for 10 to 180 minutes, depending on material and properties desired. The parts are then immediately transferred to the oxidizing salt-bath quench maintained at 650 to 750° F (345 to 400° C) for 5 to 10 minutes, followed by cooling and a water rinse. Light mechanical polishing, lapping, or vibratory finishing is performed to achieve the desired surface finish. After polishing, the parts are reimmersed into the oxidizing salt bath to improve corrosion resistance and develop the black surface finish.

CONVERSION COATINGS

Advantages and limitations. The QPQ™ process provides better corrosion protection than conventional salt-bath nitriding and, for some applications, chromium plating. The surface finish of the parts is also improved. However, certain thin parts cannot be treated in this manner because of the high heat treatment temperatures.

Applications. The QPQ™ process can be used for applications requiring corrosion and wear resistance as essential properties. Many parts in the automotive industry can be treated with the QPQ™ process. Some of the applications include shock absorber piston rods, carburetor parts, engine valves, splined drive train couplings, and hydraulic components. Other applications include firearms, golf club heads, video recorder components, clamps and bolts, and camera parts.

Blackening Baths

Some blackening baths, especially those used for blackening iron and steel, are highly concentrated solutions of caustic soda. However, alkaline-chromate oxidizing processes and fused-salt oxidizing processes are also used for corrosion and abrasion-resistance applications on steel. The blueing or browning of steel also comes under the same category as blackening of steel.

Ferrous metals. The metal surface is attacked by caustic soda to produce metal hydroxide. Because of high temperatures and the presence of oxidizing agents such as nitrates, nitrites, or chlorates, the metal hydroxide is converted to oxides of varying oxygen contents. Some baths also contain activators such as cyanides, tannates, and tartrates that remove dissolved iron by complex formation.

Nonferrous metals. Some blackening processes produce a black coating on zinc and cadmium surfaces and are based on acidic compositions. Because of the nature of the base metals,

these coatings are not abrasion resistant and provide very little corrosion protection. They are generally used for aesthetic and identification purposes. However, if they are subsequently coated with oils, waxes, or clear lacquer, their resistance to corrosion can be improved. Color of the coating ranges from dark brown to black.

PROCESSING

The complete process for chemical conversion treatment normally consists of the following steps: (1) cleaning, (2) water and/or conditioning rinsing, (3) treating with the coating solution, (4) rinsing, (5) post-treating or final rinsing, and (6) drying. In some cases the cleaning and conversion coating steps are combined. Depending on other factors, including the size and shape of the parts and the rates at which they are to be treated, additional cleaning and rinsing steps may be necessary.

EQUIPMENT

The equipment required for conversion coating depends upon the method of application. Design of the equipment is dependent on the end use of the product, quality requirements, space availability, and other similar factors.

The most commonly used methods of coating are by immersion and spray. Workpiece handling is usually done by monorail, manual, automatic, and continuous strip methods. Immersion may also be performed in a barrel-type unit. On items too large for immersion, application by brushing steam or pressure spraying is used. The method of application chosen depends upon (1) the time for completing the process, (2) the size and shape of the work, and (3) the material handling method used. Some coating processes may require 30 minutes, while others may be completed in a matter of seconds.

ANODIZING

Anodizing is the common commercial term for the electrolytic treatment of metals that forms stable films or coatings on the metal's surface. Aluminum and magnesium are anodized to the greatest extent on a commercial basis, but other metals such as zinc, beryllium, titanium, zirconium, and thorium also respond to anodic treatment to form films of varying thicknesses. The coatings on these metals are used primarily for decorative purposes, but anodic coatings on aluminum alloys are used for functional and decorative purposes or some combination of the two.

Anodizing differs from electroplating in two ways. In electroplating, the work is made the cathode, and the metallic coatings are deposited on the work. In anodizing, the work is made the anode, and its surface is converted to a form of its oxide that is integral with the metal substrate.[2] The metallic portion of the electrolytic container is made the cathode.

The first oxide layer formed is located at the interface of the anodic coating and the aluminum surface. Subsequent oxide formation is more porous than the coating formed underneath because it is in contact with the solvent action of the electrolyte longer. The type of electrolyte, its temperature, and the duration of the treatment determine the amount of solvent action. The porosity of the anodic coating located between the barrier layer and the outer surface of the coating is one of its outstanding features.

COATINGS PRODUCED

Many variations of anodizing have been developed to produce coatings for a wide range of applications. Anodic coatings produced in sulfuric acid electrolyte are generally transparent, and a wide range of properties may be obtained by varying operating techniques. Coating thicknesses range from 0.0001 to 0.003″ (2.5 to 75 μm), depending on the application. The coatings produced in a chromic acid electrolyte have an opaque, slightly iridescent appearance and are much thinner than coatings produced in sulfuric acid solutions, usually around 0.0001″ (25 μm) thick. Since the chromic acid coatings are thin, they also have a low resistance to abrasion, a high degree of flexibility, and are excellent as a base for paint, enamel, or lacquer. Anodic oxidation in oxalic acid electrolytes produces coatings that are essentially transparent but can vary in color from a light yellow to bronze. The thicknesses of these coatings are usually 0.0004-0.0015″ (10-40 μm).

Dyeing and Sealing

Anodic films are capable of being colored using a wide variety of organic dyestuff. Dense films do not dye as readily or as well as the more porous films; thus, a film formed in chromic acid is more difficult to dye than one formed in sulfuric acid. The clarity of the anodized layer is important since the brilliance and depth of color depend largely upon the ability of the clear film to reflect the underlying bright aluminum surface. Chromic anodize films, which by nature are pearly or procelain appearing, will have a muted or somewhat flat appearance after dyeing. Dyeing hard coatings black is satisfactory and results in a richer or deeper color than the natural black that can be obtained in the process.

Sealing treatments are generally used for porous anodic coatings. Barrier film coatings require no sealing treatment because they are essentially nonporous. Sealing processes make the coatings nonabsorptive and are generally performed by immersion in boiling deionized water, sodium bichromate, or nickel acetate solutions, or steam. Deionized water makeup is preferred for all sealing solutions because certain anions such as phosphates, silicates, or chlorides that retard the sealing or hydration reaction are removed.

Integral and Electrolytic Color Anodizing

In the late 1950s, a new use of anodizing was introduced based in part on the observation that integral colors could be produced when hard coatings were applied to certain alloys used largely in architectural applications. As the coating thickness increased from 0.001 to 0.004" (25 to 100 μm), the corresponding color changed from a silver gray to a bronze, deep bronze, and finally at 0.004" (100 μm) to a blackish color. Since the color is inherent in the coating and is a function of the alloying elements and thickness of the coating, it has good permanency, fade and corrosion resistance, and durability. Later developments using different electrolytes enabled room temperature operations and reduced refrigeration costs. When bronze was used in building facades and curtain walls, integral-color anodized aluminum became a direct replacement.

HARD COATING

Hard coating, often referred to as hard anodizing, is a relatively new process that was introduced in the United States in early 1952. The process is similar to conventional sulfuric anodizing but with reduced temperatures, higher unit amperages, and higher final voltages. These finishes are known commercially as Alumilite (Aluminum Company of America) hard coatings, Martin hard coatings, Sanford hard coatings, or Hardas coatings. Hard coatings have high resistance to abrasion, erosion, and corrosion, and can have thicknesses ranging from 0.001 to 0.012 (25 to 300 μm); the thicknesses of conventional chromic or sulfuric anodized finishes are in the range of 0.0001 to 0.0010" (2.5 to 25 μm), depending on the application. In practice, however, most hard coatings are 0.002-0.004" (25-200 μm) thick. This type of finish is becoming increasingly popular for parts requiring light weight in combination with high resistance to wear, erosion, and corrosion. Hard coating has also been used to salvage parts that have oversized dimensions.

APPLICATIONS

Anodizing is used for many purposes, usually with the application taking advantage of one or more of the specific properties of the anodic coating. The corrosion resistance of a painted part is largely derived from the paint system; however, paint adheres poorly to bare aluminum, and the tightly adherent anodized film acts as an intermediary for accepting the paint and binding it to the part. The anodic layer also provides a portion of the overall corrosion-resisting properties of the system. In aircraft applications, parts are usually chromic anodized, with the exterior parts given a primer and several top coats.

One limited use of chromic anodizing is based on the extraordinary penetrating ability of the chromic acid. The part to be inspected is anodized and lightly surface washed, then it is allowed to set for a period of time. If a crack is present, the chromic acid may bleed out of the crack and appear as a yellowish stain against the gray chromic-anodized background.

Commercially, sulfuric-anodized and dyed parts are used in automotive trim, cosmetic cases, aerosol caps, keys, picture frames, nameplates, and sporting goods, among other applications. The integral-color anodizing and variations of this process account for a large use of aluminum in outdoor architectural and building applications. Hard coating is increasing in usage mainly because of its sliding wear and corrosion-resistant properties. Although hard coating has a DPH of 400 to 600 hardness, the relatively thin layer does not

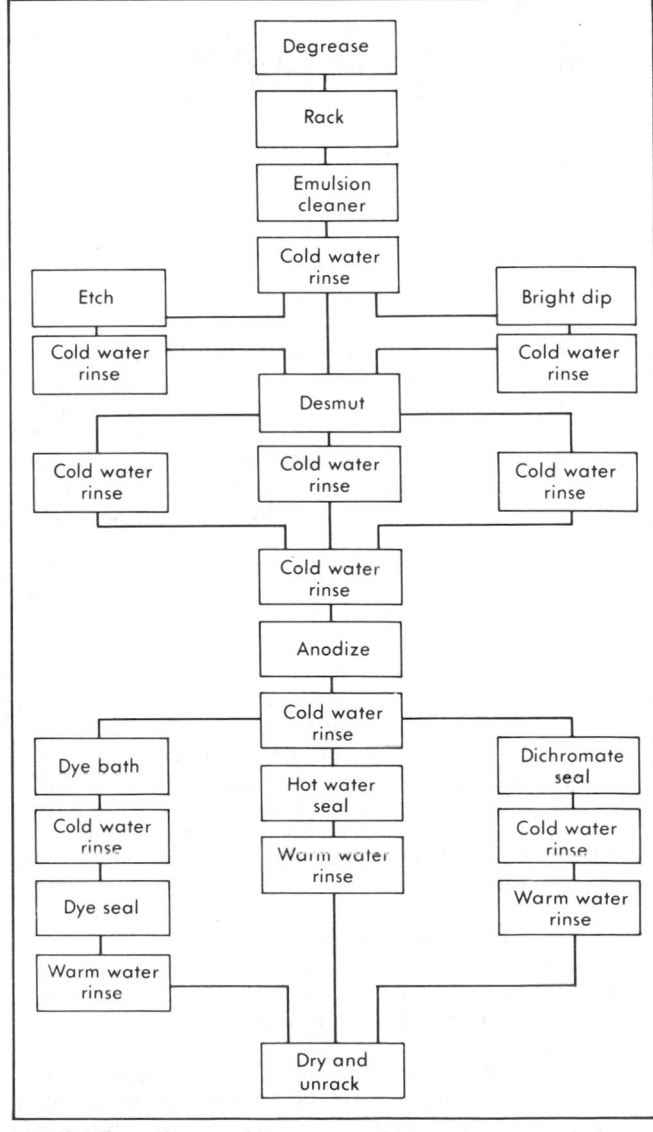

Fig. 48-1 Flow diagrams for anodic coatings produced in sulfuric and chromic acid electrolyte. (*Cidona, Inc.*)

add to the bearing strength of the underlying aluminum. Also, like most hard surfacing, hard coating reduces fatigue strength up to 50%, depending upon the alloy, thickness of coating, and the stress levels involved. In aircraft applications, where fatigue stresses are a design consideration, the hard coat is kept out of radii and other notch-sensitive areas.

Typical applications for hard coating include hydraulic cylinder bores, gun parts, and ordnance and missile components. Hard coatings are also used in laser targets, paper mill rolls, fire hose connectors, heat sinks, coarse screw threads, surveying instruments, aluminum gears, cams, torpedo hulls, textile bobbins, pots and pans, sailboat masks, davits, and pulleys.

Anodic coatings also have insulative properties. A breakdown voltage of 500V for a 0.001" to 0.002" (25 to 50 μm) thick coating when measured ground to surface is normal expectancy. The shape of the part is a factor in measuring breakdown voltage. On a flat surface, the results may be reasonably consistent; but around holes, threads, and edges, the breakdown voltage will be lower. The increase in breakdown voltage is not directly linear with anodic coating thickness. The coating thickness has a direct correlation to corrosion resistance, with tests indicating the coating thickness is the most important single factor in corrosion resistance of anodic films.

COATING PROCESS

The actual process or cycle followed in anodizing depends on the type of electrolyte being used. In general, the parts are cleaned, etched or pickled, anodized, colored, and sealed. Between each processing step, the parts are thoroughly rinsed in clean water. Figure 48-1 is a typical flow sheet for a chromic, sulfuric, or hard coat anodizing operation.

EQUIPMENT

The main components used in anodizing include tanks, racks, cathodes, agitators, a power supply, cooling coils or heat exchangers, and chillers, along with a ventilation system.[3]

THERMAL SPRAYING

Although the concept of depositing a molten metal or ceramic coating on a substrate is not new, much of the technology is new, including the precision and range of both processes and applications. The ever-increasing emphasis on cost reduction, high productivity, and more efficient manufacturing has made thermally sprayed coatings attractive for providing superior resistance to wear, corrosion, or erosion, as well as for reclaiming worn or mismachined components.

Thermal spraying is the process of depositing molten or semimolten materials such as metals, alloys, or ceramic coatings on substrate materials so that they solidify and bond to the substrate (see Fig. 48-2). The process is also called metallizing and flame or metal spraying. The coating improves surface characteristics, but does not usually change the properties of the structural component. Thus basic structural design considerations must be maintained.

The spray materials can be in the form of wire, rod, cord, or powder. As the materials pass through the spray unit, they are heated to a molten or semimolten state and then atomized and/or projected onto the substrate. Heating can be accomplished by an electric arc, gas flame, or detonation of a combustible gas mixture. In some devices, the hot particles are conveyed from the spray equipment to the substrate by an air jet, which also accomplishes atomization and particle acceleration. As the sprayed particles impinge on the substrate, they cool and build up, particle by particle, into a cast-like structure. As they strike the surface, the particles flatten and form thin platelets that conform to the irregularities of the previously prepared surface, as well as to each other (see Fig. 48-3).

MATERIALS DEPOSITED

Most metals, oxides, cermets (ceramic plus metal), and metallic compounds, some carbides and organic plastics, and certain glasses can be deposited by one or more of the thermal spraying processes.

The deposited structure of thermally sprayed coatings differs from that of the same material in the wrought or cast form because of the incremental nature of the coating buildup as well as the reaction with the hot process gases or the surrounding atmosphere. In the case of metals, because of intermetallic and other valency compounds, the deposited coating tends to be harder, more brittle, and more porous than the original material.

With most thermally sprayed deposits, adhesion to the substrate is mainly mechanical and surface preparation by roughening is necessary for good bonding. Important exceptions are found in some metal coatings such as molybdenum and certain composites and alloys containing aluminum and titanium, which form a metallurgical bond with certain metal and alloy substrates. Metallurgical bonds are often higher than the interparticle strength of the sprayed deposit; consequently, when coatings are tested to destruction, failure occurs within the coatings.

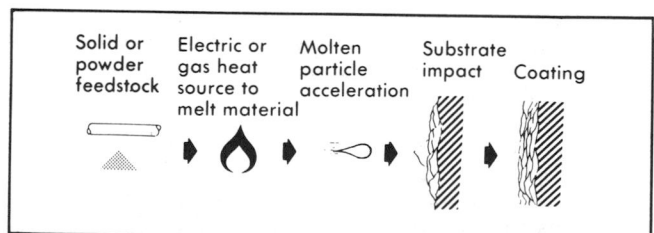

Fig. 48-2 The thermal spray process. (*TAFA, Inc.*)

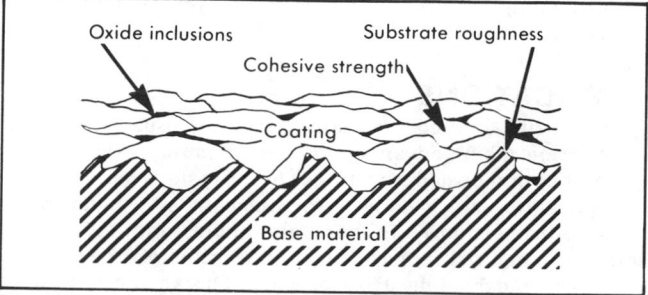

Fig. 48-3 Cross section of typical thermal spray coating. (*TAFA, Inc.*)

Bond coats are especially useful when hard metals, which cannot be roughened effectively, need to be coated. In some cases, bond coatings can be applied directly to relatively smooth, technically clean surfaces, thus eliminating the need for surface roughening, which is customarily a costly step. After initial preparation, a thin coating, normally about 0.002-0.005″ (0.05-0.12 mm) thick, of a suitable bond material is thermally sprayed prior to the application of the primary deposit.

Arc-sprayed bond coatings usually have significantly higher bond strengths than flame-sprayed coatings because of the higher temperature at which the atomized particles hit the substrate; at higher temperatures, some microwelding and diffusion also occurs. For example, aluminum sprayed on mild steel with a gas flame gun yields 1400 psi (9.6 MPa) tensile bond strength, while arc spray yields 4900 psi (34 MPa).

PROCESSES

Several processes are used to thermally deposit the coating material on the substrate, and they can be divided into two basic categories: (1) combustion flame spray and (2) electric (thermal) arc spraying. Each process has specific advantages and limitations that require the process to be carefully matched to the application.

Combustion Flame Spraying

The combustion flame spraying process is the oldest of the thermal spray techniques and includes specific equipment to apply metallic and ceramic coatings from wire, powder, or rod materials. Acetylene is generally employed as the gas, but propane, Mapp, hydrogen, or natural gas have also been used.

The tensile bond strength of coatings applied by combustion flame processes generally do not exceed 1000 psi (7 MPa) on steel substrates, unless the material is exothermic or an intermediate bond coat is employed. Most often, a nickel-aluminum exothermic material or molybdenum is used to ensure adequate bond strength.

Powder flame spray. Powder flame spraying is a type of flame spraying that involves the application of metals and other materials in the powder form. The powder materials may be held in a hopper on top of the spray gun and then gravity fed into the gun where they are picked up by the oxyacetylene (or hydrogen) gas mixtures and carried to the gun nozzle (see Fig. 48-4). Another gun design has the hopper located in a separate location, and an air aspiration carburetor system is used to feed the powder to the gun nozzle.

Powder flame spray/fusing. Powder flame spray/fusing operations incorporate the addition of a high-temperature fusion treatment in the overall process. Nickel or iron-based metals, containing small amounts (approximately 1.0-5.0%) of boron and silicon, are deposited on metallic substrates and simultaneously or subsequently fused. These materials develop hardnesses ranging from $R_C 20$ to $R_C 68$ and often contain moderate percentages of crushed tungsten carbide as an additive. The fusing operation results in a totally metallurgical-bond coating that is usually impervious to any corrosive liquid.

Wire flame spray. In wire spraying or metallizing, the flame is only used to melt the wire material. Spraying is accomplished by surrounding the flame with a coaxial stream of air in order to disintegrate the molten material and propel it onto the workpiece (see Fig. 48-5). Spray rates for materials like stainless steel are in the range of 1 to 20 lb (0.5 to 9 kg) per hour.

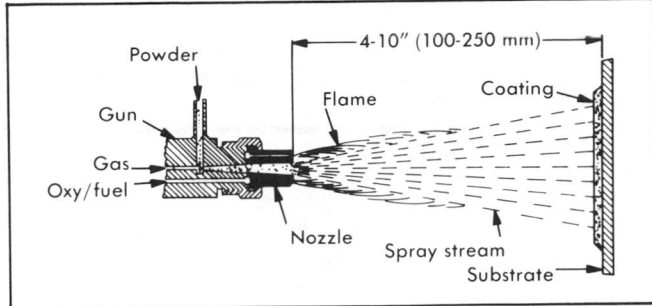

Fig. 48-4 Cross section of powder-fed combustion flame spraying torch. (*Metco, Inc.*)

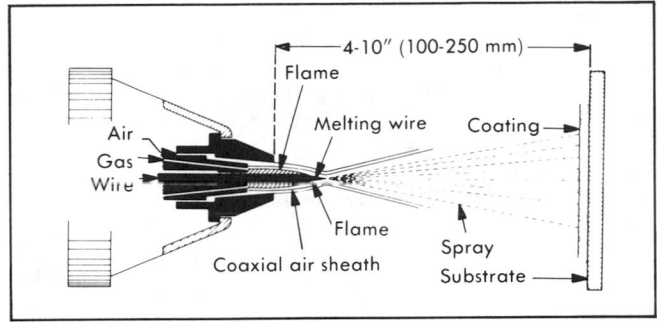

Fig. 48-5 Cross section of combustion rod spray torch. (*TAFA, Inc.*)

Wire spraying is a fast and low-cost method of applying a wide variety of metal coatings and some ceramics. (Ceramic coatings are formed into wire using plastic binders.) Carbon steels, stainless steels, brass, bronze, zinc, aluminum, and other metals can be applied over a grit-blasted, nickel-aluminum bond-coated substrate. Such coatings are often used for shaft buildup and general restoration of worn or mismatched parts.

Combustion rod spraying. Combustion rod spraying generally uses a 1/4″ (6 mm) diam rod and will cover approximately 60-65 in.^{2} (385-420 cm^2) of substrate in about four minutes. Larger diameter rods, 3/8″ (9 mm), are available for higher deposition rates. This process is often used to apply ceramic coatings such as alumina, alumina-titania, and chromium oxide. Since these coating materials are porous, the microstructure can be filled with tetrafluoroethylene (PTFE) and other organic lubricants.

Detonation gun spraying. Detonation gun spraying employs the controlled detonation of an oxyacetylene gas mixture to produce high temperatures and extremely high particle velocities. In this process, a mixture of oxygen and acetylene is fed into a combustion chamber in the rear of a long-barreled gun (see Fig. 48-6). The coating material is added to the gases, and the gaseous powder mixture is then ignited by a spark plug. The resulting detonation produces a high-velocity shock front that travels down the length of the barrel at 10 times the speed of sound. The powder particles are heated to a plastic state by the detonation and are accelerated to a velocity of approximately 2600 fps (790 m/s). The high kinetic energy of each powder particle is converted to additional heat upon impact with the work surface, thereby producing a very strong bond.

Unlike other combustion and arc spray torches that operate continuously, the detonation gun fires four to eight times a second, thereby forming a lamellar coating on the workpiece. The suc-

THERMAL SPRAYING

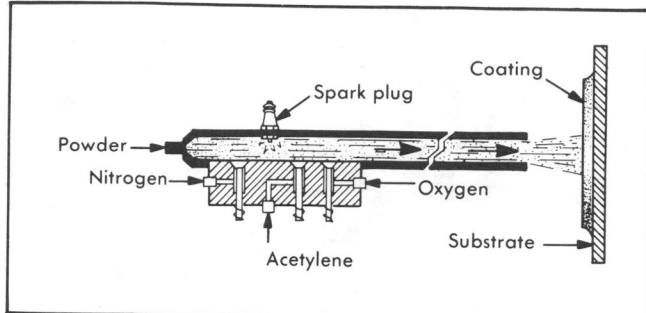

Fig. 48-6 Schematic of detonation gun thermal spraying.[4]

cessive detonations can build up coatings to maximum thicknesses approaching 0.020-0.030″ (0.5-0.8 mm), but 0.005-0.010″ (0.12-0.25 mm) is more common. As with other thermal spraying techniques, auxiliary cooling is employed to maintain workpiece temperatures between 150 and 300°F (65 and 150°C).

A variety of coatings may be applied with the detonation gun process, including tungsten carbide, aluminum oxide, and chromium carbide. However, because of the high velocity of this coating technique, it is limited to the plating of metallic substrates. Nonmetallic surfaces such as plastics and graphite or ceramics may be eroded by the high velocity of the particles.

Supersonic combustion. The supersonic combustion system is the most recent combustion flame spraying process. It reportedly yields hypersonic flame velocities and particle velocities estimated at about 2500 fps (760 m/s). The concept is essentially that of a rocket engine in which powders are injected into the burning gases and accelerated in a manner similar to the principles stated for the detonation gun. Unlike the detonation gun, however, the supersonic system is a continuous process that is easily used manually or in automatic fixtures. A high noise level, approximately 150 dB, is produced during operation, and large quantities of gas are used.

The supersonic combustion system has been used for depositing carbide coatings where microhardness in excess of 1200 Vickers with a 300 g load have been reported. Coating thicknesses are usually up to 0.015″ (380 μm); thicker coatings tend to peel away from the base substrate due to extensive cold working. At this time, supersonic combustion does not appear to be a practical process for depositing ceramic materials since the combustion temperature is not hot enough to melt the ceramic material. It does appear to lend itself to other metallic coatings; and because of its compact size, may be a versatile system for on-site applications of various hard facings and corrosion-control coatings.

Electric-Arc Spraying

Electric-arc spraying processes include a wire-arc and a nontransferred plasma arc process. In the nontransferred plasma arc process, the inert gas is heated to the plasma state by an arc within the plasma arc gun. (In the transferred plasma arc process, the arc occurs between a nonconsumable cathode and the workpiece.) The nontransferred arc process can be performed in the natural environment or in a controlled environment depending on the application.

Wire-arc gun. The two-wire-arc gun is used for electric-arc spraying of metals or other conductive materials and achieves high deposition rates. Two wires or rods of the material to be deposited are fed through electrical contacts to form positive and negative electrodes (see Fig. 48-7). These wires are driven through the unit using compressed-air turbines or electric motors. When the wires form a narrow gap, an arc is created, resulting in temperatures of 4000 to 10,000°F (2200 to 5530°C), depending on the material sprayed. The wires are melted, and then the liquid drops are atomized and carried to the substrate by a blast of compressed air or inert gas. Spray-stream geometry and spray particle size can be changed with different atomizing heads and wire intersection angles.

Nontransferred plasma arc. Nontransferred plasma arc spraying is an extremely versatile thermal spraying process. Figure 48-8 shows the cross section of a plasma arc gun. In operation, a nontransferred, high-intensity arc is struck between the gun body (anode) and a tungsten cathode. An inert gas, such as argon, is passed through this arc, where it is heated to the plasma state [up to 30,000°F (16 650°C)] and sometimes accelerated to supersonic speed. Other gases such as helium, nitrogen, and various additions to argon are used in the processing of materials. The coating material in powder form is injected into the plasma stream, where it is heated to a molten state, accelerated, and carried to the workpiece. Auxiliary cooling can maintain the workpiece temperature at less than 150°F (65°C), reducing the chance for distortion or change in the metallurgical properties of the substrate material. Air or liquid carbon dioxide is most often used for cooling, although water-cooled substrate mounts are sometimes beneficial. A wide range of substrates can be coated using the nontransferred plasma arc, including graphite, carbon, glass, ceramic, some plastics, cement, wood, and even certain papers.

Inert chamber plasma or wire arc. Inert chamber spraying places the plasma or wire-arc gun and workpiece in a chamber containing an inert atmosphere. The gun can be manipulated either by hand or mechanically. This technique is generally used for refractory metals and other material systems where oxygen atmospheres are detrimental. The process characteristics remain the same as previously described for nontransferred plasma arc spraying.

Vacuum plasma arc. Vacuum plasma spraying further enhances the characteristics of the deposit. Both the workpiece and gun are mounted within the confines of an evacuated chamber. Low chamber pressures, in the range of 15 to 60 torr (2 to 8 kPa), enhance the velocity of the molten particles and remove much of the heat loss associated with operation of the plasma stream in an air environment. The workpiece-to-gun distance is much longer because of the nature of the plasma, and the overall effective diameter of deposition expands to several inches. In this environment, the motion between the gun and the workpiece must be completely mechanically controlled. Molten particle velocities in excess of 3000 fps (900 m/s) are reported,

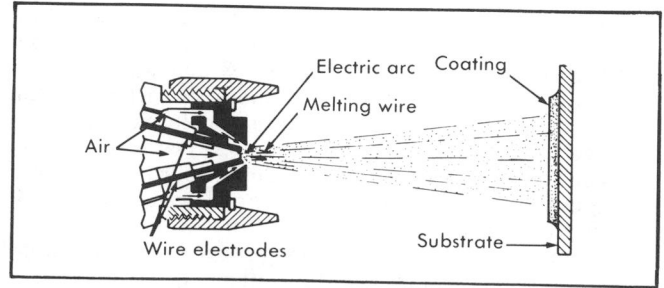

Fig. 48-7 Cross section of two-wire-arc gun.[5]

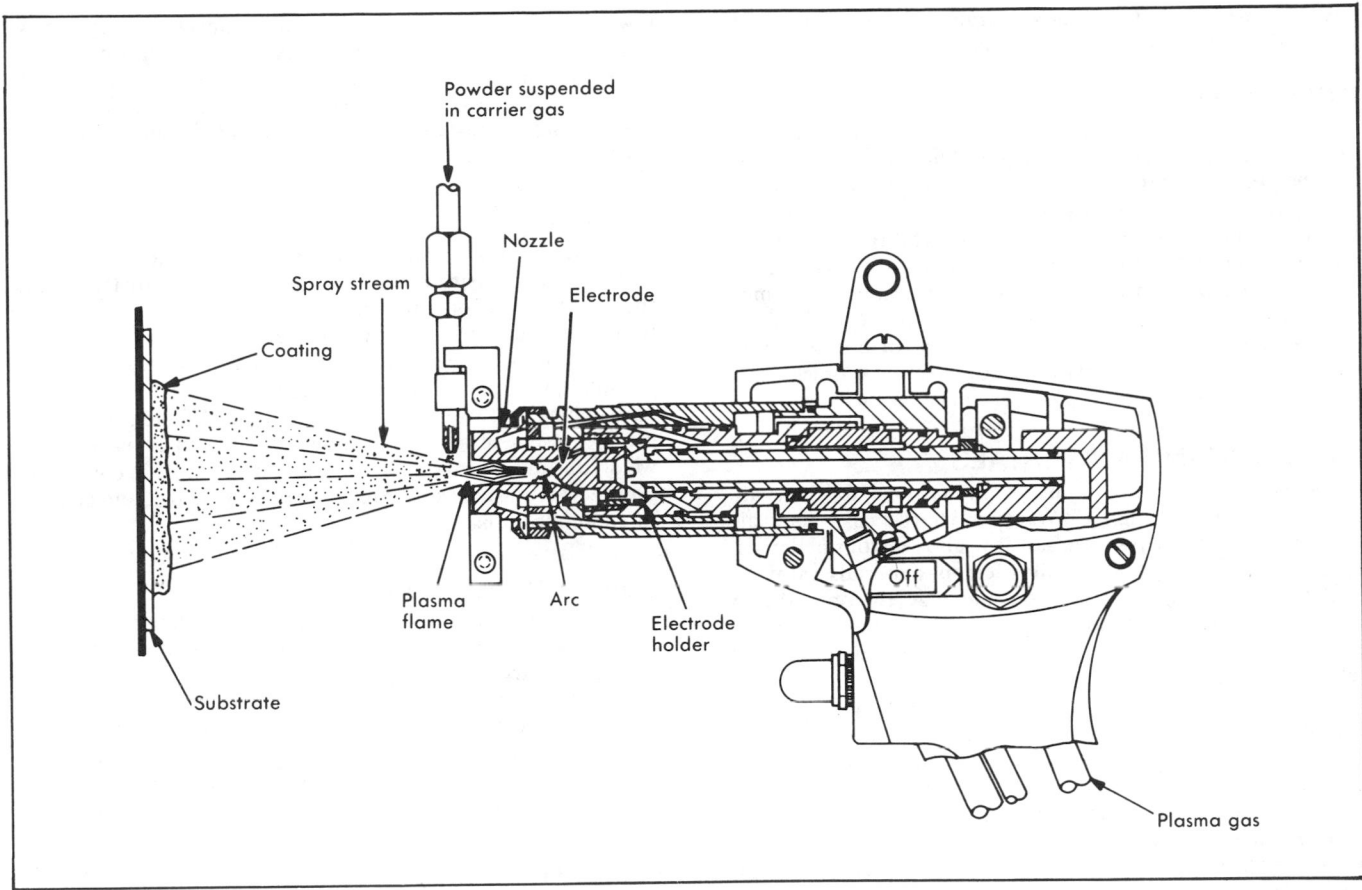

Fig. 48-8 Cross section of plasma spray gun. (*Metco, Inc.*)

and metallurgical bonding is often noted.

The vacuum plasma arc process is generally used for coatings of a critical nature, when maximum density and bond strengths are essential. Since the process is confined in an evacuated chamber, transferred arcs between the anode and the workpiece are sometimes employed to bring about additional heating of the substrate, which enhances the bond and can improve deposit metallurgy.

APPLICATIONS

The original use of thermal spraying was for rebuilding worn parts and for mismachined components. In recent years, the refinement of techniques and modern equipment have permitted the manufacture and rebuilding of highly stressed components such as gas turbine aircraft engines. Now these refined techniques and equipment have been used to extend the process into production engineering to impart desirable surface characteristics, such as wear and corrosion resistance, and electrical properties to new components.

HARD FACING

Surfacing is defined as the deposition of filler material on a metal surface to obtain desired properties or dimensions. It is usually employed to extend the life of a part that may not otherwise have all the properties necessary for an engineering application, or to replace metal that has worn or corroded away. The overlay may contribute corrosion resistance, wear resistance, toughness, or antifriction properties exactly where they are needed most.[6] When the filler material is primarily used to improve wear resistance, the process is generally referred to

as hard facing. The filler material adheres to the base metal by fusion or metallurgical bonding. Some of the advantages of hard facing include increased productivity through less downtime for repair and replacement, increased efficiency by permitting use of higher applied loads, reduced maintenance costs through reclamation of worn parts, and optimum compromise between wear and toughness through the use of less expensive, tougher base metals.[7]

Wear-resistant coatings are also applied by thermal spraying;

HARD FACING

however, the bond between the substrate and filler is sometimes mechanical rather than metallurgical.

APPLICATIONS

Hard-facing overlays are used in a wide variety of applications requiring wear resistance on particular surfaces. The wear may be due to hard particles or projections forced against and moved relative to a surface (abrasive wear), such as occurs in rock crushers and pulverizers, or may be metal-to-metal wear as takes place in control valves. Hard facing is also used to control combinations of wear and corrosion as encountered by mud seals, plows, knives in the food processing industry, valves, and pumps handling corrosive liquids or slurries. In most instances, parts are made of either plain carbon steel or stainless steel, materials that provide little wear resistance on their own.[8]

HARD-FACING MATERIALS

Many alloys, ceramics, and combinations of these are available for hard facing.[9] Conventional hard-facing materials are normally classified as steels or low-alloy ferrous materials, chromium white irons or high-alloy ferrous materials, carbides, nickel-based alloys, or cobalt-based alloys. A few copper-based alloys are sometimes used for hard-facing applications. Another group of alloys that is becoming increasingly popular are the self-fluxing alloys.

Selection of these alloys is based primarily on wear and cost considerations. In addition, it is necessary to take into consideration manufacturing and environmental considerations such as base metal composition, application method, and impact, corrosion, oxidation, and thermal requirements.

Hard-facing alloys are available in the form of rods (bare and coated), cored wire, strip, or powders. Fluxes may be in the central core portion of wire, on the surface of covered electrodes, introduced as a granular blanket, or mixed with powdered filler metal.[10]

Cobalt-Based Alloys

There are two types of cobalt-based alloys: those that contain carbides and those that contain the hard, intermetallic Laves phases. Resistance to abrasive wear is imparted primarily by the carbides or Laves phases, and resistance to corrosion and/or elevated temperature hardness is imparted by the matrix. The matrix also controls metal-to-metal wear and cavitation erosion properties. Alloys containing the Laves phases are less abrasive to mating materials than carbide-containing alloys in metal-to-metal wear applications.

Nickel-Based Alloys

Most nickel-based hard-facing alloys are divided into boride-containing or carbide-containing alloys, and alloys containing the Laves phases. The boride-containing alloys were first commercially produced as spray-and-fuse powders. These alloys are currently available from most manufacturers of hard-facing products under various trade names and in a variety of forms such as bare cast rod, cored wires, and powders, to suit a variety of welding processes.

Iron-Based Alloys

Iron-based hard-facing alloys are more widely used than cobalt and/or nickel-based hard-facing alloys and constitute the largest volume of hard-facing alloys. Iron-based alloys offer low cost and a broad range of desirable properties. They do not wear as well as nickel-based alloys of equal hardness, but thicker deposits can be applied to compensate for the reduction in wear resistance. Iron-based alloys can be divided into pearlitic steels, austenitic steels, martensitic steels, and high-alloy irons.

Carbides

The amount of carbides used for hard-facing applications is small compared to iron-based alloys, but carbides are important for severe abrasion and cutting applications. Historically, tungsten-based carbides were used exclusively; but, recently, carbides of other elements such as titanium, molybdenum, tantalum, vanadium, and chromium have also proved useful in hard-facing applications. The carbide hard-facing alloys are often inserted in a steel or alloy tube, which is used as the weld-consumable material, and are also available in composite powders for plasma transferred arc, spray-and-fuse, and puddle-torch applications.

Copper-Based Alloys

The copper-based hard-facing alloys, which are similar to bronzes, are used as overlays of low-carbon steel instead of having the part made entirely of the copper-based alloy. They are used for applications requiring resistance to corrosion, cavitation erosion, and metal-to-metal wear, as in bearing materials. These hard-facing alloys have poor resistance to corrosion by sulfur compounds, poor abrasive wear, and poor elevated temperature creep; they are also more difficult to weld.

Self-Fluxing Alloys

Self-fluxing alloys are generally nickel-based powdered alloys, although carbide-based alloys are sometimes used, containing chromium, carbon, and boron to provide hard-phase carbides, nitrides, and corrosion resistance. Silicon is also added to provide a wide range of fusion temperatures so that the alloys behave like glass and not like metallic material, which has a true melting point. The compositions of these powders provide coatings ranging in hardness from R_C15 to R_C65; the higher the alloy content, the harder the coating. Fusion temperatures vary between 1900 and 2050° F (1040 and 1120°C); the lower the alloy content, the higher the fusion temperature. Self-fluxing alloys are usually applied by oxyacetylene welding methods and are typically used in the glass and oil well industries.

APPLICATION METHODS

Hard-facing alloys are usually applied by a variety of welding methods such as oxyacetylene, shielded metal arc, open arc, submerged arc, gas tungsten arc, plasma arc, and laser.

The selection of the method is based on the size of the workpiece, metallurgical properties of the substrate, the form and composition of the metal being deposited, weld characteristics desired, welder skill, and the cost of the welding operation.

Manual, semiautomatic, and automatic techniques may all be used. In most semiautomatic welding, the deposit is positioned by means of a handheld gun, and the wire is fed by rollers on a variable-speed motor. In some machines, the motor is controlled by the voltage drop across the arc. In automatic welding, both the arc and the work are positioned mechanically.

Oxyacetylene Welding

Gas welding is used widely for hard facing because of its flexibility and portability, precision deposit placements, minimum dilution from the base metal, and minimum thermal stress due to slower heating and cooling rates. Operator skill is important for high-grade results, however; and it is not the lowest cost procedure. The overlay metal is usually in the form of a conventional welding rod, steel wires filled with carbide granules, or powders. Deposit thicknesses are generally between 1/32 and 1/8″ (0.8 and 3.2 mm).

Shielded Metal Arc and Open Arc

Shielded metal arc (SMAW) and open arc welding are the most economical methods for hard facing. High deposition rates can be attained, but thermal stresses are also high, resulting in distortion or residual stresses. The first layer of arc weld may be diluted as much as 50% by melted base metal. Dilution is the interalloying of the base metal with the hard-facing alloy. A dilution of 50% means that the deposit contains 50% of the base metal and 50% of the hard-facing alloy. Generally, hardness and wear resistance decrease as dilution increases.

Submerged Arc Welding

Submerged arc welding (SAW) with a single electrode is the most widely used automated technique for hard facing. Because of its high deposition rate, submerged arc hard facing can result in deposits made at lower costs than by other methods; however, distortion may occur due to the high heat input. Because of dilution, two or three layers are generally required to achieve good wear-resistant properties. Hard facing by submerged arc welding is limited to flat or cylindrical workpieces. For some applications, as many as six electrodes can be used; however, single or double-electrode methods are more common.

Gas Tungsten Arc

Gas tungsten arc welding (GTAW), also referred to as tungsten inert gas (TIG), is a nonconsumable-electrode arc method that shields both the molten hard-facing alloy and the nonconsumable electrode with an inert gas. The TIG method is commonly used for applying hard facing on titanium-stabilized stainless steels and aluminum-bearing, nickel-based alloys. It is also more adaptable to hard facing small, intricate parts, and generally produces higher quality deposits than several other hard-facing processes. Gas tungsten arc welding generally produces hard-facing deposits with minimal base metal dilution.

Plasma Arc

In the plasma arc process, an arc is struck between a nonconsumable cathode and a conductive workpiece. The hard-facing material, usually in the form of powder or wire, is fed into the plasma stream, where it is melted and then puddled on the surface of the workpiece. Deposits are from 0.020 to 0.250″ (0.50 to 6.4 mm) thick in a single pass. Low dilutions are achievable at relatively high deposition rates; however, most deposits are generally applied in at least two-layer thicknesses. Up to 0.75″ (19 mm) can be deposited with multiple passes. This hard-facing process offers the greatest flexibility in the selection of the coating material and also offers excellent robotics control for hard facing complex shapes.

Lasers

Laser hard facing is a method in which a high-intensity beam of light is focused on the surface of the part, then rapidly scanned over the area while injecting the powder into the interaction zone. This method allows for the hard facing of irregular shapes and deposits powder only where it is needed. Deposits of 0.010 to 0.10″ (0.25 to 2.5 mm) are attainable in a single pass. Due to the speed of the process and the localized heat, distortion and dilution are minimized. Rapid solidification of the hard facing permits the formation of previously unattainable microstructures.

PORCELAIN ENAMELING

Porcelain enamels can be defined as highly durable, alkaliborsilicate glass coatings that are bonded by fusion to various metal substrates at temperatures above 800° F (425° C).[11] They are distinguished from other ceramic coatings by their predominantly vitreous nature and by the types of applications for which they are used, and from paint by their inorganic composition and the temperature at which the coating matrix is fused to the substrate metal.

Porcelain enamels were used initially in making jewelry and ceremonial objects. Today these coatings are widely used for industrial products, household appliances, plumbing fixtures, signs and architectural applications. They are also used in jet engine components as a protective metal coating to extend service life and for many types of industrial and chemical process equipment requiring resistance to extreme heat and corrosion. Normally, porcelain enamels are selected for products or components requiring chemical resistance, corrosion protection, weather resistance, specific mechanical or electrical properties, appearance or color needs, cleanability, or thermal shock capability.

Porcelain enamels for sheet steel and cast iron are classified as either ground coat or cover coat enamels. A ground coat enamel contains oxides that promote adherence of the enamel to the metal substrate and may be used as a single functional coat or as a base for additional cover coats. Cover coat enamels are applied over ground coats to improve the appearance and chemical and physical properties of the coating. Cover coats may also be applied directly to properly prepared decarburized steel substrates. The color of ground coats is limited to various shades of blue, black, brown, and gray. Cover coats, however, may be clear, semiopaque, opaque, or pigmented to take on a great variety of colors; colors may also be smelted into the basic coating material. Opaque cover coats are usually white.

For aluminum, neither ground coats nor adherence-promoting oxides are required. Single-coat systems are used for most applications. When two coats are desired, the first coat can be of any color. Porcelain enamels for aluminum are usually transparent and can be pigmented and opacified inorganically to produce the desired appearance.

Porcelain enamels are not designated by composition because

PORCELAIN ENAMELING

all are varieties of silicate glass. Selection is made on the basis of end use and processing requirements. Some common designations for porcelain enamels with particular characteristics are acid resistant, alkali resistant, heat resistant, glossy, low gloss, and matte. Specifications usually include the main requirements for quality and the processing parameters.

PROPERTIES OF PORCELAIN ENAMELS

Porcelain enamels are prepared to ensure satisfactory properties for specific environments.

Chemical Resistance

Porcelain enamel is extensively used because of its resistance to household chemicals and foods. Mild alkaline or acid environments are generally involved in household applications. Table 48-1 presents examples of corrosive environments in which porcelain enamels are widely used for long periods of service.

Weather Resistance

The important factors that determine the weather resistance of porcelain enamels are chemical durability, color stability, cleanability, and continuity of coating. Gloss and enamel texture do not necessarily affect weather resistance.

Appearance For Indoor Exposure

Where corrosive attack is unlikely to limit the life of a given part, and attractive appearance is the principal requirement, enamel selection and processing are directed toward providing reproducible color matching along with optimum gloss and smoothness.

Service Temperatures

The temperature to which porcelain enamels can be exposed is limited by the softening of the glassy matrix. The softening releases gases remaining from reactions between the enamel and ferrous metal, producing random defects known as *reboil*.

METAL SUBSTRATES

Porcelain enamels are primarily applied to products made of sheet iron or steel, cast iron, aluminum, or aluminum-coated steel to impart selected chemical, physical, and aesthetic properties.

THE PORCELAIN ENAMELING PROCESS

Porcelain enamel is applied to steel by dipping, flow coating, spraying of wet slip, electrostatic powder spraying, and electrodeposition. Cast iron is porcelain enameled by a dry process (nonelectrostatic) or by the same wet process as used for

TABLE 48-1
Applications in Which Porcelain Enamels are Used
for Resistance to Corrosive Environments

Application	Corrosive Environment		
	Temperature, °F (°C)	pH	Corrosive Media
Bathtubs	to 120 (49)	5-9	Water, cleansers
Chemical ware	to 212 (100)	12	Alkaline solutions
	to 212 (100)	1-2	All acids except hydrofluoric
	350-450 (175-230)	1-2	Concentrated sulfuric acid, nitric acid, and hydrochloric acid
Home laundry equipment	to 160 (71)	11	Water, detergents, and bleach
Dishwashers	to 180 (82)	8-12	Water, strong detergents
Range exteriors	70-150 (21-66)	2-10	Food acids, cleaners
Range oven liners: Conventional	70-600 (20-315)	2-10	Food acids, cleaners
Pyrolytic	70-1000 (20-540)	2-10	Food acids, cleaners
Range burner grates	70-1100 (20-595)	2-10	Food acids, cleaners
Refrigerators	0-70 (-18 to 20)	2-10	Food acids, cleaners
Kitchen sinks, lavatories	to 160 (71)	2-10	Food acids, water, and cleansers
Water heaters	to 160 (71)	5-8	Water

(American Society for Metals)

enameling sheet steel. The wet process permits easier part handling since the part is cold, and more uniform coats of enamel can be applied than with the dry process; however, it is

difficult to enamel large articles, such as sanitary ware, by the wet process. Porcelain enamel slips for aluminum are usually applied by spraying.

HOT DIPPING

Hot dipping is a process by which a metal is coated onto the surface of a metal product by immersion in a bath of molten metal. During the coating process, an intermetallic compound layer is formed that provides the adherence to join the coating metal to the base metal. There are a number of coating metals used to hot dip steel, the most important being zinc, aluminum, tin, and lead. The corrosion rates of these metals are substantially less than that of steel. Thus, metallic coatings on steel preserve the useful properties of the base metal while producing a composite material having greater utility than either base or coating alone.

The two major corrosion protection mechanisms provided by hot-dip coatings are barrier and sacrificial protection. In barrier protection, the coating isolates the substrate from the corrosive environment. A major limitation of barrier protection is that the protection ceases the instant the barrier is broken; barrier damage can be caused by a scratch, abrasion, impact, shaping, forming, or other mechanical removal. Coatings providing only barrier protection should generally be used in areas where mechanical damage is not likely to occur; these coatings are also painted to provide additional protection. Tin and lead are two common metallic coatings that provide barrier protection to the substrate.

ZINC HOT DIPPING (GALVANIZING)

Zinc hot dipping or galvanizing is a process by which a coating of zinc and zinc-iron alloy is developed on the surface of steel products by immersing the properly prepared base metal in a bath of molten zinc. It is the most widely used of the zinc coating processes and has been employed commercially for almost two hundred years.

Zinc hot dipping is applied primarily to finished parts and semifabricated parts in batch galvanizing; whereas sheet, strip, wire, and tube are commonly galvanized on the continuous, automated lines of the steel producers. The amount of zinc used in continuous galvanizing in comparison to batch galvanizing is approximately 4:1.

Coating Characteristics

The batch galvanized coating consists of a series of layers. Starting from the steel surface, each successive layer contains a higher proportion of zinc until the outer layer is pure zinc. There is no real line of demarcation between the iron and the zinc, but a gradual transition occurs through the series of zinc-iron alloys that provides a powerful bond between the basis metal and the coating. The temperature of the bath has little effect on the nature of the coating as long as the temperature is maintained between 810 and 880°F (430 and 470°C).

Batch Galvanizing

Batch galvanizing is hot-dip galvanizing applied to prefabricated steel items. The advantage to galvanizing after fabrication

is that the zinc completely seals edges, overlaps, rivets, and welds; establishes liquid tightness; and prevents corrosion from starting. Iron and steel in all shapes and sizes can be coated with zinc by batch galvanizing. The process is simple, extremely versatile, and has been used to provide protection to articles ranging from small items, such as bolts, nuts, and miscellaneous hardware, to large items like structural beams for bridges or buildings. The virtually unrestricted size range of parts that can be galvanized and the ability to bolt or weld prefabricated sections after galvanizing enables almost any structure to be built from galvanized steel. Shape is not a restriction to batch galvanizing. Tubes, open vessels, drums, tanks, and complicated shapes such as large heat exchangers are readily galvanized on the inside and outside in one operation.

Continuous Galvanizing

Hot-dipped galvanized coatings are also applied to a variety of mill products by highly mechanized mass production methods at speeds of over 300 fpm (90 m/min). Several designs of galvanizing lines have been developed for commercial use by the steel suppliers. Most steel suppliers can produce galvanized coils (sheets) in widths of 10 to 72" (250 to 1830 mm) and thicknesses of 0.017 to 0.164" (0.43 to 4.17 mm). Typical applications for mill coated sheets are roofing and siding panels, guardrails, appliance cabinets, automotive body parts, and ductwork. Galvanized pipe and tubing is used for fencing, sign poles, playground equipment, and plumbing.

The coatings applied by continuous galvanizing contain more aluminum than batch galvanized coatings to minimize the formation of the brittle zinc-iron alloy and permit deep drawing and bending without damage to the coating. Coating weights vary from 0.5 to 2.75 oz/ft^2 (152.5 to 840 g/m^2). The zinc coating may be on one side of the sheet only, of equal weight on both sides of the sheet, or differentially applied (one side has a thicker coating than the other side).

ALUMINUM HOT DIPPING

Although zinc is well established as a coating material, aluminum is gaining in popularity. In normal or mild industrial environments, aluminum hot-dipped coatings provide good barrier protection against corrosion. The process of applying a hot-dipped aluminum coating to various substrates is also referred to as aluminizing. The coating process creates a strong metallurgical bond between the coating and steel base, and provides a uniform coating thickness and matte surface finish.

Two types of aluminum coatings are commercially available and can be applied using both batch and continuous processes. The specifications and standards for these coatings are given in ASTM Specification A 463. The first type of coating (Type 1) contains 5-10% silicon with the remainder being aluminum. These coatings are generally used in applications requiring good corrosion and heat resistance, and can generally be used to temperatures as high as 1250°F (675°C). The other coating

HOT DIPPING

(Type 2) is pure aluminum and is used in applications requiring good corrosion resistance. In most corrosive environments, aluminum coatings perform better than zinc coatings; research has shown that Type 2 aluminum coatings will outlast zinc coatings 5:1 in bold atmospheric exposure.

Batch Aluminizing

The batch aluminizing process is similar to the batch galvanizing process (see Fig. 48-9). The process consists of cleaning, heating, fluxing, and coating. Organic soils can be removed from the parts to be coated by alkaline cleaning and water rinsing. Steel parts are then descaled by abrasive blasting or acid pickling, followed by rinsing and drying. Gray or malleable iron parts are cleaned in molten salt in order to remove carbon smut.[12]

Continuous Aluminizing

The aluminum dip coating of continuous steel strip, sheet, or tubing is produced on continuous in-line equipment similar to that used for galvanizing. The process consists of surface preparation, heat treatment, and immersion coating with aluminum. Surface preparation may take place in an oxidizing furnace or in a nonoxidizing preheater; if an oxidizing furnace is used, the surface oxides are reduced in a suitable atmosphere. The immersion time, the temperature of the steel before and after immersion, and the temperature of the molten aluminum must be controlled to prevent the formation of an excess of iron-aluminum interfacial alloy.

HOT-DIP TINNING (TINPLATING)

In hot-dip tinning or tinplating, a thin coating of molten tin is applied to the surface of iron or steel substrates. The tin provides a nontoxic, protective, or decorative coating for food handling, packaging, or dairy equipment; facilitates the soldering of a variety of components used in electronic and electrical equipment; and assists in bonding another metal to the basis metal.[13] The production and consumption of tinplate for food cans in the U.S. has dropped dramatically over the years due to the more popular electrolytic processes. A modern hot-tinning line may produce approximately 1100 tons (1000 t) of hot-dipped tinplate per month, whereas an electrolytic line may produce that much in a day. Changes in effluent standards for electroplating wastes, however, may revive hot dipping to some extent.[14]

Coating Characteristics and Specifications

Three grades of tin are used in hot-dip tinning: standard tin containing 99% tin, refined tin with over 99.8% tin, and high-purity tin with over 99.9% tin. The amount of impurities that can be present in these grades is covered by ASTM Specification B 339; lead is the most common impurity and may cause the coating to be spangled. Military Specification MIL-T-10727-B covers pretreatment processing of base metals and the coating characteristics of hot-dip tinned coatings. The majority of the hot-dip tinning applications use grade A tin (99.8% tin). Standard tin is used in applications that only require soldering and do not come in contact with food. Coating weights range from 0.05 to 0.15 oz/ft^2 (15 to 45 g/m^2).

The term *hot tin dip* has also been used generically when a hot solder dip coating is applied to a workpiece; the coating generally consists of 60% tin and 40% lead. While this type of coating offers corrosion protection similar to pure tin, it is used primarily on electronic parts that must be soldered after assembly and when a corrosive-type flux cannot be tolerated.

Process Description[15]

In a typical hot-tinning process, individual steel sheets are pickled with hydrochloric acid or sulfuric acid, possibly with cathodic polarization, and then rinsed. On entering the bath of molten tin, the steel passes through a zinc chloride/ammonium chloride, aqueous flux cover that floats on the bath. It then passes through the molten tin, which is held at about 450°F (230°C) in an indirectly heated pot, and leaves the bath through the flux cover. Thicker coatings may be achieved by inserting the steel in a second pot of tin. The tin thickness is regulated by passage through wipers, where about 90% of the excess molten tin is wiped off the part and drops back into the bath. The tin coating thickness is related to a number of factors including contour of the tinning wipers, the wiper pressure, speed, bath temperature, and surface condition of the steel sheet before tinning. The drainage of the coating during solidification may result in a "list" or "drip" edge on the sheet, which must normally be removed by trimming.

LEAD ALLOY HOT DIPPING (TERNE COATING)

The term *terneplate* or *terne coating* is used to describe a hot-dipped coating of an alloy of lead and tin on a steel substrate. Since lead alone does not adhere to steel, a small amount of tin in the molten bath forms a thin layer of FeSn$_2$ compound, thus providing an adherent base for the terne coating. Tin also assists in the formation of a relatively continuous coating and adds to the solderability of the coating. Tin content is usually in the range of 2 to 15%. Terne coatings conform to ASTM Specification A 308.

Terne coatings are the most economical of the metallic coatings applied to steel; and, unlike the other coatings, the coating adherence does not deteriorate as the coating weight increases. However, since the terne coating is not sacrificial, it will show "pinhole" corrosion more rapidly than zinc or

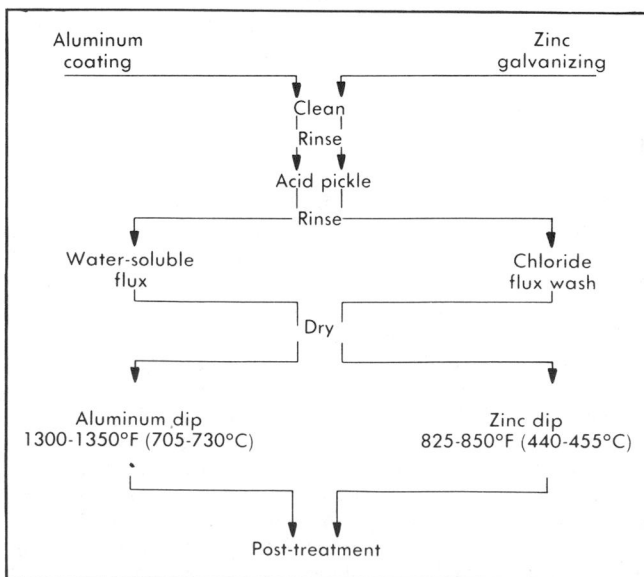

Fig. 48-9 Comparison of aluminum hot-dip coating with galvanizing.

aluminum-coated steel in accelerated tests and in harsh atmospheric exposure; but as the steel rusts, iron oxide fills the pinholes and resists further corrosion until the terne in the area is consumed.

Terne coatings are usually applied over carbon steel substrates having commercial quality, drawing quality, or drawing quality special-killed steel designations. Terne-coated stainless steel is also available.

Batch Lead Alloy Hot Dipping

In hot dipping formed and fabricated parts with a lead alloy, the steel is first cleaned of oils and greases using the appropriate solvents or detergents, followed by pickling in a sulfuric acid or hydrochloric acid solution. Before hot dipping, the parts are immersed in a zinc chloride or zinc-ammonium chloride flux.

The lead alloy bath is usually maintained at 620 to 675° F (325 to 390° C). The bath temperature and immersion time are determined by part weight. After the parts are withdrawn from the bath, they may be placed in a centrifuge or shaken to remove any excess coating. The part may then be quenched in water to solidify the coating.

Continuous Lead Alloy Hot Dipping

The production of terneplate is essentially the same process as that of hot-dipped tinplate.[16] Two general classifications of terneplate are produced: short ternes and long ternes. Short ternes are used only for roofing applications and are always painted to provide additional corrosion protection. Short ternes are heavier than long ternes and are produced from sheet material rather than coils.

CHEMICAL VAPOR DEPOSITION

Chemical vapor deposition (CVD) is a distinctly different coating process than vacuum evaporation, ion plating, or sputtering. A heat-activated process, CVD relies on the reaction of gaseous chemical compounds with suitably heated and prepared substrates.

The primary reactive vapor can be either a metal halide (chloride, bromide, iodide, or fluoride) or a metal carbonyl, $M(CO)_x$, although some hydrides and organometallic compounds are used. In general, deposition of a pure metal from the halide can occur either by hydrogen reduction at a given temperature or by direct pyrolytic decomposition at a higher temperature. The reduction method is illustrated in Fig. 48-10.

Whenever carbides, nitrides, or borides are the desired CVD products, the metal halide vapor is accompanied by an additional reactive species such as methane, nitrogen, or boron trichloride respectively. The addition of a reactive species lowers the free energy of the reaction products so that the compound is formed in preference to the pure metal. However, manipulation of reactor pressure, temperature, and/or reactant composition can also influence the deposition products.

ADVANTAGES AND LIMITATIONS

The versatility of the CVD process has been demonstrated by the wide variety of geometrical configurations into which it forms refractory metals, alloys, and refractory compounds. Users of CVD maintain that the process compares favorably with other methods of plating and forming in its ability to produce high-density materials, high-purity materials, high-strength materials, and complex shapes. The extraordinary throwing power of the CVD technique is such that very intricate coatings may be formed on substrates of complex geometry.

Materials in excess of 99.9% of theoretical density are commonly produced by this process. Thin structures made by CVD are used for applications in which vacuum tightness is required; in some cases, such structures could not be made by any other process. For example, as little as 0.002″ (50 μm) of a vapor-deposited material is commonly used to seal a vacuum of 10^{-8} torr (13.3 x 10^{-6} Pa), even at temperatures of 3630° F (2000° C).

Engineering materials can be deposited at considerably higher purity levels than is possible with other manufacturing means because of CVD's ability to purify the precursors. The strength of CVD materials is dependent on crystal structure and

size, purity, density, and internal stress, much the same as that of materials formed by other processes. Generally the CVD materials are more ductile because of their purity and can have comparable or higher mechanical strength than wrought material, providing that they are dense and have a fine equalized grain structure.

Not all deposited materials exhibit high strength; certain materials, such as pure tantalum and pure columbium, which are weak in their fully annealed condition, have low-yield strengths and high ductility in the vapor-deposited condition. However, when pure rhenium, pure columbium, tantalum alloys, and most rhenium alloys are formed by CVD, they have higher strengths.

Metals that are readily electroplated or electroformed commercially are generally not well-suited to chemical vapor deposition. In the case of the former, CVD processes are precluded owing to the unsuitable or hazardous properties of potential reactants. For example, electroplated metals such as lead, tin, and copper, and alloys such as brass are available as cyanides and fluoroborates and not as CVD-compatible halide salts.[17] With electroforming, in general, the electroformed part is the

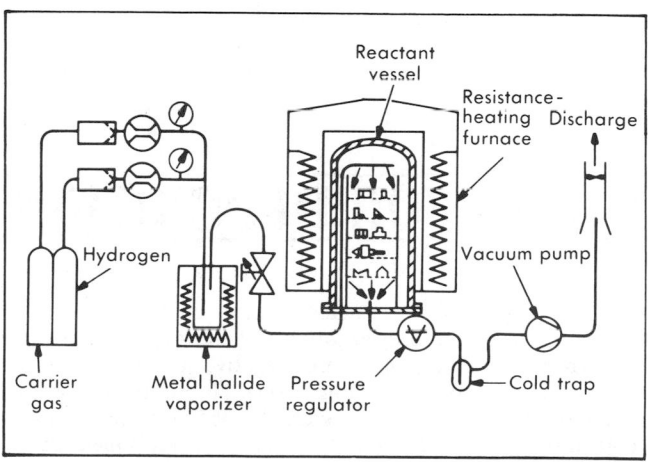

Fig. 48-10 Typical components used in the reduction method of chemical vapor deposition. (*Sylvester-Bernex Corp.*)

CHEMICAL VAPOR DEPOSITION

product desired and not the coating-substrate combination. However, molds for forming plastics that are vapor formed from nickel carbonyl are available for commercial use when their longer life justifies the higher costs.

A closed system is usually required when depositing the materials because of the corrosive, toxic, or moisture-sensitive characteristics of most reactants. Within the control volume, low pressures reduce the likelihood of homogeneous (gas-phase) nucleation and induce conditions favorable for heterogeneous (gas-to-solid) nucleation. Moreover, closed systems tend to normalize gas compositions while preventing the formation of undesirable species. Material utilization can be low, and reactant cost may be high, which may increase the overall cost of the process. In addition, the high temperature of the reaction can cause distortion of the parts being coated.

COATINGS DEPOSITED

A variety of pure metals or carbides, nitrides, borides, silicides, and oxides of metals can be deposited by CVD processes.[18] Coating thicknesses are usually in the range of 0.0002 to 0.050″ (5 to 1270 μm). The codeposition of titanium carbide (TiC) and titanium nitride (TiN) to form titanium carbonitride (TiC,N) by the Bernex Moderate Temperature Chemical Vapor Deposition (MTCVD) process is rapidly expanding in use.[19] Chromium deposition on steel substrates, resulting in carbides of chromium and iron, $(CrFe)_7C_3$, provides exceptional resistance to corrosion and cold welding.[20]

APPLICATIONS

The major applications of CVD take advantage of the unique characteristics of the process, such as good throwing power, the ability to deposit refractory materials at temperatures far below the normal ceramic processing temperatures, and the capability of producing materials of exceptionally high purity. Typical uses for the CVD process include the fabrication or coating of tubing, tungsten boride crucibles, decorative trim, and dinnerware.

A substantial field of CVD application exists for the hard coating of tools fabricated from high-speed steels, air-hardenable tool and stainless steels, and the cemented carbides. In particular, both titanium carbide (TiC) and titanium nitride (TiN) are regularly used to enhance the life of cemented carbide cutting tools and high-speed steel punches and dies. In the fastener industry, the vertical integration of high-temperature, low-pressure CVD of TiC and TiN into the tool manufacturing sequence has shown the greatest benefit.[21] Similarly, the incorporation of TiC and TiN in the carbide cutting tool industry has proven to be of significant commercial value.

More exotic depositions include the silicon and silicide coating of tungsten, and the platinum and rhenium coating of electronic hardware. Emitting surfaces and structures for cathodes as well as structural hardware for grids and anodes can be created by this process. Chemical vapor deposition is also the basis for several steps in the manufacture of integrated circuits for microelectronic applications and for solar cell fabrication.[22]

Chemical vapor deposition is used for depositing a refractory metal on jet aircraft turbine blades and for joining tungsten to other refractories at low temperature. Many applications are found in the nuclear power field, such as the coating of nuclear fuel particles for fission product retention or for matrix compatibility. Nuclear fuel can be contained by direct deposition of refractory metals and/or pyrolytic carbon on the surface of the fuel itself.[23] Ceramic-to-metal seals have been made by the deposition of metals, ceramics, or both; and there are many applications for composite materials that use deposited high-density oxides and metals. Tungsten and/or carbon fibers have been encapsulated with both boron carbide and silicon carbide by CVD processes.[24] The filaments have been subsequently used as reinforced composites in structural components.

The protection of chemical equipment is an obvious application of CVD. Steel with less than a 0.002″ (50 μm) deposited coating of tantalum will frequently outperform stainless steel, or Monel or Inconel (the International Nickel Co., Inc.) at a competitive cost. Cladding for abrasion resistance also warrants serious consideration. Many hard refractory-metal compounds cannot readily be formed or finished by mechanical means. On the other hand, hard coatings such as silicon carbide, tungsten carbide, tantalum carbide, or titanium diboride are readily applied by chemical vapor deposition to resist abrasion and corrosion on devices such as pump impellers, valves, and nozzles. Superficial coatings of such materials may be particularly adherent and of high density, and they have been measured at hardnesses above 2500 Vickers hardness using a 200 g weight.

PROCESS FACTORS

Some important factors in CVD processes are the thermodynamic combinations of gas pressure, temperature, and velocity, and reactant composition; composition material; substrate cleanliness and temperature; the gas storage, flow, and recovery systems; scrubber systems for the by-products; and the composition and construction of the reaction vessel.

ION VAPOR DEPOSITION

The IVD process takes place in an evacuated chamber in which an inert gas (usually argon) is added to raise the pressure and to become ionized when a high negative potential is applied to the parts to be coated (see Fig. 48-11). The positively charged argon ions bombard the negatively charged parts, providing a final cleaning. The metal that will coat the parts is melted and vaporized. Some metal vapor is ionized, accelerating it to the parts where the coating is formed.

ADVANTAGES AND LIMITATIONS

The IVD process offers a number of advantages over other coating methods. It produces a dense, adherent, and uniform coating that is not limited to line-of-sight deposition. Thus, coating uniformity is maintained even on complex shapes. It is a nontoxic and nonpolluting process, eliminating the need for pollution control and waste disposal equipment and procedures.[25]

Since the IVD process does not introduce hydrogen, hydro-

ION VAPOR DEPOSITION

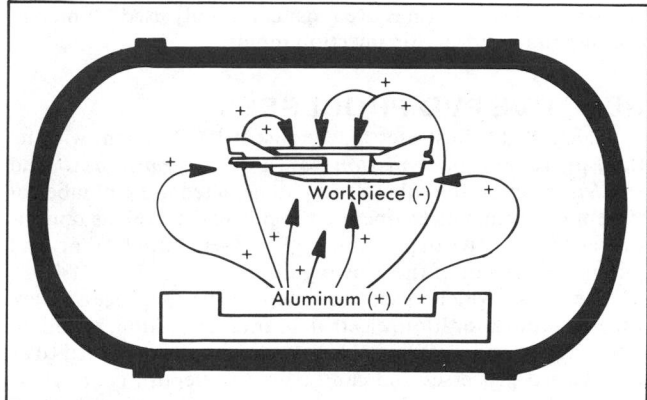

Fig. 48-11 Schematic diagram of the Ion vapor deposition process. (*McDonnell Aircraft Co.*)

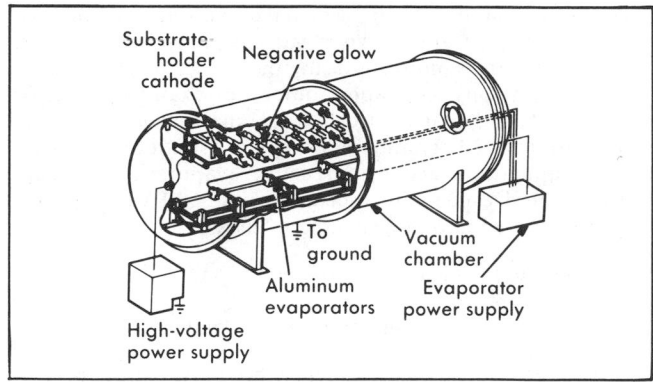

Fig. 48-12 Schematic diagram of large-parts rack coater. (*McDonnell Aircraft Co.*)

gen embrittlement is not a consideration, and therefore the process can be used on steels at any strength level. Ion vapor deposition also eliminates solid-metal embrittlement of titanium and does not reduce the fatigue properties of aluminum alloys—both problems related to other coating processes.[26] With a chromate conversion coating, the IVD aluminum coating provides excellent electrical conductivity.

Use of the IVD process is limited by the initial expense of the equipment and its capacity, which is similar to other vacuum coatings or metallizing processes. However, recent developments have increased product throughput significantly.

APPLICATIONS

The major use of the IVD process is to coat alloy steel, titanium, or aluminum alloys with pure aluminum. The aluminum coating is generally applied per military standard MIL-C-83488,[27] which provides for three classes of thicknesses, from 0.0003 to 0.0010″ (8 to 25 μm) minimum, and two types of finished coatings, either chromated or nonchromated.

Some specific applications for IVD aluminum are as follows:

- Aircraft applications: alloy steel details of all strength levels; fatigue-critical aluminum alloy structures; alloy steel, corrosion-resistant steel, and titanium fasteners.
- Aluminum alloy fuel and pneumatic line fittings.
- Electromagnetic interference (EMI) applications.
- Powder metallurgy details.
- High-temperature applications to 925° F (496° C).
- Depleted uranium substrates.
- Marine applications.

EQUIPMENT

The basic equipment needed for the IVD process consists of a vacuum chamber, a vacuum pumping system, an evaporation

source, a parts-holding rack, and a high-voltage power supply capable of 2 kV and 2.5 A. In addition, conventional supporting equipment may include a vapor degreaser, grit blasting equipment, inert gas storage and supply, glass-bead peening equipment, a chromate treatment line, and a system for stripping aluminum coating.

The first production system was used by the Naval Air Rework Facility in San Diego, California in 1974.[28] Since then, a number of systems have been fabricated for production use. These systems are available as racked parts coaters, barrel coaters, or combinations that can be converted for either racked parts or barrel coating. Schematic diagrams of the two basic systems are shown in Fig. 48-12 and Fig. 48-13.

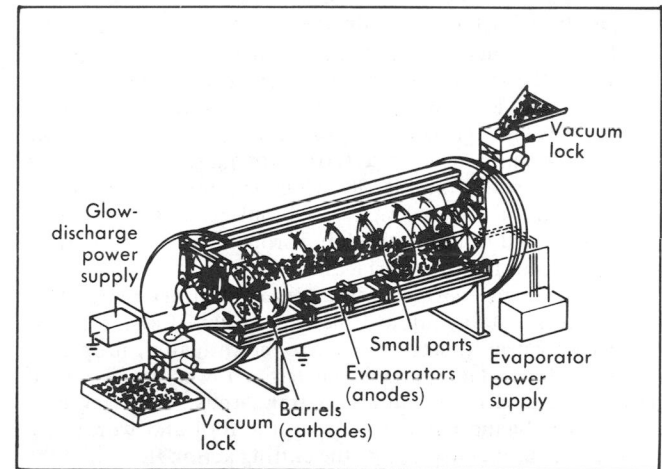

Fig. 48-13 Schematic diagram of small-parts barrel coater. (*McDonnell Aircraft Co.*)

PHYSICAL VAPOR DEPOSITION OF HARD COATINGS

Physical vapor deposition (PVD) covers a broad class of vacuum coating processes in which material is physically removed from a source by evaporation or sputtering, transported through a vacuum or partial vacuum by the energy of the vapor particles, and condensed as a film on the surfaces of

appropriately placed parts or substrates. Chemical compounds are deposited by either using a similar source material, or by introducing a gas (nitrogen, oxygen, or simple hydrocarbons) containing the desired reactants, which react with metal(s) from the PVD source.

PHYSICAL VAPOR DEPOSITION OF HARD COATINGS

A myriad of PVD processes have evolved over the last twenty years. They are known by various phrases or acronyms that are sometimes more confusing than descriptive. Most are named for the physical vapor source; for example, diode or triode sputtering, planar or cylindrical magnetron sputtering, direct current (DC) or radio frequency (RF) sputtering, electron beam evaporation, activated reactive evaporation, and arc evaporation. Despite any name confusion, all PVD processes can be separated into three distinct phases:

1. *Emission* from a vapor source.
2. Vapor *transport* in vacuum.
3. *Condensation* on substrates to be coated.

Historically, PVD processes have been relatively expensive as the result of slow deposition rates, expensive vacuum equipment, and throughput limitations. Painting, electroplating, thermal spraying, and chemical vapor deposition (CVD) are typically less expensive coating processes. Additional information on painting, electroplating, thermal spraying, and CVD can be found in the designated chapters of this volume. In recent years, the use of PVD methods has expanded at an extremely rapid rate owing to reduced costs and, more importantly, because of increased demand for high-performance materials and coatings that cannot be produced by other methods.

COATINGS DEPOSITED

A broad spectrum of metals, alloys, and electrically conductive, semiconductive, and insulating compounds are deposited commercially using PVD methods. Physical vapor deposition methods are used almost exclusively to deposit films that are 1-200 μin. (0.03-5 μm) thick. Thicker films are sometimes deposited, but the cost-benefit ratio usually acts as a barrier, dictating the use of films thinner than 200 μin. (5 μm).

The use of reactive PVD hard coatings, especially titanium nitride (TiN), to improve the performance of metalcutting tools, as well as a wide variety of other tools and wear components, has grown at an exceptionally high rate since 1980. Titanium nitride is a refractory material that has a hardness of greater than R_C80, which is approximately three times harder than typical high-speed tool steels. The increased hardness, in addition to antiwelding properties, reduces the rate of wear for most cutting surfaces.

A TiN coating provides resistance to chemical deterioration because it is a stable (almost inert) material. It also prevents chip welding in cutting tools owing to the antigalling properties of the coating. Titanium nitride has a lower coefficient of friction than hard chromium coatings, thus improving chip flow and reducing friction between the tool and workpiece. Most of the heat generated by the cutting action flows into the chips rather than into the cutting tool.

APPLICATIONS

Physical vapor deposition coatings are an integral part of many products ranging from conductive, resistive, or insulating coatings for microelectronic devices to heat-reflective and decorative coatings on architectural glass; from photoelectric and antireflective coatings in solar cells to corrosion-resistant coatings on aircraft fasteners; and from decorative coatings on pens and watchcases to wear-resistant coatings on metalcutting tools.

Titanium nitride hard coatings are widely used in the automotive, tractor, gear, bearing, fabrication, aircraft, and oil industries. These coatings are most commonly used on metalworking tools and plastic injection molds.

REACTIVE PVD PROCESSES

Figure 48-14 illustrates a generalized PVD system with its three phases of vapor *emission* from a source, *transport* to, and *condensation* on the substrate. Also depicted are a number of system requirements to operate the process, as well as options that enable reactive deposition, a plasma-enhanced vapor, and ion bombardment of the growing film.

The most widely used commercial PVD processes are vacuum arc evaporation, electron beam evaporation, and high-rate magnetron sputtering. These are commonly referred to as ion-assisted processes and can be used to deposit coatings by nonreactive and reactive means.

Reactive PVD

In reactive PVD, carbides, nitrides, oxides, carbonitrides, and many other compound types are deposited by introducing a reactive gas (simple hydrocarbons such as CH_4, C_2H_6, nitrogen, oxygen, and other gases) into the physical vapor stream. Reactions between the gas and physical vapor can occur at the source surface, in transit, or at the substrate surface, as well as on the chamber walls and other surfaces.

In most processes, reactions at the vapor source are minimal owing to the nature of the process and/or the desires of the process designer. In vacuum arc evaporation, surface reactions often take place at the source; these reactions do not significantly affect the vaporization rates because most of the vapor release comes from beneath the source surface. With electron beam evaporation, the maximum operating pressure at the source is too low at typical evaporation rates for significant reactions to occur. For reactive planar magnetron sputtering, cathode vaporization rates are often reduced by a factor of 10 or more at a given power input when oxide, nitride, or carbide layers form on the sputtering surface.

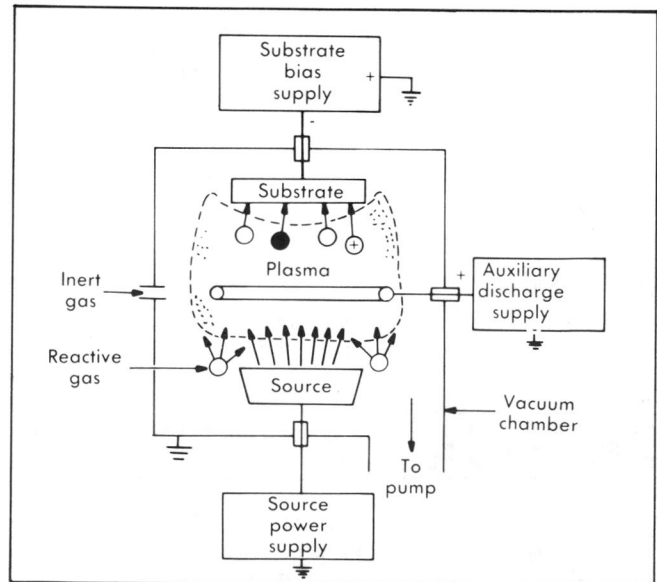

Fig. 48-14 Schematic of generalized PVD system. (*Multi-Arc Vacuum Systems, Inc.*)

PHYSICAL VAPOR DEPOSITION OF HARD COATINGS

Plasma Enhancement

Plasma enhancement refers to various methods of increasing the number of ions, electrons, fragmented molecules, and excited neutrons in a gas or vapor. To employ plasma enhancement, inert and/or reactive gases must be present at pressures suitable for maintaining a gas discharge. When used in conjunction with a negative substrate bias, the increased ion bombardment resulting from plasma enhancement is an important factor that generally results in improved film properties. In reactive PVD, plasma enhancement produces excited and ionized atoms, molecules, and molecular fragments that react more readily with the surface of the growing film.

Ion Bombardment

When energetic ion bombardment of a growing film is present, the process is referred to as ion-bombardment-assisted deposition, or simply ion-assisted deposition. Ion-assisted deposition processes are very successful in many applications because they produce films with extremely high adherence and good physical properties.

In most ion-assisted PVD processes, ions gain energy as a result of a negative bias voltage that is applied to the substrates. For nonconductive substrates or coatings, a high-frequency or RF bias voltage is applied; positive ions are accelerated to the substrates during the negative phase, and charging of the substrates is neutralized by electrons during the positive phase of each cycle.

Ion Plating Processes

Ion plating is the name given by Mattox in 1964 to the PVD process illustrated in Fig. 48-15.[29] In this process, substrates are heated and sputtered clean by argon ions from a glow discharge that is supported by a negatively biased substrate; the negative bias is between -2000 to -5000 V. During deposition, molecules from a thermal evaporation source pass through the glow discharge on their way to the substrate. The vapor condensing on the substrate is accompanied by the bombardment of metal and argon ions as well as energetic molecules. This process produces highly adherent coatings with a relatively uniform thickness on irregularly shaped substrates due to gas scattering and sputtering-recondensation effects.

In addition to its use in the original ion plating process, ion bombardment is employed for surface cleaning and conditioning in many contemporary PVD processes. Although this procedure is not an economical substitute for thorough cleaning prior to loading in the coating chamber, it provides a very effective final touch that is an important factor in achieving good film adhesion. In the wake of a large number of PVD processes that utilize energetic particle bombardment of growing films, the term "ion plating" is gradually being replaced by the more general and descriptive term "ion assisted deposition."

Vacuum Arc Evaporation

In processes employing vacuum arc evaporation, shown in Fig. 48-15, metal vapor is evaporated from a cathode source as a result of intense localized heating by arc spots that move more or less randomly across the cathode surface. Distinguishing features of arc evaporation processes are that the vapor source remains solid while a major fraction of the metal vapor is ionized.

Because arc melting is highly localized, cathodes may be used in any orientation, allowing greater flexibility in designing systems with multiple sources for coating very large parts or large quantities of smaller parts. With judicious source placement, uniform coatings can be applied to a variety of substrates through the use of very simple fixturing and rotation devices.

Electron Beam Reactive Deposition

The electron beam reactive deposition processes in current industrial use are thermionically-enhanced-triode ion plating, hollow cathode discharge, and coaxial. In each process, metal heated by an electron beam evaporates from a molten pool. The

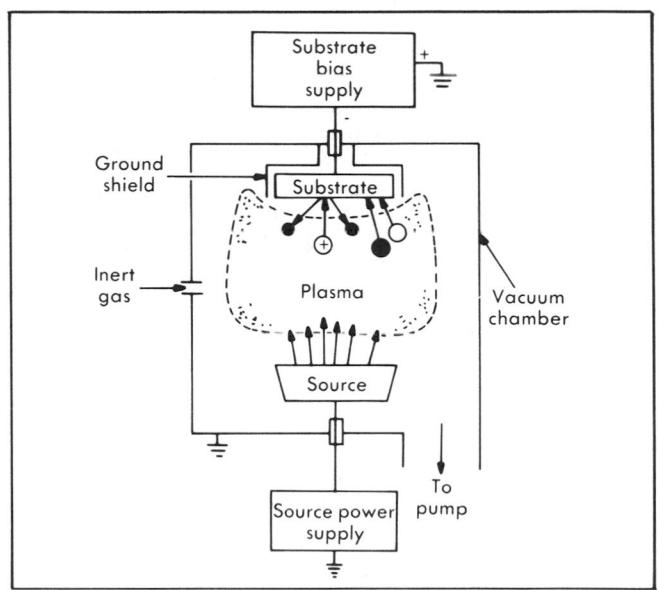

Fig. 48-15 Schematic of classical ion plating system. (*Multi-Arc Vacuum Systems, Inc.*)

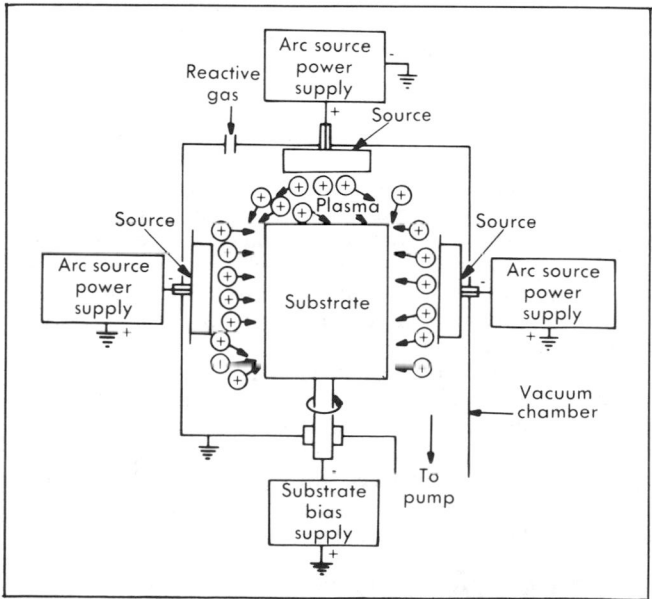

Fig. 48-16 Schematic of components in a vacuum arc reactive system. (*Multi-Arc Vacuum Systems, Inc.*)

VACUUM METALLIZING

substrates are oriented to collect vapor from bottom-mounted sources. Substrate rotation is commonly used to increase the uniformity of the film thickness and part capacity. The reactive gas pressure must be closely controlled to achieve good film stoichiometry.

High-Rate Reactive Magnetron Sputtering

In high-rate reactive magnetron sputtering, metal vapor is sputtered from cathode sources by an intense inert gas discharge that is largely confined to a region within 4" (100 mm) of the cathode source; magnetron sources may be used in any orientation. Compared to evaporation sources in general, the vaporization rates per unit area are relatively low; but large single sources can be used, as well as multiple sources, to compensate for the low rates. To maintain maximum sputtering rates during reactive deposition, the components and process controls must be arranged to prevent the formation of reaction products on the cathode surface. Magnetron sputtering is well

suited for applying uniform coatings on large, planar surfaces and for use in continuous in-line systems.

PROCESS CONSIDERATIONS

Although PVD methods typically require more expensive equipment, more parts preparation, more system maintenance, and greater processing times than many alternate processes, PVD is a viable coating process for hard coatings. In some instances, PVD is the only method capable of depositing a coating of the desired material. The overall cost of PVD can often be less than other coating methods when all factors are taken into account. The primary considerations that must be evaluated before selecting a PVD process include desired end result, substrate properties, cleaning and preparation, fixturing, temperature, and coating rates. When alternative means of achieving the end result are available, total costs must be compared among the alternatives; total cost would include equipment cost and operating environment.

VACUUM METALLIZING

In vacuum metallizing, a metal or metal compound is evaporated at high temperature in a closed, evacuated chamber and then allowed to condense on a workpiece within the chamber. The workpiece is usually at room or a relatively low temperature. The coating can be deposited on flexible substrates and on discrete objects. When the coatings are deposited on rolled flexible substrates, the process is referred to as roll or semicontinuous metallizing; when deposited on discrete or solid objects, the process is called batch metallizing.

ROLL METALLIZING

Vacuum metallizing of flexible substrates, while involving the same vacuum deposition process as used in batch metallizing, requires additional process operations and controls. In general, no substrate cleaning or preparation is required, although certain film and paper grades are more suitable for roll metallizing. In the basic vacuum deposition process, the pressure in the vacuum chamber is reduced to a pressure of approximately 1×10^{-4} torr (0.013 Pa) or lower. The evaporation source heats the coating material to a temperature such that the vapor pressure exceeds the chamber pressure, permitting the coating material to be deposited on the substrate. The substrate is then transported above the evaporation source at a high rate of speed as it is rewound onto the rewind shaft. The substrate is normally held in contact with a chilled drum when it is exposed to the evaporation source to protect it from thermal shock due to infrared radiation from the source and the heat of condensation from the evaporant.

The metallized products manufactured by roll metallizing are used in a wide range of applications. Products include hot stamping foils, laminated film products, capacitors, solar control products, reflective insulation, packaging materials, labels, decals, optical products, decorative materials, wrapping papers and films, protective fabrics, magnetic coatings, and many other types of functional products.

BATCH METALLIZING

In batch metallizing, the parts are loaded on fixturing racks and then placed in the vacuum work chamber; as many as

several thousand parts may be coated in one load. The smallest part size that can be processed is approximately 1/8" (3 mm) in diameter by 1/4" (6 mm) long; smaller parts are more difficult to grip individually. Maximum size is limited only by the size of the metallizer.[30] Coating rates are typically 50 μin./min (1.3 μm/min) and higher for aluminum, and from 5 to 20 μin./min (0.13 to 0.56 μm/min) for most other materials.

The substrates upon which metallic vapor can be deposited include glass, plastics, and metallic materials. The primary requirement of the material to be coated is that it be stable in vacuum. It must not evolve gas or vapor when exposed to the metal vapor.[31]

Coatings Deposited

Virtually all metals, many alloys and semimetallic elements, and innumerable compounds can be deposited by vacuum metallizing. A limiting factor is that as the vapor pressure of the coating material drops, vaporization becomes progressively more difficult because a better vacuum is required and the design and material problems of the vapor source become increasingly complex.

In practice, only a small group of coatings are commonly deposited by vacuum metallizing. Aluminum is the most widely used material because of its high vapor pressure, excellent reflectivity, and attractive appearance. After aluminum, some of the more commonly used materials, in order of decreasing vapor pressure, are selenium, cadmium, silicon monoxide, silver, and copper. Gold, chromium, nickel chromium, palladium, titanium, and magnesium fluoride are also deposited.

Applications

Vacuum metallizing is most commonly used to deposit decorative aluminum coatings onto plastics and metal substrates. The two types of decorative coatings are referred to as first-surface and second-surface coatings. First-surface coatings are deposited on the outer or front surface of the part and are generally used for applications that require wear or corrosion resistance. For typical application examples such as automotive instrument panels or television control bezels and knobs, a thin, transparent coating is applied over the aluminum to provide wear and corrosion resistance.

Vacuum metallizing is also used for depositing functional coatings in the optical, electrical/electronic, and corrosion-resistance fields. In the optical field, these coatings are selected primarily for their reflective or antireflective characteristics. They are used for mirrors varying from rearview mirrors and sealed-beam headlamps to optical components of scientific instruments, such as microscopes, monochromators, and tele-scopes. In other optical applications, the absorption property of the metal film is used, serving as light attenuators or neutral-density filters to reduce intensity levels. Typical product applications of these coatings are sunglasses and specially graded filters to provide uniform illumination of wide-angle lenses.

A variety of metals and alloys are deposited for use in the electrical/electronics industry as conductors, resistors, and capacitors. Cadmium and aluminum, in thicknesses of 0.25 to 1.0 mil (6 to 25 μm), are used for corrosion resistance.

SPUTTERING

Sputtering is the deposition of materials under vacuum onto prepared substrates to produce specific films for both decorative and functional applications. Sputtering differs from vacuum metallizing (evaporation) in that the material is removed from a solid cathode or target instead of being vaporized by a heating source. Rapidly moving gas ions in the vacuum chamber strike a negatively biased target causing metal atoms to be ejected through a transfer of momentum (Fig. 48-17). Subsequently, the ejected target atoms strike and adhere to the substrate surface forming a thin coating that has the same composition as the target.

Because the coating material is passed into the vapor phase by a mechanical process rather than a chemical or thermal process, virtually any material is a candidate for coating.[41] Virtually all types of metals can be successfully sputtered, including chromium, stainless steel, titanium, aluminum, copper, brass, tungsten, molybdenum, gold, silver, and tantalum. Alloys and compounds can also be sputtered without altering their original compositions. New compounds can be created by sputtering with a gas background that reacts with a metal or metal alloy to form new materials such as oxides, carbides, and nitrides. Semiconducting and insulating materials may be sputtered by applying a radio frequency potential to the target.

Sputtered coatings can be deposited on both conductive and nonconductive substrates; some metals and nylons may require a primer or pretreatment before sputtering. Base coats are generally applied to the substrates when a bright finish is required. Most sputtered deposits are from 2 to 40 μin. (0.05 to 1 μm) thick.

ADVANTAGES AND LIMITATIONS

Sputtering is a nonpolluting, controllable process and a versatile tool for both decorative and functional finishing. As previously stated, a wide variety of metals and alloys can be successfully deposited. The coatings adhere better than conventional vacuum-metallized coatings. The primary limitation to sputtering is the slow deposition rate, but newer sputtering methods have resulted in faster rates.

APPLICATIONS

Sputtered coatings are used in decorative, decorative/functional, and functional applications. In decorative applications, the coatings are primarily for aesthetic purposes. Typical parts include toys, cosmetic caps, and picture frames. In decorative/functional applications, the coatings provide aesthetic value along with resistance to corrosion and impact, reflectivity, durability, and adhesion. These coatings are often used for appliance endcaps; automotive grills, wheelcovers, and hubcaps; fixtures for plumbing, marine, and electrical use; and knobs, buttons, and door hardware. Typical functional applications include electromagnetic interference shielding, semiconductor fabrication, transparent conductors, printed circuit boards, optical and magnetic storage media, electrical connections, architectural windows, solar control film, and barrier coats.

SPUTTERING METHODS

The sputtering process may be used as a method for either surface coating or etching. Some of the more common coating methods are planar diode, triode, magnetron, and ion gun sputtering. Direct current discharges are generally used for sputtering conductive substrates; a radio frequency (RF) potential must be applied to the target to sputter nonconducting substrates.[32] Reactive sputtering can be performed with the addition of small, controlled quantities of a reactive gas, such as oxygen, to the argon stream.

Planar Diode Sputtering[33]

A planar diode is a two-component system. The sputtering target is the cathode, and the substrate to be coated is the anode (see Fig. 48-18). When a negative potential of several hundred to a few thousand volts is applied to the cathode, a glow discharge (plasma) ignites within the vacuum chamber after the appropriate pressure level is reached. The plasma usually consists of argon gas ions.

With this simple arrangement, deposition rates are low, and it is difficult to avoid contamination in the film. In order to produce results that can be duplicated, it is necessary to control residual gas pressure. Because of the low deposition rates, the base pressure required before backfilling should be less than 1 x 10^{-7} torr (1.3 x 10^{-5} Pa). However, the low base pressure is not practical in a production environment. The advantages of diode sputtering are as follows:

- Refractory films can be deposited.
- Insulating films can be deposited.

The limitations of diode sputtering are:

- Good film adhesion is only possible with a few materials.
- Low base pressures are required.
- The source material must be available in sheet form.
- Special holders are required to maintain low substrate temperatures.
- The deposition rates are usually less than 4 +in./min (0.1 +m/min).

SPUTTERING

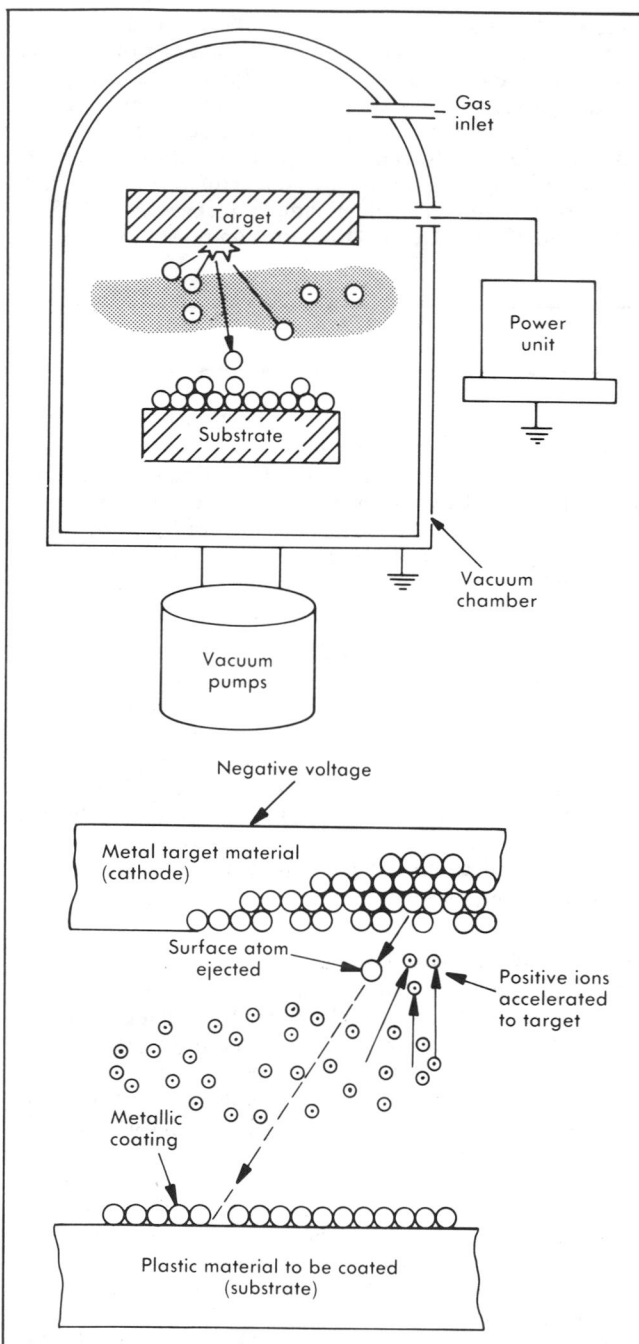

Fig. 48-17 Principles of sputtering operation. (*General Electric*)

Triode Sputtering[34]

In triode sputtering, the apparatus consists of three electrodes, an anode and target, and an additional electron source (see Fig. 48-19). The chamber is held at the required pressure, and electrons are generated by a thermionically heated filament. The electrons are accelerated toward the anode where they ionize a larger portion of the gas molecules. The process that takes place in the triode system is known as electron-supported discharge because it relies on the abundance of electrons generated by the heated filament to ensure sufficient ionizing collisions. The

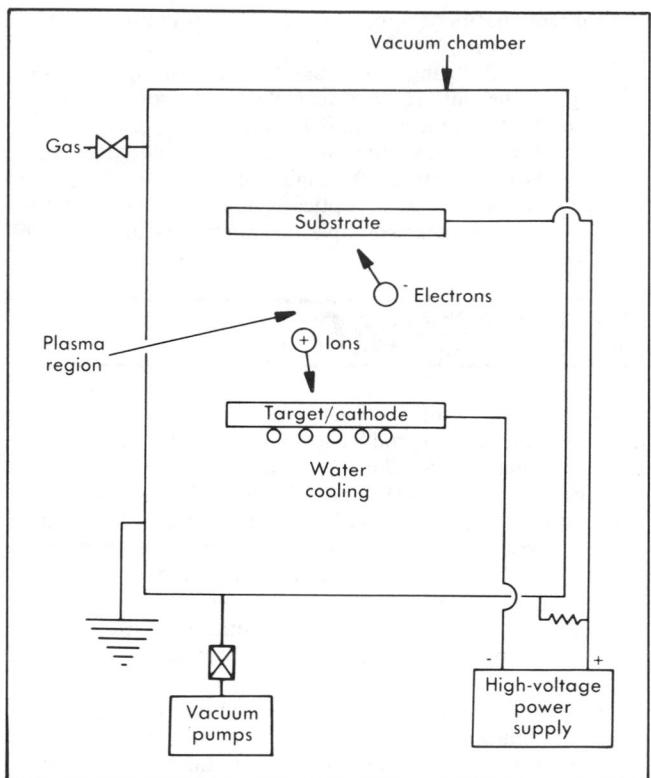

Fig. 48-18 Schematic of planar diode sputtering. (*Technical Enterprises, Inc.*)

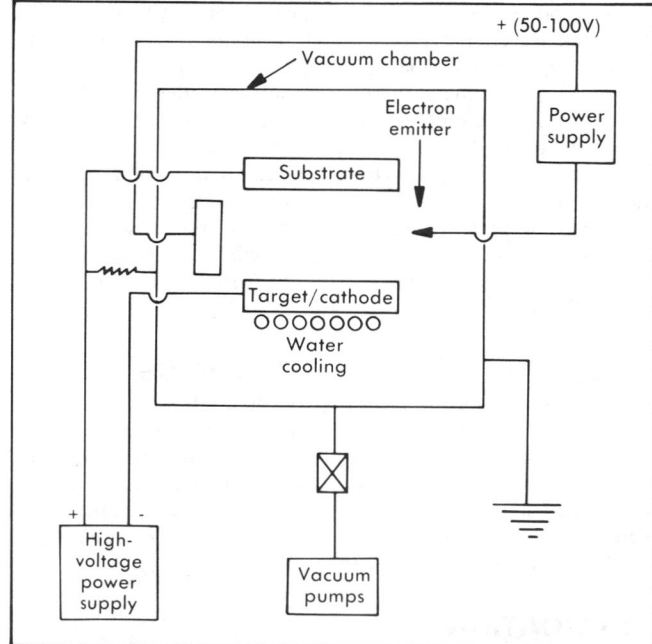

Fig. 48-19 Schematic of triode sputtering.)

abundance of electrons allows the plasma to operate and sputter material at pressures considerably lower than diode sputtering.

The advantages of low-pressure triode sputtering over diode sputtering are:

- Higher deposition rates.
- Decreased ratio of sputtering gas molecules to sputtered atoms, which means that the film density and purity are enhanced.
- More consistent straight-line deposition from target to substrate, making it possible to use masks to define film patterns.

However, the use of the heated element as a source of free electrons creates the following limitations when compared with diode sputtering:

- The thermionic elements make reactive sputtering with chemically reactive gas impractical or even dangerous.
- The filament contributes to contamination and is subject to burnout.

Magnetron Sputtering

In magnetron sputtering, a magnetic field is applied over the sputtering target to confine the high-density plasma. The argon ions in the plasma are accelerated to the target, which is negatively biased. The collision of the ions with the cathode ejects particles of the target material with mean kinetic energies of 4 to 6 eV. The substrate to be coated is positioned in front of the target, and the particles that strike the substrate condense to form an adherent coating (see Fig. 48-20). A number of target configurations are commercially available, such as planar magnetron and cylindrical-post magnetron; planar targets are more suitable for in-line or semicontinuous process operations, and cylindrical targets are more suitable for batch processes.

High sputtering rates and efficiency are possible with magnetron sputtering because a greater percentage of the current flow is carried by the argon gas. Because of the higher sputtering rates, the sputtered material can be made to cover larger areas. Magnetron sputtering typically takes place at pressures midway between diode and triode sputtering methods.

Ion Gun Sputtering

Ion gun sputtering is a method that extracts ions from a Kaufman source and impinges them on a target that becomes eroded; the eroded atoms are then deposited on the substrate.

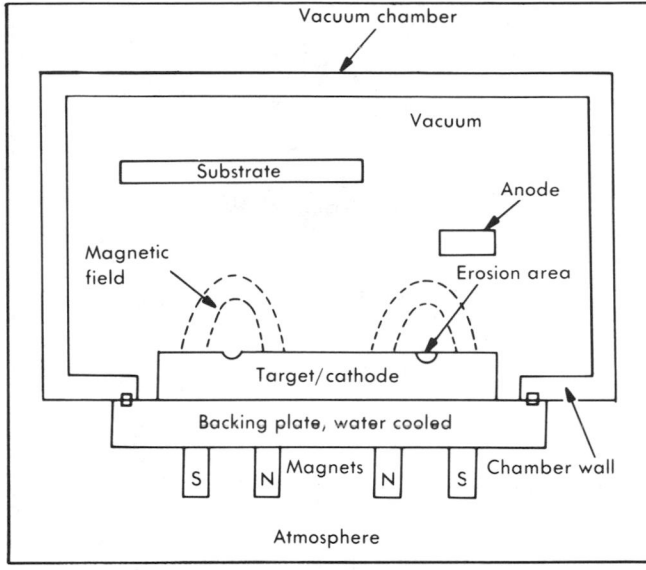

Fig. 48-20 Schematic of magnetron sputtering.

The Kaufman source uses a magnetically enhanced low-voltage discharge that is similar to a cold-cathode gage.

The ions are extracted through a series of screen grids and dumped into a low-gas-density chamber where they can be further accelerated at the target. Since the gas density or pressure is low, few if any collisions take place, resulting in higher energy ions striking the target. Because the background pressure is low, less argon is included in the coating. This method is used for sputtering, etching, and ion implantation; however, it has not been used for production applications.

PROCESS DESCRIPTION

Sputtering is performed on both rigid and flexible substrates. Rigid substrates are sputtered in batch or in-line multichamber equipment, whereas flexible substrates are sputtered in semicontinuous equipment.

FLEXIBLE OVERLAYS

A new process has recently been developed for applying hard facing to workpiece surfaces that are susceptible to wear. The process consists of applying both a flexible clothlike material containing a hard, wear-resistant metal or ceramic powder and a cloth containing a brazing alloy to the surface of a workpiece. During the heating cycle, the metal powders are fused to the surface of the workpiece.

ADVANTAGES AND LIMITATIONS

The major advantage of the flexible overlay process is the ability to coat selected areas of the workpiece while retaining excellent dimensional control of the coating. Another important advantage is flexibility in the selection of coating materials since the process is not constrained by powder chemistry, particle shape, or size distribution. In addition, material utilization is high since there is no overspray and cloth remnants can be easily recycled with no loss in coating properties. Finally, the micro-

structure of the coating is homogeneous and does not contain the slag, entrapped oxide, or unmelted particles that are sometimes associated with thermal spray processes.

The major limitation of the flexible overlay process is its inability to lay down thin coatings. Coating thicknesses are usually 0.01 to 0.1" (0.25 to 2.5 mm). Another limitation of this new process involves the high temperatures required for the brazing cycle. Since the whole workpiece is heated, grain growth and loss of temper may occur. The brazing furnace capacity also limits the size of the workpiece that can be hard faced.

APPLICATIONS

Flexible overlays can be used for applications requiring high abrasive resistance, erosion resistance, and/or impact resistance. Examples of such applications are debarkers and chain saw teeth in the forest products industry. High-volume production of coated components for business machines is routinely

FLEXIBLE OVERLAYS

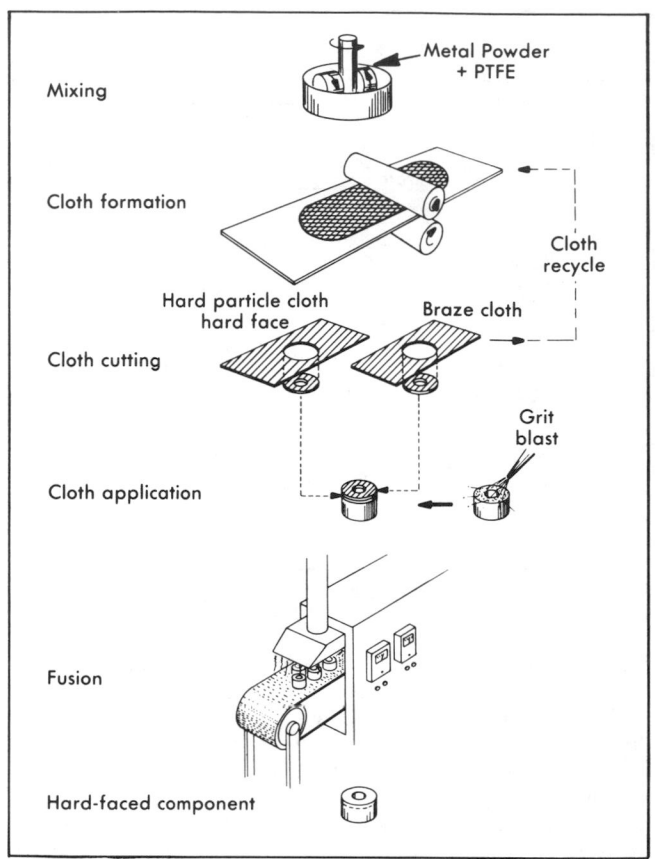

Fig. 48-21 Flexible overlay process (Conforma Clad®) for applying hard-facing coatings. (*Imperial Clevite, Inc.*)

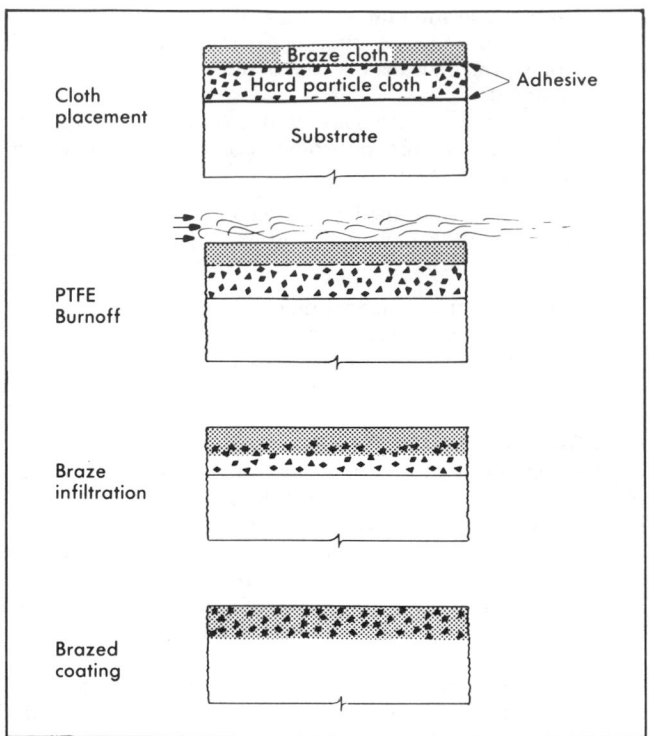

Fig. 48-22 Sequence involved in the infiltration of the brazing alloy in composite coatings. (*Imperial Clevite, Inc.*)

handled through resistance fusion. In the oil drilling and mining industries, rock bits, attack points, driveshaft caps, and drill collars have been successfully coated. Other applications for flexible overlays include extrusion dies and screws, combustion fan liners, valves, turbine tips, rocker arms, agricultural fan blades, and wear tiles.

AVAILABLE COATINGS

Various composite coatings for hard-facing applications are available, with the hard particles generally being tungsten carbide and/or tungsten carbide with cobalt; the brazing alloy is generally nickel-based. By varying the proportion of brazing alloy and carbide, or by changing the carbide volume fraction using particle size control, coatings can be offered with hardnesses up to R_C72. The performance characteristics of the coating can also be changed by varying the toughness of the carbide particles or by changing the brazing alloy composition. The intercarbide particle spacing is another variable that can be controlled to provide a coating with specific properties. Generally, for the low end of hardnesses (R_C 40-60), single-alloy

coatings made from a cobalt-based or a nickel-based alloy are preferred. Within the composite coatings family, a chromium carbide hard particle coating is also offered, with a nickel-based alloy matrix. Experimental coatings have also been developed containing molybdenum tungsten carbide or tungsten titanium carbide.

PROCESS

The flexible overlay process, illustrated in Figs. 48-21 and 48-22, uses a two-cloth approach developed by Imperial Clevite, Inc. called Conforma Clad®. Figure 48-21 presents a breakdown of the process in intermediate steps. Figure 48-22 depicts how the metal-impregnated cloth is fused to the surface of the workpiece. A variation of the two-cloth technique uses a single cloth made from a mixture of brazing alloy and hard particle powders. Instead of the composite coating, which is comprised of hard particles dispersed within a brazing matrix, single alloy coatings can also be used. The control of the coating geometry becomes more demanding during fusion with the single-alloy materials than with the composite materials when dimensional control is dictated by the relatively inert refractory material, such as tungsten carbide. Flexible overlay coatings have been fused on plain-carbon steels, high-alloy steels, stainless steels, nickel-based superalloys, and cast irons.

STEAM TREATING

Treating parts in a steam atmosphere is an older process that is being increasingly used by present-day metalworkers owing to the escalating production costs of other processes. During steam treating, a tightly adherent oxide film (Fe_3O_4) is formed on the surface of ferrous parts. The film is usually a blue-black color and approximately 0.0002" (5 μm) thick.

ADVANTAGES AND LIMITATIONS

Steam treating is a clean and safe process that requires only heat and steam to produce the coating on parts. Supervision and labor during the process are minimal. Further, steam treating can be combined with other heat processing operations.

The materials being treated must be capable of withstanding the processing temperatures, usually 400 to 1200°F (200 to 650°C). Since stainless steels do not react to the steam atmosphere, they cannot be treated by the process. Finally, steam treating is usually limited to parts that can be treated in a batch process.

APPLICATIONS

Steam treating can be used in both ferrous and nonferrous applications. In most nonferrous applications, the steam provides a protective atmosphere during annealing or aging operations. Generally, the natural color of the metal is retained.

PROCESS DESCRIPTION

Steam treating is performed in heat treating furnaces. The actual process cycle for ferrous parts is different than for nonferrous parts. Before loading the parts into the furnace, it is important that the parts are dry to produce a clean and scale-free coating.

ION IMPLANTATION

Ion implantation is a process by which atoms of virtually any element can be injected into the near-surface region of any solid. The implantation process involves forming a beam of charged ions of the desired element and then accelerating them at high energies towards the surface of the solid, which is held under high vacuum. The atoms penetrate into the solid to a depth of 0.01 to 1.0 μin. (0.25 to 25 nm). This process differs from coating processes such as electroplating in that it does not produce a discrete coating; rather, it alters the chemical composition near the surface of the solid.[35] Some of the material properties influenced by ion implantation are conductivity, hardness, and wear and corrosion resistance.

PROCESS DESCRIPTION

In ion implantation, atoms of a desired element are ionized and accelerated using an electric field, then the ionized atoms are scanned across the solid to obtain a uniform deposition. The energy imparted to the ionized atoms determines the depth of their penetration into the solid; their concentration throughout the surface can be accurately predicted using rather well-documented theories and experimental data based on energy loss and stoppage of energetic particles in matter.

As ions enter the solid, they transfer energy through excitation of electrons and by collisions with the nuclei of the solid. Ions of elements with small nuclear charges lose most of their energy to the solid through electronic excitation, while heavier elements lose more energy to target atoms through collision cascades. As might be expected, all of the ions do not penetrate to the same depth. Some make collisions near the surface, while others go deeper, transferring energy along the way and eventually coming to rest. At some point between the surface and the deepest ion, there is a peak in the distribution of ions. The depth of this peak is referred to as the *projected range* (R_p). The cross section of ions coming to rest in a solid roughly follows a Gaussian distribution for specific species of ions implanted at specific energies; thus, range concentration curves can be described, and projected ranges calculated for given elements at various energies. A plot for boron ions implanted into silicon is presented in Fig. 48-23. The standard deviation of the projected range is ΔR_p.

Projected range data for ions penetrating crystalline solids such as silicon can be different than the calculated range concentration due to an effect called *channeling*. Channeling

occurs when most of the ions are steered away from the closely packed rows or planes of atoms in the crystal, thereby avoiding collisions with the atoms until near the end of the path. Ions entering the solid in a direction that is parallel to a row or plane of atoms (channeling direction) will have a deeper distribution because only electronic collision will have occurred along their path. Since it is often important to control the depth of ion penetration, it is necessary to direct most of the ions in a channeling direction, or prevent channeling entirely, by tilting the crystal to a relatively nonchanneled direction before implanting.

ADVANTAGES AND LIMITATIONS

The successful use of ion implantation in semiconductor production has led to the development of equipment for use in other areas. For example, experiments have shown that ion implantation can be used to improve the functional capability of materials in a variety of applications. A report by the National Materials Advisory Board cited the following advantages of ion implantation.[36]

- A variety of ion species can be implanted with the same basic apparatus. Almost all elements of the periodic table have been implanted.
- Ion implantation is a low-temperature process. It can often be added to the end of a production line without affecting existing operations.
- The surface of finished products can be treated without introducing significant dimensional changes and without changing bulk properties.
- The process is easily controlled through the electrical signals applied to the ion accelerator.
- Novel nonequilibrium structures and metallurgical phases with properties that cannot be duplicated in bulk material can be produced at the surface.
- Ion implantation creates no problems for disposal of waste products, as does electroplating.
- The absence of a discontinuous interface between the implanted surface layer and the bulk leads to excellent adhesion of the implanted layer.

In addition to the advantages previously described, ion implantation offers new opportunities for metallurgical research. Some of the unusual properties or characteristics that can be produced are as follows:

ION IMPLANTATION

- New metallurgical phases with new properties can be formed. In certain cases, such as heavy implantations of tantalum in copper or phosphorus in iron, amorphous or glassy phases can be formed.
- If the implanted atoms are mobile, precipitates or inclusions can be formed. For example, implanted argon and helium atoms are insoluble in metals and may form bubbles; nitrogen in titanium may form titanium nitride.

- The composition of a surface layer can be changed by differential sputtering caused by the implanted ions.
- Damage and high concentrations of lattice defects, resulting from atomic displacements produced by the incident atoms, can change the chemical reactivity and mechanical characteristics of a treated surface.
- Implantation can enhance the diffusion of impurities already deposited in a substrate, presumably through the motion of the high concentrations of lattice defects produced by the incident ions.
- Cooperative effects of two implanted species can occur; for example, implantation of both molybdenum and sulfur into steels seem to have an effect similar to lubrication with molybdenum disulfide.
- Surface layers, either contaminants or deliberately deposited layers, can be driven into the substrate by impinging atoms.
- Surface layers with conventional (in the sense that they are the same as in bulk material of the same composition) chemical, optical, magnetic, and mechanical properties may be produced.

The primary limitation of ion implantation is the present cost of ion-implanting equipment capable of providing a few hundred kilovolts of acceleration potential. Ion implantation is also limited to line-of-sight applications; surfaces such as the interior of a gun barrel are difficult to implant. Further, mechanical manipulators are required to ensure a uniform deposition on all the exterior surfaces of a part. The depth of the implanted layer may also be a limiting factor in some applications because the implanted ions may diffuse away from the surface layer when the part is exposed to high temperatures.

APPLICATIONS

The major industrial applications of ion implantation techniques currently include fabrication of semiconductor devices (computer microcircuitry) and modification of the surface performance characteristics of tools, dies, and other metal

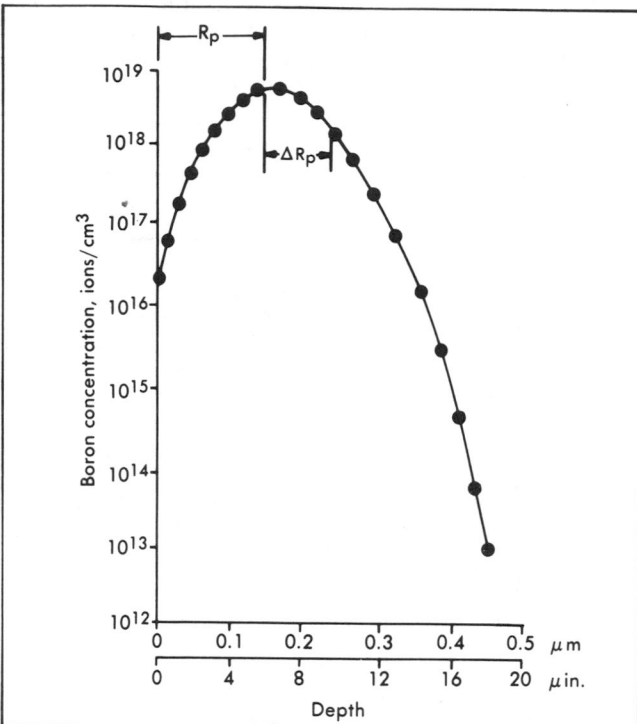

Fig. 48-23 Projected range plot of boron implanted in silicon; the dose of boron ions is $10^{14}/cm^2$, and the implant energy is 50 keV.

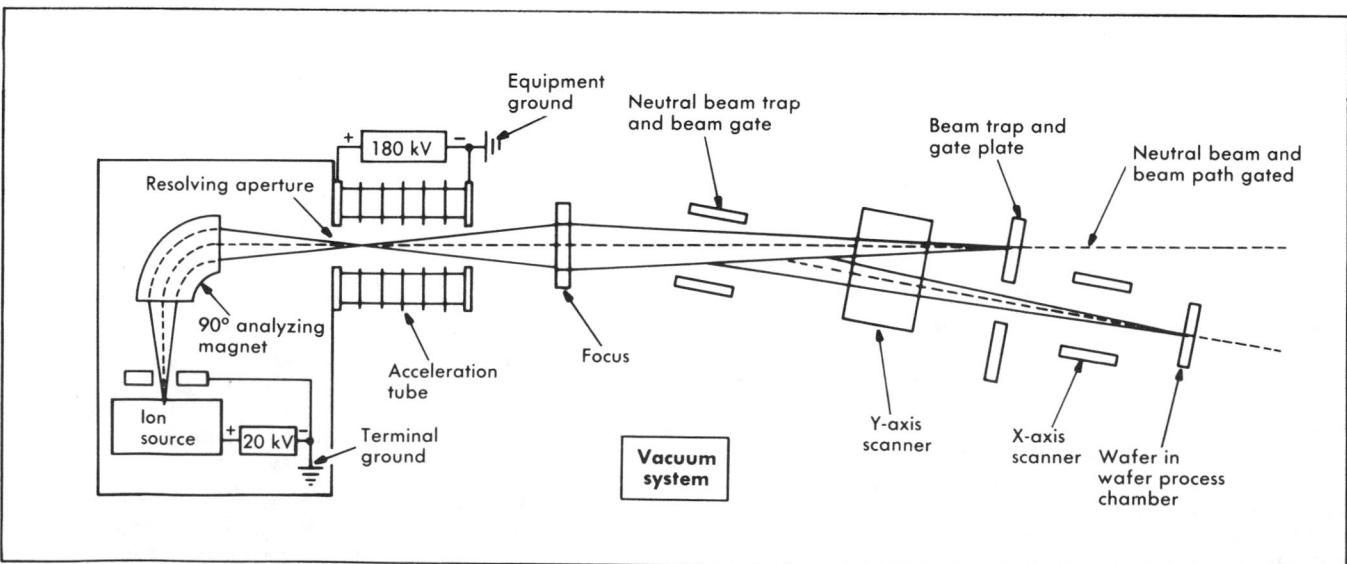

Fig. 48-24 Typical ion implantation equipment. (*Ion Implant Services*)

components. At the same time, researchers are investigating other areas where ion implantation can be used.

EQUIPMENT

As illustrated in Fig. 48-24, present-day semiconductor ion implanters have the following components:[37]

- An ion source.
- A magnetic mass-analyzing system to select the isotope of the atom to be implanted.
- An accelerating stage or stages that can bring the ions up to energies of hundreds of kilovolts.
- A beam scanner or "wobbler" to obtain beam uniformity.
- A target chamber that can be instrumented to handle large numbers of planar structures, rotate samples in and out of the beam, and make use of complicated masks.
- Electronics that provide readouts of mass analysis, beam current, beam profile, and vacuum conditions in the machine and at or near the implantation site.

Ion implantation systems designed for processing metal components are configured much like those designed for semiconductor fabrication. In the system most widely used for nitrogen implantation of metals, the magnetic mass-analyzing system is eliminated by using prepurified nitrogen gas in the ion source.

References

1. Fred W. Eppensteiner and Melvin R. Jenkins, "Chromate Conversion Coatings," *Metal Finishing—Guidebook Directory Issue* (January 1984), pp.488 and 490.
2. Frederick A. Lowenheim, *Electroplating* (New York: McGraw-Hill Book Co., 1978), p. 452.
3. David Thomas, "Anodizing Aluminum," *Metal Finishing Guidebook and Directory Issue* (1983), p. 512.
4. Merle L. Thorpe, "Thermal Spraying Becomes A Design Tool," *Machine Design* (November 24, 1983), p. 72.
5. *Ibid.*
6. Stanley T. Walter, ed., *Welding Handbook*, 6th ed., sec. 3A (Miami, FL: American Welding Society, 1970), p. 44.3.
7. Joseph R. Davis, ed., *Metals Handbook*, 9th ed., vol. 6 (Metals Park, OH: American Society for Metals, 1983), p. 772.
8. *Ibid.*, p. 771.
9. *Ibid.* pp. 773-777.
10. Walter, *op. cit.*, p. 44.6.
11. Lennard G. Kruger, ed., *Metals Handbook*, 9th ed., vol. 5 (Metals Park, OH: American Society for Metals, 1982), pp. 509-531.
12. *Ibid.*, p. 337.
13. Daniel Maykuth, "Hot Dip Tin Coating of Steel and Cast Iron," *Metals Handbook*, 9th ed., vol. 5 (Metals Park, OH: American Society for Metals, 1982), p. 351.
14. Martin Grayson, ed., *Encyclopedia of Composite Materials and Components* (NY: John Wiley & Sons, Inc., 1983), p.804.
15. International Tin Research Institute, *Guide to Tinplate*, ITRI Publication No. 622 (Columbus, OH: 1983), p. 15.
16. American Welding Society, Inc., *Soldering Manual*, 2nd ed., (Miami, FL: 1978).
17. A. Kenneth Graham, "Plating Bath Compositions and Operating Conditions," *Electroplating Engineering Handbook*, 3rd ed. (New York: Van Nostrand Reinhold Co., 1971), Chap. 6.
18. John M. Blocher, Jr.,"Chemical Vapor Deposition," *Metals Handbook*, 9th ed., vol. 5 (Metals Park, OH: American Society for Metals, 1982), pp. 381-386.
19. M. Bonetti-Lang, et. al., "Carbonitride Coatings at Moderate Temperatures Obtained from Organic C/N-Compounds," *Proceedings of the 8th International CVD Conference* (Pennington, NJ: The Electrochemical Society, 1981).
20. W. Hanni and H. E. Hintermann, "Chemical Vapor Deposition of Chromium," *Proceedings of the International Conference—Metallurigical Coatings*, 1976, Vol. II (Lausanne, Switzerland: Elsevier Sequoia, S.A.) pp. 107-114.
21. Richard P. Vento, *Low Pressure-High Temperature Chemical Vapor Deposition—An Applications Guide*, SME Technical Paper No. AD83-870 (Dearborn, MI: Society of Manufacturing Engineers, 1983).
22. B. O. Seraphin, "Chemical Vapor Deposition of Thin Semiconductor Films for Solar Energy Conversion," *Proceedings of the International Conference—Metallurgical Coatings*, 1976, Vol. I (Lausanne, Switzerland: Elsevier Sequoia, S.A.), pp. 87-94.
23. E. Fitzer and D. Kehr, "Carbon, Carbide and Silicide Coatings," *Proceedings of the International Conference—Metallurgical Coatings*, 1976, Vol. I (Lausanne, Switzerland: Elsevier Sequoia, S.A.), pp. 55-67.
24. Fitzer, *loc. cit.*
25. M. J. Paleen, *Summary of Tests on Ivadizer® Aluminum Coated Fasteners*, MDC Report No. A 5517 (St. Louis, MO: McDonnell Aircraft Co., April 4, 1979).
26. E. R. Fannin, "Aluminum Coated Fasteners by Ion Vapor Deposition," *Fastener Technology* (August 1978), pp. 25-29.
27. Military Specification MIL-C-83488, "Coating, Aluminum, Ion Vapor Deposition."
28. E. R. Fannin, *Ion Vapor Deposited Aluminum Coatings for Improved Corrosion Protection*, Presented at AGARD meeting in Florence, Italy, 26-28 September 1978, MCAir Report No. 78-007 (St. Louis, MO: McDonnell Aircraft Co., September 1978).
29. D. M. Mattox, "Film Deposition Using Accelerated Ions," *Electrochemical Technology* (September-October 1964), p. 1385.
30. David V. Rigney, "Vacuum Coating," *Metals Handbook*, 9th ed., vol. 5 (Metals Park, OH: American Society for Metals, 1982), p. 397.
31. *Ibid.*, p. 396.
32. John A. Thorton, and Wolf-Dieter Munz, "Sputtering," *Metals Handbook*, 9th ed., vol. 5 (Metals Park, OH: American Society for Metals, 1982), p. 412.
33. Russel J. Hill, *Physical Vapor Deposition* (Berkeley, CA: Airco Temescal, 1976), pp. 104-105.
34. *Ibid.*, pp. 105-106.
35. National Materials Advisory Board, *Ion Implantation as a New Surface Treatment Technology*, NMAB-349 (Washington, DC: 1979), p. 3.
36. *Ibid.*, pp. 4-5.
37. *Ibid.*, p. 33.

ORGANIC COATINGS

Organic surface coatings are complex mixtures of materials that are designed to enhance the appearance of and/or to protect a substrate. The coating itself is normally composed of a number of ingredients including (1) the polymer (binder), which is designed to provide the major properties of the coating; (2) solvents, which are used to adjust the viscosity of the coating primarily for application; (3) pigments, which are designed to hide the substrate, provide decorative color, and enhance specific desired properties in the coating, such as corrosion resistance; and (4) additives, which include materials such as thickeners, flow agents, catalysts, inhibitors, and stabilizers.

BINDERS

Binders are defined as liquid polymeric or resinous materials that are used in coatings to hold the pigment and various additives together, to provide adhesion, and to supply the major properties of the coating.

CLASSIFICATIONS

As used in the coatings industry, polymers can be divided into various classes depending on the type of material and the type of crosslinking required to generate the final properties of the polymer. Polymers are most commonly used in such coating systems as lacquers, auto-oxidation film former, nonauto-oxidation film formers, radical polymerization-curable film formers, and emulsion-type vehicles.

Lacquers

Lacquers are polymers dissolved in a solvent and require simple solvent evaporation to yield the final-film properties of the polymer. Because polymeric properties generally improve as the molecular weight of the polymer increases, lacquers are limited to polymers of reasonably high molecular weight. In addition, since high-molecular-weight polymers are very viscous in solvents, these materials are normally available at very low solids concentrations. Concentrations as low as 20% are not unusual. Since the volatile organic content of lacquers is high, these materials generate large amounts of organic volatiles, considered harmful to the environment, during film formation.

Auto-Oxidation Film Formers

Auto-oxidation film formers are low-molecular-weight polymers, primarily alkyds, natural oils, and/or epoxy esters, containing carbon-carbon double bonds that allow the materials to oxidize in the presence of atmospheric oxygen to form crosslinked systems. The concept of crosslinking is an especially useful concept in the coatings industry since it allows low-molecular-weight products with relatively poor properties to be crosslinked into high-molecular-weight materials with extremely good properties. In crosslinking, lower molecular-weight materials can be applied to the substrate at high-solids concentrations in solvents. Curing occurs on the substrate after the solvent has evaporated, producing highmolecular-weight materials with excellent properties.

Nonauto-Oxidation Film Formers

Nonauto-oxidation film formers are low-molecular-weight polymers containing functional groups that are useful in crosslinking reactions. Unlike the auto-oxidation film formers that react with oxygen, these materials react with a crosslinking agent to form high-molecular-weight products. Similar to the auto-oxidation film formers, these materials are usually of lower molecular weight and are available without solvent or at higher solids concentration in solvents. Baking alkyds using melamine or urea-formaldehyde resins as crosslinking agents are examples of polymeric materials of this type.

Radical Polymerization-Curable Film Formers

Radical polymerization-curable film formers are low-molecular-weight materials supplied in reactive diluents that can be cured by exposure to radiation. This radiation can take the form of ultraviolet radiation (UV), electron beam radiation (EB), gamma radiation (γ), or other radiation sources. Since both the polymeric materials and diluents are reactive, these materials can be fully cured into highly crosslinked systems without the liberation of large amounts of volatile organic compounds. As such, radical polymerization-curable film formers are considered to be 100% nonvolatile. Materials normally found in this classification possess acrylic and methacrylic properties that permit chemical reactions to occur.

Emulsion-Type Film Formers

Emulsion-type film formers are extremely high-molecular-weight polymers that are dispersed as particles of polymers in a nonsolvent phase. Two types of emulsion systems exist: (1) the aqueous type, which is more commonly used in latex paints, and (2) the nonaqueous dispersion type, which is commonly abbreviated as NAD paint. In emulsion-type systems, the nonsolvent phase is considered to be the continuous phase of the media, and the polymeric particles are considered to be the dispersed phase of the media. Film formation in both instances occurs by the evaporation of the nonsolvent, either water or an organic nonsolvent, followed by coalescence of the polymeric particles into a continuous coating. Numerous polymers are useful in these systems, including acrylics and vinyls.

CHAPTER 49

BINDERS

TYPES OF BINDERS

Various polymeric materials or binders of many chemical types are used in coatings, depending on the end use of the material or the curing cycle required for the system. The binders most commonly used are natural oils or vegetable oils, alkyds, polyesters, aminoplast resins, phenolic resins, polyurethane resins, epoxy resins, silicone resins, acrylic resins, vinyl resins, cellulosics, and fluorocarbons.

Natural Oils

Natural drying oils are polyunsaturated fatty acid esters of glycerol that can be crosslinked into protective coatings by reaction with oxygen in the air. In their natural form, oils are mixtures of different fatty materials containing different levels of unsaturation.

Based on the composition of natural oils, the coatings industry has divided oils into drying, semidrying, and nondrying classes. These classifications are based on how rapidly or easily the oil reacts with oxygen present in the air.

Alkyd Resins

Although oils are quite flexible and cure by reacting with oxygen in the air, they lack the hardness and fast drying speed required in many applications where coatings are used. Alkyd resins, essentially polyesters modified by reaction with fatty acids, do not exhibit the hardness of polyesters, but have flexibility and drying properties superior to oils.

Polyester Resins

Polyesters are the reaction products of polyfunctional carboxylic acids and polyfunctional alcohols. They are divided into saturated and unsaturated polyesters. Saturated polyesters are basically oil-free alkyds with crosslinking occurring after blending with co-reactants such as melamine-formaldehyde resins or isocyanate prepolymers. Unsaturated polyesters use a separate reaction, normally after the coating application, to convert the lower molecular-weight polyester, as synthesized, into higher molecular-weight crosslinked products.

Aminoplast Resins

Aminoplast resins are condensation products of urea, melamine, or benzoguanamine and formaldehyde. As initially synthesized, these materials are rather unstable and prone to self-condensation. They are stabilized quite readily, however, by reaction with alcohols to form alkylated aminoplast resins. In this form, aminoplast resins are used extensively as thermally initiated crosslinking agents for use with hydroxyl-containing polymers.

Phenolic Resins

Although the early types of phenol-formaldehyde resins found only limited application in varnishes, recent modifications allow them to be used in more general applications. Specifically, resinous materials are used as modifying agents in phenol-formaldehyde resins to achieve improved solubility. Alkyl-substituted phenol-formaldehyde resins are dissolved in oil to generate varnishes and printing-ink bases. The most important application of phenolic resins is in the area of air drying and baking metal primers and spar varnishes.

Polyurethane Resins

By using polyfunctional reactants, it is possible to synthesize the polymeric materials known as polyurethanes. Polyfunctional reactants are formed by reacting compounds containing two or more isocyanate groups with compounds containing two or more hydroxyl groups. Polyurethane resins are especially noted for their abrasion resistance, toughness, and flexibility. They are resistant to chemicals, possess excellent electrical properties, and crosslink or cure at very low temperatures.

Epoxy Resins

Most of the epoxy resins used in this country are derived from a series of prepolymers that are based on bisphenol A and epichlorohydrin. A number of epoxy resins exist with different molecular weights and different epoxy contents. The important properties of cured epoxy resins include:

- Chemical resistance in corrosive environments.
- Excellent adhesion to a wide variety of materials including metal, wood, concrete, glass, ceramic, and many plastics.
- Low shrinkage during curing resulting in good dimensional stability and excellent adhesion.
- Ease of fabrication, which is inherent in systems that can be cured at room temperature.
- Good physical properties such as toughness, flexibility, and abrasion resistance.
- Excellent performance at elevated temperatures.

Silicone Resins

Silicone resins differ considerably from the carbon-hydrogen polymers that have been discussed previously because they contain only silicon and oxygen in the basic building block of the polymer. They are used primarily for high-temperature applications, such as for ovens, stacks, exhaust systems, and space heaters. In recent years, however, silicone-modified resins have found application as decorative coatings when improved weather resistance is required. In addition, they possess other useful properties such as a low coefficient of friction (slip), water-repellent action, and antifoam properties.

Acrylic Resins

Acrylics are divided into thermoplastic dispersions, thermoplastic solutions, and thermosetting acrylics. Although the word *acrylic* technically refers to polymers produced exclusively from acrylic monomers, over the years *acrylics* has come to include virtually any thermosetting or thermoplastic materials that are based on acrylic monomers or any other monomers that will easily copolymerize with them. The properties of acrylic polymers are greatly dependent on the monomers used in the synthesis of the polymer.

The major use of acrylics today is in the emulsion field. Basically, there are two different types of emulsions, the aqueous emulsions and the nonaqueous dispersions, which are commonly abbreviated NAD's. The aqueous emulsions are commonly known as latex paint vehicles. Both emulsions form continuous coatings by the evaporation of the nonsolvent. In the case of aqueous emulsions, the nonsolvent is water; in nonaqueous dispersions, the nonsolvent is organic. The process by which the continuous coating forms is called coalescence and is typical for both aqueous and nonaqueous systems.

Vinyl Resins

Vinyl resins are produced by the polymerization of certain monomers containing a double bond between adjacent carbon atoms; for example, the polymerization of vinyl chloride to form polyvinyl chloride. Although there are many resins and plastics that could fit into the vinyl classification of coating resins, a number of them, such as polyethylene, acrylic, and styrene-butadiene, are generally not included. Some of the common types of vinyl polymers and copolymers used in organic coatings include polyvinyl chloride, vinyl chloride-acetate copolymer, polyvinyl butyral, polyvinyl formal, and polyvinyl alcohol.

The resins produced from vinyl chloride have limited solubility in practical paint solvents, so they find limited use in solution-type coatings. However, there is a substantial, growing use of vinyl chloride resins in organosol and plastisol coatings.

Cellulosics

The cellulosic polymers used in organic coatings are esters and ethers of cellulose. Perhaps the best known polymer to the average user of paints is nitrocellulose, which is used in many fast-drying lacquers. Other polymers include cellulose acetate, cellulose acetate butyrate, ethyl cellulose, methyl cellulose, and carboxymethyl cellulose. The last two polymers are water soluble and thus are not included among the lacquer resins. Cellulosic polymers are produced in different molecular weights and varying degrees of solubility.

The cellulosics are good film-forming materials and form the basis for fast-drying lacquers; however, they require modification for specific properties.

Fluorocarbons

The fluorocarbon resins are unique materials that are noted for their lubricity and antistick properties as well as their weatherability, which is three to five times greater than other commonly used resins. The principal fluorocarbon polymers available today are prepared from the following monomers: tetrafluoroethylene, chlorotrifluoroethylene, vinyl fluoride, and vinylidene fluoride. These polymers are extremely inert materials and require special techniques in preparing their resins for application as coatings, generally as dispersions. The continuous coating is formed by fusing the dispersed particles of resin into a continuous film.

PIGMENTS

Paint pigments are solid grains or particles of uniform and controlled size that are permanently insoluble in the vehicle of the coating.[1] They are generally dispersed in the vehicle by some type of grinding operation, usually performed by the paint manufacturer. Pigments are dispersed in a coating to hide or enhance the appearance or protection of a substrate. In addition, pigments have a positive effect on a number of properties including strength, adhesion, durability, gloss, flow, and corrosion resistance.

One very important factor in pigment dispersion is the pigment volume concentration (PVC).[2] The PVC is defined as the volume percent of the dry film that is actually pigment, as opposed to binder or additives. When the pigment particles are in contact with each other in the vehicle, the concentration is referred to as critical pigment volume concentration (CPVC). Exceeding the CPVC results in a deterioration in the resistance properties of the paint.

PIGMENT CLASSES

The four commonly recognized classes of pigments are: (1) colored pigments; (2) white pigments, which include the primary and extender pigments; (3) metallic powders; and (4) functional pigments. The first class is available in both inorganic and organic compounds. The other classes are mostly inorganic materials. Functional pigments provide corrosion resistance, antifouling protection, slip resistance, or many other desired properties.

PIGMENT PROPERTIES

The important pigment properties include tinting strength, light fastness, bleed characteristics, hiding power, transparency, particle size and shape, chemical and thermal stability, physical properties, rheological properties, and oil absorption.

SOLVENTS

Although solvents are defined as liquids that dissolve other substances, there are many materials used in the coating industry that are solvents for one type of resin but not solvents for another type of resin. In order to distinguish various solvents, the coatings chemist recognizes three types of solvent materials: (1) active solvents, (2) diluents, and (3) thinners. Active solvents are defined as liquids that dissolve binders and rapidly reduce the viscosity of the coating material. A diluent is a liquid that extends a solution but definitely acts to weaken the solvent power of the active solvent. The diluent must be completely miscible with the active solvent used. When using a diluent, it is quite common to have the viscosity actually increase as the solvency power of the active solvent is reduced. A thinner is a liquid that also extends a solution but does not materially impair the solvent power of the active solvent. It should be recognized that materials can function as active solvents, diluents, or thinners depending on the polymer system that is being dissolved.

Although there are many ways to classify solvents, solvents are generally divided into (1) hydrocarbons consisting of both aliphatic and aromatic hydrocarbons, (2) alcohols and amines, (3) active solvents such as esters and ketones, and (4) chlorinated solvents. The use of solvents in surface coatings is best illustrated by examining their function in various coating systems in which the selection of the solvent or solvent combination depends to a great extent on the type of resin, the method of application, and the drying time or the evaporation time required for the coating system. In addition, the solvent

SOLVENTS

chosen must be suitable for the entire coating system, which might contain plasticizers and various additives such as pigments.

The application methods must also be considered in selecting the solvents or solvent combination. For example, paints applied by spraying require fast-evaporating solvents in order to ensure that a large proportion of the solvent is evaporated during the spraying process. The solvent evaporation prevents sagging of the film on vertical surfaces and allows quick setup of the coating. However, if the coating is to be applied by brushing, slow-evaporating solvents are required to ensure adequate flow and to avoid lap marks. Dipping or roll coating applications require slow-evaporating solvents so that solvent loss from the dipping bath or coater is minimized and coating flowout is enhanced.

Air-drying paints and fast-drying enamels are normally based on alkyd resins that require aromatic solvents and mineral spirits for the solvent combination. Aliphatic and aromatic solvents are commonly used. Baking enamels, primers, and automotive primers with alkyd resins are usually based on short-oil alkyd resins that require toluene and/or xylene as the solvent(s) for spray applications. Epoxy resins such as epoxy esters, which have been discussed previously, require both aromatic and aliphatic solvents for solubility. Nitrocellulose and vinyl resins normally require ketones to generate soluble systems. Latex paints, which are primarily waterborne, incorporate solvents as coalescing aids; glycol ethers are frequently used, also.

ADDITIVES

Additives are materials that, when added to a coating system in very small concentrations, exhibit a profound influence on the physical and chemical properties of the coating. Additives include such materials as surfactants, colloids and thickeners, biocides and fungicides, freeze/thaw stabilizers, coalescing agents, defoamers, plasticizers, flattening agents, flow modifiers, stabilizers, catalysts, and antiskinning agents. Each of these additives imparts special properties to the coating without which it would be impossible, in many cases, to develop a useable formulation.

SURFACTANTS

Surfactants are among the most versatile of the additives in the chemical industry, appearing in such diverse products as motor oils, pharmaceuticals, and detergents, as well as coatings.

By definition, a surface-active agent (surfactant) is a substance that when present at a low concentration has the ability of adsorbing at the interface of a system and altering—usually reducing—the interfacial free energy. Surface-active agents have a characteristic molecular structure consisting of a group, known as the lyophilic group, that has very little attraction for the solvent, together with a group, called the lyophobic group, that has a very strong attraction for the solvent. When the solvent is water, these groups are referred to as hydrophilic or hydrophobic, respectively.

PROTECTIVE COLLOIDS
AND THICKENERS

Protective colloids and thickeners are essentially water-soluble resins that are used in emulsion-type paints at levels ranging from 0.1 to 1% by weight. They aid in pigment dispersion by increasing the viscosity of the paint system, preventing coagulation and settling, and controlling the flow and leveling of the final paint system. Materials commonly used as protective colloids and thickeners include starches, cellulosics, polyvinyl alcohols, sodium polyacrylates, and natural gums.

The disadvantages in using protective colloids and thickeners in coating formulations include the facts that they are water soluble, sometimes expensive, incompatible with the dry resin, and, in some cases, cause flocculation in coatings, especially if these colloids and thickeners possess a different charge than the surfactant used to disperse the resin. Colloids and thickeners are also prone to attack by bacteria and fungi.

BIOCIDES AND FUNGICIDES

Microbial growth can occur in paint systems when temperatures are between 72 and 100° F (22 and 38°C), when oxygen is readily available, and when sufficient water is available at neutral pH levels. The enzymes produced by microorganisms promote degradation of the stabilizers in the polymeric system.

Biocides and fungicides function in water-reducible coatings as inhibitors to prevent the formation of microbial growth. Specifically, biocides function to inhibit microbial growth in aqueous uncured systems, whereas fungicides inhibit microbial growth in dry paint systems. Materials commonly used as biocides and/or fungicides include mercuric compounds and sodium salts of pentachlorophenol.

FREEZE/THAW STABILIZERS

Freeze and/or thaw stabilizers, commonly of the glycol or glycol ether types, are useful in water-based systems in which freezing is particularly destructive to the emulsion. Freeze/thaw stabilizers essentially function to reduce the freezing point of the aqueous system much like antifreeze functions in the radiator of a car.

COALESCING AGENTS

Coalescing agents are essentially high-boiling solvents, normally of the glycol ether or polyethylene oxide type, that are added to water-soluble systems to aid in coalescing the polymer particles as the water evaporates from the system.

DEFOAMERS

Foaming is commonly caused by the presence of surfactants and various additives such as solvents and amines. Foaming causes cratering in the paint film and may occur during or after paint application. Defoamers function by displacing surfactants from the surface of the foam, thereby increasing the surface tension and breaking the foam.

PLASTICIZERS

A plasticizer is defined as a substance that is added to a polymer or a paint system to increase the flexibility of the finished product. In the coating industry, plasticizers are used to lower the glass transition temperature (T_g) of the polymer.

FLATTENING AGENTS

Flattening agents are materials that are basically added to a paint or coating to reduce the gloss or angular sheen of the dry coating. Materials commonly available that can be used as flattening agents include a great variety of synthetic silicas and zinc stearate.

FLOW MODIFIERS

Flow modifiers are used in coatings to impart thixotropy to the coating system. Thixotropy is the property possessed by certain gels or dispersions that enables the viscosity to decrease when the liquid is shaken, brushed, or mechanically disturbed, but increase when left in an undisturbed state. This property is necessary when the coating must be applied at low viscosity; yet after application, the coating must thicken rapidly to prevent sagging. Various materials can be added to paint systems to impart thixotropy.

STABILIZERS

Polymers are prone to degradation under the influence of ultraviolet light and heat. To avoid degradation, stabilizers are added to coating systems containing polymers. Stabilizers come in many forms depending on the role they play in stabilizing the polymer.

CATALYSTS

Catalysts are used in chemical applications to lower the energy at which chemical reactions, such as crosslinking, take place. Catalysts are normally metallic driers such as divalent salts of carboxylic acids, strong acids such as sulfonic acids, and weaker acids such as carboxylic acids, amines, and polyamides. The catalysts used in coating applications are fairly specific to the particular application involved. Driers are used exclusively in promoting the oxidative crosslinking of alkyds, epoxy esters, and other materials containing unsaturation in the form of natural oils. Sulfonic acids are commonly used in thermal crosslinking of polymers to promote the reaction between aminoplast crosslinkers and hydroxyl and carboxyl-containing polymers. Amines and polyamides are used with epoxy-resin systems.

ANTISKINNING AGENTS

Alkyd coatings and other coating materials containing unsaturated natural oils are especially prone to surface oxidation in open containers, leading to the formation of a polymeric skin on the surface of the paint. Antiskinning agents prevent the paint from forming a skin while in storage. Oxime and phenolic compounds, when used as additives, are especially helpful in preventing skinning in alkyd coating systems.

FORMULATIONS

When developing a formulation, the basic prerequisite is a broad knowledge of the properties of the raw materials that are used in coatings and how these materials interact with each other, as well as an understanding of all the components that make up a coating including the polymer, the pigments, the additives, and the solvents. The coatings chemist must also be aware of both the costs involved in putting these materials together and the processing costs. Other essential information includes the application method, the substrates on which the coating will be used, the kind of exposure that the paint will be required to endure, and the viscosity, evaporation rate, color, and hiding power required.

CORROSION-PREVENTIVE MATERIALS

The corrosion-preventive function of a coating is to prevent the onset of corrosion or to control the spread of corrosion from the initial site of corrosion. Coatings have been developed that function as barrier coatings, conversion coatings, or sacrificial coatings. Sacrificial coatings are primarily inorganic zinc systems containing between 80 and 90% zinc. The zinc oxidizes preferentially to the iron, providing corrosion protection of the metal.

BARRIER COATINGS

The permeation of coatings by water requires the surface of the metal to be constantly exposed to moisture. If oxygen and electrolytes are available, rapid corrosion can form on the surface. However, organic coatings exhibit low permeability to ionic species (electrolytes) dissolved in water. Consequently, the concentration of the electrolyte at the surface is minimal, making it difficult to set up a conductive cell as long as the coating remains intact. Barrier coatings are normally optimized by applying thick films of materials to the substrates to be coated. No coating, however, is completely impermeable to moisture and any electrolytes that might be dissolved in the

moisture, and corrosion will occur regardless of the thickness of the coating. The tendency for corrosion to occur is simply reduced as the thickness of the barrier coating is increased.

CONVERSION-TYPE PIGMENTS

Many paints use inorganic pigments that inhibit the corrosion of the metal by processes similar to those of conversion coatings. These inorganic pigments, primarily phosphates or chromates, passivate the surface of the metal. The solubility of inorganic pigments in water is important because a pigment must not be too soluble or it will be washed rapidly from the metal surface. However, if the pigment is too insoluble, there will not be enough pigment migrating to the surface in the form of an aqueous solution to passivate the metal.

Chromates are the most effective inorganic pigments, with zinc yellow or basic zinc chromate being the most commonly used. The various molybdates are fairly expensive but are also effective inhibitors. Compounds of lead and chromium are considered to possess a certain degree of toxicity, and hence efforts are under way to replace these traditional corrosion-inhibiting pigments with other materials.

RADIATION-CURABLE COATINGS

RADIATION-CURABLE COATINGS

Radiation-curable coatings have been developed over the past fifteen years primarily as clear (nonpigmented) coatings for use on floor tile, beverage containers, building products, and packaging. These coatings are acrylic or methacrylic functional polymers diluted with reactive diluents containing the same type of functionality as the polymer. They are also epoxy functional polymers diluted with diluents containing epoxy functionality. Both types of coatings can be crosslinked under ultraviolet light, with the acrylic/methacrylic coatings using photoinitiators to promote radical crosslinking and the epoxy coatings using organic salts such as diphenyliodonium fluoroborate to initiate cationic crosslinking of the epoxy groups.

VAPOR CURE COATINGS

Vapor cure coatings are the latest type of coatings produced by the coatings industry. These coatings utilize the rapid crosslinking reaction that occurs between isocyanates and polyester alcohols when catalyzed by tertiary amines. The earliest vapor cure coatings required premixing the isocyanate prepolymer and the polyester alcohol, applying this mixture to the part to be coated, and then exposing the coating to a low concentration of tertiary amine gas in an inert carrier gas. Recent advances in vapor cure coatings enable all the components to be mixed with a less volatile amine. Coatings prepared by this process show many, if not all, of the properties of standard urethane coatings.

SPRAY COATING

Spray coating is the process of applying a liquid coating by causing the liquid coating material to be broken up or atomized into a fine mist or spray that is then deposited onto the part surface. The individual droplets of material flow together on the surface to form the coating film. The three basic methods of breaking up or atomizing liquid coatings are: (1) conventional or air atomization, (2) airless or hydraulic atomization, and (3) rotary (centrifugal) atomization. There are also two adaptations of these basic methods that are gaining noted use today. In the newest adaptation, the primary atomization is with hydraulic pressure, while air pressure is used to control the spray pattern. This method is normally referred to as air-assisted airless. The application of an electrostatic charge to the basic methods of atomization can aid in the efficiency of the droplet transfer to the part being painted. This method is usually referred to as electrostatic spraying.

THE LIQUID COATING MATERIAL

In painting operations, there are two viscosities that affect the resulting finish of the material on the part: the viscosity of the material when it is atomized and the viscosity of the material when it reaches the part. The viscosity of the material when it is atomized is critical because it determines the fineness of the material particle. The viscosity of the material when it reaches the part can cause sags and runs, but it can be controlled by the quantity of material applied. The difference between these two viscosities is the result of solvent evaporation as the particle goes to the part.

CONVENTIONAL AIR SPRAY

In conventional air spray, the material is usually supplied from a container in one of two ways. In the first way, the container may use pressure, up to 100 psi (690 kPa), to force the material to the spraying equipment via a pressure vessel or a pumping device. The other method of material supply uses a vacuum created by the spraying device to pull the material from the container to the atomizing area. The method using pressure to force the material to the spray device is called pressure feed, and the method using the vacuum to draw the material is called suction feed.

A typical air-atomizing spray system consists of: (1) an air pressure source, probably a compressor; (2) an air regulator, to control the flow of air to the spray equipment; (3) an air line to the spray equipment; (4) a material supply, either suction or pressure feed, and a material supply line to the spray device; and (5) a spray device, usually a spray gun. The spray gun is generally categorized by the method used to control the air and fluid flow or by the design of the air nozzle.

A type of spray gun that controls only the fluid flow is known as a bleeder-type spray gun because the air constantly bleeds from the gun as it is being used. This type of equipment is common on small portable compressors since they need to maintain constant airflow to avoid possible damage. The other type of spray gun, known as a nonbleeder, controls the air and the fluid by the action of the trigger. These nonbleeder-type spray guns use a mechanical method to ensure that the air comes on before the fluid begins flowing and shuts off after the fluid flow has stopped. Known as lead-lag, this mechanical method helps the spray gun to keep clean and eliminates spitting.

The air nozzles, referred to as air caps, are the most important part of the air spray gun. They direct the air to the material and cause atomization and pattern development. The two basic types of air spray systems used are external mixing and internal mixing. External mixing systems (see Fig. 49-1) mix the air and the fluid outside of the air cap. This type of cap is used on both bleeder and nonbleeder types of spray guns and can be either siphon or pressure fed. External mixing systems are the most common type used in production.

Internal mixing systems (see Fig. 49-2) mix the air and the fluid inside the air cap before being released. The air cap's exit-hole shape controls the pattern of the material spray, which cannot be varied with the gun controls. Internal mixing equipment must be pressure fed, and the air and fluid balance must be closely maintained. This type of air spray system is generally used for applying heavy-bodied coating materials since low pressures are normally used and the resulting finish is very coarse. Internal mixing equipment is hard to keep clean and requires additional maintenance.

AIRLESS (HYDRAULIC) SPRAYING

Airless spraying is a method of spray application that uses hydraulic pressure to atomize the fluid. The fluid is pumped to the spray device at high pressures, 500-4500 psi (3500-31 000 kPa), and then forced through a very small orifice at the spray nozzle. As the fluid is released from the nozzle at these high pressures, it is atomized into small droplets, resulting in a fine spray. The material is discharged at such a high velocity that after atomization the particles travel to the workpiece by their initial momentum. The pressures that are required to atomize various materials depend upon the material's viscosity and solids makeup, the distance of fluid travel, and the size of the orifice tip in the spray gun.

Advantages and Limitations

Airless spraying is generally used to apply a large volume of paint to a large area in a short period of time. Materials can be applied to the surface as fast as the operator can move and control the spray device. The degree of atomization is typically not as fine as in air spray, but fluid delivery is much higher. Because of this, airless spraying is generally not used for fine finish work or for coating metal substrates. The spray pattern is also very defined, which causes overlapping to be difficult.

Airless spraying typically is cleaner and faster than air spray due to its reduction in overspray and bounce-back. The main advantage of airless spraying is its ability to spray a variety of coating materials without reduction in viscosity; even high-viscosity materials can be sprayed successfully with little or no reduction in viscosity.

The main limitation with airless equipment is that, unlike air spray equipment, it can only vary the pressure and cannot be throttled. Greater operator skill is also necessary with airless equipment than with air equipment when spraying in difficult-

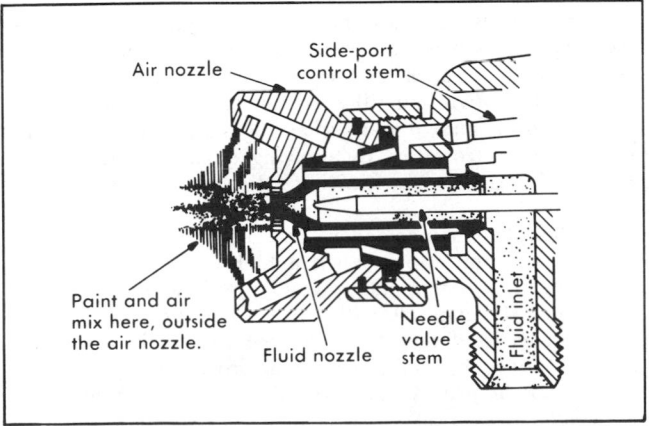

Fig. 49-1 Cross section of a spray gun with an external-mix nozzle. (*Binks Manufacturing Co.*)

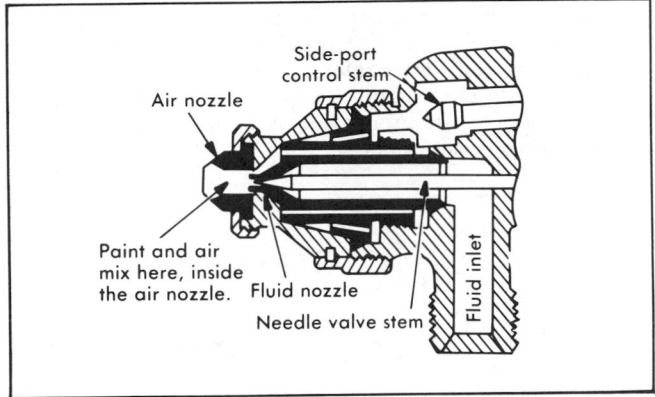

Fig. 49-2 Cross section of a spray gun with an internal-mix nozzle. (*Binks Manufacturing Co.*)

to-reach areas because the full material flow comes from the spray device whenever the trigger is pulled.

Spray Equipment

The airless spray gun is specifically designed for use with high fluid pressures. The pressurized fluid enters the gun either at the base of the handle or at the back of the nozzle. Some spray guns use a tungsten carbide ball and seat in the fluid shutoff as well as a tungsten carbide tip for maximum wear resistance and service life. A fluid filter may be inserted in the gun when fine filtration is required. Reversible tips are also available to help reduce downtime due to tip plugging.

ROTARY ATOMIZATION

Rotary atomizers differ greatly in their operation from that of either air spray or airless equipment. The atomization takes place by adding energy to the coating material through the high-speed rotation of a disc or cup-shaped part onto which the material is pumped. The material is pumped by a pressure source to a nozzle, either at the center of the rotating part or close to the center but off to the side. These methods of material feeding are referred to as center feed and side feed respectively.

As previously mentioned, there are two forms of rotating members. A flat platelike member is referred to as a disc and can vary from 4 to 14" (100 to 350 mm) diam. It is normally rotated at 2000 to 20,000 rpm and can be driven by either an electric motor or an air turbine. A disc almost always has a side-feed type of material discharge. The material is pumped onto the surface of the rotating disc and is formed into a fine spray by the flinging action of the rotation. Figure 49-3 illustrates this type of an arrangement.

When the rotating member is in the shape of a cup or bowl, it is referred to as a bell atomizer. This type of atomizer also uses the rotational force to cause the atomization, but the bell arrangement directs the spray created to a smaller area. Bells use a ring of small, directed holes or air jets (referred to as shaping air) to control the pattern size and direction of the atomized particles. The bells are usually 2-4" (50-100 mm) diam and operate at speeds from 20,000 to 60,000 rpm. The bell can be either center feed or side feed. A handheld bell is shown in Fig. 49-4.

The rotary method of material atomization is the most efficient method of transforming the material into an atomized

SPRAY COATING

form. It requires little material reduction and can handle a variety of material viscosities, as well as a wide range of fluid flow rates. Typically, these rotary methods of atomization are coupled with an electrostatic charge to improve the transfer efficiency. Electrostatic atomization is discussed subsequently, in the section on electrostatic spraying.

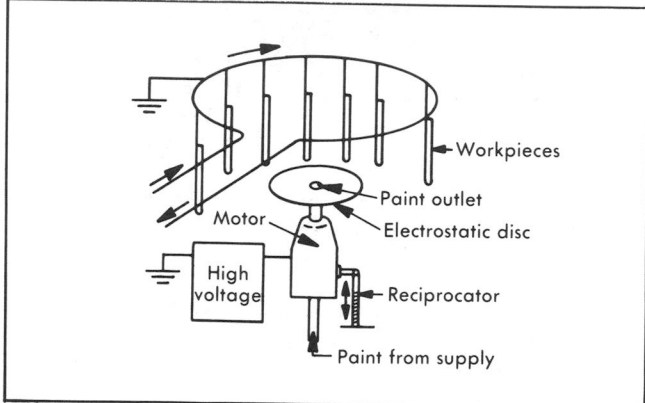

Fig. 49-3 Schematic of an atomization disc with an electrostatic charge.

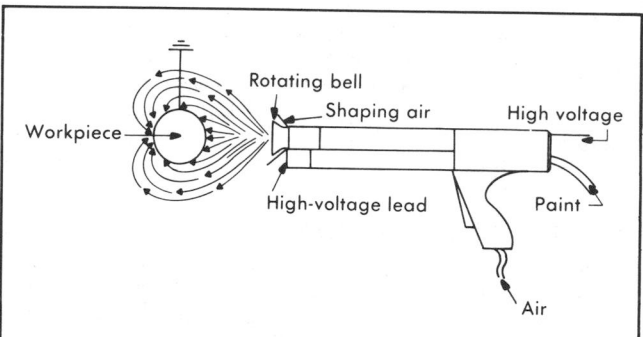

Fig. 49-4 Schematic of a handheld electrostatic bell atomizer.

AIR-ASSISTED AIRLESS SPRAY

An adaptation of airless spraying has recently become an accepted method of high transfer efficiency in spray coating. This method uses the principle of airless (hydraulic) atomization but adds a concentrated airflow to control the atomized particles. In general, a material can be broken into fine particles (atomized) at a relatively low pressure, 300-1000 psi (2000-7000 kPa). However, higher pressures are needed to complete the pattern forming. The air-assisted airless principle uses the low hydraulic pressure to provide the initial atomization, but then uses a low-pressure air to further atomize the tails and complete the pattern forming. This method also allows the pattern width to be adjusted somewhat by adding air to jets that act to compress the fan pattern.

Air-assisted airless spraying overcomes some of the problems of both air spray and airless spraying. The quality of the atomization approaches that of air spray but does not require the material reduction needed with air spray. The fluid delivery is higher than air spray, allowing faster coverage without bounce-back or overspray, which are common with conventional air spray. The use of low hydraulic pressure improves pump life, reduces maintenance cost, and is much safer to

operate. Air-assisted airless spray produces a finish comparable to that of air spray with the speed of airless equipment.

HOT SPRAYING

Hot spraying is a technique in which the coating material is heated to a temperature of 120 to 160°F (50 to 70°C) before spraying. The increased temperature lowers the viscosity of the material, permitting materials to be atomized easier. The hot spraying technique can be used for all forms of spray application.

The coating material can be heated using electrically heated coils or a hot-water heat exchanger. Two types of heating systems are in common use, a recirculation system and a nonrecirculation system. In the recirculating system, the material is continually recirculated between the gun and the heater. In the nonrecirculating system, the material is only circulated through the heater one time, subjecting the material to cooling, which is dependent on hose length and application conditions.

When properly prepared materials are used, hot spraying has several advantages over unheated spraying. Since the viscosity is controlled by the temperature, little or no solvent is used for thinning, reducing labor costs, solvent costs, and solvent emissions. The coating material can also be stored in unheated areas or at a lower temperature than materials used for unheated methods. The disadvantages of the hot spraying method, however, are notable. A material heater and possibly a special gun are required, thereby increasing the initial cost. Application techniques are more critical with hot spraying than with unheated methods to minimize overspray losses as the cost of the material is higher than solvent-thinned material. In addition, many types of materials are affected by heat, so care must be used to limit the amount of heat used. The material supplier can provide additional information regarding the benefits and limitations of the hot spray method for certain coating materials.

ELECTROSTATIC SPRAYING

As the basic methods of material atomization have advanced, it has been found that the addition of an electrostatic charge to the atomized particles causes a dramatic increase in the material-to-part transfer efficiency. This application of electrostatic charges to the material particles causes them to act like small magnets when placed in the vicinity of a grounded object. During the spraying process, the part to be painted is grounded. As the material is sprayed at the part, the magnetic action of the charged particles causes the particles, which would normally be lost due to bounce-back or blow-by, to be attracted back to the part by actually wrapping the part in material particles. This phenomenon is known as *wrap* and is the prime force in the move to use electrostatics. By applying an electrostatic charge to the material particles, transfer efficiencies of 60 to 90% are possible.

Another phenomenon achieved with electrostatics is actual electrostatic atomization. When a high-voltage potential is created on a thin film of material and it is allowed to be free in atmosphere, the material, with all the same types of charges, tries to repel itself and forms a type of atomization. The particles formed by this atomization process maintain their charge, and the process may continue if the initial charge is high enough.

There are a few limitations to the use of electrostatics. Electrostatic attraction is greater on outside edges and hole-edge areas due to what is known as edge phenomenon. It is known that magnetic forces are concentrated on the outside surfaces of an object and that any sharp edge is a collection point. This concentration of magnetic forces causes a heavy buildup of material on the edges of a part. The buildup can be controlled, however, by the application method and the charge used. Another problem associated with electrostatic application methods involves the Faraday cage effect. The Faraday cage effect is caused by the focused concentration of the charge resulting in low levels of material getting into recessed areas. Application methods can help in overcoming this problem, but normally a separate application using conventional air spray will ensure the proper coverage, while still maintaining the large savings in material for the major part of the application process.

AUTOMATED SPRAYING

In manual spraying, the operator selects the system variables such as fluid flow rate, atomizing pressure, fan shape, paint temperature, and the sweep of the gun. In unmanned spraying processes, these parameters are preset to coat a preselected number or type of parts, with the operator checking that the parameters stay within the specified tolerances.

Two methods of unmanned spraying are in current use, automated booths and robotic systems. A part identification system is necessary for both. These systems size the part with mechanical fingers, limit switches, photocells, magnetic strips, bar codes, or by visual observation. A color-change system is also required for unmanned spraying processes; in it, a manual or automatic signal interacts with the color-change mechanism, which ejects the paint, cleans the paint line with solvent and air, and then refills the line with the newly selected paint. The time required for the color change varies with the paint viscosity and length of supply lines. In addition, unmanned systems require the parts to be hung uniformly since missing or improperly hung parts cannot be detected. Conveyors must also operate smoothly because these systems cannot compensate for swaying parts or other unforeseen motion.

Automated spraying methods ensure greater uniformity of finish from part to part as well as from day to day, while reducing the amount of manpower required. In addition, ventilation can be reduced; unmanned booths may require as little as 1/3 the amount of air as manned booths.

POWDER COATING

Like all other industrial surface coatings, powder coatings are individually formulated to meet the industrial user's specific finishing needs. Individual formulation means matching color and film performance requirements, all within the particular restrictions of the finisher's operation. As with the selection of any industrial finish, therefore, a close relationship must be developed between the user of the coating and the coatings supplier so that exacting requirements are thoroughly understood and the correct type of finishing material is supplied.

Powder coating is a dry painting process in which powder particles are applied directly to the surface to be coated without the use of solvents or water. Each powder particle contains the resin, pigments, modifiers, and, if it is a reactive system, the curing agent. Most powders are formulated to provide the color and properties required by the manufacturer.

The most common limitations of powder coating are problems with film appearance and powder handling. For example, powder coatings often have more "orange peel" defects than conventional films because of the high melt viscosity of the powder. Flow modifiers are used to achieve an acceptable smoothness for most applications. Changing colors may also present a problem because of the necessity to collect and reuse overspray if powder coating is to be economically feasible. To reuse overspray effectively, powder particles of each color must be kept separated if a booth is to be used for more than one color. To avoid handling problems, it is important to maintain a clean, dry air supply when transporting the powder particles.

THERMOPLASTIC POWDERS

A thermoplastic powder coating is one that melts and flows with the application of heat, but maintains the same chemical composition when it solidifies on cooling. Thermoplastic powder coatings are based on thermoplastic resins of high molecular weight. These tough and resistant resins tend to be difficult and also expensive to grind into the very fine particles necessary for the fusion of thin paintlike film thicknesses. Consequently, thermoplastic resin systems are used more as thick-film functional coatings and are applied mainly by the fluidized-bed application technique.

THERMOSETTING POWDERS

Thermosetting powder coatings are quite different from thermoplastic powder coatings in that they are based on lower molecular-weight solid resins, which, on melting and flowing, chemically crosslink within themselves or with other reactive components to form a higher molecular-weight reaction product. The coating film formed by this reaction is heat stable and will not soften back to a liquid on further exposure to heat.

APPLICATION METHODS

Several methods have been developed to apply powder coatings to the workpiece. The most commonly used method is electrostatic powder spraying. Some of the other methods include the fluidized bed, the electrostatic fluidized bed, and powder flocking. The particular method is selected based on the required coating properties and coating thickness, the size and shape of the parts, the rate of production, and the material handling techniques employed.

Electrostatic Powder Spraying

In electrostatic powder spraying, dry powder is pneumatically fed from a supply reservoir to a spray gun where a low-amperage, high-voltage charge is imparted to the powder

POWDER COATING

particles (see Fig. 49-5).[3] The parts to be coated are electrically grounded so that the charged particles projected at them are firmly attracted to the part's surface and held there until melted and fused into a smooth finish in a baking oven.

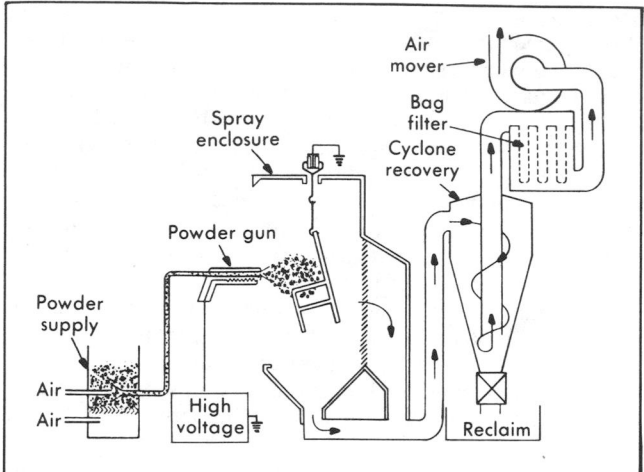

Fig. 49-5 Typical components in an electrostatic powder spray system.

Fluidized Bed

Fluidized-bed coating is a method for applying thermosetting or thermoplastic materials in the form of fine powders to preheated metal parts. The powders are placed in the upper chamber of a dip tank. Pressurized air flows through a diffuser plate into a powder chamber, causing the powder to become suspended (fluidized) in the airstream. In this state, the air-powder mixture resembles a boiling liquid. The part to be coated is heated to a temperature above the powder's melting point and then immersed in the air-powder mixture (see Fig. 49-6). The powder particle that contact the hot surface begin to fuse and form a film on the surface. Uniform distribution of the particles over the surface is enhanced by vibrating the part while it is in the powder chamber. After the part is removed from the chamber, it is generally reheated to achieve good fusion and film properties; in the case of thermosetting powders, reheating is performed to cure the coating.

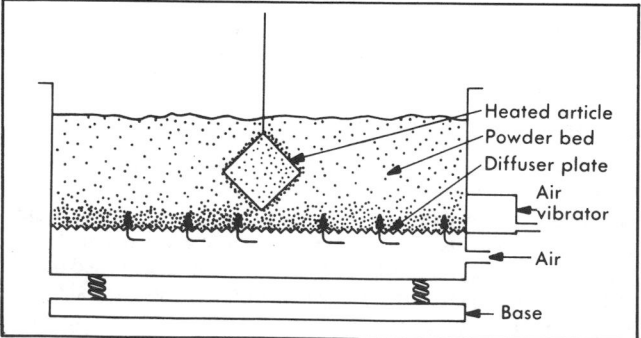

Fig. 49-6 Schematic diagram of a fluidized powder bed.

Advantages and limitations. Fluidized-bed coating is widely used to apply films in the range of 6 to 60 mils (0.15 to 1.50 mm) thick. Variables used to control film thickness are preheat oven temperature, dwell time in the preheat oven, dip time, powder density, and part motion. Flat areas, recessed areas, and edges are all coated during the process, thereby improving corrosion protection. Actual immersion times are relatively short, from 4 to 10 seconds; and the part does not have to be withdrawn at a specified rate as in dipping.

Although most parts can be coated with this method, parts with low mass are difficult to coat due to the rapid loss of heat between the preheat oven and the powder chamber. Films less than 6 mils (0.15 mm) thick are also difficult to obtain by this method. In addition, films are generally applied to both sides of the part rather than to just one side because masking costs would make fluidized-bed coating less competitive with the other powder coating methods. Fluidized-bed coating also requires a greater amount of powder than the other powder coating methods so that the parts can be completely immersed in the air-powder mixture.

Electrostatic Fluidized Bed

The electrostatic fluidized-bed coating method combines the principles of the fluidized-bed process with those of electrostatic deposition.[4] An illustration of a typical electrostatic fluidized bed is found in Fig. 49-7. The powder particles are placed in the fluidized bed, which has special charging electrodes built into the diffuser plate, to a depth of approximately 1 to 3″ (25 to 75 mm). When a high-voltage source of a given potential and polarity is applied, the powder particles become charged; the charged powder particles repel each other and form a cloud over the bed.

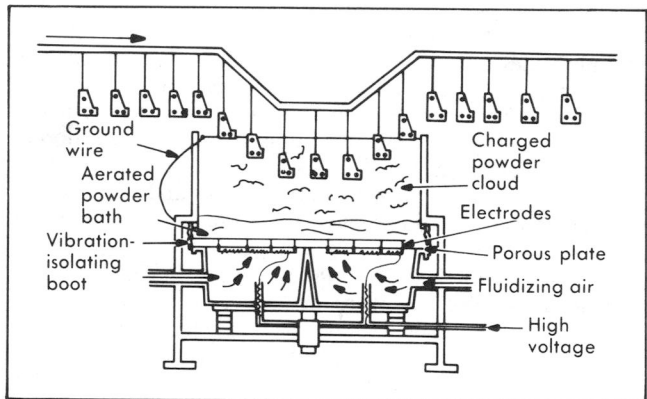

Fig. 49-7 Schematic of typical electrostatic fluidized bed.

Parts to be coated are grounded and then transported over the cloud where the powder is electrostatically attracted to the parts. If the part is cold, the powder will collect on the surface until the accumulated surface charge is sufficient to repel further collection (in essence, the part is insulated). The part can then be transported to an oven where the collected powder is fused to the surface of the part. If the part is preheated and then transported over the particle cloud, the powder will fuse as it collects. Since the fused particles lose their charge, the powder will continue to be attracted to the part as long as it is held in place over the cloud or until the powder ceases to fuse to the part due to cooling.

Not all powder materials that are normally associated with product finishes can be applied using the electrostatic fluidized-bed method. Some of the materials that have been successfully applied are epoxy, cellulose acetate butyrate, polyester, poly-propylene, polyethylene, and acrylic. Polyvinyl chlorides and polyamides are not suited for this method.

Powder Flocking

Powder flocking combines the fluidizing feature of the fluidized-bed process with the flexibility of the flocking process. The basic steps in this coating method are part preparation, preheating, spraying, and postheating. Generally, most parts are prepared using conventional methods such as cleaning and priming. The parts are then heated to a temperature slightly higher than the melting point of the coating material. Spraying of the powder onto the parts can be performed either manually or automatically. After spraying, the parts are heated to cause the coating to flow and then to cure the coating film. Overspray is collected and reprocessed for future use.

Powder flocking has advantages over other powder coating methods that are often overlooked when choosing a powder coating method. One advantage is the low cost of coating equipment. Powder flocking is also capable of applying a full range of coating thicknesses, as well as providing good penetration into cavities; however, it is difficult to control the uniformity of film thickness.

Powder flocking has limitations due to its design. For example, the compressed air used to transport the powder cools the parts during coating, thereby requiring the part to be heated to a higher temperature than with the fluidized-bed method. Compared with the electrostatic powder spraying method, powder flocking does not provide a wrap effect when coating circular or irregularly shaped parts.

ELECTROCOATING

Electrocoating is a process for applying organic coatings through the use of film-forming organic macro-ions; the process resembles metal plating.[5] The part to be coated is electrically activated and then immersed in a bath of paint that has been given an electrical charge of the opposite polarity. The resin and pigment migrate to the part, and a uniform film is deposited. The part is then removed from the paint bath, rinsed to remove any excess material, and baked to cure the finish.

Electrocoating is not a panacea for the painting industry, but it does offer several advantages over other coating methods. Some of the advantages are as follows:[6]

- Approximately 90% of the paint adheres to the work.
- Water-based paints are used, resulting in fewer fire hazard and solvent air pollution problems.

- Sags, runs, and tears are eliminated.
- Uniform film thickness; film thickness can also be accurately controlled.
- Sharp edges, points, angles, and welding seams can be successfully painted.

Electrocoating is limited, however, to one-coat applications; and separate tanks are required for each color used. Large, flat surfaces can be electrocoated, but the equipment must be designed for the particular application.

Electrocoating was first used approximately 20 years ago for single coats to prime automotive bodies with alkyd and epoxy primers. Currently, electrocoating is used to apply primers and one-coat or topcoat finishes to a diverse range of automotive, furniture, appliance, industrial, and consumer products.

AUTODEPOSITION

Autodeposition is a coating process that has been in commercial use since 1973.[7] The film is deposited chemically, rather than electrolytically as in electrocoating. The film has a slightly textured, matte appearance. One of the most important characteristics of autodeposition is that it does not require a metal conversion coating because the adhesion of the deposited coating is extremely good due to the strong interaction between the metal and the organic film. The elimination of a phosphate stage leads to savings in floor space and operating costs.[8]

Some of the advantages of autodeposition are:[9]

- Minimum overall energy requirements for the complete coating process.
- Uniform, self-limiting film thickness.
- Uniform coverage on interior and exterior surfaces (excellent throwing power).
- Excellent adhesion and impact resistance, and good salt-spray resistance after baking.
- No solvents required, minimizing fire hazards.
- Minimum rack stripping required.
- Minimum air and water pollution.
- High system efficiency.
- High production rates.

- Low coating cost per unit area of steel coated.

However, autodeposition does have limitations. The color and polymer selection is limited because color capability is under development; currently, only black is available. In addition, only one company offers commercial autodeposition systems.

So far, autodeposited coatings have been commercially applied on automotive components such as engine mounts, lamp housing stampings, and axle housings.[10] The process is not limited, however, to the automotive industry. Autodeposition can be used whenever 200-500 hours of salt-spray resistance is required on steel substrates. The coating can serve as a primer or as a final finish on parts that are not highly visible after assembly. The quality level depends upon the type of steel substrate being coated and the process selection. Part size is not a critical factor.

The autodeposition bath is composed of a resin in the form of a latex (a water-dispersible resin), hydrofluoric acid, hydrogen peroxide, and deionized water. Theoretically, the percentage of solids in the bath may vary widely; but for commercial applications, the range is generally from 3 to 6% by volume.[11] The bath is acidic and operates at a pH of 2.6 to 3.5.

When a part is immersed in the bath, the proton attack on the substrate produces ionic species such as ferrous ions (Fe^{+2}).

DIP, FLOW AND CURTAIN COATING

Hydrogen peroxide in the bath oxidizes the ferrous ions, producing ferric ions (Fe^{+3}). The ferric ions act as destabilizing agents for the colloidal latex particles in the bath, causing their deposition on the metal surface. As long as the environment at the liquid-metal interface contains the proper ions for producing destabilizing agents, the film continues to grow.

DIP, FLOW AND CURTAIN COATING

The common feature of dip, flow, and curtain coating methods is that the parts are coated with a large volume of coating material and the excess is allowed to drain off. In the case of curtain coating, however, the excess is the material that is not deposited on the part; whereas in the other two methods, the coating material contacts the surface and then flows off. Electrodeposition, autodeposition, and fluidized-bed powder coating (all of which have been discussed previously in this chapter) also use the drainoff principle.

DIP COATING

In its simplest form, dip coating is the complete immersion of a part in an open tank of a liquid coating material, the withdrawal of the part from the liquid, the supporting of the part over the tank or drainboard until it has completely drained, and finally the drying or curing of the coating. Although supporting and dipping the part manually is possible, mass production systems normally employ conveyors to transport and support the parts during the coating cycle. As shown in Fig. 49-8, a dip in the conveyor lowers the parts into the tank. During the period of time in which the part is immersed in the coating material, the conveyor moves evenly and smoothly to minimize withdrawal lines and improve film characteristics on the finished part. The controlled withdrawal also permits the meniscus of the reservoir to pull off the excess coating material, thereby reducing the drainage time. Since draining requires time, conveyorized systems incorporate a drainboard that extends under the conveyor to catch the excess material.

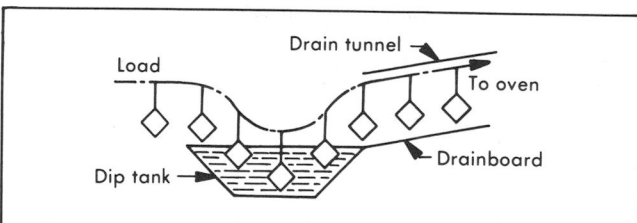

Fig. 49-8 Conveyor movement in dip coating.

Dip coating is widely used in industry for rough finishes, for applying a prime coat, and to coat the internal and external surfaces of a part. Dipping is generally efficient in its use of materials; up to 90% of the material is used, whereas only 50% of the material is used in spraying. Material loss is due to drag-out and drainage. One disadvantage of dip coating is that the coatings tend to be heavier on the bottom of the part than at the top. This difference in coating thickness is called wedging. To achieve more uniform film thicknesses, it is necessary to coordinate the solvent evaporation rate with the conveyor speed. Another disadvantage is that color changes can only be economically accomplished through the use of separate tanks.

FLOW COATING

In the flow coating process, the part is hung on a conveyor and carried through an enclosure, as illustrated in Fig. 49-9. Inside the enclosure, a series of nozzles connected to a pump that draws the coating material from a reservoir are suitably positioned with respect to the part. On some flow coaters, the

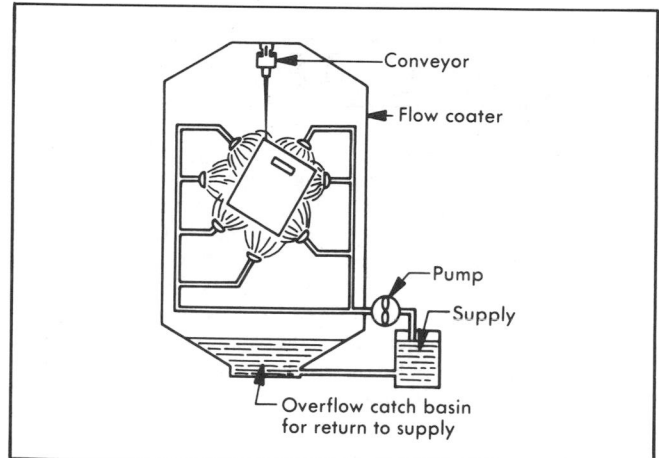

Fig. 49-9 Cross section of typical flow coating enclosure.

nozzles are mounted on a manifold tube that oscillates in the enclosure. The liquid material leaves the nozzles as a shower, coating the entire surface of the part. The excess material flows from the part surface to the bottom of the enclosure and then back to the supply reservoir. After passing through the shower, the part is carried by a conveyor over a drainboard until drainage stops and is then transported to the curing oven. In large industrial installations, extensive flow tunnels outside the application enclosure keep the area around the part saturated with solvent to improve flowout (drainage and uniform film formation).

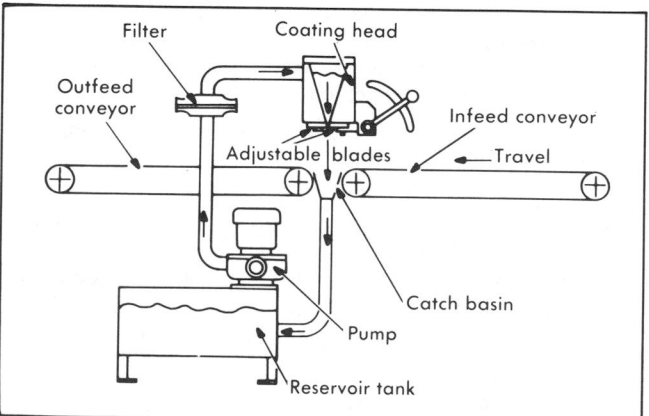

Fig. 49-10 Pressure head-type curtain coater designed for coating sheet products. (*Koating Machinery Company, Inc.*)

Three types of flow coating are currently being used: high pressure, low pressure, and centrifugal. In the high-pressure method, the individual nozzles regulate the pressure of the coating material. In the low-pressure method, the pressure is regulated at the reservoir tank and rarely exceeds 10 psi (70 kPa). In the centrifugal method, the coating material flows out of nozzles mounted at the end of a rotating arm.

CURTAIN COATING

Curtain coating is a specialized type of flow coating in which the flat surface to be coated is passed through a continuous sheet or curtain of material. A typical curtain coater contains a coating system and a conveyor system. The coating system consists of a coating head, reservoir tank, variable-speed pump,

filter, and a catch basin or return through (see Fig. 49-10). The conveyor system consists of an infeed and an outfeed conveyor with a variable-speed drive; speeds range from 0 to 600 fpm. A heating system may also be incorporated in the curtain coater to maintain the coating material at a specified temperature.

Curtain coating is most readily applied to flat surfaces and is widely used in the coating of sheets such as plywood and chipboard surfaces, floor tiles, cabinet doors, corrugated boxes, and mirror backings. Curtain coaters are capable of coating sheets in widths from 12 to 144″ (300 to 3650 mm). Some curtain coaters have been designed to coat rolls (webs) of materials; the coatings produced are smooth and uniform in thickness. Edges are not easily coated by this method if they are at right angles to the main surface.

ROLLER COATING

Roller coating is a high-speed machine painting process used for the continuous coating of flat panels or coils (webs) of metal, plastics, paper, film, and fabric. The process consists of transferring an organic coating from a revolving applicator roller to the surface of the material as it passes through the machine. Depending on the equipment design, the top, bottom, or both surfaces can be coated in one pass.[12] Most organic coating materials can be applied by roller coating. In addition, roll coaters are used to apply filler materials to porous or rough surfaces prior to applying the topcoat. Paints are usually thinned with slow-evaporating solvents and are applied at higher viscosities than in other application methods, permitting close control of paint flow and film thickness.[13]

When the material and the rollers travel in the same direction and at the same speed, the process is called direct roller coating. When the roller motion is in the opposite direction to the motion of the material, the process is called reverse roller coating.[14] When direct or reverse roll coaters are used to apply a coating to a continuous strip of metal, the process is commonly referred to as coil coating.

A direct roll coater consists of a coating roll, a doctor roll located next to the coating roll, and a feed roll beneath the

coating roll (see Fig. 49-11).[15] The rolls are usually made from ethylene propylene rubber of various hardnesses to provide resiliency. The coating and feed rolls turn at the same surface speed, which is about six times the speed of the doctor roll, to obtain smooth coatings.

Another type of roll coater is the precision roll coater, which is a modified direct roll coater. Instead of the surface of the doctor roll being smooth, it has an engraved pattern on it that allows a definite deposit to remain on the coating roll. The doctor roll is also in direct contact with the coating roll and thus turns at the same speed. The pattern on the doctor roll determines, to a great extent, the thickness of the coating film on the substrate.

A reverse roll coater is essentially a direct roll coater with the bottom feed roll turning in the opposite direction to the coating roll (see Fig. 49-12). The opposite turning direction serves to wipe the coating material onto the substrate. The coating roll is also made from metal that has been chromium plated instead of being made from a resilient material; the doctor and feed rolls are generally made from a resilient material. Reverse roll coaters are commonly used for coating material in coil (web) form; the coil is held in contact with the coating roll by two smaller rolls, one on either side of the coating roll. The coating

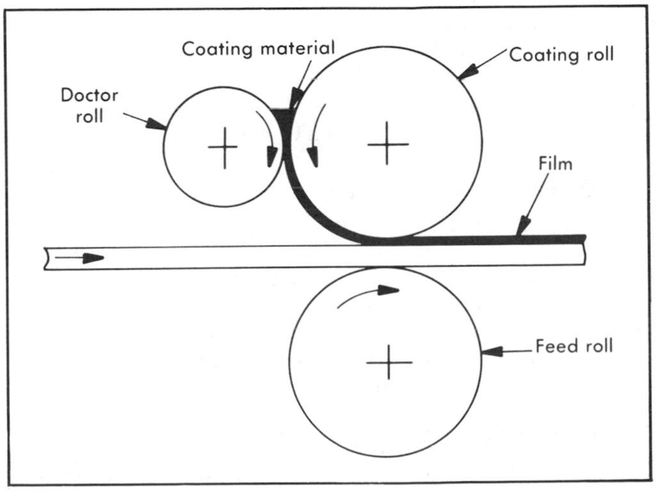

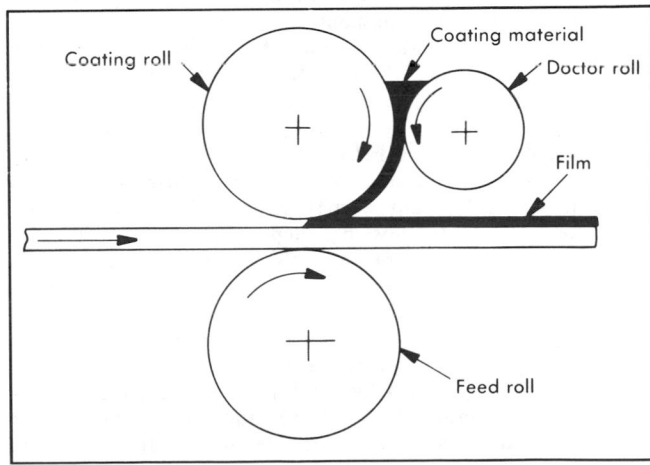

Fig. 49-11 Schematic of direct roll coater. (*The Black Bros. Co.*)

Fig. 49-12 Schematic of reverse roll coater. (*The Black Bros. Co.*)

CURING METHODS

film applied by reverse roll coaters is thicker than the film applied by direct roll coaters.

A fourth type of roll coater, referred to as a combination roll coater, combines a direct roll coater with a reverse roll coater in the same machine frame.[16] At the first station (direct roll coater), an excess amount of coating material is applied to the surface. The second station wipes off the excess material from the surface and then applies a smooth, uniform film across the entire surface. The combination roll coater is commonly used to apply opaque base coats to hardboard surfaces.

CURING METHODS

While the terms *drying* or *baking* are commonly used in the painting industry when referring to curing, there is a distinction between the processes of drying (baking) and curing. A paint film can be dry, but not cured. Dry can refer to the film resulting from the loss of solvent from a paint; the solvent is gone, but the resin is unchanged. To be cured, however, the resin must be converted to a new resin. An incompletely cured film may be dry to the touch, but fail in use.

All organic coating films, as they occur on a surface as a finish, are polymers containing large numbers of molecular units of the same chemical form, bound together to create a solid, continuous film. To produce such film structures, it is necessary that the chemical resin components are in a form such as a liquid so that application is possible. Once the material is applied, it is allowed to level and convert to the desired solid film.

AMBIENT TEMPERATURE DRYING

The process of air drying basically involves a physical change and is therefore reversible; formed films can be redissolved by the use of proper solvents. Nitrocellulose lacquers dry by solvent evaporation, as do other coatings—vinyls, vinyl copolymers, acrylic resins, shellac, styrene copolymers, and solutions of bitumens. Certain acrylic resins and styrene copolymers require baking. Other coating materials, such as drying oils and oleoresinous varnishes, are liquids or soft, sticky solids that form films by both solvent evaporation and combination with oxygen taken from the air. Oxygen take-up is a chemical process and irreversible.

Air drying is an energy-saving process and therefore quite desirable. Air-drying paints, however, require large quantities of solvents for reduction to a viscosity low enough to allow brushing, spraying, or other methods of application. Paints having high contents of volatile organic compounds have to be avoided because of environmental reasons. However, it is possible to replace some of the objectionable solvents with so-called "compliance solvents," like 1,1,1-trichloroethane and/or metylene chloride.

CATALYTIC CURING

The polymerization or curing of many coating materials is brought about chemically. Two types of polymer linkage (linear and crosslinkage) are possible, depending upon the type of chemical agent used to promote the polymerization reaction and the resin. Catalytic agents are used to trigger a reaction between molecules of resin materials to create larger molecules. Reactive agents, when used, themselves combine with one or more resin molecules to form larger molecules. Whether the polymerization is caused by catalysis or by reaction, heat is given off as the molecules crosslink, and the heat accelerates curing. For some types of metal protection, catalyzed conversion coatings are unsurpassed.

Epoxy materials are the most frequently used catalytic conversion coating materials for metals exposed to corrosive chemical environments. Other types of catalyzed conversion coatings include alkyd-urea, alkyd-triazines, two-package urethanes, and polyester finishes.

Several types of resins are marketed in the form of two-liquid components that are intended to be mixed and then applied and allowed to chemically react to form a film. These components are carefully metered and mixed because the rate at which they react is determined by the mix ratio. The allowable time before use is called pot life and varies from minutes to as long as hours. Widely used representatives of this group are the two-component epoxies and polyurethanes.

ELEVATED TEMPERATURE CURING

With some materials, the polymerization reaction can be accelerated by raising the temperature of the applied coating. The accelerated, molecular crosslinking produced by heating is often called baking. In addition to the actual polymerization of a film, a certain amount of drying by evaporation takes place as solvents are liberated. In the case of oil-based and oleoresinous paints, oxidation (another chemical polymerization process) also takes place. Oxidation likewise occurs to some degree with all alkyds. In fact, with most paints, the curing process is a combination of evaporation, oxidation, and polymerization. Heating increases the rate of all three processes.

VAPOR CURING

A comparatively new technique for bringing about the polymerization of an applied coating is referred to as vapor curing. Amine-vapor-curable polyurethanes are the coating materials that are cured by this technique, but the method has had only limited application. Paints to be used are prepared by mixing a liquid polyol resin with a liquid polymeric, crosslinking isocyanate resin and all other ingredients required, like pigments. Two methods of curing these paints when they have been applied to product surfaces are: vapor permeation curing (VPC) and vapor injection curing (VIC).[17]

Vapor Permeation Curing (VPC)

A curing line for the VPC coating system is designed specifically for a given application. It consists of four basic components: a tertiary amine gas generator, a curing chamber, a scrubber, and analytical instrumentation to monitor amine and oxygen levels. The process is amenable to almost all coating application methods, including gravure coating, curtain coating, conventional spray, electrostatic spray, and airless spray.

Vapor Injection Curing (VIC)

A new vapor curing process has recently been developed that eliminates the need for a curing chamber. This process is called the vapor injection curing (VIC) coating process. It is particularly applicable to large automotive parts, such as reaction injection molding (RIM) fascias, sheet molding compound (SMC) hoods, grill panels, lift gates, and similar parts.

RADIATION CURING

Radiation curing is the process by which specifically formulated inks, coatings, and adhesives are dried and converted to a useable coating by means of high-energy electrons or short wavelengths of light. Several ranges of radiating energy are widely used for the drying and curing of paint. These include microwaves and infrared radiation having waves longer than visible light, ultraviolet radiation of shorter wavelength than visible light, and the still shorter waves of electron beams.

Process Advantages and Limitations

A major advantage of the radiation curing process is the short time required for curing. All the other curing processes previously discussed require curing times several orders of magnitude greater than that required by radiation curing. Short curing times are economically favorable in several ways. For example, short curing times allow reductions of in-process inventory and processing space, and they also allow simplified and improved line control.

The radiation curing process makes possible the maintenance of product dimensional stability, better quality control of finishes, lower utility costs, immediate startup and shutdown, and easier product handling. Some coatings contain little or no volatile organic components (VOC) and therefore do not contribute to air pollution. Solventless monomers can be used for zero VOC emission.

The radiation curing process is not always applicable to all substrate shapes. Radiation usually follows a straight line from the source to the part surface. As a result, reentrant angles and very deep recesses may cause insufficient curing. However, when high-speed electron curing is used, electron scattering can be depended on to provide a sufficiently uniform dosage to cure most injection molded or stamped metal contours encountered in production. The low impact strength of parts made from some plastics is another limitation to the use of radiation curing.

Applications

For a coating to be radiation curable and also have commercially acceptable properties for the intended product, the unsaturation of the material should approximate one-half to three double bonds per 1000 molecular weight. Below this range, the coating cannot be suitably cured; above it, the film tends to be brittle. However, certain applications requiring high hardness can employ coatings with as much as five double bonds per 1000 molecular weight.

Radiation-curable coatings are formulated to be applied by one of the common industrial coating methods. All the standard pigments and fillers may be used to provide specific properties to the coating. Polymers that can be formulated to cure by crosslinking, such as polyesters, acrylics, silicones, and various combinations and modifications of these, are suitably cured by radiation. These resins are combined, when appropriate, with various monomers to make a complete coating binder.

Electron Beam (EB) Curing

A radiation curing installation using electron beams (EB) generally consists of integrated line operations, including substrate preparation, coating, curing, further finishing if necessary, and preparation for distribution. The entire operation can be automated, with the required cure dose electronically coordinated with line speed.

Electron-accelerator positioning and part indexing may be used to take maximum advantage of process parameters. External shielding is required to protect against the X rays produced when high-speed electrons impinge on the substrate. Maximum shielding compactness is obtainable with lead and steel, but concrete vault construction with labyrinth accesses may also be used.

Costs are not sufficiently established by experience to determine which applications for radiation curing with electron beams will be economically competitive. It is clear, however, that high-speed, high-volume production installations to cure large panels, continuous sheet or strip, and relatively simple contoured parts are the first to take economic advantage of the process. Curing with EB is also useful for substrates that are temperature sensitive and for special applications in which the high cost of the equipment can be justified.

References

1. Guy E. Weismantel, ed., *Paint Handbook* (New York: McGraw-Hill Book Co. 1981), pp.1-18.
2. Gerald L. Schneberger, *Understanding Paint and Painting Processes*, 2nd ed. (Wheaton, IL: Hitchcock Publishing Co.) p. 7.
3. The Powder Coating Institute, *Powder Coatings* (Greenwich, CT: 1983).
4. Daniel R. Savage, *The Electrostatic Fluidized Bed—Theory, Design and Application*, SME Technical Paper FC72-935 (Dearborn, MI: Association for Finishing Processes of SME, 1972).
5. George E. F. Brewer, ed., *Electrodeposition of Coatings* (Washington, DC: American Chemical Society, 1973).
6. Robert W. Whitehall, *Electrocoating Equipment*, SME Technical Paper FC75-564 (Dearborn, MI: Association for Finishing Processes of SME 1975).
7. Harry M. Leister, *Processing With Autodeposition*, SME Technical Paper FC81-248 (Dearborn, MI: Association for Finishing Processes of SME, 1981).
8. M. J. Johnson and N. R. Roobol, "An Evaluation of Autodeposition," *Plating and Surface Finishing* (July 1984), pp. 58-62.
9. Joseph W. Prane, "Organic Coatings Technology, A Review—Part II," *Metal Finishing* (October 1983), pp. 75-78.
10. Harry M. Leister, "Autodeposition of Organic Coatings," *Plating and Surface Finishing* (July 1982), pp. 46-48.
11. Johnson, *loc. cit.*
12. Melvin H. Sandler, et. al., "Painting," *Metals Handbook*, 9th ed., vol. 5 (Metals Park, OH: American Society for Metals, 1982), p. 482.
13. *Ibid.*, p. 483.
14. Carl Izzo, "Paint Finishing Materials and Equipment Guide," *Products Finishing*, 1984 Directory (September 1983), p. 36.
15. Donald T. Jones, "Roll Coating Equipment—Applications and Limitations," *Radiation Curing V Proceedings*, September 23-25, 1980, Boston, MA (Dearborn, MI: Association for Finishing Processes of SME, 1980), pp. 401-412.
16. Donald T. Jones, "Latest Roll Coater Technology for Improved Panel Finishing," *Finishing '83 Conference Proceedings*, October 10-13, 1983, Cincinnati, OH (Dearborn, MI: Association for Finishing Processes of SME, 1983), pp. 3-15 to 3-23.
17. Michael G. Cobb, *The Development of Vapor Permeation Cure (VPC) Coatings for RIM and SMC Substrates*, presentation at AFP/SME clinic "Finishing Automotive Plastics," Dearborn, MI, October 23-25, 1984.

OCCUPATIONAL SAFETY AND HEALTH

SAFETY LEGISLATION

The Occupational Safety and Health Act of 1970 and the Federal Mine Safety Act of 1977 are the two most significant pieces of federal legislation on occupational safety affecting the manufacturing community. The OSHA legislation will be given attention here.

THE OCCUPATIONAL SAFETY AND HEALTH ACT

Occupational Safety and Health Act (OSHAct) was enacted to assure safe and healthy working conditions for every working man and woman in the United States. The Act applies to every employer in the U.S. or in U.S. possessions who has any number of employees and who engages in a business affecting commerce. Federal employees are covered by this Act, but employees of state and local government are excluded. Operators of mines covered by the federal Mine Safety and Health Act of 1977 are excluded from the OSHAct. Also excluded are operations where a federal agency (other than the Department of Labor) has authority to dictate or enforce occupational safety and health regulations or standards.

Employers covered by the Act have the obligation of complying with the safety and health standards connected with the Act. Also, the OSHAct has a "general-duty clause" that obligates employers to provide employees with a workplace free from recognized hazards that are likely to cause death or serious physical harm to the employees. This legislation makes on-thejob safety and health a management responsibility. The law places on every employee the duty to comply with safety standards; however, final responsibility for compliance remains with the employer.

OCCUPATIONAL SAFETY AND HEALTH ADMINISTRATION

The administration and enforcement of the Occupational Safety and Health Act are vested with the Secretary of Labor and the Occupational Safety and Health Review Commission. Investigation and prosecution are performed by the Secretary of Labor, and the Review Commission makes decisions in contested cases during the enforcement procedure. The National Institute for Occupational Safety and Health (NIOSH), established within the Department of Health and Human Services (DHHS), carries out safety and health research and related functions. Statistical data relating to injuries and illnesses are compiled by the Bureau of Labor Statistics within the Department of Labor.

The Occupational Safety and Health Administration (OSHA) has the authority to institute and revoke safety and health standards, conduct inspections and investigations, issue citations and penalties, place requirements for recordkeeping of safety and health data, and to petition the courts to act against employers with dangerously hazardous work environments. OSHA also has the authority to provide employer and employee training, implement voluntary protection programs including injury prevention consultation, grant funds to states for the operation of safety and health programs, grant funds to private organizations to develop safety and health training programs, and develop and maintain occupational safety and health statistics programs.

NATIONAL INSTITUTE FOR OCCUPATIONAL SAFETY AND HEALTH

The National Institute for Occupational Safety and Health (NIOSH) is part of the Department of Health and Human Services' Centers for Disease Control. NIOSH is engaged in research, education, and training related to occupational health and safety. NIOSH develops criteria and recommendations for health and safety standards, conducts safety research experiments and demonstrations, and conducts educational programs to train personnel to carry out the OSHAct. The OSHAct also requires NIOSH to annually publish a listing of all known toxic substances and their toxic thresholds.

NIOSH offers the following technical services to employers through its Division of Technical Services in Cincinnati:

1. On-site hazard evaluation of potentially toxic substances.
2. Technical information concerning health and safety issues in the workplace.
3. Technical assistance in reducing on-the-job injuries by evaluating problem areas and offering corrective techniques.
4. Technical assistance in industrial hygiene and recommendations for engineering controls.
5. Assistance in solving workplace problems in occupational medical and nursing areas.

EMPLOYER AND EMPLOYEE DUTIES UNDER THE OSHAct

It is the employer's duty to abide by the applicable safety and health standards promulgated by OSHA. The *Code of Federal Regulations* (CFR), published in paperback volumes every year, contains the rules and regulations that have been released. The CFR is divided into 50 different titles,

SAFETY LEGISLATION

representing broad subject areas of federal regulations, and each title is further divided into parts and subparts covering specific regulatory areas.

OSHA can promulgate emergency temporary standards if employees are exposed to grave hazards. These emergency standards take effect immediately on publication in the Federal Register and serve as a proposed rule for a final standard, which is required to be published within six months. Any person has the right to challenge a standard issued by OSHA by petitioning the U.S. Court of Appeals within 60 days after its release.

It is possible, on some occasions, for employers to be unable to meet the standards that are in place. The OSHAct empowers OSHA to grant variances from the standards when the purposes of the Act are fulfilled. A variance may be temporary or permanent. The variance is granted if the employer demonstrates with actual evidence that alternative measures will provide a place of employment that is as safe and healthful as that provided by the standard. Affected employees must be given notice of the variance application, as well as an opportunity to participate in a hearing.

OSHA HAZARD COMMUNICATION STANDARD

On November 25, 1985, the OSHA hazard communication standard (29 CFR 1910.1200) took effect, requiring chemical manufacturers and importers to assess the hazards of chemicals they sell, affix warning labels to containers they ship, and provide material safety data sheets (MSDS) to their clients in the manufacturing sector.

The manufacturing manager who wishes to know how best to comply with the standard should read the entire standard— the preamble, the summary, and the guidelines prepared for compliance officers—or consult professionals in the field. The manager can find OSHA's definitions to key terms within the standard.

By the standard, manufacturers must compile a list of hazardous materials in the workplace and cross reference them to their MSDS by chemical and common names. The written material handling procedures must outline methods to inform workers about the hazards of tasks not performed often and the hazards associated with chemicals in piping systems. Manufacturers must also inform contractors and employees about the hazardous materials in the workplace and their proper handling procedures. This written information must be available to employees and OSHA inspectors on request.

Manufacturers must label bags, boxes, drums, storage tanks, and the like that are used with hazardous chemicals. The label must contain the identity of the hazardous chemical and appropriate warnings. The label should be a link to the more comprehensive material safety data sheet. Manufacturers are also responsible for how well the workplace hazards have been communicated to the employees. This calls for a suitable training and educational program. Training of individual employees should be based on actual and potential exposure within their work areas.

OSHA has compiled official interpretations of the hazard communication standard. This document reprints letters requesting interpretations or clarifications of key provisions of the standard, along with the responses by OSHA. The order number for this document is PB86-220456, and it can be obtained from the National Technical Information Service (5285 Port Royal Road, Springfield, Va., 22161).

OSHA RECORDKEEPING REQUIREMENTS

The OSHAct requires most employers to maintain in each establishment records consisting of a log of occupational injuries and illnesses, a supplementary record of each occupational illness and injury, and an annual summary of occupational injuries and illnesses. To relieve small businesses of recordkeeping requirements, OSHA has ruled that an employer who had 10 or less employees at any time during the calendar year need not follow the recordkeeping requirements.

No employer, however, is relieved of the obligation to report any fatalities or multiple hospitalization accidents to OSHA. Within 48 hours after the occurrence of an accident (that is fatal to any employee(s) and/or requires hospital treatment of at least 5 employees due to one single incident), the employer must report the occurrence orally or in writing to the nearest OSHA Area Director. The report must relate the circumstances of the accident and the extent of fatalities and injuries.

These records must be available for inspection and copying by OSHA compliance officers during any inspection, investigation, or for statistical computations.

WORKPLACE INSPECTION

OSHA inspections are almost always conducted without prior notice. An employer representative and employee representative can accompany the compliance officer during an inspection. These representatives can also participate in the opening and closing conferences. The OSHA priorities for investigations are as follows:

1. *Imminent danger investigation.* An imminent danger is a condition or practice within a place of employment that could reasonably be expected to cause death or serious physical harm before the danger can be removed through the enforcement procedures of the OSHAct. Except in extreme situations, a health hazard is not normally an imminent danger. Imminent danger allegations will ordinarily provoke an inspection within 24 hours of notification.
2. *Catastrophic or fatal accident investigation.* An accident will be investigated if it is of the type that requires OSHA reporting, or draws significant publicity, or is of the type that calls for investigation under an OSHA special program.
3. *Employee complaint investigation.* Investigating priority is given first to those complaints of imminent danger, then to serious situations. The inspection by the compliance officer is normally restricted to the area of complaint. However, the officer is required to cite any other violations observed during the inspection.
4. *High hazard industry inspections.* Industry classifications with high death, injury, and illness incidence rates receive priority for inspection.
5. *Reinspections.* Employers who have been cited for alleged serious violations are normally reinspected to determine if the hazard has been controlled.

VIOLATIONS

There are four types of violations:

- *Imminent danger.* The OSHAct defines imminent danger as "any condition or practice in any phase of employment which is such that a danger exists which could reasonably be expected to cause death or serious physical harm immediately." An employer will be seen as having abated an imminent danger if employees are removed from the danger area until the hazard is eliminated or if the hazardous operation is removed altogether. When the employer voluntarily eliminates the danger, an imminent danger procedure is not instituted and no Notice of Imminent Danger is issued. If the employer does not abate the alleged imminent danger, the CSHO will inform the employer and employees that a civil action will be recommended to shut down the operation.

- *Serious violation.* A serious violation is one where there is a strong probability of death or serious harm from a hazard and that the employer knew or should have known about it.
- *Nonserious violation.* A nonserious violation is one where a condition exists that is likely to cause an injury but not a death or serious physical harm, or that the employer did not know of the hazard.
- *De Minimis violation.* A violation of a standard without having a direct relationship to safety or health. An example is compliance with a more recent issue of a voluntary consensus standard that is referenced in an OSHA standard, resulting in equal or greater protection to the employee.

CITATIONS AND PENALTIES

An employer may receive a written citation from the OSHA Area Director if an inspection reveals a condition that is alleged to be a violation of the standards. The citation would state the standard allegedly violated, specifically how the condition violates that standard, and the time allowed for correction. A penalty may not be proposed when a violation is not a serious one, but proposed penalties always accompany a serious violation.

A nonserious violation may have a penalty of up to $1000 for each violation. A penalty assessment of up to $1000 per violation must be brought against the employer who has received a serious violation. For willful or repeated violations, a penalty of up to $10,000 may be proposed. In cases of imminent danger, penalties may be proposed even if the employer immediately corrects the situation. An employer may receive criminal penalties if a standard is willfully violated and this violation causes death to an employee. Any employer who fails to correct an uncontested citation within the abatement period may receive a proposed penalty of a maximum of $1000 per day for each day that the violation continues beyond the abatement period.

EMPLOYER PREPARATION FOR A CONTESTED CASE

If an employer feels that an OSHA response is unjustified, then the action can be contested, whether it be a proposed penalty, a notice of failure to correct a violation, the correction time allowed, or a combination of any of these. Before contesting a citation, the employer should seek professional counsel and/or attempt to resolve the matter informally with the OSHA Area Director or Assistant Regional Director. An informal conference may be requested within 15 working days after the receipt of a citation.

Should an employer decide to contest a proposed penalty or an alleged serious violation, the site or organization safety officer is in many cases the key to successful preparation of an OSHA case. Many cases are based on a question of feasibility—of how the workplace should be made safer, how much safer it should be made, at what cost, and by what timetable. Usually, the safety professional has the training and experience to identify the relevant facts, determine their importance in the workplace under question, and evaluate the possible alternatives. Employees familiar with the operation involved may offer significant insight into the details of the process as well as possible solutions.

MANAGEMENT POLICY TOWARD SAFETY

Every organization, no matter what the size, should make a written safety policy statement and follow it. It should publicize the policy to everyone in the organization, from all supervisory levels to employees. All top-level managers must agree with the policy, and each level of management must understand who is responsible for safety. The safety policy statement should be succinct and reflect the attitude of management. The effectiveness of any safety policy depends directly on the active support of management. The policy comes from the president of the company or the person with final responsibility, such as the plant manager. The policy will lay out a plan for making a safe workplace. It should require the keeping of accident investigation records and direct that a training program will be in place for employees and supervisors. Specific goals should be set forth, and personnel responsible for safety matters must have access to company and government standards. An example of a corporation's safety policy is summarized in Fig. 50-1.

The OSHAct spells out minimum standards for safety and health and does not give details of safe treatment of all workfacturing, sales, marketing, cost control, and customer service. If the health and safety program within the organization is

place hazards. Hazardous conditions or practices that are not covered by specific OSHA standards are covered by the general-duty clause of the Act. This clause says: "Each employer shall furnish to each of his employees employment and a place of employment which are free from recognized hazards that are causing or are likely to cause death or serious physical harm to his employees." In all cases, recognized hazards need to be eliminated in the workplace. If the intent of the law is being met, a variance from the applicable standard can be requested from OSHA. Active support from management means enforcing the policy, recognizing good safety performance, continuously reviewing safety performance, and setting a good example. A safety program must always start at the top management level, and each level must accept their responsibility for their role in the company's safety objectives. Employees will usually commit to safety at the minimum level displayed by their supervisors.

ECONOMIC REASONS FOR SAFETY PROGRAM

The employer should give the health and safety program equal importance with other business functions such as manu-

MANAGEMENT POLICY

The Du Pont Safety Philosphy:
"We will not make, handle, use, sell, transport or dispose of a product unless we can do so safely and in an environmentally sound manner."

Ten Principles of Safety:

1. All injuries and occupational illnesses can be prevented. At Du Pont, we believe that this is a realistic goal and not just a theoretical objective. Our safety performance proves that this goal is achievable, as we have plants with over 1000 employees that have operated for over ten years without a lost-time injury.

2. Management is directly responsible for preventing injuries and illnesses, with each level accountable to the one above and responsible for the level below. This includes all levels, from the chairman, who is also the chief safety officer, through to the first line supervisor.

3. Safety is a condition of employment; each employee must assume responsibility for working safely. In Du Pont, safety is as important as production, quality, and cost control.

4. Training is an essential element for safe workplaces. Safety awareness does not come naturally—management must teach, motivate and sustain employee safety knowledge to eliminate injuries. This includes establishing procedures and safety performance standards for each job or function.

5. Safety audits must be conducted. Management must audit performance in the workplace to assess the effectiveness of facilities and programs, and to detect areas for improvement.

6. All deficiencies must be corrected promptly, either through modifying facilities, changing procedures, bettering employee training or disciplining constructively and consistently. Follow-up audits are used to verify effectiveness.

7. It is essential to investigate all unsafe practices and incidents with injury potential, as well as all injuries.

8. Safety off the job is just as important as safety on the job. Du Pont was a pioneer in tracking the off-the-job safety of employees beginning in 1953. As a result, the Company initiated programs to dramatically improve off-the-job performance.

9. It's good business to prevent illnesses and injuries. Serious illnesses and injuries involve tremendous costs—direct and indirect. The highest cost is human suffering.

10. People are the most critical element in the success of a safety and health program. Management responsibility must be complemented by employees' suggestions and their active involvement in keeping workplaces safe.

Fig. 50-1 Example of corporate directive stating the safety policies and management commitment to employee safety. (*E.I. DuPont de Nemours & Co., Inc.*)

---

facturing, sales, marketing, cost control, and customer service. If the health and safety program within the organization is effective in the prevention of accidents and illnesses, it can save money for the company.

Accidents cost an organization money in insured and uninsured costs. The *insured costs* (also called "direct" costs) are covered by the employer's liability insurance premium and include medical treatment costs, cost of lost work time for the injured person, and cost of payment to the injured person. The *uninsured* (or *hidden*) costs (also called "indirect" costs) of accidents can be outlined as follows:

1. Cost of an accident investigation.
2. Cost of replacement labor.
3. Cost of business interruption.
4. Cost of damage repair.
5. Cost of damaged product.
6. Miscellaneous cost of photographs, transport, administrative overhead, and so on.

An effective health and safety program also helps the organization save money in addition to reducing pain and suffering.

MANAGEMENT STRATEGIES FOR SAFETY

Regardless of the size of a manufacturing organization, the integration of the safety ethic throughout the business is essential if the safety function is to be effective. If safety is a separate function, its effectiveness is doomed. Safety is not a concern for only the manufacturing personnel; it is a necessity for the engineering, marketing, accounting, shipping, industrial relations, and customer service groups. Participation within the safety function must be obtained across plant political or organizational lines.

Management within a moderately sized organization or larger must admit the necessity for a safety staff function. Safety and health programs are becoming increasingly complicated. Safety and health standards are becoming voluminous and difficult to interpret. No organization can afford to rely on existing personnel within the site and trained in other disciplines for competent and expert safety advice. A safety staff group should be present in the large company, and a staff position should be present in the small company. In a small company, a competent individual may be assigned the responsibility for safety in addition to other duties. Even with the presence of staff safety professionals, the individual who delegates responsibility is still accountable for the results. Although safety functions are performed by the site safety group, the ultimate authority and responsibility for safety must rest with their immediate supervisors.

A prominent function of the safety staff is to identify safety and health hazards and to recommend countermeasures. The identification of hazards with respect to existing regulations is to be uncovered by staff through plant inspections. The identification of hazards unique to system idiosyncrasies is the responsibility of the line manager. The staff personnel cannot be as intimately familiar with the various operations as the line manager. Staff safety personnel can implement special countermeasures beyond the normal operational controls for a hazard, once they are made aware of them.

RESPONSIBILITIES OF MANAGEMENT

There should be an unbroken chain of accountability for safety, from the line supervisor to the president or owner of a company. A manager at each level should be able to evaluate the safety efforts of each subordinate manager. A good system can operate in accordance with the following assignment of safety responsibility:

- The *supervisor* is accountable for the safety of all subordinates and for the safe condition of the work area under his or her responsibility.
- The *department head* is responsible for the establishment of good housekeeping practices in the department and for the safety training and development of each supervisor.
- The *superintendent's* safety commission is to see that the corporation's safety program is administered at the plant level. He or she is responsible for all safety activities in his or her administration.
- The *plant manager*, who is generally accountable to a vice president at the corporate level, is vested with the responsibility for safety performance at the plant. The plant manager should see that members of the staff complete safety training, which will continue to develop safety awareness. The plant manager must establish the corporate safety program within the plant and, if necessary, clearly spell out the specific safety duties of subordinates.

HEALTH AND SAFETY PROGRAM FUNDAMENTALS

In addition to humanitarian concern and a natural desire to obey the law, there are purely economic incentives for organizing and maintaining safety and health programs in any organization. Escalating worker's compensation costs and potential civil litigation are two significant reasons. As previously stated, the safety program must have the backing and commitment of management at all levels. The boss's attitude toward job safety and health will be reflected by the employees.

Two main features of any safety program are accident and illness prevention and controlling potential losses. The keys to minimizing accidents are to have engineered hazard-eliminating features on plant machinery and to have employee training programs with instruction of general work practices. Scheduled periodic inspections can identify and lead to correction of unsafe conditions and work practices. Communicating safety and health information is effectively done through joint labor-management safety and health committees. Should an accident occur, an accident response procedure must be in place to discover the cause, take corrective action to prevent future injuries, and break the cascading nature of accident-related costs. Maintaining good relations with injured workers is essential to preventing increased losses.

SAFETY TRAINING

It is management's duty to see that safety training programs are developed for all employees—from the director level to the shop-floor worker. There are numerous types and aspects of employee training programs. Employees should:

- Understand the need for constant attention to their work environment.
- Know how hazardous substances encountered affect the body.
- Be instructed in proper procedures for handling, storing, mixing, and disposing of hazardous substances.
- Be trained in the proper use of protective equipment.
- Be aware of plant emergency and evacuation procedures.
- Understand the importance of good housekeeping practices. (Good housekeeping can reduce accidents and fire hazards.)

- Be trained in the use of plant equipment.
- Be instructed in the use of portable fire extinguishers.
- Be instructed in the safe technique for lifting.
- Be thoroughly aware of general plant safety policies.

NEW EMPLOYEE TRAINING

An effective new employee orientation program will include safety training of the general and overall safety policies. Before the employee actually begins work, while he or she is forming initial attitudes about the company, a good safety indoctrination will lay a foundation for initial and continued safe performance. To have a good start in safety training, management needs to stress the following:

- Management is very interested in keeping every employee in the workplace safe.
- It is possible to prevent accidents.
- Unsafe conditions should be immediately reported.
- If unsafe procedures or equipment are recognized, then management is willing to make immediate corrections.
- No employee should perform a job without the proper training and a clear understanding of any potential hazard.
- All injuries, no matter how small, should be reported at once.

OSHA TRAINING REQUIREMENTS

OSHA has published voluntary training guidelines that follow a model consisting of:[1]

1. Determining if training is needed.
2. Identifying training needs.
3. Identifying goals and objectives.
4. Developing learning requirements.
5. Conducting the training.
6. Evaluating program effectiveness.
7. Improving the program.

Copies of the guidelines can be obtained from OSHA, Office of Training and Education (1555 Time Drive, Des Plaines, IL 60018).

HAZARD ANALYSIS AND ACCIDENT PREVENTION PROGRAMS

Accidents are caused by unsafe acts, unsafe conditions, or a combination of both. On occasion, an accident is caused by a series of errors. This should be considered when an accident is being scrutinized for its cause. An employee's mental state should also be considered. Ignorance and improper attitudes frequently contribute to accidents. In addition, management must recognize that internal faults, such as weak leadership, failure to enforce rules, and poor maintenance, may also be contributing factors when the unexpected happens. Because management defines the system in which production takes place, they must bear the major responsibility for accidents.

Unsafe acts, in more cases than unsafe conditions, are the cause of accidents. An "unsafe act" is a human action that deviates from a standard or written job procedure, safety rule or regulation, instruction, or job safety analysis. Most times, unsafe acts are done because the worker did not receive proper instruction, lacked attention to the job, was looking for a shortcut, or was poorly coordinated, distracted, or under stress. An "unsafe condition" is an arrangement that increases the odds of an employee having an accident. The actions of employees themselves are the greatest contributor to unsafe conditions.

"Unsafe acts and conditions" are often referred to as "hazardous acts and conditions," or simply "hazards." There are three steps in the proper management of hazards: (1) recognition, (2) evaluation, and (3) control. Supervision at all levels has a responsibility to eliminate unsafe acts and conditions, or hazards. This means management has a responsibility to recognize, evaluate, and control hazards that could cause injury or damage.

HAZARD ANALYSIS

The first step toward controlling a hazard is to recognize the hazard. Management must work with the site safety professional to determine locations with a high accident potential as well as to identify severe hazards with a low occurrence likelihood. When specific hazards are being evaluated, both the probability of accident occurrence and the severity of injury or property damage are factored in. Once this is done, it becomes possible to rate hazards across a site to determine the priority of corrective action. This is also useful in cost-effectiveness evaluations. As hazards are being evaluated, countermeasures should be considered. Immediate action, unencumbered by procedure, should take place to eliminate hazards when the remedies are known and cost is not a factor.

COST EFFECTIVENESS WITH GENERAL HAZARD EVALUATION

The main purpose of cost-effectiveness evaluations is to stimulate rational thinking and decision making on the part of management. There are numerous procedures for performing cost-effectiveness evaluations. One will be discussed here. Whatever the technique used, it is essential that several alternatives for resolving each hazard be suggested and that reasonable constraints be placed on the problem. The selection of alternatives that will provide the greatest degree of safety in the face of recognized hazards within given budget constraints will be given careful consideration. With careful consideration, several countermeasures can be employed and cost effectiveness becomes useful.

WORKPLACE HAZARD ANALYSIS

To identify occupational health hazards with a specific task, a job health hazard analysis can be made. A job health hazard analysis survey, like the one shown in Fig. 50-2, can be used. The survey should list the substances used, the number of employees at risk, entry routes, hazardous byproducts, and methods of controlling exposure. Activities, such as maintenance or service operations, should be examined when the survey is done to determine other health hazard potential. After completing the survey, evaluate all exposure substances for hazard potential. Determine if the existing controls are adequate and, if not, then any required controls should be provided.

Job Hazard Analysis Survey for Spray Painting Operation

Operation:_____   Page:_____
                               Date:_____

Number of employees	Job title	Exposure substance	Form[1]	Route of entry[2]	Control[3]
4	Spray painter	No. 4 red primer	M	I	LV
			V	I	LV
			L	S	G (rubber)
				S	O (apron)
		Xylene	L	S	G (rubber)
					O (apron)
			V	I	LV
			M	I	LV

1. Form: D = dust, L = liquid, V = vapor, G = gas, F = fume, M = mist.
2. Route of entry: S = skin, I = inhalation.
3. Control: LV = local ventilation, GV = general ventilation, R = respirator (type), G = gloves (type), F = face protection, O = other protection (type).

Fig. 50-2 Job hazard analysis survey for spray painting operation. (Copied from Health and Safety Guide for Textile Machinery Manufacturers. *NIOSH, U.S. Department of Health, Education, and Welfare (January 1978), p.11*)

CONTROL OF HAZARDS

A continued program of hazard control is a necessary part of the management process. Management commitment toward the control of hazards is expressed through evaluations, procedures, and audits. A hazard control program, with predefined specifics, assures that sound design and operating procedures, operator training, test programs, inspections, and hazard communications are addressed. The hazard control program must emphasize shared responsibilities among departments of a facility. This is possible only if supervisors cooperate.

HAZARD CONTROL METHODS

Various means can be used to reduce or prevent employee exposure to hazards. Some of these methods are listed below, in order of preference. These methods can be used singly or in combination:

1. Eliminate the source of the hazards.
2. Substitute a less hazardous equivalent.
3. Reduce the hazards at the source.
4. Remove the employee from the hazards (i.e., automating the process).
5. Isolate the hazards (i.e., by enclosure).
6. Dilute the hazards (i.e., ventilation).
7. Reduce employee's exposure to hazard by administrative control such as employee rotation.
8. Use personal protective equipment.
9. Train employees in the proper methods used for hazard avoidance.
10. Practice good housekeeping.

SAFETY INSPECTIONS

Inspection, a vital management tool, is an essential part of hazard control. Inspection is the organization's monitoring activity to locate and report hazards that may cause accidents. The purposes of safety inspections are: (1) to detect potential hazards for correction before an accident takes place, (2) to increase operational efficiency, and (3) to improve profitability.

For safety inspections to be effective, corrective steps must take place when hazards are located. The following are several types of safety inspections:

- *Ongoing inspection* is conducted as part of the job responsibilities of supervisors and maintenance personnel. Also, continuous inspection by all employees of personal protective equipment is important. Continuous inspection is a feature of successful health and safety programs. Supervisors can do well in spotting hazards by having another supervisor audit the area. For example, inspections at the start of the shift and immediately after lunch are particularly effective.

- *Planned periodic inspection* is an inspection that is conducted at scheduled intervals, like the monthly inspection. In facilities where the accident potential is high, formal inspections should be more frequent. The advantage of planned periodic inspection is that it covers a preselected area and is scheduled regularly to correct hazards either before or shortly after they occur.

- *Intermittent inspections* are made at irregular intervals. These unscheduled safety inspections are done as the need arises. They can be made when a new piece of equipment is installed, when a process change is instituted, or when a health hazard is suspected.

- A *general inspection* is a planned inspection of an area that is not inspected regularly, like overhead areas, fencing, and the parking lot.

ACCIDENT INVESTIGATIONS AND REPORTS

If and when an accident takes place, its circumstances must be investigated so that steps can be taken to keep history from repeating itself. Investigation of an accident is a means to uncover the direct and indirect cause, document the occurrence and follow-up action, provide cost information, and stress safety. Management should include accident investigating as a part of the organization's approach to hazard control.

The primary reason for investigating an accident is not to identify a scapegoat, but to determine the cause of the accident. The investigation concentrates on gathering factual information about the details that led to the incident. If investigations are conducted properly, there is the added benefit of uncovering problems that did not directly lead to the accident. This information benefits the ongoing effort of reducing the likelihood of accidents. As problems are revealed during the investigation, action items and improvements that can prevent similar accidents from happening in the future will be easier to identify than at any other time.

A report, which is a tool of management personnel to implement corrections, is generated after the investigation. It documents the facts involved in an accident that can be useful in compensation matters and litigation. The report produced becomes the permanent record of facts surrounding the accident and allows the reconstruction of an accident situation. It also contains information that is useful in determining the direct and indirect costs of the accident.

Accident investigation indicates management's sense of accountability for accidents and the organization's concern for a safe work environment. When the investigation is a cooperative effort between management and labor, it further demonstrates management's commitment to safety.

WHEN TO INVESTIGATE

Supervisory personnel must take a serious approach to investigating an accident, no matter how trivial it seems. All accidents, no matter how small the consequences, are candidates for thorough scrutiny. Management must be aware that serious accidents arise from the identical hazards as minor accidents. Therefore, an immediate, on-the-scene investigation is best. This will prevent other important nonrelated matters from prolonging the investigation, and the facts generated will be most accurate and useful. The longer the time elapsed prior to examining an accident scene, the greater the possibility of gathering incomplete or erroneous information. The scene of the accident changes, people involved forget, and witnesses

ACCIDENT INVESTIGATIONS

change their stories to agree with someone else's interpretation. Besides these reasons for a prompt investigation, the swift investigation expresses management's concern for the safety and well-being of employees.

WHAT TO INVESTIGATE

During an investigation, many questions need to be answered. It is best to have a prepared procedure to help direct an investigation. It is also best to have a supervisor lead the investigating team. If at all possible, sketches should be made and photographs taken during the investigative work. Table 50-1 contains a list of questions that are generally applicable in most accident investigations.

THE ACCIDENT REPORT

The accident report should be impartial and objective and should accurately present the facts in a clear fashion. All of the facts should be presented; nothing should be omitted. It should say which unsafe acts and unsafe conditions specifically caused or contributed to the accident. Ambiguous terminology should not be used because it may mean something different to various people. The accident report is the product of the investigation, and it should be carefully prepared to adequately justify the conclusions and corrective action being suggested. The report should be understandable to anyone who reads it. Also, it must be issued soon after the accident.

The report should receive circulation through the supervisory arm of the organization. Supervisors can then keep workers informed of the findings and preventive measures executed. The report may be summarized, mentioning the causes and recommended action, and posted throughout the facility. The actual report should be maintained on file for at least 5 years. This report ought to be used by management as a tool to boost the safety program. Past mistakes can be used to improve future operations.

TABLE 50-1
Accident Investigation Checklist

The following list of concerns can be used for consideration in accident investigations:

1. What type of work was the injured performing? Precisely what was he doing at the time of the accident?
2. Was the injured person familiar with the task that he was engaged in? Was he authorized to work on the equipment or process?
3. Were there other workers in the vicinity at the time of the accident? If so, what were they doing?
4. Was the task being performed properly? Proper equipment being used? Proper energy sources locked out?
5. Was the injured employee new on the job? Is the process/ operation/task new?
6. Was the injured person being supervised? What role did supervisory personnel play? Was this role adequate?
7. Had the injured employee received adequate or proper training?
8. Is it apparent that any site safety rules were being violated?
9. Where did the accident take place? What was the condition of the area at the time of the accident?
10. What could have prevented the accident? Short-term solution? Long-term solution?
11. Has an accident like this occurred before? Was there any corrective action recommended? If so, was it adopted?

SUPERVISORY PLANS FOR EMERGENCIES

The management of any organization should assess the potential emergencies that could occur at the establishment and put these into a plan of action. There must be written procedures in connection with fire, first aid, toxic release, explosion, and other possible emergencies. It is sometimes necessary to involve employees in this planning process. The procedure must be well documented and must be communicated to all employees through training.

FIRE

In all premises, employees should be instructed what to do in the event of fire. They should understand fire precautions and have regular fire drills. Written fire emergency instructions should cover the following:

1. What to do if a fire is discovered.
2. Location of fire alarm boxes and how they are triggered.
3. How to call the fire brigade. (Emergency telephone numbers and the conditions under which they should be dialed.)
4. What to do if a fire alarm is heard.
5. The location and use of firefighting equipment. If firefighting equipment is used, hands-on training, with periodic refresher training, must be conducted.

6. Proper escape routes that are clear of obstruction for emergency egress.
7. The need to keep fire doors closed.
8. How to shut down machines and processes that could be dangerous if unattended or otherwise left operating or in service.
9. Isolating appropriate power supplies.

Fire emergency procedures should be prominently displayed at conspicuous points throughout the workplace. Practice fire drills should take place at least once a year, and practice drills simulating a blocked escape route are a good practice. Also, fire emergencies in the light of new equipment installations should be examined during new equipment safety audits. Fire alarms should be tested on a monthly basis, and an audibility test should be taken to be certain that they can be heard when equipment is operating. Also, portable fire extinguishers should be inspected monthly.

FIRST AID [2]

First aid programs in industry are required under OSHAct/70. A physician should help develop and direct the program, including approving the first aid supplies (as required by the OSHA rules), selecting the ambulance services to be used, planning routines for handling the various types of injuries and illnesses that may occur, and overseeing the records that will be needed.

Smaller companies may want to consider part-time medical service to provide not only first aid and injury care, but to bring to the company and its people the broader benefits of an occupational health program.

First Aid Training

First aid is the early treatment that is given until the injured or ill employee can obtain professional medical care. Emphasis in first aid training is placed on getting the individual to medical care. Because the law permits only licensed practitioners to provide definitive medical care, the first aider is limited as to scope of care provided. The first aider should provide immediate, temporary care within the scope of his or her training to relieve pain and suffering and enhance recovery. The first aider should not engage in any continuing treatment.

Acceptable first aid training can be provided by the American Red Cross through one of its local chapters. At least two employees on each shift should be trained, one to be assigned the primary responsibility and the other to assist as needed and to cover when the primary first aider is absent or otherwise unavailable.

Some companies have provided supervisors and a major segment of the employees with training in first aid and cardiopulmonary resuscitation (CPR). This provides additional trained support personnel, and it assures that actions by workers at the scene before the responsible first aider arrives will be helpful and not harmful.

The Consulting Physician

OSHA regulations require "...the ready availability of medical personnel for advice and consultation on matters of plant health." Further required are "First aid supplies approved by the consulting physician..." These two requirements of OSHA are an expression of the logic of involving a physician in the beginning of emergency planning in an occupational health program.

It is necessary to find a physician who not only can assist in devising the emergency plan, but also provide or arrange for the needed care. If the medical resource is a local clinic, a group practice, or a hospital, it is important for management to ascertain which specific physician is to be designated as the "consulting physician." Otherwise, the individual industrial case is likely to become submerged in the flow of clinical cases.

First Aid Facility, Equipment and Supplies

The kind of first aid facility that is appropriate depends on such factors as the size of the company, number of employees, severity of accident and illness hazards, and the distance to a clinic or hospital.

The facility should include a cabinet for first aid supplies, a sink with hot and cold running water, a chair, an adjustable light, a basin, covered waste container, paper towels with dispenser, and paper cups with dispenser.

Maintenance of the first aid facility should be an assigned responsibility of the first aiders on each shift. Additional equipment and supplies should be obtained in accordance with the recommendations of the consulting physician.

If the size of the company warrants it, consideration should be given to setting aside a separate first aid room to accommodate a bed or cot and other equipment that the consulting physician deems appropriate.

The basic first aid supplies would include: a first aid manual, adhesive tape, bandage strips, bandage scissors, gauze bandage rolls, sterile gauze squares, antibacterial soap, elastic bandages, triangular bandages, safety pins, splinter forceps, and ammonia inhalants. Additional first aid kits should be available to field crews, either by assigning a kit to one worker or by placing the kit in the crew vehicle when it remains on the site.

Emergency Transportation

Emergency planning should include the investigation and evaluation of ambulance or medical services in the communities. Many communities have a comprehensive emergency transportation system—the ambulances carry sophisticated equipment and are staffed with emergency medical technicians capable of assessing needs and initiating prompt emergency care in the ambulance, if indicated. Communication with the emergency care physician in the hospital or clinic is readily available for advice and guidance.

Awareness of other community services that are available, such as the fire department, rescue squad, and burn center, should also be considered in the emergency care planning.

Names and telephone numbers of the ambulance service, rescue squad, fire department, hospital, and consulting physician should be posted in appropriate places throughout the plant or building, in addition to being posted at the first aid facilities.

First Aid Records

A record should be kept of all persons receiving first aid. These records may have worker's compensation implications and may be used to verify worker's compensation claims. These records can also be used to identify patterns of injury occurrence. OSHA Form 200 must be kept for cases involving time lost from work, temporary limited work assignments, and cases referred to the physician for continuing care.

The Occupational Health Nurse

Companies with sufficient numbers of employees to warrant it should consider part-time or full-time in-house nursing services. The nurse will assume responsibilities beyond taking care of injuries. The scope of the occupational health nurse's function could include the health assessment of new and present employees, conducting or arranging for medical monitoring procedures, educating workers to the exposures and measures for protecting themselves from injury or illness, and maintaining the medical record system.

The Role of the Insurance Carrier

The responsibility for providing a safe workplace is solely that of the employer. The worker's compensation insurance carriers have traditionally provided assistance to policyholder management in safety matters, and so it has been logical for policyholders to look to their carrier for guidance in the safety aspects. The occupational health aspects are now receiving increasing attention, and the worker's compensation insurance carrier can provide guidance to policyholder management in setting up an adequate occupational health program.

OTHER EMERGENCY PROCEDURES

Management of every organization should be certain that

WORKER'S COMPENSATION

effective plans are in place for all foreseeable emergencies. Possible emergency situations are bomb threat, chemical spill, toxic gas release, natural disaster, loss of power, civil disturbance, plane crash, explosion, or out-of-control production process. The emergency instructions should incorporate procedures to deal with the cause of the emergency, evacuation of nonessential personnel away from the danger, arrangements for the coordination of emergency services, news releases to the public, and restoration of operations.

In facilities where extreme hazards exist, an emergency control center should be predesignated. Information kept at the control center must include the following:

- Telephone numbers of emergency services.
- Telephone numbers of essential personnel.
- Layout drawings of the facilities identifying power lines, water mains, emergency services, and so on.
- Hazardous material information and material safety data sheets (MSDS).
- List of explosive and toxic materials and indication of their locations.

AN OVERVIEW OF WORKER'S COMPENSATION

The first worker's compensation law in the United States was passed in 1908 and applied only to federal employees. The first state worker's compensation law was enacted in 1911. In 1916, the U.S. Supreme Court declared worker's compensation laws to be constitutional.

MODERN WORKER'S COMPENSATION

Generally, worker's compensation is a no-fault arrangement. The employee's negligence does not affect the determination of liability. A compromise was reached with the worker's compensation system; for the compensation, the employees have given up their right to legally pursue the employer for unlimited damages due to pain and suffering. The aims of worker's compensation benefits are to rehabilitate the worker and minimize his or her losses because of the reduced ability to compete in the labor market.

It should be noted that many states consider each physical or chemical-related disability as a bodily injury by disease. This is commonly referred to as "occupational diseases." Disorders that are the result of an extended, long-term attack on the body may be called cumulative injuries. According to the California Labor Code, Sec. 3208.1, a cumulative injury is defined as "occurring as repetitive mentally or physically traumatic activities extending over a period of time, the combined effect of which causes any disability or need for medical treatment."

A difficulty associated with the cumulative injury claim is that the disability usually manifests itself as a disease rather than a wound. Many disorders due to occupational overexposures involve the joints and may appear similar to symptoms of aging. Therefore, a portion of the solution to the difficulties presented by the cumulative injury claim relies on the safety and health professional. If a worker's compensation claim goes to court, it is vital that a close liaison be established by the safety and health professional with the physician and attorney involved in the case to ensure a just and equitable settlement as well as to rehabilitate or return the disabled employee to gainful employment.

Because a cumulative injury-type claim has a long time in which to develop, it is even more important to identify its origin (usually a poorly designed work operation) and correct it before the worker's health is affected.

OBJECTIVES AND CHARACTERISTICS OF WORKER'S COMPENSATION

The commonly accepted objectives of worker's compensation are the following:

1. *Replacement of income.* This is the first major objective of worker's compensation—to replace the lost wages that a job-related injury or illness causes. This replacement should be prompt and adequate. The program should replace the present and projected lost earnings, minus taxes and commuting costs. Most state statutes mandate a two-thirds income replacement ratio, but the program must treat all workers fairly. All workers should have the same proportion of their wages replaced. The employer's worker's compensation program should provide income replacement as soon as possible after disability. The employee should know in advance what he or she would receive if he or she were to become disabled on the job. These benefits are to continue even if the employer's business were to discontinue.
2. *Restoration of an injured worker.* A second objective is rehabilitation, both medical and vocational, to return the employee to the workforce. Medical care should be provided for the employee at no cost until he or she is restored as fully as possible. The program should attempt to positively motivate the employee to return to work.
3. *Prevention of accidents.* Safety programs should reward good safety practices and discourage dangerous operations. A third objective of worker's compensation is occupational accident prevention and reduction.
4. *Cost allocation.* A fourth objective of worker's compensation is to allocate the costs of worker's compensation programs in accordance with the employers and industries responsible for the losses. Because this allocation tends to shift resources from hazardous employers and industries to safe employers and industries, it motivates safety improvements.

Who is Covered?

Most state worker's compensation laws fail to cover all forms of employment. It is also important to realize that the laws vary greatly between states. An employer can reject worker's compensation coverage in states where laws are elective and can relinquish indemnity to common law defenses. This gives an employee a legal action in negligence against an employer, and the employer may not plead defenses of assumed risk, fellow servant negligence, or contributory negligence. Many laws contain exemptions, such as employment at charitable or religious institutions. Others not protected by worker's compensation are volunteers, unpaid family workers, and the self-employed. Compensation benefits, for those who are covered, are limited to injury caused by conditions arising out of and in the course of employment.

Benefits

Benefits are paid by three methods: commercial insurance policies, state insurance funds, and self-insured employers. Benefits include the following:

- Medical service.
- Cash payments to the worker while disabled.
- Burial allowance should the worker die.
- Allowances to the worker's dependents.
- Allowances for a nursing attendant (some states).
- Special costs for prosthesis (some states).

Income Replacement

Although a large percentage of worker's compensation cases are for temporary total disablement, these cases account for one fourth of cash benefits. Income benefits to workers for permanent partial disabilities account for nearly two thirds of the total dollar amount. Cash benefits are payable as a wage-related benefit.

ADMINISTRATION OF WORKER'S COMPENSATION

Almost all of the states have agencies to handle the administrative responsibilities of worker's compensation. Worker's compensation claims may be contested or uncontested. The administrative agency usually has jurisdiction over contested cases. It is the agency's responsibility to supervise the processing of all cases. Administration by a division within the labor department, by a board, or by a commission can effectively operate to assure compliance with the law and guarantee an injured worker's rights. The state agency sees to it that worker's compensation payments commence promptly. It also sees that the worker gets the full benefit that is due. Some states require signed receipts with every compensation payment, or the filing of final receipts, to permit an audit of individual payments.

POTENTIAL EMPLOYER LIABILITIES

In the case of some possible workplace injuries, the employer may be liable beyond worker's compensation. The following is a listing of potential employer liabilities:

1. *Criminal liability* should the employer fail to train employees about on-the-job hazards, neglect to furnish adequate protective equipment against hazards, or disregard complaints of hazardous working conditions.
2. *Liable for aggravation of injuries (dual capacity)* should the employer negligently aggravate a workplace injury when performing functions other than an employer, as in providing improper medical treatment.
3. *Product liability (dual capacity)* should the employee become injured from the use of a faulty product that the employer manufactured.
4. *Liable for intentional assault* should the worker become injured as a result of physical attack by a manager.
5. *Liable for damages to immediate family* should the employee's injury cause loss of consortium, loss of companionship, and negligent mental suffering to the injured worker's immediate family.
6. *Liable corporate subsidiaries.* A California court (Gigax v. Ralston Purina Co., 136 Cal App 3d 591 1982) ruled that "a host of cases hold an employee of a wholly owned subsidiary, who has obtained worker's compensation benefits from the subsidiary, may obtain an action in tort against the parent corporation and this is so even though the parent and subsidiary are covered by the same worker's compensation policy."

INFORMATION SOURCES

Management personnel can find up-to-date specialized information on the various topics covered in this chapter from several sources. Various information sources are listed in Table 50-2. Professional societies, trade associations, and standards organizations are also sources of helpful information, although this listing is by no means complete.

TABLE 50-2
Organizations and Professional Societies Offering Information on Occupational Safety and Health Concerns

SERVICE ORGANIZATIONS

American Red Cross 17th & D Streets, N.W. Washington, DC 20006 (202) 737-8300	Industrial Health Foundation 34 Penn Circle W. Pittsburgh, PA 15206 (412) 363-6600	National Safety Council 4444 North Michigan Avenue Chicago, IL 60611 (312) 527-4800	National Society to Prevent Blindness 79 Madison Avenue New York, NY 10016 (212) 684-3505

STANDARDS GROUPS

American National Standards
  Institute
1430 Broadway
New York, NY 10018
(212) 354-3300
	American Society for Testing
	  and Materials
	655 15th Street, N.W.
	Washington, DC 20005
	(202) 639-4025

(continued)

INFORMATION SOURCES

TABLE 50-2—*Continued*

FIRE PROTECTION ORGANIZATIONS

Factory Mutual Engineering
and Research
1151 Boston-Providence
Turnpike
Norwood, MA 02062
(617) 762-4300

National Fire Protection
Association
Batterymarch Park
Quincy, MA 02269
(617) 770-3000

Underwriters Laboratories
333 Pfingsten Road
Northbrook, IL 60062
(312) 272-8800

PROFESSIONAL SOCIETIES WITH SAFETY CONCERNS

American Association of
Occupational Health Nurses
3500 Piedmont Road, N.E.
Atlanta, GA 30305
(404) 262-1162

American Board of Industrial
Hygiene
302 S. Waverly Road
Lansing, MI 48917
(517) 321-2638

American Conference of
Governmental Industrial
Hygienists
6500 Glenway Avenue
Cincinnati, OH 45211
(513) 661-7881

American Industrial Hygiene
Association
475 Wolf Ledges Parkway
Akron, OH 44311
(216) 762-7294

American Occupational Medical
Association
2340 S. Arlington Heights Road
Arlington Heights, IL 60005
(312) 228-6850

American Public Health
Association
1015 15th Street, N.W.
Washington, DC 20005
(202) 789-5600

American Society of Safety
Engineers
1800 East Oakton Street
Des Plaines, IL 60016
(312) 692-4121

Board of Certified Safety
Professionals
208 Burwash Avenue
Savoy, IL 61874
(217) 359-9263

Board of Hazard Control
Management
8009 Carita Ct.
Bethesda, MD 20817

Health Physics Society
1340 Old Chain Bridge Road,
Suite 300
McLean, VA 22101
(703) 790-1745

Human Factors Society
P.O. Box 1369
Santa Monica, CA 90406
(213) 394-1811

International Healthcare Safety
Professional Certification
Board
5010 A Nicholson Lane
Rockville, MD 20852
(301) 984-8969

National Safety Management
Society
3871 Piedmont Avenue
Oakland, CA 94611
(415) 653-4148

SAFE Association
15723 Vanowen Street, Suite 246
Van Nuys, CA 91406
(818) 994-6495

Society of Fire Protection
Engineers
60 Batterymarch Street
Boston, MA 02110
(617) 482-0686

System Safety Society
14252 Culver Drive, Suite A-261
Irvine, CA 92714
(714) 551-2463

Veterans of Safety
203 N. Wabash Avenue,
Suite 2206
Chicago, IL 60601
(312) 346-3835

MACHINE SHOP SAFETY

In the machine shop, mechanical safety is usually the first safety consideration and is obtained through the use of guarding, controls, and awareness systems. Because some of the most serious injury problems arise from an operator's being caught by or pinched between moving machine components, placing mechanical safety foremost in a safety program is appropriate. Builders and users of modern machinery have laminated many of these problems through guarding drives, shafts, pulleys, couplings, and other machine components. The point of operation generally pinpoints the particular problem of concern, enabling the employer to rectify it. However, this has not always been the case.

BASICS OF MACHINE SAFEGUARDING

A good rule is: Any machine part, function, or process that may cause injury must be safeguarded. When the operation of a machine or accidental contact with it can injure the operator or others in the vicinity, the hazard must be either controlled or eliminated. To protect workers against mechanical hazards, safeguards must meet the following minimum general requirements:

1. *Prevent contact.* The guard must prevent hands, arms, or any other part of a worker's body from making contact with dangerous moving parts.
2. *Secure.* Workers should not be able to easily remove or tamper with the safeguard. Guards and safety devices should be made of durable material that withstands conditions of normal use. They must be firmly secured to the machine or, in some instances, to the tooling.
3. *Protect from falling objects.* The guard must ensure that no objects can fall into moving parts. A small tool or loose machine part dropped into a cycling machine could become a projectile that may strike and injure someone.
4. *Create no new hazards.* A safeguard defeats its purpose if it creates a hazard of its own, such as a shear point, a

jagged edge, or an unfinished surface that can cause a laceration. The edges of guards, for instance, should be rolled or deburred and smoothed to eliminate sharp edges and pinch points.

5. *No interference.* Any safeguard that impedes a worker from performing the job quickly and comfortably might soon be overridden or disregarded.

6. *Safe lubrication.* Employees should be able to lubricate the machine without removing safeguards. Locating oil reservoirs outside the guard, with a line leading to the lubrication point, reduces the need for the operator or maintenance worker to enter the hazardous area.

METHODS OF SAFEGUARDING

There are many ways to safeguard machinery. The type of operation, the size or shape of stock, the method of handling, the physical layout of the work area, the type of material, and production requirements or limitations help to determine the appropriate safeguarding method for the individual machine.

In general, power transmission apparatus is best protected by fixed guards that enclose the danger area. For hazards at the point of operation, where moving tools perform work on stock (workpieces) several methods of safeguarding are possible. The most effective and practical means should be used. Safeguards can be grouped in the following five general classifications:

1. Guards:
   - Fixed.
   - Interlocked.
   - Adjustable.
   - Self-adjusting.
2. Safety devices.
3. Location/distance.
4. Feeding and Ejection Methods:
   - Loading and Unloading.
   - Safety Considerations.
5. Safety aids:
   - Awareness Barriers.
   - Shields.
   - Signs.
   - Signals.
   - Color.
   - Personal Protection.
   - Expendable Tools.

GUARDS

Guards are barriers that prevent entry of any part of the body into hazardous machine areas. The use of guards can be an effective method of protecting employees from machine hazards if the guards are designed and used properly. Although guards are sometimes referred to as shields, that reference is inaccurate. Shields are barriers that prevent chips, oil, and coolant from striking employees.

For many general purpose machines, the design of guards and shields depends upon the specific parameters of the operation to be performed. For this reason, manufacturers of general purpose machines are often unable to provide suitable guards and shields for all applications. In these cases, employers have a particular responsibility to select and install guards and shields for their applications. In addition, the guards must be removable so that various operations can be accomplished.

On dedicated, highly automated machines, guards and shields can be installed on a more permanent basis than is possible on general purpose machines. In addition, it is often advisable that the guard or shield be interlocked with the machine controls.

SAFETY DEVICES

A safety device may perform one of several functions. It may (1) stop the machine if a hand or any part of the body is inadvertently placed in the danger area; (2) restrain or withdraw the operator's hands from the danger area during operation; (3) require the operator to use both hands on machine controls, thus keeping hands and body out of danger; or (4) provide a barrier synchronized with the operating cycle of the machine, thereby preventing entry to the danger area during a hazardous part of a cycle.

LOCATION/DISTANCE

A thorough hazard analysis of each machine and particular situation is essential before the principle of safeguarding by location/distance can be applied.

To safeguard a machine by location, a machine or its dangerous moving parts must be so positioned that hazardous areas are not accessible and do not present a hazard to a worker during normal operation. This may be accomplished by locating the machine so that a plant design feature, such as a wall, protects the worker and other personnel. Additionally, enclosure walls or fences can restrict access to machines. Another possible solution is to locate dangerous parts high enough to be out of the normal reach of any worker.

A feeding process can be safeguarded by location if a safe distance can be maintained to protect the worker's hands. The dimensions of the stock being worked on may provide adequate safety. For instance, if the stock is several feet long and only one end of the stock is being worked on, the need for the operator to hold the opposite end while the work is being performed may provide built-in protection. However, depending upon the machine, protection might still be required for other personnel.

The positioning of the operator's control station provides another potential approach to safeguarding by location. Operator controls may be located a safe distance from the machine, if there is no reason for the operator to tend it.

FEEDING AND EJECTION METHODS

The method of loading or unloading a machine should be carefully evaluated, and training should be provided when necessary. Often there is more than one way to manually load a part into a machine. By loading one way, the operator's hand is subjected to a hazard; by loading another way, no hazard exists or the hazard is greatly reduced.

For improved safety, many feeding and ejection methods do not require the operator to place hands in the danger area. As noted above, operator training can aid in avoiding a hazard. In some cases, no operator involvement is necessary after the machine is set up. In other situations, operators can manually feed the stock with the assistance of a feed mechanism. Properly designed ejection methods do not require any operator involvement after the machine starts to function.

Some feeding and ejection methods may create hazards themselves. For instance, a robot may eliminate the need for an operator to be near the machine, but may create a new hazard by the movement of its arm.

Using these feeding and ejection methods does not eliminate the need for guards and devices. Guards and devices must be used when necessary, to protect workers from hazards.

MACHINE SHOP SAFETY

SAFETY AIDS

Consideration may be given to a number of miscellaneous safety aids. While these aids do not give complete protection from machine hazards, they may provide the operator with an extra margin of safety. Sound judgment is needed in their application.

Awareness Barriers

The "awareness barrier" does not provide physical protection, but serves only to remind a person that he or she is approaching the danger area. Generally, awareness barriers are not considered adequate when continual exposure to the hazard exists. A rope may be used as an awareness barrier on the rear of a machine. Although the barrier does not physically prevent a person from entering the danger area, it calls attention to the potential danger in the area. Light or electronic barriers are becoming widely used. These provide a light or electronic beam whereby, if the beam is passed or the continuity of the beam is broken, the machine will not operate. These types of devices should be designed and installed in such a manner that, should they fail, the machine is stopped in a fail-safe condition.

Shields

Shields are barriers that are used to provide protection from flying particles, splashing cutting oils, or coolants.

Signs

Signs notify employees of certain types of hazards. "No Smoking" signs are used for flammable or combustible materials, and warning signs are placed on tanks containing various chemical solutions. Warning sign should be posted on all potentially hazardous machine operations.

Signals

Audio or visual signals are used as warnings of potential hazards. For example, they are used prior to starting a long conveyor when employees would be injured if they were not aware of its starting. They are also used as warnings of an approaching overhead crane or powered industrial truck.

Color

Color is used as notification of a hazard. For instance, red containers may designate flammable materials and orange paint on the side of guards, tools, or other areas may indicate that a mechanical hazard exists.

Personal Protection

Personal protective equipment must be depended upon to protect employees. For example, gloves should be worn when sharp, hot, or contaminated objects are being handled.

Expendable Tools

Expendable tools frequently are used to avoid a point-of-operation hazard. A typical use is for reaching into the danger area of a machine to place or remove stock or workpieces.

NONMECHANICAL HAZARDS

While concentrating attention on concepts and techniques for safeguarding mechanical motion, it should be recognized that there are a variety of other hazards that cannot be ignored. Among these are nonmechanical hazards such as circumstances and events other than those created by moving parts.

All power sources for machinery are potential sources of danger. When electrically powered or controlled machines are used, for instance, the equipment as well as the electrical system itself must be properly grounded. Replacing frayed, exposed, or old wiring also helps to protect the operator and others from electrical shocks or electrocution. High pressure systems, too, need careful inspection and maintenance to prevent possible failure from pulsation, vibration, or leaks. Such a failure could cause explosions or flying objects.

MACHINE LOCKOUT

One of the first procedures for the maintenance person is to disconnect and lock out the machine from its power sources whether the source is electrical, mechanical, pneumatic, hydraulic, or a combination of these. Energy accumulation devices must be "bled down."

PRACTICAL MACHINING SAFETY[3]

Basic to the development of safe, productive machining practices is a fundamental respect for the capabilities of modern metalcutting equipment—and its potential dangers. It should be recognized, for example, that hot chips flying from workpiece can cause severe skin burns or blindness; also, with today's high spindle speeds and feed rates, shattered insert fragments can be projected at speeds capable of serious injury. Such awareness is essential, since it stimulates constant alertness to potential dangers at and around the machine, and leads to careful observance of safety-related tool maintenance and setup procedures.

Machine Grounding and Emergency Shut-Off

In addition to adequate safeguarding, every machine tool must meet two basic electrical safety requirements before it is used. It must be electrically grounded, and it must have an emergency stop device within easy reach of the operator.

Workpiece Retention

Among precautions which should be taken for a safe machine setup, secure workpiece retention is perhaps the single most important consideration, whether the workpiece is rotating or fixed. In rotating-tool operations, it is mandatory to use properly designed workholding fixture or securing device. Effective workholding power can be achieved by first lubricating such fixtures or devices. In tightening fixture clamps, care must be taken to ensure that pressure is applied equally and that the workpiece is centered and not distorted.

As a precaution in turning operations, chuck jaws should be periodically checked to make sure they have sufficient gripping force. Checks should also be made to ensure that the workpiece is butting up against the shoulder of the jaws or some other positive stop. Such precautions are especially important when turning barstock supported on a center. In these operations it is critical that the cutting forces on the workpiece be balanced by the grip of the chuck jaws. If they are not, the barstock can work its way toward the headstock, causing it to slip off the center and fly out from the machine.

Insert Retention

Secure retention of indexable inserts is highly important to safe machining—especially when cutting tools are used under high loads and at high temperatures. To properly secure insert, it is important that the right tools be used. For many turning and boring tools, an ordinary hex wrench is appropriate. If special adjustment tool is supplied by the cutting tool manufa turer, it should be used. Inserts on milling cutters with wedge-type insert retention are best secured with a preset torque wrench. This ensures both that required force is applied and that screws are not over-torqued.

Insert pockets of toolholders, boring tools, and milling cutters should always be clean and in good repair to provide optimum insert support. Special attention should be given to clamps, screws, shims, and pocket seating surfaces. Pocket surfaces are especially critical. They must be flat, clean, and undamaged to prevent insert failure and potential high-speed ejection of insert fragments. To further ensure insert retention, insert-holding screws must be well lubricated and properly tightened.

Machining Precautions

Chipmaking and control. Unsafe and inefficient machining is often indicated by the production of long, stringy chips. When this condition develops, the machine should be shut down immediately. The condition calls for prompt correction, because stringy chips can clog the cutting action, creating a hazard to the operator and causing damage to the machine, tooling, or workpiece. In addition, stringy chips can hinder productivity. It sometimes takes longer to remove such chips wrapped around tooling or the workpiece than it does to perform the machining operation that produces them. By contrast, well-formed chips of the characteristic "C" or "figure-6" shape are thrown free of the cutting action and generally indicate a safe and productive metalcutting operation.

During the machining operation, chips should be directed away from the operator and other personnel in the area—and, if the machine is so equipped, down into the chip-disposal pan. Shields used to block the chip spray and direct the flow must be in place whenever metalcutting is in progress.

When chips are in the disposal pan, they must never be grasped by hand—not even with gloves. Since chips often have sharp edges and may still be hot, they can cause severe injury to the hands. Safe chip removal is accomplished with a hook, tongs, shovel, or mechanical chip conveyor.

Tool sharpening. Removal of hazardous material is also an important concern in the sharpening of any brazed-carbide tools that may be used. As with all other machining, grinding operations must be performed in strict accordance with accepted safety standards. These operations, however, require an important additional safety precaution. Dust and mist produced by grinding cemented carbide cutting tools contain metallic particles that can be harmful if inhaled. Therefore, adequate ventilation and an effective means of collecting this residue must be provided. OSHA regulations should be consulted to determine allowable exposure.

Cutting fluids. Like the control of chips and grinding dust, the control of cutting fluids or coolants is an important safety concern. Most coolants is use today are composed of a soluble oil mixed at a ratio of 30 to 60:1 with plain water. Coolant flow should always be contained within the machine, since coolant splashed from the workpiece onto the floor creates a slip-and-fall hazard for the operator and other plant personnel. Where coolant splash is a problem, shielding should be provided to cause the coolant to flow back into the machine. It is important, too, that coolants flow into a clean chip-disposal pan. Chip pans should never be used as garbage containers for litter, refuse, or debris. When they are, recycled coolant is contaminated and its lubricating and cooling capacities are impaired.

Contaminated coolant is also a breeding ground for odorous bacteria that can cause inflammation of the skin.

Overhang and chatter. In any machining operation, tool overhang should never be so great as to produce tool chatter. Besides resulting in a poor surface finish, prolonged chatter can cause inserts to shatter—spraying fragments dangerously into the work area. Chatter can also loosen tool clamps and hold-down screws, causing holders or inserts to be broken and thrown out of the machine. In addition, the scrap parts and damaged tools caused by chatter are costly.

Siren and cord. On multistation transfer lines, there are usually two built-in safeguards with which employees should be thoroughly acquainted. The first is a start-up alert system—usually a siren or Klaxon-type horn, and sometimes a flashing light or rotating beacons—which warns everyone on the line that operations are about to begin. (Whenever possible, the employee starting up the line should walk around it and alert others in the immediate area.) The second built-in safeguard is a total-system-shut-off cord stretching throughout the transfer line system. This cord can be used by an employee to cancel the start-up announced by the alert or, in case of an emergency while the line is active, to terminate all metalcutting operations and other machine motions at once.

Housekeeping and precautions. Around an imposing transfer line, nearly everyone is impressed with the need for extra caution. Unfortunately, the same attitude does not always prevail around smaller machines and in the work area surrounding them. Yet, small machining areas can also be either safe and productive or dangerous depending on the respect and alertness with which operations are approached and performed. Proper respect for the job to be done is especially important as a basis for observing housekeeping practices and personal safety precautions.

Good housekeeping simply means maintaining an orderly work area, including clean floors and safe tool and part storage. Slippery conditions on the floor caused by coolant spray can be remedied by shielding and periodic sweepings with oil-absorptive or grease-absorptive materials. Sweeping also rids the floor of sharp chips that can cause serious cuts in the event of a fall. The floor area of a work station should be kept free of obstructions, and provision should be made for the safe storage and handling of tooling and parts that could be dislodged and fall. In this connection, it is especially important that large tooling, such as heavy boring tools and milling cutters, be stored on low shelving.

Good housekeeping is closely related to precautions involving personal apparel. When a machining operation is in progress, nothing worn by the operator should be susceptible to snagging in moving parts or tools.

Personal protection. Engineering controls, which eliminate the hazard at the source and do not rely on the worker's behavior for their effectiveness, offer the best and most reliable means of safeguarding. Therefore, engineering controls should be the employer's first choice for eliminating machinery hazards. When an extra measure of protection is necessary, however, operators should wear protective clothing or personal protective equipment.

If it is to provide adequate protection, the protective clothing and equipment selected must be:

1. Suitable for the user.
2. Appropriate for the particular hazards.

MACHINE SHOP SAFETY

3. Maintained in good condition.
4. Properly stored when not in use.
5. Kept clean and sanitary.

Training

Even the most elaborate safeguarding system cannot offer effective protection unless the worker knows how to use it and why it should be used. Specific and detailed training is therefore a crucial part of any effort to provide safeguarding against machine-related hazards. Thorough operator training should involve instruction or hands-on training in the following:

1. A step-by-step method of operating the machine, including startup, shutdown, parts handling, and all pertinent precautions.
2. A description and identification of the hazards associated with particular machines.
3. The safeguards themselves—how they provide protection and the hazards for which they are intended.
4. How to use the safeguards and why they should be used.
5. How and under what circumstances safeguards can be removed and who should remove them (in most cases, repair or maintenance personnel only).
6. What to do (e.g., contact the supervisor) if a safeguard is damaged, missing, or unable to provide adequate protection.
7. What to do in an emergency, such as the occurrence of a workpiece misalignment, jam-up, or unusual sound.

This kind of safety training is necessary when operators and maintenance or setup personnel are new, when any new or altered safeguards are put into service, or when workers are assigned to a new machine or operation.

FIRE PROTECTION

A serious fire is a dangerous and devastating hazard. When a fire becomes out of control, the danger to people and the destruction of property can be severe. Fire prevention and control thus are of crucial importance, and proper training of responsible people can avoid fires or greatly reduce their damaging effects. In essence, the training on fire should cover: what it is; how to prevent it; and how to control and extinguish it.

Classification of Fires

The types of combustible materials consumed by fire are classified into four categories. This is done primarily to identify particular kinds of fires with the specific extinguishing agents used to put them out. As shown in Fig. 50-3, each of the four fire classifications is assigned a color-coded symbol to identify the appropriate extinguisher for that particular kind of fire.

- *Class A (green triangle):* Fires in ordinary combustible materials, such as wood, paper, plastic, and cloth, for which the cooling and quenching effects of water, or

solutions containing large percentages of water, are effective. Other extinguishers use the coating effects of certain dry chemicals that retard combustion, or the interrupting of the combustion chain reaction by halogenated agents.

- *Class B (red square):* Fires in flammable liquids and greases, including oil, gasoline, paint, and some lubricants for which a blanketing effect is essential. The fire is put out by excluding air (oxygen), inhibiting release of combustible vapors, or interrupting the combustion chain reaction. It should be noted that some burning plastics manifest the characteristics of flammable liquids.
- *Class C (blue circle):* Fires in electrical equipment, such as motors, switches, and wiring, for which a nonconductive extinguishing agent is required to smother the fire. Carbon dioxide and special dry chemical extinguishers (sodium bicarbonate and salts of potassium) are suitable, and vaporizing liquid agents (liquefied gases and Halons) also can be used.
- *Class D (yellow star):* Fires in flammable metals, such as magnesium, sodium, and lithium, for which sodium chloride, powdered graphite, and other specially prepared dry powder extinguishants are used. These dry powders act as a heat-absorbing medium that does not react with the burning metals.

Detectors and Alarms

Various factors should be considered in selecting the appropriate detector/alarm and installation procedures for a particular location. These factors include:

- Primary purpose of the device (for example, to warn people or protect equipment).
- Potential sources of ignition.
- Types of materials that ignite first.
- Type of building construction.
- Environmental conditions.

Fire detectors function by means of a variety of fire "signatures"; that is, the effects of fires that change normal ambient conditions. These include ionization; unusual concentrations of gaseous combustion products; a rapid rise in temperature; a high temperature; the flicker of a flame; infrared light; the obscuring of light by smoke; and the presence of smoke particles.

Suppression Devices

Fire suppressants control and extinguish fires mainly by removing or reducing one of the three necessary elements of the "fire triangle" (fuel, oxidant, and heat). Suppressants extract heat to cool the reaction zones, usually by wetting; render inert or dilute the oxygen-bearing surroundings by smothering the area and removing the oxidant; or isolate the fuel vapor source from the surrounding air by means of inert blanketing.

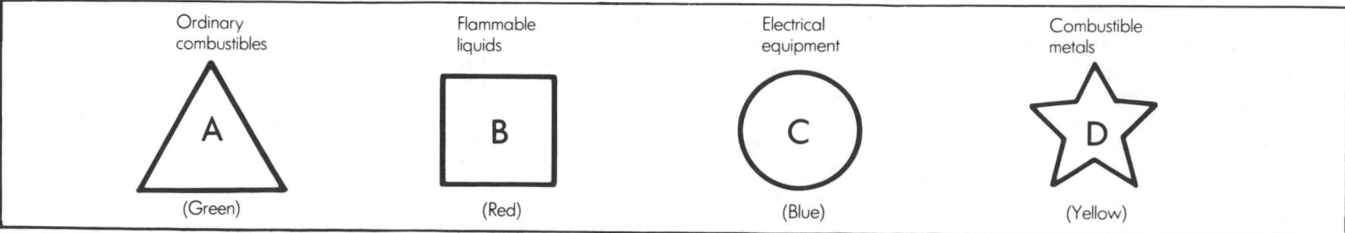

Fig. 50-3 These symbols identify extinguishers according to the type of fire for which they are suited.

Automatic. Most automatic sprinkler system heads contain a heat detector. This is a fusible element that operates when the rated temperature is reached and starts the flow of water. Sprinklers must have an adequate supply of water, which often calls for a system of pipes and sometimes a special tank or reservoir. Various types of fire detectors can activate foam generators or dry chemical or carbon dioxide automatic suppression systems. For EDM operations, in which dielectric oil fires are a potential hazard, automatic fire extinguisher and alarm systems are activated by heat sensors. The system emits Halon gas, which extinguishes the fire and sounds a bell or horn alarm.

Manual. Hose lines, blankets, and manually operated extinguishers are essential to control small fires before they spread. An adequate supply of these devices should be available and easily accessible.

Portable Fire Extinguishers

The previously noted classifications (A, B, C, and D) apply to fire extinguishers. Hence, it is necessary to identify the code letters and color symbols to assure that the correct extinguisher is used when a fire starts. Extinguishers containing water, dry chemical powders, compressed gases, or foam are available in many different portable and mobile forms. Employees should be familiar with locations of fire extinguishers and should be instructed regarding their usage.

Planning for Fire Emergency

When fires start, they can quickly get out of control if effective action is not taken promptly. A fire is most easily controlled during its beginning stage. Often, in a fire emergency, the first few minutes determine whether the fire can be controlled or will lead to serious consequences. This means that planning for fire emergencies is essential. Supervisors and workers should know what to do in dealing with outbreak of a fire. Typically, an employee-manned fire brigade is organized and trained, with emergency assignments prearranged so that an effective firefighting crew is available at all times.

Computer Fire Protection

Computer fires. The widespread and growing use of CAD/CAM and computer systems has brought an additional consideration into the provisions for machine shop fire protection. A relatively small fire in computer areas can cause a disproportionate amount of damage and loss of time.

What causes fires in computers and ancillary systems? With their continual demand for heavy power loads, the supply wiring can overheat; and unless air cooling equipment is functioning properly, a fire can result. Careless discarding of printout paper and other trash can provide fuel. Arcing, worn insulation, faulty tape, or disk drives also can cause fires. Some fires are started by careless use of cigarettes.

Considerable heat is generated by computerized system operations. The air handling systems normally maintain temperatures within a safe operating range. Careful attention to avoid overheating and to prevent or extinguish incipient fires is warranted, because sustained temperatures above 140° F (60° C) can cause malfunctioning of some parts in the system. Temperatures over 185° F (85° C) can permanently damage transistors and diodes. Temperatures from 300° F to 500° F (150° C-260° C) can impair reliability of system components. Also, smoke and acids produced by fire adversely affect operation of computer equipment and magnetic elements.

Kinds of protection. Several types of extinguishing systems are suitable for use on computer location fires. Among these are the automatic sprinkler, carbon dioxide, and Halons. Figure 50-4 compares advantages and disadvantages of these systems.

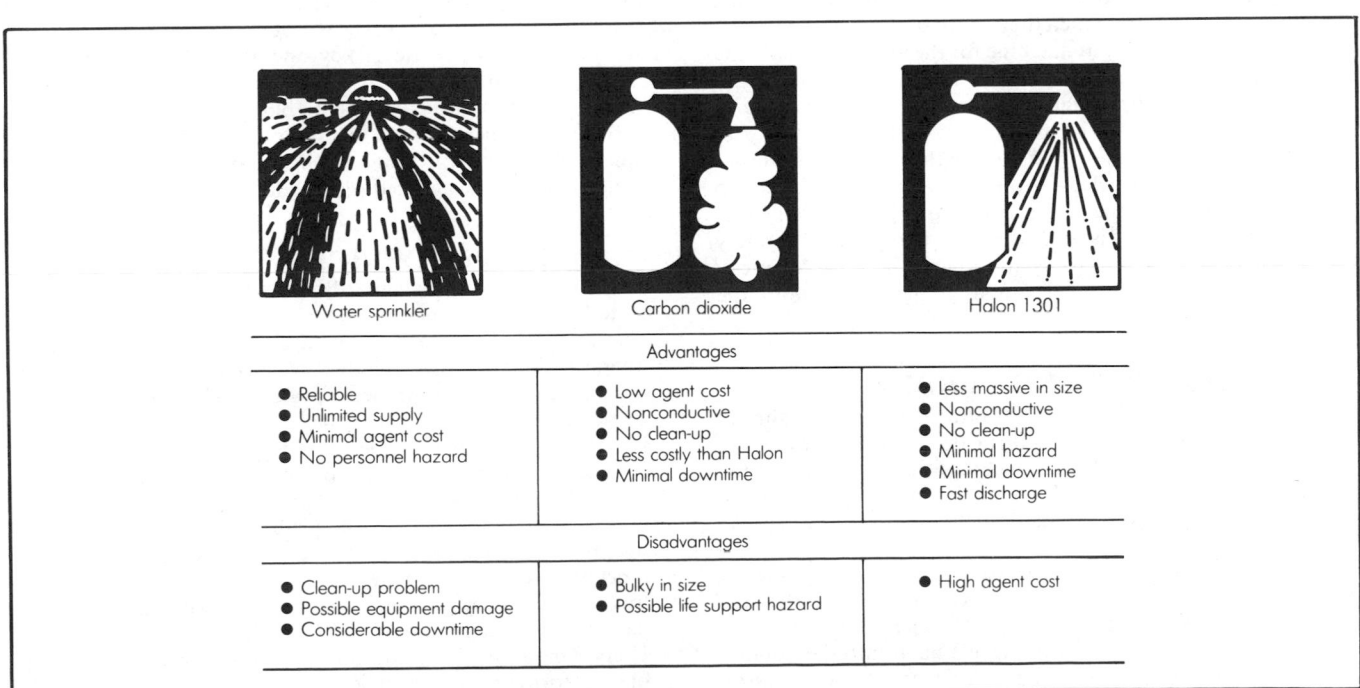

Water sprinkler	Carbon dioxide	Halon 1301
Advantages		
• Reliable • Unlimited supply • Minimal agent cost • No personnel hazard	• Low agent cost • Nonconductive • No clean-up • Less costly than Halon • Minimal downtime	• Less massive in size • Nonconductive • No clean-up • Minimal hazard • Minimal downtime • Fast discharge
Disadvantages		
• Clean-up problem • Possible equipment damage • Considerable downtime	• Bulky in size • Possible life support hazard	• High agent cost

Fig. 50-4 Comparison of computer automatic fire protection systems.

METAL FORMING SAFETY

METALFORMING SAFETY

Amputations and bone fractures are among the most common types of injuries. Typically, an accident occurs when the worker reaches into the machine's point of operation while loading, unloading, or holding a part in process. In many instances, the machine is not stopped for loading or unloading and there is insufficient space or distance for the worker to safely handle the part while loading it into or removing it from the machine.

Failure to use a brush or an appropriate hand tool is a major cause of finger amputations. Frequently, gloves, loose sleeves, and bulky jackets are caught in the tooling, resulting in injury. Whenever the operator is handling stampings, gloves should be worn to protect the hands from cuts caused by burrs and sharp edges.

When determining the most appropriate safeguarding means to be applied to metalforming equipment, consideration must be given to the job requirements and, in particular, to the level of skill needed to perform the task. In one accident study, analysis showed that only a minority of the injured workers were considered journeymen. The majority were in the general category of "operator."[4]

Experience has shown that a thorough, systematic approach must be taken in controlling employee injuries on machines, since no single accident control measure (alone) can be effective. In a given plant situation—taking account of variations in type of forming machine, operation, and workers—specific guidelines for machine safeguarding can be developed by considering key factors such as machine design, provision for "hands out of danger area," machine controls, and guards.

MACHINE DESIGN AND USE

The machine and the associated equipment must be well designed for the job for which they are to be used. Selecting the proper size and capacity of machine for the job is essential. The machine must have adequate capacity and strength and should be operated within the design capacity. When there is a choice of machines available for performing a specific job, full consideration should be given to whether optimum worker protection can be provided on the machine selected. The job should be so well planned that neither overloading nor over-speeding of the machine is likely to occur. In regard to the safety requirements for machine tools, the B11 series of the American National Standards provides good guidance for both the manufacturer and the user.

HANDS OUT OF DANGER AREA

Whenever possible, metalforming operations should be planned to eliminate the need for the worker to reach into the point of operation. This is accomplished through the use of well-designed tooling and alternative methods of feeding, part removal, and scrap removal, including the use of special hand tools.

Particularly with power presses, press brakes, shears, hammers and other machines that can be cycled, the first objective for safe operation is to plan the operation so that it is unnecessary for the operator to place a hand into the point of operation. The second objective is to prevent the operator, through the application of effective safeguarding methods,

from placing a hand in the point of operation when the slide or ram is closing.

To avoid an operational requirement that could endanger the operator's hands, the job designer or process engineer should plan the material feeding, part removal, scrap removal, and tooling lubrication to eliminate, whenever possible, the need for workers to reach into the danger area. Various feeding methods commonly used include automatic feeding (requiring no manual operation other than replacing of stock); semi-automatic feeding by means of manually operated feeding devices; hand-tool feeding (permitting hands to be kept away from the point of operation); and manual feeding of large pieces of such size or shape that when holding them, the hands are positioned well away from the point of operation or danger area. The die and the forming system should be designed to facilitate a "hands out of the die" operation.

MACHINE CONTROLS

The design and location of machine controls can have a major bearing on safe operation of the machine. Operating controls should be convenient; should be identifiable as to their function; and except for stopping controls, should be protected against accidental actuation. Stopping or deactivation controls must be convenient and obvious. Location of machine controls is critical for two reasons. First, the machine control should be conveniently located so that the operator need not reach into or be unnecessarily close to a danger area to operate the controls. Secondly, the machine controls should be placed so that the operator can control the machine, yet be in a safe location outside the danger area.

Pendant controls allow good visibility and control and help the operator to remain in a safe location. There should be supervisory control over certain modes of operation or control stations through the use of key-operated selector switches to obtain the optimum level of employee safety. Not only should the stop buttons be convenient, but also there should be a sufficient number of them to allow quick stopping in case of emergency. Electrical foot switches that are used as operator controls should be covered or guarded.

GUARDS AND DEVICES

A wide variety of safeguarding methods can be applied to metalforming machines to reduce the inherent exposures to employee injuries. The hazards are primarily at the point of operation, but can also include drive mechanisms and the loading and unloading equipment. Figure 50-5 shows a diagrammatic representation of the principles applicable to safeguarding power press point of operation for operator safety.

The type and extent of application of safeguarding is dependent upon several factors, including the exposure to injury and the experience-based probability of injury. All press operations should be safeguarded. As stated previously, the type of safeguarding depends upon the machine type, the tooling, the part size and configuration, the feeding method, the part removal method, and the provisions for scrap disposal. Users of multifunctional equipment should consider all elements of the forming system when selecting point of operation safeguarding or when determining safe methods of operation.

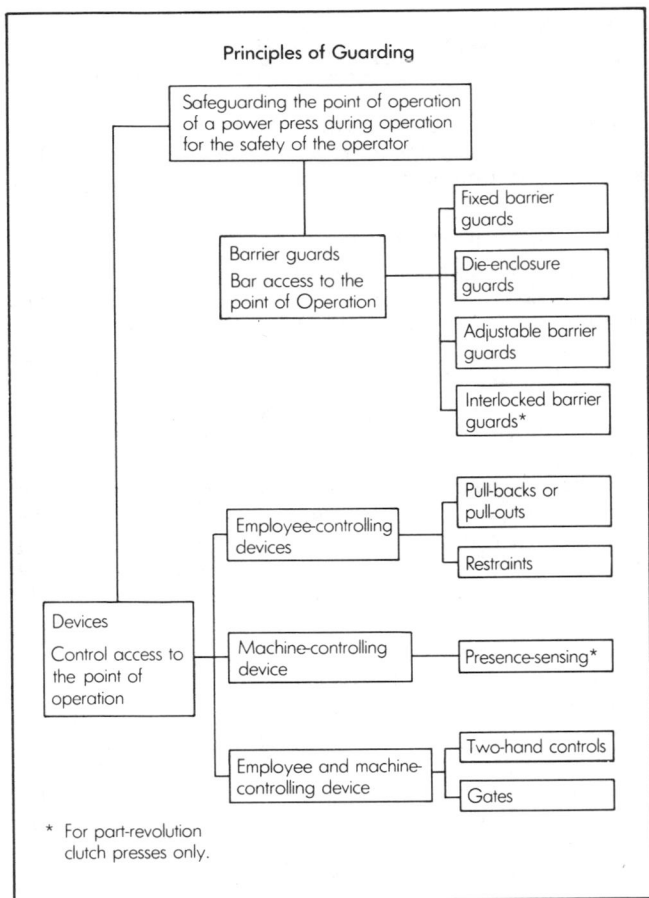

Principles of Guarding

* For part-revolution
clutch presses only.

Fig. 50-5 This diagrammatic overview identifies basic principles of machine safeguarding and shows their interrelationships. (*E. W. Bliss Division, Gulf & Western Manufacturing Company*)

PREVENTIVE MAINTENANCE

Along with the machines on which they are installed, guards and safety devices should be the object of a regular preventive maintenance program. This includes proper adjustment, regular inspection, replacement of critical parts before failure when that may be anticipated, and maintenance of reasonable records. Trained personnel should be designated to carry out the program to ensure that the standards as established by management are maintained.

LOCKOUT/TAGOUT

Means must be provided for locking out all power and releasing all stored energy when maintenance and repair activities are in progress. The power disconnects should be convenient for shutting off and locking out all power, including air, electric, hydraulic, and steam. Unexpected startup of machines must be prevented through the use of an effective lockout/tagout program. Additional information on lockout practices may be obtained from ANSI Z244.1 "Safety Standard for Lockout/Tagout of Energy Sources."

ENVIRONMENTAL HAZARD

Areas surrounding machines should be kept clear of slip, trip, and fall hazards. Good working surfaces of the nonslip type should be provided on all platforms surrounding machines. Lighting and good layout of machines with room for material movement are important items to consider.

WORKER/JOB DEMANDS

It is important to evaluate the physical as well as the mental requirements for performing metalforming machine tasks. The job should be designed to fit the worker. Adequate provision must be made for handling of heavy, sharp, or bulky materials to reduce the exposure to muscle strain and other employee injuries.

SAFE CLOTHING AND EQUIPMENT

Unrestrained long hair should not be allowed around moving machinery. Hair should be restrained, such as under a cap; and jewelry, such as rings and watches, should not be allowed. Short sleeves are generally preferable to long sleeves when operating machine tools. Eye protection should be provided and worn.

TRAINING

Operators, helpers, and maintenance and setup personnel should be well trained in safe work practices through the application of a well-planned training program. Machine manufacturers are good sources for training materials.

Particular attention must be given to new employees. Immediately upon starting work, new employees begin to learn things and form attitudes about their company, their job, their boss, and other employees. They do so whether or not the employer makes an effort to train them. If people are trained during the first few hours and days to do things the right way, considerable losses over a period of time can be avoided.

Attention must, however, be paid to all employees. Old habits can be wrong habits. An employee who continues to repeat an unsafe procedure is not working safely, even if an accident has not resulted from this condition.

Some general indicators that might show a need for training or retraining are:

- Excessive waste or scrap.
- High labor turnover.
- An increase in the number of "near misses" which could have resulted in accidents.
- A recent upswing in actual accident experience.
- High injury and illness incidence.
- Expansion of business and/or new employment.
- A change in manufacturing process, or introducing a new process.

SUPERVISION

After workers have been trained, the level and quality of supervision should be such that the applicable guards and devices are utilized along with the previously taught safe work practices and procedures.

While every employee's attitude should be one of determination that accidents can be prevented, one thing more may be needed. Management should stress the responsibility assigned to the person in charge of the job—as well as to all other supervisors—to be sure that there is a concerted effort to follow every safe work procedure and health practice applicable to that job. It should be explained to the supervisors that they must not silently condone unsafe or unhealthy activity in or around the workplace.

PAINTING SAFETY REGULATORY COMPLIANCE

PAINTING SAFETY REGULATORY COMPLIANCE

The finishing industry is required to comply with the Clean Air Act as administered by the Environmental Protection Agency (EPA) and the Occupational Safety and Health Act as administered by the Occupational Safety and Health Administration (OSHA). Regulations issued by EPA, OSHA, and state and local authorities establish limits for the following:

- Solvent emissions to the atmosphere.
- Levels of certain contaminants in liquid effluents.
- Restraints on the use of certain solvents and chemicals.
- Standards for minimizing hazards that might produce physical injuries to workers.
- Permissible levels of noise.

Due to regional variations that characterize state and local laws, only a rough outline of the general requirements for the finishing industry can be presented here. Environmental laws are in constant flux, and amendments are frequently issued. It is therefore incumbent on the reader to understand and comply with the rules and requirements of the latest laws and amendments.

SOLVENT EMISSION REGULATIONS

Solvents, called volatile organic compounds (VOC) by law, are photochemically reactive and give rise to objectionable ozone formation. As a result, these VOC emissions have to be held to a minimum. The accomplishable minimum VOC emission is called the reasonably available control technology (RACT). Large appliances, like washers, driers, and similar products, used to be spray painted with enamels containing 30% nonvolatiles (NV) and 70% volatile organic compounds (VOC) by volume, which is 0.3 gal (1.1 L) NV plus 0.7 gal (2.6 L) VOC. If it is assumed the solvent has a density of 7.25 lb/gal (0.87 kg/L), then the paint has 5.1 lb of VOC per gal of VOC + NV (0.61 kg/L). This unit, however, cannot be immediately related to the production of coatings; it first has to be converted to lb VOC/gal NV (kg/L), as follows:

$$\frac{5.1 \text{ lb VOC}}{0.3 \text{ gal NV}} = 17 \text{ lb VOC/gal NV (2.04 kg/L)}$$

Waterborne Paints

It seems reasonable that the paint discussed in the preceding paragraph can be replaced by a waterborne spray paint having a composition of 30% NV, 14% VOC, and 56% water, by volume. This content can be converted to the mass of VOC as follows:

0.14 gal (0.53 L) x 7.25 lb/gal (0.87 kg/L) = 1.0 lb (0.46 kg) of VOC, and:
1.0 lb (0.46 kg) of VOC divided by 0.44 gal (1.67 L) of NV gives VOC = 2.27 lb of VOC per gal (0.28 kg per L) of paint minus water; or 1.06 lb (0.46 kg) of VOC divided by 0.3 gal (1.14 L) of NV = 3.3 lb of VOC per gal (0.4 kg/L) of NV.

One gallon of nonvolatiles covers about 1604 ft² (149 m²) of surface with a film thickness of 1 mil (0.03 mm). Thus, the ratio of VOC emissions for the waterborne paint versus the solvent-borne paint discussed is 3.3 lb (1.5 kg) of VOC (for the waterborne paint) divided by 17 lb (7.7 kg) of VOC (for the solvent-borne paint), which equals 0.19. In other words, the solvent emission with the waterborne paint is only 19% of that with the solvent-borne paint.

High Solids and Electrocoating

High-solids paint can be used for appliance painting with a reduction in VOC emissions. A typical high-solids paint may have a composition of 68% NV and 32% VOC, by volume, with 2.3 lb of VOC per gal (0.28 kg/L), NV + VOC. The 2.3 lb of VOC divided by 0.68 gal of NV equals 3.4 lb of VOC per gal of NV (0.4 kg/L). This amount represents an 80% reduction in VOC emissions compared with the conventional solvent-borne paint.

Electrocoating materials are another reasonable replacement for solvent-borne paints to reduce VOC emissions. Some electrocoating materials contain 1.8 lb of VOC per gal (0.2₂ kg/L), NV + VOC, or 2.4 lb of VOC per gal of NV (0.29 kg/L)—an 86% reduction in VOC emissions.

Emission Limitations

Regulators have decided that the use of paints containing 2.4 lb of VOC/gal (0.29 kg/L), minus water, is a reasonably available control technology (RACT). Through similar considerations in other finishing fields, the EPA proposed to state governments the solvent emission limitations listed in Table 50-3. If paints are used that contain more solvent (VOC) than mandated by law, the emitted vapors have to be reduced by 90% through vapor adsorption or incineration.

TABLE 50-3
Emission Limitations with Respect to
Volatile Organic Compounds (VOC) for Surface Coatings

Affected Product or Facility	VOC, lb (kg) VOC + NV, gal (L)
Automotive:	
Prime	1.9 (0.23)
Topcoat	2.8 (0.34)
Repair	4.8 (0.58)
Cans:	
Sheet and exterior	2.8 (0.34)
Interior	4.2 (0.50)
Side seam	5.5 (0.66)
Sealer	3.7 (0.44)
Coating:	
Coil	2.6 (0.31)
Fabric	2.9 (0.35)
Vinyl	3.8 (0.46)
Paper	2.9 (0.35)
Large Appliances:	
Prime and interior	2.4 (0.29)
Topcoat	3.7 (0.44)
Magnet Wire	Incineration

VOC = volatile organic compounds.
NV = nonvolatiles.

SELECTING PAINTS AND PROCESSES FOR COMPLIANCE

Any change to different coating materials or processes to meet emission limitations should be made by combining environmental desirability with lower cost and quality improvement whenever possible. This, however, may entail a sizeable capital investment.

Allowable Options

The range of organic volatiles per gallon of paint, minus water, was tabulated in 1979 and is presented as a bar graph in Fig. 50-6.[5] In addition, the coatings field was resurveyed in March 1981 and 10 important breakthroughs were noted and have been inserted on the graph. If a vertical line (parallel to the ordinate) is drawn intersecting the abscissa at the required VOC [for instance, 3.0 lb VOC/gal (VOC + NV) (0.36 kg/L)], then the right half of the graph is the area containing paints that generally have an unallowably high VOC content. It can be seen, however, that the VOC content of newly developed paints is in the allowable area, and thus the study of these materials is important to paint users.

Much progress has been made in the design of electrostatic spray equipment, which can increase transfer efficiency from 40% (for hand spray) to 95% (for centrifugal electrostatic atomization). In other words, a change of spray equipment can reduce the VOC emission by 50% and may make otherwise outlawed paints "equivalent" to allowable paints, as discussed later in this section.

Other ways of complying with solvent emission laws include the use of less than the allowable amount of VOC in one operation to compensate for excess VOC emission in another operation. This approach is called the bubble concept or banking the saved amount of emission for future use, discussed later in this section. In addition, solvent emission can be reduced through incineration or carbon adsorption (add-on controls), autophoretic coating, and the use of radiation curing, as well as other methods. In all, numerous options are open to the finishing industry.

The selection process for coatings and processes that are in compliance with VOC emission regulations consists of three main steps and several substeps, as listed in Table 50-4.

TABLE 50-4
Steps in Selecting Coatings and Processes
for Compliance with VOC Emission Regulations

Step	Action
1	Compute weight of VOC:
1a	Currently emitted.
1b	EPA mandated.
2	Compute weight of VOC reduced through:
2a	Transfer efficiency (equivalence).
2b	Pooling (bubble concept).
2c	Cooperation (banking).
2d	Different materials or processes.
3	Select most favorable option.

Equivalence Principle

Spray painting is the most widely used method of industrial painting. The transfer efficiency (te) of this method of painting is officially estimated at 40%, meaning that 60% of the expended paint is wasted as overspray. The transfer efficiency of spray painting can be markedly improved, however, through the application of an electric charge (see Table 50-5).

If, for instance, a certain paint applied at 40% te uses twice the allowable amount of VOC, then it will use not more than the allowable amount if applied at 80% te. In this case, the paint actually used has become "equivalent" to an allowable paint. In general, if conventional air-atomized spray is replaced by an electrostatic spray, the emission of VOC is reduced by approximately one half. The cost of buying paint is also reduced by one half.

TABLE 50-5
Estimated Transfer Efficiencies for
Painting Automobiles and Light-Duty Trucks*

Application Method	Transfer Efficiency (te), %
Air-atomized spray	40
Manual electrostatic spray	75
Automatic electrostatic spray	95
Electrodeposition	100

* Federal Register, October 5, 1970, p. 57792.

The Bubble Approach

Some proposed state laws define the bubble approach approximately as follows: "...compliance may be achieved on a source-wide basis...provided that...all applicable facilities are

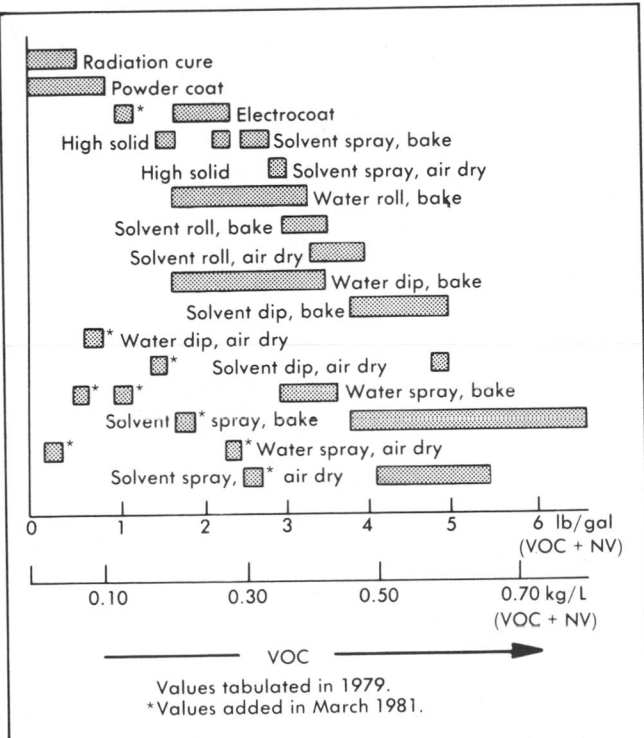

Fig. 50-6 Range of organic volatiles in paint, minus nonpolluting solvents.

PAINTING SAFETY REGULATORY COMPLIANCE

within the same source...The total VOC emissions do not exceed the sum of the allowable emissions from each facility..." Thus, the bubble approach offers the possibility of compensating for excess VOC emission from one operation by lowering the VOC emission from other operations to a level below the allowable limit.

Banking and Using VOC Emissions

The banking concept allows a company to store air quality credits earned through the emission of less than the allowable amount of VOC. The stored or banked credits can be used later by the company if needed to achieve compliance in new operations. The banked credits can also be given or even sold to other VOC-emitting parties. This offsetting policy seems to have been first used in Pennsylvania when the state agreed to reduce hydrocarbon emissions from its highway paving operations to offset the expected pollution from a proposed Volkswagen plant.

Maryland's Economic and Community Development Department has proposed a statewide program for banking and marketing anti-air-pollution credits. This concept deserves attention as an effort to encourage industrial growth while still making progress toward clean air goals. Thus, emitting less than the allowable quantity of waste may create marketable assets and encourage the use of improved methods and materials.

Using Different Materials and Processes

In addition to the paints and processes identified in Fig. 50-6, consideration should be given to certain chlorinated hydrocarbons that can be used without VOC emission restrictions. Many states offer the possibility of replacing some of the VOC in a given formulation with chlorinated solvents. Thus, a paint that exceeds the allowable VOC content can be converted into a compliance paint, virtually without change in pigment or binder and even without change in application equipment. Other methods that should be seriously considered to accomplish compliance are the autodeposition materials and add-on controls, such as incineration and carbon adsorption.

SAFETY OF PERSONNEL

As to the specific safety of personnel, the hazard and degree of exposure should first be determined. Suppliers of chemical materials provide safety data sheets listing flammability, reactivity, spill control, and suitable respiratory protection. These data sheets should be used by an industrial hygienist to develop safe procedures for the handling and the use of materials. Free or reasonably priced consultation is often available from state governments, funded by OSHA, and from workmen's compensation insurance carriers.

Industrial hygiene experts warn that an improper respirator gives employees a false sense of security, which may result in greater exposure to harmful materials. For instance, dust respirators do not protect against solvent vapors; usually, air-purifying masks or chemical cartridge respirators are required. The preferred means of minimizing toxic vapor exposure, however, include limitation of exposure duration and adequate exhaust ventilation.

As an example of adequate ventilation, the design of paint spray booths may be cited. For such equipment, the law demands solvent vapor concentrations not exceeding 50 to 200 parts per million by volume. One large spray booth emits 1245 lb (565 kg) of VOC per hour, using a solvent mixture having an average molecular weight of 82. Since 1 gram

molecular weight of vapor equals 22.4 L, evaporation of 21 lb (9.5 kg) per minute creates 91 ft³ (2.5 m³) per minute. As a result, an airflow of 910,000 ft³/min (25 480 m³/min) is required.

References

1. *Voluntary Training Guidelines*, 49FR30290 (Des Plaines, IL: OSHA, Office of Training and Education, 1984).
2. *First Aid and Emergency Plans*, Report to Management No. 4 (Schaumburg, IL: The Alliance of American Insurers, 1981).
3. *A Guide to Machining Safety*, Valenite Div., The Valeron Corp., Detroit, 1980.
4. Joseph W. Hart, "Safeguarding Metalcutting Machines," *Professional Safety* (January 1983), pp. 13-16.
5. George E. F. Brewer, *The Technique of Complying with Paint Solvent Emission Regulations*, AFP/SME Technical Paper FC81-416 (Dearborn, MI: Society of Manufacturing Engineers, 1981).

INDEX

D

X

Z